German-English English-German Dictionary

Berlitz Publishing Company, Inc.

Princeton Mexico City Dublin Eschborn Singapore

Editor: Anne Dahl

Published by arrangement with Random House Reference & Information Publishing, a division of Random House, Inc.

Trademarks
A number of entered words which we have reason to believe constitute trademarks have been designated as such. However, no attempt has been made to designate as trademarks or service marks all terms or words in which proprietary rights might exist. The inclusion, exclusion, or definition of a word or term is not intended to affect, or to express a judgement on, the validity or legal status of the word or term as a trademark, service mark, or other proprietary term.

ISBN 2-8315-7123-5

Printed in Canada

Foreword

The user of this dictionary will find useful lists and tables concerning pronunciation, verbs, abbreviations, etc., in the front, middle, and back of the book. The German spelling follows most of the regulations implemented by the cultural ministers of the various states of the Federal Republic of Germany in 1995. Subsequent regulations have not been incorporated into this volume, since they are still controversial; although the newest spelling rules are taught in schools, they are not applied to printed matter. It is permissible to follow the old as well as the new spelling rules until the year 2005. For the English spelling we have adopted the American version.

A Brief Summary of the New Spelling Regulations

The new regulations seek to expand the basic spelling principles and diminish the exceptions to them. The new rules regarding the *Umlaut* and double consonants aim to retain the word's linguistic roots. For example, the verb *schneuzen* becomes *schnäuzen*, according to its root *Schnauze*; *nummerieren* now has a double consonant, from the root word *Nummer*. If a word combination results in three consecutive consonants, they are written out (*Schifffahrt*). However, it is acceptable to separate the words with a hyphen. The *ss* is substituted for *ß* if it follows a short vowel (*daß* becomes *dass*). Foreign words are either written in their original form or may be altered according to common use. For example, *g* may replace *gh* or *f* may replace *ph* (*Jogurt, Fotografie*).

The rules for the capitalization of a noun have been expanded. When used with a preposition or verb, a noun is generally capitalized (*auf Basis von, Ball spielen*). Adjectives which are always used with a specific preposition or article are also capitalized (*das Beste*). In forms of address, only the formal forms of *Sie* and *Ihr* are capitalized; the informal *du* and *euer* are written in lower case.

Formerly combined words composed of noun and verb, verb and verb, or participle and verb are now generally written as two words (*Rad fahren, hinaus gehen, liegen bleiben*). However, all words combined with *irgend-* are written as one (*irgendjemand*). While the spelling reform of 1995 permits the use of a hyphen when combining words, the newest ruling permits such use only in the case of connecting a word with a number or single letter, or when the combined word is otherwise difficult to read.

When dividing words at the end of a line, it is now acceptable to separate the letters *st* but not the letters *ck* (*lis-tig, si-ckern*). If a word begins with a single vowel, it may stand alone at the end of a line (*a-ber*).

Main clauses that are connected with *und* or *oder* no longer need to be separated by a comma. A comma is necessary if an infinitive or participle group is introduced or referred to, or if such a construction is inserted into the sentence. In addition, a comma may be placed to facilitate clarity of sentence structure and meaning. The newest rule to use a comma after a direct quotation that ends with an exclamation or question mark is still controversial.

Vorwort

Dieser Band ist Teil der Reihe zweisprachiger Wörterbücher von Random House. Er ist eine neubearbeitete Ausgabe des in 1997 herausgegebenen Random House Deutsch-Englisches Englisch-Deutsches Wörterbuchs. Für den Benutzer dieses Wörterbuchs sind hilfreiche Tabellen betreffend Aussprache, Verben, Abkürzungen, u.s.w., am Anfang, in der Mitte, und am Ende des Buches zu finden. Die deutsche Rechtschreibung folgt den meisten Regeln der 1995 von der Kulturministerkonferenz anerkannten Rechtschreibreform. Die darauffolgenden Neuregelungen sind, da noch umstritten, nicht in diesem Wörterbuch aufgenommen worden: diese neuesten Regeln sind zwar in Schulen unterrichtet, werden aber nicht in Druckmaterialien eingesetzt. Insgesamt gilt, daß bis zum Jahr 2005 die neue wie auch die alte Orthographie anwendbar ist. Die englische Rechtschreibung ist aus dem Amerikanischen übernommen worden.

Eine Zusammenfassung der Neuen Rechtschreibung

Die Basis der Rechtschreibreform beruht auf der Erweiterung von Grundregeln und der Verminderung von Ausnahmen. Die neuen Regelungen für Umlaut und Verdopplung der Konsonate ermöglichen es, den Wortstamm zu erhalten. Somit wird *schneuzen* zu *schnäuzen*, nach dem Wortstamm *Schnauze*. *Nummerieren* enthält einen doppelten Konsonant, laut Wortstamm *Nummer*. Entstehen beim Zusammenschreiben von Wörtern drei Konsonanten, werden sie ausgeschrieben, wie z. B. bei *Schifffahrt*. Es ist aber auch erlaubt, die Wörter mit einem Bindestrich zu trennen. Das *ss* ersetzt das *ß* wenn es einem kurzen Vokal folgt (*daß* wird *dass*). Fremdwörter werden entweder in ihrer herkünftigen Form geschrieben, oder es darf, je nach bisherigem Gebrauch, z. B. *g* für *gh* oder *f* für *ph* ersetzt werden (*Jogurt*, *Fotografie*).

Die Regeln für die Großschreibung sind erweitert worden. Substantive in Verbindung mit einer Präposition oder einem Verb werden generell großgeschrieben (*auf Basis von*, *Ball spielen*). Auch Adjektive die mit bestimmten Artikeln oder Präpositionen gebraucht werden, werden großgeschrieben (*das Beste*). Bei Anreden werden nur noch die Höflichkeitsformen von *Sie* und *Ihr* großgeschrieben, *du* und *euer* werden klein geschrieben.

Beim Getrenntschreiben gilt generell, daß die Verbindung von Substantiv und Verb, Verb und Verb, sowie Partizip und Verb getrennt geschrieben wird (*Rad fahren*, *hinaus gehen*, *liegen bleiben*). Allerdings werden alle Verbindungen mit *irgend-* zusammengeschrieben (*irgendjemand*). Während die Rechtschreibreform von 1995 den Bindestrich bei der Zusammenschreibung grundsätzlich erlaubt, lässt die neueste Regelung den Bindestrich nur noch bei Zahlen, Einzelbuchstaben, und wenn ein Wort ansonsten schwer lesbar ist, zu.

Bei der Silbentrennung am Zeilenende ist die Trennung von *st* aber nicht von *ck* erlaubt (*lis-tig*, *si-ckern*). Ein Vokal am Wortanfang darf bei der Zeilentrennung alleine stehen (*a-ber*).

Hauptsätze die mit *und* oder mit *oder* verbunden sind, müssen nicht mehr mit einem Komma getrennt werden. Ein Komma ist dann zu setzen, wenn die Infinitiv- oder Partizip- Gruppe angekündigt wird, wenn auf sie verwiesen wird, oder wenn sie in den Satz eingeschoben ist. Zusätzlich wird das Komma benutzt, um eine klare Satzstruktur zu vermitteln und um Missverständnisse zu vermeiden. Eine noch umstrittene Regelung ist das Setzen des Kommas in Aussagesätzen nach Ausrufe- und Fragezeichen.

Contents/Inhalt

Inhalt/Contents

Notes on German Pronunciation

As very few German sounds are exactly like the corresponding English sounds, the English equivalents given below represent in most cases only approximately the sounds of the German vowels and consonants.

A. Vowels

Simple vowels are either long or short in German.

They are always long when doubled or followed by *h*, and mostly long when followed by a single consonant.

They are, as a rule, short when followed by a group of consonants.

All long vowels are simple sounds in German, e.g. long *e* in *Fee* is like the first part of the English *a* in *mane*, but does not shift to *i*; long *o* is like the English *o* in *no*, without shifting to *u*.

Short *i* is like *i* in *it*, e.g. *mit*.
Long *i* " " *i* in *machine*, e.g. *dir*.
Short *e* " " *e* in *let*, e.g. *fett*.
Long *e* " " *a* in *late*, e.g. *Fee*.
Long *a* " " *a* in *alms*, e.g. *Tal*.
Short *o* " " *o* in *not*, e.g. *flott*.
Long *o* " " *o* in *no*, e.g. *rot*.
Short *u* " " *u* in *put*, e.g. *und*.
Long *u* " " *u* in *rude*, e.g. *Mut*.
Short *ä* " " *e* in *fell*, e.g. *fällt*.
Long *ä* " " *a* in *mare*, e.g. *fährt*.

The letters *ie* always represent the long English *ee* sound as in *field*, e.g. *sie*.

ö is pronounced like German *e* with rounded and protruded lips.

ü is pronounced like German *i* with rounded and protruded lips.

Final *e* is always pronounced in German words, e.g. *fette* like English *fetter* (without the *r*-sound).

B. Diphthongs

äu and *eu* resemble the *oi*-sound in *boy*, e.g., *Mäuse, Heu.*

ei } are like { *ei* in height } e.g. *Ei.*
ai } { *ai* in aisle } *Mai.*

au is like *ow* in *how*, e.g. *lau*.

C. Consonants

b, d = English *b, d* at the beginning of a word or syllable, e.g. *Boden*.

b, d = English *p, t* in all other cases, e.g. *Lob, Abt, und.*

ch = (1) Scottish *ch* in 'loch' after *a, o, u*, e.g. *ach, doch, Tuch.*

= (2) first sound of 'hew' after the remaining vowels, and consonants, e.g. *ich, echt, Mächte, reich, euch, Gretchen.*
= (3) *k* before 's', e.g. *Fuchs, wachsen, Ochs,* and in some words of Greek origin, e.g. *Christ, Chor, Charakter.*
ck = *k*, e.g. *Lack, wecken.*
g = (1) English *g* at the beginning of a word or syllable, e.g. *gar, legen.*
= (2) *ch* (1) or (2) in all other cases, e.g. *zag, selig, lugte, Berg.* This *g* may also be pronounced like English *g* or *k*, except after *i* and *n*.
ng = English *ng* in *long*, e.g. *lang, singen.*
j = English *y* in *yes*, e.g. *ja, jeder.*
r = There are two regionally different pronunciations: the frontal *r* like the Scottish *r* in *girl*, e.g. *roh, Herr*; and the uvular *r*, nonexistent in English.
s = (1) English *z*, at the beginning of a word or between vowels; e.g. *so, Rose.*
= (2) English voiceless *s* in *hiss*, in all other cases, e.g. *es, ist.*
ss = English voiceless *s* in *hiss*, e.g. *lassen, grösser.*
sp, st = English *shp, sht*, at the beginning of a word, e.g. *spät, Stuhl*; in all other cases like English *sp, st.*
th = English *t*, e.g. *Theater.*
v = English *f*, e.g. *vor, Vetter*; in words of Latin origin like English *v*, e.g. *Viktoria.*
w = English *v*, e.g. *wer, wir, Löwe.*
x = English *ks* (never like *gs*), e.g. *Max.*
y = mostly like *ü*, e.g. *Symphonie*, sometimes like *i*.
z, tz = English *ts*, e.g. *zu, Reiz, Sitz, Katze.*
-tion = *-tsyon*, e.g. *Nation.*

Stress

The principal stress in German words rests on the root syllable which is usually the first syllable, e.g. *sa'gen, el'terlich.*

Exceptions are *Forel'le, Holun'der, Wa'cholder, leben'dig,* nouns ending in *-ei*, like *Bettelei'*, and verbs ending in *-ieren*, e.g. *spazier'en.*

The prefixes *be-, ge-, er-, ver-, ent-, zer-*, are unstressed.

The prefix *ant-* always has, and the prefix *un-* usually has the principal stress, e.g. *ant'worten, un'ruhig.*

Exceptions are *unmög'lich, unend'lich.*

Words borrowed from foreign languages retain their original stress, e.g. *Natur', Dok'tor, Doktor'en, Universität'.*

Compound adverbs have their principal stress on the second part, e.g. *hervor', dahin', zusam'men.*

Bemerkungen zur Aussprache des Englischen

Lautzeichen und Lautwerte decken sich im Englischen noch viel weniger als im Deutschen. Derselbe Laut kann durch ganz verschiedene Buchstaben wiedergegeben werden, und derselbe Buchstabe kann ganz verschiedene Laute bezeichnen. Die Schreibweise ist also durchaus kein Führer für die Aussprache. Dennoch dürften einige allgemeine Hinweise nützlich sein.

A. Vokale

Langes *a* ist wie im deutschen *kam*, z.B. *car*, *alms*.

Kurzes *a* liegt zwischen dem deutschen *a* und *ä*, doch ist der Raum zwischen Zunge und Gaumen grösser als beim deutschen *a*, z.B. *rat*, *can*.

Ausserdem gibt es ein kurzes dunkles *a*, wobei die zurückgezogene Zunge sich gegen den weichen Gaumen hebt, z.B. *but*, *some*.

Langes *e* ist ein Diphthong, der mit *e* beginnt und nach *i* hin ausklingt, z.B. *may*= *mee-i*.

Langes halboffenes *o* ist ein Diphthong, der mit *o* beginnt und nach *u* hin ausklingt, z.B. *no*= *noo-u*.

Langes offenes *o* liegt zwischen *a* und *o* (der Laut des *o* in *Gott* verlängert), z.B. *all*, *or*.

Kurzes offenes *o* klingt nach *a* hin, z.B. *not*, *god*.

Langes offenes *ö* in Wörtern wie *fir*, *girl*, *learn*. Die Zunge bleibt flach in mittlerer Lage und der Unterkiefer wird gesenkt.

Auslautendes *e* ist immer stumm im Englischen.

B. Konsonanten

b, *d*, und *g* werden auch am Ende einer Silbe stimmhaft, d.h. wie am Anfang gesprochen, z.B. *bib*, *dead*, *gag*.

j ist ein stimmhaftes *sch* wie in *Genie*, mit einem *d* davor, z.B. *Jew*; derselbe Laut wird oft durch *g* bezeichnet, z.B. *gin*.

r vor Vokalen wird mit der Zungenspitze hervorgebracht, aber nicht gerollt, z.B. *rid*, *proud*.

s im Anlaut ist immer stimmlos wie im deutschen *ist*, z.B. *so*. Zwischen Vokalen wird es stimmhaft, z.B. *rose*, wie im deutschen *Rose*.

sp und *st* sind niemals wie deutsches *schp* und *scht* zu sprechen.

th ist ein Reibelaut (wie *s*), bei dem sich die Zunge an die oberen Schneidezähne legt. Es ist entweder stimmlos, z.B. *thick*, oder stimmhaft, z.B. *them*.

w ist ein mit den Lippen gebildetes deutsches *w* mit der Zungenstellung für *u*.

z ist immer der stimmhafte s-Laut (wie im deutschen *sie*), z.B. *zest*, *lazy*.

Abbreviations Used in the Dictionary

Verzeichnis der im Wörterbuch gebrauchten Abkürzungen

a. = adjective, Adjektiv.
adv. = adverb, Adverb, Umstandswort.
Am. = Americanism, Amerikanismus.
ar. = arithmetic, Arithmetik.
arch. = architecture, Baukunst, Architektur.
art. = article, Artikel, Geschlechtswort.
astro. = astronomy, Astronomie.
avi. = aviation, Aviation.
bes. = besonders, especially.
bio. = biology, Biologie.
bot. = botany, Botanik.
c. = conjunction, Konjunktion, Bindewort.
chem. = chemistry, Chemie.
com. = commercial, Handel.
comp. = computer, Computer.
cp. = compare, vergleiche.
cul. = culinary, Kochkunst.
def. = defective, defektiv.
elek. = electricity, Elektrizität.
etw. = something, etwas.
f. = feminine, weiblich.
fam. = familiär, colloquial.
fig. = figuratively, figurativ.
frz. = französisch, French.
geol. = geology, Geologie.
geom. = geometry, Geometrie.
gram. = grammar, Grammatik.
her. = heraldry, Heraldik.
hist. = history, Geschichte.
hunt. = hunting, Jagdwesen.
i. = interjection, Empfindungswort.
ir. = irregular, unregelmäßig.
jn. = jemanden, someone.
jm. = jemandem, someone.
jur. = jurisprudence, Rechtswissenschaft.
ling. = linguistics, Linguistik.
lit. = literally, wörtlich.
liter. = literature, Literatur.

m. = masculine, männlich.
math. = mathematics, Mathematik.
mech. = mechanics, Maschinenwesen.
med. = medicine, Medizin.
met. = meteorology, Meteorologie.
mil. = military, Militär.
min. = mining, Bergbau.
mot. = motoring, Autofahren.
mus. = music, Musik.
n. = neuter, sächlich.
nav. = navigation, Schiffahrt.
obs. = obsolete, veraltet.
od. = or, oder.
opt. = optics, Optik.
o.s. = oneself, sich selbst.
p. = participle, Partizipium.
pej. = pejorative, abwertend.
phot. = photography, Photographie.
phys. = physics, Physik.
pl. = plural, Mehrzahl.
pn. = pronoun, Fürwort.
pol. = politics, Politik.
pr. = preposition, Verhältniswort.
print. = printing, Druckereibetrieb.
r. = regular, regelmäßig.
rail. = railway, Eisenbahn.
rel. = religion, Religion.
s. = substantive, Hauptwort.
s.b., sb. = somebody, jemand.
sl. = slang, Slang.
sp. = sports, Sport.
st. = strong, stark.
s.th., sth. = something, etwas.
subj. = subjunctive, Konjunktiv.
theat. = theater, Theater.
tech. = technical, Technik.
tel. = telegraphy, Telegraphie.
tel. = telephone, Fernsprechwesen, Telefon.
typ. = typography, Buchdruck.
u. = and, und.
v.i. = intransitive verb, intransitives Zeitwort.
v.imp. = impersonal verb, unpersönliches Zeitwort.
v.refl. = reflexive verb, rückbezügliches Zeitwort.
v.t. = transitive verb, transitives Zeitwort.
vulg. = vulgar, vulgär.
Zus. = Zusammensetzung(en), compound word(s).
zool. = zoology, Zoologie.

Notes on Signs

0 Indicates that a German noun has no plural form.

(-,) Indicates that a German noun remains unaltered in the genitive or plural.

(*s*) Indicates that the German verb is conjugated with *sein*.

(*h*, *s*) Indicates that the German verb is conjugated with either *haben* or *sein*. (Where neither of these is mentioned, the verb is conjugated with *haben*.)

~ Indicates the main word at the beginning of each separate entry.

Bemerkungen zu den Zeichen

0 Zeigt an, daß ein deutsches Substantiv keine Pluralform hat.

(-,) Zeigt an, daß ein deutsches Substantiv im Genitiv oder Plural unverändert bleibt.

(*s*) Zeigt an, daß das deutsche Zeitwort mit *sein* konjugiert wird.

(*h*, *s*) Zeigt an, daß beide Hilfszeitwörter (*haben* und *sein*) zulässig sind. (Wo eine Angabe fehlt, versteht sich die Verbindung mit *haben* von selbst.)

~ Zeigt das Stichwort am Anfang des betreffenden Artikels an.

German–English Dictionary

A, a *n.* the letter A or a; (*mus.*) A.
AA *Auswärtiges Amt,* Foreign Office; *Anonyme Alkoholiker,* Alcoholics Anonymous.
Aal *m.* **(-[e]s, -e)** eel.
aalen *v.r.* to loaf about; to laze.
aalglatt *a. pej.* slippery.
a.a.O. *am angeführten Orte,* in the abovementioned place.
Aas *n.* **(-es, Äser)** carcass, carrion.
Aasfresser *m.* **(-s, -)** scavenger.
Aasgeier *m.* **(-s, -)** vulture.
ab *adv,* off; down; (away) from; *~ und zu,* from time to time; occasionally; *auf und ~,* up and down; *Hut ~!* hats off!; *pr.* from.
abändern *v.t.* to alter; (*Gesetz*) to amend.
Abänderung *f.* **(-, -en)** alteration; (*Gesetz*) amendment.
abarbeiten *v.r.* to overwork oneself; to work off; to wear out.
Abart *f.* **(-, -en)** variety.
abartig *a.* abnormal; perverse.
Abartigkeit *f.* **(-, -en)** abnormality.
Abb. *Abbildung,* illustration, ill.
Abbau *m.* **(-[e]s, 0)** working (of a mine); retrenchment; dismantling; cutback; *Preis ~,* reduction in prices.
abbaubar *a.* degradable.
abbauen *v.t.* to work (a mine); to dismantle; to reduce; *Stellen ~,* to abolish; *Beamte ~,* to dismiss.
abbehalten *v.t.st. den Hut ~,* to remain uncovered.
abbeißen *v.t.st.* to bite off.
abbekommen *v.t.st.* to get a share in; *etwas ~,* to get hit, to get hurt.
abberufen *v.t.st.* to call back, to recall.
Abberufung *f.* **(-, -en)** recall.
abbestellen *v.t.* to cancel.
abbezahlen *v.t.* to pay off, to pay up.
abbiegen *v.t. & i.st.* to bend off; to turn off, to branch off.
Abbiegespur *f.* **(-, -en)** turnoff lane.
Abbild *n.* **(-[e]s, -er)** copy, image.
abbilden *v.t.* to copy, to portray; *nach dem Leben ~,* to draw from life.
Abbildung *f.* **(-, -en)** picture, illustration.
Abbitte *f.* **(-, -en)** apology; *~ leisten, ~ tun,* to apologize.
abblasen *v.t.st.* to blow off; to sound (a retreat); to call off (a strike).
abblättern *v.i.* to shed petals; to flake off.
abblenden *v.t.* (*mot.*) to dim.
Abblendlicht *n.* **(-s, -er)** low beam.
abblitzen *v.i. jn. ~ lassen,* to send sb. packing.
abblühen *v.i. (h, s)* to cease flowering; to wither.
abbrechen *v.t.st.* to break off, to pluck off; to cut off; to demolish, to pull down (*Häuser etc.*); *kurz ~,* to cut short; *~ v.i.st.* to break off, to leave off; to drop a subject.
abbremsen *v.t.* to brake, to slow down.
abbrennen *v.t.ir.* to burn off (away, down); (*Feuerwerk*) to set off; *~ v.i.ir. (s)* to be burnt down; to lose one's property by fire.
abbringen *v.t.ir.* to dissuade; to divert.
abbröckeln *v.t. & i. (s)* to crumble away.
Abbruch *m.* **(-[e]s, -brüche)** demolition; breaking off; pulling down; damage; injury, detriment.
abbuchen *v.t.* (*Bank*) to debit.
Abbuchung *f.* **(-, -en)** debit entry.
Abbuchungsauftrag *m.* **(-s, -träge)** debit order.
abbürsten *v.t.* to brush off, to brush.
abbüßen *v.t.* to atone for, to expiate; to serve (*Strafe*).
ABC-Waffen *pl.* ABC weapons (atomic, biological, chemical).
abdämmen *v.t.* to dam up; to embank.
abdampfen *v.i.* (*fam.*) to set off.
abdanken *v.i.* to resign, to abdicate.
Abdankung *f.* **(-, -en)** resignation, abdication.
abdecken *v.t.* to uncover; to unroof; to flay; (*den Tisch*) to clear.
Abdecker *m.* **(-s, -)** knacker.
abdichten *v.t.* to seal; to plug.
abdienen *v.t.* to pay off by service, to work off; to serve one's time.
abdrängen *v.t.* to force (sb.) away.
abdrehen *v.t.* (*Gas*) to turn off; (*Elek., Licht, Radio*) to switch off.
abdriften *v.i.* to be blown off course, to drift.
abdrosseln *v.t.* to throttle.
Abdruck *m.* **(-[e]s, -drücke),** impression; copy; (*phot.*) print; (*Abguß*) cast, stamp, mark.
abdrucken *v.t.* to make a copy, to publish.
abdrücken *v.t.* to pull the trigger, to fire.
abdüsen *v.i.* (*fam.*) to zoom off.
abebben *v.i.* to recede.
Abend *m.* **(-s, -e)** evening, night; West *m.; am ~,* in the evening; *gestern ~,* last night; *heute ~,* tonight; *morgen ~,* tomorrow night.
Abendanzug *m.* **(-[e]s, -züge), Abendkleid** *n.* **(-[e]s,-er)** evening attire.
Abendblatt *n.* evening paper.
Abendbrot *n.* supper.
Abenddämmerung *f.* twilight, dusk.
Abendessen *n.* supper.
Abendland *n.* West, Occident.
abendländisch *a.* Western.
abendlich *a.* evening...
Abendmahl *n. das heilige ~,* the Lord's Supper; *das ~ empfangen,* to take the sacrament.
Abendrot *n.* sunset glow.
abends *adv.* in the evening.
Abendstern *m.* evening star, Hesperus.
Abenteuer *n.* **(-s, -)** adventure.
abenteuerlich *a.* adventurous; strange.
Abenteurer *m.* **(-s, -)** adventurer.
aber *c.* but; *~ doch,* but yet; *~ adv.* however.
Aberglaube *m.* **(-ns, 0)** superstition.
abergläubisch *a.* superstitious.
aberkennen *v.t.ir.* to deprive of *or* disallow by legal verdict.
Aberkennung *f.* **(-, -en)** deprivation.
abermalig *a.* reiterated, repeated.
abermals *adv.* again, once more.
abernten *v.t.* to reap (a field).
Aberwitz *m.* **(-es, 0)** insanity.
aberwitzig *a.* insane.
Abf. *Abfahrt,* departure, dep.
abfahren *v.t.st.* to cart away; *~ v.i.ir. (s)* to depart, to start, to leave; *auf jn. ~,* (*fam.*) to be

crazy about sb.; *jn.* ~ *lassen,* (*fam.*) to send sb. packing.
Abfahrt *f.* **(-, -en)** departure, start; (*Schiff*) sailing.
Abfall *m.* **(-[e]s, -fälle)** falling off; decrease; garbage, waste, offal, refuse; apostasy; defection.
abfallen *v.i.st.* to fall off; to slope; to desert, to apostatize; *es fällt dabei etwas für mich ab,* I profit by it.
Abfallentsorgung *f.* **(-, 0)** waste management.
abfällig *a.* derogatory.
Abfallprodukt *n.* **(-s, -e)** by-product.
Abfallverwertung *f.* **(-, 0)** recycling.
abfangen *v.t.st.* to catch; to intercept.
Abfangjäger *m.* **(-s, -)** (*mil.*) interceptor (plane).
abfärben *v.i.* to lose color, to come off (of colors); to stain.
abfassen *v.t.* to compose, to draw up, to draft.
Abfassung *f.* **(-, -en)** composition, wording.
abfaulen *v.i.* to rot off.
abfedern *v.t.* to absorb, to cushion.
abfegen *v.t.* to wipe, to sweep (off).
abfeilen *v.t.* to file off.
abfertigen *v.t.* to dispatch, to send off; *kurz* ~, to snub, to put down.
Abfertigung *f.* **(-, -en),** dispatch; clearance.
abfeuern *v.t.* to fire off, to discharge.
abfinden *v.t.st.* to satisfy, to pay off; ~ (*mit*) *v.r.* to put up with.
Abfindung *f.* **(-, -en)** indemnity.
Abfindungssumme *f.* compensation.
abflachen *v.i.* to flatten.
abflauen *v.i.* (*Wind*) to drop; to die down; to subside.
abfliegen *v.i.st.* (*avi.*) to take off.
abfließen *v.i.st.* *(s)* to flow off.
Abflug *m.* **(-[e]s, -flüge)** takeoff; departure.
Abfluß *m.* (-flusses, -flüsse) flowing off; discharge; gutter, drain, wastepipe.
Abflußrohr *n.* **(-s, -e)** drainpipe.
abfordern *v.t.* to call away; to demand.
abfragen *v.t.* to test (*quiz*), to inquire of; to retrieve (*comp.*); *eine Lektion* ~, to give a test on a lesson.
abfressen *v.t.st.* to eat bare, to strip bare.
abfrieren *v.i.st.* to be frostbitten; *Mir frieren die Ohren ab.* My ears are freezing. ~ *v.r.* (*fam.*) *sich einen* ~, to be freezing to death.
Abfuhr *f.* **(-, -en)** removal; rebuff.
abführen *v.t.* to carry away; (*med.*) to purge; (*Schuld*) to discharge.
abführend *a.* (*med.*) aperient.
Abführmittel *n.* purgative, laxative.
abfüllen *v.t.* to decant, to bottle.
abfüttern *v.t.* to feed; to line (*coat*).
Abgabe *f.* **(-, -en)** delivery, surrender; tax, duty.
Abgang *m.* **(-[e]s, -gänge)** departure; (*com.*) deficiency, tare; diminution; (*von Waren*) sale; (*theat.*) exit.
Abgangsprüfung *f.* final examination.
Abgangszeugnis *n.* certificate of completion.
Abgas *n.* **(-es, -e)** waste gas, exhaust gas.
abgearbeitet *a.* worn out.
abgeben *v.t.st.* to deliver up, to give up, to turn in; *sich* ~ *mit,* to concern oneself about, to keep company with.
abgebrannt *a.* (*fam.*) broke.
abgebrüht *a.* (*fam.*) hardened.
abgedroschen *a.* trite, hackneyed.
abgefeimt *a.* cunning, crafty.
abgegriffen *p. & a.* well-thumbed.
abgehackt *a.* clipped, chopped.
abgehangen *a.* hung.
abgehärmt *a.* haggard.
abgehärtet *a.* tough, hardened.
abgehen *v.i.st.* *(s)* to go off, to depart; (*Schiff*) to sail; to come off; *es geht mir ab,* I lack.
abgehetzt *a.* run down.
abgekämpft *a.* worn out, exhausted.
abgekartet *a.* (*fam.*) prearranged.
abgeklärt *a.* (*fig.*) detached.
abgelagert *a.* seasoned, mature.
abgelegen *a.* remote, outlying.
abgelten *v.t.st.* to satisfy, to settle.
abgemacht *a.* settled; ~*!* done! agreed!
abgemagert *a.* emaciated.
abgemessen *a.* disinclined.
abgeneigt *a.* measured; formal.
Abgeneigtheit *f.* **(-, 0)** disinclination, aversion.
abgenutzt *a.* worn out, used up; threadbare.
Abgeordnete(r) *m.* **(-n, -n)** deputy, representative; Member of Parliament.
Abgeordnetenhaus *n.*, **Abgeordnetenkammer** *f.* House of Representatives; House of Commons.
abgepackt *p. & a.* prepacked.
abgerechnet *p.* not counting, exclusive (of), deducting.
abgerissen *p. & a.* ragged; (*fig.*) abrupt.
abgesagt *a.* cancelled.
Abgesandte(r) *m.* **(-n, -n)** messenger.
Abgesang *m.* farewell, swan song.
abgeschieden *a.* secluded; retired; deceased.
abgeschmackt *a.* tasteless; absurd.
abgesehen *p.* ~ *von,* apart from; ~ *auf,* aimed at.
abgespannt *a.* (*fig.*) exhausted, run down.
abgestanden *p. & a.* stale, flat.
abgestorben *a.* dead, numb.
abgestumpft *a.* blunted; (*fig.*) dull, insensitive.
Abgestumpftheit *f.* **(-, 0)** dullness.
abgetakelt *a.* (*fig.*) worn out.
abgetan *a.* done with, settled; dispatched.
abgetragen *a.* (*Kleider*) threadbare, worn out.
abgewinnen *v.t.st.* to win from; *Geschmack* ~, to get a taste for.
abgewogen *a.* balanced.
abgewöhnen *v.t.* to wean from; ~ *v.r. sich etw.* ~, to give up.
abgezehrt *a.* emaciated.
abgießen *v.t.ir.* to pour off, to decant.
Abglanz *m.* **(-es, 0)** reflection, image.
Abgott *m.* **(-[e]s, -götter)** idol.
Abgötterei *f.* **(-, 0)** idolatry.
abgöttisch *a.* itolatrous.
abgraben *v.t.st.* to drain off.
abgrämen *v.r.* to pine away.
abgrasen *v.t.* to graze.
abgrenzen *v.t.* to delimit, to differentiate.
Abgrund *m.* **(-[e]s, -gründe)** abyss; precipice.
abgründig *a* inscrutable, dark.
abgucken *v.t.* to learn through observation, to copy.
Abguß *m.* **(-gusses, -güsse)** cast, copy.
Abh. *Abhandlung,* treatise.
abhacken *v.t.* to chop off.
abhaken *v.t.* to unhook, to check off.
abhalftern *v.t.* to undo the halter; (*fig.*) to criticize.
abhalten *v.t.st.* to detain; to prevent; to keep off; (*Versammlung*) to hold.

abhandeln *v.t.* (*vom Preise*) to beat down; to discuss, to treat.
abhanden *adv.* not at hand; ~ *kommen,* to be missing, to get lost.
Abhandlung *f.* **(-, -en)** treatise, paper.
Abhang *m.* **(-[e]s, Abhänge)** declivity, slope.
abhängen *v.t. & i.* to take down; to depend; to shake off.
abhängig *a.* dependent; addicted; ~ *von,* subject to.
Abhängigkeit *f.* **(-en, 0)** dependence.
abhärmen *v.r.* to pine away, to grieve.
abhärten *v.t.* to harden; to toughen.
abhaspeln *v.t.* to reel off.
abhauen *v.t.* to chop off, to cut off, to beat it.
abhäuten *v.t.* to skin.
abheben *v.t.st.* (*Karten*) to cut; (*Geld*) to withdraw; to take off; ~ *v.r.* to stand out (against).
abheften *v.t.* to file.
abheilen *v.i.* to heal.
abhelfen *v.t.st.* to remedy, to redress.
abhetzen *v.t.* to rush.
Abhilfe *f.* **(-, 0)** redress, remedy, relief.
abhobeln *v.t.* to plane off.
abhold *a.* averse, ill-disposed (toward).
abholen *v.t.* to fetch, to go for, to call for; *einen vom Bahnhof* ~, to meet sb. at the station; ~ *lassen,* to send for.
Abholung *f.* **(-, -en)** collection.
abholzen *v.t.* to clear a wood.
abhorchen *v.t.* to sound (chest, lungs).
abhören *v.t.* to listen in, to monitor, to tap, to bug.
abirren *v.t.* *(s)* to deviate, to stray.
Abirrung *f.* **(-, -en)** deviation, aberration.
Abitur *n.* **(-s, 0)** school-leaving examination.
Abiturient *m.* **(-en, -en)** candidate for the leaving examination of a secondary school.
abjagen *v.t.* to retrieve; to override, overdrive (a horse); to snatch.
Abk. *Abkürzung,* abbreviation, abbr.
abkanten *v.t.* to bevel.
abkanzeln *v.t.* (*fig.*) to rebuke.
abkapseln *v.r.* to cut os. off.
abkarten *v.t.* to prearrange; *abgekartete Sache,* put-up job, plot, collusion.
abkaufen *v.t.* to buy from.
Abkehr *f.* **(-, 0)** falling away, desertion.
abkehren *v.r.* to fall away, to desert.
abklappern *v.t.* (*fam.*) to scour (shops), to do (museums).
Abklatsch *m.* **(-es, -e)** poor imitation.
abklemmen *v.t.* to disconnect, to clamp.
abklingen *v.i.st.* to abate, to ease, to subside.
abklopfen *v.t.* to tap.
abknabbern *v.t.* to nibble off.
abknallen *v.t.* (*fam.*) to shoot down.
abkneifen *v.t.ir.* to pinch (off), to nip (off).
abknicken *v.t.* to snap off; to bend.
abknöpfen *v.t.* to unbutton; (*fam.*) to get sth. out of sb.
abkochen *v.* to boil.
abkommandieren *v.t.* to detail, to send.
abkommen *v.i.st.* *(s)* to deviate; to fall into disuse; *ich kann nicht* ~, I am busy.
Abkommen *n.* **(-s, -)** agreement.
abkömmlich *a.* available.
Abkömmling *m.* **(-s, -e)** descendant.
abkoppeln *v.t.* to uncouple.
abkratzen *v.t.* to scrape off, to scratch off, (*fig. fam.*) to kick the bucket.
abkriegen *v.t.* to get (a share of); *etwas* ~, to be in for a scolding.
abkühlen *v.t.* to cool; ~ *v.r.* to cool down, to get cool.
Abkühlung *f.* **(-, -en)** cooling; (*chem.*) refrigeration.
Abkunft *f.* **(-, 0)** descent, origin; *von guter* ~, of good family.
abkuppeln *v.t.* to uncouple.
abkürzen *v.t.* to shorten, to abridge, to abbreviate; (*math.*) to reduce.
Abkürzung *f.* **(-, -en)** abbreviation.
Abkürzungsweg *m.* shortcut.
abküssen *v.t.* to kiss and hug.
abladen *v.t.st.* to unload, to dump.
Ablage *f.* **(-, -n)** file; storage.
ablagern *v.t.* to deposit.
Ablagerung *f.* **(-, -en)** sediment; (*geol.*) deposit.
Ablass *m.* **(-lasses, -lässe)** (*rel.*) indulgence; *vollkommener* ~, plenary indulgence.
ablassen *v.t.st.* (*vom Preise etwas*) to abate, to take off; (*einen Teich*) to drain; ~ *v.t.st.* to cease, to leave off.
Ablativ *m.* **(-[e]s, -e)** ablative.
Ablauf *m.* **(-[e]s, 0)** course, lapse, expiration.
ablaufen *v.t.st.* *(s)* to flow down; to end, to expire; to become due; ~ *v.t.ir.* to wear off by walking; (*den Rang*) **~,** to outdo; ~ *lassen,* to snub; *schlecht* ~, to end ill.
ablauschen *v.t.* to overhear.
Ableben *n.* **(-s, 0)** decease, death.
ablecken *v.t.* to lick off.
ablegen *v.t.* to file, to lay aside; to take off, to put down; (*einen Eid*) to take (an oath); (*ein Kleid*) to take off, to cease wearing; (*Rechenschaft*) to account for; *Zeugnis* ~, to bear witness.
Ableger *m.* **(-s, -)** layer, shoot, cutting.
ablehnen *v.t.* to decline, to refuse, to turn down; (*Richter, Geschworene*) to challenge.
Ablehnung *f.* **(-, -en)** refusal; (*Richter, Geschworene*) challenge.
ableisten *v.t.* to serve, to perform duly.
ableiten *v.t.* to divert; to derive.
Ableitung *f.* **(-, -en)** derivation; diversion.
ablenken *v.t.* to avert, to divert, to turn off; (*phys.*) to deflect.
ablernen *v.t.* to learn from.
ablesen *v.t.st.* to read.
Ablesung *f.* **(-, -en)** reading.
ableugnen *v.t.* to deny, to disown.
Ableugnung *f.* **(-, -en)** denial, abnegation.
ablichten *v.t.* to copy.
abliefern *v.t.* to deliver.
Ablieferung *f.* **(-, -en)** delivery.
abliegen *v.i.st.* *(s)* to be at a distance.
ablocken *v.t.* to get by coaxing.
ablöschen *v.t.* to wipe.
ablösen *v.t.* to loosen; to take off; to detach; (*die Wache*) to relieve; ~ *v.r.* to peel off; to alternate.
Ablösung *f.* **(-, -en)** loosening; redemption; relief.
abluchsen *v.t.* (*fam.*) *jm. etw.* ~, to get sth. out of sb.
abmachen *v.t.* to undo, to loosen; to arrange, to stipulate.
Abmachung *f.* **(-, -en)** arrangement, stipulation.
abmagern *v.i.* *(s)* to fall away, to grow lean, thin.

Abmagerungskur *f.* **(-, -en)** weight-loss diet.
abmähen *v.t.* to mow.
abmalen *v.t.* to paint, to portay; to depict.
Abmarsch *m.* **(-[e]s, -märsche)** (*mil.*) marching off.
abmarschieren *v.i.* *(s)* to march off.
abmartern *v.t.* to torture; to vex; to worry.
abmatten *v.t.* to fatigue, to tire out.
abmelden *v.t.* & *v.r.* to give notice, to report a person's departure; to cancel.
abmessen *v.t.st.* to measure, to survey.
Abmessung *f.* **(-, -en)** measurement; proportion, dimension.
abmontieren *v.t.* (*mech.*) to dismantle.
abmühen *v.r.* to exert oneself; to struggle.
abmurksen *f.* (*fam.*) to do sb. in.
abnabeln *v.t.* to cut the umbilical cord.
abnagen *v.t.* to gnaw, to nibble.
Abnäher *m.* **(-s, 0)** tuck.
Abnahme *f.* **(-, -n)** decrease; (*einer Maschine*) acceptance.
abnehmen *v.t.st.* to take off *or* away; ~ *v.i.ir.* to decrease, to diminish; to lose weight.
Abnehmer *m.* **(-s, -)** buyer.
Abneigung *f.* **(-, -en)** disinclination, aversion, dislike.
abnorm *a.* abnormal.
Abnormität *f.* **(-, -en)** abnormality, monstrosity.
abnötigen *v.t.* to force (from), to extort (from).
abnungslos *a.* unsuspecting.
abnutzen *v.t.* to wear out; ~ *v.r.* to wear off.
Abnutzung *f.* **(-, -en)** wear and tear.
Abo. *Abonnement*, subscription.
Abonnement *n.* **(-s, -s)** subscription; season ticket; *Jahres* ~, annual subscription; *Monats* ~, monthly subscription; *ein* ~ *aufgeben*, to discontinue a subscription.
Abonnent *m.* **(-en, -en)** subscriber.
abonnieren *v.t.* to subscribe to.
abordnen *v.t.* to delegate; (*mil.*) to detail.
Abordnung *f.* **(-, -en)** delegacy, delegation, deputation.
Abort *m.* **(-[e]s, -e)** lavatory; toilet; miscarriage.
abpachten *v.t.* to rent, to farm.
abpacken *v.t.* to pack, to wrap.
abpassen *v.t.* to watch for; to choose a fitting time, to time.
abpausen *v.t.* to trace.
abpfeifen *v.t.st.* (*sp.*) to blow the whistle in order to stop the game.
Abpfiff *m.* **(-[e]s, -e)** (*sp.*) final whistle.
abpflücken *v.t.* to pluck off; to pick.
abplacken, abplagen *v.r.* to tire oneself out, to drudge.
abplatten *v.t.* to flatten.
abplatzen *v.i.* to flake off.
abprallen *v.i.* *(s)* to rebound; to bounce off; to ricochet.
abpumpen *v.t.* to pump out; to extract (milk).
abputzen *v.t.* to clean, to polish.
abquälen *v.t.* to torment, to worry.
abrackern *v.r.* to slave, to toil.
abraten *v.t.st.* to dissuade (from), to warn (against).
abräumen *v.t.* to clear, to take away, to remove.
abrauschen *v.i.* (*fam.*) to rush off.
abreagieren *v.t.* to work off; ~ *v.r.* (*fam.*) to let off steam.
abrechnen *v.t.* to deduct; ~ *v.i.* to settle (accounts).
Abrechnung *f.* **(-, -en)** settlement; *auf* ~, on account.
Abrechnungstag *m.* (*Börse*) settling day.
Abrede *f.* **(-, -n)** agreement; *in* ~ *stellen*, to deny, to dispute.
abreiben *v.t.st.* to rub off, to rub down; to grind (colors).
Abreise *f.* **(-, -n)** departure.
abreisen *v.i.* *(s)* to depart, to set out, to start.
abreißen *v.t.st.* to tear off; (*Häuser*) to pull down; ~ *v.i.st.* to break off, to snap off.
abrichten *v.t.* (*Pferd*) to break (in); (*Hund*) to train.
abriegeln *v.t.* to bolt.
abringen *v.t.st.* to twist off; (*fig.*) to wrest (sth.) from.
abrinnen *v.i.st.* *(s)* to flow down.
Abriß *m.* **(-risses, -risse)** sketch, abstract; demolition.
abrollen *v.i.* *(s)* to roll off; ~ *v.t.* to unroll.
abrücken *v.t.* & *i.* to move away, to move off.
Abruf *m.* **(-[e]s, -e)** recall; (*com.*) *auf* ~, on call.
abrufen *v.t.st.* to call away or off.
abrunden *v.t.* (*Zahlen*) to correct, to round off.
abrupfen *v.t.* to pluck off.
abrupt *a.* & *adv.* abrupt, abruptly.
abrüsten *v.t.* to disarm.
Abrüstung *f.* **(-, -en),** disarmament.
abrutschen *v.i.* to glide down, to slip.
Abs. *Absatz*, paragraph, par.; *Absender*, sender.
Absage *f.* **(-, -n)** refusal.
absagen *v.t.* & *i.* to cancel (one's engagement).
absägen *v.t.* to saw off.
absahnen *v.t.* (*fam.*) to skim.
absatteln *v.t.* to unsaddle.
Absatz *m.* **(-es, -sätze)** (*Treppen*~) landing; (*Waren*~) sale, market; (*Stiefel*~) heel; (*im Druck*) paragraph; *schnellen* ~ *finden*, to sell quickly.
Absatzbewegung *f.* (*mil.*) disengagement.
Absatzgenossenschaft *f.* marketing association.
Absatzmarkt *m.* outlet, market.
absaugen *v.t.* to suck off, to vacuum.
abschaben *v.t.* to scrape off.
abschaffen *v.t.* to abolish, to remove.
Abschaffung *f.* **(-, -en)** abolition.
abschälen *v.t.* to peel, to pare.
abschalten *v.t.* to turn off.
abschatten *v.t.* to shade.
abschätzen *v.t.* to value; to assess, to estimate.
Abschätzung *f.* **(-, -en)** estimate, valuation.
Abschaum *m.* **(-[e]s, -schäume)** scum; dross; (*fig.*) *pl.* dregs.
abschäumen *v.t.* to scum, to skim.
abscheiden *v.t.st.* to secrete; ~ *v.i.* *(s)* to die.
Abscheu *m.* **(-[e]s, 0)** abhorrence, horror.
abscheuern *v.t.* to scrub off.
abscheulich *a.* abominable, detestable.
abschicken *v.t.* to send off, to dispatch.
abschieben *v.t.st.* to shove off; (*fam.*) to move off; to deport.
Abschiebung *f.* **(-, -en)** (*jur.*) deportation.
Abschied *m.* **(-[e]s, -e)** discharge; departure, leave; ~ *nehmen*, to bid farewell, to take leave; *einem den* ~ *geben*, to dismiss someone; *seinen* ~ *nehmen*, to resign.
Abschiedsgesuch *n.* resignation.
abschießen *v.t.st.* to shoot off; to fire, to discharge; (*avi.*) to shoot down.

abschinden *v.t.st.* to flay, to skin; ~ *v.r.* to tire oneself to death.
abschirmen *v.t.* to shield; to screen off.
abschirren *v.t.* to unharness.
abschlachten *v.t.* to slaughter, to butcher.
abschlaffen *v.i.* (*fam.*) to wilt; to sag.
Abschlag *m.* **(-[e]s, -schläge)** (*im Preise*) decline; *auf* ~, on account, in partial payment.
abschlagen *v.t.st.* to refuse, to deny; (*den Feind*) to repel; (*sein Wasser*) to make water.
abschlägig *a.* negative; ~*e Antwort f.* refusal, denial.
Abschlagszahlung *f.* payment on account.
abschleifen *v.t.st.* to grind off, to polish, to sand.
Abschleppdienst *m.* **(-[e]s, -e)** towing service.
abschleppen *v.t.* to tow away; to drag off; ~ *v.r.* to exert oneself in carrying.
abschließen *v.t.st.* to close, to lock; (*einen Handel*) to conclude (*or* strike) a bargain.
abschließend *a.* definitive, final.
Abschluß *m.* **(-schlusses, -schlüsse)** close, settlement, conclusion.
Abschlußprüfung *f.* **(-, -en)** final exam.
Abschlußzeugnis *n.* **(-ses, -se)** diploma.
abschmecken *v.t.* to taste; to season.
abschmieren *v.t.* to grease, (*fam.*) to copy from.
abschminken *v.t.* to remove makeup; (*fam.*) *das kannst du dir* ~, forget it.
abschnallen *v.t.* to unbuckle.
abschneiden *v.t.st.* to cut off, to clip; to pare; ~ *v.i.* to take a short cut; *gut* ~, to come off well.
abschnellen *v.t.* to let fly suddenly; ~ *v.i. (s)* to fly off suddenly.
Abschnitt *m.* **(-[e]s, -e)** cut; section; division; chapter, part, (*geom.*) segment.
abschnittweise *adv.* in paragraphs, piece by piece.
abschnüren *v.t.* to cut off.
abschöpfen *v.t.* to skim.
abschrägen *v.t.* (*mech.*) to bevel.
abschrauben *v.t.* to unscrew.
abschrecken *v.t.* to frighten, to deter.
Abschreckung *f.* **(-, -en)** deterrence.
Abschreckungsmittel *n.* **(-s, -)** deterrent, determent.
abschreiben *v.t.* to transcribe, to copy; to write off; ~ *v.t.* to cancel an engagement in writing.
Abschreibung *f.* **(-en)** amortization.
abschreiten *v.t.st.* to measure by steps; (*mil.*) to review.
Abschrift *f.* **(-, -en)** copy, transcript; *die Richtigkeit der* ~ *wird bezeugt*, certified true copy.
abschriftlich *adv.* in a copy.
abschrubben *v.t.* to scrub off.
abschuppen *v.t.* to scale.
abschürfen *v.t.* to graze; to chafe.
Abschuß *m.* **(-sses, -schüsse)** shooting; discharge, launching; ~ *rampe f.* **(-, -n)** launching pad.
abschüssig *a.* steep, precipitous.
abschütteln *v.t.* to shake off.
abschwächen *v.t.* to weaken.
abschwatzen *v.t.* to talk out of.
abschweifen *v.i. (s)* to stray; to digress.
Abschweifung *f.* **(-, -en)** digression.
abschwellen *v.t.* (*med.*) to go down; (*Lärm*) to die down.
abschwenken *v.i. (s)* to wheel, to turn aside.
abschwindeln *v.t.* to swindle out of.
abschwören *v.t.st.* to abjure, to forswear.
Abschwung *m.* **(-s, -schwünge)** downward trend; (*sp.*) dismount.
absegeln *v.i. (s)* to set sail, to put out to sea.
absehbar *a.* within sight, foreseeable.
absehen *v.t.st.* to predict, to foresee; to learn by observation; ~ *auf*, to aim at; ~ *von*, to disregard.
abseifen *v.t.* to soap down.
abseilen *v.t.* to lower with a rope.
abseits *adv.* aside, apart.
Abseits *n.* **(-, -)** (*sp.*) offside.
absenden *v.t.ir.* to send away, to dispatch.
Absender *m.* **(-s, -)** sender, consignor.
Absendung *f.* **(-, -en)** sending, dispatch.
abservieren *v.i.* to clear away; (*fam.*) to throw out.
absetzbar *a.* deductible.
absetzen *v.t.* to depose; to dismiss; to remove; (*Waren*) to sell; ~ *v.r.* (*mil.*) to disengage.
Absetzung *f.* **(-, -en)** removal, deposition.
absichern *v.t.* to make safe; (*comp.*) to save.
Absicht *f.* **(-, -en)** view, intention, purpose; *mit der* ~, with a view (to).
absichtlich *a.* intentional, deliberate, ~ *adv.* on purpose.
absichtslos *adv.* unintentionally.
absingen *v.t.st.* to sing, to chant.
absinken *v.i.st.* to sink; (*fig.*) to decline.
absitzen *v.i.st. (s)* to dismount, ~ *v.t.* to sit out (a given time).
absolut *a.* absolute, positive; ~ *adv.* absolutely, perfectly.
Absolution *f.* **(-, -en)** (*rel.*) absolution.
Absolutismus *m.* **(-, 0)** absolutism.
absolvieren *v.t.* (*Schule*) to graduate from.
absonderlich *a.* particular; singular, odd.
absondern *v.t.* to separate; to set apart; (*med.*) to secrete; ~ *v.r.* to seclude oneself, to withdraw; to dissolve a partnership.
Absonderung *f.* **(-, -en)** separation; seclusion, retirement; (*med.*) secretion.
absorbieren *v.t.* to absorb.
abspalten *v.t.* to split off.
abspannen *v.t.* (horse) to unharness.
Abspannung *f.* **(-, 0)** fatigue.
absparen *v.t. sich* ~, to pinch oneself.
abspeisen *v.t.* to feed; (*fig.*) to put off, to palm off.
abspenstig *a.* ~ *machen*, to alienate; ~ *werden*, to fall off.
absperren *v.t.* to shut off, to cut off; to block; *polizeilich* ~, to cordon off.
Absperrung *f.* **(-, -en)** isolation; blockage, closure, barrier.
abspielen *v.refl.* to play; to take place, to come off; to pass.
absplittern *v.t.* to splinter; ~ *v.i.* to come off in splinters.
Absprache *f.* **(-, -n)** agreement, arrangement.
absprechen *v.t.* to deny; ~ *v.i.* to criticize rashly; ~ *v.r.* to come to an agreement.
abspringen *v.i.st. (s)* to leap off, to jump off; to rebound; (*fig.*) to shift, to digress.
Absprung *m.* **(-[e]s, -sprünge)** (downward) leap, jump; (*sp.*) takeoff.
abspulen *v.t.* to wind off, to unwind.
abspülen *v.t.* to wash up.
abstammen *v.i. (s)* to descend; to be derived from.
Abstammung *f.* **(-, -en)** descent; derivation.

Abstammungslehre *f.* **(-, -n)** theory of evolution.
Abstand *m.* **(-[e]s, -stände)** distance; interval; compensation; ~ *nehmen,* to desist from.
abstatten *v.t.* to render; (*Besuch*) to pay a visit.
abstauben *v.t.* to dust.
abstechen *v.t.st.* to stab; to kill; ~ *v.i. (h, s)* to contrast (with).
Abstecher *m.* **(-s, -)** excursion, trip.
abstecken *v.t.* to mark out, to plot (the course); to define.
abstehen *v.i.st.* to stick out; to give up; (*schal werden*) to get stale.
Absteige *f.* **(-, -n)** flophouse.
absteigen *v.i.st. (s)* to get off; (*Hotel*) to put up at, to stop at.
Absteiger *m.* **(-s, -)** (s) relegated team.
abstellen *v.t.* to stop (*machine*); to turn off (*gas*); to put; to park.
abstempeln *v.t.* to stamp; (*fig.*) to label.
absterben *v.i.st. (s)* to die away, out; (*med.*) to mortify; to fade; to go numb.
Absterben *n.* **(-s, 0)** death, demise, decrease.
Abstieg *m.* **(-[e]s, -e)** descent; decline; (*sp.*) relegation.
abstillen *v.t.* to wean.
abstimmen *v.i.* to vote, to coordinate; ~ *lassen über etw.,* to put sth. to the vote; ~ *v.t.* to tune.
Abstimmung *f.* **(-, -en)** voting, ballot.
abstinent *a.* abstinent.
Abstinenz *f.* total abstinence.
Abstinenzler *m.* **(-s, -)** total abstainer, nondrinker.
abstoppen *v.t.* to stop; (*sp.*) to time.
abstoßen *v.t.st.* to thrust off; (*fig.*) to repel; to reject.
abstoßend *a.* revolting, repulsive.
Abstoßung *f.* **(-, -en)** repulsion.
abstottern *v.t.* (*fam.*) to pay in installments.
abstrahieren *v.t.* to abstract.
abstrakt *a.* abstract; *adv.* abstractly.
abstreifen *v.t.* to strip off, to slip off.
abstreiten *v.t.st.* to dispute, to deny.
Abstrich *m.* **(-[e]s, -e)** deduction; (*med.*) smear; (*mus.*) down-bow.
abstufen *v.t.* to grade, to gradate.
Abstufung *f.* **(-, en)** gradation.
abstumpfen *v.t.* to blunt; to deaden; ~ *v.r.* to grow blunt or dull.
Absturz *m.* **(-es, -stürze)** precipice; (*avi.*) crash.
abstürzen *v.i.* to fall; (*avi.*) to crash.
abstützen *v.t.* to support.
absuchen *v.t.* to search, to comb, to screen.
Absud *m.* **(-[e]s, -e)** decoction.
absurd *a.* absurd; ~ *adv.* absurdly.
Abt *m.* **(-[e]s, Äbte)** abbot.
Abt. *Abteilung,* department, dept.
abtakeln *v.t.* to lay up, dismantle.
abtasten *v.t.* to feel; to palpate.
abtauen *v.t. & i.* to melt away, to thaw, to defrost.
Abtei *f.* **(-, -en)** abbey.
Abteil *n.* or *m.* **(-es, -e)** compartment.
abteilen *v.t.* to divide; to partition off.
Abteilung *f.* **(-, -en)** division; partition; compartment; department; (*Soldaten*) detachment.
abtippen *v.t.* (*fam.*) to type out.
Äbtissin *f.* **(-, -nen)** abbess.
abtönen *v.t.* (*Farbe, Ton*) to shade.
abtöten *v.t.* to mortify; to destroy; to deaden.
abtragen *v.t.st.* (*Kleider*) to wear out; (*Gebäude*) to demolish, to pull down; (*Hügel*) to level; (*Schuld*) to pay; *den Tisch* ~, to clear away.
abträglich *a.* detrimental, derogatory.
abtrainieren *v.t.* to work off.
Abtransport *m.* **(-s, -e)** transport, removal.
abtransportieren *v.t.* to take away; to dispatch; to remove.
abtreiben *v.t.st.* to drive off; (*med.*) to abort; ~ *v.i.* to drift off.
Abtreibung *f.* **(-, -en)** abortion.
abtrennen *v.t.* to separate; to detach; to sever.
abtreten *v.t.st.* to cede, to make over; ~ *v.i. (s)* to retire.
Abtretung *f.* **(-, -en)** abdication, cession.
Abtritt *m.* **(-[e]s, -s)** exit; (*Abort*) toilet, urinal.
abtrocknen *v.t.* to dry.
abtröpfeln *v.i. (s)* to drip off.
abtropfen *v.i.* to drip off.
abtrotzen *v.t. jm. etw.* ~, to bully sth. out of sb.
abtrünnig *a.* renegade, rebellious, apostate.
Abtrünnig(er) *m.* **(-n, -n)** deserter, renegade.
abtun *v.t.st.* to take off; to dismiss; to settle, to finish; to kill.
abtupfen *v.t.* to dab.
aburteilen *v.i.* to criticize harshly.
abverlangen *v.t.* to demand.
abwägen *v.t.st.* to weigh, to weigh out.
abwählen *v.t.* to vote out.
abwälzen *v.t.* to shift; (*Schuld*) to exculpate.
abwandeln *v.t.* to adapt, to modify; (*gram.*) to decline, to conjugate.
Abwandlung *f.* **(-, -en)** modification; (*gram.*) declension, conjugation.
abwarten *v.t.* to await, to wait for.
abwärts *adv.* downward.
abwärtsgehen *v.i.st.* to get worse.
Abwärtstrend *m.* **(-s, -s)** downward trend.
Abwasch *m.* **(-s, 0)** dishes to be washed.
abwaschbar *a.* washable.
abwaschen *v.t.st.* to wash off.
Abwasser *n.* **(-s, -wässer)** waste water, sewage.
abwechseln *v.t.* to alternate; to vary; ~ *v.i.* to come *or* go by turns.
abwechselnd *a. & adv.* alternate; by turns, in rotation.
Abwechslung *f.* **(-, -en)** change; variation; *zur* ~, for a change.
abwechslungsreich *a.* varied; eventful.
Abweg *m.* **(-e[s], -e)** wrong way; *auf ~e geraten,* to go astray.
abwegig *a.* erroneous.
Abwehr *f.* **(-, 0)** defense; (*mil.*) counterintelligence; hostility.
abwehren *v.t.* to ward off; to avert.
Abwehrhaltung *f.* **(-, -en)** (*psych.*) defensiveness.
Abwehrkräfte *pl.* **(-)** (*med.*) resistance.
Abwehrmechanismus *m.* **(-, -en)** defense mechanism.
Abwehrreaktion *f.* **(-, -en)** defensive reaction.
Abwehrspieler *m.* **(-s, -)** (*sp.*) defender, defense.
Abwehrstoffe *pl.* **(-)** (*med.*) antibodies.
abweichen *v.i.st. (s)* to deviate, to differ.
abweichend *a.* anomalous, different, divergent; *~e Meinung,* (*jur.*) dissenting opinion.
Abweichler *m.* **(-s, -)** deviationist.
Abweichung *f.* **(-, -en)** deviation; deflection; divergence; *zugelassene* ~ (*mech.*) tolerance.
abweisen *v.t.st.* to turn away; to refuse; to reject; to dismiss; to repel.

Abweisung *f.* **(-, -en)** refusal, rejection; (*jur.*) nonsuit.

abwelken *v.i.* *(s)* to wither, to fade away.

abwenden *v.t.ir.* to turn away; to prevent; to avert; ~ *v.r.ir.* to turn away, to abandon.

abwerfen *v.t.st.* to drop, to throw off, to cast off; (*Gewinn*) to yield a profit; (*Bomben*) to release.

abwerten *v.t.* to devalue.

abwertend *a.* derogatory.

Abwertung *f.* **(-, -en)** devaluation.

abwesend *a.* absent; ~ *ohne Urlaub,* (*mil.*) absent without leave.

Abwesender *m.* absentee.

Abwesenheit *f.* **(-, -en)** absence.

abwetzen *v.t.* to wear off; to rub off.

abwickeln *v.t.* to unwind; to do (business).

Abwicklung *f.* **(-, -en)** handling.

abwiegeln *v.t.* to calm down (crowd); ~ *v.i.* (*pej.*) to appease.

abwiegen *v.t.st.* to weigh out.

abwimmeln *v.t.* to get rid of.

abwinken *v.i.* to wave off; to refuse.

abwirtschaften *v.i.* to become run down.

abwischen *v.t.* to wipe (off).

abwracken *v.t.* to break up, to scrap.

Abwurf *m.* **(-[e]s, -würfe)** (*avi.*) (*Bomben*) release.

abwürgen *v.t.* to strangle; to stall.

abzahlen *v.t.* to pay off.

abzählen *v.t.* to tell; to count out.

Abzahlung *f.* **(-, -en)** installment.

abzapfen *v.t.* to tap; *Blut* ~, to draw blood.

abzäumen, *v.t.* to unbridle.

Abzeichen *n.* **(-s, -n)** badge; ~ *pl.* insignia.

abzeichnen *v.t.* to mark (out); to draw; to copy a drawing.

Abziehbild *n.* **(-[e]s, -er)** sticker.

abziehen *v.t.st.* to pull off; to distill; to deduct; to subtract; (*phot.*) to print; (*die Aufmerksamkeit*) to divert; to sharpen; to skin; ~ *v.i.st.* *(s)* to march off.

abzielen *v.i.* to aim at.

abzirkeln *v.t.* to measure with compasses.

Abzug *m.* **(-[e]s, -züge)** departure; discount, deduction; (*phot.*) print; (*typ.*) proof.

abzüglich *pr.* (*com.*) less, deducting.

abzugsfähig *a.* deductible.

Abzugsgraben *m.* drain, conduit.

abzwacken *v.t.* to pinch off.

abzweigen *v.i.* *(s)* to branch off; ~ *v.r.* to branch off, to turn off.

Abzweigung *f.* **(-, -en)** turnoff.

abzwicken *v.t.* to nip off.

abzwingen *v.t.st.* to extort (from).

ach! *i.* alas! ah!

a.Ch. *ante Christum,* before Christ, B.C.

Achat *m.* **(-[e]s, -e)** agate.

Achse *f.* **(-, -n)** axle, axletree; axis.

Achsel *f.* **(-, -n)** shoulder; *die ~n zucken,* to shrug one's shoulders.

Achselhöhle *f.* armpit.

Achselklappe *f.* shoulder strap.

Achselzucken *n.* **(-s, 0)** shrug.

acht *a.* eight; ~ *Tage,* a week.

Acht *f.* **(-, 0)** ban, outlawry; attention, care; *sich in ~ nehmen,* to be careful; ~ *geben,* to pay attention.

achtbar *a.* respectable.

achteckig *a.* octagonal.

Achtel *n.* **(-s, -)** eighth part, eighth.

Achtelnote *f.* eighth note.

achten *v.t.& i.* to mind; to attend to; to consider; to esteem.

ächten *v.t.* to outlaw, to proscribe.

achtenswert *a.* estimable.

Achterdeck *n.* (*nav.*) quarterdeck.

achtern *adv.* aft.

achtfach *a.* eightfold.

achtgeben *v.i.st.* to take care; to pay attention.

achtlos *a.* careless, negligent.

achtsam *a.* attentive, mindful.

Achtstundentag *m.* eight-hour day.

achttägig *a.* for eight days; weekly.

Achtung *f.* **(-, 0)** attention; esteem, regard.

Ächtung *f.* **(-, -en)** ostracism, proscription, ban.

achtungswert *a.* estimable, respectable.

achtzehn *a.* eighteen.

achtzig *a.* eighty.

Achtziger *m.* **(-s, -)** octogenarian.

ächzen *v.i.* to groan.

Acker *m.* **(-s, -Äcker)** field, soil.

Ackerbau *m.* farming, agriculture.

Ackerland *n.* arable land.

ackern *v.t.* to plow, to till; (*fam.*) to work hard.

a.D. *außer Dienst,* retired.

adäquat *a.* appropriate, adequate, suitable.

addieren *v.t.* to sum up, to add up.

Addition *f.* **(-, -en)** addition; **~szeichen** *n.* plus sign.

ade! *i.* adieu! good-bye! farewell!

Adel *m.* **(-s, 0)** nobility, peerage; (*fig.*) nobleness.

adelig *a.* titled.

adeln *v.t.* (*fig.*) to ennoble, to give sb. a title.

Ader *f.* **(-, -n)** vein; artery; grain, streak; *zur ~ lassen,* to bleed.

Aderlaß *m.* **(-lasses, -lässe)** bleeding, bloodletting, phlebotomy.

adieu *adv.* adieu; ~ *sagen,* to bid farewell

Adjektiv *n.* **(-s, -e)** adjective.

Adjutant *m.* **(-en, -en)** adjutant, aide-de-camp.

a.d.L. *an der Lahn,* on the Lahn.

Adler *m.* **(-s, -)** eagle.

Adlernase *f.* aquiline *or* hooked nose.

adlig *a.* noble; *die Adligen, m.pl.* the nobles, the nobility.

Admiral *m.* **(-[e]s, -e)** admiral.

Admiralität *f.* **(-, -en)** Board of Admiralty.

a.d.O. *an der Oder,* on the Oder.

adoptieren *v.t.* to adopt.

Adoptivkind *n.* **(-[e]s, -er)** adopted child.

Adr. *Adresse,* address.

Adressat *m.* **(-en, -en)** addressee.

Adreßbuch *n.* **(-[e]s, -bücher)** directory.

Adresse *f.* **(-, -n)** address, direction; *per ~,* care of (c/o).

adressieren *v.t.* to address, to direct.

adrett *a.* smart.

Adria *f.* Adriatic.

a.d.S. *an der Saale,* on the Saale.

Adverb *n.* **(-s, -ien)** adverb.

Advokat *m.* **(-en, -en)** lawyer, counsel.

Aerodynamik *f.* **(-, 0)** aerodynamics.

Affäre *f.* **(-, -n)** affair.

Affe *m.* **(-n, -n)** ape, monkey.

Affekt *m.* **(-s, -e)** passion; affection; *im ~,* in the heat of the moment.

Affekthandlung *f.* **(-, -en)** emotive act.

affektieren *v.t.* to affect.

affektiert *a.* (*pej.*) affected.

Affenliebe *f.* blind love.
Affenschande *f.* **(-, 0)** great shame.
Äffin *f.* **(-, -nen)** female ape.
affizieren *v.t.* to affect, to influence.
Afghane *m.* **(-n, -n); Afghanin** *f.* **(-, -nen); afghanisch** *a.* Afghan; **Afghanistan** *n.* **(-s)** Afghanistan.
Afrika *n.* **(-s,)** Africa; **Afrikaner** *(m.)* **(-s, -); Afrikanerin** *f.* **(-, -nen); afrikanisch** *a.* African.
After *m.* **(-s, -)** anus.
A.G. *Aktien-Gesellschaft,* stock corporation.
Ägäis *f.* Aegean.
Agent *m.* **(-en, -en), Agentin** *f.* **(-, -nen)** representative, agent.
Agentur *f.* **(-, -en)** agency.
Aggregat *n.* **(-s, -e)** *(tech.)* unit; set.
Aggression *f.* **(-, -en)** aggression.
Aggressionstrieb *m.* **(-s, -e)** aggressive impulse.
aggressiv *a.* aggressive.
Aggressivität *f.* **(-, -en)** aggressiveness.
Aggressor *m.* **(-s, -en)** aggressor.
Ägide *f.* **(-, 0)** aegis; *pl.* auspices.
agieren *v.i.* to act.
Agio *n.* **(-s, 0)** agio, premium.
Agitation *f.* **(-, -en)** agitation.
agitieren *v.i.* to agitate.
Agonie *f.* **(-, -n)** agony.
Agraffe *f.* **(-, -n)** clasp, brooch.
Agrarland *n.* **(-es, -länder)** agrarian country.
Agrarpolitik *f.* **(-, 0)** agricultural policy.
Agronom *m.* **(-en, -en)** agronomist.
Ägypten *n.* **(-s)** Egypt; **Ägypter** *m.* **(-s, -); Ägypterin** *f.* **(-, -en); ägyptisch** *a.* Egyptian.
ah! *i.* ah! ha!
ahd. *althochdeutsch,* Old High German, O.H.G.
Ahle *f.* **(-, -n)** awl.
Ahn *m.* **(-s, -en)** ancestor, forefather.
ahnden *v.t.* to punish; to avenge.
Ahne *f.* **(-, -n)** ancestress.
ähneln *v.i.* to resemble.
ahnen *v.i.* to have a presentiment or premonition.
Ahnherr *m.* ancestor.
ähnlich *a.* resembling, similar, alike.
Ähnlichkeit *f.* **(-, -en)** resemblance, likeness.
Ahnung *f.* **(-, -en)** premonition, foreboding, presentiment, suspicion, inkling; *keine* ~, not the slightest idea.
ahnungsvoll *a.* ominous, awe-inspiring.
Ahorn *m.* **(-s, -e)** maple.
Ähre *f.* **(-, -n)** *(bot.)* ear; head; *~n lesen,* to glean.
Aids *n.* **(-, 0)** AIDS.
Akademie *f.* **(-, -en)** academy.
Akademiker *m.* **(-s, -); Akademikerin** *f.* **(-, -nen)** university graduate, academician.
akademisch *a.* academic.
Akazie *f.* **(-, -n)** acacia.
Akklamation *f.* **(-, -en)** acclamation.
akklimatisieren *v.t.* to acclimatize.
Akkord *m.* **(-[e]s, -e)** *(mus.)* chord; accord, contract, agreement.
Akkordarbeit *f.* piecework; *im Akkord arbeiten,* to do piecework.
Akkordlohn *m.* piece(work) rates.
akkreditieren *v.t.* to accredit.
Akkreditierung *f.* **(-, -en)** accreditation.
Akkumulator *m.* **(-s, -en)** accumulator, storage battery; battery.
akkurat *a.* precise; meticulous; neat.
Akkusativ *m.* **(-s, -e)** accusative.
Akne *f.* **(-, -n)** acne.
Akquisiteur *m.* **(-s, -e)** agent, canvasser.
Akribie *f.* **(-, 0)** meticulousness.
Akrobat *m.* **(-s, -en); Akrobatin** *f.* **(-, -nen)** acrobat.
Akrobatik *f.* **(-, 0)** acrobatics.
akrobatisch *a.* acrobatic.
Akt *m.* **(-[e]s, -e)** act; deed; *(art)* the nude.
Akte *f.* **(-, -n)** file.
Akten *pl.* acts, deeds, instruments, official documents, dossier.
Aktendeckel *m.* file; folder.
Aktenklammer *f.* paper clip.
Aktenstück *n.* document.
Aktentasche *f.* briefcase.
Aktenzeichen *n.* file number, reference number.
Aktie *f.* **(-, -n)** share, stock.
Aktiengesellschaft *f.* joint-stock company.
Aktienkapital *n.* share capital.
Aktion *f.* **(-, -en)** drive, project.
Aktionar *m.* **(-[e]s, -e)** shareholder.
aktiv *a.* active; *~er Teilhaber* *(com.)* working partner.
Aktiv *n.* **(-s, -e)** *(gram.)* active voice.
Aktiva *n. pl.* assets.
aktualisieren *v.t.* to update.
Aktualität *f.* **(-, -en)** relevance (to the present).
aktuell *a.* current.
Akupunktur *f.* **(-, -en)** acupuncture.
Akustik *f.* **(-, 0)** acoustics, *pl.*
akustisch *a.* acoustic.
akut *a.* acute; urgent.
AKW *Atomkraftwerk,* nuclear power plant.
Akzent *m.* **(-s, -e)** stress, accent.
akzentuieren *v.t.* to stress, to accentuate.
Akzept *n.* **(-[e]s, -e)** *(com.)* acceptance.
akzeptabel *a.* acceptable.
akzeptieren *v.t.* to accept, to honor.
Alabaster *m.* **(-s, 0)** alabaster.
Alarm *m.* **(-s, 0)** alarm.
alarmieren *v.t.* to sound the alarm.
Alaun *m.* **(-[e]s, -e)** alum.
Albaner *m.* **(-s, -,); Albanerin** *f.* **(-, -en); albanisch** *a.* Albanian; **Albanien** *n.* **(-s, 0)** Albania.
albern *a.* silly, foolish.
Alchimie *f.* **(-, 0)** alchemy.
Alexandriner *m.* **(-s, -)** *(poet.)* Alexandrine.
Alge *f.* **(-, -n)** seaweed.
Algebra *f.* **(-, 0)** algebra.
Algerien *n.* **(-s, 0)** Algeria; **Algerier** *(m.)* **(-s, -); Algerierin** *f.* **(-, -nen); algerisch** *a.* Algerian.
Alibi *n.* *(jur.)* alibi; *sein ~ nachweisen,* to prove one's alibi.
Alimente *n.pl.* alimony; *(Scheidungs-) ~*, separation allowance.
alkalisch *a.* alkaline.
Alkohol *m.* **(-s, -e)** alcohol.
alkoholfrei *a.* nonalcoholic.
Alkoholika *pl.* alcoholic beverages.
Alkoholiker *m.* **(-s, -); Alkoholikerin** *f.* **(-, -nen)** alcoholic.
alkoholisch *a.* alcoholic.
alkoholisieren *v.t.* alcoholize.
Alkoholismus *m.* **(-, 0)** alcoholism.
Alkoven *m.* **(-s, -)** alcove; recess.
All *n.* **(-s, 0)** space; universe.
allbekannt *a.* notorious.
alle *adv.* *~ sein,* to be gone, to be spent.
Allee *f.* **(-, -[e]n)** avenue.

Allegorie *f.* **(-, -[e]n)** allegory.
allein *a.* single; alone; ~ *c.* only, but.
Alleinerziehende *m.f.* **(-n, -n)** single parent.
Alleingang *m.* **(-s, -gänge)** solo; single-handed action.
Alleinherrschaft *f.* **(-, -en)** autocracy.
alleinig *a.* sole, exclusive.
Alleinsein *n.* **(-s, 0)** loneliness.
alleinstehend *a.* detached, isolated; single, unmarried.
Alleinunterhalter *m.* **(-s, -)** solo entertainer.
Alleinvertreter *m.* sole agent.
allemal *adv.* always, every time; *ein für ~*, once and for all.
allenfalls *adv.* at most, if need be; perhaps.
allenthalben *adv.* everywhere.
all(er), alle, alles *a.* all; whole; every.
alleräußerst *a.* farthest, worst.
allerdings *adv.* indeed, to be sure, however, I admit.
allererst, zu allererst *adv.* first of all.
Allergie *f.* **(-, -n)** allergy.
allergisch *a.* allergic.
allerhand *a.* of all kinds.
Allerheiligen(fest) *f.* **(-festes, -feste)** Allhallows, All Saints' Day.
allerlei *a.* of all kinds.
allerletzt *a.* last of all.
allerliebst *a.* charming, exquisite.
allermeist *a.* & *adv.* most, most of all; chiefly, mostly.
Allerseelentag *m.* All Souls' Day.
allerseits *adv.* on every side, everywhere.
allerwärts *adv.* everywhere.
Allerweltskerl *m.* **(-s, -e)** jack-of-all-trades.
allerwenigst *a.* least.
allesamt *adv.* one and all.
Allesfresser *m.* **(-s, -)** omnivore.
Alleskleber *m.* **(-s, -)** all-purpose glue.
Alleskönner *m.* **(-s, -)** person of many talents.
allezeit *adv.* always; (at) any time.
allg. *allgemein,* general, gen.
Allgegenwart *f.* **(-, 0)** omnipresence.
allgegenwärtig *a.* omnipresent, ubiquitous.
allgemein *a.* universal, general, common; *im ~en,* in general; ~ *adv.* generally.
Allgemeinbegriff *m.* **(-s, -e)** general notion.
Allgemeinbesitz *m.* **(-es, 0)** common property.
Allgemeinbildung *f.* **(-, 0)** all-around education.
allgemeingültig *a.* generally valid.
Allgemeinheit *f.* **(-, -en)** universality, generality; general public.
Allgemeinmedizin *f.* **(-, 0)** general medicine.
Allgemeinplatz *m.* **(-es, -plätze)** platitude, cliché.
Allgemeinwohl *n.* **(-s, 0)** public welfare.
Allgewalt *f.* **(-, 0)** omnipotence.
Allheilmittel *n.* panacea.
Allianz *f.* **(-, -en)** alliance.
alliiert *a.* allied.
Alliierte *m.* **(-n, -n)** ally.
alljährlich *a.* yearly, annual; ~ *adv.* yearly, annually.
Allmacht *f.* **(-, 0)** omnipotence.
allmächtig *a.* omnipotent, almighty.
allmählich *a.* gradual.
Allotria *pl.* tomfoolery.
Allparteienregierung *f.* **(-, -en)** multiparty government.
Allradantrieb *m.* **(-s, -e)** four-wheel drive.
allseitig *a.* in all respects; universal, versatile; ~ *adv.* on all sides.
Alltag *m.* **(-s, 0)** weekday; daily routine.
alltäglich *a.* daily; (*fig.*) trite, everyday, commonplace.
Alltagstrott *m.* **(-s, 0)** daily grind.
allwissend *a.* omniscient, all-knowing.
allzu *adv.* too, much too.
Allzweck- all-purpose.
Alm *f.* **(-, -en)** Alpine pasture.
Almanach *m.* **(-[e]s, -e)** almanac.
Almosen *n.* **(-s, -)** alms, charity.
Alp *m.* **(-[e]s, -e), Alpdrücken** *n.* nightmare, incubus.
Alpen *pl.* **(-)** Alps.
Alphabet *n.* **(-[e]s, -e)** alphabet.
alphabetisch *a.* & *adv.* alphabetic(al); ~ **anordnen** *v.t.* to aphabetize.
Alphabetisierung *f.* **(-)** alphabetization; teaching of literacy skills.
Alptraum *m.* **(-s, -träume)** nightmare.
Alraun *m.* **(-[e]s, -e), Alraune** *f.* mandrake.
als *c.* than; as; like; when; but; *sowohl ~ auch,* as well as; *~ ob,* as if.
alsbald *adv.* forthwith, directly.
alsdann *adv.* then.
also *adv.* thus, so; ~ *c.* consequently.
alt *a.* old, ancient; aged; stale.
Alt *m.* **(-[e]s, -e)** contralto; ~ *n.* **(-s, 0)** dark beer.
Altan *m.* **(-[e]s, -e)** balcony.
Altar *m.* **(-[e]s, -, Altäre)** altar.
Altarbild *n.* altarpiece.
altbacken *a.* stale; outdated.
Altbau *m.* **(-s, -ten)** old building.
Alte *m., f.* **(-n, -n) der ~,** the old man; **die ~,** the old woman; **die ~n,** the elderly; the ancients.
Altenheim *n.* **(-s, -e)** old people's home.
Altenpfleger *m.* **(-s, -)** geriatric nurse.
Altentagesstätte *f.* **(-, -n)** senior day center.
Alter *n.* **(-s, 0)** age; old age; *vor alters,* of old, in olden days.
älter *a.* elderly.
altern *v.i.* *(h, s)* to grow old, to age.
alternativ *a.* alternative.
Alternativbewegung *f.* **(-, -en)** alternative movement.
Alternative *f.* **(-, -n)** alternative.
Alterserscheinung *f.* sign of old age.
Altersgrenze *f.* age limit.
Altersheim *n.* home for the aged.
Altersklasse *f.* (*mil.*) age class, age group.
Altersrente *f.* old-age pension.
Altersschwäche *f.* decrepitude.
Altersversicherung *f.* old-age insurance.
Altertum *n.* **(-s, -tümer)** antiquity.
altertümlich *a.* old-fashioned; antique.
altertumsforschung *f.* **(-, 0)** archaeology.
Altistin *f.* **(-, -nen)** alto.
altklug *a.* precocious.
ältlich *a.* elderly, oldish.
altmodisch *a.* old-fashioned.
Altphilologie *f.* **(-, 0)** classical studies.
altruistisch *a.* altruistic.
Altstadt *f.* **(-, -städte)** old town.
Altvordern *pl.* ancestors, progenitors, forbears.
Altweibersommer *m.* Indian summer.
Aluminium *n.* **(-s, 0)** aluminum.
am = an dem.
a.M. *am Main,* on the Main.
amalgamieren *v.t.* to amalgamate.

Amazone *f.* **(-, -n)** Amazon.
Amboß *m.* **(-bosses, -bosse)** anvil.
ambulanter Kranker *m.* outpatient.
Ambulanz *f.* **(-, -en)** ambulance; outpatient department.
Ameise *f.* **(-, -n)** ant.
Ameisenhaufen *m.* anthill.
Ameisensäure *f.* formic acid.
Amerika *n.* **(-s, -s)** America; **Amerikaner** *m.* **(-s, -)**; **Amerikanerin** *f.* **(-, -nen)**; **amerikanisch** *a.* American.
Amme *f.* **(-, -n)** wet nurse.
Ammenmärchen *n.* nursery tale.
Ammer *f.* & *m.* **(-, -n)** yellow-hammer, bunting.
Ammoniak *n.* **(-s, 0)** ammonia.
Amnestie *f.* **(-, -[e]n)** amnesty.
Amor *m.* **(-, 0)** Cupid.
amortisieren *v.t.* to pay off, to redeem (a debt).
Ampel *f.* **(-, -n)** traffic light.
Ampere: ~meter *m.* (*el.*) ammeter; **~stunde** *f.* ampere-hour.
Amphibie *f.* **(-, -n)** amphibian.
Amphitheater *n.* **(-s, -)** amphitheater.
Ampulle *f.* **(-, -n)** ampule.
amputieren *v.t.* to amputate.
Amsel *f.* **(-, -n)** blackbird.
Amt *n.* **(-[e]s, Ämter)** position; charge, employment; office.
Amtfrau *f.* **(-, -en)** female senior civil servant.
amtieren *v.i.* to officiate.
amtl. *amtlich*, official, off.
amtlich *a.* official.
Amtmann *m.* **(-s, -männer)** male senior civil servant, bailiff, rural magistrate.
Amtsanmassung *f.* unauthorized assumption of authority.
Amtseid *m.* oath of office.
Amtsenthebung *f.* discharge from office.
Amtsführung *f.* administration.
Amtsgeheimnis *n.* official secret.
Amtsgericht *n.* local court.
Amtshandlung *f.* official act.
Amtsinhaber *m.* officeholder.
Amtspflicht *f.* official duty.
Amtsrichter *m.* district judge.
Amtsstunden *f.pl.* office hours.
amtswegen *adv.* *von* ~, officially, ex officio.
Amtszeit *f.* term of office.
Amulett *n.* **(-s, -e)** amulet, charm.
amüsant *a.* amusing.
amüsieren *v.t.* to amuse; *sich* ~, to enjoy oneself.
an *pr.* on, by, near, of, against, about, to, at.
Anabolikum *n.* **(-s, -lika)** anabolic steroid.
Analgesikum *n.* **(-s, -sika)** analgesic.
analog *a.* analogous.
Analogie *f.* **(-, -n)** analogy.
Analphabet *m.* **(-en, -en)** illiterate.
Analphabetentum *n.* illiteracy.
Analyse *f.* **(-, -n)** analysis.
analysieren *v.t.* to analyse.
analytisch *a.* analytical.
Anämie *f.* **(-, -n)** anemia.
Ananas *f.* **(-, -&-nasse)** pineapple.
Anarchie *f.* **(-, -n)** anarchy.
anarchistisch *a.* anarchistic.
Anästhesie *f.* **(-, -n)** anesthesia.
Anatolien *n.* **(-s, 0)** Anatolia.
Anatom *m.* **(-en, -en)** anatomist.
Anatomie *f.* **(-, -[e]n)** anatomy; dissecting room, anatomical institute.
anatomisch *a.* anatomical.
anbahnen *v.t.* to pave the way for.
Anbau *m.* **(-[e]s, -e)** cultivation, culture; extension, wing.
anbauen *v.t.* to cultivate; to add.
Anbeginn *m.* **(-s, 0)** beginning, outset.
anbehalten *v.t.st.* to keep on.
anbei *adv.* herewith, enclosed, attached.
anbeissen *v.t.* & *i.st.* to bite.
anbelangen *v.t.* *was mich anbelangt*, for my part.
anbellen *v.t.* to bark at.
anberaumen *v.t.* to appoint, to fix (a day).
anbeten *v.t.* to adore, to worship.
Anbetracht *m.* *in* ~, considering, seeing.
anbetteln *v.t.* to ask alms of, to importune.
Anbetung *f.* **(-, -en)** adoration, worship.
anbiedern *v.r.* to ingratiate oneself.
anbieten *v.t.st.* to offer.
anbinden *v.t.st.* to tie; to bind, to fasten; ~ *v.i.* (*mit einem*) to pick a quarrel; *kurz angebunden sein*, to be abrupt.
anblasen *v.t.st.* to blow at *or* on.
anbleiben *v.i.st.* to stay on.
Anblick *m.* **(-[e]s, -e)** view, aspect, sight; *beim ersten* ~, at first glance.
anblicken *v.t.* to look at.
anblinzeln *v.t.* to blink at.
anbohren *v.t.* to bore, to pierce, to drill.
anbrechen *v.t.st.* to break, to begin to cut off; ~ *v.i. (s)* to break, to begin, to appear.
anbrennen *v.i.ir.* to burn; *angebrannt schmecken*, to taste burned.
anbringen *v.t.ir.* to apply, to fix; to sell; to lodge (a complaint).
Anbruch *m.* **(-[e]s, -brüche)** beginning, ~ *der Nacht*, nightfall.
anbrüllen *v.t.* to roar at; to bellow.
anbrummen *v.t.* to growl at.
Anciennität *f.* seniority.
Andacht *f.* **(-, -en)** devotion, prayers *pl.*
andächtig *a.* devout, attentive.
Andalusien *n.* **(-s, 0)** Andalusia.
andauern *v.i.* to last.
andauernd *a.* constant, continual, continuous.
Anden *pl.* Andes.
Andenken *n.* **(-s, -)** souvenir; memory.
ander *a.* other, second; next.
andererseits *adv.* on the other hand.
andermal *adv.* another time.
ändern *v.t.* to alter, to change; *ich kann es nicht* ~, I cannot help it; ~ *v.r.* to change, to vary.
andernfalls *adv.* otherwise, else.
andernorts *adv.* elsewhere.
anders *adv.* otherwise, else.
anderseits *adv.* on the other side *or* hand.
anderswo *adv.* elsewhere.
anderthalb *a.* one and a half.
Änderung *f.* **(-, -en)** change, alteration.
anderweitig *a.* & *adv.* other; in another way.
andeuten *v.t.* to signify, to hint; to intimate.
Andeutung *f.* **(-, -en)** intimation, suggestion, hint.
andichten *v.t.* to impute falsely.
Andrang *m.* **(-[e]s, 0)** crowd, throng, rush.
andrängen *v.i.st.* *(s)* to press forward.
andrehen *v.t.* to turn on; to screw; (*pej.*) to sell.
androhen *v.t.* to threaten, to menace.
Androhung *f.* **(-, -en)** threat.

andrücken *v.t.* to press toward *or* against.
anecken *v.i. bei jm.* ~, to give offense to sb.
aneignen *v.r.* to appropriate.
aneinander *adv.* together; one another.
Anekdote *f.* **(-, -n)** anecdote.
anekeln *v.t.* to disgust.
Anerbieten *n.* **(-s, -)** offer, tender.
anerkennen *v.t.ir.* to acknowledge, to recognize; *Schuld nicht* ~, to repudiate a debt.
anerkennenswert *a.* commendable.
Anerkennung *f.* **(-, -en)** acknowledgement, recognition; appreciation.
anfachen *v.t.* to blow into a flame; (*fig.*) to kindle.
anfahren *v.t.* to convey, to carry; (*fig.*) to snub.
Anfahrt *f.* **(-, -en)** approach.
Anfall *m.* **(-[e]s, -fälle)** fit, seizure, attack.
anfallen *v.t.st.* to attack; to accrue; ~*de Zinsen, pl.* accrued interest.
anfällig *a.* (*fig.*) susceptible; prone.
Anfang *m.* **(-[e]s, -fänge)** commencement, beginning, opening.
anfangen *v.t.st.* to begin, to commence; to start; ~ *v.i.* to begin; to open.
Anfänger *m.* **(-s, -)** beginner.
anfangs *adv.* in the beginning.
Anfangsbuchstabe *m.* initial (letter).
Anfangsgründe *m.pl.* elements, rudiments.
anfassen *v.t.* to take hold of, to seize.
anfauchen *v.t.* to spit at; (*fig.*) to snap at.
anfaulen *v.i.* *(s)* to begin to rot, to go bad; **angefault** *a.* half rotten.
anfechtbar *a.* contestable, disputable, open to criticism.
anfechten *v.i.st* to contest; to challenge; to tempt; to trouble.
Anfechtung *f.* **(-, -en)** temptation.
anfeinden *v.t.* to attack, to persecute.
anfertigen *v.t.* to manufacture, to make.
anfeuchten *v.t.* to moisten, to dampen.
anfeuern *v.t.* to inflame, to spur on.
anflehen *v.t.* to implore, to beseech.
anfliegen *v.t.st.* to fly to, to land at; ~ *v.i.st.* to approach.
Anflug *m.* **(-[e]s, -flüge)** approach; blush, flush; tinge, smattering.
anfordern *v.t.* (*mil.*) to request, to order, to ask for.
Anforderung *f.* **(-, -en)** demand; (*mil.*) requisition.
Anfrage *f.* **(-, -n)** inquiry, application.
anfragen *v.t.* to inquire, to call for.
anfressen *v.t.st.* to gnaw; to corrode; to eat into.
anfreunden *v.r.* to become friends.
anfügen *v.t.* to join to; to enclose, to annex, to subjoin.
anfühlen *v.t.* to touch, to feel.
anführen *v.t.* to lead, to conduct, to command; to impose upon, to dupe; to cite, to quote.
Anführer *m.* **(-s, -)** leader, commander.
Anführung *f.* **(-, 0)** leadership; command; quotation.
Anführungszeichen *n.* quotation mark.
anfüllen *v.t.* to fill; to replenish.
Angabe *f.* **(-, -n)** declaration, statement; instruction; (*com.*) entry; (*Tennis*) service.
angänglich *a. & adv.* initial, incipient; at first, at the outset, originally.
angeben *v.t.st.* to specify; to suggest; to declare, to assert; to denounce; *den Ton* ~, (*fig.*) to set the fashion; ~ *v.i.st.* to brag, to boast.
Angeber *m.* **(-s, -)** boaster.
Angeberei *f.* **(-, -en)** bragging, showing off.
angeberisch *a.* boastful, pretentious.
angeblich *a.* pretended, purported, alleged; ~ *adv.* supposedly, allegedly.
angeboren *a.* innate, inborn, congenital.
Angebot *n.* **(-[e]s, -e)** offer; bid; supply; (*com.*) tender; ~ *und Nachfrage,* supply and demand.
angebracht *a.* proper, appropriate.
angebunden *a.* tied to; *kurz* ~, abrupt.
angedeihen (lassen) *v.i.st.* to bestow upon.
angegossen *a.* *wie* ~ *sitzen/passen,* to fit like a glove.
angegraut *a.* graying.
angegriffen *a.* (*Gesundheit*) delicate, weakened, strained.
angeheiratet *a.* by marriage.
angeheitert *a.* tipsy.
angehen *v.t.st.* to apply to; to have to do with, to concern; (*einen um etwas*) to solicit; ~ *v.i.st.* to begin; to be tolerable; to be practicable; *es geht nicht an,* it won't do.
angehend *a.* incipient, prospective.
angehören *v.i.* to belong to.
Angehörige *m.pl.* relatives, relations; *abhängige* ~, dependents.
Angeklagte[r] *m.* **(-n, -n)** defendant, accused.
Angel *f.* **(-, -n)** fishing rod; (*archaic*) hinge.
angelegen *v.r.* ~ *sein lassen,* to be concerned about.
Angelegenheit *f.* **(-, -en)** affair, matter; *kümmere dich um deine eigenen* ~*en,* mind your own business.
angeln *v.t.* to fish, to angle; (*fig.*) to fish for (compliments).
Angelpunkt *m.* pivot.
Angelrute *f.* fishing rod.
Angelsachse *m., f.* Anglo-Saxon.
angelsächsisch *a.* Anglo-Saxon.
Angelschnur *f.* fishing line.
angemessen *a.* appropriate, suitable, fit, adequate.
angenehm *a.* agreeable, pleasant, acceptable.
angenommen *c.* ~ *daß,* supposing that, assuming that.
angepaßt *a.* well-adjusted.
angeregt *adv.* lively, animated.
angeschlagen *a.* groggy, weakened.
angeschlossen *p.p.* connected.
angeschmutzt *a.* soiled.
angesehen *a.* distinguished, respected.
angesessen *a.* settled, resident.
Angesicht *n.* **(-[e]s, -er)** face, countenance; *von* ~, by sight.
angesichts *pr.* in the face of, considering.
angespannt *a.* tense, tight, close.
angestammt *a.* hereditary, ancestral.
Angestellte[r] *m.* **(-n, -n)** employee.
angestrengt *a.* concentrated.
angetan *a.* ~ *sein von,* to be taken with.
angetrunken *a.* tipsy.
angewandt *a.* applied.
angewiesen (auf) *a.* dependent (on).
angewöhnen *v.t.* to accustom; ~ *v.r.* to get into the habit of.
Angewohnheit *f.* **(-, -en)** habit, custom.
angleichen *v.t.st.* to assimilate.
angliedern *v.t.* to attach.

Anglikaner *m.* **(-s, -); anglikanisch** *a.* Anglican.
Anglist *m.* **(-en, -en); Anglistin** *f.* **(-, -nen)** English scholar, Anglicist.
Anglistik *f.* **(-, 0)** English language and literature.
Anglizismus *m.* **(-, -men)** anglicism.
anglotzen *v.t.* (*fam.*) to stare at.
Angola *n.* **(-s, 0)** Angola; **Angolaner** *m.* **(-s, -); Angolanerin** *f.* **(-, -nen); angolanisch** *a.* Angolan.
angreifbar *a.* vulnerable, contestable.
angreifen *v.t.st.* to attack; to undertake, (*fig.*) to fatigue, to tell upon, to affect.
Angreifer *m.* **(-s, -)** aggressor.
angrenzen *v.i.* to border on.
angrenzend *a.* adjacent, contiguous.
Angriff *m.* **(-[e]s, -e)** attack, assault; aggression; *in ~ nehmen,* to start (on).
Angriffskrieg *m.* war of aggression.
angrinsen *v.t.* to grin at.
Angst *f.* **(-, Ängste)** anxiety, anguish, fright, fear.
ängstigen *v.t.* to frighten, to scare; ~ *v.r.* to be frightened; to feel alarmed.
ängstlich *a. & adv.* anxious, uneasy; anxiously; scrupulously.
angstvoll *a.* anxious.
angucken *v.t.* to look at, to peep at.
angurten *v.t.* to strap in, to buckle up; ~ *v.r.* to fasten one's seat belt.
Anh. *Anhang,* appendix, app.
anhaben *v.t.st.* to have on, to wear; *sie können ihm nichts ~,* they can't do him any harm.
anhaften *v.t.* to stick to, to cling to.
Anhalt *m.* **(-[e]s, -e)** support, hold; clue.
anhalten *v.t.st.* to stop, to arrest; ~ *v.i.st.* to last; *~ um,* to propose (to); to pull up, to draw up.
anhaltend *a.* constant, continuous.
Anhalter *m.* **(-s, -); Anhalterin** *f.* **(-, -nen)** hitchhiker.
Anhaltspunkt *m.* evidence, clue.
anhand *pr.* with the help of.
Anhang *m.* **(-[e]s, -hänge)** appendix; supplement; adherents.
anhängen *v.t.* to hang on; to join, to annex, to affix, to add.
Anhänger *m.* **(-s, -)** supporter, adherent, follower.
Anhängewagen (Anhänger) *m.* trailer.
anhängig *a.* (*Prozeß*) pendent, pending; **~ machen,** to bring (an action against).
anhänglich *a.* attached.
Anhängsel *n.* **(-s, -)** appendage.
anhauchen *v.t.* to breathe on, to blow on.
anhäufen *v.t. & v.r.* to heap up; to accumulate.
Anhäufung *f.* **(-, -en)** accumulation.
anheben *v.t. & i.st.* to begin; to lift, to raise.
Anhebung *f.* **(-, -en)** increase.
anheften *v.t.* to tack on; to stitch to.
anheimelnd *a.* homely, cozy.
anheimfallen *v.i.st. (s)* to fall to.
anheimstellen *v.t.* to leave to; to submit (to).
anheischig *a. sich ~ machen,* to pledge oneself, to undertake.
anheizen *v.t.* to fire, to fuel, to heat up.
anheuern *v.t.* to sign on.
Anhöhe *f.* **(-, -n)** elevation, hill.
anhören *v.t.* to listen to, to attend; *sich ~,* to sound.
Anhörung *f.* **(-, -en)** hearing.
Anilin *n.* **(-s, 0)** aniline.
animalisch *a.* animal, bestial.
Animateur *m.* **(-s, -e)** animator.
animieren *v.t.* to encourage.
Animosität *f.* **(-, -en)** animosity.
Anis *m.* **(-es, -e)** anise, aniseed.
Ank. *Ankunft,* arrival, arr.
ankämpfen (gegen) *v.i.* to struggle against.
Ankauf *m.* **(-[e]s, -käufe)** purchase.
ankaufen *v.t.* to purchase, to buy; ~ *v.r.* to buy land, to settle.
Anker *m.* **(-s, -)** anchor; (*el.*) armature; *vor ~ gehen,* to cast anchor; *~ lichten,* to weigh anchor.
ankern *v.t.* to anchor.
Anker: ~platz *m.* anchorage; **~winde** *f.* windlass, capstan.
anketten *v.t.* to chain (to).
Anklage *f.* **(-, -n)** accusation, charge; *f. öffentliche ~,* (*jur.*) arraignment; *unter ~ stehen,* (*jur.*) to be on trial, to stand trial.
Anklagebank *f.* **(-, -bänke)** dock.
Anklagebehörde *f.* prosecution.
anklagen *v.t.* to accuse, to impeach.
Anklagepunkt *m.* count (of an indictment).
Anklageschrift *f.* indictment.
Anklagevertreteter *m.* counsel for the prosecution.
anklammern *v.r.* to cling (to).
Anklang *m.* **(-[e]s, -klänge)** (*fig.*) approval, kind reception; *Anklänge (an etwas),* reminiscence (of sth.).
ankleben *v.t. & i.* to paste on; to stick on; to stick to, to adhere.
ankleiden *v.t.* to dress, to attire; ~ *v.r.* to get dressed.
Ankleidezimmer *n.* dressing room.
anklingen *v.i.st.* (*fig.*) to remind.
anklopfen *v.i.* to knock.
anknabbern *v.t.* to nibble.
anknipsen *v.t.* to switch on.
anknüpfen *v.t.* (*ein Gespräch*) to enter (into a conversation); *Bekanntschaft ~,* to make the acquaintance of.
Anknüpfungspunkt *m.* link, starting point.
ankommen *v.i.st. (s)* to arrive; *auf etwas ~,* to depend on sth.; *es darauf ~ lassen,* to take a chance; *es kommt nicht darauf an,* it does not matter.
Ankömmling *m.* **(-s, -e)** newcomer.
ankoppeln *v.t.* to couple, to hitch, to dock.
ankreiden *v.t. jm. etwas ~,* to blame sb.; to make sb. pay.
ankreuzen *v.t.* to mark with a cross.
ankündigen *v.t.* to announce.
Ankündigung *f.* **(-, -en)** announcement.
Ankunft *f.* **(-, 0)** arrival.
Ankunftszeit *f.* **(-, -en)** time of arrival.
ankuppeln *v.t.* to hitch, to dock.
ankurbeln *v.t.* to put into gear, to crank up; (*fig.*) to start; to boost.
Anl. *Anlage,* enclosure, encl.
anlächeln *v.t.* to smile at.
anlachen *v.t.* to smile at, to laugh with.
Anlage *f.* **(-, -n)** (*von Kapital*) investment; (*von Strassen, Gärten*) layout; (*Park*) park, grounds *pl.*; (*fig.*) talent, disposition; (*Fabrik*) plant; (*in Brief*) enclosure.
anlangen *v.i. (s)* to arrive; ~ *v.t.* to concern.
Anlaß *m.* **(-lasses, -lässe)** occasion.
anlassen *v.t.st.* to keep on; to start, to turn on; ~ *v.r.* to promise.
Anlasser *m.* **(-s, -)** starter.
anläßlich *pr. mit. Gen.* on the occasion of.

anlasten *v.t.* to accuse, to blame.
Anlauf *m.* **(-[e]s, -läufe)** run, start, rush.
anlaufen *v.i.st. (s)* to run against; (*sich trüben*) to tarnish.
Anlaut *m.* **(-s, -e)** initial sound.
Anlegehafen *m.* port of call.
anlegen *v.t.* (*Kleider, etc.*) to put on; (*Gewehr*) to take aim; to found, to establish; (*Kapital*) to invest; (*Garten*) to lay out; (*Hand*) to set to work; ~ *v.i.* (*nav.*) to land.
Anleger *m.* **(-s, -)** investor.
Anlegestelle *f.* landing place.
anlehnen *v.t.* to lean on or upon; (*Tür*) to leave ajar.
Anleihe *f.* **(-, -n)** loan; *eine ~ machen,* to make a loan.
anleimen *v.t.* to glue on.
anleinen *v.t.* to put on a leash.
anleiten *v.t.* to guide, to instruct.
Anleitung *f.* **(-, -en)** instruction.
anlernen *v.t.* to train.
Anliegen *n.* **(-s, -)** concern, request.
anliegend *a.* adjacent, tight-fitting.
Anlieger *m.* **(-s, -)** resident, ~ *frei!* residents only!
anlocken *v.t.* to lure; to attract.
anlöten *v.t.* to solder.
anlügen *v.t.st.* to lie to.
Anm. *Anmerkung,* note.
anmachen *v.t.* e to fasten to; (*Feuer*) to light; (*Salat*) to dress; (*fam.*) to turn on; to snap at.
anmalen *v.t.* to paint.
Anmarsch *m.* **(-[e]s, -märsche)** approach (of an army).
anmassen *v.r.* to assume, to arrogate, to usurp; to pretend to.
anmassend *a.* arrogant.
Anmassung *f.* **(-, -en)** assumption, usurpation, arrogance.
anmelden *v.t.* to enroll, to announce; ~ *v.r.* (*polizeilich*) to register; to notify.
Anmeldung *f.* **(-, -en)** enrollment, registration.
anmerken *v.t.* **(-, -en)** to remark, to note.
Anmerkung *f.* **(-, -en)** note, footnote, remark.
Anmut *f.* **(-, 0)** sweetness, charm, grace.
anmuten *v.t.* to seem, to appear.
anmutig *a.* graceful, charming.
annageln *v.t.* to nail to.
annähen *v.t.* to sew on.
annähern *v.r.* to approach.
annähernd *a.* approximate; *adv.* almost, nearly.
Annäherung *f.* **(-, -en)** approach.
Annäherungsversuch *m.* **(-s, -e)** advance.
Annahme *f.* **(-, -n)** acceptance; (*an Kindes Statt*) adoption; (*Meinung*) assumption.
Annahmestelle *f.* receiving office.
Annalen *pl.* annals
annehmbar *a.* acceptable, admissible, plausible
annehmen *v.t.st.* to accept; to assume; (*als ausgemacht*) to take for granted; ~ *v.r.* to take care of, befriend.
Annehmlichkeit *f.* **(-, -en)** comfort, amenity.
annektieren *v.t.* to annex.
Annexion *f.* **(-, -en)** annexation.
anno, Anno in the year.
Annonce *f.* **(-, -n)** advertisement.
annoncieren *v.t.* to advertise.
annullieren *v.t.* to annul; (*jur.*) to set aside.
Anode *f.* **(-, -n)** anode.
anöden *v.t.* (*fam*) to bore to death.
anomal *a.* anomalous, abnormal.
Anomalie *f.* **(-, -n)** anomaly, abnormality.
anonym *a.* anonymous.
Anonymität *f.* **(-, en)** anonymity.
Anorak *m.* **(-s, -s)** anorak.
anordnen *v.t.* to order, to dispose, to arrange.
Anordnung *f.* **(-, -en)** order; arrangement, disposition, alignment.
anorganisch *a.* inorganic.
anormal *a.* abnormal.
anpacken *v.t.* to grasp, to seize.
anpassen *v.t.* to fit to; to try on; to adapt, to accommodate.
Anpassung *f.* **(-, 0)** adaptation.
anpassungsfähig *a.* adaptable.
Anpassungsfähigkeit *f.* adaptability.
anpeilen *v.t.* to take a bearing on; to aim at.
anpfeifen *v.t.st.* to whistle for the start; (*fam.*) to scold.
Anpfiff *m.* **(-s, -e)** starting whistle; *einen ~ kriegen,* to get ticked off.
anpflanzen *v.t.* to plant.
anpöbeln *v.t.* to molest, to mob.
anpochen *v.i.* to knock.
Anprall *m.* **(-[e]s, 0)** impact; (*mil.*) shock.
anprallen *v.i. (s)* to crash.
anprangern *v.t.* to denounce.
anpreisen *v.t.* to commend, to extol.
Anprobe *f.* **(-, -en)** fitting.
anproben, anprobieren *v.t.* to try on, to fit on.
anpumpen *v.t.* to borrow money from.
Anrainer *m.* **(-s, -)** neighbor.
anrasen *v.i.* to come racing along or up.
anraten *v.t. st.* to advise.
anrechnen *v.t.* to count; to charge; to rate; to impute; ~ *gegen,* to set off against.
Anrecht *n.* **(-[e]s, -e)** right, claim, title.
Anrede *f.* **(-, -n)** address; (*Brief*) salutation.
anreden *v.t.* to address, to accost.
anregen *v.t.* to suggest; to stimulate; to mention.
anregend *a.* stimulating.
Anregung *f.* **(-, -en)** incitement, stimulation; suggestion.
anreichern *v.t.* to enrich.
anreihen *v.r.* to join.
Anreise *f.* **(-, -n)** journey there or here; arrival.
anreisen *v.i.* to travel there or here.
Anreiz *m.* **(-s, -e)** incitement; stimulus.
anreizen *v.t.* to incite, to instigate.
anrempeln *v.t.* to jostle against.
anrennen *v.i.st. (s)* to run against.
Anrichte *f.* **(-, -n)** dresser, sideboard.
anrichten *v.t.* to prepare; to arrange; to serve up, to dish up; (*fig.*) to cause, to occasion.
anrüchig *a.* disreputable.
anrücken *v.i.* to approach, to move up.
Anruf *m.* **(-s, -e)** call.
Anrufbeantworter *m.* **(-s, -)** answering machine.
anrufen *v.t.st.* to call (to); (*tel.*) to phone; to call.
Anrufer *m.* **(-s, -); Anruferin** *f.* **(-, -nen)** caller.
Anrufung *f.* **(-, -en)** invocation.
anrühren *v.t.* to touch, to handle.
ans = an das.
ansagen *v.t.* to announce; (*Kartenspiel*) to bid.
Ansager *m.* **(-s, -)** announcer.
ansammeln *v.r.* to gather, to collect.
Ansammlung *f.* **(-, -en)** collection; pile; crowd.
ansässig *a.* resident, settled, domiciled; *~e Briten,* British residents.

Ansatz *m.* **(-es, -sätze)** start; approach; deposit; (*math.*) statement.
ansatzweise *adv.* to some extent.
ansaufen *v.r. einen* ~, to get plastered.
ansaugen *v.t.* to suck in.
anschaffen *v.t.* to provide, to procure, to buy.
Anschaffung *f.* **(-, -en)** procurement; purchase.
anschalten *v.t.* to switch on.
anschauen *v.t.* to look at, to view; to contemplate; ~ *v.r.* to look over.
anschaulich *a.* clear; evident; graphic, lucid.
Anschauung *f.* **(-, -en)** view; experience.
Anschein *m.* **(-s, 0)** appearance, semblance.
anscheinend *a.* apparent, seeming.
anschicken *v.r.* to get ready; to prepare; to set about.
anschieben *v.t.st.* to push.
anschießen *v.t.st.* to shoot and wound.
anschirren *v.t.* to harness.
Anschiß *m.* **(-, -e)** (*fam.*) scolding.
Anschlag *m.* **(-[e]s, -schläge)** (*Mauer*~) poster; (*Schätzung*) estimate; (*Komplott*) plot; (*auf das Leben*) attempt.
anschlagen *v.t.st.* to affix; (*Zettel*) to post; (*Saite*) to strike; ~ *v.i.* to prove effectual.
anschleichen *v.r.st.* to creep up.
anschleppen *v.t.* to drag along.
anschließen *v.t.st.* annex; to fasten with a lock; ~ *v.r.* to join (a company).
anschließend *adv.* afterward.
Anschluß *m.* **(-schlusses, -schlüsse)** (*rail., el.*) connection; ~ **dose,** *f.* socket.
Anschlußzug *m.* **(-s, -züge)** connecting train.
anschmiegen *v.r.* to nestle, to snuggle up.
anschmiegsam *a.* affectionate.
anschmieren *v.t.* to smear, to daub; (*pej.*) to cheat.
anschnallen *v.t.* to buckle.
anschnauzen *v.t.* (*fam.*) to shout at.
anschneiden *v.t.st.* to cut; to raise (*question*).
Anschnitt *m.* **(-[e]s, -e)** first cut.
anschreiben *v.t.st.* to write (down); to score up; *gut angeschrieben,* favorably known.
Anschrift *f.* **(-, -en)** address.
Anschuldigung *f.* **(-, -en)** accusation, charge.
anschwärzen *v.t.* to blacken; (*fig.*) to slander.
anschwellen *v.i.st.* *(s)* to swell.
anschwemmen *v.t.* to wash ashore.
Anschwemmung *f.* **(-, -en)** deposit (of flood).
anschwindeln *v.t.* (*fam.*) to lie.
ansehen *v.t.st.* to look at; to consider; to regard.
Ansehen *n.* **(-s, 0)** appearance; (*Achtung*) esteem, credit, reputation, authority; *von* ~, by sight
ansehnlich *a.* considerable, sizable; good-looking.
ansetzen *v.t.* to put on; (*Preis*) to fix; (*schätzen*) to rate, to estimate; (*Blätter*) to put forth.
Ansicht *f.* **(-, -en)** sight, view; inspection; (*Meinung*) opinion; *zur* ~, on approval.
Ansichts(post)karte *f.* picture postcard.
ansiedeln *v.t.* & *v.r.* to settle.
Ansiedler *m.* **(-s, -)** settler, colonist.
Ansied(e)lung *f.* **(-, -en)** settlement.
Ansinnen *n.* **(-s, -)** demand, request.
anspannen *v.t.* to stretch; (*Pferde*) to hitch up; (*fig.*) to exert, to strain.
Anspannung *f.* **(-, -en)** exertion, strain.
anspielen *v.i.* to hint at, to allude to.
Anspielung *f.* **(-, -en)** allusion, hint; (*pej.*) insinuation.
Ansporn *m.* **(-s, 0)** incentive.
anspornen *v.t.* to spur; (*fig.*) to incite.
Ansprache *f.* **(-, -en)** address, speech.
ansprechen *v.t.st.* to address, to accost; to please, to appeal to.
ansprechend *a.* appealing; attractive.
Ansprechpartner *m.* **(-s, -)** contact (person).
anspringen *v.i.st.* to start; *v.t.st.* to jump at.
Anspruch *m.* **(-[e]s, -sprüche)** claim, pretension, title.
anspruchslos *a.* unassuming, unpretentious.
anspruchsvoll *a.* demanding, exacting, fastidious.
anspucken *v.t.* to spit at.
anspülen *v.t.* to wash ashore, to deposit.
anstacheln *v.t.* to spur on, to prick, to goad.
Anstalt *f.* **(-, -en)** institution, establishment; ~*en treffen* od. *machen,* to make arrangements; to arrange.
Anstand *m.* **(-[e]s, -stände)** decorum, decency, polite manners; (*Beanstandung*) objection.
anständig *a.* proper; respectable, decent.
Anständigkeit *f.* **(-, -en)** propriety, decency.
Anstandsdame *f.* chaperon.
anstandslos *adv.* without hesitation.
anstarren *v.t.* to stare at.
anstatt *pr.* instead of; ~ *daß, c.* instead of.
anstauen *v.t.* to dam up; ~ *v.r.* to accumulate, to build up.
anstaunen *v.t.* to gaze at.
anstechen *v.t.st.* to prick; to puncture; (*ein Faß*) to tap.
anstecken *v.t.* to stick on; to pin; (*mit Krankheit*) to infect; (*Licht*) to light; (*Feuer*) to make a fire.
ansteckend *a.* contagious, catching; infectious; communicable.
Ansteckung *f.* **(-, -en)** contagion, infection.
anstehen *v.t.st.* to stand in line; to line up; to suit.
ansteigen *v.i.st.* *(s)* to ascend, to rise.
anstelle *pr.* instead.
anstellen *v.t.* to appoint; to arrange; (*Versuch*) to make; ~ *v.r.* to behave; to feign, to make believe.
anstellig *a.* handy, skillful.
Anstellung *f.* **(-, -en)** appointment; (*Stelle*) job, place, situation.
Anstieg *m.* **(-[e]s, -e)** rise, increase.
anstiften *v.t.* to contrive, to cause; to instigate, to set upon.
Anstifter *m.* **(-s, -)**; **Anstifterin** *f.* **(-, -nen)** instigator.
Anstiftung *f.* **(-, -en)** incitement.
anstimmen *v.t.* to sing, to strike up.
Anstoß *m.* **(-es, -stöße)** impulse, stimulus; (*fig.*) offense; (*Fußball*) kickoff; *Stein des* ~*es, m.* stumbling block.
anstoßen *v.t.st.* to push or strike against; ~ *v.i.st.* to stumble; to give offense; (*mit den Gläsern*) clink glasses; (*mit der Zunge*) to lisp.
anstößig *a.* offensive, scandalous, shocking.
anstrahlen *v.t.* to illuminate, to floodlight.
anstreben *v.t.* & *i.* to aspire to.
anstreichen *v.t.st.* to paint, to stain.
Anstreicher *m.* **(-s, -)** house painter.
anstrengen *v.t.* to make an effort; to strain; to exert; (*Klage*) to bring an action; ~ *v.r.* to exert oneself.
anstrengend *a.* strenuous, demanding, fatiguing.
Anstrengung *f.* **(-, -en)** exertion, effort.
Anstrich *m.* **(-[e]s, -e)** color, painting, paint, coat; (*fig.*) appearance, tinge, air.
Ansturm *m.* **(-s, -stürme)** rush, attack.

anstürmen *v.i. (s)* to attack, to storm, to pounce upon.
ansuchen *v.t.* to apply for, to petition for.
Ansuchen *n.* **(-s, -)** request, application.
Antagonismus *m.* **(-, -men)** antagonism.
antanzen *v.i.* (*fam.*) to show up.
antarktisch *a.* Antarctic.
antasten *v.t.* to touch, to handle; to break into (savings).
Anteil *m.* **(-[e]s, -e)** share, portion; contribution; lot; (*fig.*) interest; ~ *nehmen,* to sympathize.
anteilig *a. & adv.* proportional(ly).
Anteilnahme *f.* **(-, 0)** participation; interest; sympathy.
antelephonieren *v.t.* to phone, to call.
Antenne *f.* **(-, -n)** (radio) aerial, antenna.
Antezedentien *f.pl.* antecedents.
Anthrazit *m.* **(-s, 0)** anthracite.
Anthropologe *m.* **(-n, -n); Anthropologin** *f.* **(-, -nen)** anthropologist.
Anthroposoph *m.* **(-en, -en); Anthroposophin** *f.* **(-, -nen)** anthroposophist.
Antialkoholiker *m.* **(-s, -)** teetotaler.
antiautoritär *a.* antiauthoritarian.
Antibiotikum *n.* **(-s, -tika)** antibiotic.
Antiblockiersystem, ABS *n.* antilock braking system.
antik *a.* antique.
Antike *f.* **(-, 0)** classical antiquity.
Antillen *pl.* **(-)** Antilles.
Antilope *f.* **(-, -n)** antelope.
Antipathie *f.* **(-, -n)** antipathy.
antippen *v.t.* to touch lightly, to tap.
Antiqua *f.* **(-, 0)** (*Druck*) Roman type.
Antiquar *m.* **(-[e]s, -e)** antiquary; secondhand bookseller.
Antiquariat *n.* **(-s, -e)** antiquarian *or* secondhand bookshop.
antiquarisch *a. & adv.* secondhand.
Antiquität *f.* **(-, -en)** antique, curiosity.
Antiquitätenhändler *m.* antique dealer.
Antiquitätenladen *m.* **(-s, -läden)** antique shop.
Antisemit *m.* **(-en, -en)** anti-Semite.
antisemitisch *a.* anti-Semitic.
antiseptisch *a.* antiseptic.
antizipieren *v.t.* to anticipate.
Antlitz *n.* **(-es, -e)** face, countenance.
Antrag *m.* **(-[e]s, -träge)** application, proposition, proposal; motion; bill.
Antragsformular *n.* application form.
Antragsteller *m.* applicant.
antreffen *v.t.st.* to find, to come across.
antreiben *v.t.st.* to drive; to power; to impel; to step up.
antreten *v.t.st.* (Reise) to set out upon; *Dienst* ~, to assume duty; ~ *v.i.st. (s)* to fall in.
Antrieb *m.* **(-[e]s, -e)** drive, impulse, motive, propulsion.
Antriebskraft *f.* **(-, kräfte)** power.
Antritt *m.* **(-e[s], 0)** entrance, beginning.
Antrittsrede *f.* inaugural address.
antun *v.t.st.* to put on; (*fig.*) to inflict; *einem etw.* ~, to do sth. to sb.
Antwort *f.* **(-, -en)** answer, reply.
antworten *v.t.* to answer, to reply.
Antwortschein *m.* (*Post*) reply coupon.
anvertrauen *v.t.* to entrust to, to confide in.
anvisieren *v.t.* to aim at.
anwachsen *v.i.st. (s)* to grow to; to grow up; to increase; to swell.
anwählen *v.t.* to dial.
Anwalt *m.* **(-[e]s, -e & -wälte); Anwältin** *f.* **(-, -nen)** agent; (*Rechts*~) solicitor, advocate, lawyer, attorney, counsel.
anwandeln *v.t.* to befall, to seize.
Anwandlung *f.* **(-, -en)** fit, attack; touch.
Anwärter *m.* **(-s, -)** candidate, expectant.
Anwartschaft *f.* **(-, -en)** candidacy, expectancy; reversion.
anweisen *v.t.st.* to instruct, to direct; to advise; *auf sich selbst angewiesen sein,* to be left to one's own devices.
Anweisung *f.* **(-, -en)** assignment; instruction, directive; (*Geld*~) money order, check, draft.
anwendbar *a.* applicable; practical.
anwenden *v.t.r. & st.* to apply to; to bestow upon; to make use of, to employ.
Anwendung *f.* **(-, -en)** application, practice, use.
anwerben *v.t.st.* to enlist, to enroll, to hire, to recruit; *sich* ~ *lassen,* to sign on.
Anwerbung *f.* **(-, -en)** recruitment.
Anwesen *n.* **(-s, -)** estate, property.
anwesend *a.* present.
Anwesenheit *f.* **(-, 0)** presence.
Anwesenheitsliste *f.* **(-, -n)** attendance list.
anwetzen *v.i.* (*fam.*) to run toward.
anwidern *v.t.* to incite loathing, to disgust.
Anwurf *m.* **(-[e]s, -würfe)** accusation.
anwurzeln *v.i.* to take root.
Anzahl *f.* **(-, 0)** number; quantity.
anzahlen *v.t.* to make a deposit.
Anzahlung *f.* **(-, -en)** deposit, down payment.
anzapfen *v.t.* to tap.
Anzeichen *n.* **(-s, -)** sign, symptom.
Anzeige *f.* **(-, -n)** (*Inserat*) advertisement; report (police).
Anzeigeblatt *n.* newspaper advertisement, flyer.
anzeigen *v.t.* to report; to indicate; to notify; (*einen*) to denounce; (*Meßapparat*) to read.
anzetteln *v.t.* to plot, to contrive.
anziehen *v.t.st.* to pull; (*spannen*) to tighten, to stretch; (*Kleider*) to put on; (*fig.*) to attract; ~ *v.r.* to dress.
anziehend *a.* attractive, interesting.
Anziehung *f.* **(-, 0)** attraction.
Anziehungskraft *f.* (*fig.*) appeal.
Anzug *m.* **(-[e]s, -züge)** (*Herren*~) suit; (*Damen*~) costume, dress.
anzüglich *a.* insinuating; suggestive, personal.
Anzüglichkeit *f.* **(-, -en)** insinuating nature; insinuating remark.
anzünden *v.t.* to light; to kindle; to set fire to.
Anzünder *m.* **(-s, -)** lighter.
anzweifeln *v.t.* to doubt.
anzwinkern *v.t.* to wink at.
apart *a.* out of the ordinary, unusual.
Apartment *n.* **(-s, -s)** studio apartment.
Apathie *f.* **(-, 0)** apathy.
apathisch *a.* apathetic.
Apfel *m.* **(-s, Äpfel)** apple.
Apfelmus *n.* applesauce.
Apfelsine *f.* **(-, -n)** orange.
Apfelwein *m.* cider.
Aphorismus *m.* **(-, -men)** aphorism.
aphoristisch *a.* aphoristic.
Apologet *m.* **(-en, -en)** apologist.
Apostel *m.* **(-s, -)** apostle.
Apostelgeschichte *f.* The Acts of the Apostles *pl.*
Apostroph *m.* **(-s, -e)** apostrophe.
Apotheke *f.* **(-, -n)** drugstore; pharmacy.

Apotheker *m.* **(-s, -); Apothekerin** *f.* **(-, -nen)** pharmacist.
Apparat *m.* **(-[e]s, -e)** apparatus, telephone, extension, appliance.
Appell *m.* **(-s, -e)** roll call; (*fig.*) appeal.
Appellation *f.* **(-, -en)** appeal.
Appellationsgericht *n.* court of appeal.
appellieren *v.i.* to appeal.
Appetit *m.* **(-[e]s, -e)** appetite.
appetitanregend *a.* appetizing; stimulating the appetite.
appetitlich *a.* appetizing.
appetitlos *a.* without any appetite.
Appetitlosigkeit *f.* **(-, 0)** lack of appetite.
applaudieren *v.t.* to applaud.
Applaus *m.* **(-es, 0)** applause.
apportieren *v.i.* (*von Hunden*) to retrieve.
Appretur *f.* **(-, -en)** finish, dressing.
approbiert *a.* (*Arzt*) certified.
Apr. *April,* April, Apr.
Aprikose *f.* **(-, -n)** apricot.
April *m.* **(-[e]s, -e)** April; *in den ~ schicken,* to make a fool of.
apropos *adv.* by the way.
Aquädukt *m. od. n.* **(-s, -e)** aqueduct.
Aquarell *n.* **(-[e]s, -e)** watercolor.
Aquarellist *m.* **(-en, -en)** watercolorist.
Äquator *m.* **(-s, 0)** equator.
Äquatortaufe *f.* **(-, -n)** crossing-the-line ceremony.
äquivalent *a.* equivalent.
Äquivalent *n.* **(-[e]s, -e)** equivalent.
Äquivalenz *f.* **(-, -en)** equivalence.
Ära *f.* **(-, 0)** era.
Araber *m.* **(-s, -); Araberin** *f.* **(-, -nen)** Arab; **Arabien** *p.* **(-s, 0)** Arabia; **arabisch** *a.* Arabian, Arab, Arabic.
arabische Ziffern *f.pl.* arabic numerals.
Arbeit *f.* **(-, -en)** labor, work, toil; task; (*Bearbeitung*) workmanship; (*Leistung*) performance.
arbeiten *v.i.* to labor, to work; (*Maschine*) to operate; *~ mit,* to work with; ~ *v.t.* to make, to manufacture.
Arbeiter *m.* **(-s, -)** worker, workman, laborer, hand, workingman.
Arbeiterbewegung *f.* labor movement.
Arbeiterfamilie *f.* working-class family.
Arbeitergewerkschaft *f.* labor union.
Arbeiterin *f.* **(-, -nen)** workingwoman.
Arbeitgeber *m.; **Arbeitgeberin** *f.* **(-, -nen)** employer.
Arbeitnehmer *m.* employee.
Arbeits: ~amt *n.* employment office; **~anzug** *m.* overalls; **~belastung** *f.* workload; **~beschaffung** *f.* creation of employment; **~dienst** *m.* labor service; **~dienstpflicht** *f.* compulsory labor service; **~einkommen** *n.* earned income; **~einsatz** *m.* manpower allocation; **~einstellung** *f.* strike; **~erlaubnis** *f.* work permit; **~fähig** *a.* able-bodied, fit to work; *in arbeitsfähigem Zustand,* in operating condition; *arbeitsfähige Mehrheit,* working majority; **~gang** *m.* (*mech.*) operation; **~gebiet** *n.* field; **~gemeinschaft** *f.* workers' association; **~gericht** *n.* industrial court; **~leistung** *f.* rate of output; (*einer Maschine*) service; **~los** *a.* out of work, unemployed; **~losenunterstützung** *f.* unemployment benefit, dole; **~losenversicherung** *f.* unemployment insurance; **~losigkeit** *f.* unemployment; **~minister** *m.* Secretary of Labor; **~scheu** *a.* lazy, shirking; **~streit** *m.* industrial dispute; **~stück** *n.* job; **~stunden** *f.pl.* working hours, hours of work; **~stunde** *f.* **pro Kopf** man-hour; **~unfähig** *a.* incapable of work; **~unfähigkeit** *f.* disablement; **~verhältnis** *n.* employment; **~zeit** *f.* working hours; **~zeitverkürzung** *f.* reduction of working hours; **~zimmer** *n.* workroom; study.
arbeitsam *a.* laborious, industrious.
Archäologe *m.* **(-n, -n); Archäologin** *f.* **(-, -nen)** archaeologist.
Archäologie *f.* **(-, 0)** archaeology.
archäologisch *a.* archaeologic(al).
Arche *f.* **(-, -n)** ark.
Archipel *m.* **(-s, -e)** archipelago.
Architekt *m.* **(-en, -en); Architektin** *f.* **(-, -nen)** architect.
Architektur *f.* **(-, -en)** architecture.
Archiv *n.* **(-[e]s, -e)** archives, record office.
Archivar *m.* **(-[e]s, -e)** archivist.
archivieren *v.t.* to archive.
Areal *n.* **(-[e]s, -e)** area, surface.
arg *a.* arrant; bad; mischievous.
Arg *n.* (0) malice.
ärgen *v.t.* to annoy; to make angry; to vex; *sich ~ über,* to be annoyed at.
Ärger *m.* **(-s, 0)** annoyance, vexation, anger, worry, irritation.
ärgerlich *a.* annoying, provoking, vexatious; angry.
Ärgernis *n.* **(-nisses, -nisse)** offense, scandal; vexation.
Arglist *f.* **(-, 0)** deceit, cunning.
arglos *a.* inoffensive, harmless.
Argument *n.* **(-s, -e)** argument.
Argumentation *f.* **(-, -en)** argumentation.
argumentieren *v.i.* argue.
Argwohn *m.* **(-[e]s, 0)** suspicion.
argwöhnen *v.t.* to suspect.
argwöhnisch *a.* suspicious, distrustful.
a.Rh. *am Rhein,* on the Rhein.
Arie *f.* **(-, -n)** aria.
Arier *m.* **(-s, -), arisch** *a.* Aryan.
Aristokrat *m.* **(-en, -en); Aristokratin** *f.* **(-, -nen)** aristocrat.
Aristokratie *f.* **(-, -[e]n)** aristocracy.
aristokratisch *a.* aristocratic.
Arithmetik *f.* **(-, 0)** arithmetic.
Arithmetiker *m.* **(-s, -); Arithmetikerin** *f.* **(-, -nen)** arithmetician.
arithmetisch *a.* arithmetical.
Arkade *f.* **(-, -n)** arcade.
Arktis *f.* **(-, 0)** Arctic.
arktisch *a.* arctic.
arm *a.* poor.
Arm *m.* **(-[e]s, -e)** arm; (*Fluß*) branch.
Armatur *f.* **(-, -en)** armature; fittings; instrument (car).
Armaturenbrett *n.* **(-s, -en)** instrument panel; dashboard.
Armband *n.* bracelet; **~uhr** *f.* wristwatch.
Armbinde *f.* band; sling.
Armbrust *f.* crossbow.
Arme *m.* & *f.* **(-n, -n)** poor man/woman.
Armee *f.* **(-, -n)** army.
Ärmel *m.* **(-s, -)** sleeve.
Armen: ~haus *n.* poorhouse; **~pflege** *f.* poor relief; **~recht** *n.* legal aid.
Armenien *n.* **(-s, 0)** Armenia; **Armenier** *m.* **(-s, -); Armenierin** *f.* **(-, -nen); armenisch** *a.* Armenian.
Armlehne *f.* arm (of an armchair).

Armleuchter *m.* chandelier.
ärmlich *a.* poor, miserable.
Armreif *m.* **(-s, -en)** bangle.
armselig *a.* needy, miserable; paltry; pathetic.
Armsessel *m.* **(-s, -); Armstuhl** *m.* **(-s, -stühle)** armchair.
Armut *f.* **(-, 0)** poverty, indigence.
Aroma *n.* **(-s, -s** *or* **-ta)** flavor, aroma, fragrance.
aromatisch *a.* aromatic.
Arrak *m.* **(-s, 0)** arrack.
Arrangement *m.* **(-s, -s)** arrangement.
arrangieren *v.t.* to arrange.
Arrest *m.* **(-[e]s, -e)** detention, arrest, seizure.
Arrestant *m.* **(-en, -en)** prisoner.
arretieren *v.t.* to detain, to arrest, to take into custody.
arrivieren *v.i.* to arrive, to achieve.
Arrivierte *m.* & *f.* **(-n, -n)** (*pej.*) parvenu.
arrogant *a.* arrogant.
Arroganz *f.* **(-, 0)** arrogance.
Arsch *m.* **(-es, Ärsche)** ass, arse, backside, buttocks.
Arschbacke *f.* buttock.
Arsch: ~kriecher *m.* (*vulg.*) ass-kisser; **~kriecherei** *f.* (*vulg.*) ass-kissing; **~loch** *n.* (*vulg.*) asshole.
Arsenal *n.* **(-[e]s, -e)** arsenal.
Arsenik *m.* **(-s, 0)** arsenic.
Art *f.* **(-, -en)** (*Geschlecht*) species, race, stock; (*Sorte*) sort, kind; (*Weise*) way, manner; (*Lebensart*) *pl.* manners; *auf diese ~*, in this way.
Art. *Artikel*, article, art.
Arterie *f.* **(-, -en)** artery.
Arterienverkalkung *f.* **(-, -en)** arteriosclerosis.
artesisch *a.* Artesian.
artfremd *a.* (*bio.*) alien, foreign.
artig *a.* well-behaved, civil, polite.
Artigkeit *f.* **(-, -en)** politeness, courtesy.
Artikel *m.* **(-s, -)** article; (*com.*) item.
artikulieren *v.t.* articulate.
Artillerie *f.* **(-, -[e]n)** artillery, ordnance.
Artillerist *m.* **(-en, -en)** artillery man, gunner.
Artischocke *f.* **(-, -n)** artichoke.
Artist *m.* **(-en, -en); Artistin** *f.* **(-, -nen)** artist (circus).
Arznei *f.* **(-, -en)** medicine.
Arzneikunde *f.* pharmaceutics *pl.*.
Arzt *m.* **(-es, Ärzte); Ärztin** *f.* **(-, -nen)** physician, doctor.
Arzthelferin *f.* doctor's receptionist.
ärztlich *a.* medical; **~es Attest** *n.* medical certificate; **~e Betreuung** *f.* medical care.
Arztpraxis *f.* **(-, -xen)** doctor's office.
As *n.* **(Asses, Asse)** ace.
As *n.* **(-, -)** (*mus.*) A flat.
Asbest *m.* **(-es, -e)** asbestos.
Asche *f.* **(-, -n)** *pl.* ashes.
Aschenbecher *m.* ashtray.
Aschenbrödel *n.* Cinderella.
Aschermittwoch *m.* Ash Wednesday.
Asiat *m.* **(-en, -en); Asiatin** *f.* **(-, -nen); asiatisch** *a.* Asian.
Asien *n.* **(-s, -)** Asia.
Askese *f.* **(-, 0)** asceticism.
Asket *m.* **(-en, -en)** ascetic.
asozial *a.* antisocial; asocial.
Asoziale *m.* & *f.* **(-n, -n)** social misfit.
Aspekt *m.* **(-s, -e)** aspect.
Asphalt *m.* **(-[e]s, -e)** asphalt.
asphaltieren *v.t.* to asphalt.
Aspirant *m.* **(-en, -en)** candidate.
Assessor *m.* **(-s, -en)** assessor; assistant judge.
assimilieren *v.t.* to assimilate.
Assistent *m.* **(-en, -en); Assistentin** *f.* **(-, -nen)** assistant.
Assistenzarzt *m.* **(-es, -ärzte); Assistenzärztin** *f.* **(-, -nen)** junior doctor.
assoziieren *v.r.* to enter into partnership; ~ *v.t.* to associate.
Ast *m.* **(-es, Äste)** bough, branch; (*im Holze*) knot.
Aster *f.* **(-, -n)** aster.
Ästhetik *f.* **(-, 0)** aesthetics *pl.*
ästhetisch *a.* aesthetic.
Asthma *n.* **(-s, 0)** asthma.
Asthmatiker *m.* **(-s, -); Asthmatikerin** *f.* **(-, -nen)** asthmatic.
Astloch *n.* knothole.
Astrologe *m.* **(-n, -n)** astrologer.
Astrologie *f.* **(-, 0)** astrology.
Astronom *m.* **(-en, -en)** astronomer.
Astronomie *f.* **(-, 0)** astronomy.
astronomisch *a.* astronomical.
Astrophysik *f.* **(-, 0)** astrophysics.
Asyl *n.* **(-[e]s, -e)** asylum.
Asylant *m.* **(-en, -en); Asylantin** *f.* **(-, -nen)** person seeking asylum.
asymmetrisch *a.* asymmetrical.
asynchron *a.* asynchronous.
A.T. *Altes Testament*, Old Testament.
Atelier *n.* **(-s, -s)** (artist's) studio.
Atem *m.* **(-s, 0)** breath, breathing; *ausser ~*, out of breath; *den ~ anhalten*, to hold one's breath.
atemlos *a.* breathless.
Atemnot *f.* shortness of breath.
Atempause *f.* breathing space.
Atemzug *m.* breath.
Atheismus *m.* **(-,0)** atheism.
Atheist *m.* **(-en, -en)** atheist.
Äther *m.* **(-s, 0)** ether.
ätherisch *a.* ethereal, aerial.
Äthiopien *n.* **(-s, 0)** Ethiopia; **Äthiopier** *m.* **(-s, -); Äthiopierin** *f.* **(-, -nen); äthiopisch** *a.* Ethiopian.
Athlet *m.* **(-en, -en)** athlete.
Athletik *f.* **(-, 0)** athletics.
Atlantik *m.* **(-s, 0)** Atlantic.
Atlas *m.* **(-ses, Atlanten)** atlas.
Atlas *m.* **(-lasses, -lasse)** (*Stoff*) satin.
atmen *v.t.* & *i.* to breathe, to respire.
Atmosphäre *f.* **(-, -n)** atmosphere.
atmosphärisch *a.* atmospheric.
Atmung *f.* **(-, 0)** respiration.
Atom *n.* **(-[e]s, -e)** atom; particle.
Atom... atomic.
atomar *a.* atomic.
Atombombe *f.* atomic bomb.
atomisieren *v.t.* to atomize.
Atom: ~kern *m.* atomic nucleus; **~kraft** *f.* nuclear power; **~kraftwerk** *n.* nuclear power plant; **~krieg** *m.* nuclear war; **~macht** *f.* nuclear power; **~müll** *m.* nuclear waste; **~rakete** *f.* nuclear missile; **~sprengkopf** *m.* nuclear warhead; **~waffe** *f.* nuclear weapon; **~waffensperrvertrag** *m.* Nuclear Nonproliferation Treaty; **~zeitalter** *n.* nuclear age.
Attaché *m.* **(-s, -s)** attaché.
Attacke *f.* **(-, -n)** attack.
Attentat *n.* **(-[e]s, -e)** assassination; assassination attempt.
Attentäter *m.* **(-s, -)** assassin.

Attest *n.* **(-[e]s, -e)** certificate.
attestieren *v.t.* to certify.
attraktiv *a.* attractive.
Attrappe *f.* **(-, -n)** dummy; sham.
Attribut *n.* **(-[e]s, -e)** attribute.
atypisch *a.* atypical.
ätzen *v.t.* (*med.*) to cauterize; (*Kunst*) to etch.
ätzend *a.* corrosive; (*fig.*) caustic.
Ätzmittel *n.* corrosive; (*med.*) cautery.
au! *i.* oh!
Aubergine *f.* eggplant.
auch *c.* also, too, even, likewise; ~ *nicht,* neither, nor; *sowohl... als* ~, as well... as..., both... and.
Audienz *f.* **(-, -en)** audience.
Auditorium *n.* **(-s, -rien)** lecture hall, auditorium.
Auerhahn *m.* capercaillie.
Auerochs *m.* bison, auerochs.
auf *pro.* on, upon, in, at, to, up, into, after; ~ *adv.* up, upward; **~!** *i.* arise; ~ *daß,* in order that; ~ *und ab,* up and down; ~ *einmal,* all at once, suddenly.
aufarbeiten *v.t.* to catch up; to refurbish; to work up.
aufatmen *v.i.* to breathe again.
aufbahren *v.t.* to lay out.
Aufbahrung *f.* **(-, 0)** lying in state.
Aufbau *m.* **(-[e]s, -e)** erection, structure, construction; organization.
aufbauen *v.t.* to erect, to build up.
aufbäumen *v.r.* to rear up.
aufbauschen *v.t. & i.* to billow; to puff, to swell up, to exaggerate.
aufbegehren *v.i.* to rise up *or* revolt.
aufbehalten *v.t.st.* to keep on.
aufbekommen *v.t.st.* to get open (door).
aufbessern *v.t.* (*Gehalt*) to raise.
aufbewahren *v.t.* to preserve, to keep, to take charge of.
Aufbewahrung *f.* **(-, 0)** preservation.
aufbieten *v.t.st.* to raise, to summon; (*fig.*) to exert oneself; (*Verlobte*) to publish banns of marriage.
aufbinden *v.t.st.* to untie, to loosen.
aufblähen *v.t.* to puff up; to inflate; to expand.
aufblasbar *a.* inflatable.
aufblasen *v.t.st.* to blow up, to inflate.
aufbleiben *v.i.st. (s)* to stay up; to remain open.
aufblenden *v.t. & i* to switch to high beam.
aufblicken *v.i.* to look up.
aufblinken *v.i.* to flash; to glint.
aufblitzen *v.i.* to flash; to sparkle.
aufblühen *v.i.* to bloom; to blossom.
aufbrauchen *v.t.* to consume, to use up.
aufbrausen *v.i. (s)* to flare up; to roar; to effervesce; (*fig.*) to fly out.
aufbrausend *a.* hot-tempered.
aufbrechen *v.t.st.* to break open; ~ *v.i.st. (s)* to burst open; to set out.
aufbringen *v.t.ir.* (*Truppen, Geld*) to raise; (*erzürnen*) to provoke; (*Kosten*) to defray.
Aufbruch *m.* **(-[e]s, 0)** departure.
aufbrühen *v.t.* to brew [up].
aufbügeln *v.t.* to iron, to do up.
aufbürden *v.t.* to burden.
aufdecken *v.t.* to uncover; to disclose.
aufdrängen *v.t.* to thrust upon; ~ *v.r.* to impose oneself.
aufdrehen *v.t.* to turn on.
aufdringen *v.t.st.* to force upon.
aufdringlich *a.* obtrusive; pushy; importunate; insistent.
aufdröseln *v.t.* to unravel.
aufdrücken *v.t.* to impress.
aufeinander *adv.* one after another, one upon another.
Aufenthalt *m.* **(-[e]s, -e)** stay; residence; (*Verzögerung*) delay; (*rail.*) stop.
Aufenthaltsort *m.* place of residence.
auferlegen *v.t.* to impose.
auferstehen *v.i.st. (s)* to rise from the dead.
Auferstehung *f.* **(-, 0)** resurrection.
auferwecken *v.t.* to raise from the dead, to resuscitate.
aufessen *v.i.st. (s)* to eat (up), to finish.
auffahren *v.i.st. (s)* to ascend; to start (up).
Auffahrt *f.* **(-, -en)** (*vor Palästen*) drive, approach.
auffallen *v.i.st. (s)* (*einem*) to strike (*fig.*); to stand out.
auffallend, auffällig *a.* striking.
auffangen *v.t.st.* to catch.
Auffanglinie *f.* (*mil.*) holding line.
auffassen *v.t.* to understand, to take in, to conceive; to interpret (*role*).
Auffassung *f.* **(-, -en)** comprehension, perception; opinion.
auffindbar *a.* traceable.
auffinden *v.t.st.* to find.
auffischen *v.t.st.* (*fam.*) to fish out.
aufflackern *v.i.* to flicker up; to flare up.
aufflammen *v.i. (s)* to flame, to blaze.
auffliegen *v.i.* to fly up.
auffordern *v.t.* to ask, to invite, to request.
Aufforderung *f.* **(-, -en)** summons; invitation.
aufforsten *v.t.* to reforest.
auffressen *v.t.st.* to eat up, to devour.
auffrischen *v.t.* to refresh; to brush up; to touch up.
Auffrischung *f.* brushing up; (*mil.*) rehabilitation.
aufführen *v.t.* to perform; to represent; (*Einzelnes*) to list, to specify; ~ *v.r.* to behave.
Aufführung *f.* **(-, -en)** performance, representation; behavior.
auffüllen *v.t.* to fill up.
Aufgabe *f.* **(-, -n)** delivery; (*Brief*~) posting; (*Schul*~) lesson; task, problem; surrender, resignation.
Aufgang *m.* **(-[e]s, -gänge)** stairs; steps; ascent.
aufgeben *v.t.st.* to give up, to deliver; (*Brief*) to mail; (*Gepäck*) to check; (*Frage, Rätsel*) to propose; (*Plan, Stelle*) to abandon, to resign, to give up.
aufgeblasen *a.* puffed up.
Aufgebot *n.* **(-[e]s, -e)** (*mil.*) contingent; levy; banns of marriage *pl.*
aufgebracht *a.* angry, furious.
aufgedreht *a.* (*fam.*) in high spirits.
aufgedunsen *a.* bloated, swollen, sodden.
aufgehen *v.i.st.* (*Sonne*) to rise; (*Blüten*) to open; (*Knoten*) to become loose, to come undone; (*Fenster, etc.*) to come open; (*Genähtes*) to give way; (*math.*) to leave no remainder.
aufgeklärt *a.* enlightened; explained.
aufgekratzt *a.* (*fam.*) in high spirits.
aufgelegt *a.* disposed (for), -minded.
aufgelöst *a.* distraught.
aufgeräumt *a.* merry, in good humor.
aufgeregt *a.* excited, flustered.
Aufgeregtheit *f.* **(-, 0)** excitement; agitation.

aufgeschlossen *a.* open-minded, approachable.
Aufgeschlossenheit *f.* open-mindedness.
aufgeschmissen *a.* (*fam.*) ~ *sein*, to be stuck.
aufgeweckt *a.* bright, clever.
aufgießen *v.t.st.* to make (tea, coffee); to brew.
aufgliedern *v.t.* to subdivide, to break down into parts.
aufgreifen *v.t.st.* to take up; to pick up.
aufgrund *pr.* on the basis of.
Aufguß *m.* **(-gusses, -güsse)** infusion.
aufhaben *v.t.st.* to have on; to have to do (schoolwork).
aufhaken *v.t.* to unhook, to unclasp.
aufhalsen *v.t.* to saddle (with).
aufhalten *v.t.st.* to hold up; to delay, to detain; ~ *v.r.* to reside, to stay; (*über etwas*) to find fault with sth.
aufhängen *v.t.* to hang up; to hang upon; ~ *v.r.* to hang oneself.
Aufhänger *m.* loop (clothes); tab; peg (article).
aufhäufen *v.t.* to heap up, to pile; ~ *v.r.* to accumulate.
Aufhäufung *f.* **(-, -en)** accumulation.
aufheben *v.t.st.* to pick up; (*bewahren*) to keep, to preserve; (*sparen*) to save; (*Gesetz*) to abrogate; (*Belagerung*) to raise.
Aufheben *n.* **(-s, 0)** *viel ~s machen*, to make a big fuss.
Aufhebung *f.* **(-, -en)** (*eines Gesetzes*) abolition; repeal, rescission.
aufheitern *v.t.* to clear up; to cheer up; ~ *v.r.* to clear up (weather); (*fig.*) to grow cheerful.
Aufheiterung *f.* **(-, -en)** clearing up.
aufheizen *v.t.* to heat up, to inflame.
aufhelfen *v.t.st.* to help up.
aufhellen *v.t.* to brighten; ~ *v.r.* to clear up.
aufhetzen *v.t.* to stir up; to incite.
aufholen *v.i.* to catch up (with); to make up.
aufhorchen *v.i.* to listen.
aufhören *v.i.* to cease, to leave off, to stop; *da hört alles auf*, that's the limit.
aufjauchzen *v.i.* to shout with joy.
aufkaufen *v.t.* to buy up.
Aufkäufer *m.* **(-s, -)** forestaller.
aufkeimen *v.i.* to sprout; to burgeon.
aufklappen *v.t.* to open; to fold back.
aufklären *v.t.* to clear up; (*fig.*) to explain; to enlighten; (*mil.*) to reconnoiter.
Aufklärung *f.* **(-, -en)** clearing up; enlightenment; explanation; reconnoitering.
aufkleben *v.t.* to paste upon, to stick on.
Aufkleber *m.* **(-s, -)** sticker.
aufknacken *v.t.* to crack open.
aufknöpfen *v.t.* to unbutton.
aufknoten *v.t.* to undo; to untie.
aufknüpfen *v.t.* to untie; to hang.
aufkochen *v.t.* to bring to a boil.
aufkommen *v.i.st.* *(s)* to come into use; (*für*) to be responsible (for); to prevail.
aufkrempeln *v.t.* to roll up (sleeves).
aufkriegen *v.t.* to get sth. open.
aufkündigen *v.t.* to renounce; (*Kapital*) to recall; to cancel.
Aufl. *Auflage*, edition, ed.
aufladen *v.t.st.* to load; (*fig.*) to impose, to saddle.
Auflage *f.* **(-, -n)** impost, duty, tax; (*eines Buches*) edition; (*einer Zeitung*) circulation.
Auflagenhöhe *f.* number of copies printed.
auflassen *v.t.st.* to leave open.
auflauern *v.t.* to lie in wait for, to waylay.
Auflauf *m.* **(-[e]s, -läufe)** crowd; tumult, riot; (*Speise*) soufflé.
auflaufen *v.i.st.* *(s)* (*nav.*) to run aground; (*anwachsen*) to accumulate; *aufgelaufene Summe*, aggregate amount.
aufleben *v.i.* *(s)* to revive.
auflegen *v.i.* to put on; to publish.
auflehnen *v.r.* (*gegen*) to rebel (against), to oppose.
Auflehnung *f.* **(-, -en)** insurrection, mutiny.
auflesen *v.t.st.* to pick up, to glean.
aufleuchten *v.i.* to light up.
aufliegen *v.i.st.* to lie; to rest; ~ *v.r.* to become bedsore.
auflisten *v.i.* to list.
auflockern *v.t.* to loosen.
Auflockerung *f.* **(-, -en)** loosening.
auflodern *v.i.* *(s)* to blaze up.
auflösbar *a.* soluble.
auflösen *v.t.* to loosen, to untie; to dissolve, to melt; (*Rätsel*) to solve; (*Brüche*) to reduce; (*mil. Einheiten*) to disband; ~ *v.r.* to dissolve, to break up.
Auflösung *f.* **(-, -en)** solution; (*mil.*) disbandment, deactivation.
aufmachen *v.t.* to open; to unpack; ~ *v.r.* to set out.
Aufmachung *f.* **(-, -en)** style; presentation; layout.
Aufmarsch *m.* **(-es, -märsche)** (*mil.*) review; deployment.
aufmarschieren *v.i.* *(s)* to march up, to deploy.
aufmerken *v.i.* to attend to.
aufmerksam *a.* attentive; ~ *machen auf*, to draw attention to.
Aufmerksamkeit *f.* **(-, -en)** attention, attentiveness.
aufmöbeln *v.t.* to do up; to pep up, to cheer up.
aufmotzen *v.t.* to soup up.
aufmucken *v.i.* (*fam.*) to balk at.
aufmuntern *v.t.* to encourage, to cheer.
Aufmunterung *f.* **(-, -en)** encouragement.
aufmüpfig *a. & adv.* (*fam.*) rebellious.
aufnähen *v.t.* to sew on.
Aufnahme *f.* **(-, -n)** reception, admission; survey; photographing; shooting (film); recording; photo, snapshot.
Aufnahme: ~gebühr *f.* entrance fee; **~prüfung** *f.* entrance examination.
aufnehmen *v.t.st.* to take up; to pick up; to receive; to admit; (*abbilden*) to photograph; (*messen*) to survey; (*Geld*) to borrow; (*Gäste*) to receive.
aufnötigen *v.t.* to force upon.
aufoktroyieren *v.t.* to impose.
aufopfern *v.t.* to sacrifice.
aufopfernd *a. & adv.* self-sacrificing.
Aufopferung *f.* **(-, -en)** sacrifice.
aufpäppeln *v.t.* (*fam.*) to fatten up.
aufpassen *v.i.* to attend, to look out, to take notice.
Aufpasser *m.* **(-s, -)** spy, guard.
aufpeitschen *v.t.* to whip up; to inflame.
aufpflanzen *v.t.* (*Seitengewehr*) to fix; ~ *v.r.* to plant oneself.
aufpflügen *v.t.* to plow up.
aufpfropfen *v.t.* to graft on.
aufpicken *v.t.* (*fam.*) to pick up.
aufplatzen *v.i.* to burst open; to open up;

aufplustern *v.t.* to ruffle up; to puff up; ~ *v.r.* to ruffle its feathers; (*fig.*) to show off.
aufpolieren *v.t.* to polish up.
Aufprall *m.* **(-s, -e)** impact.
aufprallen *v.i.* to hit; to collide.
Aufpreis *m.* **(-es, -e)** extra charge.
aufpumpen *v.t.* to pump up, to inflate.
aufputschen *v.t.* (*pej.*) to stimulate; to arouse.
Aufputschmittel *n.* **(-s, -)** stimulant.
Aufputz *m.* **(-es, -e)** finery, dress.
aufquellen *v.i.* to swell up.
aufraffen *v.r.* to pull oneself together; to bring oneself to do sth.; to recover; (*fig.*) to pluck up courage.
aufrappeln *v.r.* (*fam.*) to struggle to one's feet.
aufrauhen *v.t.* to roughen up.
aufräumen *v.t.* to tidy, to remove, to set in order; to clear; *mit etwas* ~, to make a clean sweep of sth.
aufrecht *a.* & *adv.* upright, erect; ~ *erhalten*, to maintain.
Aufrechthaltung *f.* **(-, 0)** maintenance.
aufrechtstehend *a.* on end, on edge.
aufregen *v.t.* to stir up, to rouse; to incite, to excite; (*nervös*) to flutter.
Aufregung *f.* **(-, -en)** excitement, agitation.
aufreiben *v.t.st.* to rub open, to gall; (*fig.*) to worry; (*vertilgen*) to destroy.
aufreihen *v.t.* to string.
aufreißen *v.t.st.* to tear open; (*Tür*) to fling open; ~ *v.i.st.* to burst, to split.
aufreizen *v.t.* to rouse, to excite.
aufreizend *v.t.* provocative.
Aufreizung *f.* **(-, -en)** provocation; incitement.
aufrichten *v.t.* to set up; to erect; to straighten up; (*fig.*) to comfort; ~ *v.r.* to sit up.
aufrichtig *a.* sincere, frank.
Aufrichtigkeit *f.* **(-, 0)** sincerity.
aufriegeln *v.t.* to unbolt.
Aufriß *m.* **(-risses, -risse)** sketch.
aufrollen *v.t.* to roll up; to unroll.
aufrücken *v.i.* to move up.
Aufruf *m.* **(-[e]s, -e)** call, summons.
aufrufen *v.t.st.* to call up, to summon.
Aufruhr *m.* **(-[e]s, -e)** uproar, insurrection, rebellion.
aufrühren *v.t.* to stir up.
Aufrührer *m.* **(-s, -)** rebel, mutineer.
aufrührerisch *a.* rebellious.
aufrunden *v.t.* to round off.
aufrüsten *v.i.* & *t.* to arm.
Aufrüstung *f.* **(-, 0)** armament.
aufrütteln *v.t.* to shake up, to rouse.
aufs = auf das.
aufsagen *v.t.* to recite.
aufsammeln *v.t.* to pick up, to gather.
aufsässig *a.* recalcitrant, refractory, adverse.
Aufsatz *m.* **(-es, -sätze)** essay, article; top; (*Tafel*~) centerpiece; essay, paper.
aufsaugen *v.t.st.* to vacuum; to suck up; to absorb.
aufschauen *v.i.* to look up.
aufscheuchen *v.t.* to frighten, to scare.
aufscheuern *v.t.* to chafe.
aufschichten *v.t.* to pile up, to stack.
aufschieben *v.t.st.* to postpone, to delay, to defer, to put off; to adjourn.
aufschießen *v.i.* to shoot up; to leap up.
Aufschlag *m.* **(-[e]s, -schläge)** (*Rock*~) cuff, facings; *Preis*~, rise, advance; (*mil. Geschoß*) impact; (*Tennis*) service.
aufschlagen *v.t.st.* (*die Augen*) to cast up; (*Gerüst*) to put up; (*Buch*) to open; (*Wort*) to look up; (*Zelt*) to pitch; ~ *v.i.* (*s*) (*im Preise*) to raise; (*tennis*) to serve.
aufschließen *v.t.st.* to unlock.
aufschlitzen *v.t.* to slit, to slash open; to rip up.
Aufschluß *m.* **(-schlusses, -schlüsse)** (*fig.*) explanation.
aufschlüsseln *v.t.* to break down, to classify.
aufschlußreich *a.* informative; revealing.
aufschnallen *v.t.* to unbuckle; to buckle on.
aufschnappen *v.t.* (*fam.*) to pick up.
aufschneiden *v.t.st.* to cut open; (*Buch*) to cut the pages; ~ *v.i.st.* to swagger, to brag.
Aufschneider *m.* **(-s, -)** swaggerer, braggart.
Aufschnitt *m.* **(-[e]s, -e)** *kalter* ~, slices of cold meat.
aufschnüren *v.t.* to unlace.
aufschrauben *v.t.* to unscrew; to screw on.
aufschrecken *v.t.* to startle; ~ *v.i.* (*s*) to start, to jump.
Aufschrei *m.* **(-[e]s, -e)** scream, shriek, outcry.
aufschreiben *v.t.st.* to write down, to take down, to put down.
aufschreien *v.i.st.* to cry out, to scream.
Aufschrift *f.* **(-, -en)** inscription; direction, address.
Aufschub *m.* **(-[e]s, -0)** delay, adjournment.
aufschürfen *v.t.* to graze; to scrape.
aufschürzen *v.t.* to tuck up.
aufschütteln *v.t.* to shake up, to rouse.
aufschütten *v.t.* to heap up; to pour upon.
aufschwatzen, aufschwätzen *v.t.* to talk into.
aufschwingen *v.r.* to soar, to rise.
Aufschwung *m.* **(-[e]s, -schwünge)** upswing; recovery; boom; rise, progress.
Aufsehen *n.* **(-s, 0)** looking up; (*fig.*) stir, sensation.
aufsehenerregend *a.* sensational.
Aufseher *m.* **(-s, -)** guard; inspector.
auf sein *v.i.ir* (*s*) to be up (out of bed); to be open.
aufsetzen *v.t.* (*Hut, Miene*) to put on; (*schriftlich*) to draw up; ~ *v.r.* to sit up.
Aufsicht *f.* **(-, 0)** inspection, supervision, superintendence, charge.
aufsichtführend *a.* in charge; on duty.
Aufsichts supervisory; **~behörde** *f.* inspectorate; **~rat** *m.* board of directors.
aufsitzen *v.i.st.* (*s*) to sit up; to mount (a horse).
aufspalten *v.t.* & *i.st.* to split, to cleave.
Aufspaltung *f.* **(-, -en)** split.
aufspannen *v.t.* (*Schirm*) to open up; (*Segel*) to spread; *Saiten* ~, to string.
aufsparen *v.t.* to save, to lay up.
aufsperren *v.t.* to open wide, to throw wide; (*Schlösser*) to pick; (*das Maul*) to gape.
aufspielen *v.r.* to swagger; to set up for; ~ *v.i.* to play (music).
aufspießen *v.t.* to spit, to pierce; to impale; to skewer.
aufsprengen *v.t.* to burst open.
aufspringen *v.i.st.* (*s*) to leap up; to crack; (*Hände*) to chap.
aufsprühen *v.t.* to spray on.
aufspulen *v.t.* to wind up.
aufspüren *v.t.* to trace out, to track down.
aufstacheln *v.t.* to goad, to incite.

aufstampfen *v.i.* to stamp.
Aufstand *m.* **(-[e]s, -stände)** rebellion; insurrection, uproar, sedition.
aufständisch *a.* rebellious, seditious.
aufstapeln *v.t.* to pile up.
aufstechen *v.t.st.* to prick; to pick open; (*Geschwür*) to lance.
aufstecken *v.t.* to pin up, to put up (hair); to give up; (*fam.*) to retire.
aufstehen *v.i.st. (s)* to get up, to rise; (*aufrecht*) to stand up.
aufsteigen *v.i.st. (s)* to rise.
aufsteigend *a.* ascending.
Aufsteiger *m.* social climber; parvenu; (*sport*) promoted team.
aufstellen *v.t.* to set up, to put up, to erect; (*mil.*) to activate; (*Behauptung*) to make (an assertion); (*Grundsatz*) to lay down; (*Kandidaten*) to nominate.
Aufstellung *f.* **(-, -en)** (*mil.*) disposition; (*eines Kandidaten*) nomination.
Aufstieg *m.* **(-[e]s, -e)** ascent, rise; promotion.
aufstöbern *v.t.* (*fig.*) to put up; to track down; to ferret out.
aufstocken *v.t.* to raise; to increase.
aufstöhnen *v.i.* to groan.
aufstören *v.t.* to stir, to disturb, to rouse.
aufstoßen *v.t.st.* to push open; ~ *v.i.st. (s)* to occur to, to meet with; (*Speisen*)(*fam.*) to belch, to burp.
aufstrebend *a.* rising; ambitious.
aufstreichen *v.t.st.* to lay on, to spread.
Aufstrich *m.* (*Brot*~) spread.
aufstülpen *v.t.* to turn up, to cock.
aufstützen *v.t.* to prop up; ~ *v.i.* to lean (upon).
aufsuchen *v.t.* to visit, to look up.
auftakeln *v.t.* to rig out.
Auftakt *m.* **(-es, -e)** upbeat, anacrusis; (*fig.*) prelude, preliminaries *pl.*
auftanken *v.t. & i.* to fill up; to refuel.
auftauchen *v.t.* to emerge, to appear.
auftauen *v.t. & i.* to thaw.
aufteilen *v.t.* to divide, to parcel out.
Aufteilung *f.* **(-, -en)** dividing; sharing.
auftischen *v.t.* to serve up.
Auftrag *m.* **(-[e]s, -träge)** commission, task, order, mandate; (*mil.*) assignment, mission; *Aufträge annehmen* (*com.*) to accept orders.
auftragen *v.t.st.* to carry up; (*Speise*) to serve up; (*einem etwas*) to charge someone with; (*Farbe*) to lay on; (*Kleider*) to wear out.
Auftraggeber *m.* client, customer (who gives an order).
auftreiben *v.t.st.* (*Geld*) to raise; (*finden*) (*fam.*) to get hold of.
auftrennen *v.t.* to rip up; to undo.
auftreten *v.i.st. (s)* to appear, to come forth; to behave.
Auftreten *n.* manner, appearance.
Auftrieb *m.* **(-[e]s, -e)** buoyancy, lift; impetus (energy).
Auftritt *m.* **(-[e]s, -e)** (*theat.*) scene, appearance; entrance.
auftrocknen *v.t. & i.* to dry up.
auftrumpfen *v.i.* (*fig.*) to fight back.
auftun *v.r.st.* to open; (*fig.*) to open up; ~ *v.t.st.* to find; (*servieren*) to help.
auftürmen *v.t.* to pile up; ~ *v.r.* to tower up.
aufwachen *v.i. (s)* to wake up.
aufwachsen *v.i.st. (s)* to grow up.
Aufwallung *f.* **(-, -en)** bubbling; ebullition; (*fig.*) emotion, transport.
Aufwand *m.* **(-[e]s, -0)** expense, display.
aufwärmen *v.t.* to warm up.
aufwarten *v.i.* to wait on; to serve; to visit; ~ *mit,* to offer.
aufwärts *adv.* upward.
Aufwärtsentwicklung *f.* **(-, -en)** upward trend.
Aufwartung *f.* **(-, -en)** (*Bedienung*) attendance; ~ *machen,* to pay a visit.
aufwaschen *v.t.st.* to wash up.
aufwecken *v.t.* to wake up.
aufweichen *v.t.* to moisten, to soak.
aufweisen *v.t.st.* to show, to produce, to exhibit.
aufwenden *v.t.* to spend.
aufwendig *a.* costly, expensive; *adv.* lavishly.
aufwerfen *v.t.st.* (*Frage*) to raise; *sich ~ zu,* to set up for.
aufwerten *v.t.* to revalue, to revalorize.
Aufwertung *f.* **(-, -en)** revaluation, revalorization.
aufwickeln *v.t.* to wind up.
aufwiegeln *v.t.* to incite, to stir up.
aufwiegen *v.t.st.* to outweigh; to counterbalance.
Aufwind *m.* upwind; *im ~ sein,* to be on the upswing.
aufwirbeln *v.t.* to swirl up, to raise.
aufwischen *v.t.* to wipe up.
aufwühlen *v.t.* to agitate; to churn up; to stir.
aufzählen *v.t.* to enumerate.
Aufzählung *f.* **(-, -en)** enumeration, listing; list.
aufzäumen *v.t.* to bridle.
aufzehren *v.t.* to consume.
aufzeichnen *v.t.* to record; to draw.
Aufzeichnung *f.* **(-, -en)** note, record.
aufzeigen *v.t.* to point out; to demonstrate, to highlight.
aufziehen *v.t.st.* to draw up, to pull up; (*Uhr*) to wind up; (*Vorhang*) to draw; (*Kinder*) to rear, to bring up; (*Pflanzen*) to cultivate, to grow, to rear; (*foppen*) to rally, to chaff; *v.i. (s)* to march up.
Aufzug *m.* **(-[e]s, -züge)** hoist; (*Fahrstuhl*) elevator; (*theat.*) act; (*Gewand*) attire.
aufzwingen *v.t.st.* to force upon.
Aug. *August,* August, Aug.
Augapfel *m.* eyeball; (*fig.*) apple of one's eye, darling.
Auge *n.* **(-s, -n)** eye; *unter vier ~n,* between us, in private; *aus dem ~ verlieren,* to lose sight of; (*mil.*) *~n geradeaus,* eyes front; *~n rechts,* eyes right.
äugen *v.i.* to peer.
Augenarzt *m.* ophthalmologist.
Augenblick *m.* moment, twinkling.
augenblicklich *a.* instantaneous, momentary; ~ *adv.* instantly.
Augenbraue *f.* eyebrow; **~nstift** *m.* eyebrow pencil.
Augenglas *n.* eyeglass; (*des Fernrohrs*) eyepiece.
Augenhöhle *f.* eye socket.
Augenlicht *n.* eyesight.
Augenlid *n.* eyelid.
Augenmaß *n.* estimate, eye.
Augenmerk *n.* attention.
Augennerv *m.* optic nerve.
Augenschein *m.* appearance; view, inspection.
augenscheinlich *a.* evident, apparent.
Augenspiegel *m.* ophthalmoscope.
Augenwimper *f.* eyelash.
Augenzeuge *m.* eyewitness.
Augenzwinkern *n.* wink.

-äugig *a.* -eyed.
August *m.* **(-[e]s, -e)** (*Monat*) August.
Auktion *f.* **(-, -en)** public sale, auction.
Auktionator *m.* **(-s, -en)** auctioneer.
Aula *f.* **(-, -s)** assembly hall, auditorium.
aus *pr.* out of, from, through, about, on, upon, in by; ~ *adv.* out, over, up, finished, consumed.
Aus *n. der Ball ging ins* ~, the ball was out of bounds.
ausarbeiten *v.t.* to elaborate, to perfect, to compose.
ausarten *v.i. (s)* to degenerate.
ausatmen *v.t.* to breathe out, to exhale.
ausbaden *v.t.* (*fig.*) to suffer for, (*sl.*) to take the rap for.
ausbaggern *v.t.* to excavate; to dredge.
ausbalancieren *v.t.* to balance (out).
Ausbau *m.* **(-es, 0)** extension, completion.
ausbauen *v.t.* to extend; to finish; (*fig.*) to improve.
ausbedingen *v.t.st.* to stipulate, to reserve.
ausbessern *v.t.* to fix; to mend; to repair.
Ausbesserung *f.* **(-, -en)** repair, reparation.
ausbeulen *v.t.* to make baggy; to bulge.
Ausbeute *f.* **(-, 0)** yield; gain, profit.
ausbeuten *v.t.* to exploit.
Ausbeutung *f.* **(-, 0)** exploitation.
ausbezahlen *v.t.* to pay (out, off).
ausbilden *v.t.* to form; to school, to train, to cultivate; ~ *v.r.* to improve one's mind.
Ausbilder *m.* instructor.
Ausbildung *f.* **(-, 0)** training; *in der* ~ *sein*, to be in training, under training.
Ausbildungsförderung *f.* provision of (education) grants.
Ausbildungsplatz *m.* trainee post; apprenticeship.
Ausbildungsstelle *f.* training center.
ausbitten *v.t.st.* to request, to beg for; *sich* ~, to insist on.
ausblasen *v.t.st.* to blow out.
ausbleiben *v.i.st.* (*s*) to stay away, to fail to appear.
Ausbleiben *n.* **(-s, 0)** absence.
ausblenden *v.t.* to fade out.
Ausblick *m.* **(-[e]s, -e)** view, prospect, preview.
ausbomben *v.t.* to bomb out.
ausbooten *v.t.* (*fam.*) to get rid of.
ausborgen *v.t.* (*fam.*) to borrow.
ausbrechen *v.t.st.* to break out; ~ *v.i.st. (s)* to break out.
ausbreiten *v.t.* to spread, to extent; to propagate; ~ *v.r.* to gain ground.
Ausbreitung *f.* **(-, -en)** spreading, propagation.
ausbrennen *v.i.* to burn out.
Ausbruch *m.* **(-[e]s, -brüche)** outbreak; (*Vulkan*) eruption; outburst.
ausbrüten *v.t.* to hatch; (*fig.*) to breed; to plot.
Ausbuchtung *f.* **(-, -en)** bulge.
ausbuddeln *v.t.* to dig up.
ausbügeln *v.t.* to iron out; (*fig.*) to make good.
ausbuhen *v.t.* to boo.
Ausbund *m.* **(-[e]s, -bünde)** best, paragon.
Ausbürgerung *f.* **(-, -en)** expatriation.
ausbürsten *v.t.* to brush.
Ausdauer *f.* **(-, 0)** perseverance, endurance.
ausdauernd *a.* persevering, tenacious.
ausdehnbar *a.* expandable, extensible.
ausdehnen *v.t.* to extend, to stretch; (*fig.*) to prolong.
Ausdehnung *f.* **(-, -en)** extension, expansion, extent; dimension.
ausdenken *v.t.ir.* to contrive, to devise; to imagine.
ausdeuten *v.t.* to interpret, to explain.
Ausdeutung *f.* **(-, -en)** interpretation.
ausdienen *v.i. ausgedient haben*, to be used up.
ausdiskutieren *v.t.* to discuss thoroughly.
ausdörren *v.t.* to parch; to dry up.
ausdrehen *v.t.* (*das Gas*) to turn off; (*elektr. Licht*) to switch off.
Ausdruck *m.* **(-[e]s, -drücke)** expression; term.
ausdrücken *v.t.* to express; ~ *v.r.* to express oneself.
ausdrücklich *a.* express, explicit.
ausdruckslos *a.* blank, vacant.
ausdrucksvoll *a.* expressive, significant.
Ausdrucksweise *f.* mode of expression.
ausdunsten, ausdünsten *v.i. & t* to evaporate; (*schwitzen*) to perspire.
Ausdünstung *f.* **(-, -en)** evaporation; exhalation; (*Schweiss*) perspiration.
auseinander *adv.* apart, asunder; separately.
auseinandernehmen *v.t.* to disassemble.
Auseinandersetzung *f.* **(-, -en)** examination; argument; dispute; discussion.
auserkoren *a.* chosen, elect.
auserlesen *v.t.st.* to choose, to select; ~ *a.* select, choice; exquisite.
ausersehen *v.t.st.* to single out.
ausfahren *v.t.st.* (*Flotte*) to put out, to put to sea.
Ausfahrt *f.* **(-, -en)** exit; departure; drive; (*Tor*) gateway.
Ausfall *m.* **(-[e]s, -fälle)** falling out; deficiency; (*Ergebnis*) result; (*mil.*) sally; (*im Fechten*) thrust, pass; failure; breakdown.
ausfallen *v.i.st. (s)* fall out, (*gut oder schlecht*) to turn out; (*Haar*) to come off; not to take place; (*mil.*) to make a sally; (*im Fechten*) to lunge.
ausfallend *a.* aggressive, abusive (verbally).
Ausfallstraße *f.* main road.
ausfechten *v.t.st.* to fight out.
ausfegen *v.t.* to sweep (out).
ausfeilen *v.t.* to file down; to polish.
ausfertigen *v.t.* to issue; to dispatch; (*Rechnung*) to make out; (*Urkunde*) to execute.
Ausfertigung *f.* **(-, -en)** dispatch; execution.
ausfindig machen *v.t.* to find out.
ausfliegen *v.i.* to fly out.
ausflippen *v.i.* (*fam.*) to freak out.
Ausflucht *f.* **(-, -flüchte)** evasion, subterfuge, poor excuse.
Ausflug *m.* **(-[e]s, -flüge)** outing, trip, excursion.
Ausflügler *m.* **(-s, -)** excursionist.
Ausflugs: ~dampfer *m.* pleasure steamer; **~lokal** *n.* restaurant for excursionists; **~ziel** *n.* destination of an excursion.
Ausfluß *m.* **(-flusses, -flüsse)** flowing out; (*Loch, etc.*) outlet; (*Mündung*) mouth; (*med.*) discharge; (*phys.*) emanation.
ausformen *v.t.* to shape.
ausformulieren *v.t.* to formulate; to flesh out.
ausforschen *v.t.* to search out.
ausfragen *v.t.* to examine.
ausfransen *v.t.* to fray.
ausfressen *v.t.* to erode; *etw.* ~, to be up to sth.
Ausfuhr *f.* **(-, -en)** exportation, export.
ausführbar *a.* practicable, feasible.
ausführen *v.t.* (*Waren*) to export; (*vollenden*) to perform, to execute; to set forth.

Ausfuhrhandel *m.* export trade.
ausführlich *a.* detailed, ample, full; ~ *adv.* in detail, fully.
Ausfuhr: ~stelle *f.* export control office; **~zoll** *m.* export duty.
Ausführung *f.* **(-, -en)** (*fig.*) execution; statement.
Ausführungsbestimmung *f.* executive regulation.
ausfüllen *v.t.* to fill out; (*Formular*) to complete, to fill in.
Ausgabe *f.* **(-, -n)** (*eines Buchs*) edition; (*Kosten*) expense; (*Papiergeld*) issue.
Ausgang *m.* **(-[e]s, -gänge)** going out; (*Ergebnis*) issue, event; (*Ende*) end, conclusion; (*Tür*) way out, exit.
Ausgangs: ~lage *f.* initial situation; **~punkt** *m.* starting point; **~sperre** *f.* curfew; **~stellung** *f.* starting position.
ausgeben *v.t.st.* to distribute; (*Buch*) to publish, to edit; (*Geld*) to spend; (*Papiergeld*) to issue; *sich ~ für,* to pass oneself off as.
ausgebrannt *a.* gutted.
ausgebreitet *a.* extensive.
ausgebucht *a.* booked up.
ausgebufft *a.* (*fam.*) canny; crafty.
Ausgeburt *f.* **(-, -en)** product, creature.
ausgedehnt *a.* extensive.
ausgedient *a.* superannuated; (*sl.*) worn out; beat up.
ausgefallen *a.* unusual.
ausgeglichen *a.* balanced, harmonious.
ausgehen *v.i.st.* *(s)* to go out; *~ von,* to originate with, to assume; (*Haare, Farbe*) to come out *or* off, to fade; (*zu Ende gehen*) to run out; *es ist uns ausgegangen,* we have run out of it.
ausgehungert *a.* starving.
Ausgehverbot *n.* curfew; *~ aufheben,* to lift the curfew.
ausgelassen *a.* frisky, exuberant; boisterous.
Ausgelassenheit *f.* exuberance; boisterousness.
ausgemacht *a.* downright, agreed; *~e Sache,* foregone conclusion.
ausgenommen *pr.* & *adv.* except, save.
ausgeprägt *a.* clear-cut, distinctive.
ausgerechnet *adv.* *~ heute,* today of all days.
ausgeschlafen *a.* wide awake.
ausgeschlossen *a.* out of the question.
ausgeschnitten *a.* low-cut.
ausgesprochen *a.* marked, decided.
ausgestalten *v.t.* to arrange; to formulate.
ausgestorben *a.* extinct; deserted.
ausgestreckt *a.* outstretched.
ausgesucht *a.* choice, exquisite; (*com.*) picked.
ausgewachsen *a.* full-grown.
ausgewogen *a.* balanced.
ausgezeichnet *a.* excellent, first-rate.
ausgiebig *a.* abundant.
ausgießen *v.t.st.* to pour out.
Ausgleich *m.* **(-[e]s, -e)** settlement; (*el.*) compensation.
ausgleichen *v.t.st.* to equalize, to compensate; to offset; to balance; (*Streit*) to make up.
ausgleiten *v.t.st.* *(s)* to slip.
ausgraben *v.t.st.* to excavate; to dig out; (*Leichnam*) to exhume.
Ausgrabung *f.* **(-, -en)** excavation; exhumation.
Ausguck *m.* lookout post.
Ausguß *m.* **(-gusses, -güsse)** sink; gutter; (*Tülle*) spout.
aushaken *v.t.* to unhook; *~ v.i.* (*fam.*) to have a mental block; to lose patience.
aushalten *v.t.st.* to hold out; to last; (*pers.*) to hold out, to persevere; ~ *v.t.st.* to endure, to bear, to stand.
aushandeln *v.t.* to negotiate.
aushändigen *v.t.* to hand over.
Aushang *m.* **(-s, -hänge)** notice.
aushängen *v.t.* to hang out; to unhinge.
Aushängeschild *n.* signboard.
ausharren *v.i.* to persevere, to hold out.
aushauchen *v.i.* & *t.* to breathe out, to expire; to exhale.
ausheben *v.t.st.* to lift out; (*Tür*) to unhinge; (*mil.*) to conscript.
Aushebung *f.* **(-, -en)** conscription.
aushecken *v.t.* to hatch; (*fig.*) to devise.
ausheilen *v.t.* to heal completely.
aushelfen *v.i.st.* to help out; to aid.
Aushilfe *f.* **(-, -n)** help, assistance, aid; (*Notbehelf*) makeshift, expedient.
aushöhlen *v.t.* to hollow out, to excavate.
ausholen *v.i.* to strike out; (*fig.*) to go far back.
aushorchen *v.t.* to sound, to pump.
aushören *v.t.* to hear to the end.
Aushülfe = Aushilfe.
aushungern *v.t.* to starve, to famish.
auskämmen *v.t.* to comb (out).
auskämpfen *v.t.* to fight out.
auskehren *v.t.* to sweep (out), to brush.
auskennen *v.r.* to be at home in; to be knowledgeable.
auskernen *v.t.* (*Früchte*) to stone.
auskippen *v.t.* to empty.
ausklammern *v.t.* (*math.*) to place outside the brackets; to exclude.
auskleiden *v.t.* to undress; ~ *v.r.* to undress oneself.
ausklingen *v.i.st.* to die away (sound).
ausklopfen *v.t.* to beat.
ausklügeln *v.t.* to figure out.
auskneifen *v.t.st.* *(s)* (*fam.*) to make oneself scarce.
ausknipsen *v.t.* to turn off.
ausknobeln *v.t.* to figure out.
auskochen *v.t.* to boil; to sterilize; to extract by boiling.
auskommen *v.i.st.* to manage, to get by; (*mit etwas*) to make both ends meet; (*mit einem*) to get on well.
Auskommen *n.* **(-s, 0)** livelihood.
auskömmlich *a.* sufficient.
auskosten *v.t.* to enjoy to the full.
auskratzen *v.t.* to scratch out.
auskundschaften *v.t.* to explore, to spy out.
Auskunft *f.* **(-, -künfte)** information.
Auskunftei *f.* **(-, -en)** inquiry office.
Auskunfts: ~bureau *n.* information office; **~mittel** *n.* expedient.
auskuppeln *v.i.* to disengage the clutch.
auskurieren *v.t.* to heal completely.
auslachen *v.t.* to laugh at, to make fun of.
Ausladebahnhof *m.* railhead.
ausladen *v.t.st.* to unload, to discharge; (*fam.*) to cancel an invitation.
Auslage *f.* **(-, -n)** disbursement; (*Kosten*) expenses; outlay; (*Schaufenster*) shop window.
Auslagerung *f.* **(-, -en)** dispersal of industry.
Ausland *n.* **(-[e]s, -0)** foreign country; *im od. ins ~*, abroad.
Ausländer *m.* **(-s, -); Ausländerin** *f.* **(-, -nen)** foreigner; alien; *feindliche ~*, enemy alien.

ausländisch *a.* foreign.
Auslandsgespräch *n.* (*tel.*) international call.
auslangen *v.t.* to leach (soil); to drain, exhaust.
auslassen *v.t.st.* to omit; to melt; (*Wut*) to give vent; *v.r.* to speak one's mind.
Auslassung *f.* **(-, -en)** omission.
Auslassungszeichen *n.* **(-s, -)** apostrophe.
auslasten *v.t.* to use to full capacity.
Auslauf *m.* space to run around; exercise.
auslaufen *v.i.st.* *(s)* to run out; to leak; (*nav.*) to put to sea.
Ausläufer *m.* **(-s, -)** foothill; (*met.*) ridge, trough.
ausleben *v.t.* to live fully; ~ *v.r.* to live it up.
auslecken *v.t.* to lick out.
ausleeren *v.t.* to empty, to clear.
auslegen *v.t.* to lay out; (*erklären*) to interpret; (*Geld*) to disburse, to advance.
Auslegung *f.* **(-, -en)** interpretation.
ausleiern *v.i.* to become baggy.
ausleihen *v.t.st.* to lend.
Auslese *f.* **(-, -n)** selection.
auslesen *v.t.st.* **(-, -n)** to select; (*Buch*) to read through.
ausliefern *v.t.* to deliver, to give up.
Auslieferung *f.* **(-, -en)** delivery; extradition.
ausliegen *v.i.st.* (*Zeitungen*) to display.
auslöschen *v.t.* to extinguish, to quench; to efface; ~ *v.i.* to go out.
auslosen *v.t.* to draw lots; to draw.
auslösen *v.t.* to trigger; to provoke; to redeem, to ransom.
Auslöser *m.* **(-s, -)** (*phot.*) release; trigger.
Auslosung *f.* **(-, -en)** draw.
Auslösung *f.* **(-, en)** ransom; redemption; (*phot.*) release.
ausloten *v.t.* to sound the depth of; (*fig.*) to sound out.
auslüften *v.t.* to air, to ventilate.
auslutschen *v.t.* to suck out.
ausmachen *v.t.* (*Feuer*) to put out; (*betragen*) to come to, to constitute; *es macht nichts aus,* it does not matter.
ausmalen *v.t.* to paint; to illuminate.
ausmarschieren *v.i.* *(s)* to march out.
Ausmaß *n.* **(-es, -e)** extent; measurement.
ausmauern *v.t.* to line with brickwork *or* masonry.
ausmergeln *v.t.* to emaciate.
ausmerzen *v.t.* to eradicate, to eliminate.
ausmessen *v.t.st.* to measure.
ausmisten *v.t. & i.* to muck out; (*fig.*) to clean out.
ausmustern *v.t.* to reject; to discharge.
Ausnahme *f.* **(-, -n)** exception; *keine ~ zulassen,* to make no exception; *~gesetz, n.* emergency law.
ausnahmsweise *adv.* by way of exception.
ausnehmen *v.t.st.* to take out; (*Geflügel*) to draw; (*fig.*) to except, to exclude; ~ *v.r.* to show, to look.
ausnehmend *adv.* exceedingly.
ausnutzen, ausnützen *v.t.* to take advantage of; to utilize fully; to use up.
auspacken *v.t.* to unpack, to open.
auspeitschen *v.t.* to whip.
auspfeifen *v.t.* to hiss.
ausplaudern *v.t.* to blab, to let out.
ausplündern *v.t.* to plunder, to pillage, to sack.
auspolstern *v.t.* to stuff.
ausposaunen *v.t.* to trumpet forth, to cry out.
ausprägen *v.r.* to develop; to become more pronounced.
auspressen *v.t.* to press out, to squeeze.
ausprobieren *v.t.* to test.
ausprügeln *v.t.* to cudgel.
Auspuff *m.* **(-s, -püffe)** exhaust.
Auspuff: ~klappe *f.* exhaust valve; **~rohr** *n.* exhaust pipe.
auspumpen *v.t.* to pump (out).
auspusten *v.t.* to blow out.
ausputzen *v.t.* to clean; to prune; (*schmücken*) to trim, to deck out.
ausquartieren *v.t.* to dislodge.
ausquetschen *v.t.* to squeeze (out).
ausradieren *v.t.* to erase.
ausrangieren *v.i.* to discard.
ausrasten *v.r.* to have a rest; (*sl.*) to have a fit.
ausrauben *v.t.* to rob.
ausräuchern *v.t.* to fumigate, to perfume.
ausraufen *v.t.* to tear out.
ausräumen *v.t.* to remove, to clear away.
ausrechnen *v.t.* to calculate, to compute.
Ausrechnung *f.* **(-, -en)** calculation, computation.
Ausrede *f.* **(-, -n)** excuse, subterfuge, evasion.
ausreden *v.t. & i.* to finish speaking; (*einem etwas*) to dissuade sb.; ~ *v.r.* to shuffle, to beat about the bush.
ausreiben *v.t.st.* to rub out.
ausreichen *v.i.* to suffice.
ausreichend *a.* sufficient.
ausreifen *v.i.* to ripen fully.
Ausreise *f.* **(-, -n)** departure to a foreign country; **~erlaubnis** *f.* exit permit.
ausreisen *v.i.* to leave the country.
ausreißen *v.t.st.* to tear out, to pull out; ~ *v.i.st.* (*fig.*) to run away, to decamp; to desert.
Ausreißer *m.* **(-s, -)** runaway, deserter.
ausreiten *v.i.st.* *(s)* to ride out, to go for a ride.
ausrenken *v.t.* to dislocate.
ausrichten *v.t.* to achieve; (*mil.*) to dress; *eine Botschaft ~*, to give a message; *etwas ~ lassen,* to leave a message.
Ausritt *m.* **(-s, -e)** ride.
ausrollen *v.t.* to roll out.
ausrotten *v.t.* to root out or up; (*fig.*) to exterminate, to extirpate.
Ausrottung *f.* **(-, -en)** extirpation, extermination.
ausrücken *v.i.* to march out; to decamp.
Ausruf *m.* **(-[e]s, -e)** cry, exclamation; proclamation.
ausrufen *v.i.st.* to cry out, to call out; ~ *v.t.st.* to proclaim.
Ausrufezeichen, Ausrufungszeichen *n.* exclamation point.
ausruhen *v.i.* to rest, to repose.
ausrupfen *v.t.* to pluck out.
ausrüsten *v.t.* to equip; to furnish; to fit out.
Ausrüstung *f.* **(-, -en)** outfit; equipment.
ausrutschen *v.i.* *(s)* to slip; to skid.
Aussaat *f.* **(-, -en)** sowing; seed.
aussäen *v.t.* to sow; to disseminate.
Aussage *f.* **(-, -n)** declaration, statement; deposition; (*gram.*) predicate.
aussagen *v.t.* to say, to declare; (*als Zeuge*) to depose, to give evidence.
Aussagesatz *m.* **(-es, -sätze)** affirmative clause.
Aussatz *m.* **(-es, 0)** leprosy; scab.
aussätzig *a.* leprous.
Aussätzige[r] *m.* **(-n, -n)** leper.

aussaugen *v.t.st. or weak* to suck out; (*fig.*) to exhaust, to impoverish.
Aussauger *m.* **(-s, -)** bloodsucker, extortionist.
ausschaben *v.t.* (*med.*) to curette.
Ausschabung *f.* (*med.*) currettage.
ausschachten *v.i.* to sink.
ausschalten *v.t.* to switch off (light); to eliminate.
Ausschank *m.* **(-[e]s, -0)** bar; counter; retail license.
ausschauen *v.i.* to look out; to look.
ausscheiden *v.t.st.* to separate; to secrete; ~ *v.i.st. (s)* to withdraw.
Ausscheidung *f.* **(-, -en)** excretion; elimination; excreta; (*sp.*) qualifier.
Ausscheidungsorgan *n.* **(-s, -)** excretory organ.
Ausscheidungsspiel *n.* **(-s, -e)** qualifying game.
ausschenken *v.t.* to pour out; to retail.
ausscheren *v.i.* to pull out; to deviate.
ausschiffen *v.t. & i.* to disembark, to land.
ausschimpfen *v.t.* to scold; to carry on.
ausschlachten *v.t.* to exploit.
ausschlafen *v.i.st.* to have a good sleep.
Ausschlag *m.* **(-[e]s, -schläge)** (*Krankheit*) rash; (*Entscheidung*) decision.
ausschlagen *v.t.st.* (*Geschenk*) to decline, to refuse; ~ *v.i.st. (s)* (*von Pferden*) to kick; (*Knospen*) to bud, to shoot; (*gut, schlecht*) to turn out, to prove.
ausschlaggebend *a.* decisive, deciding.
ausschließen *v.t.* to exclude; to expel.
ausschließlich *a.* exclusive.
ausschlüpfen *v.i.* to hatch; to emerge.
ausschlürfen *v.t.* to sip noisily; to suck.
Ausschluß *m.* **(-schlusses, -schlüsse)** exclusion, exemption.
ausschmücken *v.t.* to adorn, to decorate; to embellish.
ausschneiden *v.t.st.* to cut out.
Ausschnitt *m.* **(-[e]s, -e)** cutting (newspaper); cut; low neck; (*math.*) sector.
ausschöpfen *v.t.* to scoop out; (*fig.*) to exhaust.
ausschrauben *v.t.* to unscrew.
ausschreiben *v.t.st.* to write out, to spell out; (*Landtag, etc.*) to convene, to summon; (*Steuern*) to impose; (*Stelle*) to advertise.
Ausschreibung *f.* **(-, -en)** announcement; calling; invitation to apply.
Ausschreitung *f.* **(-, -en)** excess.
Ausschuß *m.* **(-schusses, -schüsse)** *pl.* damaged goods; (*Komitee*) committee, board, panel; *dem ~ angehören,* to be on the committee.
ausschütteln *v.t.* to shake out.
ausschütten *v.t.* to pour out; (*fig.*) to unburden (one's heart); to pay (dividend).
ausschwärmen *v.i. (s)* to swarm out; (*mil.*) to extend.
ausschwatzen *v.t.* to blab; to talk of.
ausschweifend *a.* dissolute, licentious.
Ausschweifung *f.* **(-, -en)** debauchery.
ausschweigen *v.r.st.* to remain silent.
ausschwenken *v.t.* to rinse.
ausschwitzen *v.t.* to exude.
aussehen *v.i.st.* to look; (*nach*) to look out (for).
Aussehen *n.* **(-s, 0)** appearance, look.
aus sein *v.i.ir. (s)* to be out; to be over.
außen *adv.* on the outside, without; *nach ~*, outward.
Außenbordmotor *m.* outboard motor.
aussenden *v.t.ir.* to send out.
Außenhandel *m.* foreign trade.
Außenpolitik *f.* **(-, 0)** foreign politics, foreign policy.
Außenseite *f.* outside, exterior.
Außenseiter *m.* outsider.
Außenstände *m.pl.* outstanding debts.
Außenwelt *f.* outer world.
außer *pr.* without, out of; except; besides; but; ~ *c.* unless, except that, but that.
außeramtlich *a.* unofficial.
außerdem *adv.* besides, moreover.
Außerdienststunden *f.pl.* off-duty hours.
äußere *a.* outer, exterior, external.
Äußere *n.* **(-n, 0)** external appearance; *Minister des Äußern,* Secretary of State.
außerehelich *a.* extramarital, illegitimate.
außergerichtlich *adv.* out of court.
außergewöhnlich *a.* extraordinary.
außerhalb *adv.* outside, outwardly.
äußerlich *a.* external, outward; ~ *adv.* (*med.*) for external use only!
Äußerlichkeit *f.* **(-, -en)** formality.
äußern *v.t.* to utter, to express; ~ *v.r.* to express oneself.
außerordentlich *a.* extraordinary; *~er Professor,* assistant (associate) professor.
außerplanmäßig *a.* unscheduled; unbudgeted.
äußerst *a.* outermost; extreme, utmost; ~ *adv.* extremely.
außerstande *a.* unable.
Äußerung *f.* **(-, -en)** remark; comment, utterance, pronouncement.
aussetzen *v.t.* (*Kind*) to expose; (*Belohnung*) to promise; (*Summe*) to settle; (*Tätigkeit*) to suspend; (*rügen*) to find fault (with); ~ *v.i.* to intermit; (*mit etwas*) to discontinue.
Aussetzung *f.* **(-, -en)** suspension; (*Summe*) settlement.
Aussicht *f.* **(-, -en)** view, prospect.
aussichtslos *a.* without prospects.
Aussichtsturm *m.* watchtower.
aussieben *v.t.* to sift out; to screen.
aussiedeln *v.t.* to resettle; to evacuate.
Aussiedler *m.* **(-s, -)**; **Aussiedlerin** *f.* **(-, -nen)** emigrant.
aussinnen *v.t.st.* to contrive.
aussöhnen *v.t.* to reconcile; ~ *v.r.* to become reconciled (to).
Aussöhnung *f.* **(-, -en)** reconciliation.
aussondern *v.t.* to single out.
aussortieren *v.t.* to assort, to sort (out).
ausspähen *v.t.* to spy out; ~ *v.i.* to look out (for).
ausspannen *v.t.* to relax; to have a break; to stretch, to extend; (*Pferd*) to unharness; ~ *v.i.* to take a rest.
aussparen *v.t.* to leave out; to leave blank.
ausspeien *v.t.st.* to spit (out).
aussperren *v.t.* to shut out; to lock out.
Aussperrung *f.* **(-, -en)** lockout.
ausspielen (gegen) *v.t.* to play off against.
ausspionieren *v.t.* to spy out.
Aussprache *f.* **(-, -n)** pronunciation, accent; talk.
aussprechen *v.t.st.* to pronounce; (*äussern*) to declare, to utter; ~ *v.r.* to speak one's mind.
aussprengen *v.t.* (*fig.*) to divulge, to report.
Ausspruch *m.* **(-[e]s, -sprüche)** remark; utterance; sentence, verdict.
ausspucken *v.t.* to spit out.
ausspülen *v.t.* to rinse.
ausstaffieren *v.t.* to equip, to fit out; to dress up, to rig out.

Ausstand *m.* **(-[e]s, -stände)** outstanding debts, arrears *pl.;* (*von Arbeitern*) strike.
ausständig *a.* outstanding (money); (*Arbeiter*) on strike.
ausstatten *v.t.* to endow; to provide with; (*Töchter*) to portion off.
Ausstattung *f.* **(-, -en)** outfit; dowry; (*von Büchern*) getup.
ausstäuben *v.t.* to beat (carpets), to dust.
ausstechen *v.t.st.* to cut out; (*Augen*) to put out; (*fig.*) to supplant.
ausstehen *v.t.st.* to endure, to undergo; (*fig.*) to tolerate.
aussteigen *v.i.st. (s)* to get out, to get off, to alight; (*vom Schiffe*) to disembark.
Aussteiger *m.* **(-s, -)**; **Aussteigerin** *f.* **(-, -nen)** dropout.
ausstellen *v.t.* (*auf einer Ausstellung*) to exhibit; (*Wechsel*) to draw; (*tadeln*) to find fault (with).
Aussteller *m.* **(-s, -)** (*Wechsel*~) drawer; (*Industrie*~) exhibitor.
Ausstellung *f.* **(-, -en)** exhibit; (*Industrie*~) industrial exhibition; (*Tadel*) objection.
Ausstellungsraum *m.* **(-[e]s, -räume)** showroom.
aussterben *v.i.st. (s)* to die out; to become extinct.
Aussteuer *f.* **(-, -n)** dowry, portion, trousseau.
aussteuern *v.t.* to portion, to endow; (*tech.*) to modulate; to control the level.
Ausstieg *m.* **(-s, -e)** exit; (*fig.*) opting out.
ausstopfen *v.t.* to stuff.
ausstoßen *v.t.st.* to expel; to drive out; (*Schrei*) to utter.
ausstrahlen *v.t. & i (s)* to radiate.
Ausstrahlung *f.* radiation; charisma; transmission.
ausstrecken *v.t.* to stretch (out).
ausstreichen *v.t.st.* to cross out; to delete; to strike out.
ausstreuen *v.t.* to scatter, to spread.
ausströmen *v.i.* to stream forth; to escape; to emanate.
Ausströmen *n.* **(-s, 0)** (*von Gas*) leakage (of gas).
aussuchen *v.t.* to select; to pick out.
Austausch *m.* **(-[e]s, -e)** exchange, barter.
austauschbar *a.* interchangeable; replaceable.
austauschen *v.t.* to exchange, to barter; to trade.
austeilen *v.t.* to distribute, to issue; (*Gnaden*) administer.
Auster *f.* **(-, -n)** oyster.
austilgen *v.t.* to extirpate; to obliterate.
Austilgung *f.* **(-, -en)** extirpation.
austoben *v.r.* to let off steam.
austragen *v.t.st.* to carry out; (*Briefe*) to deliver; (*Streit*) to fight out.
Australien *n.* **(-s, 0)** Australia; **Australier** *m.;* **Australierin** *f.;* **australisch** *a.* Australian.
austreiben *v.t.st.* to exorcize; to drive out; to expel.
Austreibung *f.* exorcism; expulsion.
austreten *v.t.st.* to stamp out; ~ *v.i.st. (s)* (*Fluß*) to overflow; (*verlassen*) to retire.
austricksen *v.t.* (*fam.*) to trick.
austrinken *v.t.st.* to drink up.
Austritt *m.* **(-[e]s, -e)** stepping out; retirement, leaving.
austrocknen *v.t. & i. (s)* to dry up; to drain.
austüfteln *v.t.* to work out.
ausüben *v.t.* to exercise, to practice.
Ausübung *f.* **(-, 0)** exercise, practice.
ausufern *v.i.* to get out of hand.
Ausverkauf *m.* **(-[e]s, -käufe)** clearance sale, selling off.
ausverkauft *a.* sold out.
auswachsen *v.t.* to grow out of.
Auswahl *f.* **(-, -en)** choice, selection; *eine ~ treffen,* to make a choice.
auswählen *v.t.* to choose, to select.
auswalzen *v.t.* to roll out.
Auswanderer *m.* **(-s, -)** emigrant.
auswandern *v.i. (s)* to emigrate.
Auswanderung *f.* **(-, -en)** emigration.
auswärtig *a.* foreign; **~e Beziehungen** *pl.* international relations *pl.*
Auswärtiges Amt *n.* State Department.
auswärts *adv.* outward; abroad.
auswaschen *v.t.st.* to wash (out).
auswechselbar *a.* interchangeable.
auswechseln *v.t.* to exchange.
Ausweg *m.* **(-[e]s, -e)** way out; outlet; (*fig.*) expedient.
ausweglos *a. & adv.* hopeless(ly).
Ausweglosigkeit *f.* hopelessness.
ausweichen *v.i.st. (s)* to make way for; to avoid, to evade; (*von Wagen*) to turn aside.
ausweichend *a.* evasive.
ausweiden *v.t.* to eviscerate, to draw.
ausweinen *v.r.* to have a good cry.
Ausweis *m.* **(-es, -e)** ID, identification; **~papier** identification papers, certificate of identity.
ausweisen *v.i.st.* to expel, to banish; (*erweisen*) to prove; *sich ~,* to prove one's identity.
Ausweisung *f.* **(-, -en)** expulsion, banishment.
ausweiten *v.t.* to widen, to stretch.
auswendig *a.* outer, exterior; ~ *adv.* by heart.
auswerfen *v.t.st.* to cast; (*Gehalt*) to appoint.
auswerten *v.t.* to analyze and evaluate; to make full use of.
Auswertung *f.* **(-, -en)** analysis and evaluation; utilization.
auswickeln *v.t.* to unwrap.
auswiegen *v.t.st.* to weigh.
auswirken *v.r.* to affect.
Auswirkung *f.* effect; consequence.
auswischen *v.t.* to wipe out.
auswringen *v.t.st.* to wring out.
Auswuchs *m.* **(-wuchses, -wüchse)** growth; excrescence; abuse.
auswuchten *v.t.* to balance (tires).
Auswurf *m.* **(-[e]s, -würfe)** sputum; excretion, expectoration; (*fig.*) refuse, dregs *pl.*
auszahlen *v.t.* to pay out.
auszählen *v.t.* to count out.
Auszahlung *f.* **(-, -en)** payment.
Auszählung *f.* **(-, -en)** counting.
auszehren *v.t.* to exhaust.
Auszehrung *f.* **(-, -en)** consumption.
auszeichnen *v.t.* to mark (out), to distinguish; to honor.
Auszeichnung *f.* **(-, -en)** distinction.
ausziehbar *a.* extendible; telescopic.
ausziehen *v.t.st.* to draw *or* pull out; (*chem.*) to extract; (*dehnen*) to stretch, to extend; (*Kleider*) to take off; ~ *v.i.st.* to move out; to remove; (*mil.*) to march out; *sich ~,* to undress.
Ausziehtisch *m.* extendable table.
Auszubildende *m./f.* **(-n, -n)** trainee; apprentice.
Auszug *m.* **(-[e]s, -züge)** (*Wohnungs*~) removal; (*aus einem Buche*) abstract; (*fig.*) extract, summary, digest.

auszugsweise *adv.* in excerpts *or* extracts.
auszupfen *v.t.* to pluck out; to pull out.
autark *a.* self-sufficient.
Autarkie *f.* **(-, 0)** self-sufficiency.
authentisch *a.* & *adv.* authentic(ally).
Auto *n.* **(-s, -s)** car, automobile.
Autoatlas *m.* road atlas.
Autobahn *f.* **(-, -en)** highway, freeway.
Autobiographie *f.* autobiography.
autobiographisch *a.* autobiographical.
Autodidakt *m.* **(-en, -en)** autodidact, self-taught person.
Autofahrer *m.* **(-s, -)**; **Autofahrerin** *f.* **(-, -nen)** driver.
autogen *a.* autogenous; ~ **Training** *n.* autogenic training, autogenics.
Autogramm *n.* **(-[e]s, -e)** autograph.
Autohaltestelle *f.* cab rank, taxi stand.
Autokino *n.* drive-in movie.
Autoknacker *m.* car thief.
Autokolonne *f.* convoy.
autokratisch *a.* autocratic.
Automat *m.* **(-en, -en)** machine; automaton.
Automatik *f.* **(-, -en)** automatism; automatic system *or* transmission.
automatisch *a.* & *adv.* automatic(ally).
automatisieren *v.t.* automate.
Automatisierung *f.* **(-, -en)** automation.
Automatismus *m.* **(-, -men)** automatism.
Automechaniker *m.* mechanic.
Automobil *n.* **(-s, -e)** automobile; motor car.
Automobilist *m.* driver.
autonom *a.* autonomous.
Autonummer *f.* registration number.
Autopapiere *pl.* car documents.
Autopsie *f.* **(-, -[e]n)** autopsy.
Autor *m.* **(-s, -en)**; **Autorin** *f.* **(-, -nen)** author, writer.
Autorennen *n.* **(-s, -)** car race.
autorisieren *v.t.* to authorize.
autoritär *a.* authoritarian.
Autorität *f.* **(-, -en)** authority.
Autorschaft *f.* **(-, 0)** authorship.
Autostrasse *f.* highway.
Autoverleih *m.*, **Autovermietung** *f.* car rental.
Autowerkstatt *f.* garage.
Autozubehör *n.* car accessories.
Auwald *m.* riverside forest.
avancieren *v.i.* to rise, to get promoted.
avisieren *v.t.* to advise, to inform.
Avitaminose *f.* **(-, -n)** (*med.*) avitaminosis.
Axt *f.* **(-, Äxte)** axe, hatchet.
Az. *Aktenzeichen,* file number.
Azalie *f.* **(-, -n)** azalea.
Azetylen *n.* **(-s, 0)** acetylene.
Azteke *m.* **(-n, -n)**; **Aztekin** *f.* **(-, -nen)** Aztec.
Azubi *m.* & *f.* trainee; apprentice.
azurblau, azurn *a.* azure.

B

B, b *n.* the letter B or b; (*mus.*) B flat.
b. *bei,* near.
B. *Bundesstraße,* major road.
babbeln *v.t.* & *i.* to babble.
Baby *n.* **(-s, -s)** baby.
Babyausstattung *f.* layette.
babylonisch *a.* Babylonian; **~es Sprachgewirr** *n.* a babel of languages.
Babysprache *f.* baby talk.
Bach *m.* **(-[e]s, Bäche)** brook, rivulet.
Bache *f.* **(-, -n)** (*hunt.*) wild sow.
Bachstelz *f.* **(-, -n)** wagtail.
Backblech *n.* **(-s, -e)** baking sheet.
Backbord *n.* larboard, port.
Backe *f.* **(-, -n)** cheek; jaw; (*mech.*) jaw; buttock.
backen *v.t.* to bake; (*Fische*) to fry; (*Ziegel*) to burn.
Backenbart *m.* whiskers *pl.*; beard.
Backenknochen *m.* cheekbone.
Backenzahn *m.* molar.
Bäcker *m.* **(-s, -)** baker.
Bäckerbursche *m.* **(-s, -)** baker's apprentice.
Bäckerei *f.* **(-, -en)** bakery.
Backfisch *m.* fried fish.
Backobst *n.* dried fruit.
Backofen *m.* baking oven.
Backpfanne *f.* drying pan.
Backpulver *n.* baking powder.
Backstein *m.* brick.
Bad *n.* **(-es, Bäder)** bath; (*Ort*) watering place, spa; (*Handlung*) bathe.
Badeanstalt *f.* baths *pl.*; public pool.
Badeanzug *m.* bathing suit.
Badekur *f.* spa treatment.
Bademantel *m.* dressing gown, bathrobe.
baden *v.t.* & *i.* to bathe.
Badeofen *m.* bathroom water heater.
Badeort *m.* spa.
Badetuch *n.* bath towel.
Badewanne *f.* bath, bathtub.
Badezimmer *n.* bathroom
baff *a.* **~sein** to be flabbergasted.
Bagage **(-, 0)** *f.* (*fig.*) (*pej.*) bunch, rabble.
Bagatelle *f.* **(-, -n)** trifle.
bagatellisieren *v.t.* to play down.
Bagger *m.* **(-s, -)** excavator; ~ **maschine** *f.* dredger, dredging machine.
baggern *v.t.* to excavate, to dredge.
Bahn *f.* **(-, -en)** road, path; course; (*Eisen~*) railway, railroad; (*fig.*) career; *mit der ~*, by train.
bahnbrechend *a.* pioneering.
Bahnbrecher *m.* **(-s, -)** pioneer.
Bahndamm *m.* **(-s, -dämme)** railroad embankment.
bahnen *v.t.* to clear, open (up); *einen Weg ~*, to clear a path; (*fig.*) to pave the way.
Bahnhof *m.* railroad station.
Bahnhofsvorsteher *m.* stationmaster.
Bahnlinie *f.* line (of railway).
Bahnsteig *m.* platform.
Bahnsteigkarte *f.* platform ticket.
Bahnübergang *m.* level crossing.
Bahre *f.* **(-, -n)** stretcher, bier.
Bai *f.* **(-, -en)** bay.
Baisse *frz. f.* fall in prices, slump; *auf ~ spekulieren,* to bear (i.e., to buy stocks at a low price).
Bajonett *n.* **(-[e]s, -e)** bayonet.
Bakterie *f.* **(-, -n)** bacterium.
bakteriell *a.* bacterial.
bakteriologisch *a.* bacteriological.

balancieren *v.t. & i.* to balance.
bald *adv.* soon, shortly; nearly, almost; ~ *hier,* ~ *dort,* now here, now there.
Baldachin *m.* **(-[e]s, -e)** canopy.
in Bälde soon.
baldig *a.* quick, speedy, early.
Baldrian *m.* **(-s, 0)** valerian.
Balearen *pl.* the Balearic Islands.
Balg *m.* **(-[e]s, Bälge)** skin; (*fig.*) brat.
balgen *v.r.* to fight; to romp, to scuffle.
Balgerei *f.* **(-, -en)** fight; scuffle.
Balkan *m.* **(-s, 0)** the Balkans; the Balkan Mountains.
Balken *m.* **(-s, -)** beam; rafter.
Balkon *m.* **(-s, -e & -s)** balcony.
Ball *m.* **(-[e]s, Bälle)** ball; globe.
Ballade *f.* **(-, -n)** ballad.
Ballast *m.* **(-es, -e)** ballast.
ballen *v.t.* to form into a ball; *die Faust* ~, to clench one's fist; ~ *v.r.* to cluster; to gather.
Ballen *m.* **(-s, -)** bale, pack; (*Fuß*) ball, bunion.
Ballett *n.* **(-[e]s, -e)** ballet.
Ballon *m.* **(-s, -s)** balloon.
Ballsaal *m.* ballroom.
Ballspiel *n.* ballgame.
Ballungs: ~gebiet *n.;* **~raum** *m.;* **~zentrum** *n.* conurbation; area of industrial concentration.
Balsam *m.* **(-[e]s, -e)** balm, balsam.
balsamich *a.* balmy.
Balz *f.* **(-, -n)** (*Auerhahn*) courting; mating season.
balzen *v.i.* to court, to mate.
Bambus *m.* bamboo; **~rohr** *n.* bamboo shoot
Bammel *m.* (*fam.*) fear.
banal *a.* trite, banal.
Banalität *f.* banality.
Banane *f.* **(-, -n)** banana.
Banause *m.* **(-n, -n)** Philistine, lowbrow.
Band *n.* **(-[e]s, Bänder)** band; (*Seiden~*) ribbon; (*Zwirn~*) tape; (*anat.*) ligament; (*fig.*) tie, bond.
Band *m.* **(-es, Bände)** (*Buch*) volume; (*Einband*) binding; cover.
Bandage *f.* **(-, -n)** bandage, truss.
bandagieren *v.t.* to bandage.
Bande *f.* **(-, -n)** band, gang; cushions (billiard).
Bande *n.pl.* fetters, chains; ties *pl.*
bändigen *v.t.* to tame; (*Pferd*) to break (in); (*fig.*) to subdue.
Bandit *m.* **(-en, -en)** bandit.
Bandscheibe *f.* (*intervertebral*) disc.
Bandwurm *m.* tapeworm.
bange *a.* afraid, alarmed, uneasy.
bangen *v.imp.* to be afraid of; (*nach*) to long for.
Bangigkeit *f.* **(-, -en)** anxiety.
Bank *f.* **(-, Bänke)** bench; (*Schul~*) form; *auf die lange ~ schieben,* to put off; *durch die* ~, without exception.
Bank *f.* **(-, Banken)** (*Geld~*) bank.
Bankett *n.* **(-s, -e)** banquet.
Bankier *m.* **(-s, -s)** banker.
Bankkonto *n.* banking account.
Banknote *f.* bank note, bank bill.
bankrott *a.* bankrupt.
Bankrott *m.* **(-[e]s, -e)** bankruptcy; *betrügerische~*, fraudulent bankruptcy.
Bankrottierer *m.* **(-s, -)** bankrupt.
Bann *m.* **(-[e]s, 0)** ban, excommunication.
bannen *v.t.* to banish; (*Geister*) to exorcise.
Banner *n.* **(-s, -)** banner.
bar *a.* bare; cash, ready money; *gegen* ~, for cash; *~bezahlen,* to pay cash.
Bar *f.* **(-, -s)** bar; nightclub.
Bär *m.* **(-en, -en)** bear; *der Grosse* ~, The Great Bear.
Baracke *f.* **(-, -n)** shed, hut.
Barbar *m.* **(-en, -en)** barbarian.
Barbarei *f.* **(-, -en)** barbarity; vandalism.
barbarisch *a.* barbarous.
bärbeissig *a.* grumpy.
Barbier *m.* **(-[e]s, -e)** barber, hairdresser.
barbieren *v.t.* to shave; to cheat.
Barchent *m.* **(-[e]s, -e)** cotton flannel.
Barde *m.* **(-n, -n)** bard.
Bärenhaut *f.* bearskin; *auf der ~ liegen,* to be idle.
Barett *n.* **(-s, -e)** cap.
barfuß, barfüßig *a. & adv.* barefoot.
Bargeld *n.* ready money, cash.
barhäuptig *a.* bareheaded.
Bariton *m.* **(-s, -e)** baritone.
Barkasse *f.* **(-, -n)** launch.
Barke *f.* **(-, -n)** barge.
barmherzig *a.* merciful, compassionate; *~e Schwester,* sister of mercy.
Barmherzigkeit *f.* **(-, 0)** mercy, compassion.
Barmixer *m.* barman; barkeeper.
Barock *m. & a.* baroque.
Barometer *n. & m.* **(-s, -)** barometer; *das ~ steigt,* the glass is going up.
Baron *m.* **(-[e]s, -e)** baron.
Baronin *f.* **(-, -nen)** baroness.
Barren *m.* **(-s, -n)** (*Metall*) pig, ingot; (*Turnen*) parallel bars.
Barriere *f.* **(-, -n)** barrier.
Barrikade *f.* **(-, -n)** barricade.
barsch *a.* harsh, rude, abrupt.
Barsch *m.* **(-es, -e & Bärsche)** perch.
Barschaft *f.* **(-, -en)** cash, ready money.
Bart *m.* **(-[e]s, Bärte)** beard.
bärtig *a.* bearded.
bartlos *a.* beardless.
Barzahlung *f.* cash payment.
Basalt *m.* **(-[e]s, -e)** basalt.
Basar *m.* **(-s, -e)** bazaar.
Base *f.* **(-, -n)** (*obs.*) cousin (female), (*chem.*) base.
basieren *v.i.* to base; ~ *auf,* to be based on.
Basilika *f.* **(-, -ken)** basilica.
Basilikum *n.* basil.
Basis *f.* **(-, 0)** basis.
Baskenmütze *f.* **(-, -n)** beret.
Baß *m.* **(Basses, Basse)** bass; bass viol.
Baßgeige *f.* bass viol.
Bassist *m.* **(-en, -en)** bass singer, basso.
Baßschlüssel *m.* (*mus.*) bass clef.
Bast *m.* **(-es, -e)** bast, inner bark of trees.
Bastard *m.* **(-[e]s, -e)** bastard.
Bastelei *f.* **(-, -en)** handicraft work.
basteln *v.i.* to do handicraft.
BAT *Bundesangestelltentarif,* salary scale for public employees.
Bataillon *n.* **(-s, -e)** battalion.
Batist *m.* **(-[e]s, -e)** cambric.
Batterie *f.* **(-, -[e]n)** battery.
Bau *m.* **(-es, -e)** building, structure; edifice; (*Körper*) build, frame; cultivation; (*von Tieren*) den, earth; *im* ~, under construction.
Bauamt *n.* Board of Works.
Bauarbeiten *pl.* construction work.
Baubataillon *n.* (*mil.*) construction battalion.

Bauch *m.* **(-[e]s, Bäuche)** belly, stomach; (*Schiffs*~) bottom.
Bauchentzündung *f.* peritonitis.
Bauchfell *n.* peritoneum.
bauchig *a.* bellied, bulgy.
Bauchklatscher *m.* belly flop.
Bauchlandung *f.* (*avi.*) belly landing.
Bauchnabel *m.* belly button.
Bauchredner *m.* ventriloquist.
Bauchweh *n.* colic, stomacheache.
bauen *v.t.* to build; to till; (*Getreide*) to grow; (*Pflanzen*) to cultivate; *auf jn.* ~, to rely on sb.
Bauer *m.* **(-n** *or* **-s, -n)** peasant, farmer; (*im Schach*) pawn; (*Karte*) jack.
Bauer *m.* & *n.* **(-s, -)** cage (birds).
Bäuerin *f.* **(-, -nen)** peasant farmer (woman).
bäu(e)risch *a.* rustic; (*fig.*) boorish.
bäuerlich *a.* farming; rural.
Bauernfänger *m.* (*fam.*) con man.
Bauernhof *m.* farmhouse.
Bauernkrieg *m.* peasant war.
Bauersfrau *f.* **(-, -en)** farmer's wife.
Baufach *n.* **(-[e]s, 0)** architecture.
baufällig *a.* dilapidated, tumbledown.
Baufälligkeit *f.* **(-, 0)** disrepair.
Bauführer *m.* overseer (at building works).
Baugerüst *n.* scaffolding.
Bauholz *n.* timber.
Baukasten *m.* box of bricks.
Baukunst *f.* architecture.
baulich *a.* architectural.
Baum *m.* **(-[e]s, Bäume)** tree; (*nav.*) boom.
Baumast *m.* knot.
Baumeister *m.* architect; master builder.
baumeln *v.i.* to dangle, to bob.
bäumen *v.r.* to prance, to rear.
Baumgrenze *f.* timberline.
Baumkrone *f.* treetop.
Baumrinde *f.* bark.
Baumschere *f.* pruning shears. *pl.*
Baumschule *f.* nursery.
Baumstamm *m.* trunk.
Baumwolle *f.* cotton.
baumwollen *a.* (made of) cotton.
Baumwollgarn *n.* cotton yarn.
Baumwollspinnerei *f.* cotton mill.
Bauplatz *m.* building plot.
Baupolizei *f.* buildings department.
Baurat *m.* government surveyor (of works).
Bausch *m.* **(-es, Bäusche)** bolster, pad; compress; *in ~ und Bogen,* in bulk.
bauschen *v.i.* to bag; to bulge, to swell out.
bauschig *a.* baggy, puffed out; swollen.
Bausparkasse *f.* savings and loan association.
Baustein *m.* building stone.
Baustelle *f.* building site.
Baustelle! persons at work!
Baustil *m.* architectural style.
Baustoff *m.* building material.
Bauteil *n.* component.
Bauunternehman *n.* building firm.
Bauunternehmer *m.* building contractor.
Bauvorhaben *n.* building project.
Bauweise *f.* method of building.
Bauwerk *n.* building, structure.
Bauxit *m.* **(-[e]s, -e)** bauxite.
Bauzaun *m.* **(-s, -zäune)** site fence.
Bayer *m.;* **Bayerin** *f.;* **bay(e)risch** *a.* Bavarian; **Bayern** *n.* Bavaria.
Bazillus *m.* **(-, Bazillen)** bacillus.
Bd. *Band,* volume, vol.
Bde. *Bände,* volumes, vols.
B-Dur *n.* (*mus.*) B flat major.
BE *Broteinheit,* bread unit.
beabsichtigen *v.t.* to intend.
beachten *v.t.* to observe; to follow (rule); to pay attention to.
beachtenswert *a.* noteworthy.
beachtlich *a.* considerable; notable.
Beachtung *f.* observance, following; consideration.
Beamte[r] *m.* **(-en, -en); Beamtin** *f.* **(-, -nen)** official; civil servant; *höherer* ~, senior official.
beängstigen *v.t.* to alarm.
beängstigend *a.* worrying, alarming; unsettling.
beanspruchen *v.t.* to claim, to demand.
Beanspruchung *f.* **(-, -en)** demand; stress.
beanstanden *v.t.* to object to; to complain about.
beantragen *v.t.* to apply; to propose.
beantworten *v.t.* to answer, to reply to.
Beantwortung *f.* **(-, -en)** reply, answer.
bearbeiten *v.t.* to work; to process; (*Angelegenheit*) to attend to, to deal with; (*fig.*) *jn.* ~, to influence sb.
Bearbeitung *f.* **(-, -en)** reworking; revision; treatment.
Bearbeitungsgebühr *f.* **(-, -en)** handling charge.
Beatmung *f.* **(-, 0)** respiration; *künstliche* ~, artificial respiration.
beaufsichtigen *v.t.* to supervise, to control.
Beaufsichtigung *f.* **(-, -en)** supervision.
beauftragen *v.t.* to charge.
Beauftragte *f.* & *m.* representative; commissioner.
beäugen *v.t.* to eye; to inspect.
bebauen *v.t.* to build on; to cultivate.
Bebauung *f.* development; buildings, cultivation.
beben *v.i.* to quake, to shake, to shiver.
bebildern *v.t.* to illustrate.
Becher *m.* **(-s, -)** cup, goblet; (*ohne Fuß*) tumbler; *Würfel*~, dice box.
bechern *v.i.* (*fam.*) to booze.
Becken *n.* **(-s, -)** basin; (*mus.*) cymbal; (*anat.*) pelvis.
Bedacht *m.* **(-[e]s, 0)** consideration; *mit* ~, deliberately.
bedacht *a.* ~ *sein auf,* to be intent on.
bedächtig *a.* considerate, prudent, circumspect.
Bedächtigkeit *f.* **(-, 0)** caution, circumspection.
bedachtsam *a.* circumspect.
Bedachung *f.* **(-, -en)** roofing.
bedanken *v.r.* to thank; to decline.
Bedarf *m.* **(-[e]s, 0)** need, want.
Bedarfsartikel *m.pl.* requisites.
bedauerlich *a.* deplorable.
bedauerlicherweise *adv.* regrettably, unfortunately.
bedauern *v.t.* to pity; to regret.
bedauernswert *a.* deplorable, pitiable.
bedecken *v.t.* to cover; ~ *v.r.* to put on one's hat.
Bedeckung *f.* **(-, -en)** covering; (*mil.*) escort, convoy.
bedenken *v.t.ir.* to consider, to mind, to reflect upon; (*im Testament*) to remember; ~ *v.r.ir.* to deliberate; *sich anders* ~, to change one's mind.
Bedenken *n.* **(-s, -)** doubt; hesitation, scruple.
bedenkenlos *a.* unhesitating; unscrupulous.
bedenkenswert *a.* worthy of consideration.
bedenklich *a.* doubtful, risky; scrupulous.

Bedenkzeit *f.* time for reflection.
bedeuten *v.t.* to signify, to mean; to indicate; *es hat nichts zu ~*, it is of no consequence.
bedeutend *a.* important, considerate.
bedeutsam *a.* significant.
Bedeutung *f.* **(-, -en)** meaning, significance, sense; consequence, importance.
bedeutungslos *a.* insignificant.
bedienen *v.t.* to serve, to attend; (*Maschinen*) to operate; ~ *v.r.* to make use of; (*bei Tische*) to help oneself.
Bedienstete[r] *m./f.* **(-n, -n)** employee.
Bediente[r] *m.* **(-en, -en)** servant.
Bedienung *f.* **(-, -en)** service, attendance; ~ *inbegriffen,* tip included.
Bedienungs: ~anleitung *f.* operating instructions; **~komfort** *m.* ease of operation.
bedingen *v.t.* to stipulate, to involve; to require.
bedingt (durch) *a.* conditional (on).
Bedingung *f.* **(-, -en)** condition; stipulation; terms *pl.*
bedingungslos *a.* unconditional.
Bedingungssatz *m.* conditional clause.
bedrängen *v.t.* to press hard; to oppress, to afflict.
Bedrängnis *f.* **(-, -nisse)** oppression; affliction; distress.
bedrohen *v.t.* to threaten, to menace.
bedrohlich *a.* threatening.
Bedrohung *f.* **(-, -en)** threat, menace.
bedrucken *v.t.* to print.
bedrücken *v.t.* to depress, to oppress.
bedrückend *a.* depressing; oppressive.
bedruckt *a.* printed.
bedrückt *a.* depressed.
Bedrückung *f.* **(-, -en)** depression.
Beduine *m.* **(-n, -n); Beduinen** *f.* **(-, -nen)** Bedouin.
bedürfen *v.t. & i.ir* to require; to need, to want.
Bedürfnis *n.* **(-nisses, nisse)** want, need; *pl.* **Bedürfnisse** *pl.* necessaries.
Bedürfnisanstalt *f.* comfort station.
bedürfnislos *a.* modest, simple.
Bedürfnislosigkeit *f.* lack of needs.
bedürftig *a.* needy, indigent.
Bedürftigkeit *f.* neediness.
beehren *v.t.* to honor.
beeiden *v.t.* to swear to.
beeilen *v.r.* to hurry up, to make haste.
beeindrucken *v.t.* to impress.
beeindruckend *a.* impressive.
beeinflussen *v.t.* to influence.
beeinträchtigen *v.t.* to impair.
beenden, beendigen *v.t.* to finish, to terminate.
Beendigung *f.* **(-, -en)** conclusion.
beengen *v.t.* to restrict, to narrow, to cramp.
beerben *v.t.* to be someone's heir.
beerdigen *v.t.* to inter, to bury.
Beerdigung *f.* **(-, -en)** funeral, burial.
Beere *f.* **(-, -en)** berry.
Beet *n.* **(-[e]s, -e)** bed, border.
befähigen *v.t.* to enable, to qualify.
befähigt *a.* capable, qualified.
Befähigung *f.* **(-, -en)** qualification; capacity; caliber.
befahrbar *a.* passable, navigable.
befahren *v.t.st.* to pass over.
befallen *v.t.st.* to befall; to attack.
befangen *a.* biased; self-conscious.
Befangenheit *f.* **(-, -en)** prejudice; self-consciousness.
befassen *v.r.* to occupy oneself, to engage.
befehden *v.t.* to make war upon.
Befehl *m.* **(-[e]s, -e)** command, order; *auf ~ von,* by order of.
befehlen *v.t.st.* to command, to order; to commit.
befehligen *v.t.* to command.
Befehlsausgabe *f.* (*mil.*) briefing.
Befehlshaber *m.* commanding officer.
Befehlston *m.* peremptory tone.
Befehlsweg *m.* chain of command.
befestigen *v.t.* to fasten; to fortify.
Befestigung *f.* **(-, -en)** consolidation; fortification.
befinden *v.t.st.* to find; to deem; ~ *v.r.* to be; *wie ~ Sie sich?* how are you?; *für tauglich befunden werden,* to be passed as fit.
Befinden *n.* **(-s, 0)** health; opinion.
befindlich *a.* being; contained.
beflaggen *v.t.* to deck with flags.
beflecken *v.t.* to stain, to spot; (*fig.*) to pollute.
befleissigen *v.r.* to take pains; to apply oneself.
beflissen *a.* keen, eager, studious, intent (upon).
beflügeln *v.t.* to inspire.
befolgen *v.t.* to follow, to obey; (*Gesetz*) to abide by, to comply with.
Befolgung *f.* **(-, 0)** observance; adherence.
befördern *v.t.* to further, to promote, to advance; to upgrade; (*verschicken*) to forward, to dispatch; to convey.
Beförderung *f.* **(-, -en)** furtherance, promotion, advancement; forwarding.
Beförderungsmittel *n.* means of transport.
befrachten *v.t.* to load, to charge.
befragen *v.t.* to question, to examine.
Befragung *f.* questioning, examination.
befreien *v.t.* to free, to deliver, to liberate, to release; *vom Erscheinen befreit,* excused from appearing.
Befreier *m.* **(-s, -)** liberator.
befreit *a.* relieved.
Befreiung *f.* **(-, -en)** deliverance; exemption.
befremden *v.t.* to appear strange, to surprise.
Befremden *n.* **(-s, 0)** surprise, displeasure.
befremdlich *a.* strange, odd, surprising.
befreunden *v.r.* to make friends.
befrieden *v.t.* to bring peace to.
befriedigen *v.t.* to content, to satisfy.
befriedigend *a.* satisfactory.
befriedigt *a.* satisfied.
Befriedigung *f.* **(-, -en)** satisfaction.
befristen *v.t.* to set a time limit.
befristet *a.* limited in time.
befruchten *v.t.* to impregnate; to fertilize; to pollinate.
Befruchtung *f.* **(-, -en)** impregnation, fertilization; pollination.
Befugnis *f.* **(-, -nisse)** authority.
befugt *a.* authorized, competent.
befühlen *v.t.* to feel, to touch.
befummeln *v.t.* (*fam.*) to paw; to grope.
Befund *m.* **(-[e]s,-)** finding; result.
befürchten *v.t.* to fear, to apprehend.
Befürchtung *f.* **(-, -en)** fear, apprehension.
befürworten *v.t.* to recommend; to support.
Befürworter *m.;* **Befürworterin** *f.* supporter.
Befürwortung *f.* support.
begabt *a.* gifted, talented.
Begabung *f.* **(-, -en)** endowment, gift, talent.
begaffen *v.t.* (*fam. pej.*) to gawk, to stare.

begatten *v.r.* to pair, to copulate.
Begattung *f.* **(-, -en)** copulation, mating.
begeben *v.t.st.* (*Wechsel*) to negotiate; ~ *v.r.st.* to proceed to; (*geschehen*) to come to pass, to happen.
Begebenheit *f.* **(-, -en)** event, occurrence.
begegnen *v.i.* *(s)* to meet (with); to happen (to), to befall.
Begegnung *f.* **(-, -en)** meeting.
begehen *v.t.st.* (*feiern*) to celebrate; (*verüben*) to commit.
Begehren *n.* **(-s, 0)** desire, wish.
begehren *v.t.* to desire; to request.
begehrenswert *a.* desirable.
begehrlich *a.* desirous, covetous, greedy.
begehrt *a.* much sought after.
Begehung *f.* **(-, -en)** perpetration; (*Feier*) celebration.
begeistern *v.t.* to inspire, to fill with enthusiasm.
begeistert *a.* enthusiastic.
Begeisterung *f.* **(-, -en)** enthusiasm.
Begier, Begierde *f.* **(-, Begierden)** desire, appetite.
begierig *a.* desirous; eager.
begießen *v.t.st.* to water; to baste.
Beginn *m.* **(-[e]s, 0)** beginning, origin.
beginnen *v.t.* & *i.st.* to begin; to undertake.
beglaubigen *v.t.* to certify, to attest, to confirm, to authenticate; to accredit.
Beglaubigung *f.* **(-, -en)** certification, attestation.
Beglaubigungsschreiben *n.* letter of accreditation, credentials *pl.*
begleichen *v.t.* to settle; to pay.
Begleitbrief *m.* cover(ing) letter.
begleiten *v.t.* to accompany, to attend.
Begleiter *m.* **(-s, -)** companion, attendant.
Begleiterscheinung *f.* concomitant symptom.
Begleitung *f.* **(-, -en)** company, attendants; (*mil.*) escort; retinue; (*mus.*) accompaniment.
beglücken *v.t.* to bless, to make happy.
beglückt *a.* happy, delighted.
beglückwünschen *v.t.* to congratulate.
begnadet *a.* highly gifted.
begnadigen *v.t.* to pardon.
Begnadigung *f.* **(-, -en)** pardon; amnesty.
begnügen *v.r.* to content oneself, to be satisfied, to acquiesce.
begraben *v.t.st.* to bury.
Begräbnis *n.* **(-nisses, -nisse)** burial, funeral; tomb, grave.
begreifen *v.t.st.* to include, to contain, to comprise; (*fig.*) to understand, to conceive, to comprehend.
begreiflich *a.* conceivable, intelligible.
begreiflicherweise *adv.* understandably.
begrenzen *v.t.* to bound, to border; to limit.
begrenzt *a.* limited, restricted.
Begrenztheit *f.* **(-, 0)** limitation.
Begrenzung *f.* **(-, -en)** boundary, restriction, delimitation.
Begriff *m.* **(-[e]s, -e)** idea, notion, concept, conception; *im* ~, about to, on the point of.
begrifflich *a.* conceptual.
Begriffsbestimmung *f.* definition.
begriffsstutzig *a.* dense, slow-witted.
begründen *v.t.* to found, to establish; to confirm, to prove.
Begründer *m.* founder.
begründet *a.* well-founded, reasonable.
Begründung *f.* reason; founding; establishment.
begrüßen *v.t.* to greet, to salute.
Begrüßung *f.* greeting; welcome.
begucken *v.t.* to look at.
begünstigen *v.t.* to favor, to patronize.
Begünstiger *m.* **(-s, -)** (*jur.*) accessory after the fact.
Begünstigung *f.* **(-, -en)** encouragement, patronage; advantage, privilege.
begutachten *v.t.* to give an opinion on.
begütert *a.* wealthy, well-to-do.
begütigen *v.t.* to placate; to mollify; to pacify.
behaart *a.* hairy; hirsute.
behäbig *a.* sedate; portly; stout.
behaftet *a.* affected, infected, to be marked.
behagen *v.imp.* to please, to suit.
Behagen *n.* **(-s, 0)** pleasure, comfort.
behaglich *a.* comfortable, pleasing, snug.
behalten *v.t.st.* to keep; to retain.
Behälter *m.* **(-s, -)** container, receptacle.
behandeln *v.t.* to handle; to deal with; to treat; (*Arzt*) to attend; (*chem.*) to process.
Behandlung *f.* **(-, -en)** management, treatment.
behangen *a.* decorated (tree).
behängen *v.t.* to hang.
beharren (bei) *v.i.* to persist in, to stick to.
beharrlich *a.* constant, steady, persevering.
Beharrlichkeit *f.* doggedness; persistence.
behauen *v.t.* to hew.
behaupten *v.t.* to assert, to maintain; ~ *v.r.* to keep one's ground.
Behauptung *f.* **(-, -en)** assertion, statement.
Behausung *f.* **(-, -en)** lodging, habitation.
beheben *v.t.* to clear away.
beheimatet *a.* to come from a place or country.
beheizbar *a.* heatable.
beheizen *v.t.* to heat.
Behelf *m.* **(-[e]s, -e)** expedient, shift.
behelfen *v.r.* to get by; ~ *ohne etwas*, to do without sth
behelfsmäßig *a.* makeshift; temporary.
behelligen *v.t.* to trouble, to importune.
behend[e] *a.* quick, agile, nimble.
Behendigkeit *f.* **(-, 0)** agility, nimbleness.
beherbergen *v.t.* to accommodate, to put up, to lodge, to shelter.
Beherbergung *f.* accommodation.
beherrschen *v.t.* to reign over, to rule over; to govern; (*Sprache*) to master; ~ *v.r.* to control oneself.
Beherrscher *m.* **(-s, -)** ruler.
beherrscht *a.* & *adv.* self-controlled.
Beherrschtheit *f.* self-control.
Beherrschung *f.* **(-, 0)** control; domination, rule, sway; mastery.
beherzigen *v.t.* to take to heart, to mind.
beherzt *a.* courageous, bold.
behexen *v.t.* to bewitch.
behilflich *a.* helpful, serviceable.
behindern *v.t.* to hinder, to hamper, to impede; to obstruct.
behindert *a.* handicapped.
Behinderte *m.* & *f.* **(-n, -n)** handicapped person.
Behörde *f.* **(-, -n)** authority.
Behördeneigentum *n.* government property.
behördlich *a.* official.
Behuf *m.* **(-[e]s, 0)** *zu diesem* ~, for this purpose.
behufs *pr.* for the purpose of.
behüten *v.t.* to guard, to preserve; to protect; *Gott behüte!* God forbid!
behutsam *a.* careful, cautious, wary.

Behutsamkeit *f.* care, caution.
bei *pr.* at, by, about, near; beside, with, to, in, upon, on.
beibehalten *v.t.st.* to keep, to retain.
Beiboot *n.* **(-s, -e)** ship's boat.
beibringen *v.t.ir.* to bring forward; (*Verluste*) to inflict; *jm. etwas* ~, to teach sth. to sb.
Beichte *f.* **(-, -n)** confession; ~ *hören,* to hear confession.
beichten *v.t.* to confess.
Beichtkind *n.* penitent.
Beichtstuhl *m.* confessional.
Beichtvater *m.* father confessor.
beide *a.* both, either.
beiderlei *a.* both, of both sorts.
beiderseits *adv.* on both sides.
beidseitig *a.* mutual.
Beifahrer *m.;* **Beifahrerin** *f.* (front-seat) passenger.
Beifall *m.* **(-[e]s, 0)** approbation, applause; ~ *klatschen,* to applaud.
beifällig *a.* approving, favorable.
beifolgend *a.* annexed, enclosed.
beifügen *v.t.* to add, to enclose.
beigeben *v.t.st. klein* ~, to give in.
Beigeschmack *m.* **(-[e]s, 0)** aftertaste.
Beihilfe *f.* **(-, 0)** assistance; subsidy; ~ *leisten* (*jur.*) to aid and abet.
beikommen *v.i.st. (s)* (*fig.*) to match, to come up to, to approach.
Beil *n.* **(-[e]s, -)** hatchet.
beil. *beiliegend,* enclosed, encl.
Beilage *f.* **(-, -n)** addition; (*eines Briefes*) enclosure; (*Gemüse*) vegetables *pl.;* (*einer Zeitung*) supplement.
beiläufig *a.* casual, incidental; ~ *adv.* by the way, casually, incidentally.
beilegen *v.t.* to add, to enclose; (*Streit*) to settle, to make up; (*zuschreiben*) to attribute.
Beilegung *f.* **(-, -en)** settlement.
beileibe ~ *nicht,* not for the world.
Beileid *n.* **(-[e]s, 0) Beileidsbezeigung** *f.* condolence.
beiliegen *v.i.st.* to be enclosed.
beiliegend *a.* enclosed, attached.
beim = bei dem.
beimessen *v.t.st.* to impute, to attribute.
beimischen *v.t.* to mix with.
Beimischung *f.* **(-, -en)** admixture.
Bein *n.* **(-[e]s, -e)** leg; (*Knochen*) bone; *zweibeinig, dreibeinig,* two-legged, three-legged.
beinahe *adv.* almost, nearly.
Beiname *m.* **(-ns, -n)** epithet, surname.
Beinbruch *m.* fracture (of a leg).
beinern *a.* made of bone, bony.
Beinfreiheit *f.* legroom.
Beinkleider *n.pl.* (*obs.*) trousers.
Beinschiene *f.* shin pad; splint.
Beipackzettel *m.* instruction leaflet.
beipflichten *v.t.* to agree (with).
Beirat *m.* **(-[e]s, -räte)** adviser; advisory board.
beirren *v.t.* to confuse; to divert from.
beisammen *adv.* together.
Beischlaf *m.* **(-[e]s, 0)** sexual intercourse.
Beisein *n.* **(-s, 0)** presence.
beiseite, beiseits *adv.* aside, apart.
beisetzen *v.t.* (*Leiche*) to bury.
Beisitzer *m.* **(-s, -)** assessor; assistant judge or magistrate.
Beispiel *n.* **(-[e]s, -e)** *n.* example; *zum* ~, for instance.
beispielhaft *a.* exemplary.
beispiellos *a.* unparalleled.
beispielshalber *adv.;* **beispielsweise** *adv.* for example; for instance.
beispringen *v.i.st. (s)* to assist, to succor.
beißen *v.t. & i.st.* to bite.
beißend *a.* pungent, hot; mordant.
Beißzange *f.* pincers, pliers.
Beistand *m.* **(-[e]s, -stände)** assistance.
beistehen *v.i.st.* to stand by; to assist, to support.
Beistelltisch *m.* sidetable.
Beisteuer *f.* **(-, -n)** contribution.
beisteuern *v.t.* to contribute (to).
beistimmen *v.i.* to agree with.
Beistrich *m.* comma.
Beitrag *m.* **(-[e]s, -träge)** contribution, subscription; share.
beitragen *v.t.st.* to contribute.
beitragsfrei *a.* noncontributory.
beitragspflichtig *a.* requiring contributions.
beitreiben *v.t.st.* to collect (money); to recover.
beitreten *v.i.st. (s)* to accede, to assent; (*einer Gesellschaft*) to join.
Beitritt *m.* **(-[e]s, 0)** accession; joining.
Beiwagen *m.* **(-s, -)** sidecar.
Beiwerk *n.* **(-[e]s, -e)** *pl.* accessories.
beiwohnen *v.i.* to be present at, to attend; to cohabit.
Beize *f.* **(-, -n)** (*Mittel*) caustic; wood stain.
beizeiten *adv.* in time.
beizen *v.t.* (*chem.*) to corrode; (*Fleisch*) to pickle; (*Holz*) to stain; (*med.*) to cauterize.
bejahen *v.t.* to answer in the affirmative.
bejahend *a.* affirmative.
bejahrt *a.* aged, elderly.
Bejahung *f.* **(-, -en)** affirmation; acceptance.
bejammern *v.t.* to lament, to bemoan, to bewail.
bejammernswert *a.* lamentable, deplorable.
bejubeln *v.t.* to cheer; to acclaim.
bekämpfen *v.t.* to fight against, to combat.
bekannt *a.* well known; acquainted (with).
Bekannte[r] *m. & f.* **(-en, -en)** acquaintance.
Bekanntgabe *f.* **(-, -n)** announcement.
bekanntgeben *v.t.* to announce.
Bekanntheitsgrad *m.* name recognition.
bekanntlich *adv.* as is well known.
bekanntmachen *v.t.* to announce.
Bekanntmachung *f.* **(-, -en)** notice.
Bekanntschaft *f.* **(-, -en)** acquaintance.
bekanntwerden *v.i.st.* to become known.
bekehren *v.t.* to convert.
Bekehrte[r] *m. & f.* **(-en, -en)** convert.
Bekehrung *f.* **(-, -en)** conversion.
bekennen *v.t.st.* to admit, to confess; ~ *v.r.ir.* to profess; to acknowledge.
Bekenntnis *n.* **(-nisses, -nisse)** confession, avowal.
Bekenntnisfreiheit *f.* religious freedom.
Bekenntnisschule *f.* denominational school.
bekifft *a.* (*sl.*) stoned.
beklagen *v.t.* to lament, to deplore, to pity; ~ *v.r.* to complain.
beklagenswert *a.* lamentable, pitiable.
Beklagte[r] *m. & f.* **(-en, -en)** defendant.
beklatschen *v.t.* to applaud.
bekleben *v.t.* to paste on.
bekleckern *v.t.* to stain; ~ *v.r.* to spill on oneself.

bekleiden *v.t.* to clothe, to attire; (*fig.*) to invest (with); (*Amt, Stelle*) to hold, to fill.
Bekleidung *f.* **(-, -en)** clothing, clothes *pl.*; (*fig.*) investiture.
beklemmend *a. & adv.* oppressive(ly).
Beklemmung *f.* **(-, -en)** oppression; anxiety; (*fig.*) anguish.
beklommen *a.* oppressed, anxious.
beknackt *a.* (*fam.*) lousy; stupid.
beknien *v.t.* to beg.
bekommen *v.t.st.* to obtain, to get, to receive; ~ *v.i.st. (s) jm. wohl ~*, to agree with sb.; *jm. nicht gut ~*, to disagree with sb.
bekömmlich *a.* beneficial; digestible.
beköstigen *v.t.* to board, to feed.
bekräftigen *v.t.* to confirm, to corroborate.
bekränzen *v.t.* to wreathe, to crown.
bekreuzen *v.t.* to make the sign of the cross.
bekreuzigen *v.r.* to cross oneself.
bekritzeln *v.t.* to scribble on.
bekümmern *v.t.* to afflict; ~ *v.r.* to concern oneself with.
Bekümmernis *f.* **(-, -nisse)** affliction.
bekunden *v.t.* to express, to manifest.
belächeln *v.t.* to smile at.
beladen *v.t.st.* to load; (*fig.*) to burden, to charge.
beladen *a.* loaded, laden.
Belag *m.* **(-[e]s, -läge)** coating; film; surface; (*Zunge*) fur.
belagern *v.t.* to besiege, to beleaguer.
Belagerung *f.* **(-, -en)** siege.
Belang *m.* **(-[e]s, -e)** interest.
belangen *v.t.* to concern, to relate to; (*vor Gericht*) to sue.
belanglos *a.* unimportant, trifling.
Belanglosigkeit *f.* **(-, -en)** unimportance; triviality.
Belangung *f.* **(-, -en)** prosecution.
belassen *v.t.st.* to let be; to leave.
belastbar *a.* tough, resilient, strong.
Belastbarkeit *f.* ability to withstand stress; load-bearing capacity.
belasten *v.t.* to load, to charge; (*com.*) to debit; *erblich belastet*, tainted by hereditary disease.
belastend *a.* incriminating.
belästigen *v.t.* to trouble, to bother; to molest.
Belästigung *f.* **(-, -en)** molestation.
Belastung *f.* **(-, -en)** charge, load; strain; debit.
Belastungsprobe *f.* **(-, -n)** endurance test; stress test.
Belastungszeuge *m.* witness for the prosecution.
belauern *v.t.* to watch carefully.
belaufen *v.r.* to amount to, to run to.
belauschen *v.t.* to watch, to overhear.
beleben *v.t.* to animate; to enliven.
belebt *a.* lively, animated; crowded.
Belebung *f.* **(-, -en)** animation, revival.
belecken *v.t.* to lick.
Beleg *m.* **(-[e]s, -e)** receipt, voucher, proof.
belegbar *a.* verifiable.
belegen *v.t.* to lay on or over; (*Platz*) to reserve, to secure; (*mit Beweisen*) to prove.
Belegschaft *f.* **(-, -en)** staff.
belegt *a.* (*Zunge*) furred, coated; *~e Brötchen, n.* sandwich.
belehnen *v.t.* to invest.
belehren *v.t.* to inform, to instruct.
belehrend *a.* instructive, didactic.
Belehrung *f.* **(-, -en)** instruction, lecture.
beleibt *a.* corpulent, stout.
beleidigen *v.t.* to offend, to insult.
beleidigt *a.* insulted, offended.
Beleidigte[r] *m.* (*jur.*) offended party.
Beleidigung *f.* **(-, -en)** offense, insult, slander; *tätliche ~* (*jur.*), assault; *schwere tätliche ~*, assault and battery.
beleihen *v.t.* to grant a loan on the security of.
belesen *a.* well read.
beleuchten *v.t.* to illumine, to illuminate, to light; (*fig.*) to illustrate.
Beleuchtung *f.* **(-, -en)** lighting, illumination.
Beleuchtungskörper *m.* light fixture.
beleumdet *a.*; **beleumundet** *a. übel od. gut ~ sein*, to have a good or bad reputation.
Belgien *n.* **(-s, 0)** Belgium; **Belgier** *m.*; **Belgierin** *f.*; **belgisch** *a.* Belgian.
belichten *v.t.* (*phot.*) to expose.
Belichtung *f.* **(-, -en)** (*phot.*) exposure; **~smesser** *m.* light meter.
belieben *v.t.* to like; ~ *v.i.* to please.
Belieben *n.* **(-s, 0)** pleasure, liking.
beliebig *a.* (with *ein*) any.
beliebt *a.* popular.
Beliebtheit *f.* **(-, 0)** popularity.
beliefern *v.t.* to supply.
Belieferung *f.* **(-, -en)** supply.
bellen *v.i.* to bark.
Belletristik *f.* **(-, 0)** fiction; **belletristisch** *a.* belletristic.
belobigen *v.t.* to praise.
Belobigung *f.* **(-, -en)** praise.
belohnen *v.t.* to reward, to recompense.
Belohnung *f.* **(-, -en)** reward, recompense.
belüften *v.t.* to ventilate.
Belüftung *f.* ventilation.
belügen *v.t.* to lie to.
belustigen *v.t.* to amuse, to divert.
belustigt *a.* amused.
Belustigung *f.* **(-, -en)** amusement, diversion.
bemächtigen *v.r.* to take possession of, to seize.
bemäkeln *v.t.* (*fam.*) to criticize.
bemalen *v.t.* to paint (over).
bemängeln *v.t.* to find fault with.
bemannen *v.t.* to man, to equip.
Bemannung *f.* **(-, -en)** crew.
bemänteln *v.t.* to cover up; (*fig.*) to palliate.
bemerken *v.t.* to remark, to observe; to perceive, to note.
bemerkenswert *a.* remarkable.
Bemerkung *f.* **(-, -en)** remark, observation, comment.
bemessen *v.t.* to measure according to.
bemitleiden *v.t.* to pity.
bemitleidenswert *a.* pitiable.
bemittelt *a.* well off, independent.
bemogeln *v.t.* (*fam.*) to cheat.
bemühen *v.t.* to make an effort; ~ *v.r.* to take pains, to endeavor.
Bemühung *f.* **(-, -en)** trouble, pains *pl.*; effort.
bemüssigt *adv.* obliged; *sich ~ fühlen*, to feel obliged.
bemuttern *v.t.* to mother.
benachbart *a.* neighboring.
benachrichtigen *v.t.* to inform, to advise.
Benachrichtigung *f.* **(-, -en)** information, advice.
benachteiligen *v.t.* to discriminate against; to put at a disadvantage.
Benachteiligung *f.* **(-, -en)** prejudice, detriment.
benagen *v.t.* to gnaw at.
benebeln *v.t.* to fog, to befuddle, to cloud.

benehmen *v.r.* to behave.
Benehmen *n.* **(-s, 0)** behavior, conduct.
beneiden *v.t.* to envy, to grudge.
beneidenswert *a.* enviable.
benennen *v.t.ir.* to name, to nominate.
Benennung *f.* **(-, -en)** name, appellation.
benetzen *v.t.* to moisten, to wet.
Bengel *m.* **(-s, -)** young rascal.
benommen *a.* benumbed, dazed.
benötigen *v.t.* to be in want of, to want.
Benotung *f.* **(-, -en)** grading; grade.
benutzen *v.t.* to make use of, to take advantage of.
Benutzer *m.* user.
Benutzung *f.* use.
Benzin *n.* **(-s, -e)** benzine; gasoline; petrol; **~stelle** *f.* gas station.
Benzol *n.* **(-s, -e)** benzol(e), benzene.
beobachten *v.t.* to observe, to watch; to keep, to perform.
Beobachter *m.* **(-s, -)** observer.
Beobachtung *f.* **(-, -en)** observation; observance.
beordern *v.t.* to order, to command.
bepacken *v.t.* to load, to charge.
bepflanzen *v.t.* to plant.
bequatschen *v.t.* (*fam.*) to persuade.
bequem *a.* convenient; apt, fit, commodious, comfortable; easygoing.
bequemen *v.r.* to comply with, to submit.
Bequemlichkeit *f.* **(-, -en)** convenience, comfort, ease; indolence.
berappen *v.t.* (*fam.*) to pay.
beraten *v.t.st.* to advise; ~ *v.r.* to consult, to deliberate.
beratend *a.* advisory.
Berater *m.;* **Beraterin** *f.* consultant; adviser.
beratschlagen *v.i.* & *v.r.* to discuss; to deliberate, to take counsel.
Beratung *f.* **(-, -en)** advice, council, conference; consultation.
Beratungstelle *f.* counseling center; advice bureau.
berauben *v.t.* to rob.
Beraubung *f.* robbery.
berauschen *v.t.* to intoxicate; ~ *v.r.* to get drunk; **~de Getränke** *n.pl.* intoxicating liquors.
berauschend *a.* intoxicating.
berechenbar *a.* calculable, predictable.
berechnen *v.t.* to compute, to calculate; (*anschreiben*) to charge; *der Kaffee wird besonders berechnet*, coffee will be extra.
berechnend *a.* (*pej.*) calculating.
Berechnung *f.* **(-, -en)** computation, calculation.
berechtigen *v.t.* to entitle, to authorize.
berechtigt *a.* justified, legitimate; authorized.
Berechtigung *f.* **(-, -en)** right; authorization; qualification.
bereden *v.t.* to talk over; discuss.
beredsam *a.* & *adv.* eloquent(ly).
Beredsamkeit *f.* **(-, 0)** eloquence.
beredt *a.* eloquent.
Bereich *m.* & *n.* **(-[e]s, -e)** reach, area, range; sphere, orbit.
bereichern *v.t.* to enrich; (*fig.*) to enlarge.
Bereicherung *f.* enrichment.
bereifen *v.t.* (*Faß*) to hoop; (*mot.*) to put tires on (a car).
bereinigen *v.t.* to settle.
bereisen *v.t.* to travel around.
bereit *a.* ready, prepared, prompt.
bereiten *v.t.* to prepare, to dress.
bereithalten *v.t.* to have ready; to keep ready.
bereits *adv.* already.
Bereitschaft *f.* **(-, -en)** readiness, preparedness.
bereitstehen *v.i.st.* to be ready.
bereitstellen *v.t.* to provide; to make available.
Bereitung *f.* **(-, -en)** preparation.
bereitwillig *a.* ready, willing; ~ *adv.* willingly.
Bereitwilligkeit *f.* **(-, 0)** willingness.
bereuen *v.t.* to repent; to regret.
Berg *m.* **(-[e]s, -e)** mountain, hill; *hinter dem ~e halten*, to hold in reserve; *zu ~ stehen*, to stand on end (hair).
bergab *adv.* downhill.
Bergakademie *f.* mining academy.
Bergamt *n.* mining bureau.
bergan, bergauf *adv.* uphill.
Bergbau *m.* mining.
bergen *v.t.st.* to save; to salvage; to conceal, to contain.
bergig *a.* mountainous, hilly.
Bergkette *f.* mountain chain or range.
Bergleute *pl.* miners.
Bergmann *m.* miner.
Bergpredigt *f.* Sermon on the Mount.
Bergsteiger *m.* mountaineer, alpinist.
Bergung *f.* **(-, -en)** rescue, saving; salvage.
Bergwacht *f.* mountain rescue service.
Bergwanderung *f.* hike in the mountains.
Bergwerk *n.* mine.
Bericht *m.* **(-[e]s, -e)** report, account.
berichten *v.t.* to inform, to send word, to report.
Berichterstatter *m.* reporter.
berichtigen *v.t.* to set right, to correct; (*Rechnung*) to settle.
Berichtigung *f.* **(-, -en)** correction.
beriechen *v.t.* to smell, to sniff.
berieseln *v.t.* to irrigate; *sich von Musik ~ lassen*, constantly have music on in the background.
Berieselung *f.* irrigation; (*fig.*) constant exposure.
beritten *a.* mounted.
berlinern *v.i.* to speak Berlin dialect.
Bermudainseln *f.pl.* Bermudas.
Bernhardiner *m.* **(-s, -)** St. Bernard (dog).
Bernstein *m.* **(-[e]s, 0)** amber.
bersten *v.i.st.* (*s*) to break, to burst, to crack.
berüchtigt *a.* notorious, ill-reputed.
berücken *v.t.* to fascinate.
berücksichtigen *v.t.* to regard, to respect, to allow for, to consider.
Berücksichtigung *f.* **(-, -en)** regard, consideration.
Beruf *m.* **(-[e]s, -e)** vocation; calling, trade, profession.
berufen *v.t.st.* to call; to appoint to an office; (*zusammenrufen*) to convene, to convoke; ~ *v.r.* to refer to, to invoke.
berufen *a.* competent.
beruflich *a.* professional, vocational.
Berufs... occupational, professional.
Berufsberatung *f.* vocational guidance.
Berufsdiplomat *m.* career diplomat.
Berufsspieler *m.* professional.
Berufung *f.* **(-, -en)** appointment; vocation; appeal; *~ einlegen*, to lodge an appeal; *einer ~ stattgeben*, to allow an appeal; *eine ~ zurückweisen*, to dismiss an appeal; **~sgericht** *n.* court of appeal, appelate court.
beruhen *v.i.* *~ auf*, to be based on; to rest upon; to depend on.

beruhigen *v.t.* to quiet, to calm; ~ *v.r.* to compose oneself.
Beruhigung *f.* **(-, -en)** reassurance.
Beruhigungs: ~mittel *n.*, **~pille** *f.* sedative, tranquilizer.
berühmt *a.* famous, celebrated.
Berühmtheit *f.* **(-, -en)** fame, celebrity; renown.
berühren *v.t.* to touch, to handle.
Berührung *f.* **(-, -en)** contact, touch.
bes. *besonders,* especially, esp.
besagen *v.t.* to mean, to signify.
besagt *a.* aforementioned.
besänftigen *v.t.* to soften, to soothe; to mitigate; to placate.
besät *a.* covered with.
Besatz *m.* **(-es, -sätze)** trimming.
Besatzung *f.* **(-, -en)** garrison, crew; occupation; **~szone** *f.* zone of occupation.
besaufen *v.r.* to get drunk.
Besäufnis *n.* **(-ses, -se)** (*fam.*) blast.
beschädigen *v.t.* to hurt, to damage.
Beschädigung *f.* **(-, -en)** damage, hurt.
beschaffen *v.t.* to obtain, to get.
beschaffen *a.* constituted, conditioned; ~ *v.t.* to procure.
Beschaffenheit *f.* **(-, -en)** properties, condition, quality, constitution.
Beschaffung *f.* **(-, 0)** obtaining, finding.
beschäftigen *v.t.* to employ, to occupy.
beschäftigt *a.* occupied, busy.
Beschäftigte *m./f.* **(-n, -n)** employee.
Beschäftigung *f.* **(-, -en)** occupation, employment.
beschälen *v.t.* to horse (a mare).
beschämen *v.t.* to shame.
beschämend *a.* shameful, humiliating.
beschämt *a.* ashamed.
Beschämung *f.* **(-, 0)** shame.
beschatten *v.t.* to shade, to shadow.
beschauen *v.t.* to look at, to view, to inspect.
beschaulich *a.* contemplative.
Beschaulichkeit *f.* **(-, -en)** contemplation.
Beschauung *f.* **(-, -en)** contemplation.
Bescheid *m.* **(-[e]s, -e)** decision; information; answer; ~ *wissen,* to know.
bescheiden *v.t.st. zu sich* ~, to send for; ~ *v.r.* to acquiesce.
bescheiden *a.* modest, unassuming.
Bescheidenheit *f.* **(-, 0)** modesty, discretion.
bescheinen *v.t.* to shine.
bescheinigen *v.t.* to attest, to certify.
Bescheinigung *f.* **(-, -en)** certificate.
bescheißen *v.t.* (*vulg.*) to rip off.
beschenken *v.t.* to present with.
bescheren *v.t.* to give (presents).
Bescherung *f.* **(-, -en)** distribution of presents; *eine schöne* ~, a nice mess.
bescheuert *a.* (*fam.*) crazy.
beschickert *a.* (*fam.*) tipsy.
beschießen *v.t.st.* to fire at.
Beschießung *f.* **(-, -en)** bombardment.
beschimpfen *v.t.* to insult, to swear at.
Beschimpfung *f.* **(-, -en)** insult, abuse (verbal).
beschirmen *v.t.* to protect, to defend.
Beschiß *m.* **(-es, 0)** (*vulg.*) rip-off.
beschissen *a.* (*vulg.*) lousy, shitty.
beschlafen *v.t.st. eine Sache* ~, to sleep on sth.
Beschlag *m.* **(-[e]s, -schläge)** (*metal*) mounting; (*gerichtlicher*) sequestration, seizure, confiscation; (*eines Pferdes*) shoeing; *in* ~ *nehmen, mit* ~ *belegen,* to seize, to sequester.
beschlagen *v.t.st.* to mount; (*Pferde*) to shoe; (*mit Nägeln*) to nail, to stud.
beschlagen *a.* (*fig.*) versed, skilled.
Beschlagnahme *f.* **(-, -en)** seizure, sequestration; (*nav.*) embargo; ~ *aufheben,* to derequisition.
beschlagnahmen *v.t.* to impound, to seize.
beschleichen *v.t.* to creep up on; to creep over.
beschleunigen *v.t.* to hasten, to accelerate, to speed up.
Beschleunigung *f.* acceleration; speeding up.
beschließen *v.t.st.* to resolve, to determine.
Beschluß *m.* **(-schlusses, -schlüsse)** resolution; decree.
beschlußfähig *a.* ~ *sein,* to have a quorum; ~*e Anzahl,* quorum.
Beschlußfähigkeit *f.* quorum.
beschmeißen *v.t.st.* (*fam.*) to pelt (sb.) with.
beschmieren *v.t.* to smear; to spread (sandwich); to grease.
beschmutzen *v.t.* to dirty, to soil.
beschneiden *v.t.st.* to cut, to clip; (*med.*) to circumcise; to prune, (*fig.*) to curtail.
Beschneidung *f.* **(-, -en)** circumcision; trimming, pruning.
beschönigen *v.t.* to palliate, to gloss over.
beschönigend *a.* palliative.
beschränken *v.t.* to restrict; to circumscribe; to limit; to reduce to.
beschränkt *a.* narrow; dull; half-witted.
Beschränktheit *f.* **(-, 0)** narrowness; (*fig.*) narrow-mindedness.
Beschränkung *f.* **(-, -en)** limitation, restriction.
beschreiben *v.t.st.* to describe.
Beschreibung *f.* **(-, -en)** description.
beschreiten *v.t.st.* to walk along, to step over.
beschriften *v.t.* to label; to inscribe.
beschuldigen *v.t.* to charge with, to accuse of.
Beschuldigte *m./f.* accused.
Beschuldigung *f.* **(-, -en)** charge, accusation; impeachment.
beschummeln *v.t.* (*fam.*) to cheat.
Beschuß *m.* shelling; shooting.
beschützen *v.t.* to protect, to defend.
Beschützer *m.* **(-s, -)** protector, patron.
beschwatzen *v.t.* to persuade; to talk into.
Beschwerde *f.* **(-, -n)** trouble; (*Mühe*) hardship; (*Klage*) grievance, complaint; (*Leiden*) complaint; ~ *führen,* to complain (of).
Beschwerdeführer *m.* complainant.
beschweren *v.t.* to burden, to charge; ~ *v.r.* to complain.
beschwerlich *a.* laborious, troublesome; ~ *fallen,* to molest, to inconvenience.
Beschwerlichkeit *f.* **(-, -en)** trouble, inconvenience.
beschwichtigen *v.t.* to soothe, to allay.
Beschwichtigung *f.* pacification, mollification.
beschwindeln *v.t.* to cheat, to swindle.
beschwingt *a.* elated, lively.
beschwipst *a.* tipsy.
beschworen *a.* sworn (to).
beschwören *v.t.st.* to confirm by oath; (*bitten*) to entreat; to conjure; (*bannen*) to exorcise.
Beschwörer *m.* **(-s, -)** conjuror, exorcist.
Beschwörung *f.* **(-, -en)** confirmation by oath; *Geister* ~, exorcism.
beseelen *v.t.* to animate, to inspirit.
besehen *v.t.st.* to look at, to view.

beseitigen *v.t.* to eliminate, to remove.
beseligen *v.t.* to bless, to enrapture.
Besen *m.* **(-s, -)** broom.
Besenstiel *m.* broomstick.
besessen *a.* possessed.
besetzen *v.t.* to occupy; (*Stelle*) to fill; (*Platz*) to engage; (*mit Spitzen, etc.*) to trim, to border.
besetzt *a.* busy, occupied; *die Leitung ist* ~, (*tel.*) the line is busy.
Besetztzeichen *n.* busy signal.
Besetzung *f.* **(-, -en)** (*von Stellen*) appointment; occupation.
besichtigen *v.t.* to see, to view, to inspect.
Besichtigung *f.* **(-, -en)** inspection.
besiedeln *v.t.* to settle in, to colonize.
Besiedlung *f.* settlement.
besiegeln *v.t.* to seal.
besiegen *v.t.* to defeat, to vanquish, to conquer.
besingen *v.t.st.* to celebrate, to sing.
besinnen *v.r.* to recollect, to call to mind; to consider, to reflect.
besinnlich *a.* contemplative.
Besinnung *f.* **(-, 0)** reflection, consciousness.
besinnungslos *a.* insensible, unconscious.
Besitz *m.* **(-es, 0)** possession, property; *in ~ haben,* to be in possession of.
Besitzanspruch *m.* **(-s, -sprüche)** claim to ownership.
besitzanzeigend *a.* (*ling.*) possessive.
besitzen *v.t.st.* to possess, to own.
Besitzer *m.* **(-s, -)** proprietor, owner.
Besitzergreifung, Besitznahme *f.* occupation.
besitzlos *a.* destitute.
Besitzstand *m.* standard of living.
Besitzung *f.* **(-, -en)** possession, estate.
Besitzurkunde *f.* title, deed.
besoffen *a.* (*sl.*) drunk, smashed.
besohlen *v.t.* to sole.
besolden *v.t.* to pay.
besoldet *a.* salaried.
Besoldung *f.* **(-, -en)** salary; pay, stipend.
besonder *a.* separate; peculiar, particular, special.
besonders *adv.* particularly, especially.
besonnen *a.* cautious, discreet.
Besonnenheit *f.* **(-, 0)** circumspection; calmness.
besorgen *v.t.* to provide; (*befürchten*) to fear.
Besorgnis *f.* **(-, -nisse)** concern, care; apprehension.
besorgniserregend *a.* alarming.
besorgt *a.* worried, apprehensive, anxious.
Besorgung *f.* **(-, -en)** commission.
bespannen *v.t.* to cover; to harness; to string.
bespielbar *a.* playable.
bespielen *v.t.* to record.
bespitzeln *v.t.* to spy on.
Bespitzelung *f.* spying.
bespötteln *v.t.* to mock, to ridicule.
besprechen *v.t.st.* to discuss, to talk over; (*bösen Geist*) to conjure; ~ *v.r. ~ mit,* to confer with.
Besprechung *f.* **(-, -en)** discussion, conference; review.
besprengen *v.t.* to sprinkle, to water.
bespritzen *v.t.* to splash.
besprühen *v.t.* to spray.
bespucken *v.t.* to spit at.
besser *a. & adv.* better; *um so ~,* so much the better.
bessergehen *v.i.* to feel better.
bessern *v.t.* to better; to improve, to mend, to repair.
Besserung *f.* **(-, -en)** improvement; recovery.
best *a.* best; *der erste ~e,* the first comer; *zum ~en,* for the benefit; *aufs ~e,* in the best manner; *jn. zum ~en haben,* to make fun of sb.
Bestallung *f.* **(-, -en)** appointment.
Bestand *m.* **(-[e]s, -stände)** continuance; amount, number, stock.
beständig *a.* constant, continual; steady.
Bestandsaufnahme *f.* stocktaking.
Bestandteil *m.* constituent (part), component.
bestärken *v.t.* to confirm.
bestätigen *v.t.* to confirm; to ratify, to sanction; (*Empfang*) to acknowledge; ~ *v.r.* to be confirmed.
Bestätigung *f.* **(-, -en)** confirmation; acknowledgment.
bestatten *v.t.* to bury, to inter.
Bestattung *f.* **(-, -en)** burial.
Bestattungsunternehmen *n.* funeral parlor.
bestäuben *v.t.* to pollinate.
Bestäubung *f.* **(-, -en)** pollination.
bestaunen *v.t.* to marvel at; to gaze at.
bestechen *v.t.st.* to corrupt, to bribe.
bestechend *a.* captivating, tempting.
bestechlich *a.* corruptible.
Bestechung *f.* **(-, -en)** corruption, bribery.
Bestechungsgeld *n.* **(-es, -er)** bribe.
Besteck *n.* **(-[e]s, -e)** (*Tisch~*) cutlery; instruments; (*nav.*) *das ~ machen,* to determine a ship's position.
bestehen *v.i.st.* (*aus etwas*) to consist of; (*auf etwas*) to insist on; (*dauern*) to continue, to last; ~ *v.t.st.* to undergo, to endure, to stand; *die Prüfung ~,* to pass; *die Prüfung nicht ~,* to fail.
Bestehen *n.* **(-s, 0)** existence.
bestehend *a.* existing, current.
bestehlen *v.t.st.* to rob, to steal from.
besteigen *v.t.st.* to step upon; to ascend; to mount.
Besteigung *f.* **(-, -en)** ascent.
bestellen *v.t.* to order; (*Briefe*) to deliver; (*Plätze*) to book; (*das Feld*) to till; (*einen*) to send for; (*Zeitung*) to subscribe to a paper; (*ernennen*) to appoint.
Bestellschein *m.* order form.
Bestellung *f.* **(-, -en)** order, command; (*des Feldes*) tillage; *auf ~,* to order; *eine ~ aufnehmen,* to take an order.
bestenfalls *adv.* at best.
bestens *adv.* very well.
besteuern *v.t.* to tax.
Besteuerung *f.* **(-, -en)** taxation.
bestialisch *a.* bestial; brutal.
Bestialität *f.* bestiality; brutality.
besticken *v.t.* to embroider.
Bestie *f.* **(-, -n)** beast, brute.
bestimmen *v.t.* to determine; to appoint; to define; to destine.
bestimmend *a.* decisive, determining.
bestimmt *a.* fixed; (*entschlossen*) decided; (*gewiß*) certain, positive.
Bestimmung *f.* **(-, -en)** destination; destiny; regulation, provision; definition.
Bestleistung *f.* **(-, -en)** best performance.
bestmöglich *a.* best possible.
Best.-Nr. *Bestellnummer,* order number, ord. no.
bestrafen *v.t.* to punish; to chastise; to penalize.
Bestrafung *f.* **(-, -en)** punishment; penalty.
bestrahlen *v.t.* to irradiate; (*med.*) to treat with X-rays.

Bestrahlung *f.* **(-, -en)** exposure to rays; (*med.*) X-ray treatment; radiotherapy.
bestreben *v.r.* to endeavor.
Bestreben *n.* **(-s, 0), Bestrebung** *f.* **(-, -en)** endeavor, exertion.
bestreichen *v.t.ir.* to spread over.
bestreiken *v.t.* to go on strike.
bestreitbar *a.* disputable.
bestreiten *v.t.st.* to contest, to dispute; *die Kosten ~*, to defray expenses.
bestreuen *v.t.* to strew, to sprinkle.
bestricken *v.t.* to charm.
bestürmen *v.t.* to storm, to assail; (*fig.*) to importune.
bestürzen *v.t.* to dismay, to perplex, to confound.
bestürzend *a.* dismaying.
bestürzt *a.* dismayed.
Bestürzung *f.* **(-, 0)** dismay.
Besuch *m.* **(-[e]s, -e)** visit; company, visitors *pl.*
besuchen *v.t.* to call upon, to visit; (*Lokale etc.*) to frequent, to attend.
Besucher *m.* **(-s, -)** visitor.
besucht *a.* attended (performance), frequented (restaurant).
besudeln *v.t.* to soil, to dirty.
betagt *a.* aged, elderly.
betasten *v.t.* to touch, to handle, to finger.
betätigen *v.t.* to practice; to manifest; *sich ~*, to take an active part.
betäuben *v.t.* to stun; (*med.*) to anesthetize.
Betäubung *f.* **(-, -en)** (*fig.*) stupor, bewilderment, daze; (*med.*) anesthetization, anesthesia.
Betäubungsmittel *n.* anesthetic.
beteiligen *v.t.* to give sb. his share; *beteiligt sein*, to have a share; *die Beteiligten*, those concerned; *~ v.r.* (*com.*) to participate; to have an interest in.
beteiligt *a.* involved; *am Gewinn ~ sein*, to have a share in the profits.
Beteiligung *f.* participation; involvement; share.
beten *v.i.* to pray; to say one's prayers.
beteuern *v.t.* to assert; to protest.
Beteuerung *f.* assertion; protestation.
betiteln *v.t.* to give a title, to style.
Beton (*frz.*) *m.* **(-s, -s)** concrete.
betonen *v.t.* to stress; to accent, (*fig.*) to emphasize.
Betonung *f.* **(-, -en)** stress; accentuation.
betören *v.t.* to infatuate; to bewitch.
Betr. *Betreff, betrifft*, regarding, re.
Betracht *m.* **(-[e]s, 0)** consideration, regard; *in ~ ziehen*, to take into consideration or account.
betrachten *v.t.* to look at; to consider.
beträchtlich *a.* considerable, important.
Betrachtung *f.* **(-, -en)** contemplation; examination.
Betrachtungsweise *f.* **(-, -n)** way of looking at things.
Betrag *m.* **(-[e]s, -träge)** amount.
betragen *~ v.t.st.* to amount to; *~ v.r.* to behave.
Betragen *n.* **(-s, 0)** behavior, conduct.
betrauen *v.t.* to entrust.
betrauern *v.t.* to mourn for.
Betreff *m.* **(-[e]s, 0)** subject, re; with regard to.
betreffen *v.t.st.* to concern; *was das betrifft*, as far as that is concerned.
betreffend *a.* concerning.
Betreffende *m./f.* person concerned; **~n** *pl.* people concerned.
betreffs *p.* with respect to, concerning.
betreiben *v.t.st.* to urge; (*Geschäft*) to manage, to carry on, to run; (*Beruf*) to pursue.
betreten *v.t.st.* to step on, to enter.
betreten *a.* disconcerted, embarrassed.
betreuen *v.t.* to look after, to take care of.
Betreuung *f.* **(-, 0)** care.
Betrieb *m.* **(-[e]s, -e)** management; establishment, works; (*öffentlicher*) service; *in ~ sein*, to operate; *außer ~ setzen*, to put out of action.
betrieblich *a.* internal; company-related.
betriebsam *a.* busy, industrious, active.
Betriebskapital *n.* working capital.
Betriebskosten *pl.* working expenses.
Betriebsleiter *m.* manager.
Betriebsrat *m.* shop steward, works council.
Betriebsvorrat *m.* stock-in-trade.
betrinken *v.r.* to get drunk.
betroffen *a.* dismayed, struck, perplexed.
Betroffene *m./f.* person affected; **~n** *pl.* people affected.
Betroffenheit *f.* dismay, consternation.
betrüben *v.t.* to afflict; *~ v.r.* to grieve.
Betrug *m.* **(-[e]s, 0)** fraud, deceit.
betrügen *v.t.st.* to cheat, to deceive; to defraud; to doublecross.
Betrüger *m.* **(-s, -)** swindler, fraud, deceiver.
Betrügerei *f.* **(-, -en)** deception; cheating; swindling.
betrügerisch *a.* fraudulent; deceitful.
betrunken *a.* drunk, tipsy, intoxicated.
Betrunkene *m./f.* drunk.
Betrunkenheit *f.* **(-, 0)** drunkenness.
Bett *n.* **(-[e]s, -en)** bed.
Bettbelag *m.* bedspread.
Bettdecke *f.* blanket; duvet, quilt.
Bettelei *f.* **(-, -en)** begging; solicitation.
bettelhaft *a.* beggarly.
Bettelmönch *m.* mendicant friar.
betteln *v.t.* to beg.
bettlägerig *a.* bedridden.
Bettler *m.* **(-s, -)** beggar.
Bettstelle *f.* bedstead.
Bettüberzug *m.* bedcover.
Bettuch *n.* sheet.
Bettwäsche *f.* bed linen.
Bettzeug *n. pl.* bedclothes
betucht *a.* well off.
betulich *a.* fussy; unhurried.
betupfen *v.t.* to dab.
beugen *v.t.* to bend, to bow; (*fig.*) to humble; (*gram.*) to inflect.
Beugung *f.* **(-, -en)** inflection.
Beule *f.* **(-, -en)** bump, bruise.
Beulenpest *f.* bubonic plague.
beunruhigen *v.t.* to disquiet, to harass, to worry.
Beunruhigung *f.* **(-, -en)** worry, concern.
beurkunden *v.t.* to document, to authenticate, to prove.
beurlauben *v.t.* to grant or to give leave of absence; *~ v.r.* to take leave.
Beurlaubung *f.* leave of absence.
beurteilen *v.t.* to judge; to criticize.
Beurteilung *f.* **(-, -en)** judgment; appraisal, assessment; (*mil.*) efficiency rating.
Beute *f.* **(-, 0)** booty, spoil, prey.
Beutel *m.* **(-s, -)** bag, pouch; purse.
beuteln *v.t.* to shake up.
Beutelratte *f.* opossum.
Beuteltier *n.* marsupial.
Bev. *Bevölkerung*, population, pop.

bevölkern *v.t.* to people, to populate.
Bevölkerung *f.* **(-, -en)** population.
Bevölkerungsdichte *f.* population density.
bevollmächtigen *v.t.* to authorize.
Bevollmächtigte[r] *m.* **(-en, -en)** authorized representative, (*Gesandte*) plenipotentiary.
Bevollmächtigung *f.* **(-, -en)** authorization; (*jur.*) power of attorney.
bevor *c.* before.
bevormunden *v.t.* to impose one's will on sb.
bevorstehen *v.i.st.* to impend, to be imminent.
bevorstehend *a.* imminent, coming.
bevorzugen *v.t.* to prefer, to favor, to privilege.
Bevorzugung *f.* **(-, -en)** preferential treatment.
bewachen *v.t.* to watch over, to guard.
bewachsen *a.* overgrown, cover.
Bewachung *f.* **(-, -en)** escort, guard.
bewaffnen *v.t.* to arm.
bewaffnet *a.* armed.
Bewaffnung *f.* **(-, -en)** arming, armament.
bewahren *v.t.* to preserve; to guard, to keep; *Gott bewahre!* God forbid!
bewähren ~ *v.r.* to prove oneself; to stand the test.
bewahrheiten *v.t.* to prove true.
bewährt *a.* proven, tried.
Bewährung *f.* **(-, 0)** (*jur.*) probation, verification.
Bewährungsfrist *f.* (period of) probation; *eine ~ von zwei Jahren erhalten,* to get two years' probation.
bewaldet *a.* woody.
bewältigen *v.t.* to overcome, to master.
bewandert *a.* knowledgeable, versed, skilled.
Bewandtnis *f.* **(-, -nisse)** condition, explanation.
bewässern *v.t.* to irrigate.
Bewässerung *f.* **(-, -en)** irrigation.
bewegen *v.t.& st.* to move; to stir, to induce; ~ *v.r.* to move.
Beweggrund *m.* **(-[e]s, -gründe)** motive.
beweglich *a.* mobile; movable; versatile; agile; *~es Vermögen,* movables, movable property, personal estate.
Beweglichkeit *f.* **(-, 0)** mobility; agility.
bewegt *a.* eventful, turbulent.
Bewegung *f.* **(-, -en)** motion; movement; commotion; exercise; emotion.
bewegungslos *a.* motionless.
beweinen *v.t.* to weep for, to deplore.
Beweis *m.* **(-weises, -weise)** proof; evidence; argument; *zum ~ von,* in proof of; *~ antreten,* to produce evidence; *~ liefern,* to furnish proof; *als ~ zulassen,* to admit as evidence.
beweisbar *a.* provable.
beweisen *v.t.st.* to prove; to demonstrate.
Beweisgrund *m.* argument.
Beweislast *f.* burden of proof.
bewenden *v.i.ir. es dabei ~ lassen,* to let the matter rest there.
bewerben *v.r.* to apply.
Bewerber *m.* **(-s, -); Bewerberin** *f.* **(-, -en)** applicant.
Bewerbung *f.* **(-, -en)** application.
Bewerbungsschreiben *n.* letter of application.
bewerkstelligen *v.t.* to manage.
bewerten *v.t.* to assess, to estimate, to value.
Bewertung *f.* assessment, evaluation; grading.
Bewertungsmaßstab *m.* criterion of assessment.
bewilligen *v.t.* to consent to, to grant, to concede; *bewilligte Mittel* approved funds.
Bewilligung *f.* **(-, -en)** concession; grant; consent; (*von Geldern*) appropriation of funds.
bewirken *v.t.* to effect, to cause, to bring about.
bewirten *v.t.* to entertain, to treat.
bewirtschaften *v.t.* to manage, to run (business), to cultivate.
Bewirtung *f.* food and service.
bewohnbar *a.* habitable.
bewohnen *v.t.* to inhabit.
Bewohner *m.* **(-s, -)** inhabitant; (*eines Hauses*) resident, inmate.
bewohnt *a.* occupied; inhabited.
bewölken *v.r.* to become overcast.
bewölkt *a.* cloudy, overcast.
Bewölkung *f.* **(-, 0)** clouds; *zunehmende ~,* increasing cloudiness.
Bewunderer *m.* **(-s, -); Bewunderin** *f.* **(-, -nen)** admirer.
bewundern *v.t.* to admire.
bewundernswert, bewundernswürdig *a.* admirable.
Bewunderung *f.* **(-, 0)** admiration.
bewußt *a.* conscious; in question.
bewußtlos *a.* unconscious.
Bewußtlosigkeig *f.* **(-, 0)** unconsciousness.
bewußtmachen *v.t. jm. etw. ~,* to make sb. realize sth.
Bewußtsein *n.* **(-s, 0)** consciousness.
Bewußtseinsspaltung *f.* split consciousness, schizophrenia.
Bez. *Bezeichnung,* designation; *Bezirk,* district, dist.
bezahlbar *a.* affordable.
bezahlen *v.t.* to pay, to discharge; (*Wechsel*) to honor.
Bezahlung *f.* **(-, 0)** payment, pay; *gegen ~,* for payment.
bezähmen *v.t.* to tame; (*fig.*) to restrain, to subdue.
bezaubern *v.t.* to enchant, to bewitch, to charm.
bezaubernd *a.* enchanting.
bezeichnen *v.t.* to mark, to denote; to signify; **~d,** *a.* characteristic, significant.
Bezeichnung *f.* **(-, -en)** note, mark, designation.
bezeigen *v.t.* to show, to manifest.
bezeugen *v.t.* to testify.
bezichtigen *v.t.* to charge, to accuse.
Bezichtigung *f.* accusation.
beziehen *v.t.st.* to cover; (*Instrument*) to string; (*Geld*) to draw; (*Waren*) to obtain; (*Zeitung*) to take; (*Wohnung*) to move into; (*Hochschule*) to enter; ~ *v.r. ~ auf,* to refer to; to relate to; (*Himmel*) to become cloudy.
Bezieher *m.* **(-s, -)** subscriber.
Beziehung *f.* **(-, -en)** relation, connection; respect; *mit guten ~en,* well connected.
beziehungsweise *adv.* respectively.
beziffern *v.r.* to amount to.
Bezirk *m.* **(-[e]s, -e)** district, area.
Bezug *m.* **(-[e]s, -züge)** case; (*Waren*) supply; reference; *in ~ auf,* with respect to.
bezüglich *a.* respecting, referring to.
Bezugnahme *f.* **(-, -n)** reference.
Bezugsbedingungen *f. pl.* terms of delivery.
Bezugsquelle *f.* source of supply.
bezuschussen *v.t.* to subsidize.
bezw., bzw. *beziehungsweise,* respectively.
bezwecken *v.t.* to aim at.
bezweifeln *v.t.* to doubt.
bezwingen *v.t.st.* to subdue, to vanquish.

B.G.B. *Bürgerliches Gesetzbuch,* Civil Code.
BGH *Bundesgerichtshof,* Federal Supreme Court.
Bhf. *Bahnhof,* station.
bibbern *v.i.* to shiver, to shake, to tremble.
Bibel *f.* **(-, -n)** Bible, Scripture.
Bibelspruch *m.* biblical saying.
Biber *m.* **(-s, -)** beaver.
Bibliograph *m.* **(-en, -en)** bibliographer.
Bibliographie *f.* **(-, -n)** bibliography.
Bibliothek *f.* **(-, -en)** library.
Bibliothekar *m.* **(-s, -e); Bibliothekarin** *f.* **(-, -nen)** librarian.
biblisch *a.* biblical, scriptural.
bieder *a.* unsophisticated; honest, straightforward.
Biedermann *m.* **(-es, -männer)** (*pej.*) petty bourgeois.
biegen *v.t. & i.st.* to bend, to bow; to curve; to turn; ~ *v.r.* to bend, to warp.
biegsam *a.* flexible; supple, pliant.
Biegsamkeit *f.* flexibility.
Biegung *f.* **(-, -en)** bend, curve.
Biene *f.* **(-, -n)** bee.
Bienenkönigin *f.* queen bee.
Bienenkorb *m.* beehive.
Bienenschwarm *m.* swarm of bees.
Bienenstock *m.* beehive.
Bienenwachs *n.* beeswax.
Bienenzucht *f.* bee-keeping, apiculture.
Bier *n.* **(-[e]s, -e)** beer; (*englisches*) ale.
Biest *n.* **(-e(s), -er)** creature; beast.
bieten *v.t.st.* to bid; to offer.
Bigamie *f.* **(-, -n)** bigamy.
Bigamist *m.* **(-en, -en)** bigamist.
bigott *a.* bigoted, overly devout.
Bilanz *f.* balance sheet.
Bild *n.* **(-[e]s, -er)** image; picture.
Bildband *m.* **(-es, -bände)** illustrated book.
Bildbeilage *f.* **(-, -n)** illustrated supplement.
bilden *v.t.* to form; to shape, to model; to cultivate, to improve; to constitute; (*fig.*) to improve one's mind.
bildend *a.* instructive; *~e Künste,* fine arts.
Bilderbuch *n.* picture book.
Bildergalerie *f.* picture gallery.
Bilderrahmen *m.* picture frame.
Bilderstürmer *m.* iconoclast.
Bildhauer *m.* **(-s, -); Bildhauerin** *f.* **(-, -nen)** sculptor.
Bildhauerkunst *f.* sculpture.
bildlich *a.* figurative; *~e Darstellung,* pictorial representation.
Bildnis *n.* **(-nisses, -nisse)** portrait.
Bildplatte *f.* videodisc; **~nspieler** *m.* videodisc player.
Bildregie *f.* camera work.
bildsam *a.* plastic.
Bildsäule *f.* statue.
Bildschirm *m.* **(-s, -e)** screen; (*comp.*) monitor.
Bildschnitzer *m.* woodcarver.
bildschön *a.* very beautiful, dazzling.
Bildstörung *f.* interference (TV).
Bildung *f.* **(-, -en)** formation; constitution; culture; training, education.
Bildungschancen *f.pl.* educational opportunities.
Bildungspolitik *f.* educational policy.
Bildungsurlaub *m.* educational leave.
Bildunterschrift *f.* **(-, -en)** caption.
Billard *n.* **(-s, -s)** *pl.* billiards; billiard table.
Billardstock *m.* cue.
Billett *n.* **(-[e]s, -e or -s)** (*Fahrkarte*) ticket; *ein ~ lösen,* to buy a ticket.
billig *a.* equitable, just, fair, reasonable; (*im Preise*) cheap.
billigen *v.t.* to approve (of).
Billigkeit *f.* **(-, 0)** fairness; cheapness.
Billigung *f.* **(-, 0)** sanction, approval.
Bimsstein *m.* pumice stone.
Binde *f.* **(-, -n)** band; (neck) tie; bandage, sling; sanitary napkin.
Bindeglied *n.* connecting link.
Bindehaut *f.* conjunctiva; **~entzündung** *f.* conjunctivitis.
Bindemittel *n.* binder.
binden *v.t.st.* to bind; to tie, to fasten; (*mil.*) to tie down, to contain; (*fig.*) to engage; ~ *v.r.* to commit oneself.
bindend *a.* binding, definite.
Binder *m.* tie.
Bindestrich *m.* (*gram.*) hyphen.
Bindewort *n.* conjunction.
Bindfaden *m.* string, packthread, twine.
Bindung *f.* **(-, -en)** binding; (*mus.*) ligature; (*fig.*) obligation; restriction.
binnen *pr.* within.
Binnenhafen *m.* inland harbor, inland port; basin (of a port).
Binnenhandel *m.* home trade.
Binnenland *n.* inland, interior.
Binnenmeer *n.* inland sea.
Binse *f.* **(-, -n)** rush.
Binsenweisheit *f.* **(-, -en)** truism.
Biochemie *f.* biochemistry.
Biograph *m.* **(-en, -en)** biographer.
Biographie *f.* **(-, -en)** biography.
Biologe *m.* **(-en, -en); Biologin** *f.* **(-, -nen)** biologist.
Biologie *f.* **(-, -n)** biology.
biologisch *a.* biological; natural; *aus ~em Anbau,* organically produced.
Biomasse *f.* **(-, 0)** biomass.
Biotop *n.* **(-s, -e)** biotope.
Biowissenschaften *pl.* life sciences.
Birke *f.* **(-, -n)** birch, birch tree.
Birnbaum *m.* pear tree.
Birne *f.* **(-, -n)** pear; (*el.*) (light)bulb.
Birnenfassung *f.* light bulb socket.
bis *pr.* to, up to, as far as, till, until; ~ *c.* till, until; *~ dahin, ~ jetzt,* so far.
Bisam *m.* **(-[e]s, -e)** musk; **~ratte** *f.* muskrat.
Bischof *m.* **(-[e]s, -schöfe)** bishop.
bischöflich *a.* episcopal.
Bischofsmütze *f.* mitre.
Bischofssitz *m.* episcopal see.
Bischofsstab *m.* crosier.
Bisexualität *f.* bisexuality.
bisexuell *a.* bisexual.
bisher *adv.* hitherto, till now.
bisherig *a.* previous, hitherto, existing.
Biskaya *f.* Biscay; *der Golf von ~,* the Bay of Biscay.
Biskuit *m. or n.* **(-s, -s & -e)** biscuit; sponge cake.
bislang *adv.* until now.
Biß *m.* **(Bisses, Bisse)** bite, sting.
bißchen *a.* **(-s, 0)** *ein ~,* a little.
Bissen *m.* **(-s, -)** morsel, mouthful.
bissig *a.* biting, sarcastic; (*Hund*) snappish.
Bistum *n.* **(-[e]s, -tümer)** bishopric.
bisweilen *adv.* sometimes, now and then.
Bittbrief *m.* **(-s, -e)** letter of request.

Bitte *f.* **(-, -n)** request, entreaty, prayer.
bitten *v.t.st.* to beg, to request; to pray; to invite; **bitte** please.
bitter *a.* bitter, stinging.
bitterböse *a.* very wicked; extremely angry.
Bitterkeit *f.* **(-, -en)** bitterness.
bitterlich *a.* slightly bitter; ~ *adv.* bitterly.
Bittermandel *f.* bitter almond.
Bittersalz *n.pl.* Epsom salts.
Bitt: ~gesuch *n.* petition.
Bitt: ~schrift *f.* petition, supplication.
Bitt: ~steller *m.* petitioner, supplicant.
Biwak *n.* **(-s, -e)** bivouac.
bizarr *a.* strange, odd.
Bizeps *m.* **(-, -e)** biceps.
blähen *v.t.* to billow; to inflate, to cause flatulency.
blähend *a.* flatulent.
Blähung *f.* **(-, -en)** flatulence.
blamabel *a.* shameful, disgraceful.
Blamage *f.* (*frz.*) **(-, -n)** exposure to ridicule, disgrace.
blamieren *v.t.* to disgrace; to expose to ridicule; ~ *v.r.* to make a fool of oneself.
blanchieren *v.t.* to blanch.
blank *a.* blank; smooth, polished, bright.
blanko *a.* blank; ~ *Scheck*, blank check.
Blankvers *m.* blank verse.
Blase *f.* **(-, -n)** bladder; bubble; blister; flaw (in glass).
Blasebalg *m. pl.* bellows.
blasen *v.t. & i.st.* to blow; to sound.
Blasenkatarrh *m.* (*med.*) cystitis.
Bläser *m.*; **Bläserin** *f.* wind player.
blasiert *a.* blasé, cloyed.
Blasinstrument *n.* wind instrument.
Blaskapelle *f.*, **Blasorchester** *n.* brass band.
Blasphemie *f.* blasphemy.
blasphemisch *a.* blasphemous.
Blasrohr *n.* blowpipe.
blaß *a.* pale, wan, pallid.
Blässe *f.* **(-, 0)** paleness, pallor.
Bläßhuhn *n.* coot.
Blatt *n.* **(-[e]s, Blätter)** leaf; sheet; blade; newspaper; *vom* ~, at sight; *das* ~ *wendet sich*, the tide turns.
Blatter *f.* **(-, -n)** blister, pustule; **~n** *pl.* smallpox.
blättern *v.i.* to leaf through a book.
Blatternarbe *f.* pockmark.
Blätterteig *m.* puff pastry.
Blattgold *n.* gold leaf.
Blattlaus *f.* greenfly.
Blattpflanze *f.* foliage plant.
Blattsäge *f.* wide-blade saw.
Blattsalat *m.* green salad.
blau *a.*, **Blau** *n.* **(-s, 0)** blue; *ins Blaue*, at random.
Blaubeere *f.* **(-, -en)** blueberry.
bläulich *a.* bluish.
Blaupause *f.* (*mech.*) blueprint.
Blausäure *f.* Prussic acid.
Blaustift *m.* blue pencil.
Blaustrumpf *m.* (*pej.*) bluestocking.
Blech *n.* **(-[e]s, -e)** sheet metal; tin plate, tin; (*fam.*) stuff, nonsense.
blechen *v.t. & v.i.* (*fam.*) to pay for.
Blechmusik *f.* brass-band music.
blecken *v.t. die Zähnen* ~, to bare one's teeth.
Blei *n.* **(-s, -e)** lead; (*fam.*) pencil.
bleiben *v.i.st.* (*s*) to remain, to stay; to rest; to continue, to keep; ~ *lassen*, to let alone.
bleibend *p. & a.* lasting, permanent.
bleich *a.* pale, wan; faint.
Bleiche *f.* **(-, -n)** paleness; (*obs.*) bleaching-(ground).
bleichen *v.t.* to bleach, to whiten; ~ *v.i.* to get bleached.
Bleichgesicht *n.* paleface.
Bleichmittel *n.* bleaching agent.
Bleichsucht *f.* anemia, chlorosis.
bleichsüchtig *a.* anemic, chlorotic.
bleiern *a.* leaden; (*fig.*) heavy, dull.
bleifrei *a.* unleaded.
Bleistift *m.* pencil; **~spitzer** *m.* pencil sharpener.
Blende *f.* **(-, -n)** blind, folding screen; shutter; (*Pferde*~) blinker; (*nav.*) *pl.* deadlights; (*opt.*) diaphragm, aperture.
blenden *v.t.* to blind, to blindfold; to make blind; (*fig.*) to dazzle.
Blendeneinstellung *f.* (*photo.*) aperture setting.
blendenskala *f.* aperture ring.
Blendung *f.* dazzling; blinding.
Blendwerk *n.* delusion, illusion.
Blesse *f.* blaze.
Blick *m.* **(-[e]s, -e)** glance, look; view; *auf den ersten* ~, at first glance.
blicken *v.i.* to glance, to look.
Blickfang *m.* eye-catcher.
Blickfeld *n.* field of vision.
Blickkontakt *m.* eye contact.
Blickpunkt *m.* visual focus; point of view.
Blickwinkel *m.* angle of vision; point of view.
blind *a.* blind; dull; ~*er Alarm*, false alarm; ~ *machen*, to render harmless, defuse (granade).
Blinddarm *m.* appendix; **~entzündung** *f.* appendicitis.
Blinde *m. & f.* blind person.
Blindekuh *f.* blindman's buff.
Blindgänger *m.* dud.
Blindheit *f.* **(-, 0)** blindness.
blindlings *adv.* blindly, blindfolded.
Blindschleiche *f.* **(-, -n)** blindworm.
blinken *v.i.* to glitter, to gleam, to twinkle.
Blinker *m.* turn signal; spoon bait (fishing).
Blinkfeuer *m.* intermittent light.
blinzeln, blinzen *v.i.* to blink, to wink; to twinkle.
Blitz *m.* **(-es, -e)** lightning; *wie ein* ~ *aus heiterem Himmel*, out of the blue.
Blitzableiter *m.* lightning conductor; lightning rod.
blitzen *v.i.* to flash, to sparkle.
Blitzgerät *n.* (*photo.*) flash.
Blitzkrieg *m.* blitzkrieg.
Blitzlicht *n.* flashlight.
blitzschnell *a.* swift as lightning.
Block *m.* **(-[e]s, Blöcke)** block; log.
Blockade *f.* **(-, -n)** blockade; *die* ~ *brechen*, to run the blockade; **~brecher** *m.* blockade-runner.
Blockhaus *n.* log cabin.
blockieren *v.t.* to block up, to blockade.
Blockschokolade *f.* baking chocolate.
Blockschrift *f.* block letters.
Blockstunde *f.* double period (school).
blöd[e] *a.* stupid, imbecile.
Blödsinn *m.* nonsense, trash.
blöken *v.i.* to bleat (sheep); to low (cattle).
blond *a.* fair, blond.
blondieren *v.t.* to dye blond.

Blondine *f.* **(-, -n)** blonde.
bloß *a.* naked, bare; uncovered; mere; ~ *adv.* merely, only; ~ *stellen,* to expose.
Blöße *f.* **(-, -n)** nakedness, bareness; weak side.
bloßlegen ~ *v.t.* to uncover; to expose; to reveal.
bloßliegen ~ *v.i.* to be exposed.
bloßstellen ~ *v.t.* to show up.
Bluff *m.* **(-s, -s)** bluff.
bluffen *v.i.* to bluff.
blühen *v.i.* to bloom, to flower, to blossom; (*fig.*) to flourish.
Blume *f.* **(-, -n)** flower; *Wein*~, bouquet; *durch die* ~, figuratively, allusively.
Blumenausstellung *f.* flower show.
Blumenbeet *n.* flower bed.
Blumenblatt *n.* petal.
Blumenhändler *m.* florist.
Blumenkohl *m.* cauliflower.
Blumenspende *f.* floral tribute.
Blumenstock *m.* flowering pot plant.
Blumenstrauß *m.* bunch of flowers, bouquet.
Blumentopf *m.* flowerpot.
Blumenzucht *f.* floriculture.
Blumenzwiebel *f.* bulb.
blumig *a.* flowery; (*fig.*) florid.
Bluse *f.* **(-, -n)** blouse.
Blut *n.* **(-[e]s, 0)** blood.
Blutader *f.* vein; blood vessel.
Blutalkohol *m.* blood alcohol level.
Blutarmut *f.* anemia.
Blutbahn *f.* bloodstream.
Blutbild *n.* blood count.
Blutbuche *f.* copper beech, bronze beech.
Blutdruck *m.* blood pressure.
blutdürstig *a.* bloodthirsty.
Blüte *f.* **(-, -n)** blossom, bloom; (*fig.*) prime, heyday.
Blutegel *m.* leech.
bluten *v.i.* to bleed.
Blütenkelch *m.* calyx.
blütenknospe *f.* bud.
Blütenstaub *m.* pollen.
Bluter *m.* **(-s, -)** hemophiliac.
Bluterguß *m.* hematoma, bruise.
Bluterkrankheit *f.* hemophilia.
Blütezeit *f.* prime, golden age.
Blutfarbstoff *m.* hemoglobin.
Blutgefäß *n.* blood vessel.
Blutgerinnsel *n.* blood clot.
blutgierig *a.* sanguinary, bloodthirsty.
Blutgruppe *f.* blood group.
Bluthochdruck *m.* **(-s, 0)** high blood pressure.
blutig *a.* bloody; sanguinary.
blutjung *a.* very young.
Blutkonserve *f.* unit of stored blood.
Blutkörperchen *n.* blood corpuscle.
Blutkrebs *m.* leukemia.
Blutkreislauf *m.* blood circulation.
Blutlache *f.* pool of blood.
blutleer, blutlos *a.* bloodless, anemic.
Blutprobe *f.* blood test; blood sample.
Blutrache *f.* vendetta.
blutrünstig *a.* bloody.
Blutsauger *m.* vampire; (*fig.*) extortionist, skinflint.
Blutschande *f.* incest.
blutschänderisch *a.* incestuous.
Blutschuld *f.* (*lit.*) bloodguilt; capital crime.
Blutspender *m.* blood donor.
blutstillend *a.* hemostatic, styptic.
Blutsturz *m.*, **Blutung** *f.* hemorrhage.
blutsverwandt *a.* consanguineous.
Blutsverwandter *m.* blood relation.
Blutsverwandtschaft *f.* consanguinity; blood relationship.
Blutübertragung *f.* blood transfusion.
blutunterlaufen *a.* bloodshot.
Blutvergießen *n.* bloodshed.
Blutvergiftung *f.* food poisoning.
Blutwurst *f.* black pudding; blood sausage.
BLZ *Bankleitzahl,* bank code.
b-Moll *n.* B flat minor.
BND Bundesnachrichtendienst, Federal Intelligence Service.
Bö *f.* **(-, en)** gust.
Bob *m.* **(-, -s)** bobsled.
Bobbahn *f.* bobsled run.
Bobfahrer *m.;* **Bobfahrerin** *f.* bobsledder.
Bock *m.* **(-[e]s, Böcke)** ram; (*andere Tiere*) buck; trestle; high stool; *einen* ~ *schiessen,* to make a blunder.
bockbeinig *a.* stubborn.
Bockgestell *n.* trestle.
bockig *a.* stubborn; pigheaded.
Bockleder *n.* buckskin.
Bockshorn *n. jn. ins* ~ *jagen,* to intimidate sb.
Boden *m.* **(-s, Böden)** ground; soil; bottom; garret, loft; (*eines Fasses etc.*) head; floor.
Bodenfenster *n.* dormer window.
Bodenkammer *f.* garret, attic.
bodenlos *a.* bottomless.
Bodenrente *f.* base rent.
Bodensatz *m.* sediment, *pl.* dregs.
Bodenschätze *m.pl.* mineral resources.
bodenständig *a.* native.
Bogen *m.* **(-s, -)** arch, vault; blow; (*math.*) arc; (*Geigen*~) bow; sheet (paper); *in Bausch und* ~, wholesale.
Bogengang *m.* arcade.
Bogenlampe *f.* arc lamp.
Bogenschütze *m.* archer.
Bohème (*frz.*) *f.* Bohemia.
Bohèmien *m.* Bohemian.
Bohle *f.* **(-, -n)** board, plank.
bohlen *v.t.* to board, to plank.
Böhme *m.;* **Böhmin** *f.;* **böhmisch** *a.* Bohemian; *das sind mir* ~*e Dörfer,* that is Greek to me.
Böhmen *n.* Bohemia.
Bohne *f.* **(-, -n)** bean; *dicke* ~*n,* broad beans; *grüne* ~*n,* French beans, runner beans.
Bohnenstange *f.* beanpole.
bohnern *v.t.* to wax.
bohren *v.t.* to bore, to drill; *ein Schiff in den Grund* ~, to sink a ship.
bohrend *a.* gnawing; piercing; probing.
Bohrer *m.* **(-s, -)** drill.
Bohrinsel *f.* oil rig.
Bohrmaschine *f.* boring machine, drilling machine.
Bohrturm *m.* derrick.
Bohrung *f.* drilling; hole.
böig *a.* gusty.
Boiler *m.* water heater; boiler.
Boje *f.* **(-, -n)** buoy.
Bolivianer *m.;* **Bolivianerin** *f.;* **bolivianisch** *a.* Bolivian.
Bolivien *n.* Bolivia.
Böller *m.* **(-s, -)** small mortar.
Böllerschuß *m.* gun salute.

Bollwerk *n.* bastion, bulwark.
bolzen *v.i.* (*fam.*) to play soccer.
Bolzen *m.* **(-s, -)** bolt; arrow.
Bolzplatz *m.* soccer field (children's).
Bombardement *n.* **(-s, -s)** bombardment.
bombardieren *v.t.* to bombard, to shell, to pound.
Bombardierung *f.* **(-, -en)** bombing.
Bombast *m.* **(-es, 0)** bombast.
bombastisch *a.* bombastic, inflated.
Bombe *f.* **(-, -n)** bomb, shell.
Bomben: ~angriff *m.* bomb attack, bombing raid; **~anschlag** *m.*, **~attentat** *n.* bomb attack; **~drohung** *f.* bomb threat; **~erfolg** *m.* (*fam.*) smash hit; **~flugzeug** *n.* bomber; **~punktwurf** *m.* pinpoint bombing; **~schacht** *m.* bomb rack; **~sicher** *a.* bombproof; **~zielgerät** *n.* bombsight.
Bomber *m.* bomber.
Bon *m.* **(-s, -s)** voucher; coupon; sales slip.
Bonbon (frz.) *n.* **(-s, -s)** sweet.
bonbonfarben *a.* candy-colored.
Bonmot *n.* **(-s, -s)** bon mot.
Bonus *m.* **(-, -se)** discount; bonus point.
Bonze *m.* **(-n, -n)** (*pej.*) bigwig; big wheel.
Boom *m.* **(-s, -s)** boom.
Boot *n.* **(-[e]s, -e)** boat.
Boots: ~fahrt *f.* boat trip; **~mann** *m.* boatswain; **~steg** *m.* landing stage; **~verleih** *m.* boat rental.
Bord *n.* **(-s, -e)** shelf.
Bord *m.* **(-[e]s, -e)** board; *an ~*, aboard; *über ~*, overboard.
Bordbuch *n.* logbook.
Bordell *n.* **(-[e]s, -e)** brothel.
Bordfunk *m.* radio.
Bordfunker *m.* (*avi.*) radio operator.
Bordpersonal *n.* cabin crew.
Bordstein *m.* curb; **~kante** *f.* edge of the curb.
Bordüre *f.* **(-, -n)** edging.
borgen *v.t.* to borrow; to lend.
Borke *f.* **(-, -n)** bark.
Borkenkäfer *m.* bark beetle.
borniert *a.* narrow-minded.
Borniertheit *f.* narrow-mindedness.
Borretsch *m.* **(-[e]s, 0)** borage.
Borsalbe *f.* boric acid ointment.
Börse *f.* **(-, -n)** purse; (*com.*) stock exchange.
Börsen: ~bericht *m.* market report; **~kurs** *m.* quotation; **~makler** *m.* stockbroker.
Borste *f.* **(-, -n)** bristle.
borstig *f.* **(-, -n)** bristly.
Borte *f.* **(-, -n)** lace trim.
Borwasser *n.* boric acid lotion.
bösartig *a.* malignant; malicious, vicious.
Bösartigkeit *f.* maliciousness, viciousness.
Böschung *f.* **(-, -en)** embankment, scarp, slope.
böse *a.* bad; evil, ill, wicked; angry.
Bösewicht *m.* **(-[e]s, -e[r])** villain.
boshaft *a.* spiteful, malicious.
Bosheit *f.* **(-, -n)** malice, spite.
Boskop *m.* russet (apple).
Boss *m.* (*fam.*) boss.
böswillig *a.* malevolent, wicked.
Böswilligkeit *f.* malice, maliciousness.
Botanik *f.* **(-, 0)** botany.
Botaniker *m.* **(-s, -)** botanist.
botanisch *a.* botanic(al).
botanisieren *v.i.* to botanize.
Bote *m.* **(-n, -n)** messenger.
Botengang *m.* errand.
Botschaft *f.* **(-, -en)** message; news; embassy.
Botschafter *m.* **(-s, -)** ambassador.
Böttcher *m.* **(-s, -)** cooper.
Bottich *m.* **(-[e]s, -e)** vat, coop, tub.
Bouillon *f.* bouillon broth; **~würfel** *m.* bouillon cube.
Bowle *f.* **(-, -n)** punch; (*Getränk*) spiced wine, claret cup, iced cup.
Bowling *n.* bowling; **~bahn** *f.* bowling alley.
boxen *v.i.* to box.
Boxer *m.* **(-s, -)** boxer, pugilist, prizefighter.
Boykott *m.* boycott.
boykottieren *v.t.* to boycott.
brabbeln *v.i.* (*fam.*) to mumble, to mutter; to bubble.
brach *a.* fallow, unplowed.
Brachfeld *n.* fallow (ground).
brachial *a.* violent.
Brachialgewalt *f.* brute force.
Brachland *n.* fallow; uncultivated land.
brachliegen *v.i.* to lie fallow.
brackig *a.* brackish.
Brahmane *m.* Brahman; **Brahmanin** *f.* Brahmanee.
bramarbasieren *v.i.* (*sl.*) to swagger, to bully.
Bramsegel *n.* topsail.
Branche *f.* **(-, -n)** branch, line (of business).
Branchenverzeichnis *n.* classified directory, yellow pages.
Brand *m.* **(-[e]s, Brände)** combustion; fire, conflagration; fuel; firebrand; (*med.*) gangrene; (*bot.*) blight, mildew; *in ~ stecken*, to set on fire.
Brandbombe *f.* incendiary bomb.
Brandbrief *m.* urgent letter.
branden *v.i.* to surge, to break.
brandig *a.* blighted, blasted; smelling as if burnt; (*med.*) gangrenous.
Brandlegung *f.* **(-, -en)** incendiarism.
Brandmal *n.* **(-[e]s, -e)** stigma.
brandmarken *v.t.* to brand.
Brandmauer *f.* fireproof wall.
Brandschaden *m.* damage by fire.
brandschatzen *v.t.* to plunder.
Brandstifter *m.* incendiary.
Brandstiftung *f.* arson, incendiarism.
Brandung *f.* **(-, -en)** *pl.* breakers; surf, surge.
Brandungswelle *f.* **(-, -n)** breaker.
Brandwunde *f.* burn, scald.
Branntwein *m.* **(-[e]s, -e)** *pl.* spirits.
Branntweinbrenner *m.* distiller.
Brasil *f.* Brazil cigar.
Brasilianer *m.*; **Brasilianerin** *f.*; **brasilianisch** *a.* Brazilian; **Brasilien** *n.* Brazil.
braten *v.t.st.* to roast; to broil, to grill; (*in der Pfanne*) to fry.
Braten *m.* **(-s, -)** roast meat.
Bratenfett *n.* drippings.
Bratensoße *f.* gravy.
Bratkartoffel *f.* fried potato.
Bratofen *m.* roasting oven.
Bratpfanne *f.* frying pan.
Bratrost *m.* gridiron, grill.
Bratsche *f.* **(-, -n)** viola, bass viol, double bass.
Bratspieß *m.* spit.
Bratwurst *f.* sausage.
Brauch *m.* **(-[e]s, Bräuche)** usage, custom.
brauchbar *a.* useful, serviceable.
brauchen *v.t.* to use, to employ; to need, to want.
brauen *v.t.* to brew.
Brauer *m.* **(-s, -)** brewer.
Brauerei *f.* **(-, -en)** brewery.

braun *a.* brown, tawny; (*Pferd*) bay; **Braune** *m.* bay horse.
Bräune *f.* **(-, 0)** tan; brownness.
bräunen *v.t.* to get a tan; to brown.
Braunkohle *f.* lignite.
bräunlich *a.* brownish.
Braunsche Röhre *f.* cathode-ray tube.
Braus *m.* *in Saus und ~ leben,* to live in luxury.
Brausebad *n.* shower.
brausen *v.i.* to roar; to buzz; to race, to effervesce.
Brausepulver *n.* effervescent powder.
Braut *f.* **(-, Bräute)** fiancée; (*am Hochzeitstage*) bride.
Brautaussteuer *f.* trousseau.
Brautführer *m.* man who gives away the bride.
Bräutigam *m.* **(-s, -e)** fiancé; (*am Hochzeitstage*) bridegroom.
Brautjungfer *f.* bridesmaid.
Brautkleid *n.* wedding dress.
Brautkranz *m.* bridal wreath.
Brautnacht *f.* wedding night.
Brautpaar *n.* bride and groom.
brav *a.* honest, good, brave, courageous.
bravo! *i.* bravo! well done!
Bravour *f.* stylishness; *mit ~,* brilliantly.
Bravourleistung *f.* brilliant performance.
bravourös *a. & adv.* brilliant(ly).
Bravourstück *n.* piece of bravura.
BRD *Bundesrepublik Deutschland,* Federal Republic of Germany, FRG.
Brecheisen *n.* crowbar.
brechen *v.st.* to break; (*Knochen*) to fracture; (*Lichtstrahlen*) to be refracted; to vomit.
Brechmittel *n.* emetic.
Brechreiz *m.* retching; nausea.
Brechung *f.* **(-, -en)** (*opt.*) refraction.
Brei *m.* **(-[e]s, -e)** porridge; pulp, mush.
breiig *a.* mushy.
breit *a.* broad; wide, large; *weit und ~,* far and wide; *~ schlagen,* to persuade.
Breite *f.* **(-, -n)** breadth; width; (*geographische*) latitude.
Breitengrad *m.* degree of latitude.
breitspurig *a.* bumptious.
Bremsbacke *f.* brake shoe.
Bremsbelag *m.* brake lining.
Bremse *f.* **(-, -n)** brake; gadfly.
bremsen *v.t.* to brake.
Bremsflüssigkeit *f.* brake fluid.
Bremshebel *m.* brake arm.
Bremsklotz *m.* brake pad.
Bremslicht *n.* brake light.
Bremsscheibe *f.* brake disc.
Bremsspur *f.* skid mark.
Bremstrommel *f.* brake drum.
Bremsung *f.* braking.
Bremsweg *f.* braking distance.
brennbar *a.* combustible, inflammable.
brennen *v.t.ir.* to burn, to scorch; (*med.*) to cauterize; (*Kaffee*) to roast; (*Kohlen*) to char; (*Branntwein*) to distill; (*Ziegel*) to bake; ~ *v.i.st.* to burn, to be on fire; (*Wunde*) to smart; (*Nessel*) to sting.
Brennerei *f.* **(-, -en)** distillery.
Brennessel *f.* stinging nettle.
Brennholz *n.* firewood.
Brennmaterial *n.* fuel.
Brennpunkt *m.* focus.
Brennstoff *m.* fuel.
brenzlig *a.* dangerous, risky.
Bresche *f.* **(-, -n)** breach; gap.
Bretagne *f.* Brittany.
Brett *n.* **(-[e]s, -er)** board; plank; *mit Brettern verschlagen,* to board up.
Bretterboden *m.* wooden floor.
Bretterbude *f.* hut, shack.
Bretterverschlag *m.* shed.
Bretterwand *f.* wooden wall.
Bretterzaun *m.* wooden fence.
Brettspiel *n.* **(-s, -e)** board game.
Brevier *n.* **(-s, -e)** breviary.
Brezel *f.* **(-, -n)** pretzel.
Brief *m.* **(-[e]s, -e)** letter, epistle; *unter ~ und Siegel,* under hand and seal.
Briefbeschwerer *m.* paperweight.
Briefdrucksache *f.* printed paper.
Brieffreund *m.;* **Brieffreundin** *f.* pen pal.
Briefkasten *m.* mailbox.
Briefkopf *m.* letterhead.
brieflich *a. & adv.* by letter.
Briefmarke *f.* (postage) stamp; **~nsammler** *m.* stamp collector.
Briefpapier *n.* stationery.
Briefporto *n.* postage.
Briefschaften *f.pl.* letters, papers, documents *pl.*
Brieftasche *f.* wallet.
Brieftaube *f.* carrier pigeon.
Briefträger *m.;* **Briefträgerin** *f.* letter carrier.
Briefumschlag *m.* envelope.
Briefwaage *f.* postage scale.
Briefwechsel *m.* correspondence.
Bries *n.* **(-es, -e)** (*cul.*) sweetbreads.
Brigade *f.* **(-, -n)** brigade.
Brigg *f.* **(-, -s)** brig.
Brikett *n.* **(-s, -s)** briquette.
Brillant *m.* **(-en, -en)** brilliant, cut diamond.
brillant *a. & adv.* brilliant(ly).
Brillanz *f.* **(-, 0)** brilliance.
Brille *f.* **(-, -n)** *pl.* (pair of) spectacles; *pl.* glasses; *pl.* goggles.
Brillenetui *n.;* **Brillenfutteral** *n.* eyeglass case.
Brillengestell *n.* eyeglass frame.
brillieren *v.i.* to shine.
Brimborium *n.* **(-s, 0)** (*fam. pej.*) hoo-ha.
bringen *v.t.ir.* to bring; to carry; to take; to convey; to conduct; to give, to present; *in Gang ~,* to set going; *zustand(e) ~,* to bring about; *es weit ~,* to get on in the world; *um etwas ~,* to deprive; *ums Leben ~,* to kill, to murder; *ein Opfer ~,* to make a sacrifice.
brisant *a.* (*fig.*) explosive.
Brisanz *f.* **(-, 0)** (*fig.*) explosiveness.
Brise *f.* **(-, -n)** breeze.
Britannien *n.* **(-s, 0)** Britain; Britannia; **Brite** *m.* **(-n, -n);** **Britin** *f.* **(-, -nen);** Briton; **britisch** *a.* British.
bröck[e]lig *a.* crumbling.
bröckeln *v.t. & i.* to crumble.
Brocken *m.* **(-s, -)** fragment; morsel; crumb.
brodeln *v.i.* to bubble.
Brokat *m.* **(-[e]s, -e)** brocade.
Brom *m.* **(-s, 0)** bromine.
Brombeere *f.* blackberry.
Brombeerstrauch *m.* bramble.
Bronchialkatarrh *m.* bronchitis.
Bronchie *f.* **(-, -n)** bronchial tube; *pl.* bronchus.
Bronze *f.* **(-, -n)** bronze, brass.
Bronzezeit *f.* Bronze Age.
Brosame *f.* **(-, -n)** crumb.

Brosche *f.* **(-, -n)** brooch.
broschiert *a.* paperbacked, paperbound.
Broschüre *f.* **(-, -n)** pamphlet, booklet.
Brösel *m.* **(-s, -)** crumb.
bröselig *a.* crumbly.
bröseln *v.i.* to crumble.
Brot *n.* **(-[e]s, -e)** bread; loaf.
Brotaufstrich *m.* sandwich spread.
Brötchen *n.* **(-s,-)** roll.
Broterwerb *m.* way to earn a living.
Brotkasten *m.* breadbox.
Brotkrümel *m.* breadcrumb.
Brotlaib *m.* loaf.
brotlos *a.* unprofitable.
Brotmaschine *f.* bread slicer.
Brotrinde *f.* crust (bread).
Bruch *m.* **(-[e]s, Brüche)** breach, rupture; (*Bein* ~) fracture; (*med.*) rupture, hernia; (*ar.*) fraction; *gemeiner* ~, common fraction; *in die Brüche gehen*, to break up.
Bruchband *n.* truss.
Bruchbude *f.* (*fam. pej.*) hovel, dump.
brüchig *a.* full of cracks, brittle.
Bruchlandung *f.* (*avi.*) crash landing.
Bruchstrich *m.* fraction line.
Bruchstück *n.* fragment.
Bruchteil *m.* fraction.
Brücke *f.* **(-, -n)** bridge.
Brückengeländer *n.* railing.
Brückenkopf *m.* bridgehead.
Brückenpfeiler *m.* pier.
Bruder *m.* **(-s, Brüder)** brother; (*Mönch*) friar.
Bruderkrieg *m.* fratricidal war.
brüderlich *a. & adv.* fraternal.
Brudermord *m.* fratricide.
Brüderschaft *f.* **(-, -en)** brotherhood.
Brühe *f.* **(-, -n)** broth, gravy, sauce.
brühen *v.t.* brew; to make (tea).
brühheiß, brühwarm *a.* boiling hot.
brüllen *v.i.* to roar; to bellow, to low.
Brummbär *m.* (*fam.*) grouch.
brummeln *v.i.* (*fam.*) to mumble, to mutter.
brummen *v.i.* to growl, to grumble; to hum; to mumble.
Brummer *m.* (*fam.*); **Brummi** *m.* (*fam.*) truck.
brummig *a.* grumpy.
Brünette *f.* **(-, -n)** brunette.
Brunft *f.* **(-, 0)** rut, rutting time.
Brunnen *m.* **(-s, -)** spring, well; fountain; *pl.* mineral waters.
Brunnenkresse *f.* watercress.
Brunst *f.* **(-, 0)** rut, sexual desire, heat.
brünstig *a.* ardent, fervent; in heat.
Brunszeit *f.* rutting season, heat.
brüsk *a.* brusque.
brüskieren *v.t.* to snub.
Brust *f.* **(-, Brüste)** breast; bosom, chest.
Brustbild *n.* half-length portrait.
brüsten *v.r.* to boast, to brag about.
Brustfellentzündung *f.* pleurisy.
Brustkasten *m.* chest, thorax.
Brustkorb *m.* chest, thorax.
Brustschwimmen *n.* breaststroke.
Brüstung *f.* **(-, -en)** parapet, balustrade.
Brustwarze *f.* nipple.
Brustwehr *f.* parapet.
Brustwickel *m.* chest compress.
Brut *f.* **(-, -en)** brood, hatch; (*Fische*) fry; (*Vögel*) covey; (*fig.*) set, pack.
brutal *a.* brutish, brutal.
Brutalität *f.* brutality.
Brutapparat *m.* incubator.
brüten *a.* to brood, to hatch, to sit (on eggs).
Brüter *m.* breeder (nuclear power).
Bruthenne *f.* **(-, -n)** sitting hen.
Brutkasten *m.* incubator.
Brutstätte *f.* breeding place; hotbed.
brutto *adv.* gross.
Bruttogewicht *n.* **(-[e]s, -e)** gross weight.
bsd. *besonders*, especially, esp.
bst! *i.* hush! hist!
Btx. *Bildschirmtext*, view data.
Bube *m.* **(-n, -n)** boy, lad; knave, rogue; (*in der Karte*) jack.
Bubenstreich *m.* childish prank.
Bubikopf *m.* bobbed hair.
Buch *n.* **(-[e]s, Bücher)** book; (~ *Papier*) quire; *die Bücher führen*, to keep the books.
Buchbesprechung *f.* book review.
Buchbinder *m.* bookbinder.
Buchdeckel *m.* book cover.
Buchdruck *m.* printing.
Buchdrucker *m.* printer.
Buche *f.* **(-, -n)** beech, beech tree.
Buchecker *f.* **(-, -n)** beechnut.
buchen *v.t.* to book, to enter.
Bücherbrett *n.* bookshelf.
Bücherei *n.* library.
Bücherschrank *m.* bookcase.
Bücherstütze *f.* bookend.
Buchfink *m.* chaffinch.
Büchführung *f.* bookkeeping.
Buchhalter *m.* bookkeeper.
Buchhandel *m.* book trade.
Buchhändler *m.* bookseller.
Buchhandlung *f.* bookstore.
Buchladen *m.* bookstore.
Buchmesse *f.* book fair.
Buchprüfer *m.* auditor.
Buchrücken *m.* spine.
Buchsbaum *m.* **(-[e]s, -bäume)** box tree.
Buchschuld *f.* **(-, -en)** book debt.
Buchse *f.* **(-, -n)** (*elek.*) socket; (*tech.*) bush, liner.
Büchse *f.* **(-, -n)** box, case; tin; (*Flinte*) rifle, shotgun.
Büchsenfleisch *n.* canned meat.
Büchsenöffner *m.* can opener.
Buchstabe *m.* **(-n[s], -n)** letter, character; type.
buchstabengetreu *a. & adv.* literal(ly); to the letter.
buchstabieren *v.t.* to spell.
buchstäblich *a.* literal, verbatim; ~ *adv.* literally.
Buchstütze *f.* bookend.
Bucht *f.* **(-, -en)** creek, bay, inlet, cove.
Buchtitel *m.* title.
Buchung *f.* **(-, -en)** entry; booking.
Buchweizen *m.* **(-s, 0)** buckwheat.
Buchzeichen *n.* bookmark.
Buckel *m.* **(-s, -)** hunchback, hump.
buckeln *v.i.* (*fam. pej.*) to bow and scrape, to kowtow.
bücken *v.r.* to bend, to stoop, to bow.
bucklig *a.* hunchbacked.
Bucklige *m./f.* hunchback.
Bückling *m.* **(-s, -e)** (smoked) herring.
buddeln *v.i.* (*fam.*) to dig.
Buddhismus *m.* Buddhism.

Buddhist *m.;* **Buddhistin** *f.;* **buddhistisch** *a.* Buddhist.
Bude *f.* **(-, -n)** booth, stall.
Budget *n.* **(-s, -s)** budget.
Büffel *m.* **(-s, -)** buffalo.
büffeln *v.i.* to cram, to grind.
Büffet *n.* **(-s, -s)** sideboard; bar.
Bug *m.* **(-[e]s, -e)** bow (ship).
Bügel *m.* **(-s, -)** hanger; earpiece (glasses), hoop, bow.
Bügelbrett *n.* ironing board.
Bügeleisen *n.* iron.
Bügelfalte *f.* crease.
bügeln *v.t.* to iron, to smoothe.
Buggy *m.* stroller.
bugsieren *v.t.* (*fam.*) to shift, to steer.
Bugspriet *n.* **(-[e]s, -e)** bowsprit.
buhen *v.i.* (*fam.*) to boo.
Buhle *m.* **(-n, -n)** & *f.* **(-, -n)** lover.
buhlen *v.i.* to court.
Buhmann *m.* bogeyman.
Bühne *f.* **(-, -n)** stage; scaffold; platform; *zur ~ gehen,* to go on the stage.
Bühnenanweisung *f.* stage direction.
Bühnenarbeiter *n.* stagehand.
Bühnenautor *m.;* **Bühnenautorin** *f.* playwright.
Bühnenbearbeitung *f.* stage adaptation.
Bühnenbeleuchtung *f.* stage lighting.
Bühnenbild *n.* (stage) set; **~ner** *m.;* **~nerin** *f.* set designer.
Bühnenleiter *m.* stage manager.
Bühnenregisseur *m.;* **Bühnenregisseurin** *f.* (stage) director.
Bühnenstück *n.* (stage) play.
Buhruf *m.* boo.
Bukett *n.* **(-s, -s)** bouquet, bunch of flowers.
Bulette *f.* **(-, -n)** meatball.
Bulgare *m.;* **Bulgarin** *f.;* **bulgarisch** *a.* Bulgarian; **Bulgarien** *n.* **(-s, 0)** Bulgaria.
Bullauge *n.* circular porthole.
Bulle *m.* **(-en, -en);** *f.* **(-, -n)** (*rel.*) bull.
bullig *a.* beefy, stocky, chunky, hefty.
Bummel *m.* **(-s, -)** stroll.
Bummelei *f.* **(-, -en)** dawdling.
bummeln *v.i.* to stroll; to loaf.
Bummelstreik *m.* slowdown (strike).
bums! bang.
bumsen *v.i.* (*fam.*) to crash; to bang; to bash; (*vulg.*) to screw.
Bund *m.* **(-[e]s, Bünde)** band, tie; league, alliance, confederacy; covenant.
Bund *n.* **(-[e]s, -e)** bundle, bunch, truss.
Bündel *n.* **(-s, -)** bundle, bunch, truss, wisp (of straw).
Bundes... federal.
Bundesbürger *m.;* **~bürgerin** *f.* citizen of the Federal Republic.
Bundesebene *f.* federal or national level.
Bundesgenosse *m.* confederate, ally.
Bundesgrenzschutz *m.* Federal Border Police.
Bundeshaus *n.* Federal Parliament Building.
Bundeskabinett *n.* Federal Cabinet.
Bundeskanzler *m.* Federal Chancellor; **~amt** *n.* Federal Chancellery.
Bundeslade *f.* Ark of the Covenant.
Bundesland *n.* (federal) state; province (Austria).
Bundesliga *f.* national league.
Bundespräsident *m.* (Federal) President.
Bundesrat *m.* Upper House (of Parliament).
Bundesregierung *f.* Federal government.
Bundesrepublik *f.* Federal Republic.
Bundesstaat *m.* Federal State.
Bundestag *m.* Lower House (of Parliament); **~sabgeordnete** *m./f.* member of the Bundestag; **~swahl** *f.* general election.
Bundeswehr *f.* (Federal) Armed Forces.
bundesweit *a.* & *adv.* nationwide.
bündig *a.* concise, terse; convincing.
Bündnis *n.* **(-nisses, -nisse)** alliance.
bündnisfrei *a.* nonaligned.
Bündnispartner *m.* ally.
Bundweite *f.* waist (size).
Bunker *m.* **(-s, -)** air-raid shelter; bunker.
bunt *a.* colorful, colored, variegated; motley, particolored, spotted; *das ist zu ~,* that is too much.
Buntdruck *m.* **(-[e]s, -e)** color printing.
Buntsandstein *m.* red sandstone.
Buntspecht *m.* spotted woodpecker.
Buntwäsche *f.* colored wash.
Bürde *f.* **(-, -n)** burden, load.
Bureau *n.* **(-s, -s** *u.* **-x)** office.
Bureaukratie *f.* bureaucracy.
Burg *f.* **(-, -en)** castle, stronghold.
Bürge *m.* **(-n, -n)** bail, guarantee, surety.
bürgen *v.i.* to stand bail, to answer for, to warrant.
Bürger *m.* **(-s, -)** citizen, townsman.
Bürgerinitiative *f.* citizens' action group.
Bürgerkrieg *m.* civil war.
bürgerlich *a.* civil, civic; **~es Gesetzbuch** *n.* code of Civil Law.
Bürgerliche *m./f.* **(-n, -n)** commoner.
Bürgermeister *m.* mayor.
Bürgerrecht *n.* civil rights.
Bürgerschreck *m.* bogey of the middle class.
Bürgerstand *m.* middle class.
Bürgersteig *m.* sidewalk, pavement.
Bürgertum *n.* **(-[e]s, 0)** middle class.
Burgfriede *m.* truce.
Burggraben *m.* moat.
Bürgschaft *f.* **(-, -en)** bail, surety, security; guarantee, guaranty; *gegen ~ freilassen,* to release on bail; *~ leisten,* to set bail; *~ zulassen,* to admit to bail.
Burgund *n.* **(-s, 0)** Burgundy.
burlesk *a.* burlesque.
Büro *n.* **(-s, -s)** office.
Büroarbeit *f.* paperwork.
Büroartikel *m.pl.* office appliances.
Bürobedarf *m.* office supplies.
Bürogebäude *n.* office building.
Büroklammer *f.* paper clip.
Bürokrat *m.* bureaucrat; **Bürokratie** *f.* bureaucracy; **bürokratisch** *a.* bureaucratic.
Büropersonal *n.* office staff.
Bürostunden *pl.* office hours.
Bürozeit *f.* office hours.
Bursch(e) *m.* **(-en, -en)** fellow, lad.
Burschenschaft *f.* (*Studenten*) fraternity.
burschikos *a.* pert.
Bürste *f.* **(-, -n)** brush.
bürsten *v.t.* to brush.
Bürstenbinder *m.* brushmaker.
Bus *m.* **(-ses, -se)** bus.
Busbahnhof *m.* bus station.
Busch *m.* **(-[e]s, Büsche)** bush; thicket.
Büschel *m.* **(-s, -)** tuft; bunch; cluster.
buschig *a.* bushy.
Buschmann *m.* Bushman.

Buschmesser *n.* machete.
Buschwindröschen *n.* wood anemone.
Busen *m.* **(-s, -)** bosom; breast; heart.
busenfrei *a.* topless.
Busenfreund *m.;* **Busenfreundin** *f.* bosom buddy.
Busfahrer *m.* bus driver.
Bushaltestelle *f.* bus stop.
Buslinie *f.* bus route.
Bussard *m.* **(-s, -e)** buzzard.
Buße *f.* **(-, -n)** penance, penitence; (*Geld*~) fine, penalty.
büßen *v.t.* to atone for; ~ *v.t.* to suffer, to expiate.
Büßer *m.* **(-s, -)** penitent.
bußfertig *a.* penitent, repentant.
Bußgeld *n.* fine; **~bescheid** *m.* notice of fine due.
Bußtag *m.* day of penance.
Büste *f.* **(-, -n)** bust.
Büstenhalter *m.* **(-s, -)** bra, brassiere.
Busverbinding *f.* bus service; bus connection.
Busverkehr *m.* bus service.
Butt *m.* flounder.
Bütte *f.* **(-, -n)** tub.
Büttenpapier *n.* handmade paper.
Butter *f.* **(-, 0)** butter.
Butterblume *f.* buttercup.
Butterbrotpapier *n.* greaseproof paper.
Butterfaß *n.* churn.
Buttermilch *f.* buttermilk.
buttern *v.t.* to butter; to churn.
Buttersemmel *f.* roll and butter.
butterweich *a.* very soft; (*fig.*) vague.
Button *m.* **(-s, -s)** badge.
Butzenscheibe *f.* bull's eye window pane.
Bw. *Bundeswehr,* Federal Armed Forces.
b.w. *bitte wenden,* please turn over, p.t.o.
Byte *n.* (*comp.*) byte.
bzgl. *bezüglich,* with reference to.
bzw. *beziehungsweise,* respectively, resp.

C

C, c *n.* the letter C or c; (*mus.*) C.
C. *Celsius,* Celsius, centigrade, C.
ca. *circa,* about, ca.
Café *n.* **(-s, -s)** coffeehouse, café.
Cafeteria *f.* cafeteria.
campen *v.i.* to camp.
Camper *m.;* **Camperin** *f.* camper.
Camping *n.* camping.
Camping: ~bus *m.* camper; **~platz** *m.* campground.
Campus *m.* campus.
Caravan *m.* station wagon; trailer.
CB-Funk *m.* CB radio.
CD *f.* CD.
CD-Spieler *m.* CD player.
CDU *Christlich-Demokratische Union,* Christian Democratic Union.
C-Dur *n.* C major.
Cellist *m.* **(-en, -en)** cellist.
Cello *n.* **(-[s], -s)** cello.
Ces *n.* **(-, 0)** (*mus.*) C flat.
C-Flöte *f.* soprano recorder.
Chamäleon *n.* **(-s, -s)** chameleon.
Champagner *m.* **(-s, -)** champagne.
Champignon *m.* **(-s, -s)** mushroom.
Champion *m.* champion.
Chance (*frz.*) *f.* **(-, -n)** chance.
Chancengleichheit *f.* equal opportunities.
changieren *v.i.* to shimmer.
Chaos *n.* **(-, 0)** chaos.
chaotisch *a.* chaotic.
Characterzug *m.* **(-es, züge)** characteristic.
Charakter *m.* **(-s, Charaktere)** character.
Charaktereigenschaft *f.* characteristic; trait.
charakterfest *a.* firm.
charakterisieren *v.t.* to characterize.
Charakteristik *f.* **(-, -en)** characteristic.
charakteristisch *a.* characteristic.
charakterlos *a.* unprincipled.
Charisma *n.* charisma.
charismatisch *a.* charismatic.
charmant *a.* charming.
Charme *m.* charm.
Charta *f.* charter.
Charterflug *f.* charter flight.
Chartermaschine *f.* charter plane.
chartern *v.t.* to charter, to hire.
Chassis *n.* chassis.
Chauffeur (*frz.*) *m.* **(-s, -e)** chauffeur.
Chaussee *f.* **(-, -n)** high road.
Chauvi *m.* (*fam. pej.*) male chauvinist.
Chauvinismus *m.* **(-, 0)** chauvinism.
Chauvinist *m.* **(-en, -en)** chauvinist.
chauvinistisch *a.* chauvinistic.
checken *v.t.* to check, to examine; (*fam.*) check out.
Chef *m.* **(-s, -s)** head, principal, boss.
Chefarzt *m.* head physician.
Chefin *f.* **(-, -nen)** head, leader, boss.
Chefredakteur *m.;* **Chefredakteurin** *f.* editor in chief.
Chefsekretärin *f.* director's secretary.
Chemie *f.* **(-, 0)** chemistry.
Chemiefaser *f.* synthetic fiber.
Chemikalien *n.pl.* chemicals.
Chemiker *m.* **(-s, -)** (analytical) chemist.
chemisch *a. & adv.* chemical; **~e Reinigung** *f.* dry cleaning; **~e Wirkung** *f.* chemical action.
Cherub *m.* **(-s, -im)** cherub.
Chesterkäse *m.* cheddar cheese.
Chicoree *m.* endive.
Chiffre *(frz.) f.* **(-, -n)** cipher.
Chiffretelegramm *n.* code telegram, cipher.
chiffrieren *v.t.* to cipher, to code.
Chile *n.* **(-s, 0)** Chile.
Chilene *m.;* **Chilenin** *f.;* **chilenisch** *a.* Chilean.
China *n.* **(-s, 0)** China.
Chinese *m.;* **Chinesin** *f.;* **chinesisch** *a.* Chinese.
Chinin *n.* **(-s, 0)** quinine.
Chiropraktiker *m.;* **Chiropraktikerin** *f.* chiropractor.
Chirurg *m.* **(-en, -en);** **Chirurgin** *f.* **(-, -nen)** surgeon.
Chirurgie *f.* **(-, 0)** surgery.
chirurgisch *a.* surgical.
Chitinpanzer *m.* chitinous exoskeleton.
Chlor *n.* **(-[e]s, 0)** chlorine.
chloren *v.t.* to chlorinate.

Chlorkalium *n.* potassium chloride.
Chlorkalk *m.* chloride of lime.
Chlorkalzium *n.* calcium chloride.
chloroformieren *v.t.* to chloroform.
Cholera *f.* **(-, 0)** cholera.
cholerisch *a.* choleric.
Chor *m.* **(-s, Chöre)** chorus; choir.
Choral *m.* **(-[e]s, Choräle)** chorale.
Choreograph *m.;* **Choreographin** *f.* choreographer.
Choreographie *f.* **(-, -n)** choreography.
Chorhemd *n.* surplice, alb.
Chorknabe *m.* choirboy.
Chorleiter *m.* choirmaster.
Chormusik *f.* choral music.
chorsänger *m.* chorister.
Chorstuhl *m.* (cathedral) stall.
Chr. *Christus,* Christ.
Christ *m.;* **Christin** *f.* Christian.
Christbaum *m.* Christmas tree.
Christdemokrat *m.* (*pol.*) Christian Democrat.
Christengemeinde *f.* Christian community.
Christenheit *f.* **(-, 0)** Christendom.
Christentum *n.* **(-s, 0)** Christianity.
Christkind *n.* infant Jesus.
christlich *a.* Christian.
Christliche Wissenschaft *f.* **(-, O)** Christian Science.
Christmesse *f.* Christmas Mass; midnight service on Christmas eve.
Christnacht *f.* Christmas night.
Christus *m.* Christ.
Chrom *n.* **(-s, 0)** chromium, chrome.
chromatisch *a.* chromatic.
Chromosom *n.* **(-s, -en)** chromosome.
Chronik *f.* **(-, -en)** chronicle.
chronisch *a.* chronic.
Chronist *m.* **(-en, -en)** chronicler.
Chronologie *f.* **(-, -[e]n)** chronology.
chronologisch *a.* chronological.
Chrysantheme *f.* chrysanthemum.
circa, **zirca** *adv.* about, nearly.
Cis *n.* **(-, 0)** (*mus.*) C sharp.
City *f.* **(-, -s)** downtown, city center.
clever *a.* clever, smart; shrewd.
Clou *m.* main point.
cm *zentimeter,* centimeter.
Co. *Compagnie,* company, co.
Comeback *n.* comeback.
Comicheft *n.* comic.
Computer *m.* **(-s, -)** computer; *auf ~ umstellen,* to computerize.
Conférencier (*frz.*) *m.* emcee.
Container *m.* container.
Copyright *n.* **(-s, -s)** copyright.
Cord *m.* corduroy.
Couch *f.* **(-, -es)** couch.
Couchgarnitur *f.* three-piece suite.
Couchtisch *m.* coffee table.
Coup *m.* coup.
Coupé *n.* **(-s, -s)** *(mot.)* coupé compartment.
Couplet (*frz.*) *n.* **(-s, -s)** comic song.
Coupon *m.* **(-s, -s)** coupon, voucher.
Courage *f.* courage, pluck.
couragiert *a.* courageous.
Cousin *m.* **(-s, -s)** (male) cousin.
Cousine *f.* **(-, -n)** (female) cousin.
Crême (*frz.*) *f./m.* **(-, 0)** cream.
cremig *a.* creamy.
Crew *f.* team, crew.
C-Schlüssel *m.* (*mus.*) C clef.
CSU *Christlich-Soziale Union,* Christian Social Union.
Cutter *m.;* **Cutterin** *f.* editor (film, TV).
CVJM *Christlicher Verein Junger Männer,* Young Men's Christian Association, YMCA.

D

D, d *n.* the letter D or d; (*mus.*) D.
da *adv.* there; then; ~ *c.* when; because, as, since; *wer ~?* who goes there?
da capo *i.* encore.
d.Ä. *der Ältere,* senior, Sen. Snr., Sr.
DAAD *Deutscher Akademischer Austauschdienst,* German Academic Exchange Service.
dabehalten *v.t.st.* to keep (here).
dabei *adv.* thereby, near it; on this occasion; *~ bleibt es,* that is agreed; *was ist ~?* what harm is there in that?
dabeibleiben *v.i.st.* to stick to; to stay there.
dabeihaben *v.t.st.* to have with one.
dabeisein *v.i.st.* to be there; to take part.
dabeisitzen *v.i.st.* to sit there.
dabeistehen *v.i.st.* to stand by.
dableiben *v.i.st. (s)* to stay, to remain.
Dach *n.* **(-[e]s, Dächer)** roof.
Dachbalken *m.* rafters *pl.*
Dachboden *m.* loft, garret.
Dachdecker *m.* roofer, slater, tiler.
Dachgarten *m.* roof garden.
Dachgepäckträger *m.* roof-rack.
Dachgeschoss *n.* attic.
Dachkammer *f.* garret, attic.
Dachpappe *f.* roofing, roofing felt.
Dachrinne *f.* gutter.
Dachs *m.* **(-es, e)** badger.
Dachshund *m.* dachshund.
Dachstuhl *m.* framework of a roof.
Dachziegel *m.* tile.
Dackel *m.* dachshund.
dadurch *adv.* thereby.
dafür *adv.* for that, for it; instead; *ich kann nichts dafür,* I cannot help it.
Dafürhalten *n. nach meinem ~,* in my opinion.
DAG *Deutsche Angestelltengewerkschaft,* Trade Union of German Employees.
dagegen *adv.* against that, in return, on the other hand.
dagegenhalten *v.t.st.* to counter, to object.
dagegenstellen *v.r.* to oppose.
daheim *adv.* at home.
daher *adv.* thence; therefore; along.
dahin *adv.* thither, to that place; gone; lost.
dahinab *adv.* down there.
dahinauf *adv.* up there.
dahinaus *adv.* out there.
dahinbringen *v.t.ir.* to manage, to persuade, to prevail upon.
dahindämmern *v.i.* to be semiconscious.
dahineilen *v.i.* to hurry along; to pass quickly.

dahinein *adv.* in there.
dahingehen *v.i.st.* to pass, to go by.
dahinjagen *v.i.* to race along.
dahinkommen *v.i.st. (s)* to come so far.
dahinstellen *v.t. dahingestellt sein lassen,* to leave undecided.
dahinten *adv.* over there.
dahinter *adv.* behind that, after it; *es steckt nichts ~,* there is nothing in it.
dahinterklemmen *v.r.* to buckle down to it.
dahinterstehen *v.i.st.* to support.
dahinziehen *v.i.st.* to drift by; to pass along.
Dahlie *f.* dahlia.
dalassen *v.t.st.* to leave there.
daliegen *v.i.st.* to lie there.
damalig *a.* then, of that time.
damals *adv.* then, at that time.
Damast *m.* **(-es, -e)** damask.
Dame *f.* **(-, -n)** lady, gentlewoman; (*im Kartenspiel*) queen; (*beim Tanzen*) partner; checkers, drafts.
Damenbinde *f.* sanitary napkin.
damenhaft *a.* lady-like.
Damenmannschaft *f.* women's team.
Damensattel *m.* sidesaddle.
Damenschneider *m.* ladies' tailor.
damit *adv. & c.* with that; in order that.
dämlich *a.* (*fam.*) foolish.
Damm *m.* **(-[e]s, Dämme)** levee, dam, dike; causeway; (*rail.*) embankment; (*fig.*) barrier.
Dammbruch *m.* bursting of a dike; rupture of the perineum.
dämmen *v.t.* to dam.
Dämmerlicht *n.* twilight; dim light.
dämmern *v.i.* to grow dusky, to dawn.
Dämmerung *f.* **(-, -en)** twilight, dusk, dawn.
dämmrig *a.* dim; *es wird ~,* day is breaking; night is falling.
Dämon *m.* **(-s, -en)** demon.
dämonisch *a.* demoniac(al).
Dampf *m.* **(-[e]s, Dämpfe)** vapor; steam; fume.
Dampfdruckmesser *m.* steam pressure gauge.
dampfen *v.i.* to steam.
dämpfen *v.t.* to dampen; (*fig.*) to quell; (*Speisen*) to stew.
Dampfer *m.* **(-s, -)** steamer.
Dämpfer *m.* **(-s, -)** damper.
Dampfkessel *m.* boiler.
Dampfkochtopf *m.* pressure cooker.
Dampfmaschine *f.* steam engine.
Dampfschiff *n.* steam vessel, steamer.
Dampfschiffahrt *f.* steam navigation.
Dampfwalze *f.* steamroller.
Damwild *n.* **(-es, 0)** fallow deer.
danach *adv.* after that; accordingly; *~ aussehen,* to look like.
Däne *m.;* **Dänin** *f.* Dane.
daneben *adv.* near it; besides.
Dänemark *n.* **(-s, 0)** Denmark.
danieder *adv.* on the ground; down; **~liegen** *v.i.* to lie prostrate, to be depressed.
dänisch *a.* Danish.
Dank *m.* **(-es, 0)** thanks *pl.;* acknowledgment; gratitude; vote of thanks.
dankbar *a.* thankful, grateful; profitable.
Dankbarkeit *f.* **(-, 0)** gratitude.
danke! thank you; *~ nein,* no, thanks.
danken *v.i.* to thank; ~ *v.t.* (*einem etwas*) to be indebted to sb. for sth.
dankenswert *a.* deserving of thanks.
Dankeschön *n.* thank you.
Dankfest *n.* Thanksgiving Day.
Danksagung *f.* **(-, -en)** thanksgiving.
Dankschreiben *n.* letter of acknowledgment.
dann *adv.* then; *~ und wann,* now and then.
daran *adv.* thereon, thereat; by, of, about it; *es ist nichts ~,* it is not true; *er ist ~,* it is his turn.
darankommen *v.i.st. ich komme daran,* it is my turn.
darauf *adv.* thereupon, thereon; on that; after that.
daraus *adv.* out of that, therefrom; thence; *es wird nichts ~,* it won't come to anything.
darben *v.i.* to suffer want; to starve.
darbieten *v.t.st.* to perform, to offer, to present.
Darbietung *f.* presentation, performance.
darbringen *v.t.ir.* to tender, to render, to offer up.
darein *adv.* into it, therein.
darin(nen) *adv.* therein; in it, in this.
darlegen *v.t.* (*fig.*) to explain, to prove.
Darlehen *n.* **(-s, -)** loan.
Darlehnskasse *f.* lending bank.
Darm *m.* **(-[e]s, Därme)** gut; bowels, intestines *pl.*
Darm... enteric.
Darmsaite *f.* catgut.
Darmspiegelung *f.* enteroscopy.
Darmträgheit *f.* constipation.
Darmverschluß *m.* obstruction of the bowels.
darreichen *v.t.* to reach, to hand, to present.
darstellen *v.t.* exhibit; to represent; to act; (*chem.*) to produce.
Darsteller *m.* **(-s, -); Darstellerin** *f.* **(-, -nen)** performer.
Darstellung *f.* **(-, -en)** presentation, representation, exhibition.
dartun *v.t.st.* to demonstrate.
darüber *adv.* over it, about it; concerning that; above, upwards.
darüberliegen *v.i.st.* to be higher.
darüberstehen *v.i.st.* to be above such things.
darum *adv.* around that; therefore, for that reason; *~ kommen,* to lose.
darunter *adv.* under that, beneath it; below that; among them, between them.
darunterfallen *v.i.st.* to be included; to be in the same category.
darunterliegen *v.i.st.* to be lower.
daruntersetzen *v.t.* to put (signature) to it.
das *art. pn.* the; that; which.
dasein *v.i.ir. (s)* to be present; to exist.
Dasein *n.* **(-, 0)** existence; presence.
Daseinsberechtigung *f.* right to exist.
daselbst *adv.* there, in that place.
dasitzen *v.i.st.* to sit there.
daß *c.* that; *~ nicht,* lest.
Datei *f.* **(-, -en)** data file.
Daten *pl.* data, facts.
Datenbank *f.* data bank.
Datenerfassung *f.* data collection.
Datenmissbrauch *m.* data abuse.
Datennetz *n.* data network.
Datenschutz *m.* data protection.
Datenspeicherung *f.* data storage.
Datentechnik *f.* data systems engineering.
Datenübermittlung *f.* data transfer.
Datenverarbeitung *f.* data processing.
datieren *v.t.* to date.
Dativ *m.* **(-[e]s, -e)** (*gram.*) dative (case).
Dattel *f.* **(-, -n)** date.

Datum *n.* **(-[s], Daten)** date; *ohne ~*, undated.
Dauer *f.* **(-, 0)** duration; continuance; *auf die ~*, in the long run.
dauerhaft *a.* durable, lasting.
Dauerkarte *f.* season ticket.
dauern *v.i.* to last, to continue; to abide; *er dauert mich,* I pity him; *es dauert mich,* I regret it.
dauernd *a. & adv.* constant(ly), permanent(ly).
Dauerwelle *f.* perm; permanent wave.
Daumen *m.* **(-s, -)** thumb.
Daumenschraube *f.* thumbscrew.
Daune *f.* **(-, -n)** down.
Daunendecke *f.* **(-, -n)** duvet.
davon *adv.* thereof, therefrom, of that; off, away.
davonkommen *v.i.st.* to get away.
davontragen *v.t.st.* to obtain, to win.
davor *adv.* before that; for that.
dazu *adv.* thereto, to that, to it; in addition to that; for that purpose.
dazukommen *v.i.st.* to arrive; to turn up.
dazuverdienen *v.t.* to earn on the side.
dazwischen *adv.* between them, among them.
dazwischenfahren *v.i.st.* to step in.
dazwischenkommen *v.i.st.* to intervene.
dazwischenliegen *v.i.st.* to lie in between.
dazwischenreden *v.i.* to interrupt.
dazwischentreten *v.i.st.* to intervene.
DB *Deutsche Bundesbahn,* German Federal Railway.
DBP *Deutsche Bundespost,* German Federal Postal Services.
dealen *v.t.* to sell drugs.
Debatte *f.* **(-, -n)** debate.
debattieren *v.i.* to debate.
Debüt *n.* **(-s, -s)** debut; first appearance.
debütieren *v.i.* to make one's debut.
dechiffrieren *v.t.* to decipher; to decode.
Deck *n.* **(-[e]s, -e)** deck.
Deckadresse *f.* cover address.
Deckbett *n.* **(-s, -en)** duvet.
Deckblatt *n.* cover page; (*Zigarren*) wrapper.
Decke *f.* **(-, -n)** cover; blanket, coverlet, quilt; (*eines Zimmers*) ceiling; *unter einer ~ stecken,* to conspire.
Deckel *m.* **(-s, -)** cover; lid; top.
decken *v.t.* to cover, to roof; (*com.*) to reimburse, to refund; *den Tisch ~*, to lay the table.
Deckengemälde *n.* ceiling painting.
Deckmantel *m.* (*pej.*) cover.
Deckname *m.* pseudonym.
Deckoffizier *m.* warrant officer.
Deckung *f.* **(-, -en)** (*com.*) reimbursement; (*mil.*) cover; *Gold~* gold backing; *Zahlungsmittel mit Dollardeckung,* dollar-backed instruments.
deckungsgleich *a.* (*geom.*) congruent.
Deckweiß *n.* opaque white.
Deckwort *n.* codeword.
deduktiv *a.* deductive.
de facto *adv.* de facto, in reality.
Defätismus *m.* defeatism.
Defätist *m.* **(-en, -en)** defeatist.
Defekt *m.* **(-[e]s, -e)** defect, deficiency; **~** *a.* defective, incomplete.
defensiv *a.* defensive.
Defensive *f.* **(-, 0)** defensive; *in die ~gehen,* to go over to the defensive.
defilieren *v.i. (s)* to march past.
definierbar *a.* definable.
definieren *v.t.* to define.
definitiv *a.* final.
Defizit *n.* **(-s, -e)** deficit, deficiency.
Deformation *f.* deformation; deformity.
deformieren *v.t.* to distort, to deform.
deftig *a.* solid; crude, coarse (speech).
Degen *m.* **(-s, -)** sword.
degenerieren *v.i.* to degenerate.
degradieren *v.t.* to downgrade; to demote; *zum Gemeinen ~*, to reduce to the ranks.
dehnbar *a.* elastic; (*Begriff*) vague.
dehnen *v.t.* to stretch, to extend.
Dehnung *f.* stretching; lengthening (pronunciation).
Deich *m.* **(-[e]s, -e)** dike, dam.
Deichsel *f.* **(-, -n)** pole, shaft.
dein *pn.* your.
deinerseits *adv.* on/for your part.
deinesgleichen the likes of you.
deinetwegen, deinethalben *adv.* on your account, for your sake.
deinetwillen *adv. um ~*, for your sake.
de jure *adv.* de jure, legally.
Dekade *f.* **(-, -n)** decade.
dekadent *a.* decadent.
Dekadenz *f.* decadence.
Dekan *m.* **(-s, -e)** dean.
Dekanat *n.* **(-s, -e)** dean's office.
Deklamation *f.* **(-, -en)** declamation.
deklamieren *v.t.* to recite, to declaim.
deklarieren *v.t.* to declare.
Deklination *f.* **(-, -en)** declension.
deklinieren *v.t.* to decline.
Dekolleté *n.* neckline.
dekolletiert *s.* low (-necked).
Dekor *n.* **(-s, -e)** decoration.
Dekorateur *m.*; **Dekorateurin** *f.* window dresser; interior decorator.
Dekoration *f.* **(-, -en)** decoration.
dekorieren *v.t.* to decorate; *neu ~*, to redecorate.
Dekret *n.* **(-[e]s, -e)** decree.
dekretieren *v.t.* to decree.
Delegation *f.* **(-, -en)** delegation.
delegieren *v.t.* to delegate.
Delegierte *m./f.* **(-n, -n)** delegate.
delikat *a.* delicious, delicate.
Delikatesse *f.* **(-, -n)** delicacy, treat.
Delikt *n.* **(-[e]s, -e)** crime, offence.
Deliquent *m.* **(-en, -en)** offender.
delirieren *v.i.* to be delirious.
Delirium *n.* **(-s, -rien)** delirium.
Delle *f.* dent.
Delphin *m.* **(-[e]s, -e)** dolphin.
Delta *n.* **(-s, -s)** delta.
dem *art. dative* the.
Demagog[e] *m.* **(-en, -en)** demagogue.
demagogisch *a.* demagogic(al).
Demarkationslinie *f.* demarcation line.
demaskieren *v.t.* to unmask.
Dementi *n.* **(-s, -s)** denial.
dementieren *v.t.* to deny.
dementsprechend *adv.* accordingly.
demgegenüber *adv.* in contrast.
demgemäss *adv.* accordingly.
demnach *c.* therefore, consequently.
demnächst *adv.* soon after; in the near future.
Demo *f.* demo.
demobilisieren *v.t. & v.i.* to demobilize.
Demographie *f.* demography.

demographisch *a.* demographic.
Demokrat *m.* **(-en, -en)** democrat.
Demokratie *f.* **(-, 0)** democracy.
demokratisch *a.* democratic.
demokratisieren *v.t.* democratize.
Demokratisierung *f.* democratization.
demolieren *v.t.* to demolish.
Demonstrant *m.;* **Demonstrantin** *f.* demonstrator.
Demonstration *f.* **(-, -en)** demonstration.
demonstrieren *v.t.* demonstrate.
Demontage *n.* **(-, -n)** dismantling.
demontieren *v.t.* to dismantle.
demoralisieren *v.t.* to demoralize.
Demoskop *m.;* **Demoskopin** *f.* opinion pollster.
Demoskopie *f.* opinion research.
demoskopisch *a.* **~e Umfrage** *f.* opinion poll.
Demut *f.* **(-, 0)** humility, meekness.
demütig *a.* humble; submissive.
demütigen *v.t.* to humble, to humiliate.
Demütigung *f.* **(-, -en)** humiliation.
demzufolge *adv.* consequently.
den *art. accusative* the.
denkbar *a.* conceivable, imaginable.
denken *v.i.st.* to think (of).
Denken *n.* **(-s, 0)** thinking; thought.
Denker *m.* thinker.
denkfaul *a.* mentally lazy.
Denkfehler *m.* flaw in one's reasoning.
Denkmal *n.* **(-[e]s, -mäler)** monument.
Denkmünze *f.* medal.
Denkschrift *f.* memorial; memoir.
Denkweise *f.* way of thinking.
denkwürdig *a.* memorable.
Denkwürdigkeiten *f.pl.* memoirs.
Denkzettel *m.* refresher, reminder.
denn *c. & adv.* for; then; than.
dennoch *c.* yet, nevertheless.
Denunziant *m.* **(-en, -en)** informer.
denunzieren *v.t.* to denounce, to inform against.
Deo *n.* **Deodorant** *n.* **(-s, -s)** deodorant.
Depesche *f.* **(-, -n)** dispatch, telegram, wire.
deplaciert, deplaziert *a.* out of place.
Deponie *f.* **(-, -n)** dump.
deponieren *v.t.* to deposit, to depose.
deportieren *v.t.* to deport.
Deportierter *m.* deportee.
Depositen *n.pl.* deposits; **~kasse** *f.* (*Bank*) branch office.
Depot *n.* depot, warehouse.
Depp *m.* fool, idiot.
Depression *f.* **(-, -en)** depression.
depressiv *a.* depressive.
deprimieren *v.t.* to depress.
deprimierend *a.* depressing.
deprimiert *a.* depressed.
Deputierte[r] *m.* **(-en, -en)** deputy.
der, die, das, *art.* the; **der, die, das,** *pn.* that, who, which.
derartig *a.* such, of the kind.
derb *a.* compact; coarse.
Derbheit *f.* crudity, coarseness.
derenthalben, derentwegen, derentwillen *adv.* on their (her, whose) account.
dergestalt *adv.* in such a manner, thus.
dergleichen *adv.* such, such like.
Derivat *n.* **(-[e]s, -e)** (*chem.*) derivative.
derjenige, diejenige, dasjenige *pn.* that, this, he.
derlei *a.* of that kind.
dermaßen *adv.* in such a degree *or* manner, so much.
derselbe, dieselbe, dasselbe *pn.* the same; he, she, it; that.
derweil(en) *adv.* while.
Derwisch *m.* **(-[e]s, -e)** dervish.
derzeit *adv.* at the moment.
derzeitig *a.* for the time being.
Des *n.* (*mus.*) D flat.
Desaster *n.* disaster.
desavouiren *v.t.* to disavow.
Deserteur *m.* **(-[e]s, -e)** deserter.
desertieren *v.i.* (s) to desert.
deshalb *c.* therefore.
Design *n.* **(-s, -s)** design.
Designer *m.;* **Designerin** *f.* designer.
desillusionieren *v.t.* to disillusion.
Desinfektion *f.* disinfection.
desinfizieren *v.t.* to disinfect.
Desinformation *f.* disinformation.
Desinteresse *n.* lack of interest.
desinteressiert *a.* uninterested.
desodorierend *a.* deodorant.
desolat *a.* wretched.
Despot *m.* **(-en, -en)** despot, tyrant.
Despotie *f.* **(-, -n)** despotism.
despotisch *a.* despotic.
Despotismus *m.* **(-, 0)** despotism.
dessentwegen, dessentwillen *adv.* on that account.
dessenungeachtet *adv.* notwithstanding.
Dessert *n.* **(-s, -s)** dessert.
destillieren *v.t.* to distill.
desto *adv.* the; ~ *besser,* so much the better.
Destruktion *f.* **(-, -en)** destruction.
destruktiv *a. & adv.* destructive(ly).
deswegen *adv. & c.* therefore.
Detail *n.* **(-s, -s)** detail, particulars *pl.*
Detailhandel *m.* retail trade.
detaillieren *v.t.* to detail, to itemize; to retail.
Detektiv *m.* **(-s, -e); Detektivin** *f.* **(-, -nen)** detective.
Detektor *m.* **(-s, -en)** detector.
Detonation *f.* detonation, blast.
detonieren *v.i.* to detonate.
Deut *m.* **(-[e]s, -e)** doit; farthing.
deuteln *v.t. & i.* to subtilize, to twist the meaning.
deuten *v.i.* to point; ~ *v.t.* to interpret, to explain.
deutlich *a.* clear, distinct; evident, plain.
Deutlichkeit *f.* clarity; distinctness.
deutsch *a.* German.
Deutsch(e) *n.* German (language).
Deutsche *m./f.* **(-n, -n)** German.
Deutschland *n.* Germany.
Deutschtum *n.* **(-s, 0)** Germanness.
Deutung *f.* **(-, -en)** interpretation.
Devise *f.* **(-, -n)** motto; foreign exchange; **~nzwangswirtschaft,** *f.* foreign exchange control.
devot *a.* obsequious.
Dez. *Dezember,* December, Dec.
Dezember *m.* **(-s, -)** December.
dezent *a.* quiet, subdued, discreet; ~ *adv.* unostentatiously.
dezentralisieren *v.t.* to decentralize.
Dezentralisierung *f.* decentralization.
Dezernat *n.* **(-[e]s, -e)** government department.

Dezernent *m.* **(-en, -en)** head of a government department.
dezimal *a.* decimal.
dezimieren *v.t.* to decimate.
DFB *Deutscher Fußballbund,* German Football Association.
DGB *Deutscher Gewerkschaftsbund,* Federation of German Trade Unions.
dgl. *dergleichen, desgleichen,* the like.
d.Gr. *der Große,* the Great.
d.h. *das heißt,* that is, i.e.
d.i. *das ist,* that is, i.e.
Di. *Dienstag,* Tuesday, Tues.
Dia *n.* **(-s, -s)** slide.
Diabetiker *m.;* **Diabetikerin** *f.* diabetic.
diabolisch *a.* diabolic.
Diadem *n.* **(-s, -e)** diadem, tiara.
Diagnose *f.* **(-, -n)** diagnosis.
diagnostizieren *v.t.* to diagnose.
Diagonale *f.* **(-, -n)** diagonal.
Diagramm *n.* graph, diagram.
Diakon *m.* **(-s, -e)** deacon.
Diakonissin *f.* **(-, -nen)** deaconess.
Dialekt *m.* **(-[e]s, -e)** dialect.
Dialog *m.* **(-[e]s, -e)** dialogue.
Dialyze *f.* dialysis.
Diamant *m.* **(-en, -en)** diamond.
Diamantschleifer *m.* diamond cutter.
diametral *a.* diametrical.
Diarrhöe *f.* **(-, -n)** diarrhea.
Diät *f.* **(-, 0)** special diet.
Diäten *f.pl.* daily allowance.
Diätetik *f.* dietetics.
Diätetiker *m.* **(-s, -);** **Diätetikerin** *f.* **(-, -nen)** dietician.
dicht *a.* dense, solid, compact, close; tight.
Dichte *f.* density.
dichten *v.t.* to make watertight, to caulk.
dichten *v.t. & i.* to write poetry.
Dichter *m.* **(-s, -);** **Dichterin** *f.* **(-, -nen)** poet.
dichterisch *a.* poetic(al).
dichtgedrängt *a.* tightly packed.
dichthalten *v.i.st.* (*fam.*) to keep one's mouth shut.
Dichtkunst *f.* poetry.
Dichtung *f.* **(-, -en)** poetry; (*mech.*) sealing, gasket.
Dichtungsring *m.* washer.
dick *a.* thick; stout; large, bulky; (*Milch*) curdled.
Dickdarm *m.* large intestine.
Dicke *f.* **(-, 0)** thickness, bigness, bulk.
dickflüssig *a.* sticky.
Dickhäuter *m.* pachyderm.
dickhäutig *a.* thick-skinned, callous, dull.
Dickicht *n.* **(-[e]s, -e)** thicket.
Dickkopf *m.* mule; pig-headed person.
dickköpfig *a.* stubborn, obstinate.
Didaktik *f.* didactics; teaching method.
die *art. & pn.* the; that; which.
Dieb *m.* **(-[e]s, -e);** **Diebin** *f.* **(-, -nen)** thief.
diebisch *a.* thievish; (*Freude*) devilish.
Diebs (Diebes): **~bande** *f.* gang of thieves.
Diebstahl *m.* **(-[e]s, -stähle)** theft, robbery.
Diele *f.* **(-, -n)** board, plank, deal; hall.
dienen *v.i.* to serve; to be serviceable.
Diener *m.* **(-s, -),** **Dienerin** *f.* **(-, -nen)** servant.
dienern *v.i.* (*pej.*) to bow.
Dienerschaft *f.* **(-, -en)** servants, domestics *pl.*
dienlich *a.* serviceable, useful.
Dienst *m.* **(-[e]s, -e)** service; employment, office; *im ~,* on duty; *ausser ~,* off duty, retired; *~ leisten,* to render service.
Dienstag *m.* **(-[e]s, -e)** Tuesday.
dienstags *adv.* on Tuesdays.
Dienstalter *n.* seniority.
dienstälter *a.* senior.
Dienstantritt *m.* assumption of duty.
dienstbar *a.* subject; subservient; tributary.
Dienstbezüge *pl.* salary.
Dienstbote *m.* domestic servant.
Diensteid *m.* oath of office.
diensteifrig *a.* zealous, officious, eager to serve.
dienstfrei *a.* exempt from service; off duty.
Dienstgeheimnis *n.* professional secret.
Dienstgrad *m.* (*nav.*) rank.
Dienstleistung *f.* service; **~sbetrieb** *m.* business in the service sector.
dienstlich *a.* (*amtlich*) official.
Dienstliste *f.* (*mil.*) roster.
Dienstmädchen *n.* servant girl, maidservant.
Dienstpflicht *f.* compulsory military service.
dienstpflichtig *a.* liable to service.
Dienstreise *f.* business trip.
Dienstsache *f.* official matter.
Dienststelle *f.* agency.
Dienststunden *f.pl.* duty hours.
diensttauglich *a.* fit for service.
diensttuend *a.* on duty.
Dienstturnus *m.* work rotation.
dienstunfähig *a.* unfit for work, disabled, invalid.
Dienstwohnung *f.* official residence.
Dienstzeit *f.* working hours.
diesbezüglich *a.* referring to this.
Dieselmotor *m.* diesel engine.
dieser, diese, dieses *pn.* this; the latter.
diesjährig *a.* of this year, this year's.
diesmal *adv.* this time, for this once.
diesmalig *a.* present.
diesseitig *a.* on this side.
diesseits *adv.* (on) this side.
Diesseits *n.* **(-, 0)** this world.
Dietrich *m.* **(-[e]s, -e)** picklock, burglar; skeleton key.
diffamieren *v.t.* to slander; to defame.
Diffamierung *f.* defamation.
Differentialrechnung *f.* differential calculus.
Differenz *f.* **(-, -en)** difference.
differenzieren *v.t.* (*math.*) to differentiate; ~ *v.i.* to differentiate, to make a distinction.
differieren *v.i.* to differ.
diffus *a.* diffuse; vague.
digitalisieren *v.t.* to digitalize.
Diktat *n.* **(-s, -e)** dictation.
Diktator *m.* dictator.
diktatorisch *a.* dictatorial.
Diktatur *f.* **(-, -en)** dictatorship.
diktieren *v.t.* to dictate.
Dilettant *m.* **(-en, -en);** **Dilettantin** *f.* **(-, -nen)** (*pej.*) amateur.
Dill (-[e]s, -e) (*bot.*) dill.
Dimension *f.* dimension.
DIN *Deutsches Institut für Normung,* German Institute for Standardization.
Ding *n.* **(-[e]s, -e[r])** thing, matter; creature; *guter ~e sein,* to be in high spirits.
dingen *v.t.st.* to hire.
dingfest *a.* *~ machen,* to arrest.
dinglich *m.* (*jur.*) real.

Dinkel *m.* **(-s, 0)** spelt.
Dinosaurier *m.* **(-s, -)** dinosaur.
Dioxyd *n.* **(-s, -e)** dioxide.
Diözese *f.* **(-, -n)** diocese.
Diphtheritis *f.* **(-, 0)** diphtheria.
Diphthong *m.* **(-s, -e)** diphthong.
Dipl. *Diplom,* diploma, Dip., Dipl.
Diplom *n.* **(-[e]s, -e)** diploma, patent.
Diplomat *m.* **(-n, -en)** diplomat.
Diplomatie *f.* **(-, 0)** diplomacy.
diplomatisch *a.* diplomatic.
Dir. *Direktor,* director, dir.
direkt *a.* direct.
Direktheit *f.* directness.
Direktion *f.* **(-, -en)** direction, management; board of directors.
Direktive *f.* **(-, -n)** instruction.
Direktor *m.* **(-s, -en); Direktorin** *f.* **(-, -nen)** director, manager; headmaster.
Direktsendung *f.*, **Direktübertragung** *f.* live broadcast.
Direktwahl *f.* direct election.
Dirigent *m.* **(-en, -en)** (*mus.*) conductor.
Dirigentenpult *n.* conductor's rostrum.
Dirigentenstab *m.* baton.
dirigieren *v.t.* to direct; (*mus.*) to conduct.
Dirne *f.* **(-, -n)** maid, lass, prostitute.
Dis *n.* **(-, 0)** (*mus.*) D sharp.
Disharmonie *f.* **(-e, -[e]n)** disharmony.
Diskant *m.* **(-[e]s, -e)** treble, soprano.
Diskette *f.* **(-, -n)** (*comp.*) floppy disc.
Diskettenlaufwerk *n.* **(-s, -e)** disc drive.
Diskont, Diskonto *m.* **(-s, -s & -i)** discount.
diskontieren *v.t.* to discount.
Diskontsatz *m.* discount rate.
Diskothek *f.*, **Disko** *f.* disco.
diskreditieren *v.t.* to bring into disrepute.
Diskrepanz *f.* discrepancy.
diskret *a.* & *adv.* discreet; discreetly.
Diskretion *f.* **(-, 0)** discretion.
diskriminieren *v.t.* to discriminate against, to disparage.
diskriminierend *a.* disparaging.
Diskriminierung *f.* discrimination.
Diskussion *f.* **(-, -en)** discussion.
diskutieren *v.t.* to debate, to discuss.
Dispens *m.* **(-es, -e)** dispensation, license.
dispensieren *v.t.* to dispense, to excuse, to exempt.
Disponent *m.* **(-en, -en)** manager.
disponieren *v.i.* to make plans, to plan ahead.
Disposition *f.* **(-, -en)** arrangement, disposition.
Disput *m.* **(-[e]s, -e)** dispute.
disputieren *v.i.* to dispute; to argue.
disqualifizieren *v.t.* to disqualify.
Dissertation *f.* **(-, -en)** thesis, dissertation.
Dissident *m.* **(-en, -en); Dissidentin** *f.* **(-, -nen)** dissident.
Dissonanz *f.* **(-, -en)** dissonance, discord.
Distanz *f.* **(-, -en)** distance.
distanzieren *v.r.* to dissociate oneself.
Distel *f.* **(-, -n)** thistle.
distinguiert *a.* distinguished, distinguished-looking.
Distrikt *m.* **(-[e]s, -e)** district.
Disziplin *f.* **(-, -en)** discipline.
Disziplinar... disciplinary.
Disziplinargewalt *f.* disciplinary power.
Disziplinarverfahren *n.* disciplinary action *or* proceedings.
disziplinieren *v.t.* to discipline; ~ *v.r.* to discipline oneself.
dito *adv.* (*com.*) ditto.
Dividende *f.* **(-, -n)** dividend.
dividieren *v.t.* to divide.
Division *f.* **(-, -en)** (*auch mil.*) division.
Diwan *m.* **(-s, -s)** divan, sofa.
d.J. *dieses Jahres,* of this year; *der Jüngere,* Junior, Jun., Jr.
DJH *Deutsches Jugendherbergswerk,* German Youth Hostel Asssociation.
DKP *Deutsche Kommunistische Partei,* German Communist Party.
DM *Deutsche Mark,* German mark.
d.M. *dieses Monats,* of this month, inst.
d.O. *der Obige,* the above.
do. *ditto,* ditto, do.
Do. *Donnerstag,* Thurs., Thursday.
doch *c.* yet; however; but, nevertheless; *ja ~!* yes, to be sure!; *nicht ~!* certainly not! don't!; yes (after neg. clause).
Docht *m.* **(-[e]s, -e)** wick.
Dock *n.* **(-s, -s & -e)** dock, dockyard.
Dogge *f.* **(-, -n)** Great Dane; mastiff.
dogmatisch *a.* & *adv.* dogmatic, dogmatically.
Dohle *f.* **(-, -n)** jackdaw.
Doktor *m.* **(-s, -en)** doctor; physician.
Doktor: ~arbeit *f.* dissertation; **~würde** *f.* doctorate.
Doktrinär *m.* **(-s, -e)** doctrinaire, theorist.
Dokument *n.* **(-[e]s, -e)** document.
Dokumentarfilm *m.* documentary.
dokumentieren *v.t.* to document.
Dolch *m.* **(-[e]s, -e)** dagger, poniard, dirk.
Dolde *f.* (*bot.*) umbel.
doll *a.* (*fam.*) great; amazing.
Dollar *m.* **(-(s), -s)** dollar.
dolmetschen *v.t.* to interpret.
Dolmetscher *m.* **(-s, -); Dolmetscherin** *f.* **(-, -nen)** interpreter.
Dom *m.* **(-[e]s, -e)** cathedral.
Domäne *f.* **(-, -n)** domain, crown land.
domestizieren *v.t.* to domesticate.
Domherr *m.* canon, prebendary.
dominant *a.* dominant.
Dominante *f.* (*mus.*) dominant (chord).
Dominanz *f.* dominance.
dominieren *v.i.* to domineer.
Dominikaner *m.*; **Dominikanerin** *f.*; **dominikanisch** *a.* Dominican.
Dominikanische Republik *f.* Dominican Republic.
Domino: ~spiel *n.* dominoes *pl.*; **~stein** *m.* domino.
Domizil *n.* domicile, residence.
Domkapitel *n.* cathedral chapter.
Dompteur *m.*; **Dompteuse** *f.* tamer.
Donau *f.* Danube.
Donner *m.* **(-s, -)** thunder; *von ~ gerührt,* thunderstruck.
donnern *v.i.* to thunder.
Donnerschlag, *m.* thunderclap.
Donnerstag *m.* **(-[e]s, -e)** Thursday.
donnerstags *adv.* Thursdays.
Donnerwetter *n.*, **~!** *i.* wow!; damn it!
doof *a.* stupid, dumb.
Doofheit *f.* stupidity.
dopen *v.t.* to dope.
Doping *n.* doping.

Doppel *n.* **(-s, -)** duplicate copy; doubles.
Doppeldecker *m.* biplane.
doppeldeutig *a.* ambiguous.
Doppelfenster *n.* double window.
Doppelflinte *f.* double-barrelled gun.
Doppelgänger *m.* double.
doppelläufig *a.* double-barrelled.
Doppelmoral *f.* double standard.
Doppelname hyphenated name.
Doppelpunkt *m.* colon.
doppelseitige Lungenentzündung *f.* double pneumonia.
doppelsinnig *a.* ambiguous.
Doppelspiel *n.* (tennis) doubles; (*fig.*) double game.
doppelt *a.* double, twofold; *~e Buchführung,* book-keeping by double entry.
doppelzüngig *a.* two-faced.
Doppelzüngigkeit *f.* **(-, -en)** duplicity.
Dorf *n.* **(-[e]s, Dörfer)** village.
Dorfbewohner *m.* **(-s, -)**; **Dorfbewohnerin** *f.* **(-, -nen)** villager.
dörflich *a.* village; rural.
Dorn *m.* **(-[e]s, -en & -e)** thorn, prickle.
dornig *a.* (*fig.*) thorny.
dörren *v.t.* to dry.
Dörrobst *n.* **(-[e]s, 0)** dried fruit.
Dorsch *m.* **(-[e]s, -e)** cod; torsk, codling.
dort *adv.* there, yonder.
dortbleiben *v.i.st.* to stay there.
dorther *adv.* from there.
dorthin *adv.* there; **~ab** *adv.* down there; **~auf** *adv.* up there; **~aus** *adv.* out there.
dortig *a.* of that place; residing there.
Dose *f.* **(-, -n)** can; box; snuffbox.
Dosenöffner *m.* can opener.
dosieren *v.t.* to dose.
Dosis *f.* **(-, Dosen)** dose; *zu starke ~,* overdose.
dotieren *v.t.* to endow.
Dotter *m.* or *n.* **(-s, -)** yolk.
Dotterblume *f.* marsh marigold.
Double *n.* stand-in; double.
Doz. *Dozent(in),* lecturer.
Dozent *m.* **(-en, -en); Dozentin** *f.* **(-, -nen)** lecturer, university teacher.
dpa *Deutsche Presse-Agentur,* German Press Agency.
Drache *m.* **(-n, -n)** dragon; (paper) kite.
Drachenfliegen *n.* hang gliding.
Dragoner *m.* **(-[e]s, -)** dragoon.
Draht *m.* **(-[e]s, Drähte)** wire; cable.
Drahtbürste *f.* wirebrush.
drahten *v.t.* to wire.
Drahtgeflecht *n.* wire netting.
drahtlos *a.* wireless.
Drahtseil *n.* wire rope; **~bahn** *f.* cable railway.
Drahtverhau *n.* wire entanglement.
Drahtzange *f.* pliers *pl.*
Drahtzieher *m.* wirepuller.
drakonisch *a.* Draconian.
drall *a.* strapping; full; rounded.
Drama *n.* **(-[e]s, Dramen)** drama; (*fig.*) disaster.
Dramatiker *m.* **(-s, -)** dramatist, playwright.
dramatisch *a.* dramatic.
Dramaturg *m.*; **Dramaturgin** *f.* dramaturge.
Dramaturgie *f.* dramaturgy.
dran = daran.
Dränage *f.* **(-, -n)** drainage.
dranbleiben *v.i.* to hold (tel.); to stick at (work).
Drang *m.* **(-[e]s, 0)** urge; pressure; impulse.
drängen *v.t.* to throng, to press; to urge.
Drangsal *f.* **(-, -e)** hardship; distress, misery.
drangsalieren *v.t.* to worry, to torment.
dränieren *v.t.* to drain.
drastisch *a.* drastic; strong.
drauf = darauf.
Draufgänger *m.* daredevil.
draufgängerisch *a.* daring, audacious.
draufgehen *v.i.st.* (*fam.*) to be killed; to be lost (money).
draufkriegen *v.t. einen ~,* to get a beating.
drauflegen *v.t.* to pay extra.
drauflos *adv.* straight ahead; right away.
draufmachen *v.t. einen ~,* to have a ball.
draufstehen *v.i.st.* to be on it.
draußen *adv.* outside, out of doors.
Drechselbank *f.* turner's lathe.
drechseln *v.t.* to turn (on a lathe).
Drechsler *m.* **(-s, -)** turner.
Drechslerarbeit, Drechslerei *f.* turnery.
Dreck *m.* **(-[e]s, 0)** dirt, filth.
dreckig *a.* dirty, muddy, filthy.
Drecksack *m.* (*vulg.*) bastard.
Dreckschwein *n.* (*fam.*) filthy swine.
Dreckskerl *m.* swine.
Drehbank *f.* (turner's) lathe.
Drehbrücke *f.* swing bridge.
Drehbuch *n.* (*film*) script.
drehen *v.t.* to turn; (*Film*) to shoot; **~** *v.r.* to turn, to rotate, to revolve; *sich drehen um,* to pivot round.
Dreher *m.* **(-s, -)** (*mech.*) lathe operator.
Drehkreuz *n.* turnstile.
Drehorgel *f.* barrel organ.
Drehpunkt *m.* pivot.
Drehschalter *m.* (*el.*) rotary switch.
Drehscheibe *f.* potter's wheel; (*rail.*) turntable.
Drehstrom *m.* three-phase current.
Drehstuhl *m.* swivel chair.
Drehtür *f.* revolving door.
Drehung *f.* **(-, -en)** turn; revolution.
drei *a.* three.
Dreiachteltakt *m.* **(-[e]s, -e)** (*mus.*) three-eighth time.
dreibeinig *a.* three-legged.
dreidimensional *a.* three-dimensional.
Dreieck *n.* **(-[e]s, -e)** triangle.
dreieckig *a.* triangular, three-cornered.
Dreiecksverhältnis *n.* love triangle.
dreierlei *a.* of three kinds.
dreifach *a.* threefold, treble; *~e Ausfertigung,* triplicate.
Dreifaltigkeit *f.* **(-, 0)** Trinity.
Dreifuß *m.* **(-es, -füsse)** tripod; trivet.
dreijährig *a.* three years old; triennial.
Dreiklang *m.* **(-[e]s, 0)** (*mus.*) triad.
Dreikönigsfest *n.* Twelfth Night; Epiphany.
Dreimächte... tripartite.
dreimal *adv.* three times, thrice.
drein = darein.
Dreirad *n.* **(-[e]s, -räder)** tricycle.
Dreisatz *m.* (*math.*) rule of three.
dreisilbig *a.* trisyllabic.
dreispurig *a.* three-laned.
dreißig *a.* thirty.
Dreißiger *m.* **(-s, -)** thirty year old man.
dreißiger *a. die ~ Jahre,* the thirties.
dreißigjährig *a.* thirty-year.

dreist *a.* bold, brazen.
Dreistigkeit *f.* **(-, -en)** boldness, brazenness.
Dreivierteltakt *m.* **(-[e]s, 0)** triple time *or* measure.
Dreizack *m.* **(-[e]s, -e)** trident.
dreizehn *a.* thirteen.
dreschen *v.t.st.* to thresh, to thrash, to wallop, to bang.
Dreschflegel *m.* flail.
Dreschmaschine *f.* threshing machine.
Dreschtenne *f.* threshing floor.
dressieren *v.t.* to break in (horses); to train dogs, etc.
Dressman *m.* male model.
Dressur *f.* **(-, -en)** breaking in; training.
Drillbohrer *m.* drill.
drillen *v.t.* to drill.
Drillich *m.* **(-[e]s, -e)** ticking.
Drillichanzug *m.* fatigue dress.
Drilling *m.* **(-[e]s, -e)** triplet; lantern wheel; three-barrelled gun.
drin = darin.
dringen *v.t. & i.st.* to urge; to penetrate.
dringend *a.* urgent.
dringlich *a.* urgent, pressing.
Dringlichkeit *f.* urgency.
drinnen *adv.* inside, within.
dritte *a.* third; ~ *Person,* (*jur.*) third party.
Drittel *n.* **(-s, -)** third part, third.
drittens *adv.* thirdly.
Dritte Welt *f.* Third World.
drittletzt *a.* third from last, antepenultimate.
Dr.jur. *Doktor der Rechte,* Doctor of Laws, LLD.
Dr.med. *Doktor der Medizin,* Doctor of Medicine, MD.
droben *adv.* above, on high, overhead.
Drogen *pl.* drugs *pl.*.
drogenabhängig *a.* addicted to drugs.
Drogenabhängige *m./f.* **(-, -n)** drug addict.
Drogenabhängigkeit *f.* drug addiction.
Drogerie *f.* **(-, -n)** drugstore, pharmacy.
Drogist *m.* **(-en, -en)** druggist.
Drohbrief *m.* threatening letter.
drohen *v.i.* to threaten, to menace.
drohend *a.* threatening.
Drohne *f.* **(-, -n)** drone.
dröhnen *v.i.* to boom, to roar.
Drohung *f.* **(-, -en)** threat, menace.
drollig *a.* droll, odd, funny.
Dromedar *n.* dromedary.
Droschke *f.* **(-, -n)** hackney carriage.
Drossel *f.* **(-, -n)** thrush.
drosseln *v.t.* to throttle; to reduce.
Dr.phil. *Doktor der Philosophie,* Doctor of Philosophy, Ph.D.
Dr.rer.nat. *Doktor der Naturwissenschaften,* Doctor of Science, Sc.D., D.Sc.
Dr.theol. *Doktor der Theologie,* Doctor of Theology, Th.D.
drüben, da drüben *adv.* over there.
drüber = darüber.
Druck *m.* **(-[e]s, -e & Drücke)** pressure, compression; oppression; print, impression; ~ *auf einen ausüben,* to put pressure on someone.
Druck: ~abfall *m.* drop in pressure; **~bogen** *m.* proof (sheet); **~buchstabe** *m.* printed letter.
Druckbogen *m.* proof (sheet).
Druckbuchstabe *f.* printed letter.
Drückeberger *m.* **(-s, -)** shirker.
druckempfindlich *a.* pressure-sensitive.
drucken *v.t.* to print.
drücken *v.t.* to press, to squeeze; (*Schuhe*) to pinch; (*Preise*) to bring down; ~ *v.r.* to shirk.
drückend *a.* burdensome; heavy; oppressive.
Drucker *m.* **(-s, -)** printer.
Drücker *m.* **(-s, -)** trigger; latch.
Druckerei *f.* **(-, -en)** printing plant.
Druckerpresse *f.* printing press.
Druckerschwärze *f.* printer's ink.
Druckfehler *m.* misprint.
druckfertig *a.* ready for the press.
druckfest *a.* pressure-resistant.
Druckknopf *m.* patent fastener.
Drucksache *f.* printed matter.
Druckschrift *f.* print.
drum = darum.
drunten *adv.* there below.
drunter und drüber upside down.
Drüse *f.* **(-, -n)** gland.
Dschungel *m.* **(-s, -)** jungle.
dt. *deutsch,* German.
Dtz. *Dutzend,* dozen.
du *pn.* you.
Dübel *m.* dowel, peg.
dübeln *v.t.* to dowel.
Dublee *n.* gold plate.
ducken *v.t.* to duck; to humble; ~ *v.r.* to submit, to stoop.
Duckmäuser (-s, -) *m.* sneak, cringer.
dudeln *v.i.* (*fam.*) to tootle.
Dudelsack *m.* **(-[e]s, -säcke)** bagpipes.
Dudelsackpfeifer *m.* bagpiper.
Duell *n.* **(-[e]s, -e)** duel.
duellieren *v.r.* to fight a duel.
Duett *n.* **(-[e]s, -e)** duet.
Duft *m.* **(-[e]s, Düfte)** scent, fragrance.
duften *v.i.* to smell.
duftend *a.* fragrant.
Duftstoff *m.* aromatic substance.
Duftwasser *n.* perfume, scent.
Duftwolke *f.* cloud of perfume.
dulden *v.t.* to endure; to tolerate.
duldsam *a. & adv.* tolerant(ly); patient.
Duldsamkeit *f.* tolerance; patience.
Duldung *f.* tolerance.
dumm *a.* dull, stupid.
dummerweise *adv.* unfortunately; annoyingly.
Dummheit *f.* **(-, -en)** stupidity; blunder.
Dummkopf *m.* **(-[e]s, -köpfe)** idiot; blockhead.
dümmlich *a.* simpleminded.
dumpf *a.* hollow, dull; close, musty.
Düne *f.* **(-, -n)** sandhill, dune.
düngen *v.t.* to manure.
Dünger *m.* **(-s, -)** dung, manure; fertilizer.
dunkel *a.* dark, dusky, gloomy; obscure; mysterious.
Dunkel *n.* darkness.
Dünkel *m.* **(-s, 0)** conceit, arrogance.
dünkelhaft *a.* arrogant, conceited.
Dunkelheit *f.* **(-, -en)** darkness; obscurity.
Dunkelkammer *m.* (*phot.*) darkroom.
dunkeln *v.i. es dunkelt,* it is growing dark.
Dunkelziffer *f.* estimated number of unknown cases.
dünken *v.t.imp.* to seem, to appear; to think.
dünn *a.* thin, fine, slender; (*Getränk*) weak; (*Luft*) rare.
Dünndruckpapier *n.* **(-s, -e)** India paper, Bible paper.

Dünne *f.* **(-, 0)** thinness; sparseness.
Dunst *m.* **(-es, Dünste)** haze; mist; vapor; steam; fume (of wine).
Dunstabzug *m.* extractor, range hood.
dünsten *v.t.* to stew, to steam, to braise.
Dunstglocke *f.* blanket of smog.
dunstig *a.* vaporous; hazy.
Duo *n.* (*mus.*) duet; duo.
düpieren *v.t.* to dupe.
Duplikat *n.* **(-[e]s, -e)** duplicate.
Dur *n.* (*mus.*) major.
durch *pr.* through, by; ~ *a.* well-done; ~ *und* ~, thoroughly; ~ *und* ~ *nass,* wet through.
durcharbeiten *v.t.* to work through.
durchaus *adv.* by all means, absolutely; ~ *nicht,* by no means.
durchbeißen *v.r.* (*fig.*) to fight one's way through; ~ *v.t.st.* to bite through.
durchblättern *v.t.* to skim (a book).
Durchblick *m. den* ~ *haben,* to know what's going on.
durchblicken to look through; ~ *lassen,* to give to understand.
durchbohren *v.t.* to pierce; to perforate.
durchboxen *v.r.* to fight one's way through.
durchbrechen *v.t. & i.st. (s)* to break through.
durchbrennen *v.i.ir. (s)* (*el.*) to blow, to fuse; (*fig.*) to run away, to abscond.
durchbringen *v.t.ir.* to squander; to get past/through/accepted.
durchbrochen *a.* open (pierced) work.
Durchbruch *m.* **(-[e]s, -brüche)** breach; (*mil.*) breakthrough.
durchchecken *v.t.ir.* to check thoroughly.
durchdenken *v.t.ir.* to think over.
durchdrängen *v.r.* to force one's way through.
durchdrehen *v.i.* to mince; (*fig.*) to flip; to panic.
durchdringen *v.t.st.* to come through; to penetrate; ~ *v.i.st. (s)* (*fig.*) to prevail.
durchdringend *a.* piercing, penetrating, sharp.
durchdrücken *v.t.* to press sth. through; to straighten (leg); to manage to get (benefits).
durcheinander *adv.* in a mess; confused.
Durcheinander *n.* **(-s, 0)** muddle; confusion, mess.
durchfahren *v.i.st.* to pass through.
Durchfahrt *f.* **(-, -en)** passage, thoroughfare, gateway; transit.
Durchfall *m.* **(-[e]s, -fälle)** diarrhea.
durchfallen *v.i.st. (s)* to fall through; to fail; to flunk (an examination).
durchfinden *v.t.st.* to find one's way.
durchfließen *v.i.st. (s) & v.t.st.* to flow through.
durchfluten *v.t.* to flood (through).
durchforschen *v.t.* to explore.
Durchforschung *f.* **(-, -en)** exploration.
durchforsten *v.t.* to sift through.
durchfragen *v.r.* to ask one's way.
durchfressen *v.t.st.* to eat through; to corrode.
durchfrieren *v.i. durchgefroren sein,* to be frozen stiff.
Durchfuhr *f.* **(-, 0)** transit.
durchführbar *a.* practicable; feasible.
Durchführbarkeit *f.* practicability; feasibility.
durchführen *v.t.* to accomplish, to implement, to carry out.
durchfurchen *v.t.* to furrow, to wrinkle; to plow (the sea).
durchfüttern *v.t.* to feed; (*fig.*) to support.
Durchgang *m.* **(-[e]s, -gänge)** passage, transit; **~slager** *n.* transit camp; **~sverkehr** *m.* transit traffic; **~szoll** *m.* transit duty.
durchgängig *a.* general, common; ~ *adv.* in all cases, generally.
durchgehen *v.t.st.* to peruse, to go through; ~ *v.i.st. (s)* to abscond; to bolt.
durchgehend *a.* (*Zug, Fahrkarte*) non-stop.
durchgehends *a.* generally, universally.
durchgeistigen *v.t.* to spiritualize.
durchgreifen *v.i.st.* to crack down; to take energetic action.
durchgreifend *a.* determined, energetic.
durchhalten *v.t.* to hold out; ~ *v.i.* to stick it out.
durchhängen *v.i.st.* to sag.
durchhauen *v.t.ir.* to cut through; to flog.
durchhecheln *v.t.* to criticize.
durchhelfen *v.i.st.* to support; ~ *v.r.* to get by.
durchkämpfen *v.t.* to fight out.
durchkommen *v.i.st. (s)* to get through; (*Prüfung*) to pass; to succeed; to recover.
durchkönnen *v.i.ir.* to be able to pass.
durchkreuzen *v.t.* to cross; to thwart.
durchlassen *v.t.st.* to let pass, to let through.
durchlässig *a.* permeable.
Durchlässigkeit *f.* permeability.
Durchlaucht *f.* **(-, -en)** Serene Highness.
Durchlauf *m.* run; flow.
durchlaufen *v.i.st. (s)* to run through; ~ *v.t.st.* to wear out; to run over.
durchlaufend *a.* continuous; in sequence.
Durchlauferhitzer *m.* instantaneous water heater.
durchleben *v.t.* to live through.
durchlesen *v.t.st.* to read through, to peruse.
durchleuchten *v.t.* to screen, to X-ray; to investigate.
durchlöchern *v.t.* to perforate; to riddle.
durchmachen *v.t.* to go through.
Durchmarsch *m.* **(-es, -märsche)** (troops) transit.
durchmessen *v.t.st.* to cross, to traverse.
Durchmesser *m.* **(-s, -)** diameter.
durchmogeln *v.r.* to cheat one's way through.
durchmüssen *v.i.ir.* to have to pass through.
durchmustern *v.t.* to scan, to review.
durchnässen *v.t.* to soak, to wet through.
durchnehmen *v.t.st.* to deal with, to go over.
durchpausen *v.t.* to trace.
durchpeitschen *v.t.* to thrash; (*fig.*) to rush through.
durchprügeln *v.t.* to thrash.
durchqueren *v.t.* to cross.
durchrechnen *v.t.* to calculate, to examine.
durchreiben *v.t.st.* to rub a hole in.
Durchreise *f.* **(-, -n)** passage, passing through.
durchreisen *v.i (s)* to travel through.
durchreißen *v.t.st.* to tear in half.
durchringen *v.r.* to make up one's mind.
durchrosten *v.i.* to rust through.
durchs = durch das.
Durchsage *f.* announcement.
durchsäuern *v.t.* to leaven thoroughly.
durchschaubar *a.* transparent.
durchschauen *v.i.* to look through; ~ *v.t.* (*fig.*) to see through.
durchscheinen *v.i.st. (s)* to shine through; to be transparent.
durchscheinend *a.* translucent.
durchscheuern *v.t.* to wear through.
durchschimmern *v.i.* to shimmer/gleam through.
Durchschlag *m.* **(-[e]s, -schläge)** (carbon) copy.

durchschlagen *v.i.st.* to penetrate; (*fig.*) to tell, to have effect; ~ *v.r.* to rough it.
durchschlagend *a.* resounding (success); decisive.
durchschlüpfen *v.i. (s)* to slip through.
durchschneiden *v.r.* to cut through.
Durchschnitt *m.* **(-[e]s, -e)** cut; average.
durchschnittlich *a. & adv.* average; on average.
durchschreiten *v.t.st.* to stride through.
durchschwitzen *v.t.* to soak with sweat.
durchsehen *v.t.st.* to revise, to look over.
durchseihen *v.t.* to filter, to strain.
durchsein *v.i.ir. (s)* to be done with.
durchsetzen *v.t.* (*fig.*) to carry through; to mix with.
durchsetzt (mit) *a.* honeycombed with.
Durchsetzungskraft *f.*, **Durchsetzungsvermögen** *n.* self-assertion.
Durchsicht *f.* **(-, -en)** revision, perusal.
durchsichtig *a.* transparent.
durchsickern *v.i. (s)* to trickle through, to ooze through; (*fig.*) to leak through.
durchsieben *v.t.* to sift, to sieve.
durchspielen *v.t.* to play through (a piece of music).
durchsprechen *v.t.st.* to talk over.
durchstehen *v.t.st.* to stand; to come through; to get over (illness).
durchstellen *v.i.* to put through (call).
Durchstich *m.* **(-[e]s, -e)** (*rail.*) cutting, excavation.
durchstöbern *v.t.* to rummage, to ransack.
durchstossen *v.t.st.* to break by thrusting; to pierce, to run through the body.
durchstreichen *v.t.st.* to cross out; to delete.
durchstreifen *v.t.* to roam through.
durchströmen *v.t.* to flow through.
durchsuchen *v.t.* to search, to ransack.
Durchsuchung *f.* **(-, -en)** search.
Durchsuchungsbefehl *m.* search warrant.
durchtränken *v.t.* to soak with.
durchtrennen *v.t.* to cut, to sever.
durchtrieben *a.* sly; arrant, cunning.
durchwachsen *a.* (*vom Fleisch*) streaked, streaky; (*fig.*) mixed.
Durchwahl *f.* direct dialing.
durchwählen *v.i.* to dial direct.
durchwärmen *v.t.* to warm thoroughly.
durchweg *adv.* throughout.
durchweichen *v.t.* to soak thoroughly, to drench; ~ *v.i. (s)* to become soft.
durchwinden *v.t.st.* to entwine; ~ *v.r.* to struggle through.
durchwischen *v.i. (s)* to slip away.
durchwühlen *v.i.* to root up; (*fig.*) to ransack.
durchzählen *v.t.* to count up.
durchzucken *v.t.* to flash across; to flash through.
Durchzug *m.* **(-[e]s, -züge)** passage, march through; draft.
dürfen *v.i.ir.* to be allowed; *darf ich?* may I?; *du darfst nicht,* you must not.
dürftig *a.* needy, indigent; scanty, insufficient.
dürr *a.* dry, arid; withered; barren; lean; *~e Worte,* plain language.
Dürre *f.* **(-, -n)** drought.
Durst *m.* **(-es, 0)** thirst.
dursten, dürsten *v.i.* to thirst, to be thirsty; to yearn.
durstig *a.* thirsty.
durstlöschend *a.*, **durststillend** *a.* thirst-quenching.
Durststrecke *f.* (*fig.*) lean period.
Dusche *f.* **(-, -n)** shower.
duschen *v.t. & i.r.* to take a shower.
Düse *f.* **(-, -n)** nozzle; jet.
Dusel *m.* luck, ~ *haben,* to be lucky.
düsen *v.i.* (*fam.*) to zoom.
Düsenantrieb *m.* jet propulsion.
Düsenflugzeug *n.* jet plane.
Düsenjäger *m.* jet fighter.
Düsentriebwerk *n.* jet engine.
Dussel *m.* dope.
dusselig *a.* stupid.
düster *a.* gloomy.
Düsterkeit *f.* darkness; gloom.
Dutzend *n.* **(-s, -e)** dozen.
dutzendweise *adv.* by the dozen.
duzen *v.t.* to call sb. "du"; *sich* ~, to call each other "du."
d.Vf. *der Verfasser,* the author.
Dynamik *f.* **(-, 0)** dynamics *pl.*
dynamisch *a.* dynamic; *adv.* dynamically.
Dynamit *m.* **(-s, 0)** dynamite.
Dynamomaschine *f.* dynamo.
Dynastie *f.* **(-, -en)** dynasty.
dynastisch *a.* dynastic(al).
DZ *Doppelzimmer,* double room.
D-Zug *m.* **(-[e]s, -züge)** *Durchgangszug,* fast train, corridor train.

E

E, e *n.* the letter E or e; (*mus.*) E.
E *Eilzug,* fast train; *Europastraße,* European Highway.
Ebbe *f.* **(-, -n)** ebb, low tide.
ebben *v.i.* to ebb.
ebd. *ebenda,* in the same place, ibid.
eben *a.* even, level; flat; (*math.*) plane; ~ *adv.* just; precisely; ~ *erst,* just now; *ebenso,* just so, quite as.
Ebenbild *n.* **(-[e]s, -er)** image; likeness.
ebenbürtig *a.* equal.
Ebene *f.* **(-, -n)** plain; (*math.*) plane, level.
ebenerdig *a. & adv.* (at) ground level.
ebenfalls *adv.* likewise, too, also.
Ebenholz *n.* **(-es, 0)** ebony.
Ebenmaß *n.* **(-es, -e)** symmetry, regularity.
ebenmäßig *a.* regular, well-proportioned.
ebenso *adv.* just as.
Eber *m.* **(-s, -)** boar.
Eberesche *f.* mountain ash, roan tree.
ebnen *v.t.* to level, to smoothe.
Echo *n.* **(-s, -s)** echo.
Echolot *n.* echo sounder.
Echse *f.* **(-, -n)** saurian.
echt *a.* genuine; true; authentic; (*Farben*) fast; (*Perle, Diamant*) real.
Echtheit *f.* genuineness, authenticity.
Ecke *f.* **(-, -n)** corner; nook; *an allen ~n und En-*

den, everywhere; *um die ~ gehen,* (*fig.*) to go west.
Ecker *f.* **(-, -n)** acorn.
Eckhaus *n.* corner-house.
eckig *a.* angular; (*fig.*) awkward.
Eckplatz *m.* corner seat.
Eckstein *m.* corner-stone.
Eckstoß *m.* corner kick.
Eckzahn *m.* canine tooth.
Economyklasse *f.* economy class.
Ed. *Edition, Ausgabe,* edition, ed.
edel *a.* noble; well-born; generous; precious; *die edlen Teile,* the vital parts.
Edelmann *m.* nobleman.
Edelmetall *n.* rare metal, precious metal.
Edelmut *m.* **(-[e]s, 0)** generosity.
edelmütig *a.* generous.
Edelstahl *m.* stainless steel.
Edelstein *m.* precious stone.
Edeltanne *f.* silver fir, pitch pine.
Eden *n.* **der Garten ~,** the Garden of Eden.
Edikt *n.* **(-[e]s, -e)** edict.
EDV *elektronische Datenverarbeitung,* electronic data processing, EDP.
EEG *Elektroenzephalogramm,* electroencephalogram, EEG.
Efeu *m.* **(-s, 0)** ivy.
Effekt *m.* effect.
Effekten *m.pl.* (*com.*) securities.
effektiv *a.* effective; real.
Effektivität *f.* effectiveness.
Effektivlohn *m.* real wage.
effektvoll *a.* effective; dramatic.
effizient *a.* & *adv.* efficient(ly).
e.G. *eingetragene Gesellschaft,* incorporated company.
EG *Europäische Gemeinschaft,* European Community, EC.
egal *a.* equal, all the same.
Egel *m.* leech.
Egge *f.* **(-, -n)** harrow.
eggen *v.t.* to harrow.
Ego *n.* ego.
Egoismus *m.* **(-, 0)** selfishness, egoism.
Egoist *m.* **(-en, -en); Egoistin** *f.* **(-, -nen)** selfish person, egoist.
egoistisch *a.* selfish, egoistic(al).
Egozentriker *m.;* **Egozentrikerin** *f.* egocentric.
egozentrisch *a.* egocentric.
ehe *c.* before.
Ehe *f.* **(-, -n)** marriage, wedlock; *aus erster ~,* from the first marriage; *wilde ~,* concubinage.
Eheberatung *f.* marriage counseling.
ehebrechen *v.i.st.* to commit adultery.
Ehebrecher *m.* **(-s, -)** adulterer.
Ehebrecherin *f.* **(-, -nen)** adulteress.
ehebrecherisch *a.* adulterous.
Ehebruch *m.* adultery; (law) misconduct.
ehedem *adv.* formerly.
Ehefrau *f.* wife.
Ehegatte *m.* husband; spouse.
Ehegattin *f.* wife, spouse.
Ehehälfte *f.* (*fam.*) better half, spouse.
Ehehindernis *n.* (marriage) impediment.
Eheleute *pl.* married people, spouses.
ehelich *a.* matrimonial; legitimate.
ehelichen *v.t.* to marry.
ehelos *a.* unmarried, single.
Ehelosigkeit *f.* **(-, 0)** celibacy, unmarried state.
ehemalig *a.* former; late.
ehemals *adv.* formerly.
Ehemann *m.* husband.
Ehepaar *n.* married couple.
eher *adv.* sooner; rather.
Eherecht *n.* matrimonial law.
ehern *a.* brazen.
Ehescheidung *f.* divorce.
Ehestand *m.* married state, wedlock.
Ehetrennung *f.* separation.
Ehevermittlungsinstitut *n.* marriage bureau.
Ehevertrag *m.* marriage settlement.
Eheweib *n.* (*obs*) spouse, wife.
Ehrabschneider *m.* slanderer.
ehrbar *a.* respectable; honorable.
Ehre *f.* **(-, -n)** honor, reputation.
ehren *v.t.* to honor, to respect.
Ehrenamt *n.* honorary post.
ehrenamtlich *a.* honorary, unpaid.
Ehrenbürger *m.* (honorary) citizen.
Ehrenbürgerrecht *n.* freedom of the city.
Ehrengericht *n.* court of honor.
ehrenhaft *a.* honorable.
ehrenhalber *adv.* honorarily.
Ehrenhandel *m.* affair of honor.
Ehrenkränkung *f.* affront, libel, defamation.
Ehrenmann *m.* man of honor.
Ehrenmitglied *n.* honorary member.
ehrenrührig *a.* defamatory, calumnious.
ehrenvoll *a.* honorable, creditable.
Ehrenwache *f.* guard of honor.
ehrenwert *a.* respectable.
Ehrenwort *n.* word of honor.
ehrerbietig *a.* respectful, reverential.
Ehrerbietung *f.* **(-, 0)** reverence.
Ehrfurcht *f.* **(-, 0)** reverence, awe.
Ehrgefühl *n.* sense of honor.
Ehrgeiz *m.* ambition.
ehrgeizig *a.* ambitious.
ehrlich *a.* honest, fair, faithful.
Ehrlichkeit *f.* **(-, 0)** honesty, faithfulness.
ehrlos *a.* disgraceful, dishonorable, infamous.
Ehrlosigkeit *f.* **(-, 0)** infamy.
ehrwürdig *a.* venerable, reverend.
Ei *n.* **(-[e]s, -er)** egg; *gekochtes ~,* boiled egg (*hartgekocht,* hardboiled, *weichgekocht,* soft-boiled); *frischgelegtes ~,* newlaid egg.
ei! *i.* ah! why!; indeed!
Eibe *f.* **(-, -n)** yew(tree).
Eichamt *n.* **(-s, -ämter)** Bureau of Standards.
Eiche *f.* **(-, -n)** oak.
Eichel *f.* **(-, -n)** acorn; glans; (*Karten*) club.
eichelförmig *a.* acorn-shaped.
eichen *v.t.* to adjust, to calibrate, to gauge.
eichen *a.* oaken, oak.
Eichenlaub *n.* oak leaves *pl.*
Eichhörnchen *n.* **(-s, -)** squirrel.
Eichkätzchen *n.* **(-s, -)** squirrel.
Eichmaß *n.* standard.
Eid *m.* **(-es, -e)** oath; *einen ~ leisten,* to take an oath; *unter ~,* on oath; *an Eides statt, eidesstattlich,* in lieu of an oath.
eidbrüchig *a.* perjured, forsworn.
Eidechse *f.* **(-, -n)** lizard.
Eiderdaunen *f.pl.* eiderdown.
Eidesformel *f.* wording of an oath.
eidesstattliche Erklärung *f.* statutory declaration.
Eidgenosse *m.;* **Eidgenossin** *f.* Swiss.

Eidgenossenschaft *f.*, **die Schweizerische ~** the Swiss Confederation.
eidgenössisch *a.* Swiss.
eidlich *a.* by oath, upon oath, sworn; *~e Versicherung f.*, affidavit; *eine ~e Versicherung abgeben*, to make an affidavit.
Eidotter *m.* or *n.* yolk.
Eierbecher *m.* egg cup.
Eierkuchen *m.* omelette.
eierlegend *a.* oviparous.
Eierschale *f.* eggshell.
Eierstock *m.* ovary.
Eifer *m.* **(-s, 0)** zeal, ardor; passion.
Eiferer *m.* zealot.
eifern *v.i.* to be zealous.
Eifersucht *f.* **(-, 0)** jealousy.
Eifersüchtelei *f.* **(-, -en)** petty jealousy.
eifersüchtig *a.* jealous.
eiförmig *a.* egg-shaped.
eifrig *a.* zealous; ardent, eager.
eig., eigtl. *eigentlich*, properly.
Eigelb *n.* yolk.
eigen *a.* own; singular, strange, odd.
Eigenart *f.* peculiarity; originality.
eigenartig *a.* original, peculiar.
Eigenbrötler *m.* **(-s, -)** loner, crank.
Eigendünkel *m.* **(-s, 0)** self-conceit.
eigenhändig *a.* with one's own hand.
Eigenheim *n.* house of one's own.
Eigenheit *f.* **(-, -en)** peculiarity, singularity; idiosyncrasy.
eigenmächtig *a.* arbitrary, autocratic.
Eigenname *m.* **(-ns, -n)** proper name.
Eigennutz *m.* **(-es, 0)** self-interest.
eigennützig *a.* self-seeking, selfish.
eigens *adv.* particularly, (e)specially.
Eigenschaft *f.* **(-, -en)** quality, property; attribute; (*chem.*) property; *in seiner Eigenschaft als...*, in his capacity as.
Eigenschaftswort *n.* adjective.
Eigensinn *m.* **(-[e]s, 0)** obstinacy.
eigensinnig *a. & adv.* obstinate(ly), stubborn(ly).
eigenständig *a. & adv.* independent(ly).
eigensüchtig *a. & adv.* selfish(ly).
eigentlich *a.* actual, proper; real; peculiar; true; ~ *adv.* actually, properly; exactly.
Eigentum *n.* **(-[e]s, -tümer)** property.
Eigentümer *m.* **(-s, -)** owner, proprietor.
eigentümlich *a.* peculiar; proper.
Eigentümlichkeit *f.* **(-, -en)** peculiarity.
Eigentumsrecht *n.* right of possession; copyright.
eigenwillig *a.* self-willed.
eignen *v.r.* to suit, to be fit, to be adapted for.
Eignung *f.* suitability, aptitude.
Eignungsprüfung *f.*, **Eignungstest** *m.* aptitude test.
Eilbestellung *f.* urgent order.
Eilbote *m.* courier, express messenger.
Eilbrief *m.* express letter.
Eile *f.* **(-, 0)** haste, speed, hurry.
Eileiter *m.* fallopian tube; oviduct.
eilen *v.i.* to hasten, to make haste; *die Sache eilt (nicht)*, the matter is (not) urgent; there is (no) hurry.
eilend, eilends *a. & adv.* speedy; hastily.
eilfertig *a.* hasty, precipitate, speedy.
Eilgut *n.* express goods; *als ~* or *mit Eilboten schicken*, to send express.
eilig *a.* hasty, speedy; *ich habe es sehr ~*, I am in a hurry.
Eilmarsch *m.* forced march.
Eilzug *m.* fast train.
Eimer *m.* **(-s, -)** bucket.
ein *adv.* in; *ich weiss nicht, wo ~ und aus*, I am at my wits' end.
ein, eine, ein *art.* a, an; *unser ~er*, people like us; *~er nach dem andern*, one by one; *~s*, one; *in ~em zu*, continuously.
Einakter *m.* one-act play.
einander *a.* one another, each other; *nach ~*, in succession, one after another.
einarbeiten *v.r.* to familiarize oneself, to get used to a job.
einarmig *a.* one-armed.
einäschern *v.t.* to cremate.
einatmen *v.t.* to inhale, to breathe.
einäugig *a.* one-eyed.
Einbahnstraße *f.* one-way street.
Einbahnverkehr *m.* one-way traffic.
einbalsamieren *v.t.* to embalm.
Einband *m.* **(-[e]s, -bände)** cover, binding; *in Leinwand ~*, clothbound; *in Leder ~*, leatherbound.
einbändig *a.* in one volume.
einbauen *v.t.* to build in; to fit; to install.
einbegreifen *v.t.st.* to include.
einbehalten *v.t.st.* to keep back.
einbeinig *a.* one-legged.
einberufen *v.t.st.* to summon (a meeting); (*mil.*) to call up.
Einberufung *f.* summoning; draft.
einbetten *v.t.* to embed.
Einbettzimmer *n.* single room.
einbeulen *v.t.* to dent.
einbeziehen *v.t.* to include.
Einbeziehung *f.* **(-, -en)** inclusion.
einbiegen *v.t.* to bend inward; ~ *v.i.* to turn into.
einbilden *v.r.* to imagine, to fancy; *sich etwas (viel) ~*, to think a good deal of oneself.
Einbildung *f.* **(-, -en)** imagination, fancy; conceit.
Einbildungs: ~kraft *f.*; **~vermögen** *n.* imagination, imaginative powers.
einbinden *v.t.st.* to bind (a book).
einblenden *v.t.* to insert; ~ *v.r.* to go over to.
Einblick *m.* **(-s, -e)** insight.
einbrechen *v.i.st. (s)* to break into; to set in.
Einbrecher *m.* **(-s, -)** burglar.
einbrennen *v.t.ir.* to burn in; to brand.
einbringen *v.t.ir.* to bring in; to yield; *wieder ~*, to recoup.
Einbruch *m.* **(-[e]s, -brüche)** burglary; (*mil.*) penetration; *~ der Nacht*, nightfall.
einbruchsicher *a.* burglarproof.
Einbuchtung *f.* **(-, -en)** bay, recess; dent.
einbürgern *v.t.* to naturalize.
Einbürgerung *f.* naturalization.
Einbuße *f.* **(-, -n)** loss.
einbüßen *v.t.* to suffer loss; to lose.
einchecken *v.t. & i.* to check in.
eincremen *v.t.* to put cream on.
eindämmen *v.t.* to dam up, to embank, to contain.
eindecken *v.r.* to stock up; ~ *v.t.* to swamp.
Eindecker *m.* **(-s, -)** monoplane.
eindellen *v.t.* to dent.
eindeutig *a.* unambiguous, univocal.
eindeutschen *v.t.* to Germanize.
eindimensional *a.* one-dimensional.
eindösen *v.i.* to doze off.
eindringen *v.i.st. (s)* to penetrate.

eindringlich *a.* impressive.
Eindringlichkeit *f.* urgency; impressiveness; forcefulness.
Eindringling *m.* **(-s, -e)** intruder.
Eindruck *m.* **(-[e]s, -drücke)** impression.
eindrücken *v.t.* to smash in; to press/push in.
eindrucksvoll *a.* impressive.
einebnen *v.t.* to level.
Einebnung *f.* leveling.
Einehe *f.* monogamy.
eineiig *a.* identical (twins).
eineinhalb one and a half.
einengen *v.t.* to restrict; to confine; to cramp.
Einer *m.* **(-s, -)** (*ar.*) unit; single number, digit.
einerlei *a.* of the same kind, the same; *es ist mir ~*, it's all the same to me.
Einerlei *n.* monotony, sameness.
einerseits *adv.* on the one hand.
einfach *a.* single, simple; plain; *~e Buchführung f.* bookkeeping by single entry.
Einfachheit *f.* **(-, 0)** simplicity.
einfädeln *v.t.* to thread; (*fig.*) to contrive, to scheme.
einfahren *v.i.* *(s)* to enter; to descend (into a mine).
Einfahrt *f.* **(-, -en)** entrance.
Einfall *m.* **(-[e]s, -fälle)** invasion; idea, whim, fancy.
einfallen *v.i.st.* *(s)* to fall in; to interrupt; to invade; to occur; *es will mir nicht ~*, I can't think of it; *(das) fällt mir gar nicht ein!* catch me doing that!
einfallslos *a.* unimaginative.
einfallsreich *a.* imaginative.
Einfalt *f.* **(-, 0)** simple-mindedness.
einfältig *a.* simple; silly; naïve.
Einfamilienhaus *n.* one-family house.
einfangen *v.t.st.* to catch, to seize.
einfärben *v.t.* to dye.
einfarbig *a.* of one color; plain.
einfassen *v.t.* to set; to mount.
Einfassung *f.* **(-, -en)** setting; foil.
einfetten *v.t.* to oil, to grease; to lubricate.
einfinden *v.r.st.* to turn up.
einflechten *v.t.st.* to mention casually.
einfliegen *v.t.st.* to fly in.
einfließen *v.i.st.* (*eine Bemerkung, ein Wort*) *~ lassen*, to slip in (a remark, a word).
einflößen *v.t.* to imbue, to inspire.
Einfluß *m.* **(-flusses, -flüsse)** influence.
einflußreich *a.* influential.
einflüstern *v.t.* to whisper to, to suggest.
einfordern *v.t.* to call in.
einförmig *a.* uniform; monotonous.
Einförmigkeit *f.* **(-, -en)** uniformity, monotony.
einfrieden, einfriedigen *v.t.* to enclose.
einfrieren *v.t.st.* *(s)* to freeze.
einfügen *v.t.* to insert.
einfühlen *v.r.* *in jmdn. ~*, to empathize with sb.
einfühlsam *a.* understanding, sensitive.
Einfuhr *f.* **(-, -en)** importation, import.
einführen *v.t.* to import; to introduce.
Einführung *f.* **(-, -en)** introduction.
Einführungsbesprechung *f.* general orientation.
Einfuhrzoll *m.* import duty.
einfüllen *v.t.* to fill; to pour into.
Eingabe *f.* **(-, -n)** petition; memorial.
Eingang *m.* **(-[e]s, -gänge)** entrance, entry; way in; preamble.
eingängig *a.* catchy.
eingangs *adv.* at the beginning.
eingeben *v.t.st.* (*comp.*) to feed in.
ein: ~gebildet *a.* imaginary; conceited; **~geboren** *a.* native; innate.
Eingebung *f.* **(-, -en)** inspiration.
eingedenk *a.* mindful of.
eingefallen *a.* gaunt (face); sunken, hollow.
eingefleischt *a.* inveterate; confirmed.
eingehen *v.i.st.* *(s)* (*Brief*) to come to hand; (*Ehe*) to contract; *eine Wette ~*, to make a bet; to consent to; to decay; to shrink.
eingehend *a.* thorough, exhaustive; (*Post, etc.*) incoming.
eingekeilt *a.* wedged in; hemmed in.
eingeklemmt *a.* trapped.
Eingemachte[s] *n.* **(-n, 0)** preserves *pl.*; (*in Essig*) pickles *pl.*
eingemeinden *v.t.* to incorporate.
eingenommen *a.* *~ sein von*, to be taken; *von sich ~ sein*, to be full of oneself.
eingerostet *a.* rusty.
eingeschnappt *a.* (*fam.*) huffy.
eingeschneit *a.* snowed in.
eingeschränkt *a.* restrained, limited.
eingeschrieben *a.* registered, enrolled.
eingeschworen *a.* confirmed.
eingestandenermaßen *adv.* avowedly.
Eingeständnis *n.* **(-ses, -se)** confession, avowal.
eingestehen *v.t.st.* to admit, to confess, to avow.
eingestellt *a.* *fortschrittlich ~*, progressively minded.
Eingeweide *n.* **(-s, -)** entrails, intestines, bowels *pl.*
eingewöhnen *v.r.* to get used to, to accustom oneself to.
eingießen *v.t.st.* to pour in; (*ein Glas*) to pour out.
eingipsen *v.t.* to fix in with plaster, to put in plaster.
eingleisig *a.* single-track.
eingliedern *v.t.* to incorporate, to include; to rehabilitate.
Eingliederung *f.* integration.
eingraben *v.t.st.* to bury; to sink; *~ v.r.* (*mil.*) to entrench.
eingravieren *v.t.* to engrave.
eingreifen *v.i.st.* to intervene; (*von Zahnrädern*) to interlock; to interfere.
Eingriff *m.* **(-[e]s, -e)** intervention; interference; (*med.*) operation; (*mech.*) mesh.
Einhalt *m.* **(-[e]s, 0)** *~ gebieten*, to stop.
einhalten *v.t.st.* to observe; to stop.
Einhaltung *f.* observance.
einhämmern *v.i.* to hammer (on sth.); *~ v.t.* to drum (into somebody).
einhandeln *v.t.* to purchase, to buy.
einhändig *a.* one-handed, single-handed.
einhändigen *v.t.* to hand (over).
einhängen *v.t.* to hang (up); to take sb.'s arm.
einhauchen *v.t.* to inspire.
einheften *v.t.* to file.
einhegen *v.t.* to enclose.
einheimisch *a.* indigenous; native.
einheimsen *v.t.* (*fam.*) to rake in.
einheiraten *v.i.* to marry into.
Einheit *f.* **(-, -en)** unity; (*ar.*) unit.
einheitlich *a.* unified, uniform, standardized.
Einheits: ~format *n.* standard size; **~front** *f.* united front; **~gewerkschaft** *f.* general trade un-

ion; **~preis** *m.* uniform price; **~staat** *m.* unitary state; **~tarif** *m.* flat rate.
einheizen *v.t.* to light a fire; (*fig.*) to give sb. hell.
einhellig *a.* unanimous.
einher *adv.* forth, along, on.
einholen *v.t.* to catch up with; to collect, to get.
Einhorn *n.* **(-[e]s, -hörner)** unicorn.
einhüllen *v.t.* to wrap up; to cover.
einig *a.* united; ~ *sein,* to agree.
einigen *v.t.* to unite; ~ *v.r.* to come to an agreement.
einige[r], einiges *pn.* some, any; **einige** *pl.* some, a few; ~ *hundert,* a hundred odd.
einigermaßen *adv.* to a certain extent.
Einigkeit *f.* **(-, 0)** union, unanimity, concord.
Einigung *f.* **(-, -en)** agreement, union; unification.
einimpfen *v.t.* to inoculate.
einjagen *v.t.* *einem einen Schrecken* ~, to frighten someone.
einjährig *a.* one year old.
einkalkulieren *v.t.* to take into account.
einkassieren *v.t.* to cash.
Einkauf *m.* **(-[e]s, -käufe)** purchase; *Einkäufe machen,* to go shopping.
einkaufen *v.t.* to buy, to purchase; to shop.
Einkaufspreis *m.* purchase price, wholesale price.
Einkaufswagen *m.* shopping cart.
einkehren *v.i.* *(s)* to stop off.
einkerben *v.t.* to notch.
einkerkern *v.t.* to imprison.
einklagen *v.t.* to sue for.
einklammern *v.t.* to put in brackets.
Einklang *m.* **(-[e]s, 0)** unison, harmony; *im ~ stehen,* to be in unison, to agree.
einkleiden *v.t.* to clothe; (*Gedanken*) to put into words.
einklemmen *v.t.* to squeeze in, to jam, to wedge in.
einknicken *v.t.* to bend, to snap.
einkochen *v.t.* (*Frucht*) to preserve, to bottle.
Einkommen *n.* **(-s, -)** income, revenue.
Einkommensteuer *f.* income tax; **~erklärung** *f.* income tax return.
einkreisen *v.t.* to encircle; to circumscribe, (*mil.*) to envelop.
Einkreisung *f.* **(-, -en)** encirclement.
Einkünfte *f.pl.* income, revenue, rent.
einladen *v.t.st.* to invite, to bid; (*Güter*) to load.
einladend *a.* inviting, appetizing.
Einladung *f.* **(-, -en)** invitation.
Einlage *f.* **(-, -n)** (*Brief*) enclosure; (*Bank*) deposit; (*Schuh*) arch support; (*Zahn*) filling; (*Schneiderei*) wadding.
einlagern *v.t.* to store, to warehouse.
Einlaß *m.* **(-lasses, 0)** admission; inlet.
einlassen *v.t.st.* to let in; to admit; ~ *v.r.* to engage in.
Einlaßkarte *f.* ticket of admission.
Einlauf *m.* **(-s, -läufe)** enema.
einlaufen *v.i.st.* *(s)* to shrink; (*Schiff*) to make *or* enter a port; (*Briefe, Gelder*) to come to hand; **nicht einlaufend** *a.* unshrinkable; ~ *v.r.* to warm up.
einleben *v.r.* to accustom oneself.
Einlegearbeit *f.* inlaid work, intarsia.
einlegen *v.t.* to lay in, to put in; to inlay; to deposit; (*Früchte etc.*) to preserve, to pickle; (*Berufung*) to lodge; *ein Wort für einen ~,* to intercede for someone.
einleiten *v.t.* to introduce; (*Maßnahmen*) to initiate.
einleitend *a.* introductory.
Einleitung *f.* **(-, -en)** introduction.
einlenken *v.i.* to relent.
einleuchten *v.i.* to be evident.
einleuchtend *a.* plausible.
einliefern *v.t.* to mail; to take sb. to the hospital.
einliegend *a.* enclosed, herewith.
einlochen *v.t.* (*fam.*) to put sb. away, imprison.
einlösen *v.t.* to redeem (a pledge); (*Wechsel*) to honor, to take up; (*Scheck*) to cash.
Einlösung *f.* **(-, -en)** redemption.
einlullen *v.t.* to lull to sleep.
einmachen *v.t.* to pickle, to preserve.
Einmachglas *n.* preserving jar.
einmal *adv.* once; *auf ~,* all at once, suddenly; *nicht ~,* not even.
Einmaleins *n.* **(-, -)** multiplication table.
Einmalhandtuch *n.* disposable towel.
einmalig *a.* unique.
Einmannbetrieb *m.* one-man business.
Einmarsch *m.* **(-[e]s, -märsche)** entry.
einmarschieren *v.i.* *(s)* to march in.
einmauern *v.t.* to wall in.
einmengen *v.r.* to meddle (with), to interfere (in).
einmieten *v.r.* rent an apartment or room.
einmischen *v.r.* to interfere (in), to meddle (with).
Einmischung *f.* **(-, -en)** intervention, interference.
einmonatig *a.* one-month (duration).
einmonatlich *a.* monthly.
einmotorig *a.* single-engined.
einmumme(l)n *v.t.* to wrap up.
einmünden *v.i.* to flow into, to debouch.
Einmündung *f.* junction (streets).
einmütig *a.* unanimous.
Einmütigkeit *f.* **(-, 0)** concord, unanimity.
einnähen *v.t.* to sew in.
Einnahme *f.* **(-, -n)** receipt, income, revenue; capture, taking; *Einnahmen und Ausgaben,* revenue and expenditure.
Einnahmequelle *f.* source of income/revenue.
einnehmen *v.t.st.* to take; (*fig.*) to charm, to captivate; (*den Kopf*) to disturb.
einnehmend *a.* engaging, charming.
Einnehmer *m.* **(-s, -)** receiver, collector.
einnicken *v.i.* *(s)* to nod off.
einnisten *v.r.* to nest; to install oneself.
Einöde *f.* **(-, -n)** desert, solitude.
einölen *v.t.* to oil, to grease.
einordnen *v.t.* to arrange; to classify; to file.
einpacken *v.t.* to pack up.
einparken *v.t.* to park.
einpauken *v.t.* (*Studenten*) to coach, to bone up.
einpferchen *v.t.* to be crammed together.
einpflanzen *v.t.* to plant; (*med.*) to implant.
einplanen *v.t.* to plan; to include; to allow for.
einpökeln *v.t.* to salt, to pickle.
einprägen *v.t.* to impress; to stamp.
einprägsam *a.* easily remembered; catchy.
einprogrammieren *v.t.* (*comp.*) to program in.
einquartieren *v.t.* to quarter, to billet.
Einquartierung *f.* **(-, -en)** soldiers' quarters *pl.*
einquetschen *v.t.* to squeeze.
einrahmen *v.t.* to frame.
einrasten *v.i.* to engage, to click into place.
einräumen *v.t.* to clear away; to concede.

einrechnen *v.t.* to include (in an account).
Einrede *f.* **(-, -n)** objection, exception; (*jur.*) plea.
einreden *v.t.* to talk into; ~ *v.i.* to remonstrate.
einregnen *v.i. eingeregnet sein,* to be caught in the rain; *es regnet sich ein,* the rain is settling in.
einreiben *v.t.st.* to rub into.
einreichen *v.t.* to hand in, to submit; *ein Gesuch* ~, to file *or* present a petition.
einreihen *v.t.* to range, to enroll.
einreihig *a.* (*Rock*) single-breasted.
Einreise *f.* **(-, -n)** entry; **~erlaubnis** *f.* entry permit.
einreisen *v.i.* to enter (country).
einreissen *v.t.st.* to pull down, to tear, to rend; ~ *v.i.st.* to become a habit.
einreiten *v.i.st.* to ride in; to break in.
einrenken *v.t.* to set (a bone); to arrange.
einrennen *v.t.st.* to force open by running against.
einrichten *v.t.* to arrange, to settle; (*Wohnung*) to furnish.
Einrichtung *f.* **(-, -en)** arrangement, institution; furniture.
Einrichtungsgegenstände *m.pl.* furnishings.
einritzen *v.t.* to carve.
einrosten *v.i. (s)* to get rusty.
einrücken *v.i. (s)* to march in(to), to enter; ~ *v.i.* to indent; to insert.
einrühren *v.t.* to stir in.
eins *a.* one.
Eins *f.* **(-, Einsen)** one, grade A.
einsacken *v.i.* to bag; to pocket; to sink in.
einsalzen *v.t.st.* to salt, to cure.
einsam *a.* lonely, solitary.
Einsamkeit *f.* **(-, 0)** solitude, loneliness.
einsammeln *v.t.* to pick up, to gather in, to collect.
Einsatz *m.* **(-[e]s, -sätze)** stake, pool; (*mil.*) commitment, employment.
Einsatzbefehl *m.* combat order.
Einsatzkommando *n.* task force.
Einsatzleiter *m.* head of operations.
Einsatzplan *m.* plan of action.
Einsatzzentrale *f.* operations center.
einsaugen *v.t.st.* to suck in; to absorb.
einsäumen *v.t.* to hem; to border.
einschalten *v.t.* to insert; (*el.*) to switch on; (*anderen Gang*) to put in another gear.
Einschaltquote *f.* ratings.
einschärfen *v.t.* (*fig.*) to impress.
einschätzen *v.t.* to assess; to estimate.
Einschätzung *f.* assessment, estimation.
einschäumen *v.t.* to lather.
einschenken *v.t.* to pour out, to fill; *einem reinen Wein* ~, to tell sb. the plain truth.
einscheren *v.i.* to move into a lane.
einschicken *v.t.* to send in.
einschieben *v.t.st.* to put in, to insert.
einschießen *v.r.st.* (*mil.*) to get the range.
einschiffen *v.t.* & *v.r.* to embark.
Einschiffung *f.* **(-, -en)** embarkation.
einschl. *einschließlich,* inclusive, incl.
einschlafen *v.i.st. (s)* to go to sleep, to fall asleep.
einschläfern *v.t.* to lull to sleep.
einschläfernd *a.* soporific.
Einschlag *m.* **(-[e]s, -schläge)** woof, weft; tuck; touch.
einschlagen *v.t.st.* to beat in; to break; to wrap up; *einen Weg* ~, to take a road; ~ *v.i.st.* (*Blitz*) to strike.
einschlägig *a.* relevant.
einschleichen *v.r.st.* to creep in.
einschleifen *v.t.* to cut in.
einschleppen *v.t.* (*Krankheit*) to introduce.
einschleusen *v.t.* to infiltrate.
einschließen *v.t.st.* to lock up; to enclose; (*fig.*) to include.
einschließlich *a.* inclusive.
Einschluß *m.* **(-schlusses, -schlüsse)** inclusion; *mit* ~ *von,* inclusive of, including.
einschmeicheln *v.r.* to ingratiate oneself.
einschmelzen *v.t.st.* to melt down.
einschmieren *v.t.* to cream; to grease, to oil.
einschmuggeln *v.t.* to smuggle.
einschnappen *v.i.* to click shut (lock or door); (*fig.*) to get into a huff.
einschneiden *v.i.st.* to cut; **~d** *a.* incisive, thorough.
einschneien *v.i.* to get snowed in.
Einschnitt *m.* **(-[e]s, -e)** incision; notch.
einschränken *v.t.* to confine; to restrain; ~ *v.r.* to retrench.
Einschränkung *f.* **(-, -en)** limitation, restriction; retrenchment.
einschrauben *v.t.* to screw in.
Einschreibe: ~brief *m.* registered letter; **~gebühr** *f.* registration fee.
einschreiben *v.t.st.* to register; ~ *v.r.* to enroll.
Einschreibung *f.* registration; enrollment.
einschreiten *v.i.st. (s)* to intervene.
einschrumpfen *v.i. (s)* to shrink up.
Einschub *m.* **(-[e]s, -schübe)** insertion.
einschüchtern *v.t.* to intimidate.
einschulen *v.t.* to start school.
Einschuss *m.* **(-es, -schüsse)** bullet wound.
einschütten *v.t.* to pour in.
einschweißen *v.t.* to weld in; to shrink-wrap.
einschwenken *v.i.* (*mil.*) to turn in.
einsegnen *v.t.* to consecrate; to confirm.
Einsegnung *f.* **(-, -en)** consecration, blessing; confirmation.
einsehen *v.t.st.* to look into, to look over; to understand, to see.
Einsehen *n.* **(-s, 0)** *ein* ~ *haben,* to be reasonable.
einseifen *v.t.* to soap; (*den Bart*) to lather; (*fig.*) to take in.
einseitig *a.* unilateral; partial, one-sided; biased.
einsenden *v.t.ir.* to send in.
einsetzen *v.t.* (*mil.*) to commit, to employ; (*Pflanze*) to set up; to insert; (*Geld*) to stake; (*Kraft*) to use; (*einen*) to appoint, to install; *einen zum Erben* ~, to make sb. one's heir; ~ *v.i.* to begin, to set in; ~ *v.r.* (*für*) to work hard (for).
Einsicht *f.* **(-, -en)** insight; intelligence.
einsichtig *a.* sensible, well-advised.
einsickern *v.i.* to seep in.
Einsiedler *m.* **(-s, -)** hermit, anchorite.
einsilbig *a.* monosyllabic; (*fig.*) taciturn.
einsinken *v.i.st. (s)* to sink in, to fall in.
einsitzig *a.* single-seated.
einspannen *v.t.* (*Pferde*) to harness.
einspännig *a.* drawn by one horse.
einsparen *v.t.* to save, to economize.
einspeichern *v.t.* (*comp.*) to feed in, to input.
einsperren *v.t.* to lock up; to imprison.
einsprachig *a.* monolingual.

einspringen *v.i.* *(s)* *helfend* ~, to lend a hand; *als Stellvertreter* ~, to step in for someone.
einspritzen *v.t.* to inject.
Einspritzmotor *m.* fuel-injection engine.
Einspritzung *f.* **(-, -en)** injection.
Einspruch *m.* protest, objection; appeal.
einsprühen *v.t.* to spray.
einspurig *a.* single-lane.
einst *adv.* once.
einstampfen *v.t.* to pulp.
Einstand *m.* start of a new job; debut (sports); deuce (tennis).
einstecken *v.t.* to pocket; to mail; to put in.
einstehen *v.i.st.* to answer for, to guarantee.
einsteigen *v.i.st.* *(s)* to get in; to get into, to enter; **~!** *i.* take your seats!
einstellbar *a.* (*mech.*) adjustable.
einstellen *v.t.* (*mech.*) to adjust; (*mil.*) to enlist; (*Radio*) to tune; (*Zahlungen*) to stop; *die Arbeit* ~, to strike; ~ *v.r.* to appear, to turn up.
einstellig *a.* one position.
Einstellplatz *m.* parking space.
Einstellung *f.* **(-, -en)** (*der Feindseligkeiten*) cessation; ~ *der Arbeit,* strike; enlistment; (*Zahlungen*) suspension; attitude, mentality.
Einstellungsgespräch *n.* job interview.
Einstich *m.* puncture, prick.
Einstieg *m.* entrance, entry; (*fig.*) start, beginning.
einstig *a.* future; ancient, former.
einstimmig *a.* unanimous; unison.
Einstimmigkeit *f.* **(-, 0)** unanimity.
einstmals *adv.* once, formerly.
einstöckig *a.* one-story.
einstoßen *v.t.st.* (*Tür*) to smash.
einstreichen *v.t.st.* to pocket.
einstreuen *v.t.* to intersperse.
einströmen *v.i.* to pour into.
einstudieren *v.t.* (*Theater*) to produce, to rehearse.
einstufen *v.t.* to classify; to categorize.
Einstufung *f.* categorization; classification.
einstündig *a.* one hour (duration).
einstürmen *v.t.* (*auf*) to assail.
Einsturz *m.* **(-es, -stürze)** collapse.
einstürzen *v.i.* *(s)* to collapse; to fall in.
einstweilen *adv.* for the time being; meanwhile.
einstweilig *a.* provisional, temporary; ~*e Verfügung f.* interim order.
eintägig *a.* one-day.
Eintänzer *m.* **(-s, -)** gigolo.
eintauchen *v.t.* to immerse, to dip, to steep; ~ *v.i.* to dive.
eintauschen *v.a.* to exchange.
einteilen *v.t.* to divide, to distribute.
Einteilung *f.* **(-, -en)** division; distribution; classification.
eintippen *v.t.* to type in; to key in.
eintönig *a.* monotonous.
Eintönigkeit *f.* monotony.
Eintopf *m.*, **Eintopfgericht** *n.* stew.
Eintracht *f.* **(-, 0)** concord; harmony.
einträchtig *a.* harmonious.
Eintrag *m.* **(-[e]s, -träge)** entry (in a book).
eintragen *v.t.st.* to enter, to yield.
einträglich *a.* profitable, lucrative.
Eintragung *f.* **(-, -en)** entry, registration.
eintreffen *v.i.st.* *(s)* to arrive; to happen.
Eintreffen *n.* arrival.
eintreiben *v.t.st.* (*Geld*) to call in, to collect.
eintreten *v.i.st.* *(s)* to enter, to join; (*für einen*) to intercede; (*Hindernisse*) to arise, to crop up.
eintrichtern *v.t.* to drum sth. in.
Eintritt *m.* **(-[e]s, 0)** entry, entrance; setting in; *freier* ~, free admission.
Eintrittsgeld *n.* admission fee.
Eintrittskarte *f.* ticket.
eintrocknen *v.i.* *(s)* to dry up, to shrivel.
eintrudeln *v.i.* (*fam.*) to drift in.
eintunken *v.t.* to dip, to steep.
einüben *v.t.* to practice, to drill, to train.
einverleiben *v.t.* to annex; to absorb.
Einverleibung *f.* **(-, -en)** annexation.
Einvernehmen *n.* **(-s, 0)** understanding; agreement; *im besten* ~ *mit einem,* on the best of terms with sb.
einverstanden *a.* agreed; *mit etwas* ~ *sein,* to agree to sth.
Einverständnis *n.* **(-ses, -se)** agreement, understanding.
Einwand *m.* **(-[e]s, -wände)** objection.
Einwanderer *m.* **(-s, -)** immigrant.
einwandern *v.i.* *(s)* to immigrate.
Einwanderung *f.* **(-, -en)** immigration.
einwandfrei *a.* flawless; perfect; unobjectionable; ~ *adv.* beyond doubt.
einwärts *adv.* inward, inwards.
einwechseln *v.t.* to change; to substitute (sports).
einwecken *v.t.* to preserve.
Einweckglas *n.* preserving jar.
Einwegflasche *f.* nonreturnable bottle.
Einwegspritze *f.* disposable syringe.
einweichen *v.t.* to soak.
einweihen *v.t.* to inaugurate, to consecrate; to initiate.
Einweihung *f.* **(-, -en)** opening.
einweisen *v.t.st.* to send; to hospitalize; to brief; to direct (car).
Einweisung *f.* admission to a hospital; introduction (work).
einwenden *v.t.ir.* to object; to reply.
einwerfen *v.t.st.* (*Scheiben*) to smash, to break; (*fig.*) to object; to insert (coin); to throw in (remark).
einwickeln *v.t.* to wrap up, to envelop; to take in.
einwilligen *v.t.* to consent, to agree.
Einwilligung *f.* **(-, -en)** consent, assent.
einwinken *v.t.* to guide in (plane); to direct (car).
einwirken *v.t.* to influence.
einwöchig *a.* one-week (duration); week-old.
Einwohner *m.* **(-s, -)**; **Einwohnerin** *f.* **(-, -nen)** inhabitant.
Einwohnermeldeamt *n.* residents' registration office.
Einwohnerschaft *f.* population.
Einwurf *m.* **(-[e]s, -würfe)** objection; insertion (mail); (*des Briefkastens*) slit, slot.
einwurzeln *v.i.* *(s)* to take root.
Einzahl *f.* **(-, 0)** singular (number).
einzahlen *v.t.* to pay in.
Einzahlung *f.* **(-, -en)** payment.
einzäunen *v.t.* to fence in.
Einzäunung *f.* **(-, -en)** enclosure, fence.
einzeichnen *v.t.* to mark.
einzeilig *a.* one-line; single-spaced.
Einzel *n.* **(-s, -)** singles (sports).
Einzelaktion *f.* independent action.
Einzelanfertigung *f.* custom-made article.
Einzelaufstellung *f.* itemized list.

Einzelausgabe *f.* separate edition.
Einzelbett *n.* single bed.
Einzelerscheinung *f.* isolated occurence.
Einzelexemplar *n.* unique speciman.
Einzelfall *m.* particular case.
Einzelgänger *m.;* **Einzelgängerin** *f.* loner
Einzelhaft *f.* **(-, 0)** solitary confinement.
Einzelhandel *m.* retail trade.
Einzelheit *f.* **(-, -en)** detail; particulars *pl.*
Einzelkind *n.* only child.
einzeln *a.* odd; single; individual; isolated.
Einzelstück *n.* individual piece.
Einzelverkauf *m.* **(-e[e]s, -verkäufe)** selling by retail.
Einzelwesen *n.* **(-s, -)** individual.
Einzelzelle *f.* single cell.
Einzelzimmer *n.* single-room.
Einziehdecke *f.* duvet.
einziehen *v.t.st.* to draw in; (*zur Strafe*) to confiscate; (*Münzen etc.*) to call in, to withdraw; (*Erkundigungen*) to make (inquiries); ~ *v.i.st. (s)* to march in; (*Haus*) to move into.
Einziehung *f.* **(-, -en)** confiscation; collection.
einzig *a.* only; single; sole; ~ *in seiner Art,* unique.
einzigartig *a. & adv.* unique(ly).
Einzigartigkeit *f.* uniqueness.
Einzimmerwohnung *f.* one-room apartment.
Einzug *m.* **(-[e]s, -züge)** entry, entrance; moving in.
Einzugsbereich *m.;* **Einzugsgebiet** *n.* catchment area; drainage basin.
Einzugsermächtigung *f.* standing order for a direct debit.
einzwängen *v.t.* to squeeze in.
Eis *n.* **(-es, 0)** ice; ice cream.
Eisbahn *f.* skating rink.
Eisbär *m.* polar bear.
Eisbein *n.* pig's knuckles.
Eisberg *m.* iceberg.
Eisbeutel *m.* ice bag.
Eisblume *f.* frost flower.
Eisbrecher *n.* icebreaker.
Eischnee *m.* beaten egg white.
Eisdiele *f.* **(-, -n)** ice-cream parlor.
Eisen *n.* **(-s, -)** iron.
Eisenbahn *f.* railway, railroad; **~abteil** *n.* railroad compartment; **~damm** *m.* embankment; **~endpunkt** *m.* railhead; **~netz** *n.* railroad network; **~schaffner** *m.* railroad conductor; **~wagen** *m.* railroad car.
Eisenbergwerk *n.* iron mine.
Eisenbeton *m.* ferroconcrete, reinforced concrete.
Eisenerz *n.* iron ore.
Eisengießerei *f.* iron-foundry.
Eisenkonstruktion *f.* steel frame.
Eisenmangel *m.* iron deficiency.
Eisensäge *f.* hacksaw.
Eisenstange *f.* iron bar.
Eisenträger *m.* iron girder.
Eisenwaren *pl.* hardware.
Eisenwarengeschäft *n.* hardware store.
Eisenzeit *f.* Iron Age.
eisern *a.* iron, of iron; **~er Vorhang** *m.* Iron Curtain.
Eisfach *n.* freezing compartment.
Eisgang *m.* icedrift.
eisig *a.* icy, glacial; chilly.
eiskalt *a.* icy cold.
Eiskübel *m.* ice bucket.
Eiskunstlauf *m.* figure skating.
Eislauf *m.* skating.
Eispickel *m.* ice pick.
Eisprung *m.* ovulation.
Eisregen *m.* sleet.
Eisrevue *f.* ice show.
Eisscholle *f.* ice floe.
Eisschrank *m.* refrigerator.
Eisstadion *n.* ice rink.
Eistanz *m.* ice dancing.
Eiswürfel *m.* ice cube.
Eiszapfen *m.* icicle.
Eiszeit *f.* ice age, glacial period.
eitel *a. & adv.* vain.
Eitelkeit *f.* **(-, -en)** vanity.
Eiter *m.* **(-s, 0)** pus.
eitern *v.i.* to suppurate.
eitrig *a.* suppurating.
Eiweiß *n.* **(-es, 0)** egg white, albumen; protein.
Eiweißbedarf *m.* protein requirement.
eiweißhaltig *a.* albuminous.
Eiweißmangel *m.* protein deficiency.
eiweißreich *a.* rich in protein.
Eizelle *f.* egg cell; ovum.
Ejakulation *f.* ejaculation.
Ekel *m.* **(-s, 0)** disgust; revulsion; ~ *n.* nasty person.
ekelerregend *a.* repulsive.
ekelhaft *a.* loathsome, disgusting.
ekeln *v.r.* to feel disgusted.
EKG *Elektrokardiogramm,* electrocardiogram, EKG, ECG.
Eklat *m.* sensation; scandal.
eklatant *a.* striking; scandalous.
eklig *a.* disgusting; nauseating.
Eklipse *f.* eclipse.
Ekstase *f.* **(-, -n)** ecstasy.
Ekzem *n.* **(-[e]s, -e)** eczema.
Elan *m.* verve; energy.
elastisch *a.* elastic.
Elastizität *f.* elasticity; suppleness.
Elch *m.* **(-[e]s, -e)** elk; moose.
Elefant *m.* **(-en, -en)** elephant.
elegant *a.* elegant, stylish; civilized.
Eleganz *f.* **(-, 0)** elegance.
Elegie *f.* **(-, -n)** elegy.
elegisch *a.* elegiac; mournful.
elektrifizieren *v.t.* to electrify.
Elektriker *m.* **(-s, -)** electrician.
elektrisch *a.* electric(al).
elektrisieren *v.t.* to electrify.
Elektrizität *f.* **(-, 0)** electricity.
Elektrizitätsversorgung *f.* power supply.
Elektrizitätswerk *n.* power station.
Elektroantrieb *m.* electric drive.
Elektroauto *n.* electric car.
Elektrode *f.* **(-, -n)** electrode.
Elektroenzephalogramm *n.* EEG; electroencephalogram.
Elektro: ~gerät *n.* electrical appliance; **~installateur** *m.* electrician; **~kardiogramm** *n.* EKG, electrocardiogram; **~konzern** *m.* electrical company; **~lyse** *f.* electrolysis; **~lyt** *m.* electrolyte;
Elektron *n.* **(-s, -en)** electron.
Elektronen: ~blitz *m.* electronic flash; **~hirn** *n.* electronic brain.
Elektronik *f.* electronics.
Elektrotechnik *f.* electrical engineering; **~er** *m.* electrical engineer.

Element *n.* **(-[e]s, -e)** element; rudiment; (*el.*) cell.
elementar *a.* elementary; primary.
Elementarkenntnisse *pl.* elementary knowledge.
Elementarteilchen *pl.* (*phys.*) elementary particle.
Elementarunterricht *m.* elementary instruction.
Elend *n.* **(-[e]s, 0)** misery; affliction.
elend *a.* miserable, wretched.
Elendsquartier *n.; **Elendsviertel** n.* slum.
Eleve *m.;* **Elevin** *f.* student (theater, ballet).
elf *a.* eleven.
Elfe *f.* **(-, -n)** elf, fairy.
Elfenbein *n.* **(-[e]s, 0)** ivory; **~turm** *m.* ivory tower.
Elfmeter *m.* penalty (soccer).
elftens *adv.* in the eleventh place.
eliminieren *v.t.* to eliminate.
elisabethanisch *a.* Elizabethan.
elitär *a.* elitist.
Elite *f.* elite.
Elitedenken *n.* elitism.
Elitetruppen *f.pl.* (*mil.*) crack troops.
Ellbogen *m.* **(-s, -)** elbow.
Elle *f.* **(-, -n)** ulna (anatomical); cubit (about 17 to 21 inches.).
ellenlang *a.* (*fam.*) interminable.
Ellipse *f.* **(-, -n)** ellipse; ellipsis.
elliptisch *a.* elliptical.
Elsaß *n.* **(-, 0)** Alsace.
Elsässer *m.;* **Elässerin** *f.;* **elsässisch** *a.* Alsatian.
Elster *f.* **(-, -n)** magpie.
elterlich *a.* parental.
Eltern *pl.* parents *pl.*
Eltern: ~abend *m.* parent-teacher meeting; **~beirat** *m.* parents association; **~teil** *m.* parent.
Email *n.* **(-s, 0)** enamel.
emaillieren *v.t.* to enamel.
Emanzipation *f.* emancipation.
Emanzipationsbewegung *f.* liberation movement.
emanzipieren *v.t.* to emancipate.
emanzipiert *a.* emancipated.
Embargo *n.* embargo.
Embolie *f.* embolism.
Embryo *m.* **(-s, -nen)** embryo.
embryonal *a.* embryonic.
Emigrant *m.;* **Emigrantin** *f.* emigrant; emigré.
emigrieren *v.i.* to emigrate.
Emission *f.* **(-, -en)** (*Finanz*) issue.
e-Moll *n.* E minor.
Emotion *f.* **(-, -en)** emotion.
emotional *a.* emotional.
Emotionalität *f.* emotionalism.
Empfang *m.* **(-[e]s, -pfänge)** reception, receipt.
empfangen *v.t.st.* to receive; ~ *v.i.st.* to conceive.
Empfänger *m.* **(-s, -); Empfängerin** *f.* **(-, -nen)** receiver, recipient; addressee; consignee.
empfänglich *a.* receptive; susceptible.
Empfängnis *f.* **(-, 0)** conception.
Empfängnisverhütung *f.* contraception; **empfängnisverhütendes Mittel** *n.* contraceptive.
Empfangs: ~dame *f.* receptionist; **~schein** *m.* receipt; **~zimmer** *n.* reception room, drawing room.
empfehlen *v.t.st.* to recommend; ~ *v.r.st.* to take leave; *~ Sie mich Ihrem Herrn Vater,* please remember me to your father.
empfehlenswert *a.* recommendable.
Empfehlung *f.* **(-, -en)** recommendation.
Empfehlungsbrief *m.;* **~Empfehlungsschreiben** *n.* letter of recommendation.
empfinden *v.t.st.* to feel, to perceive, to be sensible.
empfindlich *a.* sensible; sensitive, touchy; delicate; painful, grievous.
empfindsam *a.* sentimental; sensitive.
Empfindsamkeit *f.* sensitivity; sentimentality.
Empfindung *f.* **(-, -en)** perception, sensation, feeling.
empfindungslos *a.* insensible, unfeeling.
emphatisch *a.* emphatic(al).
empirisch *a.* empirical.
empor *adv.* upwards, on high, up, aloft.
emporarbeiten *v.r.* to work one's way up.
Empore *f.* gallery.
empören *v.t.* to revolt, to shock; ~ *v.r.* to rebel.
empörend *a.* outrageous; shocking.
Empörer *m.* **(-s, -)** insurgent, rebel.
emporkommen *v.i.st.* to rise in the world.
Emporkömmling *m.* **(-[e]s, -e)** upstart.
emporragen *v.i.* to tower; to rise up.
emporsteigen *v.i.st.* to rise aloft; to climb up.
empört *a.* outraged.
Empörung *f.* **(-, -en)** rebellion, revolt; indignation.
emsig *a.* assiduous, industrious, busy.
Emsigkeit *f.* industriousness, sedulousness.
E-Musik *f.* serious music.
en gros (*frz.*) *adv.* wholesale.
Endabrechnung *f.* final account.
Ende *n.* **(-s, -n)** end; close, conclusion; *zu ~ gehen,* to draw to an end.
Endeffekt *m. im ~,* in the end.
endemisch *a.* endemic.
enden *v.i.* & *v.r.* to end, to finish, to terminate, to conclude.
Endergebnis *n.* **(-ses, -se)** final result.
Endgeschwindigkeit *f.* **(-, -en)** terminal velocity.
endgültig *a.* definitive, final.
endigen *v.t.* to end, to finish.
Endivie *f.* **(-, -n)** chicory, endive.
Endkampf *m.* final battle.
Endlagerung *f.* ultimate disposal (of nuclear waste).
endlich *a.* finite; final, ultimate; ~ *adv.* at last, finally.
endlos *a.* endless, infinite.
endogen *a.* endogenous.
Endoskop *n.* endoscope.
Endphase *f.* final stages.
Endpunkt *m.* final point; terminus.
Endrunde *f.* final.
Endspurt *m.* final spurt.
Endstadium *n.* final stage; terminal stage.
Endstation *f.* terminus.
Endung *f.* **(-, -en)** ending, termination.
Endverbraucher *m.* end user.
Endzweck *m.* final purpose.
Energie *f.* **(-, -n)** energy.
Energie: ~bedarf *m.* energy requirement; **~gewinnung** *f.* energy production; **~haushalt** *m.* energy balance; **~quelle** *f.* energy source; **~verbrauch** *m.* energy consumption; **~verschwendung** *f.* waste of energy; **~versorgung** *f.* energy supply; **~wirtschaft** *f.* energy industry.
energisch *a.* energetic, vigorous.
eng *a.* narrow, tight, strait; strict.
engagieren *v.t.* to engage; ~ *v.r.* to commit os.; to become involved.

engagiert *a.* committed; involved.
enganliegend *a.* tight(-fitting).
Enge *f.* **(-, -n)** narrowness, tightness; *in die ~ treiben,* to drive into a corner.
Engel *m.* **(-s, -)** angel.
Engelsgeduld *f.* patience of a saint.
engherzig *a.* small-minded.
engl. *englisch,* English.
England *n.* **(-s, -)** England, Britain.
Engländer *m.* (*mech.*) monkey wrench; ~ *m.* **(-s, -)** Englishman; **Engländerin** *f.* **(-, -nen)** Englishwoman; **englisch** *a.* English, British.
Englisch *n.* **(-, 0)** English, the English language.
englisch-deutsch *a.* Anglo-German; English-German (dictionary).
Engpaß *m.* **(-es, -pässe)** pass; (*fig.*) bottleneck.
Engrospreis *m.* wholesale price.
engstirnig *a.* narrow-minded.
Engstirnigkeit *f.* narrow-mindedness.
Enkel *m.* **(-s, -)** grandson, grandchild.
Enkelin *f.* **(-, -nen)** granddaughter.
Enklave *f.* **(-, -n)** enclave.
enorm *a.* enormous, immense, huge.
en passant *adv.* in passing.
Ensemble *n.* ensemble; company; outfit.
entarten *v.i.* *(s)* to degenerate.
entartet *p. & a.* degenerate.
Entartung *f.* **(-, -en)** degeneration, degeneracy.
entäußern *v.r.* to renounce, to give up.
entbehren *v.t.* to lack, to be without; to want, to miss; to do without.
entbehrlich *a.* unnecessary, dispensable.
Entbehrung *f.* **(-, -en)** privation.
entbinden *v.t.st.* to deliver (a woman); to disengage; (*fig.*) to release.
Entbindung *f.* **(-, -en)** childbirth, delivery, confinement; disengagement.
Entbindungsklinik *f.* maternity clinic.
entblättern *v.t.* to take the leaves off; ~ *v.r.* to shed the leaves; (*fig.*) to strip.
entblößen *v.t.* to uncover.
entbrennen *v.i.st.* to break out, to flare up.
entdecken *v.t.* to discover, to detect.
Entdeckung *f.* **(-, -en)** discovery.
Ente *f.* **(-, -n)** duck; (*Zeitungs-*) canard.
entehren *v.t.* to dishonor; to violate.
entehrend *a.* disgraceful, degrading.
enteignen *v.t.* to expropriate.
Enteignung *f.* **(-, -en)** expropriation.
enteisen *v.t.* to de-ice.
Entenbraten *n.* roast duck.
Entenküken *n.* duckling.
Ententeich *m.* duck pond.
enterben *v.t.* to disinherit.
Enterhaken *m.* grapnel.
Enterich *m.* **(-s, -e)** drake.
entern *v.t.* to board, to grapple.
entfachen *v.t.* to kindle.
entfahren *v.i.st.* *(s)* to escape (sigh).
entfallen *v.i.st.* *(s)* ~ *auf jdn.* to be someone's share; *es ist mir ~,* I cannot remember.
entfalten *v.t.* to unfold; to develop; ~ *v.r.* to open, to expand.
entfärben *v.r.* to lose color; ~ *v.t.* to get the color out.
entfernen *v.t.* to remove; ~ *v.r.* to withdraw.
entfernt *a.* remote, distant; far from.
Entfernung *f.* **(-, -en)** removal; distance.
entfesseln *v.t.* to unchain, to let loose; to unleash.
entfetten *v.t.* to skim.
entflammen *v.t.* to inflame, to kindle.
entflechten *v.t.st.* to disentangle; to break up.
entfliehen *v.i.st.* *(s)* to run away; to escape.
entfremden *v.t.* to estrange, to alienate.
Entfremdung *f.* **(-, -en)** estrangement, alienation.
entfrosten *v.t.* to defrost.
entführen *v.t.* to hijack; to abduct; to elope with; (*Kinder*) to kidnap; *sich ~ lassen,* to elope (with sb.).
Entführer *m.* kidnapper, hijacker.
Entführung *f.* kidnapping; hijacking; abduction.
entgegen *pr.* against, contrary to, in opposition to.
entgegenarbeiten *v.t.* to counteract.
entgegengehen *v.i.st.* (*s*) to go to meet.
entgegengesetzt *a.* opposite, contrary.
entgegenhalten *v.t.st.* to object.
entgegenkommen *v.i.st.* *(s)* to come to meet; (*fig.*) to meet (half way).
entgegenkommend *a.* accommodating.
Entgegennahme *f.* **(-, 0)** receipt.
entgegennehmen *v.t.st.* to accept, to receive.
entgegensehen *v.i.st.* to look forward to.
entgegensetzen *v.t.* to oppose, to contrast.
entgegenstehen *v.i.st.* to be opposed.
entgegenstellen *v.t.* to oppose.
entgegentreten *v.i.st.* *(s)* (*fig.*) to oppose.
entgegenwirken *v.i.* to counteract.
entgegnen *v.i.* to reply, to retort.
Entgegnung *f.* **(-, -en)** reply; retort.
entgehen *v.i.st.* *(s)* to escape, to get off.
entgeistert *a.* dumbfounded; aghast.
Entgelt *n.* **(-[e]s, 0)** remuneration.
entgelten *v.t.st.* to pay for.
entgleisen *v.i.* *(s)* to run off the rails; (*fig.*) to make a slip.
Entgleisung *f.* **(-, -en)** derailment; slip.
entgleiten *v.i.st.* *(s)* to slip from.
entgräten *v.t.* to bone.
enthaaren *v.t.* to depilate, to remove hair.
enthalten *v.t.st.* to contain; ~ *v.r.st.* to abstain (from), to forbear.
enthaltsam *a.* abstemious, abstinent, continent.
Enthaltsamkeit *f.* **(-, 0)** abstinence.
Enthaltung *f.* abstention.
enthärten *v.t.* to soften.
enthaupten *v.t.* to behead, to decapitate.
enthäuten *v.t.* to skin.
entheben *v.t.st.* to remove (from office).
enthemmend *a.* disinhibitory.
enthemmt *a.* uninhibited.
enthüllen *v.t.* to unveil; to reveal.
Enthüllung *f.* **(-, -en)** unveiling (of a statue); (*fig.*) exposure, revelation.
enthülsen *v.t.* to shell.
Enthusiasmus *m.* enthusiasm.
enthusiastisch *a.* enthusiastic.
entjungfern *v.t.* to deflower.
entkalken *v.t.* to decalcify.
entkernen *v.t.* to core, to stone.
entkleiden *v.t.* to undress.
entkommen *v.i.st.* *(s)* to escape.
entkorken *v.t.* to uncork, to open.
entkräften *v.t.* invalidate; to refute; to weaken.
Entkräftung *f.* debility; exhaustion; refutation.
entkrampfen *v.t.* to ease; to relax.
entladen *v.t.st.* to unload; ~ *v.r.* to go off, to burst.

entlang *adv.* along.
entlarven *v.t.* to unmask; to expose.
entlassen *v.t.st.* to dismiss, to discharge.
Entlassung *f.* **(-, -en)** dismissal; *seine ~ nehmen,* to resign (one's office); *seine ~ beantragen,* to tender one's resignation.
entlasten *v.t.* to unburden, to exonerate, to credit.
Entlastung *f.* **(-, -en)** exoneration; defense.
Entlastungszeuge *m.* witness for the defense.
entlauben *v.t.* to strip (branch); to defoliate.
entlaufen *v.i.st. (s)* to run away.
entledigen *v.r.* to get rid (of); to acquit oneself (of one's duty).
entleeren *v.t.* to empty.
entlegen *a.* remote.
entlehnen *v.t.* to borrow.
entleihen *v.t.st.* to borrow (of, from).
Entleiher *m.* **(-s, -)** borrower.
entlocken *v.t.* to elicit, to draw from.
entlohnen *v.t.* to pay off.
entlüften *v.t.* to ventilate; (*tech.*) to bleed (brakes).
entmachten *v.t.* to deprive of power.
Entmachtung *f.* deprivation of power.
entmannen *v.t.* to castrate.
entmenscht *a.* inhuman, brutish.
entmilitarisieren *v.t.* to demilitarize.
Entmilitarisierung *f.* demilitarization.
entmündigen *v.t.* (*jur.*) to incapacitate; to disenfranchise.
Entmündigung *f.* incapacitation.
entmutigen *v.t.* to discourage.
Entmutigung *f.* discouragement.
Entnahme *f.* taking (samples); withdrawal (money); removal (organs).
entnehmen *v.t.st.* to take from; to gather (from); (*com.*) to draw upon.
entnerven *v.t.* to enervate.
entnervend *a.* nerve-racking.
entpuppen *v.r.* (*als*) to turn out to be.
enträtseln *v.t.* to decipher; to unriddle, to make out.
entrechten *v.t.* to deprive sb. of his/her rights.
entreißen *v.t.st.* to snatch away (from).
entrichten *v.t.* to pay.
entriegeln *v.t.* to unbolt.
entrinnen *v.i.st. (s)* to escape; *knapp ~,* to have a narrow escape.
entrollen *v.t.* to unroll, to unfurl.
entrosten *v.t.* to derust.
entrückt *a.* carried away; enraptured.
entrümpeln *v.t.* to clear out.
entrüsten *v.t.* to provoke, to exasperate; ~ *v.r.* to get indignant, to get angry.
Entrüstung *f.* **(-, 0)** indignation.
entsaften *v.t.* to extract the juice from.
Entsafter *m.* juicer.
entsagen *v.i.* to renounce, to waive.
Entsagung *f.* **(-, -en)** renunciation.
entschädigen *v.t.* to indemnify, to compensate; (*fig.*) to make up for.
Entschädigung *f.* **(-, -en)** compensation; indemnity; *~ leisten,* to make compensation for.
entschärfen *v.t.* to deactivate; to defuse; to tone down.
Entschärfung *f.* defusing; deactivation.
entscheiden *v.t.st.* to decide; ~ *v.r.st.* to come to a decision.
entscheidend *a.* decisive.
Entscheidung *f.* **(-, -en)** decision; ruling; *zur ~ bringen,* to bring to a head.
entschieden decided; resolute; definite.
Entschiedenheit *f.* **(-, 0)** determination; decisiveness.
entschlacken *v.t.* to purge; to purify.
entschlafen *v.i.st.* to pass away.
entschließen *v.r.st.* to resolve, to make up one's mind.
Entschließung *f.* **(-, -en)** resolution.
entschlossen *a.* resolute, determined.
Entschlossenheit *f.* determination; resolution.
entschlummern *v.i.* to fall asleep.
entschlüpfen *v.i. (s)* to escape; to slip out.
Entschluß *m.* **(-schlusses, -schlüsse)** resolution.
entschlüsseln *v.t.* to decipher; to decode.
Entschlüsselung *f.* deciphering; decoding.
entschuldbar *a.* excusable; pardonable.
entschuldigen *v.t.* to excuse; ~ *v.r.* to apologize.
Entschuldigung *f.* **(-, -en)** excuse, apology; *um ~ bitten,* to beg pardon.
entschwinden *v.i.st.* to vanish.
entsenden *v.t.ir.* to send off, to despatch.
entsetzen *v.t.* to depose; to relieve; ~ *v.r.* to be shocked.
Entsetzen *n.* **(-s, 0)** terror, horror.
entsetzlich *a.* horrible, terrible, dreadful.
entseuchen *v.t.* to decontaminate.
entsichern *v.t.* to release the safety catch.
entsiegeln *v.t.* to open, to unseal.
entsinnen *v.r.st.* to remember; to recall.
entsorgen *v.t.* to dispose of (waste).
Entsorgung *f.* waste disposal.
entspannen *v.i. or r.* to relax.
Entspannung *f.* **(-, 0)** relaxation; détente.
entspr. *entsprechend,* corresponding.
entsprechen *v.i.st.* to correspond to; to answer, to suit (a purpose).
entsprechend *a.* corresponding; suitable.
Entsprechung *f.* correspondence.
entspringen *v.i.st. (s)* to escape; to arise, to rise.
entstammen *v.i. (s)* to descend from.
entstehen *v.i.st. (s)* to begin, to originate, to arise; to result, to spring (from).
Entstehung *f.* **(-, -en)** origin, rise.
entsteinen *v.t.* to stone.
entstellen *v.t.* to disfigure, to deface; to misrepresent.
Entstellung *f.* **(-, -en)** distortion.
enttäuschen *v.t.* to disappoint.
Enttäuschung *f.* **(-, -en)** disappointment.
entthronen *v.t.* to dethrone.
entvölkern *v.t.* to depopulate.
entwachsen *v.i.st. (s)* to outgrow.
entwaffnen *v.t.* to disarm.
Entwarnung *f.* **(-, -en)** (*Luftschutz*) "all-clear" signal.
entwässern *v.t.* to drain.
Entwässerung *f.* drainage.
entweder *c.* *~... oder...,* either... or...
entweichen *v.i.st. (s)* to escape.
entweihen *v.t.* to profane, to desecrate.
entwenden *v.t.* to purloin, to embezzle.
entwerfen *v.t.st.* to sketch, to design.
entwerten *v.t.* to cancel; to devalue.
Entwertung *f.* **(-, -en)** cancellation, devaluation.
entwickeln *v.t.* to develop.
Entwicklung *f.* **(-, -en)** development; evolution; (*phot.*) developing.
Entwicklungs: ~abteilung *f.* planning depart-

ment; **~dienst** *m.* development aid service; **~geschichte** *f.* developmental history; evolution; **~hilfe** *f.* development aid; **~land** *n.* developing country; **~störung** *f.* developmental disturbance.

entwirren *v.t.* to unravel, to disentangle.

entwischen *v.i. (s)* to escape.

entwöhnen *v.t.* to disaccustom; to wean (a child).

entwölken *v.r.* to clear up.

entwürdigen *v.t.* to disgrace, to degrade.

Entwurf *m.* **(-[e]s, -würfe)** sketch, draft, blueprint; *erster ~*, rough draft.

entwurzeln *v.t.* to uproot.

entziehen *v.t.st.* to take away; to deprive of; ~ *v.r.* to withdraw.

Entziehung *f.* withdrawal.

Entziehungskur *f.* withdrawal treatment.

entzifferbar *a.* decipherable.

entziffern *v.t.* to decipher.

entzücken *v.t.* to delight; to enrapture, to charm.

Entzücken *n.* delight.

entzückt *a.* delighted.

Entzückung *f.* **(-, -en)** transport.

Entzug *m.* withdrawal.

Entzugserscheinung *f.* withdrawal symptom.

entzündbar *a.* inflammable.

entzünden *v.t.* to kindle, to set on fire; (*fig.*) to inflame; ~ *v.r.* to catch fire.

entzündlich *a.* inflammable; (*med.*) inflammatory.

Entzündung *f.* **(-, -en)** inflammation.

entzwei *adv.* in two, in pieces; broken.

entzweien *v.t.* to disunite, to set at variance; ~ *v.r.* to fall out.

entzweigehen *v.i.st.* to break (down).

Enzian *m.* **(-[e]s, -e)** (*bot.*) gentian.

Enzyklopädie *f.* encyclopedia.

enzyklopädisch *a.* encyclopedic.

Enzym *n.* enzyme.

Epaulett *n.* **(-s, -s)** épaulet.

Epheu = Efeu *n.* ivy.

Epidemie *f.* **(-, -[e]n)** epidemic.

epidemisch *a.* epidemic.

Epigramm *n.* **(-s, -e)** epigram.

Epik *f.* epic poetry.

Epilepsie *f.* **(-, 0)** epilepsy.

epileptisch *a.* epileptic.

Epilog *m.* **(-[e]s, -e)** epilogue.

episch *a.* epic.

Episkopat *n.* episcopate.

Episode *f.* **(-, -n)** episode.

episodenhaft *a.* episodic.

Epistel *f.* **(-, -n)** epistle.

Epizentrum *n.* epicenter.

epochal *a.* epochal; epoch-making.

Epoche *f.* **(-, -n)** epoch.

epoche-machend *a.* epoch-making.

Epos *n.* **(-, Epen)** epic poem; epos.

Equipage *f.* **(-, -n)** carriage.

er *pn.* he; ~ *selbst*, he himself.

erachten *v.t.* to consider, to think, to judge.

Erachten *n.* **(-s, 0)** opinion; *meines ~s*, in my opinion, for all I know.

erahnen *v.t.* to suspect; to imagine.

erarbeiten *v.t.* to obtain by labor.

erb. *erbaut*, built.

Erbanlage *f.* hereditary disposition.

erbarmen *v.r.* to pity.

Erbarmen *n.* **(-s, 0)** mercy; commiseration, pity.

erbarmenswert, erbarmenswürdig *a.* pitiable.

erbärmlich *a.* wretched; miserable, pitiful.

erbarmungslos *a.* merciless; pitiless, remorseless.

erbauen *v.t.* to build, to erect; (*fig.*) to edify; ~ *v.r.* to be edified; *sich ~ an etw.*, to find pleasure in sth.

Erbauer *m.* **(-s, -)** builder, founder.

erbaulich *a.* edifying.

erbberechtigt *a.* entitled to inherit.

Erbe *m.* **(-n, -n)** heir; *gesetzlicher ~*, legal heir; heir-at-law; *mutmaßlicher ~*, heir presumptive; ~ *n.* **(-s, 0)** inheritance; heritage.

erbeben *v.i.* to tremble, to shake.

Erbeigenschaft *f.* hereditary characteristic.

erben *v.t.* to inherit, to succeed to.

erbetteln *v.t.* to get by begging.

erbeuten *v.t.* to capture.

Erbfall *m.* case of succession, heritage.

Erbfolge *f.* hereditary succession.

Erbforschung *f.* genetics.

Erbgut *n.* hereditary make-up.

erbieten *v.r.* to volunteer.

Erbin *f.* **(-, -nen)** heiress.

erbitten *v.t.st.* to request, to solicit.

erbittern *v.t.* to exasperate, to provoke.

erbittert *a. & adv.* bitter.

Erbitterung *f.* **(-, -en)** exasperation, bitterness.

Erbkrankheit *f.* hereditary disease.

erblassen *v.i. (s)* to turn pale, to pale.

Erblasser *m.* **(-s, -)** testator.

erbleichen *v.i.st. (s)* to pale.

erblich *a.* hereditary.

erblicken *v.t.* to see, to discover.

erblinden *v.i. (s)* to go blind.

erblühen *v.i. (s)* to bloom; to blossom.

Erbmasse *f.* genotype; genetic make-up; (*jur.*) estate.

erbost *a.* angry; furious.

Erbpacht *f.* hereditary lease.

erbrechen *v.t.st.* to break open; ~ *v.r.* to vomit.

Erbrechen *n.* **(-s, 0)** vomiting.

Erbrecht *n.* law of inheritance.

erbringen *v.t.ir.* to produce.

Erbschaden *m.* hereditary defect.

Erbschaft *f.* **(-, -en)** inheritance.

Erbschaftssteuer *f.* estate/death duties.

Erbschleicher *m.* legacy hunter.

Erbse *f.* **(-, -n)** pea.

Erbstück *n.* heirloom.

Erbsünde *f.* original sin.

Erbteil *n.* portion (of an inheritance).

Erdanziehung *f.* earth's gravity.

Erdapfel *m.* potato.

Erdball *m.* globe.

Erdbeben *n.* earthquake.

Erdbeere *f.* strawberry.

Erdboden *m.* ground, soil; earth.

Erde *f.* **(-, -n)** earth; world; ground, soil; (*fam.*) floor; (*fig.*) dust, clay; (*el.*) earth, ground.

erden *v.t.* to earth, to ground.

Erdenbürger *m.* earth dweller.

erdenken *v.t.ir.* to imagine.

erdenklich *a.* imaginable, conceivable.

Erdgas *n.* natural gas.

Erdgeschoß *n.* ground floor.

erdichten *v.t.* to invent, to feign.

Erdkabel *n.* underground cable.

Erdkreis *m.* globe.

Erdkugel *f.* globe.

Erdkunde *f.* geography.

Erdnuß *f.* peanut; groundnut.
Erdöl *n.* petroleum.
erdolchen *v.t.* to stab.
Erdölraffinerie *f.* oil refinery.
Erdreich *n.* earth; soil.
erdreisten *v.r.* to make bold.
erdrosseln *v.t.* to strangle, to throttle.
erdrücken *v.t.* to crush; to overwhelm.
erdrückend *a.* overwhelming.
Erdrutsch *m.* landslide; land slip.
Erdteil *m.* continent.
Erdtruppen *f.pl.* ground forces.
erdulden *v.t.* to suffer, to endure.
Erdumdrehung *f.* rotation of the earth.
Erdumfang *m.* circumference of the earth.
Erdumlaufbahn *f.* orbit.
Erdung *f.* grounding.
Erdzeitalter *n.* geological era.
ereifern *v.r.* to get excited.
ereignen *v.r.* to happen, to occur.
Ereignis *n.* **(-ses, -se)** occurrence, event.
ereignislos *a.* uneventful.
ereignisreich *a.* eventful.
ereilen *v.t.* to catch up.
Erektion *f.* erection.
Eremit *m.* **(-en, -en)** hermit.
ererben *v.t.* to inherit.
erfahren *v.t.st.* to experience, to suffer; to learn, to hear; ~ *a.* experienced, expert; conversant (with).
Erfahrung *f.* **(-, -en)** experience; knowledge; practice; *in ~ bringen,* to learn, to be informed, to find out.
erfassen *v.t.* to comprehend, to grasp; to catch.
Erfassung *f.* registration.
erfinden *v.t.st.* to invent; to make up.
Erfinder *m.* **(-s, -)** inventor.
erfinderisch *a.* inventive.
Erfindung *f.* **(-, -en)** invention.
Erfindungsgabe *f.* inventiveness.
erfindungsreich *a.* imaginative.
erflehen *v.t.* to implore.
Erfolg *m.* **(-[e]s, -e)** result, effect, success.
erfolgen *v.i. (s)* to take place; to happen.
erfolglos *a.* unsuccessful, vain.
erfolgreich *a.* successful.
erfolgversprechend *a.* promising.
erforderlich *a.* necessary, required.
erfordern *v.t.* to demand, to require.
Erfordernis *n.* **(-ses, -se)** requirement, demand.
erforschen *v.t.* to explore, to investigate.
Erforschung *f.* **(-, -en)** exploration.
erfragen *v.t.* to ascertain by inquiry.
erfreuen *v.t. & r.* to rejoice; to cheer, to please.
erfreulich *a.* pleasant; encouraging.
erfreulicherweise *adv.* fortunately.
erfrieren *v.i.st. (s)* to freeze (to death).
Erfrierung *f.* frostbite.
erfrischen *v.t.* to refresh.
erfrischend *a.* refreshing.
Erfrischung *f.* **(-, -en)** refreshment.
erfüllen *v.t.* to fulfil; to accomplish; *seine Pflicht ~,* to do one's duty; *ein Versprechen ~,* to keep a promise.
Erfüllung *f.* **(-, 0)** fulfilment, accomplishment; *in ~ gehen,* to come true.
Erfüllungsort *m.* settling place.
ergänzen *v.t.* to complete, to supply.
ergänzend *a.* supplementary.
Ergänzung *f.* **(-, -en)** supplement; supplementation.
ergattern *v.t.* to get hold of.
ergeben *v.t.st.* to yield, to produce; ~ *v.r.* to surrender; to result; to devote oneself.
ergeben *a.* devoted, addicted; obedient.
ergebenst *adv.* very truly yours.
Ergebnis *n.* **(-ses, -se)** result.
ergebnislos *a.* without result.
Ergebung *f.* **(-, 0)** surrender; submission, resignation.
ergehen *v.i.st. es wird ihm schlimm ~,* he will suffer for it; *~ lassen,* to issue, to promulgate; *über sich ~ lassen,* to submit to.
ergiebig *a.* productive; fertile, rich.
ergießen *v.r.* to fall (into); to pour.
ergötzen *v.t.* to amuse, to delight; ~ *v.r.* to enjoy oneself.
ergötzlich *a.* delightful, amusing.
ergrauen *v.i.* to turn grey.
ergreifen *v.t.st.* to seize, to take up; (*Flucht*) to take to flight; (*Partei*) to side with; to affect.
ergreifend *a.* moving.
Ergreifung *f.* capture; seizure.
ergriffen *a.* moved; struck, affected.
ergründen *v.t.* to get to the bottom of.
Erguß *m.* **(-gusses, -güsse)** (*fig.*) effusion; *Blut ~,* bruise; *Samen ~,* ejaculation.
erhaben *a.* raised, elevated; sublime.
Erhalt *m.* receipt.
erhalten *v.t.st.* to maintain; to sustain; to preserve; to receive, to get; to obtain; ~ *v.r.* to live *or* subsist on.
erhältlich *a.* obtainable.
Erhaltung *f.* **(-, 0)** preservation, conservation; maintenance.
erhängen *v.r.* to hang oneself.
erhärten *v.t.* to substantiate; to strengthen.
erhaschen *v.t.* to catch, to seize.
erheben *v.t.st.* to lift up; to elevate, to raise; to extoll, to praise; ~ *v.r.st.* to rise; *ein Geschrei ~,* to raise an outcry; *die Frage ~,* to raise the question; *Geld ~,* to raise money; *ins Quadrat ~,* to square.
erheblich *a.* considerable.
Erheblichkeit *f.* **(-, 0)** relevance.
Erhebung *f.* **(-, -en)** elevation; promotion; (*Steuer*) levy; (*Nachforschung*) inquiry; (*Aufstand*) insurrection.
erheitern *v.t.* to cheer, to exhilarate.
Erheiterung *f.* **(-, -en)** amusement, diversion.
erhellen *v.t.* to light up, to clear up; ~ *v.i.* to become evident.
erheucheln *v.t.* to feign.
erhitzen *v.t.* to heat; ~ *v.r.* to grow hot; (*fig.*) to get angry.
erhoffen *v.t.* to hope for.
erhöhen *v.t.* to heighten; to enhance; to raise, to increase.
Erhöhung *f.* **(-, -en)** rise, increase.
erholen *v.r.* to recover.
erholsam *a.* restful.
Erholung *f.* **(-, -en)** recovery; recreation.
Erholungsstätte *f.* rest center.
erhören *v.t.* to hear; to grant.
erigieren *v.i.* to become erect.
Erika *f.* (*bot.*) heather.
erinnerlich *a. soviel mir ~ ist,* so far as I can recollect.

erinnern *v.t.* to remind; ~ *v.r.* to remember; to recollect.
Erinnerung *f.* **(-, -en)** remembrance; reminiscence.
Erinnerungslücke *f.* gap in one's memory.
Erinnerungswert *m.* sentimental value.
erjagen *v.t.* to get (by hunting).
erkalten *v.i. (s)* to cool down.
erkälten *v.r.* to catch (a) cold.
Erkältung *f.* **(-, -en)** cold.
erkämpfen *v.t.* to gain by fighting.
erkennbar *a.* recognizable; visible; discernible.
erkennen *v.t.st.* to perceive; to discern; to realize, to see; to know; to recognize; to decide.
erkenntlich *a.* grateful.
Erkenntnis *f.* **(-ses, -se)** knowledge; cognition; perception.
Erkennungs: ~dienst *m.* police records department; **~melodie** *f.* theme music; signature tune; **~zeichen** *n.* sign.
Erker *m.* **(-s, -)** oriel; **~fenster** *n.* bay window.
erklärbar *a.* explicable.
erklären *v.t.* to explain, to interpret; to declare; to account for; ~ *v.r.* to declare oneself.
erklärend *a.* explanatory.
erklärlich *a.* explicable; *leicht* ~, easily accounted for, easily explained.
erklärt *a.* professed; sworn.
erklärtermaßen *adv.* professedly.
Erklärung *f.* **(-, -en)** explanation; declaration.
erklecklich *a.* considerable.
erklettern *v.t.* to climb to the top.
erklimmen *v.t.* to climb.
erklingen *v.i.st. (s)* to resound, to ring.
erkranken *v.i. (s)* to fall ill, to become sick.
Erkrankung *f.* **(-, -en)** illness, sickness, disease.
erkühnen *v.r.* to dare.
erkunden *v.t.* to explore; to find out; (*mil.*) to reconnoiter.
erkundigen *v.r.* to make inquiries.
Erkundigung *f.* **(-, -en)** inquiry.
erlahmen *v.i. (s)* to get tired or weak.
erlangen *v.t.* to attain; to obtain.
Erlaß *m.* **(-lasses, -lasse)** remission, pardon; decree.
erlassen *v.t.st.* to issue; (*Gesetz*) to enact; (*nachlassen*) to remit.
erlauben *v.t.* to permit, to allow.
Erlaubnis *f.* **(-, 0)** permission, leave; *mit* ~ *von,* by permission of.
erläutern *v.t.* to illustrate, to elucidate; to explain; to annotate.
Erläuterung *f.* **(-, -en)** explanation; illustration.
Erle *f.* **(-, -n)** alder.
erleben *v.t.* to live to see; to experience.
Erlebnis *n.* **(-ses, -se)** experience.
erledigen *v.t.* to deal with; carry out; to settle; ~ *v.r.* to be settled.
erledigt *a.* finished; settled.
Erledigung *f.* **(-, -en)** settlement; execution (of work); errand.
erlegen *v.t.* to kill.
erleichtern *v.t.* to facilitate; to lighten, to ease; to alleviate.
Erleichterung *f.* **(-, -en)** relief; facilitation; (*von Bestimmungen*) relaxation.
erleiden *v.t.st.* to suffer, to bear.
erlernen *v.t.* to learn.
erlesen *a.* select, choice.
erleuchten *v.t.* to illuminate; to enlighten.
Erleuchtung *f.* **(-, -en)** illumination.
erliegen *v.i.st. (s)* to succumb.
erlogen *a.* false, untrue, forged.
Erlös *m.* **(-ses, -se)** proceeds *pl.*
erlöschen *v.t.* to extinguish; ~ *v.i.st. (s)* to go out; to become void.
erlösen *v.t.* to redeem, to deliver.
Erlöser *m.* **(-s, -)** Redeemer, Saviour.
Erlösung *f.* **(-, -en)** redemption.
ermächtigen *v.t.* to empower, to authorize.
Ermächtigung *f.* **(-, -en)** authorization; **~sgesetz** *n.* enabling act.
ermahnen *v.t.* to admonish.
Ermahnung *f.* **(-, -en)** admonition, exhortation.
ermangeln *v.i.* to be wanting; to fail.
Ermangelung *f.* **(-, 0)** *in* ~ *von,* in default of.
ermäßigen *v.t.* to abate, to reduce; *zu ermässigten Preisen,* at reduced rates.
Ermäßigung *f.* **(-, -en)** reduction; abatement.
ermatten *v.i. (s)* to grow tired, to slacken.
ermessen *v.t.st.* to measure; to judge.
Ermessen *n.* **(-s, 0)** judgment; *nach meinem* ~, in my opinion.
Ermessens: ~frage *f.* matter of opinion; **~spielraum** *m.* latitude.
ermitteln *v.t.* to find out, to ascertain.
Ermittlung *f.* **(-, -en)** inquiry.
Ermittlungs: ~beamte *m.;* **~beamtin** *f.* investigating officer.
ermöglichen *v.t.* to enable; to render possible.
ermorden *v.t.* to murder; (*pol.*) to assassinate.
Ermordung *f.* **(-, -en)** murder; (*pol.*) assassination.
ermüden *v.t.* to tire, to fatigue; ~ *v.i. (s)* to get tired.
ermüdend *a.* tiring.
Ermüdung *f.* **(-, -en)** exhaustion.
ermuntern *v.t.* to encourage; to animate.
ermutigen *v.t.* to encourage.
ermutigend *a.* encouraging.
Ermutigung *f.* **(-, -en)** encouragement.
ernähren *v.t.* to nourish; to support.
Ernährer *m.;* **Ernährerin** *f.* provider; supporter.
Ernährung *f.* **(-, -en)** nutrition.
Ernährungsweise *f.* diet.
Ernährungswissenschaft *f.* dietetics.
ernennen *v.t.st.* to nominate, to appoint.
Ernennung *f.* **(-, -en)** appointment.
erneuen, erneuern *v.t.* to renew, to renovate; to replace.
Erneuerung *f.* **(-, -en)** renovation; replacement; renewal; revival.
erneut *a.* renewed; once again.
erniedrigen *v.t.* to lower; to humble; ~ *v.r.* to degrade oneself.
erniedrigend *a.* humiliating.
Erniedrigung *f.* humiliation.
Ernst *m.* **(-es, 0)** seriousness.
ernst *a.* earnest, serious, grave, stern; *etwas* ~ *nehmen,* to take sth. seriously.
Ernstfall *m.* emergency; (*mil.*) case of war; *im* ~, in case of emergency.
ernstgemeint *a.* serious; sincere.
ernsthaft *a.* serious, grave.
Ernsthaftigkeit *f.* seriousness.
ernstlich *a.* earnest, serious.
Ernte *f.* **(-, -n)** harvest; (*Ertrag*) crop.
Ernte: ~ausfall *m.* crop failure; **~dankfest** *n.* harvest festival; **~ertrag** *m.* yield; **~maschine** *f.* harvester.

ernten *v.t.* to reap, to harvest.
ernüchtern *v.t.* to sober, to disillusion.
Ernüchterung *f.* disillusionment.
Eroberer *m.* **(-s, -); Eroberin** *f.* **(-, -nen)** conqueror.
erobern *v.t.* to conquer.
Eroberung *f.* **(-, -en)** conquest.
eröffnen *v.t.* to open, to begin; to inaugurate; (*fig.*) to disclose, to make known.
Eröffnung *f.* **(-, -en)** opening, beginning; communication.
Eröffnungsausprache *f.* opening speech.
Eröffnungsfeier *f.* opening ceremony.
erogen *a.* erogenous.
erörtern *v.t.* to discuss.
Erörterung *f.* **(-, -en)** discussion.
Erosion *f.* **(-, -en)** erosion.
Erotik *f.* eroticism.
erotisch *a.* erotic.
Erpel *m.* drake.
erpicht *a.* keen on; bent (on).
erpressen *v.t.* to blackmail; to extort.
erpresserisch *a.* blackmailing.
Erpressung *f.* **(-, -en)** extortion; blackmail.
erproben *v.t.* to try, test.
Erprobung *f.* testing.
erquicken *v.t.* to refresh.
erraten *v.t.* to guess, to divine.
errechnen *v.t.* to compute.
erregbar *a.* excitable; irritable.
erregen *v.t.* to stir up, to arouse; to excite; to provoke; to produce.
erregend *a.* exciting; arousing.
Erreger *m.* (*med.*) pathogen.
erregt *a.* excited; aroused.
Erregung *f.* (**-, -en**) excitement; arousal.
erreichbar *a.* attainable; within reach.
erreichen *v.t.* to attain, to reach.
erretten *v.t.* to save, to rescue (from).
Erretter *m.* savior.
Errettung *f.* **(-, -en)** deliverance.
errichten *v.t.* to build; to erect; to establish.
Errichtung *f.* **(-, -en)** erection; establishment.
erringen *v.t.st.* to gain; to win.
erröten *v.i.* *(s)* to blush.
Errungenschaft *f.* **(-, -en)** achievement; acquisition.
Ersatz *m.* **(-es, 0)** substitute; compensation, reparation; amends *pl.*
Ersatz: ~anspruch *m.* right of compensation; **~batterie** *f.* spare battery; **~handlung** *f.* (psych.) displacement activity; **~rad** *n.* (*mot.*) spare wheel; **~reifen** *m.* spare tire; **~stoff** *m.* substitute; **~teil** *m.* spare (part).
ersaufen *v.i.st.* (*fam.*) to drown.
ersäufen *v.t.* to drown.
erschaffen *v.t.st.* to create.
Erschaffung *f.* **(-, 0)** creation.
erschauern *v.i.* to tremble; to shudder.
erscheinen *v.i.st.* *(s)* to appear; (*Buch*) to come out.
Erscheinung *f.* **(-, -en)** appearance; apparition; phenomenon; symptom.
Erscheinungsjahr *n.* year of publication.
erschellen *v.i.* to sound.
erschießen *v.t.st.* to shoot (dead).
Erschießung *f.* shooting; (*mil.*) execution.
Erschießungskommando *n.* firing squad.
erschlaffen *v.i.* *(s)* to slacken.
erschlagen *v.t.st.* to slay.
erschlichen *a.* surreptitious.
erschließen *v.t.st.* to make accessible.
erschöpfen *v.t.* to exhaust.
erschöpfend *a.* exhaustive.
erschöpft *a.* exhausted.
Erschöpfung *f.* **(-, 0)** exhaustion.
erschrecken *v.t.* to frighten, to startle; ~ *v.i.st.* *(s)* to be frightened.
erschrocken *a.* frightened, terrified.
erschüttern *v.t.* to shake, to shock.
erschütternd *a.* deeply distressing; shocking.
Erschütterung *f.* **(-, -en)** shock; (*fig.*) emotion.
erschweren *v.t.* to aggravate.
erschwerend *a.* complicating; aggravating.
erschwindeln *v.t.* to swindle.
erschwingen *v.t.st.* to afford.
erschwinglich *a.* reasonable; affordable.
ersehen *v.t.st.* to see, to find; to choose.
ersehnen *v.t.* to long for.
ersetzbar *a.* replaceable.
ersetzen *v.t.* to replace, to repair, to compensate; to refund.
Ersetzung *f.* reimbursement; compensation (damage).
ersichtlich *a.* evident, apparent.
ersinnen *v.t.st.* to devise.
ersparen *v.t.* to spare, to save.
Ersparnis *f.* **(-ses, -se)** savings *pl.*
ersprießlich *a.* useful, beneficial.
erst *adv.* first, at first; not until, only.
erstarken *v.i.* *(s)* to grow strong.
erstarren *v.i.* *(s)* to grow stiff *or* numb.
erstatten *v.t.* to reimburse; *Bericht* ~, to report (on).
Erstattung *f.* **(-, -en)** reimbursement.
Erstaufführung *f.* **(-, -en)** premiere; opening night.
erstaunen *v.i.* *(s)* to amaze; to be astonished.
Erstaunen *n.* **(-s, 0)** amazement; astonishment.
erstaunlich *a.* astonishing, amazing.
erstaunlicherweise *adv.* amazingly.
erstaunt *a.* astonished; amazed.
erstechen *v.t.st.* to stab.
erstehen *v.i.st.* *(s)* to arise; ~ *v.t.st.* to buy.
Erste-Hilfe-Ausrüstung *f.* first-aid kit.
ersteigen *v.t.st.* to ascend, to climb.
ersteigern *v.t.* to buy at an auction.
Ersteigung *f.* ascent.
erstens *adv.* firstly, in the first place.
erstgeboren *a.* firstborn.
Erstgeburt *f.* **(-, -en)** primogeniture.
ersticken *v.t.* to suffocate, to choke; ~ *v.i.* *(s)* to be suffocated.
Erstickung *f.* suffocation; asphyxiation.
erstklassig *a.* first-rate.
erstlich *adv.* firstly, at first.
Erstling *m.* first work.
erstmalig *a.* first; ~ *adv.* for the first time.
erstrahlen *v.i.* to shine.
erstreben *v.t.* to strive after.
erstrebenswert *a.* desirable.
erstrecken *v.r.* to extend; to stretch.
Erstschlag *m.* first strike.
erstürmen *v.t.* to take by storm.
ersuchen *v.t.* to request, to beg.
ertappen *v.t.* to surprise, to catch; *bei der Tat* ~, to catch in the act.
erteilen *v.t.* to impart, to confer; (*Verweis*) to administer.

Erteilung *f.* granting.
ertönen *v.i. (s)* to (re)sound.
Ertrag *m.* **(-[e]s, -träge)** produce, yield; proceeds *pl.;* returns *pl.*
ertragen *v.t.st.* (*fig.*) to bear, to endure.
Ertragfähigkeit *f.* productiveness.
erträglich *a.* tolerable, endurable.
ertränken *v.t.* to drown.
erträumen *v.r.* to dream of.
ertrinken *v.i.st. (s)* to drown.
Ertrinkende *m./f.* drowning person.
Ertrunkene *m./f.* drowned person.
ertüchtigen *v.t.* to train.
erübrigen *v.t.* to save, to spare; to remain; ~ *v.r.* to be unnecessary.
eruieren *v.t.* to find out.
Erw. *Erwachsene,* adults.
Erwachen *n.* awakening.
erwachen *v.i. (s)* to awake.
erwachsen *v.i.st. (s)* to accrue; ~ *a.* grown-up.
Erwachsenenbildung *f.* adult education.
Erwachsene[r] *m.* **(-n, -n)** adult, grown-up person.
erwägen *v.t.st.* (*fig.*) to weigh, to consider.
Erwägung *f.* **(-, -en)** consideration; *in ~ ziehen,* to take into consideration; *in ~ daß,* considering, seeing that...
erwählen *v.t.* to choose, to elect.
erwähnen *v.t.* to mention.
erwähnenswert *a.* worth mentioning.
Erwähnung *f.* **(-, -en)** mention.
erwärmen *v.t.* to warm, to heat.
erwarten *v.t.* to expect; to wait for, to await.
Erwartung *f.* **(-, -en)** expectation.
erwartungs: ~gemäß *a.* as expected; **~voll** *a.* expectant.
erwecken *v.t.* to awaken.
Erweckung *f.* **(-, -en)** awakening.
erwehren *v.r.* to fend off.
erweichen *v.t.* to soften, to mollify.
erweisen *v.t.st.* to prove, to render; (*eine Gunst*) to bestow upon; *sich ~ als,* to turn out to be.
erweitern *v.t.* to widen, to enlarge; to expand; to extend, to amplify.
Erweiterung *f.* **(-, -en)** enlargement; amplification, expansion; extension.
Erwerb *m.* **(-[e]s, 0)** acquisition; gain, earnings *pl.;* living.
erwerben *v.t.st.* to acquire, to gain.
erwerbsfähig *a.* able-bodied, capable of earning one's living.
Erwerbsleben *n.* working life.
erwerbslos *a.* unemployed.
Erwerbslosenunterstützung *f.* **(-, 0)** unemployment benefit, dole.
Erwerbslosigkeit *f.* **(-, 0)** unemployment.
erwerbsunfähig *a.* unable to work.
Erwerbung *f.* **(-, -en)** acquisition.
erwidern *v.t.* to return; to reply.
Erwiderung *f.* **(-, -en)** return; reply.
erwiesen *a.* proved.
erwiesenermaßen *adv.* as has been proved.
erwirken *v.t.* to procure.
erwirtschaften *v.t.* to make.
erwischen *v.t.* to catch.
erwünscht *a.* desired, welcome.
erwürgen *v.t.* to strangle, to throttle.
Erz *n.* **(-es, -e)** ore.
erzählen *v.t.* to tell, to narrate, to relate.
erzählend *a.* narrative.
erzählerisch *a.* narrative.
Erzählkunst *f.* narrative art.
Erzählung *f.* **(-, -en)** narrative, tale, story.
Erzbergbau *m.* ore mining.
Erzbergwerk *n.* ore mine.
Erzbischof *m.* archbishop.
erzbischöflich *n.* archiepiscopal.
Erzbistum *n.* archbishopric.
Erzengel *m.* archangel.
erzeugen *v.t.* to beget, to engender, to produce; (*Dampf*) to generate.
Erzeuger *m.* producer; father.
Erzeugerland *n.* country of origin.
Erzeugerpreis *m.* manufacturer's price.
Erzeugnis *n.* **(-ses, -se)** (*der Natur*) produce; (*des Geistes*) product.
Erzeugung *f.* **(-, -en)** generation; production.
Erzfeind *m.* arch enemy.
Erzgießer *m.* brass founder.
Erzherzog *m.* archduke.
Erzherzogin *f.* archduchess.
erziehen *v.t.st.* to bring up, to educate.
Erzieher *m.* teacher, tutor.
Erzieherin *f.* **(-, -nen)** governess.
Erziehung *f.* **(-, 0)** upbringing; education.
Erziehungs: ~anstalt *f.* approved school; **~berater** *m.* educational adviser; **~beratung** *f.* child guidance; **~berechtigte** *m./f.* parent; guardian; **~wissenschaft** *f.* educational science.
erzielen *v.t.* to obtain; to produce.
erzittern *v.i.* to shake; to tremble.
erzkonservativ *a.* ultraconservative.
erzürnen *v.t.* to anger; ~ *v.r.* to grow angry.
erzwingen *v.t.st.* to force, to enforce.
es *pn.* it; sb.
Es *n.* **(-, 0)** E flat.
E-saite *f.* E-string.
Esche *f.* **(-, -n)** ash (tree).
Esel *m.* **(-s, -)** ass; donkey; (*fam.*) idiot.
Eselsbrücke *f.* mnemonic (aid).
Eselsohr *n.* (*fig.*) (*im Buche*) dog-ear.
Eskalation *f.* escalation.
eskalieren *v.i.* to escalate.
Eskapade *f.* escapade.
Eskorte *f.* escort.
eskortieren *v.t.* to escort.
esoterisch *a.* esoteric.
Espe *f.* **(-, -n)** aspen, quaking aspen.
Espenlaub *n.* aspen leaves *pl.*
Esprit *m.* wit.
Eßapfel *m.* eating apple.
Essay *m.* essay.
eßbar *a.* edible.
Eßbesteck *n.* knife, fork and spoon.
Esse *f.* **(-, -n)** smithy; chimney.
essen *v.t. & i.st.* to eat; to dine; to feed.
Essen *n.* **(-s, 0)** food; dinner, meal; *ohne ~ sein,* to go without food.
Essenszeit *f.* mealtime.
essentiell *a.* essential.
Essenz *f.* **(-, -en)** essence.
Eßgewohnheiten *pl.* eating habits.
Essig *m.* **(-[e]s, -e)** vinegar.
Essig: ~gurke *f.* gherkin; **~sauer** *a.* acetic; acetate of; **~saure Tonerde** *f.* aluminium acetate; **~säure** *f.* acetic acid.
Eßkastanie *f.* chestnut.
Eßlöffel *m.* tablespoon; *ein ~voll,* one tablespoonful of.

Eßlokal *n.* restaurant.
Eß-Service *n.* dinnerware.
Eßstäbchen *n.* chopstick.
Eßtisch *m.* dining table, dinner table
Eßwaren *pl.* edibles, victuals *pl.*
Eßzimmer *n.* dining room.
Este *m.* **(-n, -n); Estin** *f.* **(-, -nen)** Estonian; **Estland** *n.* **(-s, 0)** Estonia.
estnisch *a.* Estonian.
Estragon *m.* tarragon.
Estrich *n.* **(-[e]s, -e)** floor.
etablieren *v.t.* to establish; ~ *v.r.* to settle; to set up in business.
Etablissement *n.* **(-s, -s)** establishment.
Etage *f.* **(-, -n)** story, floor, apartment.
Etagenbett *n.* bunk bed.
Etagenwohnung *f.* apartment.
Etappe *f.* **(-, -n)** stage; (*mil.*) rear.
Etat (*frz.*) *m.* **(-s, -s)** budget, estimate.
Etatkürzung *f.* cut in the budget.
Ethik *f.* **(-, 0)** ethics *pl.*
ethisch *a.* ethical.
ethnisch *a.* ethnic.
Ethnologe *m.;* **Ethnologin** *f.* ethnologist.
Ethnologie *f.* ethnology.
ethnologisch *a.* ethnological.
Etikett *n.* **(-s, -s)** label.
Etikette *f.* **(-, -n)** etiquette.
etliche *a.pl.* quite a number of, several.
Etrusker *m.;* **Etruskerin** *f.;* **etruskisch** *a.* Etruscan.
Etui *n.* **(-s, -s)** case, box.
etwa *adv.* perhaps, nearly, about; say.
etwaig *a.* eventual.
etwas *pn.* something; some, any; ~ *adv.* somewhat.
Etymologie *f.* **(-, -en)** etymology.
etymologisch *a.* etymological.
euch *pn.* you.
euer *pn.* your; yours; **euresgleichen,** people like you.
Eugenik *f.* **(-, -en)** eugenics *pl.*
Eule *f.* **(-, -n)** owl, owlet.
Euphemismus *m.* **(-, -men)** euphemism.
Euphorie *f.* euphoria.
euphorisch *a.* euphoric; ~ *adv.* euphorically.
Eurasien *n.* Eurasia.
eurethalben, euretwegen, um euretwillen, *adv.* for your sake.
eurige (*der, die, das*) *pn.* yours.
Europa *n.* **(-s, 0)** Europe.
Europäer *m.;* **Europäerin** *f.;* **europäisch** *a.* European.
Europäische Gemeinschaft *f.* European Community.
Europaparlament *n.* European Parliament.
Europarat *m.* Council of Europe.
Euroscheck *m.* Eurocheque.
Euter *n.* **(-s, -)** udder, dug.
Euthanasie *f.* euthanasia.
ev. *evangelisch,* Protestant, Prot.
e.V. *eingetragener Verein,* registered society, incorporated, inc.
evakuieren *v.t.* to evacuate.
Evakuierte *m./f.* evacuee.
Evakuierung *f.* evacuation.
evangelisch *a.* evangelical; Protestant.
Evangelist *m.* **(-en, -en)** evangelist.
Evengelium *n.* **(-s, Evangelien)** gospel.
eventuell *a. & adv.* possible, possibly, in a certain contingency.
evident *a.* obvious.
Evolution *f.* evolution.
evolutionär *a.* evolutionary.
evtl. *eventuell,* possibly, poss.
ewig *a.* eternal, everlasting, perpetual; *auf* ~, in perpetuity.
Ewigkeit *f.* **(-, -en)** eternity.
EWS *Europäisches Währungssystem,* European Monetary System, EMS.
exakt *a.* exact, accurate; ~*e Wissenschaften,* exact sciences.
exaltiert *a.* overexcited, exaggerated, effusive.
Examen *n.* **(-s, Examina)** examination; *ein ~ bestehen,* to pass an examination.
Examinator *m.* **(-s, -en)** examiner.
examinieren *v.t.* to examine.
exekutieren *v.t.* to execute.
Exempel *n.* **(-s, -)** example.
Exemplar *n.* **(-[e]s, -e)** (*eines Buches*) copy; sample, specimen.
exemplarisch *a.* exemplary.
exerzieren *v.t. & i.* to exercise, to drill.
Exerzierplatz *m.* drill ground.
Exhibitionismus *m.* exhibitionism.
exhibitionistisch *a.* exhibitionist.
exhumieren *v.t.* to exhume.
Exil *n.* exile.
Exilant *m.;* **Exilantin** *f.* exile.
Existentialismus *m.* existentialism.
existentiell *a.* existential.
Existenz *f.* **(-, -en)** existence, livelihood.
Existenzminimum *n.* subsistence level.
existieren *v.i.* to exist, to subsist.
exkl. *exklusive,* not included.
exklusiv *a. & adv.* exclusive(ly).
Exklusivität *f.* exclusiveness, exclusivity.
Exkurs *m.* digression; excursus.
exmatrikulieren *v.t. & r.* to remove sb.'s name from the university register.
Exorzismus *m.* exorcism.
exotisch *a.* exotic.
expandieren *v.i.* to expand.
expansiv *a.* expansionist; expansionary.
expedieren *v.t.* to dispatch, to forward.
Expedition *f.* **(-, -en)** expedition.
Experiment *n.* **(-[e]s, -e)** experiment.
experimentieren *v.t.* to experiment.
Experte *m.;* **Expertin** *f.* expert.
Expertise *f.* expert's report.
explizit *a.* explicit.
explodieren *v.i. (s)* to explode.
Explosion *f.* **(-, -en)** explosion.
Explosionsmotor *m.* internal combustion engine.
explosiv *a.* explosive.
Explosivität *f.* explosiveness.
Exponat *n.* exhibit.
exponiert *a.* exposed.
Export *m.* **(-[e]s, -e)** export, exportation.
Exporthandel *m.* export trade.
exportieren *v.t.* to export.
Exposé *n.* exposé; outline.
expreß *a. & adv.* express(ly).
Expressionismus *m.* expressionism.
expressionistisch *a.* expressionist; *adv.* expressionistically.
exquisit *a. & adv.* exquisite(ly).
extensiv *a. & adv.* extensive(ly).

extern *a.* external.
Exterritorialität *f.* extraterritoriality.
extra *adv.* extra, besides, over and above; (*fam.*) especially, separately.
Extraausgabe *f.* special edition; additional expense.
Extrablatt *n.* special edition.
Extrakt *m.* **(-s, -e)** extract.
Extraration *f.* extra ration.
extraterrestrisch *a.* extraterrestrial.
extravagant *a.* flamboyant.
Extravaganz *f.* flamboyance.
Extrem *n.* **(-[e]s, -e)** extreme.
Extremfall *m.* extreme case.
Extremismus *m.* extremism.
extremistisch *a.* extremist.
Extremitäten *f.pl.* extremities *pl.*
extrovertiert *a.* extrovert(ed).
Exzellenz *f.* **(-, -en)** Excellency.
Exzentriker *m.*; **Exzentrikerin** *f.* eccentric.
exzentrisch *a.* eccentric.
Exzeß *m.* **(-es, -e)** excess.
EZ *Einzelzimmer,* single room.

F

F, f *n.* the letter F or f; (*mus.*) F.
Fa. *Firma,* firm.
Fabel *f.* **(-, -n)** fable, fiction; plot.
fabelhaft *a.* fabulous, amazing.
Fabrik *f.* **(-, -en)** factory, mill, works *pl.*
Fabrikanlage *f.* factory plant.
Fabrikant *m.* **(-en, -en)** factory owner; manufacturer.
Fabrikat *n.* **(-[e]s, -e)** product; make.
Fabrikation *f.* **(-, -sarten)** production.
Fabrikgebäude *n.* factory building.
Fabrikgelände *n.* factory site.
fabrikmäßig *a.* & *adv.* by machinery.
Fabrikware *f.* manufactured goods *pl.*
fabrizieren *v.t.* to manufacture, to make.
Facette *f.* **(-, -en)** facet.
facettieren *v.t.* to cut in facets.
Fach *n.* **(-[e]s, Fächer)** compartment, partition; drawer, box, shelf; panel; (*im Schreibtisch*) pigeonhole; (*fig.*) province, department; branch, line; (*Lehrfach*) subject.
Facharbeiter *m.* skilled worker
Fachausdruck *m.* technical term.
Fachberater *m.* technical adviser or consultant.
Fachbildung *f.* professional education.
fächeln *v.t.* to fan.
Fächer *m.* **(-s, -)** fan.
Fachfrau *f.* expert.
Fachgelehrte *m./f.* specialist.
fachkundig *a.* knowledgeable.
Fachlehrer *m.*; **Fachlehrerin** *f.* subject teacher.
Fachleute *pl.* experts.
fachlich *a.* specialized.
Fachliteratur *f.* specialized/technical literature.
Fachmann *m.* expert.
fachmännisch *a.* expert, specialist, professional.
fachmäßig *a.* & *adv.* professional(ly).
Fachrichtung *f.* field.
Fachschule *f.* technical school.
Fachsimpelei *f.* shoptalk.
Fachstudium *n.* professional study.
Fachwerk *n.* half-timbering.
Fachwissenschaft *f.* special branch of science.
Fackel *f.* **(-, -n)** torch.
Fackelzug *m.* torchlight procession.
fade *a.* flat, tasteless; insipid, dull.
Faden *m.* **(-s, Fäden)** thread; fathom.
Fadenkreuz *n.* cross-hairs.
Fadennudeln *f.pl.* vermicelli.
fadenscheinig *a.* threadbare; flimsy.
Fagott *n.* **(-[e]s, -e)** bassoon.
fähig *a.* capable, able; fit, qualified.
Fähigkeit *f.* **(-, -en)** capacity; ability, faculty, talent.
fahl *a.* pale, ashen; drab; livid.
fahnden *v.i. nach einem* ~, to search for sb.
Fahne *f.* **(-, -n)** standard, colors *pl.*, flag, banner.
Fahnenabzug *m.* (*typ.*) galley (-proof).
Fahneneid *m.* oath of allegiance.
Fahnenflucht *f.* desertion.
Fahnenstange *f.* flagpole.
Fahnenträger *m.* standard-bearer.
Fähnrich *m.* **(-[e]s, -e)** ensign; ~ *(zur See)* midshipman.
Fahrausweis *m.* ticket; (*mil.*) travel order, travel permit.
Fahrbahn *f.* road, lane.
fahrbar *a.* practicable (*Straße*); mobile (*Kantine, etc.*).
Fähre *f.* **(-, -n)** ferry(boat).
fahren *v.t.st.* to drive; to cart, to wheel; to convey; ~ *v.i.st. (s)* to ride; to sail; to travel; to go; *aus der Haut* ~, to jump out of one's skin.
fahrend *a.* itinerant.
Fahrer *m.* **(-s, -)**; **Fahrerin** *f.* **(-, -nen)** driver.
Fahrerlaubnis *f.* driver's license.
Fahrgast *m.* passenger.
Fahrgeld *n.* fare.
Fahrgemeinschaft *f.* car pool.
Fahrgestell *n.* (*avi.*) chassis.
fahrig *a.* fidgety.
Fahrkarte *f.* **(-, -n)** (*rail.*) ticket.
Fahrkartenausgabe *f.* ticket office.
Fahrkartenautomat *m.* ticket machine.
Fahrkartenkontrolle *f.* ticket inspection.
Fahrkartenschalter *m.* ticket office.
fahrlässig *a.* negligent, careless.
Fahrlässigkeit *f.* **(-, -en)** negligence.
Fährmann *m.* ferryman.
Fahrordnung *f.* **(-, -en)** rule of the road.
Fahrplan *m.* timetable, schedule.
fahrplanmäßig *a.* regular; ~ *adv.* on time; scheduled, on schedule.
Fahrpreis *m.* fare.
Fahrrad *n.* cycle, bicycle, (*fam.*) bike.
Fahrschein *m.* ticket.
Fahrschule *f.* driving school.
Fahrstuhl *m.* elevator.
Fahrt *f.* **(-, -en)** ride (in a vehicle), drive; journey; (sea) voyage; row; course; *in voller* ~, at full speed.
fahrtauglich *a.* fit to drive.
Fahrtbefehl *m.* (*mil.*) travel order.
Fährte *f.* **(-, -n)** track, scent; *auf falscher* ~, on the wrong track.

Fahrtenmesser *n.* sheath knife.
Fahrtrichtung *f.* direction.
fahrtüchtig *a.* fit to drive.
Fahrtunterbrechung *f.* stopover.
Fahrtwind *m.* **(-es, -e)** airflow.
Fahrunterricht *m.* (*mot.*) driving instruction.
Fahrwasser *n.* track; channel.
Fahrweg *m.* wagon road; driveway.
Fahrzeug *n.* vehicle.
Faible *n.* **(-s, -s)** liking; weakness.
fair *a.* fair.
faktisch *a. & adv.* actual(ly).
Faktor *m.* **(-s, -en)** factor.
Faktur, Faktura *f.* **(-, -ren)** invoice.
Fakultät *f.* **(-, -en)** faculty.
fakultativ *a.* optional.
falb *a.* fallow, sorrel, dun.
Falke *m.* **(-n, -n)** falcon, hawk.
Falkner *m.* falconer.
Fall *m.* **(-[e]s, Fälle)** *m.* fall, accident; case; *im ~e daß,* in case; *den ~ setzen,* to suppose; *auf jeden ~*, at all events; *auf keinen ~*, on no account; *zu ~ bringen,* to ruin, to seduce.
Fallbeil *n.* guillotine.
Falle *f.* **(-, -n)** trap, snare; (*fig.*) pitfall.
fallen *v.i.st. (s)* to fall, to drop; (*Preise*) to decline; (*com.*) to fail, to break; (*Schuß*) to be heard; *in die Augen ~*, to catch *or* strike the eye; *ins Gewicht ~*, to be of great weight; *in Ohnmacht ~*, to swoon, to faint; *es fällt mir schwer,* I find it hard.
fällen *v.t.* to fell; to cut down; *ein Urteil ~*, to pass a sentence.
fallenlassen *v.t.st.* to abandon; to drop; to let fall.
Fallgeschwindigkeit *f.* rate of fall.
Fallgrube *f.* trap.
Fallhammer *m.* pile driver.
fällig *a.* due, payable; ~ **werden,** to become due; *sofort ~e Schulden,* liquid debts.
Fälligkeit *f.* **(-, -en)** maturity (*com.*).
Fallobst *n.* windfall.
falls *adv.* in case (that).
Fallschirm *m.* **(-s, -e)** parachute.
Fallschirm: ~absprung *m.* parachute jump; **~abwurf** *m.* airdrop; **~jäger** *m.* (*mil.*) paratrooper; **~springen** *n.* parachute jumping; (*sp.*) sky diving; **~springer** *m.* parachutist; **~leuchtbombe** *f.* parachute flare; **~truppen** *pl.* paratroops.
Fallstrick *m.* trap, snare.
Fallstudie *f.* case study.
Falltür *f.* trapdoor.
falsch *a.* false, wrong; forged, counterfeit; (*fig.*) faithless, deceitful; ~ **singen,** to sing out of tune; ~ **spielen,** to cheat at play.
Falschaussage *f.* false testimony.
Falscheid *m.* false oath.
fälschen *v.t.* to falsify; to adulterate; (*Wechsel, Scheck*) to forge; (*Geld*) to counterfeit; *gefälschte Stelle,* surreptitious passage.
Fälscher *m.* forger; counterfeiter.
Falschgeld *n.* counterfeit money.
Falschheit *f.* **(-, -en)** falsehood, falseness; deceitfulness.
fälschlich *a.* false; ~ *adv.* falsely.
fälschlicherweise *adv.* by mistake; mistakenly.
Falschmeldung *f.* false report; hoax.
Falschmünzer *m.* **(-s, -)** forger; counterfeiter.
Falschspieler *m.* **(-s, -)** cardsharp.
Fälschung *f.* **(-, -en)** fake; forgery.
Falsett *n.* (*mus.*) falsetto.
Faltblatt *n.* leaflet; insert (newspaper).
Faltboot *n.* collapsible boat.
Falte *f.* **(-, -n)** fold, pleat, crease.
fälteln *v.t.* to pleat.
falten *v.t.* to fold, to pleat; *die Stirn ~*, to knit one's brow; (*Hände*) to join.
Faltenbildung *f.* folding; wrinkling.
Faltengebirge *n.* fold mountains.
faltenlos *a.* unwrinkled, uncreased.
Faltenrock *m.* pleated skirt.
Faltenwurf *n.* drapery.
Falter *m.* **(-s, -)** (*Nacht~*) moth; (*Tag~*) butterfly.
faltig *a.* creased; wrinkled; lined.
Falz *f.* fold.
Falzbein *n.* (paper) folder.
falzen *v.t.* to fold; to flute; to groove.
Fam. *Familie,* family.
familiär *a.* familiar, intimate.
Familie *f.* **(-, -n)** family.
Familienangehörige *m./f.* member of the family.
Familienangelegenheit *f.* family affair/matter.
Familienbetrieb *m.* family business.
Familienfeier *n.* family party.
Familienkrach *m.* family quarrel.
Familienleben *n.* family life.
Familienname *m.* family name.
Familienstand *m.* marital status.
Familienunterstützung *f.* (*mil.*) separation allowance.
Familienzulage *f.* family allowance.
famos *a.* (*fam.*) first-rate, prime.
Fanatiker *m.* **(-s, -)** fanatic.
fanatisch *a.* fanatic(al).
Fanatismus *m.* **(-, 0)** fanaticism.
Fanfare *f.* **(-, -n)** fanfare; flourish of trumpets.
Fang *m.* **(-[e]s, Fänge)** catch, capture; fang, tusk; claw, talon; thrust, stab.
fangen *v.t.st.* to catch; to seize, to take; ~ *v.r. st.* to rally; to recover.
Fangen *n.* **~spielen** to play tag.
Fangfrage *f.* trick question.
Fangopackung *f.* mud pack.
Farbband *n.* **(-[e]s, -bänder)** typewriter ribbon.
Farbe *f.* **(-, -n)** color; dye, paint; hue, complexion.
farbecht *a.* colorfast.
färben *v.t.* to color, to tinge; to dye.
farbenblind *a.* color-blind.
Farbendruck *m.* color printing.
Färber *m.* **(-s, -)** dyer, stainer.
farbig *a.* colored.
Farbkasten *m.* **(-s, -kästen)** color box.
farblich *a.* colored; *adv.* in color.
farblos *a.* colorless.
Farbschicht *f.* layer of paint.
Farbskala *f.* color chart.
Farbstift *m.* **(-s, -e)** crayon.
Farbstoff *m.* dye; coloring.
Färbung *f.* **(-, -en)** coloration, coloring; tinge, shade.
Farce *f.* **(-, -n)** farce.
Farn *m.*, **Farnkraut** *n.* fern.
Fasan *m.* **(-[e]s, -e[n])** pheasant.
Fasching *m.* **(-s, -e)** carnival.
Faschismus *m.* **(-, 0)** fascism.
Faschist *m.* **(-en, -en)** fascist.
faschistisch *a.* fascist.
faseln *v.i.* (*pej.*) to drivel, to twaddle.

Faser *f.* **(-, -n), Faserstoff** *m.* fiber; **Faserbrett** *n.* fiberboard.
faserig *a.* fibrous; stringy.
fasern *v.r.* to fray.
Faß *n.* **(Fasses, Fässer)** barrel, cask; (*offenes*) tub, vat; *Bier vom* ~, beer on tap.
Fassade *f.* **(-, -n)** façade; front.
faßbar *a.* tangible, comprehensible.
fassen *v.t.* to lay hold of, to seize; to contain; to conceive, to comprehend; ~ *v.r.* to compose oneself; *sich kurz* ~, to be brief; *Edelsteine* ~, to set, to mount; *in Worte* ~, to put into words; *einen Entschluß* ~, to come to a decision.
faßlich *a.* intelligible, easy to understand.
Fasson *f.* **(-, -en)** shape.
Fassung *f.* **(-, -en)** setting (of stones); version; wording, draft; composure.
fassungslos *a.* beside oneself; stunned.
Fassungsvermögen *n.* capacity.
fast *adv.* almost, nearly.
fasten *v.i.* to fast.
Fastenzeit *f.* Lent; time of fasting.
Fastnacht *f.* Mardi Gras, Shrove Tuesday; Shrovetide; carnival.
Fasttag *m.* day of fasting.
Faszination *f.* fascination.
faszinieren *v.t.* to fascinate.
fatal *a.* unlucky, disagreeable; odious.
Fatalismus *m.* fatalism.
Fatalist *m.;* **Fatalistin** *f.* fatalist.
fatalistisch *a.* fatalistic.
Fata Morgana *f.* Fata Morgana; illusion.
Fatzke *m.* (*pej.*) jerk.
fauchen *v.i.* to hiss; to snarl.
faul *a.* putrefied, rotten; lazy, idle, slothful.
faulen *v.i. (s)* to rot, to putrefy.
faulenzen *v.i.* to idle, to loaf; to laze around.
Faulenzer *m.* **(-s, -)** idler, lazybones.
Faulenzerei *f.* idleness, laziness.
Faulheit *f.* idleness, laziness.
faulig *a.* stagnating; putrefying; rotting; foul, putrid (smell).
Fäulnis *f.* **(-, 0)** rottenness, putrefaction.
Faulpelz *m.* lazybones.
Faultier *n.* sloth.
Fauna *f.* **(-, -nen)** fauna.
Faust *f.* **(-, Fäuste)** fist.
Fäustchen *n.* **(-s, -)** *sich ins* ~ *lachen,* to laugh in one's sleeve.
Fausthandschuh *m.* mitten.
Fäustling *f.* mitten.
Faustregel *f.* rule of thumb.
Faustschlag *m.* punch.
Fauxpas *m.* faux pas.
favorisieren *v.t.* to favor.
Favorit *m.;* **Favoritin** *f.* favorite.
Fax *n.* **(-, -e)** fax.
faxen *v.t.* to fax.
Faxen *pl.* nonsense; ~ **machen,** to make faces, to clown around.
Fazit *n.* **(-s, -s or -e)** result, sum total.
FCKW *Fluorchlorkohlenwasserstoff,* chlorofluorocarbon, CFC.
F.D.P. *Freie Demokratische Partei,* Liberal Democratic Party.
F-Dur *n.* F-major.
Feature *n.* feature.
Feb(r). *Februar,* February, Feb.
Februar *m.* **(-s, -e)** February.
fechten *v.i.st.* to fight; (*kunstgerecht*) to fence; (*fig.*) to beg.
Fechter *m.* **(-s, -)** swordsman, fencer.
Feder *f.* **(-, -n)** feather; pen; spring.
Federball *m.* badminton; shuttlecock.
Federbett *n.* feather bed.
Federbusch *m.* plume; crest.
Federhalter *m.* fountain pen.
federleicht *a.* light as a feather.
Federlesen *n.* *nicht viel* ~*s machen,* to make short work of.
Federmesser *n.* **(-s, -)** penknife.
federn *v.i.* to rebound; to be elastic.
Federstrich *m.* stroke of the pen.
Federung *f.* springs; suspension (car).
Federzeichnung *f.* pen and ink drawing.
Fee *f.* **(-, -n)** fairy.
feenhaft *a.* fairy-like.
Fegefeuer *n.* **(-s, 0)** purgatory.
fegen *v.t.* to sweep.
Fehde *f.* **(-, -n)** quarrel, feud; challenge.
Fehdehandschuh *m.* gauntlet.
Fehl *m.* **(-s, 0)** blemish.
fehl *adv.* amiss, wrong.
fehlbar *a.* fallible.
Fehlbesetzung *f.* miscast.
Fehlbetrag *m.* deficit.
Fehldiagnose *f.* incorrect diagnosis.
Fehleinschätzung *f.* misjudgment.
fehlen *v.i.* to be missing; ~ *v.t.* to miss; *was fehlt dir?,* what is the matter with you?
fehlend *a.* missing; absent.
Fehlentscheidung *f.* wrong decision.
Fehlentwicklung *f.* undesirable development.
Fehler *m.* **(-s, -)** fault, defect; error, mistake, blunder.
fehlerfrei *a.* faultless.
fehlerhaft *a.* faulty, incorrect.
fehlerlos *a.* flawless.
Fehlerquelle *f.* source of error.
Fehlerquote *f.* error rate.
Fehlerzahl *f.* number of errors.
Fehlgeburt *f.* miscarriage.
fehlgehen *v.i.st. (s)* to go wrong.
fehlgreifen *v.i.st.* to make a mistake.
Fehlgriff *m.* mistake; blunder.
Fehlkonstruktion *f.* *eine* ~ *sein* to be badly designed.
Fehlleistung *f.* *Freudsche* ~ (Freudian) slip.
Fehlschlag *m.* miss; failure.
fehlschlagen *v.i.st.* to miscarry, to fail.
Fehlschluß *m.* fallacy.
Fehlstart *m.* false start.
Fehltritt *m.* false step; (*fig.*) error, mistake.
Fehlurteil *n.* **(-s, -e)** miscarriage of justice.
Fehlzündung *f.* misfire.
Feier *f.* **(-, 0)** party, celebration; festival; rest.
Feierabend *m.* end of work, closing time.
feierlich *a.* festive, solemn; ceremonious.
Feierlichkeit *f.* **(-, -en)** celebration, festivity, ceremony.
feiern *v.i.* to rest from labor; ~ *v.t.* to solemnize; to celebrate.
Feierschicht *f.* cancelled shift.
Feiertag *m.* holiday; *gesetzlicher* ~, public holiday.
feig(e) *a.* cowardly.
Feige *f.* **(-, -n)** fig.
Feigheit *f.* **(-, -en)** cowardice.

Feigling *m.* **(-[e]s, -e)** coward.
feil *a.* for sale, venal; mercenary.
feilbieten *v.t.st.* to offer for sale.
Feile *f.* **(-, -n)** file.
feilen *v.t.* to file; to refine, to polish.
feilschen *v.t.* to bargain, to haggle.
fein *a.* fine; delicate, elegant, refined; polite, genteel; subtle; *extra* ~, super-fine.
Feinarbeit *f.* detailed work; precision work.
feind *a.* hostile, inimical.
Feind *m.* **(-[e]s, -e); Feindin** *f.* **(-, -nen)** enemy; adversary, foe.
feindlich *a.* inimical, hostile, adverse.
Feindschaft *f.* **(-, -en)** enmity, hostility.
feindselig *a.* hostile, malevolent.
Feindseligkeit *f.* **(-, -en)** hostility.
feinfühlig *a.* sensitive.
Feingefühl *n.* sensitivity.
Feingehalt *m.* **(-[e]s, -e)** standard (of coins, gold, etc.)
Feinheit *f.* fineness, delicacy, subtlety.
feinkörnig *a.* fine-grained.
Feinkost *f.* **(-, 0)** delicatessen.
feinmachen *v.r.* (*fam.*) to dress up.
feinmaschig *a.* finely meshed.
Feinschmecker *m.* **(-s, -)** gourmet.
feinsinnig *a.* delicate, sensitive.
feist *a.* fat, obese, stout.
feixen *v.i.* (*fam.*) to smirk.
Feld *n.* **(-[e]s, -er)** field; plain; panel; (*Schach*) square.
Feldarbeit *f.* work in the fields; field work.
Feldbahn *f.* field railway.
Feldbett *n.* camp bed.
Feldgeistlicher *m.* army chaplain.
Feldgeschrei *n.* war cry.
Feldherr *m.* general.
Feldküche *f.* field kitchen.
Feldlazarett *n.* field hospital.
Feldmarschall *m.* field marshal.
Feldmesser *m.* surveyor.
Feldpolizei *m.* provost marshal.
Feldpost *f.* army post.
Feldpostamt *n.* Army Post Office (APO).
Feldspat *m.* feldspar.
Feldstuhl *m.* camp stool.
Feld-Wald-und-Wiesen- (*fam.*) run-of-the-mill; common or garden variety.
Feldwebel *m.* sergeant-major.
Feldzug *m.* campaign.
Felge *f.* **(-, -n)** rim.
Fell *n.* **(-[e]s, -e)** fur; hide; skin; coat; *ein dickes ~ haben,* to be thick-skinned.
Fels *m.* **(-en, -en),** *see* **Felsen** *m.* **(-s, -)** rock, crag.
Felsblock *m.* rock, boulder.
Felsen *m.* **(-s, -)** rock, cliff.
felsenfest *a.* firm as a rock.
Felsenklippe *f.* rocky cliff.
Felsenriff *n.* rocky reef.
felsig *a.* rocky.
Felsspalte *f.* crevice.
Felsvorsprung *m.* rock ledge.
Felswand *f.* rock face.
Feme *f.* Vehmgericht; kangaroo court.
Fememord *m.* lynching.
feminin *a.* feminine, effeminate.
Femininum *n.* **(-s, -na)** feminine noun.
Feminismus *m.* feminism.
Feminist *m.;* **Feministin** *f.* feminist.
feministisch *a.* feminist.
Fenchel *m.* fennel.
Fenster *n.* **(-s, -)** window.
Fensterbank *n.* window sill.
Fensterbrett *n.* window sill.
Fensterkitt *m.* putty.
Fensterladen *m.* shutter.
Fensterputzer *m.* window cleaner.
Fensterrahmen *m.* window frame.
Fensterscheibe *f.* windowpane.
Ferien *pl.* vacation, holidays *pl.; in den* ~, on vacation.
Ferienkolonie *f.* holiday/vacation camp.
Ferkel *n.* **(-s, -)** piglet.
Ferkelei *f.* filthy behavior; dirty remark.
ferkeln *v.t.* to farrow.
Ferment *n.* enzyme; ferment.
fern *a. & adv.* far, remote, distant.
Fernaufklärung *f.* (*mil.*) long-range reconnaissance.
Fernbedienung *f.* remote control.
fernbleiben *v.i.st.* to stay away.
Ferne *f.* **(-, -n)** distance.
ferner *a.* farther, further; ~ *adv.* further, moreover.
fernerhin *adv.* henceforward, henceforth.
Fernfahrer *m.* trucker.
Ferngespräch *n.* long-distance call.
ferngesteuert *a.* remote-controlled.
Fernglas *n.* telescope, binoculars.
fernhalten *v.t.st.* to keep off.
Fernheizung *f.* long-distance heating.
fernhin *adv.* at a distance, far away.
Fernkampfartillerie *f.* long-range artillery.
Fernrohr *n.* telescope.
Fernschreiben *n.* teletype.
Fernschreiber *m.* teletype.
Fernsehapparat *m.* television set.
Fernsehen *n.* television.
Fernsicht *f.* prospect, panorama.
Fernsprechamt *n.* telephone exchange.
Fernsprecher *m.* **(-s, -)** telephone.
Fernsteuerung *f.* remote control.
Fernsteuerwaffe *f.* guided missile.
Ferse *f.* **(-, -n)** heel.
fertig *a.* ready; ready-made; finished; *ich bin* ~, I have (am) done; *mit etw.* ~ *werden,* to finish sth., to get over sth.
Fertigbau *m.* prefabricated building; **~weise** *f.* prefabricated construction.
fertigen *v.t.* to manufacture, to make.
Fertiggericht *n.* ready-to-serve meal.
Fertighaus *n.* prefabricated house.
Fertigkeit *f.* **(-, -en)** skill, dexterity; fluency.
Fertigstellung *f.* completion.
Fertigteil *n.* prefabricated part.
Fertigungsstraße *f.* production line.
Fertigwaren *f.pl.* finished (*or* manufactured) goods.
Fes *m.* fez.
fesch *a.* smart; dashing; stylish.
Fessel *f.* **(-, -n)** fetter, shackel; (*des Pferdes*) fetlock, pastern; **~ballon** *m.* captive balloon.
fesseln *v.t.* to tie up, to chain up; to fetter; (*fig.*) to captivate; (*Blick*) to arrest.
fest *a. & adv.* fast; firm; solid; settled, fixed; fortified; **~er Schlaf,** sound sleep; ~ **Körper,** solid; **sich ~halten,** to hold on; **sich ~legen,** to commit oneself; **~legen,** to fix, lay down; **~machen,** to

fasten; **~nehmen,** to arrest; **~setzen, ~stellen,** to establish; **... fest** *a.* resisting.
Fest *n.* **(-es, -e)** feast, festival.
Festbeleuchtung *f.* illumination.
Feste *f.* **(-, -n)** fastness, stronghold.
Festessen *n.* banquet.
festhalten *v.t.st.* to hold on to.
festigen *v.t.* to strengthen; to consolidate.
Festigkeit *f.* **(-, 0)** firmness; solidity; constancy; (*Metall*) strength.
Festigung *f.* strengthening; consolidation.
Festival *n.* festival.
fest: ~klammern *v.r.* to cling to; **~klemmen** *v.i.* to be stuck; **~** *v.t.* to wedge.
Festkörper *m.* (*phys.*) solid.
Festland *n.* continent.
Festlandsockel *m.* continental shelf.
festlegen *v.t.st.* to fix, to arrange; **~** *v.r.st.* to commit oneself.
festlich *a.* festive, festival; solemn.
Festlichkeit *f.* **(-, -en)** festivity, solemnity.
festliegen *v.i.st.* to be stuck; to be tied up (money).
festmachen *v.t.* to fix; to arrange (appointment); to moor.
Festnahme *f.* arrest.
Festplatte *f.* (*comp.*) hard disk.
Festplatz *m.* fairground.
Festpreis *m.* fixed price.
Festrede *f.* (ceremonial) address.
Festschrift *f.* commemorative publication.
festsetzen *v.t.* to fix, to settle, to appoint.
Festspiel *n.* festival.
feststellen *v.t.* to ascertain; to establish.
Festtag *m.* feast, holiday.
Festung *f.* **(-, -en)** fortress.
Festungs: ~anlage *f.* fortification; **~mauer** *f.* wall of a fortress.
Festzelt *n.* marquee.
Festzug *m.* procession, pageant.
Fete *f.* **(-, -n)** (*fam.*) party.
Fetisch *m.* **(-es, -e)** fetish.
Fetischismus *m.* fetishism.
fett *a.* fat; greasy; (*von Speisen*) rich; bold (print).
Fett *n.* **(-[e]s, -e)** fat; grease.
Fettdruck *m.* bold face.
Fettflecken *m.* grease-spot.
fettgedruckt *a.* bold.
Fettgewebe *n.* fatty tissue.
fettig *a.* greasy, fatty.
fettleibig *a.* obese.
Fettleibigkeit *f.* obesity.
Fettsack *m.* (*fam.*) fatso.
Fettsäure *f.* fatty acid.
Fettschicht *f.* layer of fat.
Fettwanst *m.* (*fam.*) paunch.
Fetus *m.* **(-, -se)** fetus.
Fetzen *m.* **(-s, -)** shred, tatter, rag.
feucht *a.* moist, wet; damp.
Feuchtigkeit *f.* **(-, -en)** moisture, humidity.
Feuchtigkeitsmesser *m.* hygrometer.
feuchtigkeitssicher *a.* damp-proof.
feudal *a.* feudal; aristocratic; plush.
Feuer *n.* **(-s, -)** fire; (*fig.*) ardor; (*für Zigarren*) light.
Feuerbekämpfung *f.* fire fighting.
Feuerbestattung *f.* cremation.
Feuereifer *m.* enthusiasm; zest.
feuerfest *a.* fireproof.
Feuergefahr *f.* danger of fire.
feuergefährlich *a.* (in)flammable, combustible.
Feuergitter *n.* (*am Kamin*) fireguard.
Feuerkraft *f.* (*mil.*) fire power.
Feuerleiter *f.* fire escape; ladder.
Feuerlöscher *m.* fire extinguisher.
Feuermelder *m.* fire alarm.
feuern *v.i.* to fire.
feuerrot *a.* fiery red, red-hot.
Feuersbrunst *f.* **(-, brünste)** fire, conflagration.
Feuerschein *m.* glow of fire.
Feuerschlucker *m.* fire-eater.
feuersicher *a.* fireproof.
Feuerspritze *f.* fire hose.
Feuerstein *m.* flint.
Feuerstelle *f.* fireplace, hearth.
Feuerteufel *m.* firebug.
Feuertod *m.* (death at) the stake, death by fire.
Feuerung *f.* **(-, -en)** fuel; firing.
Feuerversicherung *f.* fire insurance.
Feuerwache *f.* fire station.
Feuerwehr *f.* fire brigade; **~mann** *m.*; **~frau** *f.* fire fighter.
Feuerwerk *n.* fireworks *pl.*
Feuerzange *f.* tongs *pl.*
Feuerzeug *n.* lighter.
Feuilleton *n.* arts and leisure section (newspaper).
feurig *a.* fiery; ardent.
ff. *folgende,* following.
FF *Französischer Franc,* French franc, FF.
FH *Fachhochschule,* technical college.
Fiasko *n.* **(-[s], -s)** failure; **~ machen,** to fail.
Fibel *f.* **(-, -n)** primer, spelling book.
Fiber *f.* **(-, -n)** fiber, filament.
Fichte *f.* **(-, -n)** spruce; pine (-tree).
ficken *v.t.* (*vulg.*) to fuck.
fidel *a.* (*fam.*) merry, jolly.
Fidschiinseln *pl.* the Fiji Islands.
Fieber *n.* **(-s, -)** fever; ~ *haben,* to have a temperature.
fieberhaft *a.* feverish.
fieberkrank *a.* feverish.
fiebern *v.i.* have a fever.
fiebrig *a.* feverish.
Fiedel *f.* **(-, -n)** fiddle.
Fiedelbogen *m.* fiddlestick, bow.
fiedeln *v.t. & i.* to fiddle; to scrape.
fiepen *v.i.* to whimper; to cheep.
fies *a.* nasty, mean.
Fig. *Figur,* figure, fig.
Figur *f.* **(-, -en)** figure; diagram; (*Schach*) chessman.
figurativ *a. & adv.* figurative(ly).
figürlich *a.* figured; figurative.
Fiktion *f.* fiction.
fiktiv *a.* fictitious.
Filet *n.* **(-s, -s)** netting; fillet of beef.
Filiale *f.* branch (establishment).
Filigranarbeit *f.* filigree.
Film *m.* **(-s, -)** film; movie, motion picture.
Filmatelier *n.* film studio.
Filmemacher *m.*; **Filmemacherin** *f.* film-maker.
filmen *v.t.* to film, to shoot.
filmisch *a.* cinematic.
Filmverleih *m.* film distribution.
Filter *m. or n.* **(-s, -)** filter.
filtern, filtrieren *v.t.* to filter, to strain.
Filz *m.* **(-es, -e)** felt; (*fig.*)miser, niggard.

filzen *v.i.* to felt; (*fig.*) to search, to frisk.
Filzhut *m.* felt hat.
filzig *a.* felt-like; (*fig.*) stingy, niggardly.
Filzlaus *f.* crab louse.
Filzokratie *f.* (*fam. pej.*) corruption, graft.
Filzstift *m.* felt-tip pen; marker.
Fimmel *m.* craze.
Finale *n.* final; (*mus.*) finale.
Finalsatz *m.* final clause.
Finanzamt *n.* internal revenue office.
Finanzausschuß *m.* finance committee.
Finanzen *f.pl.* finances *pl.*; revenue.
finanziell *a.* financial.
finanzieren *v.t.* to finance.
Finanzierung *f.* financing.
Finanzjahr *n.* fiscal year.
Finanzmann *m.* financier.
Finanzminister *m.* Secretary of the Treasury.
Findelhaus *n.* foundling hospital.
Findelkind *n.* foundling.
finden *v.t.st.* to find; to discover; to meet with; to think, to deem; ~ *v.r.st.* to be found; *Vergnügen ~ an,* to take pleasure in; *Geschmack ~ an,* to like, to relish; *es wird sich ~*, we shall see; *sich ~ in,* to put up with.
Finderlohn *m.* reward to the finder.
findig *a.* shrewd, ingenious.
Findling *m.* **(-[e]s, -e)** foundling.
Finesse *f.* finesse, trick.
Finger *m.* **(-s, -)** finger; *einem auf die ~ sehen,* to watch sb. closely; *durch die ~ sehen,* to wink at.
Fingerabdruck *m.* fingerprint.
Fingerfertigkeit *f.* dexterity.
Fingerhakeln *n.* finger wrestling.
Fingerhandschuh *m.* glove.
Fingerhut *m.* thimble; (*bot.*) fox glove.
Fingerknöchel *m.* knuckle.
Fingerkuppe *f.* fingertip.
fingern *v.t.* to finger.
Fingernagel *m.* fingernail.
Fingersatz *m.* (*mus.*) fingering.
Fingerspitze *f.* fingertip.
Fingerspitzengefühl *n.* feeling.
Fingerzeig *m.* hint.
fingieren *v.t.* to fake.
Fink[e] *m.* **(-en, -en)** finch.
Finne *m.*; **Finnin** *f.* Finn; **finnisch** *a.* Finnish.
Finnland *n.* **(-s, 0)** Finland.
finster *a.* dark, obscure; gloomy, dim.
Finsternis *f.* **(-, se)** darkness, obscurity; eclipse.
Finte *f.* **(-, -n)** feint; pretense; fib.
Firlefanz *m.* (*fam. pej.*) frippery; nonsense.
firm *a.* (*fam.*) knowledgeable.
Firma *f.* **(-, Firmen)** firm.
Firmament *n.* **(-[e]s, -e)** firmament, sky.
Firmen: ~inhaber *m.* owner of a company; **~name** *m.* trade name; **~sitz** *m.* headquarters; **~wagen** *m.* company car; **~zeichen** *n.* logo.
Firmung *f.* **(-, -en)** confirmation.
Firnis *m.* **(-nisses, -nisse)** varnish.
firnissen *v.t.* to varnish.
First *m.* **(-es, -e)** & *f.* **(-, -en)** top; ridge of a roof.
Fis *n.* **(-, 0)** (*mus.*) F sharp.
Fisch *m.* **(-es, -e)** fish.
Fisch: ~angel *f.* fish hook; **~bein** *n.* whalebone.
fischen *v.t.* to fish, to angle; *im Trüben ~*, to fish in troubled waters.
Fischer *m.* **(-s, -)** fisherman, angler.
Fischerboot *n.* fishing boat.
Fischerei *f.* fishing.
Fisch: ~fang *m.* fishing; **~grätenmuster** *n.* herringbone pattern; **~gründe** *pl.* fishing grounds; **~händler** *m.* fishmonger; **~konserve** *f.* canned fish; **~kutter** *m.* fishing trawler; **~laich** *m.* spawn; **~mehl** *n.* fishmeal; **~zucht** *f.* fish farming.
fiskalisch *a.* fiscal.
Fiskus *m.* **(-, 0)** treasury; government.
Fistel *f.* **(-, -n)** fistula; (*als Stimme*) falsetto.
Fitness center *n.* health club, gym.
Fittich *m.* **(-[e]s, -e)** wing, pinion.
Fitzelchen *n.* (*fam.*) scrap.
fix *a.* fixed, firm; (*fig.*) quick, sharp; ~ **und fertig,** worn out, exhausted.
fixen *v.i.* to fix.
Fixer *m.*; **Fixerin** *f.* fixer.
fixieren *v.t.* to fix, to settle; (*phot.*) to fix; (*einen*) to stare at; **Fixierbad, Fixierlösung** (*phot.*) fixing solution.
Fixstern *m.* **(-[e]s, -e)** fixed star.
Fjord *m.* fiord.
FKK *Freikörperkultur,* nudism.
FKK-Strand *m.* nudist beach.
flach *a.* flat; plain, level; shallow.
Fläche *f.* **(-, -n)** plain, surface; plane.
Flächen: ~inhalt *m.* area; **~maß** *n.* square measure; **~raum** *m.* area.
Flachland *n.* lowland.
flach: ~legen *v.r.* to lie down; **~liegen** to be flat on one's back.
Flachrelief *n.* bas relief, low relief.
Flachs *m.* **(-es, -e)** flax.
flackern *v.i.* to flare, to flicker.
Fladen *m.* flat cake; cowpat; **Fladenbrot** *n.* flat loaf of bread.
Flagge *f.* **(-, -n)** flag, colors *pl.*
flaggen *v.i.* to hoist the flag(s).
Flair *n.* aura, flair.
Flak *f.* anti-aircraft gun, AA gun.
Flakon *n.od.m.* little bottle.
flambieren *v.t.* to flame.
Flame *m.*; **Flämin** *f.* Fleming.
flämisch *a.* Flemish.
Flamme *f.* **(-, -n)** flame, blaze; (*Liebchen*) love, sweetheart.
flammen *v.i.* to flame, to blaze.
flammend *a.* flaming.
Flammenwerfer *m.* flame thrower.
Flandern *n.* Flanders.
Flanell *m.* **(-[e]s, -e)** flannel.
flanieren *v.i.* to stroll.
Flanke *f.* **(-, -n)** flank.
Flankenspiel *n.* (*mech.*) backlash.
flankieren *v.t.* to flank.
flapsig *a.* loutish.
Flasche *f.* **(-, -n)** bottle flask; *auf ~n ziehen,* to bottle.
Flaschen: ~bier *n.* bottled beer; **~gestell** *n.* bottle-rack; **~öffner** *m.* bottle opener.
Flaschenzug *m.* pulley, tackle.
flatterhaft *a.* unsteady, fickle.
Flatterhaftigkeit *f.* fickleness.
flattern *v.i.* to flit, to flutter; (*Fahne*) to wave, to stream.
flau *a.* flat, insipid; faint; (*com.*) dull.
Flaum *m.* **(-[e]s, 0)** down.
flaumig *a.* downy.
flauschig *a.* fluffy.
Flause *f.* silly idea.

Flaute *f.* lull; slack period.
Flechte *f.* **(-, -n)** twist, plait, braid; (*med.*) eczema; (*Pflanze*) lichen.
flechten *v.t.st.* to twist, to plait; (*Kranz*) to wreathe; to weave.
Flechtwerk *n.* wickerwork.
Fleck *m.* **(-[e]s, -e)** spot; place; patch; blot, stain; tripe.
flecken *v.t.* to stain.
Flecken *m.* **(-s, -)** spot, stain; blemish; (*Ort*) market town, hamlet.
Fleckfieber *n.* typhus.
fleckig *a.* spotted, speckled, stained.
fleddern *v.t.* to blunder, to rob.
Fledermaus *f.* bat.
Flegel *m.* **(-s, -)** lout.
Flegelei *f.* **(-, -en)** loutish behavior.
flegelhaft *a.* loutish.
Flegeljahre *pl.* awkward age.
flehen *v.i.* to implore, to beseech.
flehend *a.* suppliant.
flehentlich *a.* & *adv.* imploring(ly), urgent(ly).
Fleisch *n.* **(-es, 0)** flesh; meat; (*des Obstes*) pulp.
Fleischbeschauer *m.* meat inspector.
Fleischbrühe *f.* broth, beef-tea; gravy.
Fleischer *m.* **(-s, -)** butcher.
Fleischerei *f.;* **Fleischerladen** *m.* butcher's shop.
Fleischeslust *f.* carnal appetite.
Fleischextrakt *m.* extract of meat.
Fleischfarbe *f.* flesh-color.
fleischfressend *a.* carnivorous.
fleischig *a.* plump; fleshy.
Fleischkäse *m.* meat loaf.
Fleischkloß *m.* meatball.
Fleischkonserve *f.* can of meat.
fleischlich *a.* carnal.
fleischlos *a.* meatless.
Fleischpastete *f.* pâté.
Fleischwolf *m.* mincer.
Fleiß *m.* **(-es, 0)** diligence, application, industry.
fleißig *a.* diligent; industrious.
flektieren *v.t.* to inflect.
fletschen *v.t.* to snarl.
flexibel *a.* & *adv.* flexible, flexibly.
Flexibilität *f.* flexibility.
Flexion *f.* inflection.
flicken *v.t.* to mend, to patch, to botch.
Flickendecke *f.* patchwork quilt.
Flickschuster *m.* cobbler.
Flickwerk *n.* patch-up job.
Flickzeug *n.* repair kit.
Flieder *m.* **(-s, -)** (*spanischer*) lilac.
Fliege *f.* **(-, -n)** fly.
fliegen *v.i.st.* *(s)* to fly; to rush, to dash; **~lassen,** to fly (a kite), to wave (a flag).
Flieger *m.* **(-s, -); Fliegerin** *f.* **(-, -nen)** flyer, aviator; pilot.
Fliegerabwehr... anti-aircraft-.
Fliegeralarm *m.* air-raid warning.
fliehen *v.i.st.* *(s)* to flee; ~ *v.t.st.* to avoid, to shun.
fliehend *a.* sloping (forehead); receding (chin).
Fliehkraft *f.* centrifugal force.
Fliese *f.* **(-, -n)** tile.
Fließband *n.* assembly line.
fließen *v.i.st.* *(s)* to flow; (*vom Papier*) to blot.
fließend *a.* & *adv.* fluent(ly); *~es warmes Wasser,* hot running water.
Fließpapier *n.* blotting paper.
flimmern *v.i.* to twinkle, to flicker.
flink *a.* brisk, quick, nimble.
Flinte *f.* **(-, -n)** gun, musket; *die ~ ins Korn werfen,* to give in, to throw in the towel.
Flipper *m.;* **Flipperautomat** *m.* pinball machine.
flippern *v.i.* to play pinball.
Flittchen *n.* (*fam. pej.*) floozie.
Flitter *m.* frippery.
Flitterwochen *f.pl.* honeymoon.
Flocke *f.* **(-, -n)** flock; flake (of snow).
flockig *a.* fluffy.
Floh *m.* **(-[e]s, Flöhe)** flea.
Flor *m.* **(-[e]s, -e)** (*Trauer-*) crepe, gauze.
Florett *n.* **(-[e]s, -s & -e)** (fencing) foil.
florieren *v.i.* to flourish, to thrive.
Floskel *f.* **(-, -n)** flourish (of rhetoric), tirade, phrase; cliché.
floskelhaft *a.* cliché-ridden.
Floß *n.* **(-es, Flöße)** raft.
Flosse, Floßfeder *f.* **(-, -n)** fin; flipper; (*fam.*) paw.
flößen *v.t.* to float.
Flöte *f.* **(-, -n)** flute.
Flotille *f.* **(-, -n)** squadron, flotilla.
Flötist *m.;* **Flötistin** *f.* flautist, flute player.
flott *a.* afloat, floating; slick; lively, fast; *wieder ~ machen,* to refloat; *~ leben,* to lead a fast life.
Flotte *f.* **(-, -n)** fleet, navy.
Flotten: ~stützpunkt *m.* naval base; **~verband** *m.* naval unit.
Flöz *n.* **(-es, -e)** layer, stratum; seam.
Fluch *m.* **(-[e]s, Flüche)** curse, malediction; (*aus Gewohnheit*) oath.
fluchen *v.t.* to curse; to swear.
Flucht *f.* **(-, 0)** flight, escape; (*wilde*) rout; (*Reihe*) range, row.
fluchtartig *a.* & *adv.* hurried(ly), hasty, hastily.
flüchten *v.i.* *(s)* & *r.* to flee, to take to flight; ~ *v.t.* to secure, to carry to a place of safety.
flüchtig *a.* fugitive; (*oberflächlich*) careless, slight, fleeting.
Flüchtigkeit *f.* cursoriness.
Flüchtigkeitsfehler *m.* slip; careless mistake.
Flüchtling *m.* **(-[e]s, -e)** refugee.
Flüchtlingslager *n.* refugee camp.
Fluchtversuch *m.* escape attempt.
Flug *m.* **(-[e]s, Flüge)** flight.
Flugbahn *f.* trajectory.
Flugbegleiter *m.;* **Flugbegleiterin** *f.* flight attendant.
Flugblatt *n.* leaflet.
Flügel *m.* **(-s, -)** wing; grand piano; leaf (of a door); blade (of a propeller).
Flügeltür *f.* double door.
Fluggast *m.* air passenger.
flügge *a.* fully fledged.
Flug: ~geschwindigkeit *f.* flying speed; **~gesellschaft** *f.* airline; **~hafen** *m.* airport; **~lotse** *m.* air traffic controller; **~platz** *n.* airfield, airport; **~preis** *m.* air fare.
flugs *adv.* quickly, instantly.
Flug: ~sand *m.* quicksand; **~schneise** *f.* approach corridor; **~schreiber** *m.* flight recorder, black box; **~schrift** *f.* pamphlet; **~zeug** *n.* aircraft, airplane; **~zeughalle** *f.* hangar; **~zeugträger** *m.* (*nav.*) aircraft carrier.
Flugzeug: ~absturz *m.* plane crash; **~besatzung** *f.* crew; **~entführer** *m.* hijacker; **~entführung** *f.* hijacking.
Flugziel *n.* destination.

Fluidum *n.* aura.
fluktuieren *v.i.* to fluctuate.
Flunder *m.* **(-s, -n)** & *f.* **(-, -n)** flounder.
Flunkerer *m.* **(-s, -)** liar.
flunkern *v.i.* to brag, to tell fibs.
Flunsch *m.* pout.
Fluoreszenz *f.* fluorescence.
Flur *f.* **(-, -en)** field, tilled plain; ~ *m.* **(-[e]s, -e)** (*Haus*~) entrance hall; corridor.
Fluß *m.* **(Flusses, Flüsse)** flow; river, stream; flux.
Fluß: ~abschnitt *m.* reach; **~bett** *n.* channel, river bed; **~gebiet, ~becken** *n.* river basin; **~krebs** *m.* crayfish; **~landschaft** *f.* fluvial topography; **~mündung** *f.* river mouth; **~pferd** *n.* hippopotamus; **~übergang** *m.* river crossing; **~ufer** *n.* riverbank.
flüssig *a.* fluid, liquid.
Flüssigkeit *f.* **(-, -en)** fluidity; fluid, liquid.
flüstern *v.t.* to whisper.
Flüster: ~propaganda *f.* underground propaganda; **~ton** *m.* whisper; **~tüte** *f.* megaphone; **~witz** *m.* underground joke.
Flut *f.* **(-, -en)** flood; high tide; (*fig.*) torrent, spate.
fluten *v.i.* to flow.
Flutlicht *n.* floodlight.
Flutwelle *f.* tidal wave.
Fockmast *m.* **(-es, -e)** foremast.
Focksegel *n.* foresail.
Föderalismus *m.* federalism.
föderalistisch *a.* federalist.
Föderation *f.* federation.
föderativ *a.* federal.
fohlen *v.i.* foal.
Fohlen *n.* **(-s, -)** foal, colt.
Föhn *m.* **(-[e]s, -e)** föhn, foehn (a warm, dry mountain wind).
Föhre *f.* **(-, -n)** pine tree.
Fol., fol. *Folio,* page, folio.
Folge *f.* **(-, -n)** succession, series; consequence; (*Zeit*) future, sequel; ~ **leisten,** to comply with; *infolge,* in consequence of, pursuant to; *zufolge,* according to.
Folgeerscheinung *f.* consequence.
folgen *v.i. (s)* to follow, to succeed; to result, to ensue; to obey; *im Folgenden,* hereinafter.
folgendermaßen *adv.* in the following manner.
folgenreich *a.* momentous.
folgenschwer *a.* portentous, serious.
folgerecht, folgerichtig *a.* consistent; logical.
Folgerichtigkeit *f.* logicality.
folgern *v.t.* to conclude, to infer.
Folgerung *f.* **(-, -en)** deduction, conclusion, inference.
Folgeschaden *m.* consequential damage.
folgewidrig *a.* inconsistent.
Folgezeit *f.* time to come, after-ages *pl.*
folglich *adv.* consequently, therefore.
folgsam *a.* obedient; obsequious.
Foliant *m.* **(-en, -en)** folio (volume).
Folie *f.* **(-, -n)** foil.
Folio *n.* **(-[s], -s & Folien)** folio.
folkloristisch *a.* folklore.
Follikel *m.* follicle.
Follikelsprung *m.* ovulation.
Folter *f.* **(-, -n)** rack, torture.
foltern *v.t.* to torture; (*fig.*) to torment.
Folterung *f.* torture.
Fön *m.* hair dryer.
Fond *m.* rear compartment, back.
Fonds *m.* **(-, -)** fund, capital, stock.
fönen *v.t.* to blow-dry.
Fontäne *f.* fountain.
foppen *v.t.* to put sb. on; to hoax.
Förder: ~anlage *f.* conveyor; **~band** *n.* conveyor belt.
Förderer *m.;* **Förderin** *f.* patron.
förderlich *a.* useful, beneficial.
fordern *v.t.* to demand, to claim, to call for; to require; (*zum Duell*) to challenge.
fördern *v.t.* to further, to forward; to promote; (*Bergwerk*) to haul; *zu Tage* ~, to bring to light, to unearth.
förderndes Mitglied *n.* sponsoring member.
Förderschacht *f.* engine shaft.
Forderung *f.* **(-, -en)** demand, claim; challenge.
Förderung *f.* **(-, -en)** furtherance; promotion; hauling, output.
Forelle *f.* **(-, -n)** trout.
forensisch *a.* forensic.
Form *f.* **(-, -en)** shape, form, figure; fashion; model, pattern; mold.
formal *a.* formal.
Formalität *f.* **(-, -en)** formality, form.
Format *n.* **(-[e]s, -e)** (*Buch*) size; format, form, shape.
formbar *a.* malleable; soft; pliable.
Formel *f.* **(-, -n)** formula, form.
formell *a.* & *adv.* formal(ly), in due form.
formen *v.t.* to form, to shape, to mold.
Formenlehre *f.* morphology.
Form: ~fehler *m.* irregularity; faux pas; **~frage** *f.* formality; **~gebung** *f.* design.
formieren *v.t.* to form.
Formierung *f.* formulation.
förmlich *a.* formal, in due form; ceremonious, stiff; explicit; regular, downright; ~ *adv.* actually; formally.
Förmlichkeit *f.* **(-, -en)** formality.
formlos *a.* shapeless; informal; rude.
Formular *n.* **(-[e]s, -e)** (printed) form, schedule.
formulieren *v.t.* to formulate; *neu* ~, to restate.
Formulierung *f.* formulation.
formvollendet *a.* perfectly shaped.
forsch *a.* (*fam.*) vigorous, self-assertive.
forschen *v.i.* to do research, to search, to inquire.
Forscher *m.* **(-s, -)** researcher, investigator, scholar.
Forschung *f.* **(-, -en)** research, investigation; **~sreisender** *m.* explorer.
Forst *m.* **(-es, -e)** forest.
Forstakademie *f.* school of forestry.
Forstamt *n.* Forestry Commission.
Förster *m.* **(-s, -)** forester, ranger.
fort *adv.* on; off, gone, away; *in einem* ~, without interruption; *und so* ~, and so on.
fortan *adv.* henceforth.
fortarbeiten *v.i.* to keep on working.
fortbegeben *v.r.st.* to leave.
Fortbestand *m.* continuation; continued existence.
fortbestehen *v.i.st.* to continue to exist.
fortbewegen *v.t.* & *r.* to move on.
fortbilden *v.r.* to continue studying.
Fortbildung *f.* continuing education.
Fortbildungsschule *f.* school for continuing education.
fortbleiben *v.i.st. (s)* to stay away.
fortbringen *v.t.ir.* to carry away; to help forward.
Fortdauer *f.* **(-, 0)** continuance.

fortdauern *v.i.* to continue, to last.
fortdürfen *v.i.ir.* to be permitted to go.
fortentwickeln *v.t.* to develop sth. further.
fortfahren *v.i.st. (h)* to continue, to go on.
fortführen *v.t.* to carry on.
Fortgang *m.* **(-[e]s, 0)** progress, success.
fortgehen *v.i.st. (s)* to go away.
Fortgeschrittener *m.* advanced student.
fortgesetzt *a. & adv.* continual(ly), constant(ly).
fortjagen *v.t.* to expel; to chase away.
fortkommen *v.i.st. (s)* to prosper; *gut, schlecht ~*, to do well, ill.
Fortkommen *n.* **(-s, 0)** progress, success.
fortlassen *v.t.st.* to allow to go.
fortlaufen *v.i.st. (s)* to run away.
fortlaufend *a.* continuous, continual.
fortleben *v.i.* to live on.
fortmachen *v.i. & v.r.* to make off.
fortmarschieren *v.i. (s)* to march off or on.
fortmüssen *v.i.ir.* to be obliged to go.
fortpflanzen *v.t. & v.r.* to reproduce; to propagate; to transmit; (*Krankheit*) to spread.
Fortpflanzung *f.* **(-, 0)** propagation, reproduction.
Fortpflanzungs... reproductive *a.*
fortreisen *v.i. (s)* to depart.
fortrennen *v.i.ir. (s)* to run off.
fortrücken *v.t. (h) & i. (s)* to move on, to remove; to advance, to make progress.
Forts. *Fortsetzung*, continuation.
fortschaffen *v.t.* to carry off, to remove.
fortschicken *v.t.* to send away.
fortschleppen *v.r.* to drag oneself on.
fortschreiten *v.t.st. (s)* to proceed, to make progress; to improve.
fortschreitend *a.* progressive.
Fortschritt *m.* **(-[e]s, -e)** progress.
fortschrittlich *a.* progressive.
fortsetzen *v.t.* to continue, to pursue.
Fortsetzer *m.* **(-s, -)** continuer.
Fortsetzung *f.* **(-, -en)** continuation, sequel.
Fortsetzungsroman *m.* serialized novel.
forttragen *v.t.st.* to carry away.
fortwährend *a. & adv.* continual(ly).
fortwirken *v.i.* to continue to operate.
fortwollen *v.i.ir.* to want to go.
fortziehen *v.t.st.* to draw away; ~ *v.i.st. (s)* to move off; to leave (a house).
fossil *a.* fossilized, fossil.
Fossil *n.* **(-[e]s, -ien)** fossil.
Foto *n.* photo, picture.
Foto: ~apparat *m.* camera; **~atelier** *n.* photographic studio.
fotogen *a.* photogenic.
Fotograf *m.* **(-en, -en); Fotografin** *f.* **(-, -nen)** photographer.
fotographieren *v.t. & i.* to photograph, to take pictures.
fotographisch *a.* photographic.
Fotokopie *f.* photocopy.
Fotokopierer *m.*, **Fotokopiergerät** *n.* photocopier.
Fotothek *f.* photographic library.
Fötus *m.* fetus.
Foul *n.* foul.
Foyer *n.* lounge, foyer.
Fr. *Frau*, Mrs., Ms; *Freitag*, Friday, Fri.
Fracht *f.* **(-, -en)** freight; load; cargo; ~ **geld,** freight; ~ **bezahlt,** freight paid.
Fracht: ~brief *m.* waybill; **~dampfer** *m.* cargo steamer.
Frachter *m.* freighter, cargo ship.
frachtfrei *a.* freight prepaid; carriage-paid.
Frack *m.* **(-[e]s, Fräcke)** tailcoat; **~hemd** *n.* dress shirt.
Frage *f.* **(-, -n)** question; issue; *eine ~ stellen*, to ask a question; *in ~ stellen*, to question; *ohne ~*, unquestionably.
Fragebogen *m.* questionnaire.
fragen *v.t.* to ask, to demand; *es fragt sich*, it is doubtful, the question is whether...
Frage: ~wort *n.* interrogative; **~zeichen** *n.* question mark.
fragil *a.* fragile.
fraglich *a.* questionable; doubtful.
fragwürdig *a.* questionable; dubious.
Fraktion *f.* **(-, -en)** parliamentary party; faction.
fraktionslos *a.* independent.
Fraktionszwang *m.* obligation to vote according to party policy.
Frakturschrift *f.* Gothic type.
frank *a.* free, frank, ingenuous.
Franken *n.* Franconia.
frankieren *v.t.* to stamp.
frankiert, franko *a.* prepaid.
Frankreich *n.* France.
Franse *f.* **(-, -n)** fringe.
fransig *a.* fringed, frayed.
Franziskaner *m.* **(-s, -)** Franciscan.
Franzose *m.* Frenchman; **Französin** French woman.
französisch *a.* French.
Französisch *n.* French.
frappant *a.* striking.
frappieren *v.t.* to astonish.
frappierend *a.* astonishing, remarkable.
Fräse *f.* milling machine; molding machine; rotary cultivator.
Fraß *m.* food (animals); muck.
fraternisieren *v.i.* to fraternize.
Fratz *m.* **(-es, -en)** brat, naughty child; (little) rascal.
Fratze *f.* **(-, -n)** grimace; caricature.
Frau *f.* **(-, -en)** woman; wife; lady; (*auf Briefen*) Mrs. (=Mistress).
Frauen: ~arzt *m.* gynecologist; **~bewegung** *f.* women's movement; **~feind** *m.* misogynist; **~haus** *n.* battered wives' refuge; **~held** *m.* womanizer; **~kloster** *n.* nunnery; **~zimmer** *n.* (*fam.*) woman, female.
Fräulein *n.* **(-s, -)** Miss (title); young lady, single lady.
fraulich *a.* feminine; womanly.
Fraulichkeit *f.* femininity; womanliness.
frech *a.* insolent, saucy, shameless.
Frechheit *f.* **(-, -en)** impudence.
Freesie *f.* freesia.
Fregatte *f.* **(-, -n)** frigate.
Fregattenkapitän *m.* commander.
frei *a.* free; disengaged; exempt; vacant; *im Freien*, outdoors, in the open air; *es steht dir ~*, you are at liberty (to); *es einem ~ stellen*, to leave sb. at liberty (to); ~ **Eisenbahn,** free on rail; ~ **Schiff,** free on board; **~e Berufe** *pl.* the independent professions; **~e Fahrt** (*mot.*) clear road ahead; **~e Wirtschaft,** private enterprise; *aus ~er Hand*, off-hand; *aus ~em Willen*, of one's own free will.
Freibad *n.* outdoor swimming pool.
freibekommen *v.i.st.* to get time off.
freiberuflich *a.* self-employed; freelance.

Freibetrag *m.* allowance.
Freibrief *m.* charter.
Freidenker *m.* freethinker.
freien *v.t. & i.* to court, to woo; to marry.
Freier *m.* **(-s, -)** wooer, suitor.
Freiexemplar *n.* free copy, presentation copy.
Freifrau *f.* baroness.
Freigabe *f.* release.
freigeben *v.t.* st. to set free, to release.
freigebig *a.* liberal, generous.
Freigeist *m.* freethinker.
Freihafen *m.* free port.
Freihandel *m.* free trade.
Freihandzeichnen *n.* freehand drawing.
Freiheit *f.* **(-, -en)** freedom, liberty; *in* ~, at large.
freiheitlich *a.* liberal.
Freiheitsberaubung *f.* wrongful detention.
Freiheitsbewegung *f.* liberation movement.
Freiheitsentzug *m.* imprisonment.
Freiheitskämpfer *m.* freedom fighter.
Freiheitsrechte *pl.* civil rights.
Freiheitsstrafe *f.* imprisonment.
freiheraus *adv.* openly, frankly.
Freiherr *m.* baron.
freiherrlich *a.* baronial.
Freiin *f.* **(-, -nen)** baron's daughter.
freikaufen *v.t.* to ransom.
freikommen *v.i.st.* to be released.
Freikörperkultur *f.* nudism.
freilassen *v.t.st.* to set free, to release.
Freilauf *m.* freewheel.
freilebend *a.* living in the wild.
freilegen *v.t.* to uncover.
freilich *adv.* indeed, certainly, to be sure, it is true, I admit.
Freilichtbühne *f.* open-air theater.
Freilichttheater *n.* open-air theater.
freimachen *v.t.* to stamp; ~ *v.r.* to free sb.; to arrange to be free; to take off one's clothes.
Freimaurer *m.* freemason.
Freimut *m.* frankness, candor.
freimütig *a.* candid, frank.
Freiraum *m.* (*psych.*) space to be oneself.
freischaffend *a.* freelance.
Freischärler *m.* **(-s, -)** guerilla.
freisinnig *a.* liberal.
freisprechen *v.t.st.* to acquit.
Freisprechung *f.* acquittal.
Freistaat *m.* republic; free state.
Freistätte *f.* refuge, asylum.
Freistelle *f.* scholarship (in a school).
Freitag *m.* Friday.
Freitreppe *f.* outside stairs.
Freiübungen *f.pl.* calisthenics, light gymnastics *pl.*
Freiwild *n.* fair game.
freiwillig *a.* voluntary, spontaneous.
Freiwillige *m./f.* **(-n, -n)** volunteer.
Freizeichen *n.* dial tone.
Freizeit *f.* free/leisure time.
Freizeit: ~beschäftigung *f.* leisure time activity; **~kleidung** *f.* casual wear.
freizügig *a.* generous, liberal, permissive.
Freizügigkeit *f.* **(-, 0)** generosity, liberalness, right of settlement.
fremd *a.* strange, foreign, outlandish.
fremdartig *a.* strange, odd.
Fremde *m./f.* stranger, foreigner; alien.
Fremde *f.* foreign parts; away from home.
Fremdenamt *n.* visitors' bureau.
Fremdenbuch *n.* visitors' book; hotel register.
fremdenfeindlich *a.* xenophobic.
Fremdenfeindlichkeit *f.*, **Fremdenhaß** *m.* xenophobia.
Fremdenführer *m.* guide.
Fremdenlegion *f.* foreign legion.
Fremdenverkehr *m.* tourist traffic.
fremdgehen *v.i.st.* (*fam.*) to be unfaithful.
Fremdheit *f.* strangeness.
Fremdherrschaft *f.* **(-, -en)** foreign domination.
Fremdkörper *m.* foreign body.
Fremdling *m.* **(-[e]s, -e)** stranger.
Fremdsprache *f.* foreign language.
Fremdsprachen: ~korrespondent *m.*; **~korrespondentin** *f.* foreign-language correspondent **~sekretär** *m.*; **~sekretärin** *f.* bilingual/multilingual secretary.
Fremdwort *n.* **(-[e]s, -wörter)** foreign word.
frenetisch *a.* frenetic.
frequentieren *v.t.* to frequent, to use.
Frequenz *f.* (*elek.*) frequency.
Fresko *n.* **(-s, Fresken)** fresco (-painting).
fressen *v.t.st.* to eat (animals); to devour.
Fressen *n.* **(-s, -)** food, meal.
Fresserei *f.* guzzling, stuffing.
Frettchen *n.* **(-s, -)** ferret.
Freude *f.* **(-, -n)** joy; enjoyment, pleasure, delight.
Freudenfest *n.* celebration.
Freudenfeuer *n.* bonfire.
Freudentaumel *m.* transport of delight.
freudestrahlend *a.* beaming with joy.
freudetrunken *a.* overjoyed, enraptured.
freudig *a.* joyful, joyous, cheerful.
freudlos *a.* joyless, cheerless.
freuen *v.t.* to please; to give pleasure; *das freut mich,* I am glad of that; ~ *v.r.* (*über*) to be glad of; (*auf*) to look forward to.
Freund *m.* **(-[e]s, -e)** friend.
Freundeskreis *m.* circle of friends.
Freundin *f.* **(-, -nen)** (female) friend.
freundlich *a.* kind, friendly; (*Ort*) cheerful.
freundlicherweise *adv.* kindly.
Freundlichkeit *f.* **(-, -en)** kindness.
Freundschaft *f.* **(-, -en)** friendship.
freundschaftlich *a.* amicable, friendly.
Freundschafts: ~besuch *m.* goodwill visit; **~vertrag** *m.* treaty of friendship.
Frevel *m.* **(-s, -)** crime; outrage.
frevelhaft *a.* mischievous, criminal.
freveln *v.i.* to commit an outrage.
Frevler *m.* **(-s, -)** transgressor; offender.
Friede[n] *m.* **(-dens, 0)** peace; *im* ~*n*, at peace.
Friedensbewegung *f.* peace movement.
Friedensbruch *m.* violation of the peace.
Friedensnobelpreis *m.* Nobel Peace Prize.
Friedensrichter *m.* Justice of the peace, J.P.
Friedensschluß *m.* conclusion of peace.
Friedensstifter *m.* peacemaker.
Friedenstruppe *f.* peace-keeping force.
Friedensverhandlungen *pl.* peace talks.
Friedensvertrag *m.* peace treaty.
friedfertig *a.* peaceful, peaceable.
Friedhof *m.* church-yard, cemetery, graveyard.
friedlich *a.* peaceable, peaceful.
friedliebend *a.* peaceable.
frieren *v.i.st.* to freeze; to feel cold.
Fries *m.* **(-es, -e)** (*arch.*) frieze; (*Zeug*) baize.
frigide *a.* frigid.

Frikadelle *f.* meatball.
Frikassee *n.* fricassee.
Friktion *f.* friction.
frisch *a.* fresh; new; (*fig.*) brisk; bright; vigorous; hale.
Frische *f.* **(-, 0)** freshness; vigor.
Frischzellentherapie *f.* living-cell therapy.
Friseur *m.* **(-[e]s, -e); Friseuse** *f.* **(-, -n)** hairdresser.
frisieren *v.t.* to dress the hair.
Frist *f.* **(-, -en)** time limit; deadline.
fristen *v.t.* (*das Leben*) to get by somehow.
frist: ~gemäß, ~gerecht *a.* in time.
fristlos *a.* & *adv.* without notice.
Frisur *f.* **(-, -en)** hair style, hair do.
Friteuse *f.* deep fryer.
frivol *a.* & *adv.* frivolous(ly).
Frl. *Fräulein,* Miss, Ms.
froh *a.* joyous, glad, joyful.
frohgelaunt *a.* cheerful.
frohgemut *a.* happy; ~ *adv.* in good spirits.
fröhlich *a.* joyous; merry, cheerful.
Fröhlichkeit *f.* cheerfulness.
frohlocken *v.i.* to rejoice; to exult.
Froh: ~natur *f.* cheerful person; **~sinn** *m.* cheerfulness, gaiety.
fromm *a.* pious, religious.
Frömmelei *f.* **(-, -en)** sanctimoniousness.
Frömmigkeit *f.* **(-, 0)** piety.
Frondienst *m.*, **Fron(e)** *f.* **(-, -n)** enforced labor; (*hist.*) corveé.
frönen *v.i.* to indulge in.
Fronleichnamsfest *n.* Corpus Christi Day.
Front *f.* **(-, -en)** front, façade; face.
frontal *a.* frontal; head-on.
Frontal: ~angriff *m.* frontal attack; **~zusammenstoß** *m.* head-on collision.
Frontantrieb *m.* front-wheel drive (car).
Frosch *m.* **(-es, Frösche)** frog.
Froschkönig *m.* Frog Prince.
Froschperspektive *f.* worm's eye view.
Froschschenkel *m.* frog's leg.
Frost *m.* **(-es, Fröste)** frost; chill; cold.
Frostbeule *f.* chillblain; frostbite.
frösteln *v.i.* to shiver, to feel chilly.
frostig *a.* frosty; chilly; frigid.
frottieren *v.t.* (*med.*) to rub.
Frotzelei *f.* teasing remark.
frotzeln *v.t.* to tease.
Frucht *f.* **(-, Früchte)** fruit; (*fig.*) result, effect.
fruchtbar *a.* fruitful, productive, fertile.
Fruchtbarkeit *f.* **(-, 0)** fruitfulness, fertility; fecundity.
Fruchtblase *f.* amniotic sac.
Früchtchen *n.* (*fam.*) good-for-nothing.
Fruchteis *n.* sorbet.
fruchten *v.i.* (*fig.*) to be effectual.
fruchtlos *a.* fruitless; ineffectual.
Fruchtsaft *m.* fruit juice.
Fruchtsalat *m.* fruit salad.
Fruchtwasser *n.* amniotic fluid.
Fruchtwechsel *m.* rotation of crops.
Fruchtzucker *m.* fructose.
früh *a.* & *adv.* early; in the morning.
Früh: ~aufsteher *m.* early bird; **~dienst** *m.* early duty.
Frühe *f.* **(-, 0)** early morning; *in aller ~,* early in the morning.
Früherkennung *f.* early diagnosis/recognition.
frühestens *adv.* at the earliest.
Frühgeburt *f.* premature birth.
Frühjar *n.* spring.
Frühling *m.* **(-s, -e)** spring.
frühreif *a.* precocious.
Frühschicht *f.* early shift.
Frühschoppen *m.* morning drink.
Frühstadium *n.* early stage.
Frühstart *m.* early start.
Frühstück *n.* breakfast; ~ **anrichten,** to make *or* serve breakfast.
frühstücken *v.i.* to breakfast.
frühzeitig *a.* early, premature; untimely.
Frust *m.* (*fam.*), **Frustration** *f.* frustration.
frustrieren *v.t.* to frustrate.
frz. *französisch,* French, Fr.
Fuchs *m.* **(Fuchses, Füchse)** fox, sorrel horse; (*Student*) freshman.
fuchsen *v.t.* to annoy; ~ *v.r.* to be annoyed.
Füchsin *f.* vixen.
Fuchsjagd *f.* fox hunt.
Fuchsschwanz *m.* foxtail; (*mech.*) pad saw.
fuchsteufelswild *a.* hopping mad.
Fuchtel *f.* **(-, -n)** ferule, rod; *unter der ~ stehen,* to be under the thumb.
fuchteln *v.i.* to fidget.
Fuder *n.* **(-s, -)** cartload.
Fug *m.* **(-[e]s, 0)** *mit ~ und Recht,* with good cause.
Fuge *f.* **(-, -n)** juncture, joint; groove; (*mus.*) fugue; *aus den ~n sein,* to be out of joint.
fügen *v.t.* to join, to unite; ~ *v.r.* to be suitable, to be convenient; to submit (to), to conform (to); to chance, to happen.
fügsam *a.* accommodating, docile.
Fügung *f.* **(-, -en)** contingency; divine Providence.
fühlbar *a.* sensible, perceptible.
fühlen *v.t.* to feel; to be sensible or aware of.
Fühler *m.* **(-s, -)** antenna, feeler, tentacle.
Fühlung *f.* **(-, -en)** contact (*mil.*) touch; *~ haben mit jm.,* to be in touch with sb.
Fuhre *f.* **(-, -n)** conveyance; cartload.
führen *v.t.* to convey, to conduct; to lead, to guide; to manage; (*Bücher*) to keep; (*Waren*) to keep, to deal in; (*betreiben*) to carry on; *die Aufsicht ~ über,* to superintend; *den Beweis ~,* to show proof; *das Wort ~,* to be spokesman; *wohin soll das ~?* what we are coming to?
Führer *m.* **(-s, -)** leader; conductor; guide; pilot; guidebook.
Führerprinzip *n.* leadership principle.
Führerschaft *f.* **(-, 0)** leadership.
Führerschein *m.* (*mot.*) driver's license.
Fuhrmann *m.* wagoner, carrier.
Führung *f.* **(-, -en)** guidance, conduct; direction, management; (*mil.*) generalship.
Führungsaufgabe *f.* management/leadership function.
Führungsanspruch *m.* claim to leadership.
Führungskraft *f.* executive.
Führungsspitze *f.* top echelons.
Führungszeugnis *n.* certificate of good conduct.
Fuhrwerk *n.* carriage, vehicle.
Fülle *f.* **(-, 0)** plenty; abundance; *in Hülle und ~,* enough and to spare.
füllen *v.t.* to fill (up); to stuff; (*Zahn*) to stop.
Füllen *n.* **(-s, -)** foal, colt, filly.
Füller, Füllfeder *f.* fountain pen.
Füllgewicht *n.* net weight.
füllig *a.* corpulent; portly; ample.

Füllung *f.* **(-, -en)** stuffing, filling; panel.
Füllwort *n.* filler; expletive.
Fummelei *f.* twiddling; petting (erotic).
fummeln *v.i.* (*fam.*) to fumble around; to pet (erotic).
Fund *m.* **(-[e]s, -e)** find.
Fundament *n.* **(-[e]s, -e)** foundation.
Fundbüro: *n.* lost and found office.
Fundgrube *f.* (*fig.*) treasure trove.
fünf *a.* **Fünf** *f.* **(-, -en)** five.
Fünfeck *n.* **(-[e]s, -e)** pentagon.
fünfeckig *a.* pentagonal.
fünferlei *a.* of five kinds.
fünffach, fünffältig *a.* fivefold, quintuple.
fünfhundert, five hundred.
Fünfhundertjahrfeier *f.* quincentenary.
Fünfkampf *m.* pentathlon.
Fünfkämpfer *m.*; **Fünfkämpferin** *f.* pentathlete.
Fünflinge *pl.* quintuplets *pl.*
fünfte Kolonne *f.* fifth column.
fünftens *adv.* fifth(ly); in the fifth place.
fünfzehn *a.* fifteen.
fünfzig *a.* fifty.
Fünfziger *m.* **(-s, -)** quinquagenarian, man of fifty.
fungieren *v.i.* to act as.
Funk *m.* **(-s, 0),** radio.
Funkamateur *m.* radio ham.
Funkaufklärung *f.* **(-, -en)** radio intelligence.
funkeln *v.i.* to sparkle, twinkle, blaze.
funkelnagelneu *a.* brand-new.
funken *v.i. & t.* to radio, to send out.
Funke[n] *m.* **(-ken[s], -ken)** spark, sparkle.
Funker *m.* **(-s, -)** radio operator.
Funkgerät *n.* radio set.
Funkmeßgerät *n.* radar.
Funkpeilung *f.* radio direction finding.
Funkspruch *m.* walkie-talkie/radio message.
Funktelegramm *n.* radio-telegram; radio.
Funktion *f.* function; functioning, working.
funktional *a.* functional.
Funktionär *m.*; **Funktionärin** *f.* official.
funktionieren *v.i.* to function, to work.
Funkturm *m.* radio tower.
Funkverbindung *f.* radio contact.
Funkverkehr *m.* radio communication.
für *pr.* for; instead of; (*im Interesse von*) on behalf of; *an und ~ sich,* in itself; *Tag ~ Tag,* day by day; *~ sich leben,* to live by oneself; *er ~ seine Person,* he, for one; *~ und wider,* pro and con.
Fürbitte *f.* **(-, -n)** intercession.
Furche *f.* **(-, -n)** furrow.
furchen *v.t.* to furrow; (*fig.*) to wrinkle.
Furcht *f.* **(-, 0)** fear, fright, dread.
furchtbar *a.* terrible, dreadful; awful.
furchteinflößend *a.* frightening, fearsome.
fürchten *v.t.* to fear, to apprehend, to dread; ~ *v.r.* to be afraid.
fürchterlich *a.* terrible, frightful.
furchterregend *a.* frightening.
furchtlos *a.* fearless, intrepid.
Furchtlosigkeit *f.* fearlessness.
furchtsam *a.* timid, nervous, shy.
Furchtsamkeit *f.* timidity; fearfulness.
füreinander *adv.* for each other, for one another.
Furie *f.* **(-, -n)** fury.
Furnier *n.* **(-s, -e)** veneer.
furnieren *v.t.* to veneer.
Furore *f.* **~machen** cause a sensation.
Fürsorge *f.* care; welfare.
fürsorgend, fürsorglich *a.* caring, thoughtful, considerate.
Fürsorglichkeit *f.* considerateness, thoughtfulness.
Fürsprache *f.* **(-, -n)** support; intercession, good offices *pl.*
Fürsprecher *m.* **(-s, -)** intercessor, mediator.
Fürst *m.* **(-en, -en)** prince, sovereign.
Fürstenhaus *n.* dynasty.
Fürstentum *n.* principality.
Fürstin *f.* **(-, -nen)** princess.
fürstlich *a.* princely; sumptuous.
Furt *f.* **(-, -en)** ford.
Furunkel *m.* furuncle.
Fürwort *n.* **(-[e]s, -wörter)** (*gram.*) pronoun.
Furz *m.* (*vulg.*) fart.
furzen *v.i.* (*vulg.*) to fart.
Fusel *m.* rotgut.
Fusion *f.* **(-, -en)** fusion; merger.
fusionieren *v.t.* to amalgamate; to merge.
Fuß *m.* **(-es, Füsse)** foot; base; footing, style; (*Münz~*) standard; *zu ~,* on foot, afoot; *auf gutem, gespanntem ~ mit einem stehen,* to be on good, strained terms with sb.
Fußabstreifer *m.* doormat.
Fußangel *f.* mantrap; trap.
Fußball *m.* soccer, football; **~toto** *m.* football pool.
Fußboden *m.* floor.
Fussel *n.* lint.
fusselig *a.* linty; *sich den Mund ~ reden,* to talk one's head off.
fußen *v.i.* to rely upon.
Fußgänger *m.* pedestrian; **~zone** *f.* pedestrian precinct.
Fußgelenk *n.* ankle.
Fußleiste *f.* baseboard.
Fußmatte *f.* doormat.
Fußnote *f.* footnote.
Fußpflege *f.* chiropody.
Fußpilz *m.* athlete's foot.
Fußsohle *f.* sole.
Fußstapfe *f.* footstep, trace, track.
Fußtritt *m.* kick.
Fußweg *m.* footpath.
futsch *a.* (*fam.*) broken.
Futter *n.* **(-s, -)** lining; food, fodder.
Futteral *n.* **(-[e]s, -e)** case.
Futterkrippe *f.* manger.
Futtermittel *n.pl.* feed, fodder.
futtern, füttern *v.t.* to line; to feed.
Fütterung *f.* **(-, -en)** feeding; lining.
Futur (um) *n.* **(-s, -a)** future tense.
futuristisch *a.* futuristic.

G

G, g *n.* the letter G or g; (*mus.*) G.
g. *Gramm*, gram.
Gabe *f.* **(-, -n)** gift, present; donation; alms; talent; (*med.*) dose.
Gabel *f.* **(-, -n)** fork; (*bot.*) tendril; (*eines Wagens*) thill, shafts *pl.*.
gabeln *v.r.* to fork, to bifurcate.
Gabelstapler *m.* forklift.
Gabelung *f.* fork (streets).
Gabentisch *m.* table for presents.
gackern *v.i.* to cluck; to cackle.
gaffen *v.i.* to gape, to stare, to gaze at.
Gag *m.* gag; gimmick.
Gage *f.* **(-, -n)** salary, pay.
gähnen *v.i.* to yawn.
Gala *f.* **(-, 0)** gala.
Gala: ~abend *m.* gala; **~diner** *n.* formal dinner; **~empfang** *m.* gala; formal reception.
Galakleid *n.* full dress, court dress.
galaktisch *a.* galactic; **~er Nebel** *m.* nebula.
galant *a.* polite, courteous; gallant.
Galanterie *f.* **(-, -[e]n)** gallantry, courtesy.
Galanteriewaren *f.pl.* trinkets, fancy articles *pl.*
Galaxie *f.* galaxy.
Galeere *f.* **(-, -n)** galley.
Galerie *f.* **(-, -[e]n)** gallery.
Galgen *m.* **(-s, -)** gallows, gibbet.
Galgenfrist *f.* (*fam.*) respite, short delay.
Galgenstrick *m.* rogue.
Galgenvogel *m.* rogue.
Galionsfigur *f.* figurehead.
Gallapfel *m.* **(-s, -äpfel)** gall nut.
Galle *f.* **(-, 0)** gall; bile.
Gallenblase *f.* gall bladder.
Gallenstein *m.* gall stone.
Gallerist *m.*; **Galleristin** *f.* gallery owner.
Gallert(e) *f.* **(-, -n)** jelly; gelatin.
gallertartig *a.* gelatinous.
gallig *a.* bilious.
Galopp *m.* **(-[e]s, -e)** gallop.
Galoppbahn *f.* race track.
galoppieren *v.i.* to gallop.
galvanisch *a.* galvanic.
galvanisieren *v.t.* to galvanize.
Galvanismus *m.* **(-, 0)** galvanism.
Galvanostegie *f.* electroplating.
Gamaschen *f.* **(-, -n)** gaiters; spats.
Gambe *f.* viola da gamba.
Gammastrahlen *pl.* (*phys.*) gamma rays.
gammelig *a.* rotten; scruffy.
gammeln *v.i.* to bum around.
Gammler *m.*; **Gammlerin** *f.* bum.
Gang *m.* **(-[e]s, -Gänge)** walk, turn; gait; (*Maschine*) movement; alley, passage, corridor; (*Speisen*) course; (*Verlauf*) progress, course; (*Pferd*) pace; *im ~ sein*, to be in progress; *in vollem ~*, in full swing; *in ~ bringen*, to set going, to start.
gang und gäbe *a.* usual, common.
Gangart *f.* way of walking; gait.
gangbar *a.* passable.
Gängelband *n.* **(-[e]s, -bänder)** leading-strings *pl.*
gängeln *v.t.* to lead by the nose.
gängig *a.* usual, common; popular.
Gangräne *f.* **(-, 0)** gangrene.
Gangschaltung *f.* gearshift.
Gangster *m.* gangster; **~bande** *f.* gang.
Gangway *f.* (avi.) steps; gangway.
Gangwerk *n.* **(-[e]s, -e)** mechanism, movement.
Ganove *m.* (*fam.*) crook.
Gans *f.* **(-, Gänse)** goose. *es überläuft mich eine ~haut*, my flesh creeps.
Gänseblume *f.* daisy.
Gänsebraten *m.* roast goose.
Gänsefüßchen *n.pl.* quotation marks, inverted commas.
Gänseklein *n.* (*goose*) giblets *pl.*
Gänsemarsch *m.* single file.
Gänserich, Ganser[t] *m.* **(-s, -e)** gander.
Gänseschmalz *n.* goose dripping.
ganz *a.* whole, entire, all; complete; **~** *adv.* quite, entirely, wholly; *eine ~e Note*, a semibreve, whole note; **~e Zahl,** integer; *im ~en*, on the whole.
Ganze *n.* **(-n, 0)** whole; totality.
Gänze *f.* *zum ~* in its totality.
gänzlich *a.* whole, total; **~** *adv.* totally, wholly.
ganzmetall *a.* all metal.
ganztägig *a.* all day.
ganztags *adv.* all day; full-time.
ganzwolle *a.* all wool.
ganzzeitlich *a.* full-time.
gar *a.* (*gekocht*) done, sufficiently cooked; **~** *adv.* quite, very, fully; even; **~ nicht,** not at all, by no means.
Garage *f.* **(-, -n)** garage.
Garantie *f.* **(-, -[e]n)** guarantee, warranty; security.
garantieren *v.t.* to warrant, guarantee.
Garaus *m.* **(-, 0)** knockout blow; *den ~ machen*, to ruin, to do someone in.
Garbe *f.* **(-, -n)** sheaf.
Garde *f.* **(-, -n)** guard.
Garderobe *f.* **(-, -n)** wardrobe; checkroom, cloakroom; clothes *pl.*
Gardine *f.* **(-, -n)** curtain.
Gardinen: ~leiste *f.*, **~stange** *f.* curtain rail.
garen *v.t. & i.* to cook.
gären *v.i.st.* to ferment; (*fig.*) to seethe.
Garn *n.* **(-[e]s, -e)** yarn, thread; *ins ~ gehen*, to fall into the net; *ins ~ locken*, to decoy.
Garnele *f.* **(-, -n)** shrimp.
garnieren *v.t.* to garnish, to trim.
Garnierung *f.* garnish; garnishing.
Garnison *f.* **(-, -en)** garrison.
Garnitur *f.* **(-, -en)** set; (*Besatz*) trimming.
Garnknäuel *n.* ball of thread.
Garnrolle *f.* reel; bobbin.
garstig *a.* nasty; naughty.
Garten *m.* **(-s, Gärten)** garden.
Gartenarbeit *f.* gardening.
Gartenbau *m.* horticulture.
Gartenfest *n.* garden party.
Gartenhaus *n.* summer house.
Gartenlokal *n.* beer garden.
Gartenmesser *n.* pruning knife.
Gärtner *m.* **(-s, -); Gärtnerin** *f.* gardener.
Gärtnerei *f.* **(-, -en)** nursery.
Gärung *f.* **(-, 0)** fermentation.
Gas *n.* **(-es, -e)** gas.
Gasanzünder *m.* gas lighter.

gasartig *a.* gaseous.
Gasbeleuchtung *f.* gas-lighting.
Gasbrenner *m.* burner.
gasförmig *a.* gaseous.
Gasfußhebel *m.* (*mot.*) accelerator.
Gashahn *m.* gas tap.
Gasmaske *f.* gas mask.
Gasmesser *m.* gas meter.
Gasometer *m.* **(-s, -)** gasometer.
Gaspedal *n.* (*mot.*) accelerator.
Gasrohr *n.* gas pipe.
Gasse *f.* **(-, -n)** street; lane.
Gassenbube *m.* street-boy.
Gassenhauer *m.* popular song.
Gassenjunge *m.* street urchin.
Gast *m.* **(-[e]s, Gäste)** guest; visitor; stranger; customer; *Gäste haben,* to have company; *zu ~ bitten,* to invite (to dinner *or* supper).
gastfrei, gastfreundlich *a.* hospitable.
Gastfreundschaft *f.* hospitality.
Gastgeber *m.* host.
Gastgeberin *f.* hostess.
Gasthaus *n.* restaurant, inn.
Gasthof *m.* hotel.
Gasthörer *m.* auditor.
gastlich *a.* hospitable.
Gastlichkeit *f.* hospitality.
Gastmahl *n.* banquet, dinner party.
Gastprofessor *m.;* **Gastprofessorin** *f.* visiting professor.
Gastrecht *n.* right to hospitality.
Gastritis *f.* gastritis.
Gastrolle *f.* guest role *or* appearance.
Gastronom *m.* restaurant owner.
Gastronomie *f.* restaurant trade, gastronomy.
Gastronomin *f.* restaurant owner.
Gastronomisch *a.* gastronomic.
Gastspiel *n.* guest performance; **~reise** *f.* tour.
Gaststätte *f.* restaurant.
Gastvorlesung *f.* guest lecture.
Gastwirt *m.* host, landlord; **~schaft** *f.* inn.
Gatte *m.* **(-n, -n)** husband, spouse, consort.
Gatter *n.* **(-s, -)** grate, lattice; railing.
Gattin *f.* **(-, -nen)** wife, spouse.
Gattung *f.* **(-, -en)** kind, sort; (*liter.*) genre; (*Naturgeschichte*) species, family genus.
Gattungsname *m.* appellative, generic name.
Gau *m.* **(-[e]s, -e)** district; county.
GAU *größter anzunehmender Unfall,* maximum credible accident, MCA.
Gaudi *f.* (*fam.*) fun.
Gaukelei *f.* **(-, -en)** juggling; (*fig.*) trick, imposture.
gaukeln *v.i.* to juggle; to sway to and fro, to dangle.
Gaukelspiel *n.* **(-[e]s, -e)** delusion.
Gaukler *m.* **(-s, -)** conjurer, juggler.
Gaul *m.* **(-[e]s, Gäule)** horse, nag.
Gaumen *m.* **(-s, -)** palate.
Gaumen: ~freude *f.,* **~kitzel** *m.;* **~schmaus** *m.* delicacy.
Gauner *m.* **(-s, -)** cheat, crook, swindler.
Gaze *f.* **(-, -n)** gauze.
Gazelle *f.* **(-, -n)** gazelle.
geachtet *a.* respected.
Geächtete[r] *m.* **(-n, -n)** outlaw.
Geächze *n.* **(-s, 0)** groaning.
geädert *a.* veined, veiny.
geartet *a.* disposed; *gut ~,* good-natured.
Geäst *n.* branches.
geb. *geboren,* born, b.
Gebäck *n.* **(-[e]s, -e)** pastry.
Gebälk *n.* **(-[e]s, -e)** beams; rafters; timber-work, frame.
geballt *a.* concentrated; clenched.
Gebärde *f.* **(-, -n)** gesture.
gebärden *v.r.* to behave.
Gebärdensprache *f.* sign language.
gebaren *v.r.* to behave.
gebären *v.t.st.* to bear (a child), to give birth to.
Gebaren *n.* behavior, conduct.
Gebärmutter *f.* womb, uterus.
Gebäude *n.* **(-s, -)** building, edifice.
Gebein *n.* **(-[e]s, -e)** bones *pl.;* skeleton.
Gebell *n.* **(-[e]s, 0)** barking.
geben *v.t.st.* to give; to produce; to act, to perform; (*Karten*) to deal; *es gibt,* there is, there are; ~ *v.r.st.* to abate; *Achtung ~,* to pay attention; *Nachricht ~,* to send word; *sich Mühe ~,* to take pains; *nichts auf einen ~,* to make no account of sb.; *sich zufrieden ~,* to rest content (with).
Geber *m.;* **Geberin** *f.* donor; giver.
Gebet *n.* **(-[e]s, -e)** prayer.
Gebetbuch *n.* prayer book.
Gebiet *n.* **(-[e]s, -e)** district, territory; department; (*fig.*) province, sphere.
gebieten *v.t.st.* to command, to order; ~ *v.i.st.* (*über*) to rule; to control; to possess, to dispose of.
Gebieter *m.* master; **Gebieterin** *f.* mistress.
gebieterisch *a.* imperious, peremptory.
Gebietsanspruch *m.* territorial claim.
Gebilde *n.* **(-s, -)** structure, organization; form; image.
gebildet *a.* cultured; educated.
Gebirge *n.* **(-s, -)** (range of) mountains.
gebirgig *a.* mountainous.
Gebirgsausläufer *m.* foothill.
Gebirgsbach *m.* mountain stream.
Gebirgskamm *m.* mountain ridge.
Gebirgskette *f.* mountain chain.
Gebirgsmassiv *n.* massif.
Gebirgspaß *m.* mountain pass.
Gebirgszug *m.* mountain range.
Gebiß *n.* **(-bisses, -bisse)** set of teeth; (*künstliches*) denture.
Gebläse *n.* (*tech.*) fan; blower.
Geblödel *n.* (*fam.*) silly chatter; silly things.
geblümt *a.* flowered.
Geblüt *n.* blood, descent.
geboren *p. & a.* born; *ein ~er Leipziger,* a native of Leipzig; *sie ist eine ~e N.,* her maiden name is N., neé N.
geborgen *a.* saved, secure.
Geborgenheit *f.* security.
Gebot *n.* **(-[e]s, -e)** command(ment), order; (*com.*) offer, bid; *zu ~ stehen,* to be at (someone's) disposal.
Gebotsschild *n.* mandatory sign (traffic).
Gebr. *Gebrüder,* Brothers, Bros.
Gebräu *n.* **(-s, -e)** mixture, concoction.
Gebrauch *m.* **(-[e]s, -bräuche)** use, usage; custom; rite; *außer ~ sein,* to be obsolete; *außer ~ kommen,* to fall into disuse.
gebrauchen *v.t.* to use, to employ.
gebräuchlich *a.* usual, customary; **~er** more widely used.
Gebrauchsanweisung *f.* directions for use.

gebrauchsfertig *a.* ready-made.
Gebrauchsgegenstand *m.* item of practical use.
gebraucht *a.* second-hand; used.
Gebrauchtwagen *m.* used/second-hand car.
Gebrechen *n.* **(-s, -)** disability, handicap, infirmity.
gebrechlich *a.* fragile; infirm, weak.
gebrochen *p. & a.* broken, fractured; *mit ~em Herzen,* broken-hearted.
Gebrüder *m.pl.* brothers *pl.*
Gebrüll *n.* **(-[e]s, 0)** roar; lowing.
gebückt *a.* stooping; bending forward.
Gebühr *f.* **(-, -en)** duty, due; fee; tax; *eine ~ erheben,* to charge a fee; *nach ~,* deservedly; *über ~,* unduly.
gebühren *v.i. & v.r.* to be due; to be proper, to be met.
gebührend *a. & adv.* appropriate(ly).
Gebühreneinheit *f.* (*tel.*) unit.
Gebührenerhöhung *f.* increase in charges/fees.
Gebührenermäßigung *f.* reduction of charges/fees.
gebührenfrei *a.* free of charges, post-free.
gebührlich *a.* due, suitable, proper.
Geburt *f.* **(-, -en)** delivery, childbirth; birth; extraction.
Geburtenkontrolle *f.* birth-control.
Geburtenziffer *f.* birthrate.
gebürtig *a.* born, a native of.
Geburtsdatum *n.* date of birth.
Geburtshelfer *m.*; **Geburtshelferin** *f.* midwife; obstetrician.
Geburtshilfe *f.* midwifery; obstetrics *pl.*
Geburtsland *n.* native country.
Geburtsort *m.* native place, birthplace.
Geburtsschein *m.* birth certificate.
Geburtstag *m.* birthday.
Geburtsurkunde *f.* birth certificate.
Gebüsch *n.* **(-[e]s, -e)** bushes, shrubbery, underwood.
Geck *m.* **(-en, -en)** dandy, fop.
geckenhaft *a.* foppish, dandyish.
Gedächtnis *n.* **(-nisses, 0)** memory.
Gedächtnislücke *f.* gap in one's memory.
Gedächtnisschwund *m.* loss of memory; amnesia.
Gedächtnisstütze *f.* memory aid, mnemonic.
gedämpft *a.* subdued; muted; muffled; low.
Gedanke *m.* **(-ns, -n)** thought, idea.
Gedankenblitz *m.* (*fam.*) brainwave.
Gedankenfreiheit *f.* freedom of thought.
Gedankengang *m.* train of thought.
Gedankenlesen *n.* mind reading.
gedankenlos *a.* thoughtless.
Gedankenlosigkeit *f.* thoughtlessness.
Gedankenstrich *m.* dash.
Gedankenübertragung *f.* telepathy.
gedankenverloren *a.* lost in thought.
gedankenvoll *a.* thoughtful, pensive.
gedanklich *a.* intellectual.
Gedärm *n.* **(-[e]s, -e)** intestines, bowels *pl.*
Gedeck *n.* **(-[e]s, -e)** tablecloth; plate; cover (at table), knife and fork.
gedeihen *v.i.st. (s)* to thrive; to prosper.
Gedeihen *n.* **(-s, 0)** prosperity.
gedeihlich *a.* prosperous; wholesome.
gedenken *v.i. & t.ir.* to think of; to remember; to intend.
Gedenkfeier *f.* commemoration.
Gedenkminute *f.* minute's silence.
Gedenkstätte *f.* memorial.
Gedenktag *m.* commemoration day.
Gedicht *n.* **(-[e]s, -e)** poem.
gediegen *a.* solid; pure; sterling.
Gedränge *n.* **(-s, 0)** crowd, throng.
gedrängt *a.* crowded; condensed.
gedrückt *a.* depressed.
gedrungen *a.* compact; square-built.
Gedudel *n.* (*pej.*) tootling; noise.
Geduld *f.* **(-, 0)** patience.
gedulden *v.r.* to have patience.
geduldig *a.* patient.
Geduldsfaden *m.* *mir reißt der ~* my patience is wearing thin.
Geduldsprobe *f.* trial of one's patience.
Geduldsspiel *n.* puzzle.
gedungen *a.* hired.
gedunsen *a.* bloated, sodden.
geehrt *a.* honored.
geeignet *a.* fit, adapted, suitable.
Gefahr *f.* **(-, -en)** danger, peril, risk; **~ laufen,** to run a risk; *auf eigene ~,* at one's own risk; *auf Ihre ~,* at your peril.
gefährden *v.t.* to endanger, to jeopardize, to imperil.
gefährdet *a.* at risk.
Gefährdung *f.* endangering; jeopardizing.
Gefahrenbereich *m.* danger area.
Gefahrenherd *m.* source of danger.
Gefahrenquelle *f.* source of danger.
Gefahrenzulage *f.* danger money.
gefährlich *a.* dangerous.
Gefährlichkeit *f.* dangerousness; riskiness.
gefahrlos *a.* free from danger; safe.
Gefährt *n.* vehicle.
Gefährte *m.* **(-n, -n); Gefährtin** *f.* **(-, -nen)** companion, comrade, associate, mate.
gefahrvoll *a.* perilous.
Gefälle *n.* **(-s, -)** fall, slope, grade; *starkes ~,* (*mot.*) steep downhill.
gefallen *v.i.st.* to please, to like; *sich ~ lassen,* to tolerate.
Gefallen *m.* **(-s, 0)** pleasure; liking; *einen ~ erweisen,* to do a favor.
Gefallene *m.* soldier killed in action.
gefällig *a.* pleasing; agreeable, obliging.
Gefälligkeit *f.* **(-, -en)** favor.
gefälligst *adv.* please (ironic; hidden order).
gefallsüchtig *a.* coquettish.
gefangen *a.* imprisoned; captured, captive; **~nehmen,** to take prisoner; **~setzen,** to imprison; *sich ~ geben,* to surrender, to give oneself up.
Gefangene[r] *m./f.* **(-n, -n)** prisoner, captive.
Gefangennahme *f.* **(-, 0)** imprisonment; *ungesetzliche ~,* false imprisonment.
Gefangenschaft *f.* **(-, 0)** captivity.
Gefängnis *n.* **(-ses, se)** prison, jail; *ein Jahr ~,* one year's imprisonment; **~strafe** *f.* prison sentence; **~wärter** *m.* warder; **~wärterin** *f.* wardress.
Gefasel *n.* **(-s, 0)** drivel.
Gefäß *n.* **(-es, -e)** vessel.
gefaßt *a.* composed, collected, calm; **~ auf,** prepared, ready for; *sich ~ machen,* to prepare oneself.
Gefecht *n.* **(-[e]s, -e)** fight, combat, engagement.
gefedert *a.* (*mech.*) sprung.
gefeit (gegen) *a.* immune to.
Gefieder *n.* **(-s, -)** plumage.

gefiedert *a.* feathered.
Gefilde *n.* **(-s, -)** plain, fields *pl.*
Geflecht *n.* **(-[e]s, -e)** texture; wickerwork.
gefleckt *a.* speckled, spotted.
geflissentlich *a.* intentional, wilful.
geflochten *a.* plaited.
Geflügel *n.* **(-s, 0)** poultry, fowl *pl.*
Geflügelhändler *m.* poulterer.
geflügelt *a.* winged; **~es Wort** *n.* familiar quotation.
Geflüster *n.* **(-s, 0)** whisper(ing).
Gefolge *n.* **(-s, -)** entourage, retinue, suite, attendants *pl.*
Gefolgschaft *f.* **(-, -en)** followers *pl.*
Gefolgsmann *m.* vassal; supporter, follower.
gefragt *a.* in demand, in request.
gefräßig *a.* voracious, gluttonous, greedy.
Gefräßigkeit *f.* greediness, gluttony, voracity.
Gefreite[r] *m.* **(-n, -n)** private first class; lance-corporal.
gefrieren *v.i.st. (s)* to freeze.
Gefrierfleisch *n.* frozen meat.
Gefrierpunkt *m.* **(-[e]s, 0)** freezing point, zero.
Gefrier: schrank *m.* freezer; **~truhe** *f.* (chest) freezer.
Gefüge *n.* **(-s, 0)** structure; texture, tissue.
gefügig *a.* pliant; (*fig.*) docile.
Gefühl *n.* **(-[e]s, -e)** feeling, sensation.
gefühllos *a.* numb, unfeeling, insensitive.
gefühlsarm *a.* (emotionally) cold.
Gefühlsausbruch *m.* outburst of emotion.
gefühlsbetont *a.* emotional.
Gefühlsduselei *f.* (*pej.*) sentimentality.
gefühlsmäßig *a.* emotional (reaction).
Gefühlsregung *f.* emotion.
gefühlvoll *a.* sensitive, feeling, tender.
gefüllt *a.* filled; stuffed.
gefurcht *a.* lined; wrinkled.
gefürchtet *a.* dreaded, feared.
gegeben *a.* given.
gegebenenfalls *adv.* should the occasion arise.
Gegebenheit *f.* condition; fact.
gegen *pr.* towards; against; versus; to; in exchange for; contrary to; about, nearly; *~ bar,* for cash.
Gegenangriff *m.* counterattack.
Gegenantrag *m.* counter-motion; counterproposal.
Gegenbesuch *m.* return visit.
Gegenbewegung *f.* countermovement.
Gegend *f.* **(-, -en)** region; country.
Gegendarstellung *f.* correction; reply (news).
gegeneinander *adv.* against each other; against one another.
Gegenentwurf *m.* alternative draft.
Gegenfahrbahn *f.* opposite lane.
Gegenforderung *f.* counterclaim.
Gegengewicht *n.* counterweight.
Gegengift *n.* antidote.
Gegenkandidat *m.* rival candidate.
Gegenleistung *f.* return; equivalent.
Gegenlicht *n.* back-lighting.
Gegenmaßregel *f.* preventative measure.
Gegenmittel *n.* antidote, remedy.
Gegenpapst *m.* antipope.
Gegenpartei *f.* opposite party.
Gegenprobe *f.* counter-test.
Gegensatz *m.* contrast, opposition, antithesis.
gegensätzlich *a.* contrary, opposite.
Gegenschlag *m.* counter stroke.
Gegenseite *f.* opposite side; opponent.
gegenseitig *a.* mutual, reciprocal.
Gegen: ~seitigkeit *f.* reciprocity; **~stand** *m.* object; subject.
gegenständlich *a.* representational (art).
gegenstandslos *a.* invalid; unsubstantiated, unfounded.
Gegenstimme *f.* vote against, objection.
Gegenstoß *m.* counterthrust.
Gegenstück *n.* counterpart.
Gegenteil *n.* contrary, reverse; *im ~*, on the contrary.
gegenteilig *a.* opposite.
gegenüber *adv. & pr.* opposite (to).
Gegenüber *n.* **(-s, 0)** person opposite.
Gegenüberstellung *f.* confrontation.
Gegenverkehr *m.* oncoming traffic.
Gegenvorschlag *m.* counterproposal.
Gegenwart *f.* **(-, 0)** presence; (*Zeit*) the present.
gegenwärtig *a.* current, present; ~ *adv.* at present.
Gegenwartsliteratur *f.* contemporary literature.
gegenwartsnahe *a.* topical.
Gegenwartsprobleme *pl.* current problems.
Gegenwehr *f.* defense, resistance.
Gegenwert *m.* equivalent.
Gegenwind *m.* headwind.
Gegenwirkung *f.* reaction; countereffect.
gegenzeichnen *v.t.* to countersign.
Gegenzug *m.* countermove.
gegliedert *a.* jointed; organized, structured.
Gegner *m.* **(-s, -)** opponent, adversary; *sich zum ~ machen,* to antagonize.
gegnerisch *a.* antagonistic, adverse.
Gegnerschaft *f.* **(-, -en)** antagonism; opposition *pl.*
gegr. *gegründet,* established, est.
Gegröle *n.* raucous singing; bawling.
Gehackte *n.* ground meat.
Gehalt *m.* **(-[e]s, 0)** contents *pl.;* value, merit; (*chem.*) proportion of; ~ *n.* **(-[e]s, Gehälter)** salary, wages *pl.*
Gehaltsliste *f.* payroll.
Gehaltsskala *f.* **(-, skalen)** salary scale.
Gehaltsvorschuß *m.* advance (on one's salary).
Gehaltszulage *f.* **(-, -n)** increase of salary.
gehaltvoll *a.* nourishing, substantial.
Gehänge *n.* **(-s, -)** festoon, garland.
geharnischt *a.* armor-clad; (*fig.*) angry, aggressive.
gehäßig *a.* malicious, spiteful.
Gehäßigkeit *f.* **(-, -en)** animosity, spitefulness.
gehäuft *a.* heaped.
Gehäuse *n.* **(-s, -)** case; capsule (*Obst*) core; shell.
gehbehindert *a.* disabled.
Gehege *n.* preserve; enclosure.
geheim *a.* secret; clandestine; *ganz ~, ~e Kommandosache,* top secret.
Geheimbund *m.* **(-[e]s, -bünde)** secret alliance, society.
Geheimdienst *m.* secret service.
Geheimhaltung *f.* secrecy.
Geheimmittel *n.* **(-s, -)** nostrum, patent medicine.
Geheimnis *n.* **(-ses, se)** secret, mystery, arcanum.
Geheimniskrämer *m.* secret-monger.
geheimnisvoll *a.* mysterious.
Geheimpolizei *f.* secret police.
Geheimschrift *f.* **(-, -en)** cipher; code.
Geheimsprache *f.* **(-, -n)** secret language.

Geheimtuerei *f.* **(-, -en)** secretiveness.
Geheiß *n.* **(-es, 0)** order, command.
gehemmt *a.* inhibited.
gehen *v.i.st. (s)* to go, to walk; to sell *(v.i.)*; (*Maschinen*) to work; *zum Fischen* ~, to go fishing; *wie geht es Ihnen?*, how are you?; *es geht nicht*, it won't do!; *vor sich* ~, to take place; *sich* ~ *lassen*, to indulge one's humor.
Geher *m.;* **Geherin** *f.* walker.
geheuer *a.* safe; *nicht* ~, haunted; unsafe.
Geheul *n.* **(-[e]s, 0)** howl(ing).
Gehilfe *m.* **(-n, -n)** assistant.
Gehirn *n.* **(-[e]s, -e)** brain, brains *pl.*
Gehirnerschütterung *f.* concussion of the brain.
Gehirnerweichung *f.* softening of the brain.
Gehirnhautentzündung *f.* meningitis.
Gehirnschlag *m.* stroke, apoplexy.
Gehöft *n.* **(-[e]s, -e)** homestead.
Gehölz *n.* **(-es, -e)** wood, copse.
Gehör *n.* **(-[e]s, 0)** hearing; *sich* ~ *verschaffen*, to make oneself heard; ~ *finden*, to be heard; *ein gutes* ~, a good ear.
gehorchen *v.i.* to obey.
gehören *v.i.* to belong; to appertain; ~ *v.r.* to be proper.
Gehörgang *m.* auditory duct.
Gehörhilfe *f.* hearing aid.
gehörig *a.* belonging, appertaining; proper, due; ~ *adv.* duly, soundly.
gehörlos *a.* deaf.
Gehörnerv *m.* auditory nerve.
gehörnt *a.* horned; antlered; (*fig.*) cuckolded.
Gehörorgan *n.* organ of hearing.
Gehörrohr *n.* **(-s, -e)** ear trumpet.
gehorsam *a.* obedient.
Gehorsam *m.* **(-[e]s, 0)** obedience.
Gehorsamsverweigerung *f.* (*mil.*) insubordination.
Gehörsinn *m.* sense of hearing.
Gehsteig *m.* sidewalk.
Gehverwundete *m.* **(-n, -n)** walking wounded.
Geier *m.* **(-s, -)** vulture.
Geifer *m.* **(-s, 0)** slaver, slobber; (*fig.*) venom.
geifern *v.i.* to slaver; to foam.
Geige *f.* **(-, -n)** violin, fiddle.
geigen *v.i.* to play the violin, to fiddle.
Geigenbogen *m.* fiddlestick, bow.
Geigenkasten *m.* violin case.
Geiger *m.* **(-s, -)** violinist, fiddler.
Geigerzähler *m.* (*phys.*) Geiger counter.
geil *a.* (*fam.*) terrific; randy, horny.
Geisel *m.* **(-s, -n)** hostage.
Geiß *f.* **(-, -en)** goat; roe.
Geiß: ~blatt *n.* honeysuckle; **~bock** *m.* he-goat.
Geißel *f.* **(-, -n)** whip, lash, scourge.
geißeln *v.t.* to castigate, to scourge, to whip.
Geißelung *f.* castigation; scourging.
Geist *m.* **(-es, -er)** spirit; wit; mind, intellect; specter, ghost.
Geisterbahn *f.* ghost train.
Geisterfahrer *m.* driver going against traffic.
Geistergeschichte *f.* ghost story.
geisterhaft *a.* spectral, ghostly.
geistesabwesend *a.* absentminded.
Geistesabwesenheit *f.* absentmindedness.
Geistesblitz *m.* brainwave.
Geistesgegenwart *f.* presence of mind.
Geistesgeschichte *f.* intellectual history; history of ideas.
Geisteshaltung *f.* attitude.
geisteskrank *a.* mentally ill, insane, of unsound mind.
Geisteskranker *m.* mental patient, mental case.
geistesschwach *a.* feeble-minded, imbecile.
Geistesstörung *f.* mental disorder.
Geisteswissenschaften *f.pl.* humanities.
Geisteszustand *m.* mental condition.
geistig *a.* (*Getränke*) alcoholic; intellectual, mental; spiritual.
geistlich *a.* sacred; spiritual; ecclesiastical, clerical.
Geistliche[r] *m.* **(-n, -n)** clergyman, minister.
Geistlichkeit *f.* **(-, 0)** clergy; priesthood.
geistlos *a.* spiritless, flat, dull.
geistreich *a.* witty, gifted, racy, spirited.
geistvoll *a.* ingenious, witty, bright.
Geiz *m.* **(-es, 0)** meanness, stinginess, avarice.
geizen *v.i.* to be stingy.
Geizhals *m.* miser, niggard.
geizig *a.* avaricious, stingy.
Gejammer *n.* **(-s, 0)** lamentation.
gek. *gekürzt*, abridged, abr.
Gekicher *n.* giggling.
Geklapper *n.* **(-s, 0)** clatter, rattling.
Geklimper *n.* tinkling.
Geklingel *n.* **(-s, 0)** tinkling, jingling.
geknickt *a.* (*fam.*) downcast.
Geknister *n.* rustling; crackling.
gekonnt *a.* accomplished.
Gekreisch *n.* **(-s, 0)** shrieking, screaming.
Gekritzel *n.* scribble.
gekünstelt *a.* artificial, affected.
Gel *n.* gel.
Gelaber *n.* (*fam. pej.*) babbling.
Gelächter *n.* **(-s, 0)** laughter.
geladen *a.* loaded; charged; furious.
Gelage *n.* **(e[e]s, -e)** feast; banquet.
Gelähmte *m./f.* paralytic.
Gelände *n.* **(-s, -)** terrain; **~abschnitt** *m.* (*mil.*) sector.
Gelände: ~fahrt *f.* cross-country drive; **~fahrzeug** *n.* cross-country vehicle.
Geländer *n.* **(-s, -)** railing, balustrade, banisters *pl.*
gelangen *v.i. (s)* to arrive at; to attain.
gelassen *a.* composed, resigned, quiet, calm.
Gelassenheit *f.* calmness; composure.
Gelatine *f.* gelatin.
geläufig *a.* fluent; common; familiar.
gelaunt *a.* disposed, humored.
Geläute *n.* **(-s, -)** ringing, peal (of bells).
gelb *a.* yellow: (*Ei*) ~ *n.* yolk; **~es Fieber,** yellow fever.
gelblich *a.* yellowish.
Gelbsucht *f.* jaundice.
Geld *n.* **(-[e]s, -er)** money; *bares* ~, cash.
Geld: ~angelegenheit *f.* financial matter; **~anlage** *f.* investment; **~automat** *m.* cash dispenser; **~betrag** *m.* sum, amount; **~beutel** *m.* purse; **~geber** *m.* financial backer; sponsor; **~gier** *f.* greed; **~institut** *n.* financial institution; **~schrank** *m.* safe; **~strafe** *f.* fine; **~stück** *n.* coin; **~wechsel** *m.* exchange.
geldlich *a.* financial.
Geld: ~mittel *pl.* financial resources; funds; **~prämie** *f.* cash bonus; **~quelle** *f.* source of income; **~schein** *f.* bill.
Gelee *n.* jelly.
gelegen *a.* situated; convenient.

Gelegenheit *f.* **(-, -en)** occasion, opportunity; ~ *ergreifen,* to take an opportunity.
Gelegenheits: ~arbeiter *m.* casual worker; **~arbeiten** *pl.* odd jobs; **~kauf** *m.* bargain.
gelegentlich *a.* occasional.
gelehrig *a.* docile, tractable.
Gelehrsamkeit *a.* **(-, 0)** learning, erudition.
gelehrt *a.* scholarly; learned, erdudite; *die ~en Berufe, pl.* the scholarly professions.
Gelehrte *m./f.* **(-n, -n)** scholar.
Geleise *n.* **(-s, -)** track; (*rail.*) rails *pl.*
Geleit *n.* **(-[e]s, -e)** escort, safe conduct.
geleiten *v.t.* to conduct, to escort; to convoy.
Geleitzug *m.* (*nav.*) convoy.
Gelenk *n.* **(-[e]s, -e)** joint, articulation; link.
Gelenkentzündung *f.* arthritis.
gelenkig *a.* agile, flexible, supple.
Gelenkrheumatismus *m.* articular rheumatism.
gelernter Arbeiter(in) *m.(f.)* skilled worker.
Geliebte *m./f.* **(-n, -n)** lover; sweetheart; mistress.
gelieren *v.t.* to jell.
gelind[e] *a.* mild, soft.
gelingen *v.i.st. (s)* to succeed, to prosper; *es gelang ihm,* he succeeded (in).
Gelingen *n.* **(-s, 0)** success.
gellen *v.t.* to yell, to shrill.
gellend *a.* piercing, shrill.
geloben *v.t.* to vow, to promise solemnly.
Gelöbnis *n.* **(-ses, -se)** vow.
gelöst *a.* relaxed.
gelt *i.* (*fam.*) is it not so? right?
gelten *v.i.st.* to be worth, to be valid; to have influence; **~ für,** to pass for; **~ lassen,** to let pass, to admit; **das gilt nicht!,** that's not fair!
geltend *p. & a.* in force; ~ *machen,* to assert.
Geltung *f.* **(-, 0)** value; recognition; *zur ~ bringen,* to enforce, to assert; *zur ~ kommen,* to get into favor.
Geltungs: ~bedürfnis *n.*, **~drang** *m.*, **~sucht** *f.* craving for recognition.
Gelübde *n.* **(-s, -)** vow, solemn promise.
gelungen *a.* (*fam.*) amusing.
gelüsten *v.i.* to long for.
gemach *i.* peace!
Gemach *n.* **(-[e]s, -mächer)** apartment, chamber.
gemächlich *a.* easy, comfortable.
Gemahl *m.* **(-[e]s, -e)** consort, husband.
Gemahlin *f.* **(-, -nen)** consort, wife.
Gemälde *n.* **(-s, -)** picture, painting.
Gemäldegalerie *f.* picture gallery.
gemäß *a.& p.* according to.
gemäßigt *a.* (*Klima*) temperature; moderate.
Gemäuer *n.* **(-s, -)** walls *pl.*
Gemecker *n.* bleating, griping, grousing.
gemein *a.* common; low, vulgar, coarse; mean; *der ~e Mann,* the common people; *der ~e Soldat,* the simple soldier.
Gemeinde *f.* **(-, -n)** community; (*Stadt*) municipality; parish; congregation.
Gemeinde... communal.
Gemeinde: ~rat *m.* city council; **~steuer** *f.* community tax, rate.
gemeingefährlich *a.* dangerous to the public.
Gemeingut *n.* common property.
Gemeinheit *f.* **(-, -en)** vulgarity; baseness; dirty trick.
gemeinhin *adv.* commonly.
gemeinnützig *a.* of public utility; **~e Organisation** *f.* nonprofit organization.
Gemeinplatz *m.* commonplace, truism.
gemeinsam *a.* common; mutual, joint.
Gemeinsamkeit *f.* common feature; point in common.
Gemeinschaft *f.* **(-, -en)** community.
gemeinschaftlich *a.* common, joint.
Gemeinschaftsarbeit *f.* joint work.
Gemeinschaftsgefühl *n.* community spirit.
Gemeinsinn *m.* public spirit.
gemeint *a.* intended.
gemeinverständlich *a.* generally intelligible, popular.
Gemein: ~wesen *n.* commonwealth; **~wohl** *n.* public welfare.
Gemenge *n.* **(-s, -)** mixture, medley; (*fig.*) crowd.
gemessen *a.* measured; formal.
Gemetzel *n.* **(-e, -0)** slaughter, butchery.
Gemisch *n.* **(es, -e)** mixture.
gemischtes Doppel *n.* (Tennis) mixed doubles.
Gemme *f.* **(-, -n)** gem.
Gemotze *n.* (*fam.*) grouching.
Gemse *f.* **(-, -n)** chamois.
Gemunkel *n.* **(-s, 0)** secret talk, gossip.
Gemurmel *n.* **(-s, 0)** murmur(ing).
Gemüse *n.* **(-s, -)** greens, vegetables *pl.*
Gemüsegarten *m.* vegetable garden.
Gemüsehändler *m.* greengrocer.
Gemüt *n.* **(-[e]s, -er)** mind, soul, heart, feeling, disposition, nature.
gemütlich *a.* good-natured; cozy, snug.
Gemütlichkeit *f.* **(-,0)** good nature; coziness; comfort.
Gemütsbewegung *f.* emotion.
Gemütskrankheit *f.* mental disorder.
Gemütsmensch *m.* good-natured person.
Gemütsregung *f.* emotion.
Gemütsruhe *f.* peace of mind.
gemütvoll *a.* warm-hearted; sentimental.
Gen *n.* (*bio.*) gene.
genagelt *a.* (*Schuhe*) hobnailed.
genau *a.* close; strict, precise; exact, accurate; *es ~ nehmen,* to be particular.
genaugenommen *adv.* strictly speaking.
Genauigkeit *f.* **(-, 0)** accuracy, precision, exactness.
Gendarm *m.* **(-en, -en)** gendarme.
Gendarmerie *f.* rural police.
Genealogie *f.* **(-, -n)** genealogy.
genehm *a.* convenient, acceptable.
genehmigen *v.t.* to approve of.
Genehmigung *f.* **(-, -en)** approval; assent, sanction; ratification.
geneigt *a.* inclined; prone; favorable.
General *m.* **(-[e]s, -e)** general; **~ der Flieger,** air marshal.
General: ~agent *m.* agent-general; **~baß** *m.* (*mus.*) basso continuo; **~direktor** *m.* general manager; **~konsul** *m.* consul-general; **~probe** *f.* final dress rehearsal; **~stab** *m.* general staff; **~stabskarte** *f.* ordnance survey map; **~versammlung** *f.* general meeting; **~vollmacht** *f.* general power of attorney.
Generation *f.* **(-, -en)** generation.
Generationskonflikt *m.* generation gap, new generation; (*bio.*) alteration of generations.
Generator *m.* generator.
generell *a. & adv.* general(ly).
genesen *v.i.st. (s)* to recover, to be restored to health.
Genesung *f.* **(-, -en)** convalescence, recovery; **~sheim** *n.* convalescent home.

Genetik *f.* genetics.
genetisch *a. & adv.* genetical(ly).
Genf *n.* **(-s, 0)** Geneva; *der ~er See,* Lake Geneva.
genial *a.* inspired, gifted, brilliant.
Genialität *f.* genius, brilliancy.
Genick *n.* **(-[e]s, -e)** nape, back of the neck.
Genie *n.* **(-s, -s)** genius; man of genius.
genieren *v.t.* to molest, to bother; ~ *v.r.* to feel embarrassed.
genießbar *a.* edible; palatable.
genießen *v.t.st.* to enjoy; to eat or drink.
Genießer *m.* bon vivant.
genießerisch *a. & adv.* appreciative(ly).
Genitalien *pl.* genitals.
Genitiv *m.* **(-s, -e)** genitive case.
Genius *m.* **(-, -Genien)** genius.
Genosse *m.* **(-n, -n) Genossin** *f.* **(-, -nen)** companion, comrade, partner, mate.
Genossenschaft *f.* **(-, -en)** cooperative.
genossenschaftlich *a.* cooperative; collective.
Genre *n.* **(-s, -s)** genre.
Gen: technik *f.;* **~technologie** *f.* genetic engineering.
genug *a. & adv.* enough, sufficient.
Genüge *f.* **(-, 0)** *zur ~,* sufficiently; ~ *tun,* to satisfy.
genügen *v.i.* to suffice; to satisfy; *sich ~ lassen,* to be satisfied (with).
genügend *a.* sufficient, enough.
genügsam *a.* modest; easily satisfied; frugal.
Genugtuung *f.* **(-, -en)** satisfaction.
Genus *n.* **(-, Genera)** gender.
Genuß *m.* **(-nusses, -nüsse)** consumption; enjoyment; pleasure, delight; use, profit; eating, drinking.
genüßlich *a. & adv.* appreciative(ly).
genußsüchtig, *a.* pleasure-seeking.
Geograph *m.* **(-en, -en)** geographer.
Geographie *f.* **(-, 0)** geography.
geographisch *a.* geographical.
Geologe *m.* **(-en, -en)** geologist.
Geologie *f.* geology.
geologisch *a.* geological.
Geometer *m.* **(-s, -)** geometrician; surveyor.
Geometrie *f.* **(-, -n)** geometry.
geometrisch *a.* geometrical.
Gepäck *n.* **(-[e]s, -e)** luggage, baggage.
Gepäckabfertigung *f.* baggage check-in; baggage office.
Gepäckaufbewahrungsstelle *f.* check-room.
Gepäckaufgabeschein *m.* check slip.
Gepäcknetz *n.* luggage rack.
Gepäcktrager *m.* carrier; porter.
Gepäckwagen *m.* baggage car.
Gepard *m.* cheetah.
gepflegt *a.* neat, cultured, stylish.
Gepflogenheit *f.* **(-, -en)** custom, habit.
Geplänkel *n.* **(-s, 0)** skirmishing, banter.
Geplapper *n.* **(-s, 0)** babbling, chatter.
Geplätscher *n.* **(-s, 0)** splashing, plashing; babbling, chit-chat.
Geplauder *n.* **(-s, 0)** small-talk.
Gepolter *n.* clatter; grumbling.
Gepräge *n.* **(-s, -)** impression, stamp, coinage.
Gepränge *n.* **(-s, 0)** pomp, ceremony, pageantry.
gepunktet *a.* spotted; dotted.
gequält *a.* forced, pained.
Gequassel *n.*, **Gequatsche** *n.* jabbering.
gerade *a.* straight; direct, right; upright, honest; (*Zahl*) even; **~aus** *adv.* straight on; **~heraus** *adv.* frankly.
gerade *adv.* just, exactly.
Gerade *f.* straight line; straight arm punch.
geradezu *adv.* bluntly; actually, no less than.
gerad: ~linig *a.* straight, rectilineal, rectilinear; **~sinnig** *a.* upright, straightforward.
Gerangel *n.* scrapping, wrangling.
Geraschel *n.* rustling.
Gerassel *n.* **(-s, 0)** rattling, din.
Gerät *n.* **(-[e]s, -e)** tool, implement, appliance, utensil.
geraten *v.i.st. (s)* to come, to get (into); to succeed, to turn out well, to prosper; *in Brand ~,* to catch fire; *ins Stocken ~,* to come to a standstill.
geraten *a.* advisable.
Geräteschuppen *m.* toolshed.
Geräteturnen *n.* apparatus gymnastics.
Geratewohl *n. aufs ~,* haphazard.
Gerätschaften *f.pl* tools, implements *pl.*
geraum *a.* long; **~e Zeit,** (for) a long time.
geräumig *a.* spacious, roomy, ample.
Geräusch *n.* **(-[e]s, -e)** noise, sound, bustle.
geräusch: ~los *a.* noiseless, silent; **~voll,** noisy.
gerben *v.t.* to tan; to refine.
Gerber *m.* **(-s, -)** tanner.
Gerberei *f.* tannery.
Gerbsäure *f.* **(-, 0) Gerbstoff** *m.* **(-[c]s, -e)** tannic acid, tannin.
gerecht *a.* just; righteous, impartial.
gerechtfertigt *a.* justified.
Gerechtigkeit *f.* **(-, 0)** justice.
Gerechtigkeitsgefühl *n.* sense of justice.
gerechtigkeitsliebend *a.* having a love for justice; fair-minded.
Gerede *n.* **(-s, 0)** talk, rumor.
geregelt *a.* regular, steady.
gereizt *a. & p.* irritated, angry.
Gereiztheit *f.* **(-, 0)** irritation, anger.
gereuen *v.imp. es gereut mich,* I repent (of it), I regret (it).
Gericht *n.* **(-[e]s, -e)** court of justice, tribunal; judgment; dish, food; *das jüngste ~,* Doomsday, the Last Judgment; *vor ~ stellen,* to bring to trial, to try.
Gerichtbarkeit *f.* jurisdiction; *streitige ~,* contentious jurisdiction.
gerichtlich *a.* judicial, legal; forensic; *~ vorgehen gegen,* to take proceedings against.
Gerichtsbeschluß *m.* courtorder.
Gerichtsentscheidung *f.* ruling.
Gerichtsferein *pl.* recess, vacation.
Gerichtsgebäude *n.* court-house.
Gerichtshof *m.* court of justice.
Gerichtskosten *pl.* court costs.
Gerichts: ~medizin *f.* forensic medicine; **~saal** *m.* courtroom; **~schreiber** *m.* clerk of the court; **~stand** *m.* venue; **~vollzieher** *m.* marshal, bailiff; **~wesen** *n.* judiciary, judicature.
geriffelt *a.* corrugated, fluted, ribbed.
gering *a.* small, little, mean; scanty, slight, unimportant; inferior, poor; *nicht im ~sten,* not in the least.
geringelt *a.* curly, with horizontal stripes.
geringfügig *a.* unimportant, slight; trifling.
Geringfügigkeit *f.* triviality; insignificance.
geringschätzen *v.t.* to think little of.
geringschätzig *a.* disdainful, contemptuous.

Geringschätzung *f.* **(-, 0)** disdain, contempt, scorn.
gerinnen *v.i.st. (s)* to coagulate, to curdle.
Gerinnsel *n.* clot.
Gerippe *n.* **(-s, -)** skeleton; framework.
gerippt *a.* ribbed, fluted, laid.
gerissen *a.* cunning, crafty.
Germane *m.;* **Germanin** *f.* Teuton.
germanisch *a.* Teutonic; Germanic.
germanisieren *v.t.* to germanize.
Germanist *m.;* **Germanistin** *f.* Germanist, German scholar.
Germanistik *f.* German studies.
gern *adv.* with pleasure, willingly, readily, easily; **~haben** to be fond of; **~sehen** to like; **nicht ~ gesehen** unwelcome.
Geröll *n.* **(-[e]s, -e)** rubble, boulders *pl.*
Gerste *f.* **(-, -n)** barley.
Gerstengraupen *pl.* pearl barley.
Gerstenkorn *n.* barleycorn; (*med.*) sty.
Gerte *f.* **(-, -n)** switch, rod.
Geruch *m.* **(-[e]s, -rüche)** smell; scent, odor.
geruchlos, *a.* odorless, unscented.
Geruchs: ~organ *n.* olfactory organ; **~sinn** *m.* sense of smell.
Gerücht *n.* **(-[e]s, -e)** rumor, report, news *pl.; es geht das ~,* it is rumored.
geruhen *v.i.* to be pleased, to deign.
gerührt *a.* touched; moved.
geruhsam *a.* peaceful; leisurely.
Gerümpel *n.* **(-s, 0)** junk; trash.
Gerundium *n.* **(-s, -dien)** gerund.
Gerüst *n.* **(-[e]s, -e)** scaffold, stage, scaffolding, frame(work).
Ges *n.* **(-, 0)** (*mus.*) G flat.
Ges. *Gesellschaft,* company, co., society, soc.
gesalzen *a.* salted; (*fig.*) (prices, etc.) steep; (*fig.*) biting, smart.
gesammelt *a.* concentrated; **~e Werke** *pl.* collected works.
gesamt *a.* whole, total, aggregate.
Gesamt: ~auflage *f.* total edition; total circulation; **~ausgabe** *f.* complete edition; **~betrag** *m.* sum total; **~eindruck** *m.* overall impression, **~ergebnis** *n.* overall result; **~gewicht** *n.* total weight.
Gesamtheit *f.* **(-, 0)** totality.
Gesandte *m./f.* **(-n, -n)** minister, envoy.
Gesandtschaft *f.* **(-, -en)** legation.
Gesandtschaftsrat *m.* counsellor of legation.
Gesang *m.* **(-[e]s, -sänge)** singing; song, air; canto (of a long poem).
Gesangbuch *n.* hymnbook.
Gesang: ~lehrer *m.;* **~lehrerin** *f.* singing teacher, voice teacher; **~unterricht** *m.* singing lesson, voice lesson; **~verein** *m.* choral society.
Gesäß *n.* **(-es, -e)** bottom, buttocks.
gesättigt *a.* (*chem.*) saturated; full.
gesch. *geschieden,* divorced, div.
Geschädigte *m.* (*jur.*) the injured party.
Geschäft *n.* **(-[e]s, -e)** business; employment, occupation; shop, establishment; transaction.
Geschäftemacher *m.* (*pej.*) profit seeker.
geschäftig *a.* busy, bustling, active.
geschäftlich *a.* business, commercial; *~e Verbindung haben mit,* to do (transact) business with.
Geschäfts: ~abschluß *m.* transaction; **~aufsicht** *f.* legal control; **~bedingungen** *pl.* terms of trade; **~bericht** *m.* company report; **~brief** *m.* business letter; **~bücher** *n.pl* the books (of a firm); **~fähigkeit** *f.* (*jur.*) legal capacity; **~führer** *m.* manager; **~mann** *m.* business man; **~nummer** *f.*, **~zeichen** *n.* reference (number); **~ordnung** *f.* rules of procedure; standing order; **~papiere** *pl.* (*Post*) commercial papers; **~reise** *f.* business trip; **~stunden** *f.pl* office hours; **~träger** *m.* chargé d'affaires; **~verkehr** *m.* business dealings *pl.;* **~zeit** *f.* office hours *pl.;* **~zweig** *m.* branch of business.
gescheckt *a.* spotted; pinto.
geschehen *v.i.st. (s)* to come to pass, to occur, to happen; **~ lassen,** to permit; *es geschieht ihm recht,* it serves him right.
Geschehen *n.* events; action.
gescheit *a.* clever, intelligent.
Geschenk *n.* **(-[e]s, -e)** gift, present.
Geschichte *f.* **(-, -n)** history; story; (*fam.*) affair.
geschichtlich *a.* historic(al).
Geschichtschreiber *m.* historian.
Geschichtsschreibung *f.* historiography.
Geschichtswissenschaftler *m.;* **Geschichtswissenschaftlerin** *f.* historian.
Geschick *n.* **(-[e]s, -e)** dexterity, skill; destiny, fate.
Geschicklichkeit *f.* **(-, -en)** dexterity, adroitness, skill.
geschickt *a.* fit, apt, clever; skilled.
geschieden *a.* divorced.
Geschiedene *m.* divorcé; *f.* divorcée
Geschirr *n.* **(-[e]s, -e)** vessel; (*Silber*) plate; (*irdenes*) crockery, earthenware; tools *pl.;* (*Pferde~*) harness.
Geschirr: ~schrank *m.* cupboard; **~spüler** *m.* dishwasher; **~tuch** *n.* dishtowel.
Geschlecht *n.* **(-[e]s, -er)** sex; kind, race; lineage; generation; (*gram.*) gender.
geschlechtlich *a.* sexual.
Geschlechts: ~krankheit *f.* venereal disease; **~reife** *f.* sexual maturity; **~teile** *m.pl* genitals *pl.;* **~trieb** *m.* sexual drive; **~verkehr** *m.* intercourse; **~wort** *n.* (*gram.*) article.
geschliffen *a.* polished; (*Glas*) cut.
geschlossen *a.* closed, close, compact; concentrated; solid, in a body.
Geschlossenheit *f.* unity; uniformity.
Geschmack *m.* **(-[e]s, -schmäcke)** taste; flavor; liking.
geschmacklos *a.* tasteless; in bad taste.
Geschmacklosigkeit *f.* **(-, -en)** bad taste.
Geschmacksfrage *f.*, **Geschmacksache** *f.* matter of taste.
Geschmacksverirrung *f.* lapse of taste.
geschmackvoll *a.* tasteful, elegant.
Geschmeide *n.* **(-s, -)** jewels *pl.*
geschmeidig *a.* flexible, pliant, supple.
Geschmeiß *n.* **(-es, 0)** (*sl. pej.*) low rabble; vermin.
Geschnatter *n.* cackling; chatter.
geschniegelt *a.* spruce, trim.
Geschöpf *n.* **(-[e]s, -e)** creature; creation.
Geschoß *n.* **(-schosses, -schosse)** projectile, missile; story, floor.
geschraubt *a.* stilted; pretentious.
Geschrei *n.* **(-es, -e)** screaming; yelling; shouting.
Geschütz *n.* **(-es, -e)** cannon, gun.
Geschütz: ~feuer *n.* gunfire; **~stand** *m.* emplacement.
geschützt *a.* protected; *m.* turret.
Geschwader *n.* **(-s, -)** squadron; (*avi.*) wing;

Geschützturm *~kommandeur* *m.* wing commander.
Geschwafel *n.* (*pej.*) waffle.
Geschwätz *n.* **(-es, 0)** gossip; prattle.
geschwätzig *a.* talkative, garrulous.
geschweift *a.* curved; **~e klammern** *pl.*, parentheses.
geschweige denn, not to mention, let alone.
geschwind *a.* quick, fast, swift.
Geschwindigkeit *f.* **(-, -en)** quickness, speed; velocity.
Geschwindigkeits: ~begrenzung *f.* speed limit; **~kontrolle** *f.* speed check; **~messer** *m.* speedometer.
Geschwirr *n.* **(-[e]s, 0)** whirr, buzz.
Geschwister *pl.* brothers and sisters *pl.*; siblings.
geschwisterlich *a.* brotherly; sisterly.
geschwollen *a.* swollen; pompous, bombastic.
geschworen *a.* sworn.
Geschworene *m./f.* **(-n, -n)** jury member, juror.
Geschworenengericht *n.* jury.
Geschwulst *f.* **(-, -schwülste)** tumor; swelling.
geschwungen *a.* curved.
Geschwür *n.* **(-[e]s, -e)** ulcer, abscess.
Gesell, Geselle *n.* **(-[e]n, -[e]n)** journeyman; companion, comrade.
gesellen *v.r.* to join (with).
gesellig *a.* social, sociable, convivial; **~e Zusammenkunft** *f.*, social gathering.
Geselligkeit *f.* **(-, 0)** sociability.
Gesellschaft *f.* **(-, -en)** society; company; party; *eine ~ gründen,* to form a company.
Gesellschafter *m.*; **(-s, -) Gesellschafterin** *f.* **(-, -nen)** companion; associate; (*com.*) partner; shareholder.
gesellschaftlich *a.* social.
Gesellschaftsanzug *m.* evening dress.
Gesellschaftsform *f.* social system.
Gesellschaftskritik *f.* social criticism.
Gesellschaftsordnung *f.* social order.
Gesellschaftspolitik *f.* social policy.
Gesellschaftsreise *f.* conducted tour.
Gesellschaftsspiel *n.* society game, parlor game.
Gesellschaftstanz *m.* ballroom dancing.
Gesellschaftsvertrag *m.* deed of partnership.
Gesetz *n.* **(-es, -e)** law, statute; rule.
Gesetzblatt *n.* law gazette.
Gesetz: ~buch *n.* code; **~entwurf** *m.* bill.
Gesetzeskraft *f.* force of law, legal force.
gesetzgebend *a.* legislative; **~e Körperschaft** *f.* legislative body.
Gesetz: ~geber *m.* legislator; **~gebung** *f.* legislation; legislature.
gesetzlich *a.* lawful, legal, statutory; **~geschützt** *a.* legally registered, proprietary.
gesetzlos *a.* lawless, illegal.
Gesetzlosigkeit *f.* **(-, -en)** anarchy.
gesetzmäßig *a.* lawful, legitimate; legal.
gesetzt *a.* steady; sedate; **~daß,** suppose, supposing that.
gesetzwidrig *a.* illegal, unlawful, contrary to law.
gesichert *a.* safe, secured.
Gesicht *n.* **(-[e]s, -er)** face; countenance, mien; apparition, vision.
Gesichtsausdruck *m.* expression, look.
Gesichtsfarbe *f.* complexion.
Gesichtskreis *m.* horizon; (*fig.*) intellectual horizon.
Gesichtspunkt *m.* point of view.
Gesichtszug *m.* feature.
Gesims *n.* **(-es, e)** shelf; cornice; mantlepiece.
Gesinde *n.* **(-s, 0)** servants, domestics *pl.*
Gesindel *n.* **(-s, 0)** mob, rabble.
gesinnt *a.* minded, disposed.
Gesinnung *f.* **(-, -en)** intention; disposition, opinion; mind; conviction.
Gesinnungs: ~genosse *m.*; **~genossin** *f.* like-minded person; **~losigkeit** *f.* lack of principle; **~wandel** *m.* change of heart.
gesittet *a.* well-behaved; well-mannered.
Gesittung *f.* **(-, 0)** civilization.
Gesöff *m.* (*pej.*) muck.
gesondert *a.* separate.
gesonnen *a.* disposed, resolved.
Gespann *n.* **(-[e]s, -e)** team; yoke (of oxen).
gespannt *a.* & *p.* strained; intent, wrought up; anxious to know; *auf ~em Fuß,* on bad terms.
Gespenst *n.* **(-es, -er)** specter, ghost.
Gespenster: ~geschichte *f.* ghost story; **~stunde** *f.* witching hour.
gespenstisch *a.* ghostly; eerie.
gesperrt *a.* closed; (*Druck*) spaced; *~ für Zutritt,* out of bounds, off-limits.
Gespött *n.* **(-[e]s, 0)** mockery, ridicule.
Gespräch *n.* **(-[e]s, -e)** conversation, talk.
gesprächig *a.* talkative, communicative.
Gesprächs: ~bereitschaft *f.* readiness for discussion; **~fetzen** *m.* fragment of conversation; **~stoff** *m.* topics of conversation.
gespreizt *a.* pompous; stilted.
gesprenkelt *a.* speckled.
Gespritzte *m.* wine spritzer.
Gespür *n.* feeling; nose.
gest. *gestorben,* died, d.
Gestade *n.* **(-s, -)** shore, beach, bank.
Gestalt *f.* **(-, -en)** form, figure, shape; frame; size, stature; fashion, manner.
gestalten *v.t.* to form, to shape; **~** *v.r.* to turn out.
gestaltlos *a.* shapeless; formless.
Gestaltung *f.* **(-, -en)** shaping; fashioning; formation; configuration; condition.
Gestaltungsprinzip *n.* formal principle.
Gestammel *n.* stammering, stuttering.
geständig *a.* confessing; **~sein,** to confess.
Geständnis *n.* **(-ses, se)** confession.
Gestank *m.* **(-[e]s, -stänke)** stink, stench.
gestatten *v.t.* to permit, to allow.
Geste *f.* **(-, -n)** gesture.
Gesteck *n.* flower arrangement.
gestehen *v.t.st.* to confess, to avow, to admit.
Gestehungskosten *pl.* prime cost, cost price.
Gestein *n.* **(-[e]s, -e)** rock.
Gesteinskunde *f.* petrology.
Gestell *n.* **(-[e]s, -e)** frame; rack, stand; trestle.
gestelzt *a.* stilted; affected.
gestern *adv.* yesterday.
gestiefelt *a.* booted.
Gestik *f.* gestures.
gestikulieren *v.i.* to gesticulate.
Gestirn *n.* **(-[e]s, -e)** star; constellation.
gestirnt *a.* starred, starry.
gestört *a.* disturbed.
Gestotter *n.* **(-s, 0)** stammering, stuttering.
Gesträuch *n.* **(-[e]s, -e)** thicket, shrubs *pl.*
gestreift *a.* striped.
gestreng *a.* strict, severe, rigorous.
gestrichen *a.* painted; deleted; level (measure).
gestrig *a.* yesterday's.

Gestrüpp *n.* **(-[e]s, -e)** undergrowth.
Gestühl *n.* seats.
Gestüt *n.* **(-[e]s, -e)** stud farm.
Gesuch *n.* **(-[e]s, -e)** application, request; **~ einreichen,** to make an application; *ein ~ bewilligen,* to grant (approve) an application.
gesucht *a.* in demand; affected; sought-after.
Gesumm *n.* buzzing, humming.
gesund *a.* sound, healthy; well, in good health; (*Ansicht*) sane; (*Speisen, etc.*) wholesome; (*Klima*) salubrious.
gesunden *v.i. (s)* to recover (health), to get well.
Gesundheit *f.* **(-, 0)** health; sanity; **~!** Bless you!
gesundheitlich *a.* physical; sanitary.
Gesundheits: ~pflege *f.* hygiene.
gesundheitsschädlich *a.* unhealthy.
Gesundheitswesen *n.* public health service.
gesund: ~schrumpfen *v.r.* to pare down (business); **~stoßen** *v.r.* to make a pile (business).
Gesundung *f.* recovery.
getäfelt *a.* wainscoted, tiled.
Getier *n.* animals.
getigert *a.* striped; patterned like a tiger.
Getöse *n.* **(-s, 0)** noise, din.
getragen *a.* used (clothes); solemn, measured.
Getrampel *n.* **(-s, 0)** trampling.
Getränk *n.* **(-[e]s, -e)** beverage, drink.
Getränkeautomat *m.* drinks dispenser.
Getränkekarte *f.* list of beverages; wine list.
Getratsche *n.* (*fam.*) gossip, gossiping.
getrauen *v.r.* to dare, to venture; *ich getraue mich nicht hinein,* I dare not go in.
Getreide *n.* **(-s, -)** corn, grain.
Getreidespeicher *m.* grain silo.
getrennt *a. & adv.* separate(ly).
getreu *a.* faithful, true, trusty; loyal.
getreulich *a. & adv.* faithful(ly).
Getriebe *n.* **(-s, -)** gears; (*Uhr, Klavier*) works; bustle; **~kasten** *m.* gear box.
getrost *a.* confident.
Getto *n.* **(-s, -s)** ghetto.
Getue *n.* **(-s, 0)** fuss.
Getümmel *n.* **(-s, 0)** bustle.
getupft *a.* speckled.
Getuschel *n.* whispering, gossiping.
geübt *a.* experienced; practised, expert.
Gewächs *n.* **(-es, -e)** plant, vegetable; (*Wein*) vintage; (*med.*) growth.
gewachsen *a.* equal to, a match for.
Gewächshaus *n.* greenhouse.
gewagt *a.* risky; daring; risqué.
gewählt *a.* refined, select, choice.
gewahr *a.* aware (of).
Gewähr *f.* **(-, 0)** guarantee; *ohne ~*, subject to correction.
gewahren *v.t.* to perceive.
gewähren *v.t.* to give, to allow, to grant; *einen ~ lassen,* to let a person alone.
gewährleisten *v.t.* to guarantee.
Gewahrsam *m.* **(-s, 0)** safe keeping, safe custody; *in ~*, under restraint.
Gewährsmann *m.* informant; authority.
Gewalt *f.* **(-, -en)** power, authority; force, violence; *höhere ~*, act of God.
Gewalt: ~akt *m.* act of violence; **~anwendung** *f.* use of violence.
Gewaltenteilung *f.* separation of powers.
Gewaltherrschaft *f.* tyranny; despotism.
gewaltig *a.* mighty, enormous; tremendous; powerful.
gewaltlos *a.* nonviolent.
Gewaltmarsch *m.* forced march.
gewaltsam *a.* forcible, violent; *eines ~en Todes sterben,* to die a violent death.
gewalttätig *a.* violent, outrageous.
Gewalttätigkeit *f.* **(-, -en)** violence; rowdyism.
Gewaltverbrechen *n.* crime of violence.
Gewaltverbrecher *m.* violent criminal.
Gewaltverzichtsabkommen *n.* nonaggression treaty.
Gewand *n.* **(-[e]s, Gewänder)** robe, garment; vestment; drapery.
gewandt *a.* dexterous, smart, agile.
gewärtigen *v.t.* to expect.
Gewäsch *n.* **(-es, 0)** twaddle.
Gewässer *n.* **(-s, -)** waters *pl.*
Gewebe *n.* **(-s, -)** texture, tissue, fabric.
Gewehr *n.* **(-[e]s, -e)** gun, rifle.
Gewehrkolben *m.* butt.
Gewehrlauf *m.* rifle barrel.
Geweih *n.* **(-[e]s, -e)** antlers *pl.*
geweiht *a.* consecrated.
Gewerbe *n.* **(-s, -)** trade; calling; industry.
Gewerbe: ~freiheit *f.* freedom of trade; **~ordnung** *f.* trade regulations *pl.; ~***schein** *m.* trading license; **~schule** *f.* technical school; **~steuer** *f.* tradetax; **~treibende** *m./f.* person practicing a trade.
gewerbetreibend *a.* manufacturing.
gewerblich *a.* industrial, commercial.
gewerbsmäßig *a.* professional.
Gewerkschaft *f.* **(-, -en)** labor union.
Gewerkschafter *m.;* **Gewerkschafterin** *f.* labor unionist.
gewerkschaftlich *a.* (labor) union.
Gewerkschaftsbund *m.* federation of labor unions.
Gewerkschaftsmitglied *n.* member of a labor union.
Gewicht *n.* **(-[e]s, -e)** weight.
Gewichtheben *n.* weight-lifting.
gewichtig *a.* weighty, important.
Gewichts: ~klasse *f.* (*sp.*) weight (class); **~verlust** *m.* loss of weight; **~zunahme** *f.* increase of weight.
gewillt *a.* wiling, disposed.
Gewimmel *n.* **(-s, 0)** swarm, crowd.
Gewimmer *n.* whimpering.
Gewinde *n.* **(-s, -)** thread.
Gewindebohrer *m.* (*mech.*) tap.
Gewinn *m.* **(-[e]s, -e)** gain, profit, advantage; *mit ~*, at a profit; **~ und Verlustkonto** *n.* profit and loss account; **~ beteiligung** *f.* profit sharing.
Gewinnanteil *m.* dividend.
gewinnbringend *a.* profitable.
gewinnen *v.i. & t.st.* to win; to gain, to get, to earn.
gewinnend *a.* winning, engaging.
Gewinner *m.;* **Gewinnerin** *f.* winner.
gewinnlos *adj.* profitless, unprofitable.
Gewinnnummer *f.* winning number.
Gewinnspanne *f.* profit margin.
Gewinnstreben *n.* pursuit of profit.
Gewinnsucht *f.* greed for profit.
gewinnsüchtig *a.* profiteering.
Gewinnung *f.* mining, extraction, recovery.
Gewinsel *n.* **(-s, 0)** whimpering, whining.
Gewirr *n.* **(-[e]s, 0)** confusion; criss-cross; tangle.
Gewisper *n.* **(-s, -)** whispering.

gewiß *a.* certain; sure; constant, fixed; ~ *adv.* certainly, no doubt.

Gewissen *n.* **(-s, -)** conscience.

gewissenhaft *a.* conscientious.

Gewissenhaftigkeit *f.* conscientiousness.

gewissenlos *a.* unscrupulous.

Gewissenlosigkeit *f.* unscrupulousness.

Gewissens: ~biß *m.* remorse; **~freiheit** *f.* freedom of conscience; **~konflikt** *m.* moral conflict.

gewissermaßen *adv.* so to speak.

Gewißheit *f.* **(-, -en)** certainty, surety.

Gewitter *n.* **(-s, -)** (thunder)storm.

gewitz *a.* smart, clever.

gewogen *a.* favorable, kindly disposed.

gewöhnen *v.t.* to accustom.

Gewohnheit *f.* **(-, -en)** custom; habit.

gewohnheitsmäßig *a.* habitual.

Gewohnheits: ~recht *n.* common law; **~tier** *n.* creature of habit; **~verbrecher** *m.* habitual criminal.

gewöhnlich *a.* usual; common, vulgar; ~ *adv.* usually, as a rule.

gewohnt *a.* usual, accustomed, habitual; in the habit of...; *es ~ sein,* to be used to.

Gewöhnung *f.* habituation; addiction.

Gewölbe *n.* **(-s, -)** vault, arch.

gewölbt *a.* vaulted, arched.

Gewühl *n.* **(-[e]s, 0)** throng, crowd.

gewunden *a.* & *p.* tortuous.

gewürfelt *a.* checked.

Gewürz *n.* **(-es, -e)** spice; seasoning.

Gewürznelke *f.* clove.

Geysir *m.* **(-s, -e)** geyser.

gez. *gezeichnet,* signed.

Gezänk *n.* **(-[e]s, -e), Gezanke** *n.* **(-s, 0)** quarrel, squabble.

Gezappel *n.* wriggling.

gezeichnet *a.* (*gez.*) signed.

Gezeiten *pl.* tides.

Gezeitenkraftwerk *n.* tidal power station.

Gezeter *n.* **(-s, 0)** scalding, nagging.

gezielt *a.* specific, deliberate, well-directed.

geziemen *v.i. jm.* ~, to become, to befit sb.; ~ *v.r. es geziemt sich nicht,* it's not fitting, it's not considered proper.

geziemend *a.* proper, befitting.

geziert *a.* affecting, finicking, finicky.

Gezirpe *n.* chirping.

Gezwitscher *n.* **(-s, 0)** chirping, twitter.

gezwungen *a.* constrained, forced.

gezwungenermaßen *adv.* of necessity.

GG *Grundgesetz,* constitution.

gg(f)s. *gegebenenfalls,* if necessary, if applicable.

Gicht *f.* **(-, 0)** gout.

Giebel *m.* **(-s, -)** gable, gable-end.

Gier *f.* **(-, 0)** desire, greed(iness).

gierig *a.* eager, greedy.

Gießbach *m.* torrent.

gießen *v.t.st.* to pour; (*Blumen*) to water; (*Metall*) to cast, to found; *Öl ins Feuer ~,* to add fuel to the fire.

Gießerei *f.* **(-, -en)** foundry.

Gießkanne *f.* watering can.

Gift *n.* **(-[e]s, -e)** poison; venom (snake); (*fig.*) spite.

giftfrei *a.* nontoxic; nonpoisonous.

giftgrün *a.* garish green.

giftig *a.* poisonous; venomous; toxic; (*fig.*) angry.

Gift: ~müll *m.* toxic waste; **~mülldeponie** *f.* toxic waste dump; **~pflanze** *f.* poisonous plant.

Gigant *m.* **(-en, -en)** giant.

gigantisch *a.* gigantic.

Gilde *f.* **(-, -n)** guild; corporation.

Ginster *m.* **(-s, -)** broom, furze; gorse.

Gipfel *m.* **(-s, -)** summit, peak; top; (*fig.*) height, acme.

gipfeln *v.i.* to culminate.

Gips *m.* **(-es, -e)** gypsum, plaster of Paris.

Gipsabdruck *m.* **Gipsabguß** *m.* plaster cast.

Gipsverband *m.* plaster cast.

Giraffe *f.* **(-, -n)** giraffe.

girieren *v.t.* to endorse (a bill of exchange); to circulate.

Girlande *f.* garland.

Giro *n.* **(-[s], -s)** endorsement.

Giro: ~konto *n.* bank account; **~verkehr** *m.* clearinghouse business.

girren *v.i.* to coo.

Gis *n.* **(-, 0)** G sharp.

Gischt *m.* **(-[e]s, -e)** foam (wave), spray.

Gitarre *f.* **(-, -n)** guitar.

Gitter *n.* **(-s, -)** trellis, grating, grille, lattice.

Glacéhandschuh *m.* kid-glove.

Gladiole *f.* gladiolus.

Glanz *m.* **(-es, 0)** luster, gloss; polish, sheen; brightness, splendor.

glänzen *v.i.* to glitter; to shine.

glänzend *a.* shining, bright, brilliant.

Glanz: ~leder *n.* patent leather; **~leistung** *f.* brilliant performance; **~papier** *n.* glossy paper; **~stück** *n.* pièce de résistance; **~zeit** *f.* heyday.

Glas *n.* **(-es, Gläser)** glass; *buntes ~,* stained glass.

Glasbläser *m.* glassblower.

Glaser *m.* **(-s, -)** glazier.

gläsern *a.* glassy, of glass.

Glas: ~glocke *f.* glass shade; bell-glass; **~hütte** *f.* glassworks *pl.*

glasieren *v.t.* to glaze; to varnish.

Glaskörper *m.* (*biol.*) vitrious body.

Glassplitter *m.* splinter of glass.

Glasur *f.* **(-, -en)** glazing.

Glasware *f.* glassware.

glatt *a.* smooth, sleek; **~rasiert** *a.* clean-shaven.

Glätte *f.* smoothness; slipperiness.

Glatteis *n.* **(-es, 0)** glare ice; icy ground, icy roads.

glätten *v.t.* to smooth; (*mech.*) to face.

glattgehen *v.i.st.* to go smoothly.

Glatze *f.* **(-, -u)** bald head.

Glaube *m.* **(~ns, 0)** faith, belief, credit; religion; *auf Treu und ~,* in good faith, on trust; *in gutem ~n* (*jur.*) bona fide, in good faith.

glauben *v.t.* to believe, to trust; to think, to suppose.

Glaubens: ~artikel *m.* article of faith; **~bekenntnis** *n.* confession of faith, creed; **~freiheit** *f.* religious freedom; **~genosse** *m.* co-religionist; **~satz** *m.* dogma; **~streit** *m.* religious dispute.

glaubhaft *a.* credible, believable.

Glaubhaftigkeit *f.* credibility.

gläubig *a.* believing; faithful; devout.

Gläubige *m./f.* **(-n, -n)** (true) believer.

Gläubiger *m.* **(-s, -)** creditor.

glaublich *a.* credible; probable.

glaubwürdig *a.* credible; authentic.

Glaukom *n.* glaucoma.

glazial *a.* glacial.

gleich *a.* same, equal, like; ~ *adv.* equally, just,

alike; at once, directly; *meinesgleichen,* my equals *pl.*, people like me.
gleichartig *a.* homogeneous.
gleichbedeutend *a.* synonymous, equivalent.
Gleichberechtigung *f.* **(-, 0)** equal rights.
gleichbleibend *a.* constant, steady.
gleichen *v.i.st.* to be alike, to resemble; to equal.
gleichermaßen *adv.* equally.
gleicherweise *adv.* likewise.
gleichfalls *adv.* likewise, also, equally.
gleichförmig *a.* uniform; conform.
gleichgeschlechtlich *a.* homosexual.
gleichgesinnt *a.* like-minded, congenial.
Gleichgewicht *n.* **(-[e]s, 0)** balance, equilibrium; *das ~ halten,* to keep one's balance.
gleichgültig *a.* indifferent; irrelevant; **~ wie,** no matter how.
Gleichgültigkeit *f.* **(-, 0)** indifference.
Gleichheit *f.* **(-, 0)** equality; likeness.
Gleichheitszeichen *n.* (*mus.*) equal sign.
gleichlaufend *a.* parallel.
gleich: ~lautend *a.* identical; **~machen** *v.t.; dem Boden ~machen,* to level; **~macherisch** *a.* (*pej.*) egalitarian.
Gleichmaß *n.* (*es, 0*) symmetry, proportion.
gleichmäßig *a.* uniform, regular.
Gleichmut *m.* **(-[e]s, 0)** equanimity.
gleichmütig *a.* calm, even-tempered.
gleichnamig *a.* bearing the same name.
Gleichnis *n.* **(-ses,-e)** parable.
gleichordnen *v.t.* to coordinate.
gleichrangig *a.* equally important; of equal rank.
Gleichrichter *m.* **(-s, -)** (*elek.*) rectifier.
gleichsam *adv.* as it were, as if.
Gleichschaltung *f.* (political) co-ordination.
gleichschenk(e)lig *a.* (*geom.*) isosceles.
Gleichschritt *m.* marching in step.
gleichseitig *a.* equilateral.
Gleichstellung *f.* **(-, -en)** equalization.
Gleichstrom *m.* (*elek.*) direct current (D.C.).
Gleichung *f.* **(-, -en)** equation.
gleichviel *adv.* no matter, all the same.
gleichwertig *a.* equivalent.
gleichwie *c.* as, even as.
gleichwink(e)lig *a.* equiangular.
gleichwohl *c.* yet, however.
gleichzeitig *a.* contemporary; simultaneous.
gleichziehen *v.i.st.* to catch up, to draw level.
Gleis *n.* track; rails; line.
gleißen *v.i.* to blaze.
gleiten *v.i.st. (s)* to glide; to slide.
gleitend *a.* sliding; **~e Arbeitszeit** *f.* flexible working hours, flextime.
Gleit: ~flug *m.* glide; **~flugzeug** *m.* glider; **~klausel** *f.* (*jur.*) escalator clause; **~mittel** *n.* lubricant; **~schutz** *m.* antiskid device; **~sichtgläser** *pl.* multifocal lenses.
Gleitzeit *f.* flextime; flexible working hours; **~karte** *f.* time card.
Gletscher *m.* **(-s, -)** glacier.
Gletscherspalte *f.* crevasse.
Glied *n.* **(-[e]s, -er)** limb; member; link; rank, file (of soldiers); *männliches ~,* penis.
Gliederfüßer *m.* (*bio.*) arthropod.
gliedern *v.t.* to articulate; to organize; to structure.
Gliederpuppe *f.* jointed doll; lay-figure.
Gliederschmerz *m.* rheumatic pains.
Gliederung *f.* **(-, -en)** (*auch mil.*) organization; structure.
Gliedmaßen *pl.* limbs *pl.*
Gliedsatz *m.* subordinate clause.
glimmen *v.i.* to glimmer, to glow.
Glimmer *m.* **(-s, 0)** glimmer; mica.
glimpflich *a.* gentle, mild, lenient.
glitschen *v.i. (s)* to slide, to glide.
glitschig *a.* slippery.
glitzern *v.i.* to twinkle; to glitter, to sparkle.
global *a.* global, world-wide; general, overall.
Globus *m.* **(-, -ben)** globe.
Glocke *f.* **(-, -n)** bell.
Glocken: ~blume *f.* bellflower; **~schlag** *m.* stroke; **~spiel** *n.* chimes *pl.;* **~turm** *m.* bell tower, belfry.
glockig *a.* bell-shaped.
Glöckner *m.* bellringer.
Glorie *f.* **(-, 0)** glory; **~nschein** *m.* halo.
glorifizieren *v.t.* to glorify.
Glorifizierung *f.* glorification.
Gloriole *f.* glory; halo, aura.
glorreich *a.* glorious.
Glossar *n.* **(-s, -e)** glossary.
Glosse *f.* **(-, -n)** gloss, commentary.
Glotzaugen *pl.* goggle eyes.
Glotze *f. (fam.)* (boob) tube.
glotzen *v.i.* to stare; to goggle.
Glück *n.* **(-[e]s, 0)** luck, good luck; happiness, prosperity; fortune; *~ haben,* to be in luck; *kein ~ haben,* to be unlucky; *viel ~!* good luck!; *es war ein ~,* it was fortunate; *~ wünschen,* to wish good luck.
glückbringend *a.* lucky.
Glucke *f.* sitting hen; (*fig.*) mother hen.
glucken *v.i.* to cluck; to brood.
glücken *v.i.(s)* to succeed, to prosper.
gluckern *v.i.* to glug; to gurgle.
glücklich *a.* happy, fortunate; lucky.
glücklicherweise *adv.* fortunately; luckily.
glücklos *a.* luckless; unhappy (existence).
Glücksbringer *m.* mascot, lucky charm.
Glückseligkeit *f.* **(-, -en)** bliss, happiness.
glucksen *v.i.* to chuckle.
Glücks: ~fall *m.* stroke of luck; **~göttin** *f.* goddess of fortune; Fortune; **~spiel** *n.* game of chance; **~strähne** *f.* lucky streak.
glückstrahlend *a.* radiant.
Glückwunsch *m.* congratulation.
Glühbirne *f.* light bulb.
glühen *v.i.* to glow.
glühend *a.* glowing; red-hot; ardent; burning.
Glühwürmchen *n.* glowworm; firefly.
Glut *f.* **(-, -en)** fire, heat; embers; (*fig.*) fervor, ardor.
G.m.b.H. *Gesellschaft mit beschränkter Haftung,* limited liability company, Ltd.
Gnade *f.* **(-, -n)** grace, favor; pardon, mercy.
Gnadengesuch *n.* clemency plea, petition for clemency *or* mercy.
gnadenlos *a.* merciless.
Gnaden: ~schuß *m;* **~stoß** *m.* coup de grâce; **~tod** *m.* mercy killing.
gnädig *a.* gracious; *~e Frau,* madam.
Gnom *m.* gnome.
Gobelin *m.* **(-s, -s)** tapestry.
Gockel *m.* (*fam.*) rooster; cock.
Golanhöhen *pl.* Golan Heights.
Gold *n.* **(-[e]s, 0)** gold.
Goldbarren *m.* gold bar, ingot.
golden *a.* gold; (*fig.*) golden.
goldhaltig *a.* auriferous.

goldig *a.* (*fam.*) sweet, cute.
Gold: ~regen *m.* (*bot.*) laburnum; **~schmied** *m.* goldsmith; **~schnitt** *m.* gilt edges; **~standard** *m.*, **~währung** *f.* gold standard.
Golf *m.* **(-[e]s, -e)** gulf; (*Spiel*) golf.
Golf: ~platz *m.* golf course, golf links; **~spieler** *m.* golfer; **~schläger** *m.* golf club.
Golfstrom *m.* Gulf Stream.
Gondel *f.* **(-, -n)** gondola.
gönnen *v.t.* not to envy, not to grudge; to allow, to grant.
Gönner *m.* **(-s, -)** patron.
gönnerhaft *a.* patronizing.
Gonorrhöe *f.* gonorrhea.
Göre *f.* child, kid; brat.
Gorilla *m.* **(-s, -s)** gorilla.
Gosse *f.* **(-, -n)** gutter.
Gotik *f.* **(-, 0)** Gothic style.
gotisch *a.* Gothic.
Gott *m.* **(-s, Götter)** God; *um ~es willen,* for God's sake; **~sei Dank!** thank God, thank goodness!; *leider Gottes!* alas!
göttergleich *a.* god-like.
Götterspeise *n.* food of the gods; jelly.
Gottesdienst *m.* public worship, divine service.
gottesfürchtig *a.* pious, God-fearing.
Gotteslästerung *f.* blasphemy.
Gottesurteil *n.* trial by ordeal.
gott: ~gefällig *a.* pleasing to God; **~gewollt** *a.* ordained by God.
Gottheit *f.* **(-, -en)** deity; divinity.
Göttin *f.* **(-, -nen)** goddess.
göttlich *a.* divine; godlike.
Göttlichkeit *f.* **(-, 0)** divinity; divine origin.
gottlos *a.* godless, impious, wicked.
Gottvater *m.* God the Father.
gott: ~verdammt *a.*, **~verflucht** *a.* goddamned; **~verlassen** *a.* godforsaken.
Gottvertrauen *n.* trust in God.
gottvoll *a.* divine; (*fam.*) capital, grand.
Götze *m.* **(-n, -n)** idol.
Götzendienst *m.* idolatry.
Gouvernante *f.* **(-, -n)** governess.
Gouverneur *m.* **(-s, -e)** governor.
Grab *n.* **(-[e]s, Gräber)** grave, tomb, sepulcher.
Graben *m.* **(-s, Gräben)** ditch, trench; moat.
graben *v.t.st.* to dig; to engrave, to cut.
Grab: ~mal *n.* tomb, sepulchre; **~rede** *f.* funeral sermon; **~schrift** *f.* epitaph; **~stätte** *f.*, **~stelle** *f.* grave, tomb; **~stein** *m.* tombstone, gravestone.
Grabung *f.* excavation.
Graburne *f.* funeral urn.
Gracht *f.* canal.
Grad *m.* **(-[e]s, -e)** degree; grade; rate; *in hohem ~*, highly; *im höchsten ~*, exceedingly, to the last degree.
Gradeinteilung *f.* **(-, -en)** graduation, scale.
graduieren *v.i.* to graduate.
Graf *f.* **(-en, -en)** count; (*englischer*) earl.
Gräfin *f.* **(-, -nen)** countess.
Grafschaft *f.* **(-, -en)** earldom; county.
Gram *m.* **(-[e]s, 0)** grief, sorrow.
grämen *v.r.* to grieve, to be grieved, to fret, to pine.
grämlich *a.* sullen, morose.
Gramm *n.* **(-[e]s, -e)** gram.
Grammatik *f.* **(-, -en)** grammar.
Grammatiker *m.* **(-s, -)** grammarian.
grammatisch *a.* & *adv.* grammatical(ly).
Grammophon *n.* **(-s, -e)** gramophone, phonograph; **~platte** *f.* record.
Granat *m.* garnet.
Granatapfel *m.* pomegranate.
Granate *f.* **(-, -n)** grenade, shell.
Granattrichter *m.* (shell) crater.
Granatwerfer *m.* mortar.
grandios *a.* terrific.
Granit *m.* **(-[e]s, -e)** granite.
grantig *a.* grumpy, bad-tempered.
Granulat *n.* granules.
Grapefruit *f.* **(-, -s)** grapefruit.
Graphik *f.* **(-, -en)** graphic art; engraving.
Graphiker *m;* **Graphikerin** *f.* graphic designer.
graphisch *a.* graphic; **~e Darstellung** *f.* graphic representation, graph; **~es Zeichen** *n.* symbol.
Graphit *m.* **(-[e]s, -e)** graphite.
Graphologe *m.* **(-en, -en)** graphologist.
Gras *n.* **(-es, Gräser)** grass, herbage; (*fam.*) *ins ~ beißen,* to bite the dust.
Grasbüschel *n.* tuft of grass.
grasen *v.i.* to graze.
Grashalm *m.* blade of grass.
Grashüpfer *m.* grasshopper.
grassieren *v.i.* to spread, to rage.
gräßlich *a.* ghastly, dreadful, horrible.
Grat *a.* **(-[e]s, -e)** edge, ridge; (*mech.*) burr.
Gräte *f.* **(-, -n)** fish bone.
grätenlos *a.* boneless.
Grätenmuster *n.* herringbone pattern.
Gratifikation *f.* bonus.
grätig *a.* full of (fish-)bones.
gratis *adv.* free of charge.
Grätsche *f.* straddle.
Gratulation *f.* **(-, -en)** congratulation.
gratulieren *v.i.* to congratulate (on).
Gratwanderung *f.* ridge walk; (*fig.*) balancing act.
grau *a.* gray, grey; grizzled; **~er Star,** cataract.
grauen *v.imp.* to shudder (at); to dawn.
Grauen *n.* **(-s, 0)** dread, horror.
grauenhaft, grauenvoll *a.* horrifying, terrible.
gräulich *a.* grayish.
graumeliert *a.* graying.
Graupe *f.* **(-, -n)** groats *pl.;* pearl barley.
Graupel *f.* **(-s, -n)** sleet.
graupeln *v.i.imp.* to sleet.
Graus *m.* **(-[e]s, 0)** horror, dread.
grausam *a.* cruel.
Grausamkeit *f.* **(-, -en)** cruelty.
Grauschimmel *m.* gray horse; gray mold.
grausen *v.i.imp.* to shudder (at).
Grausen *n.* horror.
grausig *a.* dreadful, gruesome, awful.
Grau: ~tier *n.* ass; donkey; mule; **~zone** *f.* (*fig.*) grey area.
Graveur *m.* **(-[e]s, -e)** engraver.
gravieren *v.t.* to engrave.
gravierend *a.* serious, important.
Gravitation *f.* gravitation.
Gravitations: ~feld *n.* gravitational field; **~gesetz** *n.* law of gravitation.
gravitätisch *a.* grave, solemn.
Grazie *f.* **(-, -n)** grace, gracefulness; *pl.* Graces.
graziös *a.* graceful, pretty.
Greif *m.* **(-[e]s, -e)** griffin.
greifbar *a.* tangible, palpable; on hand.
greifen *v.t.st.* to seize, to lay hold on; to grasp, to catch.

Greifer *m.* (*tech.*) grab, gripper.
Greif: ~vogel *m.* bird of prey; **~zange** *f.* tongs.
greis *a.* very old.
Greis *m.* **(-es, -e); Greisin** *f.* **(-, -nen)** old person.
Greisenalter *n.* old age.
greisenhaft *a.* senile.
Greisenhaftigkeit *f.* senility.
grell *a.* (*Licht, Farbe*) glaring, dazzling.
Gremium *n.* committee.
Grenadier *m.* **(-s, -e)** grenadier.
Grenz: ~abfertigung *f.* passport control and custom clearance; **~berichtigung** *f.* **(-, -en)** frontier readjustment.
Grenze *f.* **(-, -n)** border, frontier, boundary; limit.
grenzen *v.i.* to border, to adjoin.
grenzenlos *a.* boundless; immense.
Grenzfall *m.* borderline case.
Grenzformalitäten *pl.* passport and customs formalities.
Grenzkontrolle *f.* border check.
Grenzlinie *f.* border.
Greuel *m.* **(-s, -)** horror, abomination, outrage.
Greueltat *f.* atrocity.
greulich *a.* horrible, heinous.
Grieche *m.*; **Griechin** *f.*; **griechisch** *a.* Greek.
Griechenland *n.* **(-s, 0)** Greece.
Griesgram *m.* **(-[e]s, -e)** grumbler.
griesgrämig *a.* morose, sullen, grumbling.
Grieß *m.* **(-sses, -sse)** semolina *pl.*
Griff *m.* **(-[e]s, -e)** grip, grasp, hold.
griffbereit *a.* ready to hand.
Griffbrett *n.* (*Geige*) fret-board, neck.
Griffel *m.* **(-s, -)** (*bot.*) style; slate pencil.
griffig *a.* handy.
Grill *m.* barbecue.
Grille *f.* **(-, -n)** cricket (insect); (*fig.*) whim, caprice, fad.
grillen *v.t.* to grill.
Grimasse *f.* **(-, -n)** grimace, wry face.
grimm *a.* grim, furious.
Grimm *m.* **(-[e]s, 0)** fury, rage, wrath.
grimmig *a.* grim, furious.
Grind *m.* **(-[e]s, -e)** scab, scurf.
grinsen *v.i.* to grin, to smirk.
Grippe *f.* **(-, 0)** (*med.*) influenza, (*fam.*) flu.
Grips *m.* (*fam.*) brains.
grob *a.* coarse, gross, thick; clumsy; rude, insolent; rough; **~e Berechnung** *f.* rough calculation.
grobgemahlen *a.* coarsely ground.
Grobheit *f.* rudeness; coarseness.
Grobian *m.* **(-s, -e)** lout, boor.
gröhlen, grölen *v.i.* to scream, to squall.
Groll *m.* **(-[e]s, 0)** rancor, grudge, resentment.
grollen *v.i.* to bear a grudge *or* ill-will; (*Donner*) to rumble.
Gros *n.* **(-, 0)** bulk.
groß *a.* large: (*dick*) big; (*Wuchs*) tall; (*fig.*) great; high, eminent; **~er Buchstabe** *m.* capital (letter); *~ tun,* to brag, to give oneself airs.
groß: ~sprecherisch *a.* swaggering, vain-glorious.
Großstadt *f.* large city.
Großstädter *m.* inhabitant of a large city.
großartig *a.* grand, sublime.
Großbetrieb *m.* large undertaking.
Größe *f.* **(-, -n)** size; (*fig.*) greatness, magnitude; quantity.
Großeinkauf *m.* bulk purchase.
Großeltern *pl.* grandparents *pl.*
Großenkel *m.* great-grandson.
großenteils *adv.* in large measure.
Größenwahn *m.* megalomania.
Großgrundbesitzer *m.* large estate owner.
Großhandel *m.* wholesale business.
Grosßhändler *m.* wholesale merchant.
großherzig *a.* magnanimous.
Großherzog *m.* grand-duke.
Großindustrie *f.* big industry *pl.*
Grossist *m.*; **Grossistin** *f.* wholesaler.
großjährig *a.* of age.
Großkampfschiff *n.* capital ship.
Großmacht *f.* great power.
Großmaul *n.* (*fam.*) big mouth.
Großmut *f.* magnanimity, generosity.
großmütig *a.* magnanimous, generous.
Groß: ~mutter *f.* grandmother; **~neffe** *m.* grandnephew; **~nichte** *f.* grandniece; **~sprecher** *m.* swaggerer, braggart; **~sprecherei** *f.* big talk.
großstädtisch *a.* big city (attrib.).
Groß: ~tat *f.* achievement, exploit; **~vater** *m.* grandfather.
größtenteils *adv.* for the most part.
großzügig *a.* on a large scale, generous.
grotesk *a.* grotesque.
Grotte *f.* **(-, -n)** grotto.
Grübchen *n.* dimple.
Grube *f.* **(-, -n)** pit; mine; (*fig.*) grave.
Grübelei *f.* **(-, -en)** pondering; musing.
grübeln *v.i.* to brood, to ponder.
Gruben: ~klotz *m.* prop; **~licht** *n.* miner's lamp.
Grübler *m.* meditative person.
Gruft *f.* **(-, Grüfte)** tomb, vault.
grummeln *v.i.* to rumble; to mumble.
grün *a.* green; fresh; (*fig.*) unripe; *~er Tisch,* bureaucracy.
Grün *n.* **(-s, 0)** green color; verdure.
Grund *m.* **(-[e]s, Gründe)** ground; bottom; foundation; reason, motive; argument; *auf ~ von,* on the strength of; *von ~ aus,* thoroughly; *im ~e,* after all, at bottom; *auf ~ laufen,* to run aground; *zu ~e richten,* to ruin; *zu ~e gehen,* to perish.
Grundbedingung *f.* main condition.
Grundbegriff *m.* fundamental notion.
Grundbesitz *m.* landed property, real estate.
Grundbesitzer *m.* landowner.
Grundbestandteil *m.* main element, essential ingredient.
Grundbuch *n.* land register; real estate register.
Grundbuchamt *n.* land registry.
Grunddienstbarkeit *f.* (*law*) encumbrance.
Grundeigentum *n.* landed property.
Grundeigentümer *m.* landowner.
gründen *v.t.* to establish, to found, to promote, to float; ~ *v.r.* to rest (upon).
Gründer *m.* **(-s, -)** founder.
grundfalsch *a.* radically wrong *or* false.
Grundfarbe *f.* ground color, priming.
Grundfläche *f.* base, basis.
Grundgedanke *m.* fundamental idea.
Grundgehalt *m.* basic salary.
Grundgesetz *n.* fundamental law.
grundieren *v.t.* to prime.
Grundirrtum *m.* fundamental error.
Grundkapital *n.* initial capital, stock.
Grundlage *f.* foundation, groundwork, substructure, base.
Grundlegung *f.* foundation.
gründlich *a.* profound, thorough; solid.
Grundlinie *f.* basis; base line.
Grundlohn *m.* basic wage.

grundlos *a.* bottomless; groundless.
Gründonnerstag *m.* Maundy Thursday.
Grundrechte *n.pl* fundamental rights.
Grundregel *f.* basic rule.
Grundrente *f.* basic pension, ground-rent.
Grundriß *m.* ground plan; (*Buch*) outline.
Grundsatz *m.* principle; maxim.
grundsätzlich *a.* fundamental; ~ *adv.* on principle.
Grundschule *f.* primary school.
Grundstein *m.* foundation-stone.
Grundsteuer *f.* property tax.
Grundstock *m.* basis, foundation, nucleus.
Grundstück *n.* real estate.
Grundton *m.* key-note.
Gründung *f.* **(-, -en)** foundation, establishment.
Grundursache *f.* original cause.
grundverschieden *a.* radically different.
Grundwasser *n.* ground water.
Grundzahl *f.* cardinal number.
Grundzins *m.* ground-rent.
Grundzug *m.* main feature.
Grüne *n.* green, countryside.
Grüne *m./f.* member of the Green Party.
grünen *v.i.* to grow green.
Grünen *pl.* the Greens.
grünlich *a.* greenish.
Grünschnabel *m.* greenhorn, sucker.
Grünspan *m.* verdigris.
grunzen *v.i.* to grunt.
Grünzeug *n.* **(-es, 0)** greens *pl.*
Gruppe *f.* **(-, -n)** group; (*avi.*) group.
Gruppen: ~arbeit *f.* group work; **~dynamik** *f.* group dynamics; **~kommandeur** *m.* (*avi.*) group commander; **~therapie** *f.* group therapy.
gruppieren *v.t.* to group.
Gruppierung *f.* **(-, -en)** grouping (*pol.*) faction.
Gruselgeschichte *f.* horror story.
gruselig *a.* uncanny, creepy.
gruseln *v.t.imp. mich gruselt,* my flesh creeps, I shudder.
Gruß *m.* **(-es, Grüsse)** salutation, greeting; salute; compliment.
grüßen *v.t.* to greet; to salute; ~ **lassen,** to send one's regards.
grußlos *a.* without a word of greeting.
Grütze *f.* **(-, 0)** groats *pl.*; (*fig.*) brains.
Guatelmateke *m.*; **Guatelmatekin** *f.* Guatemalan.
Guatemala *n.* **(-s, 0)** Guatemala.
gucken *v.i.* to peep, to look.
Guckloch *n.* spy-hole; peephole.
Guerilla *f.* **(-, -s)** guerilla war; guerilla unit; **~kämpfer** *m.* guerilla.
Gulasch *n./m.* goulash.
Gulden *m.* **(-s, -)** florin; (*holländischer*) guilder.
Gully *m.* drain.
gültig *a.* valid, available; good, current; ~ **machen,** to validate.
Gültigkeit *f.* **(-, 0)** validity, legality.
Gummi *n.* **(-s, 0)** eraser, rubber.
Gummiband *n.* elastic.
gummieren *v.t.* to gum.
Gummiknüppel *m.* truncheon.
Gummiparagraph *m.* elastic clause.
Gummischuhe *m.pl.* galoshes *pl.*
Gummistiefel *m.* rubber boot.
Gummizelle *f.* padded cell.
Gunst *f.* **(-, 0)** favor, kindness; *zu ~en,* in favor of.
günstig *a.* favorable.
Günstling *m.* **(-[e]s, -e)** favorite.
Gurgel *f.* **(-, -n)** throat, gullet.
gurgeln *v.i.* to gargle.
Gurke *f.* **(-, -n)** cucumber; (*fig.*) lemon; *saure ~,* pickled cucumber, gherkin.
gurren *v.i.* to coo.
Gurt *m.* **(-[e]s, -e)** strap; seat belt.
Gürtel *m.* **(-s, -)** belt; (*geog.*) zone.
Gürtel: ~linie *f.* waistline; **~reifen** *m.* radial tire; **~rose** *f.* (*med.*) shingles *pl.*; **~schnalle** *f.* belt buckle; **~tier** *n.* armadillo.
gürten *v.t.* to gird, to girdle.
GUS *Gemeinschaft unabhängiger Staaten,* Commonwealth of Independent States, CIS.
Guß *m.* **(Gusses, Güsse);** casting, founding; gush, shower; downpour; (*cul.*) icing.
Guß: ~eisen *n.* cast iron; **~stahl** *m.* cast steel.
gut *a.* good; well; *~heißen,* to approve of; *es ~ haben,* to have a good time; *~schreiben,* to credit, to place to one's credit; *einem etwas zu ~e halten,* to make allowance for a thing; *sich etwas zu ~e tun,* to pride oneself upon; *kurz und ~,* in short; *mit einem ~ stehen,* to be on good terms with a person.
Gut *n.* **(-[e]s, Güter)** good; property estate; (*com.*) commodity, article, goods *pl.*
Gutachten *n.* **(-s, -)** expert opinion *or* evidence.
gutartig *a.* good-natured; (*med.*) benign.
Gutdünken *n.* judgment, discretion.
Güte *f.* **(-, 0)** goodness; (*com.*) (good) quality.
Güter: ~bahnhof *m.* goods-station, goods-yard, freight yard; **~gemeinschaft** *f.* joint property; **~recht** *n.* property law; **~trennung** *f.* separation of property; **~verkehr** *m.* goods traffic; **~wagen** *m* (*rail.*) truck, freight-car; **~zug** *m.* goods train, freight train.
gut: ~gelaunt *a.* good-humored; **~gesinnt** well disposed; **~gläubig,** bona fide, in good faith; credulous.
Gutgläubigkeit *f.* credulity; gullibility.
Guthaben *n.* **(-s, -)** (credit) balance.
gutheißen *v.t.st.* to approve of.
gutherzig *a.* kind-hearted.
gütig *a.* kind, benignant.
gütlich *a.* amicable.
gutmachen *v.t.* to make good; to correct.
gutmütig *a.* good-natured.
Gutmütigkeit *f.* **(-, 0)** good-nature.
Gutsbesitzer *m.* **(-s, -)** landowner.
Gutschein *m.* **(-s, -e)** voucher, coupon.
gutschreiben *v.t.* to enter to one's credit.
Gutschrift *f.* credit.
Gutshof *m.* farmyard.
gutsituiert *a.* well-to-do, well-off.
Gutsverwalter *m.* bailiff.
guttun *v.i.st.* to do good.
gutwillig *a.* obliging; willing; friendly.
Gymnasial: ~bildung *f.* secondary-school education; **~direktor** *m.* principal of a secondary school; **~lehrer** *m.* secondary-school teacher.
Gymnasiast *m.* **(-en, -en); Gymnasiastin** *f.* high-school student.
Gymnasium *n.* **(-s, -ien)** secondary school.
Gymnastik *f.* **(-, 0)** gymnastics *pl.*
gymnastisch *a.* gymnastic.
Gynäkologe *m.*; **Gynäkologin** *f.* gynecologist.
Gynäkologie *f.* gynecology.
gynäkologisch *a.* gynecological.
H, h *n.* the letter H or h; (*mus.*) B.

ha *Hektar*, hectare.
Haar *n.* **(-[e]s, -e)** hair; *die ~e standen ihm zu Berge*, his hair stood on end; *einander in die ~e geraten*, to come to blows; *sich die ~e machen*, to do one's hair.
Haar: ~ausfall *m.* loss of hair; **~bürste** *f.* hairbrush; **~büschel** *n.* tuft of hair.
haaren *v.i.* to moult, to shed (hair); ~ *v.r.* to lose one's hair.
Haaresbreite *f. um* ~ by a hair's breadth.
haarig *a.* hairy; *kurz~*, short-haired; *lang~*, long-haired.
Haarklammer *f.* hair clip.
haarklein *a.* (*fam.*) detailed; ~ *adv.* minutely, in great detail.
Haarklemme *f.* hair clip.
Haarnadel *f.* hairpin, bodkin.
haarscharf *a.* very subtle, very keen.
Haarschleife *f.* bow; hair ribbon.
Haarschopf *m.* shock of hair.
Haarspalterei *f.* (*fig.*) hair-splitting.
haarsträubend *a.* revolting, shocking.
Haar: ~wasser *n.* hair-lotion; **~wuchsmittel** *n.* hair tonic
Habe *f.* **(-, 0)** property, effects *pl.; Hab' und Gut*, goods and chattels *pl.*
haben *v.t.ir.* to have; *da ~ wir's!* there we are! *was hast du denn?* what's the matter with you?
Haben *n.* **(-s, -)** (*com.*) credit.
Haben: ~seite *f.* credit side; **~zinsen** *pl.* interest on deposits.
Habgier *f.* **(-, 0)** covetousness, greediness.
habgierig *a.* covetous, greedy.
habhaft *a.* **~ werden,** to get hold of.
Habicht *m.* **(-[e]s, -e)** hawk.
Habilitation *f.* postdoctoral lecturing qualification; **~sschrift** *f.* postdoctoral thesis.
habilitieren ~ *v.r.* to be admitted as lecturer at a German university; ~ *v.t.* to confer university lecturing status on.
Habsburger *m.* Habsburg.
Habseligkeiten *pl.* meager belongings *pl.*, effects *pl.*
Habsucht *f.* **(-, 0)** avarice, covetousness.
habsüchtig *a.* avaricious, covetous.
Hack: ~beil *n.* chopper, hatchet; **~block** *m.* chopping block; **~brett** *n.* chopping board; (*mus.*) dulcimer.
Hacke *f.* **(-, -n)** hoe, pick(axe), heel.
hacken *v.t.* to chop, to hack, to cleave; to mince; to hoe.
Hackfleisch *n.* ground meat.
Hackordnung *f.* (*fig.*) pecking order.
Häcksel *m.* or *n.* **(-s, 0)** chaff.
Hacksteak *n.* hamburger.
Hader *m.* **(-s, -n)** quarrel, brawl.
hadern *v.i.* to quarrel, to wrangle.
Hafen *m.* **(-s, Häfen)** harbor, port, haven.
Hafen: ~anlagen *pl.* docks; **~arbeiter** *m.* dockworker; **~gebühren** *f.pl* harbor dues, port dues; **~stadt** *f.* port; **~viertel** *n.* dock area.
Hafer *m.* **(-s, 0)** oats *pl.*
Hafer: ~brei *m.* porridge; **~mehl** *n.* oatmeal; **~schleim** *m.* gruel.
Haft *f.* **(-, 0)** custody, arrest.
Haftanstalt *f.* prison.
haftbar *a.* liable, responsible.
Haftbefehl *m.* arrest warrant.
haften *v.i.* to stick, to adhere; ~ *für*, to be liable for.
haftenbleiben *v.i.st.* to stick.
Häftling *m.* **(-s, -e)** detainee, prisoner.
Haftpflicht *f.* liability.
haftpflichtig *a.* liable.
Haftung *f.* adhesion, grip; liability; *(un)beschränkte ~*, (un)limited liability.
Hagebutte *f.* **(-, -n)** rose-hip.
Hagedorn *m.* hawthorn.
Hagel *m.* **(-s, 0)** hail.
Hagelkorn *n.* hailstone.
hageln *v.i.imp.* to hail.
Hagel: ~schaden *m.* damage caused by hail; **~schaden-Versicherung** *f.* hail insurance; **~wetter** *n.* hailstorm.
hager *a.* lean, gaunt, meager.
Häher *m.* **(-s, -)** jay.
Hahn *m.* **(-[e]s, Hähne)** cock, rooster; faucet; (gun) hammer.
Hähnchen *n.* chicken.
Hahnen: ~fuß *m.* buttercup; **~kamm** *m.* cockscomb; **~kampf** *m.* cockfight; **~schrei** *m.* cockcrow; **~trittmuster** *n.* hound's-tooth check.
Hahnrei *m.* **(-[e]s, -e)** cuckold.
Hai(fisch) *m.* **(-[e]s, -e)** shark.
Hain *m.* **(-[e]s, -e)** grove, wood.
Häkchen *n.* **(-s, -)** small hook.
Häkelarbeit *f.* crochet work.
Häkelgarn *n.* crochet yarn.
Häkelmuster *n.* crochet pattern.
häkeln *v.t. & i.* to crochet.
Häkelnadel *f.* crochet needle.
Haken *m.* **(-s, -)** hook, clasp; *das hat einen ~*, there's a snag somewhere.
Hakenkreuz *n.* swastika.
halb *a. & adv.* half; *~e Note f.* (*mus.*) half note; **~er Ton** *m.* semitone; *auf ~em Weg*, halfway.
halbamtlich *a.* semi-official.
Halbbruder *m.* **(-s, -brüder)** half-brother.
Halbdunkel *n.* dusk, twilight.
Halbedelstein *m.* semi-precious stone.
halbfertig *a.* half-finished.
Halbfinale *n.* semifinal.
halbgar *a.* underdone, rare.
Halbgott *m.* demigod.
Halbheit *f.* **(-, -en)** half-measure.
halbherzig *a. & adv.* half-hearted(ly).
halbieren *v.t.* to halve; to bisect.
Halbinsel *f.* peninsula.
halbjährig *a.* lasting six months; six months old.
halbjährlich *a.* semi-annual; ~ *adv.* semi-annually.
Halb: ~kreis *m.* semicircle; **~kugel** *f.* hemisphere.
halblaut *a. & adv.* in a low voice, in an undertone.
Halbleinen *n.* half-linen.
Halbleiter *m.* semiconductor.
halbmast *adv. auf ~ stehen*, fly at half-mast.
Halbmesser *m.* radius.
Halbmond *m.* half-moon, crescent.
halboffen *a.* ajar, half-open.
Halbschlaf *m.* light sleep.
Halbschuh *m.* (low) shoe.
halbseiden *a.* half-silk; (*fig.*) dubious.
halbsteif *a.* semi-stiff.
Halbstiefel *m.* (*Damen*) ankle boot.
halbstündig *a.* half-hour.
halbstündlich *a.* half-hourly.
halbtags *a.* part-time.
Halbtagsarbeit *f.* part-time job.
Halbtagskraft *f.* part-timer.

halbwegs *adv.* to some extent; reasonably.
Halbwelt *f.* demimonde.
Halbwüchsige *m./f.* adolescent; teenager.
Halbzeit *f.* half-time.
Halde *f.* **(-, -n)** declivity, slope; dump.
Hälfte *f.* **(-, -n)** half; middle.
Halfter *m.* & *n.* **(-s, -)** halter; *f.* **(-, -n)** holster.
halftern *v.t.* to halter, to put a halter on.
Hall *m.* **(-[e]s, -e)** reverberation; echo.
Halle *f.* **(-, -n)** hall; lobby; foyer.
hallen *v.i.* to sound, to resound, to reverberate, to echo.
Hallenbad *n.* indoor pool.
Hallig *f.* **(-, -en)** small island off the North Sea coast.
hallo! *i.* hello!
Halluzination *f.* hallucination.
Halm *m.* **(-[e]s, -e)** stalk, straw.
Hals *m.* **(Halses, Hälse)** neck; throat; *vom Halse,* off one's hands; *bis zum Halse,* neck-deep; *~ über Kopf,* in a rush/hurry; *einen auf dem ~e haben,* to be encumbered with sb.; *sich vom ~e schaffen,* to get rid of; *um den ~ fallen,* to embrace.
Hals-Nasen-Ohren-Arzt *m.;* **-Ärztin** *f.* ear, nose, and throat specialist.
Hals: ~abschneider *m.* cutthroat; **~band** *n.* necklace; collar; choker.
halsbrecherisch *a.* breakneck.
Halsentzündung *f.* sore throat.
Halsschlagader *f.* carotid artery.
halsstarrig *a.* stubborn, obstinate.
Hals: ~tuch *n.* scarf, neckerchief; **~- und Beinbruch!** Break a leg! **~weh** *n.* sore throat; **~weite** *f.* collar size; **~wirbel** *m.* cervical vertebra.
Halt *m.* **(-[e]s, -e)** hold, footing; halt, stop; support, stay.
halt! *i.* hold! stop!
haltbar *a.* nonperishable; durable; *das ist vier Wochen ~,* that will keep for four weeks.
halten *v.t. & i.st.* to hold; to keep; to contain; to deem, to estimate; (*mil.*) to hold on to; ~ *v.r.* to keep (well); to hold one's own; *länger ~* (*von Sachen*), to have longer wear; *viel auf einen ~,* to think highly of sb.; *den Mund ~,* to hold one's tongue; *eine Predigt ~,* to preach a sermon; *eine Rede ~,* to make a speech; *im Zaume ~,* to keep a tight hand on; *Wort ~,* to keep one's word; *sich an etw. ~,* to have recourse to sth.
Halter *m.* **(-s, -)** keeper; owner; holder.
Halterung *f.* holding device; mounting.
Halte: ~schild *n.* stop sign; **~signal** *n.* stop signal; **~stelle** *f.* station, stop; **~verbot** *n.* no stopping; **~verbotsschild** *n.* no-stopping sign.
haltlos *a.* unsteady, fickle.
haltmachen *v.i.* to stop.
Haltung *f.* **(-, -en)** attitude; bearing, position; *Körper~ f.* posture.
Halunke *m.* **(-n, -n)** scoundrel, rascal.
hämisch *a.* malicious, sneering.
Hammel *m.* **(-s, -)** wether; mutton; (*fig.*) idiot.
Hammel: ~braten *m.* roast mutton; **~fleisch** *n.* mutton; **~keule** *f.* leg of mutton; **~sprung** *m.* (*parl.*) division.
Hammer *m.* **(-s, Hämmer)** hammer.
hämmerbar *a.* malleable.
hämmern *v.t.* to hammer; ~ *v.i.* to pound, to thump.
Hammerwerfer *m.* hammer thrower.
Hämorrhoiden *f.pl* piles *pl.*, hemorrhoids *pl.*
Hampelmann *m.* jumping jack; (*pej.*) puppet, doormat, sucker.
hampeln *v.i.* to jump about.
Hamster *m.* **(-s, -)** hamster, marmot.
Hamsterer *m.* **(-s, -)** hoarder.
Hamster: ~fahrt *f.* foraging trip; **~kauf** *m.* panic buying.
hamstern *v.t.* to hoard.
Hand *f.* **(-, Hände)** hand; *mit der ~,* by hand; *zu Händen,* attention; *sich die Hände reiben,* to rub one's hands (together); *die ~ drücken,* to shake hands; *aus der ~ in den Mund leben,* to live from hand to mouth; *die Hände in den Schoß legen,* to remain idle; *unter der ~,* underhand, secretly; *die Hände im Spiel haben,* to have a finger in the pie; *bei der ~, zur Hand,* at hand.
Hand: ~akten *pl.* personal files; **~arbeit** *f.* handicraft, craft work; **~bibliothek** *f.* reference library.
handbreit *a.* of a hand's breadth.
Handbremse *f.* handbrake.
Handbuch *n.* manual, handbook.
Hände: ~druck *m.* handshake; **~klatschen** *n.* applause.
Handel *m.* **(-s, 0)** trade, traffic, commerce; bargain; affair; *einen* ~ **abschließen,** to strike a bargain; *~ treiben,* to trade; *pl.* **Händel,** quarrel(s).
handeln *v.i.* to act; to deal; to trade, to do business; to bargain, to chaffer; *es handelt sich um...,* it's a question of...
Handels: ~abkommen *n.* trade agreement; **~adressbuch** *n.* commercial directory; **~bilanz** *f.* balance of trade; **~einig werden,** to come to terms; **~flotte** *f.* merchant fleet; **~gesellschaft** *f.* trading company; *offene ~gesellschaft,* (general) partnership; **~gesetzbuch** *n.* commercial code; **~hochschule** *f.* business school; **~kammer** *f.* chamber of commerce; **~recht** *n.* commercial law; **~schiff** *n.* merchant ship; **~schiffahrt** *f.* merchant marine; **~schule** *f.* commercial school; **~teil** (*einer Zeitung*) *m.* business section; **~vertrag** *m.* commercial treaty.
handeltreibend *a.* trading.
händeringend *adv.* despairingly.
Händeschütteln *n.* handshake.
Handfertigkeit *f.* manual skill.
handfest *a.* strong, stout, strapping.
Handfeuerwaffe *f.* handgun; **~n** *pl.* small arms.
Handfläche *f.* palm of the hand.
Handgelenk *n.* wrist; *etw. aus dem ~ machen,* to do sth. with one's little finger.
handgemein *a.* at close quarters; *mit einem ~ werden,* to come to blows with sb.
Handgemenge *n.* scuffle, fight.
Handgepäck *n.* hand luggage.
handgeschneidert *a.* hand-tailored.
Hand: ~granate *f.* hand grenade; **~griff** *m.* grasp; handle; (*fig.*) knack; **~habe** *f.* handle.
handgreiflich obvious, palpable, blatant; violent; *er wurde ~,* he used his fists.
handhaben *v.t.* to handle; to manage.
Handikap *n.* **(-s, -s)** handicap.
Handkoffer *m.* suitcase.
Handlanger *m.* laborer.
Händler *m.* **(-s, -)** dealer, tradesman.
handlich *a.* handy; manageable.
Handlung *f.* **(-, -en)** act, action, deed; trade; (*lit.*) plot.
Handlungs: ~fähigkeit *f.* ability to act; **~freiheit** *f.* freedom of action; **~reisende(r)** *m.* traveling

salesman, representative; **~spielraum** *m.* scope of action; **~unfähigkeit** *f.* inability to act; **~weise** *f.* way of acting, mode of dealing.
Handrücken *m.* the back of one's hand.
Handschelle *f.* handcuff.
Handschlag *m.* handshake.
Handschrift *f.* handwriting; manuscript.
handschriftlich *a.* in manuscript, written.
Hand: ~schuh *m.* glove; **~streich** *m.* surprise attack; coup de main; **~tasche** *f.* attaché case, handbag; **~teller** *m.* palm of one's hand; **~tuch** *n.* towel; **~umdrehen** *n.*, *im ~*, in no time; **~voll** *f.* handful; **~werk** *n.* craft, trade, small business.
Handwerker *m.* **(-s, -)** craftsman, artisan, mechanic.
Handwerksbetrieb *m.* workshop.
Handwerkszeug *n.* implements, tools *pl.*
Handwörterbuch *n.* concise dictionary.
Handzettel *m.* leaflet; handout.
hanebüchen *a.* outrageous.
Hanf *m.* **(-[e]s, 0)** hemp.
hänfen *a.* hempen.
Hänfling *m.* **(-[e]s, -e)** linnet.
Hanfzwirn *m.* hemp yarn.
Hang *m.* **(-[e]s, 0)** slope, declivity; propensity, bias, bent.
Hängebacke *f.* flabby cheek.
Hängebauch *m.* paunch.
Hängebrücke *f.* suspension bridge.
Hängebrust *f.*; **Hängebusen** *m.* sagging breasts.
Hängelampe *f.* ceiling lamp.
Hängematte *f.* hammock.
hängen *v.t. & i.* to hang; to suspend.
hängend *a.* hanging.
Hansdampf *m. ~ in allen Gassen,* jack of all trades.
Hanse *f.* Hanseatic League, Hansa.
hänseln *v.t.* to tease.
Hansestadt *f.* Hanseatic town.
Hanswurst *m.* clown, harlequin; buffoon.
Hanteln *f.pl* dumbbells *pl.*
hantieren *v.t.* to handle, to manage.
hapern *v.i.impers.* to stick, to be amiss; to be lacking.
Happen *m.* **(-s, -)** morsel, snack.
happig *a.* (*fam.*) excessive, steep; **~e Preise** *pl.* high prices.
Härchen *n.* tiny hair cilium.
Harem *m.* harem.
Häretiker *m.* heretic.
Harfe *f.* **(-, -n)** harp.
Harfenist *m.* **(-en, -en)** harpist.
Harke *f.* **(-, -n)** rake.
harken *v.t.* to rake.
Harlekin *m.* **(-s, -e)** harlequin.
Harm *m.* **(-[e]s, 0)** grief, sorrow; injury.
härmen *v.r.* (*um*) to grieve, to pine (for).
harmlos *a.* harmless.
Harmlosigkeit *f.* harmlessness; mildness.
Harmonie *f.* **(-, -n)** harmony; concord.
harmonieren *v.i.* to agree, to harmonize.
Harmonik *f.* (*mus.*) harmony.
Harmonika *f.* **(-, -s)** accordion.
harmonisch *a.* harmonious; harmonic.
Harn *m.* **(-[e]s, 0)** urine.
Harnblase *f.* bladder.
harnen *v.i.* to make water, to urinate.
Harnisch *m.* **(-[e]s, -e)** armor.
Harnröhre *f.* urethra.
Harnsäure *f.* uric acid.
harntreibend *a.* diuretic.
Harnuntersuchung *f.* urinalysis.
Harnwege *pl.* urinary tract.
Harpune *f.* **(-, -n)** harpoon.
harren *v.i.* to wait.
harsch *a.* harsh; rough, stiff.
Harsch *n.* crusted snow.
hart *a.* hard; stiff; severe, austere; cruel.
Härte *f.* **(-, -n)** hardness; severity; cruelty.
Härtefall *m.* case of hardship.
Härtegrad *m.* degree of hardness.
härten *v.t.* to harden; (*Stahl*) to temper, to chill.
Hartfaserplatte *f.* fiberboard.
Hartgummi *m.* hard rubber.
hart: ~herzig *a.* hard-hearted; **~näckig** *a.* stubborn; headstrong, obstinate.
Hartplatz *m.* hard court.
Hartwurst *f.* dry sausage.
Harz *n.* **(-es, -e)** resin, rosin.
harzig *a.* resinous.
Hasardspiel *n.* game of chance; gamble.
Hasch *n.* hash.
Haschee *n.* (*cul.*) hash.
haschen *v.t.* to snatch, to seize, to snap up; *~ v.i.* (*nach*) to aspire to; to smoke hash.
Haschisch *n.* hashish.
Hase *m.* **(-n, -n)** hare.
Haselnuß *f.* hazelnut.
Hasenfuß *m.* coward.
Hasenscharte *f.* harelip.
Haspel *f.* **(-, -n)** reel, windlass.
haspeln *v.t. & i.* to reel, to wind on a reel; to splutter.
Haß *m.* **(Hasses, 0)** hate, hatred.
hassen *v.t.* to hate.
hassenswert *a.* hateful.
haßerfüllt *a.* filled with hatred.
häßlich *a.* ugly; nasty; hateful.
Häßlichkeit *f.* ugliness; nastiness.
Haßliebe *f.* love-hate relationship.
Hast *f.* **(-, 0)** haste, hurry, rush.
hasten *v.i.* to hasten, to hurry.
hastig *a.* hasty, hurried.
hätscheln *v.t.* to coddle, to caress; to pamper.
Haube *f.* **(-, -n)** cap; hood.
Haubitze *f.* **(-, -n)** howitzer.
Hauch *m.* **(-[e]s, -e)** breath, whiff; (*fig.*) aura, hint.
hauchdünn *a.* wafer-thin; flimsy.
hauchen *v.i.* to breathe; to aspirate.
hauchfein *a.* extremely fine.
Hauchlaut *m.* aspirate.
hauchzart *a.* extremely delicate (fabric).
Haudegen *m.* warhorse.
Haue *f.* **(-, -n)** hoe; spanking; *~ pl.* blows.
hauen *v.t.ir.* to hew, to cut; to strike; *einen übers Ohr ~*, to make sb. pay through the nose.
Hauer *m.* **(-s, -)** (mine) faceworker; fang, tusk.
Haufen *m.* **(-s, -)** heap; pile; crowd, rabble; *über den ~ werfen,* to overthrow.
häufen *v.t. & r.* to accumulate, to pile up.
haufenweise *adv.* in heaps.
Haufenwolke *f.* cumulus cloud.
häufig *a.* frequent; copious, abundant; *~ adv.* frequently.
Häufigkeit *f.* **(-, 0)** frequency.
Häufung *f.* **(-, 0)** accumulation.

Haupt *n.* **(-[e]s, Häupter)** head; (*fig.*) chief, chieftain.
Haupt... chief, main, principal.
Hauptaktionär *m.* principal shareholder.
Hauptbahnhof *m.* main *or* central station.
Hauptbuch *m.* ledger.
Hauptfach *n.* main subject, major.
Hauptgeschäftsstelle *f.* headquarters, main office.
Hauptgeschäftszeit *f.* peak business hours.
Hauptinhalt *m.* summary, substance.
Häuptling *m.* **(-[e]s, -e)** chieftain.
Hauptlinie *f.* main line, trunk line.
Hauptmann *m.* captain.
Hauptmast *m.* mainmast.
Hauptnenner *m.* (*ar.*) common denominator.
Hauptprobe *f.* dress-rehearsal.
Hauptquartier *n.* headquarters *pl.*
Hauptrolle *f.* principal *or* leading part.
Hauptsache *f.* main point.
hauptsächlich *a.* chief, principal; ~ *adv.* chiefly, principally.
Hauptsaison *f.* high season.
Hauptsatz *m.* (*gram.*) principal clause.
Hauptschlagader *f.* aorta.
Hauptschlüssel *m.* master key.
Hauptschule *f.* intermediate school.
Hauptsendezeit *f.* TV prime time.
Hauptsorge *f.* main concern.
Hauptspeicher *m.* (*comp.*) main memory.
Hauptstadt *f.* capital; metropolis.
Hauptstraße *f.* main street.
Haupttäter *m.* (*jur.*) principal.
Haupttribüne *f.* main stand.
Hauptverhandlung *f.* (*jur.*) main hearing.
Hauptverkehrszeit *f.* rush hour.
Hauptwohnsitz *m.* main residence.
Hauptwort *n.* noun, substantive.
Haus *n.* **(-es, Häuser)** house; *zu Hause,* at home; *ich bin für niemanden zu* ~*e,* I am not in for anybody; *nach* ~*e,* home; *von* ~ *aus,* originally.
Hausangestellte *m./f.* domestic servant.
Hausarbeiten *pl.* homework.
Hausarzt *m.* family doctor.
hausbacken *a.* unadventurous, boring.
Hausbau *m.* house construction.
Hausbesetzer *m.* squatter.
Hausbesetzung *f.* squatting; occupation.
Hausbesitzer *m.* landlord.
Hausbesitzerin *f.* landlady.
Hausbrand *m.* heating fuel.
Häuschen *n.* **(-s, -)** *dim. of Haus; aus dem* ~ *sein,* to be wild.
hausen *v.i.* to dwell; to keep house.
Häusermakler *m.* real estate agent.
Hausflur *f.* vestibule, hall.
Hausfrau *f.* housewife.
Hausfriedensbruch *m.* illegal entry into sb.'s home.
Hausgebrauch *m.* domestic use.
hausgemacht *a.* homemade.
Hausgemeinschaft *f.* house community; household.
Haushalt *m.* household; *den* ~ *führen,* to keep house.
haushalten *v.i.* to economize.
Haushälter(in) *m.(f.)* housekeeper.
haushälterisch *a.* economical, thrifty.
Haushalts... housekeeping...
Haushalts: **~ausschuß** *m.* budget committee; **~jahr** *n.* fiscal year, financial year; **~kunde** *f.* domestic subjects *pl.;* **~plan** *m.* budget; **~voranschlag** *m.* budget estimates; **~vorstand** *m.* head of the household.
haushoch *a.* as high as a house.
hausieren *v.i.* to peddle, to hawk.
Hausierer *m.* **(-s, -)** peddler, hawker.
Hauskleid *n.* house dress; hostess gown.
Hauslehrer(in) *m.(f.)* private tutor.
häuslich *a.* domestic; economical, frugal.
Häuslichkeit *f.* **(-, 0)** home, family life; domesticity.
Hausmacherart *f.* homemade style.
Hausmacht *f.* power base.
Hausmädchen *n.* housemaid.
Hausmarke *f.* house wine; own label.
Hausmeister *m.* custodian; caretaker.
Hausrat *m.* household goods; **~versicherung** *f.* household contents insurance.
Hausschlüssel *m.* front-door key.
Hausschuh *m.* slipper.
Hausse *f.* bull market; boom.
Haussuchung *f.* house search.
Haussuchungsbefehl *m.* search warrant.
Haustier *n.* domestic animal.
Haustür *f.* front door.
Hausvater *m.* father of the family.
Hausverwalter *m.* house manager.
Hauswesen *n.* household.
Haut *f.* **(-, Häute)** skin, hide; (*auf Flüßigkeit*) film; (*anat.*) membrane; (*fam.*) *gute, ehrliche* ~, good fellow; *aus der* ~ *fahren,* to lose all patience; *sich seiner* ~ *wehren,* to defend one's own life.
Haut: **~abschürfung** *f.* graze; **~arzt** *m.;* **~ärztin** *f.* dermatologist; **~ausschlag** *m.* rash.
Häutchen *n.* **(-s, -)** cuticle, pellicle; film.
häuten *v.t. & r.* to skin; to shed or change one's skin; to peel.
hauteng *a.* skin-tight.
Hautevolee *f.* **(-, 0)** upper crust.
Hautfarbe *f.* complexion, skin color.
hautfarben *a.* flesh-colored; skin-colored.
Hautkrankheit *f.* skin disease.
hautnah *a.* immediate, vivid; very close.
Haut: **~pflege** *f.* skin care; **~pilz** *m.* fungal infection; **~schere** *f.* cuticle scissors; **~transplantation** *f.* skin graft(ing).
Häutung *f.* shedding; sloughing.
Hautwasser *n.* lotion.
Havarie *f.* **(-, -en)** damage.
Hbf. *Hauptbahnhof,* main station, main sta.
H-Bombe *f.* H-bomb.
h.c. *honoris causa, ehrenhalber,* honorary, hon.
hd. *hochdeutsch,* High German, H.G.
Hebamme *f.* **(-, -n)** midwife.
Hebebock *m.* (*mech.*) jack.
Hebebühne *f.* car lift.
Hebel *m.* **(-s, -)** lever.
Hebel: **~gesetz** *n.* principle of the lever: **~kraft** *f.* **~wirkung** *f.* leverage.
heben *v.t.st.* to raise, to lift; to elevate; ~ *v.r.* to lift, to rise.
hebräisch *a.* Hebrew.
Hebung *f.* **(-, -en)** lifting, raising; (*fig.*) improvement.
hecheln *v.t.* to pant; to heckle, to taunt; to gossip.
Hecht *m.* **(-[e]s, -e)** pike.
hechten *v.i.* to do a pike-dive; to dive full-length.

Heck *n.* **(-[e]s, -e)** (*nav.*) stern; rear, back; (*avi.*) tail.
Heckantrieb *m.* rear-wheel drive.
Hecke *f.* **(-, -n)** hedge; thicket.
Heckenrose *f.* dogrose, wild rose.
Heckenschütze *m.* (*mil.*) sniper.
heda! *i.* hello! hey there!
Heer *n.* **(-[e]s, -e)** army; host; great number; *stehende(s)* ~, standing army.
Heer(es)dienst *m.* military service.
Heerführer *m.* general, army commander.
Heerschau *f.* military review, parade.
Hefe *f.* **(-, -n)** yeast; (*fig.*) dregs *pl.*
Heft *n.* **(-[e]s, -e)** haft, handle, hilt; (*Schule*) notebook.
heften *v.t.* to fasten; to pin; to stitch; to tack.
Hefter *m.* file.
heftig *a.* violent, vehement.
Heft: ~klammer *f.* paper clip; staple; **~maschine** *f.* stapling machine; **~pflaster** *n.* adhesive plaster; **~verband** *m.* adhesive bandage.
Hegemonie *f.* **(-, -n)** hegemony.
hegen *v.t.* to foster, to cherish; (*Zweifel*) to entertain.
Hehl *n.* **(-[e]s, 0)** concealment; *kein ~ daraus machen,* to make no secret of.
Hehler *m.* **(-s, -)** receiver (of stolen goods).
hehr *a.* sublime, august.
Heide *f.* **(-, -n)** heath; (*Kraut*) heather.
Heide *m.* **(-n, -n); Heidin** *f.* **(-, -nen)** pagan, heathen; gentile.
Heidekraut *n.* heather.
Heidelbeere *f.* blueberry; bilberry; whortleberry.
Heidelerche *f.* woodlark.
Heiden: ~angst *f.* (*fam.*) *eine ~ haben,* to be scared to death; **~geld** *n.* no end of money.
Heidentum *n.* **(-[e]s, 0)** paganism.
heidnisch *a.* heathenish, pagan.
heikel, heiklig *a.* fastidious, delicate, ticklish, thorny.
heil *a.* unhurt; *mit ~er Haut davonkommen,* to get off scot-free.
Heil *n.* **(-[e]s, 0)** salvation; *~! i.* hail!; *sein ~ versuchen,* to try one's luck.
Heiland *m.* **(-[e]s, -e)** Savior, Redeemer.
Heilanstalt *f.* medical establishment, sanatorium.
Heilbad *n.* watering place, spa.
heilbar *a.* curable.
heilbringend *a.* salutary.
Heilbutt *m.* halibut.
heilen *v.t.* to cure, to heal; ~ *v.i.* to heal.
heilfroh *a.* (*fam.*) very glad.
heilig *a.* holy; (*geweiht*) sacred; *Heiliger Abend,* Christmas Eve; *~ halten,* to keep holy, to observe religiously.
Heilige *m./f.* **(-n, -n)** saint.
heiligen *v.t.* to sanctify, to hallow.
Heiligenschein *m.* gloriole, aureole; halo.
Heiligkeit *f.* **(-, 0)** holiness; sanctity; sacredness.
heiligsprechen *v.t.* to canonize.
Heiligtum *n.* **(-[e]s, -tümer)** sanctuary, shrine.
Heiligung *f.* **(-, 0)** sanctification.
Heilkraft *f.* healing power.
heilkräftig *a.* healing, curative.
Heilkunde *f.* medicine.
heillos *a.* dreadful.
Heil: ~mittel *n.* remedy, medicine; **~quelle** *f.* mineral spring.
heilsam *a.* wholesome, salutary.
Heilsarmee *f.* Salvation Army.
Heilserum *n.* **(-s, 0)** antitoxic serum.
Heilung *f.* **(-, -en)** cure.
Heilverfahren *n.* **(-s, -)** medical treatment.
heim *adv.* home.
Heim *n.* **(-[e]s, -e)** home, homestead.
Heimarbeit *f.* homework, outwork.
Heimarbeiter *m.*; **Heimarbeiterin** *f.* homeworker.
Heimat *f.* **(-, -en)** homeland, home, native place *or* country.
Heimat: ~adresse *f.* home address; **~dichter** *m.*, **~dichterin** *f.* regional writer; **~erde** *f.* native soil; **~film** *m.* (sentimental) regional film; **~hafen** *m.* homeport, port of registry; **~kunde** *f.* local history, geography, and natural history; **~land** *n.* homeland, home country.
heimatlich *a.* native; homelike.
heimatlos *a.* homeless.
Heimat: ~museum *n.* museum of local history; **~ort** *m.* home town/village; **~stadt** *f.* home town; **~vertriebene** *m./f.* expellee.
heimbegleiten *v.t.* to take *or* see sb. home; **heimbringen** *v.t.st.* to take home; to bring home.
Heimchen *n.* **(-s, -)** (*zool.*) cricket.
Heimcomputer *m.* home computer.
heimelig *a.* cozy.
Heimfahrt *f.* return, homeward journey.
heimführen *v.t.* to lead home; (*obs.*) to marry.
Heimgang *m.* decease.
heimgehen *v.i.st. (s)* to go home.
heimisch *a.* domestic, homelike, homely; native, indigenous.
Heimkehr *f.* return; homecoming.
heimkehren *v.i. (s)* to return home.
Heimkind *n.* institution child.
Heimkunft *f.* return home.
heimlich *a.* secret, clandestine, furtive; private.
Heimlichkeit *f.* **(-, -en)** secrecy.
Heimlichtuer(in) *m.(f.)* (*pej.*) secretive person.
Heimmannschaft *f.* home team.
Heimreise *f.* return, journey home..
heimsuchen *v.t.* to visit; to afflict; to punish.
Heimsuchung *f.* **(-, -en)** affliction.
Heimtücke *f.* **(-, 0)** malice; treachery.
heimtückisch *a.* malicious; insidious; treacherous.
heimwärts *adv.* homeward(s).
Heim: ~weg *m.* way home, return; **~weh** *n.* home-sickness, nostalgia; ~ **haben,** to be homesick.
Heimwerker(in) *m.(f.)* handyman; do-it-yourselfer.
heimzahlen *v.t. einem etwas ~,* to get even with sb.
Heinzelmännchen *n.* goblin, brownie, imp.
Heirat *f.* **(-, -en)** marriage; match.
heiraten *v.t.* to marry; ~ *v.i. & r.* to get married.
Heiratsantrag *m.* offer *or* proposal of marriage.
heiratsfähig *a.* marriageable.
Heirats: ~schwindler *m.* marriage imposter; **~urkunde** *f.* marriage certificate; **~vermittlung** *f.* marriage bureau.
heischen *v.t.* to demand, to require.
heiser *a.* hoarse, husky; raucous.
Heiserkeit *f.* **(-, 0)** hoarseness, raucousness.
heiß *a.* hot; (*Zone*) torrid; fervent, ardent.
heißblütig *a.* hot-blooded, passionate.
heißen *v.t.st.* to call; to bid, to command; *etwas gut ~,* to approve of a thing; ~ *v.i.st.* to be called; to signify, to mean; *wie heißt das auf*

französisch? what do you call this in French?; *das heißt,* that is to say.
heißersehnt *a.* ardently longed-for.
heißgeliebt *a.* dearly loved.
Heißhunger *m.* ravenous hunger; (sudden) craving.
heißhung(e)rig *a.* ravenous, voracious.
heißlaufen *v.i.st.* to run hot; to overheat.
Heiß: ~luftballon *m.* hot-air balloon; **~mangel** *f.* rotary ironer; **~sporn** *m.* hothead, firebrand.
heißumkämpft *a.* fiercely disputed.
heißumstritten *a.* highly controversial.
Heißwasserbereiter *m.* water heater.
heiter *a.* cheerful, serene; clear, bright; fair.
Heiterkeit *f.* **(-, 0)** cheerfulness; serenity; hilarity.
Heizanlage *f.* heating system.
heizbar *a.* heatable; with heat.
Heizdecke *f.* electric blanket.
heizen *v.t.* to heat, to make a fire (in), to stoke; ~ *v.i.* to heat, give (off) heat.
Heizer *m.* **(-s, -)** (*rail.*) fireman, stoker.
Heiz: ~gerät *n.* heater; **~kessel** *m.* boiler; **~kissen** *n.* heating pad; **~körper** *m.* radiator; **~material** *n.* fuel; **~öl** *n.* fuel oil; *elektrische ~vorrichtung f.* electric heater.
Heizung *f.* **(-, -en)** heating, firing.
Hektar *m.* or *n.* **(-e, -e)** hectare.
Hektik *f.* hectic rush, hectic pace.
Hektograph *m.* mimeograph.
Held *m.* **(-en, -en)** hero.
Helden: ~dichtung *f.* epic/heroic poetry; **~epos** *n.* heroic epic.
heldenhaft, heldenmütig *a.* heroic.
Heldensage *f.* heroic legend, heroic saga.
Heldentod *m.* hero's death, heroic death.
Heldentum *n.* heroism.
Heldin *f.* **(-, -nen)** heroine.
helfen *v.i.st.* to help; to aid, to assist; to avail, to do good, to remedy.
Helfer *m.* **(-s, -)**; **Helferin** *f.* **(-, -nen)** helper, assistant.
Helfershelfer *m.* (*pej.*) accomplice.
hell *a.* light, clear, bright; *am ~en Tage,* in broad daylight; **~er Wahnsinn,** sheer madness.
hellblau *a.* light blue.
Helldunkel *a.* chiaroscuro.
Heller *m.* **(-s, -)** farthing, doit; *bei ~ und Pfennig,* to the last cent.
Helligkeit *f.* **(-, 0)** clearness, brightness.
hellodernd *a.* blazing.
hellsehen *v.i.* (*infinitive only*) to be clairvoyant.
Hellseher(in) *m.(f.)* clairvoyant.
hellsichtig *a.* clear-sighted.
hellwach *a.* wide-awake; bright, intelligent.
Helm *m.* **(-[e]s, -e)** helmet.
Helmbusch *m.* crest, plume.
Hemd *n.* **(-[e]s, -en)** shirt; *Frauen~* chemise.
Hemdärmel *m.* shirt-sleeve.
Hemisphäre *f.* hemisphere.
hemmen *v.t.* to slow, to hinder, to check.
Hemm: ~nis *n.* check, obstruction, obstacle.
hemmschuh *m.* obstacle, hindrance.
Hemmung *f.* **(-, -en)** inhibitions.
Hengst *m.* **(-[e]s, -e)** horse, stallion.
Hengstfohlen *n.* colt, (male) foal.
Henkel *m.* **(-s, -)** handle; ear.
henken *v.t.* to hang.
Henker *m.* **(-s, -)** hangman; executioner.
Henne *f.* **(-, -n)** hen.
her *adv.* hither, here; ~ **damit!** out with it! give that here!; *hin und ~,* to and fro; *nicht weit ~ (sein),* not much to boast of.
herab *adv.* down; downward.
herablassen ~ *v.r.* to condescend.
herablassend *a.* condescending.
Herablassung *f.* **(-, 0)** condescension.
herabmindern *v.t.* to reduce; to belittle, to disparage.
herabregnen *v.i.* to rain down.
herabsehen *v.i.st.* to look down.
herabsenken ~ *v.r.* to fall (night); to settle.
herabsetzen *v.t.* to disparage; to reduce.
Herabsetzung *f.* **(-, 0)** disparagement; reduction, lowering.
herabsteigen *v.i.st.* *(s)* to descend; (*vom Pferde*) to dismount.
herabwürdigen *v.t.* to abase; to disparage; ~ *v.r.* to demean oneself.
Heraldik *f.* **(-, 0)** heraldry.
heran *adv.* on, up, near.
heranbilden *v.t.* to train, to educate.
heranführen *v.t.* (*mil.*) to bring up, to move up.
herangehen *v.i.st.* to go up; to tackle (a problem).
herankommen *v.i.st.* *(s)* to come up to; to approach.
heranmachen *v.r.* (*an*) to get going on; to have a go at; to sidle up to.
herannahen *v.i.* *(s)* to approach.
heranreifen *v.i.* *(s)* to ripen, to come to maturity.
heranrücken *v.i.* *(s)* to advance.
heranwachsen *v.i.st.* *(s)* to grow up.
herauf *adv.* up, upward.
heraufbeschwören *v.t.* to conjure up, to precipitate.
heraufsetzen *v.t.* (*Preis*) to increase, to raise.
heraufziehen *v.i.st.* to pull up; ~ *v.i.st.* *(s)* to be approaching.
heraus *adv.* out; ~! come out!; *er hat's ~,* he has got the knack of it.
herausbekommen *v.i.st.* to get back (change); to find out.
herausbringen *v.t.ir.* to bring out; to find or make out.
herausfinden *v.t.* to find out.
herausfordern *v.t.* to challenge; to provoke.
Herausforderung *f.* **(-, -en)** challenge; provocation.
Herausgabe *f.* **(-, 0)** handing over, delivery; publication.
herausgeben *v.t.st.* to give up, to deliver up; to give change; to publish; to edit.
Herausgeber *m.* **(-s, -)** (*Leiter*) editor; publisher.
herauskommen *v.i.st.* *(s)* to come out; to transpire; *auf eins ~,* to come to the same thing; *dabei kommt nichts heraus,* it's no use, it doesn't pay.
herausnehmen *v.r.st.* (*etwas*) to take out, to remove.
herausplatzen *v.i.* *(s)* (*mit*) to burst out, to blurt out.
herausputzen *v.t.* to dress up, to rig out.
herausreden *v.r.* to talk one's way out.
herausrücken *v.i.* *(s)* (*mit dem Geld*) to fork out, to cough up; (*mit der Sprache*) to speak frankly.
herausschlagen *v.t.st.* to make money.
herausstellen *v.t.* to emphasize; ~ *v.r. imp.* to turn out, to become apparent.
herausstreichen *v.t.st.* to delete; to point out.
heraustreten *v.i.st.* *(s)* to step out; to protrude.

herb *a.* sharp; astringent; dry; tangy; (*fig.*) harsh, austere.
herbei *adv.* hither, near; on.
herbeiführen *v.t.* to bring about, to entail.
herbeischaffen *v.t.* to produce, to procure.
Herberge *f.* **(-, -n)** hostel; inn.
Herbergs: ~mutter *f.;* **~vater** *m.* warden of a youth hostel.
herbestellen *v.t.* to appoint, to send for.
herbitten *v.t.st.* to invite.
herbringen *v.t.ir.* to bring (hither).
Herbst *m.* **(-es, -e)** autumn, fall.
herbstlich *a.* autumnal.
Herbstzeitlose *f.* **(-, -n)** (*bot.*) meadow saffron.
Herd *m.* **(-[e]s, -e);** stove; fireplace; kitchen range; (*einer Epidemie*) center.
Herde *f.* **(-, -n)** (*Schafe*) flock; herd.
Herdentier *n.* gregarious animal.
Herdentrieb *m.* herd instinct.
Herdplatte *f.* hotplate.
herein *adv.* in; **~!** *i.* come in!.
hereinbitten *v.i.st.* to invite in.
hereinbrechen *v.i.st.* to befall; to close in.
hereindürfen *v.i.ir.* to be allowed in.
Hereinfall *m.* (*fam.*) hoax; failure.
hereinfallen *v.i.* to be taken in, to be sold.
hereinlassen *v.t.* to let in.
hereinplatzen *v.i.* to burst in.
hereinschneien *v.i.* to snow in; to turn up out of the blue.
hereinsehen *v.i.st.* to look in; to drop in.
hereinstürmen *v.i.* to dash in; to storm in.
herfallen *v.i.st.* (*über*) to fall (upon); to attack.
Hergang *m.* **(-[e]s, -gänge)** proceedings *pl.*, course of events, circumstances *pl.*
hergeben *v.t.st.* to surrender, to give up; **~** *v.r.* (*zu, für*) to lend oneself, to be a party (to).
hergebracht *a.* traditional, established.
hergehen *v.i.st.* to happen; (*lustig, etc.*) to be going on.
hergehören *v.t.* to belong here; to be relevant.
hergelaufen *a.* *ein* *~er Mensch,* undesirable newcomer; upstart; adventurer.
herholen *v.t.* to fetch.
Hering *m.* **(-[e]s, -e)** herring.
herkommen *v.i.st.* *(s)* to come near; to come from; to originate in.
herkömmlich *a.* customary, conventional, traditional.
Herkunft *f.* **(-, 0)** descent, origin.
herlegen *v.t.* to put down (here).
herleiern *v.t.* to reel off.
herleiten *v.t.* to conduct; to derive.
hermachen **~** *v.r.* (*über*) to fall upon; to set about.
Hermelin *n.* **(-[e]s, -e)** ermine.
hermetisch *a.* & *adv.* hermetic(ally).
hernach *adv.* afterwards.
hernehmen *v.t.st.* to take from.
heroben *adv.* up here.
Heroin *n.* **(-s, 0)** heroin.
heroisch *a.* & *adv.* heroic(ally).
Herold *m.* **(-[e]s, -e)** herald.
herplappern *v.t.* & *i.* to rattle off; to rattle on.
Herr *m.* **(-n, -en)** master; lord; gentleman; Lord; *Herr Braun,* Mr. (Mister) B.; *~ werden,* to master, to overcome.
Herreise *f.* **(-, 0)** journey here.
herreisen *v.i.* *(s)* to travel here.
Herren: ~abend *m.* stag evening; **~ausstatter** *m.* men's outfitter; **~haus** *n.* manor house, hall.
herrenlos *a.* stray.
Herrenreiter *m.* gentleman rider.
Herrgott *m.* (*fam.*) the Lord, God.
Herrgottsfrühe *f.* *in aller ~*, at the crack of the dawn.
herrichten *v.t.* to get ready, to arrange.
Herrin *f.* **(-, -nen)** mistress, lady.
herrisch *a.* imperious, peremptory.
herrlich *a.* magnificent, splendid.
Herrlichkeit *f.* **(-, -en)** magnificence, splendor, glory; excellence.
Herrschaft *f.* **(-, -en)** dominion, mastery; master and mistress; *meine ~en,* ladies and gentlemen.
herrschaftlich *a.* high-class.
Herrschaftsform *f.* system of government.
herrschen *v.i.* to rule, to govern; to prevail.
herrschend *a.* ruling; reigning; prevailing.
Herrscher *m.* **(-s, -)** ruler, sovereign.
Herrscherfamilie *f.* dynasty.
Herrschsucht *f.* thirst for power, domineering nature.
herrschsüchtig *a.* domineering.
herrücken *v.i.* to move near.
herrühren *v.i.* to originate in.
hersagen *v.t.* to recite, to repeat.
herschaffen *v.t.* to procure, to produce.
herstellen *v.t.* to manufacture, to produce, to turn out; to restore (to health).
Hersteller *m.* producer; manufacturer.
Herstellung *f.* production; manufacture.
herüben *adv.* over here.
herüber *adv.* over, across, on this side.
herüberkommen *v.i.st.* to come over.
herum *adv.* round; about; *hier ~*, hereabout(s); *die Reihe ~*, each one in his turn.
herumalbern *v.i.* to fool around.
herumärgern *v.r.* to be plagued (by), to struggle (with).
herumfahren *v.i.st.* *(s)* to travel *or* drive around.
herumführen *v.t.* to show around; *an der Nase ~*, to lead by the nose.
herumkommen *v.i.st.* *(s)* (*um*) to get out (of), to get around, to avoid; *weit ~*, to see the world.
herumlaufen *v.i.* to run around.
herumliegen *v.i.* to lie around.
herumlungern *v.i.* to loaf around.
herumnörgeln *v.i.* to moan; to grumble.
herumpfuschen *v.i.* (*an*) to tamper (with).
herumreichen *v.t.* to hand round.
herumschlagen *v.t.st.* to wrap around; **~** *v.r.* (*mit*) to scuffle (with).
herumstehen *v.i.* (things) to lie around; (people) to stand around.
herumtreiben *v.r.st.* to hang around; to gad about.
Herumtreiber(in) *m.(f.)* tramp, vagabond.
herumtrödeln *v.i.* to dawdle.
herumziehend *a.* ambulatory; wandering.
herunter *adv.* down, off; (*fam.*) low, weak.
herunterbringen *v.t.ir.* to bring down; to reduce; to ruin.
herunterkommen *v.i.st.* *(s)* to come down; to decay, to go bad.
herunterlassen *v.t.* to lower.
heruntermachen *v.t.* to run down, to take down.
herunterreißen *v.t.st.* to tear down, to pull off, to tear off.
herunterschlucken *v.t.* to swallow.

heruntersteigen *v.i.st. (s)* to descend, to climb down.
hervor *adv.* forth, out.
hervorbrechen *v.i.st. (s)* to burst out, to break through.
hervorbringen *v.t.ir.* to bring forth, to produce; to effect; (of words) to utter.
hervorgehen *v.i.st. (s)* to proceed; to result; to emerge.
hervorheben *v.t.st.* to emphasize; to set off.
hervorragen *v.i.* to stand out; to project.
hervorragend *a.* outstanding.
hervorrufen *v.t.st.* to call forth, to cause.
hervorstechen *v.i.st.* to be prominent; to stand out.
hervorstechend *a.* striking.
hervorstehen *v.i.st.* to protrude; to stick out.
hervortreten *v.i.st. (s)* to step out, to emerge, to bulge; (*fig.*) to excel, to stand pre-eminent.
hervortun *v.r.st.* to distinguish oneself.
Herweg *m.* **(-[e]s, -e)** way here.
Herz, *n.* **(-ens, -en)** heart; breast; (*Kern*) core; (*fig.*) courage; *ans ~ legen,* to urge, to enjoin; to entrust; *es ging mir bis ins ~*, it cut me to the quick; *es liegt mir am ~en,* I am very concerned about it; *es zerreißt mir das ~*, it breaks my heart; *mit ganzem ~en,* wholeheartedly; *von ~en,* with all my heart; *(sich) etwas zu ~en nehmen,* to take sth. to heart.
Herz... cardiac....
Herzanfall *m.* heart attack.
Herzbeschwerden *pl.* heart trouble.
Herzbeutel *m.* pericardium.
herzbrechend *a.* heart-rending.
Herzbube *m.* jack of hearts.
Herzchen *n.* darling, sweetheart.
Herzdame *f.* queen of hearts.
herzen *v.t.* to hug, to caress.
Herzensangelegenheit *f.* affair of the heart.
Herzensbedürfnis *n.* sth. very important *or* very dear to sb.
Herzensbrecher *m.* lady-killer.
herzensgut *a.* kind-hearted, good-hearted.
Herzensleid *n.* heartache, grief, anguish.
Herzenslust *f.* nach ~, to one's heart's content.
Herzenswunsch *m.* fondest wish.
herzerfreuend *a.* heartwarming.
herzerfrischend *a.* refreshing.
Herzerweiterung *f.* dilation of the heart.
Herzfehler *m.* heart defect.
herzhaft *a.* courageous, bold; hearty; strong, firm.
herzig *a.* lovely, sweet, dear.
Herzinfarkt *m.* heart attack; cardiac infarction.
Herzkammer *f.* ventricle.
Herzklappe *f.* heart valve.
Herzklopfen *n.* heartbeat; palpitation; *mit ~*, with one's heart in one's mouth.
Herzkönig *m.* king of hearts.
Herzkranzgefäß *n.* coronary vessel.
Herzleiden *n.* heart disease.
herzlich *a.* hearty; heartfelt; sincere.
Herzlichkeit *f.* warmth, kindness, sincerity.
herzlos *a.* heartless, callous.
Herzog *m.* **(-[e]s, Herzöge)** duke.
Herzogin *f.* **(-, -nen)** duchess.
herzoglich *a.* ducal.
Herzogtum *n.* **(-[e]s, -tümer)** dukedom, duchy.
Herzschlag *m.* heartthrob; heart failure.
Herzschrittmacher *m.* pacemaker.
Herzstillstand *m.* cardiac arrest.
Herzversagen *n.* heart failure.
herzzerreißend *a.* heart-rending, heartbreaking.
heterogen *a.* heterogeneous.
Heterosexualität *f.* heterosexuality.
heterosexuell *a.;* **Heterosexuelle** *m./f.* heterosexual.
Hetze *f.* **(-, -n)** hunt, chase; (*fig.*) hurry, rush; agitation; persecution, baiting.
hetzen *v.t.* to hunt; to set on; to agitate; to incite; to bait.
Hetzer *m.* **(-s, -)** agitator.
Hetzerei *f.* inflammatory propaganda; agitation.
hetzerisch *a.* inflammatory.
Hetzjagd *f.* hunt (with hounds); chase; mad rush.
Heu *n.* **(-[e]s, 0)** hay; (*sl.*) grass (marijuana).
Heuboden *m.* hay loft.
Heuchelei *f.* **(-, -en)** hypocrisy.
heucheln *v.t.* to feign, to put on, simulate; ~ *v.i.* to dissemble.
Heuchler *m.* **(-s, -); Heuchlerin** *f.* **(-, -nen)** hypocrite.
heuchlerisch *a.* hypocritical.
heuer *adv.* this year.
Heuer *f.* pay, (sailors) wages.
Heu: ~ernte *f.* hay-time, hay-making; **~gabel** *f.* pitchfork; **~haufen** *m.* haystack.
Heulboje *f.* whistling buoy; (*pej.*) pop singer.
heulen *v.i.* to howl; to cry, to whine.
Heulsuse *f.* (*fam. pej.*) crybaby.
heurig *a.* this year's.
Heuschnupfen *m.* **(-s, 0)** hay fever.
Heuschrecke *f.* **(-, -n)** grasshopper.
heute *adv.* today; these days.
heutig *a.* today's, present-day.
heutzutage *adv.* nowadays.
Hexe *f.* **(-, -n)** witch.
hexen *v.i.* to practice witchcraft.
Hexen: ~jagd *f.* witch-hunt; **~kessel** *m.* (*fig.*) pandemonium; inferno; **~meister** *m.* sorcerer; **~schuß** *m.* lumbago; **~verfolgung** *f.* witch-hunt.
Hexerei *f.* **(-, -en)** sorcery, witchcraft.
HGB *Handelsgesetzbuch,* Commercial Code.
Hickhack *m.* (*fam.*) squabbling; bickering.
hie *adv.* **~und da,** here and there; now and then.
Hieb *m.* **(-[e]s, -e)** blow, lash, cut, stroke; (*fig.*) hit.
hiebfest *a.* *~- und stichfest,* watertight; cast-iron.
hienieder *adv.* here below.
hier *adv.* here; present.
Hierarchie *f.* **(-, -[e]n)** hierarchy.
hierarchisch *a.* hierarchical.
hierauf *adv.* hereupon; after this.
hieraus *adv.* from this; hence.
hierbei *adv.* in this connection; on this occasion; doing this.
hierbleiben *v.i.* to stay here.
hierdurch *adv.* by this, hereby.
hierfür *adv.* for this.
hiergegen *adv.* against this.
hierher *adv.* hither, this way; *bis ~*, so far, hitherto.
hierherum *adv.* around here, hereabouts.
hierhin *adv.* this way, here.
hierin *adv.* in this.
hiermit *adv.* with this, herewith.
hiernach *adv.* after this, according to this.
Hieroglyphe *f.* **(-, -n)** hieroglyph.
hierorts *adv.* in this place.
Hiersein *n.* **(-s, 0)** presence, stay here.

hierüber *adv.* over here; about this.
hierum *adv.* about this.
hierunter *adv.* under this, among these.
hiervon *adv.* of, from this; about this.
hierwider *adv.* against this.
hierzu *adv.* to this; ~ *kommt noch,* add to this.
hierzulande *adv.* (here) in this country, over here.
hiesig *a.* of this place.
hieven *v.t.* to heave.
Hilfe *f.* **(-, -n)** help, aid, assistance, relief; *erste ~,* first aid; *zu ~ kommen,* to come to the rescue; *~ leisten,* to aid, to assist.
Hilfeleistung *f.* assistance.
Hilferuf *m.* cry for help.
Hilfestellung *f.* support.
hilflos *a.* helpless.
Hilflosigkeit *f.* helplessness.
hilfreich *a.* helpful; benevolent.
Hilfsaktion *f.* relief action.
Hilfsarbeiter *m.* laborer, unskilled worker.
hilfsbedürftig *a.* in need; needy.
Hilfsbedürftigkeit *f.* need; neediness.
hilfsbereit *a.* helpful; ready to help.
Hilfs: ~fonds *m.* relief fund; **~mittel** *n.* resource, expedient; **~quelle** *f.* resource; **~truppen** *pl.* auxiliary troops *pl.;* **~unterstützung** *f.* grant-in-aid; **~verb, ~zeitwort** *n.* auxiliary (verb).
Himalaja *m.* the Himalayas.
Himbeere *f.* **(-, -n)** raspberry.
Himmel *m.* **(-s, -)** heaven; heavens *pl.;* (*sichtbarer*) sky; (*eines Bettes*) canopy; (*im Auto*) roof.
Himmelbett *n.* four-poster (bed).
himmelblau *a.* azure, sky-blue.
Himmelfahrt *f.* Ascension.
Himmelfahrtskommando *n.* suicide squad.
Himmelfahrtstag *m.* Ascension Day.
himmelhoch *a.* sky-high.
Himmelreich *n.* kingdom of heaven.
himmelschreiend *a.* crying to heaven; outrageous, appalling.
Himmels: ~gewölbe *n.* firmament; **~körper** *m.* celestial body; **~richtung** *f.* direction; **~schrift** *f.* skywriting.
himmelwärts *adv.* heavenward.
himmelweit *a. & adv.* vast.
himmlisch *a.* celestial, heavenly.
hin *adv.* thither, there, along; gone, lost; *~ und her,* to and fro, backwards and forwards; *~ und wieder,* now and then; *~ und zurück,* there and back.
hinab *adv.* down.
hinarbeiten *v.i.* to aim at.
hinauf *adv.* up, up to; upstairs.
hinaufarbeiten *v.r.* to work one's way up.
hinaufsteigen *v.i.st.* *(s)* to ascend, to step up, to climb up.
hinaus *adv.* out; *darüber ~,* beyond that.
hinausgehen *v.i.st.* *(s)* to go out; (*auf*) to open into; to surpass, to exceed, to go beyond.
hinauskommen *v.i.st.* *(s)* to go beyond, to get beyond; *auf dasselbe ~,* to come to the same thing.
hinauslaufen *v.i.st.* *(s)* (*aus*) to run out (of sth.); (*auf*) to amount (to sth.); *auf dasselbe ~,* to come to the same thing.
hinausschieben *v.t.st.* (*fig.*) to defer, to put off, to postpone.
hinauswerfen *v.t.st.* to throw out.
hinauswollen *v.i.ir.* to want to get out; (*auf*) to be driving (at).
hinbegeben *v.r.st.* to go to.
Hinblick *m.* **(-[e]s, 0)** consideration; *im ~ auf,* with a view to, in consideration of.
hinbringen *v.t.ir.* to carry to; (*Zeit*) to pass, to spend.
hinderlich *a.* hindering, in the way.
hindern *v.t.* to hinder, to prevent, to impede.
Hindernis *n.* **(-nisses, -nisse)** hindrance, impediment, obstacle, fence.
Hindernis: ~lauf *m.,* **~rennen** *n.* steeplechase.
Hinderung *f.* **(-, -en)** hindrance.
hindeuten *v.i.* to point to *or* at.
Hindu *m.* Hindu.
Hinduismus *m.* Hinduism.
hinduistisch *a.* Hindu.
hindurch *adv.* through, throughout; across.
hinein *adv.* in; *in den Tag ~,* at random.
hineinarbeiten *v.r.* to familiarize oneself with.
hineinbegeben *v.r.st.* to enter, to go in.
hineindenken *v.r.ir.* to transfer oneself mentally into.
hineinfahren *v.i.* to run into.
hineinfinden *v.r.* to make the best of sth.
hineingeh(e)n *v.i.st.* to enter.
hineinstecken, hineintun *v.t.* to put into.
hineinsteigern *v.r.* to get worked up.
hineinwagen *v.r.* to venture in.
hineinziehen *v.t.st.* to pull into, to drag into.
hinfahren *v.i.st.* *(s)* to go there, to drive there, to sail there.
Hinfahrt *f.* **(-, -en)** journey to, drive, passage to; outward journey.
hinfallen *v.i.st.* *(s)* to fall down.
hinfällig *a.* frail, weak.
hinführen *v.t.* to conduct (to), to lead (to).
Hingabe *f.* **(-, 0)** devotion, dedication; surrender; abandon.
Hingang *m.* **(-[e]s, 0)** decease.
hingeben *v.t.st.* to give up; **~** *v.r.* to devote oneself (to); to indulge (in).
hingebend *a.* devoted, fond.
Hingebung *f.* **(-, 0)** resignation; devotion.
hingebungsvoll *a.* devoted; *adv.* devotedly; with abandon.
hingegen *adv.* on the other hand.
hingehen *v.i.st.* *(s)* to go; to pass; **~ lassen,** to wink at, to let pass.
hingerissen *a.* carried away; spellbound.
hinhalten *v.t.st.* to hold out (to sb.); to put off, to delude with hopes.
hinken *v.i.* to limp; to be clumsy.
hinkommen *v.i.st.* *(s)* to come to, to get to.
hinlänglich *a.* sufficient, adequate.
hinnehmen *v.t.st.* to put up with.
hinraffen *v.t.* (*fig.*) to carry off, to cut off (in the prime of life).
hinreichen *v.t.* to hand, to offer; **~** *v.i.* to suffice.
hinreichend *a.* sufficient.
Hinreise *f.* **(-, -n)** journey to, voyage out.
hinreisen *v.i.* *(s)* to travel to.
hinreißen *v.t.st.* to enthrall.
hinreißend *a.* charming, ravishing.
hinrichten *v.t.* to execute.
Hinrichtung *f.* **(-, -en)** execution.
hinschaffen *v.t.* to convey to.
hinscheiden *v.i.st.* to depart (life).
hinschlachten *v.t.* to massacre.
hinschlagen *v.i.st.* to fall down.

hinschlendern *v.i. (s)* to saunter.
hinschwinden *v.i.st. (s)* to dwindle.
hinsehen *v.i.* to look (at).
hinsein *v.i.st. (s)* to be lost, to be gone; to be shattered.
hinsetzen *v.t.* to seat; to set down; ~ *v.r.* to sit down.
Hinsicht *f.* **(-, -en)** respect; *in ~ auf,* with regard to.
hinsichtlich *a.* with regard to.
hinsiechen *v.i.* (*h, s*) to pine away, to waste away.
Hinspiel *n.* (*sp.*) first leg.
hinsterben *v.i.st. (s)* to die away.
hinstrecken *v.t.* (*fig.*) to knock down; ~ *v.r.* to lie down; to stretch out.
hintan: ~setzen; ~stellen *v.t.* to put last; to neglect.
hinten *adv.* behind; in the back; (*nav.*) aft; **~nach,** afterwards.
hinten: ~drauf *adv.* (*fam.*) on the back; **~über** *adv.* backwards.
hinter *pr.* behind, after; **~einander,** one after another; *~s Licht führen,* to dupe; *etwas ~ sich haben,* to have gotten over sth.
Hinter: ~achse *f.* rear/back axle; **~ansicht** *f.* rear/back view; **~ausgang** *m.* rear/back exit; **~bänkler** *m.* backbencher; **~bein** *n.* hind leg.
Hinterbliebene *f./m.* **(-n, -n)** survivor; **~n** *pl.* the bereaved; surviving dependents.
hinterbringen *v.t.st.* to inform.
Hinterdeck *n.* afterdeck.
hinterdrein *adv.* afterwards, after; too late.
hintere[r] *a.* hind, hinder, back.
Hintere[r] *m.* **(-n, -n)** rear; backside.
hintereinander *adv.* one behind the other; one after another.
hinterfragen *v.t.* to question; to scrutinize; to analyze.
Hinterfuß *m.* hind foot.
Hintergedanke *m.* ulterior motive.
hintergehen *v.t.st.* to deceive.
Hintergrund *m.* background.
hintergründig *a.* enigmatic; cryptic; profound.
Hinterhalt *m.* **(-[e]s, -e)** ambush.
hinterhältig *a.* underhand(ed); crafty.
Hinterhand *f.* hindquarters (animals) *pl.*
Hinterhaus *n.* back building (accessible through a courtyard); outhouse.
hinterher *adv.* behind; afterwards; **~sein** *v.i.st. jm. ~,* to pursue diligently; *~ mit,* to be behind with (sth.).
Hinterkopf *m.* back of the head; back of one's mind; occiput.
Hinterland *n.* hinterland.
hinterlassen *v.t.st.* to leave (behind); to leave word; to bequeath; **~e Werke,** posthumous work.
Hinterlassene *m./f.* **(-n, -n)** survivor.
Hinterlassenschaft *f.* **(-, -en)** inheritance; estate.
hinterlegen *v.t.* to deposit.
Hinterlist *f.* fraud, deceit, cunning.
hinterlistig *a.* cunning, deceitful.
Hintermann *m.* person behind (sb.); **~männer** *pl.* brains behind the operation.
Hintermannschaft *f.* (*sp.*) defense.
Hintern *m.* **(-, -)** behind, backside; bottom.
Hinterpfote *f.* **(-, -n)** hind paw.
Hinterrad *n.* rear wheel; **~antrieb** *m.* rear-wheel drive.
hinterrücks *adv.* from behind, insidiously.
hintersinnig *a.* with a deeper meaning, subtle.
Hintersitz *m.* back seat.
hinterste[r] *a.* hindmost.
Hinter: ~teil *n.* behind; backside; (*nav.*) stern; **~treppe** *f.* back stairs *pl.*
hintertreiben *v.t.st.* to frustrate.
Hinter: ~tür *f.* back door; loophole; **~wäldler** *m.* **(-s, -)** backwoodsman, hillbilly.
hinterziehen *v.t.st.* to evade (taxes).
hintun *v.t.* to put.
hinüber *adv.* over, across.
Hin- und Rück: ~fahrt *f.,* **~flug** *m.,* **~reise** *f.,* **~weg** *m.* round trip.
hinunter *adv.* down; downstairs.
hinunter: ~schlucken *v.t.* to swallow; **~würgen** *v.t.* to gulp down; to choke back tears.
hinwagen ~ *v.r.* to dare to go somewhere.
hinweg *adv.* away off; **~!** begone; *über etwas ~gehen,* to pass lightly over sth.; *~sehen über etwas,* to overlook a thing; *sich über etwas ~setzen,* not to mind a thing, to make light of it; **~raffen,** to cut off, to sweep away.
Hinweg *m.* **(-[e]s, -e)** way there.
Hinweis *m.* **(-es, -e)** hint; tip; reference.
hinweisen *v.i.st.* (*auf*) to point (out); to refer (to).
hinweisend *a.* (*gram.*) demonstrative.
Hinweis: ~schild *n.* sign; road sign; **~tafel** *f.* information board.
hinwerfen *v.t.st.* to throw down; to fling to; to dash off, to utter carelessly.
hinwieder *adv.* again; on the other hand.
hinwirken *v.i.* (*auf*) to work toward.
hinziehen *v.t.st.* to draw to, to protract; ~ *v.r.* to drag on.
hinzielen *v.i.* to aim at; (*fig.*) to have in view.
hinzu *adv.* to it; in addition; near.
hinzudenken *v.t.ir.* to supply mentally.
hinzufügen *v.t.* to add; to subjoin.
hinzukommen *v.i.st. (s)* to come to; to be added.
Hinz *m.* **~und Kunz** (*fam. pej.*) every Tom, Dick and Harry; *von ~ zu Kunz,* from pillar to post.
hinzurechnen *v.t.* to add to.
hinzusetzen *v.t.* to add, to subjoin.
hinzuziehen *v.t.st.* to include, to add; (*einen Arzt*) to consult.
Hiob *m.* Job.
Hiobspost *f.* **(-, -en)** bad news.
Hirn *n.* **(-[e]s, -e)** brain, brains *pl.*
Hirngespinst *n.* **(-[e]s, -e)** fantasy, chimera.
Hirnhautentzündung *f.* meningitis.
hirnlos *a.* brainless, hare-brained.
hirnrissig *a.* (*fam.*) crazy, mad.
Hirnschale *f.* skull, cranium.
hirnverbrannt *a.* mad.
Hirsch *m.* **(-[e]s, -e)** stag, hart; deer; venison.
Hirsch: ~brunft *f.;* **~brunst** *f.* rut; **~fänger** *m.* hunting knife; **~geweih** *n.* antlers *pl.,* hartshorn; **~kalb** *n.* fawn; **~käfer** *m.* stag-beetle; **~kuh** *f.* hind, doe; **~leder** *n.* buckskin.
Hirse *f.* **(-, 0)** millet.
Hirsebrei *m.* millet gruel.
Hirte *m.* **(-en, -en)** shepherd.
Hirtenbrief *m.* pastoral letter.
Hirtin *f.* shepherdess.
His (*mus.*) B sharp.
hissen *v.t.* to hoist (up).
Historiker *m.* **(-s, -); Historikerin** *f.* **(-, -en)** historian.

historisch *a.* historical.
Hitze *f.* **(-, 0)** heat; hot weather; (*fig.*) ardor, passion; *fliegende* ~, hot flashes.
hitzebeständig *a.* heat-resistant.
Hitzebläschen *a.* heat spot.
hitzeempfindlich *a.* sensitive to heat.
hitzefrei *a.* **~ haben** to have time off from school because of hot weather.
Hitzewelle *f.* heat wave.
hitzig *a.* hot; ardent, passionate; fevered; heated.
Hitzkopf *m.* spitfire, hothead.
hitzköpfig *a.* hotheaded.
Hitzschlag *m.* sunstroke, heatstroke.
Hj. *Halbjahr,* half-year.
hl *hektoliter,* hectoliter.
hl. *heilig,* holy.
Hobby *n.* **(-s, -s)** hobby.
Hobel *m.* **(-s, -)** plane; (vegetable) slicer.
Hobelbank *f.* carpenter's bench.
Hobelmaschine *f.* **(-, -n)** planer.
hobeln *v.t.* to plane.
Hobelspäne *f.pl.* shavings *pl.*
hoch *a.*, **hohe (-r, -s),** *comp.* **höher,** *superl.* **höchste** highly; lofty, sublime; eminent; *drei Mann* ~, three men strong; *hohe See,* high seas; *hohe Strafe,* heavy penalty; *wenn es ~ kommt,* at most; *hoch lebe!* long live!;
Hoch *n.* (*Wetterkunde*) high.
hochachten *v.t.* to esteem, to respect, to value.
Hochachtung *f.* **(-, 0)** esteem, respect.
hochachtungsvoll *adv.* yours faithfully.
Hochamt *n.* high mass.
Hochbahn *f.* elevated railroad.
Hochbau *m.* superstructure; structural engineering.
Hochburg *f.* stronghold.
hochdeutsch *a.* standard *or* High German.
Hochdruck *m.* high pressure; **~gebiet** *n.* high-pressure area.
Hochebene *f.* plateau, tableland.
hochfahrend *a.* haughty; arrogant.
hochfein *a.* superfine; of high quality.
hochfliegend *a.* (*fig.*) ambitious, lofty.
Hochfrequenz *f.* high frequency.
Hochgebirge *n.* high mountain region.
Hochgefühl *n.* elation.
Hochgenuß *m.* treat, delight.
Hochglanz *m.* high gloss; high polish.
hochglänzend *a.* very shiny; glossy; highly polished.
hochgradig *a.* extreme; absolute; utter.
hochhackig *a.* high-heeled.
Hochhaus *n.* high-rise building.
hoch: ~herzig *a.* high-minded, magnanimous; **~kirchlich** *a.* High Church.
Hochkonjunktur *f.* boom (economy).
Hochland *n.* **(-[e]s, -e** *u* **-länder)** highland.
Hochleistung *f.* outstanding performance; **~ssport** *m.* competitive sport.
höchlich *adv.* highly.
Hochmittelalter *n.* High Middle Ages.
Hochmut *a.* arrogance, haughtiness.
hochmütig *a.* haughty, proud.
hochnäsig *a.* conceited; stuck-up; snooty.
Hochofen *m.* blast-furnace.
hochragen *v.i.* to rise up, to tower up.
Hochrechnung *f.* (*Statistik*) projection.
hochrot *a.* bright red, crimson.
Hochsaison *f.* **(-, -s)** peak season.
hochschätzen *v.t.* to esteem highly.
Hoch: ~schätzung *f.* high esteem; **~schule** *f.* university, college.
hochschwanger *a.* far advanced in pregnancy.
Hoch: ~seefischerei *f.* deep-sea fishing; **~seeschlepper** *m.* sea-going tug.
Hochseilakt *m.* tightrope act.
Hochsitz *m.* raised hide.
Hochsommer *m.* midsummer.
Hochspannung *f.* high tension *or* voltage.
Hochspannungsleitung *f.* power line.
hochspielen *v.t.* to blow up *or* play up (an incident).
Hochsprache *f.* **(-, -n)** standard language.
Hochsprung *m.* high jump.
höchst *a.* & *adv.* highest; extremely; **~e Zeit,** high time.
Hochstapler *m.* **(-s,); Hochstaplerin** *f.* **(-, -nen)** swindler, confidence trickster, fraud.
Höchstbelastung *f.* maximum load.
hochstehend *a.* of high standing; advanced; highly intellectual; superior.
höchstenfalls *adv.* at most; at the very most.
höchstens *adv.* at most, at best.
Höchst: ~fall *m.* *im* ~, at the very most; **~form** *f.* top form.
Höchstgeschwindigkeit *f.* maximum *or* top speed; *zulässige* ~, speed limit.
Höchstgrenze *f.* ceiling, upper limit.
hochstilisieren *v.t.* to build up.
Hochstimmung *f.* festive mood; high spirits.
Höchst: ~leistung *f.* best performance, record; **~preis** *m.* maximum price; **~strafe** *f.* maximum penalty.
höchstwahrscheinlich *adv.* very probably.
hoch: ~trabend *a.* pretentious; high-sounding, bombastic; **~verdient** *a.* of great merit; **~verehrt** *a.* highly respected, esteemed.
Hochverrat *n.* high treason.
Hochwasser *n.* high tide; flood
hochwertig *a.* high grade, high-quality.
hochwürdig *a.* reverend.
Hochzeit *f.* wedding, marriage.
hochzeitlich *a.* nuptial, bridal.
Hochzeitsreise *f.* honeymoon.
hocken *v.i.* to squat.
Hocker *m.* **(-s, -)** stool.
Höcker *m.* **(-s, -)** bump.
höckerig *a.* uneven; hunchbacked.
Hoden *m.* **(-s, -)** testicle.
Hodensack *m.* scrotum.
Hof *m.* **(-[e]s, Höfe)** yard; court; farm; (*um den Mond*) halo; (*opt.*) cornea; *einem den ~ machen,* to court sb.
Hofdame *f.* lady-in-waiting.
Hoffart *f.* **(-, 0)** pride, haughtiness.
hoffen *v.i.* (*auf*) to hope (for); to expect.
hoffentlich *adv.* I hope, hopefully.
Hoffnung *f.* **(-, -en)** hope; expectation; *sich ~ machen,* to indulge in the hope of; *guter ~ sein* (*von Frauen*) to be expecting a baby.
hoffnungslos *a.* hopeless, past hope.
Hoffnungslosigkeit *f.* hopelessness; despair.
Hoffnungsschimmer *m.* glimmer of hope.
hoffnungsvoll *a.* hopeful; promising.
hofhalten *v.i.* to hold court.
Hofhund *m.* watchdog.
hofieren *v.i.* to court, to flatter.
höfisch *a.* courtly, courtier-like.
höflich *a.* courteous, polite.

Höflichkeit *f.* **(-, -en)** courteousness, courtesy, politeness.

Höflichkeits: ~besuch *m.* courtesy visit; **~floskel** *f.*, **~formel** *f.* polite phrase.

Höfling *m.* **(-s, -e)** courtier; sycophant.

Hof: ~mann *m.* courtier; **~marschall** *m.* major-domo; **~narr** *m.* jester; **~schranze** *m.* (*pej.*) fawning courtier; **~staat** *m.* royal *or* princely household.

Höhe *f.* **(-, -n)** height; hill; (*Luft, Geogr.*) altitude; (*der Preise*) level; *auf der ~*, up to date; *Ehre sei Gott in der ~*, glory to God in the highest; *nicht ganz auf der ~*, not quite up to the mark; *auf der ~ von*, (*nav.*) off.

Hoheit *f.* **(-, -en)** grandeur; (*Titel*) Highness; sovereignty.

Hoheitsabzeichen *n.* national emblem.

Hoheitsgewässer *n.* territorial waters *pl.*

Hoheitsrecht *n.* sovereign jurisdiction.

Hohelied *n.* Song of Solomon.

Höhen: ~angst *f.* fear of heights; **~krankheit** *f.* altitude sickness: **~kurort** *m.* high-altitude health resort; **~lage** *f.* high altitude; **~luft** *f.* mountain air; **~messer** *m.* (*avi.*) altimeter; **~sonne** *f.* mountain sun; sun lamp; **~steuer** *n.* (*avi.*) elevator; **~zug** *m.* mountain range.

Höhepunkt *m.* climax, acme, peak.

hohl *a.* hollow; concave.

Höhle *f.* **(-, -n)** cave, cavern.

Höhlen: ~forscher *m.*; **~forscherin** *f.* speleologist; **~forschung** *f.* speleology; **~malerei** *f.* cave painting; **~mensch** *m.* cave dweller.

Hohl: ~kopf *m.* idiot; dimwit; **~maß** *n.* capacity measure; **~raum** *m.* cavity; **~saum** *m.* hemstitch; **~spiegel** *m.* concave mirror.

Höhlung *f.* **(-, -en)** hollow, cavity.

Hohlweg *m.* ravine.

Hohn *m.* **(-[e]s, 0)** scorn; derision.

höhnen *v.t.* to sneer (at).

Hohngelächter *n.* derisive laughter.

höhnisch *a.* scornful, sneering.

hohnlächeln *v.i.* to sneer, to smile scornfully.

hohnlachen *v.i.* to laugh scornfully.

hohnsprechen *v.i.* to scorn; to make a mockery.

hökern *v.i.* to huckster.

Hokuspokus *m.* **(-, 0)** hocus-pocus.

hold *a.* fair, lovely, propitious.

holdselig *a.* charming, lovely.

holen *v.t.* to fetch; *~ v.r. etwas ~*, to catch sth. (disease); *Atem ~*, to breathe, to catch one's breath; **~lassen,** to send for.

holl. *holländisch*, Dutch.

holla! *i.* hello!

Holland *n.* **(-s, 0)** Holland; The Netherlands *pl.*

Holländer *m.* **(-s, -)** Dutchman; Dutch cheese; **Holländerin** *f.* **(-, -nen)** Dutchwoman.

holländisch *a.* Dutch.

Hölle *f.* **(-, 0)** hell.

Höllenangst *f.* mortal fright.

Höllen: ~lärm *m.* diabolical noise; **~maschine** *f.* infernal machine; **~pein** *f.*, **~qual** *f.* agony; **~qualen** *pl.* *~ leiden* to suffer the torments of hell; **~tempo** *n.* breakneck speed.

höllisch *a.* hellish, infernal.

Hollywoodschaukel *f.* swinging garden bench.

Holm *m.* (*sp.*) bar; beam; small island.

holpern *v.i.* to jolt, to be uneven.

holp(e)rig *a.* bumpy, rough, rugged; rude.

holterdiepolter *adv.* helter-skelter.

Holunder *m.* **(-s, -)** elder.

Holz *n.* **(-[e]s, Hölzer)** wood, lumber, timber; bush, forest.

Holz: ~arbeit *f.* woodwork; **~arbeiter** *m.* woodworker.

Holz: ~bläser *m.*, **~bläserin** *f.* woodwind player; **~blasinstrument** *n.* woodwind instrument.

Holzbock *m.* sawing-block, trestle.

hölzern *a.* wooden; (*fig.*) clumsy, awkward.

Holzfäller *m.* lumberjack; wood cutter.

Holzfaser *f.* wood fiber; **~stoff** *m.* wood cellulose; wood pulp.

Holzhacker *m.* woodchopper.

Holzhammer *m.* mallet.

Holzhammermethode *f.* (*fam.*) sledgehammer method.

Holzhandel *m.* timber trade.

Holzhändler *m.* timber merchant.

holzig *a.* woody, wooded; stringy, tough.

Holzklotz *m.* log; block of wood.

Holzkohle *f.* charcoal.

Holzpflock *m.* peg.

Holzscheit *m.* stick of wood.

Holzschnitt *m.* woodcut.

Holzschnitzer *m.* wood carver.

Holzschnitzerei *f.* woodcarving.

Holzschuh *m.* clog.

Holzspan *m.* wood shaving.

Holzstoß *m.* pile of wood.

Holzweg *m.* logging path; *auf dem ~ sein*, to be on the wrong track.

Homo *m.* gay, homo, queer.

homogen *a.* homogeneous.

Homöopathie *f.* **(-, 0)** homeopathy.

Homosexualität *f.* homosexuality.

homosexuell *a.* homosexual.

Homosexuelle *m./f.* homosexual.

Honig *m.* **(-s, 0)** honey.

Honigmelone *f.* honeydew melon.

Honigwabe *f.* honeycomb.

Honorar *n.* **(-s, -e)** fee; royalty (author); *ein ~ berechnen*, to charge a fee.

Honoratioren *pl.* notabilities; local dignitaries.

honorieren *v.t.* to pay a fee.

Hopfen *m.* **(-s, 0)** (*bot.*) hop, hops; *an ihm ist ~ und Malz verloren*, he is a lost cause.

Hopfenstange *f.* hop-pole; (*fam. von Menschen*) beanpole.

hopp! *i.* quick!, chop-chop!

hoppeln *v.i.* to hop.

hopsen *v.i.* *(s)* to jump, to hope, to skip.

hopsgehen *v.i.st.* (*fam.*) to get broken; to kick the bucket.

hörbar *a.* audible.

horch! *i.* hark!

horchen *v.i.* to listen, to eavesdrop.

Horcher *m.* eavesdropper.

Horde *f.* **(-, -n)** horde; mob, gang.

hören *v.t.* to hear; to listen; *schwer ~*, to be hard of hearing; *hören Sie mal*, listen here! *das läßt sich ~*, that sounds fair; *bei einem Professor ~*, to attend a professor's lectures.

Hörensagen *n.* hearsay; *vom ~*, by hearsay.

Hörer *m.* **(-s, -)** (*Radio*) listener; (*univ.*) student; (*tel.*) receiver; headphone(s).

Hörerschaft *f.* **(-, -en)** audience.

hörig *a.* enslaved; bond.

Hörigkeit *f.* **(-, 0)** bondage; serfdom.

Horizont *m.* **(-[e]s, -e)** horizon.

Hormon *n.* **(-, -e)** hormone; **~drüse** *f.* ductless gland.

hormonal *a.* hormonal.
Horn *n.* **(-[e]s, Hörner)** horn; French horn, bugle.
Hornbläser *m.;* **Hornbläserin** *f.* horn player.
Hornbrille *f.* hornrimmed glasses.
Hörnchen *n.* (*Gebäck*) crescent, croissant.
hörnern *a.* (made of) horn.
Hornhaut *f.* cornea (*Auge*); callous.
Hornisse *f.* **(-, -n)** hornet.
Hornist *m.* **(-en, -en)** horn player; bugler.
Horoskop *n.* **(-es, -e)** horoscope.
horrend *a.* horrendous.
Hörrohr *n.* ear trumpet.
Horror *m.* horror.
Hörsaal *m.* lecture hall.
Hörspiel *n.* radio play.
Horst *m.* **(-es, -e)** eyrie, nest (of a bird of prey).
Hörsturz *m.* (*med.*) sudden deafness.
Hort *m.* **(-[e]s, -e)** hoard; (*fig.*) stronghold, retreat; protector; *Kinder*~, day nursery.
Hortensie *f.* **(-, -n)** hydrangea.
Hörweite *f.* hearing range; earshot.
Hose *f.* **(-, -n)** trousers *pl.*, pants; *Knie*~, breeches *pl.*, knickerbockers, plus-fours *pl.*
Hosen: ~aufschläge *pl.* cuffs; **~boden** *m.* seat (of pants); **~schlitz** *m.* fly; **~träger** *pl.* suspenders.
Hospital *n.* **(-[e]s, Hospitäler)** hospital.
Hostie *f.* **(-, -n)** host, holy wafer.
Hotel *n.* **(-s, -s)** hotel; **~apartement** *n.* suite; **~ garni** bed-and-breakfast hotel.
Hotelhalle *f.* lobby.
HP *Halbpension,* half board.
Hr. *Herr,* Mr.
h(rs)g. *herausgegeben,* edited.
H(rs)g. *Herausgeber,* editor, ed.
Hs. *Handschrift,* manuscript, MS; **Hss.** *Handschriften,* MSS.
Hub *m.* **(-es, Hübe)** hoisting capacity; lift; (*Kolben*) stroke.
Hubbel *m.* bump.
hubbelig *a.* bumpy.
hüben *adv.* on this side; **~ und drüben,** on each (either) side.
Hubraum *m.* cubic capacity.
hübsch *a.* pretty, fair; proper; *das ist nicht ~ von ihm,* that's not very nice of him.
Hubschrauber *m.* **(-s, -)** helicopter; **~landeplatz** *m.* heliport; helicopter pad.
huckepack *adv.* piggyback.
hudeln *v.t.* to bungle, to work sloppily.
Huf *m.* **(-[e]s, -e)** hoof.
Hufbeschlag *m.* (horse)shoeing.
Hufeisen *n.* horseshoe.
Hufschmied *m.* blacksmith, farrier; **~e** *f.* smithy.
Hüftbein *n.* hip bone.
Hüfte *f.* **(-, -n)** hip; haunch.
Hüftgelenk *n.* hip joint.
Huftier *n.* hoofed animal; ungulate.
Hügel *m.* **(-s, -)** hill, hillock.
Hügelgrab *n.* barrow; tumulus.
hugelig *a.* hilly
Hügelkette *f.* chain *or* range of hills.
Hugenotte *m.;* **Hugenottin** *f.* Huguenot.
Huhn *n.* **(-[e]s, Hühner)** chicken; fowl; hen.
Hühnchen *n.* **(-s, -)** chicken; *Brat*~ *n.* (young) roast chicken.
Hühner: ~auge *n.* corn (on the foot); **~braten** *m.* roast chicken; **~futter** *n.* chickenfeed; **~korb** *m.* chicken coop; **~stall** *m.* henhouse; **~stange, ~steige,** *f.* chicken roost.
Huld *f.* **(-, 0)** grace, favor.
huldigen *v.i.* to pay, render, *or* do homage; to hold (an opinion); to indulge in.
Huldigung *f.* **(-, -en)** homage, tribute.
huldvoll *a.* benevolent, gracious.
Hülle *f.* **(-, -n)** cover, case, holder, wrapper; *~ und Fülle,* abundance, more than enough.
hüllen *v.t.* to cover, to wrap.
Hülse *f.* **(-, -n)** hull; husk; (*Patronen*) case, shell, cartridge.
Hülsenfrucht *f.* legume; pulse.
human *a.* humane, considerate, decent.
humanisieren *v.t.* to humanize.
Humanisierung *f.* humanization.
Humanismus *m.* **(-, 0)** humanism.
humanitär *a.* humanitarian.
Humanität *f.* **(-, 0)** humanity, humaneness.
Humanmedizin *f.* human medicine.
Humbug *m.* **(-s, 0)** humbug, nonsense.
Hummel *f.* **(-, -n)** bumblebee.
Hummer *m.* **(-s, -)** lobster.
Hummerkrabbe *f.* king prawn.
Humor *m.* **(-s, -e)** humor.
Humoreske *f.* **(-, -n)** humorous sketch.
humorig *a.* humorous; genial.
Humorist(in) *m.(f.)* humorist; comedian.
humoristisch *a.* humorous.
humpeln *v.i.* **(h, s)** to hobble, to limp.
Humpen *m.* **(-s, -)** tankard.
Hund *m.* **(-[e]s, -e)** dog, hound; *auf den ~ kommen,* to go to the dogs; *du blöder ~,* (*sl.*) you stupid *or* silly bastard.
hundeelend *a.* (*fam.*) wretched, lousy.
Hunde: ~halsband *n.* dog collar; **~hütte** *f.* kennel; **~kälte** *f.* bitter cold; **~kuchen** *m.* dog biscuit; **~leben** *n.* dog's life; **~rasse** *f.* breed of dog.
hundert *a.* hundred.
Hunderter *m.* hundred-mark note.
hunderterlei *a.* a hundred and one.
hundertfach *a.* hundredfold.
Hundertjahrfeier *f.* centenary; centennial.
Hundertjährige *m./f.* centenarian.
hundertmal *adv.* hundred times.
hundertste *a.* hundredth.
Hundertstel *n.* hundredth.
Hündin *f.* **(-, -nen)** bitch.
hündisch *a.* doglike; servile; mean; sycophantic.
Hundstage *m.pl.* dog days *pl.*
Hüne *m.* **(-n, -n)** giant.
Hünengrab *n.* megalithic tomb; barrow.
Hunger *m.* **(-s, 0)** hunger; *~bekommen,* to get hungry; *~ haben,* to be hungry; *~ leiden,* to starve; *~s sterben,* to die of hunger, to starve to death.
Hungerlohn *m.* starvation wages, pittance.
hungern *v.i.imp.* to hunger, to be hungry, to go hungry, to starve.
Hungersnot *f.* famine.
Hunger: ~streik *m.* hunger strike; **~tod** *m.* death from starvation.
hungrig *a.* hungry.
Hunne *m.* Hun.
Hupe *f.* **(-, -n)** horn.
hupen *v.i.* to hoot, to honk, to sound the horn.
hüpfen *v.i.* *(s)* to hop, to skip.
Hupzeichen *n.* horn signal.
Hürde *f.* **(-, -n)** hurdle; pen, fold.
Hure *f.* **(-, -n)** prostitute, whore.
huren *v.i.* to whore, to fornicate.
Hurerei *f.* **(-, 0)** whoring, whoredom.

hurra *i.* hurrah!
hurtig *a.* quick, swift, nimble, agile.
Husar *m.* **(-en, -en)** hussar.
husch *i.* quick!
huschen *v.i. (s)* to scurry, to dart, to flit; to flash.
hüsteln *v.i.* to have a slight cough.
Husten *m.* **(-s, 0)** cough; ~ **haben,** to have a cough.
husten *v.i.* to cough.
Hut *m.* **(-[e]s, Hüte)** hat, bonnet; (*Zucker*) loaf.
Hut *f.* **(-, 0)** keeping, care, charge, guard; *auf der ~ sein,* to be on one's guard.
Hutablage *f.* hat rack.
hüten *v.t.* to guard, to watch, to tend, to keep; ~ *v.r.* (*nach + dat.*) to be on one's guard (against), to beware (of); *das Bett, das Zimmer ~,* to be confined to one's bed, room.
Hüter *m.* **(-s, -)** keeper, guardian.
Hutkrempe *f.* brim (of a hat).
Hutmacher *m.* hatter, millener.
Hutschachtel *f.* hat-box.
Hütte *f.* **(-, -n)** hut, cabin; shack; (*Werkhaus*) foundry, smelting works, forge.
Hütten: ~industrie *f.* iron and steel industry; **~käse** *m.* cottage cheese; **~schuh** *m.* slipper-sock; **~werk** *n.* metallurgical plant.
Hüttenwesen *n.* metallurgy.
Hyäne *f.* **(-, -n)** hyena.
Hyazinthe *f.* **(-, -n)** hyacinth.
Hydraulik *f.* hydraulics *sing.*
hydraulisch *a.* hydraulic.
hydrieren *v.t.* to hydrogenate.
Hydrokultur *f.* hydroponics.
Hygiene *f.* **(-, 0)** hygiene.
hygienisch *a.* hygienic.
Hymne *f.* **(-, -n)** hymn.
Hyperbel *f.* **(-, -n)** hyperbole; (*geom.*) hyperbola.
hyperbolisch *a.* hyperbolical.
hyperkorrekt *a.* (*fam.*) hypercorrect.
Hypnose *f.* **(-, -n)** hypnosis.
hypnotisieren *v.t.* to hypnotize.
Hypochonder *m.* **(-s, -)** hypochondriac.
Hypochondrie *f.* **(-, 0)** hypochondria.
hypochondrisch *a.* hypochondriac.
Hypothek *f.* **(-, -en)** mortgage; *eine ~ für verfallen erklären,* to foreclose a mortgage; **~enschuld** *f.* mortgage debt.
hypothekarisch *a. & adv. das Haus ist ~ belastet,* the house is mortgaged; **~er Kredit,** mortgage credit.
Hypothese *f.* **(-, -n)** hypothesis.
hypothetisch *a.* hypothetical.
Hysterie *f.* **(-, 0)** hysteria.
hysterisch *a.* hysterical.
Hz *Hertz,* hertz, Hz.

I

I, i *n.* the letter I or i.
I. *im, in,* in.
i.A. *im Auftrag,* per procurationem, p.p., by proxy.
i. allg. *im allgemeinen,* in general, gen.
iambisch *a.* iambic.
i.b. *im besonderen,* in particular.
iberisch *a.* Iberian; **Iberische Halbinsel** *f.* Iberian Peninsula.
IC *Intercity(-Zug),* inter-city (train).
ICE *Intercity-Expreßzug,* intercity express (train).
ich *pn.* I, I myself.
Ich *n.* self, ego.
ichbezogen *a.* egocentric.
Ichbezogenheit *f.* egocentricity.
Ich-Form *f.* first person.
i.D. *im Dienst,* on duty; *im Durchschnitt,* on average, on av.
Ideal *n.* **(-[e]s, -e)** ideal; ~ *a.* ideal.
idealisieren *v.t.* to idealize.
Idealisierung *f.* idealization.
Idealismus *m.* idealism.
idealistisch *a.* idealistic.
Idee *f.* **(-, -n)** idea, notion; *die ~ zu etwas,* the idea for sth.; *wie kommst du denn auf die ~,* whatever gave you that idea? *einen auf die ~ bringen, etwas zu tun,* to give sb. the idea of doing sth.
ideell *a.* nonmaterial, spiritual.
ideenreich *a.* full of ideas; inventive.
Identifikation *f.* identification.
identifizierbar *a.* identifiable.
identifizieren *v.t.* to identify; ~ *v.r.* to identify (oneself) (with).
identisch *a.* (*mit*) identical (with).
Identität *f.* **(-, -en)** identity; **~skrise** *f.* identity crisis; **~sverlust** *m.* loss of identity.
Ideologe *m.;* **Ideologin** *f.* ideologue.
Ideologie *f.* **(-, -n)** ideology.
ideologisch *a.* ideological.
Idiom *n.* idiom.
idiomatisch *a.* idiomatic.
Idiot *m.* idiot, fool.
idiotensicher *a.* foolproof.
Idiotie *f.* idiocy.
Idiotin *f.* idiot, fool.
idiotisch *a.* idiotic; stupid.
Idol *n.* idol.
Idyll *n.* **(-s, -en)** idyll, idyllic spot.
Idylle *f.* idyll.
idyllisch *a.* idyllic.
i.e. *im einzelnen,* in detail.
IFO *Institut für Wirtschaftsforschung,* Institute for Economic Research.
IG *Industriegewerkschaft,* industrial union.
Igel *m.* **(-s, -)** hedgehog.
Iglu *m./n.* **(-s, -s)** igloo.
Ignorant *m.* **(-en, -en)** (*fam.*) ignoramus.
Ignoranz *f.* ignorance.
ignorieren *v.t.* to ignore.
IHK *Industrie- und Handelskammer,* Chamber of Industry and Commerce.
ihm *pn.* (to) him; (to) it.
ihn *pn.* him, it.
ihnen *pn.* (to) them.
ihr *pn.* (to) her, their; **ihrer** *pn.* of her, of them.
Ihr *pn.* your; **Ihrer** *pn.* of you.
ihrerseits *adv.* on their (her) part.
ihresgleichen *pn.* people like her/them; **Ihresgleichen** people like you.
ihrethalben, ihretwegen, ihretwillen *adv.* for her, their sake; **Ihrethalben, etc.** for your sake.
ihrige *pn.* hers, theirs; *Ihrige,* yours.
i.J. *im Jahre,* in the year.

Ikone *f.* icon.
illegal *a.* illegal.
Illegalität *f.* illegality.
Illumination *f.* illumination.
illuminieren *v.t.* to illuminate; to color.
illusionär *a.* illusory; illusionary.
illustrieren *v.t.* to illustrate.
Illustrierte *f.* magazine.
Iltis *m.* **(-tisses, -tisse)** polecat.
im = in dem.
i.M. *im Monat,* in the month.
imaginär *a.* imaginary.
Imbiß *m.* **(-bisses, -bisse)** snack; light meal.
Imbißraum *m.;* **Imbißstube** *f.* snack bar.
imitieren *v.t.* to imitate.
Imker *m.* **(-s, -)** beekeeper.
Imkerei *f.* beekeeping; apiary.
immanent *a.* inherent; immament.
Immatrikulation *f.* (university) registration.
immatrikulieren *v.t.* & *r.* to register; to matriculate.
immens *a.* & *adv.* immense(ly).
immer *adv.* always, ever; *noch* ~, still; **~ besser,** better and better; **~ wieder,** again and again, over and over again; **~zu,** continually.
immerdar *adv.* for ever.
immerfort *adv.* for ever and ever, continually, the whole time.
Immergrün *n.* **(-s, 0)** evergreen.
immerhin *adv.* at least; anyhow; at any rate; still, yet.
immermehr *adv.* more and more.
immerwährend *a.* perpetual.
Immigrant *m.;* **Immigrantin** *f.* immigrant.
immigrieren *v.i.* to immigrate.
Immobilien *pl.* immovables *pl.;* real estate.
Immobilienmakler *m.* realtor.
immun *a.* *(gegen)* immune (against).
immunisieren *v.t.* to immunize.
Immunisierung *f.* immunization.
Immunität *f.* **(-, -en)** immunity.
Immunkörper *m.* **(-s, -)** antibody.
Immunschwäche *f.* immunodeficiency.
Imperativ *m.* **(-s, -e)** imperative.
Imperfekt *n.* imperfect tense.
Imperialismus *m.* imperialism.
imperialistisch *a.* imperialistic.
Imperium *n.* **(-s, -rien)** empire.
impertinent *a.* impertinent, impudent.
Impetus *m.* impetus; verve; zest.
impfen *v.t.* to vaccinate, to inoculate.
Impfschein *m.* certificate of vaccination.
Impfstoff *m.* vaccine, serum.
Impfung *f.* **(-, -en)** vaccination, inoculation.
Implantat *n.* **(-s, -e)** (*med.*) implant.
implantieren *v.t.* to implant.
Implikation *f.* **(-, -en)** implication.
implizieren *v.t.* to implicate; (*stillschweigend*) to imply.
implizit *a.* implicit.
Imponderabilien *pl.* imponderables *pl.*
imponieren *v.i.* to impress, to overawe; **~d** *a.* impressive, imposing.
Imponiergehabe *n.* (*zool.*) display behavior; (*fig.*) exhibitionism.
Import *m.* **(-s, -en)** import; imports.
Importeur *m.* importer.
importieren *v.t.* to import.
imposant *a.* imposing; impressive.
Impotenz *f.* **(-, 0)** impotence.
imprägnieren *v.t.* to impregnate; to waterproof.
imprägniert *a.* waterproofed.
Imprägnierung *f.* impregnation, waterproofing.
Impression *f.* impression.
Impressionismus *m.* impressionism.
Impressum *n.* imprint; masthead (newspaper).
Improvisation *f.* improvization.
improvisieren *v.i.* to improvise.
Impuls *m.* impulse, impetus, momentum.
impulsiv *a.* impulsive.
Impulsivität *f.* impulsiveness.
imstande *a.* able.
in *pr.* in, into; at; within.
inadäquat *a.* & *adv.* inadequate.
inakzeptabel *a.* unacceptable.
Inangriffnahme *f.* beginning, start.
Inanspruchnahme *f.* **(-, -n)** strain; demands.
Inbegriff *m.* perfect example, epitome, embodiment.
inbegriffen *a.* included, inclusive of.
Inbetrieb: ~nahme *f.;* **~setzung** *f.* **(-, -en)** opening, inauguration, putting into operation.
Inbrunst *f.* **(-, 0)** fervor; ardor.
inbrünstig *a.* ardent, fervent.
indem *c.* while, when; as, because.
Inder *m.;* **Inderin** *f.* Indian.
indes, indessen *c.* meanwhile, in the meantime.
Indianer *m.;* **Indianerin** *f.* (American) Indian; Native American.
indianisch *a.* Indian.
Indien *n.* **(-s, -)** India.
Indienststellung *f.* **(-, -en)** (*Kriesgsschiff*) commissioning.
indigniert *a.* indignant.
Indikativ *m.* **(-s, -e)** indicative (mood).
indikativisch *a.* indicative.
Indikator *m.* **(-s, -en)** indicator.
Indio *m.* **(-s, -s)** Indian (Central/South America).
indirekt *a.* indirect.
indisch *a.* Indian.
indiskret *a.* indiscreet, ill-advised.
Indiskretion *f.* **(-, -en)** indiscretion.
indisponiert *a.* indisposed.
Individualismus *m.* individualism.
individualistisch *a.* individualistic.
Individualität *f.* **(-, -en)** individuality, individual characteristic.
individuell *a.* individual.
Individuum *n.* **(-s, -duen)** individual.
Indiz *n.* **(-es, -zien)** indication, sign.
Indizienbeweis *m.* circumstantial evidence.
indoeuropäisch *a.* Indo-European.
indoktrinieren *v.t.* to indoctrinate.
Indonesien *n.* **(-s, 0)** Indonesia.
Indonesier *m.;* **Indonesierin** *f.;* **indonesisch** *a.* Indonesian.
Indossant *m.* **(-en, -en)** endorser.
Indossat *m.* **(-en, -en)** endorsee.
indossieren *v.t.* to endorse.
Induktion *f.* **(-, -en)** induction.
industrialisieren *v.t.* to industrialize.
Industrie *f.* **(-, -[e]n)** industry.
Industrie- und Handelskammer *f.* Chamber of Industry and Commerce.
industriell *a.* industrial.
Industrielle *m./f.* industrialist.
induzieren *v.t.* to induce.
ineinander *adv.* in one another; in each other.

ineinandergreifen *v.i.* to mesh, to interlock.
Ineinanderspiel *n.* **(-[e]s, 0)** interplay.
infam *a.* infamous, scandalous.
Infamie *f.* **(-, 0)** infamy, enormity.
Infanterie *f.* **(-, 0)** infantry.
Infanterist *m.* **(-en, -en)** foot-soldier.
infantil *a.* infantile.
Infarkt *m.* infarct, coronary thrombosis.
Infekt *m.;* **Infektion** *f.* infection.
Infektionsgefahr *f.* risk of infection.
Infektionsherd *m.* locus of the infection.
Infektionskrankheit *f.* contagious disease.
infektiös *a.* infectious.
infernalisch *a.* infernal.
infiltrieren *v.t.* to infiltrate.
Infinitiv *m.* **(-s, -e)** infinitive.
infizieren *v.t.* to infect.
Inflation *f.* inflation.
inflationär *a.* inflationary.
Info *n.* **(-s, -s)** (*fam.*) (*Informationsblatt*) handout.
Info *f.* **(-, -s)** (*fam.*) (*Information*) info.
infolge *pr.* owing to, in consequence of; **~dessen** *adv.* consequently, as a result of that.
Informant *m.;* **Informantin** *f.* informant.
Informatik *f.* **(-, 0)** computer science, information studies *pl.*
Informatiker(in) *m.(f.)* computer scientist.
Information *f.* **(-, -en)** information.
Informations: ~austausch *m.* exchange of information; **~fluß** *m.* flow of information; **~quelle** *f.* source of information; **~schalter** *m.*, **~stand** *m.* information desk.
informativ *a.* informative.
informell *a.* informal.
informieren *v.t.* to inform.
infrarot *a.* infra-red.
Infrastruktur *f.* infrastructure.
Infusion *f.* **(-, -en)** infusion.
Infusorien *pl.* infusoria.
Ing. *Ingenieur,* engineer, eng.
Ingenieur *m.* **(-s, -e)** engineer; **~büro** *n.* engineering office.
Ingrimm *m.* **(-[e]s, 0)** anger, spite, wrath.
ingrimmig *a.* angry, wrathful.
Ingwer *m.* **(-s, 0)** ginger.
Inh. *Inhaber,* proprietor, prop.; *Inhalt,* contents, cont.
Inhaber *m.* **(-s, -)** possessor, holder; proprietor; occupant; (*eines Wechsels*) payee, bearer.
Inhaberaktie *f.* bearer share.
inhaftieren *v.t.* to imprison.
Inhaftierung *f.* **(-, -en)** detention, arrest, imprisonment.
Inhalation *f.* inhalation.
inhalieren *v.t.* to inhale.
Inhalt *m.* **(-[e]s, -e)** contents, tenor, substance; volume; *eine Nachricht des ~s, daß...* a message to the effect that....
inhaltlich *a. & adv.* material; in substance.
Inhaltsangabe *f.* summary, synopsis.
inhalt[s]leer, inhalt[s]los *a.* empty, meaningless.
Inhaltsverzeichnis *n.* table of contents, index.
inhibieren *v.t.* to inhibit, to prevent.
inhuman *a.* inhuman; inhumane.
Initiale *f.* **(-, -n)** initial.
Initialzündung *f.* detonation.
Initiative *f.* **(-, 0)** initiative; *die ~ ergreifen,* to take the initiative.
Initiator *m.;* **Initiatorin** *f.* initiator.
initiieren *v.t.* to initiate.
Injektion *f.* **(-, -en)** injection; **~snadel** *f.* hypodermic needle; **~sspritze** *f.* hypodermic syringe.
injizieren *v.t.* to inject
Injurie *f.* **(-, -n)** insult.
Inkarnation *f.* incarnation.
Inkasso *n.* **(-, -s)** cashing, collection.
inkl. *inklusive,* included, incl.
inklusive pr. inclusive of; including.
inkompetent *a.* incompetent.
inkonsequent *a.* inconsistent.
Inkonsequenz *f.* **(-s, -en)** inconsistency.
Inkrafttreten *n.* **(-s, 0)** coming into force.
Inkubation *f.* incubation; **~szeit** *f.* incubation period.
Inkunabel *f.* **(-, -n)** incunabula.
Inland *n.* **(-[e]s, 0)** inland, interior; *im In- und Ausland,* at home and abroad.
Inländer *m.* **(-s, -); Inländerin** *f.* **(-, -nen)** native.
inländisch *a.* domestic; native, inland; indigenous.
Inlaut *m.* **(-s, -e)** medial sound.
Inlett *n.* **(-s, -e)** tick, ticking; cambric.
inliegend *a.* enclosed.
inmitten pr. in the midst/middle of.
innehaben *v.t.ir.* to possess.
innehalten *v.i.st.* to stop, to pause.
innen *adv.* within, inside, indoors; *nach ~,* inwards, inwardly; *von ~,* (from) within, from the heart, on the inside; *von ~ und aussen kennen,* to know the ins and outs of.
Innen: ~dekoration *f.* interior decoration; **~hof** *m.* inner courtyard, quadrangle; **~leben** *n.* inner life; **~politik** *f.* domestic politics *or* policy; **~raum** *m.* interior space *or* room(s).
Innenseite *f.* inside, inner side.
Innenstadt *f.* city center, center of town.
inner *a.* interior, internal, inner.
Innere *n.* **(-[e]s, 0)** inside, interior; Department of the Interior.
Innereien *pl.* entrails; (*cul.*) offal.
innerhalb pr. within; inside.
innerlich *a.* inward; internal, intrinsic.
innerparteilich *a.* within the party.
innerst *a.* inmost, innermost.
innerstaatlich *a.* internal, domestic.
innewerden *v.r.st.* to become aware of.
innewohnen *v.i.* to be inherent.
innig *a.* hearty, heartfelt; intimate; profound.
Innigkeit *f.* **(-, 0)** cordiality, fervor, depth, sincerity.
Innung *f.* **(-, -en)** corporation, guild.
inoffiziell *a.* unofficial.
in petto *adv. etw. ~ haben* to have sth. up one's sleeve.
in puncto *pr.* as regards.
ins = in das.
Insasse *m.* **(-n, -n)** occupant, inmate (*Haus*); (*Schiff, Abteil*) passenger.
insbesondere *adv.* especially.
Inschrift *f.* **(-, -en)** inscription.
Insekt *n.* **(-[e]s, -en)** insect.
Insektenlehre *f.* entomology.
Insektenpulver *n.* insect powder.
Insektenstich *m.* insect sting (bee); insect bite (mosquito).
Insektizid *n.* insecticide.
Insel *f.* **(-, -n)** island, isle.
Inserat *n.* **(-[e]s, -e)** advertisement.
inserieren *v.t. & i.* to advertise.
insgeheim *adv.* privately, secretly.

insgemein *adv.* generally, commonly, on the whole, by and large.
insgesamt *adv.* altogether, collectively, all in all.
Insignien *pl.* insignia *pl.*, badge of office.
insofern *adv.* (*als*) insofar (as); in this respect.
insolvent *a.* insolvent.
Insolvenz *f.* **(-, -en)** insolvency.
insoweit *adv.* (in)sofar.
Inspektion *f.* inspection; service; *das Auto zur ~ bringen,* to take the car in for service.
inspirieren *v.t.* to inspire.
inspizieren *v.t.* to inspect, to examine.
Installateur *m.* **(-s, -e)** plumber; electrician *or* gas fitter.
installieren *v.t.* to install; ~ *v.r.* to install oneself.
Instandesetzung *f.* restoration, overhaul.
instandhalten *v.t.st.* to maintain; to service.
Instandhaltung *f.* **(-, -en)** maintenance, servicing, upkeep.
inständig *a.* instant, urgent, fervent.
instandsetzen *v.t.* to enable; to repair, to restore.
Instanz *f.* **(-, -en)** court; appeal; authority; judgment; *höhere ~,* superior court; *höchste ~,* highest court of appeal; *in der letzten ~,* in the last resort; *im ~enweg,* through (official) channels.
Instinkt *m.* **(-[e]s, -e)** instinct.
instinktiv *a. & adv.* instinctive(ly).
instinktmäßig *a. & adv.* instinctive(ly).
Institut *n.* **(-[e]s, -e)** institute.
Institution *f.* **(-, -en)** institution.
institutionalisieren *v.t.* to institutionalize.
institutionell *a.* institutional.
instruieren *v.t.* to instruct; to inform.
instruktiv *a.* instructive; informative.
Instrument *n.* **(-[e]s, -e)** instrument; tool, implement.
Instrumentarium *n.* **(-s, -rien)** equipment; instruments; apparatus.
instrumentieren *v.t.* (*mus.*) to orchestrate.
Insuffizienz *f.* **(-, -en)** insufficiency.
inszenieren *v.t.* to stage, to produce (a play); to direct.
Inszenierung f **(-, -en)** staging; direction; production; (*pej.*) engineering.
intakt *a.* intact; in working condition.
Intarsie *f.* **(-, -n)** marquetry, inlay.
integer *a.* *eine ~e Persönlichkeit,* a person of integrity.
Integralrechnung *f.* integral calculus.
Integration *f.* **(-, -en)** integration.
integrieren *v.t.* to integrate.
Integrierung *f.* **(-, -en)** integration.
Integrität *f.* integrity.
Intellekt *m.* **(-s, 0)** intellect.
intellektuell *a.* intellectual.
Intellektuelle *m./f.* intellectual.
intelligent *a.* intelligent.
Intelligenz *f.* **(-, 0)** intelligence.
Intelligenzprüfung *f.* intelligence test.
Intelligenzquotient *m.* **(-s, -en)** intelligence quotient, IQ.
Intendant *m.* **(-en, -en)** (*theat.*) manager and artistic director.
intendieren *v.t.* to intend; *ein Kritik hatte ich damit nicht intendiert,* I didn't intend that as a criticism.
Intensität *f.* intensity.
intensiv *a.* intensive; intense.
intensivieren *v.t.* to intensify.
Intensivierung *f.* intensification.
Intensivpflege *f.* intensive care.
Intensivstation *f.* intensive care unit.
Intention *f.* intention.
Intercity *m.* inter-city, IC; ~ **Express** *m.* intercity-express (train), ICE.
interdisziplinär *a.* interdisciplinary.
interessant *a.* interesting; *sich ~ machen,* to attract attention to oneself.
Interesse *n.* **(-s, -n)** interest.
Interessenssphäre *f.* sphere of influence.
Interessent *m.* **(-en, -en)** prospective customer.
interessieren *v.t.* to interest, to concern; ~ *v.r.* (*für*) to be interested (in).
interessiert *a.* interested.
interimistisch *a.* temporary.
Interimsregierung *f.* interim government; caretaker *or* provisional government.
Interkontinentalflug *m.* **(-s, -flüge)** intercontinental flight.
Interkontinentalrakete *f.* intercontinental balistic missile.
Intermezzo *n.* **(-[e]s, -s)** interlude; (*mus.*) intermezzo.
intern *a.* internal.
Internat *n.* **(-[e]s, -e)** boarding school.
international *a.* international.
internationalisieren *v.t.* to internationalize.
internieren *v.t.* to intern.
Internierte *m./f.* **(-ten, -ten)** internee.
Internierung *f.* **(-, -en)** internment.
Internierungslager *n.* internment camp.
Internist *m.;* **Internistin** *f.* internist.
interparlamentarisch *a.* interparliamentary.
Interpret *m.;* **Interpretin** *f.* performer, singer; intrepreter.
interpretieren *v.t. & i.* to interpret.
Interpunktion *f.* **(-, -en)** punctuation; **~szeichen** *n.* punctuation mark.
interrogativ *a.* interrogative.
Intervall *n.* interval.
intervenieren *v.i.* to intervene.
Intervention *f.* intervention.
interviewen *v.t.* to interview.
Interviewer *m.;* **Interviewerin** *f.* interviewer.
Interviewte *m./f.* interviewee.
Inthronisation *f.* enthronement.
intim *a.* intimate.
Intimbereich *m.* genital area; private parts.
Intimität *f.* intimacy.
Intimsphäre *f.* private life; *jds. ~ verletzen,* to invade sb.'s privacy.
Intimverkehr *m.* intimate relations; intimacy.
intolerant *a.* intolerant.
Intoleranz *f.* **(-, 0)** intolerance.
intonieren *v.t.* to start to sing/to play (music).
intransitiv *a.* intransitive.
intravenös *a.* intravenous.
Intrige *f.* intrigue.
intrigieren *v.i.* to plot, to intrigue.
Intrigrant *m.;* **Intrigrantin** *f.* schemer, intriguer.
introvertiert *a.* introverted.
Intuition *f.* intuition.
intuitiv *a. & adv.* intuitive(ly).
Invalide *m.* **(-n, -n)** invalid, disabled person.
Invalidenversicherung *f.* disability insurance.
invariabel *a.* invariable.
Invasion *f.* invasion.
Inventar *n.* **(-s, -e)** inventory; *das ~ aufnehmen,* to take stock, to inventory.

inventarisieren *v.t.* to inventory.
Inventur *f.* **(-, -en)** stock-taking.
Inversion *f.* inversion.
investieren *v.t. & i.* to invest.
Investierung *f.* **(-, -en), Investition** *f.* **(-, -en)** investment.
Investitionsgüter *pl.* capital goods.
Investmentfonds *m.* investment fund.
inwendig *a.* interior, inner; ~ *adv.* inside, within.
inwiefern, inwieweit *adv.* how far, to what extent, in what way.
Inzest *m.* incest.
Inzucht *f.* **(-, 0)** inbreeding; intermarriage.
inzwischen *adv.* meanwhile, in the meantime, since (then).
ionisiert *a.* (*elek.*) ionized.
Ionosphäre *f.* ionosphere.
I-Punkt *m.* dot over the i.
IQ *Intelligenz Quotient,* intelligence quotient, IQ.
i.R. *im Ruhestand,* retired, ret.
Irak *m.* **(-s, 0)** Iraq.
Iraker *m.;* **Irakerin** *f.;* **irakisch** *a.* Iraqi.
Iran *m.* Iran.
Iraner *m.;* **Iranerin** *f.;* **iranisch** *a.* Iranian.
irden *a.* earthen.
irdisch *a.* earthly; temporal; worldly.
Ire *m.* **(-n, -n)** Irishman.
irgend *adv.* at all, possibly; any(where); *wenn ~ möglich,* if at all possible; *~ etwas,* anything, something; *~ jemand,* anybody, somebody.
irgendein *pn.* any(one), anybody, (*attr.*) some.
irgendwann *adv.* some time.
irgendwas *pn.* something.
irgendwer *pn.* somebody.
irgendwie *adv.* anyhow, somehow.
irgendwo *adv.* anywhere, somewhere.
irgendwoher *adv.* from some place (or other).
irgendwohin *adv.* (to) anywhere, somewhere
Irin *f.* **(-, -nen)** Irishwoman.
irisch *a.* Irish.
irisieren *v.i.* to iridesce; **~d** *a.* iridescent.
IRK *Internationales Rotes Kreuz,* International Red Cross, IRC.
Irland *n.* **(-s, 0)** Ireland.
Ironie *f.* **(-, 0)** irony.
ironisch *a. & adv.* ironical(ly).
ironisieren *v.t.* to ironize.
irrational *a. & adv.* irrational(ly).
Irrationalität *f.* irrationality.
irre *a. & adv.* mad, astray, wrong; insane; **~werden (an),** to lose confidence (in); **~gehen,** to lose one's way; **~führen,** to lead astray; *sich nicht ~machen lassen,* not to be easily put out or perplexed; *wie ~,* like crazy; *das macht ihn ganz ~,* that drives him mad.
Irre *m./f.* **(-n, -n)** madman, lunatic.
Irre *f. in die ~ gehen,* to go astray; to make a mistake; *jn. in die ~ führen,* to lead sb. astray.
irreal *a.* unreal.
irreführen *v.t.* to mislead; **~d** *a.* misleading.
irrelevant *a.* irrelevant.
irremachen *v.t.* to disconcert, confuse, muddle.
irren *v.i.* to err; to go astray; ~ *v.r.* to be mistaken.
Irrenanstalt *f.* lunatic asylum, mental institution.
Irrenhaus *n.* (*fig.*) madhouse.
irreparabel *a.* irreparable.
Irrfahrt *f.* odyssey, wandering, vagary.
Irrgarten *m.* maze, labyrinth.
Irrglaube *m.* misconception; heretical belief.
irrgläubig *a.* heretical.
irrig *a.* erroneous, wrong, false.
Irritation *f.* irritation.
irritieren *v.t. & i.* to irritate; to annoy; to put off.
Irrlehre *f.* heresy; false doctrine.
Irrlehrer *m.* heretic.
Irrlicht *n.* will-o'-the-wisp, jack o' lantern.
Irrsinn *m.* madness, insanity.
irrsinnig *a.* insane, deranged.
Irrsinnigkeit *f.* madness, insanity.
Irrtum *m.* **(-[e]s, -tümer)** error, mistake; fallacy.
irrtümlich *a.* wrong; mistaken, erroneous; ~ *adv.* by mistake.
irrtümlicherweise *adv.* erroneously, by mistake.
Irrung *f.* **(-, -en)** error; misunderstanding, mistake.
Irrwahn *m.* delusion.
ISBN *Internationale Standardbuchnummer,* international standard book number, ISBN.
Ischias *f.* **(-, 0)** sciatica.
Ischiasnerv *m.* sciatic nerv.
Islam *m.* **(-(s), 0)** Islam.
islamisch *a.* Islamic.
Island *n.* **(-s, 0)** Iceland.
Isländer *m.* **(-s, -); Isländerin** *f.* **(-, -nen)** Icelander.
isländisch *a.* Icelandic.
Isobare *f.* **(-, -n)** isobar.
Isolation *f.* isolation, insulation, **~shaft** *f.* solitary confinement.
Isolator *m.* **(-s, -en)** insulator.
Isolierband *n.* (*elek.*) insulating tape.
isolieren *v.t.* to isolate; to insulate (electric wire).
Isolierstation *f.* (*med.*) isolation ward.
Isolierung *f.* isolation; insulation; soundproofing.
Isotherme *f.* **(-, -n)** isotherm.
Isotop *n.* **(-s, -e)** isotope.
Israel *n.* **(-s, 0)** Israel.
Israeli *m./f.* **(-s, -s); israelisch** *a.* Israeli.
Israelit *m.* **(-en, -en); Israelitin** *f.* **(-, -nen); israelitisch** *a.* Israelite.
Ist-Bestand *m.* cash in hand; actual stock.
Ist-Stärke *f.* **(-, -n)** actual strength.
Italien *n.* **(-s, 0)** Italy.
Italiener *m.* **(-s, -); Italienerin** *f.* **(-, -nen); italienisch** *a.* Italian.
I-Tüpfelchen *n.* **(-s, -)** dot over the i; finishing touch.
i.V. *in Vertretung,* on behalf of, by proxy, p.p.; *in Vorbereitung,* in preparation, in prep.
IWF *Internationaler Währungsfonds,* International Monetary Fund, IMF.

J

J, j *n.* the letter J *or* j.
J *Joule,* joule.
ja *adv.* yes; aye; even; *er ist ~ mein Bruder,* he is my brother, you know.
Jacht *f.* **(-, -en)** yacht.
Jacke *f.* **(-, -n)** jacket; cardigan.
Jackett *n.* **(-s, -e)** jacket.
Jagd *f.* **(-, -en)** chase; hunt; shoot; *auf die ~ gehen,* to go hunting, shooting.
Jagd: ~beute *f.* bag; kill; **~falke** *m.* falcon; **~flinte** *f.* shotgun; **~flugzeug** *n.* fighter; **~frevel** *m.* poaching; **~gesellschaft** *f.* hunting party; **~gesetz** *n.* game law; **~haus** *n.* hunting lodge; **~hund** *m.* hunting dog; hound; **~hütte** *f.* shooting box; **~saison** *f.* open season; **~schein** *m.* hunting *or* shooting license; **~zeit** *f.* hunting season.
jagen *v.t.* to chase, to hunt; *ins Bockshorn ~,* to bully, to intimidate; **~** *v.i. (s)* to rush.
Jäger *m.* **(-s, -)** hunter, sportsman.
Jägerin *f.* **(-, -nen)** huntress.
Jägerlatein *n.* tall stories *pl.*
jäh *a.* steep, precipitous; sudden.
jählings *adv.* suddenly, abruptly.
Jahr *n.* **(-[e]s, -e)** year; *übers ~,* a year hence; *von ~ zu ~,* & one year after another; *~ ein, ~ aus,* year in, year out.
Jahrbuch *n.* yearbook.
jahrelang *a.* & *adv.* (lasting) for years.
jähren *v.r.* to have happened a year ago.
Jahres ~ausgleich *m.* end-of-year adjustment; **~bericht** *m.* annual report; **~frist** *f.* a year's time; **~tag** *m.* anniversary; **~urlaub** *m.* annual leave, vacation; **~wende** *f.*, **~wechsel** *m.* New Year; **~zahl** *f.* (date of the) year; **~zeit** *f.* season.
Jahrgang *m.* year; annual volume; *~ 1950,* persons born in 1950; (*Wein*) vintage.
Jahrhundert *n.* **(-s, -e)** century.
Jahrhundertfeier *f.* centennial.
Jahrhundertwende *f.* turn of the century.
jährlich *a.* yearly, annual; *adv.* annually.
Jahrmarkt *m.* street festival; fair.
Jahrtausend *n.* **(-s, -e)** millennium.
Jahrzehnt *n.* **(-[e]s, -e)** decade.
Jähzorn *m.* violent anger, fit, outburst.
jähzornig *a.* hot-tempered.
Jakob *m.* Jacob, James.
Jakobiner *m.* **(-s, -)** Jacobin.
Jalousie *f.* **(-, -n)** Venetian blind.
Jamaika *n.* Jamaica.
Jamaikaner *m.* **(-s, -); Jamaikanerin** *f.* **(-, -nen); jamaikanisch** *a.* Jamaican.
jambisch *a.* iambic.
Jambus *m.* **(-, -ben)** iambus; iamb.
Jammer *m.* **(-s, 0)** lamentation; misery.
Jammer: ~bild *n.* miserable sight; **~gestalt** *f.* pitiful creature; **~lappen** *m.* (*fig.*) coward.
jämmerlich *a.* pathetic, pitiful, miserable, wretched.
jammern *v.i.* to lament; to complain; to moan; **~** *v.t. sie jammert mich,* I feel sorry for her.
jammerschade *a. es ist ~,* it's such a shame.
Jammertal *n.* vale of tears.
jammervoll *a.* deplorable, piteous.
Jan. *Januar,* January, Jan.
Januar *m.* **(-s, -e)** January.
Japan *n.* **(-s, 0)** Japan.
Japaner *m.* **(-s, -); Japanerin** *f.* **(-, -nen); japanisch** *a.* Japanese.
japsen *v.i.* to pant.
Jargon *m.* jargon; slang.
Jasager *m.* yes-man.
Jasmin *m.* **(-s, -e)** jasmine, jessamine.
Jaspis *m.* **(-ses, -se)** jasper.
Jastimme *f.* yes-vote.
jäten *v.t.* to weed.
Jauche *f.* **(-, -n)** liquid manure.
jauchzen *v.i.* to cheer, to shout, to exult.
jaulen *v.i.* to howl, to yowl.
Jause *f.* **(-, -n)** snack.
jawohl *adv.* yes (indeed).
Jawort *n.* consent.
Jazz *m.* jazz; **~band** *f.* jazzband.
je *adv.* ever; *~ nachdem,* that depends; *~ nach,* according to; *~ zwei,* two at a time, every two; *~ zwei Mark,* two marks each; *~ mehr desto besser,* the more the better.
Jeans *f./pl.* jeans.
jedenfalls *adv.* at all events, at any rate.
jeder, jede, jedes *pn.* every, each, everybody.
jedermann *pn.* **(-[e]s)** every one, everybody.
jederzeit *adv.* always, at any time.
jedesmal *adv.* every *or* each time; *~ wenn,* whenever.
jedoch *c.* yet, however, nevertheless.
jedweder *pn.* each, everyone.
jeglicher, jegliche, jegliches *pn.* every, each.
jeher *adv. seit ~, von ~,* always; from time immemorial.
jemals *adv.* ever, at any time.
jemand *pn.* **(-es)** somebody, anyone.
Jemen *n./m.* Yemen.
jener, jene, jenes *pn.* that, that one, the former.
jenseitig *a.* being on the other side, opposite.
jenseit(s) *pr.* beyond, over, on the other side.
Jenseits *n.* **(-, 0)** the other world; hereafter.
Jesuit *m.* **(-en, -en)** Jesuit.
Jesuitisch *a.* Jesuitical.
Jet *m.* **(-[s], -s)** jet.
jetten *v.i.* to jet.
jetzig *a.* present, now existing; current.
jetzt *adv.* now, at present; *für ~,* for the present time; *von ~ an,* henceforth, from this time forward.
Jetzt *n.* the present.
jeweilig *a.* particular; respective.
jeweils *adv.* **~ zwei,** two at a time; **~ am Montag,** each Monday.
JH *Jugendherberge,* youth hostel, Y.H.
Jh. *Jahrhundert,* century, c., cent.
jhrl. *jährlich,* yearly, annual(ly), ann.
jiddisch *a.* Yiddish.
Job *m.* **(-s, -s)** job.
jobben *v.i.* to do odd jobs.
Joch *n.* **(-[e]s, -e)** yoke; (*Brücken~*) arch; mountain ridge.
Jod *n.* **(-[e]s, 0)** iodine.
jodeln *v.t.* & *i.* to yodel.
Jodler *m.* **(-s, -)** yodeler; yodeling song.
Joga *m./n.* yoga.

Jogaübung *f.* yoga exercise.
joggen *v.i.* to jog.
Joghurt *n.* yoghurt.
Johannisbeere *f.* red currant.
Johanniswürmchen *n.* glowworm.
johlen *v.i.* to yell; to howl.
Joint *m.* joint, marijuana cigarette.
Jolle *f.* **(-, -n)** dinghy.
Jongleur *m.* **(-s, -e)** juggler, conjurer.
jonglieren *v.i.* to juggle.
Joppe *f.* **(-, -n)** jacket.
Jordanien *n.* **(-s, 0)** Jordan.
Jordanier *m.* **(-s, -); Jordanierin** *f.* **(-, -nen); jordanisch** *a.* Jordanian.
Jota *n.* **(-[s], -s)** iota.
Journal *n.* **(-es, -e)** journal, magazine, periodical; (*com.*) daily ledger.
Journalismus *m.* journalism.
Journalist *m.* **(-en, -en); Journalistin** *f.* **(-, -nen)** journalist.
jovial *a.* jovial.
Jovialität *f.* joviality.
jr., jun. *junior,* junior, Jun., jun., Jr.
Jubel *m.* **(-s, 0)** jubilation; cheering.
Jubelfeier *f.* jubilee.
jubeln *v.i.* to cheer; to jubilate, to exult.
Jubilar *m.* **(-s, -e); Jubilarin** *f.* **(-, -nen)** aged person or official of long service celebrating his/her jubilee.
Jubiläum *n.* **(-s, -äen)** anniversary; jubilee.
jubilieren *v.i.* to jubilate.
Juchtenleder *n.* Russian leather.
juchzen *v.i.* to shout with joy.
Juchzer *m.* shout of joy.
jucken *v.i.* to itch.
Judaist *m.* **(-s, -); Judaistin** *f.* **(-, -nen)** specialist in Jewish studies.
Judaistik *f.* Jewish studies.
Jude *m.* **(-n, -n); Jüdin** *f.* **(-, -nen)** Jew; *der Ewige* ~, the Wandering Jew.
Judenhaß *m.* anti-Semitism.
Judenhetze *f.* Jew-baiting.
Judenschaft *f.* **(-, 0)** Jewry.
Judenstern *m.* star of David.
Judentum *n.* **(-s, 0)** Judaism.
Judenverfolgung *f.* persecution of Jews.
Judenviertel *n.* Jewish quarter.
jüdisch *a.* Jewish.
Judo *n.* judo.
Jugend *f.* **(-, 0)** youth; young people.
Jugendalter *n.* adolescence.
Jugendgericht *n.* juvenile court.
Jugendherberge *f.* youth hostel.
jugendlich *a.* youthful, young, juvenile.
Jugendliche *m./f.* juvenile.
Jugendlichkeit *f.* youthfulness.
Jugendrichter *m.* juvenile court judge.
Jugendstil *m.* art nouveau.
Jugendsünde *f.*, **Jugendtorheit** *f.* youthful folly.
Jugendzeit *f.* youth; early life.
Jul. *Juli,* July, Jul.
Juli *m.* **(-s, -[s])** July.
Jun. *Juni,* June, Jun.
jung *a.* young; new, recent; (*fig.*) green.
Jungbrunnen *m.* fountain of youth.
Junge *m.* **(-n, -n)** boy, lad.
Junge *n.* **(-n, -n)** (*zool.*) cub.
jungenhaft *a.* boyish.
Jungenstreich *m.* boyish prank.
Jünger *m.* **(-s, -)** disciple.
Jungfer *f.* **(-, -n)** maid, spinster, virgin.
Jungfern: ~kranz *m.* bridal wreath; **~rede** *f.* maiden speech.
Jungfernschaft *f.* **(-, 0)** virginity.
Jungfrau *f.* **(-, -en)** maid, virgin.
jungfräulich *a.* virgin, maidenly, maiden.
Junggesell[e] *m.* bachelor.
Jüngling *m.* **(-[e]s, -e)** young man, youth.
Jünglingsalter *n.* adolescence.
jüngst *adv.* lately, newly, of late.
jüngst *a.* youngest, last; *der Jüngste Tag,* doomsday, day of the Last Judgment.
Jungsteinzeit *f.* Neolithic period; New Stone Age.
Jungwähler *m.* **(-s, -)** first-time voter.
Juni *m.* **(-[s], -[s])** June.
junior *a.* junior.
Junker *m.* **(-s, -)** squire.
Junkerei *f.*, **Junkertum** *n.* squirearchy.
Junta *f.* junta.
Jura *pl.* the law; ~ **studieren,** to study law.
Jura: ~student *m.;* **~studentin** *f.* law student.
Jurastudium *n.* law studies.
Jurist *m.* **(-en, -en); Juristin** *f.* **(-, -nen)** jurist, legal practitioner, barrister, lawyer; law student.
juristisch *a.* legal, juridical; **~e Person,** legal entity.
Jury *f.* **(-, -s)** jury.
just *adv.* just, exactly; just now, but just.
justieren *v.t.* to adjust.
Justitiar *m.* **(-s, -e); Justitiarin** *f.* **(-, -nen);** company lawyer.
Justiz *f.* **(-, 0)** justice.
Justiz: ~beamte[r] *m.* judicial officer; **~gebäude** *n.* law courts *pl.;* **~gewalt** *f.* judiciary power; **~minister** *m.* attorney general; Minister of Justice; Lord Chancellor; (*UK*). **~mord** *m.* judicial murder.
Jute *f.* **(-, 0)** jute.
Juwel *n.* **(-[e]s, -en)** jewel, gem.
Juwelier *m.* **(-s, -e)** jeweler.
Jux *m.* **(-es, -e)** joke, lark, hoax.

K

K, k *n.* the letter K or k.
Kabale *f.* **(-, -n)** cabal, intrigue.
Kabarett *n.* **(-[e]s, -e)** cabaret, nightclub.
Kabel *n.* **(-s, -)** cable; **~fernsehen** *n.* cable TV.
Kabeljau *m.* **(-s, -e)** cod(fish).
kabeln *v.t.* to cable.
Kabelrundfunk *m.* cable broadcasting.
Kabine *f.* **(-, -n)** cabin.
Kabinett *n.* **(-[e]s, -e)** cabinet; closet.
Kabinettsmitglied *n.* cabinet member.
Kabinettsstück(chen) *n.* tour de force.
Kabrio *n.* **(-s, -s); Kabriolett** *n.* **(-s, -s)** convertible.
Kabuff *n.* **(-s, -s)** (*fam.*) cubbyhole.
Kachel *f.* **(-, -n)** tile.
kacheln *v.t.* to tile.

Kachelofen *m.* tiled stove.
Kachelwand *f.* tiled wall.
Kacke *f.* (*vulg.*) shit.
kacken *v.i.* (*vulg.*) to shit.
Kadaver *m.* **(-s, -)** carcass; (*med.*) corpse; **~gehorsam** *m.* blind obedience.
Kadenz *f.* cadence; cadenza.
Kader *n.* **(-s, -)** cadre, skeleton staff.
Kadett *m.* **(-en, -en)** cadet.
Kadetten: ~anstalt *f.*, **~haus** *n.* military academy; **~schiff** *n.* training ship.
Käfer *m.* **(-s, -)** beetle; chafer.
Kaffee *m.* **(-s, -s)** coffee.
Kaffee: ~bohne *f.* coffee bean; **~geschirr** *n.* coffee set; **~haus** *n.* café; **~kanne** *f.* coffee pot; **~mühle** *f.* coffee mill; **~satz** *m.* coffee grounds.
Käfig *m.* **(-s, -e)** (bird)cage.
kahl *a.* bald; (*fig.*) bare, naked.
Kahlkopf *m.* bald head.
kahlköpfig *a.* bald-headed.
Kahn *m.* **(-[e]s, Kähne)** boat, punt.
Kai *m.* **(-s, -s)** quay.
Kaiman *m.* caiman; alligator.
Kaiser *m.* **(-s, -)** emperor.
Kaiserin *f.* **(-, -nen)** empress.
kaiserlich *a.* imperial.
Kaiserreich *n.* empire.
Kaiserschnitt *m.* Cesarean section.
Kaisertum *n.* **(-s, 0)** empire; imperial dignity.
Kajüte *f.* **(-, -n)** cabin; *erste* ~, first class saloon; **~nbett** *n.* berth.
Kakadu *m.* **(-[e]s, -s)** cockatoo.
Kakao *m.* **(-[s], -s)** cocoa.
Kakerlak *m.* **(-s, -en)** cockroach.
Kaktus *m.* **(-, Kakteen)** cactus.
Kalauer *m.* **(-s, -)** (*fam.*) joke, pun.
Kalb *n.* **(-[e]s, Kälber)** calf; (*cul.*) veal.
kalben *v.i.* to calve.
Kalb: ~fell *n.* calf's skin; (*fig.*) drum; **~fleisch** *n.* veal; **~leder** *n.* calfskin.
Kalbs: ~braten *m.* veal roast; **~haxe** *f.* shank of veal; **~keule** *f.* leg of veal.
Kaldaunen *pl.* tripe; entrails *pl.*
Kaleidoskop *n.* **(-s, -e)** kaleidoscope.
Kalender *m.* **(-s, -)** calendar, almanac.
Kalesche *f.* **(-, -n)** light carriage.
kalfatern *v.t.* (*nav.*) to caulk.
Kali *n.* **(-s, 0)** potash.
Kaliber *n.* **(-s, -)** caliber; sort.
Kalif *m.* **(-en, -en)** caliph.
Kalifornien *n.* California.
Kalium *n.* **(-s, 0)** potassium.
Kalk *m.* **(-[e]s, -e)** lime; (*gebrannter*) quicklime; (*gelöschter*) slaked lime; (*schwefelsaurer*) carbonate of lime.
Kalkablagerung *f.* calcareous deposit.
Kalkboden *m.* lime soil.
kalken *v.t.* to whitewash.
Kalkerde *f.* lime, quicklime.
kalkhaltig *a.* limy, calcareous.
Kalkmangel *m.* calcium deficiency; deficiency of lime.
Kalkofen *m.* limekiln.
Kalkstein *m.* limestone.
Kalkstickstoff *m.* calcium cyanamide.
Kalkül *n./m.* **(-s, -e)** calculation.
Kalkulation *f.* calculation.
kalkulieren *v.i.* & *t.* to calculate, to compute; *falsch* ~ to miscalculate.
kalkweiß *a.* white as chalk; deathly pale.
Kalorie *f.* **(-, -n)** calorie.
kalorien: ~arm *a.* low-calorie; **~reich** *a.* high-calorie.
kalt *a.* cold; frigid, indifferent; *~es Fieber,* ague; *~er Brand,* mortification; *das läßt mich* ~, that leaves me cold; **~stellen** ~*v.t.* to keep cold, to refrigerate.
Kaltblüter *m.* cold-blooded animal.
kaltblütig *a.* cool, cold-blooded; ruthless; ~ *adv.* in cold blood.
Kaltblütigkeit *f.* **(-, 0)** cold-bloodedness; presence of mind.
Kälte *f.* **(-, 0)** cold; coldness, frigidity.
kältebeständig *a.* resistant to cold.
kälteempfindlich *a.* sensitive to cold.
Kälteperiode *f.* cold spell.
Kaltmiete *f.* rent exclusive of heating charges.
Kaltschale *f.* **(-, -n)** cold soup.
kaltschnäuzig *a.* (*fam.*) insensitive; impertinent.
kaltsinnig *a.* indifferent, cold.
Kaltwasserheilanstalt *f.* hydropathic establishment.
Kaltwasserkur *f.* cold-water treatment.
Kalvinismus *m.* Calvinism.
Kalzium *n.* calcium.
Kambodscha *n.* **(-s, 0)** Cambodia.
Kambodschaner *m.* **(-s, -); Kambodschanerin** *f.* **(-, -nen); kambodschanisch** *a.* Cambodian.
Kamee *f.* **(-, -n)** cameo.
Kamel *n.* **(-[e]s, -e)** camel; (*fam.*) blockhead.
Kamelie *f.* **(-, -n)** camellia.
Kamera *f.* **(-, -s)** camera.
Kamerad *m.* **(-en, -en); Kameradin** *f.* **(-, -nen)** companion; comrade; mate.
Kameradschaft *f.* **(-, -en)** fellowship; comradeship.
kameradschaftlich *a.* & *adv.* friendly; companionable; comradely.
Kameraführung *f.* camerawork.
Kameramann *m.* cameraman.
Kameratasche *f.* camera case.
Kamerun *n.* Cameroon.
Kameruner *m.* **(-s, -); Kamerunerin** *f.* **(-, -nen)** Cameroonian.
Kamille *f.* **(-, -n)** camomile.
Kamin *m.* **(-[e]s, -e)** chimney; fireplace.
Kamin: ~feger, ~kehrer *m.* chimney sweep; **~sims** *m.* mantlepiece; **~vorleger** *m.* hearthrug; **~vorsetzer** *m.* fender.
Kamm *m.* **(-[e]s, Kämme)** comb; (*Hahn*) crest; (*Gebirge*) ridge.
kämmen *v.t.* to comb; (*Wolle*) to card.
Kammer *f.* **(-, -n)** room, chamber; (*pol.*) chamber.
Kammerdiener *m.* valet.
Kämmerer *m.* treasurer.
Kammerherr *m.* gentleman in waiting.
Kammerjäger *m.* exterminator.
Kammerkonzert *n.* chamber concert.
Kammermusik *f.* chamber music.
Kammerzofe *f.* chambermaid.
Kammgarn *n.* worsted yarn.
Kampagne *f.* campaign.
Kämpe *m.* **(-n, -n)** warrior, champion.
Kampf *m.* **(-[e]s, Kämpfe)** combat, fight, conflict; struggle; ~ *ums Dasein,* struggle for existence.
Kampbahn *f.* arena; ring.
kämpfen *v.t.* to combat, to fight; to struggle.
Kampfer *m.* **(-s, 0)** camphor.
Kämpfer *m.* **(-s, -); Kämpferin** *f.* **(-, -nen)** fighter; champion.

kämpferisch *a.* belligerent; aggressive.
Kämpfernatur *f.* fighter.
Kampfflugzeug *n.* (*mil.*) bomber.
Kampfgebiet *n.* battle arena; combat zone.
Kampfplatz *m.* battlefield; arena.
Kampfpreis *m.* prize.
Kampfrichter *m.* umpire, referee.
Kampfstoff *m.* (*mil.*) chemical warfare agent.
kampfunfähig *a.* disabled; out of action.
kampieren *v.i.* to camp, to camp out.
Kanada *n.* **(-s, 0)** Canada.
Kanadier *m.* **(-s, -); Kanadierin** *f.* **(-, -nen); kanadisch** *a.* Canadian.
Kanaille *f.* scoundrel.
Kanal *m.* **(-s, Kanauml;le)** canal; channel; sewer, drain; the Channel; **~deckel** *m.* manhole cover.
Kanalisation *f.* **(-, -en)** (*Stadt*) sewerage; (*Fluß*) canalization.
kanalisieren *v.t.* to drain; to canalize.
Kanapee *n.* **(-s, -s)** sofa.
Kanaren *pl.* the Canaries.
Kanarienvogel *m.* (*zool.*) canary.
Kanarische Inseln *pl.* the Canary Islands.
Kandare *f.* **(-, -n)** (horse) bit.
Kandelaber *m.* **(-s, -)** candelabrum; chandelier.
Kandidat *m.* **(-en, -en); Kandidatin** *f.* **(-, -nen)** candidate.
Kandidatur *f.* candidacy.
kandidieren *v.i.* to be a candidate for; to run; *in einem Wahlkreis ~*, to contest a seat, to campaign.
kandieren *v.t.* to candy.
Kandis *m.*; **~zucker** *m.* rock candy.
Känguruh *n.* **(-s, -s)** kangaroo.
Kaninchen *n.* **(-s, -)** rabbit; **~stall** *m.* rabbit hutch.
Kanne *f.* **(-, -n)** can; *Kaffee~*, coffeepot.
kannelieren *v.t.* to channel, to flute.
Kannibale *m.* **(-n, -n)** cannibal.
Kanon *m.* **(-s, -s)** (*mus.*) canon.
Kanonade *f.* **(-, -n)** bombardment.
Kanone *f.* **(-, -n)** cannon, gun.
Kanonen: ~boot *n.* gunboat; **~futter** *n.* cannon fodder; **~kugel** *f.* cannonball; **~rohr** *n.* barrel of a cannon; **~stiefel** *m.pl.* jackboots *pl.*
Kanonier *m.* **(-s, -e)** gunner.
kanonieren *v.t.* to cannonade.
kanonisch *a.* canonical.
Kantate *f.* **(-, -n)** cantata.
Kante *f.* **(-, -n)** corner, edge; brim; list, border.
kantig *a.* angular, edged.
Kantine *f.* **(-, -n)** canteen.
Kanton *m.* **(-s, -e)** canton, district.
kantonal *a.* cantonal.
Kantor *m.* **(-s, -en)** choirmaster and organist.
Kanu *n.* **(-s, -s)** canoe.
Kanüle *f.* **(-, -n)** (*med.*) cannula; needle.
Kanute *m.* **(-n, -n); Kanutin** *f.* **(-, -nen)** canoeist.
Kanzel *f.* **(-, -n)** pulpit; cockpit.
kanzerogen *a.* carcinogenic.
Kanzlei *f.* **(-, -en)** office.
Kanzlei: ~beamter *m.* clerk; **~diener** *m.* office attendant.
Kanzler *m.* **(-s, -)** chancellor; **~amt** *n.* Chancellery; **~kandidat** *m.* candidate for the chancellorship.
Kap *n.* **(-s, -s)** cape, promontory.
Kap. *Kapitel*, chapter, ch.
Kapaun *m.* **(-[e]s, -e)** capon.
Kapazität *f.* **(-, -en)** capacity; expert.
Kapelle *f.* **(-, -n)** chapel; (*mus.*) band.
Kapellmeister *m.* conductor; bandmaster.
Kaper *m.* **(-s, -)** privateer; (*Beere*) caper.
Kaperei *f.* **(-, -en)** privateering.
kapern *v.t.* to capture, to seize.
Kaperschiff *n.* privateer.
kapieren *v.t.* (*fam.*) to understand.
kapital *a.* (*fam.*) major, capital.
Kapital *n.* **(-es, -e & ien)** capital; principal.
Kapital: ~abgabe *f.* capital levy; **~anlage** *f.* investment; **~verbrechen** *n.* capital crime.
Kapitalismus *m.* capitalism.
Kapitalist *m.* **(-en, -en)** capitalist.
kapitalistisch *a.* capitalist(ic).
Kapitän *m.* **(-s, -e)** captain.
Kapitel *n.* **(-s, -)** chapter.
Kapitell *n.* **(-[e]s, -e)** (*arch.*) capital.
kapitulieren *v.i.* to capitulate.
Kaplan *m.* **(-es, Kapläne)** chaplain.
Kappe *f.* **(-, -n)** cap, hood.
kappen *v.t.* to cut; to cut back or off; to castrate.
Kapriole *f.* **(-, -n)** caper, leap.
kapriziös *a.* capricious.
Kapsel *f.* **(-, -n)** capsule.
kaputt *a.* broken; out of order.
Kapuze *f.* **(-, -n)** cowl, hood.
Kapuziner *m.* **(-s, -)** Capuchin (friar).
Karabiner *m.* **(-s, -)** carbine; rifle.
Karabinerhaken *m.* snaphook; spring hook, carabiner.
Karaffe *f.* **(-, -n)** carafe, decanter.
Karambolage *f.* **(-, -n)** crash; collision.
Karamel *m.* caramel.
Karamelle *f.* caramel, toffee.
Karat *n.* **(-[e]s, -e)** carat.
karätig *a.* *22 ~es Gold*, 22 carat gold.
Karavelle *f.* caravel.
Karawane *f.* **(-, -n)** caravan.
Karbid *n.* **(-s, -e)** (*chem.*) carbide.
Karbolsäure *f.* carbolic acid.
Karbunkel *m.* **(-s, -)** carbuncle.
Kardinal *m.* **(-s, -äle)** cardinal.
Kardiogramm *n.* cardiogram.
Karenzzeit *f.* waiting period.
Karfreitag *m.* Good Friday.
Karfunkel *m.* **(-s, -)** carbuncle.
karg *a.* meager; frugal; scant; sparse.
kargen *v.i.* to be parsimonious, stingy.
kärglich *a.* sparing, poor.
Karibik *f.* the Caribbean.
karibisch *a.* Caribbean.
kariert *a.* checkered; tartan.
Karies *f.* tooth decay; dental caries.
Karikatur *f.* **(-, -en)** cartoon, caricature; **~streifen** *m.* comic strip.
Karikaturist *m.* **(-en, -en)** (*pol.*) cartoonist.
karikieren *v.t.* to caricature.
kariös *a.* decayed.
karitativ *a.* charitable.
Karmeliter *m.* **(-s, -)** Carmelite.
Karmin *n.* **(-[e]s, 0)** crimson.
Karneval *m.* **(-s, -s & -e)** carnival.
Karnickel *n.* **(-s, -)** (*fam.*) rabbit, bunny; dummy.
Kärnten *n.* Carinthia.
Karo *n.* **(-[s], -s)** square; (*Spielkarten*) diamonds *pl.*
Karo: ~as *n.* ace of diamonds; **~bube** *m.* jack of diamonds; **~dame** *f.* queen of diamonds; **~könig** *m.* king of diamonds.

Karolinger *m.* Carolingian.
Karosserie *f.* (*mot.*) body work.
Karotin *n.* carotene.
Karotte *f.* **(-, -n)** carrot.
Karpaten *pl.* Carpathian Mountains.
Karpfen *m.* **(-s, -)** carp.
Karpfenteich *m.* carp pond; *er ist Hecht im ~,* he is the wolf in the sheepfold.
Karre *f.* **(-, -n); Karren** *m.* **(-s, -)** cart.
Karree *n.* **(-s, -s)** square.
karren *v.t.* to cart.
Karriere *f.* **(-, -n)** career.
Karrierist *m.* **(-en, -en); Karrieristin** *f.* **(-, -nen)** careerist.
Karsamstag *m.* Holy Saturday.
Karst *m.* **(-[e]s, -e)** karst.
Kartätsche *f.* **(-, -n)** canister-shot, grape-shot.
Kartause *f.* **(-, -n)** Carthusian monastery.
Kartäuser *m.* **(-s, -)** Carthusian friar.
Karte *f.* **(-, -n)** card; map; chart; ticket; *Speise~* menu; *ein Spiel ~n,* pack of cards; *alles auf eine ~ setzen,* to stake everything on one throw.
Kartei *f.* **(-, -en)** cardfile index.
Kartell *n.* **(-s, -e)** cartel.
Karten: ~haus *n.* house of cards; **~legerin, ~schlägerin** *f.* fortune-teller; **~maßstab** *m.* map scale; **~netz** *n.* grid; **~spiel** *n.* game at cards; pack of cards; **~vorverkauf** *m.* advance ticket sale.
Karthager *m.* Carthaginian.
Karthago *n.* Carthage.
Kartoffel *f.* **(-, -n)** potato; *~n in der Schale, Pell~n,* potatoes in jackets; **~käfer** *m.* Colorado beetle; **~püree** *n.* mashed potatoes; *Brat~ n.* home-fried potatoes; *Salz~ n.* boiled potatoes; *geröstete ~streifen* (*pommes frites*), French fries.
Kartograph *m.* **(-en, -en); Kartographin** *f.* **(-, -nen)** cartographer.
Kartographie *f.* cartography.
Karton *m.* **(-s, -s)** cardboard; cardboard box.
kartonieren *v.t.* to bind in board.
Kartothek *f.* **(-, -en)** card index; filing cabinet.
Karussell *n.* **(-[e]s, -s & -e)** merry-go-round; carousel.
Karwoche *f.* **(-, 0)** Holy Week.
Karzer *m.* **(-s, -)** prison.
karzinogen *a.* carcinogenic.
Karzinom *n.* **(-s, -e)** carcinoma.
Kaschemme *f.* (*pej.*) dive, joint.
kaschieren *v.t.* to conceal.
Kaschmir *m.* **(-s, 0)** cashmere.
Käse *m.* **(-s, -)** cheese.
Käsebrot *n.* cheese sandwich.
Kasematte *f.* **(-, -n)** (*hist.*) casemate.
Käseplatte *f.* assorted cheeses.
Käserei *f.* cheese dairy.
Kaserne *f.* **(-, -n)** barracks *pl.*; *unter ~narrest,* confined to barracks.
käsig *a.* cheesy.
Kasino *n.* (*mil.*) officers' mess; casino.
Kaskade *f.* cascade.
Kaskoversicherung *f.* comprehensive insurance.
Kasper *m.* **(-s, -)** clown, fool.
Kasperletheater *n.* Punch and Judy show.
Kaspisches Meer *n.* Caspian Sea.
Kasse *f.* **(-, -n)** cash register; box office; cash, ready money; *gut/schlecht bei ~ sein,* to have plenty/be short of money.
Kassen: ~arzt *m.* health-plan doctor; **~bestand** *m.* cash in hand; **~patient** *m.* health-plan patient.
Kassette *f.* **(-, -n)** box; case; cassette.
Kassettenrekorder *m.* cassette recorder.
Kassier[er] *m.* **(-s, -); Kassiererin** *f.* **(-, -nen)** cashier.
kassieren *v.t.* to take in (money); to cashier; (*Urteil*) to quash.
Kastagnette *f.* **(-, -n)** castanet.
Kastanie *f.* **(-, -n)** chestnut.
Kästchen *n.* **(-s, -)** little box.
Kaste *f.* **(-, -n)** caste.
kasteien *v.t.* to chastise; to mortify (the flesh).
Kastell *n.* **(-s, -e)** fort; castle.
Kasten *m.* **(-s, Kästen)** chest, case, box.
Kastrat *m.* **(-en, -en)** eunuch; castrate.
kastrieren *v.t.* to castrate.
Kasuistik *f.* **(-, 0)** casuistry.
Kasus *m.* **(-, -)** case.
Katakomben *f.pl.* catacomb.
Katalog *m.* **(-[e]s, -e)** catalog.
katalogisieren *v.t.* to catalog.
Katalysator *m.* **(-s, -en)** (*chem.*) catalyst; catalytic converter.
Katapult *n./m.* catapult.
Katarakt *m.* rapids; cataract.
Katarrh *m.* **(-s, -e)** catarrh, cold.
Kataster *n.* **(-s, -)** land register.
Katasteramt *n.* land registry.
katastrophal *a.* catastrophic.
Katastrophe *f.* **(-, -n)** catastrophe; disaster.
Katastrophenalarm *m.* emergency alert.
Katastrophendienst *m.* emergency service.
Katastrophengebiet *n.* disaster area.
Katechismus *m.* **(-, -men)** catechism.
Kategorie *f.* **(-, -n)** category.
kategorisch *a.* categorical.
kategorisieren *v.t.* to categorize.
Kater *m.* **(-s, -)** tomcat; (*fam.*) hangover.
kath. *katholisch,* Catholic, C(ath).
Katheder *n.* **(-s, -)** lectern.
Kathedrale *f.* **(-, -n)** cathedral.
Katheter *m.* **(-s, -)** (*med.*) catheter.
Kathode *f.* **(-, -n)** (*elek.*) cathode; **~nstrahlen,** cathode rays.
Katholik *m.* **(-en, -en); Katholikin** *f.* **(-, -nen)** Roman-Catholic.
katholisch *a.* Roman Catholic.
Katholizismus *m.* Catholicism.
Kattun *m.* **(-[e]s, -e)** calico, print.
katzbuckeln *v.i.* to cringe.
Katze *f.* **(-, -n)** cat; *die ~ im Sack kaufen,* to buy a pig in a poke.
Katzenjammer *m.* hangover.
Katzenklo *n.* cat box.
Katzensprung *m.* (*fig.*) a stone's throw; *nur einen ~ entfernt,* just around the corner.
Katzenstreu *f.* cat litter.
Katzenwäsche *f.* (*fig.*) a lick and a promise.
Kauderwelsch *n.* **(-s, 0)** gibberish.
kauen *v.t.* to chew.
kauern *v.i.* to cower, to crouch.
Kauf *m.* **(-[e]s, Käufe)** purchase, bargain.
kaufen *v.t.* to buy, to purchase.
Käufer *m.* **(-s, -); Käuferin** *f.* **(-, -nen)** buyer, customer.
Kauffrau *f.* businesswoman.
Kaufhaus *n.* department store.
Kaufkraft *f.* purchasing power.
Kaufleute *pl.* merchants; shopkeepers.
käuflich *a.* for sale; venal.

Kaufmann *m.* businessman, merchant; shopkeeper.
kaufmännisch *a.* mercantile, commercial.
Kaufvertrag *m.* contract of sale.
Kaugummi *n.* **(-s, -s)** chewing gum.
Kaukasus *m.* Caucasus.
Kaulquappe *f.* **(-, -n)** tadpole.
kaum *adv.* scarcely, hardly.
kausal *a.* causal.
Kausalität *f.* **(-, -en)** causality.
kaustisch *a.* caustic, sarcastic.
Kautabak *m.* chewing tobacco.
Kaution *f.* **(-, -en)** security, bail.
Kautschuk *m.* **(-s, -e)** rubber.
Kauz *m.* **(-es, Käuze)** screech-owl; (*fig.*) oddball.
kauzig *a.* odd, queer; funny.
Kavalier *m.* **(-es, -e)** cavalier, gentleman.
Kavallerie *f.* **(-, -n)** cavalry.
Kavallerist *m.* **(-en, -en)** horseman.
Kaviar *m.* **(-s, 0)** caviar(e).
KB *Kilobyte,* kilobyte, KB.
keck *a.* bold, daring; saucy, pert.
Kegel *m.* **(-s, -)** cone; *pl.* bowling pins; *Kegelschieben,* to go bowling; *Kind und ~,* lock, stock, and barrel.
Kegelbahn *f.* bowling alley.
kegelförmig *a.* conical, cone shaped.
kegeln *v.i.* to bowl.
Kegelschnitt *m.* conic section.
Kehle *f.* **(-, -n)** throat, gorge; *aus voller ~,* at the top of one's voice.
kehlig *a.* guttural; throaty.
Kehlkopf *m.* larynx.
Kehlkopfspiegel *m.* laryngoscope.
Kehllaut *m.* gutteral sound.
Kehraus *m.* **(-, 0)** last dance; (*fig.*) end.
Kehre *f.* **(-, -n)** turn, bend.
kehren *v.t.* to sweep, to brush; to turn; ~ *v.r.* (*an etwas*) to mind (sth.); *vor seiner eignen Tür ~,* to mind one's own business; *kehrt!* (*mil.*) about face!
Kehricht *m.* & *n.* **(-s, 0)** sweepings; garbage.
Kehrreim *m.* refrain.
Kehrseite *f.* reverse, back; seamy side.
kehrtmachen *v.i.* to turn back.
keifen *v.i.* to scold; to nag.
Keil *m.* **(-[e]s, -e)** wedge; (*mech.*) key.
Keilerei *f.* **(-, -en)** (*sl.*) free fight, row.
keilförmig *a.* wedge-shaped; cuneiform.
Keil: ~kissen *n.* wedge-shaped bolster; **~riemen** *m.* (*mech.*) drivebelt; fanbelt; **~schrift** *f.* cuneiform characters.
Keim *m.* **(-[e]s, -e)** germ; bud, sprout; *im ~ ersticken,* to nip in the bud.
Keim: ~blatt *n.* cotyledon; seed leaf; **~drüse** *f.* gonad.
keimen *v.i.* to germinate, to bud; to sprout.
keimfrei *a.* sterile, aseptic.
Keimling *m.* **(-s, -e)** embryo.
keimtötend *a.* germicidal; antiseptic.
Keimträger *m.* germ carrier.
Keimzelle *f.* germ cell; (*fig.*) nucleus.
kein (keiner, keine, kein[e]s) *a.* no, no one, not any, none.
keinerlei *a.* no... at all; no... whatsoever.
keinesfalls *adv.* on no account.
keineswegs *adv.* by no means.
keinmal *adv.* not once, never.
Keks *m., n.* **(-es, -e)** biscuit; cookie.
Kelch *m.* **(-[e]s, -e)** goblet; chalice; (*bot.*) calyx; **~blatt** *n.* sepal.
Kelle *f.* **(-, -n)** trowel; ladle; (*rail.*) signaling disk.
Keller *m.* **(-s, -)** cellar, basement.
Kellerassel *f.* sow bug.
Kellerei *f.* **(-, -en)** winery.
Kellergeschoß *n.* basement.
Kellner *m.* **(-s, -)** waiter.
Kellnerin *f.* **(-, -nen)** waitress.
kellnern *v.i.* to work as waiter/waitress.
Kelte *m.* Celt.
Kelter *f.* **(-, -n)** winepress.
keltern *v.t.* to tread (grapes), to press.
keltisch *a.* celtic.
Kenia *n.* **(-s, 0)** Kenya.
Kenianer *m.* **(-s, -); Kenianerin** *f.* **(-, -nen)** Kenyan.
kennbar *a.* recognizable, distinct.
kennen *v.t.ir.* to know; to be acquainted with; **~lernen,** to become acquainted with, to get introduced to.
Kenner *m.* **(-s, -)** connoisseur, expert, authority.
Kennerblick *m.* expert eye.
Kennkarte *f.* identity card.
kenntlich *a.* recognizable.
Kenntlichmachung *f.* labeling.
Kenntnis *f.* **(-, -se)** knowledge; *~ von etwas nehmen,* to take note or cognizance of sth.; *in ~ setzen,* to inform; *ohne ~ von,* unaware of; *zur ~nahme,* for information.
kenntnisreich *a.* knowledgable, well-informed, learned.
Kennwort *n.* motto; password.
Kennzeichen *n.* mark, badge, label; characteristic, criterion.
kennzeichnen *v.t.* to label, to mark; to characterize.
kentern *v.i.* to capsize.
Keramik *f.* **(-, -en)** ceramics *pl.;* pottery.
Kerbe *f.* **(-, -n)** notch.
Kerbel *m.* **(-s, 0)** (*bot.*) chervil.
kerben *v.t.* to notch, to indent.
Kerker *m.* **(-s, -)** prison, jail, dungeon.
Kerl *m.* **(-[e]s, -e)** fellow; chap.
Kern *m.* **(-[e]s, -e)** kernel; stone; nucleus; (*fig.*) core.
kerngesund *a.* thoroughly healthy.
kernig *a.* pithy, solid.
Kernkraft *f.* nuclear power.
Kernkraft: ~gegner *m.* opponent of nuclear power; **~werk** *n.* nuclear power plant.
kernlos *a.* seedless.
Kernobst *n.* stone fruit.
Kernphysik *f.* nuclear physics.
Kernteilung *f.* nuclear fission.
Kerntruppen *pl.* crack troops.
Kernwaffe *f.* **(-, -n)** nuclear weapon.
kernwaffenfrei *a.* nuclear-free.
Kerosin *n.* **(-s, 0)** kerosene.
Kerze *f.* **(-, -n)** candle.
kerzeng[e]rade *a.* (*fig.*) bolt-upright.
Kerzenhalter *m.* candlestick.
Kerzenlicht *n.* candlelight.
Kerzenständer *m.* candlestick.
kess *a.* pert; jaunty, cheeky.
Kessel *m.* **(-s, -)** kettle, cauldron; hollow; *Dampf~,* boiler; (*mil.*) pocket.
Kesselstein *m.* scale, fur.
Kesseltreiben *n.* hunt; witchhunt.

Kette *f.* **(-, -n)** chain; necklace; (*Weberei*) warp; (*mil.*) track; *Berg*~ range.
ketten *v.t.* to chain, to bind.
Ketten: ~brücke *f.* suspension bridge; **~glied** *n.* (chain) link; **~hemd** *n.* coat of chain mail; **~hund** *m.* watchdog; **~rauchen** *n.* chain-smoking.
Ketzer *m.* **(-s, -); Ketzerin** *f.* **(-, -nen)** heretic.
Ketzerei *f.* **(-, -en)** heresy.
ketzerisch *a.* heretical.
keuchen *v.i.* to pant, to puff.
Keuchhusten *m.* whooping cough.
Keule *f.* **(-, -n)** club; leg (of mutton, etc.).
keusch *a.* chaste, pure.
Keuschheit *f.* **(-/0)** chastity.
Kffr. *Kauffrau,* businesswoman.
Kfm. *Kaufmann,* businessman.
Kfz *Kraftfahrzeug,* motor vehicle.
kg *Kilogramm,* kilogramme, kg.
KG *Kommanditgesellschaft,* limited partnership.
kgl. *königlich,* royal.
Kibbuz *m.* **(-, -im & -e)** kibbutz.
Kichererbse *f.* chickpea.
kichern *v.i.* to giggle.
kicken *v.t.* (*fam.*) to kick; ~ *v.i.* to play soccer.
kidnappen *v.t.* to kidnap.
Kiebitz *m.* **(-[e]s, -e)** lapwing, peewit; looker-on.
Kiefer *f.* **(-, -n)** pine (tree); ~ *m.* **(-s, -)** jawbone.
Kiefernholz *n.* pinewood.
Kiefernzapfen *m.* pinecone.
Kieferorthopädie *f.* orthodontics.
kieken *v.i.* (*fam.*) to look.
Kiel *m.* **(-[e]s, -e)** quill; (*nav.*) keel.
Kielwasser *n.* wake.
Kieme *f.* **(-, -n)** gill.
Kies *m.* **(-es, -e)** gravel.
Kiesel *m.* **(-s, -)** flint, pebble.
Kiesgrube *f.* (*fam.*) gravel pit.
kiffen *v.i.* to smoke pot.
kikeriki cock-a-doodle-doo.
killen *v.t.* to do in, to kill.
Kilo: ~gramm *n.* kilogram; **~hertz** *n.* kilohertz.
Kilometer *m.* kilometer; **~geld** *n.* mileage allowance; **~stand** *m.* mileage reading; **~zähler** *m.* odometer.
Kind *n.* **(-[e]s, -er)** child; *kleines* ~, infant, baby; *an* ~*es Statt annehmen,* to adopt.
Kindbett *n.* childbed; ~*fieber n.* puerperal fever.
Kinderarzt *m.;* **Kinderärztin** *f.* pediatrician.
Kinderbett *n.* crib.
Kinderei *f.* **(-, -en)** childishness; childish prank.
kinderfeindlich *a.* hostile to children; anti-children.
kinderfreundlich *a.* fond of children; suitable for children.
Kinderfürsorge *f.* child welfare.
Kindergarten *m.* nursery school.
Kindergärtnerin *f.* preschool teacher.
Kinderhort *m.* day-care center.
Kinderkrippe *f.* day-care for infants.
Kinderlähmung *f.* infantile paralysis; polio(myelitis).
kinderleicht *a.* very easy.
kinderlos *a.* childless.
Kindermädchen *n.* nanny.
Kindersicherung *f.* childproof lock.
Kinderspiel *n.* child's play.
Kindersterblichkeit *f.* infant mortality.
Kinderstube *f.* nursery; manners.
Kindertagesstätte *f.* daycare center.
Kinderwagen *m.* baby carriage.
Kinderzulage *f.* family allowance.
Kindes: ~alter *n.* childhood, infancy; **~entführung** *f.* kidnapping, child abduction; **~mißhandlung** *f.* child abuse; **~tötung** *f.* infanticide.
kindgemäß *a.* suitable for children.
Kindheit *f.* **(-, 0)** childhood.
kindisch *a.* childish.
kindlich *a.* infantile; childlike.
Kindskopf *m.* (*fam.*) (big) child.
Kindtaufe *f.* christening.
Kinetik *f.* kinetics.
Kinkerlitzchen *n. pl.* trifles.
Kinn *n.* **(-[e]s, -e)** chin.
Kinn: ~backen *m.* jaw(bone); **~haken** *m.* (*sp.*) uppercut; **~lade** *f.* jaw.
Kino *n.* **(-s, -s)** movie theater, cinema.
Kino: ~karte *f.* movie ticket; **~kasse** *f.* movie box-office; **~programm** *n.* movie guide.
Kippe *f.* **(-, -n)** stub, butt; seesaw; dump (garbage).
kippen *v.t. & i.* to tilt, to tip over.
Kipper *m.* **(-s, -)** dump truck.
Kippfenster *n.* tilting window.
Kipp: ~frequenz *f.* (*elek.*) sweep frequency; **~schalter** *m.* (*elek.*) toggle switch.
Kirche *f.* **(-, -n)** church.
Kirchen: ~buch *n.* parish register; **~geschichte** *f.* ecclesiastical history; **~lied** *n.* hymn; **~raub** *m.* sacrilege; **~recht** *n.* canon law; **~schiff** *n.* nave; **~staat** *m.* Papal States *pl.;* **~steuer** *f.* church tax; **~stuhl** *m.* pew; **~vater** *m.* Father (of the church).
kirchlich *a.* ecclesiastical.
Kirchturm *m.* steeple; **~spitze** *f.* spire.
Kirchweih *f.* parish fair.
Kirmes *f.* **(-, -sen)** village fair.
kirre *a.* tame.
Kirsch: ~baum *m.* cherry-tree; **~blüte** *f.* cherry-blossom; **~branntwein** *m.* cherry-brandy.
Kirsche *f.* **(-, -n)** cherry.
Kirschkern *m.* cherry stone.
Kirschwasser *n.* kirsch.
Kissen *n.* **(-s, -)** cushion, pillow.
Kissen: ~bezug *m.* pillowcase; cushion cover; **~schlacht** *f.* pillow fight.
Kiste *f.* **(-, -n)** box, chest, case.
Kitsch *m.,* **(-es, 0)** trash, kitsch.
kitschig *a.* kitschy.
Kitt *m.* **(-[e]s, -e)** putty; glue.
Kittchen *n.* **(-s, -)** (*fam.*) jail, clink, jug.
Kittel *m.* **(-s, -)** smock.
kitten *v.t.* to cement; (*fig.*) to patch up.
Kitz *n.* **(-es, -e)** *Reh*~ fawn; *Ziegen*~, *Gemsen*~ kid.
Kitzel *m.* **(-s, 0)** tickle, itch; thrill.
kitzeln *v.t.* to tickle.
Kitzler *m.* clitoris.
kitzlig *a.* ticklish; (*fig.*) difficult.
k.k. *kaiserlich-königlich,* imperial and royal.
KKW *Kernkraftwerk,* nuclear power station.
Kl. *Klasse,* class, cl.
Klacks *m.* dollop; blob.
Kladde *f.* **(-, -n)** rough copy; scribbling book; (*com.*) log.
Kladderadatsch *m.* **(-es, 0)** crash, clash.
klaffen *v.i.* to gape, to yawn.
kläffen *v.i.* to yap.

Kläffer *m.* **(-s, -)** yapping dog; (*fig.*) brawler, wrangler.
Klafter *f.* **(-, -n)** fathom; (*Holz*) cord of wood.
Klage *f.* **(-, -n)** complaint; lament; (*gerichtliche*) suit, action; charge.
klagen *v.i.* to complain, to lament; (*jur.*) to take action, to sue.
Kläger *m.* **(-s, -); Klägerin** *f.* **(-, -nen)** plaintiff; prosecuting party; petitioner.
Klageschrift *f.* statement of claim; writ.
kläglich *a.* lamentable; pitiful.
Klamauk *m.* **(-s, -e)** fuss, hullabaloo.
klamm *a.* numb, clammy.
Klamm *f.* **(-e,-en)** narrow gorge.
Klammer *f.* **(-, -n)** clip; staple; grip; brace; cramp, peg; bracket, parenthesis; paper clip, clamp.
klammern *v.t.* to clip; to staple; to peg; ~ *v.r.* to cling (to).
klammheimlich *a.* on the quiet.
Klamotte *f.* **(-, -n)** rags, clobber; junk; slapstick movie.
Klang *m.* **(-[e]s, Klänge)** sound; ring; tone.
Klangfarbe *f.* timbre.
Klangfülle *f.* sonority.
klanglich *a.* tonal.
klanglos *a.* toneless.
klangvoll *a.* sonorous, rich.
Klappbett *n.* folding bed.
Klappe *f.* **(-, -n)** flap; valve; (*mus.*) key; (*fig.*) mouth.
klappen *v.i.* to clap, to clatter; (*fig.*) to go well, to tally.
Klappentext *m.* blurb.
Klapper *f.* **(-, -n)** rattle.
klapp[e]rig *a.* rattling; shaky.
klappern *v.i.* to clatter, to rattle; (*Zähne*) to chatter.
Klapperschlange *f.* rattlesnake.
Klappfenster *n.* top-hung window.
Klappmesser *n.* jackknife.
Klappsitz *m.* folding seat.
Klappstuhl *m.* folding chair.
Klapptisch *m.* folding table.
Klappverdeck *n.* (*mot.*) folding top.
Klaps *m.* **(-es, -e)** flap, smack.
Klapsmühle *f.* (*sl.*) nut house.
klar *a.* clear; (*Wasser*) limpid; evident.
Kläranlage *f.* sewage (purification) plant.
Klärbecken *n.* settling basin.
klarblickend clear-sighted.
klären *v.t.* to clear; to clarify; to purify.
klargehen *v.t.st.* to be all right.
Klarheit *f.* **(-, -en)** clearness; evidence.
Klarinette *f.* **(-, -n)** clarinet.
klarkommen *v.i.st.* to manage, to cope.
klarsehen *v.t.st.* to understand.
Klarsicht: ~folie *f.* plastic wrap; **~packung** *f.* transparent pack.
klarspülen *v.t.* to rinse.
klarstellen *v.t.* to clear up.
Klarstellung *f.* clarification.
Klasse *f.* **(-, -n)** class, form; order, rank; grade.
Klassen: ~arbeit *f.* (class) test; **~kamerad** *m.*, **~kameradin** *f.* classmate; **~kampf** *m.* class struggle; **~lehrer** *m.*, **~lehrerin** *f.* homeroom teacher.
klassenlos *a.* classless.
klassifizieren *v.t.* to classify, to break down.
Klassifizierung *f.* **(-, -en)** classification.
Klassik *f.* (*Antike*) classical antiquity; classical period/age.
Klassiker *m.* **(-s, -)** classic (author).
klassisch *a.* classical.
Klassizismus *m.* classicism.
klassizistisch *a.* classicistic.
klatsch *i.* crack! smack!
Klatsch *m.* **(-es, -e)** slap; (*fig.*) gossip; scandal.
Klatschbase *f.* gossip, chatterbox.
klatschen *v.i.* to smack; to flap; to splash; (*fig.*) to gossip; *Beifall* ~, to applaud.
Klatscher *m.* **(-s, -)** clapper.
Klatscherei *f.* **(-, -en)** chitchat, gossip.
klatschhaft *a.* talkative, gossiping.
Klatsch: ~spalte *f.* gossip column; **~tante** *f.*, **~weib** *n.* (*pej.*) gossiper.
klauben *v.t.* to pick, to carp at.
Klaue *f.* **(-, -n)** claw, talon, paw; clutch.
klauen *v.t.* to steal.
Klause *f.* **(-, -n)** cell hermitage.
Klausel *f.* **(-, -n)** clause, proviso.
Klausner *m.* **(-s, -)** hermit, recluse.
Klausurarbeit *f.* examination; test paper.
Klausurtagung *n.* closed meeting.
Klaviatur *f.* **(-, -en)** keyboard.
Klavier *n.* **(-[e]s, -e)** piano.
Klavier: ~auszug *m.* piano arrangement; **~begleitung** *f.* piano accompaniment; **~hocker** *m.* piano stool; **~konzert** *n.* piano concerto; piano recital; **~sonate** *f.* piano sonata; **~spieler** *m.*, **~spielerin** *f.* pianist; piano player; **~stimmer** *m.* piano tuner; **~stunde** *f.* piano lesson; **~unterricht** *m.* piano lessons.
Klebeband *n.* adhesive tape.
Klebefolie *f.* adhesive film.
kleben *v.t.* to paste, to glue, to stick; ~ *v.i.* to adhere, to stick.
Kleber *m.* **(-s, -)** glue.
kleb[e]rig *a.* sticky, viscous; glutinous.
Klebstoff *m.* adhesive, glue.
Klebstreifen *m.* adhesive tape.
kleckern *v.i.* to spill; to drip; to splash.
kleckerweise *adv.* (*fam.*) in dribs and drabs.
Klecks *m.* **(-es, -e)** blot, ink spot, staining, blob.
klecksen *v.i.* to blot, to blotch; to daub.
Klee *m.* **(-s, 0)** clover.
Kleeblatt *n.* clover leaf; (*fig.*) trio.
Kleid *n.* **(-[e]s, -er)** garment; gown, dress; coat; **~er** *pl.* clothes *pl.*
kleiden *v.t.* to dress, to clothe; (*passen*) to fit, to become; ~ *v.r.* to dress.
Kleiderablage *f.* coat rack.
Kleiderbügel *m.* hanger.
Kleiderbürste *f.* clothes brush.
Kleidergröße *f.* size.
Kleiderschrank *m.* wardrobe.
Kleiderständer *m.* clothes tree; coat stand.
Kleiderstange *f.* clothes rail.
kleidsam *a.* becoming.
Kleidung *f.* **(-, -en)** clothing, dress, clothes *pl.*
Kleidungsstück *n.* garment; **~e** *pl.* wearing apparel.
Kleie *f.* **(-, -n)** bran.
klein *a.* little; small; petty, mean; *~es Geld*, small change; *kurz und ~*, in splinters; ~ *adv.* (*Gas*) *~ drehen*, to turn down.
Kleinbahn *f.* local railway, narrow-gauge railway.
Kleinbuchstabe *m.* lowercase letter.
Kleinbürger petty bourgeois.
Kleinbürgertum *n.* petite bourgeoisie.

Kleine *m./f.* **(-n, -n)** little boy; little girl.
Kleinfamilie *f.* nuclear family.
Kleingeld *n.* small change.
Kleinhandel *m.* retail trade.
Kleinheit *f.* smallness; small size.
Kleinholz *n.* firewood.
Kleinigkeit *f.* **(-, -en)** small matter, trifle, detail.
Kleinigkeitskrämer *m.* pettifogger, stickler.
kleinkariert *a.* small-checked; (*fig.*) narrow-minded.
Kleinkind *n.* infant.
kleinlaut *a.* subdued, disheartened.
kleinlich *a.* mean, petty, fussy.
kleinmütig *a.* faint-hearted, timid.
Kleinod *n.* **(-[e]s, -e)** jewel, treasure.
Kleinstaat *m.* small state.
Kleinstadt *f.* small town.
kleinstädtisch *a.* provincial.
Kleinstlebewesen *n.* microorganism.
kleinstmöglich *a.* smallest possible.
Kleinwagen *m.* small car.
kleinwüchsig *a.* small, short.
Kleister *m.* **(-s, 0)** paste.
kleistern *v.t.* to paste.
Klemme *f.* **(-, -n)** clamp; straits *pl.*, fix, difficulty.
klemmen *v.t.* to pinch; to squeeze; ~ *v.r.* to jam one's finger.
Klempner *m.* **(-s, -)** plumber, tinner.
Klepper *m.* **(-s, -)** nag, hack.
Kleptomane *m.* **(-n, -n); Kleptomanin** *f.* **(-, -nen)** kleptomaniac.
Kleptomanie *f.* kleptomania.
klerikal *a.* clerical.
Kleriker *m.* **(-s, -)** clergyman, priest.
Klerus *m.* clergy.
Klette *f.* **(-, -n)** bur.
klettern *v.i.* to climb, to clamber.
Kletterpflanze *f.* climber, creeper.
Klettverschluß *m.* Velcro.
klicken *v.i.* to click.
Klient *m.* **(-en, -en); Klientin** *f.* **(-, -nen)** client.
Klima *n.* **(-s, -s & -te)** climate.
Klimaanlage *f.* air-conditioning.
Klimakterium *n.* menopause, climacteric.
klimatisch *a.* climatic.
klimatisieren *v.t.* to air-condition.
Klimatologie *f.* climatology.
klimmen *v.i.st. (s)* to climb.
Klimmzug *m.* **(-s, -züge)** pull-up.
klimpern *v.i.* to jingle; to strum.
Klinge *f.* **(-, -n)** blade; sword.
Klingel *f.* **(-, -n)** doorbell.
Klingelbeutel *m.* (church) offering, collection bag.
Klingelknopf *m.* bell-push.
klingeln *v.i.* to ring (the bell), to tinkle; **es klingelt,** the doorbell is ringing.
Klingelschnur *f.* bellpull.
klingen *v.t.st.* to ring, to clink, to sound.
Klinik *f.* **(-, -en)** hospital, clinic.
Klinikum *n.* clinic complex.
klinisch *a.* clinical.
Klinke *f.* **(-, -n)** latch, door-handle.
Klinker *m.* **(-s, -)** clinker.
klipp, *adv.* (*fam.*) ~ *und klar* quite plainly.
Klippe *f.* **(-, -n)** reef, rock.
klirren *v.i.* to clink, to clatter, to crash.
Klischee *n.* **(-s, -s)** cliché; (stereotype) block.
Klistier *n.* **(-s, -e)** enema; **~spritze** *f.* enema syringe.
Klitoris *f.* **(-, -)** clitoris.
klitzeklein *a.* teeny-weeny.
Klo *n.* **(-s, -s)** (*fam.*) toilet, john.
Kloake *f.* **(-, -n)** sewer.
klobig *a.* coarse, rude, clumsy.
klopfen *v.t.* to knock, to beat, to rap, to tap.
Klopfer *m.* **(-s, -)** knocker, beater, rapper.
Klöppel *m.* **(-s, -)** clapper; drumstick; bobbin, lace-bone.
klöppeln *v.t.* to make bone lace.
Klöppelspitze *f.* bone lace.
Klöppler *m.* **(-s, -), Klöpplerin** *f.* **(-, -nen)** lace maker.
Klops *m.* **(-es, -e)** mincemeat dumpling.
Klosett *n.* **([e]s, -e & -s)** toilet.
Klosettbrille *f.* **(-, -n)** toilet seat.
Kloss *m.* **(-es, Klösse)** clod; dumpling.
Kloster *n.* **(-s, Klöster)** cloister; monastery; convent, nunnery.
Klosterbruder *m.* friar.
Klosterfrau *f.* nun.
klösterlich *a.* monastic.
Klosterschule *f.* convent-school.
Klotz *m.* **(-es, Klötze)** block, log, trunk.
klotzig *a.* loglike; rude; enormous.
Klub *m.* **(-s, -s)** club.
Kluft *f.* **(-, Klüfte)** chasm, ravine, gulf.
klug *a.* prudent; intelligent; clever; sharp; *aus etwas nicht ~ werden,* to be puzzled by sth.
klugerweise *adv.* wisely.
Klugheit *f.* **(-, 0)** prudence, shrewdness.
Klugscheißer *m.* (*vulg.*) smart ass.
Klumpen *m.* **(-s, -)** lump, clod.
Klumpfuß *m.* club foot.
klumpig *a.* lumpy, clotted.
Klüngel *m.* **(-s, 0)** clique.
Klunker *m.* **(-s, -)** (*fam.*) rock (jewels).
km *Kilometer,* kilometer, km.
knabbern *v.t. & i.* to nibble, to gnaw.
Knabe *m.* **(-n, -n)** boy, lad.
Knabenalter *n.* boyhood.
knabenhaft *a.* boyish.
Knäckebrot *n.* crispbread.
knacken *v.t.* to crack; ~ *v.i.* to break.
Knacker *m.* **(-s, -)** *alter ~* (*fam.*) old fogy.
knackig *a.* crisp; crunchy; (*fig.*) delectable.
Knall *m.* **(-[e]s, -e)** clap, crack; bang, detonation; *~ und Fall,* all of a sudden.
Knallbonbon *m./n.* cracker.
Knalleffekt *m.* stage effect.
knallen *v.t.* to crack (a whip); ~ *v.i.* to detonate, to pop.
knallig *a.* loud; gaudy.
Knallkopf *m.* (*fam.*) jerk.
knallrot *a.* glaring red.
knapp *a.* close, tight, narrow; scarce, scanty; (*Stil*) concise; *jn. ~ halten,* to keep sb. short.
Knappe *m.* **(-n, -n)** page; miner.
Knappheit *f.* **(-, -en)** shortage; scarcity.
knarren *v.i.* to creak, to jar.
Knast *m.* **(-s, Knäste)** (*fam.*) clink; jug; prison.
knattern *v.i.* to rattle, to clatter.
Knäuel *m./n.* **(-s, -)** clue, ball of thread; throng.
Knauf *m.* **(-[e]s, Knäufe)** head, knob.
Knauser *m.* **(-s, -)** miser, tightwad.
Knauserei *f.* **(-, -en)** stinginess.
knauserig *a.* stingy, close.

knausern *v.i.* to be stingy.
knautschen *v.t. & i.* to crumple; to crease; to get creased.
Knebel *m.* **(-s, -)** gag.
knebeln *v.t.* to gag; to muzzle.
Knecht *m.* **(-[e]s, -e)** farm hand; (*fig.*) slave.
knechten *v.t.* to enslave; to oppress.
knechtisch *a.* slavish, servile.
Knechtschaft *f.* **(-, 0)** servitude, slavery.
kneifen *v.t.st.* to pinch, to nip.
Kneifer *m.* **(-s, -)** pince-nez.
Kneifzange *f.* pincers *pl.*
Kneipe *f.* **(-, -n)** tavern; pub; bar.
kneten *v.t.* to knead; to massage; to mold.
Knick *m.* **(-[e]s, -e)** sharp bend; kink; crease.
knicken *v.t.* to snap; to bend; to crease.
Knickerei *f.* **(-, -en)** stinginess.
knickerig *a.* stingy.
knickern *v.i.* to be stingy.
Knicks *m.* **(-es, -e)** curtsy.
knicksen *v.i.* to curtsy.
Knie *n.* **(-s, -)** knee.
Kniebeuge *f.* kneebend.
Kniebeugung *f.* genuflection.
kniefällig *a.* upon one's knees.
Kniehose *f.* breeches, knickerbockers, plus fours *pl.*
Kniekehle *f.* **(-, -n)** hollow of the knee.
knien *v.i.* to kneel.
Kniescheibe *f.* kneecap.
Kniff *m.* **(-[e]s, -e)** pinch; trick, dodge.
kniffig *a.* clever, shrewd.
knifflig *a.* tricky; intricate.
knipsen *v.i.* to snap one's fingers; ~ *v.t.* (*Fahrkarte*) to punch; (*phot.*) to snap.
Knirps *m.* **(-es, -e)** little guy; folding umbrella.
knirschen *v.i.* to grate; to creak.
knistern *v.i.* to crackle.
knitterfrei *a.* noncrease.
knittern *v.i.* to crease; *nicht knitternd,* wrinkle resisting.
knobeln *v.i.* to play at dice; to puzzle.
Knoblauch *m.* **(-[e]s, 0)** *m.* garlic; **~zehe** *f.* **(-, -n)** clove of garlic.
Knöchel *m.* **(-s, -)** knuckle; joint; ankle.
Knochen *m.* **(-s, -)** bone.
Knochen: ~arbeit *f.* back-breaking work; **~brüch** *m.* fracture (of a bone); **~gerüst** *n.* skeleton; **~mark** *n.* (bone) marrow; **~mehl** *n.* bone-meal; **~splitter** *m.* bone splinter.
knöchern *a.* bony.
knochig *a.* bony.
Knödel *m.* **(-s, -)** dumpling.
Knolle *f.* **(-, -n)** tuber; bulb.
Knollen *m.* **(-s, -)** clod, lump; (*fam.*) parking ticket.
Knollenblätterpilz *m.* death cup.
Knollennase *f.* bulbous nose.
knollig *a.* bulbous; knobby.
Knopf *m.* **(-es, Knöpfe)** button.
knöpfen *v.t.* to button.
Knopfloch *n.* buttonhole.
Knorpel *m.* **(-s, -)** cartilage, gristle.
knorpelig *a.* cartilaginous, gristly.
Knorren *m.* **(-s, -)** knot, gnarl.
knorrig *a.* gnarled; gruff.
Knospe *f.* **(-, -n)** bud, eye.
knospen *v.i.* to bud.
knoten *v.t.* to knot.
Knoten *m.* **(-s, -)** knot; node; (*med.*) lump.
Knotenpunkt *m.* (*rail.*) junction; intersection.
knotig *a.* knotty.
knuffen *v.t.* to poke.
knüllen *v.t.* to rumple, to crumple.
Knüller *m.* (*fam.*) sensation.
knüpfen *v.t.* to tie; to knot, to unite, to connect.
Knüppel *m.* **(-s, -)** cudgel, stick; club.
knurren *v.i.* to growl, to snarl; to grumble.
knusp[e]rig *a.* (*Gebäck*) crisp, short, crusty, crunchy.
knuspern *v.t.* to nibble, to munch.
Knute *f.* **(-, -n)** knout.
knutschen *v.t.* (*fam.*) to smooch with; to neck with; to pet.
Knutschfleck *m.* (*fam.*) hickey; love bite.
Knüttelvers *m.* doggerel (line).
Koalition *f.* **(-, -en)** coalition.
Kobalt *m.* **(-s, -e)** cobalt.
Kobold *m.* **(-[e]s, -e)** goblin; gnome.
Kobra *f.* **(-, -s)** (*zool.*) cobra.
Koch *m.* **(-[e]s, Köche)** (male) cook, chef.
Kochbuch *n.* cookbook.
kochen *v.t.* to boil, to cook; ~ *v.i.* to boil; to be cooking.
kochendheiß *a.* boiling hot.
Kocher *m.* **(-s, -)** cooker.
Köcher *m.* **(-s, -)** quiver.
kochfertig *a.* ready to cook.
Kochgelegenheit *f.* cooking facility.
Köchin *f.* **(-, -nen)** (female) cook.
Kochkunst *f.* culinary art.
Kochlöffel *m.* wooden spoon.
Kochnische *f.* kitchenette.
Kochrezept *n.* recipe.
Kochsalz *n.* table salt; sodium chloride.
Kochsalzlösung *f.* saline solution.
Kochtopf *m.* saucepan, cooking-pot.
Kochwäsche *f.* laundry to be boiled.
Köder *m.* **(-s, -)** bait, lure.
ködern *v.t.* to bait, to allure, to decoy.
Kodex *m.* **(-, Kodizes)** code.
kodieren *v.t.* to code; to encode.
Koeffizient *m.* **(-en, -en)** coefficient.
Koexistenz *f.* **(-, 0)** coexistence.
Koffein *n.* caffeine.
koffeinfrei *a.* decaffeinated.
Koffer *m.* **(-s, -)** suitcase.
Kofferraum *m.* trunk.
Kognak *m.* **(-s, -s)** brandy, cognac.
Kohl *m.* **(-[e]s, 0)** cabbage; kale; (*fam.*) twaddle, humbug.
Kohle *f.* **(-, -n)** charcoal; coal; carbon; (*fam.*) dough (money).
Kohlehydrat *n.* carbohydrate.
Kohlehydrierung *f.* hydrogenation.
Kohlekraftwerk *n.* coal power plant.
kohlen *v.t.* to char, to carbonize; (*nav.*) to coal.
Kohlenbergwerk *n.* coal mine, colliery.
Kohlendioxyd *n.* carbon dioxide.
Kohlengrube *f.* coalpit, colliery.
Kohlenschiff *n.* collier.
Kohlenschuppen *m.* coal shed.
Kohlenstoff *m.* carbon.
kohlenstoffhaltig *a.* carbonaceous.
Kohlenwasserstoff *m.* hydrocarbon.
Kohlepapier *n.* carbon paper.
Köhler *m.* **(-s, -)** charcoal burner.
Kohletablette *f.* charcoal tablet.
Kohlezeichnung *f.* charcoal drawing.

Kohlmeise *f.* great tit.
Kohlrabi *m.* **(-, -[s])** kohlrabi.
Kohlrübe *f.* turnip; rutabaga.
Koitus *m.* **(-, -)** coitus.
Koje *f.* **(-, -n)** berth, cabin.
Kokain *n.* cocaine.
Kokarde *f.* **(-, -n)** cockade.
kokett *a.* coquettish.
Kokette *f.* **(-, -n)** coquette, flirt.
Koketterie *f.* **(-, -n)** coquetry, flirtation.
kokettieren *v.i.* to flirt.
Kokolores *m.* (*fam.*) rubbish, nonsense.
Kokon *m.* **(-s, -s)** cocoon.
Kokos: ~flocken *pl.* shredded coconut; **~nuß** *f.* coconut, **~palme** *f.* coconut tree.
Koks *m.* **(-es, 0)** coke.
Kolben *m.* **(-s, -)** piston; flask; spike; cob.
Kolbenfresser *m.* jamming of the piston.
Kolbenhub *m.* piston stroke.
Kolbenring *m.* piston ring.
Kolbenstage *f.* piston rod.
Kolibakterie *f.* **(-, -n)** colibacillus.
Kolibri *m.* **(-s, -s)** hummingbird.
Kolik *f.* **(-, 0)** colic.
kollabieren *v.i.* to collapse.
Kollaborateur *m.* **(-s, -e)** collaborator.
Kollaboration *f.* **(-, 0)** collaboration.
kollaborieren *v.i.* to collaborate.
Kollaps *m.* collapse.
Kolleg *n.* **(-s, -ien)** course of lectures.
Kollege *m.* **(-n, -n); Kollegin** *f.* **(-, -nen)** colleague.
kollegial *a.* cooperative; helpful.
Kollegialität *f.* cooperativeness.
Kollegium *n.* **(-s, -ien)**; faculty; staff (of teachers).
Kollekte *f.* **(-, -n)** (church) collection; (*Gebet*) collect.
Kollektion *f.* collection, range.
kollektiv *a.* collective; *~e Sicherheit f.* collective security.
Kollektivshuld *f.* collective guilt.
Koller *m.* **(-s, 0)** rage, madness.
kollern *v.t. & i.* to roll.
kollidieren *v.i.* to collide; to clash.
Kollier *n.* **(-s, -s)** necklace.
Kollision *f.* collision; conflict; clash.
Kolloquium *n.* **(-s, -ien)** colloquium.
kölnisch Wasser, Kölnisches-wasser *n.* eau de Cologne.
kolonial *a.* colonial.
Kolonialismus *m.* colonialism.
Kolonie *f.* **(-, -n)** colony.
kolonisieren *v.t.* to colonize.
Kolonist *m.* **(-en, -en)** colonist, settler.
Kolonne *f.* **(-, -n)** column.
Kolophonium *n.* **(-s, 0)** colophony.
Koloratur *f.* **(-, -en)** coloratura.
kolorieren *v.t.* to color.
Kolorit *n.* **(-s, 0)** coloring.
Koloss *m.* **(-es, -e)** colossus.
kolossal *a.* colossal, huge.
kolportieren *v.t.* to hawk; to spread.
Kolumbianer *m.* **(-s, -); Kolumbianerin** *f.* **(-, -nen); kolumbianisch** *a.* Columbian.
Kolumbien *n.* **(-s, 0)** Columbia.
Kolumne *f.* **(-, -n)** column (newspaper).
Koma *n.* **(-s, 0)** coma.
Kombi *m.* **(-s, -s)** station wagon.
Kombination *f.* **(-, -en)** combination.
kombinieren *v.t.* to combine.
Kombiwagen *m.* station wagon.
Komet *m.* **(-en, -en)** comet.
kometenhaft *a.* meteoric.
Komfort *m.* **(-s, 0)** comfort; *mit allem ~*, with all modern conveniences.
komfortabel *a.* comfortable.
Komik *f.* **(-, 0)** comic effect, element, aspect.
Komiker *m.* **(-s, -)** comic actor.
komisch *a.* comical; strange, odd, funny.
komischerweise *adv.* strangely enough.
Komitee *n.* **(-s, -s)** committee.
Komma *n.* **(-[s], -s ~ -ta)** comma.
Kommandant *m.* **(-en, -en)** commander.
kommandieren *v.t.* to command.
Kommanditgesellschaft *f.* limited partnership (with shares).
Kommando *n.* **(-s, -s)** command; detachment (of soldiers); **~brücke** *f.* (*nav.*) bridge; **~zentrale** *f.* control center.
kommen *v.i.st. (s)* to come; to happen; to arrive at, to get to; *woher kommt das?* what is the cause of this? how is it that...?; *~ lassen*, to send for, to write for; *~ sehen*, to foresee; *abhanden ~* to get lost, to be mislaid; *einem gleich ~*, to equal sb.; *zu kurz ~*, to lose; *teuer, hoch zu stehen ~*, to cost a fortune; *wenn es hoch kommt*, at most, in extreme cases; *auf etwas ~* to think of; *ich konnte gestern nicht dazu ~*, I could not find time for it yesterday; *nicht zu Worte ~*, to be unable to put in a word; *um etwas ~*, to lose sth.; *sich etwas zu Schulden ~ lassen*, to be guilty of sth.
Kommentar *m.* **(-s, -e)** commentary, comment.
Kommentator *m.*; **Kommentatorin** *f.* commentator.
kommentieren *v.t. & i.* to comment (on).
Kommerz *m.* (*pej.*) business interests.
kommerzialisieren *v.t.* to commercialize.
kommerziell *a.* commercial.
Kommilitone *m.* **(-n, -n); Kommilitonin** *f.* **(-, -nen)** fellow student.
Kommissar *m.* **(-s, -e)** commissioner, captain of police; superintendent.
Kommode *f.* **(-, -n)** chest of drawers.
kommunal *a.* local; communal, municipal.
Kommunalbehörden *f. pl.* local authorities.
Kommunalverwaltung *f.* local government.
Kommune *f.* **(-, -n)** local authority, municipality; commune.
Kommunikation *f.* **(-, -en)** communication.
Kommunikations: ~mittel *pl.* means of communication; **~wissenschaft** *f.* communication science.
kommunikativ *a.* communicative.
Kommunismus *m.* **(-, 0)** communism.
Kommunist *m.* **(-en, -en); Kommunistin** *f.* **(-, -nen)** communist.
kommunizieren *v.i.* to communicate.
Komödiant *m.* **(-en, -en); Komödiantin** *f.* **(-, -nen)** actor, actress, comedian.
Komödie *f.* **(-, -n)** comedy; play.
Kompa(g)nie *f.* **(-, -n)** company.
Kompagnon *m.* **(-s, -s)** associate; partner.
Komparativ *m.* **(-s, -e)** comparative.
Komparse *m.*; **Komparsin** *f.* (film) extra.
Kompaß *m.* **(-sses, -sse)** compass.
kompatibel *a.* compatible.
Kompensation *f.* **(-, -en)** compensation.

kompensieren *v.t.* to compensate.
kompetent *a.* competent; authorized.
Kompetenz *f.* **(-, -en)** competence; authority.
komplementär *a.* complementary.
Komplementärfarbe *f.* complementary color.
komplett *a.* complete.
komplettieren *v.t.* to complete.
komplex *a.* complex.
Komplex *m.* **(-es, -e)** complex.
Komplexität *f.* **(-, -en)** complexity.
Komplikation *f.* **(-s, -e)** complication.
Kompliment *n.* compliment.
Komplize *m.* **(-n, -n); Komplizin** *f.* **(-, -nen)** accomplice.
kompliziert *a.* complicated.
Komplott *n.* **(-s -e)** plot; conspiracy.
Komponente *f.* **(-, -n)** component.
komponieren *v.t.* to compose, (*mus.*) to set.
Komponist *m.* **(-en, -en); Komponistin** *f.* **(-, -nen)** composer.
Komposition *f.* **(-, -en)** (*mus.*) composition, setting.
Kompositum *n.* **(-s, -ta)** compound (word).
Komposthaufen *m.* compost heap.
Kompott *n.* **(-[e]s, -e)** stewed fruit.
Kompresse *f.* **(-, -en)** compress; pad.
Kompressor *m.* **(-s, -en)** (*mot.*) compressor, supercharger.
komprimieren *v.t.* to compress.
komprimiert *a.* condensed.
Kompromiß *m.* **(-sses, -ss)** compromise.
kompromißlos *a.* uncompromising.
kompromittieren *v.t.* to compromise; ~ *v.r.* to expose oneself.
kondensierte Milch *f.* condensed milk.
Kondition *f.* **(-, -en)** condition; trim; shape.
Konditions: ~schwäche *f.* lack of fitness; **~training** *n.* fitness training.
Konditor *m.* **(-s, -en)** confectioner; pastry cook.
Konditorei *f.* **(-, -en)** confectioner's (shop); pastry shop.
kondolieren *v.i.* to offer one's condolences.
Kondom *n.* **(-s, -e)** condom.
Konfekt *n.* **(-[e]s, -e)** sweets; candy; chocolates.
Konfektion *f.* **(-, 0)** off-the-rack clothes; garments.
Konferenz *f.* **(-, -en)** meeting, conference.
konferieren *v.i.* to confer.
Konfession *f.* **(-, -en)** denomination, religion.
konfessionell *a.* denominational.
konfessionslos *a.* non-denominational.
Konfirmand *m.* **(-en, -en); Konfirmandin** *f.* **(-, -nen)** confirmand.
konfirmieren *v.t.* to confirm.
konfiszieren *v.t.* to confiscate.
Konfitüre *f.* **(-, -n)** jam.
Konflikt *m.* **(-s, -e)** conflict.
Konfliktstoff *m.* cause of conflict.
Konföderation *f.* **(-, -en)** confederation.
konform *a.* conforming.
Konformist *m.*; **Konformistin** *f.*; **konformistisch** *a.* conformist.
konfus *a.* confused, scatterbrained.
Kongreß *m.* **(-es, -e)** congress; Congress.
Kongreßmitglied *n.* Congressman, Congresswoman.
Kongruenz *f.* congruence.
König *m.* **(-s, -e)** king.
Königin *f.* **(-, -nen)** queen.
königlich *a.* royal, regal.
Königreich *n.* kingdom.
Königtum *n.* **(-[e]s, -tümer)** royalty, kingship.
konisch *a.* conical.
Konjugation *f.* conjugation.
konjugieren *v.t.* to conjugate.
Konjunktion *f.* **(-, -en)** conjunction.
Konjunktiv *m.* **(-s, -e)** subjunctive.
Konjunktur *f.* **(-, -en)** economic activity; economy.
Konjunkturabschwächung *f.* downswing.
Konjunkturaufschwung *m.* upswing.
Konjunkturbericht *m.* economic report.
Konjunkturforschung *f.* market research.
Konjunkturschwankungen *pl.* economic fluctuation.
konkav *a.* concave.
Konkordat *n.* **(-[e]s, -e)** concordat.
konkret *a.* concrete.
konkretisieren *v.t.* to put in concrete terms.
Konkubinat *n.* **(-[e]s, -e)** concubinage.
Konkurrent *m.* **(-en, -en)** competitor.
Konkurrenz *f.* **(-, -en)** competition.
konkurrenzfähig *a.* competitive.
konkurrieren *v.i.* to compete.
Konkurs *m.* **(-es, -e)** bankruptcy, insolvency; ~ *machen*, to become *or* go bankrupt.
Konkurs: ~masse *f.* bankrupt's assets; **~ordnung** *f.* bankruptcy law; **~verfahren** *n.* proceedings in bankruptcy.
können *v.i.ir.* to be able, can, to know, to understand; *ich kann*, I can, I may; *ich kann nichts dafür*, it's no fault of mine, I can't help it.
Können *n.* **(-s, 0)** ability; skill.
Könner *m.* **(-s, -)** expert.
konsekutiv *a.* consecutive.
konsequent *a.* consistent, logical.
Konsequenz *f.* **(-, -en)** consistency; consequence.
konservativ *a.* conservative.
Konservative *m./f.* conservative.
Konservatorium *n.* **(-s, -ien)** conservatory.
Konserve *f.* **(-, -n)** canned food.
Konservenbüchse *f.* **(-, -n)** tin, can.
konservieren *v.t.* to preserve, to keep.
Konsistenz *f.* consistency.
konsolidieren *v.t.* to consolidate.
Konsolidierung *f.* consolidation.
Konsonant *m.* **(-en, -en)** consonant.
Konsorte *n.* **(-n, -n)** associate.
Konsortium *n.* **(-s, -ien)** group, syndicate.
Konspiration *f.* conspiracy.
konspirativ *a.* conspiratorial.
konspirieren *v.i.* to conspire; to plot.
konstant *a.* constant.
konstatieren *v.t.* to state, to notice.
Konstellation *f.* combination, constellation.
konsterniert *a.* filled with consternation.
Konsternierung *f.* consternation.
konstituieren *v.t.* to constitute.
Konstitution *f.* **(-, -en)** constitution.
konstitutionell *a.* constitutional.
konstruieren *v.t.* to construct.
Konstrukteur *m.* **(-s, -e); Konstrukteurin** *f.* **(-, -nen)** designer; design engineer.
Konstruktionsbüro *n.* design office.
Konstruktionsfehler *m.* design error.
konstruktiv *a.* constructive; constructional.
Konsul *m.* **(-s, -n); Konsulin** *f.* **(-, -nen)** consul.
Konsulat *m.* **(-s, -e)** consulate.
konsultieren *v.t.* to consult.

Konsum *m.* **(-s, 0)** consumption.
Konsumartikel *m.* **(-s, -)** consumer item.
Konsument *m.* **(-en, -en); Konsumentin** *f.* **(-, -nen)** consumer.
Konsumgesellschaft *f.* consumer society.
Konsumgüter *pl.* consumer goods.
Konsumterror *m.* pressure to buy.
Kontakt *m.* **(-s, -e)** contact.
kontaktfreudig *a.* sociable.
Kontaktlinse *f.* **(-, -n)** contact lens.
Kontamination *f.* contamination.
kontaminieren *v.t.* to contaminate.
Konteradmiral *m.* rear-admiral.
Konterbande *f.* contraband.
Konterrevolution *f.* counterrevolution.
Kontext *m.* context.
Kontinent *m.* **(-s, -e)** continent.
Kontinentalverschiebung *f.* continental drift.
Kontingent *n.* **(-[e]s, -e)** quota, contingent.
kontinuierlich *a.* steady; continuous.
Kontinuität *f.* continuity.
Konto *n.* **(-s, -en & -s)** account; *Depositen* ~, deposit account; *fiktives* ~, fictitious account; *laufendes* ~, current account; *ein* ~ *eröffnen,* to open an account; **~auszug** *m.* account statement; **~inhaber** *m.* account holder.
Kontor *n.* **(-s, -e)** office.
Kontostand *m.* account balance.
kontra *pr.* contra; against.
Kontrabass *m.* double bass.
Kontrahent *m.* **(-en, -en)** adversary; opponent.
Kontrakt *m.* **(-es, -e)** contract.
kontraktlich *a. & adv.* by contract, contractual; ~ *verpflichtet* under contract.
Kontrapunkt *m.* (*mus.*) counterpoint.
konträr *a.* contrary, opposite.
Kontrast *m.* **(-s, -s)** contrast.
kontrastieren *v.t. & i.* to contrast.
Kontrastmittel *n.* radiopaque material.
Kontrollabschnitt *m.* stub.
Kontrolle *f.* **(-, 0)** control, surveillance, check, inspection.
Kontrolleur *m.* **(-s, -e)** inspector.
kontrollieren *v.t.* to control, to check.
Kontroll: ~kasse *f.* cash register; **~marke** *f.* check; **~punkt** *m.* checkpoint.
kontrovers *a.* conflicting, controversial.
Kontroverse *f.* controversy.
Kontur *f.* **(-, -en)** outline.
Konvention *f.* convention.
Konventionalstrafe *f.* (*jur.*) liquidated damages.
konventionell *a.* conventional.
Konversation *f.* conversation.
Konversationslexikon *n.* encyclopedia.
Konversion *f.* conversion.
konvertierbar *a.* convertible.
konvertieren *v.t.* to convert.
Konvertit *m.* **(-en, -en)** convert.
konvex *a.* convex.
Konvoi *m.* **(-s, -s)** convoy.
Konzentrat *n.* **(-s, -e)** concentrate.
Konzentration *f.* concentration.
Konzentrationslager *n.* concentration camp.
konzentrieren *v.t.* to concentrate, to focus.
konzentriert *a.* concentrated, focused.
Konzept *n.* **(-[e]s, -e)** (rough) draft, sketch.
Konzeption *f.* central ideal; conception.
konzeptionslos *a.* haphazard; without a clear plan.
Konzern *m.* **(-[e]s, -e)** group, conglomerate.
Konzert *n.* **(-s, -e)** concert, concerto; **~agentur** *f.* concert agency; **~besucher** *m.*, **~besucherin** *f.* concertgoer; **~flügel** *m.* concert grand; **~meister** *m.*, **~meisterin** *f.* concertmaster; **~saal** *m.* concert hall.
Konzession *f.* **(-, -en)** concession; license; *sich eine* ~ *beschaffen,* to take out a franchise; *mit Regierungs*~, under license from the government; **~sinhaber** *m* licensee, franchisee.
konzessionsbereit *a.* prepared to make concessions.
Konzessivsatz *m.* concessive clause.
Konzil *n.* **(-s, -e)** (*rel.*) council.
konzipieren *v.t.* to conceive; to draft; *konzipiert für,* designed for.
Kooperation *f.* cooperation.
kooperativ *a.* cooperative.
kooperieren *v.t.* to cooperate.
Koordination *f.* coordination.
koordinieren *v.t.* to coordinate.
Köper *m.* **(-s, -)** twill.
Kopf *m.* **(-es, Köpfe)** head; (*fig.*) mind; (*Pfeifen*~) bowl; *aus dem* ~, from memory; *Hals über* ~, head over heels; *einen vor den* ~ *stossen,* to offend; *sich auf den* ~ *stellen,* to resist; *sich den* ~ *über etwas zerbrechen,* to rack one's brains about; *den* ~ *hängen lassen,* to hang one's head, to be dispirited.
Kopfarbeit *f.* brain work, intellectual work.
köpfen *v.t.* to behead.
Kopfhaut *f.* scalp.
Kopfhörer *m.* earphone, headphone.
Kopfkissen *n.* pillow.
kopflos *a.* brainless, confused.
Kopfnicken *n.* nod.
Kopfrechnen *m.* mental arithmetic.
Kopfsalat *m.* lettuce.
kopfscheu *a.* skittish, shy.
Kopfschmerz *m.* headache.
Kopfschmuck *m.* headdress.
Kopfschuppen *pl.* dandruff.
Kopfschütteln *n.* shake of the head.
Kopfsprung *m.* header, head dive.
Kopfstand *m.* headstand.
Kopfsteinpflaster *n.* cobblestones.
Kopfsteuer *f.* poll tax.
Kopfstütze *f.* headrest.
Kopftuch *n.* headscarf, kerchief.
kopfüber *adv.* head first; (*fig.*) headlong.
Kopfverband *m.* head bandage.
Kopfverletzung *f.* head injury.
Kopfwäsche *f.* hair-wash; shampoo.
Kopfweh *n.* headache.
Kopfzerbrechen *n.* concentration; worry.
Kopie *f.* **(-, -n)** copy; duplicate.
kopieren *v.t.* to copy; (*phot.*) to print.
Kopierer *m.*, **Kopiergerät** *n.* copier; copy machine.
Koppel *f.* **(-, -n)** paddock.
koppeln *v.t.* to couple, to link; to dock.
Koproduktion *f.* coproduction.
Kopulation *f.* copulation.
kopulieren *v.i.* to copulate.
Koralle *f.* **(-, -n)** coral.
Korb *m.* **(-[e]s, Körbe)** basket, hamper, crate; *einen* ~ *bekommen,* to meet with a refusal.
Korbblütler *m.* (*bot.*) composite flower.
Korbflechtwaren *pl.* wickerwork.
Korbflechter *m.* basketmaker.
Korbmacher *m.* basketmaker.

Korbmöbel *n. pl.* wicker furniture.
Kord *m.* **(-s, -e)** corduroy, cord.
Kordel *f.* **(-, -n)** cord, string.
Kordsamt *m.* cord velvet.
Korea *n.* **(-s, 0)** Korea.
Koreaner *m.* **(-s, -)**; **Koreanerin** *f.* **(-, -nen)**; **koreanisch** *a.* Korean.
Korinthe *f.* **(-, -n)** currant.
Kork *m.* **(-[e]s, -e)**; **Korken** *m.* **(-s, -)** cork; stopper; float (fishing).
korken *v.t.* to cork.
Korkenzieher *m.* corkscrew.
Kormoran *m.* **(-s, -e)** cormorant.
Korn *n.* **(-[e]s, Körner)** corn; grain; **Korn** *m.* brandy.
Kornblume *f.* cornflower.
körnen *v.t. & i.* to granulate.
Kornfeld *n.* grainfield.
körnig *a.* grainy, granular.
Kornkammer *f.* granary.
Korona *f.* corona; (*fig.*) crowd.
Körper *m.* **(-s, -)** body; (*toter*) corpse; (*phys.*) solid.
Körperbau *m.* physique.
Körperbeherrschung *f.* body control.
Körperbehinderung *f.* physical handicap.
Körperbeschädigung *f.* bodily harm or injury.
Körperchen *n.* **(-s, -)** corpuscle.
Körperfülle *f.* corpulence.
Körpergeruch *m.* body odor, (*fam.*) BO.
Körperhaltung *f.* posture.
Körperkontakt *m.* physical contact.
Körperkraft *f.* physical strength.
körperlich *a.* corporal, bodily; physical.
Körperpflege *f.* hygiene.
Körperschaft *f.* corporation; **~ssteuer** *f.* corporation tax.
Körpersprache *f.* body language.
Korps *n.* **(-, -)** (*mil.*) corps; body.
Korpulenz *f.* corpulence.
korrekt *a.* correct.
Korrektheit *f.* correctness.
Korrektor *m.* **(-s, -en)** proofreader.
Korrektur *f.* **(-, -en)** correction; proofreading, revise; **~bogen** *m.* (*typ.*) proof; **~fahnen** *pl.* (*typ.*) galleys.
Korrelat *n.* **(-[e]s, 0)** correlate.
Korrespondent *m.* **(-en, -en)** (*com.*) correspondent.
Korrespondenz *f.* **(-, -en)** correspondence.
korrespondieren *v.i.* to correspond.
Korridor *m.* **(-s, -e)** passage, corridor.
korrigieren *v.t.* to correct.
korrumpieren *v.t.* to corrupt.
Korruption *f.* corruption.
Korsar *m.* **(-s, -en)** corsair, pirate.
Korsett *n.* **(-[e]s, -e & -s)** corset.
Kortison *n.* **(-s, 0)** cortisone.
Koryphäe *m.* **(-n, -n)** authority.
koscher *a.* kosher.
kosen *v.i.* to caress.
Kosename *m.* pet name.
Kosinus *m.* (*math.*) cosine.
Kosmetik **(-, 0)** beauty care; cosmetics.
Kosmetiker *m.* **(-s, -)**; **Kosmetikerin** *f.* **(-, -nen)** cosmetician, beautician.
Kosmetikkoffer *m.* vanity box/case.
Kosmetiksalon *m.* beauty parlor.
Kosmetikum *n.* **(-s, -ka)** cosmetic.
kosmetisch *a.* cosmetic.
kosmetische Chirurgie *f.* cosmetic surgery.
kosmisch *a.* cosmic.
Kosmonaut *m.* **(-s, -en)**; **Kosmonautin** *f.* **(-, -nen)** cosmonaut.
Kosmopolit *m.*; **Kosmopolitin** *f.* cosmopolitan.
kosmopolitisch *a.* cosmopilitan.
Kosmos *m.* **(-, 0)** cosmos.
Kost *f.* **(-, 0)** fare, food; board; *in ~ sein bei,* to board with.
kostbar *a.* costly, precious; valuable.
Kostbarkeit *f.* **(-, -en)** preciousness; valuables *pl.*
kosten *v.t.* to taste; to cost; to require.
Kosten *pl.* cost, costs, charges, expenses *pl.*; *die ~ tragen,* to bear the expenses.
kostenlos *a.* free of charge.
Kosten-Nutzen-Analyse *f.* cost-benefit analysis.
Kostenpunkt *m.* question of cost.
Kostenvoranschlag *m.* **(-s, -schläge)** estimate.
Kostgänger *m.* boarder.
Kostgeld *n.* board; allowance.
köstlich *a.* precious; delicious.
Köstlichkeit *f.* **(-, -en)** delicacy.
Kostprobe *f.* **(-, -n)** sample, taste.
kostspielig *a.* expensive, costly.
Kostüm *n.* **(-s, -e)** costume, dress, suit; **~bildner** *m.*; **(-s, -)**; **~bildnerin** *f.* **(-, -nen)** costume designer; **~fest** *n.* costume ball.
kostümieren *v.r.* to dress up.
Kostümprobe *f.* dress rehearsal.
Kostümverleih *m.* costume rental.
Kot *m.* **(-[e]s, 0)** excrement; feces.
Kotelett *f.* **(-s, -s)** cutlet, chop.
Koteletten *pl.* sideburns.
Köter *m.* **(-s, -)** cur, dog.
Kotflügel *m.* fender.
Kotze *f.* **(-, 0)** (*vulg.*) vomit.
kotzen *v.i.* (*vulg.*) to vomit; to puke.
Krabbe *f.* **(-, -n)** crab; shrimp; prawn
krabbeln *v.i.* to crawl.
Krach *m.* **(-[e]s, -e)** noise, crash; quarrel; row.
krachen *v.i.* to crack, to crash; to creak.
Kracher *m.* banger.
krächzen *v.i.* to croak, to caw.
Kräcker *m.* cracker.
kraft *pr.* by virtue of.
Kraft *f.* **(-, Kräfte)** strength; power; vigor; (*Natur*) force; *in ~,* in force; *in ~ setzen,* to put into operation; *außer ~ setzen,* to repeal, to countermand; *in ~ treten,* to come into force; *aus Leibeskräften,* with might and main.
Kraftakt *m.* feat of strength.
Kraftausdruck *m.* swearword.
Kraftbrühe *f.* bouillon, clear soup.
Kräfteverfall *m.* loss of strength.
Kräfteverhältnis *n.* balance of power.
Kräfteverschleiß *m.* waste of energy.
Kraftfahrer *m.* driver; motorist.
Kraftfahrzeug *n.* **(-s, -e)** motor vehicle; **~brief** *m.* vehicle registration document; **~mechaniker** *m.* car mechanic; **~schein** *m.* vehicle registration document; **~steuer** *f.* automobile tax.
Kraftfeld *n.* (*phys.*) energy field.
kräftig *a.* strong; powerful; vigorous; nourishing.
kräftigen *v.t.* to strengthen; to fortify; to invigorate.
Kräftigungsmittel *n.* **(-s, -)** tonic.
kraftlos *a.* weak, feeble; impotent.
Kraftmeier *m.* (*pej.*) muscleman.
Kraftprobe *f.* trial of strength.
Kraftprotz *m.* (*pej.*) muscleman.

Kraftstoff *m.* fuel.
Kraftstoffverbrauch *m.* fuel consumption.
kraftvoll *a.* vigorous; powerful.
Kraftwagen *m.* motor vehicle.
Kraftwerk *n.* power station.
Kragen *m.* **(-s, -)** collar; **~weite** *f.* collar size.
Krähe *f.* **(-, -n)** crow.
krähen *v.i.* to crow.
Krake *m.* **(-n, -n)** (*zool.*) octopus; kraken.
krakeelen *v.i.* to make a racket.
Krakeeler *m.* **(-s, -)** quarreler, brawler.
Krakel *m.* **(-s, -)** (*fam.*) scrawl.
krakeln *v.t.* & *i.* (*fam.*) to scrawl, to scribble.
Kralle *f.* **(-, -n)** claw.
krallen *v.t.* to dig one's finger into; ~ *v.r.* to cling to, to dig one's claws into.
Kram *m.* **(-[e]s, Kräme)** junk; stuff.
kramen *v.i.* to rummage.
Krämer *m.* **(-s, -)** shopkeeper, grocer; (*fig.*) stingy person.
Kramladen *m.* (*pej.*) junk shop.
Krampf *m.* **(-[e]s, -ämpfe)** cramp; spasm, convulsion.
Krampfader *f.* varicose vein.
krampfhaft *a.* spasmodic, convulsive, frantic.
krampflösend *a.* spasmolytic.
Kran *m.* **(-[e]s, -äne)** crane; hoist.
Kranich *m.* **(-s, -e)** (*zool.*) crane.
krank *a.* ill, sick; ~ *werden,* to fall ill; *sich ~ stellen,* to feign illness, to malinger; ~ *im Bett liegen,* to be ill in bed; *sich ~ melden,* to call in sick.
kränkeln *v.i.* to be ailing, to be in poor health.
kranken *v.i.* to suffer from.
kränken *v.t.* & *r.* to vex, to mortify; (*fig.*)to injure, to hurt.
Kranken: ~appell *m.* (*mil.*) sick-call; **~bett** *n.* sickbed; **~blatt** *n.* medical record; **~geld** *n.* sick pay; **~geschichte** *f.* medical history; **~gymnast** *m.*, **~gymnastin** *f.* physiotherapist; **~gymnastik** *f.* physiotherapy; **~haus** *n.* hospital; *ins ~haus überführen,* to hospitalize; **~kasse** *f.* health insurance; **~pflege** *f.* nursing; **~pfleger** *m.*, **~schein** *m.* health insurance certificate; **~schwester** *f.* hospital nurse; **~träger** *m.* stretcher-bearer; **~urlaub** *m.* sick leave; **~versicherung** *f.* health insurance; **~wagen** *m.* ambulance; **~wärter** *m.* male nurse.
Kranke[r] *m./f.* **(-n, -n)** patient.
krankhaft *a.* morbid; abnormal; pathological.
Krankheit *f.* **(-, -en)** disease, sickness.
Krankheitsbild *n.* clinical picture.
Krankheitserreger *m.* pathogen.
Krankheitserscheinung *f.* symptom.
Krankheitsfall *m.* case of illness.
krankheitshalber *adv.* owing to illness.
Krankheitsherd *m.* focus of disease.
Krankheitskeim *m.* germ.
Krankheitsüberträger *m.* carrier.
kränklich *a.* sickly, ailing.
Krankmeldung *f.* **(-, -en)** notification of illness.
Kränkung *f.* **(-, -en)** insult, mortification.
Kranz *m.* **(-es, -änze)** wreath, garland.
kränzen *v.t.* to wreathe, to crown.
Krapfen *m.* **(-s, -)** doughnut.
kraß *a.* coarse, gross; blatant.
Krater *m.* **(-s, -)** crater.
Kratzbürste *f.* wire brush; (*fig.*) vicious person.
kratzbürstig *a.* (*fig.*) bad-tempered, hostile.
Krätze *f.* **(-, 0)** scabies.
kratzen *v.t.* to scratch, to scrape; (*Wolle*) to card; ~ *v.i.* (*von Federn*) to spurt.
Kratzer *m.* **(-s, -)** scratch; scraper.
kratzig *a.* scratchy, itchy.
Kraul *n.* **(-s, 0)** (*sp.*) crawl.
kraulen *v.i.* to crawl.
kraus *a.* curl, frizzy.
Krause *f.* **(-, -n)** ruff, ruffle; frill, frizziness.
kräuseln *v.t.* to curl, to frizz.
Krauskopf *m.* curly head.
Kraut *n.* **(-[e]s, -äuter)** herb; plant; cabbage.
Krautsalat *m.* coleslaw.
Krawall *m.* **(-[e]s, -e)** row, riot; **~macher** *m.* rowdy.
Krawatte *f.* **(-, -n)** (neck)tie, **~nnadel** *f.* tie pin.
kraxeln *v.i.* (*fam.*) to climb; to clamber.
Kreation *f.* **(-, -en)** creation (fashion).
kreativ *a.* creative.
Kreativität *f.* creativity.
Kreatur *f.* **(-, -en)** creature.
Krebs *m.* **(-es, -e)** crayfish; crab; (*med.*) cancer.
krebsartig *a.* cancerous.
krebserregend, krebserzeugend *a.* carcinogenic.
Krebs: ~forschung *f.* cancer research; **~gang** *m.* retrogressive; **~geschwulst** *f.* cancerous growth/tumor; **~geschwür** *n.* cancerous ulcer; (*fig.*) cancer; **~kranke** *m./f.* cancer patient.
kredenzen *v.t.* to offer, to serve.
Kredit *m.* **(-[e]s, -e)** credit; trust; reputation.
Kredit: ~anstalt *f.* credit institution; **~brief** *m.* letter of credit; **~geber** *m.* lender; **~hai** *m.* (*fam. pej.*) loan shark; **~institut** *n.* credit bank; **~karte** *f.* credit card; **~kauf** *m.* purchase on credit; **~nehmer** *m.* borrower.
kreditfähig *a.* creditworthy, sound.
kreditieren *v.t.* to credit.
kreditwürdig *a.* creditworthy.
Kreditwürdigkeit *f.* creditworthiness.
Kredo *n.* credo.
Kreide *f.* **(-, -n)** chalk; crayon.
kreidebleich *a.* as white as a sheet.
Kreidezeit *f.* cretaceous period.
kreieren *v.t.* to create.
Kreis *m.* **(-es, -e)** circle, cycle; orbit; sphere; county district.
Kreisabschnitt *m.* segment.
Kreisausschnitt *m.* sector.
Kreisbahn *f.* orbit.
Kreisbogen *m.* arc of a circle.
kreischen *v.i.* to scream; to shriek.
Kreisel *m.* **(-s, -)** top; gyroscope.
kreiseln *v.i.* to turn like a top.
kreisen *v.i.* to revolve.
Kreisfläche *f.* circular surface.
kreisförmig *a.* circular.
Kreislauf *m.* circulation; cycle; **~kollaps** *m.* circulatory collapse; **~mittel** *n.* circulatory medicine, **~störungen** *pl.* circulatory trouble.
Kreislinie *f.* circumference of a circle.
Kreissäge *f.* circular saw.
kreißen *v.i.* to be in labor.
Kreißsaal *m.* delivery room.
Krematorium *n.* **(-s, -ien)** crematorium.
Krempe *f.* **(-, -n)** brim (of a hat).
Krempel *m.* **(-s, 0)** junk; stuff.
krempeln *v.t.* to turn up.
krepieren *v.i.* *(s)* to die a miserable death; (*Geschoß*) to burst, to explode.
Krepp *m.* **(-s, 0)** crepe.
Kresse *f.* **(-, -n)** (water)cress.

Kretin *m.* cretin; imbecile.
Kreuz *n.* **(-es, -e)** cross; crucifix; (*Spielkarten*) club; (*fig.*) cross, tribulation; *kreuz und quer,* right and left, in all directions.
Kreuzband *n.* crucial ligament.
kreuzen *v.t.* to cross; to interbreed; ~ *v.i.* (*nav.*) to cruise; ~ *v.r.* to intersect; *die beiden Briefe kreuzten sich,* the two letters crossed.
Kreuzer *m.* **(-s, -)** (*nav.*) cruiser.
Kreuzfahrer *m.* crusader.
Kreuzfahrt *f.* crusade.
Kreuzfeuer *n.* crossfire.
kreuzfidel *a.* very cheerful.
kreuzförmig *a.* cross-shaped; cruciform.
Kreuzgang *m.* cloister.
kreuzigen *v.t.* to crucify.
Kreuzigung *f.* crucifixion.
Kreuzkönig *m.* king of clubs.
Kreuzotter *f.* viper.
Kreuzschlüssel *m.* four-way wheel brace.
Kreuzschmerzen *pl.* lower back pain.
Kreuzspinne *f.* garden spider.
Kreuzstich *m.* cross-stitch.
Kreuzung *f.* **(-, -en)** junction; crossroads; cross-breeding.
Kreuzverhör *n.* cross examination.
Kreuzwegstationen *pl.* stations of the cross.
kreuzweise *adv.* across, crosswise.
Kreuzworträtsel *n.* crossword puzzle.
Kreuzzeichen *n.* sign of the cross.
Kreuzzug *m.* crusade.
kribbelig *a.* fidgety, edgy.
kribbeln *v.i.* to tickle, to itch.
Kricket *n.* cricket.
kriechen *v.t.st.* *(h. & s.)* to creep, to crawl; (*fig.*) to cringe, to fawn, to toady.
Kriecher *m.* **(-s, -)** (*fig.*) toady; yes-man.
Kriecherei *f.* **(-, -en)** toadyism, servility.
kriecherisch *a.* crawling, groveling.
Kriech: ~spur *f.* slow lane; **~tier** *n.* reptile.
Krieg *m.* **(-[e]s, -e)** war.
kriegen *v.t.* (*fam.*) to get, to obtain.
Krieger *m.* **(-s, -)** warrior.
Kriegerdenkmal *n.* war memorial.
kriegerisch *a.* warlike, martial.
kriegführend *a.* warring; belligerent.
Kriegführung *f.* warfare.
Kriegs: ~artikel *pl.* articles of war; **~ausbruch** *m.* outbreak of war; **~beschädigte[r]** *m.* disabled veteran; **~blind** *a.* war-blinded; **~brücke** *f.* military bridge; **~dienst** *m.* military service; **~dienstverweigerer** *m.* conscientious objector; **~einsatz** *m.* war effort; **~entschädigung** *f.* reparations; **~erklärung** *f.* declaration of war; **~fall** *m.* *im ~* in the event of war; **~flotte** *f.* navy; **~gebiet** *n.* war zone; **~gefangene[r]** *m.* prisoner of war; **~gefangenschaft** *f.* captivity; **~gericht** *n.* court martial; **~gewinnler** *m.* war-profiteer; **~gliederung** *f.* order of battle; **~hafen** *m.* naval base; **~hetzer** *m.* warmonger; **~list** *f.* stratagem; **~material** *n.* materiel; **~ministerium** *n.* War Office; **~potential** *n.* war potential; **~recht** *n.* military law; **~risiko** *n.* war risk; **~schauplatz** *m.* theater of war; **~schiff** *n.* warship; **~spiel** *n.* (*mil.*) map maneuver; **~verbrechen** *n.* war crime; **~verbrecher** *m.* war criminal; **~wichtiges Ziel** *n.* military target *or* objective; **~wissenschaft** *f.* military science; **~zeit** *f.* wartime.
Krimi *m.* **(-s, -s)** (*fam.*) crime thriller; detective story.
Kriminalbeamte *m.* **(-n, -n); Kriminalbeamtin** *f.* **(-, -nen)** detective.
Kriminalfilm *m.* crime film; thriller.
kriminalisieren *v.t.* to criminalize.
Kriminalität *f.* **(-, 0)** criminality; crime rate; delinquency.
Kriminalkommissar *m.*; **Kriminalkommissarin** *f.* detective superintendent.
Kriminalpolizei *f.* criminal investigation department; detective police.
Kriminalroman *m.* crime novel; thriller; detective novel.
kriminell *a.* criminal.
Kriminelle *m./f.* **(-n, -n)** criminal.
Kriminologe *m./f.* **(-n, -n)** criminologist.
Krimskrams *m.* (*fam.*) stuff.
Kringel *m.* (small)ring; round squiggle.
kringeln *v.t. & r.* to curl.
Krippe *f.* **(-, -n)** crib, manger; day nursery; crèche.
Krippenspiel *n.* nativity play.
Krise, Krisis *f.* **(-, -sen)** crisis.
kriseln *v.i.* imp. to go through a crisis.
krisenanfällig *a.* crisis prone.
krisenfest *a.* stable.
Krisengebiet *n.* crisis area.
krisengeschüttelt *a.* crisis ridden.
Krisenherd *m.* trouble spot.
Krisenzeit *f.* time of crisis.
Kristall *m.* **(-[e]s, -e)** crystal.
kristallen *a.* crystalline.
Kristallglas *n.* crystal.
kristallisieren *v.i.* to crystallize.
Kriterium *n.* **(-s, -ien)** criterion.
Kritik *f.* **(-, -en)** criticism; critique, review; *unter aller ~,* below contempt.
Kritiker *m.* **(-s, -); Kritikerin** *f.* **(-, -nen)** critic.
kritiklos *a.* uncritical.
kritisch *a.* critical.
kritisieren *v.t.* to criticize; to review.
Krittelei *f.* **(-, -en)** fault-finding; carping.
kritteln *v.i.* to find fault; to carp.
Kritzelei *f.* **(-, -en)** scribbling, doodling.
kritzeln *v.t.* to doodle; to scribble.
Krokodil *n.* **(-[e]s, -e)** crocodile.
Krokus *m.* **(-, - & -se)** crocus.
Krone *f.* **(-, -n)** crown; coronet; crest.
krönen *v.t.* (*also fig.*) to crown.
Kronleuchter *m.* chandelier.
Kronprinz *m.* crown prince.
Krönung *f.* **(-, -en)** coronation.
Kronzeuge *m.* chief witness; *~ werden,* to turn state's evidence.
Kröpf *m.* **(-[e]s, öpfe)** crop; goiter.
kroß *a.* crisp.
Kröte *f.* **(-, -n)** toad.
Krücke *f.* **(-, -n)** crutch.
Krückstock *m.* walking stick.
Krug *m.* **(-[e]s, Krüge)** pitcher; jug; *Henkel~,* mug.
Krume *f.* **(-, -n)** crumb; (*Acker*) mold.
Krümel *m.* **(-s, -)** crumb.
krümelig *a.* crumbling, crummy.
krümeln *v.i. & r.* to crumble.
krumm *a.* crooked; curved; bent; *etwas ~ nehmen,* to resent sth.
krummbeinig *a.* bow-legged.
krümmen *v.t.* to bend, to crook; ~ *v.r.* to cringe, to stoop; (*vor Schmerz*) to writhe; (*Fluß*) to bend,

to wind; *einem kein Haar* ~, not to hurt a hair of a person's head.
Krummstab *m.* crosier.
Krümmung *f.* **(-, -en)** curvature; curve.
Krüppel *m.* **(-s, -)** cripple.
krüppelhaft, krüppelig *a.* crippled, lame.
Kruste *f.* **(-, -n)** crust.
Krustentier *n.* crustacean.
Kruzifix *n.* **(-es, -e)** crucifix.
Krypta *f.* **(-, Krypten)** crypt.
KSZE *Konferenz über Sicherheit und Zusammenarbeit in Europa,* Conference on security and cooperation in Europe, CSCE.
Kto. *Konto,* account, acct, a/c.
Kübel *m.* **(-s, -)** tub; pail.
Kubikwurzel *f.* cube root.
Kubikzahl *f.* cube (number).
kubisch *a.* cubical; cube-shaped; cubic.
Kubismus *m.* cubism.
Küche *f.* **(-, -n)** kitchen; cooking, cookery, cuisine; *kalte* ~, cold meal.
Kuchen *m.* **(-s, -)** cake, pastry.
Küchenabfälle *pl.* kitchen scraps.
Küchenartikel *m.* kitchen utensil.
Kuchenbäcker *m.* pastry cook.
Kuchenblech *n.* baking sheet.
Küchenchef *m.* chef.
Kuchenform *f.* cake tin.
Küchengerät *n.* kitchen appliance.
Küchenschabe *f.* cockroach.
Küchlein *n.* **(-s, -)** (*zool.*) chick.
Kuckuck *m.* **(-s, -e)** cuckoo.
Kuddelmuddel *m.* **(-s, 0)** (*fam.*) muddle; confusion.
Kufe *f.* **(-, -n)** skid, runner.
Küfer *m.* **(-, -)** cooper.
Kugel *f.* **(-, -n)** ball; (*Flinte*) bullet; (*math.*) sphere, globe; bowl.
kugelfest *a.* bullet-proof.
kugelförmig *a.* spherical.
Kugelgelenk *n.* socket joint; (*mech.*) ball and socket.
Kugellager *n.* ball bearing.
kugeln *v.t. & i.* to roll, to bowl.
Kugelschreiber *m.* ballpoint pen.
kugelsicher *a.* bullet-proof.
Kugelstoßen *n.* shotput(ting).
Kugelstoßer *m.* **(-s, -)**; **Kugelstoßerin (-, -nen)** *f.* shotputter.
Kuh *f.* **(-, Kühe)** cow.
Kuhdorf *n.* (*pej.*) one-horse town.
Kuhfladen *m.* cowpat.
Kuhhandel *m.* (*pej.*) horse trading.
kuhhaut *f.* cowhide.
kühl *a.* cool, fresh.
Kühle *f.* **(-, 0)** coolness.
kühlen *v.t.* to cool; ~ *v.i.* to grow cool.
Kühler *m.* **(-s, -)** (*mot.*) radiator; **~haube** *f.* hood.
Kühlflüssigkeit *f.* **(-, -en), Kühlmittel** *n.* **(-s, -)** (*mech.*) coolant.
Kühlraum *m.* cold storage.
Kühlschrank *m.* **(-s, -schänke)** refrigerator.
Kühltasche *f.* **(-s, -n)** cool box.
Kühltruhe *f.* (chest) freezer.
Kühlung *f.* **(-, -en)** cooling.
Kühlwagen *m.* refrigerator car (train); refrigerator truck.
Kühlwasser *n.* cooling water.
Kuhmilch *f.* cow's milk.
Kuhmist *m.* cow dung.
kühn *a.* bold, daring, audicious.
Kühnheit *f.* **(-, 0)** boldness; daringness; audacity.
Kuhstall *m.* cow-shed.
Küken *n.* **(-s, -)** chicken; (*fam.*) chick.
kulant *a.* fair.
Kuli *m.* **(-s, -s)** coolie; ballpoint pen.
Kulisse *f.* **(-, n);** scenery; backdrop; wing, side-scene; *hinter den* ~*n,* behind the scenes.
kullern *v.i.* to roll.
Kult *m.* **(-s, -e)** cult.
Kultfigur *f.* cult figure.
Kulthandlung *f.* ritual act.
kultisch *a.* ritual, cultic.
kultivieren *v.t.* to cultivate; to culture.
kultiviert *a.* cultivated; cultured; refined; civilized.
Kultstätte *f.* **(-, -n)** center of worship.
Kultur *f.* **(-, -en)** culture; civilization; cultivation.
Kulturbanause *m.* **(-n, -n)**; philistine.
Kulturbanausin *f.* **(-, -nen)**; philistine.
Kulturbeutel *m.* cosmetic bag.
kulturell *a. & adv.* cultural(ly).
Kulturfilm *m.* documentary film.
Kulturgeschichte *f.* history of civilization; cultural history.
Kulturgut *n.* cultural asset(s).
Kulturhoheit *f.* autonomy in cultural and educational matters.
Kulturkreis *m.* cultural area.
Kulturpolitik *f.* cultural and educational policy.
Kultus *m.* **(-, -te)** (public) worship.
Kultusminister *m.;* **Kultusministerin** *f.* secretary of education.
Kümmel *m.* **(-s, -)** caraway; *Kreuz*~, *m.* cumin.
Kummer *m.* **(-s, 0)** grief, sorrow, distress.
kümmerlich *a.* miserable, scanty.
kümmern *v.r.* to care for, to mind.
kummervoll *a.* sorrowful, grievous, afflicted.
Kumpan *m.* **(-[e]s, -e); Kumpanin** *f.* **(-, -nen)** buddy; companion, pal.
Kumpel *m.* **(-s, -)** miner; buddy.
kumpelhaft *a.* matey; chummy.
kund *a.* ~ *tun,* to notify, to give notice; *sich* ~ *geben,* to manifest oneself.
kündbar *a.* terminable; subject to notice.
Kunde *f.* **(-, -n)** knowledge; information;
Kunde *m.* **(-n, -n); Kundin** *f.* **(-, -nen)** customer, client.
künden *v.t.* to make known.
Kundgebung *f.* **(-, -en)** demonstration.
kundig *a.* skilled, versed (in).
kündigen *v.i.* to give notice; ~ *v.t.* to cancel.
Kündigung *f.* **(-, -en)** notice, cancellation; termination; dismissal; warning; *auf monatliche* ~, at a month's notice.
Kündigungsfrist *f.* period of notice.
Kündigungsgrund *m.* grounds for giving notice.
Kündigungsschreiben *n.* letter of notice/dismissal.
Kündigungsschutz *m.* protection against unlawful dismissal.
Kundschaft *f.* **(-, -en)** customers; patronage.
kundschaften *v.i.* to reconnoiter.
Kundschafter *m.* **(-s, -)** scout; spy.
künftig *a.* future, to be, next; ~ *adv.* in future.
Kunst *f.* **(-, Künste)** art; skill.
Kunstakademie *f.* academy of fine arts.
Kunstausstellung *f.* art exhibition.
Kunstbanause *m.* **(-n, -n)** philistine.
Kunstdünger *m.* chemical fertilizer.

Künstelei *f.* **(-, -en)** affectation.
Kunstfertigkeit *f.* skill; skillfulness.
Kunstgegenstand *m.* work of art.
kunstgerecht *a.* (technically) correct, workmanlike; expert.
Kunstgeschichte *f.* art history.
Kunstgewerbe *n.* arts and crafts.
Kunstgriff *m.* trick, artifice.
Kunsthändler *m.* art dealer.
Kunsthandlung *f.* art dealer's.
Kunsthandwerk *n.* arts and crafts.
Kunstkenner *m.* connoisseur
Kunstkritik *f.* art criticism.
Kunstleder *n.* imitation letter.
Künstler *m.* **(-s, -); Künstlerin** *f.* **(-, -nen)** artist.
künstlerisch *a.* artistic.
Künstlername *m.* stage name.
künstlich *a.* artificial; artful.
Kunstliebhaber *m.* **(-s, -)**; **Kunstliebhaberin** *f.* **(-nen)** art lover, collector.
kunstlos *a.* artless, plain.
Kunstrichtung *f.* trend in art.
Kunstsammlung *f.* art collection.
Kunstschule *f.* school of art.
Kunstseide *f.* artificial silk, rayon.
kunstsinnig *a.* art-loving.
Kunstspringen *n.* springboard diving.
Kunststoff *m.* synthetic material, plastic.
Kunststopferei *f.* invisible mending.
Kunststück *n.* feat, trick, stunt.
Kunsttischler *m.* cabinet maker.
Kunstturnen *n.* gymnastics.
kunstverständig *a.* expert.
Kunstvoll *a.* artistic, elaborate.
Kunstwerk *n.* work of art.
Kunstwissenschaft *f.* of fine arts.
kunterbunt *a.* & *adv.* colorful; untidy.
Kupfer *n.* **(-s, -)** copper.
Kupferbergwerk *n.* copper mine.
Kupferblech *n.* sheet copper.
Kupferdruck *m.* copper plate.
Kupfermünze *f.* copper (coin).
kupfern *a.* copper.
Kupferplatte *f.* copperplate.
kupferrot *a.* copper-colored.
Kupferschmied *m.* coppersmith, brazier.
Kupferstecher *m.* engraver (in copper).
Kupferstich *m.* engraving, copperplate, print.
Kuppe *f.* **(-, -n)** curved top, summit; tip (finger).
Kuppel *f.* **(-, -n)** cupola, dome.
Kuppelbau *m.* domed building.
Kuppelei *f.* **(-, -en)** procuration, (*pej.*) match making.
kuppeln *v.t.* to couple, to link, to join; ~ *v.i.* to procure.
Kuppler *m.* **(-s, -)** pander, pimp.
Kupplerin *f.* **(-, -nen)** procuress, bawd.
Kupplung *f.* **(-, -en)** coupling; clutch.
Kur *f.* **(-, -en)** medical treatment.
Kür *f.* free program (ice skating); optional exercises (gymnastics).
Kürassier *m.* **(-[e]s, -e)** cuirassier.
Kuratel *f.* **(-, -en)** guardianship, trusteeship.
Kurator *m.* **(-s, -en)** guardian, trustee.
Kuratorium *n.* board of trustees.
Kuraufenthalt *m.* stay at a spa.
Kurbad *n.* spa; health resort.
Kurbel *f.* **(-, -n)** crank, winder.
kurbeln *v.t.* to crank; (*film*) to reel off.
Kurbelwelle *f.* (*mech.*) crankshaft.
Kürbis *m.* **(-ses, -se)** gourd, pumpkin.
küren *v.t.* to choose.
Kurfürst *m.* elector.
Kurfürstentum *n.* electorate.
Kurfürstin *f.* electress.
kurfürstlich *a.* electoral.
Kurgast *m.* visitor at a health resort or spa.
Kurhaus *m.* pump room; casino (of a spa).
Kurie *f.* **(-, -n)** curia.
Kurier *m.* **(-[e]s, -e)** courier.
Kurierdienst *m.* messenger service.
kurieren *v.t.* to cure.
kurios *a.* curious, odd, strange.
Kuriosität *f.* **(-, -en)** strangeness, oddity, peculiarity; curiosity, curio.
Kuriositätenkabinett *n.* gallery of curios.
Kurort *m.* health-resort, spa, watering place.
Kurpfuscher *m.* quack.
Kurs *m.* **(-es, -e)** (rate of) exchange; price; (*nav.*) course; *außer* ~ (*Geld, Briefmarke*), out of circulation.
Kursänderung *f.* change of course.
Kursanstieg *m.* rise in the exchange rate; rise in prices (stock market).
Kursbuch *n.* railway guide, time tables *pl.*
Kürschner *m.* **(-s, -); Kürschnerin** *f.* **(-, -nen)** furrier, skinner.
kursieren *v.i.* to circulate.
kursiv *a.* italics; ~ *gedruckt,* printed in italics.
Kursivschrift *f.* italics *pl.*
Kurskorrektur *f.* course correction.
Kursleiter *m.* **(-s, -), Kursleiterin** *f.* **(-s, -)** instructor.
Kursnotierung *f.* quotation.
Kursrückgang *m.* fall in exchange rates; fall in prices (stock market).
Kursschwankung *f.* fluctuation in prices (stock market); fluctuation in exchange rates.
Kursteilnehmer *m.*, **Kursteilnehmerin** *f.* participant in a class.
Kursus *m.* **(-, Kurse)** course (of lessons); class.
Kurtaxe *f.* visitors' tax (spa).
Kurve *f.* **(-, -n)** curve, bent.
kurven *v.i.* to drive *or* ride around.
Kurvenbild *n.* graph, diagram.
Kurvenlage *f.* (*mot.*) curve handling.
kurvenreich *a.* winding, twisting.
Kurverwaltung *f.* administrative offices at a spa.
kurz *a.* short; brief, abrupt; ~ *adv.* in short, briefly; ~ *und gut,* in a word; ~ *um,* in short; ~ *weg,* briefly, in brief; ~ *und bündig,* concise(ly), terse(ly); *in* ~ *em,* shortly, soon; *vor* ~ *em,* recently, the other day; *über* ~ *oder lang,* sooner or later; *zu* ~ *kommen,* to get short measure; *den kürzeren ziehen,* to get the worst of it.
Kurzarbeit *f.* part-time work.
Kurzarbeiter *m.*, **Kurzarbeiterin** *f.* part-time worker.
kurzatmig *a.* short-winded.
Kurzbiographie *f.* profile.
Kurze *m.* **(-n, -n)** (*fam.*) short (circuit); schnapps.
Kürze *f.* **(-, 0)** shortness; brevity.
Kürzel *n.* **(-s, -)** abbreviation; shorthand symbol.
kürzen *v.t.* to shorten, to curtail; (*Schriftliches*) to abridge.
kurzerhand *adv.* without further ado.
kürzertreten *v.i.st.* to take things easier, to spend less; to cut back.
Kurzfassung *f.* shortened/abridged version.

Kurzfilm *m.* short film.
kurzfristig *a.* short-term.
Kurzgeschichte *f.* short story.
kürzlich *adv.* lately, recently.
Kurzschluß *m.* short circuit; fallacy.
Kurzschlußhandling *f.* sudden irrational act.
Kurzschrift *f.* shorthand (writing).
kurzsichtig *a.* near-sighted, short-sighted, narrow-minded.
Kurzstreckenflug *m.* short-haul flight.
Kurzstreckenläufer(in) *m.(f.)* sprinter.
Kürzung *f.* **(-, -en)** abridgement; curtailment, cut.
Kurzwaren *pl.* notions.
Kurzweil *f.* **(-, 0)** pastime.
kurzweilig *a.* merry, diverting, amusing.
Kurzwelle *f.* **(-, -n)** short wave.
kuschelig *a.* cozy.
kuscheln *v.r.* to snuggle.
kuschen *v.i.* (*Hund*) to crouch, to lie down; *kusch (dich)!* lie down!
Kusine *f.* **(-, -n)** cousin.
Kuß *m.* **(Kusses, Küsse)** kiss.
küssen *v.t.* to kiss.
Kußhand *f.* blown kiss.
Küste *f.* **(-, -n)** coast, shore.
Küstenschiffahrt *f.* coastal shipping.
Küstenwache *f.* coastguard.
Küster *m.* **(-s, -)** sexton, verger.
Kustos *m.* **(-, oden)** curator, custodian.
Kutsche *f.* **(-, -n)** carriage, coach.
Kutscher *m.* **(-s, -)** coachman, driver.
kutschieren *v.i.* to drive a coach.
Kutte *f.* **(-, -n)** cowl; monk's habit.
Kutteln *pl.* tripe.
Kutter *m.* **(-s, -)** (*nav.*) cutter.
Kuvert *n.* **(-s, -e)** envelope; (*Gedeck*) cover.
Kuvertüre *f.* chocolate coating.
Kuwait *n.* **(-s, 0)** Kuwait.
Kuwaiti *m./f.*; **kuwaitisch** *a.* Kuwaiti.
Kux *m.* **(-es, -e)** mining share.
kW *Kilowatt,* kilowatt.
kWh *Kilowattstunde,* kilowatt-hour.
Kybernetik *f.* **(-, 0)** cybernetics.
Kybernetiker *m.*; **~in** *f.* cyberneticist.
kybernetisch *a.* cybernetic.
kyrillisch *a.* Cyrillic.
KZ *Konzentrationslager,* concentration camp.
KZ-Häftling *m.* concentration camp prisoner.

L

L, l *n.* the letter L or l.
l *Liter,* liter.
l. *links,* left, l.
labb(e)rig *a.* (*fam.*) wishy-washy; floppy; limp.
laben *v.t.* to refresh, to comfort; ~ *v.r.* to refresh oneself.
labern *v.t.* (*fam. pej.*) to babble.
labil *a.* unstable; delicate.
Labilität *f.* delicateness; frailness; instability.
Labor *n.* **(-s, -e & -s), Laboratorium** *n.* **(-s, -rien)** laboratory.
Laborant *m.*, **Laborantin** *f.* lab assistant.
Labsal *n.* **(-[e]s, -e)** refreshment.
Labyrinth *n.* **(-s, -e)** maze, labyrinth.
Lachanfall *m.* **(-s, -anfälle)** laughing fit.
Lache *f.* **(-, -n)** pool, puddle; (*fam.*) laugh.
lächeln *v.i.* to smile.
Lächeln *n.* **(-s, 0)** smile.
lachen *v.i.* to laugh.
Lachen *n.* **(-s, 0)** laughter, laugh.
Lacher *m.* **(-s, -)** laughter.
lächerlich *a.* laughable, ridiculous; ludicrous.
Lächerlichkeit *f.* **(-, -en)** ridiculousness, ludicrousness.
Lachgas *n.* laughing gas.
lachhaft *a.* ridiculous, laughable.
Lachkrampf *m.* convulsive laughter.
Lachs *m.* **(-es, -e)** salmon.
Lachsschinken *m.* **(-s, -)** fillet of smoked ham.
Lack *m.* **(-[e]s, -e)** varnish, lacquer, paint.
Lackaffe *m.* (*fam. pej.*) dandy.
lackieren *v.t.* to varnish, to lacquer, to spray.
Lackmus *n.* **(-, 0)** litmus.
Lackstiefel *m.* patent leather boots.
Lade *f.* **(-, -n)** drawer.
Ladegerät *n.* (*elek.*) charger.
laden *v.t.st.* to load, to charge; to summon, to cite; to invite.
Laden *m.* **(-s, Läden)** shop; store.
Ladendieb *m.* shoplifter.
Ladendiebstahl *f.* shoplifting.
Ladenfenster *n.* store.
Ladenhüter *m.* unsalable merchandise.
Ladenpreis *m.* retail price; (*Buch*) publication price.
Ladentisch *m.* counter.
Lader *m.* (*avi.*) supercharger.
Laderampe *f.* loading ramp.
Laderaum *m.* baggage space; hold.
lädieren *v.t.* to damage; to harm.
Ladung *f.* **(-, -en)** freight, cargo, shipment; (*Gewehr*~), (*elek.*) charge.
Lage *f.* **(-, -n)** situation, position; location; condition; layer, stratum; (*mech.*) thickness; **~karte** *f.* (*mil.*) map of area; **~meldung** *f.* (*mil.*) situation report.
Lager *n.* **(-s, -)** couch, bed; warehouse; (*von Tieren*) lair; (*Vorrat*) stock; (*Erz*) deposit; (*mil.*) camp.
Lagerbier *n.* lager.
Lagergebuhr *f.* storage (charge).
Lagergeld *n.* storage.
Lagerhaus *n.* warehouse.
Lagerist *m.* stockkeeper.
lagern *v.t.* to lay, to store, to warehouse; ~ *v.i.* to (en)camp; to be stored; ~ *v.r.* to lie down.
Lagerstätte *f.* resting place; depot.
Lagerung *f.* storage.
Lagune *f.* **(-, -n)** lagoon.
lahm *a.* lame, halt.
Lahme *m./f.* **(-n, -n)** cripple.
lahmen *v.i.* to be lame.
lähmen *v.t.* to lame, to paralyze.
lahmlegen *v.t.* to paralyze.
Lähmung *f.* **(-, -en)** paralysis.
Laib *m.* **(-[e]s, -e)** loaf.
Laich *m.* **(-[e]s, 0)** spawn.
laichen *v.i.* to spawn.
Laie *m.* **(-n, -n)** layman.
Laienbruder *m.* lay brother.

Laientheater *n.* **(-s, -)** amateur theater.
Lakai *m.* **(en, -en)** footman, lackey.
Lake *f.* **(-, -n)** brine, pickle.
Laken *n.* **(-s, -)** sheet.
lakonisch *a. & adv.* laconic(ally).
Lakritz *m.* **(-es, -e), Lakritze** *f.* **(-, -n)** licorice.
lallen *v.t. & i.* to stammer.
Lama *n.* **(-s, -s)** llama.
Lamelle *f.* **(-, -n)** (*elek.*) lamina.
lamentieren *v.i.* to moan, to complain.
Lamm *n.* **(-[e]s, Lämmer)** lamb.
Lammbraten *m.* roast lamb.
Lammfell *n.* lambskin.
Lammfleisch *n.* lamb.
Lammkeule *f.* leg of lamb.
Lammkotelett *n.* lamb chop.
Lampe *f.* **(-, -n)** lamp.
Lampenfieber *n.* stage fright.
Lampenschirm *m.* lampshade.
Lampion *m.* **(-s, -s)** Chinese lantern.
lancieren *v.t.* (*fig.*) to launch.
Land *n.* **(-[e]s, Länder *or poet.* Lande)** land; country; territory; *zu ~*, by land; *auf dem ~*, in the country.
Landadel *m.* landed aristocracy.
Landarbeiter *m.* farm worker.
Landarzt *m.* country doctor.
Landauer *m.* **(-s, -)** landau.
Landbesitz *m.* landed property.
Landbevölkerung *f.* rural population.
Landeanflug *m.* (*avi.*) landing approach.
Landebahn *f.* runway.
Landeerlaubnis *f.* permission to land.
Landefähre *f.* landing module.
landeinwärts *adv.* (further) inland.
Landeklappe *f.* landing flap.
landen *v.t. (h) & i. (s)* to land; to get ashore, to disembark.
Landenge *f.* isthmus.
Landepiste *f.* landing strip.
Landeplatz *m.* airstrip; landing pad.
Länderei *f.* **(-, -en)** landed property; estate.
Länderkunde *f.* geography.
Landesfarben *pl.* national colors.
Landesherr *n.* sovereign.
Landeskirche *f.* national or established church.
Landestracht *f.* national costume.
landesüblich *a.* customary, usual.
Landesverrat *m.* treason.
Landesverteidigung *f.* defense.
Landfriede[n] *m.* the king's peace.
Landgericht *n.* county court.
Landgut *n.* estate, manor.
Landhaus *n.* country house.
Landkarte *f.* map.
Landkrieg *m.* land warfare.
landläufig *a.* in current use.
ländlich *a.* rural.
Landmaschine *f.* agricultural machine.
Landmesser *m.* surveyor.
Landplage *f.* plague of the country; (*fig.*) pest, nuisance.
Landratte *f.* (*fam.*) landlubber.
Landschaft *f.* **(-, -en)** landscape; scenery; countryside.
landschaftlich *a.* regional; scenic.
Landschaftspflege *f.* conservation.
Landschaftsschutz *m.* conservation; **~gebiet** *n.* nature preserve.
Landsitz *m.* country seat.
Landsknecht *m.* hired foot soldier.
Landsmann *m.* countryman, compatriot.
Landstraße *f.* country road.
Landstreicher *m.* vagrant, tramp, hobo.
Landstreitkräfte *pl.* ground forces.
Landstrich *m.* area.
Landtag *m.* state parliament.
Landtruppen *pl.* ground forces.
Landung *f.* **(-, -en)** landing, descent.
Landungsbrücke *f.* landing stage; jetty.
Landwirt *m.* farmer; agriculturist.
Landwirtschaft *f.* agriculture, farming.
landwirtschaftlich *a.* agricultural; *~er Betriebsleiter* farm manager.
Landwirtschafts: ~minister *m.*, **~ministerin** *f.* secretary of agriculture; **~ministerium** *n.* department of agriculture.
Landzunge *f.* promontory.
lang *a.* long; tall; *Tage ~*, for days in a row.
langatmig *a.* long-winded, lengthy.
lange *adv.* long; *~ her*, long ago.
Länge *f.* **(-, -en)** length; tallness; longitude; *auf die ~*, in the long run; *der ~ nach*, lengthwise.
langen *v.t.* to hand, to give, to reach; *~ v.i.* to suffice, to be enough.
Längen: ~grad *m.* degree of longitude; **~kreis** *m.* longitude; **~maß** *n.* long or linear measure.
Langeweile *f.* **(-, 0)** boredom.
langfristig *a.* long term.
langjährig *a.* of long standing.
Langlauf *m.* cross-country (skiing).
Langläufer *m.*, **Langläuferin** *f.* cross-country skier.
langlebig *a.* long-lived.
länglich *a.* oblong.
Langmut *f.* **(-, 0)** forbearance.
langmütig *a.* forbearing
längs *pr.* along.
Längsachse *f.* longitudinal axis.
langsam *a.* slow; tardy.
Langsamkeit *f.* slowness.
Langschläfer *m.*, **Langschläferin** *f.* late riser.
Längsschnitt *m.* longitudinal section.
längsseits *adv.* alongside.
längst *adv.* long since.
längstens *adv.* at the longest, at the latest.
Langstrecke *f.* long distance; long haul.
Languste *f.* spiny lobster; langouste.
langweilen *v.t.* to tire, to bore; *~ v.r.* to be bored.
Langweiler *m.* bore.
langweilig *a.* dull; *~e Person*, bore.
Langwelle *f.* (*radio*) long wave.
langwierig *a.* lengthy, protracted.
Lanze *f.* **(-, -n)** lance, spear.
Lanzette *f.* **(-, -n)** lancet.
lapidar *a. & adv.* succinct(ly); terse(ly).
Lappalie *f.* **(-, -n)** trifle.
Lappe *m.*, **Lappin** *f.* Lapp, Laplander.
Lappen *m.* **(-s, -)** rag; patch.
läppisch *a.* silly, foolish.
Lappland *n.* **(-s, 0)** Lapland.
Lärche *f.* **(-, -n)** larch.
Larifari *n.* (*fam.*) nonsense.
Lärm *m.* **(-[e]s, 0)** noise, din; *~ schlagen*, to sound the alarm.
Lärmbekämpfung *f.* noise abatement.
Lärmbelästigung *f.* noise pollution.
lärmempfindlich *a.* sensitive to noise.

lärmen *v.i.* to make a noise or row.
lärmend *a.* noisy.
Lärmpegel *m.* noise level.
Lärmschutz *m.* protection against noise.
Larve *f.* **(-, -n)** mask; larva.
lasch *a.* limp, lax.
Lasche *f.* **(-, -n)** strap; loop; flap; tongue (of shoe).
Laserstrahl *m.* laser beam.
lassen *v.t.st.* to let; to allow, to suffer; to order, to cause; to leave; *sein Leben ~*, to sacrifice one's life; *einen in Ruhe oder zufrieden ~*, to leave (let) sb. alone; *kommen ~*, to send for, to order; *machen ~*, to have done; *sehen ~*, to show; *sagen ~*, to send word; *übrig ~*, to leave; *sein Tun und Lassen*, all his doing; *laß das!* don't!; *das läßt sich hören*, it is pleasant to hear; there is something in that.
lässig *a.* casual; (*fam.*) cool.
läßlich *a.* pardonable.
Last *f.* **(-, -n)** load, charge, burden; tonnage; *zu Ihren ~en*, to your account; *zur ~ fallen*, to be a burden.
lasten *v.i.* to weigh upon, to press.
Laster *n.* **(-s, -)** vice; crime.
lasterhaft *a.* vicious, profligate.
Lästermaul *n.* slanderer, scandalmonger.
lästern *v.t.* to slander; to blaspheme.
Lästerung *f.* **(-, -n)** calumny; blasphemy.
lästig *a.* burdensome, troublesome.
Lastkraftwagen *m.* truck.
Lasttier *n.* beast of burden.
Lasur *f.* **(-, -en)** varnish, glaze.
Latein *n.* **(-s, 0)** Latin.
Lateinamerika *n.* Latin America.
lateinamerikanisch *a.* Latin American.
lateinisch *a.* Latin.
latent *a.* latent.
Laterne *f.* **(-, -n)** lantern; (street)lamp.
Laternenpfahl *m.* lamppost.
Latrine *f.* **(-, -n)** latrine.
Latsche *f.* **(-, -n)** dwarf pine.
latschen *v.i.* to shuffle along; to slouch; to trudge.
Latte *f.* **(-, -n)** lath; slat.
Lattenrost *m.* duckboards; slatted frame (bed).
Lattenzaun *m.* paling fence.
Latz *m.* **(-es, Lätze)** flap; bib.
Latzhose *f.* dungarees *pl.*
lau *a.* tepid; (*met.*) mild; (*fig.*) lukewarm.
Laub *n.* **(-[e]s, 0)** leaves *pl.*; foliage.
Laubbaum *m.* deciduous tree.
Laube *f.* **(-, -n)** arbor, bower.
Laubengang *m.* arcade.
Laubfrosch *m.* treefrog.
laubig *a.* leafy, leaved.
Laubsäge *f.* fretsaw.
Lauch *m.* **(-[e]s, -e)** leek.
Lauer *f.* **(-, 0)** lurking place; ambush; *auf der ~ sein*, to lie in wait.
lauern *v.i.* to lurk, to lie in wait.
Lauf *m.* **(-[e]s, Läufe)** course; run; race; (*Gewehr~*) barrel; leg (of game); (*mus.*) roulade.
Laufbahn *f.* course, career.
Laufbursche *m.* errand-boy, messenger boy.
laufen *v.i.st.* *(s)* to run, to flow, to leak.
laufend *a.* running; current; *auf dem ~en sein*, to be well-informed; *auf dem ~en halten*, to keep informed; *~e Arbeiten pl.* routine work; *~es Band n.* conveyor belt; *~e Nummer f.* serial number; *~es Wasser n.* running water.
laufenlassen *v.t.st.* to let sb. go.
Läufer *m.* **(-s, -)** runner, long carpet; (*Schach*) bishop; (*sp.*) halfback.
Lauferei *f.* **(-, -en)** running around.
Lauffeuer *n.*, *wie ein ~*, like wildfire.
Lauffläche *f.* tread (of tire).
Laufgitter *n.* playpen.
Laufkran *m.* traveling crane.
Laufmasche *f.* run (in stocking).
Laufschritt *m.* *im ~*, on the double.
Laufstall *m.* playpen.
Laufsteg *m.* catwalk.
Laufzeit *f.* running time; run; term.
Lauge *f.* **(-, -n)** lye, suds; (*chem.*) alkaline solution.
Laune *f.* **(-, -n)** whim, caprice; humor, temper, mood.
launenhaft *a.* temperamental; capricious; fickle.
launig *a.* humorous.
launisch *a.* capricious, wayward.
Laus *f.* **(-, Läuse)** louse (*pl.* lice).
Lausbub *m.* **(-en, -en)** scamp.
Lauscher *m.* **(-s, -)** listener.
lauschig *a.* snug, cozy, quiet.
lausig *a.* lousy, wretched.
Lausjunge, Lausekerl *m.* little rascal.
laut *a.* loud; *~ adv.* loudly; *~ pr.* as per, according to.
Laut *m.* **(-[e]s, -e)** sound.
Laute *f.* **(-, -n)** lute.
lauten *v.i.* to sound; to run, to read.
läuten *v.i. & t.* to ring.
lauter *a.* clear; pure; mere, none but, nothing but; sincere, ingenious.
Lauterkeit *f.* **(-, 0)** purity; integrity.
läutern *v.t.* to purify, to reform.
Läuterung *f.* **(-, -en)** purification.
Lautgesetz *n.* phonetic law.
lauthals *adv.* at the top of one's voice.
lautlich *a.* phonetic.
lautlos *a.* silent, mute; hushed.
Lautschrift *f.* phonetic alphabet.
Lautsprecher *m.* loudspeaker; **~wagen** *m.* loudspeaker van.
Lautstärke *f.* volume; **~einstellung** *f.* volume control.
Lautzeichen *n.* phonetic symbol.
lauwarm *a.* lukewarm; tepid; warm.
Lava *f.* **(-, Laven)** lava.
Lavendel *m.* **(-s, 0)** lavender.
lavieren *v.i.* to maneuver.
Lawine *f.* **(-, -n)** avalanche.
lax *a.* lax, loose.
Lazarett *n.* **(-[e]s, -e)** military hospital.
Lazarettschiff *n.* hospital ship.
Lazarettzug *m.* hospital train.
l.c. *loco citato*, in the place quoted.
Leasing *n.* leasing.
Lebemann *m.* man about town; epicure.
leben *v.i.* to live, to be alive; *lebe wohl!* farewell; *hoch ~ lassen*, to cheer.
Leben *n.* **(-s, -)** life; (*fig.*) animation; *am ~ bleiben*, to live; *ums ~ bringen*, to kill; *ums ~ kommen*, to perish; *sich sein ~ verdienen*, to make a living.
lebend *a.* living; alive; *~e Sprachen*, modern languages; *~e Bilder*, tableaux vivants.
lebendig *a.* living, alive; quick, lively.
Lebendigkeit *f.* liveliness.
Lebensabend *m.* old age, autumn of one's life.

Lebensabschnitt *m.* period of life.
Lebensalter *n.* age.
Lebensart *f.* way of life; manner.
Lebensbedingungen *pl.* living conditions.
lebensbedrohlich *a.* life-threatening.
Lebensbedürfnisse *pl.* necessities of life.
Lebensbejahung *f.* positive approach to life.
Lebensbeschreibung *f.* biography, life.
Lebensdauer *f.* (*auch von Dingen*) lifespan; *von langer* ~, long-lived; *mutmaßliche* ~, life expectancy.
Lebenserinnerungen *pl.* memoirs.
Lebenserwartung *f.* life expectancy.
lebensfähig *a.* capable of living, viable.
Lebensfrage *f.* vital question.
Lebensfreude *f.* joie de vivre; zest for life.
Lebensgefahr *f.* mortal danger.
lebensgefährlich *a.* perilous; ~ *verwundet od. krank,* in critical condition.
Lebensgefährte *m.*, **Lebensgefährtin** *f.* companion, partner in life.
Lebensgröße *f.* life size.
Lebenshaltung *f.* standard of living; **~skosten** *pl.* cost of living.
Lebensjahr *n.* year of one's life.
Lebenskampf *m.* struggle for survival.
Lebenskraft *f.* vitality, vigor.
lebenslang *a.* lifelong.
lebenslänglich *a.* for life, life-long; *~er Nießbrauch,* (*law*) life-interest.
Lebenslauf *m.* career; résumé; curriculum vitae.
lebenslustig *a.* cheery, enjoying life.
Lebensmittel *pl.* provisions, victuals.
lebensmittelabteilung *f.* food department.
Lebensmittelgeschäft *n.* grocery store.
Lebensmittelkarten *pl.* ration book.
Lebensmittelvergiftung *f.* food poisoning.
lebensmüde *a.* weary of life.
lebensunfähig *a.* nonviable.
Lebensunterhalt *m.* (means of) livelihood.
Lebensversicherung *f.* life insurance.
Lebenswandel *m.* conduct.
Lebensweise *f.* way of life.
Lebensweisheit *f.* practical wisdom.
lebenswert *a.* worth living.
lebenswichtig *a.* vital.
Lebenswille *m.* will to live.
Lebenszeichen *n.* sign of life.
Lebenszeit *f. auf* ~, for life.
Leber *f.* **(-, -n)** liver.
Leber: ~fleck, ~flecken *m.* mole; **~knödel** *m.* (*cul.*) liver dumpling; **~pastete** *f.* (*cul.*) liver pâté; **~tran** *m.* cod-liver oil; **~zirrhose** *f.* cirrhosis of the liver.
Lebewesen *n.* living being; creature; organism.
Lebewohl *n.* **(-[e]s, -e & -s)** farewell.
lebhaft *a.* vivid, lively, brisk, animated.
Lebhaftigkeit *f.* **(-, 0)** vivacity, animation.
Lebkuchen *m.* gingerbread.
leblos *a.* lifeless, inanimate; heavy, dull.
Lebzeiten *pl.* lifetime.
lechzen *v.i.* to pant, to languish.
leck *a.* leaky; ~ *werden,* to spring a leak.
Leck *n.* **(-[e]s, -e)** leak.
lecken *v.t.* to lick, to lap; ~ *v.i.* to leak.
lecker *a.* tasty; delicious; good.
Leckerbissen *m.* delicacy, tidbit, choice morsel.
Leckerei *f.* **(-, -en)** dainty; sweet.
led. *ledig,* single, unmarried.
Leder *n.* **(-s, -)** leather.
Lederband *m.* leatherbound book.
ledern *v.t.* to leather.
ledern *a.* leather, leathern; (*fig.*) dull.
Lederzeug *n.* leather straps and belts *pl.*
ledig *a.* unmarried, single.
lediglich *adv.* solely, only.
leer *a.* empty, void; vacant.
Leere *f.* **(-, 0)** emptiness; void, vacuum.
leeren *v.t.* to empty, to clear.
leergefegt *a.* (*fig.*) deserted.
Leerlauf *m.* **(-[e]s, 0)** idle running; neutral gear; freewheel.
leerstehend *a.* unoccupied.
Leertaste *f.* space bar.
Leerung *f.* emptying; *nächste* ~, next collection.
Lefzen *pl.* flews.
legal *a.* & *adv.* legal(ly).
legalisieren *v.t.* to legalize.
Legalität *f.* legality.
Legasthenie *f.* **(-, -n)** dyslexia.
Legastheniker *m.* **~in** *f.* dyslexic.
Legat *n.* **(-[e]s, -e)** legacy; ~ *m.* **(-en, -en)** legate.
Legehenne *f.* laying hen.
legen *v.t.* to lay, to put, to place; ~ *v.r.* to lie down; (wind) to abate; *Karten* ~, to tell fortunes from cards; *einem das Handwerk* ~, to stop one's little game; *nahe* ~, to suggest, to impress upon; *an den Tag* ~, to manifest, to evince; *sich ins Mittel* ~, to step in, to interpose.
legendär *a.* legendary.
Legende *f.* **(-, -n)** legend.
leger *a.* casual; relaxed.
legieren *v.t.* to alloy.
Legierung *f.* **(-, -en)** alloy(ing).
Legion *f.* **(-, -en)** legion.
Legionär *m.* **(-s, -e)** legionnaire.
Legislative *f.* legislature.
Legislaturperiode *f.* parliamentary term.
legitim *a.* legitimate, lawful.
Legitimationspapier *n.* certificate of identity; **~e** *pl.* identity papers.
legitimieren *v.t.* to legitimate; ~ *v.r.* to prove one's identity.
Legitimität *f.* **(-, 0)** legitimacy.
Leh(e)n *n.* **(-s, -)** fief.
Leh(e)nsrecht *n.* feudal law.
Lehm *m.* **(-[e]s, -e)** loam, clay.
Lehmboden *m.* loamy soil; clay soil.
Lehmhütte *f.* mud hut.
lehmig *a.* loamy, clayey.
Lehmziegel *m.* clay brick.
Lehne *f.* **(-, -n)** back(rest); arm(rest).
lehnen *v.t.* & *i.* & *r.* to lean (against).
Lehnsessel, Lehnstuhl *m.* armchair.
Lehramt *n.* teaching position; teaching profession.
Lehranstalt *f.* academy, school.
Lehrauftrag *m.* lectureship; teaching assignment.
lehrbar *a.* teachable.
Lehrbeauftragte *m./f.* lecturer.
Lehrbuch *n.* textbook.
Lehre *f.* **(-, -n)** doctrine; instruction; precept; moral, warning; lesson; apprenticeship; *in der* ~ *sein,* to serve one's apprenticeship; (*mech.*) gauge.
lehren *v.t.* to teach, to instruct.
Lehrer *m.* **(-s, -), Lehrerin** *f.* **(-, -nen)** teacher; tutor.
Lehrerausbildung *f.* teacher training.
Lehrerkonferenz *f.* faculty meeting.

Lehrerzimmer *n.* teachers' room.
Lehrfach *n.* subject.
Lehrfilm *m.* instructional film.
Lehrgang *m.* course.
Lehrjahre *pl.* apprenticeship.
Lehrkörper *m.* **(-s, -)** teaching staff; faculty.
Lehrling *m.* **(-[e]s, -e)** apprentice.
Lehrmeister *m.* instructor.
Lehrmittel *n.* teaching aid.
Lehrplan *m.* curriculum; syllabus.
lehrreich *a.* instructive.
Lehrsatz *m.* theorem, maxim.
Lehrstuhl *m.* (professor's) chair; professorship.
Lehrveranstaltung *f.* class; lecture.
Lehrzeit *f.* apprenticeship.
Leib *m.* **(-[e]s, -er)** body; (*Bauch*) belly; *sich vom ~ halten,* to keep at a distance.
Leibarzt *m.* private physician.
Leibbinde *f.* sash, waistband; (*med.*) truss.
Leibchen *n.* **(-s, -)** bodice.
Leibeigene[r] *m.* **(-n, -n)** serf.
Leibeigenschaft *f.* serfdom.
Leibeserben *pl.* offspring, issue.
Leibeserziehung *f.* physical education.
Leibesfrucht *f.* fetus.
Leibesübung *f.* physical exercise.
Leibgarde *f.* bodyguard.
Leibgericht *n.* favorite dish.
leibhaftig *a.* real.
leiblich *a.* physical, bodily; *~e Eltern* biological parents.
Leibrente *f.* life annuity.
Leibschmerzen *pl.* stomachache.
Leibwache *f.* bodyguard.
Leiche *f.* **(-, -n)** corpse, (dead) body.
Leichenbegängnis *n.* funeral, burial.
Leichenbeschauer *m.* coroner.
Leichenbestatter *m.* undertaker; mortician.
Leichenbestattungsinstitut *n.* funeral home.
leichenblaß *a.* deadly pale.
Leichenfeier *f.* funeral service.
Leichengift *n.* ptomaine.
Leichenhalle *f.* mortuary.
Leichenschauhaus *n.* morgue.
Leichenstarre *f.* rigor mortis.
Leichentuch *n.* shroud.
Leichenverbrennung *f.* cremation.
Leichenwagen *m.* hearse.
Leichnam *m.* **(-[e]s, -e)** corpse; carcass.
leicht *a.* light; easy, slight; mild; *~ adv.* easily.
Leichtathlet *m.,* **Leichtathletin** *f.* (track and field) athlete.
Leichtathletik *f.* athletics; track and field.
leichtblütig *a.* sanguine.
leichtfertig *a.* careless; ill-considered; frivolous.
Leichtgewicht *n.* (*sp.*) lightweight.
leichtgläubig *a.* gullible; credulous.
leichtherzig *a.* lighthearted.
leichthin *adv.* lightly.
Leichtigkeit *f.* **(-, -en)** ease, facility.
leichtlebig *a.* easygoing.
Leichtmetall *n.* light metal.
Leichtsinn *m.* carelessness, levity, frivolity.
leichtsinnig *a.* careless, frivolous, lighthearted, heedless.
Leid *n.* **(-[e]s, 0)** grief, sorrow; pain, harm; *einem etwas zu ~e tun,* to harm, to wrong, to hurt sb.; *es tut mir leid,* I am sorry.
leiden *v.t. & i.st.* to suffer, to endure; to tolerate; *ich kann ihn nicht ~,* I can't stand him.
Leiden *n.* **(-s, -)** suffering; disease.
leidend *a.* ailing, suffering.
Leidenschaft *f.* **(-, -en)** passion.
leidenschaftlich *a.* passionate, vehement.
Leidensgefährte *m.,* **~gefährtin** *f.;* **~genosse** *m.,* **~genossin** *f.* fellow sufferer.
Leidensgeschichte *f.* Christ's Passion; sad story.
Leidensmiene *f.* doleful expression.
leider *adv.* unfortunately; *~ i.* alas!
leidig *a.* tiresome, unpleasant.
leidlich *a.* tolerable; passable.
Leidtragende *m./f.* victim; bereaved; mourner.
leidvoll *a.* sorrowful.
Leidwesen *n.* regret.
Leier *f.* **(-, -n)** lyre; *die alte ~,* the old story.
Leierkasten *m.* hurdy-gurdy; barrel-organ.
leiern *v.i.* to drone; to reel, to rattle off.
Leihbibliothek *f.* lending library.
leihen *v.t.st.* to lend; to borrow.
Leih: ~gabe *f.* loan; **~gebühr** *f.* rental charge; borrowing fee; **~haus** *n.* pawnbroker's shop; **~mutter** *f.* surrogate mother; **~wagen** *m.* rental car.
leihweise *adv.* on loan, by way of loan.
Leim *m.* **(-[e]s, -e)** glue; *aus dem ~ gehen,* to get out of joint; *auf den ~ gehen,* to fall into the trap.
leimen *v.t.* to glue; (*Papier*) to paste; to take sb. in.
Leine *f.* **(-, -n)** line, cord, rope; leash.
leinen *a.* linen.
Leinen *n.* **(-s, -)** linen (goods).
Leinenband *m.* clothbound book.
Leinöl *n.* linseed oil.
Leinsamen *m.* linseed.
Leinwand *f.* **(-, 0)** linen; *Maler~,* canvas; screen.
leise *a.* quiet, low, soft, gentle; *~ adv.* softly, in a low voice; *~r reden,* to lower one's voice.
Leiste *f.* **(-, -n)** ridge, ledge; strip; trim; rail.
leisten *v.t.* to do, to perform; (*Dienst*) to render; (*Eid*) to take; (*Großes*) to achieve (great things); *Gesellschaft ~,* to keep (sb.) company; *ich kann mir das ~,* I can afford it.
Leisten *m.* **(-s, -)** last, form; shoe tree.
Leisten: ~bruch *m.* (*med.*) hernia; **~gegend** *f.* (*med.*) groin.
Leistung *f.* **(-, -en)** performance; accomplishment.
leistungs: ~berechtigt *a.* entitled to claim; **~bezogen** *a.* performance-oriented.
Leistungs: ~denken *n.* performance-oriented outlook; **~druck** *m.* pressure to achieve.
leistungsfähig *a.* efficient; productive.
Leistungsfähigkeit *f.* **(-, 0)** efficiency; productivity; power, (working) capacity.
Leistungs: ~gesellschaft *f.* performance-oriented society; **~prämie** *f.* productivity bonus.
leistungsschwach *a.* inefficient; low-performance.
Leistungssport *m.* competitive sport(s).
leistungsstark *a.* efficient; high-performance.
Leitartikel *m.* editorial, lead article, leader.
Leitartikler *m.* **(-s, -)** editorial writer.
Leitbild *n.* model.
leiten *v.t.* to lead, to guide, to conduct; to manage, to direct.
Leiter *m.* **(-s, -),** **Leiterin** *f.* **(-, -nen)** manager; leader, conductor; (*elek.*) conductor.
Leiter *f.* **(-, -n)** ladder; steps.

Leit: ~fähigkeit *f.* (*elek.*) conductivity; **~faden** *m.* (*Buch*) manual; **~gedanke** *m.* central theme; **~hammel** *m.* bellwether; (*fig.*) leader.
Leit: ~linie *f.* guideline; **~motiv** *n.* **(-s, -e)** leitmotiv; central theme; **~planke** *f.* crash barrier, guardrail; **~satz** *m.* guiding principle; **~spruch** *m.* motto.
Leitung *f.* **(-, -en)** guidance; management, direction; (*Röhre*) conduit; (*elek.*) line; *die ~ von etwas haben*, to be in charge of.
Leitungswasser *n.* tap water.
Lektion *f.* **(-, -en)** lesson; (*fig.*) lecture.
Lektor *m.*, **Lektorin** *f.* editor.
Lektüre *f.* **(-, 0)** reading; books *pl.*
Lende *f.* **(-, -n)** loin; haunch, thigh.
Lendenbraten *m.* sirloin; rump of beef.
Lendenschurz *m.* loincloth.
lenken *v.t.* to direct, to rule; to steer.
Lenker *m.*, **Lenkerin** *f.* driver.
Lenker *m.* handlebar.
Lenkrad *n.* steering wheel.
Lenksäule *f.* (*mot.*) steering column.
Lenkstange *f.* **(-, -n)** handlebar.
Lenkung *f.* control; governing; steering.
Lenz *m.* **(-es, -e)** spring.
Leopard *m.* **(-en, -en)** leopard.
Lepra *f.* leprosy.
Lerche *f.* **(-, -n)** lark, skylark.
lernbar *a.* learnable.
lernbegierig *a.* eager to learn; keen.
lernbehindert *a.* learning disabled.
Lerneifer *m.* eagerness to learn.
lernen *v.t.* to learn, to study; to train.
Lernende *m./f.* learner.
lernfähig *n.* able to learn.
Lernmittel *n.* **(-s, -)** learning aid.
Lesart *f.* reading, variant.
lesbar *a.* legible; (*fig.*) readable.
Lesbe *f.* **(-, -n) Lesbierin** *f.* **(-, -nen)** lesbian.
lesbisch *a.* lesbian.
Lese *f.* **(-, -n)** grape harvest, vintage.
Lesebrille *f.* reading glasses.
Lesebuch *n.* reader.
Lesegerät *n.* (*comp.*) scanner.
lesen *v.t. & i.st.* to gather, to glean; to read; to lecture; (*Messe*) to say.
lesenswert *a.* worth reading.
Leser *m.* **(-s, -), Leserin** *f.* **(-, -nen)** reader; gleaner.
Leseratte *f.* bookworm.
Leserbrief *m.* letter to the editor.
leserlich *a.* legible.
Leserstift *m.* (*comp.*) scanner.
Lesesaal *m.* reading room.
Lesezeichen *n.* bookmark.
Lesung *f.* **(-, -en)** reading.
Lethargie *f.* lethargy.
lethargisch *a.* lethargic.
Lette *m.*, **Lettin** *f.* Latvian; Lett.
Letter *f.* **(-, -n)** letter, type.
lettisch *a.* Latvian; Lettish (language).
Lettland *n.* Latvia.
letzen *v.r.* *~ an*, to enjoy, to relish.
letzt *a.* last, final; *~e Ölung*, last rites; *zu guter Letzt*, finally.
letztemal *adv.* *das ~* last time.
letztere[r] *a.* latter.
letzthin *adv.* lately, the other day.
letztlich *adv.* lastly.
letztwillig *a.* testamentary.
Leuchte *f.* **(-, -n)** lamp, lantern; (*fig.*) shining light.
leuchten *v.i.* to shine; to beam.
leuchtend *a.* shining bright.
Leuchter *m.* **(-s, -)** candlestick; chandelier.
Leuchtfarbe *f.* luminous paint.
Leuchtfeuer *n.* beacon; runway light.
Leuchtkäfer *m.* glowworm.
Leuchtkugel *f.* fireball.
Leuchtturm *m.* lighthouse.
Leuchtuhr *f.* luminous watch.
leugnen *v.t.* to deny, to disown.
Leukämie *f.* **(-, 0)** leukemia.
Leumund *m.* reputation.
Leute *pl.* people, persons *pl.;* servants *pl.*
Leuteschinder *m.* slavedriver.
Leutnant *m.* **(-[e]s, -s)** second lieutenant.
leutselig *a.* affable.
Leviten *pl.* *jm. die ~ lesen*, to read sb. the riot act.
Levkoje *f.* **(-, -n)** stock, gilly flower.
lexikalisch *a.* lexical.
Lexikographie *f.* lexicography.
Lexikon *n.* **(-s, Lexika)** encyclopedia.
lfd. *laufend*, current, running.
Lfrg. *Lieferung*, delivery; part.
Libanese *m.*, **Libanesin** *f.*, **libanesisch** *a.* Lebanese.
Libanon *n./m.* Lebanon.
Libelle *f.* **(-, -n)** dragonfly.
liberal *a.* liberal; generous.
Liberale *m./f.* liberal.
liberalisieren *v.t.* to liberalize.
Liberalisierung *f.* **(-, -n)** liberalization.
Liberalismus *m.* liberalism.
Libero *m.* sweeper (soccer).
Libyen *n.* Libya.
Libyer *m.;* **Libyerin** *f.;* **libysch** *a.* Libyan.
licht *a.* light, bright; lucid; clear; *~e Höhe f.* overhead clearance.
Licht *n.* **(-[e]s, -er & -e)** light; candle; *bei ~e*, (*fig.*) closely; *ungeschütztes ~*, naked light; *einem ein ~ aufstecken*, to open sb.'s eyes; *hinters ~ führen*, to dupe, to impose on; *ans ~ bringen*, to bring to light; *ins rechte ~ setzen*, to show in its true colors.
Lichtbild *n.* photograph; **~ervortrag** *m.* slide lecture.
Lichtblick *m.* ray of hope.
Lichtbogen *m.* electric arc.
lichtempfindlich *a.* (*photo*) sensitive.
lichten *v.t.* (*Wald*) to clear, to thin; *den Anker ~*, to weigh anchor.
lichterloh *a.* blazing.
Lichtgeschwindigkeit *f.* speed of light.
Lichthupe *f.* (*mot.*) flasher.
Lichtmaschine *f.* dynamo, generator.
Lichtschalter *m.* light switch.
lichtscheu *a.* shade-loving; (*fig.*) shunning publicity.
Lichtseite *f.* bright side (of things).
Lichtspieltheater *m.* cinema, movies.
Lichtstrahl *m.* ray of light; beam.
Lichtung *f.* **(-, -en)** clearing, glade.
lichtvoll *a.* luminous, lucid.
Lid *n.* **(-[e]s, -er)** eyelid.
Lidschatten *m.* eyeshadow.
lieb *a.* dear, beloved; agreeable.
liebäugeln *v.i.* to have one's eye on s.th.
Liebe *f.* **(-, 0)** love; (*christliche*) charity.

liebebedürftig *a.* in need of love.
Liebelei *f.* **(-, -en)** flirtation.
lieben *v.t.* to love; to like; ~ *v.i.* to be in love.
liebend *a.* loving.
Liebende *m./f.* **(-n, -n)** lover.
liebenswert *a.* lovable; amiable.
liebenswürdig *a.* sweet; kind.
liebenswürdigerweise *adv.* kindly.
Liebenswürdigkeit *f.* **(-, -en)** kindness; winning ways *pl.*
lieber *adv.* rather, sooner.
Liebes: ~dienst *m.* act of kindness; **~paar** *n.* lovers; **~roman** *m.* romantic novel.
liebestoll *a.* love-crazed.
liebevoll *a.* loving.
liebgewinnen *v.t.st.* to grow fond of.
liebhaben *v.t.st.* to love, to be fond of.
Liebhaber *m.* **(-s, -), Liebhaberin** *f.* **(-, -nen)** lover; amateur.
Liebhaberei *f.* **(-, -en)** hobby.
Liebhaberstück *m.* collector's item.
Liebhaberwert *m.* sentimental value.
liebkosen *v.t.* to caress, to fondle.
lieblich *a.* lovely; charming, sweet.
Liebling *m.* **(-[e]s, -e)** favorite, pet, darling.
Lieblingsbuch *n.* favorite book.
lieblos *a.* unkind, uncharitable.
liebreich *a.* kind, loving.
Liebreiz *m.* charm, attraction.
liebreizend *a.* charming, lovely.
Liebste *m./f.* **(-n, -n)** love, sweetheart.
Lied *n.* **(-[e]s, -er)** song, air; *Kirchen* ~, hymn.
Liederabend *m.* song recital.
liederlich *a.* loose, dissolute, immoral; messy.
Liedermacher *m.*, **Liedermacherin** *f.* singer-songwriter.
Lieferant *m.* **(-en, -en)** supplier.
Lieferanteneingang *m.* tradesman's entrance.
lieferbar *a.* available.
Lieferbedingungen *pl.* terms of delivery.
Lieferfrist *f.* delivery time.
liefern *v.t.* to deliver; to furnish; to supply; *eine Schlacht* ~, to give battle.
Lieferschein *m.* delivery note.
Liefertermin *m.* delivery date.
Lieferung *f.* **(-, -en)** delivery, supply; number, part (of a book).
Liefervertrag *m.* supply contract.
Lieferwagen *m.* delivery van.
Lieferzeit *f.* term of delivery.
Liege *f.* couch; campbed; sunbed.
Liegegeld *n.* (*nav.*) demurrage.
Liegekur *f.* rest cure.
liegen *v.t.st.* to lie; to be situated; *vor Anker* ~, to ride at anchor; ~ *lassen*, to leave (behind); to leave alone, to give up; ~ *bleiben*, to be left (unfinished, unsettled); *es liegt an mir*, it is my fault; *es liegt nichts daran*, it's of no consequence; *die Sache liegt ganz anders*, the case is altogether different.
Liegenschaften *pl.* real estate.
Liegeplatz *m.* mooring.
Liegesitz *m.* reclining seat.
Liegestuhl *m.* deck chair.
Liegestütz *m.* pushup.
Liegewagen *m.* (*rail*) couchette car.
Liegewiese *f.* lawn (at a pool).
Lift *m.* **(-s, -e u -s)** elevator; lift (ski).
liften *v.t. sich* ~ *lassen* to have a face-lift.
Liga *f.* **(-, -gen)** league.
liieren *v.r.* to team up; to start an affair.
Likör *m.* **(-[e]s, -e)** liqueur.
lila *a.* lilac.
Lilie *f.* **(-, -n)** lily; (*Wappen*) fleur-de-lis.
Liliputaner *m.*; **Liliputanerin** *f.* dwarf, midget.
Limit *n.* **(-s, -s)** limit.
limitieren *v.t.* to limit, to restrict.
Limonade *f.* **(-, -n), Limo** *f.* **(-, -s)** lemonade.
Limone *f.* **(-, -n)** lime.
Limousine *f.* **(-, -n)** sedan; limousine.
lind *a.* & *adv.* soft(ly), mild(ly).
Linde *f.* **(-, -n)** lime tree, linden.
lindern *v.t.* to soften, to mitigate; to alleviate.
Linderung *f.* **(-, 0)** relief; alleviation.
Lineal *n.* **(-[e]s, -e)** ruler, straightedge.
Linguist *m.*, **Linguistin** *f.* linguist.
Linguistik *f.* linguistics.
linguistisch *a.* & *adv.* linguistic; linguistically.
Linie *f.* **(-, -n)** line; lineage, descent; *in absteigender* ~, in the descending line; *in aufsteigender* ~, in the ascending line; *in gerader* ~, in the direct line.
Linien: ~bus *m.* scheduled bus; **~flug** *m.* scheduled flight; **~richter** *m.* (*sp.*) linesman; line judge; touch judge; **~papier** *n.* ruled paper; **~verkehr** *m.* (transportation) scheduled services.
linieren *v.t.* to rule.
liniert *a.* ruled, lined.
link *a.* left; left-wing; underhand(ed), shady.
Linke *f.* **(-n, 0)** left hand or side; (*pol.*) left.
Linke *m./f.* left-winger; leftist.
linkisch *a.* awkward.
links *adv.* to the left; on the left-hand side; ~ *um, kehrt!*, left face!
Linksabbieger *m.* (vehicle) turning left.
Linksaußen *m.* (*sp.*) left wing; outside left.
Linksextremismus *m.* left-wing extremism.
Linkshänder *m.*, **Linkshänderin** *f.* left-hander.
linkshändig *a.* left-handed.
Linksliberale *m./f.* left-wing liberal.
Linksradikalismus *m.* left-wing radicalism.
Linksruck *m.* shift to the left.
Linse *f.* **(-, -n)** lentil; (*opt.*) lens.
Lippe *f.* **(-, -n)** lip.
Lippenbekenntnis *n.* empty talk.
Lippenstift *m.* lipstick.
liquidieren *v.t.* to liquidate, to wind up.
lispeln *v.i.* to lisp.
List *f.* **(-, -en)** cunning, craft; trick, stratagem.
Liste *f.* **(-, -n)** list, roll; catalogue; *von der* ~ *streichen*, to cross off the list.
listig *a.* cunning, crafty, sly, artful.
Litanei *f.* **(-, -en)** litany.
Litauen *n.* **(-s, 0)** Lithuania.
Litauer *m.*, **Litauerin** *f.*, **litauisch** *a.* Lithuanian.
Liter *n.* **(-s, -)** liter.
Literarhistoriker *m.* literary historian.
literarisch *a.* literary.
Literat *m.* **(-en, -en)** man of letters.
Literatur *f.* **(-, -en)** literature, letters *pl.*
Literatur: ~angabe *f.* reference; **~gattung** *f.* literary genre; **~geschichte** *f.* history of literature; **~kritik** *f.* literary criticism; **~verzeichnis** *n.* list of references; **~wissenschaft** *f.* literary studies.
Litfaßsäule *f.* advertising pillar.
Lithograph *m.* **(-en, -en)** lithographer.
Lithographie *f.* **(-, -n)** lithography; lithograph.
Liturgie *f.* **(-, -n)** liturgy.
Litze *f.* **(-, -n)** lace, tape, braid; (*elek.*) cord.
Litzenbesatz *m.* piping.

Live-Sendung *f.* live program; live broadcast.
Livree *f.* **(-, -n)** livery.
Lizenz *f.* **(-, -en)** license; **~ausgabe** *f.* licensed edition; **~gebühr** *f.* royalty.
Lizenzinhaber, Lizenzträger *m.* licensee.
Lkw *Lastkraftwagen,* truck.
LKW-Fahrer *m.* trucker.
Lob *n.* **(-[e]s, 0)** praise; commendation.
loben *v.t.* to praise, to commend.
lobenswert *a.* praiseworthy.
Lobgesang *m.* song of praise.
lobhudeln *v.t.* to flatter, to heap praise on.
löblich *a.* laudable, commendable.
Lobrede *f.* eulogy.
Lobredner *m.* eulogist.
Loch *n.* **(-[e]s, Löcher)** hole; dungeon.
lochen *v.t.* to perforate, to punch.
Locher *m.* **(-s, -)** punch.
löcherig *a.* full of holes, in holes.
löchern *v.t.* to pester.
Lochkarte *f.* punch card.
Lochstreifen *m.* ticker tape.
Locke *f.* **(-, -n)** curl, ringlet.
locken *v.t.* to lure, to entice.
Lockenwickler *m.* curler.
locker *a.* relaxed, loose; licentious, dissolute.
lockern *v.t.* to loosen; to relax.
Lockerung *f.* loosening; relaxation.
lockig *a.* curled, curly.
Lockmittel *n.* lure, bait.
Lockung *f.* temptation.
Loden *m.* **(-s, -)** loden.
lodern *v.i.* to blaze; (*fig.*) to glow (with).
Löffel *m.* **(-s, -)** spoon; ladle.
löffeln *v.t.* to spoon (up); to ladle.
löffelweise *adv.* by the spoonful.
Log *n.* **(-s, -s)** (*nav.*) log.
Logarithmus *m.* **(-, men)** logarithm.
Loge *f.* **(-, -n)** box; (*Freimaurer*) lodge.
Logenschließer *m.* (theater) usher.
Loggia *f.* **(-, -ien)** balcony.
logieren *v.i.* to stay.
Logik *f.* **(-, 0)** logic.
Logiker *m.* **(-s, -)** logician.
logis *n.* room (for rent).
logisch *a.* logical.
logischerweise *adv.* logically.
lohen *v.t.* to tan (leather); ~ *v.i.* to blaze.
Lohn *m.* **(-[e]s, Löhne),** reward; wages *pl.*, pay; salary, fee.
Lohnabhängige *m./f.* wage earner.
Lohnbuchhalter *m.* payroll accountant.
Lohnempfänger *m.* wage earner.
lohnen *v.t. & i.* to reward, to recompense, to pay; *es lohnt (sich) nicht (der Mühe),* it is not worthwhile.
lohnend *a.* rewarding; lucrative.
Lohnerhöhung *f.* pay raise.
Lohnschreiber *m.* literary hack.
Lohnsteuer *f.* income tax; **~jahresausgleich** *m.* annual adjustment of income tax; **~karte** *f.* income tax card.
Lohntarif *m.* wage scale.
Lohntüte *f.* pay envelope.
Lohnzettel *m.* pay slip.
Loipe *f.* **(-, -n)** (cross-country) trail.
Lok *f.* **(-, -s)** engine, locomotive.
lokal *a.* local.
Lokal *n.* **(-[e]s, -e)** locality, place, shop, premises *pl.*; (*Gastwirtschaft*) tavern, café.
Lokalanästhesie *f.* local anaesthesia.
lokalisieren *v.t.* to locate; to prevent from spreading.
Lokalkolorit *n.* local color.
Lokalpatriotismus *m.* local patriotism.
Lokaltermin *m.* visit to the scene (of the crime).
Lokalverbot *n.* ban (from a bar).
Lokomotive *f.* **(-, -n)** (locomotive) engine.
Lokomotivführer *m.* engineer.
Lokus *m.* john; **~papier** *n.* toilet paper.
Lorbeer *m.* **(-s, -en)** laurel, bay; **~blatt** *n.* bayleaf; **~kranz** *m.* laurel wreath.
Lore *f.* **(-, -n)** lorry, load.
Lorgnette *f.* **(-, -n)** eyeglass, lorgnette.
los *a.* loose, untied; *was ist ~?* what is the matter?; *ich bin es ~,* I am rid of it; *etwas ~ haben,* to have the knack; *etwas ~ kriegen,* to get the hang of sth.
los let's go!, go!; *Achtung, fertig, ~,* ready, set, go.
Los *n.* **(-, -)** lot, destiny, fate; lottery ticket; *das große ~,* the first prize.
lösbar *a.* soluble.
losbinden *v.t.st.* to untie.
losbrechen *v.t.st.* to break loose *or* off; ~ *v.i.st. (s)* to burst out.
Lösch: ~blatt *n.* blotting paper; **~eimer** *m.* fire bucket.
löschen *v.t.* to extinguish; to quench; to slake; to unload.
Lösch: ~fahrzeug *n.* fire engine; **~papier** *n.* blotting paper.
lose *a.* loose; dissolute.
Lösegeld *n.* ransom.
losen *v.i.* to cast *or* draw lots.
lösen *v.t.* to loosen, to untie; to free, to deliver, to solve; to buy (a ticket).
Losentscheid *m. durch ~* by drawing lots.
losfahren *v.i.st.* to set off, to drive off.
losgehen *v.i.st. (s)* to come off; to get loose; to go off; to rush upon, to fight; to begin, to commence.
loskaufen *v.t.* to redeem, to ransom.
loskommen *v.t.st.* (*s*) to get away.
loslassen *v.t.st.* to let go.
löslich *a.* soluble.
losmachen *v.t.* to disengage, to free.
losplatzen *v.i. (s)* to blurt out.
losreißen *v.t.st.* to tear off; to separate; ~ *v.r.* to tear oneself away.
lossagen *v.r.* to renounce.
losschlagen *v.t.st.* to knock off; (*verkaufen*) to dispose of, to sell off; ~ *v.i.* to begin to fight.
lossprechen *v.t.st.* to absolve.
Lossprechung *f.* **(-, -en)** absolution.
lossteuern (auf) *v.i.* to make for.
Lostrommel *f.* lottery drum.
Losung *f.* **(-, -en)** (*mil.*) password; watchword.
Lösung *f.* **(-, -en)** solving, loosening; solution.
loswerden *v.t.* to get rid of.
loswickeln *v.t.* to reel off.
losziehen *v.i.st. (s)* (*fig.*) to set off.
Lot *n.* **(-[e]s, -e)** plumb line, lead; perpendicular; solder.
loten *v.i.* to take soundings.
löten *v.t.* to solder.
Lötkolben *m.* soldering iron.
Lötlampe *f.* blowlamp.

Lotos *m.* (*bot.*) lotus.
lotrecht *a.* perpendicular, vertical.
Lötrohr *n.* blowpipe.
Lotse *m.* **(-n, -n)** pilot; guide.
lotsen *v.t.* to pilot; (*fig.*) to take in tow.
Lotsengebühr *f.* pilotage.
Lotterie *f.* **(-, -n)** lottery.
Lotterielos *n.* lottery ticket.
Lotto *n.* national lottery.
Löwe *m.* **(-n, -n)** lion.
Löwen: **~anteil** *m.* lion's share; **~maul** *n.* (*bot.*) snapdragon; **~zahn** m. (*bot.*) dandelion.
Löwin *f.* **(-, -nen)** lioness.
Loyalität *f.* loyalty.
lt. *laut,* according to, acc. to.
Luchs *m.* **(-es, -e)** lynx.
Lücke *f.* **(-, -n)** gap; (*fig.*) space, void, blank; omission, deficiency, hiatus.
Lückenbüßer *m.* **(-s, -)** stopgap.
lückenhaft *a.* defective, fragmentary; sketchy.
lückenlos *a.* without a gap; complete.
Luder *n.* **(-s, -)** wretch, hussy.
Luft *f.* **(-, Lüfte)** air; breath; breeze; *frische ~ schöpfen,* to get some air; *in die ~ sprengen,* to blow up.
Luftangriff *m.* air raid.
Luftaufklärung *f.* aerial reconnaissance.
Luftbild *n.* aerial photograph.
Luftbrücke *f.* airlift.
Lüftchen *n.* **(-s, -)** breeze.
luftdicht *a.* airtight, hermetic.
Luftdruck *m.* atmospheric pressure.
Luftdruckbremse *f.* pneumatic brake.
lüften *v.t.* to air, to ventilate; to raise, to tip (hat).
Luftfahrt *f.* aviation.
Luftfahrtgesellschaft *f.* airline.
Luftgeschwindigkeitsmesser *m.* airspeed indicator.
Lufthoheit *f.* air sovereignty.
luftig *a.* airy; (*dress*) thin; well ventilated.
Luftkissen: **~boot** *n.*, **~fahrzeug** *n.* hovercraft.
Luftkurort *m.* health resort.
luftleer *a.* void of air; *~er Raum,* vacuum.
Luftlinie *f.* *100 km ~*, 100 kilometers as the crow flies.
Luftloch *n.* air pocket.
Luftpirat *m.* (airplane) hijacker.
Luftpost *f.* airmail.
Luftröhre *f.* windpipe, trachea.
Luftschiff *n.* airship; **~fahrt** *f.* aeronautics.
Luftschloß *n.* (*fig.*) castle in the air.
Luftschraube *f.* propeller; **~nblatt** *n.* propeller blade.
Luftschutz *m.* civil air defense; **~keller** *m.* air raid shelter; **~wart** *m.* air raid warden.
Luftspiegelung *f.* mirage.
Luftstörungen *pl.* (*radio*) atmospherics.
Lüftung *f.* **(-, -en)** airing, ventilation.
Lüftungsklappe *f.* ventilation flap.
Luftveränderung *f.* change of air.
Luftverpestung *f.*, **Luftverschmutzung** *f.* air pollution.
Luftwaffe *f.* air force.
Luftweg *m.* *auf dem ~*, by air.
Luftzufuhr *f.* air supply.
Luftzug *m.* breeze; draft.
Lug *m.* **(-[e]s, 0)** *~ und Trug* lies and deceit.
Lüge *f.* **(-, -n)** lie, falsehood.
lugen *v.i.* to look out, to peep.
lügen *v.t.st.* to lie, to tell a lie.
lügenhaft *a.* lying, false, mendacious.
Lügner *m.* **(-s, -), Lügnerin** *f.* **(-, -nen)** liar.
Luke *f.* **(-, -n)** skylight (roof); trap-door; (*nav.*) hatch(way).
lukrativ *a.* lucrative.
Lulatsch *m.* lanky fellow.
lullen *v.t. & i.* to lull (to sleep).
Lümmel *m.* **(-s, -)** ruffian, lout.
lümmelhaft *a.* loutish.
Lump *m.* **(-[e]s, -e)** rascal, rogue.
Lumpen *m.* **(-s, -)** rag, tatter.
Lumpensammler *m.* ragpicker.
Lumperei *f.* **(-, -en)** trash.
lumpig *a.* (*fig.*) shabby, paltry.
Lunge *f.* **(-, -n)** lung[s]; lights (of animals) *pl.*
Lungen: **~entzündung** *f.* pneumonia; **~flügel** *m.* (lobe of the) lung; **~schwindsucht** *f.* tuberculosis.
lungern *v.i.* to idle, to lounge, to skulk.
Lunte *f.* **(-, -n)** fuse; *~ riechen* (*fam.*) to smell a rat.
Lupe *f.* **(-, -n)** magnifying glass.
lupenrein *a.* flawless.
Lupine *f.* **(-, -n)** (*bot.*) lupin.
Lurch *m.* **(-s, -e)** amphibian.
Lusche *f.* **(-, -n)** low card (card game).
Lust *f.* **(-, Lüste)** joy, delight; inclination; desire, lust; *~ haben, etw. zu tun,* to feel like doing sth.
Lustbarkeit *f.* **(-, -en)** amusement, sport.
Lüster *m.* chandelier.
lüstern *a.* greedy (for); lecherous, lascivious, lustful.
lustig *a.* gay, merry, cheerful; funny, droll; *sich über jn. ~ machen,* to make fun of sb.
Lüstling *m.* lecher.
lustlos *a.* unenthusiastic; listless.
Lustmord *m.* rape and murder.
Lustschloß *n.* summer residence.
Lustspiel *n.* comedy.
lustwandelen *v.i.* (*h & s*) to stroll.
lutherisch *a.* Lutheran.
Luthertum *n.* **(-s, 0)** Lutheranism.
lutschen *v.i.* to suck.
Lutscher *m.* lollipop.
Luvseite *f.* (*nav.*) windward.
Luxemburg *n.* Luxembourg.
luxuriös *a.* luxurious.
Luxus *m.* **(-, 0)** luxury.
Luxuszug *m.* luxury train.
Luzerne *f.* **(-, -n)** (*bot.*) lucerne.
Luzifer *m.* Lucifer.
Lymph: **~drüse** *f.*, **~knoten** *m.* lymph node/gland.
Lymphe *f.* **(-, -n)** lymph.
lynchen *v.t.* to lynch.
Lynchjustiz *f.* lynch law.
Lyra *f.* **(-, Lyren)** lyre.
Lyrik *f.* **(-, 0)** lyric poetry.
Lyriker *m.* **(-s, -)** lyric poet.
lyrisch *a.* lyric.
Lyzeum *n.* **(-s, -een)** high school for girls.
LZB *Landeszentralbank,* State Central Bank.

M

M, m *n.* the letter M or m.
m *Meter,* meter.
Maat *m.* **(-[e]s, -e)** (*nav.*) (ship)mate, petty officer.
Machart *f.* **(-, -en)** style.
Mache *f.* **(-, 0)** show.
machen *v.t.* to make; to do; *was macht das?* how much is it?; *das macht nichts,* that does not matter; *die Rechnung macht so und so viel,* it comes to so much in all; *Licht ~,* to turn on a light; *Ernst ~,* to mean it; *zu Geld ~,* to sell, to turn into money; *sich auf den Weg ~,* to set out; *sich daraus nichts ~,* not to care about sth.
Machenschaften *pl.* intrigues *pl.*
Macher *m.* (*fig.*) doer.
Macho *m.* macho.
Macht *f.* **(-, Mächte)** power; might; forces.
Machtbefugnis *f.* power, authority, competence.
Machtbereich *m.* sphere of power.
Machtergreifung *f.* seizure of power.
Machtgier *f.* craving for power.
Machthaber *m.* **(-s, -)** potentate, ruler.
mächtig *a.* powerful; mighty.
Machtkampf *m.* power struggle.
machtlos *a.* powerless.
Machtlosigkeit *f.* powerlessness, helplessness.
Machtpolitik *f.* power politics.
Machtprobe *f.* trial of strength.
Machtstreben *n.* striving for power.
Machtvollkommenheit *f.* absolute power, authority.
Machtwechsel *m.* change of government.
Machtwort *n.* word of command.
Machwerk *n.* concoction; (*fam.*) lousy job.
Macke *f.* defect; (*fig.*) kink.
Macker *m.* guy.
MAD *Militärischer Abschirmdienst,* Military Counter-Intelligence Service.
Mädchen *n.* **(-s, -)** girl; maid, lass; servant; *~ für alles,* girl *or* gal Friday.
mädchenhaft *a.* girlish.
Mädchen: ~handel *m.* white slave traffic; **~name** *m.* (*der Frau*) maiden name; **~schule** *f.* girls' school.
Made *f.* **(-, -n)** maggot, larva; mite.
Magazin *n.* **(-[e]s, -e)** depot; (*Zeitschrift*) magazine.
Magd *f.* **(-, Mägde)** maid-servant, (*female*) farmhand.
Magen *m.* **(-s, -)** stomach.
Magenbeschwerden *pl.* indigestion, dyspepsia.
Magenbitter *m.* bitters.
Magengeschwür *n.* stomach ulcer.
magenleidend *a.* suffering from a disorder of the stomach.
Magensaft *m.* gastric juice.
Magensaüre *f.* gastric acid.
Magenschmerzen *pl.* stomachache.
mager *a.* lean, thin; meager.
Magerheit *f.* thinness; meagerness.
Magerkäse *m.* low-fat cheese.
Magermilch *f.* skim milk.
Magie *f.* **(-, 0)** magic.
Magier *m.* **(-s, -)** magician.
magisch *a.* magical.
Magistrat *m.* **(-[e]s, -e)** city council.
Magma *n.* **(-s, -men)** magma.
Magnat *m.* **(-en, -en)** magnate.
Magnet *m.* **(-[e]s, -e)** magnet.
magnetisch *a.* magnetic.
magnetisieren *v.t.* to magnetize.
Magnetismus *m.* **(-, 0)** magnetism.
Magnetnadel *f.* magnetic needle.
Magnetzünder *m.* (*mot.*) coil.
Magnolie *f.* **(-, -n)** magnolia.
Mahagoni *n.* **(-s, 0)** mahogany.
Mähdrescher *m.* combine harvester.
mähen *v.t.* to mow.
Mahl *n.* **(-[e]s, -e & Mähler)** meal, repast.
mahlen *v.t.* to grind.
Mahlzeit *f.* meal, repast.
Mähmaschine *f.* mower, reaping machine.
Mahn: ~bescheid *m.* order to pay; **~brief** *m.* reminder; **~gebühr** *f.* fine.
Mähne *f.* **(-, -n)** mane.
mahnen *v.t.* to urge, to remind, to admonish.
Mahnung *f.* **(-, -en)** reminder; admonition.
Mähre *f.* **(-, -n)** mare; (*Schind~*) jade.
Mai *m.* **(-[e]s, -e)** May.
Maibaum *m.* maypole; birch.
Maid *f.* **(-, -en)** (*poet.*) maid.
Maiglöckchen *n.* lily of the valley.
Maikäfer *m.* cockchafer, Maybug.
Maikraut *m.* woodruff.
Maikundgebung *f.* May Day rally.
Mais *m.* **(-es, 0)** corn.
Maiskolben *m.* ear of corn.
Majestät *f.* **(-, -en)** majesty.
majestätisch *a.* majestic.
Major *m.* **(-[e]s, -e)** major.
Majoran *m.* marjoram.
Majorat *n.* **(-[e]s, -e)** entail(ed estate); primogeniture.
Majorität *f.* **(-, -en)** majority.
makaber *a.* macabre.
Makel *m.* **(-s, -)** spot; blemish; (*fig.*) stigma.
makellos *a.* unblemished; perfect, immaculate.
mäkeln *v.i.* to find fault (with); to carp.
Make-up *n.* **(-s, -s)** makeup.
Makkaroni *pl.* macaroni.
Makler *m.* **(-s, -)** broker; realtor; middleman.
Maklergebühr *f.* brokerage charges.
Makrele *f.* **(-, -n)** mackerel.
makrobiotisch *a.* macrobiotic.
Makrone *f.* **(-, -n)** macaroon.
Makulatur *f.* **(-, -en)** wastepaper, trash.
Mal *n.* **(-[e]s, -e)** time; mark, sign, monument; (on the skin) mole; *einmal,* once; *noch einmal,* once more; *auf einmal,* at once; *ein für allemal,* once for all.
mal *adv.* once, just.
Malachit *m.* **(-s, -e)** malachite.
Malaie *m.*, **Malaiin** *f.*, **malaiisch** *a.* Malaysian.
Malaria *f.* malaria.
Malbuch *n.* coloring book.
malen *v.t.* to paint; to portray; *sich ~ lassen,* to sit for one's portrait.
Maler *m.* **(-s, -)**; **Malerin** *f.* **(-, -nen)** painter, artist.
Malerei *f.* **(-, -en)** painting; picture.

malerisch *a.* picturesque.
Malermeister *m.* master painter.
Malkasten *m.* paint box.
malnehmen *v.i.st.* to multiply.
Malpinsel *m.* paintbrush.
malträtieren *v.t* to mistreat.
Malve *f.* mallow.
Malz *n.* **(-es, 0)** malt.
Malzeichen *n.* multiplication sign.
malzen *v.i.* to malt.
Mälzer *m.* **(-s, -)** maltster.
Mama *f.* **(-, -s)** mamma; (*fam.*) ma, mom.
Mammographie *f.* mammography.
Mammon *m.* mammon.
Mammut *n.* **(-s, -s)** mammoth.
mampfen *v.t.* to munch.
man *pn.* they, people, one.
Management *n.* management.
Manager *m.* **(-s, -)**, **Managerin** *f.* **(-, -nen)** manager.
Managerkrankheit *f.* executive stress.
mancher, manche, manches *pn.* many a, many a man; **manche** *pl.* some.
mancherlei *a.* various.
manchmal *adv.* sometimes.
Mandant *m.* **(-en, -en)**; **Mandantin** *f.* **(-, -nen)** (*jur.*) client.
Mandarine *f.* tangerine.
Mandat *n.* **(-[e]s, -e)** mandate, commission, seat.
Mandel *f.* **(-, -n)** almond; (*anat.*) tonsil.
Mandelentzündung *f.* tonsillitis.
Mandeloperation *f.* tonsillectomy.
Mandoline *f.* **(-, -n)** mandolin.
Manege *f.* ring (circus); arena.
Mangan *n.* **(-[e]s, 0)** manganese.
Mangel *m.* **(-s, Mängel)** lack; want; deficiency; defect; shortage.
Mangel: ~beruf *m.* labor shortage.
Mangel: ~erscheinung *f.* deficiency symptom.
mangelhaft *a.* incomplete; defective.
mangeln *v.i.* to want, to lack.
mangels *pr.* for lack of.
Mangelware *f.* goods in short supply *pl.*
Mangrove *f.* **(-, -n)** mangrove forest.
Manie *f.* **(-, -n)** mania.
Manier *f.* **(-, -en)** manner.
manieriert *a.* affected, mannered.
Manierismus *m.* mannerism.
manierlich *a.* mannerly, polite, civil.
Manifest *n.* **(-[e]s, -e)** manifesto.
manifestieren *v.i.* to manifest.
Manipulation *f.* **(-, -en)** manipulation.
manipulierbar *a. leicht ~* easy to manipulate.
manipulieren *v.t.* to manipulate.
manisch *a.* manic; **~-depressiv** *a.* manic-depressive.
Manko *n.* **(-s, -s)** shortcoming, handicap.
Mann *m.* **(-[e]s, Männer)** man; husband.
Männchen *n.* **(-s, -)** (*von Tieren*) male; (*von Vögeln*) cock.
Mannesalter *n.* manhood.
Manneskraft *f.* virility.
mannhaft *a.* manly, manful.
mannigfach, mannigfaltig *a.* manifold; diverse.
Mannigfaltigkeit *f.* **(-, -en)** variety; diversity.
Manniküre *f.* manicure; manicurist.
Mannikuren *v.t.* to manicure.
männlich *a.* male; (*gram.*) masculine; (*fig.*) manly.
Mannschaft *f.* **(-, -en)** (*nav.*) crew, (*sp.*) team.
Mannschaftstransportwagen *m.* (*mil.*) personnel carrier.
mannshoch *a.* as tall as a man.
mannstoll *a.* nymphomaniac.
Manöver *n.* **(-s, -)** maneuvers; exercise.
Manöverkritik *f.* post mortem.
manövrieren *v.i.* to maneuver.
Mansarde *f.* **(-, -n)** attic, garret; mansard roof.
manschen *v.i.* to dabble, to paddle; to mix.
Manschette *f.* **(-, -n)** cuff.
Manschettenknopf *m.* cuff link.
Mantel *m.* **(-s, Mäntel)** overcoat, mantle; cloak.
manuell *a.* manual.
Manufaktur *f.* **(-, -en)** manufactory.
Manuskript *n.* **(-[e]s, -e)** manuscript.
Maoismus *m.* Maoism.
Mäppchen *n.* pencil case.
Mappe *f.* **(-, -n)** briefcase, portfolio.
Marathon *m.* marathon.
Märchen *n.* **(-s, -)** (fairy)tale; fable, fiction; (*Lüge*) fib.
märchenhaft *a.* fabulous, legendary.
Märchenland *n.* fairyland.
Märchenprinz *m.* (*fig.*) Prince Charming.
Marder *m.* **(-s, -)** marten.
Margarine *f.* **(-, -n)** margarine.
Margerite *f.* **(-, -n)** marguerite.
Marienkäfer *m.* ladybird.
Marihuana *n.* marijuana.
Marinade *f.* marinade; dressing.
Marine *f.* **(-, -n)** marine, navy.
Marine: ~minister *m.* Navy Minister; **~offizier** *m.* naval officer; **~stützpunkt** *m.* naval base; **~werft** *f.* navy-yard.
marinieren *v.t.* to marinate; to pickle.
Marionette *f.* **(-, -n)** puppet; marionette.
Marionettentheater *n.* puppet show.
Mark *f.* **(-, -en)** border, marches *pl.*; district; (*Münze*) Mark.
Mark *n.* **(-[e]s, 0)** marrow, pith.
markant *a.* striking.
Marke *f.* **(-, -n)** brand; *Brief~* (postage) stamp; *Spiel~* counter, chip.
Markenartikel *m.* brand-name product.
Markenzeichen *n.* trademark.
Marketenderin *f.* **(-, -nen)** (*mil.*) camp follower.
Marketing *n.* marketing.
markieren *v.t.* to mark; (*fig.*) to sham (illness).
markig *a.* pithy, marrowy.
Markise *f.* **(-, -n)** awning.
Markstein *m.* boundary stone.
Markt *m.* **(-e[s], Märkte)** market; marketplace; *auf den ~ bringen,* to place on the market; *auf den ~ kommen,* to come into the market.
Marktbericht *m.* market report.
Marktflecken *m.* market town.
marktgängig *a.* current.
marktschreierisch *a.* loud.
Marktwirtschaft *f.* market economy.
Marmelade *f.* **(-, -n)** jam; *Apfelsinen~*, orange marmalade.
Marmor *m.* **(-s, 0)** marble.
marmoriert *a.* marbled.
marmorn *a.* marble.
marode *a.* rotten, degenerate.
Marodeur *m.* **(-s, -e)** marauder.
Marokkaner *m.*; **Marokkanerin** *f.*; **marokkanisch** *a.* Moroccan.
Marokko *n.* **(-s, 0)** Morocco.

Marone *f.* **(-, -n)** edible chestnut.
Maroquin *m.* **(-s, 0)** morocco (leather).
Marotte *f.* **(-, -n)** fad.
Marquise *f.* **(-, -n)** marchioness.
Mars *m.* Mars.
Marsbewohner *m.* Martian.
marsch! *i.* march!; be off! get out!.
Marsch *m.* **(-es, Märsche)** march.
Marsch *f.* **(-, -en)** (salt)marsh, fen.
Marschall *m.* **(-[e]s, schälle)** marshal.
Marschallsstab *m.* marshal's baton.
Marschbefehl *m.* marching order.
marschieren *v.i. (h & s)* to march.
Marstall *m.* **(-[e]s, ~ställe)** royal stables *pl.*
Marter *f.* **(-, -n)** torture; (*fig.*) torment.
Marterkammer *f.* torture chamber.
martern *v.t.* to rack, to torture.
Marterpfahl *m.* stake.
martialisch *a.* martial.
Martinshorn *n.* siren.
Märtyrer *m.* **(s, -); Märtyrerin** *f.* **(-, -nen)** martyr.
Martyrium *n.* **(-s, 0)** martyrdom.
Marxismus *m.* Marxism.
marxistisch *a.* Marxist.
März *m.* **(- & -es, -e)** March.
Marzipan *m.* **(-s, -e)** marzipan.
Masche *f.* **(-, -n)** mesh; stitch (in knitting).
Maschendraht *m.* wire netting.
Maschine *f.* **(-, -n)** machine, engine.
maschinegeschrieben *a.* typed; typewritten.
maschinell *a.* mechanical; machine...
Maschinenbauer *m.* mechanical engineer.
Maschinengewehr *n.* machine gun.
Maschinenpistole *f.* submachine gun, tommy gun.
Maschinenschlosser *m.* fitter.
Maschinenschrift *f.* typewriting, typescript.
Maschinerie *f.* **(-, -n)** machinery.
Maschinist *m.* **(-en, -en)** machinist.
Masern *pl.* measles *pl.*
masern *v.t.* to vein, to grain.
Maserung *f.* **(-, -en)** grain; vein; patterning.
Maske *f.* **(-, -n)** mask; makeup.
Maskenball *m.* masked ball; masquerade.
Maskerade *f.* **(-, -n)** masquerade; costume.
maskieren *v.t. & r.* to mask; to disguise oneself; to dress up.
Maskottchen *n.* **(-s, -)** mascot.
maskulin *a.* masculine.
Maskulinum *n.* **(-s, -lina)** masculine noun.
Masochismus *m.* masochism.
Masochist *m.*; **Masochistin** *f.* masochist.
masochistisch *a.* masochistic.
Maß *n.* **(-es, -e)** measure; (*fig.*) moderation; ~ *halten,* to observe moderation; *nach* ~, to measure; ~ *nehmen,* to take a person's measurement(s).
Maß *f.* **(-, -e)** quart, pot.
Massage *f.* massage.
Massaker *n.* **(-s, -)** massacre.
Maßarbeit *f.* made to measure; precision work.
Masse *f.* **(-, -n)** mass, bulk; large quantity, multitude.
Maßeinheit *f.* unit of measurement.
Massenartikel *pl.* staple goods.
Massenerzeugung *f.* mass production.
massenhaft *a.* wholesale, on a huge/massive scale.
Massenproduktion *f.* mass production.
massenweise *adv.* in large quantities.
Masseur *m.* **(-s, -e)** masseur.
Masseuse *f.* **(-, -n)** masseuse.
Maßgabe *f. nach* ~, according to.
maßgearbeitet *a.* made to measure; custom-made.
maßgebend *a.* authoritative; standard.
massieren *v.t.* to massage.
massig *a.* massive; bulky.
mäßig *a.* moderate; frugal; *~e Preise,* reasonable prices.
mäßigen *v.t.* to moderate; to temper.
Mäßigkeit *f.* **(-, 0)** temperance, frugality.
Mäßigung *f.* **(-, 0)** moderation; self-control.
massiv *a.* massive, solid.
Massiv *n.* **(-s, -e)** massif.
Maßkrug *m.* quart, tankard; stein.
maßlos *a.* immoderate, boundless.
Maßlosigkeit *f.* excessiveness; intemperance.
Maßnahme *f.* measure; *~n treffen,* to take measures; to discipline.
Maßregel *f.* rule; guideline.
maßregeln *v.t.* to take measures; to discipline.
Maßstab *m.* measure; scale; standard.
maßstabsgerecht *a.* (true) to scale.
maßvoll *a.* moderate, measured.
Mast *m.* **(-es, -en)** mast; (*elec.*) pylon; pole.
Mast *f.* **(-, -en)** fattening feed.
Mastbaum *m.* mast.
Mastdarm *m.* rectum.
mästen *v.t.* to feed, to fatten.
Mastkorb *m.* (*nav.*) top, masthead, crow's nest.
Masturbation *f.* masturbation.
masturbieren *v.i. & t.* to masturbate.
Mastvieh *n.* beef cattle.
Matchball *m.* tennis match point.
Material *n.* **(-[e]s, -ien)** material.
Materialismus *m.* **(-, 0)** materialism.
Materialist *m.* **(-en, -en)** materialist.
materialistisch *a.* materialistic.
Materie *f.* **(-, -n)** matter; subject.
materiell *a.* material; wordly.
Mathematik *f.* **(-, 0), Mathe** *f.* **(-, 0)** mathematics *pl.*
Mathematiker *m.* **(-s, -)** mathematician.
mathematisch *a.* mathematical.
Matinée *f.* matinée.
Matratze *f.* **(-, -n)** mattress.
Mätresse *f.* **(-, -n)** mistress.
Matriarchat *n.* **(-s, -e)** matriarchy.
Matrikel *f.* **(-, -n)** register, roll.
Matrize *f.* **(-, -n)** matrix.
Matrose *m.* **(-n, -n)** sailor, mariner.
Matsch *m.* **(-[e]s, 0)** mud; sludge; mush.
matschig *a.* muddy; slushy.
matt *a.* matt; tired; feeble, languid, faint; (*Gold*) dull; (*Schach*) (check)mate; ~ *setzen,* to checkmate.
Matte *f.* **(-, -n)** mat; alpine meadow.
Mattglas *n.* frosted glass.
mattherzig *a.* faint-hearted.
Mattigkeit *f.* **(-, -0)** weakness; weariness.
Mattscheibe *f.* (*fam.*) tube (TV).
Mauer *f.* **(-, -n)** wall.
Mauerblümchen *n.* wallflower.
mauern *v.t.* to make a wall, to build.
Mauersegler *m.* (*zool.*) swift;
Mauervorsprung *m.* projecting section of a wall.
Mauerwerk *n.* stonework; masonry walls.

Maul *n.* **(-[e]s, Mäuler)** mouth (animals); gob; *das ~ halten,* (*pej.*) to shut up.
Maulbeere *f.* mulberry.
maulen *v.i.* to grouse, to moan.
Maulesel *m.* mule; hinny.
Maulkorb *m.* muzzle.
Maultier *n.* mule.
Maul- und Klauenseuche *f.* foot-and-mouth disease.
Maulwurf mole.
Maufwurfshaufen, Maulwurfshügel *m.* molehill.
Maurer *m.* **(-s, -)** mason, bricklayer.
Maurerkelle *f.* brick trowel.
Maurermeister *m.* master bricklayer.
Maus *f.* **(-, Mäuse)** mouse.
mauscheln *v.i.* to engage in shady business.
mäuschenstill *a.* stock still.
Mausefalle *f.* mousetrap.
mausen *v.t.* to pilfer; ~ *v.i.* to catch mice, to mouse.
mausern *v.r.* to moult.
Maut *f.* toll.
mauzen *v.i.* to meow plaintively.
m.a.W. *mit anderen Worten,* in other words.
Maxime *f.* **(-, -n)** maxim.
maximieren *v.t.* to maximize.
Maximierung *f.* maximization.
Mayonnaise *f.* mayonnaise.
Mäzen *m.* **(-[e]s, -e); Mäzenin** *f.* **(-, -nen)** patron of arts.
MB *Megabyte,* megabyte, mb.
mbH *mit beschränkter Haftung,* with limited liability.
MdB *Mitglied des Bundestages,* Member of the Bundestag.
MdL *Mitglied des Landtags,* Member of the Landtag.
mdl. *mündlich,* verbal, oral.
m.E. *meines Erachtens,* in my opinion.
Mechanik *f.* **(-, -en)** mechanics *pl.*; mechanism.
Mechaniker *m.* **(-s, -); Mechanikerin** *f.* **(-, -nen)** mechanic.
mechanisch *a. & adv.*, mechanical(ly); by rote.
Mechanismus *m.* mechanism.
meckern *v.i.* to bleat; (*fig.*) to grumble.
Medaille *f.* **(-, -n)** medal.
Medaillon *n.* **(-s, -s)** locket; medallion.
Medikament *n.* **(-[e]s, -e)** medicine.
medikamentös *a.* with drugs (treatment).
Meditation *f.* **(-, -en)** meditation.
meditieren *v.i.* to meditate.
Medium *n.* **(-s, -dien)** medium.
Medizin *f.* **(-, -en)** medicine.
Mediziner *m.* **(-s, -); Medizinerin** *f.* **(-, -nen)** doctor *or* medical student.
medizinisch *a.* medical; medicinal;
medizinisches Gutachten *n.* medical opinion.
Meer *n.* **(-[e]s, -e)** sea, ocean; *offenes ~,* high sea.
Meer: ~busen *m.* bay, gulf; **~enge** *f.* straits *pl.*
Meerenge *f.* straits. *pl.*
Meeresbiologie *f.* marine biology.
Meeresboden *m.* seabed.
Meeresfrüchte *pl.* seafood.
Meeresklima *n.* maritime climate.
Meeresspiegel *m.* sea level.
Meerjungfrau *f.* mermaid.
Meerkatze *f.* guenon.
Meerrettich *m.* horseradish.
Meerschaum *m.* meerschaum.
Meerschweinchen *n.* guinea pig.
Meerwasser *n.* seawater.
Megaphon *n.* **(-s, -e)** megaphone.
Mehl *n.* **(-[e]s, 0)** meal; flour.
Mehlbrei *m.* porridge.
mehlig *a.* mealy.
Mehlspeise *f.* farinaceous food; sweet dish (Austria).
mehr *a. & adv.* more; *um so ~,* so much the more; *nicht ~,* no more, no longer; *immer ~,* more and more; *nicht ~ als,* not exceeding.
Mehr *n.* **(-s, 0)** *ein ~ an,* more of.
Mehrbedarf *m.* extra requirement.
Mehrbetrag *m.* surplus.
mehrdeutig *a.* ambiguous.
Mehreinnahme *f.* increased revenue.
mehren *v.t.* to increase, to augment; ~ *v.r.* to multiply.
mehrere *a.pl.* several, various.
mehrfach *a. & adv.* repeated(ly).
Mehrfamilienhaus *n.* multiple dwelling.
Mehrheit *f.* **(-, -en)** majority, plurality.
mehrheitlich *a.* majority; of the majority.
Mehrheitsentscheidung *f.* majority decision.
Mehrheitswahlrecht *n.* majotity vote system.
mehrjährig *a.* lasting several years; several years.
Mehrkosten *pl.* extra expense.
mehrmalig *a.* repeated.
mehrmals *adv.* several times.
Mehrparteiensystem *n.* multiparty system.
mehrseitig *a.* multilateral.
mehrstimmig *a.* (*mus.*) arranged for several voices.
Mehrwertsteuer *f.* value-added tax; sales tax.
Mehrzahl *f.* plural; majority.
meiden *v.t.st.* to avoid, to shun.
Meile *f.* **(-, -n)** mile.
Meilenstein *m.* **(-s, -e)** milestone.
meilenweit *adv.* for miles; miles off.
Meiler *m.* **(-s, -)** charcoal pile.
mein, meine, mein *pn.* my; mine; *~esgleichen,* people like me.
Meineid *m.* perjury.
meineidig *a.* perjured.
meinen *v.t.* to mean, to think.
meinethalben, meinetwegen *adv.* because of me; as far as I'm concerned.
meinige (*der, die, das*) *a.* mine.
Meinung *f.* **(-, -en)** opinion; meaning; intention; *nach meiner ~,* in my opinion.
Meinungsforschung *f.* opinion research.
Meinungsfreiheit *f.* freedom of opinion.
Meinungsumfrage *f.* opinion poll.
Meinungsverschiedenheit *f.* divergence of opinion.
Meise *f.* **(-, -n)** titmouse.
Meißel *m.* **(-s, -)** chisel.
meißeln *v.t.* to chisel, to carve.
meist *adv.* most, mostly.
Meistbegünstigungsklausel *f.* most-favorednation clause.
Meistbietende *m./f.* **(-n, -n)** highest bidder.
meistens *adv.* mostly, generally.
meistenteils *adv.* for the most part.
Meister *m.* **(-s, -)** master; master craftsman; (*sp.*) champion.
meisterhaft *a.* masterly.
Meisterin *f.* master craftswoman; (*sp.*) champion.
meistern *v.t.* to master; to surpass.

Meisterschaft *f.* **(-, -en)** mastery, perfection; (*sp.*) championship.
Meisterstück, Meisterwerk *n.* masterpiece.
Meistgebot *n.* **(-es, -e)** highest bid.
Melancholie *f.* **(-, 0)** melancholy.
melancholisch *a.* melancholy.
Melanom *n.* melanoma.
Melasse *f.* **(-, 0)** molasses *pl.*
Meldeamt *n.* police registration office.
Meldeformular *n.* registration form.
melden *v.t.* to notify, to announce; ~ *v.r.* to register; *sich* ~ *lassen,* to send one's name; *sich zu etwas* ~, to enter for.
Meldepflicht *f.* obligatory registration; duty of notification.
meldepflichtig *a.* subject to registration; notifiable.
Meldung *f.* **(-, -en)** report; mention, announcement, notification; entry.
Melhtau *m.* **(-s, 0)** mildew, blight.
meliert *a.* mottled.
melken *v.t.st.* to milk.
Melodie *f.* **(-, -n)** melody; tune; air.
Melodik *f.* melodic features; theory of melody.
melodisch *a.* melodic; melodious, tuneful.
Melone *f.* **(-, -n)** melon; bowler (hat).
Membran *f.* **(-, -e)** membrane.
Memoiren *pl.* memoirs.
Menagerie *f.* **(-, -n)** menagerie.
Menge *f.* **(-, -n)** multitude; quantity; great deal, lots *pl.;* a great many.
mengen *v.t.* to mix, to mingle.
Mengenlehre *f.* set theory.
mengenmäßig *a.* quantitative.
Mengenrabatt *m.* bulk discount.
Meningitis *f.* meningitis.
Meniskus *m.* **(-, -ken)** meniscus.
Mennig *m.* **(-s, 0)** red-lead, minium.
Mensa *f.* **(-, -s & -sen)** canteen; cafeteria (university).
Mensch *m.* **(-en, -en)** man, human being.
Menschenaffe *m.* ape; anthropoid.
Menschenauflauf *m.* crowd.
Menschenfeind *m.* misanthropist.
Menschenfresser *m.* cannibal; maneater.
Menschenfreund philanthropist.
menschenfreundlich *a.* humane, philanthropic.
Menschen: ~gedenken *n. seit* ~, within living memory; **~haß** *m.* misanthropy; **~kenner** *m.* judge of human nature.
menschenleer *a.* deserted.
Menschenliebe *f.* philanthropy, charity.
menschenmöglich *a.* in the power of man.
Menschenopfer *n.* human sacrifice.
menschenscheu *a.* shy, unsociable.
Menschenschlag *m.* **(-s, 0)** breed of people.
Menschenverstand *m. gesunder* ~ common sense.
Menschenwürde *f.* human dignity.
Menschheit *f.* **(-, 0)** human race, humankind; humanity.
Menschheitsentwicklung *f.* evolution of humankind.
menschlich *a.* human; humane.
Menschlichkeit *f.* **(-, 0)** humanity.
Menstruation *f.* menstruation.
Mensur *f.* **(-, -en)** students' fencing match.
Mentalität *f.* **(-, -en)** mentality.
Menü *n.* **(-s, -s)** menu.
Menuett *n.* **(-[e]s, -e)** minuet.
Mergel *m.* **(-s, -)** marl.
Meridian *m.* **(-s, -e)** meridian.
merkbar *a.* perceptible; noticeable.
Merkblatt *n.* instructional pamphlet, booklet.
merken *v.t.* to notice; to note, to perceive; to remember; ~ *lassen,* to betray, to show.
merklich *a.* noticeable.
Merkmal *n.* **(-[e]s, -e)** mark, sign; feature.
merkwürdig *a.* strange, odd; curious.
Merkwürdigkeit *f.* **(-, -en)** curiosity.
meschugge *a.* (*fam.*) meshuga, crazy.
Mesner *m.* **(-s, -)** sexton.
Meßband *n.* tape measure.
meßbar *a.* measurable.
Meßbuch *n.* missal.
Messe *f.* **(-, -n)** mass; fair; (*nav. & mil.*) mess; *stille* ~, low mass; ~ *lesen,* to say mass.
messen *v.t.st.* to measure.
Messer *n.* **(-s, -)** knife.
Messer: ~schmied *m.* cutler; **~stiel** *m.* knife-handle.
Messestand *m.* **(-s, -stände)** exhibition booth.
Messias *m.* Messiah.
Messing *n.* **(-s, 0)** brass.
Messung *f.* **(-, -en)** measurement.
Mestize *m.* **Mestin** *f.* mestizo.
Met *m.* **(-[e]s, 0)** mead.
Metall *n.* **(-[e]s, -e)** metal.
metallen *a.* (of) metal.
Metaller *m.* **(-s, -); Metallerin** *f.* **(-, -nen)** metalworker.
Metallfutter *n.* (*mech.*) bush.
metallisch *a.* metallic.
Metallsäge *f.* (*mech.*) hacksaw.
Metallurgie *f.* metallurgy.
Metallverarbeitung *f.* metal processing.
Metallwaren *f. pl.* hardware.
Metamorphose *f.* **(-, -n)** metamorphosis.
Metapher *f.* **(-, -n)** metaphor.
Metaphorik *f.* imagery; metaphors.
metaphorisch *a.* metaphorical.
Metaphysik *f.* **(-, 0)** metaphysics *pl.*
metaphysisch *a.* metaphysical.
Meteor *m.* **(-s, -e)** meteor.
Meteorologe *m.* **(-en, -en); Meteorologin** *f.* **(-, -nen)** meteorologist.
Meteorologie *f.* meteorology.
meteorologisch *a.* meteorological.
Meter *n. & m.* **(-s, -)** meter.
Metermaß *n.* tape measure.
Meterware *f.* fabric/material sold by the meter.
Methode *f.* **(-, -n)** method.
Methodik *f.* methodology.
methodisch *a.* methodological, methodical.
Metier *n.* **(-s, -s)** profession.
Metrik *f.* **(-, 0)** meter; prosody.
metrisch *a.* metrical; **~es System** *n.* metric system.
Metronom *n.* metronome.
Metropole *f.* **(-, -n)** metropolis.
Metrum *n.* **(-s, -tra & -tren)** meter.
Mettwurst *f.* smoked sausage.
Metzelei *f.* **(-, -en)** massacre, butchery
metzeln *v.t.* to massacre, to butcher.
Metzger *m.* **(-s, -)** butcher.
Metzgerei *f.* butcher's shop.
Meuchel: ~mord *m.* assassination; **~mörder** *m.* assassin.
meuchlings *adv.* treacherously.

Meute *f.* **(-, -n)** pack of hounds.
Meuterei *f.* **(-, -en)** mutiny.
Meuterer *m.* **(-s, -)** mutineer.
meuterisch *a.* mutinous.
meutern *v.i.* to mutiny, to revolt.
Mexikaner *m.*; **Mexikanerin** *f.*; **mexikanisch** *a.* Mexican.
Mexiko *n.* **(-s, 0)** Mexico.
M.E.Z. *Mitteleuropäische Zeit,* Central European Time, CET.
mg *Milligramm,* milligram.
mhd. *mittelhochdeutsch,* Middle High German, M. H.G.
Mi. *Mittwoch,* Wednesday, Wed.
miauen *v.i.* to meow.
mich *pn.* me.
mickrig *a.* miserable; measly; puny.
Mieder *n.* **(-s, -)** bodice.
Miederwaren *pl.* lingerie.
Mief *m.* **(-s, 0)** (*fam.*) stink; stuffy atmosphere.
miefen *v.i.* to stink.
Miene *f.* **(-, -en)** mien, air, countenance; ~ *machen,* to threaten (to do).
Mienenspiel *n.* facial expression.
mies *a.* (*sl.*) bad, rotten.
Miesmacher *m.* **(-s, -)** defeatist.
Miesmuschel *f.* **(-, -n)** mussel.
Miete *f.* **(-, -n)** rent, hire.
mieten *v.t.* to hire, to rent; to take; to charter.
Mieter *m.* **(-s, -)**; **Mieterin** *f.* **(-, -nen)** tenant, lodger.
mietfrei *a.* rent-free.
Mietsflugzeug *n.* charter plane;
Mietstruppen *pl.* hired troops, mercenaries.
Mietsumme *f.* rental fee.
Mietvertrag *m.* lease.
mietweise *adv.* on lease.
Miet(s)wohnung *f.* rented apartment;
Mietzins rental (fee).
Mieze *f.* (*fam.*) puss; pussy; chick.
Migräne *f.* **(-, 0)** migraine.
Mikado *n.* pick-up sticks.
Mikrobe *f.* **(-, -n)** microbe.
Mikrophon *n.* **(-s, -e)** microphone.
Mikroskop *n.* **(-[e]s, -e)** microscope.
mikroskopisch *a.* microscopic(al).
Mikrowellenherd *m.* microwave oven.
Milbe *f.* **(-, -n)** mite.
Milch *f.* **(-, 0)** milk; milt.
Milchmädchenrechung *f.* naive reasoning.
Milchstraße *f.* Milky Way, galaxy.
Milchzahn *m.* baby *or* milk tooth.
mild *a.* mild, soft, gentle; liberal, charitable.
Milde *f.* **(-, 0)** softness, mildness.
mildern *v.t.* to mitigate, to soften.
mildernd *a.* extenuating; ~*e Umstände pl.* extenuating circumstances.
Milderung *f.* **(-, -en)** mitigation.
mildtätig *a.* charitable.
Milieu *n.* milieu; environment.
militant *a.* militant.
Militär *n.* **(-[e]s, 0)** military, armed forces.
Militär *m.* **(-[e]s, -s)** soldier.
Militärdienst *m.* military service.
Militärdiktatur *f.* military dictatorship.
militärisch *a.* military.
Militarisierung *f.* militarization.
Militarist *m.* **(-en, -en)** militarist.
militaristisch *a.* (*pej.*) militarist; militaristic.
Militärjunta *f.* military junta.
Militärregierung *f.* military government.
Militärstrafgesetzbuch *n.* military code.
Miliz *f.* **(-, -en)** militia.
Mill., Mio. *Million,* million, m.
Milliardär *m.*, **Milliardärin** *f.* billionaire.
Milliarde *f.* **(-, -n)** billion.
Million *f.* **(-, -en)** million.
Millionär *m.* **(-s, -e)**; **Millionärin** *f.* **(-, -nen)** millionaire.
Milz *f.* **(-, -en)** spleen.
mimen *v.t.* to act; to play.
Mimik *f.* mimic art.
Mimikry *f.* mimicry; camouflage.
Mimose *f.* mimosa; (*fig.*) oversensitive person.
minder *a.* less; minor, inferior.
minderbegabt *a.* less gifted.
minderbemittelt *a.* less well off.
Minderheit *f.* **(-, -en)** minority.
Minderheitsregierung *f.* minority government.
minderjährig *a.* underage, minor.
mindern *v.t.* to diminish, to lessen, to abate; ~ *v.r.* to decrease.
Minderung *f.* **(-, -en)** diminution, decrease.
minderwertig *a.* (of) inferior (quality).
Minderwertigkeitsgefühl *n.* feeling of inferiority.
Minderwertigkeitskomplex *m.* inferiority complex.
Minderzahl *f.* minority.
mindest *a.* least, lowest; *zum* ~*en,* at (the) least, to say the least.
mindestens *adv.* at least.
Mindestmaß, *n.* minimum (size).
Mine *f.* **(-, -n)** mine.
Minenfeld *n.* minefield.
Minensucher *m.* minesweeper.
Mineral *n.* **(-[e]s, -e & -ien)** mineral.
mineralisch *a.* mineral.
Mineralogie *f.* **(-, 0)** mineralogy.
Mineralquelle *f.* mineral spring.
Miniaturgemälde *n.* miniature.
minieren *v.t.* to (under)mine, to sap.
Minister *m.* **(-s, -)** minister (government).
Ministerium *n.* **(-s, -ien)** ministry; department.
Ministerpräsident *m.* prime minister.
Ministerrat *m.* cabinet.
Minne *f.* **(-, 0)** courtly love.
Minnesänger *m.* **(-s, -)** minnesinger.
minus *pr.* minus.
Minus *n.* **(-s, 0)** (*fig.*) deficit; disadvantage.
Minuspunkt *m.* penalty point.
Minute *f.* **(-, -n)** minute.
Minutenzeiger *m.* minute hand.
minuziös *a.* detailed; meticulous.
Minze *f.* **(-, 0)** mint.
mir *pn.* me, to me.
Misanthrop *m.* **(-en, -en)** misanthrope.
Mischbrot *n.* bread made from wheat and rye flour.
Mischehe *f.* mixed marriage.
mischen *v.t.* to mix, to blend; (*Karten*) to shuffle.
Mischfarbe *f.* nonprimary color.
Mischling *m.* **(-s, -e)** hybrid, mongrel, half-caste.
Mischmasch *m.* **(-es, -e)** medley, hodge-podge.
Mischung *f.* **(-, -en)** mixture, blend.
miserabel *a.* wretched, miserable.
Misere *f.* **(-, -n)** misery.
Mispel *f.* **(-, -n)** medlar.
mißachten *v.t.* to disregard, to slight.

Mißachtung *f.* **(-, 0)** disregard; ~ *des Gerichtes,* contempt of court.
Mißbehagen *n.* **(-s, 0)** uneasiness.
Mißbildung *f.* **(-, -en)** deformity, malformation.
mißbilligen *v.t.* to disapprove (of).
Mißbilligung *f.* **(-, 0)** disapproval.
Mißbrauch *m.* **(-[e]s, -bräuche)** abuse; misuse.
mißbrauchen *v.t.* to misuse, to abuse.
mißdeuten *v.t.* to misinterpret.
Mißdeutung *f.* **(-, -en)** misinterpretation.
missen *v.i.* to miss, to want.
Mißerfolg *m.* **(-[e]s, -e)** failure.
Mißernte *f.* **(-, -n)** bad harvest; crop failure.
Missetat *f.* **(-, -en)** misdeed, crime.
Missetäter *m.* **(-s, -)** malefactor, criminal.
mißfallen *v.i.st.* to displease.
Mißfallen *n.* **(-s, 0)** displeasure.
mißfällig *a.* displeasing.
mißgebildet *a.* deformed.
Mißgeburt *f.* **(-, -en)** monster, freak.
Mißgeschick *n.* **(-[e]s, -e)** mishap, misfortune.
mißglücken *v.i. (s)* to fail.
mißgönnen *v.t.* to grudge, to envy.
Mißgriff *m.* **(-[e]s, -e)** mistake, blunder.
Mißgunst *f.* **(-, 0)** ill will, grudge, envy.
mißgünstig *a.* envious, jealous.
mißhandeln *v.t.* to ill-treat, to mistreat.
Mißhandlung *f.* ill-treatment, mistreatment, abuse.
Mißheirat *f.* **(-, -en)** misalliance.
Mißhelligkeit *f.* **(-, -en)** difference, misunderstanding, dissension.
Mission *f.* **(-, -en)** mission.
Missionar *m.* **(-s, -e), Missionarin** *f.* **(-, -nen)** missionary.
missionarisch *a.* missionary.
missionieren *v.i.* to do missionary work; to convert.
Mißklang *m.* **(-[e]s, -änge)** dissonance.
Mißkredit *m.* **(-[e]s, 0)** disrepute; discredit.
mißlich *a.* awkward, difficult.
mißliebig *a.* unpopular, objectionable.
mißlingen *v.i.st. (s)* to fail, to miscarry.
Mißmut *m.* **(-[e]s)** low spirits *pl.*
mißmutig *a.* discouraged, dejected.
mißraten *v.i.st. (s)* turn out badly.
Miß: ~stand *m.* **(-[e]s, -stände)** deplorable state of affairs; **~stimmung** *f.* **(-, -en)** bad temper.
Mißton *m.* **(-[e]s, -töne)** false note; note of discord.
mißtrauen *v.i.* to distrust.
Mißtrauen *n.* **(-s, 0)** distrust.
Mißtrauensvotum *n.* vote of no confidence.
mißtrauisch *a.* suspicious; distrustful.
mißvergnügt *a.* discontented.
Mißverhältnis *n.* **(-ses, -se)** disproportion; incongruity.
mißverständlich *a.* unclear; misleading.
Mißverständnis *n.* **(-ses, -se)** misunderstanding.
mißverstehen *v.t.st.* to misunderstand.
Mißwirtschaft *f.* mismanagement.
Mist *m.* **(-es, 0)** dung, manure.
Mistel *f.* **(-, -n)** mistletoe.
misten *v.t.* to manure.
Mistgabel *f.* pitchfork.
Misthaufen *m.* dung heap.
Mistkäfer *m.* dung beetle.
Miststück *n. (sl.)* bastard; bitch.
Mistwetter *n.* lousy weather.
mit *pr.* with; by, at; ~ *der Post,* by mail; ~ *der Zeit,* in time; ~*einander,* together, jointly; ~ *dabei sein,* to make one (of a party).
Mitangeklagte *m./f.* codefendant.
Mitarbeit *f.* **(-, 0)** collaboration; assistance; participation.
mitarbeiten *v.i.* to collaborate, to cooperate.
Mitarbeiter *m.,* Mitarbeiterin *f.* fellowworker, collaborator, colleague, associate.
mitbekommen *v.t.st.* to get; (*fig.*) to get, to catch.
mitbenutzen *v.t.* to share.
Mitbesitzer *m.* joint owner.
mitbestimmen *v.i.* to have a say in sth.
Mitbestimmung *f.* **(-, 0)** participation.
Mitbewerber *m.* competitor.
Mitbewohner *m.;* **Mitbewohnerin** *f.* fellow resident; roommate.
mitbringen *v.t.ir.* to bring along.
Mitbringsel *n.* **(-s, -)** (*fam.*) present; souvenir.
Mitbrüder *m.* **(-s, 0)** fellow.
Mitbürger *m.;* Mitbürgerin *f.* fellow citizen.
mitdenken *v.i.st.* to follow (the argument *or* explanation).
Miteigentümer *m.* **(-s, -)** co-owner.
miteinander *adv.* together.
Miteinander *n.* togetherness.
mitempfinden *v.t.st.* to sympathize in.
Miterbe *m.;* **Miterbin** *f.,* joint heir.
miterleben *v.t.* to witness.
Mitesser *m.* pimple, blackhead.
mitfahren *v.i.* to ride, to go with.
Mitfahrgelegenheit *f.* ride.
mitfühlen *v.i.* to sympathize (with).
Mitgefühl *n.* sympathy.
mitgehen *v.i.st. (s)* to go along (with), to come (with).
Mitgift *f.* dowry, portion.
Mitglied *n.* member; fellow.
Mitgliederversammlung *f.* general meeting.
Mitgliedsbeitrag *m.* membership subscription.
Mitgliedschaft *f.* membership.
Mitgliedskarte *f.* membership card.
mithalten *v.t.st.* to keep up.
mithelfen *v.t.st.* to lend a hand.
Mithilfe *f.* assistance, cooperation.
mithin *c.* consequently.
Mitinhaber *m.;* **Mitinhaberin** *f.* co-owner.
Mitkämpfer *m.* fellow-combatant.
mitklingen *v.t.st.* to resonate.
Mitläufer *m.* **(-s, -)** 'fellow traveler' (*einer Partei*); (*pej.*) hanger-on.
Mitlaut *m.* **(-s -e)** consonant.
Mitleid *n.* compassion, pity.
Mitleidenschaft *f.* sympathy; *in* ~ *ziehen,* to implicate, involve, affect.
mitleiderregend *a.* pitiful.
mitleidig *a.* compassionate.
mitleidlos *a.* pitiless, ruthless.
mitmachen *v.i.* to take part in.
Mitmensch *m.* fellow human being.
mitmischen *v.i.* (*fam.*) to be involved.
mitnehmen *v.t.st.* to take along; (*fig.*) to weaken, to exhaust.
mitrechnen *v.t.* to include, to count in.
mitreden *v.i.* to join in the conversation; to have one's say.
mitreißen *v.t.st.* to sweep away; (*fig.*) to carry away.
mitsamt *pr.* together with.

mitschleppen *v.t.* (*fam.*) to drag along.
mitschreiben *v.i. & t.st.* to write down (a speech, etc.).
Mitschuld *f.* complicity.
Mitschuldige *m./f.* accomplice, accessory.
Mitschüler *m.;* **Mitschülerin** *f.* classmate.
mitspielen *v.i.* to join in a game; *einem übel ~,* to treat sb. badly.
Mitspracherecht *n. ein ~ haben* to have a say.
Mittag *m.* **(-s, -e)** midday, noon; *zu ~ essen, speisen,* to have lunch.
mittags *adv.* at noon.
Mittag(s)essen *n.* **(-s, -)** lunch.
Mittäter *m.;* **Mittäterin** *f.* accomplice.
Mitte *f.* **(-, 0)** middle, midst.
mitteilbar *a.* fit to be told or printed.
mitteilen *v.t.* to communicate.
mitteilsam *a.* communicative.
Mitteilung *f.* communication, notice.
Mitteilungsbedürfnis *n.* need to talk.
Mittel *n.* **(-s, -)** medium, average, mean; means, expedient, way; remedy; (*Geld*) means; *sich ins ~ legen,* to step in.
Mittelalter *n.* Middle Ages *pl.*
mittelalterlich *a.* medieval.
Mittelamerika *n.* Central America.
mittelbar *a.* indirect.
Mittelding *n.* intermediate thing.
Mitteleuropa *n.* Central Europe.
mitteleuropäisch *a.* Central European.
Mittelfinger *m.* middle finger.
mittelgroß *a.* middle sized.
Mittelgröße *f.* medium size.
mittelgut *a.* of average quality.
mittelhochdeutsch *a.* Middle High German.
mittelländisch *a.* Mediterranean.
mittellos *a.* penniless, destitute.
mittelmäßig *a.* mediocre.
Mittelmäßigkeit *f.* mediocrity.
Mittelmeer *n.* Mediterranean.
Mittelohrentzündung *f.* inflammation of the middle ear; ear infection.
mittels, mittelst *pr.* by means of.
Mittelscheitel *m.* middle part.
Mittelschule *f.* secondary school.
Mittelsmann *m.,* **Mittelsperson** *f.* intermediary.
Mittelstand *m.* middle class(es).
Mittelsturmer *m.* (*sp.*) center forward.
Mittelweg *m.* middle course.
Mittelwelle *f.* (*radio*) medium wave.
mitten *adv.* midst; *~ im Winter,* in the depth of winter; *~ durch,* through the midst; *~ entzwei,* broken in two; *~ in,* in the middle of.
Mitternacht *f.* **(-, -nächte)** midnight.
Mittler *m.* **(-s, -)** mediator.
Mittleramt *n.* mediatorship, umpireship.
mittlere[r] *a.* middle, mean.
Mittlerrolle *f.* mediating role.
mittlerweile *adv.* meanwhile.
mittragen *v.t.st.* to bear part of; to share.
Mittsommernacht *f.* Midsummer Night.
mittun *v.t.st.* to join in doing.
Mittwoch *m.* **(-s, -e)** Wednesday.
mitunter *adv.* now and then.
mitverantwortlich *a.* jointly responsible.
Mitverantwortung *f.* joint responsibility.
mitversichern *v.t.* to include in one's insurance.
Mitw. *Mitwirkung,* assistance, participation.
Mitwelt *f.* **(-, 0)** contemporaries.
mitwirken *v.i.* to cooperate, to concur.
Mitwirkende *m./f.* participant; performer; actor.
Mitwirkung *f.* **(-, 0)** cooperation.
Mitwisser *m.;* **Mitwisserin** *f.* person who knows information *or* a secret; accessory.
mitzählen *v.t.* to count; to include.
Mixbecher *m.* (cocktail) shaker.
mm *Millimeter,* millimeter.
Mo. *Montag,* Monday, Mon.
Möbel *n.* **(-s, -)** piece of furniture.
Möbelhändler *m.* furniture dealer.
Mobëlmagazin *n.* furniture warehouse.
Mobëlschreiner ~tischler *m.* cabinetmaker.
Mobëlspedition *f.* moving company.
Mobëlwagen *m.* moving van.
mobil *a.* active, quick; *~ machen,* to mobilize.
Mobiliar *n.* furniture.
mobilisieren *v.t.* to mobilize.
Mobilmachung *f.* **(-, 0)** mobilization.
möbl. *möbliert,* furnished, furn.
möblieren *v.t.* to furnish.
Möchte-gern... would-be....
modal *a.* modal.
Modalverb *n.* modal verb.
Mode *f.* **(-, -n)** mode, fashion.
Modell *n.* **(-s, -e)** model, pattern; mold.
modellieren *v.t.* to model, to mold.
Modellversuch *n.* pilot project.
modeln *v.t.* to fashion, to form.
Moder *m.* **(-s, 0)** mold; mud; decay.
Moderator *m.;* **Moderatorin** *f.* moderator.
moderieren *v.t.* to moderate.
moderig *a.* musty, moldy.
modern *v.i.* (*s*) to molder, to decay.
modern *a.* fashionable; modern.
Moderne *f.* modern age; modern times.
modernisieren *v.t.* to modernize.
Modernisierung *f.* modernization.
Modewaren *pl.* novelties *pl.*
modifizieren *v.t.* to modify.
modisch *a.* fashionable, stylish.
Modistin *f.* **(-, -nen)** milliner, dressmaker.
Modus *m.* **(-, -di)** way; method; (*ling.*) mood.
Mogelei *f.* **(-, -en)** cheating.
mogeln *v.i.* (*sl.*) to cheat.
mögen *v.i. & t.ir.* to like, to wish; *ich mag,* I may, I can; I like; *ich möchte,* I would like; *ich möchte lieber,* I would rather.
möglich *a.* possible.
möglicherweise *adv.* perhaps; possibly.
Möglichkeit *f.* **(-, -en)** possibility.
Möglichkeiten *pl.* potentialities.
möglichst *adv.* as much as possible.
Mohammedaner *m.;* **Mohammedanerin** *f.* Muslim.
Mohn *m.* **(-[e]s, -e)** poppy, poppyseed.
Mohnsaft *m.* opium.
Mohr *m.* **(-en, -en)** Moor.
Möhre *f.,* **(-, -n) Mohrrübe** *f.* carrot.
Mohrenkopf *m.* chocolate marshmallow.
mokieren *v.r.* to mock, to scoff.
Molch *m.* **(-es, -e)** newt.
Molekül *n.* **(-s, -e)** molecule.
molekular *a.* molecular.
Molke *f.* **(-, -n), Molken** *pl.* whey.
Molkerei *f.* **(-, -en)** dairy.
moll *a.* (*mus.*) minor, flat.
mollig *a.* comfortable, snug; plump.
Molltonart *f.* **(-, -en)** (*mus.*) minor key.

Moment *m.* **(-[e]s, -e)** moment.
momentan *a.* momentary; for the present.
Momentaufnahme *f.* (*phot.*) snapshot.
Monarch *m.* **(-en, -en); Monarchin** *f.* **(-, -nen)** monarch.
Monarchie *f.* **(-, -n)** monarchy.
monarchisch *a.* monarchical.
monarchistisch *a.* monarchist; monarchistic.
Monat *m.* **(-[e]s, -e)** month.
monatelang *a. & adv.* lasting for months.
monatlich *a. & adv.* monthly.
Monatsbinde *f.* sanitary napkin.
Monatsblutung *f.* period.
Monatseinkommen *n.* monthly income.
Monatsgehalt *n.* month's salary; *dreizehntes ~*, extra month's salary.
Monatskarte *f.* monthly ticket.
Monatsrate *f.* monthly installment.
Monatsschrift *f.* monthly (magazine).
Mönch *m.* **(-es, -e)** monk, friar.
mönchisch *a.* monkish; monastic.
Mönchskloster *n.* monastery.
Mond *m.* **(-[e]s, -e)** moon.
mondän *a.* fashionable.
Mondaufgang *m.* moonrise.
Mondfinsternis *f.* eclipse of the moon.
mondhell *a.* moonlit.
Mondlandefähre *f.* lunar module.
Mondphase *f.* phase of the moon.
Mondschein *m.* moonlight.
Mondsichel *f.* crescent.
mondsüchtig *a.* somnambulant.
Monduntergang *m.* moonset.
Mongole *m.*; **Mongolin** *f.*; **mongolisch** *a.* Mongol(ian).
Mongolei *f.* **(-, 0)** Mongolia.
Mongolismus *n.* (*med.*) Down's syndrome.
mongoloid *a.* mongoloid.
monieren *v.t.* to criticize; (*com.*) to remind.
monogam *a.* monogamous.
Monogamie *f.* monogamy.
Monogramm *n.* **(-s, -e)** monogram.
Monographie *f.* **(-, -n)** monograph.
Monokultur *f.* monoculture.
monolithisch *a.* monolithic.
Monolog *m.* **(-s, -e)** monologue.
Monopol *n.* **(-[e]s, -e)** monopoly.
monopolisieren *v.t.* to monopolize.
Monotheismus *m.* monotheism.
monoton *a.* monotonous.
Monotonie *f.* **(-, 0)** monotony.
Monster *n.* **(-s, -tren)** monster.
monster *a.* mammoth
Monstranz *f.* **(-, -en)** pyx, monstrance.
monströs *a.* monstrous; hideous.
Monsun *m.* **(-s, -e)** monsoon.
Montag *m.* **(-[e]s, -e)** Monday.
Montage *f.* assembly; installation.
Montageband *n.* assembly line.
Montagehalle *f.* assembly shop.
montags *adv.* on Monday(s).
Montanaktien *pl.* mining shares.
Montanindustrie *f.* mining industry.
Monteur *m.* **(-s, -e)** mechanic; electrician; fitter.
montieren *v.t.* (*mech.*) to mount, to fit, to assemble.
Montur *f.* **(-, -en)** outfit; gear.
Monument *n.* **(-s, -e)** monument.
Moor *n.* **(-[e]s, -e)** moor, fen, bog.
Moos *n.* **(-es, -e)** moss.
moosig *a.* mossy.
Mops *m.* **(-es, Möpse)** pug(dog).
mopsen *v.t.* to pinch.
Moral *f.* **(-, 0)** moral philosophy; morality; (*einer Fabel*) moral; morals *pl.*; *doppelte ~*, double standards.
moralisch *a.* moral; virtuous.
moralisieren *v.i.* to moralize.
Morast *m.* **(-es, -e & Moräste)** morass; bog; swamp.
morastig *a.* muddy.
Moratorium *n.* **(-s, -ien)** moratorium.
Morchel *f.* **(-, -n)** morel (mushroom).
Mord *m.* **(-[e]s, -e)** murder, homicide.
morden *v.t. & i.* to murder.
Mörder *m.* **(-s, -)** murderer.
Mörderin *f.* **(-, -nen)** murderess.
mörderisch *a.* murderous.
Mordkommission *f.* homicide squad.
Mordskerl *m.* great guy.
mordsmäßig *a.* (*fam.*) tremendous.
Mordtat *f.* murder.
Mordverdacht *m.* suspicion of murder.
morgen *adv.* tomorrow; *heute ~*, this morning; *~ früh*, tomorrow morning.
Morgen *m.* **(-s, -)** morning; acre (of land).
Morgenland *n.* Orient, East.
Morgen: ~rot *n.*, **~röte** *f.* dawn, aurora, blush of dawn; **~stern** *m.* morning star.
morgens *adv.* in the morning.
morgig *a.* of tomorrow, tomorrow's.
Mormone *m.*; **Mormonin** *f.* Mormon.
Morphium *n.* **(-s, 0)** morphine.
morsch *a.* rotten, decayed.
Morsealphabet *n.* Morse (code).
Mörser *m.* **(-s, -)** mortar; (*mil.*) howitzer.
Mörserkeule *f.* pestle.
Mortalität *f.* mortality.
Mörtel *m.* **(-s, -)** mortar, cement.
Mosaik *n.* **(-[s], -en)** mosaic.
Moschee *f.* **(-, -n)** mosque.
Moschus *m.* **(-, o)** musk.
Moskito *m.* **(-s, -s)** mosquito.
Moslem *m.* **(-s, -s)** Muslim.
Most *m.* **(-es, -e)** must; *Apfel~* cider.
Mostrich *m.* **(-s, -)** mustard.
Motiv *n.* **(-s, -e)** motive; (*mus.*) motif.
Motivation *f.* motivation.
motivieren *v.t.* to motivate.
Motodrom *n.* autodrome; speedway.
Motor *m.* **(-s, -e)** motor, engine.
Motorbarkasse *f.* motor launch.
Motorboot *n.* motorboat.
Motorfahrzeug *n.* motor vehicle.
Motorhaube *f.* hood.
motorisieren *v.t.* to motorize.
Motorrad *n.* motorcycle.
Motorunterbau *m.* engine bed.
Motte *f.* **(-, -n)** moth; *von ~n zerfressen*, moth-eaten.
Mottenfraß *m.* damage caused by moths.
Mottenpulver *n.* moth powder.
Mottensicher *a.* mothproof.
Motto *n.* **(-s, -s)** motto.
motzen *v.i.* (*fam.*) to grouch.
moussieren *v.i.* to effervesce, to sparkle.
Möwe *f.* **(-, -n)** seagull.
Mrd. *Milliarde*, billion, bn.

MS, Ms. *Manuskript,* manuscript, MS, ms.
MT *Megatonne,* megaton.
mtl. *monatlich,* monthly.
Mucke *f.* **(-, -n)** caprice, whim.
Mücke *f.* **(-, -n)** gnat, midge; mosquito.
mucken *v.i.* to grumble; to mutter.
Mucks *m.* **(-es, -er)** (*fam.*) murmur.
mucksen ~ *v.r.* to make a sound.
müde *a.* weary, tired.
Müdigkeit *f.* **(-, 0)** weariness, fatigue.
Muff *m.* **(-[e]s, -e)** muff; musty smell.
muffig *a.* musty; sulky.
Mufflon *n.* **(-s, -s)** (*zool.*) mouflon.
Mühe *f.* **(-, -n)** trouble, effort; pains *pl.; sich ~ geben,* to take pains; *der ~ wert sein,* to be worthwhile.
mühelos *a.* without trouble, effortless.
mühen ~ *v.r.* to trouble oneself.
mühevoll *a.* laborious.
Mühlrad *n.* mill wheel.
Mühlstein *m.* millstone.
Mühsal *n.* **(-[e]s, -e),** *f.* **(-, -e)** tribulation; hardship.
mühsam *a.* troublesome; toilsome.
mühselig *a.* toilsome; miserable.
Mulatte *m.* **(-n, -n), Mulattin** *f.* **(-, -nen)** mulatto.
Mulde *f.* **(-, -n)** hollow
Mull *m.* **(-[e]s, 0)** gauze, mull.
Müll *m.* **(-[e]s, 0)** garbage; rubbish.
Müllabfuhr *f.* garbage collection.
Mülleimer *m.* garbage can.
Müller *m.* **(-s, -)** miller.
Müllhalde *f.* garbage dump.
Müllschlucker *m.* garbage chute.
Mülltonne *f.* garbage can.
Müllwagen *m.* garbage truck.
mulmig *a.* (*fam.*) uneasy.
Multiplikation *f.* multiplication.
multiplizieren *v.t.* to multiply.
m.ü.M. *Meter über dem Meeresspiegel,* meters above sea level.
Mumie *f.* **(-, -n)** mummy.
mumifizieren *v.t.* to mummify.
Mumm *m.* (*fam.*) guts; drive.
mummeln *v.i. &. t.* (*fam.*) to chew; to nap.
Mund *m.* **(-[e]s, Münder)** mouth; *den ~ halten,* to hold one's tongue; *von der Hand in den ~ leben,* to live from hand to mouth.
Mundart *f.* dialect.
mundartlich *a.* dialect.
Munddusche *f.* water pick.
Mündel *n.* **(-s, -)** ward.
munden *v.i.imp* to taste nice.
münden *v.i.* to flow into.
mundgerecht *a.* bite-sized.
Mundgeruch *m.* bad breath.
Mundharmonika *f.* mouth organ.
mündig *a.* of age; *~ werden,* to come of age.
Mündigkeit *f.* **(-, 0)** majority, full age.
mündlich *a.* verbal, oral.
Mundpflege *f.* oral hygiene.
Mundraub *m.* petty theft.
Mundstück *n.* mouthpiece
mundtot *a. jn ~ machen* to silence sb.
Mündung *f.* **(-, -en)** mouth; estuary; (*einer Flinte*) muzzle; orifice.
Mund-zu-Mund-Beatmung *f.* mouth-to-mouth resuscitation.
Munition *f.* **(-, -en)** ammunition.
munkeln *v.i.* to whisper, to mutter.
Münster *n., m.* **(-s, -)** minster, cathedral.
munter *a.* awake; lively, gay, brisk.
Münzautomat *m.* slot machine; payphone.
Münze *f.* **(-, -n)** coin; medal; mint; *klingende ~,* hard cash.
Münzeinheit *f.* monetary unit.
münzen *v.t.* to mint; to coin.
Münzkunde *f.* numismatics *pl.*
mürbe *a.* mellow; tender, soft.
Mürbeteig *m.* short pastry.
Murmel *f.* **(-, -n)** marble.
murmeln *v.t. & i.* to mumble; to murmur; to mutter.
Murmeltier *n.* marmot.
murren *v.i.* to grumble, to growl
mürrisch *a.* morose, surly, peevish.
Mus *n.* **(es, -e)** pulp, pap; (*Früchte*) jam.
Muschel *f.* **(-, -n)** shell, mussel.
Muse *f.* **(-, -n)** muse.
Museum *n.* **(-s, -een)** museum.
Musik *f.* **(-, 0)** music.
Musikalienhandlung *f.* music store.
musikalisch *a.* musical.
Musikalität *f.* musicality.
Musikant *m.* **(en, -en)** (inferior) musician.
Musikantenknochen *m.* funny bone
Musikbox *f.* juke box.
Musiker *m.* **(-s, -); Musikerin** *f.* **(-, -nen)** musician.
Musiklehrer *m.;* **Musiklehrerin** *f.* music teacher.
Musikwissenschaft *f.* musicology.
Musikwissenschaftler *m.,* **Musikwissenschaftlerin** *f.* musicologist.
musisch *a.* artistic; musically gifted.
musizieren *v.i.* to make music.
Muskat *m.* **(-[e]s, -e), Muskatnuß** *f.* **(-, -nüsse)** nutmeg.
Muskateller *m.* **(s, -0)** (*Wein*) muscatel.
Muskel *m.* **(-s, -n)** muscle.
Muskel: ~kater *m.* sore muscles; **~krampf** *m.* cramp; **~paket** *n.* bulging muscles; **~protz** *m.* muscleman; **~riß** *m.* torn muscle; **~schwund** *m.* muscular atrophy; **~zerrung** *f.* pulled muscle.
Muskete *f.* **(-, -n)** musket.
Musketier *m.* **(-[e]s, -e)** musketeer.
Muskulatur *f.* **(-, -en)** muscular system.
muskulös *a.* muscular.
Müsli *n.* **(-s, -s)** muesli.
Muß *n.* must.
Muße *f.* **(-, 0)** leisure; *mit ~,* at leisure.
Musselin *m.* **(-[e]s, -e)** muslin
müssen *v.i.ir.* to be obliged, to be forced, to be constrained, to have to.
Mußestunde *f.* leisure hour.
müßig *a.* unemployed, idle.
Müßiggang *m.* **(-[e]s, 0)** idleness, idling.
Müßiggänger *m.* **(-s, -)** idler, loafer.
Muster *n.* **(-s, -)** pattern; sample; design; *nach ~,* according to sample.
Muster: ~beispiel *n.* perfect example; model; **~exemplar** *n.* specimen.
mustergültig *a.* exemplary.
musterhaft *a.* exemplary, model.
mustern *v.t.* to review, to scrutinize; (*Stoffe*) to pattern.
Musterrolle *f.* muster roll.
Musterschutz *m.* copyright, patent.
Musterung *f.* **(-, -en)** examination, inspection; (*mil.*) review.

Musterzeichner *m.* designer (of patterns).
Mut *m.* **(-[e]s, 0)** courage; spirit, mettle.
Mutation *f.* **(-, -en)** mutation.
mutig *a.* courageous, brave.
mutlos *a.* discouraged, disheartened.
mutmaßen *v.t.* to conjecture.
mutmaßlich *a.* presumptive.
Mutmaßung *f.* conjecture.
Mutter *f.* **(-, Mütter)** mother; *Schrauben*~ nut; *werdende* ~, expectant mother.
Mutterboden *m.* topsoil.
Muttergesellschaft *f.* parent company.
Muttercomplex *m.* mother fixation.
Mutterkuchen *m.* placenta.
Mutterleib *m.* womb.
mütterlich *a.* motherly; maternal.
mütterlicherseits *adv.* on one's mother's side; maternal (parent).
Mütterlichkeit *f.* motherliness.
Mutterliebe *f.* motherly love.
Muttermal *n.* birthmark.
Muttermund *m.* cervix.
Mutterschaft *f.* **(-, 0)** motherhood; maternity.
Mutterschafturlaub *m.* maternity leave.
Mutterschoß *m.* womb.
Mutterschwein *n.* sow.
mutterseelenallein *adv.* all alone.
Muttersöhnchen *n.* mommy's boy, sissy.
Muttersprache *f.* mother tongue.
Mutterwitz *m.* mother wit, common sense.
Mutwille (ns, -0) willfulness; wantonness.
mutwillig *a.* willful; wanton.
Mütze *f.* **(-, -n)** cap.
MWSt. *Mehrwertsteuer,* value-added tax, VAT.
Myrrhe *f.* **(-, -n)** myrrh.
Myrte *f.* **(-, -n)** myrtle.
mysteriös *a.* mysterious.
Mysterium *n.* **(-s, -ien)** mystery.
mystifizieren *v.t.* to mystify.
Mystik *f.* **(-, 0)** mysticism.
Mystiker *m.* **(-s, -)** mystic.
mystisch *a.* mystical.
Mythe *f.* **(-, -n)** fable, myth.
mythisch *a.* mythical.
Mythologie *f.* **(-, -n)** mythology.
mythologisch *a.* mythological.
Mythos *m.* **(-, -then)** myth.

N

N, n *n.* the letter N or n.
N *Nord(en),* north, N.
n. *nach,* after.
na! *i.* well! now!
Nabe *f.* **(-, -n)** hub.
Nabel *m.* **(-s, -)** navel.
Nabelschnur *f.* umbilical cord.
nach *pr. & adv.* after, behind; according to; past; to; ~ *und* ~, little by little; ~ *Gewicht,* by weight; ~ *der Reihe,* in turn; ~ *wie vor,* as ever.
nachäffen *v.t. & i.* to ape, to mimic.
nachahmen *v.t.* to imitate; to copy.
nachahmenswert *a.* exemplary.
Nachahmer *m.* **(-s, -)** imitator.
Nachahmung *f.* **(-, -en)** imitation.
nacharbeiten *v.t.* to make up missed time; to go over (text).
Nachbar *m.* **(-s & -n, -n); Nachbarin** *f.* **(-, -nen)** neighbor.
nachbarlich *f.* neighborly.
Nachbarschaft *f.* **(-, -en)** neighborhood.
nachbarschaftlich *a.* neighborly.
Nachbehandlung *f.* follow-up treatment.
nachbestellen *v.t.* to order again.
Nachbestellung *f.* **(-, -en)** repeat order.
nachbeten *v.t.* (*fig.*) to echo.
nachbilden *v.t.* to copy, to imitate.
nachblicken *v.i.* to look after.
nachdatieren *v.t.* to postdate.
nachdem *adv.* afterward, after that; ~ *c.* after; *je* ~, according to.
nachdenken *v.i.ir.* to think; to meditate, to muse.
Nachdenken *n.* **(-s, 0)** thought; reflection.
nachdenklich *a.* thoughtful, pensive.
nachdrängen *v.i.* (*h*), **nachdringen** *v.t.st.* (*s*) to crowd after, to press in after.
Nachdruck *m.* **(-[e]s, -e)** energy, emphasis, stress; pirated edition; reprint.
nachdrucken *v.t.* to reprint; to pirate.
nachdrücklich *a.* energetic, emphatic.
Nachdrucksrecht *n.* **(-s, -e)** right of reproduction.
nacheifern *v.i.* to emulate.
Nacheiferung *f.* **(-, 0)** emulation.
nacheilen *v.i.* (*s*) to hasten after.
nacheinander *adv.* one after another.
nachempfinden *v.t.st.* to empathize; to feel.
Nachen *m.* **(-s, -)** boat, skiff.
nacherzählen *v.t.* to retell.
Nacherzählung *f.* retold story.
Nachfahr(e) *m.* **(-n, -en); Nachfahrin** *f.* **(-, -nen)** descendant
nachfahren *v.i.st.* (*s*) to follow (in a car).
nachfeiern *v.t.* to celebrate at a later date.
Nachfolge *f.* succession; imitation.
nachfolgen *v.i.* (*s*) to succeed; to imitate.
nachfolgend *a.* following, subsequent.
Nachfolger *m.* **(-s, -)** follower; successor; imitator.
Nachforderung *f.* **(-, -en)** additional claim or charge.
nachforschen *v.i.* to search after; to inquire into, to investigate.
Nachforschung *f.* **(-, -en)** search, inquiry, investigation.
Nachfrage *f.* demand, request; inquiry.
nachfragen *v.i.* to inquire after.
nachfühlen *v.t.* to feel; to empathize.
nachfüllen *v.t.* to refill.
nachgeben *v.t. & i. st.* to give in; to give way.
nachgeboren *a.* posthumous; born later.
Nachgebühr *f.* surcharge, excess postage.
Nachgeburt *f.* afterbirth.
nachgehen *v.i.st.* (*s*) to follow; (*einer Sache*) to investigate; (*Uhr*) to be slow.
nachgelassen *a.* posthumous (writings).
nachgemacht *a.* counterfeit.
nachgerade *adv.* by this time; really.
nachgeraten *v.t.st.* to take after a person.
Nachgeschmack *m.* aftertaste, tang.
nachgiebig *a.* yielding, compliant.
Nachgiebigkeit *f.* compliance, softness.
nachhaken *v.t.* (*fam.*) to follow up.

Nachhall *m.* **(-s, -e)** reverberation.
nachhallen *v.i.* to reverberate.
nachhaltig *a.* lasting, enduring.
Nachhauseweg *m.* **(-s, -e)** way home.
nachhelfen *v.t.st.* to lend a helping hand.
nachher *adv.* afterward.
nachherig *a.* subsequent.
Nachhilfe *f.* help, aid; coaching; **~stunde** *f.* tutoring lesson.
nachhinein *adv. im ~* afterward; with hindsight.
Nachholbedarf *m.* need to catch up.
nachholen *v.t.* to make up for.
Nachhut *f.* **(-, 0)** rear guard.
nachjagen *v.i. & t. (s & h)* to pursue; to chase after.
Nachklang *m.* resonance; aftereffect.
Nachkomme *m./f.* **(-n, -n)** descendant.
nachkommen *v.i.st. (s)* to come after; (*fig.*) to conform to, to obey.
Nachkommenschaft *f.* **(-, -en)** issue, descendants *pl.*, posterity.
Nachkömmling *m.* **(-s, -e)** much younger child.
Nachkriegs: ~generation *f.* post-war generation, **~zeit** *f.* post-war period.
Nachlaß *m.* **(-lasses, -lasse & -lässe)** remission; estate, inheritance; **~steuer** *f.* estate tax.
nachlassen *v.t.st.* to slacken, to relax; (*Preise*) to reduce; **~** *v.i.st.* to abate, to subside.
nachlässig *a.* negligent, careless.
Nachlässigkeit *f.* **(-, -en)** negligence.
nachlaufen *v.i.st. (s)* to run after.
Nachlese *f.* **(-, -n)** gleaning.
nachlesen *v.t.st.* to glean; to look up (a passage).
nachliefern *v.t.* to supply later.
Nachlieferung *f.* **(-, -en)** subsequent delivery.
nachlösen *v.t.* to buy a ticket (on the train).
nachm. *nachmittags,* in the afternoon, P.M.
nachmachen *v.t.* to copy; to counterfeit.
nachmalig *a.* subsequent.
nachmals *adv.* afterward, subsequently.
nachmessen *v.t.st.* to measure again; to check the measurements.
Nachmittag *m.* afternoon.
nachmittags *adv.* in the afternoon.
Nachnahme *f.* **(-, -n)** (*com.*) *per ~*, cash on delivery, COD.
Nachname *m.* **(-, -n)** last name.
nachplappern *v.t. & i.* to repeat (another's words) mechanically.
Nachporto *n.* excess postage.
nachprüfen *v.t.* to verify, to reexamine.
nachrechnen *v.t.* to check (an account).
Nachrede *f.* **(-, -n)** *üble ~*, slander
nachreden *v.t.* to repeat (another's words).
nachreichen *v.t.* to hand in late.
Nachricht *f.* **(-, -en)** advice, information, news.
Nachrichten: ~abteilung *f.* intelligence department; **~agentur** *f.* news agency; **~büro** *n.* news agency; **~dienst** *m.* intelligence service; **~sendung** *f.* news broadcast; **~stelle, zentrale** *f.* (*mil.*) message center, signal center; **~wesen** *n.* (*mil.*) communications.
nachrücken *v.i.* (*mil.*) to move up.
Nachruf *m.* obituary (notice).
Nachruhm *m.* posthumous fame.
nachrühmen *v.t.* to praise.
nachrüsten *v.i.* to close the armament gap; (*mot.*) to retrofit.
Nachrüstung *f.* rearmament.
nachsagen *v.t.* to repeat.
Nachsaison *f.* late season.
Nachsatz *m.* postscript; (*gram.*) final clause.
nachschicken *v.t.* to forward.
Nachschlag *m.* (*fam.*) second helping.
Nachschlage: ~bibliothek *f.* reference library; **~buch** *n.* reference book.
nachschlagen *v.t.st.* to look up; to refer to, to consult (a book); **~** *v.i.st.* to take after.
nachschleichen *v.i.st. (s)* to steal after.
Nachschlüssel *m.* duplicate key.
Nachschub *m.* **(-[e]s, -schübe)** (*mil.*) supply.
nachsehen *v.t. & i.st.* to look after; to pardon, to excuse; to look up (in a book).
Nachsehen *n. das ~ haben,* to be the loser.
nachsenden *v.t.ir.* (*Brief*) to forward; *bitte ~!* please forward!
nachsetzen *v.i. (s)* to pursue.
Nachsicht *f.* **(-, 0)** lenience.
nachsichtig *a.* indulgent, lenient.
Nachsilbe *f.* suffix.
nachsinnen *v.t.st.* to muse.
nachsitzen *v.t.st.* to be in detention (school).
Nachsommer *m.* Indian summer.
Nachspeise *f.* dessert; sweet.
Nachspiel *n.* sequel; epilogue; postlude.
nachspionieren *v.i.* to spy.
nachsprechen *v.t.st.* to repeat.
nachspüren *v.i.* to trace; to investigate.
nächst *pr.* nearest; next to; **~ beste[r]** *a.* second-best.
Nächste[r] *m.* **(-n, -n)** neighbor.
nachstehen *v.i.* to be inferior to.
nachstehend *a.* following.
nachstellen *v.i.* to persecute; **~** *v.t.* to readjust; (*Uhr*) to put back.
Nachstellung *f.* **(-, -en)** readjust; pursuit; postposition.
Nächstenliebe *f.* charity.
nächstens *adv.* soon, shortly.
nachstreben *v.i.* to strive for; to emulate.
nachsuchen *v.i.* to petition for.
Nacht *f.* **(-, Nächte)** night; *bei ~*, at night; *über ~*, during the night.
nachtaktiv *a.* (*zool.*) nocturnal.
nachtanken *v.t.* to refuel.
Nachtanzug *m.* nightclothes.
Nachtblindheit *f.* nightblindness.
Nachtdienst *m.* night duty.
Nachteil *m.* **(-[e]s, -e)** disadvantage.
nachteilig *a.* disadvantageous; detrimental.
nächtelang *a.* all night; night after night.
Nachtessen *n.* supper.
Nachteule *f.* night owl.
Nachtfalter *m.* moth.
Nachtfrost *m.* night frost.
Nachthemd *n.* nightshirt; (*Frauen*) nightgown.
Nachtigall *f.* **(-, -en)** nightingale.
nächtigen *v.i.* to pass the night.
Nachtisch *m.* dessert.
nächtlich *a.* nightly, nocturnal.
Nachtlokal *n.* nightclub.
Nachtportier *m.* night porter.
Nachtrag *m.* **(-[e]s, äge)** supplement.
nachtragen *v.t.st.* to add, to append; *einem etwas ~*, to bear someone a grudge.
nachtragend *a.* unforgiving.
nachträglich *a.* subsequent, supplementary.
nachtrauern *v.i.* to mourn; to cry after.
Nachtruhe *f.* sleep.
nachts *adv.* in the night, at night.

Nachtschatten *m.* (*bot.*) nightshade.
Nachttisch *m.* night table.
Nachtwache *f.* night watch.
Nachtwächter *m.* watchman.
Nachtwandler *m.* sleepwalker.
Nachuntersuchung *f.* follow-up examination.
nachvollziehbar *a.* comprehensible.
nachwachsen *v.i.st.* *(s)* to grow again.
Nachwahl *f.* special election.
Nachwehen *pl.* after pains; painful consequences *pl.*
nachweinen *v.i.* to bemoan a loss.
Nachweis *m.* **(-es, -e)** proof.
nachweisen *v.t.st.* to prove.
nachweislich *a.* demonstrable.
Nachwelt *f.* posterity.
nachwirken *v.i.* to have a lasting effect.
Nachwirkung *f.* after effect.
Nachwort *n.* concluding remarks *pl.*; afterword; epilogue.
Nachwuchs *m.* **(-es, -wüchse)** offspring; young generation.
nachzahlen *v.t.* to pay later.
nachzählen *v.t.* to count again.
Nachzahlung *f.* additional payment.
nachzeichnen *v.t.* to copy from, to draw from.
nachziehen *v.t.st.* to drag; to trace; ~ *v.i.st.* to follow.
Nachzügler *m.* **(-s, -)** straggler; latecomer.
Nackedei *m.* **(-s, -s)** naked little thing.
Nacken *m.* **(-s, -)** nape of the neck.
nackt *a.* & *adv.* naked, nude; bare.
Nackt: ~baden *n.* nude bathing; **~badestrand** *m.* nudist beach.
Nackte *m./f.* **(-n, -n)** naked person.
Nacktheit *f.* nakedness; nudity.
Nadel *f.* **(-, -n)** needle; pin.
Nadelbaum *m.* coniferous tree.
Nadel: ~kissen *n.* pincushion; **~öhr** *n.* eye of a needle; **~spitze** *f.* point of a needle *or* pin; **~stich** *m.* pinprick; **~wald** *m.* coniferous forest.
Nagel *m.* **(-s, Nägel)** nail.
Nagelbürste *f.* nailbrush.
Nagelfeile *f.* nail file.
Nagelhäutchen *n.* cuticle.
Nagellack *m.* nail polish.
nageln *v.t.* to nail.
nagelneu *a.* brand-new.
Nagelschere *f.* nail scissors.
Nagelschmied *m.* nail smith.
nagen *v.t.* & *i.* to gnaw; (*fig.*) to rankle.
nagend *a.* gnawing; nagging.
Nager *m.* **(-s, -), Nagetier** *n.* rodent.
nah[e] *a.* near, close, nigh; imminent; *das geht mir ~,* that grieves me; *einem zu ~ treten,* to hurt someone's feelings.
Nahaufklärung *f.* (*mil.*) close reconnaissance.
Nahaufnahme *f.* (*phot.*) closeup.
Nähbeutel *m.* workbag.
Nähe *f.* **(-, -n)** nearness, proximity; *in der ~,* near.
nahebei *adv.* nearby.
nahebringen *v.t.st.* to make accessible.
nahegehen *v.i.st.* to affect deeply.
nahekommen *v.i.st.* to come close; ~ *v.r.* to become close.
nahen *v.i.* *(s)* to approach.
nähen *v.t.* to sew, to stitch.
Nähere[s] *n.* details, particulars *pl.*
Näherei *f.* **(-, -en)** needlework.
Naherholungsgebiet *n.* recreational area close to a city.
Näherin *f.* **(-, -nen)** seamstress.
nähern *v.r.* to draw near.
nahestehen *v.i.st.* to be intimate with.
nahezu *adv.* almost.
Nähgarn *n.* sewing thread.
Nähkästchen *n.* sewing box.
Nähkorb *m.* sewing basket.
Nähmaschine *f.* sewing machine.
Nähnadal *f.* sewing needle.
Nährboden *m.* breeding ground, hotbed (*also fig.*)
nähren *v.t.* to feed, to nourish; to nurse; (*fig.*) to foster.
nahrhaft *a.* nutritious, nourishing; (*fig.*) profitable, lucrative.
Nahrung *f.* **(-, 0)** nourishment, food; livelihood, means of subsistence.
Nahrungs: ~mittel *n.* (article of) food; *pl.* victuals, provisions *pl.*; **~sorgen** *pl.* cares for daily bread.
Nährwert *m.* nutritional value.
Nähseide *f.* sewing silk.
Naht *f.* **(-, Nähte)** seam; suture.
nahtlos *a.* seamless.
Nahverkehr *m.* local traffic.
Nähzeug *n.* sewing kit.
Nahziel *n.* short-term goal.
naiv *a.* naive, unsophisticated.
Naivität *f.* **(-, -en)** naïveté, artlessness.
Name[n], *m.* **(-ns, -n)** name; title; (*fig.*) reputation, fame; *dem ~ nach,* by name only; nominally.
namenlos, *a.* nameless; unspeakable.
namens *adv.* in the name of, on behalf; ~ *N,* called N.
Namens: ~liste *f.* (*mil.*) roster; **~schild** *n.* nameplate; **~tag** *m.* name day; **~vetter** *m.* namesake.
namentlich *adv.* by name; particularly.
namhaft *a.* considerable, well-known; ~ *machen,* to name, to specify.
näml. *nämlich,* that is to say, viz.
nämlich *a.* the same; ~ *adv.* namely, viz.
Napf *m.* **(-[e]s, Näpfe)** basin, bowl.
Narbe *f.* **(-, -n)** scar; stigma.
narbig *a.* scarred.
Narkose *f.* **(-, -n)** anesthesia; narcosis.
narkotisch *a.* narcotic.
narkotisieren *v.t.* to anesthetize.
Narr *m.* **(-en, -en)** fool; buffoon, jester; *einem zum ~ en haben,* to fool someone.
narren *v.t.* to make a fool of, to chaff.
Narrenfreiheit *f.* fool's license.
narrensicher *a.* foolproof.
Narretei *f.* **(-, -en)** tomfoolery, buffoonery.
Närrin *f.* **(-, -nen)** fool.
närrisch *a.* foolish; mad; odd, queer.
Narzisse *f.* **(-, -n)** narcissus.
Nasal *m.* nasal (sound).
naschen *v.t.* & *i.* to eat sweets (on the sly); to nibble.
Nascherei *f.* **(-, -en)** dainties *pl.*
naschhaft *a.* fond of candies.
Nase *f.* **(-, -n)** nose; (*Tier*) snout; (*fig.*) reprimand; *die ~ rümpfen,* to turn up one's nose (at); *an der ~ herumführen,* to lead by the nose.
näseln *v.i.* to talk through the nose.
Nasenbluten *n.* **(-s, 0)** nosebleed.

Nasen: ~loch *m.* nostril; **~spitze** *f.* tip of the nose.
naseweis *a.* pert, saucy, impertinent.
Nashorn *n.* rhinoceros.
naß *a.* wet, moist.
Nässe *f.* **(-, 0)** wetness, moisture.
nässen *v.t.* to wet, to moisten.
naßkalt *a.* raw, damp and cold.
Nation *f.* **(-, -en)** nation.
national *a.* national.
Nationalhymne *f.* **(-, -n)** national anthem.
nationalisieren *v.t.* to nationalize.
Nationalismus *m.* **(-, 0)** nationalism.
nationalistisch *a.* nationalist; nationalistic.
Nationalität *f.* **(-, -en)** nationality.
NATO *Nordatlantikpakt-Organisation,* North Atlantic Treaty Organization, NATO.
Natrium *n.* **(-s, -0)** sodium.
Natron *n.* **(-s, 0)** soda; *doppeltkohlensaures* ~, (bi)carbonate of soda.
Natter *f.* **(-, -n)** adder, viper.
Natur *f.* **(-, -en)** nature; disposition; *von* ~, by nature, naturally.
Naturalien *pl.* natural produce; *in ~ bezahlen,* to pay in kind.
naturalisieren *v.t.* to naturalize; *sich ~ lassen,* to become naturalized.
Naturalismus *m.* naturalism.
naturalistisch *a.* naturalistic; naturalist.
Naturalleistung *f.* payment in kind.
Naturbursche *m.* boy of nature.
Naturdenkmal *n.* natural monument.
Naturell *n.* **(-[e]s, -e)** natural disposition.
Naturereignis *n.* natural phenomenon.
Naturerscheinung *f.* natural phenomenon.
Naturfaser *f.* natural fiber.
Naturforscher *m.*; **Naturforscherin** *f.* scientist, naturalist.
Naturgas *n.* natural gas.
naturgemäß *a. & adv.* natural, normal; in accordance with nature.
Naturgeschichte *f.* natural history.
Naturgesetz *n.* law of nature.
naturgetreu *a.* true to nature *or* life.
Naturgewalt *f.* **(-, -en)** force of nature.
Naturheilkunde *f.* naturopathy.
Naturkatastrophe *f.* natural disaster.
Naturkind *n.* child of nature.
Naturkunde *f.* science.
Naturlehrpfad *m.* nature trail.
natürlich *a.* natural; innate; unaffected; ~ *adv.* of course.
natürlicherweise *adv.* of course; naturally.
Naturrecht *n.* natural right; law of nature.
naturrein *a.* pure; no artificial ingredients.
Naturschauspiel *n.* natural spectacle.
Naturschutz *m.* conservation.
Naturschutzgebiet *n.* **(-s, -e)** nature preserve.
Naturtalent *n.* natural talent.
naturverbunden *a.* nature loving.
Naturvolk *n.* primitive people.
naturwidrig *a.* unnatural.
Naturwissenschaft *f.* (natural) science.
Naturwunder *n.* natural wonder.
Nautik *f.* **(-, 0)** art of navigation.
Navigation *f.* **(-, 0)** navigation.
Nazi *m.* **(-s, -s)** Nazi.
Nazismus *m.* **(-, 0)** Nazism.
nazistisch *a.* Nazi.
Nazizeit *f.* Nazi period.
n.Br. *nördliche Breite,* northern latitude.
n.Chr. *nach Christus,* after Christ, A.D.
Neandertaler *m.* **(-s, -)** Neanderthal man.
Nebel *m.* **(-s, -)** mist, fog; (*mil.*) smoke.
nebelhaft *a.* nebulous; misty, hazy.
neb(e)lig *a.* misty, foggy.
Nebel: ~scheinwerfer *m.* (*mot.*) fog light; **~schlußleuchte** *f.* rear fog light.
neben *pr.* near, by, beside; at, next to.
Nebenabsicht *f.* secondary intention.
nebenan *adv.* next door; close by.
Nebenanschluß *m.* (*tel.*) extension.
Nebenausgaben *pl.* incidentals, sundries.
Nebenbedeutung *f.* secondary meaning.
nebenbei *adv.* by the way; besides; ~ *bemerkt,* incidentally.
Nebenberuf *m.* sideline.
Nebenbeschäftigung *f.* sideline.
Nebenbranche *f.* sideline.
Nebenbuhler *m.*; **Nebenbuhlerin** *f.* rival.
nebeneinander *adv.* side by side, abreast.
Nebeneinander *n.* **(-s, 0)** coexistence.
Nebeneinanderschaltung *f.* (*elek.*) parallel connection.
Nebeneingang *m.* side entrance.
Nebeneinkünfte *pl.* extra income *pl.*
Nebenfach *n.* minor (subject).
Nebenfluß *m.* tributary.
Nebengebäude *n.* outbuilding; annex.
Nebengleis *n.* siding.
Nebenhandlung *f.* subplot.
nebenher *adv.* besides; by the way.
Nebenhöhle *f.* (*anat.*) paranasal sinus.
Nebenkosten *pl.* extras.
Nebenlinie *f.* collateral line; (*rail*) branchline.
Nebenmann *m.* neighbor.
Nebenperson *f.* inferior *or* secondary character.
Nebenprodukt *n.* by-product.
Nebenrolle *f.* subordinate part.
Nebensache *f.* matter of secondary importance.
nebensächlich *a.* of secondary importance.
Nebensatz *m.* subordinate clause.
Nebenstelle *f.* extension; branch.
Nebentätigkeit *f.* second job.
Nebenumstand *m.* accessory *or* accidental circumstance.
Nebenverdienst *m.* extra earnings *pl.;* perquisites, emoluments *pl.*
Nebenzimmer *n.* adjoining room.
nebst *pr.* together with, besides.
Necessaire *n.* **(-s, -s)** cosmetic kit.
necken *v.t.* to tease.
Neckerei *f.* **(-, -en)** teasing.
neckisch *a.* playful; saucy.
nee *i.* (*fam.*) no; nope
Neffe *m.* **(-n, -n)** nephew.
Negation *f.* **(-, -en)** negation.
negativ *a.* negative.
Negativ *n.* **(-s, -e)** (*phot.*) negative.
Neger *m.*, **Negerin** *f;* black person.
negieren *v.t.* to negate; to deny.
Negligé *n.* **(-s, -s)** negligee.
nehmen *v.t.st.* to take; *es genau* ~, to be very particular; *es leicht* ~, to take things easy, to make light of.
Neid *m.* **(-es, 0)** envy, jealousy.
neiden *v.t.* to envy.
Neider *m.* **(-s, -), Neidhammel** *m.* **(-s, -)** envious person.

neidisch *a.* envious.
neidlos *a.* ungrudging, without envy.
neidvoll *a.* envious.
Neige *f.* **(-, -n)** dregs *pl., auf die ~ gehen,* to be on the decline; to run short.
neigen *v.t. & i.* to incline; ~ *v.r.* to bow, to decline; to feel inclined.
Neigung *f.* **(-, -en)** inclination; bias, affection; dip, slope, gradient.
Neigungswinkel *m.* angle of inclination.
nein *adv.* no.
Nein *n.*, **Neinstimme** *f.* no vote; vote against.
Nektar *m.* **(-s, 0)** nectar.
Nektarine *f.* **(-, -en)** nectarine.
Nelke *f.* **(-, -n)** carnation.
nennen *v.t. ir.* to name, to call, to mention.
nennenswert *a.* worth mentioning.
Nenner *m.* **(-s, -)** (*ar.*) denominator.
Nennung *f.* citing; mentioning.
Nenn: ~wert *m.* nominal value; denomination; **~wort** *n.* noun.
Neofaschismus *m.* neo-fascism.
Neon *n.* **(-s, o)** neon; **~röhre,** *f.* neon tube.
Nepp *m.* (*pej.*) rip-off.
neppen *v.t.* (*sl.*) to rook; to rip off.
Nepplokal *n.* (*fam.*) clip joint.
Neptun *m.* **(-s, 0)** Neptune.
Nerv *m.* **(-es, -en)** nerve; *seine ~en verlieren* to lose one's nerve.
nerven *v.t.* (*fam.*) to get on sb.'s nerves.
Nervenarzt *m.*; **Nervenärztin** *f.* neurologist.
nervenaufreibend *a.* nerve-racking.
Nerven: ~belastung *f.* strain on the nerves; **~bündel** *n.* (*fam.*) bundle of nerves; **~fieber** *n.* typhoid fever; **~heilanstalt,** sanatorium (for nervous diseases); **~knoten** *m.* ganglion.
nervenkrank, nervenschwach *a.* suffering from a nervous disorder; mentally ill.
Nerven: ~krankheit *f.* nervous disease; **~leiden** *n.* nervous disorder; **~säge** *f.* (*fam.*) pain in the neck; **~schmerz** *m.* neuralgia.
nervenstärkend *a.* tonic.
Nervensystem *n.* nervous system.
Nervenzusammenbruch *m.* nervous breakdown.
nervig *a.* nervous; sinewy.
nervlich *a.* nervous.
nervös *a.* nervous; highly-strung.
Nervosität *f.* **(-, 0)** nervousness.
nervtötend *a.* (*fam.*) nerve-shattering.
Nerz *m.* **(-es, -e)** mink, small otter.
Nessel *f.* **(-, -en)** nettle.
Nesselausschlag *m.* nettle rash.
Nesseltuch *n.* untreated cotton fabric.
Nest *n.* **(-es, -er)** nest; (*fam.*) dump, hole.
Nesthäkchen *n.* youngest child, pet.
nett *a.* neat, fair, nice, pretty.
netterweise *adv.* kindly.
Nettigkeit *f.* kindness; goodness.
netto *adv.* (*Preis, Gewicht*) net.
Netto: ~betrag *m.* net amount; **~einnahme** *f.* net receipts *pl.;* **~ertrag** *m.* net proceeds *pl.*
Netz *n.* **(-es, -e)** net; network.
Netzanschluß *m.* (*elec.*) mains connection.
netzen *v.t.* to wet; to moisten.
netzförmig *a.* reticular.
Netzhaut *f.* retina.
neu *a.* new, recent; *aufs ~e, von ~ em,* anew, again; *~e[re] Zeit,* modern times; *~ere Sprache,* modern language.
Neuankömmling *m.* newcomer.
Neuanschaffung *f.* new acquisition.
neuartig *a.* novel.
Neuauflage *f.* new edition; repeat performance.
Neuausgabe *f.* new edition.
Neubau *m.* **(-[e]s, ~ten)** new building.
Neubearbeitung *f.* **(-, -en)** revised edition.
neubenennen *v.t. ir.* to redesignate.
Neudruck *m.* reprint.
neuerdings *adv.* lately, recently.
Neuerer *m.* **(-s, -)** innovator.
Neuerscheinung *f.* **(-, -en)** new publication; new release.
Neuerung *f.* **(-, -en)** innovation.
Neuerwerbung *f.* new acquisition.
Neufassung *f.* revised version; remake.
neuformen *v.t.* to reshape.
neugeboren *a.* new-born.
neugestalten *v.t.* to reorganize.
Neugier, Neugier[de], *f.* **(-, 0)** curiosity.
neugierig *a.* inquisitive, curious.
Neugliederung *f.* reorganization.
neugotisch *a.* neo-Gothic.
Neugründung *f.* new foundation.
neugültig machen *v.t.* to revalidate.
Neuheit *f.* **(-, -en)** newness; novelty.
Neuigkeit *f.* **(-, -en)** news.
Neujahr *n.* **(-[e]s, -s)** New Year's Day.
Neuland *m.* new territory; *~ betreten* (*fig.*) to break new ground.
neulich *adv.* recently, the other day.
Neuling *m.* **(-[e]s, -e)** novice, beginner.
neumodisch *a.* newfangled.
Neumond *m.* new moon.
neun *a.* nine.
Neunauge *n.* lamprey.
neunfach *a.* ninefold.
neunmal *adv.* nine times.
neunzehn *a.* nineteen.
neunzig *a.* ninety.
neunziger *a. die ~ Jahre* the nineties.
Neuordnung *f.* reorganization.
Neuorientierung *f.* reorientation.
Neuphilologe *m.*; **Neuphilologin** *f.* student *or* teacher of modern languages.
Neuralgie *f.* neuralgia.
neuralgisch *a.* neuralgic.
Neuregelung *f.* revision of rules.
neureich *a.* nouveau riche.
Neurologe *m.*; **Neurologin** *f.* neurologist.
Neurose *f.* neurosis.
Neurotiker *m.*; **Neurotikerin** *f.* neurotic.
neurotisch *a.* neurotic.
Neuschnee *m.* fresh snow.
Neuseeland *n.* **(-s, 0)** New Zealand.
Neuseeländer *m.*; **Neuseeländerin** *f.* New Zealander.
neuseeländisch *a.* New Zealand.
neusprachlich *a.* modern-language.
neutral *a.* neutral.
neutralisieren *v.t.* to neutralize.
Neutralität *f.* **(-, 0)** neutrality.
Neutron *n.* **(-s, -en)** neutron.
Neutronenbombe *f.* neutron bomb.
Neutrum *n.* **(-s, -ra)** (*gram.*) neuter.
neuvermählt *a.* newly married.
neuwertig *a.* as new.
Neuzeit *f.* modern times, our days *pl.*
Neuzugang *m.* new acquisition.
nhd. *neuhochdeutsch,* New High German, N.H.G.

nicht *adv.* not; *auch* ~, not; ~ *einmal,* not even; *durchaus* ~, not at all; *gar* ~, not at all, by no means; *noch* ~, not yet; ~ *mehr,* no more, no longer.
Nichtachtung *f.* disregard.
nichtalkoholische Getränke *pl.* soft drinks.
Nichtangriff *m.* nonaggression.
nichtansässig *a.* nonresident.
Nichtbeachtung *f.*, **Nichtbefolgung** *f.* **(-, 0)** inattention, noncompliance, nonobservance.
Nichte *f.* **(-, -n)** niece.
Nichteinmischung *f.* **(-, 0)** nonintervention.
Nichteisenmetall *n.* nonferrous metal.
Nichterfüllung *f.* nonfullfillment.
Nichterscheinen *n.* nonattendance.
nichtig *a.* null, void; vain, empty.
Nichtigkeit *f.* **(-, -en)** invalidity, nullity, futility; vanity, emptiness.
Nichtigkeitsklage *f.* writ of error, plea of nullity.
Nichtkriegführende *m.* nonbelligerent.
Nichtmitglied *n.* nonmember.
Nichtraucher *m.* nonsmoker; **~abteil** *m.* nonsmoking compartment.
nichtrostend *a.* non rusting; stainless.
nichts *adv.* nothing; ~ *als;* nothing but; ~ *weniger als,* anything but this; *mir* ~, *dir* ~, just like that.
Nichts *n.* **(-, 0)** nothing(ness), void.
nichtsahnend *a.* unsuspecting.
Nichtschwimmer *m.*; **Nichtschwimmerin** *f.* nonswimmer.
nichtsdestotrotz *adv.*, **nichtsdestoweniger** *adv.* nevertheless.
Nichtskönner *m.* incompetent.
Nichtsnutz *m.* **(-es, -e)** good for nothing.
nichtssagend *a.* meaningless, unmeaning.
Nichtstuer *m.* idler, loafer.
Nichtstun *m.* inactivity; idleness.
Nichtswisser *m.* ignoramus.
nichtswürdig *a.* vile, worthless.
Nichtvorhandensein *n.* nonexistence.
Nickel *m.* **(-s, -)** nickel.
Nickelbrille *f.* metal-rimmed glasses.
nicken *v.t.* to nod; to nap.
Nickerchen *n.* **(-s, -)** (*fam.*) nap; snooze.
nie *adv.* never.
nieder *a. & adv.* low, lower, nether; down; *auf und* ~, up and down.
niederbeugen *v.t.* to bend down.
niederbrennen *v.t. & i.* to burn down.
niederdeutsch *a.* Low German.
niederdrücken *v.t.* to press down; (*fig.*) to depress, to oppress.
niederfallen *v.i.st. (s)* to fall down.
Niedergang *m.* decline.
niedergehen *v.i.st.* to go down.
niedergeschlagen *a.* dejected, downcast.
niederhalten *v.t.st.* to keep down.
niederknie[e]n *v.i. (s)* to kneel down.
Niederkunft *f.* **(-, 0)** delivery.
Niederlage *f.* **(-, -n)** defeat.
Niederlande *pl.* **(-)** the Netherlands.
Niederländer *m.*; **Niederländerin** *f.* Dutch, Netherlander.
niederländisch *a.* Dutch, Netherlandish.
niederlassen *v.r.st.* to establish oneself, to settle down; to set up (in business).
Niederlassung *f.* **(-, -en)** establishment; branch office; settlement.
niederlegen *v.t.* to lay down; to retire from; (*Arbeit*) to strike, to knock off.
niedermachen *v.t.* to kill, to slay.
niedermetzeln *v.t.* to massacre.
niederreißen *v.t.st.* to pull down.
Niedersachsen *n.* Lower Saxony.
Niederschlag *m.* rain; (*chem.*) precipitation.
niederschlagen *v.t.st.* to knock down; (*Augen*) to cast down; (*jur.*) to quash (a charge); (*chem.*) to precipitate.
Niederschlagsmenge *f.* **(-, -n)** rainfall.
niederschmettern *v.t.* to crush.
niederschreiben *v.t.st.* to write down.
niederschreien *v.t.st.* to shout down.
Niederschrift *f.* **(-, -en)** writing down, copy.
niedersetzen *v.t.* to set *or* put down; ~ *v.r.* to sit down.
niederstrecken *v.t.* to fell.
niederträchtig *a.* base, abject, vile.
Niederträchtigkeit *f.* **(-, -en)** baseness.
niedertreten *v.t.st.* to trample down.
Niederung *f.* **(-, -en)** lowland.
niederwerfen *v.t.st.* to throw down; ~ *v.r.* to prostrate oneself.
niedlich *a.* cute; neat, nice.
niedrig *a.* low; mean, vile, base.
Niedrigkeit *f.* **(-, -en)** lowness; baseness.
niemals *adv.* never.
niemand *pn.* nobody.
Niemandsland *n.* no-man's-land.
Niere *f.* **(-, -n)** kidney; reins *pl.*
Nieren: **~braten** *m.* roast loin of veal; **~entzündung** *f.* nephritis; **~leiden** *n.* kidney disease; **~stein** *m.* kidney stone; renal calculus.
nieseln *v.i.* to drizzle.
niesen *v.i.* to sneeze.
Nieswurz *f.* **(-, 0)** hellebore.
Niete *f.* **(-, -n)** rivet; blank (lottery).
nieten *v.t.* to rivet.
Nihilismus *m.* nihilism.
nihilistisch *a.* nihilistic.
Nikolaustag *m.* St. Nicholas' Day.
Nikotin *n.* nicotine.
nikotinarm *a.* low-nicotine.
nikotinfrei *a.* nicotine-free.
Nikotinvergiftung *f.* nicotine poisoning.
Nilpferd *n.* hippopotamus.
Nimbus *m.* **(-, 0)** nimbus, halo; prestige.
nimmer[mehr] *adv.* never, nevermore, no more; by no means, nowise.
Nippel *m.* **(-s, -)** nipple; valve (inflatables).
nippen *v.t.* to sip.
Nippsachen *pl.* knick-nacks *pl.*
nirgend[s] *adv.* nowhere.
Nische *f.* **(-, -n)** niche.
nisten *v.i.* to nest; to build; to nestle.
Nistkasten *m.* **(-s, -kästen)** nesting box.
Nitrat *n.* **(-s, -e)** nitrate.
Nitroglyzerin *n.* nitroglycerine.
Niveau *n.* **(-s, -s)** level; *ein hohes* ~, high standards.
nivellieren *v.t.* to level.
Nixe *f.* **(-, -n)** water fairy, nixie.
N.N. *nomen nominandum,* name to be announced.
NO *Nordost(en),* northeast, NE.
No., Nr. *Numero,* number, no.
nobel *a.* noble; generous; magnificent.
Nobel: **~herberge** *f.* (*fam.*) high-class hotel; **~kutsche** *f.* flashy car.

Nobelpreis *m.* Nobel prize; **~träger** *m.*, **~trägerin** *f.* Nobel prize winner.
noch *adv.* still, yet; ~ *einmal,* once more; ~ *etwas,* something more; ~ *immer,* still; ~ *nicht,* not yet.
nochmalig *a.* repeated.
nochmals *adv.* once again.
Nockenwelle *f.* (*mech.*) camshaft.
Nomade *m.* **(-n, -n); Nomadin** *f.* **(-, -nen)** nomad.
nomadisch *a.* nomadic.
Nomen *n.* **(-s,Nomina)** noun; substantive.
Nominativ *m.* **(-s, -e)** nominative (case).
nominell *a.* nominal.
nominieren *v.t.* to nominate; to name.
Nonkonformismus *m.* nonconformism.
nonkonformistisch *a.* nonconformist, unconventional.
Nonne *f.* **(-, -n)** nun.
Nonnenkloster *n.* nunnery, convent.
Nonsens *m.* nonsense.
Noppe *f.* **(-, -n)** knop; nub; bump; pimple.
Nord[en] *m.* **(-s, 0)** North.
Nordamerika *m.* North America.
Nordamerikaner *m.*; **Nordamerikanerin** *f.* North American.
norddeutsch *a.* North German.
Norddeutschland *n.* North Germany.
Nordengland *n.* the North of England.
Nordeuropa *n.* Northern Europe.
nordisch *a.* Northern; Nordic.
Nordkap *n.* North Cape.
Nordländer *m.* **(-s, -)** northerner.
nördlich *a.* northerly, northern; arctic; ~*e Breite,* northern latitude.
Nordlicht *n.* aurora borealis; northern lights.
Nordost *m.* **(-ens, 0)** northeast.
Nord: ~pol *m.* north pole; **~polarkreis** *m.* arctic circle.
Nordrhein-Westfalen *n.* North Rhine-Westphalia.
Nordsee *f.* North Sea.
Nordsüd... *a.* north, south,
nordwärts *adv.* northward.
Nordwest *m.* **(-ens, 0)** northwest.
Nordwind *m.* north wind.
nörgeln *v.i.* to grumble, to nag.
Nörgler *m.* **(-s, -)** moaner; grumbler.
Norm *f.* **(-, -en)** standard, rule.
normal *a.* normal, standard.
Normalbenzin *n.* regular gasoline.
normalerweise *adv.* normally.
Normalfall *m.* normal case.
normalisieren *v.t.* to normalize.
Normalität *f.* **(-, 0)** normality.
Normalmaß *n.* normal size.
Normalverbraucher *m.* average consumer.
Normalzustand *m.* normal state.
Normandie *f.* Normandy.
normativ *a.* normative.
normen, normieren *v.t.* to standardize.
Normung *f.* standardization.
Norwegen *n.* **(-s, 0)** Norway.
Norweger *m.*; **Norwegerin** *f.*; **norwegisch** *a.* Norwegian.
Nostalgie *f.* nostalgia.
Not *f.* **(-, Nöte)** need, misery; necessity, distress, trouble; *zur* ~, if need be; *mit knapper* ~, barely, with great difficulty.
Not... emergency...
Nota *f.* **(-, 0)** memorandum.
Notar *m.* **(-s, -e)** notary public.
Notariat *n.* **([e]s, -s)** notary's office.
notariell *a.* notarized.
Notarzt *m.*; **Notärztin** *f.* emergency doctor.
Notausgang *m.* emergency exit.
Notbehelf *m.* shift, makeshift.
Notbremse *f.* emergency brake.
Notdurft *f.* **(-, 0)** *seine* ~ *verrichten,* to ease oneself.
notdürftig *a.* indigent; scant.
Note *f.* **(-, -n)** note; grade; bill; mark; ~ *pl.* music; *ganze* ~, whole note, semibreve; *halbe* ~, half note, minim.
Notenbank *f.* issuing bank.
Notenblatt *n.* sheet of music.
Notenlinien *pl.* staff.
Notenpapier *n.* music paper.
Notenpult *n.* music stand.
Notenschlüssel *m.* clef.
Notenschrift *f.* musical notation.
Notenständer *m.* music stand.
Notfall *m.* case of need, emergency.
notfalls *adv.* if necessary.
notgedrungen *adv.* of necessity.
Notgeld *n.* emergency money.
notieren *v.t.* to note (down); (*com.*) to quote; to be quoted.
nötig *a.* necessary; *etwas* ~ *haben,* to stand in need of, to need.
nötigen *v.t.* to compel, to force, to urge.
nötigenfalls *adv.* in case of need.
Nötigung *f.* **(-, -en)** intimidation; coercion.
Notiz *f.* **(-, -en)** notice; memorandum; *pl.* notes.
Notizblock *m.* memo pad.
Notizbuch *n.* notebook.
Notlage *f.* predicament, plight.
Notlandung *f.* forced landing.
notleidend *a.* needy.
Notlösung *f.* stopgap.
Notlüge *f.* evasive lie; white lie.
notorisch *a.* notorious.
Notpfennig *m.* savings *pl.*
Notruf *m.* emergency call *or* number.
Notsignal *n.* distress signal.
Notstand *m.* state of emergency; **~sgebiet** *n.* disaster, distressed area; **~sarbeiten** *pl.* relief work.
Notverband *m.* provisional dressing; **~skasten** *m.* first-aid kit.
Notverordnung *f.* emergency decree.
Notwehr *f.* **(-, 0)** self-defense.
notwendig *a.* necessary.
notwendigerweise *adv.* necessarily.
Notwendigkeit *f.* **(-, 0)** necessity.
Notzeit *f.* **(-, -en)** time of need.
Notzucht *f.* rape, violation.
notzüchtigen *v.t.* to rape.
Nov. *November,* November, Nov.
Novelle *f.* **(-, -n)** novella; (*jur.*) amendment.
novellieren *v.t.* to amend.
November *m.* **(-s, -)** November.
Novität *f.* **(-, -en)** novelty.
Novize *m.* **(-n, -n); Novizin** *f.* **(-, -nen)** novice.
NPD *Nationaldemokratische Partei Deutschlands,* National-Democratic Party of Germany.
N.T. *Neues Testament,* New Testament.
Nu *n.* **(-, 0)** moment; *in einem* ~, in no time.
Nuance *f.* **(-, -n)** nuance, (*fig.*) shade.
nuancieren *v.t.* to shade, to differentiate.
nüchtern *a.* fasting; sober; (*fig.*) matter-of-fact; dreary, prosaic; *noch* ~ *sein,* not to have eaten anything yet.

nuckeln *v.i.* to suck.
Nudeln *pl.* noodles.
nuklear *a.* nuclear.
Nuklearkrieg *m.* nuclear war.
null *a.* null; ~ *und nichtig,* null and void.
Null *f.* **(-, -en)** zero.
Nullpunkt *m.* zero, freezing point.
Nulltarif *m.* free transport; free admission.
Nullwachstum *n.* zero growth.
numerieren *v.t.* to number.
numerisch *a.* numerical.
Numerus *m.* **(-, ri)** number.
Numerus clausus *m.* limited admission (university).
Nummer *f.* **(-, -n)** number.
Nummernschild *n.* license plate.
nun *adv.* & *c.* now, at present; therefore; **~?** well?
nunmehr *adv.* now, by this time.
Nuntius, Nunzius *m.* **(-, -zien)** nuncio.
nur *adv.* only, but solely.
nuscheln *v.i.* to mumble.
Nuß *f.* **(-, Nüsse)** nut; *eine harte* ~, a hard nut to crack.
Nuß: ~baum *m.* walnut tree; **~holz** *n.* walnut (wood); **~knacker** *m.* nutcracker; **~schale** nutshell.
Nüster *f.* **(-, -n)** nostril.
Nutte *f.* (*fam. pej.*) hooker.
Nutz *m.* **(-es, 0)** *sich zu ~e machen,* to be useful *or* profitable.
Nutzanwendung *f.* practical use.
nutzbar *a.* useful; profitable.
nutzbringend *a.* useful, profitable.
nütze *a. zu etwas* ~ *sein,* to be of use; *zu nichts* ~ *sein,* to be of no use.
Nutzeffekt *m.* efficiency.
nutzen, nützen *v.t.* to make use of, to use, to turn to account; ~ *v.i.* to be of use, to serve.
Nutzen *m.* **(-s, 0)** use; profit, benefit.
Nutzfahrzeug *n.* commercial vehicle.
Nutzfläche *f.* usable floor space.
Nutzholz *n.* timber.
Nutzlast *f.* payload.
nutzlich *a.* useful, profitable; conducive (to).
Nützlichkeit *f.* **(-, 0)** usefulness, utility.
nutzlos *a.* useless, of no use; futile.
Nutzlosigkeit *f.* uselessness; futility.
Nutznießer *m.* **(-s, -)**; **Nutznießerin** *f.* **(-, -nen)** beneficiary; usufructuary.
Nutznießung *f.* **(-, 0)** usufruct.
Nutzung *f.* **(-, -en)** use; cultivation; exploitation.
Nutzwert *m.* practical value.
NW *Nordwest(en),* northwest, NW.
Nylon *n.* nylon.
Nymphe *f.* **(-, -n)** nymph.
Nymphomanin *f.* **(-, -nen)** nymphomaniac.

O

O, o *n.* the letter O or o.
O *Ost(en),* east, E.
o. *oben,* above; *oder,* or; *ohne,* without, w/o.
o! *i.* o! oh!; ~ **weh!** alas! oh dear!
o.a. *oben angeführt,* above (-mentioned).
o.ä. *oder ähnliche,* or the like.
Oase *f.* **(-, -n)** oasis.
ob *c.* whether; if; *als* ~, as if.
OB *Oberbürgermeister,* mayor.
o.B. *ohne Befund,* results negative.
Obacht *f.* **(-, 0)** caution, care; ~ *geben,* to pay attention.
ÖBB *Österreichische Bundesbahn,* Austrian Federal Railways.
Obdach *n.* **(-[e]s, 0)** shelter, lodging.
obdachlos *a.* homeless.
Obdachlose *m./f.* homeless person.
Obdachlosenasyl *n.* homeless shelter.
Obduktion *f.* **(-, -en)** postmortem; autopsy.
O-Beine *pl.* bow legs.
o-beinig *a.* bow-legged.
oben *adv.* above; on the surface; upstairs; *von* ~ *herab,* in a superior way; *von* ~ *bis unten,* from top to bottom; *diese Seite nach* ~, this side up; *das zweite von* ~, the second down.
obenan *adv.* at the top.
obendrauf *adv.* on top.
obendrein *adv.* besides, into the bargain.
obenerwahnt *a.* above-mentioned.
obenhin *adv.* superficially.
ober *a.* upper, higher; (*fig.*) chief; **~e rechte Ecke,** top righthand corner.
Ober *m.* **(-s, -)** (*fam.*) waiter.
Oberarm *m.* upper arm.
Oberarzt *m.* head physician.
Oberbefehl *m.* chief command; **~shaber** *m.* commander-in-chief.
Oberbegriff *m.* generic term.
Oberbett *n.* comforter.
Oberbürgermeister *m.*, **Oberbürgermeisterin** *f.* mayor.
Oberdeck *n.* upper-deck.
oberdeutsch *a.* Upper German.
Obere[r] *m.* **(-n, -n)** superior.
Oberfläche *f.* surface.
oberflächlich *a.* & *adv.* superficial(ly).
Oberflächlichkeit *f.* superficiality.
Obergeschoß *n.* upper floor.
Obergrenze *f.* upper limit, ceiling.
oberhalb *pr.* above.
Oberhand *f.* upper hand.
Oberhaupt *n.* head, chief.
Oberhaus *n.* upper house (of parliament).
Oberhemd *n.* shirt.
Oberherrschaft *f.* supremacy.
Oberhoheit *f.* supremacy.
Oberin *f.* **(-, -nen)** mother superior; matron.
oberirdisch *a.* surface; ~ *adv.* above ground.
Oberkellner *m.* headwaiter.
Oberkiefer *n.* upper jaw.
Oberklasse *f.* upper class.
Oberkommando *n.* high command.
Oberkörper *m.* upper part of the body.
Oberleder *n.* uppers *pl.*
Oberleitung *f.* (*elek.*) overhead wire, overhead cable.
Oberlicht *n.* skylight.
Oberlippe *f.* upper lip.
Obersatz *m.* (*Logik*) major term.
Oberschenkel *m.* thigh.
Oberschicht *f.* upper class.

Oberschwester *f.* head nurse.
Oberseite *f.* upper side.
oberst *a.* uppermost; supreme; top.
Oberst *m.* **(-en, -en)** colonel.
Oberstaatsanwalt *m.;* **Oberstaatsanwältin** *f.* attorney general.
Oberstleutnant *m.* lieutenant colonel.
Oberstudiendirektor *m.;* **Oberstudiendirektorin** *f.* principal.
Oberstudienrat *m.;* **Oberstudienrätin** *f.* senior teacher.
Oberwasser *n.* (*fig.*) ~ *bekommen,* to get the upper hand.
obgleich *c.* though, although.
Obhut *f.* **(-, 0)** protection, care.
obig *a.* above; foregoing.
Objekt *n.* **(-s, -e)** object; property.
objektiv *a.* objective; impartial.
Objektiv *n.* **(-s, -s)** objective; lens.
Objektivität *f.* objectivity.
Objektsatz *m.* object clause.
Oblate *f.* **(-, -n)** wafer.
obliegen *v.i.st.* to be incumbent on; to apply oneself to; *es liegt mir ob,* it is my duty.
Obliegenheit *f.* **(-, -en)** duty, obligation.
Obligation *f.* **(-, -en)** (*com.*) debenture.
obligatorisch *a.* obligatory; compulsory.
Obmann *m.* chairman.
Oboe *f.* **(-, -n)** oboe.
Obrigkeit *f.* **(-, -en)** authorities *pl.*, government.
Obrigkeitsstaat *m.* authoritarian state.
obschon *c.* (al)though, albeit.
Observatorium *n.* **(-[s], -rien)** observatory.
observieren *v.t.* to keep under surveillance; to observe.
obskur *a.* obscure.
Obst *n.* **(-es, 0)** fruit.
Obst: ~baum *m.* fruit tree; **~garten** *m.* orchard; **~händler** *m.* fruit seller; **~kern** *m.* stone, pit; **~saft** *m.* juice; **~salat** *m.* fruit salad; **~wasser** *n.* fruit brandy.
obszön *a.* obscene.
Obszönität *f.* obscenity.
obwalten *v.i.* to prevail.
obwohl *c.* though, although.
Ochs *m.* **(-en, en)** ox; bull, bullock; (*fig.*) blockhead.
Ochsenbrust *f.* brisket of beef.
Ochsenfleisch *m.* beef.
Ochsenschwanzsuppe *f.* oxtail soup.
Ochsenzunge *f.* ox-tongue.
Ocker *m.* **(-s, 0)** ocher.
od. *oder,* or.
Ode *f.* **(-, -n)** ode.
öde *a.* desert, desolate, waste; dull.
Öde *f.* **(-, -n)** desert, wilderness; wasteland.
Odem *m.* **(-s, 0)** breath.
oder *c.* or; or else.
Ödland *n.* **(-[e]s, -länder)** wasteland.
Ofen *m.* **(-s, Öfen)** stove, oven; furnace, kiln.
Ofen: ~kachel *f.* Dutch tile; **~loch** *n.* mouth of an oven; **~röhre** *f.* stove pipe; **~schirm** *m.* fire-screen; **~setzer** *m.* stove-fitter.
offen *a.* open; (*Stelle*) vacant; (*fig.*) frank; (*Wechsel*) blank check.
offenbar *a.* obvious, evident, manifest.
offenbaren *v.t.* to make known; to disclose, to reveal.
Offenbarung *f.* **(-, -en)** revelation.
Offenbarungseid *m.* oath of disclosure.
offenbleiben *v.i.st.* to remain open.
offenhalten *v.t.st.* to keep open; to reserve.
Offenheit *f.* frankness; honesty.
offenherzig *a.* sincere, candid, frank.
offenkundig *a.* notorious, public, obvious.
offensichtlich *a.* obvious.
offensiv *a.* offensive.
Offensive *f.* **(-, -n)** offensive.
offenstehen *v.i.st.* to be open; to be outstanding.
öffentlich *a.* public; **~ e Einrichtung** *f.*, public utility.
Öffentlichkeit *f.* **(-, 0)** public, publicity; *unter Ausschluß der* ~, (*jur.*) in camera; in private.
Öffentlichkeitsarbeit *f.* public relations.
öffentlich-rechtlich *a.* under public law.
offerieren *v.t.* to offer.
Offerte *f.* **(-, -n)** offer, tender.
offiziell *a.* official.
Offizier *m.* **(-[e]s, -e)** officer.
Offizierkorps *n.* officers corps.
Offiziersanwärter *m.* officer candidate.
Offizierslaufbahn *f.* officer's career.
offiziös *a.* semi-official.
öffnen *v.t. & v.r.* to open.
Öffner *m.* **(-s, -)** opener.
Öffnung *f.* **(-, -en)** opening; aperture.
Öffnungszeiten *pl.* opening hours *pl.*
Offsetdruck *m.* offset printing.
öfter *a.* frequent, repeated; **~** *adv.* more often.
öfters *adv.* repeatedly.
oft(mals) *adv.* often, frequently.
oh! *i.* oh! **oha!** *i.* oho!
Oheim, Ohm *m.* **(-s, -e)** (*obs.*) uncle.
Ohm *n.* (*elek.*) ohm.
ohne *pr.* without; but for, except; **~ weiteres,** without ceremony, without further ado; *es ist nicht* ~, (*fam.*) it is not bad.
ohnedies, ohnehin *adv.* anyhow.
ohneeinander *adv.* without each other.
ohnegleichen *a.* unparalleled.
Ohnmacht *f.* **(-[e]s, -en)** swoon, fainting fit; weakness.
ohnmächtig *a.* unconscious; powerless; fainting, in a swoon.
Ohr *n.* **(-[e]s, -en)** ear; *die* ~*en spitzen,* to prick up one's ears; *einen übers* ~ *hauen,* to make someone pay through the nose; *bis an, bis über die* ~*en,* head over heels.
Öhr *n.* **(-[e]s, Öhre)** eye (of a needle).
Ohrenarzt *m.;* **Ohrenärztin** *f.* ear specialist; otologist.
ohrenbetäubend *a.* ear-splitting; deafening.
Ohrensausen *n.* ringing/buzzing in the ears.
Ohrenschmalz *n.* earwax.
Ohrenschmerz *m.* earache.
Ohrenschützer *pl.* earmuffs.
Ohrensessel *m.* wing chair.
Ohrenzeuge *m.* ear-witness.
Ohrfeige *f.* box on the ear.
ohrfeigen *v.t.* to box a person's ears.
Ohrläppchen *n.* ear lobe.
Ohrmuschel *f.* outer ear, auricle.
Ohrring *m.* earring.
Ohrstecker *m.* earstud.
Ohrwurm *m.* earwig.
o.J. *ohne Jahr,* no date, n.d.
okkult *a.* occult.
Okkultismus *m.* **(-, 0)** occultism.
Ökologe *m.;* **Ökologin** *f.* ecologist.
Ökologie *f.* ecology.

ökologisch *a.* ecological.
Ökonom *m.* **(-en, -en)** economist.
Ökonomie *f.* **(-, -[e]n)** economy.
ökonomisch *a.* economical.
Ökosystem *n.* ecosystem.
Okt. *Oktober,* October, Oct.
Oktan *n.* **(-s, 0)** (*mot.*) octane; **~zahl** *f.* octane rating.
Oktavband *m.* octavo (volume).
Oktave *f.* **(-, -n)** (*mus.*) octave.
Oktober *f.* **(-s, -)** October.
oktroyieren *v.t.* to dictate to, to impose upon.
okulieren *v.t.* (*bot.*) to inoculate, to graft.
ökumenisch *a.* (*eccl.*) ecumenical.
Okzident *m.* **(-s, 0)** occident.
Öl *n.* **(-[e]s, -e)** oil; ~ *ins Feuer gießen,* (*fig.*) to add fuel to the fire.
ö.L. *östliche Länge,* east longitude.
Ölbaum *m.* olive tree.
Ölberg *m.* Mount of Olives.
Ölbild *n.* oil painting.
Öldruck *m.* oil pressure.
Öldruckbild *n.* chromolithograph.
Oleander *m.* **(-s, -)** oleander.
ölen *v.t.* to oil; to lubricate.
Ölfarbe *f.* oilpaint.
OLG *Oberlandesgericht,* Higher Regional Court.
Ölgemälde *n.* oil painting.
ölig *a.* oily.
Oligarchie *f.* **(-, -n)** oligarchy.
oliv *a.* olive (-green).
Olive *f.* **(-, -n)** olive.
Olivenbaum *m.* **(-s, -bäume)** olive tree.
Olivenöl *n.* olive oil.
Ölkanne *f.* oil can.
Ölkuchen *m.* oil cake.
Ölleitung *f.* oil pipe.
Ölmalerei *f.* oil painting.
Ölpest *f.* oil pollution.
Ölraffinerie *f.* oil refinery.
Ölstand *m.* oil level; **~zeiger** *m.* oil gauge.
Öltankschiff *n.* oil tanker.
Ölteppich *m.* oil slick.
Ölung *f.* **(-, -n)** oiling; lubrication; *letzte* ~, extreme unction.
Ölvorkommen *n.* oil deposit.
Ölwanne *f.* (*mot.*) oil sump.
Ölwechsel *m.* oil change.
Olymp *m.* **(-s, 0)** Mount Olympus.
Olympiade *f.* **(-, -n)** Olympic Games; Olympics.
olympisch *a.* Olympic.
Ölzeug *n.* oilskins.
Ölzweig *m.* olive branch.
Oma *f.* (*fam.*) granny, grandma.
Omelett *m.* omelet.
ominös *a.* ominous; sinister.
Omnibus *m.* **(-sses, -sse)** bus.
Omnibushaltestelle *f.* bus stop.
Onanie *f.* **(-, 0)** onanism; masturbation.
onanieren *v.i.* to masturbate.
ondulieren *v.t.* to wave.
Onkel *m.* **(-s, -)** uncle.
o.O. *ohne Ort,* no place (of publication), n.p.
OP *Operationssaal,* operating room, OR.
Opa *m.* (*fam.*) grandad; grandpa.
Opal *m.* **(-s, -e)** opal.
Oper *f.* **(-, -n)** opera.
Operateur *f.* **(-s, -e)** operator.
Operation *f.* **(-, -en)** operation.
Operationsgebiet *n.* (*mil.*) zone of operations.
Operationssaal *m.* operating room.
operativ *a.* operative.
Operette *f.* **(-, -n)** operetta, musical comedy.
operieren *v.t.* & *i.* to operate; ~ *lassen v.r.* (*med.*) to be operated on.
Opern: ~arie *f.* aria; **~glas** *n.*, **~gucker** *m.* opera glass; **~haus** *n.* opera house; **~sänger(in)** *m.(f.)* opera singer; **~text** *m.* libretto, book.
Opfer *n.* **(-s, -)** offering; sacrifice; victim; *ein* ~ *bringen,* (*fig.*) to make a sacrifice.
Opfergabe *f.* offering.
Opferlamm *n.* sacrificial lamb.
opfern *v.t.* to sacrifice.
Opferstock *m.* offertory.
Opfertier *n.* sacrificial animal.
Opferung *f.* **(-, -en)** immolation; sacrifice.
Opiat *n.* **(-s, -e)** opiate.
Opium *n.* **(-s, 0)** opium.
Opponent *m.;* **Opponentin** *f.* opponent.
opponieren *v.t.* to oppose.
opportun *a.* opportune.
Opportunist *m.;* **opportunistisch** *a.* opportunist.
Opposition *f.* opposition.
Oppositions: ~führer *m.*, **~führerin** *f.* opposition leader; **~partei** *f.* opposition party.
o.Prof. *ordentlicher Professor,* full professor, prof.
optieren *v.i.* to opt.
Optik *f.* **(-, 0)** optics *pl.*
Optiker *m.* **(-s, -)** optician.
Optimismus *m.* **(-, 0)** optimism.
Optimist *m.;* **Optimistin** *f.* optimist.
optimistisch *a.* optimistic.
optisch *a.* optical.
Orakel *n.* **(-s, -0), Orakelspruch** *m.* oracle.
orakelhaft, orakelmäßig *a.* oracular.
orakeln *v.i.* to speak oracularly.
oral *a.* & *adv.* oral(ly).
Orange *f.* **(-, -n)** orange.
orangefarben *a.* orange (-colored).
Orangenbaum *m.* orange tree.
Orangenschale *f.* orange peel.
Orangerie *f.* **(-, -[e]n)** orangery; greenhouse.
Orang-Utan *m.* **(-s, -s)** orangutan.
Oratorium *n.* **(-s, -rien)** (*mus.*) oratorio.
Orchester *n.* **(-s, -)** orchestra.
Orchestermusik *f.* orchestral music.
Orchidee *f.* **(-, -n)** orchid.
Orden *m.* **(-s, -)** order; decoration, medal.
Ordens: ~band *n.* ribbon (of an order); **~regel** *f.* monastic rule; **~schwester** *f.* sister, nun.
ordentlich *a.* orderly, tidy; ordinary, usual, regular; ~*er Professor,* (full) professor.
Ordentlichkeit *f.* tidiness, neatness.
ordinär *a.* vulgar, mean, low.
Ordinarius *m.* **(-, -rien)** (full) professor.
ordinieren *v.t.* to ordain; **~ lassen** *v.r.* to take (holy) orders.
ordnen *v.t.* to put in order; to arrange, to regulate; to classify.
Ordner *m.* file; steward.
Ordnung *f.* **(-, -en)** order, arrangement; class; *zur* ~ *rufen,* to call to order; *etwas in* ~ *bringen,* to straighten out; ~ *schaffen,* to establish order.
ordnungshalber *adv.* as a matter of form.
ordnungsmäßig *a.* orderly, regular.
Ordnungsstrafe *f.* (*jur.*) penalty for contempt of court.
ordnungswidrig *a.* irregular, illegal; **~es Benehmen** *n.* disorderly conduct.

Ordnungszahl *f.* ordinal number.
Organ *n.* **(-[e]s, -e)** organ; voice.
Organisation *f.* **(-, -en)** organization.
Organisator *m.; **Organisatorin*** *f.* organizer.
organisatorisch *a.* organizational.
organisch *a.* organic.
organisieren *v.t.* to organize.
Organismus *m.* **(-e, -men)** organism.
Organist *m.* **(-en, -en); Organistin** *f.* **(-, -nen)** organist.
Organverpflanzung *f.* organ transplantation.
Orgasmus *m.* **(-, -men)** orgasm.
Orgel *f.* **(-, -n)** organ.
Orgelbauer *m.* organ builder.
Orgel: ~konzert *n.* organ concerto; organ recital; **~pfeife** *f.* organ pipe; **~register** *n.* organ stop; **~spieler** *m.*, **~spielerin** *f.* organist.
Orgie *f.* **(-, -n)** orgy.
Orient *m.* **(-[e]s, 0)** Orient, East(ern countries).
Orientale *m.*; **Orientalin** *f.* Oriental.
orientalisch *a.* oriental.
Orientalist *m.*; **Orientalistin** *f.* specialist in oriental studies.
Orientalistik *f.* oriental studies.
orientieren *v.t.* to inform; to fill sb. in; to orient ~ *v.r.* (*fig.*) to see one's way.
Orientierung *f.* orientation; *zu Ihrer ~*, for your guidance.
orientierungslos *a.* disoriented.
Orientierungssinn *m.* sense of orientation.
original *a.* original.
Original *n.* **(-[e]s, -e)** original.
Originalfassung *f.* original version.
originalgetreu *a.* faithful (to the original).
Originalität *f.* originality; authenticity.
originell *a.* original, eccentric.
Orkan *m.* **(-[e]s, -e)** hurricane, tornado.
Ornament *n.* **(-s, -e)** ornament.
Ornat *n.* **(-[e]s, -e)** vestments, robes.
Ornithologie *f.* ornithology.
Ort *m.* **(-es, -e)** place; spot, locality; *an ~ und Stelle*, on the spot.
orten *v.t.* to find the position.
orth. *Orthodox*, Orthodox, Orth.
orthodox *a.* orthodox; rigid.
Orthographie *f.* orthography.
orthographisch *a.* orthographic.
Orthopäde *m.*; **Orthopädin** *f.* orthopedist.
Orthopädie *f.* orthopedics.
orthopädisch *a.* orthopedic.
örtlich *a.* local.
Örtlichkeit *f.* **(-, -en)** locality.
Ortsangabe *f.* statement of place.
ortsansässig *a.*, **Ortsansässige** *m./f.* resident; local.
Ortschaft *f.* **(-, -en)** village.
ortsfest *a.* (*mil.*) fixed, static.
Ortsgespräch *n.* (*tel.*) local call.
ortskundig *a.* acquainted with the locality.
Ortsnetzkennzahl *f.* area code.
Ortsverkehr *m.* local traffic.
Ortszeit *f.* local time.
Öse *f.* **(-, -n)** eye (for a hook).
Osmose *f.* osmosis.
Ost, Osten *m.* **(s, 0)** east.
ostdeutsch *a.* Eastern German.
Ostdeutschland *n.* Eastern Germany.
ostentativ *a.* ostentatious; pointed.
Osteoporose *f.* osteoporosis.
Osterei *n.* **(-s, -er)** Easter egg.
Oster: ~fest *n.* Easter; **~glocke** *f.* daffodil; **~hase** *m.* Easter bunny; **~lamm** *n.* paschal lamb.
österlich *a.* paschal, Easter.
Ostern *n. or pl.* Easter.
Österreich *n.* **(-s, 0)** Austria.
Österreicher *m.*; **Österreicherin** *f.*; **österreichisch** *a.* Austrian.
Ostertag *m.* Easter day.
Osterwoche *f.* week after Easter.
Osteuropa *n.* Eastern Europe.
Ostküste *f.* east(ern) coast.
östlich *a.* eastern, easterly; oriental.
Ostsee *f.* Baltic Sea.
ostwärts *adv.* eastward.
Ostwind *m.* east wind.
Otter *f.* **(-, -n)** adder, viper.
Otter *m.* otter.
Ottomane *f.* **(-, -0)** ottoman.
Ouvertüre *f.* **(-, -n)** (*mus.*) overture.
oval *a.* oval.
Ovation *f.* **(-, -en)** ovation.
ÖVP *Österreichische Volkspartei*, Austrian People's Party.
Ovulation *f.* ovulation.
Oxyd *n.* **(-[e]s, -e)** oxide.
oxydieren *v.t.i.* to (become) oxidize(d).
Ozean *m.* **(-s, -e)** ocean.
Ozeandampfer *m.* oceanliner.
Ozeanographie *f.* oceanography.
Ozelot *m.* **(-s, -e)** ocelot.
Ozon *n.* **(-s, 0)** ozone.
ozonhaltig *a.* ozoniferous.
Ozonloch *n.* hole in the ozone layer.
Ozonschicht *f.* ozone layer.
Ozonwerte *pl.* ozone levels.

PQ

P, p *n.* the letter P or p.
p. *per*, per, by.
p.A., p.Adr. *per Adresse*, care of, c/o.
Paar *n.* **(-[e]s, -e)** pair, couple; brace (of fowl); *ein paar*, a few.
paaren *v.t. & v.r.* to pair; to mate; to couple; to copulate.
Paarhufer *m.* **(-s, -)** eventoed, ungulate.
Paarlauf *m.*; **Paarlaufen** *n.* pair skating.
Paarung *f.* **(-, -en)** copulation; pairing.
paarweise *adv.* by pairs, in twos.
Pacht *m.* **(-[e]s, -e)** & *f.* **(-, -en)** tenure, lease; rent.
pachten *v.t.* to rent, to lease.
Pächter *m.* **(-s, -)** tenant, leaseholder.
Pacht: ~geld *m.* rental, rent; **~gut** *n.* tenant farm, leasehold estate; **~vertrag** *m.* lease.
Pachtung *f.* **(-, -en)** leaseholding.
pachtweise *adv.* on lease.
Pack *m.* **([e]s, -e)** pack, bundle, parcel; (*fig.*) ~ *n.* rabble.
Päckchen *n.* **(-s, -)** small parcel.

Packeis *n.* **(-es, 0)** pack ice.
packen *v.t.* to pack up; to lay hold of, to seize; (*ergreifen*) to affect; ~ *v.r.* to be gone.
Packen *m.* **(-s, -)** pack; bale.
packend *a.* thrilling.
Pack: ~esel *m.* pack mule; **~papier** *n.* brown paper; **~pferd** *n.* packhorse; **~sattel** *m.* packsaddle.
Packung *f.* **(-, -en)** pack, package.
Pädagoge *m.* **(-en, -en); Pädagogin** *f.* **(-, -nen)** pedagogue.
Pädagogik *f.* **(-, 0)** pedagogy; education.
pädagogisch *a.* educational.
Paddel *n.* **(-s, -)** paddle
Paddelboot *n.* **(-es, -e)** canoe.
paddeln *v.t.* & *i.* to paddle.
paffen *v.i.* to puff; to smoke.
Page *m.* **(-n, -n)** page (boy); bellboy.
Pagen: ~kopf *m.* pageboy (hairstyle); **~streich** *m.* escapade.
paginieren *v.t.* to page (a book).
pah! *i.* pshaw! pooh!
Pair *m.* **(-s, -s)** peer.
Paket *n.* **(-[e]s, -e)** packet, parcel, pile.
Paketpost *f.* parcel-post.
Paketzustellung *f.* parcel delivery.
Pakistan *n.* **(-s, 0)** Pakistan.
Pakistani *m./f.;* **pakistanisch** *a.* Pakistani.
Pakt *m.* **(-[e]s, -e)** agreement, (com)pact.
paktieren *v.i.* to come to terms, to agree (on).
Palast *m.* **(-[e]s, Paläste)** palace.
Palästina *n.* **(-s, 0)** Palestine.
Palästinenser *m.;* **Palästinenserin** *f.;* **palästinensisch** *a.* Palestinian.
Palaver *n.* **(-s, -)** (*fam.*) palaver.
Palette *f.* **(-, -n)** palette.
Palissade *f.* **(-, -n)** palisade.
Palme *f.* **(-, -n)** palm tree.
Palmenwedel *m.* **(-s, -)** palm frond.
Palmsonntag *m.* Palm Sunday.
Pampe *f.* **(-, 0)** mud; mush.
Pampelmuse *f.* **(-, -n)** grapefruit.
pampig *a.* (*fam.*) insolent; mushy.
Panama *n.* **(-s, 0)** Panama.
Panamese *m.;* **Panamesin** *f.* Panamanian.
Panier *n.* **(-[e]s, -e)** banner, standard.
panieren *v.t.* to roll in crumbs.
Paniermehl *n.* breadcrumbs.
Panik *f.* **(-, -en)** panic.
panisch *a.* panic; **~er Schrecken,** panic.
Panne *f.* **(-, -n)** breakdown; flat tire; *eine ~ haben,* to break down.
Pannendienst *m.* breakdown service.
panschen *v.t.* to water down.
Panther *m.* **(-s, -)** panther.
Pantoffel *m.* **(-s, -)** slipper; (*fig.*) *unter dem ~ stehen,* to be henpecked.
Pantoffelheld *m.* henpecked husband.
Pantoffeltierchen *n.* (*biol.*) slipper animalcule.
Pantomime *f.* **(-, -n)** pantomime
Panzer *m.* **(-s, -0)** armor; (*Schiffs~*) armor plating.
Panzer: ~abwehrkanone *f.* anti-tank gun; **~fahrer** *m.* tank driver; **~glas** *n.* bulletproof glass; **~jäger** *pl.* anti-tank troops; **~kreuzer** *m.* armored cruiser, pocket battleship.
panzern *v.t.* to armor.
Panzer: ~schrank *m.* safe; **~platte** *f.* armor plate; **~truppen** *pl.* armored troops; **~wagen** *m.* armored car; **~zug** *m.* armored train.
Päonie *f.* **(-, -n)** peony.
Papa *m.* **(-s, -s); Papi** *m.* **(-s, -s)** papa, dad.
Papagei *m.* **(-en, -en)** parrot.
Papier *n.* **(-[e]s, -e)** paper; *zu ~ bringen,* to commit to paper; *~e pl.* stocks, securities *pl.*
Papier: ~deutsch *n.* officialese; **~fabrik** *f.* papermill; **~geld** *n.* paper money; **~handlung** stationery store; *f.* **~korb** *m.* wastepaper basket; **~serviette** *f.* paper napkin.
papieren *a.* (made of) paper.
papistisch *a.* popish, papistical.
Papp: ~arbeit *f.* pasteboard work; **~band** *m.* (binding in) boards; **~deckel = Pappendeckel.**
Pappe *f.* **(-, -en)** cardboard, pasteboard.
Pappel *f.* **(-, -n)** poplar.
pappen *v.t.* to paste.
Pappen: ~deckel *m.* cardboard; **~stiel** *m.* (*fig.*) trifle.
Pappschachtel *f.* cardboard box.
Paprika *n.* **(-s, -(s))** pepper; paprika.
Papst *m.* **(-es, Päpste)** pope.
päpstlich *a.* papal; pontifical.
Papsttum *n.* **(-, 0)** papacy; pontificate.
Parabel *f.* **(-, n)** parable; (*geom.*) parabola.
Parade *f.* **(-, n)** parade; (*fig.*) display; (*mil.*) review; (*Fechten*) parry.
Parade: ~anzug *m.* full dress; **~beispiel** *n.* perfect example; **~marsch** *m.* parade step; **~platz** *m.* parade ground.
paradieren *v.t.* & *i.* to parade.
Paradies *n.* **(-es, -e)** paradise.
paradiesisch *a.* paradisiacal.
paradox *a.* paradoxical.
Paradox *n.* paradox.
paradoxerweise *adv.* paradoxically.
Paragraph *m.* **(-en, -en)** paragraph.
parallel *a.* parallel.
Parallele *f.* **(-, -n)** parallel, parallel line.
Parallelschaltung *f.* (*elec.*) parallel connection.
Paranoia *f.* **(-, 0)** paranoia.
paranoid *a.* paranoid.
Paranuß *f.* Brazil nut.
paraphieren *v.t.* to initial.
Parasit *m.* **(-en, -en)** parasite.
parasitär *a.* parasitic.
parat *a.* ready.
Paratyphus *m.* **(-, 0)** paratyphoid (fever).
Parcours *m.* **(-, -)** course.
Pardon *m.* **(-s, 0)** pardon.
Parfüm *n.* **(-s, -e)** perfume, scent.
Parfümerie *f.* perfumery.
parfümieren *v.t.* to perfume.
Pari *n.* **(-[s], 0)** par (of exchange).
pari *adv.* at par.
parieren *v.t.* to parry; ~ *v.i.* to obey.
Parität *f.* **(-, -en)** parity.
Park *m.* **(-[e]s, -e)** park.
parken *v.t.* & *i.* to park; **~ verboten,** no parking!
Parkett *m.* **(-[e]s, -e)** parquet (floor).
Park: ~gebühr *f.* parking fee; **~haus** *n.* parking garage; **~lücke** *f.* parking space; **~platz** *m.* parking lot; **~scheibe** *f.* parking token; **~uhr** *f.* parking meter.
Parlament *n.* **(-[e]s, -e)** Parliament.
Parlamentarier *m.* **(-, -)** parliamentarian; Congressman; **Parlamentarierin** *f.* parliamentarian; Congresswoman.
parlamentarisch *a.* parliamentary.
Parlaments: ~ausschuß *m.* parliamentary com-

mittee; **~sitzung** *f.* sitting (of parliament); **~wahl** *f.* parliamentary election.
Parodie *f.* **(-, -[e]n)** parody.
Parole *f.* **(-, -n)** motto; password; watchword.
Partei *f.* **(-, -en)** party, side; **~ ergreifen,** to take sides, to side (with).
Partei: ~apparat *m.* party machine; **~funktionär** *m.* party official; **~gänger** *m.* partisan.
parteiisch, parteilich *a.* partial.
Parteilinie *f.* party line.
parteilos *a.* impartial, neutral.
Parteitag *m.* party conference.
Parteiung *f.* **(-, -en)** division into parties.
Parterre *n.* **(-[s], -s)** ground floor; flowerbed; (*im Theater*) pit.
Partie *f.* **(-, -[e]n)** parcel, lot; (*Heirat*) match; (*Spiel*) game; (*Ausflug*) excursion.
partiell *a.* partial.
Partikel *f.* **(-, -n)** particle.
Partisan *m.* **(-n, -n); Partisanin** *f.* **(-, -nen)** (*mil.*) partisan; guerilla.
Partitur *f.* **(-, -en)** score.
Partizip *n.* **(-s, -zipien)** participle.
Partner *m.* **(-s, -); Partnerin** *f.* **(-, -nen)** partner.
Partnerschaft *f.* **(-, -en)** partnership.
Partnerstadt *f.* sister city/town.
partout *adv.* at all costs.
Parze *f.* **(-, -n)** Fate.
Parzelle *f.* **(-, -n)** plot (of land).
parzellieren *v.t.* to parcel out.
Pascha *m.* **(-s, -s)** pasha.
Pasquill *n.* **(-[e]s, -e)** lampoon.
Paß *m.* **(Passes, Pässe)** pass; defile; passport; (*Ritt*) amble.
Passage *f.* **(-, -n)** arcade; sequence.
Passagier *m.* **(-[e]s, -e)** passenger; *blinder ~,* stowaway.
Passagierflugzeug *n.* airliner.
Passah *n* **(-s, -s)** Passover.
Passant *m.* **(-en, -en)** passerby.
Passanten: ~hotel *n.* transient hotel; **~quartier** *n.* transient billets.
Passatwind *m.* tradewind.
passé *a.* (*fam.*) passé; out of date.
passen *v.i.* to fit, to suit, to be convenient; (*im Spiel*) to pass.
passend *a.* fitting, suitable; convenient.
passierbar *a.* passable; navigable.
passieren *v.t.* to pass, to cross; **~** *v.i.(s)* to happen.
Passierschein *m.* pass, permit.
passioniert *a.* passionate; ardent.
passiv *a.* passive; indolent, inactive.
Passiv *m.* **(-s; -e)** passive (voice).
Passiv[um] *n.* **(-s, 0)** passive voice.
Passiva, Passiven *pl.* liabilities.
Passivhandel *m.* adverse trade.
Passivität *f.* **(-, 0)** passivity.
Passivposten *m.* liability.
Paste *f.* **(-, -n)** paste.
Pastell(stift) *m.* **(-[e]s, -e)** pastel, crayon.
Pastete *f.* **(-, -n)** pie, pâté.
Pastetenbäcker *m.* pastry chef.
pasteurisieren *v.t.* to pasteurize.
Pastille *f.* **(-, -n)** lozenge, pastil.
Pastor *m.* **(-s, -en); Pastorin** *f.* **(-, -nen)** pastor, minister.
pastoral *a.* pastoral.
Pate *m.* **(-n, -n); Patin** *f.* **(-, -nen)** godfather, godmother.
Patenkind *n.* godchild.
Patent *n.* **(-[e]s, -e)** patent; (*mil.*) commission; *angemeldetes ~,* pending patent.
Patent: ~amt *n.* patent office; **~anmeldung** *f.* application for a patent; **~anwalt** *f.* patent agent or lawyer; **~beschreibung** *f.* specification; **~erteilung** *f.* patent grant.
patentieren *v.t.* to patent; *~ v.r. etwas ~ lassen,* to take out a patent for sth.
Patentinhaber *m.* patentee; **~gesellschaft** *f.* patent holding company.
Patentverlängerung *f.* renewal of a patent.
Pater *m.* **(-s, Patres)** Father.
pathetisch *a. & adv.* pathetic(ally); emotional(ly).
Pathologe *m.;* **Pathologin** *f.* pathologist.
Pathologie *f.* pathology.
pathologisch *a.* pathological.
Pathos *n.* emotionalism.
Patient *m.* **(-en, -en); Patientin** *f.* **(-, -nen)** patient.
patriarchalisch *a.* patriarchal; paternal.
Patriot *m.* **(-en, -en); Patriotin** *f.* **(-, -nen)** patriot.
patriotisch *a.* patriotic.
Patriotismus *m.* patriotism.
Patrizier *m.* **(-s, -); Patrizierin** *f.* **(-, -nen)** patrician.
Patron *m.* **(-[e]s, -e)** patron, protector, supporter.
Patronat *n.* **(-[e]s, -e)** patronage.
Patrone *f.* **(-, -n)** pattern; cartridge.
Patronentasche *f.* cartridge-box, pouch.
Patrouille *f.* **(-, -)** patrol.
patrouillieren *v.i.* to be on patrol.
Patsche *f.* **(-, -n)** (*fig.*) pickle, mess, fix.
patschen *v.i.* to splash; to slap.
Patt *n.* **(-s, -s)** stalemate.
patzen *v.i.* (*fam.*) to slip up.
Patzer *m.* **(-s, -)** (*fam.*) slip, goof.
patzig *a.* (*fam.*) snotty; smart aleck
Pauke *f.* **(-, -n)** kettledrum.
pauken *v.i.* to beat the kettledrums; (*fam.*) to bone up; to cram.
pausbackig *a.* chubby (-faced).
pauschal *a.* all inclusive; indiscriminate.
Pauschale *f.* **(-, -n)** lump sum.
Pauschalreise *f.* package tour.
Pauschalsumme *f.* lump sum.
Pause *f.* **(-, -n)** pause, stop; (*mus.*) rest; interval, break; traced design.
pausen *v.t.* to trace, to copy.
pausenlos *a.* uninterrupted; continuous.
pausieren *v.i.* to pause.
Pauspapier *n.* tracing paper.
Pavian *m.* **(-s, -e)** baboon.
Pavillon *m.* **(-s, -s)** pavilion.
Pazifik *m.* **(-, 0)** Pacific.
Pazifismus *m.* pacifism.
Pazifist *m.* **(-en, -en)** pacifist.
pazifistisch *a.* pacifist.
PDS *Partei des Demokratischen Sozialismus,* Party of the Democratic Socialism.
Pech *n.* **(-[e]s, -e)** pitch; (*fig.*) bad luck.
pechfinster *a.* pitch-dark.
pechschwarz *a.* jet-black, pitch-dark.
Pechvogel *m.* (*fig.*) unlucky person.
Pedal *n.* **(-[e]s, -e)** pedal.
Pedant *m.* **(-en, -en); Pedantin** *f.* **(-, -nen)** pedant, prig.
Pedanterie *f.* **(-, 0)** pedantry.
pedantisch *a.* pedantic; over-punctilious.
Pedell *m.* **(-es, -e)** caretaker, janitor.

PedikĂźre *f.* pedicure.
Pegel *m.* **(-s, -)** water gauge.
peilen *v.t.* (*nav.*) to sound, to take soundings, to take the bearings of.
Peilung *f.* **(-, -en)** direction finding.
Pein *f.* **(-, 0)** pain, torment.
peinigen *v.t.* to torment, to torture.
peinlich *a.* embarrassing.
Peinlichkeit *f.* embarrassment; meticulousness.
Peitsche *f.* **(-, -n)** whip, scourge.
peitschen *v.t.* to whip.
pekuniär *a.* pecuniary.
Pelikan *m.* **(-[e]s, -e)** pelican.
pellen *v.t.* to peel, to skin.
Pellkartoffeln *pl.* potatoes in jackets.
Pelz *m.* **(-es, -e)** fur, skin; pelt; fur coat.
pelzgefüttert *a.* fur-lined.
Pelzhändler *m.* furrier.
Pelzkragen *m.* fur collar.
Pelzmantel *m.* fur coat.
PelzmĂźtze *f.* fur cap.
Pendel *m.* **(-s, -)** pendulum.
pendeln *v.i.* to oscillate, to swing; to commute.
PendeltĂźr *f.* swinging door.
Pendelverkehr *m.* shuttle service.
Pendler *m.* **(-s, -); Pendlerin** *f.*, **(-, -nen)** commuter.
penetrant *a.* (*pej.*) penetrating (odor); pushy (person).
penibel *a.* fussy.
Penis *m.* **(-, -se)** penis.
Penizillin *n.* **(-s, 0)** penicillin.
Penne *f.* (*fam.*) school; flophouse.
pennen *v.i.* (*fam.*) to sleep.
Penner *m.*; **Pennerin** *f.* (*fam.*) bum; tramp.
Pension *f.* **(-, -en)** pension; board; boarding house.
Pensionär *m.* **(-[e]s, -e); Pensionärin** *f.* **(-, -nen)** pensioner.
Pensionat *n.* **(-[e]s, -e)** boarding school.
pensionieren *v.t.* to pension (off); ~ *v.r.*, ~ **lassen** to retire.
Pensionierung *f.* **(-, -en)** retirement.
pensionsberechtigt *a.* entitled to a pension.
pensionsfähig *a.* pensionable.
Pensum *n.* **(-s, Pensen)** amount of work.
Perfekt *n.* **(-s, -e)** perfect (tense).
Perfektion *f.* **(-, 0)** perfection.
perfid *a.* perfidious.
perforieren *v.t.* to perforate.
Pergament *n.* **(-[e]s, -e)** parchment.
Periode *f.* **(-, -n)** period.
periodisch *a.* & *adv.* periodical(ly).
peripher *a.* peripheral.
Peripherie *f.* **(-, -[e]n)** circumference, periphery.
Perle *f.* **(-, -n)** pearl; (*Glas*) bead.
perlen *v.i.* (s) to sparkle; to drip from.
Perl: ~graupen *f. pl.* pearl barley; **~huhn** *n.* guinea fowl; **~mutt** *n.*, **~mutter** *f.* mother-of-pearl.
Perlwein *m.* sparkling wine.
perplex *a.* baffled, puzzled.
Persianer *m.* Persian lamb.
persisch *a.* Persian.
Person *f.* **(-, -en)** person.
Personal *n.* **(-[e]s -e)** staff, personnel.
Personal... personnel-; **~abbau** *m.* reduction of staff; **~abteilung** *f.* personnel department; **~akten** *pl.* personnel file; **~ausweis** *m.* identity card; **~bĂźro** *n.* personnel office; **~chef** *m.*; **~chefin** *f.* personnel manager; **~computer** *m.* personal computer.
Personalien *pl.* particulars, personal data.
Personal: ~kosten *pl.* staff costs; **~mangel** *m.* staff shortage; **~pronomen** *n.* personal pronoun.
personell *a.* regarding staff; personnel.
Personen: ~aufzug *m.* elevator; **~beschreibung** *f.* personal description; **~gedächtnis** *n.* memory for faces; **~kult** *m.* personality cult; **~schaden** *m.* personal injury; **~verkehr** *m.* passenger traffic **~zug** *m.* (*rail.*) passenger train.
personifizieren *v.t.* to personify.
persönlich *a.* personal; **~er Wert** *m.* sentimental value; ~ *adv.* in person.
Persönlichkeit *f.* **(-, -en)** personality.
Perspektive *f.* **(-, -n)** perspective.
Peru *n.* **(-s, 0)** Peru.
Peruaner *m.* **(-s, -); Peruanerin** *f.* **(-, -nen); peruanisch** *a.* Peruvian.
PerĂźcke *f.* **(-, -n)** wig.
pervers *a.* perverse.
Pessimismus *m.* **(-, 0)** pessimism.
pessimistisch *a.* pessimistic.
Pest *f.* **(-, -en)** plague, pest(ilence).
Petersilie *f.* **(-, 0)** parsley.
Petition *f.* **(-, -en)** petition.
Petroleum *n.* **(-s, 0)** petroleum.
Petting *n.* **(-s, -s)** petting.
in petto haben, to have up one's sleeve.
Petze *f.* telltale, sneak.
Pf. *Pfennig(e)*, pfennig.
Pfad *m.* **(-es, -e)** path.
Pfadfinder *m.* **(-s, -)** boy scout; **~in** *f.* girl scout.
Pfaffe *m.* **(-n, -n)** (*pej.*) parson.
Pfahl *m.* **(-[e]s, Pfähle)** pile; post, pole.
Pfahlbau *m.* pile dwelling.
Pfand *n.* **(-[e]s, Pfänder)** pledge, pawn; security; (*Spiel*) forfeit.
pfändbar *a.* distrainable.
Pfandbrief *a.* mortgage bond.
pfänden *v.t.* to distrain, to seize.
Pfänderspiel *n.* game of forfeits.
Pfandhaus *n.* pawn shop.
Pfandleiher *m.* pawnbroker.
Pfandschuldner *m.* pledger.
Pfändung *f.* **(-, -en)** distraint, seizure; **~sbefehl** *m.* distress warrant.
Pfanne *f.* **(-, -n)** pan.
Pfannkuchen *m.* pancake.
Pfarre *f.* **(-, -n)** rectory, parsonage, vicarage; parish.
Pfarrei *f.* parish.
Pfarrer *m.* **(-s, -)** minister, pastor, priest, rector.
Pfarr: ~haus *n.* parsonage, rectory; **~kirche** *f.* parish church.
Pfau *m.* **(-[e]s & -en, -en)** peacock.
Pfauenauge *n.* peacock butterfly.
Pfd. *Pfund*, German pound.
Pfeffer *m.* **(-s, 0)** pepper.
Pfefferkuchen *m.* gingerbread.
Pfefferminze *f.* peppermint.
PfeffermĂźhle *f.* pepper mill.
pfeffern *v.t.* to pepper.
pfeffrig *a.* peppery.
Pfeife *f.* **(-, -en)** (tobacco-)pipe; whistle; *eine ~ stopfen*, to fill a pipe.
pfeifen *v.i.* & *i.st.* to pipe; to whistle.
Pfeifenreiniger *m.* pipe cleaner.
Pfeifer *m.* **(-s, 0)** piper; whistler.
Pfeil *m.* **(-[e]s, -e)** arrow; bolt, dart.

Pfeiler *m.* **(-s, -)** pillar; pier.
Pfeilspitze *f.* arrowhead.
Pfennig *m.* **(-s, -e)** small coin (penny).
Pfennigfuchser *m.* (*fam.*) penny pincher.
Pferch *m.* **(-[e]s, -e)** fold, pen.
pferchen *v.t.* to pen, to cram.
Pferd *n.* **(-[e]s, -e)** horse; (*Turnen*) vaulting-horse; *zu ~e*, on horseback.
Pferde: ~äpfel *pl.* horse droppings; **~fuß** *m.* shag; **~koppel** *f.* paddock; **~kraft** *f.* horsepower.
Pferde: ~rennbahn *f.* racetrack; **~rennen** *n.* (horse-)race; **~stall** *m.* stable; **~stärke (PS)** *f.* horsepower (H.P.); **~zucht** *f.* breeding of horses.
Pfiff *m.* **(-[e]s, -e)** whistle; trick.
Pfifferling *m.* **(-s, -e)** chanterelle.
pfiffig *a.* sly, sharp, smart.
Pfingsten *n. or f. or pl.;* **Pfingstfest** *n.* Pentecost.
Pfirsich *m.* **(-, -e)** peach.
Pflanze *f.* **(-, -n)** plant.
pflanzen *v.t.* to plant, to set.
Pflanzenfaser *f.* vegetable fiber.
Pflanzenfett *n.* vegetable fat.
Pflanzenfresser *m.* herbivore.
Pflanzenkost *f.* vegetable diet or food.
Pflanzennahrung *f.* vegetable diet or food.
Pflanzenöl *n.* vegetable oil.
Pflanzenreich *n.* vegetable kingdom.
Pflanzenschädling *m.* pest.
Pflanzenschutzmittel *n.* pesticide.
Pflanzer *m.* **(-s, -)** planter.
pflanzlich *a.* plant; vegetable; vegetarian.
Pflanzung *f.* **(-, -en)** plantation.
Pflaster *n.* **(-s, -)** plaster; pavement.
pflastern *v.t.* to pave.
Pflasterstein *m.* paving stone.
Pflaume *f.* **(-, -n)** plum; *getrocknete ~*, prune.
Pflege *f.* **(-, 0)** care, cultivation.
Pflege: ~eltern *pl.* foster parents *pl.;* **~kind** *n.* foster child; **~mutter** *f.* foster mother.
pflegen *v.t.* to foster, to nurse, to take care of, to attend to; *~ v.i.* to be accustomed, to use; *~ v.r.* to take care of one's appearance; *Umgang ~*, to see a good deal (of).
Pfleger *m.;* **Pflegerin** *f.* nurse; keeper.
Pflege: ~sohn *m.* foster son; **~tochter** *f.* foster daughter; **~vater** *m.* foster father.
pfleglich *a.* careful.
Pflegling *m.* **(-[e]s, -e)** foster child.
Pflicht *f.* **(-, -en)** duty; obligation.
pflichtbewußt *a.* conscientious; dutiful.
Pflichteifer *m.* zeal, dutifulness.
Pflichtgefühl *n.* sense of duty.
pflichtgemäß *a. & adv.* dutiful(ly).
pflichtgetreu *a.* dutiful, conscientious.
pflichtmäßig *a.* prescribed by duty.
Pflichtteil *m.* lawful portion.
pflichtvergessen *a.* undutiful.
Pflichtverletzung *f.* breach of duty.
Pflichtversäumnis *f.* neglect of duty.
Pflock *m.* **(-[e]s, Pflöcke)** plug, peg.
pflöcken *v.t.* to peg.
pflücken *v.t.* to pluck; to pick.
Pflug *m.* **(-[e]s, Pflüge)** plow.
Pflugbagger *m.* bulldozer.
pflügen *v.t.* to plow.
Pflugschar *f.* plowshare.
Pforte *f.* **(-, -n)** gate; (*nav.*) porthole.
Pförtner *m.* **(-s, -)** doorman, porter.
Pfosten *m.* **(-s, -)** post; pale, stake.
Pfote *f.* **(-, -n)** paw, claw.
Pfriem *m.* **(-[e]s, -e), Pfriemen** *m.* **(s, -), Pfrieme** *f.* **(-, -n)** awl, punch.
Pfropf *m.* **(-[e]s, -e), Pfropfen** *m.* **(-s, -)** cork, stopper; (*Holz*) plug; (*med.*) clot.
pfropfen *v.t.* to cram; (*Pflanzen*) to graft; to cork.
Pfründe *f.* **(-, -n)** (*rel.*) benefice; (*fig.*) sinecure.
Pfuhl *m.* **(-[e]s, -e)** pool, puddle, slough.
pfui! *i.* yuck! shame! ugh!
Pfuiruf *m.* **(-s, -e)** boo.
Pfund *n.* **(-[e]s, -e)** pound.
pfündig *a.* (*in Zus.*) of (so many) pounds.
pfundweise *adv.* by the pound.
pfuschen *v.i.* to bungle, to botch; *einem ins Handwerk ~*, (*fig.*) to trespass on another's field.
Pfütze *f.* **(-, -n)** puddle.
PH *Pädagogische Hochschule,* teacher's college.
Phänomen *n.* **(-s, -e)** phenomenon.
Phantasie *f.* **(-, -[e]n)** fantasy; imagination.
phantasiereich *a.* imaginative.
phantasieren *v.i.* to fantasize; (*med.*) to wander, to rave; (*mus.*) to improvise.
Phantast *m.* **(-en, -en)** dreamer; visionary.
phantastisch *a.* fantastic, (*fam.*) terrific.
Phantombild *n.* identikit picture.
Pharisäer *m.* **(-s, -)** Pharisee.
pharisäerhaft, pharisäisch *a.* pharisaical.
Pharmakologie *f.* pharmacology.
Pharmakonzern *m.* pharmaceutical company.
Pharmazeut *m.* **(-en, -en); Pharmazeutin** *f.* **(-, -nen)** pharmacist.
Pharmazie *f.* pharmaceutics.
Phase *f.* **(-, -n)** (*astr.*) phase; stage.
Philanthrop *m.* **(-en, -en)** philanthropist.
Philharmonie *f.* **(-, -n)** philharmonic orchestra; philharmonic hall.
Philippinen *pl.* Philippines.
Philister *m.* **(-s, -)** Philistine.
philisterhaft, philiströs *a.* narrow minded.
Philologe *m.* **(-en, -en); Philologin** *f.* **(-, -nen)** philologist.
Philologie *f.* **(-, 0)** philology.
philologisch *a.* philological.
Philosoph *m.* **(-en, -en); Philosophin** *f.* **(-, -nen)** philosopher.
Philosophie *f.* **(-, -[e]n)** philosophy.
philosophieren *v.i.* to philosophize.
philosophisch *a.* philosophical.
Phlegma *n.* **(-[s], 0)** phlegm.
phlegmatisch *a.* phlegmatic.
Phobie *f.* **(-, -n)** phobia.
Phonetik *f.* **(-, -en)** phonetics.
phonetisch *a.* phonetic.
Phosphat *n.* phosphate.
Phosphor *m.* **(-s, -e)** phosphorus.
phosphoreszieren *v.i.* to phosphoresce.
Phosphorsäure *f.* phosphoric acid.
Photograph *m.* **(-en, -en); Photographin** *f.* **(-, -nen)** photographer.
Photographie *f.* **(-, -[e]n)** photograph. (*fam.*) photo; (*Kunst*) photography.
photographieren *v.t.* to photograph.
Photokopie *f.* **(-, -n)** photocopy.
Photozelle *f.* photoelectric cell.
Phrase *f.* **(-, -n)** phrase, idiom.
phrasenhaft *a.* empty, grandiloquent.
pH-Wert *m.* pH(-value).
Physik *f.* **(-, 0)** physics *pl.*
physikalisch *a.* physics; physical.
Physiker *m.* **(-s, -); Physikerin** *f.* **(-, -nen)** physicist.

Physiologie *f.* physiology.
physisch *a.* physical.
Pianist *m.*; **Pianistin** *f.* pianist.
Piano(forte) *n.* **(-s, -s)** piano.
Picke *f.* **(-, -n)** pickaxe.
Pickel *m.* **(-s, -)** stonemason's hammer; pimple.
Pickelhaube *f.* spiked helmet.
picken *v.i.* to peck, to pick.
Picknick *n.* picnic.
piekfein *a.* (*fam.*) classy.
piepen, piepsen *v.i.* to chirp, to squeak; to squeal; to pipe.
piepsig *a.* squeaky.
Pietät *f.* **(-, 0)** reverence.
pietätvoll *a.* reverent, reverential.
Pietist *m.* **(-en, -en)** pietist.
Pik *n.* **(-[s], -[s])** (*in der Karte*) spade.
pikant *a.* piquant, spicy, pungent; racy.
Pikee *m.* & *n.* **(-s, -s)** (*Stoff*) quilting.
Pilger *m.* **(-s, -)** pilgrim.
Pilgerfahrt *f.* pilgrimage.
pilgern *v.i.* *(s, h)* to go on a pilgrimage.
Pille *f.* **(-, -n)** pill.
Pilot *m.* **(-en, -en)** pilot.
Pilz *m.* **(-es, -e)** fungus; mushroom; (*giftiger*) toadstool.
Pilzkrankheit *f.* mycosis; fungus (disease).
pingelig *a.* (*fam.*) nitpicking.
Pinguin *m.* penguin.
Pinie *f.* **(-, -n)** pine.
Pinkel *m.* (*fam. pej.*) *feiner* ~, snob.
pinkeln *v.i.* to pee.
Pinnwand *f.* bulletin board.
Pinscher *m.* **(-s, -)** pinscher.
Pinsel *m.* **(-s, -)** (painter's) brush; (*fig.*) simpleton.
pinseln *v.t.* to paint.
Pinzette *f.* **(-, -n)** tweezers.
Pionier *m.* (*mil.*) engineer; (*fig.*) pioneer.
Pipi *n.* ~ **machen,** to pee.
Pirat *m.* **(-en, -en)** pirate.
Piratensender *m.* pirate radio station.
Pirsch *f.* stalking.
pirschen *v.t.* to go stalking.
pissen *v.i.* to piss.
Pistazie *f.* **(-, -n)** pistachio.
Piste *f.* **(-, -n)** piste; ski run; track.
Pistole *f.* **(-, -n)** pistol, gun.
pitschnaß *a.* dripping wet.
Pizza *f.* **(-, -zzen)** pizza.
Pkw *Personenkraftwagen,* (motor) car.
Pl. *Platz,* Square, Sq.; *Plural,* plural, pl.
placken *v.t.* to harass, to pester; ~ *v.r.* to toil, to drudge.
Plackerei *f.* **(-, -en)** toil, drudgery; vexation.
plädieren *v.i.* to plead.
Plädoyer *n.* **(-s, -s)** (*jur.*) final speech.
Plage *f.* **(-, -n)** plague, torment, bother.
Plagegeist *m.* bore.
plagen *v.t.* to plague, to trouble, to vex; ~ *v.r.* to drudge, to slave.
Plagiat *n.* **(-[e]s, -e)** plagiarism, plagiary.
Plakat *n.* **(-[e]s, -e)** poster, placard, bill.
Plakatwand *f.* billboard.
Plakette *f.* badge.
Plan *m.* **(-[e]s, Pläne)** plan; design, scheme.
plan *a.* level; ~ *adv.* **~liegen,** to lie flat.
Plane *f.* **(-, -n)** tarpaulin.
planen *v.t.* to plan, to project.
Planet *m.* **(-en, -en)** planet.
planieren *v.t.* to level; to plane.
Planierraupe *f.* bulldozer.
Planke *f.* **(-, -en)** plank, board.
Plänkelei *f.* **(-, -en)** skirmishing.
plänkeln *v.i.* (*mil.*) to skirmish.
Plankton *n.* plankton.
planlos *a.* aimless, without a plan; ~ *adv.* at random.
planmäßig *a.* established, scheduled; ~ *adv.* according to plan.
Planschbecken *n.* baby pool.
planschen, plantschen *v.i.* to splash.
Planspiel *n.* (*mil.*) map exercise.
Plantage *f.* **(-, -n)** plantation.
Planwirtschaft *f.* planned economy.
plappern *v.i.* to prattle, to chatter.
plärren *v.t.* to bawl; to blare.
Plasma *n.* **(-s, -men)** plasma.
Plastik *f.* **(-, 0)** plasticity; sculpture.
Plastik *n.* plastic.
plastisch *a.* plastic; **~e Chirurgie** *f.* plastic surgery.
Platane *f.* **(-, -n)** plane tree.
Platin *n.* **(-s, 0),** platinum.
platschen *v.i.* to splash.
plätschern *v.i.* to splash, to dabble.
platt *a.* flat, level; (*fam.*) amazed.
Plättbrett *n.* ironing board.
plattdeutsch *a.* Low German.
Platte *f.* **(-, -n)** plate; bald head, pate; (*Stein*) flag, slab; (*Teller*) tray, silver; (*Tisch*) leaf; (*Grammophon*) record.
Plätteisen *n.* (flat)iron.
plätten *v.t.* to iron.
Plattenhülle *f.* record sleeve.
Plattenspieler *m.* (*Grammophon*) record player.
Platt: ~form *f.* platform; **~fuß** *m.* flat foot; **~fußeinlage** *f.* arch support, foot support.
plattfüßig *a.* flatfooted.
Plattheit *f.* **(-, -en)** flatness, platitude.
Platz *m.* **(-es, Plätze)** place; room space; public place, square; seat; ~ **machen,** to make room; ~ **nehmen,** to take a seat.
Platzangst *f.* claustrophobia; agoraphobia.
Platzanweiser *m.* usher.
Platzanweiserin *f.* usher.
Plätzchen *n.* **(-s, -)** (chocolate) drop; small cookie.
platzen *v.i.* to burst; to explode.
Platzpatrone *f.* blank cartridge.
Platzregen *m.* downpour.
Platzverweis *m.* (*sp.*) sending off.
Platzvorteil *m.* (*sp.*) home advantage.
Platzwart *m.* (*sp.*) groundsman.
Platzwunde *f.* lacerated wound.
Plauderei *f.* **(-, -en)** chat.
plaudern *v.i.* to gossip, to chat.
plausibel *a.* plausible.
Playback *n.* pre-recorded version; backing.
plazieren *v.t.* to place; to position.
Pleite *f.* **(-, -n)** (*sl.*) bankruptcy; ~ *sein,* ~ *gehen,* to fail, to go bust.
Plenarsitzung *f.* **(-, -en)** plenary session.
Plenum *n.* **(-s, 0)** plenary meeting.
Pleuelstange *f.* **(-, -n)** connecting rod.
Plexiglas *f.* safety glass.
Plissee *n.* **(-s, -s)** pleating.
Plombe *f.* **(-, -n)** lead seal; filling.
plombieren *v.t.* to seal with lead; to plug, to fill (a tooth).

plötzlich *a.* sudden; ~ *adv.* suddenly, all of a sudden.
plump *a.* plump; unwieldy, clumsy; coarse.
plumpsen *v.i.* *(s)* (*fam.*) to plump.
Plunder *m.* **(-s, 0)** junk; trash.
plündern *v.t.* to pillage, to plunder.
Plünderung *f.* **(-, -en)** plundering, looting.
Plural *m.* **(-s, -e)** plural (number).
Plüsch *m.* **(-es, -e)** plush.
Plüschtier *n.* cuddly toy.
Pluspol *m.* positive pole/terminal.
Plusquamperfekt(um) *n.* **(-s, -fekte)** pluperfect; past perfect.
Pluszeichen *n.* plus sign.
PLZ *Postleitzahl,* zip code.
Po *m.* **(-s, -s)** bottom.
Pöbel *m.* **(-s, 0)** mob, rabble, populace.
pöbelhaft *a.* vulgar, low.
pochen *v.t.* to knock; (*vom Herzen*) to beat, to throb; (*fig.*) to boast (of).
Pocken *f.pl.* smallpox.
Pockennarbe *f.* pock mark.
Podest *n./m.* rostrum.
Podium *n.* **(-s, Podien)** stage; rostrum.
Poesie *f.* **(-, -[e]n)** poetry, poem.
Poet *m.* **(-s, -en); Poetin** *f.* **(-, -nen)** poet; bard.
Poetik *f.* **(-, -en)** poetics.
poetisch *a.* & *adv.* poetical(ly); poetic.
Pointe *f.* **(-, -n)** punch line; point; curtain line.
pointiert *a.* & *adv.* pointed(ly).
Pokal *m.* **(-[e]s, -e)** goblet; (*Sport*) cup.
Pökelfleisch *n.* salt meat.
pökeln *v.t.* to pickle, to salt.
Pol *m.* **(-[e]s, -e)** pole.
Polar... *adj.* polar.
Polarkreis *m.* polar circle.
Polarstern *m.* polestar.
Pole *m.* **(-n, -n); Polin** *f.* **(-, -nen)** Pole.
Polemik *f.* **(-, 0)** controversy.
polemisieren *v.i.* to polemize.
Polen *n.* **(-s, 0)** Poland.
Police *f.* **(-, -n)** policy; **~inhaber** *m.* policyholder.
Polier *m.* **(-[e]s, -e)** foreman.
polieren *v.t.* to polish, to burnish.
Poliklinik *f.* outpatients' clinic.
Politesse *f.* traffic warden.
Politik *f.* **(-, 0)** politics *pl.*, policy.
Politiker *m.* **(-s, -); Politikerin** *f.* **(-, -nen)** politician.
politisch *a.* political; ~ **maßgebende Person** *f.* policymaker; ~ **prüfen** *v.t.* to screen.
politisieren *v.t.* to talk politics; to politicize.
Politologe *m.* **(-, -n); Politologin** *f.* **(-, -nen)** political scientist.
Politur *f.* **(-, -en)** polish.
Polizei *f.* **(-, -en)** police; police station; *sich der ~ stellen,* to give oneself up to the police; **~aufsicht** *f.* police supervision; **~einsatz** *m.* police operation; **~kontrolle** *f.* police check.
polizeilich *a.* of the police.
Polizei: ~präsident *m.*, **~präsidentin** *f.* chief of police; **~präsidium** *n.* police headquarters; **~revier** *n.* precinct; **~streife** *f.* police patrol; **~wache** *f.* police station.
polizeiwidrig *a.* contrary to police regulations.
Polizist *m.* **(-en, -en)** policeman; **Polizistin** *f.* policewoman
Pollen *m.* **(-s, -)** pollen.
polnisch *a.* Polish.
Polster *n.* **(-, -)** cushion; bolster.
Polstermöbel *pl.* upholstered furniture.
polstern *v.t.* to upholster; to stuff, to pad.
Polterabend *m.* wedding eve.
poltern *v.i.* to racket, to rattle; to bluster.
Polygamie *f.* polygamy.
Polyp *m.* **(-en, -en)** polyp(us); (*fam.*) cop.
Polytechnikum *n.* **(-[s], -techniken)** polytechnic school, engineering college.
Pomade *f.* **(-, -n)** pomade.
Pomeranze *f.* **(-, -n)** orange.
Pommern *n.* Pomerania.
Pommes frites *pl.* French fries.
Pomp *m.* **(-[e]s, 0)** pomp, splendour.
pomphaft *a.* stately, magnificent.
pompös *a.* stately, magnificent.
Ponton *m.* pontoon.
Pony *n. or m.* **(-s, -s)** pony.
Pony *m.* **(-s, -s)** bangs.
Popanz *m.* **(-es, -e)** bugbear.
popelig *a.* (*fam.*) crummy; lousy.
Popelin *m.* **(-s, -e)** poplin.
popeln *v.i.* (*fam.*) to pick one's nose.
Popmusik *f.* popmusic.
Popo *m.* **(-s, -s)** (*fam.*) backside; bottom.
populär *a.* popular.
Popularität *f.* **(-, 0)** popularity.
Pore *f.* **(-, -n)** pore.
Pornographie *f.* **(-, -n)** pornography.
pornographisch *a.* pornographic.
porös *a.* porous.
Porree *m.* **(-s, -s)** leek.
Portal *n.* **(-[e]s, -e)** portal.
Portefeuille *n.* **(-[s], -s)** portfolio.
Portemonnaie *n.* **(-s, -s)** purse.
Portier *m.* **(-s, -s)** porter, janitor; (*Hotel*) porter, desk clerk.
Portion *f.* **(-, -en)** portion, ration; *zweite ~*, second helping; *eine ~ Kaffee,* coffee for one.
Porto *n.* **(-s, -s)** postage.
portofrei *a.* postage paid.
Portospesen *pl.* postal expenses.
portraitieren *v.t.* to portray.
Porträt *n.* **(-s, -s)** portrait.
Portugal *n.* **(-s, 0)** Portugal.
Portugiese *m.* **(-n, -n); Portugiesin** *f.* **(-, -nen) portugiesisch** *a.* Portuguese.
Portwein *m.* **(-s, -e)** port.
Porzellan *n.* **(-[e]s, -e)** china, porcelain.
Posaune *f.* **(-, -n)** trombone.
posaunen *v.t.* (*fig.*) to trumpet.
Pose *f.* **(-, -n)** pose; attitude.
positiv *a.* positive.
Positur *f.* **(-, -en)** posture.
Posse *f.* **(-, -n)** jest; farce, burlesque.
possessiv *a.* possessive.
Possessivpronomen *n.* possessive pronoun.
possierlich *a.* droll, funny.
Post *f.* **(-, -en)** post, mail; post office; *mit der ~*, by mail; *gewöhnliche ~ (nicht Luftpost)*, surface mail; *mit umgehender ~, postwendend,* by return mail.
Postament *n.* **(-[e]s, -e)** pedestal, base.
Postamt *n.* post office.
Postanweisung *f.* money order.
Postbote *m.* mailcarrier.
Posten *n.* **(-s, -)** post, station, place; (*mil.*) outpost; sentry; (*com.*) item, sum; parcel, lot; entry.
Postfach *n.* post office box.
Postkarte *f.* postcard; *farbige ~*, color postcard.

Postkutsche *f.* stagecoach, mail coach.
postlagernd *a. & adv.* (*auf Briefen*) to be (kept till) called for, poste restante, general delivery.
Postleitzahl *f.* zip code.
Postministerium *n.* postmaster general's office.
Postpaket *n.* parcel sent by post.
Postscheck *m.* postal check; **~konto** *n.* postal check(ing) account.
Postsparkasse *f.* post office savings bank.
Poststempel *m.* postmark.
postum *a. & adv.* posthumous(ly).
Postversandhaus *n.* mail-order house.
postwendend *adv.* by return mail; (*fig.*) right away.
Postwurfsendung *f.* direct-mail item.
Postzustellung *f.* postal delivery.
potent *a.* potent; strong.
Potentat *m.* **(-en, -en)** potentate.
Potential *n.* **(-s, -e)** potential.
potentiell *a. & adv.* potential(ly).
Potenz *f.* **(-, -en)** potency; (*math.*) power.
potenzieren *v.t.* to raise to a higher power.
Potpourri *n.* **(-s, -s)** (*mus.*) potpourri, medley.
Präambel *f.* **(-, -n)** preamble.
Pracht *f.* **(-, 0)** splendor, pomp, state.
prächtig *a.* magnificent, splendid.
prachtvoll *a.* splendid.
prädestinieren *v.t.* to predestine.
Prädikat *n.* **(-[e]s, -e)** predicate; title; rating.
prägen *v.t.* to coin, to stamp.
pragmatisch *a.* pragmatic.
prägnant *a.* terse; pithy.
prahlen *v.i.* to boast, to brag.
Prahler *m.* **(-s, -)** braggart, boaster.
Prahlerei *f.* **(-, -en)** boasting.
prahlerisch *a.* boastful, ostentatious.
Praktik *f.* **(-, -en)** practice.
Praktikant *m.* **(-en, -en)**; **Praktikantin** *f.* **(-, -nen)** trainee, intern.
Praktiker *m.* **(-s, -)** practical man.
Praktikum *n.* **(-s, -ka)** internship; practical training.
praktisch *a.* practical; *~er Arzt, m.* general practitioner.
praktizieren *v.t.* to practice.
Prälat *m.* **(-en, -en)** prelate.
Praliné *n.* **(-s, -s)**, **Praline** *f.* **(-, -n)** (filled) chocolate; **~schachtel** *f.* box of chocolates.
prall *a.* full; firm; tight.
prallen *v.i.* to collide; to crash.
Prämie *f.* **(-, -n)** premium; prize; bonus.
prämiieren *v.t.* to award a prize.
Prämisse *f.* **(-, -n)** premise.
prangen *v.i.* to shine; to be clearly visible.
Pranger *m.* **(-s, -)** pillory.
Pranke *f.* **(-, -n)** paw.
Präparat *n.* **(-[e]s, -e)** preparation, mixture.
präparieren *v.t.* to prepare.
Präposition *f.* **(-, -en)** preposition.
Prärie *f.* **(-, -n)** prairie.
Präsens *n.* **(-, e)** present (tense).
präsent *a.* present.
präsentieren *v.t.* to present.
Präsenz *f.* **(-, -en)** presence; **~liste** *f.* list of those present; **~stärke** *f.* actual strength.
Präservativ *n.* **(-s, -e)** condom.
Präsident *m.* **(-en, -en)**; **Präsidentin** *f.* **(-, -nen)** president, chairman, chairwoman.
präsidieren *v.t. & i.* to preside over, to be in the chair.
Präsidium *n.* **(-s, -dien)** chair(man's office), presidency; directorate.
prasseln *v.i.* to crackle.
prassen *v.i.* to feast, to revel.
Prätendent *m.* **(-en, -en)** pretender.
Präteritum *n.* **(-s, -ta)** preterite, past tense.
präventiv *a.* preventive.
Praxis *f.* **(-, 0)** practice; exercise; (*Arzt, Rechtsanwalt*) office.
Präzedenzfall *m.* precedent.
präzis *a.* punctual, exact, precise.
präzisieren *v.t.* to specify.
Präzision *f.* **(-, 0)** precision; **~sarbeit** *f.* precision work; **~swerkzeug** *n.* precision tool.
predigen *v.t.* to preach.
Prediger *m.* **(-s, -)**; **Predigerin** *f.* **(-, -nen)** preacher.
Predigt *f.* **(-, -en)** sermon; lecture.
Preis *m.* **(-es, -e)** (*Belohnung*) prize; (*Wert*) price, rate, cost, figure; (*Lob*) praise, glory; *um keinen ~*, not for the world.
Preisangabe *f.* quotation (of price).
Preisausschreiben *n.* competition.
Preisbindung *f.* price-fixing.
Preiselbeere *f.* **(-, -n)** cranberry.
preisen *v.t.st.* to praise.
Preiserhöhung *f.* price increase.
Preisgabe *f.* abandonment; revelation (secret).
preisgeben *v.t.* to expose; to abandon.
preisgekrönt *a.* prize-winning.
Preisgericht *n.* jury; panel of judges.
Preislage *f.* range of prices; *in niedriger ~*, low-priced.
Preisrichter *m.* adjudicator.
Preisschild *n.* price tag.
Preissturz *m.* sudden fall of prices.
Preisträger *m.*; **Preisträgerin** *f.* winner (of a competition).
Preisüberwachung *f.* price-control.
preiswert *a.* cheap.
prekär *a.* precarious.
Prellbock *m.* buffer.
prellen *v.t.* to cheat.
Prellung *f.* **(-, -en)** (*med.*) bruise.
Premiere *f.* **(-, -n)** opening night; premiere.
Premier: ~minister *m.*, **~ministerin** *f.* prime minister.
Presse *f.* **(-, -n)** press; squeezer.
Presse: ~agentur *f.* press agency; **~bericht** *m.* press report; **~besprechung** *f.* press conference; **~empfang** *m.* press reception; **~erklärung** *f.* press release; **~freiheit** *f.* freedom of the press; **~korrespondenz** *f.* press service; **~tribüne** *f.* press gallery.
pressen *v.t.* to press, to squeeze.
Presse: ~sprecher *m.* spokesman, **~sprecherin** *f.* spokeswoman; **~zensur** *f.* censorship of the press; **~zentrum** *n.* press center.
pressierin *v.i.* to be urgent.
Preßluft *f.* compressed air; **~bohrer** *m.* pneumatic drill; **~hammer** *m.* pneumatic hammer.
Preßwehen *pl.* bearing-down pains.
Preuße *m.*; **Preußin** *f.*; **preußisch** *n.* Prussian.
preußischblau *a.* Prussian blue.
prickeln *v.t.* to prickle, to itch.
prickelnd *a.* prickling; (*fig.*) thrilling.
Priester *m.* **(-s, -)** priest.
Priesterin *f.* **(-, -nen)** priest(ess).
Priesterschaft *f.* clergy; priesthood.
Priestertum *n.* priesthood.

Priesterweihe *f.* ordination of a priest.
Prima *f.* **(-, -men)** first-class, top grade
prima *a.* (*fam.*) great; fantastic.
primär *a.* & *adv.* primary; primarily.
Primaten *pl.* primates.
Primel *f.* **(-, -n)** primrose, cowslip.
primitiv *a.* primitive.
Primzahl *f.* (*ar.*) prime number.
Prinz *m.* **(-en, -en)** prince.
Prinzessin *f.* **(-, -nen)** princess.
Prinzip *n.* **(-[e]s, -ien)** principle.
Prinzipal *m.* **(-[e]s, -e)** principal, chief.
prinzipiell *a.* in/on principle.
Priorität *f.* **(-, -en)** priority.
Prise *f.* **(-, -n)** prize; (*Schnupftabak*) pinch.
Prisma *n.* **(-s, -men)** prism.
Pritsche *f.* **(-, -n)** wooden couch, bunk.
privat *a.* private.
Privat: ~adresse *f.* home address; **~angelegenheit** private matter; **~besitz** *m.* private property.
Privatdozent *m.* university lecturer.
Privatfernsehen *n.* commercial television.
privatim *adv.* privately.
privatisieren *v.i.* to privatize; to live on one's private income.
Privatklinik *f.* private clinic.
Privatmann *m.* private person.
Privatpatient *m.*, **Privatpatientin** *f.* private patient.
Privatrecht *n.* civil law.
Privatwirtschaft *f.* private sector.
Priv.-Doz. *Privatdozent,* university lecturer.
Privileg *n.* **(-s, -ien)** privilege.
privilegieren *v.t.* to grant a privilege.
privilegiert *a.* privileged.
pro *pr.* per; **~ Jahr,** per annum.
Pro *n. das ~ und das Kontra,* the pros and cons.
pro forma *adv.* as a matter of form.
Probe *f.* **(-, -n)** experiment, trial, test; (*Waren ~*) sample; (*Theater*) rehearsal; *auf ~,* on probation; *auf die ~ stellen,* to put to the test.
probe *a.* probationary
Probe: ~dienst *m.* probationary service; **~exemplar** *n.* specimen copy; **~fahrt** *f.* trial run; **~flug** *m.* test flight.
proben *v.t.* & *i.* to rehearse.
probeweise *adv.* on a trial basis.
Probezeit *f.* term of probation, qualifying period.
probieren *v.t.* to try, to test; to taste.
Problem *n.* **(-s, -e)** problem, question.
Problematik *f.* problematic nature; problems.
problemlos *a.* problem free.
Produkt *n.* **(-s, -e)** product.
Produktenbörse *f.* produce exchange.
Produktion *f.* **(-, -en)** production.
Produktionsmittel *pl.* means of production.
Produktions: ~prozeß *m.;* **~verfahren** *n.* production process.
produktiv *a.* productive.
Produktivität *f.* productivity.
Produzent *m.* **(-en, -en)** producer.
produzieren *v.t.* to produce.
profan *a.* profane.
profanieren *v.t.* to profane, to desecrate.
Profession *f.* **(-, -en)** profession; trade.
professionell *a.* professional.
Professor *m.* **(-s, -en)**; **Professorin** *f.* **(-, -nen)** professor.
Professur *f.* **(-, -en)** professorship.
Profi *m.* **(-s, -s)** (*fam.*) pro.
Profil *n.* **(-s, -e)** profile.
profilieren *v.r.* to distinguish os.
profiliert *a.* distinguished.
Profisport *m.* professional sport.
Profit *m.* **(-s, -e)** profit; **~gier** *f.* greed for profit.
profitieren *v.i.* to profit (by).
Profitstreben *n.* profit seeking.
Prof. Ord. *Professor Ordinarius,* Professor.
profund *a.* profound.
Prognose *f.* **(-, -n)** prognosis.
Programm *n.* **(-[e]s, -e)** program.
programmgemäß *adv.* & *a.* according to program.
Programmheft *n.* **(-s, -e)** program.
programmierbar *a.* programmable.
programmieren *v.t.* to program.
Programmierer *m.* **(-s, -)**; **Programmiererin** *f.* **(-, -nen)** programmer.
Programmiersprache *f.* programming language.
Programmierung *f.* programming.
Programm: ~vorschau *f.* program preview; trailer; **~wahl** *f.* channel selection; **~zeitschrift** *f.* program guide.
Progression *f.* **(-, -en)** progression.
progressiv *a.* progressive.
Projekt *n.* **(-[e]s, -e)** project, scheme.
Projektgruppe *f.* task force.
Projektionsapparat *m.* projector.
Projektionsschirm *m.* screen.
projizieren *v.t.* to project.
proklamieren *v.t.* to proclaim.
Pro-Kopf-Einkommen *n.* per capita income.
Prokura *f.* **(-, 0)** (power of) procuration; proxy.
Prolet *m.* prole.
Proletariat *n.* **(-[e]s, 0)** proletariat.
Proletarier *m.* **(-s, -)** proletarian.
Prolog *m.* **(-[e]s, -e)** prologue.
Promenade *f.* **(-, -n)** promenade, walk.
Promille *n.* **(-s, -)** per mil; alcohol level.
Promillegrenze *f.* legal alcohol limit.
prominent *a.* prominent.
Prominente *m./f.* prominent figure.
Prominenz *f.* **(-, -en)** VIP's; celebrities.
Promotion *f.* **(-, -en)** doctorate.
promovieren *v.i.* to earn a doctorate.
prompt *a.* prompt, quick.
Pronomen *n.* **(-s, -nomina)** pronoun.
propagieren *v.t.* to propagate.
Propeller *m.* **(-s, -)** propeller.
Prophet *m.* **(-en, -en)** prophet.
prophetisch *a.* prophetic.
prophezeien *v.t.* to prophesy; to predict.
Prophezeiung *f.* **(-, -en)** prophecy.
proportional *a.* proportional; *umgekehrt ~,* inversely proportional.
Proporz *m.* **(-es, -e)** proportional representation.
Propst *m.* **(-es, Pröpste)** provost.
Prosa *f.* **(-, 0)** prose.
prosaisch *a.* prosaic; (*fig.*) prosy.
prosit! *i.* prost! cheers!
Prospekt *m.* **(-[e]s, -e)** brochure; leaflet.
Prostituierte *m./f.* **(-n, -n)** prostitute.
protegieren *v.t.* to patronize; to sponsor.
Protein *n.* **(-s, -e)** protein.
Protektorat *n.* **(-es, -e)** protectorate.
Protest *n.* **(-es, -e)** protest; **~ erheben,** to enter a protest.
Protestant *m.* **(-en, -en)**; **Protestantin** *f.* **(-, -nen)** Protestant.

protestantisch *a.* Protestant.
protestieren *v.i.* to protest.
Protest: ~kundgebung *f.* protest rally; **~welle** *f.* wave of protest.
Prothese *f.* **(-, -n)** artificial limb; dentures.
Protokoll *n.* **(-[s], -e)** minutes *pl.; ~ führen,* to keep the minutes; *zu ~ geben,* to place on record; *zu ~ nehmen,* to take down.
protokollieren *v.t.* to write the minutes of.
Protz *m.* **(-n, -n)** show-off; snob.
protzen *v.i.* to show off.
protzig *a.* showy.
Proviant *m.* **(-[e]s, 0)** provisions, stores.
Provinz *f.* **(-, -en)** province.
provinziell *a.* provincial.
Provinzler *m.* provincial.
Provision *f.* **(-, -en)** commission.
provisorisch *a.* provisional, temporary.
Provokation *f.* provocation.
provokativ *a.* provocative.
provozieren *v.t.* to provoke.
Prozedur *f.* **(-, -en)** procedure.
Prozent *n.* **(-[e]s, -e)** per cent.
Prozentsatz *m.* percentage.
Prozeß *m.* **(-zesses, -zesse)** process; lawsuit (action); proceedings *pl.; kurzen ~ machen mit,* to make short work of.
Prozeßakten *f.pl.* minutes (*pl.*) of a law case.
prozeßieren *v.i.* to go to court.
Prozession *f.* **(-, -en)** procession.
Prozeßkosten *f.pl.* legal costs *pl.*
Prozeßverfahren *n.* legal procedure.
prüde *a.* prudish, squeamish.
Prüderie *f.* **(-, 0)** prudery.
prüfen *v.t.* to try, to test; to examine; to censor; *von der Zensur geprüft,* censored.
Prüfer *m.;* **Prüferin** *f.* tester; inspector; auditor; examiner.
Prüfling *m.* **(-s, -e)** examinee; candidate.
Prüfstein *m.* touchstone.
Prüfung *f.* **(-, -en)** trial; examination; *eine ~ machen,* to take an examination *or* test; *einer ~ unterziehen, v.r.* to sit for an examination or test.
Prüfungs: ~angst *f.* exam nerves; **~kommission** *f.* examination board.
Prügel *m.* **(-s, -)** stick, cudgel; beating.
Prügelei *f.* **(-, -en)** fight, row, scuffle.
Prügelknabe *m.* (*fam.*) scapegoat.
prügeln *v.t.* to fight; to thrash.
Prügelstrafe *f.* corporal punishment.
Prunk *m.* **(-es, 0)** ostentation, splendor.
prunken *v.i.* to make a show.
prunkvoll *a.* gorgeous, splendid.
P.S. *Pferdestärke,* horse-power, hp; *Nachschrift,* postscript, P.S.
Psalm *m.* **(-es, -en)** psalm.
Pseudonym *n.* pseudonym; pen name.
pst! *i.* hush!
Psychiater *m.* **(-s, -)**; **Psychiaterin** *f.* **(-, -nen)** psychiatrist.
psychiatrisch psychiatric; *~e Klinik f.* mental hospital.
psychisch *a.* psychic(al).
Psychoanalyse *f.* psychoanalysis.
Psychoanalytiker *m.;* **Psychoanalytikerin** *f.* psychoanalyst.
psychoanalytisch *a.* psychoanalytical.
Psychologe *m.* **(-en, -en)**; **Psychologin** *f.* **(-, -nen)** psychologist.
Psychologie *f.* psychology.
psychopathisch *a.* psychopathic.
Psychopharmakon *n.* **(-s, -ka)** psychiatric drug.
Psychose *f.* psychosis.
psychosomatisch *a.* psychosomatic.
Psychotherapeut *m.;* **Psychotherapeutin** *f.* psychotherapist.
psychotherapeutisch *a.* psychotherapeutic.
Psychotherapie *f.* psychotherapy.
Pubertät *f.* **(-, 0)** puberty.
publik *a. etw. ~ machen,* to make sth. public.
Publikum *n.* **(-[s], 0)** public.
publizieren *v.t.* to publish.
Publizist *m.;* **Publizistin** *f.* publicist; journalist.
Publizistik *f.* journalism.
Pudding *m.* **(-s, -s)** pudding.
Pudel *m.* **(-s, -)** poodle.
Puder *m.* **(-s, 0)** powder.
pudern *v.t.* to powder.
Puderquaste *f.* (powder-)puff.
Puderzucker *m.* confectioners' sugar; powdered sugar.
Puff *m.* **(-[e]s, -e)** cuff, thump; puff; (*Knall*) pop, report; (*fam.*) brothel.
puffen *v.t. & i.* to cuff, to thump.
Puffer *m.* **(-s, -)** buffer.
Pulk *m.* group; crowd.
Pulle *f.* (*fam.*) bottle.
Pulli *m.;* **Pullover** *m.* sweater.
Puls *m.* **(es, -e)** pulse.
Pulsader *f.* artery.
pulsen, pulsieren *v.i.* to pulsate, to throb; (*fig.*) to pulse.
Pult *n.* **(-es, -e)** desk; lectern.
Pulver *n.* **(-s, -)** powder; gunpowder.
Pulverfaß *m.* **(-es, fässer)** barrel of gunpowder; powder keg.
pulverisieren, pulvern *v.t.* to pulverize.
Pulverkaffee *m.* instant coffee.
Pulverschnee *m.* powder snow.
pummelig *a.* chubby.
Pump *m.* **(-[e]s, -e)** credit; *auf ~,* on credit.
Pumpe *f.* **(-, -n)** pump.
pumpen *v.t.* to pump; to lend; to borrow.
Punker *m.* punk (rocker).
Punkt *m.* **(-[e]s, -e)** point, dot; (*gram.*) period; article, item; *~ 7 Uhr,* seven o'clock sharp; *der wunde ~,* the sore point *or* spot.
punktieren *v.t.* to point, to dot; to punctuate; (*med.*) to tap.
Punktion *f.* (*med.*) puncture.
pünktlich *a.* punctual; *~ adv.* punctually.
Punktsieg *m.* (*Boxen*) winning on points.
Punsch *m.* **(-es, -e & Pünsche)** punch.
Pupille *f.* **(-, -n)** (*des Auges*) pupil.
Puppe *f.* **(-, -n)** doll; puppet; chrysalis.
Puppenspiel *n.* puppet show.
Puppenspieler *m.;* **Puppenspielerin** *f.* puppeteer.
pur *a.* pure, mere.
Püree *n.* **(-s, -s)** purée.
Puritaner *m.* Puritan.
puritanisch *a.* Puritan; puritanical.
Purpur *m.* **(-s, 0)** purple; purple robe.
purpurn *a.* purple, crimson.
purpurrot *a.* purple, crimson.
Purzelbaum *m.* somersault.
purzeln *v.i.* *(s)* to tumble.
Puste *f.* (*fam.*) puff; breath.
Pustel *f.* **(-, -n)** pimple; pustule.
pusten *v.i.* *(s)* to breathe hard, to puff.

Pute, Puthenne *f.* **(-, -n)** turkey hen.
Puter *m.* **(-s, -)** turkey cock; turkey (roast).
Putsch *m.* **(-es, -e)** putsch; coup.
putschen *v.i.* to revolt; to stage a putsch.
Putte *f.* **(-, -n)** putto.
Putz *m.* **(-es, 0)** dress, finery, attire; (*Mauer*) rough-cast, plaster.
putzen *v.t.* to clean, to polish; (*die Nase*) to blow, to wipe.
Putzfimmel *m.* **(-s, -)** (*pej.*) mania for cleaning.
Putzfrau *f.* **(-, -en)** cleaning lady.
putzig *a.* droll, queer.
Putzlappen *m.* **(-s, -)** cleaning rag.
Putzmacherin *f.* **(-, -nen)** milliner.
Putzmittel *n.* **(-s, -)** cleaning agent.
Putzzeug *n.* cleaning utensils *pl.*
Puzzle *n.* **(-s, -)** jigsaw puzzle.
Pygmäe *m.* **(-n, -n)** pygmy.
Pyjama *m.* **(-s, -s)** pyjamas.
Pyramide *f.* **(-, -n)** pyramid.
pyramidenförmig *a.* pyramidal.
Pyrenäen *pl.* the Pyrenees.
Pyromane *m.* **(-n, -n)** pyromaniac.
pythagoreisch *a.* Pythagorean; *~er Lehrsatz,* Pythagorean theorem.
Q, q *n.* the letter Q or q.
qkm *Quadratkilometer,* square kilometer.
qm *Quadratmeter,* square meter.
Quacksalber *m.* **(-s, -)** quack, charlatan.
Quaderstein *m.* square or hewn stone.
Quadrat *n.* **(-[e]s, -e)** square; *im ~,* square.
quadratisch *a.* quadratic, square.
Quadratmeter *m.* squaremeter.
Quadratur *f.* quadrature; *die ~ des Kreises,* the squaring of the circle.
Quadratwurzel *f.* square root.
Quadratzahl *f.* square number.
quadrieren *v.t.* to square.
quadrophon *a.* quadrophonic.
quaken *v.i.* to croak; to quack.
quäken *v.i.* to scream, to squawk.
Quäker *m.* **(-s, -)** Quaker, Friend.
Qual *f.* **(-, -en)** pain, torment, agony.
quälen *v.t.* to torment, to vex; *~ v.r.* to toil, to drudge.
Quälerei *f.* **(-, -en)** torture; torment; annoyance.
Quälgeist *m.* (*fam.*) pest.
qualifizieren *v.t. & v.r.* to qualify.
Qualität *f.* **(-, -en)** quality.
qualitativ *a.* qualitative.
Qualitäts... quality-.
Qualle *f.* **(-, -n)** jellyfish.
Qualm *m.* **(-[e]s, 0)** thick smoke.
qualmen *v.i.* to smoke.
qualvoll *a.* very painful.
Quantität *f.* **(-, -en)** quantity.
Quantum *n.* **(-[e], -ta)** quantum; dose; share.
Quarantäne *f.* **(-, -n)** quarantine.
Quark *m.* **(-[e]s, 0)** curd cheese; (*sl.*) trifle; trash, rubbish.
Quarkkäse *m.* white cheese.
Quart *n.* **(-[e]s, -e)** quart; *in ~,* in quarto.
Quarta *f.* **(-, -ten)** third year of high school.
Quartal *n.* **(-s, -s)** a quarter of a year.
Quart: ~band *m.* quarto volume; **~blatt** *n.* quarter of a sheet.
Quart[e] *f.* **(-, -n)** (*mus.*) fourth.
Quartett *n.* **(-[e]s, -e)** quartet(te).
Quartier *n.* **(-[e]s, -e)** quarters *pl.*
Quartiermeister *m.* (*mil.*) quartermaster.
Quarz *m.* **(-es, -e)** quartz.
quasseln *v.t.* to prate, to blather.
Quasselstrippe *f.* chatterbox.
Quast *m.* **(-es, -en); Quaste** *f.* **(-, -n)** tassel, tuft; puff; mop, brush.
Quatsch *m.* **(-es, 0)** foolish talk, rubbish; nonsense.
quatschen *v.i.* to talk nonsense.
Quatschkopf *m.* silly goose.
Quecksilber *n.* quicksilver, mercury.
Quell *m.* **(-s, 0); Quelle** *f.* **(-, -n)** well, spring, source.
quellen *v.t.* to soak, to swell; *~ v.i.st. (s)* to spring, to gush, to flow; to swell.
quengelei *f.* **(-, O)** whining.
quengelig *a.* whining; fretful.
quengeln *v.i.* to whine; to carp.
quer *a.* cross; oblique, transverse; *~ adv.* across, diagonally.
Querbalken *m.* crossbeam.
querdurch *adv.* straight across.
Quere *f.* **(-, 0)** oblique direction; *der ~ nach,* crosswise; *in die ~ kommen,* to thwart.
querfeldein *adv.* across country.
Quer: ~flöte *f.* transverse flute; **~format** *n.* horizontal format; **~linie** *f.* cross-line; **~schiff** *n.* transept; **~schnitt** *m.* cross-section; **~schnittslähmung** *f.* paraplegia; **~strasse** *f.* intersection; **~stück** *n.* (*mech.*) traverse; **~summe** *f.* sum of the digits; **~treiber** *m.* (*fam.*) obstructionist.
querüber *adv.* over against, athwart.
Querulant *m.* **(-en, -en)** litigious person; grumbler.
Querverbindung *f.* cross connection; **Querverweis** *m.* cross reference.
quetschen *v.t.* to squeeze, to squash, to bruise.
Quetschung *f.* **(-, -en)** contusion, bruise.
Queue *n.* **(-s, -s)** cue.
quicklebendig *a.* lively, brisk.
quieken, quietschen *v.i.* to squeak.
quietschfidel *a.* chipper.
Quinta *f.* **(-, -ten)** fifth grade.
Quinte *f.* **(-, -n)** (*mus.*) fifth.
Quintessenz *f.* **(-, -en)** quintessence, gist.
Quintett *n.* **(-[e]s, -e)** quintet(te).
Quirl *m.* **(-[e]s, -e)** hand blender; beater.
quirlen *v.t.* to whisk.
quirlig *a.* lively.
quitt *adv.* quits, even; rid, free.
quittieren *v.t.* to receipt (a bill); to quit.
Quittung *f.* **(-, -en)** receipt.
Quittungsmarke *f.*, **Quittungsstempel** *m.* receipt stamp.
Quote *f.* **(-, -n)** quota, share.
Quotient *m.* **(-en, -en)** (*ar.*) quotient.

R

R, r *n.* the letter R or r.
r. *rechts,* right, r.
RA *Rechtsanwalt,* lawyer, attorney, att.
Rabatt *m.* **(-[e]s, 0)** abatement, discount.
Rabatte *m.* border (flowers).
Rabatz *m.* racket; din.
Rabauke *m.* (*fam.*) roughneck.
Rabbi, Rabbiner *m.* **(-s, -)** rabbi.
Rabe *m.* **(-n, -n)** raven.
Rabeneltern *pl.* uncaring parents.
rabenschwarz *a.* jet black.
rabiat *a.* violent.
Rache *f.* **(-, 0)** revenge, vengeance.
Rachen *m.* **(-s, -)** mouth (of an animal), jaws *pl.;* pharynx; (*fig.*) abyss.
rächen *v.t.* to avenge, to revenge; **~** *v.r.* to take vengeance.
Rächer *m.* **(-s, -)** avenger.
Rachitis *f.* **(-, 0)** rickets *pl.*
Rachsucht *f.* vindictiveness.
rachsüchtig *a.* vindictive.
Rad *n.* **(-[e]s, Räder)** wheel; bicycle; *fünftes ~ am Wagen sein,* to be superfluous.
Radachse *f.* axle.
Radar *n.* or *m.* radar; **~falle** *f.* speed trap; **~kontrolle** *f.* speed check.
Radau *m.* **(-[e]s, 0)** (*sl.*) noise, row.
Raddampfer *m.* paddle-steamer.
radebrechen *v.t.* to speak poorly (a language); *er radebrechte auf Deutsch, daß...,* he said in broken German that...
radeln *v.t.* to cycle, to bike.
Rädelsführer *m.* ringleader.
rädern *v.t.* to break on the wheel.
Räderwerk *n.* gearing.
radfahren *v.i.* to cycle, to wheel.
Radfahrer *m.* **(-s, -)** cyclist.
Radfahrweg *m.* cyclists' path.
radieren *v.t.* to erase; (*Kunst*) to etch.
Radiergummi *n.* eraser.
Radierung *f.* **(-, -en)** erasure; etching.
Radieschen *n.* **(-s, -)** radish.
radikal *a.* radical; drastic.
Radikale *m./f.* **(-n, -n)** radical.
Radikalismus *m.* radicalism.
Radikalität *f.* radicalness.
Radio *n.* **(-s, 0)** radio; **~apparat** *m.* radio.
radioaktiv *a.* radioactive; *~er Niederschlag, m.* fallout.
Radioaktivität *f.* radioactivity.
Radiosender *m.* radiostation.
Radiotherapie *f.* radiotherapeutics.
Radium *n.* radium.
Radius *m.* **(-, -dien)** radius.
Rad: ~kappe *f.* hubcap; **~lager** *n.* wheel bearing; **~rennen** *n.* cycle racing.
radschlagen *v.i.* to do a cartwheel.
Radweg *m.* cycle path/track.
raffen *v.t.* to snatch up; to gather.
Raffinerie *f.* refinery.
Raffinesse *f.* cleverness; subtleness.
raffinieren *v.t.* to refine.
raffiniert *p. & a.* refined; (*fig.*) ingenious, crafty, wily; exquisite.
Rage *f.* fury; rage.
ragen *v.i.* to project, to be prominent.
Ragout *m.* **(-s, -s)** stew, ragout.
Rahm *m.* **(-[e]s, 0)** cream.
Rahmen *m.* **(-s, -)** frame; *im ~ von,* within the framework of.
rahmen *v.t.* to frame.
Rahmkäse *m.* cream cheese.
Rakete *f.* **(-, -n)** rocket; missile.
Raketenwurfmaschine *f.* (*mil.*) rocket launcher.
rammen *v.t.* to ram, to drive in.
Rampe *f.* **(-, -n)** ramp, sloping drive.
Rampenlicht *n.* footlights *pl.; im ~ stehen,* to be in the limelight.
ramponieren *v.t.* to knock around, to batter.
Ramsch *m.* **(-es, -e)** trash; rubbish.
Ramschverkauf *m.* rummage sale.
Rand *m.* **(-es, Ränder)** edge; (*Hut*) brim; (*Buch*) margin; (Teller) rim; (*Wunde*) lip; (*fig.*) brink, verge; border.
Randale *f.* (*fam.*) riot.
randalieren *v.i.* to riot.
Randalierer *m.* **(-s, -)** hooligan, rioter.
Randbemerkung *f.* marginal note.
Randerscheinung *f.* peripheral phenomenon.
Randgebiet *n.* borderland; outskirts; (*fig.*) fringe area.
Randgruppe *f.* marginal group.
Randproblem *n.* side issue.
Randstreifen *m.* shoulder (street).
Rang *m.* **(-[e]s, Ränge)** rank, order; quality, rate; (*Theater*) circle, row, tier; *erster ~,* dress circle; *zweiter ~,* upper circle.
Range *m.* **(-n, -n),** *f.* **(-, -n)** naughty boy; romp; tomboy.
Rangfolge *f.* order of precedence.
Rangierbahnhof *m.* switchyard.
rangieren *v.i.* (*rail.*) to switch; **~** *v.i.* to rank.
Rangiergleis *n.* siding.
Rang: ~liste *f.* rankings; **~ordnung** *f.* (order of) precedence; pecking order; **~stufe** *f.* degree, order.
Ranke *f.* **(-, -n)** tendril, creeper.
Ränke *m.pl.* intrigues.
ranken *v.r.* to climb, to creep.
Ränkeschmied *m.* intriguer, trickster.
Ränzel *n.* **(-s, -), Ranzen** *m.* **(-s, -)** knapsack, satchel.
ranzig *a.* rancid.
Rappe *m.* **(-n, -n)** black horse.
Rappel *m.* (*fam.*) crazy mood.
Rapport *m.* **(-[e]s, -e)** report.
Raps *m.* **(-ses, 0)** rapeseed, colza.
rar *a.* rare; exquisite; scarce.
Rarität *f.* **(-, -en)** curio; rarity.
rasant *a.* fast; dynamic; dashing.
rasch *a.* speedy, swift; brisk, prompt.
rascheln *v.i.* to rustle.
Rasen *m.* **(-s, -)** turf, lawn.
rasen *v.i.* to rave, to rage; to rush.
rasend *a.* furious, frantic.
Rasenmäher *m.* lawn mower.
Rasenmähmaschine *f.* lawn mower.
Rasenplatz *m.* grass plot, lawn, green.
Rasensprenger *m.* sprinkler.
Rasenstück *n.* sod.

Raserei *f.* **(-, -en)** delirium, frenzy.
Rasierapparat *m.* **(-es, -e)** electric shaver.
rasieren *v.t.* to shave.
Rasier: ~klinge *f.* razor blade; **~messer** *n.* razor; **~seife** *f.* shaving soap; **~zeug** *n.* shaving things.
Raspel *f.* **(-, -n)** rasp; grater.
raspeln *v.t.* to grate.
Rasse *f.* **(-, -n)** breed, race; *von reiner ~*, thoroughbred.
Rassehund *m.* pedigree dog.
Rassel *f.* rattle.
rasseln *v.i.* to rattle.
Rassen... racial, *a.; **~krawall*** *m.* race riot; **~schranke** *f.* color bar; **~trennung** *f.* segregation; **~unruhen** *pl.* race riots.
Rassepferd *n.* thoroughbred.
rassig *a.* racy.
Rassismus *m.* **(-, 0)** racism.
Rassist *m.* **(-en, -en)**; **Rassistin** *f.* **(-, -nen)** racist.
rassistisch *a.* racist.
Rast *f.* (-, 0) rest; halt.
rasten *v.i.* to rest, to repose; to halt.
Raster *n.* **(-s, -)** grid; screen; framework.
Rasthaus *n.* service area (on a highway).
rastlos *a. & adv.* restless(ly).
Rastplatz *m.* rest area.
Raststätte *f.* service area.
Rasttag *m.* day of rest.
Rasur *f.* **(-, -en)** shave.
Rat *m.* **(-[e]s, Räte)** counsel, advice; consultation; council, board; (*Person*) councillor; *zu ~e ziehen*, to consult; *mit sich zu ~e gehen*, to consider; *um ~ fragen*, to ask advice; *mit ~ und Tat*, with advice and assistance.
Rate *f.* **(-, -n)** (*com.*) installment; (*Statistik*) rate; *in ~n, ratenweise*, by installments.
raten *v.t.st.* to guess, to divine; to counsel, to advise.
Ratenzahlung *f.* payment by installments.
Ratespiel *n.* guessing game.
Ratgeber *m.* adviser.
Rathaus *n.* town hall.
Ratifikation *f.*, **Ratifizierung** *f.* ratification.
ratifizieren *v.t.* to ratify.
Ration *f.* **(-, en)** ration, allowance.
rational *a.* rational.
rationalisieren *v.i.* to rationize.
rationell *a. & adv.* efficient(ly); economic(ally).
rationieren *v.t.* to ration; *nicht mehr rationiert sein*, to come off the ration; *rationiert werden*, to go on rations.
Rationierung *f.* **(-, -en)** rationing; *von der ~ befreien*, to de-ration.
ratlos *a.* perplexed, helpless, at a loss.
ratsam *a.* advisable, expedient.
Ratschlag *m.* advice, counsel.
ratschlagen *v.i.* to consult, to deliberate.
Ratschluß *m.* decree, resolution.
Rätsel *n.* **(-s, -)** riddle; enigma; mystery; problem.
rätselhaft *a.* enigmatic, mysterious.
Ratte *f.* **(-, -n)** rat.
Ratten: ~fänger *m.* rat catcher; **~gift** *m.* rat poison.
rattern *v.i.* to clatter; to rattle.
Raub *m.* **(-[e]s, 0)** robbery, piracy; prey.
rauben *v.t.* to rob; (*Kinder*) to kidnap.
Räuber *m.* **(-s, -)** robber.
Räuberbande *f.* gang of robbers.
Räuberei *f.* **(-, -en)** robbery.
räuberisch *a.* rapacious, predatory.
Raubfisch *m.* predatory fish.
Raubgier *f.* rapacity.
Raubmord *m.* murder with robbery.
Raubritter *m.* robber baron.
Raubtier *n.* beast of prey.
Raubüberfall *m.* armed robbery; hold-up.
Raubvogel *m.* bird of prey.
Raubzug *m.* raid.
Rauch *m.* **(-[e]s, 0)** smoke, fume.
rauchen *v.t. & i.* to smoke; **~ verboten,** no smoking!
Raucher *m.* **(-s, -)** smoker; *starker ~*, heavy smoker.
Räucheraal *m.* smoked eel.
Raucherabteil *n.* smoking compartment.
Räucherhering *m.* smoked herring.
räuchern *v.t.* to perfume; to cure, to smoke (dry); to fumigate.
Rauchfang *m.* chimney; flue.
rauchig *a.* smoky; husky (voice).
Rauch: ~tabak *m.* smoking tobacco; **~waren** *f.pl.* tobacco products *pl.*; furs *pl.*; **~zimmer** *n.* smoking room.
Räude *f.* **(-, 0)** mange, scab.
räudig *a.* scabbed, mangy.
Raufbold *m.* brawler, bully.
raufen *v.t.* to pluck; *~ v.r.* to scuffle, to fight.
Rauferei *f.* **(-, -en)** fight; brawl, scuffle.
rauh *a.* rough, rugged; boisterous; (*Wetter*) raw; (*im Halse*) hoarse; (*fig.*) harsh, rude.
Rauhhaardackel *m.* wire-haired dachshund.
Rauhreif *m.* **(-[e]s, 0)** hoar-frost.
Raum *m.* **(-[e]s, Räume)** room, space, place; (*Schiff*) hold; *leerer ~*, vacuum; **~ geben,** (*der Hoffnung*) to indulge in; (*dem Gedanken*) to give way to; (*der Bitte*) to grant.
räumen *v.t.* to clear away, to remove; (*Platz*) to evacuate; *aus dem Wege ~*, to put out of the way.
Raumfahrer *m.*, **Raumfahrerin** *f.* astronaut, cosmonaut.
Raumfahrt *f.* space travel; (*in compounds*) space....
Raumfahrzeug *n.* spacecraft.
Raum: ~gehalt *m.* tonnage; **~inhalt** *m.* volume, capacity; **~kunst** *f.* interior decoration.
räumlich *a.* relating to space.
Raumpfleger(in) *m.* (*f.*) cleaner.
Raumschiff *n.* spacecraft.
Raumstation *f.* space station.
Räumung *f.* **(-, -en)** clearing; removal; evacuation.
Räumungsausverkauf *m.* clearance sale.
raunen *v.t. & i.* to whisper.
Raupe *f.* **(-, -n)** caterpillar.
Raupenfahrzeuge *pl.* caterpillar (truck).
Rausch *m.* **(-es, Räusche)** drunkenness, intoxication; (*fig.*) frenzy (of love, etc.).
rauschen *v.i.* to rustle, to rust.
Rauschgift *n.* **(-[e]s, -e)** drug, narcotic; **~handel** *m.* drug traffic; **~händler** *m.*, **~händlerin** *f.* drug trafficker, dealer; **~sucht** *f.* drug addiction; **~süchtige** *m./f.* drug addict.
räuspern *v.r.* to clear one's throat, to hem and haw.
Rausschmeißer *m.* (*fam.*) bouncer.
Raute *f.* **(-, -n)** rhombus.
rautenförmig *a.* rhombic.
Razzia *f.* **(-, Razzien)** raid.
rd. *rund*, roughly.

Reagenzglas *n.* test tube.
reagieren *v.i.* to react.
reaktionär *a.* reactionary.
Reaktionär *m.* **(-[e]s, -e); Reaktionärin** *f.* **(-, -nen)** reactionary.
Reaktionsfähigkeit *f.* ability to react.
reaktionsschnell *a.* with quick reactions.
Reaktionszeit *f.* reaction time.
real *a.* real.
realisierbar *a.* realizable.
Realisierbarkeit *f.* practicability.
realisieren *v.t.* to realize; to turn into money.
Realismus *m.* realism.
Realist *m.;* **Realistin** *f.* realist.
realistisch *a.* realistic.
Realität *f.* reality.
Realschule *f.* non-classical high school.
Rebe *f.* **(-, -n)** vine.
Rebell *m.* **(-en, -en); Rebellin** *f.* **(-, -nen)** rebel, mutineer.
rebellieren *v.i.* to rebel, to mutiny.
Rebellion *f.* **(-, -en)** rebellion.
rebellisch *a.* rebellious.
Rebhuhn *n.* partridge.
Reblaus *f.* phylloxera.
Rebstock *m.* vine.
rechen *v.i.* to rake.
Rechen *m.* **(-s, -)** rake.
Rechen: ~art *f.* type of arithmetical operation; **~aufgabe** *f.* sum, mathematical problem; **~buch** *n.* arithmetic book; **~exempel** *n.* sum, arithmetical problem; **~fehler** *m.* miscalculation; **~kunst** *f.* arithmetic; **~maschine** *f.* calculator.
Rechenschaft *f.* **(-, 0)** account; *~ ablegen,* to give an account; *zur ~ ziehen,* to call to account.
Rechenschieber *m.* slide rule.
recherchieren *v.i. & t.* to investigate.
rechnen *v.t. & i.* to count, to reckon, to compute, to calculate; *auf einen ~,* to depend, to rely, to count on sb.; **~ zu,** to class with.
Rechner *m.* calculator; computer; *ein guter ~ sein,* to be good at arithmetic.
Rechnung *f.* **(-, -en)** reckoning, calculation, computation; (*Nota*) bill, account; *die ~ stimmt, trifft zu,* the account squares, is correct; *auf die ~ setzen,* to add to the bill; *in ~ stellen,* to carry to account; *auf ~ bestellen,* to order on account; *auf eigene, fremde ~,* on one's own account, for account of another; *einen Strich durch die ~ machen,* to thwart one's plans; *den Umständen ~ tragen,* to accommodate oneself to circumstances.
Rechnungs: ~abschluß *m.* balance of account; **~jahr** *n.* business year; **~prüfer** *m.* auditor; **~wesen** *n.* bookkeeping, accounts *pl.*
recht *a.* right, just; convenient, fitting; correct, proper; **~** *adv.* right, fairly; well; *ein ~er Winkel,* a right angle; **~e Seite** right-hand side; *zur ~en Zeit,* in time; **~ haben,** to be right; **rechts** *adv.* on the right hand.
Recht *n.* **(-[e]s, -e)** right; justice; title, claim; law, jurisprudence; *mit Fug und ~,* with good reason, in all conscience; *~ sprechen,* to administer justice; *die ~e studieren,* to study law, to read for the bar; *von ~s wegen,* by right, according to law.
Rechte *f.* **(-n, -n)** right hand.
Rechteck *n.* **(-s, -e)** rectangle.
rechteckig *a.* rectangular.
rechten *v.i.* to contest, to dispute.
rechtfertigen *v.i.* to justify, to vindicate.
Rechtfertigung *f.* **(-, -en)** justification.
rechtgläubig *a.* orthodox.
Rechtgläubigkeit *f.* **(-, 0)** orthodoxy.
Rechthaberei *f.* **(-, -en)** self-opinionatedness.
rechthaberisch *a.* self-opinionated, dogmatic, obstinate.
rechtlich *a.* legal, lawful.
rechtlos *a.* illegal; outlaw.
Rechtlosigkeit *f.* **(-, 0)** lack of rights.
rechtmäßig *a.* lawful, legitimate, rightful.
Rechtmäßigkeit *f.* **(-, 0)** legitimacy, legality.
rechts *adv.* on the right to the right; *~ um, kehrt!* right, face!
Rechtsanwalt *m.* lawyer, attorney; *als ~ praktizieren,* to practice law.
Rechtsanwältin *f.* lawyer, attorney.
Rechtsbeistand *m.* counsel, legal adviser.
Rechtsbeugung *f.* miscarriage of justice.
rechtschaffen *a.* righteous, honest.
Rechtschreibfehler *m.* spelling mistake.
Rechtschreibung *f.* spelling, orthography.
Rechtsextremismus *m.* right-wing extremism.
Rechtsextremist *m.;* **Rechtsextremistin** *f.* right-wing extremist.
Rechtsfall *m.* case (at law).
Rechtsfrage *f.* legal question/issue.
Rechtsgelehrter *m.* jurist.
Rechtsgrund *m.* legal argument.
Rechtgrundsatz *m.* legal principle.
rechtsgültig *a.* legal, valid.
Rechts: ~händer *m.*, **~händerin** *f.* right-hander; **~hilfe** *f.* legal aid; **~kraft** *f.* force of law.
rechtskräftig *a.* legal, valid.
Rechtslage *f.* legal situation.
Rechtslehrer *m.* professor of jurisprudence.
Rechtsmittel *n.* legal remedy, appeal.
Rechtspflege *f.* administration of justice.
Rechtsprechung *f.* administration of justice.
Rechtsradikalismus *m.* right-wing radicalism.
Rechtsruck *m.* shift to the right.
Rechtssache *f.* lawsuit, case.
Rechtsschutz *m.* legal protection.
Rechts: ~spruch *m.* legal decision; **~staat** *m.* constitutional state; **~staatlichkeit** *f.* rule of law; **~stellung** *f.* legal status; **~titel** *m.* (legal) title.
rechtswidrig *a.* contrary to law, illegal.
Rechtswissenschaft *f.* jurisprudence.
rechtwink[e]lig *a.* rectangular.
rechtzeitig *a.* well-timed; *adv.* in due time.
Reck *n.* **(-[e]s, -e)** horizontal bar; high bar.
Recke *m.* **(-n, -n)** hero, warrior.
recken *v.t.* to extend, to stretch, to rack; (*Hals*) to crane.
Redakteur *m.* **(-[e]s, -e); Redakteurin** *f.* **(-, -nen)** editor.
Redaktion *f.* **(-, -en)** editorship; editor's office; editorial staff; editing.
redaktionell *a.* editorial.
Rede *f.* **(-, -n)** speech; oration, address, *eine ~ halten,* to make a speech; *in die ~ fallen,* to interrupt; *zur ~ stellen,* to call to account; *~ stehen,* to give an account; *nicht der ~ wert,* not worth mentioning.
Rede: ~freiheit *f.* freedom of speech; **~gewandtheit** *f.* eloquence; **~kunst** *f.* rhetoric; oratory.
reden *v.t. & i.* to speak, to talk.
Redensart *f.* phrase; expression; saying; **Redensarten** *pl.* empty phrases.

Redewendung *f.* idiom; idiomatic expression.
redigieren *v.t.* to edit.
redlich *a.* honest, just, candid.
Redlichkeit *f.* honesty.
Redner *m.* **(-s, -)**; **Rednerin** *f.* **(-, -nen)** orator, speaker; lecturer.
Rednerbühne *f.* platform.
rednerisch *a.* oratorical, rhetorical.
Redoute *f.* **(-, -n)** masquerade.
redselig *a.* talkative.
Reduktion *f.* **(-, -en)** reduction.
reduzieren *v.t.* to reduce, to diminish.
Reeder *m.* **(-s, -)** shipowner.
Reederei *f.* **(-, -en)** shipping company.
reell *a.* honest, respectable, solid.
Reet *n.* **(-s, 0)** reeds.
reetgedeckt *a.* thatched.
Ref. *Referent,* referee.
Referat *n.* **(-s, -e)** paper; report; department.
Referendar *m.* **(-s, -e)**; **Referendarin** *f.* **(-, -nen)** candidate for the higher civil service.
Referenz *f.* **(-, -en)** reference.
referieren *v.t.* to report.
reffen *v.t.* to reef (the sails).
reflektieren *v.t. & i.* to reflect.
Reflex *m.* **(-es, -e)** reflex.
Reflexion *f.* **(-, -en)** reflection.
reflexiv *a.* reflexive.
Reflexivpronomen *n.* **(-s, -)** reflexive pronoun.
Reform *f.* **(-, -en)** reform.
Reformation *f.* reformation.
reformbedürftig *a.* in need of reform.
Reformhaus *n.* health food store.
reformieren *v.t.* to reform.
Refrain *m.* **(-s, -s)** refrain.
Regal *n.* **(-[e]s, -e)** shelf, shelves *pl.*
Regatta *f.* **(-, -tten)** boat race, regatta.
Reg.-Bez. *Regierungsbezirk,* administrative district.
rege *a.* stirring, brisk; active.
Regel *f.* **(-, -n)** rule, regulation; (*med.*) menses; *in der ~,* as a rule, generally.
regel: ~los *a.* irregular; **~mäßig** *a.* regular.
Regelmäßigkeit *f.* **(-, -en)** regularity.
regeln *v.t.* to regulate; to settle.
regelrecht *a.* regular, correct.
Regelung *f.* **(-, -en)** regulation, settlement.
regelwidrig *a.* contrary to rule.
regen *v.r.* to stir.
Regen *m.* **(-s, 0)** rain; (*fig.*) shower.
regenarm *a.* dry.
Regenbogen *m.* rainbow; **~farben** *f.pl.* prismatic colors *pl.*
Regenbogenhaut *f.* iris (eye).
Regendach *n.* eaves *pl.*
Regeneration *f.* regeneration; **~sfähigkeit** *f.* regenerative power.
regenerieren *v.i.* to regenerate.
Regenfälle *m.pl.* rain(fall).
Regenguß *m.* downpour.
Regenmantel *m.* raincoat.
Regenmesser *m.* rain gauge.
Regenschauer *m.* shower.
Regenschirm *m.* umbrella; **~ständer** *m.* umbrella stand.
Regent *m.* **(-en, -en)**; **Regentin** *f.* **(-, -nen)** regent.
Regentonne *f.* water butt.
Regentschaft *f.* **(-, 0)** regency.
Regenwetter *n.* rainy weather.
Regenwurm *m.* earthworm.
Regenzeit *f.* rainy season.
Regie *f.* **(-, -[e]n)** direction (performing arts); management.
regieren *v.i.* to rule, to reign; ~ *v.t.* to govern, to rule.
Regierung *f.* **(-, -en)** government; reign.
Regierungs: ~antritt *m.* accession; **~bezirk** *m.* administrative district; **~chef** *m.*, **~chefin** *f.* head of government; **~erklärung** *f.* government declaration; **~sprecher** *m.*, **~sprecherin** *f.* government spokesman/woman; **~umbildung** *f.* government reshuffle; **~wechsel** *m.* change of government; **~zeit** *f.* reign; term of office.
Regime *n.* **(-s, -)** regime.
Regimegegner *m.*; **Regimegegnerin** *f.* dissident.
Regiment *n.* **(-[e]s, -er)** regiment.
Region *f.* **(-, -en)** region.
regional *a.* regional.
Regisseur *m.* **(-s, -e)**; **Regisseurin** *f.* **(-, -nen)** director; producer.
Register *n.* **(-s, -)** register; index; (*Orgel*) stop.
registrieren *v.t.* to register.
Registrierung *f.* registration.
reglementieren *v.t.* to regulate.
Regler *m.* **(-s, -)** (*elek.*) regulator.
reglos *a.* motionless.
regnen *v.i.* to rain; *fein ~,* to drizzle.
regnerisch *a.* rainy.
Regreß *m.* **(-es, -e)** recourse; **~ nehmen,** to have recourse, to seek recovery.
regsam *a.* quick, agile, active.
regulär *a.* regular.
regulieren *v.t.* to regulate, to adjust; *die Uhr ~,* to set a watch.
Regung *f.* **(-, -en)** impulse.
regungslos *a.* motionless.
Reh *n.* **([e]s, -e)** roe deer.
rehabilitieren *v.t.* to rehabilitate.
Reh: ~bock *m.* roebuck; **~braten** *m.* venison; **~keule** *f.* haunch of venison.
Reibach *m.* **(-s, 0)** (*fam.*) *einen ~ machen,* to make a killing.
Reibeisen *n.* grater.
reiben *v.t.st.* to rub; to grate; to grind; *wund ~,* to gall, to chafe.
Reiberei *f.* **(-, -en)** provocation; friction.
Reibfläche *f.* striking surface.
Reibung *f.* **(-, -en)** friction.
Reibungsfläche *f.* (*fig.*) cause of friction.
reibungslos *a. & adv.* smooth(ly).
reich *a.* rich, opulent, wealthy; copious.
Reich *n.* **(-[e]s, -e)** empire, kingdom.
reichen *v.t.* to reach; to pass, to hand; ~ *v.i.* to reach, to extend (to); to suffice.
reichhaltig *a.* copious, comprehensive.
reichlich *a.* copious, plentiful.
Reichtum *m.* **(-s, -tümer)** riches, wealth; abundance.
Reichweite *f.* reach; range.
reif *a.* ripe; mature; *in reiferen Jahren,* advanced in years; *~ zu, ~ für,* ripe for.
Reif *m.* **([e]s, 0)** frost.
Reife *f.* **(-, 0)** maturity, ripeness.
reifen *v.t.* to mature; ~ *v.i.* to ripen, to grow ripe.
Reifen *m.* **(-s, -)** hoop, ring; tire.
Reifenpanne *f.* flat tire.
Reifeprüfung *f.* school certificate examination (*Gymnasium*).
Reifezeugnis *n.* school certificate (*Abitur*).

Reifglätte *f.* slippery frost on the road.
reiflich *a.* careful, mature; ~ *adv.* maturely, thoroughly.
Reigen *m.* **(-s, -)** round dance.
Reihe *f.* **(-, -n)** row, line; rank, range; series; turn; *in Reih und Glied,* with closed ranks; *er ist an der ~, er kommt an die ~, die ~ ist an ihm,* it is his turn; *nach der ~,* by turns.
reihen *v.t.* to range, to rank; to string.
Reihen *m.* **(-s, -)** round dance.
Reihenfolge *f.* succession, sequence, order.
Reihengeschäft *n.* chain store.
Reihenschaltung *f.* (*elek.*) series connection.
reihenweise *adv.* in rows; by files.
Reiher n. **(-s, -)** heron.
reihum *adv.* by turns.
Reim *m.* **(-[e]s, -e)** rhyme.
reimen *v.t.* to rhyme; ~ *v.r.* (*fig.*) to rhyme.
reimlos *a.* blank, unrhymed.
rein *a.* clean, pure; clear; *der ~e Zufall,* pure coincidence; *ins ~e schreiben,* to make a fair copy; *ins ~e bringen,* to settle, to arrange.
Reinertrag *m.* net proceeds *pl.*
Reinfall *m.* (*sl.*) washout; flop.
Reingewinn *m.* net profit.
Reinheit *f.* **(-, 0)** cleanness, purity.
reinigen *v.t.* to clean, to purify.
Reinigung *f.* dry cleaning; dry cleaners.
reinlich *a.* cleanly, neat; ~ *adv.* cleanly.
Reinlichkeit *f.* **(-, 0)** cleanliness.
Reinschrift *f.* fair copy.
reinweg *adv.* clean, flatly.
Reis *n.* **(-es, -er)** scion; sprig.
Reis *m.* **(-es, 0)** rice.
Reise *f.* **(-, -n)** trip, journey, tour; (*See*) voyage; travels *pl.; eine ~ antreten,* to go on a trip; *auf ~n sein,* to be traveling.
Reise: ~agent *m.* tourist agent; **~agentur** *f.* travel agency; **~andenken** *n.* souvenir; **~artikel** *pl.* travel goods; **~büro** *n.* travel agency.
reisefertig *a.* ready to start.
Reise: ~führer *m.* guide(-book); **~gepäck** *n.* baggage; **~gruppe** *f.* tourist party; **~handbuch** *n.* guide (-book); **~leiter** *m.*, **~leiterin** *f.* courier.
reisen *v.i.* (*h*) to travel, to journey; (*s*) to go (to).
Reisende *m./f.* **(-n, -n)** traveler.
Reise: ~omnibus *m.* coach; **~pass** *m.* passport; **~route** *f.* itinerary; **~scheck** *m.* traveler's check; **~tasche** *f.* traveling bag; **~veranstalter** *m.* tour operator; **~zeit** *f.* holiday season; **~ziel** *n.* destination; **~zuschuß** *m.* travel allowance.
Reisfeld *n.* paddy field.
Reisig *n.* **(-s, 0)** brushwood.
Reißaus nehmen *v.i.* (*fam.*) to take to one's heels.
Reißbrett *n.* drawing board.
reißen *v.t.st.* to tear, to rend, to pull; ~ *v.st.* to burst; to split; *entzwei ~,* to tear to pieces; *Witze ~,* to crack jokes; *an sich ~,* to take hold of; *sich um einen oder etwas ~,* to scramble for, to fight for; *das reißt in den Geldbeutel,* that runs into money; *mir reißt die Geduld,* I am losing patience; *wenn alle Stränge ~,* if worst comes to worst.
Reißen *n.* **(-s, 0)** rheumatism, ache.
reißend *a.* rapid; rapacious (animal).
Reißer *m.* **(-s, -)** (*Buch*) bestseller.
reißerisch *a.* sensational; lurid.
Reißfeder *f.* drawing pen.
Reißnagel *m.* drawing pin, thumbtack.
Reißverschluß *m.* zipper.
Reißzahn *m.* fang, canine tooth.
Reißzeug *n.* case of mathematical instruments.
Reißzwecke *f.* drawing pin; thumbtack.
Reitbahn *f.* riding arena, manège.
reiten *v.t. & i.st.* (*s & h*) to ride, to go on horseback.
Reiter *m.* **(-s, -)** rider, horseman.
Reiterei *f.* **(-, -en)** cavalry.
Reiterin *f.* **(-, -nen)** horsewoman.
Reit: ~gerte, ~peitsche *f.* riding whip; **~hose** *f.* riding breeches; **~kleid** *n.* riding habit; **~knecht** *m.* groom; **~kunst** *f.* horsemanship; **~pferd** *n.* saddle horse; **~schule** *f.* riding school; **~stiefel** *m.pl.* boots; **~turnier** *n.* riding event; **~weg** *m.* bridlepath; **~zeug** *n.* riding equipment.
Reiz *m.* **(-es, -e)** charm, attraction; incentive, stimulus; irritation.
reizbar *a.* sensitive; irritable.
Reizbarkeit *f.* irritability.
reizen *v.t.* to stimulate; to charm; to irritate, to annoy.
reizend *a.* charming.
Reizhusten *m.* dry cough.
reizlos *a.* unattractive.
Reizmittel *n.* incentive; (*med.*) stimulant.
Reizung *f.* irritability.
reizvoll *a.* attractive.
Reizwort *n.* emotive word.
rekapitulieren *v.t.* to recapitulate.
rekeln *v.r.* to lounge around.
Reklamation *f.* **(-, -en)** complaint.
Reklame *f.* **(-, -n)** advertisement; publicity; ~ **machen,** to advertise; **~wirkung** *f.* appeal.
reklamieren *v.t.* to claim; ~ *v.i.* to protest.
rekonstruieren *v.t.* to reconstruct.
Rekonstruktion *f.* reconstruction.
Rekonvaleszent *m.* **(-en, -en); Rekonvaleszentin** *f.* convalescent.
Rekord *m.* **(-[e]s, -e)** record.
Rekrut *m.* **(-en, -en)** recruit.
rekrutieren *v.t.* to recruit.
Rektor *m.* **(-s, -en); Rektorin** *f.* rector; head (-master or -mistress); principal; president (of a college).
Rektorat *n.* **(-[e]s, -e)** rectorship.
Rel. *Religion,* religion, rel.
Relais *n.* relay.
relativ *a.* relative.
relativieren *v.t.* to relativize.
Relativität *f.* **(-, -en)** relativity.
Relativitätstheorie *f.* theory of relativity.
Relativpronomen *n.* relative pronoun.
Relativsatz *m.* relative clause.
Relief *n.* **(-s, -s)** relief.
Religion *f.* **(-, -en)** religion.
Religions: ~freiheit *f.* freedom of worship; **~gemeinschaft** *f.* religious community; confession; **~zugehörigkeit** *f.* religion, religious confession.
religiös *a.* religious.
Relikt *n.* **(-[e]s, -e)** relic; (*biol.*) relict.
Reling *f.* **(-, -s/e)** rail.
Reliquie *f.* **(-, -n)** (*rel.*) relic.
Remis *n.* **(-, -)** draw (chess).
rempeln *v.t.* (*fam.*) to push; to jostle.
Renaissance *f.* **(-, -n)** Renaissance; (*fig.*) revival.
Renegat *m.* **(-en, -en)** renegade.
renitent *a.* refractory.
Rennbahn *f.* race course; racetrack.
rennen *v.i.ir.* (*s*) to run hard; to race.

Rennen *n.* **(-s, -)** race; run; heat.
Renner *m.* **(-s, -)** (*fam.*) big seller.
Rennpferd *n.* racehorse.
Rennplatz *m.* race course.
Rennsport *m.* racing, the turf.
Rennstall *m.* racing stable.
Renommee *n.* **(-s, -s)** reputation.
renommieren *v.i.* to brag, to show off.
renommiert *a.* well-known, renowned.
renovieren *v.t.* to renovate.
Renovierung *f.* renovation.
rentabel *a.* profitable, economic.
Rentabilität *f.* **(-, 0)** profitableness.
Rente *f.* **(-, -n)** annuity; pension.
Rentier *n.* **(-s, -e)** reindeer.
rentieren *v.r.* to pay.
Rentner *n.* **(-s, -); Rentnerin** *f.* **(-, -nen)** senior citizen.
Rep. *Republik,* Republic, Rep.
reparabel *a.* repairable.
Reparatur *f.* **(-, -en)** repair; **~werkstatt** *f.* repair shop.
reparieren *v.t.* to repair.
Repertoire *n.* **(-s, -s)** (*theat.*) stock, repertoire, repertory.
repetieren *v.t.* to repeat.
Replik *f.* **(-, -en)** replica; reply.
Report *m.* **(-s, -e)** report.
Reporter *m.; **Reporterin*** *f.* reporter.
Repräsentant *m.* **(-en, -en); Repräsentantin** *f.* **(-, -nen)** representative.
Repräsentantenhaus *f.* House of Representatives.
Repräsentativumfrage *f.* representative survey.
repräsentieren *v.t.* to represent.
Repressalien *pl.* reprisals *pl.*
repressiv *a.* repressive.
Reproduktion *f.* reproduction.
reproduzieren *v.t.* to reproduce.
Reptil *n.* **(-s, -ien)** reptile.
Republik *f.* **(-, -en)** republic.
Republikaner *m.* **(-s, -); Republikanerin** *f.* **(-, -nen)** republican.
republikanisch *a.* republican.
requirieren *v.t.* (*mil.*) to requisition.
Requisit *n.* **(-s, -en)** prop; property.
Reservat *n.* **(-s, -e)** reservation; reserve.
Reserve *f.* **(-, -n)** reserve.
Reserve: ~bank *f.* substitutes' bench; **~rad** *n.* spare wheel; **~reifen** *m.* spare tire; **~tank** *m.* reserve tank.
reservieren *v.t.* to reserve.
Reservist *m.* **(-en, -en)** reservist.
Residenz *f.* **(-, -en)** (monarch's) residence.
residieren *v.i.* to reside.
resignieren *v.i.* to give up.
resistent *a.* resistant.
resolut *a.* resolute.
Resolution *f.* **(-, -en)** resolution.
Resonanzboden *m.* sounding board.
resozialisieren *v.t.* to reintegrate into society.
Resozialisierung *f.* reintegration into society.
resp. *respektive,* respectively.
Respekt *m.* **(-[e]s, 0)** respect, regard.
respektabel *a.* respectable.
respektieren *v.t.* to respect, to honour.
respektlos *a.* without respect.
Respektlosigkeit *f.* **(-, -en)** disrespect.
respektvoll *a.* respectful.
Ressentiment *n.* **(-s, -s)** antipathy.
Ressort *n.* **(-s, -s)** department.
Rest *m.* **(-[e]s, -e)** rest, residue, remainder; remnant; leftovers.
Restaurant *n.* restaurant; ~ *mit Selbstbedienung* cafeteria.
Restaurateur *m.* **(-[e]s, -e)** innkeeper.
Restauration *f.* **(-, -en)** restoration; restaurant.
restaurieren *v.t.* to restore, to renovate (a building, etc.).
Restbestand *m.* remainder; residue.
Restbestand *m.* remaining stock.
Restbetrag *m.*, **Restsumme** *f.* balance.
restlich *a.* remaining.
restlos *a. & adv.* complete(ly).
Resultat *n.* **(-[e]s, -e)** result; (*Rechnung*) answer.
resultieren *v.i.* to result.
Resümee *n.* **(-s, -s)** summary.
resümieren *v.t.* to summarize.
Retorte *f.* **(-, -n)** retort, alembic.
retour *adv.* back.
Retrospektive *f.* **(-, -n)** retrospective (view).
retten *v.t.* to save, to rescue, to preserve; ~ *v.r* to save oneself.
Retter *m.* **(-s, -); Retterin** *f.* **(-, -nen)** rescuer; savior.
Rettich *m.* **(-[e]s, -e)** radish.
Rettung *f.* **(-, -en)** rescue; salvation.
Rettungs: ~boot *n.* lifeboat; **~dienst** *m.* ambulance service; rescue service; **~gürtel** *m.* life belt
rettungslos *adv.* hopeless.
Rettungs: ~ring *m.* life belt; **~schwimmer** *m.* **~schwimmerin** *f.* life saver; life guard; **~wagen** *m.* ambulance.
retuschieren *v.t.* to retouch.
Reue *f.* **(-, 0)** remorse; repentance.
reuelos *a.* impenitent; unrepentant.
reuen *v.t.imp. es reut mich,* I regret it.
reuig, reumütig *a.* repentant.
reuvoll *a.* repentant.
Revanche *f.* **(-, -n)** revenge; (*sp.*) return match fight.
revanchieren *v.r.* to return (a service, etc.); to take one's revenge.
Reverenz *f.* **(-, -en)** curtsy, bow.
revidieren *v.t.* to revise; to check.
Revier *n.* **(-[e]s, -e)** (hunting-)district; quarter district; beat; (*mil.*) sick bay, infirmary.
Revision *f.* **(-, -en)** revision; inspection; (*jur.*) review.
Revolte *f.* **(-, -n)** revolt.
revoltieren *v.i.* to revolt.
Revolution *f.* **(-, -en)** revolution.
revolutionär *a.* revolutionary.
Revolutionär *m.* **(-[e]s, -e); Revolutionärin** *f.* **(-, -nen)** revolutionist.
revolutionieren *v.t.* to revolutionize.
Revolver *m.* **(-s, -)** revolver.
Revue *f.* **(-, -n)** review; revue.
Rezensent *m.* **(-en, -en)** reviewer, critic.
rezensieren *v.t.* to review.
Rezension *f.* **(-, -en)** review.
Rezept *n.* **(-es, -e)** prescription; recipe.
rezeptfrei *a.* obtainable without a prescription.
Rezeption *f.* **(-, -en)** reception.
rezeptpflichtig *a.* obtainable only on prescription.
Rezession *f.* **(-, -en)** recession.
Rezitativ *n.* **(-s, -e)** recitative.
rezitieren *v.t.* to recite.
R-Gespräch *n.* collect call.

Rh. *Rhein,* the Rhine.
Rhabarber *m.* **(-s, 0)** rhubarb.
Rhapsodie *f.* **(-, -n)** rhapsody.
Rhein *m.* **(-s, 0)** Rhine.
rheinisch *a.* Rhenish.
Rheinland-Pfalz *n.* Rhineland-Palatinate.
Rhesusfaktor *m.* rhesus factor, Rh factor.
Rhetorik *f.* **(-, 0)** rhetoric.
rhetorisch *a.* rhetorical.
Rheuma *n.* **(-s, 0)** (*fam.*) rheumatism.
rheumatisch *a.* rheumatic.
Rheumatismus *m.* **(-, 0)** rheumatism.
Rhinozeros *n.* **(-ses, -se)** rhinoceros.
rhombisch *a.* rhombic.
rhythmisch *a.* rhythmical.
Rhythmus *m.* **(-, -men)** rhythm.
richten *v.t.* to direct; to judge; *sich* ~ *nach,* to be determined by; *eine Bitte an jn.* ~, to make a request of sb.; *zu Grunde* ~, to ruin, to destroy.
Richter *m.* **(-, -); Richterin** *f.* **(-, -nen)** judge.
richterlich *a.* judicial.
Richterspruch *m.* sentence.
Richtfest *n.* housewarming.
Richtgeschwindigkeit *f.* recommended speed.
richtig *a. & adv.* right(ly), exact(ly); correct(ly); *die Uhr geht nicht* ~, the watch does not go right.
Richtige *m./f./n.* the right one.
Richtigkeit *f.* **(-, 0)** accuracy; correctness.
richtigstellen *v.t.* to rectify.
Richtlinie *f.* guideline, directive.
Richtschnur *f.* guiding principle.
Richtung *f.* **(-, -en)** direction.
richtungweisend *a.* trendsetting.
riechen *v.t. & i.st.* to smell; to scent; ~ *nach,* to smell of.
Riegel *m.* **(-s, -)** bar, bolt.
Riemen *m.* **(-s, -)** strap, belt, thong; (*nav.*) oar.
Riese *m.* **(-n, -n)** giant.
Rieselfeld *n.* field irrigated with sewage.
rieseln *v.i.* to trickle; to fall slightly.
riesengroß, riesenhaft, riesig *a.* gigantic.
Riesen: ~rad *n.* Ferris wheel; **~schlange** *f.* boa constrictor; **~schritt** *m.* giant stride.
Riff *n.* **(-[e]s, -e)** reef, ridge.
rigoros *a.* rigorous.
Rille *f.* **(-, -n)** small groove.
Rind *n.* **(-[e]s, -er)** cow, cattle; beef; bovine.
Rinde *f.* **(-, -n)** bark, rind; (*des Brotes*) crust.
Rinder: ~braten *m.* roast beef; **~pest, ~seuche** *f.* cattle plague.
Rindfleisch *n.* beef.
Rindvieh *n.* cattle; (*sl.*) blockhead.
Ring *m.* **(-[e]s, -e)** ring; circle; link.
Ringelblume *f.* marigold.
Ringellocke *f.* ringlet.
ringeln *v.t. & v.r.* to curl.
Ringelnatter *f.* grass snake.
ringen *v.t.st.* to wring, to wrest; to struggle, to wrestle; to strive (after).
Ringer *m.* **(-s, -)** wrestler.
ringförmig *a.* circular; ring-shaped.
Ringkampf *m.* wrestling match.
rings *adv.* around.
ringsum(her) *adv.* all around.
Rinne *f.* **(-, -n)** groove, channel; gutter.
rinnen *v.i.* (*s, h*) to run; to leak.
Rinnsal *n.* **(-[e]s, -e), Rinnsel** *n.* **(-s, -)** rivulet.
Rinnstein *m.* gutter.
Rippe *f.* **(-, -n)** rib; (*arch.*) groin.
Rippen: ~fell *n.* pleura; **~fellentzündung** *f.* pleurisy.
Risiko *n.* **(-s, -s)** risk.
riskant *a.* hazardous, risky.
riskieren *v.t.* to risk.
Riß *m.* **(Risses, Risse)** crevice, chink, cleft; rent, tear; breach, schism.
rissig *a.* cracked; chapped.
Rist *m.* **(-es, -e)** instep; (*Hand*) wrist; (*eines Pferdes*) withers *pl.*
Ritt *m.* **(-[e]s, -)** ride.
Ritter *m.* **(-s, -)** knight, cavalier.
Rittergut *n.* estate, manor; **~sbesitzer** *m.* landed gentleman.
ritterlich *a.* chivalrous, knightly.
Ritterschlag *m.* knightly accolade.
Rittersporn *m.* larkspur.
rittlings *adv.* astride, astraddle.
Rittmeister *m.* cavalry captain.
rituell *a.* ceremonial.
Ritus *m.* **(-, Riten)** rite.
Ritz *m.* **(-es, -e)** scratch.
Ritze *f.* **(-, -n)** chink.
ritzen *v.t.* to scratch.
Rivale *m.* **(-n, -n); Rivalin** *f.* **(-, -nen)** rival.
rivalisieren *v.i.* to rival.
Rivalität *f.* **(-, -en)** rivalry.
Rizinusöl *n.* castor oil.
rk, r.-k. *römisch-katholisch,* Roman Catholic, RC.
Robbe *f.* **(-, -n)** seal.
robben *v.i.* to crawl.
Robe *f.* **(-, -n)** gown.
Roboter *m.* **(-s, -)** robot.
röcheln *v.i.* to rattle; to groan.
Rochen *m.* ray.
Rock *m.* **(-[e]s, Röcke)** coat; petticoat; skirt; rock (music).
Rodel: ~bahn *f.* toboganning course; **~schlitten** *m.* toboggan; (*mit Steuerung*) bobsled; luge.
rodeln *v.i.* to toboggan.
roden *v.t.* to root out; to clear (for cultivation).
Rodung *f.* **(-, -en)** clearing, cleared land.
Rogen *m.* **(-s, -)** roe, spawn.
Roggen *m.* **(-s, 0)** rye.
roh *a.* raw, crude, rude.
Roheit *f.* roughness; brutality.
Roh: ~fassung *f.* rough draft; **~gewinn** *m.* gross profit; **~gummi** *m.* crude rubber; **~kost** *f.* raw fruit and vegetables; **~material** *n.* raw material; **~öl** *n.* crude oil.
Rohr *n.* **(-[e]s, -e)** reed, cane; pipe; tube; barrel.
Rohrbruch *m.* burst pipe.
Röhre *f.* **(-, -n)** tube, pipe; funnel; conduit; (*radio*) tube.
röhrenförmig *a.* tubular.
Röhrenleitung *f.* conduit pipes *pl.*
Röhricht *n.* **(-[e]s, -e)** reed bank.
Rohrleitung *f.* pipeline.
Rohrpost *f.* pneumatic post.
Rohrstuhl *m.* cane-bottomed chair.
Rohrzucker *m.* cane sugar.
Roh: ~seide *f.* raw silk; **~stoff** *m.* raw material.
Rokoko *n.* **(-(s), 0)** rococo (period).
Rolladen *m.* **(-s, -)** roller shutters.
Rollbahn *f.* **(-, -n)** runway.
Rolle *f.* **(-, -n)** reel; roll, roller; register; (*theat. und fig.*) role; part; *Geld spielt keine* ~, money is no object.
rollen *v.t. & i.* to roll, to rumble.

Rollenbesetzung *f.* cast.
Rollenlager *n.* (*mech.*) roller bearing.
Rollenspiel *n.* role-playing.
Rollentausch *m.* reversal of roles.
Rollenverteilung *f.* casting.
Rollfeld *n.* landing field.
Rollholz *n.* rolling pin.
Rollkragen *m.* turtleneck.
Rollschuh *m.* rollerskate.
Rollstuhl *m.* wheelchair.
Rolltreppe *f.* escalator.
röm. *römisch,* Roman, Rom.
Roman *m.* **(-[e]s, -e)** novel; romance.
Romanfigur *f.* **(-, -en)** character from a novel.
Romanik *f.* **(-, 0)** Romanesque (period).
romanisch *a.* Romani; (*lang. and lit.*) Romance; Romanesque.
Romanistik *f.* Romance studies; Romance languages and literature.
Romanschreiber *m.* novelist.
Romantik *f.* romanticism; Romanticism.
romantisch *a.* romantic.
Romanze *f.* **(-, -n)** romance.
Römer *m.* **(-s, -); Römerin** *f.* **(-, -nen)** Roman.
römisch *a.* Roman.
römische Zahl *f.* Roman numeral.
römisch-katholisch *a.* Roman Catholic.
Rommé *n.* rummy.
Röntgen: ~bild *n.* radiograph; **~röhre** *f.* X-ray tube; **~strahlen** *pl.* X-rays *pl.*
rosa *a.* pink.
Rose *f.* **(-, -n)** rose.
Rosen: ~beet *n.* rose bed; **~kohl** *m.* Brussels sprouts *pl.*; **~kranz** *m.* rosary; **~montag** *m.* Monday before Lent.
rosenfarben *a.* rose-colored, rosy.
rosenrot *a.* rose-colored.
Rosenstock *m.* rose tree.
Rosette *f.* **(-, -n)** rose window; rosette.
rosig *a.* rosy, roseate.
Rosine *f.* **(-, -n)** raisin; (*kleine*) currant.
Rosmarin *n.* rosemary.
Ross *n.* **(-es, e)** horse.
Ross: ~haar *n.* horsehair; **~kastanie** *f.* horse-chestnut; **~kur** *f.* drastic cure.
Rost *m.* **(-[e]s, -e)** rust; gridiron, grate.
Rostbraten *m.* roast meat, roast beef.
rosten *v.i.* to rust, to get rusty.
rösten *v.t.* to roast, to grill; (*Brot*) to toast.
Rostfleck *m.* rust stain.
rostfrei *a.* (*Stahl*) stainless.
rostig *a.* rusty.
rot *a.* red.
Rot *n.* **(-es, 0)** red color.
rotbäckig *a.* red-cheeked.
rotbraun *a.* reddish-brown, ruddy; bay.
Rot: ~buche *f.* copper beech; **~dorn** *m.* pink hawthorn.
Röte *f.* **(-, 0)** redness; blush.
Röteln *pl.* German measles *pl.*
röten *v.t.* to redden.
rote Rübe *f.* red beet.
Rotes Kreuz *n.* Red Cross.
Rotfuchs *m.* sorrel *or* chestnut; red fox.
rotgelb *a.* orange-colored, flame-colored.
rotglühend *a.* red-hot.
Rotglut *f.* red-heat.
rothaarig *a.* red-haired, carroty.
Rot: ~haut *f.* redskin; **~hirsch** *m.* red deer.
rotieren *v.i.* to rotate; to get into a flap.
Rotkäppchen *n.* Little Red Riding Hood.
Rotkehlchen *n.* robin red-breast.
Rotkohl *m.*, **Rotkraut** *n.* red cabbage.
rötlich *a.* reddish.
Rotstift *m.* red pencil.
Rotte *f.* **(-, -n)** band, gang; (*mil.*) troop.
Rotwild *n.* red deer.
Rotz *m.* **(-es, 0)** mucus; (*vulg.*) snot; (*der Pferde*) glanders *pl.*
rotzfrech *a.* insolent, snotty.
rotzig *a.* (*fam.*) snotty.
Rotznase *f.* snotty nose.
Roulade *f.* roulade; roll.
Rouleau *n.* **(-[s], -s)** (roller-)blind.
Route *f.* route.
Routine *f.* experience; expertise; routine.
routiniert *a.* experienced; smart.
Rowdy *m.* **(-s, -s)** hooligan.
rubbeln *v.i.* (*fam.*) to rub.
Rübe *f.* **(-, -n)** (*weisse*) turnip; (*gelbe*) carrot; (*rote*) red beet.
Rubel *m.* **(-s, -)** ruble.
Rübenzucker *m.* beet sugar.
rüber *adv.* (*fam.*) over.
Rubin *m.* **(-[e]s, -e)** ruby.
Rubrik *f.* **(-, -en)** category; column; rubric.
rubrizieren *v.t.* to distribute in columns.
ruchbar *a.* notorious, rumoured.
ruchlos *a.* profligate, reprobate.
Ruck *m.* **(-[e]s, -e)** jolt, jerk, start.
Rück: ~anschrift *f.* return address; **~antwort** *f.* reply; **~blick** *m.* retrospect.
ruckartig *a.* jerky; ~ *adv.* with a jerk.
rückblickend *a.* & *adv.* retrospective(ly).
rücken *v.t.* to move, to push; ~ *v.i.* *(s)* to move, to budge; *näher* ~, to draw near; *ins Feld* ~, to take the field.
Rücken *m.* **(-s, -)** back, ridge; (*mil.*) rear; *einem den ~ kehren,* to turn one's back on sb.
Rücken: ~deckung *f.* (*mil.*) rear cover; **~flosse** *f.* dorsal fin; **~lehne** *f.* back (of a chair); **~mark** *n.* spinal cord; **~schmerz** *m.* backache; **~schwimmen** *n.* back stroke; **~stück** *n.* sirloin; **~wind** *m.* tail wind; **~wirbel** *m.* vertebra.
Rückerstattung *f.* refund.
Rückfahrkarte *f.* return ticket.
Rückfahrt *f.* return.
Rückfall *m.* relapse.
rückfällig *a.* relapsing; revertible.
Rückfrage *f.* further inquiry.
Rückführung *f.* repatriation.
Rückgabe *f.* restitution, return.
Rückgang *m.* drop, decline.
rückgängig *a.* **~ machen** to annul, to cancel.
Rückgrat *n.* backbone, spine.
rückgratlos *a.* spineless.
Rückhalt *m.* reserve; support.
rückhaltlos *a.* & *adv.* unreserved(ly).
Rückkauf *m.* redemption, buying back.
Rückkehr, Rückkunft *f.* **(-, 0)** return.
Rücklage *f.* i **(-, -n)** savings.
Rücklauf *m.* o **(-s, -läufe)** rewinding; return flow.
rückläufig *a.* decreasing; declining.
rücklings *adv.* backwards; from behind.
Rückmarsch *m.* march back; return, retreat.
Rückporto *n.* return postage.
Rückreise *f.* return journey; *auf der* ~, homeward bound.
Rückruf *m.* return call.

Rucksack *m.* backpack, rucksack.
Rückschau *f.* review.
Rückschlag *m.* setback.
Rückschluß *m.* inference, conclusion.
Rückschreiben *n.* reply, letter.
Rückschritt *m.* step backward.
rückschrittlich *a.* reactionary.
Rückseite *f.* back, reverse.
Rücksicht *f.* **(-, -en)** regard, consideration, respect; *in ~ auf,* in consideration of, with regard to; *~ nehmen auf,* to take notice of; to make allowance for.
rücksichtslos *a.* inconsiderate, reckless.
Rücksichtslosigkeit *f.* **(-, -en)** lack of consideration; recklessness.
rücksichtsvoll *a.* considerate.
Rücksitz *m.* back seat.
Rückspiegel *m.* **(s, -)** rearview mirror.
Rückspiel *n.* **(-s, -e)** return match.
Rücksprache *f.* consultation; *~ nehmen mit,* to confer with.
Rückstand *m.* arrears *pl.*; residue; backlog.
rückständig *a.* overdue; in arrears; backward.
Rückständigkeit *f.* backwardness.
Rückstau *m.* **(-s, -s)** build-up; backup.
Rückstoß *m.* recoil; repulsion.
Rückstrahler *m.* reflector.
Rücktritt *m.* withdrawal, resignation.
Rücktrittbremse *f.* coaster brake.
Rücktrittsgesuch *n.* (letter of) resignation.
Rücktrittsrecht *n.* right to rescind.
Rückübersetzung *f.* retranslation.
Rückvergütung *f.* refund.
Rückversicherung *f.* reinsurance.
rückwärtig *a.* rear; **~es Gebiet** rear area.
rückwärts *adv.* backwards; reverse.
Rückwärtsgang *m.* reverse gear.
Rückweg *m.* way back, return.
ruckweise *a. & adv.* jerky; jerkily.
rückwirkend *a.* retroactive; *mit ~er Kraft,* with retroactive effect.
Rückwirkung *f.* reaction, repercussion.
Rückzahlung *f.* repayment.
Rückzug *m.* retreat.
rüde *a.* rude, coarse.
Rudel *n.* **(-s, -)** pack; herd.
Ruder *n.* **(-s, -)** oar; rudder; (*fig.*) helm.
Ruderboot *n.* rowing boat.
Ruderer *m.* **(-s, -)** rower, oarsman.
rudern *v.t. & i.* to row.
rudimentär *a.* rudimentary.
Ruf *m.* **(-[e]s, -e)** call; shout; vocation; report; reputation; (*com.*) credit, standing; *in gutem ~e stehen,* to have a good reputation.
rufen *v.i. & t.st.* to call; to cry, to shout; *um Hilfe ~,* to cry for help; *etwas ins Leben ~,* to start sth.; **~ lassen,** to send for, to summon.
Rüffel *m.* **(-s, -)** (*fam.*) tongue-lashing.
Rufmord *m.* **(-s, -e)** character assassination.
Rufname *m.* **(-ns, -n)** first name (by which one is called).
Rufnummer *f.* **(-, -n)** telephone number.
Rufweite *f. in ~,* within earshot.
Rufzeichen *n.* exclamation mark.
Rüge *f.* **(-, -n)** censure, blame, reprimand.
rügen *v.t.* to censure, to reprimand.
Ruhe *f.* **(-, 0)** silence, rest, repose; quiet, tranquility; *sich zur ~ setzen,* to retire from business (office, active life); **~ stiften,** to make peace; **~!** hush! be quiet!; *in ~ lassen,* to let alone.
ruhebedürftig *a.* in need of rest.
ruhelos *a.* restless.
ruhen *v.i.* to rest, to repose; *ein Verdacht ruht auf ihm,* he is under suspicion.
Ruhepause *f.* break.
Ruhestand *m.* retirement; *im ~,* retired; *in den ~ versetzen,* to retire, to put on the retired list.
Ruhestörung *f.* disturbance.
Ruhetag *m.* day off.
ruhig *a.* quiet; calm; silent.
Ruhm *m.* **(-[e]s, 0)** fame, glory, renown.
rühmen *v.t.* to praise, to extol; **~** *v.r.* to boast of, to glory (in).
rühmlich *a.* inglorious.
ruhmreich *a.* glorious; celebrated.
Ruhr *f.* **(-, 0)** dysentery.
Rührei *n.* scrambled *or* buttered eggs *pl.*
rühren *v.t. & i.* to stir; to beat (the drum, eggs); **~** *v.r.* to stir, to bestir oneself; *sich nicht vom Flecke ~,* not to budge; *rührt euch!* (*mil.*) stand at ease; *rührende Worte,* touching words; *ich bin ganz gerührt,* I am deeply affected.
rührend *a.* touching.
rührig *a.* active, stirring, bustling.
rührselig *a.* sentimental.
Rührung *f.* **(-, -en)** emotion.
Ruin *m.* **(-[e]s, 0)** ruin.
Ruine *f.* **(-, -n)** ruins *pl.*
ruinieren *v.t.* to ruin, to spoil.
rülpsen *v.i.* to belch, to burp.
Rum *m.* **(-s, -s)** rum.
Rumäne *m.*; **Rumänin** *f.*; **rumänisch** *a.* Romanian.
Rumänien *n.* **(-s, 0)** Romania.
Rummel *m.* **(-s, 0)** commotion; fair.
rumoren *v.i.* to make a noise or row.
Rumpelkammer *f.* junk room.
Rumpf *m.* **(-[e]s, Rümpfe)** trunk; torso; (*Schiffs ~*) hull; (*Flugzeug*) fuselage.
rümpfen *v.t. die Nase ~,* to turn up one's nose.
rund *a.* round; plain; **~e Summe** round sum.
Rundblick *m.* panorama.
Rundbogen *m.* Roman arch.
Rundbrief *m.* circular (letter).
Runde *f.* **(-, -n)** round.
Rund: ~erlaß *m.* circular (notice); **~fahrt** *f.* tour.
Rundfunk *m.* broadcasting; **~anstalt** *f.* radio corporation; **~gebühren** *pl.* radio license fees; **~gerät** *n.* radio set; **~sender** *m.* radio station; **~sendung** *f.* radio program; **~sprecher** *m.*, **~sprecherin** *f.* radio announcer; **~übertragung** *f.* radio broadcast.
Rundgang *m.* round.
rundheraus *adv.* straight out; bluntly.
rundherum *adv.* all around.
rundlich *a.* roundish; chubby.
Rundreise *f.* (circular) tour; **~karte** *n.* roundtrip ticket.
Rundschreiben *n.* circular.
Rundung *f.* curve; bulge.
rundweg *adv.* flatly, plainly.
Rundweg *m.* circular path/walk.
runter *adv.* (*fam.*) off; down.
Runzel *f.* **(-, -n)** wrinkle; (*um die Augen*) crow's feet *pl.*
runz(e)lig *a.* wrinkled.
runzeln *v.t.* to wrinkle; *die Stirn ~,* to knit one's brows.
Rüpel *m.* **(-s, -)** lout, boor.
Rüpelei *f.* **(-, -en)** insolence.

rüpelhaft *a.* loutish; unmannerly.
rupfen *v.t.* to pluck; (*fig.*) to fleece.
Rupie *f.* **(-, -n)** rupee.
ruppig *a.* gruff; shabby; rude.
Ruß *m.* **(-es, 0)** soot.
Russe *m.* **(-n, -n); Russin** *f.* **(-, -nen); russisch** *a.* Russian.
Rüssel *m.* **(-s, -)** snout, trunk, proboscis.
rußen *v.i.* to smoke; ~ *v.t.* to blacken.
rußig *a.* sooty.
Rußland *n.* **(-s, 0)** Russia.
rüsten *v.t.* to arm; to prepare; ~ *v.i.* to prepare for war.
rüstig *a.* vigorous, robust, strong.
rustikal *a.* country-style; rustic.
Rüstung *f.* **(-, -en)** armament; armour.
Rüstungs: ~ausgaben *pl.* defense expenditure; **~begrenzung** *f.* arms limitation; **~industrie** *f.* defense industry; **~kontrolle** *f.* arms control; **~stopp** *m.* arms freeze; **~wettlauf** *m.* arms race.
Rüstzeug *n.* equipment.
Rute *f.* **(-, -n)** rod, wand, twig, switch.
Rutsch *m.* **(-es, -e)** slide, landslip.
Rutschbahn *f.* slide.
Rutsche *f.* slide; chute
rutschen *v.i.* to slide; to skid.
rutschig *a.* slippery.
rutschsicher *a.* nonslip; nonskid.
rütteln *v.t.* to shake, to jolt; to vibrate.

S

S, s *n.* the letter S or s.
S *Süd(en),* south, S; *Schilling,* shilling, s.
S. *Seite,* page, p.
s. *siehe,* see.
Sa. *Samstag,* Saturday, Sat.
Saal *m.* **(-[e]s, Säle)** hall, (large) room.
Saarland *n.* **(-s, 0)** Saarland.
Saat *f.* **(-, -en)** seed; standing corn; sowing.
Saatkorn *n.* seed-corn.
Sabbat *m.* **(-[e]s, -e)** Sabbath.
sabbern *v.i.* to slobber; to dribble.
Säbel *m.* **(-s, -)** sabre, sword.
Säbelrasseln *n.* sabre rattling.
Sabotage *f.* **(-, -n)** sabotage.
sabotieren *v.t.* to sabotage.
Sacharin *n.* **(-s, 0)** saccharine.
Sachbeschädigung *f.* property damage.
Sachbuch *n.* nonfiction book.
Sache *f.* **(-, -n)** thing, matter; affair, business; cause; (*Prozeß*) case; *es ist seine* ~, it is up to him; *das gehört nicht zur* ~, that is beside the question; *bei der* ~ *bleiben,* to stick to the point; *nicht bei der* ~, inattentive, absent-minded; *gemeinschaftliche* ~ *mit einem machen,* to make common cause with; **~nrecht** *n.* property law.
sachgemäß *a.* appropriate; relevant.
sachgerecht *a.* proper, correct.
Sach: ~kenner *m.*, **~kennerin** *f.* expert; **~kenntnis** *f.* knowledge of a subject, experience.
sachkundig *a.* expert.
Sachlage *f.* **(-, 0)** state of affairs.
Sachleistung *f.* payment in kind.
sachlich *a.* real, to the point; material (not formal); impartial, objective.
sächlich *a.* (*gram.*) neuter.
Sachlichkeit *f.* **(-, 0)** objectivity; functionalism.
Sachregister *n.* subject-index.
Sachschaden *m.* **(-s, -schäden)** material damage.
Sachse *m.;* **Sächsin** *f.;* **sächsisch** *a.* Saxon.
Sachspende *f.* **(-, -n)** donation in kind.
sacht *a.* & *adv.* soft(ly), gentle, gently.
Sachverhalt *m.* **(-[e]s, 0)** facts or bearings (of a case) *pl.*
sachverständig *a.* expert.
Sachverständige *m./f.* **(-n, -n)** expert.
Sachwalter *m.* **(-s, -)** advocate.
Sachwert *m.* real value.
Sachzwang *m.* **(-s, -zwänge)** (factual *or* material) constraints.
Sack *m.* **(-[e]s, Säcke)** bag, sack; *mit* ~ *und Pack,* bag and baggage.
Säckel *m.* **(-s, -)** (*fam. fig.*) purse.
sacken *v.i.* to sink, to slump; to plummet.
Sackgasse *f.* dead end.
Sackhüpfen *n.* sack race.
Sadismus *m.* **(-, 0)** sadism.
Sadist *m.;* **Sadistin** *f.* sadist.
sadistisch *a.* sadistic.
Sä[e]mann *m.* sower.
Sä[e]maschine *f.* sowing machine.
säen *v.t.* to sow.
Safran *m.* **(-s, 0)** saffron.
safrangelb *a.* saffron-colored.
Saft *m.* **(-[e]s, Säfte)** juice; (*der Bäume*) sap.
saftig *a.* juicy, sappy, succulent.
saftlos *a.* juiceless; (*fig.*) insipid, stale, dry.
Saftpresse *f.* squeezer; juice extractor.
Sage *f.* **(-, -n)** myth; saga; tale, legend; *die* ~ *geht,* it is rumored.
Säge *f.* **(-, -n)** saw.
Säge: ~blatt *n.* saw blade; **~bock** *m.* sawhorse; **~mehl** *n.* sawdust; **~mühle** *f.* saw-mill.
sagen *v.t.* to say, to tell; ~ *lassen,* to send word; *er läßt sich nichts* ~, he will not listen to reason; *das hat nichts zu* ~, that does not matter; *das will nicht viel* ~, there is not much in that; *so zu* ~, as it were; *Dank* ~, to return thanks.
sägen *v.i.* & *t.* to saw.
sagenhaft *a.* fabulous, legendary.
Sägespäne *m.pl.* wood shavings.
Sägewerk *n.* sawmill.
Sahne *f.* **(-, 0)** cream.
Saison *f.* **(-, -s)** season.
Saisonarbeit *f.* **(-, -en)** seasonal work.
saisonbedingt *a.* seasonal.
Saite *f.* **(-, -n)** string, chord.
Saiteninstrument *n.* stringed instrument.
Saitenspiel *n.* string music; lyre.
Sakko *m.* **(-s, -s)** jacket.
Sakrament *n.* **(-[e]s, -e)** sacrament.
Sakristan *m.* **(-[e]s, -e)** sacristan, sexton.
Sakristei *f.* **(-, -en)** vestry, sacristy.
säkularisieren *v.t.* to secularize.
Salamander *m.* **(-s, -)** salamander.
Salat *m.* **(-[e]s, -e)** salad; lettuce.
Salatsoße *f.* salad dressing.
salbadern *v.i.* to talk nonsense.
Salbe *f.* **(-, -n)** ointment.
Salbei *m.* **(-s, -e)** *f.* **(-, -en)** sage.

salben *v.t.* to anoint.
Salböl *n.* consecrated oil.
Salbung *f.* **(-, -en)** unction.
salbungsvoll *a.* unctuous.
Saldo *m.* **(-[e]s, -s & Saldi)** balance; *den ~ ziehen,* to strike a balance; *per ~ quittieren,* to receipt in full.
Saldobetrag *m.* (amount of) balance.
Saline *f.* **(-, -n)** salt-works *pl.*
Salizylsäure *f.* salicylic acid.
Salm *m.* **(-[e]s, -e)** salmon.
Salmiak *m.* **(-s, 0)** ammonium chloride.
Salmiakgeist *m.* ammonia.
Salon *m.* **(-s, -s)** drawing room; parlor.
salonfähig *a.* presentable; respectable.
salopp *a.* casual.
Salpeter *m.* **(-s, 0)** saltpeter.
salpetrig *a.* nitrous; *~e Säure, f.* nitric acid.
Salut *m.* **(-[e]s, -e)** salute.
Salve *f.* **(-, -n)** volley; salvo.
Salz *n.* **(-es, -e)** (*also fig.*) salt.
salzarm *a.* low in salt.
Salzbrühe *f.* pickle, brine.
salzen *v.t.* to salt.
Salzfaß *n.* saltshaker.
salzig *a.* salt(y), briny.
Salzkartoffeln *pl.* boiled potatoes.
salzlos *a.* saltfree.
Salzsäure *f.* hydrochloric acid.
Salzstreuer *m.* salt shaker.
Samen *m.* **(-ns, -n)** seed; sperm, semen.
Samen: ~bank *f.* sperm bank; **~erguß** *m.* ejaculation; **~faden** *m.* spermatozoon; **~leiter** *m.* vas deferens; **~spender** *m.* (sperm) donor; **~strang** *m.* spermatic cord.
Sämerei *f.* **(-, -en)** seeds (of plants) *pl.*
Sammelband *m.* anthology.
Sammelbecken *n.* reservoir; (*fig.*) gathering place.
Sammelbestellung *f.* joint order.
Sammelbüchse *f.* collecting box.
sammeln *v.t.* to gather, to collect; *~ v.r.* to assemble; (*fig.*) to collect oneself.
Sammelplatz *m.* meeting place.
Sammelpunkt *m.* rallying point.
Sammelsurium *n.* **(-[s], -surien)** omniumgatherum.
Sammet *m.* velvet.
Sammler *m.* **(-s, -); Sammlerin** *f.* **(-, -nen)** collector, gatherer.
Sammlung *f.* **(-, -en)** collection; composure.
Samstag *m.* Saturday.
samstags *adv.* on Saturdays.
samt *pr.* & *adv.* together with; *~ und sonders,* each and all.
Samt *m.* **(-s, -e)** velvet; velveteen.
samtartig *a.* velvety.
samtig *a.* velvety.
sämtlich *a.* all, entire, complete.
Sand *m.* **(-[e]s, 0)** sand; *einem ~ in die Augen streuen,* to throw dust in a person's eyes.
Sandale *f.* **(-, -n)** sandal.
Sandalette *f.* **(-, -n)** high-heeled sandals.
Sandbank *f.* sand bar, sands *pl.*
Sandburg *f.* sandcastle.
Sanddorn *m.* buckthorn.
sandig *a.* sandy.
Sandkasten *m.* sandbox.
Sandmännchen *n.* sandman.
Sandpapier *n.* sandpaper.
Sandsack *m.* sandbag.
Sandstein *m.* sandstone.
Sanduhr *f.* hourglass.
sanft *a.* soft, gentle, mild; meek.
Sänfte *f.* **(-, -n)** sedan chair, litter.
Sanftmut *f.* **(-,0)** meekness.
sanftmütig *a.* gentle, mild.
Sang *m.* **(-[e]s, Sänge)** song; *ohne ~ und Klang,* quietly.
Sänger *m.* **(-s, -); Sängerin** *f.* **(-, -nen)** singer.
Sanguiniker *m.* **(-s, -)** sanguine person.
sanguinisch *a.* sanguine.
sanieren *v.t.* to redevelop; to restore, to reorganize.
Sanitäter *m.* first-aid man; ambulance man.
Sanitäts: ~behörde *f.* Public Health Department; **~dienst** *m.* medical service; **~wache** *f.* ambulance station.
Sanktion *f.* **(-, -n)** sanction.
sanktionieren *v.t.* to sanction.
Saphir *m.* **(-s, -e)** sapphire.
Sardelle *f.* **(-, -n)** anchovy.
Sardine *f.* **(-, -n)** sardine.
Sarg *n.* **(-[e]s, Särge)** coffin.
Sarkasmus *m.* **(-, 0)** sarcasm.
sarkastisch *a.* sarcastic.
Sarkophag *m.* **(-s, -e)** sarcophagus.
Satan *m.* **(-s, -)** Satan.
satanisch *a.* satanic.
Satellit *m.* **(-en, -en)** satellite.
Satelliten: ~bild *n.*, **~foto** *n.* satellite picture; **~übertragung** *f.* (TV) satellite transmission.
Satin *m.* **(-s, -s)** satin; sateen.
Satire *f.* **(-, -n)** satire.
Satiriker *m.* **(-s, -); Satirikerin** *f.* **(-, -nen)** satirist.
satt *a.* satisfied, full; *etwas ~ haben,* to be sick of sth.; *es ~ bekommen,* to get sick of sth.
Sattel *m.* **(-s, Sättel)** saddle.
Satteldecke *f.* saddle cloth.
sattelfest *a.* (*fig.*) experienced.
satteln *v.t.* to saddle.
sättigen *v.t.* to satiate, to fill; (*chem.*) to saturate.
sättigend *a.* filling.
Sättigung *f.* **(-, -en)** (*chem.*) saturation.
Sattler *m.* **(-s, -)** saddler.
sattsam *adv.* sufficiently, enough.
Satz *m.* **(-es, Sätze)** leap, jump; *Boden~,* sediment, dregs *pl.*; (*gram.*) sentence, clause; (*mus.*) movement; (*log.*) proposition; (*Druck*) composition; (*gleichartige Dinge*) set; (*Verhältnis*) rate.
Satz: ~aussage *f.* predicate; **~ergänzung** *f.* complement; **~gefüge** *n.* complex sentence; **~gegenstand** *m.* subject; **~glied** *n.* component part (of a sentence); **~lehre** *f.* syntax; **~teil** *m.* part of a sentence.
Satzung *f.* **(-, -en)** statute, regulation.
satzungsgemäß *a.* statutory.
Satzzeichen *n.* **(-s, -)** punctuation mark.
Sau *f.* **(-, -en)** sow, hog; (*vulg.*) slut.
sauber *a.* clean, neat; fine, pretty.
sauberhalten *v.t.st.* to keep clean.
Sauberkeit *f.* **(-, 0)** cleanliness; neatness.
säuberlich *a.* & *adv.* neatly; properly.
saubermachen *v.t.* & *i.* to clean.
säubern *v.t.* to clean, to cleanse, to purge; (*mil.*) to mop up.
Säuberung *f.* **(-, -en)** cleaning; (*pol.*) purge.
Saubohne *f.* broad bean.
Sauce *f.* **(-, -n)** gravy; sauce.
Sauciere *f.* **(-, -n)** gravy boat.

Saudi *m.;* **Saudiaraber** *m.;* **Saudiaraberin** *f.* Saudi.
Saudi-Arabien *n.* **(-s, 0)** Saudi Arabia.
saudiarabisch *a.* Saudi Arabian.
saudumm *a.* (*fam.*) damned stupid.
sauer *a.* sour; acid; morose; ~ *werden,* to go sour.
Sauerampfer *m.* sorrel.
Sauerei *f.* **(-, -en)** mess, filth; obscenity, scandal.
Sauerkirsche *f.* **(-, -n)** sour cherry.
Sauerkraut *n.* pickled cabbage, sauerkraut.
säuerlich *a.* sour; acidulous.
Sauermilch *f.* curdled milk.
Sauerstoff *m.* oxygen; **~gerät** *n.* oxygen apparatus.
Sauerteig *m.* sourdough; leaven.
saufen *v.t. & i.st.* to drink to excess.
Säufer *m.* **(-s, -)**; **Säuferin** *f.* **(-, -nen)** alcoholic; boozer.
Sauferei *f.* **(-, -en)** drinking-bout, boozing.
Säuferwahnsinn *m.* delirium tremens.
Saufgelage *n.* drinking bout.
saugen *v.t. & i.st.* to suck; to vacuum.
säugen *v.t.* to suckle, to nurse.
Sauger *m.* **(-s, -)** sucker; teat; siphon.
Säuger *m.*, **Säugetier** *n.* mammal.
saugfähig *a.* absorbent.
Saugflasche *f.* feeding bottle.
Säugling *m.* **(-s, -e)** baby, infant.
Säuglings: ~alter *n.* infancy; **~nahrung** *f.* baby food; **~pflege** *f.* baby care; **~schwester** *f.* baby nurse; **~sterblichkeit** *f.* infant mortality.
Saugnapf *m.* **(-s, -näpfe)** sucker.
saukalt *a.* damned cold.
Säule *f.* **(-, -n)** pillar, column; (galvanic) pile.
Säulen: ~gang *m.* colonnade; **~halle** *f.* portico; **~schaft** *m.* shaft of a column.
Saum *m.* **(-[e]s, Säume)** border, edge, seam, hem.
Saumagen *m.* (*cul.*) stuffed pig's stomach.
saumäßig *a.* lousy; damned.
säumen *v.t.* to hem; ~ *v.i.* to delay, to tarry.
säumig *a.* tardy, late.
saumselig *a.* tardy, dilatory; negligent.
Säure *f.* **(-, -n)** (*chem.*) acid; tartness; sourness.
säurearm *a.* low in acid.
säurebeständig *a.* acid-proof.
Sauregurkenzeit *f.* silly season.
saurer Regen *m.* acid rain.
Saurier *m.* **(-s, -)** saurian.
Saus *m.* **(-ses, 0)** ~ **und Braus,** riot and revelry.
säuseln *v.i.* to rustle; to whisper; to murmur.
sausen *v.i.* to whistle, to whiz; to buzz; to rush; to roar.
Saustall *m.* pigsty; (*fig.*) mess.
Sauwetter *n.* (*fam.*) lousy weather.
sauwohl *a.* (*fam.*) *ich fühle mich* ~, I feel great.
Savanne *f.* **(-, -n)** savannah.
Saxophon *n.* **(-s, -e)** saxophone.
SB- *Selbstbedienungs-*, self-service...
S-Bahn *f.* city and suburban railroad.
Schabe *f.* **(-, -n)** cockroach.
Schabefleisch *n.* ground meat.
schaben *v.t.* to scrape; to rub.
Schabernack *m.* **(-[e]s, -e)** hoax; practical joke.
schäbig *a.* shabby; mean.
Schäbigkeit *f.* shabbiness; paltriness.
Schablone *f.* **(-, -n)** pattern; template; cliché.
Schach *n.* **(-s, 0)** chess; check!; ~ *bieten,* to give check; *einen im* ~ *halten,* to keep sb. in check.
Schach: ~brett *n.* chessboard; **~feld** *n.* square; **~figur** *f.* chessman.
Schacher *m.* **(-s, 0)** mean or unfair traffic, petty trade.
schachern *v.t.* to bargain; to haggle.
schachmatt *a.* checkmate; (*fig.*) exhausted.
Schacht *m.* **(-[e]s, Schächte)** pit, shaft.
Schachtel *f.* **(-, -n)** box; bandbox; (*fig. pej.*) *alte* ~, old bag.
schächten *v.t.* to slaughter according to Jewish law.
Schachzug *m.* move.
schade *pred. a., es ist* ~, it is a pity; *zu* ~ *für,* too good for.
Schädel *m.* **(-s, -)** skull.
Schädelbruch *m.* fracture of the skull.
schaden *v.i.* to hurt, to injure, to damage; *es schadet nichts,* it does not matter.
Schaden *m.* **(-s, Schäden)** damage, hurt; ~ *leiden* or *nehmen* or *zu* ~ *kommen,* to come to grief, to be hurt.
Schadenersatz *m.* indemnification; damages *pl.*, compensation.
Schadenfreude *f.* schadenfreude; malicious joy.
schadhaft *a.* damaged, defective, faulty.
schädigen *v.t.* to damage, to injure.
schädlich *a.* hurtful, detrimental.
Schädlichkeit *f.* harmfulness.
Schädling *m.* **(-s, -e)** (insect) pest; noxious creature.
Schädlingsbekämpfung *f.* pest control; **~smittel** *n.* pesticide.
schädlos *a. sich* ~ *halten,* to recover one's losses.
Schadstoff *m.* harmful substance; pollutant.
schadstoffarm *a.* low in harmful substances.
Schaf *n.* **(-[e]s, -e)** sheep; (*fig.*) simpleton; (*fig.*) ninny; *schwarzes* ~, black sheep.
Schafbock *m.* ram.
Schäfchen *n.* **(-s, -)** lamb.
Schäfer *m.* **(-s, -)** shepherd.
Schäferhund *m.* German shepherd.
Schäferin *f.* shepherdess.
Schäferstündchen *n.* lovers' tryst.
Schaffell *n.* sheepskin.
schaffen *v.t.st.* to create; ~ *v.t.* to afford, to procure; to convey; ~ *v.i.* to be active, to work, to do; *aus dem Wege* ~, to remove; *sich vom Halse* ~, to rid oneself of; *zu* ~ *machen,* to give trouble; *sich zu* ~ *machen,* to busy oneself.
Schaffen *n.* (creative) work; **~skraft** *f.* creative power.
Schaffleisch *n.* mutton.
Schaffner *n.* **(-s, -)**; **Schaffnerin** *f.* **(-, -nen)** (*rail.*) conductor.
Schaffung *f.* creation.
Schafgarbe *f.* yarrow.
Schafherde *f.* flock of sheep.
Schafhirt *m.* shepherd.
Schafott *n.* **(-[e]s, -e)** scaffold.
Schafschur *f.* sheep shearing.
Schafskopf *m.* blockhead.
Schaft *m.* **(-[e]s, Schäfte)** shaft; leg (of a boot); (*Baum*) trunk; (*Blumen*) stalk; (*tech.*) shank.
Schaftstiefel *m.* high boot.
Schafweide *f.* sheep pasture.
Schafzucht *f.* sheep-farming.
Schakal *m.* **(-s, -e)** jackal.
schäkern *v.i.* to fool about; to flirt.
schal *a.* stale, flat, inspid.

Schal *m.* **(-s, -s)** scarf.
Schale *f.* **(-, -n)** shell; peel; husk; pod; dish; bowl, saucer; (*Wage*) scale.
schälen *v.t.o* to shell; to peel, to pare; to husk; to bark; *v.r.* to peel off, to come off.
Schalk *m.* **(-[e]s, -e)** rogue; prankster.
schalkhaft *a.* waggish, roguish.
Schall *m.* **(-[e]s, -e)** sound.
schalldämpfend *a.* sound-deadening.
Schalldämpfer *m.* sound absorber; silencer.
Schalldämpfung *f.* sound insulation.
schalldicht *a.* soundproof.
schallen *v.i.* to sound, to ring.
Schallgeschwindigkeit *f.* sonic speed.
Schallmauer *f.* sonic/sound barrier.
Schallplatte *f.* record.
Schallwelle *f.* soundwave.
Schalotte *f.* shallot.
Schaltbrett *n.* instrument panel.
schalten *v.i.* to act, to command; to switch; ~ *und walten,* to manage.
Schalter *m.* **(-s, -)** ticket window; counter; (*elek.*) switch.
Schaltgetriebe *n.* gear box.
Schalthebel *m.* control or gear lever.
Schaltjahr *m.* leap year.
Schaltkasten *m.* switch box.
Schaltknopf *m.* button.
Schaltkreis *m.* circuit.
Schaltplan *m.* wiring diagram.
Schaltpult *n.* control desk.
Schalttag *m.* intercalary day.
Schaltung *f.* **(-, -en)** (*elek.*) connection; manual gear change; circuit.
Schaluppe *f.* **(-, -n)** sloop; yawl.
Scham *f.* **(-, 0)** shame; genitals *pl.*
schämen *v.r.* to be ashamed.
Schamgefühl *n.* sense of shame.
Schamhaare *pl.* pubic hair.
schamhaft *a.* bashful, shamefaced.
Schamlippen *pl.* labia.
schamlos *a.* shameless; indecent.
Schamlosigkeit *f.* shamelessness.
Schamotte *f.* **(-, -)** fireclay.
schamponieren *v.t.* to shampoo.
schamrot *a.* red with shame.
Schamröte *f.* blush.
Schamteile *m.pl.* genitals *pl.*
schandbar *a.* shameful; indecent.
Schande *f.* **(-, 0)** shame; disgrace; *zu ~n machen,* to destroy, to ruin.
schänden *v.t.* to violate, to rape, to defile.
Schandfleck *m.* stain, blemish.
schändlich *a.* disgraceful, shameful.
Schändlichkeit *f.* shamefulness; shameful action.
Schandtat *f.* disgraceful deed.
Schankwirtschaft *f.* public bar.
Schanze *f.* **(-, -n)** ski-jump.
Schar *f.* **(-, -en)** crowd; horde.
Scharade *f.* **(-, -n)** charade.
scharen *v.r.* to assemble, to collect, to flock together, to rally.
scharenweise *adv.* in swarms/hordes.
scharf *a.* sharp, keen; (*spitz*) acute; hot, acrid, pungent.
Scharfblick *m.* **(-[e]s, 0)** perspicacity.
Schärfe *f.* **(-, -n)** sharpness; acuteness; pungency; acrimony; severity; edge.
Scharfeinstellung *f.* focusing.
schärfen *v.t.* to sharpen; *Minen ~,* to fuse mines.
Schärfentiefe *f.* depth of focus.
Scharfmacher *m.* firebrand.
Scharfrichter *m.* executioner.
Scharfschütze *m.* marksman.
scharfsichtig *a.* sharp-sighted; perspicacious.
Scharfsinn *m.* **(-[e]s, 0)** acumen, acuteness.
scharfsinnig *a.* sagacious, shrewd.
scharfzüngig *a.* sharp-tongued.
Scharlach *m.* **(-[e]s, 0)** scarlet.
Scharlachfieber *n.* scarlet fever.
Scharlatan *m.* **(-s, -e)** charlatan, quack.
Scharmützel *n.* **(-s, -)** skirmish.
Scharnier *n.* **(-[e]s, -e)** hinge, joint.
Schärpe *f.* **(-, -n)** sash, sling.
scharren *v.t. & i.* to scrape, to scratch.
Scharte *f.* **(-, -n)** nick, notch.
schartig *a.* jagged.
Schatten *m.* **(-s, -)** shade, shadow; *in ~ stellen,* (*fig.*) to throw into the shade.
Schatten: ~bild *n.* shade, phantom; **~morelle** *f.* morello cherry; **~riß** *m.* silhouette; **~seite** *f.* shady side; (*fig.*) drawback.
schattieren *v.t.* to shade.
Schattierung *f.* **(-, -en)** shade, nuance.
schattig *a.* shady, shadowy.
Schatulle *f.* **(-, -n)** casket.
Schatz *m.* **(-es, Schätze)** treasure; (*fig.*) darling, love.
Schatzamt *n.* treasury.
Schatzanweisung *f.* **(-, -en)** treasury bond.
schätzbar *a.* valuable, estimable.
schätzen *v.t.* to value, to esteem; to estimate; *geschätzt auf,* valued at.
schätzenlernen *v.t.* to come to appreciate.
schätzenswert *a.* estimable.
Schätzer *m.* **(-s, -)** appraiser, valuer.
Schatzgraber *m.* treasure hunter.
Schatzkammer *f.* treasury.
Schatzmeister *m.;* **Schatzmeisterin** *f.* treasurer.
Schatzsuche *f.* treasure hunt.
Schätzung *f.* **(-, -en)** valuation; estimate.
Schau *f.* **(-, 0)** view; show; *zur ~ stellen,* to exhibit, to display; *zur ~ tragen,* to parade, to sport; to boast of.
Schaubild *n.* chart.
Schaubude *f.* show booth.
Schauder *m.* **(-s, -)** shudder; horror.
schauderhaft, schaudervoll *a.* horrible, dreadful, shocking.
schaudern *v.i.* to shudder, to shiver.
schauen *v.t. & i.* to look, to view, to gaze.
Schauer *m.* **(-s, -)** shivering fit; horror, awe; (*Regen~*) shower.
schauerlich *a.* awful, horrifying.
Schaufel *f.* **(-, -n)** hovel; ladle; paddle; dustpan.
schaufeln *v.t.* to shovel; to dig.
Schaufelrad *n.* paddle wheel.
Schaufenster *n.* shop window; **~dekorateur** *m.* window dresser.
Schaukasten *m.* showcase.
Schaukel *f.* **(-, -n)** swing.
schaukeln *v.t. & i.* to swing, to rock.
Schaukelpferd *n.* rocking horse.
Schaukelstuhl *m.* rocking chair.
schaulustig *a.* curious.
Schaulustige *m./f.* **(-n -n)** curious onlooker.
Schaum *m.* **(-[e]s, Schäume)** foam, froth.
Schaumbad *n.* bubble bath.

schäumen *v.i.* to foam, to froth.
Schaumgummi *m.* foam rubber.
schaumig *a.* foamy, foaming.
Schaumstoff *m.* (plastic) foam.
Schaumwein *m.* sparkling wine.
Schauplatz *m.* scene; (*fig.*) theater.
schaurig *a.* awful, horrid.
Schauspiel *n.* spectacle, sight; play, drama; **~direktor** *m.* manager of a theater; **~er** *m.*; actor, player; **~erei** *f.* hypocrisy; **~erin** *f.* actress.
schauspielerisch *a.* stagey, theatrical.
Schauspielhaus *n.* theater.
Schauspielkunst *f.* dramatic art.
Scheck *m.* check; *einen ~ sperren,* to stop payment on a check.
Scheck: ~buch *n.*, **~heft** *n.* checkbook; **~karte** *f.* check card.
scheckig *a.* piebald, dapple.
scheel *a.* squint-eyed; envious; ~ *adv.* askance.
Scheffel *m.* **(-s, -)** bushel.
scheffeln *v.t.* to rake in; to pile up.
scheffelweise *a.* & *adv.* by the bushel.
Scheibe *f.* **(-, -n)** disk, puck; target; *Glas~*, pane; (*Schnitte*) cut, slice.
Scheibenschießen *n.* target practice.
Scheibenwischer *m.* (*mot.*) windshield wiper.
Scheich *m.* **(-s, -s)** sheikh.
Scheide *f.* **(-, -n)** sheath; (*anat.*) vagina.
scheiden *v.t.st.* to divide, to separate; to divorce; ~ *v.i.* to depart, to part, to leave.
Scheidewand *f.* partition; (*fig.*) barrier.
Scheidung *f.* **(-, -en)** separation; divorce.
Scheidungsklage *f.* divorce suit.
Schein *m.* **(-[e]s, -e)** shine; luster, splendor; appearance; pretext; certificate, bill; *zum ~*, seemingly.
Scheinangriff *m.* (*mil.*) feint attack.
scheinbar *a.* apparent, ostensible.
Scheinbeweis *m.* sophism.
Scheinehe *f.* sham marriage.
scheinen *v.i.st.* to shine; to see, to appear.
Scheingeschäft *n.* fictitious transaction.
scheinheilig *a.* hypocritical; sanctimonious.
Scheinheiligkeit *f.* hypocrisy.
Scheintod *m.* apparent death, catalepsy.
Scheinwerfer *m.* searchlight; *mit ~ beleuchten,* to floodlight; **~licht** spotlight; (*mot.*) headlights.
Scheiß... (*vulg.*) fucking-.
Scheiße *f.* **(-, 0)** (*vulg.*) shit; crap.
scheißen *v.i.* (*vulg.*) to shit.
Scheit *n.* **(-[e]s, -e)** piece of wood, billet.
Scheitel *m.* **(-s, -)** (*Haar~*) part.
Scheiterhaufen *m.* funeral pyre, stake.
scheitern *v.i.* to be wrecked; (*fig.*) to fail.
Schellack *m.* **(-[e]s, -e)** shellac.
Schelle *f.* **(-, -n)** (small) bell.
schellen *v.i.* to ring.
Schellfisch *m.* haddock.
Schelm *m.* **(-[e]s, -e)** rogue, rascal.
schelmisch *a.* roguish.
Schelte *f.* **(-, -n)** scolding.
schelten *v.t.* & *i.st.* to scold, to moan about.
Schema *n.* **(-s, -s & -mata)** pattern; diagram.
schematisch *a.* mechanical; ~ *adv.* in diagram form.
Schemel *m.*, **Schemen** *m.* **(-s, -)** stool; footstool.
Schenke *f.* **(-, -n)** inn, public house.
Schenkel *m.* **(-s, -)** thigh, shank; leg; (*des Winkels*) side.
schenken *v.t.* to make a present of, to give, to grant; *die Strafe ~*, to remit a punishment.
Schenker *m.* **(-s, -)** donor.
Schenkung *f.* **(-, -en)** donation.
Schenkungsurkunde *f.* deed of gift.
Scherbe *f.* **(-, -n)**, **Scherben** *m.* **(-s, -)** broken piece; fragment; shard.
Schere *f.* **(-, -n)** scissors; (*große*) pair of shears *pl.*; *Hummer~*, claw.
scheren *v.t.st.* to shear, to clip; to fleece, to cheat; *sich um etwas ~*, to care about sth.; *sich zum Teufel ~*, to go to the devil; *das schert mich nichts,* that doesn't worry me.
Scherenschleifer *m.* knife grinder.
Schererei *f.* **(-, -en)** trouble.
Scherflein *n.* **(-s, -)** mite.
Scherz *m.* **(-es, -)** joke; ~ **beiseite,** joking apart.
scherzen *v.i.* to jest, to joke; ~ **über,** to make fun of.
scherzhaft *a.* jocular; playful, funny.
scherzweise *adv.* jestingly, in fun.
scheu *a.* shy; timid, bashful.
Scheu *f.* **(-, 0)** shyness; aversion; awe.
scheuchen *v.t.* to frighten away; to scare.
scheuen *v.t.* to shun, to avoid; ~ *v.i.* to shy (at); ~ *v.r.* to be shy.
Scheuer *f.* **(-, -n)** shed, barn.
scheuern *v.t.* to scour; to scrub.
Scheuklappe *f.*, **Scheuleder** *n.* blinker.
Scheune *f.* **(-, -n)** barn, shed.
Scheusal *n.* **(-[e]s, -e)** monster.
scheußlich *a.* frightful, hideous.
Schicht *f.* **(-, -en)** layer, bed, stratum; *Gesellschafts~*, class, rank; shift, task.
Schichtarbeiter *m.* shift worker.
schichten *v.t.* to layer, to pile up; to arrange.
Schichtwechsel *m.* change of shifts.
schichtweise *a.* & *adv.* in layers.
schick *a.* stylish, smart.
Schick *m.* **(-[e]s, 0)** style.
schicken *v.t.* to send, to dispatch; ~ *v.r.* to be suitable, to be proper.
Schickeria *f.* the chic set; the trendies.
Schickimicki *m.* (*fam.*) trendy type.
schicklich *a.* suitable, decent, proper.
Schicksal *n.* **(-[e]s, -e)** fate; destiny.
schicksalhaft *a.* fateful.
Schicksalsfrage *f.* vital question.
Schicksalsgenosse *m.*; **Schicksalsgenossin** *f.* companion in distress.
Schicksalsschlag *m.* (bad) blow.
Schiebedach *n.* sunroof.
Schiebefenster *n.* sash window.
schieben *v.t.st.* to shove, to push; (*fig.*) to act corruptly; *Kegel ~*, to bowl; *einem etwas in die Schuhe ~*, to lay the blame at someone's door.
Schieber *m.* **(-s, -)** bolt, slide; slide-valve; (*am Ofen*) damper, register; profiteer.
Schiebetür *f.* sliding door.
Schiebeventil *n.* slide-valve.
Schiebung *f.* **(-, -en)** shady deal; rigging; fixing.
Schieds: ~gericht *n.* court of arbitration; jury; **~richter** *m.* arbitrator, umpire, referee; **~spruch** *m.* award; arbitration.
schief *a.* oblique, wry, crooked; ~ *adv.* askew, awry; *~gehen v.i.* (*fig.*) to go wrong; *~e Ebene,* inclined plane.
Schiefer *m.* **(-s, -)** slate; splinter.
Schiefer: ~dach *n.* slated roof; **~decker** *m.* slater; **~platte** *f.* slab of slate; **~tafel** *f.* (school) slate.

schielen *v.i.* to squint; to leer (at).
schielend *a.* squint-eyed, squinting.
Schienbein *n.* shin(-bone).
Schiene *f.* **(-, -n)** splint; (*rail.*) rail.
schienen *v.t.* to splint.
Schienen: ~bus *m.* rail bus; **~fahrzeug** *n.* rail vehicle; **~netz** *n.* railroad system; **~verkehr** *m.* rail traffic.
schier *a.* sheer, pure; *~adv.* almost.
Schierling *m.* **(-[e]s, -e)** hemlock.
Schieß: ~befehl *m.* order to fire; **~bude** *f.* shooting gallery; **~eisen** *n.* (*fam.*) shooting-iron.
schießen *v.t. & i.st.* to shoot, to discharge, to fire; (football, *Tor ~*) to score; to rush; *die Zügel ~ lassen,* to let go the reins; *einen Bock ~*, (*fam.*) to make a blunder.
Schießerei *f.* gunfight; shooting.
Schießfertigkeit *f.* marksmanship.
Schieß: ~gewehr *n.* firearm; **~pulver** *n.* gunpowder; **~scharte** *f.* embrasure, loophole; **~scheibe** *f.* target; **~stand** *m.* shooting range.
Schiff *n.* **(-[e]s, -e)** ship, vessel, boat; (*Kirchen~*) nave; (*Weber*) shuttle.
Schiffahrt *f.* **(-, 0)** navigation.
Schiffahrts: ~linie *f.* shipping line; **~weg** *m.* shipping route.
schiffbar *a.* navigable.
Schiffbau *m.* shipbuilding.
Schiffbruch *m.* shipwreck; *~ leiden,* to be shipwrecked.
schiffbrüchig *a.* shipwrecked.
schiffen *v.i.* to navigate, to sail.
Schiffer *m.* **(-s, -)** boatman; skipper.
Schiffs: ~brücke *f.* pontoon bridge; **~junge** *m.* cabin boy; **~raum** *m.* shipping space; **~schraube** *f.* ship's screw; **~spediteur** *m.* shipping agent; **~verkehr** *n.* shipping traffic; **~werft** *f.* shipyard.
Schiite *m.* **(-n, -n)** Shiite.
Schikane *f.* chicanery, trickery.
schikanieren *v.t.* to harass, to vex.
schikanös *a.* harassing; vexatious.
Schild *m.* **(-es, -e)** shield, buckler.
Schild *n.* **(-es, -er)** road sign; sign; board; doorplate; label.
Schildbürger *m.* **(-s, -)** simpleton.
Schilddrüse *f.* thyroid gland.
schildern *v.t.* to describe, to picture.
Schilderung *f.* **(-, -en)** description.
Schildkröte *f.* turtle, tortoise.
Schildwache *f.* sentinel, sentry.
Schilf *n.* **(-[e]s, -e)** reed, rush; sedge.
Schilfgras *n.* reed grass, sedge.
Schilfrohr *n.* reed.
schillern *v.i.* to be iridescent, to glitter.
schillernd *a.* glistening, irridescent.
Schilling *m.* **(-s, -e)** (*Münze*) shilling.
Schimäre *f.* **(-, -n)** chimera, bogy.
Schimmel *m.* **(-s, -)** mold, mustiness; white horse.
schimm[e]lig *a.* moldy, musty.
schimmeln *v.i.* to get moldy, to mold.
Schimmelpilz *m.* mold.
Schimmer *m.* **(-s, -)** glitter, gleam, glimmer; (*fig.*) idea; *keinen ~*, not the slightest idea.
schimmern *v.i.* to glitter, to glisten; to gleam.
Schimpanse *m.* **(-n, -n)** chimpanzee.
Schimpf *m.* **(-[e]s, -e)** affront, insult; disgrace.
schimpfen *v.t.* to scold; to grumble; to moan.
schimpflich *a.* disgraceful.
Schimpfwort *n.* invective, insult; swearword.
Schindel *f.* **(-s, -n)** shingle.
Schindeldach *n.* shingle roof.
schinden *v.t.st.* to mistreat; (*fig.*) to oppress, to grind; *sich ~*, to slave.
Schinderei *f.* **(-, -en)** drudgery.
Schinken *m.* **(-s, -)** ham.
Schinkenspeck *m.* bacon.
Schirm *m.* **(-[e]s, -e)** screen; shade; *Regen~* umbrella; *Sonnen~* parasol; *Mützen~* peak; (*fig.*) shelter, protection.
schirmen *v.t.* to shelter, to protect.
Schirmherr *m.* patron; **~in** *f.* patroness; **~schaft** *f.* patronage.
Schirmmütze *f.* peaked cap.
Schirmständer *m.* umbrella stand.
Schisma *n.* **(-s, -s & -mata)** schism.
schismatisch *a.* schismatic.
Schiß *m.* **(-s, 0)** (*vulg.*) **~haben** to be scared stiff.
schizophren *a.* schizophrenic.
Schizophrenie *f.* **(-, -n)** schizophrenia.
Schlacht *f.* **(-, -en)** battle; *eine ~ liefern,* to fight a battle.
Schlachtbank *f.* shambles *pl.*
schlachten *v.t.* to slaughter, to kill.
Schlachtenbummler *m.* (*sp.*) fan; supporter.
Schlachter *m.*, **Schlächter** *m.* **(-s, -)** butcher.
Schlachtfeld *n.* battlefield.
Schlachtkreuzer *m.* battle cruiser.
Schlachtruf *m.* war cry.
Schlachtschiff *n.* battleship.
Schlacke *f.* **(-, -n)** dross, slag, cinders.
schlackern *v.i.* to flap; to dangle; to be baggy (pants).
Schlaf *m.* **(-[e]s, 0)** sleep; *im ~e,* asleep.
Schlafanzug *m.* pajamas.
Schläfe *f.* **(-, -n)** temple.
schlafen *v.t.st.* to sleep.
Schlafenszeit *f.* bedtime.
Schläfer *m.* **(-s, -); Schläferin** *f.* **(-, -nen)** sleeper.
schlaff *a.* limp, slack, flabby; indolent.
Schlaffheit *f.* **(-, 0)** slackness, indolence.
Schlafgast *m.* overnight guest.
Schlafgelegenheit *f.* place to sleep.
Schlafkrankheit *f.* sleeping sickness.
Schlaflied *n.* lullaby.
schlaflos *a.* sleepless.
Schlaflosigkeit *f.* sleeplessness; insomnia.
Schlafmittel *n.* soporific; sleeping pill.
Schlafmütze *f.* nightcap; (*fig.*) sleepyhead.
schläfrig *a.* sleepy, drowsy; sluggish.
Schlafrock *m.* dressing gown.
Schlafsaal *m.* dormitory.
Schlafsack *m.* sleeping bag.
Schlaftablette *f.* sleeping pill.
schlaftrunken *a.* drowsy.
Schlafwagen *n.* sleeping car, sleeper; **~schaffner** *m.* sleeping car attendant.
Schlafwandler *m.*, **Schlafwandlerin** *f.* sleepwalker.
Schlafzimmer *n.* bedroom.
Schlag *m.* **(-[e]s, Schläge)** stroke, blow; (*elek.*) shock; apoplexy, fit; (*fig.*) kind, sort; *Donner~* clap; *Puls~* beat; *~ auf ~*, in rapid succession, as thick as hail; *~ zwölf Uhr,* at twelve o'clock sharp.
Schlagader *f.* artery.
Schlaganfall *m.* stroke.
Schlagbaum *m.* barrier.
schlagen *v.t.st.* to beat, to strike; (*den Feind*) to defeat; (*Eier*) to beat; *Holz ~*, to fell wood; *eine Brücke ~*, to build a bridge; *Geld ~*, to coin

money; *ein Kreuz* ~, to make the sign of the Cross; *Alarm* ~, to sound the alarm; *ans Kreuz* ~, to crucify; *zum Ritter* ~, to knight; ~ *v.i.* (*Uhr*) to strike; *es schlägt 12 Uhr,* it strikes 12; ~ *v.r.* to fight.
schlagend *a.* cogent; conclusive.
Schlager *m.* **(-s, -)** (*theat.*) hit, pop song; best-seller.
Schläger *m.* **(-s, -)** (*Tennis*) racket, (*Kricket*) bat.
Schlägerei *f.* **(-, -en)** brawl; row.
schlagfertig *a.* quick at repartee.
Schlaginstrument *n.* percussion instrument.
Schlagkraft *f.* striking power.
Schlagloch *n.* pothole.
Schlagsahne *f.* whipped cream.
Schlagstock *m.* truncheon; cudgel.
Schlagweite *f.* striking distance.
Schlagwetter *n.* firedamp.
Schlagwort *n.* catchword; slogan.
Schlagzeile *f.* headline.
Schlagzeug *n.* drums; **~er** *m.;* **~erin** *f.* drummer.
schlaksig *a.* gangling, lanky.
Schlamassel *n.* **(-s, -)** mess.
Schlamm *m.* **(-[e]s, 0)** mud.
schlammig *a.* muddy.
Schlampe *f.* **(-, -n)** slut.
schlampen *v.i.* to be sloppy.
Schlamperei *f.* sloppiness.
schlampig *a.* slovenly, sloppy.
Schlange *f.* **(-, -n)** snake, serpent; coil; (*Reihe*) line, queue.
schlängeln *v.r.* to wind; to snake; to meander.
schlangenförmig *a.* serpentine.
Schlangenlinie *f.* wavy line.
schlank *a.* slender, slim.
Schlankheit *f.* slimness; **~skur** diet.
schlankweg *adv.* right away.
schlapp *a.* worn out; feeble; slack.
Schlappe *f.* **(-, -n)** setback.
schlappen *v.i.* to shuffle.
Schlapphut *m.* slouched hat.
schlappmachen *v.i.* to give up; to wilt.
Schlappschwanz *m.* (*fam.*) wimp.
Schlaraffenland *n.* Land of Cockaigne, land of milk and honey.
schlau *a. & adv.* sly(ly); cunning(ly), crafty(ily).
Schlauberger, Schlaukopf, Schlaumeier *m.* (*fam.*) smartie.
Schlauch *m.* **(-[e]s, Schläuche)** hose; (*Fahrrad*) tube.
Schlauch: ~boot *n.* rubber dinghy; **~mantel** *m.* cover of a tire.
schlauchen *v.t. & i.* (*fig.*) to drain.
Schläue *f.* **(-, 0)** shrewdness; astuteness.
Schlaufe *f.* **(-, -n)** loop; strap.
Schlauheit *f.* **(-, -en)** cunning, slyness.
schlecht *a.* mean, base, bad, wicked; (*Geld*) base; vile; ill; *mir ist* or *wird* ~, I feel ill; *es* ~ *haben,* to have a bad time; *es geht ihm* ~, he is unwell *or* badly off.
schlechterdings *adv.* absolutely.
schlechtgelaunt *a.* bad-tempered.
schlechtgesinnt *a.* evil-minded
schlechthin *adv.* plainly; positively.
Schlechtigkeit *f.* **(-, -en)** meanness, baseness, badness.
schlechtmachen *v.t.* to run down, to denigrate.
schlechtweg *adv.* plainly, simply.
schlecken *v.t. & i.* to lick.
Schleckerei *f.* **(-, -en)** sweets, dainties *pl.*
Schlegel *m.* **(-s, -)** mallet; leg (of mutton, etc.); drumstick.
Schlehdorn *m.* blackthorn.
Schlehe *f.* **(-, -n)** sloe.
schleichen *v.i.st.* *(s)* to sneak, to steal, to glide, to slink; *sich fort* ~, to steal away, to sneak off.
schleichend *a.* sneaking; insiduous (disease); (*fig.*) lingering.
Schleichhandel *m.* black market.
Schleichhändler *m.* black marketeer.
Schleichweg *m.* secret path.
Schleie *f.* **(-, -n)** (*Fisch*) tench.
Schleier *n.* **(-s, -)** veil.
schleierhaft *a.* mysterious; *das ist mir* ~, I don't know what to make of it.
Schleife *f.* **(-, -n)** loop; knot, bow; sledge, drag.
schleifen *v.t. & i.* to drag, to trail; to raze; to glide, to slide; ~ *v.t.st.* to grind, to polish; to cut (glass).
Schleifer *m.* **(-s, -)** grinder, polisher; *Edelstein* ~, cutter.
Schleifmittel *n.* abrasive.
Schleifstein *m.* whetstone, grindstone.
Schleim *m.* **(-[e]s, -e)** slime; phlegm; mucous; gruel.
Schleimhaut *f.* mucous membrane.
schleimig *a.* slimy, mucous.
schlemmen *v.i.* to feast, to revel.
Schlemmer *m.* **(-s, -)** gourmet.
Schlemmerei *f.* feasting.
Schlemmerlokal *n.* gourmet restaurant.
schlendern *v.i.* *(s)* to stroll.
Schlendrian *m.* **(-s, 0)** dawdling; rut.
schlenkern *v.t. & i.* to swing; to dangle.
Schleppdampfer *m.* tug boat.
Schleppe *f.* **(-, -n)** train (of a dress).
schleppen *v.t. & i.* to drag; to trail; (*nav.*) to tow, to tug.
schleppend *a.* flagging, lengthy, heavy.
Schlepper *m.* **(-s, -)** tug.
Schlepp: ~lift *m.* ski tow; **~kleid** *n.* dress with a train; **~tau** *n.* tow rope; *ins* ~ *nehmen,* to take in tow.
Schlesien *n.* **(-s, 0)** Silesia.
Schlesier *m.;* **Schlesierin** *f.* Silesian.
Schleuder *f.* **(-, -n)** sling; slingshot.
schleudern *v.t.* to sling, to throw; ~ *v.i.* to swing.
Schleuderpreis *m.* knock-down price.
Schleudersitz *m.* **(-es, -e)** ejector seat.
schleunig *a.* quick, speedy.
Schleuse *f.* **(-, -n)** sluice, lock, floodgate.
Schlich *m.* **(-[e]s, -e)** trick, dodge; *hinter die* ~*e kommen,* to be on to one's dodges *or* tricks.
schlicht *a.* plain; sleek, smooth.
schlichten *v.t.* to smooth; (*fig.*) to settle, to arrange, to adjust.
Schlichter *m.* **(-s, -)** arbitrator.
Schlichtheit *f.* simplicity; plainness.
Schlichtung *f.* **(-, 0)** settling (of differences); **~samt** *n.* conciliation board; **~sausschuß** *m.* court of arbitration.
Schlick *m.* **(-[e]s, 0)** slit.
Schließe *f.* **(-, -n)** buckle; clasp.
schließen *v.t. & i.st.* to shut, to close, to bolt; to conclude; (*Ehe*) to contract; *in sich* ~, to include.
Schließfaß *n.* post office box; safe deposit box; locker.
schließlich *adv.* lastly, finally.
Schließmuskel *m.* sphincter.

Schließung *f.* **(-, -en)** closure.
Schliff *m.* **(-[e]s, -e)** (*fig.*) polish; cutting; sharpening.
schlimm *a.* bad, evil, serious.
schlimmstenfalls *adv.* if the worst comes to the worst.
Schlinge *f.* **(-, -n)** noose, knot; loop, snare; (*med.*) sling.
Schlingel *m.* **(-s, -)** rascal; naughty boy.
schlingen *v.t. & i.st.* to swallow, to gulp (down); to twist, to entwine; ~ *v.r.* to wind, to twine (round).
schlingern *v.i.* (*nav.*) to roll.
Schlingpflanze *f.* creeper.
Schlips *m.* **(-es, -e)** (neck-)tie.
Schlipsnadel *f.* tie pin.
Schlitten *m.* **(-s, -)** sledge, sleigh; (*kleiner*) toboggan; (*mech.*) slide, carriage.
Schlittenfahrt *f.* sleigh ride.
schlittern *v.i.* to slide; to slip; to skid.
Schlittschuh *m.* skate; ~ **laufen,** to skate.
Schlittschuhläufer *m.;* **Schlittschuhläuferin** *f.* skater.
Schlitz *m.* **(-es, -e)** slit, slash; fissure; slot.
Schlitz: **~auge** *n.* (*pej.*) slit eye; **~ohr** *n.* (*fig.*) crafty devil.
schlitzen *v.t.* to slit, to slash.
Schloß *n.* **(Schlosses, Schlösser)** lock; castle; palace; *unter ~ und Riegel,* under lock and key.
Schlosser *m.* **(-s, -)** locksmith; metal worker; fitter.
Schlot *m.* **(-[e]s, -e)** chimney.
schlotterig *a.* wobbling.
schlottern *v.i.* to wobble, to hang loose.
Schlucht *f.* **(-, -en)** cleft, ravine.
schluchzen *v.i.* to sob.
Schluchzer *m.* **(-s-)** sob.
Schluck *m.* **(-[e]s, Schlucke)** swallow; mouthful; gulp, drink.
Schluckauf *m.* **(-s, 0)** hiccups.
schlucken *v.i. & t.* to gulp (down), to swallow; (*fig.*) to swallow.
Schlucker *m.* **(-s, -)** hiccup; *armer ~,* poor wretch.
Schluckimpfung *f.* oral vaccination.
schludern *v.i.* to work sloppily.
schludrig *a. & adv.* sloppy; sloppily.
Schlummer *m.* **(-s, 0)** slumber; doze.
schlummern *v.i.* to slumber, to doze.
Schlund *m.* **(-[e]s, Schlünde)** throat, gullet; gulf, abyss.
schlüpfen *v.i.* *(s)* to slip, to slide.
Schlüpfer *m.* **(-s, -)** panties.
Schlupf: **~loch** *n.* loophole; hiding place; **~winkel** *m.* hiding place.
schlüpfrig *a.* slippery; prurient, obscene.
schlurfen *v.i.* to shuffle.
schlürfen *v.t.* to sip, to slurp.
Schluß *m.* **(Schlusses, Schlüsse)** conclusion, end; (*log.*) inference; closure.
Schlußabstimmung *f.* final vote.
Schlußakkord *m.* final chord.
Schlußakte *f.* final communiqué.
Schlüssel *m.* **(-s, -)** key; (*mus.*) key.
Schlüssel: **~anhänger** *m.* key chain; **~bein** *n.* collar bone; **~blume** *f.* cowslip, primrose; **~bund** *m.* bunch of keys; **~erlebnis** *n.* crucial experience; **~figur** *f.* key figure; **~kind** *n.* latchkey child; **~loch** *n.* keyhole; **~ring** *m.* keyring; **~roman** *m.* roman à clef; **~stellung** *f.* key position; **~wort** *n.* keyword; (*comp.*) password.
Schlußexamen *m.* final examination.
Schlußfeier *f.* (*Schule*) commencement; speech day.
Schlußfolgerung *f.* inference, conclusion.
schlüssig *a.* conclusive; *sich (dat.) ~ werden,* to make up one's mind.
Schlußlicht *n.* rear lamp or light; (*fig.*) last one.
Schlußnotierung *f.* closing price.
Schlußsatz *m.* concluding sentence; (*mus.*) finale.
Schlußstein *m.* keystone.
Schlußverkauf *m.* (end of season) sale.
Schmach *f.* **(-, 0)** ignominy; insult.
schmachten *v.i.* to languish, to long for, to pine.
schmachtend *a.* soulful.
schmächtig *a.* slight; thin.
schmachvoll *a.* ignominious; disgraceful.
schmackhaft *a.* savory, tasty.
schmähen *v.t.* to revile.
schmählich *a.* shameful; despicable.
Schmähschrift *f.* libel, lampoon.
Schmähung *f.* **(-, -en)** abuse, invective.
schmal *a.* narrow; small; scanty; slim.
schmälern *v.t.* to lessen; to belittle.
Schmalspur *f.* narrow gauge; (*fig.*) lightweight.
Schmalz *n.* **(-es, 0)** lard; (*pej.*) schmaltz.
schmalzig *a.* greasy; (*fig.*) sentimental.
schmarotzen *v.i.* to sponge (off others).
Schmarotzer *m.* **(-s, -)** parasite; (*fig.*) sponger.
schmatzen *v.t. & i.* to smack one's lips.
Schmaus *m.* **(-ses, Schmäuse)** feast, treat.
schmausen *v.i.* to feast, to banquet.
schmecken *v.t. & i.* to taste (*nach,* of); to savor; to taste good; *wie schmeckt es dir...?* how do you like...?
Schmeichelei *f.* **(-, -en)** flattery.
schmeichelhaft *a.* flattering.
schmeicheln *v.i.* to flatter.
Schmeichler *m.;* **Schmeichlerin** *f.* flatterer.
schmeichlerisch *a.* flattering, fawning.
schmeißen *v.t.st.* to chuck, to fling.
Schmeißfliege *f.* **(-, -n)** bluebottle; blowfly.
Schmelz *m.* **(-es, -e)** enamel; (*fig.*) mellowness.
Schmelze *f.* **(-, -n)** melting.
schmelzen *v.t.st.* to melt; (*Erze*) to smelt; to fuse; ~ *v.i.st.* to melt (away).
schmelzend *a.* melodious; languishing.
Schmelzkäse *m.* soft cheese.
Schmelzpunkt *m.* melting point.
Schmelztiegel *m.* crucible; (*fig.*) melting pot.
Schmerbauch *m.* paunch.
Schmerle *f.* **(-, -n)** loach.
Schmerz *m.* **(-es, -en)** pain, ache; grief.
schmerzempfindlich *a.* sensitive to pain.
schmerzen *v.t. & i.* to hurt, to grieve.
Schmerzensgeld *n.* compensation; punitive damages.
schmerzfrei *a.* painless.
schmerzhaft *a.* painful, grievous.
schmerzlich *a.* painful.
schmerzlos *a.* painless.
schmerzstillend *a.* anodyne; soothing, pain-killing.
Schmerztablette *f.* pain-killer; analgesic tablet.
schmerzverzerrt *a.* distorted with pain.
Schmetterling *m.* **(-[e]s, -e)** butterfly.
schmettern *v.i.* (*von Trompeten*) to bray, to blare; (*von Singvögeln*) to warble.

Schmetterschlag *m.* (*Tennis*) smash.
Schmied *m.* **(-[e]s, -e)** (black-)smith.
Schmiede *f.* **(-, -n)** forge, smithy.
Schmiede: ~eisen *n.* wrought iron; **~hammer** *m.* sledge(-hammer).
schmieden *v.t.* to forge; (*fig.*) to plan, to frame, to concoct.
schmiegen *v.r.* to nestle, to snuggle.
schmiegsam *a.* (*fig.*) pliant, supple.
Schmiere *f.* **(-,-n)** grease; salve; (*sl.*) low theater.
schmieren *v.t. & i.* to grease, to lubricate; (*Butter*) to spread; (*sudeln*) to scrawl; (*fig.*) to bribe; *es geht wie geschmiert*, things go like clockwork; (*fam.*) *jn.* ~, to grease sb.'s palm.
Schmierenkomödiant *m.* ham actor.
Schmiererei *f.* scrawling, scribbling.
Schmierfink *m.* (*fam.*) hack.
schmierig *a.* greasy; dirty; (*fig.*) sordid.
Schmiermittel *n.* lubricant.
Schmierpapier *n.* scrap paper.
Schmierseife *f.* soft soap.
Schminkdose *f.*, **Schminktopf** *m.* rouge pot.
Schminke *f.* **(-, -n)** paint, rouge, makeup.
schminken *v.t.* to paint; ~ *v.r.* to put on make up.
Schmirgel *m.* **(-s, 0)** emery board; sandpaper.
schmirgeln *v.t.* to rub down; to sand.
Schmiß *m.* **(Schmisses, Schmisse)** stroke, blow; cut, slash; (*fig.*) smartness.
schmissig *a.* snappy.
Schmöker *m.* **(-s, -)** (*fam.*) old book; light novel.
schmollen *v.i.* to pout, to sulk.
Schmorbraten *m.* braised beef.
schmoren *v.t. & i.* to braise, to stew.
Schmu *m.* **(-s, 0)** (*fam.*) unfair gain.
schmuck *a.* neat, spruce, trim, natty.
Schmuck *m.* **(-[e]s, 0)** ornament, jewels *pl.*
schmücken *v.t.* to adorn; to trim; to decorate; ~ *v.r.* to dress up.
Schmuckkasten *m.* jewelry box.
schmucklos *a.* plain, unadorned.
Schmucksachen *f.pl.* jewelry.
Schmuckstück *n.* ornament; piece of jewelry.
schmuddelig *a.* (*fam.*) messy; grubby.
Schmuggel *m.* **(-s, 0)** smuggling.
schmuggeln *v.t.* to smuggle.
Schmuggelware *f.* contraband.
Schmuggler *m.*; **Schmugglerin** *f.* smuggler.
schmunzeln *v.i.* to smile.
Schmus *m.* **(-es, 0)** (*fam.*) soft soap.
schmusen *v.i.* (*fam.*) to cuddle.
Schmutz *m.* **(-s, 0)** dirt, soil, filth.
schmutzen *v.t. & i.* to soil; to get dirty.
Schmutz: ~fink *m.* (*fam.*) pig; **~fleck** *m.* stain; (*fig.*) blot.
schmutzig *a.* dirty, filthy; sordid; obscene.
Schnabel *m.* **(-s, Schnäbel)** bill, beak; gob.
Schnake *f.* **(-, -n)** mosquito.
Schnakenstich *m.* (*fig.*) mosquito bite.
Schnalle *f.* **(-, -n)** buckle.
schnallen *v.t.* to buckle.
schnalzen *v.i.* to smack; to snap; to crack (a whip).
schnappen *v.i.* to snap, to snatch; *nach Luft* ~, to gasp for breath.
Schnappschloß *n.* springlock.
Schnaps *m.* **(-es, Schnäpse)** schnapps; strong liquor; dram.
Schnapsidee *f.* (*fig.*) crazy idea.
schnarchen *v.i.* to snore.
Schnarcher *m.*; **Schnarcherin** *f.* snorer.
Schnarre *f.* **(-, -n)** rattle.
schnarren *v.i.* to rattle; to buzz.
schnattern *v.i.* to cackle; chatter.
schnauben v.i. to snort.
schnaufen *v.i.* to puff; to pant.
Schnauzbart *m.* moustache.
Schnauze *f.* **(-, -n)** snout, muzzle.
schnauzen *v.t. & i.* to bark; to snarl.
Schnauzer *m.* schnauzer; moustache.
Schnecke *f.* **(-, -n)** snail; slug; (*Gebäck*) sweetroll.
schneckenförmig *a.* spiral, helical.
Schnecken: ~haus *n.* snail shell; **~tempo** *n.* snail's pace.
Schnee *m.* **(-[e]s, 0)** snow.
Schneeball *m.* snowball.
Schneeballschlacht *f.* snowball fight.
Schneebesen *m.* (*cul.*) whisk.
schneeblind *a.* snow-blind.
Schneebrille *f.* goggles *pl.*
Schneeflocke *f.* snowflake.
Schneegestöber *n.* snow flurry.
Schneeglätte *f.* packed snow.
Schneeglöckchen *n.* snowdrop.
Schneegrenze *f.* snowline.
Schneeketten *f.pl.* snow-chains.
Schneemann *m.* snowman.
Schneematsch *m.* slush.
Schneepflug *m.* snowplow.
schneeräumgerät *n.* snow blower.
Schneeschmelze *f.* thaw.
Schneetreiben *n.* snow flurry.
Schneeverwehungen *f.* snowdrift.
Schneewetter *n.* snowy weather.
Schneewittchen *n.* Snow White.
Schneid *m.* **(-s, 0)** (*fam.*) guts. *pl.*
Schneide *f.* **(-, -n)** (cutting) edge; blade.
schneiden *v.t.st.* to cut; to carve; to saw; to reap; to pull (faces); ~ *v.r.* (*math.*) to intersect.
schneidend *a.* cutting, caustic, trenchant.
Schneider *m.* **(-s, -)**, **Schneiderin** *f.* **(-, -nen)** tailor, dressmaker.
schneidern *v.i.* to make clothes, to tailor.
Schneider: ~puppe *f.* tailor's dummy; **~sitz** *m.* cross-legged position.
Schneidezahn *m.* incisor.
schneidig *a.* plucky, dashing.
schneien *v.i.* to snow.
Schneise *f.* **(-, -n)** glade; air corridor.
schnell *a.* quick, swift, speedy, fast; rapid; prompt.
Schnellbahn *f.* municipal railroad.
Schnellboot *n.* speedboat.
schnellen *v.t.* to let fly, to jerk, to toss; ~ *v.i.* *(s)* to spring.
Schnellfeuer *n.* rapid fire; **~geschütz** *n.* automatic weapon.
Schnellgang *m.* (*mot.*) overdrive.
Schnellgericht *n.* quick meal; court of summary jurisdiction.
Schnelligkeit *f.* **(-, 0)** quickness, velocity, rapidity, speed.
Schnellimbiß *m.* snack (bar).
Schnellkraft *f.* elasticity.
Schnellverfahren *n.* (*law*) summary proceeding.
schnellwirkend *a.* fast-acting.
Schnellzug *m.* fast train, express.
Schnepfe *f.* **(-, -n)** snipe; woodcock.
schnetzeln *v.t.* to cut into thin strips.
schneuzen *v.r.* to blow one's nose.

Schnickschnack *m.* (*fam.*) trinkets; frills; drivel.
schniefen *v.i.* to sniffle.
schniegeln *v.r.* to spruce oneself up.
Schnippchen *n.* **(-s, -)** *ein ~ schlagen,* to trick.
schnippeln *v.t. & i.* to snip.
schnippen *v.i.* to snap (fingers); to flap.
schnippisch *a.* pert.
Schnipsel *m./n.* scrap; shred.
Schnitt *m.* **(-[e]s, -e)** cut; incision; *Buch~,* edge; fashion, pattern; section.
Schnittchen *n.* open sandwich.
Schnitte *f.* **(-, -n)** slice, steak, cut.
Schnitter *m.* **(-s, -)** reaper.
schnittfest *a.* firm.
schnittig *a.* stylish; racy.
Schnitt: ~lauch *m.* chives *pl.;* **~muster** *n.* pattern; **~punkt** *m.* intersection; **~wunde** *f.* cut; gash.
Schnitzel *n.* **(-s, -)** chip, shred; escalope; cutlet.
Schnitzeljagd *f.* paper chase.
schnitzen *v.t.* to carve, to cut.
Schnitzer *m.* **(-s, -)** carver; blunder.
Schnitzerei *f.* **(-, -en)** carved work.
schnoddrig *a.* snotty; brash.
schnöde *a.* scornful; base, vile.
Schnorchel *m.* snorkel.
Schnörkel *m.* **(-s, -)** (*arch.*) scroll; flourish.
schnorren *v.t.* to scrounge.
Schnorrer *m.* scrounger.
Schnösel *m.* snot-nose.
schnucklig *a.* (*fam.*) cuddly.
schnüffeln *v.i.* to sniff; to pry.
Schnüffler *m.* **(-s, -)** spy.
Schnuller *m.* pacifier.
Schnulze *f.* tear-jerker.
schnupfen *v.t. & i.* to take snuff; to sniff.
Schnupfen *m.* **(-s, 0)** cold (in the head); *sich den ~ holen,* to catch cold.
Schnupftabak *m.* snuff; **~sdose** *f.* snuff-box.
Schnupftuch *n.* (pocket-) handkerchief.
schnuppern *v.i.* to sniff, to snuffle.
Schnur *f.* **(-, Schnüre)** string, cord.
Schnürchen *n.* **(-s, -)** *wie am ~,* like clockwork.
schnüren *v.t.* to lace; to cord, to tie up.
schnurgerade *a.* straight.
Schnurrbart *m.* moustache.
schnurren *v.i.* to hum, to whiz, to whir; (*von Katzen*) to purr.
Schnurrhaar *n.* whiskers.
schnurrig *a.* droll, funny.
Schnür: ~senkel *m.* shoelace, bootlace; **~schuh, ~stiefel** *m.* lace-up boot.
schnurstracks *adv.* directly.
Schnute *f.* **(-, -n)** mouth; gob.
Schober *m.* **(-s, -)** stack, rick; open-sided barn.
Schock *m.* **(-s, -s)** shock.
schocken *v.t.* (*fam.*) to shock.
schockieren *v.t.* to shock.
schofel *a.* mean, paltry.
Schöffe *m.* **(-n, -n)** juror, juryman, lay-judge.
Schöffengericht *n.* lowest court of law.
Schokolade *f.* **(-, -n)** chocolate.
Schokoladeneis *m.* chocolate icing.
Scholle *f.* **(-, -n)** clod, floe; (*Fisch*) plaice.
schon *adv.* already; surely.
schön *a.* fine, fair, beautiful, handsome; **~e Künste** *pl.* fine arts.
schonen *v.t.* to spare, to save; **~** *v.r.* to take good care of oneself.
Schoner *m.* **(-s, -)** schooner.
Schönfärberei *f.* **(-, -en)** embellishment, glossing over the facts.
Schonfrist *f.* period of grace; period of convalescence.
Schöngeist *m.* wit, aesthete.
schöngeistig *a.* aesthetic.
Schönheit *f.* **(-, -en)** beauty.
Schönheits: ~chirurgie *f.* cosmetic surgery; **~fehler** *m.* blemish; flaw; **~salon** *m.* beauty parlor; **~wettbewerb** *m.* beauty contest.
Schonkost *f.* light diet.
Schonung *f.* **(-, -en)** forbearance, indulgence; rest; protection; sparing; nursery for young trees.
schonungslos *a.* unsparing, relentless.
Schonzeit *f.* (*Jagd*) close time *or* season.
Schopf *m.* **(-[e], Schöpfe)** shock of hair.
schöpfen *v.t.* to draw (water); to obtain, to get; *Luft ~,* to get some air; *Verdacht ~,* to conceive a suspicion; *Hoffnung ~,* to be reanimated by hope.
Schöpfer *m.* **(-s, -); Schöpferin** *f.* **(-, -nen)** creator; author.
schöpferisch *a.* creative, productive.
Schöpferkraft *f.* creative power.
Schöpf: ~kelle *f.,* **~löffel** *m.* ladle, scoop.
Schöpfung *f.* **(-, -en)** creation; work.
Schoppen *m.* **(-s, -)** pint.
Schorf *f.* **(-[e]s, -e)** scab.
schorfig *a.* scabby.
Schorle *m.* **(-, -n)** spritzer.
Schornstein *m.* chimney; funnel; smokestack.
Schornsteinfeger *m.* chimney sweep.
Schoß *m.* **(-es, Schösse)** lap; (*fig.*) womb; *Rock~,* flap, skirt, coattail; *die Hände in den ~ legen,* to sit with folded hands.
Schoß: ~hund *m.* lapdog; **~kind** *n.* darling, pet child.
Schößling *m.* **(-[e]s, -e)** shoot, sprout.
Schote *f.* **(-, -n)** husk; pod.
Schott *n.* **(-[e]s, -e)** (*nav.*) bulkhead.
Schotte *m.* **(-n, -n)** Scotsman, Scot.
Schottenrock *m.* tartan skirt; kilt.
Schotter *m.* **(-s, -)** gravel; metal.
Schottin *f.* **(-, -nen)** Scotswoman, Scot.
Schottisch *a.* Scottish; **~er Whisky** *m.* Scotch whiskey.
Schottland *n.* **(-s, 0)** Scotland.
schraffieren *v.t.* to hatch.
schräg *a.* oblique, slanting; tilted; **~er Anschnitt** *m.* (*mech.*) bevel.
Schräge *f.* **(-, 0)** slant; slope.
Schramme *f.* **(-, -n)** scratch, slight wound.
schrammen *v.t.* to scratch, to graze.
Schrank *m.* **(-[e]s, Schränke)** cupboard; wardrobe; cabinet; closet.
Schranke *f.* **(-, -n)** bar, barrier, bound, limit; (*Eisenbahn*) gate.
schrankenlos *a.* boundless.
Schrankenwärter *m.* gatekeeper.
Schraube *f.* **(-, -n)** screw; bolt; *Dampfer~,* propeller.
schrauben *v.t.* to screw.
Schrauben: ~gewinde *n.* thread of a screw; **~mutter** *f.* nut; **~schlüssel** *m.* wrench; **~zieher** *m.* screwdriver.
Schraubstock *m.* vise.
Schrebergarten *m.* allotment (garden).
Schreck *m.* **(-[e]s, -)** fright, terror.
Schreckbild *n.* bugbear, fright.

schrecken *v.t.* to frighten.
Schrecken *m.* **(-s, -)** fright, terror; *ein blinder ~*, a false alarm.
schreckenerregend *a.* horrific.
Schreckensherrschaft *f.* reign of terror, terrorism.
schreckhaft *a.* easily frightened.
schrecklich *a.* awful, dreadful, terrible.
Schreckschuß *m.* warning shot.
Schrei *m.* **(-[e]s, -e)** cry, shriek, scream.
Schreibarbeit *f.* paperwork.
Schreibblock *m.* writing pad, writing tablet.
schreiben *v.t.st.* to write; to compose; *richtig ~*, to spell correctly; *falsch ~*, to misspell; *mit der Maschine ~*, to type; *den Namen unter etw. ~*, to sign something; *ins Reine ~*, to copy out neatly; *einem auf die Rechnung ~*, to put down to one's account.
Schreiben *n.* **(-s, -)** letter, epistle; (art of) writing.
Schreiber *m.* **(-s, -)**; **Schreiberin** *f.* **(-, -nen)** writer; clerk, copyist.
Schreib: ~feder *f.* pen; **~fehler** *m.* slip of the pen, spelling mistake; **~heft** *n.* exercise book; **~kraft** *f.* typist; **~maschine** *f.* typewriter; **~papier** *n.* writing paper; **~pult** *n.* writing desk; **~stube** *f.* (*mil.*) orderly room; **~tisch** *m.* desk; writing table; **~waren** *f.pl.* stationery; **~warenhändler** *m.* stationer; **~weise** *f.* spelling; **~zeug** *n.* writing things.
schreien *v.t. & i.st.* to cry, to scream; to yell; to screech.
schreiend *a.* loud; blatant; glaring.
Schreier *m.* **(-s, -)**, **Schreihals** *m.* crier; bawler; squalling child.
Schrein *m.* **(-[e]s, -e)** shrine.
Schreiner *m.* **(-s, -)** joiner, cabinetmaker; carpenter.
schreiten *v.i.st.* *(s)* to stride, to step.
Schrift *f.* **(-, -en)** writing; handwriting; script; type; book; Scripture, Bible.
Schriftdeutsch *n.* written German.
Schriftführer *m.* secretary.
Schriftgießerei *f.* typefoundry.
Schriftleiter *m.* editor.
schriftlich *a.* written; ~ *adv.* in writing, by letter; **~er Lehrkurs** *m.* correspondence course.
Schriftsatz *m.* (*jur.*) written statement.
Schriftsetzer *m.* typesetter.
Schriftsprache *f.* written language.
Schriftstelle *f.* Scripture text.
Schriftsteller(in) *m.(f.)* writer, author.
schriftstellerisch *a.* literary.
Schriftstellername *m.* penname.
Schriftstück *n.* document, letter.
Schriftwechsel *m.* exchange of letters.
Schriftzeichen *n.* character.
schrill *a.* shrill, piercing.
Schritt *m.* **(-[e]s, -e)** step, stride, pace; gait; demarche; *~ vor (für) ~*, step by step; *für einen ~e tun,* to take steps on behalf of sb.; *im ~ gehen,* to walk, to pace; *~ mit einem halten,* to keep pace with sb.; *aus dem ~ kommen,* to fall out of time; *~ reiten, fahren,* to pace, to walk.
Schrittempo *n.* walking pace.
Schrittmacher *m.* pacemaker.
schrittweise *adv.* step by step.
schroff *a.* steep, rugged; (*fig.*) gruff.
schröpfen *v.t.* to cup; (*fig.*) to fleece.
Schrot *n.* **(-[e]s, -e)** due weight (of a coin); small shot; whole grain.
Schrotflinte *f.* shotgun.
Schrotkugel *f.* pellet.
Schrott *m.* **(-, 0)** scrap(iron); **~platz** *m.* scrap yard; **~wert** *m.* scrap value.
schrubben *v.t.* to scrub.
Schrulle *f.* **(-, -n)** cranky idea; whim.
schrullenhaft *a.* whimsical.
schrullig *a.* cranky.
schrumpelig *a.* (*fam.*) wrinkled.
schrumpeln *v.i.* (*fam.*) to wrinkle.
schrumpfen *v.i.* *(s)* to shrink, to shrivel.
Schrumpfkopf *m.* shrunken head.
Schub *m.* **(-[e]s, Schübe)** shove, push; thrust; phase.
Schub: ~fach *n.* drawer; **~fenster** *n.* sash window; **~karren** *m.* wheelbarrow; **~lade** *f.* drawer.
Schubs *m.* (*fam.*) push, shove.
schubsen *v.t.* (*fam.*) to push, to shove.
schubweise *adv.* in batches.
schüchtern *a.* shy, coy, bashful.
Schüchternheit *f.* shyness.
Schuft *m.* **(-[e]s, -e)** blackguard, scoundrel.
schuften *v.i.* (*sl.*) to slave.
schuftig *a.* base, abject.
Schuh *m.* **(-[e]s, -e)** shoe; (*fig.*) *einem etwas in die ~e schieben,* to lay the blame at someone's door.
Schuhband *n.* shoelace.
Schuheinlage *f.* insole, sock.
Schuhflicker *m.* cobbler.
Schuhleisten *m.* shoetree.
Schuhlitze *f.* shoelace.
Schuhlöffel *m.* shoehorn.
Schuhmacher *m.* shoemaker.
Schuhputzer *m.* bookblack.
Schuhriemen *m.* bootlace.
Schuhsohle *f.* sole.
Schuhwichse *f.* shoe polish.
Schulabgänger *m.*, **~abgängerin** *f.* school leaver.
Schulabschluß *m.* school leaving certification.
Schulalter *n.* school age.
Schulbehörde *f.* education authority.
Schulbeispiel *n.* textbook example.
Schulbesuch *m.* school attendance.
Schulbildung *f.* education.
Schulbuchverlag *m.* educational publisher.
Schuld *f.* **(-, -en)** guilt, fault; debt; *einem ~ geben,* to blame sb.; *sich etwas zu ~en kommen lassen,* to be guilty of sth.; *ich bin daran ~*, it is my fault; *eine ~ abtragen,* to pay off a debt.
Schuldbekenntnis *n.* confession (of guilt).
schuldbewußt *a.* guilty.
schulden *v.t.* to owe, to be indebted to.
Schulden *f.pl.* debts; *~ eingehen, machen,* to contract *or* incur debts.
schuldenfrei *a.* debt-free; unmortgaged.
Schuldentilgung *f.* liquidation of debts.
Schuldforderung *f.* claim, demand.
Schuldgefühl *n.* feeling of guilt.
schuldig *a.* guilty, culpable; due; indebted, owing; *einen etwas ~ bleiben,* to remain in debt to sb. for sth.; *einen ~ sprechen,* to find a person guilty.
Schuldige *m./f.* guilty person; guilty party.
Schuldigerklärung *f.* (law) conviction.
Schuldigkeit *f.* **(-, 0)** obligation, duty.
Schuldirektor(in) *m.(f.)* principal.
Schuldklage *f.* action for debt.
schuldlos *a.* guiltless; innocent.
Schuldner *m.* **(-s, -)** debtor.

Schuldschein *m.*, **Schuldverschreibung** *f.* promissory note, I.O.U. (I owe you).
Schuldspruch *m.* verdict of guilt.
Schule *f.* **(-, -n)** school; school-house; *eine ~ besuchen, in die ~ gehen, auf der ~ sein,* to go to school, to be at school.
schulen *v.t.* to school; to train.
Schulentlassungsalter *n.* school-leaving age.
Schüler *m.* **(-s, -); Schülerin** *f.* **(-, -nen)** student, schoolboy, schoolgirl; pupil.
Schüleraustausch *m.* student exchange.
Schülerlotse *m.* student acting as a school crossing guard.
Schülermitverwaltung *f.* student council.
Schülerzeitung *f.* school newspaper.
Schulfach *n.* school subject.
Schulfall *m.* test case.
Schulferien *pl.* vacation.
schulfrei *a.* ~ **haben** have a day off from school.
Schulfreund(in) *m.(f.)* friend from school.
Schulgelände *f.* campus, premises.
Schulgeld *n.* tuition.
Schulheft *n.* exercise book.
Schulhof *m.* schoolyard.
schulisch *a.* at school; school.
Schuljahr *n.* school year.
Schulkamerad *m.* schoolfriend.
Schulleiter *m.*, **Schulleiterin** *f.* principal.
Schulmappe *f.* bookbag.
schulmeistern *v.t. & i.* (*pej.*) to lecture, to censure.
Schulordnung *f.* school rule.
Schulpflicht *f.* required school attendance.
schulpflichtig *a.* required to attend school; *~es Alter,* school age.
Schulschiff *n.* training ship.
Schulschluß *m.* end of school.
Schulschwänzer *m.* truant.
Schulsprecher(in) *m.(f.)* students' representative.
Schulstunde *f.* period.
Schultasche *f.* bookbag.
Schulter *f.* **(-, -n)** shoulder.
Schulterblatt *n.* shoulder blade.
schulterfrei *a.* off-the-shoulder.
schultern *v.t.* to shoulder.
Schultertasche *f.* shoulder bag.
Schulung *f.* **(-, -en)** training, practice.
Schulunterricht *m.* lessons, classes.
Schulweg *m.* way to school.
Schulwesen *n.* school system.
Schulzeit *f.* schooldays.
Schulzeugnis *n.* report card, grades.
Schulzwang *m.* compulsory education.
schummeln *v.i.* to cheat.
schummerig *a.* (*fam.*) dim.
Schund *m.* **(-[e]s, 0)** trash, rubbish.
schunkeln *v.i.* to rock; to sway.
Schuppe *f.* **(-, -n)** scale; dandruff.
schuppen *v.r.* to scale.
Schuppen *m.* **(-s, -)** shed; (*fam.*) joint (restaurant).
schuppig *a.* scaly.
Schur *f.* **(-, -en)** shearing; fleece.
schüren *v.t.* to stoke; (*fig.*) to stir up.
schürfen *v.t.* to scratch, to cut; to prospect (*nach,* for); to open a mine.
Schürfwunde *f.* **(-, -n)** graze, abrasion.
Schurke *m.* **(-n, -n)** rogue, rascal, villain.
Schurkenstreich *m.* villainy.
schurkisch *a.* knavish, rascally.
Schurwolle *f.* virgin wool.
Schurz *m.* **(-es, -e)** apron.
Schürze *f.* **(-, -n)** apron.
schürzen *v.t.* to tuck up; to purse (lips).
Schürzenjäger *m.* (*fam.*) womanizer.
Schuß *m.* **(Schusses, Schüsse)** shot.
Schüssel *f.* **(-, -n)** dish, platter.
Schußfeld *n.* range.
Schuß: ~waffe *f.* firearm; **~weite** *f.* range; **~wunde** *f.* gunshot wound.
Schuster *m.* **(-s, -)** shoemaker.
schustern *v.i.* to cobble.
Schutt *m.* **(-[e]s, 0)** rubble.
Schüttelfrost *m.* shivering fit.
schütteln *v.t.* to shake, to toss; *einem die Hand ~,* to shake hands with sb.; *aus dem Ärmel ~,* to produce offhand.
schütten *v.t. & i.* to shed, to pour; to heap.
Schutz *m.* **(-es, 0)** protection, shelter; *in ~ nehmen,* to take under one's protection.
Schutz: ~befohlene *m./f.* protégé, client; **~blech** *n.* mudguard; **~brille** *f.* goggles.
Schütze *m.* **(-n, -n)** shot, marksman; (*mil.*) rifleman.
schützen *v.t.* to protect, to guard, shelter.
Schutzengel *m.* guardian angel.
Schützengraben *m.* trench.
Schützenregiment *m.* rifle regiment.
Schutz: ~frist *f.* term of copyright; **~haft** *f.* protective custody; **~helm** *m.* helmet; **~herr** *m.* patron, protector; **~impfung** *f.* immunization.
Schützling *m.* **(-[e]s, -e)** protégeé.
schutzlos *a.* defenseless, unprotected.
Schutz: ~mann *m.* policeman, constable; **~marke** *f.* trade-mark; **~raum** *m.* (*Luftschutz*) shelter; **~rücken** *m.* (*Buch*) cover; **~umschlag** *m.* (publisher's) jacket, dust cover; **~zoll** *m.* protection; **~zöllner** *m.* protectionist.
schwabbelig *a.* (*fam.*) flabby; wobbly.
schwabbeln *v.i.* (*fam.*) to wobble.
Schwabe *m.;* **Schwäbin** *f.;* **schwäbisch** *a.* Swabian.
schwäbeln *v.i.* (*fam.*) to speak Swabian.
Schwaben *n.* Swabia.
schwach *a.* weak, feeble, infirm; *mir wird ~,* I feel faint.
Schwäche *f.* **(-, -)** weakness, feebleness.
schwächen *v.t.* to weaken, to enfeeble.
Schwachheit *f.* **(-, -en)** weakness, frailty, infirmity.
Schwachkopf *m.* simpleton, idiot.
schwachköpfig *a.* idiotic.
schwächlich *a.* infirm, feeble, sickly.
Schwächling *m.* **(-s, -e)** weakling.
Schwachsinn *m.* mental deficiency.
schwachsinnig *a.* feeble-minded, mentally deficient *or* defective.
Schwachstrom *m.* low-voltage.
Schwächung *f.* **(-, -en)** weakening.
Schwaden *m.* **(-s, 0)** cloud; vapor, steam.
Schwadron *f.* **(-, -en)** squadron, squad.
schwadronieren *v.i.* to bluster.
Schwafelei *f.* **(-, -en)** nonsense, gibberish.
schwafeln *v.i.* (*fam.*) to talk nonsense, to babble.
Schwager *m.* **(-s, Schwäger)** brother-in-law.
Schwägerin *f.* **(-, -nen)** sister-in-law.
Schwalbe *f.* **(-, -n)** swallow.
Schwall *m.* **(-[e]s, 0)** gush, flood.
Schwamm *m.* **(-[e]s, Schwämme)** sponge; mushroom, fungus; *Haus~,* dry rot.

schwammig *a.* spongy; bloated; woolly; ~ *adv.* vaguely.
Schwan *m.* **(-[e]s, Schwäne)** swan.
schwanen *v.i. & imp.* to sense.
Schwanengesang *m.* swansong.
schwanger *a.* pregnant.
Schwangere *f.* **(-n, -n)** pregnant woman.
schwängern *v.t.* to make pregnant; (*fig.*) to impregnate.
Schwangerschaft *f.* **(-, -en)** pregnancy.
Schwangerschaftsunterbrechung *f.* abortion, termination of pregnancy.
Schwank *m.* **(-[e]s, Schwänke)** merry tale; (*theatr.*) farce.
schwanken *v.i.* to totter, to stagger; (*fig.*) to waver; to fluctuate; to hesitate.
Schwankung *f.* **(-, -en)** fluctuation
Schwanz *m.* **(-es, Schwänze)** tail; (*vulg.*) cock, prick.
schwänzeln *v.i.* to wag its tail.
schwänzen *v.t.* (*die Schule, etc.*) to play hooky.
Schwanzflosse *f.* tail fin.
schwappen *v.i.* to splash; to slosh.
Schwäre *f.* abscess, ulcer.
schwären *v.i.* to fester, to suppurate.
Schwarm *m.* **(-[e]s, Schwärme)** swarm.
schwärmen *v.i.* to swarm; to riot, to revel; ~ *für*, to be mad about.
Schwärmer *m.* **(-s, -)** dreamer; enthusiast.
Schwärmerei *f.* **(-, -en)** enthusiasm.
schwärmerisch *a.* enthusiastic, fanatic.
Schwarte *f.* **(-, -n)** rind (bacon).
schwarz *a.* black; *es wird ihm ~ vor den Augen*, his head begins to swim; *ins Schwarze treffend*, to hit the mark; ~ *auf weiß*, in black and white; **~e Liste** *f.* black list; **~es Brett** *n.* notice board, bulletin board.
Schwarz *n.* **(-es, 0)** black (color).
Schwarzarbeit *f.* moonlighting.
Schwarzbrot *n.* rye bread.
Schwarzdorn *m.* blackthorn.
Schwarze *m./f.* black person.
Schwarze *n.* bull's eye (target).
Schwärze *f.* **(-, -n)** blacking; (printer's) ink.
schwärzen *v.t.* to black(en); to black out.
Schwarzfahrer *m.*; **Schwarzfahrerin** *f.* fare-dodger.
Schwarzhandel *m.* black marketeering.
schwärzlich *a.* blackish.
Schwarzmarkt *m.* black market.
Schwarzseher *m.* pessimist.
Schwarzwald *m.* the Black Forest.
schwarzweiß *a.* black-and-white.
Schwarzwurzel *f.* black salsify.
Schwatz *m.* chat; natter.
schwatzen, schwätzen *v.i.* to chatter, to talk idly.
Schwätzer *m.* **(-s, -); Schwätzerin** *f.* chatterbox, blabber.
schwatzhaft *a.* talkative, garrulous.
Schwebe *f.* **(-, 0)** suspense; *in der ~ sein*, to be undecided.
Schwebebahn *f.* suspension railway.
Schwebebalken *m.* **(s-, -)** balance beam.
schweben *v.i.* to hover, to float; to be suspended; (*fig.*) to be pending; *in Gefahr ~*, to be in danger; *die Sache schwebt noch*, the matter is still pending.
Schwede *m.*; **Schwedin** *f.* Swede.
Schweden *n.* **(-s, 0)** Sweden.
schwedisch *a.* Swedish.
Schwefel *m.* **(-s, -)** sulfur.
schwefelig *s.* sulfurous.
schwefeln *v.t.* to sulphurize.
Schwefelsäure *f.* sulphuric acid.
Schwefelwasserstoff *m.* hydrogen sulfide.
Schweif *m.* **(-[e]s, -e)** tail; (*fig.*) train.
schweifen *v.i. (s)* to roam, to stray.
Schweigegeld *n.* hush money.
Schweigemarsch *m.* silent march.
Schweigeminute *f.* minute of silence.
schweigen *v.i.st.* to be silent, to hold one's tongue.
Schweigen *n.* **(-s, 0)** silence.
schweigsam *a.* taciturn, silent; quiet.
Schwein *n.* **(-[e], -e)** pig, hog, swine; pork; (*fam.*) luck.
Schweine: ~braten *m.* roast pork; **~fett** *n.* lard; **~fleisch** *n.* pork; **~hirt** *m.* swineherd.
Schweinehund *m.* (*pej.*) bastard.
Schweinerei *f.* **(-, -en)** filth, mess; (*fig.*) obscenity.
Schweinestall *m.* pigsty, pigpen.
schweinisch *a.* swinish, filthy.
Schweins: ~borste *f.* hog's bristle; **~hachse, ~haxe** *f.* knuckle of pork; **~keule** *f.* leg of pork; **~leder** *n.* pig-skin.
Schweiß *m.* **(-es, 0)** sweat; perspiration.
schweißen *v.t.* to weld.
Schweißer *m.* **(-s, -); Schweißerin** *f.* **(-, -nen)** (*mech.*) welder.
schweißgebadet *a.* soaked with sweat.
schweißtreibend *a.* sudorific; ~ **sein,** make one sweat.
Schweiz *f.* **(-, 0)** Switzerland.
Schweizer *m.* **(-s, -); Schweizerin** *f.* **(-, -nen); schweizerisch** *a.* Swiss.
schweizerdeutsch *a.* Swiss German.
Schweizer Käse *m.* Swiss cheese.
Schwelbrand *m.* smoldering fire.
schwelen *v.i.* to smolder.
schwelgen *v.i.* to revel, to feast.
schwelgerisch *a.* luxuriant; sumptuous.
Schwelle *f.* **(-, -n)** threshold, sill; (*rail.*) sleeper.
schwellen *v.i. (s)* to swell.
Schwellenangst *f.* fear of entering a place.
Schwellung *f.* **(-, -en)** swelling, to become swollen.
Schwemme *f.* **(-, -n)** glut; watering place.
schwemmen *v.t.* to wash (*an Land*) ashore.
Schwemmland *n.* alluvial land.
Schwengel *m.* **(-s, -)** *Glocken~*, clapper; *Pumpen~*, handle.
Schwenk *m.* **(-s, -s)** swing; pan (film).
schwenken *v.t.* to swing; to wave; to pan; ~ *v.i.* to wheel.
schwer *a.* heavy, weighty; difficult, hard; grave; grievous; (*Wein*) strong; **~e Artillerie** medium artillery; *ein Pfund ~*, weighing one pound; *es fällt mir ~*, I find it hard.
Schwer: ~arbeit *f.* heavy work; **~behinderte** *m./f.* severely handicapped person; **~beschädigter** *m.* seriously disabled man.
schwerbewaffnet *a.* heavily armed.
Schwere *f.* **(-, 0)** gravity; heaviness.
schwerelos *a.* weightless.
Schwerelosigkeit *f.* weightlessness.
Schwerenöter *m.* **(-s, -)** ladykiller.
schwerfällig *a.* ponderous; unwieldy; clumsy.
Schwergewicht *n.* weight; (Boxer) heavyweight.

schwerhörig *a.* hard of hearing.
Schwerindustrie *f.* heavy industry.
Schwerkraft *f.* gravitation.
schwerlich *adv.* hardly, scarcely.
Schwermut *f.* melancholy.
schwermütig *a.* melancholic.
Schwerpunkt *m.* center of gravity.
schwerste Artillerie *f.* heavy artillery.
Schwert *n.* **(-[e]s, -er)** sword; **~fisch** *m.* swordfish; **~lilie** *f.* iris.
Schwerverbrecher *m.* serious offender.
schwerverdaulich *a.* hard to digest.
schwerverletzt *a.* seriously injured.
schwer: ~verständlich *a.* hard to understand, abstruse; **~verwundet** *a.* severely wounded.
Schwester *f.* **(-, -n)** sister; nun; nurse.
schwesterlich *a.* sisterly.
Schwieger: ~eltern *pl.* parents-in-law *pl.*; **~mutter** *f.* mother-in-law; **~sohn** *m.* son-in-law; **~tochter** *f.* daughter-in-law; **~vater** *m.* father-in-law.
Schwiele *f.* **(-, -n)** callus.
schwielig *a.* callused, horny.
schwierig *a.* hard, difficult.
Schwierigkeit *f.* **(-, -en)** difficulty.
Schwierigkeitsgrad *m.* degree of difficulty.
Schwimm: ~anzug *m.* swimsuit; **~bad** *n.* swimming pool; **~dock** *n.* floating dock.
schwimmen *v.t.st.* to swim; to float.
Schwimmen *n.* **(-s, 0)** swimming.
Schwimmer *m.* **(-s, -)** swimmer; float.
Schwimmerin *f.* **(-, -nen)** swimmer.
Schwimm: ~flosse *f.* flipper; fin; **~gestell** *n.* (*avi.*) float; **~gürtel** *m.* lifebelt; **~vogel** *m.* web-footed bird; **~weste** *f.* life jacket.
Schwindel *m.* **(-s, 0)** giddiness, dizziness, vertigo; swindle, cheat, humbug, bubble.
Schwindelei *f.* swindle, fraud; lies *pl.*
schwindelerregend *a.* vertiginous; meteoric.
schwindelfrei *a.* **~ sein,** to have a good head for heights; *nicht ~ sein,* to be afraid of heights.
schwindelhaft *a.* fraudulent.
schwind(e)lig *a.* dizzy, giddy.
schwindeln *v.i.* to swindle, to cheat, **~** *v.imp.* to be giddy.
Schwindelpreis *m.* extortionate price.
schwinden *v.t.st.* (s) to disappear, to vanish; (*Radio*) to fade.
Schwindler *m.* **(-s, -)** swindler, cheat.
schwindlerisch *a.* swindling.
Schwindsucht *f.* consumption, tuberculosis.
schwindsüchtig *a.* consumptive, tubercular.
Schwinge *f.* **(-, -n)** wing.
schwingen *v.t. & i.st.* to brandish; to swing; to vibrate, to oscillate.
Schwingtür *f.* swing door.
Schwingung *f.* **(-, -en)** vibration, oscillation.
Schwips *m.* **(-es, e)** *einen ~ haben,* to be tipsy.
schwirren *v.i.* to whir; to buzz.
Schwitzbad *n.* steam bath, Turkish bath.
schwitzen *v.i.* to sweat, to perspire.
schwitzig *a.* sweaty.
schwören *v.t.st.* to swear; *einen Eid ~,* to take an oath; *auf etwas ~, bei etwas ~,* to swear by; *falsch ~,* to swear falsely.
schwul *a.* gay, homosexual.
schwül *a.* sultry, muggy.
Schwule *m.* **(-n, -n)** (*fam.*) gay man.
Schwüle *f.* **(-, 0)** sultriness.
Schwulst *m.* **(-es, 0)** bombast.
schwülstig *a.* bombastic, inflated.
Schwund *m.* **(-[e]s, 0)** decrease, decline; fading; atrophy.
Schwung *m.* **(-[e]s, Schwünge)** swing, vibration; momentum; flight, strain; rapture; *etwas ist im ~, kommt in ~,* sth. is in full swing, is coming into vogue.
schwunghaft *a.* flourishing, spirited; thriving.
schwunglos *a.* spiritless, lifeless.
Schwungrad *m.* flywheel.
schwungvoll *a.* full of fire.
Schwur *m.* **(-[e]s, Schwüre)** oath.
Schwurgericht *n.* jury court; **~sverhandlung** *f.* trial by jury.
s.d. *siehe dort,* see above *or* there.
sechs *a.* six.
Sechs *f.* **(-, 0)** number six; lowest grade (in German school).
Sechsachteltakt *m.* (*mus.*) six-eight time.
Sechseck *n.* **(-[e]s, -e)** hexagon.
sechserlei *a.* of six kinds.
sechsfach *a.* sixfold.
sechsmal *adv.* six times.
sechsmonatlich *a.* half-yearly.
sechsseitig *a.* hexagonal.
sechstens *adv.* sixthly.
sechzehn *a.* sixteen.
Sechzehntel *n.* **(-s, -)** sixteenth part; note *f.*, (*mus.*) sixteenth note.
sechzig *a.* sixty; *ein Mann in den ~ern, ein Sechziger,* a sexagenarian.
See *m.* **(-[e]s, -[e]n)** lake; **~** *f.* **(-, 0)** sea; *zur ~,* at sea; *hohe (offene) ~,* high *or* open sea; *in ~ gehen,* to put to sea.
Seeadler *m.* sea eagle.
Seebad *n.* seaside resort.
Seefahrt *f.* voyage, cruise; navigation.
seefest *a.* seaworthy; *~ sein,* to be a good sailor.
Seegang *m.* motion of the sea.
Seegefecht *n.* naval battle.
Seegras *n.* seaweed.
Seehafen *m.* seaport.
Seehandel *m.* maritime trade.
Seeherrschaft *f.* naval supremacy.
Seehund *m.* seal.
Seeigel *m.* sea urchin.
Seekadett *m.* naval cadet.
Seekarte *f.* chart.
Seeklima *n.* maritime climate.
seekrank *a.* seasick.
Seekrankheit *f.* seasickness.
Seekrieg *m.* naval war.
Seeküste *f.* seacoast.
Seelachs *m.* pollack; sea salmon.
Seele *f.* **(-, -n)** soul; mind; *mit Leib und ~,* body and soul.
Seelenamt *n.* office for the dead.
Seelenfriede *m.* peace of mind.
seelenfroh *a.* heartily glad.
Seelengröße *f.* magnanimity.
Seelenheil *n.* spiritual welfare.
Seelenhirt *m.* pastor.
Seelenmesse *f.* requiem.
Seelenruhe *f.* composure, calmness.
seelenruhig *a.* calm; unruffled.
seelenvergnügt *a.* thoroughly happy.
Seelenwanderung *f.* transmigration of souls.
Seeleute *pl.* seamen, mariners *pl.*
seelisch *a.* mental; psychological.
Seelöwe *m.* sea lion.

Seelsorge *f.* pastoral care; **~r** *m.* pastor.
seelsorgerisch *a.* pastoral.
Seeluft *f.* sea air.
Seemacht *f.* maritime power.
Seemann *m.* sailor, mariner.
Seemeile *f.* nautical mile; knot.
Seenot *f.* distress.
Seeoffizier *m.* naval officer.
Seepferd *n.* sea horse.
Seeräuber *m.* pirate, corsair; **~ei** *f.* piracy.
Seerecht *n.* maritime law.
Seereise *f.* voyage, cruise.
Seerose *f.* water lily.
Seeschiffahrt *f.* ocean navigation.
Seeschlacht *f.* naval battle.
Seesieg *m.* naval victory.
Seesoldat *m.* marine.
seetüchtig *a.* seaworthy.
Seeufer *n.* shore, beach.
Seewarte *f.* naval observatory.
seewärts *adv.* seaward, outward.
Seeweg *m.* sea route; *auf dem ~e,* by sea.
Seewesen *n.* naval affairs *pl.*
Seezunge *f.* (*Fisch*) sole.
Segel *m.* **(-s, -)** sail; **~ setzen,** to set sail; **~ streichen,** to strike sail.
Segelboot *n.* sailboat.
Segel: ~flug *m.* gliding; **~flieger** *m.* glider; **~jacht** *f.* sailing yacht.
segeln *v.i. (s, h)* to sail.
Segel: ~regatta *f.* sailing regatta; **~schiff** *n.* sailing vessel; **~tuch** *n.* canvas.
Segen *m.* **(-s, -0)** blessing, benediction; abundance.
segensreich *a.* blessed.
segensvoll *a.* blessed, fruit-bearing.
Segenswunsch *m.* blessing, kind wishes *pl.*
Segler *m.* **(-s, -)** sailor, yachtsman.
Seglerin *f.* **(-, -nen)** sailor, yachtswoman.
segnen *v.t.* to bless.
Segnung *f.* **(-, -en)** blessing, benediction.
sehen *v.i. & t.st.* to see, to look, to behold; *einem auf die Finger ~*, to watch one closely; *durch die Finger ~*, to connive, to wink at; *ungern ~*, to dislike; *ähnlich ~*, to look like, to resemble; *~ nach,* to look for; (*sorgen*) to look after; *vom ~*, by sight.
sehenswert *a.* worth seeing.
Sehenswürdigkeit *f.* **(-, -en)** sight, place of interest.
Seher *m.* **(-s, -)** seer, prophet.
Sehergabe *f.* gift of prophecy.
Seherin *f.* **(-, -nen)** seer, prophetess.
Sehfehler *m.* eye defect.
Sehfeld *n.* range of vision.
Sehkraft *f.* visual faculty, eyesight.
Sehne *f.* **(-, -n)** sinew, tendon; *Bogen~*, string; (*math.*) chord.
sehnen *v.r.* (*nach*) to long (for); to yearn.
Sehnenzerrung *f.* pulled tendon.
Sehnerv *m.* optic nerve.
sehnig *a.* sinewy; wiry; stringy (meat).
sehnlich *a.* ardent, fervent; **~** *adv.* eagerly, ardently.
Sehnsucht *f.* **(-, 0)** intense longing; yearning.
sehnsüchtig *a.* longing, yearning.
sehr *adv.* very, much, greatly.
Sehschärfe *f.* visual power, (eye) sight.
Sehschwäche *f.* poor (eye) sight.
Sehstörung *f.* impaired vision.
Sehtest *m.* eye test.
seicht *a.* shallow, flat, superficial.
Seide *f.* **(-, 0)** silk.
Seidel *m.* **(-s, -)** beer mug (pint).
seiden *a.* silk(en).
Seiden: ~händler *m.* silk merchant; **~papier** *n.* tissue paper; **~raupe** *f.* silkworm.
seidenweich *a.* silky.
seidig *a.* silky.
Seife *f.* **(-, -n)** soap.
seifen *v.t.* to soap.
Seifen: ~blase *f.* soap bubble; **~lauge** *f.* soapsuds; **~pulver** *n.* soap powder; **~schale** *f.* soap dish; **~schaum** *m.* lather.
seifig *a.* soapy.
seihen *v.t.* to strain, to filter.
Seiher *m.* **(-s, -)** strainer.
Seihtuch *n.* straining cloth.
Seil *n.* **(-[e]s, -e)** rope, cord, line.
Seilbahn *f.* cableway.
Seiltänzer *m.*; **Seiltänzerin** *f.* tightrope walker.
sein *pn.* his, of him; its, of it; *das Seine,* his property; *die Seinen,* his people.
sein *v.i.ir. (s)* to be, to exist.
Sein *n.* **(-s, 0)** being, existence.
seinerseits *adv.* on his part.
seinerzeit *adv.* in its time, in those days.
seinethalben, seinetwegen, um seinetwillen *adv.* on his account, for his sake.
Seinige *n.* **(-n, 0)** his; *die ~n pl.* his family.
Seismograph *m.* seismograph; **Seismologe** *m.*, **Seismologin** *f.* seismologist.
seit *pr. & c.* since; for.
seitdem *adv.* since then.
Seite *f.* **(-, -n)** side, part, flank; page; party; *schwache ~*, weak point; *bei ~*, aside; *sich auf jemandes ~ stellen,* to side with sb.; *bei ~ schaffen,* to put out of the way, to make away with; *auf jemandes ~ stehen,* to take sb.'s part.
Seitenangriff *m.* flank attack.
Seitenansicht *f.* profile, side view.
Seitenausgang *m.* side exit.
Seitenblick *m.* sidelong glance.
Seiteneingang *f.* side entrance.
Seitenflügel *m.* side aisle, wing.
Seitenhieb *m.* (*fig.*) sideswipe.
seitenlang *a.* of many pages; **~** *adv.* for pages and pages.
Seitenlinie *f.* collateral line; sideline; touchline.
Seitenloge *f.* side box.
seitens *pr.* on the part of.
Seitenschiff *n.* aisle.
Seitensprung *f.* escapade.
Seitenstechen *n.* pain in the side, stitch.
Seitensteuer *n.* rudder.
Seitenstreifen *m.* shoulder (highway).
Seitentür *f.* side door.
Seitenverwandte *m./f.* collateral relation.
seither *adv.* since (that time)
seitlich *a.* lateral, collateral.
seitwärts *adv.* sideways, aside.
Sek., sek. *sekunde,* second, sec., s.
Sekret *n.* **(-s, -e)** secretion.
Sekretär *m.* **(-s, -e); Sekretärin** *f.* **(-, -nen)** (secretary's) office.
Sekt *m.* **(-[e]s, -e)** sparkling wine; champagne.
Sekte *f.* **(-, -n)** sect.
Sektierer *m.* **(-s, -)** sectarian.
Sektion *f.* **(-, -en)** section; postmortem (examination).

Sektor *n.* **(-s, -en)** field; sector.
Sekunda *f.* **(-, -den)** second grade.
Sekundant *m.* **(-en, -en)** second.
sekundär *a.* secondary.
Sekunde *f.* **(-, -n)** second; *Bruchteil einer* ~, split-second.
Sekundenschnelle *f. in* ~, in a matter of seconds.
Sekundenzeiger *m.* second hand (of a watch).
selber *pn.* myself, himself, etc., personally (*cp. derselbe*).
selbst *pn.* self; myself, etc.; ~ *adv.* even.
Selbstachtung *f.* self-respect.
selbständig *a.* independent.
Selbständigkeit *f.* **(-, 0)** independence.
Selbstauslöser *m.* self-timer.
Selbstbedienung *f.* self-service.
Selbstbefriedigung *f.* masturbation.
Selbstbehauptung *f.* self-assertion.
Selbstbeherrschung *f.* self-control.
Selbstbestimmung *f.* self-determination.
Selbstbetrug *m.* self-deception.
selbstbewußt *a.* self-confident.
Selbstbewußtsein *n.* self-confidence.
Selbsterhaltung *f.* self-preservation.
Selbsterkenntnis *f.* self-knowledge.
selbstgefällig *a.* smug, self-complacent.
Selbstgefälligkeit *f.* complacency.
selbstgenügsam *a.* self-sufficient.
selbstgerecht *a.* self-righteous.
Selbstgespräch *n.* monologue, soliloquy. *ein* ~ *führen,* to talk to oneself.
selbstherrlich *a. & adv.* high-handed(ly).
Selbsthilfe *f.* self-help.
Selbstjustiz *f.* self-administered justice.
Selbstklebefolie *f.* self-adhesive plastic sheeting.
Selbstkostenpreis *m.* cost-price.
Selbstkritik *f.* self-criticism.
Selbstlaut *m.* vowel.
selbstlos *a.* unselfish, disinterested.
Selbstlosigkeit *f.* unselfishness, altruism.
Selbstmord *m.* suicide; ~ *begehen,* to commit suicide.
Selbstmörder *m.* suicide.
selbstmörderisch *a.* suicidal.
selbstredend *a.* self-evident; ~ *adv.* of course.
Selbstschuß *m.* spring-gun.
selbstsicher *a.* self-confident.
Selbstsucht *f.* **(-, 0)** selfishness.
selbstsüchtig *a.* selfish, egotistic.
selbsttätig *a.* spontaneous; automatic.
Selbsttäuschung *f.* self-delusion.
Selbstüberwindung *f.* self-control.
Selbstverleugnung *f.* self-denial.
selbstverständlich *a.* self-evident; ~ *adv.* of course; needless to say, obviously, it goes without saying.
Selbstvertrauen *m.* self-confidence, self-reliance.
Selbstverwaltung *f.* self-government.
Selbstzufriedenheit *f.* self-satisfaction.
Selbstzweck *m.* end in itself.
Selen *n.* **(-s, 0)** selenium.
selig *a.* blessed, blissful; (*obs.*) deceased, late.
Seligkeit *f.* **(-, -en)** salvation; perfect happiness.
seligmachend *a.* beatific; saving.
seligsprechen *v.t.* to beatify.
Seligsprechung *f.* **(-, -en)** beatification.
Sellerie *m.* **(-s, -s)** celery.
selten *a.* rare, scarce; ~ *adv.* seldom, rarely.
Seltenheit *f.* **(-, -en)** rarity, scarcity; curiosity, curio.
Selterswasser *n.* seltzer (water).
seltsam *a.* singular, strange, odd.
seltsamerweise *adv.* strangely enough.
Semantik *f.* **(-, 0)** semantics.
semantisch *a.* semantic; *adv.* semantically.
Semester *m.* **(-s, -)** academic term; semester.
Seminar *n.* **(-s, -e)** training college; seminary.
Seminar: ~arbeit *f.* seminar paper; **~schein** *m.* credits for a seminar.
Semit *m.* **(-en, -en); Semitin** *f.* **(-, -nen)** semite.
semitisch *a.* semitic.
Semmel *f.* **(-, -n)** roll; **~brösel** *pl.* bread crumbs; **~knödel** *m.* bread dumpling.
sen. *senior,* senior, Sen., Sr.
Senat *m.* **(-s, -e)** senate.
Sendbote *m.* emissary.
Sendebereich *m.* transmitting area.
senden *v.t.ir.* to send, to dispatch; to broadcast; *nach einem* ~, to send for sb.; *Waren mit der Post* ~, to send goods by mail; to broadcast.
Sender *m.* **(-s, -)** transmitter; broadcasting station.
Senderaum *m.* (*Radio*) studio.
Sendestation *f.* radio *or* broadcasting station.
Sendung *f.* **(-, -en)** mission; consignment, parcel; broadcast.
Senf *m.* **(-[e]s, -e)** mustard.
Senfkorn *n.* mustard-seed.
sengen *v.t.* to singe, to scorch; to scald; ~ *und brennen,* to lay waste by fire.
senil *a.* senile.
Senilität *f.* senility.
Senior *m.; **Seniorin*** *f.* senior; senior partner; senior citizen.
Seniorenheim *n.* home for the elderly.
Senkblei *n.* plumb.
senken *v.t.* to let down, to lower; ~ *v.r.* to sink.
Senkgrube *f.* cesspit.
senkrecht *a.* perpendicular; vertical.
Senkrechtstarter *m.* vertical takeoff aircraft; (*fig.*) whiz-kid.
Senkung *f.* **(-, -en)** sinking; depression; (*Preise*) reduction; lowering; unstressed syllable.
Senner *m.* **(-s, -)** (Alpine) herdsman and dairyman.
Sennerei (-, -en), Sennhütte *f.* Alpine cheese dairy.
Sennerin *f.* **(-, -nen)** (Alpine) dairymaid.
Sensation *f.* sensation.
sensationell *a.* sensational.
Sense *f.* **(-, -n)** scythe.
sensibel *a.* sensitive.
Sensibilität *f.* sensitivity.
Sensor *m.* **(-s, -en)** sensor.
sentimental *a.* sentimental.
Sentimentalität *f.* sentimentality.
separat *a.* separate.
Separatismus *m.* separation.
Sept. *September,* September, Sept.
September *m.* **(-s, -)** September.
Septime *f.* seventh (music).
sequestrieren *v.t.* to sequestrate.
Serail *n.* **(-s, -s)** seraglio.
Serbe *m.;* **Serbin** *f.* Serb.
Serbien *n.* Serbia.
serbisch *a.* Serbian.
Serenade *f.* serenade.
Sergeant *m.* **(-en, -en)** sergeant.
Serie *f.* **(-, -n)** series.

serienmäßig *a.* standard; fitted as standard.
Seriennummer *f.* serial number.
Serienproduktion *f.* series production.
seriös *a.* respectable; trustworthy.
Serum *n.* **(-s, -ra & -ren)** serum.
Service *n.* service, set.
Service *m.* service; serve (tennis).
servieren *v.t.* to serve.
Serviererin *f.* waitress.
servierfertig, *a.* ready-to-serve.
Serviette *f.* **(-, -n)** napkin.
Sessel *m.* **(-s, -)** easy chair, arm chair.
Sessellift *m.* chairlift.
seßhaft *a.* settled; sedentary resident.
Setzei *n.* fried egg.
setzen *v.t.* to set, to put, to place; to stake; to compose; ~ *v.i.* to leap; ~ *v.r.* to sit down; to settle; *alles auf eine Karte* ~, to stake everything on one card; *aufs Spiel* ~, to stake, to risk; *instand* ~, to enable; to repair; *in Schrecken* ~, to frighten; *unter Wasser* ~, to inundate; *alles daran* ~, to risk everything; *sich zur Ruhe* ~, to retire into private life; *sich zur Wehr* ~, to offer resistance; *über den Fluß* ~, to cross the river; *gesetzt den Fall,* put the case, suppose.
Setzer *m.* **(-s, -); Setzerin** *f.* **(-, -nen)** typesetter.
Setzling *m.* **(-s, -e)** seedling.
Seuche *f.* **(-, -n)** epidemic; pestilence.
seuchenartig *a.* epidemic, contagious.
Seuchenbekämpfung *f.* epidemic control.
seufzen *v.i.* to sigh, to groan.
Seufzer *m.* **(-s, -)** sigh, groan; ~ *ausstoßen,* to heave sighs, to utter groans.
Sex *m.* **(-es, 0)** sex.
Sexismus *m.* sexism.
sexistisch *a.* sexist.
Sexta *f.* **(-, -ten)** first year in a German high school.
Sextett *n.* **(-[e]s, -e)** sextet(te).
Sexualerziehung *f.* sex education.
Sexualhormon *n.* sex hormone.
Sexualität *f.* sexuality.
sexuell *a.* sexual.
Sezessionskrieg *m.* American Civil War.
sezieren *v.t.* to dissect.
Seziermesser *n.* dissecting knife.
SFr., sfr *Schweizer Franken,* Swiss Franc, SF, sfr.
Sg. *Singular,* singular, sing.
sg., sog. *sogenannt,* so-called.
Show *f.* **(-, -s)** show.
Siam *n.* Siam.
Siamese *m.;* **Siamesin** *f.* Siamese.
Sibirien *n.* Siberia.
Sibylle *f.* **(-, -n)** Sibyl, prophetess.
sich *pn.* oneself, himself, etc.; each other; *an und für* ~, in itself; *wieder zu* ~ *kommen,* to come to, to regain consciousness; *es hat nichts auf* ~, it is of no consequence.
Sichel *f.* **(-, -n)** sickle; *Mond*~, crescent.
sicher *a.* sure, certain; secure, safe; ~ *adv.* for sure, for certain; ~ *wissen,* to be sure; ~*e Hand,* steady hand; ~*es Geleit,* safe-conduct; ~ *v.r.* ~ *stellen,* to secure (oneself).
Sicherheit *f.* **(-, -en)** security; surety, safety; *in* ~ *bringen,* to secure; ~ **leisten,** to stand bail, to give security; *in* ~, in (a place of) safety.
Sicherheitsabstand *m.* safe distance.
Sicherheitsglas *n.* shatterproof glass, safety glass.
sicherheitshalber *adv.* as a precaution.
Sicherheitskontrolle *f.* security check.
Sicherheitslampe *f.* safety lamp.
Sicherheitsmaßregeln *pl.* precautions.
Sicherheitsnadel *f.* safety pin.
Sicherheitsrat *m.* Security Council.
Sicherheitsschloß *n.* safety lock.
Sicherheitsventil *n.* safety valve.
Sicherheitszündholz *m.* safety match.
sicherlich *adv.* surely, certainly.
sichern *v.t.* to secure.
Sicherung *f.* **(-, -en)** (*am Gewehr*) safety bolt; (*elek.*) fuse.
Sicherungskasten *m.* fusebox.
Sicht *f.* **(-, 0)** sight; *auf* ~, at or on sight; *nach* ~, after sight; *auf kurze* ~, at short date; *auf 8 Tage* ~, seven days after sight;' *auf 2 Monate* ~, at two months' sight; *ausser* ~ *sein,* to be out of sight.
sichtbar *a.* visible; (*fig.*) evident.
sichten v.t. to sift; (*nav.*) to sight.
sichtlich *a.* obvious, perceptible.
Sichtverhältnisse *pl.* visibility.
Sichtvermerk *m.* **(-s, -e)** visa.
Sichtweite *f.* visual range.
sickern *v.i.* to trickle, to ooze.
sie *pn.* she, her; they, them.
Sie *pn.* you.
Sieb *n.* **(-[e]s, -e)** sieve; strainer.
sieben *v.t.* to sift, to strain.
sieben *a.* seven, *es ist halb* ~, it is half-past six.
siebenerlei *a.* of seven kinds.
siebenfach, siebenfältig *a.* sevenfold.
siebenmal *adv.* seven times.
Siebenmeilenstiefel *pl.* seven-league boots *pl.*
Siebensachen *pl.* one's belongings.
siebzehn *a.* seventeen.
siebzig *a.* seventy.
Siebziger *m.* **(-s, -)** septuagenarian.
siech *a.* sick, sickly, infirm.
Siechbett *n.* sickbed.
siechen *v.i.* to be sickly; to pine away.
Siechtum (-s, 0) *n.* protracted sickness.
Siedehitze *f.* boiling heat.
siedeln *v.i. & t.* to colonize, to settle.
sieden *v.t. & i.st.* to seethe, to boil; to simmer.
siedeheiß *a.* scalding hot.
Siedepunkt *m.* boiling point.
Siedler *m.* **(-s, -); Siedlerin** *f.* **(-, -nen)** settler.
Siedlung *f.* **(-, -en)** settlement.
Sieg *m.* **(-[e]s, -e)** victory; triumph.
Siegel *n.* **(-s, -)** seal; *sein* ~ *auf etwas drücken,* to set one's seal to sth.
Siegel: ~abdruck *m.* imprint (of a seal); **~lack** *m.* sealing wax.
siegeln *v.t.* to seal.
Siegelring *m.* signet ring.
siegen *v.i.* to conquer, to win, to be victorious (over).
Sieger *m.* **(-s, -); Siegerin** *f.* **(-, -nen)** conqueror, victor; (*Sport*) winner.
siegreich *a.* victorious, triumphant.
sieh! *i.* see! lo!; ~ **einmal!** ~ **da!** look there!
siezen *v.t.* to use the polite "Sie."
Signal *n.* **(-[e]s, -e)** signal.
signalisieren *v.t.* to signal.
Signalwächter *m.* (*rail.*) signalman.
Signatur *f.* **(-, -en)** initials; abbreviated signature; autograph; mark, brand; (*fig.*) stamp.
signieren *v.t.* to sign; to autograph.
Silbe *f.* **(-, -n)** syllable.
Silbenschrift *f.* syllabary.

Silbenteilung *f.* syllabication.
Silber *n.* **(-s, 0)** silver; *gediegenes* ~, solid silver.
Silberbarre *f.*, **Silberbarren** *m.* ingot of silver.
Silbergeschirr *n.* (silver-)plate, silverware.
silbern *a.* (of) silver; **~e Hochzeit** *f.* silver wedding anniversary.
Silberpappel *f.* white poplar.
Silberstreifen *m.* silver lining.
Silberwährung *f.* silver standard.
Silberwaren *pl.* silverware, silverplate.
Silberzeug *n.* silver plate.
Silentium! *i.* silence!
Silhouette *f.* **(-, -n)** silhouette.
Silikat *n.* silicate.
Silikon *n.* silicone.
Silvesterabend *m.* New Year's Eve.
Simbabwe *n.* **(-s, 0)** Zimbabwe.
simpel *a.* simple, plain.
Simpel *m.* **(-s, -)** simpleton.
Sims *m.* & *n.* **(-es, -e)** ledge; sill; mantelpiece.
Simulant *m.* **(-en, -en)**; **Simulantin** *f.* **(-, -nen)** malingerer.
simulieren *v.t.* to malinger, to simulate (illness).
simultan *a.* simultaneous.
Simultandolmetscher *m.*; **Silumtandolmetscherin** *f.* simultaneous interpreter.
Sinaihalbinsel *f.* Sinai Peninsula.
Sinekure *f.* **(-, -n)** sinecure.
Sinfonie *f.* **(-, -n)** symphony.
Sinfonieorchester *n.* symphony orchestra.
sinfonisch *a.* symphonic.
singen *v.i.* & *t.st.* to sing; *vom Blatt,* ~ to sight-read; *nach Noten* ~, to sing from notes.
Single *f.* single (recording).
Single *m.* single (person).
Single *n.* singles (tennis, etc.).
Singsang *m.* sing-song.
Singspiel *n.* singspiel.
Singstimme *f.* vocal part.
Singular *m.* singular.
Singvogel *m.* songbird.
Singweise *f.* melody, tune.
sinken *v.i.st (s)* to sink, to decline; *den Mut* ~ *lassen,* to get discouraged.
Sinn *m.* **(-[e]s, -e)** sense; mind; liking, taste (for, *für*); meaning; *im* ~ *haben,* to intend; *nicht nach meinem* ~, not to my mind; *die fünf* ~*e,* the five senses; *bei* ~*en sein,* to have one's wits about one.
Sinnbild *n.* symbol, emblem; allegory.
sinnbildlich *a.* symbolic(al), emblematic.
sinnen *v.t.st.* to meditate, to reflect, to muse; *anders gesinnt sein,* to be otherwise inclined; *nicht gesonnen sein,* to feel disinclined; *all sein Sinnen und Trachten,* all his thoughts and aspirations.
Sinnengenuß *m.* sensual pleasure.
Sinnenlust *f.* sensuality.
sinnentstellend *a.* distorting (meaning).
sinnentstellt *a.* distorted.
Sinnenwelt *f.* external world.
Sinnesänderung *f.* change of mind.
Sinnesart *f.* disposition, character.
Sinneseindruck *m.* sensation.
Sinnesorgan *n.* sense organ, sensory organ.
Sinnestäuschung *f.* illusion; hallucination; delusion.
Sinneswandel *m.* change of mind.
Sinneswerkzeug *n.* sense organ.
Sinngedicht *n.* epigram.
sinngemäß *a.* conveying the general meaning.
sinnig *a.* thoughtful; sensible.
sinnlich *a.* sensual; sensuous, material.
Sinnlichkeit *f.* **(-, 0)** sensuality.
sinnlos *a.* senseless; irrational; useless.
Sinnlosigkeit *f.* senselessness; pointlessness.
sinnreich *a.* ingenious; clever.
Sinnspruch *m.* maxim, motto, device.
sinnverwandt *a.* synonymous.
sinnvoll *a.* sensible; meaningful.
sinnwidrig *a.* nonsensical.
Sintflut *f.* (great) flood, deluge.
sintflutartig *a.* torrential; ~ *adv.* in torrents.
Sinus *m.* **(-, -)** sine.
Sippe *f.* **(-, -n)**, **Sippschaft** *f.* clan; tribe, family.
Sirene *f.* **(-, -n)** siren.
Sirenengeheul *n.* wail of sirens.
Sirup *m.* **(-s, -e)** molasses; syrup.
Sitte *f.* **(-, -n)** custom, usage, fashion.
Sitten *n.pl.* manners; morals *pl.*
Sittendezernat *n.* vice squad.
Sittengeschichte *f.* history of life and customs.
Sittengesetz *n.* moral law.
Sittenlehre *f.* moral philosophy, ethics *pl.*
sittenlos *a.* immoral.
Sittenlosigkeit *f.* **(-, 0)** immorality.
sittenrein *a.* (morally) pure.
Sittenstrenge *f.* austerity.
sittlich *a.* moral.
Sittlichkeit *f.* **(-, 0)** morality.
Sittlichkeitsverbrechen *n.* sex crime.
Sittlichkeitsverbrecher *m.* sex offender.
Sittlichkeitsvergehen *n.* indecent assault.
sittsam *a.* modest; demure.
Situation *f.* **(-, -en)** situation.
situiert *a. gut* ~, well-off.
Sitz *m.* **(-es, -e)** seat; residence; chair.
Sitzbad *n.* hip bath, sitz bath.
sitzen *v.i.st.* to sit; to fit; to be imprisoned; *gut* ~, to fit well; *auf sich* ~ *lassen,* to pocket; *ein Mädchen* ~ *lassen,* to jilt a girl; ~ *bleiben,* to remain a spinster; (*in der Schule*) to be held back; *das Kleid sitzt gut,* the dress is a good fit; *sitzende Lebensweise,* sedentary life.
Sitzfleisch *n.* (*fam.*) perseverance.
Sitzgelegenheit *f.* seating accommodation.
Sitzplatz *m.* seat.
Sitzstreik *m.* sit-down strike.
Sitzung *f.* **(-, -en)** meeting, conference; sitting, session.
Sitzungsbericht *m.* minutes, (report of) proceedings *pl.*
Sitzungssaal *m.* **(-s, -säle)** conference hall; court room.
Sizilianer *m.*; **Sizilianerin** *f.* Sicilian.
Sizilien *n.* Sicily.
Skala *f.* **(-, -len)** scale; range.
Skalp *n.* **(-s, -s)** scalp.
Skalpell *n.* **(-s, -s)** scalpel.
skalpieren *v.t.* to scalp.
Skandal *m.* **(-[e]s, -e)** scandal; row.
skandalös *a.* scandalous.
skandieren *v.t.* to scan; to chant.
Skat *m.* **(-[e]s, -e)** skat, a German card game.
Skelett *n.* **(-[e]s, -e)** skeleton.
Skepsis *f.* scepticism.
Skeptiker *m.* **(-s, -)**; **Skeptikerin** *f.* **(-, -nen)** sceptic.
skeptisch *a.* sceptical.
Ski *m.* **(-s, -er)** ski.
Ski: **~bindung** *f.* ski binding; **~lauf** *m.*, **~laufen**

n. skiing; **~läufer** *m.*, **~läuferin** *f.* skier; **~stock** *m.* ski pole.
Skizze *f.* **(-, -n)** sketch; outline.
Skizzenbuch *n.* sketch book.
skizzieren *v.t.* to sketch.
Sklave *m.* **(-n, -n); Sklavin** *f.* **(-, -nen)** slave.
Sklaven: ~halter *m.* slave owner; **~handel** *m.* slave trade; **~händler** *m.* slave trader.
Sklaverei *f.* **(-, 0)** slavery.
sklavisch *a.* slavish, servile.
Sklerose *f.* sclerosis.
Skonto *m.* **(-[s], 0)** discount.
Skorbut *m.* **(-[e]s, 0)** scurvy.
Skorpion *m.* **(-[e]s, -e)** scorpion; Scorpio (astrology).
skrupellos *a.* unscrupulous.
Skrupeln *pl.* scruples *pl.; sich keine ~ machen,* to have no scruples.
skrupelös *a.* scrupulous.
Skulptur *f.* **(-, -en)** sculpture.
skurril *a.* absurd; bizarre.
S-Kurve *f.* **(-, -n)** hairpin curve.
Slalom *m.* **(-s, -s)** slalom.
Slawe *m.* **(-n, -n); Slawin** *f.* **(-, -nen)** Slav.
slawisch *a.* Slav; Slavonic.
Slip *m.* **(-s, -s)** briefs.
Slogan *m.* **(-s, -s)** slogan.
Slowake *m.* **(-n, -n); Slowakin** *f.* **(-, -nen)** Slovak.
Slowakei *f.* **(-, 0)** Slovakia.
slowakisch *a.* Slovak; Slovakian.
Slowene *m.* **(-n, -n); Slowenin** *f.* **(-, -nen)** Slovene, Slovenian.
Slowenien *n.* **(-s, 0)** Slovenia.
slowenisch *a.* Slovene; Slovenian.
Slum *m.* **(-, -s)** slum.
Smaragd *m.* **(-[e]s, -e)** emerald.
Smog *m.* **(-s, -s)** smog; **~alarm** *m.* smog warning.
Smoking *m.* **(-s, -s)** tuxedo; dinner jacket.
Snob *n.* **(-s, -s)** snob.
Snobismus *m.* snobbery; snobbishness.
snobistisch *a.* snobbish.
so *adv. & c.* so, thus, in such a manner, like this; *~ und ~ viel,* so and so much; *~ reich er auch ist,* rich as he may be; *~ sehr auch, wenn auch noch ~ sehr,* however much, if... ever so much; *~ ein Mann,* such a man; *~ etwas,* such a thing; *um ~ besser,* so much the better.
SO *Südost(en),* southeast, SE.
So *Sonntag,* Sunday, Sun.
s.o. *siehe oben,* see above.
sobald *c.* *~ (als)* as soon as.
Socke *f.* **(-, -n)** sock.
Sockel *m.* **(-s, -)** plinth; base.
Sockenhalter *m.* garter.
Soda *f.* **(-, 0)** soda.
sodann *adv.* then.
Sodawasser *n.* soda(-water).
Sodbrennen *n.* heartburn; pyrosis.
soeben *adv.* just now, this minute.
Sofa *n.* **(-s, -s)** sofa.
sofern *c.*, if; inasmuch as, so far as.
sofort *adv.* at once, immediately.
Sofortbildkamera *f.* instant camera.
Soforthilfe *f.* immediate aid.
sofortig *a.* immediate, instantaneous.
Sofortmaßnahme *f.* immediate measure.
Soft-Eis *n.* soft ice cream.
Software *f.* **(-, -s)** software.
Sog *m.* **(-s, -e)** suction; current; wake (ship); slipstream (plane).
sogar *adv.* even.
sogenannt *a.* so-called.
sogleich *adv.* immediately, directly.
Sohle *f.* **(-, -n)** sole.
sohlen *v.t.* to sole.
Sohn *m.* **(-[e]s, Söhne)** son; *der verlorene ~,* the prodigal son.
Soja: ~bohne *f.* soybean; **~soße** *f.* soy sauce.
solange als, as long as.
solar *a.* solar.
Solarium *n.* **(-s, -rien)** solarium.
Solar: ~technik *f.* solar technology; **~zelle** *f.* solar cell.
solcher, solche, solch[es] *pn.* such; the same.
solchergestalt *a.* thus, in such manner.
solcherlei *a.* of such a kind.
Sold *m.* **(-[e]s, 0)** (military) pay; (*fig.*) wages; *in ~ stehen,* to be the hireling of.
Soldat *m.* **(-en, -en); Soldatin** *f.* **(-, -nen)** soldier; **~ werden,** to enlist.
Soldatenfriedhof *m.* war cemetery.
Soldateska *f.* **(-, 0)** (brutal) soldiery.
soldatisch *a.* soldier-like, military.
Soldliste *f.* (*mil.*) payroll.
Söldner *m.* **(-s, -)** mercenary, hireling.
Sole *f.* **(-, -n)** saltwater, brine.
solidarisch *a.* united.
Solidarität *f.* **(-, 0)** solidarity.
solide *a.* solid, strong; (*fig.*) respectable, steady, safe, solvent.
Solidität *f.* **(-, 0)** solidity; (*com.*) respectability, acknowledged standing.
Solist *m.* **(-en, -en); Solistin** *f.* **(-, -nen)** soloist.
Soll *n.* **(-[e]s, -[s])** debit; *~ und Haben,* debit and credit.
sollen *v.i.ir.* shall, to be to; to be said, be supposed to; *was soll das?* what does this mean?
Solo *n.* **(-s, -s & Soli)** solo.
Solquelle *f.* saline spring.
somatisch *a.* somatic.
somit *adv.* therefore; consequently.
Sommer *m.* **(-s, -)** summer.
Sommeranfang *f.* beginning of summer.
Sommeraufenthalt *m.* summer vacation.
Sommerfäden *m.pl.* gossamer.
Sommerfahrplan *m.* summer service timetable.
Sommerfrische *f.* summer vacation.
Sommergäste *m.pl.* visitors.
sommerlich *a.* summerlike.
Sommerschlußverkauf *m.* summer sale.
Sommersemester *n.* **(-s, -)** summer term/semester.
Sommersprosse *f.* freckle.
sommersprossig *a.* freckled.
Sommerzeit *f.* summertime.
somnambul *a.* somnambulistic.
sonach *adv.* therefore, accordingly.
Sonate *f.* **(-, -n)** sonata.
Sonde *f.* **(-, -n)** (*med.*) probe; sonde.
Sonderangebot *n.* **(-s, -e)** special offer.
Sonderausgabe *f.* special edition.
sonderbar *a.* strange, singular, odd.
Sonderberichterstatter *m.* special correspondent.
Sonderfall *m.* special case; exception.
sondergleichen *a. & adv.* without equal.
Sonderinteresse *n.* special interest.
sonderlich *a.* special, particular; important.
Sonderling *m.* **(-[e]s, -e)** odd character.
sondern *v.t.* to separate, to sever; *~ c.* but; *nicht nur..., ~ auch,* not only..., but also.

Sonder: ~nummer *f.* special edition/issue; **~recht** *n.* privilege; **~stellung** *f.* unique or exceptional position; **~zug** *m.* special train.
sondieren *v.t.* (*med.*) to probe; to sound; (*fig.*) to explore, to feel one's way.
Sonett *n.* **(-[e]s, -e)** sonnet.
Sonnabend *m.* **(-s, -e)** Saturday.
Sonne *f.* **(-, -n)** sun.
sonnen *v.r.* to sunbathe.
Sonnenaufgang *m.* sunrise.
Sonnenbad *n.* sunbath.
Sonnenblume *f.* sunflower.
Sonnenbrand *m.* sunburn.
Sonnenbrille *f.* sunglasses.
Sonnenenergie *f.* solar energy.
Sonnenfinsternis *f.* solar eclipse.
Sonnenfleck *m.* sunspot.
Sonnenjahr *n.* solar year.
sonnenklar *a.* as clear as daylight.
Sonnenkollektor *m.* solar collector.
Sonnenlicht *n.* sunlight.
Sonnenschein *m.* sunshine.
Sonnenschirm *m.* parasol, sunshade.
Sonnenspektrum *n.* solar spectrum.
Sonnenstich *m.* sunstroke.
Sonnenstrahl *m.* sunbeam.
Sonnensystem *n.* solar system.
Sonnenuhr *f.* sundial.
Sonnenuntergang *m.* sunset, sundown.
sonnenverbrannt *a.* sunburnt.
Sonnenwende *f.* solstice.
sonnig *a.* sunny, sunshiny.
Sonntag *m.* **(-s, -e)** Sunday.
sonntäglich *a.* Sunday.
sonntags *adv.* on Sunday(s).
sonst *adv.* else, otherwise; besides; formerly; ~ *etwas,* anything else; ~ *jemand,* anybody else; ~ *nichts,* nothing else; ~ *nirgends,* nowhere else; ~ *wo,* elsewhere.
sonstig *a.* other, remaining; former.
Sophistik *f.* **(-, 0)** sophistry.
sophistisch *a.* sophistic(al).
Sopran *m.* **(-[e]s, -e)** soprano, treble.
Sopranist *m.* **(-en, -en); Sopranistin** *f.* **(-, -nen)** soprano.
Sorge *f.* **(-, -n)** care; worries *pl.; sich ~ machen um,* to be concerned about.
sorgen *v.i.* to worry; to care, provide; *sich um etwas ~,* to be concerned about sth.; ~ *für,* to provide for, to see to, to look after, to take care of.
sorgenfrei, sorgenlos *a.* carefree.
Sorgenkind *n.* problem child.
sorgenschwer *a.* anxious, uneasy.
sorgenvoll *a.* anxious, uneasy.
Sorgfalt *f.* **(-, 0)** care(fulness).
sorgfältig *a.* careful, heedful.
Sorgfältigkeit *f.* carefulness.
sorglos *a.* careless, thoughtless.
sorgsam *a.* careful.
Sorte *f.* **(-, -n)** sort, kind.
sortieren *v.t.* to (as)sort.
Sortierer *m.* **(-s, -0)** sorter.
Sortimenter *m.* **(-s, -), Sortimentsbuchhändler** *m.* retail bookseller.
sosehr *conj.* however much.
Soße *f.* **(-, -n)** sauce; gravy; dressing.
Souffleur *m.* **(-[e]s, -e); Souffleuse** *f.* **(-, -n)** prompter.
Souffleurkasten *m.* prompter's box.
soufflieren *v.i.* to prompt.
Souterrain *n.* **(-[e]s, -s)** basement.
Souvenir *n.* **(-s, -s)** souvenir.
souverän *a.* sovereign.
Souverän *m.* **(-[e]s, -e)** sovereign.
Souveränität *f.* **(-, 0)** sovereignty.
soviel *c.* as far as; as soon as.
soweit *c.* as far as.
sowenig *c.* however; *n.* ~ *wie möglich,* as little as possible.
sowie *c.* as well as; as soon as.
sowieso *adv.* anyhow, anyway.
sowohl *c.* **~... als auch,...** as well as both...and.
sozial *a.* social.
Sozialabgaben *pl.* social contributions.
Sozialamt *n.* social welfare office.
Sozialarbeiter *m.,* **Sozialarbeiterin** *f.* social worker.
Sozialdemokrat *m.* **(-en, -en); Sozialdemokratin** *f.* **(-, -nen)** Social Democrat.
Sozialdemokratie *f.* social democracy.
sozialdemokratisch *a.* social-democratic.
Sozialhilfe *f.* social welfare.
sozialisieren *v.t.* to socialize.
Sozialismus *m.* **(-, 0)** socialism.
Sozialist *m.;* **Sozialistin** *f.* socialist.
sozialistisch *a.* socialist.
Sozialkunde *f.* social studies.
Sozialleistungen *pl.* social welfare benefits.
Sozialpolitik *f.* social policy.
Sozialprestige *f.* social status.
Sozialprodukt *n.* national product.
Sozialstaat *m.* welfare state.
Sozialversicherung *f.* social security.
Sozialwissenschaft *f.* sociology.
Sozialwohnung *f.* public housing unit.
Soziologie *f.* **(-, 0)** sociology.
soziologisch *a.* sociological.
Sozius *m.* **(-, Sozii)** (*com.*) partner.
sozusagen *adv.* as it were, so to speak.
Spachtel *m.* putty knife; paint-scraper.
Spachtelmasse *f.* filler.
spachteln *v.t.* to fill; to smooth over.
Spagat *m.* **(-[e]s, -e)** splits.
spähen *v.i. & t.* to spy, to peer.
Späher *m.* **(-s, -)** spy, scout.
Spähtrupp *m.* patrol; **~tätigkeit** *f.* patrol activity.
Spalier *n.* **(-[e]s, -e)** espalier, trellis; (*fig.*) lane.
Spalierobst *n.* wall fruit.
Spalt *m.* **(-[e]s, -e), Spalte** *f.* **(-, -n)** opening; crack, crevice, fissure; *Spalte* (newspaper) column.
spalten *v.t.* to split, to cleave, to slit; ~ *v.r.* to divide; to bifurcate.
spaltig *a.* fissured, cracked.
Spaltung *f.* **(-, -en)** division, cleavage, schism; (*Atomkern, Zelle*) fission.
Span *m.* **(-[e]s, Späne)** chip, splinter; **Späne** *pl.* shavings, chips *pl.*
Spanferkel *n.* sucking pig.
Spange *f.* **(-, -n)** buckle, clasp; bracelet.
Spaniel *m.* spaniel.
Spanien *n.* **(-s, 0)** Spain.
Spanier *m.* **(-s, -); Spanierin** *f.* **(-, -nen)** Spaniard.
spanisch *a.* Spanish; **~e Wand** *f.* folding screen.
Spankorb *m.* wire or wood basket.
Spann *m.* **(-[e]s, -e)** instep.
Spanne *f.* **(-, -n)** span; (*fig.*) short space; (*com.*) margin.
spannen *v.t.* to stretch, to strain; to extend; to

span; (*den Bogen*) to bend; (*das Gewehr*) to cock; *seine Forderungen zu hoch* ~, to set one's stakes too high; *einen auf die Folter* ~, to keep sb. in suspense.
spannend *a.* exciting; deeply interesting, thrilling.
Spanner *m.* **(-s, -)** press; shoetree; (*fig.*) peeping Tom.
Spannfeder *f.* spring.
Spannkraft *f.* elasticity.
Spannung *f.* **(-, -en)** tension; (*elek.*) voltage; strained relations *pl.*
Spannungsgebiet *n.* area of (political) tension.
spannungsgeladen *a.* tense.
spannungslos *a.* (*elek.*) dead.
Spannweite *f.* spread; span.
Spanplatte *f.* chipboard.
Sparbuch *n.* savings book.
Sparbüchse *f.* money box.
Spareinlage *f.* savings deposit.
sparen *v.t.* to save, to spare; ~ *v.i.* to economize.
Spargel *m.* **(-s, -)** asparagus.
Sparkasse *f.* savings bank.
spärlich *a.* scanty, meager, frugal.
Sparmaßnahmen *pl.* economy measures.
Sparren *m.* **(-s, -)** rafter.
sparsam *a.* economical, thrifty.
Sparsamkeit *f.* **(-, 0)** thrift, economy.
Sparschein *m.* savings certificate.
Sparschwein *n.* piggy bank.
spartanisch *a.* Spartan.
Sparte *f.* **(-, -n)** department, branch.
Spaß *m.* **(-es, Spässe)** jest, joke, sport; *das macht mir* ~, it amuses me; *das ist kein* ~, this is no laughing matter; *zum* ~, for fun.
spaßen *v.i.* to jest, to joke.
spaßeshalber *adv.* for the fun of it.
spaßhaft *a.* waggish, funny, jocular.
spaßig *a.* funny, amusing.
Spaßmacher, Spaßvogel *m.* comedian, clown.
spastisch *a.* spastic.
Spat *m.* **(-[e], -e)** (*Mineral*) spar.
spät *a.* & *adv.* late; *wie* ~ *ist es?* what time is it? *früher oder* ~*er*, sooner or later; ~ *am Tage, im Jahre*, late in the day, in the year.
Spaten *m.* **(-s, -)** spade.
späterhin *adv.* later on.
spätestens *adv.* at the latest.
Spätherbst *m.* late autumn.
Spätlese *f.* late vintage.
Spätobst *n.* late fruit.
Spätschicht *f.* late shift.
Spätsommer *m.* late summer.
Spatz *m.* **(-en, -en)** sparrow.
spazieren *v.i.* *(s)* to take a walk, to stroll; **~gehen** to go for a walk.
Spazier: ~fahrt *f.* drive, ride; **~gang** *m.* walk, stroll; promenade; **~stock** *m.* walking-stick; **~weg** *m.* walk, promenade.
SPD *Sozialdemokratische Partei Deutschlands*, Social Democratic Party of Germany.
Specht *m.* **(-[e]s, -e)** woodpecker.
Speck *m.* **(-[e]s, 0)** bacon; blubber (whales); (*fam.*) fat.
speckig *a.* greasy.
Speck: ~schwarte *f.* bacon rind; **~seite** *f.* side of bacon; **~stein** *m.* (mineral) soapstone.
spedieren *v.t.* to dispatch, to forward.
Spediteur *m.* **(-s, -)** forwarding agent, carrier; furniture remover.
Speditionsfirma *f.* forwarding/shipping company; moving company.
Speditionskosten *pl.* transport *or* forwarding charges.
Speer *m.* **(-[e]s, -e)** spear; javelin.
Speiche *f.* **(-, -n)** spoke.
Speichel *m.* **(-s, 0)** spittle, saliva.
Speichellecker *m.* (*pej. fam.*) toady.
Speichelleckerei *f.* (*pej. fam.*) sucking up.
Speicher *m.* **(-s, -)** granary; warehouse; attic.
speichern *v.t.* to store.
speien *v.t.* & *t.st.* to spit; to vomit.
Speise *f.* **(-, -n)** food, meat; dish.
Speisegaststätte *f.* restaurant.
Speisekammer *f.* larder, pantry.
Speisekarte *f.* menu, bill of fare.
speisen *v.t.* to feed; ~ *v.i.* to eat; to dine.
Speiseöl *n.* salad oil.
Speiseröhre *f.* gullet, esophagus.
Speisesaal *m.* dining room.
Speisewagen *m.* dining car; **~schaffner** *m.* dining-car attendant.
Speisezimmer *n.* dining room.
Spektakel *m.* & *n.* **(-s, -)** noise, row.
spektakulär *a.* spectacular.
Spektralanalyse *f.* spectrum analysis.
Spektrum *n.* **(-s, -tren)** spectrum.
Spekulant *m.* **(-en, -en)** speculator.
Spekulation *f.* **(-, -en)** speculation.
spekulieren *v.i.* to speculate (in, on).
Spelunke *f.* **(-, -n)** (*fam.*) dive.
Spelze *f.* **(-, -n)** husk.
spendabel *a.* generous.
Spende *f.* **(-, -n)** donation.
spenden *v.t.* to contribute (to), to donate.
Spender *m.* **(-s, -)**; **Spenderin** *f.* **(-, -nen)** donor.
spendieren *v.t.* to give liberally.
Spengler *m.* **(-s, -)** plumber.
Sperber *m.* **(-s, -)** sparrow-hawk.
Sperling *m.* **(-s, -e)** sparrow.
Sperma *n.* **(-s, -men)** sperm; semen.
Sperrad *n.* ratchet (wheel).
sperrangelweit *a.* wide open.
Sperrbezirk *m.* restricted area.
Sperre *f.* **(-, -n)** bar, barrier; (*nav.*) embargo, blockade; (*Straßen*~) block; *ich habe eine* ~, I have a mental block.
sperren *v.t.* to shut up, to bar, to stop; (*Druck*) to space; (*Straße*) to block; ~ *v.r.* to turn restive.
Sperrfeuer *n.* barrage.
Sperrholz *n.* plywood.
Sperrkonto *n.* blocked account.
Sperrsitz *m.* (*theat.*) orchestra seat.
Sperrung *f.* **(-, -en)** closing (off); disconnection; embargo, blockade.
Spesen *f.pl.* charges, expenses *pl.*
Spezerei *f.* **(-, -en)** grocery; spices *pl.*
Spezialarzt *m.* specialist.
spezialisieren *v.t.* to specialize, to detail.
Spezialist *m.* **(-en, -en)**; **Spezialistin** *f.* **(-, -nen)** specialist.
Spezialität *f.* **(-, -en)** specialty; special line.
speziell *a.* specific, special.
spezifisch *a.* specific; **~es Gewicht,** *n.* specific gravity.
spezifizieren *v.t.* to specify.
Sphäre *f.* **(-, -n)** sphere; province, range.
sphärisch *a.* spherical.
spicken *v.t.* to lard.
Spickzettel *m.* (*fam.*) crib, pony.

Spiegel *m.* **(-s, -)** mirror.
Spiegelbild *n.* reflected image.
Spiegelei *n.* fried egg.
Spiegelfechterei *f.* shadow boxing.
Spiegelfläche *f.* smooth surface.
Spiegelglas *n.* mirror glass.
spiegelglatt *a.* smooth as a mirror.
spiegeln *v.i.* to glitter, to shine; ~ *v.t.* to reflect; ~ *v.r.* to be reflected.
Spiegel: ~reflexkamera *f.* reflex camera; **~schrift** *f.* mirror writing.
Spiegelung *f.* **(-, -en)** reflection; mirage.
Spiel *n.* **(-[e]s, -e)** play; game; *auf dem ~e stehen,* to be at stake; *aufs ~ setzen,* to risk, to stake; *etwas anderes ist dabei im ~,* there is something else in the case; *die Hand dabei im ~ haben,* to have a finger in the pie; *einen aus dem ~ lassen,* to let sb. alone.
Spiel: ~art *f.* variety; (*Biol.*) sport; **~ball** *m.* (*fig.*) sport, plaything; **~bank** *f.* casino.
spielen *v.t. & i.* to play; to gamble; to act, to perform; *falsch ~,* to cheat at play; *vom Blatte ~,* to play at sight; *einen Streich ~,* to play a trick.
spielend *a. & adv.* (*fig.*) easy; easily.
Spieler *m.* **(-s, -); Spielerin** *f.* **(-, -nen)** player; gambler.
Spielerei *f.* **(-, -en)** child's play, sport.
spielerisch *a.* playful, sportive.
Spielfilm *m.* (feature) film.
Spielhölle *f.* gambling den.
Spielkarte *f.* playing card.
Spielleiter *m.* stage manager.
Spielplan *m.* (*theat.*) program.
Spielplatz *m.* playground.
Spielraum *m.* elbow room, play, scope.
Spielregel *m.* rule of a game.
Spielsache *f.* plaything, toy.
Spielverderber *m.* spoilsport.
Spielzeug *n.* plaything(s), toy(s).
Spieß *m.* **(-es, -e)** spear, pike; *Brat~,* spit, skewer; *den ~ umkehren,* (*fig.*) to turn the tables (on).
Spießbürger *m.* petty bourgeois; Philistine.
spießbürgerlich *a.* petit bourgeois; humdrum, Philistine.
Spießer *m.* **(-s, -) = Spießbürger.**
Spieß: ~geselle *m.* accomplice; **~ruten** *f.pl.* *~ laufen,* to run the gauntlet.
spießig *a.* **= spießbürgerlich.**
Spike *m.* **(-s, -s)** spike; stud (tire).
Spill *n.* **(-s, -e)** capstan.
Spinat *m.* **(-[e]s, 0)** spinach.
Spind *n.* **(-es, -e)** locker.
Spindel *f.* **(-, -n)** spindle; distaff; (*mech.*) mandrel.
spindeldürr *a.* skinny.
Spinett *n.* **(-[e]s, -e)** spinet, harpsichord.
Spinne *f.* **(-, -n)** spider.
spinnen *v.i. & t.st.* to spin; (*fam.*) to be crazy.
Spinnennetz *n.* spider's web.
Spinner *m.*; **Spinnerin** *f.* spinner; (*fam.*) idiot.
Spinnerei *f.* **(-, -en)** spinning mill.
Spinn: ~maschine *f.* spinning jenny; **~rad** *n.* spinning wheel.
Spinnwebe *f.* cobweb.
Spion *m.* **(-[e]s, -e); Spionin** *f.* **(-, -nen)** spy.
Spionage *f.* **(-, 0)** espionage.
Spionageabwehr *f.* counter-espionage; counter-intelligence.
spionieren *v.i.* to spy.
Spirale *f.* **(-, -n)** spiral (line); coil (contraceptive).
Spiralfeder *f.* spiral spring.
spiralförmig *a.* spiral.
Spiritismus *m.* **(-, 0)** spiritualism.
Spiritist *m.* **(-en, -en); Spiritistin** *f.* **(-, -nen)** spiritualist.
Spirituosen *pl.* spirits *pl.*
Spiritus *m.* **(-, 0)** spirit, alcohol.
Spiritusbrennerei *f.* distillery.
Spital *n.* **(-[e]s, -täler), Spittel** *m. & n.* **(-s, -)** hospital.
spitz *a.* pointed; (*math.*) acute; (*fig.*) sharp, shrill; cutting; ~ **zulaufen,** to taper.
Spitz *m.* **(-es, -e)** Pomeranian dog.
Spitzbart *n.* goatee; pointed beard.
Spitzbogen *m.* (*arch.*) pointed *or* Gothic arch.
Spitzbube *m.* scoundrel; rascal.
spitzbübisch *a.* mischievous.
Spitze *f.* **(-, -n)** point; top; (*Gewebe*) lace; (*Feder~*) tip; (*mil.*) spearhead; *auf die ~ treiben,* to carry to extremes; *an der ~ stehen,* to be at the head (of).
Spitzel *m.* **(-s, -)** police, informer.
spitzen *v.t.* to point; to sharpen; *die Ohren ~,* to prick up one' ears.
Spitzen: ~geschwindigkeit *f.* top speed; **~kandidat** *m.*, **~kandidatin** *f.* frontrunner.
Spitzenklöppel *m.* lace bobbin.
Spitzentechnologie *f.* state-of-the-art technology.
Spitzer *m.* (pencil) sharpener.
spitzfindig *a.* subtle; shrewd; cavilling.
Spitzfindigkeit *f.* **(-, -en)** subtlety, sophistry.
Spitzhacke *f.* pickaxe.
spitzig *a.* pointed, sharp; poignant.
Spitzname *m.* nickname.
Spitzwegerich *m.* ribwort.
spitzwinklig *a.* acute-angled.
spitzzüngig *a.* sharp-tongued.
Spleen *m.* **(-s, -e)** (*fam.*) tic; quirk.
spleißen *v.t. & i.st.* to splice.
splitten *v.t.* to split.
Splitter *m.* **(-s, -)** splinter, chip.
Splitterbruch *m.* chip fracture.
Splittergruppe *f.* splinter group.
splittern *v.i.* to splinter, to shatter.
splitternackt *a.* stark naked.
Splitterpartei *f.* splinter party.
splittersicher *a.* splinter-proof.
SPÖ *Sozialistische Partei Österreichs,* Austrian Socialist Party.
sponsern *v.t.* to sponsor.
Sponsor *m.* **(-s, -en); Sponsorin** *f.* **(-, -nen)** sponsor.
spontan *a.* spontaneous.
sporadisch *a. & adv.* sporadic(ally).
Spore *f.* **(-, -n)** (*bot.*) spore.
Sporenpflanze *f.* cryptogamous plant.
Sporentierchen *n.* sporozoan.
Sporn *m.* **(-[e]s, Sporen)** spur.
spornen *v.t.* to spur.
spornstreichs *adv.* directly.
Sport *m.* **(-s, -s)** sport; physical education.
Sportanlage *f.* sports complex.
Sportkleidung *f.* sportswear.
Sportler *m.* **(-s, -); Sportlerin** *f.* **(-, -nen)** athlete.
sportlich, sportsmäßig *a.* sporting, sporty, sportsmanlike.
Spott *m.* **(-[e], 0)** derision, ridicule, mockery, scorn.
spottbillig *a.* dirt cheap.
Spöttelei *f.* **(-, -en)** sneer, taunt, gibe.

spötteln *v.i.* to mock, to sneer at.
spotten *v.i.* to mock, to deride; *das spottet aller Beschreibung,* it defies description.
Spötter *m.* **(-s, -)** mocker, scoffer.
spöttisch *a.* satirical, ironical, scoffing.
Sprachbegabung *f.* gift for languages.
Sprache *f.* **(-, -n)** language, tongue; speech, voice; *zur ~ bringen,* to bring sth. up; *zur ~ kommen,* to be mentioned.
Sprach[en]kunde *f.* linguistics *pl.*
Sprachfehler *m.* speech defect/impediment.
Sprachforscher *m.* linguist; philologist.
Sprachforschung *f.* linguistics; philology.
Sprachführer *m.* phrase book.
Sprachgebrauch *m.* usage (in language).
Sprachlehre *f.* grammar.
sprachlich *a.* linguistic.
sprachlos *a.* speechless; (*fig.*) dumb.
Sprachrohr *n.* speaking tube; (*fig.*) mouthpiece.
sprachwidrig *a.* ungrammatical.
Sprachwissenschaft *f.* linguistics.
sprechen *v.t. & i.st.* to speak; to talk; *er ist nicht zu ~,* you cannot see him now.
sprechend *a. & adv.* striking(ly).
Sprecher *m.* **(-s, -); Sprecherin** *f.* **(-, -nen)** spokesman/spokeswoman; announcer.
Sprechfilm *m.* talking film, talkie.
Sprechstunden *pl.* office hours; (*Stellen*) interviewing hours.
Sprechzimmer *n.* consulting room.
spreizen *v.t.* to spread open, to stretch, to straddle.
Spreizfuß *m.* splayfoot.
Sprengel *m.* **(-s, -)** diocese; parish.
sprengen *v.t. & i.* to sprinkle, to water; to burst open; (*Bank*) to break; to blow up, to blast; to gallop.
Spreng: ~geschoß *n.* explosive, shell; **~kapsel** *f.* detonator; **~kraft** *f.* explosive power; **~ladung** *f.* explosive charge; **~stoff** *m.* high explosive.
Sprenkel *m.* **(-s, -)** spot; dot; speckle.
sprenkeln *v.t.* to sprinkle.
Spreu *f.* **(-, 0)** chaff.
Sprichwort *n.* proverb.
sprichwörtlich *a. & adv.* proverbial(ly).
sprießen *v.t.st. (s, h)* to sprout, to shoot.
Spring: ~brett *n.* spring board; **~brunnen** *m.* fountain, jet.
springen *v.i.st. (s,& h)* to spring; to leap, to jump; to crack, to burst; *entzwei ~,* to burst asunder; *in die Augen ~,* to be obvious.
Springer *m.* **(-s, -)** (*im Schachspiel*) knight.
Spring: ~feder *f.* spring; **~federmatratze** *f.* spring mattress; **~flut** *f.* spring tide; **~kraft** *f.* elasticity; **~quelle** *f.* spring, fountain.
Sprint *m.* sprint.
sprinten *v.i.* to sprint.
Sprinter *m.;* **Sprinterin** *f.* sprinter.
Sprit *m.* **(-s, 0)** alcohol; gas.
Spritze *f.* **(-, -n)** syringe; injection; spray; fire-engine.
spritzen *v.t.* to spray; to water; to spout, to squirt.
Spritzer *m.* **(-s, -)** splash; drop.
spritzig *a.* sparkling; peppy.
Spritzmittel *n.* spray.
Spritzpistole *f.* spray gun.
Spritztour *f.* **(-, -en)** spin (car).
spröde *a.* brittle; (*Haut*) rough; (*fig.*) coy, reserved, prim.
Sprödigkeit *f.* **(-, 0)** brittleness; coyness.
Sproß (Sprosses, Sprossen) shoot, sprout; scion, offspring.
Sprosse *f.* **(-, -n)** step, round, rung.
Sprossenwand *f.* wall bars.
Sprößling *m.* **(-[e]s, -e)** sprout, shoot, (*fig.*) offspring.
Sprotte *f.* **(-, -n)** sprat.
Spruch *m.* **(-[e]s, Sprüche)** maxim, saying; (*Bibel~*) verse.
Sprücheklopfer *m.* **(-s, -)** big mouth.
spruchreif *a. es ist noch nicht ~,* it hasn't been decided yet.
Sprudel *m.* **(-s, -)** sparkling mineral water.
sprudeln *v.i.* to bubble; to sputter.
Sprühdose *f.* spray can.
sprühen *v.t.* to spray; to sprinkle, to emit; ~ *v.i.* to emit sparks, to scintillate.
Sprühregen *m.* drizzle.
Sprung *m.* **(-[e]s, Sprünge)** spring; leap jump; dive; chink, crack, fissure; *auf dem ~e sein, stehen,* to be on the point of.
Sprung: ~brett *n.* springboard; diving board; **~feder** *f.* (coil) spring.
sprunghaft *a.* erratic; disjointed.
Sprungschanze *f.* ski jump.
Sprungtuch *n.* safety blanket.
Sprungturm *m.* diving platform.
sprungweise *adv.* by leaps.
Spucke *f.* **(-, 0)** spittle.
spucken *v.i.* to spit.
Spucknapf *m.* spittoon.
Spuk *m.* **(-[e]s, -e)** apparition, specter.
spuken *v.i.* to haunt; to be haunted.
Spukgeschichte *f.* ghost story.
Spülbecken *n.* sink.
Spule *f.* **(-, -en)** spool, bobbin; (*Feder*) quill; (*elek.*) coil.
spulen *v.t.* to spool, to reel.
spülen *v.t.* to rinse; to wash.
Spül: ~maschine *f.* dishwasher; **~mittel** *n.* dishwashing liquid.
Spülung *f.* rinse; irrigation; douche; flush.
Spülwasser *n.* dishwater.
Spulwurm *m.* roundworm.
Spund *m.* **(-[e]s, Spünde)** bung, stopper.
Spundloch *n.* bunghole.
Spur *f.* **(-, -en)** track, trace; vestige; (*Wagen~*) rut; *keine ~ von,* not an idea or inkling of.
spürbar *a.* noticeble; perceptible; evident.
spüren *v.t.* to track, to trace; to perceive, to feel.
Spürhund *m.* tracker dog; (*fig.*) spy.
spurlos *adv.* without leaving a trace.
Spürnase *f.,* **Spürsinn** *m.* good nose.
sputen *v.r.* to hurry.
s.R. *siehe Rückseite,* see overleaf.
SS *Sommersemester,* summer term.
St. *Sankt,* Saint, St.; *Stück,* piece.
Staat *m.* **(-es, -en)** state; pomp, show.
Staatenbund *m.* confederation.
staatlich *a.* state-..., public; politic(al).
staatlich unterstützt, state-subidized.
Staatsamt *n.* public office.
Staatsangehörige *m./f.* national, citizen, subject.
Staatsangehörigkeit *f.* nationality; citizenship.
Staatsanleihe *f.* government loan.
Staatsanwalt *m.* public prosecutor; **~schaft** *f.* public prosecutor's office.
Staatsanzeiger *m.* official gazette.
Staatsbeamte *m./f.* civil servant.

Staatsbesitz *m. im* ~, state-owned.
Staatsbürger *m.* subject, citizen.
Staatsdienst *m.* public *or* civil service.
Staatseinkünfte *pl.* revenue
Staatsgesetz *n.* law of the land, statute law.
Staatsgewalt *f.* supreme *or* executive power.
Staatshaushalt *m.* budget.
Staatskirche *f.* established church.
Staatskunst *f.* statesmanship.
Staatsmann *m.* **(-[e]s, -männer)** statesman.
staatsmännisch *a.* statesmanlike.
Staatsminister *m.* minister of state.
Staatsoberhaupt *n.* head of state.
Staatspapiere *n.pl.* stocks, public funds *pl.*
Staatsrecht *n.* public law.
Staatsschuld *f.* national debt.
Staatssekretär *m.* Secretary of State.
Staatsstreich *m.* coup d'état.
Staatsverfassung *f.* constitution.
Staatsverwaltung *f.* government, public administration.
Staatswesen *n.* state politics.
Staatswissenschaft *f.* political science, politics.
Stab *m.* **(-[e]s, Stäbe)** staff, stick; bar; rod.
Stabhochspringer *m.* pole vaulter.
Stabhochsprung *m.* pole vaulting.
stabil *a.* stable; sturdy.
stabilisieren *v.t.* to stabilize.
Stabilität *m.* stability; sturdiness.
Stabreim *m.* alliteration.
Stabs: ~arzt *m.* medical officer; **~offizier** *m.* field officer.
Stachel *m.* **(-s, -)** (*Insekten~*) spine; sting; prickle, thorn.
Stachel: ~beere *f.* gooseberry; **~draht** *m.* barbed wire.
stach(e)lig *a.* prickly, thorny.
Stachelschwein *n.* porcupine.
Stadion *n.* **(-s, -dien)** stadium.
Stadium *m.* **(-[s], -dien)** stage.
Stadt *f.* **(-, Städte)** town; city.
Stadt: ~amt *n.* municipal office; **~bahn** *f.* municipal railroad.
Städtebau *m.* city planning.
Städtepartnerschaft *f.* sister city relationship.
Städter *m.* **(-s, -); Städterin** *f.* **(-, -nen)** city dweller; town dweller.
Stadtgespräch *n.* talk of the town; (*tel.*) local call.
städtisch *a.* municipal; urban.
Stadt: ~kämmerer *m.* city treasurer; **~mauer** *f.* city wall; **~rat** *m.* municipal council; city councillor; **~verordnete[r]** *m.* city councillor; **~viertel** *n.* quarter (of a town).
Staffel *f.* **(-, -n)** step, rung; degree; (*Sport*) relay; (*mil.*) echelon; (*avi.*) squadron.
Staffelei *f.* **(-, -en)** easel.
Staffel: ~kapitän *m.* squadron leader; **~lauf** *m.* relay race.
staffeln *v.t.* to grade; to stagger; *gestaffelte Ferien, pl.* staggered holidays.
Staffelung *f.* staggering; progressive rates.
Stagnation *f.* stagnation.
stagnieren *v.i.* to stagnate.
Stahl *m.* **(-[e]s, Stähle)** steel; (*mech.*) tool.
Stahl: ~bau *m.* steel construction; **~beton** *m.* reinforced concrete; **~blech** *n.* sheet steel.
stählen *v.t.* to temper, to harden.
stählern *a.* (of) steel; steely.
Stahl: ~helm *m.* steel helmet; **~werk** *n.* steelworks *pl.;* **~wolle** *f.* steel wool.
staken *v.t.* to pole, to punt.
Stalagmit *m.* stalagmite.
Stalaktit *m.* stalactite.
Stall *m.* **(-[e]s, Ställe)** stable.
Stallbursche *m.* groom.
Stallung *f.* **(-, -en)** stable; cowshed; pigsty.
Stamm *m.* **(-[e]s, Stämme)** stem, stalk; trunk, body; stock, race, family, tribe; (*gram.*) root.
Stammaktie *f.* common stock.
Stammbaum *m.* family tree; pedigree.
Stammbuch *n.* album.
stammeln *v.t. & i.* to stammer, to stutter.
Stammeltern *pl.* progenitors *pl.*
stammen *v.i. (s)* to originate, to proceed; to descend from; to be derived.
Stammesgeschichte *f.* phylogenesis.
Stammeshäuptling *m.* tribal chief.
Stammgast *m.* regular customer.
Stammhalter *m.* son and heir.
stämmig *a.* stout, strong.
Stammkapital *n.* nominal capital.
Stammler *m.* **(-s, -)** stammerer, stutterer.
Stamm: ~personal; *n.* regular staff; **~tisch** *m.* table reserved for regular customers; **~vater** *m.* ancestor.
stampfen *v.i. & t.* to stamp; to pound.
Stand *m.* **(-[e]s, Stände)** state, condition; *Verkaufs~*, stand, stall; station, situation; rank, profession, order, class; (*im Stall*) stall; (*Barometer, etc.*) reading; *neu in ~ setzen,* to recondition.
Standard *m.* **(-s, -s)** standard.
standardisieren *v.t.* to standardize.
Standardisierung *f.* standardization.
Standarte *f.* **(-, -n)** standard.
Standbild *n.* statue.
Ständchen *n.* **(-s, -)** serenade.
Stände *m.pl.* estates (*pl.*) of the realm.
Ständer *m.* **(-s, -)** stand, upright; (*elek.*) stator.
Standesamt *n.* registry office.
standesamtlich *a.* before the registrar.
Standesbeamte[r] *m.* registrar.
standesgemäß *a.* in accordance with one's rank.
standhaft *a.* firm, steady, steadfast; constant.
Standhaftigkeit *f.* **(-, 0)** constancy, steadfastness.
standhalten *v.t.st.* to hold one's ground.
ständig *a.* permanent, constant.
ständisch *a.* corporate.
Standlicht *n.* sidelights.
Standort *m.* location.
Standpunkt *m.* point of view; standpoint.
Standrecht *n.* martial law.
standrechtlich *a.* according to martial law.
Standspur *f.* hard shoulder (street).
Stange *f.* **(-, -n)** pole, perch; bar; stick; **~nbohne** *f.* string bean.
Stänkerei *f.* **(-, -en)** quarrel, row.
stänkern *v.i.* (*fig.*) to quarrel, to pick quarrels; to find fault.
Stanniol *n.* **(-[e]s, 0)** tinfoil.
stanzen *v.t.* to stamp, to punch.
Stapel *m.* **(-s, -)** heap, pile; staple, emporioum; *vom ~ lassen,* to launch (a ship, an enterprise).
Stapellauf *m.* launching.
stapeln *v.t.* to pile up.
stapfen *v.i.* to trudge.
Star *m.* **(-[e]s, -e)** star (celebrity); starling; (*med.*) *grauer ~* cataract; *grüner ~*, glaucoma.

stark *a.* strong, robust; stout, fat; intense; *~e Seite,* strong point.
starkbesetzt *a.* well-attended, crowded.
Stärke *f.* **(-, 0)** strength, force, vigor; starch; thickness.
stärkehaltig *a.* containing starch.
Stärkemehl *n.* cornstarch.
stärken *v.t.* to strengthen; to corroborate; to comfort; to starch.
stärkend *a.* strengthening, invigorating.
Starkstrom *m.* high voltage current.
Stärkung *f.* **(-, -en)** strengthening; consolation; refreshment, food.
Stärkungsmittel *n.* tonic.
starr *a.* stiff, rigid; fixed; *~ sein vor Erstaunen,* to be dumb with astonishment.
starren *v.i.* to stare; *von Schmutz ~,* to be stiff with dirt; (*von Fehlern, etc.*) to bristle with.
Starrheit *f.* stiffness, rigidity; obstinacy.
Starrkopf *m.* stubborn fellow.
starrköpfig *a.* stubborn, headstrong.
Starr: ~krampf *m.* tetanus; **~sinn** *m.* stubbornness.
starrsinnig *a.* stubborn, headstrong.
Start *m.* start.
Startbahn *f.* (*avi.*) runway.
starten *v.i. & t.* to start.
Startplatz *m.* starting place.
Startrampe *f.* launching pad.
Statik *f.* **(-, 0)** statics.
Station *f.* **(-, -en)** station; stopping place, stage.
stationär *a.* stationary; steady; (*med.*) inpatient.
stationieren *v.t.* (*mil.*) to station; to deploy.
Stations: ~arzt *m.,* **~ärztin** *f.* ward doctor; **~schwester** *f.* floor nurse; **~vorsteher** *m.* station-master.
statisch *a.* static.
Statist *m.* **(-en, -en); Statistin** *f.* **(-, -nen)** (*theat.*) extra.
Statistik *f.* **(-, -en)** statistics.
statistisch *a.* statistic(al).
Stativ *n.* **(-s, -e)** stand; (*phot.*) tripod.
statt *pr.* instead of, in lieu of; *~ dessen,* instead of this.
Statte *f.* **(-, 0)** place, stead; *an meiner ~,* in my place; *an Kindes ~ annehmen,* to adopt.
Stätte *f.* **(-, -n)** place, site.
stattfinden *v.i.st.* to take place.
stattgeben *v.i.st.* to grant.
statthaben *v.i.st.* to take place.
statthaft *a.* admissible, allowable, lawful.
Statthalter *m.* governor.
stattlich *a.* considerable; imposing; impressive.
Statue *f.* **(-, -n)** statue.
Statuette *f.* **(-, -n)** statuette.
Statur *f.* **(-, -en)** stature, size.
Status *m.* **(-, -)** status.
Statut *n.* **(-[e]s, -e)** statute, regulation.
statutenmäßig *a.* statutory.
Stau *m.* **(-s, -s)** accumulation; congestion; traffic jam.
Staub *m.* **(-[e]s, 0)** dust; powder; *sich aus dem ~e machen,* to make off, to abscond.
Stäubchen *n.* **(-s, -)** speck of dust.
Staubecken *n.* reservoir.
stauben *v.i.* to give off dust, to be dusty.
staubig *a.* dusty.
Staubsauger *m.* vacuum cleaner.
Staubtuch *n.* duster.
Staubwedel *m.* feather duster.
Staudamm *m.* dam.
Staude *f.* **(-, -n)** shrub; bush.
stauen *v.t.* to dam up, to bank up; *das Wasser staut sich,* the water is dammed up.
Staumauer *f.* dam (wall).
staunen *v.i.* to be astonished, to be surprised, to be amazed.
Staunen *n.* amazement; astonishment.
staunenswert *a.* amazing, marvellous.
Staupe *f.* **(-, 0)** *Hunde~,* distemper.
Stausee *m.* reservoir.
Std. *Stunde,* hour, hr., h.
stdl. *stündlich,* hourly.
stechen *v.t.st.* to sting, to prick; to stab; (*Torf*) to cut; *~ v.t.st.* (*Sonne*) to burn; *in die Augen ~,* to catch one's eye; *in See ~,* to put to sea, to set sail.
stechend *a.* penetrating; piercing.
Stech: ~karte *f.* timecard; **~mücke** *f.* mosquito; **~palme** *f.* holly; **~schritt** *m.* goose step; **~uhr** *f.* time clock; **~zirkel** *m.* dividers.
Steckbrief *m.* "wanted" poster.
steckbrieflich *a. & adv. einen ~ verfolgen,* to issue a warrant against someone.
Steckdose *f.* socket.
stecken *v.t.* to stick; *~ v.t.st.* to stick, to be fixed; **~bleiben,** to stick fast; *was steckt dahinter?* what can be at the bottom of it? *Geld in ein Unternehmen ~,* to invest money in an undertaking; *mit einem unter einer Decke ~,* to play into each other's hands.
Stecken *m.* **(-s, -)** stick, staff.
Steckenpferd *n.* hobbyhorse; (*fig.*) hobby, fad.
Stecker *m.* **(-s, -)** plug.
Steckling *m.* **(-s, -e)** cutting.
Stecknadel *f.* pin; **~kopf** *m.* pinhead.
Steckrübe *f.* turnip.
Steg *m.* **(-[e]s, -e)** path; small bridge; (*Geigen~*) bridge.
Stegreif *m. aus dem ~e,* extempore, offhand; *aus dem ~ sprechen,* to extemporize.
Stehaufmännchen *n.* tumbling figure.
stehen *v.t.st.* to stand; to suit (well, ill); to be; *es steht fest,* it is beyond doubt; *frei ~,* to be permitted; *es steht Ihnen frei,* you are at liberty to; *es steht in der Zeitung,* it says in the paper; *Modell ~,* to serve as model (to); *wie steht's?* how are you? *sich gut ~,* to be well off; *die Aktien ~ auf...,* the shares stand at...; *seinen Mann ~,* to hold one's own; *~bleiben,* to stop, to pause; *Geld bei einem ~ haben,* to have deposited money with someone; *sich den Bart ~ lassen,* to let one's beard grow; *es steht zu erwarten,* it is to be expected; *zum ~ bringen,* to bring to a stand.
stehend *a.* standing; *~es Heer,* standing army; *~e Redensart,* stock phrase.
Stehkragen *m.* stand-up collar.
Stehlampe *f.* floor lamp.
stehlen *v.t.st.* to steal; to pilfer; *sich aus dem Hause ~,* to steal out of the house.
Stehplatz *m.* standing room.
Stehpult *n.* standing desk.
steif *a.* stiff; rigid; awkward, formal; *~ werden,* to stiffen; *~ und fest behaupten,* to maintain obstinately; *~er Grog,* strong grog.
Steifheit *f.* **(-, -en)** stiffness; (*fig.*) formality, pedantry.
Steig *m.* **(-[e]s, -e)** path.
Steigbügel *m.* **(-s, -)** stirrup.
steigen *v.i.st.* *(s)* to mount, to ascend, to rise; to

increase; to climb; *die Haare ~ mir zu Berge,* my hair stands on end; *die Aktien ~,* the shares are going up.
Steiger *m.* **(-s, -)** pit foreman.
steigern *v.t.* to raise (the price), to enhance, to increase.
Steigerung *f.* **(-, -en)** rise, increase, gradation; (*gram.*) comparison.
Steigerungsform *f.* comparative form.
Steigerungsgrad *m.* (*gram.*) degree of comparison.
Steigung *f.* **(-, -en)** rising, ascent; (*rail.*) gradient; (*mot.*) (steep) hill (up).
steil *a.* steep, stiff.
Steil: ~hang *m.* steep slope; **~küste** *f.* cliffs.
Stein *m.* **(-[e]s, -e)** stone; (*im Schachspiele*), piece; *~ des Anstosses,* stumbling block; *~ der Weisen,* philosophers' stone; *es fällt mir ein ~ vom Herzen,* a great weight is taken off my mind; *wie ein Tropfen auf einen heißen ~,* altogether insufficient.
Steinbild *n.* statue.
Steinbock *m.* ibex; (*Sternbild*) Capricorn.
Steinbruch *m.* quarry.
Steinbutt *m.* turbot.
Steindruck *m.* lithography.
steinern *a.* (of) stone; (*fig.*) stony.
Steingut *n.* earthenware, crockery.
steinhart *a.* hard as stone, stony.
steinig *a.* stony, rocky.
steinigen *v.t.* to stone.
Steinigung *f.* **(-, -en)** stoning.
Steinkohle *f.* hard coal.
Steinmetz *m.* stonemason.
Steinobst *n.* stone fruit.
Steinöl *n.* petroleum.
Steinpilz *m.* cep.
Steinplatte *f.* slab, flagstone.
steinreich *a.* enormously rich.
Steinschlag *m.* falling rocks.
Steinsetzer *m.* paver, pavior.
Steinwurf *m.* stone's throw.
Steinzeit *f.* Stone Age.
Steiß *m.* **(-[e]s, -e)** backside, rump, buttocks *pl.*
Steißbein *n.* coccyx.
Stelldichein *n.* **(-[e]s, -)** rendezvous.
Stelle *f.* **(-, -n)** place, spot; situation, office; (*Buch~*) passage; *an höchster ~,* on top level; *auf der ~ treten,* to mark time; *nicht von der ~ kommen,* not to get anywhere; *sich nicht von der ~ rühren,* not to move an inch; *an Ort und ~ sein,* to be on the spot; *an ~ von,* in lieu of; *sich zu einer ~ melden,* to apply for a situation; *auf der ~,* at once, on the spot.
stellen *v.t.* to put, to place, to set; to regulate; *~ v.r.* to step, to stand; (*Preis*) to amount to; to dissemble, to make believe; *bereit ~,* to make available; to get ready; *sich krank ~,* to feign sickness; *sich ~ als ob,* to pretend, to make believe; *eine Uhr richtig ~,* to set a watch; *einem ein Bein ~,* to trip someone up; *nach dem Leben ~,* to attempt one's life; *einen Antrag ~,* to move.
Stellenangebot *n.* job offer.
Stellenbesetzung *f.* placement.
Stellengesuch *n.* (*Zeitung*) situation wanted.
Stellensuche *f.* job hunting, search for a job.
Stellenvermittlungsbüro *n.* employment agency.
stellenweise *a.* sporadically, in parts.
Stellung *f.* **(-, -en)** position; situation; (*Körper~*) posture.
Stellungnahme *f.* comment(s); statement; opinion.
Stellungskrieg *n.* trench warfare.
stellungslos *a.* unemployed.
stellvertretend *a.* acting; deputy.
Stellvertreter *m.* deputy; substitute.
Stellwerk *n.* signal box; switch tower.
Stelze *f.* **(-, -n)** stilt.
stelzen *v.i.* to stalk; to strut.
Stelzfuß *m.* wooden leg.
Stemmeisen *n.* chisel.
stemmen *v.t.* (*Flut, usw.*) to stem; *~ v.r.* to lean (against); to resist; *die Hände in die Seiten ~,* to set one's arms akimbo; *sich gegen etwas ~,* to press against; to resist.
Stempel *m.* **(-s, -)** stamp; (*bot.*) pistil; post mark.
Stempelkissen *n.* ink pad.
Stempelmarke *f.* stamp.
stempeln *v.t.* to stamp, to mark; **~gehen** *v.i.* to be on welfare.
Stengel *m.* **(-s, -)** stalk, stem.
Steno *f.*, **Stenographie (-, -en)** shorthand.
stenographieren *v.t. & i.* to write (in) shorthand.
Stenotypistin *f.* **(-, -nen)** shorthand typist.
Steppdecke *f.* quilt, eiderdown.
Steppe *f.* **(-, -n)** steppe.
steppen *v.t. & i.* to backstitch; to tapdance.
Steptanz *m.* tapdance.
Sterbebett *n.* deathbed.
Sterbefall *m.* (case of) death.
Sterbehilfe *f.* euthanasia.
sterben *v.i.st. (s)* to die; *eines natürlichen Todes ~,* to die a natural death; *vor Scham ~,* to die of shame.
Sterben *n.* **(-s, -)** dying, epidemic; *im ~ liegen,* to be dying.
sterbend *a.* moribund.
Sterbensangst *f.* mortal fear.
sterbenskrank *a.* mortally ill.
Sterbenswörtchen *n.* a single word, a syllable; *kein ~,* not a word.
Sterbesakramente *pl.* the last rites.
sterblich *a.* mortal; **~ verliebt,** desperately in love.
Sterblichkeit *f.* **(-, 0)** mortality; **~sziffer** *f.* death rate, mortality.
Stereo: ~anlage *f.* stereo system; **~aufnahme** *f.* stereo recording; **~ton** *m.* stereo sound.
stereotyp *a.* stereotyped.
stereotypieren *v.t.* to stereotype.
steril *a.* sterile.
sterilisieren *v.t.* to sterilize.
Stern *m.* **(-[e]s, -e)** star; (*im Druck*) asterisk.
Sternbild *n.* constellation.
Sternchen *n.* **(-s, -)** little star; asterisk.
Sterndeuter *m.* **(-s, -)** astrologer.
Sternen: ~banner *n.* stars and stripes; **~himmel** *m.* starry sky; **~licht** *n.* starlight.
Sternfahrt *f.* (*mot.*) motor rally.
sternförmig *a.* star-shaped.
sternhell *a.* starlit, starry.
Sternhimmel *m.* firmament, starry sky.
Sternkunde *f.* astronomy.
Sternschnuppe *f.* shooting star.
Sternwarte *f.* observatory.
Sternzeichen *n.* zodiac sign.
Sterz *m.* **(-es, -e)** tail.
stet *a.* steady, constant, continued.

Stethoskop *n.* **(-s, -e)** stethoscope.
stetig *a.* steady, contintual, continuous.
Stetigkeit *f.* **(-, 0)** continuity, constancy, stability.
stets *adv.* continually, always, ever.
Steuer *n.* **(-s, -)** wheel; rudder.
Steuer *f.* **(-, -n)** (*Staats*) tax; (*Gemeinde*) rate; (*Zoll*) duty.
steuerbar *a.* assessable, liable to duty.
Steuerbeamter *m.* tax collector, revenue officer.
Steuerbehörde *f.* internal revenue authorities.
Steuerbord *n.* starboard.
Steuereinnehmer *m.* tax collector.
Steuererklärung *f.* income tax return.
Steuererlaß *m.* tax remission.
steuerfrei *a.* exempt from taxes, duty-free.
Steuerfreibetrag *m.* tax allowance.
Steuerfreiheit *f.* exemption from taxes.
Steuerhinterziehung *f.* tax evasion.
Steuerklasse *f.* tax category.
Steuerknüppel *m.* control lever; joystick.
steuerlich *a.* tax.
Steuermann *m.* helmsman; steersman.
Steuermarke *f.* revenue stamp.
steuern *v.t.* to steer; to pilot; ~ *v.i.* to steer; (*einem Dinge*) to check, to repress.
Steuernachlaß *m.* tax remission.
Steuern hinterziehen to evade taxes.
steuerpflichtig *a.* dutiable, subject to taxation.
Steuerpolitik *f.* fiscal policy.
Steuerrad *n.* (*mot.*) steering wheel.
Steuerrückvergütung *f.* tax refund.
Steuerruder *n.* helm, rudder.
Steuersatz *m.* rate of assessment.
Steuerschuld *f.* tax arrears.
Steuersenkung *f.* tax cut, tax reduction.
Steuerung *f.* **(-, -en)** (*mech.*) control.
Steuerveranschlagung *f.* assessment.
Steuerzahler *m.* taxpayer.
Steven *m.* **(-s, -)** (*nav.*) posts at bow or stern.
StGB *Strafgesetzbuch*, criminal code.
stibitzen *v.t.* (*fam.*) to pinch.
Stich *m.* **(-[e]s, -e)** puncture; stab; (*Nadel*) prick; sting; *Näh*~, stitch; engraving; ~ **halten,** to hold good; *im* ~ *lasssen*, to leave in the lurch.
Stichelei *f.* **(-, -en)** taunt, raillery, sneer.
sticheln *v.i.* (*auf einen*), to taunt.
Stichflamme *f.* **(-, -n)** jet of flame.
stichhaltig *a.* valid, sound.
Stichprobe *f.* **(-, -n)** spotcheck; ~ *machen*, to spotcheck.
Stichtag *m.* deadline.
Stichwahl *f.* second ballot.
Stichwort *n.* cue; headword; catchword.
sticken *v.t.* to embroider.
Stickerei *f.* **(-, -en)** embroidery.
Stickerin *f.* **(-, -nen)** embroideress.
stickig *a.* stuffy.
Stick: ~luft *f.* stuffy air; **~muster** *n.* pattern for embroidering, sampler; **~rahmen** *m.* embroidery-frame; **~stoff** *m.* nitrogen.
stickstoffhaltig *a.* nitrogenous.
Stickstoffverbindung *f.* nitrous compound.
Stiefbruder *m.* step-brother, half-brother.
Stiefel *m.* **(-s, -)** boot.
Stiefelknecht *m.* bootjack.
Stiefelputzer *n.* bootblack.
Stiefeltern *pl.* step-parents *pl.*
Stief: ~geschwister *pl.* step-brother[s] and sister[s]; **~kind** *n.* step-child; **~mutter** *f.* step-mother; **~mütterchen** *n.* (*bot.*) pansy.
stiefmütterlich *a.* ~ **behandeln,** to treat badly.
Stief: ~schwester *f.* step-sister; **~sohn** *m.* step-son; **~tochter** *f.* step-daughter; **~vater** *m.* step-father.
Stiege *f.* **(-, -n)** staircase, stairway.
Stieglitz *m.* **(-es, -e)** goldfinch.
Stiel *m.* **(-[e]s, -e)** handle, helve; (*bot.*) stem, stalk, pedicle; *mit Stumpf und* ~, root and branch.
Stier *m.* **(-[e]s, -e)** bull; (*astrol.*) Taurus.
stieren *v.i.* to stare.
Stier: ~kampf *m.* bullfight; **~kämpfer** *m.*; **~kämpferin** *f.* bullfighter.
stiernackig *a.* bullnecked.
Stift *m.* **(-[e]s, -e)** peg; pencil, crayon; (*fam.*) office boy.
Stift *n.* **(-[e]s, -e)** (charitable) foundation; home for old people; chapterhouse; college.
stiften *v.t.* to establish; to found; *Gutes, Nutzen* ~, to do good, to be useful.
Stifter *m.* **(-s, -); Stifterin** *f.* **(-, -nen)** founder, donor.
Stiftung *f.* **(-, -en)** foundation; endowment; institution.
Stiftungsfest *n.* founder's day.
Stil *m.* **(-[e]s, -e)** style; manner.
Stilblüte *f.* howler, stylistic lapse.
Stilebene *f.* style level.
stilecht *a.* period.
Stilett *n.* stiletto.
stilisieren *v.t.* to stylize.
Stilistik *f.* **(-, -en)** theory of style; stylistics.
stilistisch *a.* relating to style.
still *a.* still, silent; calm, quiet, tranquil; **~!** hush!; *im* ~*en*, quietly; **~halten,** to keep still; **~schweigen,** to be silent, to keep silence; **~sein,** to be quiet; **~stehen,** to stand still; *der* ~*e Ozean*, the Pacific; **~er Teilhaber** *m.* silent partner.
Stille *f.* **(-, 0)** silence, tranquillity; *in aller* ~, secretly.
Stilleben *n.* still life.
stillegen *v.t.* to close down.
Stillegung *f.* **(-, -en)** shut down.
stillen *v.t.* to quiet, to appease, to quench; (*Blut*) to staunch; (*Begierden*) to gratify; (*ein Kind*) to feed, to nurse.
stillgestanden! (*mil.*) attention.
stilliegend *a.* dormant; ~*e Fabrik*, idle factory.
stillos *a.* lacking in style.
Stillschweigen *n.* silence.
stillschweigend *a.* silent, tacit.
Stillstand *m.* standstill, stop, deadlock.
stillstehen *v.i.* to stand still.
Stillzeit *f.* lactation period.
Stilmittel *n.* **(-s, -)** stylistic device.
Stilmöbel *n.pl.* period furniture.
stilvoll *a.* in style; stylish.
Stimmband *n.* vocal chord.
stimmberechtigt *a.* entitled to vote.
Stimmbruch *m.* breaking of the voice.
Stimme *f.* **(-, -n)** voice; *Wahl*~, vote; (*mus.*) part; *seine* ~ *abgeben*, to cast one's vote.
stimmen *v.t.* to tune; (*fig.*) to dipose; *das stimmt!* that's true enough; ~ *v.t.* to vote; *die Rechnung stimmt*, the account is square or correct; *er ist heute schlecht gestimmt*, he is in a bad mood today.
Stimm(en)abgabe *f.* voting.
Stimmengleichheit *f.* equality of votes, tie.
Stimmenmehrheit *f.* majority of votes.

Stimmenthaltung *f.* **(-, -en)** abstention.
Stimmer *n.* **(-s, -)** tuner.
stimmfähig *a.* entitled to vote.
Stimmgabel *f.* tuning fork.
stimmhaft *a.* voiced.
stimmlos *a.* voiceless.
Stimmrecht *n.* right to vote; *allgemeines ~* , universal suffrage.
Stimmung *f.* **(-, -en)** mood, humour, disposition; (*mil.*) morale, general feeling.
Stimmwechsel *m.* breaking of the voice.
Stimmzettel *m.* paper ballot.
stinken *v.i.st.* to stink (of).
Stipendiat *m.* **(-en, -en); Stipendiatin** *f.* **(-, -nen)** person receiving a scholarship.
Stipendium *n.* **(-[e]s, -dien)** scholarship, exhibition.
stippen *v.t.* to dip, to steep.
Stirn *f.* **(-, -en)** forehead; front; (*fig.*) insolence; *einem die ~ bieten,* to defy someone.
Stirn: ~band *n.* headband; **~runzeln** *n.* frown(ing).
stöbern *v.i.* (*nach*) to rummage (for).
stochern *v.t.* to poke, to stir.
Stock *m.* **(-[e]s, Stöcke)** stick; staff; cane; log, block, trunk; (*Stockwerk*) story, floor.
stockdumm *a.* utterly stupid.
stockdunkel *a.* pitch dark.
Stöckelschuh *m.* **(-s, -e)** high-heeled shoe.
stocken *v.i.* to stop; (*gerinnen*) to curdle; (*fig.*) to hesitate; *die Geschäfte ~*, business is at a standstill.
Stocken *n.* **(-s, 0)** *ins ~ geraten,* to come to a standstill.
stockfinster *a.* pitch dark.
Stockfisch *m.* dried cod.
stocksteif *a.* stiff as a poker.
stocktaub *a.* stone-deaf, deaf as a post.
Stockung *f.* **(-, -en)** stagnation; interruption, block; (*med.*) congestion.
Stockwerk *n.* floor, story.
Stoff *m.* **(-[e]s, -e)** stuff, material, fabric; matter, subject.
stofflich *a.* material.
Stoffwechsel *m.* (*med.*) metabolism.
stöhnen *v.i.* to groan.
Stoiker *m.* **(-s, -)** stoic.
stoisch *a.* stoic(al).
Stoizismus *m.* **(-, 0)** stoicism.
Stola *f.* **(-, -en)** stole.
Stollen *m.* **(-s, -)** fruit-loaf; (mining) adit, gallery.
stolpern *v.i. (s)* to stumble, to trip.
stolz *a.* proud; stately.
Stolz *m.* **(-es, 0)** pride; *~ in etwas setzen,* to take pride in sth.
stolzieren *v.i. (s)* to flaunt, to strut.
stopfen *v.t.* to stop; to stuff, to cram; to fill (a pipe); to obstruct; (*mit Garn*) to darn; (*med.*) to constipate.
Stoppel *f.* **(-, -n)** stubble.
Stoppel: ~bart *m.* stubble; **~feld** *n.* stubble field.
stoppelig *a.* stubbly.
stoppen *v.t.* (*nav.*) to stop.
Stopper *m.* **(-s, -)** center-half (soccer).
Stoppschild *n.* stop sign.
Stoppuhr *f.* stopwatch.
Stöpsel *m.* **(-s, -)** plug; stopper, cork.
stöpseln *v.t.* to cork, to plug.
Stör *m.* **(-[e]s, -e)** sturgeon.
Storch *m.* **(-[e]s, Störche)** stork.
stören *v.t.* to disturb, to trouble; (*Radio*) to jam; *~ v.i.* to be in the way.
Störenfried *m.* **(-[e]s, -e)** troublemaker.
stornieren *v.t.* to cancel; to reverse.
Stornierung *f.*, **Storno** *n.* cancellation; reversal.
störrisch *a.* stubborn, refractory.
Störsender *m.* jamming station.
Störung *f.* **(-, -en)** disturbance, interruption; **~en,** (*Radio*) atmospherics *pl.*
Stoß *m.* **(-es, Stöße)** thrust, push; shock; punch; (*Fuß*) kick; jolt; (*phys.*) impact; (*Billiard*) stroke; (*Haufen*) pile, heap; *Akten ~*, file, bundle.
Stoßdämpfer *m.* shock absorber (car).
Stößel *m.* **(-s, 0)** pestle.
stoßempfindlich *a.* sensitive to shock.
stoßen *v.t.* to thrust, to push; to kick, to knock; (*im Mörser*) to pound; *~ v.t.st.* (*Wagen*) to jolt; to butt; (*an etwas*) to border (on); to strike against; (*auf etwas*) to come across; *~ v.r.* to knock against; to hurt oneself; *einen vor den Kopf ~*, to offend sb.; *über den Haufen ~*, to overturn; *sich an etwas ~*, to take offense at sth.
stoßfest *a.* shock-resistant.
Stoß: ~seufzer *m.* deep sigh; **~stange** *f.* bumper; **~verkehr** *m.* rush hour traffic.
stoßweise *adv.* by fits and starts; intermittently.
Stoßzahn *n.* tusk.
Stoßzeit *f.* rush hour.
stottern *v.i.* to stutter, to stammer.
StPO *Strafprozeßordnung,* Code of Criminal Procedure.
Str. *Straße,* street, st.
stracks *adv.* straightaway, immediately.
Straf... *a.* punitive
Staf: ~anstalt *f.* prison; **~antrag** *m.* (*jur.*) demand for punishment; **~arbeit** *f.* extra work; **~bank** *f.* (*sp.*) penalty bench.
strafbar *a.* punishable; *~* **sein,** to be liable to prosecution.
Straf: ~befugnis *f.* right to impose penalties; **~bestimmung** *f.* clause in penal code; **~buch** *n.* book of fines.
Strafe *f.* **(-, -n)** punishment; (*Geld*) fine, penalty; *seine ~ erleiden,* to undergo one's punishment; *es ist bei ~ verboten,* it is forbidden on pain of (the law, a fine, etc.); *seine ~ absitzen,* to serve one's sentence.
strafen *v.t.* to punish, to chastise; (*an Geld*) to fine; *einen Lügen ~*, to give someone the lie.
Strafentlassene *m./f.* ex-convict.
Straferlaß *m.* remission; amnesty.
straff *a.* tight, tense; (*nav.*) taut.
straffällig *a. ~* **werden,** to commit an offense.
straffen *~ v.t. & v.r.* to tighten; to tauten.
straffrei *a.* unpunished.
Straffreiheit *f.* immunity from prosecution.
Strafgefangene *m./f.* convict.
Strafgericht *n.* judgment.
Strafgesetz *n.* penal law; **~buch** *n.* penal code.
Strafkolonie *f.* penal settlement.
sträflich *a.* criminal.
Sträfling *m.* **(-[e]s, -e)** convict; prisoner.
straflos *adv.* unpunished.
Strafmandat *n.* ticket.
Strafmaß *n.* sentence.
Strafporto *n.* surcharge.
Strafpredigt *f.* stern lecture, reprimand.
Strafprozeß *m.* crinimal case; criminal procedure; **~ordnung** *f.* code of criminal procedure.
Strafpunkt *m.* (*Sport*) penalty.

Strafrecht *n.* criminal law; **~spflege** *f.* criminal justice; **~sreform** *f.* penal reform.
strafrechtlich *a.* criminal, penal.
Strafregister *n.* criminal register.
Strafrichter *m.* criminal judge.
Strafsache *f.* criminal case.
Strafsumme *f.* penalty, fine.
Straftat *f.* criminal offense.
Strafumwandlung *f.* commutation of sentence.
Strafurteil *n.* sentence.
Strafverfahren *n.* criminal proceedings.
Strafvollstreckung *f.* penal administration.
Strafzeit *f.* prison term.
Strafzettel *m.* ticket.
Strahl *m.* **(-[e]s, -en)** beam, ray flash; *Wasser~*, jet.
strahlen *v.t. & i.* to radiate, to beam; to shine.
Strahlenbelastung *f.* radioactive contamination.
Strahlenbrechung *f.* refraction.
strahlend *a.* radiant, shining.
Strahlendosis *f.* radiation dose.
strahlenförmig *a.* radial.
Strahlentherapie *f.* radiotherapy.
Strahlenunfall *m.* radiation accident.
Strahlung *f.* radiation.
Strähne *f.* **(-, -n)** strand; streak.
strähnig *a.* straggly.
stramm *a.* tight; sturdy, strapping; erect; (*im Dienst*) strict.
strammstehen *v.i.* to stand to attention.
Strampelhöschen *n.* rompers.
strampeln *v.i.* to kick, to struggle.
Strand *m.* **(-[e]s, -e)** strand, shore, beach; *auf den ~ laufen,* to run ashore.
stranden *v.i. (s)* to strand, to be stranded.
Strand: ~gut *n.* jetsam, flotsam; **~korb** *m.* wicker chair for the beach.
Strang *m.* **(-[e]s, Stränge)** rope; *Galgen~*, noose; (*Schienen~*) track.
strangulieren *v.t.* to strangle.
Strapaze *f.* **(-, -n)** strain; fatigue, over-exertion.
strapazieren *v.t.* to strain, to exhaust, to be hard on.
Strapazierfähigkeit *f.* resistance to wear.
strapaziös *a.* wearing.
Straße *f.* **(-, -n)** road, highway; street; (*Meeresenge*) straits *pl.*
Straßen: ~bahn *f.* streetcar; **~bahnwagen** *m.* streetcar, trolley; **~bau** *m.* road construction; **~gabel** *f.* fork; **~karte** *f.* road map; **~kreuzung** *f.* intersection, crossing, crossroads; **~laterne** *f.* streetlamp; **~pflaster** *n.* pavement; **~raub** *m.* highway robbery; **~schild** *n.* street sign; **~sperre** *f.* (*mil.*) roadblock; **~unterbau** *m.* roadbed; **~verkehrsordnung** *f.* rule of the road; **~verkäufer** *m.* street vendor.
Stratege *m.* **(-en, -en)** strategist.
Strategie *f.* **(-, 0)** strategy.
strategisch *a.* strategic(al).
sträuben *v.t.* to bristle; ~ *v.r.* to struggle.
Strauch *m.* **(-[e]s, Sträuche[r])** bush, shrub.
straucheln *v.i. (s)* to stumble.
Strauß *m.* **(-es -e)** ostrich; (*pl. Sträuße*) bunch, bouquet.
streben *v.i.* to strive, to aspire.
Streben *n.* **(-s, -0)** effort, endeavour.
Strebepfeiler *m.* buttress.
Streber *m.* **(-s, -)** grind.
strebsam *a.* active, industrious.
Strebsamkeit *f.* industriousness.
Strecke *f.* **(-, -n)** extent, distance; (*rail.*) section.
strecken *v.i.* to stretch; to extend; *die Waffen ~*, to lay down one's arms; *zu Boden ~*, to fell.
Streckennetz *n.* railroad network.
streckenweise *adv.* in sections; at times.
Streich *m.* **(-[e]s, -e)** stroke, blow, lash; trick; *auf einen ~*, at one blow; *einem einen ~ spielen,* to play a trick on someone; *ein dummer ~*, a foolish trick; *ein lustiger ~*, a prank.
streicheln *v.t.* to stroke, to caress.
streichen *v.t.st.* to rub; (*Butter*) to spread; (*die Flagge*) to strike; (*Segel*) to lower; (*ausstreichen*) to strike out, to erase; ~ *v.i. (s)* to rove, to stroll.
Streicher *pl.* (*mus.*) the strings.
Streich: ~holz, ~hölzchen *n.* match; **~holzschachtel** *f.* matchbox; **~instrument** *n.* string instrument; **~musik** *f.* string music; **~riemen** *m.* strop.
Streichquartett *n.* string quartet.
Streichung *f.* **(-, -en)** cut, deleted passage.
Streife *f.* **(-, -n)** patrol.
streifen *v.t.* to graze, to touch slightly, to brush; to stripe, to streak; ~ *v.i. (s)* to ramble, to rove; (*h*) (*an etwas*) to border or verge (upon); *(die Ärmel) in die Höhe ~*, to roll up (one's sleeves).
Streifen *m.* **(s, -)** stripe, streak; strip.
Streifen: ~dienst *m.* patrol duty; **~wagen** *m.* patrol car.
streifig *a.* striped; streaky (bacon).
Streif: ~schuß *m.* grazing shot; **~zug** *m.* expedition; prowl (animals).
Streik *m.* **(-s, -e)** strike (of workmen).
Streikbrecher *m.* **(-s, -)** strikebreaker.
streiken *v.i.* to strike.
streikend *a.* on strike.
Streikende *m./f.* striker.
Streik: ~kasse *f.* strikefund; **~posten** *m.* picket.
Streit *m.* **(-[e]s, -e)** fight; contest, dispute, quarrel; conflict; *in ~ geraten,* to fall out, to get into a quarrel.
Streitaxt *f.* battleaxe.
streitbar *a.* valiant.
streiten *v.t.st.* to fight; to dispute, to quarrel; to disagree; *darüber lässt sich ~*, that is a matter of opinion; *die streitenden Parteien,* the contending parties.
Streitfrage *f.* moot point, controversial question.
Streitgegenstand *m.* matter in dispute.
Streithandel *m.* dispute.
streitig *a.* contested, controversial; *einem etwas ~ machen,* to contest someone's right to sth.
Streitigkeit *f.* **(-, -en)** contention; controversy; quarrel.
Streitkräfte *pl.* (military) forces.
Streitlust *f.* argumentative disposition.
streitlustig *a.* argumentative; contentious, litigious.
Streitpunkt *m.* point at issue.
Streitschrift *f.* polemic treatise.
Streitsucht *f.* contentiousness.
streitsüchtig *a.* litigious, quarrelsome.
streng *a.* severe, stern; (*Charakter*) austere; strict, stringent.
Strenge *f.* **(-, 0)** severity; austerity; rigor (of climate).
strenggenommen *adv.* strictly speaking.
strenggläubig *a.* strict.
Streß *m.* **(-es, -e)** stress.
stressen *v.t.* (*fam.*) to put under stress.
stressig *a.* (*fam.*) stressful.

Streu *f.* **(-, -en)** litter.
Streubüchse *f.* shaker (salt, sugar).
streuen *v.t.* to strew; to scatter, to spread; to sprinkle.
streunen *v.i.* to roam around; **~de Hunde** stray dogs.
Streuzucker *m.* confectioners' sugar.
Strich *m.* **(-[e]s, -e)** stroke, line, dash; *Land~*, tract; *in einem ~*, at a stretch; *das macht einen ~ durch die Rechnung*, that upsets the whole plan; *gegen oder wider den ~*, against the grain.
stricheln *v.i.* to sketch in; to hatch; **eine gestrichelte Linie** a broken line.
Strich: ~junge *m.* young male prostitute; **~mädchen** *n.* hooker.
Strichpunkt *m.* semicolon.
strichweise *adv.* here and there.
Strick *m.* **(-[e]s, -e)** cord, rope.
Strickbeutel *m.* knitting bag.
stricken *v.t.* to knit.
Strickerei *f.* **(-, -en)** knitting.
Strick: ~jacke *f.* cardigan; **~leiter** *f.* rope ladder; **~nadel** *f.* knitting needle; **~waren** *pl.* knitwear.
Striegel *m.* **(-s, -)** currycomb.
striegeln *v.t.* to groom.
Striemen *m.* **(-s, -), Strieme** *f.* **(-, -n)** stripe, weal.
strikt *a.* strict.
Strippe *f.* **(-, -n)** string; strap, band.
strippen *v.i.* to strip; to do a striptease.
Striptease *m./n.* **(-, 0)** striptease.
strittig *a.* contentious; disputed.
Stroh *n.* **(-[e]s, 0)** straw.
Strohdach *n.* thatch.
Stroh: ~halm *m.* straw; **~hut** *m.* straw hat; **~hütte** *f.* thatched hut; **~sack** *m.* straw mattress; palliasse; **~witwe** *f.* grass widow; **~witwer** *m.* grass widower.
Strolch *m.* **(-[e]s, -e)** tramp.
strolchen *v.i.* *(s)* to loaf or prowl about.
Strom *m.* **(-[e]s, Ströme)** large river; (*elek. usw.*) current; (*fig.*) torrent, flood; *gegen den ~, mit dem ~ schwimmen*, to swim against, with the stream or the tide.
stromabwärts *adv.* downstream.
stromaufwärts *adv.* upstream.
strömen *v.i.* *(s)* to stream, to flow; to pour.
Stromer *n.* **(-s, -)** vagabond, tramp.
Strom: ~kreis *m.* circuit; **~linienförmig,** *a.* streamlined; **~schnelle** *f.* rapid; **~stärke** *f.* amperage.
Strömung *f.* **(-, -en)** current, drift.
Stromverbrauch *m.* power consumption.
Stromversorgung *f.* power supply.
Stromzähler *m.* electric meter.
Strophe *f.* **(-, -n)** stanza, verse; strophe.
strophisch *a.* strophic, in stanzas.
strotzen *v.i.* to be full of.
Strudel *m.* **(-s, -)** whirlpool.
Struktur *f.* **(-, -en)** structure.
strukturell *a.* structural.
strukturieren *v.t.* to structure.
Strumpf *m.* **(-[e]s, Strümpfe)** stocking; *Glüh~*, mantle.
Strumpf: ~band *n.* garter; **~halter** *m.* garter; **~hose** *f.* pantyhose; **~ware** *f.* hosiery.
Strunk *m.* **(-s, Strünke)** stalk.
struppig *a.* touseled, shaggy (dog).
Struwwelkopf *m.* tousle-head.
Strychnin *m.* **(-[e]s, 0)** strychnine.
Stube *f.* **(-, -n)** (living) room, chamber.
Stuben: ~arrest *m.* confinement in one's own room; **~hocker** *m.* stay-at-home; **~mädchen** *n.* chambermaid.
stubenrein *a.* clean; housebroken.
Stuck *m.* **(-[e]s, 0)** stucco(-work).
Stück *n.* **(-[e]s, -e)** piece, bit, morsel; fragment; (*Theater*) piece, play; (*Zucker*) lump; *~ für ~*, piece by piece; *im ~*, by the piece; *grosse ~e auf einen halten*, to think much of someone; *aus freien ~en*, of one's own accord; *in allen ~en*, in every respect.
Stückeschreiber *m.* playwright.
Stücklohn *m.* piece rate.
Stückpreis *m.* unit price.
stückweise *adv.* by the piece, piecemeal.
Stückzucker *m.* lump-sugar.
Student *m.* **(-en, -en); Studentin** *f.* **(-, -nen)** student, undergraduate.
Studentenschaft *f.* **(-, 0)** students.
Studentenverbindung *f.* fraternity.
studentisch *a.* student-like, student.
Studie *f.* **(-, -n)** *Maler~*, painter's study; essay, sketch.
Studien: ~aufenthalt *m.* study visit; **~direktor** *m.* principal (of a secondary school); **~fach** *n.* subject; **~gang** *m.* course of study; **~gebühr** *f.* tuition fee; **~kopf** *m.* study of a head; **~rat** *m.*, **~rätin** *f.* tenured teacher at secondary school.
studieren *v.t. & i.* to study; to read.
Studier: ~lampe *f.* reading lamp; **~stube** *f.* study.
Studio *n.* studio.
Studiobühne *f.* studio theater.
Studiosus *m.* **(-, -sen)** student, undergraduate.
Studium *n.* **(-s, Studien)** study.
Stufe *f.* **(-, -n)** step; stair; degree.
stufenartig *a.* gradual, graduated.
Stufen: ~barren *m.* asymmetric bars; **~leiter** *f.* scale; (*fig.*) gradation.
stufenweise *adv.* gradually, by degrees.
stufig *a.* layered.
Stuhl *m.* **(-[e]s, Stühle)** chair, seat; (*ohne Lehne*) stool; *Kirchen~*, pew; *der apostoliche ~*, the Holy See; *sich zwischen zwei Stühle setzen*, (*fig.*) to fall between two stools.
Stuhl: ~bein *n.* leg of a chair; **~drang** *m.* need to relieve the bowels; **~gang** *m.* bowel movement, (*med.*) stool; **~lehne** *f.* back of a chair.
Stukkateur *m.* **(-s, -e)** stucco worker.
Stukkatur *f.* **(-, -en)** stucco(-work).
Stulle *f.* **(-, -n)** slice of bread and butter.
stülpen *v.t.* to cock (a hat); to tilt, to turn up; to put over.
Stulp[en]stiefel *m.* top boot.
stumm *a.* dumb, mute, silent; *~er Film*, silent film.
Stumme *m./f.* mute.
Stummel *m.* **(-s, -)** stump, cigar butt; stub (pencil).
Stümper *m.* **(-s, -)** botcher; bungler.
Stümperei *f.* **(-, -en)** botching; bungling.
stümperhaft *a.* bungling.
stümpern *v.t.* to bungle, to botch.
stumpf *a.* obtuse; blunt; dull; *~er Winkel*, obtuse angle.
Stumpf *m.* **(-[e]s, Stümpfe)** stump, trunk.
Stumpfsinn *m.* dullness; apathy.
stumpfsinnig *a.* stupid, dull.
Stunde *f.* **(-, -n)** hour; lesson.
stunden *v.t.* to grant a delay for sth.

Stunden: ~geld *n.* fee for a lesson; **~glas** *n.* hour-glass.
stundenlang *a.* lasting for hours.
Stunden: ~plan *m.* timetable; **~zeiger** *m.* hour-hand.
stündlich *a. & adv.* hourly; every hour.
Stundung *f.* **(-, -en)** delay (of payment), respite.
Stundungsfrist *f.* (*com.*) days of grace.
stupide *a.* dull; moronic.
Stups *m.* **(-es, -e)** (*fam.*) push; shove.
stupsen *v.t.* (*fam.*) to push; to shove.
Stupsnase *f.* snubnose.
stur *a.* stubborn; obstinate.
Sturheit *f.* stubbornness; obstinacy.
Sturm *m.* **(-[e]s, Stürme)** gale, storm; tempest; (*mil.*) assault.
Sturm: ~angriff *m.* assault; **~warnung** *f.* gale warning.
stürmen *v.t. & i.* to storm; to rush; to assault.
Stürmer *m.* **(-s, -)** (*Fußball*) forward.
Sturmflut *f.* storm tide.
stürmisch *a.* stormy, tempestuous.
Sturmwind *m.* heavy gale.
Sturz *m.* **(-es, Stürze)** rush; fall, ruin; plunge; (*fig.*) overthrow.
Sturzbach *m.* torrent.
stürzen *v.t.* to plunge; to plummet; to shoot; (*fig.*) to overthrow, to ruin; ~ *v.i. (s)* to fall; to tumble down; to rush; *sich in Gefahren ~*, to rush into dangers; *sich in Schulden, Kosten ~*, to plunge into debt, to incur heavy expenses; *ins Elend ~*, to plunge into misery; *ins Verderben ~*, to undo, to ruin.
Sturzflug *m.* (*avi.*) nosedive.
Sturzhelm *m.* **(-s, -e)** crash helmet.
Stute *f.* **(-, -n)** mare.
Stütze *f.* **(-, -n)** prop, stay; support.
stutzen *v.t.* to curtail; to prune; to crop (ears); to clip, to lop, to trim; ~ *v.i.* to be startled; to stop short.
stützen *v.t.* to prop, to support; to base on; ~ *v.r.* to rely upon, to lean against; to refer to.
Stutzer *m.* **(-s, -)** dandy.
stutzerhaft *a.* dandified.
Stutzflügel *m.* baby grand (piano).
stutzig *a.* ~ **machen,** to startle.
Stützpunkt *m.* point of support; (*des Hebels*) fulcrum; (*mil.*) base.
Stutzschwanz *m.* bobtail.
StVO *Straßenverkehrsordnung,* traffic regulations.
s.u. *siehe unten,* see below.
subaltern *a.* subaltern, inferior.
Subdominante *f.* subdominant.
Subjekt *n.* **(-[e]s, -e)** subject; (*fam.*) person, fellow.
subjektiv *a.* subjective.
Subjektivität *f.* subjectivity.
Subjektsatz *m.* subject clause.
Subkultur *f.* **(-, -en)** subculture.
subordinieren *v.t.* to subordinate.
Subsidiengelder *pl.* subsidies.
subskribieren *v.t.* to subscribe (to).
Subskription *f.* **(-, -en)** subscription.
Substantiv *n.* **(-s, -e)** noun.
Substanz *f.* **(-, -en)** substance.
Substrat *n.* **(-[e]s, -e)** substratum.
subtil *a.* subtle.
subtrahieren *v.t.* to subtract.
Subtraktion *f.* subtraction.
subtropisch *a.* subtropic(al).
subventionieren *v.t.* to subsidize.
Subventionierung *f.* **(-, -en)** subsidy.
Suche *f.* **(-, -n)** search; *auf der ~ sein,* to be in search (of).
suchen *v.t.* to seek, to look for; (*versuchen*) to endeavour, to try; *er hat hier nichts zu ~*, he has no business here; *gesucht,* wanted; affected; far-fetched.
Sucher *m.* **(-s, -)** (*phot.*) viewfinder.
Suchhund *m.* tracker dog.
Sucht *f.* **(-, 0)** addiction.
süchtig *a.* addicted.
Süchtige *m./f.*, **Suchtkranke** *m./f.* addict.
Südafrika *n.* South Africa.
Südafrikaner *m.;* **Südafrikanerin** *f.;* **südafrikanisch** *a.* South African.
Südamerika *n.* South America.
Sudan *m./n.* Sudan.
süddeutsch *a.* South German.
Sudelei *f.* **(-, -en)** mess.
sudeln *v.t.* to make a mess.
Süden *m.* **(-s, 0)** south.
Südfrüchte *pl.* fruits grown in the south.
Südküste *f.* south coast.
südlich *a.* south(ern).
Südost[en] *m.* southeast.
südöstlich *a.* southeast(ern).
Süd: ~pol *m.* South Pole; **~see** *f.* South Sea; **~seite** *f.* south side.
südwärts *adv.* southward.
südwestlich *a.* southwest(ern).
Südwind *m.* south/southerly wind.
Suff *m.* **(-[e]s, 0)** (*vulg.*) boozing.
süffig *a.* drinkable.
süfisant *a.* smug.
suggerieren *v.t.* to suggest.
suggestiv *a.* suggestive.
suhlen *v.r.* to wallow.
Sühne *f.* **(-, -n)** expiation, atonement.
sühnen *v.t.* to expiate, to atone for.
Suite *f.* **(-, -n)** retinue; suite.
sukzessiv *a.* gradual.
Sulfat *n.* sulfate.
Sulfonamid *n.* sulfonamide.
Sultan *m.* **(-[e]s, -e)** sultan.
Sultanine *f.* **(-, -n)** sultana (raisin).
Sülze *f.* **(-, -n)** brawn; aspic.
Summa *f.* **(-, Summen)** sum (total).
summarisch *a.* summary.
Summe *f.* **(-, -n)** sum; sum total.
summen *v.i.* to buzz, to hum.
summieren *v.t. & r.* to add up (to).
Sumpf *m.* **(-[e]s, Sümpfe)** marsh, swamp, (*fig.*) morass.
Sumpfhuhn *n.* moorhen.
sumpfig *a.* marshy, swampy.
Sund *m.* **(-[e], -e)** straits *pl.*, sound.
Sünde *f.* **(-, -n)** sin.
Sünden: ~bock *m.* scapegoat; **~fall** *m.* Fall (of man); **~vergebung** *f.* remission of sins.
Sünder *m.* **(-s, -); Sünderin** *f.* **(-, -nen)** sinner.
sündhaft *a.* sinful.
sündig *a.* sinful.
sündigen *v.i.* to sin.
sündlos *a.* sinless.
Super *n.* premium (gas).
superklug *a.* (*fam.*) overwise.
Superlativ *m.* **(-s, -e)** superlative.
Supermarkt *m.* supermarket.

Suppe *f.* **(-, -n)** soup; *jm. eine ~ einbrocken,* to do sb. a bad turn.
Suppen: ~fleisch *n.* meat for soup; **~löffel** *m.* tablespoon, soup ladle; **~schüssel** *f.* soup tureen; **~würfel** *m.* bouillon cube.
Surfbrett *n.* surfboard.
surfen *v.i.* to surf.
Surrealismus *m.* surrealism.
surrealistisch *a.* surrealist; surrealistic.
surren *v.i.* to hum, to buzz.
Surrogat *n.* **(-[e]s, -e)** substitute.
suspekt *a.* suspicious.
suspendieren *v.t.* to suspend; to dismiss.
süß *a.* sweet.
Süße *f.* **(-, 0)** sweetness.
süßen *v.t.* to sweeten.
Süßigkeit *f.* **(-, -en)** sweet; sweetness; **Süßigkeiten** *f.pl.* sweets *pl.*
süßlich *a.* sweetish; on the sweet side; mawkish.
Süßwasser *n.* fresh water.
SW *Südwest(en),* southwest, SW.
Syllogismus *m.* **(-, -gismen)** syllogism.
Sylphe *f.* **(-, -n)** sylph.
Sylvester[abend] *m.* New Year's Eve.
Symbol *n.* **(-[e]s, -e)** symbol.
symbolhaft *a. & adv.* symbolic(ally).
Symbolik *f.* **(-, 0)** symbolism.
symbolisch *a.* symbolic.
symbolisieren *v.t.* to symbolize.
Symbolismus *m.* symbolism; Symbolism (art).
Symmetrie *f.* **(-, -[e]n)** symmetry.
symmetrisch *a.* symmetrical.
Sympathie *f.* **(-, -[e]n)** sympathy.
Sympathisant *m.* **(-en, -en); Sympathisantin** *f.* **(-, -nen)** sympathizer.
sympathisch *a.* congenial, likeable; nice.
sympathisieren *v.i.* to sympathize (with).
Symphonie *f.* **(-, -[e]n)** symphony.
Symptom *n.* **(-[e]s, -e)** symptom.
symptomatisch *a.* symptomatic (of).
Synagoge *f.* **(-, -n)** synagogue.
synchronisieren *v.t.* to dub; to synchronize.
Syndikat *n.* **(-es, -e)** syndicate.
Syndikus *m.* **(-, -dizi)** company lawyer.
Syndrom *n.* **(-s, -e)** syndrome.
Synkope *f.* **(-, -n)** syncopation.
synkopieren *v.t.* to syncopate.
Synode *f.* **(-, -n)** synod.
synonym *a.* synonymous.
Synonym *n.* synonym.
syntaktisch *a.* syntactic.
Syntax *f.* **(-, 0)** syntax.
Synthese *f.* **(-, -n)** synthesis.
synthetisch *a.* synthetic.
Syphilis *f.* **(-, 0)** syphilis.
Syrer *m.;* **Syrerin** *f.;* **syrisch** *a.* Syrian.
Syrien *n.* **(-s, 0)** Syria.
Syrup *m.* **(-s, 0)** syrup, molasses.
System *n.* **(-[e]s, -e)** system.
systematisch *a.* systematic.
Szenario *n.* **(-, -s)** scenario.
Szene *f.* **(-, -n)** scene.
Szenerie *f.* **(-, -en)** scenery; setting.
Szepter *n.* = **Zepter.**

T

T, t *n.* the letter T or t.
t. *Tonne,* ton.
Tabak *m.* **(-[e]s, -e)** tobacco.
Tabaks: ~beutel *m.* tobacco pouch; **~dose** *f.* snuff box.
tabellarisch *a.* tabular, tabulated.
Tabelle *f.* **(-, -n)** table(s), schedule.
Tabellenführer *m.* top team/player.
Tablett *n.* **(-s, -e)** tray.
Tablette *f.* **(-, -n)** tablet.
Tacho *m.* (*fam.*), **Tachometer** *n.* **(-s, -)** speedometer.
Tadel *m.* **(-s, -)** blame, censure; fault, blemish.
tadelhaft *a.* blameable.
tadellos *a.* impeccable; blameless, faultless, perfect.
tadeln *v.t.* to rebuke; to blame.
tadelnswert *a.* reprehensible.
Tadler *m.* **(-s, -)** faultfinder.
Tafel *f.* **(-, -n)** (dining)table; slab; plate; slate; bar (of chocolate); *Wand~,* blackboard.
tafelfertig *a.* ready to serve.
tafelförmig *a.* tabular, table-shaped.
Tafelgeschirr *n.* dinner service.
tafeln *v.i.* to dine, to feast.
täfeln *v.t.* to panel.
Täfelung *f.* **(-, -en)** panelling.
Tafelwasser *n.* mineral water.
Tafelwein *m.* table wine.
Taft *m.* **(-[e]s, -e)** taffeta.
Tag *m.* **(-[e]s, -e)** day; light; *es ist heller ~,* it is broad daylight; *an den ~ kommen,* to come to light; *bei ~,* in the daytime; *heute über acht ~e,* a week from today; *in den ~ hineinleben,* to live one day at a time.
tagaus *adv.* **~, tagein** day in, day out.
Tagebau *m.* stripmining.
Tagebuch *n.* diary, journal; (*com.*) daybook.
Tagegeld *n.* per diem allowance.
tagelang *a. & adv.* for days together.
Tagelohn *m.* daily wages *pl.*
Tagelöhner *m.* day laborer.
tagen *v.i.* to dawn; ~ *v.i.* (of assemblies) to meet, to sit.
Tagereise *f.* day's journey.
Tagesablauf *m.* day; daily.
Tagesanbruch *m.* daybreak.
Tagesangriff *m.* (*mil.*) daylight attack.
Tagesbefehl *m.* (*mil.*) order of the day; routine.
Tagesgespräch *n.* topic of the day.
Tageslicht *n.* daylight; *ans ~ kommen,* to come to light.
Tagesordnung *f.* agenda, order of the day.
Tageszeit *f.* time of day.
tageweise *adv.* by the day.
Tagewerk *n.* day's work, day's task.
taghell *a.* light as day.
täglich *a.* daily; **~es Geld,** call money.
tags *adv.* by day; **~zuvor** the day before; **~darauf** the day after.
Tagschicht *f.* day shift.
tagtäglich *adv.* every day.
Tagträumer *m.* daydreamer.
Tag- und Nachtgleiche *f.* equinox.

Tagung *f.* **(-, -en)** conference, rally, session.
Tagungsort *m.* conference venue.
Taifun *m.* **(-s, -e)** typhoon.
Taille *f.* **(-, -n)** waist; waistline.
tailliert *a.* waisted.
Takel *n.* **(-s, -)** (*nav.*) tackle.
Takelage *f.* rigging.
takeln *v.t.* to tackle, to rig.
Takelwerk *n.* rigging.
Takt *m.* **(-es, -e)** time, measure; bar; (*fig.*) tact; **~ halten,** to keep time; **~ schlagen,** to beat time; *im ~*, in time.
Taktgefühl *n.* sense of tact.
Takt[ier]stock *m.* baton; **~strich** *m.* (*mus.*) bar.
Taktik *f.* **(-, -en)** tactics *pl.*
Taktiker *m.* **(-s, -); Taktikerin** *f.* **(-, -nen)** tactician.
taktisch *a.* tactical.
taktlos *a.* tactless.
Taktlosigkeit *f.* **(-, -en)** tactlessness.
taktvoll *a.* tactful; discreet.
Tal *n.* **(-[e]s, Täler)** valley, dale, glen.
Talar *m.* **(-[e]s, -e)** robe.
Talent *n.* **(-[e]s, -e)** talent; gift, aptitude.
talentiert *a.* talented.
talentvoll *a.* talented, gifted.
Talg *m.* **(-[e]s, e)** tallow, suet.
Talglicht *n.* tallow candle.
Talisman *m.* talisman; mascot.
Talsohle *f.* valley floor; (*fig.*) depression.
Talsperre *f.* dam; reservoir.
Talstation *f.* valley station.
Tambour *m.* **(-s, -e)** drummer.
Tamburin *n.* **(-[e]s, -e)** tambourine.
Tampon *n.* **(-s, -s)** tampon; plug.
Tand *m.* **(-[e]s, 0)** knicknacks *pl.*, toy(s).
tändeln *v.t.* to trifle, to toy, to dandle.
Tang *m.* **(-[e]s, -e)** seaweed.
Tangens *m.* **(-, -)** tangent.
Tangente *f.* **(-, -n)** tangent.
tangieren *v.t.* to affect; (*math.*) to be tangent to.
Tank *m.* **(-[e]s, -s)** tank; **~dampfer** *m.* tanker.
tanken *v.i.* to fill up; to refuel.
Tankstelle *f.* **(-, -n)** gas station.
Tankwart *m.* gas station attendant.
Tanne *f.* **(-, -n)** fir (-tree), silver-fir.
Tannennadel *f.* fir needle.
Tannenzapfen *m.* pine cone, fir cone.
Tannin *m.* **(-[e]s, 0)** tannic acid, tannin.
Tante *f.* **(-, -n)** aunt.
Tantieme *f.* **(-, -n)** royalty.
Tanz *m.* **(-es, Tänze)** dance.
tänzeln *v.i.* to prance; to skip.
tanzen *v.i.* to dance.
Tänzer *m.* **(-s, -); Tänzerin** *f.* **(-, -nen)** dancer.
Tanz: ~lehrer, ~lehrerin dancing instructor; **~sport** *m.* ballroom dancing; **~stunde** *f.* dancing lesson.
Tapet *n.* **(-[e]s, -e)** (*fig.*) *aufs ~ bringen,* to broach *or* to introduce (a subject).
Tapete *f.* **(-, -n)** wallpaper.
tapezieren *v.t.* to paper; to hang with tapestry.
Tapezier[er] *m.* **(-s, -)** paper-hanger, upholsterer.
tapfer *a.* brave, valiant.
Tapferkeit *f.* **(-, 0)** valor, bravery.
tappen *v.i.* to grope; to patter.
täppisch *a.* awkward, clumsy.
tapsen *v.i.* to lurch along.
tapsig *a.* awkward, clumsy.
Tara *f.* **(-, 0)** (*Gewicht*) (*com.*) tare.
Tarantel *f.* **(-, -n)** tarantula; *wie von der ~ gestochen,* like one possessed.
Tarif *m.* **(-s, -e)** tariff; scale of wages; railway rate.
Tarif: ~gruppe *f.* wage group; salary group; **~lohn** *m.* standard wage; **~vertrag** *m.* collective agreement.
tarnen *v.i.* (*mil.*) to camouflage.
Tarnung *f.* **(-, -en)** camouflage.
Tarock *m.* *& n.* **(-s, 0)** taroc.
Tasche *f.* **(-, -n)** pocket; bag; *Schul~*, satchel.
Taschen: ~ausgabe *f.* pocket edition; **~buch** *n.* paperback; **~dieb** *m.* pickpocket; **~format** *n.* pocket-size; **~geld** *n.* pocket money; **~krebs** *m.* crab; **~lampe** *f.* flashlight; **~messer** *n.* pocket-knife; **~spiel** *n.* juggling, sleight-of-hand; **~spieler** *m.* conjurer, juggler; **~tuch** *n.* handkerchief; **~uhr** *f.* pocket watch.
Tasse *f.* **(-, -n)** cup.
Tastatur *f.* **(-, -en)** (*mus.*) keyboard, keys *pl.*
Taste *f.* **(-, -n)** (*mus.*) key.
tasten *v.t. & i.* to grope, to feel, to touch.
Tasten: ~instrument *n.* keyboard instrument; **~telefon** *n.* push button telephone.
Taster *m.* **(-s, -)** feeler, antenna.
Tastsinn *m.* (sense of) touch, feeling.
Tat *f.* **(-, -en)** action, deed, fact, act; *in der ~*, indeed, as a matter of fact; *auf frischer ~*, in the very act; *mit Rat und ~*, by word and deed.
Tatbestand *m.* facts of the case *pl.*
Tatendrang, Tatendurst *m.* desire for action.
tatenlos *a.* inactive.
Täter *m.* **(-s, -); Täterin** *f.* **(-, -nen)** culprit; offender.
tätig *a.* active; busy, industrious.
tätigen *v.t.* to effect, to carry out.
Tätigkeit *f.* **(-, -en)** activity; *außer ~ setzen,* to suspend.
Tatkraft *f.* energy.
tatkräftig *a.* energetic.
tätlich *a.* violent; **~werden,** to become violent; **~e Beleidigung,** assault and battery.
Tatort *m.* crime scene.
tätowieren *v.t.* to tattoo.
Tatsache *f.* **(-, -n)** fact.
tatsächlich *a. & adv.* actual(ly), as a matter of fact, in point of fact.
tätscheln *v.t.* to pat.
tatte(e)rig *a.* shaky.
tatverdächtig *a.* suspected.
Tatze *f.* **(-, -n)** paw, claw.
Tau *n.* **(-[e]s, -e)** cable rope.
Tau *m.* **(-[e]s, 0)** dew.
taub *a.* deaf.
Taube *f.* **(-, -n)** pigeon, dove.
Taube *m./f.* deaf person.
Taubenschlag *m.* pigeon loft.
Taubheit *f.* **(-, 0)** deafness.
Taubnessel *f.* deadnettle.
taubstumm *a.* deaf-mute.
Taubstumme *m./f.* deaf-mute.
tauchen *v.t.* to dip, to steep, to duck; **~** *v.i.* to dive, to plunge.
Taucher *m.* **(-s,-); Taucherin** *f.* **(-, -nen)** diver; skin diver.
Taucher: ~anzug *m.* diving suit; **~brille** *f.* diving goggles; **~glocke** *f.* diving bell; **~maske** *f.* diving mask.
Tauchsieder *m.* immersion heater.

tauen *v.i.imp.* to thaw; to melt.
Taufbecken *n.* (baptismal) font.
Taufbuch *n.* parish register.
Taufe *f.* **(-, -n)** baptism, christening.
taufen *v.t.* to christen, to baptize.
Täufer *m.* **(-s, -)** *Johannes der ~*, St. John the Baptist.
Täufling *m.* **(-[e]s, -e)** child (*or* person) to be baptized.
Taufname *m.* Christian name.
Taufpate *m.* godfather.
Taufpatin *f.* godmother.
Taufschein *m.* certificate of baptism.
taugen *v.i.* to be good *or* fit for; *nichts ~*, to be good for nothing.
Taugenichts *m.* **(-, -e)** good-for-nothing.
tauglich *a.* fit, able, qualified; (*mil.*) able-bodied.
Taumel *m.* **(-s, 0)** dizziness; ecstasy, passion.
taumeln *v.i. (s)* to reel, to stagger.
Tausch *m.* **(-es, -e)** exchange, barter.
tauschen *v.t.* to exchange, to barter.
täuschen *v.t.* to deceive, to delude; ~ *v.r.* to be deceived; *sich durch etwas ~ lassen,* to be deceived by a thing.
täuschend *a.* deceptive; striking.
Tauschhandel *m.* barter; *~ treiben,* to barter.
Täuschung *f.* **(-, -en)** deception; delusion, illusion; *optische ~*, optical illusion.
tauschweise *adv.* by way of exchange.
tausend *a.* thousand; *zu Tausenden,* by thousands, in the thousands.
Tausend *n.* **(-s, -e)** thousand.
Tausender *m.* **(-s, -)** thousand, figure denoting the thousand.
tausenderlei *a.* of a thousand kinds.
tausendfach, tausendfältig *a.* thousand-fold.
Tausendfüßler *m.* millipede.
tausendjährig *a.* millennial.
tausendmal *adv.* a thousand times.
Tautropfen *m.* dewdrop.
Tauwetter *n.* thaw.
Tauziehen *n.* tug-of-war.
Taxe *f.* **(-, -n)** fee, fixed scale of charges; taxi.
Taxi *n.* **(-s, -s)** taxi.
taxieren *v.t.* to estimate; to value.
Taxi: ~fahrer *m.*; **~fahrerin** *f.* taxi driver; **~stand** *m.* taxi stand.
Taxushecke *f.* yew hedge.
Taxwert *m.* estimated value.
Tb *Tuberkulose,* TB, tuberculosis.
Tb-Kranke *m./f.* Tuberculosis patient.
Team *n.* **(-s, -s)** team; **~arbeit** *f.*, **~work** *n.* team work.
Technik *f.* **(-, -en)** technology; (*in der Kunst*) technique, execution.
Techniker *m.* **(-s, -)**; **Technikerin** *f.* **(-, -nen)** technical expert.
Technikum *n.* **(-s, -ken)** technical school.
technisch *a.* technical.
technischer Berater *m.* consulting engineer.
Technokrat *m.* **(-en, -en)**; **Technokratin** *f.* **(-, -nen)** technocrat.
Technologie *f.* technology.
technologisch *a.* technological.
Teckel *m.* **(-s, -)** dachshund.
Tedeum *n.* **(-[e]s, -[e]s)** Te Deum.
Tee *m.* **(-s, -s)** tea.
Tee: ~beutel *m.* teabag; **~gesellschaft** *f.* tea party; **~kanne** *f.* teapot; **~kessel** *m.* teakettle; **~löffel** *m.* teaspoon.
Teenager *m.* **(-s, -)**; **Teenagerin** *f.* **(-, -nen)** teenager.
Teer *m.* **(-[e]s, -e)** tar.
teeren *v.t.* to tar.
Teesieb *n.* strainer.
Teestube *f.* tearoom.
Teetasse *f.* teacup.
Teich *m.* **(-[e]s, -e)** pond.
Teig *m.* **(-[e]s, -e)** dough, pastry; batter.
Teigwaren *pl.* pasta.
Teil *m./n.* **(-[e]s, -e)** share, part, portion; division; *~nehmen an,* to take part in; *beide ~e,* both parties; *zu gleichen ~en,* in equal shares; *ich für meinen ~*, I, for one; for my part; *zum ~*, partly.
teilbar *a.* divisible.
Teilchen *n.* **(-s, -)** particle.
teilen *v.t.* to divide; to share.
Teiler *m.* **(-s, -)** (*mus.*) divisor.
teilhaben *v.i.* to share.
Teilhaber *m.* **(-s, -)**; **Teilhaberin** *f.* **(-, -nen)** partner.
Teilhaberschaft *f.* partnership.
teilhaft(ig) *a.* participating in; *~ werden,* to partake of, to share.
Teilkaskoversicherung *f.* insurance with partial coverage.
Teilnahme *f.* **(-, 0)** participation; interest, sympathy.
teilnahms: ~los indifferent; **~voll** compassionate.
Teilnahmslosigkeit *f.* **(-, 0)** indifference.
teilnehmend *a.* sympathetic.
Teilnehmer *m.* **(-s, -)**; **Teilnehmerin** *f.* **(-, -nen)** participant, contestant; (*tel.*) subscriber.
teils *adv.* partly.
Teilstrecke *f.* stretch; stage.
Teilstück *n.* piece, section.
Teilung *f.* **(-, -en)** division, partition.
teilw. *teilweise,* partly.
teilweise *adv.* in part(s), partially.
Teilzahlung *f.* partial payment, installment.
Teilzeitarbeit *f.* part-time work.
Teint *m.* **(-s, -s)** complexion.
Tel. *Telefon,* telephone, tel.
Telefon *n.* **(-s, -e)** telephone.
Telefon: ~anruf *m.* (tele)phone call; **~apparat** *m.* telephone.
Telefonat *n.* **(-s, -e)** telephone call.
Telefon: ~buch *n.* directory; **~gebühr** *f.* telephone charge; **~hörer** *m.* receiver.
telefonieren *v.i.* to make a phone call; *mit jm. ~*, to talk to sb. on the phone.
Telefonist *m.* **(-en, -en)**; **Telefonistin** *f.* **(-, -nen)** switchboard operator.
Telefon: ~karte *f.* phonecard; **~nummer** *f.* phone number; **~zelle** *f.* (tele)phone booth.
Telegraf *m.* **(-en, -en)** telegraph.
Telegrafen: ~leitung *f.* telegraph wire or line; **~linie** *f.* telegraph line; **~stange** *f.* telegraph pole.
Telegrafie *f.* **(-, 0)** telegraphy; *drahtlose ~*, wireless (telegraphy).
telegrafieren *v.t.* to telegraph, to wire; to cable.
telegrafisch *a. & adv.* telegraphic; by wire, by telegram.
Telegramm *n.* **(-s, -e)** telegram, wire.
Telegrammadresse *f.* telegraphic address.
Teleobjektiv *n.* telephoto lens.
Telepathie *f.* telepathy.
Teleskop *n.* **(-s, -e)** telescope.
Teller *m.* **(-s, -)** plate.

Tempel *m.* **(-s, -)** temple.
Temperafarbe *f.* distemper; tempera.
Temperament *n.* **(-[e]s, -e)** temper.
temperamentlos *a.* spiritless; lifeless.
temperamentvoll *a.* fiery, spirited; lively.
Temperatur *f.* **(-, -en)** temperature; *~ nehmen,* to take the temperature.
Temperatur: ~anstieg *m.* rise in temperature; **~rückgang** *m.* drop in temperature; **~sturz** *m.* sudden drop in temperature.
temperieren *v.t.* to temper.
Tempo *n.* **(-s, -s)** (*mus.*) time; movement; pace; speed.
Tempolimit *n.* speed limit.
temporär *a.* temporary.
Tempus *n.* **(-, Tempora)** (*gram.*) tense.
Tendenz *f.* **(-, -en)** tendency; bias; slant.
tendenziös *a.* biased, tendentious.
Tender *m.* **(-s, -)** (engine-)tender.
tendieren *v.i.* to tend, be inclined.
Tenne *f.* **(-, -n)** threshing floor.
Tennis *n.* **(-, 0)** tennis; **~platz** *m.* tennis court; **~schläger** *m.* racket.
Tenor *m.* **(-[e]s, -e)** tenor (voice).
Teppich *m.* **(-[e]s, -e)** rug; carpet.
Teppich: ~boden wall-to-wall carpeting; **~fliese** *f.* carpet tile; **~kehrer** *m.* carpet sweeper; **~klopfer** *m.* carpet beater.
Termin *n.* **(-[e]s, -e)** term, time limit, deadline; *einen ~ anberaumen,* (*jur.*) to fix a hearing.
Termindruck *m.* time pressure.
termingemäß *a. & adv.* on schedule.
Termingeschäft *n.* futures trading.
Terminkalender *m.* appointment calendar.
Terminologie *f.* **(-, -[e]n)** terminology.
Termite *f.* **(-, -n)** termite.
Terpentin *m.* or *n.* **(-s, 0)** turpentine.
Terrain *n.* **(-s, -s)** ground.
Terrarium *n.* **(-s, -rien)** terrarium.
Terrasse *f.* **(-, -n)** terrace.
terrassenförmig *a.* terraced.
Terrine *f.* **(-, -n)** tureen.
Territorium *n.* **(-[s], -rien)** territory.
Terror *m.* **(-s, 0)** terror.
Terroranschlag *m.* terrorist attack.
terrorisieren *v.t.* to terrorize.
Terrorismus *m.* terrorism.
Terrorist *m.* **(-en, -en); Terroristin** *f.* **(-, -nen)** terrorist.
Tertia *f.* **(-, -tien)** fourth year of German high school.
Terz *f.* **(-, -en)** (*mus.*) third; *grosse ~,* major third; (fencing) tierce.
Terzett *n.* **(-[e]s, -e)** terzetto, trio.
Test *m.* **(-s, -s & -e)** test.
Testament *n.* **(-[e]s, -e)** testament, will.
testamentarisch, testamentlich *a.* testamentary, by will.
Testamentsvollstrecker *m.* executor.
testen *v.t.* to test.
testieren *v.i.* to make a will; to bequeath; to testify.
Tetanus *m.* **(-, 0)** tetanus.
teuer *a.* expensive; *wie ~ ist das?* how much is this?
Teuerung *f.* **(-, -en)** rise in prices.
Teufel *m.* **(-s, -)** devil.
teuflisch *a.* devilish, diabolical.
Text *m.* **(-es, -e)** text; context; (*Lied~*) words; (*Opern~*) libretto.
Textbuch *n.* libretto, words *pl.*
texten *v.t.* to write.
Texter *m.* **(-s, -)** writer; copywriter (advertising).
Textilbranche *f.* textile industry.
Textilien *pl.* textiles.
Textilindustrie *f.* textile industry.
Textstelle *f.* passage of a text.
Textverarbeitung *f.* word processing.
Textverarbeitungssystem *n.* word processor.
tgl. *täglich,* daily.
TH *Technische Hochschule,* school of technology.
Thailand *n.* Thailand.
Thailänder *m.*, **Thailänderin** *f.* Thai.
Theater *n.* **(-s, -)** theater; stage.
Theater: ~besucher *m.*, **~besucherin** *f.* theater goer; **~dichter** *m.* dramatist, playwright; **~direktor** *m.* theatrical manager; **~kasse** *f.* box office; **~loge** *f.* box; **~stück** *n.* play; **~zettel** *m.* playbill.
theatralisch *a.* theatrical, stagey.
Theismus *m.* **(-, 0)** theism.
Theist *m.* **(-en, -en)** theist.
Theke *f.* counter.
Thema *n.* **(-s, Themen)** theme, subject, topic.
Thematik *f.* complex theme.
thematisch *a.* thematic.
Theologe *m.* **(-n -n); Theologin (-, -nen)** *f.* theologian; divinity student.
Theologie *f.* **(-, -[e]n)** theology, divinity.
theologisch *a.* theological.
Theoretiker *m.* **(-s, -)** theorist; theoretician.
theoretisch *a.* theoretical.
Theorie *f.* **(-, -[e]n)** theory.
Theosophie *f.* theosophy.
Therapeut *m.; **Therapeutin*** *f.* therapist.
therapeutisch *a.* therapeutic.
Therapie *f.* **(-, -en)** therapy.
Thermalbad *n.* **(-s, -bäder)** thermal spa.
Thermik *f.* thermionics.
Thermodynamik *f.* thermodynamics.
Thermometer *n.* *(m.)* **(-s, -)** thermometer.
Thermosflasche *f.* thermos or vacuum flask.
These *f.* **(-, -n)** thesis.
Thron *m.* **(-[e]s, -e)** throne.
thronen *v.i.* to sit enthroned; to reign.
Thron: ~erbe *m.*, **~erbin** *f.;* **~folger** *m.*, **~folgerin** *f.* heir to the throne; **~rede** *f.* King's speech.
Thunfisch *m.* tuna.
Thüringen *n.* **(-s, 0)** Thuringia.
Thymian *m.* **(-s, -e)** thyme.
Tiara *f.* **(-, Tiaren)** tiara, triple crown.
Tibet *n.* Tibet.
Tibeter *m.;* **Tibeterin** *f.;* **tibetisch** *a.* Tibetan.
Tick *m.* **(-[e]s, -e)** quirk; tic.
ticken *v.i.* (*von Uhren*) to tick.
tief *a.* deep; profound; low; (*von Farben*) dark.
Tief *n.* **(-[e]s, -e)** (*Wetterkunde*) low.
Tief: ~bau *m.* deep mining; underground constructions *pl.;* road construction; **~blick** *m.* keen insight.
tiefblickend *a.* perceptive.
Tiefdruck *m.* low pressure.
Tiefe *f.* **(-, -n)** depth; profundity.
Tiefebene *f.* lowlands.
Tiefgang *m.* draft (of a ship), depth.
Tiefgarage *f.* underground garage.
tiefgreifend *a.* profound; far-reaching.
tiefgründig *a.* profound.
tiefkühlen *v.t.* to deep freeze.

Tiefkühl: ~kost *f.* frozen food; **~schrank** *m.* freezer.
Tiefland *n.* lowlands.
tiefliegend *a.* deep-set, sunken.
Tiefpunkt *m.* nadir.
Tiefsinn *m.* melancholy; profoundness.
tiefsinnig *a.* thoughtful, pensive; profound.
Tiefstand *m.* low level.
Tiegel (-s, -) crucible; saucepan.
Tier *n.* **(-[e]s, -e)** animal; *Haus*~, pet.
Tier: ~art *f.* animal species; **~arzt** *m.* veterinarian, vet; **~garten** *m.* zoological gardens, zoo; **~handlung** *f.* pet shop.
tierisch *a.* animal; brutish, bestial.
Tier: ~kreis *m.* zodiac; **~liebe** *f.* love of animals; **~quälerei** *f.* cruelty to animals; **~reich** *n.* animal kingdom; **~schutzverein** *m.* society for the prevention of cruelty to animals.
Tiger *m.* **(-s, -)** tiger.
Tigerin *f.* tigress.
Tilde *f.* **(-, -n)** tilde.
tilgbar *a.* redeemable; extinguishable.
tilgen *v.t.* to extinguish, to annul, to cancel; (*eine Schuld*) to repay.
Tilgung *f.* **(-, -en)** cancelling, repayment.
timen *v.t.* to time.
Tinktur *f.* **(-, -en)** tincture.
Tinte *f.* **(-, -n)** ink; *in der ~ sitzen*, to be in a nice pickle.
Tinten: ~faß *n.* inkstand; **~fisch** *m.* cuttlefish, sepia; **~fleck, ~klecks** *m.* blot, ink spot; **~stift** *m.* indelible pencil.
Tip *m.* **(-[e]s, -e)** tip.
tippen *v.t.* to touch gently, to tap; to type.
Tirade *f.* **(-, -n)** flourish, tirade.
Tirol *n.* **(-s, 0)** Tyrol.
Tisch *m.* **(-es, -e)** table; board; (*fig.*) dinner; *bei ~e*, at table; *zu ~e*, to dinner; *den ~ decken*, to lay the table; *reinen ~ machen*, to make a clean slate.
Tischdecke *f.* tablecloth.
Tischgebet *n.* grace.
Tischgesellschaft *f.* dinner party.
Tischler *m.* **(-s, -)** carpenter, cabinet-maker.
Tischlerei *f.* **(-, -en)** carpentry.
tischlern *v.i.* to do woodwork.
Tischmanieren *pl.* table manners.
Tischplatte *f.* table top.
Tischrücken *n.* table turning.
Tischtennis *n.* table tennis.
Tischtuch *n.* tablecloth.
Tischzeug *n.* table linen.
titanenhaft, titanisch *a.* titanic.
Titel *m.* **(-s, -)** title; style.
Titel: ~anwärter *m.*, **~anwärterin** *f.* title contender; **~bild** *n.* frontispiece; **~blatt** *n.* title page; **~kampf** *m.* final; **~rolle** *f.* title role; **~verteidiger** *m.*, **~verteidigerin** *f.* title holder.
titulieren *v.t.* to call, to title.
Toast *m.* **(-es, -e)** toast; *einen ~ ausbringen*, to drink someone's health.
toasten *v.t.* to toast.
toben *v.i.* to rage, to storm.
Tobsucht *f.* raving madness, frenzy.
Tochter *f.* **(-, Töchter)** daughter.
Tochtergesellschaft *f.* subsidiary (company).
Tod *m.* **(-[e]s, 0)** death, decease.
todbringend *a.* deadly, lethal; fatal.
Todes: ~angst *f.* agony, mortal fear; **~anzeige** *f.* obituary (notice); **~art** *f.* manner of death; **~fall** *m.* death, decease; (*mil.*) fatal casualty; **~kampf** *m.* agony; **~stoß** *m.* death-blow; **~strafe** *f.* capital punishment; *bei ~*, on pain of death; **~urteil** *n.* death sentence.
Todesfall *m.* death; *im ~*, in the event of death.
Todfeind *m.* deadly enemy.
todkrank *a.* fatally ill.
tödlich *a.* mortal, deadly.
todmüde *a.* dead-tired.
Todsünde *f.* mortal sin.
Toilette *f.* **(-, -n)** toilet, lavatory; **~ngarnitur** *f.* toilet set; **~nseife** *f.* toilet soap.
tolerant *a.* tolerant.
Toleranz *f.* **(-, 0)** tolerance.
toll *a.* great, fantastic, mad, frantic.
tollen *v.i.* (*fam.*) to romp, to fool about.
Toll: ~haus *n.* madhouse, bedlam.
Tollheit *f.* **(-, -en)** madness.
Tollkirsche *f.* deadly nightshade.
tollkühn *a.* foolhardy.
Tollwut *f.* rabies.
Tolpatsch *m.* **(-es, -e)** awkward person.
Tölpel *m.* **(-s, -)** awkward person.
tölpelhaft, tölpisch *a.* clumsy, awkward.
Tomate pf. **(-, -n)** tomato.
Tombola *f.* **(-, -s)** raffle.
Ton *m.* **(-[e]s, Töne)** sound; tone; note; key; stress, accent; shade, tint; *guter, feiner ~;* "good form"; *einen anderen ~ anschlagen*, (*fig.*) to change one's tune; *den ~ angeben*, to set the fashion.
Ton *m.* **(-[e]s, -e)** clay, potter's earth.
tonangebend *a.* setting the tone; predominant.
Tonart *f.* (*mus.*) key.
Tonband *n.* tape.
Tonbandaufnahme *f.* tape recording.
Tonbandgerät *n.* tape recorder.
Tondichter *m.* musical composer.
tönen *v.t.* to sound; to resound; to tint.
Tonerde *f.* clay.
tönern *a.* (of) clay, earthern.
Tonfall *m.* tone; intonation.
Tonfilm *m.* sound film, talkie.
Tonkunst *f.* music, musical art.
Tonleiter *f.* scale.
tonlos *a.* toneless, feeble; unaccented (syllable).
Tonne *f.* **(-, -n)** (*Schiffs~*) ton; barrel, tun.
Tonnen: ~gehalt *n.* tonnage; **~gewölbe** *n.* barrel-vault.
Tonspur *f.* (*Film*) soundtrack.
Tonsur *f.* **(-, -en)** tonsure.
Tontechniker *m.* sound technician.
Tönung *f.* **(-, -en)** tint, shading.
Topas *m.* **(Topases, Topase)** topaz.
Topf *m.* **(-[e]s, Töpfe)** pot, saucepan; *alles in einen ~ werfen*, (*fig.*) to treat all alike.
Töpfer *m.* **(-s, -); Töpferin** *f.* **(-, -nen)** potter.
Töpferei *f.* pottery.
töpfern *v.i. & t.* to make pottery.
Töpferscheibe *f.* potter's wheel.
Tor *n.* **(-[e]s, -e)** gate; (*Fußball*) goal.
Tor *m.* **(-n, -en)** fool.
Torf *m.* **(-[e]s, 0)** peat.
Torheit *f.* folly, foolishness.
Torhüter *m.* goalkeeper; goalie.
töricht *a.* foolish, silly.
torkeln *v.i.* *(s)* to stagger, to reel.
Tormann *m.* goalkeeper.
Tornister *m.* **(-s, -)** knapsack, pack.
Torpedo *m.* **(-[e]s, -e),** torpedo.

Torpedo: ~boot *n.* torpedo-boat.
Torso *m.* **(-s, -s)** torso, trunk.
Torte *f.* **(-, -n)** layer cake; fruit tart.
Tortur *f.* **(-, -en)** torture, rack.
Torwächter *m.* goalkeeper.
Torwart *m.* (*Fußball*) goalkeeper.
Torweg *m.* gateway.
tosen *v.i.* to roar, to rage.
tot *a.* dead, deceased; **~es Kapital,** idle capital; **~schlagen,** to slay; to kill (time); **~schießen,** to shoot dead; **~schweigen,** to hush up (an affair); ~ *v.r.* **~lachen,** to die laughing; **~geboren,** stillborn.
total *a.* total.
Total: ~ausfall *m.* total loss; **~betrag** *m.* aggregate amount.
Totalschaden *m.* **(-s, -schäden)** write-off.
Tote *m./f.* **(-n, -n)** dead person, dead man/woman; *die ~n,* the dead.
töten *v.t.* to kill; (*Nerv*) to deaden.
Toten: ~amt *n.* requiem; **~bahre** *f.* bier.
totenblaß, totenbleich *a.* deadly pale.
Toten: ~feier *f.* funeral service; **~gedenktag** *m.* memorial day; **~gräber** *m.* gravedigger; **~hemd** *n.* shroud; **~kopf** *m.* skull; death's head; **~messe** *f.* requiem, mass for the dead; **~schein** *m.* death certificate.
totenstill *a.* silent as the grave.
Totenstille *f.* deathly silence.
Totgeburt *f.* stillbirth.
Toto *n./m.* football pool; **~schein** *m.* pool ticket.
Totschlag *m.* manslaughter.
totschlagen *v.t.st.* to beat to death.
totschweigen *v.t.st.* to hush up; to leave unmentioned.
totsicher *a.* cocksure.
totstellen *v.r.* to play dead.
tottreten *v.t.st.* to trample to death.
Tötung *f.* **(-, -en)** killing, slaying.
Toupet *n.* **(-s, -s)** toupee.
toupieren *v.t.* to backcomb.
Tour *f.* **(-, -en)** tour, trip.
Tourismus *m.* tourism.
Tourist *m.* **(-en, -en); Touristin** *f.* **(-, -nen)** tourist.
Tournee *f.* **(-, -n)** tour.
Trab *m.* **(-[e]s, 0)** trot; **~ reiten,** to trot.
Trabant *m.* **(-en, -en)** satellite.
traben *v.i. (s)* to trot.
Trabrennen *n.* trotting race.
Tracht *f.* **(-, -en)** fashion, costume; *eine ~ Prügel,* a thrashing.
trachten *v.i.* to strive.
trächtig *a.* pregnant (of animals).
Tradition *f.* **(-, -en)** tradition.
traditionell *a.* traditional.
Trag: ~bahre *f.* stretcher, litter; **~balken** *m.* beam, transom.
tragbar *a.* portable; tolerable.
Trage *f.* **(-, -n)** stretcher, litter.
träge *a.* lazy, inert, idol, indolent.
tragen *v.t.st.* to bear; to carry; (*Kleider*) to wear; ~ *v.r.* to wear (well, etc.); *bei sich ~,* to carry on one's person; *kein Bedenken ~,* not to hesitate; *die Kosten ~,* to bear the expense; *sich mit etwas ~,* to have one's mind occupied with sth.
tragend *a.* supporting; basic; leading.
Träger *m.* **(-s, -)** bearer; carrier, porter; wearer; (*arch.*) beam, girder.
Tragetasche *f.* carrier bag.
Tragfähigkeit *f.* capacity.
tragfertig *a.* ready-to-wear.
Tragfläche *f.* (*avi.*) wing.
Trägheit *f.* **(-, 0)** laziness; (*phys.*) inertia.
Tragik *f.* tragedy.
Tragiker *m.* **(-s, -)** tragic poet; tragedian.
tragikomisch *a.* tragicomic(al).
Tragikomödie *f.* tragicomedy.
tragisch *a.* tragic; ~ *adv.* tragically.
Tragkraft *f.* load.
Tragöde *m.* **(-n, -n)** tragic actor.
Tragödie *f.* **(-, -n)** tragedy.
Tragriemen *m.* sling, strap.
Tragweite *f.* range; (*fig.*) bearing, significance.
Trainer *m.* **(-s, -); Trainerin** *f.* **(-, -nen)** coach.
trainieren *v.t.* to train, to practice; to coach.
Training *n.* **(-s, -s)** training, practice.
Trainingsanzug *m.* track suit.
Trakt *m.* **(-s, -e)** section; wing.
Traktat *m.* or *n.* **(-[e]s, -e)** treatise.
Traktor *m.* **(-s, -en)** tractor.
trällern *v.t.* to warble.
Trambahn *f.* tramway.
trampeln *v.i.* to trample.
trampen *v.i.* to hitchhike.
Tramper *m.*; **Tramperin** *f.* hitchhiker.
Trampolin *n.* trampoline.
Tran (-[e]s, -e) train oil; blubber.
tranchieren *v.t.* to carve meat.
Tranchiermesser *n.* carving knife.
Träne *f.* **(-, -n)** tear.
tränen *v.i.* to water.
Tränen: ~drüse *f.* tear gland; **~gas** *n.* tear gas.
tränenlos *a.* tearless.
Trank *m.* **(-[e]s, Tränke)** drink, beverage; potion, decoction.
Tränke *f.* **(-, -n)** watering place (for animals).
tränken *v.t.* to water (cattle), to give to drink; to soak.
Transaktion *f.* **(-, -en)** transaction.
transatlantisch *a.* transatlantic.
Transformator *m.* **(-s, -en)** (*elek.*) transformer; adapter.
Transit: ~handel *m.* transit trade.
transitiv *a.* transitive.
Transitverkehr *m.* transit traffic.
Transmission *f.* **(-, -en)** transmission.
Transparent *n.* **(-[e]s, -e)** banner; transparency.
Transparenz *f.* transparency.
transpirieren *v.i.* to perspire.
Transplantation *f.* **(-, -en)** transplant; graft (skin).
Transport *m.* **(-[e]s, -e)** transport, haulage; *auf dem ~,* in transit.
Transport(mittel), *n.* transportation.
Transporteur *m.* **(-s, -e)** carrier.
transportfähig *a.* transportable.
transportieren *v.t.* to transport.
Transportunternehmer *m.* haulage contractor.
Transvestit *m.* **(-en, -en)** transvestite.
transzendental *a.* transcendental.
Transzendenz *f.* **(-, 0)** transcendency; transcendence.
Trapez *n.* **(-es, -e)** (*math.*) trapezium; (*Gymnastik*) trapeze.
Trasse *f.* route, line.
trassieren *v.i.* to draw.
Tratsch *m.* **(-(e)s, 0)** (*fam.*) gossip.
tratschen *v.i.* to gossip.

Traualtar *m.* (marriage-)altar.
Traube *f.* **(-, -n)** bunch of grapes; cluster.
Traubenzucker *m.* glucose.
trauen *v.t.* to marry, to join in wedlock; ~ *v.i.* to trust, to confide in; ~ *v.r.* to venture, to dare; *sich ~ lassen,* to get married.
Trauer *f.* **(-, 0)** mourning; mourning dress; affliction; ~ **haben um,** to be in mourning for.
Trauer: ~fall *m.* death, mournful event; **~flor** *m.* mourning band; **~geleit** *n.* funeral procession; **~kleid** *n.* mourning (dress); **~marsch** *m.* funeral march.
trauern *v.i.* to mourn; to be in mourning (for).
Trauer: ~spiel *n.* tragedy; **~weide** *f.* weeping willow; **~zug** *m.* funeral procession.
Traufe *f.* **(-, -n)** eaves *pl.;* gutter; water dripping from the eaves; *aus dem Regen in die ~ kommen,* to drop from the frying pan into the fire.
träufeln *v.t. & i.* to drip, to trickle.
traulich *a.* cordial, intimate; cozy.
Traum *m.* **(-[e]s, Träume)** dream.
Trauma *n.* **(-s, -men)** trauma.
träumen *v.t. & i.* to dream.
Träumer *m.* **(-s, -); Träumerin** *f.* **(-, -nen)** dreamer.
Träumerei *f.* **(-, -en)** reverie; daydream.
träumerisch *a.* dreamy; wistful.
traumhaft *a.* dreamlike.
traurig *a.* mournful, sad, dismal.
Traurigkeit *f.* sadness; sorrow.
Trauring *m.* wedding ring.
Trauschein *m.* marriage certificate.
Trauung *f.* **(-, -en)** wedding ceremony.
Trauzeuge *m.;* **Trauzeugin** *f.* witness to a marriage.
Travestie *f.* **(-, -n)** travesty.
Treff *n.* **(-s, 0)** meeting place; (*Kartenspiel*) club.
treffen *v.t.st.* to hit; to meet (with); to befall; *ihn trifft die Schuld,* it is his fault; *sein Bild ist gut getroffen,* his portrait is a good likeness; *es trifft sich gut,* it is lucky; *Anstalten, Vorkehrungen ~,* to take measures, precautions; ~ *v.r.* to happen; to meet.
Treffen *n.* **(-s, -)** encounter; meeting.
treffend *a.* apt.
Treffer *m.* **(-s, -)** hit; blow; goal; prize (in a lottery).
trefflich *a.* excellent, exquisite.
Treffpunkt *m.* meeting place, venue.
Treibeis *n.* drift ice.
treiben *v.t.st.* to drive, to propel; (*fig.*) to urge, to impel, to incite; (*Gewerbe*) to carry on, to do, to exercise; (*Blätter*) to put forth; ~ *v.t.st.* to float, to drift; *auf die Spitze, aufs Äußerste ~,* to carry to excess; *in die Enge ~,* to drive into a corner; *die Preise in die Höhe ~,* to send or force the prices up; *Musik ~,* to study or practice music; *alte Sprachen ~,* to work at Latin and Greek; *Aufwand ~,* to live in great style; *sein Wesen ~,* to be at it (again).
Treibhaus *n.* hothouse, greenhouse; **~effekt** *m.* greenhouse effect.
Treib: ~holz *n.* driftwood; **~jagd** *f.* drive, roundup; (*fig.*) witch hunt; **~rad** *n.* driving wheel; **~riemen** *m.* driving belt; **~sand** *m.* quicksand *pl.;* **~stoff** *m.* fuel.
tremulieren *v.t.* to quaver, to trill.
Trend *m.* **(-s, -s)** trend.
trennbar *a.* separable.
trennen *v.t.* to separate, to sever; to disunite; ~ *v.r.* to part.
Trennung *f.* **(-, -en)** separation; parting.
Trennungs: ~linie *m.* dividing line; **~strich** *m.* hyphen.
trepanieren *v.t.* to trepan.
Treppe *f.* **(-, -n)** staircase, stairway; stairs; flight of stairs; *treppauf, treppab,* up and down the stairs; *eine, zwei ~n hoch wohnen,* to live on the first, second floor.
Treppen: ~absatz *m.* landing; **~geländer** *n.* banisters *pl.;* **~haus** *n.* staircase; **~stufe** *f.* stair; step.
Tresen *m.* bar; counter.
Tresor *m.* **(-s, -s)** safe, vault.
treten *v.i.st.* to tread; to step; to trample (upon); *einem zu nahe ~,* to hurt someone's feelings; *an die Spitze ~,* to take the lead; *an die Stelle eines ~,* to take another's place; *aus den Ufern ~,* to overflow its banks; *in den Vordergrund ~,* to come to the front.
Tretmühle *f.* treadmill.
treu *a.* faithful, true; *zu ~en Händen,* in trust.
Treubruch *m.* breach of faith.
treubrüchig *a.* faithless, perfidious.
Treue *f.* **(-, 0)** faithfulness, fidelity; allegiance, loyalty; *auf Treu und Glauben,* on trust.
Treueid *m.* **(-s, -e)** oath of allegiance; ~ **schwören,** to swear allegiance.
Treuhand *f.* trust; **~gesellschaft** *f.* trust company.
Treuhänder *m.* trustee.
treuherzig *a.* naive, artless.
treulos *a.* faithless, perfidious.
Treulosigkeit *f.* infidelity; disloyalty; faithlessness.
Triangel *m.* **(-s, -)** triangle.
Tribunal *n.* **(-[e]s, -e)** tribunal.
Tribüne *f.* **(-, -n)** platform; (grand-) stand (at races).
Tribut *m.* **(-[e]s, -e)** tribute; *jdm ~ entrichten, zollen,* to pay tribute to sb.
tributpflichtig *a.* tributary.
Trichine *f.* **(-, -n)** trichina.
Trichter *m.* **(-s, -)** funnel; (*Granat~*) crater.
Trick *m.* **(-s, -s)** trick, dodge.
Trickfilm *m.* cartoon film.
Trieb *m.* **(-[e]s, -e)** sprout, shoot; impulse, bent, instinct.
Trieb: ~feder *f.* motive; **~rad** *n.* driving wheel; **~wagen** *m.* (*rail.*) rail car; **~werk** *n.* engine.
triefen *v.i.st.* to drip, to trickle; *seine Augen ~,* his eyes run.
triefnaß *a.* dripping wet.
Triennium *n.* **(-[e]s, -nien)** period of three years.
triftig *a.* weighty, cogent, forcible.
Trikot *m.* **(-s, -s)** tights, leotard.
Trikotagen *pl.* knitted goods.
Triller *m.* **(-s, -)** trill; quaver; shake.
trillern *v.i.* to trill, to quaver; (*Vogel*) to warble.
Trillion *f.* **(-, -en)** quadrillion.
Trilogie *f.* **(-, -n)** trilogy.
Trimester *n.* term.
Trimm-dich-Pfad *m.* fitness trail.
trimmen *v.t.* to trim; to train; ~ *v.r.* to keep fit.
Trinität *f.* **(-, 0)** Trinity.
trinkbar *a.* drinkable, potable.
Trinkbecher *m.* mug.
trinken *v.t. & i.st.* to drink; to imbibe; *er trinkt,* he is a drunkard.

Trinker *m.* **(-s, -); Trinkerin** *f.* **(-, -nen)** alcoholic; drunkard.
Trinkgelage *n.* drinking bout.
Trinkgeld *n.* gratuity, tip.
Trinkhalm *m.* drinking straw.
Trinkwasser *n.* drinking water.
Trio *n.* **(-[e]s, -s)** trio.
trippeln *v.i.* to trip; to patter; to mince.
Tripper *m.* **(-s, -)** (*med.*) gonorrhea.
Triptychon *n.* triptych.
trist *a.* dreary; sad.
Tritt *m.* **(-[e]s, -e)** tread, step, pace; kick; (*Spur*) footstep; steps; **~ halten,** to keep pace; *im ~,* in step.
Tritt: ~brett *n.* step; (*mot.*) running board; **~leiter** *f.* stepladder.
Triumph *m.* **(-[e]s, -e)** triumph.
Triumphbogen *m.* triumphal arch.
triumphieren *v.i.* to triumph.
Triumphzug *m.* triumphal procession.
Triumvirat *n.* **(-[e]s, -e)** triumvirate.
trivial *a. & adv.* trite, trivial(ly).
Trivialität *f.* **(-, -en)** triviality, triteness; (*konkret*) banality.
Trochäus *m.* **(-, chäen)** trochee.
trocken *a.* dry, arid; barren; (*fig.*) plain; prosy; *auf dem Trockenen sitzen,* to be stuck.
Trocken: ~dock *n.* dry dock; **~gebiet** *n.* arid region; **~haube** *f.* hairdrier.
Trockenheit *f.* **(-, 0)** dryness; drought; (*fig.*) barrenness, aridity, dullness.
trockenlegen *v.t.* to change (a baby); to drain.
Trockenlegung *f.* drainage, draining.
Trockenzeit *f.* dry season.
trocknen *v.t. & i.* to dry, to dry up.
Troddel *f.* **(-, -n)** tassel.
Trödel *m.* **(-s, 0)** lumber, junk.
Trödelei *f.* **(-, -en)** (*fig.*) dawdling.
Trödel: ~laden *m.* junk shop; **~markt** *m.* flea market.
trödeln *v.i.* to dawdle.
Trödler: *m.;* **Trödlerin** *f.* junk dealer; dawdler.
Trog *m.* **(-[e]s, Tröge)** trough.
trollen *v.r.* to go off.
Trommel *f.* **(-, -n)** drum.
Trommel: ~fell *m.* (*Ohr*) eardrum; drumskin; **~feuer** *n.* barrage.
trommeln *v.i.* to drum, to play the drums.
Trommel: ~schlag *m.* drumbeat; **~schlegel** *m.* drumstick; **~wirbel** *m.* drum roll.
Trommler *m.* **(-s, -); Trommlerin** *f.* **(-, -nen)** drummer.
Trompete *f.* **(-, -n)** trumpet.
trompeten *v.i.* to (sound the) trumpet.
Trompeter *m.* **(-s, -); Trompeterin** *f.* **(-, -nen)** trumpeter.
Tropen *f.pl.* tropics; **~helm** *m.* sun helmet.
Tropf *m.* **(-[e]s, Tröpfe)** simpleton, dunce; (*med.*) intravenous feeding, *am ~ hängen* to be on intravenous.
tröpfeln, tropfen *v.t. & i.* to drop; to trickle, to drip.
Tropfen *m.* **(-s, -)** drop; bead (of perspiration).
tropfenweise *adv.* by drops.
tropfnaß *a.* dripping wet.
Tropfstein *m.* stalactite; stalagmite.
Trophäe *f.* **(-, -n)** trophy.
tropisch *a.* tropical.
Troposphäre *f.* troposphere.
Troß *m.* **(Trosses, Trosse)** baggage-(train); retinue.
Trosse *f.* **(-, -n)** cable, hawser.
Trost *m.* **(-es, 0)** consolation, comfort; *schwacher ~,* cold comfort; *nicht recht bei ~e sein,* to be not all there.
trost: ~bedürftig *a.* in need of consolation; **~bringend** *a.* consolatory.
trösten *v.t.* to console; **~** *v.r. über etwas ~,* to get reconciled to a thing.
tröstlich *a.* comforting, consoling.
trostlos *a.* inconsolable, hopeless.
trostreich *a.* comforting, consoling.
Tröstung *f.* **(-, -en)** consolation.
Trott *m.* **(-[e]s, 0)** trot; routine.
Trottel *m.* **(-s, 0)** fool, idiot.
trotten *v.i.* *(s)* to trot, to trudge.
Trottoir *n.* **(-[e]s, -e & -s)** (foot-) pavement, sidewalk.
trotz *pr.* in spite of; **~ alledem,** for all that.
Trotz *m.* **(-es, 0)** defiance.
trotzdem *adv.* nevertheless; ~ *(daß),* although.
trotzen *v.i.* to brave, to defy.
trotzig *a.* defiant; pig-headed; sulky.
trüb(e) *a.* troubled, murky, muddy, thick; dim, dull; *im trüben fischen,* (*fig.*) to fish in troubled waters.
Trubel *m.* **(-s, 0)** hubbub, bustle.
trüben *v.t.* to trouble, to dim.
Trübsal *f.* **(-, -e)** affliction, calamity.
trübselig *a.* woeful, doleful.
Trübsinn *m.* melancholy; dejection.
Trüffel *f.* **(-, -n)** truffle.
Trug *m.* **(-[e]s, 0)** deceit, fraud; delusion.
Trugbild *n.* phantom.
trügen *v.t. & i.st.* to deceive, to delude.
trügerisch, trüglich *a.* deceptive, deceitful, illusory.
Trugschluß *m.* logical fallacy, non sequitur.
Truhe *f.* **(-, -n)** chest, trunk.
Trümmer *pl.* fragments; ruins *pl.;* rubble.
Trümmer: ~feld *n.* expanse of rubble; **~haufen** *m.* heap of rubble.
Trumpf *m.* **(-[e]s, Trümpfe)** trump.
trumpfen *v.t.* to trump.
Trumpfkarte *f.* trump card.
Trunk *m.* **(-[e]s, Trünke)** potion; drink.
trunken *a.* drunken; tipsy.
Trunkenbold *m.* **(-[e]s, -e)** drunkard.
Trunkenheit *f.* drunkenness.
Trunksucht *f.* alcoholism.
Trupp *m.* **(-[e]s, -s)** troop, band; flock.
Truppe *f.* **(-, -n)** troop.
Truppen *f.pl.* troops, forces *pl.*
Truppen: ~gattung *f.* arm *or* branch of service; **~parade** *f.* military parade; **~übungsplatz** *m.* troop training ground.
truppweise *adv.* in troops, in flocks.
Truthahn *m.* turkey (-cock).
Trutz *m.* **(-es, 0)** defiance, attack.
Tschako *m.* **(-s, -s)** shako.
Tscheche *m.* **(-n, -n); Tschechin** *f.* **(-, -nen);**
Tschechische Republik *f.* Czech Republic.
tschilpen *v.i.* to chirp.
tschüs (*fam.*) bye.
TU *Technische Universität,* Technical University.
Tuba *f.* **(-, -ben)** tuba.
Tube *f.* **(-, -n)** tube.
tuberkulös *a.* tubercular, tuberculous.
Tuberkulose *f.* **(-, 0)** tuberculosis.

Tuch *n.* **(-[e]s, Tücher)** cloth; shawl.
Tuch: ~händler *m.* cloth merchant, draper; **~muster** *n.* swatch.
tüchtig *a.* able, apt, fit; excellent; ~ *adv.* thoroughly.
Tüchtigkeit *f.* industry; ability.
Tücke *f.* **(-, -n)** deceit; treachery.
tückisch *a.* deceitful; treacherous.
Tuff *m.* **(-[e]s, -e), Tuffstein** *m.* tufa, tuff.
tüfteln *v.i.* to fiddle; to puzzle.
Tugend *f.* **(-, -en)** virtue.
tugendhaft *a.* virtuous.
tugendsam *a.* virtuous.
Tüll *m.* **(-[e]s, -e)** tulle.
Tulpe *f.* **(-, -n)** tulip.
Tulpenzwiebel *f.* tulip bulb.
tummeln *v.r.* to bestir oneself.
Tummelplatz *m.* playground.
Tumor *m.* **(-s, -en)** tumor.
Tümpel *m.* **(-s, -)** pool, puddle.
Tumult *m.* **(-[e]s, -e)** tumult, riot.
tumultuarisch *a.* tumultuous, riotous.
tun *v.t. & i.st.* to do, to make; to perform, to act; ~ *als ob,* to make as if, to pretend...; *mit einem schön* ~, to cajole; *er tut nur so,* it's all a sham, it's all make-believe; *es tut nichts,* it does not matter; *es tut mir leid,* I am sorry; *ich kann nichts dazu* ~, I cannot help it; *das hat damit nichts zu* ~, that has nothing to do with it; *es ist mir sehr darum zu* ~, I feel very anxious about it.
Tun *n.* **(-s, 0)** doing; activity.
Tünche *f.* **(-, -n)** distemper; whitewash.
tünchen *v.t.* to distemper; whitewash.
Tunesien *n.* **(-s, 0)** Tunisia.
Tunesier *m.;* **Tunesierin** *f.;* **tunesisch** *a.* Tunisian.
Tunichtgut *m.* **(-s, -es)** ne'er-do-well.
Tunke *f.* **(-, -n)** gravy; sauce.
tunken *v.t.* to dip, to steep.
tunlichst *adv.* as far as possible.
Tunnel *m.* **(-s, -[s])** tunnel.
Tüpfelchen *n.* dot.
tüpfeln *v.t.* to dot.
tupfen *v.t.* to swab; to dot.
Tür *f.* **(-, Türen)** door.
Türangel *f.* door hinge.
Turban *m.* **(-[e]s, -e)** turban.
Turbine *f.* **(-, -n)** turbine.
Türflügel *m.* leaf of a door.
Türfüllung *f.* door panel.
Türhüter *m.* doorkeeper.
Türke *m.* **(-n, -n); Türkin** *f.* **(-, -nen)** Turk.
Türkei *f.* Turkey.
Türkis *m.* **(-es, -e)** turquoise.
türkisch *a.* Turkish; **~er Weizen,** maize, corn.
Türklinke *f.* latch, door handle.
Türklopfer *m.* knocker.
Turm *m.* **(-[e]s, Türme)** tower; turret; (*im Schach*) rook; castle.
türmen *v.t.* to run away; ~ *v.r.* to pile up; to stack up.
turmhoch *a.* towering, very high.
Turnanstalt *f.* gymnasium.
turnen *v.t. & i.* to practise gymnastics or athletics.
Turnen *n.* **(-s, 0)** gymnastics.
Turner *m.* **(-s, -); Turnerin** *f.* **(-, -nen)** gymnast.
Turn: ~halle *f.* (covered) gymnasium; **~hose** *f.* shorts *pl.*
Turnier *n.* **(-[e]s, -e)** tournament, joust.
turnieren *v.i.* to joust, to tilt.
Turnierplatz *m.* the lists *pl.*
Turn: ~schuh *m.* gymshoe; **~übung** *f.* gymnastic exercise; gymnastics.
Tür: ~pfosten *m.* doorpost; **~rahmen** *m.* door frame; **~schild** *n.* doorplate; **~schwelle** *f.* threshold.
Turteltaube *f.* turtledove.
Türvorleger *m.* doormat.
Tusch *m.* **(-es, -e)** fanfare.
Tusche *f.* **(-, -n)** India ink.
tuscheln *v.i.* to whisper.
tuschen *v.t. die Wimpern* ~, to put mascara on.
Tüte *f.* **(-, -n)** bag.
tuten *v.t. & i.* to toot; (*mot.*) to honk.
TÜV *Technischer Überwachungsverein,* Technical Control Board.
Typ *m.* **(-s, -en), Type** *f.* **(-, -n)** type; crank.
Typhus *m.* **(-, 0)** typhoid.
typisch *a.* typical.
Typographie *f.* typography.
typographisch *a.* typographical.
Typus *m.* **(-, Typen)** type.
Tyrann *m.* **(-en, -en)** tyrant.
Tyrannei *f.* **(-, -en)** tyranny.
tyrannisch *a.* tyrannic(al).
tyrannisieren *v.t.* to tyrannize, to oppress; to bully.

U

U, u the letter U or u; *einem ein X für ein* ~ *machen,* to bamboozle, to hoodwink someone.
u. *und,* and.
u.a. *unter anderem,* among other things; *und andere,* and others.
u.ä. *und ähnliche(s),* and the like.
u.A.w.g. *um Antwort wird gebeten,* R.S.V.P.
U-Bahn *f. Untergrundbahn,* subway.
U-Bahnhof *m.,* **U-Bahn-Station** *f.* subway station.
übel *a.* evil, bad; sick; ~ *adv.* ill, badly; *wohl oder* ~, willy-nilly; ~*nehmen,* to take ill or amiss; ~ *daran sein,* to be in a sad plight; *mir wird* ~, I feel sick.
Übel *n.* **(-s, -)** evil; disease; injury.
Übelbefinden *n.* indisposition.
übelgelaunt *a.* bad-tempered.
übelgesinnt *a.* evil-minded; hostile.
Übelkeit *f.* **(-, -en)** sickness, nausea.
übellaunig *a.* ill-humored, cross.
übelnehmen *v.t.st.* to take offense.
übelriechend *a.* foul-smelling.
Übel: ~stand *m.* inconvenience, nuisance; drawback; **~tat** *f.* misdeed, crime; **~täter** *m.* wrong doer; criminal.
übelwollend *a.* malevolent.
üben *v.t.* to exercise; to practise; (*mil.*) to drill, to train; *geübt sein in,* to be versed in.
über *pr.* over, above; about; across, beyond; by, on, upon; more than; ~ *und* ~, all over; ~ *Ber-*

lin reisen, to travel via Berlin; *Fehler ~ Fehler* blunder upon blunder; *heute ~ 8 Tage,* a week from today; *~ zwanzig,* more than twenty; *10 Minuten ~ 4 Uhr,* ten minutes past four; *~ kurz oder lang,* sooner or later; *~ Nacht,* over night; *tags~,* during daytime; *einem ~ sein,* to surpass someone.
überall *adv.* everywhere, throughout; *von ~her,* from everywhere; *~hin,* in all directions.
Überangebot *n.* excessive supply.
überängstlich *a.* overanxious.
überanstrengen *v.t.* to strain; ~ *v.r.* to over-exert oneself.
Überanstrengung *f.* over-exertion.
überarbeiten *v.t.* to revise; to rework; ~ *v.r.* to overwork oneself.
Überarbeitung *f.* revision; reworking.
überaus *adv.* extremely.
überbacken *v.t.st.* to brown sth. in the oven.
Überbau *m.* superstructure.
überbeanspruchen *v.t.* to strain; to overburden; to overload.
überbelegt *a.* overcrowded.
überbelichten *v.t.* (*phot.*) to overexpose.
Überbeschäftigung *f.* overemployment.
überbesetzt *a.* overstuffed.
überbewerten *v.t.* to overvalue.
überbieten *v.t.st.* to outbid; to outdo.
Überbleibsel *n.* **(-s, -)** remnant; relic.
Überblick *m.* general view; survey.
überblicken *v.t.* to survey.
überbringen *v.t.st.* to deliver, to bring.
Überbringer *m.* bearer.
überbrücken *v.t.* to bridge.
Überbrückungskredit *m.* (*com.*) short term credit, bridging loan.
überbuchen *v.t.* to overbook.
überdachen *v.t.* to roof in.
überdauern *v.t.* to outlast.
überdenken *v.t.st.* to think over.
überdies *adv.* besides, moreover.
überdosieren *v.t.* to overdose.
Überdosis *f.* overdose.
überdreht *a.* (*fam.*) wound up; crazy.
Überdruck *m.* excess pressure.
Überdruß *m.* **(-sses, 0)** disgust.
überdrüssig *a.* disgusted with.
überdurchschnittlich *a.* above average.
übereignen *v.t.* to transfer.
übereilen *v.t.* to precipitate; ~ *v.r.* to be over-hasty.
übereilt *a.* precipitate, over-hasty.
Übereilung *f.* **(-, -en)** precipitation, rush.
übereinander *adv.* one upon another.
übereinkommen *v.i.st. (s)* to agree.
Übereinkommen *n.* **(-s, -)** agreement; *ein ~ treffen,* to make an agreement.
Übereinkunft *f.* **(-, -künfte)** agreement.
übereinstimmen *v.t.* to agree.
übereinstimmend *a.* in conformity with.
Übereinstimmung *f.* **(-, -en)** agreement.
überempfindlich *a.* oversensitive; (*med.*) hypersensitive.
überessen *v.r.st.* to overeat.
überfahren *v.t.* to run over.
Überfahrt *f.* crossing; passage.
Überfall *m.* sudden attack; raid.
überfallen *v.t.st.* to surprise, to attack suddenly; (*Nacht*) to overtake.
überfällig *a.* overdue.
Überfallkommando *n.* flying squad.
überfein *a.* over-refined, fastidious.
überfliegen *v.t.st.* to fly over; to glance over (a book).
überfließen *v.i.st. (s)* to overflow.
überflügeln *v.t.* to outstrip.
Überfluß *m.* abundance, profusion.
überflüssig *a.* superfluous, needless.
überfluten *v.t.* to flood; to overflow.
überfordern *v.t.* to overcharge; to demand too much.
überführen *v.t.* to conduct; to convict.
Überführung *f.* **(-, -en)** transportation; conviction.
Überfülle *f.* superabundance.
überfüllen *v.t.* to cram, to glut.
überfüllt *a.* overcrowded.
Überfüllung *f.* overcrowding, congestion; repletion.
überfüttern *v.t.* to overfeed.
Übergabe *f.* handing over; delivery; surrender.
Übergang *m.* passage; change, transition; crossing; *~ für Fahrzeuge,* vehicle crossing: *~ für Fußgänger,* pedestrian crossing.
Übergangs: ~bestimmungen *pl.* temporary regulations; **~zeit** *f.* period of transition, transition stage.
übergeben *v.t.st.* to deliver (up), to hand over, to turn over; (*mil.*) to surrender; ~ *v.r.* to vomit; to surrender.
übergehen *v.t.st.* to pass over; to omit; to skip, to revise; *mit Stillschweigen ~,* to pass over in silence; ~ *v.i. (s)* (*mil.*) to go over.
übergenau *a.* overmeticulous.
Übergewicht *n.* overweight, excess weight; preponderance.
überglücklich *a.* overjoyed.
übergreifen *v.i.* to spread.
Übergriff *m.* encroachment.
übergroß *a.* huge, oversized.
Überguß *m.* icing.
überhand *adv.* *~ nehmen,* to gain the upperhand; to get out of control.
überhäufen *v.t.* to overload.
überhaupt *adv.* in general; at all.
überheben *v.t.st.* to lift over; ~ *v.r.* to be overbearing.
überheblich *a.* arrogant.
Überheblichkeit *f.* arrogance.
überheizen *v.t.* to overheat.
überhin *adv.* superficially.
überhitzen *v.t.* to overheat.
überhöht *a.* excessive.
überholen *v.t.* to overhaul; to overtake, to pass (*Verkehr*).
Überhol: ~manöver *n.* passing maneuver; **~spur** *f.* passing lane; **~verbot** *n.* No Passing.
überhören *v.t.* to miss a word; to overhear.
überirdisch *a.* celestial; supernatural.
überkandidelt *a.* (*fam.*) affected.
überkippen *v.i. (s)* to tilt over.
überkleben *v.t.* to paste over.
Überkleid *n.* outer garment; overall.
überklug *a.* overwise, conceited.
überkochen *v.i. (s)* to boil over.
überkommen *v.t.st.* to receive; *die Angst überkam ihn,* he was overcome by fear.
überladen *v.t.st.* to overload.
überlagern *v.t.* to superimpose; to overlap.
Überlandreise *f.* overland journey.

überlappen *v.t.* to overlap.
überlassen *v.t.st.* to cede; ~ *v.r.* to give oneself up to.
Überlassung *f.* **(-. -en)** cession, abandonment.
überlasten *v.t.* to overburden; to overwork.
überlaufen *v.t.st.* to overrun; to importune; *es überläuft mich,* I shudder; ~ *v.i.st. (s)* to go over.
überlaufen *a.* overcrowded.
Überläufer *m.* defector.
überlaut *a.* too or very loud, noisy.
überleben *v.t.* to outlive, to survive; *diese Sache hat sich überlebt,* the thing is out of date altogether.
Überlebende *m./f.* survivor.
überlebensgroß *a.* more than lifesize.
überlegen *v.t. & r.* to reflect upon, to consider, to think over; ~ *a.* superior.
Überlegenheit *f.* **(-, 0)** superiority.
überlegt *a.* carefully considered.
Überlegung *f.* **(-, -en)** reflection; consideration.
überleiten *v.t.* lead over.
Überleitung *f.* **(-, -en)** transition.
überlesen *v.t.st.* to read over; to overlook.
überliefern *v.t.* to surrender; to hand down (to posterity, etc.)
Überlieferung *f.* tradition.
überlisten *v.t.* to outwit, to dupe.
Übermacht *f.* superiority; superior force.
übermächtig *a.* overpowering; superior.
übermalen *v.t.* to paint over.
übermannen *v.t.* overpower.
Übermaß *n.* excess.
übermäßig *a.* exorbitant, excessive.
Übermensch *m.* superman.
übermenschlich *a.* superhuman.
übermitteln *v.t.* to transmit.
übermorgen *adv.* the day after tomorrow.
Übermüdung *f.* **(-, 0)** over-fatigue.
Übermut *m.* high spirits.
übermütig *a.* high-spirited; in high spirits.
übernachten *v.i.* to pass the night.
übernächtigt *a.* overtired; worn out.
Übernachtung *f.* overnight stay; ~ *und Frühstück,* bed and breakfast.
Übernachtungsmöglichkeit *f.* overnight accommodation.
Übernahme *f.* **(-, 0)** taking possession of, taking charge of.
übernatürlich *a.* supernatural.
übernehmen *v.t.st.* to take possession of, to take upon oneself; ~ *v.r.* to overdo; to overwork.
überordnen *v.t.* to place or set over.
Überproduktion *f.* overproduction.
überprüfen *v.t.* to check; to inspect; to examine.
Überprüfung *f.* check up; examination.
überquellen *v.t.st.* to spill over.
überqueren *v.t.* to cross.
überragen *v.t.* to surpass; to outclass.
überragend *a.* outstanding.
überraschen *v.t.* to surprise.
überraschend *a.* surprising, unexpected.
Überraschung *f.* **(-, -en)** surprise.
überreden *v.t.* to persuade.
Überredung *f.* **(-, -en)** persuasion.
überreich *a.* abundant; lavish.
überreichen *v.t.* to hand over, to present.
überreif *a.* over-ripe.
überreizen *v.t.* to over-excite; to strain.
überrennen *v.t.* to overrun.
Überrest *m.* remains, residue, remnant.
überrumpeln *v.t.* to (take by) surprise.
überrunden *v.t.* to lap; to outstrip.
übersät *a.* covered.
übersättigen *v.t.* oversaturate.
Überschall *m.* supersonic.
überschatten *v.t.* to overshadow.
überschätzen *v.t.* to overrate; to overestimate.
Überschau *f.* **(-, 0)** review, survey.
überschauen *v.t.* to survey, to overlook.
überschäumen *v.i.* to froth over.
Überschlag *m.* estimate, rough calculation; (*am Rock*) facing; somersault, handspring.
überschlagen *v.t.st.* to estimate.
überschnappen *v.i. (s.)* to squeak; (*fig.*) to turn crazy.
überschneiden *v.r.* to overlap partially; to cross.
überschreiben *v.t.st.* to transfer; to entitle.
Überschreibung *f.* transfer.
überschreien *v.t.st.* to cry down; ~ *v.r.st.* to overstrain one's voice.
überschreiten *v.t.st.* to pass, to exceed; to go beyond; to cross.
Über: ~schrift *f.* heading; title; headline; **~schuh** *m.* galoshes *pl.*
überschuldet *a.* overburdened with debt.
Überschuß *m.* surplus, excess.
überschüssig *a.* surplus (money, etc.).
überschütten *v.t.* to cover (with).
Überschwang *m.* exuberance.
überschwappen *v.i.* to slop over.
überschwemmen *v.t.* to flood, to inundate, to submerge.
Überschwemmung *f.* inundation, flood.
überschwenglich *a.* exuberant; effusive.
Übersee *n.* oversea(s).
überseeisch *a.* transatlantic, overseas.
übersehbar *a.* assessable.
übersehen *v.t.st.* to omit; to overlook; to disregard; to let pass; to survey.
übersein *v.ir.* (*fam.*) *das ist mir über,* I am sick of it; *er ist dir über,* he has the better of you.
übersenden *v.t.st.* to send.
Übersendung *f.* transmission.
übersetzen *v.t.* to ferry across; to translate; ~ *v.i. (s)* to leap over; to pass over, to cross.
Übersetzer *m.*; **Übersetzerin** *f.* translator.
Übersetzung *f.* **(-, -en)** translation, version; (*Fahrrad*) gear; *grosse* ~, high gear; *kleine* ~, low gear.
Übersicht *f.* **(-, -en)** survey; summary; overall view.
übersichtlich *a.* well arranged; open.
Übersichtstafel *f.* chart.
übersiedeln *v.i. (s)* to move (to).
übersinnlich *a.* supernatural.
überspannen *v.t.* to span; to overstrain; (*fig.*) to exaggerate.
überspannt *a.* (*fig.*) eccentric.
überspielen *v.t.* to cover up; to smooth over.
überspitzen *v.t.* to push sth. too far.
überspringen *v.t.st.* to leap over; (*fig.*) to skip.
übersprudeln *v.i.* to bubble over.
überstehen *v.t.st.* to get over; to survive; (*einen Sturm*) to weather, to ride out.
übersteigen *v.t.st.* to surmount; to surpass, to exceed.
überstellen *v.t.* to hand over.
übersteuern *v.t.* to oversteer; to overmodulate.
überstimmen *v.t.* to outvote.
überstrahlen *v.t.* to outshine; to shine upon.

überströmen *v.t.* to flood, to overwhelm; ~ *v.i. (s)* to overflow; to abound.
Überstunden *pl.* overtime; ~ *machen,* to work overtime.
überstürzen *v.t.* to hasten, to precipitate; ~ *v.r.* to act rashly.
überstürzt *a.* hurried; over-hasty.
übertäuben *v.t.* to stun, to deafen.
überteuert *a.* overpriced.
übertölpeln *v.t.* to dupe, to take in.
übertönen *v.t.* to drown out.
Übertrag *m.* **(-[e]s, -träge)** sum carried over; carry over.
übertragbar *a.* transferable; negotiable; (*med.*) infectious.
übertragen *v.t.st.* to translate; to transfer; to carry over; to confer (an office upon); (*Befugnis*) to delegate; (*Schrift*) to transcribe; (*Blut*) to transfuse; ~ *a.* figurative, metaphorical.
Übertragung *f.* **(-, -en)** transfer, cession; translation; (*tech.*) transmission.
Übertragungswagen *m.* broadcasting van.
übertreffen *v.t.st.* to surpass, to excel.
übertreiben *v.t.st.* to exaggerate; to overdo, to overact.
Übertreibung *f.* **(-, -en)** exaggeration.
übertreten *v.t.st.* to transgress, to trespass (against), to infringe; ~ *v.i.st. (s)* to go over.
Übertretung *f.* **(-, -en)** violation, transgression.
übertrieben *a.* excessive, exaggerated.
Übertritt *m.* (*Kirche*) conversion; change.
übertrumpfen *v.t.* to outdo.
übertünchen *v.t.* to whitewash.
übervölkern *v.t.* to overpopulate.
Übervölkerung *f.* **(-, 0)** overpopulation.
übervoll *a.* overfull.
übervorteilen *v.t.* to cheat.
überwachen *v.t.* to keep under surveillance; to supervise.
Überwachung *f.* supervision, control, surveillance.
überwältigen *v.t.* to overpower; to overwhelm.
überwältigend *a.* overwhelming; stunning.
überwechseln *v.i.* to cross over; to change (sides; lanes).
überweisen *v.t.st.* to refer, to transfer.
Überweisung *f.* transfer, remittance.
überwerfen *v.t.st.* to slip on (clothing); ~ *v.r.st.* to fall out (with).
überwiegen *v.t.st.* to predominate (over).
überwiegend *a.* predominant.
überwinden *v.t.st.* to overcome, to vanquish; ~ *v.r.st.* to bring oneself (to do).
Überwindung *f.* **(-, -en)** conquest; effort; (*Selbst*~) willpower.
überwintern *v.i.* to spend the winter; to hibernate (animals).
überwölken *imp.* to get overcast.
überwuchern *v.t.* to overgrow.
Überwurf *m.* shawl.
Überzahl *f.* **(-, 0)** numerical superiority.
überzählig *a.* surplus.
überzeugen *v.t.* to convince.
überzeugend *a.* convincing, conclusive.
Überzeugung *f.* **(-, -en)** conviction.
überziehen *v.t.st.* to cover; (*Bett*) to put fresh sheets on; (account) to overdraw; ~ *v.r. (insep.) st.* to become overcast.
Überzieher *m.* **(-s, -)** overcoat, topcoat.
überzüchtet *a.* overbred.
überzuckern *v.t.* to candy, to ice.
Überzug *m.* cover, coat(ing); pillowcase.
üblich *a.* usual, customary, in use.
U-Boot *n.* submarine; **U-Boot Bunker** *m.* submarine pen.
übrig *a.* remaining, left; ~*bleiben,* to be left; *im übrigen,* for the rest; ~*sein,* to be left; ~*behalten,* to keep, to spare; ~*haben,* to have... left or to spare; ~*lassen,* to leave; *das Übrige, die Übrigen,*the rest.
übrigens *adv.* by the way.
übriglassen *v.t.st.* to leave.
Übung *f.* **(-, -en)** exercise, practice; (*mil.*) drill(ing); *aus der* ~, out of practice.
u.dergl.m. *und dergleichen mehr,* and more of the kind.
u.d.M. *unter dem Meeresspiegel,* below sea level.
ü.d.M. *über dem Meeressspiegel,* above sea level.
Ufer *n.* **(-s, -)** (*Fluß*~) bank; (*See*~) shore, beach; **~böschung** *f.* embankment.
uferlos *a.* boundless.
UFO, Ufo *n.* **(-s, -s)** *unbekanntes Flugobjekt,* unidentified flying object, UFO.
Uganda *n.* **(-s, 0)** Uganda.
Ugander *m.;* **Uganderin** *f.* Ugandan.
U-Haft *Untersuchungshaft,* custody.
Uhr *f.* **(-, -en)** clock; (*Taschen*~) watch; *wieviel* ~ *ist es?* what time is it?; *es ist halb drei (*~*),* it is half past two; *eine* ~ *aufziehen,* to wind a watch; *eine* ~ *stellen,* to set a clock *or* watch; *die* ~ *ist abgelaufen,* the watch has stopped.
Uhr: ~band *n.* watchstrap; **~blatt** *n.* face.
Uhrenarmband *n.* watchband.
Uhr: ~gehäuse *n.* watch-case; **~macher** *m.* watchmaker, clockmaker; **~werk** *n.* clockwork.
Uhrzeiger *m.* hand; *im* ~*sinn,* clockwise; *entgegen dem* ~*sinn,* counterclockwise.
Uhu *m.* **(-s, -s)** eagle owl.
Ukraine *f.* **(-, 0)** Ukraine.
Ukrainer *m.;* **Ukrainerin** *f.;* **ukrainisch** *a.* Ukrainian.
UKW-sender *m.* FM station.
Ulk *m.* **(-[e]s, -e)** (*fam.*) spree, lark, hoax.
ulkig *a.* funny.
Ulme *f.* **(-, -en)** elm.
Ultimatum *n.* **(-s, -ten)** ultimatum.
Ultimo *m.* **(-s, -s)** last day of the month.
Ultrakurzwelle *f.* (*Radio*) ultra-short wave; very high frequency, VHF.
Ultraschall *m.* ultrasound.
ultraviolett *a.* ultraviolet.
um *pr.* about, round; at; by; for; ~ *3 Uhr,* at three (o'clock); *es ist gerade* ~, it is just past; ~ *so besser,* all the better; ~ *etwas kommen,* to lose something; ~ *zu,* in order to.
umackern *v.t.* to plow up.
umadressieren *v.t.* to redirect
umändern *v.t.* to change, to alter.
Umänderung *f.* change, alteration.
umarbeiten *v.t.* to rework, to remodel.
umarmen *v.t.* to embrace, to hug.
Umarmung *f.* **(-, -en)** embrace.
umbauen *v.t.* to rebuild; to alter; to change.
umbehalten *v.t.st.* to keep on.
umbenennen *v.t.* to rename.
umbesoldet *a.* unsalaried, unpaid.
umbiegen *v.t.st.* to bend, to double up.
umbilden *v.t.* to transform; to reshuffle.
Umbildung *f.* transformation; reshuffle.
umbinden *v.t.st.* to tie round, to put on.

umblättern *v.t.* to turn over.
umblicken *v.r.* to look around.
umbringen *v.t.st.* to kill.
Umbruch *m.* (*typ.*) page-proof; radical change.
umbuchen *v.t.* to transfer (money); to change (flight).
umdenken *v.i.st.* to rethink.
umdisponieren *v.i.* to rearrange.
umdrehen *v.t.* to turn, to twist, to wring; ~ *v.r.* to turn round; to rotate, to revolve.
Umdrehung *f.* turn; rotation; (*mech.*) revolution.
umfahren *v.t.st.* to run down; to circumnavigate.
umfallen *v.t.st.* to fall over.
Umfang *m.* **(-[e]s, -fänge)** circumference, size; compass, extent.
umfangen *v.t.st.* to encircle; to embrace; to encompass.
umfangreich *a.* extensive; voluminous.
umfassen *v.t.* to grasp; to comprise, to include, to embrace; (*mil.*) to envelop.
umfassend *a.* comprehensive.
Umfassung *f.* enclosure; embrace, grasp.
Umfeld *n.* milieu.
umfliegen *v.t.st.* to circle round.
umformen *v.t.* to remodel, to recast; to transform.
Umformer *m.* (*elek.*) converter.
Umfrage *f.* survey.
umfrieden *v.t.* to fence, to hedge in.
umfüllen *v.t.* to transfuse; to decant.
Umgang *m.* contact; dealings; handling.
umgänglich *a.* sociable, conversable.
Umgangssprache *f.* colloquial speech.
umgarnen *v.t.* (*fig.*) to ensnare.
umgeben *v.t.st.* to surround.
Umgebung *f.* **(-, -en)** environs, surroundings *pl.*; environment; (*Personen*) entourage.
Umgegend *f.* **(-, 0)** neighborhood; surroundings.
umgehen *v.t.st.* to evade, to elude, to bypass; ~ *v.i.st.* *(s)* to associate (with); *es geht in dem Schloß um,* the castle is haunted; *mit einem umzugehen wissen,* to know how to deal with someone; *umgehend antworten,* to answer immediately.
Umgehung *f.* (*Gesetz*) evasion.
Umgehungsstraße *f.* bypass road.
umgekehrt *a.* opposite, contrary, reverse; inverse; the other way round.
umgestalten *v.t.* to transform, to recast.
umgraben *v.t.st.* to dig (up).
umgrenzen *v.t.* to circumscribe.
umgruppieren *v.t.* to regroup, to realign.
Umgruppierung *f.* (*mil.*) regrouping.
umgucken *v.r.* to look around.
umgürten *v.t.* to buckle on (a sword); (*fig.*) to encircle.
umhaben *v.i.st.* to have on or about one.
Umhang *m.* **(-[e]s, -hänge)** cape.
umhängen *v.t.* to put on.
umhauen *v.t.st.* to fell, to cut down.
umher *adv.* around, (round) about.
umherschweifen *v.t.* (s) to rove, to wander.
umherziehend *a.* ambulatory; vagrant.
umhin *adv. ich kann nicht* ~, I cannot help.
umhören *v.* to ask around.
umhüllen *v.t.* to wrap (up), to shroud.
Umhüllung *f.* **(-, -en)** cover, wrapping, veil.
U/min *Umdrehungen pro Minute,* revolutions per minute, r.p.m.
Umkehr *f.* **(-, 0)** return; complete change, revulsion (of feeling).
umkehren *v.t.* to turn (round), to invert; (*mech.*) to reverse; ~ *v.i.* *(s)* to turn back; *in umgekehrtem Verhältnis stehen,* to be in inverse ratio (to).
Umkehrung *f.* **(-, -en)** reversal.
umkippen *v.i.* *(s)* to tilt over; ~ *v.t.* to upset, to overturn.
umklammern *v.t.* to clasp, to cling to; to clutch.
Umkleide: ~kabine *f.* changing cubicle; **~raum** *m.* changing room; (*sp.*) locker room.
umkleiden *v.r.* to change one's clothes.
umknicken *v.i.* to sprain one's ankle; *v.t.* to fold over (paper); to break (flower).
umkommen *v.i.st.* *(s)* to perish; to die; to get killed.
Umkreis *m.* compass, circle; circumference; *im* ~ *von,* within a radius of...
umkreisen *v.t.* to circle, to orbit, to revolve.
umkrempeln *v.t.* to roll up; to turn inside out.
umladen *v.t.st.* to reload.
Umlagen *pl.* utilities.
umlagern *v.t.* to besiege.
Umlauf *m.* circulation (of coins, words); *in* ~ *bringen, setzen,* to circulate; to issue; *im* ~ *sein,* to circulate.
Umlaut *m.* umlaut, mutation.
umlegen *v.t.* to put round *or* on; to fell; to fold down; (*fam.*) to kill.
umleiten *v.t.* (*Verkehr*) to divert.
Umleitung *f.* diversion; detour; **~sschild** *n.* detour sign.
umlenken *v.t.* to divert.
umlernen *v.t.* to change one's views.
umliegend *a.* surrounding, neighboring.
ummauern *v.t.* to wall in.
umnachten *v.t.* to wrap in darkness.
Umnachtung *f.* derangement.
umnebeln *v.t.* to dim.
umpacken *v.t.* to repack.
umpflanzen *v.t.* to transplant.
umpflügen *v.t.* to plow up.
umprägen *v.t.* to recoin.
umquartieren *v.t.* to reaccommodate; to remove to other quarters.
umrahmen *v.t.* to frame, to encircle.
umrändern *v.t.* to border, to edge.
umranken *v.t.* to twine around.
umräumen *v.t.* to rearrange.
umrechnen *v.t.* to convert.
Umrechnungskurs *m.* exchange rate.
umreißen *v.t.st.* to pull down; to sketch the outlines of; to outline.
umrennen *v.t.ir.* to run down or over.
umringen *v.t.* to encircle, to surround.
Umriß *m.* **(-[ss]es, -[ss]e)** sketch, outline, contour.
umrühren *v.t.* to stir.
umrüsten *v.t.* to convert; to reequip (army).
umsatteln *v.i.* (*fig.*) to change one's profession.
Umsatz *m.* **(-es, 0)** turnover; **~steuer** *f.* value added sales tax.
umsäumen *v.t.* to hem; (*fig.*) to surround.
umschalten *v.t.* to switch (on), to reverse (the current).
Umschalter *m.* switch, commutator.
umschatten *v.t.* to shade.
Umschau *f.* **(-, 0)** survey; ~ *halten,* to look round.
umschauen *v.r.* to look back or around.
umschiffen *v.t.* to circumnavigate.

Umschlag *m.* **(-[e]s, -schläge)** envelope, wrapper; poultice, compress; sudden change, turn; (*Ärmel*) cuff, tuck; (*Waren*) trans-shipment.
umschlagen *v.t.st.* (*Saum*) to turn up; (*Kragen*) to turn down; (*Blatt*) to turn over; (*Ärmel*) to roll up; to wrap around; to buy and sell; ~ *v.i.st. (s)* to capsize; to change suddenly; to turn sour; (*Stimme*) to break.
umschleichen *v.t.st.* to prowl around.
umschließen *v.t.st.* to enclose.
umschlingen *v.t.st.* to embrace.
umschmeißen *v.t.st.* to overturn.
umschnallen *v.t.* to buckle on.
umschreiben *v.t.st.* to transcribe; to transfer; (*Wechsel*) to reindorse; (*mit Worten*) to paraphrase; (*math.*) to circumscribe.
Umschreibung *f.* **(-, -en)** paraphrase; description; definition.
Umschrift *f.* **(-, -en)** (*phonetische*), phonetic transcription.
Umschuldung *f.* debt conversion.
umschulen *v.t.* to retrain; to transfer to another school.
Umschulung *f.* retraining.
umschütten *v.t.* to spill, to pour (into another container).
umschwärmen *v.t.* to idolize; to adore.
Umschweif m **(-[e]s, -e)** digression; *ohne ~e*, without beating about the bush.
umschwenken *v.i. (h. s)* to wheel round.
Umschwung *m.* **(-[e]s, -schwünge)** revolution; reversal, the turning of the tide.
umsehen *v.r. st..* to look around *or* back; (*nach*) to look out for; (*in*) to become acquainted (with).
um sein *v.i.st.* to be over.
umseitig *adv.* overleaf; *Fortsetzung ~*, continued over.
umsetzen *v.t.* (*Pflanzen*) to transplant; to turn over; *in Taten ~*, to translate into deeds.
Umsichgreifen *n.* **(-s, 0)** spread, proliferation.
Umsicht *f.* **(-, 0)** circumspection.
umsichtig *a.* circumspect.
umsiedeln *v.t.* to resettle.
Umsiedlung *f.* **(-, -en)** resettlement.
umsinken *v.i.st. (s)* to drop, to faint.
umsonst *adv.* gratis, for nothing; in vain; *nicht ~*, not without good reason.
umspannen *v.i.* to span, to encompass.
umspringen *v.i.st. (s)* to veer (round), to turn; *~ mit*, to manage, to handle.
Umstand *m.* **(-[e]s, -stände)** circumstance; **Umstände** *pl.* ceremonies, fuss; particulars *pl.; in anderen Umständen sein (von Frauen)*, to be in the family way; to be expecting.
umständlich *a.* involved, awkward.
Umstandskleid *n.* maternity dress.
Umstandswort *n.* adverb.
umstehend *a.* next (page); standing round.
Umstehende[n] *m.pl.* bystanders *pl.*
umsteigen *v.i.st. (s)* to change (trains, etc.).
umstellen *v.t.* to transpose; to surround.
Umstellung *f.* **(-, -en)** inversion; changeover.
umstimmen *v.t.* to bring (one) round.
umstoßen *v.t.st.* to knock down.
umstricken *v.t.* (*fig.*) to ensnare.
umstritten *a.* controversial; disputed.
umstrukturieren *v.t.* to restructure.
umstülpen *v.t.* to turn inside out.
Umsturz *m.* **(-es. -stürze)** overthrow; revolution; coup.
umstürzen *v.t.* to throw down, to overturn; ~ *v.i. (s)* to be upset.
Umstürzler *m.* **(-s, -)** revolutionary.
Umsturzversuch *m.* attempted coup.
umtaufen *v.t.* to rename.
Umtausch *m.* **(-[e]s, 0)** exchange, barter.
umtauschen *v.t.* to exchange.
Umtrieb *m.* **(-[e]s, -e)** intrigue.
umtun *v.t.st.* to put on; *sich nach etwas ~*, to look for.
U-Musik *f.* (*Unterhaltungsmusik*) light music.
umwälzen *v.t.* to revolutionize; to circulate.
Umwälzung *f.* **(-, -en)** revolution.
umwandeln *v.t.* to change, to convert (into); to commute (sentence).
Umwandlung *f.* **(-, -en)** change, transformation; conversion; commutation (sentence).
umwechseln *v.t.* to (ex)change.
Umweg *m.* **(-[e]s, -e)** detour.
umwehen *v.t.* to blow down.
Umwelt *f.* **(-, 0)** environment.
Umwelt: ~belastung *f.* environmental pollution; **~forschung** *f.* ecology
umweltfreundlich *a.* environmentally-friendly; nonpolluting; biodegradable.
Umwelt: ~katastrophe *f.* catastrophe for the environment; **~kriminalität** *f.* environmental crime; **~ministerium** *n.* Department of the Environment; **~schäden** *pl.* environmental damage.
umweltschädlich *a.* polluting; harmful to the environment.
Umwelt: ~schutz *m.* environmental protection; **~verschmutzung** *f.* pollution (of the environment); **~zerstörung** *f.* destruction of the environment.
umwenden *v.t.st.* to turn round.
umwerben *v.t.st.* to court.
umwerfen *v.t.st.* to overthrow; to knock over.
Umwertung *f.* **(-, -en)** revaluation.
umwickeln *v.t.* to wrap up.
umwölken *v.t. & r.* to get cloudy; (*fig.*) to darken.
umzäunen *v.t.* to hedge, to fence.
Umzäunung *f.* **(-, -en)** enclosure, fence.
umziehen *v.i.st. (s)* to move, to relocate, *v.t.st. (h) jn. ~*, to change somebody's clothes; ~ *v.r. st.* to change (one's clothes).
umzingeln *v.t.* to encircle, to surround.
Umzug *m.* **(-[e]s, -züge)** procession; (*Wohnungswechsel*) move.
unabänderlich *a.* irrevocable.
unabdingbar *a.* indispensable.
unabhängig *a.* independent.
Unabhängigkeit *f.* **(-, 0)** independence.
unabkömmlich *a.* indispensable.
unablässig *a.* incessant; unremitting.
unabsehbar *a.* immeasurable, unbounded.
unabsichtlich *a.* unintentional.
unabwendbar *a.* inevitable.
unachtsam *a.* inadvertent; careless.
Unachtsamkeit *f.* **(-, -en)** inadvertency.
unähnlich *a.* unlike, dissimilar.
unanfechtbar *a.* incontestable.
unangebracht *a.* inappropriate; out of place.
unangefochten *a.* unchallenged; unmolested.
unangekündigt *a.* unannounced.
unangemeldet *a. & adv.* without (previous) notice; unannounced.

unangemessen *a.* inadequate, unsuitable.
unangenehm *a.* disagreeable, unpleasant.
unangetastet *a.* untouched.
unangreifbar *a.* unassailable.
unannehmbar *a.* unacceptable.
Unannehmlichkeit *f.* **(-, -en)** inconvenience.
unansehnlich *a.* unsightly, poor-looking; plain.
unanständig *a.* indecent; improper.
unantastbar *a.* inviolable.
unappetitlich *a.* unsavory, unappetizing.
Unart *f.* **(-, -en)** bad habit.
unartig *a.* naughty, rude.
unartikuliert *a.* inarticulate.
unästhetisch *a.* unpleasant, disgusting.
unauffällig *a.* inconspicuous; discreet.
unauffindbar *a.* undiscoverable.
unaufgefordert *a.* unasked; ~ *eingesandte Manuskripte,* unsolicited manuscripts.
unaufhaltsam *a.* irresistible.
unaufhörlich *a.* incessant.
unauflöslich *a.* indissoluble.
unaufmerksam *a.* inattentive.
unaufrichtig *a.* insincere.
unaufschiebbar *a.* urgent, pressing.
unaufspürbar *a.* untraceable.
unausbleiblich *a.* inevitable.
unausführbar *a.* impracticable.
unausgeglichen *a.* unstable; unsettled.
unausgesetzt *a.* uninterrupted.
unauslöschlich *a.* indelible.
unaussprechlich *a.* unpronounceable; (*fig.*) unspeakable.
unausstehlich *a.* insufferable.
unausweichlich *a.* inevitable.
unbändig *a.* boisterous; unbridled.
unbarmherzig *a.* merciless.
unbeabsichtigt *a.* unintentional.
unbeachtet *a.* unnoticed.
unbeanstandet *a.* approved.
unbeaufsichtigt *a.* unattended.
unbedacht, unbedächtig, unbedachtsam *a.* inconsiderate, rash.
unbedenklich *a.* unhesitating; unobjectionable; ~ *adv.* without hesitation.
unbedeutend *a.* insignificant, trifling.
unbedingt *a.* unconditional, absolute; implicit; ~ *adv.* by all means.
unbeeinflust *a.* uninfluenced.
unbefangen *a.* unprejudiced; unembarrassed; candid, natural.
unbefleckt *a.* immaculate, pure.
unbefriedigend *a.* unsatisfactory.
unbefriedigt *a.* unsatisfied.
unbefristet *a.* indefinite; unlimited.
unbefugt *a.* unauthorized; incompetent.
unbegreiflich *a.* incomprehensible, inconceivable.
unbegreiflicherweise *adv.* inexplicably.
unbegrenzt *a.* unbounded, unlimited.
unbegründet *a.* unfounded, groundless.
unbegütert *a.* not rich, without landed property.
Unbehagen *n.* uneasiness, discomfort.
unbehaglich *a.* uneasy, uncomfortable.
Unbehaglichkeit *f.* discomfort.
unbehelligt *a.* unmolested.
unbeherrscht *a.* uncontrolled.
Unbeherrschtheit *f.* lack of self-control.
unbehindert *a.* unrestrained, unhindered.
unbeholfen *a.* awkward, clumsy.
unbek. *unbekannt,* unknown.
unbekannt *a.* unknown.
Unbekannte *m./f.* unknown/unidentified person.
unbekehrbar *a.* inconvertible.
unbekümmert *a.* unconcerned (about).
unbelebt *a.* inanimate; lifeless, dull.
unbeleckt *a.* untouched, untainted.
unbeleuchtet *a.* unlit.
unbeliebt *a.* unpopular.
unbemerkt *a.* unnoticed, unperceived.
unbemittelt *a.* poor, without means.
unbenannt *a.* anonymous.
unbenommen *a.* *es bleibt dir* ~, you are quite free to...
unbenutzt *a.* unused.
unbeobachtet *a.* unobserved.
unbequem *a.* uncomfortable.
unberechenbar *a.* unpredictable; incalculable.
unberechtigt *a.* unauthorized; unlawful.
unberichtigt *a.* uncorrected; (*Rechnung*) unpaid.
unberücksichtigt *a.* unconsidered.
unberührt *a.* untouched.
unbeschadet *adv.* without prejudice to.
unbeschädigt *a.* unhurt, uninjured.
unbescheiden *a.* immodest; presumptuous.
unbescholten *a.* blameless.
Unbescholtenheit *f.* blameless reputation.
unbeschränkt *a.* unlimited.
unbeschreiblich *a.* indescribable.
unbeschrieben *a.* blank; empty.
unbeschwert *a.* carefree; light.
unbeseelt *a.* inanimate.
unbesehen *a.* unseen, unexamined; ~ *adv.* without hesitation.
unbesetzt *a.* unoccupied, vacant.
unbesiegbar *a.* invincible.
unbesiegt *a.* unbeaten.
unbesonnen *a.* thoughtless, rash; impulsive.
unbesorgt *a.* unconcerned; easy.
unbeständig *a.* inconstant, fickle.
Unbeständigkeit *f.* instability, fickleness.
unbestätigt *a.* unconfirmed.
unbestechlich *a.* incorruptible.
unbestellbar *a.* not deliverable.
unbestimmt *a.* indeterminate.
unbestreitbar *a.* indisputable.
unbestritten *a.* uncontested.
unbeteiligt *a.* not concerned.
unbetont *a.* unstressed.
unbeträchtlich *a.* inconsiderable.
unbeugsam *a.* inflexible.
unbewacht *a.* unguarded; unwatched.
unbewaffnet *a.* unarmed; *mit ~em Auge,* with the naked eye.
unbewältigt *a.* unmastered; uncompleted.
unbewandert *a.* unversed in.
unbeweglich *a.* motionless; immovable; real (property); (*fig.*) inflexible.
Unbeweglichkeit *f.* immobility.
unbewiesen *a.* unproved.
unbewohnbar *a.* uninhabitable.
unbewohnt *a.* uninhabited.
unbewußt *a.* unconscious (of); unknown.
unbez. *unbezahlt,* unpaid.
unbezahlbar *a.* priceless.
unbezahlt *a.* unpaid.
unbezähmbar *a.* indomitable.
unbezeugt *a.* unattested, not proved.
unbezweifelt *a.* undoubted.

unbezwingbar *a.* invincible, impregnable.
unbiegsam *a.* not pliant; inflexible.
Unbill *f.* **(-, -bilden)** injury, wrong; (*des Wetters*) inclemency.
unblutig *a.* bloodless.
unbotmäßig *a.* unruly, refractory.
unbrauchbar *a.* useless, unusable.
unbußfertig *a.* impenitent.
und *c.* and; ~ *wenn,* even if; ~ *so weiter,* and so on; etc.; *der* ~ *der,* so and so.
Undank *m.* **(-[e]s, 0)** ingratitude.
undankbar *a.* ungrateful; thankless.
undatiert *a.* undated.
undefinierbar *a.* undefinable.
undenkbar *a.* inconceivable.
undenklich *a.* immemorial.
undeutlich *a.* indistinct; inarticulate.
undicht *a.* not tight, leaking.
Unding *n.* absurdity.
undiszipliniert *a.* undisciplined.
unduldsam *a.* intolerant.
undurchdringlich *a.* impenetrable.
undurchführbar *a.* impracticable.
undurchlässig *a.* impermeable; waterproof.
undurchsichtig *a.* opaque.
Undurchsichtigkeit *f.* opacity.
uneben *a.* uneven, rugged.
unecht *a.* not genuine; spurious, counterfeit, sham.
unehelich *a.* illegitimate.
unehrenhaft *a.* dishonorable.
unehrerbietig *a.* irreverent, disrespectful.
unehrlich *a.* dishonest.
uneigennützig *a.* disinterested.
uneingeschränkt *a.* unrestricted.
uneingeweiht *a.* uninitiated.
uneinig *a.* discordant, divided.
Uneinigkeit *f.* disagreement, discord
uneinnehmbar *a.* impregnable.
uneins *a.* divided; ~ **sein** to be at variance.
uneinträglich *a.* unprofitable, barren.
unempfänglich *a.* unreceptive.
unempfindlich *a.* insensitive, indifferent.
unendlich *a.* endless, infinite.
Unendlichkeit *f.* infinity; infinite space.
unentbehrlich *a.* indispensable.
unentgeltlich *a.* gratuitous; free (of charge); ~ *adv.* gratis.
unenthaltsam *a.* incontinent, intemperate.
unentrinnbar *a.* inevitable, unavoidable.
unentschieden *a.* undecided; irresolute.
Unentschieden *n.* **(-, -)** (*Sport*) tie; draw.
unentschlossen *a.* undecided; irresolute.
Unentschlossenheit *f.* indecision; irresolution.
unentschuldbar *a.* inexcusable.
unentwegt *a.* steady.
unentwickelt *a.* undeveloped.
unentwirrbar *a.* inextricable.
unerbittlich *a.* inexorable.
unerfahren *a.* inexperienced.
Unerfahrenheit *f.* **(-, 0)** inexperience.
unerfindlich *a.* inexplicable.
unerforschlich *a.* inscrutable.
unerfreulich *a.* unpleasant.
unerfüllbar *a.* not to be fulfilled or complied with, unrealizable.
unergiebig *a.* unproductive.
unergründlich *a.* unfathomable.
unerheblich *a.* inconsiderable; irrelevant.
unerhört *a.* unheard of, unprecedented.
unerkannt *a.* unrecognized.
unerkennbar *a.* unrecognizable.
unerkenntlich *a.* ungrateful.
unerklärlich *a.* inexplicable.
unerläßlich *a.* indispensable.
unerlaubt *a.* illicit, unlawful.
unerledigt *a.* unattended, not dispatched.
unermeßlich *a.* immeasurable; immense.
Unermeßlichkeit *f.* **(-, 0)** immensity.
unermüdlich *a.* untiring, tireless.
unerörtert *a.* undiscussed; undecided.
unerquicklich *a.* unpleasant, unedifying.
unerreichbar *a.* unattainable.
unerreicht *a.* unequalled.
unersättlich *a.* insatiable.
unerschlossen *a.* undeveloped.
unerschöpflich *a.* inexhaustible.
unerschrocken *a.* intrepid, undaunted.
unerschütterlich *a.* unshakable, imperturbable, firm, unshaken.
unerschwinglich *a.* beyond one's means; ~*er Preis,* prohibitive price.
unersetzlich *a.* irreparable; irreplaceable.
unersprießlich *a.* unprofitable.
unerträglich *a.* intolerable.
unerwähnt *a.* unmentioned; ~ *lassen,* to pass over (in silence).
unerwartet *a.* unexpected.
unerwidert *a.* unanswered; unreturned.
unerwiesen *a.* not proved.
unerwünscht *a.* undesirable.
unerzogen *a.* naughty.
unfähig *a.* incapable, inefficient.
Unfähigkeit *f.* incompetence; inability.
Unfall *m.* accident; mischance.
Unfall: ~station *f.* ambulance station, **~versicherung** *f.* accident insurance; **~wagen** *f.* ambulance.
unfaßbar *a.* inconceivable.
unfehlbar *a.* infallible.
Unfehlbarkeit *f.* **(-, 0)** infallibility.
unfein *a.* ill-mannered; coarse.
unfern *adv.* not far off; ~ *pr.* near, not far from.
unfertig *a.* unfinished, not ready.
unflätig *a.* filthy; obscene.
unfolgsam *a.* disobedient.
Unfolgsamkeit *a.* disobedience.
unförmig *a.* shapeless.
unfrankiert *a.* unstamped.
unfrei *a.* not free.
unfreiwillig *a.* involuntary; compulsory.
unfreundlich *a.* unfriendly; unkind; harsh.
Unfreundlichkeit *f.* unfriendliness; unkindness.
Unfriede *m.* discord, dissension.
unfruchtbar *a.* infertile; barren, sterile.
Unfruchtbarkeit *f.* infertility; sterility, barrenness.
Unfug *m.* **(-[e]s, 0)** mischief, nuisance, *grober* ~, gross misdemeanor.
unfügsam *a.* uncomplying, intractable.
ungangbar *a.* (*Weg*) impassable.
Ungar *m.* **(-n, -n); Ungarin** *f.* **(-, -nen); ungarisch** *a.* Hungarian.
Ungarn *n.* **(-s, 0)** Hungary.
ungastlich *a.* inhospitable.
ungeachtet *pr.* notwithstanding.
ungeahnt *a.* unexpected, unthought of.
ungebändigt *a.* untamed, unsubdued.
ungebärdig *a.* unruly.

ungebeten *a.* uninvited.
ungebildet *a.* uneducated, uncultured.
ungebleicht *a.* unbleached.
ungeboren *a.* unborn.
ungebräuchlich *a.* unusual; obsolete.
ungebraucht *a.* unused; new.
ungebrochen *a.* unbroken.
ungebührlich *a.* improper, unmannerly.
ungebunden *a.* unbound; (*Bücher*) in sheets; (*fig.*) loose, licentious; *~e Rede,* prose; *~es Wesen,* dissolute ways *pl.*
ungedeckt *a.* uncovered; (*com.*) unpaid; *~er Kredit,* unsecured credit.
ungedruckt *a.* unprinted.
Ungeduld *f.* impatience.
ungeduldig *a.* impatient.
ungeeignet *a.* unsuitable (for).
ungefähr *a.* approximate; ~ *adv.* about, nearly; *von ~,* by chance.
ungefährlich *a.* harmless, safe.
ungefärbt *a.* undyed, uncolored.
ungehalten *a.* angry, indignant.
ungeheißen *a.* spontaneous, unbidden.
ungeheizt *a.* unheated.
ungehemmt *a.* unchecked, uninhibited.
ungeheuchelt *a.* unfeigned.
ungeheuer *a.* immense, prodigious, huge.
Ungeheuer *n.* **(-s, -)** monster.
ungeheuerlich *a.* monstrous.
Ungeheuerlichkeit *f.* **(-, -en)** monstrosity.
ungehindert *a.* unimpeded.
ungehobelt *a.* unplaned; (*fig.*) coarse.
ungehörig *a.* improper; unsuitable.
ungehorsam *a.* disobedient.
Ungehorsam *m.* disobedience.
ungeimpft *a.* unvaccinated.
ungekämmt *a.* uncombed, unkempt.
ungeklärt *a.* unsolved; unknown.
ungekünstelt *a.* unaffected.
ungekürzt *a.* unabridged.
ungeladen *a.* uninvited; unloaded.
ungeläufig *a.* unfamiliar.
ungelegen *a.* inconvenient, inopportune.
Ungelegenheit *f.* inconvenience, trouble.
ungelehrig *a.* unteachable, unintelligent.
ungelehrt *a.* unlettered, unlearned.
ungelenk *a.* stiff; clumsy, awkward.
ungelernt *a.* unskilled.
Ungemach *n.* **(-[e]s, -e)** discomfort, adversity; trouble, hardship.
ungemein *a.* uncommon; extraordinary.
ungemildert *a.* unmitigated.
ungemütlich *a.* uncomfortable.
ungenannt *a.* unnamed.
ungenau *a.* inaccurate, inexact.
Ungenauigkeit *f.* inaccuracy.
ungeniert *a.* uninhibited.
ungenießbar *a.* unpalatable.
ungenügend *a.* insufficient; inadequate.
ungenutzt *a.* unused, unemployed.
ungeöffnet *a.* unopened.
ungeordnet *a.* unarranged; unsettled.
ungerade *a.* (*Zahl*) odd; uneven.
ungeraten *a.* (*Kind*) spoiled.
ungerecht *a.* unjust.
Ungerechtigkeit *f.* injustice.
ungereimt *a.* (*Vers*) unrhymed; blank; (*fig.*) absurd, preposterous.
Ungereimtheit *f.* **(-, -en)** (*fig.*) absurdity.
ungern *adv.* unwillingly, reluctantly.
ungerufen *a.* uncalled.
ungerügt *a.* uncensured, unpunished.
ungesagt *a.* unsaid.
ungesalzen *a.* unsalted; fresh.
ungeschehen *a.* undone; *~ machen,* to undo.
Ungeschicklichkeit, Ungeschicktheit *f.* awkwardness, ineptitude.
ungeschickt *a.* awkward, clumsy.
ungeschliffen *a.* (*von Edelsteinen*) rough; (*fig.*) unpolished, rude, unmannerly.
ungeschmälert *a.* undiminished.
ungeschminkt *a.* without makeup, unvarnished.
ungeschoren *a.* unshorn; undisturbed.
ungesellig *a.* unsociable.
ungesetzlich *a.* illegal.
Ungesetzlichkeit *f.* illegality.
ungesetzmäßig *a.* illegal, unlawful.
ungesittet *a.* unmannerly.
ungestalt(et) *a.* ill-shaped, misshapen.
ungestillt *a.* unquenched, unslaked.
ungestört *a.* undisturbed.
ungestraft *a.* unpunished; ~ *adv.* with impunity.
ungestüm *a.* impetuous.
Ungestüm *n.* **(-[e]s, 0)** impetuosity.
ungesund *a.* unwholesome; unhealthy.
ungeteilt *a.* undivided.
ungetreu *a.* faithless.
ungetrübt *a.* cloudless, untroubled.
Ungetüm *m.* **(-[e]s, -e)** monster.
ungeübt *a.* unpracticed.
ungewiß *a.* uncertain.
Ungewißheit *f.* uncertainty.
ungewöhnlich *a.* unusual, uncommon.
ungewohnt *a.* unaccustomed, unfamiliar.
ungewollt *a.* unwanted; unintentional.
ungezählt *a.* unnumbered, untold.
ungezähmt *a.* untamed; (*fig.*) uncurbed.
Ungeziefer *n.* vermin.
ungezogen *a.* ill-bred, rude; naughty.
ungezügelt *a.* unbridled.
ungezwungen *a.* unaffected, easy.
Unglaube *m.* disbelief; (*kirchlich*) unbelief.
unglaubhaft *a.* unbelievable.
ungläubig *a.* unbelieving, infidel.
Ungläubige(r) *m.* infidel, unbeliever.
unglaublich *a.* incredible.
unglaubwürdig *a.* unreliable.
ungleich *a.* unequal; unlike, dissimilar, uneven; odd; ~ *adv.* (by) far, much.
ungleichartig *a.* heterogeneous.
ungleichförmig *a.* not uniform.
Ungleichheit *f.* inequality, dissimilarity.
ungleichmäßig *a.* uneven.
Unglück *n.* misfortune; adversity; bad luck.
unglücklich *a.* unlucky, unhappy, unfortunate.
unglücklicherweise *a.* unfortunately.
unglückselig *a.* miserable; disastrous.
Unglücks(fall) *m.* misfortune; accident; **~vogel** *m.* poor devil.
Ungnade *f.* disgrace, disfavor.
ungnädig *a.* ungracious, unkind, angry.
ungrammatisch *a.* ungrammatical.
ungültig *a.* invalid, void; (*Fahrkarte*) not available; *für ~ erklären, ~ machen,* to annul, to invalidate, to void.
Ungunst *f.* disfavor; (*Wetter*) inclemency.
ungünstig *a.* unfavorable.
ungut *a.* *nichts für ~!* no offense!

unhaltbar *a.* untenable.

Unheil *m.* **(-[e]s, 0)** harm; calamity.

unheilbar *a.* incurable.

unheilig *a.* unholy, profane, unhallowed.

unheilvoll *a.* calamitous, disastrous.

unheimlich *a.* uncanny; eerie.

unhistorisch *a.* unhistoric.

unhöflich *a.* impolite, uncivil, rude.

Unhöflichkeit *f.* rudeness, incivility.

Unhold *m.* **(-[e]s, -e)** monster; fiend.

unhörbar *a.* inaudible.

unhygienisch *a.* insanitary; unhygienic.

Uniform *f.* **(-, -en)** uniform.

Unikum *n.* **(-[e]s, -ka)** unique object.

uninteressant *a.* uninteresting.

uninteressiert *a.* uninterested.

Union *f.* **(-, -en)** union.

universal *a.* universal.

Universalerbe *m.* sole heir.

Universität *f.* **(-, -en)** university.

Universum *n.* **(-[s], 0)** universe.

unkenntlich *a.* unrecognizable.

Unkenntnis *f.* **(-, 0)** ignorance.

unkeusch *a.* unchaste.

unklar *a.* confused, unintelligible; *im ~ sein,* to be in the dark (about).

unklug *a.* imprudent, indiscreet.

unkompliziert *a.* uncomplicated.

unkontrollierbar *a.* uncontrollable.

unkontrolliert *a.* uncontrolled.

Unkosten *pl.* charges, expenses *pl.; laufende ~,* overhead expenses.

Unkraut *n.* **(-[e]s, 0)** weeds.

unkritisch *a.* uncritical.

unkultiviert *a.* uncultivated.

Unkultur *f.* **(-, 0)** lack of civilization.

unkündbar *a.* permanent (position).

unkundig *a.* ignorant (of).

unlängst *adv.* lately, the other day.

unlauter *a.* dishonest; unfair; *~er Wettbewerb,* unfair competition.

unleidlich *a.* intolerable.

unlenksam *a.* unmanageable, unruly.

unlesbar *a.* unreadable.

unleserlich *a.* illegible.

unleugbar *a.* undeniable.

unlieb *a.* disagreeable.

unliebsam *a.* unpleasant.

unlogisch *a.* illogical.

unlösbar *a.* unsolvable.

unlöslich *a.* insoluble.

Unlust *f.* **(-, 0)** disinclination.

unmanierlich *a.* unmannerly.

Unmasse *f.* (*fam.*) vast quantity.

unmaßgeblich *a.* without authority.

unmäßig *a.* immoderate; intemperate.

Unmäßigkeit *f.* intemperance; excess.

Unmenge *f.* vast quantity *or* number.

Unmensch *m.* monster, brute.

unmenschlich *a.* inhuman, cruel.

Unmenschlichkeit *f.* inhumanity, cruelty.

unmerklich *a.* imperceptible.

unmethodisch *a.* unmethodical.

unmittelbar *a.* immediate, direct.

unmöbliert *a.* unfurnished.

unmodern *a.* old-fashioned; outmoded.

unmöglich *a.* impossible.

Unmöglichkeit *f.* impossibility.

unmoralisch *a.* immoral.

unmotiviert *a.* without any motive.

unmündig *a.* under age.

Unmündigkeit *f.* (*jur.*) minority.

unmusikalisch *a.* unmusical.

Unmut *m.* ill-humor, discontent.

unmutig *a.* ill-humoured.

unnachahmlich *a.* inimitable.

unnachgiebig *a.* intransigent; unyielding.

unnachsichtlich *a.* unrelenting.

unnahbar *a.* unapproachable.

Unnatur *f.* unnaturalness, affectation.

unnatürlich *a.* unnatural; affected.

unnennbar *a.* ineffable, unutterable.

unnötig *a.* unnecessary, needless.

unnütz *a.* useless, unprofitable.

unordentlich *a.* disorderly, untidy.

Unordnung *f.* disorder, untidiness.

unparteiisch, unparteilich *a.* impartial.

Unparteiische *m./f.* umpire.

Unparteilichkeit *f.* impartiality.

unpassend *a.* unbecoming; improper.

unpäßlich *a.* indisposed, unwell.

Unpäßlichkeit *f.* **(-, 0)** indisposition.

unpatriotisch *a.* unpatriotic.

unpersönlich *a.* impersonal.

unpolitisch *a.* apolitical.

unpopulär *a.* unpopular.

unpraktisch *a.* unpractical.

unproduktiv *a.* unproductive.

unpünktlich *a.* unpunctual.

unqualifiziert *a.* unqualified.

unrasiert *a.* unshaven.

Unrast *f.* **(-, 0)** restlessness.

Unrat *m.* **(-[e]s, 0)** dirt, rubbish.

unratsam *a.* inadvisable.

unrecht *a.* wrong; unjust.

Unrecht *n.* wrong, injustice, injury; *~ haben,* to be wrong; *~ setzen,* to put in the wrong.

unrechtmäßig *a.* unlawful, illegal.

unredlich *a.* dishonest.

Unredlichkeit *f.* dishonesty.

unregelmäßig *a.* irregular.

unreif *a.* unripe; (*fig.*) immature.

Unreife *f.* **(-, 0)** immaturity; unripeness.

unrein *a.* unclean, impure.

unreinlich *a.* unclean.

unrentabel *a.* unprofitable.

unrettbar *a.* past help, past recovery; *~ verloren sein,* to be irretrievably lost.

unrichtig *a.* wrong, incorrect.

unritterlich *a.* unchivalrous.

Unruhe *f.* disquiet, trouble; disturbance; alarm; noise; restlessness.

unruhig *a.* restless; uneasy; turbulent.

unrühmlich *a.* inglorious.

uns *pn.* us, to us; ourselves.

unsachgemäß *a.* improper.

unsachlich *a.* unobjective.

unsäglich *a.* unspeakable.

unsanft *a.* hard, harsh, rough.

unsauber *a.* unclean, slovenly; shady, unfair.

unschädlich *a.* harmless, innocuous.

unschätzbar *a.* inestimable, invaluable.

unscheinbar *a.* inconspicuous.

unschicklich *a.* improper, unseemly.

unschlüssig *a.* undecided; irresolute; *~ sein,* to hesitate.

unschön *a.* plain, homely, not nice.

Unschuld *f.* innocence.

unschuldig *a.* innocent.
unschwer *adv.* easily.
unselbständig *a.* dependent, unable to act or judge by oneself.
unselig *a.* luckless, unfortunate, fatal.
unser *pn.* our, ours; *~einer, ~eins,* the likes of us.
unseretwegen *adv.* for our sake; as far as we are concerned.
unsicher *a.* unsafe; uncertain, dubious.
Unsicherheit *f.* insecurity; uncertainty.
Unsicherheitsfaktor *m.* element of uncertainty.
unsichtbar *a.* invisible.
unsigniert *a.* unsigned.
Unsinn *m.* **(-[e]s, 0)** nonsense.
unsinnig *a.* nonsensical, absurd.
Unsitte *f.* bad habit.
unsittlich *a.* indecent.
unsolide *a.* dissipated, loose; unreliable.
unsozial *a.* antisocial.
unsrige (der, die, das) *pn.* ours.
unstatthaft *a.* inadmissible; illicit.
unsterblich *a.* immortal.
Unsterblichkeit *f.* **(-, 0)** immortality.
Unstern *m.* **(-[e]s, 0)** evil star, bad luck.
unstet *a.* unsteady, unsettled.
unstillbar *a.* insatiable, unquenchable.
Unstimmigkeit *f.* inconsistency; discrepancy.
unstreitig *a.* unquestionable.
Unsumme *f.* (*fam.*) immense number.
unsymmetrisch *a.* unsymmetrical.
unsympatisch *a.* disagreeable; unpleasant; *mir ist es ~,* I do not like it.
untadelhaft, untadelig *a.* blameless.
Untat *f.* crime, misdeed.
untätig *a.* inactive; idle.
Untätigkeit *f.* **(-, 0)** inactivity.
untauglich *a.* unsuitable; unfit; *für ~ erklären,* to condemn.
unteilbar *a.* indivisible.
unten *adv.* below; downstairs; at the bottom; *nach ~,* down(wards); *von oben bis ~,* from top to bottom; *weiter ~,* lower down; *der zweite von ~,* the second from the bottom.
untendrunter *adv.* (*fam.*) underneath.
unter *pr.* under, below; among, between; beneath; during; *~ uns,* among ourselves; *~ uns gesagt,* between you and me.
unter *a.* inferior, lower.
Unterabteilung *f.* subdivision.
Unterarm *m.* forearm.
Unterart *f.* subspecies.
Unterbau *m.* foundation, groundwork; (*rail.*) substructure.
unterbelichten *v.t.* to underexpose.
unterbeschäftigt *a.* underemployed.
unterbesetzt *a.* understaffed.
unterbewerten *v.t.* to undervalue; to underrate.
unterbewußt *a.* subconscious.
Unterbewußtein *n.* subconscious; *im ~,* subconsciously.
unterbieten *v.t.st.* to undercut.
unterbinden *v.t.st.* to ligature (an artery); to stop; to cut off (supplies, etc.).
unterbleiben *v.i.st. (s)* to be left undone; not to take place.
unterbrechen *v.t.st.* to interrupt.
Unterbrechung *f.* **(-, -en)** interruption.
unterbreiten *v.t.* to submit (to).
unterbringen *v.t.st.* to put up, to accommodate; to provide for; (*Waren*) to dispose of; to place (a loan); (*Wechsel*) to negotiate.
unterdes, unterdessen *adv.* meanwhile, in the meantime.
unterdrücken *v.t.* to oppress; to suppress, to crush.
Unterdrücker *m.* **(-s, -)** oppressor.
Unterdrückung *f.* **(-, -en)** oppression; suppression.
unterdurchschnittlich *a.* below average.
untereinander *adv.* one below the other; among one another.
unterentwickelt *a.* underdeveloped.
unterernährt *a.* underfed.
Unterernährung *f.* malnutrition.
Unterfangen *n.* **(-s, 0)** venture; undertaking.
Unterführung *f.* underpass.
Untergang *m.* **(-[e]s, 0)** decline; fall, ruin, destruction.
untergeben *a.* inferior (to).
Untergebene *m./f.* **(-n, -n)** subaltern, subordinate.
untergehen *v.i.st. (s)* to go down, to set; to sink; to drown.
untergeordnet *a.* subordinate, inferior.
Untergeschoß *n.* basement.
Untergestell *n.* truck, frame.
untergliedern *v.t.* to subdivide.
untergraben *v.t.st.* to undermine, to sap.
Untergrund *m.* subsoil; foundation; underground; **~bahn** *f.* subway.
unterhalb *pr.* below.
Unterhalt *m.* **(-[e]s, 0)** maintenance; livelihood; living.
unterhalten *v.t.st.* to maintain, to support, to keep (up); to amuse, to entertain; ~ *v.r.st.* to converse, to talk; to enjoy oneself.
unterhaltend *a.*, **unterhaltsam** *a.* entertaining, amusing.
Unterhaltung *f.* **(-en, -en)** entertainment; maintenance; conversation.
Unterhaltungs: ~branche *f.* entertainment industry; **~literatur** *f.* light fiction; **~musik** *f.* light music; **~wert** *m.* entertainment value.
Unterhändler *m.* negotiator, agent.
Unterhaus *n.* lower house of parliament.
Unterhemd *n.* undershirt.
unterhöhlen *v.t.* to hollow out; to erode.
Unterholz *n.* undergrowth.
Unterhose *f.* underpants; panties.
unterirdisch *a.* underground; subterranean.
unterjochen *v.t.* to subjugate, to subdue.
Unterkiefer *m.* lower jaw.
unterkommen *v.i.st. (s)* to find lodgings, employment, etc.
Unterkommen *n.* **(-s, 0)** shelter, accommodation, lodging; place, employment.
unterkriegen *v.t.* (*fam.*) to get the better of.
Unterkühlung *f.* hypothermia.
Unterkunft *f.* **(-, 0)** accommodation; shelter, (*mil.*) quarters.
Unterlage *f.* deskpad, mat; padding; (*Beweis*) evidence; **~n** *pl.* documentation.
Unterlaß *m.* **(-lasses, 0)** intermission.
unterlassen *v.t.st.* to refrain from; to fail to do sth.
Unterlassung *f.* **(-, -en)** omission.
Unterlauf *m.* lower course (of a river).
unterlaufen *v.t.st.* to occur; to evade; *mir ist ein Fehler ~,* I made a mistake.

unterlegen *v.t.* to lay or put under; (*fig.*) to put (a construction) upon; *einer Melodie einen Text, Worte* ~, to adapt words to a melody.
unterlegen *a.* inferior.
Unterleib *m.* lower abdomen.
unterliegen *v.i.st.* *(s)* to succumb; to be defeated; to admit of (doubt).
Unterlippe *f.* lower lip.
unterm = unter dem
Untermalung *f.* accompaniment; background music.
untermauern *v.t.* to underpin; to support.
untermengen *v.t.* to mix in; to mingle.
Untermiete *f.* subtenancy; sublease.
Untermieter *m.* subtenant.
unterminieren *v.t.* to undermine.
untern = under den
unternehmen *v.t.st.* to undertake, to take upon oneself.
Unternehmen *n.* **(-s, -)** enterprise; (*mil.*) operation.
unternehmend *a.* enterprising, bold.
Unternehmer *m.* **(-s, -)** contractor; employer; entrepreneur.
Unternehmung *f.* **(-, -en)** enterprise.
unternehmungslustig *a.* active; enterprising.
unternormal *a.* subnormal.
Unteroffizier *m.* non-commissioned officer, corporal.
unterordnen *v.t.* to subordinate.
Unter: ~ordnung *f.* subordination; **~pfand** *n.* pledge; pawn, mortgage.
Unterproduktion *f.* underproduction.
unterreden *v.r.* to converse.
Unterredung *f.* conversation; conference.
Unterricht *m.* **(-[e]s, 0)** instruction, teaching, lessons *pl.*
unterrichten *v.t.* to instruct, to teach; to inform.
Unterrichts: ~fach *n.* subject; **~ministerium** *n.* Department of Education.
unterrühren *v.t.* to stir in.
unters = unter das.
untersagen *v.t.* to forbid, to prohibit.
Untersatz *m.* stand, support.
unterschätzen *v.t.* to underrate, to underestimate.
Unterschätzung *f.* **(-, 0)** undervaluation.
unterscheiden *v.t.* & *i.st.* to distinguish, to discern; to discriminate; ~ *v.r.* to differ.
unterscheidend *a.* distinctive.
Unterscheidung *f.* distinction.
Unterschenkel *m.* shank, lower leg.
unterschieben *v.t.st.* to push under; (*fig.*) to accuse falsely.
Unterschiebung *f.* **(-, -en)** false accusation.
Unterschied *m.* **(-[e]s, -e)** difference.
unterschiedlich *a.* distinct, various.
unterschiedslos *a.* indiscriminate.
unterschlagen *v.t.st.* (*Geld*) to embezzle; to intercept; to misappropriate.
Unterschlagung *f.* **(-, -en)** embezzlement; interception (of letters); misappropriation.
Unterschlupf *m.* shelter; hide-out.
unterschreiben *v.t.st.* to subscribe; to sign.
unterschreiten *v.t.st.* to fall below.
Unterschrift *f.* signature.
unterschwellig *a.* subliminal.
Unterseeboot *n.* submarine.
unterseeisch *a.* submarine.
Unterseekabel *n.* submarine cable.
Untersetzer *m.* mat; coaster (glass).
untersetzt *a.* stocky.
untersinken *v.i.st.* *(s)* to go down, to sink.
unterspülen *v.t.* to wash away.
Unterspülung *f.* washout.
unterst *a.* lowest, undermost.
Unterstaatssekretär *m.* Under-Secretary of State.
Unterstand *m.* (*mil.*) dug-out.
unterstehen *v.r.st.* to dare, to venture; *einem* ~, to be under another's orders.
unterstellen *v.t.* to place or put under; to insinuate, to impute; *v.r.* to take shelter.
Unterstellung *f.* **(-, -en)** insinuation; allegation.
unterstreichen *v.t.st.* to underline; to emphasize.
Unterströmung *f.* undercurrent.
unterstützen *v.t.* to support; to assist.
Unterstützung *f.* **(-, -en)** aid, support; assistance, relief.
untersuchen *v.t.* to search; to examine, to investigate.
Untersuchung *f.* **(-, -en)** inquiry, examination, investigation; (*chem.*) analysis.
Untersuchungshaft *f.* pretrial detention; *in* ~ *nehmen,* to commit for trial; ~ *anrechnen,* to make allowance for the period of custody.
Untersuchungsrichter *m.* examining magistrate.
untertags *adv.* by day.
untertan *a.* subject, obedient.
Untertan *m.* **(-s & -en, -en)** subject.
untertänig *a.* subservient; submissive.
Untertasse *f.* saucer.
untertauchen *v.t.* & *i.* *(s)* to dip, to immerse, to duck; to dive.
Unterteil *n.* & *m.* lower part.
unterteilen *v.t.* to subdivide.
Unterteilung *f.* **(-, -en)** subdivision.
Untertitel *m.* **(-s, -)** subtitle
Unterton *m.* undertone.
untertreiben *v.t.st.* to understate.
Untertreibung *f.* **(-, -en)** understatement.
untervermieten *v.t.* & *i.* to sublet.
Untervermietung *f.* subletting.
unterwandern *v.t.* to infiltrate.
Unterwäsche *f.* underwear.
unterwegs *adv.* on the way; in transit, en route.
unterweisen *v.t.st.* to instruct, to teach.
Unterweisung *f.* **(-, -en)** instruction.
Unterwelt *f.* underworld.
unterwerfen *v.t.st.* to subject; to subjugate, to subdue; ~ *v.r.st.* to submit.
Unterwerfung *f.* **(-, 0)** subjection; submission; resignation (to).
unterwühlen *v.t.* to undermine.
unterwürfig *a.* submissive.
unterzeichnen *v.t.* to subscribe; to sign.
Unterzeichner *m.* **(-s, -)** signatory.
Unterzeichnete *m./f.* **(-n, -n)** undersigned.
Unterzeichnung *f.* **(-, -en)** signing; ratification (of a treaty).
unterziehen *v.r.st.* to undergo; ~ *v.t.st.* to put on underneath.
Untiefe *f.* shallow place, shoal.
Untier *n.* monster.
untilgbar *a.* (*Schuld*) irredeemable.
untragbar *a.* unbearable.
untrennbar *a.* inseparable.
untreu *a.* unfaithful; disloyal.
Untreue *f.* unfaithfulness; disloyalty.
untröstlich *a.* disconsolate, inconsolable.
untrüglich *a.* infallible, unmistakable.

untüchtig *a.* unfit, incapable.
Untugend *f.* vice; bad habit.
unüberlegt *a.* rash, inconsiderate.
unübersehbar *a.* vast, immense; obvious.
unübersichtlich *a.* badly arranged; confusing.
unübertrefflich *a.* unequalled, unrivalled.
unübertroffen *a.* unbeaten, unsurpassed.
unüberwindlich *a.* invincible; insurmountable.
unumgänglich *a.* indispensable; *adv.* absolutely.
unumschränkt *a.* unlimited, absolute.
unumstößlich *a.* irrefutable; irrevocable.
unumwunden *a.* frank, plain.
ununterbrochen *a.* uninterrupted; ~ *adv.* without interruption.
unveränderlich *a.* unchangeable; unchanging.
unverändert *a.* unaltered, unchanged.
unverantwortlich *a.* irresponsible.
unveräußerlich *a.* inalienable.
unverb. *unverbindlich,* not binding.
unverbesserlich *a.* incorrigible.
unverbindlich *a.* not binding; *adv.* without any commitment.
unverblümt *a.* plain, frank, blunt.
unverbrüchlich *a.* inviolable.
unverbürgt *a.* unconfirmed.
unverdächtig *a.* unsuspicious.
unverdaulich *a.* indigestible.
unverdaut *a.* undigested.
unverdient *a.* underserved, unmerited.
unverdorben *a.* uncorrupted, unspoilt.
unverdrossen *a.* indefatigable.
unvereidigt *a.* unsworn.
unvereinbar *a.* incompatible (with).
unverfälscht *a.* unadulterated, genuine.
unverfänglich *a.* innocuous, harmless.
unverfroren *a.* (*fam.*) impudent, insolent.
unvergänglich *a.* imperishable; immortal.
unvergessen *a.* unforgotten.
unvergeßlich *a.* unforgettable.
unvergleichlich *a.* incomparable.
unverhältnismäßig *a.* disproportionate.
unverheiratet *a.* unmarried.
unverhofft *a.* unexpected.
unverhohlen *a.* unconcealed, open.
unverkäuflich *a.* unsal(e)able.
unverkauft *a.* unsold.
unverkennbar *a.* unmistakable.
unverletzbar, unverletzlich *a.* inviolable.
unverletzt *a.* intact, uninjured.
unvermeidlich *a.* inevitable.
unvermindert *a.* undiminished, unabated.
unvermittelt *a.* sudden, abrupt.
Unvermögen *n.* inability; impotence.
unvermögend *a.* unable; penniless.
unvermutet *a.* unexpected.
unvernehmlich *a.* inaudible, indistinct.
Unvernunft *f.* unreasonableness.
unvernünftig *a.* unreasonable; irrational.
unveröffentlicht *a.* unpublished.
unverrichtet *a.* unperformed; *~er Sache,* unsuccessfully; with empty hands.
unverschämt *a.* impudent; impertinent.
Unverschämtheit *f.* impudence; impertinence.
unversehens *adv.* unexpectedly.
unversehrt *a.* safe, uninjured, intact.
unversiegbar *a.* inexhaustible, perennial.
unversiegelt *a.* unsealed.
unversöhnlich *a.* irreconcilable.
unversorgt *a.* unprovided for.
Unverstand *m.* folly.
unverständig *a.* ignorant; unable to understand.
unverständlich *a.* unintelligible.
Unverständnis *f.* **(-isses, 0)** incomprehension.
unversucht *a.* untried.
unverträglich *a.* unsuitable; quarrelsome; incompatible.
unvertretbar *a.* unjustifiable.
unverwandt *a.* steadfast, fixed.
unverwechselbar *a.* unmistakable.
unverwehrt *a.* *es ist dir ~ zu...,* you are quite free to...
unverweilt *adv.* without delay.
unverwundbar *a.* invulnerable.
unverwüstlich *a.* indestructible.
unverzagt *a.* intrepid, undaunted.
unverzeihlich *a.* unpardonable; inexcusable.
unverzinslich *a.* & *adv.* non-interest-bearing.
unverzollt *a.* duty unpaid.
unverzüglich *a.* & *adv.* immediate; without delay, immediately.
unvollendet *a.* unfinished.
unvollkommen *a.* imperfect.
Unvollkommenheit *f.* imperfection.
unvollst. *unvollständig,* incomplete.
unvollständig *a.* incomplete.
unvollzählig *a.* incomplete.
unvorbereitet *a.* unprepared.
unvorhergesehen *a.* unforeseen.
unvorhersehbar *a.* unforeseeable.
unvorsichtig *a.* careless, heedless.
Unvorsichtigkeit *f.* **(-, -en)** imprudence.
unvorstellbar *a.* inconceivable.
unvorteilhaft *a.* unattractive; unprofitable.
unwahr *a.* untrue, false, feigned.
Unwahrheit *f.* **(-, -en)** untruth, falsehood.
Unwahrscheinlichkeit *f.* **(-, -en)** improbability.
unwandelbar *a.* immutable, invariable.
unwegsam *a.* impassable.
unweigerlich *a.* & *adv.* inevitable; inevitably.
unweit *pr.* not far from, near.
unwert *a.* unworthy.
Unwesen *n.* **(-s, 0)** nuisance; *sein ~ treiben,* to be up to one's tricks.
unwesentlich *a.* immaterial, irrelevant.
Unwetter *n.* storm.
unwichtig *a.* unimportant.
unwiderlegbar, unwiderleglich *a.* irrefutable.
unwidersprochen *a.* unchallenged.
unwiderstehlich *a.* irresistible.
unwideruflich *a.* irrevocable.
unwiederbringlich *a.* irretrievable.
Unwille *m.* displeasure, indignation.
unwillig *a.* & *adv.* indignant(ly), reluctant(ly).
unwillkommen *a.* unwelcome.
unwillkürlich *a.* involuntary; spontaneous.
unwirklich *a.* unreal.
unwirksam *a.* ineffective.
unwirsch *a.* morose, surly, harsh.
unwirtlich *a.* inhospitable.
unwirtschaftlich *a.* uneconomical.
Unwissen *n.* ignorance.
unwissend *a.* ignorant.
Unwissenheit *f.* **(-, 0)** ignorance.
unwissenschaftlich *a.* unscientific.
unwissentlich *adv.* unknowingly.
unwohl *a.* indisposed, unwell; ~ *v.r.* *~ fühlen,* to feel unwell.
Unwohlsein *n.* **(-s, 0)** indisposition.

unwohnlich *a.* uninhabitable.
unwürdig *a.* **(-, 0)** unworthy; undeserving.
Unzahl *f.* **(-, 0)** immense number.
unzählbar, unzählig *a.* innumerable, uncountable; countless.
unzähmbar *a.* untameable.
unzart *a.* indelicate, rude.
Unze *f.* **(-, -n)** ounce.
Unzeit *f. zur* ~, inopportunely.
unzeitgemäß *a.* old-fashioned.
unzeitig *a.* untimely, unseasonable.
unzensiert *a.* uncensored.
unzerbrechlich *a.* unbreakable.
unzerreißbar *a.* untearable; (*fig.*) indisoluble.
unzerstörbar *a.* indestructible.
unzertrennlich *a.* inseparable.
unzivilisiert *a.* uncivilized, uncultured.
Unzucht *f.* **(-, 0)** sexual offense.
unzüchtig *a.* obscene; indecent.
unzufrieden *a.* discontented, dissatisfied.
Unzufriedene *m./f.* **(-n, -n)** malcontent.
Unzufriedenheit *f.* discontent, dissatisfaction.
unzugänglich *a.* inaccessible.
unzulänglich *a.* insufficient, inadequate.
Unzulänglichkeit *f.* **(-, -en)** insufficiency, inadequacy.
unzulässig *a.* inadmissible.
unzumutbar *a.* unreasonable.
unzurechnungsfähig *a.* not responsible for one's actions.
unzureichend *a.* insufficient.
unzusammenhängend *a.* incoherent.
unzuständig *a.* not competent.
unzuträglich *a.* disadvantageous; unhealthy; bad for.
unzutreffend *a.* inappropriate; incorrect.
unzuverlässig *a.* unreliable.
Unzuverlässigkeit *f.* unreliability.
unzweckmässig *a.* unsuitable.
unzweideutig *a.* unequivocal.
unzweifelhaft *a.* undoubted; indubitable; ~ *adv.* doubtless, without doubt, indubitably.
üppig *a.* luxurious; luxuriant, opulent, sumptuous.
Üppigkeit *f.* **(-, -en)** lushness; luxuriance.
Ur *m.* **(-[e]s, -en)** aurochs.
Urabstimmung *f.* strike ballot.
Urahn *m.* ancestor.
uralt *a.* very old, very ancient.
Uran *n.* uranium.
Uraufführung *f.* **(-, -en)** première, first night.
urbar *a.* arable; ~ **machen,** to bring under cultivation.
Urbeginn *m.* first beginning.
Urbevölkerung *f.* native population.
Urbild *a.* prototype.
Urchristentum *n.* primitive Christianity.
ureigen *a.* very own; original.
Ureinwohner *m.* original inhabitant.
Ureltern *pl.* ancestors.
Urenkel *m.* great-grandson.
Urenkelin *f.* great-granddaughter.
Urform *f.* archetype.
Urgeschichte *f.* primitive history.
Urgestalt *f.* archetype, prototype.
Urgroßmutter *f.* great-grandmother.
Urgroßvater *m.* great-grandfather.
Urheber *m.* **(-s, -)** author, originator.
Urheberrecht *n.* copyright.
Urheberschaft *f.* **(-, -en)** authorship.
Urin *m.* **(-[e]s, 0)** urine; ~ **lassen** *v.i.* to urinate.
urinieren *v.i.* to urinate.
Urinprobe *f.* urine specimen.
Urknall *m.* big bang.
urkomisch *a.* extremely funny.
Urkunde *f.* **(-, -n)** record, document.
Urkundenbeweis *m.* documentary evidence.
urkundlich *a.* authentic; documentary.
Urlaub *m.* **(-[e]s, -e)** vacation; holiday; leave (of absence).
Urlauber *m.* **(-s, -); Urlauberin** *f.* **(-, -nen)** vacationer.
Urmensch *m.* primitive man.
Urne *f.* **(-, -n)** urn.
Urologe *m.;* **Urologin** *f.* urologist.
urplötzlich *a.* very sudden.
Ursache *f.* **(-, -n)** cause; reason; motive.
ursächlich *a.* causal; causative.
Urschrei *m.* primal scream.
Urschrift *f.* original (text).
urspr. *ursprünglich,* originally.
Ursprung *m.* **(-[e]s, -sprünge)** source, origin; *seinen* ~ *haben od. nehmen von,* to originate in.
ursprünglich *a.* original, primitive.
Ursprungsland *n.* country of origin.
Urteil *n.* **(-[e]s, -e)** judgment; sentence, verdict; *einem das* ~ *sprechen,* to pass sentence on someone.
urteilen *v.t. & i.* judge.
Urteilsbegründung *f.* reasons for the verdict
Urteilskraft *f.* (power of) judgment.
Urteilsspruch *m.* sentence.
Urtext *m.* original (text).
Ururgroßmutter *f.* great-great grandmother.
Ururgroßvater *m.* great-great grandfather.
Urwald *m.* primeval forest; jungle
urweltlich *a.* primeval.
urwüchsig *a.* original, native; rough.
Urzeit *f.* primeval times.
Urzustand *m.* original state.
USA *Vereinigte Staaten (von Amerika),* United States (of America), US(A).
usf., usw. *und so fort, und so weiter,* and so forth, etc.
Usurpator *m.* **(-s, -toren)** usurper.
Usus *m.* **(-, 0)** usage, custom.
Utensilien *pl.* utensils, implements *pl.*
Utilitarier *m.* **(-s, -)** utilitarian.
Utopie *f.* **(-, -n)** utopia, utopian scheme.
utopisch *a.* utopian.
u.U. *unter Umständen,* perhaps, perh.; if need be.
UV *Ultraviolett,* ultraviolet, UV.
UV-strahlen *pl.* UV rays.
Ü-Wagen *m.* outside broadcast van.
uzen *v.t.* to tease, to chaff, to mock.

V

V, v *n.* the letter V or v.
V *Volt,* volt, V.
V. *Vers,* verse, v.
v. *von,* of, from; *versus,* versus, v., vs.
vag *a.* vague, loose.
Vagabond *m.* **(-en, -en)** vagabond.
vagabundieren *v.i.* to tramp (about).
vage *a.* vague.
Vagina *f.* **(-, -nen)** vagina.
vakant *a.* vacant.
Vakanz *f.* **(-, -en)** vacancy.
Vakuum *n.* **(-s, -kuen)** vacuum.
Valuta *f.* **(-, -uten)** currency.
Vamp *m.* **(-s, -s)** vamp.
Vampir *m.* **(-[e]s, -e)** vampire.
Vandalismus *m.* **(-, 0)** vandalism.
Vanille *f.* **(-, -n)** vanilla.
variabel *a.* variable.
Variable *f.* variable.
Variante *f.* **(-, -n)** variant; variation.
Varieté *n.* **(-s, -s)** music hall, vaudeville (theater).
variieren *v.t. & i.* to vary; to fluctuate.
Vasall *m.* **(-en, -en)** vassal.
Vasallenstaat *m.* satellite state.
Vase *f.* **(-, -en)** vase.
Vaselin *n.* **(-s, -e)** vaseline.
Vater *m.* **(-s, Väter)** father.
Vater: ~haus *n.* parental house, home; **~land** *n.* native country, fatherland.
vaterländisch *a.* patriotic.
Vaterlandsliebe *f.* patriotism.
väterlich *a.* fatherly; paternal.
Vater: ~mord *m.* patricide; **~mörder** *m.* patricide.
Vaterschaft *f.* **(-, 0)** paternity; fatherhood; **~sklage** *f.* paternity suit.
Vaterstadt *f.* native town.
Vaterunser *n.* **(-s, -)** Lord's prayer.
VB *Verhandlungsbasis,* or nearest offer, o.n.o.
v. Chr. *vor Christus,* before Christ, B.C.
v.D. *vom Dienst,* on duty.
Vefassungsrecht *n.* constitutional law.
Vegetarier *m.* **(-s, -); Vegetarierin** *f.* **(-, -nen)** vegetarian.
vegetarisch *a.* vegetarian.
Vegetation *f.* **(-, -en)** vegetation.
vegetieren *v.i.* to vegetate.
vehement *a. & adv.* vehement(ly).
Veilchen *n.* **(-s, -)** violet.
veilchenblau *a.* violet (-colored).
Veilheit *f.* **(-, -en)** multitude; plurality.
Veitstanz *m.* St. Vitus' dance.
Vektor *m.* **(-s, -en)** vector.
Vene *f.* **(-, -n)** vein.
Venenentzündung *f.* (*med.*) phlebitis.
venerisch *a.* venereal.
Ventil *n.* **(-[e]s, -e)** valve
Ventilaton *f.* **(-, -en)** ventilation.
Ventilator *m.* **(-s, -en)** ventilator, fan.
ventilieren *v.t.* to ventilate.
Venus *f.* Venus.
verabfolgen *v.i.* & t. to deliver.
verabreden *v.t. & r.* to agree upon; to make an appointment.
Verabredung *f.* **(-, -en)** appointment; *nach ~,* by appointment; *eine ~ treffen,* to make an appointment.
verabreichen *v.t.* to administer, to give.
verabsaümen *v.t.* to neglect, to omit.
verabscheuen *v.t.* detest.
verabscheuungswürdig *a.* detestable; abominable.
verabschieden *v.t.* to say goodbye; to discharge; to adopt (plan); to pass (law); *~ v.r.* to say goodbye.
Verabschiedung *f.* **(-, -en)** leave-taking; retirement; adoption (plan); passing (law).
verachten *v.t.* to despise, to scorn, to disdain.
Verächter *m.* **(-s, -)** scorner, opponent.
verächtlich *a.* contemptible, despicable; *(verachtend)* contemptuous.
Verachtung *f.* contempt, scorn.
veralbern *v.t.* to make fun of.
verallgemeinern *v.t.* to generalize.
Verallgemeinerung *f.* generalization.
veralten *v.i. (s)* to become obsolete.
veraltet *a.* obsolete, antiquated.
Veranda *f.* **(-, -den)** porch; veranda.
veränderlich *a.* variable; changeable.
Veränderlichkeit *f.* changeability; variability.
verändern *v.t.* to alter; to change.
Veränderung *f.* **(-, -en)** change, alteration.
verängstigen *v.t.* to frighten; to scare.
verankern *v.t.* (*nav.*) to anchor; (*fig.*) to establish firmly; (*mech.*) to stay.
veranlagen *v.t.* to assess (taxes); *gut veranlagt,* gifted, clever.
Veranlagung *f.* **(-, -en)** disposition; assessment; talent, aptitude (for).
veranlassen *v.t.* to occasion; to cause; to induce (one to do something).
Veranlassung *f.* **(-, -en)** occasion.
veranschaulichen *v.t.* to illustrate.
Veranschaulichung *f.* **(-. -en)** illustration.
veranschlagen *v.t.* to estimate (at).
veranstalten *v.t.* to arrange, to organize.
Veranstaltung *f.* **(-, -en)** function; (*Sport*) event.
verantworten *v.t.* to answer for; to take responsibility; *~ v.r.* to justify or defend oneself.
verantwortlich *a.* responsible, accountable.
Verantwortung *f.* **(-, 0)** responsibility; *zur ~ ziehen,* to call to account.
verantwortungsbewußt *a.* responsible.
Verantwortungsgefühl *n.* sense of responsibility.
verantwortungsvoll *a.* involving great responsibility, responsible.
verarbeiten *v.t.* to process, to digest; to assimilate (film); to come to terms with.
verargen *v.t.* to blame sb. for.
verärgert *a.* annoyed.
verarmen *v.i. (s)* to become poor.
verarmt *a.* impoverished.
verästeln *v.r.* to ramify.
Verästelung *f.* **(-, -en)** ramification.
verausgaben *v.t.* to overspend; *~ v.r.* to run out of money; to exhaust oneself.
veräußern *v.t.* to dispose of; to sell.
Verb *n.* **(-s, -en)** verb.

verbal *a.* & *adv.* verbal(ly).
verballhornen *v.t.* to corrupt, to distort.
Verband *m.* **(-[e]s, -bände)** association, federation, union; (*einer Wunde*) dressing, bandage.
Verbandplatz *m.* first aid station.
Verbandskasten *m.* first aid kit.
Verbandzeug *n.* first aid.
verbannen *v.t.* to banish.
Verbannte *m./f.* **(-n, -n)** exile.
Verbannung *f.* **(-, 0)** banishment, exile.
verbarrikadieren *v.t.* to barricade.
verbauen *v.t.* (*fig.*) to obstruct.
verbeißen *v.t.st.* (*fig.*) to suppress.
verbergen *v.t.st.* to conceal, to hide.
verbessern *v.t.* to correct; to improve.
Verbesserung *f.* improvement.
verbesserungsfähig *a.* capable of improvement.
verbeugen *v.r.* to bow (to).
Verbeugung *f.* **(-, -en)** bow.
verbeulen *v.t.* to dent.
verbiegen *v.t.st.* to bend out of shape.
verbieten *v.t.st.* to forbid, to prohibit, to ban.
verbilligen *v.t.* to lower (prices).
verbinden *v.t.st.* to dress (a wound); to join; to connect; (*Telephon*) to put through; to join.
verbindlich *a.* obliging; obligatory, binding.
Verbindlichkeit *f.* **(-, -en)** obligation, liability, engagement; civility, obligingness.
Verbindung *f.* **(-, -en)** connection; union, alliance; junction; society, club; communication; (*chem.*) compound; *in ~ bleiben,* to keep in touch; ~ *v.r. in ~ setzen,* to get in touch.
Verbindungs: ~glied *n.* connecting link; **~linie** *f.* line of communication; **~offizier** *m.* liaison officer.
verbissen *a.* dogged, obstinate.
verbitten *v.r.st.* to refuse to tolerate, to object, to decline, to deprecate.
verbittern *v.t.* to embitter, to exasperate.
verblassen *v.i.* *(s)* to fade; to turn pale.
Verbleib *m.* **(-[e]s, 0)** whereabouts.
verbleiben *v.i.st.* *(s)* to remain.
verblenden *v.t.* to delude; to blind.
Verblendung *f.* infatuation.
verblichen *a.* faded; deceased.
verblüffen *v.t.* to amaze; to baffle.
verblühen *v.i.* *(s)* to wither, to fade.
verblümt *a.* allusive; ~ *adv.* by innuendo.
verbluten *v.r.* to bleed to death.
verbohren *v.t.* & *r. in etwas ~,* to become obsessed.
verborgen *a.* concealed, secret.
Verbot *n.* **(-[e]s, -e)** prohibition; (*amtlich*) ban.
verbrämen *v.t.* to border, to trim.
verbrannte Erde (*mil.*) scorched earth.
Verbrauch *m.* **(-[e]s, 0)** consumption, use; expenditure.
verbrauchen *v.t.* to consume.
Verbraucher *m.* **(-s, -); Verbraucherin** *f.* **(-, -nen)** consumer.
Verbraucher: ~schutz *m.* consumer protection; **~umfrage** *f.* consumer survey.
Verbrauchsgüter *pl.* consumer goods.
Verbrauchsteuer *f.* excise duty.
verbraucht *a.* used.
verbrechen *v.t.st.* to commit (a crime); to perpetrate (a joke).
Verbrechen *n.* **(-s, -)** crime, offence.
Verbrecher *m.* **(-s, -); Verbrecherin** *f.* **(-, -nen)** criminal, convict.
verbrecherisch *a.* criminal.
verbreiten *v.t.* to spread, to diffuse, to disseminate; ~ *v.r.* to spread; (*fig.*) to enlarge upon.
verbreitern *v.t.* to widen.
Verbreitung *f.* **(-, 0)** propagation; diffusion.
verbrennbar *a.* combustible.
verbrennen *v.t.ir.* to burn; ~ *v.i.ir.* *(s)* to be burnt (down); ~ *v.r.* to burn or scald oneself.
Verbrennung *f.* **(-, 0)** burning; incineration; combustion.
verbriefen *v.t.* to document, guarantee; *verbriefte Rechte pl.* vested rights *pl.*
verbringen *v.t.st.* to pass, to spend.
verbrüdern *v.r.* to fraternize.
Verbrüderung *f.* **(-, -en)** fraternization.
verbrühen *v.t.* to scald.
verbuchen *v.t.* to book.
verbummeln *v.t.* (*fam.*) to idle away; to forget.
verbunden *a.* obliged; connected.
verbünden *v.r.* to ally oneself (to or with).
Verbündete *m./f.* **(-n, -n)** ally.
verbürgen *v.t.* to warrant; ~ *v.r.* ~ *für,* to vouch for, to guarantee.
verbüßen *v.t.* to serve one's time.
verchromt *a.* chromium-plated.
Verdacht *m.* **(-[e]s, 0)** suspision; *über allen ~ erhaben,* above suspicion.
verdächtig *a.* suspect, suspicious.
verdächtigen *v.t.* to suspect; to cast suspicion on.
Verdächtigung *f.* **(-, -en)** suspicion; insinuation.
Verdachtsperson *f.*, **Verdächtiger** *m.* suspect.
verdammen *v.t.* to condemn; to damn.
verdammlich *a.* damnable.
Verdammnis *f.* **(-, 0)** damnation.
verdammt *adv.* damned.
Verdammung *f.* **(-, -en)** damnation; condemnation.
verdampfen *v.i.* *(s)* to evaporate.
verdanken *v.t.* to owe, to be indebted for.
verdauen *v.t.* to digest.
verdaulich *a.* digestible.
Verdauung *f.* **(-, 0)** digestion.
Verdauungs: ~beschwerden *pl.* indigestion; **~kanal** *m.* digestive tract; **~system** *n.* digestive system.
Verdeck *n.* **(-[e]s, -e)** top; hood (car).
verdecken *v.t.* to cover, to hide.
verdenken *v.t.st. ich kann es ihr nicht ~,* I can't blame her.
verderben *v.t.st.* to spoil; to corrupt; ~ *v.i.st.* *(s)* to be spoiled, to go bad; *sich den Magen ~,* to upset one's stomach; *es mit einem nicht ~ wollen,* not want to quarrel with sb.
Verderben *n.* (**-s, 0**) ruin; downfall.
verderblich *a.* pernicious; (*Waren*) perishable; fatal.
Verderbnis *n.* **(-nisses, -nisse)** corruption; decay.
verdeutlichen *v.t.* to make plain.
verdeutschen *v.t.* to translate into German.
verdichten *v.t.* to condense.
verdicken *v.t.* & *r.* to thicken.
verdienen *v.t.* to earn; to deserve, to merit.
Verdienst *m.* **(-es, 0)** gain, profit; earnings *pl.*
Verdienst *n.* **(-es, -e)** merit, desert.
Verdienstausfall *m.* lost earnings.
verdienstvoll *a.* deserving, able.
verdient *a.* deserving, meritorious; (*Strafe*) deserved.
Verdikt *n.* **(-[e]s, -e)** verdict.
verdolmetschen *v.t.* to interpret.

verdonnern *v.t.* (*fam.*) to sentence.
verdoppeln *v.t.* to double.
verdorben *a.* spoiled; depraved; *~er Magen*, upset stomach.
verdorren *v.i.* *(s)* to dry up, to wither.
verdrängen *v.t.* to displace.
Verdrängung *f.* displacement; repression, suppression; inhibition.
verdrehen *v.t.* to twist; (*fig.*) to misrepresent, to distort.
verdreht *a.* distorted; (*fig.*) cracked, flighty.
Verdrehung *f.* **(-, -en)** distortion.
verdreifachen *v.t.* to triple; to treble.
verdreschen *v.t.st.* to thrash.
verdrießen *v.t.imp.st.* to vex, to annoy, to grieve.
verdrießlich *a.* tiresome, annoying; vexed; peevish, morose.
verdrossen *a.* sullen, unwilling.
Verdrossenheit *f.* moroseness; sullenness.
verdrücken *v.t.* (*fam.*) to polish off; to crumple (fabric); ~ *v.r.* to slip away.
Verdruß *m.* **(-sses, 0)** annoyance, trouble.
verduften *v.i.* (*fam.*) to slip away; to clear off.
verdummen *v.t.* to make stupid; to stultify; ~ *v.i.* *(s)* to become stupid.
verdunkeln *v.t.* to darken; to obscure; (*fig.*) to eclipse.
Verdunkelung *f.* **(-, -en)** darkening; (*Luftschutz*) blackout.
verdünnen *v.t.* to dilute.
Verdünnung *f.* dilution.
verdunsten *v.i.* to evaporate.
verdursten *v.i.* to die of thirst.
verdüstern *v.r.* to darken.
verdüstert *a.* (*fig.*) gloomy.
verdutzt *a.* baffled; nonplussed.
veredeln *v.t.* to improve, to refine.
verehelichen *v.t.* & *r.* to marry.
verehren *v.t.* to venerate, to revere; to worship, to adore.
Verehrer *m.* **(-s. -); Verehrerin** *f.* **(-, -en)** worshipper; admirer.
Verehrung *f.* **(-, 0)** veneration; worship.
verehrungswürdig *a.* venerable.
vereidigen *v.t.* to administer an oath to; to swear in.
Vereidigung *f.* **(-, -en)** swearing in.
Verein *m.* **(-s, -e)** union, society, club; *im ~ mit meinem Freunde*, jointly with my friend.
vereinbar *a.* compatible, consistent.
vereinbaren *v.t.* to agree; to arrange.
Vereinbarung *f.* **(-, -en)** agreement.
vereinen *v.t.* to unite; to reconcile; ~ *v.r.* to unite.
vereinfachen *v.t.* to simplify.
vereinheitlichen *v.t.* to standardize.
vereinigen *v.t.* to unite; to merge, to combine.
vereinigt *a.* united; *die Vereinigten Staaten*, the United States.
Vereinigung *f.* **(-, -en)** association; organization.
vereinnahmen *v.t.* to receive, to take.
vereinsamen *v.t.* to become lonely.
vereinzelt *a.* sporadic; occasional.
Vereinzelung *f.* **(-, 0)** isolation.
vereisen *v.i.* to freeze over; to ice over.
vereiteln *v.t.* to frustrate; to prevent.
vereitert *a.* septic.
verekeln *v.t.* to render loathsome.
verenden *v.i.* *(s)* to die.
verengen *v.t.* to narrow, to contract.
vererbbar *a.* inheritable.
vererben *v.t.* to bequeath, to leave; to transmit (disease); ~ *v.r.* to be hereditary, to run in the family.
Vererbung *f.* **(-, 0)** heredity; hereditary transmission.
verewigen *v.t.* to immortalize.
Verf., Vf. *Verfasser*, author.
verfahren *v.i.st.* *(s)* to proceed, to go to work, to act; ~ *v.t.st.* to bungle; ~ *v.r.* to lose one's way.
verfahren *a.* muddled.
Verfahren *n.* **(-s, -)** method, procedure; (*chem.*) process; (*law*) proceedings; *beschleunigtes ~*, summary proceedings.
Verfahrensfrage *f.* procedural question.
Verfall *m.* **(-[e]s, 0)** decay, decline, ruin; forfeiture; (*eines Wechsels*) maturity.
verfallen *v.i.st.* to decay; to decline; (*von Wechseln*) to fall due; (*Rechte*) to lapse; to expire; *auf einen Gedanken ~*, to hit upon an idea; *das Pfand ist ~*, the pledge is forfeited.
Verfalltag *m.* day of maturity.
verfälschen *v.t.* to falsify; to adulterate.
verfangen *v.t.st.* to take effect, to tell; *das verfängt bei mir nicht*, that will get you nowhere with me; to get entangled.
verfänglich *a.* risky, awkward.
verfärben *v.r.* to change color; to discolor.
verfassen *v.t.* to compose, to write.
Verfasser *m.* **(-s, -), Verfasserin** *f.* **(-, -nen)** author; writer.
Verfassung *f.* **(-, -en)** constitution; state.
verfassunggebend *a.* constituent.
verfassungsmäßig *a.* constitutional.
verfassungswidrig *a.* unconstitutional.
verfaulen *v.i.* *(s)* to rot, to putrify.
verfechten *v.t.st.* to advocate; to champion.
verfehlen *v.t.* to miss.
verfehlt *a.* unsuccessful, abortive.
Verfehlung *f.* **(-, -en)** misdemeanour.
verfeinden *v.t.* to set (one) against (another); ~ *v.r.* to fall out with.
verfeinern *v.t.* to refine, to polish.
verfertigen *v.t.* to make, to manufacture.
verfestigen *v.t.* & *r.* to harden, to strengthen.
Verfettung *f.* **(-, 0)** adiposis.
verfilmen *v.t.* to film, to make a film of.
verfilzen *v.i.* to become felted/matted.
verfinstern *v.t.* & *r.* to darken; to eclipse.
Verfinsterung *f.* **(-, -en)** eclipse.
verflachen *v.t.* to flatten, to level.
verflechten *v.t.st.* to interlace; to entangle in.
verfliegen *v.i.st.* *(s)* to evaporate, to vanish.
verflossen *a.* (*fam.*) former.
verfluchen *v.t.* to curse, to execrate.
verflucht *a.* damned; cursed.
verflüchtigen *v.i.* & *r.* to evaporate, to vanish.
verfolgen *v.t.* to pursue; to persecute; (eine Sache) to follow up; *gerichtlich ~*, to prosecute at law.
Verfolger *m.* **(-s, -); Verfolgerin** *f.* **(-, -nen)** pursuer.
Verfolgte *m./f.* victim of persecution; *politisch ~*, victim of political persecution.
Verfolgung *f.* **(-, -en)** pursuit; persecution; *strafrechtliche ~*, prosecution.
Verfolgungswahn *m.* persecution mania.
verfrachten *v.t.* to freight; to load; to ship.
verfressen *a.* greedy.
verfroren *a.* frozen; sensitive to cold.

verfrüht *a.* premature.

verfügbar *a.* available.

verfügen *v.t.* to order; ~ *v.i.* to dispose (of).

Verfügung *f.* **(-, -en)** disposition, disposal; order, decree, injunction; (*gerichtlich*) rule; **~srecht** *n.* power of disposal.

verführen *v.t.* to tempt; to seduce.

Verführer *m.* **(-s, -)** seducer.

Verführerin *f.* **(-, -nen)** seductress.

verführerisch *a.* tempting, seductive.

Verführung *f.* **(-, -en)** temptation; seduction.

verfüttern *v.t.* to feed; to use as animal food.

vergällen *v.t.* (*fig.*) to spoil.

vergammeln *v.i.* (*fam.*) to rot; ~ *v.t.* to waste (time).

vergammelt *a.* (*fam.*) scruffy; rotten.

vergangen *a.* past, last, bygone.

Vergangenheit *f.* **(-, 0)** the past, time past; (*gram.*) past tense.

vergänglich *a.* transient; transitory; ephemeral.

Vergänglichkeit *f.* transience; transitoriness.

Vergaser *m.* **(-s, -)** carburetor.

vergeben *v.t.st.* to forgive, to pardon; to give away, to dispose of; *seiner Ehre etwas* ~, to compromise one's honor.

vergebens *adv.* in vain, vainly.

vergeblich *a.* futile; vain, fruitless.

Vergeblichkeit *f.* futility.

Vergebung *f.* **(-, 0)** forgiveness, pardon.

vergegenwärtigen *v.r.* to figure, to represent, to visualize; to realize.

vergehen *v.i.st.* *(s)* to pass away, to elapse; to vanish; ~ *v.r.* to offend; to violate.

Vergehen *n.* **(-s, -)** fault, offense; misdemeanor.

vergeistigen *v.t.* to spiritualize.

vergelten *v.t.st.* to requite, to return, to repay.

Vergeltung *f.* **(-, 0)** repayment; (*feindliche*) retaliation, reprisal.

vergessen *v.t.st.* to forget; ~ *v.r.* to forget oneself.

Vergessenheit *f.* **(-, 0)** oblivion.

vergeßlich *a.* forgetful.

Vergeßlichkeit *f.* forgetfulness.

vergeuden *v.t.* to squander, to waste.

Vergeudung *f.* **(-, -en)** squandering; waste.

vergewaltigen *v.t.* to violate; to rape; to oppress.

Vergewaltigung *f.* **(-, -en)** rape; violation.

vergewissern *v.r.* to ascertain, to make sure of.

Vergewisserung *f.* **(-, 0)** confirmation.

vergießen *v.t.st.* to spill; to shed.

vergiften *v.t.* to poison; (*fig.*) to envenom, to embitter.

Vergiftung *f.* **(-, -en)** poisoning.

vergilbt *a.* yellowed.

Vergißmeinnicht *n.* **(-s, -)** forget-me-not.

vergittern *v.t.* to bar, to lattice.

verglasen *v.t.* to glaze; to vitrify.

Vergleich *m.* **(-[e]s, -e)** comparison; arrangement, compromise, agreement.

vergleichbar *a.* comparable.

vergleichen *v.t.st.* to compare; *sich ~ mit,* to compete with.

vergleichsweise *adv.* comparatively.

vergnügen *v.t.* to amuse; ~ *v.r.* to enjoy oneself, to take pleasure in.

Vergnügen *n.* **(-s, -)** pleasure; diversion; *~ finden an,* to delight in.

vergnüglich *a.* amusing; entertaining.

vergnügt *a.* pleased, cheerful.

Vergnügung *f.* pleasure, amusement.

Vergnügungspark *m.* amusement park.

Vergnügungssteuer *f.* entertainment tax.

Vergnügungsviertel *n.* night-life district.

vergolden *v.t.* to gild.

vergönnen *v.t.* to grant, to allow; not to grudge.

vergöttern *v.t.* to deify; (*fig.*) to idolize.

Vergötterung *f.* **(-, -en)** deification.

vergr. *vergriffen,* out of print.

vergraben *v.t.st.* to bury.

vergrämt *a.* careworn.

vergraulen *v.t.* (*fam.*) to scare off.

vergreifen *v.r.st.* to make a mistake; (*an Geld*) to embezzle.

vergriffen *a.* sold out; out of print.

vergrößern *v.t.* to magnify; (*phot.*) to enlarge; to extend; to increase.

Vergrößerung *f.* **(-, -en)** (*Mikroskop, etc.*) magnification; (*phot.*) enlargement; extension; increase.

Vergrößerungsglas *n.* magnifying glass.

Vergünstigung *f.* **(-, -en)** favor, privilege.

vergüten *v.t.* to compensate; (*Auslagen*) to reimburse.

Vergütung *f.* **(-, -en)** remuneration; reimbursement.

verh. *verheiratet,* married, mar.

verhaften *v.t.* to arrest.

Verhaftete *m./f.* person under arrest.

Verhaftung *f.* **(-, -en)** arrest.

verhallen *v.i.* *(s)* to die away.

verhalten *v.t.st.* to retain, to keep back; (*das Lachen*) to restrain; ~ *v.r.* to stand; to behave; *wie verhält sich die Sache?* how does the matter stand?; *sich ruhig ~,* to keep quiet.

verhalten *a.* restrained.

Verhalten *n.* **(-s, 0)** conduct, behavior.

Verhaltensmaßregel *f.* rule of conduct.

Verhaltensweise *f.* **(-, -n)** behavior.

Verhältnis *n.* **(-nisses, -nisse)** proportion, rate, ratio; circumstance; state, condition; relationship, love affair; *im ~ zu,* in proportion to.

verhältnismäßig *adv.* relatively.

Verhältniswahl *f.* proportional representation.

verhältniswidrig *a.* disproportionate.

Verhältniswort *n.* preposition.

verhandeln *v.t. & i.* to negotiate, to treat; *gerichtlich ~,* to try, to hear a case; *erneut ~,* to retry.

Verhandlung *f.* **(-, -en)** negotiation; (*jur.*) trial, hearing; *nochmalige Verhandlung,* rehearing, retrial; **~en aufnehmen,** to enter into negotiations.

verhängen *v.t.* (*Strafe*) to inflict.

Verhängnis *n.* **(-nisses, -nisse)** fate, destiny.

verhängnisvoll *a.* fatal, fateful.

verhärmt *a.* careworn.

verharren *v.i.* to persist (in); to remain.

verhärten *v.t., v.i. & (sich)* ~ *v.r.* to harden.

verhaßt *a.* hated, odious.

verhätscheln *v.t.* to pamper, to spoil.

verhauen *v.t.st.* (*fam.*) to thrash; ~ *v.r.st.* to plunder.

verheddern *v.r.* to tangle.

verheeren *v.t.* to devastate, to lay waste.

verheerend *a.* devastating; disastrous.

Verheerung *f.* **(-, -en)** devastation.

verhehlen *v.t.* to conceal, to hide.

verheilen *v.i.* to heal up.

verheimlichen *v.t.* to keep a secret; to conceal.

Verheimlichung *f.* **(-, -en)** concealment.

verheiraten *v.t.* to give in marriage; ~ *v.r.* to marry, to get married.

verheißen *v.t.st.* to promise.

Verheißung *f.* **(-, -en)** promise.
verheißungsvoll *a.* promising.
verheizen *v.t.* to burn; to use as fuel.
verhelfen *v.t.st.* to help to.
verherrlichen *v.t.* to glorify; to extol.
Verherrlichung *f.* **(-, -en)** glorification.
verhetzen *v.t.* to instigate, to set (against).
Verhetzung *f.* **(-, -en)** instigation.
verhexen *v.t.* to bewitch.
verhindern *v.t.* to prevent.
Verhinderung *f.* **(-, -en)** prevention.
verhohlen *a.* & *adv.* secret(ly).
verhöhnen *v.t.* to mock; to ridicule; to deride.
Verhöhnung *f.* **(-, -en)** derision, mockery.
Verhör *n.* **(-[e]s, -e)** trial; examination; *ins ~ nehmen,* to examine.
verhören *v.t.* to question, to interrogate; ~ *v.r.* to mishear.
verhüllen *v.t.* to wrap up, to veil.
Verhüllung *f.* **(-, -en)** disguise.
verhundertfachen *v.i.* & *r.* to increase a hundredfold; to centuple.
verhungern *v.i.* to starve.
verhunzen *v.t.* to spoil.
verhüten *v.t.* to prevent, to avert.
Verhütung *f.* **(-, 0)** prevention; *Empfängnis~* *f.* contraception.
verirren to get lost; to lose one's way.
verirrt *a.* stray(ing), erring; misled.
Verirrung *f.* **(-, -en)** aberration.
verjagen *v.t.* to chase away.
verjähren *v.i.* to come under the statute of limitations.
verjährt *a.* cancelled by the statute of limitations; (*Schulden*) superannuated.
Verjährung *f.* **(-, -en)** prescription, limitation; **~sfrist** *f.* period of limitation.
verjüngen *v.t.* to rejuvenate; to reduce in size; ~ *v.r.* to grow young again; to taper.
Verjüngung *f.* **(-, -en)** rejuvenation; tapering.
verkabeln *v.t.* to connect by cable (TV).
verkalken *v.i.* to calcify; to become calcified/hardened; to become senile.
Verkalkung *f.* **(-, -en)** calcification; hardening; senility.
verkannt *a.* misjudged, misunderstood.
verkappt *a.* disguised.
verkatert *a.* (*fam.*) hung-over.
Verkauf *m.* **(-[e]s, -käufe)** sale.
verkaufen *v.t.* to sell, to dispose of.
Verkäufer *m.* **(-s, -)** seller, (*jur.*) vendor; salesman, sales assistant, sales clerk; **~in** *f.* saleswoman.
verkäuflich *a.* sal(e)able; marketable.
Verkaufpreis *m.* retail price.
Verkaufssteuer *f.* sales tax.
Verkehr *m.* **(-s, 0)** traffic; contact; intercourse; *starker ~*, heavy traffic.
verkehren *v.t.* to invert; (*fig.*) to pervert; ~ *v.i.* to associate (with); to frequent (a place).
Verkehrs: ~ampel *f.* traffic light; **~amt** *n.* tourist office; **~aufkommen** *n.* volume of traffic; **~delikt** *f.* traffic offense; **~flugzeug** *n.* commercial or passenger plane; **~insel** *f.* traffic island; **~minister** *m.* Secretary of Transportation; **~mittel** *f.* means of transport; **~ordnung** *f.* traffic regulations; **~regeln** *pl.* traffic code; **~regelung** *f.* traffic regulation; **~schild** *n.* traffic sign; road-sign; **~schutzmann** *m.* traffic cop; **~stau** *f.* traffic jam; **~störung** *f.* traffic hold-up; **~zeichen** *n.* traffic sign.
verkehrt *a.* inverted, upside down; wrong.
verkennen *v.t.st.* to misjudge; to undervalue; to deny, to disbelieve.
Verkennung *f.* **(-, -en)** misjudgment, underestimation.
verketten *v.t.* to link together.
Verkettung *f.* **(-, -en)** chain; concatenation.
verkitten *v.t.* to cement.
verklagen *v.t.* to sue, to bring an action against; to accuse.
verklären *v.t.* to glorify, to transfigure.
Verklärung *f.* **(-, -en)** transfiguration.
verklauseln, verklausulieren *v.t.* to limit by provisos, (*fig.*) to express in a roundabout way.
verkleben v.t. to paste up or over.
verkleiden *v.t.* to line; to disguise; (*arch.*) to face.
Verkleidung *f.* **(-, -en)** disguise.
verkleinern *v.t.* to diminish; to reduce; (*fig.*) to belittle, to derogate from.
Verkleinerung *f.* **(-, -en)** (*phot.*) reduction.
Verkleinerungsform *f.* diminutive form.
verkleistern *v.t.* to paste up, to glue up.
verklingen *v.i.st.* to die away.
Verknappung *f.* **(-, 0)** shortage.
verkneifen *v.t.* & *r.st.* (*sl.*) to do without sth.; to repress sth.
verknöchern *v.i.* to ossify.
verknüpfen *v.t.* to connect; to join, to combine.
Verknüpfung *f.* **(-, -en)** connection.
verkommen *v.i.st.* to be neglected, to perish, to decay.
verkorksen *v.t.* to mess up.
verkörpern *v.t.* to embody.
Verkörperung *f.* **(-, -en)** embodiment.
verköstigen *v.t.* to board, to feed.
verkrachen *v.r.* to fall out.
verkrampfen *v.r.* to cramp; to tense up.
verkriechen *v.r.st.* to crawl away, to sneak off, to hide.
verkrümmt *a.* crooked.
verkrüppeln *v.t.* to cripple, to stunt.
verkrusten *v.i.* to form a crust/scab.
verkümmern *v.i.* to pine away, to waste away; to atrophy; to be stunted, to starve.
verkünden *v.t.* to announce; to pronounce; to promulgate (law).
verkündigen *v.t.* to preach; to announce, to proclaim.
Verkündigung *f.* **(-, -en)** preaching; announcement, proclamation; *Maria ~*, Annunciation Day.
Verkündung *f.* announcement; pronouncement; promulgation.
verkuppeln *v.t.* to pair off.
verkürzen *v.t.* to shorten; to abridge.
Verkürzung *f.* **(-, -en)** shortening.
Verl. *Verlag,* publishing house.
verlachen *v.t.* to deride, to laugh at.
verladen *v.t.st.* to load; to ship; to embark.
Verladung *f.* loading.
Verlag *m.* **(-[e]s, -lage)** publishing house.
verlagern *v.t.* to shift.
Verlagerung *f.* shifting.
Verlags: ~buchhändler *m.* publisher; **~buchhandlung** *f.* publishing house; **~recht** *n.* copyright.
verlangen *v.t.* to demand; to desire.
Verlangen *n.* **(-s, 0)** desire; request, demand.

verlängern *v.t.* to lengthen, to prolong; ~ *v.r.* to be extended.
Verlängerung *f.* **(-, -en)** extension; prolongation.
verlangsamen *v.t.* to slow down.
Verlangsamung *f.* **(-, -en)** slow-down.
Verlaß *m. es ist auf ihn kein ~,* he is not to be relied on.
verlassen *v.t.st.* to leave; to desert; ~ *v.r. ~ auf,* to rely or depend on; ~ *a.* deserted.
Verlassenheit *f.* **(-, 0)** loneliness.
verläßlich *a.* reliable.
Verläßlichkeit *f.* reliability.
Verlauf *m.* **(-[e]s, 0)** course; lapse.
verlaufen *v.i.st. (s)* to elapse; ~ *v.r.* to lose one's way; *wie ist die Sache ~?* how has the matter turned out?
verlautbaren *v.t.* to make known; ~ *v.imp.* to be divulged.
Verlautbarung *f.* **(-, -en)** announcement.
verlauten *v.imp.* to be reported.
verleben *v.t.* to spend, to pass.
verlebt *a.* dissipated.
verlegen *v.t.* to remove; to mislay; (*Weg*) to bar; (*aufschieben*) to put off; (*Buch*) to publish, to bring out; *sich ~ auf,* to go in for, to apply oneself to.
verlegen *a.* embarrassed.
Verlegenheit *f.* **(-, -en)** self-consciousness, embarrassment, dilemma.
Verleger *m.* **(-s, -)** publisher.
Verlegung *f.* **(-, -en)** removal, transfer; postponement.
verleiden *v.t. jdm etw. ~,* to spoil sth. for sb.
Verleih *m.* hiring out; distribution (film).
verleihen *v.t.st.* to lend, to let out; to confer upon, to grant; to invest with.
verleiten *v.t.* to induce/entice.
verlernen *v.t.* to unlearn, to forget.
verlesen *v.t.st.* to read out; ~ *v.r.* to read wrong.
verletzbar, verletzlich *a.* vulnerable.
verletzen *v.t.* to injure; to violate; to infringe; to offend.
verletzlich *a.* vulnerable.
Verletzlichkeit *f.* vulnerability.
Verletzte *m./f.* injured person.
Verletzung *f.* **(-, -en)** hurt, injury; (*med.*) lesion; violation, infraction.
verleugnen *v.t.* to deny, to disown.
Verleugnung *f.* **(-, 0)** denial; abnegation.
verleumden *v.t.* to slander; to libel; to calumniate.
Verleumder *m.* **(-s, -); Verleumderin** *f.* **(-, -nen)** slanderer; libeler.
verleumderisch *a.* slanderous.
Verleumdung *f.* **(-, -en)** calumny, slander.
verlieben *v.r.* to fall in love (with).
verliebt *a.* in love, enamored; amorous.
Verliebte *m./f.* lover.
Verliebtheit *f.* being in love.
verlieren *v.t.st.* to lose; *aus den Augen ~,* to lose sight of; ~ *v.i.* to be a loser; ~ *v.r.* to lose one's way; to disappear gradually.
Verlierer *m.* **(-s, -); Verliererin** *f.* **(-, -nen)** loser.
Verlies *n.* **(-es, -e)** dungeon.
verloben *v.t.* to betroth; ~ *v.r.* to become engaged (to).
Verlöbnis *n.* **(-nisses, -nisse)** betrothal, engagement.
verlobt *a.* engaged (to be married).
Verlobte *m.* **(-n, -n)** fiancé.
Verlobte *f.* **(-n, -n)** fiancée.
Verlobung *f.* **(-, -en)** engagement; *die ~ auflösen,* to break off the engagement.
Verlobungsring *m.* engagement ring.
verlocken *v.t.* to entice, to allure.
verlockend *a.* tempting; enticing.
Verlockung *f.* temptation; enticement.
verlogen *a.* given to lying, mendacious.
Verlogenheit *f.* falseness; mendacity; lying.
verlohnen *v.t. es verlohnt sich der Mühe,* it is worth while.
verloren *a. & p.* lost.
verlöschen *v.t.* to extinguish; ~ *v.i.st.* to go out.
verlosen *v.t.* to raffle.
Verlosung *f.* **(-, -en)** lottery, raffle.
verlottern *v.i. (s)* to go downhill.
Verlust *m.* **(-es, -e)** loss; *~ und Gewinnkonto n.* profit and loss account.
verlustig *a.* ~ **gehen,** to lose.
Verlustliste *f.* list of casualties.
vermachen *v.t.* to bequeath.
Vermächtnis *n.* **(-nisses, -nisse)** legacy, bequest.
vermählen *v.r.* to marry, to get married.
Vermählung *f.* **(-, -en)** marriage; wedding.
vermauern *v.t.* to wall up; to close.
vermehren *v.t.* to augment, to increase; ~ *v.r.* to multiply.
Vermehrung *f.* **(-, -en)** increase; (*bio.*) reproduction.
vermeidbar *a.* avoidable.
vermeiden *v.t.st.* to avoid, to shun.
vermeidlich *a.* avoidable.
Vermeidung *f.* **(-, 0)** avoidance.
vermeinen *v.t.* to suppose, to think.
vermeintlich *a.* supposed, pretended.
vermengen *v.t.* to mix, to intermingle; to confound.
Vermengung *f.* **(-, -en)** mingling; mixture, medley; confusion, mistake.
Vermerk *m.* **(-[e]s. -e)** entry, note.
vermerken *v.t.* to make a note of.
vermessen *v.t.st.* to measure; to survey; ~ *a.* audacious, presumptuous.
Vermessenheit *f.* **(-, -en)** presumption.
Vermessung *f.* **(-, -en)** measuring; survey.
vermieten *v.t.* to let (out), to lease; *zu ~,* for rent.
Vermieter *m.* **(-s, -)** landlord; (*jur.*) lessor.
Vermieterin *f.* **(-, -nen)** landlady.
Vermietung *f.* renting (out); hiring (out).
vermindern *v.t.* to diminish; to reduce; ~ *v.r.* to decrease.
vermindert *a.* diminished; *~e Zurechnungsfähigkeit, f.* diminished responsibility.
Verminderung *f.* **(-, -en)** diminuition.
vermischen *v.t.* to (inter)mix, to mingle.
Vermischung *f.* **(-, -en)** mixture.
vermissen *v.t.* to miss.
Vermißte *m./f.* **(-n, -n)** missing person.
vermitteln *v.t.* to mediate; (*Zwist*) to make up; (*Frieden, Anleihen*) to negotiate.
Vermittler *m.* **(-s, -)** mediator.
Vermittlung *f.* **(-, -en)** mediation.
vermodern *v.i. (s)* to molder, to rot.
vermögen *v.t.ir.* to be able to do.
Vermögen *n.* **(-s, -)** ability, faculty; power; fortune, property; *über mein ~,* beyond my power or reach.
vermögend *a.* rich, wealthy.
Vermögens: ~abgabe *f.* capital levy; **~bestand**

m. assets *pl.*; **~einkommen** *n.* unearned income; **~steuer** *f.* property tax; **~umstände** *pl.*, **~verhältnisse** *n.pl.* financial circumstances.
vermummen *v.t.* to mask; to wrap up.
vermuten *v.t.* to conjecture, to suspect.
vermutlich *a.* presumable; presumptive.
Vermutung *f.* **(-, -en)** supposition; conjecture.
vernachlässigen *v.t.* to neglect.
Vernachlässigung *f.* **(-, -en)** neglect.
vernähen *v.t.* to sew up.
vernarben *v.i.* to scar; to heal.
vernarrt *a.* infatuated (with).
vernebeln *v.t.* to shroud in fog.
vernehmbar *a.* audible.
vernehmen *v.t.st.* to understand, to hear; to interrogate, to examine.
vernehmlich *a.* audible, distinct.
Vernehmung *f.* **(-, -en)** interrogation, examination.
vernehmungsfähig *a.* fit to be questioned.
verneigen *v.r.* to bow.
Verneigung *f.* **(-, -en)** bow, curtsy.
verneinen *v.t.* to answer in the negative.
verneinend *a.* negative; **~ antworten,** to answer in the negative.
Verneinung *f.* **(-, -en)** negation; denial.
vernichten *v.t.* to annihilate, to destroy; to wipe out.
Vernichtung *f.* **(-, 0)** destruction; annihilation.
verniedlichen *v.t.* to trivialize; to play down.
Vernunft *f.* **(-, 0)** reason; sense, judgment.
vernunftbegabt *a.* endowed with reason; rational.
Vernunftehe *f.* marriage of convenience.
vernunftgemäß *a.* reasonable, rational.
vernünftig *a.* reasonable; rational; sensible.
Vernunftmensch *m.* rational person.
vernunftwidrig *a.* irrational.
veröden *v.i. (s)* to become deserted.
veröffentlichen *v.t.* to publish.
Veröffentlichung *f.* **(-, -en)** publication.
verordnen *v.t.* to decree, to ordain; (*med.*) to prescribe.
Verordnung *f.* **(-, -en)** decree; ordinance, regulations *pl.*; (*med.*) prescription.
verpachten *v.t.* to lease (land).
verpacken *v.t.* to pack; to wrap up.
Verpackung *f.* **(-, -en)** wrapping; packing.
verpäppeln *v.t.* to pamper.
verpassen *v.t.* to miss (bus, etc.).
verpesten *v.t.* to infect, to pollute.
verpfänden *v.t.* to pawn, to pledge; to mortgage.
verpflanzen *v.t.* to transplant.
Verpflanzung *f.* **(-, 0)** transplantation.
verpflegen *v.t.* to feed, to board.
Verpflegung *f.* **(-, -en)** catering; maintenance; (*mil.*) provisioning; *volle ~*, full board; *teilweise ~*, partial board; **~sgeld** *n.* subsistence allowance.
verpflichten *v.t.* to oblige, to engage,to obligate; *~ v.r.* to pledge oneself, to undertake; *einen eidlich ~*, to bind sb. by oath.
verpflichtend *a.* obligatory.
Verpflichtung *f.* **(-, -en)** obligation, engagement; (*Diplomatie*) commitment; (*Geld*) liability; *seinen ~en nachkommen,* to meet one's obligations; *eine ~ eingehen,* to incur an obligation.
verpfuschen *v.t.* to make a mess of.
verplanen *v.t.* to book up (time); to commit (money).
verplappern *v.r.* to blab.
verplempern *v.t.* (*fam.*) to waste.
verpönt *a.* scorned; taboo.
verprassen *v.t.* to squander.
verprügeln *v.t.* to beat up, to thrash.
verpuffen *v.i.* (*fig.*) to fizzle out; to blow up.
verpuppen *v.r.* to pupate.
Verputz *m.* **(-es, 0)** plaster.
verputzen *v.t.* to plaster (walls).
verquer *a.* crooked; angled; weird.
verquicken *v.t.* to amalgamate.
verrammeln *v.t.* to barricade, to bar.
verrannt *a.* obsessed.
Verrat *m.* **(-[e]s, 0)** treason; treachery; betrayal.
verraten *v.t.st.* to betray; to disclose.
Verräter *m.* **(-s, -); Verräterin** *f.* traitor.
verräterisch *a.* treacherous; traitorous.
verrauchen *v.i.* to go up in smoke, to evaporate; (*fig.*) to cool, to pass away.
verräuchern *v.t.* to fill with smoke.
verraucht *a.* smoke-filled; smoky.
verrauschen *v.i.* to pass away, to die away, (music; festivity).
verrechnen *v.t.* to take into account; to credit to another account; *~ v.r.* to miscalculate; to be mistaken.
Verrechnung *f.* **(-, -en)** settlement; *nur zur ~*, (*Scheck*) not negotiable; **~sscheck** *m.* non-negotiable check.
verrecken *v.i. (s)* (*von Tieren*) to die; (*fam.*) to kick the bucket.
verregnen *v.t.* to spoil by rain.
verreisen *v.i. (s)* to go on a journey.
verreissen *v.t.* to tear into pieces.
verreist *a.* away on travel.
verrenken *v.t.* to dislocate, to sprain.
Verrenkung *f.* **(-, -en)** dislocation.
verrennen *v.r.st.* **~ in,** (*fig.*) to become obsessed with.
verrichten *v.t.* to do, to perform, to execute, to achieve; *seine Notdurft ~*, to relieve oneself; *sein Gebet ~*, to say one's prayers.
Verrichtung *f.* **(-, -en)** carrying out; performance.
verriegeln *v.t.* to bolt, to bar.
verringern *v.t. & r.* to diminish, to lessen.
verrinnen *v.i.st.* to run off *or* out.
verrohen *v.t. & i.* to brutalize; to grow brutal.
verrosten *v.i.* to rust.
verrostet *a.* rusty.
verrottet *a.* rotten.
verrucht *a.* infamous.
verrücken *v.t.* to displace, to remove.
verrückt *a.* deranged, crazy, mad.
Verrückte *m./f.* lunatic, madman, madwoman.
Verrücktheit *f.* **(-, -en)** craziness; madness.
Verruf *m.* **(-[e]s, 0)** *in ~ kommen,* to fall into disrepute.
verrufen *a.* ill reputed; disreputable.
verrühren *v.t.* to stir together.
verrußt *a.* sooted up.
verrutschen *v.i.* to slip.
Vers *m.* **(Verses, Verse)** verse.
versagen *v.t. & i.* to deny, to refuse; *~ v.i.* to misfire; (*Stimme*) to fail.
Versager *m.;* **Versagerin** *f.* failure.
versalzen *v.t.* to oversalt.
versammeln *v.t.* to gather; to assemble; *~ v.r.* to assemble, to congregate, to meet.
Versammlung *f.* **(-, -en)** assembly, meeting; *eine*

~ *auf 10 Uhr einberufen,* to call a meeting for 10 o'clock.
Versand *m.* **(-[e]s, 0)** dispatch
versanden *v.i.* to silt up; (*fig.*) to peter out.
Versandhaus *n.* mail-order firm.
versauen *v.t.* (*sl.*) to make a mess of.
versauern *v.t.* to embitter.
versaufen *v.t.st.* to waste in drink.
versäumen *v.t.* to miss, to neglect.
Versäumnis *f.* **(-, -nisse)** omission; **~urteil** *n.* judgment by default.
verschaffen *v.t.* to procure, to provide; ~ *v.r.* to procure, to secure, to acquire.
verschalen *v.t.* to board over.
Verschalung *f.* **(-, -en)** wooden covering.
verschämt *a.* bashful, shamefaced.
verschandeln *v.t.* to disfigure, to spoil.
verschanzen *v.t.* to entrench, to fortify.
Verschanzung *f.* **(-, -en)** fortification.
verschärfen *v.t.* to intensify; to increase; to aggravate.
verscharren *v.t.* to bury (without ceremony).
verscheiden *v.i.st.* to expire, to die.
verschenken *v.t.* to give away.
verscherzen *v.t.* to forfeit, to lose.
verscheuchen *v.t.* to scare away.
verschicken *v.t.* to dispatch.
verschieben *v.t.st.* to shift, to displace; to delay, to put off, to postpone.
verschieden *a.* different; various; diverse; deceased.
verschiedenartig *a.* various, heterogeneous.
verschiedenerlei *a.* of various kinds.
verschiedenfarbig *a.* in different colors.
Verschiedenheit *f.* **(-, -en)** diversity.
verschiedentlich *adv.* on various occasions.
verschießen *v.t.st.* to shoot.
verschiffen *v.t.* to ship; to export.
verschimmeln *v.i.* to go moldy.
verschimmelt *a.* moldy
verschlafen *v.t.st.* to sleep away; ~ *v.r.* to oversleep.
verschlafen *a.* half-asleep; sleepy.
Verschlag *m.* **(-[e]s, -schläge)** shed; hutch.
verschlagen *v.t.st.* to mishit (tennis); *es hat mir den Atem ~*, it took my breath away.
verschlagen *a.* cunning, sly, crafty.
Verschlagenheit *f.* **(-, 0)** cunning; slyness.
verschlechtern *v.t.* to impair; ~ *v.r.* to deteriorate.
Verschlechterung *f.* deterioration, worsening.
verschleiern *v.t.* to veil; to screen.
verschleiert *a.* veiled; misty.
Verschleierung *f.* veiling; covering up.
Verschleimung *f.* **(-, -en)** mucus congestion.
Verschleiß *m.* **(-es, -e)** wear and tear.
verschleißen *v.t.st.* to wear out.
verschleppen *v.t.* to mislay; to abduct; (*Krankheiten*) to spread; (*fig.*) to protract, to put off, to delay.
Verschleppung *f.* **(-, -en)** protraction; kidnapping; delaying.
verschleudern *v.t.* to waste; to sell dirt cheap.
verschließbar *a.* closable; lockable; *luftdicht ~*, sealable.
verschließen *v.t.st.* to shut, to close; to lock; ~ *v.r.* to lock oneself off or up.
verschlimmern *v.t.* to make worse; to aggravate; ~ *v.r.* to get worse, to worsen; to deteriorate.
Verschlimmerung *f.* **(-, 0)** change for the worse; worsening.
verschlingen *v.t.st.* to (inter)twine; to interlace; to swallow (up), to devour.
verschlossen *a. & p.* locked up, shut; (*fig.*) reticent, reserved, close.
Verschlossenheit *f.* **(-, 0)** (*fig.*) reserve.
verschlucken *v.t.* to swallow; ~ *v.r.* to choke, to swallow the wrong way.
Verschluß *m.* **(-sses, -üsse)** lock; (*phot.*) shutter; *unter ~*, under lock and key.
verschlüsseln *v.t.* to encode.
verschmachten *v.i.* to pine away.
verschmähen *v.t.* to disdain, to scorn.
verschmelzen *v.t.st.* to blend; ~ *v.i.st.* to be blended.
verschmerzen *v.t.* to get over (a loss).
verschmieren *v.t.* to smear; to smudge, to blur.
verschmitzt *a.* cunning, sly, artful.
verschmutzen *v.t.* to dirty, to soil; ~ *v.i.* to get dirty.
Verschmutzung *f.* **(-, -en)** pollution; soiling.
verschnaufen *v.r.* to have/take a breather.
Verschnaufpause *f.* rest; breather.
verschneiden *v.t.st.* to adulterate (wine).
verschneit *a.* snow-covered.
Verschnitt *m.* **(-es, -e)** blend.
verschnörkelt *a.* ornate.
verschnupfen *v.t. & i.* to offend; *~ sein,* to have a cold; (*fig.*) to feel offended.
verschnüren *v.t.* to tie up.
verschollen *a.* forgotten; presumed dead or lost.
verschonen *v.t.* to spare.
verschönern *v.t.* to embellish.
verschossen *a.* faded, discolored.
verschränken *v.t.* to cross (one's arms); to interlace, to entwine.
verschreiben *v.t.st.* (*med.*) to prescribe; ~ *v.r.st.* to make a slip of the pen.
Verschreibung *f.* **(-, -en)** prescription.
verschreibungspflichtig *a.* available only on prescription.
verschroben *a.* eccentric, strange.
verschroten *v.t.* to grind (up).
verschrotten *v.t.* to scrap.
verschrumpeln *v.i.* (*fam.*) to shrivel (up).
verschüchtern *v.t.* to intimidate.
verschulden *v.t.* to be guilty of, to commit; to get into debt.
Verschulden *n.* **(-, 0)** fault, guilt.
Verschuldung *f.* **(-, -en)** indebtedness; offense, fault.
verschütten *v.t.* to spill; *verschüttet werden,* to be buried alive.
verschwägert *a.* related by marriage.
verschweigen *v.t.st.* to keep a secret, to conceal; to suppress.
verschwenden *v.t.* to squander, to dissipate, to waste.
Verschwender *m.* **(-s, -)**; **Verschwenderin (-, -nen)** *f.* spendthrift; squanderer.
verschwenderisch *a.* wasteful, lavish; (*reichlich*) profuse.
Verschwendung *f.* **(-, -en)** waste; extravagance.
verschwiegen *a.* discreet, reticent.
Verschwiegenheit *f.* **(-, 0)** secrecy, discretion.
verschwimmen *v.i.st.* *(s)* to become indistinct or blurred.
verschwinden *v.i.st.* to disappear, to vanish.
verschwistert *a.* ~ **sein** to be siblings.

verschwitzen *v.t.* to make (clothing) sweaty; (*fam.*) to forget.
verschwitzt *a.* sweaty.
verschwollen *a.* swollen.
verschwommen *a.* indistinct, blurred.
verschwören *v.r.st.* to plot, to conspire.
Verschwörer *m.* **(-s, -); Verschwörerin** *f.* **(-, -nen)** conspirator.
Verschwörung *f.* **(-, -en)** conspiracy, plot.
versehen *v.t.* to provide, to supply; (*Dienst*) to perform; ~ *v.r.* to make a mistake; *ehe ich mir's versehe,* before I am aware of it.
Versehen *n.* **(-s, -)** oversight; slip; *aus* ~, inadvertently.
versehentlich *adv.* by mistake; inadvertently.
versehrt *a.* disabled.
Versehrte *m./f.* **(-n, -n)** disabled person.
verselbständigen *v.r.* to become independent.
versenden *v.t.st.* to dispatch, to ship.
Versendung *f.* **(-, -en)** dispatch; sending.
versengen *v.t.* to singe, to scorch.
versenken *v.t.* to sink, to submerge.
Versenkung *f.* sinking; lowering; *in der* ~ *verschwinden,* to vanish from the scene.
versessen *a.* ~ **sein auf** to be crazy about.
versetzen *v.t.* to displace; to transplant; to pawn; to promote (to a higher grade); to mix, to alloy; ~ *v.i.* to reply, to rejoin; *einem einen Schlag, Hieb* ~, to deal someone a blow, a cut.
Versetzung *f.* **(-, -en)** transfer (*eines Beamten*); removal; promotion (school, etc.); transplanting.
Versetzungszeugnis *n.* end-of-year report.
verseuchen *v.t.* to contaminate.
Versfuß *m.* (metrical) foot, meter.
Versicherer *m.* insurer.
versichern *v.t.* to assure, to affirm; to insure; *das Leben seiner Frau* ~, to take out a policy on the life of one's wife; ~ *v.r.* to make sure of, to ascertain; to secure.
Versicherte *m./f.* **(-n, -n)** insured (person).
Versicherung *f.* **(-, -en)** assurance, affirmation; insurance; *eine* ~ *abschließen,* to take out insurance.
Versicherungs: ~anspruch *m.* insurance claim; **~beitrag** *m.* premium; **~fähig** *a.* insurable; **~makler** *m.* insurance broker; **~nehmer** *m.* policy holder; **~police** insurance policy; **~prämie** *f.* insurance premium.
versickern *v.i.* to drain away.
versiegeln *v.t.* to seal (up).
Versiegelung *f.* seal; sealing.
versiegen *v.i.* to dry up, to be drained.
versilbern *v.t.* to (silver)-plate; (*fig.*) to convert into money.
Versilberung *f.* **(-, -en)** silver-plating; conversion.
versinken *v.i.st. (s)* to sink; (*fig.*) ~ **in** to become immersed.
versinnbildlichen *v.t.* to symbolize.
Version *f.* **(-, -en)** version.
versklaven *v.t.* to enslave.
Versmaß *n.* meter.
versoffen *a.* drunken.
versöhnen *v.t.* to reconcile.
versöhnlich *a.* placable, conciliatory.
Versöhnung *f.* **(-, -en)** reconciliation.
versonnen *a.* dreamy; lost in thought.
versorgen *v.t.* to provide with, to supply; to provide for, to take care of, to maintain.
Versorger *m.* **(-s, -); Versorgerin** *f.* **(-, -nen)** provider; breadwinner (for).
Versorgung *f.* **(-, -en)** provision; supply(ing).
verspannen *v.r.* to tense up.
verspannt *a.* tense; cramped.
verspäten *v.t., v.r.* to be late.
verspätet *a.* late.
Verspätung *f.* **(-, -en)** delay, lateness.
verspeisen *v.t.* to consume.
verspekulieren *v.t.* to lose by speculation.
versperren *v.t.* to block up, to obstruct.
verspielen *v.t.* to gamble away.
verspielt *a.* playful; fanciful.
versponnen *a.* eccentric; odd.
verspotten *v.t.* to mock; to ridicule.
Verspottung *f.* **(-, -en)** mockery, derision.
versprechen *v.t.st.* to promise; ~ *v.r.st.* to make a slip of the tongue.
Versprechen *n.* **(-s, -)** promise.
Versprecher *m.* **(-s, -)** slip of the tongue.
Versprechung *f.* **(-, -en)** promise.
versprengen *v.t.* to disperse; to sprinkle.
versprühen *v.t.* to spray.
verspüren *v.t.* to perceive, to feel.
verstaatlichen *v.t.* to nationalize.
verstädtern *v.i.* to become urbanized.
Verstädterung *f.* urbanization.
Verstand *m.* **(-[e]s, 0)** understanding, intellect; (good) sense; *gesunder* ~, common sense; *den* ~ *verlieren,* to go out of one's mind.
verstandesmäßig *a.* intellectual, rational.
verständig *a.* intelligent, sensible.
verständigen *v.t.* to inform; to notify; *sich mit einem* ~, to come to an understanding with someone.
Verständigung *f.* **(-, -en)** arrangement, agreement; information; communication.
verständlich *a.* intelligible; *allgemein* ~, popular, within the reach (comprehension) of everyone.
verständlicherweise *adv.* understandably.
Verständnis *n.* **(-nisses, -nisse)** comprehension; understanding.
verständnislos *a.* uncomprehending.
Verständnislosigkeit *f.* **(-, 0)** lack of understanding; incomprehension.
verständnisvoll *a.* understanding.
verstärken *v.t.* to strengthen, to reinforce; to intensify; (*radio*) to amplify.
Verstärker *m.* amplifier.
verstärkt *a.* increased; reinforced.
Verstärkung *f.* **(-, -en)** reinforcement, strengthening.
verstauben *v.i.* to get dusty.
verstaubt *a.* dusty; (*fig.*) old-fashioned.
verstauchen *v.t.* to sprain; to dislocate.
Verstauchung *f.* **(-, -en)** spraining; dislocation.
Versteck *m.* **(-[e]s, -e)** hiding-place; ~*en spielen,* to play hide-and-seek.
verstecken *v.t.* to hide, to conceal.
versteckt *a.* hidden; concealed; veiled.
verstehen *v.t.st.* to understand; to comprehend; to know (how); to mean; *falsch* ~, to misunderstand.
versteifen *v.t.* to stiffen; ~ *v.r.* to harden (*Börse*); (*fig.*) to insist upon.
versteigen *v.r.st. zu einer Behauptung* ~, to go as far as to maintain that...
versteigern *v.t.* to auction.
Versteigerung *f.* **(-, -en)** auction, public sale.
versteinert *a.* petrified.
Versteinerung *f.* **(-, -en)** petrifaction, fossil.
verstellbar *a.* adjustable.

verstellen *v.t.* to misplace; to shift; (*den Weg*) to bar; ~ *v.r.* to dissemble, to feign.
Verstellung *f.* **(-, -en)** pretense; disguising.
versterben *v.t.st.* to die; to pass away.
versteuern *v.t.* to pay excise *or* duty on.
verstiegen *a.* high-flown, extravagant.
verstimmen *v.t.* to put in a bad mood.
verstimmt *a.* out of tune; (*fig.*) out of humor, put out.
Verstimmtheit, Verstimmung *f.* **(-, -en)** (*fig.*) bad humor, ill-humor, ill-feeling.
verstocken *v.t.* to harden.
verstockt *a.* obdurate, hardened.
Verstocktheit *f.* obduracy; stubbornness.
verstohlen *a.* surreptitious, stealthy.
verstopfen *v.t.* to block, to stop; (*med.*) to constipate.
Verstopfung *f.* **(-, -en)** stopping, obstruction; constipation.
verstorben *a.* deceased, defunct; *mein ~er Mann,* my late husband
verstört *a.* distraught; troubled, haggard.
Verstoß *m.* **(-es, -stösse)** violation; fault, offense, mistake.
verstoßen *v.i.st.* to cast off, to expel; ~ *v.t.st.* ~ **gegen,** to offend against, to transgress.
verstrahlen *v.t.* to radiate; to contaminate with radiation.
verstreichen *v.i.st.* to elapse; to spread.
verstreuen *v.t.* to scatter, to disperse.
verstricken *v.t.* (*fig.*) to entangle, to ensnare; ~ *v.r.* to become involved.
Verstrickung *f.* involvement.
verstümmeln *v.t.* to mutilate, to mangle.
Verstümmelung *f.* **(-, -en)** mutilation.
verstummen *v.i.* to fall silent; to fade away.
Versuch *m.* **(-[e]s, -e)** experiment; trial, attempt; test.
versuchen *v.t.* to try, to attempt; to taste.
Versucherin *f.* **(-, -nen)** temptress.
Versuchs: ~anordnung *f.* set-up for an experiment; **~ballon** *m.* trial balloon; **~fabrik** *f.* pilot plant; **~kaninchen** *n.* guinea pig; **~objekt** *n.* test object; **~person** *f.* test person; **~reihe** *f.* series of tests; **~tier** *n.* laboratory animal.
versuchsweise *adv.* by way of experiment.
Versuchung *f.* **(-, -en)** temptation.
versündigen *v.r.* to sin (against).
Versündigung *f.* **(-, -en)** sin; grave offense.
Versunkenheit *f.* **(-, 0)** absorption; contemplation.
versüßen *v.t.* to sweeten.
vertagen *v.t.* to adjourn; ~ *v.r.* to adjourn.
Vertagung *f.* **(-, -en)** adjournment.
vertändeln *v.t.* to fritter away.
vertauschen *v.t.* to exchange.
Vertauschung *f.* **(-, -en)** exchange, reversal; switching.
verteidigen *v.t.* to defend.
Verteidiger *m.* **(-s, -); Verteidigerin** *f.* **(-, -nen)** defender; (*jur.*) counsel for the defense; (*Fußball*) back.
Verteidigung *f.* **(-, -en)** defense.
verteilen *v.t.* to distribute, to apportion.
Verteiler *m.* **(-s, -)** (*auf Akten*) distribution list.
Verteilung *f.* **(-, -en)** distribution.
verteuern *v.t.* to make more expensive.
verteufeln *v.t.* to condemn.
verteufelt *a.* (*fam.*) devilish.
vertiefen *v.t.* to deepen; ~ *v.r.* to be absorbed in.
Vertiefung *f.* **(-, -en)** deepening; strengthening; hollow.
vertikal *a.* vertical.
Vertikale *f.* **(-, -n)** vertical (line).
vertilgen *v.t.* to exterminate; to consume.
vertippen *v.r.* to make a typing mistake; to get it wrong (lotto); ~ *v.t.* to mistype.
vertonen *v.t.* to set to music.
Vertonung *f.* **(-, -en)** setting to music.
vertrackt *a.* odd, strange; confounded, intricate.
Vertrag *m.* **(-[e]s, -träge)** contract, agreement; (*Staats~*) treaty; *mündlicher ~,* verbal agreement.
vertragen *v.t.st.* to bear, to stand, to endure; to digest; *ich kann kein Bier ~,* beer does not agree with me; ~ *v.r.* to get along well (together).
vertraglich *a.* contractual.
verträglich *a.* digestible; social, peaceable; compatible.
Vertraglichkeit *f.* digestibility; good nature.
Vertragsabschluß *m.* conclusion of a contract.
Vertragsbedingungen *pl.* terms of the contract.
Vertragsbruch *m.* breach of contract.
Vertragsentwurf *m.* draft contract.
Vertragspartei *f.* contracting party.
Vertragsrecht *n.* contract law.
vertragswidrig *a.* contrary to a contract or treaty.
vertrauen *v.t.* to entrust, to confide; ~ *v.i.* to confide, to rely upon.
Vertrauen *n.* **(-s, 0)** confidence; trust; *im ~,* privately, confidentially.
vertrauenerweckend *a.* inspiring confidence.
Vertrauensbruch *m.* breach of trust.
vertrauens: ~selig *a.* too confiding; gullible; rashly trustful; **~voll** *a.* confiding, trusting, trustful; **~würdig** *a.* trustworthy.
Vertrauensstellung *f.* position of trust.
vertraulich *a.* confidential, intimate.
Vertraulichkeit *f.* **(-, -en)** familiarity, intimacy.
verträumen *v.t.* to dream away.
verträumt *a.* dreamy.
vertraut *a.* intimate, familiar; conversant (with), versed (in); *auf ~em Fuß stehen,* to be on intimate terms.
Vertraute *m./f.* **(-n, -n)** confidant; close friends.
Vertrautheit *f.* **(-, 0)** familiarity.
vertreiben *v.t.st.* to drive away, to expel, to banish; to sell; to pass (time).
Vertreibung *f.* **(-, -en)** expulsion.
vertretbar *a.* defensible; tenable; justifiable.
vertreten *v.t.st.* to represent.
Vertreter *m.* **(-s, -); Vertreterin** *f.* **(-, -nen)** representative
Vertretung *f.* **(-, -en)** representation; substitution; *in ~ von,* acting for or as representative of; by proxy.
Vertrieb *m.* **(-[e]s, 0)** sale, distribution.
Vertriebene *m./f.* **(-n, -n)** exile.
vertrinken *v.t.st.* to spend on drink.
vertrocknen *v.i.* to dry up, to wither.
vertrödeln *v.t.* to trifle away; to waste time.
vertrösten *v.t.* to put off.
vertun *v.t.st.* to waste, to squander.
vertuschen *v.t.* to hush up; to suppress (news).
verübeln *v.t.* to take amiss.
verüben *v.t.* to commit, to perpetrate.
verulken *v.t.* to make fun of.
verunglimpfen *v.t.* to denigrate; to revile.
verunglücken *v.i.* (*s*) to be involved in an accident.

verunreinigen *v.t.* to soil, to contaminate; (*Wasser*) to pollute; (*Lust*) to infect; (*fig.*) to defile.
Verunreinigung *f.* **(-, -en)** defilement, contamination.
verunsichern *v.t.* to make unsure/uncertain.
Verunsicherung *f.* feeling of insecurity.
verunstalten *v.t.* to disfigure, to deface.
Verunstaltung *f.* **(-, -en)** disfigurement.
veruntreuen *v.t.* to embezzle.
Veruntreuung *f.* **(-, -en)** embezzlement.
verunzieren *v.t.* to disfigure, to mar.
verursachen *v.t.* to cause; to occasion.
Verursacher *m.* **(-s, -)** person responsible; cause.
verurteilen *v.t.* to condemn; to convict, to sentence.
Verurteilte *m./f.* convicted person.
Verurteilung *f.* **(-, -en)** condemnation.
vervielfältigen *v.t.* to multiply; to duplicate.
Vervielfältigung *f.* **(-, -en)** reproduction; duplication; copying.
vervierfachen *v.t.* to quadruple.
vervollkommen *v.t.* to perfect.
vervollständigen *v.t.* to complete, to complement.
Vervollständigung *f.* completion.
Verw. *Verwaltung,* administration, adm.
verwachsen *v.i.st. (s)* to grow together.
verwachsen *a.* deformed, crippled.
verwählen *v.r.* to dial the wrong number.
verwahren *v.t.* to keep; *sich gegen etwas* ~, to protest against.
verwahrlost *a.* neglected, unkempt.
Verwahrlosung *f.* **(-, -en)** neglect.
Verwahrung *f.* **(-, -en)** keeping, custody; protest; *in ~ nehmen,* to take into custody.
verwaisen *v.i. (s)* to become an orphan.
verwaist *a.* orphaned; (*fig.*) deserted.
verwalten *v.t.* to administer.
Verwalter *m.* **(-s, -); Verwalterin** *f.* **(-, -nen)** administrator.
Verwaltung *f.* **(-, -en)** administration, management.
Verwaltungs: ~gericht *n.* administrative court; **~recht** *n.* administrative law.
verwandelbar *a.* convertible.
verwandeln *v.t.* to change, to transform, to convert, to turn; (*Strafe*) to commute; ~ *v.r.* to be changed.
Verwandlung *f.* **(-, -en)** change, transformation; changing, turning.
verwandt *a.* related, akin to; (Begriffe) cognate.
Verwandte *m./f.* **(-n, -n)** relation, relative, kinsman, kinswoman; *nächste* ~, next-of-kin.
Verwandtschaft *f.* **(-, -en)** relationship; relations *pl.*; (*fig.*) affinity.
verwandtschaftlich *a.* relational.
verwarnen *v.t.* warn; to caution.
verwaschen *a.* washed-out, faded.
verwässern *v.t.* to dilute, to drown.
verweben *v.t.* to interweave.
verwechselbar *a.* mistakable.
verwechseln *v.t.* to mistake (for), confuse.
Verwechslung *f.* **(-, -en)** mistake, confusion.
verwegen *a.* audacious, daring, bold.
Verwegenheit *f.* audacity; daring.
verwehen *v.t.* to blow away.
verwehren *v.t.* to hinder, to prohibit.
verweichlichen *v.t.* to make soft; to render effeminate.
verweigern *v.t.* to refuse.
Verweigerung *f.* **(-, -en)** denial, refusal.
verweilen *v.i.* to stay; to sojourn; (*fig.*) to dwell (on).
verweint *a.* tearstained.
Verweis *m.* **(-es, -e)** rebuke, reprimand; (*im Buch*) (cross) reference.
verweisen *v.t.st.* to refer to; *einen des Landes oder aus dem Land* ~, to exile, to banish someone; (*einem etwas* ~), to rebuke someone for sth.
Verweisung *f.* **(-, -en)** reference; banishment, exile; **~szeichen** reference.
verwelken *v.i.* to wither, to fade.
verweltlichen *v.t.* to secularize.
verwendbar *a.* usable; applicable.
Verwendbarkeit *f.* usability.
verwenden *v.t.st.* to use; to apply (to), to spend (on), to employ (in); *sich ~ für,* to intercede on behalf of.
Verwendung *f.* **(-, -en)** application, use, employment.
verwendungsunfähig *a.* unemployable.
verwerfen *v.t.st.* to reject; to quash; to condemn.
verwerflich *a.* reprehensible.
Verwerfung *f.* **(-, -en)** rejection; condemnation.
verwertbar *a.* utilizable; usable.
Verwertbarkeit *f.* usability.
verwerten *v.t.* utilize.
Verwertung *f.* utilization; exploitation.
verwesen *v.t.* to administer; ~ *v.i.* to rot, to decay; to decompose.
verweslich *a.* perishable.
Verwesung *f.* **(-, -en)** decomposition.
verwickeln *v.t.* to entangle; to complicate, to implicate; to involve; ~ *v.r.* to become complicated; to get involved.
verwickelt *a.* complicated, intricate.
Verwicklung *f.* **(-, -en)** entanglement, complication; plot (of a play).
verwiegend *adv.* mainly.
verwildern *v.i.* to become overgrown (garden); to go wild.
verwildert *a.* overgrown (garden); wild.
verwirken *v.t.* to forfeit.
verwirklichen *v.t.* to realize; ~ *v.r.* to be *or* become realized, to materialize.
Verwirklichung *f.* **(-, -en)** realization.
verwirren *v.t.* to confuse; to perplex.
verwirrt *a.* confused; bewildered.
Verwirrung *f.* **(-, -en)** confusion.
verwirtschaften *v.t.* to waste (by mismanagement).
verwischen *v.t.* to wipe out, to blot out; (*fig.*) to become blurred.
verwittern *v.i.* to become disintegrated, dilapidated.
verwittert *a.* weather-beaten.
verwitwet *a.* widowed.
verwöhnen *v.t.* to spoil, to pamper.
verworfen *a.* abandoned, depraved; (*fig.*) immoral.
verworren *a.* intricate, confused.
verwundbar *a.* vulnerable.
Verwundbarkeit *f.* vulnerability.
verwunden *v.t.* to wound, to hurt.
verwunderlich *a.* strange, odd.
verwundern *v.r.* to be surprised.
verwundert *a.* astonished, surprised.
Verwunderung *f.* surprise; astonishment.

verwundet *a.* wounded, injured.
Verwundete *m./f.* wounded person; casualty.
Verwundung *f.* **(-, -en)** wound; injury.
verwunschen *a.* enchanted.
verwünschen *v.t.* to curse, to execrate.
Verwünschung *f.* **(-, -en)** curse.
verwüsten *v.t.* to devastate, to lay waste.
Verwüstung *f.* **(-, -en)** devastation.
verzagen *v.i.* to lose courage, to despair.
verzagt *a.* discouraged, despondent.
verzählen *v.r.* to count wrong; to miscount.
Verzahnung *f.* **(-, -en)** *(Holz)* dovetailing.
verzärteln *v.t.* to coddle, to pamper.
verzaubern *v.t.* to bewitch, to enchant; to cast a spell.
Verzauberung *f.* **(-, -en)** enchantment; spell.
Verzehr *m.* **(-s, 0)** consumption.
verzehren *v.t.* to consume; to eat.
verzeichnen *v.t.* to list; to note down; to specify.
Verzeichnis *n.* **(-nisses, -nisse)** list, catalogue; index.
verzeihen *v.t.st.* to pardon, to forgive.
verzeihlich *a.* pardonable; excusable; forgivable.
Verzeihung *f.* **(-, 0)** pardon; forgiveness; *um ~ bitten,* to beg pardon.
verzerren *v.t.* to distort.
verzetteln *v.t.* to fritter away.
Verzicht *m.* **(-[e]s, -e)** renunciation; *~ leisten auf,* to renounce.
verzichten *v.i.* to renounce, to resign.
Verzichtleistung *f.* renunciation.
verziehen *v.t.st.* to distort; *~ v.i. ein Kind ~,* to spoil a child; *in die Stadt ~,* to move into town; *~ v.r.* to go out of shape; to disperse.
verzieren *v.t.* to decorate, to adorn.
Verzierung *f.* **(-, -en)** decoration, ornament.
verzinsen *v.t.* to pay interest on; *~ v.r.* to bear *or* yield interest.
verzinslich *a.* bearing interest.
verzogen *a.* spoiled (child); no longer at this address.
verzögern *v.t.* to delay, to protract.
Verzögerung *f.* **(-, -en)** delay; **~staktik** *f.* delaying tactics.
verzollbar *a.* durable.
verzollen *v.t.* to pay duty on.
verzuckern *v.t.* to sugar over; to put too much sugar in.
verzückt *a.* enraptured; ecstatic.
Verzückung *f.* **(-, -en)** rapture; ecstasy.
Verzug *m.* **(-[e]s, 0)** delay.
verzweifeln *v.i.* to despair (of/at).
verzweifelt *a.* desperate; despairing.
Verzweiflung *f.* **(-, 0)** despair, desperation.
verzweigen *v.r.* to branch out; to ramify.
verzweigt *a.* branching.
verzwickt *a.* odd, strange; intricate.
Vesper *f.* **(-, -n)** vespers *pl.*
vespern *v.i.* to have supper.
Vestalin *f.* **(-, -en)** vestal.
Veteran *m.* **(-en, -en)** veteran.
Veterinär *m.* **(-s, -e)** veterinary surgeon.
Veto *n.* **(-[s], -s)** veto.
Vetter *m.* **(-s, -n)** (male) cousin; *~ zweiten Grades,* second cousin.
Vetternwirtschaft *f.* nepotism.
vexieren *v.t.* to tease, to banter; to quiz, to puzzle, to mystify.
vgl. *vergleiche,* compare, cf.
v.H. *vom Hundert,* per cent.
via *pr.* via, by way (of).
Viadukt *m.* **(-[e]s, -e)** viaduct.
Vibration *n.* **(-, -en)** vibration.
vibrieren *v.i.* to vibrate.
Video *n.* **(-s, -s)** video.
Video: ~band *n.* videotape; **~gerät** *n.* video recorder; **~kassette** *f.* video cassette; **~recorder** *m.* video recorder; **~spiel** *n.* video game; **~text** *m.* teletext.
Videothek *f.* **(-, -en)** video tape library.
Vieh *n.* **(-[e]s, 0)** beast; cattle; livestock.
Vieh: ~futter *n.* fodder; **~händler** *m.* cattle dealer.
viehisch *a.* beastly, brutal, bestial.
Vieh: ~seuche *f.* cattle plague, rinderpest; foot-and-mouth disease; **~zucht** *f.* cattle breeding; **~züchter** *m.* stock farmer, cattle breeder.
viel *a. & adv.* a lot; plenty; much, a great deal; **~e** *pl.* many; *gleich ~,* as many or much; no matter; just the same.
vielbändig *a.* in many volumes.
vielbeschäftigt *a.* busy, much occupied.
vieldeutig *a.* ambiguous.
vieldiskutiert *a.* much-discussed.
Vieleck *n.* **(-[e]s, -e)** polygon.
vielerlei *a.* different, various.
vielfach, vielfältig *a. & adv.* manifold, multiple; multifarious; repeatedly.
Vielfraß *m.* **(-es, -e)** glutton.
vielgeliebt *a.* much-loved.
vielgepriesen *a.* much-vaunted.
vielgestaltig *a.* multiform.
Vielgötterei *f.* **(-, 0)** polytheism.
vielköpfig *a.* many-headed.
vielleicht *adv.* perhaps, maybe.
vielmalig *a.* repeated, frequent.
vielmals *adv.* many times, frequently.
vielmehr *adv.* rather; on the contrary.
vielsagend *a.* significant, expressive; meaningful.
vielseitig *a.* multilateral; *(fig.)* many-sided, versatile.
Vielseitigkeit *f.* **(-, 0)** versatility.
vielsilbig *a.* polysyllabic.
vielsprachig *a.* polyglot.
vielstimmig *a.* *(mus.)* polyphonic; for many voices; many-voiced.
vielverheissend *a.* promising.
Vielvölkerstaat *m.* multiethnic state.
Vielweiberei *f.* **(-, 0)** polygamy.
vier *a.* four; *auf allen ~en,* on all fours; *unter ~ Augen,* in private, between you and me.
Vier *f.* **(-, -en)** the number/figure/grade four.
vierbeinig *a.* four-footed, four-legged.
vierblättrig *a.* four-leaved.
Viereck *n.* **(-[e]s, -e)** square, quadrangle.
viereckig *a.* quadrangular, square.
viererlei *a.* of four sorts.
vierfach, vierfältig *a.* fourfold.
vierfüßig *a.* four-footed.
Vierfüßler *m.* **(-s, -)** quadruped.
vierhändig *a.* four-handed; *~ (Klavier) spielen* to play four-handed.
vierhundert *a.* four hundred.
vierjährig *a.* four years old.
Vierlinge *pl.* quadruplets.
Viermächte *pl.* quadripartite *a.*
viermal *adv.* four times; *~ so viel,* four times as much, four times the number.
viermalig *a.* repeated four times.
viermotorig *a.* four-engined(d).

Vierradbremse *f.* four-wheel brakes.
vierrädrig *a.* four-wheeled.
vierschrötig *a.* square-built, robust.
vierseitig *a.* four-sided; quadrilateral.
Viersitzer *m.* four-seater.
viersitzig *a.* four-seated.
vierspännig *a.* four-horse(d).
vierstimmig *a.* for four voices *or* parts.
vierteilen *v.t.* to quarter.
Viertel *n.* **(-s, -)** fourth part; quarter; (*Stadt*) quarter.
Vierteljahr *n.* quarter.
vierteljährig *a.* quarterly.
vierteljährlich *adv.* every three months, quarterly.
Vierteljahrsschrift *f.* quarterly (journal).
Viertel: ~note *f.* quarter note; **~stunde** *f.* quarter of an hour.
viertelstündlich *a.* every quarter of an hour.
viertens *adv.* fourthly, in the fourth place.
Viervierteltakt *m.* (*mus.*) common time.
vierzehn *a.* fourteen; ~ *Tage,* a fortnight; fourteen days.
vierzig *a.* forty.
Vierziger *m.* **(-s, -); Vierzigerin** *f.* **(-, -nen)** quadraganarian; forty-year-old.
Vietnam *n.* **(-s, 0)** Vietnam.
Vietnamese *m.* **(-n, -n); Vietnamesin** *f.* **(-, -nen); vietnamesisch** *a.* Vietnamese.
Vietnamkrieg *m.* Vietnam War.
Vikar *m.* **(-s, -e)** curate, assistant.
viktorianisch *a.* Victorian.
Viktualien *pl.* victuals, eatables *pl.*
Villa *f.* **(-, Villen)** villa; residence; country house.
Villenviertel *n.* residential area.
Viola *f.* **(-, -len)** viola.
violett *a.* purple; violet.
Violinbogen *m.* bow.
Violine *f.* **(-, -n)** violin.
Violinist *m.* **(-en, -en); Violinistin** *f.* **(-, -nen); Violinspieler** *m.;* **Violinspielerin** *f.* violinist.
Violin: ~konzert *n.* violin concerto; **~saite** *f.* string; **~schlüssel** *m.* treble-clef.
Violon *n.* **(-s, -s)** bass-viol.
Violoncello *n.* **(-[s], -cellos u. -celli)** cello, violoncello.
Viper *f.* **(-, -n)** viper.
Virtuose *m.* **(-n, -n); Virtuosin** *f.* **(-, -nen)** virtuoso.
Virtuosität *f.* **(-, -en)** virtuosity.
Virus *n.* /m. **(-, Viren)** virus.
Visier *n.* **(-[e]s, -e)** visor; (*am Gewehr*) back sight.
visieren *v.t.* to aim; to gauge.
Vision *f.* **(-, -en)** vision.
visionär *a.* visionary.
Visite *f.* **(-, -n)** doctor's round.
Visitenkarte *f.* (visiting)-card.
visuell *a.* visual.
Visum *n.* **(-s, Visa)** visa.
vital *a.* vital; energetic.
Vitalität *f.* vitality.
Vitamin *n.* **(-s, -e)** vitamin.
vitaminarm *a.* low in vitamins.
Vitaminmangel *m.* vitamin deficiency.
vitaminreich *a.* rich in vitamins.
Vitrine *f.* **(-, -n)** display case; glass cupboard.
Vize: vice...; **Vizekönig** *m.* viceroy.
v.J. *vorigen Jahres,* of last year.
v.M. *vorigen Monats,* of last month.
v.o. *von oben,* from the top.
Vogel *m.* **(-s, Vögel)** bird; (*Huhn*) fowl; *einen ~ haben,* (*fig.*) to have a screw loose; *den ~ abschiessen,* to carry off the prize.
Vogelbauer *m.* birdcage.
vogelfrei *a.* outlawed.
Vogel: ~haus *n.* aviary; **~kunde** *f.* ornithology; **~perspektive** *f.* bird's-eye view; **~schau** *f.* bird's-eye view; *aus der ~,* a bird's-eye view of; **~scheuche** *f.* scarecrow; **~warte** *f.* ornithological station.
Vöglein *n.* **(-s, -)** little bird.
Vogt *m.* **(-[e]s, Vögte)** steward; bailiff.
Vokabel *f.* **(-, -n)** word.
Vokal *m.* **(-[e]s, -e)** vowel.
Vokalmusik *f.* vocal music, singing.
Vokativ *m.* **(-s, -e)** vocative.
Volk *n.* **(-[e]s, Völker)** people, nation.
Völker: ~bund *m.* League of Nations; **~kunde** *f.* ethnology; **~mord** *m.* genocide; **~recht** *n.* international law.
völkerrechtlich *a.* relating to international law.
Völkerschaft *f.* **(-, -en)** tribe, people.
Völkerwanderung *f.* migration of nations.
volkreich *a.* populous.
Volks... ethnic *a.*
Volks: ~abstimmung *f.* plebiscite, referendum; **~bibliothek** *f.* public library; **~charakter** *m.* national character; **~entscheid** (*über*) *m.* referendum (on); **~fest** *n.* public festival; **~hochschule** *f.* adult education center; **~kunde** *f.* folklore; **~lied** *n.* popular song, folksong.
Volks: ~menge *f.* multitude, throng; **~partei** *f.* people's party; **~redner** *m.* popular speaker; **~schule** *f.* elementary school; **~schullehrer** *m.* elementary teacher; **~schulwesen** *n.* system of national education; **~stamm** *m.* tribe; **~tracht** *f.* national dress or costume.
Volkstum *n.* **(-s, 0)** nation(ality); national character.
volkstümlich *a.* popular; national.
Volks: ~unterricht *m.* public instruction; **~versammlung** *f.* public meeting; **~vertreter** *m.* representative of the people; **~vertretung** *f.* popular representation; national assembly, parliament; **~wirtschaft** *f.* national economy; economics.
volkswirtschaftlich *a.* economic.
Volkszählung *f.* census.
voll *a.* full; entire; (*vulg.*) drunk; *~ ausgeschrieben,* in full; *es war ~ im Theater,* the house was crowded; *nicht für ~ ansehen,* not to take seriously; *das Maß ~ machen,* to fill up the measure, to top it all; *um das Unglück ~ zumachen,* to make things worse; *~ pfropfen,* to cram, to stuff.
vollauf *adv.* completely; fully.
vollautomatisch *a.* fully automatic.
Vollbart *m.* beard.
Vollbesitz *m.* full possession.
Vollblut, Vollblutpferd *n.* thoroughbred (horse).
vollbringen *v.t.st.* to accomplish.
Volldampf *m.* full steam.
vollenden *v.t.* to finish; to accomplish.
vollendet *a.* perfect.
vollends *adv.* altogether, wholly; finally.
Vollendung *f.* **(-, 0)** completion, perfection.
Völlerei *f.* **(-, 0)** gluttony.
vollführen *v.t.* to execute, to accomplish.
Vollgefühl *n.* feeling of fullness.
Vollgehalt *m.* full or entire contents *pl.*
Vollgenuß *m.* full enjoyment.

vollgepfropft, vollgerüttelt *a.* crammed (with), chockfull.
vollgültig *a.* full value.
völlig *a.* entire, whole; ~ *adv.* fully.
volljährig *a.* of age.
Volljährigkeit *f.* **(-, 0)** majority.
vollkommen *a.* perfect; consummate.
Vollkommenheit *f.* **(-, -en)** perfection.
Vollkraft *f.* **(-, 0)** full vigour, energy.
Vollmacht *f.* **(-, -en)** full power; power of attorney; letter of attorney.
Vollmatrose *m.* able-bodied seaman.
Vollmilch *f.* whole milk.
Vollmond *m.* full moon.
Vollpension *f.* (full) board and lodging.
vollständig *a.* complete, full, integral; ~ *adv.* completely, in full.
Vollständigkeit *f.* completeness.
vollstreckbar *a.* executable; (*jur.*) enforceable.
vollstrecken *v.t.* to execute, to carry out.
Vollstreckung *f.* execution.
Vollstreckungsbefehl *m.* writ of execution.
volltanken *v.t.* to fill up.
volltönend *a.* sonorous, full-toned.
Volltreffer *m.* direct hit.
Vollversammlung *f.* general assembly.
vollwertig *a.* of full value.
Vollwertkost *f.* macrobiotic food.
vollzählig *a.* complete (in number).
vollziehen *v.t.st.* to execute; to carry out; to consummate (marriage); (*Testament*) to administer; *~de Gewalt,* executive (power).
Vollziehung *f.* **(-, -en), Vollzug** *m.* **(-[e]s, 0)** execution, consummation.
Volontär *m.* **(-s, -s); Volontärin** *f.* **(-, -nen)** unpaid trainee.
Volontariat *n.* **(-s, -e)** period of training; traineeship.
Volt *n.* **(-s, -)** volt.
Voltmeter *n.* **(-s, -)** volt-meter.
Volumen *n.* **(-s, -mina)** volume.
vom = von dem
von *pr.* of; from; by; upon; on; *~... an,* since, from... upwards (downwards, forward); *~... her,* from; *~ herab,* from; *~ selbst,* of itself, of its own accord, automatically.
voneinander *a.* from each other.
vonnöten *a.* necessary.
vonstatten gehen *v.i.* to proceed.
vor *pr.* before, in front of; above; prior to; since, ago; ~ *adv.* before; *nach wie ~,* now as before; *~ allem,* above all; *vor 8 Tagen,* a week ago; *10 Minuten vor 8 Uhr,* ten minutes to eight; *Gnade ~ Recht ergehen lassen,* to let mercy overrule justice.
vorab *adv.* beforehand.
Vorabend *m.* eve.
Vorahnung *f.* premonition; presentiment.
voran *adv.* before, in front; on, ahead.
vorangehen *v.i. (s)* to go before, to lead the way; to precede; *mit gutem Beispiel ~,* to lead by example.
Vorankündigung *f.* advance announcement.
Voranschlag *m.* previous estimate.
Vorarbeit *f.* preliminary work.
vorarbeiten *v.i.* to prepare the ground (for).
Vorarbeiter *m.* foreman.
voraus *adv.* before; beforehand, in advance; ahead of; *im (zum) ~,* beforehand, in anticipation.
vorausahnen *v.t.* to anticipate.
vorausbestellbar *a.* bookable in advance.
vorausbestellen *v.t.* to order in advance.
Vorausbestellung *f.* booking.
vorausbezahlen *v.t.* to pay in advance, to prepay.
vorauseilen *v.i.* to hurry on in advance.
vorausgehen *v.t.st.* to lead the way.
voraushaben *v.t.st.* to have an advantage over; to have in advance.
vorausnehmen *v.t.st.* to anticipate.
voraussagen *v.t.* to foretell, to predict.
vorausschicken *v.t.* to send before *or* in advance; (*fig.*) to premise.
voraussehen *v.t.st.* to foresee.
voraussetzen *v.t.* to suppose, to presuppose, to presume; to take for granted.
Voraussetzung *f.* **(-, -en)** prerequisite; supposition; *unter der ~ daß,* on the understanding that.
Voraussicht *f.* foresight, prudence.
voraussichtlich *a.* prospective; ~ *adv.* probably, presumably.
Vorauszahlung *f.* advance payment.
Vorbau *m.* **(-s, -ten)** porch; front part.
vorbauen *v.i.* (*fig.*) to prevent, to preclude, to guard against.
vorbedacht *a.* premeditated.
Vorbedacht *m.* **(-[e]s, 0)** premeditation; *mit ~,* intentionally; deliberately.
Vorbedeutung *f.* omen, portent.
Vorbedingung *f.* **(-, -en)** precondition.
Vorbehalt *m.* **(-[e]s, -e)** reservation; *unter ~,* with the proviso that.
vorbehalten *v.t.st.* to reserve; *alle Rechte ~,* all rights reserved; ~ *v.r.* to reserve to oneself.
vorbehaltlich *a.* conditional; ~ *pr. & adv.* with the proviso that (of), subject to.
vorbehaltlos *a.* unreserved.
vorbehandeln *v.t.* to pretreat.
vorbei *adv.* by, past; over; finished.
vorbeifahren *v.t.st.* to drive past.
vorbeigehen *v.i.st. (s)* to pass by.
vorbeilassen *v.t.st.* to let pass.
vorbeischießen *v.t.st.* to miss (one's mark); (*s*) to shoot past, to rush past.
vorbelastet *a.* handicapped.
Vorbemerkung *f.* preliminary remark.
vorbereiten *v.t.* to prepare.
vorbereitend *a.* preparatory.
Vorbereitung *f.* **(-, -en)** preparation.
Vorbesitzer *m.*; **Vorbesitzerin** *f.* previous owner.
vorbestellen *v.t.* to order in advance.
Vorbestellung *f.* **(-, -en)** reservation.
vorbestraft *a.* previously convicted; *nicht ~,* no criminal record; *nicht ~er Verbrecher,* first offender.
vorbeten *v.t. & i.* to lead prayers.
vorbeugen *v.i.* (*fig.*) to prevent, to preclude, to guard against; ~ *v.r.* to bend forward.
Vorbeugung *f.* prevention, preventing.
Vorbild *n.* model, standard; (proto-)type.
vorbildlich *a.* exemplary; model.
Vorbildung *f.* **(-, 0)** previous training.
Vorbote *m.* harbinger; forerunner.
vorbringen *v.t.ir.* to bring forward, to advance; to utter.
vorchristlich *a.* pre-Christian.
Vordach *n.* canopy.
vordatieren *v.t.* to antedate.

vordem *adv.* formerly.
vordemonstrieren *v.t.* to demonstrate.
vorder *a.* anterior, fore-, front-.
Vorderachse *f.* front axle.
Vorderansicht *f.* front view.
Vorderarm *m.* forearm.
Vorderfuß *m.* forefoot.
Vordergebäude *n.* front building.
Vordergrund *m.* foreground.
vorderhand *adv.* for the present.
Vordermann *m.* man in front.
Vorderrad *n.* front wheel; **~antrieb** *m.* front-wheel drive.
Vorderseite *f.* front (face).
Vordersitz *m.* front seat.
vorderst *a.* foremost.
Vorderteil *n.* forepart.
Vordertür *f.* front door.
vordrängen *v.t.v.r.* to press or push forward.
vordringen *v.i.st. (s)* to advance.
vordringlich *a.* urgent.
Vordruck *m.* printed form.
vorehelich *a.* premarital.
voreilig *a.* hasty, forward, rash.
voreinander *adv.* one in front of the other.
voreingenommen *a.* prejudiced, biased.
Voreingenommenheit *f.* **(-, 0)** bias.
vorenthalten *v.t.st.* to withhold (from).
Vorentscheidung *f.* preliminary decision.
vorerst *adv.* for the time being.
vorerwähnt *a.* aforementioned.
Vorfahr[e] *m.* **(-s & -en, -en)** ancestor.
vorfahren *v.i.st. (s)* to drive up to a house; (*Verkehr*) to pass; to move foreward.
Vorfahrt *f.* priority; right of way.
Vorfall *m.* occurrence, incident; (*med.*) prolapse.
vorfallen *v.i.st. (s)* to occur, to happen.
vorfinden *v.t.st.* to find, to meet with.
Vorfrage *f.* preliminary question.
Vorfreude *f.* anticipated joy.
Vorfrühling *m.* early spring.
vorfühlen *v.t.* to sound out.
vorführen *v.t.* to show; to present; to perform.
Vorführraum *m.* (*Lichtbilder, etc.*) projection room.
Vorführung *f.* **(-, -en)** performance; presentation; demonstration; ~ *vor Gericht,* arraignment.
Vorführwagen *n.* demonstration car.
Vorgabe *f.* **(-, -en)** handicap.
Vorgang *m.* occurrence, incident.
Vorgänger *m.* **(-s, 0); Vorgängerin** *f.* **(-, -nen)** predecessor.
Vorgarten *m.* front garden.
vorgaukeln *v.t. einem etwas* ~, to deceive s.o.
vorgeben *v.t.st.* to pretend.
Vorgebirge *n.* foothills.
vorgeburtlich *a.* prenatal.
vorgefaßt *a.* preconceived.
vorgefertigt *a.* prefabricated.
Vorgefühl *n.* presentiment, misgiving.
vorgehen *v.i.st. (s)* to go before; (*Uhr*) to be fast; to proceed, to act; to occur, to happen.
Vorgehen *n.* proceedings *pl.*
vorgenannt *a.* aforementioned.
Vorgeschichte *f.* prehistory.
vorgeschichtlich *a.* prehistoric.
Vorgeschmack *m.* foretaste.
Vorgesetzte *m./f.* **(-n, -n)** superior.
vorgesetzte Stelle *or* **Behörde** *f.* superior authority, headquarters.
vorgestern *adv.* the day before yesterday.
vorgreifen *v.t.st.* to anticipate.
Vorgriff *m. im* ~ *auf,* in anticipation of.
vorhaben *v.t.ir.* to intend, to plan.
Vorhaben *n.* **(-s, -)** design, intention.
Vorhalle *f.* entrance hall.
vorhalten *v.t.st.* to reproach, to rebuke; ~ *v.i.* to last, to hold out.
Vorhaltung *f.* reproach.
Vorhand *f.* forehand.
vorhanden *a.* at hand; on hand, in stock; ~ *sein,* to exist; to be at hand.
Vorhang *m.* **(-[e]s, -hänge)** curtain; *den* ~ *zuziehen,* to draw the curtain.
Vorhängeschloß *n.* padlock.
Vorhangstange *f.* curtain rod.
Vorhaut *f.* foreskin, prepuce.
vorher *adv.* before(hand), previously.
vorherbestimmen *v.t.* to predestine; to predetermine.
Vorherbestimmung *f.* predestination.
vorhergehen *v.i.st. (s)* to go before, to precede.
vorhergehend *a.* preceding, previous.
vorherig *a.* prior; preceding.
Vorherrschaft *f.* supremacy; dominance.
vorherrschen *v.i.* to predominate.
Vorhersage *f.* prediction; forecast.
vorhersagen *v.t.* to forecast, to predict.
vorhersehen *v.t.st.* to foresee.
vorhin *adv.* before; a short time ago.
Vorhof *m.* (outer-)court, entry.
Vorhut *f.* **(-, 0)** vanguard.
vorig *a.* former, preceding, last; ~*e Woche,* last week.
Vorjahr *n.* preceding year.
vorjährig *a.* of last year.
Vorkämpfer *m.* pioneer.
vorkauen *v.t.* (*fig.*) to repeat over and over again.
Vorkaufsrecht *n.* first refusal.
Vorkehrung *f.* **(-, -en)** preventive measure, precaution; preparation; ~*en treffen,* to make provisions.
Vorkenntnisse *f.pl.* preliminary knowledge.
vorklassisch *a.* pre-classical.
vorkommen *v.i.st. (s)* to occur, to happen; to seem, to appear.
Vorkommen *n.* **(-s, -)** occurrence; deposit.
Vorkommnis *n.* **(-nisses, -nisse)** occurrence; incident.
Vorkriegs.. .pre-war.
vorladen *v.t.st.* to cite, to summon.
Vorladung *f.* citation, summons.
Vorladungsschreiben *n.* writ of summons, subpoena.
Vorlage *f.* draft, bill; model, pattern (for drawing *or* writing).
Vorläufer *m.* forerunner, precursor.
vorläufig *a.* provisional, preliminary; temporary.
vorlaut *a.* pert, forward.
Vorleben *n.* **(-s, -)** former life; *gutes, schlechtes* ~, good, bad record.
Vorlegemesser *n.* carving knife.
vorlegen *v.t.* to present; to produce, to exhibit; to propose, to submit (a plan).
Vorleger *m.* **(-s, -)** mat; rug.
Vorlegeschloß *n.* padlock.
vorlesen *v.t.st.* to read (to); to read aloud.

Vorlesung *f.* **(-, -en)** lecture; course of lectures; **~en halten,** to lecture.
Vorlesungsraum *m.* lecture room.
Vorlesungsverzeichnis *f.* course catalogue.
vorletzt *a.* last but one, penultimate.
vorleuchten *v.i.* to shine before.
Vorliebe *f.* predilection.
vorliebnehmen *v.i.* to put up with.
vorliegen *v.t.st.* to lie before.
vorliegend *a.* in question; present.
vorlügen *v.t.st.* (*einem etwas*) to tell lies *or* stories (to sb.).
Vorm. *Vormittag,* forenoon, A.M.
vormachen *v.t.* to demonstrate; *einem etwas oder blauen Dunst ~*, to deceive someone.
Vormacht *f.* leading power; supremacy.
Vormachtstellung *f.* position of supremacy.
vormalig *a.* former.
vormals *adv.* formerly, heretofore.
Vormarsch *m.* advance.
vormerken *v.t.* to book.
vormilitärisch *a.* premilitary.
Vormittag *m.* morning.
vormittägig *a.* in the morning.
vormittags *adv.* in the morning; a.m. (*ante meridiem*)
Vormund *m.* **(-[e]s, -e & -münder)** guardian.
Vormundschaft *f.* guardianship; *unter ~ stellen,* to place under the care of a guardian.
vormundschaftlich *a.* custodial.
Vormundschaftsgericht *n.* Surrogate Court.
vorn *adv.* before, in front; (*nav.*) fore; *von ~*, facing, head...; from the beginning over again, anew; *von ~ herein,* from the first.
Vorname *m.* Christian name, first name.
vornehm *a.* distinguished.
vornehmen *v.t.st.* to take in hand; to examine; ~ *v.r.* to resolve on, to intend.
Vornehmen *n.* **(-s, 0)** intention.
Vornehmheit *f.* **(-, 0)** rank, distinction.
vornehmlich *adv.* chiefly, principally.
Vorort *m.* suburb.
Vorortszug *m.* commuter train.
Vorplatz *m.* forecourt; hall; vestibule.
Vorposten *m.* outpost.
vorpredigen *v.t.* to preach to.
vorpreschen *v.i.* (*fig.*) to rush ahead.
Vorprogramm *n.* supporting program.
vorprogrammieren *v.t.* to preprogram.
Vorprüfung *f.* preliminary examination.
Vorrang *m.* **(-s, 0)** precedence, priority.
vorrangig *a.* priority.
Vorrat *m.* **(-[e]s, -räte)** store, stock, provision, supply; stockpile; (*Erz*) resources.
vorrätig *a.* in stock, on hand.
Vorratskammer *f.* pantry; larder.
Vorraum *m.* anteroom.
vorrechnen *v.t.* to calculate s.th. (for demonstration).
Vorrecht *n.* prerogative, privilege.
Vorrede *f.* preface, foreword; prologue.
Vorredner *m.*; **Vorrednerin** *f.* previous speaker.
Vorrichtung *f.* **(-, -en)** device.
vorrücken *v.t.* to advance; ~ *v.i. (s)* to march on, to advance.
Vorrücken *n.* **(-s, 0)** advance.
Vorruhestand *m.* early retirement.
Vorrunde *f.* qualifying round.
Vors. *Vorsitzende(r),* chairperson.
vorsagen *v.t.* to prompt; to tell sb. the answer.
Vorsaison *f.* early season.
Vorsänger *m.*; **Vorsängerin** *f.* leader of a choir.
Vorsatz *m.* **(-es, -sätze)** purpose, design, intention; *mit ~*, intentionally, on purpose.
vorsätzlich *a.* premediated, wilful; ~ *adv.* on purpose.
Vorschau *f.* **(-, -en)** preview.
Vorschein *m.* *zum ~ kommen,* to come forth, to appear.
vorschicken *v.t.* to send forward.
vorschieben *v.t.st.* to shove *or* push forward; to plead as an excuse; to slip (a bolt).
vorschießen *v.t.st.* to advance (money).
Vorschlag *m.* proposal, offer.
vorschlagen *v.t.st.* to propose.
Vorschlaghammer *m.* sledgehammer.
vorschnell *a.* precipitate, hasty, rash.
vorschreiben *v.t.st.* to prescribe.
Vorschrift *f.* direction, instruction.
vorschriftsmäßig *a.* according to rule; regulation; *~es Verfahren, n.* (*mil.*) standard operating procedure (SOP).
Vorschub *m.* **(-[e]s, 0) ~ leisten,** to promote; to support.
Vorschule *f.* kindergarten; preschool.
Vorschuß *m.* payment in advance.
vorschützen *v.t.* (*fig.*) to pretend.
vorschweben *v.i.* to be on one's mind.
vorsehen *v.r.st.* to take care, to guard (against).
Vorsehung *f.* **(-, 0)** Providence.
vorsetzen *v.t.* to put before.
Vorsicht *f.* **(-, 0)** caution; **~!** (*auf Kisten*) with care!
vorsichthalber *adv.* as a precaution.
vorsichtig *a.* cautious, careful; *~e Schätzung,* conservative estimate.
Vorsichtsmaßnahme *f.* precaution; *~n treffen,* to take precautions.
Vorsilbe *f.* prefix.
vorsingen *v.t.st.* to sing to; to audition.
vorsintflutlich *a.* antediluvian.
Vorsitz *m.* **(-es, 0)** chair, chairmanship; *den ~ führen,* to be in the chair.
vorsitzen *v.t.st.* to be in the chair.
Vorsitzender *m.* chairman; *stellvertretender ~*, vice-chairman.
Vorsorge *f.* foresight; precaution; **~untersuchung** *f.* (preventive) medical checkup.
vorsorgen *v.i.* to make provisions.
vorsorglich *a.* careful; provident.
Vorspann *m.* opening credits (film, TV).
Vorspeise *f.* hors d'oeuvre.
vorspiegeln *v.t.* to make a false show of.
Vorspiegelung *f.* **(-, -en)** pretence; *~ falscher Tatsachen,* false pretences.
Vorspiel *n.* prelude; prologue; foreplay.
vorspielen *v.t.* to play to; to audition (theater).
vorsprechen *v.t.st.* to call on; to audition (theater).
vorspringen *v.i.st. (s)* to project.
Vorsprung *m.* **(-[e]s, -sprünge)** advantage, start, lead.
Vorstadt *f.* suburb.
vorstädtisch *a.* suburban.
Vorstand *m.* **(-[e]s, -stände)** (*Firma*) executive committee *or* board, management; (*Krankenhaus, etc.*) governing body; principal, head.
Vorstandsmitglied *n.* board member.
Vorstandssitzung *f.* board meeting.
vorstehen *v.t.st.* to preside over.

vorstehend *a.* preceding; ~ *adv.* above.
Vorsteher *m.* **(-s, -)**, **Vorsteherin** *f.* **(-, -nen)** head; chairman.
Vorsteherdrüse *f.* prostate (gland).
vorstellbar *a.* imaginable.
vorstellen *v.t.* to introduce; to represent; to act; (*eine Uhr*) to put forward; ~ *v.r.* to imagine.
Vorstellung *f.* **(-, -en)** introduction, presentation; performance; conception, idea; expostulation.
Vorstellungs: ~gespräch *n.* (job) interview; **~kraft** *f.*, **~vermögen** *n.* power of imagination.
Vorstoß *m.* advance.
vorstoßen *v.t.st.* to push forward.
Vorstrafe *f.* previous conviction.
Vorstrafenregister *n.* criminal records.
vorstrecken *v.t.* to stretch forward, to thrust *or* poke out; (*fig.*) to advance, to lend (money).
Vorstufe *f.* preliminary stage.
Vortag *n.* day before.
vortanzen *v.t.* to demonstrate; ~ *v.i.* to audition (ballet).
vortäuschen *v.t.* to feign.
Vorteil *m.* **(-[e]s, -e)** advantage, profit.
vorteilhaft *a.* advantageous, profitable.
Vortrag *m.* **(-[e]s, -träge)** elocution; recitation; lecture; (*Musik*) recital; (*com.*) balance carried forward; *einen ~ halten,* to deliver a lecture, to read a paper.
vortragen *v.t.st.* to carry forward; to recite; to declaim; to lecture (on), to deliver (a speech); (*mus.*) to execute.
Vortragende *m./f.* speaker; lecturer.
Vortragskunst *f.* elocution.
Vortragsreihe *f.* series of lectures/talks.
Vortragsreise *f.* lecture tour.
vortrefflich *a.* excellent, superior.
vortreten *v.i.st. (s)* to step forward.
Vortritt *m.* **(-[e]s, 0)** precedence.
vorüber *adv.* by; past, over, finished.
vorübergehen *v.t.st.* (s) to pass by.
vorübergehend *a.* transitory, temporary.
Vorübergehende *m./f.* passerby.
Vorübung *f.* preliminary exercise.
Voruntersuchung *f.* preliminary examination.
Vorurteil *n.* prejudice.
vorurteilslos *a.* unprejudiced.
Vorvergangenheit *f.* past perfect; pluperfect.
Vorverhör *n.* preliminary examination.
Vorverkauf *m.* (*theat.*) booking in advance; advance sale.
vorverlegen *v.t.* to move up (appointment).
Vorwahl *f.* preliminary election; primary; area code.
Vorwand *m.* **(-[e]s, -wände)** pretence, pretext.
vorwärmen *v.t.* to preheat.
vorwärts *adv.* ahead, forward(s), on; *~ marsch!* forward march!; *~ kommen,* to get on, to make one's way.
Vorwäsche *f.* prewash.
vorweg *adv.* before(hand).
vorwegnehmen *v.t.st.* to anticipate.
vorweisen *v.t.st.* to produce.
vorwerfen *v.t.st.* (*einem etwas*) to accuse sb. of sth.; to reproach with.
vorwiegen *v.i.* to prevail.
Vorwissen *n.* **(-s, 0)** preliminary knowledge.
vorwitzig *a.* impertinent; prying.
Vorwort *n.* **(-[e]s, -wörter)** foreword, preface.
Vorwurf *m.* **(-[e]s, -würfe)** reproach; accusation.
vorwurfsfrei, vorwurfslos *a.* irreproachable.
vorwurfsvoll *a.* reproachful.
Vorzeichen *n.* omen, token, portent; (*mus.*) signature; (*math.*) sign.
vorzeichnen *v.t.* to trace out, to sketch (a plan).
vorzeigen *v.t.* to produce; to show.
Vorzeit *f.* **(-, 0)** prehistory.
vorzeitig *a.* premature; precocious.
vorziehen *v.t.st.* to prefer.
Vorzimmer *n.* anteroom, antechamber.
Vorzug *m.* preference; advantage, privilege.
vorzüglich *a.* superior, excellent, exquisite; ~ *adv.* chiefly, especially.
Vorzüglichkeit *f.* **(-, -en)** superiority, excellence.
Vorzugs... preferential *a.*
Vorzugsaktie *f.* preferred stock.
Vorzugsbehandlung *f.* preferential treatment.
Vorzugstarif *m.* preference.
vorzugsweise *adv.* preferably.
votieren *v.t. & i.* to vote.
Votum *n.* **(-[s], -ta & -ten)** vote, suffrage.
VP *Vollpension,* full board.
v.T. *vom Tausend,* per thousand.
v.u. *von unten,* from the bottom.
vulgär *a.* vulgar.
Vulkan *m.* **(-[e]s, -e)** volcano.
vulkanisch *a.* volcanic.
vulkanisieren *v.t.* to vulcanize.

W

W, w *n.* the letter W or w.
W *West(en),* west, W; *Watt,* watt, w.
w. *wenden,* turn over, T.O.
WAA *Wiederaufbereitungsanlage,* reprocessing plant.
Waage *f.* **(-, -n)** scales; balance.
waagerecht *a.* horizontal.
Waagschale *f.* **(-, -n)** scale; *in die ~ werfen,* to bring sth. to bear.
wabbeln *v.i.* to wobble.
wabb(e)lig *a.* flabby.
Wabe *f.* **(-, -n)** honeycomb.
wach *a.* awake, alert.
Wachablösung *f.* changing of the guard; (*fig.*) transfer of power.
Wachdienst *m.* guard duty.
Wache *f.* **(-, -en)** guard, watch; guard room; sentry; *auf ~ sein,* to be on guard.
wachen *v.i.* to be awake; to watch over.
wachhabend *a.* on duty, on guard.
wachhalten *v.t.* (*fig.*) to keep alive.
Wachhund *m.* watchdog.
Wacholder *m.* **(-s, -)** juniper.
Wacholderbranntwein *m.* gin.
Wachs *n.* **(-es, -e)** wax.
wachsam *a.* watchful, vigilant.
Wachsamkeit *f.* vigilance.
wachsen *v.i.st.* to grow; *einem gewachsen sein,* to be a match for someone; *einer Sache gewachsen sein,* to be equal to a task; ~ *v.t.* to wax.
wächsern *a.* waxen, made of wax.
Wachsfigurenkabinett *n.* waxworks *pl.*

Wachsleinwand *f.* oil cloth.
Wachstuch *m.* oil cloth.
Wachstum *n.* **(-[e]s, 0)** growth; increase.
wachstums: **~fördernd** *a.* growth-inducing; **~hemmend** *a.* growth-retarding.
Wacht *f.* **(-, -en)** guard, watch.
Wachtel *f.* **(-, -n)** quail.
Wächter *m.* **(-s, -)** watchman; keeper.
Wachtposten *m.* post, sentinel, sentry.
wack(e)lig *a.* shaky, rickety, tottering.
wackeln *v.i.* to wobble, to totter.
wacker *a.* stout, gallant, brave, valiant.
Wade *f.* **(-, -en)** calf (of the leg).
Waffe *f.* **(-, -n)** weapon; arm.
Waffel *f.* **(-, -n)** waffle, wafer.
Waffeleisen *n.* waffle iron.
Waffenbesitz *m.* possession of firearms.
Waffenfabrik *f.* arms factory.
Waffengattung *f.* branch of the service.
Waffengewalt *f.* *mit ~*, by force of arms.
Waffenhandel *m.* arms trade.
Waffenkammer *f.* armory.
waffenlos *a.* unarmed.
Waffenruhe *f.* ceasefire.
Waffenschein *m.* gun license.
Waffenschmied *m.* armorer.
Waffenschmuggel *m.* gunrunning.
Waffenstillstand *m.* armistice; ceasefire; truce.
wägbar *a.* ponderable.
Wagehals *m.* daredevil.
wagen *v.t.* to venture, to dare, to risk; *sich ~*, to venture.
Wagen *m.* **(-s, -)** vehicle; car; (*Last~*) wagon, cart, carriage, coach.
wägen *v.t.st.* to weigh.
Wagen: **~heber** *m.* jack; **~ladung** *f.* truckload, wagonload; **~pflege** *f.* car maintenance; **~typ** *m.* model.
Waggon *m.* **(-s, -s)** railway-carriage; (*Güter~*) truck, van.
waghalsig *a.* foolhardy, rash.
Wagnis *n.* **(-nisses, -nisse)** venture.
Wahl *f.* **(-, -en)** choice, selection, option; (*politisch*) election.
wählbar *a.* eligible.
Wählbarkeit *f.* **(-, 0)** eligibility.
wahlberechtigt *a.* entitled to vote.
Wahlbeteiligung *f.* (voter) turnout.
Wahlbezirk *m.* electoral district.
wählen *v.t.* to choose; to select; (*politisch*) to elect; ~ *v.i.* (*politisch*) to vote; (*Telephon*) to dial.
Wähler *m.* **(-s, -)**; **Wählerin** *f.* **(-, -nen)** voter, constituent, elector.
Wahlergebnis *n.* election returns or result.
wählerisch *a.* particular, fastidious.
Wählerschaft *f.* **(-, 0)** electorate; constituency.
wahlfähig *a.* eligible; entitled to vote.
wahlfrei *a.* optional.
Wahlgang *f.* ballot.
Wahlheimat *f.* adopted country.
Wahlkampf *m.* election campaign.
Wahlkreis *m.* constituency.
Wahllokal *n.* polling station.
Wahlrecht *n.* right to vote, franchise; (*allgemeines*) universal suffrage.
Wählscheide *f.* dial.
Wahlspruch *m.* motto.
Wahlurne *f.* ballot box.
Wahlzettel *m.* paper ballot.
Wahn *m.* **(-[e]s, 0)** illusion, error.
Wahnbild *n.* phantasm, delusion.
wähnen *v.t.* to imagine.
Wahnsinn *m.* **(-, 0)** insanity, madness, frenzy.
wahnsinnig *a.* insane, mad, frantic.
Wahnsinnige *m./f.* maniac; madman, madwoman; lunatic.
wahnwitzig *a.* insane, mad, frantic.
wahr *a.* true; real; genuine; *so ~ ich lebe!* as sure as I live!; *~ machen*, to bear out; to prove, to fulfil; *nicht ~?* isn't it? don't you think so?
wahren *v.t.* to guard; *das Gesicht ~*, to save face.
währen *v.i.* to last.
während *pr.* during; ~ *c.* while.
währenddessen *adv.* in the meantime; meanwhile.
wahrhaft *a.* true, veracious, truthful, real.
wahrhaftig *a.* genuine; ~ *adv.* truly.
Wahrhaftigkeit *f.* **(-, 0)** veracity.
Wahrheit *f.* **(-, -en)** truth; *einem die ~ sagen*, to tell sb. off.
wahrheitsgemäß *a.* veracious.
wahrheitsgetreu *a.* truthful.
Wahrheitsliebe *f.* love of truth.
wahrlich *adv.* truly, verily.
wahrnehmbar *a.* perceptible.
wahrnehmen *v.t.st.* to perceive, to observe.
Wahrnehmung *f.* **(-, -en)** perception, observation; care (of).
wahrsagen *v.i.* to tell fortunes.
Wahrsager *m.* **(-s, -)**; **Wahrsagerin** *f.* **(-, -nen)** fortuneteller, soothsayer.
wahrscheinlich *a.* likely, probable.
Wahrscheinlichkeit *f.* **(-, -en)** likelihood, probability.
Wahrung *f.* **(-, 0)** preservation; maintenance.
Währung *f.* **(-, -en)** currency.
Währungsausgleichfonds *m.* exchange stabilization fund.
Wahrzeichen *n.* symbol; landmark (city).
Waise *f.* **(-, -n)** orphan.
Waisenhaus *n.* orphanage.
Wal *m.* **(-[e]s, -e)** whale.
Wald *m.* **(-[e]s, Wälder)** wood, forest.
Waldarbeiter *m.* forestry worker.
Waldbrand *m.* forest fire.
Waldgebiet *n.* wooded area, woodland.
Waldgegend *f.* wooded area, woodland.
Waldhorn *n.* French horn.
waldig *a.* wooded, woody.
Waldmeister *m.* (*bot.*) woodruff.
waldreich *a.* wooded.
Waldsterben *n.* dying of the forest.
Waldung *f.* **(-, -en)** woodland; forest.
Waldweg *m.* forest path.
Walfang *m.* whaling.
Walfänger *m.* **(-s, -)** whaler.
Walfisch *m.* whale.
Waliser *m.* **(-s, -)** Welshman.
Waliserin *f.* **(-, -nen)** Welshwoman.
walisisch *a.* Welsh.
Walküre *f.* **(-, -n)** Valkyrie.
Wall *m.* **(-[e]s, Wälle)** rampart; mound.
Wallach *m.* **(-[e]s, -e)** gelding.
wallen *v.i.* to boil (up), to bubble.
wallfahren *v.i.* *(s)* to go on a pilgrimage.
Wallfahrer *m.* **(-s. -)** pilgrim.
Wallfahrt *f.* pilgrimage.
Wallung *f.* **(-, -en)** ebullition; agitation.
Walnuß *f.* walnut.

Walroß *n.* **(-rosses, -rosse)** walrus.
walten *v.i.* to rule, to manage; *seines Amtes* ~, to perform the duties of one's office, to officiate.
Walze *f.* **(-, -n)** roller, cylinder; (*Schreib-*) platen.
walzen *v.t.* to roll; ~ *v.i.* to waltz.
wälzen *v.i.* to roll, to turn about; ~ *v.r.* to wallow, to welter.
walzenförmig *a.* cylindrical.
Walzer *m.* **(-s, -)** waltz.
Walzwerk *n.* rolling mill.
Wampe *f.* **(-, -n)** (*fam.*) pot belly.
Wand *f.* **(-, Wände)** wall, partition; *spanische* ~, folding screen.
Wandalismus *m.* vandalism.
Wandehalle *f.* lobby.
Wandel *m.* **(-s, 0)** change, mutation.
wandelbar *a.* variable.
wandeln *v.r.* to change; ~ *v.i.* to stroll.
Wanderausstellung *f.* touring exhibition.
Wanderbühne *f.* touring company.
Wanderer *m.* **(-s, -)**; **Wanderin** *f.* **(-, -nen)** hiker.
Wandergewerbe *f.* itinerant trade.
Wanderheuschrecke *f.* migratory locust.
wandern *v.t.* (s) to wander, to hike; to ramble.
Wanderpokal *m.* challenge cup.
Wanderschaft *f.* **(-, 0)** *auf der* ~ *sein,* to be traveling.
Wanderung *f.* **(-, -n)** walking tour.
Wanderweg *m.* footpath.
Wandgemälde *n.* wall-painting, mural.
Wandkarte *f.* wall-map.
Wandlung *f.* **(-, -en)** change; (*Religion*) transubstantiation.
wandlungsfähig *a.* flexible; versatile.
Wandschirm *m.* folding screen.
Wandtafel *f.* blackboard.
Wanduhr *f.* clock.
Wange *f.* **(-, -n)** cheek.
Wankelmut *m.* fickleness.
wankelmütig *a.* fickle, inconstant.
wanken *v.i.* to totter, to stagger; to waver.
wann *adv.* when; *dann und* ~, now and then, occasionally.
Wanne *f.* **(-, -en)** bathtub; tub.
Wanst *m.* **(-es, Wänste)** belly, paunch.
Wanze *f.* **(-, -n)** bug, bedbug.
Wappen *m.* **(-s, -)** (coat of) arms.
wappnen *v.t.* to arm.
Ware *f.* **(-, -n)** merchandise, ware, goods *pl.*, commodity.
Waren: ~haus *n.* department store; **~lager** *n.* warehouse, stock-in-trade; **~probe** *f.* sample; **~sendung** *f.* shipment, consignment; **~zeichen** *n.* trademark.
warm *a.* warm; hot.
warmblütig *a.* warm-blooded.
Wärme *f.* warmth, heat; *Blutwärme, Körperwärme, etc.*, blood heat, body heat.
wärmebeständig *a.* heat-resistant.
Warme: ~dämmung *f.* heat insulation; **~kraftwerk** *n.* thermoelectric powerplant; **~lehre** *f.* thermodynamics.
wärmen *v.t.* to warm, to heat.
Wärmepumpe *f.* heat pump.
wärmesicher *a.* heatproof.
Wärmflasche *f.* hot-water bottle.
warmherzig *a.* warm hearted.
Warnanlage *f.* warning device.
warnen *v.t.* to warn.
Warn: ~schild *n.* warning sign; **~schuß** *m.* warning shot; **~signal** *n.* warning signal; **~streik** *m.* token strike.
Warnung *f.* **(-, -en)** warning, caution.
Warnzeichen *n.* warning sign.
Warte *f.* **(-, -en)** watchtower; observatory.
Warteliste *f.* waiting list.
warten *v.t.* to tend, to nurse; ~ *v.i.* to wait, to stay; to attend to; ~ *lassen,* to keep waiting.
Wärter *m.* **(-s. -)** attendant; keeper.
Wärterin *f.* **(-, -nen)** nurse; attendant.
Warte: ~saal *m.* waiting room (at a station); **~zimmer** *n.* (physician's) waiting room.
Wartung *f.* **(-, -en)** service; attendance; (*Wagen*) maintenance.
warum *adv.* why.
Warze *f.* **(-, -n)** wart; *Brust*~, nipple.
was *pn.* what; which; something; ~ *immer,* whatever; ~ *für ein,* what (kind of).
Waschanstalt *f.* laundry.
waschbar *a.* washable.
Waschbär *m.* racoon.
Waschbecken *n.* wash-(*or* hand)basin.
Wäsche *f.* **(-, -n)** washing, linen; laundry; *schmutzige* ~, soiled, dirty linen.
waschecht *a.* fast (colors); (*fig.*) genuine.
Wäscheklammer *f.* clothes-pin.
Wäschekorb *m.* linen basket.
Wäscheleine *f.* clothesline.
waschen *v.t. & i.* to wash; to launder; ~*v.r.* to wash oneself.
Wäscherei *f.* **(-, -en)** laundry.
Wäscheschleuder *f.* spin drier.
Wäscheständer *m.* drying rack.
Wäschetrockner *m.* drier.
Waschgelegenheit *f.* washing facilities.
Waschlappen *m.* flannel, washcloth.
Waschmaschine *f.* washing machine.
Waschmittel *n.* detergent.
Waschsalon *m.* laundromat.
Waschseife *f.* laundry soap.
Waschstraße *f.* car wash.
Waschtag *m.* washday.
Waschtisch *m.* washing-stand.
Wasser *n.* **(-s, -)** water; ~*abschlagen,* to make water; *fliessendes* ~, running water; *unter* ~ *setzen,* to submerge, to flood; *zu* ~ *und zu Lande,* by sea and land.
wasserabstoßend *a.* water-repellent.
wasserarm *a.* dry, arid.
Wasseraufbereitungsanlage *f.* water treatment plant.
Wasserball *m.* beach ball; water polo ball.
wasserblau *a.* marine-blue, light-blue.
Wasserdampf *m.* steam.
wasserdicht *a.* waterproof, tight.
Wasserdruck *m.* hydraulic pressure.
Wasserfahrzeug *n.* watercraft; vessel.
Wasserfall *m.* waterfall, cataract, cascade.
Wasserfarbe *f.* watercolor.
Wasserglas *n.* water glass.
Wassergraben *m.* ditch, moat.
Wasserhahn *m.* faucet.
wäss(e)rig *a.* watery; (*fig.*) insipid, flat.
Wasserkessel *m.* kettle.
Wasserkopf *m.* hydrocephalus.
Wasserkraft *f.* water power; **~werk** *n.* hydroelectric station.
Wasserleitung *f.* water pipe; watermain.
Wassermann *m.* (*als Sternbild*) Aquarius.
Wassermelone *f.* melon.

wässern *v.t.* to water, to irrigate.
Wasserpflanze *f.* aquatic plant.
wasserreich *a.* abounding in water.
Wasser: ~röhre *f.* water pipe; **~scheide** *f.* watershed.
Wasserschaden *m.* water damage.
wasserscheu *a.* afraid of water.
Wasserschildkröte *f.* turtle.
Wasserspiegel *m.* surface of the water, water-level.
Wassersport *m.* aquatic sports.
Wasserspülung *f.* flush.
Wasserstand *m.* water level; **~messer** *m.* water gauge.
Wasserstelle *f.* watering place.
Wasserstoff *m.* hydrogen.
Wasserstoffsuperoxyd *n.* hydrogen peroxide.
Wasserstrahl *m.* jet of water.
Wasserstraße *f.* waterway.
Wassersucht *f.* dropsy.
Wassertier *n.* aquatic animal.
Wasserturm *m.* watertower.
Wasserverschmutzung *f.* water pollution.
Wasserversorgung *f.* water supply.
Wasserwage *f.* level.
Wasserwerk *n.* waterworks.
Wasserzeichen *n.* watermark.
waten *v.i.* to wade.
watscheln *v.i.* to waddle.
Watt *n.* **(-[e]s, -e)** mud flats; (*elek.*) watt.
Watte *f.* **(-, -n)** (absorbent) cotton.
wattieren *v.t.* to wad, to pad.
wauwau! *i.* bow-wow!
wbl. *weiblich,* female, fem.
WC *Wasserklosett,* toilet, WC.
Wdh. *Wiederholung,* repetition, repeat.
weben *v.t.st.* to weave.
Weber *m.* **(-s, -); Weberin** *f.* **(-, -nen)** weaver.
Weberei *f.* weaving mill; weaving (product).
Webstuhl *m.* weaver's loom, frame.
webtreiben *v.t.st.* to drive away.
Wechsel *m.* **(-s. -)** change, vicissitude; exchange; bill of exchange; (*auf Sicht*) bill payable at sight; (*gezogener*) draft.
Wechsel: ~balg *m.* changeling; **~beziehung** *f.* mutual relation, correlation; **~fall** *m.* vicissitudes *pl.;* **~geld** *n.* bank money; change; **~geschäft** *n.* exchange office, banking business; **~gläubiger** *m.* holder *or* bearer of a bill of exchange; **~inhaber** *m.* holder of a bill of exchange; **~jahre** *pl.* menopause; **~klage** *f.* action on *or* about a bill of exchange; **~konto** *n.* exchange account, bill-account; **~kredit** *m.* discount credit; **~kurs** *m.* rate of exchange; **~makler** *m.* exchange broker.
wechseln *v.t.* to change, to exchange; ~ *v.i.* to alternate; *Briefe* ~, to correspond.
wechselnd *a.* alternating.
wechselseitig *a.* reciprocal, mutual.
Wechselseitigkeit *f.* reciprocity.
Wechsel: ~strom *m.* alternating current; **~verhältnis** *n.* reciprocal relation *or* proportion.
wechselvoll *a.* changeable, varied.
wechselweise *adv.* alternately; mutually.
Wechselwirkung *f.* interaction.
wecken *v.t.* to wake, to awaken, to rouse.
Wecken *n.* **(-s, 0)** waking, awaking; ~ *m.* **(-s, 0)** small loaf.
Wecker *m.* **(-s. -)** alarm clock.
wedeln *v.i.* to wag (the tail); to fan.
weder *c.* neither; **~... noch**.. .neither..., nor...
weg *adv.* away; gone; off; *das Buch ist* ~, the book is gone, missing; *über etwas* ~ *(hinweg) sein,* to be above a thing; *in einem* ~, at a stretch, at a sitting; *kurzweg,* briefly, curtly; *schlechtweg,* simply, unceremoniously.
Weg *m.* **(-[e]s, -e)** way, path; (*Gang*) road; course; errand; (*fig.*) manner, means; *auf gütlichem* ~, amicably; *auf halbem* ~*e,* halfway, midway; *verbotener* ~*!* no thoroughfare!; *sich auf den* ~ *machen,* to set out, to start; *auf bestem* ~ *sein,* to be in a fair way to; *im* ~*e sein, stehen,* to be in the way.
wegbegeben *v.r.st.* to go away.
Wegbereiter *m.;* **Wegbereiterin** *f.* forerunner.
wegblasen *v.t.st.* to blow away.
wegbleiben *v.i.st.* *(s)* to stay away *or* out; to be omitted.
wegbringen *v.t.st.* to remove.
wegdenken *v.t.st.* *etw.* ~, to imagine s.th. is not there.
wegdürfen *v.i.st.* to be permitted to go.
wegeilen *v.i.* *(s)* to hasten away.
Wegelagerer *m.* **(-s, -)** highwayman.
wegen *pr.* on account of, because of; *von Rechts* ~, by right.
Wegerecht *n.* right of way.
Wegerich *m.* plantain.
wegessen *v.t.st.* to eat away, to eat up.
wegfahren *v.t.st.* to carry away; ~ *v.i.st.* *(s)* to drive off, to start.
Wegfall *m.* omission; *in* ~ *kommen,* to be abolished or omitted, to cease.
wegfallen *v.i.st.* *(s)* to be omitted.
wegfangen *v.t.st.* to catch.
wegfliegen *v.i.st.* *(s)* to fly away *or* off.
wegführen *v.t.* to lead or carry away.
Weggang *m.* **(-[e]s, 0)** departure.
weggeben *v.t.st.* to give away.
weggehen *v.i.st.* *(s)* to go away, to leave; *über etwas* ~, to pass over.
weggetreten! dismissed!
weggießen *v.t.st.* to pour out.
weghaben *v.t.ir.* *sein Teil* ~, to have gotten one's share.
weghelfen *v.t.st.* to help to get away.
wegholen *v.t.* to take *or* carry away.
wegjagen *v.t.* to chase away.
wegkommen *v.i.st.* *(s)* to get away; to come off.
wegkönnen *v.i.ir.* to be able to go *or* get away.
weglassen *v.t.st.* to let go; to leave out, to omit.
weglaufen *v.i.st.* *(s)* to run off *or* away.
weglegen *v.t.* to put away, to lay aside.
wegleugnen *v.t.* to deny flatly.
weglocken *v.t.* to entice away.
wegmachen *v.r.* (*fam.*) to go away; ~ *v.t.* to remove.
wegmüssen *v.i.st.* to be obliged to leave.
Wegnahme *f.* **(-, 0)** seizure; capture.
wegnehmen *v.t.st.* to take away, to seize.
wegraffen *v.t.* to sweep off.
wegräumen *v.t.* to clear away.
wegreisen *v.i.* *(s)* to depart.
wegreißen *v.t.st.* to tear *or* snatch away.
wegrücken *v.t.* to remove; ~ *v.i.* *(s)* to move aside.
wegrufen *v.t.st.* to call away.
wegschaffen *v.t.* to remove.
wegschenken *v.t.* to give away.
wegscheuchen *v.t.* to frighten away.
wegschicken *v.t.* to send away *or* off.

wegschieben *v.t.st.* to shove away.
wegschleichen *v.r.st.* to steal *or* sneak away.
wegschleppen *v.t.* to drag *or* force away.
wegschmeißen *v.t.st.* to throw away.
wegschnappen *v.t.* to snatch away.
wegschneiden *v.t.st.* to cut away *or* off.
wegsehen *v.t.st.* to look away; (*über etwas*) to overlook.
weg sein *v.i.st.* *(s)* to be gone, to be absent; to be lost; *über etwas* ~, to be above (minding) sth.; *ganz* ~, to be enraptured.
wegsenden *v.t.ir.* to send away.
wegsetzen *v.i.* *(s)* (*über etwas*) to leap (over), to clear; *sich über etwas* ~, not to mind sth.
wegspringen *v.i.st.* *(s)* to leap away; to run away, to escape.
wegspülen *v.t.* to wash away.
wegstehlen *v.t.st.v.r.* to steal away.
wegstellen *v.t.* to put away *or* aside.
wegsterben *v.i.st.* *(s)* to die off.
wegstoßen *v.t.st.* to push away.
wegstreichen *v.t.st.* to strike out.
wegtragen *v.t.st.* to bear *or* carry away.
wegtreten *v.t.st.* to step aside.
wegtun *v.t.st.* to put away, to remove.
wegwälzen *v.t.* to roll away.
Wegweiser *m.* **(-s, -)** roadsign.
wegwerfen *v.t.st.* to throw *or* cast away; ~ *v.r.* to degrade oneself.
wegwerfend *a.* disparaging.
Wegwerf: ~flasche *f.* disposable bottle; **~gesellschaft** *f.* throwaway society.
wegwollen *v.i.ir.* to want to go away.
wegwünschen *v.t.* to wish away.
wegzaubern *v.t.* to spirit away.
wegziehen *v.t.st.* to pull away; ~ *v.i.st.* *(s)* to march away; (*aus einer Wohnung*) to move.
weh, wehe *i.* wo! woe!
weh *a.* painful, sore; **~tun** *v.i.* to cause pain; ~ *v.r.* to hurt oneself.
Weh *n.* **(-[e]s, 0)** woe, pain, grief; *Wohl und* ~, wealth and woe.
Wehe *f.* drift.
wehen *v.t. & i.* to blow.
Wehen *f.pl.* labor pains.
Wehgeschrei *n.* lamentations, wailings *pl.*
Wehklage *f.* lamentation, wailing.
wehklagen *v.i.* to lament, to wail.
wehleidig *a.* plaintive; whining.
Wehmut *f.* sadness, (*sweet*) melancholy.
wehmütig *a.* sad, melancholy; nostalgic.
Wehr *f.* **(-, -en)** defense; *sich zur* ~ *setzen,* to offer resistance.
Wehr *n.* **(-[e]s, -e)** weir; dam, dike.
Wehrdienst *m.* military service.
Wehrdienstverweigerer *m.* conscientious objector.
wehren *v.t. & i.* to restrain; to hinder; ~ *v.r.* to defend oneself.
Wehrersatzdienst *m.* obligatory service for conscientious objectors.
wehrfähig *a.* fit for military service.
wehrhaft *a.* ready to defend; fortified.
wehrlos *a.* defenseless, weak.
Wehrlosigkeit *f.* defenselessness.
Wehr: ~paß *m.* service record; **~pflicht** *f.* compulsory military service, conscription.
wehrpflichtig *a.* liable to military service.
Weib *n.* **(-es, -er)** woman, female; wife.
Weibchen *n.* **(-s, -)** (*pej.*) little woman; (*von Tieren*) female.
Weiberfeind *m.* woman-hater, misogynist.
weiberhaft *a.* womanlike, womanish.
Weiberheld *m.* lady-killer.
weibisch *a.* womanish; effeminate.
weiblich *a.* female; womanly, feminine.
Weiblichkeit *f.* **(-, 0)** femininity.
Weibsbild *n.* (*fam. pej.*) female, wench, hussy.
weich *a.* soft, mellow; tender (-hearted).
Weiche *f.* **(-, -n)** softness; side; flank; (*rail.*) points *pl.;* (*elek.*) switch, shunt.
weichen *v.t.* to steep, to soak, to soften; ~ *v.i.* to soak, to soften.
weichen *v.i.st.* to give way, to yield; *von der Stelle* ~, to budge, to stir.
weichgekocht *a.* soft-boiled.
weichherzig *a.* tender-hearted.
weichlich *a.* soft; weak, effeminate.
Weichling *m.* **(-[e]s, -e)** weakling.
Weichmacher *m.* softener.
Weichspüler *m.* (fabric) softener.
Weichteile *pl.* soft parts.
Weichtier *n.* mollusc.
Weide *f.* **(-, -n)** pasture(-ground); pasturage; (*Baum*) willow.
Weideland *n.* pastureland.
weiden *v.t.* to feed, to tend; ~ *v.i.* to pasture, to graze; ~ *v.r.* ~ *(an etwas),* to delight (in), to gloat (over).
Weidengeflecht *n.* wicker-work.
weidlich *adv.* thoroughly.
Weidmann *m.* huntsman.
weidmännisch *a.* huntsmanlike.
weigern *v.r.* to refuse.
Weigerung *f.* **(-, -en)** refusal, denial.
Weih: ~becken *n.* holy water font; **~bischof** *m.* suffragan bishop.
Weihe *f.* **(-, -n)** consecration; ordination.
weihen *v.t.* to consecrate, to ordain; (*fig.*) to dedicate, to devote; *sich* ~ *lassen,* to take (holy) orders.
Weiher *m.* **(-s, -)** (fish-)pond.
weihevoll *a.* sacred, hallowed, solemn.
Weihnachten *f.pl.* Christmas, Xmas.
Weihnachts: ~abend *m.* Christmas Eve; **~baum** *m.* Christmas tree; **~(feier)tag** *m.* Christmas Day; **~lied** *n.* Christmas carol *or* hymn; **~mann** *m.* Father Christmas, Santa Claus.
Weihrauch *m.* **(-[e]s, 0)** incense.
Weihrauchfaß *n.* censer.
Weihwasser *n.* holy water.
weil *c.* because, since, as.
weiland *adv.* formerly; late, deceased.
Weilchen *n.* **(-s, 0)** little while.
Weile *f.* **(-, 0)** while, time; leisure; *eine* ~, for a while.
weilen *v.i.* to tarry, to stay.
Weiler *m.* **(-s, -)** hamlet.
Wein *m.* **(-[e]s, -e)** wine; (*bot.*) vine; *einem reinen* ~ *einschenken,* to tell one the plain truth, not to mince matters; *wilder* ~, Virginia creeper.
Wein: ~bau *m.* viticulture; **~bauer** *m.;* **~bäuerin** *f.* wine grower; **~berg** *m.* vineyard; **~brand** *m.* brandy.
weinen *v.i.* to weep (for, at, over), to cry.
weinerlich *a.* tearful; weepy; whining.
Wein: ~essig *m.* (wine-)vinegar; **~geist** *m.* spirit of wine; **~handel** *m.* wine trade; **~händler** *m.* wine-merchant; **~jahr** *n.* *gutes* ~, good vintage;

~karte *f.* wine list; **~keller** *m.* wine cellar; **~kenner** *m.* connoisseur of wine; **~lese** *f.* grape harvest; **~säure** *f.* acidity of wine, tartaric acid; **~stein** *m.* tartar; **~stock** *m.* vine; **~stube** *f.* wine tavern; **~traube** *f.* (bunch of) grapes.

weise *a.* wise.

Weise *m./f.* **(-n, -n)** sage, philosopher, wise man or woman; *Stein der ~n,* philosopher's stone.

Weise *f.* **(-, -n)** manner, way; method, fashion; habit; tune, melody; *auf keine ~,* no way, by no means.

weisen *v.t.st.* to point out, to show, to direct; *an einem ~,* to refer to sb.; *von sich ~,* to reject, to refuse; to repudiate; *etwas von der Hand ~,* to dismiss.

Weisheit *f.* **(-, -en)** wisdom, prudence.

Weisheitszahn *m.* wisdom tooth.

weislich *adv.* wisely, prudently.

weismachen *v.t. jdm etw ~* to make sb. believe sth.

weiß *a.* white; clean.

Weiß *n.* **(-es, 0)** white.

weissagen *v.t.* to prophesy, to foretell.

Weissager *m.* **(-s, -)** fortune-teller, prophet.

Weissagerin *f.* **(-, -nen)** prophetess; fortune-teller.

Weissagung *f.* **(-, -en)** prophecy.

Weißblech *n.* tinplate, white metal.

Weißbrot *n.* white bread.

Weissdorn *m.* hawthorn.

Weiße *f.* **(-, 0)** whiteness, white; (*fam.*) glass of Berlin pale beer.

Weiße *m./f.* white man/woman.

weißen *v.t.* to whiten; to whitewash.

Weißfisch *m.* whiting; whitebait.

weißglühend *a.* white-hot.

Weißglut *f.* white heat.

Weißherbst *m.* rosé wine.

Weißkohl *m.*, **Weißkraut** *n.* white cabbage.

weißlich *a.* whitish.

Weißmetall *n.* white metal.

Weißnäherin *f.* seamstress.

Weißwein *m.* white wine.

Weißwurst *f.* veal sausage.

Weißzeug *n.* linen.

Weisung *f.* **(-, -en)** direction, instruction.

weit *a.* distant, remote, far, far off, wide; large; *~ adv.* far; widely; *zwei Meilen ~,* two miles off; *bei ~em,* by far; *von ~em,* from afar; *~ und breit,* far and wide; *nicht ~ kommen,* to make no great progress; *mit etwas ~ sein,* to have got well into sth.; *die Sache ist noch lange nicht so ~,* the matter has not got nearly so far as that; *nicht ~ her sein,* (*fam.*) not much to speak of; *es ~ bringen,* to get on in the world; *das geht zu ~,* that is going too far; *es zu ~ treiben,* to carry things too far; *einen ~ übertreffen,* to surpass someone by far; *~ gefehlt!,* very wide of the mark!; *(in)-soweit,* so far; *soweit (als),* so far as.

weitaus *adv.* by far.

weitblickend *a.* (*fig.*) far-sighted.

Weite *f.* **(-, -n)** width; distance; capacity.

weiten *v.t.* to widen; **~** *v.r.* to widen, to expand.

weiter *adv.* further; forward, on; *und so ~,* and so on, etc.; *~ nichts,* nothing else; *~! i.* go on! proceed!; *~ niemand,* no one else *or* besides; *~lesen,* to go on reading; *~kommen,* to get on, to proceed; *bis auf ~es,* until further notice, advice or orders; *ohne ~es,* without much ado.

Weiterbeförderung *f.* forwarding; *zur ~ an,* to be forwarded *or* sent on to.

Weiterbestand *m.* continued existence.

weiterentwickeln *v.t. & r.* to develop further.

weitergeben *v.t.st.* to pass on.

weitergehen *v.i.st. (s)* to proceed.

weiterhin *adv.* further.

weiterleiten *v.t.* to pass on.

Weiterreise *f.* journey onwards.

weiterverarbeiten *v.t.* to process.

weiterverfolgen *v.t.* to follow up.

weiterziehen *v.t.st.* to move on.

weitgehend *a.* far-reaching; extensive.

weitgereist *a.* widely-traveled.

weitgreifend *a.* far-reaching.

weither *adv.* from afar; *~ geholt,* far-fetched.

weitherzig *a.* generous.

weithin *adv.* to a great distance, far off.

weitläufig *a.* ample, spacious; detailed; *sie sind ~ verwandt,* they are distantly related.

weit: ~maschig *a.* wide-meshed; **~reichend** *a.* far-reaching: **~schweifig** *a.* prolix, lengthy, tedious.

weitsichtig *a.* long-sighted; (*fig.*) far-sighted.

Weitsprung *m.* broad jump.

weittragend *a.* far-reaching, portentous; **~ verzweigt** *a.* extensive; with many branches.

Weitwinkelobjektiv *a.* wide-angle lens.

Weizen *m.* **(-s, -)** wheat.

welcher, welche, welches *pn.* who, which, that; some, any.

welk *a.* withered, faded, flabby.

welken *v.i. (s)* to wither, to fade.

Wellblech *n.* corrugated iron.

Welle *f.* **(-, -n)** wave, billow; shaft, axletree.

wellen *v.t.* (*Haar*) to wave.

Wellen: ~band *n.* (*Radio*) waveband; **~brecher** *n.* breakwater.

wellenförmig *a.* wavy, undulating.

Wellenlänge *f.* wavelength.

Wellenlinie *f.* wavy line.

Wellenreiten *n.* surfing.

wellig *a.* wavy.

Wellpappe *f.* corrugated cardboard.

Welpe *m.* **(-n, -n)** whelp; pup; cub.

Wels *m.* **(Welses, Welse)** catfish.

Welsche *m.* **(-n, -n)** Italian; Frenchman.

Welt *f.* **(-, -en)** world; universe; people; *alle ~,* all the world, everybody; *zur ~ bringen,* to give birth to; *aus der ~ schaffen,* to do away with; *um alles in der ~ nicht,* not for the world.

Weltall, Weltenall *n.* **(-s, 0)** universe.

Welt: ~anschaulich *a.* ideological; **~anschauung** *f.* world-view; **~ausstellung** *f.* international exhibition.

welt: ~bekannt *a.*, **~berühmt** *a.* world-famous.

Weltbürger *m.*; **Weltbürgerin** *f.* cosmopolitan.

Weltenbummler *m.* **(-s, -)** globetrotter.

welterfahren *a.* experienced.

welterschütternd *a.* earthshaking.

weltfremd *a.* unworldly; naive.

Welt: ~frieden *m.* world peace; **~geschichte** *f.* world history.

weltgeschichtlich, welthistorisch *a.* historical.

weltgewandt *a.* experienced in the world.

Welt: ~handel *m.* international trade; **~herrschaft** *f.* world supremacy; **~karte** *f.* map of the world; **~kenntnis** *f.* knowledge of the world; **~krieg** *m.* world war; **~lage** *f.* international situation; **~lauf** *m.* way of the world.

weltlich *a.* worldly, mundane; temporal, secular.
Welt: ~literatur *f.* world literature; **~macht** *f.* world power or empire.
weltmännisch *a.* urbane.
Welt: ~markt *m.* international market; **~meister** *m.* world champion; **~meisterschaft** *f.* world championship.
Welt: ~raum *m.* space; **~reich** *n.* great empire; **~schmerz** *m.* weariness of life, pessimistic melancholy; **~sprache** *f.* universal language; **~stadt** *f.* cosmopolitan city; **~stellung** *f.* position in the world; **~teil** *m.* part of the world; **~untergang** *m.* end of the world; **~verkehr** *m.* international trade.
wem *pn.* to whom; he to whom.
Wemfall *m.* dative (case).
wen *pn.* whom; he whom.
Wende *f.* **(-, -n)** turn, turning point.
Wendekreis *m.* tropic.
Wendeltreppe *f.* spiral staircase.
wenden *v.t. & st. & reg.* to turn; ~ *v.r.* to turn; (*an einen*) to address, to apply to; *bitte ~!* please turn over!
Wendepunkt *m.* turning point.
wendig *a.* nimble; easy to steer.
Wendung *f.* **(-, -en)** turn; *eine ~ zum Schlimmeren,* a change for the worse.
Wenfall *m.* accusative (case).
wenig *a. & adv.* little; some; **~e,** few; *ein ~*, a little.
weniger *a.* less; fewer.
Wenigkeit *a.* **(-, 0)** small quantity, trifle; *meine ~* (*hum.; obs.*), yours truly.
wenigstens *adv.* at least.
wenn *c.* when; if; *~ anders, ~nur,* provided that; *es ist als ~*, it is as if; *außer ~*, unless, except when (if); *~ auch,* though, although; *selbst ~, und ~*, even when (if); *~ anders,* if.. .at all, if really; *~ schon, denn schon, (fam.)* in for a penny, in for a pound; *~ auch noch so,* if.. .ever so.
wenngleich, wennschon *c.* though, although, albeit.
wer *pn.* who; he who; which; whoever, whosoever; **~ da?** who goes there?
Werbe... (*in Zus.*) advertising...
Werbe: ~abteilung *f.* advertising department; **~agentur** *f.* advertising agency; **~fachmann** *m.* publicity agent; **~fernsehen** *n.* commercial TV; **~geschenk** *n.* free gift.
werben *v.t.st.* to apply for, to sue, to court; to canvass, to make propaganda; ~ *v.t.st.* to recruit, to enlist; *~ um,* to court, to woo, to sue for.
Werber *m.* **(-s, -)** wooer, suitor.
Werbe: ~slogan *m.* advertising slogan; **~spot** *m.* commercial.
Werbung *f.* **(-, -en)** recruiting; courtship; (*com.*) advertising, public relations.
Werdegang *m.* career.
werden *v.i.st.* to become; to grow, to turn, to get; *zuteil ~*, to fall to one's share; *was soll aus ihm ~?* what is to become of him?; *die Sache wird,* things are coming along; *es wird schon!,* we are getting on well!; *wird's bald?* will you have it done soon?
Werden *n.* **(-s, 0)** genesis; *im ~ sein,* to be in progress, to be in the making.
werfen *v.t.st.* to throw, to cast, to fling; (*von Tieren*) to bring forth; ~ *v.r.st.* (*Holz*) to warp; *Verdacht ~ auf,* to cast suspicion on.
Werft *m.* **(-[e]s, -e)** shipyard, dockyard.
Werg *n.* **(-es, 0)** tow.
Werk *n.* **(-[e]s, -e)** work; action, deed; clockwork; mechanism; *ins ~ setzen,* to set going; *im ~e sein,* to be going on; *ans ~ gehen,* to go to work; *Hand ans ~ legen,* to set to work; *sich ans ~ machen,* to begin work; *zu ~e gehen,* to set about sth., to go to work.
Werkbank *f.* workbench, shop-counter.
Werk: ~führer *m.* foreman; **~führerin** *f.* forewoman; **~meister** *m.* foreman; **~schutz** *m.* factory guard; **~statt, ~stätte** *f.* workshop; **~stattauftrag** *m.* work order; **~stoff** *m.* material; **~student** *m.* working student; **~tag** *m.* workday.
Werkt. *Werktags,* weekdays.
werktäglich *a.* workaday, everyday.
werktags *adv.* on weekdays.
werktätig *a.* active, industrious.
Werkzeug *n.* instrument, tool; **~kasten** *m.* tool box; **~maschine** *f.* machine tool.
Wermut *m.* **(-[e]s, 0)** wormwood; vermouth.
wert *a.* worth, worthy; valuable; dear; *der Mühe ~*, worthwhile; **~achten, ~schätzen,** to hold dear, to prize highly.
Wert *m.* **(-[e]s, -e)** value, worth; rate, price; **~ auf etwas legen,** to attach value to.
Wert: ~angabe *f.* declaration of value; **~arbeit** *f.* high-quality workmanship.
wertbeständig *a.* of fixed value.
Wertbestimmung *f.* valuation.
Wertbetrag *m.* value in money.
Wertbrief *m.* insured letter.
Wertgegenstand *m.* valuable.
Wertigkeit *f.* (*chem.*) valency; significance.
wertlos *a.* worthless.
Wertmaßstabe *m.* standard of value.
Wertpaket *n.* insured package.
Wertpapiere *n.pl.* securities *pl.*
Wertsachen *pl.* valuables.
wertschätzen *v.t.* to esteem highly.
Wertschätzung *f.* **(-, 0)** esteem, regard.
Wertsendung *f.* parcel containing money or valuables.
Wertsteigerung *f.* increase in value.
Werturteil *n.* value judgment.
wertvoll *a.* valuable; precious.
Wertzuwachs *m.* capital gains; **~steuer** *f.* capital gains tax.
Werwolf *m.* **(-[e]s, -wölfe)** wer(e)wolf.
wes *pn.* whose (*obs. poet.*).
Wesen *n.* **(-s, -)** being, entity; essence; substance, nature, character; ado, hubbub, noise; *sein ~ treiben,* to be at it (again); *viel ~s aus etwas machen,* to make a good deal of fuss or much ado about a thing; *Finanzwesen,* finances; *Kriegswesen,* military affairs; *Schulwesen,* educational affairs.
Wesenheit *f.* **(-, 0)** essence, nature.
wesenlos *a.* unsubstantial, unreal.
Wesens: ~art *f.* nature, character; **~zug** *m.* characteristic.
wesentlich *a.* fundamental, essential; substantial.
Wesfall *m.* genitive (case).
weshalb, weswegen *adv.* wherefore, why.
Wespe *f.* **(-, -en)** wasp; yellow jacket.
Wespenstich *m.* wasp sting.
wessen *pn.* whose.
West (without article) west; West.
westdeutsch *a.;* **Westdeutsche** *m./f.* West German.

Weste *f.* **(-, -n)** vest.
Westen *m.* **(-s, 0)** west, Occident.
Westentasche *f.* vest pocket.
Westindien *n.* the West Indies.
westl. *westlich,* western.
westlich *a.* western, westerly.
Westmächte *pl.* Western Powers.
Westseite *f.* western side.
westwärts *adv.* westward.
Westwind *m.* west wind.
wett *a.* equal, (*fam.*) quits; *etwas ~ machen,* to even the score.
Wettbewerb *m.* competition; contest.
Wettbewerber *m.* competitor.
Wettbüro *m.* betting office.
Wette *f.* **(-n, -n)** bet, wager; *um die ~ laufen,* to race; *eine ~ eingehen, machen,* to lay a wager, to make a bet.
Wetteifer *m.* competition; rivalry.
wetteifern *v.i.* to vie, to contend with.
wetten *v.t.* to wager, to bet, to lay a wager; *es läßt sich 100 gegen eins ~,* you can bet or lay 100 to one; *auf ein Pferd ~,* to back a horse.
Wetter *n.* **(-s, -)** weather; *schlechtes ~,* bad weather; *schönes ~,* fine *or* fair weather; *bei gutem ~,* weather permitting.
Wetter: ~amt *n.* meteorological office; **~aussichten** *pl.* weather outlook; **~bericht** *m.* weather report; **~dienst** *m.* meteorological service; **~fahne** *f.* weather vane; (*fig.*) turncoat.
wetterfest *a.* weather-proof.
Wetter: ~karte *f.* meteorological chart; **~kunde** *f.* meteorology.
Wetterlage *f.* weather conditions.
Wetterleuchten *n.* summer lightning.
wettern *v.i.* to storm, to swear.
Wetter: ~vorhersage *f.* weather forecast; **~warte** *f.* weather bureau.
wetterwendisch *a.* changeable, fickle.
Wetterwolke *f.* thunder cloud.
Wettkampf *m.* contest; prize fight, match.
Wettlauf *m.* race.
wettlaufen *v.i.st.* *(s)* to run a race; *~ gegen,* to race against.
Wettläufer *m.* runner (in a race).
Wettrennen *n.* horse race; racing.
Wettrudern *n.* boat race.
Wettstreit *m.* contest, contention, match.
wetzen *v.t.* to whet, to sharpen.
Wetzstein *m.* whetstone.
WEZ *Westeuropäische Zeit,* Greenwich Mean Time, GMT.
WG *Wohngemeinschaft,* people sharing an apartment.
Whg. *Wohnung,* apartment.
Whiskey *m.;* **Whisky** *m.* whiskey, whisky.
Wichse *f.* **(-, -en)** blacking, polish.
wichsen *v.t.* to black, to polish; ~ *v.i.* (*vulg.*) to wank; to jerk off.
Wicht *m.* **(-[e]s, -e)** little imp; creature.
Wichtel *m.* **(-s, -)** gnome; goblin.
wichtig *a.* important.
Wichtigkeit *f.* **(-, 0)** importance.
Wichtigtuer *m.* pompous ass.
wichtigtuerisch *a.* pompous; self-important.
Wicke *f.* vetch, sweet pea.
Wickel *m.* **(-s, -)** compress.
Wickel: ~kind *n.* child in swaddling clothes, baby; **~kommode** *f.* changing table.
wickeln *v.t.* to wind (up); to wrap up; to roll, to curl; to swathe, to change (a diaper), to swaddle; *auseinander ~,* to unwrap, to undo, to unfold.
Wicklung *f.* **(-, -en)** (*elek.*) winding.
Widder *m.* **(-s, -)** ram; (*Sternbild*) Aries.
wider *pr.* against, contrary to; versus; *~ Willen,* unwillingly; *das Für und Wider,* the pros and cons.
widerborstig *a.* unruly; rebellious.
widerfahren *v.i.st.* *(s)* to happen to, to befall; *einem Gerechtigkeit ~ lassen,* to do sb. justice.
Widerhaken *m.* barbed hook; barb (of an arrow or hook).
Widerhall *m.* **(-[e]s, -e)** echo.
widerhallen *v.i.* to echo.
Widerholung *f.* **(-, -en)** repetition.
widerlegen *v.t.* to refute, to disprove.
Widerlegung *f.* **(-, -en)** refutation.
widerlich *a.* disgusting, repulsive.
widernatürlich *a.* contrary to nature.
Widerpart *m.* **(-[e]s, -e)** opponent.
widerraten *v.t.st.* to dissuade.
widerrechtlich *a.* unlawful.
Widerrede *f.* contradiction.
Widerruf *m.* revocation; recantation.
widerrufen *v.t.st.* to revoke; to recant, to retract.
widerruflich *a.* revocable; ~ *adv.* on probation.
Widerrufung *f.* **(-, -en)** revocation.
Widersacher *m.* **(-s, -); Widersacherin** *f.* **(-, -nen)** adversary.
Widerschein *m.* reflection, reflex.
widersetzen *v.r.* to resist.
widersetzlich *a.* refractory.
Widersinn *m.* nonsense, absurdity.
widersinnig *a.* nonsensical, absurd.
widerspenstig *a.* refractory, obstinate.
widerspiegeln *v.t.* to reflect.
widersprechen *v.t.st.* to contradict, to gainsay, ~ *v.r.* to contradict oneself; *sich ~d,* contradictory.
Widerspruch *m.* contradiction.
widersprüchlich *a.* contradictory.
widerspruchslos *a.* unprotesting, uncontradicting.
Widerstand *m.* resistance, opposition; (*elek.*) resistance; ~ **leisten,** to offer resistance; **~sbewegung** *f.* resistance; underground movement.
widerstandsfähig *a.* robust; capable of resistance.
Widerstandskämpfer *m.* resistance fighter.
Widerstandskraft *f.* resistance.
widerstandslos *a.* without resistance.
widerstehen *v.t.st.* to resist, to withstand; to be repugnant (to).
widerstreben *v.i.* to oppose, to resist; *das widerstrebt mir,* I am uncomfortable with that.
Widerstreben *n.* reluctance.
widerstrebend *a. & adv.* reluctant(ly).
Widerstreit *m.* conflict, clash.
widerstreiten *v.i.* to conflict.
widerstreitend *a.* conflicting.
widerwärtig *a.* repulsive, revolting; offensive.
Widerwille *m.* aversion, repugnance.
widerwillig *a.* reluctant, unwilling.
widmen *v.t.* to dedicate, to inscribe; to devote.
Widmung *f.* **(-, -en)** dedication.
widrig *a.* contrary; adverse; offensive.
Widrigkeit *f.* **(-, -en)** adversity.
wie *adv.* how; *~ c.* as, like; *~ so?* how do you mean?; *~ wenn,* as if, as though; *~ glücklich er*

auch sein mag, however happy he may be; *~dem auch sei,* be that as it may.
wieder *adv.* again, anew, afresh; back, in return; *hin und ~,* now and then; *~gutmachen,* to redress, to make reparations for.
wiederabdrucken *v.t.* to reprint.
Wiederaufbau *m.* reconstruction.
wiederaufbauen *v.t.* to rebuild.
Wiederaufbereitung *f.* reprocessing; **~sanlage** *f.* reprocessing plant; recycling plant.
wiederaufleben *v.i. (s)* to revive.
Wiederaufnahme *f.* resumption.
Wiederaufnahmeverfahren *n.* (*jur.*) retrial.
wiederaufnehmen *v.t.st.* to resume.
wiederauftauchen *v.i.* to turn up again.
Wiederbeginn *m.* recommencement; resumption.
wiederbekommen *v.t.st.* to get back.
wiederbeleben *v.t.* to revive, to resuscitate.
Wiederbelebungsversuch *m.* attempt to revive.
wiederbringen *v.t.st.* to return.
wiedereinführen *v.t.* to reintroduce, to reimport.
wiedereinlösen *v.t.* to redeem.
Wiedereinreiseerlaubnis *f.* reentry permit.
wiedereinsetzen *v.t.* to reinstate.
wiederentdecken *v.t.* to rediscover.
wiedererkennen *v.t.st.* to recognize.
wiedererlangen *v.t.* to recover.
wiedererobern *v.t.* to reconquer.
wiedereröfnen *v.t.* to reopen.
Wiedererstattung *f.* repayment.
wiedererzählen *v.t.* to recount.
wiederfinden *v.t.st.* to find again.
Wiedergabe *f.* reproduction, rendering.
wiedergeben *v.t.st.* to give back; to reproduce, to render; interpret (music, etc.).
Wiedergeburt *f.* regeneration, new birth.
wiedergenesen *v.i.st. (s)* to recover (one's health).
wiedergewinnen *v.t.st.* to regain.
Wiedergutmachung *f.* reparation.
wiederhaben *v.t.st.* to have back.
wiederherstellen *v.t.* to restore; to cure.
Wiederherstellung *f.* restoration.
wiederholen *v.t.* to repeat, to reiterate.
Wiederholungsaufführung *f.* repeat performance.
Wiederholungskurs *m.* refresher course.
wiederkäuen *v.t. & i.* (*auch fig.*) to ruminate, to chew the cud.
Wiederkäuer *m.* ruminant.
Wiederkehr *f.* **(-, 0)** return.
wiederkehren *v.i. (s)* to return.
wiederkommen *v.i.st. (s)* to come again *or* back, to return.
wiedersehen *v.t.st.* to see *or* meet again.
Wiedersehen *n.* **(-s, 0)** meeting after a separation; *auf ~!* so long!, I'll be seeing you.
Wiedertäufer *m.* anabaptist.
wiederum *adv.* again, anew, afresh.
wiedervereinigen *v.t.* to reunite.
Wiedervereinigung *f.* reunification.
wiederverheiraten *v.t.* to remarry.
Wiederverheiratung *f.* remarriage.
Wiederverkauf *m.* resale.
Wiederwahl *f.* re-election.
wiederwählen *v.t.* to re-elect.
Wiederzulassung *f.* readmission; relicensing (car).
Wiege *f.* **(-, -n)** cradle.
wiegen *v.t. & i.st.* to rock; to mince; to weigh.
Wiegen: ~fest *n.* birthday; **~lied** *n.* lullaby.
wiehern *v.i.* to whinny; to neigh.
Wiener *f.* **(-, -)** wiener (wurst).
wienerisch *a.* Viennese.
wienern *v.t.* to polish.
Wiese *f.* **(-, -n)** meadow.
Wiesel *n.* **(-s, -)** weasel.
wieso *adv.* why.
wieviel *interrogativ pn.* how much; how many.
wievielmal *adv.* how many times.
wievielte *a.* which of the number; *der ~?* what day of the month?
wieweit *adv.* to what extent.
wiewohl *c.* though, although.
Wikinger *m.* **(-s, -)** Viking.
wild *a.* wild; savage, uncultivated; fierce, ferocious; turbulent; unmanageable.
Wild *n.* **(-[e]s, 0)** game; deer.
Wild: ~bret *n.* venison, game; **~dieb** *m.* poacher.
Wilde *m./f.* **(-n, -n)** savage.
Wilderei *f.* poaching.
Wilderer *m.* **(-s, -)** poacher.
wildern *v.i.* to poach.
Wildfang *m.* **(-[e]s, -fänge)** romp.
wildfremd *a.* completely strange.
Wildheit *f.* **(-, 0)** wildness, savageness.
Wildleder *n.* suede.
Wildnis *f.* **(-, -nisse)** wilderness.
Wildpark *m.* deer park.
Wildschwein *n.* wild boar.
wildwachsend *a.* growing wild.
Wildwechsel *m.* game path; game crossing.
Wille *m.* **(-ns, -n)** will; mind, wish; design, intention, purpose; *letzter ~,* last will; *um meinetwillen,* for my sake; *~s sein,* to intend, to have a mind; *einem zu ~ sein,* to do someone's will or pleasure; *aus freiem ~,* of one's own accord, voluntarily; *wider ~,* unwillingly.
willenlos *a.* irresolute, weak.
Willensfreiheit *f.* freedom of will.
Willenskraft *f.* will-power.
willensschwach *a.* weak-willed.
willensstark *a.* strong-willed.
willfährig *a.* compliant, complaisant.
willig *a.* willing, docile, cooperative.
Willkomm(en) *n.* **(-s, 0)** welcome.
willkommen *a. & i.* welcome; *~ heißen,* to welcome.
Willkür *f.* **(-, 0)** arbitrariness; (*Belieben*) discretion; *nach ~,* at one's pleasure; **~akt** *m.* arbitrary act; **~herrschaft** *f.* tyranny.
willkürlich *a.* arbitrary.
wimmeln *v.i.* to swarm (with).
wimmern *v.i.* to whimper, to whine.
Wimpel *f.* **(-, -n)** pennant.
Wimper *f.* **(-, -n)** eyelash.
Wimperntusche *f.* mascara.
Wind *m.* **(-[e]s, -e)** wind, breeze.
Windbeutel *m.* (*Backwerk*) cream puff; (*fig.*) swaggerer, windbag.
Windbö(e) *f.* **(-, -n)** gust of wind.
Winde *f.* **(-, -n)** winch; (*bot.*) bindweed.
Windel *f.* **(-, -n)** diaper.
windelweich *a. einen ~ schlagen,* to beat someone to a pulp.
winden *v.t.st.* to wind; to twist; *~ v.r.* to wind, to meander; to writhe.
Windeseile *f. mit ~,* in no time.
Wind: ~fahne *f.* vane; **~hose** *f.* water spout; **~hund** *m.* greyhound.

windig *a.* windy; doubtful, shaky.
Wind: ~jacke *f.* wind breaker; **~mühle** *f.* windmill; **~pocken** *pl.* chicken-pox; **~rose** *f.* compass card.
windschief *a.* crooked.
Windschutzscheibe *f.* (*mot.*) windshield.
windstill *a.* calm.
Wind: ~stille *f.* calm; **~stoß** *m.* gust, squall.
Windsurfen *n.* windsurfing.
Windung *f.* **(-, -en)** winding, coil; spire, whorl (of a shell); worm (of a screw).
Wink *m.* **(-[e]s, -e)** sign, nod; (*fig.*) hint; tip.
Winkel *m.* **(-s, -)** angle; corner; nook.
Winkeladvokat *m.* (*fam.*) shyster.
winkelförmig *a.* angular.
wink(e)lig *a.* angular; crooked.
Winkelmaß *n.* (carpenter's) square, iron rule.
Winkelmesser *m.* protractor.
Winkelzug *m.* shady trick/move.
winken *v.i.* to beckon to, to nod; *mit den Augen ~*, to wink.
winseln *v.i.* to whimper, to whine.
Winter *m.* **(-s, -)** winter.
Winterhalbjahr *n.* winter term.
winterlich *a.* wintry.
Winterschlaf *m.* hibernation.
Winterzeit *f.* wintertime.
Winzer *m.* **(-s, -)** wine grower.
winzig *a.* tiny.
Wipfel *m.* **(-s, -)** treetop.
Wippe *f.* **(-, -n)** see-saw.
wippen *v.i.* to see-saw; to bob.
wir *pn.* we.
Wirbel *m.* **(-s, -)** whirl, eddy, whirlpool; (*phys.*) vortex; crown (of the head); vertebra; (drum) roll.
wirbellos *a.* invertebrate.
wirbeln *v.i.* to whirl, to eddy; *mir wirbelt der Kopf,* my head is swimming.
Wirbelsäule *f.* spine, spinal column.
Wirbelsturm *m.* cyclone, tornado.
Wirbeltier *n.* vertebrate.
Wirbelwind *m.* whirlwind; tornado.
wirken *v.t.* to weave; to effect; to work, to produce; ~ *v.i.* to act (upon), to operate, to influence.
wirkend *a.* active, efficient, operative.
wirklich *a.* real, actual; effective; ~ *adv.* really, actually, positively; **~?,** really?
Wirklichkeit *f.* **(-, -en)** reality.
wirksam *a.* efficient, effective; (*med*) operative; **~ werden (law),** to take effect.
Wirksamkeit *f.* **(-, 0)** effectiveness; efficiency; (*eines Gesetzes*) operation.
Wirkstoff *m.* **(-s, -e)** active agent.
Wirkstuhl *m.* loom.
Wirkung *f.* **(-, -en)** effect, operation, action; *mit sofortiger ~*, effective immediately; *mit ~ vom 1 Juni,* effective June 1.
Wirkungs: ~kraft *f.* efficiency; efficacy; **~kreis** *m.* sphere of activity.
wirkungslos *a.* ineffective.
wirkungsvoll *a.* effective.
Wirkungsweise *f.* operation; function; action.
wirr *a.* confused; **~es Haar,** dishevelled hair.
Wirren *f.pl.* turmoil.
wirrköpfig *a.* muddle-headed.
Wirrnis *f.* **(-nisses, -nisse), Wirrsal** *n.* **(-[e]s, -e)** confusion, jumble.
Wirrwarr *m.* **(-s, 0)** confusion, jumble.
Wirsing *m.* **(-s, 0), Wirsingkohl** *m.* savoy (cabbage).
Wirt *m.* **(-[e]s, -e)** host, landlord, innkeeper.
Wirtin *f.* **(-, -nen)** hostess, landlady.
Wirtschaft *f.* **(-, -en)** economy; public house, inn; *freie ~*, private enterprise.
wirtschaften *v.i.* to manage, to keep house; to economize.
Wirtschafterin *f.* **(-, -nen)** housekeeper.
wirtschaftlich *a.* economic(al), thrifty.
Wirtschaftlichkeit *f.* profitability; economic efficiency.
Wirtschafts: ~betrieb *m.* management (of household, inn, etc.); **~gebäude** *pl.* domestic quarters; **~geld** *n.* housekeeping money; **~krieg** *m.* economic warfare; **~krise** *f.* economic crisis; **~politik** *f.* economic policy; **~minister** *m.*, **~ministerin** *f.* minister for economic affairs; secretary of commerce; **~ministerium** *n.* Board of Trade; **~wissenschaft** *f.* economics; **~wissenschaftler** *m.*, **~wissenschaftlerin** *f.* economist; **~zeitung** *f.* financial newspaper; **~zweig** *m.* economic sector.
Wirtshaus *n.* inn; tavern.
Wirts: ~leute *pl.* host and hostess; **~stube** *f.* inn parlor; common room.
Wisch *m.* **(-es, -e)** piece of paper.
wischen *v.t.* to wipe, to rub.
Wischer *m.* **(-s, -)** wiper.
Wischlappen *m.* dish cloth; duster.
Wisent *m.* **(-s, -e)** bison
Wismut *m.* **(-[e]s, 0)** bismuth.
wispern *v.i.* to whisper.
wiss. *wissenschaftlich,* academic.
Wißbegierde *f.* thirst for knowledge.
wißbegierig *a.* eager for knowledge; curious.
wissen *v.t. & i.* st. to know; to be aware of; *einem Dank ~*, to owe, to feel indebted to sb.; *er will von uns nichts ~*, he will have nothing to do with us.
Wissen *n.* **(-s, 0)** knowledge; learning; *meines ~s,* as far as I know, to my knowledge; *nach bestem ~ und Gewissen,* to the best of my knowledge and belief.
wissend *a.* knowing.
Wissenschaft *f.* **(-, -en)** knowledge; science; learning; *die schönen ~en,* belles-lettres, the humanities.
Wissenschaftler *m.;* **Wissenschaftlerin** *f.* scholar, scientist.
wissenschaftlich *a.* scientific, scholarly; learned.
Wissensdrang, Wissensdurst, Wissenstrieb *m.* desire for knowledge.
wissenswert *a.* worth knowing.
wissentlich *a.* knowing, willful.
wittern *v.t.* to scent, to smell.
Witterung *f.* **(-, -en)** weather; scent.
Witwe *f.* **(-, -en)** widow.
Witwer *m.* **(-s, -)** widower.
Witz *m.* **(-es, -e)** joke, witticism.
Witzblatt *n.* comic paper.
Witzbold *m.* **(-[e]s, -e)** joker.
Witzelei *f.* **(-, -en)** teasing; jokes.
witzeln *v.i.* to joke.
witzig *a.* funny; amusing; witty; *~er Einfall,* flash of wit.
w.L. *westliche Länge,* Western longitude, W long.
wo *adv.* where; somewhere; when; *~ nicht,* if not, unless; *~ nur,* wherever.
w.o. *wie oben,* as above.

wö. *wöchentlich*, weekly.
woanders *adv.* somewhere else.
wobei *adv.* at, by, in, with, which *or* what, in which case.
Woche *f.* **(-, -n)** week.
Wochen: ~bett *n.* childbed.
Wochenende *n.* weekend.
wochenlang *a. & adv.* for weeks together.
Wochenlohn *m.* weekly wages.
Wochenschau *f.* newsreel.
Wochenschrift *f.* weekly.
Wochentag *m.* weekday.
wochentags *adv.* on weekdays.
wöchentlich *a. & adv.* weekly.
wodurch *adv.* by which, through what or which.
wofür *adv.* for what or which.
Woge *f.* **(-, -n)** wave; *die ~n glätten,* pour oil on troubled waters.
wogegen *adv.* against what *or* which; (in return) for what *or* which.
wogen *v.i.* to wave; to fluctuate; to heave; to surge.
woher *adv.* where from, from what place.
wohin *adv.* where to.
wohingegen *c.* whereas.
wohl *adv.* well; indeed; possibly, probably; *wieder ~ sein,* to be all right again; *~ oder übel,* willy-nilly, come what may; *mir ist ~,* I feel comfortable.
Wohl *n.* **(-[e]s, 0)** welfare, good, benefit.
wohlan! *i.* now then! well!
wohlauf! *i.* now then! up!; *er ist ~,* he is in good health.
wohlbedacht *a.* well-considered, well-advised.
Wohlbefinden *n.* good health.
Wohlbehagen *n.* comfort, ease.
wohlbehalten *a.* safe (and sound).
wohlbekannt *a.* well-known.
wohlbeliebt *a.* corpulent, stout.
wohlbeschaffen *a.* in good condition.
wohlbesetzt *a.* well-filled, well-stored.
wohlbewandert *a.* well-versed, well up (in).
wohlerfahren *a.* experienced, well skilled.
Wohlergehen *n.* **(-s, 0)** welfare.
wohlerhalten *a.* in good condition, well-preserved, safe.
wohlerwogen *a.* well-considered.
wohlerworben *a.* duly acquired.
wohlerzogen *a.* well-bred.
Wohlfahrt *f.* welfare.
Wohlfahrtspflege *f.* welfare work.
wohlfeil *a.* cheap.
wohlgebildet *a.* well-formed, well-shaped.
Wohlgefallen *n.* pleasure, delight; *sein ~ haben an,* to take delight in; *sich in ~ auflösen,* to end satisfactorily.
wohlgefällig *a.* pleasant; pleased, complacent.
wohlgelaunt *a., adv.* cheerful(ly).
wohl: ~gelitten *a.* well-liked; **~gemeint** *a.* well-meant; **~gemut** *a.* cheerful, merry; **~genährt** *a.* well-fed; **~geordnet** *a.* well-ordered; **~geraten** *a.* fine; successful.
Wohlgeruch *m.* perfume, fragrance.
Wohlgeschmack *m.* flavor, relish.
wohlgesinnt *a.* well-meaning.
wohlgesittet *a.* well-mannered.
wohlgestaltet *a.* well-shaped.
wohlgewogen *a.* kind.
wohlhabend *a.* well off, well-to-do.
Wohlhabenheit *f.* **(-, 0)** wealth, affluence.
wohlig *a.* comfortable, snug, cozy.
Wohlklang, Wohllaut *m.* euphony, harmony; harmonious sound.
wohlklingend *a.* sweet (-sounding), harmonious, euphonious.
Wohlleben *n.* life of luxury.
wohlmeinend *a.* well-meaning.
wohlriechend *a.* sweet-scented, fragrant.
wohlschmeckend *a.* tasty.
Wohlsein *n.* good health.
Wohlstand *m.* prosperity, comfort.
Wohltat *f.* benefit; kindness, good action.
Wohltäter *m.* benefactor.
Wohltäterin *f.* benefactress.
wohltätig *a.* charitable, salutary.
Wohltätigkeit *f.* charity, benevolence; **~sverein** *f.* charitable society.
wohltuend *a.* beneficial, salutary.
wohltun *v.t.st.* to do good, to benefit.
wohlverbürgt *a.* well authenticated.
wohlverdient *a.* well-deserved; deserving.
Wohlverhalten *n.* good conduct.
wohlverstanden *a.* well understood.
wohlweislich *adv.* prudently.
wohlwollen *v.i.st.* to wish well.
Wohlwollen *n.* goodwill, kindness
wohlwollend *a.* benevolent, kind.
Wohn... residential, *a.*
wohnen *v.i.* to dwell, to live, to reside; to lodge, to stay.
Wohngebäude *n.* residential building.
wohnhaft *a.* resident.
Wohnhaus *n.* residential building.
wohnlich *a.* comfortable.
Wohn: ~ort, ~platz, ~sitz *m.* place of residence.
Wohnung *f.* **(-, -en)** apartment.
Wohnungs: ~amt *n.* housing office; **~mangel** *m.*, **~not** *f.* housing shortage; **~wechsel** *m.* change of residence.
Wohnviertel *n.* residential district.
Wohnwagen *m.* trailer, mobile home.
Wohnzimmer *n.* living room.
wölben *v.t.* to vault, to arch.
Wölbung *f.* **(-, -en)** vault(ing).
Wolf *m.* **(-[e]s, Wölfe)** wolf.
wölfisch *a.* wolfish.
Wolfram *m.* **(-s, 0)** tungsten; **~erz** *n.* wolfram.
Wolfs: ~hund *m.* German shepherd; **~hunger** *m.* ravenous appetite.
Wolke *f.* **(-, -n)** cloud.
Wolkenbruch *m.* cloudburst.
Wolkenkratzer *m.* skyscraper.
wolkenlos *a.* cloudless, serene.
wolkig *a.* cloudy, clouded.
Wolldecke *f.* (woollen) blanket.
Wolle *f.* **(-, -n)** wool.
wollen *a.* woolen; worsted; **~** *v.i.st.* to be willing, to intend, to wish, to want; *lieber ~,* to prefer.
Wollen *n.* will; volition (*phil.*).
Wollgarn *n.* worsted.
wollig *a.* woolly.
Wolljacke *f.* cardigan.
Wollkleid *n.* woolen dress.
Wollknäuel *n.* ball of wood.
Wollstoff *m.* woolen cloth.
Wollust *f.* **(-, -lüste)** lust, voluptuousness, sensuality.
wollüstig *a.* voluptuous; lustful; sensual.
Wollüstling *m.* **(-[e]s, -e)** lecher.
womit *adv.* with which or what.

womöglich *adv.* possibly.
wonach *adv.* after what or which.
Wonne *f.* **(-, -n)** delight, bliss, rapture.
wonnetrunken *a.* enraptured.
wonnig *a.* delightful, blissful; lovely.
woran *adv.* on what or which; ~ *liegt es?* how is it that?
worauf *adv.* whereupon.
woraus *adv.* wherefrom.
worein *adv.* in(to) what or which.
worin *adv.* wherein, in which or what.
Wort *n.* **(-[e]s, -e & Wörter)** word, term; *mit anderen ~en,* in other words; *ich bitte ums ~,* I request permission to speak; *sein ~ brechen, halten,* to break, keep one's word; *das ~ haben,* to have the floor; *ins ~ fallen,* to interrupt.
Wortbildung *f.* word formation.
Wortbruch *m.* breach of faith.
wortbrüchig *a.* **~ werden** to break one's word.
Wörterbuch *n.* dictionary.
Wortführer *m.* spokesman.
Wortführerin *f.* spokeswoman.
wortgetreu *a.* literal.
wortkarg *a.* laconic; taciturn.
Wortklauberei *f.* hairsplitting.
Wortlaut *m.* wording, text.
wörtlich *a.* verbal, literal; ~ *adv.* literally, word for word, verbatim.
wortlos *a.* wordless; unspoken.
wortreich *a.* verbose, wordy, voluble.
Wort: ~schatz *m.* vocabulary; **~schöpfung** *f.* coinage; neologism; **~schwall** *m.* bombast; volley of words; **~sinn** *m.* literal sense; **~spiel** *n.* pun; **~stellung** *f.* order of words; **~streit** *m.* dispute (about words), quarrel; **~wechsel** *m.* dispute, argument; **~witz** *m.* pun.
worüber *adv.* over what.
worum *adv.* about what or which.
worunter *adv.* under or among which or what.
wovon *adv.* from where; ~ *leben sie?* what do they live on?
wovor *adv.* before, of what or which.
wozu *adv.* to what; what for.
Wrack *n.* **(-[e]s, -e)** wreck.
wringen *v.t.st.* to wring (out).
WS *Wintersemester,* winter term.
Wucher *m.* **(-s, 0)** usury, profiteering.
Wucherer *m.* **(-s, -)** usurer.
wucherhaft, wucherisch *a.* usurious.
wuchern *v.i.* (*von Pflanzen*) to proliferate.
Wucherpreis *m.* extortionate price.
Wucherung *f.* **(-, -en)** growth.
Wuchs *m.* **(-es, Wüchse)** growth; figure, stature, shape, size.
Wucht *f.* **(-, 0)** weight; force, impact.
wuchten *v.t.* to heave.
wuchtig *a.* heavy, ponderous.
Wühlarbeit *f.* subversive activities *pl.*
wühlen *v.i. & t.* to dig (up); (*fig.*) to agitate, to stir up; to wallow.
Wulst *m.* **(-s, Wülste)** roll; pad.
wulstig *a.* bulging; thick (lip).
wund *a.* sore, wounded; *ein ~er Punkt,* a sore spot.
Wundbrand *m.* gangrene.
Wunde *f.* **(-, -n)** wound, cut.
Wunder *n.* **(-s, -)** wonder, marvel; miracle; *es nimmt mich wunder,* I wonder at it.
wunderbar *a.* wonderful, miraculous, marvelous, strange.
Wunder: ~ding *n.* wonderous thing; **~doktor** *m.* miracle doctor.
wunderhübsch *a.* simply lovely.
Wunder: ~kind *n.* child prodigy; **~kraft** *f.* miraculous power; **~kur** *f.* miraculous cure.
wunderlich *a.* strange, odd, peculiar.
wundern *v.r.* to wonder, to be amazed; *es wundert mich,* I wonder at it, I am surprised.
wunderschön *a.* wonderful, beautiful.
Wundertäter *m.;* **Wundertäterin** *f.* miracle worker.
wundervoll *a.* wonderful, marvellous.
Wunderwerk *n.* marvel.
Wundfieber *n.* wound fever.
wundgelaufen *a.* footsore.
wundliegen *v.r.st.* to get bedsores.
Wundmal *n.* scar, cicatrice; stigma.
Wundstarrkrampf *m.* tetanus.
Wunsch *m.* **(-es, Wünsche)** wish, desire; *auf ~,* at the request of; *nach ~* according to one's wish; *ein frommer ~,* a vain desire or wish.
Wunschdenken *n.* wishful thinking.
Wünschelrute *f.* divining rod.
Wünschelrutengänger *m.* dowser; diviner.
wünschen *v.t.* to wish (for); to desire, to long for; *Glück ~,* to congratulate.
wünschenswert *a.* desirable.
wunschgemäß *adv.* as desired.
Wunschkind *n.* wanted child.
Wunschkonzert *n.* request program.
wunschlos *a.* contented.
Wunschtraum *m.* pipe dream.
Wunschzettel *m.* list of presents.
Würde *f.* **(-, -n)** dignity; honor; office.
würdelos *a.* undignified.
Würdenträger *m.* dignitary.
würdevoll *a.* dignified, grave.
würdig *a.* worthy; deserving (of).
würdigen *v.t.* to appreciate, to value.
Würdigung *f.* **(-, -en)** appreciation.
Wurf *m.* **(-[e]s, Würfe)** cast, throw; litter, brood.
Würfel *m.* **(-s, -)** die; (*math.*) cube.
Würfelbecher *m.* dice box.
würfelförmig *a.* cubic(al).
würfeln *v.i.* to throw the dice; to play dice; to dice (vegetables).
Würfel: ~spiel *n.* game of dice; **~zucker** *m.* cube-sugar.
Wurfgeschoß *n.* missile, projection.
Wurflinie *f.* trajectory.
Wurfmaschine *f.* catapult.
Wurfspeer *m.* javelin.
Wurfspieß *m.* javelin.
würgen *v.t.* to strangle, to throttle; to retch; to choke on.
Würger *m.* **(-s, -)** murderer, cut-throat.
Wurm *m.* **(-[e]s, Würmer)** worm.
Wurm *n.* little mite.
wurmartig *a.* vermicular, worm-like.
wurmen *v.t.* to vex, to annoy.
Wurmfortsatz *m.* (*med.*) appendix.
wurmig *a.* wormy; worm-eaten.
Wurst *f.* **(-, Würste)** sausage; *das ist mir (ganz) ~,* I couldn't care less.
Wurstigkeit *f.* **(-, 0)** (*sl.*) to-hell-with-it attitude.
Würze *f.* **(-, -n)** spice, seasoning.
Wurzel *f.* **(-, -n)** root; carrot; *~ fassen (schlagen),* to take root.
wurzeln *v.t.* to root, to be rooted.
Wurzelwerk *n.* roots, root system.

Wurzelzeichen *n.* (*math.*) radical sign.
würzen *v.t.* to season, to spice.
würzhaft, würzig *a.* aromatic, spicy.
wuschelig *a.* frizzy; fuzzy.
Wuschelkopf *m.* shock of frizzy/fuzzy hair.
Wust *m.* **(-es, -e)** chaos; jumble
wüst *a.* waste, desert, wilderness.
Wüste *f.* **(-, -en)** desert, wilderness.
Wüstenei *f.* **(-, -en)** desert, wasteland.
Wüstling *m.* **(-[e]s, -e)** libertine, rake.
Wut *f.* **(-, 0)** rage, fury.
Wutanfall *m.* fit of rage.
wüten *v.i.* to rage, to rave.
wütend, wutentbrannt *a.* furious, enraged.
Wüterich *m.* **(-s, -e)** brute.
wütig *a.* enraged, furious.
wutschnaubend *a.* infuriated.
Wutschrei *m.* cry of rage.
Wz. *Warenzeichen,* trademark, TM.

XYZ

X, x *n.* the letter X or x; *einem ein X für U (vor-) machen,* to fool sb.; to dupe sb.
Xanthippe *f.* (*pej.*) shrew; battle axe.
X-Beine *n.pl.* knock-knees *pl.*
x-beinig *a.* knock-kneed.
x-beliebig *a.* any...(you like).
X-Chromosom *n.* X chromosome.
x-fach *adv.* x times.
x-mal *adv.* (number of) times; many times.
Xylophon *n.* **(-s, -e)** xylophone.
Y, y *n.* the letter Y or y.
Yacht *f.* **(-, -en)** yacht.
Y-Chromosom *n.* Y chromosome.
Yoga *m./n.* yoga.
Ypsilon *n.* y, Y; upsilon (in the Greek alphabet).
Z, z *n.* *von A bis Z,* from beginning to end; ~ *n.* the letter Z or z.
Z. *Zeile,* line; *Zoll,* inch.
z. *zu, zum, zur,* to, at.
Zack *auf ~ sein,* to be on the ball.
Zacke *f.* **(-, -n), Zacken** *m.* **(-s, -)** tooth, spike, prong; (*Felsen ~*) jag.
zacken *v.t.* to tooth, to indent.
zackig *a.* pronged, indented; jagged.
zagen *v.i.* to hesitate; to be afraid.
zaghaft *a.* timid; hesitant; cautious.
zäh *a.* tough; sticky; tenacious.
Zäheit *f.* toughness; heaviness; viscosity.
zähflüssig *a.* viscous; heavy.
Zähflüssigkeit *f.* **(-, 0)** viscosity.
Zähigkeit *f.* tenacity, toughness.
Zahl *f.* **(-, -en)** number; figure, digit.
Zählapparat *m.* counter; meter (gas).
zahlbar *a.* payable, due.
zählbar *a.* numerable, countable.
zahlen *v.t.* to pay; *Kellner ~!* the check, please!
zählen *v.t.* to count, to number
zahlender Gast *m.* paying guest.
zahlenmäßig *a.* numerical.
Zahlenschloß *n.* combination lock.
Zahlenwert *m.* numerical value.
Zahler *m.* **(-s, -)** payer.
Zähler (*math*) numerator; (*gas, elek.*) meter.
zahllos *a.* numberless, innumerable.
Zahlmeister *m.* paymaster.
zahlreich *a.* numerous.
Zahl: ~stelle *f.* pay office; **~tag** *m.* pay day.
Zahlung *f.* **(-, -en)** payment; *als ~,* in settlement; *~en einstellen,* to stop *or* suspend payment.
Zahlungs: ~anweisung *f.* money order; **~bedingungen** *pl.* terms of payment; **~befehl** *m.* payment order; **~einstellung** *f.* suspension of payment; **~empfänger** *m.* payee.
zahlungsfähig *a.* solvent, able to pay.
Zahlungs: ~fähigkeit *f.* solvency; **~frist** *f.* time of payment; **~mittel** *n.* (legal) tender; **~ort** *m.* place of payment; **~termin** *m.* date of payment.
zahlungsunfähig *a.* insolvent.
Zahlungs: ~unfähigkeit *f.* insolvency; **~verbindlichkeit** *f.* liability (to pay).
Zahlwort *n.* numeral.
Zahlzeichen *n.* numeral; figure; digit (0-9).
zahm *a.* tame, domesticated; (*fig.*) gentle.
zähmen *v.t.* to tame, to domesticate.
Zahn *m.* **(-[e]s, Zähne)** tooth; cog (of a wheel); *Haare auf den Zähnen haben,* to know what's what; to be a Tartar.
Zahnarzt *m.;* **Zahnärztin** *f.* dentist.
Zahnbelag *m.* plaque.
Zahnbürste *f.* toothbrush.
Zahncreme *f.* toothpaste.
Zähnefletschen *n.* **(-s, 0)** showing one's teeth.
Zähneklappern *n.* **(-s, 0)** chattering of teeth.
Zähneknirschen *n.* gnashing of teeth.
zahnen *v.i.* to teethe, to cut one's teeth.
zähnen to indent, to tooth, to notch.
Zahn: ~erzatz *m.* dentures; **~fäule** *f.* tooth decay; caries; **~fleisch** *n.* gums *pl.;* **~füllung** *f.* filling; **~heilkunde** *f.* dentistry; **~krone** *f.* crown; **~laut** *m.* dental (sound).
zahnlos *a.* toothless.
Zahnlücke *f.* gap between two teeth.
Zahn: ~medizin *f.* dentistry; **~paste** *f.* toothpaste; **~pflege** *f.* dental hygiene; **~prothese** *f.* dentures; **~pulver** *n.* tooth powder; **~rad** *n.* gear, pinion, cog wheel; **~radbahn** *f.* cog railroad; **~schmerzen** *m.* toothache; **~seide** *f.* dental floss; **~stein** *m.* tartar; **~stocher** *m.* toothpick; **~techniker** *m.* dental technician; **~weh** *n.* toothache.
Zaire *n.* **(-s, 0)** Zaire.
Zange *f.* **(-, -en)** pincers; tongs; pliers *pl.*
Zank *m.* **(-[e]s, 0)** quarrel, squabble.
Zankapfel *m.* (*fig.*) bone of contention.
zanken *v.i.* to quarrel, to wrangle; ~ *v.r.* to quarrel, to dispute.
zänkisch *a.* quarrelsome.
Zank: ~lust, ~sucht *f.* quarrelsomeness.
zanksüchtig *a.* quarrelsome.
Zäpfchen *n.* **(-s, -)** (*anat.*) uvula; (*med.*) suppository.
Zapfen *m.* **(-s, -)** cone, pin, peg; (*Faß*) tap.
zapfen *v.t.* to draw, to tap.
Zapfenstreich *m.* taps; *der Grosse ~,* tattoo.
Zapfhahn *m.* tap.
Zapfsäule *f.* gasoline pump.
zappeln *v.i.* to sprawl, to kick, to struggle, to flounder; to fidget.
zapp(e)lig *a.* fidgety, restless, fussy.
Zar *m.* **(-en, -e)** czar, tsar.

Zarin (-, nen) *f.* czarina, tsarina.
zart *a.* tender; delicate; frail.
zartbesaitet *a.* highly sensitive.
zartbitter *a.* bittersweet.
zartfühlend *a.* considerate, sensitive.
Zartgefühl *n.* delicacy of feeling.
Zartheit *f.* **(-, -en)** tenderness; delicacy.
zärtlich *a.* tender, delicate, fond.
Zärtlichkeit *f.* **(-, -en)** tenderness; fondness; **~en** *pl.* caresses *pl.*
Zartsinn *m.* delicacy.
Zäsur *f.* **(-, -en)** caesura.
Zauber *m.* **(-s, -)** magic, charm, enchantment, spell, fascination.
Zauberei *f.* **(-, -en)** magic, witchcraft.
Zauberer *m.* **(-s, -)** magician, sorcerer.
Zauberformel *f.* magic spell; magic formula.
zauberhaft *a.* magical, enchanting.
Zauberin *f.* **(-, -nen)** sorceress, witch.
zauberisch *a.* magical; enchanting.
Zauberkraft *f.* magic power.
Zauberkunst *f.* magic.
Zauberkünstler *m.* magician, conjurer.
zaubern *v.i.* to practise magic, to conjure.
Zauberstab *m.* magic wand.
Zaubertrick *m.* conjuring trick.
zaudern *v.i.* to hesitate, to waver.
Zaum *m.* **(-[e]s, Zäume)** bridle; *im ~e halten,* to bridle, to check.
zäumen *v.t.* to bridle; (*fig.*) to restrain.
Zaumzeug *n.* bridle.
Zaun *m.* **(-[e]s, Zäune)** hedge, fence.
Zaungast *m.* onlooker.
Zaunkönig *m.* wren.
Zaunpfahl *m.* fence post; *ein Wink mit dem ~,* a broad hint.
z.B. *zum Beispiel,* for instance.
Zebra *n.* **(-[s], -s)** zebra.
Zebrastreifen *m.* pedestrian crossing.
Zechbruder *m.* (*sl.*) boozer.
Zeche *f.* **(-, -n)** tab (in a bar); (*Bergwerk*) mine, colliery; *die ~ bezahlen* (*fig.*) to pick up the tab.
zechen *v.i.* to tipple, to drink hard, to carouse.
Zechgelage *n.* drinking bout.
Zechkumpan *m.* drinking companion.
Zech: ~preller *m.* cheat, swindler.
Zecke *f.* **(-, -n)** tick.
Zeder *f.* **(-, -n)** cedar.
zedieren *v.t.* to cede, to surrender.
Zehe *f.* **(-, -n), Zeh** *m.* **(-en, -en)** toe; *die grosse ~,* the big toe; *auf den ~n gehen,* to walk on tiptoe.
Zehennagel *m.* toenail.
Zehenspitze *f.* tiptoe; point of the toe.
zehn *a.* ten.
Zehner *m.* **(-s, -)** ten.
zehnerlei *a.* of ten sorts.
zehnfach, zehnfältig *a.* tenfold.
zehnjährig *a.* ten years old, of ten years.
Zehnkampf *m.* decathlon.
Zehnkämpfer *m.* decathlete.
zehnmal *adv.* ten times.
Zehnmarkschein *m.* ten mark bill.
Zehnpfennigbriefmarke *f.* ten pfennig stamp
Zehnpfennigstück *n.* ten pfennig piece.
zehnt *a.* tenth.
Zehnte *m.* **(-n, -n)** tithe.
Zehntel *n.* **(-s, -)** tenth.
zehntens *adv.* tenthly.
zehren *v.i.* (*an, von*) to live on, to feed on.
Zeichen *n.* **(-s, -)** sign, token, mark; (*com.*) reference(-number); *seines ~s ist er Schuster,* he is a shoemaker by trade.
Zeichen: ~block *m.* sketch pad; **~brett** *n.* drawing board; **~erklärung** *f.* legend; **~setzung** *f.* punctuation; **~sprache** *f.* sign language; **~tinte** *f.* marking ink; **~trickfilm** *m.* animated cartoon.
zeichnen *v.t.* to draw, to design; to mark; to sign, to subscribe; (*Anleihe*) to subscribe for.
Zeichner *m.* **(-s, -)** graphic artist; draftsman; subscriber.
Zeichnung *f.* **(-, -en)** drawing, design, sketch, diagram; subscription.
zeichnungsberechtigt *a.* authorized to sign.
Zeichnungsliste *f.* subscription list.
Zeigefinger *m.* forefinger, index.
zeigen *v.t.* to show, to point out, to demonstrate; *~ v.r.* to appear; *es muß sich zeigen,* it remains to be seen.
Zeiger *m.* **(-s, -)** hand (of a clock); pointer.
Zeigestock *m.* pointer.
zeihen *v.t.st.* to accuse (of).
Zeile *f.* **(-, -n)** line; **einzeilig** *a.* single-spaced; **zweizeilig** *a.* double-spaced.
Zeilen: ~abstand *m.* spacing; **~anzeige** *f.* line display; **~drucker** *n.* (*comp.*) line printer.
Zeisig *m.* **(-[e]s, -e)** siskin.
Zeit *f.* **(-, -en)** time; season; age; era, period; tide; *zur ~,* at present; *mit der ~,* in the course of time; *vor ~en,* in former times; *in rechter ~, zur rechten ~,* in (good) time; *zu ~en,* at times; *eine ~lang,* for a while, for some time; **~ (seines) Lebens,** (in) (all) his life; *sich ~ lassen,* to take (one's) time; *sich die ~ vertreiben,* to pass the time with.
Zeit: ~ablauf *m.* lapse of time; **~abschnitt** *m.* epoch, period; **~alter** *n.* age, era; **~bombe** *f.* time-bomb; **~dauer** *f.* duration, lapse of time; **~form** *f.* (*gram.*) tense; **~geist** *m.* spirit of the age.
zeitgemäß *a.* modern.
zeitgen. *zeitgenössisch,* contemporary.
Zeitgenosse *m.*; **Zeitgenossin** *f.* contemporary.
zeitgenössisch *a.* contemporary.
Zeitgeschehen *n.* current events.
zeitgleich *a.* simultaneous.
zeitig *a.* early, timely; ripe; *~ adv.* early, in (due) time.
zeitigen *v.t.* to produce; to yield; to provoke.
Zeitkarte *f.* season or weekly ticket.
Zeitlang *f.* *eine ~,* for a while.
zeitlebens *adv.* for life; during life.
zeitlich *a.* temporal, temporary, earthly.
Zeitlichkeit *f.* **(-, 0)** earthly life.
Zeit: ~lupe *f.* slow motion; **~lupenaufnahme** *f.* slow-motion picture; **~punkt** *f.* moment; **~raffer** *m.* time lapse; quick motion.
zeitraubend *a.* time consuming.
Zeit: ~raum *m.* space of time, period; **~rechnung** *f.* chronology; era; **~schrift** *f.* periodical, journal, magazine.
Zeitung *f.* **(-, -en)** newspaper, gazette.
Zeitungs: ~anzeige *f.* advertisement; **~ausschnitt** *m.* newspaper cutting *or* clipping; **~ente** *f.* canard; **~inserat** *n.* advertisement; **~kiosk** *m.* newsstand; **~papier** *n.* newsprint; **~verkäufer** *m.* newsvendor; **~wesen** *n.* journalism, the press.
Zeitvergeudung *f.* waste of time.
Zeit: ~verhältnisse pl. circumstances; **~verlauf**

m. lapse of time; **~verschwendung** *f.* waste of time; **~vertreib** *m.* pastime, diversion.
zeitvertreibend *a.* diverting, amusing.
zeitweilig *a.* temporary; **~er Dienst,** (*mil.*) temporary duty.
zeitweise *adv.* at times.
Zeit: ~wort *n.* verb; **~zeichen** *n.* (*Radio*) time signal.
Zeitzünder *m.* time fuse.
zelebrieren *v.t.* to celebrate.
Zelle *f.* **(-, -n)** cell.
Zellgewebe *n.* cell tissue.
Zellkern *m.* nucleus.
Zellophan *n.* **(-s, 0)** cellophane.
Zellstoff *m.* cellulose; pulp.
zellular *a.* cellular.
Zellulitis *f.* cellulitis.
Zelluloid *n.* **(-s, 0)** celluloid.
Zellulose *f.* **(-, 0)** cellulose; pulp.
Zellwolle *f.* rayon.
Zelot *m.* **(-en, -en)** zealot.
Zelt *n.* **(-[e]s, -e)** tent, awning; pavilion.
Zeltdach *n.*, **Zeltdecke** *f.* marquee.
zelten *v.i.* to camp.
Zelter *m.* **(-s, -)** ambler, palfrey (horse).
Zeltlager *n.* tent camp.
Zeltplane *f.* tarpaulin.
Zeltplatz *m.* campsite.
Zement *m.* **(-es, -)** cement.
Zementboden *m.* concrete floor.
zementieren *v.t.* to cement.
Zenit *m.* **(-[e]s, 0)** zenith.
zensieren *v.t.* to mark; to criticize; to censure.
Zensor *m.* **(-s, -en)** censor.
Zensur *f.* censorship; (school-)report, mark, grade.
Zensus *m.* **(-, 0)** census.
Zentigramm *n.* centigram.
Zentimeter *m. or n.* **(-s, -)** centimeter.
Zentner *m.* **(-s, -)** hundredweight; centner.
Zentnerlast *f.* heavy burden.
zentnerschwer *a.* very heavy, ponderous, oppressive.
zentral *a.* central.
Zentrale *f.* **(-, -n)** central office *or* station; headquarters.
Zentralheizung *f.* central heating; *mit* ~, centrally heated.
zentralisieren *v.t.* to centralize.
Zentralismus *m.* centralism.
Zentralverriegelung *f.* central locking system (car).
zentrieren *v.t.* to center.
Zentrifugalkraft *f.* centrifugal force.
Zentripetalkraft *f.* centripetal force.
zentrisch *a.* centric.
Zentrum *n.* **(-s, -tren)** center; bull's eye; ~ *der Stadt,* downtown.
Zepter *n.* & *m.* **(-s, -)** sceptre; mace.
zerbeißen *v.t.st.* to bite into pieces.
zerbersten *v.i.st.* to burst.
zerbrechen *v.t.st.* to break (to pieces); ~ *v.r. den Kopf* ~, to rack one's brains; ~ *v.i.st.* to break.
zerbrechlich *a.* fragile, brittle.
zerbröckeln *v.i.* to crumble.
zerdrücken *v.t.* to crush; to bruise.
Zeremonie *f.* **(-, -n)** ceremony.
Zeremoniell *n.* **(-s, -e)** ceremonial.
zeremoniös *a.* ceremonious.
zerfahren *a.* thoughtless, incoherent.
Zerfall *m.* **(-[e]s, 0)** ruin, decay, disintegration; decomposition.
zerfallen *v.i.st.* to fall to pieces; to decay; (*fig.*) to fall out (with one).
Zerfalls: ~produkt *n.* decomposition product; **~zeit** *f.* decomposition period.
zerfasern *v.t.* to ravel out.
zerfetzen *v.t.* to slash, to tatter.
zerfleischen *v.t.* to tear to pieces; to mangle.
zerfließen *v.i.st.* to dissolve, to melt.
zerfressen *v.t.st.* to corrode.
zergehen *v.i.st.* to dissolve.
zergliedern *v.t.* to dissect, to dismember.
Zergliederung *f.* **(-, -en)** dissection; (*fig.*) analysis.
zerhacken *v.t.* to chop, to mince.
zerhauen *v.t.st.* to chop up; to cut up, to slash.
zerinnen *v.i.st.* to dissolve, to melt.
zerkauen *v.t.* to chew.
zerkleinern *v.t.* to chop (wood).
zerklüftet *a.* fissured; craggy.
zerknirscht *a.* contrite.
Zerknirschung *f.* **(-, 0)** contrition.
zerknittern, zerknüllen *v.t.* to crumple.
zerkratzen *v.t.* to scratch.
zerkrümeln *v.t.* to crumble.
zerlassen *v.t.st.* to dissolve, to melt.
zerlegbar *a.* divisible, dissectible.
zerlegen *v.t.* to take to pieces; to carve.
zerlumpt *a.* ragged, tattered.
zermahlen *v.t.st.* to grind (to powder).
zermalmen *v.t.* to bruise, to crush.
zermürben *v.t.* to wear down.
zernagen *v.t.* to gnaw to pieces.
zerpflücken *v.t.* to pick to pieces.
zerplatzen *v.i.* to burst.
zerquetschen *v.t.* to crush, to squash.
Zerrbild *n.* caricature; distorted picture.
zerreiben *v.t.st.* to grind to powder.
zerreißbar *a.* tearable.
zerreißen *v.t.st.* to tear, to rend; ~ *v.i.st.* to be torn.
zerren *v.t.* to pull, to tug.
Zerrissenheit *f.* **(-, 0)** raggedness, disruption; *innere* ~, inner conflicts.
Zerrung *f.* strain.
zerrütten *v.t.* to unsettle, to ruin, to shatter; (*den Geist*) to unhinge.
Zerrüttung *f.* **(-, -en)** disorder, ruin; (*Geistes*~) derangement.
zersägen *v.t.* to saw to pieces.
zerschellen *v.i.* to be dashed to pieces.
zerschlagen *v.t.st.* to shatter, to smash, to break (by striking); ~ *v.r.* to come to nothing; ~ *a.* shattered.
zerschmettern *v.t.* to crush, to shatter.
zerschneiden *v.t.st.* to cut to pieces.
zersetzen *v.t.* to decompose.
zersetzend *a.* submersive.
Zersetzung *f.* **(-, -en)** decomposition.
zerspalten *v.t.* to cleave, to split.
zersplittern *v.t.* to split, to shiver; to fritter away.
zersprengen *v.t.* to disperse, to scatter.
zerspringen *v.i.st.* to burst; (*Glas*) to crack; (*Kopf*) to split.
zerstäuben *v.t.* to spray.
zerstechen *v.t.st.* to sting all over; to puncture.
zerstieben *v.i.st.* to vanish, to fly asunder.
zerstörbar *a.* destructible.
zerstören *v.t.* to destroy, to ruin.

Zerstörer *m.* **(-s, -)** (*nav.*) destroyer.
zerstörerisch *a.* destructive.
Zerstörung *f.* **(-, -en)** destruction.
zerstoßen *v.t.st.* to pound, to crush.
zerstreuen *v.t.* to scatter, to disperse; to dispel; ~ *v.r.* to divert oneself, to seek diversion.
zerstreut *a.* (*fig.*) absent-minded; (*Licht*) diffused.
Zerstreutheit *f.* **(-, 0)** absentmindedness.
Zerstreuung *f.* **(-, -en)** dispersion; diversion.
Zerstückelung *f.* **(-, -en)** dismemberment, parcelling (out).
zerstückeln *v.t.* to dismember; to cut up, to parcel out.
zerteilbar *a.* divisible.
zerteilen *v.t.* to divide, to disperse, to dismember; (*math.*) to resolve (into factors).
zertrennen *v.t.* to take apart; to rip up.
zertreten *v.t.st.* to crush.
zertrümmern *v.t.* to destroy, to wreck.
Zervelatwurst *f.* salami.
zerwühlen *v.t.* to churn up; to make a mess of.
Zerwürfnis *n.* **(-nisses, -nisse)** difference, discord, quarrel, dissension.
zerzausen *v.t.* to ruffle, to tousle.
Zeter *n.* *~ über einen schreien,* raise a hue and cry after sb.
zetern *v.i.* to wail; to nag.
Zettel *m.* **(-s, -)** slip of paper, note; label; poster.
Zeug *n.* **(-[e]s, -e)** stuff; matter; cloth; rubbish, trash; *das ~ haben zu etwas,* (*fig.*) to have the makings of; *sich ins ~ legen,* to launch out; *dummes ~,* stuff and nonsense.
Zeuge *m.* **(-n, -n)** witness; *einen ~n beibringen,* to produce a witness.
zeugen *v.t.* to father; ~ *v.i.* to witness, to testify, to depose.
Zeugen: ~aussage *f.* testimony; **~beweis** *n.* evidence; **~bank** *f.* witness box; **~stand** *m.* witness stand; **~verhör** *n.*, **~vernehmung** *f.* examination of witnesses; **~vorladung** *f.* witness summons.
Zeughaus *n.* arsenal.
Zeugin *f.* (female) witness.
Zeugnis *n.* **(-nisses, -nisse)** testimony, evidence; character, certificate; (*Schul~*) reportcard; **~ ablegen,** to give evidence; to bear witness.
Zeugung *f.* **(-, -en)** fathering, procreation, generation.
zeugungsfähig *a.* fertile.
zeugungsunfähig *a.* impotent, sterile.
ZH *Zentralheizung,* central heating, centr. heat.
z.H. *zu Händen,* at *or* on hand; care of.
Zi. *Zimmer,* room, rm; *Ziffer,* figure, fig., number, no.
Zichorie *f.* **(-, -n)** chicory.
Zicke *f.*, **Zicklein** *n.* **(-s, -)** kid.
zickig *a.* prim; prudish.
Zickzack *m.* **(-[e]s, -e)** zigzag.
Ziege *f.* **(-, -n)** goat, she-goat.
Ziegel *m.* **(-s, -)** tile; brick.
Ziegelbrenner *m.* brickmaker.
Ziegelbrennerei *f.* brickworks *pl.*
Ziegel: ~dach *n.* tiled roof; **~decker** *m.* tiler.
Ziegelei *f.* **(-, -en)** brickworks.
Ziegelstein *m.* brick.
Ziegen: ~bock *m.* he-goat; **~fell** *n.* goatskin; **~hirt** *m.* goatherd; **~leder** *n.* goatskin.
Ziegenpeter *m.* **(-s, -)** (*fam.*) mumps *pl.*
Ziehbrunnen *m.* well.
ziehen *v.t.st.* to draw; to pull; to cultivate, to grow, to breed; (*Schiff*) to tow; to extract (a tooth, a root of a number); ~ *v.r.* to extend; (*Holz*) to warp; ~ *v.i.* *(h)* (*im Schach*) to move; (*aus der Wohnung*) to move, to remove; *die Bilanz ~,* to draw up the balance sheet; *Nutzen aus etwas ~,* to derive profit from; *in den Schmutz ~,* (*fig.*) to blacken, to asperse; *in Betracht, in Erwähung ~,* to take into consideration, to consider; *ins Geheimnis, ins Vertrauen ~,* to take into confidence; *Gesichter ~,* to make faces; *den kürzeren ~,* to get the worst of it; *in die Länge ~,* to spin out; *in Zweifel ~,* to (call in) question, to doubt; *Folgen nach sich ~,* to entail consequences; *das Stück zieht,* the play draws large audiences; *der Tee muß noch ~,* the tea hasn't brewed yet; *es zieht hier,* there's a draft here.
Zieh: ~harmonika *f.* accordion, concertina; **~kind** *n.* foster-child.
Ziehung *f.* **(-, -en)** drawing (of the lottery).
Ziel *n.* **(-[e]s, -e)** aim, goal, mark; (*Luftkrieg*) target, objective; (*Reise*) destination; *ein ~ setzen,* to aim at.
zielbewußt *a.* purposeful; determined.
zielen *v.i.* to aim, to take aim, to sight; (*fig.*) to drive at.
Zielgerade *f.* home stretch.
zielgerichtet *a.* goal directed.
Zielgruppe *f.* target group.
Ziellinie *f.* finishing line.
ziellos *a.* aimless.
Zielscheibe *f.* target.
Zielsetzung *f.* objective; target.
zielsicher *a.* unerring.
Zielsprache *f.* target language.
zielstrebig *a.* purposeful, determined.
Zielstrebigkeit *f.* determination.
ziemen *v.i.* to become, to be suitable.
ziemlich *a.* suitable, fit; fair, moderate, passable, middling; *adv.* rather; quite.
Zier *f.* **(-, -en)** ornament, decoration.
Zierat *m.* **(-[e]s, -en)** ornament; decoration.
Zierde *f.* **(-, -n)** ornament; decoration.
zieren *v.t.* to adorn, to decorate; ~ *v.r.* to be coy; *sie ziert sich nicht,* she doesn't mince words.
zierlich *a.* delicate; neat.
Ziffer *f.* **(-, -n)** figure; digit; cipher; numeral.
Zifferblatt *n.* dial, (clock-) face.
ziffer(n)mäßig *a.* by figures, in number.
Zigarette *f.* **(-, -n)** cigarette.
Zigaretten: ~etui *n.* cigarette case; **~stummel** *m.* cigarette butt.
Zigarre *f.* **(-, -n)** cigar.
Zigarren: ~spitze *f.* cigar holder; tip (of a cigar); **~tasche** *f.* cigar case.
Zigeuner *m.* **(-s, -); Zigeunerin** *f.* **(-, -nen)** gipsy.
Zikade *f.* **(-, -n)** cicada, cigala.
Zimbel *f.* **(-, -n)** cymbal.
Zimmer *n.* **(-s, -)** room, chamber.
Zimmer: ~kellner *m.* room waiter; **~mädchen** *n.* chambermaid; **~mann** *m.* carpenter.
zimmern *v.t.* to construct (of wood); to do carpentry.
Zimmervermieter(in) *m.(f.)* landlord.
zimperlich *a.* prim, prudish, mincing.
Zimt *m.* **(-[e]s, -e)** cinnamon.
Zink *n.* **(-[e]s, 0)** zinc; spelter.
Zinke *f.* **(-, -n)** prong; (*mus.*) cornet.
Zinkgießer *m.* zinc-founder.
Zinn *n.* **(-[e]s, 0)** tin; (*für Geräte*) pewter.
Zinnbergwerk *n.* tin mine, stannary.

Zinne *f.* **(-, -n)** battlement; pinnacle.
Zinngeschirr *n.* pewter(utensils *pl.*).
Zinngießer *m.* pewterer.
Zinnober *m.* **(-s, 0)** cinnabar, vermilion; (*fam. fig.*) rubbish, fuss.
zinnoberrot *a.* vermilion.
Zins *m.* **(-es, -en)** rent; interest.
zinsbringend *a.* bearing interest.
Zinsen *f.pl.* interest; ~ *tragen,* to bear interest.
Zinseszins *m.* compound interest.
zinsfrei *a.* free of interest, rent-free.
Zinsfuß *m.* interest rate.
Zinssatz *m.* interest rate.
Zionismus *m.* zionism.
Zipfel *m.* **(-s, -)** tip, corner.
Zipfelmütze *f.* tasselled cap.
Zipperlein *n.* **(-s, 0)** gout.
zirka *adv.* approximately.
Zirkel *m.* **(-s, -)** circle (of people); pair of compasses *or* dividers.
zirkulieren *v.t. & i.* to circulate.
Zirkumflex *m.* **(-es, -e)** circumflex (accent).
Zirkus *m.* **(-, -kusse)** circus.
zirpen *v.i.* to chirp.
zischeln *v.i.* to whisper.
zischen *v.i.* to hiss; to whiz.
Zischlaut *m.* hissing sound; sibilant.
ziselieren *v.t.* to chase.
Zisterne *f.* **(-, -n)** cistern.
Zitadelle *f.* **(-, -n)** citadel.
Zitat *n.* **(-[e]s, -e)** quotation.
Zither *f.* **(-, -n)** zither.
zitieren *v.t.* to cite; to quote.
Zitronat *n.* candied lemon peel.
Zitrone *f.* **(-, -n)** lemon.
zitronengelb *a.* lemon-colored.
Zitronen: ~saft *m.* lemon-juice; **~säure** *f.* citric acid; **~schale** *f.* lemon peel; **~wasser** *n.* lemonade.
zittern *v.i.* to tremble, to quake, to shiver.
zittrig *a.* shaky; doddery.
Zitze *f.* **(-, -n)** teat, nipple.
zivil *a.* civil; **Zivil** *n.* **(-s, 0)** civilian clothes; *in* ~, in plain clothes, in mufti.
Zivil: ~bevölkerung *f.* civilian population; **~courage** *f.* courage of one's convictions; **~dienst** *m.* alternative service for conscientious objectors; **~dienstleistende** *m.* conscientious objectors doing alternative service.
Zivilehe *f.* civil marriage.
Zivilisation *f.* **(-, -en)** civilization.
Zivilisationskrankheit *f.* disease caused by modern civilization.
zivilisatorisch *a.* civilizing.
zivilisieren *v.t.* to civilize.
Zivilist *m.* **(-en, -en)** civilian.
Zivilklage *f.* (law) civil action.
Zivilprozeßordnung *f.* civil law.
Zivilsache *f.* civil case.
Zlg. *Zahlung,* payment.
Zobel *m.* **(-s, -)** sable.
Zofe *f.* **(-, -n)** (lady's) maid.
Zoff *m.* (*fam.*) trouble.
zögerlich *a.* hesitant, tentative.
zögern *v.i.* to hesitate, to delay.
Zögling *m.* **(-[e]s, -e)** pupil.
Zölibat *n.* **(-es, 0)** celibacy.
Zoll *m.* **(-[e]s, -)** inch; **Zölle** *pl.* duty, tariff, customs; (*fig.*) tribute.
Zollabfertigung *f.* customs clearance.
Zollamt *n.* customs house; customs station.
Zollbeamte *m./f.* customs officer.
Zolleinnehmer *m.* customs agent.
zollen *v.t.* to pay, to give.
Zollerklärung *f.* customs declaration.
zollfrei *a.* duty-free.
Zollgrenze *f.* customs-frontier.
Zollhaus *n.* customs house.
Zollkontrolle *f.* customs check.
zollpflichtig *a.* liable to duty.
Zollrevision *f.* customs examination or inspection.
Zollschranke *f.* customs barrier.
Zollstock *m.* folding rule.
Zolltarif *m.* tariff.
Zollverband *m.* customs union.
Zollverein *m.* customs union.
Zollverschluß *m.* customs seal; *unter* ~, in bond.
zollweise *adv.* by inches.
Zone *f.* **(-, -n)** zone.
Zonen... zonal, *a.*
Zonentarif *m.* zone tariff.
Zoo *m.* zoo.
Zoohandlung *f.* pet shop.
Zoologe *m.* **(-n, -n); Zoologin** *f.* **(-, -nen)** zoologist.
Zoologie *f.* **(-, 0)** zoology.
zoologisch *a.* zoological.
Zoowärter *m.* zookeeper.
Zopf *m.* **(-[e]s, Zöpfe)** pigtail; (*Mädchen* ~) plait.
Zorn *m.* **(-[e]s, 0)** wrath, anger, ire.
Zornausbruch *m.* fit *or* burst of anger.
zornentbrannt *a.* angry.
zornig *a.* furious; wrathful, angry.
Zote *f.* **(-, -n)** dirty joke; obscenity.
zotenhaft, zotig *a.* smutty, obscene.
Zotte, Zottel *f.* **(-, -n)** tuft, lock; *pl.* straggly hair.
zottig *a.* shaggy, ragged; matted.
z.T. *zum Teil,* partly.
Ztr. *Zentner,* German hundredweight, cwt.
Ztschr. *Zeitschrift,* periodical.
zu *pr.* to, at, by, in, on, for; ~ *adv.* too; shut; ~ *Land,* by land, on (dry) land; ~*r See,* by sea; ~*m Beispiel,* for instance; ~ *Not,* if need be; ~ *zweien,* two of us (them, etc.); ~ *Hunderten,* by hundreds, in the hundreds; ~ *dritt,* three of them (us, etc.); *Tür* ~*!,* shut the door, please.
zuallererst *adv.* first of all.
zuallerletzt *adv.* last of all.
Zub. *Zubehör,* accessories.
zubauen *v.t.* to block; to obstruct.
Zubehör *n.* accessories; attachments.
Zubehörteile *pl.* accessories.
zubeißen *v.i.st.* to bite or snap.
Zuber *m.* **(-s, -)** (two-handled) tub.
zubereiten *v.t.* to prepare, to cook.
Zubereitung *f.* preparation; cooking.
zubilligen *v.t.* to grant.
zubinden *v.t.st.* to tie up; (*die Augen*) to blindfold.
zubleiben *v.t.st.* to remain closed.
zublinzeln *v.i.* to wink.
zubringen *v.t.ir.* to pass, to spend (time).
Zubringer *m.* access road; shuttle.
Zubrot *n.* (*sl.*) extra income.
zubuttern *v.t. & i.* (*fam.*) to chip in.
Zuchtbuch *n.* stud book.
Zucht *f.* **(-, 0)** breeding, breed; discipline, education; modesty.

züchten *v.t.* to breed; to grow, to cultivate; to train.
Züchter *m.* **(-s, -)** breeder (of animals); grower (of plants).
Zuchthaus *n.* penitentiary; (*Strafe*) penal servitude; *lebenslängliches* ~, life imprisonment.
züchtig *a.* modest, chaste.
züchtigen *v.t.* to punish; to beat.
Züchtigung *f.* **(-, -en)** punishment.
zuchtlos *a.* undisciplined; disorderly.
Zuchtlosigkeit *f.* indiscipline.
Zuchtperle *f.* cultured pearl.
Zuchtpferd *n.* pedigree horse.
Züchtung *f.* **(-, -en)** breeding; (*von Pflanzen*) cultivation; training.
Zuchtvieh *n.* breeding cattle.
zucken *v.i.* to twitch; to wince; ~ *v.t.* to shrug.
zücken *v.t.* to draw, to pull out (a sword).
Zucker *m.* **(-s, 0)** sugar.
Zucker: ~bäcker *m.* confectioner; **~bäckerei** *f.* confectioner's shop; **~dose** *f.* sugar bowl; **~fabrik** *f.* refinery; **~guß** *m.* (sugar) icing, frosting; **~hut** *m.* sugar loaf; **~kranker** *m.* diabetic; **~krankheit** *f.* diabetes.
zuckern *v.t.* to sugar (over).
Zucker: ~rohr *n.* sugar cane; **~rübe** *f.* sugar beet.
zuckersüß *a.* as sweet as sugar.
Zucker: ~watte *f.* cotton candy; **~werk** *n.* sweets *pl.*, confectionery; **~zange** *f.* sugar tongs *pl.*
Zuckung *f.* **(-, -en)** convulsion.
zudecken *v.t.* to cover (up).
zudem *adv.* besides, moreover.
Zudrang *m.* **(-[e]s, 0)** rush, run (on).
zudrehen *v.t.* to shut off, to turn off; *einem den Rücken* ~, to turn one's back on someone.
zudringlich *a.* obtrusive; importunate; pushy.
zudrücken *v.t.* to close (by pressure); *ein Auge bei etwas* ~, to connive *or* wink at a thing.
zueignen *v.t.* to dedicate.
Zueignung *f.* **(-, -en)** dedication.
zueilen *v.i.* *(s)* to hasten (up) to.
zueinander *adv.* to each other; to one another.
zuerkennen *v.t.ir.* to award, to adjudicate; to sentence (one) to.
zuerst *adv.* first, at first.
zufahren *v.t.st.* *auf einen,* ~, to head toward someone.
Zufahrt *f.* access; driveway.
Zufahrtsstraße *f.* access road.
Zufall *m.* chance, hazard, accident.
zufallen *v.i.st.* *(s)* to shut by itself, to close; *jm.* ~, to fall to sb.
zufällig *a.* casual, accidental.
zufälligerweise *adv.* by chance.
Zufalls: ~auswahl *f.* random selection; **~bekanntschaft** *f.* chance acquaintance; **~treffer** *m.* lucky hit.
zufassen *v.i.* to grab.
zufliegen *v.i.st.* *(s)* to fly to *or* towards; (*Tür*) to slam.
zufließen *v.i.st.* *(s)* to flow to or towards; *einem etwas* ~ *lassen,* to make something come somebody's way.
Zuflucht *f.* **(-, 0)** refuge; recourse; *seine* ~ *nehmen zu,* to have recourse to.
Zufluchtsort *m.*, **Zufluchtsstätte** *f.* place of refuge, asylum.
Zufluß *m.* **(-flusses, -flüsse)** influx; inflow; supply; tributary.
zuflüstern *v.t.* to whisper to.
zufolge *pr.* according to.
zufrieden *a.* content(ed), satisfied; ~*stellen,* to satisfy, to content.
zufriedengeben *v.r. st.* to content o.s.
Zufriedenheit *f.* **(-, 0)** contentment; satisfaction.
zufriedenstellend *a.* satisfactory.
zufrieren *v.i.st.* *(s)* to freeze over or up.
zufügen *v.t.* to do, to inflict, to cause.
Zufuhr *f.* **(-, -en)** (*mil.*) provisions *pl.*, supply.
zuführen *v.t.* to lead to, to bring to; to introduce; to import, to supply; (*mech.*) to feed.
Zug *m.* **(-[e]s, Züge)** pull; draft, current (of air); procession; (*im Schach*) move; (*Eisenbahn*~) stroke; (*Neigung*) bent, impulse; (*mil.*) platoon; ~ *Pferde,* team of horses; (*Gebirgs*~) mountain range; *der Ofen hat keinen guten* ~, the stove draws badly; *in einem* ~, *auf einen* ~, at one stroke; *in den letzten Zügen liegen,* to be breathing one's last.
Zugabe *f.* addition, adjunct; (*theat.*) encore.
Zugang *m.* access, approach; entrance.
zugänglich *a.* accessible; (*fig.*) affable.
Zuganschluß *m.* (train) connection.
Zugbrücke *f.* drawbridge.
zugeben *v.t.st.* to add; to permit; to admit, to grant.
zugegebenermaßen *adv.* admittedly.
zugegen *a.* present.
zugehen *v.i.st.* *(s)* to shut; to go up to, to move towards; to come to hand; to come to pass, to happen; *einem etwas* ~ *lassen,* to send, to forward, to transmit something to someone.
zugehören *v.i.* to belong to.
zugehörig *a.* belonging to.
Zugehörigkeit *f.* **(-, 0)** membership (of a company, union, club, etc.).
zugeknöpft *a.* buttoned up; (*fig.*) tight-lipped.
Zügel *m.* **(-s, -)** rein, bridle.
zügellos *a.* (*fig.*) unbridled.
zügeln *v.t.* to bridle; to curb, to check.
zugesellen *v.t.* to associate, to unite.
Zugeständnis *n.* concession.
zugestehen *v.t.st.* to concede, to grant, to admit.
zugetan *a.* attached.
Zugewinn *m.* gain.
Zugfestigkeit *f.* tensile strength.
zugießen *v.t.st.* to pour more, to add.
zugig *a.* drafty; windy.
Zugkraft *f.* power of traction; (*fig.*) attractiveness.
zugkräftig *a.* attractive.
zugleich *adv.* at the same time, together.
Zugluft *f.* draft (of air).
zugreifen *v.i.st.* to seize, to help oneself (at the table).
Zugriff *m.* grasp; access.
zugrunde *adv.* ~ *gehen,* to perish; ~ *richten,* to ruin.
zugucken *v.i.* to look on.
Zugunglück *n.* train crash.
zugunsten *adv.* in favor of.
zugute *adv.* ~ *halten,* to make allowances for; ~ *kommen lassen,* to give the benefit of; *sich etwas auf eine Sache* ~ *tun,* to be proud of something.
zuguterletzt *adv.* finally, ultimately.
Zugverbindung *f.* railroad service.
Zugverkehr *m.* train services.
Zugvieh *n.* draft cattle.
Zugvogel *m.* migratory bird; (*fig.*) drifter.
Zugzwang *m.* *in* ~ *geraten,* to be forced to act.

zuhaben *v.i.* to be closed.
zuhalten *v.t.st.* to keep closed, to stop.
Zuhälter *m.* **(-s, -)** pimp.
zuhängen *v.t.st.* to hang over *or* in front of.
zuhauen *v.i.st.* to hew, to shape; ~ *v.t.st.* to shut; to slam; to strike.
Zuhause *n.* home.
zuheilen *v.i. (s)* to heal up, to close.
Zuhilfenahme *f.* **(-, 0)** *unter oder mit* ~ *von,* with the aid of.
zuhinterst *adv.* at the very end.
zuhorchen *v.i.* to listen to.
zuhören *v.i.* to listen.
Zuhörer *m.* **(-s, -)**; **Zuhörerin** *f.* **(-, -nen)** listener.
Zuhörerraum *m.* lecture room, auditorium.
Zuhörerschaft *f.* **(-, 0)** audience.
zujauchzen, zujubeln *v.i.* to cheer.
zukehren *v.t.* to turn (towards).
zuklappen *v.t. & i.* to close; to fold; to shut.
zukleben, zukleistern *v.t.* to glue or paste up.
zuknallen *v.t.* to slam.
zukneifen *v.t.st.* to squeeze; to shut tight.
zuknöpfen *v.t.* to button up.
zukommen *v.i.st. (s)* to come to hand; to belong to; to befit, to be due *or* suitable; to fall to one's share; *einem etwas* ~ *lassen,* to let someone... have.
Zukunft *f.* **(-, 0)** future, time to come; *in* ~, in the future.
zukünftig *a.* future; next; intended.
Zukünftige *m./f.* (*fam.*) *mein* ~*r/meine* ~, my husband/wife to be.
Zukunfts: ~aussichten *pl.* future prospects; **~forschung** *f.* futurology.
Zukunftsroman *m.* science fiction novel.
zukunftsweisend *a.* advanced.
zul. *zulässig,* permissible.
zulächeln *v.i.* to smile at.
Zulage *f.* **(-, -n)** extra pay, allowance.
zulangen *v.i.* to help oneself.
zulänglich *a.* sufficient.
zulassen *v.t.st.* to permit; to admit.
zulässig *a.* admissible, allowable.
Zulassung *f.* **(-, 0)** admission, admittance; permission; registration (car).
Zulauf *m.* **(-[e]s, 0)** run (of customers); *grossen* ~ *haben,* to be in vogue.
zulaufen *v.i.st. (s)* to run on; to run to; *spitz* ~, to taper.
zulegen *v.t.* to add, to increase; *sich etwas* ~, to provide oneself with something.
zuleide *adv.* ~ **tun,** to do harm.
zuleiten *v.t.* to direct to; to supply; to send.
zulernen *v.t. & i.* to enlarge one's knowledge, to live and learn.
zuletzt *adv.* (at) last, finally, after all.
zuliebe *adv.* for the sake of.
zumachen *v.t.* to shut, to close, to fasten.
zumal *adv.* especially, chiefly; especially as.
zumauern *v.t.* to wall or brick up.
zumeist *adv.* for the most part, mostly.
zumindest *adv.* at least.
zumutbar *a.* reasonable.
Zumutbarkeit *f.* reasonableness.
zumute *a.* ~ **sein,** to feel.
zumuten *v.t.* to expect.
Zumutung *f.* **(-, -en)** (unreasonable) demand; imposition.
zunächst *adv.* first, above all.
zunageln *v.t.* to nail up.
zunähen *v.t.* to sew up.
Zunahme *f.* **(-, 0)** increase, growth.
Zuname *m.* surname, family name.
zündeln *v.i.* to play with fire.
zünden *v.i.* to catch fire; (*fig.*) to take, to catch on; ~ *v.t.* to kindle.
zündend *a.* stirring.
Zunder *m.* **(-, 0)** tinder.
Zünder *m.* **(-s, -)** fuse, match, igniter.
Zündholz *n.* match; *ein* ~ *anzünden,* to strike a match.
Zündkerze *f.* spark plug.
Zündschnur *f.* fuse.
Zündung *f.* **(-, -en)** ignition.
zunehmen *v.t.st.* to increase, to grow; to put on weight.
zuneigen *v.t.* to bend or incline (towards).
Zuneigung *f.* inclination, affection.
Zunft *f.* **(-, Zünfte)** guild.
zünftig *a.* proper; competent.
Zunge *f.* **(-, -n)** tongue.
züngeln *v.t.* (*von Flammen*) to flicker; to dart.
Zungenbelag *m.* coating of the tongue.
Zungenbrecher *m.* tongue twister.
zungenfertig *a.* glib.
Zungenkuß *m.* French kiss.
Zungenspitze *f.* tip of the tongue.
zunichte *adv.* undone, ruined.
zunicken *v.i.* to nod to.
zunutzemachen *v.t.* to make use of
zuoberst *adv.* at the top, uppermost.
zuordnen *v.t.* to classify with.
zupfen *v.t.* to pull, to tug, to pluck, to pick.
zupflastern *v.t.* to pave or plaster over.
zuprosten *v.i.* raise one's glass to.
zur. *zurück,* back.
zuraten *v.t.st.* to advise.
zuraunen *v.t.* to whisper.
zurechnen *v.t.* to attribute.
zurechnungsfähig *a.* of sound mind.
Zurechnungsfähigkeit *f.* soundness of mind; (*jur.*) responsibility.
zurecht *adv.* in time; ready.
zurechtbringen *v.t.st.* to put to rights, to restore, to adjust.
zurechtfinden *v.r. st.* to find *or* see one's way.
zurechtkommen *v.i.st. (s)* to succeed, to get on well; (*mit einem*) to get on (with), to agree (with); (*der Zeit nach*) to arrive in (the nick of) time.
zurechtlegen *v.t.* to arrange, to lay out in order; ~ *v.r.* to explain to oneself.
zurechtmachen *v.t.* to prepare; ~ *v.r.* to get ready.
zurechtschneiden *v.t.st.* to trim.
zurechtsetzen *v.t.* to set or put right.
zurechtweisen *v.t.st.* to reprimand.
Zurechtweisung *f.* reprimand; rebuke.
zureden *v.i.* to persuade, to encourage.
zureichend *a.* sufficient.
zureiten *v.t.st.* to break in (a horse).
zurichten *v.t.* (*fam.*) to injure; to make a mess.
zuriegeln *v.t.* to bolt.
zürnen *v.i.* to be angry.
Zurschaustellung *f.* exhibition, display.
zurück *adv.* back, backwards; ~ *sein* (*fig.*) to be back/behind; ~*!* stand back!; *ich werde bald* ~ *sein,* I'll be back soon.
zurückbegeben *v.r.st.* to go back, to return.
zurückbehalten *v.t.st.* to keep back.

zurückbekommen *v.t.st.* to get back.
zurückberufen *v.t.st.* to recall.
zurückbezahlen *v.t.* to repay, to reimburse.
zurückbleiben *v.i.st.* *(s)* to remain behind; to lag behind.
zurückblicken *v.i.* to look back.
zurückbringen *v.t.st.* to bring back, to return.
zurückdatieren *v.t.* to antedate; ~ *v.i.* to date back.
zurückdenken *v.t.st.* *(an)* to think back.
zurückdrängen *v.t.* to repress.
zurückerhalten *v.t.st.* to get back.
zurückerstatten *v.t.* to give back, to return.
zurückfahren *v.t.st.* to drive back; *(fig.)* to recoil.
zurückfinden *v.r.* to find one's way back.
zurückfordern *v.t.* to demand back.
Zurückforderung *f.* reclamation.
zurückführen *v.t.* to lead back; *(ar.)* to reduce (to); to trace (back) (to).
zurückgeben *v.t.st.* to give back, to return, to restore.
zurückgehen *v.i.st.* *(s)* to go back; to decrease; *(Preis)* to decline.
zurückgezogen *a.* retired; secluded.
Zurückgezogenheit *f.* **(-, 0)** retirement; seclusion.
zurückgreifen *v.t.st.* *(auf)* to fall back (on).
zurückhaben *v.t.ir.* to have back.
zurückhalten *v.t.st.* to hold back, to restrain; *mit etwas* ~, to be reserved concerning sth.
zurückhaltend *a.* reserved; cautious.
Zurückhaltung *f.* **(-, 0)** reserve.
zurückkaufen *v.t.* to buy back, to buy in.
zurückkehren *v.i.* *(s)* to return.
zurückkommen *v.i.st.* *(s)* to come back, to return.
zurückkönnen *v.i.st.* to be able to return.
zurücklassen *v.t.st.* to leave (behind).
zurücklegen *v.t.* to put by, to save; *(Weg)* to travel.
Zurücknahme *f.* revocation, withdrawal.
zurücknehmen *v.t.st.* to take back; to withdraw, to retract.
zurückprallen *v.i.* *(s)* to rebound.
zurückrufen *v.t.st.* to call back.
zurückschaudern *v.i.* *(s)* to recoil (from).
zurückschlagen *v.t.st.* to beat back, to repulse.
zurückschrecken *v.t.st.* *(s)* to recoil; to start back.
zurücksehnen *v.r.* to long to be back.
zurücksetzen *v.t.* to put back; to reduce the price of; to slight, to neglect.
Zurücksetzung *f.* **(-, -en)** neglect, slight.
zurücksinken *v.i.st.* *(s)* to relapse (into).
zurückspringen *v.i.st.* *(s)* to rebound.
zurückstehen *v.t.st.* to be inferior (to).
zurückstellen *v.t.* to put back; to shelve; *(mil.)* to defer.
Zurückstellung *f.* **(-, -en)** *(mil.)* deferment.
zurückstrahlen *v.t.* to reflect, to throw back.
zurücktreiben *v.t.st.* to drive back, to thrust back, to repulse, to repel.
zurücktreten *v.i.st.* *(s)* to step back; *(vom Amt)* to resign office.
zurückübersetzen *v.t.* to retranslate.
zurückverlangen *v.t.* to demand *or* ask back; ~ *v.i.* to desire to go back (to).
zurückversetzen *v.t.* put back, restore; ~ *v.r. sich in eine Zeit* ~, to go back to a time.
zurückweichen *v.i.st.* *(s)* to fall back, to recede, to give away, to yield.
zurückweisen *v.t.st.* to reject, to repel, to decline.
Zurückweisung *f.* **(-, -en)** repulse, repudiation.
zurückwerfen *v.t.st.* to throw back.
zurückzahlen *v.t.* to pay back, to repay.
zurückziehen *v.t.st.* to withdraw; ~ *v.r.* to withdraw (from); to retreat; to retire.
Zuruf *m.* **(-[e]s, -e)** acclamation; call.
zurufen *v.t.st.* to call to, to shout to; *Beifall* ~, to cheer, to applaud.
zurzeit *adv.* for the time being.
zus. *zusammen,* together, tog.
Zusage *f.* **(-, -n)** promise; assent; acceptance.
zusagen *v.t.* to promise; ~ *v.i.* to promise to come; to suit, to please.
zusammen *adv.* together; jointly.
Zusammenarbeit *f.* cooperation.
zusammenarbeiten *v.i.* to collaborate, to cooperate.
zusammenballen *v.t.* to conglomerate.
zusammenbeißen *v.t.st.* to clench (one's teeth).
zusammenbinden *v.t.st.* to bind or tie together.
zusammenbleiben *v.i.st.* to stay together.
zusammenbrechen *v.i.st.* *(s)* to break down, to collapse.
zusammenbringen *v.t.ir.* to bring together; to collect.
Zusammenbruch *m.* collapse.
zusammendrängen *v.t.* to compress; to condense; ~ *v.r.* to crowd together.
zusammendrücken *v.t.* to compress.
zusammenfahren *v.i.st.* *(s)* to start, to wince.
zusammenfallen *v.i.st.* *(s)* to collapse; to coincide.
zusammenfalten *v.t.* to fold (together, up), to double up.
zusammenfassen *v.t.* to collect; to sum up, to summarize.
Zusammenfassung *f.* summary.
zusammenfinden *v.r.st.* to meet.
zusammenflicken *v.t.* to patch together, to botch up.
Zusammenfluß *m.* **(-flusse, -flüsse)** confluence; concourse, crowd.
zusammenfügen *v.t.* to join, to unite.
zusammengehen *v.i.st.* *(s)* to coincide; to cooperate; to match.
zusammengehören *v.i.* to belong together, to be of the same kind.
zusammengesetzt *a.* composed, compound; composite.
Zusammenhalt *m.* **(-[e]s, 0)** cohesion.
zusammenhalten *v.t.st.* to hold together; ~ *v.t.st.* to assist one another.
Zusammenhang *m.* **(-[e]s, -hänge)** connection, coherence; *ohne* ~, incoherent; *aus dem* ~, out of context.
zusammenhängen *v.t.st.* to cohere; to be connected (with).
zusammenhangslos *a.* incoherent.
zusammenkauern *v.r.* to huddle up.
zusammenketten *v.t.* to chain together.
zusammenkitten *v.t.* to cement together.
Zusammenklang *m.* accord, harmony.
zusammenklappen *v.t.* to fold together, to shut; ~ *v.i.* *(fig.)* to break down.
zusammenkommen *v.i.st.* *(s)* to meet.
Zusammenkunft *f.* **(-, -künfte)** meeting.
zusammenlaufen *v.i.st.* *(s)* to flock together; to shrink; to curdle; *(math.)* to converge.

Zusammenleben *n.* **(-s, 0)** social life; (*eheliches*) cohabitation.
zusammenleben *v.i.* to live together.
zusammenlegbar *a.* folding, collapsible.
zusammenlegen *v.t.* to lay together, to fold up; (*Geld*) to club together.
zusammenleimen *v.t.* to stick together.
zusammennehmen *v.t.st.* to summon; ~ *v.r.st.* to pull oneself together; *seine Gedanken gehörig* ~, to collect one's thoughts.
zusammenpacken *v.t.* to pack up.
zusammenpassen *v.i.* to go together; to be well matched.
zusammenpferchen *v.t.* to herd together.
zusammenprallen *v.i.* to collide, to clash.
zusammenpressen *v.t.* to squeeze/press together.
zusammenraffen *v.t.* to collect hurriedly; ~ *v.r.* to muster courage; *seine Kräfte* ~, to collect all one's strength.
zusammenrechnen *v.t.* to add up.
zusammenreißen *v.r.st.* to pull o.s. together.
zusammenrotten *v.r.* to band together; to gang up; to form a mob.
zusammenrücken *v.t.* to join together, to put close together; ~ *v.i. (s)* to draw together.
zusammenscharen *v.r.* to flock together.
zusammenschießen *v.t.st.* to put a bullet through sb.
zusammenschlagen *v.t.st.* to beat up; to smash; *die Hände über dem Kopf* ~, to throw up one's arms in astonishment; ~ *v.i. (s) die Wogen schlugen über ihm zusammen,* the waves crashed over him.
zusammenschließen *v.t.st.* to lock together; to unite; ~ *v.r.st.* to merge; to line up (against).
Zusammenschluß *m.* union, fusion, merger.
zusammenschnüren *v.t.* to tie up.
zusammenschrecken *v.i. (s)* to startle.
zusammenschrumpfen *v.i. (s)* to shrivel up, to dwindle; to wrinkle.
zusammensetzen *v.t.* to compose; (*mech.*) to assemble; ~ *v.r.* to consist of.
Zusammensetzung *f.* **(-, -en)** composition; compound.
zusammensinken *v.i.st. (s)* to collapse.
Zusammenspiel *n.* **(-[e]s, -e)** (*sport*) team work.
zusammenstellen *v.t.* to put together; to make up, to compile.
Zusammenstellung *f.* **(-, -en)** combination; (*fig.*) compilation.
zusammenstimmen *v.t.* to accord, to chime in, to agree; to harmonize.
zusammenstoppeln *v.t.* to piece together.
Zusammenstoß *m.* **(-es, -stöße)** collision; (*mil.*) encounter; (*fig.*) clash, conflict.
zusammenstoßen *v.i.st. (s)* to collide; to adjoin each other; ~ *v.t.* to knock together; (*Gläser*) to clink.
zusammenströmen *v.i. (s)* to flock together.
zusammenstürzen *v.i. (s)* to tumble down; to collapse.
zusammentreffen *v.i.st. (s)* to meet; to coincide, to clash; to encounter.
zusammentreten *v.i.st. (s)* to meet.
zusammentrommeln *v.t.* (*fam.*) to drum up; (*Geld*) to raise by hook and by crook.
zusammentun *v.r.* to combine.
zusammenwachsen *v.i.st.* to grow together.
zusammenwerfen *v.t.st.* to jumble *or* throw together, to pool, to confound.
zusammenwirken *v.i.* to collaborate, cooperate.
zusammenzählen *v.t.* to add up.
zusammenziehen *v.t.st.* to draw together, to contract; to gather, to concentrate; to abridge; ~ *v.r.* to shrink up; to gather.
zusammenziehend *a.* astringent.
Zusatz *m.* **(-es, -sätze)** addition, supplement; alloy, admixture; codicil; postscript.
zusätzlich *a.* additional.
zuschanzen *v.t.* (*fam.*) *einem etwas* ~, to make something come somebody's way.
zuschauen *v.i.* to look on.
Zuschauer *m.* **(-s, -); Zuschauerin** *f.* **(-, -nen)** spectator, onlooker.
Zuschauerraum *m.* auditorium.
zuschicken *v.t.* to send (to).
zuschieben *v.t.st.* to push towards; shut gently.
zuschießen *v.t.st.* to contribute.
Zuschlag *m.* **(-[e]s, -schläge)** surcharge; supplement; (*Steuer*) surtax; *Teuerungs*~, bonus.
zuschlagen *v.i.st.* to slam (a door); to knock down (to a bidder); ~ *v.t.st.* to strike hard, to hit away.
Zuschlagporto *n.* surcharge.
zuschließen *v.t.st.* to lock (up).
zuschmeißen *v.t.st.* (*fam.*) to bang.
zuschneiden *v.t.st.* to cut out.
Zuschneider *m.* **(-s, -)** cutter.
Zuschnitt *m.* **(-[e]s, -e)** cut; style.
zuschnüren *v.t.* to lace; to tie up.
zuschrauben *v.t.* to screw on.
zuschreiben *v.t.st.* to ascribe, to impute; (*com.*) to put to one's credit.
zuschreiten *v.i.st. (s)* to step up to.
Zuschrift *f.* **(-, -en)** letter.
Zuschuß *m.* **(-usses, -üsse)** additional allowance; grant.
zuschütten *v.t.* to fill up; to pour on.
zusehen *v.i.st.* to look on; to suffer; to see to, to take care.
zusehends *adv.* visibly.
zusein *v.i.st.* to be shut.
zusenden *v.t.st.* to send (to).
Zusendung *f.* sending.
zusetzen *v.t.* to add; ~ *v.i.* (*einem*) to pressure on.
zusichern *v.t.* to promise.
Zusicherung *f.* **(-, -en)** assurance.
zusperren *v.t.* to lock, to bar.
Zuspiel *n.* passing; pass.
zuspielen *v.t.* to pass (the ball).
zuspitzen *v.t.* to point; ~ *v.r.* to taper; (*fig.*) to come to a crisis.
Zusprache *f.* **(-, -n)** encouragement.
zusprechen *v.i.st.* to exhort; to comfort, to encourage; ~ *v.t.st.* to award, to adjudge; to do justice to (a dish).
Zuspruch *m.* **(-[e]s, -sprüche)** encouragement; run of customers.
Zustand *m.* **(-[e]s, -stände)** condition, situation, state (of affairs).
zustande *adv.* ~ *bringen,* to accomplish, to bring about; ~ *kommen,* to come about, to be realized.
zuständig *a.* competent; responsible.
Zuständigkeit *f.* **(-, 0)** competence; responsibility.
zustatten kommen *v.i.* to prove useful.
zustecken *v.t.* to pin up; *einem etwas* ~, to convey something secretly to someone.

zustehen *v.t.st.* to be due; to belong; (*jur.*) to be vested in; *das steht mir zu,* I'm entitled to it.
zustellen *v.t.* to deliver, to hand to.
Zustellung *f.* service; delivery.
zustimmen *v.t.* to agree to.
Zustimmung *f.* **(-, -en)** consent, approval.
zustopfen *v.t.* to plug; to darn.
zustoßen *v.i.st. (s)* to happen, to befall.
zuströmen *v.i. (s)* to flow towards; to crowd in (upon one).
zustutzen *v.t.* to trim, to fashion.
zutage *adv.* to light; to the surface.
Zutat *f.* **(-, -en)** ingredient, addition; (*Schneiderei*) trimmings *pl.*
zuteil *adv.* ~ *werden,* to be granted; ~ *werden lassen,* to allot to.
zuteilen *v.t.* to allot, to assign.
Zuteilung *f.* **(-, -en)** quota, allowance.
Zuteilungsperiode *f.* ration period.
zutragen *v.t.st.* to carry to; to report; ~ *v.r.* to happen.
zuträglich *a.* wholesome; conducive (to).
zutrauen *v.t.* (*einem etwas*) to believe someone capable of something.
Zutrauen *n.* **(-s,0)** trust, confidence, faith.
zutraulich *a.* confiding, trustful.
zutreffen *v.t.st.* to prove right; to come true.
zutreffend *a.* correct, applicable.
zutreiben *v.t.st.* to drive towards; ~ *v.i.st. (s)* to drift towards.
zutrinken *v.t.st.* to drink to, to pledge.
Zutritt *m.* **(-[e]s, -e)** access, admission; ~ *verboten,* no entrance, no entry; *Unbeschäftigten* ~ *verboten,* no admittance except on business.
Zutun *n.* **(-s, 0)** aid, interference.
zuungunsten *pr.* to the disadvantage of.
zuunterst *adv.* at the (very) bottom.
zuverlässig *adv.* reliable, trustworthy, dependable.
Zuverlässigkeit *f.* **(-, 0)** reliability.
Zuversicht *f.* **(-, 0)** confidence, trust.
zuversichtlich *a.* confident.
zuviel *indef.pn.* too much.
zuvor *adv.* before(hand), previously.
zuvorkommen *v.i.st. (s)* to get the start of; to prevent; to anticipate.
zuvorkommend *a.* obliging; courteous.
Zuvorkommenheit *f.* courteousness; courtesy.
zuvortun *v.t.st. es einem* ~, to outdo someone.
Zuwachs *m.* **(-ses, 0)** increase.
zuwachsen *v.t.st.* to become overgrown.
Zuwanderung *f.* **(-, -en)** immigration.
zuwarten *v.t.* to wait.
zuwege bringen *v.t.st.* to bring something off; to achieve.
zuweilen *adv.* sometimes.
zuweisen *v.t.st.* to assign to.
zuwenden *v.t.st.* to turn *or* direct towards; to procure (for).
Zuwendung *f.* grant; allowance; love; loving care; attention.
zuwenig *indef.pn.* too little.
zuwider *a.* repugnant, odious.
zuwiderhandeln *v.i.* to contravene.
Zuwiderhandelnde *m./f.* **(-n, -n)** offender.
Zuwiderhandlung *f.* **(-, 0)** non-compliance.
zuwiderlaufen *v.i.st. (s)* to run counter to.
zuwinken *v.i.* to wave to.
zuzahlen *v.t.* to pay extra.
zuziehen *v.t.st.* to pull shut; to draw together or tight; to draw (a curtain); to call in (another physician); ~ *v.r.* to incur; to catch.
Zuzug *m.* **(-[e]s, -züge)** influx.
zuzüglich *pr.* plus.
zuzwinkern *v.i.* to wink at.
zw. *zwischen,* between, bet.
Zwang *m.* **(-[e]s, 0)** constraint, compulsion, coercion; force.
zwängen *v.t.* to force, to press (into).
zwanglos *a.* unconstrained; informal.
Zwangsanleihe *f.* forced loan.
Zwangsarbeit *f.* forced *or* hard labor.
Zwangsjacke *f.* straitjacket.
Zwangsläufig *n.* automatic.
Zwangsmaßnahme *f.* coercive measure.
Zwangsmittel *n.* coercive measure.
Zwangsverkauf *m.* forced sale.
Zwangsverschleppter *m.* displaced person (DP).
Zwangsversteigerung *f.* forced sale.
Zwangsverwaltung *f.* sequestration.
Zwangsvollstreckung *f.* (*law*) execution.
zwangsweise *adv.* by compulsion *or* force.
Zwangswirtschaft *f.* government control.
zwanzig *a.* twenty; a score; *in den Zwanzigern sein, stehen,* to be between twenty and thirty (years of age).
zwar *adv.* it is true, no doubt.
Zweck *m.* **(-[e]s, -e)** aim, purpose, object, end; *es hat keinen* ~, there is no point in.
zweckdienlich *a.* relevent; useful.
Zwecke *f.* **(-, -n)** hob-nail, tack, thumbtack.
zweckentsprechend *a.* suitable.
zweckentfremden *v.t.* to use for another purpose.
zwecklos *a.* useless; purposeless, aimless.
zweckmäßig *a.* expedient, suitable.
zwecks *pr.* for the purpose of.
zweckwidrig *a.* unsuitable, inexpedient.
zwei *a.* two.
Zwei *f.* **(-, en)** number *or* figure of two; (*im Spiel*) deuce.
zweiarmig *a.* two-armed.
zweibeinig *a.* two-legged.
Zweibettzimmer *n.* double room.
zweideutig *a.* ambiguous, equivocal.
Zweideutigkeit *f.* **(-, -en)** ambiguity.
zweierlei *a.* of two sorts; different.
zweifach *a.* double, twofold; *in* ~*er Ausfertigung,* in duplicate.
Zweifel *m.* **(-s, -)** doubt.
zweifelhaft *a.* doubtful; dubious.
zweifellos *a.* undoubtedly; doubtless.
zweifeln *v.i.* to doubt, to question.
Zweifelsfall *m.* case of doubt; *im* ~ *zu eines Gunsten entscheiden,* to give someone the benefit of the doubt.
zweifelsohne *adv.* doubtless.
Zweifler *m.* **(-s, -); Zweiflerin** *f.* **(-, -nen)** sceptic, doubter.
zweifüßig *a.* two-footed, biped.
Zweig *m.* **(-[e]s, -e)** branch, bough; twig.
Zweigespann *n.* team of two (horses).
Zweiggeschäft *n.* branch (establishment).
zweigleisig *a.* double track (*rail.*)
zweihändig *a.* two handed.
zweijährig *a.* two years old, of two years.
Zweikammersystem *n.* two-chamber system of government.
Zweikampf *m.* single combat, duel.
zweimal *adv.* twice.

zweimalig *a.* done twice.
zweimonatlich *a.* bimonthly.
zweimotorig *a.* (*avi.*) twin engined.
Zweirad *n.* bicycle; (*sl.*) bike.
zweirädrig *a.* two wheeled.
zweireihig *a.* double-breasted (coat).
zweischneidig *a.* double-edged.
zweisilbig *a.* disyllabic.
zweisitzig *a.* having two seats.
zweispaltig *a.* in double columns.
zweispännig *a.* drawn by two horses.
zweisprachig *a.* bilingual.
zweiseitig *a.* two-sided, bilateral.
zweistimmig *a.* for two voices.
zweistündig *a.* (lasting) two hours.
zweiteilig *a.* two-part; *~er Anzug,* two-piece suit.
zweitens *adv.* secondly.
zweite[r] *a.* second; *jeden ~n Tag,* every other day; *~s Gesicht,* second sight; *der ~ beste,* the second-best; *der zweitletzte,* the next to last.
zweitjüngst *a.* next to youngest.
Zweiunddreißigstelnote *f.* thirty-second note.
zweiwöchentlich *a.* biweekly.
Zwerchfell *n.* diaphragm.
Zwerg *m.* **(-[e]s, -e)** dwarf, pygmy, midget.
zwergartig, zwerghaft *a.* dwarfish.
Zwetsche, Zwetschge *f.* **(-, -n)** plum.
Zwgst. *Zweigstelle,* branch.
Zwickel *m.* **(-s, -)** clock (of a stocking); gusset (of a shirt); (*arch.*) spandrel.
zwicken *v.t.* to pinch, to nip.
Zwicker *m.* **(-s, -)** pince-nez.
Zwickmühle *f.* (*Spiel*) double-mill; (*fig.*) dilemma.
Zwieback *n.* **(-[e]s, -e)** biscuit, rusk.
Zwiebel *f.* **(-, -n)** onion; *Blumen~* bulb.
zwiefach, zwiefältig *a.* twofold.
Zwiegespräch *n.* dialogue.
Zwielicht *n.* twilight.
zwielichtig *a.* shady, dubious.
Zwiespalt *m.* **(-[e]s, -e)** inner conflict, dissension, discord.
zwiespältig *a.* (*fig.*) conflicting, discordant.
Zwietracht *f.* **(-, 0)** discord.
Zwilling *m.* **(-[e]s, -e)** twin.
zwingen *v.t.st.* to constrain, to compel, to force; *gezwungen,* forced, constrained.
zwingend *a.* compelling; imperative; urgent.
Zwinger *m.* **(-s, -)** kennel; dungeon.
Zwingherrschaft *f.* despotism, tyranny.
zwinkern *v.i.* to twinkle, to blink.
Zwirn *m.* **(-[e]s, -e)** thread; twine.
Zwirnfaden *m.* thread.
zwischen *pr.* between.
Zwischenakt *m.* intermission.
Zwischenbemerkung *f.* incidental remark; digression.
zwischendurch *adv.* at intervals, in between.
Zwischenfall *m.* incident, episode.
Zwischenglied *n.* connecting link.
Zwischenhandel *m.* commission business.
Zwischenhändler *m.* middleman.
Zwischenlandung *f.* stopover.
zwischenliegend *a.* intermediate.
Zwischenlösung *f.* interim solution.
Zwischenraum *m.* interval, interstice, intermediate space.
Zwischenruf *m.* interruption; **~er** *m.* heckler.
Zwischensatz *m.* parenthesis.
Zwischenspiel *n.* interlude.
Zwischenzeit *f.* intervening time, meantime.
Zwischenzonen... interzonal, *a.*
Zwist *m.* **(-[e]s, -e)** dispute, quarrel.
Zwistigkeit *f.* **(-, -en)** discord, quarrel.
zwitschern *v.i.* to chirp, to twitter.
Zwitter *m.* **(-s, -)** hermaphrodite; (*bot.*) hybrid.
zwo *a.* two.
zwölf *a.* twelve.
zwölferlei *a.* of twelve sorts.
Zwölffingerdarm *m.* duodenum.
zwölfjährig *a.* twelve years old.
zwölftens *adv.* twelfthly.
Zyankali *n.* **(-s, -)** cyanide of potassium.
zyklisch *a.* cylindrical.
Zyklon *m.* **(-s, -e)** cyclone.
Zyklus *m.* **(-, -len)** cycle.
Zylinder *m.* **(-s, -)** cylinder; (*Hut*) silk hat, top hat.
zylindrisch *a.* cylindrical.
Zyniker *m.;* **Zynikerin** *f.* cynic.
zynisch *a.* cynical.
Zynismus *m.* **(-, -men)** cynicism.
Zypern *n.* **(-s, 0)** Cyprus.
Zypresse *f.* **(-, -n)** cypress.
Zypriot *m.;* **Zypriotin** *f.;* **zypriotisch** *a.* Cypriot.
Zyste *f.* **(-, -n)** cyst.
z.Z. *zur Zeit,* at the moment.
zzgl. *zuzüglich,* plus.

Geographical Names*

Aachen *n.* Aix-la-Chapelle.
Abessinien *n.* Abyssinia.
Abruzzen *pl.* Abruzzi.
Admiralitätsinseln *f.pl.* the Admiralty Islands.
Adrianopel *n.* Adrianople.
Adriatische(s) Meer *n.* Adriatic Sea.
Afrika *n.* Africa.
Afrikaner(in) *m.* (*f.*), **afrikanisch** *a.* African.
Ägäische(s) Meer *n.* Aegean Sea.
Ägypten *n.* Egypt.
Ägypter(in) *m.* (*f.*), **ägyptisch** *a.* Egyptian.
Akko *n.* Acre.
Albanese *m.* Albanian.
Albanien *n.* Albania.
Algier *n.* Algeria (*Land*); Algiers (*Stadt*).
Alpen *pl.* Alps.
Alpen . . . *a.* Alpine.
Amazonenstrom *m.* Amazon (river).
Amerika *n.* America.
Amerikaner(in) *m.* (*f.*), **amerikanisch** *a.* American.
Anatolien *n.* Anatolia.
Andalusien *n.* Andalusia.
Andalusier(in) *m.* (*f.*), **andalusisch** *a.* Andalusian.
Anden *pl.* Andes.
Angelsachse *m.* Anglo-Saxon.
Ansbach *n.* Anspach.
Antillen *pl.* Antilles.
Antwerpen *n.* Antwerp.
Apenninen *pl.* Apennines.
Apulien *n.* Apulia.
Araber(in) *m.* (*f.*) Arab.
Arabien *n.* Arabia.
Aragonien *n.* Aragon.
Aragonier(in) *m.* (*f.*), **aragonisch** *a.* Aragonese.
Ardennen *pl.* Ardennes.
Arktis *f.* Arctic.
Armenien *n.* Armenia.
Armenier(in) *m.* (*f.*), **armenisch** *a.* Armenian.
Asiat(in) *m.* (*f.*), **asiatisch** *a.* Asiatic.
Asien *n.* Asia.
Asowsche(s) Meer *n.* Sea of Azov.
Athen *n.* Athens.
Athener(in) *m.* (*f.*), **athenisch** *a.* Athenian.
Äthiopien *n.* Ethiopia.
Atlantische(s) Meer *n.* Atlantic.
Ätna *m.* Mount Etna.
Australien *n.* Australia.
Azoren *pl.* Azores.

Balkanstaaten *pl.* Balkan States.
Balte *m.*, **Baltin** *f.* native of the Baltic States.
baltisch *a.* Baltic.
Baltische(s) Meer *n.* Baltic Sea.
Balearen *pl.* Balearic Isles.
Basel *n.* Basle, Bâle.
Baske *m.*, **Baskin** *f.*, **baskisch** *a.* Basque.
Bayer(in) *m.* (*f.*), **bayrisch** *a.* Bavarian.
Bayern *n.* Bavaria.
Beduine *m.* Bedouin.
Behringstraße *f.* Bering Strait.
Belgien *n.* Belgium.
Belgier(in) *m.* (*f.*), **belgisch** *a.* Belgian.
Belgrad *n.* Belgrade.
Bengale *m.*, **Bengalin** *f.*, **bengalisch** *a.* Bengali.
Bengalen *n.* Bengal.
Berberei *f.* Barbary States *pl.*
Bessarabien *n.* Bessarabia.
Birma *n.* Burma; **Birmane** *m.*, **birmanisch** *a.* Burmese.
Biskaya *f.* Biscay.
Blindheim *n.* Blenheim.
Bodensee *m.* Lake Constance.
Böhme *m.*, **Böhmin** *f.*, **böhmisch** *a.* Bohemian.

* Names of countries, places and peoples in -er, generally take -es (or -[e]s) in the Gen. Sing. [*Asien, Asiens*; *Athen, Athens*; *Afrika, Afrikas*; *Gent, Gents*; *Rußland, Rußlands*; *Hessen, Hessens*; also: *der Holländer, des Holländers*] (Nom. Sing. and Plur. always alike). Names of peoples in -e take -n in the Gen. Sing. and Nom. Plur.; feminine names in -in take -nen in the Nom. Plur. [*der Pole*, Gen. Sing. *des Polen* Nom. Plur. *die Polen*; *die Polin, die Polinnen*] (Masc. Gen. Sing. always like the Nom. Plur.).

Böhmen *n.* Bohemia.
Böotien *n.* Boeotia.
Bosnien *n.* Bosnia.
Bosporus *m.* Bosphorus.
Bottnischer Meerbusen *m.* Gulf of Bothnia.
Brasili(an)er(in) *m.* (*f.*), **brasilianisch** *a.* Brazilian.
Brasilien *n.* Brazil.
Braunschweig *n.* Brunswick.
Bretagne *f.* Brittany.
Britannien *n.* Britain.
britisch *a.* British.
Brite *m.*, **Britin** *f.* Briton.
Brügge *n.* Bruges.
Brüssel *n.* Brussels.
Bukarest *n.* Bucharest.
Bulgare *m.*, **Bulgarin** *f.*, **bulgarisch** *a.* Bulgarian.
Bulgarien *n.* Bulgaria.
Bundesrepublik Deutschland *f.* Federal Republic of Germany.
Burgund *n.* Burgundy.
Burgunder(in) *m.* (*f.*), **burgundisch** *a.* Burgundian.
Byzanz *n.* Byzantium.

Cadix *n.* Cadiz.
Chaldäer *m.*, **chaldäisch** *a.* Chaldean.
Chilene *m.*, **Chilenin** *f.* Chilian.
Chinese *m.*, **Chinesin** *f.*, **chinesisch** *a.* Chinese.

Dahome *n.* Dahomey.
Dalmatien *n.* Dalmatia.
Dalmatiner(in) *m.* (*f.*), **dalmatinisch** *a.* Dalmatian.
Däne *m.*, **Dänin** *f.* Dane.
Dänemark *n.* Denmark.
dänisch *a.* Danish.
Danzig *n.* Dantzig, Danzig.
Dardanellenstraße *f.* (Straits of) the Dardanelles.
Dauphiné *f.* Dauphiny.
Delphi *n.* Delphos.
Den Haag *m.* The Hague.
deutsch *a.*, **Deutsche** *m.*, *f.* German.
Deutschland *n.* Germany.
Dnjeper *m.* Nieper, Dnieper.
Dnjester *m.* Niester, Dniester.
Donau *f.* Danube.
Drau *f.* River Drave.
Düna *f.* River Dwina.
Dünkirchen *n.* Dunkirk.

Eismeer *n.* Polar Sea; *Nördliches* ~, Arctic Sea; *Südliches* ~, Antarctic Sea.
Elsaß *n.* Alsace.
Elsässer(in) *m.* (*f.*), **elsässisch** *a.* Alsatian.
Engländer(in) *m.* (*f.*) Englishman; Englishwoman.
englisch *a.* English.
Epirus *m.* Epiros.
Estland *n.* Estonia.
Etsch *f.* Adige.
Euphrat *m.* Euphrates.
Europa *n.* Europe.
Europäer(in) *m.* (*f.*), **europäisch** *a.* European.

Felsengebirge *n.* Rocky Mountains *pl.*
Ferne Osten, Fernost *m.* Far East.
Feuerland *n.* Tierra del Fuego.
Fidschiinseln *pl.* Fiji Islands.
Finnland *n.* Finland.
Finnländer(in), Finne *m.* (*f.*) Finlander.
Flame *m.*, **Flamin** *f.* Fleming; **flämisch** *a.* Flemish.
Flandern *n.* Flanders.
Florentiner(in) *m.* (*f.*), **florentinisch** *a.* Florentine.
Florenz *n.* Florence.
Franke *m.*, **fränkisch** *a.* Franconian, Frank.
Franken *n.* Franconia.
Frankfurt *n.* Frankfort.
Frankreich *n.* France.
Franzose *m.* Frenchman; *die ~n*, the French.
Französin *f.* Frenchwoman.
französisch *a.* French.
Freiburg *n.* Friburg.
Freundschaftsinseln *pl.* Tonga (or Friendly Islands).
Friese *m.*, **Friesin** *f.*, **Friesländer(in)** *m.* (*f.*) Frisian; **friesisch** *a.* Frisian.

Galiläa *n.* Galilee.
gälisch *a.* Gaelic.
Galizien *n.* Galicia.
Gallen, St. *n.* St. Gall.
Gascogne *f.* Gascony.
Genf *n.* Geneva.
Genfer(in) *m.* (*f.*), **genferisch** *a.* Genevese.
Gent *n.* Ghent.
Genua *n.* Genoa.

Genuese(rin) *m.* (*f.*), **genuesisch** *a.* Genoese.
Germane *m.* Teuton; **Germanin** *f.* Teuton woman; **germanisch**, Germanic, Teutonic.
Golanhöhen *f.* Golan Height.
Gote *m.* Goth; **gotisch** *a.* Gothic.
Graubünden *n.* the Grisons *pl.*
Grieche *m.*, **Griechin** *f.* Greek; **griechisch** *a.* Greek, Hellenic.
Griechenland *n.* Greece.
Grönland *n.* Greenland.
Grönländer(in) *m.* (*f.*) Greenlander.
Grossbritannien *n.* Great Britain.
Grosse(r) Ozean *m.* Pacific (Ocean).

Haag *m.* The Hague.
Hamelin *n.* Hamelin.
Hannover *n.* Hanover.
Hansastädte *pl.* Hanse Towns, Hanseatic Towns *pl.*
Harz *m.* Hartz Mountains *pl.*
Havanna *n.* Havana.
Hebräer *m.*, **hebräisch** *a.* Hebrew.
Hebriden *pl.* Hebrides.
Helgoland *n.* Heligoland.
Helsingör *n.* Elsinore.
Hennegau *m.* Hainault.
Herzegowina Herzegovina.
Hesse *m.*, **Hessin** *f.*, **hessisch** *a.* Hessian.
Hessen *n.* Hesse.
Hinterindien *n.* Indo-China.
Hochland, schottische(s) *n.* Highlands *pl.*
Holländer(in) *m.* (*f.*) Dutchman; Dutchwoman.
holländisch *a.* Dutch.

Iberische Halbinsel *f.* Iberian Peninsula.
Illyrien *n.* Illyria.
Inder(in) *m.* (*f.*) Indian.
Indianer(in) *m.* (*f.*) Indian, Native American.
Indien *n.* India.
indisch *a.* Indian.
indo: **~europäisch** *a.* Indo-European; **~germanisch** *a.* Indo-Germanic.
ionisch *a.* Ionian.
Irak *m.* Iraq.
irisch, irländisch *a.* Irish.
Irland *n.* Ireland.
Irländer(in) *m.* (*f.*) Irishman; Irishwoman.
Island *n.* Iceland.
Isländer(in) *m.* (*f.*) Icelander; **isländisch** *a.* Icelandic.
Istanbul *n.* Istanbul.
Istrien *n.* Istria.
Italien *n.* Italy.
Italiener(in) *m.* (*f.*), **italienisch** *a.* Italian.

Japaner *m.*, **Japanerin** *f.*, **japanisch,** Japanese.
Joppe *n.* Jaffa.
Jugoslavien *n.* Yugoslavia.

Kalabrien *n.* Calabria.
Kalifornien *n.* California.
Kalvarienberg *m.* Mount Calvary.
Kamerun *n.* Cameroon.
Kanada *n.* Canada.
Kanadier(in) *m.*(*f.*), **kanadisch** *a.* Canadian.
Kanal *m.* Channel.
Kanarische(n) Inseln *f.pl.* Canaries *pl.*
Kap der guten Hoffnung *n.* Cape of Good Hope.
Kärnten *n.* Carinthia.
Karpaten *pl.* Carpathians.
Kaschmir *n.* Kashmir.
Kaspische(s) Meer *n.* Caspian Sea.
Kastilien *n.* Castile.
Kaukasus *m.* Caucasus.
Kelte *m.* Celt; **keltisch** *a.* Celtic.
Kleinasien *n.* Asia Minor.
Kleve *n.* Cleves.
Köln *n.* Cologne.
Korse *m.*, **Korsin** *f.*, **korsisch** *a.* Corsican.
Kosak *m.* Cossack.
Krakau *n.* Cracow.
Kreta *n.* Crete.
Krim *f.* the Crimea.
Kroate *m.*, **Kroatin** *f.*, **kroatisch** *a.* Croatian.
Kroatien *n.* Croatia.

Lakedämon *n.* Lacedaemonian.
Lakedämonier(in), *m.* (*f.*), **lakedämonisch** *a.* Lacedaemonian.
Lappe, Lappländer(in) *m.* (*f.*) Laplander; **lappländisch** *a.* Lapp.
Lausitz *f.* Lusatia.
Lausitzer(in) *m.* (*f.*), **lausitzisch** *a.* Lusatian.
Levante *f.* Levant.
Libanon *m.* Lebanon.

libysch *a.* Libyan.
Lille *n.* Lisle.
Liparische Inseln *pl.* Lipari Islands.
Lissabon *n.* Lisbon.
Litauen *n.* Lithuania.
Litauer(in) *m.* (*f.*), **litauisch** *a.* Lithuanian.
Livland *n.* Livonia.
Livländer(in) *m.* (*f.*), **livländisch** *a.* Livonian.
Livorno *n.* Leghorn.
Lofoten *pl.* Lofoden Islands.
Lombardo *m.*, **Lombardin** *f.*, **lombardisch** *a.* Lombard.
Lombardei *f.* Lombardy.
Lothringen *n.* Lorraine.
Löwen *n.* Louvain.
Ludwigsburg *n.* Lewisburg.
Luganer See *m.* Lake Lugano.
Lüttich *n.* Liège.
Luzern *n.* Lucerne.
Lyon *n.* Lyons.

Maas *f.* Meuse.
Mähre *m.*, **Mährin** *f.*, **mährisch** *a.* Moravian.
Mähren *n.* Moravia.
Mailand *n.* Milan.
Malaie *m.* Malay; **malaiisch** *a.* Malayan.
Malteser(in) *m.* (*f.*), **maltesisch** *a.* Maltese.
Mandschurei *f.* Manchuria.
Mark *f.* the Marches.
Marmarameer *n.* Sea of Marmara.
Marokko *n.* Morocco.
Marseille *n.* Marseilles.
Maure *m.* Moor.
maurisch *a.* Moorish.
Mazedonien *n.* Macedonian.
Mazedonier(in) *m.* (*f.*), **mazedonisch** *a.* Macedonian.
Mecheln *n.* Malines.
Meerbusen: der Arabische ~, the Gulf of Arabia; *der Bengalische* ~, the bay of Bengal; *der Finnische* ~, the Gulf of Finland; *der Persische* ~, the Persian Gulf.
Mittel..., Central...
Mittelamerika *n.* Central America.
Mittelmeer *n.* Mediterranean.
Mittlere Osten *m.* Middle East.
Moldau *f.* (*Land*) Moldavia.
Molukken, molukkische Inseln *pl.* Moluccas.
Mongole *m.*, **Mongolin** *f.*, **mongolisch,** Mongol.
Mongolei *f.*, *n.* Mongolia.
Mosel *f.* Moselle.
Moskau *n.* Moscow.
Mülhausen *n.* Mulhouse.
München *n.* Munich.

Neapel *n.* Naples.
Neapolitaner(in) *m.* (*f.*), **neapolitanisch** *a.* Neapolitan.
Neufundland *n.* Newfoundland.
Neuschottland *n.* Nova Scotia.
Neuseeland *n.* New Zealand.
Niederlande *pl.* the Netherlands.
Niederländer(in) *m.* (*f.*) Dutchman; Dutchwoman.
niederländisch *a.* Dutch.
Niederrhein *m.* Lower Rhine.
Nil *m.* Nile.
Nimwegen *n.* Nijmegen.
Nizza *n.* Nice.
Nordafrika *n.* North Africa.
Nordamerika *n.* North America.
nordisch *a.* Norse; Nordic.
Nordsee *f.* North Sea.
Normandie *f.* Normandy.
Normanne *m.*, **normannisch** *a.* Norman.
Norwegen *n.* Norway.
Norweger(in) *m.* (*f.*), **norwegisch** *a.* Norwegian.
Nubien *n.* Nubia.
Nubier(in), *m.* (*f.*), **nubisch** *a.* Nubian.
Nürnberg *n.* Nuremberg.

Ober..., Upper...
Olymp *m.* Olympus.
Oranien *n.* Orange.
Oranjefreistaat *m.* Orange Free State.
Orkaden (*Inseln*) *pl.* Orkneys.
Osmanische(s) Reich *n.* Ottoman Empire.
Ostasien *n.* Eastern Asia, Far East.
Osteuropa *n.* Eastern Europe.
Ostende *n.* Ostend.
Ostfriesland *n.* East Frisia.
Ostindien *n.* East Indies *pl.*
Ostindische(r) Archipel *m.* Malay Archipelago.
Österreich *n.* Austria.
Österreicher(in) *m.* (*f.*), **österreichisch** *a.* Austrian.
Ostsee *f.* Baltic (Sea).
Ozeanien *n.* Oceania.

Palästina *n.* Palestine.
Parnaß *m.* (**Parnasses**) Parnassus.
Peloponnes *m.* Peloponnese.
Perser(in) *m.* (*f.*), **persisch** *a.* Persian.
Persien *n.* Persia.
Persische Golf *m.* Persian Gulf.
Pfalz *f.* the Palatinate.
Pfälzer(in) *m.* (*f.*), **pfälzisch** *a.* Palatine.
Philippinen *pl.* Philippines.
Piemont *n.* Piedmont.
Piemontese(rin) *m.* (*f.*), **piemontesisch** *a.* Piedmontese.
Polen *n.* Poland.
polnisch *a.* Polish.
Pommern *n.* Pomerania.
Portugiese *m.*, **Portugiesin** *f.*, **portugiesisch** *a.* Portuguese.
Prag *n.* Prague.
Preuße *m.*, **Preußin** *f.*, **preußisch** *a.* Prussian.
Preußen *n.* Prussia.
Pyrenäen *pl.* Pyrenees.

Regensburg *n.* Ratisbon.
Rhein *m.* Rhine.
rheinisch, rheinländisch *a.* Rhenish.
Rhodier(in) *m.* (*f.*) Rhodian.
Rhodus *n.* Rhodes.
Rom *n.* Rome.
Römer(in) *m.* (*f.*), **römisch** *a.* Roman.
Rumänien *n.* Romania.
Rumänier(in) *m.* (*f.*), **rumänisch** *a.* Romanian.
Rumelien *n.* Roumelia.
Russe *m.*, **Russin** *f.*, **russisch** *a.* Russian.
Rußland *n.* Russia.

Sachse *m.*, **Sächsin** *f.*, **sächsisch** *a.* Saxon.
Sachsen *n.* Saxony.
Saloniki *n.* Thessalonica.
Sambia *n.* Zambia.
Sansibar *n.* Zanzibar.
Sarde *m.*, **Sardinier(in)** *m.* (*f.*), **sardinisch** *a.* Sardinian.
Sardinien *n.* Sardinia.
Sauerland *n.* Southern Westphalia.
Savoyarde *m.*, **Savoyer(in)** *m.* (*f.*), **savoyisch** *a.* Savoyard.
Savoyen *n.* Savoy.
Schelde *f.* Scheldt.
Schlesien *n.* Silesia.
Schlesier(in) *m.* (*f.*), **schlesisch** *a.* Silesian.
Schotte *m.*, **Schottin** *f.* Scotsman; Scotswoman.
schottisch *a.* Scottish.
Schottland *n.* Scotland.
Schwabe *m.*, **Schwäbin** *f.*, **schwäbisch** *a.* Swabian.
Schwaben *n.* Swabia.
Schwarze(s) Meer *n.* Black Sea.
Schwarzwald *m.* Black Forest.
Schwede *m.*, **Schwedin** *f.* Swede.
Schweden *n.* Sweden.
schwedisch *a.* Swedish.
Schweiz *f.* Switzerland.
Schweizer(in) *m.* (*f.*), **schweizerisch** *a.* Swiss.
Seeland *n.* Zealand.
Serbe *m.*, **Serbin** *f.*, **serbisch** *a.* Serb.
Serbien *n.* Serbia.
Sevilla *n.* Seville.
Sibirien *n.* Siberia.
sibirisch *a.* Siberian.
Siebenbürgen *n.* Transylvania.
Simbabwe *n.* Zimbabwe.
Sizili[an]er(in) *m.* (*f.*), **sizil[ian]isch** *a.* Sicilian.
Sizilien *n.* Sicily.
Skandinavien *n.* Scandinavia.
Slave *m.*, **Slavin** *f.* Slav.
slavisch *a.* Slavonic, Slav.
Slavonien *n.* Slavonia.
Slavonier(in), Slavone *m.* (*f.*), **slavonisch** *a.* Slavonian.
Slowake *m.*, **Slowakin** *f.*, **slowakisch** *a.* Slovak.
Slowene *m.*, **Slowenin** *f.*, **slowenisch** *a.* Slovenian.
Sowjets *pl.* Soviets.
Spanien *n.* Spain.
Spanier(in) *m.* (*f.*) Spaniard.
spanisch *a.* Spanish.
Steiermark *f.* Styria.
Steiermärker(in) *m.* (*f.*), **steiermärkisch, steirisch** *a.* Styrian.
Stille(r) Ozean *m.* Pacific.
Südafrika *n.* South Africa.
Südamerika *n.* South America.
Sudeten *pl.* Sudetes.
Südsee *f.* South Sea.
Sund *m.* The Sound.
Syrakus *n.* Syracuse.
Syrien *n.* Syria, **syrisch** *a.* Syrian.

Tafelberg *m.* Table Mountain.
Tajo *m.* Tagus.

Tanger *n.* Tangier.
Tartare *m.*, **tartarisch** *a.* Tartar.
Tartarei *f.* Tartary.
Taurien, Tauris *n.* Taurie Chersonese.
Themse *n.* Thames.
Thermopylen *pl.* Thermopylae.
Thessalien *n.* Thessaly.
Thessal(i)er(in) *m.* (*f.*), **thessalisch** *a.* Thessalian.
Thrazien *n.* Thrace.
Thüringen *n.* Thuringia.
Thüringer(in) *m.* (*f.*), **thüringisch** *a.* Thuringian.
Thüringer Wald *m.* Thuringian Forest.
Tirol *n.* Tyrol.
Tiroler(in) *m.* (*f.*), **tirolisch** *a.* Tyrolese.
Toskana *n.* Tuscany.
Tote(s) Meer *n.* Dead Sea.
Trient *n.* Trento.
Trier *n.* Treves.
Tripolis *n.* Tripoli.
Troja *n.* Troy.
Trojaner(in) *m.* (*f.*), **trojanisch** *a.* Trojan.
Tschad *m.* Chad.
Tscheche *m.*, **tschechisch** *a.* Czech.
Tschechien Czech Republic.
Tschechoslovakei *f.* Czechoslovakia.
Türke *m.*, **Türkin** *f.* Turk.
Türkei *f.* Turkey.
türkisch *a.* Turkish.
Tyrrhenische(s) Meer *n.* Tyrrhenian Sea.

Ungar(in) *m.* (*f.*), **ungarisch** *a.* Hungarian.
Ungarn *n.* Hungary.

Venedig *n.* Venice.
Venetianer(in) *m.* (*f.*), **venetianisch** *a.* Venetian.
Vereinigte Arabische Emirate *pl.* United Arab Emirates.
Vereinigte Staaten *pl.* United States.
Vesuv *m.* Vesuvius.
Vierwaldstätter See *m.* Lake Lucerne.
Vogesen *pl.* Vosges.
Voralpen *pl.* Lower Alps.
Vorderasien *n.* Middle East.
Vorderindien *n.* India.

Walachei *f.* Wallachia.
Wallis *n.* Valais.
Waliser *m.* Welshman.
walisisch *a.* Welsh.
Wallone *m.* Walloon.
Warschau *n.* Warsaw.
Wasgau, Wasgenwald *m.* the Vosges *pl.*
Weichsel *f.* Vistula.
Weißrußland *n.* Belarus, Belorussia.
Westeuropa *n.* Western Europe.
Westfalen *n.* Westphalia; **Westfale** *m.*, **westfälisch** *a.* Westphalian.
Westindien *n.* West Indies *pl.*
Wien *n.* Vienna.
Wiener(in) *m.* (*f.*), **wienerisch** *a.* Viennese.
Württemberg *n.* Würtemberg.

Zentralafrikanische Republik *f.* Central African Republic.
Zürich *n.* Zurich.
Zweibrücken *n.* Deux-Ponts.
Zypern *n.* Cyprus; **zyprisch** *a.* Cyprian.

Table of German Strong and Irregular Verbs

Forms in parentheses are less common but acceptable.

Infinitive	Indicative Present	Preterite	Participle Past
backen	ich backe, du bäckst (backst), er bäckt (backt)	ich buk*	gebacken
befehlen	ich befehle, du befiehlst, er befiehlt	ich befahl	befohlen
beginnen	ich beginne	ich begann	begonnen
beißen	ich beisse, du beißt, er beißt etc.	ich biß	gebissen
bergen	ich berge, du birgst, er birgt	ich barg	geborgen
bersten	ich berste, du berstest u. birst, er birst (berstet)	ich barst	geborsten
besinnen sich	ich besinne mich	ich besann mich	besonnen
besitzen	ich besitze, du besitzest u. besitzt	ich besaß	besessen
betrügen	ich betrüge	ich betrog	betrogen
bewegen†	ich bewege	ich bewog	bewogen
biegen	ich biege	ich bog	gebogen
bieten	ich biete	ich bot	geboten
binden	ich binde	ich band, du band(e)st	gebunden
bitten	ich bitte	ich bat, du bat(e)st	gebeten
blasen	ich blase, du bläst, er bläst	ich blies, du bliesest	geblasen
bleiben	ich bleibe	ich blieb, du bliebst	geblieben
braten	ich brate, du brätst, er brät	ich briet	gebraten
brechen	ich breche, du brichst, er bricht	ich brach	gebrochen
brennen	ich brenne	ich brannte	gebrannt
bringen	ich bringe	ich brachte	gebracht
denken	ich denke	ich dachte	gedacht
dingen	ich dinge	ich dang	gedungen
dreschen	ich dresche, du drischst, er drischt	ich drosch (drasch)	gedroschen
dringen	ich dringe	ich drang	gedrungen
dünken	mich dünkt, deucht	mich deuchte, dünkte	gedeucht
dürfen**	ich darf, du darfst, er darf; wir dürfen	ich durfte	gedurft (dürfen)
empfangen	ich empfange, du empfängst, er empfängt	ich empfing	empfangen
empfehlen	ich empfehle, du empfiehlst, er empfiehlt	ich empfahl	empfohlen
empfinden	ich empfinde	ich empfand	empfunden
erbleichen	ich erbleiche	ich erblich	erblichen
erfrieren	ich erfriere	ich erfror	erfroren
erlöschen	ich erlösche, du erlischst, er erlischt	ich erlosch	erloschen
erscheinen	ich erscheine	ich erschien	erschienen
erschrecken††	ich erschrecke, du erschrickst, er erschrickt	ich erschrak	erschrocken
ertrinken	ich ertrinke	ich ertrank	ertrunken

* The German verbs and tenses marked by one asterisk (*) are more commonly used in their regular form.

** The past participle of a modal auxiliary verb (*dürfen, können, mögen, müssen, sollen, wollen*) is replaced by its infinitive in the perfect tenses when it is immediately preceded by a dependent infinitive (e.g., *Ich habe in die Stadt gehen müssen*). This principle also applies to the following verbs when used as auxiliaries with dependent infinitives: *heißen, helfen, hören, lassen, lehren, lernen*, and *sehen*.

† The verb "*bewegen*" "to move" is regular, "to induce" strong.

†† The verb "*erschrecken*" in its transitive sense "*einen erschrecken*" is regular.

Table of German Strong and Irregular Verbs—*continued*

Infinitive	Indicative Present	Preterite	Participle Past
erwägen	ich erwäge	ich erwog	erwogen
essen	ich esse, du ißt, er ißt	ich aß	gegessen
fahren	ich fahre, du fährst, er fährt	ich fuhr, du fuhrst	gefahren
fallen	ich falle, du fällst, er fällt	ich fiel	gefallen
fangen	ich fange, du fängst, er fängt	ich fing	gefangen
fechten	ich fechte, du fichtst, er ficht	ich focht	gefochten
finden	ich finde	ich fand	gefunden
flechten	ich flechte, du flichtst*, er flicht*	ich flocht	geflochten
fliegen	ich fliege	ich flog	geflogen
fliehen	ich fliehe	ich floh	geflohen
fließen	ich fliesse	ich floß	geflossen
fragen	ich frage, du fragst, er fragt	ich fragte	gefragt
fressen	ich fresse, du frißt, er frißt	ich fraß	gefressen
frieren	ich friere	ich fror	gefroren
gären	ich gäre	ich gor u. gärte	gegoren, gegärt
gebären	ich gebäre, du gebierst, sie gebiert	ich gebar	geboren
geben	ich gebe, du gibst, er gibt	ich gab	gegeben
gebieten	ich gebiete	ich gebot	geboten
gedeihen	ich gedeihe	ich gedieh	gediehen
gefallen	ich gefalle, du gefällst, er gefällt	ich gefiel	gefallen
gehen	ich gehe, du gehst	ich ging	gegangen
gelingen	es gelingt	es gelang	gelungen
gelten	ich gelte, du giltst, er gilt	ich galt, du galt(e)st	gegolten
genesen	ich genese, du genesest u. genest, er genest	ich genas, du genasest	genesen
genießen	ich geniesse	ich genoß	genossen
geraten	ich gerate, du gerätst, er gerät	ich geriet	geraten
geschehen	es geschieht, sie geschehen	es geschah	geschehen
gewinnen	ich gewinne	ich gewann, du gewannst	gewonnen
gießen	ich giesse, du gießt	ich goß	gegossen
gleichen	ich gleiche	ich glich, du glichst	geglichen
gleiten	ich gleite	ich glitt	geglitten
glimmen	ich glimme	ich glomm*	geglommen*
graben	ich grabe, du gräbst, er gräbt	ich grub, du grubst	gegraben
greifen	ich greife	ich griff, du griffst	gegriffen
haben	ich habe, du hast, er hat, wir haben, ihr habt, sie haben	ich hatte	gehabt
halten	ich halte, du hältst, er hält	ich hielt	gehalten
hängen†	ich hänge, du hängst, er hängt	ich hing, du hing(e)st	gehangen*
hauen	ich haue, du haust	ich hieb, (haute) du hiebst	gehauen
heben	ich hebe	ich hob	gehoben
heißen**	ich heisse, du heißt, er heißt	ich hieß	geheissen
helfen**	ich helfe, du hilfst, er hilft	ich half	geholfen
kennen	ich kenne	ich kannte	gekannt
klimmen	ich klimme	ich klomm*	geklommen
klingen	es klingt	es klang	geklungen
kneifen	ich kneife	ich kniff	gekniffen
kommen	ich komme	ich kam	gekommen

† **hängen** *v.i.* is regular.

Table of German Strong and Irregular Verbs—*continued*

Infinitive	Indicative Present	Preterite	Participle Past
können**	ich kann, du kannst, er kann	ich konnte	gekonnt (können)
kriechen	ich krieche	ich kroch	gekrochen
laden	ich lade, du lädst, er lädt	ich lud	geladen
lassen**	ich lasse, du läßt, er läßt	ich ließ	gelassen (lassen)
laufen	ich laufe, du läufst, er läuft	ich lief	gelaufen
leiden	ich leide	ich litt	gelitten
leihen	ich leihe	ich lieh	geliehen
lesen	ich lese, du liest, er liest	ich las	gelesen
liegen	ich liege	ich lag	gelegen
lügen	ich lüge	ich log	gelogen
mahlen	ich mahle	ich mahlte	gemahlen
meiden	ich meide	ich mied	gemieden
melken	ich melke	ich molk*	gemolken
messen	ich messe, du [missest] u. mißt, er mißt	ich maß	gemessen
mißfallen	ich mißfalle, du mißfällst, er mißfällt	ich mißfiel	mißfallen
mögen**	ich mag, du magst, er mag, wir mögen, ihr mög(e)t, sie mögen	ich mochte	gemocht (mögen)
müssen**	ich muß, du mußt, er muß; wir müssen, ihr müßt, sie müssen	ich mußte	gemußt (müssen)
nehmen	ich nehme, du nimmst, er nimmt	ich nahm	genommen
nennen	ich nenne	ich nannte	genannt
pfeifen	ich pfeife	ich pfiff	gepfiffen
pflegen†	ich pflege	ich pflog*	gepflogen*
preisen	ich preise	ich pries	gepriesen
quellen	ich quelle, du quillst, er quillt	ich quoll	gequollen
raten	ich rate, du rätst, er rät	ich riet	geraten
reiben	ich reibe	ich rieb	gerieben
reißen	ich reisse	ich riss	gerissen
reiten	ich reite	ich ritt	geritten
rennen	ich renne	ich rannte	gerannt
riechen	ich rieche	ich roch	gerochen
ringen	ich ringe	ich rang	gerungen
rinnen	ich rinne	ich rann	geronnen
rufen	ich rufe	ich rief	gerufen
salzen	ich salze	ich salzte	gesalzen, gesalzt††
saufen	ich saufe, du säufst, er säuft	ich soff	gesoffen
saugen	ich sauge	ich sog*	gesogen (gesaugt)
schaffen†††	ich schaffe	ich schuf, du schufst	geschaffen
schallen	es schallt	schallte u. scholl	geschallt
scheiden	ich scheide	ich schied	geschieden
scheinen	ich scheine	ich schien	geschienen
scheißen	ich scheisse	ich schiß	geschissen
schelten	ich schelte, du schiltst, er schilt	ich schalt, du schalt(e)st	gescholten
scheren	ich schere, du scherst u. schierst, er schert u. schiert	ich schor*	geschoren
schieben	ich schiebe	ich schob	geschoben
schießen	ich schiesse, du schiessest u. schießt	ich schoß, du schossest	geschossen

† The verb "*pflegen*" in the sense of *to nurse, to attend to,* is regular.
†† In compounds and fig. use only *(ge)salzen.*
††† "*schaffen*" when used in the sense of *arbeiten* is regular.

Table of German Strong and Irregular Verbs—*continued*

Infinitive	Indicative Present	Preterite	Participle Past
schinden	ich schinde	ich schund*, du schund(e)st*	geschunden
schlafen	ich schlafe, du schläfst, er schläft	ich schlief	geschlafen
schlagen	ich schlage, du schlägst, er schlägt	ich schlug	geschlagen
schleichen	ich schleiche	ich schlich	geschlichen
schleifen	ich schleife	ich schliff	geschliffen
schließen	ich schliesse, du schliessest u. schließt	ich schloß	geschlossen
schlingen	ich schlinge	ich schlang	geschlungen
schmeißen	ich schmeisse, du schmeißt	ich schmiß	geschmissen
schmelzen†	ich schmelze, du schmilzt, er schmilzt	ich schmolz, du schmolzest	geschmolzen
schnauben	ich schnaube	ich schnob*	geschnoben
schneiden	ich schneide	ich schnitt	geschnitten
schrecken	ich schrecke	ich schrak	geschreckt
schreiben	ich schreibe	ich schrieb	geschrieben
schreien	ich schreie	ich schrie	geschrie[e]n
schreiten	ich schreite	ich schritt	geschritten
schweigen	ich schweige	ich schwieg	geschwiegen
schwellen	ich schwelle, du schwillst, er schwillt	ich schwoll	geschwollen
schwimmen	ich schwimme	ich schwamm	geschwommen
schwinden	ich schwinde	ich schwand	geschwunden
schwingen	ich schwinge	ich schwang	geschwungen
schwören	ich schwöre	ich schwor	geschworen
sehen**	ich sehe, du siehst, er sieht	ich sah	gesehen
sein	ich bin, du bist, er ist; wir sind, ihr seid, sie sind. *Subjunctive* ich sei, du seist, er sei; wir seien, ihr seiet, sie seien	ich war	gewesen
senden	ich sende	ich sandte*	gesandt (gesendet)
sieden	ich siede	ich sott*	gesotten
singen	ich singe	ich sang	gesungen
sinken	ich sinke	ich sank	gesunken
sinnen	ich sinne	ich sann	gesonnen
sitzen	ich sitze	ich saß	gesessen
sollen**	ich soll, du sollst, er soll	ich sollte	gesollt (sollen)
spalten	ich spalte, du spaltest	ich spaltete	gespalten, gespaltet
speien	ich speie	ich spie	gespie(e)n
spinnen	ich spinne	ich spann	gesponnen
sprechen	ich spreche, du sprichst, er spricht	ich sprach	gesprochen
sprießen	ich spriesse, du spriessest u. sprießt	ich sproß	gesprossen
springen	ich springe	ich sprang	gesprungen
stechen	ich steche, du stichst, er sticht	ich stach	gestochen
stecken††	ich stecke	ich stak u. steckte	gesteckt
stehen	ich stehe, du stehst	ich stand, du standst	gestanden
stehlen	ich stehle, du stiehlst, er stiehlt	ich stahl	gestohlen
steigen	ich steige	ich stieg	gestiegen
sterben	ich sterbe, du stirbst, er stirbt	ich starb	gestorben
stieben	ich stiebe	ich stob	gestoben

† The verb "*schmelzen*" is regular in its transitive sense.
†† The verb "*stecken*" meaning *to put to, to fix*, is regular and transitive.

Infinitive	Indicative Present	Preterite	Participle Past
stinken	ich stinke	ich stank	gestunken
stoßen	ich stosse, du stößt, er stößt	ich stieß, du stiessest	gestossen
streichen	ich streiche	ich strich	gestrichen
streiten	ich streite	ich stritt	gestritten
tragen	ich trage, du trägst, er trägt	ich trug	getragen
treffen	ich treffe, du triffst, er trifft	ich traf	getroffen
treiben	ich treibe	ich trieb	getrieben
treten	ich trete, du trittst, er tritt	ich trat	getreten
triefen	ich triefe, du triefst	ich troff*	getroffen, getrieft
trinken	ich trinke	ich trank	getrunken
trügen	ich trüge	ich trog	getrogen
tun	ich tue, du tust, er tut	ich tat	getan
verbergen	ich verberge, du verbirgst, er verbirgt	ich verbarg	verborgen
verbieten	ich verbiete	ich verbot	verboten
verbleiben	ich verbleibe	ich verblieb	verblieben
verbleichen	ich verbleiche	ich verblich	verblichen
verderben†	ich verderbe, du verdirbst, er verdirbt	ich verdarb	verdorben
verdrießen	es verdrießt	es verdroß	verdrossen
vergessen	ich vergesse, du vergißt, er vergißt	ich vergaß	vergessen
verlieren	ich verliere	ich verlor	verloren
verlöschen	ich verlösche, du verlischt, er verlischt	ich verlosch*	verloschen*
verschallen	verschallt	verschallte, verscholl	verschollen
verschleißen	ich verschleisse	ich verschliß	verschlissen
verschwinden	ich verschwinde	ich verschwand	verschwunden
verzeihen	ich verzeihe	ich verzieh	verziehen
wachsen	ich wachse, du wächst, er wächst	ich wuchs	gewachsen
wägen	ich wäge, du wägst, er wägt	ich wog	gewogen
waschen	ich wasche, du wäsch(e)st, er wäscht	ich wusch	gewaschen
weben	ich webe, du webst	ich webte (wob)	gewebt (gewoben)
weichen††	ich weiche	ich wich	gewichen
weisen	ich weise, du weist	ich wies, du wiesest	gewiesen
wenden	ich wende	ich wandte*	gewandt*
werben	ich werbe, du wirbst, er wirbt	ich warb	geworben
werden	ich werde, du wirst, er wird	ich wurde u. ward, du wurdest u. wardst, er wurde u. ward	geworden (worden)
werfen	ich werfe, du wirfst, er wirft	ich warf	geworfen
wiegen†††	ich wiege, du wiegst, er wiegt	ich wog	gewogen
winden	ich winde	ich wand	gewunden
wissen	ich weiß, du weißt, er weiß, wir (sie) wissen, ihr wißt	ich wußte	gewußt
wollen**	ich will, du willst, er will	ich wollte	gewollt (wollen)
zeihen	ich zeihe	ich zieh	geziehen
ziehen	ich ziehe	ich zog	gezogen
zwingen	ich zwinge	ich zwang	gezwungen

† The verb "*verderben*" is irregular in the sense of *to spoil*, but its participle is regular when used in the sense of *to corrupt*.

†† Compounds meaning *to soften, to mollify*, are regular.

††† "Wiegen" in the sense of *to rock a cradle* or *to mince* is regular.

German Abbreviations

AA, *Auswärtiges Amt,* Foreign Office; *Anonyme Alkoholiker,* Alcoholics Anonymous.
a.a.O., *am angeführten Orte,* in the above-mentioned place.
Abb., *Abbildung,* illustration, ill.
Abf., *Abfahrt,* departure, dep.
Abh., *Abhandlung,* treatise.
Abk., *Abkürzung,* abbreviation, abbr.
Abo., *Abonnement,* subscription.
Abs., *Absatz,* paragraph, par.; *Absender,* sender.
Abt., *Abteilung,* department, dept.
a.Ch., *ante Christum,* before Christ, B.C.
a.D., *außer Dienst,* retired.
Adr., *Adresse,* address.
A.G., *Aktien-Gesellschaft,* stock corporation.
ahd., *althochdeutsch,* Old High German, O.H.G.
a.d.L., *an der Lahn,* on the Lahn.
AKW, *Atomkraftwerk,* nuclear power plant.
allg., *allgemein,* general, gen.
a.M., *am Main,* on the Main.
amtl., *amtlich,* official, off.
Anh., *Anhang,* appendix, app.
Ank., *Ankunft,* arrival, arr.
Anl., *Anlage,* enclosure, encl.
Anm., *Anmerkung,* note.
a.d.O., *an der Oder,* on the Oder.
Apr., *April,* April, Apr.
a.Rh., *am Rhein,* on the Rhein.
Art., *Artikel,* article, art.
a.d.S., *an der Saale,* on the Saale.
A.T., *Altes Testament,* Old Testament.
Aufl., *Auflage,* edition, ed.
Aug., *August,* August, Aug.
Az., *Aktenzeichen,* file number.

b., *bei,* near.
B., *Bundesstraße,* major road.
BAT, *Bundesangestelltentarif,* salary scale for public employees.
Bd., *Band,* volume, vol.
Bde., *Bände,* volumes, vols.
BE., *Broteinheit,* bread unit.
beil., *beiliegend,* enclosed, encl.
bes., *besonders,* especially, esp.
Best.-Nr., *Bestellnummer,* order number, ord. no.
Betr., *Betreff, betrifft,* regarding, re.
Bev., *Bevölkerung,* population, pop.
Bez., *Bezeichnung,* designation; *Bezirk,* district, dist.
bez., *bezüglich,* with reference to.
bezw., bzw., *beziehungsweise,* respectively.
B.G.B., *Bürgerliches Gesetzbuch,* Civil Code.
BGH, *Bundesgerichtshof,* Federal Supreme Court.
Bhf., *Bahnhof,* station.
BLZ, *Bankleitzahl,* bank code.
BND, *Bundesnachrichtendienst,* Federal Intelligence Service.
Bq., *Becquerel,* becquerel, bq.
BRD., *Bundesrepublik Deutschland,* Federal Republic of Germany, FRG.
bsd., *besonders,* especially, esp.
Btx., *Bildschirmtext,* view data.
Bw., *Bundeswehr,* Federal Armed Forces.
b.w., *bitte wenden,* please turn over, p.t.o.
bzgl., *bezüglich,* with reference to.
bzw., *beziehungsweise,* respectively, resp.

C., *Celsius,* Celsius, centigrade C.
ca., *circa,* about, ca.
CDU, *Christlich-Demokratische Union,* Christian Democratic Union.
Chr., Christus.
cm, *zentimeter,* centimeter.
Co., *Compagnie,* company, co.
CSU, *Christlich-Soziale Union,* Christian Social Union.
CVJM, *Christlicher Verein Junger Männer,* Young Men's Christian Association, YMCA.

d.Ä., *der Ältere,* senior, Sen., Snr., Sr.
DAAD, *Deutscher Akademischer Austauschdienst;* German Academic Exchange Service.
DAG, *Deutsche Angestelltengewerkschaft,* Trade Union of German Employees.
DB, *Deutsche Bundesbahn,* German Federal Railway.

DBP, *Deutsche Bundespost,* German Federal Postal Services.
Dez., *Dezember,* December, Dec.
DFB, *Deutscher Fußballbund,* German Football Association.
DGB, *Deutscher Gewerkschaftsbund,* Federation of German Trade Unions.
dgl., *dergleichen, desgleichen,* the like.
d.Gr., *der Grosse,* the Great.
d.h., *das heißt,* that is, i.e.
d.i., *das ist,* that is, i.e.
Di., *Dienstag,* Tuesday, Tues.
DIN, *Deutsches Institut für Normung,* German Institute for Standardization.
Dipl., *Diplom,* diploma, Dip., Dipl.
Dir., *Direktor,* director, dir.
d.J., *dieses Jahres,* of this year; *der Jüngere,* Junior, Jun., Jr.
DJH, *Deutsches Jugendherbergswerk,* German Youth Hostel Association.
DKP, *Deutsche Kommunistische Partei,* German Communist Party.
DM, *Deutsche Mark,* German mark.
d.M., *dieses Monats,* of this month, inst.
d.O., *der Obige,* the above.
do., *ditto,* ditto, do.
Do., *Donnerstag,* Thurs., Thursday.
Doz., *Dozent(in),* lecturer.
dpa, *Deutsche Presse-Agentur,* German Press Agency.
Dr. jur., *Doktor der Rechte,* Doctor of Laws, LLD.
Dr. med., *Doktor der Medizin,* Doctor of Medicine, MD.
Dr. phil., *Doktor der Philosophie,* Doctor of Philosophy, Ph.D.
Dr. rer. nat., *Doktor der Naturwissenschaften,* Doctor of Science, Sc.D, D.Sc.
Dr. theol., *Doktor der Theologie,* Doctor of Theology, Th.D.
dt., *deutsch,* German.
Dtz., *Dutzend,* dozen.
d.Vf., *der Verfasser,* the author.
DZ, *Doppelzimmer,* double room.
D-Zug., *Durchgangszug,* corridor train.

E, *Eilzug,* fast train; *Europastraße,* European Highway.
ebd., *ebenda,* in the same place, ibid.
Ed., *Edition, Ausgabe,* edition, ed.
EDV, *elektronische Datenverarbeitung,* electronic data processing, EDP.
EEG, *Elektroenzephalogramm,* electroencephalogram, EEG.
e.G., *eingetragene Gesellschaft,* incorporated company.
EG, *Europäische Gemeinschaft,* European Community, EC.
eig., eigtl., *eigentlich,* properly.
einschl., *einschließlich,* inclusive, incl.
EKG, *Elektrokardiogramm,* electrocardiogram, EKG, ECG.
engl., *englisch,* English.
entspr., *entsprechend,* corresponding.
erb., *erbaut,* built.
Erw., *Erwachsene,* adults.
ev., *evangelisch,* Protestant, Prot.
e.V., *eingetragener Verein,* registered society, incorporated, inc.
evtl., *eventuell,* possibly, poss.
EWS, *Europäisches Währungssystem,* European Monetary System, EMS.
exkl., *exklusive,* not included.
EZ, *Einzelzimmer,* single room.

Fa., *Firma,* firm.
Fam., *Familie,* family.
FCKW, *Fluorchlorkohlenwasserstoff,* chlorofluorocarbon, CFC.
F.D.P., *Freie Demokratische Partei,* Liberal Democratic Party.
Feb(r)., *Februar,* February, Feb.
ff., *folgende,* following.
FF, *Französischer Franc,* French franc, FF.
FH, *Fachhochschule,* technical college.
Fig., *Figur,* figure, fig.
FKK, *Freikörperkultur,* nudism.
Fol., fol., *Folio,* page, folio.
Forts., *Fortsetzung,* continuation.
Fr., *Frau,* Mrs., Ms.; *Freitag,* Friday, Fri.
Frl., *Fräulein,* Miss, Ms.
frz., *französisch,* French, Fr.

g., *Gramm,* gram.
GAU, *größter anzunehmender Unfall,* maximum credible accident, MCA.
geb., *geboren,* born, b.
Gebr., *Gebrüder,* Brothers, Bros.
gegr., *gegründet,* established, est.
gek., *gekürzt,* abridged, abr.
Ges., *Gesellschaft,* company, co., society, soc.
gesch., *geschieden,* divorced, div.
gest., *gestorben,* died, d.

gez., *gezeichnet*, signed.
GG, *Grundgesetz*, constitution.
ggf(s)., *gegebenenfalls*, if necessary, if applicable.
G.m.b.H., *Gesellschaft mit beschränkter Haftung*, limited liability company, Ltd.
GUS, *Gemeinschaft unabhängiger Staaten*, Commonwealth of Independent States, CIS.

ha, *Hektar*, hectare.
Hbf., *Hauptbahnhof*, main station, main sta.
h.c., *honoris causa, ehrenhalber*, honorary, hon.
HGB, *Handelsgesetzbuch*, Commercial Code.
Hj., *Halbjahr*, half-year.
hl, *hektoliter*, hectoliter.
hl., *heilig*, holy.
hd., *hochdeutsch*, High German, H.G.
holl., *holländisch*, Dutch.
HP, *Halbpension*, half board.
Hr., *Herr*, Mr.
h(rs)g., *herausgegeben*, edited.
H(rs)g., *Herausgeber*, editor, ed.
Hs., *Handschrift*, manuscript, MS.; **Hss.,** *Handschriften*, MSS.
Hz, *Hertz*, hertz, Hz.

i., *im, in* in.
i.A., *im Auftrag*, per procurationem, p.p., by proxy.
i. allg., *im allgemeinen*, in general, gen.
i.b., *im besonderen*, in particular.
IC, *Intercity(-Zug)*, inter-city (train).
ICE, *Intercity-Expreßzug*, intercity express (train).
i.D., *im Dienst*, on duty; *im Durchschnitt*, on average, on av.
i.e., *im einzelnen*, in detail.
IFO, *Institut für Wirtschaftsforschung*, Institute for Economic Research.
IG, *Industriegewerkschaft*, industrial union.
IHK, *Industrie-und Handelskammer*, Chamber of Industry and Commerce.
i.J., *im Jahre*, in the year.
i.M., *im Monat*, in the month.
Ing., *Ingenieur*, engineer, eng.
Inh., *Inhaber*, proprietor, prop.; *Inhalt*, contents, cont.
inkl., *inklusive*, included, incl.
IQ, *Intelligenz quotient*, intelligence quotient, IQ.
i.R., *im Ruhestand*, retired, ret.
IRK, *Internationales Rotes Kreuz*, International Red Cross, IRC.
ISBN, *Internationale Standardbuchnummer*, international standard book number, ISBN.
i.V., *in Vertretung*, on behalf of, by proxy, p.p.; *in Vorbereitung*, in preparation, in prep.
IWF, *Internationaler Währungsfonds*, International Monetary Fund, IMF.

J, *Joule*, joule.
Jan., *Januar*, January, Jan.
JH, *Jugendherberge*, youth hostel, Y.H.
Jh., *Jahrhundert*, century, c., cent.
jhrl., *jährlich*, yearly, annual(ly), ann.
jr., jun., *junior*, junior, Jun., jun., Jr.
Jul., *Juli*, July, Jul.
Jun., *Juni*, June, Jun.

Kap., *Kapitel*, chapter, ch.
kath., *katholisch*, Catholic, C(ath).
KB, *Kilobyte*, kilobyte, KB.
Kffr., *Kauffrau*, businesswoman.
Kfm., *Kaufmann*, businessman.
Kfz, *Kraftfahrzeug*, motor vehicle.
kg, *Kilogramm*, kilogramme, kg.
KG, *Kommanditgesellschaft*, limited partnership.
kgl., *königlich*, royal.
k.k., *kaiserlich-königlich*, imperial and royal.
KKW, *Kernkraftwerk*, nuclear power station.
Kl., *Klasse*, class, cl.
km, *Kilometer*, kilometer, km.
KSZE, *Konferenz über Sicherheit und Zusammenarbeit in Europa*, Conference on security and cooperation in Europe, CSCE.
Kto., *Konto*, account, acct, a/c.
kW, *Kilowatt*, kilowatt.
kWh, *Kilowattstunde*, kilowatt-hour.
KZ, *Konzentrationslager*, concentration camp.

l, *Liter*, liter.
l., *links*, left, l.
l.c., *loco citato*, in the place quoted.
led., *ledig*, single, unmarried.
lfd., *laufend*, current, running.
Lfrg., *Lieferung*, delivery; part.
Lkw, *Lastkraftwagen*, truck.

lt., *laut,* according to, acc. to.
luth., *lutherisch,* Lutheran, Luth.
LZB, *Landeszentralbank,* State Central Bank.

m, *Meter,* meter.
MAD, *Militärischer Abschirmdienst,* Military Counter-Intelligence Service.
m.a.W., *mit anderen Worten,* in other words.
MB, *Megabyte,* megabyte, mb.
mbH, *mit beschränkter Haftung,* with limited liability.
MdB, *Mitglied des Bundestages,* Member of the Bundestag.
MdL, *Mitglied des Landtags,* Member of the Landtag.
mdl., *mündlich,* verbal, oral.
m.E., *meines Erachtens,* in my opinion.
M.E.Z., *Mitteleuropäische Zeit,* Central European Time, CET.
mg, *Milligramm,* milligram.
mhd., *mittelhochdeutsch,* Middle High German, M.H.G.
Mi., *Mittwoch,* Wednesday, Wed.
Mill., Mio., *Million,* million, m.
Mitw., *Mitwirkung,* assistance, participation.
mm, *Millimeter,* millimeter.
Mo., *Montag,* Monday, Mon.
möbl., *möbliert,* furnished, furn.
Mrd., *Milliarde,* billion, bn.
MS, Ms., *Manuskript,* manuscript, MS, ms.
MT, *Megatonne,* megaton.
mtl., *monatlich,* monthly.
m.ü.M., *Meter über dem Meeresspiegel,* meters above sea level.
MWSt., *Mehrwertsteuer,* value-added tax, VAT.

N, *Nord(en),* north, N.
n., *nach,* after.
nachm., *nachmittags,* in the afternoon, P.M.
näml., *nämlich,* that is to say, viz.
NATO, *Nordatlantikpakt-Organisation,* North Atlantic Treaty Organization, NATO.
n.Br., *nördliche Breite,* northern latitude.
n.Chr., *nach Christus,* after Christ, A.D.
nhd., *neuhochdeutsch,* New High German, N.H.G.
N.N., *nomen nominandum,* name to be announced.
NO, *Nordost(en),* northeast, NE.
No., Nr., *Numero,* number, no.
Nov., *November,* November, Nov.
NPD, *Nationaldemokratische Partei Deutschlands,* National-Democratic Party of Germany.
N.T., *Neues Testament,* New Testament.
NW, *Nordwest(en),* northwest, NW.

O, *Ost(en),* east, E.
o., *oben,* above; *oder,* or; *ohne,* without, w/o.
o.a., *oben angeführt,* above (-mentioned).
o.ä., *oder ähnliche,* or the like.
OB, *Oberbürgermeister,* mayor.
o.B., *ohne Befund,* results negative.
ÖBB, *Österreichische Bundesbahn,* Austrian Federal Railways.
od., *oder,* or.
o.J., *ohne Jahr,* no date, n.d..
Okt., *Oktober,* October, Oct.
ö.L., *östliche Länge,* east longitude.
OLG, *Oberlandesgericht,* Higher Regional Court.
o.O., *ohne Ort,* no place (of publication), n.p.
OP, *Operationssaal,* operating room, OR.
o.Prof., *ordentlicher Professor,* full professor, prof.
orth., *Orthodox,* Orthodox, Orth.
ÖVP, *Österreichische Volkspartei,* Austrian People's Party.

p., *per,* per, by.
p.A., p.Adr., *per Adresse,* care of, c/o.
PDS *Partei des Demokratischen Sozialismus,* Party of Democratic Socialism.
Pf., *Pfennig(e),* pfennig.
Pfd., *Pfund,* German pound.
PH, *Pädagogische Hochschule,* teachers' college.
Pkw, *Personenkraftwagen,* (motor) car.
Pl., *Platz,* Square, Sq.; *Plural,* plural, pl.
PLZ, *Postleitzahl,* zip code.
Priv.-Doz., *Privatdozent,* university lecturer.

Prof. Ord., *Professor Ordinarius,* Professor.
P.S., *Pferdestärke,* horse-power, hp; *Nachschrift,* postscript, P.S.

qkm, *Quadratkilometer,* square kilometer.
qm, *Quadratmeter,* square meter.

r., *rechts,* right, r.
RA, *Rechtsanwalt,* lawyer, attorney, att.
rd., *rund,* roughly.
Ref., *Referent,* referee.
Reg.-Bez., *Regierungsbezirk,* administrative district.
Rel., *Religion,* religion, rel.
Rep., *Republik,* Republic, Rep.
resp., *respektive,* respectively.
Rh., *Rhein,* the Rhine.
rk, *r.-k., römisch-katholisch,* Roman Catholic, RC.
röm., *römisch,* Roman, Rom.

S, *Süd(en),* south, S; *Schilling,* shilling, s.
S., *Seite,* page, p.
s., *siehe,* see.
Sa., *Samstag,* Saturday, Sat.
s.d., *siehe dort,* see above *or* there.
SB-, *Selbstbedienungs-,* self-service . . .
Sek., sek., *sekunde,* second, sec., s.
sen., *senior,* senior, Sen., Sr.
Sept., *September,* September, Sept.
SFr., *sfr, Schweizer Franken,* Swiss Franc, SF, sfr.
Sg., *Singular,* singular, sing.
sg., sog., *sogenannt,* so-called.
SO, *Südost(en),* southeast, SE.
So, *Sonntag,* Sunday, Sun.
SPD, *Sozialdemokratische Partei Deutschlands,* Social Democratic Party of Germany.
SPÖ, *Sozialistische Partei Österreichs,* Austrian Socialist Party.
s.o., *siehe oben,* see above.
s.R., *siehe Rückseite,* see overleaf.
SS, *Sommersemester,* summer term.
St., *Sankt,* Saint, St.; *Stück,* piece.
Std., *Stunde,* hour, hr., h.
stdl., *stündlich,* hourly.
StGB, *Strafgesetzbuch,* criminal code.
StPO, *Strafprozeßordnung,* Code of Criminal Procedure.
Str., *Straße,* street, st.
StVO, *Straßenverkehrsordnung,* traffic regulations.
s.u., *siehe unten,* see below.
SW, *Südwest(en),* southwest, SW.

t., *Tonne,* ton.
tgl., *täglich,* daily.
Tb, *Tuberkulose,* TB, tuberculosis.
teilw., *teilweise,* partly.
Tel., *Telefon,* telephone, tel.
TH, *Technische Hochschule,* school of technology.
TU, *Technische Universität,* Technical University.
TÜV, *Technischer Überwachungsverein,* Technical Control Board.

u., *und,* and.
u.a., *unter anderem,* among other things; *und andere,* and others.
u.ä., *und ähnliche(s),* and the like.
u.A.w.g., *um Antwort wird gebeten,* R.S.V.P.
U-Bahn, *Untergrundbahn,* subway.
u.dergl.m., *und dergleichen mehr,* and more of the kind.
u.d.M., *unter dem Meeresspiegel,* below sea level.
ü.d.M., *über dem Meeresspiegel,* above sea level.
UFO, *unbekanntes Flugobjekt,* unidentified flying object, UFO.
U-Haft, *Untersuchungshaft,* custody.
UKW, *Ultrakurzwelle,* frequency modulation, FM.
U/min, *Umdrehungen pro Minute,* revolutions per minute, r.p.m.
U-Musik, *Unterhaltungsmusik,* light music.
unbek., *unbekannt,* unknown.
unbez., *unbezahlt,* unpaid.
unverb., *unverbindlich,* not binding.
unvollst., *unvollständig,* incomplete.
urspr., *ursprünglich,* originally.
USA, *Vereinigte Staaten (von Amerika),* United States (of America), US(A).
usf., usw., *und so fort, und so weiter,* and so forth, etc.
u.U., *unter Umständen,* perhaps, perh.; if need be.
UV, *Ultraviolett,* ultraviolet, UV.

V, *Volt,* volt, V.
V., *Vers,* verse, v.
v., *von,* of, from; *versus,* versus, v., vs.

VB, *Verhandlungsbasis,* or nearest offer, o.n.o.
v. Chr., *vor Christus,* before Christ, B.C.
v.D., *vom Dienst,* on duty.
Verf., Vf., *Verfasser,* author.
vergr., *vergriffen,* out of print.
verh., *verheiratet,* married, mar.
Verl., *Verlag,* publishing house.
Verw., *Verwaltung,* administration, adm.
vgl., *vergleiche,* compare, cf.
v.H., *vom Hundert,* per cent.
v.J., *vorigen Jahres,* of last year.
v.M., *vorigen Monats,* of last month.
v.o., *von oben,* from the top.
Vorm., *Vormittag,* forenoon, A.M.
Vors., *Vorsitzende(r),* chairperson.
VP, *Vollpension,* full board.
v.T., *vom Tausend,* per thousand.
v.u., *von unten,* from the bottom.

W, *West(en),* west, W; *Watt,* watt, w.
w., *wenden,* turn over, T.O.
WAA, *Wiederaufbereitungsanlage,* reprocessing plant.
wbl., *weiblich,* female, fem.
WC, *Wasserklosett,* toilet, WC.
Wdh., *Wiederholung,* repetition, repeat.
Werkt., *Werktags,* weekdays.
westl., *westlich,* western.
WEZ, *Westeuropäische Zeit,* Greenwich Mean Time, GMT.
WG, *Wohngemeinschaft,* people sharing an apartment.
Whg., *Wohnung,* apartment.
wiss., *wissenschaftlich,* academic.
w.L., *westliche Länge,* Western longitude, W long.
w.o., *wie oben,* as above.
wö., *wöchentlich,* weekly.
WS, *Wintersemester,* winter term.
Wz., *Warenzeichen,* trademark, TM.

Z., *Zeile,* line; *Zoll,* inch.
z., *zu, zum, zur,* to, at.
z.B., *zum Beispiel,* for instance.
zeitgen., *zeitgenössisch,* contemporary.
ZH, *Zentralheizung,* central heating, centr. heat.
z.H., *zu Händen,* at *or* on hand; care of.
Zi., *Zimmer,* room, rm; *Ziffer,* figure, fig., number, no.
Zlg., *Zahlung,* payment.
z.T., *zum Teil,* partly.
Ztr., *Zentner,* German hundredweight, cwt.
Ztschr., *Zeitschrift,* periodical.
Zub., *Zubehör,* accessories.
zul., *zulässig,* permissible.
zur., *zurück,* back.
zus., *zusammen,* together, tog.
zzgl., *zuzüglich,* plus.
zw., *zwischen,* between, bet.
Zwgst., *Zweigstelle,* branch.
z.Z., *zur Zeit,* at the moment.

English–German Dictionary

A, a *s.* der Buchstabe A oder a *n.; (mus.)* **A, a, A-sharp** Ais, ais, **A-flat** As, as.
a(n) *art.* ein, eine, ein.
A *answer,* Antwort, Antw.; *ampere,* Ampere, A.
A.B. *able bodied,* dienstfähiger Matrose *m.; Bachelor of Arts,* Bakkalaureus der Philosophie.
aback *adv. taken* ~, bestürzt, verblüfft.
abandon *v.t.* aufgeben; verlassen, preisgeben.
abandoned *p. & a.* verlassen, aufgegeben.
abandonment *s.* Aufgeben *n.;* Verlassenheit *f.;* Hingabe *f.*
abase *v.t.* erniedrigen.
abasement *s.* Erniedrigung *f.*
abash *v.t.* beschämen, verlegen machen.
abashed *a.* beschämt, verlegen.
abate *v.t. & i.* vermindern, herabsetzen; nachlassen; fallen (vom Preise).
abatement *s.* Verminderung *f.;* Abnahme *f.;* Rabatt *m.,* Abzug *m.*
abbess *s.* Äbtissin *f.*
abbey *s.* Abtei *f.*
abbot *s.* Abt *m.*
abbr. *abbreviation,* Abkürzung, Abk.
abbreviate *v.t.* abkürzen.
abbreviation *s.* Abkürzung *f.*
abdicate *v.t. & i.* abdanken, zurücktreten.
abdication *s.* Abdankung *f.*
abdomen *s.* Unterleib *m.*
abdominal *a.* Unterleibs...
abduct *v.t.* entführen, wegführen.
abduction *s.* Wegführung, Entführung *f.*
aberration *s.* Abweichung *f.;* geistige Verwirrung *f., (phys.)* Aberration *f.*
abet *v.t.* unterstützen.
abettor *s.* Anstifter *m.,* Mitschuldige *m./f.*
abeyance *s.* Unentschiedenheit *f.; to fall into* ~, außer Kraft treten, außer Gebrauch kommen.
abhor *v.t.* verabscheuen.
abhorrence *s.* Abscheu *m.*
abhorrent *a.* widerlich; abscheulich.
abide *v.t. & i.st.* bleiben, warten; aushalten; *to ~ by,* befolgen (Gesetze).
abiding *a.* dauernd.
ability *s.* Fähigkeit *f.;* **abilities** *pl.* Geisteskräfte *f.pl.; to the best of one's* ~, nach bestem Vermögen.
abject *a.,* **~ly** *adv.* elend, erbärmlich; demütig, verworfen.
abjuration *s.* Abschwörung *f.*
abjure *v.t.* abschwören; entsagen.
ablative *s.* Ablativ *m.*
ablaze *adv.* in Flammen, flammend.
able *a.* fähig, geschickt; *to be* ~, imstande sein; **~-bodied,** dienstfähig.
able(-bodied) seaman *s.* Vollmatrose *m.*
ablution *s.* Abwaschung *f.*
abnegate *v.t.* ableugnen.
abnegation *s.* Selbstverleugnung.
abnormal *a.* abnorm, anormal, ungewöhnlich.
abnormality *s.* Abnormität *f.;* Unregelmäßigkeit *f.*
abnormally *adv.* anormal, abnorm.
aboard *pr. & adv.* an Bord.
abode *s.* Wohnort *m.;* Aufenthalt *m.*
abolish *v.t.* abschaffen, vernichten.
abolition *s.* Abschaffung *f.*
A-bomb *s.* Atombombe *f.*
abominable *a.,* **~bly** *adv.* abscheulich.
abominate *v.t.* verabscheuen.
abomination *s.* Abscheu *f.;* Greuel *m.; to hold in* ~, verabscheuen.
aboriginal *a.* ursprünglich.
Aborigine *s.* Ureinwohner(in) *m.(f.)*
abort *v.t.* abbrechen; abtreiben; ~ *v.i.* Fehlgeburt haben.
abortion *s.* Fehlgeburt *f.;* Mißgeburt *f.;* Abtreibung *f.; to have an* ~, abtreiben.
abortive *a.,* **~ly** *adv.* fehlgeschlagen; mißlungen.
abound *v.i.* Überfluß haben an, reichlich vorhanden sein.
about *pr. & adv.* um, herum; *(fig.)* über; etwa, ungefähr, bei, an, auf; wegen; *to be ~ to,* im Begriff sein; *round* ~, ringsumher; ~ *face,* kehrt.
above *pr. & adv.* oben, über, mehr als; ~ *all,* vor allem; ~ *board,* frank und frei, ehrlich; **~-mentioned,** obenerwähnt; over and ~, außer, über, obendrein.
abrasion *s.* Abschabung *f.*
abrasive *s.* Scheuermittel *n.*
abreast *adv.* nebeneinander.
abridge *v.t.* (ab)kürzen.
abridgment *s.* Abkürzung *f.,* Kürzung *f.*
abroad *adv.* im Ausland; *from abroad,* vom Ausland.
abrogate *v.t.* abschaffen; aufheben (Gesetz).
abrupt *a.,* **~ly** *adv.* jäh; barsch.
abscess *s.* Abszeß *m.*
abscond *v.t.* (plötzlich und heimlich) weggehen.
absence *s.* Abwesenheit *f.; leave of* ~, Urlaub *m.*
absent *a.* abwesend; ~ *without leave,* abwesend ohne Urlaub; **~-minded,** geistesabwesend, zerstreut; ~ *v.r.* sich entfernen, fernbleiben.
absentee *s.* Abwesende *m./f.* (bes. von der Arbeit).
absolute *a.,* **~ly** *adv.* unbeschränkt, unbedingt; schlechthin.
absolution *s.* Lossprechung *f.*
absolutism *s.* Absolutismus *m.*
absolve *v.t.* freisprechen.
absorb *v.t.* einsaugen; in Anspruch nehmen.
absorbent *a.* einsaugend; ~ *s.* aufsaugendes Mittel *n.*
absorption *s.* Aufsaugen *n.,* Einsaugung *f.*
abstain *v.i.* sich enthalten.
abstemious *a.,* **~ly** *adv.* enthaltsam.
abstention *s.* Enthaltung *f.*
abstinence *s.* Enthaltsamkeit *f.; day of* ~, Fasttag *m.*
abstinent *a.,* **~ly** *adv.* enthaltsam, mäßig.
abstract *v.t.* abziehen; wegnehmen.
abstract *a.* abstrakt; abgesondert; ~ *s.* Zusammenfassung *f.,* Inhaltsangabe *f.,* Auszug *m.; in the* ~, theoretisch.

abstraction *s.* Abstraktion *f.;* abstrakter Begriff *m.;* Zerstreutheit *f.*
abstruse *a.*, **~ly** *adv.* abstrus.
absurd *a.*, **~ly** *adv.* absurd.
absurdity *s.* Absurdität *f.*
abundance *s.* Überfluß *m.*, Menge *f.*
abundant *a.*, **~ly** *adv.* überflüssig, reichlich.
abuse *v.t.* mißbrauchen; betrügen; schmähen; schänden, verführen; ~ *s.* Mißbrauch *m.;* Beschimpfung *f.*
abusive *a.*, **~ly** *adv.* mißbräuchlich; schimpfend.
abut *v.i.* ~ *on* angrenzen; stoßen an.
abutment *s.* Strebe-, Stützpfeiler *m.*
abysmal *a.*, abgrundtief; katastrophal.
abyss *s.* Abgrund *m.*
AC *alternating current,* Wechselstrom.
A.C. *ante Christum,* vor Christi Geburt.
a/c *account,* Rechnung.
acacia *s.* Akazie *f.*
academic(al) *a.*, **~ly** *adv.* akademisch.
academy *s.* Akademie *f.*
accede *v.i.* beitreten, beipflichten.
accelerate *v.t.* beschleunigen.
acceleration *s.* Beschleunigung *f.*
accelerator *s.* (*mot.*) Gashebel *m.*, Gaspedal *n.*
accent *s.* Betonung *f.;* Tonzeichen *n.;* Nachdruck *m.*, Aussprache *f.;* ~ *v.t.* betonen, hervorheben.
accentuate *v.t.* betonen.
accept *v.t.* annehmen; (einen Wechsel) akzeptieren.
acceptability *s.* Angemessenheit *f.;* Annehmbarkeit *f.*
acceptable *a.*, **~bly** *adv.* annehmbar.
acceptance *s.* Annahme *f.;* Akzept (eines Wechsels) *n.;* Abnahme (von Maschinen) *f.*
accepted *a.* allgemein anerkannt.
access *s.* Zugang *m.;* Zuwachs, *m.; easy* ~, leicht zugänglich.
accessible *a.* zugänglich.
accession *s.* Amtsantritt *m.;* Thronbesteigung *f.*
accessory *a.* hinzukommend; Neben-; ~ *s.* Mitschuldige *m./f.;* **accessories** *pl.* Beiwerk, Zubehör *n.*
access road *s.* Zufahrtstraße *f.*
accident *s.* Unfall *m.;* Zufall *m.; by* ~, zufällig; ~ **insurance,** Unfallversicherung *f.* **~-prone** *a.* unfallgefährdet.
accidental *a.*, **~ly** *adv.* zufällig.
acclaim *v.t.* feiern.
acclamation *s.* Zuruf, Beifall *m.*
acclimatization *s.* Akklimatisierung *f.*
acclimatize *v.t.* akklimatisieren.
accommodate *v.t.* unterbringen, versorgen.
accommodating *a.* gefällig.
accommodation *s.* Anpassung *f.;* Vergleich *m.;* Unterkommen (für die Nacht) *n.*, Unterkunft *f.;* **~-bill** *s.* Gefälligkeitswechsel *m.*
accompaniment *s.* (*mus.*) Begleitung *f.*
accompanist *s.* (*mus.*) Begleiter *m.*
accompany *v.t.* begleiten; mitspielen.
accomplice *s.* Mitschuldige *m./f.*, Komplize *m.*, Komplizin *f.*
accomplish *v.t.* vollenden, erreichen.
accomplished *a.* fähig, vorzüglich.
accomplishment *s.* Ausführung *f.;* Fertigkeit *f.;* Vollendung *f.*, Leistung *f.;* **~s** *pl.* Talente *n.pl.*
accord *s.* Abkommen *n.;* Eintracht *f.;* Vergleich *m.;* ~ *v.t. & i.* übereinstimmen.
accordance *s.* Übereinstimmung *f.*
according (to) *pr.* gemäß.
accordingly *adv.* demgemäß, folglich; entsprechend.
accordion *s.* Akkordeon *n.*, Ziehharmonika *f.*
accost *v.t.* ansprechen.
account *s.* Rechnung *f.;* Rechenschaft *f.;* Bericht *m.;* Rücksicht *f.;* Konto *n.;* **~-book,** Kontobuch *n.;* **~-holder,** Kontoinhaber *m.; current* ~, laufende Rechnung *f.*, laufendes Konto *n.; deposit* ~, Depositenkonto *n.; fictitious* ~, fiktives Konto *n.; on* ~, auf Rechnung; *on* ~ *of,* wegen; *to call to* ~, zur Rechenschaft ziehen; *to keep* ~, Buch führen; *to open an* ~, ein Konto eröffnen; ~ *v.t.* schätzen, halten für; *to* ~ *for,* Rechenschaft ablegen von; erklären.
accountable *a.* verantwortlich; *to hold sb.* ~, jn. verantwortlich machen.
accountant *s.* Buchhalter(in) *m.(f.);* Steuerberater(in) *m.(f.)*
accounting *s.* Buchführung *f.*
accredit *v.t.* beglaubigen.
accrue *v.i.* auflaufen, zufallen; *accrued interest,* angefallene Zinsen *m.pl.*
accumulate *v.t. & i.* sammeln; aufhäufen; sich häufen; *accumulated interest,* aufgelaufene Zinsen *m.pl.*
accumulation *s.* Ansammeln *n.*, Anhäufung *f.*
accumulative *a.* sich anhäufend.
accumulator *s.* Akkumulator *m.*
accuracy *s.* Genauigkeit, *f.*
accurate *a.*, **~ly** *adv.* genau, sorgfältig.
accursed *p. & a.* verflucht, verwünscht.
accusation *s.* Anklage, Beschuldigung *f.*
accusative *s.* Akkusativ *m.*
accuse *v.t.* anklagen; beschuldigen.
accused *s.* (*jur.*) Angeklagte *m./f.*
accustom *v.t.* gewöhnen.
accustomed *a.* gewohnt.
ace *s.* As, *n.;* Eins (auf Würfeln) *f.;* (*avi.*) Fliegerheld.
acetylene *s.* Acetylen *n.*
ache *s.* Schmerz *m.;* ~ *v.i.* schmerzen.
achieve *v.t.* zustandebringen; erwerben.
achievement *s.* Vollendung *f.;* Leistung *f.*
acid *a.*, sauer; ~ *s.* Säure *f.;* **~-proof,** säurefest; ~ **rain** *s.* Sauerregen *m.*
acidic *a.* säuerlich.
acidity *s.* Säure, Schärfe *f.*
acknowledge *v.t.* anerkennen; bestätigen; *to* ~ *receipt,* den Empfang bestätigen.
acknowledgment *s.* Anerkennung *f.;* Empfangsbestätigung *f.*
acme *s.* Gipfel, höchster Punkt *m.*
acne *s.* Akne *f.*
acorn *s.* Eichel *f.*
acoustic *a.* akustisch; ~ **guitar** *s.* Akustikgitarre *f.;* ~ **nerve** *s.* Gehörnerv *m.*
acoustics *s. pl.* Schallehre, Akustik *f.*
acquaint *v.t.* bekannt machen, *to be* ~*ed with sb.*, mit jm. bekannt sein.
acquaintance *s.* Bekanntschaft *f.;* Bekannte *m./f.*
acquiesce *v.t.* einwilligen.
acquiescence *s.* Einwilligung, Fügung *f.*
acquiescent *a.* fügsam; ergeben.

acquire *v.t.* erwerben, erlangen.
acquirement *s.* Erwerbung *f.*; Fertigkeit *f.*; **~s** *pl.* Kenntnisse *f.pl.*
acquisition *s.* Erwerbung *f.*; Errungenschaft *f.*
acquisitive *a.*, **~ly** *adv.* habsüchtig.
acquit *v.t.* freisprechen; *refl.* (gut, schlecht) machen.
acquittal *s.* Freisprechung *f.*
acre *s.* Morgen (Land) *m.*, Acker *m.*
acreage *s.* Ackerfläche *f.*
acrimonious *a.*, **~ly** *adv.* scharf, beißend.
acrimony *s.* Schärfe *f.*
acrobat *s.* Akrobat(in) *m.(f.)*
acrobatic *a.* akrobatisch.
acrobatics *s.* Akrobatik *f.*
across *adv.* kreuzweise; **~** *pr.* quer durch, quer hinüber; *to come* ~, zufällig finden, begegnen.
act *v.t.* spielen, darstellen; **~** *v.i.* handeln; **~** *s.* Handlung, Tat *f.*; (*theat.*) Aufzug, Akt *m.*; Gesetz *n.*; *Act of God,* höhere Gewalt *f.*; *Act of Parliament,* Parlamentsakte *f.*; *in the very* ~, auf frischer Tat; *Acts of the Apostles,* Apostelgeschichte *f.*
acting *p.* & *a.* stellvertretend; **~** *s.* Schauspielerei.
action *s.* Handlung, Wirkung *f.*; Klage *f.*; Gefecht *n.*; *to bring an* ~ *against sb.*, gegen jn. Klage anstrengen, jn. verklagen; *to put out of* ~, (*mil.*) außer Gefecht setzen; (*mech.*) außer Betrieb setzen; *to take* ~, Maßnahmen ergreifen; (*jur.*) klagen.
activate *v.t.* in Gang setzen; aktivieren.
active *a.*, **~ly** *adv.* tätig, wirksam, lebhaft, rührig; (*com.*) gesucht, belebt; (*mil.*) aktiv; **~ voice,** (*gram.*) Aktiv *n.*
activity *s.* Aktivität *f.*; Lebhaftigkeit *f.*
actor *s.* Schauspieler *m.*
actress *s.* Schauspielerin *f.*
actual *a.*, **~ly** *adv.* eigentlich; **~ stock,** Ist-Bestand *m.*; **~ strength,** (*mil.*) Ist-Stärke *f.*
actuate *v.t.* antreiben; auslösen.
acumen *s.* Scharfsinn *m.*
acupuncture *s.* Akupunktur *f.*; **~** *v.t.* akupunktieren.
acute *a.*, **~ly** *adv.* scharf, spitz; scharfsinnig; (*med.*) akut, hitzig; **~-angled,** spitzwink[e]lig.
ad *s.* (*fam.*) Annonce, Anzeige *f.*
A.D. *anno Domini,* im Jahre des Herrn, nach Christus, n. Chr.
adamant *a.*, **~ly** *adv.* fest, unerbittlich unnachgiebig.
Adam's apple *s.* Adamsapfel *m.*
adapt *v.t.* anpassen; adaptieren.
adaptability *s.* Anpassungsfähigkeit *f.*
adaptable *a.* anpassungsfähig.
adaptation *s.* Anpassung *f.*
adapter, adaptor *s.* Adapter *m.*
add *v.t.* & *i.* hinzutun; addieren.
addendum *s.* Nachtrag *m.*
adder *s.* Natter *f.*
addict *s.* Süchtige *m./f.*; *drug* ~, Rauschgiftsüchtige *m./f.*
addicted *s.* süchtig.
addiction *s.* Sucht *f.*
addictive *a. to be* ~ süchtig machen.
adding machine *s.* Rechenmaschine *f.*
addition *s.* Hinzusetzung *f.*; (*ar.*) Addition *f.*; Zusatz *m.*; *sign of* ~, Additionszeichen *n.*
additional *a.* weiter; zusätzlich; Neben-, Zusatz-; **~ claim, ~ charge,** Nachforderung *f.*
additive *s.* Zusatz *m.*
address *s.* Adresse, Anschrift *f.*; Anrede *f.*; **~** *v.t.* anreden; richten, adressieren; *to* ~ *oneself to sb.*, sich an jn. wenden.
address book *s.* Adreßbuch *n.*
addressee *s.* Adressat(in), Empfänger(in) *m./f.*
address label *s.* Adressenaufkleber *m.*
adept *a.* geschickt.
adequacy *s.* Angemessenheit *f.*
adequate *a.*, **~ly** *adv.* angemessen; adäquat.
adhere *v.i.* anhängen; ankleben.
adherence *s.* Anhänglichkeit *f.*
adherent *a.*, **~ly** *adv.* anhängend; **~** *s.* Anhänger(in) *m./f.*
adhesion *s.* Anhaften *n.*
adhesive *a.*, **~ly** *adv.* anhaftend; klebrig; **~ dressing,** Heftverband *m.*; **~ envelopes** *s. pl.* gummierte Briefumschläge; **~ bandage** *s.* Heftpflaster *n.*; Klebstoff *m.*, Klebemittel *n.*
adj. *adjective,* Adjektiv, Adj.
adjacent *a.* anliegend, angrenzend.
adjective *s.* Adjektiv, Eigenschaftswort *n.*
adjoin *v.t.* anfügen; **~** *v.i.* angrenzen.
adjourn *v.t.* & *i.* vertagen; sich vertagen; unterbrechen.
adjournment *s.* Vertagung *f.*, Unterbrechung *f.*
adjudge *v.t. to* ~ *sb. to be sth.* jn. für etw. erklären.
adjudication *s.* Beurteilung *f.*; Entscheidung *f.*
adjudicator *s.* Preisrichter *m.*
adjunct *s.* Zusatz *m.*; Attribut *n.*; **~ position** stundenweise Anstellung an Universitäten.
adjure *v.t.* beschwören.
adjust *v.t.* ordnen; berichtigen; einstellen; ausgleichen; eichen.
adjustable *a.* einstellbar, verstellbar, anpassungsfähig.
adjustment *s.* Ausgleich *m.*; Beilegung *f.*; Anpassung *f.*
adjutant *s.* Adjutant *m.*
ad-lib *a.* aus dem Stegreif.
Adm. *Admiral,* Admiral *m.*
adman *s.* Werbefachmann *m.*
administer *v.t.* verwalten; (Verweis) erteilen; *to* ~ *an oath,* einen Eid abnehmen; *to* ~ *a will,* ein Testament vollziehen.
administration *s.* Verwaltung, Regierung *f.*; Austeilung (der Sakramente); ~ *of justice,* Rechtspflege *f.*
administrative *a.* verwaltend **~ court,** Verwaltungsgericht *n.*; **~ law,** Verwaltungsrecht *n.*
administrator *s.* Verwalter *m.*; Testamentsvollstrecker *m.*
admirable *a.* bewunderungswürdig.
admiral *s.* Admiral *m.*; *rear* ~, Konteradmiral *m.*
admiralty *s.* Marineministerium *n.*
admiration *s.* Bewunderung *f.*
admire *v.t.* bewundern.
admirer *s.* Bewunderer *m.*, Bewunderin *f.*
admissible *a.*, **~bly** *adv.* zulässig.
admission *s.* Zulassung *f.*, Eintritt *m.*; Zugeständnis *n.*; **~ ticket,** Eintrittskarte *f.*
admit *v.t.* zulassen, zugeben.

admittance *s.* Zulassung *f.; no* ~! Zutritt verboten.
admittedly *adv.* zugestandenermaßen.
admixture *s.* Beimischung *f.*
admonish *v.t.* ermahnen, warnen.
admonition *s.* Ermahnung, Warnung *f.*
ad nauseam *adv.* bis zum Überdruß.
ado *s.* Getue *n.*; Aufheben *n.*
adobe *s.* Backstein *m.*
adolescence *s.* judgendliches Alter *n.*
adolescent *a.* heranwachsend; ~ *s.* Heranwachsende *m./f.*
adopt *v.t.* annehmen; adoptieren.
adoption *s.* Adoption *f.*; Annahme *f.*
adoptive *a.* adoptiert.
adorable *a.*, **~bly** *adv.* anbetungswürdig; bezaubernd.
adoration *s.* Anbetung *f.*
adore *v.t.* anbeten; innig lieben.
adorn *v.t.* schmücken.
adornment *s.* Verschönerung *f.*, Verzierung *f.*
Adriatic *s.* Adria *f.*
adrift *adv.* treibend, schwimmend; *cast* ~, in die weite Welt gestoßen.
adroit *a.*, **~ly** *adv.* gewandt.
adulate *v.t.* schmeicheln.
adulation *s.* Schmeichelei *f.*
adulator *s.* Schmeichler(in) *m.(f.)*
adulatory *a.* schmeichlerisch.
adult *a.* erwachsen; ~ *s.* Erwachsene *m./f.*
adulterate *v.t.* verfälschen.
adulterer *s.* Ehebrecher *m.*
adulteress *s.* Ehebrecherin *f.*
adulterous *a.* ehebrecherisch.
adultery *s.* Ehebruch *m.*
adulthood *s.* Erwachsenenalter.
adumbrate *v.t.* flüchtig skizzieren; hindeuten auf.
adv. *adverb*, Adverb, Adv.
advance *s.* Fortschritt *m.*; Vorschuss *m.*; Steigen (der Preise) *n.*; *in* ~, im Voraus; **~s** *pl.* Auslagen *f.pl;* ~ *v.t. & i.* vorrücken; befördern; vorschießen; Fortschritte machen; im Preise steigen; *to* ~ *a claim*, eine Forderung geltend machen; *to* ~ *an opinion*, eine Meinung vorbringen.
advanced *a.* fortgeschritten.
advancement *s.* Beförderung, Verbesserung *f.*
advantage *s.* Vorteil, Vorzug *m.*; Überlegenheit *f.*; *to take* ~ *of*, sich etwas zunutze machen.
advantageous *a.*, **~ly** *adv.* vorteilhaft.
advent *s.* Advent *m.*
adventitious *a.*, **~ly** *adv.* zufällig.
adventure *s.* Abenteuer *n.*; ~ *v.t. & i.* wagen.
adventurer *s.* Abenteuerer *m.*
adventuress *s.* Abenteuerin *f.*
adventurous *a.*, **~ly** *adv.* abenteuerlich.
adverb *s.* Umstandswort *n.*, Adverb *n.*
adverbial *a.* adverbial.
adversary *s.* Gegner *m.*; Widersacher(in) *m.(f.)*
adverse *a.*, **~ly** *adv.* widrig; (Bilanz) passiv.
adversity *s.* Not *f.*, Widrigkeit *f.*
advertise *v.t.* inserieren, annoncieren.
advertisement *s.* Anzeige *f.*; Reklame *f.*; Inserat *n.*
advertiser *s.* Inserent(in) *m.(f.)*, Auftraggeber(in) *m.(f.)*
advertising *s.* Werbung *f.*; ~ **agency** *s.* Werbeagentur *f.*
advice *s.* Rat *m.*; Bericht *m.*
advisable *a.* ratsam.
advise *v.t.* raten; benachrichtigen; ~ *v.i.* sich beraten.
advisedly *adv.* bewußt.
adviser *s.* Ratgeber(in) *m.(f.)*
advisory board, ~ council *s.* Beirat *m.*
advocacy *s.* Befürwortung *f.*
advocate *s.* Verteidiger, Anwalt *m.*; ~ *v.t.* verteidigen; befürworten.
advt. *advertisement*, Inserat.
Aegean *s.* Ägäis *f.*
aegis *s.* Schirmherrschaft *f.*
aerial *a.* Luft...; ~ *s.* (*radio*) Antenne *f.*; ~ **photograph,** Luftbild *n.*, Luftaufnahme *f.*
aerobics *s.* Aerobic *n.*
aerodynamic *a.* aerodynamisch.
aeronautics *s.* Aeronautik *f.*
aerosol *s.* Spray *m.*, *n.*
aerospace *s.* Weltraum *m.*
aesthetic *a.*, **~ally** *adv.* ästhetisch.
aesthetics *s.* Ästhetik *f.*
afar *adv.* fern, von fern.
affability *s.* Leutseligkeit.
affable *a.*, **~ly** *adv.* leutselig, gesprächig; freundlich.
affair *s.* Angelegenheit *f.*
affect *v.t.* betreffen; beeinflussen.
affectation *s.* Ziererei *f.*; Affektiertheit *f.*
affected *p. & a.* gerührt; geziert.
affecting *a.* rührend, ergreifend.
affection *s.* Zuneigung *f.*
affectionate *a.* liebend zugetan; liebevoll.
affidavit *s.* beeidigte Erklärung *f.*; *to make an* ~, eine eidliche Versicherung abgeben.
affiliated *a. to be* ~ *with* angegliedert sein an; verbunden sein mit.
affiliation *s.* Angliederung *f.*
affinity *s.* Verschwägerung, Verwandtschaft *f.*; (*chem.*) Affinität *f.*
affirm *v.t.* bestätigen, beteuern.
affirmation *s.* Bekräftigung *f.*
affirmative *a.*, **~ly** *adv.* bejahend; ~ *s.* Bejahung *f.*; *in the* ~, bejahend.
affix *v.t.* anheften; ~ *s.* Affix.
afflict *v.t.* betrüben; plagen; heimsuchen.
affliction *s.* Kummer *m.*, Mißgeschick *n.*
affluence *s.* Reichtum *m.*; Überfluß *m.*
affluent *a.*, **~ly** *adv.* reich.
afflux *s.* Zufluß *m.*
afford *v.t.* sich leisten können.
affordable *a.* erschwinglich.
afforest *v.t.* aufforsten.
afforestation *s.* Aufforstung *f.*
affray *s.* Schlägerei *f.*; Auflauf *m.*
affront *v.t.* beleidigen; ~ *s.* Affront *m.*, Beleidigung *f.*
Afghan *a.* afghanisch; ~ *s.* Afghane *m.*, Afghanin *f.*
Afghanistan *s.* Afghanistan *n.*
afield *adv.* in der Ferne.
aflame *adv.* in Flammen.
AFL-CIO *American Federation of Labor & Congress*

of Industrial Organizations, Gewerkschaftsverband.
afloat *adv.* schwimmend.
afoot *adv.* zu Fuß; im Gange.
aforementioned *a.* vorerwähnt.
afraid *a.* besorgt, bange.
afresh *adv.* von neuem.
Africa *s.* Afrika *n.*
African *a.* afrikanisch; Afrikaner(in) *m.(f.)*
after *pr.* nach, hinter; zufolge; ~ **all,** am Ende, alles wohl erwogen, schließlich; ~ *adv.* hinterher, darauf; ~ *c.* nachdem.
afterbirth *s.* Nachgeburt *f.*
aftercare *s.* Nachbehandlung *f.*, Nachsorge *f.;* Resozialisierungshilfe *f.*
after-dinner speech *s.* Tischrede *f.*
aftereffect *s.* Nachwirkung *f.*
afterlife *s.* Leben *n.* nach dem Tode.
aftermath *s.* Nachwirkungen *f. pl.*
afternoon *s.* Nachmittag *m.*
aftertaste *s.* Nachgeschmack *m.*
afterthought *s.* nachträglicher Einfall *m.*
afterwards *adv.* nachher.
again *adv.* wieder, zurück; *~ and ~,* immer wieder.
against *pr.* wider, gegen.
agape *adv.* gaffend.
agate *s.* Achat *m.*
age *s.* Alter *n.;* Zeitalter *n.; to be of ~,* mündig sein; ~ **class,** ~ **group** Altersklasse *f.;* ~ **limit,** Altersgrenze *f.; old ~,* Greisenalter *n.; under ~,* unmündig, minderjährig; *not seen for ages,* seit einer Ewigkeit nicht gesehen; ~ *v.i.* altern, alt werden.
aged *a.* bejahrt; *~ 9 years,* neun Jahre alt.
agency *s.* Wirkung *f.;* Vermittlung *f.;* Agentur *f.;* Dienststelle *f.*
agenda *s.* Tagesordnung *f.*
agent *s.* Agent *m.;* Mittel *n.*
age-old *a.* uralt.
agglomerate *v.i.* sich klumpen.
agglutinate *v.t.* zusammenkleben; agglutinieren.
aggrandizement *s.* Vergrößerung *f.*
aggravate *v.t.* erschweren; ärgern.
aggravating *a.* ärgerlich; ~ **circumstances,** (*jur.*) erschwerende Umstände *m. pl.*
aggravation *s.* Verschlimmerung *f.;* Ärger *m.*
aggregate *s.* Haufen *m.;* Ganze *n.;* Aggregat *n.;* ~ *a.,* **~ly** *adv.* gehäuft; ~ **amount,** aufgelaufene Summe *f.;* ~ *v.t.* verbinden, ansammeln.
aggregation *s.* Ansammlung *f.;* Aggregation *f.*
aggression *s.* Angriff, Anfall *m.; war of ~,* Angriffskrieg *m.*
aggressive *a.* angreifend.
aggressiveness *s.* Aggressivität.
aggressor *s.* Angreifer *m.*
aggrieve *v.t.* kränken.
aggrieved *a.* verärgert; gekränkt.
aghast *a.* erschrocken, bestürzt.
agile *a.* behend, flink.
agility *s.* Beweglichkeit, Behendigkeit *f.*
agitate *v.t.* aufregen, beunruhigen.
agitation *s.* Bewegung, Hetzerei *f.*
agitator *s.* Agitator *m.*
aglow *a. & adv.* glühend.
agnostic *s.* Agnostiker(in) *m.(f.);* ~ *a.* agnostisch.
ago *adv.* vor; *a year ~,* vor einem Jahr; *long ~,* lange her.
agog *a. & adv., all ~,* ganz erpicht.
agonize *v.t.* martern, ~ *v.r.* quälen.
agony *s.* Qual *f.;* Seelenangst *f.;* Pein *f.*
agrarian *s.* Agrarier *m.;* ~ *a.* agrarisch.
agree *v.i.* übereinstimmen; sich vergleichen; vereinbaren; zuträglich, sein; zustimmen; *that does not ~ with me,* das bekommt mir nicht.
agreeable *a.* angenehm; erfreulich; einverstanden.
agreed *a.* einig, vereinbart.
agreement *s.* Übereinstimmung *f.;* Vergleich *m.;* Vertrag *m.; to come to an ~,* sich verständigen, sich vergleichen; *to enter into an ~, to make an ~,* ein Übereinkommen treffen.
agricultural *a.* landwirtschaftlich.
agriculture *s.* Landwirtschaft *f.*
aground *adv.* gestrandet; *to go ~, to run ~,* auf Grund laufen.
ague *s.* kaltes Fieber *n.*
ahead *adv.* voran; *go ~!* vorwärts!
aid *v.t.* helfen; *to ~ and abet,* (*jur.*) Beihilfe leisten; ~ *s.* Hilfe *f.*
aide *s.* Berater(in) *m.(f.)*
aide-de-camp (*frz.*) Adjutant *m.*
AIDS *s.* (*acquired immune deficiency syndrome*) Aids *n.*
ail *v.t.* plagen.
ailing *a.* kränklich.
ailment *s.* Unpäßlichkeit f; Gebrechen *n.*
aim *vt. & i* zielen, trachten; richten; ~ *s.* Ziel *n.*, Richtung *f.;* Absicht *f.*
aimless *a.*, **~ly** *adv.* ziellos.
air *v.t.* lüften; ~ *s.* Luft *f.;* Luftzug, Wind *m.;* Melodie *f.;* Miene *f.;* Schein *m.; by ~,* auf dem Luftweg; *open ~,* freie Luft.
airbase *s.* Luftwaffenstützpunkt.
airborne troops *s. pl.* (*mil.*) Luftlandetruppen *f.pl.*
aircraft *s.* Flugzeug *n.;* ~ **carrier** *s.* (*nav.*) Flugzeugträger *m.*
airfield *s.* Flugplatz *m.*
airgun *s.* Luftgewehr.
airing *s., to take an ~,* frische Luft schöpfen.
airless *a.* stickig; windstill.
airlift *s.* Luftbrücke.
airline *s.* Flugverkehrsgesellschaft *f.*, Fluglinie *f.*
airliner *s.* Verkehrs-, Linienflugzeug *n.*
airmail *s.* Luftpost; *by ~,* mit Luftpost.
airman *s.* Flieger *m.*
airplane *s.* Flugzeug *n.*
airpocket *s.* (*avi.*) Luftloch *n.*
air pollution *s.* Luftverschmutzung *f.*
airport *s.* Flughafen *m.*
air raid *s.* Luftangriff *m.*
air-raid protection (ARP) *s.* Luftschutz *m.*
air-reconnaissance *s.* (*mil.*) Luftaufklärung *f.*
air-raid warning *s.* Fliegeralarm *m.*
airship *s.* Luftschiff *n.*
air-speed indicator *s.* (*avi.*) (Luft-) Geschwindigkeitsmesser *m.*
airtight *a.* luftdicht.
air traffic *s.* Flugverkehr *m.;* ~ **control** *s.* Flugleitung *f.*
airworthy *a.* flugtüchtig.

airy *a.* luftig; leicht, flüchtig, lebhaft.
aisle *s.* Gang *m.;* Seitenschiff *n.;* Chorgang *m.*
ajar *adv.* halb offen, angelehnt.
akimbo *adv.* mit eingestemmten Armen.
akin *a.* verwandt.
alabaster *s.* Alabaster *m.*
alacrity *s.* Bereitwilligkeit *f.*
alarm *v.t.* alarmieren; beunruhigen, erschrecken; ~ *s.* Alarm, Larm, Aufruhr *m.;* Besorgnis *f.*
alarmclock *s.* Weckuhr *f.*
alarming *a.* alarmierend.
alarmist *s.* Panikmacher *m.;* Bangemacher *m.*
alas *i.* ach! o weh! leider!
Albania *s.* Albanien *n.*
Albanian *a.* albanisch; ~ *s.* Albanier(in) *m.(f.)*
albatross *s.* Albatros *m.*
albeit *c.* obschon.
albino *s.* Albino *m.*
album *s.* Album *n.*
albumen *s.* Albumin *n.*
alchemy *s.* Alchimie *f.*
alcohol *s.* Alkohol *m.*
alcoholic *a.* alkoholisch, spiritusartig.
alcoholism *s.* Alkoholismus *m.*, Trunksucht *f.*
alcove *s.* Alkoven *m.;* Nische *f.*
alder *s.* Erle *f.*
alderman *s.* Ratsherr *m.*, Stadtrat *m.*
ale *s.* helles englisches Bier *n.*
alert *a.*, **-ly** *adv.* wachsam, flink; *on the* ~, auf der Hut, wach.
alga *s.* **-e** *pl.* Alge *f.*
algebra *s.* Algebra *f.*
algebraic *a.* algebraisch.
Algeria *s.* Algerien *n.*
Algerian *a.* algerisch; ~ *s.* Algerier(in) *m.(f.)*
algorithm *s.* Algorithmus.
alias *s.* alias; falscher Name *m.*
alibi *s.* (*jur.*) Alibi *n.; to prove one's* ~, sein Alibi nachweisen.
alien *a.* fremd; ~ *s.* Ausländer(in) *m.(f.)*
alienate *v.t.* entfremden, veräußern.
alienation *s.* Entfremdung.
alight *v.i.* sich niederlassen; aussteigen; ~ *a.* brennend, angezündet.
align *v.t.* in eine Linie bringen, richten.
alignment *s.* Aufstellung in einer Linie *f.;* Richtung *f.*
alike *a. & adv.* gleich, ähnlich; ebenso.
alimentary *a.* Nahrungs..., nahrhaft.
alimony *s.* Unterhaltszahlung *f.*
alive *a.* lebendig; (*fig.*) munter; (*elek.*) geladen.
alkali *s.* Laugensalz *n.;* Alkali *n.*
alkaline *a.* laugensalzig; alkalisch.
all *a.* aller, alle, alles; ~ *adv.* gänzlich; *at* ~, überhaupt; **~ at once,** auf einmal; **~ but,** fast; *by ~ means,* auf jeden Fall; *on ~ fours,* auf allen Vieren; *not at* ~, ganz und gar nicht; *once and for* ~, ein für allemal; **~ the better,** desto besser; **~ the same,** trotzdem, doch; **~ right!,** ganz recht! in Ordnung; **~ of a sudden,** urplötzlich; **~ along,** die ganze Zeit.
all-around *a.* vielseitig; Allround...
allay *v.t.* lindern, beruhigen.
all-clear signal *s.* (*mil.*) Entwarnung *f.*
allegation *s.* Angabe *f.;* Behauptung *f.*
allege *v.t.* behaupten.
alleged *a.* angeblich.
allegiance *s.* Loyalität *f.;* Untertanenpflicht *f.; to swear* ~, den Treueid schwören.
allegoric(al) *a.* sinnbildlich; allegorisch.
allegory *s.* bildliche Rede *f.;* Allegorie *f.*
all-embracing *a.* alles umfassend.
allergic *a.* allergisch.
allergy *s.* Allergie.
alleviate *v.t.* erleichtern.
alley *s.* Gäßchen *n.*
alliance *s.* Bündnis *n.;* Allianz *f.*
allied *a.* verbündet; verwandt.
alligator *s.* Alligator.
alliteration *s.* Stabreim *m.*
allocate *v.t.* zuteilen; anweisen.
allocation *s.* Anweisung, Zuteilung *f.*
allot *v.t.* zuteilen, zuerkennen.
allotment *s.* Anteil *m.;* Zuteilung *f.;* Landparzelle *f.;* Schrebergarten *m.*
all-out *a.* mit allen Mitteln; kompromißlos.
allow *v.t.* erlauben, bewilligen; zugestehen; vergüten; abrechnen.
allowable *a.* zuläßig.
allowance *s.* Erlaubnis *f.;* Taschengeld, Kostgeld *n.;* Ration *f.;* Nachsicht *f.;* Abzug *m.;* Zulage *f.; family* ~, Familienzulage *f.*
alloy *s.* Legierung *f.; to* ~ *v.t.* (Metalle) vermischen, legieren.
all-powerful *a.* allmächtig.
all-purpose *a.* Allzweck...
All Saints' Day *s.* Allerheiligen *n.*
all-time *a.* beispiellos; unerreicht.
allude (to) *v.i.* anspielen (auf).
allure *v.t.* anlocken; faszinieren; ~ *s.* Verlockung *f.*
allusion *a.* Anspielung *f.*
allusive *a.* anspielend.
alluvial *a.* angeschwemmt.
all-weather *a.* Allwetter...
all-wool *a.* Ganzwolle...
ally *s.* Bundesgenosse *m.*, Allierte *m.;* ~ *v.t.* verbünden; verbinden (mit).
almanac *s.* Almanach *m.*
almighty *a.* allmächtig.
almond *s.* Mandel *f.*
almost *adv.* beinahe, fast.
alms *s.pl.* Almosen *n.*
aloe *s.* Aloe *f.*
aloft *adv.* hoch, empor.
alone *a.*, *adv.* allein; *to let* ~, in Ruhe lassen.
along *pr.* längs, an... entlang; *adv.* entlang; weiter.
alongside *adv.* daneben; längsseits, Bord an Bord.
aloof *adv.* weit ab; *to keep ~ from,* sich fernhalten von.
aloofness *s.* Zurückhaltung *f.*
aloud *adv.* laut.
alphabet *s.* Alphabet *n.;* Abc *n.*
alphabetical *a.* alphabetisch.
Alpine *a.* von den Alpen, alpinisch.
Alps *s.pl.* Alpen pl.
already *adv.* schon, bereits.
Alsace *s.* Elsaß *n.*
Alsatian *a.* elsässisch; ~ *s.* Elsässer(in) *m.(f.);* ~ **dog** Schäferhund *m.*

also *adv.* auch, ebenfalls.
altar *s.* Altar *m.*
altar cloth *s.* Altardecke *f.*
altarpiece *s.* Altargemälde *n.*
alter *v.t. & i.* ändern; sich ändern.
alterable *a.* veränderlich.
alteration *s.* Änderung *f.*
altercate *v.i.* streiten.
altercation *s.* Zank *m.;* Auseinandersetzung *f.*
alternate *v.t. & i.* abwechseln; ~ *a.*, **~ly** *adv.* abwechselnd.
alternative *s.* Alternative *f.;* ~ *a.* abwechselnd; alternativ.
alternator *s.* Wechselstromgenerator.
although *c.* obgleich.
altimeter *s.* (*avi.*) Höhenmesser *m.*
altitude *s.* Höhe (*Luft, geographisch*) *f.*
alto *s.* Alt *m.;* Altist(in) *m.(f.)*
altogether *adv.* völlig; gänzlich, ganz und gar.
altruism *s.* Altruismus *m.;* Uneigennützigkeit *f.*
altruistic *a.* altruistisch, uneigennützig.
alum *s.* Alaun *m.*
aluminum *s.* Aluminium *n.*
aluminum acetate *s.* essigsaure Tonerde *f.*
always *adv.* immer.
AM *amplitude modulation,* Kurz-, Mittel-, u. Langwelle.
a.m. *ante meridiem,* vormittags.
amalgam *s.* Amalgam *n.*
amalgamate *v.t. & i.* verschmelzen; vereinigen.
amalgamation *s.* Vereinigung, Fusion *f.*
amass *v.t.* anhäufen.
amateur *s.* Amateur, Dilettant *m.*
amateurish *a.* (*pej.*) amateurhaft, laienhaft.
amaze *v.t.* erstaunen, in Erstaunen setzen; verwundern.
amazement *s.* Erstaunen *n.*, Verwunderung *f.*
amazing *a.*, **~ly** *adv.* erstaunlich.
Amazon *s.* Amazone *f.; the* ~, der Amazonas.
ambassador *s.* Botschafter(in) *m.(f.)*
amber *s.* Bernstein *m.*
ambidextrous *a.* beidhändig.
ambience *s.* Ambiente *n.*
ambient *a.* umliegend.
ambiguity *s.* Zweideutigkeit *f.*
ambiguous *a.*, **~ly** *adv.* zweideutig.
ambiguousness *s.* Zweideutigkeit.
ambition *s.* Ehrgeiz *m.*, Ambition *f.*
ambitious *a.*, **~ly** *adv.* ehrgeizig, begierig.
ambivalent *a.* ambivalent.
amble *s.* Paßgang *m.;* ~ *v.i.* paßgehen; schlendern.
ambrosia *s.* Ambrosia *f.*
ambulance *s.* Krankenwagen.
ambulatory *a.* gehfähig.
ambush *s.* Hinterhalt *m.* ~ *v.t.* im Hinterhalt auflauern.
ameliorate *v.t.* verbessern.
amen *adv.* amen; ~ *s.* Amen *n.*
amenable *a.* zugänglich; verantwortlich.
amend *v.t. & i.* bessern; (Gesetzentwurf) ändern od. ergänzen; sich bessern.
amendment *s.* Verbesserung *f.;* Verbesserungsantrag *m.*
amends *s.pl.* Ersatz *m.*
amenity *s.* Annehmlichkeit *f.*, Attraktivität *f.;* Reiz *m.*
America *s.* Amerika *n.*
American *a.* amerikanisch; ~ *s.* Amerikaner(in) *m.(f.)*
Americanism *s.* Amerikanismus *m.*
Americanize *v.t.* amerikanisieren.
amiability *s.* Liebenswürdigkeit *f.*
amiable *a.*, **~bly** *adv.* liebenswürdig.
amicable *a.*, **~bly** *adv.* freundschaftlich.
amidships *adv.* mittschiffs.
amid(st) *pr.* mitten in, mitten unter.
amino acid *s.* Aminosäure *f.*
amiss *adv.* unrecht, verkehrt, fehlerhaft; *to take* ~, übelnehmen.
amity *s.* gutes Einvernehmen *n.*
ammeter *s.* (*elek.*) Strommesser, Amperemeter *m.*
ammonia *s.* Ammoniak; *liquid* ~, Salmiakgeist *m.*
ammonite *s.* Ammonshorn *n.*
ammunition *s.* Munition *f.*, Kriegsvorrat *m.*
amnesia *s.* Amnesie *f.*
amnesty *s.* Amnestie *f.;* ~ *v.t.* begnadigen.
amoeba *s.* Amöbe *f.*
among(st) *pr.* unter, zwischen.
amoral *a.* amoralisch.
amorous *a.*, **~ly** *adv.* verliebt.
amorphous *a.* amorph, gestaltlos.
amortization *s.* Tilgung (einer Schuld) *f.*
amortize *v.t.* tilgen, amortisieren.
amount *s.* Betrag *m.;* ~ *v.i.* sich belaufen (auf).
ampere *s.* (*elek.*) Ampere *n.; ampere-hour,* Amperestunde *f.*
amphetamine *s.* Amphetamin *f.*
amphibian, amphibious *a.* amphibisch; ~ *s.* Amphibie *f.;* **~ tank,** (*mil.*) Schwimmpanzer *m.*
amphitheater *s.* Amphitheater *n.*
ample *a.* groß, weit; reichlich.
amplification *s.* Verstärkung, Erweiterung *f.*
amplifier *s.* (*radio, elek.*) Verstärker *m.*
amplify *v.t.* verstärken; erweitern.
amplitude *s.* Umfang *m.*
amply *adv.* ausreichend; reichlich.
ampoule *s.* Ampulle *f.*
amputate *v.t.* amputieren.
amputation *s.* Amputation *f.*
amputee *s.* Amputierte *m./f.*
amuck *adv., to run* ~ *(against or at),* Amok laufen.
amulet *s.* Amulett *n.*
amuse *v.t.* unterhalten, ergötzen.
amusement *s.* Unterhaltung *f.*
amusing *a.*, **~ly** *adv.* unterhaltsam.
an *art.* ein, eine, ein.
anabaptist *s.* Wiedertäufer *m.*
anachronism *s.* Anachronismus *m.*
anagram *s.* Anagramm *n.*
analogous *a.*, **~ly** *adv.* ähnlich.
analogy *s.* Ähnlichkeit *f.*
analysis *s.* Analyse, Auflösung *f.*
analyst *s.* Analytiker(in) *m.(f.)*
analytic(al) *a.*, **~ly** *adv.* analytisch.
analyze *v.t.* analysieren.
anarchic(al) *a.* anarchisch.
anarchist *s.* Anarchist *m.*

anarchy *s.* Anarchie *f.*, Gesetzlosigkeit *f.*
anathema *s. to be ~ to sb.* jm. verhaßt sein.
anatomical *a.* anatomisch.
anatomist *s.* Anatom *m.*
anatomize *v.t.* zergliedern.
anatomy *s.* Anatomie *f.*
ancestor *s.* Ahn(in) *m.(f.);* Vorfahre *m.*
ancestral *a.* ererbt, angestammt.
ancestry *s.* Abstammung *f.;* Herkunft *f.;* Ahnen *m. pl.*
anchor *s.* Anker *m.;* (Radio, TV) Moderator(in) *m.(f.); to cast ~,* vor Anker gehen; *to weigh ~,* Anker lichten; ~ *v.t. & i.* vor Anker legen; vor Anker liegen; (Radio, TV) moderieren.
anchorage *s.* Ankerplatz *m.*
anchovy *s.* Sardelle, Anschovis *f.*
ancient *a.* alt; **~ly** *adv.* vor alters; *the ancients,* die Alten.
ancillary *a.* dienstbar, untergeordnet.
and *c.* und.
Andes *pl.* die Anden.
anecdotal *a.* anekdotisch; anekdotenhaft.
anecdote *s.* Anekdote *f.*
anemia *s.* Anämie, Blutarmut *f.*
anemic *a.* anämisch, blutarm.
anemone *s.* Anemone *f.*
anesthesia *s.* Anästhesie *f.*, Betäubung *f.*
anesthetic *a.* (*med.*) (Schmerz) betäubend; ~ *s.* Betäubungsmittel *n.*
anesthetist *s.* Anesthetist(in) *m.(f.);* Narkosearzt *m.*, Narkoseärztin *f.*
anesthetize *v.t.* betäuben.
anew *adv.* von neuem.
angel *s.* Engel *m.*
angelic *a.* engelgleich.
anger *v.t.* erzürnen, ärgern; ~ *s.* Zorn, Ärger *m.*
angina *s.* Angina *f.*, Halsentzündung *f.*
angle *s.* Winkel *m.; right ~,* rechter Winkel *m.;* ~ *v.i.* angeln.
Anglican *a.* anglikanisch.
Anglicism *s.* Anglizismus *m.*
Anglicize *v.t.* anglisieren.
Anglo-American *s.* Angloamerikaner(in) *m.(f.);* ~ *a.* angloamerikanisch.
anglophile *s.* Englandfreund *m.*
anglophobe *s.* Englandfeind *m.*
Anglo-Saxon *s.* Angelsachse *m.;* ~ *a.* angelsächsisch.
angry *a.* zornig.
anguish *s.* Seelenangst *f.;* Qual *f.*
angular *a.*, **~ly** *adv.* winkelig, eckig.
aniline *s.* Anilin *n.*
animal *s.* Tier *n.;* ~ *a.* animalisch, tierisch; ~ **fat,** tierisches Fett *n.;* ~ **lover** *s.* Tierfreund(in) *m.(f.)*
animate *v.t.* beseelen; beleben; ~ *a.* beseelt.
animated *a.* lebhaft; ~ **cartoon** *s.* Zeichentrickfilm *m.*
animation *s.* Lebhaftigkeit *f.*
animosity *s.* Feindseligkeit *f.*
aniseed *s.* Aniskorn *n.*
ankle *s.* Fußknöchel *m.*, Fußgelenk *n.*
annals *s.pl.* Annalen *pl.*
anneal *v.t.* ausglühen; kühlen (Glas).
annex *v.t.* anhängen; annektieren; ~ *s.* Anhang *m.;* Nebengebäude *n.*
annexation *s.* Einverleibung, Annexion *f.*
annihilate *v.t.* vernichten, zerstören.
annihilation *s.* Vernichtung, Zerstörung *f.*
anniversary *s.* Jahrestag *m.;* Jubiläum *n.; wedding ~,* Hochzeitstag.
annotate *v.t.* mit Anmerkungen versehen.
annotation *s.* Anmerkung *f.;* Kommentar *m.*
announce *v.t.* ankündigen.
announcement *s.* Ankündigung *f.*
announcer *s.* Ansager *m.*
annoy *v.t.* ärgern, belästigen.
annoyance *s.* Plage *f.;* Verdruß *m.*
annoyed *a.* ärgerlich; verärgert.
annoying *a.* ärgerlich; lästig.
annual *a.*, **~ly** *adv.* jährlich; ~ **leave,** Jahresurlaub *m.; ~ report,* Jahresbericht *m.*
annuity *s.* Jahresrente *f.*
annul *v.t.* annullieren.
annular *a.* ringförmig.
annulment *s.* Annullierung *f.*
Annunciation *s.* Verkündigung *f.;* Mariä Verkündigung *f.*
anode *s.* Anode *f.*
anodyne *a.* schmerzstillend; ~ *s.* schmerzstillendes Mittel; (*fig.*) Linderungsmittel *n.*
anoint *v.t.* salben.
anointment *s.* Salbung *f.*
anomalous *s.* abweichend, unregelmäßig.; anomal.
anomaly *s.* Anomalie *f.*
anon *adv.* sogleich.
anon. *anonymous,* anonym.
anonymity *s.* Anonymität *f.*
anonymous *a.*, **~ly** *adv.* anonym.
anorak *s.* Anorak *m.*
anorexia *s.* Anorexie *f.*
another *a.* ein anderer; *one another,* einander.
answer *s.* Antwort *f.;* Resultat (einer Rechnung), *n.;* ~ *v.t. & i.* antworten; verantwortlich sein für; entsprechen; (*com.*) sich rentieren; *to ~ for,* bürgen; *to ~ the bell (door),* nach der Tür sehen; *to ~ the telephone,* ans Telephon gehen; *to ~ to a name,* auf einen Namen hören.
answerable *a.* verantwortlich.
answering machine *s.* Anrufbeantworter *m.*
ant *s.* Ameise *f.*
antagonism *s.* Widerstreit *m.*
antagonist *s.* Gegner *m.*
antagonistic *a.* feindlich; gegensätzlich; antagonistisch.
antagonize *v.t.* verärgern.
antarctic *a.* antarktisch.
Antarctic *s.* Antarktis *f.*
Antarctica *s.* die Antarktis *f.*
anteater *s.* Ameisenfresser.
antecedent *a.*, **~ly** *adv.* vorhergehend; ~ *s.* Vorhergehender *m.;* **antecedents** *pl.* frühere Lebensumstände.
antechamber *s.* Vorzimmer *n.*
antedate *v.t.* vordatieren; ~ *s.* Vordatierung *f.*
antediluvian *a.* vorsintflutlich.
antelope *s.* Antilope *f.*
antenatal *a.* vorgeburtlich; ~ **care** *s.* Schwangerschaftsfürsorge *f.*
antenna *s.* (*radio*) Antenne *f.*
anterior *a.* vorherig; älter.
anthem *s.* Hymne *f.*

anthill *s.* Ameisenhaufen *m.*
anthology *s.* Anthologie *f.;* Auslese *f.*
anthracite *s.* Anthrazit *m.*
anthrax *s.* Milzbrand *m.*
anthropoid *s.* Anthropoid *m.;* Menschenaffe *m.*
anthropological *a.* anthropologisch.
anthropologist *s.* Anthropologe *m.*
anthropology *s.* Anthropologie *f.*
anti *a.* (in Zus.) gegen...
anti-aircraft *a.* Fliegerabwehr...
antibiotic *s.* Antibiotikum *n.*
antibody *s.* Antikörper *m.*
antic *a.,* **~ly** *adv.* lächerlich; ~ *s.* Posse *f.;* Possenreißer *m.*
anticipate *v.t.* vorwegnehmen; zuvorkommen; voraussehen.
anticipation *s.* Vorwegnahme *f.;* Erwartung *f.;* Vorgeschmack *m.*
anticlimax *s.* Abstieg *m.,* Abfall *m.;* Antiklimax *f.*
anticyclone *s.* Hochdruckgebiet *n.;* Antizyklone *f.*
antidote *s.* Gegengift *n.*
antifreeze *s.* Frostschutzmittel *n.*
anti-nuclear *a.* Anti-Atomkraft...
antipathetic *a.* antipathisch, zuwider.
antipathy *s.* natürliche Abneigung *f.*
antipodes *s.pl.* Gegenfüßler *m. pl.*
antiquarian *a.* antiquarisch.
antiquary *s.* Altertumsforscher *m.*
antiquated *a.* veraltet.
antique *a.* antik; altertümlich; ~ *s.* Antiquität *f.;* ~ **dealer,** Antiquitätenhändler *m.;* ~ *furniture,* antike Möbel.
antiquity *s.* Vorzeit *f.,* Altertum *n.*
anti-Semite *s.* Antisemit *m.*
anti-Semitic *a.* antisemitisch.
antiseptic *a.* antiseptisch; ~ *s.* Antiseptikum.
antisocial *a.* asozial.
antitank *a.* Antitank...; ~ **ditch,** Panzergraben *m.;* ~**-gun,** Panzerabwehrkanone; ~**-troops,** Panzerjäger *m. pl.*
antithesis *s.* Antithese *f.;* Entgegenstellung *f.*
antithetic, antithetic(al) *a.* antithetisch; gegensätzlich.
antitoxin *s.* Gegengift *n.*
antler *s.* Geweih *n.;* Sprosse *f.* (am Hirschgeweih).
antonym *s.* Antonym *n.*
anus *s.* After *m.*
anvil *s.* Amboß *m.*
anxiety *s.* Angst *f.;* Beklemmung *f.*
anxious *a.,* **~ly** *adv.* ängstlich; begierig.
any *a.* jeder, jede; irgendein, -eine, -ein; *anybody,* ~ **one,** irgend jemand; *anything,* etwas, irgend etwas; *anyhow,* irgendwie, immerhin; jedenfalls; *anywhere,* irgendwo.
a/o *account of,* auf Rechnung von.
aorta *s.* Aorta *f.;* Hauptschlagader *f.*
AP *Associated Press,* amerikanische Nachrichten Agentur.
apace *adv.* hurtig, zusehends.
apart *adv.* beiseite, für sich; ~ **from,** abgesehen von.
apartment *s.* Wohnung *f.*
apathetic *a.* apathisch, stumpf.
apathy *s.* Gleichgültigkeit *f.,* Apathie *f.*
ape *s.* Menschenaffe *m.;* Nachäffer *m.;* ~ *v.t.* nachäffen.
aperient *a.* (*med.*) abführend; ~ *s.* Abführmittel *n.*
aperture *s.* Öffnung *f.*
apex *s.* Spitze *f.,* Gipfel *m.*
aphorism *s.* Aphorismus *m.*
apiece *adv.* pro Stück.
apish *a.,* **~ly** *adv.* affenartig.
aplomb *s.* Aplomb *m.;* Fassung *f.*
apocalypse *s.* Apokalypse *f.*
apocalyptic *a.* apokalyptisch.
apocryphal *a.* apokryph.
apodictic(al) *a.,* **~ly** *adv.* apodiktisch.
apolitical *a.* apolitisch.
apologetic(al) *a.,* **~ly** *adv.* entschuldigend.
apologize *v.i.* sich entschuldigen.
apology *s.* Rechtfertigung *f.;* Entschuldigung *f.*
apoplectic(al) *a.* apoplektisch.
apoplexy *s.* Schlaganfall *m.*
apostasy *s.* Abtrünnigkeit *f.*
apostate *a.* abtrünnig.
apostatize *v.i.* abtrünnig werden.
apostle *s.* Apostel *m.*
apostrophe *s.* Anrede *f.;* Apostroph *m.*
apothecary *s.* Apotheker *m.*
apotheosis *s.* Vergötterung, Apotheose *f.*
appal *v.t.* erschrecken.
appalling *a.* schrecklich, entsetzlich.
apparatus *s.* Gerät *n.;* Apparat *m.*
apparel *s.* Kleidung *f.;* ~ *v.t.* ankleiden.
apparent *a.,* **~ly** *adv.* augenscheinlich; *heir* ~, rechtmäßiger Thronerbe *m.*
apparently *adv.* offensichtlich; scheinbar.
apparition *s.* Erscheinung *f.;* Gespenst *n*
appeal *v.i.* appellieren, Berufung einlegen; gefallen; ~ *v.t.* anrufen; ~ *s.* Ruf *m.,* Bitte *f.;* Anziehungskraft *f.;* Reklamewirkung *f.;* (*jur.*) Berufung *f.,* Rechtsmittel *n.;* *court of* ~, Berufungsgericht *n.;* *to allow an* ~, einer Berufung stattgeben; *to dismiss an* ~, eine Berufung zurückweisen; *to lodge an* ~, Berufung einlegen.
appealing *a.* flehend, ansprechend, verlockend.
appear *v.i.* erscheinen, scheinen.
appearance *s.* Erscheinung *f.;* Anschein *m.;* *to keep up* ~*s,* den Schein wahren; *to put in an* ~, sich blicken lassen; *outward* ~, äußere Erscheinung; **~s** Äußerlichkeiten *f. pl.;* *to judge by* ~*s,* allem Anschein nach.
appease *v.t.* besänftigen.
appeasement *s.* Besänftigung *f.;* Beruhigung *f.*
appellant *s.* Berufungskläger *m.*
appendage *s.* Anhang *m.,* Zubehör. *n., m.*
appendicitis *s.* Blinddarmentzündung *f.*
appendix *s.* Anhang *m.;* Blinddarm *m.*
appertain *v.i.* gehören.
appetite *s.* Appetit *m.;* Eßlust *f.,* Verlangen *n.*
appetizer *s.* Appetitanreger *m.*
appetizing *a.* appetitlich; lecker.
applaud *v.t.* Beifall spenden *or* klatschen.
applause *s.* Beifall *m.*
apple *s.* Apfel *m.*
applepie *s.* Apfelpastete *f.*
applesauce *s.* Apfelmus *n.*
appliance *s.* Vorrichtung, Anwendung *f.;* Gerät *n.*
applicable *a.* anwendbar; geeignet.

applicant *s.* Bewerber(in) *m.(f.)*
application *s.* Bewerbung *f.;* Anwendung *f.;* Gesuch *n.;* (*med.*) Verband *m.;* Fleiß *m.;* Aufmerksamkeit *f.;* *to make an* ~, ein Gesuch einreichen; *to grant an* ~, ein Gesuch bewilligen; ~ **form,** Antragsformular *n.*
apply *v.t. & i.* anwenden; sich bewerben um; sich wenden an; *for particulars* ~ *to...*, Näheres zu erfragen bei...
appoint *v.t.* bestimmen, ernennen; *at the appointed time,* zur verabredeten Zeit, zur festgesetzten Zeit.
appointment *s.* Festsetzung *f.;* Verabredung *f.;* Ernennung *f.;* *by* ~, nach Verabredung; *to make an* ~, eine Verabredung treffen.
apportion *v.t.* einverteilen, zuteilen.
apposite *a.* passend; treffend.
apposition *s.* Zusatz *m.*, Apposition *f.*
appraisal *s.* Beurteilung *f.*
appraise *v.t.* abschätzen, bewerten.
appreciable *a.* nennenswert.
appreciate *v.t.* schätzen, zu würdigen wissen.
appreciation *s.* Würdigung, Schätzung *f.*
apprehend *v.t.* ergreifen; begreifen; fürchten.
apprehensible *a.* begreiflich.
apprehension *s.* Verhaftung *f.;* Besorgnis *f.;* Auffassung *f.;* Ansicht *f.*
apprehensive *a.*, **~ly** *adv.* besorgt.
apprentice *s.* Lehrling *m.* Auszubildende *m./f.;* ~ *v.t.* in die Lehre geben.
apprenticeship *s.* Lehrzeit *f.*
approach *v.t. & i.* nähern; sich nähern; sich wenden an; ~ *s.* Annäherung *f.;* Zutritt *m.;* Auffahrt *f.;* Ansatz *m.*
approbation *s.* Billigung *f.*, Beifall *m.*, Zustimmung *f.*
appropriate *v.t.* sich aneignen; zu einem Zwecke bestimmen; **~d funds,** bewilligte Gelder; ~ *a.* angemessen.
appropriation *s.* Aneignung *f.;* Bewilligung (von Geldern) *f.;* **~s** *s. pl.* bewilligte Gelder *n. pl.*
approval *s.* Billigung f; Genehmigung *f.*
approve *v.t.* billigen, genehmigen.
approving *a.* zustimmend; beipflichtend.
approx. *approximately,* ungefähr.
approximate *v.t. & i.* nahe bringen; sich nahen; ~ *a.* annähernd.
approximation *s.* Annäherung *f.*
appurtenance *s.* Zubehör *n.*
Apr. *April,* April, Apr.
apricot *s.* Aprikose *f.*
April *s.* April *m.;* ~ **Fool's Day** der 1. April.
apron *s.* Schürze *f.;* Schurzfell *n.*
apronstring *s.* Schürzenband *n.*
apropos *adv.* beiläufig.
apse, apsis *s.* (*arch.*) Apsis *f.*
apt *a.*, **~ly** *adv.* geschickt; geneigt; fähig.
apt. *apartment,* Wohnung, Wng.
aptitude, aptness *s.* Begabung *f.;* Tauglichkeit *f.*
aquarelle *s.* Aquarell *n.*
aquarium *s.* Aquarium *n.*
Aquarius *s.* Wassermann *m.*
aquatic *a.* Wasser...; **~s** *s. pl.* Wassersport *m.*
aqueduct *s.* Wasserleitung *f.*
aquiline *a.* adlerartig.
Arab *s.* Araber(in) *m.(f.);* ~ *a.* arabisch.
Arabia *s.* Arabien *n.*
Arabian *a.* arabisch.
Arabic *a.* arabisch, **~numeral** *s.* arabische Ziffer *f.*
arable *a.* kultivierbar.
arbiter *s.* (Schieds)richter *m.*
arbitrariness *s.* Willkür *f.*
arbitrary *a.*, **~ily** *adv.* willkürlich.
arbitrate *v.t. & i.* schlichten.
arbitration *s.* Schiedsspruch *m.;* (*com.*) Arbitrage *f.;* *court of* ~, Schiedsgericht *n.*, Schlichtungsausschuß *m.*
arbitrator *s.* Schiedsrichter *m.;* **~'s award,** Schiedsspruch *m.*
arbor *s.* Laube *f.*
arc *s.* (*geom.*) Bogen *m.*
arcade *s.* Bogengang *m.*
Arcadian *a.* idyllisch, ländlich, einfach.
arcane *a.* geheimnisvoll, verborgen.
arch *a.*, **~ly** *adv.* schlau; schalkhaft; ~ *a.* (in Zus.) Erz...; ~ *v.t.* wölben; ~ *s.* Bogen *m.;* Gewölbe *n.;* **~support,** Plattfußeinlage *f.*
archaeologic(al) *a.* archäologisch.
archaeologist *s.* Altertumsforscher *m.*, Archäologe *m.*, Archäologin *f.*
archaeology *s.* Altertumskunde, Archäologie, *f.*
archaic *a.* veraltet; altertümlich.
archaism *s.* veraltete Sprachwendung *f.;* Archaismus.
archangel *s.* Erzengel *m.*
archbishop *s.* Erzbischof *m.*
archduchess *s.* Erzherzogin *f.*
archduchy *s.* Erzherzogtum *n.*
archduke *s.* Erzherzog *m.*
archer *s.* Bogenschütze *m.*
archery *s.* Bogenschießen *n.*
archetypal *a.* archetypisch; typisch.
archetype *s.* Archetyp *m.;* Prototyp *m.*
archiepiscopal *a.* erzbischöflich.
archipelago *s.* Archipel *m.*, Inselmeer *n.*
architect *a.* Baumeister *m.*
architecture *s.* Baukunst *f.*
archives *s. pl.* Archiv *n.*
archway *s.* Bogengang *m.*
arclamp *s.* Bogenlampe.
arctic *a.* arktisch, nördlich, Polar...
Arctic *s.* Arktis *f.*
arcwelding Lichtbogenschweißung *f.*
ardent *a.*, **~ly** *adv.* heiß; inbrünstig.
ardor *s.* Hitze *f.*, Eifer *m.*
arduous *a.* anstrengend; schwierig.
area *s.* Fläche *f.*, Flächenraum *m.;* Bezirk *m.*
arena *s.* Kampfplatz *m.*, Arena *f.*
Argentina *s.* Argentinien.
Argentine *a.* argentinisch.
Argentinian *a.* argentinisch; ~ *s.* Argentinier(in) *m.(f.)*
arguable *a.* bestreitbar, fragwürdig.
arguably *adv.* möglicherweise.
argue *v.i.* Gründe anführen; streiten; ~ *v.t.* beweisen.
argument *s.* Beweisgrund *m.;* Streitfrage *f.;* Inhalt *m.*
argumentation *s.* Beweisführung *f.*
argumentative *a.* beweisend; streitsüchtig.
aria *s.* Arie *f.*

arid *a.* dürr.
aridity *s.* Trockenheit *f.*
Aries *s.* Widder *m.*
aright *adv.* gerade, richtig.
arise *v.i.st.* aufsteigen; entstehen.
aristocracy *s.* Aristokratie *f.*
aristocrat *s.* Aristokrat(in) *m.(f.)*
aristocratic *a.*, **~ally** *adv.* aristokratisch.
arithmetic *s.* Rechnen *n.; mental ~,* Kopfrechnen *n.*
arithmetical *a.*, **~ly** *adv.* arithmetisch.
ark *s.* Arche *f.*
arm *s.* Arm *m.; to keep at arm's length,* in gehöriger Entfernung halten; ~ *v.t. & i.* bewaffnen; sich rüsten.
armadillo *s.* Gürteltier *n.*
armament *s.* Rüstung *f.*
armature *s.* Rüstung *f.;* Armatur *f.;* Anker (*elek.*) *m.*
armchair *s.* Lehnsessel *m.*
armed *a.* bewaffnet; ~ **conflict** *s.* bewaffnete Auseinandersetzung *f.;* ~ **forces** *s.* Streitkräfte *f.*
armful *s.* Armvoll *m.*
armistice *s.* Waffenstillstand *m.*
armor *s.* Rüstung *f.;* Panzer *m.*
armored *a.* Panzer...; ~ **troops,** Panzertruppen *f.pl.*
armorer *s.* Waffenschmied *m.*
armorial *a.* Wappen...
armory *s.* Waffenfabrik *f.*
armpit *s.* Achselhöhle *f.*
arms *s. pl.* Waffen *f. pl.;* Wappen *n.; small ~,* Handwaffen *pl.*
army *s.* Heer *n.*
army list *s.* Rangliste der Offiziere *f.*
aroma *s.* Wohlgeruch *m.*
aromatic(al) *a.* würzig.
around *adv.* ringsherum.
arousal *s.* Aufwachen *n.;* Erregung *f.*
arouse *v.t.* wecken, aufwecken; erregen.
arr. *arrival,* Ankunft, Ank.
arrack *s.* Reisbranntwein *m.;* Arrak *m.*
arraign *v.t.* anklagen, vor Gericht stellen.
arraignment *s.* (*jur.*) öffentliche Anklage *f.*, Vorführung vor Gericht *f.*
arrange *v.t.* ordnen, einrichten; anordnen (Stühle usw.); schlichten.
arrangement *s.* Beilegung *f.*, Vergleich *m.;* Anordnung *f.*
array *s.* Reihe *f.;* Anzug *m.;* ~ *v.t.* anordnen; ankleiden.
arrear *s.* (Zahlungs-)Rückstand *m.; in ~s,* rückständig; *interest on ~s,* Verzugszinsen *m.pl.*
arrest *s.* Verhaftung *f.;* Festnahme *f.; under ~,* in Verhaft, in Gewahrsam; ~ *v.t.* hemmen; verhaften; (*fig.*) fesseln.
arrival *s.* Ankunft *f.;* Ankömmling *m.*
arrive *v.t.* ankommen; gelangen
arrogance *s.* Überheblichkeit *f.;* Arroganz *f.*
arrogant *a.*, **~ly** *adv.* anmaßend.
arrogate *v.t.* sich anmassen.
arrow *s.* Pfeil *m.;* **~head** *s.* Pfeilspitze *f.*
arsenal *s.* Zeughaus *n.*
arsenic *s.* Arsenik *n.*
arson *s.* Brandstiftung *f.*
arsonist *s.* Brandstifter(in) *m.(f.)*
art *s.* Kunst *f.;* List *f.;* **~dealer,** Kunsthändler *m.*
arterial *a.* Pulsader...; ~ **road,** Hauptverkehrsstraße *f.*
artery *s.* Pulsader *f.*
artesian *a.* artesisch.
art form *s.* Kunstgattung *f.*, Kunstform *f.*
artful *a.*, **~ly** *adv.* schlau, listig; künstlich.
art gallery *s.* Kunstgallerie *f.*
arthritis Gelenkentzündung *f.*
artichoke *a.* Artischocke *f.*
article *s.* Artikel *m.*
articulate *a.*, **~ly** *adv.* gegliedert; vernehmlich; ~ *v.t.* artikulieren; zusammenfügen.
articulation *s.* Aussprache *f.;* Artikulation *f.*
artifice *s.* Kunstgriff *m.;* List *f.*
artificial *a.*, **~ly** *adv.* künstlich,; ~ **insemination** *s.* künstliche Befruchtung *f.;* ~ **intelligence** *s.* künstliche Intelligenz *f.*
artificiality *s.* Künstlichkeit *f.*
artificial respiration *s.* künstliche Beatmung.
artillery *s.* Artillerie *f.; long-range ~,* Fernkampfartillerie *f.*
artilleryman *s.* Artillerist, Kanonier *m.*
artisan *s.* Handwerker *m.*
artist *s.* Künstler(in) *m.(f.)*
artiste *s.* Artist(in) *m.(f.)*
artistic *a.* künstlerisch.
artless *a.* kunstlos; naiv.
art nouveau *s.* Jugendstil *m.*
as *c.* als, da, so, sowie, sofern, wenn; wie; weil; indem; ~... ~..., (eben) so... wie; ~ **for,** ~ **to,** was betrifft; ~ **it were,** sozusagen; ~ **if,** ~ **though,** als ob, wie wenn; ~ **far** ~ soweit als; ~ **long ~,** solange; ~ **soon ~,** sobald (als); ~ **yet,** noch, bisher.
asbestos *s.* Asbest *m.*
ascend *v.t. & i.* hinaufsteigen; ersteigen.
ascendancy *s.* Vorherrschaft *f.;* Überlegenheit *f.*
ascendant *a.* aufsteigend; überlegen; *~s.* Aszendent *m.*
ascension *s.* Aufsteigen *n.*, Besteigung *f.;* ~ **Day** *s.* Himmelfahrtstag *m.*
ascent *s.* Aufstieg *m.*
ascertain *v.t.* feststellen, ermitteln.
ascertainable *a.* feststellbar.
ascetic *a.* asketisch; ~ *s.* Asket(in) *m.(f.)*
asceticism *s.* Askese *f.*
ASCII *American Standard Code for Information Interchange,* standardisierter Code zur Darstellung alphanumerischer Zeichen.
ascribe *v.t.* zuschreiben.
aseptic *a.* keimfrei, aseptisch.
asexual *a.* asexuell.
ash *s.* Esche *f.;* Asche *f.*
ashamed *a.* beschämt.
ashen *a.* aschfarben; aschfahl.
ashes *s.pl.* Asche *f.*
ashore *adv.* am Ufer; *to get ~,* landen.
ashtray *s.* Aschenbecher *m.*
Ash Wednesday *s.* Aschermittwoch *m.*
Asia *s.* Asien *n.;* ~ **Minor** Kleinasien *n.*
Asian *a.* asiatisch; *s.* Asiat(in) *m.(f.)*
aside *adv.* beiseite, abseits; ~ *s.* beiseite gesprochene Worte *n.pl.*
asinine *a.* eselhaft; Esel...

ask *v.t. & i.* fordern, fragen, bitten; *to be had for the asking,* umsonst zu bekommen.
askance *adv. to look ~ at,* schief, schräg ansehen.
askew *adv.* schief; *to go ~,* schiefgehen.
aslant *adv.* schräg, quer.
asleep *adv.* schlafend; *to fall ~,* einschlafen.
asparagus *s.* Spargel *m.*
aspect *s.* Anblick *m.;* Aussicht *f.*
aspen *s.* Espe *f.*
asperity *s.* Rauheit *f.*
asperse v.t. besprengen; verleumden.
aspersion *s.* Verleumdung *f.*
asphalt *s.* Asphalt *m.*
asphyxiate *v.t.* ersticken.
asphyxiation *s.* Erstickung *f.*
aspirant *s.* Bewerber(in) *m.(f.); ~ a.* aufstrebend.
aspirate *v.t.* aspirieren.
aspiration *s.* Streben *n.;* Sehnsucht *f.*
aspire *v.i.* streben, heftig verlangen.
aspirin *s.* Aspirin *n.*
aspiring *a.* aufstrebend.
ass *s.* Esel *m.;* (*vulg.*) Arsch *m.*
assail *v.t.* anfallen, angreifen.
assailant *s.* Angreifer *m.*
assassin *s.* Meuchelmörder(in) *m.(f.),* Mörder(in) *m.(f.)*
assassinate *v.t.* ein Attentat verüben auf.
assassination *s.* Meuchelmord *m.,* Mord *m.* Attentat *n.*
assault *s.* Angriff, Sturm *m.;* (*jur.*) tätliche Beleidigung *f.;* ~ **and battery,** schwere tätliche Beleidigung *f.; indecent ~,* Sittlichkeitsvergehen *n.; ~ v.t.* angreifen, anfallen.
assay *s.* Probe *f.,* Prüfung *f.; ~ v.t.* prüfen, probieren.
assemblage *s.* Zusammenkunft *f.;* Zusammensetzen *n.*
assemble *v.t. & i.* sammeln; sich versammeln; (*mech.*) zusammensetzen, montieren.
assembly *s.* Versammlung *f.*
assembly line *s.* Montagefließband *n.*
assembly plant *s.* Montagewerkstatt *f.*
assent *s.* Genehmigung *f.; ~ v.i.* beipflichten.
assert *v.t.* behaupten, verfechten.
assertion *s.* Behauptung *f.*
assertive *a.* ausdrücklich, bestimmt.
assess *v.t.* abschätzen, besteuern.
assessable *a.* steuerbar.
assessment *s.* Einschätzung *f.*
asset *s.* Aktivposten *m.;* (*fig.*) Vorteil *m.;* **~s** *pl.* (*com.*) Activa *pl.*, Vermögen *n.*
asseveration *s.* Beteuerung *f.*
assiduity *s.* Emsigkeit *f.*
assiduous *a.*, **~ly** *adv.* emsig.
assign *v.t.* anweisen; abtreten; *to ~ to a unit,* (*mil.*) einer Einheit unterstellen.
assignment *s.* Anweisung *f.;* (*mil.*) Auftrag *m.*
assimilate *v.t.* angleichen; in sich aufnehmen; *~ v.i.* ähnlich werden.
assimilation *s.* Angleichung *f.*
assist *v.t.* beistehen; *~ v.i.* zugegensein, teilnehmen (an).
assistance *s.* Beistand *m.*
assistant *a.* behilflich; *~ s.* Helfer(in) *m.(f.);* Gehilfe *m.;* Assistent(in) *m.(f.);* ~ **master** Studienrat *m.*
associate *s.* Genosse *m.;* Teilhaber *m.;* Mitarbeiter *m.; ~ v.t. & i.* zugesellen; umgehen mit.
association *s.* Vereinigung *f.*, Verband *m.*
assort *v.t.* aussuchen, sortieren; *~ v.i.* übereinstimmen.
assorted *a.* gemischt; sortiert.
assortment *s.* Auswahl *f.;* Sortiment *n.*
asst. *assistant,* Assistent(in), Asst.
assuage *v.t.* besänftigen.
assume *v.t.* annehmen, sich anmaßen; *to ~ duty,* Dienst antreten.
assumption *s.* Annahme *f.;* (*jur.*) ~ **of authority** Dienstanmaßung *f.*
assurance *s.* Vertrauen *n.;* Selbstsicherheit *f.;* Versicherung *f.*
assure *v.t.* versichern, sicher stellen.
assured *a.*, **~ly** *adv.* gewiß.
asterisk *s.* Sternchen *n.*
astern *adv.* achtern; achteraus.
asthma *s.* (*med.*) Asthma *n.*
asthmatic(al) *a.* asthmatisch.
astir *adv.* rege, wach.
astonish *v.t.* erstaunen, in Erstaunen setzen.
astonishing *a.* **~ly** *adv.* erstaunlich.
astonishment *s.* Erstaunen *n.*
astound *v.t.* in Staunen versetzen; verblüffen.
astounding *a.* erstaunlich.
astraddle *adv.* rittlings.
astray *adv.* in der Irre; *to go ~,* irregehen.
astride *adv.* sperrbeinig, rittlings.
astringent *a.* (*med.*) zusammenziehend; adstringent, blutstillend.
astrologer *s.* Astrologe *m.*, Astrologin *f.*
astrological *a.* astrologisch.
astrology *s.* Astrologie.
astronaut *s.* Astronaut(in) *m.(f.)*
astronautical *a.* astronautisch.
astronautics *s.* Raumfahrt *f.*
astronomer *s.* Astronom(in) *m.(f.)*
astronomical *a.* astronomisch.
astronomy *s.* Sternkunde *f.;* Astronomie *f.*
astute *a.* schlau; scharfsinnig.
astuteness s Scharfsinnigkeit.
asunder *adv.* auseinander, entzwei.
asylum *s.* Zufluchtsort *m.; lunatic ~ s.* Irrenhaus *n.*
asymmetric, asymmetrical *a.* asymmetrisch.
asymmetry *s.* Asymmetrie *f.*
at *pr.* an, zu, bei, auf, in, gegen; *~ first,* zuerst; *~ last,* endlich; *~ least,* wenigstens; *~ length,* schließlich; *~ once,* auf einmal.
atheism *s.* Gottesleugnung *f.*
atheist *s.* Atheist(in) *m.(f.)*
athlete *s.* Athlet(in) *m.(f.)*
athletic *a.* athletisch; kraftvoll.
athletics *s.pl.* Leichtathletik *f.*
athwart *pr.* querüber.
Atlantic *a.* atlantisch; ~ **Ocean** *s.* Atlantik *m.*, Atlantischer Ozean *m.*
atlas *s.* Atlas *m.*
atmosphere *s.* Atmosphäre *f.*
atmospheric(al) *a.* atmosphärisch, Luft...; ~ **pressure,** Luftdruck *m.*
atmospherics *s.pl.* (*radio*) Luftstörungen *f.pl.*

atoll *s.* Atoll *n.*
atom *s.* Atom *n.*
atomic *a.* Atom..., atomar; ~ **bomb** *s.* Atombombe *f.*; ~ **energy** *s.* Atomenergie *f.*; ~ **power** *s.* Atomkraft; ~ **waste** *s.* Atommüll *m.*
atomizer *s.* Zerstäuber *m.*
atone *v.i.* sühnen; büßen.
atonement *s.* Sühne *f.*; Buße.
atop *adv.* obenauf.
atrocious *a.*, **~ly** *adv.* abscheulich.
atrocity *s.* Abscheulichkeit, Gräßlichkeit *f.*; Greueltat *f.*
atrophy *s.* Abzehrung, Verkümmerung *f.*
attach *v.t.* anhängen, anheften; beilegen; fesseln; verhaften; ~ *v.i.* verknüpft sein mit.
attaché *s.* Attaché *m.*; **~case** *s.* Aktentasche *f.*
attached *a.* beiliegend, angeschlossen.
attachment *s.* Anhänglichkeit, Ergebenheit *f.*; Anhängsel *n.*
attack *v.t.* angreifen; ~ *s.* Angriff *m.*; Anfall *m.*
attain *v.t.* & *i.* erreichen, erlangen.
attainable *a.* erreichbar.
attainment *s.* Erreichung *f.*; Verwirklichung *f.*; Leistung *f.*
attempt *s.* Versuch *m.*; Angriff *m.*; Attentat *n.*; ~ *v.t.* versuchen; angreifen.
attend *v.t.* begleiten; aufmerken; aufwarten, pflegen; ~ *v.i.* achthaben; besorgen; zugegen sein; besuchen; *to* ~ *to,* bearbeiten (Angelegenheit).
attendance *s.* Bedienung *f.*; Gefolge *n.*
attendant *a.* begleitend; ~ *s.* Diener *m.*; Aufwärter *m.*
attention *s.* Aufmerksamkeit *f.*; *to call (draw) a person's* ~ *to a thing,* einen auf etwas aufmerksam machen; *attention Mr. Smith,* zu Händen Herrn Smith; *attention!,* stillgestanden!; *to stand to* ~, stramm stehen.
attentive *a.*, **~ly** *adv.* aufmerksam.
attentiveness *s.* Aufmerksamkeit *f.*
attenuate *v.t.* verdünnen, vermindern.
attest *v.t.* bezeugen; beglaubigen.
attestation *s.* Beglaubigung; Bescheinigung.
attic *s.* Dachstube *f.*; Dachgeschoß *n.*
attire *s.* Anzug, Putz *m.*; ~ *v.t.* ankleiden, putzen.
attitude *s.* Stellung *f.*, Haltung *f.*
attn. *attention (of),* zu Händen (von), z. Hdn.
attorney *s.* Bevollmächtigter, Anwalt *m.*; *power of* ~, schriftliche Vollmacht *f.*; **~-general** *s.* Oberstaatsanwalt *m.*
attract *v.t.* anziehen, reizen.
attraction *s.* Anziehung *f.*; Reiz *m.*
attractive *a.*, **~ly** *adv.* anziehend.
attribute *v.t.* beilegen, beimessen; ~ *s.* Abzeichen *n.*; Merkmal *n.*
attribution *s.* Zuordnung *f.* Zurückführung *f.*
attributive *a.* zueignend.
attrition *s.* Zermürbung *f.*; Zerknirschung *f.*; Reduzierung (Personal) *f.*
attune *v.t.* einstimmen, gewöhnen.
auburn *a.* nußbraun, kastanienbraun.
auction *s.* Versteigerung *f.*; Auktion *f.*; *to sell by* ~, versteigern; ~ *v.t.* versteigern.
auctioneer *s.* Auktionator(in) *m.(f.)*
audacious *a.*, **~ly** *adv.* keck, kühn.
audacity *s.* Keckheit, Kühnheit *f.*
audibility *s.* Hörbarkeit *f.*
audible *a.*, **~bly** *adv.* hörbar.
audience *s.* Publikum *n.*, Audienz *f.*; Zuhörer *m.pl.*
audio-visual *a.* audio visuell.
audit *s.* Rechnungsprüfung *f.*; ~ *v.t.* Rechnungen prüfen.
audition *s.* Hörvermögen *n.*, Gehör *n.*; Vorspielen, *n.*, Vorsingen *n.*, Vorsprechen *n.*, Vortanzen *n.*; ~ *v.t.* & *i.* vorsingen, vorsprechen, vorspielen, vortanzen.
auditor *s.* Buchprüfer(in) *m.(f.)*
auditorium *s.* Zuhörerraum, *m.* Vortragssaal *m.*, Konzerthalle *f.*
Aug. *August,* August, Aug.
augment *v.t.* vermehren.
augmentation *s.* Vermehrung *f.*
augur *v.t.* vorhersagen; weissagen.
augury *s.* Wahrsagung *f.*; Vorzeichen *n.*
august *a.* erhaben, hehr.
August *s.* (*Monat*) August *m.*
aunt *s.* Tante *f.*
aura *s.* Fluidum *n.*
auricle *s.* Ohrmuschel *f.*
auricular *a.*, **~ly** *adv.* Ohren...; ~ **confession** *s.* Ohrenbeichte *f.*
aurora *s.* Morgenröte *f.*; ~ **borealis,** Nordlicht *n.*
auspices *s.* Vorbedeutung *f.*; (*fig.*) Schutz *m.*
auspicious *a.*, **~ly** *adv.* günstig.
austere *a.*, **~ly** *adv.* herb, streng.
austerity *s.* Strenge *f.*
Australia *s.* Australien *n.*
Australian *a.* australisch; *s.* Australier(in) *m.(f.)*
Austria *s.* Österreich *n.*
Austrian *a.* österreichisch; ~ *s.* Österreicher(in) *m.(f.)*
authentic(al) *a.*, **~ly** *adv.* glaubwürdig, echt.
authenticate *v.t.* beurkunden.
authentication *s.* Bestätigung *f.*
authenticity *s.* Echtheit *f.*
author *s.* Verfasser(in) *m.(f.)*, Urheber(in) *m.(f.)*, Schriftsteller(in) *m.(f.)*, Autor(in) *m.(f.)*
authoritarian *a.* autoritär.
authoritative *a.*, **~ly** *adv.* gebieterisch; bevollmächtigt; maßgebend.
authority *s.* Ansehen *n.*; Glaubwürdigkeit *f.*; Gewährsmann *m.*, Autorität *f.*; Befugnis, Vollmacht *f.*; **authorities** *pl.* Behörden *f.pl.*
authorization *s.* Bevollmächtigung *f.*; Genehmigung *f.*
authorize *v.t.* bevollmächtigen; ermächtigen.
authorship *s.* Autorschaft *f.*
autistic *a.* autistisch.
autobiographic(al) *a.* autobiographisch.
autobiography *s.* Selbstbiographie *f.*
autocracy *s.* Selbstherrschaft *f.*; Autokratie *f.*
autocrat *s.* Selbstherrscher *m.*; Autokrat *m.*
autocratic(al) *a.* selbstherrlich.
autograph *s.* Handschrift *f.*, Autograph *n.*; Autogramm *n.*; ~ *v.t.* signieren.
autographic *a.* eigenhändig.
automat *s.* Automat *m.*
automate *v.t.* automatisieren.
automatic *a.* automatisch, selbsttätig.
automation *s.* Automation *f.*; Automatisierung *f.*
automaton *s.* Automat *m.*

automobile *s.* Automobil *n.*
automotive *a.* Kraftfahrzeug...; ~ **industry** *s.* Automobilindustrie *f.*
autonomous *a.* autonom.
autonomy *s.* Selbstregierung, Autonomie *f.*
autopsy *s.* Autopsie *f.*, Obduktion *f.*
autumn *s.* Herbst *m.*
autumnal *a.* herbstlich.
auxiliaries *s.pl.* Hilfstruppen *f.pl.*
auxiliary *a.* Hilfs...; ~ *s.* Hilfsverb.
av. *average,* Durchschnitt.
avail *s.* Vorteil *m.; of no* ~, vergeblich; ~ *v.t. & i.* helfen, nützen; *to* ~ *oneself of a thing,* sich etwas zunutze machen.
availability *s.* Verfügbarkeit *f.*
available *a.* verfügbar.
avalanche *s.* Lawine *f.*
avarice *s.* Geiz *m.*, Habsucht *f.*
avaricious *a.*, **~ly** *adv.* geizig, habsüchtig.
Ave. *Avenue,* Allee.
avenge *v.t.* rächen.
avenger *s.* Rächer(in) *m.(f.)*
avenue *s.* Allee *f.;* Zugang *m.*
aver *v.t.* behaupten.
average *s.* Durchschnitt *m.;* Havarie *f.; on an* ~, durchschnittlich; ~ *v.t. & i.* durchschnittlich fertig bringen, liefern, betragen.
averse *a.*, **~ly** *adv.* abgeneigt.
aversion *s.* Widerwille *m.*, Abneigung *f.*
avert *v.t.* abwenden, wegwenden.
aviary *s.* Vogelhaus *n.*
aviation *s.* Fliegen *n.;* Flugwesen *n.*
aviator *s.* Flieger(in) *m.(f.)*
avid *a.* begeistert; passioniert.
avoid *v.t.* vermeiden.
avoidable *a.* vermeidlich.
avoidance *s.* Vermeidung *f.*
avoirdupois weight *s.* Handelsgewicht *n.* (*pound* = 16 Unzen).
avouch *v.t.* behaupten, bekräftigen.
avow *v.t.* anerkennen, eingestehen.
avowal *s.* Geständnis *n.*
avowedly *adv.* eingestandenermaßen.
avuncular *a.* onkelhaft.
await *v.t.* erwarten.
awake *v.t.st.* aufwecken; ~ *v.t.st.* aufwachen; ~ *a.* wach.
awaken *v.t.* erwecken.
awakening *s.* Erwachen *n.*; *a rude* ~, ein böses Erwachen.
award *s.* Urteil *n.;* Spruch *m.;* Auszeichnung *f.*, Preis *m.;* Stipendium *n.;* ~ *v.t.* zuerkennen; gewähren.
award-winning *a.* preisgekrönt.
aware *a.* gewahr, bewußt; *I am* ~ *of it,* ich weiß es.
awareness *s.* Bewußtsein *n.;* Kenntnis *f.*
away *adv.* weg, fort; abwesend.
awe *s.* Ehrfurcht *f.;* Scheu *f.;* ~ *v.t.* in Furcht halten; Ehrfurcht einflößen.
awe-inspiring *a.* ehrfurchtgebietend.
awesome *a.* überwältigend.
awe-struck *a.* von Ehrfurcht ergriffen.
awful *a.*, **~ly** *adv.* (*fam.*) schrecklich.
awhile *adv.* eine Zeitlang.
awkward *a.*, **~ly** *adv.* linkisch; ungelegen.
awkwardness *s.* Unbeholfenheit *f.;* Peinlichkeit *f.*
awl *s.* Ahle *f.*, Pfriem *m.*
awning *s.* Markise *f.;* Zeltdecke *f.*
awry *adv.* schief; verkehrt.
axe *s.* Axt *f.;* Beil *n.*
axiom *s.* Axiom *n.*, Grundsatz *m.*
axiomatic(al) *a.* axiomatisch, unumstößlich.
axis *s.* (*math.*) Achse *f.*
axle *s.* Achse *f.;* **~tree** *s.* Radachse *f.*
aye *s.* Jastimme *f.*
azalea *s.* (*bot.*) Azalee *f.*
azure *a.* himmelblau.

B

B, b *s.* der Buchstabe B oder b *n.;* (*mus.*) H, h; **B flat** Das B, b.
b. *born,* geboren, geb.
B.A. *Bachelor of Arts,* Bakkalaureus der Philosophie.
babble *v.i.* schwatzen; ~ *s.* Geschwätz *n.*
baboon *s.* Pavian *m.*
baby *s.* Baby *n.*, kleines Kind *n.*
babycarriage *s.* Kinderwagen *m.*
baby food *s.* Babynahrung *f.*
baby grand (*piano*) *s.* Stutzflügel *m.*
babyhood *s.* Säuglingsalter *n.*
babyish *a.* kindisch; kindlich.
babysit *v.i.* babysitten, kinderhüten.
babysitter *s.* Babysitter(in), Kinderhüter(in) *m.(f.)*
baby snatcher *s.* Kindesentführer(in) *m.(f.)*
baby talk *s.* Babysprache *f.*
bachelor *s.* Junggeselle *m.;* ~ **of Arts,** Bakkalaureus Artium (erster akademischer Grad) *m.*
bachelorhood *s.* Junggesellentum *n.*
bacillus *s.* Bacillus *m.*
back *s.* Rücken *m.;* Rückseite *f.;* Rücksitz (Wagen) *m.;* (Fußball) Verteidiger *m.;* ~ **of,** hinter; ~ *v.t.* unterstützen; ~ **up,** zurückfahren; *to* ~ *a horse,* auf ein Rennpferd wetten; *gold backing,* Golddeckung *f.; dollar-backed instruments,* Zahlungsmittel mit Dollardeckung; ~ *adv.* hinterwärts, zurück.
backache *s.* Rückenschmerzen *m. pl.*
backbite *v.t.st.* lästern; verleumden.
backbone *s.* Rückgrat *n.*
back-breaking *a.* äußerst mühsam; anstrengend.
backdate *v.t.* zurückdatieren.
backdoor *s.* Hintertür *f.*
backer *s.* Unterstützer *m.*
backfire *v.i.* fehlzünden, fehlschlagen.
backgammon *s.* Backgammon *n.*
background *s.* Hintergrund *m.*
backhand *s.* Rückhandschlag *m.*
backlash *s.* Rückstoß *m.;* Gegenreaktion *f.*
backless *a.* rückenfrei.
backlog *s.* Rückstand *m.*

back-number *s.* frühere Nummer *(f.)* einer Zeitschrift oder Zeitung.
backpack *s.* Rucksack *m.*
backpedal *v.i.* rückwärts treten.
backside *s.* Rückseite *f.*; Hintere *m.*
backslide *v.i.* rückfällig werden.
backstage *s.* hinter den Kulissen.
backstairs *s.pl.* Hintertreppe *f.*
backstitch *s.* Steppstich *m.*
backstroke *s.* Rückenschwimmen *n.*
backtrack *v.i.* wieder zurückgehen; eine Kehrtwendung machen.
backward *adv.* zurück, rücklings; ~ *a.*, **~ly** *adv.* langsam; rückständig; spät.
backwardness *s.* Zurückhaltung *f.*; Rückständigkeit *f.*
backwards *adv.* nach hinten.
backwash *s.* Rückströmung *f.*; *(fig.)* Auswirkungen *pl.*
backwater *s.* Stauwasser *n.*; totes Wasser *n.*
backwoodsman *s.* Hinterwäldler *m.*
backyard *s.* Garten *m.*; Hinterhof *m.*
bacon *s.* Speck *m.*
bacterial *a.* bakteriell.
bacteriological *a.* bakteriologisch, Baktieren...
bacterium *s.* Bakterie *f.*
bad *a.*, **~ly** *adv.* schlecht; böse; schlimm; *to be badly off,* übel daran sein.
badge *s.* Abzeichen, Ehrenzeichen *n.*
badger *s.* Dachs *m.*; ~ *v.t.* hetzen.
bad-tempered *a.* griesgrämig, schlechtgelaunt.
baffle *v.t.* vereiteln; verwirren; vor ein Rätsel stellen.
bafflement *s.* Verwirrung *f.*
baffling *a.* rätselhaft.
bag *s.* Sack, Beutel *m.*; Handtasche *f.*; ~ *v.t.* einsacken; ~ *v.i.* bauschen.
bagatelle *s.* Kleinigkeit, Lappalie *f.*
baggage *s.* Gepäck *n.*; ~ **allowance** *s.* Freigepäck *n.*; ~ **car** *s.* Gepäckwagen *m.*; **~check** *m.* Gepäckschein *m.* **~insurance** *s.* Reisegepäckversicherung *f.*
baggy *a.* bauschig, ausgebeult.
bagpipe *s.* Dudelsack *m.*
bail *s.* Kaution *f.*; Bürgschaft *f.*; Bürge *m.*; *to allow* ~, Bürgschaft zulassen; *to give* ~, einen Bürgen stellen; *to release on* ~, gegen Bürgschaft freilassen; ~ *v.t.* sich verbürgen für; freibürgen; *to* ~ *out, v.i.* *(avi.)* mit Fallschirm abspringen.
bailiff *s.* Gerichtsvollzieher *m.*
bairn *s.* Kind *n.*
bait *s.* Köder *m.*; ~ *v.t.* & *i.* ködern; hetzen.
baiting *s.* Hetze *f.*
bake *v.t.* & *i.* backen (im Ofen).
baker *s.* Bäcker(in) *m.(f.)*
bakery *s.* Bäckerei *f.*
baking: ~ **dish** *s.* Auflaufform *f.*; ~ **powder** *s.* Backpulver *n.*; ~ **sheet** *s.* Backblech *n.*; ~ **soda** *s.* Natron *n.*
balance *s.* Wage *f.*; Gleichgewicht *n.*; Bilanz *f.*; Bankguthaben *n.*; Rest *m.*; Saldo *m.*; *(fig.)* Unschlüssigkeit *f.*; Unruhe (in der Uhr) *f.*; ~ **of power** *s.* politisches Gleichgewicht der Mächte; ~ **of trade** *s.* Handelsbilanz *f.*
balance sheet *s.* Bilanz *f.* ~ *v.t.* wägen, wiegen, balanzieren; erwägen; ~ *v.i.* sich ausgleichen, sich balanzieren.
balcony *s.* Balkon *m.*
bald *a.* kahl.
balderdash *s.* dummes Zeug *n.*
bald-headed *a.* glatzköpfig.
balding *a.* mit beginnender Glatze.
baldly *adv.* offen; direkt; umverblümt.
baldness *s.* Kahlheit *f.*, Knappheit *f.*
bale *s.* Ballen *m.*
baleful *a.*, **~ly** *adv.* unheilvoll.
balk *s.* Balken *m.*; *(fig.)* Querstrich *m.*; ~ *v.t.* vereiteln; ~ *v.i.* scheuen (vor).
Balkan *s.* Balkan *m.*
ball *s.* Ball *m.*; Kugel *f.*; ~ **joint,** *(Tanz)* Ball *m.* *to have a* ~, sich riesig amüsieren. ~ **and socket joint** *s.* Kugelgelenk *n.*; ~ **of wool** *s.* Wollknäuel *m.*; ~ *v.i.* sich ballen; ~ *v.t.* zusammenballen.
ballad *s.* Ballade *f.*, Volkslied *n.*
ballast *s.* Ballast *m.*; Schotter *m.*
ball-bearing *s.* Kugellager *n.*
ballet *s.* Ballett *n.*
ballistics *s.* Ballistik.
balloon *s.* Luftballon *m.*; **hot-air ~,** Heißluftballon.
ballot *s.* Abstimmung *f.*; Wahl durch Stimmzettel; ~ *v.t.* & *i.* abstimmen; *s.* Stimmzettel *m.*
ballot box *s.* Wahlurne *f.*
ballpoint pen *s.* Kugelschreiber *m.*
ballroom *s.* Ballsaal *m.* ~ **dancing** *s.* Gesellschaftstanz *m.*
ballyhoo *s.* Wirbel *m.*; Tamtam *s.*
balm *s.* Balsam *m.*; Salböl *n.*; ~ *v.t.* balsamieren.
baloney *s.* *(fam.)* Quatsch *m.*
balsam *s.* Balsam *m.*
balsamic *a.* balsamisch.
Baltic *s.* Ostsee *f.*; ~ *a.* baltisch; *the* ~ *Sea* *s.* Ostsee *f.*; the ~ **States,** Baltikum *n.*
baluster *s.* Geländerpfosten *m.*
balustrade *s.* Geländer *n.*
bamboo *s.* Bambus *m.*
bamboozle *v.t.* hintergehen; verwirren; verblüffen.
ban *s.* öffentliche Ächtung *f.*; Bann *m.*; amtliches Verbot *n.*; ~ *v.t.* in den Bann tun, verbieten.
banality *s.* Trivialität *f.*
banana *s.* Banane *f.*
band *s.* Band *n.*; Binde *f.*; Bande *f.*; Musikkapelle *f.*; ~ *v.t.* binden, sich verbinden.
bandage *s.* Verband *m.*
bandaid *s.* Heftpflaster *n.*
bandit *s.* Bandit *m.*
bandy *v.t.* (den Ball) schlagen; wechseln; *to* ~ *about,* (Gerücht) verbreiten; ~ *v.i.* wettstreiten.; ~ *a.* krumm.
bandy legs *s.pl.* O-Beine *n.pl.*; **~-legged** *a.* o-beinig.
bane *s.* Verderben *n.*; Ruin *m.*
bang *s.* Schlag, Stoß, Knall *m.*; *big* ~ *s.* Urknall *m.*; *i.* bums!; *to go* ~, explodieren, zuschlagen; ~ *v.t.* knallen, schlagen; zuschlagen.
bangle *s.* Armreif *m.*
banish *v.t.* verbannen.
banishment *s.* Verbannung *f.*
banister *s.* Geländer *n.*
banjo *s.* Banjo *n.*
bank *s.* Ufer *n.*; Damm *m.*; Bank *f.*; ~ **account** *s.*

Bankkonto *n.;* ~ **balance** *s.* Kontostand *m.;* ~ **card** *s.* Scheckkarte *f.;* ~ *v.t.* eindämmen.
banker *s.* Bankier *m.*
bank hold-up *s.* Banküberfall *m.*
banking *s.* Bankwesen *n.*
bank: ~ **manager** *s.* Zweigstellenleiter(in) *m.(f.);* ~**note** *s.* Banknote *f.;* ~ **rate** *s.* Bankdiskont *m.;* ~ **robber** *s.* Bankräuber; ~**robbery** *s.* Bankraub *m.*
bankrupt *a.* bankrott; *to go* ~, Konkurs machen; ~ *s.* Bankrotteur *m.;* ~ **estate** *s.* Konkursmasse *f.;* ~ *v.t.* bankrott machen.
bankruptcy *s.* Bankrott *m.; fraudulent* ~, betrügerischer Bankrott.
bank statement *s.* Kontoauszug *m.*
banner *s.* Standarte *f.;* Banner *n.;* Spruchband *n.*
banns *s.pl.* Aufgebot (vor der Heirat) *n.*
banquet *s.* Festmahl *n.;* Bankett *n.*
bantam *s.* Zwerghuhn *n.;* ~ **weight** *s.* Bantamgewicht (Boxen).
banter *v.t.* zum besten haben; ~ *s.* Scherz, Spott *m.*
baptism *s.* Taufe *f.; certificate of* ~, Taufschein *m.*
baptismal *a.,* ~ **font,** Taufstein *m.*
baptize *v.t.* taufen.
bar *s.* Barre, Stange *f.;* Riegel, Balken, Schlagbaum *m.;* Schranken *f.pl.;* Schenktisch *m.;* Gericht *n.;* Anwaltschaft *f.;* Taktstrich *m.;* Takt (eines Musikstücks) *m.; to practice at the* ~, als Anwalt tätig sein; *to call to the* ~, zum Anwalt berufen; ~ *v.t.* verriegeln; hindern, schließen.
barb *s.* Widerhaken *m.*
barbarian *a.* barbarisch; ~ *s.* Barbar *m.*
barbaric *a.* barbarisch.
barbarism *s.* Barbarei *f.*
barbarity *s.* Grausamkeit *f.*
barbarous *a.,* ~**ly** *adv.* roh, grausam.
barbecue *s.* Grill *m.;* Grillfest *n.;* Barbecue *n.;* ~ *v.t.* grillen; auf dem Rost braten.
barbed *a.* ~ **wire** *s.* Stacheldraht *m.*
barber *s.* Barbier *m.*
barbiturate *s.* Barbiturat *n.*
bard *s.* Barde, Dichter *m.*
bare *a.* bloß; nackt; ~ *v.t.* entblößen.
bareback *a.* ungesattelt; ohne Sattel.
barefaced *a.* (*fig.*) unverschämt.
barefoot(ed) *a.* barfüßig.
bareheaded *a.* barhäuptig.
barely *adv.* kaum; knapp; spärlich.
bargain *s.* Handel *m.;* Kauf *m.;* Gelegenheitskauf *m.; into the* ~, obendrein. ~ *v.t. & i.* handeln, feilschen.
bargaining *s.* Handel *n.;* Verhandlungen *f. pl.*
barge *s.* Barke *f.;* Boot *n.*
baritone *s.* Bariton *m.;* Baritonstimme *f.*
bark *s.* Baumrinde *f.;* Borke *f.;* (Schiff) Barke *f.;* ~ *v.t.* abrinden; ~ *v.i.* bellen; ~ *s.* Bellen *n.*
barley *s.* Gerste *f.*
barley-corn *s.* Gerstenkorn *n.*
barmaid *s.* Bardame *f.*
barman *s.* Barmann *m.*
barmy *a.* hefig; blödsinnig, verdreht.
barn *s.* Scheune *f.*
barn owl *s.* Schleiereule *f.*
barnyard *s.* Wirtschaftshof *m.*
barometer *s.* Barometer *n.*
barometric *a.* barometrisch; ~ **pressure** Luftdruck *m.*
baron *s.* Freiherr, Baron *m.; press* ~ Pressezar *m.*
baroness *s.* Baronin *f.;* Freifrau *f.*
baronet *s.* Baronet *m.*
baronetcy *s.* Baronetswürde *f.*
baroque *s.* (Kunst) Barock *m.; a.* barock.
barrack *s.* Hütte *f.;* ~**s** *pl.* Kaserne *f.*
barrage *s.* Talsperre *f.;* Damm *m.,* Wehr *n.;* (*mil.*) Sperrfeuer *n.*
barrel *s.* Faß *n.;* Lauf *m.*
barrel organ *s.* Drehorgel *f.*
barren *a.,* ~**ly** *adv.* unfruchtbar.
barrette *s.* Haarspange *f.*
barricade *s.* Barrikade *f.;* ~ *v.t.* verrammeln; hindern.
barrier *s.* Schlagbaum *m.;* Barriere *f.;* Grenze *f.;* (*fig.*) Hindernis *n.;* ~**s** *s.pl.* Schranken *f.pl.*
barring *pr.* ausgenommen; außer im Fall.
barrister *s.* (vor Gericht auftretender) Rechtsanwalt *m.*
barroom *s.* Bar *f.*
barrow *s.* Trage *f.;* Schiebkarren *m.*
bartender *s.* Barkeeper *m.*
barter *v.t. & i.* tauschen; ~ *s.* Tauschhandel *m.*
basalt *s.* Basalt *m.*
base *a.,* ~**ly** *adv.* niedrig; verächtlich; (von Metallen) unedel; ~ *s.* Grundfläche *f.;* Grundlinie (des Dreiecks), *f.;* Grund *m.;* Fußgestell *n.;* (*mil.*) Stützpunkt *m.;* (*chem.*) Basis *f.*
baseball *s.* Baseball *n.*
baseboard *s.* Fußleiste *f.*
baseless *a.* grundlos.
basement *s.* Kellergeschoß *n.*
base pay *s.* Grundgehalt *n.*
bash *v.t.* verprügeln; schlagen; ~ *s.* Party *f.*
bashful *a.,* ~**ly** *adv.* schamhaft.
basic *a.* grundlegend; (*chem.*) basisch-; ~ **salary** *s.* Grundgehalt *n.*
basically *adv.* im Grunde.
basics *s.* Grundlagen pl., Wesentliches *n.*
basil *s.* Basilikum *n.*
basilica *s.* Basilika *f.*
basin *s.* Becken *n.;* Schale *f.*
basis *s.* Grundlage *f.;* Basis *f.;* Grundbestandteil *m.*
bask *v.t. & i.* sonnen; sich sonnen.
basket *s.* Korb *m.*
basque *s.* Baske *m.;* Baskin *f.;* ~ *a.* baskisch.
bas-relief *s.* Basrelief *n.*
bass *s.* (*mus.*) Baß *m.;* (fish) Barsch *m.*
bassoon *s.* Fagott *n.*
bast *s.* Bast *m.*
bastard *s.* Bastard *m.*
baste *v.t.* mit Fett begießen.
bastion *s.* Bollwerk *n.*
bat *s.* Fledermaus *f.;* Knüttel *m.;* Schlagholz *n.,* Schläger (im Baseball) *m.*
batch *s.* Stapel *m.;* Bündel *n.;* Sendung *f.*
bate *v.t.* (Preis) ablassen, verringern; *with* ~*d breath,* mit angehaltenem Atem.
bath *s.* Bad *n.;* Badewanne *f.;* ~**chair** *s.* Rollstuhl *m.*
bathe *v.t.* baden; ~ *v.i.* ein Bad nehmen; ~ *s.* Bad (Handlung) *n.*

bathing cap *s.* Badehaube *f.*
bathing suit *s.* Badeanzug *m.*
bathmat *s.* Badematte *f.*
bathrobe *s.* Bademantel *m.*
bathroom *s.* Badezimmer *n.*, Toilette *f.*
bath salts *s.pl.* Badesalz *n.*
bath towel *s.* Badetuch *n.*
bathtub *s.* Badewanne *f.*
batiste *s.* Batist *m.*
baton *s.* Taktstock *m.*, Stab *m.*
batsman *s.* Schläger *m.*, Schlagmann *m.*
battalion *s.* Bataillon *n.*
batten *s.* Latte *f.*, Leiste *f.*
batter *v.t.* schlagen, zerschlagen, mißhandeln, ~ *s.* Backteig *m.*; Eierkuchenteig *m.*
battery *s.* Angriff *m.*; Batterie *f.*; eine ganze Reihe.
battery-charger *s.* Aufladegerät *n.*
battery-operated *a.* batteriebetrieben.
battle *s.* Schlacht *f.*; Schlägerei *f.*; ~ *v.i.* kämpfen, fechten.
battleaxe *s.* Streitaxt *f.*; (*pej.*) Schreckschraube *f.*
battle-cruiser *s.* (*nav.*) Schlachtkreuzer *m.*
battlefield *s.* Schlachtfeld *n.*
battlement *s.* Zinne *f.*
battleship *s.* (*nav.*) Schlachtschiff *n.*
battue *s.* Treibjagd *f.*
bauble *s.* Spielzeug *n.*; Tand *m.*
bauxite *s.* Bauxit *m.*
Bavaria *s.* Bayern *n.*
Bavarian *a.* bayrisch; ~ *s.* Bayer(in) *m.(f.)*
bawdy *a.* zweideutig; obszön.
bawl *v.t.* & *i.* laut schreien; ausrufen.
bay *a.* rotbraun; ~ *s.* Bucht *f.*; Fach *m.*; Nische, Abteilung *f.*, Erker *m.*; Lorbeer *m.*; *to stand at* ~, gestellt sein, in Bedrängnis; ~ *v.i.* bellen; blöken; ~ *v.t.* jagen.
bay horse *s.* Braune *m.*
bayleaf *s.* Lorbeerblatt *n.*
bayonet *s.* Bajonett *n.*; ~ *v.t.* mit dem Bajonett erstechen.
bay window *s.* Erkerfenster *n.*
bazaar *s.* Basar *m.*
B&B *bed and breakfast,* Übernachtung mit Frühstück.
B.C. *before Christ,* vor Christus.
B.D. *Bachelor of Divinity,* Bakkalaureus der Theologie.
be *v.i.ir.* sein; (*pass.*) werden; *to* ~ *off,* sich fortmachen; *to* ~ *in,* zuhause sein.
B/E *bill of exchange,* Wechsel.
beach *s.* Strand *m.*; Gestade *n.*; ~ *v.t.* auf den Strand setzen.
beach ball *s.* Wasserball *m.*
beachhead *s.* (*mil.*) Landkopf *m.*
beacon *s.* Leuchtfeuer *n.*; Bake *f.*
bead *s.* Kügelchen *n.*; Perle *f.*
beadle *s.* Pedell *m.*; Büttel *m.*
beak *s.* Schnabel *m.*; Tulle *f.*; Hakennase *f.*
beaker *s.* Becher *m.*
beam *s.* Balken *m.*; Strahl *m.*; Deichsel *f.*; ~ *v.i.* strahlen.
beaming *a.* strahlend.
bean *s.* Bohne *f.*; *green* ~, grüne Bohne *f.*; *broad* ~, Saubohne *f.*
bean: ~bag *s.* Knautschsessel *m.*; **~pole** *s.* Bohnenstange; **~sprout** *s.* Sojabohnenkeim *m.*; **~stalk** *s.* Bohnenstengel *m.*
bear *s.* Bär m; ~ *v.t.* & *i.st.* tragen, bringen; dulden; gebären; *to* ~ *company,* Gesellschaft leisten; *to* ~ *in mind,* nicht vergessen; *to* ~ *on,* Bezug haben, wirken auf; *to* ~ *out,* bestätigen; *to* ~ *witness,* Zeugnis ablegen.
bearable *a.* erträglich.
beard *s.* Bart *m.*
bearded *a.* bärtig.
beardless *a.* bartlos.
bearer *s.* Träger *m.*; Wechselinhaber *m.*
bearing *s.* Tragweite *f.*; Lage, Haltung *f.*; Stütze, Höhe *f.*; Peilung *f.*; *to get one's* ~*s,* sich orientieren.
bearish *a.* bärenhaft.
bear market *s.* flauer Markt.
bearskin *s.* Bärenfell *n.*
beast *s.* Vieh, Tier *n.*; Bestie *f.*; Biest *n.*
beastly *a.* (*fig.*) scheußlich, niederträchtig.
beat *v.t.* & *i.st.* schlagen; besiegen; klopfen; *to* ~ *off,* zurückschlagen; *to* ~ *time,* den Takt schlagen; *to* ~ *up,* verprügeln; ~ *s.* Schlag *m.*; Revier *n.*, Runde *f.*
beatification *s.* Seligsprechung *f.*
beatify *v.t.* seligsprechen.
beating *s.* Schläge *pl.*; Prügel *pl.*
beatitude *s.* Seligkeit *f.*
beau *s.* Stutzer *m.*; Verehrer *m.*
beautician *s.* Kosmetiker(in) *m.(f.)*
beautiful *a.*, **~ly** *adv.* schön.
beautify *v.t.* verschönern.
beauty *s.* Schönheit *f.*
beauty contest *s.* Schönheitswettbewerb *m.*
beauty parlor *s.* Schönheitssalon *m.*
beauty salon *s.* Schönheitssalon *m.*
beaver *s.* Biber *m.*
becalm *v.t.* besänftigen.
because *c.* weil; ~ **of,** wegen.
beck *s. at a person's* ~ *and call,* jm. zur Verfügung stehen.
beckon *v.t.* & *i.* winken; locken.
becloud *v.t.* umwölken.
become *v.i.* & t.st. werden; sich schicken; anstehen.
becoming *a.*, **~ly** *adv.* anständig.; vorteilhaft.
bed *s.* Bett *n.*; Beet *n.*; Schicht *f.* (*mech.*) Bett *n.*, Unterbau *m.*; ~ *v.t.* betten.
bedaub *v.t.* besudeln.
bedbug *s.* Wanze *f.*
bedclothes *s.* Bettzeug *n.*
bedding *s.* Bettzeug *n.*; ~ **plant** *s.* Freilandpflanze *f.*
bedeck *v.t.* schmücken.
bedevil *v.t.* durcheinanderbringen.
bedfellow *s.* Schlafkamerad *m.*
bedjacket *s.* Bettjacke *f.*
bedlam *s.* Tollhaus *n.*
bedlinen *s.* Bettwäsche *f.*
Bedouin *s.* Beduine *m.*; Beduinin *f.*
bed: ~pan *s.* Bettpfanne *f.*; **~post** *s.* Bettpfosten *m.*
bedraggled *a.* verschmutzt.
bedridden *a.* bettlägerig.
bedrock *s.* Felssohle *f.*; Basis *f.*
bedroom *s.* Schlafzimmer *n.*

bedsore *s.* wundgelegene Stelle.
bedspread *s.* Tagesdecke *f.*
bedstead *s.* Bettstelle *f.*
bedtime *s.* Schlafenszeit *f.*
bee *s.* Biene *f.*
beech *s.* Buche *f.*
beechnut *s.* Buchecker *f.*
beef *s.* Rindfleisch *n.*; Rind *n.*; **~cattle,** Mastvieh *n.*
beefsteak *s.* Beefsteak *n.*
beefy *a.* muskulös; bullig.
beehive *s.* Bienenstock *m.*
beekeeper *s.* Imker *m.*
beep *s.* Piepton *m.*; ~ *v.i.* piepen.
beeper *s.* Funkrufempfänger *m.*
beer *s.*, Bier *n.*; *small* ~, Kleinigkeiten *pl.*
beeswax *s.* Bienenwachs *n.*
beet *s.* (rote) Rübe *f.*
beetle *s.* Käfer *m.*
beet: ~root *s.* Runkelrübe *f.*; ~ **sugar,** Rübenzucker *m.*
befall *v.t.st.* zustoßen, widerfahren; ~ *v.i.* sich ereignen.
befit *v.t.* sich schicken.
before *pr.* vor; ~ *c.* bevor, ehe; ~ *adv.* vorn; früher; schon einmal.
beforehand *adv.* voraus, im voraus.
befoul *v.t.* besudeln.
befriend *v.t.* sich anfreunden mit; sich annehmen.
beg *v.t.* bitten, betteln; *to* ~ *the question,* die Streitfrage als bewiesen voraussetzen; *I* ~ *your pardon?,* Verzeihung, entschuldigen Sie, bitte!; ~ *v.i.* betteln gehen; sich erlauben.
beget *v.t.st.* zeugen, erzeugen.
beggar *s.* Bettler *m.*; Lump *m.*; ~ *v.t.* zum Bettler machen.
beggarly *a.* bettelhaft; ärmlich.
beggary *s.* Bettelei *f.*; *to reduce to* ~, an den Bettelstab bringen.
begin *v.t.* & *i.st.* anfangen.
beginner *s.* Anfänger(in) *m.(f.)*
beginning *s.* Anfang *m.*; **~s** *pl.* Anfangsgründe *m.pl.*
begone *i.* fort! packe dich!
begonia *s.* Begonie *f.*, Schiefblatt *s.*
begrudge *v.t.* mißgönnen.
beguile *v.t.* betören; verführen; betrügen.
behalf *s. on* ~, im Namen, behufs, wegen; *in* ~ *of,* im Interesse von, für.
behave *v.i.* sich benehmen, sich verhalten; sich betragen.
behavior *s.* Betragen *n.*
behaviorism *s.* Behaviorismus.
behead, *v.t.* enthaupten.
behest *s.* Befehl *m.*
behind *pr.* & *adv.* hinter, zurück; ~ *s.* Hintern *m.*
behindhand *a.* im Rückstande.
behold *v.t.st.* erblicken, betrachten.
beholden *a.* verpflichtet.
behoove *v.i.* sich ziemen.
being *s.* Dasein *n.*; Wesen, Geschöpf *n.*
belabor *v.t.* jn. bearbeiten; jm. zusetzen.
Belarus *s.* Weißrußland *n.*
belated *a.* verspätet.
belch *v.i.* & *t.* rülpsen; ~ *s.* Rülpser *m.*
beleaguer *v.t.* belagern.
belfry *s.* Glockenturm. *m.*
Belgian *s.* Belgier(in) *m.(f.)*; *a.* belgisch.
Belgium *s.* Belgien *n.*
belie *v.t.* Lügen strafen; enttäuschen; widersprechen.
belief *s.* Glaube *m.*
believable *a.* glaubhaft; glaubwürdig.
believe *v.t.* & *i.* glauben, vertrauen; *to* ~ *in,* glauben an.
believer *s.* Gläubige *m./f.*
belittle *v.t.* herabsetzen, (boshaft) verkleinern.
bell *s.* Glocke *f.*; Klingel *f.*; *to ring the* ~, klingeln; *to answer the* ~, auf das Klingeln öffnen.
bellicose *a.* kriegerisch.
belligerent *a.* kriegführend; kriegerisch; aggressiv.
bellow *v.i.* brüllen.
bellows *s.pl.* Blasebalg *m.*
bellpush *s.* Klingel *f.*; Klingelknopf *m.*
bellrope *s.* Klingelzug *m.*
belltower *s.* Glockenturm *m.*
bellwether *s.* Leithammel *m.*
belly *s.* Bauch *m.*; ~ *v.t.* schwellen.
belly: ~ache *s.* Bauchschmerzen *m. pl.*; ~ **button** *s.* Nabel *m.*; ~ **dancer** *s.* Bauchtänzerin *f.*; **~landing** *s.* Bauchlandung *f.*
belong *v.i.* gehören; betreffen.
belongings *s.pl.* Habe *f.*
Belorussia *s.* Weißrußland *n.*
Belorussian *s.* Weißrusse *m.*; Weißrussin *f.*; ~ *a.* weißrussisch.
beloved *a.* geliebt.
below *pr.* unter; ~ *adv.* unten.
belt *s.* Gürtel *m.*; Gehenk *n.*; Treibriemen *m.*; ~ *v.t.* umgürten.
bemoan *v.t.* beklagen, beweinen.
bemused *a.* verwirrt; gedankenverloren.
bench *s.* Bank *f.*; Richterbank *f.*; Werkbank.
benchmark *s.* Maßstab *m.*
bend *v.t.st* biegen; ~ *v.i.* sich biegen; ~ *s.* Biegung *f.*; Kurve *f.*
beneath pr. unter; ~ *adv.* unten.
benediction *s.* Segen *m.*
benefactor *s.* Wohltäter *m.*
benefactress *s.* Wohltäterin *f.*
benefice *s.* Pfründe *f.*
beneficence *s.* Wohltätigkeit *f.*
beneficent *a.* wohltätig.
beneficial *a.*, **~ly** *adv.* heilsam; wohltuend; vorteilhaft.
beneficiary *s.* Nutznießer.
benefit *s.* Wohltat *f.*; Vorteil *m.*; Benefizvorstellung *f.*; Vorrecht *m.*; (Versicherung) Unterstützung *f.*; Geld *n.*; ~ *v.t.* & *i.* Vorteil bringen; heilsam sein; *to* ~ *by,* Nutzen ziehen von.
benevolence *s.* Wohlwollen *n.*; Gunst *f.*
benevolent *a.*, **~ly** *adv.* wohlwollend.
benign *a.*, **~ly** *adv.* gütig, mild; (*med.*) gutartig.
benignant *a.* gütig, wohltätig.
bent *a.* gebogen; ~ **on,** versessen auf; ~ *s.* Biegung *f.*; Neigung *f.*
benumb *v.t.* betäuben, erstarren.
benzene (-ine) *s.* Benzin *n.*
benzole (-line) *s.* Benzol *n.*
bequeath *v.t.* vermachen.

bequest *s.* Vermächtnis *n.*
bereave *v.t.st.* & *r.* berauben.
bereavement *s.* Verlust *m.;* Trauerfall *m.*
bereft *a. to be ~ of sth.*, etw. verloren haben.
beret *s.* Baskenmütze *f.*
bergamot *s.* Bergamotte (Birne) *f.*
berry *s.* Beere *f.*
berserk *a.* rasend; *to go ~* durchdrehen.
berth *s.* Ankerplatz *m.;* (*nav.*) Koje *f.*, Schiffsbett *n.*, Kajütenbett *n.;* Posten *m.*
beseech *v.t.st.* bitten, anflehen.
beseechingly *adv.* flehentlich.
beseem *v.t.* sich schicken.
beset *v.t.st.* heimsuchen; plagen.
beside *pr.* neben; *~ oneself,* außer sich; *~ the mark,* weit vom Ziel.
besides *pr.* außer; ~ *adv.* außerdem.
besiege *v.t.* belagern.
besmear *v.t.* beschmieren.
besmirch *v.t.* besudeln.
bespectacled *a.* bebrillt.
bespoke tailor *s.* Maßschneider *m.*
best *p.* & *adv.* best; aufs beste; am besten; ~ *s.* Beste *n.; to make the ~ of,* mit etwas tun was man kann; *to do one's ~*, tun was man kann; *as ~ he could,* so gut er konnte; *to the ~ of one's abilities,* nach besten Kräften.
bestial *a.*, **~ly** *adv.* tierisch; barbarisch; bestialisch.
bestiality *s.* Bestialität *f.n.*
bestir *v.r.* sich rühren, sich regen.
best man *s.* Trauzeuge *m.*
bestow *v.t.* verleihen.
bestowal *s.* Verleihung *f.*
bestseller *s.* Reißer (Buch) *m.;* Bestseller *m.*
bet *s.* Wette *f.;* ~ *v.t.* wetten.
betray *v.t.* verraten; verführen.
betrayal *s.* Verrat *m.*
betroth *v.t.* verloben.
betrothal *s.* Verlobung *f.*
better *p.* & *adv.* besser; lieber; mehr; *so much the ~*, desto besser; *you had ~ go,* Sie tun wohl am besten, hinzugehen; *to think ~ of it,* sich eines Bessern besinnen; ~ *s.* Vorteil; *to get the ~ of a person,* einem den Vorteil abgewinnen; **~s** *pl.* Vorgesetzte *m.pl.;* ~ *v.t.* & *i.* verbessern; besser werden.
betterment *s.* Verbesserung *f.*
betting *s.* Wetten *n.*
between *pr.* zwischen; *they did it ~ them,* sie taten es zusammen; *~ you and me,* unter uns.
bevel *a.* schräg, schief; ~ *s.* Schräge *f.*, schräger Anschnitt *m.*, (*mech.*) Fase *f.;* **~-gear** *s.* (*mech.*) Kegelrad *n.;* ~ *v.t.* abschrägen, facettieren.
beverage *s.* Getränk *n.*
bevy *s.* Schar *f.;* Gesellschaft *f.*
bewail *v.t.* betrauern; beklagen.
beware *v.i.* sich hüten.
bewilder *v.t.* verwirren, bestürzt machen.
bewildering *a.* verwirrend.
bewilderment *s.* Verwirrung.
bewitch *v.t.* behexen, bezaubern; verzaubern.
bewitching *a.* bezaubernd.
beyond *pr.* über, jenseits; ~ *adv.* darüber hinaus.
bias *s.* Neigung *m.;* Vorurteil *n.;* ~ *v.t.* auf eine Seite neigen.
bib *s.* Lätzchen *n.*
Bible *s.* Bibel *f.*
biblical *a.* biblisch.
bibliographer *s.* Bibliograph(in) *m.(f.)*
bibliography *s.* Bibliographie *f.*
bibliophile *s.* Bücherfreund *m.*
bicarbonate, ~ of soda, Natronbikarbonat *n.*
bicker *v.i.* streiten, zanken; glitzern.
bickerings *s.pl.* Gezänk *n.*
bicycle *s.* Fahrrad *n.*, Zweirad *n.*
bid *v.t.st.* befehlen; einladen; wünschen, bieten; (Kartenspiel) ansagen; *to ~ fair,* Aussicht geben auf; ~ *s.* (Auktions-)Gebot; *no ~*, ich passe (Kartenspiel).
bidder *s.* Bieter *m.; highest ~ s.* Meistbietender *m.*
bidding *s.* Befehl *m.;* (*com.*) Gebot *n.*
bide *v.t.* ertragen; ~ *v.i.* abwarten.
biennial *a.* zweijährig.
bier d. Bahre *f.*
biff *s.* Klapps *m.; v.t.* hauen.
bifocal *a.* Bifokal-; ~ *s.pl.* Bifokalgläser *pl.*
bifurcated *a.* gabelförmig gespalten.
big *a.* groß, stark, dick; *to talk ~*, prahlen.
bigamist *s.* Bigamist *m.;* Bigamistin *f.*
bigamy *s.* Bigamie *f.*, Doppelehe *f.*
Big Bang *s.* Urknall *m. n.*
bigheaded *a.* eingebildet.
bighearted *a.* großherzig.
bight *s.* Bai, Bucht *f.*
bigmouth *s.* Großmaul *n.*
bigot *s.* blinder Anhänger; Frömmler *m.*
bigoted *a.* bigott; eifernd.
bigotry *s.* Frömmelei *f.*
big top *s.* Zirkuszelt *n.*
big-wig *s.* (*fig.*) großes Tier *n.*
bike *s.* Fahrrad *n.*
bilateral *a.* zweiseitig; bilateral.
bilberry *s.* Heidelbeere *f.*
bile *s.* Galle *f.*
bilingual *a.* zweisprachig.
bilious *a.* gallig.
bilk *v.t.* beschwindeln, betrügen.
bill *s.* Schnabel *m.;* Hippe *f.;* Rechnung *f.;* Wechsel *m.;* Zettel *m.;* Gesetzentwurf *m.;* **~ of exchange,** Wechsel *m.;* **~ of lading,** Konnossement *n.*, Frachtbrief *m.*
billboard *s.* Reklametafel *f.*
billet *s.* Quartierzettel *n.;* Quartier *n.;* Schein *m.;* ~ *v.t.* einquartieren.
billfold *s.* Brieftasche *f.*
billiard cue *s.* Queue *n.*
billiards *s.pl.* Billiard(spiel) *n.*
billiard table *s.* Billiardtisch *m.*
billow *s.* Welle *f.;* ~ *v.i.* anschwellen.
billy goat *s.* Ziegenbock *m.*
bimonthly *a.* zweimonatlich.
bin *s.* Behälter *m.*, Kasten *m.*
bind *v.t.* binden; verpflichten; *to ~ over,* (*jur.*) durch Gerichtsbeschluß verpflichten; *to be bound over for two years,* zwei Jahre Bewährungsfrist erhalten; *clothbound,* in Leinen (Kaliko) gebunden; *leatherbound,* in Leder gebunden.
binder *s.* (Buch)Binder *m.*, Binde *f.*
binding *s.* Einband *m.;* ~ *a.* bindend.
bindweed *s.* (*bot.*) Winde *f.*

binge *s.* Gelage *n.*
binocular *s.pl.* Fernglas *n.*
biochemical *a.* biochemisch.
biochemist *s.* Biochemiker(in) *m.(f.)*
biochemistry *s.* Biochemie *f.*
biographer *s.* Biograph(in) *m.(f.)*
biographical *a.* biographisch.
biography *s.* Biographie *f.*, Lebensbeschreibung *f.*
biological *a.* biologisch; **~warfare** *s.* biologische Kriegsführung. *f.*
biologist *s.* Biologe *m.*, Biologin *f.*
biology *s.* Biologie *f.*
biotechnology *s.* Biotechnologie *f.*
bipartite *a.* zweiteilig; Zweimächte...
biplane *s.* Doppeldecker *m.*
birch *s.* Birke *f.*; Rute *f.*
bird *s.* Vogel *m.*; **~ of passage,** Zugvogel *m.*; **~ of prey,** Raubvogel *m.*
birdcage *s.* Vogelbauer *m.*; Vogelkäfig *m.*
birdhouse *s.* Nistkasten *m.*
birdie *s.* Vögelchen *n.*
bird's nest *s.* Vogelnest *n.*
bird sanctuary *s.* Vogelschutzgebiet *n.*
bird's eye *s.* aus der Vogelschau gesehen; **~ view** *s.* Vogelperspektive *f.*
bird-watcher *s.* Vogelbeobachter(in) *m.(f.)*
birth *s.* Geburt *f.*
birth certificate *s.* Geburtsurkunde *f.*
birth control *s.* Geburtenkontrolle, Geburtenbeschränkung, Empfängnisverhütung. *f.*
birthday *s.* Geburtstag *m.*
birthmark *s.* Muttermal *n.*
birthplace *s.* Geburtsort *m.*
birth rate *s.* Geburtenziffer *f.*
biscuit *s.* Keks *m.*; kleines Brötchen *n.*
bisect *v.t.* halbieren.
bisexual *a.* bisexuell.
bishop *s.* Bischof *m.*; Läufer (im Schach) *m.*
bishopric *s.* Bistum *n.*
bismuth *s.* Wismut *m.*
bison *s.* Bison *n.*; Wisent *n.*
bit *s.* Bißchen *n.*; Stückchen *n.*; Pferdegebiß *n.*; Schlüsselbart *m.*; (*comp.*) Bit *n.*
bitch *s.* Hündin *f.*; (*pej.*) Miststück *n.*
bite *v.t.st.* beißen; **~** *v.t.st.* greifen; **~** *s.* Biß *m.*
biting *a.* beißend; bissig.
bitter *a.*, **~ly** *adv.* bitter; erbittert.
bitterness *s.* Bitterkeit *f.*; Gram *m.*
bitumen *s.* Bitumen *f.*
bituminous *a.* bituminös.
bivouac *s.* Biwak *n.*, Beiwacht *f.*; **~** *v.i.* biwakieren.
biweekly *a.* zweiwöchentlich.
bizarre *a.* bizarr.
bk *book,* Buch; *bank,* Bank.
B.L. *Bachelor of Law,* Bakkalaureus der Rechte.
B/L *bill of lading,* Frachtbrief.
bl. *barrel,* Faß; *bale,* Ballen.
blab *v.t.* & *i.* ausschwatzen.
black *a.* schwarz, dunkel; finster; **~** *s.* Schwärze *f.*; Trauer *f.*; Schwarze *m./f.*; **~** *v.t.* schwärzen; (Stiefel) wichsen.
blackball *s.* schwarze Wahlkugel *f.*; **~** *v.t.* hinausballotieren.
blackberry *s.* Brombeere *f.*
blackbird *s.* Amsel *f.*
blackboard *s.* Wandtafel *f.*
blacken *v.t.* & *i.* schwärzen; schwarz werden.
blackhead *s.* Mitesser *m.*
black hole *s.* schwarzes Loch *n.*
blackish *a.* schwärzlich.
blackleg *s.* Gauner *m.*; Streikbrecher *m.*
blacklist *s.* schwarze Liste; **~** *v.t.* auf die schwarze Liste setzen.
blackmail *s.* Erpressung *f.*; **~** *v.t.* Geld erpressen von.
black market *s.* schwarzer Markt *m.*
blackness *s.* Schwärze *f.*; Finsternis *f.*
blackout *s.* (Luftschutz) Verdunkelung *f.*
black pudding *s.* Blutwurst *f.*
blacksmith *s.* Schmied *m.*
blackthorn *s.* Schlehdorn *m.*
black tie *s.* schwarze Fliege (zum Smoking).
black widow *s.* schwarze Witwe.
bladder *s.* Blase *f.*
blade *s.* Blatt, Halm *m.*; Klinge *f.*
blame *v.t.* tadeln; **~** *s.* Tadel *m.*; Schuld *f.*
blameable *a.*, **~bly** *adv.* tadelhaft.
blameless *a.*, **~ly** *adv.* untadelhaft.
blameworthy *a.* tadelnswürdig.
blanch *v.t.* weiß machen, bleichen.
blancmange *s.* Flammeri *m.*
bland *a.* sanft, gütig; glattzüngig.
blandishment *s.* Schmeichelei.
blandness *s.* Verbindlichkeit *f.*; Freundlichkeit *f.*
blank *a.*, weiß; unbeschrieben, leer; verwirrt; reimlos; (*com.*) Blanko; **~** *s.* Weiße *n.*; leeres Blatt *n.*; leerer Raum *m.*; Niete *f.*; **~ cartridge,** Platz-patrone *f.*; **~ check** Blankoscheck *m.*; **~ verse,** reimloser Vers *m.*
blanket *s.* Decke *f.*; **~** *v.t.* bedecken.
blankly *a.* verdutzt.
blare *v.i.* blöken, brüllen; schmettern.
blasé *a.* blasiert.
blaspheme *v.t.* (Gott) lästern.
blasphemous *a.*, **~ly** *adv.* gotteslästerlich.
blasphemy *s.* Gotteslästerung *f.*
blast *s.* Windstoß *m.*; Schall, Trompetenstoß *m.*; Explosion *f.*; **~** *v.t.* sprengen; versengen; zerstören.
blast furnace *s.* Hochofen *m.*
blast off *s.* Abschuß *m.*, Abheben *n.*
blatant *a.* offensichtlich, unverhohlen.
blaze *s.* Lichtstrahl *m.*; Flamme *f.*; weißer Fleck, Blesse *f.*; **~** *v.i.* flammen, leuchten; **~** *v.t.* ausposaunen.
blazer *s.* farbige Flanelljacke *f.*
blazon *s.* Wappenschild *n.*; **~** *v.t.* schildern; ausposaunen.
blazonry *s.* Wappenkunde *f.*; Zurschaustellung *f.*
bleach *v.t.* & *i.* bleichen; weiß werden.
bleak *a.*, **~ly** *adv.* öde; rauh, kalt.
bleary *a.* trübe.
bleary-eyed *a.* triefäugig.
bleat *v.i.* blöken; **~** *s.* Blöken *n.*
bleed *v.i.st.* bluten; **~** *v.t.st.* zur Ader lassen.
bleeding *s.* Blutung *f.*
bleep *s.* Piepen *n.*; **~** *v.t.* piepen.
blemish *s.* Schandfleck *m.*; Schande *f.*; **~** *v.t.* verunstalten, entehren.
blend *v.t.* & *i.* vermischen; sich mischen; **~** *s.* Mischung *(f.)* von Tee, Kaffee, Tabaken, etc.

blender *s.* Mixer *m.;* Mixgerät *n.*
bless *v.t.* segnen, beglücken.
blessed *a.* gesegnet, selig; verwünscht.
blessing *s.* Segen *m.*
blight *s.* Melhtau *m.;* Fäule *f.*, Schandfleck *m.;* ~ *v.t.* verderben.
blind *a.* blind; ~ **alley,** Sackgasse *f.;* ~ *s.* Blende *f.;* Vorwand *m.;* Rouleau *n.;* Venetian ~ *s.* Jalousie *f.;* ~ *v.t.* blind machen; blenden.
blindfold *a.* & *adv.* blindlings; ~ *v.t.* die Augen verbinden.
blinding *a.* blendend; grell.
blindman's-bluff *s.* Blindekuh(spiel) *n.*
blindness *s.* Blindheit *f.*
blindworm *s.* Blindschleiche *f.*
blink *s.* Blinken *n.;* ~ *v.i.* blinzeln; ~ *v.t.* nicht sehen wollen.
blinker *s.* Scheuklappen *f. pl.*
bliss *s.* Wonne, Seligkeit *f.*
blissful *a.*, **~ly** *adv.* wonnevoll, selig.
blister *s.* Blase *f.;* Bläschen *n.;* ~ *v.t.* & *i.* Blasen bekommen.
blistering *a.* ätzend; vernichtend (Kritik).
blithe *a.*, **~ly** *adv.* munter, lustig.
blitz *s.* Luftangriff *m.;* Blitzkrieg *m.;* ~ *v.t.* bombardieren.
blizzard *s.* Blizzard *m.*, Schneesturm *m.*
bloat *v.t.* & *i.* aufschwellen.
bloated *a.* aufgedunsen; (*fig.*) aufgeblasen.
blob *s.* Tropfen *m.;* Klecks *m.*
bloc *s.* (*pol.*) Block *m.*
block *s.* Block, Klotz *m.;* Häuserviereck *n.;* Versperrung, Stockung *f.;* ~ *v.t.* versperren, blockieren, verstopfen; **~ed account,** Sperrkonto *n.*
blockade *s.* Blockade *f.;* *to run the* ~, die Blockade brechen; **~runner** *s.* Blockadebrecher *m.;* ~ *v.t.* blockieren.
blockage *s.* Block *m.;* (Röhre) Verstopfung *f.*
block: ~buster *s.* Knüller *m.;* **~capital** *s.* Blockbuchstabe; **~head** *s.* Dummkopf *m.*
blockish *a.*, **~ly** *adv.* tölpisch.
block letters *s.pl.* Blockschrift *f.*
bloke *s.* (*fam.*) Kerl *m.*
blond(e) *a.* blond; ~ *s.* Blondine *f.*
blood *s.* Blut *n.;* *related by* ~, blutsverwandt.
blood bank *s.* Blutbank *f.*
bloodbath *s.* Blutbad *n.*
blood cell *s.* Blutkörperchen *n.*
bloodclot *s.* Blutgerinnsel *n.*
blood count *s.* Blutbild *n.*
bloodcurdling *a.* grauenerregend.
blood donor *s.* Blutspender *m.*
blood group *s.* (*med.*) Blutgruppe *f.*
bloodhorse *s.* Vollblutpferd *n.*
bloodhound *s.* Bluthund *m.*
bloodless *a.* blutlos; unblutig.
blood-orange *s.* Blutorange *f.*
blood poisoning *s.* Blutvergiftung *f.*
blood pressure *s.* Blutdruck *m.*
blood pudding *s.* Blutwurst *f.*
blood-relation *s.* Blutsverwandter *m.*
blood-relationship *s.* Blutsverwandtschaft *f.*
bloodshed *s.* Blutvergießen *n.*
bloodshot *a.* blutunterlaufen (Augen).
bloodthirsty *a.* blutdurstig.
blood transfusion *s.* Blutübertragung, Bluttransfusion *f.*
blood vessel *s.* Blutgefäß *n.*
bloody *a.* blutig; blutdurstig; (*sl.*) verdammt!
bloom *s.* Blüte, Blume *f.;* ~ *v.i.* blühen.
bloomer *s.* (*sl.*) Schnitzer, Fehler *m.*
blooming *a.* blühend; verfixt.
blossom *s.* Blüte *f.;* *to be in* ~, in Blüte sein, blühen; ~ *v.i.* blühen.
blot *s.* Klecks *m.;* Schandfleck *m.;* ~ *v.t.* klecksen; *to* ~ *out*, auslöschen.
blotch *s.* Fleck *m.;* Hautfleck *m.;* ~ *v.t.* beklecksen.
blotter *s.* Schreibunterlage *f.*
blotting pad *s.* Löscher *m.*
blotting paper *s.* Löschpapier *n.*
blouse *s.* Bluse *f.*
blow *s.* Schlag, Stoß *m.;* Hieb *m.;* ~ *v.t.st.* wehen; schnauben; schallen; blühen; ~ *v.t.* blasen, hauchen; *to* ~ *one's nose*, sich schneuzen; *to* ~ *over*, vorübergehen, sich legen; *to* ~ *up*, sprengen; *to* ~ *a kiss*, eine Kußhand zuwerfen.
blower *s.* Gebläse *n.*
blowgun *s.* Blasrohr *n.*
blowlamp *s.* Lötlampe *f.*
blowpipe *s.* Blasrohr, Lötrohr *n.*
blowy *a.* windig.
blowzy *a.* rotbäckig, pausbäckig; schlampig.
blubber *s.* Walfischspeck *m.;* ~ *v.i.* plärren, schluchzen.
bludgeon *s.* Knüppel *m.*
blue *a.* blau; ~ *s.* Blau *m.;* *the blues, s.pl.* Trübsinn *m.;* *out of the* ~, aus heiterem Himmel; ~ *v.t.* blau färben.
blueberry *s.* Blaubeere *f.*
blue: ~bottle *s.* Schmeißfliege *f.*, **~cheese** *s.* Blauschimmelkäse *m.;* **~collar (worker)** *s.* Arbeiter(in) *m.(f.)*
bluedevils *s.pl.* Trübsinn *m.*
bluejacket *s.* Blaujacke *f.*, Matrose *m.*
blueness *s.* Bläue *f.*
blue pencil *s.* Blaustift.
blueprint *s.* Entwurf *m.;* Blaupause *f.*, technische Zeichnung *f.*
bluestocking *s.* (*fig.*) Blaustrumpf *m.*
bluff *a.* grob; steil; barsch; ~ *s.* Irreführung *f.;* Täuschungsmanöver *n.*, ~ *v.t.* irreführen.
bluish *a.* bläulich.
blunder *s.* Fehler *m.;* Schnitzer *m.;* ~ *v.i.* einen Schnitzer machen.
blunt *a.*, **~ly** *adv.* stumpf; grob, plump; ~ *v.t.* abstumpfen.
bluntness *s.* Stumpfheit *f.;* Unverblümtheit *f.;* Direktheit *f.*
blur *s.* Klecks, Flecken *m.;* ~ *v.t.* besudeln; verwischen.
blurb *s.* Klappentext *m.;* Waschzettel *m.*
blurt *v.t.* (*out*) unbesonnen heraussagen.
blush *v.i.* erröten; ~ *s.* Schamröte *f.*
bluster *v.i.* toben; großtun; ~ *s.* Ungestüm *n.;* Prahlerei *f.*
blustery *a.* stürmisch.
Blvd. *Boulevard*, Boulevard.
B.M. *Bachelor of Medicine*, Bakkalaureus der Medizin.
B.Mus. *Bachelor of Music*, Bakkalaureus der Musik.

BO *branch office*, Filiale.
boa *s.* Boa *f.*; Pelzboa *f.*
boar *s.* Eber *m.*, Keiler *m.*
board *s.* Brett *n.*; Planke *f.*; Bohle *f.*; Bord *m.*; Tafel, Kost *f.*; Behörde *f.*; Direktorium *n.*; Kostgeld *n.*; *full* ~, volle Verpflegung *f.*; *partial* ~, teilweise Verpflegung *f.*; ~ **of directors,** Aufsichtsrat *m.*; ~ **of Trade,** Handelsministerium *n.*; ~ *v.t.* dielen; in die Kost tun, beköstigen; entern; *to* ~ *up*, mit Brettern verschlagen; ~ *v.i.* in der Kost sein.
boarder *s.* Kostgänger *m.*; Enterer *m.*
board game *s.* Brettspiel *n.*
boarding: ~ **pass** *s.* Bordkarte *f.*; ~ **house** *s.* Pension *f.*; ~ **school** *s.* Internat *n.*
board: ~**meeting** *s.* Aufsichtsratsitzung *f.*; Vorstandssitzung *f.*; ~**room** *s.* Sitzungssaal *m.*
boast *v.i.* & t. prahlen.
boastful *a.* prahlerisch.
boat *s.* Boot *n.*; Schiff *n.*; Dampfer *m.*
boater *s.* Bootsfahrer(in) *m.(f.)*
boatswain *s.* (Hoch)bootsmann *m.*
bob *s.* Gehänge *n.*; Ruck *m.*; Büschel *n.*; ~ *v.i.* baumeln; mit dem Kopfe nicken; ~ *v.t.* stutzen; *bobbed hair*, Bubikopf *m.*
bobbin *s.* Spule *f.*; Klöppel *m.*
bobby *s.* (*sl.*) Polizist *m.*; ~**pin** *s.* Haarsprange *f.*
bobsled *s.* Rennschlitten *m.*; Bob *m.*
bobtail *s.* Stutzschwanz *m.*
bode *v.t.* vorbedeuten, ahnen.
bodice *s.* Oberteil, Mieder *n.*
bodiless *a.* unkörperlich.
bodily *a.* körperlich; wirklich, ganz und gar; ~ *harm*, ~ *injury*, Körperverletzung *f.*
body *s.* Leib, Körper *m.*; Körperschaft *f.*; Wagenkasten *m.*, (*mot.*) Karosserie *f.*; (*mil.*) Abteilung *f.*; ~ **corporate,** juristische Person *f.*; *in a* ~, geschlossen, sämtlich; ~ *v.t.* formen; verkörpern.
bodyguard *s.* Leibwächter *m.*; Leibgarde *f.*
body language *s.* Körpersprache *f.*
body odor *s.* Körpergeruch *m.*
bodywork *s.* Karosserie *f.*
bog *s.* Sumpf *n.*, Moor *m.*; ~ **down** *v.i.* steckenbleiben, sich festfahren.
boggle *v.i.* sprachlos/fassungslos werden.
boggy *a.* sumpfig.
bogus *a.* unecht, falsch; Schwindel...
bogy *s.* Kobold *m.*, Popanz *m.*
Bohemia *s.* Böhmen *n.*
Bohemian *s.* Böhme *m.*; ~ *a.* böhmisch.
boil *s.* Furunkel, *m.*; Geschwür *n.*; ~ *v.t. & i.* kochen, wallen; ~*ed beef*, Suppenfleisch *n.*; ~*ed egg*, gekochtes Ei *n.* (*hard-boiled*, hartgekocht; *soft-boiled*, weichgekocht); ~*ed shirt*, Hemd mit steifem Einsatz.
boiler *s.* Kochkessel *m.*; Dampfkessel *m.*
boilermaker *s.* Kesselschmied *m.*
boiling point *s.* Siedepunkt *m.*
boisterous *a.*, ~**ly** *adv.* ausgelassen.
bold *a.*, ~**ly** *adv.* kühn; dreist; *to make* ~, sich erkühnen.
boldface *s.* (*typ.*) Fettdruck *m.*
boldness *s.* Kühnheit *f.*; Dreistigkeit *f.*
Bolivia *s.* Bolivien *n.*
Bolivian *s.* Bolivianer(in) *m.(f.)*; ~ *a.* bolivianisch.
bolster *s.* Polster *n.*; Kompresse *f.*; ~ *v.t.* polstern; unterstützen.
bolt *s.* Bolzen *m.*; Pfeil *m.*; Riegel *m.*; Blitzstrahl *m.*; ~ *v.t.* verriegeln; beuteln, sieben; gierig hinunterschlingen; ~ *v.i.* davonlaufen, durchgehen.
bomb *s.* Bombe *f.*; ~ *v.t.* mit Bomben belegen; bombardieren.
bombard *v.t.* bombardieren.
bombardment *s.* Bombardieren *n.*
bombast *s.* Schwulst *m.*
bombastic *a.* schwülstig.
bomber *s.* Bombenflugzeug *m.*, Kampfflugzeug *n.*
bombing *s.* Bombardierung *f.*
bomb-proof *a.* bombenfest.
bombshell *s.* Bombe *f.*
bona fide (*jur.*) in gutem Glauben, gutgläubig.
bond *s.* Band, Seil *n.*; Fessel *f.*; Schuldverschreibung; *in* ~, unter Zollverschluß.
bondage *s.* Knechtschaft *f.*
bonded goods *s.pl.* Güter unter Zollverschluß *n.pl.*
bonded warehouse *s.* Zollspeicher *m.*
bone *s.* Knochen *m.*; Gräte *f.*; ~ *v.t.* entknochen, entgräten; (*med.*) ~**-grafting,** Knochenübertragung *f.*
bonelace *s.* Spitzen *f.pl.*
bonelazy *a.* stinkfaul.
bonemeal *s.* Knochenmehl *n.*
bonfire *s.* Freudenfeuer *n.*; Feuer im Freien.
bonkers *a.* (*fam.*) übergeschnappt.
bonnet *s.* Mütze *f.*; Barett *n.*; Frauenhut *m.*
bonny *a.* munter; hübsch.
bonus *s.* Zulage *f.*; Zuschlag *m.*; Bonus *m.*
bony *a.* knochig.
boo *i.* buh; ~ *s.* Buhruf *m.*; ~ *v.t.* ausbuhen.
booby *s.* Töpel *m.*
book *s.* Buch *n.*; Heft *n.*; *to keep the* ~ *s*, die Bücher führen; ~ *v.t.* eintragen, buchen; ~ *v.i.* (einen Platz) bestellen; eine Fahrkarte lösen (auf der Eisenbahn); *bookable in advance*, vorausbestellbar.
bookbinder *s.* Buchbinder *m.*
bookcase *s.* Bücherschrank *m.*
book club *s.* Buchclub *m.*
bookend *s.* Bücherstütze *f.*
bookie *s.* Buchmacher *m.*
booking *s.* Buchung *f.*; Vorbestellung *f.*
booking office *s.* Fahrkartenschalter *m.*; Kasse *f.*
bookish *a.* belesen; papieren (Stil).
bookkeeper *s.* Buchhalter *m.*
bookkeeping *s.* Buchführung *f.*; ~ *by double (single) entry*, doppelte (einfache) Buchführung *f.*
booklet *s.* Broschüre *f.*
bookmaker *s.* Buchmacher (Sport) *m.*
bookmark *s.* Buchzeichen *n.*
book review *s.* Buchbesprechung, Rezension *f.*
bookseller *s.* Buchhändler *m.*
bookshelf *s.* Regal, Bücherbrett *n.*
bookstall *s.* Bücherstand (an Bahnhöfen) *m.*
bookstore *s.* Buchhandlung *f.*
booktrade *s.* Buchhandel *m.*
bookworm *s.* Bücherwurm *m.*
boom *s.* Ausleger *m.*; Stange *f.*; Aufschwung *m.*, (Börse) Hausse *f.*; ~ *v.i.* dumpf dröhnen; in die Höhe treiben; anpreisen.

boomerang *s.* Bumerang *m.*
boon *s.* Gabe, Wohltat *f.*; **~companion** *m.* Zechkumpan *m.*
boor *s.* Lümmel *m.*
boorish *a.*, **~ly** *adv.* bäuerisch, rüpelhaft.
boost *v.t.* ankurbeln; steigern; erhöhen; ~ *s.* Auftrieb *m.*; Erhöhung *f.*
boot *s.* Stiefel *m.*; ~ *v.t.* treten, kicken; (*comp.*) laden.
bootblack *s.* Stiefelputzer *m.*
booted *a.* gestiefelt.
booth *s.* Bude *f.*; Telefonzelle *f.*; Kabine *f.*
bootjack *s.* Stiefelknecht *m.*
bootlegger *s.* Alkoholschmuggler *m.*
bootless *a.* unnütz, vergeblich.
boots *s.* Hausknecht *m.*
booty *s.* Beute *f.*
booze *v.t.* zechen; ~ *s.* Sauferei *f.*
boozy *a.* versoffen.
borax *s.* (*chem.*) Borax *m.*
border *s.* Rand, Saum *m.*; Grenze *f.*; ~ *v.i.* grenzen; ~ *v.t.* einfassen.
borderer *s.* Grenzbewohner *m.*
borderland *s.* Grenzgebiet *n.*
borderline case *s.* Grenzfall *m.*
bore *v.t.* bohren, eindringen; langweilen; ~ *s.* Bohrer *m.*; Bohrloch *n.*; Kaliber *n.*; langweilige Person *f.*
boredom *s.* Langeweile *f.*
borehole *s.* Bohrloch *n.*
boring *s.* langweilig.
born *p.* & *a.* geboren.
borough *s.* Stadtgemeinde *f.*; Stadt *f.*
borrow *v.t.* borgen; leihen.
borrower *s.* Kreditnehmer(in) *m.*(*f.*)
borrowing *s.* Kreditaufnahme *f.*
bosh *s.* Unsinn *m.*
bosom *s.* Busen *m.*; (*fig.*) Schoß *m.*
boss *s.* Buckel, Knopf *m.*; Meister, Herr, Prinzipal, Chef *m.*; ~ *v.t. to ~ around*, herumkommandieren.
bossy *a.* (*fam.*) herrisch.
botanical *a.* botanisch.
botanist *s.* Botaniker *m.*
botany *s.* Botanik *f.*
botch *v.t.* flicken; verpfuschen; ~ *s.* Flickwerk *n.*; Pfuscherei *f.*
botcher *s.* Flickschneider *m.*; Pfuscher *m.*
both *a.* beide; beides; *both... and c.* sowohl... als auch.
bother *v.t.* plagen, quälen; ~ *s.* Last, Plage *f.*
bottle *s.* Flasche *f.*; ~ *v.t.* in Flaschen abfüllen; *bottled beer*, Flaschenbier *n.*
bottleneck *s.* Flaschenhals *m.*; (*fig.*) Engpaß *m.*
bottleopener *s.* Flaschenöffner *m.*
bottom *s.* Boden *m.*; Grund *m.*; Schiff *n.*; Ende *n.*; Steiß *m.*; *at the ~*, unten, am unteren Ende, im Grunde; ~ *a.* untere.
bottomless *a.* bodenlos.
bottomline *s.* Fazit *n.*; Endergebnis *n.*
bough *s.* Ast *m.*
bouillon cube *s.* Bouillonwürfel *m.*
boulder *s.* Felsbrocken *m.*
bounce *s.* Knall *m.*; Rückprall *m.*; Prahlerei *f.*; ~ *v.i.* aufspringen; anprallen; prahlen.
bouncer *s.* (*fam.*) Rausschmeißer *m.*
bouncing *a.* stramm.
bound *s.* Sprung *m.*; Prall *m.*; ~ *v.i.* springen, prallen; ~ *s.* Grenze *f.*; *out of ~s.*, gesperrt, Zutritt verboten; ~ *v.t.* begrenzen, einschränken; ~ *a.* bestimmt, auf der Reise (nach); *north-~*, in nördlicher Richtung fahrend.
boundary *s.* Grenze *f.*
boundless *a.* grenzenlos.
bountiful *a.* freigebig, großzügig.
bounty *s.* Prämie *f.*
bouquet *s.* Strauß *m.*, Blume (des Weins) *f.*
bourbon *s.* Bourbon *m.*
bourgeois *s.* Bürger(in) *m.*(*f.*); Spießer(in) *m.*(*f.*); ~ *a.* bürgerlich.
bourgeoisie *s.* Bürgertum *n.*; Bourgeoisie *f.*
bout *s.* Gelage *n.*; (*fencing*) Gang *m.*; Anfall *m.*
bovine *a.* zum Rind gehörig, Rind...; (*fig.*) träge.
bow *v.t.* & *i.* biegen, bücken; sich verbeugen; ~ *s.* Verbeugung *f.*; Bogen *m.*; Schleife *f.*; (*naut.*) Bug *m.*
bowdlerize *v.t.* Buchtext verstümmeln.
bowel *s.* Darm *m.*; Innere *n.*
bowels *s.pl.* Eingeweide *n.pl.*
bowl *s.* Becken *n.*; Pfeifenkopf *m.*; Schüssel *f.*; Kugel *f.*; *to play at ~s*, Kegel schieben; ~ *v.i.* kegeln, rollen.
bowlegs *s.pl.* O-Beine *n.pl.*
bowler *s.* Bowlingspieler(in) *m.*(*f.*)
bowler hat *s.* Melone *f.*
bowling *s.* Bowling *n.*; **~alley** *s.* Kegelbahn *f.*
bowsprit *s.* (*nav.*) Bugspriet *n.*
bowstring *s.* Bogensehne *f.*
bowtie *s.* Fliege *f.*; Schleife *f.*
bow window *s.* Bogenfenster, vorspringendes Fenster *n.*
bow wow *s.* Wauwau *m.*
box *s.* Büchse *f.*; Kasten *m.*; Schachtel *f.*; Verschlag *m.*; Schließfach *n.*; Kutschersitz, Bock *m.*; Loge *f.*; Koffer *m.*; Buchsbaum *m.*; Schlag *m.*; ~ **on the ear,** Ohrfeige *f.*; ~ *v.t.* ohrgeigen; ~ *v.i* boxen.
boxcar *s.* (*rail.*) Güterwagen *m.*
boxer *s.* Boxer *m.*
boxing *s.* Boxen *n.*; **~gloves** *pl.* Boxhandschuhe *m.pl.*; **~match** *s.* Boxkampf *m.*
box office *s.* Kartenausgabe *f.*, Kasse *f.*
boxwood *s.* Buchsbaumholz *n.*
boy *s.* Junge *m.*
boycott *v.t.* boykottieren, in Verruf erklären; ~ *s.* Boykott *m.*
boyfriend *s.* Freund *m.*
boyhood *s.* Knabenalter *n.*
boyish *a.*, **~ly** *adv.* knabenhaft, kindisch.
bra *s.* BH *m.*; Büstenhalter *m.*
brace *s.* Schnalle *f.*; Strebe *f.*; Klammer *f.*; Stütze *f.*; (*nav.*) Brasse; (Federwild) Paar *n.*; (*mus.*) Ligaturbogen *m.*; ~ *v.t.* schnüren, spannen, anschnallen; erfrischen.
bracelet *s.* Armband *n.*
brachial *a.* Arm...
bracing *a.* stärkend, gesund.
bracken *s.* Farnkraut *n.*
bracket *s.* Klammer *f.*; Wandarm *m.*; Gasarm *m.*; (*arch.*) Träger *m.*; *in the lower ~ -s*, in den unteren Einkommensklassen; ~ *v.t.* einklammern.
brackish *a.* salzig (vom Wasser); brackig.

brag *v.i.* prahlen; ~ *s.* Prahlerei *f.*
braggart *s.* Prahler *m.*; ~ *a.* prahlerisch.
Brahman *s.* Brahmane *m.*; Brahmanin *f.*
braid *v.t.* flechten; ~ *s.* Flechte *f.*; Litze *f.*
Braille *s.* Blindenschrift *f.*
brain *s.* Gehirn *n.*; ~ *s.* Verstand *m.*
brain: ~child *s.* Geistesprodukt *n.*; ~ **death** *s.* Hirntod *m.*; ~ **drain** *s.* Abwanderung *f.* (von Wissenschaftlern).
brainless *a.* unbesonnen; hirnlos.
brain: ~storm *s.* Anfall geistiger Umnachtung; **~storming** *s.* Brainstorming *n.*; **~washing** *s.* Gehirnwäsche *f.*
brainwave *s.* Eingebung *f.*, Geistesblitz *m.*
brainy *a.* gescheit.
braise *v.t.* schmoren.
brake *s.* Bremse *f.*; ~ *v.t.* brechen (Flachs); bremsen.
brake: ~drum *s.* Bremstrommel *f.*; **~fluid** *s.* Bremsflüssigkeit *f.*; **~light** *s.* Bremslicht *n.*
bramble *s.* Brombeerstrauch *m.*
bran *s.* Kleie *f.*
branch *s.* Zweig *m.*; Abschnitt *m.*; Fach *n.*; Filiale *f.*, Zweigstelle *f.*; ~ *v.t.* in Zweige teilen; ~ *v.i.* Zweige treiben; abzweigen.
branchline *s.* Nebenstrecke *f.*
brand *s.* Brandmal *n.*; Sorte *f.*; Handelsmarke *f.*; ~ *v.t.* brandmarken.
brandish *v.t.* schwingen; schwenken.
brandname *s.* Markenname.
brand-new *a.* brandneu, nagelneu.
brandy *s.* Weinbrand *m.*
brash *a.* dreist; auffällig.
brass *s.* Messing *n.*; Unverschämtheit *f.*; *the* ~ (*mus.*) das Blech; die Blechbläser; (*fam.*) Knete *f.* (Geld).
brass band *s.* Blasorchester *n.*
brassiere *s.* Büstenhalter *m.*
brassplate *s.* Messingschild *n.*
brat *s.* Balg *m.*, Kind *n.*
bravado *s.* Mut *m.*
brave *a.* tapfer, edel; stattlich; ~ *v.t.* herausfordern, trotzen.
bravery *s.* Tapferkeit *f.*; Pracht *f.*
bravo *s.* Bandit *m.*; bravo.
brawl *v.i.* schlagen; zanken; ~ *s.* Schlägerei *f.*, Zank *m.*
brawn *s.* Muskelstärke *f.*; Pressülze *f.*
brawny *a.* fleischig; muskelstark.
bray *s.* Eselsgeschrei *n.*; ~ *v.i.* schreien, schmettern.
brazen *a.*, **~ly** *adv.* ehern; unverschämt.
brazen-faced *a.* unverschämt.
brazier *s.* Kupferschmied *m.*; Kohlenbecken *n.*
Brazil *s.* Brasilien *n.*
Brazilian *s.* Brasilianer(in) *m.(f.)*; ~ *a.* brasilianisch.
Brazil nut *s.* Paranuß *f.*
breach *s.* Verstoß *m.*; Bruch *m.*; Bresche *f.*; Uneinigkeit *f.*; ~ **of promise,** Bruch des Eheversprechens *m.*
bread *s.* Brot *n.*; ~ **and butter,** Butterbrot *n.*; ~ **and cheese,** Käsebrot *n.*
breadcrumb *s.* Brotkrume *f.*; *pl.* Paniermehl *n.*
breadspread *s.* Brotaufstrich *m.*
breadth *s.* Breit *f.*; Weite *f.*
breadwinner *s.* Ernährer(in) *m.(f.)*
break *v.t.* & *i.* brechen; bersten; anbrechen vernichten; bankrott werden; umschlagen (Wetter); (ein Pferd) zureiten; *to* ~ *down,* zusammenbrechen, versagen, nicht funktionieren (Maschine), eine Panne haben (Motor); klassifizieren; *to* ~ *in,* anlernen; *to* ~ *off,* abbrechen *to* ~ *out,* ausbrechen; *to* ~ *up,* (bes. *mil.*) zersprengen, sich auflösen, auseinandergehen; ~ *s* Bruch *m.*; Lücke *f.*; Absatz *m.*; Pause *f.*; Anbruch *m.*; ~ *in the weather,* Witterungsumschlag *m.* ~*ing of the voice,* Stimmbruch *m.*
breakable *a.* zerbrechlich.
breakage *s.* Bruch (der Waren) *m.*
breakdown *s.* Zusammenbruch *m.*; (Betriebs-)störung *f.*; Panne *f.*; Klassifizierung *f.*
breaker *s.* Brecher *m.*
breakfast *v.i.* frühstücken; ~ *s.* Frühstück *n.*; *to make* ~, das Frühstück anrichten.
breakfast cereal *s.* Frühstücksflocken *f.pl.*
break-in *s.* Einbruch *m.*
breaking-point *s.* Belastungsgrenze *f.*
breakneck *a.* halsbrecherisch.
breakthrough *s.* (*mil.*) Durchbruch *m.*
break-up *s.* Auflösung *f.*, Bruch *m.*; Trennung *f.*
breakwater *s.* Wellenbrecher *m.*
breast *s.* Brust *f.*; Busen *m.*; ~ *v.t.* die Stirn bieten; **~bone** *s.* Brustbein *n.*; ~ **cancer** *s.* Brustkrebs; ~ **feed** *v.t.* & *i.* stillen.
breast pin *s.* Anstecknadel *f.*
breaststroke *s.* Brustschwimmen *m.*
breastwork *s.* Brustwehr *f.*
breath *s.* Atem *m.*; Hauch *m.*; *to hold one's* ~ den Atem anhalten; *out of* ~, außer Atem.
breathalyzer *s.* Röhrchen *n.*
breathe *v.t.* & *i.* atmen; äußern.
breather *s.* (*fam.*) Atem-, Verschnaufpause *f.*
breathing *s.* Atmen *n.*; ~ **apparatus** *s.* Beatmungsgerät *n.*; ~ **space** *s.* Atempause *f.*
breathless *s.* atemlos.
breathlessness *s.* Atemlosigkeit *f.*
breathtaking *a.* atemberaubend.
breeches *s.pl.* Kniehosen *f.pl.*
breed *v.t.* & *i.* zeugen; züchten; ~ *s.* Zucht *f.* Schlag *m.*; Tierrasse *f.*; **~dog,** Rassehund *m.*
breeder *s.* Erzeuger *m.*; Züchter *m.*
breeding *s.* Züchten *n.*; Erziehung *f.*
breeze *s.* frischer Wind *m.*; Brise *f.*
breezy *a.* windig, luftig; jovial.
brethren *s.pl.* (*Bibl.*) Brüder *m.pl.*
breviary *s.* Brevier *n.*
brevity *s.* Kürze *f.*
brew *v.t.* brauen; mischen; ~ *s.* Gebräu *n.*
brewer *s.* Brauer *m.*
brewery *s.* Bräuerei *f.*
briarable *a.* bestechlich.
bribe *s.* Bestechung *f.*; ~ *v.t.* bestechen.
bribery *s.* Bestechung *f.*
bric-à-brac *s.* Nippsachen *f.pl.*
brick *s.* Backstein *m.*; ~ *v.t.* mit Ziegelsteinen mauern; *to* ~ *up,* zumauern.
bricklayer *s.* Maurer *m.*
bridal *a.* hochzeitlich, bräutlich.
bride *s.* Braut (am Hochzeitstag) *f.*
bridegroom *s.* Bräutigam *m.*
bridesmaid *s.* Brautjungfer *f.*

bridesman *s.* Brautführer *m.*
bridge *s.* Brücke *f.* (auch Zahnbrücke); Steg *m.* (der Geige); Bridge *n.; ~ v.t.* überbrücken.
bridgehead *s.* (*mil.*) Brückenkopf *m.*
bridging loan *s.* Überbrückungskredit *m.*
bridle *s.* Zaum *m.; ~ v.t.* aufzäumen; bändigen.
bridle path *s.* Reitweg *m.*
brief *a.,* **~ly** *adv.* kurz; knapp; ~ *s.* Aktenauszug *m.;* schriftlicher Auftrag *m.;* (*jur.*) Schriftsatz *m.*
briefcase *s.* Aktentasche *f.*
briefing *s.* (*mil.*) Befehlsausgabe *f.*
briefs *s.pl.* Slip *m.*
brier *s.* Dornstrauch *m.,* wilde Rose *f.*
brig *s.* (*nau.*) Zweimaster *m.,* Brigg *f.*
brigade *s.* Brigade *f.*
brigadier *s.* Brigadeführer *m.*
brigand *s.* Straßenräuber *m.*
brigandage *s.* Räuberwesen *n.,* Räuberei *f.*
bright *a.,* **~ly** *adv.* hell; gescheit.
brighten *v.i.* hell werden, glänzen; ~ *v.t.* glänzend machen; aufheitern.
brightness *s.* Glanz *m.;* Scharfsinn *m.*
brilliance, brilliancy *s.* Glanz *m.*
brilliant *a.,* **~ly** *adv.* glänzend; hervorstehend; ~ *s.* Brilliant *m.*
brim *s.* Rand *m.;* Krempe *f.; ~ v.t.* bis an den Rand füllen; ~ *v.i.* voll sein.
brimful *a.,* **~ly** *adv.* ganz voll.
brimstone *s.* Schwefel *m.*
brindled *a.* scheckig, gestreift.
brine *s.* Salzwasser *n.;* Sole *f.*
bring *v.t. ir.* bringen; *to ~ about,* zustande bringen; *to ~ forth,* hervorbringen, gebären; *to ~ round,* wieder zu sich bringen; *to ~ to bear,* anwenden, zur Wirkung bringen; *to ~ up,* erziehen, aufziehen; (*mil.*) heranführen; *to ~ up the subject,* den Gegenstand zur Sprache bringen.
brink *s.* Rand *m.*
briny *a.* salzig.
briquette, briquet *s.* Preßkohle *f.,* Brikett *n.*
brisk *a.,* **~ly** *adv.* frisch, lebhaft, feurig, stark; ~ *v.t.* (*up*), aufmuntern.
brisket *s.* Bruststück (Speise) *n.*
bristle *s.* Borste *f.; ~ v.t.* (die Borsten) aufrichten; ~ *v.i.* starren.
bristly *a.* borstig; stoppelig.
Brit *s.* Brite *m.;* Britin *f.*
Britain *s.* Britannien *n.*
Britanny *s.* Bretagne *f.*
British *s.* Brite *m.;* Britin *f.; ~ a.* britisch.
Britisher *s.* (*fam.*) Brite *m.*
British Isles *pl.* Britische Inseln *pl.*
Briton *s.* Brite *m.,* Britin *f.*
brittle *a.* zerbrechlich; spröde.
broach *s. ~ v.t.* anspießen; (ein Faß) anzapfen; (*fig.*) vorbringen; anfangen.
broad *a.,* **~ly** *adv.* breit, groß; grob; schlüpfrig; derb; **~ day,** heller Tag *m.*
broad bean *s.* Saubohne *f.*
broadcast *v.t.* rundfunken; **broadcasting** *s.* Rundfunk *m.*
broadcloth *s.* feines Tuch *n.*
broaden *v.t.* weiten; verbreitern.
broadly *a.* allgemein.
broad-minded *a.* tolerant; großzügig.
broadside *s.* (*nav.*) Breitseite, volle Lage *f.*
broadsword *s.* Säbel *m.*
brocade *s.* Brokat *m.*
broccoli *s.* Brokkoli *m.*
brochure *s.* Broschüre (eines Hotels u.dgl.) *f.*
brogue *s.* starker Schuh *m.;* irländische Aussprache *f.*
broil *s.* Lärm, Aufruhr *m.; ~ v.t. & i.* vor dem Feuer rösten.
broke *a.* (*fam.*) pleite.
broken *p. & a.* gebrochen (auch *fig.*); zerrissen; unterbrochen.
broken ground *s.* unebenes Gelände *f.*
brokenhearted gebrochenen Herzens, gramvoll.
broken stones *s.* Schotter *m.*
broker *s.* Makler *m.;* Trödler *m.*
brokerage *s.* Maklergebühr *f.*
bromide *s.* Bromsalz *n.;* Bromid *n.*
bromine *s.* Brom *n.*
bronchial *a.* bronchial; Bronchial...; zur Luftröhre gehörig; **~ tube** *s.* Luftröhre *f.*
bronchitis *s.* Luftröhrenentzündung *f.*
bronze *s.* Bronze *f.; ~ v.t.* bronzieren.
brooch *s.* Brosche *f.*
brood *v.i.* brüten; ~ *v.t.* ausbrüten; ~ *s.* Brut *f.*
brook *s.* Bach *m.; ~ v.t.* ertragen.
broom *s.* Ginster *m.;* Besen *m.*
broomstick *s.* Besenstiel *m.*
Bros. *brothers,* Gebrüder *pl.,* Gebr.
broth *s.* Fleischbrühe *f.*
brothel *s.* Bordell *n.*
brother *s.* Bruder *m.*
brotherhood *s.* Brüderschaft *f.*
brother-in-law *s.* Schwager *m.*
brotherly *a.* brüderlich.
brow *s.* Augenbraue *f.;* Stirn *f.*
browbeat *v.t.* st. einschüchtern.
brown *a.* braun.; ~ *v.i.* (*cul.*) bräunen; braun werden.
brownie *s.* Heinzelmännchen *n.;* kleiner Schokoladenkuchen *m.*
brownish *a.* bräunlich.
brown-paper *s.* Packpapier *n.*
browse *s.* junger Sproß *m.; ~ v.t.* abweiden; ~ *v.i.* weiden; flüchtig lesen.
bruise *v.t.* quetschen, zerstoßen; ~ *s.* blauer Fleck *m.,* Druckstelle *f.*
brunch *s.* Brunch *m.,* spätes Frühstück *n.*
brunette *a.* brünett; ~ *s.* Brünette *f.*
brunt *s. to bear the ~* die Hauptlast tragen.
brush *s.* Bürste *f.;* Pinsel *m.;* Schwanz *(m.)* des Fuchses; ~ *v.t.* bürsten; fegen; streifen; *to ~ up, v.t.* auffrischen; zusammenfegen.
brush: ~ off *s.* Abfuhr *f.;* **~stroke** *s.* Pinselstrich *m.*
brushwood *s.* Gestrüpp, Buschholz *n.*
brusque *a.* barsch, trotzig.
Brussels sprouts *s.pl.* Rosenkohl *m.*
brutal *a.,* **~ly** *adv.* viehisch; roh; brutal.
brutality *s.* rohes Wesen *n.,* Brutalität *f.*
brutalize *v.t.* verrohen.
brute *a.* tierisch, wild; ~ *s.* Vieh *n.;* roher Kerl *m.,* (*fam.*) Scheusal *n.*
brutish *a.,* **~ly** *adv.* viehisch, grob.
B.Sc. *Bachelor of Science,* Bakkalaureus der Naturwissenschaften.
bubble *s.* Blase *f.;* Seifenblase *f.;* Wasserblase *f.;*

leerer Schein *m.*; Betrug, Schwindel *m*; ~ *v.i.* sprudeln; *to* ~ *over v.i.* überschäumen.
bubble bath *s.* Schaumbad *n.*
bubbly *a.* sprudelnd, schäumend.
buccaneer *s.* Seeräuber *m.*
buck *s.* Bock *m.*; männliches Tier *n.*; Stutzer *m.*; (*fam.*) Dollar *m.*; *to pass the* ~ einem andern die Verantwortung zuschieben; ~ *v.i.* bocken; *to* ~ *up*, Mut machen, anfeuern.
bucket *s.* Eimer *m.*
bucketful *s.* ein Eimer voll *m.*
buckle *s.* Schnalle *f.*; Spange *f.*; ~ *v.t.* schnallen; sich biegen; *to* ~ *up*, sich anschnallen.
buckram *s.* Steifleinwand *f.*
buckskin *s.* Hirschleder *n.*; (Stoff) Buckskin *m.*
bucktooth *s.* vorstehender Zahn *m.*; Raffzahn *m.*
buckwheat *s.* Buchweizen *m.*
bucolic *a.* bukolisch.
bud *s.* Knospe *f.*; ~ *v.i.* sprossen, blühen; ~ *v.t.* pfropfen.
Buddhism *s.* Buddhismus *m.*
Buddhist *s.* Buddhist *m.*, Buddhistin *f.*; ~ *a.* buddhistisch.
buddy *s.* (*fam.*) Kumpel *m.*
budge *v.i.* sich.
budget *s.* Budget *n.*; Haushaltsplan *m.*, Etat *m.*; ~ **estimate,** Haushaltsvoranschlag *m.*
buff *a.* mattgelb; ~ *v.t.* polieren; putzen.
buffalo *s.* Büffel *m.*
buffer *s.*, Puffer *m.*, Stoßkissen *n.*; Prellbock *m.*
buffet *s.* Anrichte(tisch) *f.*; Schenktisch *m.*; Wirtschaftsbetrieb *m.*, Buffet *n.*; ~ *v.t.* puffen, schlagen.
buffoon *s.* Possenreißer *m.*
buffoonery *s.* Possen *f.pl.*
bug *s.* Wanze *f.*; Insekt *n.*, Käfer *m.*; Bazillus *m.*; ~ *v.t.* abhören; (*fam.*) nerven; beunruhigen.
bugbear *s.* Popanz *m.*
buggy *s.* leichter, zweirädriger Wagen *m.*
bugle *s.* Wald-, Signalhorn *n.*
bugs *s.pl.* Ungeziefer *n.*
build *v.t.* & *i.* bauen; ~ *s.* Bauart *f.*
builder *s.* Bauunternehmer *m.*; Erbauer *m.*
building *s.* Bauen *n.*; Gebäude *n.*
building contractor *s.* Bauunternehmer *m.*
built-up *a.* bebaut.
bulb *s.* Zwiebel *f.*; Thermometerkugel *f.*; *light* ~, Glühlampe, Birne *f.*
Bulgaria *s.* Bulgarien *n.*
Bulgarian *s.* Bulgare *m.*, Bulgarin *f.*; ~ *a.* bulgarisch.
bulge *s.* Ausbeulung *f.*; ~ *v.i.* anschwellen, vorragen.
bulk *s.* Umfang *m.*; Masse *f.*; Hauptteil *m.*; ~ *v.i.* vorragen.
bulkhead *s.* (*nav.*) Schott *n.*
bulk-purchase *s.* Großeinkauf *m.*
bulky *a.* groß, schwer; sperrig.
bull *s.* Bulle, Stier *m.*; Schnitzer *m.*; Haussier *m.*; päpstliche Bulle *f.*
bulldog *s.* Bullenbeißer *m.*, Bulldogge *f.*
bulldozer *s.* Planierraupe *f.*
bullet *s.* Kugel *f.*
bullet-hole *s.* Einschuß *m.*, Einschußloch *n.*
bulletin *s.* Tagesbericht *m.*; **~-board** *s.* schwarzes Brett *n.*
bullet-proof *a.* kugelfest; ~ **glass** *s.* Panzerglas *n.*
bull fight *s.* Stierkampf *m.*
bullfighter *s.* Stierkämpfer *m.*
bull frog *s.* Ochsenfrosch, Brüllfrosch *m.*
bullion *s.* Gold- oder Silberbarren *m.*
bull market *s.* Haussemarkt *m.*
bullock *s.* Ochse *m.*
bullring *s.* Stierkampfarena *f.*
bull's-eye *s.* Schwarze (in der Scheibe) *n.*
bullshit *s.* (*vulg.*) Scheiße *f.*
bully *s.* (feige) Tyrann *m.*; grober Flegel *m.*; ~ *v.t.* einschüchtern; tyrannisieren.
bulrush *s.* glatte Binse *f.*
bulwark *s.* Bollwerk *n.*
bum *s.* Penner, Gammler *m.*
bumble-bee *s.* Hummel *f.*
bump *s.* Schlag *m.*; Beule *f.*; ~ *v.t.* puffen, (*boat*) überholen; *to* ~ *into*, zufällig treffen.
bumper *s.* Stoßstange *f.*; Puffer *m.*
bumper car *s.* Autoskooter *m.*
bumpkin *s.* Tölpel *m.*
bumptious *a.* aufgeblasen, anmaßend.
bumpy *a.* holperig; uneben.
bun *s.* süßes Bröchen *n.*
bunch *s.* Bündel *n.*; Büschel *m.*; Strauß *m.*; ~ **of grapes,** Weintraube *f.*; ~ **of keys,** Schlüsselbund *m.*; ~ *v.i.* schwellen, strotzen.
bundle *s.* Bündel *n.*; (*fig.*) Bürde *f.*; ~ (*up*), *v.t.* einpacken.
bung *s.* Spund *m.*; ~ *v.t.* zuspunden.
bungalow *s.* Bungalow *m.*
bungle *v.t.* & *i.* verpfuschen; stümpern.
bungler *s.* Stümper *m.*
bungling *a.* stümperhaft.
bunion *s.* Schwellung (am Fuß) *f.*
bunk *s.* (*nav.*) Bettgestell *n.*; Blech *n.*, Unsinn *m.*
bunk-bed *s.* Etagenbett *n.*
bunker *s.* (*nav.*) Bunker *m.*, Kohlenbehälter *m.*
bunny *s.* Häschen *n.*
bunting *s.* Flaggentuch *n.*; Wimpel *m.*
buoy *s.* Boje, Bake *f.*; ~ *v.t.* & *i.* schwimmen; über Wasser halten.
buoyancy *s.* Auftrieb *m.*; (*fig.*) Schwungkraft *f.*
buoyant *a.* schwimmend; (*fig.*) leicht, heiter.
bur *s.* Klette *f.*
burble *v.i.* quasseln, drummeln.
burden *s.* Bürde *f.*; Ladung *f.*; (*fig.*) Last *f.*; Refrain *m.*, Kehrreim *m.*; ~ **of proof,** (*jur.*) Beweislast *f.*; ~ *v.t.* aufbürden.
burdensome *a.* beschwerlich.
bureau *s.* Büro *n.*, Geschäftszimmer *f.*; Schreibtisch *m.*; Kommode *f.*
bureaucracy *s.* Bürokratie *f.*
bureaucrat *s.* Bürokrat(in) *m.(f.)*
bureaucratic *a.* bürokratisch.
burgeon *s.* Knospe *f.*; ~ *v.i.* knospen.
burgher *s.* Bürger *m.*
burglar *s.* Einbrecher *m.*
burglar alarm *s.* Alarmanlage *f.*
burglarize *v.t.* einbrechen.
burglary *s.* Einbruch *m.*
Burgundy *s.* Burgunder *m.*
burial *s.* Begräbnis *n.*
burlesque *a.* possenhaft; ~ *s.* Burleske *f.*
burly *a.* stämmig.
Burma *s.* Birma *n.*

Burmese *s.* Birmane *m.*, Birmanin *f.*; ~ *a.* birmanisch.
burn *v.t.* & *i. ir.* brennen; strahlen; ~ *s.* Brand, Brandschaden *m.*
burner *s.* Brenner *m.*
burnish *v.a.* polieren; ~ *s.* Glanz *m.*
burnous *s.* Burnus *m.*
burr *s.* (*mech.*) Grat *m.*; gerolltes R *n.*
burrow *s.* Kaninchenbau *m.*; ~ *v.i.* sich eingraben, wühlen.
bursar *s.* Kassenwart *m.*; Stipendiat *m.*
bursary *s.* Kasse *f.*; Stipendium *n.*
burst *v.i.* bersten; ~ *v.t.* sprengen; ~ *s.* Riß *m.*; Ausbruch *m.*
bury *v.t.* begraben; vergraben.
bus *s.* Omnibus *m.*, Bus *m.*
bush *s.* Busch *m.*, Strauch *m.*; (*mech.*) Metallfutter *n.*
bushel *s.* Bushel *m.* (36 Liter).
bushey *a.* buschig.
business *s.* Geschäft *n.*; Handel *m.*; (*fam.*) Geschichte *f.*; *small* ~, Kleingeschäft *n.*; Kleingewerbe *n.*; *line of* ~, Geschäftszweig *m.*; *to do (transact)* ~ *with*, in geschäftlicher Verbindung stehen mit; *to go into* ~, Kaufmann werden; *mind your own* ~, kümmere dich um deine eigenen Angelegenheiten; *what* ~ *have you to...*, wie kommst du dazu...?; **~like** *a.* geschäftsmäßig.
businessman *s.* Geschäftsmann *m.*
businesswoman *s.* Geschäftsfrau *f.*
buskin *s.* Kothurn *m.*, Halbstiefel *m.*
bus stop *s.* Haltestelle *f.*
bust *s.* Büste *f.*
bustle *s.* Lärm, Auflauf *m.*; ~ *v.i.* sich rühren, geschäftig sein.
bustling *a.* belebt, geschäftig.
busy *a.* geschäftig; unruhig; ~ *v.t.* beschäftigen; *to be* ~, zu tun haben; *the line is busy*, (*tel.*) die Verbindung ist besetzt.
busybody *s.* Wichtigtuer *m.*
but *c.* aber, sondern; doch; nur; als; wenn nur; ~ *pr.* außer.
butcher *s.* Fleischer(in), Metzger(in) *m.(f.)*; ~ *v.t.* schlachten.
butchery *s.* Metzelei *f.*
butler *s.* Diener *m.*
butt *s.* dickes Ende *n.*; Stoß *m.*; Zielscheibe *f.*; Faß *n.*; Tonne *f.*; (*sl.*) Hintern *m.*; ~ *v.t.* stoßen.
butter *s.* Butter *f.*; ~ *v.t.* buttern.
buttercup *s.* Butterblume *f.*
butterdish *s.* Butterdose *f.*
butter-fingers *s.* Tolpatsch *m.*
butterfly *s.* Schmetterling *m.*; ~ **stroke** *s.* Schmetterlingsstil *m.*
buttermilk *s.* Buttermilch *f.*
buttock *s.* Hinterteil *n.*
button *s.* Knopf *m.*; ~ *v.t.* zuknöpfen.
buttonhole *s.* Knopfloch *n.*; Sträußchen (fürs Knopfloch) *n.*; ~ *v.t.* (*fig.*) zu fassen kriegen.
buttress *s.* Strebepfeiler *m.*
buxom *a.*, **~ly** *adv.* drall; kräftig.
buy *v.t.st.* kaufen.
buyer *s.* Käufer(in) *m.(f.)*
buzz *v.i.* summen, flüstern; ~ *s.* Gesumse, Geflüster *n.*
buzzard *s.* Bussard *m.*
buzzer *s.* summer *m.*
buzzword *s.* Modewort *n.*
B/W *black and white*, schwarz-weiß, s/w.
by *pr.* von, zu, nach, auf, neben, bei; ~ *adv.* nahe, vorbei; **~ and ~,** nach und nach; **~ no means,** keinesfalls, keineswegs; **~ all means,** freilich, auf jeden Fall; **~ myself, ~ yourself, etc.,** allein; **~ nine o'clock,** bis neun Uhr; **~ that time,** bis dahin.
by-election *s.* Nachwahl *f.*
bygone *a.* vergangen.
bylaw *s.* Ortstatut *n.*; Verordnung *f.*
by-name *s.* Beiname, Spitzname *m.*
bypass *s.* Entlastungs-, Umgehungsstraße *f.*; Bypass *m.*; ~ *v.t.* umgehen.
by-product *s.* Nebenprodukt *n.*
bystander *s.* Zuschauer *m.*
byte *s.* Byte *n.*
byway *s.* Nebenweg, Umweg *m.*
byword *s.* Inbegriff *m.*
Byzentine *a.* byzantinisch.

C

C, c der Buchstabe C oder c, *n.*; (*mus.*) C, c, **C-sharp** Cis, cis, **C-flat** Ces, ces.
C. *centigrade*, Grad Celsius.
c. *cent*, Cent; *century*, Jahrhundert, jh.
ca. *circa*, etwa.
cab *s.* Taxi *n.*; Fahrerhaus *n.*; (*rail.*) Führerstand *m.*
cabaret *s.* Kabarett *n.*; Variété *n.*
cabbage *s.* Kohl *m.*
cabby, cabbie, cab-driver *s.* Taxifahrer(in) *m.(f.)*
cabin *s.* Kajüte *f.*; Hütte *f.*; Kabine *f.*; ~ *v.t.* einsperren.
cabinboy *s.* Kabinensteward *m.*
cabincruiser *s.* Kabinenkreuzer *m.*
cabinet *s.* Kabinett *n.*; Schrank *m.*
cabinet-maker *s.* Kunsttischler *m.*
cable *s.* Kabel *n.*; ~ *v.t.* kabeln.
cable: ~ **car** *s.* Kabine *f.* (Seilbahn); ~ **television** *s.* Kabelfernsehen *n.*
caboodle *s. the whole* ~ der ganze Kram.
cabstand *s.* Taxistand *m.*
cacao *s.* Kakaobaum *m.*
cache *s.* geheimes Vorrats-, Schatzlager *n.*
cackle *v.i.* gackern; kichern; ~ *s.* Geschnatter *n.*
cacophony *s.* Kakophonie *f.*; Mißklang *m.*
cactus *s.* Kaktus *m.*
cad *s.* Knote *m.*
cadaver *s.* Kadaver *m.*
caddie *s.* Junge (beim Golfspiel) *m.*
caddy *s.* Teekästchen *n.*, Büchse *f.*
cadence *s.* Tonfall *m.*
cadet *s.* Kadett *m.*
café *a.* Kaffeehaus *n.*
cafeteria *s.* Cafeteria *f.*; Mensa *f.*

caffeine *s.* Koffein *n.*
cage *s.* Käfig *m.;* ~ *v.t.* einsperren.
cagey *a.* vorsichtig, schlau.
caginess *s.* Vorsicht *f.*
cajole *v.t.* beschwatzen.
cajolery *s.* Schmeichelei *f.*
cake *s.* Kuchen *m.;* ~ **of soap,** Stück Seife *n.;* ~ *v.t.* zusammenbacken.
calamitous *a.* unheilvoll.
calamity *s.* Unglück *n.;* Trübsal *f.*
calcareous *a.* kalkartig; kalkig.
calciferous *a.* kalkhaltig.
calcify *v.i.* verkalken.
calcium *s.* Kalzium *n.*
calculable *a.* berechenbar.
calculate *v.t.* berechnen; ~ *v.i.* rechnen.
calculated *a.* vorsätzlich; bewußt.
calculation *s.* Berechnung *f.*
calculator *s.* Rechner *m.*
calculus *s.* (*math.*) Rechnung *f.*
calendar *s.* Kalender *m.*
calender *s.* Tuchpresse *f.;* ~ *v.t.* warm pressen.
calf *s.* **calves** *pl.* Kalb *n.;* Kalbleder *n.;* Wade *f.; in* ~, trachtig (Kuh).
caliber *s.* Kaliber *n.;* Beschaffenheit *f.;* Befähigung *f.;* Format *n.*
calibrate *v.t.* kalibrieren, eichen.
calico *s.* Kattun *m.*
California *s.* Kalifornien *n.*
caliph *s.* Kalif *m.*
call *v.t. & i.* rufen, nennen; wecken; (*tel.*) anrufen; anlegen (Schiff); heißen; besuchen; *to* ~ *for,* abholen; erfordern; *to* ~ *to account,* zur Rechenschaft ziehen; *to* ~ *to mind,* sich erinnern; *to* ~ *off* absagen; *to* ~ *up,* anrufen (*tel.*); ~ *s.* Ruf *m.;* Aufforderung *f.;* Besuch *m.;* Telephongespräch *n.; local* ~, Ortsgespräch *n., long distance* ~, Ferngespräch *n.; on* ~, auf Abruf, auf tägliche Kündigung.
caller *s.* Besucher(in) *m.(f.),* Anrufer(in) *m.(f.)*
calligraphy *s.* Kalligraphie *f.*
calling *s.* Rufen *n.;* Beruf, Stand *m.*
callipers *s.pl.* (*mech.*) Kaliberzirkel, Tastzirkel *m.pl.*
call money *s.* tägliches Geld *n.,* Geld auf Abruf *n.*
callosity *s.* Schwiele *f.,* Hautverhärtung *f.*
callous *a.* schwielig; (*fig.*) unempfindlich.
callow *a.* nicht flügge; (*fig.*) unreif.
call-up *s.* Einberufung *f.*
calm *a.,* **~ly** *adv.* ruhig; ~ *s.* Windstille, Ruhe *f.;* ~ *v.t.* besänftigen.
calmness *s.* Ruhe *f.,* Stille *f.*
calorie *s.* Kalorie *f.*
calorific *a.* wärmeerzeugend.
calumniate *v.t.* verleumden.
calumny *s.* Verleumdung *f.*
calve *v.i.* kalben.
cam *s.* (*mech.*) Nocken *m.*
camber *v.t. & i.* wölben; ~ *s.* Wölbung.
cambric *s.* Batist *m.*
camcorder *s.* Videokamera *f.*
camel *s.* Kamel *n.*
cameo *s.* Kamee *f.*
camera *s.* Kamera *f.,* Photoapparat *m.;* (*jur.*) *in* ~, unter Ausschluß der Öffentlichkeit.
cameraman *s.* Kameramann *m.*
Cameroon *s.* Kamerun *n.*
camomile *s.* Kamille *f.* ~ **tea** *s.* Kamillentee *m.*
camouflage *s.* (*mil.*) Tarnung *f.;* ~ *v.t.* tarnen.
camp *s.* Lager *n.;* ~ *v.i.* kampieren.
campaign *s.* Feldzug *m.;* Kampagne *f.*
campaigner *s.* Vorkämpfer(in) *m.(f.);* Veteran *m.;* alter Kämpfer *m.*
camp bed *s.* Feldbett *n.*
campfire *s.* Lagerfeuer *n.*
camp followers *s.pl.* Troßpersonen *f.pl.*
campground *s.* Lagerplatz *m.;* Zeltplatz *m.;* Campingplatz *m.*
camphor *s.* Kampfer *m.*
campsite *s.* Campingplatz *m.*
campstool *s.* Klappstuhl *m.*
campus *s.* Campus *m.;* Hochschulgelände *n.*
camshaft *s.* Nockenwelle *f.*
can *s.* Kanne *f.;* Konservenbüchse *f.;* Dose *f.;* ~ *v. i.ir.* (*be able*) können; ~ *v.t.* in Büchsen einmachen.
Can. *Canada,* Kanada.
Canada *s.* Kanada *n.*
Canadian *s.* Kanadier(in) *m.(f.);* ~ *a.* kanadisch.
canal *s.* Kanal *m.;* Rinne *f.*
canalization *s.* Kanalisierung *f.*
canalize *v.t.* kanalisieren.
canard *s.* Zeitungsente *f.*
canary *s.* Kanarienvogel *m.*
Canary Islands *pl.* Kanarische Inseln *f.pl.*
cancel *v.t.* absagen, ausstreichen, tilgen; ungültig machen; widerrufen.
cancellation *s.* Absage, Aufhebung *f.;* Widerruf *m.;* Tilgung *f.*
cancer *s.* Krebs *m.*
cancerous *a.* krebsartig.
candelabra, candelabrum *s.* Armleuchter *m.,* Kandelaber *m.*
candid *a.,* **~ly** *adv.* aufrichtig, offen.
candidacy *s.* Kandidatur *f.;* Bewerbung *f.*
candidate *s.* Kandidat *m.;* Bewerber *m.*
candle *s.* Licht *n.;* Kerze *f.;* **~light** *s.* Kerzenlicht *n.*
candlestick *s.* Leuchter *m.*
candor *s.* Redlichkeit, Offenheit *f.*
candy *v.t.* überzuckern; kandieren; ~ *s.* Süßigkeiten *f.pl.;* Bonbon *n.*
cane *s.* Rohr *n.;* Stock *m.;* ~ *v.t.* durchprügeln.
cane chair *s.* Rohrstuhl *m.*
cane sugar *s.* Rohrzucker *m.*
canine *a.* hündisch; Hunds...
canister *s.* Büchse *f.,* Dose *f.;* Kanister *m.*
canker *s.* Lippengeschwür *n.*
cannabis *s.* Cannabis *m.*
cannibal *s.* Menschenfresser *m.;* Kannibale *m.;* ~ *a.* kannibalisch.
cannibalism *s.* Kannibalismus *m.*
cannibalize *v.t.* ausschlachten (Auto).
cannily *adv.* schlau, vorsichtig.
cannon *s.* Kanone *f.*
cannonade *s.* Kanonade *f.*
cannonball *s.* Kanonenkugel *f.*
cannon fodder *s.* Kanonenfutter *n.*
canny *a.* schlau, vorsichtig.
canoe *s.* Kanu *n.*
canoeing *s.* Paddeln *n.;* Kanusport *m.*

canoeist *s.* Kanute *m.;* Kanutin *f.;* Paddelbootfahrer(in) *m.(f.)*
canon *s.* Regel *f.;* Kanon *m.;* Domherr *m.*
canonical *a.* kanonisch, kirchlich.
canonize *v.t.* heiligsprechen.
canon law *s.* kanonisches Recht *n.*
can-opener *s.* Dosenöffner *m.*
canopy *s.* Traghimmel *m.;* Baldachin *m.;* Vordach *n.;* ~ *v.t.* mit einem Baldachin bedecken.
cant *s.* Schrägung *f.;* Zunftsprache *f.;* Heuchelei *f.;* ~ *v.i.* kanten; kauderwelschen; scheinheilig reden.
cantankerous *a.* rechthaberisch.; streitsüchtig.
cantata *s.* Kantate *f.*
canteen *s.* Feldflasche *f.;* Kantine *f.;* ~ *of cutlery,* Messerwarenkoffer *m.*
canter *s.* kurzer Galopp *m.;* Kanter *m.;* ~ *v.i.* im kurzen Galopp reiten.
cantilever *s.* (*arch.*) Dielenkopf *m.;* Konsole *f.;* Träger *m.*
canto *s.* Gesang *m.*
canton *s.* Kanton *m.*
canvas *s.* Kanevas *m.;* Leinwand *f.;* Segeltuch *n.;* Gemälde *n.; under* ~, in Zelten.
canvass *s.* Bewerbung (um Wahlstimmen) *f.;* ~ *v.t.* prüfen, erörtern; ~ *v.i.* sich bewerben, Stimmen sammeln.
canyon *s.* Felsental *n.*, Klamm *f.;* Cañon *m.*
cap *s.* Mütze *f.*, Kappe *f.;* Deckel *m.;* ~ *v.t.* mit einer Kappe bedecken; übertreffen.
capability *s.* Fähigkeit *f.*
capable *a.* fähig; ~ **of work,** arbeitsfähig.
capacious *a.*, **~ly** *adv.* geräumig.
capacitate *v.t.* befähigen.
capacitor *s.* Kondensator *m.*
capacity *s.* Umfang *m.;* Fähigkeit *f.;* Eigenschaft *f.;* Inhalt *m.;* Leistungsfähigkeit *f.;* Aufnahmefähigkeit *f.; legal* ~, Rechtsfähigkeit, Geschäftsfähigkeit *f.;* ~ **measures,** Hohlmaße *n.pl.*
caparison *s.* Pferdedecke *f.*
cape *s.* Kap *n.;* Umhang *m.;* Cape *n.*
caper *s.* Kaper *f.;* Luftsprung *m.;* ~ *v.i.* Luftsprünge machen.
capful *s.* Inhalt einer Verschlußkappe.
capillary *a.* haarfein.; Kapillar...; *s.* Kapillare *f.*
capital *a.*, **~ly** *adv.* Haupt...; vorzüglich; ~ *s.* Hauptstadt *f.;* Kapital *n.;* großer Buchstabe *m.*
capital assets *s.pl.* Kapitalvermögen *n.*
capital gains tax *s.* Kapitalgewinnsteuer *f.*
capitalism *s.* Kapitalismus *m.*
capitalist *s.* Kapitalist(in) *m.(f.)*
capitalize *v.t.* kapitalisieren; mit großen Buchstaben schreiben.
capital letter *s.* Großbuchstabe *m.*
capital punishment *s.* Todesstrafe *f.*
capitulate *v.i.* kapitulieren.
capon *s.* Kapaun *m.;* ~ *v.t.* verschneiden.
caprice *s.* Grille *f.;* Eigensinn *m.*
capricious *a.*, **~ly** *adv.* launenhaft.
Capricorn *s.* (*astr.*) Steinbock *m.*
capriole *s.* Luftsprung, Gaukelsprung *m.*
capsize *v.t.* (*nav.*) zum Kentern bringen; ~ *v.i.* kentern.
capstan *s.* (*nav.*) Winde *f.*, Gangspill *n.*
capsule *s.* Kapsel *f.*
Capt. *Captain,* Kapitän; Hauptmann.
captain *s.* Hauptmann *m.;* (Schiffs-)kapitän *m.;* Kapitän *m.*
captaincy *s.* Hauptmanns-, Kapitänsstelle *f.*
caption *s.* Überschrift *f.*
captious *a.*, **~ly** *adv.* trügerisch, spitzfindig; tadelsüchtig.
captivate *v.t.* (*fig.*) einnehmen, fesseln.
captive *a.* gefangen; ~ **balloon,** Fesselballon *m.;* ~ *s.* Gefangene *m./f.*
captivity *s.* Gefangenschaft *f.*
captor *s.* Eroberer *m.;* Fänger *m.*
capture *s.* Festnahme *f.;* Fang *m.;* Prise *f.;* ~ *v.t.* erbeuten; kapern.
capuchin *s.* Kapuziner *m.*
car *s.* Auto *n.;* Wagen *m.;* Eisenbahnwagen *m.*
caracole *s.* (*mil.*) halbe Schwenkung *f.;* ~ *v.i.* schwenken.
carafe *s.* Karaffe *f.;* Wasserflasche *f.*
caramel *s.* gebrannter Zucker *m.;* Karamelle *f.*
carat *s.* Karat *n.*
caravan *s.* Karawane *f.;* (großer) Wohnwagen *m.*
caraway *s.* Kümmel (Pflanze) *m.*
carbide *s.* Karbid *n.*
carbine *s.* Karabiner *m.*
carbohydrate *s.* Kohlenhydrat *n.*
carbolic acid *s.* Karbolsäure *f.*
car bomb *s.* Autobombe *f.*
carbon *s.* Kohlenstoff *m.;* Durchschlag *m.*
carbonaceous *a.* kohlenstoffhaltig, kohleführend.
carbonate *s.* kohlensaures Salz *n.*
carbon-copy *s.* Durchschlag *m.;* **~-paper** *s.* Kohlepapier *n.*
carbon dioxide *s.* Kohlendioxid *n.*
carbonic acid *s.* Kohlensäure *f.*
carbonize *v.t.* verkohlen.
carbuncle *s.* Karfunkel *m.;* (*med.*) Karbunkel *m.*
carburetor *s.* Vergaser *m.*
carcass *s.* Gerippe *n.;* toter Körper *m.*
carcinogen *s.* Karzinogen *n.;* Krebserreger *m.*
carcinogenic *a.* karzinogenisch; krebserregend.
car crash *s.* Autounfall *m.*
card *s.* Karte *f.;* Visitenkarte *f.;* Seekarte *f.;* Wollkratze *f.;* ~ *v.t.* krempeln, aufkratzen; *house of* ~*s,* Kartenhaus *n.*
cardboard *s.* Pappendeckel *m.*, Pappe *f.*
card game *s.* Kartenspiel *n.*
cardiac *a.* Herz...; ~ **arrest** *s.* Herzstillstand *m.*
cardigan *s.* Wollweste *f.*
cardinal *a.* vornehmst, Haupt...; hochrot; ~ *s.* Kardinal *m.*
cardinal numbers *s.pl.* Grundzahlen *f.pl.*
card index *s.* Kartei *f.;* Katalog *m.*
cardiogram *s.* Kardiogramm.
cardiology *s.* Kardiologie *f.*
card-sharp *s.* Betrüger im Kartenspiel *m.*
card table *s.* Spieltisch *m.*
care *s.* Sorge *f.;* Vorsicht, Pflege *f.;* ~ *of (c/o) Mrs. S.*, (auf Briefen) per Adresse, bei; *to take* ~ *(to),* dafür sorgen, daß; *to take* ~ *(of),* sich einer Sache oder Person annehmen; ~ *v.i.* sorgen; *to* ~ *for,* gern haben.
career *s.* Laufbahn *f.;* Lauf *m.;* Beruf *m.;* ~ *v.i.* rennen.
career adviser *s.* Berufsberater(in) *m.(f.)*
career diplomat *s.* Berufsdiplomat *m.*
carefree *a.* sorgenfrei; pflegeleicht.

careful *a.*, **~ly** *adv.* besorgt, sorgfältig; vorsichtig; *to be ~*, sich in Acht nehmen.
careless *a.*, **~ly** *adv.* sorglos; unvorsichtig; nachlässig; gedankenlos.
carelessness *s.* Nachlässigkeit *f.*; Gedankenlosigkeit *f.*
caress *v.t.* liebkosen; ~ *s.* Liebkosung *f.*
caretaker *s.* Hausmeister(in) *m.(f.)*; Verwalter(in) *m.(f.)*
careworn *a.* abgehärmt.
car ferry *s.* Autofähre *f.*
cargo *s.* Schiffsladung *f.*; ~ **boat** *s.* Frachtschiff; ~ **steamer** *s.* Frachtdampfer *m.*
Caribbean *s.* Karibik *f.*; ~ *a.* karibisch.
caribou *s.* Karibu *m.*
caricature *s.* Karikatur *f.*; Zerrbild *n.*; ~ *v.t.* lächerlich darstellen, karikieren.
caricaturist *s.* Karikaturist(in) *m.(f.)*
caries *s.* Karies *f.*; Knochenfraß *m.*
carillon *s.* Carillon; Glockenspiel *n.*
carious *a.* kariös.
carjack *s.* Wagenheber *m.*
carjacking *s.* Autodiebstahl *m.*
carload *s.* Wagenladung *f.*
carmelite *s.* Karmeliter *m.*
carmine *s.* Karmin *m.*
carnage *s.* Blutbad *n.*; Gemetzel *n.*
carnal *a.*, **~ly** *adv.* fleischlich.
carnation *s.* Gartennelke *f.*
carnival *s.* Karneval, Fasching *m.*
carnivore *s.* Fleischfresser *m.*; fleischfressende Pflanze *f.*
carnivorous *a.* fleischfressend.
carol *s.* Lobgesang *m.*; Weihnachtslied *n.*; ~ *v.t. & i.* lobsingen, jubeln.
carotid *a.*, ~ **artery** *s.* Halsschlagader *f.*
carousal *s.* Gelage *n.*, Fest *n.*
carouse *v.i.* zechen; ~ *s.* Gelage *n.*
carousel *s.* Karussel *n.*
carp *s.* Karpfen *m.*; ~ *v.i.* bekritteln; herumnörgeln.
carpenter *s.* Zimmermann *m.*
carpentry *s.* Zimmerhandwerk *n.*
carpet *s.* Teppich *m.*; Teppichboden *m.*
carpet sweeper *s.* Teppichkehrmaschine *f.*
carphone *s.* Autotelefon *n.*
carpool *s.* Fahrgemeinschaft *f.*
carport *s.* Einstellplatz *m.*
carriage *s.* Kutsche *f.*; Fuhre *f.*; Fracht *f.*; Wagen *m.*; Eisenbahnwagen *m.*; (*mech.*) Schlitten *m.*; Fuhrlohn *m.*; Frachtkosten *f.pl.*; Haltung *f.*
carriage-free, carriage-paid *a.* frachtfrei.
carrier *s.* Transportunternehmen *n.*; Überbringer *m.*; Träger *m.*; Gepäckhalter (Fahrrad) *m.*
carrier pigeon *s.* Brieftaube *f.*
carrier wave *s.* (*radio*) Trägerwelle *f.*
carrion *s.* Aas *n.*
carrot *s.* gelbe Rübe, Möhre *f.*
carry *v.t. & i.* führen, fahren, fortbringen; befördern; tragen; sich betragen; *to ~ forward*, (*com.*) übertragen; *to ~ a motion*, einen Antrag durchbringen; *to ~ on*, treiben, weiterführen; *to ~ on one's person*, bei sich tragen; *to ~ out*, ausführen, durchführen; *to ~ through*, durchführen; *to ~ on v.i.* sein Wesen treiben, fortfahren.
carsick *a.* übel (vom Autofahren).
carsickness *s.* Übelkeit beim Autofahren *f.*
cart *s.* Wagen, Karren *m.*; ~ *v.t.* karren, auf dem Karren fahren.
cartage *s.* Fuhrlohn *m.*; Fahren *n.*
carte blanche *s.* unbeschränkte Vollmacht *f.*
cartel *s.* Kartell *n.*
cart horse *s.* Zugpferd *n.*
Carthusian *s.* Kartäusermönch *m.*
cartilage *s.* Knorpel *m.*
cart load *s.* Fuhre, *f.* Karrenladung *f.*
carton *s.* Kartonschachtel *f.*
cartoon *s.* Cartoon *m.*; politische Karikatur *f.*; Zeichentrickfilm *m.*
cartoonist *s.* Karikaturist(in) *m.(f.)*; Cartoonist(in) *m.(f.)*
cartridge *s.* Patrone *f.*; Kassette *f.*; ~ **box** Patronentasche *f.*
cartwheel *s.* Wagenrad *n.*; *to do ~s*, radschlagen.
carve *v.t.* tranchieren; aushauen; in Kupfer stechen; schnitzen; vorschneiden.
carving *s.* Schnitzerei *f.*, Schnitzwerk *n.*; Stich *m.*
cascade *s.* Wasserfall *m.*; Kaskade *f.*
case *s.* Fall *m.*; Futteral, Gehäuse *n.*; Kiste *f.*; Schriftkasten *m.*; Rechtsfall *m.*; (*gram.*) Fall *m.*; Koffer *m.*; Aktentasche *f.*; *glass ~*, Glaskasten *m.*; *civil ~*, (*jur.*) Zivilsache *f.*; *criminal ~*, Strafsache *f.*; *the ~ for*, die Argumente zu Gunsten; *in ~*, im Falle, falls; *in any ~*, auf jeden Fall.
case-harden *v.t.* (*mech.*) einsatzhärten, oberflächenhärten.
case history *s.* Krankengeschichte *f.*; (*jur.*) Vorgeschichte *f.*
casement *s.* Fensterflügel *m.*
casestudy *s.* Fallstudie *f.*
caseworker *s.* (mit Einzelnen arbeitender) Sozialarbeiter(in) *m.(f.)*
cash *s.* Kasse *f.*; Bargeld *n.*; *for ~*, gegen bar; ~ **on delivery,** per Nachnahme; ~ *v.t.* einlösen (Scheck); einkassieren; ~ **register** *s.* Kasse *f.*
cash dispenser *s.* Geldautomat *m.*
cashier *s.* Kassierer(in) *m.(f.)*; ~ *v.t.* absetzen; kassieren.
cashmere *a.* Kaschmir....
casing *s.* Futteral *n.*, Gehäuse *n.*
cask *s.* Faß *n.*
casket *s.* Schmuckkästchen *n.*, Sarg *m.*
Caspian Sea *s.* Kaspisches Meer *n.*
casserole *s.* kleiner Kochtopf *m.*, Kasserolle *f.*
cassette *s.* Kassette *f.*
cassette: ~ deck *s.* Kassettendeck *n.*; ~ **recorder** *s.* Kassettenrekorder *m.*
cassia *s.* Kassia *f.*, Zimt *m.*
cassock *s.* Soutane *f.*
cast *v.t.ir.* (aus-, ent-, weg-)werfen; ausrechnen; gießen; (Rollen) verteilen; *to ~ up*, addieren; *to ~ one's skin*, sich häuten; *to ~ a vote*, eine Stimme abgeben; ~ **down** *a.* niedergeschlagen; ~ *s.* Wurf, Guß *m.*; Form *f.*; Gattung *f.*; Probe *f.*; angeborene Manier *f.*; Blick *m.*; Rollenverteilung *f.*, Rollenbesetzung *f.*
castanet *s.* Kastagnette *f.*
castaway *a.* weggeworfen; ~ *s.* Schiffbrüchiger *m.*
caste *s.* (in Indien) Kaste *f.*; *to lose ~*, den gesellschaftlichen Rang verlieren.

castigate *v.t.* züchtigen.
castigation *s.* Züchtigung *f.*
casting *s.* Guß(stück *n.*) *m.*; Rollenbesetzung *f.*
casting vote *s.* entscheidende Stimme *f.*
cast iron *s.* Gußeisen *n.*
castle *s.* Burg *f.*; Schloß *n.*; Turm (im Schach) *m.*
cast-off *a.* abgeworfen, abgelegt.
castor *s.* Biber *m.*; Kastorhut *m.*; Streubüchse; **~-oil,** Rizinusöl *n.*
castor sugar *s.* Streuzucker *m.*
castrate *v.t.* kastrieren; entmannen.
castration *s.* Kastration *f.*
casual *a.*, **~ly** *adv.* ungezwungen; lässig; flüchtig; zufällig; **~ laborer,** Gelegenheitsarbeiter *m.*
casualty *s.* Verletzter *m.*; Tote(s) *m.*; (*mil.*) Verlust *m.*
casuistic *a.* kasuistisch.
casuistry *s.* Kasuistik *f.*
cat *s.* Katze *f.*; **~ burglar,** Fassadenkletterer *m.*
cataclysm *s.* (Natur)katastrophe *f.*
cataclysmic *a.* katastrophal, verheerend.
catacomb *s.* Katakombe *f.*
catalepsy *s.* (*med.*) Katalepsie, Starrsucht *f.*
cataleptic *a.* starrsüchtig.
catalog *s.* Katalog *m.*; Verzeichnis *n.*; **~** *v.t.* katalogisieren.
catalyst *s.* (*chem.*) Katalysator *m.*
catapult *s.* Katapult *n.*
cataract *s.* Wasserfall *m.*; grauer Star (im Auge) *m.*
catarrh *s.* Schnupfen *m.*; Katarrh *m.*
catastrophe *s.* Katastrophe *f.*
catastrophic *a.* katastrophal.
cat call *s.* schrilles Pfeifen (als Mißbilligung) *n.*; Pfiff *m.*
catch *v.t.* & *i.ir.* fangen, überfallen; einnehmen; anstecken; *to ~ a cold,* sich erkälten; *to ~ the train,* den Zug erreichen; *to ~ up with,* aufholen. **~** *s.* Fang *m.*; Beute *f.*; Rundgesang *m.*; Kniff *m.*
catching *a.* ansteckend; packend.
catchment *s.* Reservoir *n.*
catchphrase *s.* Slogan *m.*
catchword *s.* Schlagwort *n.*
catchy *a.* eingängig.
catechism *s.* Katechismus *m.*
catechize *v.t.* katechisieren.
categorical *a.*, **~ly** *adv.* kategorisch.
category *s.* Kategorie *f.*; Klasse *f.*
cater *v.i.* Speisen und Getränke liefern.
caterer *s.* Lieferant *m.*, Einkäufer *m.*, Caterer *m.*
caterpillar *s.* Raupe *f.*
caterwaul *v.i.* miauen; **~** *s.* Katzengeschrei *n.*
catgut *s.* Darmsaite *f.*
cathedral *a.* Dom...; **~** *s.* Dom(kirche *f.*) *m.*
catheter *s.* (*med.*) Katheter *m.*
cathode *s.* Kathode *f.*; **~-rays** *s.pl.* Kathodenstrahlen *m.pl.*; **~-ray tube** *s.* Braunsche Röhre *f.*
catholic *a.* katholisch; **~** *s.* Katholik *m.*
Catholicism *s.* katholischer Glaube *m.*
catkin *s.* (*bot.*) Kätzchen *n.*
cattle *s.* Vieh, Rindvieh *n.*
cattle-breeding *s.* Rinderzucht *f.*
cattle-dealer *s.* Viehhändler *m.*
cattle-plague *s.* Rinderpest *f.*
cattle-show *s.* Tierschau *f.*
catwalk *s.* Laufsteg *m.*
cauldron *s.* Kessel *m.*
cauliflower *s.* Blumenkohl *m.*
causal *a.*, **~ly** *adv.* ursächlich, kausal.
causation *s.* Verursachung *f.*
cause *s.* Ursache *f.*; Rechtssache *f.*; Sache *f.*, Umstand *m.*; **~** *v.t.* verursachen.
causeless *a.*, **~ly** *adv.* grundlos.
causeway *s.* Dammweg *m.*
caustic *a.* ätzend; beißend; **~** *s.* Ätzmittel *n.*
cauterize *v.t.* ätzen, ausbrennen.
cautery *s.* Brenneisen *n.*
caution *s.* Vorsicht *f.*; Behutsamkeit *f.*; Warnung *f.*; **~** *v.t.* warnen.
cautionary *a.* warnend.
cautious *a.*, **~ly** *adv.* vorsichtig.
cavalcade *s.* Reiterzug *m.*
cavalier *s.* Reiter *m.*; Ritter *m.*
cavalry *s.* Reiterei *f.*
cave *s.* Höhle *f.*; **~** *v.i.* (*in*) einsinken.
cave-dweller *s.* Höhlenbewohner(in) *m.(f.)*
cavern *s.* Höhle *f.*
cavernous *a.* höhlenartig.
caviar *s.* Kaviar *m.*
cavil *v.i.* spitzfindig tadeln; **~** *s.* Spitzfindigkeit, Schikane *f.*
cavity *s.* Höhlung, Höhle *f.*; Zahnloch *n.*
cavort *v.i.* (*fam.*) herumtollen.
caw *v.i.* krächzen, schreien.
cayenne-pepper *s.* Cayenne Pfeffer *m.*
CB *Citizens Band,* CB-Funk.
C.C. *City Council,* Stadtrat.
CD *compact disc,* CD *f.*; *corps diplomatique,* diplomatisches Korps, CD.
CD player *s.* CD-Spieler *m.*
C.E. *Civil Engineer,* Ingenieur.
cease *v.i.* aufhören, nachlassen; **~** *v.t.* aufhören machen, einstellen.
cease-fire *s.* (*mil.*) Waffenruhe *f.*, Waffenstillstand *m.*
ceaseless *a.* unaufhörlich.
cedar *s.* Zedar *f.*
cede *v.t.* & *i.* abtreten; nachgeben.
ceiling *s.* Zimmerdecke *f.*; Höchstgrenze *f.*
celebrate *v.t.* preisen; feiern.
celebrated *a.* berühmt.
celebration *s.* Feier *f.*
celebrity *s.* Berühmtheit *f.*
celery *s.* Stangensellerie *m.* & *f.*
celestial *a.*, **~ly** *adv.* himmlisch.
celibacy *s.* eheloser Stand *m.*; Zölibat *n.*
celibate *a.* unverheiratet.
cell *s.* (*elek.*) Element *n.*; Zelle *f.*
cellar *s.* Keller *m.*
cellist *s.* Cellist(in) *m.(f.)*
cello *s.* Cello *n.*
cellophane *s.* Zellophanpapier *n.*
cell therapy *s.* Zelltherapie *f.*
cellular *a.* zellular; porös; luft durchlässig; **~ phone** *s.* Mobiltelefon *n.*
celluloid *s.* Zelluloid *n.*
cellulose *s.* Zellstoff *m.*; **~ wool** *s.* Zellwolle *f.*
Celt *s.* Kelte *m.*; Keltin *f.*
Celtic *a.* keltisch.

cement *s.* Zement *m.;* Kitt *m.;* (*fig.*) Band *n.;* ~ *v.t. & i.* verkitten.
cemetery *s.* Friedhof *m.*
cenotaph *s.* Ehren(grab)mal *n.*
censer *s.* Weihrauchfaß *n.*
censor *s.* Zensor *m.;* ~ *v.t.* der Zensur unterwerfen, prüfen; **~ed** *a.* geprüft.
censorious *a.*, **~ly** *adv.* tadelsüchtig.
censorship *s.* Zensur *f.*
censure *s.* Verweis *m.;* Tadel *m.; vote of* ~, Mißtrauensantrag *m.;* ~ *v.t.* tadeln, verurteilen.
census *s.* Volkszählung *f.;* Schätzung *f.*
cent *s.* Cent *m.; per* ~, Prozent *n.*
centaur *s.* Kentaur *m.*
centenarian *s.* Hundertjähriger(in) *m.(f.)*
centenary *s.* Hundertjahrfeier *f.*
centennial *a.* hundertjährig.
center *s.* Zentrum *n.;* Mittelpunkt *m.;* ~ **of gravity,** Schwerpunkt *m.* ~ *v.t.* in den Mittelpunkt stellen; ~ *v.i.* im Mittelpunkte zusammenlaufen.
centerpiece *s.* Tafelschmuck *m.;* Kernstück *n.*
centigrade *a.* Celsius *n.*
centimeter *s.* Zentimeter *m.*
centipede *s.* Hundertfüßler *m.*
central *a.*, **~ly** *adv.* zentral, Zentral
Central: America *s.* Zentralamerika *n.;* ~ **Europe** *s.* Mitteleuropa *n.*
central heating *s.* Zentralheizung *f.; centrally heated,* mit Zentralheizung.
centralize *v.t.* zentralisieren.
central: ~locking *s.* Zentralverriegelung *f.;* ~ **nervous system** *s.* Zentralnervensystem *n.;* ~ **station** *s.* Hauptbahnhof *m.*
centric(al) *a.* zentrisch, im Mittelpunkte befindlich.
centrifugal *a.* vom Mittelpunkte wegstrebend; zentrifugal.
centrifuge *s.* Zentrifuge *f.*
centripetal *a.* zum Mittelpunkte hinstrebend; zentripetal.
centuple *a.* hundertfältig.
centurion *s.* Zenturio *m.*
century *s.* Jahrhundert *n.;* Hundert *n.*
ceramic *a.* keramisch.
ceramics *s.* Keramik *f.*
cereal *a.* Getreide...; **~s** *s.pl.* Getreidearten *pl.*, Getreideflocken *pl.*
cerebral *a.* Gehirn...; zerebral.
ceremonial *a.*, **~ly** *adv.* förmlich, umständlich; ~ *s.* Zeremoniell *n.*
ceremonious *a.*, **~ly** *adv.* feierlich; förmlich.
ceremony *s.* Feierlichkeit *f.*
cert. *certificate,* Bescheinigung.
certain *a.* gewiß, zuverlässig; *for* ~, bestimmt.
certainly *adv.* gewiß, allerdings, freilich.
certainty *s.* Gewißheit *f.*
certifiable *a.* nachweislich; überprüfbar.
certificate *s.* Bescheinigung *f.;* Zeugnis *n.;* ~ *of good conduct,* Führungszeugnis *n.;* ~ *v.t.* ein Zeugnis ausstellen; bescheinigen.
certify *v.t.* bescheinigen; **certified** *a.* staatlich anerkannt od. geprüft; ~ *true copy,* die Richtigkeit der Abschrift wird bezeugt.
certitude *s.* Gewißheit *f.*
cerulean *a.* nachtblau.
cervical *a.* Hals..., Nacken...
cervix *s.* Gebärmutterhals *m.*
Cesarean section *s.* (*med.*) Kaiserschnitt *m.*
cessation *s.* Aufhören *n.*
cession *a.* Abtretung *f.*
cesspool *s.* Senkgrube *f.*
CET *Central European Time,* mitteleuropäische Zeit, MEZ.
cf. *confer,* vergleiche, vgl.
ch. *Chapter,* Kapitel, Kap.
chafe *v.t.* wund reiben; ärgern; ~ *v.i.* sich ärgern.
chaff *s.* Spreu *f.;* Neckerei *f.;* ~ *v.t.* necken, foppen.
chaffinch *s.* Buchfink *m.*
chagrin *s.* Verdruß, Ärger *m.*
chain *s.* Kette *f.;* Kettenglied *n.;* ~ *of command,* (*mil.*) Befehlsweg *m.;* ~ *of reasoning,* Schlußkette *f.;* ~ *v.t.* anketten.
chain reaction *s.* Kettenreaktion *f.*
chain smoker *s.* Kettenraucher(in) *m.(f.)*
chain store *s.* Kettenladen *m.*
chair *s.* Stuhl *m.;* Lehrstuhl *m.;* Vorsitz *m.; to take the* ~, die Sitzung eröffnen; *to be in the* ~, den Vorsitz führen (in einer Versammlung).
chair bottom *s.* Stuhlsitz *m.*
chairman *s.* Vorsitzender *m.*
chairmanship *s.* Vorsitz *m.*
chairperson *s.* Vorsitzender(in) *m.(f.)*
chairwoman *s.* Vorsitzende *f.*
chalice *s.* Kelch *m.*
chalk *s.* Kreide *f.*
challenge *v.t.* herausfordern; ablehnen (Richter od. Geschworene); ~ *s.* Herausforderung *f.;* (*mil.*) Anruf *m.;* Verwerfung, Ablehnung (von Richtern od. Geschworenen) *f.*
challenger *s.* Herausforderer *m.*, Herausforderin *f.*
challenging *a.* herausfordernd, faszinierend.
chamber *s.* Zimmer *n.;* Kammer *f.*
chamber concert *s.* Kammerkonzert *n.;*
chambermaid *s.* Zimmermädchen *n.*
chamber music *s.* Kammermusik *f.*
chamber of commerce *s.* Handelskammer *f.*
chameleon *s.* Chamäleon *n.*
chamois *s.* Gemse *f.;* Gemsleder *n.*
champ *v.t. & i.* kauen; verschlingen.
champagne *s.* Champagner *m.;* Sekt *m.*
champion *s.* Kämpe, Vorkämpfer *m.;* (Sport) Meister *m.;* preisgekröntes Rassetier *n.;* ~ *v.t.* verteidigen; verfechten.
championship *s.* (Sport) Meisterschaft *f.*
chance *s.* Zufall *m.;* Schicksal *n.;* Glück *n.;* Aussicht *f.;* Chance *f.;* Gelegenheit *f.; by* ~, von ungefähr; *to give a person a* ~, jm. eine Chance geben; *to take a* ~, es darauf ankommen lassen; *to take no* ~*s,* es nicht darauf ankommen lassen; ~ *v.i.* sich zutragen.
chancellery *s.* Kanzlei *f.*
chancellor *s.* Kanzler *m.;* ~ **of the Exchequer,** britischer Finanzminister *m.*
chancy *a.* gewagt, riskant.
chandelier *s.* Armleuchter *m.*
change *v.t.* ändern, wechseln, tauschen; herausgeben (auf); ~ *v.i.* sich ändern; sich umziehen; (Eisenbahn) umsteigen; ~ *s.* Veränderung *f.;* Tausch, Wechsel *m.;* Kleingeld *f.;* Agio *n.;* Börse *f.;* ~ **of clothes (linen),** Anzug (Wäsche) zum Wechseln; *small* ~, Kleingeld *n.; a* ~ *for the*

worse, eine Wendung zum Schlimmeren *f.; for a ~,* zur Abwechslung.
changeable *a.*, **~ly** *adv.* veränderlich.
changeless *a.* unveränderlich.
changeover *s.* Umstellung *f.*
changing *a.* wechselnd; sich ändernd.
changingroom *s.* Umkleideraum *m.;* Umkleidekabine *f.*
channel *s.* Kanal *m.;* Rinne *f.;* Flußbett *n.;* (*fig.*) Weg *m.; through official ~s,* im Instanzenweg; ~ *v.t.* aushöhlen, in Kanäle leiten.
chant *s.* Gesang *m.;* ~ *v.t.* singen.
chaos *s.* Chaos *n.;* Wirrwarr *m.*
chaotic *a.* chaotisch.
chap *s.* Spalte *f.;* Riß *m.;* Kinnbacken von Tieren *m.;* Kerl, Bursche *m.*
chapel *s.* Kapelle *f.*
chaperon *s.* Anstandsdame *f.;* Aufsichtsperson *f.;* ~ *v.t.* begleiten.
chaplain *s.* Kaplan *m.*, Feldprediger *m.*
chaplet *s.* Kranz *m.;* Rosenkranz *m.*
chapter *s.* Kapitel *n.;* Domkapitel *n.*
char *v.t.* verkohlen; ~ *v.i.* um Tagelohn dienen; ~ *s.* Tagearbeit *f.*
char-a-banc *s.* Gesellschaftswagen *m.*
character *s.* Merkmal *n.;* Schriftzug *m.;* Charakter *m.;* Original *n.;* Sonderling *m.;* Stand *m.;* Rolle *f.;* Zeugnis *n.; the characters,* die handelnden Personen (in einem Stück oder Roman).
characteristic *a.* charakteristisch; ~ *s.* Kennzeichen *n.*
characterize *v.t.* charakterisieren.
charade *s.* Silbenrätsel *n.*
charcoal *s.* Holzkohle *f.;* Zeichenkohle *f.*
charge *v.t.* laden, beladen; beauftragen; beschuldigen; angreifen; anrechnen; debitieren, einschärfen; ~ *s.* Last *f.;* Ladung *f.;* Auftrag *m.;* Beschwerde *f.;* Aufsicht *f.;* Amt *n.;* Kosten *f. pl.;* Mündel *n.;* Ermahnung *f.;* Beschuldigung, Anklage *f.;* Angriff *m.; to be in ~ of,* die Leitung von etwas haben; *to take ~ of,* die Sorge für etwas übernehmen; *free of ~,* kostenfrei; **~s** *pl.* Spesen *pl.*
chargeable *a., to be ~ to sb.* auf jemandes Kosten gehen.
chargé d'affaires, *s.* chargé d'affaires *m.*
charger *s.* Schlachtroß *n.;* Ladegerät *n.*
chariot *s.* (Triumph-, Kriegs-)wagen *m.*
charisma *s.* Charisma *n.*
charismatic *a.* charismatisch.
charitable *a.*, **charitably** *adv.* wohltätig.
charity *s.* Barmherzigkeit *f.;* christliche Liebe *f.;* Mildtätigkeit *f.;* Wohltätigkeitseinrichtung *f.;* milde Gabe *f.;* Almosen *n.*
charlatan *s.* Scharlatan *m.*
charm *v.t.* bezaubern; ~ *s.* Zauber, Charme *m.*
charming *a.* bezaubernd, reizend.
charnel house *s.* Beinhaus *n.*
chart *s.* Seekarte *f.;* Tabelle *f.;* Übersichtstafel *f.*
charter *s.* Charta *f.;* Gründungsbrief *m.;* Urkunde *f.;* ~ *v.t.* (ein Schiff) mieten, chartern.
chartered accountant *s.* beeidigter Bücherrevisor *m.;* Wirtschaftsprüfer *m.*
charwoman *s.* Scheuerfrau *f.*
chary *a.* sorgsam; karg; vorsichtig.
chase *v.t.* jagen, verfolgen; ziselieren; einfassen; ~ *s.* Jagd *f.; to give ~,* Jagd machen.
chasm *s.* Kluft *f.;* Schlund *m.*
chassis *s.* Rahmen (eines Wagens) *m.*
chaste *a.*, **~ly** *adv.* keusch.
chasten *v.t.* züchtigen, läutern; demütigen.
chastening *a.* ernüchternd.
chastise *v.t.* züchtigen; bestrafen.
chastisement *s.* Züchtigung *f.*
chastity *s.* Keuschheit *f.*
chat *s.* Plauderei *f.;* ~ *v.i.* plaudern.
chattels *s.pl.* bewegliche Habe *f.*
chatter *v.i.* plaudern; klappern; ~ *s.* Gerede *f.;* Geschnatter *n.;* Gezwitscher *n.*
chatterbox *s.* Quasselstrippe *f.*, Plappermaul *n.*
chatty *a.* gesprächig.
chauffeur *s.* Chauffeur, Führer *m.*
chauvinism *s.* Chauvinismus *m.*
chauvinist *s.* Chauvinist, Chauvi *m.;* Chauvinistin *f.*
chauvinistic *a.* chauvinistisch.
cheap *a.*, **~ly** *adv.* wohlfeil, billig.; (*fig.*) schäbig.
cheapen *v.t.* verbilligen.
cheapness *s.* Billigkeit *f.*
cheat *s.* Betrug *m.;* Betrüger(in) *m.(f.);* ~ *v.t.* betrügen.
check *s.* Anstoß *m.;* Einhalt *m.;* Hindernis *n.;* Kontrolle *f.;* Gepäckschein *m.;* Kontrollmarke *f.;* Scheck *m.;* Rechnung *f.;* ~ *v.t.* zurückhalten, hemmen; kontrollieren; nachprüfen; ~ *v.i.* Schach bieten; *to ~ out,* Hotel verlassen, (Buch) ausleihen; ~ **room** Gepäckaufbewahrung *f.*
checkbook *s.* Scheckbuch *n.*
checked *a.* kariert.
checker *s.* Damestein *m.;* Kassierer(in) *m.(f.)*
checkerboard *s.* Schachbrett *n.*
checkers *s.pl.* Damespiel *n.*
check-in *s.* Anmeldung *f.;* Einchecken *n.*
checking account *s.* Girokonto *n.*
checklist *s.* Checkliste *f.*, Kontrolliste *f.*
checkmate *s.* Schachmatt *n.;* ~ *v.t.* matt setzen.
checkpoint *s.* Kontrollpunkt *m.*
check-up *s.* Untersuchung *f.;* Überprüfung *f.*
cheek *s.* Backe, Wange *f.;* (*fam.*) Unverschämtheit *f.*
cheek bone *s.* Backenknochen *m.*
cheeky *a.* frech.
cheep *v.i.* piepsen.
cheer *s.* Bewirtung *f.;* Frohsinn *m.;* Beifallsruf *m.; of good ~,* guter Laune; ~ *v.t. & i.* erheitern; mit lautem Ruf begrüßen.
cheerful *a.*, **~ly** *adv.* fröhlich.
cheerfulness, cheeriness *s.* Heiterkeit *f.*
cheerily *adv.* fröhlich.
cheering *a.* jubelnd; fröhlich stimmend.
cheerless *a.* mutlos; freudlos.
cheery *a.* heiter, lustig.
cheese *s.* Käse *m.*
cheese: ~ board *s.* Käseplatte *f.*
cheesecake *s.* Käsekuchen *f.*
cheesecloth *s.* Baumwollstoff *m.*
cheesy *a.* käsig.
cheetah *s.* Gepard *m.*
chef *s.* Küchenchef, Koch *m.*
chemical *a.* chemisch; **~ action,** chemische Wirkung *f.;* (*mil.*) **~ warfare,** Gaskrieg *m.*, chemischer Krieg *m.;* **~ warfare agent,** Kampfstoff *m.;* **~s** *s.pl.* Chemikalien *f.pl.*

chemise *s.* (Frauen-)hemd *n.*
chemist *s.* Drogist *m.;* Chemiker *m.*
chemistry *s.* Chemie *f.*
chemotherapy *s.* Chemotherapie *f.*
cheque *s.* (*Brit.*) Scheck, Bankschein *m.*
cherish *v.t.* pflegen, hegen; liebkosen.
cherry *s.* Kirsche *f.*
cherry brandy *s.* Kirschlikör *n.*
cherry pit *s.* Kirschkern *m.*
cherub *s.* Cherub *m.*
chess *s.* Schach(spiel) *n.*
chess board *s.* Schachbrett *n.*
chess man *s.* Schachfigur *f.*
chess player *s.* Schachspieler(in) *m.(f.)*
chest *s.* Lade, Kiste *f.;* Brust *f.;* ~ **of drawers,** Kommode *f.*
chestnut *s.* Kastanie *f.;* ~ *a.* kastanienbraun.
chew *v.t. & i.* kauen; (*fig.*) überlegen.
chewing gum *s.* Kaugummi *m.*
chewing tobacco *s.* Kautabak *m.*
chewy *a.* zäh.
chic *s.* Eleganz *f.;* Schick *m.;* ~ *a.* schick, elegant.
chicane *s.* Schikane *f.;* ~ *v.t.* schikanieren.
chicanery *s.* Schikane *f.*
chick *s.* Küken *n.*
chicken *s.* (junges) Huhn *n.*, Hähnchen *n.*
chickenhearted *a.* feig.
chickenpox *s.* Windpocken *pl.*
chicory *s.* Zichorie *f.;* Endiviensalat *m.*
chide *v.t. & i.* schelten.
chief *a.*, **~ly** *adv.* vornehmst; hauptsächlich; ~ *s.* Erste *m.;* Oberhaupt *n.;* ~ *of staff,* Generalstabschef *m.*
chiefly *adv.* hauptsächlich; vor allem.
chieftain *s.* Anführer, Häuptling *m.*
chiffon *s.* Chiffon *m.*
chilblain *s.* Frostbeule *f.*
child *s.* Kind *n.*
childbirth *s.* Geburt *f.*, Gebären *n.*
childhood *s.* Kindheit *f.*
childish *a.*, **~ly** *adv.* kindisch; kindlich.
childishness *s.* kindisches Benehmen *n.*
childless *a.* kinderlos.
childlike *a.* kindlich.
child prodigy *s.* Wunderkind *n.*
childproof *a.* kindersicher.
children *pl. of* **child.**
Chile *s.* Chile *n.*
Chilean *a.* chilenisch; ~ *s.* Chilene *m.;* Chilenin *f.*
chill *a.* frostig; ~ *s.* Kälte *f.;* Verkühlung *f.; to take the ~ off,* leicht anwärmen; ~ *v.t.* kühlen; mutlos machen.
chilling *a.* ernüchternd; frostig.
chilly *a.* etwas kalt, frostig, kühl.
chime *s.* Glockenspiel *n.;* ~ *v.i.* läuten; ertönen; (*fig.*) übereinstimmen, harmonieren.
chimera *s.* Chimära *f.*
chimerical *a.*, **~ly** *adv.* schimärisch.
chimney *s.* Schornstein *m.;* Kamin *m.*
chimneypiece *s.* Kaminsims *m.*
chimneysweep(er) *s.* Schornsteinfeger *m.*
chimpanzee *s.* Schimpanse *m.*
chin *s.* Kinn *n.*
china *s.* Porzellan *n.*
China *s.* China *n.*
Chinese *a.* chinesisch; ~ *s.* Chinese *m.*, Chinesin *f.;* ~ **lantern** *s.* Lampion *m.*
chink *s.* Ritze *f.;* Spalt *m.;* ~ *v.t. & i.* klimpern; sich spalten.
chintz *s.* Chintz *m.*, Möbelkattun *m.*
chip *v.t.* schnitzeln; abraspeln; ~ *s.* Span *m.;* Schnitzel *n.*
chipboard *s.* Spanplatte *f.*
chipmunk *s.* Chipmunk *n.*, Streifenhörnchen *n.*
chippings *s. pl.* Splitt *m.*
chiropodist *s.* Fußpfleger(in) *m.(f.)*
chiropractor *s.* Chiropraktiker(in) *m.(f.)*
chirp *v.i.* zwitschern; ~ *s.* Gezwitscher *n.*
chirrup *s.* Zwitschern *n.*
chisel *s.* Meißel *m.;* ~ *v.t.* meißeln.
chit *s.* Schein *m.*, Schriftstück *n.;* Notiz *f.*
chitchat *s.* Plauderei *f.*
chivalrous *a.* ritterlich.
chivalry *s.* Ritterlichkeit *f.;* Rittertum *n.*
chive *s.* Schnittlauch *m.*
chloride *s.* Chlorid *n.*
chlorinate *v.t.* chloren.
chlorine *s.* Chlor *n.*
chloroform *s.* Chloroform *n.;* ~ *v.t.* chloroformieren.
chlorophyll *s.* Chlorophyll *n.*
chock *s.* Bremsklotz *m.;* ~ *v.t.* festkeilen.
chock-full *a.* gestopft voll.
chocolate *s.* Schokolade *f.;* **~s** *s.pl.* Pralinen *f.pl.; box of ~s,* Pralinenschachtel *f.*
choice *s.* Wahl *f.;* Auswahl *f.;* ~ *a.*, auserlesen, sehr schön.
choir *s.* Chor *m.*
choke *v.t.* ersticken; verstopfen.
choking *a.* stickig; erstickt.
cholera *s.* Cholera *f.*
choleric *a.* cholerisch; hitzig.
choose *v.t. & i.st.* wählen, aussuchen.
choosy *a.* (*fam.*) wählerisch.
chop *v.t. & i.* spalten; ~ *s.* Hieb *m.;* Röstrippchen, Kotelett *n.*
chopper *s.* Hackbeil *n.;* (*fam.*) Hubschrauber *m.*
chopping-block *s.* Hackblock *m.*
chopping-knife *s.* Hackmesser *n.*
choppy *a.* unstet; hohl (*sea*).
chopstick *s.* Eßstäbchen *n.*
choral *a.* chorartig, Chor...; ~ *s.* Choral *m.*
chord *s.* Saite *f.;* Akkord *m.*
chore *s.* Hausarbeit *f.*
choreographer *s.* Choreograph(in) *m.(f.)*
choreography *s.* Choreographie *f.*
chorister *s.* Chorsänger *m.*
chorus *s.* Chor *m.*
chorus girl *s.* Revuegirl *n.*
chowder *s.* dicke Suppe mit Kartoffeln u. Milch.
christen *v.t.* taufen.
Christendom *s.* Christenheit *f.*
christening *s.* Taufe *f.*
Christian *a.*, **~ly** *adv.* christlich; ~ *s.* Christ *m.;* Christin *f.;* ~ **name** *s.* Vorname *m.*
Christianity *s.* Christentum *n.*
christianize *v.t.* christianisieren.
Christmas *s.* Weihnachten.
Christmas carol *s.* Weihnachtslied *n.*
chromatic *a.* chromatisch.

chrome *a.* chromgelb.
chromium *s.* Chrom *n.;* **~-plated** *a.* verchromt.
chromosome *s.* Chromosom *n.*
chronic *a.* chronisch; langwierig.
chronicle *s.* Chronik *f.;* ~ *v.t.* aufzeichnen.
chronicler *s.* Chronist *m.*
chronological *a.,* **~ly** *adv.* chronologisch.
chronology *s.* Zeitrechnung *f.;* Chronologie *f.*
chrysalis *s.* (Insekten) Puppe *f.*
chrysanth, chrysanthemum *s.* Chrysantheme *f.*
chubby *a.* pummelig; pausbäckig.
chuck *v.i.* glucken; sanft stoßen; (*fam.*) wegwerfen; ~ *s.* Glucken *n.;* (*mech.*) Spannfutter *n.*
chuckle *v.i.* schmunzeln, kichern.
chug *s.* Tuckern *n.;* ~ *v.i.* tuckern.
chum *s.* Stubengenosse *m.;* Kamerad *m.*
chump *s.* Klotz *m.*
chunk *s.* Kloben, Klumpen *m.*
church *s.* Kirche *f.;* ~ **attendance,** Kirchenbesuch *m.*
churchwarden *s.* Kirchenvorsteher *m.*
churchyard *s.* Kirchhof *m.*
churl *s.* Bauer *m.;* Grobian *m.*
churlish *a.,* **~ly** *adv.* grob; mürrisch.
churn *v.i.* buttern; ~ *s.* Butterfaß *n.*
chute *s.* Schütte *f.;* Rutsche *f.*
CIA *Central Intelligence Agency,* (US-Geheimdienst).
cicada *s.* Zikade, Baumgrille *f.*
cider *s.* Apfelwein *m.*
cigar *s.* Zigarre *f.*
cigar-case *s.* Zigarrentasche *f.*
cigarette *s.* Zigarette *f.;* **~-case** *s.* Zigarettenetui *n.;* **~-butt,** *s.* Zigarettenstummel *m.;* **~-lighter** *s.* Feuerzeug *n.*
cigar-holder *s.* Zigarrenspitze *f.*
C in C *Commander in Chief,* Oberbefehlshaber.
cinch *s.* Klacks *m.;* Kinderspiel *n.*
cinder *s.* Löschkohle *f.;* Schlacke *f.*
Cinderella *s.* Aschenbrödel *n.*
cindertrack *s.* Aschenbahn *f.*
cinema *s.* Kino *n.*
cinematography *s.* Kinematographie *f.*
cinnamon *s.* Zimt *m.*
cipher *s.* Ziffer *f.;* Null *f.;* Geheimschrift *f.;* ~ *v.i.* rechnen; ~ *v.t.* mit Chiffern schreiben.
circa *pr.* zirka.
circle *s.* Kreis *m.;* Kreislinie *f.;* ~ *v.t.* einschließen; ~ *v.i.* umkreisen.
circuit *s.* Umkreis *m.;* (*elek.*) Stromkreis *m.; short* ~, Kurzschluß *m.;* Bezirk *m.;* Rundreise der Richter *f.*
circuitous *a.* weitschweifig, Um...
circular *a.,* **~ly** *adv.* kreisförmig; ~ *s.* Rundschreiben *n.*
circularize *v.t.* Zirkulare herumschicken an.
circulate *v.t.* in Umlauf bringen; ~ *v.i.* umlaufen; *circulating library s.* Leihbibliothek *f.*
circulation *s.* Kreislauf, Umlauf *m.;* Auflage (einer Zeitung) *f.*
circulatory *a.* Kreislauf...
circumcise *v.t.* beschneiden.
circumcision *s.* Beschneidung *f.*
circumference *s.* Umfang *m.*
circumflex *s.* Zirkumflex (Akzent) *m.*
circumlocution *s.* Umschreibung *f.;* Umschweif *m.*
circumnavigate *v.t.* umschiffen.
circumscribe *v.t.* umschreiben; einschränken.
circumscription *s.* Begrenzung *f.*
circumspect *a.,* **~ly** *adv.* umsichtig.
circumspection *s.* Umsicht, Vorsicht *f.*
circumstance *s.* Umstand, Zufall *m.*
circumstanced *a.* beschaffen.
circumstantial *a.,* **~ly** *adv.* zufällig; eingehend; ~ **evidence** *s.* (*jur.*) Indizienbeweis *m.*
circumvent *v.t.* umgehen; überlisten.
circus *s.* Zirkus *m.*
cirrus *s.* Federwolke *f.;* Zirruswolke *f.*
Cistercian *a.* zisteriensisch.
cistern *s.* Wasserbehälter *m.;* Zisterne *f.*
citadel *s.* Festung *f.;* Zitadelle *f.*
citation *s.* Vorladung *f.;* Zitat *n.*
cite *v.t.* vorladen; (Stellen) anführen; zitieren.
citizen *s.* Bürger(in) *m.(f.)*
citizenship *s.* Staatsbürgerschaft *f.*
citric *a.,* ~ **acid** *s.* Zitronensäure *f.*
citrus *s.* Zitrusgewächs *n.*
city *s.* Stadt *f.*
civic *a.* bürgerlich.
civil *a.,* **~ly** *adv.* bürgerlich; höflich;
civil action *s.* (*law*) Ziviklage *f.*
civil code *s.* bürgerliches Gesetzbuch *n.*
civilian *s.* Zivilist, Bürger *m.*
civility *s.* Höflichkeit *f.*
civilization *s.* Kultur, Zivilisation *f.*
civilize *v.t.* zivilisieren; verfeinern.
civilized *a.* zivilisiert, buttiviert.
civil: ~law *s.* Zivilrecht *n.*
civil rights *s.pl* Bürgerrechte *n.pl*
civil servant *s.* Staatsbeamter *m.*
civil service Staatsdienst *m.*
civil war Bürgerkrieg *m.*
cl. *centiliter,* Zentiliter; *class,* Klasse, Kl.
clack *s.* Geklapper *n.;* Geplauder *n.;* ~ *v.i.* klappern; plaudern.
clad *p.* gekleidet.
claim *v.t.* Anspruch machen, fordern; ~ *s.* Anspruch *m.;* Forderung *f.*
claimant *s.* Antragsteller(in) *m.(f.);* Forderer *m.*
clairvoyant *s.* Hellseher(in) *m.(f.)*
clam *s.* eßbare Muschel *f.*
clamber *v.i.* klettern.
clammy *a.* klamm.
clamor *s.* lautes Geschrei *n.,* Lärm *m.*
clamorous *a.* schreiend, tobend.
clamp *s.* Schraubzwinge *f.;* Klammer *f.;* ~ *v.t.* verklammern, verzapfen.
clan *s.* Stamm *m.;* Sippschaft *f.*
clandestine *a.,* **~ly** *adv.* heimlich.
clang *s.* Schall *m.;* ~ *v.i.* schallen.
clank *s.* Geklirr *n.;* ~ *v.i.* klirren.
clap *v.t.* klappern; beklatschen; ~ *v.i.* zusammenschlagen; ~ *s.* Klaps, Schlag *m.;* Klatschen *n.*
clapper *s.* Klöppel (Glocke) *m.;* Schwengel *m.*
clapping *s.* Beifall *m.;* Applaus *m.*
claptrap *s.* Phrasen *f.pl.;* Getue *n.*
claret *s.* Rotwein, Bordeaux *m.*
clarification *s.* Abklärung *f.*

clarify *v.t.* abklären; aufhellen; ~ *v.i.* sich aufklären.
clarinet *s.* Klarinette *f.*
clarion *s.* Trompete *f.*
clash *v.t.* & *i.* zusammenstoßen; rasseln; widerstreiten; ~ *s.* Stoß *m.;* Geklirr *n.;* Widerspruch *m.;* (*mil.*) Zusammenstoß *m.*
clasp *s.* Haken *m.;* Schnalle *f.;* Spange *f.;* Umarmung *f.;* ~ *v.t.* zuhaken; sich anklammern, umarmen.
class *s.* Klasse *f.;* Gesellschaftsschicht *f.;* Seminar *n.;* ~ *v.t.* klassifizieren.
class-conscious *a.* klassenbewußt.
class consciousness *s.* Klassenbewußtsein *n.*
classic(al) *a.* klassisch; ~ *s.* Klassiker *m.*
classicist *s.* Altphilologe *m.*, Altphilologin *f.*
classifiable *a.* klassifizierbar.
classification *s.* Einteilung in Klassen *f.*
classified *a.* gegliedert, unterteilt; ~ **advertisement** *s.* Kleinanzeige *f.*
classify *v.t.* klassifizieren, einordnen.
classless *a.* klassenlos.
classmate *s.* Klassenkamerad(in) *m.(f.)*
classroom *s.* Klassenzimmer *n.*
class struggle, class war *s.* Klassenkampf *m.*
clatter *v.t.* & *i.* klappern; ~ *s.* Getöse *n.*
clause *s.* Klausel *f.;* (*gram.*) Satzglied *n.*, (Neben-) satz *m.*
claustrophobia *s.* Klaustrophobie *f.*
clavicle *s.* Schlüsselbein *n.*
claw *s.* Klaue, Pfote *f.;* ~ *v.t.* kratzen.
clay *s.* Ton, Lehm *m.;* ~ *v.t.* mit Tonerde mischen, düngen.
clayey, clayish *a.* tonig, lehmig.
clean *a.* rein, sauber, blank; ~ *v.t.* reinigen.
clean-cut *a.* klar (umrissen).
cleaner *s.* Raumpfleger(in) *m.(f.);* Reinigungsmittel *n.*
cleanliness *s.* Sauberkeit *f.*
cleanly *a.* rein, sauber; ~ *adv.* reinlich.
cleanness *s.* Sauberkeit *f.*
cleanse *v.t.* reinigen, scheuern.
cleanser *s.* Reinigungsmittel *n.;* Reinigungscreme *f.*
clean-shaven *a.* glattrasiert.
cleansing cream *s.* Reinigungscreme *f.*
clear *a.*, **~ly** *adv.* klar, rein, hell; deutlich; schuldlos; *in the ~*, vom Verdacht gereinigt; frei; ~ *v.t.* reinigen; aufklären; befreien; abräumen; springen über; ~ *v.i.* hell, frei werden.
clearance *s.* Freilegung, Räumung *f.;* Abfertigung *f.;* Spielraum *m.;* ~ **order** *s.* Räumungsbefehl *m.;* ~ **sale,** Ausverkauf *m.*
clear-cut *a.* klar umrissen; scharf.
clear-headed *a.* klardenkend.
clearing *s.* Lichtung *f.;* Abrechnung *f.*
clear-sighted *a.* scharfsichtig.
cleat *s.* Klampe *f.*
cleavage *s.* Spaltung *f.*
cleave *v.i.* ankleben; ~ *v.t.st.* spalten.
clef *s.* (*mus.*) Schlüssel *m.*
cleft *s.* Spalte *f.;* Kluft *f.;* ~ **palate** *s.* Wolfsrachen *m.*
clemency *s.* Gnade, Milde *f.;* *~ plea, petition for ~*, (*jur.*) Gnadengesuch *n.*
clement *a.* sanft, mild.
clench *v.t.* zusammenpressen; umklammern.
clergy *s.* Geistlichkeit *f.*
clergyman *s.* Geistlicher *m.*
cleric *s.* Kleriker *m.*
clerical error *s.* Schreibfehler *m.*
clerical staff *s.* Büropersonal *n.*
clerk *s.* Angestellter *m.;* Angestellte *f.*
clerkship *s.* Schreiberstelle.
clever *a.*, **~ly** *adv.* gewandt, gescheit.
clew *s.* Knäuel *m.*
cliché *s.* Klischee *n.;* Gemeinplatz *m.*
click *s.* Ticken (einer Uhr) *m.;* Türklinke *f.;* ~ *v.i.* ticken.
client *s.* Klient(in) *m.(f.)*, Kunde *m.*, Kundin *f.;* (*jur.*) Mandant(in) *m.(f.)*
clientele *s.* Klientel *f.*, Kundschaft *f.*
cliff *s.* Klippe *f.*
climacteric *a.* klimakterisch; ~ *s.* Wechseljahre *pl.;* Klimakterium *n.*
climate *s.* Klima *n.*
climatic *a.* klimatisch.
climax *s.* Höhepunkt *m.;* Orgasmus *m.*
climb *v.i.* klettern; ~ *v.t.* ersteigen.
climber *s.* Bergsteiger(in) *m.(f.);* Kletterpflanze *f.*
clinch *v.t.* anpacken; (die Faust) ballen; nieten; befestigen; entscheiden, erledigen; ~ *s.* Vernietung *f.;* Klinke *f.*
cling *v.i.* anklammern, ankleben.
clinic *s.* Klinik *f.*
clinical *a.* klinisch.
clink *v.i.* & t. klingen, klirren; (Gläser) anstoßen; ~ *s.* Geklirr *n.*, Klirren *n.*
clip *v.t.* beschneiden; (Billette) lochen; klammern; ~ *s.* Zwicke *f.;* Hosenklammer *f.*
clipped *a.* abgehackt.
clipper *s.* Schnellsegler *m.*
clipping *s.* Schnipsel *m.*, Ausschnitt *m.*
clique *s.* Clique *f.*, Klüngel *m.*
clitoris *s.* Kitzler *m.*, Klitoris *f.*
cloak *s.* Mantel *m.;* (*fig.*) Deckmantel *m.;* **~room** *s.* Garderobe *f.;* ~ *v.t.* einhüllen; bemänteln.
clock *s.* Uhr *f.;* Schlaguhr *f.;* Wanduhr *f.;* ~ **face** Zifferblatt *n.;* ~ **tower** *s.* Uhrturm *m.*
clockwise *adv.* im Uhrzeigersinn.
clockwork *s.* Uhrwerk *n.*
clod *s.* Erdkloß, Klumpen *m.*
clog *v.t.* verstopfen, blockieren, hemmen; ~ *v.i.* gerinnen; ~ *s.* Hindernis *n.;* Klotz *m.;* Holzschuh *m.*
cloister *s.* Kloster *n.;* Kreuzgang *m.*
clone *s.* Klon *m.;* Kopie *f.;* ~ *v.t.* klonen.
close *v.t.* verschließen; beschließen; vereinigen; *to ~ up*, abschließen; *to ~ down*, (Betrieb) einstellen, stillegen; ~ *v.i.* sich schließen; übereinkommen; ~ *s.* Einzäunung *f.;* Schluß, Beschluß, *m.;* Ruhepunkt *m.;* ~ *a.* verschlossen; verschwiegen; knapp; dicht, steif; bündig; trübe; drückend (Luft); einsam; geizig; ~ **prisoner,** strengbewachter Gefangener *m.;* ~ **quarters,** Handgemenge *n.*
closed season *s.* Schonzeit *f.*
closely *adv.* geschlossen; genau, streng; verborgen; sparsam.
closeness *s.* Nähe, Enge *f.*
closet *s.* Schrank *m.;* Kabinett *n.;* Verschlag *m.;* *water ~*, Klosett *n.* (*W.C.* = *water closet*); ~ *v.t.* einschließen.

close-up *s.* (*film*) Nahaufnahme *f.*; Großaufnahme *f.*
closing *s.* Vertragsabschluß (Hauskauf) *m.*; ~ **date** *s.* Einsendeschluß *m.*; Meldefrist *f.*
closure *s.* Einschließung *f.*; Schließung *f.*; Schluß der Debatte *m.*
clot *a.* Klumpen *m.*; ~ *v.i.* gerinnen; klumpen; *blood* ~ *s.* Blutgerinnsel *n.*
cloth *s.* Zeug, Tuch *n.*; Tischtuch *n.*; Leinwand *f.*; *bound in* ~, in Leinwand gebunden.
clothe *v.t.* bekleiden; ~ *v.i.* sich kleiden.
clothes *s.pl.* Kleider *n.pl.*; Wäsche *f.*
clothes basket *s.* Wäschekorb *m.*
clothes brush *s.* Kleiderbürste *f.*
clothesline *s.* Wäscheleine *f.*
clothespin *s.* Wäscheklammer *f.*
clothing *s.* Kleidung *f.*
cloud *s.* Wolke *f.*; (*fig.*) Gewühl *n.*; ~ *v.t.* bewölken, verdunkeln; ~ *v.* sich umwölken.
cloudburst *s.* Wolkenbruch *m.*
cloudless *a.* unbewölkt.
cloudy *a.*, **cloudily** *adv.* wolkig.
clout *s.* Schlag *m.*; (*fig.*) Einfluß *m.*
clove *s.* Gewürznelke *f.*; ~ **of garlic** *s.* Knoblauchzehe *f.*
cloven *a.* gespalten.
clover *s.* Klee *m.*; (*fig.*) *in* ~, üppig.
clown *s.* Clown, Hanswurst *m.*
clownish *a.*, **~ly** *adv.* bäuerisch, grob.
cloy *v.t.* überladen; sättigen.
club *s.* Keule *f.*; Kreuz, Treff (der Karte) *n.*; Klub *m.*; Verein *m.*; ~ *v.t. & i.* beitragen; sich vereinigen.
club foot *s.* Klumpfuß *m.*
cluck *v.i.* glucken.
clue *s.* Leitfaden *m.*; (*fig.*) Schlüssel *m.*; Anhaltspunkt *m.*
clump *s.* Klumpen *m.*; Gruppe *f.*
clumsy *a.*, **clumsily** *adv.* plump, ungeschickt.
cluster *s.* Büschel *m.*; Traube *f.*; Haufen *m.*; ~ *v.t.* häufen; ~ *v.i.* in Büscheln wachsen.
clutch *v.t.* greifen; packen; umspannen; ~ *s.* Griff *m.*; Kupplung *f.*
clutter *s.* Verwirrung *f.*; ~ *v.i.* verworren rennen.
cm. *centimeter*, Zentimeter.
Co. *Company*, Gesellschaft; *County*, Verwaltungsbezirk.
c/o *care of*, bei, per Adresse, p.A.
coach *s.* Kutsche *f.*; Eisenbahnwagen *m.*; Überlandomnibus *m.*; (*pers.*) Einpauker *m.*; (*Sport*) Trainer *m.*; *a* ~ *and four*, vierspännige Kutsche *f.*; ~ *v.t.* einpauken; trainieren.
coachman *s.* Kutscher *m.*
coachtour *s.* Omnibusreise *f.*
coadjutor *s.* Mitgehilfe *m.*
coagulate *v.t.* gerinnen machen; ~ *v.i.* gerinnen.
coal *s.* Kohle *f.*; ~ *v.i.* zu Kohle werden; Kohlen einnehmen.
coal dust *s.* Kohlenstaub *m.*
coalesce *v.i.* verschmelzen.
coalfield *s.* Kohlenlager *n.*; Kohlenfeld *n.*
coalition *s.* Vereinigung *f.*
coal mine, coal pit *s.* Kohlengrube *f.*
coarse *a.*, **~ly** *adv.* grob, gemein.
coast *s.* Küste *f.*; ~ *v.i.* längs der Küste hinfahren; einen Abhang hinabfahren.
coastal *a.* Küsten...
coaster *s.* Untersetzer *m.*; *roller* ~, *s.* Achterbahn *f.*
coat *s.* Mantel, Rock *m.*; Fell, *n.*; Schicht *f.*; ~ **of arms,** Wappenschild *n.*; ~ **of mail,** Panzerhemd *n.*; ~ *v.t.* bekleiden.
coated *a.* überzogen, bedeckt; belegt (Zunge).
coating *s.* Schicht *f.*; Anstrich *m.*
co-author *s.* Mitautor(in) *m.(f.)*
coax *v.t.* überreden, beschwatzen.
cob *s.* Kolben *m.*
cobalt *s.* Kobalt *m.*
cobble *s.* Kopfstein, Pflasterstein *m.*; ~ *v.t.*, flicken; pflastern.
cobbler *s.* Schuster *m.*
cobra *s.* Kobra *f.*
cobweb *s.* Spinngewebe *n.*
cocaine *s.* Kokain *n.*
cock *s.* Hahn *m.*; Männchen *n.*; (*vulg.*) Penis *m.*; ~ *v.t.* (den Hahn) spannen; aufstellen; ~ *v.i.* stolzieren.
cockade *s.* Kokarde *f.*
cock-a-doodle-doo kikeriki!
Cockaigne *s.* Schlaraffenland *n.*
cockatoo *s.* Kakadu *m.*
cockatrice *s.* Basilisk *m.*
cockchafer *s.* Maikäfer *m.*
cocked *a.* ~ **hat** *s.* dreieckiger Hut *m.*
cockerel *s.* junger Hahn *m.*
cock-eyed *a.* schief.
cockfight *s.* Hahnenkampf *m.*
cockle *v.t.* runzeln; ~ *s.* Herzmuschel *f.*
cockney *s.* Londoner *m.*
cockpit *s.* (*avi.*) Führersitz *m.*, Cockpit *n.*
cockroach *s.* Schabe *f.*
cocksure *a.* todsicher.
cocktail *s.* Cocktail *m.*
coco *s.* Kokospalme *f.*
cocoa *s.* Kakao *m.*
coconut *s.* Kokosnuß *f.*
cocoon *s.* Seidenraupenpuppe *f.*, Kokon *m.*
cod *s.* Kabeljau *m.*; **~-liver oil,** Lebertran *m.*
C.O.D. *cash on delivery*, per Nachnahme.
coddle *v.t.* verhätscheln.
code *s.* Gesetzbuch *n.*; (Telegramm) Schlüssel *m.*; Chiffre *f.*; ~ **of civil procedure,** Zivilprozeßordnung *f.*; ~ **of criminal procedure,** Strafprozeßordnung *f.*; *commercial* ~, Handelsgesetzbuch *n.*; ~ **name** *s.* Deckname *m.*; ~ *v.t.* chiffrieren.
codicil *s.* Kodizill *n.*
codification *s.* Kodifizierung *f.*
codify *v.t.* kodifizieren.
coeducation *s.* Koedukation *f.*
coefficient *a.* mitwirkend; ~ *s.* Koeffizient *m.*
coerce *v.t.st.* zwingen.
coercion *s.* Zwang *m.*
coercive *a.* zwingend, Zwangs...
coeval *a.* gleichalt, gleichzeitig.
coexist *v.i.* zugleich da sein; koexistieren.
coexistent *a.* gleichzeitig.
coffee *s.* Kaffee *m.*
coffee bean *s.* Kaffeebohne *f.*
coffee grinder *s.* Kaffeemühle.
coffee grounds *s.pl.* Kaffeesatz *m.*
coffeepot *s.* Kaffeekanne *f.*

coffee roaster *s.* Kaffeebrenner *m.*
coffee shop *s.* Imbißraum *m.*
coffee table *s.* Couchtisch *m.*
coffin *s.* Sarg *m.*
cog *s.* Zahn (am Rad) *m.*
cogency *s.* zwingende Kraft *f.*
cogent *a.*, **~ly** *adv.* zwingend, triftig.
cogitate *v.i.* denken, erwägen.
cognate *a.* verwandt.
cognition *s.* (Er)kenntnis *f.*
cognizance *s.* Kenntnis *f.*
cognizant *a.* wissend.
cogwheel *s.* Zahnrad, Kammrad *n.*
cohabit *v.i.* bei(sammen)wohnen.
cohabitation *s.* (eheliche) Beiwohnung *f.*; Beisammenwohnen *n.*
coheir *s.* Miterbe *m.*
coheiress *s.* Miterbin *f.*
cohere *v.i.* zusammenhängen; zusammenhalten.
coherence *s.* Zusammenhang *m.*
coherent *s.* zusammenhängend.
cohesion *s.* Kohäsion *f.*; Zusammenhang *m.*
cohesive *a.* zusammenhaltend.
cohort *s.* Kohorte *f.*
coil *v.t.* aufwickeln; ~ *s.* (Draht) Rolle, *f.*; Windung *f.*; Schlinge *f.*
coin *s.* Münze *f.*; *false* ~, falsches Geld *n.*; ~ *v.t.* münzen; erdichten; prägen.
coinage *s.* Geld *n.*; Gepräge *n.*
coincide *v.i.* zusammentreffen.
coincidence *s.* Zusammentreffen *n.*; Zufall *m.*
coincident *a.* übereinstimmend; zusammentreffend.
coincidental *a.* zufällig.
coincidentally *adv.* zufälligerweise.
coitus *s.* Koitus *m.*, Beischlaf *m.*
coke *s.* Koks *m.*
Col. *Colonel,* Oberst.
col. *column,* Spalte, Sp.
colander *s.* Sieb *n.*
cold *a.*, **~ly** *adv.* kalt; ~ *s.* Kälte, Erkältung *f.*; *to catch a* ~, sich erkälten, einen Schnupfen bekommen.
coldness *s.* Kälte *f.*
cold storage *s.* Kühllagerung *f.*
coleslaw *s.* Krautsalat *m.*
colic *s.* Bauchkrampf *m.*, Kolik *f.*
collaborate *v.i.* zusammenarbeiten.
collaboration *s.* Mitarbeiterschaft *f.*
collaborator *s.* Mitarbeiter(in) *m.(f.)*
collapse *v.i.* zusammenfallen; ~ *s.* Zusammenbruch *m.*
collapsible *a.* zusammenlegbar, zusammenklappbar; ~ **boat** *s.* Faltboot *n.*
collar *s.* Halsband *n.*; Kragen *m.*; ~ **bone** *s.* Schlüsselbein *n.*; ~ *v.t.* beim Kragen fassen.
collate *v.t.* vergleichen; verleihen; zusammenstellen (Daten).
collateral *a.*, **~ly** *adv.* Seiten..., neben; gleichlaufend; ~ *s.* Sicherheiten (Anleihe) *pl.*; **~s** *s.pl.* Seitenverwandte *m.*
colleague *s.* Kollege *m.*, Kollegin *f.*
collect *v.t.* sammeln; einkassieren; ~ *s.* Kollekte *f.*
collected *a.* ruhig, gefaßt.
collection *s.* Sammlung *f.*; Abholung *f.*; Leerung der Briefkästen *f.*
collective *a.* gesammelt; Kollektiv...; ~ **agreement,** Tarifvertrag *m.*; ~ **security,** kollektive Sicherheit *f.*
collector *s.* Sammler *m.*
college *s.* Kollegium *n.*; höhere Lehranstalt *f.*, College *n.*
collide *v.i.* zusammenstoßen (von Schiffen etc.).
collier *s.* Kohlenarbeiter *m.*; Kohlenschiff *n.*
colliery *s.* Kohlenbergwerk *n.*; Zeche *f.*
collision *s.* Zusammenstoß *m.*
collocation *s.* Stellung, Ordnung *f.*
colloquial *a.* umgangssprachlich; in der Umgangssprache üblich.
colloquialism *s.* Ausdruck der Umgangssprache *m.*
colloquy *s.* Gespräch *n.*; Kolloquium *n.*
collusion *s.* heimliches Einverständnis *n.*; Verdunkelung *f.*
Colombia *s.* Kolumbien *n.*
Colombian *a.* kolumbianisch; ~ *s.* Kolumbianer(in) *m.(f.)*
colon *s.* Doppelpunkt *m.*; (*anat.*) Dickdarm *m.*
colonel *s.* Oberst *m.*
colonelcy *s.* Oberstenstelle *f.*
colonial *a.* Kolonial...; kolonial.
colonialism *s.* Kolonialismus *m.*
colonist *s.* Kolonist(in), Siedler(in) *m.(f.)*
colonization *s.* Kolonisierung *f.*
colonize *v.t.* besiedeln, kolonisieren.
colonnade *s.* Säulengang *m.*
colony *s.* Kolonie *f.*
colophony *s.* Geigenharz *n.*
color *s.* Farbe *f.*; Schein *m.*; Vorwand *m.*; **~s** *pl.* Fahne *f.*; *to show a person in his true* ~*s*, jemand nach dem Leben malen; ~ *v.t.* färben; beschönigen; ~ *v.i.* erröten.
coloration *s.* Färbung *f.*
color-blind *a.* farbenblind.
color-box *s.* Malkasten *m.*
coloring *s.* Färben, Beschönigen *n.*
colorless *a.* farblos.
colors *s.pl.* Fahne *f.*; *with the* ~*s*, bei der Wehrmacht.
colossal *a.* kolossal, riesig.
colossus *s.* Koloß *m.*
colt *s.* Füllen *n.*; (*fig.*) Wildfang *m.*
columbine *s.* (*bot.*) Akelei *f.*
column *s.* Säule *f.*; (*print.*) Spalte *f.*; Kolonne *f.*
columnar *a.* säulenförmig.
columnist *s.* Kommentator(in) (in der Presse) *m.(f.)*; Kolumnist(in) *m.(f.)*
coma *s.* Koma *n.*
comb *s.* Kamm *m.*; Striegel *m.*; ~ *v.t.* kämmen, striegeln.
combat *s.* Kampf *m.*; Gefecht *n.*; *single* ~, Zweikampf *m.*; ~ *v.i.* kämpfen; ~ *v.t.* bekämpfen.
combatant *s.* Kombattant *m.*; Kämpfer *m.*
combative *a.* streitsüchtig.
combed *a.* gekämmt.
combination *s.* Verbindung *f.*
combine *v.t.* verbinden; (*mil.*) *combined operations,* Operationen der verbundenen Waffen; ~ *v.i.st.* sich verbinden; ~ *s.* Zusammenschluß, Verband, Konzern *m.*; Mähdrescher *m.*
combined *a.* vereint.

combustible *a.* brennbar; ~ *s.* Brennmaterial *n.*
combustion *s.* Verbrennung *f.*
come *v.t.st.* kommen; werden; *to ~ about,* sich wenden; sich zutragen; *to ~ by,* etwas bekommen; vorbeikommen; *to ~ for,* holen kommen, kommen um...; *to ~ off,* zustande kommen; davonkommen; loskommen; *to ~ of age,* mündig werden; *to ~ round,* sich anders besinnen; sich erholen; *to ~ to pass,* geschehen, sich ereignen.
comeback *s.* Comeback *n.*
comedian *s.* Komödiant *m.*
comedienne *s.* Komikerin *f.*
comedown *s.* Abstieg *m.*
comedy *s.* Komödie *f.*, Lustspiel *n.*
comely *a.* hübsch; artig.
comestibles *pl.* Nahrungsmittel *n.pl.*
comet *s.* Komet *m.*
comfort *v.t.* trösten; erquicken; ~ *s.* Trost *m.;* Erquickung *f.;* Bequemlichkeit *f.;* Behaglichkeit *f.; cold ~,* schwacher Trost *m.*
comfortable *a.,* **~bly** *adv.* tröstlich, erfreulich; bequem, behaglich.
comforter *s.* Tröster *m.;* Deckbett *n.*
comforting *a.* beruhigend; tröstend.
comfortless *a.* trostlos; unbequem.
comic(al) *a.,* **~ly** *adv.* komisch; ~ **strip** *s.,* **comics** *s.pl.* Comics *pl.*
comma *s.* Komma *n.; inverted ~,* Anführungszeichen *n.*
command *v.t. & i.* befehlen; anführen, herrschen; bestellen; ~ *s.* Befehl *m.;* Beherrschung *f.;* Herrschaft *f.;* Bestellung *f.*
commandant *s.* Befehlshaber *m.*
commandeer *v.t.* requirieren.
commander *s.* Befehlshaber *m.;* (*nav.*) Fregattenkapitän *m.;* Handramme *f.;* **~-in-chief,** Oberbefehlshaber *m.*
commanding *a.* gebieterisch, imposant.
commandment *s.* Befehl *m.;* Gebot *n.*
commando *s.* Kommando *n.;* Kommandotrupp *m.*
commemorate *v.t.* feiern, gedenken.
commemoration *s.* Gedächtnisfeier *f.*
commemorative *a.* erinnernd, Erinnerungs...
commence *v.t. & i.* anfangen; beginnen.
commencement *s.* Anfang *m.*
commend *v.t.* empfehlen, loben.
commendable *a.,* **~bly** *adv.* empfehlenswert.
commendation *s.* Lob *n.;* Belobigung *f.;* Auszeichnung *f.*
commendatory *a.* empfehlend.
commensurable *a.* kommensurabel.
commensurate *a.,* **~ly** *adv.* entsprechend; angemessen.
comment *v.i.* erläutern, auslegen; ~ *s.* Auslegung *f.;* **~s** *s.pl.* Bemerkungen *f.pl.;* Stellungnahme *f.*
commentary *s.* Kommentar *m.*
commentate *v.i.* kommentieren.
commentator *s.* Kommentator(in), Reporter(in) *m.(f.)*
commerce *s.* Handel, Verkehr *m.;* Gewerbe *n.*
commercial *a.* kaufmännisch, Handels...; ~ **directory,** Handelsadreßbuch *n.;* ~ **law,** Handelsrecht *n.;* ~ **papers** *s.pl.* Geschäftspapiere *n.pl.* (Post); ~ **traveler,** Handlungsreisender *m.;* ~ **treaty,** Handelsvertrag *m.*
commercialize *v.t.* kommerzialisieren.
commingle *v.t. & i.* vermischen.
commiserate *v.t.* bemitleiden.
commiseration *s.* Mitgefühl *n.;* Teilnahme *f.*
commission *s.* Auftrag *m.;* Vollmacht *f.;* Ausschuß *m.;* Begehung (von Sünden) *f.;* Offizierspatent *n.;* Provision *f.;* ~ *v.t.* einen Auftrag geben, bevollmächtigen; in Dienst stellen.
commissioner *s.* Bevollmächtigter, Kommissar *m.*, Kommissionsmitglied *n.*
commit *v.t.* begehen; übergeben, anvertrauen; verüben; verpflichten, festlegen; (*mil.*) einsetzen (Truppen); *to ~ oneself,* sich binden; *to ~ to prison,* einsperren.
commitment *s.* Verpflichtung *f.;* (*mil.*) Einsatz *m.; without any ~,* unverbindlich.
committee *s.* Ausschuß *m.; to be on the ~,* dem Ausschuß angehören.
commodity *s.* Ware *f.*
commodore *s.* Kommodore *m.*
common *a.,* **~ly** *adv.* gemein, gewöhnlich; gemeinschaftlich; ~ **law,** Gewohnheitsrecht *n.;* ~ **room,** Konversationszimmer *m.;* ~ **time** *s.* (*mus.*) gerader Takt *m.;* ~ *s.* Gemeindeweide *f.;* **~s** *pl.* Gemeinen *m.pl.;* Volk *n.;* Kost *f.; House of Commons,* Unterhaus (in England) *n.*
commoner *s.* Bürgerliche *m.*
commonplace *a.* gewöhnlich.
common sense *s.* gesunder Menschenverstand *m.*
common stock *s.* Stammaktien *f.pl.*
Commonwealth *s.* Commonwealth *m.*
commotion *s.* Erschütterung *f.;* Aufruhr *m.*
communal *a.* Gemeinde...
commune *s.* Gemeinde *f.;* Kommune *f.*
communicable *a.* mitteilbar.
communicate *v.t.* mitteilen; ~ *v.i.* Gemeinschaft haben; kommunizieren.
communication *s.* Mitteilung *f.;* Umgang *m.;* Verbindung *f.;* **~s satellite** *s.* Nachrichtensatellit *m.*
communicative *s.* mitteilsam.
communion *s.* Gemeinschaft *f.;* Umgang *m.;* Abendmahl *n.*
communiqué *s.* Kommuniqué *n.*
communism *s.* Kommunismus *m.*
communist *s.* Kommunist *m.*
community *s.* Gemeinschaft, Gemeinde *f.;* Allgemeinheit *f.;* Staat *m.;* ~ **of goods,** (*jur.*) Gütergemeinschaft *f.*
community center *s.* Gemeinschaftszentrum *n.*
community service *s.* (freiwilliger) sozialer Dienst.
commutable *a.* vertauschbar.
commutation *s.* Vertauschung *f.;* Auswechslung *f.;* ~ **of a sentence,** (*jur.*) Strafumwandlung *f.*
commute *v.t.* täglich in die Stadt fahren, pendeln; umtauschen, auswechseln; ersetzen; (*jur.*) (Strafe) umwandeln od. mildern.
commuter *s.* Pendler(in) *m.(f.)*
compact *s.* Vertrag *m.;* ~ *a.,* **~ly** *adv.* dicht, gedrängt, bündig; ~ *v.t.st.* festverbinden.
compact disk *s.* Compact Disc *f.;* Kompaktschallplatte *f.*
companion *s.* Gefährte *m.*, Gefährtin *f.*
companionable *a.,* **~bly** *adv.* gesellig, umgänglich.
companionship *s.* Gesellschaft *f.*
company *s.* Gesellschaft *f.;* (*mil.*) Kompanie; Zunft *f.;* Trupp *m.*

comparable *a.*, **~bly** *adv.* vergleichbar; vergleichsweise.
comparative *a.*, **~ly** *adv.* vergleichend; verhältnismäßig; ~ *s.* (*gram.*) Komparativ *m.*
compare *v.t.* vergleichen.
comparison *s.* Vergleich *m.*
compartment *s.* Abteilung *f.*; Fach *n.*; (*rail.*) Abteil *n.*
compass *v.t.* umgeben, einschließen; erreichen; ~ *s.* Bereich *m.*; Umfang *m.*; Kompaß *m.*; (*pair of*) *~es pl.* Zirkel *m.*
compassion *s.* Mitleid *n.*
compassionate *a.* mitfühlend; ~ **leave** *s.* Familienurlaub *m.*
compatibility *s.* Vereinbarkeit *f.*
compatible *a.*, **~bly** *adv.* vereinbar.
compatriot *s.* Landsmann *m.*, Landsmännin *f.*
compeer *s.* Genosse, Gevatter *m.*
compel *v.t.* zwingen, nötigen.
compelling *a.* bezwingend.
compendium *s.* Auszug *m.*; Kompendium *n.*
compensate *v.t.* ersetzen, entschädigen.
compensation *s.* Ersatz *m.*; Entschädigung *f.*; (*elek.*) Ausgleich *m.*; *to make ~ for,* Entschädigung leisten für...
compensatory *a.* ausgleichend.
compete *v.i. v.r.* mitbewerben, konkurrieren.
competence, competency *s.* behagliches Auskommen *n.*; Befugnis, Kompetenz *f.*; Befähigung *f.*
competent *a.* hinlänglich; kompetent.
competition *s.* Mitbewerbung, Konkurrenz *f.*; Preisausschreiben *n.*; Wettbewerb *m.*; *unfair ~,* unlauterer Wettbewerb *m.*
competitive *a.* wetteifernd; Konkurrenz...; ~ **price,** konkurrenzfähiger Preis *m.*
competitor *s.* Mitbewerber(in), Konkurrent(in) *m.(f.)*
compilation *s.* Zusammenstellung *f.*
compile *v.t.* zusammentragen; zusammenstellen.
compiler *s.* Kompilator(in) *m.(f.)*
complacence, complacency *s.* Wohlgefallen *n.*; Selbstgefälligkeit *f.*
complacent *a.* gefällig, selbstzufrieden.
complain *v.i. & r.* beklagen.
complainant *s.* Beschwerdeführer(in) *m.(f.)*
complaint *s.* Beschwerde *f.*; Klage *f.*; *to lodge a ~,* eine Beschwerde einlegen.
complaisance *s.* Nachgiebigkeit *f.*
complaisant *a.* gefällig, höflich.
complement *s.* Ergänzung *f.*; volle Zahl *f.*, volle Besetzung *f.*; ~ *v.t.* vervollständigen.
complementary *a.* ergänzend.
complete *a.*, **~ly** *adv.* vollständig, vollendet; gänzlich; ~ *v.t.* vervollständigen, ergänzen; *to ~ a form,* ein Formular ausfüllen.
completion *s.* Ergänzung *f.*; Vollendung *f.*
complex *s.* Komplex *m.*; *a.*, **~ly** *adv.* zusammengesetzt, verwickelt.
complexion *s.* Aussehen *n.*; Gesichtsfarbe *f.*
complexity *s.* Verwickeltheit, Kompliziertheit *f.*
compliance *s.* Willfährigkeit *f.*; Einwilligung *f.*; Unterwürfigkeit *f.*
compliant *a.*, **~ly** *adv.* willfährig; unterwürfig.
complicate *v.t.* verwickeln.
complicated *a.* kompliziert, verwickelt.
complication *s.* Verwicklung *f.*
complicity *s.* Mitschuld *f.*
compliment *s.* Kompliment *n.*; **~s** *pl.* Gruß *m.*; ~ *v.t.* grüßen; beglückwünschen; einem Komplimente machen.
complimentary *a.* höflich; ~ **dinner,** Festessen *n.*
comply *v.i. & r.* fügen; *to ~ with* (Gesetze) befolgen.
component *s.* Bestandteil *m.*; ~ *a.* Teil...
compose *v.t.* zusammensetzen, verfassen; komponieren; (*print.*) setzen; beruhigen, ordnen; schlichten, beilegen; *to ~ oneself, v.r.* fassen, *v.r.* beruhigen.
composed *a.*, **~ly** *adv.* ruhig, gesetzt.
composer *s.* Komponist(in) *m.(f.)*
composite *a.* zusammengesetzt.
composition *s.* Zusammensetzung *f.*; Aufsatz *m.*; Schriftsatz *m.*; Tonsatz *m.*; Komposition *f.*
compositor *s.* Schriftsetzer(in) *m.(f.)*
compost *s.* Dünger *m.*; ~ *v.t.* düngen; ~ **heap,** ~ **pile** *s.* Komposthaufen *m.*
composure *s.* Gemütsruhe, Fassung *f.*
compote *s.* Kompott *n.*
compound *v.t.* zusammensetzen; beilegen; ~ *v.i. v.r.* vergleichen; ~ *a.* zusammengesetzt; ~ **eye** *s.* Facettenauge *n.*; ~ **interest** *s.* Zinseszins *m.*; ~ **fraction** *s.* (*math.*) Doppelbruch *m.*; ~ **fracture** *s.* (*med.*) komplizierter Bruch *m.*; ~ **word** *s.* zusammengesetztes Wort *n.*; ~ *s.* Mischung *f.*; (*chem.*) Verbindung *f.*; Zusammensetzung *f.*; Einzäunung *f.*, Gelände *n.*
comprehend *v.t.* zusammenfassen; begreifen.
comprehensible *a.*, **~bly** *adv.* begreiflich, verständlich.
comprehension *s.* Verständnis *n.*; Fassungskraft *f.*; Umfang *m.*
comprehensive *a.*, **~ly** *adv.* umfassend; gedrängt.
compress *v.t.* zusammendrücken.
compressed air s. Druck-, Preßluft *f.*
compressible *a.* zusammendrückbar.
compression *s.* Zusammendrückung *f.*, Kompression *f.*
compressor *s.* (*mot.*) Kompressor, Verdichter *m.*
comprise *v.t.* in *v.r.* fassen, enthalten.
compromise *s.* Kompromiß *n.*; ~ *v.t.* durch Vergleich beilegen; *to ~ oneself, v.r.* kompromittieren.
compulsion *s.* Zwang *m.*
compulsory *a.*, **~ily** *adv.* Zwangs...
compunction *s.* Gewissensangst *f.*
computation *s.* Berechnung *f.*
compute *v.t.* rechnen, berechnen.
computer *s.* Computer *m.*
computerize *v.t.* computerisieren.
computer: ~-operated *a.* computergesteuert; ~ **program** *s.* Computerprogramm *n.*; ~ **programmer** *s.* Programmierer(in) *m.(f.)*
comrade *s.* Gefährte *m.*, Gefährtin *f.*; Kamerad(in) *m.(f.)*
comradeship *s.* Kameradschaft *f.*
con *v.t.* ~ *adv. pro and ~,* für und wider; ~ *s.* Gegenstimme *f.*; ~ **man** Hochstapler(in) *m.(f.)*; Betrüger(in) *m.(f.)*
concatenation *s.* Verkettung *f.*
concave *a.*, **~ly** *adv.* hohlrund, konkav.
concavity *s.* Hohlrundung *f.*
conceal *v.t.* verhehlen.

concealed *a.* verdeckt; ~ **lighting** indirekte Beleuchtung *f.*
concealment *s.* Verheimlichung *f.;* Verbergen *n.*
concede *v.t.* einräumen, gestatten.
conceit *s.* Einbildung *f.*, Dünkel *m.;* Witzelei *f.*
conceited *a.* eingebildet, dünkelhaft.
conceivable *a.*, **~bly** *adv.* denkbar.
conceive *v.t.* & *i.* begreifen; erdenken; meinen; empfangen, schwanger werden.
concentrate *v.t.* zusammenziehen, konzentrieren.
concentration *s.* Zusammenziehung, Konzentrierung *f.;* **~camp** Konzentrationslager *n.*
concentric *a.* konzentrisch.
concept *s.* Begriff *m.*
conception *s.* Empfängnis *f.;* Auffassung *f.;* Begriff *m.;* Meinung *f.*
conceptual *a.* begrifflich.
concern *v.t.* betreffen; beunruhigen; *to ~ oneself about,* sich kümmern um; ~ *s.* Angelegenheit *f.;* Belang *m.;* Unternehmen *n.;* Anteil *m.;* Unruhe *f.;* Geschäft *n.*
concerned *p.* & *a.* bekümmert; interessiert; *those ~,* die Beteiligten *m.pl.*
concerning *pr.* betreffend.
concert *s.* Einverständnis *n.;* *(mus.)* Konzert *n.;* *in ~,* gemeinsam, zusammen.
concerted *a.* gemeinsam; ~ **action** *s.* gemeinsames Vorgehen *n.;* konzertierte Aktion *f.*
concert-goer *s.* Konzertbesucher(in) *m.(f.)*
concert hall *s.* Konzertsaal *m.*
concertina *s.* Ziehharmonika *f.*
concerto *s.*, **concerti** *pl.* *(mus.)* Konzert *n.*
concert pianist *s.* Konzertpianist(in) *m.(f.)*
concert pitch *s.* Kammerton *m.*
concession *s.* Zugeständnis *n.;* Konzession *f.*
concessionnaire *s.* Konzessionär *m.*
conciliate *v.t.* versöhnen; ausgleichen.
conciliation *s.* Versöhnung *f.;* **~board,** Schlichtungsamt *n.;* **~proceedings** *s.pl.* *(jur.)* Sühneverfahren *n.*
conciliator *s.* Vermittler *m.*
conciliatory *a.* vermittelnd, versöhnlich.
concise *a.*, **~ly** *adv.* kurz, gedrängt.
conclave *s.* Konklave *n.;* geheime Beratung *f.*
conclude *v.t.* & *i.* folgern, schließen; sich entschließen; beschließen.
conclusion *s.* Schluß *m.;* Beschluß *m.;* Ende *n.;* Folgerung *f.;* Abschluß (eines Vertrags) *m.*
conclusive *a.*, **~ly** *adv.* entscheidend; endgültig; schlüssig, überzeugend.
concoct *v.t.* schmieden, anzetteln.
concoction *s.* Gebräu *n.;* Ausbrütung *f.*
concomitant *a.*, **~ly** *adv.* begleitend.
concord *s.* Eintracht *f.;* *(gram.)* Übereinstimmung *f.*
concordance *s.* Übereinstimmung *f.;* Konkordanz *f.*
concordant *a.* übereinstimmend.
concordat *s.* Konkordat *n.*
concourse *s.* Zusammenfluß *m.;* Menge *f.*, Auflauf *m.*
concrete *v.i.* sich verdichten; **~ly** *adv.* konkret, bestimmt; ~ *s.* Beton *m.*
concubine *s.* Konkubine *n.*
concupiscence *s.* Begierde, Wollust *f.*
concur *v.i.* zusammentreffen; übereinstimmen; mitwirken.
concurrence *s.* Zusammentreffen *n.;* Mitwirkung *f.;* Einverständnis *n.*
concurrent *a.* mitwirkend; begleitend; übereinstimmend.
concuss *v.t.* *to be ~ed* eine Gehirnerschütterung haben.
concussion *s.* Erschütterung *f.;* *(med.)* Prellung *f.;* Quetschung *f.*
condemn *v.t.* verdammen, verurteilen; tadeln; verwerfen; (Ware) beschlagnahmen, (Ware) für untauglich erklären.
condemnation *s.* Verurteilung *f.*
condemnatory *a.* verdammend.
condensation *s.* Verdichtung *f.;* Kurzfassung *f.;* Kondensation *f.*
condense *v.t.* verdichten; einen Auszug machen von; ~ *v.i.* sich verdichten.
condensed milk *s.* kondensierte Milch *f.*
condenser *s.* Kondensator (Dampfmaschine od. elek.) *m.*
condescend *v.t.* sich herablassen; **~ingly** *adv.* herablassend.
condescension *s.* Herablassung *f.*
condign *a.* gehörig, verdient.
condiment *s.* Gewürz *n.*
condition *s.* Zustand *m.;* Beschaffenheit *f.;* Bedingung *f.;* Stand *m.;* Stellung *f.;* ~ *v.t.* bedingen; *(mech.)* in guten Zustand bringen (Maschinen usw.)
conditional (on) *a.* bedingt (durch).
conditionally *adv.* bedingungsweise, unter Bedingungen.
conditioned *a.* bedingt; abhängig; konditioniert.
condole *v.t.* & *i.* Beileid bezeigen.
condolence *s.* Beileid *n.*
condom *s.* Kondom *n.*
condominium *s.* Appartementhaus *n.;* Eigentumswohnung *f.*
condone *v.t.* vergeben, verzeihen.
conduce *v.i.* dienlich sein, fördern.
conducive *a.* förderlich, behilflich.
conduct *s.* Führung *f.;* Geleit *n.;* Aufführung *f.;* Verwaltung *f.;* ~ *v.t.* führen; verwalten; *(mus.)* dirigieren; *(phys.)* leiten; *to ~ onself,* sich aufführen; *conducted tour s.* Gesellschaftsreise *f.*
conductivity *s.* *(elek.)* Leitfähigkeit *f.*
conductor *s.* Schaffner, Kondukteur *m.;* Leiter *m.;* *(mus.)* Dirigent *m.*
conduit *s.* Röhre *f.;* Wasserleitung *f.*
cone *s.* Kegel *m.;* Tannenzapfen *m.*
confabulation *s.* vertrauliches Gespräch *n.*
confection *s.* Zuckerwerk *n.;* Konfekt *n.*
confectionary *s.* Zuckerwerk *n.;* Konditorei *f.*
confectioner *s.* Konditor *m.*
confederacy *s.* Bündnis *n.*
confederate *v.t.* & *i.* (sich) verbünden; ~ *a.* verbündet; ~ *s.* Bundesgenosse *m.*
confederation *s.* Bündnis *n.;* Bund *m.*
confer *v.t.* vergleichen; verleihen; ~ *v.i.* verhandeln.
conference *s.* Verhandlung, Beratschlagung *f.;* Konferenz *f.*
confess *v.t.* & *i.* bekennen, gestehen; beichten; kundgeben.

confession *s.* Geständnis *n.;* Bekenntnis *n.;* Beichte *f.*
confessional *s.* Beichtstuhl *m.*
confessor *s.* Bekenner *m.;* Beichtvater *m.*
confidant *s.* Vertraute *m./f.*
confide *v.t.* & *i.* anvertrauen; vertrauen.
confidence *s.* Vertrauen *n.;* Zuversicht *f.;* ~ **game** *s.* Trickbetrug *m.;* ~**-trickster** *s.* Hochstapler *m.*
confident *a.,* **~ly** *adv.* vertrauend.
confidential *a.,* **~ly** *adv.* vertraulich.
confidentiality *s.* Vertraulichkeit *f.*
configuration *s.* Gestaltung, Bildung *f.*
confine *s.* Grenze *f.;* ~ *v.t.* begrenzen; beschränken; einsperren; *to be confined,* in den Wochen liegen; *confined to barracks,* unter Kasernenarrest.
confinement *s.* Haft *f.;* Wochenbett *n.;* Niederkunft *f.; solitary* ~, Einzelhaft *f.*
confirm *v.t.* bestätigen, bewähren; einsegnen, konfirmieren.
confirmation *s.* Bestätigung *f.;* Konfirmation *f.;* Firmung *f.*
confirmatory *a.* bekräftigend.
confirmed *a.* unverbesserlich; eingefleischt.
confiscate *v.t.* beschlagnahmen.
confiscation *s.* Beschlagnahme *f.*
conflict *s.* Kampf *m.,* Streit *m.,* Konflikt *m.;* ~ *v.i.* kämpfen; widerstreiten.
conflicting *a.* widersprüchlich.
confluence *s.* Zusammenfluß *m.*
confluent *a.* zusammenfließend.
conform *v.t.* gleichförmig machen; ~ *v.i.* sich richten.
conformable *a.,* **~bly** *adv.* übereinstimmend.
conformism *s.* Anpassung *f.;* Konformismus *m.*
conformist *s.* Konformist(in) *m.(f.)*
conformity *s.* Übereinstimmung *f.;* Konformität *f.; in* ~ *with,* gemäß; gleichlaufend.
confound *v.t.* verwirren; verwechseln; zerstören.
confounded *a.* bestürzt; verwünscht.
confront *v.t.* & *i.* gegenüberstellen; gegenüberstehen.
confrontation *s.* Gegenüberstellung *f.;* Konfrontation *f.*
confuse *v.t.* verwirren; verwechseln.
confused *a.,* **~ly** *adv.* verworren.
confusion *s.* Verwirrung *f.;* Verwechslung *f.*
confutation *s.* Widerlegung *f.*
confute *v.t.* widerlegen.
congeal *v.t.* zum Gefrieren bringen; gerinnen lassen; ~ *v.i.* gefrieren.
congenial *a.* sympathisch, zusagend; geistesverwandt.
congenital *a.* angeboren.
congeries *s.* Masse *f.;* Gemenge *n.*
congest *v.t.* verstopfen.
congested *a.* überfüllt (Straßenverkehr, Bevölkerung); *(med.)* mit Blut überfüllt.
congestion *s.* Überfüllung *f.;* Blutandrang *m.;* Stauung *f.*
conglomeration *s.* Zusammenhäufung *f.*
congratulate (on) *v.t.* & *i.* gratulieren, Glück wünschen (zu).
congratulations *s.* Glückwunsch *m.*
congratulatory *a.* beglückwünschend.
congregate *v.t.* & *i.* (sich) versammeln.
congregation *s.* Gemeinde *f.*
congress *s.* Kongreß *m.*
congressional *a.* Kongress...
congressman *s.* Kongreßabgeordneter *m.*
congresswoman *s.* Kongreßabgeordnete *f.*
congruence *s.* Übereinstimmung *f.*
congruent *a.* übereinstimmend.
congruity *s.* Übereinstimmung *f.*
congruous *a.,* **~ly** *adv.* übereinstimmend, angemessen.
conic(al), *a.,* **~ly** *adv.* konisch; kegelförmig; ~ **section** *s.* Kegelschnitt *m.*
conifer *s.* Nadelbaum *m.*
coniferous *a.* Nadelholz...
conjectural *a.,* **~ly** *adv.* mutmaßlich.
conjecture *s.* Mutmaßung *f.;* ~ *v.t.* mutmaßen.
conjoin *v.t.* & *i.* verbinden.
conjoint *a.,* **~ly** *adv.* vereinigt.
conjugal *a.,* **~ly** *adv.* ehelich.
conjugate *v.t.* konjugieren.
conjugation *s.* Konjugation *f.*
conjunction *s.* Verbindung *f.;* Bindewort *n.;* Konjunktion *f.*
conjunctiva *s.* Bindehaut *f.*
conjunctive *a.,* **~ly** *adv.* verbindend; ~ *s. (gram.)* Konjunktiv *m.*
conjunctivitis *s.* Bindehautentzündung *f.*
conjuncture *s.* Zusammentreffen *n.*
conjuration *s.* Beschwörung *f.*
conjure *v.t.* & *i.* beschwören; bezaubern; zaubern; bannen.
conjurer *s.* Zauberer *m.;* Taschenspieler *m.*
connect *v.t.* verbinden, verknüpfen; ~ *v.i.* verbunden sein; *well-connected a.* mit guten Beziehungen.
connecting-rod *s. (mech.)* Pleuelstange *f.*
connection, *s.* Zusammenhang *m.;* Verbindung *f.; (rail.)* Anschluß *m.; (tel.)* Anschluß *m.;* Praxis (Arzt, Rechtsanwalt) *f.; (elek.)* Schaltung *f.;* Anschluß *m.;* ~ **box** *(elek.)* Anschlußdose *f.*
conning tower *s.* Kommandoturm *m.*
connivance *s.* Nachsicht *f.;* stillschweigende Einwilligung *f.*
connive *v.i.* sich verschwören, stillschweigend dulden.
connoisseur *s.* Kenner *m.*
connotation *s.* Mitbezeichnung *f.;* Konnotation *f.*
connote *v.t.* mitbezeichnen.
conquer *v.t.* & *i.* erobern, (be)siegen.
conqueror *s.* Eroberer, Sieger *m.*
conquest *s.* Eroberung *f.;* Sieg *m.*
consanguineous *a.* blutsverwandt.
consanguinity *s.* Blutsverwandtschaft *f.*
conscience *s.* Gewissen *n.*
conscientious *a.,* **~ly** *adv.* gewissenhaft.
conscientiousness *s.* Gewissenhaftigkeit *f.*
conscientious objector *s.* Kriegsdienstverweigerer *m.*
conscious *a.,* **~ly** *adv.* bewußt; wissentlich.
consciousness *a.* Bewußtsein *n.*
conscript *s.* ausgehobener Rekrut *m.;* Einberufene *m./f.;* ~ *a.* ausgehoben; einberufen.
conscription *s.* Einberufung *f.;* Aushebung *f.;* allgemeine Wehrpflicht *f.*
consecrate *v.t.* weihen; einsegnen.
consecration *s.* Einsegnung.

consecutive *a.*, **~ly** *adv.* aufeinander folgend; folglich; konsekutiv.
consensus *s.* Übereinstimmung *f.*
consent *s.* Einwilligung *f.*; *age of ~*, (*jur.*) Mündigkeitsalter *n.*; ~ *v.i.* einwilligen, einstimmen.
consequence *s.* Folge *f.*; Einfluß *m.*; Wichtigkeit *f.*
consequent *a.*, **~ly** *adv.* folgend; folglich; konsequent.
consequential *a.* konsequent.
conservation *s.* Erhaltung *f.*
conservation area *s.* Landschaftsschutzgebiet *n.*
conservationist *s.* Naturschützer(in) *m.(f.)*
conservatism *s.* Konservati(vi)smus *m.*
conservative *a.* erhaltend; konservativ; ~ **estimate,** vorsichtige Schätzung *f.*
conservator *s.* Erhalter, Konservator *m.*
conservatory *a.* erhaltend; ~ *s.* Gewächshaus *n.*; Konservatorium *n.*
conserve *v.t.* erhalten.
consider *v.t.* & *i.* betrachten; überlegen; achten.
considerable *a.*, **~bly** *adv.* ansehnlich.
considerate *a.*, **~ly** *adv.* aufmerksam; rücksichtsvoll.
consideration *s.* Betrachtung, Überlegung *f.*; Rücksicht *f.*; Preis *m.*
considering *pr.* in Erwägung (daß); in Betracht auf.
consign *v.t.* übertragen; zusenden.
consignee *s.* Warenempfänger *m.*
consignment *s.* Übersendung *f.*; Warensendung, Konsignation *f.*
consignor *s.* Warenabsender *m.*
consist *v.i.* bestehen.
consistence, consistency *s.* Festigkeit *f.*; Folgerichtigkeit *f.*
consistent *a.*, **~ly** *adv.* dicht, fest; übereinstimmend; konsequent.
consistory *s.* Konsistorium *n.*
consolation *s.* Trost *m.*
consolatory *a.* tröstlich.
console *v.t.* trösten; ~ *s.* Tragstein, *m.*; Konsole *f.*
consolidate *v.t.* befestigen; ~ *v.i.* sich verbinden; zuheilen; sich befestigen.
consolidation *s.* Verdichtung *f.*; Verbindung *f.*; Zusammenlegung *f.*
consoling *a.* tröstlich.
consommé *a.* Kraftbrühe *f.*
consonance *s.* Einklang *m.*
consonant *a.*, **~ly** *adv.* übereinstimmend; ~ *s.* Konsonant *m.*
consort *s.* Gefährte *m.*; Gatte *m.*; Gattin *f.*; ~ *v.i.* sich gesellen, umgehen; übereinstimmen.
consortium *s.* Konsortium *n.*
conspicuous *a.*, **~ly** *adv.* auffallend; hervorragend.
conspiracy *s.* Verschwörung *f.*
conspirator *s.* Verschwörer(in) *m.(f.)*
conspiratorial *a.* verschwörerisch.
conspire *v.i.* sich verschwören.
constable *s.* Polizist, Schutzmann *m.*; *Chief ~*, Polizeipräsident *m.*
constabulary *s.* Schutzpolizei, Schupo *f.*
constancy *s.* Beständigkeit.
constant *a.*, **~ly** *adv.* standhaft, zuverlässig; dauernd; ~ **hot water,** fließendes warmes Wasser *n.*
constellation *s.* Sternbild *n.*
consternation *s.* Bestürzung *f.*
constipate *v.t.* verdichten, verstopfen.
constipation *s.* Verstopfung *f.*
constituency *s.* Wahlkreis *m.*; Wählerschaft *f.*
constituent *a.* ausmachend, wesentlich; Wahl...; verfassunggebend; ~ **body,** Wählerschaft *f.*; ~ *s.* Vollmachtgeber *m.*; Bestandteil *m.*; Wähler *m.*
constitute *v.t.* ausmachen; bilden, errichten; gründen.
constitution *s.* Einrichtung *f.*; Verfassung *f.*; Körperbeschaffenheit *f.*
constitutional *a.*, **~ly** *adv.* verfassungsmäßig; ~ *s.* Spaziergang zur Verdauung *m.*
constitutional law *s.* Verfassungsrecht *n.*
constitutive *a.* verordnend; wesentlich.
constrain *v.t.* zwingen.
constraint *s.* Zwang *m.*; Nötigung *f.*
constrict *v.t.* zusammenziehen.
constriction *s.* Zusammenziehung *f.*
constrictor *s.* Schliessmuskel *m.*
constringent *a.* zusammenziehend.
construct *v.t.* errichten, bauen; konstruieren; ersinnen.
construction *s.* Zusammensetzung *f.*; Bau *m.*; Deutung *f.*; *under ~*, im Bau; ~ **battalion** *(mil.)* Baubataillon *n.*
constructive *a.* Bau...; aufbauend; konstruktiv.
construe *v.t.* konstruieren; auslegen.
consul *s.* Konsul *m.*; ~ **general,** Generalkonsul *m.*
consular *a.* konsularisch.
consulate, consulship *s.* Konsulat *n.*
consult *v.i.* sich beraten; ~ *v.t.* konsultieren.
consultant *s.* Berater(in) *m.(f.)*
consultation *s.* Beratung, Beratschlagung *f.*; Rücksprache *f.*
consulting *a.* beratend.
consulting engineer *s.* technischer Berater *m.*
consulting hours *s.pl.* Sprechstunden (Arzt) *f.pl.*
consume *v.t.* verzehren; verbrauchen.
consumer *s.* Verbraucher(in), Konsument(in) *m.* *(f.)*; Abnehmer(in) *m.(f.)*; ~ **goods** Verbrauchsgüter *n.pl.*; ~ **protection** *s.* Verbraucherschutz *m.*
consummate *a.* vollendet; *v.t.* vollenden; vollziehen.
consummation *s.* Vollendung *f.*; Vollzug *m.*
consumption *s.* Verzehrung *f.*; Verbrauch *m.*; Schwindsucht *f.*
consumptive *a.* schwindsüchtig.
contact *s.* Berührung *f.*; *(elek.)* Kontakt *m.*; ~ *v.t.* sich in Verbindung setzen mit.
contact lens *s.* Kontaktlinse *f.*
contagion *s.* Ansteckung, Seuche *f.*
contagious *a.* ansteckend.
contain *v.t.* in sich fassen, enthalten; *(mil.)* Kräfte binden; *to ~ oneself*, sich beherrschen.
container *s.* Behälter *m.*; Container *m.*
contaminate *v.t.* verseuchen, verunreinigen, infizieren.
contamination *s.* Verunreinigung *f.*; Infizierung *f.*
cont(d). *continued*, Fortsetzung, Forts.

contemplate *v.t.* betrachten; beabsichtigen; ~ *v.i.* nachdenken.
contemplation *s.* Betrachtung *f.*
contemplative *a.*, **~ly** *adv.* beschaulich.
contemporaneous *a.* gleichzeitig.
contemporary *a.* gleichzeitig, zeitgenössisch; ~ *s.* Zeitgenosse *m.*; Zeitgenossin *f.*
contempt *s.* Verachtung *f.*; ~ **of court,** (*jur.*) Mißachtung des Gerichts *f.*
contemptible *a.*, **~bly** *adv.* verächtlich.
contemptuous *a.*, **~ly** *adv.* verachtend; überheblich.
contend *v.i.* streiten; streben; behaupten.
contender *s.* Bewerber(in) *m.(f.)*
content *a.* zufrieden; ~ *s.* Zufriedenheit *f.*; Inhalt *m.*; Zusammensetzung *f.*; ~ *v.t.* befriedigen.
contented *a.*, **~ly** *adv.* zufrieden.
contention *s.* Streit *m.*; Wetteifer *m.*; Behauptung *f.*; Argument *n.*
contentious *a.*, **~ly** *adv.* strittig; umstritten.
contentment *a.* Zufriedenheit *f.*
contest *v.t.* streiten; bestreiten, anfechten; *to ~ a seat,* in einem Wahlkreis kandidieren; ~ *v.i.* wetteifern; ~ *s.* Streit *m.*; Wettbewerb, Wettkampf *m.*
contestable *a.* anfechtbar, streitig.
contestant *s.* (Wett)bewerber(in) *m.(f.)*, Wettkämpfer(in) *m.(f.)*
context *s.* Zusammenhang *m.*
contexture *s.* Bau *m.*; Gewebe *n.*
contiguity *s.* Aneinanderstoßen *n.*
contiguous *a.*, **~ly** *adv.* anstoßend, nahe.
continence *s.* Enthaltsamkeit *f.*
continent *a.*, **~ly** *adv.* enthaltsam, mäßig; ~ *s.* Festland *n.*; Kontinent *m.*
continental *a.* festländisch; kontinental.
contingency *s.* Zufall *m.*; Möglichkeit *f.*
contingent *a.* möglich; abhängig; ~ *s.* (*mil.*) Kontingent *n.*
continual *a.*, **~ly** *adv.* fortwährend; ständig.
continuance *s.* Fortdauer *f.*
continuation *s.* Fortsetzung *f.*; ~ **school,** Fortbildungsschule *f.*
continue *v.t.* & *i.* fortsetzen; fortdauern, beharren.
continuity *s.* Zusammenhang *m.*; Kontinuität *f.*
continuous *a.* zusammenhängend; durchgehend.
continuum *s.* Kontinuum *n.*
contort *v.t.* verdrehen; verzerren.
contortion *s.* Verdrehung, Verzerrung *f.*
contour *s.* Umriß *m.*
contra *pr.* gegen, wider.
contraband *a.* Schmuggel...; ~ *s.* Schmuggelware *f.*
contraception *s.* Empfängnisverhütung *f.*
contraceptive *a.* empfängnisverhütend; ~ *s.* empfängnisverhütendes Mittel *n.*
contract *s.* Vertrag *m.*; Akkord *m.*; *law of ~,* Vertragsrecht *n.*; *to make a ~,* einen Vertrag eingehen; *under ~ to,* einem kontraktlich verpflichtet; ~ *v.t.* zusammenziehen; sich zuziehen; erlangen; *to ~ debts,* Schulden eingehen; ~ *v.i.* einschrumpfen; einen Vertrag schließen; sich verpflichten; *contracting party,* Vertragspartei *f.*
contraction *s.* Zusammenziehung *f.*; Krampf *m.*; Wehe *f.*
contractor *s.* Lieferant *m.*; Unternehmer *m.*
contractual *a.* vertragsmäßig; vertraglich.
contradict *v.t.* widersprechen.
contradiction *s.* Widerspruch *m.*
contradictory *a.*, **~ily** *adv.* widersprechend.
contralto *s.* tiefe Altstimme *f.*; Kontraalt *m.*
contrary *a.* entgegengesetzt, zuwider; widerspenstig; ~ *s.* Gegenteil *n.*; ~ **to,** im Gegensatz zu; *on the ~,* im Gegenteil.
contrast *s.* Kontrast *m.*; Gegensatz *m.* ~ *v.t.* & *i.* gegenüberstellen; abstechen von.
contrasting *a.* gegensätzlich, kontrastierend.
contravene *v.t.* zuwiderhandeln.
contravention *s.* Übertretung *f.*
contribute *v.t.* & *i.* beitragen.
contribution *s.* Beitrag *m.*, Beisteuer *f.*
contributor *s.* Beitragender *m.*; Mitarbeiter (an einer Zeitung) *m.*
contributory *a.* beitragend.
contrite *a.*, **~ly** *adv.* zerknirscht.
contrition *s.* Zerknirschung *f.*
contrivance *s.* Vorrichtung *f.*; Kunstgriff *m.*
contrive *v.t.* & *i.* ersinnen; veranstalten, fertigbringen; darauf ausgehen.
control *s.* Einschränkung *f.*; Aufsicht *f.*; Gewalt *f.*; Kontrolle *f.*; Überwachung *f.*; (*mech.*) Steuerung, Kontrollvorrichtung *f.*; ~ **center** *s.* Kontrollzentrum *n.*; ~ **desk** *s.* Schaltpult *n.*; **~office** Überwachungsstelle *f.*; ~ **room** *s.* Kontrollraum *m.*; ~ *v.t.* beaufsichtigen, überwachen; beherrschen; kontrollieren.
controllable *a.* kontrollierbar.
controller *s.* Kontrolleur *m.*, Aufseher *m.*, Leiter *m.*; Rechnungsprüfer *m.*
controversial *a.* kontrovers, strittig, streitsüchtig.
controversy *s.* Streitfrage *f.*; Streit *m.*; Kontroverse *f.*; *matter in ~,* (*jur.*) Streitgegenstand *m.*
controvert *v.t.* bestreiten.
controvertible *a.* bestreitbar, streitig.
contumacious *a.*, **~ly** *adv.* widerspenstig.
contumacy *s.* Widerspenstigkeit *f.*
contuse *v.t.* quetschen.
contusion *s.* Quetschung *f.*
conundrum *s.* Problem *n.*; Scherzrätsel *n.*
conurbation *s.* Ballungszentrum *n.*
convalesce *v.i.* genesen, rekonvaleszieren.
convalescence *s.* Genesung *f.*
convalescent *a.* genesend; **~-home,** Genesungsheim *n.*
convene *v.t.* zusammenberufen; vorladen; ~ *v.i.* zusammenkommen.
convenience *s.* Schicklichkeit, Gelegenheit, Bequemlichkeit *f.*; *at your earliest ~,* umgehend; *with all modern ~s,* mit allem Komfort.
convenient *a.*, **~ly** *adv.* bequem, praktisch.
convent *s.* (Nonnen-)Kloster *n.*
conventicle *s.* Zusammenkunft *f.*
convention *s.* Zusammenkunft *f.*, Versammlung *f.*; Vergleich *m.*; Bund *m.*; Tagung *f.*; Kongreß *m.*
conventional *a.* verabredet, vertragsmäßig; herkömmlich.
converge *v.i.* zusammenlaufen.
convergence *s.* Zusammenlaufen.
convergent *a.* konvergierend.
conversant *a.* vertraut, bewandert.
conversation *s.* Unterhaltung *f.*; Umgang *m.*

conversational *a.* Unterhaltungs...; gesprächig.
converse *a.* umgekehrt; ~ *v.i.* Umgang haben, sich unterhalten.
conversely *adv.* umgekehrt.
conversion *s.* Umwandlung *f.;* Bekehrung *f.;* Schwenkung *f.;* Konvertierung (von Staatspapieren) *f.;* Versilberung *f.; fraudulent* ~, (*jur.*) betrügerische Verwendung anvertrauten Geldes.
convert *s.* Bekehrter *m.;* ~ *v.t.* umändern; bekehren, umkehren; ~ *v.i.* sich verwandeln.
converter *s. (elek.)* Umformer *m.*
convertible *a.* umwandelbar; umsetzbar, vertauschbar; *(com.)* konvertierbar; ~ *s.* Kabriolett *n.*
convex *a.* konvex.
convexity *s.* Konvexheit *f.*
convey *v.t.* führen; befördern; übertragen; übermitteln; vermitteln.
conveyance *s.* Beförderung *f.;* Abtretung *f.*
conveyor belt *s.* Fliessband *n.;* Förderband *n.*
convict *v.t.* für schuldig erklären; überführen; ~ *s.* Strafgefangene *m.*, Verbrecher *m.*
conviction *s.* Überzeugung *f.;* Überführung *f.;* (*jur.*) Schuldigerklärung *f.*
convince *v.t.* überzeugen.
convincing *a.* überzeugend.
convivial *a.* gastlich, festlich.
convocation *s.* Zusammenberufung *f.;* Versammlung, Synode *f.*
convoke *v.t.* zusammenberufen.
convoluted *a.* verschlungen.
convoy *v.t.* geleiten; ~ *s.* Geleit *n.;* Bedeckung *f.;* *(nav.)* Geleitzug *m.*
convulse *v.t.* in Zuckungen versetzen; *to be ~d,* von Krämpfen geschüttelt werden.
convulsion *s.* Zuckung *f.;* Krampf *m.*
convulsive *a.* zuckend, krampfhaft.
coo *v.i.* gurren.
cook *s.* Koch *m.;* Köchin *f.;* ~ *v.t.* kochen; *what's ~ing?* was gibt's?
cookbook *s.* Kochbuch *n.*
cooker *s.* Kochapparat, Kochherd *m.*
cookery *s.* Kochkunst *f.*
cookie *s.* Plätzchen *n.;* Keks *m.*
cooking *s.* Kochen *n.*
cool *a.* kühl; kaltblütig; unverfroren; *(fam.)* spitze, cool; ~ *v.t.* kühlen, erfrischen; besänftigen; ~ *v.i.* erkalten.
coolant *s. (mech.)* Kühlflüssigkeit *f.*
cooler *s.* (Wein)kühler *m.*
coolie *s.* Kuli *m.*
coolly *adv.* kaltblütig; kühl; ruhig.
coolness *s.* Kühle *f.;* Kaltblütigkeit *f.*
cooper *s.* Böttcher *m.;* Küfer *m.*
cooperate *v.i.* mitwirken, teilnehmen.
cooperation *s.* Mitwirkung *f.*
cooperative *a.* mitwirkend; zur Mitarbeit bereit, willig; ~ **society** *s.* Konsumverein *m.*
cooperator *s.* Mitarbeiter *m.*
coopt *v.t.* kooptieren.
coordinate *a.*, **~ly** *adv.* beigeordnet; koordiniert; ~ *v.t.* beiordnen; gleichordnen; koordinieren.
coordination *s.* Koordinierung *f.;* Koordination *f.;* Abstimmung.
cop *s. (fam.)* Polizist, Bulle *m.*
copartner *s.* Teilhaber *m.*
cope *s.* Decke, Kuppel *f.;* Chorrock *m.;* ~ *v.t.* bedecken; ~ *v.i. to ~ with,* zurechtkommar mit.
copier *s.* Kopierer *m.;* Kopiergerät *n.*
copilot *s.* Kopilot(in) *m.(f.)*
coping *s.* Sims *m.;* ~ **stone,** Deckstein *m.*
copious *a.*, **~ly** *adv.* reichlich.
cop-out *s.* Drückebergerei *f.*
copper *s.* Kupfer *n.;* Kupfergeschirr *n.;* Kupfermünze *f.;* ~ *a.* kupfern.
copperplate *s.* Kupferplatte *f.;* Kupferstich *m.*
coppice, copse *s.* Unterholz *n.*
copula *s. (ling.)* Kopula *n.*
copulate *v.i.* kopulieren, sich begatten.
copulation *s.* Begattung *f.*
copulative *a.* verbindend, Binde...
copy *s.* Abschrift *f.;* Abdruck *m.;* Durchschlag *m.;* Exemplar *n.;* Nachahmung *f.; fair ~, clean ~,* Reinschrift *f.; rough ~,* Konzept *n.;* ~ *v.t.* kopieren; nachzeichnen, nachahmen; *to ~ out,* ins Reine schreiben.
copyist *s.* Abschreiber, Kopist *m.*
copyright *s.* Verlagsrecht, Urheberrecht *n.;* ~ **in designs,** Musterschutz *m.*
coquette, coquettish *a.* gefallsüchtig, kokett.
coral *s.* Koralle *f.*
cord *s.* Strick *m.;* Schnur *f.;* Tau *n.;* ~ *v.t.* mit Stricken befestigen.
cordial *a.*, **~ly** *adv.* herzlich; ~ *s.* Herzstärkung *f.;* Magenlikör *m.*
cordiality *s.* Herzlichkeit *f.*
cordon *s.* Truppenkette *f.; to ~ off v.t.* (polizeilich) absperren.
corduroy *s.* Kordsamt *m.*
core *s.* Mark *n.;* Herz *n.;* Kern *m.*
co-respondent *m.* Mitbeklagter im Scheidungsprozeß *m.*
coriander *s.* Koriander *m.*
cork *s.* Kork *m.;* ~ *v.t.* verkorken; *the wine is ~ed,* der Wein schmeckt nach dem Kork.
corkscrew *s.* Korkenzieher *m.*
cork tree *s.* Korkeiche *f.*
cormorant *s.* Kormoran *m.;* Scharbe *f.*
corn *s.* Korn *n.;* Getreide *n.;* Mais *m.;* Hühnerauge *n.;* **~ed beef,** Büchsenrindfleisch *n.;* **~cob** *s.* Maiskolben *m.*
cornea *s.* Hornhaut (Auge) *f.;* Cornea *f.*
corner *s.* Winkel *m.;* Ecke *f.;* **~stone,** Eckstein *m.; (fig.)* Eckpfeiler *m.;* ~ *v.t.* in eine Ecke treiben.
cornet *s.* (Eis)Tüte *f.;* Eishörnchen *n.; (mus.)* Kornett *n.*
cornflower *s.* Kornblume *f.*
cornice *s.* Karnies *n.;* Fries *m.*
cornstarch *s.* Maismehl *n.;* Stärkemehl *n.*
cornucopia *s.* Füllhorn *n.*
corny *a.* altmodisch; abgedroschen.
corollary *s.* Folgesatz *m.;* Korrollar(ium) *n.*
coronary *a. (med.)* Koronar...; ~ **vessel** *s.* Herzkranzgefäß *n.*
coronation *s.* Krönung *f.*
coroner *s.* Leichenbeschauer (bei gewaltsamem od. rätselhaftem Tode); **~'s inquest,** gerichtliche Leichenschau *f.*
coronet *s.* Adelskrone *f.*
corporal *a.*, **~ly** *adv.* körperlich, leiblich; ~ *s.* Korporal *m.*

corporal punishment *s.* Prügelstrafe *f.*
corporate *a.*, **~ly** *adv.* körperschaftlich, Gesellschafts...
corporation *s.* Gesellschaft Gemeinde, Körperschaft *f.*; ~ **profits tax,** Körperschaftssteuer *f.*
corporeal *a.* körperlich.
corps *s.* Korps *n.*
corpse *s.* Leichnam *m.*
corpulence *s.* Wohlbeleibtheit *f.*
corpulent *a.* korpulent.
Corpus Christi *s.* Fronleichnamsfest *n.*
corpuscle *s.* Blutkörperchen *n.*
corral *s.* Pferch *m.*; *v.t.* einpferchen.
correct *v.t.* verbessern; tadeln; strafen; (Zahlen) abrunden; ~ *a.*, **~ly** *adv.* fehlerfrei, richtig.
correction *s.* Verbesserung *f.*; Berichtigung *f.*; Bestrafung *f.*; *house of* ~, Besserungsanstalt *f.*; ~ **of proofs,** Korrekturlektur *f.*
corrective *a.* verbessernd; ~ *s.* Besserungsmittel *m.*
correctness *s.* Korrektheit *f.*; Richtigkeit *f.*
correlate *v.t. & i.* korrelieren; in Beziehung setzen.
correlation *s.* Beziehung *f.*, Korrelation *f.*
correlative *a.* entsprechend, korrelativ.
correspond *v.i.* in Briefwechsel stehen; entsprechen.
correspondence *s.* Briefwechsel *m.*; Übereinstimmung *f.*; ~ **course,** Fernkurs *m.*
correspondent *s.* Korrespondent(in) *m.(f.)*
corresponding *a.*, **~ly** *adv.* entsprechend.
corridor *s.* Gang *m.*; ~ **train,** D-Zug (Durchgangszug) *m.*
corroborate *v.t.* stärken; bestätigen.
corroboration *s.* Bestätigung *f.*
corroborative *a.* bestätigend.
corrode *v.t.* zernagen, zerfressen, korrodieren.
corrosion *s.* Zerfressung *f.*; Korrosion *f.*
corrosive *a.*, **~ly** *adv.* zerfressend, ätzend; ~ *s.* Ätzmittel *n.*
corrugate *v.t.* zerfurchen.
corrugated *a.* gewellt; ~ **iron,** Wellblech *n.*
corrugation *s.* Zerfurchung *f.*; Furche *f.*
corrupt *v.t.* verderben; verführen; bestechen; korrumpieren. ~ *v.i.* verderben; verfaulen; ~ *a.*, **~ly** *adv.* verfault; lasterhaft; verderbt; bestechlich, korrupt.
corruption *s.* Verdorbenheit, Fäulnis *f.*; Bestechung *f.*, Korruption *f.*
corsair *s.* Seeräuber *m.*; Raubschiff *n.*
corset *s.* Schnürleib *m.*, Korsett *n.*
cortisone *s.* Kortison *n.*
coruscate *v.t.* schimmern.
coruscation *s.* Schimmern *n.*, Lichtglanz *m.*
corvette *s.* Korvette *f.*
cosh *s.* Knüppel, Totschläger *m.*
cosine *s. (math.)* Kosinus *m.*
cosmetic *a.* kosmetisch; ~ *s.* Schönheitsmittel *n.*
cosmic(al) *a.* kosmisch, Welt...; ~ **radiation** *s.* kosmische Strahlung *f.*
cosmonaut *s.* Kosmonaut(in) *m.(f.)*
cosmopolitan, cosmopolite *s.* Weltbürger(in) *m.(f.)*; ~ *a.* weltbürgerlich, kosmopolitisch.
Cosmos *s.* Kosmos *m.*
Cossack *s.* Kosak *m.*
cosset *v.t.* verhätscheln.
cost *s.* Kosten, Unkosten *f.pl.*; Preis *m.*; Aufwand *m.*; Schaden *m.*; ~ **of living,** Lebenshaltungskosten *pl.*; **~s** *pl.* Gerichtskosten *pl.*; *to dismiss with* ~ *(jur.)* kostenpflichtig abweisen; ~ *v.i.* kosten, zustehen kommen.
cost-effective *a.* kostensparend.
costly *a.* kostspielig, kostbar.
cost price *s.* Selbstkostenpreis *m.*
costume *s.* Kostüm *n.*
cot *s.* Hütte *f.*; Kinderbett *n.*
coterie *a.* Clique, Sippschaft *f.*
cottage *s.* Hütte *f.*; Landhäuschen *n.*
cotton *s.* Baumwolle *f.*; Kattun *m.*; Garn *n.*; *(absorbent)* ~, Watte *f.*; ~ *v.t.* in Baumwolle packen; ~ *v.i.* sich vertragen, anpassen.
cotton mill *s.* Baumwollspinnerei *f.*
couch *s.* Liegesofa *n.*; Couch *f.*; ~ *v.t.* (in Worte) fassen.
cough *s.* Husten *m.*; ~ *v.i.* husten.
coughing *s.* Husten *m.*; Gehuste *n.*
cough medicine *s.* Hustenmittel *n.*
council *s.* Ratsversammlung *f.*; Rat *m.*; *Common* ~, Stadtrat *m.*
councillor *s.* Ratsmitglied *n.*, Ratsherr *m.*; Stadtverordneter *m.*
counsel *s.* Rat *m.*; Beratschlagung *f.*; Vorhaben *n.*; Anwalt *m.*; die juristischen Berater im Prozeß, *m.pl.*; ~ **for the defense,** Verteidiger; ~ **for the prosecution,** Staatsanwalt *m.*, Staatsanwaltschaft *f.*, Anklagevetreter *m.*; *to keep one's* ~, seine Gedanken bei sich behalten; ~ *v.t.* raten.
counseling *s.* Beratung *f.*
counselor *s.* Ratgeber; ~ **of legation,** Gesandtschaftsrat *m.*
count *s.* Graf *m.*; Zählung *f.*; Rechnung *f.*; Anklagepunkt *m.*; ~ *v.t.* zählen, rechnen; dafür halten; ~ *v.i.* rechnen, ~ *v.r.* verlassen; gelten.
countenance *s.* Antlitz *n.*; Miene *f.*; Fassung *f.*
counter *s.* Spielmarke *f.*; Zahltisch *m.*; Ladentisch *m.*; ~ *v.t.* entgegenwirken; ~ *adv.* zuwider; entgegen.
counteract *v.t.* entgegenwirken.
counteraction *s.* Gegenwirkung *f.*
counter-attack *s.* Gegenangriff *m.*
counterbalance *s.* Gegengewicht *n.*; ~ *v.t.* aufwiegen, ausgleichen.
counter-charge *s.* Gegenbeschuldigung *f.*
counter-claim *s.* Gegenforderung *f.*
counterclockwise *adv.* gegen den Uhrzeigersinn.
counter-espionage *s.* Spionageabwehr *f.*
counterfeit *s.* nachgemachte Sache *f.*; Fälschung *f.*; Falschgeld *n.*; ~ *a.* nachgemacht; falsch, gefälscht; ~ *v.t.* fälschen.
counterfeiter *s.* Fälscher(in) *m.(f.)*
counterfoil *s.* Kontrollabschnitt *m.*
counter-intelligence *s. (mil.)* Abwehr *f.*
countermand *v.t.* abbestellen, widerrufen.
countermeasure *s.* Gegenmaßnahme *f.*
countermove *s.* Gegenschlag *m.*
counteroffensive *s.* Gegenoffensive *f.*
counter order *s.* Gegenbefehl *m.*
counterpart *s.* Gegenstück *n.*
counterpoint *s.* Kontrapunkt *m.*
counterpoise *s.* Gegengewicht *n.*; ~ *v.t.* das Gleichgewicht halten.
counterproductive *a.* kontraproduktiv.

counterproposal *s.* Gegenvorschlag *m.*
counterrevolution *s.* Gegenrevolution *f.*
countersign *v.t.* gegenzeichnen.
countersink *v.t. (mech.)* versenken; *countersunk screw,* Senkschraube *f.*
countertenor *s.* Kontratenor *m.*
countervail *v.t.* ausgleichen, aufwiegen.
counterweight *s.* Gegengewicht *n.*
countess *s.* Gräfin *f.*
countless *a.* unzählbar.
country *s.* Land *n.;* Gegend, Landschaft *f.;* Vaterland *n.;* ~ *a.* ländlich, Land...
country dance *s.* Volkstanz *m.*
country house *s.* Landhaus *n.*
countryman *s.* Landsmann *m.;* Landmann *m.*
country seat *s.* Landsitz *m.*
countryside *s.* Gegend *f.;* Landschaft *f.*
countrywide *a.* landesweit.
countrywoman *s.* Landsmännin *f.;* Landbewohnerin *f.*
county *s.* Grafschaft *f.;* (Land)kreis *m.*
coup *s.* Schlag, Streich *m.*
coup d'état *s.* Staatsstreich *m.*
couple *s.* Paar *n.;* ~ *v.t.* koppeln.
couplet *s.* Verspaar *n.*
coupling *s.* Kuppelung *f.*
coupon *s.* Coupon, Gutschein *m.*
courage *s.* Mut *m.;* Tapferkeit *f.*
courageous *a.,* **~ly** *adv.* mutig, tapfer.
courier *s.* Kurier, Eilbote *m.*
course *s.* Lauf, Gang *m.;* Fahrt *f.;* Kurs *m.;* Gang (beim Essen) *m.; a ~ of bricks,* eine Lage Ziegel; *in due ~,* zur gehörigen Zeit; *in (the) ~ of time,* mit der Zeit, nach und nach; *the fever has run its ~,* das Fieber hat seinen Verlauf gehabt; *of ~,* natürlich, versteht sich; ~ *v.i.* laufen, rennen; ~ *v.t.* jagen, hetzen.
court *s.* Hof *m.;* Gerichtshof *m.; criminal ~,* Strafgericht *n.; commercial ~,* Handelsgericht *n.;* **~house,** Gerichtsgebäude *n.;* **~room,** Gerichtssaal *m.; out of ~,* außergerichtlich; ~ *v.t.* den Hof machen; freien; huldigen; sich bewerben um.
courteous *a.,* **~ly** *adv.* höflich, gefällig.
courtesy *s.* Artigkeit, Höflichkeit *f.; by ~ of,* mit freundlicher Genehmigung von.
courtier *s.* Höfling *m.*
court-martial *s.* Kriegsgericht *n.;* ~ *v.t.* vor ein Kriegsgericht stellen.
courtship *s.* Freien *n.;* Werben *n.*
courtyard *s.* Hof, Hofraum *m.*
cousin *s.* Vetter *m.;* Base, Kusine *f.; first ~,* Vetter ersten Grades; *second ~,* Vetter zweiten Grades.
cove *s.* Bucht *f.;* Wölbung *f.*
covenant *s.* Vertrag *m.;* Bündnis *n.;* ~ *v.i.* übereinkommen; geloben.
cover *v.t.* decken, bedecken; bemänteln; schützen; (Weg) zurücklegen; (Gelände) bestreichen; brüten; ~ *s.* Decke *f.;* Deckel *m.;* Umschlag *m.;* Kuvert *n.;* Schutzrücken (eines Buches) *m.;* Gehege *n.;* Dickicht *n.;* Schutz *m.; (mil.)* Deckung *f.;* ~ **address,** Deckadresse *f.*
coverage *s.* Berichterstattung *f.*
coverall *s.* Overall *m.*
cover charge *s.* (Preis für das) Gedeck *n.*
cover girl *s.* Covergirl *n.*
covering *s.* Deckschicht *f.*
cover letter *s.* Begleitbrief *m.*
covert *s.* Dickicht *n.;* ~ *a.* bedeckt, verborgen; **~ly** *adv.* heimlich.
cover-up *s.* Verschleierung *f.*
covet *v.t.* begehren, gelüsten.
covetous *a.,* **~ly** *adv.* habsüchtig.
cow *s.* Kuh *f.;* ~ *v.t.* einschüchtern.
coward *s.* Feigling *m.;* ~ *a.* feig.
cowardice *s.* Feigheit *f.*
cowardly *a. & adv.* feig(e).
cowboy *s.* Cowboy *m.*
cower *v.i.* niederkauern.
cowherd *s.* Kuhhirt *m.*
cowhide *s.* Ochsenziemer *m.*
cowl *s.* Kapuze *f.,* Kutte *f.*
co-worker *s.* Kollege *m.,* Kollegin *f.*
cowpox *s.* Kuhpocken *f.pl.*
cowslip *s.* (wilde) Schlüsselblume *f.*
coxcomb *s.* Stutzer, Narr *m.*
coxswain *s.* Bootführer *m.*
coy *a.,* **~ly** *adv.* schüchtern; spröde.
coyote *s.* Kojote *m.*
cozen *v.t.* täuschen; prellen.
cozenage *s.* Betrug.
cozily *adv.* bequem; gemütlich.
cozy *a.* gemütlich.
CP *Canadian Press,* (Nachrichtenagentur); *Communist Party,* Kommunistische Partei, KP.
cp. *compare,* vergleiche, vgl.
CPA *certified public accountant,* amtlich zugelassener Wirtschaftsprüfer.
crab *s.* Taschenkrebs *m.;* Krabbe *f.;* Nörgler(in) *m.(f.);* ~ *v.t.* nörgeln; verpatzen.
crabbed *a.,* **~ly** *adv.* herb; mürrisch, schwierig; unleserlich.
crack *s.* Knall *m.;* Riß *m.;* Spalte *f.;* (Rauschgift) Crack *m.;* ~ *v.t.* sprengen, aufbrechen, zerreißen; knallen; ~ *v.i.* krachen, bersten, springen, zerplatzen.
cracked *a.* geborsten; nicht recht gescheit.
cracker *s.* knuspriger Keks *m.;* Knallbonbon *m.*
crackle *v.i.* krachen; knistern.
crackling *s.* Geknister *n.;* Kruste *(f.)* des Schweinebratens.
crackpot *s.* verschrobener Mensch *m.*
cradle *s.* Wiege *f.;* ~ *v.t.* einwiegen.
craft *s.* Fertigkeit *f.;* Gewerbe, Handwerk *n.;* List *f.;* Schiff *n.*
craftsman *s.* (Kunst-)Handwerker *m.*
craftsmanship *s.* fachmännische Arbeit *f.*
crafty *a.,* **~ily** *adv.* listig.
crag *s.* Klippe *f.;* Fels *m.*
craggy *a.* schroff, felsig.
cram *v.t. & i.* stopfen, nudeln; mästen; einpauken.
cramp *s.* Krampf *m.;* Klammer *f.;* ~ *v.i.* verklammern; verzerren.
cramped *a.* eng, gedrängt.
cranberry *s.* Preiselbeere *f.*
crane *s.* Kranich *m.;* Kran *m.;* ~ *v.t.* aufwinden.
cranial *a.* Schädel...
cranium *s.* Hirnschale *f.*
crank *s.* Kurbel *f.;* Krummzapfen *m.;* grillenhafter Mensch *m.*
crankiness *s.* Verdrehtheit *f.*
crankshaft *s. (mech.)* Kurbelwelle *f.*

cranky *a.* reizbar, schlecht gelaunt.
cranny *s.* Riß, Spalt *m.*
crap *s. (fam.)* Mist *m.; Quatsch m.; Schrott m.*
crash *v.i.* krachen, platzen; ~ *s.* Bruch *m.;* Krach *m.; (avi.)* Absturz *m.*
crash: ~ **barrier** *s.* Leitplanke *f.;* ~ **course** *s.* Intensivkurs *m.;* ~ **landing** *s.* Bruchlandung *f.;* ~ **test** *s.* Crashtest *m.*
crass *a.* dick, kraß; dumm.
crate *s.* Kiste *f.*
crater *s.* Krater *m.*
crave *v.t.* dringend bitten, verlangen.
craving *s.* Begierde *f.;* Verlangen *n.;* ~ *a.* begehrlich, gierig.
crawl *v.i.* kriechen, schleichen; kraulen (schwimmen); *to* ~ *with,* wimmeln von.
crayfish *s.* Flußkrebs *m.*
crayon *s.* Farbstift *m.*
craze *v.t.* verrückt machen; ~ *s.* Grille *f.,* Manie *f.*
crazy *a.* wahnsinnig; verrückt.
creak *v.i.* knarren.
cream *s.* Rahm *m.;* Sahne *f.; (fig.)* Beste *n.;* ~ *v.t.* abrahmen.
cream cheese *s.* Frischkäse *n.*
creamery *s.* Butterei *f.;* Milchgeschäft *n.*
crease *s.* Falte, Bügelfalte *f.;* Eselsohr (im Buch) *n.;* **~-resisting,** nicht knitternd; ~ *v.t.* umbiegen, kniffen; ~ *v.i.* knittern.
create *v.t.* erschaffen; ernennen.
creation *s.* Schöpfung *f.;* Ernennung *f.*
creative *a.* schöpferisch.
creator *s.* Schöpfer *m.*
creature *s.* Geschöpf *n.;* Wesen *n.*
credentials *s.pl.* Beglaubigungsschreiben *n.*
credibility *s.* Glaubwürdigkeit *f.*
credible *a.,* **~bly** *adv.* glaubwürdig.
credit *s.* Glaube *m.;* Glaubwürdigkeit *f.;* Zeugnis *n.;* Einfluß *m.;* Ehre *f.;* Kredit *m.; to his* ~, zu seinen Gunsten; *open* ~, Blankokredit *f.; letter of* ~, Kreditbrief *m.;* ~ **balance,** Guthaben *n.;* ~ **restriction,** Kreditbeschränkung *f.;* ~ **voucher,** Kreditkassenschein *m.; on* ~, auf Kredit; *to enter to a person's* ~, einem gutschreiben; ~ *v.t.* glauben; kreditieren, gutschreiben.
creditable *a.,* **~bly** *adv.* anerkennenswert.
credit card *s.* Kreditkarte *f.*
creditor *s.* Gläubiger *m.*
creditworthy *a.* kreditwürdig.
credulity *s.* Leichtgläubigkeit *f.*
credulous *a.* leichtgläubig.
creed *s.* Glaubensbekenntnis *n.*
creek *s.* kleine Bucht *f.;* kleiner Fluß *m.,* Flüßchen *n.*
creep *v.i.* kriechen, schleichen; *my flesh* ~*s,* mich überläuft eine Gänsehaut.
creeper *s.* Schlingpflanze *f.;* Kletterpflanze *f.*
creepy *a.* gruselig; unheimlich.
cremate *v.t.* einäschern.
cremation *s.* Einäscherung *f.;* Leichenverbrennung *f.*
crematorium, crematory *s.* Krematorium *n.*
crenellated *a.* mit Zinnen gezackt.
creosote *s.* Kreosot *n.*
crêpe *s.* Krepp *m.*
crescendo *s. (mus.)* Crescendo *n.; (fig.)* Zunahme *f.*
crescent *s.* zunehmender Mond *m.;* Halbmond *m.;* ~ *a.* halbmondförmig; ~ *s.* halbmondförmige Straße *f.*
cress *s.* Kresse *f.*
crest *s.* Kamm *m.;* Mähne *f.;* Bergrücken *m.;* Helmschmuck (im Wappen) *m.*
crestfallen *a.* niedergeschlagen.
cretin *a.* Kretin *m.*
crevasse *s.* Gletscherspalte *f.*
crevice *s.* Riß *m.*
crew *s.* Besatzung (Schiff, Panzer) *f.;* Mannschaft *f.;* Personal *n.*
crib *s.* Krippe *f.;* Kinderbettchen *n.; (fig.)* Eselsbrücke *f.;* ~ *v.t.* abschreiben.
cricket *s.* Grille *f.;* Heimchen *n.;* Kricket, Schlagballspiel *n.*
crier *s.* Ausrufer *m.*
crime *s.* Verbrechen *n.; capital* ~, Kapitalverbrechen *n.*
crime rate *s.* Kriminalitätsrate *f.*
criminal *a.,* **~ly** *adv.* verbrecherisch; Straf...; ~ **code,** Strafgesetzbuch *n.;* ~ **investigation department,** Kriminalabteilung *f.;* ~ **justice,** Strafrechtspflege *f.;* ~ **law,** Strafrecht *n.;* ~ **procedure,** Strafprozeß *m.;* ~ **record,** Strafregister *n.;* ~ *s.* Verbrecher *m.; habitual* ~, Gewohnheitsverbrecher *m.*
criminally *a.* kriminell; strafrechtlich.
criminologist *s.* Kriminologe *m.*
criminology *s.* Kriminologie *f.*
crimson *s.* Karmesin *n.;* ~ *a.* karmesinrot; ~ *v.t.* rot färben.
cringe *v.i.* sich krümmen; kriechen; zusammenzucken.
cringing *a.* kriecherisch.
crinkle *v.i.* knittern, zerknittern; kranseln; ~ *s.* Kränsel *m.;* Knitterfalte *f.*
crinoline *s.* Krinoline *f.*
cripple *s.* Krüppel *m.;* ~ *a.* krüpplig; ~ *v.t.* verstümmeln; lähmen.
crippled *a.* verkrüppelt.
crisis *s.* Krise *f.;* Wendepunkt *m.*
crisp *a.* kraus; knusperig; frisch; ~ *v.t.* kräuseln; braun rösten.
crispbread *s.* Knäckebrot *n.*
crispy *a.* knusprig, knackig.
criss-cross *s.* Gewirr (von Straßen, Kanälen, usw.) *n.*
criterion *s.* Kriterium, Merkmal *n.*
critic *s.* Kritiker(in) *m.(f.)*
critical *a.* kritisch; bedenklich; entscheidend; *in* ~ *condition,* lebensgefährlich verwundet od. krank; ~ **goods** *s.pl.* Mangelware *f.*
critically *adv.* kritisch.
criticism *s.* Kritik *f.; open to* ~, anfechtbar.
criticize *v.t. & i.* beurteilen, tadeln.
critique *s.* Kritik *f.*
croak *v.i.* quaken, krächzen.
crochet *s.* Häkelarbeit *f.;* ~ *v.i.* häkeln.
crock *s.* Krug, Topf *m.*
crockery *s.* Töpferware *f.*
crocodile *s.* Krokodil *n.;* ~ **tears** Krokodilstränen *pl.*
crocus *s.* Krokus *m.*
croissant *s.* Hörnchen *n.*
crone *s.* alte Frau *f.;* Hexe *f.*
crony *s.* alte Bekannte *m./f.*

crook *s.* Haken *m.;* Schwindler *m.;* ~ *v.t.* krümmen.
crooked *a.*, **~ly** *adv.* krumm, verdreht, schief; betrügerisch.
croon *v.i.* leise singen; schmachtend singen.
crooner *s.* Schnulzensänger *m.*
crop *s.* Kropf (der Vögel) *m.;* Ernte *f.;* kurzes Haar *n.;* Jagdpeitsche, Reitgerte *f.;* ~ *v.t.* stutzen, verschneiden; abpflücken, einsammeln, ernten; ~ **up** *v.i.* auftauchen.
cropper *s.* schwerer Sturz *m.*
croquet *s.* Krocket, Kugelschlagspiel *n.*
crosier *s.* Bischofsstab *m.*
cross *s.* Kreuz *n.;* Leiden *n.;* (Rassen-)Kreuzung *f.;* ~ *a. & adv.* kreuzweise; zuwider, widrig; störrisch, mürrisch; böse; querdurch; ~ *v.t.* kreuzen; überschreiten, gehen über; widersprechen, widerstehen; ~ *v.i.* sich kreuzen; *to ~ out,* ausstreichen; *your letter ~ed mine,* unsere Briefe haben sich gekreuzt; *~ed check,* Verrechnungsscheck *m.*
crossbar *s.* Querholz *n.;* Fahrradstange *f.*
crossbow *s.* Armbrust *f.*
cross-bred *a.* hybrid.
cross-check *s.* Gegenprobe *f.*
cross-country *a.* querfeldein...
cross-dressing *s.* Transvestismus *m.*
crossed *a.* gekreuzt.
cross-examination *s.* Kreuzverhör *n.*
cross-examine *v.t.* einem Kreuzverhör unterziehen.
crossing *s.* Übergang (auf der Straße) *m.;* Kreuzung *f.;* Überfahrt *f.;* *pedestrian ~,* Übergang für Fußgänger; *vehicle ~,* Übergang für Fahrzeuge.
cross-legged *a.* mit gekreuzten Beinen.
crossly *a.* verärgert.
crossover *s.* Überführung (Straße) *f.*
cross-purpose *s.* Mißverständnis *n.*
cross reference *s.* Verweis (im Buch) *m.*
crossroads *s.pl.* Straßenkreuzung *f.*
cross section *s.* Querschnitt *n.*
crosswalk *s.* Fußgängerübergang *m.*
crosswise *adv.* kreuzweise.
crossword puzzle *s.* Kreuzworträtsel *n.*
crotchet *s.* Haken *m.*
crouch *v.i.* kriechen, ~ *v.r.* zusammenkauern; ~ *s.* Hocke *f.*
crow *s.* Krähe *f.;* *distance as the ~ flies,* Luftlinie *f.*, Kartenentfernung *f.;* ~ **bar** *s.* Brecheisen *n.*, Hebestange *f.;* ~ *v.i.* krähen.
crowd *s.* Menschenmenge *f.;* Gedränge *n.;* ~ *v.t.* drängen; vollstopfen; ~ *v.i. & r.* drängen.
crowded *a.* überfüllt.
crown *s.* Krone *f.;* Kranz *m.;* Scheitel, Gipfel *m.;* Kopf (des Hutes) *m.;* ~ *v.t.* krönen.
crown prince *s.* Kronprinz *m.*
crown princess *s.* Kronprinzessin *f.*
crown witness *s.* Kronzeuge *m.*, Kronzeugin *f.*
crow's nest *s.* Krähennest *n.;* Mastkorb *m.*
crucial *a.* entscheidend; kritisch.
crucible *s.* Schmelztiegel *m.*
crucifix *s.* Kruzifix *n.*
crucifixion *s.* Kreuzigung *f.*
cruciform *a.* kreuzförmig.
crucify *v.t.* kreuzigen.
crude *a.*, **~ly** *adv.* roh, unreif; ~ **oil** *s.* Rohöl *n.;* ~ **rubber** *s.* Rohgummi *m.*
crudity *s.* Roheit, Unreife *f.*
cruel *a.*, **~ly** *adv.* grausam.
cruelty *s.* Grausamkeit *f.;* *~ to animals,* Tierquälerei *f.*
cruise *v.i.* hin- und herfahren; mit Reisegeschwindigkeit fliegen; mit Dauergeschwindigkeit fahren. ~ *s.* Kreuzen *n.;* Seefahrt *f.*
cruise missile *s.* Marschflugkörper *m.*
cruiser *s.* *(nav.)* Kreuzer *m.*
crumb *s.* Krume *f.;* Brösel *m.*, Krümel *m.*
crumble *v.i.* zerbröckeln; krümeln.
crumbly *a.* krümelig; bröckelig.
crumple *v.t.* zerknittern; ~ *v.i.* einschrumpfen.
crunch *v.t. & i.* knirschen; zerkauen.
crunchy *a.* knusprig; knackig.
crusade *s.* Kreuzzug *m.*
crusader *s.* Kreuzfahrer *m.*
crush *s.* Gedränge *n.*, Gewühl *n.;* Schwärmerei *f.;* ~ *v.t.* quetschen; unterdrücken; vernichten.
crust *s.* Rinde *f.;* Schale *f.;* Brotkruste *f.;* ~ *v.t.* mit einer Kruste überziehen.
crustacean *s.* Krebstier *n.;* Krustentier *n.*
crusty *s.*, **~ily** *adv.* krustig, rindig; mürrisch.
crutch *s.* Krücke *f.*
crux *s.* Crux *f.;* Kernpunkt *m.*
cry *v.i.* & t. schreien; weinen; rufen; ~ *s.* Geschrei *n.;* Zuruf *m.*
crypt *s.* Gruft, Krypta *f.*
cryptic *a.* geheim, undurchsichtig.
crystal *s.* Kristall *m.;* ~ *a.* kristallen.
crystal-gazing *s.* Hellseherei *f.*
crystalline *a.* kristallen.
crystallize *v.t. & i.* kristallisieren.
cu. *cubic,* Kubik.
cub *s.* Junge *n.;* ~ *v.t.* Junge werfen.
Cuba *s.* Kuba *n.*
Cuban *a.* kubanisch; ~ *s.* Kubaner(in) *m.(f.)*
cubby *s.* Spint *m.;* Kämmerchen *n.*
cube *s.* Kubus *m.;* Würfel *m.;* *~ (-number) s.* Kubikzahl *f.;* ~ **root** *s.* Kubikwurzel *f.*
cubic *a.* kubisch; ~ **meter,** Kubikmeter *m.*
cubicle *s.* Bettnische *f.;* Kabine *f.*
cubit *s.* Unterarm *m.;* Elle *f.* (1½ Fuß).
cuckold *s.* Hahnrei *m.*
cuckoo *s.* Kuckuck *m.*
cucumber *s.* Gurke *f.;* *pickled ~,* saure Gurke *f.*
cud *s.* Futter (*n.*) im Vormagen der Tiere; *to chew the ~,* wiederkäuen.
cuddle *v.t.* hätscheln, umarmen; ~ *s.* Liebkosung *f.*
cuddly *a.* verschmust.
cudgel *s.* Prügel *m.;* ~ *v.t.* prügeln.
cue *s.* Queue *n.*, Billardstock *m.;* Stichwort *n.;* Wink *m.*
cuff *s.* Puff *m.;* Manschette *f.;* Hosenaufschlag *m.;* ~ *v.t. & i.* puffen; sich schlagen.
cuisine *s.* Küche (Art zu kochen) *f.*
culinary *a.* zur Küche gehörig.
cull *v.t.* aussuchen; auslesen.
culminate *v.i.* kulminieren; gipfeln.
culmination *s.* Gipfelpunkt *m.*
culpability *s.* Strafbarkeit, Schuld *f.*
culpable *a.*, **~culpably** *adv.* strafbar, schuldig.
culprit *s.* Schuldiger *m.;* Verbrecher *m.*

cult *s.* Kult *m.*
cultivate *v.t.* anbauen; (Pflanzen, Pilze) züchten; ausbilden; pflegen.
cultivation *s.* Anbau *m.*; Pflege *f.*
cultivator *s.* Pflanzer *m.*
cultural *a.* kulturell.
culture *s.* Anbau *m.*; Bildung *f.*; Kultur *f.*; *~d pearl* Zuchtperle *f.*
cumber *v.t.* überhäufen; hindern.
cumbersome *a.*, **~ly** *adv.* lästig, hinderlich; unbehilflich.
cumulative *a.* aufhäufend.
cuneiform *a.* keilförmig; Keilschrift...
cunning *a.*, **~ly** *adv.* listig; kundig; ~ *s.* List *f.*; Geschicklichkeit *f.*
cup *s.* Becher *m.*; Tasse *f.*; Schröpfkopf *m.*; ~ *v.t.* schröpfen.
cupboard *s.* Schrank *m.*
cupful *s.* Tasse *f.*
cupidity *s.* Begierde *f.*, Habgier *f.*
cupola *s.* Kuppel *f.*
cur *s.* Köter *m.*; Schurke *m.*
curable *a.* heilbar.
curate *s.* Hilfsgeistlicher *m.*
curative *a.* heilend.
curator *s.* Kurator(in) *m.(f.)*; Direktor(in) *m.(f.)*
curb *s.* Kandare *f.*; Bordstein, Randstein *m.*; ~ *v.t.* bändigen, zügeln.
curd *s.* Quark *m.*; dicke Milch *f.*
curdle *v.t. & i.* gerinnen machen; gerinnen; erstarren.
cure *s.* Kur *f.*; ~ **of souls,** Seelsorge *f.*; ~ *v.t.* heilen; einpökeln; räuchern.
curfew *s.* Ausgehverbot *n.*; Ausgangssperre *f.*; *to lift the ~*, das Ausgehverbot aufheben.
curio *s.* Rarität *f.*
curiosity *s.* Neugierde *f.*; Kuriostät *f.*
curious *a.*, **~ly** *adv.* neugierig; sorgfältig; zierlich; seltsam.
curl *s.* Locke *f.*; Wallung *f.* ~ *v.t.* kräuseln; winden; ~ *v.i.* sich locken.
curler *s.* Lockenwickler *m.*
curling *s.* Eisstockschießen *n.*
curling-iron *s.* Brenneisen *n.*
curly *a.* gekräuselt.
curmudgeon *s.* Geizhals, Knicker *m.*
currant *s.* Korinthe *f.*; Johannisbeere *f.*
currency *s.* Lauf, Umlauf *m.*; Währung *f.*; Kurs *m.*; Umlaufsmittel *n.*; *hard ~*, feste Währung; *soft ~*, unstabile Währung.
current *a.*, **~ly** *adv.* (um)laufend; gangbar; geläufig; ~ *s.* Lauf, Strom *m.*; Zug *m.*; elektrischer Strom *m.*; *alternating ~ (AC)*, Wechselstrom *m.*; *direct ~ (DC)*, Gleichstrom *m.*
current: ~ **account** *s.* Girokonto *n.*; ~ **events** *pl.* Tagesereignisse *pl.*; ~ **meter** *s.* Stromzähler *m.*
curriculum *s.* Lehrplan *m.*; ~ **vitae** *s.* Lebenslauf *m.*
curry *v.t.* striegeln; prügeln; *to ~ favor,* die Gunst erschleichen; ~ *s.* Curry *m.* (ostindisches Mischgewürz).
currycomb *s.* Pferdestriegel *m.*
curse *s.* Fluch *m.*; Verwünschung *f.*; ~ *v.i. & t.* fluchen; verwünschen.
cursed *a.* verflucht.
cursive *a.* laufend, Kursiv...
cursor *s.* Läufer *m.*; Cursor *m.*
cursory *a.* flüchtig, oberflächlich.
curt *a.*, **~ly** *adv.* kurz, kurz angebunden.
curtail *v.t.* stutzen, abkürzen; verstümmeln; *(fig.)* einschränken.
curtailment *s.* Beschränkung, Kürzung *f.*
curtain *s.* Vorhang *m.*; *(mil.)* Zwischenwall *m.*; *to draw the ~*, den Vorhang zuziehen; ~ *v.t.* mit Vorhängen versehen, verhüllen.
curtain-fire *s.* *(mil.)* Sperrfeuer *n.*
curtain-rod *s.* Vorhangstange *f.*
curtsy *s.* Knicks *m.*; ~ *v.i.* knicksen.
curvaceous *a.* kurvenreich.
curvature *s.* Krümmung *f.*
curve *s.* Krümmung *f.*; ~ *v.t.* krümmen, biegen.
curved *a.* krumm, gebogen.
cushion *s.* Kissen *n.*; Polster *m.*
cushy *a.* bequem, weich.
cuss *s.* Fluch *m.*; Kerl *m.*
cussed *a.* stur.
cussedness *s.* Sturheit *f.*
custard *s.* Pudding *m.*
custodial *a.* vormundschaftlich.
custodian *s.* Hüter(in) *m.(f.)*; Wächter(in) *m.(f.)*; Kustos *m.*
custody *s.* Verwahrung *f.*; Haft *f.*; Aufsicht *f.*; Obhut *f.*; *protective ~*, Schutzhaft *f.*; *to take into ~*, verhaften.
custom *s.* Gebrauch *m.*; Gewohnheit *f.*; Kundschaft *f.*; Zoll *m.*
customary *a.*, **~ily** *adv.* gebräuchlich.
customer *s.* Kunde *m.*; Kundin *f.*; *regular ~*, Stammkunde, Stammgast *m.*
custom-made *a.* spezialgefertigt; maßgeschneidert.
customs *s.pl.* Zoll *m.*; ~ **clearance,** Zollabfertigung *f.*; ~ **declaration,** Zollerklärung *f.*; ~ **house** *s.* Zollamt *n.*, ~ **inspection,** Zollrevision *f.*; ~ **officer** *s.* Zollbeamter *m.*; ~ **station** Zollamt *n.*
cut *v.t. & i. st.* schneiden, hauen; schnitzen; spalten; verstümmeln; kürzen; abheben (Karten); *to ~ a person,* einen nicht sehen wollen, schneiden; *to ~ out, (mech.)* ausschalten; *(com.)* unterbieten; *to ~ prices,* Preise herabsetzen; *to ~ teeth,* Zähne bekommen; *~ and dried,* fix und fertig; ~ *s.* Schnitt, Einschnitt *m.*; Stich, Hieb *m.*; Kürzung *f.*; *short ~*, Abkürzungsweg *m.*
cutaneous *a.* zur Haut gehörig.
cutback *s.* Kürzung *f.*
cute *a.* *(fam.)* niedlich, schlau.
cut glass *s.* Kristallglas *n.*
cuticle *s.* Oberhaut *f.*, Häutchen *n.*
cutlery *s.* Messerwaren *f.pl.*
cutlet *s.* Schnitzel *n.*
cutter *s.* Steinschneider *m.*; Schneidezeug *n.*; Zuschneider *m.*; *(mech.)* Schneider *m.*; Kutter (Schiff) *m.*; Cutter(in) *m.(f.)*
cut-throat *s.* Meuchelmörder *m.*; ~ *a.* mörderisch, gnadenlos.
cutting *s.* Einschnitt *m.*; Zeitungsausschnitt *m.*; ~ *a.* schneidend, scharf.
cuttle *s.* Tintenfisch *m.*
CV *curriculum vitae,* Lebenslauf.
C.W.O. *cash with order,* Barzahlung bei Bestellung.
cwt. *hundredweight,* Zentner *m.*

cyanide *s.* Cyanid *n.*
cyclamen *s.* Alpenveilchen *n.*
cycle *s.* Kreis *m.;* Fahrrad *n.;* Zyklus *m.*
cycler *s.* Radfahrer(in) *m.(f.)*
cycling *s.* Radfahren *n.*
cyclist *s.* Radfahrer *m.;* **~'s path,** Radfahrweg *m.*
cyclone *s.* Wirbelsturm *m.*
cygnet *s.* junger Schwan *m.*
cylinder *s.* Zylinder *m.;* Walze *f.*
cylindrical *a.* zylindrisch.
cymbal *s.* Schallbecken *n.*, Zimbel *f.*
cynic *a.* zynisch; ~ *s.* Zyniker(in) *m.(f.)*
cynicism *s.* Zynismus *m.*
cypress *s.* Zypresse *f.*
cyst *s.* Blase *f.;* Eitersack *m.*
czar *s.* Zar *m.*
Czech *a.* tschechisch; ~ *s.* Tscheche *m.*, Tschechin *f.*
Czech Republic *s.* Tschechische Republik *f.*

D

D, d der Buchstabe D oder d *n.; (mus.)* D, d; **D-sharp** Dis, dis; **D-flat** Des, des.
d. *died,* gestorben, gest.; *depth,* Tiefe, T.
DA *deposit account,* Depositenkonto.
dab *v.t.* betupfen; besudeln; ~ *s.* Tupfer *m.;* Klecks *m.*
dabble *v.i.* planschen; stümpern; ~ *v.t.* bespritzen.
dachshund *s.* Dachshund *m.*, Dackel *m.*
dad, daddy *s.* Papa, Vater *m.;* ~ **longlegs** *s.* langbeinige Mücke *f.;* Weberknecht *m.*
daffodil *s.* gelbe Narzisse *f.*
daft *a.* doof; blöd.
dagger *s.* Dolch *m.*
dahlia *s.* Dahlie *f.*
daily *a. & adv.* täglich; ~ *s.* Tageszeitung *f.*
dainty *a.*, ~ily *adv.* lecker; niedlich; zierlich, fein; geziert; heikel; ~ *s.* Leckerbissen *m.*, Naschwerk *n.*
dairy *s.* Molkerei *f.;* Milchwirtschaft *f.;* ~ **farm** Meierei *f.*
dairy produce *s.* **products** *s.pl.* Molkereiprodukte *n.pl.*
dais *s.* Podium *n.*
daisy *s.* Gänseblümchen *n.;* Margerite *f.*
dale *s.* Tal *n.*
dalliance *s.* Tändelei *f.;* Trödelei *f.;* Verzögerung *f.*
dally *v.i.* tändeln, trödeln.
dam *s.* Damm *m.;* Talsperre *f.;* Muttertier *f.;* ~ *v.t.* dämmen.
damage *s.* Schaden, Verlust *m.;* Beschädigung *f.; property* ~, Sachbeschädigung *f.;* ~ *v.t.* beschädigen.
damageable *a.* leicht zu beschädigen.
damages *s.pl.* Schadenersatz *m.*
damaging *a.* schädlich.
damask *s.* Damast *m.;* ~ *a.* damasten.
dame *s.* Dame *f.* (Adelstitel); *(fam.)* Weid *n.*
damn *v.t.* verdammen; verwerfen.
damnation *s.* Verdammung *f.*
damned *a.* verdammt, verflucht.
damning *a.* vernichtend; belastend.
damp *a.* feucht, dumpfig; ~ *s.* Feuchtigkeit *f.;* Schwaden *m.;* ~ *v.t.* befeuchten; dämpfen.
damper *s.* Dämpfer *m.*
dampness *s.* Feuchtigkeit *f.*
damp-proof *a.* feuchtigkeitssicher.
damsel *s.* Mädchen *n.;* Jungfer *f.*
dance *s.* Tanz *m.;* ~ *v.i.* tanzen; *ballroom dancing,* Gesellschaftstanz *m.*
dance master *s.* Tanzlehrer *m.*
dancer *s.* Tänzer(in) *m.(f.)*
dandelion *s. (bot.)* Löwenzahn *m.*
dandle *v.t.* schaukeln, hätscheln.
dandruff *s.* Kopfschuppen *f.pl.*
dandy *s.* Stutzer *m.*, Dandy *m.*
Dane *s.* Däne *m.;* Dänin *f.*
danger *s.* Gefahr *f.* ~ **signal** *s.* Warnzeichen.
dangerous *a.*, **~ly** *adv.* gefährlich.
dangle *v.i.* baumeln; anhängen.
Danish *a.* dänisch; ~ *s.* Däne *m.*, Dänin *f.*
dank *a.* unangenehm feucht.
Danube *s.* Donau *f.*
dapper *a.* flink, gewandt; nett.
dapple *a.* gefleckt, scheckig; ~ *v.t.* sprenkeln.
dare *v.i.* dürfen; wagen; *I ~ say,* ich denke; ~ *v.t.* trotzen.
daredevil *a.* waghalsig; ~ *s.* Draufgänger(in) *m.(f.);* Teufelskerl *m.*
daring *a.*, **~ly** *adv.* vermessen, verwegen; ~ *s.* Kühnheit *f.*
dark *a.* dunkel, trübe; *Dark Ages pl.* finsteres Mittelalter *n.;* ~ **room** *s.* Dunkelkammer *f.; after* ~, nach Eintritt der Dunkelheit; ~ *s.* Finsternis *f.*
darken *v.t. & i.* verdunkeln; dunkel werden.
darkish *a.* etwas dunkel.
darkness *s.* Dunkelheit *f.;* Verborgenheit *f.;* Unwissenheit *f.*
darling *a.* teuer; ~ *s.* Liebling *m.*
darn *v.t.* stopfen, ausbessern.
darned *a. adv.* verflixt.
darning *s.* Stopfen *n.;* ~ **needle** *s.* Stopfnadel *f.*
dart *s.* Wurfgeschoß *n.;* Pfeil *m.;* ~ *v.t.* werfen, schießen; ~ *v.i.* hinschießen, stürzen; **~s** *s.pl.* Pfeilwurfspiel *n.*
dash *v.t.* schmeißen, stoßen; vermischen; zerschmettern; vereiteln; ~ *v.i.* stoßen; stürmen, stürzen, jagen; dahinrauschen; scheitern; ~ *s.* Klatsch, Schlag, Stoß *m.;* Federzug *m.*; Gedankenstrich *m.;* Aufguß *m.;* Stückchen, Bißchen *n.;* Wagemut *m.*, Schneid *f.*
dashboard *s.* Armaturenbrett *n.*
dashing *a.* schneidig, flott.
dastard *s.* feige Memme *f.;* ~ *a.*, **~ly** *adv.* feig; abscheulich.
data *s.pl.* Daten; **~bank** *s.* Datenbank *f.;* ~ **processing** Datenverarbeitung *f.;* ~ **transmission** *s.* Datenübertragung *f.*
date *s.* Datum *n.;* Frist *f.;* Dattel *f.; what is the ~?,* den wievielten haben wir?; *up-to-~*, zeitgemäß, modern; *out of ~*, aus der Mode; ~ *v.t.* datieren; mit jemandem ausgehen.

dated *a.* altmodisch.
date palm *s.* Dattelpalme *f.*
dative *s. (gram.)* Dativ *m.*
daub *v.t.* überschmieren, sudeln.
daughter *s.* Tochter *f.;* **~-in-law,** Schwiegertochter *f.*
daunt *v.t.* entmutigen.
dauntless *a.* unerschrocken.
davit *s.* Jütte *f.*, Davit *m.*
dawdle *v.i.* trödeln; schlendern.
dawdler *s.* Tagedieb *m.*
dawn *v.i.* dämmern, tagen; ~ *s.* Dämmerung *f.*
day *s.* Tag *m.; by ~,* untertags; *the other ~,* neulich; **~s of grace** *pl.* Verzugstage *m.pl.*
daybreak *s.* Tagesanbruch *m.*
day care *s.* Kinderbetreuung.
daydream *s.* Tagtraum *m.*
daylight *s.* Tageslicht; *(avi.)* ~ **attack,** Tagesangriff *m.*
day nursery *s.* Kinderhort *m.*
day shift *s.* Tagesschicht *f.*
daytime *s.* Tageszeit *f.; in the ~,* bei Tag.
day trip *s.* Tagesausflug *m.*
daze *v.t.* benommen machen; ~ *s.* Benommenheit *f.*
dazzle *v.t.* blenden.
DC *direct current,* Gleichstrom; *District of Columbia* (Distrikt der amerikanischen Hauptstadt Washington).
D.C.L. *Doctor of Civil Law,* Doktor des bürgerlichen Rechts.
D.D. *Doctor of Divinity,* Doktor der Theologie.
D.D.S. *Doctor of Dental Surgery,* Doktor der Zahnmedizin, Dr. med. dent.
DDT *dichlorodiphenyltrichloroethane,* Dichlordiphenyl-trichloräthan, DDT.
deacon *s.* Diakon *m.*
dead *a.* tot; dumpf, schal; *(elek.)* spannungslos; *~ against,* gerade entgegen; ~ *adv.* ganz, völlig; *the ~,* die Toten *pl.*
deaden *v.t.* abstumpfen, schwächen.
dead end *s.* Sackgasse *f.*
dead letter *s.* unzustellbarer Brief *m.*
deadline *s.* Termin *m.*
deadlock *s.* Stockung *f.*, Stillstand *m.*
deadly *a. & adv.* tödlich.
deadpan *a.* ausdruckslos; trocken.
dead silence *s.* Totenstille *f.*
deaf *a.*, **~ly** *adv.* taub; dumpf; *~ and dumb,* taubstumm.
deafen *v.t.* taub machen.
deafening *a.* ohrenbetäubend.
deaf-mute *s.* Taubstummer *m.;* ~ *a.* taubstumm.
deafness *s.* Taubheit *f.*
deal *s.* Teil *m.;* Anzahl *f.;* Geschäft *f.;* Kartengeben *n.;* Fichtenholz, Brett *n.; a good ~, a great ~,* viel, sehr; ~ *v.t.* austeilen, ausstreuen; Karten geben; ~ *v.i.* handeln, verfahren; vermitteln; *to ~ with,* behandeln.
dealer *s.* Händler *m.;* Kartengeber *m.*
dealing *s.* Verfahren *n.;* Austeilen *n.;* Umgang *m.; to have ~s with sb.,* mit einem zu tun haben.
dean *s.* Dechant, Dekan *m.*
dear *a.* teuer, wert; innig; ~ *s.* Geliebter *m.*, Geliebte *f.;* ~ **me!,** meine liebe Güte!
dearth *s.* Teuerung *f.;* Mangel *m.*
death *s.* Tod *m.;* Todesfall *m.; to put to ~,* hinrichten.
deathbed *s.* Sterbebett *n.*
death blow *s.* Todesstoß *m.*
death certificate *s.* Totenschein *m.*
deathless *a.* unsterblich.
deathly *a.* tödlich, Todes...
death penalty *s.* Todesstrafe *f.*
death rate *s.* Sterblichkeitsziffer *f.*
death's head *s.* Totenkopf *m.*
death toll *s.* Zahl der Todesopfer *f.*
death warrant *s.* Todesurteil *n.*
debacle *s.* Debakel *n.*
debar *v.t.* ausschließen; verhindern.
debase *v.t.* erniedrigen; verfälschen.
debasement *s.* Erniedrigung *f.*
debatable *a.* streitig.
debate *s.* Debatte *f.;* ~ *v.t.* bestreiten, erörtern.
debauch *v.t.* verführen, verderben.
debauchee *s.* Schwelger, Wüstling *m.*
debauchery *s.* Ausschweifung *f.*
debenture *s.* Schuldschein *m.; (com.)* Obligation *f.*
debilitate *v.t.* schwächen, entkräften.
debilitation *s.* Schwächung *f.;* Entkräftung *f.*
debility *s.* Schwachheit.
debit *v.t.* belasten, debitieren; ~ *s.* Soll *n.;* Lasten *f.pl.*
debonair *a.* gefällig, höflich.
debouch *v.i.* hervorbrechen; einmünden.
debris *s.* Trümmer *pl.*
debt *s.* Schuld *f.; to go into ~,* in Schulden geraten.
debtor *s.* Schuldner(in) *m.(f.)*
debug *v.t. (fam.)* entwanzen (Abhörgeräte entfernen); Fehler beheben.
debut *s.* Debüt *n.*
debutante *s.* Debütantin *f.*
Dec. *December,* Dezember, Dez.
dec. decd., *deceased,* gestorben, gest.
decade *s.* Jahrzehnt *n.*
decadence *s.* Dekadenz *f.*, Verfall *m.*
decadent *a.* dekadent.
Decalogue *s.* Dekalog *m.*
decamp *v.i.* aufbrechen, ausreißen.
decant *v.t.* abgießen; umfüllen.
decanter *s.* Karaffe *f.*
decapitate *v.t.* köpfen.
decathlon *s.* Zehnkampf *m.*
decay *v.i.* verfallen; verwelken; ~ *s.* Verfall *m.;* Abnahme *f.*
decease *s.* Ableben *n.;* ~ *v.i.* sterben, verscheiden.
deceased *a.* verstorben; ~ *s.* Verstorbene *m.*
deceit *s.* Betrug *m.;* List *f.*
deceitful *a.*, **~ly** *adv.* betrügerisch.
deceitfulness *s.* Falschheit *f.;* Hinterlistigkeit *f.*
deceive *v.t.* betrügen, täuschen.
December *s.* Dezember *m.*
decency *s.* Anstand *m.;* Schicklichkeit *f.*
decennial *a.* zehnjährig.
decent *a.*, **~ly** *adv.* sittsam, anständig.
decentralization *s.* Dezentralisierung *f.*
decentralize *v.t.* dezentralisieren.

deception *s.* Betrug *m.*
deceptive *a.* trügerisch.
decibel *s.* Dezibel *n.*
decide *v.t.* entscheiden, bestimmen.
decided *a. & adv.* entschieden, bestimmt.
deciduous *a.* ~ **tree** laubwerfender Baum, Laubbaum *m.*
decimal *a.* dezimal; ~ *s.* Dezimale.
decimate *v.t.* dezimieren.
decipher *v.t.* entziffern.
decision *s.* Entscheidung *f.*; Entschlossenheit *f.*
decisive *a.*, **~ly** *adv.* entscheidend.
deck *s.* Deck, Verdeck *n.*; ~ *v.t.* bekleiden; schmücken.
deck chair *s.* Liegestuhl *m.*
declaim *v.t.* deklamieren; eifern.
declamation *s.* Deklamation *f.*
declamatory *s.* deklamatorisch.
declaration *s.* Erklärung *f.*
declare *v.t.* erklären, behaupten; (Zoll) deklarieren; ~ *v.i.* sich erklären.
declassify *v.t.* freigeben (Dokument).
declension *s.* *(gram.)* Deklination *f.*
declination *s.* Abweichung *f.*; Abnahme *f.*; Deklination *f.*
decline *v.i.* abweichen; abnehmen; sich weigern; fallen (im Preise); ~ *v.t.* ablehnen; deklinieren; ~ *s.* Abnahme *f.*; Verfall *m.*
declivity *s.* Abhang *m.*
declutch *v.t.* auskuppeln.
decoction *s.* Absud *m.*, Absieden *n.*
decode *v.t.* entziffern.
decompose *v.t.* zerlegen; ~ *v.i.* zerfallen, zersetzen.
decomposition *s.* Zersetzung *f.*
decompression *s.* Dekompression *f.*
decontaminate *v.t.* dekontaminieren, entseuchen.
decontamination *s.* Dekontamination *f.*; Entseuchung *f.*
decontrol *v.t.* freigeben.
decor *s.* Ausstattung *f.*
decorate *v.t.* verzieren, schmücken.
decoration *s.* Dekoration *f.*, Schmuck *m.*; Ordenszeichen *n.*
decorative *a.* schmückend.
decorator *s.* Dekorateur(in) *m.(f.)*; Tapezierer(in) *m.(f.)*
decorous *a.*, **~ly** *adv.* anständig, schicklich.
decorum *s.* Anstand *m.*, Schicklichkeit *f.*
decoy *v.t.* locken, ködern; ~ *s.* Köder *m.*
decrease *v.t.* vermindern; ~ *v.i.* abnehmen; ~ *s.* Abnahme *f.*
decree *v.t.* beschließen; verfügen; ~ *s.* Beschluß *m.*, Verordnung *f.*
decrepit *a.* altersschwach, heruntergekommen.
decrepitude *s.* Altersschwäche *f.*
decry *v.t.* herabsetzen; schlechtmachen.
dedicate *v.t.* widmen, zueignen.
dedication *s.* Widmung, Zueignung *f.*
dedicatory *a.* Widmungs...
deduce *v.t.* ableiten; schließen, folgern.
deducible *a.* ableitbar.
deduct *v.t.* abziehen, abrechnen.
deduction *s.* Abzug, Rabatt *m.*; Schlußfolge *f.*
deductive *a.*, **~ly** *adv.* deduktiv, folgernd.
deed *s.* Tat, Handlung *f.*; Urkunde *f.*; ~ **of gift,** Schenkungsurkunde *f.*; ~ **of partnership,** Gesellschaftsvertrag *m.*; ~ **of sale,** Kaufkontrakt *m.*
deem *v.t.* halten für, erachten.
deep *a.*, **~ly** *adv.* tief; geheim; schlau; ~ *s.* Tiefe *f.*; Meer *n.*
deepen *v.t.* vertiefen; ~ *v.i. & r.* vertiefen; stärker werden.
deep-freeze *s.* Tiefkühlgerät *n.*; ~ *v.t.* tiefkühlen, einfrieren.
deep-fry *v.t.* fritieren.
deep-rooted *a.* tiefverwurzelt.
deer *s.* Hirsch *m.*; Rotwild *n.*
deerskin *s.* Wildleder *n.*
deerstalking *s.* Pirschen *n.*
deface *v.t.* verunstalten, entstellen.
defalcate *v.i.* (Geld) unterschlagen.
defamation *s.* Verleumdung *f.*; Diffamierung *f.*
defamatory *a.* verleumderisch.
defame *v.t.* verleumden; verlästern.
default *s.* Versäumnis *n.*; Zahlungseinstellung *f.*; Nichterscheinen *n.*; *in ~ of,* mangels; *judgment by ~,* (*jur.*) Versäumnisurteil *n.*; ~ *v.i.* unterlassen; fehlen; im Verzug sein, Verpflichtungen nicht erfüllen.
defaulter *s.* säumiger Zahler *m.*; zum Termin nicht Erscheinender *m.*
defeat *v.t.* besiegen; schlagen; vereiteln; ~ *s.* Niederlage, Vereitelung *f.*
defeatism *s.* Miesmacherei *f.*, Defätismus *m.*
defeatist *s.* Defätist *m.*; ~ *a.* defätistisch.
defecate *v.i.* defäkieren, Darm entleeren.
defect *s.* Mangel *m.*; Gebrechen *n.*; *speech ~,* Sprachfehler *m.*
defection *s.* Überlaufen *n.*; Abtrünnigkeit *f.*; Abfall *m.*
defective *a.* mangelhaft, unvollständig.
defector *s.* Überläufer(in) *m.(f.)*; Abtrünnige *m./f.*
defend *v.t.* verteidigen.
defendant *s.* Verteidiger *m.*; (*jur.*) Angeklagter, Beklagter *m.*
defender *s.* Verteidiger(in) *m.(f.)*
defense *s.* Verteidigung (auch *jur.*) *f.*; (*mil.*) Widerstand *m.*; *witness for the ~,* Entlastungszeuge *m.*
defenseless *a.*, **~ly** *adv.* wehrlos.
defense mechanism *s.* Abwehrmechanismus *m.*
defensible *a.* zu verteidigen, haltbar.
defensive *a.*, **~ly** *adv.* Verteidigungs...; ~ *s.* (*mil.*) Defensive *f.*; *to be on the ~,* in der Defensive sein.
defer *v.t.* aufschieben, vorenthalten; (*mil.*) zurückstellen; *~ red shares,* Verzugsaktien *f.pl.*; ~ *v.i.* sich beugen, nachgeben.
deference *s.* Ehrerbietung *f.*; Nachgiebigkeit *f.*
deferential *a.*, **~ly** *adv.* ehrerbietig.
deferment *s.* (*mil.*) Aufschub *m.*; Zurückstellung *f.*
defiance *s.* Herausforderung *f.*; Trotz *m.*
defiant *a.* herausfordernd, trotzig.
deficiency *s.* Mangel *m.*
deficient *a.* unzulänglich, mangelhaft.
deficit *s.* Fehlbetrag *m.*, Defizit *n.*
defile *v.t.* beflecken; ~ *v.i.* defilieren; ~ *s.* Engpaß *m.*
defilement *s.* Befleckung *f.*
define *v.t.* festsetzen; definieren.

definite *a.* festgesetzt, bestimmt.
definitely *adv.* eindeutig; endgültig.
definition *s.* Begriffsbestimmung *f.*, Definition *f.*; (*TV*) Schärfe *f.*
definitive *a.*, **~ly** *adv.* endgültig.
deflate *v.t.* Luft rauslassen (aus Reifen), ernüchtern.
deflation *s.* Entleerung *f.*; Deflation *f.*
deflationary *a.* deflationär.
deflect *v.t.* & *i.* ablenken; abweichen.
deflection *s.* Abweichung *f.*
deform *v.t.* verunstalten, entstellen.
deformity *s.* Ungestaltheit *f.*, Gebrechen *n.*
defraud *v.t.* betrügen.
defray *v.t.* übernehmen, bezahlen.
defrost *v.t.* auftauen; enteisen.
deft *a.*, **~ly** *adv.* geschickt, gewandt.
defunct *a.* verstorben; defekt; veraltet.
defuse *v.t.* entschärfen.
defy *v.t.* herausfordern, trotzen.
deg. *degree*, Grad *m.*
degeneracy *s.* Entartung *f.*
degenerate *v.i.* entarten ~ *a.*, **~ly** *adv.* ausgeartet, schlecht, entartet.
degeneration *s.* Degeneration *f.*
degradation *s.* Erniedrigung *f.*
degrade *v.t.* herabsetzen, erniedrigen, herabwürdigen; vermindern.
degrading *a.* entwürdigend.
degree *s.* Grad *m.*; Stufe *f.*; Diplom *n.*
dehydrate *v.t.* Wasser entziehen, **~d** *a.* dehydratisiert; **~d food,** Trockennahrung *f.*
de-ice *v.t.* enteisen.
deify *v.t.* vergöttern.
deign *v.t.* geruhen; belieben.
deity *s.* Gottheit *f.*
deject *v.t.* entmutigen.
dejected *a.* niedergeschlagen.
dejection *s.* Niedergeschlagenheit *f.*
delay *v.t.* aufschieben, hinhalten; hindern; **~ed action,** (mit) Verzug *m.*; ~ *v.i.* zaudern; ~ *s.* Aufschub *m.*, Verzug *m.*
delectable *a.*, **delectably** *adv.* köstlich, angenehm.
delegacy *s.* Abordnung *f.*
delegate *v.t.* abordnen; übertragen; *to ~ authority,* Befugnis übertragen; ~ *s.* Abgeordneter *m.*
delegation *s.* Abordnung *f.*
delete *v.t.* auslöschen, tilgen.
deleterious *a.* schädlich.
deletion *s.* (*comp.*) Streichung *f.*; Löschung *f.*
deliberate *v.i.* beratschlagen; ~ *a.* absichtlich.
deliberation *s.* Beratschlagung *f.*
deliberative *a.* beratschlagend.
delicacy *s.* Schmackhaftigkeit *f.*; Leckerbissen *m.*; Zartheit *n.*
delicate *a.*, **~ly** *adv.* zart; fein; heikel.
delicatessen *pl.* Feinkostgeschäft *n.*
delicious *a.*, köstlich.
delight *s.* Vergnügen *n.*; Wonne *f.*; ~ *v.t.* ergötzen, vergnügen; ~ *v.i.* Vergnügen finden.
delighted *a.* hocherfreut.
delightful *a.*, **~ly** *adv.* entzückend.
delimit *v.t.* abgrenzen; begrenzen.
delimitation *s.* Abgrenzung *f.*
delineate *v.t.* zeichnen, entwerfen.
delinquency *s.* Vergehen *n.*; Kriminalität *f.*
delinquent *s.* Delinquent(in) *m.(f.)*; Straffällige *m.*
delirious *a.* wahnsinnig.
delirium *s.* (Fieber-) Wahnsinn *m.*
deliver *v.t.* überliefern; befreien; vortragen; entbinden; abliefern; (Angriff) ausführen.
deliverance *s.* Befreiung *f.*; Erlösung *f.*
delivery *s.* Lieferung *f.*; Befreiung *f.*; Vortrag *m.*; Entbindung *f.*; Briefbestellung *f.*
delivery note *s.* Lieferschein *m.*
delta *s.* Delta *n.*
delude *v.t.* betrügen, täuschen.
deluge *s.* Überschwemmung *f.*; Sintflut *f.*; ~ *v.t.* überschwemmen.
delusion *s.* Täuschung *f.*; Wahn *m.*
delusive *a.*, **~ly** *adv.* täuschend.
deluxe *a.* Luxus...
delve *v.t.* graben; ~ *v.i.* & *r.* vertiefen.
demagogic *a.* demagogisch.
demagogue *s.* Aufwiegler(in) *m.(f.)*; Demagoge *m.*, Demagogin *f.*
demand *v.t.* fordern; fragen; verlangen; ~ *s.* Forderung *f.*; Frage *f.*; Anspruch *m.*; Nachfrage *f.*
demanding *a.* anspruchsvoll.
demarcate *v.t.* abgrenzen.
demarcation *s.* Grenzlinie *f.*
demean *v.t.* & *r.* erniedrigen.
demeaning *a.* erniedrigend.
demeanor *s.* Betragen *n.*
demented *a.* toll, verrückt.
démenti *s.* Dementi *n.*
demi- (*prefix*) halb.
demigod *s.* Halbgott *m.*
demilitarize *v.t.* entmilitarisieren.
demise *s.* Übertragung *f.*; Ableben *n.*; ~ *v.t.* vermachen; verpachten.
demobilize *v.t.* abrüsten, demobilisieren.
democracy *s.* Demokratie *f.*
democrat *s.* Demokrat(in) *m.(f.)*
democratic *a.* demokratisch.
democratically *adv.* demokratisch.
demolish *v.t.* niederreißen, abtragen; abreißen.
demolition *s.* Niederreißen *n.*; Abriß *m.*; Zerstörung *f.*
demon *s.* Dämon *m.*; Teufel *m.*
demoniac *a.* dämonisch.
demonstrable *a.*, **~bly** *adv.* beweisbar.
demonstrate *v.t.* beweisen.
demonstration *s.* Beweis *m.*; Äußerung (des Gefühls) *f.*; Vorführung *f.*; Demonstration *f.*
demonstrative *a.*, **~ly** *adv.* beweisend; auffällig; (*gram.*) hinweisend.
demonstrator *s.* Demonstrant(in) *m.(f.)*
demoralization *s.* Demoralisierung *f.*
demoralize *v.t.* demoralisieren.
demotivate *v.t.* demotivieren.
demur *v.i.* Einwände erheben.
demure *a.*, **~ly** *adv.* betont zurückhaltend, gesetzt.
demurrer *s.* Rechtseinwand *m.*
den *s.* Höhle, Grube *f.*; (*inf.*) Bude *f.*
denial *s.* Verneinung, Verweigerung *f.*
denigrate *v.t.* verunglimpfen.
denizen *s.* Bewohner *m.*
Denmark *s.* Dänemark *n.*

denomination *s.* Benennung *f.;* Klasse *f.;* Nennwert (Banknote, Scheck) *m.;* Konfession *f.*
denominational *a.* konfessionell.
denominative *a.* benennend.
denominator *a.* (*ar.*) Nenner *m.*
denote *v.t.* bezeichnen, bedeuten.
denounce *v.t.* verklagen, anklagen; denunzieren.
dense *a.* dicht, fest; dumm.
denseness *s.* Dichte *f.;* (*fig.*) Begriffsstutzigkeit *f.*
density *s.* Dichtheit *f.*
dent *s.* Kerbe *f.*, Einschnitt *m.;* Beule *f.;* ~ *v.t.* einbeulen.
dental *a.* Zahn...
dental surgeon *s.* Zahnarzt *m.*, Zahnärztin *f.*
dentist *s.* Zahnarzt *m.*, Zahnärztin *f.*
dentistry *s.* Zahnheilkunde *f.*
dentrifrice *s.* Zahnpulver *n.*
dentures *s.* Gebiß *n.*
denude *v.t.* entblößen.
denunciate *v.t.* denunzieren.
denunciation *s.* Anzeige; Anklage *f.*
deny *v.t.* verneinen; abschlagen; (ver)leugnen.
deodorant *s.* Deodorant *n.*
deodorize *v.t.* geruchlos machen.
dep. *departure,* Abfahrt, Abf.
depart *v.i.* abreisen; weggehen; abweichen.
department *s.* Abteilung *f.;* Bezirk *m.;* Geschäftskreis *m.;* Behörde *f.;* Ministerium *n.*
department store *s.* Kaufhaus *n.*
departure *s.* Abreise *f.;* Abweichung *f.;* (*fig.*) Tod *m.; a new* ~, ein neuer Anfang *m.*
depend *v.i.* abhängen; *to* ~ *on,* sich verlassen auf; *it* ~*s,* es kommt darauf an; je nachdem.
dependable *a.* zuverlässig.
dependant *s.* Abhängige *m./f.*
dependence *s.* Abhängigkeit *f.*
dependency *s.* Besitzung, Kolonie *f.*
dependent *a.* abhängig.
depict *v.t.* darstellen.
depilatory *s.* Enthaarungsmittel *n.*
deplete *v.t.* entleeren; erschöpfen.
depletion *s.* Entleerung *f.*
deplorable *a.*, **~bly** *adv.* beklagenswert.
deplore *v.t.* beklagen, beweinen.
deploy *v.t.* aufmarschieren, Truppen einsetzen.
deployment *s.* Aufmarsch *m.;* Einsatz *m.*
deponent *s.* vereidigter Zeuge *m.*
depopulate *v.t.* entvölkern.
deport *v.t.* fortschaffen, deportieren.
deportation *s.* Deportation *f.*
deportee *s.* Deportierter *m.*
depose *v.t. & i.* niedersetzen; absetzen.
deposit *v.t.* niederlegen; ablegen; deponieren; ausleihen; ablagern; ~ *s.* Unterpfand, Pfand *n.;* Kaution *f.;* Einlage *f.;* Depot *n.*, Einzahlung *f.*, Depositum *n.;* anvertrautes Gut *n.;* Niederschlag *m.;* (Erz-)lager *n.*
depositary *s.* Verwahrer *m.*
deposition *s.* Absetzung *f.;* Zeugenaussage *f.*
depositor *s.* Einzahler, Hinterleger *m.*
depository *s.* Gewahrsam *m.;* Niederlage *f.;* Verwahrungsort *m.*
depot *s.* Lagerhaus *n.*
deprave *v.t.* verderben.
deprecate *v.t.* mißbilligen.
deprecatory *a.* mißbilligend.
depreciate *v.t.* herabsetzen, verkleinern; entwerten; abschreiben.
depreciation *s.* Wertverlust *m.;* Abschreibung *f.*
depredation *s.* Plünderung *f.;* Räuberei *f.*
depress *v.t.* niederdrücken, deprimieren.
depressant *s.* Beruhigungsmittel *n.*
depressed *a.* deprimiert.
depressed area *a.* Notstandsgebiet *n.*
depression *s.* Tief *n.;* Niedergeschlagenheit *f.;* Erniedrigung *f.;* Sinken (im Preis) *n.*
depressive *a.* deprimiert, depressiv.
deprivation *s.* Entzug *m.;* Aberkennung *f.*
deprive *v.t.* berauben; entziehen.
deprived *a.* benachteiligt.
dept. *department,* Abteilung *f.*, Abt.
depth *s.* Tiefe *f.;* ~ **charge,** Unterwasserbombe *f.*
deputation *s.* Abordnung *f.;* Delegation *f.*
depute *v.t.* abordnen.
deputy *s.* Abgeordnete *m.;* Stellvertreter(in) *m.(f.)*
derail *v.t. & i* entgleisen.
derailment *s.* Entgleisung *f.*
derange *v.t.* zerrütten.
deranged *a.* geistesgestört.
derangement *s.* Unordnung *f.;* Geisteszerrüttung *f.*
derelict *a.* verlassen, herrenlos; ~ *s.* Obdachlose *m.*
dereliction *s.* Vernachlässigung *f.;* ~ **of duty,** Pflichtvergessenheit *f.*
deride *v.t.* verlachen.
derision *s.* Verspottung *f.;* Spott *m.*
derisive *a.* spöttisch, höhnisch.
derisory *a.* lächerlich; spöttisch.
derivation *s.* Ableitung, Herleitung *f.*
derivative *a.*, **~ly** *adv.* hergeleitet; abgeleitet; ~ *s.* abgeleitetes Wort *n.*, Ableitung *f.;* (*chem.*) Derivat *n.*
derive *v.t.* ableiten; herleiten.
dermatitis *s.* Hautentzündung *f.*
dermatologist *s.* Dermatologe *m.*, Dermatologin *f.;* Hautarzt *m.*, Hautärztin *f.*
derogate *v.i.* Abbruch tun.
derogation *s.* Schmälerung *f.*
derogatory *a.* verletzend; abfällig.
derrick *s.* Hebekran *m.*
descant *s.* Diskantstimme *f.*
descend *v.i. & t.* herabsteigen; landen; abstammen; sich senken.
descendant *s.* Nachkomme *m./f.*
descent *s.* Herabsteigen *n.;* Abstieg *m.;* Senkung *f.;* Abstammung *f.*
describe *v.t.* beschreiben, schildern.
description *s.* Beschreibung *f.;* Sorte *f.*
descriptive *a.* beschreibend.
descry *v.t.* ausspähen, entdecken.
desecrate *v.t.* entweihen.
desegregate *v.t.* die Rassentrennung aufheben.
desegregation *s.* Aufhebung der Rassentrennung.
desert *a.* öde, wild; ~ *s.* Wüste *f.;* ~ *v.t. & i.* verlassen, entlaufen, desertieren.
deserted *a.* verlassen.
deserter *s.* Fahnenflüchtige *m./f.*, Deserteur *m.*
desertion *s.* Fahnenflucht *f.*
deserve *v.t.* verdienen.
deservedly *adv.* verdientermaßen.

deserving *a.*, **~ly** *adv.* verdienstvoll.
desiccated *a.* getrocknet.
desideratum *s.* Wünschenswertes *n.*
design *v.t. & i.* bestimmen; entwerfen, zeichnen; planen; ~ *s.* Absicht *f.;* Entwurf *m.;* Zeichnung *f.;* Muster *n.*
designate *v.t.* bezeichnen; ernennen.
designation *s.* Bezeichnung, Bestimmung *f.*
designer *s.* Musterzeichner(in) *m.(f.);* Designer(in) *m.(f.)*
designing *a.* hinterlistig.
desirable *a.* wünschenswert.
desire *s.* Verlangen *n.;* Wunsch *m.;* ~ *v.t.* wünschen, verlangen; bitten.
desirous *a.*, **~ly** *adv.* wünschend, begierig.
desist *v.i.* ablassen.
desk *s.* Pult *n.;* Schreibtisch *m.*
desolate *a.*, **~ly** *adv.* öde; wüst; betrübt; ~ *v.t.* verwüsten.
desolation *s.* Verwüstung, Einöde *f.*
despair *s.* Verzweiflung *f.;* ~ *v.i.* verzweifeln.
desperate *a.*, **~ly** *adv.* verzweifelt; verwegen.
desperation *s.* Verzweiflung *f.*
despicable *a.*, **~bly** *adv.* verachtenswert; verabscheuungswürdig.
despise *v.t.* verachten, verschmähen.
despite *pr.* trotz.
despoil *v.t.* plündern.
despondency *s.* Kleinmut *m.;* Niedergeschlagenheit *f.*
despondent *a.* verzagend, niedergeschlagen.
despot *s.* Gewaltherrscher, Despot *m.*
despotic *a.*, **~ly** *adv.* despotisch.
despotism *s.* Gewaltherrschaft *f.*
dessert *s.* Nachtisch *m.*
destination *s.* Bestimmung *f.;* Ziel *n.*
destine *v.t.* bestimmen.
destiny *s.* Schicksal, Verhängnis *n.*
destitute *a.* mittellos; verlassen, hilflos.
destitution *s.* Hilflosigkeit, Not *f.*
destroy *v.t.* zerstören, verwüsten.
destroyer *s.* Zerstörer (auch Schiff) *m.*
destruction *s.* Zerstörung *f.*
destructive *a.*, **~ly** *adv.* zerstörend.
desultory *a.* sprunghaft; oberflächlich.
detach *v.t.* entfernen, ablösen.
detachable *a.* abtrennbar.
detachment *s.* Ablösung *f.;* Detachement, Absonderung *f.;* (*mil.*) Abteilung *f.*, Trupp *m.*
detail *v.t.* einzeln aufführen; (*mil.*) abordnen; ~ *s.* Einzelheit *f.;* Detail *n.;* *in* ~, ausführlich; **~ed** *a.* ausführlich, genau, eingehend.
detain *v.t.* zurückhalten; abhalten; in Haft halten.
detainee *s.* Verhaftete *m./f.*
detect *v.t.* entdecken, aufdecken.
detectable *a.* feststellbar, wahrnehmbar.
detection *s.* Entdeckung *f.*
detective *s.* Geheimpolizist, Detektiv *m.*
detector *a.* (*radio*) Detektor.
detente *s.* Entspannung.
detention *s.* Haft *m.;* Festnahme *f.*
deter *v.t.* abschrecken.
detergent *s.* Reinigungsmittel *n.*
deteriorate *v.t.* verschlimmern.
deterioration *s.* Verschlimmerung.
determinate *a.*, **~ly** *adv.* bestimmt.
determination *s.* Bestimmung; Entschlossenheit *f.;* Beschluß *m.*
determinative *a.*, **~ly** *adv.* bestimmend.
determine *v.t.* festsetzen; feststellen; beendigen; ~ *v.i.* sich entschließen.
determined *a.* entschlossen.
deterrence *s.* Abschreckung *f.*
deterrent *s.* Abschreckungsmittel *n.*
detest *v.t.* verabscheuen.
detestable *a.*, **~bly** *adv.* abscheulich.
detestation *s.* Abscheu *m.*
dethrone *v.t.* entthronen.
dethronement *s.* Entthronung *f.*
detonate *v.i.* explodieren, zur Detonation bringen.
detonation *s.* Zündung *f.*, Detonation *f.*
detonator *s.* Zünder *m.;* Sprengkapsel *f.*
detour *s.* Umweg *m.;* ~ *v.t.* umleiten.
detract *v.t.* schmälern; ablenken.
detraction *s.* Beeinträchtigung *f.*
detriment *s.* Schaden, Nachteil *m.*
detrimental *a.*, **~ly** *adv.* nachteilig.
detritus *s.* Überbleibsel *n.*
deuce *s.* Zwei *f.;* Einstand *m.*
devaluation *s.* Abwertung *f.*
devalue *v.t.* abwerten.
devastate *v.t.* verwüsten.
devastating *a.* verheerend, vernichtend.
devastation *s.* Verwüstung *f.*
develop *v.t.* entwickeln, enthüllen.
developer *s.* (*phot.*) Entwickler *m.;* Bauunternehmer(in) *m.(f.)*
developing country *s.* Entwicklungsland *n.*
development *s.* Entwicklung *f.*
deviant *a.* abweichend.
deviate *v.i.* abweichen.
deviation *s.* Abweichung, Verirrung *f.*
device *s.* Kunstgriff *m.;* Vorrichtung *f.;* Wahlspruch *m.*
devil *s.* Teufel *m.*
devilish *a.* teuflisch.
devil-may-care *a.* sorglos, unbekümmert.
devilry *s.* Teufelei *f.*
devious *a.* abwegig.
devise *v.i.* ersinnen; (*by will*) vermachen.
devoid *a.* bar, frei; **~ of,** ohne.
devolution *s.* Dezentralisierung *f.;* Übertragung von Aufgaben *f.*
devolve *v.t.* (*fig.*) übertragen; ~ *(on) v.i.* zufallen, heimfallen.
devote *v.t.* widmen.
devoted *a.*, **~ly** *adv.* ergeben, fromm.
devotee *s.* Verehrer(in) *m.(f.);* Anhänger(in) *m.(f.)*
devotion *s.* Aufopferung, Hingabe *f.;* Widmung *f.;* Andacht *f.*
devotional *a.*, **~ly** *adv.* andächtig.
devour *v.t.* verschlingen.
devout *a.*, **~ly** *adv.* andächtig.
dew *s.* Tau *m.;* ~ *v.t.* betauen.
dewy *a.* taufeucht; taufrisch.
dexterity *s.* Gewandtheit, Fertigkeit *f.*
dexterous *a.*, **~ly** *adv.* gewandt, geschickt.
dextrose *s.* Traubenzucker *m.*
diabetes *s.* (*med.*) Zuckerkrankheit *f.*

diabetic *a.* zuckerkrank; ~ *s.* Zuckerkranker(in) *m.(f.)*, Diabetiker(in) *m.(f.)*
diabolic(al) *a.*, **~ly** *adv.* teuflisch.
diagnose *v.t.* diagnostizieren.
diagnosis *s.* Diagnose *f.*
diagnostic *a.* diagnostisch.
diagonal *a.*, **~ly** *adv.* schräg; diagonal; ~ *s.* Diagonale *f.*
diagram *s.* (*geom.*) Riß *m.*; Figur *f.*; graphische Darstellung *f.*
dial *s.* Zifferblatt *n.*; Wählscheibe *f.*; ~ *v.t.* (*tel.*) wählen.
dialect *s.* Mundart *f.*, Dialekt *m.*
dialectical *a.*, **~ly** *adv.* dialektisch.
dialectics *s.* Dialektik *f.*
dialogue *s.* Zwiegespräch *n.*
dial tone *s.* Freizeichen *n.*
dialysis *s.* Dialyse *f.*
diameter *s.* Durchmesser *m.*
diametrical *a.*, **~ly** *adv.* diametral; ~ **opposed,** gerade entgegengesetzt.
diamond *s.* Diamant *m.*; Karo, Rot (Karte) *n.*
diapason *s.* (*mus.*) Zusammenklang *m.*; Mensur (Orgel) *f.*
diaper *s.* Windel *f.*
diaphragm *s.* Zwerchfell *n.*; (*tel.*) Membrane *f.*; (*optics*) Blende *f.*
diarrhea *s.* Durchfall *m.*
diary *s.* Tagebuch *n.*; Terminkalender *m.*
diatetics *s.pl.* Ernährungswissenschaft *f.*, Diätetik *f.*
diatribe *s.* heftiger Angriff, Tadel *m.*
dice *s.* (*pl.* von *die*) Würfel *m.pl.*; ~ *v.i.* würfeln.
dice cup *s.* Würfelbecher *m.*
dicey *a.* riskant; heikel.
dichotomy *s.* Dichotomie *f.*
dick *s.* (*fam.*) Schnüffler *m.*; (*vulg.*) Schwanz *m.*
dickens *s.* *what the ~!* was zum Kuckuck!
dick(e)y *a.* (*fam.*) schwach, klapprig.
dictate *v.t.* diktieren; ~ *s.* Vorschrift *f.*
dictation *s.* Diktat *n.*; Geheiß *n.*
dictator *s.* Diktator(in) *m.(f.)*
dictatorial *a.* gebieterisch.
dictatorship *s.* Diktatur *f.*
diction *s.* Sprechweise *f.*, Stil *m.*, Diktion *f.*
dictionary *s.* Wörterbuch *n.*
didactic *a.* didaktisch, lehrhaft; Lehr...
diddle *v.t.* beschwindeln.
die *s.* Würfel *m.*; Stempel *m.*; Matrize *f.*; ~ *v.i.* sterben; umkommen; verwelken; sich verlieren.
diehard *s.* Unentwegter *m.*
diesel *s.* Diesel *m.*
diet *s.* Diät *f.*; Kost *f.*; ~ *v.t.* eine Diät machen.
dietary *a.* diätetisch.
dietitian *s.* Diätassistent(in) *m.(f.)*
differ *v.i.* verschieden sein, abweichen; streiten, sich unterscheiden.
difference *s.* Unterschied *m.*; Streit *m.*
different *a.*, **~ly** *adv.* verschieden, anders.
differential tariff *s.* Staffeltarif *m.*
differentiate *v.t.* & *i.* (sich) unterscheiden; differenzieren.
differing *a.* unterschiedlich.
difficult *a.* schwierig.
difficulty *s.* Schwierigkeit *f.*
diffidence *s.* Schüchternheit *f.*
diffident *a.*, **~ly** *adv.* schüchtern.; zurückhaltend.
diffuse *v.t.* ausgießen; verbreiten; zerstreuen; ~ *a.* weitläufig.
diffusion *s.* Verbreitung *f.*
dig *v.t.* & *i.st.* graben; bohren.
digest *v.t.* verdauen; überdenken; ertragen; ~ *s.* Auszug, Abriß *m.*; Übersicht *f.*; Gesetzessammlung *f.*
digestible *a.* verdaulich.
digestion *s.* Verdauung *f.*; Überlegung *f.*
digestive system *s.* Verdauungssystem *n.*
digger *s.* Gräber *m.*; Bagger *m.*
digging *s.* Graben *n.*
digit *s.* Finger *m.*; Zehe *f.*; Ziffer *f.*
digital *a.* digital.
dignified *a.* würdevoll.
dignitary *s.* Würdenträger *m.*
dignity *s.* Würde *f.*; Rang *m.*
digress *v.t.* abschweifen.
digression *s.* Abschweifung *f.*
digressive *a.* abweichend, abschweifend.
dike *s.* Deich *m.*; Graben *m.*; Damm *m.*
dilapidate *v.t.* verfallen lassen.
dilapidated *a.* baufällig; verfallen.
dilapidation *s.* Verfall *m.*
dilate *v.t.* erweitern, ausdehnen.
dilation *s.* Dilation *f.*, Ausdehnung *f.*; Erweiterung *f.*
dilatory *a.*, **~ily** *adv.* aufschiebend.
dilemma *s.* Dilemma *n.*
dilettante *s.* Dilettant(in) *m.(f.)*
diligence *s.* Fleiß *m.*; Sorgfalt *f.*
diligent *a.*, **~ly** *adv.* fleißig, emsig.
dill *s.* (*bot.*) Dille *f.*, Dill *m.*
dilly-dally *v.i.* trödeln.
dilute *v.t.* verdünnen; mildern.
dilution *s.* Verdünnung *f.*
dim *a.*, **~ly** *adv.* dunkel, trübe, matt; ~ *v.t.* verdunkeln, trüben; (*mot.*) abblenden.
dime *s.* Zehncentstück *n.*
dimension *s.* Ausdehnung *f.*; Maß *n.*
diminish *v.t.* vermindern; ~ *v.i.* abnehmen.
diminution *s.* Verkleinerung *f.*; Abnahme *f.*
diminutive *a.*, **~ly** *adv.* vermindernd; winzig; ~ *s.* Verkleinerungsform *f.*
dimple *s.* Grübchen *n.*
din *s.* Gerassel, Getöse *n.*; ~ *v.t.* & *i.* schallen; rasseln; betäuben.
dine *v.i.* speisen.
diner *s.* Gast (beim Essen) *m.*
ding-dong *s.* Klingklang *m.*; ~ **race,** schwankender heißumstrittener Kampf *m.*
dinghy *s.* flaches Boot *n.*
dingy *a.* schmutzig.
dining car *s.* Speisewagen *m.*; ~ **attendant** *s.* Speisewagenschaffner *m.*
dining room *s.* Speisesaal *m.*; Eßzimmer *n.*
dining table *s.* Eßtisch *m.*
dinner *s.* Hauptmahlzeit *f.*; ~ **jacket,** Smoking *m.*; ~ **set** Eß-Service *n.*
dinosaur *s.* Dinosaurier *m.*
dint, *by ~ of,* mittels, kraft.
diocese *s.* Diözese *f.*
dioxin *s.* Dioxin *n.*
dip *v.t.* eintauchen; ~ *v.i.* sich senken; ~ *s.* Eintauchen *n.*; Neigung *f.*; Dip *m.*

Dip., dip. *diploma,* Diplom, dipl.
diphtheria *s.* Diphtherie *f.*
diphthong *s.* Diphthong *m.*
diploma *s.* Diplom *n.*
diplomacy *s.* Diplomatie *f.*
diplomat *s.* Diplomat(in) *m.(f.)*
diplomatic(al) *a.* diplomatisch.
dipsomania *s.* Trunksucht *f.*
dipstick *s.* Meßstab *m.*
Dir., dir. *director,* Direktor, Dir.
dire *a.* gräßlich.
direct *a.* gerade, unmittelbar; ausdrücklich; **~ly** *adv.* geradezu, sogleich, direkt; ~ *v.t.* richten, anweisen; adressieren.
direction *s.* Richtung *f.*; Leitung, Anordnung *f.*; Adresse *f.*
directions for use *pl.* Gebrauchsanweisung *f.*
directive *s.* Anweisung *f.*; **~s** *pl.* Richtlinien *f.pl.*
directness *s.* Direktheit *f.*; Geradheit *f.*
director *s.* Direktor(in) *m.(f.)*, Leiter(in) *m.(f.)*
directorate *s.* Präsidium *n.*
directory *s.* Adreßbuch *n.*; Telefonbuch *n.*; Branchenverzeichnis *n.*
dirge *s.* Trauergesang *m.*
dirk *s.* Dolch *m.*
dirt *s.* Kot, Schmutz *m.*; **~-cheap,** spottbillig.
dirty *a.* schmutzig; ~ *v.t.* besudeln.
dirty word *s.* unanständiges Wort *n.*; Schimpfwort *n.*
disability *s.* Unvermögen *n.*; Unfähigkeit *f.*
disable *v.t.* unfähig machen.
disabled *a.* unfähig, untauglich; invalid.
disablement *s.* Behinderung *f.*
disabuse *v.t.* aufklären.
disadvantage *s.* Nachteil *m.*
disadvantageous *a.*, **~ly** *adv.* nachteilig.
disaffected *a.* unzufrieden.
disaffection *s.* Abneigung *f.*; Unzufriedenheit *f.*
disagree *v.i.* nicht übereinstimmen; nicht gut bekommen (von Speisen).
disagreeable *a.*, **~bly** *adv.* unangenehm.
disagreement *s.* Meinungsverschiedenheit *f.*
disallow *v.t.* & *i.* nicht gestatten; in Abrede stellen.
disappear *v.i.* verschwinden.
disappearance *s.* Verschwinden *n.*
disappoint *v.t.* vereiteln, enttäuschen.
disappointing *a.* enttäuschend.
disappointment *s.* Enttäuschung *f.*
disapprobation, disapproval *s.* Mißbilligung *f.*
disapprove *v.t.* & *i.* mißbilligen.
disapproving *a.* mißbilligend.
disarm *v.t.* entwaffnen; ~ *v.i.* abrüsten.
disarmament *s.* Abrüstung *f.*
disarming *a.* entwaffnend.
disarrange *v.t.* verwirren.
disarray *v.t.* in Unordnung bringen; ~ *s.* Verwirrung *f.*
disaster *s.* Unglück *n.*, Unfall *m.*, Katastrophe *f.*; ~ **area** *s.* Katastrophengebiet *n.*
disastrous *a.*, **~ly** *adv.* unheilvoll.
disavow *v.t.* nicht anerkennen, disavow.
disband *v.t.* verabschieden; (*mil.*) (Einheit) auflösen; ~ *v.i.* sich auflösen.
disbelief *s.* Unglaube, Zweifel *m.*
disbelieve *v.t.* nicht glauben.
disburse *v.t.* auszahlen, verschießen.
disbursement *s.* Auszahlung *f.*
disc. *discount,* Abzug *m.*, Rabatt *m.*
discard *v.t.* entfernen; abwerfen (eine Karte); ablegen (Kleider); wegwerfen.
discern *v.t.* & *i.* unterscheiden, erkennen.
discernible *a.*, **~bly** *adv.* unterscheidbar; erkennbar.
discerning *a.* scharf; kritisch; fein; urteilsfähig.
discharge *v.t.* ausladen, löschen; abfeuern; loslassen; entlassen; entlasten; freisprechen ~ *v.i.* sich entladen; eitern; ~ *s.* Entladung *f.*; Entlassung, Befreiung *f.*; Entlastung *f.*; Abfeuern *n.*; Abfluß *m.*; (*med.*) Ausfluß *m.*
disciple *s.* Schüler, Jünger *m.*, Anhänger(in) *m.(f.)*
disciplinarian *s.* Zuchtmeister *m.*
disciplinary *a.* disziplinarisch; ~ **action,** Disziplinarverfahren *n.*; ~ **power,** Disziplinargewalt *f.*; ~ **proceedings** *pl.* Disziplinarverfahren *n.*
discipline *s.* Unterweisung, Zucht *f.*; Disziplin *f.*; ~ *v.t.* züchtigen.
disciplined *a.* diszipliniert.
disc jockey *s.* Diskjockey *m.*
disclaim *v.t.* leugnen; abstreiten.
disclaimer *s.* Verzicht *m.*; Widerruf *m.*
disclose *v.t.* enthüllen; offenbaren.
disclosure *s.* Enthüllung, Mitteilung *f.*
discolor *v.t.* entfärben; entstellen.
discoloration *s.* Verfärbung *f.*; Verschießen *n.*
discomfit *v.t.* verunsichern.
discomfiture *s.* Verunsicherung.
discomfort *s.* Mißbehagen *n.*
discompose *v.t.* beunruhigen; verwirren.
discomposure *s.* Verwirrung, Verlegenheit *f.*; Verdrießlichkeit *f.*
disconcert *v.t.* außer Fassung bringen.
disconnect *v.t.* trennen; (*mech.*) entkuppeln, ausschalten.
disconnected *a.* zusammenhangslos.
disconsolate *a.*, **~ly** *adv.* trostlos, betrübt.
discontent *a.* mißvergnügt; ~ *s.* Unzufriedenheit *f.*; ~ *v.t.* mißvergnügt machen.
discontinuance *s.* Unterbrechung *f.*; Aufhören *n.*; Trennung *f.*
discontinue *v.t.* unterbrechen; abbestellen; ~ *v.i.* aufhören.
discord *s.* Mißklang *m.*; Zwietracht *f.*
discordance *s.* Uneinigkeit *f.*
discordant *a.* missklingend; verschieden; mißhellig.
discotheque *s.* Diskothek *f.*
discount *v.t.* abziehen, diskontieren; ~ *s.* Abzug *m.*; Diskonto *n.*
discountenance *v.t.* außer Fassung bringen, entmutigen; mißbilligen.
discourage *v.t.* entmutigen; abraten.
discouragement *s.* Entmutigung *f.*
discourse *s.* Diskurs *m.*; Gespräch *n.*; Vortrag *m.*; Abhandlung *f.*; ~ *v.i.* sich unterreden; sprechen.
discourteous *a.* unhöflich.
discourtesy *s.* Unhöflichkeit *f.*
discover *v.t.* entdecken, offenbaren.
discoverer *s.* Entdecker(in) *m.(f.)*
discovery *s.* Entdeckung *f.*

discredit *s.* Mißkredit *m.;* übler Ruf *m.;* ~ *v.t.* in schlechten Ruf bringen; bezweifeln.
discreditable *a.*, **~bly** *adv.* schimpflich.
discreet *a.*, **~ly** *adv.* vorsichtig; klug; verschwiegen.
discrepancy *s.* Widerspruch *m.;* Diskrepanz *f.*
discrepant *a.* widersprechend.
discretion *s.* Besonnenheit, Klugheit, Verschwiegenheit *f.;* Takt *m.;* Belieben *n.; to surrender at ~*, sich auf Gnade und Ungnade ergeben.
discriminate *v.t.* unterscheiden; unterschiedlich behandeln; diskriminieren; ~ *a.*, **~ly** *adv.* unterschieden; genau, deutlich.
discriminating *a.* diskriminierend; kritisch, fein.
discrimination *s.* Unterscheidung *f.;* Unterschied *m.;* Scharfsinn *m.*
discriminative *a.* unterscheidend.
discursive *a.* weitschweifend.
discuss *v.t.* erörtern; verzehren.
discussion *s.* Erörterung *f.;* Diskussion *f.*
disdain *s.* Verachtung *f.;* ~ *v.t.* verschmähen, verächtlich herabsetzen.
disdainful *a.*, **~ly** *adv.* geringschätzig.
disease *s.* Krankheit *f.*
diseased *a.* krank.
disembark *v.t. & i.* ausschiffen, landen.
disembarkation *s.* Ausschiffung *f.*
disembarrass *v.t.* aus der Verlegenheit bringen.
disembodied *a.* körperlos; geisterhaft.
disembowl *v.t.* ausweiden.
disenchant *v.t.* entzaubern; ernüchtern.
disenchantment *s.* Ernüchterung *f.*
disencumber *v.t.* befreien; entbinden.
disengage *v.t.* losmachen; befreien; ~ *v.i.* (*mil.*) sich absetzen.
disengaged *a.* frei, unbeschäftigt.
disengagement *s.* Entbindung *f.;* (*mil.*) Absetzungsbewegung *f.*
disentangle *v.t.* entwirren, losmachen.
disfavor *s.* Ungnade *f.;* Mißfallen *n.;* ~ *v.t.* nicht begünstigen.
disfigure *v.t.* entstellen.
disfigurement *s.* Entstellung *f.*
disfranchise *v.t.* das Wahlrecht entziehen.
disgorge *v.t.* ausspucken, ausspeien.
disgrace *s.* Ungnade *f.;* Schande *f.;* ~ *v.t.* die Gunst entziehen; entehren.
disgraceful *a.*, **~ly** *adv.* schimpflich; erbärmlich.
disgruntled *a.* unzufrieden.
disguise *v.t.* vermummen; verbergen; verkleiden; ~ *s.* Verkleidung, Verstellung *f.*
disgust *s.* Ekel, Widerwille *m.;* ~ *v.t.* anwidern; ekeln; verdrießen.
disgusting *a.* ekelhaft, widerlich.
dish *s.* Schüssel *f.;* Napf *m.;* Gericht *n.;* ~ *v.t.* (*up*) anrichten, auftragen.
dishearten *v.t.* verzagt machen; entmutigen.
disheartening *a.* entmutigend.
dishevel *v.t.* zerzausen.
disheveled *a.* zerzaust; unordentlich.
dishonest *a.*, **~ly** *adv.* unehrlich; unaufrichtig.
dishonesty *s.* Unredlichkeit *f.;* Unaufrichtigkeit *f.*
dishonor *s.* Schande *f.;* ~ *v.t.* beleidigen; nicht honorieren (Wechsel).
dishonorable *a.*, **~bly** *adv.* ehrlos.
dish: ~ **rack** *s.* Abtropfgestell *n.;* ~ **towel** *s.* Geschirrtuch *n.;* ~ **washer** *s.* Geschirrspüler *m.;* ~ **water** *s.* Spülwasser *n.*
disillusion *s.* Ernüchterung *f.;* ~ *v.t.* ernüchtern.
disillusioned *a.* desillusioniert.
disillusionment *s.* Desillusionierung *f.*
disincentive *s.* Hemmnis *n.*
disinclination *s.* Abneigung *f.*
disincline *v.t.* abgeneigt machen.
disinclined *a.* abgeneigt.
disinfect *v.t.* desinfizieren.
disinfectant *s.* Desinfizierungsmittel *n.;* ~ *a.* desinfizierend.
disinfection *s.* Desinfizierung *f.*
disingenuous *a.* unaufrichtig; hinterhältig.
disinherit *v.t.* enterben.
disintegrate *v.t. & i.* sich in Bestandteile auflösen; zerfallen.
disintegration *s.* Zerfall *m.;* Auflösung *f.*
disinter *v.t.* wieder ausgraben.
disinterested *a.*, **~ly** *adv.* uneigennützig; unvoreingenommen.
disjoin *v.t.* trennen.
disjoint *v.t.* zerlegen.
disk *s.* Scheibe *f.;* (Schall)Platte *f.; compact ~ s.* Compact Disk; *hard ~ s.* Festplatte *f.*
disk drive *s.* Diskettenlaufwerk *n.*
diskette *s.* Diskette *f.*
dislike *s.* Abneigung *f.;* Mißfallen *n.;* ~ *v.t.* mißbilligen, nicht mögen.
dislocate *v.t.* verrenken.
dislocation *s.* Verrenkung *f.;* Störung *f.*
dislodge *v.t.* vertreiben.
disloyal *a.*, **~ly** *adv.* ungetreu, treulos.
disloyalty *s.* Treulosigkeit *f.*
dismal *a.* trübe; schrecklich; traurig.
dismantle *v.t.* entblößen; niederreißen; demontieren; abtakeln.
dismantling *s.* Demontage *f.*
dismay *v.t.* erschrecken; ~ *s.* Bangigkeit *f.*, Bestürzung *f.*
dismember *v.t.* zerstückeln.
dismiss *v.t.* entlassen; abweisen; **~ed!** (*mil.*) weggetreten!
dismissal *s.* Entlassung, Abdankung *f.*
dismount *v.i.* absitzen.; absteigen (Reiter).
disobedience *s.* Ungehorsam *m.*
disobedient *a.*, **~ly** *adv.* ungehorsam.
disobey *v.t.* nicht gehorchen.
disoblige *v.t.* ungefällig begegnen.
disobliging *a.* ungefällig.
disorder *s.* Unordnung *f.;* Störung *f.;* Unpäßlichkeit *f.*
disordered *p. & a.*, **~ly** *adv.* unordentlich; liederlich.
disorderly *a.* gesetzwidrig; liederlich; ~ **conduct,** ordnungswidriges Betragen *n.*
disorganization *s.* Desorganisation *f.*
disorganize *v.t.* auflösen, zerrütten.
disorganized *a.* desorganisiert, chaotisch.
disorient *v.t.* desorientieren.
disoriented *a.* desorientiert.
disown *v.t.* verleugnen, verwerfen.
disparage *v.t.* herabsetzen, schmälern.
disparagement *s.* Herabsetzung *f.;* Beeinträchtigung *f.*
disparaging *a.* abschätzig.

disparate *a.* verschieden, disparat.
disparity *s.* Ungleichheit *f.*; Unterschied *m.*
dispassionate *a.*, **~ly** *adv.* leidenschaftslos.
dispatch *v.t.* schicken; abfertigen; befördern; erledigen; ~ *s.* Abfertigung *f.*; Absendung *f.*; Eile *f.*; Depesche *f.*; ~ **box** Depeschenmappe *f.*
dispel *v.t.* vertreiben.
dispensable *a.* entbehrlich.
dispensary *s.* Apotheke *f.*
dispensation *s.* Austeilung *f.*; Erlassung *f.*; Dispens *f.*
dispense *v.t.* austeilen; dispensieren; *to ~ with,* erlassen; entbehren können.
dispersal *s.* Zerstreuung *f.*; ~ **of industry,** Industrieauslagerung *f.*
disperse *v.t.* zerstreuen; verteilen; ~ *v.i.* sich zerstreuen.
dispersion *s.* Zerstreuung *f.*
dispirit *v.t.* entmutigen.
dispirited *a.* entmutigt.
dispiriting *a.* entmutigend.
displace *v.t.* verschieben; absetzen; verdrängen.
displaced person *s.* Zwangsverschleppte *m.*
displacement *s.* Verschiebung *f.*; Verrückung *f.*; Absetzung *f.*; Verdrängung *f.*
display *v.t.* entfalten; zur Schau stellen; ~ *s.* Schaustellung *f.*; Darstellung *f.*; Pomp *m.*; *on ~,* ausliegend.
displease *v.t. & i.* mißfallen.
displeased *p. & a.* ungehalten.
displeasure *s.* Mißfallen *n.*; Verdruß *m.*
disposable *a.* Wegwerf...; Einweg...
disposal *s.* Verfügung *f.*; Beseitigung *f.*; Entsorgung *f.*
dispose *v.t.* anordnen, einrichten, anwenden; bereit machen; verfügen; *~ of,* beseitigen; absetzen.
disposed *p. & a.* gesinnt; gelaunt.
disposition *s.* Einrichtung, Anordnung *f.*; Zustand *m.*; Neigung, Gemütsart *f.*; (*mil.*) Aufstellung *f.*
dispossess *v.t.* enteignen.
disproportion *s.* Mißverhältnis *n.*
disproportionate *a.*, **~ly** *adv.* unverhältnismäßig.
disprove *v.t.* widerlegen.
disputable *a.* strittig.
disputant *s.* Streiter, Gegner *m.*
disputation *s.* gelehrter Streit *m.*
dispute *v.i.* streiten, disputieren; ~ *v.t.* bestreiten; ~ *s.* Streit *m.*
disqualification *s.* Disqualifikation *f.*
disqualify *v.t.* disqualifizieren; untauglich machen; unfähig erklären.
disquiet *s.* Unruhe *f.*; ~ *v.t.* beunruhigen.
disregard *s.* Mißachtung *f.*; ~ *v.t.* unbeachtet lassen.
disrepair *s.* Baufälligkeit *f.*
disreputable *a.* verrufen; schimpflich.
disrepute *s.* übler Ruf *m.*; Ehrlosigkeit *f.*
disrespect *s.* Geringschätzung, Unehrerbietigkeit *f.*
disrespectful *a.* unehrerbietig, unhöflich.
disrupt *v.t.* unterbrechen; stören (Unterricht).
disruption *s.* Unterbrechung *f.*; Störung *f.*
disruptive *a.* störend.
dissatisfaction *s.* Unzufriedenheit *f.*
dissatisfied *a.* unzufrieden.
dissatisfy *v.t.* nicht befriedigen.
dissect *v.t.* zerlegen; sezieren.
dissection *s.* Zerlegung *f.*; Präparation *f.*
dissemble *v.i.* sich verstellen, heucheln; ~ *v.t.* verhehlen.
disseminate *v.t.* aussäen, ausstreuen.
dissension *s.* Uneinigkeit *f.*, Zwist *m.*; Dissens *m.*
dissent *v.i.* anderer Meinung sein; **~ing opinion,** (*jur.*) abweichende Meinung *f.*; ~ *s.* Abweichung *f.*
dissenter *s.* Andersdenkende *m./f.*
dissertation *s.* Abhandlung *f.*; Dissertation *f.*
disservice *s.* schlechter Dienst *m.*
dissever *v.t.* absondern, trennen.
dissidence *s.* Uneinigkeit *f.*
dissident *a.* verschieden; ~*s.* Andersdenkende *m./f.*; Dissident(in) *m.(f.)*
dissimilar *a.* ungleichartig.
dissimilarity *s.* Ungleichheit.
dissimulate *v.i.* sich verstellen.
dissipate *v.t.* zerstreuen; verschwenden.
dissipated *a.* ausschweifend.
dissipation *s.* Zerstreuung *f.*; Ausschweifung *f.*
dissociate *v.t.* trennen.
dissolute *a.*, **~ly** *adv.* ausschweifend.
dissolution *s.* Auflösung *f.*
dissolve *v.t.* auflösen, schmelzen; ~ *v.t.* zergehen.
dissonance *s.* Mißklang *m.*; Dissonanz *f.*
dissuade *v.t.* abraten.
dissuasion *s.* Abraten *n.*
dissuasive *a.*, **~ly** *adv.* abratend.
distance *s.* Entfernung, Weite *f.*; Abstand *m.*; Entfremdung, Kälte *f.*; ~ *v.t.* hinter sich lassen.
distant *a.* entfernt; zurückhaltend, kalt.
distaste *s.* Widerwille *m.*; Abneigung *f.*
distasteful *a.*, **~ly** *adv.* ärgerlich, widrig.
distemper *s.* Stumpe *f.* (Hunde); Temperafarbe *f.*
distend *v.t.* ausdehnen, ausstrecken.
distil *v.i. & a.* destillieren.
distillation *s.* Destillation *f.*; Destillat *n.*
distillery *s.* (Branntwein-) Brennerei *f.*
distinct *a.*, **~ly** *adv.* verschieden; unterschieden; deutlich.
distinction *s.* Unterscheidung *f.*; Unterschied *m.*; Auszeichnung *f.*
distinctive *a.* unterscheidend; **~ly** *adv.* deutlich.
distinguish *v.t.* unterscheiden; auszeichnen.
distinguishable *a.* unterscheidbar.
distinguished *a.* namhaft; angesehen.
distort *v.t.* verdrehen; verzerren.
distortion *s.* Verdrehung *f.*; Verzerrung *f.*
distract *v.t.* ablenken, zerstreuen; beunruhigen, stören, zerrütten.
distraction *s.* Zerstreuung *f.*; Kummer *m.*; Zerrüttung *f.*; Wahnsinn *m.*
distraught *a.* verstört.
distress *s.* Elend *n.*, Not *f.*; Seenot *f.*; Beschlagnahme, Pfändung *f.*; ~ **signal** (*nav.*) Notzeichen *n.*; ~ **warrant,** Pfändungsbefehl *m.*; ~ *v.t.* auspfänden; in Verlegenheit, in Not bringen.
distressed *a.* leidvoll; betrübt.
distressing *a.* erschütternd.
distribute *v.t.* verteilen, austeilen.

distribution *s.* Verteilung *f.; ~* **list,** Verteiler (auf Akten) *m.*
distributor *s.* Verteiler(in) *m.(f.);* Vertrieb *m.*
district *s.* Bezirk *m.;* Landstrich *m.;* Wahlkreis *m.; ~* **attorney** *s.* Bezirksstaatsanwalt *m.*
distrust *v.t.* mißtrauen; *~ s.* Mißtrauen *n.*
distrustful *a.*, **~ly** *adv.* mißtrauisch.
disturb *v.t.* stören.
disturbance *s.* Störung, Verwirrung *f.;* Aufruhr *m.*
disturbed *a.* besorgt; geistesgestört.
disunite *v.t.* trennen, entzweien.
disuse *s.* Nichtgebrauch *m.*
disused *a.* stillgelegt; leerstehend.
ditch *s.* Graben *m.; ~ v.t.* (*fam.*) sitzenlassen.
dither *v.t.* schwanken.
ditto *adv.* desgleichen.
ditty *s.* Liedchen *n.*, Gesang *m.*
diurnal *a.* täglich.
div. *divorced,* geschieden, gesch.; *division,* Abteilung, Abt.
divan *s.* Diwan *m.*
dive *v.i.* (unter)tauchen; eindringen.
divebomber *s.* Sturzkampfflieger *m.*
diver *s.* Taucher(in) *m.(f.);* Kunstspringer(in) *m.(f.)*
diverge *v.i.* auseinanderlaufen; abweichen.
divergence *s.* Abweichen *n.*
divergent *a.* divergierend, abweichend.
diverse *a.*, **~ly** *adv.* verschieden, mannigfaltig.
diversify *v.t.* verschieden machen.
diversion *s.* Ablenkung *f.;* Zeitvertreib *m.*
diversity *s.* Verschiedenheit *f.;* Mannigfaltigkeit *f.*
divert *v.t.* umleiten; ablenken; belustigen.
diverting *a.* unterhaltsam.
divest *v.t.* berauben.
divide *v.t.* teilen, trennen; dividieren; *~ v.i.* sich trennen; namentlich abstimmen.
dividend *s.* (*com.*) Dividende *f.;* (*ar.*) Dividend *m.*
divider *s.* Trennwand *f.*
dividers *s.pl.* Zirkel *m.*
divine *v.t.* weissagen, erraten; ahnen; *~ a.* **~ly** *adv.* göttlich; *~ s.* Geistliche *m.*
diving *s.* Kunstspringen *n.*
diving: ~ bell *s.* Taucherglocke *f.; ~* **board** *s.* Sprungbrett *n.; ~* **suit** *s.* Taucheranzug *m.*
divining rod *s.* Wünschelrute *f.*
divinity *s.* Gottheit *f.;* Theologie *f.*
divisible *a.* teilbar.
division *s.* Teilung *f.;* Trennung *f.;* Abteilung *f.;* Division *f.;* Abstimmung (durch Hammelsprung) *f.*
divisor *s.* (*mus.*) Divisor *m.;* Teiler *m.*
divorce *s.* Ehescheidung *f.; ~ v.t.* scheiden; verstoßen.
divorcee *s.* Geschiedene *m./f.*
divulge *v.t.* verbreiten; ausschwatzen.
dizzy *a.* schwindlig; unbesonnen; *~ v.t.* schwindlig machen.
DJ *disc jockey,* Disk Jockey.
D.Litt. *Doctor of Literature,* Doktor der Literatur.
D.Mus. *Doctor of Music,* Doktor der Musik.
do *v.t. & i.st.* tun, machen; ausführen; *that will ~,* das genügt; *that won't ~,* das geht nicht; *I cannot ~ without it,* ich kann es nicht entbehren; *to dh away with,* abschaffen; *to ~ up,* instand setzen; einpacken; *to ~ ill,* schlecht fortkommen; *to ~ well,* gut fortkommen.
do. *ditto,* dito, desgleichen, dgl.
docile *a.* sanft; unterwürfig.
dock *s.* (*nav.*) Dock *n.;* Stutzschwanz *m.;* Anklagebank *f.; ~ v.t.* stutzen; in ein Dock bringen, docken.
docker *s.* Hafenarbeiter *m.*
docket *s.* Liste *f.;* Zettel *m.*
dockyard *s.* Schiffswerft *n.* & *f.*
doctor *s.* Doktor *m.;* Arzt *m.; ~ v.t.* ärztlich behandeln; zustutzen; fälschen; (Tier) kastrieren.
doctorate *s.* Doktorwürde *f.*
doctrinaire *a.* doktrinär.
doctrine *s.* Lehre *f.;* Doktrin *f.*
document *s.* Urkunde *f.*, Dokument *n.*
documentary *a.* urkundlich; *~* **evidence,** Urkundenbeweis *m.; ~* **film,** Dokumentarfilm *m.*
documentation *s.* Urkundenbelege *m.pl.;* Dokumentation *f.*
dodder *v.i.* zittern; schlottern.
doddering *a.* tatterig.
dodge *v.i.* ausweichen; *~ s.* Kniff, Schlich *m.*
doe *s.* Reh *n.*
doeskin *s.* Rehleder *n.*
doff *v.t.* lüften, ziehen.
dog *s.* Hund *m.;* Gestell *n.;* Kerl *m.*
dogdays *s.pl.* Hundstage *m.pl.*
dogfight *s.* Handgemenge *n.;* (*avi.*) Kurvenkampf *m.*
dogged *a.*, **~ly** *adv.* verbissen.
doggerel *s.* Knittelvers *m.*
doghouse *s.* Hundehütte *f.*
dogma *s.* Glaubenssatz, Lehrsatz *m.*
dogmatic *a.*, **~ally** *adv.* dogmatisch.
dogmatism *s.* Dogmatismus *m.*
dogmatize *v.i.* Behauptungen aufstellen.
dog rose *s.* Heckenrose, wilde Rose *f.*
dog's ear *s.* Eselsohr (im Buche) *n.*
doing *s.* Begebenheit *f.;* Tätigkeit *f.;* Treiben *n.*
do-it-yourself *s.* Heimwerken *n.*
dol. *dollar,* Dollar.
doldrums *s.pl. in the ~* niedergeschlagen; in einer Flaute.
dole *s.* Spende *f.;* Erwerbslosenunterstützung *f.; ~ v.t.* spenden.
doleful *a.*, **~ly** *adv.* kummervoll, kläglich.
doll *s.* Puppe *f.*
dollhouse *s.* Puppenhaus *n.*
dolomite *s.* Dolomit, Bitterspat *m.*
Dolomites *s.pl.* Dolomiten *pl.*
dolorous *a.* schmerzhaft.
dolphin *s.* Delphin *m.*
dolt *s.* Tölpel *m.*
doltish *a.*, **~ly** *adv.* tölpisch, plump.
domain *s.* Gebiet *n.;* Staatsgut *n.*
dome *s.* Kuppel *f.;* Wölbung *f.*
domestic *a.* häuslich; inländisch; zahm, *~* **fuel,** Hausbrand *m.; ~* **politics,** Innenpolitik *f.; ~* **subjects** *pl.* Haushaltskunde *f.*
domesticate *v.t.* heimisch machen; zähmen; domestizieren.
domesticated *a.* domestiziert.
domesticity *s.* Häuslichkeit *f.*
domicile *s.* Wohnsitz *m.*

domiciled *a.* wohnhaft.
dominance *s.* Dominanz *f.;* Vorherrschaft *f.*
dominant *a.* herrschend.; beherrschend; dominierend.
dominate *v.t. & i.* (be)herrschen.
domination *s.* Herrschaft *f.*
domineering *a.* herrisch; herrschsüchtig.
Dominican *s.* Dominikaner *m.*
dominion *s.* Herrschaft *f.;* Dominium Kolonie *(f.)* mit Selbstverwaltung.
domino *s.* Domino *m.*
dominoes *s.* Domino(spiel) *n.*
don *s.* Universtätsdozent(in) *m.(f.); ~ v.t.* anziehen; aufsetzen.
donate *v.t.* spenden; stiften.
donation *s.* Schenkung *f.;* Stiftung *f.*
donkey *s.* Esel *m.*
donor *s.* Schenker(in) *m.(f.)*
doom *s.* Urteilsspruch *m.;* Schicksal *n.;* Verderben *n.; ~ v.t.* verurteilen.
doomsday *s.* Jüngster Tag *m.*
door *s.* Tür *f.*
doorkeeper *s.* Pförtner *m.*
doorplate *s.* Türschild *n.*
doorpost *s.* Türpfosten *m.*
doorway *s.* Eingang *m.*, Türöffnung *f.*
dope *s.* Dopingmittel *n.;* Rauschgift *n.;* Betäubungstrank *m.; ~ v.t.* betäuben.
dopey *a.* benebelt.
dormant *a.* schlafend; unbenutzt.
dormer *s.* Dachfenster *n.*
dormitory *s.* Schlafsaal *m.*
dormouse *s.* Haselmaus *f.*
dorsal *a.* Rücken...
dosage *s.* Dosierung *f.*
dose *s.* Dosis *f.; ~ v.t.* eingeben.
dossier *s.* Akte, Personalakte *f.*
dot *s.* Punkt *m.; ~ v.t.* punktieren.
dotage *s. to be in one's ~*, senil sein.
dote *v.i.* kindisch werden; vernarrt sein; abgöttisch lieben.
double *a. & adv.* doppelt; **~-barrelled gun** *s.* Doppelflinte *f.;* **~-breasted coat** *s.* zweireihiger. Rock *m.;* **~ time,** Laufschritt *m.;* **~ track** *a.* zweigleisig; **~ window,** Doppelfenster *n.; ~ s.* Doppelte *n.;* Doppelgänger *m.; ~ v.t.* verdoppeln; (Faust) ballen; umschiffen; **~ up,** zusammenklappen, zusammenfalten; *~ v.i.* sich verdoppeln.
doublecross *v.t.* betrügen.
double-dealer *s.* Betrüger *m.*
double-quick *a.* im Laufschritt.
double room *s.* Doppelzimmer *n.*
double-spaced *a.* zweizeilig.
doubly *adv.* doppelt.
doubt *v.t. & i.* (be)zweifeln; *~ s.* Zweifel *m.; to give a person the benefit of the ~*, im Zweifelsfall zu jemandes Gunsten entscheiden.
doubter *s.* Zweifler(in) *m.(f.)*
doubtful *a.*, **~ly** *adv.* zweifelhaft.
doubtless *a. & adv.* ohne Zweifel, gewiß.
dough *s.* Teig *m.*
doughnut *s.* Krapfen *m.*
doughty *a.*, **~ily** *adv.* beherzt, tapfer.
dour *a.* hartnäckig; mürrisch.
dove *s.* Taube *f.*
dovecote *s.* Taubenschlag *m.*
dovetail *v.t.* keilförmig befestigen; innig verbinden; *~ s.* Schwalbenschwanz *m.*
dowager *s.* Witwe von Stand *f.*
dowdy *a.* schlampig; *~ s.* Schlampe *f.*
dowel *s.* Dübel *m.*
dower *s.* Ausstattung, Mitgift *f.*
down *s.* Flaum *m.*, Daune *f.;* Düne *f.; ~ pr. & adv.* nieder, hinab, herunter, zu Boden; *the second ~*, der zweite von oben; *~ a.* niedergeschlagen; *~ v.t.* niederlegen.
downcast *a.* niedergeschlagen.
downfall *s.* Sturz, Untergang *m.*
downgrade *v.t.* im Rang herabsetzen; *on the ~*, im Niedergang begriffen.
downhearted *a.* mutlos.
downhill *a.* bergab.
down payment *s.* Anzahlung *f.*
downpour *s.* Regenguß *m.*
downright *a.* offen, bieder; *~ adv.* geradezu; gänzlich.
downstairs *adv.* treppab; unten, (die Treppe) hinunter.
downstream *adv.* stromabwärts.
down-to-earth *a.* nüchtern; realistisch.
downtown *a. & adv.* im Stadtzentrum; in der Innenstadt; *~ s.* Innenstadt *f.;* City *f.*
down under *adv.* nach Neuseeland; nach Australien; *~ s.* Neuseeland *n.;* Australien *n.*
downward(s) *adv.* abwärts, hinab.
downwind *a.* in Windrichtung.
dowry *s.* Mitgift *f.;* Aussteuer *f.*
dowser *m.* Wünschelrutengänger *m.*
dowsing rod *s.* Wünschelrute *f.*
doz. *dozen,* Dutzend *n.*
doze *v.i.* schlummern, dösen.
dozen *s.* Dutzend *n.*
D.Phil. *Doctor of Philosophy,* Doktor der Philosophie.
Dpt. *department,* Abteilung *f.*, Abt.
Dr. *Doctor,* Doktor *m.*, Dr.; *drive,* Fahrweg.
drab *s.* graubraun; düster; langweilig.
draft *s.* Skizze *f.;* Zeichnung *f.;* Entwurf *m.;* Aushebung *f.;* Zug *m.;* Luftzug *m.;* (Schiff) Tiefgang *m.;* Schluck *m.;* Rinne *f.;* Wehrpflicht *f. beer on ~* Bier vom Faß; *~ a.* zum Ziehen bestimmt; *~ v.t.* zeichnen, entwerfen; detachieren.
draft horse *s.* Zugpferd *n.*
draftsman *s.* Zeichner *m.*
drafty *a.* zügig.
drag *v.t. & i.* ziehen; schleppen *~ s.* Schleife *f.;* Hemmung *f.*
dragnet *s.* Schleppnetz *n.;* Netz *n.*
dragon *s.* Drache *m.;* **~fly,** Libelle *f.*
dragoon *s.* Dragoner *m.*
drain *v.t.* ablassen; austrocknen; *~ s.* Abzugsgraben *m.*
drainage *s.* Entwässerung *f.*
drainpipe *s.* Regen(fall)rohr *n.;* Abflußrohr *n.*
drake *s.* Enterich *m.*
dram *s.* Quentchen *n.;* Schluck *m.*
drama *s.* Schauspiel *n.*, Drama *n.*
dramatic *a.*, **~ally** *adv.* dramatisch.
dramatist *s.* Dramatiker(in) *m.(f.)*
dramatize *v.t.* dramatisieren.
drape *v.t.* drapieren, einhüllen; *~ s.* Tuch *n.;* Vorhang *m.*

draper *s.* Tuchhändler *m.*
drapery *s.* Tuchhandel *m.;* Draperie *f.;* Faltenwurf *m.*
drastic *a.* wirksam, durchschlagend.
draw *v.t. & i.st.* ziehen; spannen; abzapfen; zeichnen; trassieren; herleiten; locken; (Pension, Lohn) beziehen; (Geld) abheben; *to ~ up,* anhalten; aufsetzen, entwerfen, abfassen; *to ~ six feet,* sechs Fuß Tiefgang haben; *to ~ on sb.,* einen Wechsel auf jm. ziehen; ~ *s.* Ziehen *n.;* Los *n.;* unentschiedenes Spiel *n.;* Zugstück *n.*
drawback *s.* Nachteil *m.;* Schattenseite *f.*
drawbridge *s.* Zugbrücke *f.*
drawer *s.* Schublade *f.*
drawing *s.* Ziehen *n.;* Zeichnung *f.*
drawing board *s.* Reißbrett *n.*
drawing office *s.* Konstruktionsbüro *n.*
drawing pin *s.* Reißnagel *m.*
drawing room *s.* Gesellschaftszimmer *n.*
drawl *v.i.* dehnen; (die Worte) schleppen.
drawn *s.* unentschieden, verzogen (Gesicht).
dread *s.* Schrecken *m.;* ~ *a.* schrecklich; ~ *v.t.* erschrecken; ~ *v.i.* sich fürchten.
dreadful *a.* schrecklich.
dream *s.* Traum *m.;* ~ *v.t. &* träumen.
dreamer *s.* Träumer(in) *m.(f.)*
dreamy *a.* träumerisch; verträumt.
dreary *a.,* **~ily** *adv.* öde; traurig.
dredge *s.* Bagger *m.;* ~ *v.t.* ausbaggern; bestreuen (Mehl).
dregs *s.pl.* Bodensatz *m.*
drench *v.t.* tränken; durchnässen.
dress *s.* Anzug *m.;* Kleidung *f.;* Kleid *n.;* ~ **circle,** erster Rang (im Theater) *m.;* ~ **rehearsal,** *s.* Hauptprobe *f.;* ~ **shirt,** Frackhemd *n.;* ~ *v.t.* ankleiden; putzen; zurichten; anrichten; verbinden; ~ *v.i.* sich ankleiden; (*mil.*)sich richten; ~ *left,* ~*!,* nach links, richt euch!; ~ *right,* ~*!,* richt euch!
dresser *s.* Anrichtetisch *m.;* (Theater) Kostümier *m.*
dressing *s.* Ankleiden *n.;* Anzug *m.;* Verband *m.;* Füllung (Braten) *f.;* Haarsalbe *f.;* *salad ~,* Salatsoße *f.*
dressing gown *s.* Bademantel *m.*
dressing station *s.* Verbandplatz *m.;* Verbandstelle *f.*
dressing table *s.* Frisiertisch *m.*
dressmaker *s.* Schneider(in) *m.(f.)*
dribble *v.t. & i.* tröpfeln, geifern; sabbern.
dribs and drabs *s.pl. in ~,* kleckerweise.
dried *a.* Dörr..., getrocknet.
drier *s.* (Wäsche)trockner *m.;* Haartrockner *m.*
drift *s.* Trieb, Antrieb *m.;* Tendenz *f.;* Schneewehe *f.;* ~ *v.i.* sich aufhäufen; **~wood** *s.* Treibholz *n.*
drill *s.* Drillbohrer *m.;* Exerzieren *n.;* Furch *f.;* Drillich *m.;* ~ *v.t. & i.* drillen, bohren; einexerzieren.
drink *s.* Getränk *n.;* ~ *v.t.st.* trinken.
drinkable *a.* trinkbar.
drinker *s.* Trinker(in) *m.(f.)*
drinking straw *s.* Trinkhalm *m.*
drinking water *s.* Trinkwasser *n.*
drip *v.t. & i.* tröpfeln; ~ *s.* Traufe *f.*
dripping *s.* Bratenfett *n.;* Schmalz *n.*
dripping wet *a.* tropfnaß.
drive *v.t.st.* treiben; fahren; ~ *v.i.* fahren; *what he is driving at,* worauf er hinauswill; *driving belt,* (*mech.*) Treibriemen *m.;* *~r's license,* Führerschein *m.;* *driving test,* Führerprüfung *f.;* ~ *s.* (*tennis*) Treibschlag *m.;* Spazierfahrt *f.;* Fahrweg *m.;* Schwung *m.;* Energie *f.;* Aktion *f.*
drivel *v.i.* geifern; faseln; ~ *s.* Geifer *m.;* Gefasel *n.*
driver *s.* Fahrer, Kutscher *m.;* Lokomotivführer *m.;* Chauffeur *m.;* **~'s license** *s.* Führerschein *m.*
driveway *s.* Zufahrt(straße) *f.;* Auffahrt *f.*
driving: ~ instructor *s.* Fahrlehrer(in) *m.(f.);* ~ **lesson** *s.* Fahrstunde *f.*
drizzle *s.* Sprühregen *m.;* Nieseln *n.;* Nieselregen *m.*
droll possierlich, drollig.
drollery *s.* Posse, Schnurre *f.*
dromedary *s.* Dromedar *n.*
drone *s.* Drohne *f.;* Brummen *n.;* ~ *v.i.* summen.
droop *v.t.* sinken lassen; ~v.i. niederhängen; den Kopf hängen lassen.
drop *s.* Tropfen *m.;* Rückgang, Fall *m.;* ~ *v.i.* tropfen; fallen; sinken; ~ *v.t.* tropfen; fallen lassen; fahren lassen.
droplet *s.* Tröpfchen *n.*
drop out *s.* Aussteiger(in) *m.(f.);* (Schul-, Studien) Abbrecher(in) *m.(f.)*
droppings *s.pl.* Mist *m.,* tierischer Kot *m.*
drop shot *s.* Stoppball *m.*
dropsy *s.* Wassersucht *f.*
drought *s.* Trockenheit, Dürre *f.*
drove *s.* Herde *f.;* Schar *f.*
drown *v.t.* ertränken; überschwemmen; ~ *v.i.* ertrinken; *he was ~ed,* er ertrank.
drowse *v.i.* dösen.
drowsy *a.,* **~ily** *adv.* schläfrig.
drudge *s.* Arbeitstier *n.;* Kuli *m.;* Knecht *m.;* ~ *v.i.* schwere Arbeit verrichten, sich placken.
drudgery *s.* Plackerei *f.*
drug *s.* Droge, Medikament *n.;* Rauschgift *n.;* Ladenhüter *f.;* ~ *v.i.* mit Arznei versetzen, Arznei eingeben, vergiften.
drug: ~ addict *s.* Drogensüchtige *m./f.;* ~ **addiction** *s.* Drogensucht; ~ **dealer** *s.* Drogenhändler(in) *m.(f.)*
druggist *s.* Drogist *m.*
drugstore *s.* Drugstore *m.*
drum *s.* Trommel *f.;* ~ *v.t.* trommeln.
drum: ~fire, Trommelfeuer *n.;* **~head** *s.* Trommelfell *n.;* **~stick** *s.* Trommelstock *m.*
drummer *s.* Schlagzeuger(in) *m.(f.)*
drunk *a.* betrunken.
drunkard *s.* Trinker(in) *m.(f.)*
drunkenness *s.* Trunkenheit *f.*
dry *a.* trocken, dürr; durstig; (Wein) herb; ~ *v.t.* trocknen; ~ *v.i.* dürr werden.
dry cell *s.* Trockenbatterie *f.*
dry cleaning *s.* chemische Reinigung *f.*
dry dock *s.* Trockendock *n.*
dryness *s.* Trockenheit *f.*
dry run *s.* (*fam.*) Probelauf *m.*
D.Sc. *Doctor of Science,* Doktor der Naturwissenschaften, Dr. rer. nat.
dual *a.* Zwei..., doppelt.
dub *v.t.* synchronisieren.
dubious *a.,* **~ly** *adv.* zweifelhaft.
ducal *a.* herzoglich.

duchess *s.* Herzogin *f.*
duchy *s.* Herzogtum *n.*
duck *s.* Ente *f.;* ~ *v.t.* untertauchen; ~ *v.i.* sich ducken.
duckling *s.* junge Ente *f.;* Entenküken *n.*
duck pond *s.* Ententeich *m.*
duct *s.* Gang *m.;* Röhre *f.*
ductile *a.* dehnbar.; (*fig.*) fügsam.
dud *s.* Blindgänger (Granate, Bombe) *m.;* (*fig.*) Niete *f.*
dude *s.* (*fam.*) Stadtmensch *m.*
dudgeon *s.* Groll, Unwille *m.*
due *a. & adv.* schuldig, gebührend; fällig; recht, pünktlich; *to become* ~, fällig werden (Wechsel, etc); *in* ~ *course,* zur gehörigen Zeit; ~ *s.* Gebühr, Pflicht *f.;* Gerechtsame *f.;* Abgabe *f.*
duel *s.* Zweikampf *m.* ~ *v.i.* sich duellieren.
duellist *s.* Duellant *m.*
duet *s.* Duett *n.*
dugout *s.* Unterstand *m.;* (*mil.*) Einbaum *m.*
duke *s.* Herzog *m.*
dukedom *s.* Herzogtum *n.;* Herzogwürde *f.*
dull *a.* matt; stumpf; einfältig, dumm; plump, langweilig, dumpf; (*com.*) flau; ~ *v.t.* abstumpfen; dumm machen.
dullness *s.* Stumpfheit, Stumpfsinnigkeit *f.;* Flauheit *f.*
duly *adv.* gehörig, richtig.
dumb *a.,* **~ly** *adv.* stumm; dumm.
dumbbells *s.pl.* Hanteln *f.pl.*
dumbfound *v.t.* sprachlos machen; verblüffen.
dumbfounded *a.* sprachlos; verblüfft.
dumb show *s.* Gebärdenspiel *n.*
dumbwaiter *s.* Serviertisch *m.*
dummy *s.* Attrappe *f.;* (*mil.*) Blindgänger *m.;* Strohmann (im Kartenspiele) *m.;* Schein..., Schwindel...
dump *s.* Müllkippe *f.;* Müllhalde *f.;* Munitionslager *n.;* ~ *v.t.* hinwerfen; umkippen, (Waren) verschleudern.
dumping *s.* Schleuderausfuhr *f.*
dumping ground *s.* (Schutt-)abladeplatz *m.*
dumpling *s.* Kloß *m.;* Knödel *m.*
dumps *s.pl.* (*fam.*) *in the* ~, niedergeschlagen.
dumpy *a.* kurz und dick.
dun *a.* graubraun; dunkel; ~ *v.t.* mahnen.
dunce *s.* Dummkopf *m.*
dune *s.* Düne *f.*
dung *s.* Mist, Dünger *m.;* ~ *v.t.* düngen.
dungarees *s.pl.* Latzhose *f.*
dungeon *s.* Kerker *m.*
dungfork *s.* Mistgabel *f.*
dunghill *s.* Misthaufen *m.*
dunk *v.t.* eintunken, stippen.
duodenal *a.* duodenal; Zwölffingerdarm...
duodenum *s.* Duodenum *n.;* Zwölffingerdarm *m.*
dupe *s.* Geprellte *f.* /m.; Narr *m.;* ~ *v.t.* prellen.
duplex *a.* zweistöckig; doppelt, Doppel...
duplicate *a.* doppelt; ~ *s.* Duplikat *n.;* ~ *v.t.* verdoppeln; vervielfältigen.
duplication *s.* Verdoppelung *f.;* Wiederholung *f.*
duplicity *s.* Falschheit, Zweideutigkeit *f.*
durability *s.* Dauerhaftigkeit *f.*
durable *a.,* **~bly** *adv.* dauerhaft.
duration *s.* Dauer *f.*
duress *s.* Zwang *m.;* Haft *f.; under* ~, (*jur.*) durch Nötigung.
during *pr.* während.
dusk *a.* dämmerig, dunkel; ~ *s.* Dämmerung, Dunkelheit *f.*
dust *s.* Staub *m.;* ~ *v.t* abstauben.
dustbin *s.* Müll-, Kehrichtkasten *m.*
dust cart *s.* Müll-, Kehrichtwagen *m.*
dust cover *s.* Schutzumschlag (Buch) *m.;* Abdeckhaube *f.*
duster *s.* Wischlappen *m.;* Staubbesen *m.*
dustman *s.* Müllmann *m.*
dustpan *s.* Kehrschaufel *f.*
dusty *a.* staubig; verstaubt.
Dutch *a.* holländisch; ~ *s.* Holländer(in) *m.(f.)*
duteous, dutiful *a.,* **~ly** *adv.* pflichttreu.
dutiable *a.* zollpflichtig, steuerpflichtig.
duty *s.* Pflicht, Schuldigkeit *f.;* Abgabe *f.;* Zoll *m.;* Dienst *m.;* **~-free** zollfrei; *on* ~, im Dienst; *off* ~, außer Dienst; ~ **hours** *pl.* Dienststunden *f.pl.; breach of* ~, Pflichtverletzung *f.*
D.V.M. *Doctor of Veterinary Medicine,* Doktor der Tiermedizin.
dwarf *s.* Zwerg *m.;* ~ *v.t.* am Wachstum hindern.
dwarfish *a.,* **~ly** *adv.* zwergartig.
dwell *v.t. & i.* wohnen; verweilen.
dwelling *s.* Wohnort, Aufenthalt *m.*
dwindle *v.i.* einschrumpfen, abnehmen.
dye *s.* Farbstoff *m.;* **~-works** *s.pl.* Farbwerke *n.pl.;* ~ *v.t.* färben.
dyer *s.* Färber *m.*
dying *a.* sterbend.
dynamic(al) *a.* dynamisch.
dynamics *s.pl.* Dynamik *f.*
dynamite *s.* Dynamit *n.*
dynamo *s.* Dynamo(maschine *f.*) *m.*
dynastic *a.* dynastisch.
dynasty *s.* Dynastie *f.*
dysentry *s.* Ruhr *f.;* Dysenterie *f.*
dysfunction *s.* Funktionsstörung *f.*
dyslexia *s.* Dyslexie *f.;* Lesestörung *f.*
dyspepsia *s.* Verdauungsstörung *f.;* Dyspepsie *f.*

E

E, e der Buchstabe E oder e *n.;* (*mus.*) E, e; **E-sharp** Eis; **E-flat** Es.

E. *east*, Osten *m.*, O.

each *pn.* jeder, jede, jedes; ~ *other*, einander.

eager *a.*, **~ly** *adv.* eifrig; erpicht.

eagerness *s.* Eifer *m.;* Begierde *f.*

eagle *s.* Adler *m.*

eaglet *s.* junger Adler *m.*

ear *s.* Ohr *n.;* Gehör *n.;* Öhr *n.;* Henkel *m.;* Ähre *f.;* ~ **ache** *s.* Ohrenschmerzen; **~drum** *s.* Ohrentrommel *f.*

earl *s.* (englischer) Graf *m.*

earldom *s.* Grafenwürde *f.*

earlobe *s.* Ohrläppchen *n.*

early *a.* & *adv.* früh, zeitig.

earmark *s.* Ohrenzeichen (bei Schafen) *n.;* ~ *v.t.* vormerken.

earmuffs *s.pl.* Ohrenschützer *pl.*

earn *v.t.* verdienen, erwerben, gewinnen.

earnest *a.*, **~ly** *adv.* ernstlich; dringend; ~ *s.* Ernst *m.;* Eifer *m.;* Handgeld *n.;* Unterpfand *n.;* *in good* ~, in vollem Ernste.

earnings *s.pl.* Verdienst, Lohn *m.*

earphones *s.pl.* Kopfhörer *m.*

earring *s.* Ohrring *m.*

earshot *s.* Hörweite *f.*

earsplitting *a.* ohrenbetäubend.

earth *s.* Erde *f.;* (*radio*) Erdung *f.;* ~ *v.t.* (*radio*) erden.

earthen *a.* irden.

earthenware *s.* Steingut *n.*

earthly *a.* irdisch, sinnlich.

earthquake *s.* Erdbeben *n.*

earthworm *s.* Regenwurm *m.*

earthy *a.* erdig; derb.

ear trumpet *s.* Hörrohr *n.*

earwax *s.* Ohrenschmalz *n.*

earwig *s.* Ohrwurm *m.*

earwitness *s.* Ohrenzeuge *m.*

ease *s.* Ruhe, Gemächlichkeit *f.;* Erleichterung *f.;* *at* ~, gemächlich; *stand at* ~, (*mil.*) rührt euch!; ~ *v.t.* erleichtern; beruhigen; lindern.

easel *s.* Staffelei *f.*

easiness *s.* Leichtigkeit *f.*

east *s.* Osten *m.;* Orient *m.;* ~ *a.* östlich.

Easter *s.* Ostern *n. or pl.;* ~ **Sunday,** Ostersonntag *m.;* ~ **egg** *s.* Osterei *n.*

easterly *a.* & *adv.* östlich.

eastern *a.* östlich; morgenländisch.

eastward *adv.* ostwärts.

easy *a.*, **easily** *adv.* leicht, bequem, frei; willig, gefällig.

easy chair *s.* Lehnstuhl *m.*

easy-going *a.* lässig, gemütlich.

eat *v.t.* & *i.st.* essen; fressen; zerfressen.

eatable *a.* eßbar; **~s** *pl.* Eßwaren *f.pl.*

eater *s.* Esser(in) *m.(f.)*

eating apple *s.* Eßapfel *m.*

eating house *s.* Speisehaus *n.*

eaves *s.pl.* Dachtraufe *f.*

eavesdropper *s.* Horcher *m.*

ebb *s.* Ebbe *f.;* ~ *v.i.* abfließen.

ebony *s.* Ebenholz *n.*

ebullient *a.* sprudelnd; überschwenglich.

ebullition *s.* Aufwallung *f.*

eccentric *a.* exzentrisch; überspannt.

ecclesiastic(al) *a.* kirchlich, geistlich; ~ *s.* Geistliche *m.*

echelon *s.* Staffelung *f.;* *in* ~ *formation,* (*mil.*) gestaffelt.

echo *s.* Widerhall *m.;* Echo *n.;* ~ *v.i.* & *t.* widerhallen; wiederholen.

eclectic *a.* eklektisch, auswählend.

eclecticism *s.* Eklektizismus *m.*

eclipse *s.* Finsternis *f.;* ~ *v.t.* verfinstern, verdunkeln.

ecological *a.* ökologisch.

ecology *s.* Ökologie.

economic(al) *a.* wirtschaftlich; sparsam.

economics *s.pl.* Volkswirtschaftslehre *f.*

economic warfare *s.* Wirtschaftskrieg *m.*

economist *s.* Nationalökonom(in) *m.(f.);* Wirtschaftswissenschaftler(in) *m.(f.)*

economize *v.t.* haushälterisch verwalten; sparen.

economy *s.* Sparsamkeit *f.;* Anordnung *f.*, Bau *m.;* Haushaltung *f.;* Wirtschaft, Volkswirtschaft *f.;* ~ **measures** *pl.* Sparmaßnahmen *f.pl.;* *planned* ~, Planwirtschaft *f.;* *political* ~, Volkswirtschaft, Nationalökonomie *f.*

ECOSOC *Economic and Social Council,* Wirtschafts- und Sozialrat der UN.

ecstasy *s.* Verzückung *f.;* Ekstase *f.*

ecstatic *a.* verzückt; ekstatisch.

ECU *European Currency Unit,* Europäische Währungseinheit.

Ecuador *s.* Ekuador *n.*

Ecuadorian *s.* Ekuadorianer(in) *m.(f.);* ~ *a.* ekuadorianisch.

ecumenical *a.* ökumenisch.

eczema *s.* Hautausschlag *m.;* Ekzem *n.*

Ed., ed. *edited,* herausgegeben, h(rs)g.; *edition,* Auflage, Aufl.; *editor,* Herausgeber(in), H(rs)g.

eddy *s.* Wirbel *m.;* ~ *v.i.* wirbeln.

edge *s.* Schärfe, Schneide *f.;* Ecke *f.;* Kante *f.;* Rand *m.;* *on* ~, hochkant; *to be on* ~ *over,* nervös sein über; *cutting* ~ *s.*, Schneide *f.;* ~ *v.t.* schärfen; säumen, einfassen; drängen; ~ *v.i.* vordringen.

edgeways, edgewise *adv.* hochkantig.

edging *s.* Saum *m.*, Einfassung *f.*

edible *a.* eßbar; **~s,** Eßwaren *f.pl.*

edict *s.* Verordnung *f.*

edification *s.* (*fig.*) Erbauung *f.*

edifice *s.* Gebäude *n.*

edify *v.t.* (*fig.*) erbauen.

edit *v.t.* herausgeben (ein Buch); edieren; redigieren; bearbeiten.

edition *s.* Ausgabe, Auflage *f.*

editor *s.* Herausgeber(in) *m.(f.);* Redakteur(in) *m.(f.);* **~-in-chief,** Chefredakteur(in) *m.(f.)*

editorial *s.* Leitarikel *m.;* ~ *a.* Redaktions...

editorialist *s.* Leitartikler *m.*

EDP *electronic data processing,* elektronische Datenverarbeitung, EDV.
EDTA *estimated time of arrival,* Voraussichtliche Ankunftszeit.
educate *v.t.* erziehen.
educated *a.* gebildet.
education *s.* Erziehung *f.*
educational *a.* Erziehungs...
educator *s.* Erzieher(in) *m.(f.)*
E.E., e.e. *errors excepted,* Irrtümer vorbehalten.
eel *s.* Aal *m.*
eerie *a.* gespenstisch, unheimlich.
efface *v.t.* auslöschen, ausstreichen; in den Schatten stellen.
effect *s.* Wirkung *f.; in* ~, in Wirklichkeit; *to take* ~, *to go into* ~, wirksam werden (Verordnung, etc.); *with* ~ *from,* mit Wirkung von; *to the* ~ *that,* des Inhalts daß; ~ *v.t.* ausführen, bewirken; *to* ~ *a policy,* eine Versicherung abschließen.
effective *a.*, **~ly** *adv.* wirksam, kräftig; wirklich vorhanden; ~ *June 1,* mit Wirkung vom 1. Juni; ~ *immediately,* mit sofortiger Wirksamkeit.
effectiveness *s.* Wirksamkeit *f.*
effectual *a.*, **~ly** *adv.* wirklich, wirksam.
effectuate *v.t.* bewerkstelligen.
effeminacy *s.* Verweichlichung *f.*
effeminate *a.*, **~ly** *adv.* effeminiert, weichlich; üppig; ~ *v.t.* verweichlichen; ~ *v.i.* sich verweichlichen.
effervesce *v.i.* sprudeln.
effervescence *s.* Sprudeln *n.;* Überschaumen *n.*
effete *a.* entkräftet; abgenutzt.
efficacious *a.*, **~ly** *adv.* wirksam.
efficacy *s.* Wirksamkeit *f.*
efficiency *s.* Wirksamkeit *f.;* (*mech.*) Nutzeffekt *m.;* Tüchtigkeit, Brauchbarkeit, Leistungsfähigkeit *f.;* ~ **rating,** (*mil.*) Beurteilung *f.*
efficient *a.*, **~ly** *adv.* wirksam, leistungsfähig; tüchtig, brauchbar.
effigy *s.* Bildnis *n.*
effort *s.* Anstrengung *f.*
effortless *a.* mühelos.
effuse *v.t.* ausgießen.
effusion *s.* Verschwendung *f.;* (*fig.*) Erguß *f.*
effusive *a.* überschwenglich.
e.g. *exempli gratia,* zum Beispiel.
egg *s.* Ei *n.; dried* ~, Trockenei *n.; newlaid* ~, frisch gelegtes Ei *n.; bad* ~, übler Bursche *m.;* ~ *on, v.t.* anhetzen.
egg cup *s.* Eierbecher *n.*
eggplant *s.* Aubergine *f.*
egg shell *s.* Eierschale *f.*
egg whisk *s.* Schneebesen *m.*
egg white *s.* Eiweiß *n.*
egg yolk *s.* Eigelb *n.*
ego *s.* Ego *n.;* Ich *n.*
egoism *s.* Egoismus *m.*, Selbstsucht *f.*
egoist *s.* Egoist(in) *m.(f.)*
egotism *s.* Selbstsucht *f.*
egotist *s.* Egotist(in) *m.(f.)*
egotistic(al) *a.* egoistisch, selbstbezogen.
Egypt *s.* Ägypten *n.*
Egyptian *s.* Ägypter(in) *m.(f.);* ~ *a.* ägyptisch.
eh *i.* he? hoho!
eiderdown *s.* Daunendecke *f.*
eight *a.* acht.
eighteen *a.* achtzehn.
eighteenth *a.* achtzehnt...
eightfold *a.* achtfach.
eighth *a.* acht...; ~ **note** *s.* Achtelnote.
eightieth *a.* achtzigst...
eighty *a.* achtzig.
either *pn.* einer von beiden; beide; **~... or** entweder... oder.
ejaculate *v.t.* ausstoßen; ejakulieren.
ejaculation *s.* Ausstoßen *n.;* Stosseufzer *m.;* Ejakulation *f.*, Samenerguß *m.*
eject *v.t.* hinauswerfen, ausstoßen, vertreiben.
ejection *s.* Vertreibung *f.;* Ausstoßung *f.*
eke *v.t. to* ~ *out,* dehnen, verlängern; ergänzen; sich durchhelfen.
elaborate *v.t.* ausarbeiten; verfeinern; ~ *a.*, **~ly** *adv.* ausgearbeitet; verfeinert, umständlich; kunstvoll.
elapse *v.i.* verfließen, verlaufen.
elastic *a.* elastisch; ~ *s.* Gummiband *n.*
elasticity *s.* Spring-, Federkraft *f.*
elated *a.* freudig erregt.
elation *s.* gehobene Stimmung *f.;* Stolz *m.*
elbow *s.* Ellbogen *m.;* (*mech.*) Knie *n.;* ~ *v.t.* wegstoßen; verdrängen.
elbow room *s.* Spielraum *m.;* Ellbogenfreiheit *f.*
elder *a.* älter; ~ *s.* Kirchenälteste *m.;* ~ *s.* Holunder *m.* **~berry** *s.* Holunderbeere *f.*
elderly *a.* älter, bejahrt; ~ *s.pl.* ältere Menschen *pl.*
eldest *a.* älteste.
elect *v.t.* (er)wählen; ~ *a.* erwählt.
election *s.* Erwählung *f.*, Wahl *f.;* ~ **campaign** *s.* Wahlkampf *m.*
electioneering *a.* Wahl...; ~ *s.* Wahlarbeit *f.*
elective *a.*, **~ly** *adv.* wählend; Wahl...
elector *s.* Wähler(in) *m.(f.)*
electoral *a.* Wahl...
electoral district *s.* Wahlbezirk *m.*
electorate *s.* Wählerschaft *f.;* Kurfürstentum *n.*
electric *a.* elektrisch; ~ **arc** *s.* Lichtbogen *m.;* ~ **heater** *s.* elektrische Heizvorrichtung *f.*
electrical *a.*, ~ *adv.* elektrisch; ~ *engineer,* Elektroingenieur(in) *m.(f.)*
electricity *s.* Elektrizität *f.*
electric shock *s.* Stromschlag *m.*
electrify *v.t.* elektrisieren; elektrifizieren.
electrocute *v.t.* durch Stromschlag töten.
electrode *s.* Elektrode *f.*
electrolysis *s.* Elektrolyse *f.*
electrolyte *s.* Elektrolyt *m.*
electromagnetic *a.* elektromagnetisch.
electron *s.* Elektron *n.*
electronic *a.* elektronisch.
electronics *s.* Elektronik *f.*
electroplate *v.t.* galvanisieren.
elegance *s.* Eleganz *f.*
elegant *a.*, **~ly** *adv.* zierlich; geschmackvoll; elegant.
elegiac *a.* elegisch.
elegy *s.* Elegie *f.*, Trauergedicht *n.*
element *s.* Urstoff *m.;* Bestandteil *m.*, Element *n.;* **~s** *pl.* Anfangsgründe *m.pl.*
elementary *a.* elementar, Anfangs...
elementary school *s.* Grundschule *f.*

elephant *s.* Elefant *m.*
elephantine *a.* elefantenartig.
elevate *v.t.* erhöhen, erheben.
elevated *p. & a.* hoch, erhaben; stolz.
elevation *s.* Erhöhung, Erhabenheit *f.*; Höhe *f.*; Polhöhe *f.*; Aufriß *m.*
elevator *s.* Aufzug *m.*
eleven elf.
elf *s.* Elf(e) *m.(f.)*, Kobold *m.*
elicit *v.t.* entlocken, hervorlocken.
eligibility *s.* Wählbarkeit *f.*
eligible *a.* wählbar; wünschenswert.
eliminate *v.t.* ausscheiden, entfernen.
elimination *s.* Beseitigung *f.*
elite *s.* Elite *f.*
Elizabethan *a.* elisabethanisch.
elk *s.* Elch *m.*
ell *s.* Elle *f.*
ellipse *s.* Ellipse *f.*
ellipsis *s.* (*ling.*) Ellipse *f.*
elliptical *a.* elliptisch.
elm *s.* Ulme *f.*
elocution *s.* Vortragsweise *f.*; Vortragskunst *f.*
elongate *v.t.* verlängern.
elope *v.i.* (*fam.*) durchbrennen.
elopement *s.* (*fam.*) Durchbrennen *n.*
eloquence *s.* Beredsamkeit *f.*
eloquent *a.*, **~ly** *adv.* beredt.
else *adv.* anders, sonst, außerdem.
elsewhere *adv.* anderswo.
elucidate *v.t.* erläutern.
elude *v.t.* entwischen, ausweichen; entgehen; (*Gesetz*) umgehen.
elusive *a.* ausweichend; flüchtig.
emaciate *v.t.* ausmergeln, abmagern.
emaciated *a.* abgezehrt.
emanate *v.i.* ausströmen; herrühren.
emancipate *v.t.* emanzipieren.
emancipated *a.* emanzipiert.
emancipation *s.* Emanzipation *f.*
emasculate *v.t.* entmannen.
embalm *v.t.* einbalsamieren.
embank *v.t.* eindeichen, dämmen.
embankment *s.* Eindämmung *f.*; (*rail.*) Damm *m.*; Kai *m.*; Ufereinfassung *f.*
embargo *s.* Embargo *n.*, Handelsverbot *n.*
embark *v.t.* einschiffen; ~ *v.i.* (*fig.*) sich einlassen (auf).
embarkation *s.* Einschiffung *f.*
embarrass *v.t.* verlegen machen.
embarrassed *a.* verlegen.
embarrassing *a.* peinlich; unangenehm.
embarrassment *s.* Verlegenheit *f.*
embassy *s.* Botschaft *f.*
embed *v.t.* betten, lagern, legen.
embellish *v.t.* verschönern.
embellishment *s.* Verschönerung *f.*
embers *s.pl.* Glut *f.*
embezzle *v.t.* unterschlagen, veruntreuen.
embezzlement *s.* Unterschlagung *f.*
embitter *v.t.* verbittern.
emblem *s.* Sinnbild *n.*; Symbol *n.*
emblematic *a.*, **~ally** *adv.* sinnbildlich; symbolisch *a.*
embodiment *s.* Verkörperung *f.*
embody *v.t.* verkörpern; enthalten.
embolden *v.t.* anfeuern, kühn machen.
emboss *v.t.* prägen.
embrace *v.t.* umarmen; enthalten; ergreifen; ~ *s.* Umarmung *f.*
embrasure *s.* Schießscharte *f.*
embroider *v.t.* sticken; ausschmücken.
embroidery *s.* Stickerei *f.*
embroil *v.t.* verwirren, verwickeln.
embryo *s.* Embryo *m.*
embryonic *a.* Embryonisch.
emend *v.t.* emendieren; berichtigen.
emendation *s.* Verbesserung *f.*
emerald *s.* Smaragd *m.*
emerge *v.i.* auftauchen, emporkommen.
emergence *s.* Auftauchen *n.*; Hervortreten *n.*
emergency *s.* Notfall *m.*; Not...; ~ **exit**, Notausgang *m.*
emergent *a.* aufstrebend, auftauchend.
emery *s.* Schmirgel *m.*
emetic *s.* Brechmittel *n.*
emigrant *s.* Auswanderer *m.*, Auswanderin *f.*
emigrate *v.i.* auswandern.
emigration *s.* Auswanderung *f.*
eminence *s.* Höhe, Anhöhe *f.*; Auszeichnung *f.*; Eminenz (Titel) *f.*
eminent *a.*, **~ly** *adv.* hervorragend; bedeutend.
emissary *s.* Kundschafter(in) *m.(f.)*, Abgesandte *m./f.*
emission *s.* Aussendung *f.*; Ausgabe *f.*
emit *v.t.* aussenden; äußern; ausgeben.
emotion *s.* Gefühl *n.*, Emotion *f.*, Gemütsbewegung *f.*
emotional *a.* gefühlsmäßig; erregt; emotionell.
emotionally *adv.* emotionell.
emotive *a.* emotionell, gefühlsbetont.
empathy *s.* Empathie *f.*; Einfühlung *f.*
emperor *s.* Kaiser *m.*
emphasis *s.* Betonung *f.*, Nachdruck *m.*; ~ *added,* Unterstreichung zugefügt.
emphasize *v.t.* betonen, hervorheben.
emphatic(al) *a.*, **~ly** *adv.* nachdrücklich.
empire *s.* Reich *n.*
empiric *s.* Empiriker; Quacksalber *m.*
empirical *a.* erfahrungsmäßig.
employ *v.t.* anstellen, einstellen; beschäftigen.
employee *s.* Arbeitnehmer(in) *m.(f.)*
employer *s.* Arbeitgeber(in) *m.(f.)*
employment *s.* Arbeit *f.*; Beschäftigung *f.*; ~ **agency** *s.* Arbeitsamt *n.*; *creation of ~*, Arbeitsbeschaffung *f.*
empower *v.t.* ermächtigen.
empress *s.* Kaiserin *f.*
emptiness *s.* Leere *f.*
empty *a.* leer; *~-handed a.* mit leeren Händen; ~ *v.t.* ausleeren.
emulate *v.t.* nacheifern; wetteifern mit.
emulation *s.* Nacheiferung *f.*; Wetteifer *m.*
emulous *a.*, **~ly** *adv.* nacheifernd.
enable *v.t.* fähig machen, ermöglichen.
enabling act *s.* Ermächtigungsgesetz *n.*
enact *v.t.* verordnen, verfügen; (*Gesetz*) erlassen; aufführen, spielen.
enactment *s.* Verordnung, Verfügung *f.*
enamel *s.* Emaille *f.*; Schmelzglas *n.*; Zahnschmelz *m.*; ~ *v.t.* emaillieren.

enamored *a.* verliebt.
encamp *v.t. & i.* (sich) lagern.
encampment *s.*; Lager *n.*
encase *v.t.* einschließen.
enchant *v.t.* bezaubern, verzaubern.
enchanter *s.* Zauberer *m.*
enchanting *a.* entzückend, bezaubernd.
enchantment *s.* Entzücken *n.*
enchantress *s.* Zauberin *f.*
encircle *v.t.* umringen; umgeben.
enc(l). *enclosure(s),* Anlage, Anl.
enclave *s.* Enklave *f.*
enclose *v.t.* einhegen; einschließen; enthalten; (einem Brief) beilegen.
enclosure *s.* Einhegung *f.*; Einlage, Anlage (in Briefen) *f.*
encode *v.t.* verschlüsseln.
encompass *v.t.* umgeben.
encore *s.* Zugabe *f.*
encounter *s.* Zusammentreffen *n.*; Gefecht *n.*; ~ *v.t.* zusammentreffen mit; ~ *v.i.* sich begegnen.
encourage *v.t.* ermutigen; fördern.
encouragement *s.* Ermutigung *f.*; Unterstützung *f.*
encouraging *a.* ermutigend.
encroach *v.i.* Eingriff tun; übergreifen.
encroachment *s.* Eingriff, Übergriff *m.*
encumber *v.t.* verwickeln; belasten.
encumbrance *s.* Beschwerde, Last *f.*; Hindernis *n.*
encyclic(al) *s.* Enzyklika *f.*
encyclopedia *s.* Enzyklopädie *f.*
end *s.* Ende, Ziel *n.*; Absicht *f.*; Stückchen *n.*; *at an* ~, am Ende; *no* ~ *of...*, eine Unzahl von...; *on* ~, aufrechtstehend, hochkant; ~ *in itself,* Selbstzweck *m.*; ~ *v.t.* beendigen; ~ *v.i.* aufhören.
endanger *v.t.* gefährden, *~ed species s.* vom Aussterben bedrohte Art *f.*
endear *v.t.* wert machen, teuer machen.
endearment *s.* Zärtlichkeit *f.*
endeavor *s.* Bestreben *n.*, Bemühen *n.*; ~ *v.i.* sich bemühen.
endemic *a.* endemisch, verbreitet.
ending *s.* Ende *n.*; Schluß *m.*; Endung *f.*
endive *s.* Chicorée *f.*
endless *a.*, **~ly** *adv.* unendlich, endlos.
endorse *v.t.* indossieren; gutheißen.
endorsement *s.* Indossament *n.*; Unterstützung *f.*; Billigung *f.*
endow *v.t.* ausstatten; finanzieren.
endowment *s.* Begabung; Stiftung; Ausstattung *f.*; ~ **policy** *s.* abgekürzte Lebensversicherung *s.*
end-product *s.* Endprodukt *n.*, Resultat *n.*
endurable *a.* erträglich.
endurance *s.* Beharrlichkeit *f.*; Widerstandskraft *f.*; Ausdauer *f.*; ~ **test** *s.* Belastungsprobe *f.*
endure *v.t. & i.* ertragen; erdulden; dauern.
enduring *a.* dauerhaft; beständig.
enema *s.* Einlauf *m.*; Klistierspritze *f.*
enemy *s.* Feind *m.*; ~ *alien,* feindlicher Ausländer *m.*
energetic *a.* kräftig, nachdrücklich.
energetically *adv.* schwungvoll; entschieden.
energy *s.* Tatkraft *f.*, Energie *f.*
energy: ~ **crisis** *s.* Energiekrise; **~-giving** *a.* energiespendend; **~-saving** *a.* energiesparend.
enervate *v.t.* entnerven; schwächen.
enfeeble *v.t.* schwächen.
enforce *v.t.* erzwingen; durchsetzen.
enforceable *a.* durchsetzbar.
enforcement *s.* Durchsetzung *f.*
enfranchise *v.t.* das Wahlrecht verleihen.
engage *v.t.* verpflichten; anwerben; beschäftigen; angreifen; ~ *v.i.* fechten; sich einlassen; sich verloben.
engaged *p. & a.* verlobt; bestellt, besetzt; beschäftigt.
engagement *s.* Verabredung *f.*; Verpflichtung *f.*; Verbindlichkeit *f.*; Beschäftigung *f.*; Verlobung *f.*; Einladung *f.*; Gefecht *n.*; *to meet one's engagements,* seinen Verpflichtungen nachkommen; *to break off the* ~, die Verlobung auflösen.
engaging *a.* verbindlich, einnehmend; bezaubernd.
engender *v.t.* erzeugen.
engine *s.* Maschine *f.*; Motor *m.*; Lokomotive *f.*; Feuerspritze *f.*
engine driver *s.* Lokomotivführer *m.*
engineer *s.* Ingenieur *m.*; Techniker, Maschinenbauer *m.*; (*mil.*) Pioneer *m.*
engineering *s.* Ingenieurwesen *n.*; Maschinenbaukunst *f.*; *electrical* ~, Elektrotechnik *f.*
England *s.* England *n.*
English *a.* englisch; ~ *s.* Englisch *n.*; **~man,** Engländer *m.*; **~woman** Engländerin *f.*
engraft *v.t.* pfropfen; einprägen.
engrain *v.t.* tief färben; einprägen.
engrave *v.t.* stechen, gravieren.
engraver *s.* Graveur *m.*; Bildstecher *m.*
engraving *s.* Kupferstich *m.*; Holzschnitt *m.*
engross *v.t.* ganz in Anspruch nehmen.
engulf *v.t.* versenken, verschlingen.
enhance *v.t.* verbessern; erhöhen, steigern.
enhancement *s.* Verbesserung; Erhöhung; Steigerung *f.*
enigma *s.* Rätsel *n.*
enigmatic(al) *a.*, **~ly** *adv.* rätselhaft.
enjoin *v.t.* einschärfen, anbefehlen.
enjoy *v.t.* genießen; *to* ~ *oneself,* sich gut unterhalten.
enjoyable *a.* angenehm; erfreulich.
enjoyment *s.* Vergnügen *n.*
enlarge *v.t.* erweitern, vergrößern; ~ *v.i.* sich verbreiten.
enlargement *s.* Erweiterung *f.*; (*phot.*) Vergrößerung *f.*
enlighten *v.t.* aufklären, erleuchten.
enlightened *a.* aufgeklärt.
enlightenment *s.* Aufklärung *f.*
enlist *v.t.* anwerben; ~ *v.i.* Dienste nehmen.
enlistment *s.* (*mil.*) Anwerbung *f.*
enliven *v.t.* beleben, ermuntern.
enmesh *v.t.* umgarnen, verstricken.
enmity *s.* Feindschaft *f.*
ennoble *v.t.* adeln; veredeln.
enormity *s.* Ungeheuerlichkeit *f.*
enormous *a.*, **~ly** *adv.* ungeheuer; riesig; gewaltig.
enormousness *s.* ungeheure Größe *f.*; Riesenhaftigkeit *f.*
enough *a. & adv.* genug; genügend.
enounce *v.t.* verkünden; aussprechen.

enrage *v.t.* in Wut versetzen; wütend machen.
enrapture *v.t.* entzücken.
enrich *v.t.* bereichern; anreichern.
enrichment *s.* Anreicherung *f.*; Bereicherung *f.*
enroll *v.t.* einschreiben; anwerben.
enrollment *s.* Einschreibung *f.*; Immatrikulation *f.*
enshrine *v.t.* einschließen; (als Heiligtum) aufbewahren.
enslave *v.t.* zum Sklaven machen.
ensnare *v.t.* verstricken, fangen.
ensue *v.i.* folgen; sich ergeben.
ensure *v.t.* (sich) sichern.
entail *v.t.* mit sich bringen.
entangle *v.t.* verwickeln; *to become ~d,* sich verfangen.
entanglement *s.* Verwirrung, Verwicklung *f.*, Verstrickung *f.*
enter *v.t. & i.* eintreten; hineingehen; einführen; einschreiben, eintragen.
enteric *a.* enterisch, Darm...
enteritis *s.* Darmkatarrh *m.*
enterprise *s.* Unternehmung *f.*
enterprising *a.* unternehmend.
entertain *v.t.* unterhalten; bewirten; hegen (Hoffnung).
entertainer *s.* Entertainer(in) *m.(f.)*
entertaining *a.* unterhaltsam.
entertainment *s.* Unterhaltung *f.*
entertainment tax *s.* Vergnügungssteuer *f.*
enthrall *v.t.* bezaubern, fesseln.
enthrone *v.t.* inthronisieren.
enthusiasm *s.* Begeisterung *f.*, Enthusiasmus *m.*
enthusiast *s.* Schwärmer *m.*
enthusiastic *a.* schwärmerisch, begeistert.
entice *v.t.* reizen, anlocken.
enticement *s.* Anlockung *f.*; Reiz *m.*
enticing *a.* verlockend.
entire *a.*, **~ly** *adv.* ganz, ungeteilt, vollständig.
entirety *s.* Ganzheit, Gesamtheit *f.*
entitle *v.t.* betiteln; berechtigen.
entity *s.* Einheit *f.*
entomb *v.t.* begraben.
entombment *s.* Begräbnis *n.*
entomologist *s.* Entomologe *m.*; Entomologin *f.*
entomology *s.* Insektenkunde *f.*
entourage *s.* Begleitung, Gefolge *f.*
entrails *s.pl.* Eingeweide *n.pl.*
entrance *s.* Eingang *m.*; Antritt *m.*; **~ examination,** Aufnahmeprüfung *f.*; **~ fee,** Aufnahmegebühr *f.*; **~ hall** *s.* Diele *f.*; Vorsaal *m.*; *no ~,* Eintritt verboten.
entrance *v.t.* entzücken.
entrant *s.* Beitretender (zu einem Verein) *m.*; Bewerber *m.*; Teilnehmer eines Wettbewerbs *m.*
entrap *v.t.* verleiten.
entreat *v.t.* anflehen, beschwören.
entreaty *s.* Bitte *f.*; Gesuch *n.*
entree *s.* Hauptgericht *n.*
entrench *v.t.* sich festsetzen (Idee); sich verwurzeln.
entrepreneur *s.* Unternehmer(in) *m.(f.)*
entrust *v.t.* anvertrauen.
entry *s.* Eingang *m.*; Eintragung *f.*; Meldung *f.* (*Sport*); gebuchter Posten *m.*; **~ permit,** Einreiseerlaubnis *f.*; *no ~,* Eintritt verboten, Einfahrt verboten.
entwine *v.t.* sich schlingen, sich winden.
enumerate *v.t.* aufzählen.
enumeration *s.* Aufzählung *f.*
enunciate *v.t.* aussagen, berichten; formulieren.
envelop *v.t.* einhüllen, einwickeln; (*mil.*) umfassen.
envelope *s.* Hülle *f.*; (Brief)umschlag *m.*
envenom *v.t.* vergiften; erbittern.
enviable *a.* beneidenswert.
envious *a.*, **~ly** *adv.* neidisch.
environment *s.* Umgebung *f.*
environmentalist *s.* Umweltschützer(in) *m.(f.)*
environs *s.pl.* Umgebung *f.*
envisage *v.t.* ins Auge fassen; sich etw. vorstellen.
envoy *s.* Gesandte *m./f.*; Bote *m.*, Botin *f.*
envy *s.* Neid *m.*; **~** *v.t.* beneiden.
enzyme *s.* Enzym *n.*
E. & O.E. *errors and omissions excepted,* Irrtümer und Auslassungen vorbehalten.
ephemeral *a.* kurzledig, flüchtig, ephemer.
epic *a.* episch; **~** *s.* Epos *n.*
epicenter *s.* Epizentrum *n.*
epicure *s.* Epikuräer, Genußmensch *m.*
epicurean *a.* üppig lebend, epikuräisch.
epidemic *a.* epidemisch; **~** *s.* Seuche *f.*
epigram *s.* Sinngedicht *n.*, Epigramm *n.*
epilepsy *s.* Fallsucht *f.*; Epilepsie *f.*
epileptic *a.* fallsüchtig, epileptisch.
epilogue *s.* Nachwort *n.*, Epilog *m.*
Epiphany *s.* Dreikönigsfest *n.*
episcopal *a.* bischöflich.
episcopate *s.* Episkopat *n.*
episode *s.* Episode *f.*; Folge *f.*
epistle *s.* Brief *m.*; Epistel *f.*
epitaph *s.* Grabschrift *f.*
epithet *s.* Beiwort *n.*; Beiname *m.*
epitome *s.* Inbegriff *m.*
epitomize *v.t.* verkörpern.
epoch *s.* Epoche *f.*
equable *a.* ausgeglichen.
equal *a.*, **~ly** *adv.* gleich; gewachsen; **~** *v.i.* gleichen, gleichkommen.
equality *s.* Gleichheit *f.*
equalize *v.t.* gleichmachen.
equal opportunity *s.* Chancengleichheit *f.*
equals sign *s.* (*math.*) Gleicheitszeichen *n.*
equanimity *s.* Gleichmut *m.*
equate *v.t.* gleichsetzen.
equation *s.* Gleichung *f.*
equator *s.* Äquator *m.*
equatorial *a.* äquatorial.
equestrian a reitend; Reiter...
equidistant *a.* gleich weit entfernt.
equilateral *a.* (*geom.*) gleichseitig, gleichschenklig (Dreieck).
equilibrium *s.* Gleichgewicht *n.*
equinox *s.* Tagundnachtgleiche *f.*
equip *v.t.* ausrüsten.
equipment *s.* Ausrüstung *f.*
equipoise *s.* Gleichgewicht *n.*
equitable *a.*, **~bly** *adv.* gerecht; billig.
equity *s.* Billigkeit, Unparteilichkeit *f.*
equivalent *a.*, **~ly** *adv.* gleichbedeutend; **~** *s.* Gegenwert *m.*, Äquivalent *n.*

equivocal *a.*, **~ly** *adv.* zweideutig.
equivocate *v.i.* zweideutig reden; Ausflüchte gebrauchen.
equivocation *s.* Ausflucht *f.*
equivoque *s.* Zweideutigkeit *f.*
era *s.* Zeitrechnung *f.;* Ära, Zeit *f.*
eradicate *v.t.* ausrotten.
erase *v.t.* ausstreichen; ausradieren.
eraser *s.* Radiergummi *n.;* Tafelwischer *m.*
erasure *s.* Ausradierung *f.*
erect *v.t.* aufrichten; errichten; ~ *a.* aufrecht; erigiert.
erection *s.* Aufrichtung *f.;* Erhebung *f.;* Aufbau *m.;* Erektion *f.*
eremite *s.* Einsiedler *m.*
ermine *s.* Hermelin *n.* & *m.*
erode *v.t.* erodieren; auswaschen; zerfressen.
erosion *s.* Erosion *f.*, Zerfressung *f.*
erotic *a.* erotisch.
erotically *adv.* erotisch.
err *v.i.* sich verirren; abweichen; irren.
errand *s.* Botengang *m.*
errand boy *s.* Laufbursche *m.*
errant *a.* herumirrend (Ritter); umherziehend.
erratic *a.* irrend; erratisch.
erratum *s.* **errata** *pl.* Erratum *n.*
erroneous *a.*, **~ly** *adv.* irrig, irrtümlich.
error *s.* Irrtum, Fehler *m.*
erudite *a.*, **~ly** *adv.* gelehrt.
erudition *s.* Gelehrsamkeit *f.*
erupt *v.i.* ausbrechen.
eruption *s.* Ausbruch *m.*
ESA *European Space Agency,* Europäische Weltraumbehörde.
escalate *v.i.* eskalieren.
escalation *s.* Eskalation *f.*
escalator *s.* Rolltreppe *f.*
escapade *s.* Eskapade *f.*, Seitensprung *m.*
escape *v.t.* & *i.* entrinnen, entlaufen; entweichen; vermeiden; ~ *s.* Entkommen *n.;* Ausflucht *f.;* *to have a narrow* ~, mit knapper Not davonkommen.
escapism *s.* Realitätsflucht *f.*
eschew *v.t.* meiden, scheuen.
escort *v.t.* geleiten, decken; ~ *s.* Bedeckung *f.*, Geleit *a.*, Begleit...; ~ *plane,* Begleitflugzeug *n.*
esophagus *s.* Speiseröhre *f.*
esoteric *a.* esoterisch, geheim.
esp. *especially,* besonders, bes., bsd.
especial *a.*, besonder; **~ly** *adv.* besonders.
espionage *s.* Spionage *f.*
espouse *v.t.* Partei ergreifen für.
Esq. *Esquire,* Herrn.
essay *s.* Essay *m.;* Aufsatz *m.*
essence *s.* Wesen *n.;* Essenz *f.*
essential *a.*, **~ly** *adv.* wesentlich; ~ *s.* Hauptsache *f.;* wesentlicher Umstand *m.*
est. *established,* gegründet, gegr.; *estimated,* geschätzt, gesch.
establish *v.t.* errichten, einsetzen; ansiedeln; bestätigen; festsetzen.
Established Church *s.* Staatskirche *f.*
establishment *s.* Einrichtung *f.;* Niederlassung *f.;* Anlage (von Fabriken, etc.) *f.;* (*mil.*) Mannschaftsbestand *m.*, Establissement *n.*, Firma *f.*
estate *s.* Stand *m.;* Vermögen *n.;* Grundstück *n.;* Landgut *n.;* Nachlaß *m.*
esteem *v.t.* achten, schätzen; erachten; ~ *s.* Wertschätzung *f.*
estimable *a.* schätzbar, achtbar.
estimate *v.t.* schätzen; veranschlagen, berechnen; ~ *s.* Schätzung *f.;* Voranschlag *m.;* *rough* ~, ungefährer Überschlag *m.;* *budget estimates,* Haushaltsvoranschlag *m.*
estimation *s.* Schätzung *f.;* Achtung *f.*
Estonia *s.* Estland *n.*
Estonian *s.* Estländer(in) *m.(f.);* ~ *a.* estländisch.
estrange *v.t.* entfremden; entwenden.
estrangement *s.* Entfremdung *f.*
estuary *s.* Mündung *f.;* Seebucht *f.*
etc. *et cetera,* usw.
etch *v.t.* ätzen, radieren.
etching *s.* Radierung *f.*
ETD *estimated time of departure,* voraussichtliche Abflug- oder Abfahrtszeit.
eternal *a.*, **~ly** *adv.* ewig.
eternity *s.* Ewigkeit *f.*
ether *s.* Äther *m.*
ethereal *a.* ätherisch.
ethic *s.* Ethik *f.*
ethical *a.*, **~ly** *adv.* sittlich, ethisch.
ethics *s.pl.* Sittenlehre *f.*, Ethik *f.*
Ethiopia *s.* Äthiopien *n.*
Ethiopian *s.* Äthiopier(in) *m.(f.);* *a.* äthiopisch.
ethnic *a.* Volk..., ethnisch.
ethnography *s.* Völkerkunde *f.;* Ethnographie *f.*
ethyl *s.* Äthyl *n.*
etiquette *s.* (feine) Sitte, Etikette *f.*
etymology *s.* Etymologie *f.*
eucalyptus *s.* Eukalyptus *m.*
eugenics *s.pl.* Eugenik *f.*
eulogize *v.t.* loben.
eulogy *s.* Lobrede *f.*
eunuch *s.* Eunuch *m.*
euphemism *s.* Euphemismus *m.*
euphemistic *a.* euphemistisch.
euphonic *a.* wohlklingend.
euphony *s.* Wohlklang *m.*
euphoria *s.* Euphorie *f.*
euphoristic *a.* euphoristisch.
EURATOM *European Atomic Energy Community,* Europäische Atomgemeinschaft, Euratom.
Europe *s.* Europa *n.*
European *s.* Europäer(in) *m.(f.);* ~ *a.* europäisch.
European Community *s.* Europäische Gemeinschaft.
euthanasia *s.* Euthanasie *f.*
evacuate *v.t.* (*mil.*) räumen, evakuieren.
evacuation *s.* Räumung *f.;* Evakuierung *f.*
evade *v.t.* & *i.* ausweichen; umgehen; ~ *taxes,* Steuern hinterziehen.
evaluate *v.t.* zahlenmäßig berechnen.
evaluation *s.* Evaluierung *f.*
evanescent *a.* verschwindend.
evangelical *a.* evangelisch.
evangelize *v.t.* evangelisieren.
evaporate *v.i.* verdunsten, verdampfen; ~ *v.t.* verdampfen; *evaporated milk,* Trockenmilch *f.*
evasion *s.* Umgehung *f.* (eines Gesetzes); (Steuer) Hinterziehung *f.*
evasive *s.* ausweichend.

eve *s.* Abend *m.;* Vorabend *m.*
even *a.,* **~ly** *adv.* eben, glatt; gerade; unparteiisch; quitt; ~ *adv.* sogar; *not* ~, nicht einmal; ~ *now,* jetzt; ~ *though,* selbst wenn; ~ *v.t.* gleichmachen, ebnen.
even-handed *a.* unparteiisch.
evening *s.* Abend *m.;* ~ **dress,** Abendkleidung *f.*
even-numbered *a.* gerade (Zahl).
evensong *s.* Abendgottesdienst *m.*
event *s.* Begebenheit *f.;* Vorfall *m.; at all* ~*s,* auf alle Fälle.
even-tempered *a.* ausgeglichen.
eventful *a.* ereignisreich.
eventual *a.* etwaig; zufällig; **~ly** *adv.* schließlich.
eventuality *s.* Eventualität *f.,* Möglichkeit *f.,* Fall *m.*
ever *adv.* je, jemals; immer; noch so.
evergreen *a.* immergrünend; ~ *s.* Immergrün *n.*
everlasting *a.,* **~ly** *adv.* immerwährend.
evermore *adv.* auf ewig.
every *a.* jeder, jede, jedes; ~ *one,* jeder(mann), alle *pl.;* **~thing,** alles; **~where,** überall.
evict *v.t.* zur Räumung zwingen.
eviction *s.* Räumungszwang *m.*
evidence *s.* Zeugnis *n.;* Beweis *m.; to admit in* ~, als Beweis zulassen; *to give* ~, aussagen; *to produce* ~, Beweis antreten.
evident *a.,* **~ly** *adv.* augenscheinlich, klar, offensichtlich.
evil *a.,* **~ly** *adv.* übel, böse; ~ *s.* Übel, Verbrechen *n.;* Unglück *n.*
evil: ~doer Übeltäter(in) *m.(f.);* **~-minded** *a.* bösartig.
evince *v.t.* an den Tag legen; zeugen von.
evocation *s.* Hervorrufung *f.*
evocative *a.* evozierend; aufrüttelnd.
evoke *v.t.* hervorrufen; beschwören, evozieren.
evolution *s.* Entwicklung *f.;* Evolution *f.*
evolutionary *a.* evolutionär.
evolve *v.t.* entwickeln; ~ *v.i.* sich entwickeln.
ewe *s.* Mutterschaf *n.*
exacerbate *v.t.* erbittern, verschlimmern.
exact *a.,* **~ly** *adv.* genau, gewissenhaft; ~ *v.t.* fordern, erpressen.
exacting *a.* streng, genau.
exaction *s.* Eintreibung *f.*
exactitude, exactness *s.* Genauigkeit *f.*
exaggerate *v.t.* übertreiben.
exaggeration *s.* Übertreibung *f.*
exalt *v.t.* (lob)preisen.
exaltation *s.* Erhöhung, Erhebung *f.;* Überschwang *m.*
exalted *a.* hoch, erhaben; überschwenglich.
examination *s.* Prüfung *f.,* Examen *n.;* Untersuchung *f.;* (*jur.*) Verhör *n.,* Vernehmung *f.; to be under* ~, erwogen werden; ~ **board,** Prüfungskommission *f.; final* ~, Schlußexamen *n.;* ~ **papers** *pl.* Prüfungsaufgaben *f.pl.;* Klausurarbeit *f.*
examine *v.t.* prüfen; verhören.
examinee *s.* Examenskandidat(in) *m.(f.)*
examiner *s.* Untersucher, Examinator *m.*
example *s.* Beispiel, Muster *n.; for* ~, zum Beispiel.
exasperate *v.t.* verärgern, zur Verzweiflung bringen.
exasperating *a.* ärgerlich.
exasperation *s.* Ärger *m.;* Verzweiflung *f.*
excavate *v.t.* aushöhlen; ausgraben.
excavation *s.* Ausgrabung *f.*
excavator *s.* Bagger *m.*
exceed *v.t.* überschreiten, übertreffen.
exceeding *a.,* **~ly** *adv.* außerordentlich, überaus; *not* ~, nicht mehr als.
excel *v.t.* übertreffen; ~ *v.i.* hervorstechen, sich auszeichnen.
excellence *s.* Vortrefflichkeit, *f.;* hervorragende Qualität.
excellency *s.* Exzellenz *f.*
excellent *a.,* **~ly** *adv.* vortrefflich.
except *v.t.* ausnehmen; Einwendungen machen; ~ *pr.* ausgenommen, außer.
exception *s.* Ausnahme *f.;* Einwendung *f.; to admit of no* ~, keine Ausnahme zulassen; *to take* ~ *to,* sich stossen an.
exceptional *a.,* **~ly** *adv.* außergewöhnlich, ausnahmsweise.
excerpt *v.t.* exzerpieren; ~ *s.* Auszug *m.*
excess *s.* Übermaß *n.;* Ausschweifung *f.;* ~ **fare** *s.* Zuschlag *m.;* ~ **baggage** *s.* Mehrgepäck *n.*
excessive *a.,* **~ly** *adv.* übermäßig.
exchange *v.t.* wechseln, tauschen; ~ *s.* Tausch, Wechsel *m.;* Börse *f.;* ~ **rate** *s.* Wechselkurs *m.; foreign* ~, Devisen *f.pl.; foreign* ~ *control,* Devisenzwangswirtschaft *f.*
exchequer *s.* Schatzkammer *f.;* Staatskasse *f.;* Schatzamt *n.; Chancellor of the* ~, (englischer) Schatzkanzler *m.*
excise *s.* Akzise *f.* (Verbrauch-) Steuer *f.;* ~ *v.t.* besteuern; herausschneiden.
excision *s.* (*med.*) Ausschneidung *f.*
excitable *a.* reizbar; erregbar.
excite *v.t.* erregen, anfeuern, reizen.
excited *a.* aufgeregt.
excitement *s.* Begeisterung *f.;* Aufregung *f.*
exciting *a.* aufregend; spannend.
excl. *exclusive, excluding,* ausschließlich, ausschl.
exclaim *v.t.* ausrufen.
exclamation *s.* Ausruf *m.;* ~ **mark,** ~ **point** Ausrufezeichen *n.*
exclamatory *a.,* ausrufend, Ausrufungs...
exclude *v.t.* ausschließen.
exclusion *s.* Ausschluß *m.*
exclusive *a.* ausschließlich.
excommunicate *v.t.* exkommunizieren.
excommunication *s.* Exkommunikation *f.*
excrement *s.* Kot *m.,* Exkremente *pl.*
excretion *s.* Absonderung *f.*
excruciating *a.* qualvoll.
exculpate *v.t.* entschuldigen.
excursion *s.* Ausflug *m.*
excursionist *s.* Tourist(in), Ausflügler(in) *m.(f.)*
excursive *a.* abschweifend.
excusable *a.* verzeihlich, entschuldbar.
excuse *v.t.* entschuldigen, verzeihen; *excused from appearing,* vom Erscheinen befreit; ~ *s.* Entschuldigung *f.*
execrable *a.,* **~ly** *adv.* abscheulich.
execrate *v.t.* verwünschen, verabscheuen.
execration *s.* Verwünschung *f.*
execute *v.t.* ausführen, vollziehen; vortragen,

spielen (Musik, Theater); hinrichten; *to ~ a deed,* eine Urkunde ausfertigen.
execution *s.* Ausführung, Vollziehung *f.;* Vortrag *m.*, Vortragsweise *f.;* Pfändung *f.;* Hinrichtung *f.;* Verheerung *f.*
executioner *s.* Scharfrichter *m.*
executive *a.* vollziehend; *~ committee,* Vorstand *m.; ~ regulation,* Ausführungsbestimmung *f.; ~ s.* vollziehende Gewalt *f.;* leitende Angestellte *m./f.*
executor *s.* Testamentsvollstrecker *m.*
exemplary *a.* vorbildlich.
exemplify *v.t.* durch Beispiele erläutern.
exempt *a.* frei, ausgenommen; ~ *v.t.* ausnehmen, verschonen.
exemption *s.* Befreiung *f.*
exercise *s.* Übung, Ausübung *f.;* Bewegung *f.;* ~ *v.t.* ausüben; ~ *v.i.* sich üben; exerzieren.
exercise book *s.* Schreibheft *n.*, Schulheft *n.*
exert *v.t.* ausüben; geltend machen; sich anstrengen.
exertion *s.* Anstrengung, Bemühung *f.*
exhalation *s.* Ausatmen *n.;* Verströmen *n.*
exhale *v.t.* ausatmen, verströmen.
exhaust *v.t.* erschöpfen; auspumpen; ~ *s.* Auspuff *m.*
exhausted *a.* ermüdet, erschöpft.
exhausting *a.* ermüdend, anstrengend.
exhaustion *s.* Erschöpfung *f.*
exhaustive *a.* umfassend, erschöpfend.
exhaust pipe *s.* Auspuffrohr *n.*
exhibit *v.t.* darstellen; aufweisen; ausstellen; ~ *s.* ausgestellter Gegenstand *m.*
exhibition *s.* Darstellung *f.;* Ausstellung *f.*
exhibitionist *s.* Exhibitionist(in) *m.(f.)*
exhibitor *s.* Aussteller(in) *m.(f.)*
exhilarate *v.t.* aufheitern.
exhilarating *a.* erheiternd.
exhort *v.t.* ermahnen.
exhortation *s.* Ermahnung *f.*
exhumation *s.* Wiederausgrabung *f.*
exhume *v.t.* wieder ausgraben.
exigence(cy) *s.* Erfordernis *n.;* Not *f.*
exigent *a.* auspruchsvoll, dringend.
exile *s.* Verbannung *f.;* Verbannte *m./f.;* ~ *v.t.* verbannen.
exist *v.i.* existieren.
existence *s.* Dasein *n.*
existent *a.* vorhanden.
existential *a.* existentiell.
existentialism *s.* Existentialismus *m.*
existing *a.* bestehend.
exit *s.* Ausgang *m.;* Abtreten *n.;* **~permit,** Ausreiseerlaubnis *f.;* **~visa** *s.* Ausreisevisum *n.*
exodus *s.* Auszug *m.*
ex officio *a. & adv.* von Amts wegen, amtlich.
exonerate *v.t.* entlasten; entbinden (Pflicht).
exorbitant *a.*, **~ly** *adv.* maßlos; überhöht.
exorcise *v.t.* (böse Geister) bannen, austreiben.
exorcism *s.* Geisterbeschwörung *f.*
exorcist *s.* Exorzist.
exotic *a.* ausländisch, exotisch.
expand *v.t.* erweitern; ~ *v.i.* sich ausdehnen.
expanse *s.* weiter Raum *m.;* weite Fläche *f.*
expansible *s.* ausdehnbar.
expansion *s.* Ausdehnung, Vergrößerung *f.*
expansive *a.* ausgedehnt; mitteilsam, überschwenglich.
expatriate *v.t.* ausbürgern; ~ *a.* ausgebürgert; ~ *s.* Ausgebürgerte *m./f.*
expatriation *s.* Verbannung *f.;* Auswanderung *f.;* Ausbürgerung *f.*
expect *v.t.* erwarten; denken, vermuten.
expectancy *s.* Erwartung; Anwartschaft *f.; life expectancy,* Lebenserwartung *f.*
expectant *a.* erwartend; *~ mother,* werdende Mutter *f.;* ~ *s.* Anwärter *m.*
expectation *s.* Erwartung *f.*
expediency *s.* Zweckmäßigkeit *f.*
expedient *a.*, **~ly** *adv.* zweckmäßig; ~ *s.* Mittel *n.*, Ausweg *m.*
expedite *v.t.* beschleunigen; abfertigen.
expedition *s.* Abfertigung *f.;* Feldzug *m.;* Forschungsreise *f.*
expeditionary *a.* Expeditions...
expeditious *a.*, **~ly** *adv.* hurtig, förderlich.
expel *v.t.* vertreiben; verstoßen.
expend *v.t.* ausgeben; aufwenden.
expenditure *s.* Kosten *pl.;* Ausgabe *f.;* Aufwand *m.;* (*mil.*) Verbrauch (von Munition) *m.*
expense *s.* Ausgabe *f.;* Preis *m.;* Kosten *pl.; to bear the ~s,* die Kosten tragen.
expensive *a.*, teuer, kostspielig.
experience *s.* Erfahrung *f.;* Erlebnis *n.;* ~ *v.t.* erfahren; erleben.
experienced *a.* erfahren.
experiment *s.* Versuch *m.;* ~ *v.i.* Versuche anstellen, experimentieren.
experimental *a.* experimentell, erfahrungsmäßig.
experimentation *s.* Experimentieren *n.*
expert *a.*, **~ly** *adv.* erfahren, kundig; ~ *s.* Sachverständige, Fachmann *m.; ~'s opinion, ~ evidence,* Gutachten *n.*
expertise *s.* Fachkentnisse *pl.;* Können *n.*
expertly *adv.* meisterhaft; fachmännisch.
expiate *v.t.* sühnen.
expiation *s.* Sühnung *f.*
expiration *s.* Ablauf *m.;* Verfallzeit *f.*
expire *v.i.* ablaufen; fällig werden.
explain *v.t.* erklären, erläutern.
explanation *s.* Erklärung *f.*
explanatory *a.* erklärend.
expletive *s.* Fluch *m.;* Kraftausdruck *m.*
explicable *a.* erklärbar.
explicit *a.*, **~ly** *adv.* ausdrücklich.
explode *v.t.* sprengen; ~ *v.i.* platzen, ausbrechen.
exploit *s.* Heldentat *f.;* ~ *v.t.* ausbeuten; ausnutzen.
exploitation *s.* Ausbeutung *f.;* Ausnutzung *f.*
exploration *s.* Erforschung *f.*
exploratory *a.* Forschungs...; ~ **talks** Sondierungsgespräche *pl.*
explore *v.t.* erforschen, untersuchen.
explorer *s.* Entdeckungsreisende *m./f.;* Forschungsreisende *m./f.*
explosion *s.* Explosion *f.*, Ausbruch *m.*
explosive *a.* explosiv; ~ *s.* Sprengstoff *m.*
exponent *s.* Exponent(in) *m.(f.);* Vertreter(in) *m.(f.)*
export *s.* Ausfuhr *f.; ~ control office,* Ausfuhrstelle *f.;* ~ **trade,** Ausfuhrhandel *m.;* ~ *v.t.* ausführen.

exporter *s.* Exporteur *m.*
expose *v.t.* bloßstellen; entlarven; belichten.
exposed *a.* ungeschützt.
exposition *s.* Darstellung *f.;* Ausstellung *f.*
exposure *s.* Bloßstellung *f.;* (*phot.*) Belichtung *f.*
expound *v.t.* auslegen.
express *v.t.* ausdrücken; äußern; ~ *a.*, **~ly** *adv.* deutlich, ausdrücklich; ~ *letter,* Eilbrief *m.;* ~ *train s.* Schnellzug *m.; to send* ~, durch Eilboten schicken.
expression *s.* Ausdruck *m.;* Redensart *f.*
expressionism *s.* Expressionismus *m.*
expressive *a.*, **~ly** *adv.* ausdrucksvoll.
expropriate *v.t.* enteignen.
expropriation *s.* Enteignung *f.*
expulsion *s.* Vertreibung *f.*
expunge *v.t.* ausstreichen, tilgen.
expurgate *v.t.* reinigen, ausmerzen.
expurgation *s.* Reinigung *f.*
exquisite *a.*, **~ly** *adv.* auserlesen.
ex-serviceman *s.* ehemaliger Soldat *m.*
ext. *extension,* Apparat (teleph.), App.; *external, exterior,* äußerlich, Außen...
extant *a.* noch vorhanden.
extemporaneous, extemporary *a.*, **~ily** *adv.* unvorbereitet, aus dem Stegreif.
extempore *adv.* aus dem Stegreif.
extemporize *v.t.* improvisieren, aus dem Stegreif darbieten.
extend *v.t.* ausdehnen; erweisen; ~ *v.i.* sich erstrecken; *extending table,* Ausziehtisch *m.*
extension *s.* Ausdehnung *f.;* (*tel.*) Nebenanschluß *m.;* ~ **cable** *s.* Verlängerungsschnur *f.*
extensive *a.*, **~ly** *adv.* ausgedehnt.
extent *s.* Ausdehnung, Weite *f.;* Umfang *m.;* Grad *m.*
extenuate *v.t.* verdünnen; schwächen; beschönigen; ~*ing circumstances s.pl.* mildernde Umstände *m.pl.*
exterior *a.*, **~ly** *adv.* äußerlich; ~ *s.* Äußere *n.*
exterminate *v.t.* ausrotten.
extermination *s.* Ausrottung *f.*
exterminator *s.* Kammerjäger *m.*
external *a.*, **~ly** *adv.* äußerlich; ~ *s.* Äußere *n.; for* ~ *use only,* äußerlich! (von Medizinen).
extinct *a.* erloschen; ausgestorben.
extinction *s.* Aussterben *n.*
extinguish *v.t.* auslöschen; vertilgen.
extinguisher *s.* Feuerlöscher *m.*
extirpate *v.t.* ausrotten, vertilgen.
extol *v.t.* erheben, preisen.
extort *v.t.* entwinden; erpressen.
extortion *s.* Erpressung, Plackerei *f.*
extortionate *a.* erpressend.
extra *a.* Extra..., Sonder..., Neben...; *coffee will be* ~, Kaffee wird besonders berechnet; **~s** *s.pl.* Nebenkosten *pl.; no* ~*s,* keine Kosten außerdem; **film** ~ *s.* Filmstatist *m.*
ex(tra)territorial *a.* exterritorial.
ex(tra)territoriality *s.* Exterritorialität *f.*
extract *v.t.* ausziehen; ableiten; ~ *s.* Auszug *m.;* Extrakt *m.*
extraction *s.* Extraktion *f.;* Gewinnung *f.;* Herkunft *f.*
extradite *v.t.* ausliefern.
extradition *s.* Auslieferung (von Verbrechern) *f.*
extramarital *a.* außerehelich.
extraneous *a.* von außen; belanglos; nicht zur Sache gehörig.
extraordinarily *adv.* außerordentlich.
extraordinary *a.* außerordentlich.
extravagance *s.* Verschwendung *f.;* Übertriebenheit *f.;* Extravaganz *f.*
extravagant *a.*, **~ly** *adv.* verschwenderisch; übermäßig hoch; extravagant.
extreme *a.*, **~ly** *adv.* äußerst, höchst; radikal; ~ *s.* Äußerste *n.;* höchster Grad *m.*
extremist *s.* Extremist(in) *m.(f.)*
extremity *s.* Äußerste *n.;* Unglück *n.;* **extremities** *pl.* Gliedmassen *pl.*
extricate *v.t.* herauswickeln.
extrinsic *a.*, **~ally** *adv.* äußerlich, von außen.
extrovert *a.* extrovertiert.
exuberance *s.* Überfülle *f.;* Überschwang *m.*
exuberant *a.*, **~ly** *adv.* üppig; überschwenglich.
exude *v.t.* ausschwitzen.
exult *v.i.* frohlocken.
exultant *a.* frohlockend.
exultation *s.* Frohlocken *n.*
eye *s.* Auge *n.;* (Nadel-) öhr *n.;* Knospe *f.; eyes front!* (*mil.*) Augen gerade aus!; *eyes right!* (*mil.*) Augen rechts!; ~ *v.t.* ansehen.
eyeball *s.* Augapfel *m.*
eyebrow *s.* Augenbraue *f.;* ~ **pencil,** Augenbrauenstift *m.*
eyeglass *s.* Zwicker *m.*, Brille *f.*
eyelash *s.* Augenwimper *f.*
eyelid *s.* Augenlid *n.*
eye shadow *s.* Lidschatten *m.*
eyesight *s.* Sehkraft *f.*
eyesore *s.* häßlicher Anblick *m.;* Dorn im Auge *m.;* Schandfleck *m.*
eyewash *s.* Augenwasser *n.;* (*fig.*) Quatsch *m.*
eyewitness *s.* Augenzeuge *m.*, Augenzeugin *f.*

F

F, f der Buchstabe F oder f *n.;* (*mus.*) F, f; **F-sharp** Fis, fis.
F. *Fahrenheit,* Fahrenheit.
F.A. *Football Association,* Fußballverband.
fable *s.* Fabel *f.;* Märchen *n.;* ~ *v.i.* fabeln; ~ *v.t.* erdichten.
fabric *s.* Bau *m.;* Gewebe *n.;* Stoff *m.*
fabricate *v.t.* erbauen; verfertigen; fälschen; erdichten.
fabrication *s.* Erdichtung, Fälschung *f.*
fabulous *a.*, **~ly** *adv.* fabelhaft.
facade *s.* Fassade *f.*
face *s.* Gesicht *n.;* Vorderseite *f.;* Uhrblatt *n.;* Fläche, Oberfläche *f.; in the* ~ *of,* angesichts; ~ *v.t.* ansehen; gegenüber liegen od. stehen; Trotz bieten; einfassen; (*arch.*) verkleiden; (*mech.*) glätten.
faceless *a.* anonym.

facelift *s.* Facelifting *n.*
facet *s.* Facette *f.*
facetious *a.*, **~ly** *adv.* drollig, scherzhaft, witzig.
facial *a.* Gesichts...; Gesichtsmassage *f.*
facile *a.* leicht; gefällig, banal.
facilitate *v.t.* erleichtern.
facility *s.* Leichtigkeit *f.*; Erleichterung *f.*; **facilities** *s.pl.* Anlagen, Einrichtungen *f.pl.*
facing *adv.* gegenüber; (Fenster) hinausliegend; ~ *s.* Vorderseite *f.*; Aufschlag *m.*; Einfassung *f.* (Kleid).
facsimile *s.* Faksimile. *f.*
fact *s.* Tatsache *f.*
faction *s.* Splittergruppe *f.*
factitious *a.* künstlich, gekünstelt.
factor *s.* Faktor *m.*
factory *s.* Fabrik *f.*; Faktorei *f.*; ~ **guard,** Werkschutz *m.*; ~ **hand,** Fabrikarbeiter *m.*
factual *a.* sachlich.
faculty *s.* Fähigkeit *f.*; Fakultät *f.*
fad *s.* Modeerscheinung *f.*; Marotte *f.*
fade *v.i.* verwelken; verschießen; vergehen; (*radio*) schwinden.; **~-in** einblenden; **~-out** ausblenden.
fag end *s.* letztes (schlechtes) Ende *n.*
fagot, faggot *s.* Reisigbündel *n.*; ~ *v.t.* zusammenbinden.
Fahrenheit *a.* Fahrenheit.
fail *v.i.* fehlen, mangeln; versiegen; fehlschlagen; durchfallen; Bankrott machen; ~ *v.t.* verlassen, unterlassen; ~ *s.* Mangel *m.*
failed *a.* nicht bestanden; gescheitert.
failing *s.* Mangel, Fehler *m.*; ~ *pr.* in Ermangelung von.
failure *s.* Versäumnis *n.* Mangel *m.*; Mißerfolg, Fehlschlag *m.*; Bankrott *m.*; ~ *to do sth.*, Unterlassung etwas zu tun.
faint *v.i.* vergehen; in Ohnmacht fallen; ~ *a.*, **~ly** *adv.* schwach.
faintness *s.* Undeutlichkeit; Mattheit *f.*
fair *a.*, **~ly** *adv.* hübsch; rein; hell: günstig; ehrlich, aufrichtig; blond; billig; ~ **play** *s.* ehrliches Spiel *n.*; anständige Handeln *n.*; ~ *adv.* mäßig, gefällig, höflich; ~ *s.* (Handels) Messe *f.*; Jahrmarket *m.*
fairly *adv.* ziemlich, leidlich; gehörig.
fairness *s.* Gerechtigkeit *f.*; Ehrlichkeit *f.*; Billigkeit *f.*
fairy *s.* Fee *f.*; Zauberin *f.*
fairy tale *s.* Märchen *n.*
faith *s.* Glaube *m.*; Treue *f.*; *breach of* ~, Treubruch *m.*; *in good* ~, in gutem Glauben, gutgläubig.
faithful *a.*, **~ly** *adv.* gläubig, treu; ehrlich; *yours ~ly,* hochachtungsvoll.
faith healing *s.* Gesundbeten *n.*
faithless *a.* ungläubig; treulos.
fake *v.t.* Betrug, Schwindel *m.*; ~ *v.t.* betrügen.
falcon *s.* Falke *m.*
falconer *s.* Falkner *m.*
fall *v.t.st.* fallen; sich ereignen; geraten; *to ~ into,* münden in (Fluß); *to ~ off,* abfallen; vergehen; *to ~ out with,* sich verkrachen mit; *to ~ short of,* zurückbleiben hinter; ~ *s.* Fall *m.*; Abnahme *f.*; Senkung *f.*; Herbst *m.*; Wasserfall *m.*
fallacious *a.*, **~ly** *adv.* irrig.
fallacy *s.* Täuschung *f.*; Betrug *m.*; Trugschluß *m.*
fallible *a.*, **fallibly** *adv.* fehlbar.
fall-out *s.* Fallout *m.*, radioaktiver Niederschlag *m.*
fallow *a.* falb; brach; ~ *deer,* Damwild *n.*; ~ *s.* Brache *f.*; ~ *v.t.* brachen.
false *a.*, **~ly** *adv.* falsch, unecht; ~ *alarm,* blinder Alarm *m.*; ~ *key,* Nachschlüssel *m.*
falsehood *s.* Unwahrheit *f.*; Falschheit *f.*
falseness *s.* Falschheit *f.*; Treulosigkeit *f.*
falsetto *s.* Fistelstimme *f.*
falsification *s.* Verfälschung *f.*
falsify *v.t.* verfälschen; verdrehen.
falsity *s.* Falschheit *f.*
falter *v.i.* straucheln; stammeln.
fame *s.* Ruhm, Ruf *m.*
familiar *a.*, **~ly** *adv.* vertraulich; vertraut; ~ *s.* Vertraute *m.* & *f.*
familiarity *s.* Vertrautheit *f.*, Vertraulichkeit *f.*
familiarize *v.t.* vertraut machen.
family *s.* Familie *f.*; Gattung *f.*
family allowance *s.* Kindergeld *n.*
family doctor *s.* Hausarzt *m.*
family planning *s.* Familienplanung *f.*
family tree *s.* Stammbaum *m.*
famine *s.* Hungersnot *f.*
famished *a.* (*fam.*) verhungert.
famous *a.*, **~ly** *adv.* berühmt.
fan *s.* Fächer *m.*; Ventilator *m.*; Fan *m.*; ~ *v.t.* fächeln; anfachen.
fanatic(al) *a.*, **fanatically** *adv.* eifervoll; ~ *s.* Fanatiker(in) *m.(f.)*
fanaticism *s.* Fanatismus *m.*
fan belt *s.* Keilriemen *m.*
fancier *s.* Liebhaber(in), Züchter(in) (von Vögeln, Pflanzen, etc.) *m.(f.)*
fanciful *a.*, **~ly** *adv.* phantastisch.
fancy *s.* Einbildung, Phantasie *f.*; Vorliebe *f.*; (*fig.*) Grille *f.*; ~ *v.i.* sich einbilden; ~ *v.t.* Gefallen finden an; lieb haben; *a.* phantastisch; kunstvoll; elegant.
fancy dress *s.* Maskenanzug *m.*; ~ *ball,* Maskenball, Kostümball *m.*
fancy goods *s.pl.* Modeartikel *m.pl.*
fancy price *s.* Liebhaberpreis *m.*
fanfare *s.* Fanfare *f.*
fang *s.* Fangzahn, Hauer *m.*; Klaue *f.*
fantasia *s.* (*mus.*) Fantasie *f.*
fantastic(al) *a.*, **~ally** *adv.* fantastisch.
fantasy *s.* Phantasie *f.*
FAO *Food and Agriculture Organization,* Organisation für Ernährung und Landwirtschaft der UN.
far *adv.* weit, fern; ~ *a.* fern, entfernt; *by* ~, bei weitem.
far away *a.* entlegen; fern.
farce *s.* Posse *f.*; Farce *f.*
farcical *a.*, possenhaft; (*fig.*) absurd.
fare *s.* Fahrt, Reise *f.*; Fuhre *f.*; Kost *f.*; Fahrgast *m.*; Fahrpreis *m.*, Fahrgeld *n.*; *at half-fare,* zum halben Fahrpreis.
Far East *s.* **the** ~ der Ferne Osten.
Far Eastern *a.* fernöstlich.
farewell *adv.* lebe wohl; ~ *s.* Lebewohl *n.*, Abschied *m.*
far-fetched *a.* weit hergeholt.
far-flung *a.* weit ausgedehnt; weit entfernt.
farm *s.* Bauernhof *m.*; Landgut *n.*; **~yard,** Hof

m.; ~ **manager,** landwirtschaftlicher Betriebsleiter *m.;* ~ *v.t.* (ver)pachten.
farmer *s.* Landwirt(in) *m.(f.);* Bauer *m.*, Bäuerin *f.*
farmhouse *s.* Bauernhaus *n.*
farming *s.* Landwirtschaft *f.*
farmland *s.* Landarbeiter(in) *m.(f.)*
farmstead *s.* Gehöft *n.*
far-off *a.* weit entfernt.
farreaching *a.* weitreichend.
far-seeing *a.* weitblickend.
farsighted *a.* weitsichtig; weitblickend.
fart *s.* (*vulg.*) Furz *m.;* ~ *v.i.* furzen.
farther *a.* & *adv.* weiter, ferner.
farthest *a.* & *adv.* am weitesten.
Far West *s.* **the** ~ der Westen der USA.
fascinate *v.t.* bezaubern; faszinieren.
fascinated *a.* fasziniert.
fascinating *a.* faszinierend; bezaubernd.
fascination *s.* Zauber, Reiz *m.*
Fascism *s.* Faschismus *m.*
Fascist *s.* Faschist *m.*
fashion *s.* Form *f.*, Gestalt *f.;* Mode *f.;* ~ *v.t.* gestalten.
fashionable *a.*, **fashionably** *adv.* elegant, modisch; modern.
fashion show *s.* Modeschau *f.*
fast *v.i.* fasten; ~ *s.* Fasten *n.;* Fasttag *m.;* ~ *a.* & *adv.* fest; stark, sehr; geschwind; flott, leichtlebig; *the clock is* ~, die Uhr geht vor.
fasten *v.t.* befestigen; verbinden.
fastener *s.* Verschluß *m.*, Zwecke *f.*
fast-food restaurant *s.* Schnellimbiß *m.*
fastidious *a.*, **~ly** *adv.* wählerisch; pingelig; heikel.
fastness *s.* Festigkeit, Stärke *f.;* Festung *f.*
fast train *s.* Schnellzug *m.*
fat *a.* fett, dick; ~ *s.* Fett *n.*
fatal *a.*, **~ly** *adv.* verhängnisvoll; tödlich.
fatalism *s.* Fatalismus *m.*
fatalist *s.* Fatalist(in) *m.(f.)*
fatalistic *a.* fatalistisch.
fatality *s.* Verhängnis *n.;* (tödlicher) Unglücksfall *m.*
fate *s.* Schicksal *n.*, Verhängnis *n.*
fateful *a.* verhängnisvoll; entscheidend.
father *s.* Vater *m.;* Stammvater *m.*
Father Christmas *s.* Weihnachtsmann *m.*
fatherhood *s.* Vaterschaft *f.*
father-in-law *s.* Schwiegervater *m.*
fatherland *s.* Vaterland *n.*
fatherless *a.* vaterlos.
fatherly *a.* väterlich.
fathom *s.* Faden *m.;* Klafter *f.;* ~ *v.t.* umklaftern; ergründen.
fathomless *a.* unergründlich.
fatigue *s.* Müdigkeit, Mühseligkeit *f.;* ~ *v.t.* ermüden.
fatness *s.* Fettigkeit *f.;* Fett *n.*
fatten *v.t.* mästen; ~ *v.i.* fett werden.
fattening *a.* dick machend.
fatty *a.* fettig, ölig; Fett...; ~ **acid** *s.* Fettsäure *f.*
fatuity *s.* Albernheit *f.*
fatuous *a.* albern.
faucet *s.* Wasserhahn *m.*
fault *s.* Fehler, Mangel *m.; to find* ~ *with,* etwas auszusetzen finden an..., tadeln.
fault finder *s.* Nörgler(in) *m.(f.)*
faultless *a.* fehlerfrei.
faulty *a.*, **faultily** *adv.* fehlerhaft.
fauna *s.* Fauna *f.*
favor *s.* Gunst, Gewogenheit *f.;* Gefallen; *in* ~ *of,* zu Gunsten; *to do a person a* ~, einem einen Gefallen erweisen; **~s** *pl.* Gunstbezeigungen *f.pl.;* ~ *v.t.* begünstigen, beehren.
favorable *a.*, **favorably** *adv.* günstig.
favorite *s.* Günstling *m.;* ~ *a.* Lieblings...
favoritism *s.* Günstlingswirtschaft *f.*
fawn *s.* Rehkitz *n.;* Rehfarbe *f.;* ~ *a.* hellbraun; ~ *v.i.* kriechend schmeicheln.
fax *s.* (Tele)Fax *n.;* ~ *v.t.* faxen.
fax machine *s.* Faxgerät *n.*
FBI *Federal Bureau of Investigation,* US-Bundeskriminalamt.
fear *s.* Furcht *f.;* Scheu *f.;* ~ *v.t.* & *i.* fürchten; sich fürchten.
fearful *a.*, **~ly** *adv.* furchtsam.
fearless *a.*, **~ly** *adv.* furchtlos.
fearsome *a.* furchterregend.
feasibility *s.* Ausführbarkeit *f.* Machbarkeit *f.*
feasible *a.*, **feasibly** *adv.* machbar; möglich.
feast *s.* Fest *n.;* Schmauserei *f.;* ~ *v.i.* schmausen; ~ *v.t.* bewirten.
feat *s.* Meisterleistung *f.;* Meisterwerk *n.*
feather *s.* Feder *f.;* ~ *v.t.* mit Federn schmücken/polstern.
feather: ~ **bed** *s.* mit Federn gefüllte Matratze; ~ **duster** *s.* Federwisch *m.;* **~weight** *s.* Federgewicht *n.*
feathery *a.* gefiedert; locker.
feature *s.* Gesichtszug *m.;* Merkmal *n.;* ~ *v.t.* (*film*) darstellen.
featureless *a.* eintönig.
Feb. *February,* Februar, Feb.
febrile *a.* fieberhaft.
February *s.* Februar *m.*
feces *s.pl.* Fäkalien *pl.*
fecundate *v.t.* befruchten.
fecundity *s.* Fruchtbarkeit *f.*
fed. *federal,* Bundes...
federal *a.* bundesmäßig; Bundes...
federalism *s.* Föderalismus *m.*
federate *a.* verbündet.
federation *s.* Bund *m.*
fee *s.* Lohn *m.*, Honorar *n.;* Gebühr *f.;* Lehen *n.; to charge a* ~, ein Honorar berechnen, eine Gebühr erheben; ~ *v.t.* bezahlen, besolden.
feeble *a.*, **feebly** *adv.* schwach; **~-minded** *a.* geistesschwach.
feebleness *s.* Schwäche *f.*
feed *v.t.ir.* füttern; widen; ~ *v.i.* essen; (*mech.*) Material zuführen, vorschieben; sich nähren; ~ *s.* Futter *n.;* Nahrung *f.;* (*mech.*) Vorschub *m.*
feedback *s.* Feedback *n.;* Rückkoppelung *f.*
feeder *s.* Zufluß *m.*
feeding bottle *s.* Saugflasche *f.*
feeding stuffs *pl.* Futtermittel *n.pl.*
feel *v.t.* & *i. ir.* (sich) fühlen, befühlen, empfinden; ~ *s.* Gefühl *n.*
feeler *s.* Fühler *m.*, Fühlhorn *n.*

feeling *p.* & *a.*, **~ly** *adv.* fühlend, gefühlvoll; ~ *s.* Gefühl *n.*
feet *s.pl.* (von *foot*) Füsse *m.pl.*
feign *v.t.* & *i.* erdichten; heucheln, vorgeben.
feint *s.* Verstellung, Finte *f.*; (*mil.*) Scheinangriff *m.*
felicitate *v.t.* beglückwünschen.
felicitous *a.* glücklich.
felicity *s.* Glückseligkeit *f.*; Glück *n.*
feline *a.* katzenartig; ~ *s.* Katze *f.*
fell *a.* (*poet.*) grausam; ~ *s.* Fell *n.*; Haut *f.*; ~ *v.t.* fällen, hinstrecken.
felloe *s.* Felge *f.*
fellow *s.* Genosse *m.*; Mitglied *n.*; Bursche *m.*; (in Zusammensetzungen) Mit...
fellow being *s.* Mitmensch *m.*
fellow citizen *s.* Mitbürger *m.*
fellow countryman *s.* Landsmann *m.*
fellow creature *s.* Mitmensch *m.*
fellow feeling *s.* Mitgefühl *n.*; Zusammengehörigkeitsgefühl *n.*
fellowship *s.* Gemeinschaft, Genossenschaft *f.*; Stipendium *n.*
fellow traveller *s.* Mitreisende *m./f.*
felon *s.* Verbrecher *m.*
felonious *a.* verbrecherisch; treulos.
felony *s.* schweres Verbrechen *n.*
felspar *s.* Feldspat *m.*
felt *s.* Filz *m.*; ~ *v.t.* filzen.
female *a.* weiblich; ~ *s.* weibliche Person *f.*; Weibchen *n.* (von Tieren).
feminine *a.* weiblich; feminin ~ *s.* (*gram.*) Femininum *n.*
feminism *s.* Feminismus *m.*
feminist *s.* Feministin *f.*; Feminist *m.*; *a.* feministisch.
femur *s.* Oberschenkelknochen *m.*
fen *s.* Sumpf *m.*, Moor *n.*
fence *s.* Zaun *m.*; Schutzwehr *f.*; ~ *v.t.* einhegen; verteidigen; ~ *v.i.* fechten; abwehren.
fencer *s.* Fechter(in) *m.(f.)*
fencing *s.* Einhegung *f.*; Fechtkunst *f.*
fend *v.t.* abwehren; parieren.
fender *s.* Kaminschutz *m.*; Kotflügel *m.*
fennel *s.* Fenchel *m.*
ferment *v.i.* gären; ~ *s.* Gärungsmittel *n.*
fermentation *s.* Gärung *f.*
fern *s.* Farnkraut *n.*
ferocious *a.*, **~ly** *adv.* wild, grimmig.
ferocity *s.* Wildheit, Grausamkeit *f.*
ferret *s.* Frettchen *n.*; ~ *v.t.* durchsuchen; herumstöbern.
ferrous *a.* Eisen...
ferry *s.* Fähre *f.*; ~ *v.t.* übersetzen.
ferryman *s.* Fährmann *m.*
fertile *a.*, **~ly** *adv.* fruchtbar.
fertility *s.* Fruchtbarkeit *f.*
fertilization *s.* Befruchtung *f.*
fertilize *v.t.* befruchten.
fertilizer *s.* Dünger *m.*
fervency *s.* Inbrunst *f.*; Eifer *m.*
fervent *a.*, **~ly** *adv.* heiß, inbrünstig.
fervid *a.* heiß, glühend; eifrig.
fervor *s.* Leidenschaft *f.*; Inbrunst *f.*
festal, **festive** *a.* festlich.
fester *v.i.* eitern.
festival *s.* Fest *n.*; Festival *n.*
festive *a.* festlich.
festivity *s.* Festlichkeit *f.*
festoon *s.* Girlande *f.*; ~ *v.t.* schmücken.
fetal *a.* fötal; fetal.
fetch *v.t.* holen, beibringen.
fetching *a.* einnehmend, gewinnend.
fetid *a.* stinkend.
fetish *s.* Fetisch *m.*
fetishism *s.* Fetischismus *m.*
fetishist *s.* Fetischist(in) *m.(f.)*
fetter *v.t.* fesseln; ~ *s.* Fessel *f.*
fetus *s.* Fötus *m.*, Fetus *m.*
feud *s.* Fehde *f.*; Lehen *n.*
feudal *a.* feudal, Feudal...; Lehns...
feudalism *s.* Lehnswesen *n.*
fever *s.* Fieber *n.*
feverish *a.* fieberhaft.
few *a.* wenig *pl.* wenige; *a.* ~, einige.
fiancé *s.* Verlobte, Bräutigam *m.*
fiancée *s.* Verlobte, Braut *f.*
fib *s.* kleine Lüge, Schwindelei *f.*; ~ *v.i.* flunkern.
fibber *s.* Flunkerer *m.*; Schwindler(in) *m.(f.)*
fiber *s.* Faser *f.*
fiberboard *s.* Faserbrett *n.*
fibrous *a.* faserig.
fickle *a.* veränderlich, unbeständig.
fiction *s.* Erdichtung *f.*; Romandichtung *f.*, Unterhaltungsliteratur.
fictional *a.* fiktiv, erfunden.
fictitious *a.*, **~ly** *adv.* erdichtet; ~ *transaction*, Scheingeschäft *n.*
fiddle *s.* Geige, Fiedel *f.*; ~ *v.i.* geigen.
fiddler *s.* Geiger(in) *m.(f.)*
fiddlestick *s.* Fiedelbogen *m.*; **~s!** *i.* Unsinn! Larifari!
fiddlestring *s.* Violinsaite *f.*
fiddling *a.* belanglos.
fiddly *a.* knifflig; umständlich.
fidelity *s.* Treue *f.*; Klangtreue *f.*; Bildtreue *f.*
fidget *v.i.* sich ruhelos bewegen, zappeln; ~ *s.* nervöse Unruhe *f.*
fidgety *a.* unruhig, nervös.
fiduciary *a.* Vertrauens...; ~ *issue*, ungedeckte Notenausgabe *f.*; ~ *s.* Treuhänder *m.*
fie *i.* pfui!
fief *s.* Lehen *n.*
field *s.* Feld *n.*; Schlachtfeld *n.*; Arbeitsgebiet *n.*; ~ **glass,** Feldstecher *m.*; ~ **marshal** *s.* Feldmarshall *m.*; ~ **kitchen** *s.* Feldküche *f.*; ~ **officer,** Stabsoffizier *m.*; ~ **post** *s.* Feldpost *f.*
fiend *s.* Teufel *m.*; Unhold *m.*
fiendish *a.* teuflisch, ummenschlich.
fierce *a.*, **~ly** *adv.* wild, grimmig.
fiery *a.* feurig; jähzornig.
fife *s.* Querpfeife *f.*
fifteen *a.* fünfzehn.
fifth column *s.* fünfte Kolonne *f.*
fiftieth *a.* fünfzigst...
fifty *a.* fünfzig.
fig *s.* Feige *f.*
fig. *figure,* Abbildung, Abb.
fight *v.t.* & *i.st.* kämpfen, streiten; ~ *s.* Gefecht *n.*; Kampf *m.*
fighter *s.* Jagdflugzeug *n.*; Kämpfer(in) *m.(f.)*
fighting *a.* Kampf...; ~ *s.* Kämpfe *pl. m.*

figment *s.* Erdichtung *f.; ~ of the imagination,* reine Einbildung *f.*
figurative *a.*, **~ly** *adv.* bildlich.
figure *s.* Gestalt *f.;* Ziffer *f.;* Zahl, Summe *f.;* **~head** Gallionsbild *n.; (fig.)* Strohpuppe *f.; ~ of speech,* Redewendung *f.; ~ v.i.* bilden, formen; vorstellen; *~ v.i.* eine Rolle spielen, auftreten.
figured *a.* gemustert.
figure skating *s.* Eiskunstlauf *m.*
figurine *s.* Figurine *f.*
Fiji Islands *pl.* Fidschi Inseln *pl.*
filament *s.* Faser *f.;* Faden *(m.)* der Glühlampe.
filch *a.* mausen.
file *s.* Liste *f.;* Reihe *f., (mil.)* Rotte *f.;* Briefordner *m.;* Feile *f.;* Akt *m.,* Aktenbündel *n.; single ~,* Gänsemarsch *m.; ~ v.t.* aufreihen; einordnen; feilen; *to ~ a petition,* ein Gesuch einreichen.
file card *s.* Karteikarte *f.*
filial *a.*, **~ly** *adv.* kindlich.
filibuster *s.* Verschleppungstaktik *f.;* Filibuster *n.; ~ v.t.* Dauerreden halten.
filigree *s.* Filigranarbeit *f.*
filing cabinet *s.* Aktenschrank *m.*
filings *s.pl.* Feilspäne *m.pl.*
fill *v.t.* füllen; einschenken; stopfen; *to ~ out, to ~ up,* ausfüllen (Formular); *~ s.* Fülle, Genüge *f.*
filler *s.* Füllmaterial *n.*
fillet *s.* Lendenbraten *m.,* Filet *n.*
filling *s.* Füllung *f.;* Plombe *f.*
fillip *s.* Anreiz *m.*
filly *s.* Stutenfohlen *n.*
film *s.* Häutchen *n. (phot.)* Film, *m.; ~ v.t. & i.* (ver)filmen.
filter *v.t.* Filter *m. & n.; ~ v.t.* filtern.
filth *s.* Schmutz, Kot *m.*
filthy *a.*, **filthily** *adv.* kotig; unflätig.
filtrate *v.t. & i.* filtrieren.
fin, *s.*, Flosse *f.*
final *a.*, **~ly** *adv.* endlich; endgültig; *~ s. (Sport)* Schlußrunde *f.;* Endspiel *n.*
finale *s.* Finale *n.*
finalist *s.* Finalist(in) *m.(f.)*
finalize *v.t.* vollenden, abschließen.
finance *s.* Finanzwesen *n.; ~ v.t.* finanzieren; *~ s.pl.* Finanzen *pl.*
financial *a.* finanziell; *~ year,* Hautshaltsjahr *n.*
financier *s.* Finanzmann *m.*
finch *s.* Fink *m.*
find *v.t. & i.st.* finden, antreffen; bemerken; *to ~ out,* herausfinden, ausfindig machen; *the jury found him guilty,* die Geschworenen sprachen ihn schuldig; *~ s.* Fund *m.*
finder *s.* Finder(in) *m.(f.)*
finding *s.* Befund *m.,* Ergebnis *n.*
fine *a.*, **~ly** *adv.* fein, schön; zart; kostbar; schlau; *~ s.* Geldbusse *f.; ~ v.t.* klären; eine Geldstrafe auflegen.
fine arts *pl.* schöne Künste *f.pl.*
finery *s.* Staat, Putz *m.*
finesse *s.* Feinheit *f.*
finger *s.* Finger *m.; ~ v.t.* betasten.
finger bowl *s.* Fingerschale *f.*
fingering *s. (mus.)* Fingersatz *m.*
fingernail *s.* Fingernagel *m.*
fingerprint *s.* Fingerabdruck *m.*
fingertip *s.* Fingerspitze *f.; to have sth. at one's ~s,* etwas am Schnürchen haben.
finicky *a.* zimperlich, geziert; heikel.
finish *v.t.* endigen, vollenden; *~ s.* Schluß *m.;* Appretur *f.*
finished goods *pl.* Fertigwaren *f.pl.*
finite *a.*, **~ly** *adv.* begrenzt; endlich.
Finland *s.* Finnland *n.*
Finn *s.* Finne *m.;* Finnin *f.*
Finnish *a.* finnisch.
fiord *s.* Fjord *m.*
fir *s.* Tanne, Kiefer *f.*
fir cone *s.* Tannenzapfen *m.*
fire *s.* Feuer *n.;* Feuersbrunst *f.; (fig.)* Leidenschaft *f.; to set on ~,* anzünden; *~ v.t.* anzünden; anfeuern; abfeuern; *(fam.)* entlassen, herauswerfen; *~ v.i.* Feuer fangen; schießen.
fire alarm *s.* Feuermelder *m.*
firearms *s.pl.* Feuerwaffen *f.pl.*
firebrand *s.* Feuerbrand *m.;* Aufwiegler *m.*
firebrick *s.* feuerfester Ziegel *m.*
fire department *s.* Feuerwehr *f.*
fire-eater *s.* Feuerschlucker *m.*
fire engine *s.* Löschfahrzeug *n.*
fire escape *s.* Rettungsleiter *f.*
fire extinguisher *s.* Feuerlöscher *m.*
firefighting *s.* Feuerbekämpfung *f.*
firefly *s.* Leuchtkäfer *m.*
fireguard *s.* Feuergitter (Kamin) *n.*
fire insurance *s.* Feuerversicherung *f.*
fireman *s.* Feuerwehrmann *m.*
fireplace *s.* Kamin, Herd *m.*
firepower *s. (mil.)* Feuerkraft *f.*
fireproof *a.* feuerfest.
fireside *s.* Herd, Kamin *m.*
fire station *s.* Feuerwache *f.*
firewood *s.* Brennholz *n.*
fireworks *s.pl.* Feuerwerk *n.*
firing *s.* Brennen *n.* (Ton); Abfeuern *s.*
firing range *s. (mil.)* Schussweite *f.;* Schießstand *m.*
firm *a.*, **~ly** *adv.* fest, derb; entschlossen; *~ s.* Firma *f.*
firmament *s.* Himmelsgewölbe *n.*
firmness *s.* Festigkeit *f.*
first *a. & adv.* **~ly** *adv.* der, die, das erste; erstens; *at ~,* anfänglich, zuerst, zunächst; *~ of all,* vor allen Dingen; *~ come, ~ served,* wer zuerst kommt, mahlt zuerst.
first aid *s.* Erste Hilfe *f.*
first-rate *a.* erstklassig, vorzüglich.
fiscal *a.* fiskalisch; *~ year,* Haushaltsjahr *n.*
fish *s.* Fisch *m.; ~ v.t.* fischen.
fish bone *s.* Fischgräte *f.*
fisher *s.* Fischer *m.*
fisherman *s.* Fischer *m.*
fishery *s.* Fischfang *m.,* Fischerei *f.*
fishing boat *s.* Fischerboot *n.*
fishing hook *s.* Fischangel *f.*
fishing line *s.* Angelschnur *f.*
fishing rod *s.* Angelrute *f.*
fishing tackle *s.* Angelgerät *n.*
fishmonger *s.* Fischhändler *m.*
fishy *a.* fischartig; verdächtig.
fission *s.* Spaltung (Zelle, Atomkern) *f.*
fissure *s.* Spalte *f.;* Riß *m.; ~ v.t.* spalten.

fist *s.* Faust *f.*
fistful *s.* Handvoll *f.*
fistula *s.* Fistel *f.*
fit *s.* Anwandlung *f.;* Anfall *m.;* ~ *a.,* **~ly** *adv.* passend; bequem, tauglich; in guter Form; ~ *v.t.* anpassen, versehen; zurechtmachen; ~ *up,* montieren; ~ *v.i.* sich schicken.
fitful *a.* launisch.
fitness *s.* Tauglichkeit; Schicklichkeit *f.*
fitted *a.* geeignet, passend.
fitter *s.* Monteur *m.*
fitting *a.,* **~ly** *adv.* schicklich, passend; ~ *s.pl.* Zubehörteile *f.pl.;* Einrichtung *f.;* ~ *s.* Anprobe *f.* (beim Schneider).
five *a.* fünf.
fix *v.t.* befestigen, anbringen; festsetzen; bestimmen; in Ordnung bringen; (*phot.*) fixieren; ~ *v.i.* festwerden; ~ *s.* Verlegenheit, Klemme *f.*
fixation *s.* Fixierung *f.;* Festsetzung, Befestigung *f.*
fixed *p. & a.,* **~ly** *adv.* festgesetzt, unverwandt; (*mil.*) ortsfest.
fixing solution *s.* (*phot.*) Fixierbad *n.*
fixture *s.* eingebautes Teil *n.*
fizz *v.i.* sprudeln; ~ *s.* Sprudeln *n.*
fizzle *v.i.* zischen, sprühen.
fizzy *a.* sprudelnd.
fl. *floor,* Stock.
flabbergast *v.t.* völlig verblüffen.
flabby *a.* schlaff, welk.
flaccid *a.* schlapp, schlaff.
flag *s.* Fahne, Flagge *f.;* ~ *v.i.* erschlaffen.
flagellate *v.t.* geisseln.
flagon *s.* (Deckel-)kanne *f.;* Flasche *f.*
flagpole *s.* Flaggenmast *m.*
flagrant *a.,* **~ly** *adv.* offenkundig; berüchtigt; abscheulich.
flagship *s.* Flaggschiff *n.*
flagstaff *s.* Flaggenstange *f.*
flail *s.* Dreschflegel *m.*
flair *s.* Gespür *n.*
flake *s.* Flocke *f.;* ~ *v.i.* sich flocken; abblättern.
flaky *a.* blättrig, bröckelig.
flamboyance *s.* Extravaganz *f.;* Grellheit *f.*
flamboyant *a.* extravagant; grell.
flame *s.* Flamme *f.;* ~ *v.i.* flammen.
flamethrower *s.* (*mil.*) Flammenwerfer *m.*
flaming *a.* feuerrot; flammend; leidenschaftlich.
flan *s.* Torte *f.,* Törtchen *n.*
flange *s.* Flansch *m.*
flank *s.* Seite, Weiche *f.;* Flanke *f.;* ~ *v.t.* in die Flanke fallen, flankieren.
flannel *s.* Flanell *m.;* Flanell...; Waschlappen *m.;* **~s** *pl.* wollenes Unterzeug *n.;* Flanellhosen *pl.*
flap *s.* Lappen *m.;* Klaps *m.;* Rockschoß *m.;* ~ *v.t.* klapsen.
flapper *s.* Klappe *f.*
flare *v.i.* flackern; ausbrechen; ~ *s.* Lohe *f.,* Geflacker *n.*
flare path *s.* (*avi.*) Leuchtpfad *m.*
flash *s.* schnelle Flamme *f.;* Blitz *m.;* ~ *v.i.* aufblitzen, auflodern.
flashback *s.* Rückblende *f.*
flashlight *s.* Taschenlampe *f.;* Blitzlicht *n.*
flashy *a.* schimmernd; oberflächlich anziehend.
flask *s.* Flasche *f.;* Reiseflasche, Feldflasche *f.;* Pulverhorn *n.*
flat *a.,* **~ly** *adv.* platt, flach, schal; matt; rundheraus; (*com.*) flau; (*mus.*) um halben Ton erniedrigt; ~ *rate,* (*com.*) Einheitssatz *m.;* ~ *tire,* Reifenpanne *f.;* ~ *s.* Plattheit; Fläche *f.;* Untiefe *f.;* Stockwerk *n.;* Etagenwohnung *f.;* (*mus.*) das B *n.*
flat-chested *a.* flachbrüstig; flachbusig.
flatfoot *s.* Plattfuß; ~ *a.* **flatfooted** plattfüßig.
flatiron *s.* Bügeleisen *n.*
flatly *a.* rundweg, direkt.
flatness *s.* Flachheit *f.*
flatten *v.t.* flach machen; ~ *v.i.* schal werden.
flatter *v.t.* schmeicheln.
flatterer *s.* Schmeichler(in) *m.(f.)*
flattery *s.* Schmeichelei *f.*
flat tire *s.* Reifenplatte *f.;* Platte *m.*
flatulence *s.* Blähung *f.;* Nichtigkeit *f.*
flatulent *a.* blähend; schwülstig.
flaunt *v.i.* & t. protzen, zur Schau stellen.
flautist *s.* Flötist(in) *m.(f.)*
flavor *s.* Geschmack *m.;* Aroma *n.;* Blume (des Weines) *f.*
flaw *s.* Fehler *m.;* Defekt *m.*
flawless *a.* fehlerfrei; einwandfrei.
flax *s.* Flachs *m.*
flaxen *a.* flachsen.
flay *a.* (die Haut) abziehen, schinden.
flea *s.* Floh *m.;* ~ **bite** *s.* Flohbiß *m.;* (*fig.*) Kleinigkeit *f.*
fleck *s.* Fleck *m.;* Tupfen *m.;* ~ *v.t.* sprenkeln.
fledge *v.t.* befiedern.
fledged *a.* flügge, befiedert.
fledgling *s.* Jungvogel *m.*
flee *v.i.ir.* fliehen.
fleece *s.* Vlies *n.;* ~ *v.t.* scheren; (*fig.*) prellen.
fleecy *a.* flauschig; wollig.
fleet *a.* Flotte *f.*
fleeting *a.* flüchtig; vergänglich.
Flemish *a.* flämisch.
flesh *s.* Fleisch *n.*
flesh-eating *a.* fleischfressend.
flesh wound *s.* Fleischwunde *f.*
fleshy *a.* fleischig.
flex *v.t.* beugen; (Muskel) anspannen.
flexibility *s.* Biegsamkeit *f.,* Flexibilität *f.*
flexible *a.,* **flexibly** *adv.* biegsam; flexibel.
flexion *s.* Biegung *f.*
flextime *s.* Gleitzeit *f.*
flick *v.t.* schnippen, schnellen.
flicker *v.i.* flackern; flimmern (Film).
flier *s.* Flieger *m.;* Renner *m.*
flight *s.* Flucht *f.;* Flug *m.;* Schwarm *m.;* (*avi.*) Staffel *f.;* ~ *(of stairs) s.* Treppe *f.*
flight attendant *s.* Flugbegleiter(in) *m.(f.)*
flight recorder *s.* Flugschreiber *m.*
flighty *a.* flatterhaft.
flimsy *a.* locker, dünn; schwach.
flinch *v.i.* zurückschaudern.
fling *v.t.st.* werfen, schleudern; ~ *s.* Wurf, Schlag *m.;* Austoben *n.*
flint *s.* Feuerstein, Kiesel *m.*
flip *v.t. & i.* schnellen; schnipsen; ~ *s.* Schnipsen *n.*
flippancy *s.* Leichtfertigkeit *f.*

flippant *a.* leichtfertig, frivol.
flipper *s.* Flosse *f.*
flirt *v.t.* schnellen; ~ *v.i.* liebeln, kokettieren.
flirtation *s.* Liebelei *f.*, Flirt *m.*
flirtatious *a.* kokett.
flit *v.i.* flattern; huschen; ausrücken.
float *s.* Floß *m.*; Schwimmer *m.*; (*avi.*) Schwimmgestell, *n.*; ~ *v.i.* obenauf schwimmen; dahintreiben; ~ *v.t.* flößen; überfluten; flott machen; ins Leben rufen.
floating *a.* schwimmend; treibend; schwebend; ~ **debts** *pl.* schwebende Schulden *f.pl.*; ~ **dock** *s.* Schwimmdock *n.*
flock *s.* Herde *f.*; Haufen *m.*; (Woll-) flocke *f.*; ~ *v.i.* in Haufen ziehen, strömen, sich scharen.
flocky *a.* flockig.
floe *s.* Treibeis *n.*; Eisscholle *f.*
flog *v.t.* peitschen.
flogging *s.* Prügelstrafe *f.*
flood *s.* Flut *f.*; Hochwasser *n.*; ~ *v.t.* überschwemmen.
floodlight *s.* Scheinwerferlicht *n.*; ~ *v.t.* mit Scheinwerfer beleuchten.
floor *s.* Fußboden, Boden *m.*; Tenne *f.*; Stockwerk *n.*; ~ *v.t.* dielen; zu Boden schlagen.
floor lamp *s.* Stehlampe *f.*
floor leader *s.* Fraktionsführer(in) *m.(f.)*
floorshow *s.* Varietévorstellung *f.*
flop *v.i.* plumpsen; ~ *s.* Versager *m.*
floppy *a.* biegsam, weich; ~ **disk** *s.* (*comp.*) Diskette *f.*
flora *pl.* Flora *f.*
floral *a.* Blüten..., Blumen....
floral tribute *s.* Blumenspende *f.*
florid *a.*, **~ly** *adv.* verschnörkelt; blumig.
florin *s.* Gulden *m.*
florist *s.* Blumenhändler(in) *m.(f.)*
flotilla *s.* Flotille *f.*
flotsam *s.* Treibgut *n.*
flounce *v.i.* auffahren.
flounder *s.* Flunder *m.* or *f.*; ~ *v.i.* zappeln; sich abmühen.
flour *s.* Mehl *n.*
flourish *v.i.* blühen; prahlen; ~ *v.t.* schwingen; verzieren; ~ *s.* Schnörkel *m.*; Verzierung *f.*; Gepränge *m.*; Trompetenstoß *m.*
flout *v.i. & t.* mißachten.
flow *v.i.* fließen; fluten; ~ *s.* Flut *f.*; Redefluß *m.*
flowchart *s.* Flußdiagramm *n.*
flower *s.* Blume, Blüte *f.*; Beste *n.*; ~ *v.i.* blühen.
flower bed *s.* Blumenbeet *n.*
flowered *a.* geblümt.
flowerpot *s.* Blumentopf *m.*
flower shop *s.* Blumenladen *m.*
flowery *a.* blumig.
flowing *a.* fließend.
flu *s.* Grippe *f.*
fluctuate *v.i.* schwanken.
fluctuation *s.* Schwankung *f.*
flue *s.* Ofenrohr *m.* Luftkanal *m.*
fluency *s.* Fluß (der Rede) *m.*; Gewandtheit *f.*
fluent *a.*, **~ly** *adv.* fließend, flüssig; geläufig.
fluff *s.* Staubflocke, Fluse *f.*; Flaum *m.*; Fussel *f.*
fluffy *a.* weich, flauschig.
fluid *a.* flüssig; ~ *s.* Flüssigkeit *f.*
fluke *s.* (*fam.*) glücklicher Zufall *m.*
fluky *a.* glücklich, zufällig.
flunky *s.* Lakai *m.*
fluorescence *s.* Fluoreszenz *f.*
fluorescent *a.* fluoreszierend.
fluoride *a.* Fluorid *n.*
flurry *s.* Windstoß *m.*; Unruhe *f.*; ~ *v.t.* beunruhigen.
flush *s.* fliegende Röte *f.*; Aufwallung *f.*; kurzer Regenguß *m.*; ~ *v.t.* ausspülen; erröten machen; ~ *v.i.* erröten.
fluster *v.t.* aufregen; verwirren.
flute *s.* Flöte *f.*; ~ *v.t.* riefeln.
flutist *s.* Flötist(in) *m.(f.)*
flutter *v.i.* flattern; unruhig sein; ~ *v.t.* scheuchen, beunruhigen; ~ *s.* Geflatter *n.*; Unruhe *f.*
flux *s.* Fluß *m.*; Abfluß *m.*
fly *v.i.* & t.st. fliegen; fliehen; jagen; ~ *s.* Fliege *f.*; offene Droschke *f.*
fly fishing *s.* Angeln mit künstlichen Fliegen als Lockspeise *n.*
flying *a.* fliegend; ~ **boat** *s.* Flugboot *n.*; ~ **bomb** *s.* Flugbombe *f.*; ~ **saucer** *s.* fliegende Untertasse *f.*; ~ **squad** *s.* Überfallkommando *n.*; ~ **suit** *s.* Fluganzug *m.*
flyleaf *s.* Vorsetzblatt *n.*; loses Blatt *n.*
flypaper *s.* Fliegenpapier *n.*
flyswatter *s.* Fliegenklatsche *f.*
flyweight *s.* Fliegengewicht *n.*
flywheel *s.* Schwungrad *n.*
FM *frequency modulation*, Ultrakurzwellen, UKW.
fo., fol. *folio*, Folio.
foal *s.* Fohlen *n.*; ~ *v.i.* fohlen.
foam *s.* Schaum *m.*; ~ *v.i.* schäumen.
fob *v.t.* foppen, anführen.
f.o.b. *free on board*, frei (Schiff).
focal *a.* im Brennpunkt.
focus *s.* Brennpunkt *m.*; ~ *v.t.* (*phot.*) einstellen.
fodder *s.* Viehfutter *n.*; ~ *v.t.* füttern.
foe *s.* Feind *m.*
fog *s.* Nebel *n.*; ~ **signal** *s.* Nebelsignal *n.*
foggy *a.*, **foggily** *adv.* nebelig, dunkel.
foghorn *s.* Nebelhorn *n.*
fogy *s.* alter Opa *m.*, alte Oma *f.*
foible *s.* Schwäche *f.*; Eigenhert *f.*
foil *v.t.* vereiteln; ~ *s.* Foile *f.*; Laubwerk *n.*; Rapier *n.*; Metallblättchen *n.*; Einfassung *f.*
foist v.t unterschieben, zuschieben.
fold *s.* Falte *f.*; Falz *m.*; Schafhürde *f.*; ~ *v.t.* falten; pferchen; ~ *v.i.* sich schließen.
folder *s.* Falzbein *n.*; Broschüre *f.*; Aktendeckel *m.*, Mappe *f.*
folding *a.* zusammenklappbar; ~ **doors** *pl.*, Falttür *f.*
folding knife *s.* Taschenmesser *n.*
folding screen *s.* spanische Wand *f.*
foliage *s.* Laubwerk *n.*
folio *s.* Folio *n.*; Foliant *m.*
folk *s.* Volk *n.*; Leute *pl.*
folklore *s.* Volkskunde *f.*; Folklore *f.*, Überlieferung *f.*
foll. *following*, folgend, folg.
follow *v.t. & i.* (be-, nach-, ver-)folgen; *to ~ suit*, bedienen, Farbe bekennen (in der Karte); jemandes Beispiel folgen.
follower *s.* Nachfolger *m.*; Anhänger *m.*
following *a.* folgend.

folly *s.* Torheit *f.;* Ausschweifung *f.*
foment *v.t.* schüren.
fond *a.,* **~ly** *adv.* vernarrt; zärtlich; *to be ~ of,* gern haben, gern tun.
fondle *v.t.* liebkosen, verzärteln.
fondness *s.* Zärtlichkeit *f.;* Vorliebe *f.*
font *s.* Taufstein *m.;* Schriftguß *m.;* Schrifttype *f.*
food *s.* Speise *f.,* Essen *n.;* Futter *n.; to go without ~,* ohne Nahrung sein.
food hoarder *s.* Hamsterer *m.*
food poisoning *s.* Lebensmittelvergiftung *f.*
food processor *s.* Küchenmaschine *f.*
fool *s.* Narr *m.; ~ v.t.* zum besten haben.
foolery *s.* Narrheit *f.*
foolhardy *a.* tollkühn.
foolish *a.,* **~ly** *adv.* töricht, närrisch.
foolproof *a.* kinderleicht; betriebssicher.
foolscap *s.* Kanzleipapier *n.*
foot *s.* Fuß *m.;* Tritt *m.; on ~,* zu Fuß; *~ v.t. & i.* treten, fussen; zu Fuß gehen; *~ the bill,* zahlen.
foot-and-mouth-disease *s.* Maul- und Klauenseuche *f.*
football *s.* Fußball (spiel) *n.,* Rugby *n.*
football pool *s.* Fußballtoto *m.*
footbridge *s.* Steg *m.;* Brücke für Fußgänger *f.*
footfall *s.* Schritt *m.*
foothold *s.* fester Stützpunkt *m.*
footing *s.* Halt; Stützpunkt *m.; war ~,* Kriegsstand *m.*
footlights *s.pl.* Rampenlichter *n.pl.*
footlocker *s.* verschließbare Truhe *f.*
footman *s.* Lakai, Bediente *m.*
footnote *s.* Fußnote *f.*
footpace *s.* langsamer Schritt *m.*
footpath *s.* Fußweg *m.*
footprint *s.* Fußstapfe *f.*
footsore *a.* mit wunden Füssen.
footstep *s.* Schritt *m.;* Fußtritt *m.*
footstool *s.* Fußschemel *m.*
foot support *s.* Schuheinlage *f.*
footwear *s.* Schuhwerk, -zeug *n.*
footwork *s.* Beinarbeit *f.*
fop *s.* Geck *m.*
foppery *s.* Narrheit *f.;* Ziererei *f.*
foppish *a.* geziert, geckenhaft.
for *pr & c.* für, mit, nach, wegen, um... willen; aus, an, auf, zu, zufolge; denn, deswegen; *~ all that,* trotzdem; *~ and on behalf of,* per procura (p.p.).
forage *s.* Futter *n.; ~ v.t.* fouragieren; stöbern.
foray *s.* Raubzug *m.; ~ v.t.* plündern.
forbear *v.t.st.* unterlassen; Geduld haben; *~ v.t.* sich enthalten; *~ s.* Ahne *m.,* Vorfahre *m.*
forbearance *s.* Vermeidung, Unterlassung; Nachsicht *f.*
forbid *v.t.st.* verbieten, verhindern; *God ~!* Gott verhüte!
force *s.* Kraft, Gewalt, Gültigkeit *f.;* Mannschaft *f.;* **~s** *pl.* Truppen *f.pl.; to be in ~,* in Kraft sein; *to come into ~,* in Kraft treten; *~ v.t.* zwingen; Gewalt brauchen, notzüchtigen; erstürmen; *~d labor s.* Zwangsarbeit *f.; ~d loan s.* Zwangsanleihe *f.; ~d march s.* Eilmarsch *m.; ~d rate of exchange s.* Zwangskur *m.; ~d sale,* Zwangsverkauf *m.*
forceful *a.* wirkungsvoll.
forcible *a.,* **forcibly** *adv.* kräftig, gewaltsam.
ford *s.* Furt *f.; ~ v.t.* durchwaten.
fore *a.* vorder; vorherig; *~ adv.* vorn.
forebode *v.t.* vorbedeuten, ahnen.
forecast *v.t. & i.st.* voraussehen; *~ s.* Voraussage *f.*
forecastle *s.* (*nav.*) Back *f.,* Vorderdeck *n.*
foreclose *v.i.* ausschießen; vorwegnehmen.
foreclosure *s.* Verfallserklärung *f.*
foredoom *s.* Vorherbestimmung *f.; ~ v.t.* zum Untergang bestimmen.
forefather *s.* Vorfahr *m.*
forefinger *s.* Zeigefinger *m.*
forefront *s.* vorderste Reihe *f.*
forego *v.t.st.* vorhergehen.
foregone *a.* von vornherein bestimmt; *~ conclusion,* ausgemachete Sache *f.*
foreground *s.* Vordergrund *m.*
forehand *s.* Vorhand (-schlag *m.*) *f.*
forehead *s.* Stirn *f.*
foreign *a.* ausländisch; fremd; *~ bill,* Auslandswechsel *m.; ~ Office s.* Auswärtiges Amt *n.*
foreigner *s.* Ausländer(in) *m.(f.)*
foreknowledge *s.* Vorherwissen *n.*
foreland *s.* Vorgebirge *n.*
forelock *s.* Stirnhaar *n.;* Schopf *m.*
foreman *s.* Vorarbeiter *m.;* Sprecher *m.* (der Geschworenen).
foremast *s.* Fockmast *m.*
foremost *a.* vorderste, vornehmste.
forensic *a.* gerichtlich.
foreplay *s.* Vorspiel *n.*
forerunner *s.* Vorbote *m.*
foresee *v.t.st.* vorhersehen.
foreshadow *v.t.* vorausahnen lassen.
foreshorten *v.t.* verkürzen.
foresight *s.* Voraussicht *f.,* Weitblick *m.*
foreskin *s.* Vorhaut *f.*
forest *s.* Forst, Wald *m.; ~* **fire** *s.* Waldbrand *m.*
forestall *v.t.* vorwegnehmen, zuvorkommen.
forester *s.* Förster(in) *m.(f.)*
forestry *s.* Forstwirtschaft *f.*
foretaste *s.* Vorgeschmack *m.; ~ v.t.* einen Vorgeschmack haben.
foretell *v.t.st.* vorhersagen.
forethought *s.* Vorbedacht *m.*
forewarn *v.t.* vorwarnen.
forewoman *s.* Vorarbeiterin *f.*
foreword *s.* Vorwort *n.*
forfeit *s.* Geldbuße *f.;* Pfand (im Pfänderspiel) *n.; ~ v.t.* verwirken, verscherzen; *~ a.* verwirkt, verfallen.
forfeiture *s.* Verlust *m.;* Einbuße *f.*
forge *s.* Schmiede *f.; ~ v.t.* schmieden; ersinnen; fälschen; *~ ahead,* vorwärtsdrängen.
forger *s.* Fälscher(in) *m.(f.)*
forgery *s.* Fälschung *f.*
forget *v.t.st.* vergessen.
forgetful *a.* vergeßlich.
forgetfulness *s.* Vergeßlichkeit *f.*
forget-me-not *s.* Vergißmeinnicht *n.*
forgettable *a.* leicht zu vergessen.
forgive *v.t.st.* vergeben, verzeihen.
forgiveness *s.* Verzeihung *f.*
forgo *v.t.* verzichten auf, aufgeben.
fork *s.* Gabel, Zinke *f.*

forked *a.* gabelförmig.
foundation *s.* Gründung *f.;* Fundament *n.;* Stiftung *f.;* Anstalt *f.;* ~ **stone,** Grundstein *f.*
founder *s.* Stifter(in) *m.(f.);* Gründer(in) *m.(f.);* ~ *v.i.* scheitern; sinken.
foundling *s.* Findelkind *n.*
foundry *s.* Gießerei *f.*
fount = fountain.
fountain *s.* Quelle *f.;* Springbrunnen *m.;* ~**head** *s.* Urquell *m.;* ~ **pen** *s.* Füllfeder *f.*
four *a.* vier; ~ *s.* (*sport*) Vierer *m.*
four-engine(d) *a.* (*avi.*) viermotorig.
fourfold *a.* vierfach.
four-handed *a.* vierhändig.
four-in-hand *s.* Vierspänner *m.*
four poster *s.* Himmelbett *n.*
fourteen *a.* vierzehn.
fowl *s.* Vogel *m.;* Huhn *n.;* Geflügel *n.;* ~ *v.i.* Vögel fangen.
fox *s.* Fuchs *m.*
foxglove *s.* (*bot.*) Fingerhut *m.*
fox hunt *s.* Fuchsjagd *f.*
fr. *franc,* Franc, Franken.
fraction *s.* (*ar.*) Bruch; Bruchteil *m.*
fractional *a.* gebrochen, Bruch...; geringfügig.
fracture *s.* (Knochen-) bruch *m.;* ~ *v.t.* brechen.
fragile *a.* zerbrechlich, schwach.
fragility *s.* Zerbrechlichkeit *f.;* Gebrechlichkeit *f.*
fragment *s.* Bruchstück *n.*
fragmentary *a.* fragmentarisch.
fragmented *a.* bruchstückhaft.
fragrance *s.* Wohlgeruch *m.,* Duft *m.*
fragrant *a.,* ~**ly** *adv.* wohlriechend.
frail *a.* gebrechlich; schwach.
frailty *s.* Gebrechlichkeit *f.;* Fehltritt *m.;* Schwachheit *f.*
frame *s.* Rahmen *m.;* Gerüst, Gestell *n.;* Gestalt, Form *f.;* Einfassung *f.;* ~ *v.t.* einfassen; bilden; erfinden.
framework *s.* Fachwerk *n.;* (*fig.*) Bau *m.,* Rahmen *m.; within the ~ of,* im Rahmen von.
France *s.* Frankreich *n.*
franchise *s.* Wahlrecht *n.;* Gerechtsame *f.*
frank *a.,* ~**ly** *adv.* frei; aufrichtig.
frankfurt(er) *s.* Frankfurter Würstchen *n.*
frankincense *s.* Weihrauch *m.*
frankness *s.* Offenheit *f.*
frantic *a.,* ~**ally** *adv.* wahnsinnig; verzweifelt.
fraternal *a.,* ~**ly** *adv.* brüderlich.
fraternity *s.* Bruderschaft *f.;* Brüderlichkeit *f.*
fraternization *s.* Verbrüderung *f.*
fraternize *v.i.* sich verbrüdern.
fratricidal *a.* brudermörderisch.
fratricide *s.* Brudermord *m.;* Brudermörder *m.*
fraud *s.* Betrug *m.;* Enttäuschung *f.*
fraudulent *a.,* ~**ly** *adv.* betrügerisch.
fraught *p.* befrachtet; voll.
fray *s.* Schlägerei *f.;* ~ *v.t.* ausfransen; durchscheuern.
freak *s.* Mißbildung *f.;* Freak *m.*
freckle *s.* Sommersprosse *f.*
freckled, freckly *a.* sommersprossig.
free *a.,* ~**ly** *adv.* frei; offenherzig; ohne Kosten; gutwillig; *~ on board (f.o.b),* frei Schiff; *~ on rail,* frei Eisenbahn; *of my ~ will,* freiwillig; ~ *v.t.* befreien; freigeben.
freebooter *s.* Freibeuter *m.*
freedom *s.* Freiheit *f.;* Bürgerrecht *m.; ~ of association and assembly,* Koalitions- und Versammlungsfreiheit.
freedom fighter *s.* Freiheitskämpfer *m.*
free enterprise *s.* freies Unternehmertum *n.*
freehand drawing *s.* Freihandzeichnen *n.*
freehold *s.* Besitzrecht *n.*
freelance *s.* Freischaffende *m./f.; ~ journalist,* freier Journalist *m.*
free market *s.* freier Markt *m.*
freemason *s.* Freimaurer *m.*
freemasonry *s.* Freimaurerei *f.*
free port *s.* Freihafen *m.*
free-range *a.* freilaufend (Huhn).
freesia *s.* Freesie *f.*
free speech *s.* Redefreiheit *f.*
freestone *s.* Sandstein *m.*
freethinker *s.* Freigeist *m.*
free trade *s.* Freihandel *m.*
freeway *s.* Autobahn *f.*
freewheel *s.* Freilauf *m.*
freeze *v.i.st.* frieren, gefrieren; *to ~ to death,* erfrieren; ~ *v.t.* gefrieren machen; *to ~ promotions, wages,* Beförderungen aussetzen, Löhne nicht erhöhen.
freezing point *s.* Gefrierpunkt *m.*
freight *s.* Fracht *f.;* ~ **car** *s.* Güterwagen *m.;* ~ **train** *s.* Güterzug; ~ **yard** *s.* Güterbahnhof.
French *a.* französisch; ~ *s.* Franzose *m.;* Französin *f.;* Franzosen *n.pl.*
French Canadian *s.* Frankokanadier(in) *m.(f.);* ~ *a.* frankokanadisch.
French dressing *s.* Vinaigrette *f.*
french fries *pl.* Pommes frites *pl.*
French horn *s.* Waldhorn *n.*
Frenchman *m.* Franzose *m.*
French window *s.* Flügelfenster *n.,* Verandatür *f.*
Frenchwoman *f.* Französin *f.*
frenetic *a.* rasend.
frenzied *a.* wahnsinnig.
frenzy *s.* Raserei *f.*
frequency *s.* Häufigkeit *f.;* (*elek., Radio*) Frequenz *f.; high ~,* Hochfrequenz *f.*
frequent *a.,* ~**ly** *adv.* häufig, zahlreich.; ~ *v.t.* oft besuchen.
fresco *s.* Fresko *n.*
fresh *a.,* ~**ly** *adv.* frisch; kühl; neu.
freshen *v.t.* erfrischen; auffrischen; ~ *v.i.* frisch, kühl werden.
freshman *s.* Erstsemester *n.*
freshness *s.* Frische *f.*
freshwater *s.* Süßwasser *n.*
fret *s.* ~ *v.t.* abreiben; zerfressen; erzürnen; ~ *v.i.* sich grämen, ärgern.
fretful *a.,* ~**ly** *adv.* ärgerlich; verdrießlich; quengelig.
fret saw *s.* Laubsäge, Stichsäge *f.*
fretwork *s.* Gitterwerk, feines Schnitzwerk *n.,* Laubsägearbeit *f.*
Freudian *a.* Freudsche; ~ **slip** *s.* Freudsche Fehlleistung *f.*
FRG *Federal Republic of Germany,* Bundesrepublik Deutschland, BRD.
Fri. *Friday,* Freitag, Fr.
friable *a.* zerreibbar.

friar *s.* Mönch, Frater *m.*
friction *s.* Reibung *f.*
Friday *s.* Freitag *m.; Good ~,* Karfreitag *m.*
fridge *s.* Kühlschrank *m.*
friend *s.* Freund(in) *m.(f.)*
friendliness *s.* Freundlichkeit *f.*
friendly *a.* freundschaftlich; freundlich.
friendship *s.* Freundschaft *f.*
frieze *s.* Fries *m.*
frigate *s.* Fregatte *f.*
fright *s.* Entsetzen *n.;* Schreckbild *n.;* Schrecken *n.*
frighten *v.t.* erschrecken.
frightened *a.* verängstigt.
frightening *a.* furchterregend.
frightful *a.,* **~ly** *adv.* schrecklich.
frigid *a.,* **~ly** *adv.* kalt, frostig.
frigidity *s.* Kälte *f.;* Kaltsinn *m.*
frill *s.* Krause *f.*
fringe *s.* Franse *f.;* Rand *m.;* ~ *v.t.* befransen; säumen.
frippery *s.* Trödelkram *m.*
frisk *s.* Sprung *m.;* ~ *v.i.* hüpfen.
frisky *a.* lustig, munter.
fritter *v.t.* vergeuden.
frivolity *s.* Leichtfertigkeit *f.*
frivolous *a.,* **~ly** *adv.* frivol.
frizz(le) *s.* Haarlocke *f.;* ~ *v.t.* kräuseln.
fro *adv., to and ~,* hin und her.
frock *s.* Rock *m.* Frauenkleid.
frog *s.* Frosch *m.; ~ spawn s.* Froschlaich *m.*
frolic *a.* frölich; ~ *s.* Scherz *m.;* ~ *v.i.* spaßen; herumtollen.
frolicsome *a.,* **~ly** *adv.* lustig.
from *pr.* von, aus, nach, wegen; vor.
front *s.* Stirn *f.;* Vorderseite *f.,* Front *f.;* Vorder...; ~ **door** *s.* Vordertür *f.;* ~ **room** *s.* Vorderzimmer *n.;* ~ **view** *s.* Vorderansicht *f.;* ~ *v.t.* gegenüberstehen.
frontage *s.* Vorderseite *f.*
frontal *a.* Stirn..., Front...; ~ **attack** *s.* Stirnangriff *m.*
frontier *s.* Grenze *f.;* ~ **readjustments** *pl.* Grenzberichtigungen *f.pl.*
frontispiece *s.* Vorderseite (eines Gebäudes) *f.;* Titelbild *n.*
frost *s.* Frost *m.;* Reif *m.*
frostbite *s.* Frostbeulen *f.pl.*
frost-bitten *a.* vom Froste beschädigt.
frosted *a.* bereift, überfroren; ~ **glass** *s.* Mattglas *n.*
frosting *s.* Zuckerguß *m.;* Glasur *f.*
frosty *a.* frostig; bereift.
froth *s.* Schaum *m.;* ~ *v.t. & i.* schäumen.
frothy *a.* schaumig.
frown *s.* gerunzelte Stirn *f.;* ~ *v.i.* die Stirn runzeln; finster blicken.
frozen *p.* gefroren; ~ **meat** *s.* Gefrierfleisch *n.*
fructify *v.t.* befruchten.
frugal *a.,* **~ly** *adv.* sparsam; mäßig.
frugality *s.* Sparsamkeit, Mäßigkeit *f.*
fruit *s.* Frucht *f.;* Obst *n.;* Ertrag *m.*
fruiterer *s.* Obsthändler(in) *m.(f.)*
fruitful *a.,* **~ly** *adv.* fruchtbar.
fruition *s.* Genuß *m.;* Verwirklichung *f.*
fruitless *a.,* **~ly** *adv.* fruchtlos.
fruit salad *s.* Fruchtsalat *m.*
fruity *a.* fruchtartig; fruchtig; geschwollen (Ausdrucksweise); schmalzig.
frump *s.* (*pej.*) Vogelscheuche *f.*
frustrate *v.t.* vereiteln, vernichten; frustrieren.
frustration *s.* Vereitlung *f.;* Frustration *f.*
fry *s.* Fischbrut *f.; small ~,* kleines Volk *n.;* ~ *v.t.* rösten, braten; backen (Fisch); *fried egg s.* Spiegelei *n.*
frying pan *s.* Bratpfanne *f.,* Pfanne *f.*
ft. *foot, feet,* Fuß.
fth., fthm. *fathom,* Klafter.
fuck (*vulg.*) *v.t. & i.* ficken; *~you!* leck mich am Arsch.
fuddle *v.t. & i.* (fam.) (sich) berauschen, verwirren.
fudge *s.* Karamelbonbon *n.;* Unsinn *m.;* ~ *v.t.* pfuschen.
fuel *s.* Brennmaterial *n.;* Feuerung *f.*
fuel consumption *s.* Kraftstoffverbrauch *m.*
fuel oil *s.* Heizöl *n.*
fugitive *a.* flüchtig; leicht verschwindend (Farbe); ~ *s.* Flüchtling *m.*
fugue *s.* (*mus.*) Fuge *f.*
fulfill *v.t.* erfüllen, vollziehen.
fulfilment *s.* Erfüllung, Vollziehung *f.*
full *a.* voll; gänzlich; ~ *adv.* völlig, genau, recht, gerade; *in ~,* vollstandig, voll ausgeschrieben; *~ face s.* Vorderansicht (des Gesichts) *f.; ~ powers f.pl.* Vollmacht *f.; ~ stop s.* Punkt (Interpunktion) *m.;* ~ *s.* Fülle *f.*
full-blooded *a.* vollblütig.
full-blown *a.* ganz aufgeblüht; ausgewachsen.
full-bodied *a.* vollmundig.
full dress *s.* Abendkleidung *f.*
full-fledged *a.* flügge; (*fig.*) richtig.
full-length *a.* in Lebensgröße; abendfüllend.
full moon *s.* Vollmond *m.*
fullness *s.* Fülle *f.*
fulminate *v.i.* donnern; schelten.
fulsome *a.,* **~ly** *adv.* übertrieben.
fumble *v.i.&i.* tappen, betasten; stümpern.
fume *s.* Rauch *m.;* Dunst *m.;* Zorn *m.;* ~ *v.i.* rauchen, verdampfen; zornig sein; ~ *v.t.* räuchern.
fumigate *v.t.* räuchern.
fun *s.* Scherz, Spaß *m.; to make ~ of,* zum besten haben.
function *s.* Amt *n.;* Dienst *m.;* Tätigkeit *f.;* Funktion *f.;* gesellige Veranstaltung *f.;* ~ *v.i.* funktionieren; tätig sein.
functional *a.* funktionell, funktional.
fund *s.* Kapital *n.;* Fonds *m.pl.;* Vorrat *m.; public ~s pl.* Staatsschulden *f.pl.;* ~ *v.t.* finanzieren.
fundamental *s.,* **~ly** *adv.* grundlegend.
funeral *s.* Begräbnis *n. ~ march s.* Trauermarsch *m.*
funereal *a.* Trauer..., düster.
fungus *s.* Pilz *m.,* (*med.*) Fungus *m.*
funicular *a.* Drahtseil...
funk *s.* grosse Angst *f.;* ~ *v.t. & i.* sich drücken.
funnel *s.* Trichter *m.;* Schornstein *m.*
funny *a.* spaßhaft, komisch.
funny bone *s.* Musikantenknochen *m.*
fur *s.* Pelz *m.;* Belag (auf der Zunge) *m.;* Kesselstein *m.;* ~ *v.t.* mit Pelz füttern.
fur. *furlong,* Achtelmeile *f.*

furbish *v.t.* polieren; putzen.
furious *a.*, **~ly** *adv.* wütend, rasend.
furl *v.t.* aufrollen; (die Segel) aufziehen.
furlong *s.* ein Achtel engl. Meile, 201 m.
furlough *s.* Urlaub *m.*
furnace *s.* Ofen, Schmelzofen *m.*
furnish *v.t.* versehen, ausstatten, (aus-) möblieren.
furnishing *s.* Ausrüstung *f.*; **~s** *pl.* Ausrüstungsgegenstände, Einrichtungsgegenstände *m.pl.*
furniture *s.* Möbel *n.pl.*; Hausgerät *m.*
furor *s.* Furore *f.*
furred *a.* belegt (Zunge).
furrier *s.* Kürschner *m.*
furrow *s.* Furche *f.*; Runzel *f.*; ~ *v.t.* furchen.
furry *a.* pelzig; haarig.
further *a.* & *adv.* ferner, weiter; überdies; *~ to,* in weiterer Bezugnahme auf (in Briefen); ~ *v.t.* befördern.
furtherance *s.* Förderung *f.*
furthermore *adv.* ferner, ausserdem.
furthermost *a.* äußerst...; entlegenst...
furthest *a.* & *adv.* weitest; am weitesten.
furtive *a.*, **~ly** *adv.* verstohlen.
fury *s.* Tollheit *f.*, Wut *f.*
fuschia *s.* (*bot.*) Fuchsie *f.*
fuse *v.t.* & *i.* (ver)schmelzen; *to ~ mines,* Minen schärfen; ~ *s.* Zünder *m.*; (*elek.*) Sicherung *f.*
fuselage *s.* Rumpf (m.) des Flugzeuges.
fusible *a.* schmelzbar.
fusion *s.* Schmelzen *n.*; (*fig.*) Verschmelzung *f.*
fuss *s.* Lärm *m.*, Getue *n.*
fussy *a.* unruhig, übertrieben geschäftig.
futile *a.* nichtig, wertlos.
futility *s.* Nichtigkeit *f.*
future *a.* künftig; ~ *s.* Zunkunft *f.*; Futur *n.*; **~s** *pl.* Termingeschäfte *n.pl.*
futuristic *a.* futuristisch.
fuzz *s.* leichter Flaum *m.*
fuzzy *a.* flaumig; bluschelig; unscharf.

G

G, g der Buchstabe G oder g *n.*; (*mus.*) G, g; **G sharp** Gis *n.*; **G flat** Ges *n.*
g *gram,* Gramm, g.
gab *s.* Mundwerk *m.*; (*fam.*) Geschwätzigkeit *f.*
gabble *v.i.* schnattern; plaudern; ~ *s.* Geschnatter, Geschwätz *n.*
gable *s.* Giebel *m.*
gabled *a.* gegiebelt.
gad *v.i.* herumstreichen.
gadfly *s.* Bremse *f.*
gadget *s.* technische Vorrichtung *f.*; Apparat *m.*; Krimskrams *m.*
gadgetry *s.* (hochtechnisierte) Ausrüstung *f.*
Gaelic *s.* Gälisch; *a.* gälisch.
gaff *s. blow the ~* plaudern.
gaffe *s.* Fauxpas *m.*; Fehler *m.*
gag *s.* Knebel *m.*; (*fam.*) (*auf dem Theater*) Gag *m.*; witziger Einfall *m.*; ~ *v.i.* knebeln.
gaga *a.* verkalkt; vertrottelt.
gage *s.* Unterpfand *n.*; ~ *v.t.* verpfänden.
gaiety *s.* Fröhlichkeit *f.*
gaily *adv.* fröhlich.
gain *s.* Gewinn, Vorteil *m.*; ~ *v.t.* gewinnen, erlangen.
gainful *a.*, **~ly** *adv.* einträglich.
gainings *s.pl.* Gewinn *m.*
gainsay *v.t.st.* widersprechen; leugnen.
gait *s.* Gangart, Gehart *f.*
gaiter *s.* Gamasche *f.*
gal. *gallon,* Gallone (3,785 l).
gala *s.* Fest *n.*, Gala *f.*
galaxy *s.* Milchstraße *f.*; Galaxie *f.* (*fig.*) glänzende Versammlung *f.*
gale *s.* frischer Wind *m.*; Sturm *m.*; ~ **warning** *s.* Sturmwarnung *f.*
gall *s.* Galle *f.*; Gallapfel *m.*; Bitterkeit *f.*; ~ *v.t.* wund reiben; ärgern.
gallant *a.*, **~ly** *adv.* tapfer, stattlich; ~ *a.*, *adv.* höflich; galant, artig (gegen Frauen).
gallantry *s.* Tapferkeit *f.*; Galanterie *f.*
gallery *s.* Galerie *f.*; Stollen (Bergwerk) *m.*
galley *s.* Galeere *f.*; Kombüse *f.*
galley(proof) *s.* Fahnenabzug *m.* (typ.)
Gallicism *s.* Gallizismus *m.*
gallon *s.* Gallone (3,79 Liter) *f.*
gallop *v.i.* galoppieren; ~ *s.* Galopp *m.*
gallows *s.* Galgen *m.*
gallstone *s.* Gallenstein *m.*
galore *s.* adv. in Hülle und Fülle.
galosh *s.* Überschuh, Gummischuh *m.*
galvanize *v.t.* galvanisieren.
gamble *v.i.* (hoch) spielen; ~ *s.* Glücksspiel *n.*
gambler *s.* Spieler(in) *m.(f.)*
gambling *s.* Spiel(en) *n.*; Glücksspiel *n.*
gambol *s.* Luftsprung *m.*; lustiger Streich *m.*; ~ *v.i.* springen, hüpfen.
game *s.* Spiel *n.*; Scherz *m.*; Wild *n.* *~ of chance s.* Glücksspiel *n.*; ~ **law** *s.* Jagdgesetz *n.*; ~ *a.* mutig; ~ *v.i.* spielen.
gamekeeper *s.* Wildhüter *m.*
game park *s.* Wildpark.
gamester *s.* Spieler *m.*
gammon *s.* (geräucherter) Schinken *m.*
gamut *s.* Tonleiter *f.*; Skala *f.*
gander *s.* Gänserich *m.*
gang *s.* Bande *f.*; Trupp *m.*
gangrene *s.* (kalter) Brand *m.*
gangster *s.* Gangster *m.*
gangway *s.* Gangway *f.*; Durchgang *m.*; (*nav.*) Laufplanke *f.*
gantry *s.* Portal *n.*; Schilderbrücke *f.*
gap *s.* Lücke *f.*; Bresche *f.*; Riß *m.*
gape *v.i.* gaffen; gähnen; klaffen.
garage *s.* Garage *f.*
garb *s.* Gewand *n.*, Kleidung *f.*
garbage *s.* Dreck *m.*; Unrat *m.*
garbage can *s.* Mülleimer *m.*
garble *v.t.* auslesen; entstellen.
garden *s.* Garten *m.*; ~ *v.i.* Gartenbau treiben.
gardener *s.* Gärtner(in) *m.(f.)*
gardening *s.* Gärtnerei *f.*

garden shed *s.* Geräteschuppen *m.*
gargle *v.t.* gurgeln.; *s.* Gurgelmittel *n.*
gargoyle; *s.* Wasserspeier *m.*, Scheusal *n.*
garish *a.*, **~ly** *adv.* grell; prunkend.
garland *s.* Girlande *f.*
garlic *s.* Knoblauch *m.*
garment *s.* Kleidungsstück *n.;* Kleidung *f.*
garnish *v.t.* schmücken; versorgen; garnieren; **~** *s.* Verzierung *f.*
garret *s.* Dachstube *f.*
garrison *s.* Garnison *f.* **~** *v.t.* in Garnison legen; **~ town** *s.* Garnison(s)stadt.
garrulity *s.* Schwatzhaftigkeit *f.*
garrulous *a.* schwatzhaft.
garter *s.* Strumpfband *n.;* Sockenhalter *m.*
gas *s.* Gas *n.*, Benzin *n.*
gas burner *s.* Gasbrenner *m.*
gaseous *a.* gasförmig.
gash *s.* Schnittwunde *f.;* klaffende Wunde *f.;* **~** *v.t.* tief verwunden; aufritzen.
gasket *s.* (*mech.*) (Flach-)dichtung *f.*
gas lighting *s.* Gasbeleuchtung *f.*
gas meter *s.* Gasmesser *m.*
gasoline *s.* Benzin *n.;* **~ station** *s.* Tankstelle *f.*
gasometer *s.* Gasometer *m.*
gasp *v.i.* keuchen; schnappen.
gas pipe *s.* Gasrohr *n.*
gastric *a.* gastrisch, Magen...
gastronomic *a.* gastronomisch.
gastronomy *s.* Gastronomie *f.;* Kochkunst *f.*
gasworks *s.pl.* Gaswerk *n.*
gate *s.* Tor *n.;* Pforte *f.*
gate-crasher *s.* ungeladener Gast *m.*
gateway *s.* Tor *n.;* Torbogen *m.*
gather *v.t.* sammeln; pflücken, ernten; **~** *v.i.* sich versammeln.
gathering *s.* Versammlung *f.*
GATT *General Agreement on Tariffs and Trade,* Allgemeines Zoll- und Handelsabkommen.
gauche *a.* linkisch.
gaudy *a.*, **gaudily** *adv.* geputzt, bunt.
gauge *v.t.* eichen; ausmessen; abschätzen; **~** *s.* Eichmass *n.;* Spurweite (der Eisenbahn) *f.;* (*mech.*) Lehre *f.; narrow-~ railway s.* Schmalspurbahn, Kleinbahn *f.*
gaunt *a.*, **~ly** *adv.* dürr, hager.
gauntlet *s.* Fehdehandschuh *m.; to run the ~,* Spießruten laufen; *to take up the ~,* die Herausforderung annehmen.
gauze *s.* Gaze *f.*
gawk *v.t. & i.* glotzen.
gawky *a.* ungeschickt, albern.
gay *a.*, **gaily** *adv.* homosexuell; munter, lustig; bunt.
gaze *v.i.* anstaunen, anstarren; **~** *s.* starrer Blick *m.*
gazelle *s.* Gazelle *f.*
gazette *s.* Zeitung *f.*, Amtsblatt *n.;* **~** *v.t.* amtlich veröffentlichen.
gazetteer *s.* geographisches Lexikon *n.*
G.B. *Great Britain,* Großbritannien.
GDP *gross domestic product,* Bruttoinlandsprodukt, BIP.
gear *s.* Treibwerk *n.;* (*mech.*) Zahnrad *n.;* (*mech.*) Übersetzung *f.*, Gang *m.; to put in another ~,* einen anderen Gang einschalten; *high ~,* große Übersetzung (am Fahrrad) *f.; low ~,* kleine Übersetzung *f.*
gearbox *s.* (*mech.*) Getriebe *(-kasten) m.*
gearing *s.* Getriebe *n.;* Übersetzung *f.*
gear shift *s.* Gangschaltung *f.*
gear stick *s.* Schalthebel *m.*
Geiger counter *s.* Geigerzähler *m.*
gel *s.* Gel *n.*
gelatin *s.* Gallerte *f.;* Gelatine *f.*
gelatinous *a.* gallertartig.
geld *v.t.* verschneiden; kastrieren.
gelding *s.* Wallach *m.*
gem *s.* Edelstein *m.;* Juwel *n.*
Gemini *s.* (astr.) Zwillinge *pl.*
Gen. *general,* General.
gen. *generally,* allgemein.
gender *s.* Geschlecht *n.*
gene *s.* Gen *n.*
genealogical *a.* genealogisch, Stamm...
genealogy *s.* Genealogie *f.*
general *a.* allgemein; **~** *s.* General *m.;*
generality *s.* Allgemeinheit *f.*
generalization *s.* Verallgemeinerung *f.*
generalize *v.t.* verallgemeinern.
general knowledge *s.* Allgemeinwissen *n.*
generally *adv.* im allgemeinen.
general manager *s.* Direktor(in) *m.(f.)*
general meeting *s.* Generalversammlung *f.*
general practice *s.* Allgemeinmedizin *f.*
general practitioner *s.* Arzt/Ärztin (*m./f.*) für Allgemeinmedizin.
general staff *s.* Generalstab *m.*
general strike *s.* Generalstreik *m.*
generate *v.t.* erzeugen.
generation *s.* Generation *f.;* Erzeugung *f.;* Geschlecht *n.;* Zeitalter *n.*
generator *s.* Generator *m.;* Lichtmaschine *f.*
generic *a.* Gattungs...
generosity *s.* Großzügigkeit *f.;* Freigebigkeit *f.*
generous *a.*, **~ly** *adv.* großmütig; freigebig.
genesis *s.* Entstehung *f.;* Schöpfung *f.;* Genesis *f.*
genetic *a.* genetisch.
genetics *s.* Genetik *f.*
genial *a.*, **~ly** *adv.* heiter; freundlich.
geniality *s.* Freundlichkeit *f.*
genitals *s.pl.* Geschlechtsteile *pl.*,, Geschlechtsorgane *pl.*, Genitalien *pl.*
genitive *s.* Genitiv *m.; a.* genitivisch.
genius *s.* Schutzgeist *m.;* Genie *n.*
genocide *s.* Völkermord *m.*
genre *s.* Genre *n.*, Gattung *f.*
genteel *a.*, **~ly** *adv.* fein, vornehm.
gentian *s.* Enzian *m.*
gentility *s.* Vornehmheit *f.*
gentle *a.* sanft; vornehm; artig, fein; gütig; fromm (von Pferden).
gentleman *s.* Herr, Mann von Stande, feiner Mann *m.;* Gentleman *m.; gentlemen's agreement,* freundschaftliches Übereinkommen *n.*
gentlemanlike *a.* wohlgesittet, anständig.
gentleness *s.* Artigkeit, Sanftmut *f.*
gentlewoman *s.* Dame (aus gutem Hause) *f.*
gently *adv.* zärtlich; sanft; vorsichtig.
gentry *s.* niederer Adel *m.*
genuflection *s.* Kniebeugung *f.*

genuine *a.*, **~ly** *adv.* echt, rein; authentisch.
genus *s.* Gattung *f.*
geographer *s.* Geograph *m.*
geographical *a.*, **~ly** *adv.* geographisch.
geography *s.* Erdkunde *f.*
geological *a.* geologisch.
geologist *a.* Geologe, Erdkundige *m.*
geology *s.* Erdkunde *f.*
geometric *a.* geometrisch.
geometrician *s.* Geometer *m.*
geometry *s.* Geometrie *f.; plane ~*, ebene Geometrie *f.*
geranium *s.* Geranie *f.*
gerbil *s.* Wüstenmaus *f.*
geriatrics *s.* Geriatric *f.;* Altersheilkunde *f.*
germ *s.* Keim *m.*
German *a.* deutsch; *~ s.* Deutsche *m./f.*
germane *a.* verwandt; zugehörig.
Germanic d. germanisch.
Germanism *s.* Germanismus *m.*
Germany *s.* Deutschland *n.*
germfree *a.* keimfrei.
germicide *s.* bazillentötendes Mittel *n.*
germinal *a.* Keim...
germinate *v.i.* keimen, sprossen.
germination *s.* Keimung *f.*, Keimen *n.*
germ warfare *s.* Bakterienkrieg *m.*
gerund *s.* Gerundium *n.*
gestation *s.* Trächtigkeit *f.;* Schwangerschaft *f.*
gesticulate *v.i.* Gebärden machen, gestikulieren.
gesticulation *s.* Gesten *f.pl.*
gesture *s.* Gebärde, Stellung *f.*
get *v.t.st.* erhalten, bekommen; veranstalten; besorgen; erzeugen; *~ v.i.* werden; wohin geraten; sich wohin begeben; *to ~ into,* geraten; *to ~ off,* wegschaffen, entkommen; aussteigen; *to ~ on,* anziehen; vorwärts kommen; Erfolg haben; *to ~ out,* herausbringen; heraus(be)kommen; aussteigen; *to ~ over,* überwinden; *to ~ through,* durchkommen; fertig bringen; *to ~ together,* zusammenbringen; zusammenkommen; *to ~ up,* aufsteigen; sich erheben; aufstehen.
get-at-able *a.* erreichbar, zugänglich.
getup *s.* Aufmachung *f.*
geyser *s.* Geysin *m.*
Ghana *s.* Ghana *n.*
Ghanaian *a.* ghanaisch; *~ s.* Ghanaer(in) *m.(f.)*
ghastly *a.* gräßlich; geisterhaft.
gherkin *s.* Essiggurke *f.*
ghetto *s.* Ghetto *n.*
ghost *s.* Geist *m.;* Gespenst *n.*
ghostly *a.* gespenstisch.
ghost: ~ story *s.* Gespenstergeschichte *f.;* **~ town** *s.* Geisterstadt *f.;* **~writer** *s.* Ghostwriter *m.*
ghoulish *a.* teuflisch, schauerlich.
giant *s.* Riese *m.*
giant panda *s.* Riesenpanda *m.*
gibber *v.i.* plappern.
gibberish *s.* Kauderwelsch *n.*
gibe *v.t. & i.* spotten, verhöhnen; *~ s.* Hohn *m.*
giblets *s.pl.* Gänseklein *n.*
giddiness *s.* Schwindel *m.*
giddy *a.*, **giddily** *adv.* schwind[e]lig; leichtsinnig.
gift *s.* Gabe *f.;* Geschenk *n.;* **~ shop** *s.* Geschenkboutique *f.*
gifted *a.* begabt.
gift-wrap *v.t.* als Geschenk einpacken.
gig *s.* Kabriolett *n.;* leichtes Boot *n.*
gigantic *a.* riesenhaft; gigantisch.
giggle *v.i.* kichern.
gild *v.t.ir.* vergolden.
gilding, gilt *s.* Vergoldung *f.*
gill *s.* Kieme *f.*
gillyflower *s.* Goldlack *m.;* Levkoje *f.*
gilt-edged *a.* (*com.*) mündelsicher.
gimcrack *s.* Tand *m.*
gimmick *s.* Gag *m.*
gin *s.* Wacholderbranntwein *m.*, Gin *m.*
ginger *s.* Ingwer *m.;* **~ beer,** Ingwerbier *n.*
gingerbread *s.* Ingwerkuchen *m.*
gingerly *a.* sachte, zimperlich.
gipsy *s.* Zigeuner(in) m(f.)
giraffe *s.* Giraffe *f.*
gird *v.t. & i.r. & ir.* gürten; sticheln, schmähen.
girder *s.* Bindebalken *m.;* Träger *m.*
girdle *s.* Gürtel *m.;* Hüfthalter *m.; ~ v.t.* umgürten.
girl *s.* Mädchen *n.*
girlhood *s.* Mädchenjahre *n.pl.;* Mädchentum *n.*
girlish *a.*, **~ly** *adv.* mädchenhaft.
girth *s.* Gurt *m.;* Umfang *m.*
gist *s.* Wesentliche *n.;* Kern *m.*
gitt *s.* Goldauflage *f.; a.* vergoldet.
give *v.t.st.* geben; schenken; *to ~ away,* verschenken; *to ~ birth to,* gebären; *to ~ in, to ~ way,* nachgeben; *to ~ up,* abgeben; aufgeben; *to ~ oneself up,* sich freiwillig stellen; *~ v.i.* nachgeben; sich werfen (vom Holze).
give-and-take *s.* gegenseitiges Entgegenkommen *n.*
given *p.* bestimmt, festgesetzt.
gizzard *s.* (Vogel-, Fisch-) magen *m.*
glacé *a.* glasiert.
glacial *a.* eisig; Gletscher..., Eis...
glacier *s.* Gletscher *m.*
glad *a.*, **~ly** *adv.* heiter, froh; angenehm.
gladden *v.t.* erfreuen, erheitern.
glade *s.* Lichtung *f.*
gladiator *s.* Gladiator *m.*
gladiolus *s.* Gladiole *f.*
glamor *s.* Zauber *m.*, Ausstrahlung *f.*
glamorize *v.t.* verherrlichen; glorifizieren.
glamorous *a.* glanzvoll; mondän.
glance *s.* Schimmer, Blitz *m.*, Blick *m.; ~ v.t.* flüchtig anschauen; abgleiten; *~ v.i.* schimmern; strahlen.
gland *s.* Drüse *f.*
glandular *a.* drüsig, Drüsen...
glare *s.* Glanz, Schimmer *m.;* durchdringender Blick *m.; ~ v.i.* blendenden Glanz werfen; starr ansehen.
glaring *a.* grell; offenkundig.
glass *s.* Glas *n.;* Spiegel *m.;* Fernglas *n.; ~ a.* gläsern; *~ v.t.* überglasen, verglasen.
glassblower *s.* Glasbläser *m.*
glasses *pl.* Brille *f.*
glassworks *s.pl.* Glashütte *f.*
glassy *a.* gläsern, glasartig.
glaucoma *s.* Glaukoma *n.;* grüner Star *m.*
glaze *v.t.* verglasen; glätten; mit Glasscheiben versehen; *~ s.* Glasur *f.;* Lasur *f.*
glazed paper *s.* Glanzpapier *n.*

glazier *s.* Glaser *m.*
gleam *s.* Strahl, Glanz *m.;* ~ *v.i.* strahlen, glänzen.
gleaming *a.* glänzend.
glean *v.t.* nachlesen, sammeln.
glee *s.* Fröhlichkeit *f.;* Schadenfreude *f.*
gleeful *a.* freudig; vergnügt.
glib *a.*, **~ly** *adv.* glatt; zungenfertig.
glide *v.i.* gleiten, schleichen; (*avi.*) einen Gleitflug (oder Segelflug) machen; ~ *s.* Gleitflug *m.*
glider *s.* Segelflugzeug *m.*
gliding *s.* Segelfliegen *n.*
glimmer *v.i.* schimmern; ~ *s.* Schimmer *m.;* Glimmen *n.*
glimpse *s.* (kurzer) Blick *m.;* ~ *v.t.* flüchtig sehen.
glint *s.* Lichtschein *m.;* Funkeln *n.;* ~ *v.i.* glänzen; blinken.
glisten *v.i.* glitzern, glänzen.
glitter *v.i.* glänzen, glitzern.
gloaming *s.* Zwielicht *n.*
gloat *v.i. to ~ over,* sich weiden an; sich hämisch freuen.
global *a.* global, weltweit.
globe *s.* Kugel *f.;* Globus *m.; ~-trotter,* Weltenbummler(in) *m.(f.),* Globetrotter(in) *m.(f.)*
globular *a.* kugelförmig.
globule *s.* Kügelchen *n.*
gloom, gloominess *s.* Dunkelheit *f.;* Trübsinn *m.*
gloomy *a.*, **gloomily** *adv.* düster; traurig.
glorification *s.* Verherrlichung *f.*
glorify *v.t.* verherrlichen.
glorious *a.*, **~ly** *adv.* glorreich; ruhmreich.
glory *s.* Ruhm *m.;* Herrlichkeit *f.;* Stolz *m.;* ~ *v.i.* sich rühmen.
gloss *s.* Glanz *m.;* Politur *f.;* Glosse *f.;* ~ *v.t.* polieren; Glossen machen; *to ~ over,* beschönigen, bemänteln.
glossary *s.* Glossar, *n.*
glossy *a.* glänzend, glatt.
glottal stop *s.* Knacklaut *m.;* Glottisschlag *m.*
glove *s.* Handschuh *m.;* ~ **compartment** *s.* Handschuhfach *n.*
glow *v.i.* glühen; ~ *s.* Glut *f.*
glower *v.i.* finster dreinblicken.
glowing *a.* glühend, begeistert.
glowworm *s.* Glühwürmchen *n.*
glucose *s.* Glucose *f.*
glue *s.* Leim *m.;* ~ *v.t.* leimen.
glum *a.* finster, mürrisch.
glut *v.t.* überladen; ~ *s.* Überfluß *m.*
glutinous *a.* klebrig.
glutton *s.* Fresser *m.;* Vielfraß *m.*
gluttonous *a.*, **~ly** *adv.* gefräßig.
gluttony *s.* Gefräßigkeit *f.*
glycerin *s.* Glyzerin *n.*
gm *gram,* Gramm.
GMT *Greenwich Mean Time,* Westeuropäische Zeit, WEZ.
gnarled *a.* knorrig, ästig.
gnash *v.t.* knirschen.
gnat *s.* Mücke *f.*
gnaw *v.t.* nagen, zerfressen.
gnome *s.* Gnom, Erdgeist *m.*
GNP *gross national product,* Bruttosozialprodukt, BNP.
go *v.i.st.* gehen; fahren; gelten; *the sirens ~,* die Sirenen gehen an; *it goes without saying,* es versteht sich von selbst; *to ~ back on one's word,* sein Versprechen nicht erfüllen od. zurücknehmen; *to ~ down,* fallen (Preise); *to ~ fishing,* zum Fischen gehen; *to ~ in for,* sich auf etwas legen; *to ~ off,* explodieren; *to ~ on,* weitermachen, fortfahren; *to ~ sour,* sauer werden; *to ~ through,* durchsehen; durchmachen; *to ~ up,* steigen (Preise); *to ~ to law,* eine Klage anstrengen; ~ *s.* Gang, Lauf *m.;* Bewegung *f.,* Schwung, Schneid *m.*
goad *s.* Treibestachel *m.;* ~ *v.t.* stacheln; quälen.
go-ahead *a.* rührig, strebsam.
goal *s.* Mal *n.;* Grenzpfahl *m.;* Ziel *n.;* (Fußball) Tor *n.*
goalie, goalkeeper *s.* Torwart, Tormann *m.*
goat *s.* Ziege *f.; he-goat,* Ziegenbock *m.*
gobble *v.t.* gierig verschlingen.
go-between *s.* Vermittler *m.*
goblet *s.* Becher *m.*
goblin *s.* Kobold *m.*
god *s.* Gott *m.*
godchild *s.* Patenkind *n.*
goddess *s.* Göttin *f.*
godfather *s.* Pate *m.*
god-forsaken *a.* gottverlassen.
godhead *s.* Gottheit *f.*
godless *a.* gottlos.
godlike *a.* göttlich.
godly *a.* gottselig, fromm.
godmother *s.* Patin *f.*
godparent *s.* Pate *m.;* Patin *f.*
godsend *s.* Gottesgabe *f.*
go-getter *s.* Draufgänger(in) *m.(f.)*
goggle *v.i.* glotzen; die Augen verdrehen; **~s** *s.pl.* Schutzbrille *f.*
goiter *s.* Kropf *m.*
gold *s.* Gold *n.*
golden *a.* golden; ~ **eagle** *s.* Steinadler *m.;* ~ **hamster** *s.* Goldhamster *m.;* ~ **rule** *s.* goldene Regel *f.*
goldfinch *s.* Stieglitz *m.*
goldfish *s.* Goldfisch *m.*
gold leaf *s.* Goldblatt, Blattgold *n.*
gold-plated *a.* vergoldet.
goldsmith *s.* Goldschmied(in) *m.(f.)*
golf *s.* Golf *n.;* ~ **course,** ~ **links,** Golfplatz *m.;* ~ **club** *s.* Golfschläger; Golf Klub *m.*
golfer *s.* Golfspieler(in) *m.(f.);* Golfer(in) *m.(f.)*
gonad *s.* Keimdrüse *f.*
gondola *s.* Gondel *f.*
gondolier *s.* Gondolier *m.*
gone *p.* & *a.* weg, fort; vergangen.
gong *s.* Gong *m.* & *n.*
gonorrhea *s.* (*med.*) Tripper *m.*
good *a.* gut, wohl; recht; *be ~ enough,* seien Sie so freundlich; *to make ~,* vergüten, (Versprechen) erfüllen; sich durchsetzen, sich bewähren; ~ *s.* Gut *n.; this is no ~,* das ist nichts wert; **~s** *pl.* Güter *pl.;* Habe *f.;* Waren *pl.*
good-bye *adv.* & *s.* lebe wohl!; Lebewohl *n.;* auf Wiedersehen!
good-for-nothing *a.* nichtsnutzig; *~s.* Taugenichts *m.;* Nichtsnutz *m.*
Good Friday *s.* Karfreitag *m.*
good-humored *a.* gutmütig; gutgelaunt.

goodies *s. pl.* Naschereien, Süßigkeiten.
good-looking *a.* hübsch, schön.
goodly *a.* schön; beträchtlich.
good-natured *a.* gutmütig.
goodness *s.* Güte, *f.; for ~ sake,* um Himmels willen!; *~ gracious,* gütiger Himmel!; *thank ~,* Gott sei Dank!
good-tempered *a.* gutmütig; verträglich.
goodwill *s.* Wohlwollen *n.*
goof *s.* (*fam.*) Schnitzer *m.; ~ v.i.* Mist machen.
goose *s.* Gans *f.*
gooseberry *s.* Stachelbeere *f.*
gooseflesh *s.* Gänsehaut *f.*
goose pimples *s.pl. to have ~* Gänsehaut haben.
goose step *s.* Paradeschritt *m.*
gore *s.* geronnenes Blut *n.;* Zwickel *m.*
gorge *s.* Kehle, Gurgel *f.;* Felsenschlucht *f.; ~ v.t.* verschlucken; vollstopfen.
gorgeous *a.*, **~ly** *adv.* glänzend, prächtig.
gorilla *s.* Gorilla *m.*
gormandize *v.i.* schlemmen.
gorse *s.* Stechginster *m.*
gory *a.* blutig, mörderisch.
gosh (*fam.*) Gott!
gosling *s.* Gänseküken *n.;* Gössel *n.*
gospel *s.* Evangelium *n.*
gospel truth *s.* (*fig.*) absolute Wahrheit *f.*
gossamer s, Altweibersommer *m.;* Sommerfäden *m.pl.*
gossip *s.;* Klatsch *m.;* Klatschbase *f.; ~ v.i.* klatschen.
Gothic *a.* gotisch; *Gothic letters, pl.* Fraktur *f.*
gouge *v.t.* aushöhlen.
goulash *s.* Gulasch *n.*
gourd *s.* Kürbis *m.*
gourmand *s.* Gourmand, Schlemmer *m.*
gourmet *s.* Gourmet *m.*, Feinschmecker *m.*
gout *s.* Gicht *f.*
gouty *a.* gichtisch.
Gov. *government,* Regierung; *governor,* Gouverneur.
govern *v.t.* regieren, lenken, beherrschen; *~ v.i.* herrschen.
governess *s.* Erzieherin *f.*
governing body *s.* Vorstand (Krankenhaus, Schule) *m.*
government *s.* Regierungsform, Regierung *f.; ~* **property,** Behördeneigentum *n.*
governor *s.* Gouverneur *m.;* (*fam.*) Chef, Vater *m.;* Prinzipal *m.*
gown *s.* Frauenkleid *n.;* Abendtoilette *f.;* Talar *m.* (*law & univ.*)
G.P. *General Practitioner,* praktischer Arzt *m.*
G.P.O. *General Post Office,* Hauptpostamt.
grab *v.t.* plötzlich greifen, packen; *~ s.* (*fig.*) Räuberei *f.*
grace *s.* Gnade *f.;* Anmut *f.;* Tischgebet *n.; Your ~,* (Titel) Euer Gnaden; *~ v.t.* begünstigen; schmücken.
graceful *a.*, **~ly** *adv.* anmutig, gnädig, graziös, reizend.
gracefulness *s.* Anmut *f.*
gracious *a.*, **~ly** *adv.* gnädig.
gradation *s.* Steigerung *f.;* Abstufung *f.;* Ablaut *m.*
grade *s.* Grad, Rang *m.;* Klasse *f.;* Note *f. ~ v.t.* abstufen, einteilen.
gradient *s.* Steigung *f.*
gradual *a.*, **~ly** *adv.* allmählich.
graduate *v.t.* in Grade teilen; abstufen; *~ v.i.* einen Grad erlangen; *~ s.* Person *(f.)* mit akademischem Grad.
graduation *s.* Abstufung *f.;* Graduierung *f.;* Absolvieren *n.*
graffiti *s.pl.* Graffiti *pl.*
graft *s.* Pfropfreis *n.;* Transplantation *f. ~ v.t.* pfropfen; transplantieren.
grain *s.* Korn, Samenkorn *n.;* Gran *m. & n.;* Holzfaser *f.*
gram *s.* Gramm *n.*
grammar *s.* Grammatik *f.*
grammarian *s.* Grammatiker *m.*
grammatical *a.*, **~ly** *adv.* grammatisch.
gramophone *s.* Grammophon *n.*
granary *s.* Kornboden *m.;* Kornkammer *f.* Getreidesilo *m.*
grand *a.* groß, erhaben; großartig.
grandchild *s.* Enkel(in) *m.(f.)*
granddaughter *s.* Enkelin *f.*
grand duke *s.* Großherzog *m.*
grandee *s.* Grande (in Spanien) *m.;* hoher Herr *m.*
grandeur *s.* Grösse *f.;* Pracht *f.*
grandfather *s.* Großvater *m.*
grandfather clock *s.* Standuhr *f.*
grandiloquent *a.* hochtrabend.
grandiose *a.* hochtrabend; großartig.
grandly *adv.* großartig; aufwendig.
grandmother *s.* Großmutter *f.*
grandparent *s.* Großvater *m.;* Großmutter *f.;* **~s** *pl.* Großeltern.
grand piano *s.* (Konzert)Flügel *m.*
grandstand *s.* Tribüne *f.*
granite *s.* Granit *m.*
granny *s.* (*fam.*) Großmütterchen *n.*
grant *v.t.* zugestehen; bewilligen, verleihen. *~ s.* Beihilfe *f.;* Stipendium *n.*
granular *a.* gekörnt, körnig, granulient.
granulate *v.t.* (*v.i.* sich) körnen.
granulated sugar *s.* Kristallzucker *m.*
granule *s.* Körnchen *n.*
grape *s.* Weintraube Weinbeere *f.; bunch of ~s,* Weintraube *f.*
grapefruit *s.* Grapefruit *f.*, Pampelmuse *f.*
grapevine *s.* Weinstock *m.;* (*fam.*) Gerücht *n.; hear sth. on the ~,* etw. gerüchteweise hören.
graph *s.* Schaubild *n.;* Diagramm *n.;* graphische Darstellung *f.*
graphic *a.* graphisch, genau; anschaulich; *~ representation,* graphische Darstellung *f.*, Kurvenbild *n.*
graphically *adv.* plastisch, anschaulich; graphisch.
graphic arts *s.* Graphik *f.;* graphische Kunst *f.*
graphite *s.* Graphit *m.*
grapple *v.t.* packen, ergreifen; *~ v.i.* ringen (mit).
grasp *s.* Griff *m.;* Bereich *m.;* Fassungskraft *f.; ~ v.t.* greifen, fassen; *~ v.i.* haschen; streben.
grasping *a.* gierig, habsüchtig.
grass *s.* Gras *n.*
grasshopper *s.* Grashüpfer *m.*

grassland *s.* Grasland *n.;* Weideland *n.*
grass plot *s.* Rasenplatz *m.*
grassroots *s.pl.* Wurzel *f.;* (*pol.*) Basis *f.*
grass snake *s.* Ringelnatter *f.*
grass widow *s.* Strohwitwe *f.*
grass widower *s.* Strohwitwer *m.*
grassy *a.* grassig.
grate *s.* Feuerrost *m.;* ~ *v.t.* vergittern; raspeln; kränken; ~ *v.i.* knirschen.
grateful *a.*, **~ly** *adv.* dankbar; angenehm.
grater *s.* Reibe *f.*, Raspel *f.*
gratification *s.* Befriedigung *f.*
gratify *v.t.* befriedigen; willfahren.
gratifying *a.* erfreulich.
grating *s.* Gitter *n.*
gratis *a.* unentgeltlich.
gratitude *s.* Dankbarkeit *f.*
gratuitous *a.*, **~ly** *adv.* unentgeltlich; unberechtigt.
gratuity *s.* Trinkgeld *n.*
grave *a.* feierlich, ernst; tief (vom Tone); ~ *s.* Grab *n.*
gravedigger *s.* Totengräber *m.*
gravel *s.* Kies *m.*
gravestone *s.* Grabstein *m.*
graveyard *s.* Friedhof *m.*
gravitate *v.i.* gravitieren, zuneigen.
gravity *s.* Ernst *m.;* Schwere *f.;* Wichtigkeit *f.;* Schwerkraft *f.;* Gravitation *f.*
gravy *s.* Sauce *f.*, Bratensaft *m.*, Saft des Fleisches *m.;* ~ **boat** *s.* Sauciere *f.*
gray *a.* grau; ~ *s.* Grau *n.*
grayish *a.* gräulich.
gray matter *s.* (*fig.*) graue Zellen *pl.*
graze *v.i.* weiden, grasen; ~ *v.t.* abweiden; streifen; *s.* Schürfwunde *f.*
grease *s.* Fett *n.*, Schmiere *f.;* ~ *v.t.* schmieren; bestechen.
greaseproof paper *s.* Butterbrotpapier *n.;* Pergamentpapier *n.*
greasy *a.*, **greasily** *adv.* fett, schmierig.
great *a.* groß; **~-grandfather,** etc. *s.* Urgroßvater, etc.
Great Britain *s.* Großbritannien.
greatly *adv.* sehr; stark.
greatness *s.* Größe, Macht *f.*
Grecian *a.* griechisch.
Greece *s.* Griechenland *n.*
greed, greediness *s.* Gier(igkeit) *f.*
greedy *a.*, **greedily** *adv.* gierig.
Greek *a.* griechisch; ~*s.* Grieche *m.;* Griechin *f.*
green *a.*, **~ly** *adv.* grün; frisch; unreif; unerfahren; ~ *s.* Rasenplatz *m.;* **~s** *s.pl.* Gemüse *n.*
greenbelt *s.* Grüngürtel *m.*
greenery *s.* Grün *n.*
greengage *s.* Reineclaude (Pflaume) *f.*
greengrocer *s.* Gemüsehändler *m.*
greenhorn *s.* grüner Junge *m.*
greenhouse *s.* Gewächshaus *n.*
greenish *a.* grünlich.
Greenland *s.* Grönland *n.*
Green Party *s.* (*pol.*) die Grünen.
greet *v.t.* grüßen.
greeting *s.* Begrüßung *f.*, Gruß *n.;* ~ **card** *s.* Grußkarte *f.*
gregarious *a.*, **~ly** *adv.* gesellig.
gremlin *s.* Kobald *m.;* böser Geist *m.*
grenade *s.* Granate *f.*
grenadier *s.* Grenadier *m.*
greyhound *s.* Windhund *m.*
grid *s.* Bratrost *m.;* (Gitter)Netz *n.;* Raster *n.*
grief *s.* Gram, Kummer *m.*
grievance *s.* Beschwerde *f.*
grieve *v.t.* kränken; ~ *v.i.* sich grämen.
grievous *a.*, **~ly** *adv.* schmerzlich; schwer.
grill *v.t.* rösten; ~ *s.* Bratrost *m.*
grille *s.* Gitter *n.*
grim *a.*, **~ly** *adv.* grimmig.
grimace *s.* Fratze, Grimasse *f.*
grimalkin *s.* (alte) Katze *f.*
grime *s.* Schmutz *m.;* ~ *v.t.* beschmutzen.
grimy *a.* schmutzig, rußig.
grin *s.* Grinsen *n.;* ~ *v.i.* grinsen.
grind *v.t.st.* mahlen; (Orgel) drehen; (*teeth*) knirschen; schleifen; quälen.
grinder *s.* Schleifmaschine *f.;* Mühle *f.*
grindstone *s.* Schleifstein *m.*
grip *s.* Griff; ~ *v.t.* fest greifen.
gripe *v.t.* (*fam.*) meckern, schimpfen; ~ *s.* Meckern *n.;* **~s** *pl.* Bauchgrimmen *n.*
gripping *a.* packend.
grisly *a.* scheußlich.
grist *s.* Mahlgut *n.*
gristle *s.* Knorpel *m.*
grit *s.* Grieß *m.;* (*fig.*) Festigkeit *f.*
gritty *a.* sandig.
grizzled, grizzly *a.* grau; ~ **bear** *s.* Grizzlybär *m.*
groan *v.i.* seufzen, stöhnen; ~ *s.* Seufzer *m.;* Murren *n.*
grocer *s.* Lebensmittelhändler(in) *m.(f.)*
groceries *s.pl.* Lebensmittel *pl. n.*
grocery store *s.* Lebensmittelgeschäft *n.*
grog *s.* Grog *m.*
groin *s.* Leiste *f.;* Rippe *f.;* ~*ed arch,* Kreuzbogen *m.*
groom *s.* Aufwärter *m.;* Stallknecht *m.;* ~ *v.t.* ein Pferd warten.
groove *s.* Rille *f.* Nut *f.;* (*fig.*) Gleis *n.;* ~ *v.t.* auskehlen, falzen.
grope *v.i. & t.* tappen, tasten.
gross *a.*, **~ly** *adv.* dick; dumm; grob, ordinär, zotig; Brutto...; ~ **national product** *s.* Bruttosozialprodukt *n.;* ~ **weight** *s.* Bruttogewicht *n.;* ~ *s.* Ganze *n.;* Masse *f.;* Gros *n.*
grotesque *a.*, **~ly** *adv.* grotesk.
grotto *s.* Grotte *f.*
grouch *s.* Miesepeter *m.;* Spielverderber(in) *m.(f.);* ~ *v.i.* nörgeln, meckern.
grouchy *a.* nörglerisch.
ground *s.* Grund, Boden *m.;* (Beweis-) grund *m.;* (*elek.*) Erde *f.;* **~s** *pl.* Bodensatz; ~ *v.t.* gründen; (*elek.*) erden; **~breaking** *a.* bahnbrechend.
ground control *s.* Flugsicherung *f.*
ground floor *s.* Erdgeschoß *n.*
ground forces *pl.* (*mil.*) Bodentruppen *pl.f.*
ground glass *s.* (*phot.*) Mattscheibe *f.*
grounding *s.* Anfangsgründe *m.pl.;* Grundwissen *n.*
groundless *a.*, **~ly** *adv.* grundlos.
groundnut *s.* Erdnuß *f.*
ground plan *s.* Grundriß *m.*
groundswell *s.* Anschwellen *n.*

ground water *s.* Grundwasser *n.*
groundwork *s.* Grundlage *f.*
group *s.* Gruppe *f.;* (*avi.*) Gruppe *f.;* ~ **captain** *s.* Gruppenkommandeur *m.;* ~ *v.t.* gruppieren.
grouping *s.* Gruppierung *f.*
grouse *s.* schottisches Moorhuhn *n.;* ~ *v.i.* meckern.
grout *s.* Mörtel *m.*
grove *s.* Hain *m.*, Gehölz *n.*
grovel *v.i.* kriechen.
grow *v.t.st.* wachsen; werden; ~ *v.t.* bauen, kultivieren.
grower *s.* Pflanzer(in) *m.(f.);* Produzent(in) *m.(f.)*
growl *v.i.* brummen, knurren; ~ *s.* Brummen *n.*
grown-up *a.* erwachsen; ~ *s.* Erwachsene *m./f.*
growth *s.* Wachstum *n.*, Wuchs *m.;* Erzeugnis *n.;* Gewächs *n.;* ~ **industry** *s.* Wachstumsindustrie *f.*
grow up *v.i.* aufwachsen.
grub *s.* Larve, Made *f.;* Wurm *m.;* Futter *n.;* (*sl.*) Essen *n.;* ~ *v.t.* wühlen; futtern.
grudge *v.t.* mißgönnen, ungern tun; ~ *s.* Groll, Neid *m.*
grudging *a.* ~**ly** *adv.* widerwillig.
gruel *s.* Haferschleim *m.*, Grütze *f.*
grueling *a.* erschöpfend, aufreibend.
gruesome *a.* grausig.
gruff *a.*, ~**ly** *adv.* mürrisch.
grumble *v.i.* murren, brummen.
grumbler *s.* Querulant(in) *m.(f.)*
grumpy *a.* mürrisch, böse.
grunt *v.i.* grunzen; ~*s.* Grunzen *n.*
gr. wt. *gross weight,* Bruttogewicht.
gtd. *guar., guaranteed,* garantiert.
guarantee *s.* Bürge *m.*, Bürgin *f.;* Bürgschaft, Pfandsumme *f.;* ~ *v.t.* verbürgen, garantieren.
guaranty *s.* Bürgschaft *f.*
guard *s.* Wache *f.;* Schutz *m.;* Stichblatt (Degen) *n.;* Garde *f.;* Schaffner *m.; honor* ~ *s.* Ehrenwache *f.; on one's* ~, auf der Hut; *to be on* ~, Wache stehen; ~**s** *pl.* Leibwache *f.;* ~ *v.t.* bewachen, beschützen; ~ *v.i.* auf der Hut sein.
guarded *adv.* zurückhaltend; vorsichtig.
guardian *s.* Aufseher *m.;* Vormund *m.;* Beschützer *m.;* ~ **angel,** Schutzengel *m.; to place under the care of a* ~, unter Vormundschaft stellen.
guardianship *s.* Vormundschaft *f.*
guardrail *s.* Geländer *n.*
guardsman *s.* Gardist *m.*
guerilla *s.* Freischärler, Partisan *m.;* Guerillakämpfer(in) *m.(f.)*
guess *v.i. & t.* mutmassen, (er)raten; ~ *s.* Vermutung *f.*
guest *s.* Gast *m.*
guest: ~**house** *s.* Pension *f.;* ~**room** *s.* Gästezimmer *n.*
guffaw *s.* brüllendes Gelächter *n.;* ~*v.i.* laut lachen.
guidance *s.* Führung, Leitung *f.*
guide *v.t.* leiten, führen; ~ *s.* Führer(in) *m.(f.)*
guidebook *s.* Reiseführer *m.*
guided missile *s.* (*mil.*) Lenkflugkörper *m.*
guide dog *s.* Blindenhund *m.*
guided tour *s.* Führung *f.*
guidelines *s.pl.* Richtlinien *f.pl.*
guild *s.* Gilde, Innung *f.*
guilder *s.* Gulden *m.*
guile *s.* Betrug *m.;* Arglist *f.*
guileless *a.* arglos, ehrlich.
guillotine *s.* Guillotine *f.*, Fallbeil *n.*
guilt *s.* Schuld *f.*
guiltless *a.* unschuldig.
guilty *a.*, **guiltily** *adv.* schuldig.
guinea pig *s.* Meerschweinchen *n.*
guise *s.* Gewand *n.;* Maske *f.*
guitar *s.* Gitarre *f.*
guitarist *s.* Gitarrist(in) *m.(f.)*
gulch *s.* Schlucht *f.*
gulf *s.* Meerbusen *m.;* Abgrund *m.*
gull *s.* Möwe *f.*
gullet *s.* Gurgel *f.;* Schlund *m.*
gullibility *s.* Leichtgläbigkeit *f.*
gullible *a.* leichtgläubig.
gully *s.* Abfluß, *m.*, Gully *m.*
gulp *s.* Schluck, Zug *m.;* ~ *v.t.* schlucken.
gum *s.* Gummi *n.;* Zahnfleisch *n.;* ~ *v.t.* gummieren.
gumption *s.* (*fam.*) Grips *m.;* Verstand *m.*
gun *s.* Geschütz *n.;* Kanone *f.;* Flinte *f.*, Gewehr *n.;* Revolver *m.;* ~ **license** *s.* Waffenschein *m.;* ~**-running** *s.* Waffenschmuggel *m.*
gunboat *s.* Kanonenboot *n.*
gun carriage *s.* Lafette *f.*
gun cotton *s.* Schießbaumwolle *f.*
gunfight *s.* Schießerei *f.*
gunpowder *s.* Schießpulver *n.*
gunshot *s.* Schuß *m.;* Schußweite *f.*
gunsmith *s.* Büchsenmacher *m.*
gunwale *s.* (*nav.*) Schaudeck *n.*
gurgle *v.i.* gurgeln; rieseln.
guru *s.* Guru *m.*
gush *v.i.* strömen; ~ *s.* Guß *m.;* Schwall *m.;* Überschwenglichkeit *f.*
gushing *a.* reißend.
gusset *s.* Zwickel *m.;* Keil *m.*
gust *s.* Windstoß *m.;* Bö *f.*
gusto *s.* Eifer *m.*, Vernügen *n.*
gusty *a.* böig; stürmisch.
gut *s.* Darm *m.;* ~**s** *pl.* Eingeweide *n.;* ~ *v.t.* ausweiden; ausbrennen (ein Haus); **gutted** *p.* ausgebrannt.
gutter *s.* Rinne, Gosse *f.*
gutteral *a.* Kehl...; guttural; ~ *s.* Kehllaut *m.*
gutter press *s.* Sensationspresse *f.*
guy *s.* Halteseil *n.;* (*fam.*) Typ *m.*
guzzle *v.t.* verschlingen.
gym *s.* (*fam.*) Turnhalle *f.*, Turnen *n.*
gymnasium *s.* Turnhalle *f.*
gymnastic(al) *a.*, ~**ly** *adv.* gymnastisch.
gymnastics *s.pl.* Turnen *n.;* Gymnastik *f.*
gym shoe *s.* Turnschuh *m.*
gynecological *a.* gynäkologisch.
gynecologist *s.* Gynäkologe *m.*, Gynäkologin *f.*
gynecology *s.* Gynäkologie *f.;* Frauenheilkunde *f.*
gypsum *s.* Gips *m.*
gyrate *v.i.* wirbeln, kreiseln.
gyration *s.* Drehung *f.*
gyroscope *s.* Kreiselkompaß *m.;* Gyroskop *n.*

H

H, h der Buchstabe H oder h *n.*
h., hr. *hour,* Stunde *f.; hrs., hours,* Stunden; *height,* Höhe.
habeas corpus *s.* Habeaskorpusakte *f.*
haberdashery *s.* Herrenmoden geschäft *n.*
habit *s.* Gewohnheit *f.;* Zustand *m.;* Habit *m.; by* ~, aus Gewohnheit.
habitable *a.* bewohnbar.
habitat *s.* Habitat *n.;* Lebensraum *m.*
habitation *s.* Wohnung *f.*
habitual *a.,* **~ly** *adv.* gewohnt, gewohnheitsmäßig.
habituate *v.t.* gewöhnen.
habitué *s.* Stammgast *m.*
hack *v.t.* hacken; ~ *s.* Hieb *m.*
hacker *s.* (*comp.*) Hacker *m.*
hackney coach *s.* Mietskutsche *f.*
hackneyed *a.* abgedroschen.
hack saw *s.* Metallsäge *f.*
hack writer *s.* Lohnschreiber *m.*
haddock *s.* Schellfisch *m.*
haft *s.* Stiel *m.;* Heft *n.;* Griff *m.*
hag *s.* Hexe *f.*
haggard *a.,* **~ly** *adv.* wild; hager.
haggle *v.i.* feilschen.
hail *s.* Hagel *m.;* ~ *v.i.* hageln; ~ *s.* Ruf *m.;* ~*! i.* Glück! Heil!; ~ *v.t.* grüßen; anrufen; stammen; *to* ~ *a taxi,* ein Taxi herbeirufen.
hailstone *s.* Hagelkorn *n.*
hair *s.* Haar *n.; to do one's* ~, sich die Haare machen; ~*style,* ~*do,* Frisur *f.; long-*~*ed a.* langhaarig; *short-*~*ed a.* kurzhaarig.
hairbrush *s.* Haarbürste *f.*
haircut *s.* Haarschnitt *m.*
hairdresser *s.* Friseur *m.,* Friseuse *f.*
hair dryer *s.* Haartrockner *m.*
hairpin *s.* Haarnadel *f.;* ~ **turn** Haarnadelkurve *f.*
hair-raising *a.* haarsträubend.
hairsplitting *s.* Wortklauberei *f.*
hairstyle *s.* Frisur *f.*
hair tonic *s.* Haarwuchsmittel *n.*
hairy *a.* haarig, behaart; (*fig.*) schwierig.
halcyon *a.* still, friedlich.
hale *a.* heil, frisch, gesund.
half *a.* halb; ~ *past five,* halb sechs; ~ *s.* Hälfte *f.*
halfback *s.* (Fußball) Läufer *m.*
half-blood *s.* Halbblut *n.*
half-breed *s.* Mischling *m.*
half-caste *s.* Halbblut *n.*
half-hearted *a.,* halbherzig.
half pay *s.* Ruhegehalt *n.,* Pension *f.*
halfway *adv.* auf halbem Wege.
half-witted *a.* einfältig.
half-yearly *a.* halbjährlich.
halibut *s.* Heilbutt *m.*
halitosis *s.* Halitose *f.;* schlechter Mundgeruch *m.*
hall *s.* Saal *m.;* Halle *f.;* (Guts-) Herrenhaus *n.;* Hausflur *f.*
hallmark *s.* Feingehaltstempel *m.;* Kennzeichen *n.*
hallo! *i.* hallo!
hallow *v.t.* weihen, heiligen.
Halloween *s.* Abend (*m.*) vor Allerheiligen.
hall porter *s.* Portier *m.*
hall stand *s.* Kleiderständer *m.*
hallucinate *v.i.* halluzinieren.
hallucination *s.* Halluzination *f.*
hallucinogenic *a.* halluzinogen.
hallway *s.* Flur *m.;* Korridor *m.*
halo *s.* Hof (um Sonne oder Mond), *m.;* Heiligenschein *m.*
halt *i.* halt!; *s.* Halt *m.;* ~ *v.i.* anhalten; hinken; zögern.
halter *s.* Halfter *n.*
halting *a.* schleppend; zögernd.
halve *v.t.* halbieren.
ham *s.* Schenkel *m.;* Schinken *m.*
hamburger *s.* Hamburger *m.,* Hacksteak *n.*
hamlet *s.* Weiler *m.,* Dörfchen *n.*
hammer *s.* Hammer *m.;* Hahn (am Gewehr) *m.;* ~ *v.t.* hämmern, schmieden.
hammock *s.* Hängematte *f.*
hamper *v.t.* belästigen, behindern; ~*s.* (Deckel) Korb *m.*
hamster *s.* Hamster *m.*
hamstring *s.* Kniesehne *f.*
hand *s.* Hand *f.;* Handschrift *f.;* Uhrzeiger *m.;* Richtung, Seite *f.;* Arbeiter *m.;* Karten (*f.pl.*) eines Spielers; *at* ~, zur Hand, nah; *at the* ~*s of,* von Seiten; *by* ~, mit der Hand; *signed in his own* ~, eigenhändig unterschrieben; *on* ~, vorrätig, auf Lager; *to give (lend) a* ~, helfen, zugreifen; *to have on one's* ~*s,* auf dem Hals haben; *on the one* ~, *on the other* ~, einerseits, andererseits; *out of* ~, unlenkbar; *off* ~, aus dem Stegreif; *the upper* ~, die Oberhand; ~ *v.t.* einhändigen; reichen; *to* ~ *down (order, decision),* (Entscheidung) erlassen; *to* ~ *over,* übergeben, überstellen.
handbag *s.* Handtasche *f.*
hand baggage *s.* Handgepäck *n.*
handbill *s.* (Werbe-) Zettel *m.*
handbook *s.* Handbuch *n.*
hand brake *s.* Handbremse *f.*
hand-carved *a.* handgeschnitzt.
handcuff *s.* Handfessel *f.*
handful *s.* Handvoll *f.*
hand grenade *s.* Handgranate *f.*
handicap *s.* Vorgabe *f.;* Belastung *f.;* (*fig.*) Behinderung *f.;* Vorgaberennen; ~ *v.t.* belasten; hemmen.
handicapped *a.* behindert; ~ *s.* Behinderte *m./f.*
handicraft *s.* (Kunst) Handwerk *n.*
handiwork *s.* Handarbeit *f.*
handkerchief *s.* Taschentuch *n.*
handle *s.* Griff *m.;* Henkel *m.;* ~ *v.t.* anfassen; handhaben; umgehen mit.
handlebar *s.* Lenkstange *f.*
handmade *a.* handgearbeitet.
handmade paper *s.* Büttenpapier *n.*
handout *s.* Almosen *n.;* Handzettel *m.;* Handout *n.*
hand-painted *a.* handbemalt.

hand-picked *a.* handverlesen.

handrail *s.* Geländer *n.*

handset *s.* (Telefon) Hörer *m.*

handshake *s.* Händedruck *m.*

handsome *a.*, **~ly** *adv.* gutaussehend; schön, ansehnlich.

handstand *s.* Handstand *m.*

hand-tailored *a.* handgeschneidert.

hand-to-hand fighting *s.* Handgemenge *n.*

handwriting *s.* Handschrift *f.*

handwritten *a.* handgeschrieben.

handy *a.*, **handily** *adv.;* geschickt; handlich; griffbereit.

handyman *s.* Handwerker *m.*

hang *to get the ~ of it,* hinter etwas kommen, ~ *v.t.* hängen, behängen; *to ~ oneself,* sich aufhängen; ~ *v.i.* hängen, schweben.

hangar *s.* Flugzeughalle *f.*

hanger *s.* Kleiderbügel *m.;* Aufhänger *m.*

hang glider *s.* Drachenflieger(in) *m.(f.)*

hang gliding *s.* Drachenfliegen *n.*

hanging *a.* Hänge...

hangman *s.* Henker *m.*

hangover *s.* Kater *m.*, Katzenjammer *m.*

hank *s.* Strang *m.*

hanker *v.i.* sich sehnen, trachten.

hankering *s.* Verlangen *n.*

hanky *s.* Taschentuch *n.;* **~-panky** *s.* (*fam.*) Mauschelei *f.*

haphazard willkürlich; unbedacht.

hapless *a.* unglücklich.

happen *v.i.* sich ereignen; *I ~ed to be there,* ich war zufällig da.

happiness *s.* Glück *n.;* Heiterkeit *f.*

happy *a.*, **happily** *adv.* glücklich; heiter; froh.

happy ending *s.* Happy-end *n.*

happy-go-lucky *a.* sorglos.

harass *v.t.* belästigen; schikanieren.

harassment *s.* Belästigung *f.*

harbinger *s.* Vorbote *m.*

harbor *s.* Hafen *m.;* Zufluchtsort *m.;* ~ **dues** *pl.* Hafengebühren *f.pl.;* ~ *v.t.* beherbergen; hegen; ~ *v.i.* vor Anker gehen.

hard *a. & adv.* hart; mühsam; **~up,** in Not, ohne Geld; ~ **cash** *s.* klingende Münze *f.;* ~ **coal** *s.* Steinkohle *f.;* ~ **drinks** *pl.* alkoholische Getränke *n. pl.;* ~ **rubber** *s.* Hartgummi *m.*

harden *v.t.* härten; ~ *v.i.* hart werden, sich verhärten; (Preise) anziehen.

hardened *a.* verhärtet; abgehärtet.

hardening *s.* Härten *n.;* Verhärtung *f.*

hard-headed *a.* praktisch; starrköpfig.

hard-hearted *a.* hartherzig.

hard-liner *s.* Befürworter(in) *m.(f.)* einer harten Linie.

hardly *adv.* kaum.

hardness *s.* Härte *f.*

hardship *s.* Beschwerde *f.;* Ungemach *n.;* Not *f.*

hardware *s.* Metallwaren *f.pl.;* Eisenwaren.

hard-working *a.* fleißig.

hardy *a.*, **hardily** *adv.* hart, fest, stark; tapfer; kühn; abgehärtet.

hardy: ~ **annual** *s.* winterharte einjährige Pflanze *f.;* ~ **perennial** *s.* winterharte mehrjährige Pflanze *f.*

hare *s.* Hase *m.*

harebell *s.* Glockenblume *f.*

hare-brained *a.* unüberlegt.

harelip *s.* Hasenscharte *f.*

harem *s.* Harem *m.*

haricot *s.* weisse Bohne *f.*

hark *v.i.* horchen; *~! i.* horch!

harlequin *s.* Harlekin *m.*

harm *s.* Unrecht, Leid *n.;* Schaden *m.; to do ~,* schaden; ~ *v.t.* verletzen, beeintrachtigen.

harmful *a.*, **~ly** *adv.* schädlich.

harmless *a.* unschädlich, arglos, harmlos; unverletzt; *to render ~,* (Granate) blind machen.

harmonic *a.* wohlklingend.

harmonica *s.* Harmonika *f.*

harmonics *s.pl.* Harmonielehre *f.*

harmonious *a.* harmonisch.

harmonium *s.* Harmonium *n.*

harmonize *v.t.* in Einklang bringen; ~ *v.i.* übereinstimmen, harmonieren.

harmony *s.* Einklang *m.*

harness *s.* Pferdegeschirr *n.;* ~ *v.t.* anschirren.

harp *s.* Harfe *f.;* ~ *v.i.* dauernd reden; herumreiten auf.

harpist *s.* Harfenspieler(in) *m.(f.)*

harpoon *s.* Harpune *f.;* ~ *v.t.* harpunieren.

harpsichord *s.* Cembalo *n.*

Harpy *s.* Harpyie *f.*

harrow *s.* Egge *f.;* ~ *v.t.* eggen; quälen, heimsuchen.

harrowing *a.* entsetzlich; grauenhaft.

harry *v.t.* angreifen; bedrängen.

harsh *a.*, **~ly** *adv.* herb, rauh; barsch.

hart *s.* Hirsch *m.*

hartshorn *s.* Hirschhorn *n.*

harum-scarum *a.* Hals über Kopf, hastig.

harvest *s.* Ernte *f.;* ~ *v.t.* ernten.

harvester *s.* Erntemaschine *f.;* Erntearbeiter(in) *m.(f.)*

harvest home *s.* Erntefest *n.*

hash *v.t.* zerhacken; ~ *s.* gehacktes Fleisch *n.*, Haschee *n.*

hashish *s.* Haschisch *n.*

hasp *s.* Haspe *f.*

hassle *s.* Krach *m.;* Mühe *f.*

haste *s.* Eile, Hast *f.;* Eifer *m.*

hasten *v.n.* eilen; ~ *v.t.* beschleunigen.

hasty *a.*, **hastily** *adv.* eilig; hastig; hitzig.

hat *s.* Hut *m.;* ~ **box** *s.* Hutschachtel *f.; to raise one's ~ to so.,* vor einem den Hut abnehmen.

hatch *v.t.* ausbrüten; ausschlüpfen; ~ *v.i.* im Werke sein; ~ *s.* Brut *f.;* Luke *f.* *~back s.* (Auto *n.*) mit Heckklappe *f.*

hatchet *s.* Beil *n.;* Axt *f.*

hate *s.* Haß *m.;* ~ *v.t.* hassen.

hateful *a.*, **~ly** *adv.* verhaßt, gehässig.

hatred *s.* Haß *m.*

hatter *s.* Hutmacher *m.*

haughty *a.*, **haughtily** *adv.* stolz, hochmütig.

haul *v.t.* ziehen, schleppen; ~ *s.* Ziehen; Schleppen *n.;* Fang.

haulage *s.* Transport *m.;* ~ **contractor** *s.* Transportunternehmer *m.*

haunch *s.* Lendenstück *n.;* Keule *f.* *~ of venison s.* Keule *f.*

haunt *v.t.* oft besuchen; beschweren, plagen; umgehen, spuken in.

haunted *p.* & *a.* nicht geheuer; *a* ~ *house,* ein Haus, in welchem es spukt.
have *v.t.ir.* haben; halten; bekommen; lassen; ~ *to,* müssen.
haven *s.* Hafen *m.;* geschützte Anlegestelle *f.*
haversack *s.* Brotbeutel *m.*
havoc *s.* Verwüstung, Zerstörung *f.*
haw *s.* Hagebutte *f.*
Hawaii *s.* Hawaii *n.*
Hawaiian *a.* hawaiisch; *s.* Hawaiianer(in) *m.(f.)*
hawk *s.* Habicht *m.;* Falke *m.;* ~ *v.i.* mit Falken jagen; hausieren.
hawker *s.* Hausierer *m.*
hawser *s.* (*nav.*) Kabeltau *n.*, Trosse *f.*
hawthorn *s.* (*red*) Rotdorn *m.*, (*white*) Weißdorn *m.*
hay *s.* Heu *n.*
haycock *s.* Heuschober *m.*
hayfever *s.* Heuschnupfen *m.*
hayloft *s.* Heuboden *m.*
haystack *s.* Heuschober *m.*
hazard *s.* Gefahr *f.;* ~ *v.t.* aufs Spiel setzen.
hazardous *a.*, **~ly** *adv.* gefährlich.
haze *s.* Dunst *m.;* leichter Nebel *m.*
hazel *s.* Haselnußstrauch *m.* ~ *a.* hasel.
hazelnut *s.* Haselnuß *f.*
hazy *a.* nebelig; dunstig; unbestimmt.
H.B.M. *His (or Her) Britannic Majesty,* Seine (Ihre) Majestät der König (die Königin) von Großbritannien.
hdbk *handbook,* Handbuch.
he *pn.* er; ~ *s.* Männchen *n.*
HE *high explosive,* hochexplosiv.
head *s.* Haupt *n.;* Kopf *m.;* Spitze (einer Kolonne, etc.) *f.;* Gipfel *m.;* Schiffschnabel *m.;* Kapitel *n.;* Punkt *m.;* Titel (Buch, Abschnitt) *m.;* Stück *n.;* Vorsteher *m.;* Ober...; *to bring to a* ~, zur Entscheidung bringen; *he could not make* ~ *or tail of it,* er konnte daraus nicht klug werden; ~ *v.t.* & *i.* anführen, befehligen; mit einer Überschrift versehen; (*nav.*) einen Kurs nehmen.
headache *s.* Kopfweh *n.*, Kopfschmerzen *pl.*
headboard *s.* Kopfende *n.*
headdress *s.* Kopfputz *m.*
header *s.* Kopfsprung *m.*, Kopfball *m.*
headgear *s.* Kopfbedeckung *f.*
headhunter *s.* Kopfjäger *m.*
heading *s.* Überschrift *f.*
headland *s.* Landspitze *f.*
headless *a.* kopflos, unbesonnen.
headlights *pl.* Scheinwerferlicht (Auto) *n.*
headlong *a.* & *adv.* kopfüber.
headmaster *s.* Schulleiter *m.*
headmistress *s.* Schulleiterin *f.*
headphone *s.* Kopfhörer *m.*
headquarters *pl.* Hauptgeschäftsstelle, Zentrale *f.;* Hauptquartier *n.;* vorgesetzte Stelle *f.*
headstrong *a.* halsstarrig.
headwaiter *s.* Oberkellner *m.*
headway *s.* Fortschritt *m.*
headwind *s.* Gegenwind *m.*
heady *a.* berauschend.
heal *v.t.* & *i.* heilen, zuheilen.
healing *s.* Heilung *f.*
health *s.* Gesundheit *f.*
health food shop *s.* Reformhaus *n.*
health insurance *s.* Krankenversicherung *f.*
health resort *s.* Kurort *m.*
health service *s.* Gesundheitsdienst *m.*
health visitor *s.* Krankenpfleger *m.* im Sozialdienst.
healthy *a.*, **healthily** *adv.* gesund.
heap *s.* Haufen *m.;* ~ *v.t.* häufen.
hear *v.t.* & *i.ir.* hören, anhören; erfahren; verhören; *to* ~ *a case,* (*jur.*) einen Fall verhandeln.
hearing *s.* Hören *n.;* Gehör *n.;* Verhör *n.*, Verhandlung *f.* (*jur.*); Anhörung *f.;* Hearing *n.;* Hörweite *f.;* *hard of* ~, schwerhörig; ~ **aid** *s.* Hörgerät *n.;* *to fix a* ~, (*jur.*) einen Termin anberaumen.
hearsay *s.* Hörensagen *n.;* *by* ~, vom Hörensagen.
hearse *s.* Leichenwagen *m.*
heart *s.* Herz *n.;* Gemüt *n.;* *at* ~, im Grunde; *by* ~, auswendig; *to take* ~, Mut fassen; Herz (in der Karte).
heartache *s.* Qual *f.*
heart attack *s.* Herzanfall *m.*
heartbeat *s.* Herzschlag *m.*
heartbreaking *a.* herzzerreißend.
heartburn *s.* Sodbrennen *n.*
heart condition *s.* Herzleiden *n.*
hearten *v.t.* ermutigen.
heartening *a.* ermutigend.
heart failure *s.* Herzversagen *n.*
heartfelt *a.* innig empfunden, herzlich.
hearth *s.* Kamin *m.;* ~ **rug** *s.* Kaminvorleger *m.*
heartless *a.*, **~ly** *adv.* grausam; herzlos.
heartrending *a.* herzzerreißend.
heart-searching *s.* Gewissenserforschung *f.*
heart-shaped *a.* herzförmig.
heart transplant *s.* Herztransplantation *f.*
heart trouble *s.* Probleme (*n.pl.*) mit dem Herzen.
heart-warming *a.* herzerfreuend.
hearty *a.*, **heartily** *adv.* herzlich, aufrichtig.
heat *s.* Hitze *f.;* Lauf *m.*, Brunst(zeit) *f.;* (*phys.*) Wärme; *blood* ~ *s.* Blutwärme; *body* ~ *s.* Körperwärme *f.;* **~proof** *a.* wärmesicher; ~ *v.t.* heizen; erhitzen.
heated *a.* **~ly** *adv.* hitzig.
heater *s.* Ofen *m.;* Boiler *m.*
heath *s.* Heide *f.*
heathen *s.* Heide *m.*, Heidin *f.;* ~ *a.* heidnisch.
heather *s.* Heidekraut *n.*, Heide *f.*
heating *s.* Heizung *f.;* ~ **unit** *s.* Heizkörper *m.*
heat-resistant *a.* hitzebeständig.
heatstroke *s.* Hitzschlag *m.*
heat wave *s.* Hitzewelle *f.*
heave *v.t.* *st.* heben; erheben; (*nav.*) lichten; ~ *v.i.* schwellen; ~ *s.* Heben *n.;* Wogen *n.*
heaven *s.* Himmel *m.*
heavenly *a.* & *adv.* himmlisch.
heaviness *s.* Schwere *f.;* Gewicht *n.*
heavy *a.*, **heavily** *adv.* schwer; träge; ~ *artillery,* schwerste Artillerie *f.;* ~ *smoker,* starker Raucher *m.;* ~ *type,* (*typ.*) Fettdruck *m.;* ~ *traffic,* starker Verkehr *m.*
heavy-duty *a.* strapazierfähig.
heavyweight *s.* Schwergewicht (Boxen) *n.*
Hebrew *a.* hebräisch; ~ *s.* Hebräer(in) *m.(f.)*

heckle *v.t.* (einen Redner) durch Zwischenrufe unterbrechen.
hectic *a.* hektisch.
hedge *s.* Hecke *f.*; Zaun *m.*; ~ *v.t.* einhegen; *to ~ v.i.* Ausflüchte machen.
hedgehog *s.* Igel *m.*; ~ **position** *s.* (*mil.*) Igelstellung *f.*
hedgerow *s.* Hecke *f.*
heed *s.* Aufmerksamkeit *f.*; ~ *v.t.* beachten.
heedful *a.*, **~ly** *adv.* vorsichtig.
heedless *a.*, **~ly** *adv.* unachtsam.
heel *s.* Ferse *f.*; Absatz *m.*; ~ *v.t.* mit einem Absatz versehen; ~ *v.i.* sich auf die Seite legen (*nav.*).
hefty *a.* handfest, unentwegt, stramm.
hegemony *s.* Vorherrschaft *f.*
height *s.* Höhe *f.*; Gipfel *m.*
heighten *v.t.* erhöhen, verbessern.
heinous *a.*, **~ly** *adv.* abscheulich; schändlich.
heir *s.* Erbe *m.*; **~-apparent** *s.* rechtmäßiger Erbe; **~-at-law** *s.* gesetzlicher Erbe *m.*; **~-presumptive** *s.* mutmaßlicher Erbe *m.*
heiress *s.* Erbin *f.*
heirloom *s.* Erbstück *n.*; Erbe *n.*
heist *s.* Raubüberfall *m.*; ~ *v.t.* rauben.
helical *a.* schraubenfömig, Spiral...
helicopter *s.* Hubschrauber *m.*, Helikopter *m.*
heliport *s.* Heliport *m.*
helix *s.* Spirale *f.*
hell *s.* Hölle *f.*
hellfire *s.* Höllenfeuer *n.*
hellish *a.*, **~ly** *adv.* höllisch.
helm *s.* Steuerruder *n.*
helmet *s.* Helm *m.*
helmsman *s.* Steuermann *m.*
help *s.* Hilfe *f.*; ~ *v.t. & i.* helfen; (bei Tische) bedienen; ~ *yourself!* langen Sie zu; *Can I help you?* Kann ich Ihnen behilflich sein?; *I cannot ~ it,* ich kann es nicht ändern.
helper *s.* Helfer(in) *m.(f.)*
helpful *a.* behilflich, nützlich.
helping *s.* Portion (Essen), *f.*; *second ~*, zweite Portion *f.*
helpless *a.*, **~ly** *adv.* hilflos.
helpmate *s.* Gehilfe *m.*; Gehilfin *f.*
helter-skelter *adv.* Hals über Kopf; holter-die-polter.
hem *s.* Saum *m.*; Räuspern *n.*; ~ *v.t.* säumen; ~ *v.i.* sich räuspern.
hemisphere *s.* Halbkugel *f.*; Hemisphäre *f.*
hemline *s.* Saum *m.*
hemlock *s.* Schierling *m.*
hemoglobin *s.* Hämoglobin.
hemophilia *s.* Hämophilie *f.*, Bluterkrankheit *f.*
hemorrhage *s.* Blutsturz *m.*
hemorrhoids *s.pl.* Hämorrhoiden *f.pl.*
hemostatic *a.* blutstillend.
hemp *s.* Hanf *m.*; Haschisch *n.*
hemstitch *s.* Hohlsaum *m.*; ~ *v.t.* mit Hohlsaum nähen.
hen *s.* Henne *f.*; Huhn *n.*
hence *adv.* von hier; von nun an; daher.
henceforth *adv.* von nun an, von da an.
henchman *s.* (*pol.*) Anhänger *m.*; Handlanger *m.*
henpecked *p.* unter dem Pantoffel stehend.
her *pn.* sie, ihr; (*poss.*) ihr.
herald *s.* Herold *m.*; ~ *v.t.* verkünden.
heraldry *s.* Wappenkunde *f.*; Heraldik *f.*
herb *s.* Kraut *n.*; Gras *n.*
herbaceous *a.* krautartig.
herbal *a.* Kräuter...
herbalist *s.* Kräuterkenner *m.*
herbarium *s.* Herbarium *n.*
herbivore *s.* Pflanzenfresser *m.*
herbivorous *a.* pflanzenfressend.
herd *s.* Herde *f.*
herdsman *s.* Hirte *m.*
here *adv.* hier; her.
hereafter *adv.* künftig.
hereat *adv.* hierbei.
hereby *adv.* hierdurch; hiermit.
hereditary *a.*, **hereditarily** *adv.* erblich.
heredity *s.* Vererbung *f.*; Erblichkeit *f.*
herein *adv.* hierin; hier hinein.
hereinafter *adv.* im Folgenden.
hereof *adv.* hiervon.
hereon *adv.* hieran, hierauf, hierüber.
heresy *s.* Ketzerei *f.*
heretic *s.* Ketzer *m.*
heretical *a.*, **~ly** *adv.* ketzerisch.
heretofore *adv.* ehemals.
herewith *adv.* hiermit.
heritage *s.* Erbgut *n.*, Erbschaft *f.*
hermaphrodite *s.* Zwitter *m.*
hermetic *a.*, **~ally** *adv.* luftdicht.
hermit *s.* Einsiedler *m.*
hermitage *s.* Einsiedelei *f.*
hernia *s.* (*med.*) Bruch *m.*
hero *s.* Held *m.*
heroic *a.*, **~ally** *adv.* heldenhaft, heroisch.
heroine *s.* Heldin *f.*
heroism *s.* Heldenmut *m.*
heron *s.* Reiher *m.*
herpes *s.* Herpes *m.*
herring *s.* Hering *m.*
hers *pn.* der, die, das ihrige.
herself *pn.* sie selbst, ihr selbst, sich.
hesitant *a.* zögernd; unsicher.
hesitate *v.i.* zögern.
hesitation *s.* Unschlüßigkeit *f.*; Unsicherheit *f.*
heterodox *a.* heterodox; andersgläubig.
heterogeneous *a.* verschiedenartig.
heterosexual *a.* heterosexuell; ~ *s.* Heterosexuelle *m./f.*
hew *v.t.* hauen, hacken, fällen.
hex *v.t.* verhexen.
hexagon *s.* Sechseck *n.*
hexameter *s.* Hexameter *m.*
heyday *s.* Höhepunkt *m.*, Blüte *f.*
hf. *half,* halb.
hiatus *s.* Bruch *m.*; Unterbrechung *f.*
hibernate *v.i.* Winterschlaf halten.
hibernation *s.* Winterschlaf *m.*
hiccup *s.* Schluckauf *m.*; ~ *v.i.* den Schluckauf haben.
hide *s.* Hauf *f.*; Fell *n.*; ~ *v.t.st.* verstecken; ~ *v. i.st.* sich verstecken; ~ *and seek s.* Versteckspiel *n.*
hidebound *a.* engstirnig, engherzig.
hideous *a.*, **~ly** *adv.* scheußlich.
hide-out *s.* Versteck *n.*

hiding *s.* Versteck *n.; (fam.)* Tracht Prügel *f.*
hiding place *s.* Schlupfwinkel *m.*
hierarchic, hierarchical *a.;* **~ly** *adv.* hierarchisch.
hierarchy *s.* Hierarchie *f.*
hieroglyphic *a.* hieroglyphisch; **~s** *s.pl.* Hieroglyphen *f.pl.*
high *a.*, **~ly** *adv.* hoch, erhaben; (Wild) angegangen; **~ life** *s.* vornehme Welt *f.; highly strung a.* nervös, reizbar; **~** *s.* Hoch (Wetterkunde) *n.*
high altar *s.* Hochaltar *m.*
highbrow *s.* Intellektuelle *m./f.* **~** *a.* intellektuell; hochgestochen.
High Church *s.* Hochkirche *f.*
higher education *s.* Hochschulbildung *f.*
high explosive *s.* Sprengstoff *m.*
high-flown *a.* schwülstig.
high-flyer *s.* Hochbegabte *m./f.; (fam.)* Überflieger(in) *m.(f.)*
high-grade *a.* hochwertig.
high-handed *a.* selbstherrlich.
high-heeled *a.* hochhackig (Schuhe).
highland *s.* Hochland *n.*
highness *s.* Höhe *f.;* Hohheit *f.* (Titel).
high-powered *a.* Hochleistungs...; dynamisch.
high pressure *s.* Hochdruck *m.*
high priest *s.* Hohepriester *m.*
high-ranking *a.* hochrangig.
high-rise *s.* Hochhaus *n.*
high road, highway *s.* Landstraße *f.*
high school *s.* Oberschule *f.*
high seas *pl.* hohe See *f.*
high season *s.* Hochsaison *f.*
high tech *a.* High-Tech-...
high tension, high voltage *s. (elek.)* Hochspannung *f.;* **~ cable** *s.* Hochspannungsleitung *f.*
high water *s.* Hochwasser *n.*
highwayman *s.* Straßenräuber *m.*
highway robbery *s.* Straßenraub *m.*
hijack *v.t.* entführen.
hijacker *s.* Entführer(in) *m.(f.)*
hike *v.i.* wandern.
hiker *s.* Wanderer *m.*, Wanderin *f.*
hilarious *a.* heiter, aufgeheitert.
hilarity *s.* Fröchlichkeit, Heiterkeit *f.*
hill *s.* Hügel *m.*, Berg *m.*
hillbilly *s.* Hinterwäldler(in) *m.(f.)*
hillock *s.* kleiner Hügel *m.*
hillside *s.* Hang *m.*
hilltop *s.* Gipfel *m.*
hilly *a.* hügelig.
hilt *s.* Heft *n.;* Degengefäß *n.*
him *pn.* ihn, ihm; den, dem.
himself *pn.* er selbst, ihn selbst, ihm selbst; sich.
hind *a.* hinter; **~** *s.* Hirschkuh *f.*
hinder *v.t.* hindern, stören.
hindmost *a.* hinterst.
hindquarters *s.pl.* Hinterbeine (des Pferdes), *n.pl.*
hindrance *s.* Hindernis *n.*
hindsight *s.* **with ~** im nachhinein.
hinge *s.* Türangel *f.;* Scharnier *n.;* **~** *v.i. (fig.)* **~ on,** sich um etwas drehen.
hint *s.* Wink, Fingerzeig *m.;* Anspielung *f.;* **~** *v.t.* andeuten.
hinterland *s.* Hinterland *n.*, Umland *n.*
hip *s.* Hüfte *f.;* Hagebutte *f.*
hip bath *s.* Sitzbad *n.*
hipbone *s.* Hüftknochen *m.*
hip flask *s.* Flachmann *m.*
hip joint *s.* Hüftgelenk *n.*
hippie *s.* Hippie *m.*
hippodrome *s.* Rennbahn *f.*
hippopotamus *s.* Nilpferd *n.*
hire *s.* Miete *f.;* Lohn *m.; on ~,* zu vermieten; **~** *v.t.* mieten, vermieten; anwerben.
hirsute *a.* haarig, rauh.
his *pn.* sein; der, die, das seinige.
hiss *v.i.* zischen; **~** *v.t.* auszischen.; **~** *s.* Zischen *n.*
historian *s.* Geschichtsforscher(in) *m.(f.)*
historic *a.* historisch.
historical *a.*, **~ly** *adv.* geschichtlich.
historiographer *s.* Geschichtschreiber(in) *m.(f.)*
history *s.* Geschichte *f.*
histrionic *a.* dramatisch.
hit *v.t.ir.* schlagen, stossen; treffen; **~** *v.i.* anstoßen; zusammenstoßen; **~** *s.* Schlag, Stoß *m.;* Treffer, Zufall *m.; (theat.)* Schlager *m.; (mil.) direct ~,* Volltreffer *m.*
hitch *v.t. & i.* festmachen; *(sich)* ruckweise bewegen; **~** *s.* Ruck *m.; (nav.)* Knoten *m.;* Schwierigkeit *f.*
hitchhike *v.i.* per Anhalter fahren.
hitchhiker *s.* Anhalter(in) *m.(f.)*
hither *adv.* hierher; **~** *a.* diesseitig.
hitherto *adv.* bisher.
hit man *s. (sl.)* Killer *m.*
hive *s.* Bienenstock, Schwarm *m.;* **~** *v.i.* beisammen wohnen.
H.M. *His/Her Majesty,* Seine/Ihre Majestät.
H.M.S. *His/Her Majesty's Ship,* Seiner/Ihrer Majestät Schiff.
HO *head office,* Hauptgeschäftsstelle, Zentrale.
hoard *s.* Vorrat, Schatz *m.;* **~** *v.t. & i.* aufhäufen, sammeln; hamstern.
hoarder *s.* Hamsterer *m.*, Hamsterin *f.*
hoarding *s.* Bretterzaun *m.*
hoarfrost *s.* Reif *m.*
hoarse *a.*, **~ly** *adv.* heiser.
hoary *a.* eisgrau; bereift.
hoax *s.* Schwindel *m.;* Streih *m.;* blinder Alarm *m.* **~** *v.t.* foppen.
hobble *v.i.* humpeln.
hobby *s.* Steckenpferd, Hobby *n.*
hobgoblin *s.* Kobold *m.*
hobnail *s.* Nagel *m.; hobnailed boots pl.* genagelte Schuhe *m.pl.*
hobnob *v.i.* vertaulich zusammen trinken (anstoßen).
hobo *s.* Landstreicher *m.*
hock *s.* Rheinwein *m.* **~** *v.t.* versetzen.
hockey *s.* Hockey *n.*
hockey stick *s.* Hockeyschläger *m.*
hocus-pocus *s.* Taschenspielerei *f.*
hodge-podge *s.* Mischmasch *m.*
hoe *s.* Hacke *f.;* **~** *v.t.* hacken.
hog *s.* Schwein *n.*
hoggish *a.*, **~ly** *adv.* schweinisch.
hoi polloi *s.* breite Masse *f.*
hoist *v.t.* in die Höhe heben; hissen; **~** *s.* (Personen) Aufzug *m.*
hoity-toity *a.* hochnäsig; leichtsinnig.

hold *v.t.st.* halten; behalten; enthalten; meinen, schätzen; besitzen; ~ *v.i.* sich halten; beharren; *to ~ forth*, darstellen; hinreichen; vortragen; *to ~ good*, sich bestätigen; gültig sein; *to ~ off*, abhalten, ausweichen; *~ on!*, *~ the line!*, bleiben Sie am Telephon!; *to ~ on to*, (*mil.*) (eine Stellung) halten; *to ~ out*, ausstrecken; aushalten; anbieten; *to ~ up*, in die Höhe halten; aufrecht erhalten, unterstützen; *~!* halt!; ~ *s.* Halten, Fassen *n.*; Griff *m.*; Gewalt *f.*; Schiffsraum *m.*; Lager *n.*; *to get ~ of*, habhaft werden; **~-all** *s.* Reisekoffer *m.*

holder *s.* Inhaber *m.*; Halter *m.*

holding *s.* Pachtgut *n.*; Besitz *m.*; ~ **company** *s.* Dachgesellschaft *f.*; (*mil.*) **~-line** *s.* Auffanglinie *f.*

holdup *s.* Raubüberfall *m.*

hole *s.* Loch *n.*; (*fig.*) Klemme *f.*

holiday *s.* Feiertag *m.*; *public ~*, gesetzlicher Feiertag *m.*; *on ~*, in den Ferien; **~s** *pl.* Ferien *pl.*; *~s with pay*, bezahlter Urlaub *m.*

holiness *s.* Heiligkeit *f.*

Holland *s.* Holland *n.*

hollow *a.* hohl; falsch; ~ *s.* Höhle *f.*; ~ *v.t.* aushöhlen.

holly *s.* Stechpalme *f.*

hollyhock *s.* Stockrose *f.*

holm *s.* Holm, Werder *m.*; Uferland *n.*

holocaust *s.* Holocaust *m.*; Massenvernichtung *f.*

holograph *s.* eigenhändig geschriebenes Dokument *n.*

holster *s.* Halfter *f.* & *m.*

holy *a.* heilig; *~ Saturday*, Karsamstag *m.*

holy water *s.* Weihwasser *n.*

Holy Week *s.* Karwoche *f.*

homage *s.* Huldigung *f.*; *to do ~*, huldigen.

home *s.* Heimat *f.*; Wohnung *f.*; ~ *a.* heimisch; ~ **address** *s.* Heimatadresse *f.*; *~ for the elderly s.* Altersheim *n.*; ~ **rule** *s.* Selbstverwaltung *f.*; ~ **trade** *s.* Binnenhandel *m.*; ~ *adv.* heim; nach Hause; tüchtig, derb; *at ~*, zu Hause.

homeless *a.* obdachlos, heimatlos; ~ *s.* Obdachlose *m./f.*

homely *a.* & *adv.* einfach, schmucklos.

homemade *a.* zu Hause hergestellt.

homeopathic *a.* homöopathisch *f.*

homeopathy *s.* Homöopathie *f.*

homesick *a. be ~* Heimweh haben.

homesickness *s.* Heimweh *n.*

homestead *s.* Heimstätte *f.*; Gehöft *n.*

hometown *s.* Heimatstadt *f.*

homeward(s) *adv.* heimwärts; *~ bound*, auf der Rückreise.

homework *s.* Hausarbeiten, Hausaufgaben (des Schülers) *f.pl.*

homey *a.* gemütlich.

homicidal *a.* gemeingefährlich.

homicide *s.* Totschlag *m.*

homily *s.* Predigt *f.*

homing pigeon *s.* Brieftaube *f.*

homogeneous *a.* gleichartig.

homogenize *v.t.* homogenisieren.

homonym *s.* Homonym *n.*

homosexual *a.* homosexuell; *~s.* Homosexuelle *m./f.*

homosexuality *s.* Homosexualität *f.*

Hon. *Honorable*, Ehrenwert; *Honorary*, Ehren...

hone *s.* Wetzstein *m.*; ~ *v.t.* wetzen.

honest *a.*, **~ly** *adv.* anständig; redlich, ehrlich.

honesty *s.* Ehrlichkeit, Ehrbarkeit *f.*

honey *s.* Honig *m.*; Süßigkeit *f.*

honeycomb *s.* Honigwabe *f.*

honeyed *a.* honigsüß.

honeymoon *s.* Flitterwochen *f.pl.*

honeysuckle *s.* Geißblatt *m.*

honk *s.* Hupen *n.*; ~ *v.i.* hupen.

honor *s.* Ehre, Würde *f.*; ~ *v.t.* ehren, beehren; honorieren (Wechsel).

honorable *a.*, **honorably** *adv.* ehrenvoll, ehrbar, achtbar.

honorary *a.* Ehren...

hood *s.* Haube *f.*; Kapuze *f.*

hoodlum *s.* Rowdy *m.*

hoodwink *v.t.* täuschen.

hoof *s.* Huf *m.*; Klaue *f.*

hook *s.* (Angel-)haken *m.*; Gartenmesser *n.*; *by ~ or by crook*, so oder so; ~ *v.t.* anhaken.

hooked *p.* & *a.* gebogen, gekrümmt; (*fam.*) süchtig.

hooker *s.* (*fam.*) Nutte *f.*

hooligan *s.* Rowdy *m.*

hoop *s.* Reifen *m.*; Reifrock *m.*; ~ *v.t.* (ein Faß) binden; ~ *v.i.* laut rufen.

hooper *s.* Böttcher *m.*

hoot *v.i.* tuten, hupen, heulen.

hop *v.i.* hüpfen; ~ *v.t.* hopsen; ~ *s.* Hüpfen *n.*; Sprung *m.*; Hopsen *m.*; Hopfen *m.*; **~s** *pl.* (*com.*) Hopfen.

hope *s.* Hoffnung *f.*; ~ *v.i.* hoffen.

hopeful *a.*, **~ly** *adv.* hoffnungsvoll.

hopeless *a.* hoffnungslos.

horde *s.* Horde *f.*

horizon *s.* Horizont *m.*; (*avi.*) *artificial ~*, künstlicher Horizont *m.*

horizontal *a.*, **~ly** *adv.* waagerecht.

horizontal bar *s.* Reck (Turnen) *n.*

hormone *s.* Hormon *n.*

horn *s.* Horn *n.*; ~ **signal** *s.* Hupsignal *n.*

horned *a.* gehörnt.

hornet *s.* Hornisse *f.*

horn-rimmed *a. ~ spectacles, pl.* Hornbrille *f.*

horny *a.* hornig; (*vulg.*) geil.

horoscope *a.* Horoskop *n.*

horrendous *a.* schrecklich; horrend.

horrible *a.*, **horribly** *adv.* abscheulich.

horrid *a.* schrecklich.

horrific *a.* schreckenerregend.

horrify *v.t.* entsetzen.

horror *s.* Entsetzen *n.*; Greuel *m.*

horror-stricken, horror-struck *s.* von Entsetzen gepackt.

horse *s.* Pferd *n.*; *on ~back*, zu Pferde; *horseback riding s.* Reiten *n.*

horse chestnut *s.* Roßkastanie *f.*

horse drawn *s.* (*mil.*) Pferde..., bespannt; *~ artillery*, bespannte Artillerie *f.*; *~ vehicle*, Pferdefuhrwerk *n.*

horsehair *s.* Roßhaar *n.*

horseman *s.* Reiter *m.*

horsemanship *s.* Reitkunst *f.*

horseplay *s.* Balgerei *f.*

horsepower *s.* Pferdekraft *f.*

horse-race *s.* Pferderennen *n.*

horseradish *s.* Meerrettich *m.*
horseshoe *s.* Hufeisen *n.*
horse trailer *s.* Pferdeanhänger *m.*
horsewoman *s.* Reiterin *f.*
horticultural *a.* zum Gartenbau gehörig.
horticulture *s.* Gartenbau *m.*
hose *s.* Strumpf *m.;* Schlauch *m.*
hosier *s.* Strumpfwarenhändler *m.*
hosiery *s.* Strumpfwaren *f.pl.*
hospice *s.* Hospitz *n.;* Sterbeklinik *f.*
hospitable *a.*, **hospitably** *adv.* gastlich; gastfreundlich.
hospital *s.* Hospital, Krankenhaus *n.;* ~ **ship** *s.* Lazarettschiff *n.;* ~ **train** *s.* Lazarettzug *m.*
hospitality *s.* Gastlichkeit *f.*
hospitalize *v.t.* ins Krankenhaus einweisen.
host *s.* Gastgeber *m.;* Wirt *m.;* Heer *n.*, Schwarm *m.*
hostage *s.* Geisel *m.*
hostel *s.* Herberge *f.*
hostess *s.* Wirtin *f.;* Gastgeberin *f.*
hostile *a.*, **~ly** *adv.* feindlich.
hostility *s.* Feindseligkeit *f.*
hot *a.*, **~ly** *adv.* heiß; scharf (gewürzt).
hot air *s.* leeres Gerede.
hotbed *s.* Mistbeet *n.*, Frühbeet *n.;* (*fig.*) Brutstätte *f.*
hot-blooded *a.* heißblütig, hitzig.
hotchpotch *s.* Mischmasch *m.*
hotel *s.* Gasthof *m.*, Hotel *n.*
hothouse *s.* Treibhaus *n.*
hot line *s.* heißer Draht *m.*
hot plate *s.* Heizplatte *f.*
hot water bottle *s.* Wärmflasche *f.*
hound *s.* Jagdhund, Hetzhund *m.*
hour *s.* Stunde *f.*
hourglass *s.* Sanduhr *f.*
hour hand *s.* Stundenzeiger *m.*
hourly *a.* & *adv.* stündlich.
house *s.* Haus *n.;* (*theat.*) Zuschauerraum *m.;* ~ *v.t.* beherbergen; ~ *v.i.* hausen.
house agent *s.* Häusermakler *m.*
housebreaker *s.* Einbrecher *m.*
household *s.* Haushalt *m.*, Haushaltung *f.;* ~ *a.* häuslich, einfach.
householder *s.* Haushaltsvorstand *m.*
housekeeper *s.* Haushälterin *f.*
housekeeping *s.* Haushalten *n.;* ~ *a.* Haushalts...
house of correction *s.* Besserungsanstalt *f.*
house search *s.* Haussuchung *f.*
house-warming party *s.* Einzugsparty *f.*
housewife *s.* Hausfrau *f.*
housework *s.* Hausarbeit *f.*
housing *s.* Wohnungen *pl.;* Obdach *n.;* Lagern *n.;* Satteldecke *f.;* ~ **department,** ~ **office** *s.* Wohnungsamt *n.;* ~ **shortage** *s.* Wohnungsnot *f.*
hovel *s.* Schuppen *m.;* Hütte *f.*
hover *v.i.* schweben; schwanken; sich aufhalten.
hovercraft *s.* Luftkissenfahrzeug *n.*
how *adv.* wie.
however *adv.* wie dem auch sei, dennoch; aber, trotzdem; ~ *c.* wie... auch.
howitzer *s.* Haubitze *f.*
howl *v.i.* heulen; ~ *s.* Geheul *n.*
howler *s.* (*sl.*) grober Fehler *m.*
hoyden *s.* Wildfang *m.*
h.p. *horse-power,* Pferdestärke *f.*
HQ *Headquarters,* Hauptquartier.
H.S. *High School,* höhere Schule.
ht. *height,* Höhe, H.
hub *s.* Radnabe *f.;* Mittelpunkt *m.*
hubbub *s.* Tumult, Lärm *m.*
hubcap *s.* Radkappe *f.*
huckster *s.* Höker *m.;* ~ *v.i.* hökern.
huddle *s.* Verwirrung, Unordnung *f.;* ~ *v.t.* eilfertig verrichten, hudeln; ~ *v.i.* sich drängen; *to ~ oneself up,* sich zusammenkauern.
hue *s.* Farbe *f.*, Farbton *m.;* ~ *and cry,* Zetergeschrei *n.;* Hetze *f.*
huff *v.i.* keuchen, schnaufen.
hug *s.* Umarmung *f.;* ~ *v.t.* umarmen, liebkosen.
huge *a.* ungeheuer, riesig.
hulk *s.* Rumpf (des Schiffes) *m.;* Wrack *n.*
hull *s.* Schale, Hülse *f.;* Rumpf (des Schiffes) *m.;* Wanne (eines Panzers) *f.;* ~ *v.t.* schälen, enthülsen.
hullabaloo *s.* Spektakel, Klamauk *m.*
hullo *i.* hallo!
hum *s.* Gesumme, Gemurmel *n.;* ~ *i.* hm; ~ *v.i.* summen, brummen.
human *a.*, **~ly** *adv.* menschlich; ~ *s.* Mensch *m.*
human being *s.* Mensch *m.*
humane *a.*, **~ly** *adv.* liebreich, menschenfreundlich.
humanism *s.* Humanismus *m.*
humanist *s.* Humanist(in) *m.(f.)*
humanitarian *a.* humanitär; ~ *s.* Menschenfreund *m.*
humanity *s.* Menschheit *f.;* Menschlichkeit *f.;* **humanities** *pl.* klassische Wissenschaft *f.*
humanize *v.t.* vermenschlichen, humanisieren.
humankind *s.* Menschengeschlecht *n.*
humble *a.*, **humbly** *adv.* bescheiden, unterwürfig; demütig; ~ *v.t.* demütigen.
humbug *s.* Schwindel *m.;* Humbug *m.*
humdrum *a.* langweilig; eintönig.
humid *a.* feucht, naß.
humidity *s.* Feuchtigkeit *f.*
humiliate *s.* erniedrigen; demütigen.
humiliation *s.* Demütigung *f.*
humility *s.* Unterwürfigkeit *f.;* Demut *f.*
hummingbird *s.* Kolibri *m.*
hummock *s.* Hügel *m.*
humor *s.* Humor *m.;* Komik *f.;* Komische *n.;* Laune *f.*
humorist *s.* Humorist(in) *m.(f.)*
humorless *a.* humorlos.
humorous *a.*, **~ly** *adv.* humoristisch; humorvoll.
humpback *s.* Höcker, Buckel *m.*
humpbacked *a.* buck[e]lig.
humus *s.* Humus *m.*
hunch *s.* Buckel *m.;* ~ *v.t.* krümmen.
hunchback *s.* Buck[e]lige *m./f.*
hundred *a.* hundert; ~ *s.* Hundert *n.*
hundredweight *s.* (englischer) Zentner *m.* (112 Pfund; 50.8 kg.).
Hungarian *s.* Ungar(in) *m.(f.)*
Hungary *s.* Ungarn *n.*
hunger *s.* Hunger *m.;* ~ **strike** *s.* Hungerstreik *m.;* ~ *v.i.* hungern.
hungry *a.*, **hungrily** *adv.* hungrig.

hunt *v.t. & i.* hetzen, jagen; nachspüren; ~ *s.* (Hetz-) Jagd *f.*
hunter *s.* Jäger(in) *m.(f.)*; Jagdpferd *n.*
hunting *s.* (Hetz-) Jagd *f.*
hunting license *s.* Jagdschein *m.*
huntsman *s.* Jäger *m.*
hurdle *s.* Hürde *f.* ~ **race** *s.* Hürdenlauf *m.*
hurdler *s.* Hürdenläufer(in) *m.(f.)*
hurl *v.t.* werfen, schleudern.
hurly-burly *s.* Wirrwarr *m.*; Tumult *m.*
hurrah *i.* hurra!
hurricane *s.* Orkan *m.*
hurried *a.* eilig, hastig; überstürzt.
hurry *s.* Eile, Unruhe *f.*; ~ *v.t.* beschleunigen, treiben; ~ *v.i.* eilen.
hurt *s.* ~ *v.t.ir.* verletzen; ~ *v.i.ir.* schmerzen, wehtun; ~ *a.* verletzt; gekränkt.
hurtful *a.*, **~ly** *adv.* verletzend, kränkend.
husband *s.* Gatte, Ehemann *m.*; ~ *v.t.* haushalten.
husbandry *s.* Landwirtschaft *f.*; Haushaltung, Wirtschaftlichkeit *f.*
hush! *i.* still!; **~,** stillen, beruhigen; *to ~ up,* vertuschen; ~ *v.i.* schweigen; *s.* Stille *f.*; Schweigen *n.*
hushed *a.* gedämpft.
hush money *s.* Schweigegeld *n.*
husk *s.* Hülse *f.*; ~ *v.t.* aushülsen.
husky *a.* heiser, rauh; ~ *s.* Husky *m.*
hussar *s.* Husar *m.*
hussy *s.* (*pej.*). Göre *f.*; Range *f.*
hustle *v.t.* stossen, drängen; eilen.
hut *s.* Hütte; Baracke *f.*
hyacinth *s.* Hyazinthe *f.*
hybrid *s.* Bastardtier *n.*, Bastardpflanze *f.*; ~ *a.* Zwitter...
hydrangea *s.* Hortensie *f.*
hydrant *s.* Wasserhahn *m.*; Hydrant *m.*
hydraulic *a.* hydraulisch.
hydrocarbon *s.* Kohlenwasserstoff *m.*
hydrocephalus *s.* Wasserkopf *m.*
hydrochloric acid *s.* Salzsäure *f.*
hydroelectric station *s.* Wasserkraftwerk *n.*
hydrogen *s.* Wasserstoff *m.*
hydrogenation *s.* Hydrierung *f.*
hydrogen bomb *s.* Wasserstoffbombe *f.*
hydrogen peroxide *s.* Wasserstoffsuperoxyd *n.*
hydropower station *s.* Wasserkraftwerk *n.*
hyena *s.* Hyäne *f.*
hygiene *s.* Hygiene *f.*
hygienic *a.* hygienisch.
hymen *s.* Jungfernhäutchen *n.*
hymn *s.* Loblied *n.*, Hymne *f.*; **church ~,** Kirchenlied *n.*; ~ **book** *s.* Gesangsbuch *n.*
hype *s.* Reklameschwindel *m.*
hyperactive *a.* hyperaktiv.
hyperbola *s.* Hyperbel *f.*
hyperbole *s.* Übertreibung *f.*
hyperbolical *a.*, **~ly** *adv.* übertrieben.
hypercritical *a.* hyperkritisch.
hypersensitive *a.* übersensibel.
hyphen *s.* Bindestrich *m.*
hyphenated *a.* Bindestrich...
hypnosis *s.* Hypnose *f.*
hypnotic *a.* einschläfernd; hypnotisch.
hypnotism *s.* Hypnotismus *m.*
hypnotize *v.t.* hypnotisieren
hypochondria *s.* Hypochondrie *f.*
hypochondriac *s.* Hypochonder *m.*
hypocrisy *s.* Heuchelei *f.*
hypocrite *s.* Heuchler(in) *m.(f.)*
hypocritical *a.* heuchlerisch.
hypodermic *a.* subkutan.
hypothecary *a.* hypothekarisch.
hypothermia *s.* Unterkühlung *f.*
hypothesis *s.* Hypothese *f.*; Annahme *f.*
hypothetical *a.* hypothetisch.
hysterectomy *s.* Hysterektomie *f.*
hysteria *s.* Hysterie (bes. übertragen) *f.*
hysterical *a.* hysterisch.
hysterics *s.pl.* Hysterie *f.*; hysterischer Anfall *m.*

I

I, i der Buchstabe I oder i *n.*
I *pn.* ich; *it is ~*, ich bin's.
iamb *s.* Iambus *m.*
iambic *a.* iambisch.
IATA *International Air Transport Association,* Internationaler Luftverkehrsverband.
Iberia *s.* Iberien *n.*
Iberian Peninsula *s.* Iberische Halbinsel *f.*
ibex *s.* Steinbock *m.*
ib(id) *ibidem (in the same place),* ebenda, ebd.
IBRD *International Bank for Reconstruction and Development,* Internationale Bank für Wiederaufbau und Entwicklung.
IC *integrated circuit,* integrierter Schaltkreis.
ice *s.* Eis *n.*; Gefrorenes *n.*; ~ *v.t.* mit Eis kühlen; überzuckern.
ice age *s.* Eiszeit *f.*
iceberg *s.* Eisberg *m.*
ice-bound *a.* eingefroren.
icebox *s.* Kühlschrank *m.*
icebreaker *s.* Eisbrecher *m.*
ice cream *s.* Eis *n.*, Gefrorenes *n.*; ~ **parlor** *s.* Eisdiele *f.*
ice cube *s.* Eiswürfel *m.*
ice floe *s.* Eisscholle *f.*
Iceland *s.* Island *n.*
Icelander *s.* Isländer(in) *m.(f.)*
Icelandic *a.* isländisch.
ice pack *s.* Eispackung *f.*; Kühlakku *n.*
ice rink *s.* Schlittschuhbahn *f.*
ice skate *v.i.* eislaufen; Schlittschuh laufen.
ice skating *s.* Schlittschuhlaufen *n.*
icicle *s.* Eiszapfen *m.*
icing *s.* Zuckerguß *m.*; Zuckerglasur *f.*
icon *s.* Ikone *f.*
iconoclast *s.* Bilderstürmer *m.*
ICU *intensive care unit,* Intensivstation.
icy *a.* eisig.
ID *identification,* Ausweis.

idea *s.* Begriff *m.;* Idee *f.;* Vorstellung *f.;* Gedanke *m.*
ideal *a.,* **~ly** *adv.* ideal; ~ *s.* Ideal *n.*
idealism *s.* Idealismus *m.*
idealist *s.* Idealist *m.*
idealistic *a.* idealistisch.
idealize *v.t.* idealisieren.
identical *a.* identisch.
identifiable *a.* erkennbar; nachweisbar, bestimmbar.
identification *s.* Identifizierung *f.;* ~ **card** *s.* Ausweis *m.*
identify *v.t.* identifizieren.
identity *s.* Identität *f.; to prove one's ~,* sich ausweisen.
ideological *a.* ideologisch, weltanschaulich.
ideology *s.* Ideologie, Weltanschauung *f.*
idiocy *s.* Blödsinn *m.;* Idiotie *f.*
idiom *s.* Mundart *f.;* Redewendung *f.*
idiomatic a. idiomatisch.
idiosyncrasy *s.* Eigentümlichkeit *f.*
idiosyncratic *a.* eigenwillig.
idiot *s.* Dummkopf *m.;* Idiot(in) *m.(f.)*
idiotic *a.* blödsinnig; einfältig.
idle *a.,* faul; unnütz; müßig, träge; stillgelegt; stillstehend; leerlaufend. ~ **away** *v.t.* vertändeln; ~ **hours** *pl.* Mußestunden *pl.*
idleness *s.* Müßiggang *m.;* Trägheit *f.*
idol *s.* Abgott *m.;* Götzenbild *n.*
idolatrous *a.,* **~ly** *adv.* abgöttisch.
idolatry *s.* Götzendienst *m.;* Vergötterung *f.*
idolize *v.t.* vergöttern.
idyll *s.* Idylle *f.*
idyllic *a.* idyllisch.
i.e. *id est,* das heißt, d.h.
if *c.* wenn, falls; ob.
igloo *s.* Iglu *m.* od. *n.*
igneous *a.* feurig.
ignite *v.t.* anzünden, entzünden.
igniter *s.* Zünder *m.*
ignition *s.* Entzündung *f.;* Zündung *f.;* ~ **key** *s.* Zündschlüssel *m.*
ignoble *a.,* **ignobly** *adv.* unedel, gemein.
ignominious *a.,* **~ly** *adv.* schimpflich, verwerflich.
ignominy *s.* Schmach, Schande *f.*
ignoramus *s.* Nichtswisser(in) *m./f.;* Ignorant(in) *m.(f.)*
ignorance *s.* Unwissenheit *f.*
ignorant *a.,* **~ly** *adv.* unwissend.
ignore *v.t.* nicht beachten; unbeachtet lassen; ignorieren.
ilk *s. of his ~* seinesgleichen; Sorte *f.*
ill *a. & adv.* krank; unwohl; übel, böse; *~ at ease,* unbehaglich; ~ *s.* Übel *n.*
ill. *illustration,* Abbildung, Abd.
ill-advised *a.* schlechtberaten; unbedacht.
ill-behaved *a.* ungezogen.
ill-bred *a.* schlecht erzogen, unmanierlich.
illegal *a.,* **~ly** *adv.* gesetzwidrig.
illegality *s.* Gesetzwidrigkeit *f.*
illegible *a.* unleserlich.
illegitimacy *s.* uneheliche Geburt *f.*
illegitimate *a.,* **~ly** *adv.* unrechtmäßig; unehelich; gesetzwidrig.
ill-fated *a.* unglücklich.
ill-feeling *s.* Verstimmung *f.*
ill-humored *a.* schlechtgelaunt.
illiberal *a.,* **~ly** *adv.* engherzig; karg.
illicit *a.* unerlaubt.
illiteracy *s.* Analphabetentum *n.*
illiterate *a.* analphabetisch; ~ *s.* Analphabet *m.*
ill-judged *a.* unüberlegt.
ill luck *s.* Unglück *n.,* Pech *n.*
ill-mannered *a.* ungehobelt.
ill-matched *a.* schlecht zusammenpassend.
ill-natured *a.* bösartig.
illness *s.* Krankheit *f.*
illogical *a.,* **~ly** *adv.* unlogisch.
ill-tempered *a.* schlechtgelaunt; übellaunig.
ill-timed *a.* ungelegen.
ill-treat *v.t.* mißhandeln.
ill treatment *s.* Mißhandlung *f.*
illuminate *v.t.* erleuchten; illuminieren.
illuminating *a.* aufschlußreich.
illumination *s.* Festbeleuchtung *f.;* Erleuchtung *f.*
ill usage *s.* Mißhandlung *f.*
illusion *s.* Täuschung *f.*
illusive, illusory *a.* täuschend, trüglich.
illustrate *v.t.* erläutern; illustrieren.
illustration *s.* Erläuterung *f.;* Illustration, Abbildung *f.*
illustrative *a.,* **~ly** *adv.* erläuternd.
illustrator *s.* Illustrator(in) *m.(f.)*
illustrious *a.,* **~ly** *adv.* erlaucht.
ill-will *s.* Übelwollen *n.,* Böswilligkeit *f.*
image *s.* Bild *n.,* Bildnis *n.;* Image *n.*
imagery *s.* bildhafte Sprache *f.,* Bilder *pl.,* Metaphorik *f.*
imaginable *a.* denkbar.
imaginary *a.* eingebildet, imaginär.
imagination *s.* Phantasie *f.*
imaginative *a.* erfinderisch, phantasievoll.
imagine *v.t.* sich einbilden; ersinnen.
imbalance *s.* Unausgeglichenheit *f.;* Ungleichgewicht *n.*
imbecile *a.* schwachsinnig, idiotisch; ~ *s.* Idiot *m.*
imbibe *v.t.* einsaugen, aufsaugen.
imbroglio *s.* Verwicklung *f.*
imbue *v.t.* durchdringen, tränken; erfüllen.
imitate *v.t.* nachahmen, nachbilden.
imitation *s.* Nachahmung *f.*
imitative *a.* nachahmend.
imitator *s.* Nachahmer(in) *m.(f.)*
immaculate *a.,* **~ly** *adv.* makellos; unbefleckt.
immanent *a.* innewohnend.
immaterial *a.,* **~ly** *adv.* unkörperlich; unwesentlich.
immature *a.,* **~ly** *adv.* unreif; unzeitig.
immaturity *s.* Unreife *f.*
immeasurable *a.,* **immeasurably** *adv.* unermeßlich.
immediate *a.* unmittelbar; unverzüglich; **~ly** *adv.* sogleich.
immemorial *a.* undenklich; uralt.
immense *a.,* **~ly** *adv.* unermeßlich.
immensity *s.* Unermeßlichkeit *f.;* Ungeheuerlichkeit *f.*
immerse *v.t.* eintauchen, versenken.
immersion *s.* Eintauchen *n.;* ~ **heater** *s.* Tauchsieder *m.*

immigrant *s.* Einwanderer *m.*, Einwanderin *f.*
immigrate *v.i.* einwandern.
immigration *s.* Einwanderung *f.*
imminence *s.* Bevorstehen *n.*
imminent *a.* bevorstehend, drohend.
immobile *a.* unbeweglich.
immobility *s.* Unbeweglichkeit *f.*
immobilize *v.t.* unbeweglich machen; festlegen.
immoderate *a.*, **~ly** *adv.* unmäßig.
immodest *a.*, **~ly** *adv.* unbescheiden; unanständig.
immolate *v.t.* opfern.
immoral *a.* unsittlich; unmoralisch.
immorality *s.* Unsittlichkeit *f.*
immortal *a.*, **~ly** *adv.* unsterblich.
immortality *s.* Unsterblichkeit *f.*
immortalize *v.t.* unsterblich machen.
immovable *a.*, **immovably** *adv.* unbeweglich; **~s** *s.pl.* unbewegliche Güter *n.pl.*
immune *a.* geschützt (gegen).
immunity *s.* Freiheit *f.*; Befreiung *f.*; Vorrecht *n.*; Immunität *f.*
immunization *s.* Schutzimpfung *f.*
immunize *v.t.* immunisieren.
immunology *s.* Immunologie *f.*
immure *v.t.* einmauern.
immutable *a.*, **immutably** *adv.* unveränderlich.
imp *s.* Kobold *m.*; kleiner Schelm *m.*
impact *s.* Stoß, Aufprall *m.*
impair *v.t.* vermindern, beeinträchtigen.
impale *v.t.* pfählen; aufspießen.
impart *v.t.* mitteilen; verleihen.
impartial *a.*, **~ly** *adv.* unparteiisch.
impartiality *s.* Unparteilichkeit *f.*
impassable *a.* unpassierbar.
impasse *s.* Sackgasse *f.*
impassible *a.* gefühllos; unverletzlich.
impassioned *p.* leidenschaftlich.
impassive *a.* unempfindlich; ausdruckslos.
impatience *s.* Ungeduld *f.*
impatient *a.*, **~ly** *adv.* ungeduldig.
impeach *v.t.* anfechten; anklagen.
impeachment *s.* Anklage *f.*
impeccable *a.* untadelig, einwandfrei.
impecunious *a.* geldlos.
impede *v.t.* verhindern; behindern.
impediment *s.* Hindernis *n.*; **speech ~** *s.* Sprachfehler *m.*
impel *v.t.* antreiben.
impend *v.i.* (drohend) bevorstehen.
impenetrable *a.*, **impenetrably** *adv.* undurchdringlich; unerforschlich.
impenitent *a.*, **~ly** *adv.* unbußfertig.
imperative *a.*, **~ly** *adv.* gebieterisch; dringend nötig; ~ *s.* Imperativ *m.*
imperceptible *a.*, **imperceptibly** *adv.* unmerklich.
imperfect *a.*, **~ly** *adv.* unvollkommen; ~ *s.* (*gram.*) Imperfekt(um) *n.*
imperfection *s.* Unvollkommenheit *f.*
imperial *a.*, **~ly** *adv.* kaiserlich; Reichs...
imperialism *s.* Imperialismus *m.*
imperialist *s.* Imperialist(in) *m.(f.)*
imperil *v.t.* gefährden.
imperious *a.*, **~ly** *adv.* gebieterisch.
imperishable *a.* unverderblich, unvergänglich.
impermeable *a.* undurchlässig.
impermissible *a.* unzulässig.
impersonal *a.*, **~ly** *adv.* unpersönlich.
impersonate *v.t.* verkörpern; darstellen.
impersonation *s.* Verkörperung *f.*, Imitation *f.*
impersonator *s.* Imitator(in) *m.(f.)*
impertinence *s.* Anmassung *f.*; Unverschämtheit *f.*
impertinent *a.* frech.
imperturbable *a.* unerschütterlich.
impervious *a.* undurchlässig.
impetuosity *s.* Impulsivität *f.*
impetuous *a.*, **~ly** *adv.* ungestüm, impulsiv.
impetus *s.* Antrieb *m.*; Drang *m.*; Motivation *f.*
impiety *s.* Gottlosigkeit *f.*
impinge *v.i.* auftreffen; stoßen.
impious *a.*, **~ly** *adv.* gottlos.
impish *a.* schelmisch; lausbübisch.
implacable *a.*, **implacably** *adv.* unversöhnlich.
implant *v.t.* einpflanzen; einprägen.
implausible *a.* unglaubwürdig.
implement *s.* Zubehör *n.*; Gerät *n.*; ~ *v.t.* durchführen, erfüllen.
implementation *s.* Ausführung *f.*, Durchführung *f.*
implicate *v.t.* belasten; verwickeln.
implication *s.* Implikation *f.*, Verwicklung *f.*; Folgerung *f.*, Voraussetzung *f.*
implicit, *a.*, **~ly** *adv.* implizit; unbedingt; stillschweigend einbegriffen.
implode *v.i.* implodieren.
implore *v.t.* anflehen; erflehen.
imploring *a.* flehend.
imploringly *adv.* flehentlich.
imply *v.t.* implizieren, in sich schließen; besagen; stillschweigend einschließen.
impolite *a.* unhöflich.
impoliteness *s.* Unhöflichkeit *f.*
impolitic *a.*, **~ly** *adv.* unklug.
imponderable *a.* unwägbar; **~s** *pl.* unwägbare Dinge *n.pl.*
import *s.* Import *m.* Einfuhr *f.*; Wichtigkeit *f.*; ~ *v.t.* importieren; einführen; bedeuten.
importance *s.* Wichtigkeit *f.*
important *a.*, **~ly** *adv.* wichtig; bedeutend.
importer *s.* Einführer (von Waren) *m.*
importunate *a.*, **~ly** *adv.* zudringlich.
importune *v.t.* beschweren, belästigen.
importunity *s.* Zudringlichkeit *f.*
impose *v.t.* auferlegen (Arbeit), verhängen (Strafe); *to ~ upon*, aufdrängen.
imposing *a.* imponierend.
imposition *s.* Auferlegung *f.*; Auflage *f.*; Belastung *f.*
impossibility *s.* Unmöglichkeit *f.*
impossible *a.*, **impossibly** *adv.* unmöglich.
impost *s.* Steuer, Abgabe *f.*
impostor *s.* Betrüger *m.*
imposture *s.* Betrug *m.*
impotence *s.* Unvermögen *n.*; Impotenz *f.*
impotent *a.*, **~ly** *adv.* unvermögend, schwach; impotent.
impound *v.t.* beschlagnahmen; sperren.
impoverish *v.t.* arm machen.
impoverishment *s.* Verarmung *f.*

impracticable *a.* undurchführbar.
imprecate *v.t.* verfluchen, verwünschen.
imprecation *s.* Verwünschung *f.*
impregnable *a.*, **impregnably** *adv.* uneinnehmbar.
impregnate *v.t.* schwängern; sättigen; imprägnieren.
impress *v.t.* beeindrucken, eindrucken, einprägen.
impression *s.* Eindruck *m.;* Abdruck, Abzug *m.;* Auflage *f.*
impressionable *a.* beeinflußbar; eindrucksfähig.
impressive *a.*, **~ly** *adv.* beeindruckend; imponierend.
imprint *v.t.* prägen; einprägen; ~ *s.* Stempel *m.*
imprison *v.t.* gefangen halten; in Haft nehmen.
imprisonment *s.* Haft *f.; false ~,* ungesetzliche Gefangenhaltung *f.; one year's ~,* ein Jahr Gefängnis; *~ on remand,* Untersuchungshaft *f.*
improbability *s.* Unwahrscheinlichkeit *f.*
improbable *a.*, **improbably** *adv.* unwahrscheinlich.
impromptu *s.* Stück (*n.*) aus dem Stegrief; ~ *a.* aus dem Stegreif.
improper *a.*, **~ly** *adv.* uneigentlich; unpassend, unanständig; *~ assault,* (*jur.*) Sittlichkeitsvergehen *n.; ~ use,* Mißbrauch *m.*
impropriety *s.* Unrichtigkeit *f.;* Unschicklichkeit *f.*
improvable *a.*, **improvably** *adv.* verbesserungsfähig.
improve *v.t.* verbessern; ~ *v.i.* besser werden; Fortschritte machen.
improvement *s.* Verbesserung *f.*
improvident *a.*, **~ly** *adv.* unbedachtsam; sorglos.
improvise *v.t.* improvisieren.
imprudence *s.* Unklugheit *f.*
imprudent *a.*, **~ly** *adv.* unklug.
impudence *s.* Unverschämtheit *f.*
impudent *a.*, **~ly** *adv.* unverschämt.
impugn *v.t.* anfechten; bestreiten.
impulse, impulsion *s.* Antrieb *m.;* Stoß *m.;* Impuls *m.*
impulsive *a.* erregbar; antreibend.
impulsiveness *s.* Impulsivität *f.*
impunity *s.* Straflosigkeit *f.; with ~,* ungestraft.
impure *a.*, **~ly** *adv.* unrein, unkeusch.
impurity *s.* Unreinheit *f.;* Unkeuschheit *f.*
imputable *a.* zurechenbar.
imputation *s.* Anschuldigung *f.;* Zurechnung, Beimessung *f.*
impute *v.t.* Schuld geben; beimessen; unterstellen.
in *pr.* in, an, zu, bei, mit, auf; unter, während; *~ itself,* an und für sich; ~ *adv.* hinein, herein, drinnen.
in. *inches,* Zoll.
inability *s.* Unfähigkeit *f.; ~ to pay,* Zahlungsunfähigkeit *f.*
inaccessibility *s.* Unzugänglichkeit *f.*
inaccessible *a.*, **inaccessibly** *adv.* unzugänglich.
inaccuracy *s.* Ungenauigkeit *f.*
inaccurate *a.* ungenau.
inaction *s.* Untätigkeit *f.*
inactive *a.*, **~ly** *adv.* untätig.
inactivity *s.* Untätigkeit *f.;* Trägheit *f.*
inadequacy *s.* Unzulänglichkeit *f.*
inadequate *a.* unzulänglich.
inadmissible *a.* unzulässig.
inadvertence *s.* Unachtsamkeit *f.*
inadvertent *a.* unachtsam, **~ly** *adv.* aus Versehen; versehentlich.
inadvisable *a.* nicht ratsam, unratsam.
inalienable *a.* unveräußerlich.
inalterable *a.* unveränderlich.
inane *a.* leer, fad, geistlos.
inanimate *a.* unbeseelt; leblos; flau.
inapplicable *a.* unanwendbar.
inappreciable *a.* unbemerkbar.
inapproachable *a.* unzugänglich.
inappropriate *a.* unpassend.
inapt *a.* unpassend; ungeschickt.
inaptitude *s.* Untauglichkeit *f.*
inarticulate *a.*, **~ly** *adv.* undeutlich; unverständlich; unfähig, sich klar auszudrücken.
inasmuch *adv.* insofern, weil.
inattention *s.* Unaufmerksamkeit *f.;* Nichtbeachten (einer Vorschrift) *n.*
inattentive *a.*, **~ly** *adv.* unaufmerksam.
inaudible *a.* unhörbar.
inaugural *a.* einweihend; ~ **address** *s.* Antrittsrede *f.*
inaugurate *v.t.* einweihen.
inauspicious *a.*, **~ly** *adv.* ungünstig; unheilvoll.
inborn *a.* angeboren.
inbred *a.* angeboren, durch Unzucht erzeugt.
inbreeding *s.* Unzucht *f.*
Inc. *incorporated,* eingetragen.
incalculable *a.* unberechenbar.
incandescent *a.* weißglühend; leuchtend, strahlend. ~ **light** (Gas-) Glühlicht *n.*
incantation *s.* Bezauberung *f.*
incapability *s.* Unfähigkeit *f.*
incapable *a.* unfähig, untauglich.
incapacitate *v.t.* unfähig machen.
incapacity *s.* Unfähigkeit *f.*
incarcerate *v.t.* einkerkern.
incarnate *a.* fleischgeworden; personifiziert.
incarnation *s.* Menschwerdung *f.;* Verkörperung *f.*
incautious *a.*, **~ly** *adv.* unvorsichtig.
incendiary *s.* Brandstifter *m.;* Aufwiegler *m.;* ~ *a.* brandstifterisch; ~ **bomb** *s.* Brandbombe *f.*
incense *s.* Weihrauch *m.;* ~ *v.t.* entzünden; erzürnen.
incentive *s.* Anreiz *m.*
inception *s.* Anfang *m.*
inceptive *a.* Anfangs...
incertitude *s.* Ungewißheit *f.*
incessant *a.*, **~ly** *adv.* unaufhörlich.
incest *s.* Blutschande *f.*
incestuous *a.*, **~ly** *adv.* blutschänderisch.
inch *s.* Zoll *m.* (2.54 cm.)
incidence *s.* Vorkommen *n.;* (*phys.*) Einfall *m.*
incident *s.* Ereignis *n.;* Nebenumstand *m.*
incidental *a.* zufällig; *~ to,* gehörig zu, verbunden mit; **~s** *pl.* Nebenausgaben *f. pl.;* **~ly** *adv.* übrigens, nebenbei bemerkt.
incidental music *s.* Begleitmusik *f.*
incinerate *v.t.* verbrennen.
incinerator *s.* Verbrennungsofen *m.*
incipient *a.* anfangend; anfänglich.
incision *s.* Einschnitt *m.*
incisive *a.* einschneidend.

incisor *s.* Schneidezahn *m.*
incite *v.t.* anreizen, antreiben.
incitement *s.* Aufstachelung *f.;* Anstiftung *f.*
incivility *s.* Unhöflichkeit *f.*
incl. *inclusive, including,* einschließlich, einschl.
inclemency *s.* Unbarmherzigkeit *f.*
inclement *a.* umbarmherzig, rauh.
inclination *s.* Neigung *f.*
incline *v.t.* neigen; ~ *v.i.* sich neigen, geneigt sein; **~d plane** *s.* schiefe Ebene *f.;* ~ *s.* Neigung *f.*
include *v.t.* einschließen.
including *pr.* einschließlich.
inclusion *s.* Einschließung *f.;* Einbeziehung *f.*
inclusive *a.,* **~ly** *adv.* einschließlich; alles einbegriffen; *both dates* ~, beide Tage einbegriffen; ~ *terms pl.* Pensionspreis mit Licht und Bedienung *m.*
incognito *a.* inkognito.
incoherence *s.* Mangel an Zusammenhang *m.*
incoherent *a.,* **~ly** *adv.* unzusammenhängend.
incombustible *a.* unverbrennlich.
income *s.* Einkommmen *n.; earned* ~, Einkommen durch Arbeit; *unearned* ~, Einkommen aus Vermögen.
income tax *s.* Einkommensteuer *f.*
incoming *a.* einlaufend, eingehend; neu eintretend; **~s** *s.pl.* Eingänge *m. pl.*
incommensurable *a.* inkommensurabel.
incomparable *a.,* **incomparably** *adv.* unvergleichlich.
incompatibility *s.* Unverträglichkeit *f.*
incompatible *a.,* **incompatibly** *adv.* unvereinbar.
incompetence, incompetency *s.* Unbefugtheit *f.;* Unzulänglichkeit *f.*
incompetent *a.,* **~ly** *adv.* unzuständig; unfähig; unbefugt, unzulanglich.
incomplete *a.* unvollständig.
incomprehensibility *s.* Unbegreiflichkeit *f.*
incomprehensible *a.,* **incomprehensibly** *adv.* unbegreiflich.
inconceivable *a.,* **inconceivably** *adv.* unbegreiflich.
inconclusive *a.* nicht überzeugend; nicht schlüssig.
incongruity *s.* Ungereimtheit *f.*
incongruous *a.,* **~ly** *adv.* nicht passend, unvereinbar.
inconsequential *a.* belanglos.
inconsiderable *a.,* **inconsiderably** *adv.* unbedeutend, unwichtig.
inconsiderate *a.,* **~ly** *adv.* unbedachtsam, rücksichtslos.
inconsistency *s.* Inkonsequenz *f.;* Inkonsistenz *f.;* Widersprüchlichkeit *f.*
inconsistent *a.,* **~ly** *adv.* unvereinbar, ungereimt, widersprüchlich.
inconsolable *a.,* **inconsolably** *adv.* untröstlich.
inconspicuous *a.* unauffällig.
inconstant *a.* unbeständig.
incontestable *a.,* **incontestably** *adv.* unbestreitbar.
incontinence *s.* Zügellosigkeit *f.*
incontinent *s.* unmäßig; zügellos; inkontinent.
incontrovertible *a.* unbestreitbar; unwiderlegbar.
inconvenience *s.* Unbequemlichkeit, Lästigkeit *f.;* ~ *v.t.* belästigen.
inconvenient *a.,* **~ly** *adv.* unbequem, ungelegen; unpassend.
incorporate *v.t.* einverleiben; (*jur.*) zu einer Gesellschaft machen; ~ *a.* einverleibt; *~d company s.* (eingetragene) Aktiengesellschaft *f.*
incorporation *s.* Einverleibung *f.*
incorrect *a.,* **~ly** *adv.* falsch; fehlerhaft; ungenau.
incorrigible *a.,* **incorrigibly** *adv.* unverbesserlich.
incorruptible *a.,* **incorruptibly** *adv.* unbestechlich; unverderblich.
increase *v.i.* wachsen, zunehmen; ~ *v.t.* vergrößern; ~ *s.* Zunahme *f.*
increasing *a.* zunehmend; steigend.
incredible *a.,* **incredibly** *adv.* unglaublich.
incredulity *s.* Unglaube *m.*
incredulous *a.,* **~ly** *adv.* ungläubig.
increment *s.* Zuwachs *m.,* Zunahme *f.;* **~ value** *s.* Wertzuwachs *m.*
incriminate *v.t.* belasten; beschuldigen; **incriminating** *a.* belastend.
incubate *v.t.* brüten.
incubation *s.* Inkubation *f.*
incubator *s.* Brutkasten *m.*
incubus *s.* (*med.*) Alpdrücken *n.;* (*fig.*) Schreckgespenst *n.*
inculcate *v.t.* einschärfen, einprägen.
inculpate *v.t.* beschuldigen, tadeln.
incumbent *a.* obliegend; gegenwärtig.
incunabula *s.pl.* Wiegendrucke *m. pl.*
incur *v.t.* auf sich laden, sich zuziehen; *to ~ debts,* Schulden machen; *to ~ a fine,* in eine Geldstrafe verfallen; *to ~ an obligation,* eine Verpflichtung eingehen.
incurable *a.,* **incurably** unheilbar.
incursion *s.* Einfall, Streifzug *m.*
indebted *p. & a.* verschuldet; verpflichtet.
indebtedness *s.* Verschuldung *f.*
indecency *s.* Unanständigkeit *f.*
indecent *a.,* **~ly** *adv.* unanständig.
indecipherable *a.* nicht zu entziffern.
indecision *s.* Unentschlossenheit *f.*
indecisive *a.* unschlüssig; nicht entscheidend.
indecisiveness *s.* Unentschlossenheit *f.*
indecorous *a.* unanständig.
indeed *adv.* in der Tat, allerdings.
indefatigable *a.,* **indefatigably** *adv.* unermüdlich.
indefensible *a.* unhaltbar.
indefinable *a.* unbestimmbar.
indefinite *a.,* **~ly** adv. unbestimmt, unbeschränkt.
indelible *a.,* **indelibly** *adv.* unauslöschlich.
indelicacy *s.* Mangel (*m.*) an Zartgefühl.
indelicate *a.* geschmacklos; ungehörig.
indemnification *s.* Entschädigung *f.*
indemnify *v.t.* schadlos halten.
indemnity *s.* Absicherung *f.;* Schadenersatz *m.*
indent *v.t.* auszacken; einkerben; (Zeile) einrücken.
indentation *s.* Kerbe *f.;* Einschnitt *m.*
indenture *s.* Vertrag *m.;* Lehrbrief *m.;* ~ *v.t.* verdingen.
independence *s.* Unabhängigkeit *f.*
independent *a.,* **~ly** *adv.* unabhängig.

indescribable *a.* unbeschreiblich.
indestructible *a.* unzerstörbar.
indeterminate *a.*, **~ly** *adv.* unbestimmt.
index *s.* Anzeiger *m.*; Zeigefinger *m.*; Register *n.*; Index *m.*; ~ *v.t.* registrieren.
India *s.* Indien *n.*
Indian *a.* indisch; indianisch; **American** ~ *s.* Indianer(in) *m.(f.)*
Indian corn *s.* Mais *m.*
Indian Ocean *s.* Indischer Ozean *m.*
Indian summer *s.* Nachsommer *m.*; Altweibersommer *m.*
india rubber *s.* Gummi *m.* or *n.*, Kautschuk *m.*
indicate *v.t.* anzeigen; erkennen lassen.
indication *s.* Anzeichen *n.*
indicative *a.*, **~ly** *adv.* anzeigend; ~ *s.* (*gram.*) Indikativ *m.*
indicator *s.* Anzeiger *m.*
indict *v.t.* schriftlich anklagen, belangen.
indictable *a.* (*jur.*) klagbar.
indictment *s.* Anklagebeschluß *m.*
indifference *s.* Gleichgültigkeit *f.*
indifferent *a.*, **~ly** *adv.* gleichgültig; unparteiisch; leidlich; mäßig.
indigence *s.* Armut, Dürftigkeit *f.*
indigenous *a.* eingeboren.
indigent *a.*, **~ly** *adv.* dürftig; arm.
indigestible *a.* unverdaulich.
indigestion *s.* Verdauungsbeschwerde *f.*; Magenverstimmung *f.*
indignant *a.*, **~ly** *adv.* entrüstet; indigniert.
indignation *s.* Entrüstung *f.*
indignity *s.* Unwürdigkeit.
indirect *a.* mittelbar, indirekt.
indirect object *s.* indirektes Objekt *n.*
indirect speech *s.* indirekte Rede *f.*
indiscernible *a.* nicht zu unterscheiden.
indiscipline *s.* Zuchtlosigkeit *f.*
indiscreet *a.*, **~ly** *adv.* unbedachtsam; unbescheiden; indiskret.
indiscretion *s.* Unbedachtsamkeit *f.*; Unbescheidenheit *f.*; Indiskretion *f.*
indiscriminate *a.*, **~ly** *adv.* nicht unterschieden, unbedingt; ohne Unterschied.
indispensable *a.*, **indispensably** *adv.* unentbehrlich, unerlässlich.
indisposed *a.* unpässlich, abgeneigt.
indisposition *s.* Unpässlichkeit *f.*
indisputable *a.*, **indisputably** *adv.* unbestreitbar.
indissoluble *a.*, **indissolubly** *adv.* unauflöslich.
indistinct *a.*, **~ly** *adv.* undeutlich; ohne Unterschied.
indistinguishable *a.* ununterscheidbar.
indite *v.t.* abfassen, schreiben.
individual *a.*, **~ly** *adv.* einzeln, persönlich; ~ *s.* Individuum *n.*, Person *f.*
individuality *s.* Individualität *f.*
indivisible *a.*, **indivisibly** *adv.* unteilbar.
indocile *a.* ungelehrig.
indoctrinate *v.t.* indoktrinieren.
indolence *s.* Trägheit *f.*
indolent *a.*, **~ly** *adv.* träge.
indomitable *a.* unbezähmbar.
Indonesia *s.* Indonesien *n.*
Indonesian *a.* indonesisch; ~ *s.* Indonesier(in) *m.(f.)*
indoor *a.* im Hause; ~ **pool** *s.* Hallenbad *n.*
indoors *adv.* im Hause, drinnen.
indubitable *a.*, **indubitably** *adv.* unzweifelhaft.
induce *v.t.* bewegen, veranlassen; (*elek.*) induzieren.
inducement *s.* Beweggrund, Anlaß *m.*
induction *s.* Einführung *f.*; Induktion *f.*
inductive *a.*, **~ly** *adv.* bewegend; folgerungsmäßig; Induktions...
indulge *v.t.* nachsichtig sein, nachgeben; ~ *v.i.* frönen.
indulgence *s.* Nachsicht *f.*; Ablaß *m.*; *plenary* ~, vollkommener Ablaß *m.*
indulgent *a.*, **~ly** *adv.* nachsichtig.
industrial *a.* industriell, Gewerbe...; ~ *court*, Arbeitsgericht *n.*; ~ *dispute*, Arbeitsstreit *m.*; ~ *exhibition*, Gewerbeausstellung *f.*
industrious *a.*, **~ly** *adv.* fleißig.
industry *s.* Fleiß *m.*; Industrie *f.*
inebriate *v.t.* betrunken machen, (*fig.*) berauschen.
inebriated *a.* betrunken; (*fig.*) berauscht.
inebriety *s.* Trunkenheit *f.*
inedible *a.* ungenießbar.
ineffable *a.*, **ineffably** *adv.* unaussprechlich.
ineffaceable *a.* unauslöschlich.
ineffective, ineffectual *a.*, **~ly** *adv.* unwirksam.
inefficiency *s.* Unfähigkeit *f.*
inefficient *a.* unwirksam, untüchtig.
ineligible *a.* nicht wählbar.
inept *a.* unbeholfen; albern.
ineptitude *s.* Unbeholfenheit *f.*, Albernheit *f.*
inequality *s.* Ungleichheit *f.*
inequitable *a.* ungerecht.
inert *a.*, **~ly** *adv.* träge; reglos.
inertia *s.* (*phys.*) Trägheit *f.*
inescapable *a.* unausweichlich.
inessential *a.* unwesentlich.
inestimable *a.*, **inestimably** *adv.* unschätzbar.
inevitability *s.* Unvermeidlichkeit *f.*
inevitable *a.*, **inevitably** *adv.* unvermeidlich.
inexact *a.* ungenau.
inexcusable *a.*, **inexcusably** *adv.* nicht zu entschuldigen.
inexhaustible *a.* unerschöpflich.
inexorable *a.*, **inexorably** *adv.* unerbittlich.
inexpediency *s.* Unzweckmäßigkeit *f.*
inexpedient *a.* unzweckmäßig, unpassend.
inexpensive *a.* nicht kostspielig; billig, preiswert.
inexperience *s.* Unerfahrenheit *f.*
inexperienced *a.* unerfahren.
inexpert *a.* unerfahren, ungeübt.
inexplicable *a.*, **inexplicably** *adv.* unerklärlich.
inexpressible *a.* unaussprechlich.
inextinguishable *a.* unauslöschlich.
inextricable *a.* unentwirrbar.
infallibility *s.* Unfehlbarkeit *f.*
infallible *a.*, **infallibly** *adv.* unfehlbar.
infamous *a.*, **~ly** *adv.* verrufen, ehrlos.
infamy *s.* Ehrlosigkeit, Schande *f.*; Infamie *f.*
infancy *s.* frühe Kindheit *f.*
infant *s.* Säugling *m.*, (kleines) Kind *n.*; Unmündige *m.*; ~ *mortality*, Säuglingssterblichkeit *f.*
infanta *s.* Infantin *f.*
infanticide *s.* Kindesmord *m.*

infantile *a.* kindlich; kindisch; ~ *paralysis,* spinale Kinderlähmung *f.*
infantry *s.* Infanterie *f.*, Fußvolk *n.*
infatuate *v.t.* betören.
infatuated *a.* betört, bezaubert.
infatuation *s.* Verblendung, Betörung *f.*
infeasible *a.* unausführbar.
infect *v.t.* anstecken; infizieren.
infection *s.* Ansteckung *f.*; Infektion *f.*
infectious *a.*, **~ly** *adv.* ansteckend; infektiös.
infer *v.t.* schließen; folgern, herleiten.
inference *s.* Folgerung *f.*
inferior *a.* untergeordnet; niedriger; minderwertig; ~ *s.* Untergebene *m.*
inferiority *s.* Minderwertigkeit *f.*; Unterlegenheit *f.*
infernal *a.* höllisch.
inferno *s.* Inferno *n.*
infertile *a.* unfruchtbar.
infertility *s.* Unfruchtbarkeit *f.*
infest *v.t.* befallen; heimsuchen.
infidel *a.* ungläubig; ~ *s.* Ungläubige *m./f.*
infidelity *s.* Untreue *f.*; Unglaube *m.*
infighting *s.* interne Machtkämpfe *m. pl.*
infiltrate *v.i.* einsickern; infiltrieren.
infiltrator *s.* Eindringling *m.*
infinite *a.*, **~ly** *adv.* unendlich.
infinitive *s.* (*gram.*) Infinitiv *m.*
infinitude, infinity *s.* Unendlichkeit *f.*
infirm *a.* kraftlos, schwach; gebrechlich.
infirmary *s.* Krankenstube *f.*
infirmity *s.* Schwäche *f.*
inflame *v.t.* anzünden; sich entzünden.
inflammable *a.* entzündlich.
inflammation *s.* Entzündung *f.*
inflammatory *a.* entzündend; aufreizend.
inflatable *a.* aufblasbar.
inflate *v.t.* aufblasen, aufblähen.
inflated *a.* aufgeblasen; geschwollen.
inflation *s.* Aufblähung *f.*; Aufgeblasenheit *f.*; Inflation *f.*
inflationary *a.* inflationär.
inflect *v.t.* beugen; flektieren.
inflection *s.* Beugung *f.*
inflexible *a.*, **inflexibly** *adv.* unbeugsam.
inflict *v.t.* auferlegen, verhängen.
influence *s.* Einfluß *m.*; ~ *v.t.* Einfluß üben auf, einwirken, beeinflussen.
influential *a.* einflußreich.
influenza *s.* Influenza, Grippe *f.*
influx *s.* Einfließen *n.*; Zufluß *m.*
inform *v.t.* benachrichtigen; ~ *v.i.* (*against*) angeben, denunzieren.
informal *a.*, **~ly** *adv.* zwanglos; formlos.
informant *s.* Informant(in) *m.(f.)*
information *s.* Unterweisung *f.*; Nachricht *f.*; Auskunft *f.*; *for (your)* ~, zur Kenntnisnahme.
informative *a.* informativ.
informed *a.* informiert.
informer *s.* Informant(in) *m.(f.)*
infrared *a.* infrarot.
infrastructure *s.* Infrastruktur *f.*
infrequent *a.* selten, ungewöhnlich.
infringe *v.t.* übertreten, verletzen.
infringement *s.* Übertretung *f.*; Verstoß *m.*
infuriate *v.t.* wütend machen.
infuse *v.t.* aufgießen, einflößen.
infusion *s.* Aufguß (Tee) *m.*
ingenious *a.*, **~ly** *adv.* einfallsreich.
ingenuity *s.* Einfallsreichtum *m.*
ingenuous *a.* unbefangen; offen; bieder.
inglorious *a.*, **~ly** *adv.* unrühmlich.
ingot *s.* Metallbarren *m.*
ingrained *a.* eingefleischt.
ingratiate *v.t.* beliebt machen.
ingratiating *a.* schmeichlerisch.
ingratitude *s.* Undankbarkeit *f.*
ingredient *s.* Bestandteil *m.*; Zutat *f.*
inhabit *v.t.* bewohnen.
inhabitable *a.* bewohnbar.
inhabitant *s.* Einwohner *m.*
inhale *v.t.* einatmen; inhalieren.
inharmonious *a.* unharmonisch.
inhere *v.i.* anhaften, innewohnen.
inherent *a.* anhaftend; eigen.
inherit *v.t.* erben; bekommen.
inheritance *s.* Erbschaft *f.*; Erbgut *n.*; *law of* ~, Erbrecht *n.*
inhibit *v.t.* hindern; verbieten.
inhibited *a.* gehemmt.
inhospitable *a.*, **inhospitably** *adv.* ungastlich.
inhuman(e) *a.*, **~ly** *adv.* unmenschlich.
inhumanity *s.* Unmenschlichkeit *f.*
inimical *a.* schädlich.
inimitable *a.*, **inimitably** *adv.* unnachahmlich.
iniquitous *a.* unbillig, frevelhaft.
iniquity *s.* Bosheit, Ungerechtigkeit *f.*
initial *a.*, **~ly** *adv.* anfänglich; ~ *s.* Anfangsbuchstabe *m.*; ~ *v.t.* paraphieren; abzeichnen.
initiate *v.t.* einführen, einweihen; einleiten (Maßnahmen).
initiation *s.* Initiation; Einleitung; Eröffnung *f.*
initiative *a.* einleitend; ~ *s.* Initiative *f.*
inject *v.t.* einspritzen.
injection *s.* Einspritzung *f.*
injudicious *a.*, **~ly** *adv.* unverständig; unklug.
injunction *s.* Vorschrift; Verfügung *f.*
injure *v.t.* verletzen, beeinträchtigen; schädigen; *the* ~*d person,* (*jur.*) der Geschädigte *m.*
injured *a.* verletzt.
injurious *a.*, **~ly** *adv.* nachteilig.
injury *s.* Nachteil *m.*; Verletzung *f.*
injustice *s.* Ungerechtigkeit *f.*
ink *s.* Tinte *f.*; Druckerschwärze *f.*
inkling *s.* Ahnung *f.*; Wink *m.*
inkstand *s.* Tintenfaß *n.*, Schreibzeug *n.*
inky *a.* tintenbeschmiert; tintig.
inlaid *a.* eingelegt.
inland *a.* inländisch; ~ *s.* Binnenland *n.*; ~ *harbor,* ~ *port,* Binnenhafen *m.*
in-law *s.* angeheiratete Verwandte *m./f.*
inlay *v.t.ir.* einlegen.
inlet *s.* Zugang *m.*; Bucht *f.*; Einlage *f.*
inmate *s.* Insasse *m.*; Hausgenosse *m.*
inmost *a.* innerst.
inn *s.* Gasthof *m.*; Wirtshaus *n.*
innards *s. pl.* Eingeweide *pl.*; Innereien *pl.*
innate *a.*, **~ly** *adv.* angeboren.
inner *a.*, **~ly** *adv.* innerlich; geheim.
inner city *s.* Innenstadt *f.*

innermost *a.* innerst.
innkeeper *s.* Gastwirt(in) *m.(f.)*
innocence *s.* Unschuld *f.*
innocent *a.*, **~ly** *adv.* unschuldig.
innocuous *a.*, **~ly** *adv.* unschädlich.
innovate *v.i.* Neuerungen machen.
innovation *s.* Neuerung *f.*
innovator *s.* Neuerer *m.*
innuendo *s.* Wink, Fingerzeig *m.;* Andeutung *f.*
innumerable *a.*, **innumerably** *adv.* unzählig; zahllos.
inoculate *v.t.* einimpfen, impfen.
inoculation *s.* Impfung *f.*
inoffensive *a.*, **~ly** *adv.* unanstößig, arglos.
inoperative *a.* unwirksam.
inopportune *a.* ungelegen.
inordinate *a.*, **~ly** *adv.* ausschweifend.
inorganic *a.*, **~ally** *adv.* anorganisch.
in-patient *s.* stationärer Patient(in) *m.(f.)*
input *s.* (Daten) Eingabe *f.*, Input *m.;* Investition.
inquest *s.* Leichenschau *f.*
inquietude *s.* Unruhe *f.*
inquire *v.i.* sich erkundigen; untersuchen; fragen.
inquiring *a.* fragend; forschend.
inquiry *s.* Untersuchung *f.;* Nachfrage, Erkundigung *f.*
inquisition *s.* Untersuchung *f.;* Ketzergericht *n.;* Inquisition *f.*
inquisitive *a.*, **~ly** *adv.* neugierig.
inquisitiveness *s.* Neugierde *f.;* Wißbegierde *f.*
inroad *s.* Einfall *m.;* Eingriff *m.*
insane *a.*, geisteskrank, wahnsinnig.
insanitary *a.* gesundheitsschädlich, unhygienisch.
insanity *s.* Wahnsinn *m.*
insatiable *a.*, **insatiably** *adv.* unersättlich.
inscribe *v.t.* einschreiben; widmen.
inscription *s.* Inschrift *f.;* Aufschrift *f.;* Einschreibung *f.*
inscrutable *a.*, **inscrutably** *adv.* unerforschlich.
insect *s.* Insekt *n.;* **~ bite** *s.* Insektenstich *m.;* **~ repellent** *s.* Insektenpulver *n.*
insecticide *s.* Insektizid *n.*
insecure *a.*, **~ly** *adv.* unsicher.
insecurity *s.* Unsicherheit *f.*
insensate *a.* unvernünftig.
insensibility *s.* Gefühllosigkeit *f.;* Unempfindlichkeit *f.*
insensible *a.*, **insensibly** *adv.* unempfindlich; unmerklich.
insensitive *a.* unsensibel, gefühllos.
insensitiveness, insensitivity *s.* Gefühllosigkeit *f.;* Unempfindlichkeit *f.*
inseparable *a.*, **inseparably** *adv.* unzertrennlich.
insert *v.t.* einfügen, einschalten.
insertion *s.* Einfügung, Einschaltung *f.*
inset *s.* Einsatz *m.;* Einsatzbild *n.*, Einsatzkarte *f.;* Nebenbild *n.*
inshore *adv.* nahe der Küste.
inside *s.* Innenseite *f.;* *adv.* innen; *a. inner...;* Innen...; intern.
insider *s.* Insider(in) *m.(f.)*
insidious *a.*, **~ly** *adv.* hinterlistig.
insight *s.* Einsicht *f.*
insignia *s. pl.* Insignien *pl.;* Abzeichen *n. pl.*
insignificance *s.* Geringfügigkeit *f.*
insignificant *a.*, **~ly** *adv.* unbedeutend.
insincere *a.*, **~ly** *adv.* nicht aufrichtig.
insincerity *s.* Unaufrichtigkeit *f.*
insinuate *v.t.* andeuten; sich einschmeicheln.
insinuation *s.* Einschmeichelung *f.;* Unterstellung *f.;* Wink *m.*
insipid *a.*, **~ly** *adv.* geschmacklos, fade.
insist *v.i.* bestehen.
insistence *s.* Beharren, Bestehen *n.*
insole *s.* Schuheinlage *f.*
insolence *s.* Frechheit *f.*
insolent *a.* unverschämt, frech.
insoluble *a.* unlöslich; unlösbar.
insolvency *s.* Zahlungsunfähigkeit *f.*
insolvent *a.* zahlungsunfähig.
insomnia *s.* Schlaflosigkeit *f.*
inspect *v.t.* besichtigen; inspizieren; kontrollieren.
inspection *s.* Besichtigung *f.;* Inspektion *f.*
inspector *s.* Kontrolleur(in) *m.(f.)*, Inspektor(in) *m.(f.)*
inspiration *s.* Eingebung *f.;* Inspiration *f.*
inspire *v.t.* einhauchen, einflößen; begeistern; einatmen.
inspiring *a.* inspirierend.
inst. *instant, of the present month,* dieses Monats, d. M.
instability *s.* Unbeständigkeit *f.*
install *v.t.* einsetzen; installieren.
installation *s.* Installierung, Bestallung *f.;* Anlage *f.*
installment *s.* Teilzahlung *f.;* Rate *f.;* *by ~s,* in Raten.
instance *s.* dringende Bitte *f.;* Gelegenheit *f.;* Fall *m.;* Instanz *f.;* *for ~*, zum Beispiel.
instant *a.*, **~ly** *adv.* dringend; augenblicklich, sogleich; **~** *s.* Augenblick *m.*
instantaneous *a.*, **~ly** *adv.* augenblicklich.
instead *pr.* anstatt; **~** *adv.* stattdessen.
instep *s.* Spann, Rist *m.*
instigate *v.t.* aufhetzen, anstiften.
instigation *s.* Anstiftung *f.;* Initierung *f.*
instigator *s.* Anstifter(in) *m.(f.)*
instill *v.t.* einflößen.
instinct *s.* Instinkt *m.;* **~** *a.* belebt.
instinctive *a.*, **~ly** *adv.* unwillkürlich.
institute *s.* Anstalt *f.;* Institut *n.*
institution *s.* Einsetzung *f.;* Verordnung *f.;* Anstalt *f.;* Einrichtung *f.;* Institution *f.*
institutional *a.* institutionell.
instruct *v.t.* unterrichten; unterweisen; beauftragen.
instruction *s.* Unterweisung *f.;* Unterricht *m.;* Vorschrift *f.;* Auftrag *m.*
instructions *pl.* Gebrauchsanweisung *f.*
instructive *a.* lehrreich.
instructor *s.* Lehrer(in) *m.(f.)*
instrument *s.* Werkzeug *n.;* Instrument *n.*
instrumental *a.*, **~ly** *adv.* behilflich.
instrumentalist *s.* Instrumentalist(in) *m.(f.)*
insubordinate *a.* ungehorsam; aufsässig.
insubordination *s.* Ungehorsam *m.*
insubstantial *a.* dürftig; gering.
insufferable *a.*, **insufferably** *adv.* unerträglich.
insufficiency *s.* Unzulänglichkeit *f.*
insufficient a. **~ly** *adv.* unzulänglich.
insular *a.* Insel...
insularity *s.* insulare Lage *f.;* Beschränktheit *f.*

insulate *v.t.* absondern, isolieren; (*elek.*) *insulating tape*, Isolierband *n.*
insulation *s.* Isolierung *f.*
insulator *s.* Isolator *m.*
insult *v.t.* beschimpfen, beleidigen; ~ *s.* Beleidigung, Beschimpfung *f.*
insulting *a.* beleidigend.
insuperable *a.* unüberwindlich.
insupportable *a.* unerträglich.
insurable *a.* versicherungsfähig.
insurance *s.* Versicherung *f.*; ~ **broker** *s.* Versicherungsmakler *m.*; ~ **claim** *s.* Versicherungsanspruch *m.*; ~ **policy** *s.* Versicherungspolice *f.*
insure *v.t.* versichern; sichern.
insurgents *s. pl.* Aufrührer *m. pl.*
insurmountable *a.* unüberwindlich.
insurrection *s.* Aufstand *m.*
intact *a.* unberührt; unversehrt.
intake *s.* Aufnahme *f.*; Zustrom *m.*; Einlaßöffnung *f.*
intangible *a.* nicht greifbar.
integer *a.* ganze Zahl *f.*
integral *a.* ganz, vollständig.
integrate *v.t.* integrieren; eingliedern.
integration *s.* integration *f.*
integrity *s.* Vollständigkeit *f.*; Rechtschaffenheit *f.*; Integrität *f.*
intellect *s.* Verstand *m.*; Intellekt *m.*
intellectual *a.* Verstandes...; geistig; verständig; intellektuell; ~ *s.* Intellektuelle *m./f.*
intelligence *s.* Verstand *m.*, Verständnis *n.*; Einsicht *f.*; Nachricht *f.*
intelligence service *s.* Nachrichtendienst *m.*
intelligent *a.*, **~ly** *adv.* verständig, einsichtig; intelligent.
intelligible *a.*, **intelligibly** *adv.* verständlich.
intemperance *s.* Unmäßigkeit *f.*
intemperate *a.*, **~ly** *adv.* unmäßig.
intend *v.t.* beabsichtigen.
intendant *s.* Aufseher, Verwalter *m.*
intended *a.* beabsichtigt.
intending *a.* angehend; künftig.
intense *a.*, **~ly** *adv.* heftig; intensiv.
intensify *v.t.* steigern, verstärken.
intensity *s.* Heftigkeit *f.*; Intensität *f.*
intensive *a.*, **~ly** *adv.* angestrengt.
intensive care *s.* Intensivpflege *f.*
intent *a.* begierig; aufmerksam; ~ *s.* Vorhaben *n.*
intention *s.* Absicht *f.*; Intention *f.*
intentional *a.* absichtlich.
interact *v.i.* wechselwirken.
interaction *s.* Wechselwirkung *f.*
interactive *a.* interaktiv.
intercede *v.i.* dazwischen treten, vermitteln.
intercept *v.t.* abfangen; auffangen; unterbrechen.
intercession *s.* Fürsprache *f.*
interchange *v.t.* & *i.* tauschen; abwechseln; ~ *s.* Tausch, Verkehr *m.*; Abwechselung *f.*, Tauschhandel *m.*
interchangeable *a.* austauschbar.
intercom *s.* Sprechanlage *f.*
interconnect *v.t.* zusammenschalten; miteinander verbinden.
intercontinental *a.* interkontinental.
intercourse *s.* Verkehr, Umgang *m.*
interdependence *s.* gegenseitige Abhängigkeit *f.*
interdependent *a.* voneinander abhängig.
interdict *v.t.* untersagen.
interdiction *s.* Untersagung *f.*
interest *s.* Anteil *m.*; Nutzen *m.*; Zins *m.*; Zinsen *pl.*; Interesse *n.*, Belang *m.*; ~ *rate*, Zinssatz *m.*; *to bear* ~, Zinsen tragen; ~ *v.t.* angehen, beteiligen, interessieren.
interested *p.* & *a.* interessiert (*an*); eigennützig.
interesting *a.* interessant.
interface *s.* Grenzfläche *f.*; (*comp.*) Schnittstelle *f.*
interfere *v.i.* sich einmengen; stören.
interference *s.* Dazwischenkunft *f.*; Einmischung *f.*; (*phys.*) Interferenz *f.*
interim *s.* Zwischenzeit *f.*; ~ *a.* & *adv.* vorläufig, Zwischen...
interior *a.*, **~ly** *adv.* innerlich; ~ *s.* Innere *n.*; ~ **decoration** *s.* Innendekoration *f.*
interject *v.t.* einwerfen.
interjection *s.* (*gram.*) Interjektion *f.*
interlock *v.i.* ineinandergreifen.
interlope *v.i.* sich eindrängen.
interloper *s.* Eindringling *m.*
interlude *s.* Zwischenspiel *n.*
intermarriage *s.* Mischehe *f.*
intermarry *v.i.* Mischehen eingehen.
intermediary *a.* vermittelnd; ~ *s.* Vermittler *m.*
intermediate *a.*, **~ly** *adv.* dazwischenliegend, Zwischen..., Mittel...
interment *s.* Beerdigung *f.*
intermezzo *s.* (*mus.*) Intermezzo; (*fig.*) Zwischenspiel, Intermezzo *n.*
interminable *a.* unbegrenzt.
intermingle *v.t.* untermischen; ~ *v.i.* sich vermischen.
intermission *s.* Aussetzen *n.*, Pause *f.*
intermittent *a.* in Abständen auftretend.
intern *v.t.* internieren.
internal *a.*, **~ly** *adv.* innerlich; ~ *combustion engine s.* Explosionsmotor, Verbrennungsmotor *m.*
internal medicine *s.* innere Medizin *f.*
Internal Revenue Service *s.* Finanzamt *n.*
international *a.* international, zwischenstaatlich; Welt..., Völker..., ~ *call*, (*tel.*) Auslandsgespräch *n.*; ~ *law*, Völkerrecht *n.*; ~ *Monetary Fund s.* internationale Währungsfonds *m.*; ~ *relations*, *pl.* auswärtige Beziehungen *f.pl.*
internee *s.* Internierte *m.*
internment *s.* Internierung *f.*
interplay *s.* Wechselspiel *n.*
interpolation *s.* Einschiebung *f.*
interpose *v.i.* dazwischen stellen.
interpret *v.t.* dolmetschen, auslegen; interpretieren.
interpretation *s.* Auslegung *f.*; Interpretation *f.*
interpreter *s.* Dolmetscher(in) *m.(f.)*
interrelated *a.* zusammenhängend.
interrogate *v.t.* & *i.* befragen, verhören.
interrogation *s.* Verhör *n.*
interrogative *a.* fragend; ~ *s.* Fragewort *n.*
interrogatory *a.* fragend; ~ *s.* Verhör *n.*
interrupt *v.t.* unterbrechen.
interruption *s.* Unterbrechung *f.*
intersect *v.t.* & *i.* (sich) durchschneiden, sich kreuzen.
intersection *s.* Schnittpunkt *m.*; Straßenkreuzung *f.*

intersperse *v.t.* einstreuen.
interstate *a.* zwischenstaatlich.
interstice *s.* Zwischenraum *m.;* Lücke *f.*
intertwine *v.t. & i.* verflechten.
interval *s.* Zwischenraum *m.;* Pause *f.;* Abstand *m.;* Intervall *n.*
intervene *v.i.* sich einmischen; eintreten.
intervention *s.* Dazwischenkunft, Vermittlung *f.;* Einmischung, Intervention *f.*
interview *s.* Interview *n.;* Vorstellungsgespräch *n.;* Unterredung *f.;* ~ *v.t.* bei einem Besuch ausfragen, interviewen; *interviewing hours pl.* Sprechstunden (von Stellen und Behörden).
interviewee *s.* Interviewte *m./f.*
interviewer *s.* Interviewer(in) *m.(f.)*
interweave *v.t.st.* verweben.
interzonal *a.* Zwischenzonen...
intestate *adv.* ohne Testament.
intestinal *a.* intestinal; Darm...
intestine *a.* inner; **~s** *s.pl.* Eingeweide *n.*, Darm *m.*
intimacy *s.* Vertraulichkeit *f.*, Vertrautheit *f.*
intimate *s.*, **~ly** *adv.* innig; vertraut; ~ *v.t.* andeuten, anzeigen.
intimation *s.* Andeutung *f.;* Wink *m.*
intimidate *v.t.* einschüchtern.
intimidation *s.* Einschüchterung *f.*
into *pr.* in; hinein.
intolerable *a.*, **intolerably** *adv.* unerträglich.
intolerance *s.* Unduldsamkeit *f.*
intolerant *a.* unduldsam, intolerant.
intonation *s.* Tonfall *m.*
intoxicate *v.t.* berauschen; *intoxicating liquors,* berauschende Getränke *n.pl.*
intoxication *s.* Rausch *m.*
intractable *a.* unlenksam, unbändig.
intransigence *s.* Kompromißlosigkeit *f.*
intransigent *a.* unnachgiebig.
intransitive *a.* intransitiv.
intravenous *a.* intravenös.
intrepid *a.*, **~ly** *adv.* unerschrocken.
intricacy *s.* Verwicklung, Verlegenheit *f.*
intricate *a.*, **~ly** *adv.* verworren, schwierig.
intrigue *s.* Verwicklung *f.;* Intrige *f.;* ~ *v.i.* Ränke schmieden; intrigieren; faszinieren.
intriguing *a.* **~ly** *adv.* faszinierend.
intrinsic *a.*, **~ally** *adv.* inner, wesentlich.
introduce *v.t.* einführen; vorstellen.
introduction *s.* Einführung, Einleitung *f.;* Vorstellung *f.*
introductory *a.* einleitend.
introspection *s.* Selbstbeobachtung *f.*
introspective *a.* nach innen gerichtet.
introversion *s.* Introversion *f.*
introvert *s.* introvierter Mensch *m.*
introverted *a.* introvertiert.
intrude *v.i.* sich eindrängen; ~ *v.t.* aufdrängen.
intruder *s.* Eindringling *m.*
intrusion *s.* Eindringen *n.*
intrusive *a.* aufdringlich.
intuition *s.* Intuition *f.*
intuitive *a.*, **~ly** *adv.* intuitiv.
inundate *v.t.* überschwemmen.
inundation *s.* Überschwemmung *f.*
inure *v.t.* gewöhnen, abhärten.
invade *v.t.* einfallen; angreifen.
invader *s.* Angreifer(in) *m.(f.)*
invalid *a.* kränklich; dienstunfähig; ungültig; ~ *s.* Invalide *m.;* ~ **chair** *s.* Rollstuhl *m.*
invalidate *a.* ungültig machen.
invalidity *s.* Ungültigkeit *f.*
invaluable *a.* unschätzbar.
invariable *a.*, **invariably** *adv.* unveränderlich.
invasion *s.* Einfall, Angriff *m.*
invective *s.* Schmähung *f.*, Beschimpfung *f.*
inveigh *v.i.* schimpfen; schmähen.
inveigle *v.t.* verleiten, verführen.
invent *v.t.* erfinden.
invention *s.* Erfindung *f.*
inventive *a.* erfinderisch.
inventor *s.* Erfinder *m.*
inventory *s.* Verzeichnis; Inventar *n.*
inverse *a.*, **~ly** *adv.* umgekehrt.
inversion *s.* Umkehrung *f.*
invert *v.t.* umkehren; *~ed commas pl.* Anführungszeichen *n.*
invertebrate *s.* wirbelloses Tier *n.; a.* wirbellos.
invest *v.t.* bekleiden; erteilen; (eine Summe) anlegen; einschließen.; investieren.
investigate *v.t.* erforschen.
investigation before trial *s.* (*jur.*) Voruntersuchung *f.*
investigative *a.* detektivisch.
investiture *s.* Belehnung, Einsetzung *f.*
investment *s.* (Geld-) Anlage *f.;* Investition *f.*
investor *s.* Geldgeber(in) *m.(f.)*
inveterate *a.* eingefleischt; unverbesserlich; unübergehäßig; boshaft.
invidious *a.*, **~ly** *adv.* windbar.
invigorate *v.t.* stärken; beleben.
invincible *a.*, **invincibly** *adv.* unüberwindlich.
inviolable *a.*, **inviolably** *adv.* unverletzlich.
inviolate *a.* unverletzt.
invisibility *s.* Unsichtbarkeit *f.*
invisible *a.*, **invisibly** *adv.* unsichtbar.
invisible mending *s.* Kunststopferei *f.*
invitation *s.* Einladung *f.*
invite *v.t.* einladen; auffordern.
inviting *a.* einladend.
invocation *s.* Anrufung *f.*
invoice *s.* Warenrechnung, Faktura *f.;* ~ *v.t.* in Rechnung stellen.
invoke *v.t.* anrufen; sich berufen auf.
involuntary *a.*, **involuntarily** *adv.* unfreiwillig; unwillkürlich.
involve *v.t.* in sich schließen; verwickeln.
invulnerable *a.* unverwundbar.
inward *a. & adv.* **~ly** *adv.* innerlich; einwärts; ~ *s.* Innere *n.*
inwards *adv.* einwärts.
iodine *s.* Jod *n.*
ionize *v.t.* (*elek.*) ionisieren.
I.O.U. *I owe you,* ich schulde Ihnen; Schuldschein *m.*
IQ *intelligence quotient,* Intelligenzquotient, IQ.
Iran *s.* Iran *m.*
Iranian *a.* iranisch; ~ *s.* Iraner(in) *m.(f.)*
Iraq *s.* Irak *m.*
Iraqi *a.* irakisch; ~ *s.* Iraker(in) *m.(f.)*
irascible *a.* jähzornig; reizbar.
irate *a.* erzürnt, zornig.
ire *s.* Zorn *m.*

Ireland *s.* Irland *n.*
iris *s.* Regenbogenhaut, Iris *f.;* Schwertlilie *f.*
Irish *a.* irisch; **~man** *s.* Ire *m.;* **~ Republic** *s.* Irische Republik *f.;* **~ Sea** *s.* Irische See *f.;* **~woman** *s.* Irin *f.*
irk *v.t.* ärgern.
irksome *a.* ärgerlich; lästig.
iron *s.* Eisen *n.;* Bügeleisen *n.;* ~ *a.* eisern; fest; ~ *v.t.* bügeln.
ironclad *a.* gepanzert (von Schiffen).
ironic(al) *a.*, **~ally** *adv.* ironisch.
ironing board *s.* Bügelbrett *n.*
ironmonger *s.* Eisenwarenhändler *m.*
iron ore *s.* Eisenerz *n.*
ironworks *s.pl.* Eisenhütte *f.*
irony *s.* Ironie *f.*
irradiate *v.t.* bestrahlen, bescheinen.
irrational *a.*, **~ly** *adv.* unvernünftig.
irreclaimable *a.* unwiederbringlich, unverbesserlich.
irreconcilable *a.*, **irreconcilably** *adv.* unversöhnlich; unvereinbar.
irrecoverable *a.*, **irrecoverably** *adv.* unwiederbringlich; unersetzlich; **~ debts** *pl.* uneinbringliche Forderungen *f.pl.*
irredeemable *a.* unablöslich, nicht tilgbar, nicht rückzahlbar; unverbesserlich.
irreducible *a.* nicht zu verringen; nicht zu verwandeln.
irrefutable *a.*, **irrefutably** *adv.* unwiderleglich.
irregular *a.*, **~ly** *adv.* unregelmäßig.
irregularity *s.* Unregelmäßigkeit *f.*
irrelevant *a.*, **~ly** *adv.* unerheblich.
irreligion *s.* Unglaube *m.*
irreligious *a.*, **~ly** *adv.* ungläubig.
irremediable *a.*, **irremediably** *adv.* unheilbar, unersetzlich.
irremovable *a.* unabsetzbar.
irreparable *a.*, **irreparably** *adv.* nicht wiedergutzumachend; irreparabel.
irreplaceable *a.*, **irreplaceably** *adv.* unersetzlich.
irreprehensible *a.*, **irreprehensibly** *adv.* untadelhaft.
irrepressible *a.* ununterdrückbar; unbezähmbar.
irreproachable *a.*, **irreproachably** *adv.* untadelig.
irresistable *a.*, **irresistably** *adv.* unwiderstehlich.
irresolute *a.*, **~ly** *adv.* unschlüssig.
irrespective *a.*, **~ly** *adv.* ohne Rücksicht auf; ~ *of,* ungeachtet.
irresponsibility *s.* Unverantwortlichkeit *f.*
irresponsible *a.* unverantwortlich.
irretrievable *a.*, **irretrievably** *adv.* unersetzlich, unwiederbringlich.
irreverent *a.*, **~ly** *adv.* respektlos; unehrerbietig.
irrevocable *a.*, **irrevocably** *adv.* unwiderruflich.
irrigate *v.t.* bewässern.
irrigation *s.* Bewässerung *f.*
irritability *s.* Reizbarkeit *f.;* Gereiztheit *f.*
irritable *a.* reizbar.
irritant *s.* Reizmittel *n.*
irritate *v.t.* reizen; erbittern.
irritation *s.* Erbitterung *f.;* Ärger *m.*
irruption *s.* Einbruch *m.*
ISBN *international standard book number,* ISBN-Nummer.
Islam *s.* Islam *m.*
Islamic *a.* islamisch.
island *s.* Insel *f.*
islander *s.* Inselbewohner *m.*
isle *s.* Insel *f.*
isolate *v.t.* absondern; isolieren.
isolation *s.* Isolierung *f.*
isosceles *a.* gleichschenklig (Dreieck).
isotope *s.* Isotop *n.*
Israel *s.* Israel *n.*
Israeli *a.* israelisch; ~ *s.* Israeli *m.(f.)*
issuance *s.* Ausgabe *f.*
issue *s.* Ausgang *m.;* Erfolg *m.;* Notenausgabe, Emission *f.;* Nachkommen *pl.;* streitige Frage *f.;* ~ *of a paper,* Zeitungsausgabe *f.;* ~ *v.i.* herrühren, entspringen; endigen; ~ *v.t.* ergehen lassen; ausgeben, ausstellen (Wechsel).
isthmus *s.* Landenge *f.*
it *pn.* es, das; *with* ~, damit.
ital. *italics,* Kursivdruck *m.*
Italian *a.* italienisch; *s.* Italiener(in) *m.(f.)*
italic *s.* Kursivschrift *f.;* ~ *a.* kursiv.
Italy *s.* Italien *n.*
itch *s.* Jucken *n.;* Gelüst *n.;* ~ *v.i.* jucken; verlangen.
itchy *a.* juckend; kratzig.
item *adv.* desgleichen; ferner; ~ *s.* Posten *m.;* Stück *n.;* Punkt *m.*
itemize *v.t.* detaillieren.
itinerant *a.* wandernd.
itinerary *a.* reisend, wandernd; ~ *s.* Reiseroute *f.;* Reisebuch *n.*
its *pn.* sein, dessen.
itself *p.* es selbst, selbst, sich.
IUD *intrauterine device,* Intrauterinpessar.
ivory *s.* Elfenbein *n.;* ~ *a.* elfenbeinern.
ivy *s.* Epheu *m.*
Ivy League *s.* Eliteuniversitäten in USA.
IYHF *International Youth Hostel Federation,* Internationaler Jugendherbergsverband.

J

J, j der Buchstabe J oder j *n.*
J *Joule,* Joule, J.
J. *Judge,* Richter.
jab *v.t.* stossen, stechen; ~ *s.* Schlag *m.*, Stich *m.*
jabber *v.i.* schwatzen; plappern.
jack *s.* Kerl, Matrose *m.;* Bube *m.* (Karte); (*nav.*) Gösch *f.;* Sägebock *m.;* (Hand-)Winde *f.;* Bratenwender *m.;* Stiefelknecht *m.;* Flaschenzug *m.;* (*mech.*) Hebebock, Wagenheber *m.*
jackal *s.* Schakal *m.*
jackass *s.* Eselhengst *m.;* (*fig.*) Esel *m.*
jackboots *s.pl.* hohe Stiefel *m.pl.*
jackdaw *s.* Dohle *f.*
jacket *s.* Jacke *f.;* Schutzumschlag (eines Buches) *m.*

Jack-of-all-trades *s.* Hansdampf in allen Gassen; Alleskönner *m.*
jade *s.* Jade *m.*, Jadegrün *n.*; Schindmähre *f.*; **~d** *a.* erschöpft; abgestumpft; übersättigt.
jag *v.t.* kerben; ~ *s.* Kerbe *f.*; Felszacken *m.*; Zahn *m.*; Zacke *f.*
jagged *a.* zackig; zerklüftet.
jail *s.* Gefängnis *n.*; ~ *v.t.* einkerkern; einsperren.
jailbird *s.* (*fam.*) Knastbruder *m.*
jailbreak *s.* Gefängnisausbruch *m.*
jailer *s.* Gefängniswärter *m.*
jalopy *s.* (*Auto*) alte Kiste *f.*
jam *s.* Marmelade *f.*; Konfiture *f.*; *traffic* ~, Verkehrsstau *m.*; *be in a* ~, in der Klemme stecken; ~ *v.t.* zusammenpressen; (*radio*) stören.
jamboree *s.* großes Treffen *n.*; ausgelassene Feier *f.*
jam-packed *a.* vollgestopft.
Jan. *January*, Januar, Jan.
janitor *s.* Hauswart *m.*
January *s.* Januar *m.*
Japan *s.* Japan *n.*
Japanese *a.* japanisch; *s.* Japaner(in) *m.(f.)*
jape *s.* Scherz *m.*; Spaß *m.* ~*v.i.* scherzen, spaßen.
jar *v.i.* quietschen; knarren; mißtönen; ~ *s.* Krug *m.*; Topf *m.*; Ruck *m.*, Schock *m.*; Quietschen *n.*
jargon *s.* Jargon *m.*
jasmine *s.* Jasmin *m.*
jasper *s.* Jaspis *m.*
jaundice *s.* Gelbsucht *f.*
jaundiced *a.* gelbsüchtig; verbittert, zynisch.
jaunt *v.i.* herumstreifen; ~ *s.* Ausflug *m.*; Spritztour *f.*
jaunty *a.*, **jauntily** *adv.* leicht, munter.
javelin *s.* Wurfspeer *m.*
jaw *s.* Kinnbacken, Kiefer *m.*; **~s** *s.pl.* Rachen *m.*; (*mech.*) Backen *pl.*; ~ *v.t.* schimpfen, quatschen.
jawbone *s.* Kieferknochen *m.*
jay *s.* Eichelhäher *m.*; Häher *m.*
jazz *s.* Jazz *m.*; Jazzmusik *f.*; **~band** *s.* Jazzband *f.*; ~ *up*, ~ *v.t.* aufmöbeln.
JCD *Juris Civilis Doctor (Doctor of Civil Law)*, Doktor des Zivilrechts.
jealous *a.*, **~ly** *adv.* eifersüchtig; mißgünstig.
jealousy *s.* Eifersucht *f.*; Argwohn *m.*; Mißgunst *f.*; Neid *m.*
jeans *s.pl.* Jeans *pl.*
jeer *v.t. & i.* spotten; verhöhnen ~ *s.* Spott *m.*; höhnische Bemerkung *f.*; Hohngelächter *n.*; Buhruf *m.*
jejune *a.* nüchtern; fade, trocken.
jell *v.i.* gelieren; fest werden.
jelly *s.* Gallerte *f.*; Gelee *n.*; **~bean** *s.* Gelee- *or* Gummibonbon *n.*
jellyfish *s.* Qualle, Meduse *f.*
jeopardize *v.t.* gefährden; aufs Spiel setzen.
jeopardy *s.* Gefahr *f.*; *in* ~, gefährdet; *put sb./sth. in* ~, jn./etw. gefährden *or* in Gefahr bringen.
jerk *s.* Ruck *m.*; Stoß *m.*; (*fam.*) Knülch *m.*; Trottel *m.*; ~ *v.t.* ruckeln; stossen.
jerky *a.* abgehackt; holp(e)rig; ruckartig.
jerry-built *a.* unsolide *or* schlampig gebaut.
jersey *s.* Pullover *m.*; Wolljacke *f.*; Jersey *n.*
jest *s.* Scherz *m.*; ~ *v.i.* scherzen.
jester *s.* Spaßvogel *m.*; Hofnarr *m.*
Jesuit *s.* Jesuit *m.*
Jesuitical *a.*, **~ly** *adv.* jesuitisch.
jet *s.* Jet *n.*; Gagat *m.*; Wasser(Gas-)-strahl *m.*; ~ **engine** *s.* Düsentriebwerk, Strahltriebwerk *n.*; **~fighter** *s.* (*avi.*) Düsenjäger *m.*
jet black *a.* pechschwarz.
jetlag *s.* Zeitverschiebung *f.*; Jet-travel-Syndrom *n.*
jet plane *s.* Düsenflugzeug *n.*
jetsam *s.* Strandgut *n.*
jettison *v.t.* abwerfen, über Bord werfen.
jetty *s.* Hafendamm *m.*, Mole *f.*
Jew *s.* Jude *m.*; Jüdin *f.*
jewel *s.* Juwel *n.*; Edelstein *m.*, Schmuckstück *n.*
jeweler *s.* Juwelier *m.*
jewelry *s.* Juwelen *pl.*; Schmuck *n.*
Jewish *a.* jüdisch.
Jewry *s.* Judentum *n.*; das jüdische Volk *n.*
jib *s.* Fock *f.*; Ausleger *m.*; Dreharm *m.*; ~ *v.i.* bocken; scheuen.
jiff(y) *s. in a* ~, augenblicklich.
jig *s.* Gigue (Tanz) *f.*, Freudentanz *m.*; (*mech.*) (Bohr) Schablone, (Bohr) Lehre *f.*
jiggle *v.t.* wackeln; schütteln.
jilt *v.t. & i.* (den Liebhaber) sitzenlassen; (dem Liebhaber) den Laufpaß geben; **~ed** *a.* verschmäht.
jingle *v.t. & i.* klingeln, klimpern; bimmeln; ~ *s.* Geklingel *n.*; Spruch *m.*, Werbespruch *m.*
jingo *s.* Hurrapatriot, Chauvinist *m.*
jingoism *s.* Chauvinismus *m.*
jinx *s.* Pech *n.*; Unglück *n.*; Unheil *n.*; ~ *v.t.* verhexen.
jitters *s.* (*fam.*) Heidenangst *f.*; Bammel *m.*; Bibbern *n.*; Zittern *n.*
job *s.* (geringe) Arbeit *f.*; Arbeitsstück *n.*; Stelle *f.*; Job *m. odd* ~*s pl.* Gelegenheitsarbeiten *pl.*; ~ **description** *s.* Tätigkeitsbeschreibung *f.*; ~ *v.i.* Lohnarbeit tun; jobben.
jobber *s.* Stückarbeiter, Handlanger, Jobber *m.*
job hunting *s.* Arbeitssuche *f.*; (*fam.*) Stellenjagd *f.*
jobless *a.* arbeitslos, stellungslos.
jockey *s.* Jockei, Reitknecht *m.*; Betrüger *m.*; ~ *v.i.* rangeln.
jocose *a.*, **~ly** *adv.* scherzhaft.
jocular *a.*, **~ly** *adv.* spaßhaft, lustig.
jocund *a.*, **~ly** *adv.* lustig, munter.
jog *v.t.* stoßen; schütteln; ~ *v.i.* traben; joggen; ~ *s.* Schupp *m.*; Rütteln *n.*
jogger *s.* Jogger(in) *m.(f.)*
jogging *s.* Jogging *n.*; Joggen *n.*
joggle *v.t.* rütteln; ~ *v.i.* sich schütteln.
jogtrot *s.* Trott *m.*; ~ *v.i.* traben.
join *v.t.* anfügen (an), zusammenfügen, verbinden (mit), zugesellen; ~ *v.i.* sich berühren; sich verbinden; sich beteiligen; sich anschließen.
joint *a.* gemeinsam, vereinigt; ~ *s.* Verbindung *f.*; Gelenk *n.*; Fuge *f.*; Knoten *m.*; Bratenstück *n.*; ~ *v.t.* zusammenfügen; verbinden.
joint heir *s.* Miterbe *m.*
jointly *adv.* gemeinsam.
joint owner *s.* Mitinhaber *m.*
joint-stock company *s.* Aktiengesellschaft *f.*
joist *s.* Querbalken *m.*, Träger *m.*

joke *s.* Spaß, Scherz, Streich, Witz *m.;* ~ *v.i.* spaßen, Witze machen, scherzen.
jolly *a.*, **jollily** *adv.* fröhlich, lustig.
jolt *v.t. & i.* rütteln; ~ *s.* Stoß *m.*
Jordan *s.* Jordanien *n.*
Jordanian *a.* jordanisch; ~ *s.* Jordanier(in) *m.(f.)*
jostle *v.t.* anrempeln, schubsen; ~*v.i.* drängeln.
jot *s.* Iota, Pünktchen *n.;* ~ *v.t.* ~ *down* kurz niederschreiben.
jotter *s.* Notizbuch *n.*
jottings *s.* Notizen *pl.*
journal *s.* Tagebuch *n.;* Zeitschrift *f.;* Zeitung *f.*
journalism *s.* Zeitungswesen *n.;* Journalismus *m.*
journalist *s.* Journalist(in) *m.(f.)*
journey *s.* Reise *f.;* Weg *m.;* Fahrt *f.;* ~ *v.i.* reisen.
journeyman *s.* Geselle *m.*
Jove *s.* Jupiter *m.; by* ~*!* bei Gott!
jovial *a.*, **~ly** *adv.* frohsinnig, fröhlich.
joviality *s.* Frohsinnigkeit *f.*, Fröhlichkeit *f.*
jowl *s.* Backe *f.;* Hängebacke *f.;* Unterkiefer *m.; cheek by* ~, dicht zusammen.
joy *s.* Freude, Fröhlichkeit *f.*
joyful *a.* froh; freudig.
joyless *a.*, **~ly** *adv.* freudlos; griesgrämig.
joyous *a.*, **~ly** *adv.* fröhlich, erfreulich.
joystick *s.* Knüppel *m.;* Steuerknüppel *m.;* (*comp.*) Joystick *m.*
J.P. *Justice of the Peace,* Friedensrichter *m.*
Jr. *Junior,* der Jüngere, jr., jun.
jubilant *a.* frohlockend, jubelnd.
jubilation *s.* Jubel *m.*
jubilee *s.* Jubiläum *n.*
JUD *Juris Utriusque Doctor (Doctor of Canon and Civil Law),* Doktor beider Rechte.
Judaism *s.* Judaismus *m.*
judge *s.* Richter(in) *m.(f.);* Kenner(in) *m.(f.); associate* ~, Beisitzer(in) (bei Gericht) *m.(f.);* Preisrichter(in) *m.(f.);* (*sp.*) Punktrichter(in) *m.(f.)*, Kampfrichter(in) *m.(f.);* ~ *v.t. & i.* richten; (be)urteilen; entscheiden.
judgment *s.* Urteil *n.;* Urteilskraft *f.; to pronounce (pass)* ~ *on,* ein Urteil fällen.
judicature *s.* Gerichtswesen *n.*
judicial *a.*, **~ly** *adv.* gerichtlich.
judiciary *s.* Gerichtswesen *n.;* Richterstand *m.*
judicious *a.*, **~ly** *adv.* scharfsinnig, klug, umsichtig.
judo *s.* Judo *n.*
jug *s.* Krug *m.*
juggernaut *s.* (*fig.*) Moloch *m.;* schwerer Lastzug *m.*
juggle *s.* Gaukelei *f.;* ~ *v.i.* gaukeln, jonglieren; ~ *v.t.* jonglieren.
juggler *s.* Gaukler(in) *m. (f.);* Jongleur(in) *m.(f.)*
jugular *s.* Halsader *f.*, Drosselvene *f.*, Jugularvene *f.*
juice *s.* Saft *m.*
juicy *a.* saftig; (*story*) pikant; (*scandal*) gepfeffert.
jukebox *s.* Musikbox *f.*
Jul. *July,* Juli.
July *s.* Juli *m.*
jumble *v.t.* vermengen, verwirren, kunterbunt vermischen, durcheinander werfen; ~ *s.* Mischmasch *m.;* ~ **sale** *s.* Ramschverkauf *m.*
jump *v.i.* springen, hüpfen; stoßen (vom Wagen); ~ *v.t.* überspringen; ~ *s.* Sprung *m.; high* ~, Hochsprung *m.; long* ~, Weitsprung *m.*
jumper *s.* Trägerrock *m.;* Trägerkleid *n.;* Springer *m.;* ~ **cable** *s.* Starthilfekabel *n.*
jumpy *a.* nervös.
Jun. *June,* Juni.
junction *s.* Kreuzung *f.;* Vereinigung *f.;* Knotenpunkt *m.* (mehrerer Eisenbahnen).
juncture *s.* Verbindung *f.;* Gelenk *n.;* Fuge *f.;* (kritischer) Zeitpunkt *m.*
June *s.* Juni *m.*
jungle *s.* Dschungel *m.*
junior *a.* jünger; Unter...
juniper *s.* Wacholder *m.;* ~ **berry** *s.* Wacholderbeere *f.*
junk *s.* Trödel *m.;* Gerümpel *n.;* Dschunke *f.*
junta *s.* Junta *f.*
Jupiter *s.* Jupiter *m.*
juridical *a.*, **~ly** *adv.* gerichtlich, juristisch.
jurisdiction *s.* Gerichtsbarkeit *f.;* Rechtssprechung, Zuständigkeit *f.; lack of* ~, Unzuständigkeit (des Gerichts).
jurisdictional *a.* Gerichtsbarkeits..., Zuständigkeits...
jurisprudence *s.* Rechtswissenschaft *f.;* (univ.) Jura *n.*
jurist *s.* Rechtsgelehrte *m.;* Jurist *m.*
juror *s.* Geschworene *m./f.*
jury *s.* Geschworenen *m.pl.;* **~box,** Geschworenenbank *f.;* **~member** *s.* Geschworene *m./f.*
just *a.* gerecht, rechtschaffen; richtig, gehörig; vollständig; ~ *adv.* eben, bloß, gerade, fast, genau.
justice *s.* Gerechtigkeit *f.;* Recht *n.;* Justiz *f. to administer (dispense)* ~, Recht sprechen; *to bring a criminal to* ~, einen Verbrecher vor Gericht bringen.
justifiable *a.* berechtigt; **justifiably** *adv.* zu rechtfertigen, berechtigterweise.
justification *s.* Rechtfertigung, Verteidigung, Entschuldigung *f.*
justify *v.t.* rechtfertigen, verteidigen.
justly *adv.* mit Recht, zu Recht; genau, gerecht, gerechterweise.
justness *s.* Rechtmäßigkeit, Gerechtigkeit *f.*
jut *v.i.* (also ~ **out**) hervorragen, überhängen; (her)vorstehen, heranragen, hinausragen.
jute *s.* Jute *f.*
juvenile *a.* jung, jugendlich; (*pej.*) kindisch, unreif; ~ *s.* Jugendliche *m./f.;* ~ **court** *s.* Jugendgericht *n.;* ~ **delinquency** *s.* Jugendkriminalität *f.;* ~ **delinquent** *s.* jugendliche(r) Straftäter(in) *m.(f.)*
juxtapose *v.t.* nebeneinanderstellen; gegeneinanderhalten.
juxtaposition *s.* Nebeneinanderstellung *f.*

K

K, k der Buchstabe K oder k *n.*
k. *kilogram,* Kilogramm, k, kg.
kale *s.* Grünkohl *m.*
kaleidoscope *s.* Kaleidoskop *n.*
kangaroo *s.* Känguruh *n.*
kayak *s.* Kajak *m.*
K.C. *Knight Commander,* Komtur, Großmeister *m.; King's Counsel,* Justizrat *m.*
keel *s.* Kiel *m.;* Kielraum *m.;* ~ **over** *v.i.* umkippen; kentern.
keen *a.,* **~ly** *adv.* scharf, spitzig; eifrig; heftig; scharfsinnig; *~ edge,* scharfe Schneide *f.; ~ on sth.,* hinter etwas her, auf etwas erpicht.
keenness *s.* Schärfe *f.;* Eifer *m.;* Begeisterung *f.*
keep *v.t.ir.* halten; behalten; erhalten; aufbewahren; führen (Laden); hüten; unterhalten; beobachten; feiern; fortfahren; ~ *v.i.* sich halten, dauerhaft sein; sich aufhalten, bleiben; *he ~s repeating,* er wiederholt dauernd *or* immer wieder; *to ~ well,* sich weiter gut befinden, gesund bleiben; *to ~ away,* abhalten, sich fern halten, wegbleiben; *to ~ house,* den Haushalt führen; *to ~ in touch,* in Verbindung bleiben; *to ~ off,* abhalten; davonbleiben; *to ~ on,* dabei bleiben, fortfahren; aufbehalten (*hat*); anbehalten (*dress*); *to ~ up,* aufrecht erhalten; unterhalten, sich erhalten; Schritt halten.
keeper *s.* Aufseher(in) *m.(f.);* (*animal*) Wärter(in) *m.(f.);* Aufpasser(in) *m.(f.);* Hüter(in) *m.(f.)*
keeping *s.* Gewahrsam *m.; in ~ with,* in Übereinstimmung (*f.*) *or* Einklang (*m.*) mit.
keepsake *s.* Andenken *n.*
keg *s.* Fäßchen *n.*
kelp *s.* Seetang *m.*
ken *s.* Gesichtskreis *m.;* Kenntnis *f.*
kennel *s.* Hundehütte *f.;* Hundezwinger *m.;* Hundeheim *n.*
Kenya *s.* Kenia *n.*
Kenyan *a.* kenianisch; ~ *s.* Kenianer(in) *m.(f.)*
kerbstone *s.* Bordstein *m.;* Randstein *m.*
kerchief *s.* Kopf-, Halstuch *n.*
kernel *s.* Kern *m.*
kerosene *s.* Kerosin (Brennöl) *n.*
ketchup *s.* Ketchup *m.* or *n.*
kettle *s.* Kessel *m.*
kettledrum *s.* Kesselpauke *f.*
key *s.* Schlüssel *m.;* Tonart *f.;* Taste *f.;* (for map) Zeichenerklärung *f.;* (*mech.*) Keil *m.;* ~ **position,** Schlüsselstellung *f.;* **~way,** *s.* (*mech.*) Nute *f.*
keyboard *s.* Tastatur *f.;* Klaviatur *f.;* Keyboard *n.;* (of organ) Manual *n.*
keyhole *s.* Schlüsselloch *n.*
key in *v.t.* (*computer*) eintippen, eingeben.
keynote *s.* Grundton *m.;* ~ **speech** *s.* programmatische Rede *f.*
key signature *s.* (*mus.*) Vorzeichen *n.;* Tonartbezeichnung *f.*
keystone *s.* Schlußstein *m.*
keyword *s.* Schlüsselwort *n.*
kibbutz *s.* Kibbuz *m.*
kick *v.t. & i.* mit dem Fuße stoßen, treten, ausschlagen; kicken; strampeln; ~ *s.* Tritt, Stoß *m.*
kid *s.* Kitz *n.,* Zicklein *n.;* Kind *n.*
kid gloves *s.pl.* Glacéhandschuhe *m.pl.*
kidnap *v.t.* kidnappen, entführen.
kidnapper *s.* Entführer(in) *m.(f.);* Kidnapper(in) *m.(f.)*
kidnapping *s.* Entführung *f.,* Kidnapping *n.*
kidney *s.* Niere *f.*
kidney bean *s.* Weiße Bohne *f.;* Gartenbohne *f.*
kidney machine *s.* künstliche Niere *f.*
kidney stone *s.* Nierenstein *m.*
kill *v.t.* töten, schlachten; umbringen; *she was ~ed in an automobile accident,* sie ist bei einem Autounfall ums Leben gekommen; *he ~ed himself,* er brachte sich um, er nahm sich (*dat.*) das Leben; *to ~ time,* die Zeit totschlagen; *to ~ weeds,* Unkraut vernichten.
killer *s.* Mörder(in) *m.(f.)*
killer whale *s.* Schwertwal *m.*
killing *a.* tödlich; vernichtend; *~ s.* Erlegen *n.;* Tötung *f.; to make a ~,* einen Riesengewinn machen.
killjoy *s.* Spielverderber *m.*
kiln *s.* Brenn-, Darrofen *m.*
kilo *s.* Kilo *n.*
kilt *s.* Kilt *m.,* Schottenrock *m.*
kin *s.* Familie *f.,* Verwandte *f.,* Verwandtschaft *f.;* ~ *a.* verwandt.
kind *s.* Art *f.;* Gattung *f.;* Sorte *f.; payment in ~,* Naturalleistung, *f.;* ~ *a.,* **~ly** *adv.* gütig, liebreich; nett; freundlich; liebenswürdig.
kindergarten *s.* Kindergarten. *m.*
kindle *v.t.* anzünden; entwachen, wecken; ~ *v.i.* sich entzünden.
kindling *s.* Anmachholz, Anzündholz *n.*
kindly *a.* gütig, freundlicherweise, nett.
kindness *s.* Güte, Freundlichkeit *f.*
kindred *s.* Verwandtschaft, Schwägerschaft *f.;* ~ *a.* verwandt; *~ spirit,* Gleichgesinnte(r) *f.(m.)*
kinetic *a.* kinetisch.
king *s.* König *m.*
kingdom *s.* Königreich *n.;* Reich *n.*
kingfisher *s.* Eisvogel *m.*
kink *s.* Knick *m.* (im Draht); Schleife *f.* (im Tau); (*fig.*) Schrulle *f.;* Sparren *m.*
kinky *a.* abartig; schrallig; spleenig; (Haar) wellig.
kinsfolk *s.* Sippe *f.,* Verwandten *pl.*
kinship *s.* Verwandtschaft *f.*
kinsman *s.* Verwandte *m.*
kinswoman *s.* Verwandte *f.*
kipper *s.* geräucherter Bückling *m.*
kiss *v.t.* küssen; ~ *s.* Kuß *m.*
kit *s.* Ausrüstung *f.;* Werkzeug *n.;* **~bag** *s.* Tornister *m.*
kitchen *s.* Küche *f.;* ~ **appliances,** *pl.* Küchenartikel *m.pl.;* ~ **garden,** Gemüsegarten *m.;* ~ **maid,** Küchenmädchen *n.*
kitchenette *s.* Kleinküche *f.;* Kochnische *f.*
kite *s.* Gabelweih *m.;* Papierdrache *m.*
kith *s. ~ and kin,* Freunde und Verwandte; Kind und Kegel.

kitten *s.* Kätzchen *n.*
kitty *s.* Kätzchen *n.;* Mieze *f.*
km. *kilometer,* Kilometer, km.
Kn *knot,* Knoten, kn.
knack *s.* Kunstgriff *m.;* Geschick *n.*
knacker *s.* Abdecker *m.*
knapsack *s.* Tornister *m.;* Rucksack *m.*
knave *s.* Schurke *m.;* Bube (in der Karte) *m.*
knavish *a.,* **~ly** *adv.* schurkisch.
knead *v.t.* kneten, massieren.
knee *s.* Knie *n.* **~cap** *s.* Kniescheibe *f.;* **~-deep** *a.* knietief; **~ joint** *s.* Kniegelenk *n.*
kneel *v.i.ir.* knien; **~ down** niederknien, sich hinknien.
knell *s.* Totenglocke *f.*
knickerbockers *s.pl.* Kniehosen *f.pl.*
knickers *s.pl.* Schlüpfer *m.*
knick-knacks *s.pl.* Schnickschnack *m.*
knife *s.* Messer *n.;* **~ edge** *s.* Schneide *f.;* ~ *v.t.* einstechen, erstechen.
knife rest *s.* Messerbänkchen *n.*
knight *s.* Ritter *m.;* Springer (im Schach) *m.;* ~ *v.t.* adeln, zum Ritter schlagen.
knight errant *s.* fahrender Ritter *m.*
knighthood *s.* Ritterwürde *f.*
knightly *a. n. adv.* ritterlich.
knit *v.t. & r. ir.* stricken; knüpfen; runzeln; **~ together** *v.i.* verwachsen, zusammenwachsen.
knitting *s.* Stricken *n.;* Strickzeug *n.*
knitting needle *s.* Stricknadel *f.*
knitwear *s.* Strickwaren *f.pl.*
knob *s.* Knopf *m.,* Knauf *m.,* Griff *m.*
knock *v.t. & i.* klopfen, pochen; schlagen, stoßen, anstoßen; *to ~ about,* sich umhertreiben, herumziehen; *to ~ down,* umwerfen, zu Boden schlagen; zuschlagen (bei Versteigerungen); *~-down price,* äußerster Preis, Taxe (bei Versteigerungen); **~-kneed** *a.* x-beinig; **~-knees** *pl.* X-Beine *n.pl.; to ~ off,* mit der Arbeit aufhören; Schluß machen; ~ *s.* Schlag *m.;* Anklopfen *n.*
knocker *s.* Türklopfer *m.*
knoll *s.* kleiner Hügel *m.*
knot *s.* Knoten *m.;* Verspannung *f.;* Schleife *f.;* Baumast, Baumknorren *m.;* Schwierigkeit *f.;* Seemeile *f.;* ~ *v.t.* verknüpfen; verknoten.
knotty *a.,* **~ily** *adv.* knorrig; knotig; verwickelt.
know *v.t. & i.st.* wissen, kennen; erkennen; können; *to let me ~,* mich benachrichtigen; mich wissen lassen; *to get to ~,* erfahren.
know-how *s.* praktische Kenntnis *f.;* Sachkenntnis *f.*
knowing *p. & a.* bewußt, kundig, bewandert; schlau; wissend.
knowingly *adv.* wissentlich.
knowledge *s.* Wissen *n.;* Kenntnis *f.;* Wissenschaft *f.;* Erkenntnis *f.;* Bekanntschaft *f.; to the best of my ~ and belief,* nach bestem Wissen und Gewissen; *it is common ~,* es ist allgemein bekannt.
knuckle *s.* Knöchel *m.;* Hachse, Haxe *f.; ~ of veal, s.* Kalbshaxe *f.*
knuckle-duster *s.* Schlagring *m.*
KO *knockout,* Knockout, K.o.
koala *s.* Koala *m.*
kook *s.* (*fam.*) Spinner *m.*
kooky *a.* komisch, verrückt.
Koran *s.* Koran *m.*
Korea *s.* Korea *n.*
Korean *a.* koreanisch; ~ *s.* Koreaner(in) *m.(f.)*
kosher *a.* koscher.
kph *kilometer(s) per hour,* Stundenkilometer, km/h.
Kremlin *s.* Kreml *m.*
kudos *s.* Lob *n.;* Ehre *f.*
kV *kv, kilovolt,* Kilovolt, kV.
kW *kw, kilowatt,* Kilowatt, kW.

L

L, l der Buchstabe L oder l *n.*
L *large,* groß; *Lake,* See.
L., £ *libra, pound sterling,* Pfund (sterling) *n.*
l. *left,* links, l.; *line,* Zeile, z; *liter,* Liter, l.
LA *Los Angeles.*
lab *s.* Labor *n.*
label *s.* Etikett *n.;* Schild *n.;* Zettel *m.;* Aufschrift *f.;* Anhänger *m.;* Aufkleber *m.;* ~ *v.t.* mit Zettel versehen, mit Aufschrift/Schild/Anhänger/Aufkleber versehen.
labial *s.* Labial, Lippenlaut *m.;* ~ *a.* labial.
labor *s.* Arbeit *f.;* Mühe *f.;* Wehe, Geburtswehe *f.;* ~ *v.i.* arbeiten; sich abmühen; sich quälen; *to be in ~,* in den Wehen liegen; *to go into ~,* die Wehen bekommen.
laboratory *s.* Laboratorium *n.*
laborer *s.* Arbeiter *m.;* Hilfsarbeiter *m.;* landwirtschaftlicher Arbeiter, Tagelöhner *m.*
labor exchange *s.* Arbeitsamt *n.*
labor force *s.* Arbeiterschaft *f.;* Belegschaft *f.*
laborious *a.,* **~ly** *adv.* arbeitsam, mühsam; umständlich.
labor union *s.* Gewerkschaft *f.*
laburnum *s.* (*bot.*) Goldregen *m.*
labyrinth *s.* Labyrinth *n.*
lace *s.* Schnur *f.;* Spitze, Tresse *f.;* Schnürband *n.;* ~ *v.t.* zuschnüren; (Finger) ineinander verschlingen.
lacerate *v.t.* verletzen, aufreißen, zerfetzen..
laceration *s.* Rißwunde *f.;* Schnittwunde *f.;* Verletzung *f.*
lachrymal *a.* Tränen...
lachrymose *a.* weinerlich.
lack *v.i.* bedürfen, nicht haben; fehlen; ~ *s.* Mangel *m.*
lackadaisical *a.* lustlos; nachlässig.
lackey *s.* Lakai *m.*
lackluster *a.* matt; glanzlos; stumpf; langweilig.
laconic *a.* lakonisch; knapp.
lacquer *s.* Lack *m.;* ~ *v.t.* lackieren.
lacuna *s.* Lakune, Lücke *f.*
lad *s.* Bursche, Knabe, Junge *m.*
ladder *s.* Leiter *f.*
laden *a.* beladen (mit).
la-di-da *a.* affektiert; (*fam.*) affig.

ladle *s.* Schöpflöffel *m.;* ~ *v.t.* schöpfen, ausschöpfen, auslöffeln; (*fig.*) austeilen.
lady *s.* Dame *f.;* Gemahlin *f.*, Herrin *f.;* **~bug,** Marienkäfer *m.;* **~-killer** *s.* Herzensbrecher *m.*
ladylike *a.* damenhaft; wohlerzogen.
lag *v.i.* zögern; zurückbleiben; ~ *s.* Zeitabstand *m.;* Verzögerung *f.*
lager *s.* helles Bier, Lagerbier *n.*
laggard *a.* träge, langsam; ~ *s.* Zauderer *m.;* Nachzügler *m.;* Trödler *m.*
lagoon *s.* Lagune *f.*
laid-back *a.* gelassen.
lair *s.* Lager *n.;* Bau *m.;* Höhle *f.;* Unterschlupf *m.;* Schlupfwinkel *m.*
laity *s.* Laienstand *m.*, Laien *pl.*
lake *s.* See *m.*
Lake Constance *s.* Bodensee *m.*
lama *s.* Lama *n.*
lamb *s.* Lamm *n.;* ~ *v.i.* lammen.
lambaste *v.t.* (*fam.*) fertigmachen; verprügeln.
lamblike *a.* lammartig; sanft.
lame *a.* lahm; (*fig.*) faul, schwach; ~ *v.t.* lähmen.
lameness *s.* Lähmung *f.*
lament *v.i.* klagen, jammern; ~ *v.t.* beklagen, beweinen; ~ *s.* Wehklage *f.*
lamentable *a.*, **lamentably** *adv.* kläglich; beklagenswert, erbärmlich.
lamentation *s.* Wehklage *f.*, Klagelied *n.*
laminated *a.* lamelliert.
lamp *s.* Lampe *f.;* Laterne *f.;* Scheinwerfer *m.*
lampoon *s.* Schmähschrift *f.*
lamppost *s.* Laternenpfahl *m.*
lamprey *s.* Neunauge *n.*
lampshade *s.* Lampenschirm *m.*
lance *s.* Lanze *f.;* ~ **corporal** *s.* Gefreiter *m.;* ~ *v.t.* aufstechen, aufschneiden, öffnen.
lancet *s.* Lanzette *f.;* Spitzbogen *m.*
land *s.* Land *n.;* Landschaft, Länderei *f.;* Boden *m.;* Grundstück *n.;* ~ *v.t. & i.* landen.
landed *a.* Land..., Grund...
land forces *s.pl.* Landmacht *f.*, Landstreitkräfte *pl.*
landing *s.* Landung *f.;* Treppenabsatz, Flur, Gang *m.;* *forced* ~, (*avi.*) Notlandung *f.;* **~-stage** *s.* Landungsbrücke *f.;* **~-strip** Landebahn *f.*
landlady *s.* Hauswirtin; Gastwirtin *f.*
landlord *s.* Gutsbesitzer *m.;* Gastwirt *m.;* Hauswirt *m.*
landlubber *s.* Landratte *f.*
landmark *s.* Grenzstein *m.;* Markstein *m.*
landowner *s.* Grundbesitzer *m.*
land register *s.* Grundbuch *n.*
land registry *s.* Grundbuchamt *n.*
landscape *s.* Landschaft *f.*
landslide *s.* Erdrutsch *m.;* ~ **victory** *s.* überwältigender Sieg *m.*
land tax *s.* Grundsteuer *f.*
lane *s.* Heckengang *m.;* Gasse *f.;* Spur *f.;* Weg *m.;* Feldweg *m.;* Schiffahrtsweg *m.*
language *s.* Sprache *f.;* Ausdrucksweise *f.*
languid *a.*, **~ly** *adv.* matt, langsam, müde, träge, lässig.
languish *v.t.* schmachten; (*fig.*) danieder liegen.
languor *s.* Mattigkeit *f.;* Trägheit *f.;* Lauheit *f.;* Schläfrigkeit *f.;* Schwüle *f.*
languorous *a.* einschläfernd, schläfrig, schwül; (*mus.*) schmelzend.
lank, lanky *a.*, **~ly** *adv.* schlank; dünn; mager.
lantern *s.* Laterne *f.*
lap *s.* Schoß *m.;* Runde *f.;* ~ *v.t.* wickeln, einwickeln; lecken, auflecken; ~ *v.i.* plätschern.
lap dog *s.* Schoßhund *m.*
lapel *s.* Revers *n.;* Aufschlag *m.*
lapse *s.* Fehler, Fehltritt *m.;* Ablauf *m.;* Verfall *m.;* Versehen *n.;* Verlauf *m.;* time ~, Zeitablauf *m.;* ~ *v.i.* ablaufen; fallen; verfließen; verfallen.
laptop *s.* Laptop *n.*
larceny *s.* Diebstahl *m.*
larch *s.* Lärche *f.*
lard *s.* Schmalz, Schweinefett *n.;* ~ *v.t.* spicken.
larder *s.* Speisekammer *f.*, Speiseschrank *m.*
large *a.*, **~ly** *adv.* groß; weit, breit; stark; reichlich; *at* ~, in Freiheit.
lark *s.* Lerche *f.;* Schabernack *m.*
larkspur *s.* Rittersporn *m.*
larva *s.* Larve *f.*
laryngitis *s.* Kehlkopfentzündung *f.*
larynx *s.* Kehlkopf *m.*
lascivious *a.*, **~ly** *adv.* wollüstig, geil, laszig, lüstern, schlüpfrig.
laser *s.* Laser *m.*
laser beam *s.* Laserstrahl *m.*
laser printer *s.* Laserdrucker *m.*
lash *s.* Hieb, Peitschenhieb *m.;* Schnur *f.;* Geißel *f.;* Rute *f.;* Augenwimper *f.;* ~ *v.t.* peitschen; schlagen; ~ **out** *v.i.* ausschlagen.
lass *s.* Mädchen *n.*
lassitude *s.* Mattigkeit, Trägheit *f.*
last *a.* letzte, äußerste; vorig; *at* ~, endlich; **~ly** *adv.* zuletzt; schließlich; ~ *s.* Leisten *m.;* ~ *v.i.* währen, dauern; sich halten.
last-ditch *a.* allerletzt; ~ **attempt** *s.* letzter verzweifelter Versuch *m.*
lasting *p. & a.* **~ly** *adv.* dauernd; dauerhaft; haltbar; anhaltend.
lastly *adv.* zuletzt, zum Schluß.
lat. *Latitude,* Breite *f.*
latch *s.* Reigel, Schnappriegel *m.*, Schnappschloß *n.;* ~ *v.t.* verriegeln; zuklinken; einschnappen.
latchkey *s.* Wohnungsschlüssel, Hausschlüssel *m.*
late *a. & adv.* spät, letzt; (von Zügen) verspätet; *to arrive* ~ *for sth.*, zu etw. zu spät ankommen; *my friends tend to be* ~, meine Freunde haben oft Verspätung; ehemalig; neulich; verstorben; *of* ~, neulich.
latecomer *s.* Zuspätkommende *m./f.*
lately *adv.* neulich, kürzlich.
latency *s.* Latenz *n.*
lateness *s.* Verspätung *f.;* Zuspätkommen *n.;* spätes Eintreten *n.*
latent *a.* verborgen, latent; ~ **heat** *s.* gebundene Wärme *f.*
later *a. & adv.* später.
lateral *a.*, **~ly** *adv.* seitlich; Quer...
latest *a.* spätest; letzt.
lath *s.* Latte *f.;* ~ *v.t.* belatten.
lathe *s.* Drehbank *f.*
lather *s.* Seifenschaum *m.;* ~ *v.i.* schäumen; ~ *v.t.* einseifen.
Latin *a.* lateinisch; ~ *s.* Latein *n.*
Latin America *s.* Lateinamerika *n.*

Latin American *a.* lateinamerikanisch; ~ *s.* Lateinamerikaner(in) *m.(f.)*
latitude *s.* Breite *f.*; Spielraum *m.*; Freiheit *f.*
latter *a.* letztere (von zweien), spätere; *the ~ half,* die zweite Hälfte.
lattice *s.* Gitter *n.*; ~ *v.t.* vergittern.
Latvia *s.* Lettland *n.*
Latvian *a.* lettisch; ~ *s.* Lette *m.*; Lettin *f.*
laudable *a.*, **laudably** *adv.* lobenswert.
laudatory *a.* lobend.
laugh *v.i.* lachen; *to ~ off,* mit einem Lachen abtun; ~ *s.* Gelächter *n.*
laughable *a.* lächerlich, lachhaft.
laughing gas *s.* Lachgas *n.*
laughingstock *s.* Gegenstand *m.* des Gelächters *or* des Gespötts.
laughter *s.* Gelächter *m.*
launch *v.t.* schleudern; loslassen; vom Stapel lassen; in Gang setzen; ~ *v.i.* sich aufmachen; ~ *s.* Stapellauf *m.*; Barkasse *f.*; Einführung *f.*
launching: ~ **pad** *s.* Abschußrampe *f.*; ~ **site** *s.* Abschußbasis *f.*
launder *v.t.* (Wäsche) waschen.
laundromat *s.* Waschsalon *m.*
laundry *s.* Wäsche *f.*; Wäscherei *f.*
Laureate *s. poet ~,* Hofdichter
laurel *s.* Lorbeer, Lorbeerbaum *m.*
lava *s.* Lava *f.*
lavatory *s.* Toilette *f.*
lavender *s.* Lavendel *m.*
lavish *a.*, **~ly** *adv.* großzügig, üppig; reich; überschwenglich; verschwenderisch; ~ *v.t.* überhäufen, überschütten.
law *s.* Gesetz *n.*; Recht *n.*; Prozeß *m.*; Rechtswissenschaft *f.*
law-abiding *a.* gesetzestreu.
law court *s.* Gerichtshof *m.*
law firm *s.* Anwaltsfirma *f.*
lawful *a.*, **~ly** *adv.* gesetzmäßig; rechtmäßig.
lawless *a.*, **~ly** *adv.* gesetzlos; **~ness** *s.* Gesetzwidrigkeit *f.*, Gesetzlosigkeit *f.*
lawn *s.* Rasen *m.*, Rasenplatz *m.*; Batist *m.*
lawnmower *s.* Rasenmäher *m.*
lawn tennis *s.* Rasentennis *n.*
lawsuit *s.* Rechtsstreit, Prozeß *m.*; Klage *f.*
lawyer *s.* (Rechts)Anwalt *m.*, (Rechts)Anwältin *f.*
lax *a.*, **~ly** *adv.* schlaff, locker.
laxative *s.* Abführmittel *n.*; ~ *a.* abführend, laxativ.
laxity *s.* Schlaffheit *f.*
lay *v.t.* legen, stellen; verlegen; ausbreiten; *to ~ by,* zurücklegen (Geld); *to ~ in,* sich eindecken; *to ~ off,* entlassen; *to ~ out,* anlegen (Garten); *to ~ the table,* den Tisch decken; *to ~ up,* abtakeln; *to be laid up,* krank im Bett liegen; ~ *a.* weltlich, Laien...; ~ **brother,** Laienbruder *m.*
layer *s.* Lage, Schicht *f.*; Ableger *m.*
layette *s.* Babywäsche *f.*, Babyausstattung *f.*
layman *s.* Laie *m.*
layoff *s.* Entlassung *f.*; Feierschichten *n.*
layout *s.* Anlage (Garten, etc.) *f.*; Layout *n.*
laze *v.i.* faulenzen.
laziness *s.* Faulheit *f.*, Trägheit *f.*
lazy *a.*, **lazily** *adv.* faul, träge.
lazybones *s.* Faulenzer(in) *m.(f.)*, Faulpelz *m.*
lb. *libra, pound,* Pfund *n.*
l.c. *loco citato,* am angeführten Orte.
L/C *letter of credit,* Kreditbrief *m.*
LCD *liquid crystal display,* Flüssigkristallanzeige.
lea *s.* Wiese, Fläche *f.*; Wiesengrund *m.*
lead *s.* Blei *n.*; Lot, Senkblei *n.*
lead *v.t.ir.* führen, leiten; verleiten; ~ *v.i.* vorangehen; **leading** *a.* führend, erste, vornehmste, Haupt...; ~ *s.* Führung, Leitung *f.*; Vorsprung *m.*; Hinweis *m.*, Tip *m.*
leaden *a.* bleiern.
leader *s.* Führer *m.*; Leitartikel *m.*; Vorsitzende *m./f.*, Befehlshaber *m.*
leadership *s.* Führung *f.*; Leitung *f.*; Vorsitz *m.*, Führungseigenschaften *pl.*
lead-free *a.* bleifrei.
leading *a.* führend; leitend; vorderste.
leading question *s.* Suggestivfrage *f.*
lead pencil *s.* Bleistift *m.*
lead poisoning *s.* Bleivergiftung *f.*
lead story *s.* Titelgeschichte *f.*, Hauptartikel *m.*
leaf *s.* Blatt *n.*; Türflügel *m.*; **gold ~,** Blattgold *n.*; ~ *v.i.* Blätter bekommen.
leafless *s.* blätterlos.
leaflet *s.* Blättchen *n.*, Zettel *m.*
leafy *a.* belaubt.
league *s.* Bund *m.*, Bündnis *n.*; Liga *f.*; Meile *f.* (4.8 km.); ~ *v.i.* sich verbünden.
leak *s.* Leck *m.*; Durchsickern (von Geheimnissen) *n.*; ~ *v.i.* leck sein; undicht sein; ausströmen, auslaufen, tropfen; (*fig.*) *to ~ out,* durchsickern.
leakage *s.* Auslaufen *n.*; Austreten *n.*; Durchsickern *n.*
leaky *a.* leck.
lean *v.i.ir.* sich lehnen; sich neigen; tendieren; ~ *v.t.* anlehnen; ~ *a.*, **~ly** *adv.* mager, dünn, schlank.
leaning *s.* Neigung, Richtung *f.*
leanness *s.* Hagerkeit *f.*; Magerkeit *f.*
leap *v.t.st.* springen, hüpfen; ~ *s.* Sprung *m.*
leapfrog *s.* Bockspringen *n.*; ~ *v.i.* bockspringen.
leap year *s.* Schaltjahr *n.*
learn *v.i.* & t. lernen; erfahren.
learned *a.*, **~ly** *adv.* gelehrt; erfahren.
learner *s.* Lerner(in) *m.(f.)*
learning *s.* Gelehrsamkeit *f.*; Lernen *n.*
lease *s.* Pacht *f.*; Miete *f.*; ~ *v.t.* verpachten.
leasehold *s.* Pachtung *f.*; Pacht...
leash *s.* (Koppel)leine *f.*; Koppel *f.*; ~ *v.t.* koppeln.
least *a.* geringste, kleinste, wenigste; ~ *adv.* am wenigsten; *at ~,* wenigstens.
leather *s.* Leder *n.*
leathery *a.* ledern.
leave *s.* Erlaubnis *f.*; Urlaub, Abschied *m.*; ~ *v.t.ir.* lassen; verlassen; hinterlassen; ~ *v.i.ir.* aufhören; abreisen, weggehen.
leaven *s.* Sauerteig *m.*; ~ *v.t.* säuern, treiben, auflockern; **~ing** *s.* Treibmittel *n.*; Auflockerung *f.*
Lebanese *a.* libanesisch; ~ *s.* Libanese *m.*; Libanesin *f.*
Lebanon *s.* Libanon *m.*
lecherous *a.* lüstern; geil.
lechery *s.* Wollust *f.*, Lüsternheit *f.*, Geilheit *f.*
lectern *s.* Lesepult *n.*

lecture *s.* Vorlesung *f.*; Strafpredigt *f.*, Vortrag *m.*; ~ *v.t.* abkanzeln; ~ *v.i.* Vorlesungen, Vorträge halten; ~ **room,** Vorlesungsraum *m.*
lecturer *s.* Vortragende *m./f.*; Dozent(in) *m.(f.)*
ledge *s.* Leiste *f.*; Kante *f.*; Fensterbrett *n.*; Vorsprung *m.*; Sims *m.*
ledger *s.* (*com.*) Hauptbuch *n.*
lee *s.* (*nav.*) Leeseite *f.*
leech *s.* Blutegel *m.*
leek *s.* Lauch *m.*
leer *s.* anzügliches Grinsen *n.*; heimtückischer Blick *m.*; ~ *v.i.* schielen.
lees *s.pl.* Bodensatz *m.*
leeway *s.* Abtrift *f.*
left *p.* von *to leave,* übrig; *to be ~ till called for,* zur Aufbewahrung; post-lagernd; ~ *a.* link; *~-hand side,* linke Seite; ~ *s.* Linke (in der Politik) *f.*; *adv.* links.
left-handed *a.* linkshändig.
leftovers *s.pl.* Reste *pl.*; Überbleibsel *pl.*
left-wing *a.* links, dem linken Flügel angehörend.
leg *s.* Bein *n.*; Keule *f.*; Stiefelschaft *m.*; *~ of mutton, veal, etc.*, Hammelkeule, Kalbskeule *f.*; *three-legged, four-legged, etc.*, dreibeinig, vierbeinig.
legacy *s.* Vermächtnis *n.*; Erbe *n.*
legal *a.*, **~ly** *adv.* legal; gesetzlich; rechtmäßig; zulässig; ~ **action,** Klage *f.*; ~ **remedy,** Rechtsmittel *n.*, Rechtshilfe *f.*; ~ **status,** Rechtsstellung *f.*; ~ **tender,** gesetzliches Zahlungsmittel *n.*
legality *s.* Gesetzlichkeit *f.*; Rechtmäßigkeit *f.*; Legalität *f.*
legalize *v.t.* rechtskräftig machen; legalisieren.
legate *s.* (päpstlicher) Legat *m.*
legation *s.* Gesandtschaft *f.*
legend *s.* Legende *f.*; Sage *f.*; Zeichenerklärung *f.*
legendary *a.* sagenhaft; legendär.
legerdemain *s.* Taschenspielerei *f.*
leggings *s.pl.* Leggings *pl.*, Gamaschen *f.pl.*
leggy *a.* langbeinig.
legibility *s.* Lesbarkeit *f.*
legible *a.*, **legibly** *adv.* leserlich, lesbar.
legion *s.* Legion *f.*; Menge *f.*
legislation *s.* Gesetzgebung *f.*
legislative *a.* gesetzgebend; ~ **body,** gesetzgebende Körperschaft *f.*
legislator *s.* Gesetzgeber *m.*
legislature *s.* Legislative *f.*
legitimacy *s.* Legitimität *f.*; Ehelichkeit *f.*, Rechtmäßigkeit *f.*
legitimate *a.*, **~ly** *adv.* zulässig, richtig; ehelich; rechtmäßig; berechtigt; begründet.
legitimization *s.* Gültigmachung *f.*; Ausweis *m.*; Ehelichkeitserklärung *f.*
legitimize *v.t.* legitimieren.
legroom *s.* Beinfreiheit *f.*
leisure *s.* Muße *f.*; Freizeit *f.*
leisurely *a. & adv.* mit Muße, gemächlich, geruhsam.
lemon *s.* Zitrone *f.*; ~ **yellow,** Zitronengelb *n.*
lemonade *s.* Limonade *f.*
lend *v.t.ir.* leihen, verleihen, borgen.
lender *s.* Verleiher(in) *m.(f.)*
lending library *s.* Leihbibliothek *f.*
length *s.* Länge *f.*; Strecke *f.*; *at ~*, zuletzt, endlich; *a ~ of carpet,* ein Stück Teppich; *a trouser ~*, eine Hosenlänge (von Stoff).
lengthen *v.t. & i.* verlängern.
lengthwise *a.* Längen-, Längs-; ~ *adv.* der Länge nach.
lengthy *a.* lange; weitschweifig.
leniency *s.* Milde, Nachsicht *f.*
lenient *a.* nachsichtig, mild.
lens *s.* (Glas) Linse *f.*
Lent *s.* Fastenzeit *f.*
lentil *s.* Linse *f.*
leopard *s.* Leopard *m.*
leotard *s.* Trikot *n.*
leper *s.* Aussätzige *m./f.*; Leprakranke *m./f.*
leprosy *s.* Aussatz *m.*; Lepra *f.*
leprous *a.* leprös.
lesbian *s.* Lesbierin *f.*; *a.* lesbisch.
lesion *s.* (*med.*) Verletzung *f.*
less *a. & adv.* kleiner, weniger, geringer.
lessee *s.* Pächter(in) *m.(f.)*
lessen *v.t. & i.* vermindern; abnehmen.
lesser *a.* kleiner, weniger; geringer.
lesson *s.* Lektion, Stunde *f.*; Lehre *f.*; Unterricht *m.*
lessor *s.* Verpächter *m.*
lest *c.* damit... nicht; daß.
let *v.t.ir.* lassen; gestatten; vermieten, verpachten; *rooms to ~*, Zimmer zu vermieten; ~ **alone,** geschweige denn; ~ **down,** *v.t.* im Stich lassen, ~ **in** *v.t.* herein lassen; ~ **out** *v.t.* hinaus-, herauslassen; ~ **up** *v.i.* aufhören.
lethal *a.* tödlich, Toten...
lethargic *a.* lethargisch, träge.
lethargy *s.* Trägheit *f.*; Lethargie *f.*
letter *s.* Buchstabe *f.*; (*print.*) Type *f.*; Brief *m.*; *by ~*, brieflich; **~s** *s.pl.* Literatur *f.*
letter box *s.* Briefkasten *m.*
letterhead *s.* Briefkopf *m.*; Geschäfts(brief)papier *n.*
lettuce *s.* Kopfsalat *m.*
leucocyte *s.* Leukozyt *m.*; weißes Blutkörperchen *n.*
leukemia *s.* Leukämie *f.*
levee *s.* Morgenempfang *m.*; Schutzdamm (*m.*) an Flüssen.
level *a.* gleich, eben, flach; gestrichen; auf gleicher Höhe (mit); waagerecht; (meas.) ~ *s.* Fläche *f.*; Niveau *n.*; Höhenlage *f.*; Wasserwaage *f.*; Pegel *m.*; ~ *v.t.* gleichmachen; ebnen; nivellieren; richten; abreißen.
level crossing *s.* schienengleicher Bahnübergang *m.*
lever *s.* Hebel *m.*
leverage *s.* Hebelkraft *f.*
levity *s.* Leichtsinn *m.*
levy *v.t.* einziehen; auferlegen; erheben; ausheben; ~ *s.* Aushebung *f.*; Erhebung *f.*; Steuer *f.*
lewd *a.*, **~ly** *adv.* geil; lüstern; unanständig.
lexicon *s.* Wörterbuch *n.*, Lexikon *n.*
liability *s.* Verantwortlichkeit *f.*; Haftbarkeit, Haftung *f.*, Verbindlichkeit *f.*; Haftpflicht *f.*; *limited ~ s.* beschränkte Haftung *f.*; **liabilities** *pl.* Passiva *s.pl.*; *~ of kin,* Sippenhaftung *f.*
liable *a.* ausgesetzt; haftbar; *to be ~*, haften; *~ to duty,* zollpflichtig; *to render oneself ~ to prosecution,* sich strafbar machen; *we are ~ to get*

lost in the forest, wir können uns im Wald leicht verlieren.
liaison *s.* (*mil.*) Verbindung *f.;* Liaison *f.;* ~ **officer** *s.* Verbindungsoffizier *m.*
liar *s.* Lügner(in) *m.(f.)*
libel *s.* Verleumdung *f.;* ~ *v.t.* beschimpfen; verleumden.
libelous *s.* ehrenrührig, verleumderisch.
liberal *a.,* **~ly** *adv.* freisinnig; freigebig; großzügig, reichlich; liberal (polit.); ~ **arts,** geisteswissenschaftliche Fächer; ~ **education,** Allgemeinbildung *f.*
liberality *s.* Großzügigkeit *f.;* Liberalität *f.*
liberate *v.t.* befreien.
liberation *s.* Befreiung *f.*
liberator *s.* Befreier(in) *m.(f.)*
libertine *a.* ausschweifend; ~ *s.* Wüstling, Libertin *m.*
liberty *s.* Freiheit *f.*
libidinous *a.* unzüchtig, lüstern, triebhaft; libidinös.
Libra *s.* (*astro.*) Waage *f.*
librarian *s.* Bibliothekar(in) *m.(f.)*
library *s.* Bibliothek *f.,* Bücherei *f.*
libretto *s.* Libretto *n.*
Libya *s.* Libyen *n.*
Libyan *a.* libysch; *s.* Libyer(in) *m.(f.)*
license *s.* Freiheit, Erlaubnis *f.;* Genehmigung *f.;* Lizenz *f.;* Zügellosigkeit *f.;* Konzession *f.;* *under ~ from the Government,* mit Regierungskonzession; *to take out a ~,* sich eine Konzession verschaffen; **~d** *p.* mit Konzession; ~ *v.t.* genehmigen.
licensee *s.* Lizenz-, Konzessionsinhaber, Lizenzträger *m.*
licentious *a.,* **~ly** *adv.* ausschweifend.
lichen *s.* Flechte *f.*
lick *v.t.* lecken; plätschern; prügeln.
licking *s.* Tracht Prügel *f.*
licorice *s.* Süßholz *n.;* Lakritze *f.*
lid *s.* Deckel *m.;* Augenlid *n.*
lie *s.* Lüge *f.;* Lage *f.;* ~ *v.i.* lügen; ~ *v.i.st.* liegen; ruhen.
liege *s.* Lehnsherr *m.;* Lehnsmann *m.*
lien *s.* Pfandrecht *n.*
lieu *s. in ~ of,* statt, anstatt (von *or* dessen).
Lieut., Lt. *Lieutenant,* Leutnant *m.*
lieutenant *s.* Leutnant *m.;* ~ **colonel** *s.* Oberstleutnant *m.*
life *s.* Leben *n.;* Lebensbeschreibung *f.;* Lebhaftigkeit *f.;* Lebensdauer (eines Abkommens, einer Maschine, etc.); *for ~,* auf Lebenszeit; ~ **interest** (*jur.*) lebenslänglicher Nießbrauch *m.*
life annuity *s.* Lebensrente *f.*
life belt *s.* Rettungsgürtel *m.*
lifeboat *s.* Rettungsboot *n.*
lifeguard *s.* Rettungsschwimmer *m.*
life insurance *s.* Lebensversicherung *f.*
life jacket *s.* Schwimmweste *f.*
lifeless *a.,* **~ly** *adv.* leblos; (*fig.*) lahm; langweilig; teilnahmslos.
lifelong *a.* lebenslang.
lifesaving *a.* lebensrettend.
life sentence *s.* lebenslange Freiheitsstrafe *f.*
life-size *a.* lebensgroß.
life support *s.* Lebenserhaltung *f.*
lifetime *s.* Lebenszeit *f.*
lift *v.t.* heben, aufheben; erheben, hochheben; entwenden; ~ *v.i.* sich heben, sich heben lassen; *to ~ off,* starten abheben; ~ *s.* Heben *n.;* Hebewerkzeug *n.;* Aufzug, Fahrstuhl *m.,* Lift *m.*
ligament *s.* Band *n.;* Flechse *f.*
ligature *s.* Band *n.;* Bindung *f.;* Ligatur, Binde *f.*
light *s.* Licht *n.;* Beleuchtung *f.;* *will you give me a ~?,* kann ich Feuer haben?; ~ *v.t.r. & ir.* leuchten, erleuchten, anzünden; beleuchten; *to ~ on, v.i.* sich niederlassen auf; geraten auf; ~ *a. & adv.,* **~ly** *adv.* leicht; licht, hell; leichtsinnig; **~-blue, ~-brown,** hellblau, hellbraun, etc.; ~ **reading** *s.* Unterhaltungslektüre *f.*
light bulb *s.* Glühbirne *f.*
lighted *a.* brennend; beleuchtet.
lighten *v.t.* erleuchten; erleichtern; lichten; löschen.
lighter *s.* Anzünder *m.;* Feuerzeug *n.*
lightheaded *a.* benommen, angeheitert.
light-hearted *a.* fröhlich; scherzhaft; unbeschwert; heiter.
lighthouse *s.* Leuchtturm *m.*
lighting *s.* Beleuchtung *f.*
light metal *s.* Leichtmetall *n.*
lightmeter *s.* Lichtmesser, Belichtungsmesser *m.*
lightness *s.* Leichtigkeit, Leichtheit, Erleichterung *f.*
lightning *s.* Blitz *m.;* ~ **war** *s.* Blitzkrieg *m.*
lightning conductor, lightning rod *s.* Blitzableiter *m.*
lights *pl.* Lunge (der Tiere als Speise) *f.*
lightweight *s.* Leichtgewicht (Boxen) *n.;* ~ *a.* leicht.
ligneous *a.* hölzern; holzig.
lignite *s.* Braunkohle *f.,* Lignit *m.*
likable *a.* liebenswert, sympatisch.
like *a. & adv.* gleich, ähnlich; fast; *it's just ~ him,* das sieht ihm ähnlich; ~ *s.* Gleiche, Ebenbild *n.;* ~ *v.t. & i.* mögen, gefallen, belieben; gern haben.
likelihood *s.* Wahrscheinlichkeit *f.*
likely *a. & adv.* wahrscheinlich.
liken *v.t.* vergleichen (mit).
likeness *s.* Gleichheit *f.;* Ebenbild *n.*
likewise *adv.* gleichfalls.
liking *s.* Gefallen *n.,* Belieben *n.;* Geschmack *m.,* Vorliebe *f.,* Zuneigung *f.*
lilac *s.* Flieder *m.;* (color) Lila *n.;* ~ *a.* lila, fliederfarben.
lilt *s.* munterer Rhythmus *m.;* singender Tonfall *m.*
lily *s.* Lilie *f.;* *~ of the valley,* Maiglöckchen *n.*
limb *s.* Glied *n.;* Ast *m.*
limber *a.* geschmeidig; gelenkig; ~ **up** auflockern, Lockerungsübungen machen, sich warm machen.
limbo *s.* Vorhölle *f.;* Übergansstadium *n.,* Zwischenstadium *n.;* Vergessenheit *f.;* *in ~,* in der Schwebe, in der Luft.
lime *s.* Leim *m.;* Kalk *m.;* Linde *f.;* Limone *f.;* ~ **juice** Limonensaft *m.;* ~ **tree,** Lindenbaum *m.;* Limonenbaum *m.*
limelight *s. in the ~,* im Rampenlicht stehen.
limerick *s.* Limerick *m.*
limestone *s.* Kalkstein *m.*
limit *s.* Grenze *f.;* Schranke, Beschränkung, Begrenzung *f.;* (*com.*) Limite *f.;* *off ~s,* Zutritt

gesperrt; *that is the* ~, das ist die Höhe; ~ *v.t.* beschränken; ~*ed company,* Gesellschaft mit beschränkter Haftung; ~ *in scope,* von beschränktem Umfang; *there's a* ~! alles hat seine Grenzen!
limitation *s.* Beschränkung, Einschränkung *f.;* (*jur.*) Verjährung *f.; period of* ~, Verjährungsfrist *f.; statute of* ~*s,* Verjährungsgesetz *n.*
limitless *a.* grenzenlos.
limp *a.* schlaff; welk; schlapp; matt; ~ *v.i.* hinken; ~ *s.* Hinken, Humpeln *n.*
limpid *a.* klar, durchsichtig.
linchpin *s.* Kernstück *n.;* Achsennagel *m.;* Stütze *f.*
line *s.* Linie, Zeile *f.;* Eisenbahnlinie *f.;* Telephonleitung, elektrische Leitung *f.;* Leine *f.;* Reihe *f.;* Schlange *f.;* Vers *m.;* Geschäftszweig *m.;* Äquator *m.;* Stamm *m.;* Art und Weise *f.; in the direct* ~, in gerader Linie (verwandt); *in the* ~ *of communications,* (*mil.*) Zufuhrstraße, Verbindungslinie *f.;* ~ *v.t.* liniieren; einfassen, füttern; *to* ~ *up,* sich in einer Reihe aufstellen, sich zusammenschließen; *to stand in* ~, Schlange stehen; **~up** *s.* Formierung *f.;* Zusammenschluß *m.*
lineage *s.* Abstammung *f.;* Geschlecht *n.*
lineal *a.,* **~ly** *adv.* in gerader Linie; linienweise.
lineament *s.* Gesichtszug *m.*
linear *a.* Linien..., linear.
linen *s.* Leinen *n.;* Wäsche *f.;* ~ **closet** *s.* Wäscheschrank; ~ *a.* leinen.
liner *s.* Linienschiff *n.,* Passagierschiff *n.*
linesman *s.* Linienrichter *m.*
lineswoman *s.* Linienrichterin *f.*
linger *v.i.* säumen, zögern, (zurück)bleiben, sich aufhalten, verweilen.
lingo *s.* Kauderwelsch *n.;* Fachjargon *m.;* Sprache *f.*
lingual *a.* Zungen...
linguist *s.* Linguist(in) *m.(f.),* Sprachforscher(in) *m.(f.)*
linguistic *a.* sprachwissenschaftlich, sprachlich, linguistisch.
linguistics *s.* Linguistik *f.,* Sprachwissenschaft *f.*
liniment *s.* Salbe *f.;* Liniment *n.;* Einreibemittel *n.*
lining *s.* (Unter-)Futter *n.;* Belag *m.,* Auskleidung *f.*
link *s.* (Ketten)glied *n.;* Band *n.;* Verbindung *f.;* ~ *v.t.* verketten; *to* ~ *up with, v.i.* Verbindung herstellen mit.
linkage *s.* Verbindung *f.*
linnet *s.* Hänfling *m.*
linseed *s.* Leinsamen *n.*
linseed oil *s.* Leinöl *n.*
lint *s.* Mull *m.*
lintel *s.* Sturz, Türsturz *m.*
lion *s.* Löwe *m.*
lioness *s.* Löwin *f.*
lion tamer *s.* Löwenbändiger(in) *m.(f.)*
lip *s.* Lippe *f.;* Rand *m.;* Schnabel *m.*
lipstick *s.* Lippenstift *m.*
liquefy *v.t.* verflüssigen ~ *v.i.* sich verflüssigen.
liqueur *s.* Liqueur *m.;* Likör *m.*
liquid *a.* flüssig; perlend; ~ *s.* Flüssigkeit *f.*
liquidate *v.t.* (*com.*) liquidieren, bezahlen; abwickeln.
liquidation *s.* (*com.*) Liquidation, Liquidierung *f.;* Auflösung *f.*
liquidity *s.* Liquidität *f.*
liquidize *v.t.* auflösen; pürieren.
liquor *s.* alkoholisches Getränk *m.;* Alkohol *m.;* Spirituosen *pl.*
liquor store *s.* Wein- und Spirituosengeschäft *n.*
lisp *v.i.* lispeln; ~ *s.* Lispeln *n.*
lissom(e) *a.* geschmeidig, gelenkig.
list *s.* Liste *f.;* Namensregister *n.,* Zeichnis *n.,* Namensverzeichnes *n.;* (*nav.*) Schlagseite *f.; shopping* ~, Einkaufszettel *m.;* ~ *v.t.* aufschreiben; notieren; einschreiben; aufführen.
listen *v.i.* hören, zuhören; lauschen.
listener *s.* Hörer(in) *m.(f.);* Zuhörer(in) *m.(f.)*
listless *a.,* **~ly** *adv.* lustlos; verdrossen; teilnahmslos.
lit. *literally,* wörtlich.
litany *s.* Litanei *f.*
literacy *s.* Kenntnis *(f.)* des Lesens und Schreibens.
literal *a.,* **~ly** *adv.* buchstäblich; wörtlich; eigentlich.
literary *a.* literarisch; ~ **award** *s.* Literaturpreis *m.;* ~ **critic** *s.* Literaturkritiker(in) *m.(f.);* ~ **historian** *s.* Literarhistoriker(in) *m.(f.)*
literate *a. to be* ~, lesen und schreiben können; gebildet sein.
literature *s.* Literatur *f.*
lithe *a.* biegsam, geschmeidig, gelenkig.
lithograph *s.* Lithographie *f.;* Steindruck *m.;* ~ *v.t.* lithographieren.
lithographer *s.* Lithograph(in) *m.(f.)*
lithography *s.* Lithographie *f.* (Technik); Steindruck *m.*
Lithuania *s.* Litauen *n.*
Lithuanian *a.* litauisch.
litigant *s.* streitende *or* prozeßführende Partei *f.*
litigate *v.t. & i.* streiten; prozessieren; einen Prozeß führen *or* anstrengen.
litigation *s.* Prozeß *m.;* Rechtsstreit *m.*
litigious *a.,* **~ly** *adv.* streitsüchtig, prozeßsüchtig.
litmus *s.* Lackmus *n.*
Litt.D. *Litterarum Doctor (Doctor of Letters),* Doktor der Literatur.
litter *s.* Sänfte *f.;* Wurf *m.;* Abfälle *m.pl.;* Streu *f.;* ~ *v.t.* (Junge) werfen; umherstreuen.
little *a. & adv.* klein, wenig; gering; ~ *by* ~, nach und nach.
littoral *a.* Ufer...; ~ *s.* Küstenland *n.*
liturgy *s.* Liturgie *f.*
live *v.i.* leben; verleben; am Leben bleiben; wohnen; dauern; ~*v.t.* (life) führen; ~ *a.* lebend, lebendig; aktuell; (*elek.*) geladen; (Patrone) scharf; ~ **coal** *s.* glühende Kohle *f.*
livelihood *s.* Lebensunterhalt *m.*
liveliness *s.* Lebhaftigkeit *f.*
livelong *a., the* ~ *day,* den lieben langen Tag.
lively *a.* lebhaft, munter.
liver *s.* Leber *f.*
liverish *a.* mürrisch.
livery *s.* Livree *f.*
livestock *s.* Vieh(bestand) *m.*
livid *a.* bleifarbig, fahl; wütend; fuchsteufelswild.
living *s.* Auskommen *n.;* Unterhalt *m.;* Lebensunterhalt *n.;* Pfarrstelle, Pfründe *f.; to earn a* ~, sich sein Lebensunterhalt verdienen; ~*a.* lebend; ~ **room** *s.* Wohnzimmer *n.*
lizard *s.* Eidechse *f.*

ll. *lines,* Zeilen, Z.
llama *s.* Lama *n.;* Lamawolle *f.*
LL.D. *Legum Doctor,* Doktor der Rechte.
load *s.* Ladung, Last *f.;* (*elek.*) Belastung *f.;* ~ *v.t.* beladen, laden, aufladen; **~line,** Ladelinie *f.;* *~ing ramp,* Laderampe *f.*
loaded *a.* geladen, beladen; *a ~ question,* eine Fangfrage.
loaf *s.* Laib *m.,* Brot *n.;* (Zucker) Hut *m.;* ~ *v.i.* herumlungern, faulenzen.
loam *s.* Lehm *m.,* Lehmboden *m.*
loan *s.* Anleihe *f.,* Leihgabe *f.;* ~ *v.t.* leihen.
loath *a.* unwillig, abgeneigt; ungern.
loathe *v.t.* verabscheuen, hassen.
loathing *s.* Ekel *m.;* Abscheu *m.*
loathsome *a.,* **~ly** *adv.* ekelhaft, widerlich, abscheulich, verhaßt, abscheuerregend.
lob *v.t.* (Tennis) lobben.
lobby *s.* Vorsaal *m.;* Vor- *or* Eingangshalle *f.;* Vorzimmer *n.;* Wandelgang *m.;* Lobby *f.;* ~ *v.t.* seinen Abgeordneten bearbeiten; Einfluß nehmen (auf), beeinflußen.
lobe *s.* Ohrläppchen *n.*
lobster *s.* Hummer *m.*
local *a.* örtlich, Orts...; *~ authorities, pl.* Kommunalbehörden *f.pl.;* *~ government,* Kommunalverwaltung *f.;* *~ traffic,* Nahverkehr *m.*
locality *s.* Örtlichkeit *f.;* Gegend *f.*
localize *v.t.* lokalisieren.
locally *adv.* am *or* im Ort; örtlich.
locate *v.t.* ausfindig machen; legen, anlegen; *to be ~ed,* sich befinden.
location *s.* Lage *f.;* Ort *m.;* Standort *m.;* (film) Drehort *m.;* *to be on ~ in France,* bei Außenaufnahmen in Frankreich sein.
loc. cit. *loco citato (at the place already cited),* am angeführten Orte, a.a.O.
loch *s.* See *m.;* Bucht *f.*
lock *s.* Schloß *n.;* Locke *f.;* Schleuse *f.;* Verschluß *m.;* Hemmung *f.;* *under ~ and key,* hinter Schloß und Riegel; ~ *v.t.* verschließen; zuschließen; sperren; hemmen (ein Rad); ~ *v.i.* ineinander greifen, schließen.
locker *s.* Schließfach *f.;* Schrank *m.*
locket *s.* Medaillon *n.*
lockjaw *s.* Mundsperre *f.;* Wundstarrkrampf *m.*
lockout *s.* Aussperrung *f.*
locksmith *s.* Schlosser *m.,* Schlossermeister *m.*
lock-up *s.* Gefängniszelle *f.*
locomotion *s.* Fortbewegungs...
locomotive engine *s.* Lokomotive *f.*
locust *s.* Heuschrecke *f.*
locution *s.* Redensart *f.;* Ausdruck *m.,* Ausdrucksweise *f.*
lode *s.* Erzgang *m.;* Erzader *f.;* **~star,** Leitstern, Polarstern *m.*
lodge *v.i.* wohnen; steckenbleiben; ~ *v.t.* beherbergen; unterbringen; (*complaint*) einlegen; *to be ~d,* (fest)stecken; ~ *s.* Häuschen *n.;* Loge *f.;* Hütte *f.*
lodger *s.* Mieter(in), Untermieter(in) *m.(f.)*
lodging *s.* Zimmer *n.;* Unterkunft *f.*
lodgings *s.pl.* möbliertes Zimmer *n.*
loft *s.* Boden, Dachboden, Heuboden *m.;* ~ *v.t.* hochschlagen.
lofty *a.,* **loftily** *adv.* hoch, erhaben; stolz.
log *s.* Baumstamm *m.,* Block *m.;* Klotz *m.;* (*nav.*) Log *n.*
loganberry *s.* Loganbeere *f.*
logarithm *s.* Logarithmus *m.*
log book *s.* Schiffstagebuch *n.*
log cabin *s.* Blockhaus *n.*
loggerhead *s., to be at ~s,* sich in den Haaren liegen.
logging *s.* Holzeinschlag *m.;* Holzfällen *n.*
logic *s.* Logik *f.*
logical *a.,* **~ly** *adv.* logisch, folgerichtig.
logician *s.* Logiker(in) *m.(f.)*
logistics *s.pl.* Logistik *f.*
loin *s.* Lendenbraten *m.;* **~s** *s.pl.* Lenden *f.pl.*
loincloth *s.* Lendenschurz *m.*
loiter *v.i.* bummeln, zaudern, trödeln, herumlungern.
loll *v.i.* sich lümmeln, sich rekeln.
lollipop *s.* Lutscher *m.*
lone *a.,* **~ly** *adv.* einsam; einzeln; einzig; allein.
loneliness *s.* Einsamkeit *f.*
lonely, lonesome *a.* einsam.
loner *s.* Einzelgänger(in) *m.(f.)*
long *a. & adv.* lang; lange; **~-term** langfristig; *I won't be ~,* ich werde nicht lange brauchen; *so ~!,* auf Wiedersehen!; ~ *v.t.* sich sehnen.
long. *longitude,* Länge *f.*
long-distance *a.* Fern...; Langstrecken...
longevity *s.* Langlebigkeit *f.*
longhand *s.* Langschrift *f.*
longing *s.* Sehnsucht *f.*
longitude *s.* geographische Länge *f.*
longitudinal *a.,* **~ly** *adv.* der Länge nach; Längen...
long jump *s.* Weitsprung *m.*
long-lived *a.* langlebig; von langer Lebensdauer (Material).
long-range *a.* Langstrecken...; weitragend; (*missile*) Fernkampf...; mit großer Reichweite; langfristig.
longshoreman *s.* Werftarbeiter *m.,* Hafenarbeiter *m.*
long-sighted *a.* weitsichtig.
long-suffering *a.* langmütig, schwer geprüft.
long-term *a.* langfristig.
long wave *s.* Langwelle *f.* (*radio*).
long-winded *a.* langatmig, umständlich.
look *v.t. & i.* sehen, hinsehen; aussehen; *to ~ after,* betreuen; *to ~ around,* sich umsehen; *to ~ for,* suchen; *to ~ over,* sich (*dat.*) anschauen; *to ~ through,* durchsehen, durchlesen, ~ *s.* Blick *m.;* Aussehen *n.*
look-alike *s.* Doppelgänger(in) *m.(f.)*
looking-glass *s.* Spiegel *m.*
lookout *s.* Ausguck *m.;* Wache *f.*
loom *s.* Webstuhl *m.;* ~ *v.i.* sichtbar werden; *~ up,* aufragen; *~ large,* sich auftürmen.
loony *a.* (*fam.*) bekloppt; verrückt.
loop *s.* Schlaufe, (*avia.*) Looping *m.,* Schlinge *f.;* Schnürloch *n.,* Schleife.
loophole *s.* Ausflucht f; (*fig.*) Schlupfloch *n.,* Hintertürchen *n.*
loose *a.,* **~ly** *adv.* lose, los; locker; liederlich; frei; beweglich; *~-leaf notebook s.* Loseblätterbuch *n.*
loosen *v.t.* lösen, locker machen.
loot *s.* Beute *f.;* ~ *v.t.* plündern.

lop *v.t.* ausästen; abhacken.
lope *v.i.* springen; beschwingt gehen.
lopsided *a.* schief, einseitig.
loquacious *a.* schwatzhaft, redselig.
loquacity *s.* Schwatzhaftigkeit, Redseligkeit *f.*
lord *s.* Lord *m.*; Herr *m.*; Gott *m.*
lordly *a.* vornehm, stolz.
lordship *s.* Herrschaft, Lordschaft *f.*; *Your Lordship* (Titel), Euer Gnaden.
lore *s.* Kunde *f.*; Lehre *f.*; Überlieferung *f.*
lorry *s.* Lori, Lore *f.*; Lastwagen *m.*
lose *v.t.ir.* verlieren; (pursuer) abschütteln; *to ~ one's way,* sich verlaufen.
loser *s.* Verlierer(in) *m.(f.)*
loss *s.* Verlust *m.*; *at a ~,* ratlos.
lost property office *s.* Fundbüro *n.*
lot *s.* Los *n.*; Schicksal *n.*; Anteil *m.*; Haufen *m.*, Menge *f.*; Posten *m.*; Partie *f.*; Stück Land *n.*; *a ~, ~s,* viel; *to draw ~ for,* ~ *v.t.* verlosen.
lotion *s.* Hautwasser *n.*; Lotion *f.*
lottery *s.* Lotterie *f.*; ~ **ticket** *s.* Lotterielos *n.*
loud *a.*, **~ly** *adv.* laut; grell (Farben).
loudmouth Großmaul *n.*
loudness *s.* Lautstärke *f.*
loudspeaker *s.* (*radio*) Lautsprecher *m.*; ~ **van,** Lautsprecherwagen *m.*
lounge *v.i.* faulenzen; ~ *s.* (Hotel) Halle; Salon *m.* Wartesaal *m.*; Foyer *n.*
louse *s.* Laus *f.*
lousy *a.* verlaust; widerlich; mies; (*sl.*) beschissen, saumäßig; fies.
lout *s.* Lümmel, Rüpel, Flegel *m.*
loutish *a.*, **~ly** *adv.* plump, rupelhaft, flegelhaft.
lovable *a.* liebenswert.
love *v.t.* & *i.* lieben; gern haben *or* mögen; ~ *s.* Liebe *f.*; Liebchen *n.*; *in ~,* verliebt; *to fall in ~ with,* sich verlieben in; *make ~,* sich lieben; *send one's ~ to sb.,* jn. grüßen lassen; *with my ~,* mit herzlichen Grüßen; *there is no love lost between them,* sie haben nichts füreinander übrig.
love affair *s.* Liebesaffäre *f.*; Verhältnis *n.*
love-hate relationship *s.* Haßliebe *f.*
lovely *a.* liebenswürdig; lieblich; herrlich; schön.
lovemaking *s.* (körperliche) Liebe *f.*
lovematch *s.* Liebesheirat *f.*
lover *s.* Liebhaber *m.*; Geliebte *f.*, Geliebte(r) *m.*; *they are ~s,* sie lieben sich.
lovesick *a.* liebeskrank; an Liebeskummer leidend.
loving *a.*, **~ly** *adv.* liebevoll; mit viel Liebe.
low *a.* & *adv.* niedrig; leise; niedergeschlagen; ~ **brow** *a.* anspruchslos; ~ **-calorie** *a.* kalorienarm; *in a ~ voice,* leise; ~ *s.* Tief (Wetterkunde); ~ *v.i.* brüllen.
lower *a.* niedriger; tiefer; ~ *v.t.* niederlassen; senken; verringern; *to ~ a boat,* ein Boot aussetzen; *to ~ one's voice,* leiser reden; ~ *v.i.* abnehmen; sinken; fallen.
lower case *s.* Kleinbuchstabe *m.*; *a.* klein.
lower deck *s.* Unterdeck.
Lower Saxony *s.* Niedersachsen *n.*
low-fat *a.* fettarm.
low-grade *a.* geringwertig.
low-key *a.* gedämpft; zurückhaltend.
lowland *s.* Tiefland *n.*, Flachland.
lowly *a.* & *adv.* niedrig, bescheiden.
low-pressure *s.* Tiefdruck *m.*
low season *s.* Vor- *or* Nachsaison *f.*
low-spirited *a.* niedergeschlagen, mutlos.
loyal *a.*, **~ly** *adv.* treu, pflichttreu.
loyalty *s.* Treue *f.*
lozenge *s.* Raute *f.*; Pastille *f.*
LP *long playing,* Langspielplatte, LP.
l.p. *low pressure,* Tiefdruck.
Ltd. *limited (liability company),* (Gesellschaft) mit beschränkter Haftung, m.b.H.
lubber *s.* Tölpel, Grobian *m.*
lubricant *s.* Schmiermittel *n.*, Schmierstoff *m.*
lubricate *v.t.* einölen, schmieren.
lucid *a.* einleuchtend; klar, licht, durchsichtig.
luck *s.* Glück *n.*; Zufall *m.*; Schicksal, Geschick *n.*; *good ~,* Glück *n.*; *ill ~, bad ~,* Unglück *n.*
luckless *a.* glücklos.
lucky *a.*, **~ily** *adv.* glücklich; glücklicherweise.
lucrative *a.* einträglich.
lucre *s.* Gewinn *m.*, Geld *n.*; *filthy ~,* schnöder Mammon *m.*
lucubration *s.* nächtliches Studium *n.*; **~s** *pl.* gelehrte Abhandlungen *f.pl.*
ludicrous *a.*, **~ly** *adv.* lächerlich, albern.
lug *v.t.* schleppen; *to ~ something around,* etwas herum schleppen.
luggage *s.* Gepäck *n.*; *hand ~,* Handgepäck *n.*; *heavy ~,* großes Gepäck *n.*; ~ **cart** Kofferkuli *m.* ~ **office,** Gepäckabfertigung *f.*; **left-~ office,** Gepäckaufbewahrungsstelle *f.*; ~ **van,** Gepäckwagen *m.*
lugubrious *a.* schwermütig, traurig, trübsinnig.
lukewarm *a.*, **~ly** *adv.* lau.
lull *s.* Pause *f.*; Windstille *f.*; *v.t.* beruhigen; einlullen; ~ *v.i.* (wind) sich legen.
lullaby *s.* Wiegenlied *n.*
lumbago *s.* Hexenschuß *m.*
lumber *s.* Gerümpel *n.*; Plunder *m.*; Bauholz *n.*
lumberjack *s.* Holzfäller *m.*
lumber mill *s.* Sägewerk *n.*, Sagemühle *f.*
luminary *s.* Lichtkörper *m.*; (*fig.*) Leuchte *f.*
luminosity *s.* Helligkeit *f.*
luminous *a.* leuchtend; Leucht...; ~ **watch** *s.* Leuchtuhr *f.*
lump *s.* Haufen, Klumpen *m.*; Masse *f.*; *in the ~,* in Bausch und Bogen; ~ **sugar,** Stückzucker *m.*; ~ **sum,** Pauschalsumme *f.*; ~ *v.t.* im ganzen nehmen; *to ~ together,* in einen Topf werfen, alles über einen Kamm scheren.
lumpy *a.* klumpig.
lunacy *s.* Irrsinn, Wahnsinn *m.*
lunar *a.* Mond..., lunar.
lunar eclipse *s.* Mondfinsternis *f.*
lunatic *a.* irrsinnig; verrückt; wahnsinnig; ~ *s.* Irre *m./f.*; ~ **asylum** *s.* Irrenhaus *n.*, Irrenanstalt *f.*
lunch, luncheon *s.* Mittagessen *n.*, Lunch *m.*; **~-basket** *s.* Imbißkorb *m.*; ~ *v.i.* das Mittagessen einnehmen.
lunch hour *s.* Mittagspause *f.*
lunchtime *s.* Mittagszeit *f.*
lung *s.* Lunge *f.*
lunge *s.* Ausfall (beim Fechten) *m.*; Sprung (*m.*) vorwärts, Satz (*m.*) nach vorn.
lupin *s.* Lupine *f.*

lurch *s.* Ruck *m.; Schlingern n.; leave in the* ~, im Stich lassen; ~ *v.i.* taumeln.
lure *s.* Köder *m.;* Lockung *f.;* Lockmittel *n.;* Reiz *m.;* ~ *v.t.* ködern; locken; verlocken.
lurid *a.* grell; gespenstisch; schreiend; blutrünstig.
lurk *v.i.* lauern.
luscious *a.* köstlich; lecker; üppig; knackig.
lush *a.* üppig, saftig.
lust *s.* Begierde *f.;* Wollust *f.;* Gier *f.; to ~ after, to ~ for, v.i.* gelüsten (*impers.*), begehren (nach), gieren nach.
luster *s.* Glanz *m.;* Kronleuchter *m.;* Schimmer *m.*
lustful *a.* lüstern, wollustig.
lustrous *a.* glänzend, schimmernd.
lusty *a.,* **lustily** *adv.* munter; kräftig; kernig; herzhaft; kraftvoll.
lute *s.* Laute *f.;* Kitt *m.;* ~ *v.t.* verkitten.
Lutheran *a.* lutherisch; ~ *s.* Lutheraner *m.*
Luxembourg, Luxemburg *s.* Luxemburg *n.*
luxuriance *s.* Üppigkeit, Fülle, Pracht *f.*
luxuriant *a.,* **~ly** *adv.* üppig, reichlich.
luxuriate *v.i.* schwelgen.
luxurious *a.,* **~ly** *adv.* üppig; luxuriös.
luxury *s.* Üppigkeit *f.;* Luxus *m.*
LW *long wave,* Langwelle, LW.
lye *s.* Lauge *f.*
lying *a.* verlogen, lügnerisch.
lying-in *s.* Wochenbett *n.*
Lyme disease *s.* Borreliose *f.*
lymph *s.* Lymphe *f.;* Gewebsflüssigkeit *f.*
lynch *v.t.* lynchen.
lynch law *s.* Pöbeljustiz, Lynchjustiz *f.*
lynx *s.* Luchs *m.*
lyre *s.* Leier *f.;* Lyra *f.*
lyric *a.* lyrisch; ~ *poem, s.* lyrisches Gedicht *n.*
lyricism *s.* Lyrismus *m.*
lyricist *s.* Lyriker(in) *m.(f.)*

M

M, m der Buchstabe M oder m *n.*
M *medium,* mittelgroß.
m. *male, masculine,* männlich; *meter,* Meter *m.; mile,* Meile *f.; minute,* Minute *f.,* min.; *married,* verheiratet, verh.; *million,* Million, Mio., Mill.
M.A. *Master of Arts,* Magister der Philosophie.
macabre *a.* makaber.
macadam *s.* Schotter *m.*
macaroni *s.* Makkaroni *f.pl.*
macaroon *s.* Makrone *f.*
mace *s.* Keule *f.;* Streitkolben *m.;* Amtsstab *m.;* (Gewürz) Muskatblüte *f.;* chemische Keule *f.*
macerate *v.t.* (*cul.*) einlegen (Fleisch), aufweichen, einweichen.
machete *s.* Machete *f.;* Buschmesser *n.*
Machiavellian *a.* machiavellistisch.
machination *s.* (*usu. pl.*) Machenschaften *f.pl.*
machine *s.* Maschine *f.;* Apparat *m.,* ~ *v.t.* maschinell bearbeiten *od.* herstellen; **~-gun** *s.* Maschinengewehr *n.;* ~ **tool** *s.* Werkzeugmaschine *f.*
machinery *s.* Maschinerie *f.,* Maschinen *pl.*
machinist *s.* Maschinist *m.*
machismo *s.* Machismo *m.*
macho *a.* macho; *s.* Macho *m.*
mackerel *s.* Makrele *f.*
mackintosh *s.* Regenmantel *m.*
macrobiotic *a.* makrobiotisch.
macroscopic *a.* makroskopisch.
mad *a.,* **~ly** *adv.* wahnsinnig, toll; verrückt; (angry) böse, sauer.
madam *s.* gnädige Frau *f.*
madcap *s.* Tollkopf *m.;* ~ *a.* unbesonnen, wild, versponnen.
madden *v.t.* verrückt machen, ärgern.
made-to-measure *a.* Maß...
made-up *a.* erfunden; (face) geschminkt.
madhouse *s.* Tollhaus *n.;* Irrenanstalt *f.,* Irrenhaus *n.*
madman *s.* Wahnsinniger, Irrer, Verrückter *m.*
madness *s.* Wahnsinn *m.;* Tollheit *f.; sheer* ~, reiner *or* heller Wahnsinn.
madwoman *s.* Verrückte *f.*
maelstrom *s.* Strudel *m.;* Sog *m.*
Mafia *s.* Mafia *f.*
magazine *s.* Zeitschrift *f.;* Magazin *n.;* Lagerhaus *n.;* Pulvermagazin *n.*
maggot *s.* Made *f.;* (*fig.*) Grille *f.*
magic *s.* Magie *f.;* Zauber *m.,* Zauberkunst *f.;* ~ *a.* zauberhaft, magisch, Zauber...
magic carpet *s.* fliegender Teppich *m.*
magician *a.* Zauberer *m.;* Zauberin *f.*
magic wand *s.* Zauberstab *m.*
magistrate *s.* Richter(in), Friedensrichter(in) *m.(f.)*
magnanimity *s.* Großmut, Großherzigkeit *f.*
magnanimous *a.,* **~ly** *adv.* großmütig, großherzig.
magnate *s.* Magnat(in) *m.(f.)*
magnesia *s.* Magnesia *f.*
magnesium *s.* Magnesium *n.*
magnet *s.* Magnet *m.*
magnetic *a.* magnetisch.
magnetic field *s.* Magnetfeld *n.*
magnetic pole *s.* Magnetpol *m.*
magnetism *s.* Magnetismus *m.;* Anziehungskraft, Ausstrahlung *f.*
magnetize *v.t.* magnetisieren.
magneto *s.* Zündapparat, Magnetzünder *m.*
magnification *s.* Vergrößerung *f.* (Mikroskop, etc.).
magnificence *s.* Großartigkeit *f.,* Pracht *f.*
magnificent *a.,* **~ly** *adv.* prachtvoll, prächtig, großartig, herrlich, ausgezeichnet.
magnify *v.t.* vergrößern, verherrlichen.
magnifying glass *s.* Lupe *f.;* Vergrößerungsglas *n.*
magnitude *s.* Größe *f.*
magpie *s.* Elster *f.*
mahogany *s.* Mahagoni(holz) *n.*
maid *s.* Jungfer *f.;* Mädchen *n.;* Dienstmädchen *n.;* (in hotel) Zimmermädchen *n.; old* ~, alte Jungfer.

maiden *s.* Jungfer *f.;* Magd *f.;* ~ *name, s.* Mädchenname *m.;* ~ *speech, s.* Jungfernrede *f.*
maidenhead, maidenhood *s.* Jungfernschaft *f.*, Jungfernhäutchen *n.*
maidservant *s.* Hausangestellte *f.*
mail *s.* Post, *f.;* ~ *v.t.* mit der Post schicken.
mailbag *s.* Briefbeutel *m.*, Postsack *m.*
mailbox *s.* Briefkasten *m.*
mailcarrier *s.* Briefträger(in) *m.(f.)*
mailing list *s.* Adressenliste *f.*
mail-order *a.* Versand...
mail train *s.* Postzug *m.*
maim *v.t.* verstümmeln.
main *a.* hauptsächlich; Haupt...; groß; ~ *s.* Hauptrohr *n.;* Hauptleitung *f.;* Weltmeer *n.; in the* ~, hauptsächlich, im allgemeinen; *the* ~ *chance,* der eigene Vorteil.
main: ~ **beam** *s.* Aufblendlicht *n.;* ~ **clause** *s.* Hauptsatz *m.;* **~land** *s.* Festland *n.*
mainly *adv.* hauptsächlich.
main: ~ **road** *s.* Hauptstraße *f.;* **~spring** *s.* Hauptfeder, Triebfeder *f.;* **~stay** *s.* Hauptstütze *f.;* **~stream** *s.* Hauptstrom *m.;* Hauptrichtung *f.;* ~ **street** *s.* Hauptstraße *f.*
maintain *v.t.* erhalten, unterhalten; ernähren; behaupten; verfechten.
maintenance *s.* Aufrechterhaltung *f.*, Unterhalt *m.;* Instandhaltung, Unterhaltung, Wahrung, Wartung *f.;* **~-free** *a.* wartungsfrei.
maize *s.* Mais *m.*
Maj. *major,* Major.
majestic *a.*, **~ally** *adv.* majestätisch.
majesty *s.* Majestät *f.*
Maj.-Gen. *major-general,* Generalmajor.
major *a.* größer; mündig; *n.* (*mus.*) Dur; ~ *s.* Major *m.;* Obersatz *m.;* Hauptfach *n.*
majority *s.* Mehrheit *f.;* Mündigkeit *f.*, Merzahl.
majority: ~ **rule** *s.* Mehrheitsentscheidung *f.;* ~ **verdict** *s.* Mehrheitsentscheid *m.*
make *v.t.ir.* machen; (veran)lassen; *to* ~ *good,* Erfolg haben, sich bewähren; *to* ~ *out,* ausschreiben, ausstellen (Scheck, Rechnung); *to* ~ *up,* verarbeiten; sich versöhnen; ~ *v.i.* sich wenden, wohin gehen; sich stellen; *to* ~ *for,* lossteuern auf; *to* ~ *out,* ausmachen; *to* ~ *up for,* entschädigen (für);*to* ~ *up one's mind (to do sth.),* sich entschliessen; ~ *s.* Sorte, Art *f.*
make-believe *a.* Phantasie..., imaginär; *s.* Phantasie *f.*
maker *s.* Verfertiger *m.;* Schöpfer *m.;* Hersteller.
makeshift *s.* Notbehelf *m.*
make-up *s.* Schminke *f.;* Make-up *n.;* Zusammenstellung *f.;* Veranlagung *f.*
making *s.* Herstellung *f.; in the* ~, im Entstehen.
maladjusted *a.* verhaltensgestört.
maladministration *s.* Mißwirtschaft *f.*
maladroit *a.* ungeschickt; taktlos.
malady *s.* Krankheit *f.;* Leiden *n.;* Übel *n.*
malaise *s.* Unbehagen *n.*
malaria *s.* Sumpffieber *n.;* Malaria *f.*
Malay *a.* malaiisch, malanisch; ~ *s.* Malaie *m.*, Malaiin *f.*
Malaya *s.* Malaya *n.*
Malaysia *s.* Malaysia *n.*
Malaysian *a.* malaysisch; ~ *s.* Malaysier *m.;* Malaysierin *f.*
malcontent *a.*, **~ly** *adv.* unzufrieden.
male *a.* männlich; ~ *s.* Mann *m.;* Männchen *n.*
malediction *s.* Fluch *m.*
malefactor *s.* Übeltäter *m.*
malevolence *s.* Bosheit, Bösartigkeit *f.*
malevolent *a.*, **~ly** *adv.* böswillig.
malformation *s.* Mißbildung *f.*
malformed *a.* mißgebildet.
malice *s.* Bosheit *f.*, Groll *m.; with* ~ *aforethought,* (*jur.*) mit bösem Vorbedacht.
malicious *a.*, **~ly** *adv.* boshaft, tückisch.
malign *a.* schädlich; böse; bösartig; ~ *v.t.* verleumden.
malignancy *s.* Bösartigkeit *f.*
malignant *a.*, **~ly** *adv.* bösartig; böswillig.
malignity *s.* Bosheit *f.;* Schadenfreude *f.*
malinger *v.i.* simulieren.
mall *s.* Einkaufszentrum *n.;* Fußgängerzone *f.*
malleable *a.* formbar.
mallet *s.* Holzhammer *m.*
mallow *s.* Malve *f.*
malnutrition *s.* Unterernährung *f.*
malodorous *a.* übelriechend.
malpractice *s.* Amtsvergehen *n.;* (ärztlicher) Kunstfehler *m.*
malt *s.* Malz *n.;* ~ *v.t.* malzen, mälzen.
maltreat *v.t.* mißhandeln, schlecht behandeln.
maltreatment *s.* Mißhandlung *f.*
mam(m)a *s.* Mama *f.*
mammal *s.* Säugetier *n.*
mammoth *s.* Mammut *n.;* ~ *a.* riesig.
man *s.* Mensch *m.;* Mann *m.;* ~ *v.t.* bemannen.
manacle *s.usu.pl.* Handfesseln, Ketten, Handschelle *n.f.pl.;* ~ *v.t.* fesseln.
manage *v.t.* handhaben; verwalten; einrichten; leiten; fertig bringen; zureiten; ~ *v.i.* die Aufsicht führen; sich behelfen.
manageable *a.* handlich; lenksam; fügsam; zu bewältigen.
management *s.* Verwaltung *f.*, Leitung *f.*, Direktion *f.*
manager *s.* Verwalter(in) *m.(f.);* Leiter(in) *m.(f.);* Direktor(in) *m.(f.); a good* ~, ein guter Haushalter; *general* ~, Generaldirektor *m.; works* ~, Betriebsleiter *m.*
managerial *a.* leitend; geschäftlich.
managing *a.* geschäftsführend, leitend.
mandarin *s.* Hochchinesisch *n.;* Parteibonze *m.;* Bürokrat(in) *m.(f.)*
mandate *s.* Mandat *n.*, Auftrag *m.*
mandatory *a.* befehlend; Mandats...; obligatorisch.
mandolin *s.* Mandoline *f.*
mandrake *s.* Mandragore *f.*, Alraun(e) *m.(f.)*
mandrel *s.* (*mech.*) Spindel, Docke *f.*
mane *s.* Mähne *f.*
maneuver *s.* Manöver *n.;* Kunstgriff *m.;* ~ *v.t.* manövieren.
manful *a.*, **~ly** *adv.* mannhaft, tapfer.
manganese *s.* Mangan *n.*
mange *s.* Räude *f.*
manger *s.* Krippe *f.*, Trog *m.*
mangle *v.t.* verstümmeln; zerstückeln; (übel) zurichten.
mangold *s.* Mangold *m.*, Runkelrübe *f.*
mangrove *s.* Mangrovenbaum *m.;* ~ **swamp** Mangrove *f.*

mangy *a.* räudig; schäbig.
manhandle *v.t.* rauh anfassen.
manhole *s.* Einstiegsloch *n.*; Straßenschacht *m.*
manhood *s.* Mannheit *f.*; Tapferkeit *f.*; Mannesalter *n.*
manhour *s.* Arbeitsstunde *f.*
manhunt *s.* Großfahndung *f.*
mania *s.* Wahnsinn *m.*; Sucht *f.*
maniac *a.* wahnsinnig; ~ *s.* Wahnsinnige *m./f.*
manicure *s.* Maniküre *f.*; *v.t.* maniküren.
manifest *a.*, **~ly** *adv.* offenbar; ~ *s.* Ladungsverzeichnis *n.*; ~ *v.t.* offenbaren; manifest werden.
manifestation *s.* Offenbarung *f.*; Anzeichen *n.*; Bekundung *f.*
manifesto *s.* Manifest *n.*
manifold *a.*, **~ly** *adv.* vielfältig.
manikin *s.* Männlein *n.*; Gliederpuppe *f.*
manipulate *v.t.* manipulieren; handhaben.
manipulation *s.* Manipulation *f.*
manipulative *a.* manipulierend.
mankind *s.* Menschengeschlecht *f.*; Menschheit *f.*
manlike *a.* männlich; menschlich.
manly *a.* männlich; mannhaft.
man-made *a.* künstlich; von Menschen geschaffen.
manned *a.* bemannt.
mannequin *s.* Mannequin *n.*; Schaufensterpuppe *f.*
manner *s.* Art, Weise *f.*; **~s** *pl.* Sitten, Manieren *f.pl.*; *in a ~*, gewissermaßen; *in a ~ of speaking*, sozusagen.
mannered *a.* manieriert; *ill/well ~* schlechte/gute Manieren haben.
mannerism *s.* Manieriertheit *f.*
mannerly *a.* & *adv.* artig, wohlerzogen.
manometer *s.* Druckmesser *m.*
manor *s.* Rittergut *n.*; Herrenhaus *n.*
manor house *s.* Herrenhaus *n.*
manpower *s.* Arbeitspotential *n.*; Arbeitskräfte *f.pl.*; Stärke *f.*; ~ **allocation,** Arbeitseinsatz *m.*
manservant *s.* Diener *m.*
mansion *s.* Villa *f.*
manslaughter *s.* Totschlag *m.*
mantel *s.* Kaminverkleidung *f.*
mantelpiece *s.* Kaminsims *m.*
mantle *s.* Umhang *m.*; Hülle *f.*
mantrap *s.* Fußangel *f.*
manual *a.* manuell; Hand...; ~ *s.* Handbuch *n.*
manufacture *s.* Fabrikation *f.*; Herstellung *f.*; Fabrikat *n.*; ~ *v.t.* herstellen; fabrizieren; verarbeiten; **~ed articles** *pl.* Fertigwaren *f.pl.*
manufacturer *s.* Fabrikant *m.*; Hersteller *m.*
manure *v.t.* düngen; ~ *s.* Dung, Dünger; Mist *m.*
manuscript *s.* Handschrift *f.*; Manuskript *n.*
many *a.* viele, viel; mancher, manche, manches; *as ~ as*, soviele als *or* wie.
map *s.* Landkarte *f.*, Stadtplan *m.*; ~ *v.t.* in Kartenform darstellen; (*mil.*) ~ **exercise** *s.* Planspiel *n.*; (*mil.*) ~ **maneuver** *s.* Kriegspiel *n.*; **~scale** *s.* Kartenmaßstab *m.*
maple *s.* Ahorn *m.*
mar *v.t.* verderben; beschädigen.
Mar. *March*, März.
marathon race *s.* Marathonlauf *m.*
maraud *v.i.* plündern.
marauder *s.* Plünderer *m.*
marble *s.* Marmor *m.*; Murmel *f.*; ~ *a.* marmorn.
march *s.* Marsch; Zug *m.*; Mark *f.*, Grenzland *n.*; ~ *v.i.* & *t.* marschieren; *to ~ past*, vorbeimarschieren; ~ marschieren lassen.
March *s.* März *m.*
marcher *s.* Demonstrant(in) *m.(f.)*
marchioness *s.* Markgräfin *f.*, Marquise *f.*
mare *s.* Stute *f.*; *~'s nest*, (*fig.*) Windei *n.*; Zeitungsente *f.*
margarine *s.* Margarine *f.*
margin *s.* Rand *m.*; Spielraum *m.*; (*fig.*) Überschuß *m.*
marginal *a.* am Rande; Rand...; geringfügig; marginal; ~ **note** *s.* Randbemerkung *f.*
marginalize *v.t.* marginalisieren.
marigold *s.* Dotterblume *f.*
marinade *s.* Marinade *f.*
marinate *v.t.* marinieren.
marine *a.* See...; ~ *s.* Marine *f.*; Seesoldat *m.*
mariner *s.* Seemann *m.*
marionette *s.* Marionette *f.*
marital *a.* ehelich; ~ **status** *s.* Familienstand *m.*
maritime *a.* See...; zur See gehörig; ~ **law** *s.* Seerecht *n.*
marjoram *s.* Majoran *m.*
mark *s.* Fleck *m.*, Marke, Markierung *f.*; Kennzeichen, Zeichen *n.*; Spur *f.*; Schutzmarke *f.*; (Zeugnis) Note *m.*; Ziel *n.*; *not quite up to the ~*, nicht ganz auf der Höhe; *up to the ~*, den Anforderungen entsprechen; ~ *v.t.* & *i.* zeichnen; aufmerken; markieren; *to ~ off*, abstreichen; *to ~ out*, abstecken; *to ~ out for*, ausersehen für; *to ~ time*, auf der Stelle treten (*mil.* & *fig.*); *a ~d man*, ein Gezeichneter.
marked *a.*, **~ly** *adv.* deutlich; ausgeprägt; merklich.
marker *s.* Markierung *f.*; *felt-tip ~*, Filzstift *m.*
market *s.* Markt *m.*; Absatz *m.*; *to come on the ~*, auf den Markt kommen; *to place on the ~*, auf den Markt bringen.; ~ **forces** *pl.* Kräfte des Marktes; ~ **gardener** *s.* Handelsgärtner *m.*; **~ing association** *s.* Absatzgenossenschaft *f.*; **~place** *s.* Marktplatz *m.*; ~ **research** *s.* Marktforschung *f.*; *stock ~* Börse *f.*; *~ v.t.* auf den Markt bringen.
marketable *a.* absetzbar, verkäuflich, gangbar.
marking *s.* Markierung *f.*; Kennzeichen *n.* Korrektur *f.*; Musterung *f.*; Zeichnung (eines Fells) *f.*; (*mil.*) Hoheitsabzeichen *n.*; Zensieren *n.*; Benoten *n.*; **~ink** *s.* (unauslöschliche) Zeichentinte *f.*; **~iron** *s.* Brenneisen *n.*
marksman *s.* Schütze *m.*
marksmanship *s.* Schießfertigkeit, Zielsicherheit *f.*; Treffsicherheit *f.*
mark-up *s.* Preiserhöhung *f.*; Handelsspanne *f.*
marmalade *s.* Marmelade *f.*
marmot *s.* Murmeltier *n.*
maroon *a.* kastanienbraun; ~ *v.t.* aussetzen; (*fig.*) im Stich lassen.
marquee *s.* Zeltdach *n.*, Markise *f.*
marquess, marquis *s.* Marquis *m.*
marquetry *s.* eingelegte Arbeit *f.*, Marketerie *f.*
marriage *s.* Ehe, Heirat *f.*; ~ **ceremony** *s.* Trauung *f.*; **~certificate** *s.* Trauschein *m.*; ~ **counseling** *s.* Eheberatung *f.*; ~ **settlement** *s.* Ehevertrag *m.*
marriageable *a.* heiratsfähig.

married *a.* verheiratet; ~ **couple** *s.* Ehepaar *n.*
marrow *s.* Mark *n.;* **~bone** *s.* Markknochen *m.*
marry *v.t.* heiraten; verheiraten; trauen; ~ *v.i.* heiraten, sich verheiraten.
marsh *s.* Marsch *f.;* Sumpf *m.*
marshal *s.* Marschall *m.;* ~ *v.t.* ordnen; anführen.
marshland *s.* Sumpfland *n.*
marshy *a.* sumpfig.
marsupial *s.* Beuteltier *n.*
marten *s.* Marder *m.*
martial *a.* kriegerisch, militärisch; ~ **law** *s.* Standrecht, Kriegsrecht *n.*
martyr *s.* Märtyrer(in) *m.(f.);* ~ *v.t.* martern.
martyrdom *s.* Märtyrertum *n.*, Märtyrertod *m.*
marvel *s.* Wunder *n.;* ~ *v.i.* staunen, bestaunen.
marvelous *a.*, **~ly** *adv.* wunderbar, phantastisch.
Marxism *s.* Marxismus *m.*
Marxist *s.* Marxist(in) *m.(f.)*
marzipan *s.* Marzipan *n.*
masc. *masculine*, maskulin.
mascara *s.* Mascara *n.;* Wimperntusche *f.*
mascot *s.* Glücksbringer *m.*, Maskottchen *n.*
masculine *a.* männlich; (woman) maskulin; ~ *s.* (*gram.*) Maskulinum *n.*
masculinity *s.* Männlichkeit *f.*
mash *s.* Gemisch *n.;* Brei *m.;* Maische *f.;* Püree *n.;* ~ *v.t.* mengen, maischen, zerdrücken.
mashed potatoes *pl.* Kartoffelbrei *m. or* -püree.
mask *s.* Maske *f.;* ~ *v.t. & i.* maskieren; sich verstellen.
masochism *s.* Masochismus *m.*
masochist *s.* Masochist(in) *m.(f.)*
masochistic *a.* masochistisch.
mason *s.* Maurer *m.;* Freimaurer *m.*
masonic *a.* freimaurerisch.
masonry *s.* Maurerei *f.;* Mauerwerk *n.;* Freimaurertum *n.*
masque *s.* Maskenspiel *n.*
masquerade *s.* Maskerade *f.;* Maskenball *m.;* Verkleidung *f.;* ~ *v.i.* maskiert gehen.
mass *s.* Masse, Menge *f.;* Messe *f.;* **high** ~ *s.* Hochamt *n.;* **low** ~ *s.* stille Messe; ~ *v.t. & i.* (sich) anhäufen, sich sammeln, sich massieren.
massacre *s.* Metzelei *f.;* Massaker *n.;* ~ *v.t.* niedermetzeln, massakrieren.
massage *v.t.* massieren; ~ *s.* Massage *f.*
mass communication *s.* Massenkommunikation *f.*
masseur *s.* Masseur *m.*
masseuse *s.* Masseurin *f.*
massive *a.*, **~ly** *adv.* dicht, fest, massiv, riesig, enorm, wuchtig, breit.
mass media *s.pl.* Massenmedien *pl.*
mass meeting *s.* Massenversammlung *f.*
mass production *s.* Massenproduktion *f.*
mast *s.* Mast(baum) *m.;* Mast *f.*
master *s.* Meister *m.;* Herr *m.;* Magister, Lehrer *m.;* ~ *v.t.* meistern.
master builder *s.* Baumeister *m.*
masterful *a.* herrisch; meisterhaft.
master key *s.* Hauptschlüssel, Generalschlüssel *m.*
masterly *a. & adv.* meisterhaft.
mastermind *s.* führender Kopf *m.*
masterpiece *s.* Meisterstück *n.*
master switch *s.* Hauptschalter *m.*
mastery *s.* Herrschaft *f.;* Geschicklichkeit *f.;* Beherrschung *f.;* Meisterung *f.;* Oberhand *f.*
masthead *s.* Impressum *n.*
masticate *v.t. & i.* kauen.
mastiff *s.* Dogge, Bulldogge *f.;* Kettenhund, Mastiff *m.*
masturbate *v.i.* & t. masturbieren, onanieren.
masturbation *s.* Masturbation, Onanie. *f.*
mat *s.* Matte *f.;* ~ *v.t.* mit Matten bedecken; mattieren.
match *s.* Lunte *f.;* Streichholz *n.;* Gleiche *n.;* Heirat *f.;* (Spiel)Partie *f.;* Wettspiel *n.;* *to be* or *make a good* ~, gut zusammenpassen; ~ *v.t.* zusammenpassen, zusammenbringen; vergleichen; aufwiegen; ~ *v.i.* passen.
matchbox *s.* Streichholzschachtel *f.*
matchless *a.*, **~ly** *adv.* unvergleichlich.
matchmaker *s.* Ehestifter(in) *m.(f.)*
match point *s.* Matchball *m.*
mate *s.* Gefährte, Gehilfe *m.;* Geselle *m.;* Männchen, Weibchen *n.;* Arbeitskollege, Kumpel *m.;* Maat *m.;* Steuermann *m.;* Gatte *m.*, Gattin *f.;* ~ *adv.* (schach) matt; ~ *v.t. & i.* (sich) paaren; ~ *v.t.* matt setzen.
material *a.*, **~ly** *adv.* körperlich; wesentlich; materiell; ~ *s.* Material *n.*, Stoff *m.;* Kleiderstoff *m.;* *raw* ~, Rohstoff *m.*
materialism *s.* Materialismus *m.*
materialist Materialist(in) *m.(f.)*
materialistic *a.* materialistisch.
materialize *v.t.* verwirklichen; ~ *v.i.* sich ver wirklichen, zu Stande kommen.
maternal *a.*, **~ly** *adv.* mütterlich.
maternity *s.* Mutterschaft *f.;* ~ **hospital,** Entbindungsanstalt *f.*
maternity leave *s.* Mutterschaftsurlaub *m.*
mathematical *a.*, **~ly** *adv.* mathematisch.
mathematician *s.* Mathematiker *m.*
mathematics *s.pl.* Mathematik *f.*
matinée *s.* Matinee *f.*, Nachmittagsvorstellung *f.*
matins *s.pl.* Frühmesse, Frühmette *f.*, Matutin *f.*, Morgenlob *n.*
matricide *s.* Muttermord *m.*
matriculate *v.t.* einschreiben, immatrikulieren; ~ *v.i.* sich immatrikulieren.
matrimonial *a.*, **~ly** *adv.* ehelich.
matrimony *s.* Ehe *f.*
matrix *s.* Matrize *f.*, Matrix *f.*
matron *s.* Matrone; Vorsteherin *f.;* Oberschwester *f.*
matt *a.* matt, mattiert.
matted *a.* verfilzt.
matter *s.* Stoff *m.;* Sache *m.;* Gegenstand *m.;* Eiter *m.;* Matterie *f.;* (*typ.*) Satz *m.;* *business* ~*s*, geschäftliche Angelegenheiten; ~ **of course,** *s.* Selbstverständlichkeit; *as a* ~ *of fact*, tatsächlich; *matter-of-fact*, ~ *a.* sachlich, nüchtern; ~ **of opinion,** Ansichtssache *f.;* *what is the* ~*?*, was ist los? *no* ~ *how*, gleichgültig, wie...; ~ *v.i.* darauf ankommen, etwas ausmachen; bedeutsam sein, wichtig sein; *it doesn't* ~, es macht nichts; *it doesn't* ~ *to me*, es ist mir egal.
mattock *s.* Hacke *f.*, Breithacke *f.*
mattress *s.* Matratze *f.*
mature *a.*, **~ly** *adv.* reif; fällig; reiflich; ~ *v.t.* reifen; **~d** *a.* abgelagert; *to allow to* ~, ablagern lassen.

maturity *s.* Reife *f.*; Verfallzeit *f.*; Fälligkeit *f.*, Fälligkeitsdatum *n.*
maudlin *a.* weinerlich, rührlich, gefühlsselig.
maul *v.t.* stampfen; schlagen; verletzen; übelzurichten; verreißen.
maunder *v.i.* faseln.
Maundy Thursday *s.* Gründonnerstag *m.*
mausoleum *s.* Mausoleum *n.*
mauve *a.* mauve, malvenfarbig.
maverick *s.* Allein-, Einzelgänger(in) *m.(f.); Ab*trünnige(r).
maw *s.* Magen (der Tiere) *m.*; Kropf *m.*; Hals *m.*; Maul *n.*
mawkish *a.* widerlich; rührselig; kitschig; widerlich süß.
maxim *s.* Grundsatz *m.*, Maxime *f.*
maximum *s.* Höchstmaß *n.*; Höchst...; Maximum *n.*; ~ **price,** Höchstpreis *m.*
may *v.i.ir.* dürfen, mögen, können; ~ *s.* Weißdorn *m.*
May *s.* Mai *m.*
maybe *adv.* vielleicht.
May Day *s.* der erste Mai, *m.* der Maifeiertag.
mayhem *s.* Chaos *n.*
mayonnaise *s.* Mayonnaise *f.*
mayor *s.* Bürgermeister(in) *m.(f.)*
mayoralty *s.* Bürgermeisteramt *n.*
Maypole *s.* Maibaum *m.*
maze *s.* Labyrinth *n.*; Wirrwarr *m.*
MBA *Master of Business Administration,* Magister der Betriebswirtschaftslehre.
M.C. *master of ceremonies,* Zeremonienmeister, Conférencier.
M.D. *Medicinae Doctor,* Doktor der Medizin, Dr. med.
me *pn.* mich, mir.
mead *s.* Met *m.*
meadow *s.* Wiese *f.*
meager *a.*, **~ly** *adv.* mager; dürftig.
meal *s.* Schrotmehl *n.*; Mahlzeit *f.*; Essen *n.*
mealtime *s.* Essenszeit *f.*
mealy *a.* mehlig.
mealy-mouthed *a.* unaufrichtig.
mean *a.*, **~ly** *adv.* niedrig, gemein; bösartig, gehässig; geizig, knauserig; verächtlich; mittler, Durchschnitts..., mittelmäßig; *in the ~time,* inzwischen; ~ *s.* Mittel(weg) *n.*; Mitte *f.*; ~ *v.t. & i. ir.* meinen, bedeuten; beabsichtigen; *she ~s it!* sie meint das ernst!
meander *s.* Windung *f.*; ~ *v.i.* sich schlängeln; abschweifen; schlendern.
meaning *s.* Sinn *m.*; Bedeutung *f.*
meaningful *a.* sinnvoll; bedeutungsvoll.
meaningless *a.* sinnlos.
meanness *s.* Gemeinheit *f.*; Filzigkeit *f.*; Geiz *m.*, Knauserigkeit, Bösartigkeit, Gehässigkeit, Niedrigkeit *f.*
means *s.pl.* Mittel *n.*; Vermögen *n.*; ~ **of production,** Produktionsmittel *n.pl.*
meantime *s. in the ~* in der Zwischenzeit, inzwischen.
meanwhile *adv.* inzwischen.
measles *s.pl.* Masern *f.pl.*; *German ~,* Röteln *pl.*
measly *a.* (*fam. pej.*) popelig; mickrig.
measurable *a.*, **measurably** *adv.* meßbar; (*fig.*) erkennbar, deutlich.
measure *s.* Maß *n.*; Maßstab *m.*; (*mus.*) Takt *m.*; (*ar.*) Teilor, Faktor *m.*; Maßregel *f.*; Menge *f.*; Maßnahme *f.*; *to ~, a.* nach Maß; **made-to-~** *a.* maßgearbeitet; *to take ~s,* Maßnahmen ergreifen; ~ *v.t. & i.* messen, abmessen; enthalten.
measured *a.* rhythmisch, gleichmäßig; gemessen; bedacht, bedächtig.
measurement *s.* Messung *f.*; Maß *n.*; *to take a person's ~,* einem Maß nehmen.
meat *s.* Fleisch *n.*; Speise *f.*
meatball *s.* Fleischklößchen *n.*
meat pie *s.* Fleischpastete *f.*
meaty *a.* fleischig; (*fig.*) gehaltvoll.
mechanic *s.* Mechaniker *m.*
mechanical *a.*, **~ly** *adv.* mechanisch.
mechanics *s.* Mechanik *f.*; Mechanismus *m.*
mechanism *s.* Getriebe *n.*, Mechanismus *m.*
mechanize *v.t.* mechanisieren.
med. *medical,* medizinisch; *medium,* mittelgroß; *medieval,* mittelalterlich.
medal *s.* Orden *m.*; Medaille *f.*
medalist *s.* Medaillengewinner(in) *m.(f.)*
medallion *s.* Medaillon *n.*
meddle *v.i.* sich mischen, sich einmischen.
meddlesome *a.* sich einmischend.
media *s.pl.* Medien *pl.*
mediate *v.i.* vermitteln.
mediation *s.* Vermittlung *f.*
mediator *s.* Vermittler, Fürsprecher *m.*
medical *a.*, **~ly** *adv.* medizinisch; ~ **care** *s.* ärztliche Betreuung *f.*; ~ **certificate** *s.* ärztliches Attest *n.*; ~ **examination** *s.* ärztliche Untersuchung *f.*; ~ **opinion** *s.* ärztliches Gutachten *n.*; ~ **practitioner** *s.* praktischer Arzt *m.*; (*mil.*) ~ **service** *s.* Sanitätsdienst *m.*
medicate *v.t.* mit Arznei versetzen; medizinisch behandeln.
medication *s.* Medikation *f.*; Medizin *f.*; Medikament *n.*
medicinal *a.*, **~ly** *adv.* medizinisch, Heil...
medicine *s.* Arznei *f.*; Medizin *f.*
medieval *a.* mittelalterlich; *the ~ period,* Mittelalter *n.*
mediocre *a.* mittelmäßig.
mediocrity *s.* Mittelmäßigkeit *f.*
meditate *v.t. & i.* nachdenken, nachsinnen, überlegen; meditieren.
meditation *s.* Betrachtung *f.*; Meditation *f.*
Mediterranean *a.* Mittelmeer *n.*; ~ *a.* Mittelmeer..., mittelländisch; südländisch.
medium *s.* Mittel *n.*; Bindemittel (Malerei) *n.*; Mittelding *n.*; Medium *n.*; ~ *a.* Mittel..., mittlere; ~ **of exchange,** Tauschmittel *m.* **~-sized** *a.* mittelgroß; ~ **wave** *s.* (*radio*) Mittelwelle.
medley *s.* Gemenge *n.*, Mischmasch *m.*; Potpourri, Medley *n.*
meek *a.*, **~ly** *adv.* sanftmütig; demütig.
meet *v.t. & i.* ir. treffen; begegnen; entgegenkommen; versammeln; (Schuld) bezahlen; erleiden; abholen; erfüllen; sich kennenlernen.
meeting *s.* Zusammentreffen *n.*; Versammlung, Sitzung *f.*; *to call a ~ for 10 o'clock,* eine Sitzung auf 10 Uhr einberufen.
meeting place *s.* Treffpunkt *m.*
megacycle *s.* (*radio*) Megahertz *n.*
megalomania *s.* Größenwahn *m.*
megaphone *s.* Megaphon *n.*

melancholic *a.* schwermütig, melancholisch.
melancholy *s.* Schwermut *f.*; ~ *a.* schwermütig.
mellow *a.* mürbe; mild; reif; weich; ~ *v.t.* zur Reife bringen; mürbe machen; ~ *v.i.* mürbe werden; sich mildern; reif werden.
melodious *s.*, **~ly** *adv.* wohlklingend, melodisch.
melodramatic *a.* melodramatisch.
melody *s.* Melodie *f.*
melon *s.* Melone *f.*
melt *v.t.* schmelzen; ~ *v.i.* schmelzen, zerfließen; **melting point** *s.* Schmelzpunkt *m.*; **melting pot** *s.* Schmelztiegel *m.*
member *s.* Glied *n.*; Mitglied *n.*
membership *s.* Mitgliedschaft *f.*; Mitgliederzahl *f.*; ~ **card** *s.* Mitgliedskarte *f.*; ~ **subscription** *s.* Mitgliedsbeitrag *m.*
membrane *s.* Häutchen *n.*, Membran(e) *f.*
memento *s.* Andenken *n.*
memo *s.* Mitteilung *f.*, Notiz *f.*
memoir *s.* Denkschrift *f.*; **~s** *pl.* Memoiren *pl.*
memorable *a.* **~bly** *adv.* denkwürdig.
memorandum *s.* Notiz *f.*; Anmerkung *f.*; Denkschrift *f.*; Mitteilung *f.*
memorial *s.* Denkmal *n.*; Denkschrift, Bittschrift *f.*; ~ *a.* Gedächtnis...; ~ **celebration** *s.* Gedenkfeier *f.*; ~ **Day** *s.* Gedenktag für die Gefallenen.
memorize *v.t.* auswendig lernen.
memory *s.* Gedächtnis *n.*; Andenken *n.*
menace *v.t.* drohen; bedrohen; ~ *s.* Drohung *f.*
menacing *a.* drohend.
mend *v.t.* (aus)bessern; reparieren, ~ *v.i.* sich bessern.
mendacious *a.* lügenhaft.
mendacity *s.* Lügenhaftigkeit *f.*
mendicancy *s.* Bettelei *f.*
mendicant *a.* bettelnd; ~ *s.* Bettler, Bettelmönch *m.*
menfolk *s.* Männer *pl.*
menial *a.* Gesinde...; niedrig; gemein; ~ *s.* Diener *m.*
meningitis *s.* Hirnhautentzündung *f.*
menopause *s.* Wechseljahre *n. pl.*; Klimakterium *n.*
menstrual *a.* menstrual; Menstruations...
menstruation *s.* Menstruation *f.*
menswear *s.* Herrenbekleidung *f.*
mental *a.*, **~ly** *adv.* geistig, innerlich; ~ **breakdown,** Nervenzusammenbruch *m.*; ~ **case,** ~ **patient** *s.* Geisteskranker *m.*; **~ly defective** *a.* schwachsinnig; ~ **deficiency** *s.* Schwachsinn *m.*; ~ **hospital** *s.* psychiatrische Klinik *f.*; ~ **illness** *s.* Geisteskrankheit *f.*
mentality *s.* Mentalität *f.*
menthol *s.* Menthol *n.*
mention *s.* Erwähnung *f.*; ~ *v.t.* erwähnen; *don't ~ it!,* bitte!; *not to ~,* geschweige denn, nicht zu vergessen.
mentor *s.* Mentor(in) *m.(f.)*
menu *s.* Speisenfolge *f.*; Speisekarte *f.*; Menü *n.*
men working! Baustelle!
meow *v.i.* miauen; ~ *s.* Miauen *n.*
MEP *Member of the European Parliament,* Mitglied des Europaparlaments.
mercantile *a.* kaufmännisch, Handels...
mercenary *a.* gedungen; ~ *s.* Söldner *m.*
mercer *s.* Schnittwaren-, Seidenhändler *m.*
merchandise *s.* Ware *f.*
merchant *s.* Kaufmann *m.*; ~ **ship** *s.* Handelsschiff *n.*; ~ **marine** *s.* Handelsmarine *f.*
merciful *a.*, **~ly** *adv.* gnädig; barmherzig.
merciless *a.*, **~ly** *adv.* gnadenlos; unbarmherzig.
mercurial *a.* Quecksilber...; lebhaft, sprunghaft, wechselhaft.
mercury *s.* Quecksilber *n.*
mercy *s.* Barmherzigkeit, Gnade *f.*
mere *a.* bloß; lauter; **~ly** *adv.* nur.
meretricious *a.*, **~ly** *adv.* protzig; falsch; trügerisch.
merge *v.t.* zusammenlegen; fusionieren; verschmelzen; ~ *v.i.* aufgehen (in); zusammenkommen.
merger *s.* Zusammenlegung, Fusion *f.*
meridian *s.* Meridian *m.*; Höhepunkt *m.*
meringue *s.* Meringe *f.*; Baiser *n.*
merit *s.* Verdienst *n.*; Wert *m.*; Leistung *f.*; ~ *v.t.* verdienen.
meritocracy *s.* Meritokratie *f.*
meritorious *a.*, **~ly** *adv.* verdienstlich.
mermaid *s.* Meerjungfrau, Seejungfer *f.*, Nixe *f.*
merriment *s.* Fröhlichkeit, Heiterkeit, Belustigung *f.*
merry *a.*, **~ily** *adv.* lustig, fröhlich, munter; **~-go-round** *s.* Karussell *n.*
mesh *s.* Masche *f.*; Netz *n.*; ~ *v.t.* bestricken, fangen; (*mech.*) in Eingriff bringen; ~ *v.i.* (*mech.*) ineinandergreifen.
mesmerize *v.t.* hypnotisieren; faszinieren.
mess *s.* Offizierstisch *m.*; Messe *f.*; Durcheinander *n.*; Schweinerei *f.*; Unordnung *f.*; Sauerei *f.*; ~ *v.i.* zusammen speisen; ~ **up** *v.t.* verpfuschen; durcheinanderbringen.
message *s.* Botschaft *f.*; Nachricht *f.*; *to give a ~,* etwas ausrichten; *to leave a ~,* etwas ausrichten lassen; ~ **center** *s.* (*mil.*) Nachrichtenstelle, Meldesammelstelle *f.*
messenger *s.* Bote *m.*; Botin *f.*; Überbringer(in) *m.f.*; ~ **boy** *s.* Botenjunge, Laufbursche *m.*
Messiah *s.* Messias *m.*
Messrs. *Messieurs,* Herren.
mess-up *s.* Durcheinander *n.*; Kuddelmuddel *n.*
messy *a.* unordentlich; schmutzig, dreckig.
metabolism *s.* Stoffwechsel *m.*; Metabolismus *m.*
metal *s.* Metall *n.*
metal detector *s.* Metallsuchgerät *n.*
metallic *a.* metallisch.
metallurgy *s.* Metallurgie *f.*; Hüttenkunde *f.*
metamorphose *v.t.* umgestalten, verwandeln, umwandeln; ~ *v.i. sich* verwandeln.
metamorphosis *s.* Verwandlung *f.*, Metamorphose *f.*
metaphor *s.* Metapher *f.*
metaphorical *a.* bildlich, übertragen; metaphorisch.
metaphysical *a.* metaphysisch.
metaphysics *s.pl.* Metaphysik *f.*
mete ~ out *v.t.* zumessen.
meteor *s.* Meteor *n.*
meteorological *a.* meteorologisch, wetterkundlich; ~ **service** *s.* Wetterdienst *m.*
meteorology *s.* Wetterkunde *f.*; Meteorologie *f.*
meter *s.* Meßgerät *n.*; (*elek.*) Zähler *m.*; Gasuhr, Wasseruhr *f.*, Versmaß *n.*, Meter *m.*, Metrum *n.*; ~ *v.t.* messen.

meter reader *s.* Gas- oder Stromableser *m.*
method *s.* Verfahren *n.;* Ordnung *f.;* Lehrweise *f.,* Methode *f.*
methodical *a.* methodisch.
Methodist *s.* Methodist(in) *m.f.*
methodology *s.* Methodik *f.*
methyl *s.* Methyl *n.*
meticulous *a.*, **~ly** *adv.* peinlich genau, sorgfältig, exakt.
metric *s.* metrisch, Meter...; **~ system** *s.* metrisches System *n.*
metrical *a.*, **~ly** *adv.* metrisch, Vers...
metronome *s.* Metronom *n.*
metropolis *s.* Hauptstadt, Weltstadt. *f.;* Metropole *f.*
metropolitan *a.* hauptstädtisch.; *~ New York* Großraum, Weltstadt New York.
mettle *s.* Temperament *n.;* Eifer *m.*, Mut *m.; be on one's ~*, vor Eifer brennen.
mettlesome *a.* mutig, feurig, schneidig.
mew *v.i.* miauen; kreischen.
Mexican *a.* mexikanisch; ~ *s.* Mexikaner(in) *m.(f.)*
Mexico *s.* Mexiko *n.*
mfd. *manufactured,* angefertigt.
mg *milligram,* Milligramm, mg.
mica *s.* Glimmer *m.*
micro *a.* mikro..., Mikro...
microbe *s.* Mikrobe *f.*
microbiology *s.* Mikrobiologie *f.*
microchip *s.* Mikrochip *m.*
microfiche *s.* Mikrofiche *m.*
micrometer *s.* Mikrometer *n.*
microorganism *s.* Mikroorganismus *m.*
microphone *s.* Mikrophon *n.*
microprocessor *s.* Mikroprozessor *m.*
microscope *s.* Mikroskop *n.*
microscopic *a.* mikroskopisch.
microwave *s.* Mikrowelle *f.;* **~ oven** *s.* Mikrowellenherd *m.*, Mikrowellenofen *m.*
mid *a.* mitten, mittel; *in ~-air,* mitten in der Luft; *~-June,* Mitte Juni.
midday *s.* Mittag *m.*
middle *s.* Mitte *f.;* ~ *a.* Mittel...
Middle Ages *s.pl.* Mittelalter *n.*
middle class *s.* Mittelschicht *f.*, Mittelstand *m.;* ~-~ *a.* bürgerlich, Mittelstands..., Mittelständisch.
Middle East *s.* Mittlerer Osten, Naher Osten *m.*
middleman *s.* Zwischenhändler *m.*
middle-of-the-road *a.* gemäßigt.
middleweight *s.* Mittelgewicht *n.*
middling *a.* mittelmäßig.
midfield *s.* Mittelfeld *n.*
midge *s.* Mücke *f.*
midget *s.* Zwerg *m.;* Liliputaner(in) *m.(f.)*
midnight *s.* Mitternacht *f.;* ~ *a.* mitternächtlich; **~ sun** *s.* Mitternachtssonne *f.*
midshipman *s.* Seekadett *m.;* Fähnrich *m.* zur See.
midst *s.* Mitte *f.; in the midst of,* mitten in.
midsummer *s.* Sommersonnenwende *f.;* Hochsommer *m.*
midway *adv.* auf halbem Wege.
midwife *s.* Hebamme *f.*
midwifery *s.* Geburtshilfe *f.*
midwinter *s.* Wintersonnenwende *f.;* Mitte *(f.)* des Winters, Wintermitte *f.*
miff *v.t.* *(fam.)* verärgern.
might *s.* Macht, Gewalt *f.*
mighty *a.*, **~ily** *adv.* mächtig, überaus.
migraine *s.* Migräne *f.*
migrant *s.* Wanderer *m.*, Wandertier *n.;* ~ *a.* Wander...; **~ worker**, Wanderarbeiter *m.*, Gastarbeiter *m.*
migrate *v.i.* wandern, fortziehen.
migration *s.* Wanderung *f.*
migratory *a.* wandernd, Zug...
mike *s.* *(fam.)* Mikrophon *n.*
mild *a.*, **~ly** *adv.* sanft, mild, leicht.
mildew *s.* Mehltau *m.*, Schimmel *m.*
mile *s.* Meile *f.;* 1609 Meter.
mileage *s.* Meilenzahl *f.*
milestone *s.* Meilenstein *m.*
militant *a.* militant; streitend, kriegführend.
militarism *s.* Militarismus *m.*
militarize *v.t.* militarisieren.
military *a.* militärisch; **~ bridge** *s.* Kriegsbrücke *f.;* **~ code** *s.* Militärstrafgesetzbuch *n.;* **~ law** *s.* Kriegsrecht *n.;* **~ government** *s.* Militärregierung *f.;* **~ post** *s.* Standort *m.;* **~ target, ~ objective** *s.* kriegswichtiges Ziel *n.;* ~ *s.* Soldatenstand *m.*, Militär *n.*
militate *v.i.* **~ (for) against** sprechen gegen (für).
militia *s.* Milizia *f.;* Land-, Bürgerwehr *f.*
milk *s.* Milch *f.;* ~ *v.t.* melken.
milkmaid *s.* Milchmädchen *n.*
milksop *s.* Schwächling *m.*
milktooth *s.* Milchzahn *m.*
Milky Way *s.* Milchstraße *f.*
mill *s.* Mühle *f.;* Fabrik *f.;* ~ *v.t.* mahlen; (Münzen) rändeln; fräsen; walken; walzen.
millennium *s.* Millenium, Jahrtausend *n.*
miller *s.* Müller *m.*
millet *s.* Hirse *f.*
milliner *s.* Hutmacher(in) *m.(f.);* Putzmacher(in) *m.(f.)*
millinery *s.* Putzwaren *f.pl.*
milling machine *s.* Fräsmaschine *f.*
million *s.* Million *f.*
millionaire *s.* Millionär *m.;* Millionärin *f.*
mime *s.* Pantomime *f.;* Pantomime *m.;* Pantomimin *f.;* ~ *v.i.* pantomimisch darstellen.
mimeograph *s.* Mimeograph *m.;* ~ *v.t.* vervielfältigen.
mimic *a.* mimisch, Schein...; ~ *s.* Mime *m.;* ~ *v.t.* nachäffen, nachahmen.
mimicry *s.* Mimikrie *f.;* Nachahmen *n.*
minatory *a.* drohend.
mince *v.t.* kleinhacken; *to ~ one's words,* sich ein Blatt vor den Mund nehmen; ~ *v.i.* sich zieren.
mincemeat *s.* (süße) Pastetenfüllung *f.* (Fett, Rosinen, Zitrone, etc.); Hackfleisch *n.; to make ~ of (fig.)* aus jm. Hackfleisch machen.
mincingly *adv.* geziert, affektiert.
mind *s.* Gemüt *n.;* Geist, Verstand, Sinn *m.;* Neigung *f.;* Gedanken *pl.;* Gedächtnis *n.*, Meinung *f.; to make up one's ~*, sich entschließen; *to bear in ~*, sich merken; *to change one's ~*, sich anders besinnen, seine Meinung ändern; ~ *v.t.* merken; achten; sich bekümmern

um; ~ *v.i.* willens sein; *never ~!*, (es) macht nichts!
minded *a.* gesinnt, geneigt.
mindful *a.*, **~ly** *adv.* achtsam; eingedenk, denkend.
mindless *a.* hirnlos, ohne Verstand; sinnlos; geistlos.
mine *pn.* mein, meinige; ~ *s.* Bergwerk *n.*; Grube *f.*; Mine *f.*; ~ *v.t.* graben; Minen legen, Bergbau betreiben.
minefield *s.* (*mil.*) Minenfeld *n.*
miner *s.* Bergmann *m.*
mineral *s.* Mineral *n.*; ~ *a.* mineralisch; ~ **water** *s.* Mineralwasser *n.*
mineralogy *s.* Mineralogie *f.*
minesweeper *s.* Minensucher *m.*
mingle *v.t.* & *i.* mischen; sich mischen.
miniature *s.* Miniatur *f.*; Miniatur...
minimal *a.*, **~ly** *adv.* minimal.
minimize *v.t.* möglichst klein machen; auf ein Minimum reduzieren; bagatellisieren, herabsetzen.
minimum *s.* Mindestmaß, Minimum *n.*
mining *s.* Bergbau *m.*; ~ **academy** *s.* Bergakademie *f.*; ~ **bureau** *s.* Bergamt *n.*; ~ **industry** *s.* Montanindustrie *f.*
minion *s.* Günstling *m.*
miniskirt *s.* Minirock *m.*
minister *s.* Minister, Gesandte *m.*; Pastor, Pfarrer *m.*; Geistlicher *m.*; ~ *v.i.* dienen, (um einen) sich kümmern.
ministerial *a.*, **~ly** *adv.* ministeriell; geistlich.
ministration *s. usu. pl.* Pflege, Fürsorge *f.*
ministry *s.* Dienst *m.*; Ministerium *n.*; geistliche Amt; *enter the ~*, Geistlicher werden.
mink *s.* Nerz *m.*
minor *a.* kleiner, geringer; unwichtig; leicht; jünger; unmündig; (*mus.*) Moll; ~ *s.* Moll *n.*; Minderjährige(r) *m./f.*
minority *s.* Minderheit *f.*; Unmündigkeit *f.*, Minorität *f.*
minster *s.* Münster *m.* or *n.*
minstrel *s.* Spielmann *m.*; Sänger, Minnesänger *m.*
mint *s.* Münze *f.*; Fundgrube *f.*; Minze (Pflanze) *f.*; ~ *v.t.* münzen, prägen; ~ *a. in ~ condition*, in tadellosem Zustand.
mintage *s.* Prägen *n.*; Münzgebühr *f.*
mint sauce *s.* Minzsoße *f.*
minuet *s.* Menuett *f.*
minus *pr.* minus.
minuscule *a.* winzig.
minute *a.* klein; umständlich; ~ *s.* Minute *f.*; Notiz *f.*; **~s** *pl.* Protokoll *n.*; *to keep the ~s*, das Protokoll führen; ~ **hand** *s.* Minutenzeiger *m.*
minutely *adv.* genauestens, sorgfältig.
minutiae *s.pl.* Einzelheiten *f.pl.*
minx *s.* (kleines) Biest *n.*
miracle *s.* Wunder *n.*
miraculous *a.*, **~ly** *adv.* wunderbar.
mirage *s.* Luftspiegelung *f.*, Fata Morgana *f.*
mire *s.* Schlamm *m.*, Morast *n.*
mirror *s.* Spiegel *m.*; ~ *v.t.* spiegeln; ~ **image** *s.* Spiegelbild *n.*
mirth *s.* Fröhlichkeit, Freude, Lust, Heiterkeit *f.*
misadventure *s.* Mißgeschick *n.*
misalliance *s.* Mißheirat *f.*, Mesalliance *f.*
misanthrope *s.* Misanthrop *m.*, Menschenfeind *m.*
misapplication *s.* falsche Anwendung *f.*
misapply *v.t.* falsch anwenden.
misapprehend *v.t.* mißverstehen.
misapprehension *s.* Mißverständnis *n.*
misappropriate *v.t.* unterschlagen, veruntreuen.
misbehave *v.i.* sich schlecht aufführen *or* benehmen.
misbehavior *s.* schlechtes Benehmen *n.*
miscalculate *v.t.* falsch berechnen; falsch einschätzen.
miscalculation *s.* Rechenfehler *m.*; Fehleinschätzung *f.*
miscarriage *s.* Fehlgeburt *f.*; *~ of justice*, Fehlurteil *n.*, Justizirrtum *m.*
miscarry *v.i.* eine Fehlgeburt haben; mißlingen.
miscellaneous *a.* gemischt.
miscellany *s.* Gemisch *n.*; vermischte Schriften *f.pl.*
mischance *s.* unglücklicher Zufall *m.*, Mißgeschick *n.*
mischief *s.* Unsinn *m.*; Unfug *m.*
mischief-maker *s.* Unheilstifter *m.*
mischievous *a.*, **~ly** *adv.* schelmisch; spitzbübisch; boshaft; mutwillig.
misconceive *v.t.* falsch auffassen.
misconception *s.* Mißverständnis *n.*
misconduct *s.* Fehltritt *m.*; schlechte Verwaltung *f.*
misconstruction *s.* Mißdeutung *f.*
misconstrue *v.t.* mißdeuten.
miscount *v.t.* & *i.* falsch(aus)zählen, sich verzählen.
miscreant *s.* Bösewicht *m.*, Schurke *m.*
misdeed *s.* Missetat *f.*; Verbrechen *n.*
misdemeanor *s.* Vergehen *n.*
misdirect *v.t.* falsch leiten; falsch adressieren.
miser *s.* Geizhals *m.*
miserable *a.*, **miserably** *adv.* elend, unglücklich, schwer, miserabel.
miserly *a.* karg, geizig.
misery *s.* Elend *n.*, Not *f.*; Kummer *m.*; Trauer *f.*, Jammer *m.*
misfire *v.i.* versagen (Gewehr); fehlzünden (motor).
misfit *s.* Außenseiter(in) *m.(f.)*
misfortune *s.* Unglück *n.*; Mißgeschick *n.*
misgiving *s.* Befürchtung *f.*; Bedenken *pl.*
misgovern *v.t.* schlecht regieren.
misguide *v.t.* verleiten.
misguided *a.* töricht.
mishandle *v.t.* schlecht handhaben; (*fam.*) verkorxen.
mishap *s.* Mißgeschick *n.*; Unfall *m.*
mishear *v.t.* & *i.* (sich) verhören.
mish-mash *s.* Mischmasch *m.*
misinform *v.t.* falsch berichten.
misinterpret *v.t.* mißdeuten.
misinterpretation *s.* falsche Auslegung *f.*, Mißdeutung.
misjudge *v.i.* & *t.* falsch urteilen, verkennen.
mislay *v.t.st.* verlegen.
mislead *v.t.st.* verleiten; irreführen.
misleading *a.* irreführend.
mismanage *v.t.* übel verwalten.

mismanagement *s.* Mißwirtschaft *f.;* schlechte Verwaltung *f.*
misnomer *s.* falsche Bezeichnung *f.*
misogynist *s.* Frauenfeind *m.*
misogyny *s.* Misogynie *f.*
misplace *v.t.* verlegen.
misplaced *a.* deplaziert; verlegt.
misprint *v.t.* verdrucken; ~ *s.* Druckfehler *m.*
mispronounce *v.t.* falsch aussprechen.
misquotation *s.* falsches Zitat *n.*
misquote *v.t.* falsch zitieren.
misread *v.t.* falschlesen; falsch deuten.
misrepresent *v.t.* falsch darstellen.
misrepresentation *s.* falsche Darstellung *f.;* Verdrehung *f.*
misrule *s.* schlechte Regierung *f.*
miss *v.t.* missen, vermissen; verfehlen, verpassen; versäumen; übersehen; auslassen; ~ *s.* Fehlstoß, -wurf, -schuß *m.;* ~ *s.* Fräulein *n.;* Frau *f.*
misshapen *a.* mißgestaltet.
missile *s.* Wurfgeschoß *n.;* Flugkörper *m.*
missing *a.* verloren, abwesend; (*mil.*) vermißt.
mission *s.* Sendung *f.;* Gesandtschaft *f.;* Mission *f.;* (*mil.*) Auftrag *m.*
missionary *s.* Missionar *m.;* Missionarin *f.;* ~ *a.* missionarisch.
misspell *v.t.r. & st.* falsch buchstabieren, falsch schreiben.
misspend *v.t.* verschwenden.
misspent *a.* vergeudet, verschwendet.
misstate *v.t.* falsch angeben, falsch darlegen, falsch darstellen.
misstatement *s.* falsche Angabe *f.;* falsche Darstellung *f.*
mist *s.* Dunst *m.;* Nebel *m.*
mistake *v.t.st.* mißverstehen; ~ *v.i.* sich irren; ~ *s.* Irrtum *m.;* Versehen *n.;* Fehler *m.*
mistaken *a.* irrig.
mistakenly *adv.* irrtümlicherweise.
Mister (Mr.) *s.* Herr (Titel) *m.*
mistimed *a.* unzeitig.
mistletoe *s.* Mistel *f.*
mistranslate *v.t.* falsch übersetzen.
mistranslation *s.* falsche Übersetzung *f.;* Übersetzungsfehler *m.*
mistreat *v.t.* mißhandeln.
mistreatment *s.* Mißhandlung *f.*
mistress *s.* Gebieterin *f.;* Lehrerin *f.;* Herrin; Meisterin *f.;* Geliebte *f.;* **~,** (*Mrs.*) Frau (als Titel) *f.*
mistrust *s.* Mißtrauen *n.;* ~ *v.t.* mißtrauen.
mistrustful *a.,* **~ly** *adv.* mißtrauisch.
misty *a.,* **~ily** *adv.* neb(e)lig, trübe.
misunderstand *v.t.st.* mißverstehen.
misunderstanding *s.* Mißverständnis *n.*
misunderstood *a.* unverstanden; verkannt.
misuse *v.t.* mißbrauchen; ~ *s.* Mißbrauch, falscher Gebrauch *m.*
mite *s.* Milbe *f.;* Scherflein *n.;* kleines Kind *n.;* kleines bißchen.
mitigate *v.t.* lindern, mildern.
mitigation *s.* Linderung *f.;* Milderung *f.*
mitre *s.* Bischofsmütze *f.,* Mitra *f.*
mitten *s.* Fausthandschuh *m.*
mix *v.t.* mischen, vermischen; (Salat) anmachen; ~ *v.i.* sich vermischen, verkehren; *to ~ up,* durcheinanderbringen, verwechseln; **~ed doubles,** *s.* (*tennis*) gemischtes Doppel *n.* **~ed grill,** *s.* Grillteller *m.;* **~ed marriage,** *s.* Mischehe *f.*
mixer *s.* Mixer *m.;* Mischmaschine *f.*
mixture *s.* Mischung *f.*
mix-up *s.* Durcheinander *n.;* Mißverständnis *n.;* Verwechslung *f.*
mnemonic *s.* Gedächtnisstütze *f.*
mo. *month,* Monat.
M.O. *Money Order,* Postanweisung *f.*
moan *v.i.* stöhnen; ächzen; ~ *s.* Stöhnen; *n.* Ächzen *n.*
moat *s.* Burggraben *m.*
mob *s.* Pöbel *m.;* Horde, Schar *f.;* ~ *v.t.* lärmend angreifen, belästigen; herfallen über.
mobile *a.* fahrbar, beweglich.
mobile home *s.* Wohnwagen *m.*
mobility *s.* Beweglichkeit *f.*
mobilization *s.* Mobilisierung *f.*
mobilize *v.t.* mobilisieren; mobil machen (Truppen).
moccasin *s.* Mokassin *n.*
mock *a.* Pseudo... nachgemacht; ~ **turtle** *s.* falsche Schildkrötensuppe *f.;* ~ *v.i. & t.* verspotten, täuschen, nachmachen.
mockery *s.* Spott *m.,* Spötterei *f.;* Hohn *m.;* Schein *m.*
mocking *a.* spöttisch; ~ *s.* Spott *m.*
modal *a.* modal; ~ **auxiliary** *s.* Modalverb *n.*
mode *s.* Art und Weise, Sitte *f.;* Modus *m.;* Modalität *f.;* Form *f.;* ~ **of transport,** Transportmittel *n.*
model *s.* Muster, Vorbild *n.;* Modell *n.;* Model *n.;* ~ *v.t.* modellieren, entwerfen; modeln.
modeling *s.* Formung *f.;* Modellieren *n.*
modem *s.* Modem *n.*
moderate *a.,* **~ly** *adv.* mäßig; gemäßigt; mittelmäßig; ~ *v.t.* mäßigen.
moderation *s.* Mäßigung, Mäßigkeit *f.*
modern *a.* neu, modern.
modernism *s.* Modernismus *m.*
modernist *s.* Modernist(in) *m.(f.)*
modernity *s.* Modernität *f.*
modernize *v.t.* modernisieren.
modest *a.,* **~ly** *adv.* bescheiden, sittsam.
modesty *s.* Sittsamkeit; Bescheidenheit *f.*
modicum *s.* geringe Menge *f.*
modifiable *a.* modifizierbar.
modification *s.* Abänderung, Veränderung *f.;* Einschränkung *f.*
modify *v.t.* abändern, einschränken, mildern.
modular *a.* Modul...
modulate *v.t.* modulieren; anpassen.
module *s.* Modul *n.;* Bauelement *n.;* Kapsel *f.*
mohair *s.* Mohair *n.*
moiety *s.* Hälfte *f.*
moist *a.* feucht.
moisten *v.t.* anfeuchten, befeuchten.
moisture *s.* Feuchtigkeit *f.*
moisturizer *s.* Feuchtigkeits...; Feuchtigkeitscreme *f.*
molar *s.* Backenzahn *m.*
molasses *s.* Melasse *f.;* Sirup *m.*
mold *s.* Form *f.;* Gießform *f.;* Schablone *f.;* Schimmel *m.;* ~ *v.t.* formen; gießen; ~ *v.i.* schimmeln.

molder *v.i.* vermodern; zerbröckeln.
molding *s.* Fries *m.*, Simswerk *n.*
moldy *a.* schimm(e)lig, moderig.
mole *s.* Maulwurf *m.*; Muttermal *n.*
molecular *a.* molekular.
molecule *s.* Molekül *n.*
molehill *s.* Maulwurfshügel *m.*
molest *v.t.* belästigen, beschweren.
molestation *s.* Belästigung *f.*
moll *s.* Gangsterbraut *f.*
mollify *v.t.* erweichen; besänftigen.
mollusk *s.* Molluske *f.*, Weichtier *n.*
mollycoddle *s.* Weichling *m.*; ~ *v.t.* verzärteln, verpäppeln.
molt *v.i.* (sich) mausern; häuten; haaren; ~ *s.* Mauser *f.*, Haarwechsel *m.*, Häutung *f.*
molten *a.* geschmolzen, gegossen.
mom, mommy *s.* Mama, Mutti *f.*
moment *s.* Augenblick *m.*; Moment *m.*
momentary *a.*, **~ily** *adv.* einen Augenblick dauernd.
momentous *a.* wichtig, von Bedeutung, bedeutungsvoll, von großer Tragweite.
momentum *s.* Schwung *m.*; Wucht *f.*; Impuls *m.*; Triebkraft *f.*; Moment *n.*
Mon. *Monday,* Montag.
monarch *s.* Monarch(in) *m.(f.)*
monarchical *a.* monarchisch.
monarchist *s.* Monarchist(in) *m.(f.)*
monarchy *s.* Monarchie *f.*
monastery *s.* (Mönchs-) Kloster *n.*
monastic *a.*, **~ally** *adv.* klösterlich.
Monday *s.* Montag *m.*
monetarism *s.* Monetarismus *m.*
monetarist *s.* Monetarist(in) *m.(f.)*
monetary *a.* Monetär...; Währungs...; Geld...; ~ **standard** *s.* Münzfuß *m.*; ~ **unit** *s.* Geld-, Münzeinheit *f.*
money *s.* Geld *n.*; *ready* ~, ~ *in hand,* bares Geld.
moneychanger *s.* Geldwechsler *m.*
money order *s.* Postanweisung *f.*
Mongol *s.* Mongole *m.*, Mongolin *f.*
Mongolia *s.* Mongolei *f.*
Mongolian *a.* mongolisch; ~ *s.* Mongole *m.*; Mongolin *f.*
mongrel *s.* Mischling, Bastard *m.*
monitor *s.* Ermahner *m.*; Klassenordner *n.*; Monitor *m.*; Überwacher *m.*; (*comp*) Bildschirm *m.*; ~ *v.t.* abhören, mithören, überwachen.
monk *s.* Mönch *m.*
monkey *s.* Affe *m.*
monkey business *s.* Schabernack *m.*; krumme Tour *f.*; Unfug *m.*
monkish *a.* mönchisch.
monochrome *a.* einfarbig.
monocle *s.* Monokel *n.*
monogamy *s.* Einehe, Monogamie *f.*
monogram *s.* Namenszug *m.*, Monogramm *n.*
monograph *s.* Monographie *f.*
monologue *s.* Selbstgespräch *n.*; Monolog *m.*
monomania *s.* fixe Idee *f.*, Monomanie *f.*
monoplane *s.* Eindecker *m.*
monopolize *v.t.* monopolisieren; (*fig.*) an sich reißen; mit Beschlag belegen; beherrschen.
monopoly *s.* Alleinhandel *m.*, Monopol *n.*
monosyllabic *a.* einsilbig.
monosyllable *s.* einsilbiges Wort *n.*
monotonous *a.* eintönig.
monotony *s.* Eintönigkeit *f.*
monsoon *s.* Monsun *m.*
monster *s.* Ungeheuer *n.*; Riesen...
monstrance *s.* Monstranz *f.*
monstrosity *s.* Ungeheuerlichkeit *f.*
monstrous *a.*, **~ly** *adv.* ungeheuer; scheußlich.
montage *s.* Montage *f.*
month *s.* Monat *m.*
monthly *a.* & *adv.* monatlich; ~ *s.* Monatsschrift *f.*
monument *s.* Denkmal *n.*
monumental *a.*, **~ly** *adv.* Denkmal..., monumental; gewaltig.
moo *v.i.* muhen; ~ *s.* Muhen *n.*
mood *s.* Stimmung, Laune *f.*; (*gram.*) Modus *m.*
moody *a.*, **~ily** *adv.* mürrisch, launisch.
moon *s.* Mond *m.*; *once in a blue* ~, nur alle Jubeljahre.
mooncalf *s.* Mondkalb *n.*, Schwachsinnige(r) *m./f.*
moonlight *s.* Mondschein *m.*; ~ *v.i.* schwarzarbeiten.
moonshine *s.* Unsinn *m.*
moonstruck *a.* mondsüchtig.
moor *s.* Mohr *m.*; Moor *n.*; ~ *v.t.* (*nav.*) vertäuen, festmachen.
moorhen *s.* Teichhuhn, Wasserhuhn *n.*
mooring *s.* Ankerplatz *m.*
moorish *a.* maurisch; moorig.
moose *s.* Elch *m.*
moot *a.* umstritten; strittig; fraglich; ~ *v.t.* aufwerfen, vorbringen.
mop *s.* Mop, Schwammop *m.*; Scheuertuch *n.*; (*fig.*) Wuschelkopf *m.*; ~ *v.t.* wischen; ~ **up** aufwischen, säubern.
mope *v.i.* Trübsal blasen.
moraine *s.* Moräne *f.*
moral *a.*, **~ly** *adv.* sittlich; gut, moralisch; ~ *s.* Nutzanwendung *f.*; **~s** *pl.* Sitten *f.pl.*; Moral *f.*
morale *s.* Moral, Stimmung *f.*
morality *s.* Sittenlehre, Sittlichkeit *f.*; Moral, Ethik *f.*
moralize *v.i.* Sittlichkeit predigen; moralisieren.
morass *s.* Morast *m.*
moratorium *s.* Moratorium *n.*, Stundung *f.*, Zahlungsaufschub *m.*; Stopp *m.*
morbid *a.* krankhaft; makaber.
mordant *a.*, **~ly** *adv.* beißend.
more *a.* & *adv.* mehr; ferner, noch; *once* ~, noch einmal.
moreover *adv.* überdies, zudem, außerdem.
moribund *a.* sterbend; todgeweiht; (*fig.*) zum Aussterben verurteilt.
Mormon *s.* Mormone *m.*; Mormonin *f.*
morning *s.* Morgen *m.*; **~-after pill** *s.* Pille (für den Morgen) danach; ~ **coat** *s.* Cut *m.*; ~ **star** *s.* Morgenstern *m.*
Moroccan *a.* marokkanisch; ~ *s.* Marokkaner(in) *m.(f.)*
Morocco *s.* Marokko *n.*
moron *s.* Schwachkopf *m.*
morose *a.*, **~ly** *adv.* mürrisch, verdrießlich.
morphine *s.* Morphium *n.*

morphological *a.* morphologisch.
morphology *s.* Morphologie *f.*
Morse *s.* ~ **code** Morsealphabet *n.;* ~ **signal** Morsezeichen *n.*
morsel *s.* Bissen, Happen *m.*
mortal *a.*, **~ly** *adv.* sterblich, tödlich; ~ *sin,* Todsünde *f.;* ~ *s.* Sterbliche *m./f.*, Mensch *m.*
mortality *s.* Sterblichkeit *f.;* ~ **rate** Sterblichkeitsziffer *f.*
mortar *s.* Mörser *m.;* Mörtel *m.;* (*mil.*) Granatwerfer *m.;* ~ *v.t.* mörteln.
mortgage *s.* Hypothek *f.; to foreclose a* ~, eine Hypothek kündigen *or* für verfallen erklären; *debt on* ~, Hypothekenschuld *f.;* ~ **bond,** ~ **deed** *s.* Pfandbrief *m.;* ~ *credit bank,* Bodenkreditbank *f.;* ~ *v.t.* hypothekarisch *or* mit einer Hypothek belasten, verpfänden.
mortician *s.* Leichenbestatter(in) *m.(f.);* Bestattungsunternehmen *m.*
mortification *s.* Beschämung *f.;* Demütigung *f.*
mortify *v.t.* beschämen.
mortuary *a.* Begräbnis...; ~ *s.* Leichenhalle *f.*
mos. *months,* Monate.
mosaic *s.* Mosaik *n.*
Moselle *s.* Mosel *f.;* Moselwein *m.*
mosque *s.* Moschee *f.*
mosquito *s.* Moskito *m.;* Stechmücke *f.*
mosquito net *s.* Moskitonetz *n.*
moss *s.* Moos *n.*
mossy *a.* moosig; bemoost.
most *a.* meist, die meisten; ~ *adv.* meistenteils; höchst; ~ *s.* Meiste *n.; at* ~, höchstens.
mostly *adv.* meistenteils, meist, meistens; hauptsächlich; zum großen Teil.
motel *s.* Motel *n.*
motet *s.* Motette *f.*
moth *s.* Motte *f.;* Nachtfalter *m.*, ~ **ball** Mottenkugel *f.;* **~-eaten** *a.* mottenzerfressen; **~-proof** *a.* mottensicher, mottenfest.
mother *s.* Mutter *f.;* ~ *of pearl,* Perlmutter *f.;* ~ *v.t.* bemuttern.
mother country *s.* Mutterland *n.*
motherhood *s.* Mutterschaft *f.*
mother-in-law *s.* Schwiegermutter *f.*
motherland *s.* Mutterland *n.*
motherly *a.* mütterlich.
mother tongue *s.* Muttersprache *f.*
motif *s.* Motiv *n.*
motion *s.* Bewegung *f.;* Gang *m.;* Trieb *m.;* Antrag *m.*
motionless *a.* unbeweglich.
motion picture *s.* Film *m.*
motivate *v.t.* motivieren, begründen.
motivation *s.* Motivation *f.*
motive *a.* bewegend; ~ *s.* Motiv *n.*, Beweggrund *m.*
motley *a.* scheckig, bunt, kunterbunt.
motor *a.* bewegend; ~ *s.* Motor *m.*, Kraftmaschine *f.;* **~-bike** *s.* Motorrad *n.;* **~-bus** *s.* Autobus *m.;* ~ **coach** *s.* Reiseomnibus *m.;* ~ **pool** *s.* Kraftfahrpark *m.;* ~ **transport service** *s.* (*mil.*) Kraftfahrwesen *n.;* ~ **vehicle** *s.* Motorfahrzeug *n.;* ~ *v.i.* mit dem Auto fahren.
motorist *s.* Motorfahrer *m.*
motorize *v.t.* motorisieren.
mottled *a.* gesprenkelt.
motto *s.* Wahl-, Sinnspruch *m.*
mound *s.* Erdhügel *m.*
mount *s.* Berg, Hügel *m.;* Reitpferd *n.;* (*mil.*) Lafette *f.;* ~ *v.i.* (hinauf)steigen; ~ *v.t.* erheben; besteigen; beschlagen (mit Silber, etc.); montieren; (Bilder) aufziehen; (Edelsteine) fassen; *to* ~ *guard,* auf Wache ziehen.
mountain *s.* Berg *m.;* ~ **ash** Eberesche *f.*
mountaineer *s.* Bergsteiger(in) *m.(f.)*
mountaineering *s.* Bergsteigen *n.;* ~ **expedition** *s.* Bergpartie *f.*
mountainous *a.* gebirgig.
mountain: ~ **range** *s.* Gebirgszug *m.;* **~side** *s.* Bergabhang *m.;* ~ **top** *s.* Berggipfel *m.*
mounted *a.* beritten.
mourn *v.i.* trauern; ~ *v.t.* betrauern.
mourner *s.* Leidtragende *m./f.;* Trauernde *m./f.;* Trauergast *m.*
mournful *a.*, **~ly** *adv.* traurig; klagend.
mourning *s.* Trauer *f.*
mouse *s.* Maus *f.*
mouse-hole *s.* Mauseloch *n.*
mousetrap *s.* Mausefalle *f.*
moustache *s.* Schnurrbart *m.*
mousy *a.* mausgrau; schüchtern.
mouth *s.* Mund *m.;* Mündung *f.;* Maul *n.;* Rachen *m.;* ~ *v.t.* mit Lippensprache sagen; *~-to-~ resuscitation s.* Mund-zu-Mund-Beatmung *f.*
mouthful *s.* Schluck *m.;* Bissen, Happen *m.;* Zungenbrecher *m.*
mouth organ *s.* Mundharmonika *f.*
mouthpiece *s.* Mundstück *n.;* Wortführer *m.;* Sprachrohr *n.*
mouthwash *s.* Mundwasser *n.*
mouth-watering *a.* lecker.
movable *a.*, **movably** *adv.* beweglich; ~ *property,* bewegliche Habe *f.;* **~s** *pl.* bewegliche Güter *n.pl.*
move *v.t.* bewegen, fortbewegen; anregen; beantragen; überreden, erregen; ~ *v.i.* sich bewegen, sich fortbewegen, vorrücken; umziehen; *to* ~ *into a house,* ein Haus beziehen; *to* ~ *up* (*mil.*) heranführen; nachrücken; ~ *s.* Bewegung *f.;* Zug (beim Spiele) *m.;* Schritt *m.;* Maßnahme *f.*
movement *s.* Bewegung *f.;* Gangwerk (Uhr) *n.;* (*mus.*) Satz *m.;* Beförderung *f.;* Antrieb *m.*
mover *s.* Anreger *m.;* Möbelpacker *m.*
movie *s.* Film *m.;* **~s** *s.* Kino *n.; go to the ~s,* ins Kino gehen.
movie-goer *s.* Kinogänger(in) *m.(f.)*
moving *a.* beweglich; ergreifend, bewegend; Antriebs...; treibend.
mow *v.t.* mähen.
mower *s.* Mäher, Schnitter *m.*
Mozambique *s.* Mozambik *n.*
MP *Member of Parliament,* Parlamentsmitglied; *military police,* Militärpolizei.
mph *miles per hour,* Stundenmeilen.
Mr. *Mister,* Herr.
Mrs. *Mistress,* Frau *f.*
Ms. Frau, Fräulein.
MS *manuscript,* Handschrift *f.*, Ms.
M.Sc. *Master of Science,* Magister der Naturwissenschaften.
MSS. *manuscripts,* Handschriften.
Mt. *Mount,* Berg *m.*
mth *month,* Monat.

much *a. & adv.* viel; sehr; **how ~,** wieviel; **that ~,** so viel; **too ~,** zuviel; **as ~,** ebensoviel, genausoviel; **about as ~,** ungefähr soviel; **not as ~,** nicht soviel.
mucilage *s.* Pflanzenschleim *m.;* Klebstoff *m.*
muck *s.* Mist, Dünger *m.;* Dreck *m.*
mucous *a.* schleimig.
mucus *s.* Schleim *m.*
mud *s.* Schlamm, Lehm *m.;* ~ **bath** *s.* Schlammbad *n.;* **~guard** *s.* Kotflügel *m.*
muddle *v.t.* verwirren; verpfuschen; ~ *v.i.* wursteln; ~ *s.* Verwirrung *f.;* Durcheinander *n.*
muddled *a.* benebelt, verworren.
muddle-headed *a.* wirr.
muddy *a.,* **~ily** *adv.* schlammig; trübe.
mudpack *s.* Schlammpackung *f.*
mud pie *s.* Kuchen (aus Sand) *m.*
muesli *s.* Müsli *n.*
muff *s.* Muff *m.;* ~ *v.t.* verpatzen; verhauen.
muffin *s.* Muffin *n.*
muffle *v.t.* umwickeln; dämpfen (Trommel).
muffler *s.* Auspufftopf *m.;* dicke Schal *m.*
mufti *s.* Zivil *n.;* normale Kleidung *f.*
mug *s.* Krug, Becher *m.;* große Tasse *f.;* Fratze *f.* ~ *v.t.* überfallen und zusammenschlagen, herfallen über (*acc.*) und berauben.
mugger *s.* Straßenräuber(in) *m.(f.)*
mugging *s.* Straßenraub *m.*
muggy *a.* schwül; drückend.
mulatto *s.* Mulatte *m.,* Mulattin *f.*
mulberry *s.* Maulbeere *f.*
mulch *s.* Mulch *m.;* ~ *v.t.* mulchen.
mule *s.* Maultier *n.; as stubborn as a ~,* so störrisch wie ein Maulesel.
muleteer *s.* Maultiertreiber *m.*
mulish *a.* störrig, störrisch.
mull (over) *v.t.* nachdenken (über), sich (*dat.*) überlegen, überdenken, durchdenken.
mulled wine *s.* Glühwein *m.*
mullion *s.* Fensterpfosten *m.*
multicolored *a.* vielfarbig.
multifarious *a.,* **~ly** *adv.* mannigfaltig.
multiform *a.* vielförmig.
multilateral *a.* vielseitig; multilateral.
multimillionaire *s.* Multimillionär(in) *m.(f.)*
multinational *a.* multinational; ~ *s.* multinationaler Konzern *m.*
multiple *a.* vielfach; mehrfach, mehrere (*with pl.*); ~ *s.* Vielfaches *n.*
multiplicand *s.* Vervielfältigungszahl *f.;* Multiplikand *m.*
multiplication *s.* Vervielfältigung, Multiplikation *f.*
multiplication table *s.* Einmaleins *n.*
multiplicity *s.* Menge, Mannigfaltigkeit *f.*
multiply *v.t.* multiplizieren, vervielfältigen.
multi-purpose *a.* Mehrzweck...
multiracial *a.* gemischtrassig.
multitude *s.* Vielheit *f.,* Menge *f.*
mum *a.* still; **~!** *i.* still! st!; *~'s the word!* nichts verraten; *to keep ~,* den Mund halten (über + *acc.*)
mumble *v.i. & t.* nuscheln, murmeln.
mummer *s.* Schauspieler *m.*
mummy *s.* Mumie *f.*
mumps *s.pl.* (*med.*) Ziegenpeter *m.;* Mumps *m.* or *f.(sing. only).*
munch *v.t. & i.* mampfen.
mundane *a.* weltlich.
municipal *a.* Stadt..., Gemeinde...; *~ board,* Magistrat *m.*
municipality *s.* Gemeinde *f.*
munition *s.* Kriegsvorrat *m.;* Kriegsmaterial *n.*
mural *a.* Mauer...; Wandbild *n.;* Deckengemälde *n.*
murder *s.* Mord *m.; ~ with robbery,* Raubmord *m.;* ~ *v.t.* ermorden, umbringen.
murderer *s.* Mörder(in) *m.(f.)*
murderous *a.,* **~ly** *adv.* mörderisch, blutrünstig.
murky *a.* dunkel, trübe.
murmur *s.* Gemurmel *n.;* ~ *v.i.* murmeln; murren.
muscle *s.* Muskel *m.*
muscular *a.* muskulär; muskulös.
Mus.D. *Doctor of Music,* Doktor der Musik.
muse *s.* Muse *f.;* ~ *v.i.* nachdenken, nachsinnen.
museum *s.* Museum *n.*
mush *s.* Mus *n.;* Brei *m.*
mushroom *s.* Pilz *m.*
mushroom cloud *s.* Atompilz *m.;* Pilzwolke *f.*
mushy *a.* breiig.
music *s.* Musik *f.;* Noten *f.pl.*
musical *a.,* **~ly** *adv.* musikalisch, melodisch; ~ *s.* Musical *n.*
music box *s.* Spieldose *f.*
music hall *s.* Varieté *n.*
musician *s.* Musiker(in) *m.(f.)*
music lesson *s.* Musikstunde *f.*
music stand *s.* Notenpult *n.,* Notenständer *m.*
musk *s.* Moschus *m.*
musket *s.* Flinte, Muskete *f.*
musketeer *s.* Musketier *m.*
muskrat *s.* Bisamratte *f.*
musky *a.* moschusartig, Moschus...
Muslim *a.* muslimisch; ~ *s.* Muslim *m.;* Muslime *f.*
muslin *s.* Musselin *m.*
muss *v.t.* verstrubbeln; durcheinanderbringen; ~ *s.* Durcheinander *n.*
mussel *s.* Muschel *f.*
must *v.i.ir.* müssen; (in *neg.* sentences) dürfen; ~ *s.* Most *m.;* Muß *n.*
mustang *s.* Mustang *m.*
mustard *s.* Senf *m.*
muster *v.t.* mustern; einstellen; aufbringen; versammeln; zusammenrufen; ~ *s.* Musterung, Musterrolle *f.;* Trupp *m.*
mustiness *s.* Muffigkeit *f.*
musty *a.,* **~ily** *adv.* dumpfig, muffig, moderig.
mutable *a.* veränderlich.
mutant *a.* mutiert; ~ *s.* Mutant *m.*
mutate *v.t.* mutieren.
mutation *s.* Veränderung *f.;* Mutation *f.*
mute *a.,* **~ly** *adv.* stumm.
muted *a.* gedämpft.
mutilate *v.t.* verstümmeln, verschandeln.
mutilation *s.* Verstümmelung *f.*
mutineer *s.* Meuterer *m.*
mutinous *a.,* **~ly** *adv.* aufrührerisch.
mutiny *s.* Meuterei *f.;* ~ *v.i.* sich empören, meutern.

mutter *v.t. & i.* murren; murmeln; ~ *s.* Gemurmel *n.*
muttering *s.* Gemurmel *n.*
mutton *s.* Hammelfleisch *n.;* **~chop** Hammelkotelett.
mutual *a.* gegenseitig.
muzzle *s.* Maul *n.*, Maulkorb *m.;* Mündung (eines Gewehrs) *f.;* ~ *v.t.* den Maulkorb anlegen.
muzzy *a.* verschwommen.
MW *medium wave,* Mittelwelle, MW.
my *pn.* mein, meine.
myopia *s.* Myopie *f.;* Kurzsichtigkeit *f.*
myopic *a.* kurzsichtig.
myriad *s.* Myriade *f.*
myrrh *s.* Myrrhe *f.*
myrtle *s.* Myrte *f.*
myself *pn.* (ich) selbst; mich, mir.
mysterious *a.*, **~ly** *adv.* geheimnisvoll.
mystery *s.* Geheimnis *n.;* ~ **novel** *s.* Kriminalroman *m.* ~ **tour** *s.*, ~ **trip** *s.* Fahrt ins Blaue.
mystic(al) *a.*, **~ly** *adv.* mystisch; dunkel; ~ *s.* Mystiker(in) *m.(f.)*
mystification *s.* Fopperei *f.*, Verwunderung, Verwirrung *f.*
mystify *v.t.* foppen; irreführen.
myth *s.* Mythos *m.;* Mythe *f.;* Erdichtung *f.*
mythological *a.* mythologisch.
mythology *s.* Mythologie *f.*

N

N, n der Buchstabe N oder n *n.*
N. *north,* Norden, N; *Nitrogen,* Stickstoff *m.*
n. *name,* Name; *noun,* Substantiv, Subst.; *neuter,* sächlich.
nab *v.t.* (*fam.*) schnappen, erwischen; sich (*dat.*) grapschen.
nadir *s.* Nadir, Fußpunkt, Tiefpunkt *m.*
nag *s.* Klepper *m.*, (*sl.*) Gaul *m.;* ~ *v.t. & i.* nörgeln, herumnörgeln.
nagging *a.* nörglerisch; quälend, meckernd.
nail *s.* Nagel *m.;* ~ *v.t.* nageln, festnageln.
nail-biting *s.* Nagelkauen *n.*
nail brush *s.* Nagelbürste *f.*
nail file *s.* Nagelfeile *f.*
nail polish *s.* Nagellack *m.*
nail scissors *s.pl.* Nagelschere *f.*
naïve *a.* naiv, einfältig.
naïveté *s.* Naivität *f.;* Einfalt *f.*
naked *a.*, **~ly** *adv.* nackt, bloß; offen; kahl; ~ *eye,* bloßes Auge *n.*
nakedness *s.* Nacktheit, Blöße *f.*
name *s.* Name *m.;* (guter) Ruf *m.; Christian ~, first ~,* Vorname *m.; family ~,* Familienname *m.; proper ~,* Eigenname *s. of the ~ N., N. by ~,* namens N.; *in ~ only,* nur dem Namen nach; *to send in one's ~,* sich anmelden; ~ *v.t.* nennen, ernennen.
name-calling *s.* Beschimpfungen *pl.*
nameday *s.* Namenstag *m.*
nameless *a.* namenlos.
namely *adv.* nämlich.
nameplate *s.* Namensschild *n.*
namesake *s.* Namensvetter *m.*
nanny *s.* Kindermädchen *n.*
nap *s.* Schläfchen *n.;* Nickerchen *n.*
nape *s.* Genick *n.*, Nacken *m.*
napkin *s.* Serviette *f.*
napkin ring *s.* Serviettenring *m.*
narcissism *s.* Narzißmus *m.*
narcissist *s.* Narzißt(in) *m.(f.)*
narcissistic *a.* narzißtisch.
narcissus *s.* Narzisse *f.*
narcosis *s.* Narkose *f.*
narcotic *a.* betäubend, narkotisch; ~ *s.* Betäubungsmittel *n.;* Rauschgift *n.*
narcotize *v.t.* narkotisieren.
narrate *v.t.* erzählen.
narration *s.* Erzählung *f.*
narrative *a.*, **~ly** *adv.* erzählend; ~ *s.* Erzählung *f.*
narrator *s.* Erzähler(in) *m.(f.)*
narrow *a.* eng[e]; schmal; **~ly** *adv.* mit knapper Not; ~ *gauge,* schmalspurig, Schmalspur...; ~ *s.* Meerenge *f.;* ~ *v.t. & i.* (sich) verengen.
narrow-minded *a.* beschränkt; engstirnig.
nasal *a.* Nasen..., nasal; ~ *s.* (*ling.*) Nasenlaut *m.*, Nasal (laut) *m.*
nascent *a.* entstehend, werdend.
nasturtium *s.* Kapuzinerkresse *f.*
nasty *a.*, **~ily** *adv.* schmutzig; bösartig; ungünstig, unfreundlich; scheußlich; ekelhaft; widerlich; gemein; gehässig; übel.
natal *a.* Geburts...
nation *s.* Volk *n.*, Nation *f.*
national *a.*, **~ly** *adv.* national, Volks...; ~ *s.* Staatsangehöriger *m.;* Staatsangehörige *f.;* ~ **debt** *s.* Staatsschuld *f.*
nationalism *s.* Nationalismus *m.*
nationalist *a.* nationalistisch; ~ *s.* Nationalist(in) *m.(f.)*
nationalistic *a.* nationalistisch.
nationality *s.* Staatsangehörigkeit *f.*, Nationalität *f.*
nationalization *s.* Nationalisierung *f.*
nationalize *v.t.* verstaatlichen.
nationally *adv.* landesweit, im ganzen Land.
native *a.*, **~ly** *adv.* angeboren; einheimisch; Heimat...; Eingeborenen...; ~ **country** *s.* Heimat *f.;* ~ **language** *s.* Muttersprache *f.;* ~ *s.* Eingeborener *m.*
nativity *s.* Geburt *f.*
nativity play *s.* Krippenspiel *n.*
natty *a.* (*fam.*) schick; flott.
natural *a.*, **~ly** *adv.* natürlich; ~ *s.* Naturtalent *n.*
naturalism *s.* Naturalismus *m.*
naturalist *s.* Naturforscher(in) *m.(f.)*
naturalization *s.* Naturalisierung *f.*, Einbürgerung *f.*
naturalize *v.t.* einbürgern, naturalisieren.
naturally *adv.* von Natur aus; naturgetreu; natürlich.
naturalness *s.* Natürlichkeit *f.*
natural resources *s.pl.* Naturschätze *pl.*
natural science *s.* Naturwissenschaft *f.*

nature *s.* Natur *f.;* Beschaffenheit *f.; law of* ~, *natural law, s.* Naturrecht, Naturgesetz *n.*
-natured *a.* -artig; mit einem... Wesen; *good-*~, gutmütig; *ill-*~, bösartig.
nature lover *s.* Naturfreund(in) *m.(f.)*
nature reserve *s.* Naturschutzgebiet *n.*
naught *s.* Nichts *n.;* Null *f.; to come to* ~ zunichte werden; *to set at* ~, mißachten, in den Wind schlagen.
naughty *a.*, **~ily** *adv.* unartig; frech; dreist; unanständig.
nausea *s.* Übelkeit *f.*
nauseate *v.t.* sich ekeln vor; anekeln; jm. Übelkeit erregen.
nauseous *a.*, **~ly** *adv.* ekelhaft.
nautical *a.* nautisch, See...; **~ mile** *s.* Seemeile *f.*
naval *a.* Schiffs..., See...; **~ base** *s.* Kriegshafen *m.*
nave *s.* Schiff (einer Kirche) *n.;* Nabe *f.*
navel *s.* Nabel *m.*
navigable *a.* schiffbar; lenkbar.
navigate *v.i.* navigieren, steuern; **~** *v.t.* befahren, durchfahren, durchfliegen.
navigation *s.* Seemannskunst *f.;* Schiffahrt *f.;* Navigation *f.;* Steuern *n.;* ~ *light,* Positionslicht, Kennlicht *n.*
navigator *s.* Seefahrer *m.;* Navigator *m.*, Beifahrer *m.*
navvy *s.* Bauarbeiter *m.;* Strassenarbeiter *m.*
navy *s.* (Kriegs-) Flotte *f.;* Marine *f.;* **~ yard** *s.* Marinewerft *f.*
nay *s.* Gegenstimme *f.;* Neinstimme *f.*
Nazi *s.* Nazi *m.;* Nationalsozialist(in) *m.(f.)*
N.B. *nota bene (note well),* notabene, NB.
n.d. *no date,* ohne Datum.
N.E. *northeast,* Nordost, NO.
near *pr.* neben, in der Nähe von; **~** *a.* nahe; verwandt; **~** *adv.* fast, beinahe; **~** *v.t. & i.* sich nähern.
nearby *a.* nahegelegen; **~** *adv.* in der Nähe.
Near East *s.* Naher Osten *m.*
nearly *adv.* nahe, beinahe; genau.
nearness *s.* Nähe *f.*
near-sighted *a.* kurzsichtig.
neat *a.*, **~ly** *adv.* nett, sauber.
neatness *s.* Sauberkeit *f.;* Ordentlichkeit *f.*
nebulous *a.* neblig, wolkig.
necessaries *s.pl.* Bedürfnisse *n.pl.*
necessary *a.*, **~ily** *adv.* notwendig.
necessitate *v.t.* erfordern; zwingen.
necessity *s.* Notwendigkeit *f.;* Bedürfnis *n.*
neck *s.* Hals *m.*
necklace *s.* Halsband *n.*
neckline *s.* (Hals) Ausschnitt *m.*
necktie *s.* Binde, Kravatte *f.*
necromancy *s.* schwarze Kunst *f.*
necrosis *s.* *(med.)* Nekrose *f.*
nectar *s.* Nektar, Göttertrank *m.*
nectarine *s.* Nektarine *f.*
née *a.* geborene.
need *s.* Not *f.*, Mangel *m.;* Bedürfnis *n.*, Notwendigkeit *f.; in case of* ~, im Notfall; **~** *v.t.* nötig haben, bedürfen; brauchen; **~** *v.i.* nötig sein; *aux.* müssen; ~ *I wait?* muß ich warten?
needful *a.* notwendig.
needle *s.* Nähnadel *f.;* Nadel *f.*
needless *a.*, **~ly** *adv.* unnötig; ~ *to say,* selbstverständlich.
needlewoman *s.* Näherin *f.*
needlework *s.* Näharbeit *f.*
needy *a.*, **~ily** *adv.* dürftig, arm, ärmlich.
neg. *negative,* negativ, neg.
negate *v.t.* verneinen; aufheben; zunichte machen.
negation *s.* Verneinung *f.*
negative *a.*, **~ly** *adv.* verneinend; **~** *s.* Verneinung *f.;* *(phot.)* Negativ *n.; to answer in the* ~, verneinend antworten.
neglect *v.t.* vernachlässigen; **~** *s.* Vernachlässigung *f.; gross* ~, *(jur.)* grobe Fahrlässigkeit *f.;* ~ *of duty,* Pflichtversäumnis *f.*
neglectful *a.* nachlässig; unachtsam.
negligence *s.* Nachlässigkeit *f.* Unachtsamkeit *f.* *contributory* ~, mitwirkendes Verschulden.
negligent *a.*, **~ly** *adv.* nachlässig.
negligible *a.* unerheblich.
negotiable *a.* verkäuflich; begebbar; *not* ~, nur zur Verrechnung (auf Schecks).
negotiate *v.i.* handeln; unterhandeln; **~** *v.t.* verhandeln über; (Wechsel) begeben; (Hindernis) überwinden.
negotiation *s.* Handel *m.;* Unterhandlung *f.; to enter into* ~*s,* Verhandlungen aufnehmen.
negotiator *s.* Unterhändler(in) *m.(f.)*
Negro *s.* Neger *m./f.*
neigh *v.i.* wiehern; **~** *s.* Wiehern *n.*
neighbor *s.* Nachbar(in) *m.(f.);* Nächste *m.;* **~** *v.t. & i.* angrenzen.
neighborhood *s.* Nachbarschaft *f.*
neighboring *a.* benachbart; angrenzend.
neighborly *a.* nachbarlich, gefällig.
neither *pn.* keiner (von beiden); **~** *c.* weder; auch nicht; **~... nor,** weder... noch.
neo- *(in Zus.)* neo..., Neo..., neu.
neoclassical *a.* klassizistisch.
neolithic *a.* neolithisch; jung steinzeitlich.
neologism *s.* Neubildung *f.;* Neologismus *m.*
neon *s.* Neon (Edelgas) *n.;* **~lamp** *s.* Neonlampe; **~tube** *s.* Neonröhre *f.*
neophyte *s.* Neubekehrte *m. & f.*
nephew *s.* Neffe *m.*
nephritis *s.* Nierenentzündung *f.*
nepotism *s.* Vetternwirtschaft *f.*
nerve *s.* Nerv *m.;* Mut *m.;* *(fig.)* Kraft *f.; to get on sb.'s* ~*s,* jm. auf die Nerven gehen; *to lose one's* ~, die Nerven verlieren; **~** *v.t.* bestärken.
nerveless *a.* kraftlos; kaltblütig.
nerve-racking *a.* nervenaufreibend.
nervous *a.*, **~ly** *adv.* nervig; nervös.
nervous breakdown *s.* Nervenzusammenbruch *m.*
nervy *a.* unverschämt; unruhig.
nest *s.* Nest *n.;* **~ egg** *s.* Sparpfenning, Notpfennig *m.;* Nestei *n.;* **~** *v.i.* nisten.
nestle *v.t.* sich schmiegen.
nestling *s.* Nestling *m.*
net *s.* Netz *n.;* **~** *v.t.* einfangen; mit einem Netz fangen; **~** *a.* netto. **~ profit** *s.* Reingewinn *m.*
net. *netto,* netto.
nettle *s.* Nessel *f.;* **~ rash,** Nesselfieber *n.;* **~** *v.t.* ärgern, wurmen, fuchsen.
network *s.* Netzwerk, Netz *n.*

neuralgia *s.* Nervenschmerz *m.;* Neuralgie *f.*
neuritis *s.* Nervenentzündung *f.*
neurological *a.* neurologisch.
neurologist *s.* Neurologe *m.;* Neurologin *f.*
neurosis *s.* Neurose *f.*
neurotic *a.* neurotisch.
neuter *a.* geschlechtslos; (*gram.*) sächlich; ~ *s.* Neutrum *n.*
neutral *a.,* **~ly** *adv.* neutral.
neutrality *s.* Neutralität *f.*
neutralize *v.t.* neutralisieren.
neutron *s.* Neutron *n.*
neutron bomb *s.* Neutronenbombe *f.*
never *adv.* nie, niemals.
nevertheless *adv.* nichtsdestoweniger.
new *a.* neu.
newborn *a.* neugeboren; ~ *s.* Neugeborenes *n.*
newcomer *s.* Neuankömmling, Fremde *m./f.*
newfangled *a.* neumodisch.
newly *adv.* kürzlich; neu; frisch.
newlyweds *s.pl.* Jungverheiratete *pl.*
new moon *s.* Neumond *m.*
newness *s.* Neuheit *f.;* Unerfahrenheit *f.*
news *s.* Neuigkeit *f.;* Nachricht; **~-medium** *s.* Mittel der Nachrichtenverbreitung *n.*
news agent *s.* Zeitungsverkäufer *m.*
news flash *s.* Kurzmeldung *f.*
news headline *s.* Schlagzeile *f.*
newspaper *s.* Zeitung *f.;* ~ **clipping,** ~ **cutting,** Zeitungsausschnitt *m.*
newsprint *s.* Zeitungspapier *n.*
newsreel *s.* Filmwochenschau *f.*
news vendor *s.* Zeitungsverkäufer *m.*
newsworthy *a.* berichtenswert.
newt *s.* Salamander *m.;* Wassermolch *m.*
New Testament *s.* Neues Testament *n.*
New Year's Day *s.* Neujahrstag *m.*
New Year's Eve *s.* Silvester(abend) *m.*
New Zealand *s.* Neuseeland *n.*
New Zealander *s.* Neuseeländer(in) *m.(f.)*
next *a.* nächst, folgend; ~ *adv.* gleich darauf, hernach; ~ *door,* nebenan; ~ *of kin,* die nächsten Verwandten *pl.*
nib *s.* Spitze (besonders einer Schreibfeder) *f.;* Stahlfeder *f.*
nibble *v.t.* & *i.* benagen; anbeißen (von Fischen); knabbern.
Nicaragua *s.* Nicaragua *n.*
Nicaraguan *a.* nicaraguanisch; ~ *s.* Nicaraguaner(in) *m.(f.)*
nice *a.,* **~ly** *adv.* fein, nett; wählerisch; genau; schön.
niceness *s.* Feinheit.
nicety *s.* Feinheit *f.;* Genauigkeit *f.*
niche *s.* Nische *f.;* Plätzchen *n.*
nick *s.* Kerbe *f.;* rechter Augenblick *m.; Old Nick,* der Teufel; ~ *v.t.* kerben.
nickel *s.* Nickel *m.*
nickname *s.* Spitzname *m.*
nicotine *s.* Nikotin *n.*
niece *s.* Nichte *f.*
Nigeria *s.* Nigeria *n.*
Nigerian *a.* nigerisch; ~ *s.* Nigerianer(in) *m.(f.)*
niggard *s.* Filz, Knicker *m.*
niggardly *a.* karg, geizig, knauserig.
niggle *v.i.* nörgeln; herumtüfteln.
niggling *a.* belanglos; nichtssagend.
nigh *a.* nahe; ~ *adv.* nahe, beinahe.
night *s.* Nacht *f.; by* ~, nachts; *last* ~, gestern Abend; *the* ~ *before last,* vorgestern Abend; **~cap,** Schlafmütze *f.;* (*fig.*) Schlummertrunk *m.; first* ~, Erstaufführung *f.; opening* ~ *s.* Premiere *f.*
nightblindness *s.* Nachtblindheit *f.*
nightclub *s.* Nachtklub *m.,* Kabarett *n.*
nightdress *s.* Nachtkleid *n.*
nightfall *s.* Einbruch *(m.)* der Dunkelheit.
nightfighter *s.* (*avi.*) Nachtjäger *m.*
nightgown *s.* Nachthemd *n.*
nightie *s.* Nachthemd *n.*
nightingale *s.* Nachtigall *f.*
nightly *a.* nächtlich; ~ *adv.* nachts; alle Nächte.
nightmare *s.* Alpdrücken *n.;* Alptraum *m.*
nightschool *s.* Abendschule *f.*
nightshade *s.* Nachtschatten *m.*
night shift *s.* Nachtschicht *f.*
nighttime *s.* Nacht *f.*
nil *s.* nichts.
Nile *s.* Nil *m.*
nimble *a.,* **~bly** *adv.* hurtig, flink; gelenkig; beweglich.
nimbus *s.* Strahlenkranz; Nimbus *m.*
nincompoop *s.* Einfaltspinsel *m.;* Trottel *m.*
nine *a.* neun; ~ *s.* Neun *f.*
ninefold *a.* neunfach.
ninepins *s.pl.* Kegelspiel *n.*
nineteen *a.* neunzehn.
ninety *a.* neunzig.
ninny *s.* (*fam.*) Dummkopf *m.,* Trottel *m.*
ninth *a.* neunt...
nip *v.t.* kneifen; zwicken, schneiden (von der Kälte); *to* ~ *in the bud,* im Keim ersticken; ~ *s.* Kniff *m.,* Kneifen *n.;* (*fam.*) Schlückchen *n.*
nippers *s.pl.* Kneifzange *f.*
nipple *s.* Brustwarze *f.;* Sauger *m.*
nippy *a.* frisch, kühl; spritzig.
nit *s.* Nisse *f.*
niter *s.* Salpeter *m.*
nitrate *s.* salpetersaures Salz *n.;* Nitrat *n.*
nitric acid *s.* Salpetersäure *f.*
nitrogen *s.* Stickstoff *m.*
nitroglycerine *s.* Nitroglyzerin *n.*
nitty-gritty *s.* der Kern einer Sache.
nitwit *s.* (*fam.*) Trottel *m.,* Schwachkopf *m.*
NNE *north-northeast,* Nord-Nordost.
NNW *north-northwest,* Nord-Nordwest.
no *adv.* nein, nicht; ~ *a.* kein.
no. *numero,* Nummer *f.*
nobility *s.* Adel *m.*
noble *a.,* **~bly** *adv.* adlig; edel; trefflich; ~ *s.* Adlige *m./f.*
nobleman *a.* Edelmann *m.*
noblewoman *s.* Adlige *f.*
nobody *s.* niemand, keiner.
no-claim(s) bonus *s.* Schadenfreiheitsrabatt *m.*
nocturnal *a.* nächtlich, Nacht...
nod *v.t.* & *i.* nicken; ~ *s.* Nicken *n.;* Wink *m.*
nodal *a.* Knoten...
node *s.* Knoten *m.*
noise *s.* Lärm *m.;* Geräusch *n.;* ~ *v.t.* & *i.* lärmen.
noiseless *a.* geräuschlos.

noisome *a.*, **~ly** *adv.* schädlich; widrig.
noisy *a.*, **~ily** *adv.* geräuschvoll, laut.
nomad *s.* Nomade *m.*
nomadic *a.* nomadisch.
no man's land *s.* Niemandsland *n.*
nomenclature *s.* Terminologie *f.*
nominal *a.*, **~ly** *adv.* nominell; dem Namen nach; Namen..., Nenn..., Titular...; sehr gering, unwesentlich; ~ *capital*, Stammkapital *n.;* ~ *value*, Nennwert *m.*
nominate *v.t.* ernennen; vorschlagen.
nomination *s.* Ernennung, Aufstellung eines Wahlkandidaten *f.*
nominative *s.* (*gram.*) Nominativ *m.*
nominee *s.* Vorgeschlagene *m./f.*
nonacceptance *s.* Nichtannahme *f.*
nonaggression *s.* Nichtangriff *m.;* Gewaltverzicht *m.*
nonalcoholic *a.* alkoholfrei.
nonaligned *a.* blockfrei.
nonattendance *s.* Nichterscheinen *n.*
nonbelligerent *s.* Nichtkriegführender *m.;* ~ *a.* nichtkriegführend.
nonce *s. for the* ~, für das eine Mal.
nonchalance *s.* Lässigkeit *f.;* Nonchalance *f.*
noncombatant *a.* nichtkämpfend; ~ *s.* Nichtkämpfende *m./f.*
noncommissioned *a.*, ~ *officer*, Unteroffizier *m.*
noncommittal *a.* unverbindlich.
noncompliance *s.* Nichterfüllung *s.*
nonconformist *s.* Nonkonformist(in) *m.(f.)*
nondenominational *a.* konfessionslos.
nondescript *a.* unklassifizierbar, unauffällig.
none *a.* keiner, keine, keines; **~theless,** *adv.* nichtsdestoweniger.
nonentity *s.* Nichtsein *n.;* (*fig.*) Nichts *n.*
nonessential *a.* unwesentlich, unnötig.
nonevent *s.* Reinfall *m.*
nonexistence *s.* Nichtvorhandensein *n.*
nonfiction *s.* Sachbuch *n.*
nonfulfilment *s.* Nichterfüllung *s.*
nonintervention *s.* Nichteinmischung *s.*
nonmember *s.* Nichtmitglied *n.*
nonobservance *s.* Nichtbeachtung *f.*
no-nonsense *a.* nüchtern, sachlich.
nonpayment *s.* Nichtzahlung *f.*
nonplus *v.t.* verblüffen.
non-profit organization *s.* gemeinnütziges Unternehmen *n.*
nonresident *a.* nichtansässig; ~ *s.* Nichtansässige *m./f.*
nonreturnable *a.* Einweg...
nonsense *s.* Unsinn *m.*
nonsensical *a.*, **~ly** *adv.* unsinnig, albern.
nonsmoker *s.* Nichtraucher(in) *m.(f.)*
nonstop *a.* durchgehend (Zug).
nonunion *a.* nichtorganisiert.
nonviolence *s.* Gewaltlosigkeit *f.*
noodle *s.* Nudel *f.*
nook *s.* Winkel *m.;* Ecke *f.*
noon *s.* Mittag *m.*
noose *s.* Schlinge *f.*
nor *c.* noch; auch nicht; weder.
norm *s.* Regel *f.;* Muster *n.;* Norm *f.*
normal *a.* normal; *s.* Normalstand *m.*
normality *s.* Normalität *f.*
normalize *v.t.* normalisieren; ~ *v.i.* sich normalisieren.
normally *adv.* normalerweise.
north *s.* Norden *m.; a. & adv.* nördlich.
North Africa *s.* Nordafrika *n.*
North America *s.* Nordamerika *n.*
northeast *s.* Nordost(en) *m.;* ~ *a.* nordöstlich.
northeastern *a.* nordöstlich.
northerly, northern *a.* nördlich.
northern lights *s.pl.* Nordlicht *n.*
northernmost *a.* nördlichst...
northward *a. & adv.* nördlich; nordwärts.
northwest *s.* Nordwest(en) *m.;* ~ *a.* nordwestlich.
northwestern *a.* nordwestlich.
Norway *s.* Norwegen *n.*
Norwegian *a.* norwegisch; ~ *s.* Norweger(in) *m.(f.)*
nos. *numbers*, Nummern.
nose *s.* Nase *f.;* ~ *v.t.* auswittern.
nosebleed *s.* Nasenbluten *n.*
nosedive *s.* (*avi.*) Sturzflug *m.*
nosegay *s.* Blumensträußchen *n.*
nose-landing, nose-over *s.* (*avi.*) Kopfstand *m.*
nosh *s.* Bissen *m.;* Happen *m.;* ~ *v.t.* knabbern.
nostalgia *s.* Heimweh *n.*
nostalgic *a.* nostalgisch, wehmütig.
nostril *s.* Nasenloch *n.*, Nüster *f.*
nostrum *s.* Allheilmittel *n.*
not *adv.* nicht.
notable *a.*, **notably** *adv.* bemerkenswert; beträchtlich; merklich.
notary *s.* Notar *m.*
notation *s.* Notation *f.;* Notierung *f.*
notch *s.* Kerbe *f.;* ~ *v.t.* einkerben.
note *s.* Zeichen, Merkmal *n.;* Note *f.;* Schein *m.;* Anmerkung *f.;* Zettel *m.;* Briefchen *n.;* Rechnung *f.;* Wichtigkeit *f.;* Ton, Klang *m.; promissory* ~, Schuldschein *m.;* ~ *v.t.* aufzeichnen; bemerken; *be it* ~*d*, wohlgemerkt.
notebook *s.* Notizbuch *n.;* Spiralheft *n.*
noted *a.*, **~ly** *adv.* berühmt, bekannt.
notepad *s.* Notizblock *m.*
notepaper *s.* Briefpapier *n.*
noteworthy *a.* beachtenswert.
nothing *pn.* nichts; *for* ~ *(free of charge)*, umsonst; ~ **but,** nur; ~ *s.* Nichts *n.*
nothingness *s.* Nichts *n.;* Nichtigkeit *f.*
notice *s.* Bescheid *m.*, Benachrichtigung *f.*, Mitteilung *f.*, Ankündigung *f.;* Kenntnis *f.;* Bekanntmachung *f.;* Nachricht *f.;* Kündigung *f.; to give* ~, kündigen; *until further* ~, bis auf weiteres; *at (subject to) a month's* ~, auf monatliche Kündigung; *period of* ~, Kündigungsfrist *f.;* ~ *v.t.* bemerken, Acht geben auf, wahrnehmen.
noticeable *a.* merklich; wahrnehmbar.
notice board *s.* schwarzes Brett *n.*, Anschlagbrett *n.*
notifiable *a.* meldepflichtig.
notification *s.* Benachrichtigung *f.*
notify *v.t.* (an)melden; benachrichtigen, formell anzeigen.
notion *s.* Begriff *m.;* Idee *f.*, Ahnung *f.;* Meinung *f.;* Vorstellung *f.*
notoriety *s.* traurige Berühmtheit *f.*, schlechter Ruf *m.*

notorious *a.*, **~ly** *adv.* allbekannt; berüchtigt; notorisch; verrufen.
notwithstanding *c. & pr.* ungeachtet; dennoch; trotzdem.
nought *s.* Null *f.*; Nichts *n.*; *to come to* ~, sich zerschlagen.
noun *s.* Hauptwort *n.*, Substantiv *n.*
nourish *v.t. & i.* (er)nähren, unterhalten.
nourishing *a.* nahrhaft.
nourishment *s.* Nahrung *f.*
nouveau riche *s.* Neureiche *m./f.*
Nov. *November*, November, Nov.
novel *s.* Roman *m.*; ~ *a.* neu, ungewöhnlich.
novelist *s.* Romanautor(in) *m.(f.)*
novella *s.* Novelle *f.*
novelty *s.* Neuheit *f.*
November *s.* November *m.*
novice *s.* Neuling *m.*; Novize *m.*; Novizin *f.*
now *adv.* jetzt, nun; **~adays,** heutzutage; **~ and then,** zuweilen.
nowhere *adv.* nirgends, nirgendwo.
noxious *a.*, **~ly** *adv.* schädlich.
nozzle *s.* Tülle *f.*; Düse *f.*; Öffnung einer Röhre *f.*
n.s. *not specified*, nicht angegeben.
NT *New Testament*, Neues Testament, NT.
nt. wt. *net weight*, Nettogewicht.
nuance *s.* Nuance *f.*
nuclear *a.* (*phys.*) Kern...; Atom...; nuklear, atomar.
nuclear: ~ **deterrent** *s.* nukleare Abschreckung *f.*; ~ **disarmament** *s.* nukleare Abrüstung *f.*; ~ **energy** *s.* Atomenergie *f.*
nuclear family *s.* Kernfamilie *f.*; Kleinfamilie *f.*
nuclear: ~ **fission** *s.* Kernspaltung *f.*; **~-free** *a.* atomwaffenfrei; ~ **physics** *s.* Atomphysik *f.*; ~ **power** *s.* Atomkraft *f.*; ~ **power station** *s.* Kernkraftwerk *n.*; ~ **waste** *s.* Atommüll *m.*
nucleus *s.* Kern *m.*; Nukleus *m.*; *atomic* ~, Atomkern *m.*
nude *a.* nackt, bloß.
nudge *v.t.* leise anstoßen; ~ *s.* Stups *m.*
nudist *s.* Nudist(in) *m.(f.)*; Anhänger(in) der Freikörperkultur (FKK).
nudity *s.* Nacktheit *f.*
nugget *s.* Klumpen *m.*; Goldklumpen *m.*
nuisance *s.* Ärgernis *n.*, Plage *f.*; Unfug *m.*; Verdruß *m.*
nukes *s.pl.* Atomwaffen *pl.*
null *a.* nichtig, ungültig; ~ *and void*, null und nichtig.
nullify *v.t.* ungültig machen.
nullity *s.* Nichtigkeit *f.*; (*jur.*) ~ *action*, Nichtigkeitsklage *f.*; **~-appeal,** Nichtigkeitsbeschwerde *f.*
numb *a.* starr; taub; gefühllos.
number *s.* Zahl *f.*; Nummer *f.*; Lieferung *f.*; ~ *v.t.* zählen, rechnen.
numberless *a.* unzählbar.
number plate *s.* Nummernschild *n.*
numbness *s.* Gefühllosigkeit *f.*
numeral *a.* Zahl...; ~ *s.* Zahlwort *n.*; Zahlzeichen *n.*; Ziffer (des Uhrblatts) *f.*
numerator *s.* Zähler *m.*
numerical *a.*, **~ly** *adv.* numerisch.
numerous *a.* zahlreich.
numismatics *s.pl.* Münzkunde *f.*
nun *s.* Nonne *f.*
nuncio *s.* Nuntius *m.*
nunnery *s.* Nonnenkloster *n.*
nuptial *a.* hochzeitlich, ehelich.
nurse *s.* Amme *f.*; Krankenschwester *f.*, Krankenpfleger(in) *m.(f.)*; Kindermädchen *n.*; ~ *v.i.* säugen; pflegen, warten; hegen.
nursemaid *s.* Kindermädchen *n.*
nursery *s.* Kinderstube *f.*; Pflanzschule *f.*; Baumschule *f.*
nursery rhyme *s.* Kinderreim *n.*
nursery school *s.* Kindergarten *m.*; ~ **teacher** *s.* Kindergärtner(in) *m./f.*
nursing *s.* (Kranken-)Pflege *f.*; ~ **home** *s.* Pflegeheim *n.*; Genesungsheim *n.*
nursling *s.* Pflegekind *n.*
nurture *v.t.* nähren, aufziehen.
nut *s.* Nuß *f.*; Schraubenmutter *f.*
nutcracker *s.* Nußknacker *m.*
nutmeg *s.* Muskatnuß *f.*
nutrient *s.* Nährstoff *m.*
nutriment *s.* Nahrung *f.*; Futter *n.*
nutrition *s.* Ernährung *f.*; Fütterung *f.*
nutritious *a.* nährend, nahrhaft.
nuts *a.* verrückt.
nutshell *s.* Nußschale *f.*
nutty *a.* nussig; (*sl.*) verrückt.
nuzzle *v.i.* kuscheln.
NW *northwest*, Nordwest.
N.Y. *New York.*
nylon *s.* Nylon *n.*
nymph *s.* Nymphe *f.*
nymphomaniac *a.* nymphoman, mannstoll; ~ *s.* Nymphomanin *f.*
N.Z. *New Zealand*, Neuseeland.

O, o der Buchstabe O oder o *n.*
O. *Oxygen*, Sauerstoff.
oaf *s.* Tölpel, Trampel, Lümmel *m.*
oak *s.* Eiche *f.*
oaken *a.* eichen.
oar *s.* Ruder *n.*; Riemen *m.*
oarsman *s.* Ruderer *m.*
oasis *s.* Oase *f.*
oath *s.* Eid, Schwur *m.*; Fluch *m.*; *upon* ~, eidlich, unter Eid; *in lieu of an* ~, eidesstattlich, an Eides Statt; *to take an* ~, einen Eid leisten, schwören.
oatmeal *s.* Hafermehl (n.), -grütze *f.*
oats *s.pl.* Hafer *m.*
Ob. *obiit* (=*died*), gestorben, gest.
obduracy *s.* Verstocktheit *f.*
obdurate *a.*, **~ly** *adv.* verstockt.
obedience *s.* Gehorsam *m.*
obedient *a.*, **~ly** *adv.* gehorsam.
obeisance *s.* Verbeugung, Verneigung *f.*
obelisk *s.* Obelisk *m.*

obese *a.* fettleibig, feist.
obesity *s.* Fettleibigkeit *f.*
obey *v.t.* gehorchen.
obituary *s.* Todesanzeige *f.;* Nachruf *m.;* ~ *a.* Todes..., Toten...
object *s.* Gegenstand *m.;* Zweck *m.;* Objekt, Ding *n.;* Ziel *n.;* Absicht *f.; that is no* ~, das ist nebensächlich, das spielt keine Rolle; ~ *v.t.* entgegensetzen; einwenden; ~ *v.i.* dagegen sein, protestieren.
objection *s.* Einwand *m.;* Abneigung *f.;* Einspruch, Widerspruch *m.; no* ~, nichts dagegen; *to make an* ~ *to,* einen Einwand erheben gegen.
objectionable *a.* verwerflich, anstößig, unanständig, unangenehm.
objective *a.*, **~ly** *adv.* sachlich; objektiv; ~ *s.* Ziel *n.;* (*opt.*) Objektiv *n.*
objectivity *s.* Objektivität *f.*
object lesson *s.* Paradebeispiel *n.;* Veranschaulichung *f.*
objector *s.* Gegner(in) *m.(f.)*
obligate *v.t.* verpflichten.
obligation *s.* Verpflichtung *f.;* Schuldverschreibung *f.*
obligatory *a.* verpflichtend, verbindlich.
oblige *v.t.* verpflichten, verbinden.
obliging *a.*, **~ly** *adv.* verbindlich.
oblique *a.*, **~ly** *adv.* schief, schräg; mittelbar; indirekt.
obliterate *a.* auslöschen, ausstreichen.
oblivion *s.* Vergessenheit *f.;* (*jur.*) Straferlaß *m.; Act of* ~, Amnestie *f.*
oblivious *a.* vergeßlich, vergessend.
oblong *a.*, **~ly** *adv.* länglich; rechteckig.
obloquy *s.* Schmähung *f.;* Tadel *m.*
obnoxious *a.*, **~ly** *adv.* widerlich.
oboe *s.* Oboe *f.*
obscene *a.*, **~ly** *adv.* unzüchtig; obszön.
obscenity *s.* Unzüchtigkeit *f.;* Obszönität *f.*
obscure *a.*, **~ly** *adv.* dunkel; niedrig, verborgen; ~ *v.t.* verdunkeln.
obscurity *s.* Dunkelheit *f.;* Niedrigkeit *f.*
obsequies *s.pl.* Leichenbegängnis *n.*
obsequious *a.*, **~ly** *adv.* unterwürfig; kriecherisch, servil.
obsequiousness *s.* Unterwürfigkeit, Servilität *f.*
observance *s.* Beachtung *f.*, Innehaltung *f.;* Vorschrift *f.*, Regel *f.*
observant *a.* aufmerksam; achtsam.
observation *s.* Beobachtung *f.*
observatory *s.* Sternwarte *f.;* Observatorium *n.*
observe *v.t.* beobachten; bemerken.
observer *s.* Beobachter(in) *m.(f.)*
obsessed *a.* (with) besessen (von).
obsession *s.* Besessenheit *f.;* Obsession *f.;* fixe Idee, Manie *f.*
obsessive *a.* zwanghaft, obsessiv.
obsolescence *s.* Veralten *n.*
obsolescent *a.* veraltend.
obsolete *a.* veraltet.
obstacle *s.* Hindernis *n.*
obstacle race *s.* Hindernislauf *m.*, Hindernisrennen *n.*
obstetric *a.* Geburts(hilfe)...
obstetrician *s.* Geburtshelfer(in) *m.(f.)*
obstetrics *s.* Geburtshilfe *f.*
obstinacy *s.* Hartnäckigkeit *f.*
obstinate *a.*, **~ly** *adv.* hartnäckig.
obstreperous *a.*, **~ly** *adv.* lärmend; widerspenstig.
obstruct *v.t.* verstopfen; hemmen; behindern.
obstruction *s.* Verstopfung *f.;* Hindernis *n.;* Hemmung *f.*
obtain *v.t.* erlangen; erreichen; erhalten, bekommen.
obtainable *a.* erlangbar, erhältlich.
obtrude *v.t.* aufdrängen.
obtrusive *a.* aufdringlich.
obtuse *a.*, **~ly** *adv.* stumpf; dumm; **~-angled** *a.* (*geom.*) stumpfwinklig.
obviate *v.t.* vorbeugen; vermeiden.
obvious *a.* offensichtlich deutlich; einleuchtend; **~ly** *adv.* selbstverständlich.
occasion *s.* Gelegenheit *f.;* Veranlassung *f.; on this* ~, hierbei; *on that* ~, damals; *on several* ~*s*, mehrmals; ~ *v.t.* verursachen, veranlassen.
occasional *a.*, **~ly** *adv.* gelegentlich.
Occident *s.* Abendland *n.*
occidental *a.* westlich; abendländisch.
occult *a.*, **~ly** *adv.* verborgen, geheim, okkult.
occupant *s.* Inhaber(in) *m.(f.)* Insasse *m.;* Insassin *f.*
occupation *s.* Beruf *m.;* Tätigkeit *f.;* Besitzergreifung *f.;* Besetzung *f.;* Besatzung *f.;* Beschäftigung *f.*
occupational *a.* beruflich; Berufs...
occupational therapy *s.* Beschäftigungstherapie *f.*
occupier *s.* Besitzer(in) *m.(f.);* Inhaber(in) *m.(f.)*
occupy *v.t.* in Besitz nehmen; beschäftigen; innehaben, bewohnen; bekleiden (Amt); besetzen.
occur *v.i.* sich ereignen; einfallen.
occurrence *s.* Ereignis *n.;* Vorfall *m.*
ocean *s.* Weltmeer *n.;* Ozean *m.*
ocean-going *a.* hochseetüchtig; Übersee...
ocher *s.* Ocker *m.*
o'clock Uhr; *two* ~, zwei Uhr.
Oct. *October,* Oktober, Okt.
octagon *a.* Achteck *n.*
octane *s.* Oktan *n.;* ~*rating s.* Oktanzahl *f.;* Klopfwert *m.* (*mot.*)
octave *s.* Oktave *f.*
octavo *s.* Oktavformat *n.*
October *s.* Oktober *m.*
octogenarian *s.* Achtzigjährige *m./f.;* ~ *a.* achtzigjährig.
octopus *s.* Krake *m.*
ocular *a.*, **~ly** *adv.* Augen...; augenscheinlich.
oculist *s.* Augenarzt *m.*, Augenärztin *f.*
odd *a.*, **~ly** *adv.* sonderbar; seltsam; eigenartig; absonderlich; ungerade; überzählig; übrig; einzeln; wunderlich; ungefähr, etwas über; *a hundred* ~, einige hundert.
oddity, oddness *s.* Seltsamkeit *f.;* Eigentümlichkeit *f.*
odds *s.* Odds *pl.*, Gewinnquote *f.*, Kurse *pl.;* Chance(n *pl.*) *f.;* Wahrscheinlichkeit *f.;* Vorgabe *f.; to be at* ~*s with sb.*, mit einem in Streit (*m.*) liegen.
ode *s.* Ode *f.*
odious *a.*, **~ly** *adv.* verhaßt, widerlich.
odium *s.* Tadel *m.*, Vorwurf *m.*, Haß *m.*

odor *s.* Geruch, Wohlgeruch *m.*
odorless *a.* geruchlos.
odorous *a.* duftig, duftend, wohlriechend.
OECD *Organization for Economic Cooperation and Development,* Organisation für wirtschaftliche Zusammenarbeit und Entwicklung.
of *pr.* von, an, aus, vor, um, in Betreff.
off *adv. & pr.* von, ab, weg, davon; entfernt; (*nav.*) auf der Höhe von; **~!** *i.* weg! fort!
offal *s.* Abfall *m.;* Aas *n.*
off-duty hours *pl.* Außerdienststunden *f.pl.*
offend *v.t.* beleidigen; ärgern; kränken; verletzen; *the ~ed party,* der Beleidigte *m.*
offender *s.* Beleidiger *m.;* Zuwiderhandelnder *m.;* Missetäter, Täter *m.; first ~,* nicht vorbestrafter Verbrecher *m.*
offense *s.* Beleidigung *f.;* Verdruß *m.;* Ärgernis *n.;* Vergehen *n.;* Anstoß *m.; to give ~ to,* Anstoß erregen; einen beleidigen; *to take ~ at a thing,* etwas übelnehmen.
offensive *a.*, **~ly** *adv.* anstößig; beleidigend; Angriffs...; ~ *s.* Offensive *f.*
offer *v.t.* anbieten, darbringen, opfern; ~ *v.i.* sich erbieten; ~ *s.* Anerbieten *n.;* Angebot *n.;* Antrag *m.;* Offerte *f.*
offering *s.* Gabe *f.;* Angebot *n.;* Opfer *n.;* Vorstellung *f.*
offhand *a.*, **-edly** *adv.* leichthin, beilaüfig.
office *s.* Amt *n.;* Dienst *m.;* Gottesdienst *m.;* Büro *n.; head ~, main ~,* Hauptbüro *n.,* Hauptgeschäftstelle *f.; to resign ~,* vom Amt zurücktreten; *removal from ~,* Amtsenthebung *f.; oath of ~,* Diensteid *m.; term of ~,* Amtszeit; ~ **equipment, supplies** *pl.* Büroartikel *m.pl.;* **~holder,** Amtsinhaber *m.;* ~ **hours** *pl.* Amtsstunden, Geschäftsstunden *f.pl.;* ~ **worker** *s.* Büroangestellte *m./f*
officer *s.* Beamte *m.;* Offizier *m.; ~ candidate,* Offiziersanwärter *m.; ~'s mess,* Kasino, Offiziers-Kasino *n.*
official *a.*, **~ly** *adv.* amtlich, offiziell; ~ **authority,** Amtsgewalt *f.;* ~ **journey** *s.* Dienstreise *f.;* ~ *s.* Beamte *m.;* Beamtin *f.; senior ~,* höhere Beamte *m.*
officialdom *s.* Beamtentum *n.;* Bürokratie *f.*
officiate *v.i.* amtieren.
officious *a.*, **~ly** *adv.* übereifrig.
off-key *a.* verstimmt, falsch.
off-load *v.t.* abladen, ausladen, entladen.
off-peak *a.* außerhalb der Spitzenzeit; abfallend.
off-putting *a.* abstoßend, abschreckend.
offset *s.* Ausgleich *m.;* Gegenrechnung *f.;* (*arch.*) Absatz *m.;* Offsetdruck *m.;* ~ *v.t.* ausgleichen.
offshoot *s.* Sproß, Ausläufer *m.*
offspring *s.* Nachkommenschaft *f.*
offstage *adv.* in den Kulissen.
off-the-record *a. u. adv.* inoffiziell.
off-white *a.* naturweiß, gebrochen weiß.
often *adv.* oft, öfters, häufig.
ogle *v.t.* (lieb)äugeln.
ogre *s.* Menschenfresser *m.;* Unmensch *m.*
oh *i.* o, ach.
oh! *i.* oh! ach! ~ **well,** na ja!
ohm *s.* (*elek.*) Ohm *n.;* **~meter** *s.* Widerstandsmesser *m.;* **O~'s law** Ohmsches Gesetz.
O.H.M.S. *On His/Her Majesty's Service,* im Dienste Seiner/Ihrer Majestät; Dienstsache.
oil *s.* Öl *n.;* ~ *v.t.* einölen.
oilcake *s.* Ölkuchen *m.*
oilcloth *s.* Wachstuch *n.*
oil gauge *s.* (*mot., avi.*) Ölstandzeiger *m.*
oil level *s.* (*mot., avi.*) Ölstand *m.*
oil paint *s.* Ölfarbe *f.*
oil painting *s.* Ölgemälde *n.*
oil pressure *s.* Öldruck *m.*
oil refinery *s.* Ölraffinerie *f.*
oil slick *s.* Ölteppich *m.*
oil tanker *s.* Öltankschiff *n.*
oil well *s.* Ölquelle *f.*
oily *a.* ölig, fett, fettig; schmierig.
ointment *s.* Salbe *f.*
OK, okay *a.* okay, in Ordnung, einverstanden; ~ *s.* Zustimmung *f.*
old *a.* alt.
old age *s.* Alter *n.,* Greisenalter *n.;* ~ **insurance** *s.* Altersversicherung *f.;* ~ **pension** *s.* Alterspension *f.*
old-fashioned *a.* altmodisch.
oldish *a.* ältlich.
old maid *s.* alte Jungfer *f.*
old wives' tale *s.* Ammenmärchen *n.*
oleander *s.* Oleander *m.*
oleograph *s.* Öldruck *m.*
olfactory *a.* Geruchs...
oligarchy *s.* Oligarchie *f.*
olive *s.* Olive *f.;* Ölbaum *m.;* ~ **branch** *s.* Ölzweig *m.; (fig.)* Friedensangebot *n.*
olive oil *s.* Olivenöl *n.*
Olympic Games *s.pl.* Olympische Spiele *pl.*
Olympics *s.pl.* Olympiade *f.*
omelet *s.* Omelett *n.*
omen *s.* Vorbedeutung *f.,* Vorzeichen *n.*
ominous *a.*, **~ly** *adv.* bedrohlich; ominös, unheilvoll.
omission *s.* Unterlassung *f.;* Auslassung *f.*
omit *v.t.* auslassen; unterlassen.
omnibus *s.* Omnibus *m.;* Sammelausgabe *f.;* ~ *a.* allgemein, umfassend; ~ **bill,** Sammelgesetz *n.*
omnipotence *s.* Allmacht *f.*
omnipotent *a.*, **~ly** *adv.* allmächtig.
omnipresent *a.*, allgegenwärtig.
omniscient *a.* allwissend.
on *pr. & adv.* an, auf; in, zu, mit, bei, unter, von; zufolge; weiter, fort; *and so ~,* und so weiter.
once *adv.* einmal; einst, dereinst; ~ **more,** ~ **again,** noch einmal.
oncoming *a.* entgegenkommend.
one *a. & pn.* einer, eine, ein(s); man, jemand; *any~,* irgend jemand, jeder; *~ another,* einander, sich; *every ~,* jeder; *oneself,* sich selbst; *~ by ~,* einer nach dem andern.
one-armed *a.* einarmig; **one-eyed** *a.* einäugig.
onerous *a.* lästig, beschwerlich.
one-sided *a.* einseitig.
one-time *a.* ehemalig; einmalig.
one-way street *s.* Einbahnstraße *f.;* **one-way traffic** *s.* Einbahnverkehr *m.*
ongoing *a.* andauernd, laufend.
onion *s.* Zwiebel *f.*
onlooker *s.* Zuschauer(in) *m.(f.)*
only *a.* einzig; ~ *adv.* allein, nur; erst.
o.n.o. *or nearest offer,* Verhandlungsbasis, VB.
on-off *a.* ein-aus...

onset *s.* Einsetzen *n.;* Einbruch *m.;* Anfall *m.*
onslaught *s.* Angriff *m.*
onus *s.* Last *f.*
onward *a. & adv.* vorwärts.
ooze *s.* Quellen, Sickern; Schlick *m.;* ~ *v.i.* sickern; *(fig.)* ausströmen.
opal *s.* Opal *m.*
opalescent *a.* schillernd; opalisierend.
opaque *a.* dunkel, undurchsichtig; trüb; opak.
OPEC *Organization of Petroleum Exporting Countries,* Organisation der Erdöl exportierenden Länder.
open *a.* **~ly** *adv.* offen; geöffnet; öffentlich; freimütig; aufrichtig; zugänglich; *in the ~ air,* im Freien; ~ **drive** *(mot.)* freie Fahrt *f.;* ~ *v.t.* öffnen, eröffnen erschließen; ~ *v.i.* sich öffnen; *to ~ out,* aufgehen.
open-air *a.* im Freien; Openair...; ~ **swimming pool** *s.* Freibad *n.*
open-ended *a.* ohne Zeitbegrenzung.
opener *s.* Öffner *m.*
open-handed *a.* freigebig, großzügig.
open-hearted *a.* aufrichtig; herzlich.
open-heart surgery *n.* Offenherzchirurgie *f.*
opening *s.* Öffnung *f.;* Eröffnung *f.; (com.)* Absatzweg *m.;* Gelegenheit, Aussicht *f.;* ~ **ceremony** *s.* feierliche Eröffnung. ~ **hours** *pl.* Öffnungszeiten *f.pl.*
open market *s.* freier Markt *m.*
open-minded *a.* aufgeschlossen.
openness *s.* Offenheit *f.;* Empfänglichkeit *f.*
open season *s.* Jagdsaison *f.*
opera *s.* Oper *f.*
opera glasses *s. pl.* Operngucker *m.,* Opernglas *n.*
opera house *s.* Opernhaus *n.*
opera singer *s.* Opernsänger(in) *m.(f.)*
operate *v.t.* wirken, funktionieren, operieren; *(mil.)* operieren, vorgehen; *(mech.)* handhaben, bedienen (Maschine); ~ *v.i. (mech.)* betrieben werden (mit), arbeiten, in Betrieb sein (Fabrik); *in operating condition,* in arbeitsfähigem Zustand; *to be ~d on,* sich operieren lassen, operiert werden.
operatic *a.* opernmässig, Opern...
operation *s.* Funktionieren *n.,* Wirkung *f.;* Operation *s.; (chem.)* Verfahren *n.; (mech.)* Arbeitsgang *m.;* Gang, Lauf *m.;* Betrieb (einer Fabrik) *m.; (mil.)* Unternehmen *n.,* Operation *f.;* Bedienung, Handhabung *f.; in ~,* in Kraft sein, in Betrieb; *out of ~,* außer Betrieb.
operational *a. (mil.)* operativ; betriebsbereit; einsatzfähig.
operative *a.* wirksam, tätig; ~ *s.* Arbeiter(in) *m.(f.)*
operator *s.* Operateur *m.;* Vermittlung *f.;* Dame (*f.*)/Herr (*m.*) von der Vermittlung.
operetta *s.* Operette *f.*
ophthalmic *a.* Augen...; augenärztlich.
ophthalmologist *s.* Augenarzt *m.;* -ärztin *f.*
ophthalmology *s.* Ophthalmologie *f.;* Augenheilkunde *f.*
opiate *s.* Opiat *n.;* ~ *a.* einschläfernd.
opine *v.i.* meinen.
opinion *s.* Meinung; Ansicht *f.;* (*jur.*) Urteilsbegründung *f.*
opinionated, *a.* starrsinnig; eigensinnig.
opinion poll *s.* Meinungsumfrage *f.*
opium *s.* Opium *m.*
opponent *a.* widerstreitend; ~ *s.* Gegner(in) *m.(f.);* Opponent *m.*
opportune *a.,* **~ly** *adv.* günstig, gelegen.
opportunist *s.* Opportunist(in) *m.(f.)*
opportunity *s.* (gute) Gelegenheit, Möglichkeit *f.,* günstiger Augenblick *m.; to miss an ~,* die Gelegenheit verpassen; *to take an ~,* eine Gelegenheit ergreifen.
oppose *v.t.* entgegenstellen, sich widersetzen; ~ *v.i.* Widerstand leisten; einwenden.
opposed *a.* gegensätzlich, entgegengesetzt, dagegen.
opposite *a.,* **~ly** *adv.* entgegengesetzt; widerstreitend; ~ **number,** der entsprechende Beamte (eines anderen Staates); ~ *pr.* gegenüber; ~ *adv.* gegenüber; ~ *s.* Gegenteil *n.*
opposition *s.* Opposition *f.;* Gegensatz *m.;* Opposition(spartei) *f.;* Widerstand *m.*
oppress *v.t.* unterdrücken, bedrücken.
oppression *s.* Unterdrückung *f.*
oppressive *a.,* **~ly** *adv.* bedrückend; repressiv; drückend.
oppressor *s.* Unterdrücker *m.*
opprobrious *a.,* **~ly** *adv.* schimpflich.
opprobrium *s.* Schimpf *m.;* Schande *f.;* Schmach *m.;* Schmähung *f.*
opt *v.i.* sich entscheiden.
optic(al) *a.* optisch, Seh...
optician *s.* Optiker(in) *m.(f.)*
optics *s.pl.* Optik *f.*
optimism *s.* Optimismus *m.*
optimist *s.* Optimist(in) *m.(f.)*
optimistic *a.* optimistisch.
optimize *v.t.* optimieren.
optimum *s.* Optimum *n.; a.* optimal.
option *s.* Wahl *f.; first ~,* Vorkaufsrecht *n.,* Kaufoption *f.*
optional *a.* freigestellt, freiwillig, wahlfrei.
opulence *s.* Reichtum *m.*
opulent *a.* wohlhabend.
opus *s.* Opus *n.;* Werk *n.*
or *c.* oder; entweder; (w. neg.) noch; ~ **else,** sonst; *either... or,* entweder... oder.
oracle *s.* Orakel *n.*
oracular *a.* orakelhaft.
oral *a.,* **~ly** *adv.* mündlich; Mund...; oral.
orange *s.* Orange *f.;* Apfelsine *f.*
orangeade *s.* Orangenlimonade *f.*
orangutan *s.* Orang-Utan *m.*
oration *s.* Rede *f.,* Ansprache *f.*
orator *s.* Redner(in) *m.(f.)*
oratorical *a.* rednerisch.
oratorio *s.* Oratorium *n.*
oratory *s.* Redekunst *f.*
orb *s.* Kugel *f.;* Augapfel *m.;* Ball *m.;* Reichsapfel *m.*
orbit *s.* Bereich *m.;* Kreis-, Umlaufbahn *f.*
orchard *s.* Obstgarten *m.*
orchestra *s.* Orchester *n.*
orchestral *a.* Orchester...; ~ **music** *s.* Orchestermusik *f.*
orchestrate *v.t.* orchestrieren.
orchestration *s.* Orchestrierung *f.*
orchid *s.* Orchidee *f.*

ordain *v.t.* verordnen; ordinieren; *to ~ sb. priest,* einen zum Priester weihen.
ordeal *s.* Gottesurteil *n.;* Heimsuchung *f.,* Tortur *f.;* Martyrium *n.*
order *s.* Ordnung *f.;* Verordnung *f.;* Befehl *m.;* Bestellung *f.;* Auftrag *m.;* Anweisung *f.;* Gattung *f.;* Rang *m.;* Orden *m.;* Reihenfolge *f.;* Schicht *f.; in ~ to,* um zu; *by ~ of,* auf Befehl von; *higher/lower ~s,* oberen/unteren Schichten; *out of ~,* defekt, kaputt; *to ~,* auf Bestellung, nach Maß; *to call to ~,* zur Ordnung rufen; *to establish ~,* Ordnung schaffen; *to take ~s,* Aufträge, Bestellungen entgegennehmen; sich zum Priester weihen lassen; **~ blank** *s.* Bestellungsformular *n.;* **~ form** *s.* Bestellschein *m.;* **~ of battle** *s.* *(mil.)* Schlachtaufstellung *f.;* **~s** *pl.* geistlicher Stand *m.;* **~** *v.t.* ordnen, anordnen, befehlen; bestellen; *to ~ again,* nachbestellen.
orderly *a. & adv.* ordentlich, regelmäßig; gesittet; diensttuend; **~ room** *s.* *(mil.)* Schreibstube *f.; s.* Bursche *m.;* Pfleger(in) *m.(f.);* Sanitäter *m.*
ordinal *s.* Ordnungszahl *f.;* Ordinalzahl *f.*
ordinance *s.* Verordnung, Regel *f.*
ordinary *a.,* **~ily** *adv.* gewöhnlich, üblich, mittelmäßig; gemein; **~ share,** Stammaktie *f.*
ordination *s.* (Priester-) Weihe *f.*
ordure *s.* Kot, Schmutz *m.*
ore *s.* Erz, Metall *n.; high-grade ~,* hochwertiges Erz; *low-grade ~,* geringwertiges Erz.
oregano *s.* Oregano *n.*
organ *s.* Organ *n.;* Orgel *f.;* **~ stop** *s.* Orgelregister *n.*
organ grinder *s.* Orgeldreher *m.*
organic *a.,* **~ally** *adv.* organisch; biologisch; biodynamisch.
organism *s.* Organismus *m.*
organist *s.* Organist(in) *m.(f.)*
organization *s.* Organisation *f.;* Ordnung *f.;* Anordnung *f.,* Einteilung *f.*
organizational *a.,* **~ly** *adv.* organisatorisch.
organize *v.t.* einrichten, organisieren.
organized *a.* organisiert; geregelt.
organizer *s.* Organisator(in) *m.(f.)*
orgasm *s.* Orgasmus *m.*
orgy *s.* Orgie *f.*
oriel *s.* Erkerfenster *n.*
orient *a.* östlich; **~** *s.* Osten *m., to ~ oneself,* sich orientieren; **~** *v.t.* ausrichten, einführen; *the Orient s.* Orient *m.;* Morgenland *n.*
oriental *a.* östlich; orientalisch; **~** *s.* Asiate *m.;* Asiatin. *f.*
orientation *s.* Orientierung *f.; general ~,* Einführungsbesprechung *f.*
orifice *s.* Öffnung *f.;* Loch *n.*
origin *s.* Ursprung *m.;* Herkunft *f.*
original *a.,* **~ly** *adv.* ursprünglich, eigenartig; **~ sin** *s.* Erbsünde *f.;* **~** *s.* Urbild *n.;* Urschrift *f.;* Original *n.;* Urtext *m.;* Urfassung *f.*
originality *s.* Originalität *f.* Ursprünglichkeit *f.*
originate *v.t.* ins Leben rufen; schaffen; **~** *v.i.* entstehen, entspringen.
originator *s.* Urheber(in), Schöpfer(in) *m.(f.)*
ornament *s.* Verzierung *f.;* Putz *m.;* Zier, Schmuck *m.;* Schmuckstück *n.*
ornamental *a.,* **~ly** *adv.* zierend, Zier...
ornamentation *s.* Ausschmückung *f.;* Verzierung *f.*
ornate *a.* geziert, zierlich; schmuckreich.
ornithology *s.* Vogelkunde *f.*
orphan *s.* Waise *m. & f.*
orphanage *s.* Waisenhaus *n.*
orthodox *a.* rechtgläubig; üblich, landläufig.
orthodoxy *s.* Orthodoxie *f.*
orthographic(al) *a.* orthographisch.
orthography *s.* Rechtschreibung *f.*
orthopedic *a.* orthopädisch.
oscillate *v.i.* schwingen; schwanken.
oscillatiion *s.* Schwingung *f.*
osier *s.* Weide *f.*
osmosis *s.* Osmose *f.*
ossify *v.i.* ossifizieren, verknöchern.
ostensible *a.* scheinbar, vorgeblich.
ostentation *s.* Gepränge *n.;* Prahlerei *f.*
ostentatious *a.,* **~ly** *adv.* prahlerisch.
osteopath *s.* Osteopath *m.,* Knochenheilkundige *m./f.*
ostracism *s.* Ächtung *f.*
ostracize *v.t.* verbannen, ächten.
ostrich *s.* Strauß (Vogel) *m.*
O.T. *Old Testament,* Altes Testament, AT.
other *a.* ander; **every ~** jede(r,s) zweite; **~ than** außer (+ *dat.*), anders als.
otherwise *adv.* anders, sonst.
otter *s.* Fischotter *m.*
ottoman *s.* Ruhebett *n.*
ought *v.i.ir.* sollen, müssen.
ounce *s.* Unze *f.* (28.35 g.)
our *pn.* unser, unsere.
ours *pn.* unser, der unsrige.
ourself *pn.* (wir) selbst, wir.
ourselves *pn.pl.* (wir) selbst, uns.
oust *v.t.* ausstoßen, verdrängen.
out *adv.* aus; außen, draußen, außerhalb; heraus, hinaus; erloschen; *~ of,* aus, aus... hinaus; *have it ~ with sb.,* *(fig.)* die Sache mit jm. ausfechten; *be ~ of sth.,* etw. nicht mehr haben.
outbid *v.t.st.* überbieten.
outboard motor *s.* Außenbordmotor *m.*
outbreak *s.* Ausbruch *m.*
outbuilding *s.* Nebengebäude *n.*
outburst *s.* Ausbruch *m.*
outcast *p. & a.* verworfen; verbannt; **~** *s.* Verstoßene, Ausgestoßene *m./f.*
outcome *s.* Ergebnis *n.*
outcry *s.* Aufschrei *m.* (der Empörung/Entrüstung)
outdated *a.* veraltet.
outdistance *v.t.* hinter sich lassen.
outdo *v.t.st.* übertreffen, überragen, überlegen.
outdoor *a.* im Freien; Außen...; *outdoors,* im Freien.
outer *a.* äußer, Außen...
outermost *a.* äußerst.
outer space *s.* der äußere Weltraum *m.*
outfit *s.* Austrüstung *f.;* Ausstattung *f.;* Kleider *n.pl.*
outfitter *s.* Ausstatter(in) *m.(f.)*
outflow *s.* Ausfluß *m.;* Abfluß *m.*
outgoing **~s** *s.pl.* Ausgaben *f.pl.;* **~** *a.* abgehend; *the ~ president,* der ausscheidende Präsident *m.;* kontaktfreudig.
outgrow *v.t.st.* entwachsen.
outhouse *s.* Nebengebäude *n.*

outing *s.* Ausflug *m.*
outlandish *a.* seltsam, fremdartig.
outlast *v.t.* überdauern.
outlaw *s.* Geächtete, Bandit *m.;* ~ *v.t.* ächten.; verbieten.
outlay *s.* Auslage *f.;* Ausgabe *f.*
outlet *s.* Ausgang *m.;* Ventil *n.;* Absatzmarkt *m.*, Verkaufsstelle *f.*
outline *s.* Umriß, Abriß *m.;* ~ *v.t.* kurz darstellen, umreißen.
outlive *v.t.* überleben.
outlook *s.* Ausblick *m.*, Aussicht *f.*
outlying *a.* fernliegend; abgelegen.
outmaneuver *v.t.* überlisten, ausmanövrieren, ausstechen.
outmoded *a.* altmodisch.
outnumber *v.t.* an Zahl übertreffen.
outpatient *s.* ambulanter Patient(in) *m.(f.)*
outpost *s.* Vorposten *m.*
outpouring *s.* Erguß *m.*
output *s.* Ertrag *m.;* Produktion *f.*
outrage *v.t.* schmählich behandeln; hohnsprechen; empören; ~ *s.* Greueltat *f.;* Gewalttat *f.;* Unverschämtheit *f.;* Schandtat *f.*
outrageous *a.*, **~ly** *adv.* abscheulich, greulich; unverschämt; übertrieben.
outright *adv.* gänzlich, völlig, rein, total, ganz.
outrun *v.t.st.* im Laufen übertreffen, davonlaufen.
outset *s.* Anfang *m.*
outshine *v.t.st.* überstrahlen.
outside *s.* Außenseite *f.;* ~ *adv.* & *pr.* außen; außerhalb; draußen; äußerst; hinaus.
outsider *s.* Außenseiter(in) *m.(f.)*
outsized *a.* übergroß.
outskirts *s.pl.* Stadtrand *m.*, Außen-, Randgebiet *n.*
outspoken *a.* freimütig, offen, direkt.
outstanding *a.* unbezahlt; hervorragend, außerordentlich.
outstretched *p.* & *a.* ausgestreckt.
outstrip *v.t.* überholen.
outvote *v.t.* überstimmen.
outward *a.* der, die, das äußere, äußerlich; ~ *adv.* aussen, auswärts.
outwardly *adv.* äußerlich.
outward(s) *adv.* nach außen; ~ **bound** *a.* auf der Hinreise, auslaufend.
outweigh *v.t.* überwiegen.
outwit v.t überlisten.
outwork *s.* Heimarbeit *f.;* Außenwerk *n.*
oval *a.* oval, eirund; ~ *s.* Oval *n.*
ovary *s.* Eierstock *m.*
ovation *s.* Ovation *f.*, stürmischer Beifall *m.*
oven *s.* Backofen, Ofen *m.*
ovenmitt *s.* Topfhandschuh *n.*
ovenproof *a.* feuerfest.
ovenware *s.* feuerfestes Geschirr *n.*
over *pr.* & *adv.* über, darüber, hinüber, überhin; vorüber, vorbei, zu sehr, allzu; *all* ~, über und über; ganz vorbei; ~ **again,** noch einmal; *continued* ~, Fortsetzung umseitig; ~ **there,** da drüben.
over-abundant *a.* überreichlich.
overact *v.t.* & *i.* übertreiben.
overall *s.* Arbeitskittel *m.* ~ **size,** Einheitsgröße *f.* **~s** *pl.* Arbeitsanzug *m.;* ~ *a.* Gesamt..., allgemein; *adv.* im grossen und ganzen.
overawe *v.t.* in Furcht halten, überwältigen.
overbalance *v.t.* umkippen; das Gleichgewicht verlieren.
overbearing *a.* anmaßend, stolz, herrisch.
overbid *v.t.st.* überbieten.
overboard *adv.* über Bord.
overburden *v.t.* überladen.
overcast *v.t.st.* überziehen; ~ *a.* bewölkt, bedeckt.
overcharge *v.t.* überladen; zu viel berechnen; überlasten.
overcloud *v.t.* überwölken.
overcoat *s.* Überzieher *m.*, Mantel *m.*
overcome *v.t.st.* überwältigen; überwinden; bezwingen; abgewöhnen.
overconfidence *s.* Vermessenheit *f.;* übersteigertes Selbstvertrauen; zu großer Optimismus.
overconfident *a.* übertrieben selbstsicher *or* selbstbewußt.
overcrowded *a.* überfüllt.
overdo *v.t.st.* zu viel tun, übertreiben.
overdose *v.t.* überdosieren; ~ *s.* Überdosis *f.*
overdraft *s.* überzogenes Konto *n.*
overdraw *v.t.* das Bankkonto überziehen.
overdress *v.t.* sich zu elegant anziehen, zu fein kleiden.
overdue *a.* fällig; überfällig.
overeager *a.* übereifrig.
overeat *v.i.* zu viel essen.
overestimate *v.t.* überschätzen, zu hoch einschätzen.
overexcite *v.t.* zu sehr aufregen.
overexert *v.t.* sich überanstrengen.
overexpose *v.t.* überbelichten.
overexposure *s. (phot.)* Überbelichtung *f.*
overflow *v.i.* & *v.t.st.* überfließen; ~ *s.* Überlauf *m.*, Ausflußröhre *f.;* ~ **meeting,** Parallelversammlung *f.*
overgrow *v.t.st.* überwachsen, überwuchern.
overgrown *p.* & *a.* überwachsen; überwuchert.
overgrowth *s.* Überwucherung *f.*
overhang *v.t.st.* überhängen.
overhaul *v.t.* gründlich prüfen; *(nav.)* überholen.
overhead *adv.* & *a.* oben, Ober...; ~ **cable,** ~ **line,** ~ **wire,** *(elek.)* Freileitung, Oberleitung *f.;* ~ **clearance,** lichte Höhe *f.;* ~ **expenses** *pl.* laufende Ausgaben *f.pl.;* ~ **railway,** Hochbahn *f.*
overhear *v.t.ir.* zufällig hören; behorchen.
overheat *v.t.* überhitzen.
overindulge *v.t.* zu sehr frönen; ~ *v.i.* es übertreiben, zu viel genießen.
overjoyed *a.* überglücklich, äußerst erfreut.
overkill *s.* Overkill *n.*
overland *a.* Überland...
overlap *v.t.* übereinander greifen, teilweise zusammenfallen.
overlay *v.t.ir.* belegen, überlagern.
overleaf *adv.* umseitig.
overload *v.t.* überladen.
overlook *v.t.* überblicken; durchsehen, prüfen; Nachsicht haben; übersehen.
overmuch *a.* zu viel.
overnight *adv.* über Nacht; ~ **accommodation,** Übernachtungsunterkunft *f.;* ~ **stay** Übernach-

tung *f.; to stay ~ with sb.*, bei einem übernachten.
overpay *v.t.* zu reichlich bezahlen.
overpopulated *a.* überbevölkert.
overpower *v.t.* überwältigen.
overpriced *a.* zu teuer, verteuert.
overproduction *s.* Überproduktion *f.*
overprotective *a.* überfürsorglich.
overrate *v.t.* überschätzen.
overreach *v.t.* überragen; übervorteilen; *to ~ oneself*, sich übernehmen.
overreaction *s.* Überreaktion *f.*
override *v.t.* hinwegsetzen; aufheben; umstoßen; *of overriding importance*, von vorrangiger Wichtigkeit.
overripe *a.* überreif.
overrule *v.t.* als ungültig verwerfen; (Entscheidung) aufheben; abweisen.
overrun *v.t.st.* überlaufen, überrennen.
oversea *a. & adv.*, **overseas** *adv.* überseeisch.
oversee *v.t.st.* beaufsichtigen, überwachen.
overseer *s.* Aufseher *m.*
oversensitive *a.* überempfindlich.
overshadow *v.t.* überschatten.
overshoe *s.* Überschuh *m.*
overshoot *v.t.ir.* über das Ziel hinausschießen.
oversight *s.* Versehen *n.*
oversimplify *v.t.* zu stark vereinfachen.
oversleep *v.t.ir.* sich verschlafen.
overspend *v.i.* zuviel ausgeben.
overspread *v.t.st.* überdecken.
overstaff *v.t.* überbesetzen.
overstate *v.t.* übertreiben.
overstatement *s.* Übertreibung *f.*
overstay *v.t.* (Zeit) überschreiten; *to ~ a date*, über einen Termin hinaus ausbleiben; *~ing of leave*, Urlaubsüberschreitung *f.*
overstep *v.t.* überschreiten.
overstrain *v.t.* (*v.i.* sich) überanstrengen.
overstretch *v.t.* überdehnen.
overt *a.*, **~ly** *adv.* offenbar, öffentlich.
overtake *v.t.st.* einholen, überholen, ereilen.
overtax *v.t.* zu hoch besteuern; überbürden; überfordern.
overthrow *v.t.st.* umwerfen; umstürzen, vernichten; *~ s.* Umsturz *m.*
overtime *s.* Überstunden *f.pl.; to work ~*, Überstunden machen.
overture *s.* Vorschlag, Antrag, Annäherungsversuch *m.;* Ouvertüre *f.*
overturn *v.t.* umwerfen; zerstören; *~ v.i.* umkippen, umfallen; *~ s.* Umsturz *m.*
overvalue *v.t.* zu hoch schätzen.
overview *s.* Überblick *m.*
overweening *a.*, **~ly** *adv.* anmaßend.
overweight *s.* Übergewicht *n.; a.* übergewichtig.
overwhelm *v.t.* überwältigen.
overwork *v.t. & i.* (sich) überarbeiten; *~ s.* übermäßige Arbeit *f.*
oviduct *s.* Eileiter *m.*
oviparous *a.* eierlegend.
owe *v.t.* schuldig sein, verdanken.
owing *p.* schuldig; unbezahlt; *~* **to** *pr.* wegen; dank..., infolge; *how much is ~ to you?*, wieviel ist an Sie zu zahlen?
owl *s.* Eule *f.; wise old ~*, weise Eule.
own *a.* eigen; *on one's ~*, selbständig, für sich; *to come into one's ~*, zu seinem Rechte kommen; *~ v.t.* besitzen, haben.
owner *s.* Besitzer, Besitzerin *m./f.;* Eigentümer *m.; at ~'s risk*, auf eigene Gefahr.
ownership *s.* Eigentum(srecht) *n.*
ox *s.* Ochs[e] *m.;* Rindvieh *n.*
oxidation *s.* Oxydation *f.*
oxide *s.* Oxyd *n.*
oxidize *v.t. & i.* oxydieren.
oxygen *s.* Sauerstoff *m.*
oxygenate *v.t.* oxygenieren, mit Sauerstoff anreichern.
oxygen mask *s.* Sauerstoff *or* Atemmask *f.*
oxygen tank *s.* Sauerstoffbehälter *m.*
oxygen tent *s.* Sauerstoffzelt *n.*
oyster *s.* Auster *f.;* ~ **bed** *s.* Austernbank *f.*
oz. *ounce*, Unze.
ozone *s.* Ozon *n.;* ~ **layer** *s.* Ozonschicht *f.*

PQ

P, p der Buchstabe P oder p *n.*
p. *page*, Seite.
p.a. *per annum (per year)*, pro Jahr.
pace *s.* Schritt, Gang *m.;* Gangart *f.;* Tempo *n.;* **keep ~ with,** Schritt halten mit; *~ v.i.* schreiten; *~ v.t.* abschreiten.
pacemaker *s.* Schrittmacher(in) *m.(f.);* Herzschrittmacher *m.*
pachyderm *s.* Dickhäuter *m.*
pacific *a.* friedlich, friedsam.
pacification *s.* Befriedung *f.*
Pacific Ocean *s.* Pazifischer Ozean *m.;* der Pazifik *m.*
pacifism *s.* Pazifismus *m.*
pacifist *s.* Pazifist(in) *m.(f.)*
pacify *v.t.* Frieden stiften; beruhigen.
pack *s.* Packen, Ballen *m.;* Päckchen *n.;* Packung *n.* Rudel *n.*, Meute *f.;* (Karten)Spiel *n.;* Tornister *m.;* Menge *f.; a ~ of lies*, ein Haufen Lügen; **~horse** *s.* Packpferd *n.;* **~saddle** *s.* Packsattel *m.; ~ v.t.* packen; *~ v.i.* einpacken; sich packen.
package *s.* Verpackung *f.*, Packet *n.; ~ v.t.* verpacken.
package tour *s.* Pauschalreise *f.*
packaging *s.* Verpackung *f.*
packed *a.* gepackt; bepackt.
packet-boat *s.* Postschiff *n.*
packing *s.* Verpackungsmaterial *n.;* Verpacken *n.*
pack-thread *s.* Bindfaden *m.*
pact *s.* Pakt *m.*
pad *s.* Polster *n.*, Kissen *n.;* Bausch, Wulst *m.;* Unterlage *f.; ~* (of paper) Block (*m.*) Papier; *~ v.t.* polstern, wattieren.
padded *a.* gepolstert.
padding *s.* Polsterung f

paddle *s.* Paddel *n.;* Rührholz *n.;* Schaufel *f.;* ~ *v.i.* paddeln; plätschern, waten.
paddle steamer *s.* Raddampfer *m.*
paddle wheel *s.* Schaufelrad *n.*
paddling pool *s.* Plauschbekken *n.*
paddock *s.* Gehege *n.;* Koppel *f.*
padlock *s.* Vorhängeschloß *n.*
pagan *s.* Heide *m.;* ~ *a.* heidnisch.
paganism *s.* Heidentum *n.*
page *s.* Seite *f.;* Blatt *n.;* Page *m.;* Diener *m.;* ~ *v.t.* mit Seitenzahlen bezeichnen; ausrufen lassen; anpiepsen (Beeper, Telefon).
pageant *s.* Prunkaufzug, Festzug *m.; beauty* ~ Schönheitswettbewerb *m.*
pageantry *s.* Prunk *m.;* Gepränge *n.*
pager *s.* Piepser *m.*
paginate *v.t.* paginieren.
pagoda *s.* Pagode *f.*
pail *s.* Eimer *m.*
pain *s.* Schmerz *m.;* **~s** *pl.* Mühe *f.;* Leiden *n.pl.;* ~ *v.t.* Schmerzen bereiten.
painful *a.,* **~ly** *adv.* schmerzhaft; mühsam.
painkiller *s.* schmerzstillendes Mittel *n.*
painless *a.* schmerzlos.
painstaking *a.* äußerst sorgsam.
paint *v.t.* malen; anstreichen; ~ *v.i.* sich schminken; ~ *s.* Farbe *f.;* Schmink *f.*
paint box *s.* Malkasten *m.*
paintbrush *s.* Pinsel *m.*
painter *s.* Maler(in) *m.(f.)*
painting *s.* Malerei *f.;* Gemälde *n.*
pair *s.* Paar *n.;* ~ *v.t. & i.* (sich) paaren.
pajamas *s.pl.* Pyjama *m.,* Schlafanzug *m.*
Pakistan *s.* Pakistan *n.*
Pakistani *a.* pakistanisch; ~ *s.* Pakistani *m./f.;* Pakistaner(in) *m.(f.)*
pal *s. (sl.)* Kamerad, *m.* Kumpel *m.*
palace *s.* Palast *m.*
palatable *a.* schmackhaft.
palate *s.* Gaumen *m.*
palatial *a.* palastartig.
palaver *s.* Gespräch, Geschwätz *n.;* Umstrand *m.*
pale *a.,* **~ly** *adv.* blaß, bleich; **~ale** *s.* helles Bier *n.;* ~ *s.* Pfahl *m.;* ~ *v.t.* pfählen; ~ *v.i.* bleich werden.
paleness *s.* Blässe *f.*
Palestine *s.* Palästina *n.*
Palestinian *s.* palästinensisch; ~ *s.* Palästinenser(in) *m.(f.)*
palette *s.* Palette *f.*
palfrey *s.* Zelter *m.*
palisade *s.* Pfahlwerk *n.*
pall *s.* Sargtuch *n.;* ~ *v.i.* schal werden; Reiz verlieren.
pallbearer *s.* Sargträger(in) *m.(f.)*
pallet *s.* Strohsack *m.;* Palette *f.*
palliasse *s.* Strohsack *m.*
palliate *v.t.* bemänteln; lindern.
palliative *a.* beschönigend, lindernd; ~ *s.* Linderungsmittel *n.*
pallid *a.,* **~ly** *adv.* blaß, bleich.
pallor *s.* Blässe *f.*
palm *s.* Palme *f.;* Handfläche *f.;* ~ *v.t.* betasten; ~ *sth. off on sb.,* jm. etw. aufhängen.
palmistry *s.* Handlesekunst *f.*
Palm Sunday *s.* Palmsonntag *m.*
palm tree *s.* Palme *f.*
palmy *a.* palmenreich; *(fig.)* siegreich; glücklich.
palpable *a.,* **~bly** *adv.* greifbar, fühlbar; deutlich.
palpitate *v.i.* pochen (vom Herzen).
palpitation *s.* Herzklopfen *n.*
palsied *a.* gelähmt.
palsy *s.* Lähmung *f.*
paltry *a.* armselig, erbärmlich.
pamper *v.t.* verwöhnen; verhätscheln.
pamphlet *s.* Flugschrift *f.*
pamphleteer *s.* Verfasser(in) von Flugschriften *m.*
pan *s.* Kochtopf *m.;* Pfanne *f.;* ~ *v.t. & i.* (die Kamera) schwenken.
panacea *s.* Allheilmittel *n.*
Panama *s.* Panama *n.*
Panamanian *a.* panamaisch; *s.* Panamer(in) *m.(f.)*
pancake *s.* Pfannkuchen *m.*
pancreas *s.* Bauchspeicheldrüse *f.;* Pankreas *m.*
panda *s.* Panda *m.*
pandemonium *s.* Tumult *m.;* Heidenlärm *m.*
pander *s.* Kuppler *m.;* ~ *v.i.* kuppeln; Vorschub leisten.
pane *s.* Glaßscheibe *f.*
panegyrist *s.* Lobredner *m.*
panel *s.* Füllung *f.;* Fach, Feld *n.;* Geschworenenliste *f.;* Kommission *f.;* ~ **discussion** *s.* Podiumsgespräch *n.*
paneling *s.* Täfelung *f.*
panelist *s.* Mitglied (Kommission, Gremium).
pang *s.* Stich, Schreck *m.*
panic *s.* Panik *f.*
panicky *a.* beunruhigend; unruhig.
panic-stricken *a.* von Panik erfaßt.
panoply *s.* völlige Rüstung *f.*
panorama *s.* Panorama *n.*
pansy *f. (bot.)* Stiefmütterchen *n.*
pant *v.i.* schnappen (nach Luft); keuchen; lechzen; pochen.
panther *s.* Panther *m.*
panties *s.pl.* Schlüpfer *m.,* Slip *m.*
pantomime *s.* Pantomime *f.*
pantry *s.* Speisekammer *f.*
pants *s.pl.* Hosen *f.pl.;* (Herren-) Unterhosen *f.pl.*
pantyhose *s.* Strumpfhose *f.*
pap *s.* Kinderbrei *m.*
papa *s.* Papa *m.*
papacy *s.* Papsttum *n.*
papal *a.* päpstlich.
paper *s.* Papier *n.;* Zettel *m.;* Abhandlung *f.;* Zeitung *f.;* **~s** *pl.* Schriften *f.pl.;* Akten, Legitimationspapiere *pl.; to read a* ~, einen Vortrag halten; *to commit to* ~, zu Papier bringen; **~back** *s.* Taschenbuch *n.;* ~ **bag** *s.* Tüte *f.;* **~clip** *s.* Heftklammer; **~-bound** *a.* broschiert; ~ *a.* papieren; ~ *v.t.* tapezieren.
paper chase *s.* Schnitzeljagd *f.*
paperhanger *s.* Tapezier *m.*
paper mill *s.* Papiermühle *f.*
paper money *s.* Papiergeld *n.*
paper napkin *s.* Papierserviette *f.*
paperweight *s.* Briefbeschwerer *m.*
paperwork *s.* Schreibarbeit *f.*
papier-maché *s.* Papiermaché *n.*
papist *s.* Papist(in) *m.(f.)*

par *s.* Gleichheit *f.*; Pari *n.*; *at* ~, pari.
par. *paragraph,* Absatz, Abs., Abschnitt, Abschn.
parable *s.* Parabel *f.*; Gleichnis *n.*
parabola *s. (geom.)* Parabel *f.*
parabolic *a.* gleichnisweise; parabolisch.
parachute *s.* Fallschirm *m.*
parachutist *s.* Fallschirmspringer(in) *m.(f.)*
parade *s.* Gepränge *n.*; Parade *f.*; ~ *v.t.* aufziehen; ~ *v.t.* prunken mit.
parade ground *s.* Exerzierplate *m.*
paradigm *s.* Beispiel *n.*, Paradigma *n.*
paradise *s.* Paradies *n.*
paradox *s.* Paradox *n.*
paradoxical *a.*, **~ly** *adv.* paradox.
paraffin *s.* Paraffin *n.*; Petroleum *n.*
paragon *s.* Muster, Urbild *n.*
paragraph *s.* Abschnitt *m.*
parakeet *s.* Sittich *m.*
parallel *a.* parallel, gleichlaufend; entsprechend; ~ **bars** *pl.* Barren (Turnen) *m.*; *(elek.)* ~ **connection** *s.* Nebeneinanderschaltung *f.*; ~ *s.* Ähnlichkeit, Vergleich *m.* ~ *v.t.* gleichmachen; gleichkommen, vergleichen.
paralysis *s.* Lähmung *f.*
paralytic *a.* gelähmt; ~ *s.* Gelähmte *m./f.*
paralyze *v.t.* lähmen.
parameter *s.* Parameter *m.*
paramilitary *a.* paramilitärisch.
paramount *a.* oberst, höchst.
paranoia *s.* Paranoia *f.*
parapet *s.* Brustwehr *f.*; Geländer *n.*
paraphernalia *s.* Drum und Dran *n.*
paraphrase *s.* Umschreibung *f.*; ~ *v.t.* umschreiben.
paraplegia *s.* Paraplegie *f.*; Querschnittslähmung *f.*
parasite *s.* Schmarotzer *m.*
parasitic *s.* parasitisch, parasitär.
parasol *s.* Sonnenschirm *m.*
paratroops *s.pl.* Fallschirmtruppen *f.pl.*
paratyphoid *s.* Paratyphus *m.*
parboil *v.t.* halbgar kochen, ankochen.
parcel *s.* Stück *n.*; Teil *m.*; Partie, Anzahl *f.*, Posten (Ware) *m.*; Paket *n.*, Päckchen *n.*; ~ *of land,* Parzelle *f.*; ~ **post** *f.*; ~ **service** *s.* Paketfahrtgesellschaft *f.*; **~s office** Gepäckabfertigung *f.*; Paketpost ~ *v.t.* teilen, zerstückeln.
parch *v.t.* dörren; austrocknen; ~ *v.i.* verdorren.
parchment *s.* Pergament *n.*
pardon *s.* Verzeihung *f.*, Begnadigung *f.*; Vergebung *f.*; *(jur.)* *(I) beg your ~?* Verzeihung!; entschuldigen Sie bitte!; wie, bitte?; ~ *v.t.* verzeihen; begnadigen.
pardonable *a.*, **~bly** *adv.* verzeihlich.
pare *v.t.* schneiden; schälen.
parent *s.* Elternteil *m.*; Vater *m.*; Mutter *f.*; ~ **company** *s.* Muttergesellschaft; **~s** *pl.* Eltern *pl.*
parentage *s.* Abstammung *f.*
parental *a.* elterlich.
parenthesis *s.* Klammer *f.*, Parenthese *f.*
parenthetical *a.* eingeschaltet, beiläufig.
parenthood *s.* Elternschaft *f.*
paring *s.* Schale *f.*; Abfall *m.*
parish *s.* Kirchspiel *n.*; Pfarrbezirk *m.*, Gemeinde *f.* **~register** *s.* Kirchenbuch *n.*
parishioner *s.* Gemeindemitglied *n.*
parity *s.* Gleichheit *f.*; Umrechnungskurs *m.*
park *s.* Park *m.*; ~ *v.t.* (Autos) parken; *No parking!* Parken verboten!
parking: ~ **attendant** *s.* Parkplatzwächter *m.*; **~meter** *s.* Parkuhr *f.*; **~space** *s.* Parkplatz *m.*; **~ticket** *s.* Strafzettel *m.*
parlance *s.* Redeweise *f.*
parliament *s.* Parlament *n.*
parliamentary *a.* Parlaments..., parlamentarisch; ~ *division,* Wahlbezirk *m.*
parlor *s.* Wohnzimmer *n.*; Salon *m.*
parochial *a.* Pfarr..., Gemeinde...; *(fig.)* Kirchturms...
parody *s.* Parodie *f.*; ~ *v.t.* parodieren.
parole *s.* Ehrenwort *n.*; Losung *f.*; bedingte Strafaussetzung *f.*
paroxysm *s.* heftiger Anfall *m.*; Krampf *m.*
parquet *s.* Parkett *n.*
parricide *s.* Vatermord *m.*; Vatermörder *m.*
parrot *s.* Papagei *m.*; ~ *v.t.* nachplappern.
parry *v.t. & i.* abwehren, parieren.
parsimonious *a.*, **~ly** *adv.* sparsam.
parsimony *s.* Sparsamkeit *f.*
parsley *s.* Petersilie *f.*
parsnip *s.* Pastinake *f.*
parson *s.* Pfarrer *m.*; *(fam.)* Pfaffe *m.*
parsonage *s.* Pfarrei *f.*; Pfarrhaus *n.*
part *s.* Teil, Anteil *m.*; Rolle *f.*; Seite *f.*; Gegend *f.*; *(mus.)* Sing- *or* Instrumentaenabstimme *f.*; *in* ~, teilweise; Stück *n.*; *to take in good* ~, gut aufnehmen; *on my* ~, meinerseits; **~payment** *s.* Teilzahlung, Abschlagszahlung *f.*; ~ *v.t.* teilen; trennen; ~ *v.i.* sich trennen; abreisen.
partake *v.i.st.* teilnehmen, teilhaben.
partial *a.*, **~ly** *adv.* teilweise; parteiisch.
partiality *s.* Vorliebe, Parteilichkeit *f.*
participant *s.* Teilnehmer(in) *m.(f.)*
participate *v.i.* teilnehmen, teilhaben.
participle *s. (gram.)* Partizip.
particle *s.* Teilchen *n.*; Partikel *f.*
particolored *a.* buntfarbig.
particular *a.*, **~ly** *adv.* besonder; einzeln; sonderbar; seltsam; wählerisch, genau, heikel; ~ *s.*. Einzelheit *f.*; besonderer Umstand *m.*; *further* ~*s,* Näheres *n.*
particularity *s.* Besonderheit *f.*; Umständlichkeit *f.*
parting *s.* Scheiden *n.*; Scheitel *m.*; ~ *a.* Scheide...
partisan *s.* Parteigänger *m.*; Guerillakreiger, Partisan *m.*
partition *s.* Teilung *f.*; Scheidewand *f.*; ~ *v.t.* teilen, abteilen.
partitive *a.*, **~ly** *adv.* teilend, partitiv.
partly *adv.* teils, zum Teil.
partner *s.* Teilnehmer *m.*; Gefährte *m.*; Teilhaber *m.*; Tanzpartner(in) *m.(f.)*; Spielgegner *m.*; *silent* ~, stiller Teilhaber *m.*
partnership *s.* Genossenschaft *f.*; Handelsgesellschaft *f.*; Teilhaberschaft *f.*; *general* ~, offene Handelsgesellschaft *f.*; *to enter into* ~ *with,* sich assoziieren mit.
partridge *s.* Rebhuhn *n.*
part-time *a.* Teilzeit...; Halbtags...
party *s.* Partei *f.*; Gesellschaft, Partie *f.*; Teilnehmer *m.*; *to be a* ~ *to,* beteiligt sein an; **~line** *s.* Parteilinie *f.*; **~official** *s.* Parteifunktionär *m.*

parvenu *s.* Emporkömmling *m.*
paschal *a.* Oster...
pass *v.i.* gehen, vorübergehen; vergehen; fahren; felten; geschehen; *to ~ away,* sterben; *to ~ in the opposite direction, (mot.)* kreuzen; ~ *v.t.* verbringen; übertragen; überschicken; gehen lassen; bestätigen; *(Gesetz)* annehmen; verleben; passieren; überschreiten; *(mot.)* überholen; *to ~ an examination,* eine Prüfung bestehen; *to ~ sth. on,* etw. weiterleiten; ~ *s.* Paß, Weg, Durchgang *m.;* Passierschein, Ausweis *m.;* Stoß (im Fechten) *m.;* Zustand *m.;* Lage *f.*
passable *a.*, **~bly** *adv.* gangbar; mittelmäßig.
passage *s.* Durchgang *m.;* Durchfahrt *f.;* Hausflur *f.;* Gang *m.;* Überfahrt *f.;* (Buch) Stelle *f.;* Verabschiedung *f.* (eines Gesetzes).
passageway *s.* Gang *m.*
passbook *s.* Kontobuch *n.*
passenger *s.* Reisende *m./f.;* Passagier *m.; ~ train,* Personenzug *m.; ~ traffic,* Personenverkehr *m.*
passerby *s.* Passant(in) *m.(f.)*
passing *a.* vorübergehend, flüchtig; **~, ~ly** *adv.* sehr, äusserst; *in ~,* im Vorübergehen.
passion *s.* Leidenschaft *f.;* Zorn *m.; to fly into a ~,* zornig werden; *Passion of Christ,* Leiden Christi *n.*, Passion *f.*
passionate *a.*, **~ly** *adv.* leidenschaftlich.
passionflower *s.* Passionsblume *f.*
passionfruit *s.* Passionsfrucht *f.*
passive *a.*, **~ly** *adv.* leidend; untätig; passiv; ~ *s. (gram.)* Passivum *n.*
passiveness *s.*, **passivity** *s.* Passivität *f.*
Passover *s.* Passah(fest) *n.*
passport *s.* Paß *m.*
password *s.* Losung *f.;* Kennwort *n.*
past *a. & pr.* vergangen, vorbei, über... hinaus; *~ master,* Altmeister *m.;* Experte *m.;* ~ *s.* Vergangenheit *f.*
pasta *a.* Teigwaren *pl.*
paste *s.* Teig *m.;* Kleister *m.;* Paste *f.;* ~ *v.t.* kleistern, pappen.
pasteboard *s.* Pappdeckel *m.*, Karton *m.*
pastel *s.* Pastell *n.*
pastern *s.* Fessel am Pferdefuß *f.*
pasteurize *v.t.* pasteurisieren.
pastil(le) *s.* Räucherkerzchen *n.;* Pastille *f.*
pastime *s.* Zeitvertreib *m.*
pastor *s.* Pfarrer *m.*, Pastor *m.*
pastoral *s.* Hirten...; pastoral; **~letter** *s.* Hirtenbrief *m.;* ~ *s.* Schäfergedicht *n.*
pastry *s.* Backwerk *n.*, Kuchen *m.*
pastrycook *s.* Konditor *m.*
pasture *s.* Weide *f.;* ~ *v.t. & i.* weiden.
pat *s.* Schlag, Patsch *m.;* Scheibchen *n.;* ~ *a.* bequem, passend; ~ *v.t.* patschen, streicheln; klopfen.
patch *s.* Fleck *m.;* Stück *n.;* Flicken *m.;* Schönheitspflästerschen *n.;* ~ *v.t.* flicken, ausbessern
patchwork *s.* Patchwork *n.*
patchy *a.* ungleich, zusammengestoppelt.
patent *a.* offen; patentiert; *letters ~,* Freibrief *m.;* ~ *s.* Vorrecht, Patent *n.; to take out a ~ for sth.,* sich etwas patentieren lassen; *~ pending,* angemeldetes Patent; *renewal of a ~,* Patentverlängerung *f.;* ~ **lawyer** *s.* Patentanwalt *m.; f.* **~holder** *s.* Patentinhaber *m.;* **~holding company** *f.* Patentinhabergesellschaft *f.;* ~ **Office** *f.* Patentamt *n.;* ~ *v.t.* patentieren.
patent leather *s.* Lackleder *n.*
paternal *a.* väterlich.
paternity *s.* Vaterschaft *f.*
path *s.* Pfad, Fußsteig *m.;* Weg *m.*
pathetic *a.*, **~ally** *adv.* rührend, traurig.
pathological *a.*, **~ly** *adv.* pathologisch.
pathology *s.* Krankheitslehre *f.*, Pathologie *f.*
pathos *s.* Feierlichtkeit *f.;* Rührung *f.*
pathway *s.* Fußweg *m.*
patience *s.* Geduld *f.*
patient *a.*, **~ly** *adv.* geduldig; ~ *s.* Kranke *m./f.*, Patient(in) *m.(f.)*
patio *s.* Veranda *f.;* Terrasse *f.;* Patio *m.*
patriarch *s.* Patriarch *m.*
patriarchal *a.* patriarchalisch.
patrician *s.* Patrizier *m.;* ~ *a.* patrizisch.
patrimony *s.* Erbgut, Erbteil *n.*
patriot *s.* Patriot(in) *m.(f.)*
patriotic *s.* patriotisch.
patriotism *s.* Vaterlandsliebe *f.;* Patriotismus *m.*
patrol *s.* Patrouille *f.*, Spähtrupp *m.;* **~activity,** Spähtrupptätigkeit *f.;* ~ *v.i.* patrouillieren.
patron *s.* Gönner(in) *m.(f.);* Schirmherr(in) *m.(f.)*
patronage *s.* Gönnerschaft *f.;* Schutz *m.;*
patronize *v.t.* beschützen, begünstigen; als Kunde besuchen; gönnerhaft behandeln.
patter *v.i.* prasseln; trippeln.; ~ *s.* Prasseln *n.;* Trippeln *n.*
pattern *s.* Muster *n.;* Schnitt *m.*, Schnittmuster *n.*
patty *s.* Pastetchen *n.*
paucity *s.* Mangel *m.*
paunch *s.* Wanst *m.;* **~y** *a.* dickbäuchig.
pauper *s.* Arme *m./f.*
pause *s.* Ruhepunkt, Absatz *m.;* Pause *f.;* ~ *v.i.* pausieren; sich bedenken.
pave *v.t.* pflastern; bahnen.
pavement *s.* Pflaster *n.;* Bürgersteig *m.*
pavilion *s.* Zelt *n.;* Pavilion *m.*
paving stone *s.* Pflasterstein *m.*
paw *s.* Pfote, Tatze *f.;* ~ *v.t.* scharren; streicheln; *(fam.)* derb angreifen.
pawn *s.* Pfand *n.;* Bauer (im Schach) *m.;* Pranke *f.;* ~ *v.t.* verpfänden.
pawnbroker *s.* Pfandleiher *m.*
pawnshop *s.* Pfandhaus *n.;* Leihhaus *n.*
pawn ticket *s.* Pfandschein *m.*
pay *v.t.ir.* zahlen; abstatten; *to ~ attention,* achtgeben;*to ~ a call, visit,* einen Besuch abstatten; *to ~ for,* bezahlen; *to ~ down,* bar bezahlen; *to ~ in, to ~ in advance,*im voraus bezahlen; einzahlen; *to ~ off,* abzahlen (Schuld); *to ~ in advance,* im voraus bezahlen; *to ~ the piper,* die Zeche bezahlen; ~ *v.i.* sich lohnen, rentieren; ~ *s.* Bezahlung *f.;* Lohn *m.;* **~day** *s.* Zahltag *m.;* **~envelope** *s.* Lohntüte *f.*
payable *a.* zahlbar, fällig.
payee *s.* Zahlungsempfänger(in) *m.(f.)*
payer *s.* Zahler *m.;* Bezogene *m.*
paying guest *s.* zahlender Gast *m.; to take ~s,* zahlende Gäste aufnehmen.
payload *s.* Nutzlast *f.*
paymaster *s.* Zahlmeister *m.*
payment *s.* Bezahlung *f.; against ~,* gegen Be-

zahlung; ~ *on account,* Abschlagszahlung *f.;* ~ *order,* Zahlungsbefehl *m.; to stop, suspend* ~, Zahlungen einstellen.
pay phone *s.* Münzfernsprecher *m.*
pay raise *s.* Gehaltserhöhung *f.*
payroll *s.* Lohnliste *f.*
pay slip *s.* Gehaltsstreifen *m.*
PC *Personal computer,* Personal-computer, PC; *police constable,* Schutzmann.
p.c. *postcard,* Postkarte *f.;* %, *per cent,* Prozent, %.
PD *Police Department,* Polizeibehörde.
pd *paid,* bezahlt, bez.
p.d. *per diem (by the day),* pro Tag.
pea *s.* Erbse *f.; sweet* ~, Edelwicke *f.*
peace *s.* Freide *m.;* Ruhe *f.; to keep the* ~, Ruhe halten.
peaceable *a.,* **~bly** *adv.* friedfertig; friedlich.
peaceful *a.,* **~ly** *adv.* friedlich, ruhig.
peaceloving *a.* friedliebend.
peacemaker *s.* Friedensstifter(in) *m.(f.)*
peace treaty *s.* Friedensvertrag *m.*
peach *s.* Pfirsich *m.*
peacock *s.* Pfau *m.*
peahen *s.* Pfauhenne *f.*
pea jacket *s. (nav.)* Tuchjacke *f.*
peak *s.* Gipfel *m.;* Spitze *f.;* Höhepunkt *m.;* Höchststand *m.;* ~ *v.i.* den Höhepunkt erreichen.
peak hour *s.* Stoßzeit *f.*
peaky *a.* kränklich.
peal *s.* Schall *m.;* Geläut *n.;* Gekrach *n.;* ~ *v.i.* schallen, krachen.
peanut *s.* Erdnuß *f.*
pear *s.* Birne *f.*
pearl *s.* Perle *f.; real* ~, echte Perle; **~barley,** Perlgraupen *pl.;* ~ *v.i.* perlen, tropfen.
pearl oyster *s.* Perlmuschel *f.*
pear tree *s.* Birnbaum *m.*
peasant *s.* Bauer *m.*
peasantry *s.* Landvolk *n.*
peat *s.* Torf *m.*
pebble *s.* Kiesel *m.*
pebbly *a.* steinig.
peccadillo *s.* kleine Sünde *f.;* Fehler *m.*
peck *s.* Viertelscheffel *m.;* Menge *f.;* ~ *v.t.* picken, hacken.
pecking order *s.* Hackordnung *f.*
peckish *a. (fam.)* hungrig.
pectin *s.* Pektin *n.*
pectoral *a.* Brust...
peculiar *a.* eigen, eigentümlich; **~ly** *adv.* besonders.
peculiarity *s.* Eigentümlichkeit *f.*
pecuniary *a.* Geld...
pedagogic(al) *a.* pädagogisch.
pedagogue *s.* Erzieher(in) *m.(f.); (pej.)* Pedant *m.*
pedagogy *s.* Pädagogik *f.*
pedal *s.* Trittbrett *n.,* Pedal *n.*
pedant *s.* Pedant(in) *m.(f.)*
pedantic *a.* pedantisch.
pedantry *s.* Pedanterie *f.*
peddle *v.i.* hausieren; Straßenhandel betrieben.
peddler *s.* Hausierer *m.; drug* ~, Drogenhändler(in) *m.(f.)*
pedestal *s.* Sockel *m.*
pedestrian *s.* Fußgänger(in) *m.(f.)*
pedestrian crossing *s.* Fußgängerüberweg *m.*
pedicure *s.* Pediküre *f.*
pedigree *s.* Stammbaum *m.;* **~dog,** Rassehund, Zuchthund *m.*
peek *v.i.* (verstohlen) gucken; einen kurzen Blick werfen; ~ *s.* flüchtiger Blick *m.*
peel *s.* Schale, Rinde *f.;* ~ *v.t. & i.* sich schälen.
peeler *s.* (Kartoffel) Schäler *m.*
peelings *s.pl.* Schalen *pl.*
peep *v.i.* gucken, neugierig blicken; ~ *out,* zum Vorschein kommen, *(fam.)* hervorgucken; piepen; ~ *s.* Blick *m.;* Piepsen *n.;* (*sl.*). Pieps *m.*
peephole *s.* Guckloch *n.*
peer *s.* Gefährte *m.;* Gleiche *m.;* Ebenbürtige *m.;* Peer, Hochadlige *m.*
peerage *s.* Peerswürde *f.;* Peers *m.pl.*
peeress *s.* Gemahlin eines Peers *f.*
peer group *s.* Peer-group *f.;* Gleichaltrigengruppe *f.*
peerless *a.,* **~ly** *adv.* unvergleichlich.
peevish *a.,* **~ly** *adv.* verdrießlich.
peewit *s.* Kiebitz *m.*
peg *s.* Pflock; Wirbel *m.;* Holzstift *m.;* ~ *v.t.* stabilisieren, stützen.
pejorative *a.* pejorativ; abwertend.
pelican *s.* Pelikan *m.*
pellet *s.* Kügelchen *n.*
pell-mell *adv.* durcheinander.
pellucid *a.* durchsichtig.
pelt *s.* Fell *n.;* Haut *f.;* ~ *v.t.* werfen, bewerfen; ~ *v.i.* dicht fallen, stark regnen; ~*ing rain,* Platzregen *m.*
pelvis *s.* Becken *n.*
pen *s.* Schreibfeder *f.;* Füllhalter *m.;* Kugelschreiber *m.,* Pferch *m.* ~ *v.t.* niederschreiben; einpferchen.
PEN *(International Association of) Poets, Playwrights, Editors, Essayists, and Novelists,* PEN-Club, (internationaler Schriftstellerverband).
penal *a.* Straf..., strafbar; ~ *clause* (*jur.*) Strafklausel *f.;* ~ *administration,* Strafvollzug *m.;* ~ **code** *s.* Strafgesetzbuch *n.;* ~ **law** *s.* Strafgesetz *n.;* ~ **reform** *s.* Strafrechtsreform *f.;* ~ **servitude** *s.* Zuchthausstrafe *f.*
penalize *v.t.* bestrafen; benachteiligen.
penalty *s.* Strafe, Buße *f.;* **~kick** *s.* Elfmeter *m.*
penance *s.* Buße *f.*
pencil *s.* Stift *m.;* Bleistift *m.; drawing* ~, Zeichenstift *m.; colored* ~, Farbstift *m.*
pencil sharpener *s.* Bleistiftspitzer *m.*
pendant *s.* Anhänger *m.*
pendent *a.* überhängend.
pending *a.* schwebend, unentschieden; ~ *case,* (*jur.*) anhängige Sache *f.*
pendulum *s.* Pendel *m.*
penetrable *a.* durchdringlich.
penetrate *v.t. & i.* durchdringen; ergründen; *(mil.)* eindringen.
penetrating *a.* durchdringend; scharfsinnig.
penetration *s.* Durchdringung *f.,* Eindringen *n.;* Scharfsinn *m.; (mil.)* Einbruch *m.*
penguin *s.* Pinguin *m.*
pen holder *s.* Federhalter *m.*
penicillin *s.* Penizillin *n.*
peninsula *s.* Halbinsel *f.*

penis *s.* Penis *m.*
penitence *s.* Buße, Reue *f.*
penitent *a.*, **~ly** *adv.* bußfertig; ~ *s.* Büßer(in) *m.(f.)*
penitentiary *s.* Strafvollzugsanstalt *f.*, Strafanstalt *f.*
penknife *s.* Taschenmesser *n.*
penmanship *s.* Schreibekunst *f.*
penname *s.* Schriftstellername *m.*
pennant *s.* Wimpel *m.*
penniless *a.* ohne Geld; mittellos.
penny *s.* Penny *m.*
penny-pinching *s.* Pfennigfuchserei *f.*
pen pal *s.* Brieffreund(in) *m.(f.)*
pension *s.* Kostgeld *n.;* Ruhegehalt *n.;* Pension *f.;* ~ *v.t.* pensionieren.
pensionable *a.* pensionsberechtigt, pensionsfähig.
pensioner *s.* Rentner(in) *m.(f.);* Pensionär(in) *m.(f.)*
pensive *a.*, **~ly** *adv.* gedankenvoll, nachdenklich; tiefsinnig.
pent *a.* ~ *up,* aufgestaut, verhalten.
pentagon *s.* Fünfeck *n.*
pentathlon *s.* Fünfkampf *m.*
Pentecost *s.* Pfingsten *pl.*
penthouse *s.* Penthouse *n.*
penurious *a.*, **~ly** *adv.* karg; dürftig.
penury *s.* Dürftigkeit *f.;* Mangel *m.*
peony *s.* Päonie *f.*, Pfingstrose *f.*
people *s.* Volk *n.;* Leute *pl.*, (*fam.*) man; ~ *say,* man sagt; ~ *v.t.* bevölkern.
peopled *a.* bevölkert.
People's Republic of China *s.* Volksrepublik China *f.*
pep *s.* Schwung; ~ *v.t.* aufpeppen.
pepper *s.* Pfeffer *m.;* (*red, green, yellow*) rote, grüne, gelbe Paprika *m.* ~ *v.t.* pfeffern.
peppercorn *s.* Pfefferkorn *n.*
pepper mill *s.* Pfeffermühle *f.*
peppermint *s.* Pfefferminze *f.*
peppery *n.* pfeffrig; scharf.
per *pr.* durch; *as* ~, laut; ~ *annum,* pro Jahr; ~ *diem allowance,* Tagegeld *n.;* ~ **mail,** durch die Post; pound, pro Pfund; ~ *rail,* per Bahn.
perceive *v.t.* wahrnehmen; merken.
percent *s.* Prozent *n.*
percentage *s.* Prozentsatz *m.;* ~ **sign** *s.* Prozentzeichen *n.*
perceptible *a.*, **~bly** *adv.* wahrnehmbar.
perception *s.* Empfindung *f.;* Wahrnehmung *f.;* Anschauung, Vorstellung *f.*
perceptive *a.* einfühlsam; scharfsinnig.
perch *s.* Aufsitzstange, (*fam. fig.*) hoher Sitz; Hühnerstange *f.;* Barsch *m.;* Rute *f.* (5,029 *m.*); ~ *v.i.* sich setzen; aufsitzen; ~ *v.t.* setzen.
percolate *v.t.* durchsickern; durchlaufen.
percolator *s.* Kaffeemaschine *f.*
percussion *s.* Schlagzeug *n.*
peregrination *s.* Reise, Wanderschaft *f.*
peremptory *a.*, **~ily** *adv.* bestimmt; endgültig; herrisch; dogmatisch.
perennial *a.* ausdauernd; dauernd; perennierend; winterhart; ~ *s.* perennierende Pflanze.
perfect *a.*, **~ly** *adv.* vollkommen, vollendet; ~ *s.* (*gram.*) Perfekt(um) *n.;* ~ *v.t.* vervollkommnen.
perfection *s.* Vollkommenheit *f.*
perfectionism *s.* Perfektionismus *m.*
perfectionist *s.* Perfektionist(in) *m.(f.)*
perfidious *a.* treulos.
perfidy *s.* Treulosigkeit *f.*
perforate *v.t.* durchbohren.
perforation *s.* Perforation *f.;* Loch *n.*
perforator *s.* Locher, Lochapparat *m.*
perforce *adv.* notgedrungen.
perform *v.t.* vollziehen, erfüllen, verrichten, vollenden; durchführen, ausführen; ~ *v.i.* wirken; spielen (eine Rolle), aufführen; vortragen.
performance *s.* Leistung, Vollzeihung *f.;* Aufführung *f.*
performer *s.* Ausführende *m./f.*
perfume *s.* Wohlgeruch *m.;* Parfüm, *n.;* ~ *v.t.* parfümieren.
perfumery *s.* Parfümerie(n) *f.pl.*
perfunctory *a.* oberflächlich, sorglos.
perhaps *adv.* vielleicht.
peril *s.* Gefahr *f.; at your* ~, auf eigene Gefahr.
perilous *a.*, **~ly** *adv.* gefährlich.
perimeter *s.* Umkreis *m.;* Begrenzung *f.*
period *s.* Zeitraum *m.;* Periode *f.;* Punkt *m.*; (Unterrichts) Stunde *f.; (sp.)* Spielabschnitt *m.;* ~ *furniture s.* Stilmöbel *pl.*
periodic(al) *a.*, **~ly** *adv.* periodisch; ~ *s.* Zeitschrift *f.*
periodicity *s.* regelmässige Wiederkehr *f.*
periodic table *s.* Periodensystem *n.*
peripheral *a.* peripher; marginal.
periphery *s.* Peripherie *f.*
periscope *s.* Sehrohr, Periskop *n.*
perish *v.i.* umkommen.
perishable *a.* leicht verderblich.
peritonitis *s.* Bauchfellentzündung *f.*
perjure *v.t.* ~ *o.s.*, meineidig werden.
perjury *s.* Meineid *m.*
perk *v.i.* munter werden; durchlaufen (Kaffee); *to* ~ *up,* sich emporstrecken; ~ *v.t.* aufrichten.
perky *a.* lebhaft; munter; keck.
perm *s.* Dauerwelle *f.*
permanence *s.* Fortdauer *f.*
permanent *a.*, **~ly** *adv.* (fort)dauernd, beständig; planmäßig (Beamte); ~ **waves** *pl.* Dauerwellen *f.pl.*
permeable *a.* durchdringlich; durchlässig.
permeate *v.t.* durchdringen.
permissible *a.* zulässig.
permission *s.* Erlaubnis; *to ask* ~, um Erlaubnis bitten; *by* ~ *of,* mit Erlaubnis von; *by special* ~, mit besonderer Genehmigung.
permissive *a.* tolerant; großzügig; permissiv.
permit *v.t.* gestatten; ~ *s.* Erlaubnisschein *m.*
permutation *s.* Umstellung *f.* Versetzung *f.*
pernicious *a.*, **~ly** *adv.* verderblich.; bösartig; übel.
peroration *s.* Redeschluß *m.*
perpendicular *a.*, **~ly** *adv.* senkrecht; ~ *s.* senkrechte Linie *f.*, Lot *n.*
perpetrate *v.t.* verüben.
perpetrator *s.* (*jur.*) Täter(in) *m.(f.)*
perpetual *a.*, **~ly** *adv.* immerwährend.
perpetuate *v.t.* verewigen; fortsetzen.
perpetuity *s.* Ewigkeit *f.;* Fortdauer *f.; in* ~, auf ewig, für immer.
perplex *v.t.* verwirren; bestürzt machen.

perplexed *a.* verwirrt; ratlos.
perplexity *s.* Bestürzung *f.;* Verwirrung *f.*
per pro *per procurationem (by proxy),* per Prokura, pp.
perquisite *s.* Vergünstigung *f.*
persecute *v.t.* verfolgen.
persecution *s.* Verfolgung *f.*
persecutor *s.* Verfolger(in) *m.(f.)*
perseverance *s.* Beharrlichkeit *f.*
persevere *v.i.* beharren, ausdauern.
Persian *a.* persich; ~ **carpet** *s.* Perserteppich *m.;* ~ **cat** *s.* Perserkatze *f.*
persist *v.i.* beharren, bestehen.
persistence *s.* Beharrlichkeit *f.*
persistent *a.* beharrlich.
person *s.* Person *m.;* Mensch *m.; in ~,* persönlich.
personable *a.* sympathisch.
personage *s.* Persönlichkeit *f.*
personal *a.,* **~ly** *adv.* persönlich; *~ estate,* bewegliche Habe *f.;* ~ **files** *pl.* Handakten *pl.*
personality *s.* Persönlichkeit *f.*
personalize *v.t.* eine persönliche Note geben; mit Namen/Initialen versehen.
personal organizer *s.* Terminplaner *m.*
personal property *s.* bewegliches Vermögen *n.*
personification *s.* Verkörperung *f.*
personify *v.t.* verkörpern.
personnel *s.* Personal *n.;* **~carrier** *s.* Mannschaftstransportwagen *m.;* **~file** *s.* Personalakten *pl.;* **~section** *s.* Personalabteilung *f.*
perspective *s.* Perspektive, Aussicht, Fernsicht *f.;* ~ *a.,* **~ly** *adv.* perspektivisch.
perspecuity *s.* Deutlichkeit *f.*
perspicacious *a.* scharfsichtig.
perspicacity *s.* Scharfblick *m.*
perspicuous *a.,* **~ly** *adv.* durchsichtig; verständlich.
perspiration *s.* Schweiß *m.*
perspire *v.i.* ausdünsten, schwitzen.
persuadable *a.* leicht zu überreden.
persuade *v.t.* überreden, überzeugen.
persuasion *s.* Überredung *f.;* Überzeugung *f.*
persuasive *a.,* **~ly** *adv.* überredend; überzeugend.
persuasiveness *s.* Überzeugungskraft *f.*
pert *a.,* **~ly** *adv.* keck; vorlaut.
pertain *v.i.* gehören, betreffen.
pertinacious *a.,* **~ly** *adv.* hartnäckig; beharrlich.
pertinacity *s.* Beharrlichkeit *f.*
pertinence *s.* Angemessenheit *f.*
pertinent *a.,* **~ly** *adv.* angemessen, passend; treffend; relevant.
perturb *v.t.* verwirren, stören; beunruhigen.
perturbation *s.* Beunruhigung *f.*
Peru *s.* Peru *n.*
perusal *s.* Durchlesen *n.;* Durchsicht *f.*
peruse *v.t.* durchlesen; prüfen.
Peruvian *a.* peruanisch; ~ *s.* Peruaner(in) *m.(f.)*
pervade *v.t.* durchdringen.
pervasive *a.* durchdringend.
perverse *a.,* **~ly** *adv.* verkehrt; verstockt; verdorben; pervers.
perversion *s.* Verdrehung *f.;* Abkehr *f.;* Pervertierung *f.;* Perversion f
perversity *s.* Verkehrtheit *f.;* Eingensinn *m.;* Verdorbenheit *f.*
pervert *v.t.* verdrehen; verführen; pervertieren.
perverted *a.* pervertiert; verdorben.
pesky *a. (fam.)* verdammt.
pessimism *s.* Pessimismus *m.*
pessimist *s.* Pessimist *m.*
pessimistic *a.,* **~ally** *adv.* pessimistisch.
pest *s.* Plage *f.,* Plagegeist *m.;* Pflanzenschädling *m.*
pester *v.t.* belästigen, plagen.
pesticide *s.* Pestizid *n.*
pestiferous *a.* ansteckend; verpestet.
pestilence *s.* Seuche *f.;* Pest *f.*
pestilent *a.* verderblich; lästig.
pestilential *a.,* **~ly** *adv.* pestartig.
pestle *s.* Mörserkeule *f.,* Stößel *m.*
pet *s.* Haustier *n.;* Liebling *m.;* ~ *a.* Lieblings...; ~ *v.t.* hätscheln; liebkosen.
petal *s.* Blütenblatt *n.*
petard *s.* Sprengbüchse *f.*
peter out *v.i.* allmählich aufhören; versanden.
pet food *s.* Tierfutter *n.*
petit bourgeois *s.* Kleinbürger *m.*
petite *a.* zierlich.
petition *s.* Gesuch *n.;* Bittschrift *f.;* ~ *v.t.* bitten, anhalten.
petitioner *s.* Bittsteller *m.*
petrel *s.* Sturmvogel *m.*
petrifaction *s.* Versteinerung *f.*
petrify *v.i.* vesteinern.
petrol *s.* Benzin; *~ station, (mot.)* Tankstelle *f.*
petroleum *s.* Erdöl *n.;* Petroleum *n.;* ~ **jelly** *s.* Vaselin *n.*
petticoat *s.* Unterrock *m.*
petty *a.* klein; gering; kleinlich.
petulance *s.* Mutwille *m.;* Verdrießlichkeit *f.*
petulant *a.,* **~ly** *adv.* mutwillig, ärgerlich; verdrießlich.
pew *s.* Kirchenstuhl *m.*
pewter *s.* Zinn *m.*
phallic *a.* phallisch.
phantasm *s.* Traumbild, Trugbild *n.*
phantom *s.* Phantom *n.;* Gespenst *n.*
Pharaoh *m.* Pharao *m.*
Pharisee *s.* Pharisäer *m.*
pharmaceutical *a.* pharmazeutisch.
pharmaceutics *s.pl.* Arzneikunde *f.*
pharmacist *s.* Pharmazeut(in); Apotheker(in) *m.(f.)*
pharmacy *s.* Pharmazie *f.*
pharyngitis *s.* Rachenkatarrh *m.*
pharynx *s.* Rachen *m.*
phase *s.* Phase *f.*
Ph.D. *Philosophiae Doctor (Doctor of Philosophy),* Doktor der Philosophie, Dr. phil.
pheasant *s.* Fasan *m.*
phelgmatic *a.* phlegmatisch.
phenomenal *a.* phänomenal; Erscheinungs...; außerordentlich groß, etc.
phenomenon *s.* Phänomen *n.*
phial *s.* Fläschchen *n.*
philanderer *s.* Schürzenjäger *m.*
philanthropic *a.* menschenfreundlich, philanthropisch.
philanthropist *s.* Menschenfreund(in) *m.(f.),* Philanthrop(in) *m.(f.)*
philanthropy *s.* Menschenliebe *f.* Philanthropie *f.*

philatelist *s.* Briefmarkensammler(in) *m.(f.)*
philately *s.* Philatelie *f.*; Briefmarkenkunde *f.*
philharmonic *a.* philharmonisch; ~ *s.* Philharmonie *f.*
Philippines *s.pl.* Philippinen *pl.*
philistine *s.* Philister *m.*, Spießer *m.*
philological *a.* philologisch.
philologist *s.* Philologe *m.*, Philologin *f.*
philology *s.* Philologie *f.*
philosopher *s.* Philosoph(in) *m.(f.)*; *~'s stone*, Stein der Weisen *m.*
philosophic(al) *a.*, **~ly** *adv.* philosophisch.
philosophize *v.i.* philosophieren.
philosophy *s.* Philosophie *f.*
phlebitis *s.* Venenentzündung *f.*
phlegm *s.* Schleim *m.*; Phlegma *n.*
phobia *s.* Phobie *f.*
phoenix *s.* Phönix *m.*
phone *s.* Telefon *n.*; ~ *v.t.* telefonieren.
phone: ~ **book** *s.* Telefonbuch *n.*; ~ **booth** *s.* Telefonzelle *f.*; ~ **call** *s.* Anruf *m.*; ~ **card** *s.* Telefonkarte *f.*; ~ **number** *s.* Telefonnummer *f.*; ~ **tapping** *s.* Abhören *(n.)* des Telefons.
phonetic *a.*, **~ally** *adv.* phonetisch.
phonetics *s.pl.* Phonetik *f.*
phon(e)y *a.* falsch; erfunden; ~ *s.* Schwindler(in) *m.(f.)*
phonograph *s.* Grammophon *n.*
phosphate *s.* Phosphat *n.*
phosphorescent *a.* phosphoreszierend.
phosphorus *s.* Phosphor *m.*
photo *s.* Fotographie *f.*, Foto *n.*
photocopier *s.* Fotokopierer *m.*; Fotokopiergerät *n.*
photocopy *s.* Fotokopie *f.*; ~ *v.t.* fotokopieren.
photograph *s.* Fotographie *f.*, Lichtbild *n.*; ~ *v.t.* fotographieren.
photographer *s.* Fotograph(in) *m.(f.)*
photographic *s.* fotographisch.
photography *s.* Fotographie *f.*
photosensitive *a.* lichtempfindlich.
photosynthesis *s.* Photosynthese *f.*
phrase *s.* Redensart *f.*; Satz *m.*; ~ *v.t.* ausdrücken, nennen.
phraseology *s.* Redeweise *f.*
physical *a.*, **~ly** *adv.* physikalisch, physisch; körperlich, Körper...; ~ **education** *s.* Sportunterricht *m.* ~ **pecularities** *pl.* besondere Merkmale *n.pl.* **~ly disabled** *a.* körperbehindert.
physician *s.* Arzt *m.*, Ärztin *f.*
physicist *s.* Physiker(in) *m.(f.)*
physics *s.* Physik *f.*
physiognomy *s.* Gesichtsausdruck *m.*
physiological *a.* physiologisch.
physiology *s.* Physiologie *f.*
physiotherapy *a.* Physiotherapie *f.*
physique *s.* Körperbeschaffenheit *f.*, Körperbau *m.*
pianist *s.* Pianist(in) *m.(f.)*, Klavierspieler(in) *m.(f.)*
piano *s.* Klavier *n.*; *grand ~*, Flügel *m.*;
piano: ~ **player** *s.* Klavierspieler(in) *m.(f.)*; **~stool** *s.* Klavierschemel *m.*; **~tuner** *s.* Klavierstimmer(in) *m.(f.)*
piccolo *s.* Pikkoloflöte *f.*
pick *v.t.* & *i.* picken; hacken; stochern, stechen; pflücken; auflesen; wählen; zupfen; *to ~ out*, auswählen; *to ~ up*, aufheben, auflesen; (Passagiere) aufnehmen; (ab)holen; *to ~ on s.o.*, an einem herumkritisieren; *to ~ a quarrel*, mit einem anbinden; *to ~ s.o.'s pocket*, Taschendiebstahl verüben; ~ *s.* Auswahl *f.*; Spitzhammer *m.*
pickaxe *s.* Spitzhacke. *f.*
picket *s.* Streikposten *m.*
pickle *s.* Salzgurke *f.*; Gewurzgurke *f.*; Pökel *m.* Marinade *f.*; *(fam.)* mißliche Lage *f.*; ~ *v.t.* einpökeln.
picklock *s.* Dietrich *m.*
pick-me-up *s.* Stärkungsmittel *n.*
pickpocket *s.* Taschendieb *m.*
picnic *s.* Picknick *n.*; *no ~*, keine leichte Sache; ~ *v.i.* ein Picknick machen.
pictorial *a.* illustriert; bildlich; *~ representation*, bildliche Darstellung *f.*
picture *s.* Bild *n.*; Porträt *n.*; Foto *n.*; ~ *v.t.* malen; schildern.
picture: **~book** *s.* Bilderbuch *n.*; **~frame** *s.* Bilderahmen *m.*; **~gallery** *s.* Gemäldegalerie *f.*; **~hook** *s.* Bilderhaken *m.*
picturesque *a.* malerisch.
piddle *v.i.* (*fam.*) pinkeln, Pipimachen; ~ **away** zeitvertrödeln.
pidgin *s.* Pidgin *n.*
pie *s.* Pastete *f.*; Elster *f.*
piebald *a.* scheckig.
piece *s.* Stück *n.*; Scherbe *f.*; *a ~*, pro Stück; pro Person; **~goods** *pl.* Stückgüter *n.pl.*; *by the ~*, stückweise; *to take to ~s*, auseinandernehmen; ~ *v.t.* stücken; flicken.
piecemeal *a.* & *adv.* stückweise.
piecework *s.* Akkordarbeit *f.*; *to do ~*, im Akkord arbeiten; ~ **rates** *pl.* Akkordlöhne *pl.*
pier *s.* Pier *m.*; Pfeiler *m.*; Steindamm *m.*; Abfahrtsplatz *m.*, Landungsbrücke *f.*
pierce *v.t.* durchstechen; durchbohren; ~ *v.i.* eindringen; rühren.
piercing *a.* durchdringend; schneidend.
piety *s.* Frömmigkeit *f.*
pig *s.* Ferkel, Schwein *n.*; Metallbarren *m.*
pigeon *s.* Taube *f.*; **~-hole,** Fach *n.*
piggy: **~back** *adv.* huckepack; ~ **bank** *s.* Sparschwein *n.*
pig-headed *a.* dickköpfig.
pig iron *s.* Roheisen *n.*
piglet *s.* Ferkel *n.*
pigment *s.* Farbstoff *m.*
pigskin *s.* Schweinsleder *n.*
pigsty *s.* Schweinestall *m.*
pigtail *s.* Haarzopf *m.*; **~s** *pl.* Ratenschwänzchen *pl.*
pike *s.* Pike *f.*; Hecht *m.*
pilaster *s.* Wandpfeiler *m.*
pilchard *s.* Sardine *f.*
pile *s.* Pfahl *m.*; Haufen, Stoß (Papier) *m.*; **~s** *pl.* Hämorrhoiden *f.pl.*; ~ *v.t.* aufhäufen.
pile dwelling *s.* Pfahlbau *m.*
pile-up *s.* Massenkarambolage *f.*
pilfer *v.t.* & *i.* stehlen, mausen.
pilgrim *s.* Pilger(in) *m.(f.)*
pilgrimage *s.* Pilgerfahrt *f.*
pill *s.* Pille *f.*
pillage *s.* Plünderung *f.*; ~ *v.t.* plündern.
pillar *s.* Pfeiler *m.*; Säule *f.*

pillar drill *s. (mech.)* Säulenbohrmaschine *f.*
pillion *s.* Beifahrersitz *m.*
pillory *s.* Pranger *m.; ~ v.t.* an den Pranger stellen, anprangern.
pillow *s.* Kopfkissen *n.*
pillowcase *s.* Kissenüberzug *m.*
pilot *s.* Lotse *m.*, Lotsin *f.; (avi.)* Pilot(in) *m.(f.);* **~plant,** Versuchsfabrik *f.;* **~jet,** Stichflamme *f.; ~ v.t.* steuern, lotsen.
pimp *s.* Kuppler(in) *m.(f.);* Zuhälter(in) *m.(f.); ~ v.i.* kuppeln.
pimpernel *s.* Pimpernelle *f.*
pimple *s.* Pickel *m.;* Pustel *m.*
pimply *a.* pickelig.
pin *s.* Stecknadel *f.;* Stift, Pflock *m.;* Bolzen *m.;* (Instrumenten-)Wirbel *m.;* (Spiel-)Kegel *m.; ~ v.t.* anstecken; annageln; *to ~ down,* festnageln (*fig.*); *to ~ up,* anstecken.
PIN *personal identification number,* (Nummer auf Scheckkarten).
pinafore *s.* Schürze *f.*
pinball *s.* Flippern; ~ **machine** *s.* Flipper *m.*
pincers *s.pl.* Kneifzange *f.;* Scheren *pl.* (Krebs).
pinch *v.t.* kneifen, zwicken; drücken (Schuh); bedrücken, quälen; *(fam.)* klauen, stibitzen; *~ v.i.* knausern; darben; *~ s.* Zwick *m.;* Prise (Tabak) *f.;* Druck *m.;* Not, Verlegenheit *f.; in a ~,* im Notfall; *with a ~ of salt,* (*fig.*) mit Vorbehalt.
pinchbeck *s.* Tombak *m.; ~ a.* falsch, unecht.
pincushion *s.* Nadelkissen *n.*
pine *s.* Kiefer *f.*, Föhre *f.; ~ v.i.* schmachten; sich sehnen.
pineapple *s.* Ananas *f.*
pinecone *s.* Kiefernzapfen *m.*
pineneedle *s.* Kiefernnadel *f.*
ping-pong *s.* Tischtennis *n.*
pinhead *s.* Stecknadelkopf *m.*
pinion *s.* Ritzel *n.;* Zahnrad *n.; ~ v.t.* fesseln (an).
pink *a.* blaßrot, rosa.
pinkie *s.* kleiner Finger *m.*
pin money *s.* Extrageld *n.;* Taschengeld *n.*
pinnacle *s.* Gipfel *m.;* Höhepunkt *m.*
pinpoint *v.t.* genau bestimmen.
pinprick *s.* Nadelstich *m.*
pinstriped *a.* mit Nadelstreifen.
pint *s.* Pinte *f.*
pinup *s.* Pin-up-Foto *n.*
pioneer *s.* Pionier *m.;* Bahnbrecher *m.*
pious *a.,* **~ly** *adv.* fromm; *(pej.)* heuchlerisch.
pip *s.* Pips *m.;* Auge (in der Karte) *n.;* Obstkern *m.; ~ v.t.* besiegen.
pipe *s.* Röhre, *f.;* Pfeife *f.; ~ v.i.* pfeifen, flöten.
pipe cleaner *s.* Pfeifenreiniger *m.*
pipe-dream *s.* Wunschtraum *m.*
pipeline *s.* Röhrenleitung *f.;* Pipeline *f.*
piper *s.* Pfeifer(in) *m.(f.)*
pipette *s.* Pipette *f.*
piping *s.* Zierstreifen *m.* (an Kleidern), Litzenbesatz *m.;* Rohrleitungssystem *n.;* ~ **hot** *a.* siedend heiß.
piquancy *s.* Schärfe *f.; (fig.)* Pikanterie *f.*
piquant *a.,* **~ly** *adv.* beißend; pikant.
pique *s.* Groll *m.;* Gereiztheit *f.; ~ v.t.* aufreizen; sich brüsten.
piracy *s.* Seeräuberei *f.;* Plagiat *n.;* Patentverletzung *f.*
pirate *s.* Seeräuber *m.;* Raubdrucker *m.;* Raubpresser *m.; ~ v.t.* rauben; illegal nachdrucken.
piratical *a.,* **~ly** adv,. räuberisch.
pirouette *s.* Pirouette *f.; ~ v.i.* pirouettieren.
Pisces *s.pl. (astro.)* Fische *pl.*
piss *s. (vulg.)* Pisse *f.; ~ v.i.* pissen.
pissed off *a. (sl.)* stocksauer.
pistachio *s.* Pistazie *f.*
pistil *s. (bot.)* Sternpel *m.*
pistol *s.* Pistole *f.*
piston *s.* Kolben *m.;* **~rod** *s.* Kolbenstange *f.*
pit *s.* Grube *f.;* Graben *m.; (theat.)* Parkett *n.; ~ v.t.* eingraben; gegeneinander hetzen.
pitch *s.* Pech *n.;* Wurf *m.;* Grad *m.;* Tonhöhe *f.;* Stimmlage *f.;* Tonlage *f.;* Steigung *f.; ~ v.t.* befestigen; werfen; aufstellen; orden; *(mus.)* abstimmen; *~ v.i.* herabstürzen; werfen; aufschlagen.
pitch-dark *a.* pechschwarz, stockfinster.
pitched roof *s.* schräges Dach *n.*
pitcher *s.* Krug *m.;* Werfer *m.* (Baseball).
pitchfork *s.* Heugabel *f.;* Stimmgabel *f.*
piteous *a.,* **~ly** *adv.* kläglich, erbämlich.
pitfall *s.* Fallgrube, Falle *f.*
pith *s.* Mark *n.;* Kern *m.;* Kraft *f.;* Vorzüglichste *n.*
pithy *a.,* **~ily** *adv.* markig, kräftig.
pitiable *a.* erbärmlich.
pitiful *a.,* **~ly** *adv.* erbärmlich, mitleiderregend; bemitleidenswert.
pitiless *a.,* **~ly** *adv.* unbarmherzig.; mitleidlos.
pittance *s.* Hungerlohn *m.*
pity *s.* Mitleid *n.; it is a ~,* es ist schade; *~ v.t.* bemitleiden, bedauern.
pitying *a.* **~ly** *adv.* mitleidig.
pivot *s.* Zapfen *m.;* Drehpunkt *m.;* Angelpunkt *m.;* springender Punkt *m.; to ~ on, v.i.* sich drehen um.
pivotal *a.* zentral...
pixie *s.* Kobold *m.*, Elf *m.*
Pk. *Park,* Park.
Pl. *Place,* Platz, Pl.
pl. *plural,* Plural, Pl., pl.
placard *s.* (öffentlicher) Anschlag *m.*, Plakat *n.; ~ v.t.* bekanntmachen.
placate *v.t.* besänftigen.
place *s.* Platz *n.*, Stelle *f.;* Ort *m.;* Amt, *n.; to take ~,* stattfinden; *~s of interest, pl.;* Sehenswürdigkeiten *pl.; ~ v.t.* stellen, setzen; unterbringen (Kapital).
place mat *s.* Set *n.*
place name *s.* Ortsname *m.*
placenta *s.* Plazenta *f.*, Mutterkuchen *m.*
place setting *s.* Gedeck *n.*
placid *a.,* **~ly** *adv.* gelassen, sanft.
plagiarism *s.* Plagiat *n.*
plagiarist *s.* Plagiator(in) *m.(f.)*
plagiarize *v.t.* plagiieren.
plague *s.* Seuche *f.;* Plage *f.;* **~spot** *s.* Pestbeule *f.*
plaice *s. (zool.)* Scholle *f.*
plaid *s.* Plaid *n.; ~ a.* kariert.
plain *a.* eben, flach; einfach, schlicht; aufrichtig; deutlich; häßlich; **~ly** *adv.* deutlich; *~ s.* Fläche, Ebene *f.*

plain chocolate *s.* zartbittere Schokolade *f.*
plain clothes *pl.* Zivil(anzug) *n.*
plainness *s.* Klarheit *f.; Offenheit f.;*
plain-spoken *a.* ehrlich, aufrichtig.
plaint *s.* Klage *f.;* Beschwerde *f.*
plaintiff *s.* Kläger(in) *m.(f.)*
plaintive *a.*, **~ly** *adv.* klagend, kläglich.
plait *s.* Falte *f.;* Flechte *f.*, Zopf *m.; ~ v.t.* falten; verflechten.
plaited *a.* geflochten.
plan *s.* Plan, Grundriß *m.; ~ v.t.* entwerfen, modeln.
plane *s.* Fläche *f.;* Hobel *m.;* Platane *f.; ~ v.t.* ebnen, hobeln; abwärts gleiten.
planer *s.* Hobelmaschine *f.*
planet *s.* Planet *m.*
planetarium *s.* Planetarium *n.*
planetary *a.* planetarisch.
plank *s.* Planke, Bohle *f.; ~ v.t.* bohlen, dielen.
plankton *s.* (*biol.*) Plankton *n.*
planner *s.* Planer(in) *m.(f.)*
planning *s.* Planen *n.;* Planung *f.*
plant *s.* Pflanze *f.;* Werk *n.*, Fabrik *f.;* Betriebsanlage *f.; ~ v.t. & i.* pflanzen, stiften.
plantation *s.* Pflanzung, Pflanzschule *f.;* Plantage *f.*
planter *s.* Pflanzer(in) *m.(f.)*
plaque *s.* Platte *f.;* Plakette *f.*
plash *v.i.* plätschern.
plasma *s.* Plasma *n.*
plaster *s.* Pflaster *n.;* Mörtel *m.*, Verputz *m.; ~ of Paris,* Gips *m.; ~ v.t.* bepflastern; verputzen.
plasterboard *s.* Gipsplatte *f.*
plaster cast *s.* Gipsabdruck *m.;* Gipsverband *m.*.
plastered *a.* (*fam.*) voll, blau, betrunken.
plasterer *s.* Gipser *m.*
plastic *a.* plastisch, bildsam; ~ *s.* Plastik *n.;* Kunststoff *m.*
plastic surgery *s.* plastische Chirurgie *f.*
plate *s.* Metallplatte *f.;* Kupferstich, Stahlstich *m.;* (*phot.*) Platte *f.;* Teller *m.;* Silbergeschirr *n.; ~ v.t.* plattieren; (with gold) vergolden; panzern.
plateau *s.* Hochebene *f.;* Plateau *n.*
plate rack *s.* Geschirrständer *m.*
platform *s.* (*rail.*) Bahnsteig *m.;* Rednerbühne *f.;* politisches Programm *n.; ~* **ticket** *s.* Bahnsteigkarte *f.*
platinum *s.* Platin *n.*
platitude *s.* Gemeinplatz *m.;* Platitüde *f.*
platonic *a.* platonisch.
platoon *s.* (*mil.*) Zug *m.*
platter *s.* Schüssel *f.*
plaudit *s.* lauter Beifall *m.*
plausibility *s.* Glaubwürdigkeit *f.*
plausible *a.*, **~bly** *adv.* einleuchtend; glaubwürdig.
play *s.* Spiel *n.;* Schauspiel *n.*, Stück *n.;* Spielraum *m.; ~ v.t.* spielen; *to ~ off against,* ausspielen gegen; ~ *v.i.* spielen; scherzen
playable *a.* bespielbar; bühnenreif.
playbill *s.* Theaterzettel *m.*
player *s.* Spieler(in) *m.(f.);* Schauspieler(in) *m.(f.)*
playful *a.* spielend; scherzend.
play-ground *s.* Spielplatz *m.*
play group *s.* Spielgruppe *f.*
playhouse *s.* Schauspielhaus *n.*
playing field *s.* Sportplatz *m.*
playmate *s.* Spielkamerad(in) *m.(f.)*
play-off *s.* Entscheidungsspiel *n.*
play-pen *s.* Laufställchen *n.*
plaything *s.* Spielzeug *n.*
playwright *s.* Dramatiker(in) *m.(f.)*
plea *s.* Gesuch *n.;* Appell *m.;* Verteidigungsrede *f.*
plead *v.i.* vor Gericht reden; ~ *guilty,* sich schuldig bekennen; ~ *v.t.* als Beweis anführen, vorschützen; erörtern; verteidigen.
pleasant *a.*, **~ly** *adv.* angenehm; munter, lustig.
pleasantry *s.* Scherz *m.*
please *v.t. & i.* gefallen; belieben; befriedigen, besänftigen; *~!* bitte!; *~ yourself!,* wie Sie wünschen!
pleased *a.* zufrieden; erfrent.
pleasing *a.*, **~ly** *adv.* gefällig, angenehm.
pleasurable *a.*, **~bly** *adv.* angenehm, vergnüglich.
pleasure *s.* Vergnügen *n.;* Belieben *n.; ~* **cruise** *s.* Vergnügungsfahrt *f.*
pleat *s.* Falte *f.; ~ v.t.* fälteln, falten.
pleated *a.* gefältelt; Falten...
plebian *a.* pöbelhaft; ~ *s.* gemeiner Mensch *m.;* Pöbel *m.*
plebiscite *s.* Volksentscheid *m.*
plectrum *s.* Plektrum *n.*
pledge *s.* Pfand *n.;* Bürgschaft *f.; ~ v.t.* verpfänden, verpflichten; geloben.
plenary *a.*, **~ily** *adv.* vollständig, Voll..., Plenar...
plenary session *s.* Plenarsitzung *f.*
plenipotentiary *a.* bevollmächtigt; ~ *s.* Bevollmächtigte *m.*
plenitude *s.* Fülle *f.*
plentiful *a.*, **~ly** *adv.* reichlich, ergiebig.
plenty *s.* Fülle *f.;* Überfluß *m.; ~ of,* vollauf, reichlich, mehr als genug.
pleonasm *s.* Pleonasmus *m.*
plethora *s.* Überfülle *f.*
pleurisy *s.* Brustfell-, Rippenfellentzündung *f.*
pliable *a.*, **~bly** *adv.* biegsam.
pliant *a.*, **~ly** *adv.* biegsam, geschmeidig; nachgiebig.
pliers *s.pl.* Drahtzange *f.*
plight *s.* Notlage *f.*
plinth *s.* Sockel *m.*
plod *v.i.* trotten sich dahinschleppen; sich anstrengen; ochsen
plop *v.i.* plumpsen; platschen; ~ *s.* Plumps *m.;* Platsch *m.*
plot *s.* Stück (Land) *n.;* Fleck *m.;* Plan *m.;* Anschlag, Putsch *m.;* Verwicklung, Handlung *f.; ~ v.i.* sich verschwören; ~ *v.t.* aussinnen, anzetteln; *to ~ the course,* den Kurs abstecken.
plotter *s.* Verschwörer(in) *m.(f.)*
plow *s.* Pflug *m.; ~ v.t.* pflügen.
ploy *s.* Trick *m.*
pluck *s.* Zug, Ruck *m.;* (*fig.*) Mut *m.*, Schneid *m.; ~ v.t.* pflücken, rupfen; *to ~ up courage,* Mut fassen.
plucky *a.* mutig, schneidig.
plug *s.* Pflock, Stöpsel, Zapfen, Dübel *m.;* (*elek.*) Stecker *m.; ~ v.t.* zustopfen.
plum *s.* Pflaume, *f.;* Zwetsch(g)e *f.*
plumage *s.* Gefieder *n.*

plumb *s.* Bleilot *n.;* ~ *adv.* senkrecht; ~ *v.t.* sondieren; Klempnerarbeit machen.
plumber *s.* Klempner(in), Installateur(in) *m.(f.)*
plumbline *s.* Senkblei *n.*
plume *s.* (Schmuck-)Feder *f.;* ~ *v.t.* mit Federn schmücken; rupfen; ~ *v.i.* sich brüsten.
plummet *s.* Bleilot *n.;* ~ *v.i.* stürzen.
plump *a.*, **~ly** *adv.* fleischig, dick; ~ *v.i. & t.* schwellen; plumpsen; mästen.
plum tree *s.* Pflaumenbaum *m.*
plunder *s.* Beute *f.;* Raub *m.;* Plünderung *f.;* ~ *v.t.* plündern.
plunge *v.t. & i.* untertauchen; hinabstürzen; (Pferd) ausschlagen; ~ *s.* Untertauchen *n.;* Sturz *m.; (fig.)* Wagnis *n.*
pluperfect *s. (gram.)* Plusquamperfekt(um) *n.*
plural *s. (gram.)* Mehrzahl *f.*
plurality *s.* Vielzahl *f.;* Pluralität *f.*
plus *a. (ar.)* plus; ~ *adv.* zusammen mit.
plush *s.* Plüsch *m.*
plutonium *s.* Plutonium *n.*
ply *s.* Falte *f.; ~wood,* Sperrholz *n.; four~,* (Wolle) vierfach; ~ *v.t.* handhaben, treiben; ~ *v.t.* gebrauchen; nachgehen (Arbeit).
p.m. *post meridiem,* nachmittags.
pneumatic *a.* Luft..., pneumatisch.
pneumatic: **~drill** *s.* Preßluftbohrer *m.;* **~hammer** *s.* Preßlufthammer *m.*
pneumonia *s.* Lungenentzündung *f.*
P.O. *Post Office,* Postamt *n.; postal order,* Postanweisung.
poach *v.t.* im Wasserbad kochen; wildern; ~ *v.i.* wildern; **~ed eggs** *s.pl.* verlorene Eier *n.pl.*
poacher *s.* Wilddieb *m.*, Wilderer *m.*
P.O.B. *post office box,* Postfach, Pf.
pock *s.* Pocke, Blatter *f.*
pocket *s.* Tasche *f.;* Loch *n.* (Billiards); ~ *v.t.* einstecken.
pocketbook *s.* Handtasche *f.*
pocket money *s.* Taschengeld *n.*
pocket-size *a.* im Taschenformat.
pock: **~mark** *s.* Pockennarbe *f.;* ~ *a.* pockennarbig.
pod *s.* Hülse, Schale, Schote *f.*
P.O.D. *pay on delivery,* per Nachnahme; *Post Office Department,* Postministerium.
podgy *a.* dicklich; mollig.
podium *s.* Podium *n.*
poem *s.* Gedicht *n.*
poet *s.* Dichter(in) *m.(f.)*
poetic(al) *a.*, **~ly** *adv.* dichterisch.
poetics *s.pl.* Poetik *f.*
poetry *s.* Dichtkunst *f.;* Gedichte *n.pl.*, Dichtung *f.*
poignancy *s.* Schärfe *f.;* Schmerzlichkeit *f.*
poignant *a.*, **~ly** *adv.* beißend, scharf; durchdringend.
point *s.* Punkt *m.;* Spitze *f.;* Auge (in der Karte) *n.;* Zweck *m.;* Kompaßstrich *m.;* **~s** *pl. (rail.)* Weiche *f.;* **~-blank** *adv. & a.* direkt, gerade heraus; *the case in ~,* der betreffende Fall; *on the ~,* im Begriff; *there is no ~ in doing that,* es hat keinen Zweck, das zu tun; *that is beside the ~,* das hat damit nichts zu tun; *~ of view, s.* Gesichtspunkt *m.;* ~ *v.t.* hinweisen; *to ~ out,* hinweisen auf, anführen.
pointed *a.*, **~ly** *adv.* zugespitzt; spitz; punktiert; beißend.
pointer *s.* Zeiger *m.;* Zeigestock *m.;* Vorstehhund *m.*
pointless *a.*, sinnlos; belanglos; stumpf.
poise *s.* Gewicht, Gleichgewicht *n.;* Haltung *f.;* ~ *v.t.* wägen; im Gleichgewicht erhalten.
poised *a.* selbstsicher.
poison *s.* Gift *n.;* ~ *v.t.* vergiften.
poisoning *s.* Vergiftung *f.*
poisonous *a.*, **~ly** *adv.* giftig.
poke *s.* Stoß *m.;* Puff *m.;* ~ *v.t.* tappen; schüren; stoßen.
poker *s.* Schüreisen *n.;* Poker *n.*
poker-faced *a.* mit unbeweglichem Gesicht.
polar *a.* polar, Pol...
polar bear *s.* Eisbär *m.*
polarity *s.* Polarität *f.*
polarization *s.* Polarisierung *f.*
polarize *v.t.* polarisieren, spalten.
pole *s.* Pol *f.;* Stange *f.;* Mast *m.;* Pfahl *m.*
Pole *s.* Pole *m.;* Polin *f.*
poleaxe *s.* Streitaxt *f.*
polecat *s.* Iltis *m.*
polemic(al) *a.* Streit...; *m.;* **~s** *pl.* Polemik *f.*
polemicist *s.* Polemiker(in) *m.(f.)*
polestar *s.* Polarstern *m.*
pole: **~vault** *s.* Stabhochsprung; **~vaulter** *s.* Stabhochspringer(in) *m.(f.);* **~vaulting** *s.* Stabhochspringen *n.*
police *s.* Polizei *f.;* **~headquarters** *pl.* Polizeipräsidium *n.;* **~informer** *s.* Polizeispitzel *m.*
policeman *s.* Polizist, Schutzmann *m.*
police station *s.* Polizeiwache *f.*
policewoman *s.* Polizistin *f.*
policy *s.* Politik *f.;* Diplomatie *f.;* Versicherungspolice *f.;* **~-making** *a.* politisch maßgebend; **~ holder** *s.* Policeinhaber *m.; to take out a ~ on the life of his wife,* das Leben seiner Frau versichern.
polio *s.* Polio *f.;* Kinderlähmung *f.*
polish, *v.t.* glätten; zieren; ~ *s.* Glätte, Politur *f.;* Glanz *m.;* Schliff *m.*
Polish *a.* polnisch.
polite *a.*, **~ly** *adv.* höflich.
politeness *s.* Höflichkeit *f.*
politic *s.* weltklug, politisch.
political *a.*, **~ly** *adv.* politisch, staatskundig, Staats...; **~science** *s.* Politologie *f.*
politician *s.* Politiker(in) *m.(f.)*
politicize *v.t.* politisieren.
politics *s.pl.* Politik, Staatskunst *f.*
polka *s.* Polka *f.;* **~dot** *s.* Tupfen *m.*
poll *s.* Abstimmung *f.;* ~ *v.t.* Stimmen erhalten; ~ *v.i.* stimmen.
pollen *s.* Blütenstaub *m.*
pollinate *v.t.* bestäuben.
pollination *s.* Bestäubung *f.*
polling station *s.* Wahllokal *n.*
pollster *s.* Meinungsforscher(in) *m.(f.)*
poll tax *s.* Kopfsteuer *f.*
pollutant *s.* Schadstoff *m.*
pollute *v.t.* verschmutzen, verunreinigen.
pollution *s.* Verschmutzung *f.*
polo *s.* Polo *n.;* **~neck** *s.* Rollkragen *m.*
polygamist *s.* Polygamist(in) *m.(f.)*

polygamy *s.* Polygamie *f.;* Mehrehe *f.*
polyglot *a.* vielsprachig.
polygon *s.* Vieleck *n.*
polygonal *a.* vieleckig.
polyp(e) *s.* Polyp *m.*
polypus *s.* (*med.*) Polyp *m.*
polysyllabic *a.* vielsilbig.
polytechnic *a.* polytechnisch; ~ *s.* Technische Hochschule *f.*
polytheism *s.* Vielgötterei *f.*
polyvalent *a.* mehrwertig.
pomade, pomatum *s.* Pomade *f.*
pomegranate *s.* Granatapfel *m.;* Granatbaum *m.*
pommel *s.* (Degen-, Sattel-)Knopf *m.*
pomp *s.* Pracht *f.;* Gepränge *n.*
pomposity *s.* Prahlerei *f.;* Schwulst *m.*
pompous *a.*, **~ly** *adv.* hochtrabend, bombastisch.
pond *s.* Teich *m.*
ponder *v.t.* nachdenken; abwägen.
ponderable *a.* wägbar.
ponderous *a.*, **~ly** *adv.* schwer; schwerfällig.
poniard *s.* Dolch *m.;* ~ *v.t.* erdolchen.
pontiff *s.* Hohepriester *m.;* Papst *m.*
pontifical *a.*, **~ly** *adv.* päpstlich.
pontoon *s.* Brückenkahn *m.*, Ponton *m.*
pony *s.* Pony *n.*
ponytail *s.* Pferdeschwanz *m.*
P.O.O. *Post Office Order,* Postanweisung *f.*
poodle *s.* Pudel *m.*
pooh! oho! pah!
pooh-pooh *v.t.* (*fig.*) verächtlich ablehnen.
pool *s.* Pfuhl, Teich *m.;* (Spiel-)Einsatz *m.;* (*com.*) Kartell *n.;* gemeinsamer Fonds *m.;* ~ *v.t.* zusammenlegen, zusammenwerfen.
poop *s.* Heck *n.* (Schiff).
poor *a.*, **~ly** *adv.* arm, dürftig; gering.
poorly *a.* & *adv.* ärmlich; unpässlich.
poorness *s.* Armut *f.;* Dürftigkeit *f.*
poor relief *s.* Armenfürsorge *f.*
pop *s.* Puff, Knall *m.;* ~ *v.i.* knallen, paffen; huschen; ~ *v.t.* schnell bewegen, schnellen.
pop. *population,* Einwohner, Einw.
pop: **~art** *s.* Popart *f.*, **~concert** *s.* Popkonzert *n.;* **~corn** *s.* Popcorn *n.*
pope *s.* Papst *m.*
popery *s.* (*pej.*) Papisterei *f.*
pop gun *s.* Spielzeuggewehr *n.*
poplar *s.* Pappel *f.*
poplin *s.* Poplin *m.*
poppy *s.* Mohn *m.*
populace *s.* Pöbel *m.*
popular *a.* volkstümlich, beliebt, volksmäßig; Volks...
popularity *s.* Volkstümlichkeit *f.*
popularize *v.t.* populär machen, popularisieren.
popularly *adv.* allgemein; volkstümlich.
popular music *s.* Unterhaltungsmusik *f.*
populate *v.t.* bevölkern.
population *s.* Bevölkerung *f.;* ~ **explosion** *s.* Bevölkerungsexplosion *f.*
populous *a.* dichtbevölkert.
porcelain *s.* Porzellan *n.*
porch *s.* Vorhalle *f.;* Vordach *n.;* Vorbau *m.;* Veranda *f.*
porcupine *s.* Stachelschwein *n.*
pore *s.* Pore *f.;* ~ **over,** ~ *v.i.* studieren; nachdenken über.
pork *s.* Schweinefleisch *n.*
pork: ~ **chop** *s.* Schweinekotelett *n.;* ~ **sausage** *s.* Schweinswürstchen *n.*
pornographic *a.* pornographisch, Porno...
pornography *s.* Pornographie *f.*
porous *a.* porös.
porridge *s.* Haferbrei *m.*
port *s.* Hafen *m.*, Hafenstadt *f.;* (*nav.*) Pfortluke *f.;* Backbord *n.;* Portwein *m.;* ~ *of arrival,* Ankunftshafen *m.;* ~ *of call,* Anlegehafen *m.;* ~ *of destination,* Bestimmungshafen *m.;* ~ *of registry,* Heimathafen *m.;* ~ **charges,** ~ **dues** *pl.* Hafengebühren *f.pl.*
portable *a.* tragbar.
portal *s.* Portal *n.*
portcullis *s.* Fallgitter *n.*
portend *v.t.* vorbedeuten, deuten auf.
portent *s.* Vorbedeutung *f.*
portentous *a.* verhängnisvoll, fürchterlich.
porter *s.* Träger, Dienstmann *m.;* Portier *m.;* Schlafwagenschaffner *m.*
portfolio *s.* Mappe *f.;* Portefeuille *n.;* (*fig.*) Geschäftsbereich *m.*
porthole *s.* (*nav.*) Seitenfenster *n.;* Bullauge *n.*
portico *s.* Säulengang *m.*
portion *s.* Teil, Anteil *m.;* Portion *f.* Heiratsgut *n.;* *compulsory* ~, (*jur.*) Pflichtteil *n.;* ~ *v.t.* austeilen.
portly *a.* stattlich; wohlbeleibt.
portmanteau *s.* Reisekoffer *m.*
portrait *s.* Bildnis, Porträt *n.*
portraitist *s.* Porträtmaler(in) *m.(f.)*
portray *v.t.* abmalen; schildern.
Portugal *s.* Portugal *n.*
Portuguese *a.* portugiesisch; ~ *s.* Portugiese *m.*, Portugiesin *f.*
pose *s.* Pose, Stellung f; ~ *v.t.* (eine Frage, Behauptung) aufstellen.
posh *a.* (*fam.*) vornehm; nobel.
position *s.* Stellung, Lage *f.;* Stand *m.;* Standpunkt *m.;* ~ **warfare** *s.* (*mil.*) Stellungskrieg *m.;* *to hold a* ~, ein Amt bekleiden.
positive *a.*, **~ly** *adv.* ausdrücklich; sicher; bestimmt; positiv; konstruktiv.
posse *s.* (Polizei-) Aufgebot *n.*
possess *v.t.* besitzen; besetzen.
possessed *a.* besessen; ~ *s.* Besessene *m./f.*
possession *s.* Besitz *m.;* Besitzung *f.;* *to be in* ~ *of,* im Besitz von etwas sein.
possessive *a.* Besitz...; besitzergreifend (*gram.*) besitzanzeigend.
possessor *s.* Besitzer(in) *m.(f.)*
possibility *s.* Möglichkeit *f.*
possible *a.* möglich.
possibly *adv.* möglicherweise, vielleicht.
post *s.* Pfosten, Pfahl *m.;* Posten *m.;* Stelle *f.*, Anstellung *f.;* Post *f.;* *by* ~, mit der Post; *Ministry of* ~, Postministerium *n.;* ~ *v.t.* anschlagen; hinstellen; auf die Post geben, (Brief) einstecken; ~ *v.i.* mit der Post reisen, eilen.
postage *s.* Porto *n.*, Postgebühr *f.;* ~ *due,* Strafporto *n.*, Nachgebühr *f.;* ~ *paid,* franko, portofrei.
postage stamp *s.* Briefmarke *f.*
postal *a.* Post...; ~ **order** (P.O.), Postanweisung

f.; ~ **check, ~money order** *s.* Postscheck *m.*; ~ **expenses** *pl.* Portospesen *pl.*
postcard *s.* Postkarte *f.*; *color* ~, farbige Postkarte *f.*; *picture* ~, Ansichtspostkarte *f.*
post date *v.t.* nachdatieren.
poster *s.* Plakat *n.*
poste restante *adv.* postlagernd; ~ *s.* Briefaufbewahrungsstelle *f.*
posterior *a.* später; ~ *s.* Hintere *m.*
posterity *s.* Nachwelt *f.*
post-haste *adv.* in grosser Eile.
posthumous *a.* nachgeboren, hinterlasen.
postmark *s.* Poststempel *m.*
postmaster *s.* Postmeister *m.*
post-mortem *s.* nach dem Tod; ~ **examination** *s.* Obduktion *f.*, Leichenschau *f.*
post office *s.* Postamt *n.*; ~ **box** (P.O. box) *s.* Postfach *n.*; ~ *savings bank*, Postsparkasse *f.*
postpone *v.t.* verschieben; aufschieben.
postponement *s.* Aufschub *m.*; Verschiebung *f.*
postscript *s.* Nachschrift *f.*
postulate *s.* Postulat *n.*, Forderung *f.*; ~ *v.t.* fordern; als richtig annehmen.
posture *s.* Stellung, Lage *f.*; (körperliche) Haltung *f.*
post-war Nachkriegs...
posy *s.* Blumenstrauß *m.*
pot *s.* Topf, Krug *m.*; Kanne *f.*; (*sl.*) Marijuana *n.*; Pot *n.*; ~ **boiler,** Brotarbeit *f.*
potable *a.* trinkbar.
potash *s.* Pottasche *f.*; Kali *n.*
potassium *s.* Kalium *n.*
potato *s.* Kartoffel *f.*; ~ *es in jackets, pl.* Pellkartoffeln *f. boiled* ~*es, pl.* Salzkartoffeln *pl.*; *fried* ~*es, pl.* Bratkartoffeln; *mashed* ~*es,* Kartoffelbrei *m.*; ~ *blight,* Kartoffelkrankheit *f.*
pot belly *s.* Schwerbauch *m.*
potency *s.* Kraft *f.*; Wirksamkeit *f.*; Potenz *f.*
potent *a.*, **~ly** *adv.* mächtig, stark, wirksam; potent.
potentate *s.* Machthaber *m.*
potential *a.*, **~ly** *adv.* möglich, potentiell; *military* ~ *s.* Kriegspotential *n.*
potentialities *pl.* Möglichkeiten *f.pl.*
pother *s.* Lärm *m.*; ~ *v.i.* lärmen, poltern; ~ *v.t.* aufregen.
potion *s.* (Arznei-)Trank *m.*
potluck *s.* ~ **dinner** *s.* Essen, bei dem jeder etwas mitbringt.
potpourri *s.* Potpourri *n.*; Allerei *n.*
potted *a.* eingemacht.
potter *s.* Töpfer(in) *m.(f.)*
potter's wheel *s.* Töpferscheibe *f.*
pottery *s.* Töpferei *f.*; Töpferwaren *f.pl.*
potty *s.* Töpfchen *n.*; **~-trained** *a.* sauber.
pouch *s.* Tasche *f.*; Beutel *m.*; ~ *v.t.* einstecken.
poultice *s.* Wickel *m.*; (warmer) Umschlag *m.*
poultry *s.* Geflügel *n.*
pounce *s.* Sprung *m.*; Satz *m.*; ~ **on** *v.i.* herfallen über; sich stürzen auf.
pound *s.* Pfund *n.*; ~ *v.t.* zerstossen; (*mil.*) belegen mit, bombardieren ~ *v.i.* hämmern, schlagen.
pounding *s.* Schlagen *n.*; Klopfen *n.*; Stampfen *n.*
pour *v.t.* gießen; ~ *v.i.* strömen.
pouring *a.* strömend.
pout *s.* üble Laune *f.*; Schmollmund *m.*; ~ *v.i.* schmollen.
poverty *s.* Armut *f.*; Mangel *m.*
poverty: **~line** Armutsgrenze *f.*; **~-stricken** *a.* notleidend.
POW *prisoner of war,* Kriegsgefangene.
powder *s.* Pulver *n.*; Puder, Staub *m.*; ~ *v.t.* pudern; bestreuen.
power *s.* Macht, Gewalt *f.*; Kraft *f.*; Vollmacht *f.*; (*math.*) Potenz *f.*; (*elek.*) Starkstrom *m.*; ~ **cut** *s.* Stromsperre *f.*; ~ **failure** *s.* Stromausfall *m.* **~station** *s.* Kraftwerk *n.*
powerful *a.*, **~ly** *adv.* mächtig, kräftig.
powerless *a.* kraftlos, ohnmächtig.
powerloom *s.* mechanischer Webstuhl *m.*
pox *s.* Pocken *pl.*; (*fam.*) Syphilis *f.*
pp. *pages,* Seiten, *pl.*
PR *public relations,* Öffentlichkeitsarbeit.
practicable *a.*, **~bly** *adv.* ausführbar; praktikabel.
practical *a.*, **~ly** *adv.* praktisch; tatsächlich; ~ **joke** Streich *m.*
practicality *s.* Durchführbarkeit *f.*
practice *s.* Ausübung *f.*; Übung *f.*; Praxis *f.*; ~ *v.t.* üben; anwenden; ~ *v.i.* sich üben; treiben.
practiced *a.* erfahren; geübt.
practicing *a.* praktizierend.
practitioner *s.* Praktiker(in) *m.(f.)*
pragmatic *a.*, **~ally,** *adv.* pragmatisch.
prairie *s.* Prärie *f.*
praise *s.* Lob *n.*; ~ *v.t.* loben.
praiseworthy *s.*, **~ily** *adv.* lobenswert.
prance *v.i.* stolzieren; täuzeln; herumspringen.
prank *s.* Possen, Streich *m.*
prate *v.i.* schwatzen.
prattle *v.t.* schwatzen; plappern; ~ *s.* Geschwätz *n.*, Geplapper *n.*
prawn *s.* Garnele *f.*
pray *v.i.* & *t.* beten; bitten.
prayer *s.* Gebet *n.*; Bitte *f.*; *the Lord's* ~, das Vaterunser.
prayerbook *s.* Gebetbuch *n.*
preach *v.t.* & *i.* predigen.
preacher *s.* Prediger(in) *m.(f.)*
preamble *s.* Einleitung, Vorrede *f.*
prearrange *v.t.* vorher anordnen; verabreden.
precarious *a.*, **~ly** *adv.* unsicher; instabil; gefährlich; abhängig; aufkündbar.
precaution *s.* Vorsicht, Vorsichtsmaßregel *f.*; *to take* ~*s,* Vorsichtsmaßnahmen treffen.
precautionary *a.* vorbeugend, Vorsichts...
precede *v.t.* vorhergehen.
precedence *s.* Vortritt, Vorrang *m.*
precedent *s.* Präzedenzfall *m.*
precept *s.* Vorschrift, Regel *f.*
preceptor *s.* Lehrer *m.*; Tutor *m.*
precinct *s.* Viertel *n.*, Bezirk, Umfang *m.*
precious *a.*, **~ly** *adv.* kostbar; wertvoll.
precipice *s.* Abgrund *m.*
precipitate *v.t.* hinabstürzen; (*chem.*) fällen; überstürzen; heraufbeschwören; ~ *v.i.* herabstürzen; sich übereilen; vorschnell sein; ~ *a.*, **~ly** *adv.* übereilt; voreilig.
precipitation *s.* Niederschlag *m.* Herabstürzung *f.*
precipitous *a.* sehr steil; schroff.
précis *s.* kurze Inhaltsangabe *f.*, Zusammenfassung *f.*

precise *a.*, **~ly** *adv.* genau; steif.
precision *s.* Bestimmtheit *f.*; (*mech.*) ~ **worker** *s.* Präzisionsarbeiter *m.*; ~ **tool** *s.* Präzisionswerkzeug *n.*
preclude *v.t.* ausschließen.
precocious *a.* frühreif; altklug.
precocity *s.* Frühreife *f.*
preconceived *a.* vorgefaßt.
preconception *s.* Vorurteil *n.*; vorgefaßte Meinung *f.*
precondition *s.* Vorbedingung *f.*
precooked *a.* vorgekocht.
precursor *s.* Vorläufer, Vorbote *m.*
predate *v.t.* zurückdatieren.
predatory *a.* räuberisch.
predecessor *s.* Vorgänger(in) *m.(f.)*
predestination *s.* Vorherbestimmung *f.*; Gnadenwahl *f.*
predestine *v.t.* vorherbestimmen.
predestined *a.* vorherbestimmt, prädestiniert.
predicament *s.* (mißliche) Lage *f.*, Dilemma *n.*
predicate *s.* (*gram.*) Prädikat *n.*
predicative *a.* prädikativ.
predict *v.t.* vorhersagen.
predictable *a.* vorhersagbar; berechenbar.
prediction *s.* Vorhersage *f.*
predilection *s.* Vorliebe *f.*
predispose *v.t.* geneigt machen.
predisposition *s.* Neigung *f.*
predominance *s.* Übergewicht *n.*
predominant *a.*, **~ly** *adv.* vorherrschend.
predominate *v.i.* vorherrschen.
pre-eminence *s.* Vorrang *m.*
pre-eminent *a.*, **~ly** *adv.* hervorragend; herausragend.
pre-emption *s.* Vorkauf *m.*; Vorkaufsrecht *n.*
preen *v.t.* & *i.* (sich) putzen.
pre-exist *v.i.* vorher existieren.
prefab *s.* Fertighaus *n.*
prefabricated *a.* vorgefertigt.
preface *s.* Vorrede *f.*; ~ *v.t.* einleiten.
prefect *s.* Präfekt.
prefer *v.t.* vorziehen; *~red stock, s.* Vorzugsaktie *f.*
preferable *a.* vorzuziehen(d), vorzüglicher.
preferably *adv.* am besten; am liebsten; vorzugsweise.
preference *s.* Vorzug *m.*; Vorliebe *f.*
preferential *a.*, **~ly** *adv.* bevorzugt, Vorzugs...; ~ **treatment** *s.* Vorzugsbehandlung *f.*
prefigure *v.t.* sich ausmalen.
prefix *s.* Vorsilbe *f.*
pregnancy *s.* Schwangerschaft *f.* ~ **test** *s.* Schwangerschaftstest *m.*
pregnant *a.*, **~ly** *adv.* schwanger; trächtig; (*fig.*) gewichtig.
preheat *v.t.* vorheizen.
prehistoric *a.* prähistorisch, vorgeschichtlich.
prehistory *s.* Vorgeschichte *f.*
prejudge *v.t.* vorverurteilen; vorschnellbeurteilen.
prejudice *s.* Vorurteil *n.*; Nachteil *m.*; *without ~ to,* unbeschadet; ~ *v.t.* einnehmen (für/gegen); benachteiligen.
prejudicial *a.*, **~ly** *adv.* schädlich.
prelacy *s.* Prälatenwürde *f.*
prelate *s.* Prälat *m.*
preliminary *a.* vorläufig, Vor...; (*jur.*) *~ examination,* Vorverhör *n.*; ~ *s.* Vorbereitung *f.*; **~ies** *pl.* Vorverhandlungen *f.pl.*
prelude *s.* Vorspiel *n.*, Auftakt *m.*
premarital *a.* vorehelich.
premature *a.*, **~ly** *adv.* vorschnell; frühreif.
premeditate *v.t.* vorher überlegen; **~d** *p.* vorbedacht, vorsätzlich.
premeditation *s.* Vorbedacht *m.*
premier *s.* Premierminister *m.*
premiere *s.* Premiere *f.*; Erstaufführung *f.*; Uraufführung *f.*
premilitary *a.* vormilitärisch.
premise *s.* Prämisse *f.*
premises *s.pl.* Vordersätze *m.pl.*; Haus *(n.)* mit Zubehör; Grundstücke *n.pl.*
premium *s.* Preis *m.*; Versicherungsprämie *f.*; *at a ~,* über pari; sehr gesucht.
premonition *s.* Warnung, Vorahnung *f.*
prenatal *a.* vorgeburtlich, pränatal; ~ **care** *s.* Mutterschaftsfürsorge.
preoccupation *s.* Sorge *f.*; Hauptanliegen *n.*
preoccupy *v.t.* ganz in Anspruch nehmen; ausschließlich beschäftigen.
pre-packed *a.* abgepackt.
preparation *s.* Vorbereitung, Zubereitung *f.*; Präparat *n.*
preparatory *a.* vorbereitend; vorläufig.
prepare *v.t.* vorbereiten; zubereiten; ~ *v.i.* sich vorbereiten.
preparedness *s.* Bereitschaft *f.*
prepay *v.t.* vorausbezahlen; frankieren.
prepayment *s.* Vorausbezahlung *f.*
preponderance *s.* Übergewicht *n.*
preponderant *a.* überwiegend.
preponderate *v.i.* überwiegen.
preposition *s.* (*gram.*) Präposition *f.*; Verhältniswort *n.*
prepossessed *a.* eingenommen sein.
prepossessing *a.* einnehmend, anziehend.
prepossession *s.* Voreingenommenheit *f.*
preposterous *a.* unsinnig.
prerequisite *s.* Bedingung, Voraussetzung *f.*
prerogative *s.* Vorrecht *n.*
Pres. *President,* Präsident.
presage *s.* Vorbedeutung *f.*; ~ *v.t.* vorhersagen; anzeigen.
presbyterian *a.* presbyterianisch; ~ *s.* Presbyterianer *m.*
preschool *a.* Vorschul...
prescribe *v.t.* vorschreiben; ~ *v.i.* verschreiben.
prescription *s.* Vorschrift *f.*; Rezept *n.*; Verjährung *f.*
presence *s.* Gegenwart *f.*; *~ of mind,* Geistesgegenwart *f.*
present *a.* gegenwärtig; bereit; *at ~,* gegenwärtig; ~ *s.* (Zeit) Gegenwart *f.*; (*gram.*) Präsens *n.*; Geschenk *n.* ~ *v.t.* vorstellen; vorlegen, unterbreiten; einreichen; beschenken; vorschlagen, präsentieren; *to ~ a play,* ein Stück zeigen.
presentable *a.* präsentierbar.
presentation *s.* Darstellung *f.*; Vorzeigung *f.*
present-day *a.* heutig, zeitgemäß.
presenter *s.* Moderator(in) *m.(f.)*
presentiment *s.* Vorgefühl *n.*, Ahnung *f.*
presently *adv.* gleich; bald; nachher.

preservation *s.* Erhaltung, Bewahrung *f.*
preservative *a.* bewahrend; ~ *s.* Schutzmittel *n.;* Konservierungsmittel *n.*
preserve *v.t.* bewahren; einlegen, einmachen; ~ *s.* Eingemachtes *n.*
preside *v.i.* den Vorsitz führen.
presidency *s.* Vorsitz *m.;* Präsidentschaft *f.*
president *s.* Präsident(in) *m.(f.);* Vorsitzende *m./f.;* (*Univ.*) Rektor(in) *m.(f.)*
presidential *a.* Präsidenten...; ~ **campaign** *s.* Präsidentschaftswahlkampf *m.*
press *s.* Presse *f.;* Druck, Drang *m.;* Gedränge *n.;* *in the* ~, in der Presse; ~ *conference,* Pressekonferenz *f.;* ~ *v.t.* pressen; keltern; drängen; ~ *v.i.* drücken; dringen, drängen.
press gallery *s.* Pressetribüne *f.*
pressing *a.*, **~ly** *adv.* dringend.
press release *s.* Presseerklärung *f.*
pressure *s.* Druck *m.; under* ~, unter Druck (arbeiten); *to put* ~ *on s.b.*, auf jn. Druck ausüben.
pressure cooker *s.* Schnellkochtopf *m.*
pressure group *s.* Pressure-group *f.*
prestige *s.* Ansehen *n.*, Geltung *f.*
prestigious *a.* angesehen.
presumable *a.* mutmaßlich.
presume *v.t. & i.* mutmaßen; sich anmaßen; sich verlassen; *~d dead,* verschollen, mutmaßlich tot.
presumption *s.* Mutmaßung *f.;* Dünkel *m.;* Vermessenheit *f.*
presumptive *a.*, **~ly** *adv.* mutmaßlich.
presumptuous *a.*, **~ly** *adv.* anmaßend.
presuppose *v.t.* voraussetzen.
pretend *v.t.* vorgeben; erheucheln; ~ *v.i.* sich verstellen; beanspruchen.
pretended *a.* vorgetäuscht, gespielt.
pretender *s.* (Thron-) Prätendent, Beanspruchcr *m*
pretense *s.* Vorwand *m.;* Schein *m.; under false ~s,* unter Vorspiegelung falscher Tatsachen *f.*
pretension *s.* Anmaßung *f.*
pretentious *a.*, **~ly** *adv.* anspruchsvoll.
preterite *s.* (*gram.*) Präteritum *n.*
pretext *s.* Vorwand *m.*
pretty *a. & adv.* hübsch, schön, niedlich, nett; ziemlich.
pretzel *s.* Brezel *f.*
prevail *v.i.* (vor-) herrschen.
prevailing *a.* vorherrschend, aktuell.
prevalence *s.* Verbreitung *f.;* Vorhersehen *n.*
prevalent *a.*, **~ly** *adv.* vorhersehend.
prevaricate *v.i.* Ausflüchte machen.
prevarication *s.* Verdrehung, Ausflucht *f.*
prevent *v.t.* zuvorkommen; vorbeugen; verhindern.
prevention *s.* Verhütung *f.;* Vorbeugung *f.*
preventive *a.*, **~ly** *adv.* vorbeugend; ~ *s.* Verhütungsmittel *n.*
preview *s.* Vorschau *f.;* Voraufführung *f.;* Vorbesichtigung *f.*
previous *a.*, **~ly** *adv.* vorig, früher.
prewar *a.* Vorkriegs...
prey *s.* Beute *f.; bird/beast of* ~ Raubvogel *m.;* Raubtier *n.;* ~ *v.i.* rauben, plündern.
price *s.* Preis *m.;* Wert *m.;* ~ **control,** Preisüberwachung *f.; low ~d,* in niedriger Preislage.
price cut *s.* Preissenkung *f.*
priceless *a.* unschätzbar.
price: ~ **list** *s.* Preisliste *f.;* **~range** *s.* Preisspanne *f.;* **~rise** *s.* Preisanstieg *m.;* **~tag** *s.* Preisschild *n.*
prick *v.t.* stechen, anstechen; spornen; spitzen; *to ~ one's ears,* die Ohren spitzen; ~ *v.i.* stechen, prikkeln; ~ *s.* Spitze *f.;* Stich *m.;* (*vulg.*) Penis *m.*, Schwanz *m.*
prickle *s.* Stachel *m.;* Dorn *m.*
prickly *a.* dornig; stachelig.
pride *s.* Stolz *m.;* Hochmut *m.;* ~ *v.t.* ~ *o.s. on,* stolz sein auf.
priest *s.* Priester *m.*
priestess *s.* Priesterin *f.*
priesthood *s.* Priesteramt *n.;* Geistlichkeit *f.*
priestly *a.* priesterlich.
prig *s.* Tugendbold *m.*
priggish *a.* (übertrieben) tugendhaft.
prim *a.* geziert, förmlich; gesetzt.
primacy *s.* Primat *m.;* Vorrang *m.*
prima facie, auf den ersten Blick.
primary *a.* ursprünglich, Anfangs..., Haupt...; **~ily** *adv.* vornehmlich.
primary: ~ **color** *s.* Grundfarbe *f.;* ~ **election** *s.* Vorwahl *f.;* ~ **school** *s.* Grundschule *f.*
primate *s.* Primas *m.;* (*zool.*) Primat *m.*
prime *a.*, **~ly** *adv.* Haupt...; vortrefflich; **~cost** *s.* Gestehungskosten *pl.;* ~ **Minister** *s.* Ministerpräsident *m.;* ~ **number** *s.* Primzahl *f.* ~ *s.* Blüte, Vollendung *f.;* Beste *n.;* ~ *v.t.* grundieren; unterrichten.
primer *s.* Fibel *f.*, Elementarbuch *n.;* Grundierlack *m.*
primeval *a.* urzeitlich; uralt.
primitive *a.*, **~ly** *adv.* unsprünglich; einfach, primitiv.
primogeniture *s.* Erstgeburt *f.*
primrose *s.* Primel *f.;* Schlüsselblume *f.*
prince *s.* Fürst, Prinz *m.*
Prince Charming *s.* Märchenprinz *m.*
prince consort *s.* Prinzgemahl *m.*
princely *a. & adv.* prinzlich, fürstlich.
princess *s.* Prinzessin, Fürstin *f.*
principal *a.*, **~ly** *adv.* vorzüglich, Haupt..., hauptsächlich; ~ *s.* Haupt *n.;* (*jur.*)) Haupttäter *m.;* Direktor *m.;* Hauptsache *f.;* Kapital *n.*
principality *s.* Fürstentum *n.*
principally *adv.* in erster Linie.
principle *s.* Prinzip *n.;* Grundursache *f.;* Grundsatz *m.; to lay down a* ~, einen Grundsatz aufstellen.
print *v.t.* drucken, abdrucken; in grossen Buchstaben schreiben; (*phot.*) absiehen; einprägen; ~ *s.* Druck *m.;* Abdruck *m.;* (*phot.*) Abzug *m.*, Kopie *f.;* Spur *f.;* (Stahl)Stick *m.; out of* ~, vergriffen.
printable *a.* druckreif.
printed matter, **printed paper** *s.* Drucksache *f.*
printer *s.* Drucker(in) *m.(f.);* (*comp.*) Drucker *m.*
printing *s.* Drucken *n.;* ~ *house s.* Buchdruckerei *f.;* ~ *ink,* Druckerschwärze *f.*
printout *s.* Ausdruck *m.*
prior *a.* früher; ~ *to,* vor; ~ *s.* Prior *m.*
prioress *s.* Priorin *f.*
priority *s.* Priorität *f.;* Vorrang *m.*
prism *s.* Prisma *n.*
prison *s.* Gefängnis *n.*

prison camp *s.* Gefangenenlager *n.*
prisoner *s.* Gefangene *m.;* ~ **of war** *s.* Kriegsgefangene *m.*
prison guard *s.* Gefängniswärter(in) *m.(f.)*
prissy *a.* (*fam.*) zimperlich; überordentlich.
pristine *a.* ehemalig, alt.
privacy *s.* Verborgenheit *f.*
private *a.,* **~ly** *adv.* privat; geheim; nicht öffentlich; nicht amtlich; persönlich, Privat..., eigen; (*tel.*) ~ **call,** Privatgespräch *n.;* ~ **enterprise,** freie Wirtschaft *f.;* ~ *s.* gemeiner Soldat *m.; in* ~, unter vier Augen.
private parts *s.pl.* Geschlechtsteile *pl.*
private practice *s.* Privatpraxis *f.*
privation *s.* Beraubung *f.;* Mangel *m.*
privatization *s.* Privatisierung *f.*
privatize *v.t.* privatisieren.
privet *s.* (*bot.*) Liguster *m.*
privilege *s.* Vorrecht *n.;* Privileg *n.* ~ *v.t.* bevorrechten; privilegieren.
privileged *a.* privilegiert.
privy *a.* geheim, besonder; mitwissend; ~ **council** Staatsrat *m.;* ~ *s.* Abort *m.*
prize *s.* Preis *m.;* Belohnung *f.;* ~ *v.t.* würdigen, schätzen; (mit Gewalt) öffnen.
prize fighter *s.* Boxer *m.*
prize winner *s.* Preisträger(in) *m.(f.)*
probability *s.* Wahrscheinlichkeit *f.*
probable *a.,* **~bly** *adv.* wahrscheinlich.
probate *s.* Testamentsbestätigung *f.*
probation *s.* Probezeit *f.;* Bewährungsfrist *f.; on* ~, auf Probe, widerruflich.
probationary *a.* Probe...; ~ **period** *s.* Probezeit *f.*
probationer *s.* Prüfling *m.;* Anwärter(in) *m.(f.)*
probe *s.* Sonde *f.;* ~ *v.t.* sondieren.
probing *a.* forschend; durchdringend.
probity *s.* Redlichkeit *f.*
problem *s.* Aufgabe *f.,* Problem *n.*
problematic *a.,* **~ally** *adv.* zweifelhaft.; problematisch.
procedure *s.* Verfahren *n.; legal* ~, Prozeßverfahren *n.*
proceed *v.i.* fortfahren; verfahren; vorgehen; weitergehen; *to* ~ *from,* hervorgehen, herrühren; *to* ~ *to,* sich begeben nach, reisen nach.
proceeding *s.* Vorgehensweise *f.;* Verfahren; **(legal) ~s** *pl.* Prozeß *m.,* gerichtliches Verfahren *n.; to take* ~*s against,* gerichtlich vorgehen gegen.
proceeds *s.pl.* Ertrag, Gewinn *m.*
process *s.* Vorgang *m.;* Verfahren *n.;* Prozeß *m.;* ~ *v.t.* behandeln, bearbeiten (*chem.*)
procession *s.* Prozession *f.;* Umzug *m.*
processor *s.* (*comp.*) Prozessor *m.*
proclaim *v.t.* erklären
proclamation *s.* Verkündung *f.;* Bekanntmachung *f.*
proclivity *s.* Neigung *f.,* Hang *m.*
procrastinate *v.t. & i.* zandern; zögern.
procreate *v.t.* zeugen, erzeugen.
procure *v.t.* besorgen; verschaffen, liefern; ~ *v.i.* verkuppeln.
procurement *s.* Beschaffung *f.*
procurer *s.* Kuppler *m.*
procuress *s.* Kupplerin *f.*
prod *s.* Stupser *m.;* ~ *v.t.* stupsen; stoßen.
prodigal *a.,* **~ly** *adv.* verschwenderisch; ~ *s.* Verschwender(in) *m.(f.);* ~ **son** *s.* verlorener Sohn *m.*
prodigality *s.* Verschwendung *f.*
prodigious *a.,* **~ly** *adv.* ungeheuer; außerordentlich.
prodigy *s.* Wunderding, *n.;* Talent *n.; child* ~, Wunderkind *n.*
produce *v.t.* vorführen; hervorbringen; vorstellen; vorzeigen; produzieren; *to* ~ *a play,* ein Stück einstudieren; *to* ~ *a witness,* einen Zeugen beibringen; ~ *s.* Erzeugnis *n.;* Ertrag *m.;* Produkte *n.pl.;* **~exchange** *s.* Produktenbörse *f.*
producer *s.* Erzeuger(in) *m.(f.);* Produzent(in) *m.(f.)* ~ **gas** *s.* Generatorgas, Holzgas *n.*
product *s.* Erzeugnis, Produkt *n.*
production *s.* Vorführung *f.;* Erzeugnis *n.;* Vorlegung *f.;* Produktion *f.;* Erzeugung *f.*
production line *s.* Fertigungsstraße *f.;* Fließband *n.*
productive *a.* fruchtbar; schöpferisch; produktiv.
productivity *s.* Produktivität *f.*
Prof. *Professor,* Professor.
profanation *s.* Entweihung *f.*
profane *s.,* **~ly** *adv.* ungeweiht; gottlos; weltlich; ~ *v.t.* entweihen.
profanity *s.* Gottlosigkeit, Ruchlosigkeit *f.;* Fluchen *n.*
profess *v.t.* bekennen; ausüben.
professed *a.* erklärt; angeblich.
professedly *adv.* erklärtermaßen, eingestandenermaßen.
profession *s.* Bekenntnis *n.;* Beruf *m.*
professional *a.* berufsmäßig, Berufs...; Fach...; ~ *s.* (*sp.*) Berufssportler(in) *m.(f.); by* ~, von Beruf *m.*
professionalism *s.* Professionalismus *m.*
professor *s.* Professor(in) *m.(f.)*
professorship *s.* Professur *f.,* Lehrstuhl *m.*
proffer *v.t.* darbieten; anbieten; ~ *s.* Anerbieten *n.*
proficiency *s.* Können *n.;* Tüchtigkeit *f.*
proficient *a.* tüchtig, bewandert.
profile *s.* Seitenansicht *f.;* Profil *n.;* Porträt *n.; keep a low* ~, sich zurückhalten.
profit *s.* Gewinn *m.;* Vorteil *m.; at a* ~, mit Gewinn; ~ *and loss,* Gewinn und Verlust; ~ **sharing** *s.* Gewinnbeteiligung *f.;* ~ *v.t. & i.* Vorteil bringen; Nutzen ziehen; nutzen; Fortschritte machen.
profitability *s.* Rentabilität *f.*
profitable *a.,* **~bly** *adv.* einträglich.
profiteer *v.i.* sich bereichern; ~ *s.* Profitmacher(in) *m.(f.)*
profiteering *s.* Wucher *m.*
profit: **~-making** *a.* gewinnorientiert; ~ **margin** *s.* Gewinnspanne *f.,* ~ **sharing** *s.* Gewinnbeteiligung *f.*
profligacy *s.* Liederlichtkeit *f.*
profligate *a.,* **~ly** *adv.* ruchlos; liederlich; verschwenderisch.
profound *a.,* **~ly** *adv.* tief, dunkel; (*fig.*) gründlich.
profundity *s.* Tiefe *f.;* Ausmaß *n.*
profuse *a.,* **~ly** *adv.* verschwenderisch.
profusion *s.* Überfluß *m.*
progenitor *s.* Vorvater, Ahn *m.*
progeny *s.* Nachkommenschaft *f.*

prognosis *s.* Prognose *f.*, Vorhersage *f.*
prognosticate *v.t.* vorhersagen.
program(me) *s.* Programm *n.*
programmer *s.* Progammierer(in) *m.(f.)*
progress *s.* Fortschritt, Gang *m.; to be in ~*, im Gange sein; ~ *v.i.* fortschreiten.
progression *s.* Fortschritt *m.;* Zunahme *f.;* Progression *f.*
progressive *a.* fortschreitend; **~ly** *adv.* nach und nach.
progress report *s.* Tätigkeitsbericht *m.;* Lagebericht *m.*
prohibit *v.t.* verbieten, verhindern.
prohibition *s.* Verbot *n.;* Prohibition *f.*
prohibitive, prohibitory *a.* verbietend; ~ **duty** *s.* Sperrzoll *m.;* ~ **price** *s.* unerschwinglicher Preis *m.*
project *v.t.* entwerfen; ~ *v.i.* vorspringen; ~ *s.* Entwurf, Plan *m.;* Unternehmen *n.;* Aktion *f.*
projectile *a.* Wurf...; ~ *s.* Geschoß *n.*
projection *s.* Wurf *m.;* Entwurf, Riß *m.;* (*arch.*) Vorsprung *m.;* Projektion *f.;* **~room** *s.* Vorführraum *m.* (für Lichtbilder).
projectionist *s.* Filmvorführer(in) *m.(f.)*
projector *s.* Projektionsapparat *m.;* Projektor *m.*
proletarian *a.* proletarisch; Arbeiter...; ~ *s.* Proletarier(in) *m.(f.)*
proletariat *s.* Proletariat *n.*
proliferate *v.i.* sich stark vermehren; proliferieren.
proliferation *s.* starke Vermehrung *f.;* Proliferation *f.*
prolific *a.*, **~ally** *adv.* fruchtbar; produktiv.
prolix *a.*, **~ly** *adv.* weitläufig, langwierig.
prolixity *s.* Weitschweifigkeit *f.*
prolog *s.* Prolog *m.;* Eröffnungsrede *f.*
prolong *v.t.* verlängern; (*com.*) prolongieren.
prolongation *s.* Verlängerung *f.*
prolonged a lang; lang anhaltend.
promenade *s.* Spazierweg *m.;* Promenade *f.;* ~ *v.i.* spazieren(gehen).
prominence *s.* Bekanntheit *f.;* (Fels) Vorsprung *m.*
prominent *a.* hervorragend; vorspringend.
promiscuity *s.* Promiskuität *f.*
promiscuous *a.*, **~ly** *adv.* promiskuitiv.
promise *s.* Versprechen *n.;* ~ *v.t.* versprechen.
promising *a.* vielversprechend.
promontory *s.* Vorgebirge *n.*
promote *v.t.* befördern; fördern; werben für.
promoter *s.* Förderer *m.;* Förderin *f.;* Veranstalter(in) *m.(f.)*
promotion *s.* Beförderung *f.;* Förderung *f.;* (Schule) Versetzung *f.*
prompt *a.*, **~ly** *adv.* bereit; schnell; ~ *v.t.* vorsagen; anreizen; soufflieren.
prompt book *s.* Souffleurbuch *n.*
prompter *s.* Souffleur *m.*, Souffleuse *f.*
promptitude, promptness *s.* Pünklichtkeit *f.;* Schnelligkeit *f.*
promulgate *v.t.* verkünden; verbreiten.
prone *a.*, **~ly** *adv.* geneigt, hingestreckt.
prong *s.* Zinke *f.;* Spitze *f.;* Zacke *f.*
pronominal *s.* fürwörtlich; pronominal.
pronoun *s.* Fürwort *n.*
pronounce *v.t.* aussprechen; feierlich erklären.
pronounced *a.* ausgesprochen erklärt; ausgeprägt.
pronouncement *s.* Verlautbarung, Äusserung *f.;* (Urteils-) Verkündigung *f.*
pronunciation *s.* Aussprache f
proof *s.* Beweis *m.;* Probe *f.;* Korrekturbogen *m.; in ~ of*, zum Beweis von; *burden of ~*, Beweislast *f.; to furnish ~*, Beweis liefern; ~ *a.* undurchlässig; bewährt; fest; dicht.
proofread *v.t.* Korrektur lesen; **~er** *s.* Korrektor(in) *m.(f.)*
proofsheet *s.* Korrekturbogen *m.*
prop *s.* Stütze *f.*, Pfahl *m.;* Grubenklotz *m.;* Requisit *n.;* ~ *v.t.* stützen; *to ~ up*, aufstützen.
propaganda *s.* Propaganda *f.*
propagate *v.t.* fortpflanzen; ausbreiten; ~ *v.i.* sich fortpflanzen; sich vermehren.
propagation *s.* Vermehrung *f.;* Verbreitung *f.*
propel *v.t.* vorwärstreiben.
propeller *s.*, (Schiffs-, Luft-)Schraube *f.;* Propeller *m.;* **~blade** *s.* Luftschraubenblatt *n.;* **~hub** *s.* Propellernabe *f.;* **~shaft** *s.* Kardanwelle *f.*
propensity *s.* Neigung *f.;* Hang *m.*
proper *a.*, **~ly** *adv.* eigen, eigentümlich; schicklich; eigentlich; tauglich.
property *s.* Eigentum *n.;* Eigenschaft *f.;* (*chem.*) Eigenschaft *f.;* Vermögen *n.; ~ law*, Sachenrecht *n.*
prophecy *s.* Prophezeiung *f.;* Vorhersage *f.*
prophesy *v.t.* prophezeien; vorhersagen.
prophet *s.* Prophet *m.*
prophetess *s.* Prophetin *f.*
prophetic *a.*, **~ally** *adv.* prophetisch.
prophylactic *a.* vorbeugend; ~ *s.* Vorbeugungsmittel *n.*
propitiate *v.t.* versöhnen.
propitious *a.*, **~ly** *adv.* gnädig, günstig.
proponent *s.* Befürworter(in) *m.(f.);* Vorschlagende *m./f.*
proportion *s.* Verhältnis *n.;* Ebenmaß *n.;* Anteil *m.;* ~ *v.t.* ins Verhältnis bringen, anpassen; *inversely ~ed*, umgekehrt proportionell.
proportional *a.* verhältnismäßig, im Verhältnis stehend; *~ representation*, Verhältniswahl *f.*
proportionate *a.*, **~ly** *adv.* entsprechend, im Verhältnis.
proportioned *a.* proportioniert.
proposal *s.* Vorschlag *m.;* Angebot *n.;* Antrag *m.*
propose *v.t.* vorschlagen; sich vornehmen; ~ *v.i.* vorhaben; anhalten um.
proposition *s.* Vorschlag *m.;* Antrag *m.;* (*math.*) Satz *m.;* (*logic*) Aussage *f.*
propound *v.t.* darlegen; vortragen.
proprietary *a.* eigentümlich; gesetzlich geschützt; ~ **article** *s.* Markenartikel *m.;* ~ **right** *s.* Schutzrecht *n.;* ~ *s.* Eigentümer *m.pl.*
proprietor *s.* Eigentümer(in) *m.(f.);* Inhaber(in) *m.(f.)*
propriety *s.* Anstand *m.;* Richtigkeit *f.*
propulsion *s.* Antrieb *m.*
prorogation *s.* Vertagung *f.*
prorogue *v.t.* vertagen.
prosaic *a.* prosaisch.
proscribe *v.t.* ächten.
proscription *s.* Ächtung *f.;* Verbot *n.*
prose *s.* Prosa *f.*
prosecute *v.t.* verfolgen; verklagen.

prosecution *s.* Verfolgung, Anklage *f.; (jur.)* Anklagebehörde; **~ witness** *s.* Belastungszeuge *m.*
prosecutor *s.* Kläger(in) *m.(f.); public ~,* Staatsanwalt *m.*, Staatsanwaltin *f.*
proselyte *s.* Neubekehrte *m.*
prosody *s.* Prosodie *f.*
prospect *s.* Ansicht, Aussicht *f.; ~ v.i.* sich umschauen; schürfen.
prospective *a.* voraussichtlich; zukünftig; bevorstehend.
prospectus *s.* Prospekt *m.*
prosper *v.i.* gedeihen, gelingen; *~ v.t.* begünstigen; segnen.
prosperity *s.* Wohlstand *m.*, Glück *n.*
prosperous *a.*, **~ly** *adv.* glücklich, günstig.
prostitute *v.t.* prostituieren *~ s.* Dirne *f.;* Prostituierte *f.; male ~* Strichjunge *m.*
prostitution *s.* Prostitution *f.*
prostrate *a.* hingestreckt, ausgestreckt; *~ v.t.* niederwerfen.
prostration *a.* Niedergeschlagenheit *f.;* Fußfall *m.*
prosy *a.* langweilig, weitschweifig.
protect *v.t.* schützen, bewahren.
protection *s.* Schutz *m.;* Zollschutz *m.*
protective *a.* beschützend; *~ duty,* Schutzzoll *m.*
protector *s.* Beschützer(in) *m.(f.)*
protectorate *s.* Protektorat *n.*
protégé *s.* Protégé *m.;* Schützling *m.*
protein *s.* Eiweiß *n.;* Protein *n.*
protest *v.i. & t.* beteuren; sich verwahren, protestieren; zurückweisen; *~ s.* Protest *m.;* Gegenerklärung *f.*
Protestant *a.* protestantisch; *~ s.* Protestant(in) *m.(f.)*
Protestantism *s.* Protestantismus *m.*
protestation *s.* Beteurung *f.;* Protest *m.*
protester *s.* Protestierende *m.(f.);* Demonstrant(in) *m.(f.)*
protocol *s.* Protokoll *n.*
protoplasm *s.* Protoplasma *n.*
prototype *s.* Urbild, Muster *n.;* Prototyp *m.*
protract *v.t.* in die Länge ziehen; verschleppen.
protraction *s.* Verzögerung *f.*
protractor *s.* Winkelmesser *m.*
protruberance *s.* Auswuchs *m.;* Beule *f.*
protruberant *a.* (her)vorstehend.
protrude *v.i.* vordringen, hervorragen.
proud *a.*, **~ly** *adv.* stolz.
prove *v.t.* beweisen; *~ v.i.* sich bewähren, erweisen.
proven *a.* bewiesen.
proverb *s.* Sprichwort *n.*
proverbial *a.*, **~ly** *adv.* sprichwörtlich.
provide *v.t.* versehen; verschaffen, versorgen; festsetzen, bedingen, verordnen; *~ v.i.* sich vorsehen; sorgen für; *to ~ against,* unmöglich machen; *to be ~d for,* versorgt sein.
provided *c., ~ that,* vorausgesetzt daß.
providence *s.* Vorsehung *f.*
provident *a.*, **~ly** *adv.* vorsichtig; vorausblickend.
providential *a.*, **~ly** *adv.* schicksalhaft; glücklich.
provider *s.* Ernährer(in) *m.(f.);* Versorger(in) *m.(f.)*
province *s.* Gebiet *n.;* Provinz *f.*
provincial *a.* **~ly** *adv.* provinziell; Provinz...; Provinzler(in) *m.(f.)*
provision *s.* Vorsorge, Vorkehrung *f.;* Vorrat *m.;* Bestimmung *f.;* **~s** *pl.* Lebensmittel *n.pl.*, Proviant *m.;*
provisional *s.*, **~ly** *adv.* vorläufig; provisorisch.
proviso *s.* Vorbehalt *m.*
provocation *s.* Herausforderung *f.*
provocative *a.* aufreizend.
provoke *v.t.* herausfordern; provozieren.
provoking *a.*, **~ly** *adv.* empörend.
prow *s.* Bug *m.*, Vorderteil (eines Schiffes) *n.*
prowess s,. Tapferkeit *f.*
prowl *v.i.* umherstreichen.
proximity *s.* Nähe, Nachbarschaft *f.*
proxy *s.* Vollmacht *f.;* Stellvertretrer(in) *m.(f.);* Bevollmächtigte *m./f.; by ~,* in Vertretung, per procura.
prude *s.* prüder Mensch *m.*
prudence *s.* Klugheit *f.*, Vernunft *f.*
prudent *a.*, **~ly** *adv.* klug, vorsichtig.
prudential *a.* klug, Klugheits...
prudery *s.* Prüderie *f.*
prudish *a.* prüde.
prune *s.* Backpflaume *f.; ~ v.t.* (Bäume) beschneiden; putzen.
pruning shears *s.pl.* Gartenschere *f.*
prurience *s.* Lüsternheit *f.;* Geilheit *f.*
prurient *a.* lüstern.
Prussian blue *a.* preussischblau.
prussic acid *s.* Blausäure *f.*
pry *v.i.* spähen, ausforschen.
prying *a.* neugierig, naseweis.
P.S. *Postscript,* Nachschrift *f.*
psalm *s.* Psalm *m.*
pseudo *a.* Pseudo..., unecht.
pseudonym *s.* Deckname *m.;* Pseudonym *n.*
pshaw! *i.* pah!
psoriasis *s.* Schuppenflechte *f.*
psyche *s.* Psyche *f.*
psychiatric *a.* psychiatrisch.
psychiatrist *s.* Psychiater(in) *m.(f.)*
psychiatry *s.* Psychiatrie *f.*
psychic *a.* psychisch; übersinnlich.
psycho *a.* verrückt; *~ s.* Verrückte *m.(f.)*
psychoanalysis *s.* Psychoanalyse *f.*
psychoanalyst *s.* Psychoanalytiker(in) *m.(f.)*
psychoanalyze *v.t.* psychoanalysieren.
psychological *a.* psychologisch.
psychologist s,. Psychologe *m.;* Psychologin *f.*
psychology *s.* Psychologie *f.*
psychopath *s.* Psychopath(in) *m.(f.)*
psychopathic *a.* psychopathisch.
psychosis *s.* Psychose *f.*
psychosomatic *a.* psychosomatisch.
psychotherapist *s.* Psychotherapeut(in) *m.(f.)*
psychotherapy *s.* Psychotherapie *f.*
pt. *pint,* Pinte *f.; part,* Teil, T.; *payment,* Zahlung.
PTA *Parent-Teacher Association,* Eltern-Lehrer-Vereinigung.
P.T.O. *Please turn over,* bitte wenden.
pub *s.* Kneipe *f.*
puberty *s.* Entwicklungsalter *n.*, Pubertät *f.*
pubescent *a.* pubertär.
pubic *a.* Scham...

public *a.*, **~ly** *adv.* öffentlich, allgemein; Staats...; **~ relations** *pl.* Presse und Propaganda, Werbung *f.*; **~ utility** *s.* gemeinnütziges Unternehmen *n.*; ~ *s.* Publikum *n.*, Leute *pl.*
publication *s.* Bekanntmachung *f.*; Herausgabe *f.*; Veröffentlichung, Schrift *f.*; **~ price** *s.* Ladenpreis *m.*
public house *s.* Wirtshaus *n.*
publicity *s.* Öffentlichkeit *f.*; Reklame *f.*; **~ agent** *s.* Werbefachmann *m.*
publicize *v.t.* publizieren.
public library *s.* öffentliche Bücherei *f.*
public opinion *s.* öffentliche Meinung *f.*
publish *v.t.* herausgeben, verlegen.
publisher *s.* Verleger(in) *m.(f.)*; Herausgeber(in) *m.(f.)*
publishing *s.* Verlagswesen *n.*; **~ house** *s.* Verlag *m.*
pucker *v.t.* runzeln, falten ~ *v.i.* sich falten; ~ *s.* Falte *f.*
pudding *s.* Pudding *m.*
puddle *s.* Pfütze *f.*
puerile *a.* kindisch.
Puerto Rican *a.* puertoricanisch; ~ *s.* Puertoricaner(in) *m.(f.)*
Puerto Rico *s.* Puerto Rico *n.*
puff *s.* Windstoß *m.*; Hauch *m.*; Reklame *f.*; ~ *v.i.* blasen, schnauben; aufschwellen; ~ *v.t.* aufblasen; stolz machen; anpreisen.
puff pastry *s.* Blätterteig *m.*
puffy *a.* aufgebläht; schwülstig.
pug *s.* Mops *m.*
pugilist *s.* Boxer *m.*
pugnacious *a.* kampfsüchtig.
pugnacity *s.* Kampflust *f.*
puke *v.i.* (*vulg.*) kotzen; ~ *s.* Kotze *f.*
pule *v.i.* piepen; winseln.
pull *v.t.* ziehen; reißen; rudern; *~ through,* durchkommen; *~ up,* anhalten; ~ *s.* Zug, Ruck, Stoß *m.*
pullet *s.* Hühnchen *n.*
pulley *s.* Rolle *f.*, Flaschenzug *m.*
pullover *s.* Pullover *m.*
pulmonary *a.* Lungen...
pulp *s.* Brei *m.*; Zellstoff *m.*; Fleisch (vom Obst), Mark *n.*
pulpit *s.* Kanzel *f.*
pulsate *v.i.* pulsieren.
pulsation *s.* Pulsschlag *n.*
pulse *s.* Puls *m.*; Hülsenfrucht *f.*
pulverize *v.t.* pulverisieren; zu Staub machen.
pumice *s.* Bimsstein *m.*
pump *s.* Pumpe *f.* ~ *v.t.* & *i.* pumpen; (*fig.*) ausforschen.
pumpkin *s.* Kürbis *m.*
pun *s.* Wortspiel *n.*; ~ *v.i.* witzeln.
punch *s.* Stoß *m.*; Punze *f.*; Locheisen *n.*; Punsch *m.*; Hanswurst *m.*; *~ and Judy show,* Kasperletheater; ~ *v.t.* lochen; puffen, schlagen.
punching bag *s.* Sandsack *m.*
punch line *s.* Pointe *f.*
punchy *a.* doof; kräftig.
punctilio *s.* übertriebene Genauigkeit *f.*
punctilious *a.* ängstlich genau, spitzfindig.
punctual *a.*, **~ly** *adv.* pünktlich.
punctuality *s.* Pünktlichkeit *f.*
punctuate *v.t.* interpunktieren.
punctuation *s.* Interpunktion *f.*; Zeichensetzung *f.*; **~ mark** *s.* Satzzeichen *n.*
puncture *s.* Stich *m.*; Punktur *f.*; Loch *n.*, Reifenpanne *f.*; Punktion *f.*; ~ *v.t.* stechen.
pundit *s.* Experte *m.*; Expertin *f.*; Pandit, gelehrter Hindu *m.*
pungency *s.* Schärfe *f.*
pungent *a.*, **~ly** *adv.* stechend; scharf.
punish *v.t.* strafen, bestrafen.
punishable *a.* strafbar.
punishing *a.* vernichtend; mörderisch; zermürbend.
punishment *s.* Strafe, Bestrafung *f.*
punitive *a.* Straf...
punster *s.* Wortspieler *m.*
punt *s.* flacher Kahn *m.*, Schauke *f.*; ~ *v.i.* staken.
puny *a.* winzig; schwach.
pup *s.* junger Hund *m.*; *in ~*, trächtig (von Hunden).
pupa *s.* (*zool.*) Puppe *f.*
pupate *v.i.* sich verpuppen.
pupil *s.* Schüler *m.*; Mündel *n.*; Zögling *m.*; Pupille *f.*
puppet *s.* Puppe *f.*, Marionette *f.*
puppet show *s.* Puppenspiel *n.*
puppy *s.* junger Hund *m.*; Welpe *m.*
purchase *s.* Kauf *m.*; **~tax,** Verkaufssteuer *f.*; ~ *v.t.* kaufen; erwerben.
purchaser *s.* Käufer(in) *m.(f.)*
purchasing power Kaufkraft *f.*
pure *a.*, **~ly** *adv.* rein, echt; lauter.
purgation *s.* Reinigung *f.*
purgative *a.* reinigend; ~ *s.* Abführmittel *n.*
purgatory *s.* Fegefeuer *n.*
purge *v.t.* reinigen; läutern; abführen; ~ *s.* politische Säuberung *f.*
purification *s.* Reinigung.
purifier *s.* Reiniger *m.*
purify *v.t.* reinigen, klären.
purist *s.* Purist(in) *m.(f.)*
Puritan *s.* Puritaner(in) *m.(f.)*
puritanical *a.* puritanisch.
purity *s.* Reinheit, Keuschheit *f.*
purl *s.* Geriesel *n.*; Gekräusel *n.*; linke Masche *f.*; ~ *v.i.* rieseln.
purlieu *s.* Umgebung *f.*
purloin *v.t.* entwenden.
purple *s.* Purpur *m.*; ~ *a.* purpurn.
purport *s.* Inhalt *m.*; ~ *v.t.* zum Inhalt haben; scheinbar besagen; **~ed** *a.* angeblich.
purpose *s.* Absicht *f.*; Zweck *m.*; Inhalt *m.*; Tendenz *f.*; *on ~*, absichtlich; *to the ~*, zweckdienlich; *to no ~*, vergebens; ~ *v.t.* sich vornehmen.
purposeful *a.* entschlossen; zielstrebig.
purposeless *a.* zwecklos.
purposely *adv.* absichtlich.
purr *v.i.* schnurren.
purse *s.* Geldtäschchen *n.*; Börse *f.*; ~ *v.t.* rümpfen, runzeln; spitzen.
purser *s.* Zahlmeister(in) *m.(f.)*
pursuance *s.* Verfolgung *f.*, Verfolg *m.*; *in ~ of,* in Ausübung...
pursuant to *pr.* zufolge, gemäß.

pursue *v.t.* verfolgen; fortsetzen; fortfahren; (Beruf) betrieben.
pursuit *s.* Verfolgung *f.;* Trachten *n.;* **~s** *pl.* Geschäfte *n.pl.*
purulent *a.* eitrig.
purvey *v.t.* versorgen, liefern.
purveyor *s.* Lieferant(in) *m.(f.)*
purview *s.* Verfügung *f.;* Bereich *m.*
pus *s.* Eiter *m.*
push *v.t. & i.* stoßen, schieben; beschleunigen; **~** *s.* Stoß, Schub *m.*
pusher *s.* Dealer; Pusher; Streber(in) *m.(f.)*
pushing *a.* aufdringlich, streberhaft.
pusillanimity *s.* Kleinmut *m.*
pusillanimous *a.,* **~ly** *adv.* kleinmütig.
puss, pussy *s.* Mieze *f.;* Kätzchen *n.*
pustule *s.* Bläschen *n.*
put *v.t.ir.* setzen, stellen, legen; stecken; *to ~ by,* beiseitelegen; *to ~ down,* aufschreiben; *to ~ forward,* vorbringen; *to ~ in,* in den Hafen einlaufen; *to ~ into operation, effect,* ausführen; *to ~ on,* anlegen; aufsetzen; anziehen; umbinden; (*fig.*) annehmen, erheucheln; *to ~ on weight,* zunehmen; *to ~ off,* weglegen, hinhalten, aufschieben; *to ~ out,* auslöschen; ärgern; ausfahren (Flotte); ausstrecken; *to ~ to,* hinzufügen; anspannen; *to ~ together,* zusammenstellen; *to ~ up,* aufstellen, errichten, aufschlagen (Bett), einsetzen (Pflanze), heraufsetzen (Preis), verpacken; unterbringen; absteigen, einkehren; *to ~ up for sale,* meistbietend verkaufen; *to ~ up with,* sich abfinden mit; *~-up job,* abgekartete Sache *f.; to ~ through to,* (*tel.*) Verbindung herstellen mit.
putative *a.* vermeintlich; mutmaßlich.
putrefaction *s.* Zersetzung *f.;* Fäulnis *f.*
putrefy *v.i.* verfaulen; faul werden.
putrescent *a.* faulend.
putrid *a.* faul, verfault.
putty *s.* Kitt *m.* Glaserkitt *m.*
put-up job *s.* abgedartetes Spiel *n.*
puzzle *v.t.* verwirren, in Verlegenheit bringen **~** *s.* Verwirrung *f.;* Rätsel *n.;* Puzzle *n.*
puzzled *n.* ratlos.
puzzlement *s.* Verwirrung *f.*
puzzling *s.* rätselhaft.
Pvt. *private,* Gemeiner Soldat.
pygmy *s.* Zwerg(in) *m.(f.);* Pygmäe *m.,* Pygmäin *f.*
pyjamas *s.pl.* Schlafanzug *m.;* Pyjama *m.*
pylon *s.* Mast *m.*
pyramid *s.* Pyramide *f.*
pyre *s.* Scheiterhaufen *m.*
Pyrenees *s.pl.* Pyrenäen *pl.*
pyromania *s.* Pyromanie *f.*
pyromaniac *a.* Pyromane *m.;* Pyromanin *f.*
pyrotechnics *s.pl.* Feuerwerkskunst *f.*
Pyrrhic victory *s.* Pyrrhussieg *m.*
python *s.* Python *f.*
pyx *s.* Pyxis *f.;* Hostienbehälter *m.*
Q, q der Buchstabe Q oder q *n.*
qr. *quarter,* Viertel.
qt. *quart,* Quart.
qto. *quarto,* Quartformat *n.*
quack *v.i.* quacken; *~ v.t.* marktschreierisch anpreisen; **~** *s.* Quacksalber *m.;* Marktschreier *m.*
quackery *s.* Quacksalberei *f.*
quad *s.* Vierling *m.;* viereckiger Innenhof *m.*
quadrangle *s.* Viereck *n.;* Hof *m.*
quadraphonic *a.* quadrophon(isch).
quadratic *a.* quadratisch.
quadrilateral *a.* vierseitig.
quadrille *s.* Quadrille *f.;* Kontretanz *m.*
quadripartite *a.* Viermächte...
quadruped *a.* vierfüßig; **~** *s.* Vierfüßer *m.*
quadruple *a.,* **~ply** *adv.* vierfach; **~** *s.* Vierfache *n.;* **~** *v.t.* vervierfachen.
quadruplets *pl.* Vierlinge *pl.*
quaff *v.i. & t.* zechen.
quagmire *s.* Sumpf, Moorboden *m.;* Morast *m.*
quail *s.* Wachtel *f.;* **~** *v.i.* verzagen.
quaint *a.,* **~ly** *adv.* seltsam; niedlich.
quake *v.i.* zittern, beben.
Quaker *s.* Quäker(in) *m.(f.)*
qualification *s.* Eigenschaft *f.;* Befähigung *f.;* Beschränkung *f.*
qualified *a.* geeignet; qualifiziert; berechtigt; bestimmt; bedingt, eingeschränkt.
qualify *v.t.* befähigen; einschränken; bestimmen; **~** *v.i.* seine Befähigung nachweisen; *to ~ for,* Befähigung erwerben für; *~ing date,* Stichtag *m.; ~ing match s.* Qualifikationspiel *n.; ~ing period,* Probezeit *f.*
qualitative *a.* qualitativ.
quality *s.* Eigenschaft, Beschaffenheit *f.;* Qualität *f.;* (hoher) Stand, Rang *m.*
qualm *s.* Bedenken *pl.;* Zweifel *pl.*
quandary *s.* Dilemma *n.;* Ungewißheit *f.;* Verlegenheit *f.*
quantify *v.t.* quantifizieren.
quantitative *a.* der Menge nach.
quantity *s.* Menge, Anzahl *f.;* (*math.*) Grösse *f.;* Quantität *f.*
quantum *s.* Menge, Grösse *f.;* Betrag *m.;* Quant *n.*
quantum leap *s.* Quantensprung *m.*
quarantine *s.* Liegezeit, Quarantäne *f.*
quarrel *s.* Zank *m.;* Streit *m.;* **~** *v.i.* sich zanken, streiten.
quarrelsome *a.,* **~ly** *adv.* zänkisch.
quarry *s.* Steinbruch *m.;* verfolgtes Wild *n.;* Beute *f.* **~** *v.t.* Steine brechen.
quart *s.* Viertelmaß *n.*
quarter *s.* Viertel *n.;* Stadviertel *n.;* Vierteljahr *n.;* Wohnung *f.;* Quartier *n.;* **~s** *pl.* (*mil.*) Unterkunft *f.;* **~** *v.t.* vierteilen; beherbergen; einquartieren.
quarterdeck *s.* Achterdeck, Halbdeck *n.*
quarterly *a. & adv.* vierteljährlich; **~** *s.* Vierteljahrsschrift *f.*
quartermaster *s.* Quartiermeister *m.*
quarter note *s.* Viertelnote *f.*
quartet(te) *s.* Quartett *n.*
quarto *s.* Quartformat *n.;* Quartband *m.*
quartz *s.* Quarz *m.*
quasar *s.* Quasar *m.*
quash *v.t.* unterdrücken; vernichten; (Urteil) aufheben.
quasi *a. & adv.* gewissermaßen, Halb..., scheinbar.
quaver *v.i.* zittern; trillern; **~** *s.* (*mus.*) Tremolo *n.;* Achtelnote *f.*
quay *s.* Kai *m.*
queasy *a.* übel, unwohl; überempfindlich.

queen *s.* Königin *f.*
queen bee *s.* Bienenkönigin *f.*
queer *a.*, **~ly** *adv.* wunderlich, seltsam; verdächtig; unwohl, schwindlig.
quell *v.t.* dämpfen; unterdrücken; zügeln.
quench *v.t.* löschen; (den Durst) stillen.
querulous *a.*, **~ly** *adv.* reizbar; gereizt.
query *s.* Frage *f.*; ~ *v.t.* fragen, bezweifeln.
quest *s.* Suchen *n.*; Suche *f.*; Untersuchung *f.*; *in ~ of,* auf der Suche nach.
question *s.* Frage *f.*; Streitfrage *f.*; Untersuchung *f.*; Zweifel *m.*; *in ~,* fraglich, vorliegend; *~!,* zur Sache!; ~ *v.i.& t.* fragen, befragen; verhören, vernehmen; bezwiefeln.
questionable *a.* zweifelhaft, fraglich; fragwürdig.
questioning *a.* fragend; ~ *s.* Fragen *n.*; Befragung *f.*; Vernehmung *f.*
question mark *s.* Fragezeichen *n.*
questionnaire *s.* Fragebogen *m.*
queue *s.* Zopf *m.*; Schlange (von Menschen).
quibble *s.* Wortspiel *n.*; Zweideutigkeit *f.*; Ausflucht *f.*; ~ *v.i.* (spitzfindig) witzeln; ausweichen.
quick *a. & adv.*, **~ly** *adv.* schnell; lebendig; lebhaft; hurtig; scharfsinnig; **~-acting** *a.* schnellwirkend; *~ march!,* vorwärts marsch!; *~ step,* Geschwindschritt *m.*
quicken *v.t.* beleben, beschleunigen; ~ *v.i.* lebendig werden.
quicklime *s.* ungelöschter Kalk *m.*
quickness *s.* Schnelligkeit *f.*; Schärfe *f.*
quicksand *s.* Treibsand *m.*
quicksilver *s.* Quecksilber *n.*
quick-tempered *a.* hitzig.
quick-witted *a.* geistesgegenwärtig.
quid *s.* Priemchen *n.*
quid-pro-quo *s.* Gegenleistung *f.*
quiescence *s.* Ruhe *f.*
quiescent *a.* ruhend.
quiet *a.*, **~ly** *adv.* ruhig, gelassen; still, leise; ~ *s.* Ruhe *f.*; ~ *v.t.* beruhigen.
quieten *v.t.* beruhigen.
quill *s.* Federkiel *m.*; Feder *f.*
quilt *s.* Steppdecke *f.*; ~ *v.t.* steppen.
quince *s.* Quitte *f.*
quinine *s.* Chinin *n.*
quinsy *s.* Bräune (Halskrankheit) *f.*
quint *s.* Quinte *f.*
quintessence *s.* Quintessenz *f.*
quintet(te) *s.* Quintett *n.*
quintuple *a.* fünffach.
quintuplets *s.pl.* Fünflinge *pl.*
quip *s.* Stichelei *f.*; Witzelei *f.*; ~ *v.i.* sticheln, witzeln.
quirk *s.* Stichelei *f.*; Kniff *m.*; Schnörkel *m.*
quit *a.* quitt, los, frei; ~ *v.t.* verlassen; lossprechen; fahren lassen; *notice to ~,* Kündigung *f.*
quite *adv.* völlig, gänzlich.
quits *adv.* quitt, abgemacht.
quiver *s.* Köcher *m.*; ~ *v.i.* zittern.
quixotic *a.* donquichottisch.
quiz *v.t.* ausfragen; ~ *s.* Examen *n.*; Quiz *n.*
quoin *s.* Ecke (eines Hauses) *f.*; Keil *(m.)* des Setzers
quoit *s.* Wurfring *m.* (Spiel).
quondam *adv.* ehemalig.
quorum *s.* beschlußfähige Anzahl *f.*
quot. *quotation,* Kurs-Preisnotierung.
quota *s.* Anteil *m.*, Quote *f.*; Zuteilung *f.*; Kontingent *n.*
quotation *s.* Anführung *f.*; Zitat *n.*; Preisangabe *f.*; Notierung *f.*; ~ **marks** *pl.* Anführungszeichen *n.*
quote *v.t.* (Stellen) anführen; zitieren; (einen Preis) notieren, berechnen.
quotient *s.* Quotient, Teilzähler *m.*

R

R, r der Buchstabe R oder r *n.*
r. *right,* rechts, r.
rabbet *s.* Fuge *f.*; Falz *m.*; Nuthobel *m.*; ~ *v.t.* einfugen; abhobeln.
rabbi *s.* Rabbiner *m.*
rabbit *s.* Kaninchen *n.*
rabbit hutch *s.* Kaninchenstall *m.*
rabbit punch *s.* Genickschlag *m.*
rabble *s.* Pöbel, Mob *m.*
rabid *a.* wütend, rasend.
rabies *s.* Tollwut *f.*
racapitulation *s.* Zusammenfassung *f.*
race *s.* Rasse *f.*, Geschlecht *n.*; Wettlauf *m.*; Rennen *n.*; **~s** *pl.* Pferderennen *n.*; ~ *v.i.* wettrennen.
race course *s.* Rennbahn *f.*
race meeting *s.* Rennen *n.*
race track *s.* Rennstrecke *f.*
racial *a.*, **~ly** *adv.* rassisch, völkisch; Rassen...
racism *s.* Rassismus *m.*
racist *s.* Rassist(in) *m.(f.)*; ~ *a.* rassistisch.
rack *s.* Foltenbank *f.*; Raufe *f.*; *luggage ~,* Gepäcknetz *n.*; Gestell *n.*; *~ and ruin,* gänzlich zu Grunde; ~ *v.t.* strecken, foltern; *to ~ one's brains,* sich den Kopf zerbrechen.
racket *s.* Schläger *m.* (Sport); Lärm *m.*; Erpressung, Schiebung *f.*
racketeer *s.* Scheiber *m.*; Wucherer *m.*
racking *a.* quälend.
racoon *s.* Waschbär *m.*
racy *a.* rassig; flott.
radar *s.* (*mil.*) Funkmeßgerät *n.*
radial *a.*, **~ly** *adv.* strahlenförmig; Radial...
radiance *s.* Glanz *m.*; Strahlen *n.*
radiant *a.* strahlend.
radiate *v.t. & i.* ausstrahlen, strahlen.
radiation *s.* Ausstrahlung *f.*
radiator *s.* Heizkörper *m.*; (*mot.*) Kühler *m.*
radical *a.*, **~ly** *adv.* Grund...; eingewurzelt; radikal; ~ *s.* Wurzel *f.*, Grundstoff *m.*; Radikale *m.*
radio *s.* Radio *n.*, Funk *m.*; **~active** *a.* radioaktiv; **~activity** *s.* Radioaktivität *f.*, **~carbon dating** *s.* Radiokarbondatierung *f.*; **~graphy** *s.* Radiographie *f.*; **~logy** *s.* Radiologie *f.*; **~operator** *s.* Funker, Bordfunker *m.*; **~set** *s.* Radioapparat *m.*; **~station** *s.* Rundfunksender *m.*
radiotherapy Radiotherapie *f.*, Strahlentherapie *f.*

radish *s.* Radieschen *n.;* Rettich *m.*
radium *s.* Radium *n.*
radius *s.* Halbmesser *m.;* Strahl *m.;* Umkreis *m.*
radon *s.* Radon *n.*
raffia *s.* Raffiabast m.
raffle *s.* Lotterie *f.;* Tombola *f.;* ~ *v.i.* verlosen.
raft *s.* Floß *n.*
rafter *s.* Dachsparren *m.*
rag *s.* Lumpfen *m.;* Ulk *m.;* ~ *v.t.* necken.
ragamuffin *s.* Lumpenkerl *m.*
rage *s.* Wut, Raserei *f.;* Entzückung *f.;* ~ *v.i.* rasen.
ragged *a.* zerlumpt; rauh.
ragout *s.* Ragout *n.*
raid *s.* Überfall *m.;* Beutezug *m.*
raider *s.* Plünderer *m.;* Plünderin *f.;* Räuber(in) *m.(f.)*
rail *s.* Riegel *m.;* Querholz *n.;* Geländer *n.;* Schiene *f.;* (*nav.*) Reling *f.; by* ~, mit der Eisenbahn; ~ *v.t.* mit einem Gitter versehen; ~ *v.i.* schimpfen.
railing *s.* Geländer *n.;* Zaun *m.*
raillery *s.* Spöttelei *f.*
railway, railroad *s.* Eisenbahn *f.;* **~network** *s.* Eisenbahnnetz *n.;* **~shop** *s.* Eisenbahnwerkstatt *f.*
railway guide *s.* Kursbuch *n.*
raiment *s.* Kleidung *f.*
rain *s.* Regen *m.;* ~ *v.i. imp.* regen; **~coat** *s.* Regenmantel *m.;* **~fall** *s.* Niederschlagsmenge *f.;* **~soaked** *a.* vom Regen durchnäßt; **~storm** *s.* Regenguß *m.;* **~wear** *s.* Regenkleidung *f.*
rainbow *s.* Regenbogen *m.*
rainforest *s.* Regenwald *m.*
rain gauge *s.* Regenmesser *m.*
rainproof *a.* wasserdicht.
rainy *a.* regnerisch, Regen...; *for a* ~ *day,* für eine Notzeit.
raise *v.t.* aufheben, erheben; errichten; erhöhen; erregen, veranlassen; aufziehen; werben; auftreiben (Geld); ~ *s.* Lohnerhöhung *f.*
raisin *s.* Rosine *f.*
rake *s.* Rechen *m.;* Wüstling *m.;* ~ *v.t.* harken; zusammenschüren, scharren; durchstöbern;
rakish *a.*, **~ly** *adv.* flott, keß.
rally *v.t.* wieder sammeln; aufmuntern ~ *v.i.* sich wieder sammeln; sich erholen; ~ *s.* Sammlung *f.;* Tagung, Treffen, Versammlung *f.;* (Autosport) Sternfahrt *f.*
ram *s.* Widder *m.;* Schafbock *m.;* ~ *v.t.* einrammen.
RAM *random access memory,* Direktzugriffsspeicher.
ramble *v.i.* umherschweifen; abschweifen; ~ *s.* Ausflug *m.*
rambler *s.* Wanderer *m.;* Wanderin *f.*
rambling *a.* zusammenhanglos; (von Gebäuden) unregelmäßig.; verwinkelt- ~ **rose** *s.* Kletterrose *f.*
ramification *s.* Verzweigung *f.;* Auswirkungen *pl.*
ramify *v.t.* & *i.* (sich) verzweigen.
ramp *v.i.* sich drohend aufrichten (vom Tier); toben; ~ *s.* Rampe; Schwindelei *f.*
rampage *v.i.* randalieren, wüten; *go on a* ~, Randale *(f.)* machen.
rampant *a.* dreist; überhandnehmend; wuchernd; ansteigend.
rampart *s.* Wall *m.;* Wehrgang *m.*
ramshackle *a.* wack[e]lig, baufällig.
ranch *s.* Farm *f.*
rancid *a.* ranzig.
rancidity *s.* Ranzigkeit *f.*
rancor *s.* Groll *m.;* Erbitterung *f.*
rancorous *a.*, **~ly** *adv.* voller Groll, erbittert.
random *a.* zufällig, Zufalls...; willkürlich; *at* ~, aufs Geradewohl, ins Blaue.
randy *a.* (*fam.*) scharf, geil.
range *s.* Reihe *f.;* Ordnung *f.;* Küchenherd *m.;* Umfang *m.;* Bereich *m.;* Spielraum *m.;* Schußweite *f.;* ~ *of prices,* Prieslage *f.;* ~ *v.i.* sich reihen; herumstreifen; sich erstrecken; ~ *v.t.* ordnen; schweifen über.
rangefinder *s.* (*phot.*) Entfernungsmesser *m.*
ranger *s.* Aufseher(in) *m.(f.);* Förster(in) *m.(f.)*
rank *s.* Reihe *f.;* Linie *f.;* Glied *n.;* Rang *m.; to serve in the* ~*s,* (*mil.*) als gemeiner Soldat dienen; ~ *v.t.* & *i.* reihen, sich reihen; zugehören; *it* ~*s third,* es steht an dritter Stelle; ~ *a.*, **~ly** *adv.* üppig, übermäßig; ranzig; arg.
rankle *v.i.* sich entzünden; schmerzen; (*fig.*) nagen.
ransack *v.t.* plündern; durchstöbern.
ransom *s.* Lösegeld *n.;* ~ *v.t.* loskaufen.
rant *s.* schwülstige Gerede *n.* ~ *v.i.* schwülstig reden; eifern; wüten.
ranter *s.* Großsprecher *m.*
rap *v.t.* & *i.* schlagen, klopfen;- ~ *s.* Schlag *m.;* Klopfen *n.;* Nasenstüber *m.*
rapacious *a.*, **~ly** *adv.* habgierig.
rapacity *s.* Habgier *f.*
rape *s.* Notzucht *f.;* Vergewaltigung *f.;* ~ *v.i.* vergewaltigen, notzüchtigen.
rapid *a.*, **~ly** *adv.* schnell, reißend; **~s** *s.pl.* Stromschnellen *f.pl.*
rapidity *s.* Schnelligkeit *f.*
rapier *s.* Rapier *n.*
rapine *s.* Raub *m.*
rapist *s.* Vergewaltiger *m.*
rapport *s.* (harmonisches) Verhältnis *n.*
rapt *a.* hingerissen, entzückt.
rapture *s.* Entzückung *f.;* Verzückung *f.*
rapturous *a.* hinreißend; leidenschaftlich.
rare *a.*, **~ly** *adv.* selten; kostbar; dünn; nicht durchgebraten, englisch gebraten.
rarefied *a.* dünn; exklusiv.
rarefy *v.t.* verdünnen.
rareness, rarity *s.* Seltenheit *f.;* Dünnheit *f.*
raring *a.* (*fam.*) *to be* ~ *to go,* kaum abwarten können.
rascal *s.* Schurke *m.;* Schlingel *m.*
rascality *s.* Schurkerei *f.*
rash *a.*, **~ly** *adv.* übereilt, unbesonnen; ~ *s.* Hautausschlag *m.*
rasher *s.* Scheibe (Speck) *f.*
rasp *v.t.* raspeln; wehtun; ~ *s.* Raspel *f.*
raspberry *s.* Himbeere *f.*
rasping *a.* krächzend; rasselnd.
rat *s.* Ratte *f.;* Spitzel *m.*
rate *s.* Preis *m.;* Taxe *f.;* Anteil *m.*, Satz *m.*, Rate (statistisch) *f.;* bestimmtes Maß *n.;* Verhältnis *n.;* Grad, Rang *m.;* Klasse *f.; at any* ~, auf jeden Fall; ~ *v.t.* schätzen, einschätzen; tadeln; ~ *v.t.* rangieren, einen bestimmten Wert haben; *to* ~ *highly,* einen hohen Wert haben.

rather *adv.* vielmehr, lieber; ziemlich; *I had* ~, ich wollte lieber.

ratification *s.* Bestätigung *f.*; Ratifizierung *f.*

ratify *v.t.* bestätigen, ratifizieren.

rating *s.* Einschätzung *f.*; Einschaltquote *f.*; Dienstgrad *m.*

ratio *s.* Verhältnis *n.*

ration *s.* Ration *f.*, Zuteilung; ~**book** *s.* Lebensmittelkarten *pl.*; ~ *v.t.* rationieren; ~*ing,* Rationierung *f.*

rational *a.*, ~**ly** *adv.* vernünftig; rational.

rationale *s.* rationale Erklärung *f.*; logische Grundlage *f.*

rationalization *s.* Rationalisierung *f.*

rationalize *v.t.* rationalisieren.

rattle *s.* Geklapper *n.*; Knarre *f.*; Geschnatter *n.*; Röcheln *n.*; ~ *v.t. & i.* rasseln; knarren; plappern.

rattlesnake *s.* Klapperschlange *f.*

rattling *a.* rasselnd; klappernd.

ratty *a.* (*fig.*) schäbig; verkommen, abgenutzt.

raucous *a.* heiser, rauh.

ravage *v.t.* verwüsten, verheeren; ~ *s.* Verwüstung *f.*

rave *v.i.* rasen, wüten; schwärmen.

ravel *v.t.* verwickeln; ~ **out** ausfasern; ~ *v.i.* ~ **out** sich auffasern, sich entwirren.

raven *s.* Rabe *m.*

ravenous *a.*, ~**ly** *adv.* gefräßig; gierig.

ravine *s.* Schlucht *f.*

raving *a.*, ~**ly** *adv.* rasend; faselnd; (*fam.*) phantastisch.

ravish *v.t.* hinreißen, entzücken.

ravishing *a.* hinreißend.

ravishment *s.* Entzückung *f.*

raw *a.*, ~**ly** *adv.* roh; unreif; rauh; neu, unerfahren; wund; unverdünnt (von Spirituosen).

raw material *s.* Rohmaterial *n.*

ray *s.* Strahl *m.*; Rochen *m.*; ~ *v.t.* strahlen.

rayon *s.* Kunstseide *f.*

raze *v.t.* schleifen, zerstören; niederreißen.

razor *s.* Rasiermesser *n.*; Rasierapparat *m.*; Rasierer *m.*

razor blade *s.* Rasierklinge *f.*

razor edge *s.* Rasierschneide *f.*; *be on the* ~, auf des Messers Schneide stehen.

razor strop *s.* Streichriemen *m.*

razzia *s.* Razzia *f.*

RC *Roman Catholic,* römisch-katholisch, r.-k.

rcpt. *receipt,* Quittung *f.*

Rd *Road,* Straße, Str.

re *pr.* betreffend.

reach *v.t.* reichen, langen; erreichen; ~ *v.i.* sich erstrecken; streben; ~ *s.* Reichweite *f.*; Strecke *f.*; Flußabschnitt, Strombaschnitt *m.*; Raum, Bereich *m.*; Hörweite, Schußweite *f.*; Fassungskraft *f.*

reachable *a.* erreichbar.

react *v.i.* rückwirken, gegenwirken; (*chem.*) reagieren.

reaction *s.* Rückwirkung *f.*; Reaktion *f.*; (*elek.*) Rückkopplung *s.*

reactionary *a.* reaktionär; ~ *s.* Reaktionär(in) *m.(f.)*

reactor *s.* (nuclear) Kernreaktor *m.*

read *v.t. & i.ir.* lesen, vorlesen; sich lesen, lauten, klingen; anzeigen (von Meßapparaten).

readable *a.* lesbar.

readdress *v.t.* umadressieren.

reader *s.* Leser(in) *m.(f.)*; Vorleser(in) *m.(f.)*; Lektor(in) *m.(f.)*

readership *s.* Leserschaft *f.*; Leserkreis *m.*

readiness *s.* Bereitwilligkeit *f.*

reading *s.* Lektüre *f.*; Belesenheit *f.*; Lesart *f.*; Stand *m.*, Ablesung *f.* (eines Meßapparates).

reading glasses *s.pl.* Lesebrille *f.*

reading knowledge *s.* Leseverstehen *n.*

reading list *s.* Leseliste *f.*

reading room *s.* Lesezimmer *n.*

readjust *v.i.* sich umstellen; ~ *v.t.* einstellen.

readmission *s.* Wiederzulassung *f.*

readmit *v.t.* wieder zulassen.

ready *a.*, ~**ily** *adv.* bereit; fertig.

ready-made *a.* gebrauchsfertig; konfektions... **ready-to-serve** *a.* servierfertig; **ready-to-wear** *a.* Konfektions...

reaffirm *v.t.* bestätigen bekräftigen.

reagent *s.* Reagens *n.*

real *a.*, ~**ly** *adv.* echt (auch Perle, Diamant, etc.); in der Tat, wesentlich, wirklich.

real estate *s.* Grundbesitz; ~ **register** *s.* Grundbuch *n.*

realism *s.* Realismus *m.*

reality *s.* Wirklichkeit, Wesenheit *f.*

realization *s.* Verwirklichung *f.*; Verwertung *f.*

realize *v.t.* verwirklichen; erzielen; sich vorstellen; zu Geld machen.

real life *s.* wirkliches Leben *n.*

really *adv.* wirklich, in der Tat.

realm *s.* Königreich, Reich *n.*

realty *s.* Grundbesitz *m.*

ream *s.* Ries (Papier) *n.*; ~ *v.t.* (*mech.*) ausweiten, ausbohren.

reamer *s.* (*mech.*) Ausbohrwerkzeug *n.*, Aufräumer *m.*

reanimate *v.t.* wieder beleben.

reap *v.t. & i.* Korn schneiden; einernten.

reaper *s.* Schnitter *m.*; Mähmaschine *f.*

reappear *v.i.* wieder erscheinen, auftauchen.

reappearance *s.* Wiedererscheinen *n.*; Wiederauftauchen *n.*

reappraisal *s.* Neubewertung *f.*

reappraise *v.t.* bewerten.

rear *s.* hinterer Teil *m.*; Rückseite *f.* Hintergrund *m.*; Hinter... (*mil.*) rückwärtig; ~ **area** *s.* rückwärtiges Heeresgebiet *n.*; ~ **cover** *s.* Rücken deckung *f.*; ~ **light** *s.* (*mot. und cycling*) Schlußlicht, Katzenauge *n.*; ~ **wheel** *s.* Hinterrad *n.*; ~ *v.t.* heben; erziehen, aufziehen; ~ *v.i.* sich aufbäumen.

rear guard *s.* Nachhut *f.*

rearm *v.i.* wieder aufrüsten.

rearmament *s.* Aufrüstung *f.*

rearrange *v.t.* umräumen; verlegen (Termin).

rearrangement *s.* Umräumen *n.*; Verlegen *n.*

reason *s.* Vernunft *f.*; Ursache *f.*; Grund *m.*; *it stands to* ~, es ist klar; ~ *v.i.* schließen; nachdenken; streiten; ~ *v.t.* durchdenken; erörtern.

reasonable *a.*, ~**ly** *adv.* vernünftig; billig; ziemlich; ~ *prices,* mäßige Preise *pl.*

reasoned *a.* durchdacht.

reasoning *s.* Urteilskraft, Beweisführung *f.*; *line of* ~, Gedankengang *m.*

reassemble *v.t. & i.* (sich) wieder versammeln, zusammenbauen.
reassurance *s.* Bestätigung *f.*; Beruhigung *f.*
reassure *v.t.* beruhigen; bestätigen.
reassuring *a.* beruhigend.
rebate *s.* Rabatt *m.*, Abzug *m.*
rebel *v.i.* sich empören; ~ *s.* Rebell, Empörer *m.*
rebellion *s.* Aufstand *m.*, Empörung *f.*
rebellious *a.*, **-ly** *adv.* aufrührerisch; rebellisch.
rebirth *s.* Wiedergeburt *f.*
reborn *a.* wiedergeboren.
rebound *v.i.* zurückprallen; abprallen.
rebuff *s.* Rückstoß *m.*; Abweisung *f.*; ~ *v.t.* zurückstoßen; abweisen.
rebuild *v.t.st.* wieder aufbauen; umbauen.
rebuke *v.t.* tadeln; auszanken; ~ *s.* Tadel, Verweis *m.*
rebut *v.t.* widerlegen, zurückweisen.
rebuttal *s.* Widerlegung *f.*, Gegenbeweis *m.*
recalcitrant *a.* widerstrebend, störrig.
recall *s.* Zurückberufung *f.*; Widerruf *m.*; ~ *v.t.* zurückrufen; sich erinnern; kündigen.
recant *v.t. & i.* widerrufen.
recantation *s.* Widerruf *m.*
recapitulate *v.t.* kurz wiederholen.
recapture *s.* Wiederergreifung *f.*; Zurückeroberung *f.*; ~ *v.t.* wieder ergreifen; zurückerobern.
recast *v.t.* umschmelzen; umarbeiten; umformen.
recd. *received,* erhalten, erh.
recede *v.i.* zurückweichen; schwinden.
receding *a.* fliehend (Kinn, Stirn); zurückgehend.
receipt *s.* Empfang *m.*; Entgegennahme *f.*; Einnahme *f.*; Quittung *f.*; Aufnahme *f.*; Rezept *n.*; ~ *v.t. & i.* quittieren.
receive *v.t.* empfangen, annehmen.
receiver *s.* Empfänger *m.* (auch Radio); (*tel.*) Hörer *m.*; Einnehmer *m.*; ~ *of stolen goods,* Hehler *m.*; *official* ~, Konkursverwalter *m.*
recent *a.* neu; frisch; **-ly** *adv.* neulich.
receptacle *s.* Behälter *m.*
reception *s.* Aufnahme *f.*; Empfang *m.*
receptionist *s.* Empfangsdame *f.*; Empfangschef *m.*; Sprechstundenhilfe *f.*
receptive *a.* empfänglich.
recess *s.* Falte *f.*; Nische *f.*; Einbuchtung *f.*; Versteck *m.*; Pause *f.*; Ferien *pl.*; zeitweilige Unterbrechung (einer Sitzung) *f.*; ~ *v.i.* unterbrechen, sich vertagen.
recession *s.* Zurückweichen *n.*; Rezession *f.*
recharge *v.t.* aufladen; nachladen.
rechargeable *a.* wiederaufladbar.
recipe *s.* Rezept *n.*
recipient *s.* Empfänger(in) *m.(f.)*
reciprocal *a.*, **-ly** *adv.* wechselseitig.
reciprocate *v.t. & i.* abwechseln; erwidern.
reciprocity *s.* Gegenseitigkeit *f.*
recital, recitation *s.* Vortrag *m.*; Musikvortrag *m.*; Hersagen *n.*; Erzählung *f.*
recitation *s.* Rezitation *f.*
recite *v.t.* vortragen; hersagen.
reckless *a.* unbekümmert, tollkühn; rücksichtslos.
recklessness *s.* Rücksichtslosigkeit *f.*
reckon *v.t. & i.* rechnen, schätzen, achten; meinen; *to* ~ *up,* zusammenrechnen.
reckoning Rechnen *n.*; Rechnung *f.*; Berechnung *f.*
reclaim *v.t.* zurückfordern; bekehren; (Land) gewinnen.
reclamation *s.* Zurückforderung *f.*; Urbarmachung *f.*
recline *v.t. & i.* (sich) (zurück)lehnen.
recluse *s.* Einsiedler(in) *m.(f.)*
reclusive *a.* zurückgezogen.
recognition *s.* Wiedererkennen *n.*; Anerkennung *f.*
recognizable *a.* erkennbar.
recognizance *s.* schriftliche Verpflichtung *f.* (vor Gericht).
recognize *v.t.* erkennen; anerkennen.
recoil *v.i.* zurückprallen; zurückschrecken; ~ *s.* Rückstoß *m.*
recollect *v.i.* sich besinnen, sich erinnern.
recollection *s.* Erinnerung *f.*; Gedächtnis *n.*
recommend *v.t.* empfehlen.
recommendation *s.* Empfehlung *f.*
recompense *v.t.* vergelten; entschädigen; belohnen; ~ *s.* Vergeltung *f.*; Belohnung *f.*; Anerkennung *f.*
reconcilable *a.* versöhnbar; vereinbar.
reconcile *v.t.* versöhnen; vereinigen.
reconciliation *s.* Versöhnung *f.*
recondite *a.* verborgen; unverständlich.
recondition *v.t.* neu instandsetzen, überholen.
reconnaissance *s.* (*mil.*) Aufklärung *f.*; *close* ~, Nahaufklärung *f.*; *long-range* ~, Fernaufklärung *f.*
reconnoiter *v.t.* auskundschaften.
reconquer *v.t.* wiedererobern.
reconsider *v.t.* von neuem erwägen.
reconstruct *v.t.* wieder aufbauen; rekonstruieren.
record *v.t.* eintragen; ~ *s.* Verzeichnis *n.*; Urkunde *f.*; Protokoll *n.*; Bericht *m.*; Ruf *m.*; Höchstleistung *f.*; (Schall-) Platte *f.*; *good* ~, gutes Vorleben *n.*; *bad* ~, schlechtes Vorleben *n.*; *no criminal* ~, nicht vorbestraft; *the worst on* ~, der nachweisbar schlechteste; *to place on* ~, zu Protokoll geben; **-s** *pl.* Akten *pl.*; Archiv *n.*; Chronik *f.*
recorded *a.* aufgezeichnet; überliefert.
recorder *s.* Kassettenrecorder *m.*; Tonbandgerät *n.*; Blockflöte *f.*
record holder *s.* Rekordhalter(in) *m.(f.)*; Rekordinhaber(in) *m.(f.)*
recording *s.* Aufnahme *f.*; ~ **session** *s.* Aufnahme *f.*; ~ **studio** *s.* Tonstudio *n.*
recount *v.t.* erzählen.
re-count *v.t.* nachzählen.
recoup *v.t.* entschädigen; wieder einbringen.
recourse *s.* Zuflucht *f.*; (*jur.*) Regreß, Rekurs *m.*; *to have* ~ *to,* sich an einen halten; *to have* ~, Regreß nehmen; *person liable to* ~, Regreßpflichtige *m.*
recover *v.t.* wiederbekommen; zurückgewinnen; wieder gut machen; eintreiben; ~ *v.i.* sich erholen.
recoverable *a.* wiedererlangbar; *debts* ~ *by law,* klagbare Schulden.
recovery *s.* Erholung *f.*; Wiederherstellung *f.*; Genesung *f.*
recreant *a.* feigherzig; treulos, ruchlos; ~ *s.* Bösewicht *m.*; Abtrünnige *m.*
recreate *v.t. & i.* (sich) erquicken.
recreation *s.* Erholung *f.*; Freizeitbeschäftigung *f.*

recreational *a.* Unterhaltungs..., Erholungs...
recreative *a.* erquickend, ergötzlich; Unterhaltungs...
recrimination *s.* Gegenbeschuldigung *f.*
recruit *v.t. & i.* ersetzen; rekrutieren; ~ *s.* Rekrut *m.;* Neuling *m.*
recruitment *s.* Anwerbung *f.*
rectangle *s.* Rechteck *n.*
rectangular *a.* rechtwinklig, rechteckig.
rectification *s.* Berichtigung *f.*
rectify *v.t.* berichtigen, verbessern.
rectilinear *a.* geradlinig.
rectitude *s.* Redlichkeit *f.;* Rechtschaffenheit *f.*
rector *s.* Rektor(in) *m.(f.);* Pfarrer *m.*
rectory *s.* Pfarre *f.;* Pfarrhaus *n.*
rectum *s.* Mastdarm *m.;* Rektum *n.*
recumbent *a.* liegend.
recuperate *v.t.* wiederherstellen; ~ *v.i.* sich erholen.
recuperation *s.* Erholung *f.*
recur *v.i.* sich wiederholen; wiederkehren.
recurrence *s.* Wiederkehr *f.;* Wiederholung *f.*
recurrent *a.* wiederkehrend.
recycle *v.t.* wiederverwerten; recyclen.
recycling *s.* Recyling *n.* Wiedcraufbereitung *f.*
red *a.* rot; ~ **beet** *s.* rote Rübe *f.;* ~ **currant** *s.* Johannisbeere *f.;* ~ **herring** *s.* Bückling; (*fig.*) Ablenkungsversuch *m.;* ~ *tape,* Bürokratie *f.;* bürokratisch; ~ *s.* Rot *n.;* ~ *Ridinghood,* Rotkäppchen *n.*
redaction *s.* Abfassung, Neubearbeitung *f.*
redbreast *s.* Rotkehlchen *n.*
Red Cross *s.* Rotes Kreuz *n.*
redden *v.t.* röten; ~ *v.i.* erröten.
reddish *a.* rötlich.
redecorate *v.t.* neu dekorieren.
redeem *v.t.* loskaufen, auslösen, erlösen; büssen; entschädigen; einlösen; amortisieren, tilgen.
redeemable *a.* ablöslich, austilgbar.
Redeemer *s.* Erlöser *m.;* Heiland *m.*
redemption *s.* Loskaufung *f.;* Erlösung *f.;* Tilgung *f.;* Einlösung *f.;* Ablösung *f.*
red-handed *a.* auf frischer Tat.
red-headed *a.* rothaarig.
red-hot *a.* rotglühend.
redirect *v.t.* (Brief) umadressieren; weiterleiten; nachsenden.
rediscover *v.t.* wiederentdecken.
redesgnate *v.t.* neu bezeichnen, neu benennen.
redistribute *v.t.* umverteilen.
red lead *s.* Mennig *m.*
red-letter day *s.* wichtiger Kalendertag *m.;* Freudentag *m.*
red-light district *s.* Bordellviertel *n.*
redness *s.* Röte *f.*
redo *v.t.* wiederholen; erneuern; überarbeiten.
redolent *a.* stark riechend; duftend.
redouble *v.t. & i.* (sich) verdoppeln.
redoubtable *a.* furchtbar; gewaltig.
redress *v.t.* bessern; abhelfen; wiedergutmachen; ~ *s.* Abhilfe *f.;* Entschädigung *f.;* Ersatz *m.; right of* ~, Ersatzanspruch *m.*
reduce *v.t.* reduzieren; herunterbringen; verkleinern; herabsetzen; bezwingen; (*mil.*) *to* ~ *to the ranks,* zum gemeinen Soldaten degradieren; *at* ~*d rates,* zu ermäßigten Preisen.
reducible *a.* reduzierbar; zurückführbar; herabsetzbar.
reduction *s.* Herabsetzung *f.;* Bezwingung *f.;* Verminderung *f.;* Rabatt *m.;* (*phot.*) Verkleinerung *f.;* ~ *of staff,* Personalabbau *m.*
redundancy *s.* Redundanz *f.;* Überfluß *m.*
redundant *a.,* **~ly** *adv.* überflüssig.
reduplicate *v.t.* verdoppeln.
red wine *s.* Rotwein *m.*
re-echo *v.t. & i.* widerhallen.
reed *s.* Schilfrohr *n.;* Ried *n.;* Flöte *f.*
reef *s.* Riff *n.;* Reff *n.;* ~ *v.t.* reffen.
reek *s.* Gestank *m.;* ~ *v.i.* stinken.
reel *s.* Haspel *f.;* (Garn-) Rolle *f.;* Spule *f.;* ~ *v.t.* haspeln; (*Film*) kurbeln; ~ *v.i.* taumeln.
reelect *v.t.* wiederwählen.
reelection *s.* Wiederwahl *f.*
re-embark *v.t. & i.* (sich) wieder einschiffen; *to* ~ *upon,* erneut beginnen.
reenact *v.t.* wieder in Kraft setzen; nachspielen (Szene).
re-engage *v.t.* wieder beginnen; wieder anstellen; ~ *v.i.* wieder Dienste nehmen.
reenter *v.t.* wieder eintreten.
reentry permit *s.* Wiedereinreiseerlaubnis *f.*
reestablish *v.t.* wiederherstellen.
reexamine *v.t.* nachprüfen.
re-export *v.t.* wieder ausführen.
ref *s.* Ringrichter *m.*
ref. *reference,* (mit) Bezug (auf).
refashion *v.t.* umgestalten.
refectory *s.* Speisezimmer (im Kloster) *n.;* Mensa *f.*
refer *v.t.* verweisen; beziehen; ~ *v.i.* sich beziehen, sich berufen.
referee *s.* Schiedsrichter *m.*
reference *s.* Verweisung, Bezugnahme, Beziehung *f.;* Auskunftsgeber *m.;* **~number** *s.* Aktenzeichen *n.,* Aktennummer *f.,* Geschäftsnummer *f.,* Verweisungszeichen *n.;* **~s** *pl.* Referenzen, Empfehlungen *f.pl.;* Zeichenerklärung *f.;* **~date** *s.* Stichtag *m.;* **~book** *s.* Nachschlagewerk *n.;* **~library** *s.* Handbücherei, Nachschlagebibliothek *f.*
referendum (on) *s.* Volksentscheid (über) *m.;* Referendum *n.*
refill *v.t.* neu füllen; wieder füllen; *m.;* ~ *s.* Ersatzteil, Ersatzfüllung *f.;* ~ **battery** *s.* Ersatzbatterie *f.*
refine *v.t.* raffinieren, reinigen; verfeinern; ~ *v.i.* sich verfeinern; klügeln.
refined *a.* raffiniert; kultiviert.
refinement *s.* Verfeinerung *f.*
refinery *s.* Raffinerie *f.*
refit *v.t.* wiederherstellen; ausbessern.
reflect *v.t.* zurückwerfen; widerspiegeln; ~ *v.i.* ~*on sb.,* zurückfallen; ~ *(up)on sth.,* betrachten, nachdenken.
reflection *s.* Zurückstrahlung *f.;* Widerschein *m.;* Betrachtung, Überlegung *f.;* Tadel *m.*
reflective *a.* nachdenkend.
reflector *s.* Reflektor *m.*
reflex *s.* Reflex *m.;* ~ **camera** *s.* Spiegelreflexkamera *f.*
reflexive *a.* zurückwirkend; (*gram.*) reflexiv.
reflex reaction *s.* Reflexreaktion *f.*
refloat *v.t.* wieder flott machen.
reflux *s.* Rückfluß *m.*

reform *v.t.* umändern; verbessern; reformieren; ~ *v.i.* sich bessern; ~ *s.* Verbesserung, Reform *f.*
reformation *s.* Umänderung *f.*; Besserung *f.*; Reformation *f.*
reformer *s.* Reformpolitiker(in) *m.(f.)*
refract *v.t.* (Strahlen) brechen.
refraction *s.* Strahlenbrechung *f.*
refractory *a.*, **~ily** *adv.* widerspenstig.
refrain *v.t.* zügeln; ~ *v.i.* sich enthalten; ~ *s.* Kehrreim *m.*
refresh *v.t.* erfrischen; auffrischen.
refresher *s.* Erfrischung *f.*; ~ **course** *s.* Auffrischungskurs *m.*
refreshment *s.* Erfrischung *f.*;
refrigerate *v.t.* kühlen; kühl lagern.
refrigerator *s.* Kühlschrank *m.*
refuel *v.t.* & *i.* nachtanken; auftanken.
refuge *s.* Zuflucht *f.*
refugee *s.* Flüchtling *m.*; ~ **camp** *s.* Flüchtlingslager *n.*
refulgence *s.* Glanz *m.*
refulgent *a.* glänzend.
refund *v.t.* zurückzahlen; ~ *s.* Rückerstattung *f.*
refurbish *v.t.* renovieren; aufarbeiten.
refusal *s.* Verweigerung *f.*
refuse *v.t.* verweigern, abschlagen; verwerfen; ~ *s.* Abfall *m.*, Ausschuß *m.*; Auswurf *m.*; ~ **collection** *s.* Müllabfuhr *f.*
refutation *s.* Widerlegung *f.*
refute *v.t.* widerlegen.
regain *v.t.* wiedergewinnen.
regal *a.*, **~ly** *adv.* königlich.
regale *v.t.* fürstlich bewirten; erfreuen.
regalia *s.pl.* Insignien *pl.*
regard *v.t.* ansehen; achten; beobachten; Rücksicht nehmen; sich beziehen; betrachten als; ~ *s.* Blick *m.*; Achtung *f.*; Ansicht *f.*; Rücksicht, Beziehung *f.*; **~s** *pl.* Empfehlungen, Grüße *pl.*
regarding *prep.* hinsichtlich, betreffend.
regardless *adv.* ohne Rücksicht auf.
regd. *registered,* eingetragen.
regency *s.* Regentschaft *f.*
regenerate *v.t.* wiedergebären; neu beleben; ~ *a.* wiedergeboren.
regeneration *s.* Wiedergeburt *f.*
regent *a.* regierend; ~ *s.* Regent *m.*
regicide *s.* Königsmord, Königsmörder *m.*
regime *s.* Regierungssystem *n.*; Regime *n.*
regimen *s.* Lebensweise *f.*; Diät *f.*
regiment *s.* Regierung *f.*; Regiment *n.*
regimentation *s.* Reglementierung *f.*; Organisierung *f.*
region *s.* Gegend *f.*; Gebiet *n.*; Bezirk *m.*
regional *a.*, **~ly** *adv.* regional; Regional...
register *s.* Verzeichnis *n.*; Register *n.*; (Orgel-) Register *n.*; ~ *v.t.* eintragen; (einen Brief) einschreiben; (Gepäck) aufgeben.
registered *a.* eingeschrieben (Brief)
registrar *s.* Registrator *m.*; Standesbeamte *m.*; **~'s office** *s.* Standesamt *n.*
registration *s.* Registrierung *f.*; Anmeldung *f.*; Eintragung *f.*; ~ **fee** *s.* Anmeldegebühr *f.* ~ **number** *s.* polizeiliches Kennzeichen *n.*; ~ **office** *s.* Meldestelle *f.*
registry *s.* Registratur *f.*; ~ **office** *s.* Standesamt *n.*
regret *s.* Bedauern *n.*; Kummer *m.*; ~ *v.t.* bedauern; bereuen.
regretful *a.* reuevoll, bedauernd.
regrettable *a.* bedauerlich.
regroup *v.t.* & *i.* (sich) neugruppieren; umgruppieren; **~ing** *s.* Umgruppierung *f.*
Regt. *Regiment,* Regiment *n.*
regular *a.*, **~ly** *adv.* regelmäßig, ordentlich; ~ *s.* Stammkunde *m.*; Stammkundin *f.*; Stammgast *m.*, **~s** *pl.* Linientruppen *f.pl.*
regular gas *s.* Normalbenzin *n.*
regularity *s.* Regelmäßigkeit *f.*
regularize *v.t.* regeln; gesetzlich regeln *or* festlegen.
regulate *v.t.* ordnen, regeln.
regulation *s.* Einrichtung, Vorschrift *f.*; ~ *a.* vorschriftsmäßig; **~s** *pl.* Satzungen, Ausführungsbestimmungen *pl.*
regulator *s.* Regler *m.*
rehabilitate *v.t.* rehabilitieren.
rehabilitation *s.* Wiedereinsetzung in den vorigen Stand *f.*; Rehabilitation *f.*
rehash *v.t.* aufwärmen; ~ *s.* Aufguß *m.*
rehear *v.t.* (*jur.*) erneut verhandeln.
rehearsal *s.* Probe *f.*; Theaterprobe *f.*
rehearse *v.t.* proben.
rehouse *v.t.* umquartieren; neu unterbringen.
reign *v.i.* herrschen, regieren; ~ *s.* Regierung *f.*; Herrschaft *f.*
reimburse *v.t.* zurückerstatten; entschädigen.
reimbursement *s.* Entschädigung, Wiedererstattung *f.*
reimport *v.t.* wiedereinführen.
reimportation *s.* Wiedereinfuhr *f.*
rein *s.* Zügel *m.*; ~ *v.t.* zügeln.
reincarnation *s.* Reinkarnation *f.*
reindeer *s.* Rentier *n.*
reinforce *v.t.* verstärken.
reinforcement *s.* Verstärkung *f.*
reinstate *v.t.* wieder einsetzen.
reinsurance *s.* Rückversicherung *f.*
reinsure *v.t.* rückversichern.
reinterpret *v.t.* neu interpretieren.
reinvest *v.t.* wieder anlegen; **~ment** *s.* Wiederanlage *f.*
reissue *s.* Neuauflage *f.*; ~ *v.t.* neu herausbringen.
reiterate *v.t.* wiederholen.
reject *v.t.* verwerfen; ausschlagen; ablehnen.
rejection *s.* Verwerfung *f.*; Ablehnung *f.*
rejoice *v.i.* sich freuen; ~ *v.t.* erfreuen.
rejoicing *s.* Jubel *m.*; **~s** *pl.* Freudebezeugungen *f.pl.*
rejoin *v.t.* wieder vereinigen; sich wieder vereinigen mit; ~ *v.i.* erwidern.
rejoinder *s.* Erwiderung *f.*
rejuvenate *v.t.* verjüngen.
relapse *v.i.* zurückfallen, einen Rückfall bekommen; ~ *s.* Rückfall *m.*
relate *v.t.* erzählen, berichten; ~ *v.i.* sich beziehen.
related *a.* verwandt.
relation *s.* Beziehung *f.*; Verwandtschaft *f.*; Verwandte *m.* & *f.*
relationship *s.* Verwandtschaft *f.*

relative *a.*, **~ly** *adv.* sich beziehend, bezüglich; verhältnismäßig; relativ; ~ *s.* Verwandte *m.* & *f.*
relative clause *s.* Relativsatz *m.*
relative pronoun *s.* Relativpronomen *n.*
relativity *s.* Relativität *f.*
relax *v.t.* lockern, entspannen; ~ *v.i.* erschlaffen; sich entspannen.
relaxation *s.* Erschlaffung *f.*; Entspannung *f.*; Erholung *f.*; Nachlassen *n.*; Erleichterung *f.*
relaxed *a.* entspannt, gelöst.
relaxing *a.* entspannend, erholsam.
relay *s.* Schicht *f.*; Staffel *f.*; Pferdewechsel *m.*; (*elek.*) Relais *n.*; Ablösungs...; ~ *race,* Stafettenlauf *m.*; ~ *v.t.* übertragen nach (*radio*).
release *v.t.* befreien; loslassen, entlassen; (Bomben) abwerfen; ~ *s.* Freilassung, Befreiung *f.*; Entbindung, Entlastung *f.*; Freigabe *f.* (für Veröffentlichung); (Bomben-) Abwurf *m.*; (*phot.*) Auslösung *f.*; **press** ~ *s.* Presseverlautbarung.
relegate *v.t.* verweisen; absteigen.
relegation *s.* Verweisung *f.*; (*sp.*) Abstieg *m.*
relent *v.i.* nachgeben.
relentless *a.* unerbittlich, unbarmherzig.
relevance *s.* Relevanz *f.*; Bedeutung *f.*
relevant *a.* erheblich; zur Sache gehörig.
reliability *s.* Zuverlässigkeit *f.*
reliable *a.* verlässlich, zuverlässig, vertrauenswürdig.
reliance *s.* Zuversicht *f.*; Vertrauen *n.*
reliant *a.* *to be* ~ *on,* angewiesen sein auf.
relic *s.* Überrest *m.*; Reliquie *f.*
relief *s.* Erleichterung *f.*; Unterstützung *f.*; Ablösung *f.*; Relief *n.*; *low* ~, Flachrelief *n.*; **~fund** *s.* Hilfsfond *m.*; **~train** *s.* Vorzug, Entlastungszug *m.*
relieve *v.t.* erleichtern; unterstützen; ablösen; entsetzen; beruhigen; (hervor) heben.
religion *s.* Religion *f.*
religious *a.*, **~ly** *adv.* religiös, Religions...; Ordens...; (*fig.*) gewissenhaft.
relinquish *v.t.* verlassen; aufgeben.
relinquishment *s.* Verzicht *m.*
relish *s.* Geschmack *m.*; Beigeschmack *m.*; Würze *f.*; Genuß *m.*; ~ *v.t.* Geschmack finden an; schmackhaft machen; ~ *v.i.* schmecken, gefallen.
relocate *v.t.* umsiedeln, verlegen.
reluctance *s.* Widerstreben *n.*
reluctant *a.*, **~ly** *adv.* widerstrebend, zögernd, ungern.
rely *v.i.* ~ *on,* sich verlassen auf, vertrauen auf.
remain *v.i.* bleiben; übrigbleiben, verharren; *it ~s to be seen,* es muß sich zeigen.
remainder *s.* Rest *m.*; Rückstand *m.*
remaining *a.* restlich, übrig.
remains *s.pl.* (sterbliche) Reste; Überreste; Überbleibsel *pl.*; Relikte *pl.*
remake *s.* Remake *n.*; Neuverfilmung *f.*
remand *v.t.* (in Untersuchungshaft) behalten.
remark *v.t.* bemerken; wahrnehmen; ~ *s.* Anmerkung *f.*
remarkable *a.*, **~bly** *adv.* bemerkenswert; hervorragend.
remarriage *s.* Wiederverheiratung *f.*
remarry *v.i.* & *t.* wieder heiraten.
remedial *a.* heilend.
remedy *s.* Heilmittel, Hilfsmittel *n.*; Ersatz *m.*; ~ *v.t.* beilen, abhelfen.
remember *v.t.* sich erinnern; empfehlen, grüssen; gedenken; (*fam.*) behalten; *to* ~ *a person in one's will,* einen im Testament bedenken.
remembrance *s.* Erinnerung *f.*; Andenken *n.*; Gedenken *n.*
remind *v.t.* erinnern, mahnen.
reminder *s.* Mahnung *f.*
reminiscence *s.* Erinnerung *f.*
reminiscent (of) *a.* erinnernd (an).
remiss *a.*, **~ly** *adv.* schlaff; lässig.
remission *s.* Nachlassen *n.*; Milderung *f.*, Erlassung, Vergebung *f.*
remit *v.t.* remittieren, übersenden; vermindern, nachlassen; erlassen.
remittance *s.* Überweisung *f.*
remnant *a.* Überrest, Rest *m.*
remodel *v.t.* umbilden; umfassionieren (Hut, Mantel).
remold *v.t.* umgestalten.
remonstrance *s.* Einwendung *f.*; Protest *m.*
remonstrate *v.i.* Einwendungen machen.
remorse *s.* Gewissensbiß *m.*
remorseful *a.* reuig, reuevoll.
remorseless *a.*, **~ly** *adv.* hartherzig; erbarmungslos.
remote *a.*, **~ly** *adv.* entlegen, entfernt.
remote control *s.* (*mech.*) Fernsteuerung *f.*; Fernbedienung *f.*; **~led** *a.* ferngesteuert.
remount *v.t.* wieder besteigen; ~ *s.* frisches Reitpferd *n.*
removable *a.* abnehmbar; entfernbar.
removal *s.* Wegschaffung, Absetzung *f.*; Entlassung *f.*
remove *v.t.* wegräumen; versetzen; absetzen; entfernen; ~ *v.i.* sich entfernen; ~ *s.* Abstand *m.*; Grad *m.*, Stufe *f.*
remunerate *v.t.* belohnen, vergüten.
remuneration *s.* Belohnung, Vergütung *f.*
remunerative *a.* gewinnbringend.
Renaissance *s.* Renaissance *f.*
rename *v.t.* umbenennen, umtaufen.
Renascence *s.* Wiedergeburt *f.*; Renaissance *f.*
rend *v.t.* & *i.st.* zerreißen.
render *v.t.* zurückgeben; überliefern; darstellen; übersetzen; leisten; machen; *to* ~ *account,* Rechenschaft ablegen; *to* ~ *judgment,* Urteil fällen; *to* ~ *service,* Dienst leisten; *per account* ~*ed,* laut erhaltener Rechnung.
rendering *s.* Wiedergabe *f.*; Übertragung *f.*
rendezvous *s.* Stelldichein *n.*; Verabredung *f.*; Rendezvous *n.*
rendition *s.* Wiedergabe *f.*; Übertragung *f.*
renegade *s.* Abtrünnige *m./f.*
renew *v.t.* erneuern; wiederholen.
renewable *a.* verlängerbar; erneuerbar.
renewal *s.* Erneuerung *f.*; Verlängerung *f.*
renounce *v.t.* entsagen, abschwören, verzichten auf; verleugnen.
renovate *v.t.* renovieren; restaurieren.
renovation *s.* Renovierung *f.*; Restaurierung *f.*
renown *s.* Ruf, Ruhm *m.*
renowned *a.* berühmt.
rent *s.* Miete *f.*; Pacht *f.*; ~ *v.t.* (ver)mieten, (ver)pachten.
rental *s.* Miete *f.*; Mietsumme, Pachtsumme *f.*; *car* ~, Autoverleih *m.*

rent-controlled *a.* mietpreisgebunden.
renunciation *s.* Entsagung *f.;* Verzicht *m.*
reopen *v.t.* wieder eröffnen; ~ *v.i.* wieder eröffnet werden.
reorder *v.t.* nachbestellen; neu bestellen; umordnen.
reorganization *s.* Umorganisation *f.;* Umbildung *f.*, Neugliederung *f.*
reorganize *v.t.* neugestalten; umorganisieren.
reorient *v.t.* sich umorientieren, neu ausrichten.
reorientation *s.* Neuorientierung *f.*
rep *s.* (*fam.*) Vertreter(in) *m.(f.)*
repair *v.t.* ersetzen; ausbessern; ~ *s.* Ausbesserung *f.;* Reparatur *f.; to keep in good* ~, in gutem Zustand halten; *out of* ~, baufällig; **~shop** *s.* Reparaturwerkstatt *f.*
repairable *a.*, **~bly** *adv.* ausbesserungsfähig; ersetzbar.
reparation *s.* Ausbesserung *f.;* Ersatz *m.;* Entschädigung *f.*
repartee *s.* schnelle *or* treffende Antwort *f.;* Schlagfertigkeit *f.*
repast *s.* Mahlzeit *f.*
repatriate *v.t.* in die Heimat zurückbringen; repatriieren.
repatriation *s.* Rückführung, Repatriierung *f.*
repay *v.t.st.* zurückzahlen; vergelten.
repayable *a.* rückzahlbar.
repayment *s.* Rückzahlung *f.*
repeal *v.t.* widerrufen; aufheben; ~ *s.* Aufhebung *f.;* Widerruf *m.*
repeat *v.t.* wiederholen; hersagen; ~ *s.* Wiederholung *f.;* ~ *order,* Nachbestellung *f.;* ~ *performance,* Wiederholung einer Aufführung *f.*
repeatedly *adv.* wiederholt.
repel *v.t.* zurückstoßen; abstoßen; zurückschlagen.
repellent *a.* abstossend.
repent *v.t.* & *i.* bereuen, Buße tun.
repentance *s.* Reue, Buße *f.*
repentant *a.* reuig, bußfertig.
repeople *v.t.* wieder bevölkern.
repercussion *s.* Widerhall *m.*
repertoire *s.* Repertoire *n.*
repertory *s.* Sachregister *n.;* Fundgrube *f.;* Repertoire *n.;* ~ *theater,* Repertoiretheater *n.*
repetition *s.* Wiederholung *f.;* Hersagen *n.*
repetitious *a.* sich wiederholend.
repetitive *a.* eintönig.
rephrase *v.t.* umformulieren.
repine *v.i.* sich grämen; murren, klagen.
replace *v.t.* ersetzen; zurückstellen.
replacement *s.* Ersatz *m.*
replant *v.t.* umpflanzen.
replenish *v.t.* (wieder)anfüllen.
replete *a.* angefüllt, voll.
repletion *s.* Überfülle *f.*
replica *s.* Nachbildung *f.;* Abbild *n.*
reply *v.i.* erwidern; ~ *s.* Antwort *f.;* **~card,** Postkarte *(f.)* mit Antwort; **~coupon** *s.* Antwortschein *m.*
repolish *v.t.* wieder polieren.
report *v.t.* berichten, erzählen; melden, anzeigen; ~ *v.i.* sich melden; *to* ~ *out,* sich abmelden; *to* ~ *to the police,* sich bei der Polizei melden; ~ *s.* Gerücht *n.;* Ruf *m.;* Nachricht *f.;* Knall *m.;* Bericht *m.;* Schulzeugnis *n.*
reported speech *s.* indirekte Rede *f.*
reporter *s.* Berichterstatter(in) *m.(f.);* Reporter(in) *m.(f.)*
repose *v.i.* ruhen, beruhen; ~ *s.* Ruhe *f.*
repository *s.* Behältnis *n.;* Warenlager *n.*
repossess *v.t.* wieder in Besitz nehmen.
reprehend *v.t.* tadeln; rügen.
reprehensible *a.*, **~bly** *adv.* tadelnswert, sträflich.
reprehension *s.* Tadel *m.;* Rüge *f.*
reprehensive *a.* tadelnd.
represent *v.t.* darstellen, vorstellen; vertreten; verkörpern; entsprechen.
representation *s.* Vorstellung *f.;* Darstellung *f.;* Stellvertretung *f.*
representative *a.*, **~ly** *adv.* vorstellend; stellvertretend; ~ *s.* Vertreter(in) *m.(f.)*
repress *v.t.* unterdrücken; verdrängen.
repressed *a.* unterdrückt; verdrängt.
repression *s.* Unterdrückung; Verdrängung *f.*
repressive *a.* repressiv; unterdrückend.
reprieve *v.t.* Frist geben; ~ *s.* Frist *f.;* Begnadigung *f.*
reprimand *s.* Verweis, Tadel *m.;* ~ *v.t.* tadeln.
reprint *v.t.* wieder drucken; ~ *s.* Nachdruck *m.*
reprisal *s.* Wiedervergeltung *f.; in* ~ *for,* als Vergeltungsmaßnahme für.
reproach *v.t.* vorwerfen; Vorwürfe machen, tadeln; ~ *s.* Vorwurf *m.;* Tadel *m.*, tadelnd.
reproachful *a.*, **~ly** *adv.* vorwurfsvoll.
reprobate *a.* verworfen, ruchlos; ~ *s.* Halunke *m.;* ~ *v.t.* verwerfen.
reprocess *v.t.* wiederaufbereiten.
reproduce *v.t.* wieder hervorbringen; nachbilden; ~ *v.i.* sich fortpflanzen.
reproduction *s.* Nachbildung, Wiederholung *f.;* Fortpflanzung *f.;* Wiedererzeugung *f.*
reproductive *a.* wiedererzeugend; Fortpflanzungs...
reproof *s.* Vorwurf, Verweis *m.*
reprove *v.t.* tadeln, verweisen; schelten.
reptile *a.* kriechend; ~ *s.* Reptil *n.*
republic *s.* Republik *f.*
republican *a.* republikanisch; ~ *s.* Republikaner(in) *m.(f.)*
republish *v.t.* neu veröffentlichen.
repudiate *v.t.* zurückweisen, verstoßen; nicht anerkennen.
repugnance *s.* Widerwille *m.;* Abscheu *f.*
repugnant *a.* widerspenstig; zuwider; **~ly** *adv.* mit Widerwillen.
repulse *v.t.* zurückschlagen; abschlagen; ~ *s.* Zurücktreibung *f.*
repulsion *s.* Zurückstoßung *f.;* Abweisung *f.;* Abscheu *f.;* (*phys.*) Abstoßung *f.*
repulsive *a.* abstoßend, widerwärtig.
repurchase *v.t.* wiederkaufen; ~ *s.* Rückkauf *m.*
reputable *a.*, **~bly** *adv.* angesehen.
reputation *s.* Ruf *m.*
repute *v.t.* halten für, achten; ~ *s.* Ruf *m.*
reputed *a.* angeblich, bekannt; *to be* ~*d,* den Ruf haben.
request *s.* Bitte *f.;* Gesuch *n.;* Nachfrage *f.; at sb.'s* ~, auf jmds. Bitte hin; *by* ~, auf Wunsch; ~ *v.t.* bitten, ersuchen.

require *v.t.* verlangen, fordern; brauchen.
requirement *s.* Forderung *f.;* Bedarf *m.*
requisite *a.*, **~ly** *adv.* erforderlich; ~ *s.* Erfordernis *n.;* Bedarfsartikel *m.*
requisition *s.* Forderung *f.;* Beschlag *m.;* Anforderung *f.;* ~ *v.t.* anfordern, requirieren.
requital *s.* Vergeltung *f.*
requite *v.t.* vergelten.
rerun *v.t.* wiederholen; ~ *s.* Wiederholung *f.*
res. *research,* Forschungs...; *residence,* Wohnsitz.
resale *s.* Wiederverkauf *m.*
reschedule *v.t.* zeitlich neu festlegen.
rescind *v.t.* aufheben; abschaffen.
rescission *s.* Umstossung, Aufhebung (einer Verordnung) *f.*
rescue *v.t.* befreien, retten; ~ *s.* Befreiung, Rettung *f.; to come to the ~ of,* einem zu Hilfe kommen.
rescuer *s.* Retter(in) *m.(f.)*
research *s.* Forschung *f.*, Untersuchung *f.;* ~ *v.i.* erforschen, untersuchen.
research assistant *s.* wissenschaftliche Assistent(in) *m.(f.)*
researcher *s.* Forscher(in) *m.(f.)*
research fellowship *s.* Forschungsstipendium *n.*
resemblance *s.* Ähnlichkeit *f.;* Ebenbild *n.*
resemble *v.t.* ähneln; gleichen.
resent *v.t.* übelnehmen.
resentful *a.* übelnehmerisch; ärgerlich; rachgierig.
resentment *s.* Zorn *m.;* Verdruß *m.;* Groll *m.;* Unmut *m.*
reservation *s.* Aufbewahrung *f.;* Vorbehalt *m.;* Zurückhaltung *f.;* Vorbestellung *f.*, Reservierung *f.;* **~list** *s.* Warteliste *f.*
reserve *v.t.* vorbehalten, aufbewahren; reservieren; ~ *s.* Rückhalt *m.*, Reserve *f.;* Vorrat *m.;* Vorsicht *f.;* Zurückhaltung *f.*
reserved *a.*, **~ly** *adv.* zurückhaltend; vorsichtig; belegt.
reservist *s.* Reservist *m.*
reservoir *s.* Behälter *m.*
reset *v.t.* neu einfassen (Edelstein); nachstellen (Zähler, Uhr).
resettle *v.t.* umsiedeln.
resettlement *s.* Umsiedlung *f.*
reshape *v.t.* neugestalten, neuformen.
reshuffle *s.* Umbildung (der Regierung) *f.*
reside *v.i.* wohnen, sich aufhalten.
residence *s.* Aufenthalt, Wohnsitz *m.;* Wohnung *f.;* Residenz *f.; place of ~*, Aufenthaltsort *m.;* ~ **permit** *s.* Aufenthaltsgenehmigung *f.*
resident *s.* wohnhaft, ansässig; ~ *s.* Bewohner(in) *m.(f.);* Einwohner(in) *m.(f.)*
residential *a.* Wohn...; ~ **club** *s.* Wohnklub *m.;* ~ **district** *s.* Wohnviertel *n.*, Wohnbezirk *m.*
residual *a.* zurückbleibend.
residue *a.* Rest, Rückstand *m.*
residuum *s.* Rückstand *m.*
resign *v.t.* entsagen, abtreten; aufgeben, sich ergeben in; ~ *v.i.* seine Stelle aufgeben.
resignation *s.* Abtretung, Entsagung, Verzichtleistung *f.;* (Amt) Niederlegung *f.*, Rücktritt *m.;* Ergebung *f.*
resigned *a.*, **~ly** *adv.* ergeben; resigniert.
resilience *s.* Schnellkraft, Spannkraft *f.;* Elastizität *f.*
resilient *a.* spannkräftig, elastisch.
resin *s.* Harz *n.*
resinous *a.* harzig.
resist *v.t.* & *i.* widerstehen.
resistance *s.* Widerstand *m.*
resistant, resisting *a.* beständig;.. fest; *oil-~*, ölfest; *shock-~*, stoßfest.
resit *v.t.* wiederholen (Prüfung); ~ *s.* Wiederholungsprüfung *f.*
resolute *a.*, **~ly** *adv.* entschlossen.
resolution *s.* Auflösung *f.;* Entschlossenheit *f.;* Vorsatz *m.;* Beschluß *m.*, Entschließung *f.*
resolve *v.t.* auflösen; aufklären; beschließen; ~ *v.i.* sich entschließen; sich auflösen; ~ *s.* Entschluß *m.*
resonance *s.* Widerhall *m.;* Nachhall *m.;* Resonanz *f.*
resonant *a.* widerhallend; volltönend.
resonate *v.i.* mitklingen, mitschwingen.
resort *v.i.* sich begeben zu; ~ *s.* Zuflucht *f.; health ~*, Kurort *m.; ski ~*, Skiort *m.*
resound *v.i.* widerhallen.
resounding *a.* hallend; überwältigend.
resource *s.* Hilfsmittel *n.;* Zuflucht *f.;* **~s** *pl.* Geldmittel *n.pl.;* (Erz-) Vorräte *pl.;* Fähigkeiten *f.pl.*
resourceful *a.* findig; einfallsreich.
respect *v.t.* berücksichtigen; sich beziehen auf; (hoch)achten, ehren; ~ *s.* Rücksicht, Hinsicht, Beziehung *f.;* Hochachtung *f.;* **~s** *pl.* Empfehlung *f.*
respectability *s.* Achtbarkeit *f.*, Ehrbahrkeit *f.*
respectable *a.*, **~bly** *adv.* achtbar, ehrbar; ansehnlich; anständig; leidlich.
respectful *a.*, **~ly** *adv.* ehrerbietig, höflich.
respecting *pr.* hinsichtlich; bezüglich.
respective *a.* jeweilig, verschieden; **~ly** *adv.* beziehungsweise
respiration *s.* Atmen *n.;* Atmung *f.*
respirator *s.* Atmenschutzgerät *n.*
respiratory *a.* Atmungs...
respire *v.t.* & *i.* atmen, einatmen.
respite *s.* Frist *f.;* Aufschub, Stillstand *m.*
resplendent *a.*, **~ly** *adv.* glänzend; prächtig.
respond *v.i.* entsprechen; antworten.
respondent *s.* Beklagte *m./f.*
response *s.* Antwort *f.*
responsibility *s.* Verantwortlichkeit *f.*, Verantwortung *f.*
responsible *a.*, **~bly** *adv.* verantwortlich.
responsive *a.* aufgeschlossen; antwortend; empfänglich.
rest *s.* Ruhe, Rast *f.;* Ruhepunkt *m.;* Pause *f.;* Rest *m.;* die übrigen *pl.*, *the ~ of them,* sie übrigen; ~ *v.i.* ruhen, rasten; *~ against,* sich stützen gegen; *~ assured,* sich verlassen; *let a matter ~*, eine Sache auf sich beruhen lassen; ~ *v.t.* ausruhen lassen; lehnen.
restart *v.t.* wieder anlassen; wieder aufnehmen.
restate *v.t.* neu formulieren.
restaurant *s.* Restaurant *n.*
restaurant car *s.* Speisewagen *m.*
rested *a.* ausgeruht.
restful *a.* ruhig; beruhigend.
resting place *s.* Ruheplatz *m.*
restitution *s.* Wiedererstattung *f.;* Wiederherstellung *f.;* **~law** *s.* Wiedergutmachungsgesetz *n.*
restive *a.* störrisch, widerspenstig.

restless *a.*, **~ly** *adv.* ruhelos.
restoration *s.* Wiederherstellung *f.*; Restaurierung *f.*; Restauration *f.*; Zurückerstattung *f.*
restorative *a.* stärkend; ~ *s.* kräftigendes Heilmittel *n.*
restore *v.t.* wiedergeben; wiederherstellen; restaurieren.
restorer *s.* Restaurator(in) *m.(f.)*
restrain *v.t.* zurückhalten, einschränken.
restrained *a.* zurückhaltend; beherrscht.
restraint *s.* Einschränkung *f.*; Zurückhaltung *f.*; Zwang *m.*; *under* ~, in Gewahrsam.
restrict *v.t.* einschränken; **~ed** *a.* beschränkt, begrenzt.
restriction *s.* Einschränkung *f.*
restrictive *a.*, **~ly** *adv.* einschränkend.
rest room *s.* Toilette *f.*
restructure *v.t.* umstrukturieren.
restyle *v.t.* neu stylen.
result *v.i.* hervorgehen, folgen, sich ergeben; ~ *s.* Ergebnis *n.*; Folge *f.*
resume *v.t.* zurücknehmen; wieder aufnehmen; wieder anfangen; zusammenfassen.
résumé *s.* Zusammenfassung *f.*; Lebenslauf *m.*
resumption *s.* Zurückgewinnung *f.*; Wiederaufnahme *f.*
resurface *v.i.* wieder auftauchen; ~ *v.t.* (Straße) neu belegen.
resurrect *v.t.* Wiederaufleben lassen.
resurrection *s.* Auferstehung *f.*
resuscitate *v.t.* wiedererwecken; wiederbeleben.
ret., retd. *retired,* im Ruhestand, i.R., außer Dienst, a.D.
retail *v.t.* im Einzelhandel verkaufen; ~ *s.* Einzelverkauf *m.*; **~-trade** *s.* Einzelhandel *m.*; **~-price** *s.* Ladenpreis *m.*
retailer *s.* Einzelhändler(in) *m.(f.)*
retain *v.t.* behalten, beibehalten.
retainer *s.* Honorarverschuß *m.*; Verpflichtung *(f.)* eines Anwalts.
retake *v.t.st.* wiedernehmen.
retaliate *v.i.* vergelten; zurückschlagen.
retaliation *s.* Wiedervergeltung *f.*; Gegenschlag *m.*
retaliatory *a.* Vergeltungs...
retard *v.t.* aufhalten; verzögern; retardieren
retardation *s.* Verzögerung *f.*
retch *v.i.* würgen.
retention *s.* Zurückhalten *n.*; Beibehaltung *f.*; Verhaltung *f.*
retentive *a.* gut (Gedächtnis); bewahrend; (zurück)haltend.
reticence *s.* Zurückhaltung *f.*
reticent *a.* zurückhaltend.
retina *s.* Netzhaut (des Auges) *f.*
retinue *s.* Gefolge *n.*
retire *v.i.* zich zurückziehen; zu Bett gehen; in den Ruhestand treten; ~ *v.t.* in den Ruhestand versetzen.
retired *p.* & *a.*, **~ly** *adv.* zurückgezogen, eingezogen; pensioniert, im Ruhestand.
retirement *s.* Zurückgezogenheit *f.*; Ausscheiden *n.*; Pensionierung *f.*
retirement age *s.* Rentenalter *n.*; Altersgrenze *f.*
retiring *a.* zurückhaltend.
retort *v.t.* & *i.* erwidern; zurückgeben; ~ *s.* Erwiderung *f.*; Retorte *f.*
retouch *v.t.* überarbeiten; (*phot.*) retuschieren.
retrace *v.t.* wieder zeichnen; zurückgeben; zurückverfolgen.
retract *v.t.* & *i.* zurückziehen; einziehen.
retractable *a.* einziehbar.
retraction *s.* Widerruf *m.*; Einziehen *n.*; Zurücknahme *f.*
retrain *v.t.* umschulen.
retraining *s.* Umschulung *f.*
retread *v.t.* runderneueren; ~ *s.* runderneuerter Reifen *m.*
retreat *s.* Rückzug *m.*; Zufluchtsort *m.*; Eingezogenheit *f.*
retrench *v.t.* einschränken; ~ *v.i.* seine Ausgaben einschränken.
retrenchment *s.* Einschränkung *f.*; Ersparung *f.*
retrial *s.* (*jur.*) nochmalige Verhandlung *f.*; Wiederaufnahmeverfahren *n.*
retribution *s.* Vergeltung *f.*, Strafe *f.*
retrieval *s.* Rettung *f.*; Wiedergutmachung *f.*
retrieve *v.t.* wiederbekommen; wieder ersetzen; (*hunting*) apportieren.
retriever *s.* Retriever *m.*; Apportierhund *m.*
retroactive *a.* rückwirkend; *with ~ effect,* mit rückwirkender Kraft.
retrograde *a.* rückschrittlich; rückläufig.
retrogression *s.* Rückgang *m.*
retrogressive *a.* rückschrittlich.
retrospect *s.* Rückblick *m.*
retrospective *a.*, **~ly** *adv.* rückwirkend; zurückblickend.
retry *v.t.* (*jur.*) von neuem verhandeln.
return *v.i.* umkehren, wiederkommen; antworten; ~ *v.t.* erstatten; erwidern; zurückschicken, wiederbringen; melden, berichten; wählen; ~ *s.* Rückkehr *f.*; Rückgabe *f.*; Gewinn *m.*; Rückzahlung *f.*; Erwiderung *f.*; Gegendienst *m.*; Bericht, Wahlbericht *m.*; **~s** *pl.* statistische Angaben *f.pl.*; Einnahme *f.*; *many happy returns of the day,* Geburtstagsglückwunsch *m.*; *in ~,* dafür, dagegen; *by ~ of post,* postwendend.
return: ~ **address** *s.* Absenderadresse, Rückanschrift *f.*; ~ **flight** *s.* Rückflug *m.*; ~ **journey** *s.* Rückreise *f.*; ~ **postage** *s.* Rückporto *n.*
return ticket *s.* Rückfahrkarte *f.*
reunification *s.* Wiedervereinigung *f.*
reunion *s.* Wiedersehensfeier *f.*; Klassentreffen *n.*
reunite *v.t.* & *i.* (sich) wieder vereinigen.
reuse *v.t.* wiederverwenden.
rev *s.* (*fam.*) Umdrehung *f.*; ~ **counter** *s.* Drehzahlmesser *m.*; ~ *v.t.* (*up*) auf Touren bringen.
Rev. *Reverend,* Ehrwürden, Hochwürden, Ehrw.
revaluation *s.* Aufwertung *f.*
revamp *v.t.* aufmöbeln, aufpolieren.
reveal *v.t.* offenbaren; enthüllen.
revealing *a.* aufschlußreich.
reveille *s.* (*mil.*) Morgensignal *n.*
revel *v.i.* feiern; (*fig.*) schwärmen, schwelgen; ~ *s.* Gelage *n.*
revelation *s.* Offenbarung *f.*; Enthüllung *f.*
reveller *s.* Feiernde *m./f.*
revelry *s.* Feiern *n.*, lärmende Festlichkeit.
revenge *s.* Rache *f.*; ~ *v.t.* rächen.
revengeful *a.*, **~ly** *adv.* rachgierig.
revenue *s.* Einkommen *n.*; Ertrag *m.*; Staatsein-

nahmen *f.pl.*; ~ *and expenditure,* Einnahmen und Ausgaben *pl.*
reverberate *v.i.* widerhallen.
reverberation *s.* Widerhall *m.*
revere *v.t.* ehren, verehren.
reverence *s.* Ehrerbietung *f.*; Verneigung *f.*; (Titel) Ehrwürden; ~ *v.t.* verehren.
reverend *a.* ehrwürdig (Titel der Geistlichen).
reverent *a.*, **~ly** *adv.* ehrerbietig.
reverential *a.*, **~ly** *adv.* ehrerbietig.
reverie *s.* Träumerei *f.*
reversal *s.* Umstoßung (eines Urteils) *f.*; Umkehrung *f.*; Umsteuerung *f.*
reverse *v.t.* umkehren; umstoßen; umsteuern; ~ *s.* Wendung *f.*, Umschlag *m.*, Wechsel *m.*; Gegenteil *n.*; Rückseite *f.*; Schlappe *f.*; ~ *a.* Rückwärts...; **~gear** *s.* (*mech.*) Rückwärtsgang *m.*
reversible *a.* reversibel; umkehrbar.
reversion *s.* Umkehrung *f.*; Heimfall *m.*
revert *v.t.* umkehren; zurückwerfen; ~ *v.i.* zurückkehren; heimfallen.
revertible *a.* heimfallend.
review *v.t.* wieder durchsehen; mustern; rezensieren; revidieren; ~ *s.* Übersicht, Durchsicht, Rezension *f.*; kritische Zeitschrift, Rundschau *f.*, (*jur.*) Revision *f.*
reviewer *s.* Rezensent *m.*
revile *v.t.* schmähen, schimpfen.
revise *v.t.* durchsehen.
revision *s.* Durchsicht, Revision *f.*
revisit *v.t.* wieder besuchen.
revitalize *v.t.* neu beleben.
revival *s.* Wiederbelebung *f.*; Revival *n.*
revive *v.t.* wieder aufleben; ~ *v.t.* wieder beleben.
revocable *a.* widerruflich.
revocation *s.* Zurückrufung *f.*; Widerruf *m.*
revoke *v.t.* widerrufen.
revolt *v.i.* sich empören; ~ *s.* Abfall *m.*; Empörung *f.*; Aufstand *m.*
revolting *a.* abstoßend; abscheulich.
revolution *s.* Revolution *f.*; Umwälzung *f.*; Umlauf *m.*; Umdrehung *f.*
revolutionary *a.* revolutionär.
revolutionize *v.t.* revolutionieren; (gänzlich) umgestalten.
revolve *v.t.* umwälzen; erwägen; ~ *v.i.* sich drehen, umlaufen.
revolver *s.* Revolver *m.*
revolving *a.* drehbar; Dreh...
revue *s.* Revue *f.*; Kabarett *n.*
revulsion *s.* Umschwung *m.* Abscheu *m.*
reward *v.t.* vergelten, belohnen; ~ *s.* Belohnung *f.*
rewarding *a.* lohnend.
rewind *v.t.* zurückspulen; wieder aufziehen.
rewire *v.t.* neue Leitungen legen.
reword *v.t.* umformulieren.
rewrite *v.t.* umarbeiten; umschreiben.
rhapsody *s.* Rhapsodie *f.*; Schwärmerei *f.*
rhesus factor *s.* Rhesusfaktor *m.*
rhetoric *s.* Redekunst *f.*; Rhetorik *f.*; (*pej.*) Phrasen *pl.*
rhetorical *a.*, **~ly** *adv.* rednerisch; rhetorisch; (*pej.*) phrasenhaft.
rhetorician *s.* Rhetoriker(in) *m.(f.)*
rheumatic *a.* rheumatisch; ~ *s.* Rheumatiker(in) *m.(f.)*
rheumatism *s.* Rheumatismus *m.*
rhino(ceros) *s.* Nashorn *n.*; Rhinozeros *n.*
rhomboidal *a.* rautenförmig.
rhombus *s.* (*geom.*) Raute *f.*; Rhombus *m.*
rhubarb *s.* Rhabarber *m.*
rhyme *s.* Reim *m.*; Vers *m.*; ~ *v.t.* & *i.* reimen.
rhythm *s.* Rhythmus *m.*
rhythmic(al) *a.*, **~ly** *adv.* rhythmisch.
rib *s.* Rippe *f.*; (*nav.*) Inholz *n.*; Kiel *m.*; Schaft *m.*; ~ *v.t.* rippen; (*sl.*) hänseln.
ribald *a.* frech, zotig.
ribaldry *s.* zotige Sprache *f.*
ribbon *s.* Band, Ordensband *n.*; Farbband *n.*; Streifen *m.*
rice *s.* Reis *m.*; ~ **paddy** *s.* Reisfeld *n.*
rich *a.*, **~ly** *adv.* reich; kostbar; nahrhaft, fett; (Speise) schwer.
riches *s.* Reichtum *m.*
richness *s.* Reichtum *m.*; Fülle *f.*
rick *s.* (Heu) Schober *m.*
rickets *s.pl.* Rachitis *f.*
rickety *a.* rachitisch; wack[e]lig.
rickshaw *s.* Rickscha *f.*
ricochet *v.i.* (*mil.*) abprallen; ~ *s.* Abpraller *m.*
rid *v.t.st.* befreien; wegschaffen; ~ *a.* entledigt; *to get* ~ *of,* loswerden.
riddance *s.* Befreiung, Entledigung *f.*
ridden *a.* geplagt; *bed*~, bettlägerig.
riddle *s.* Rätsel *n.*; grobes Sieb *n.*; ~ *v.t.* sieben; durchlöchern.
ride *v.i.* & *t.* reiten; fahren; ~ *a bicycle,* radfahren; ~ *at anchor,* vor Anker liegen; ~ *in a train,* mit dem Zug fahren; ~ *the waves,* auf den Wellen reiten; ~ *s.* Ritt *m.*; Fahrt *f.*; Reitweg *m.*
rider *s.* Reiter(in) *m.(f.)*; Zusatzklausel *f.*
ridge *s.* Grat *m.*; Kamm *m.*; Rücken *m.*; Erhöhung *f.*, First *m.*; Furche *f.*; Bergkette *f.*; ~ *v.t.* furchen.
ridicule *s.* Spott *m.*; Lächerlichkeit *f.*; ~ *v.t.* lächerlich machen.
ridiculous *a.*, **~ly** *adv.* lächerlich.
riding *s.* Reiten *n.*; ~ *a.* Reit...; **~breeches** *pl.* Reithosen *pl.*; **~habit** *s.* Reitkleid *n.*
rife *a.*, **~ly** *adv.* häufig, weit verbreitet; ~ *with,* voll (von), angefüllt (mit); *be* ~, herrschen.
riffraff *s.* Gesindel *n.*
rifle *v.t.* rauben, plündern; riefeln; ~ *s.* Gewehr *n.*
rifleman *s.* (*mil.*) Schütze *m.*
rifle range *s.* Schießstand *m.*
rift *s.* Unstimmigkeit *f.*; Riß *m.*; Spalte *f.*; ~ *v.i.* sich spalten.
rig *s.* Streich *m.*; Takelung *f.*; Putz *m.*; ~ *v.t.* auftakeln, ausrüsten; verfälschen; manipulieren.
rigging *s.* Takelwerk *n.*; Takelung *f.*
right *a.* & *adv.*, **~ly** *adv.* gerade; recht; richtig; sehr; echt, rechtmäßig; *to be* ~, recht haben; *all* ~*!,* alles in Ordnung!; schon gut; ~*hand side,* rechte Seite; ~ *s.* Recht *n.*; rechte Seite *f.*; *by* ~, von Rechts wegen; *all* ~*s reserved,* alle Rechte vorbehalten; ~ *v.t.* berichtigen; wiedergutmachen; in Ordnung bringen; aufrichten.
right angle *s.* rechter Winkel *m.*
right-angled *a.* rechtwinkelig.
righteous *a.* gerecht, rechtschaffen.
righteousness *s.* Rechtschaffenheit *f.*

rightful *a.*, **~ly** *adv.* rechtmäßig, gerecht.
right-handed *a.* rechtshändig.
rightist *a.* rechtsgerichtet.
right-minded *a.* gerecht denkend.
right-wing *a.* (*pol.*) rechtsorienest, rechtsstehend
rigid *a.*, **~ly** *adv.* steif; starr; streng.
rigidity *s.* Steifheit *f.*, Unbiegsamkeit *f.*
rigmarole *s.* Salbaderei *f.*
rigor *s.* Strenge *f.*
rigor mortis *s.* Leichenstarre *f.*
rigorous *a.*, **~ly** *adv.* streng; genau.
rile *v.t.* (*fam.*) ärgern.
rill *s.* Bach *m.*
rim *s.* Rand *m.;* Reifen *m.*, Radkranz *m.;* Einfassung *f.*
rime *s.* Reif *m.;* Frost *m.*
rimless *a.* randlos.
rind *s.* Rinde, Schale *f.*
ring *s.* Ring *m.;* Clique *f.;* Schall *m.;* Geläute *n.;* ~ *v.t.* klingeln; ~ *v.i.* läuten; erschallen; *to ~ up*, anklingeln, anrufen.
ringing *a.* schallend; klangvoll; ~ *s.* Läuten.
ringleader *s.* Rädelsführer(in) *m.(f.)*
ringlet *s.* Ringelchen *n.;* Ringellocke *f.*
rink *s.* Eisbahn *f.;* Rollschuhbahn *f.*
rinse *v.t.* spülen, ausschwenken; ~ *s.* Spülen *n.*
riot *s.* Schwelgerei *f.;* Tumult *m.;* Aufruhr *m.;* ~ *v.i.* schwärmen, schwelgen; Aufruhr stiften.
rioter *s.* Aufrührer(in) *m.(f.)*
riotous *a.*, **~ly** *adv.* schwelgerisch; ausgelassen; aufrührerisch.
rip *v.t.* auftrennen, aufreißen; enthüllen; ~ *s.* Riß *m.*
ripe *a.*, **~ly** *adv.* reif, zeitig.
ripen *v.t. & i.* reifen.
rip-off *s.* (*fam.*) Nepp *m.*
riposte *s.* Replik *f.;* Entgegnung *f.*
ripple *v.i.* sich kräuseln; ~ *v.t.* riffeln.
rip-roaring *a.* (*fam.*) toll.
rise *v.i.* sich erheben, aufstehen; aufsteigen; aufgehen; heranwachsen; entstehen; steigen; ~ *s.* Anhöhe *f.;* Steigung *f.;* Ursprung *m.;* Steigen (im Preis) *n.*
riser: early ~ *s.* Frühaufsteher(in) *m.(f.);* **late** ~ *s.* Spätaufsteher(in) *m.(f.)*
rising *s.* Aufstand *m.;* Aufstehen *n.;* Aufbruch *m.;* Anschwellung *f.;* ~ *a.* aufgehend; steigend.
risk *s.* Gefahr *f.;* Wagnis *n.;* ~ *v.t.* wagen.
risky *a.* gewagt, gefährlich.
risqué *a.* gewagt, schlüpfrig.
rite *s.* Ritus *m.*
ritual *a.*, **~ly** *adv.* feierlich; rituell.
rival *s.* Rivale *m.;* Rivalin *f.;* Nebenbuhler(in) *m.(f.);* Konkurrent(in) *m.(f.);* ~ *a.* rivalisierend; nebenbuhlerisch; ~ *v.t. & i.* wetteifern.
rivalry *s.* Rivalität *f.;* Konkurrenz *f.*
rive *v.t. & i. st.* (sich) spalten.
river *s.* Fluß *m.;* Strom *m.;* *~ crossing,* Flußübergang *m.*
rivet *s.* Niet *m.;* Klammer *f.;* ~ *v.t.* nieten, vernieten; befestigen.
riveting *a.* fesselnd.
rivulet *s.* Bach *m.*, Flüßchen *n.*
rm. *room,* Zimmer, Zi.
roach *s.* Rotauge *n.* (Fisch); Kakerlak *f.*
road *s.* Straße, Landstraße *f.;* **~s** *pl.* Reede *f.;* **~bed** *s.* Straßenunterbau *m.;* **~block** *s.* (*mil.*) Straßensperre *f.;* **~hog** *s.* rücksichtsloser Fahrer *m.;* **~sign** *s.* Verkehrsschild *n.*
roam *v.i.* umherstreifen; ~ *v.t.* durchwandern.
roan *a.* scheckig, gefleckt ~ *s.* Schecke *f.*
roar *v.i.* brüllen; lärmen; brausen; ~ *s.* Gebrüll *n.;* Brausen *n.*
roaring *a.* dröhnend, tosend.
roast *v.t.* braten, rösten; ~ *a.* gebraten; ~ *s.* Braten *m.;* ~ **beef** *s.* Rinderbraten *m.;* ~ **chicken** *s.* Hühnerbraten *m.;* ~ **mutton** *s.* Hammelbraten *m.*
rob *v.t.* rauben, berauben, bestehlen.
robber *s.* Räuber(in) *m.(f.)*
robbery *s.* Räuberei *f.;* Raub *m.*
robe *s.* langer Rock *m.;* (*law & univ.*) Talar *m.;* Staatskleid *n.;* ~ *v.t. & i.* das Staatskleid anlegen, kleiden.
robin *s.* Rotkehlchen *n.*
robot *s.* Roboter *m.*
robust *a.* stark, rüstig; derb.
rock *s.* Felsen *m.;* ~ *v.t. & i.* rütteln; einwiegen; schaukeln.
rockery *s.* Steingarten *m.*
rocket *s.* Rakete *f.;* (*mil.*) **~launcher, ~projector,** Raketenwurfmaschine *f.*
rockfall *s.* Steinschlag *m.*
rock garden *s.* Steingarten *m.*
rocking chair *s.* Schaukelstuhl *m.*
rocking horse *s.* Schaukelpferd *n.*
rocky *a.* felsig; felsenhart.
rococo *s.* Rokoko *n.*
rod *s.* Rute *f.;* Stange *f.;* Meßrute *f.*
rodent *s.* Nagetier *n.*
roe *s.* Reh *n.;* Hirschkuh *f.;* Fischrogen *m.*
roebuck *s.* Rehbock *m.*
roger *i.* verstanden! (Funkverkehr).
rogue *s.* Schelm *m.;* Schurke *m.*
roguery *s.* Spitzbüberei, Schelmerei *f.*
roguish *a.*, **~ly** *adv.* spitzbübisch.
roister *v.i.* lärmen, poltern.
role *s.* Rolle *f.;* ~ **playing** *s.* Rollenspiel *n.;* ~ **reversal** *s.* Rollentausch *m.*
roll *v.t.* rollen, wälzen; walzen, strecken; ~ *v.i.* sich wälzen, sich drehen; schlingern; ~ *s.* Rollen *n.;* Rolle, Walze *f.;* Brötchen *n.*, Semmel *f.;* Wirbel (auf der Trommel) *m.;* Urkunde, Liste *f.;* *~ and butter,* Butterbrötchen *n.*.
roll-call *s.* Namensaufruf *m.*, (*mil.*) Appell *m.*
roller *s.* Rolle *f.;* Walze *f.;* Wickelband *n.;* ~ **skate** *s.* Rollschuh *m.*
roller-bearing *s.* (*mech.*) Rollenlager *n.*
roller-blind *s.* Rollo *n.*
roller-coaster *s.* Achterbahn *f.*
roller-skate *v.i.* Rollschuh laufen.
roller-skating *s.* Rollschuhlaufen *n.*
rollfilm *s.* (*phot.*) Rollfilm *m.*
rollick *v.i.* ausgelassen sein; **~ing** *a.* ausgelassen.
rolling-mill *s.* Walzwerk *n.*
rolling-pin *s.* Nudelholz *n.*, Teigrolle *f.*
rolling stock *s.* rollendes Material *n.*
ROM *read only memory,* Nur-Lese-Speicher.
Roman *a.* römisch; ~ **numerals** *pl.* römische Zahlen; ~ **type** *s.* Antiquaschrift *f.;* ~ **Catholic** *a.* römisch-katholisch; *s.* Katholik(in) *m.(f.)*
romance *s.* Romanze *f.;* Erdichtung *f.;* ~ *v.i.*

erdichten; aufschneiden; ~ *a.* romanisch; ~ **languages and literature** Romanistik *f.*
Romanesque *a.* (*arch.*) romanisch.
Romania *s.* Rumänien.
Romanian *a.* rumänisch; ~ *s.* Rumäne *m.;* Rumänin *f.*
romantic *a.*, **~ly** *adv.* romantisch.
Romanticism *s.* Romantik *f.*
romanticize *v.t.* romantisieren.
Romany *s.* Romani *n.* (Sprache); **~ies** *pl.* die Roma, (*fam.*) die Zigeuner.
romp *s.* Tollen, (*sp. fam.*) leichter Sieg. ~ *v.i.* ausgelassen sein, sich balgen.
rood *s.* Rute *f.*
roof *s.* Dach *n.;* Decke *f.;* **~-garden** *s.* Dachgarten *m.;* ~ *v.t.* bedachen.
roofing *s.* Bedachung *f.;* **~-felt** *s.* Dachpappe *f.*
roof-rack *s.* Dachgepäckträger *m.*
roof-top *s.* Dach *n.*
rook *s.* Saatkrähe *f.;* Turm (im Schach) *m.;* Gauner *m.*
rookery *s.* Krähenhorst *m.*
room *s.* Raum *m.;* Platz *m.;* Zimmer *n.*
roommate *s.* Zimmergenosse *m.;* Zimmergenossin *f.;* Mitbewohner(in) *m.(f.)*
roomy *a.* geräumig.
roost *s.* Hühnerstange *f.*
root *s.* Wurzel *f.;* Ursprung *m.;* ~ *v.i.* (ein) wurzeln; ~ **out** *v.t.* ausrotten; ausjäten, (Rüben) ausziehen.
rooted *a. & p.* eingewurzelt, fest.
rootless *a.* wurzellos; nichtverwurzelt.
rope *s.* Seil *n.;* Tau *n.;* Strick *m.;* ~ *v.t.* anseilen.
rope-dancer, rope-walker *s.* Seiltänzer(in) *m.(f.)*
rope-ladder *s.* Strickleiter *f.*
rope-maker *s.* Seiler *m.*
rope-walk *s.* Seilbahn *f.*
rosary *s* Rosenkranz *m.*
rose *s.* Rose *f.;* Rosette *f.*
roseate *a.* rosig, rosenfarben.
rosebud *s.* Rosenknospe *f.*
rosebush *s.* Rosenstrauch *m.*
rosemary *s.* Rosmarin *m.*
rosette *s.* Rosette (Verzierung) *f.*
rosin *s.* Harz *n.;* Kolophonium *n.*
roster *s.* Dienstplan *m.*, Namensliste *f.*
rostrum *s.* Podium *n.;* Rednerpult *n.*
rosy *a.* rosig.
rot *v.i.* faulen, modern; ~ *s.* Fäulnis *f.;* Schund *m.;* Unsinn *m.*
rota *s.* Dienstturnus *m.*
rotary *a.* rotierend; Rotations...; ~ *s.* Kreisverkehr *m.*
rotate *v.i. & t.* (sich) drehen, rotieren.
rotation *s.* Kreislauf *m.;* Umdrehung *f.;* Wechsel *m.;* ~ *of crops*, Fruchtwechsel *m.;* *in* ~, abwechselnd.
rote *s. by* ~, auswendig.
rotten *a.* verfault; verdorben; verfallen; scheußlich, übel; ~ *egg*, faules Ei *n.*
rotund *a.* rund, kreisförmig.
rotundity *s.* Rundheit *f.*
rouble *s.* Rubel *m.*
rouge *s.* Rouge *n.*
rough *a.*, **~ly** *adv.* rauh, holprig, roh; ungebildet, grob; heftig; ~ *notes pl.* flüchtige Notizen *f.pl.;* ~ *calculation*, grobe Berechnung *f.;* ~ *s.* Rohheit *f.*, ~ *v.t.* roh bearbeiten; *to* ~ *it*, primitiv leben.
roughage *s.* grobe Nahrung *f.*, Ballaststoffe *pl.*
rough-cast *s.* roher Entwurf *m.;* Rohputz *m.;* ~ *v.t.* entwerfen.
rough copy *s.* Entwurf *m.;* Konzept *n.*
rough draft *s.* erster Entwurf *m.*, Faustskizze *f.*
roughen *v.t.* rauh machen; aufrauhen.
rough neck *s.* Grobian *m.*
roughness *s.* Rauheit *f.;* Unebenheit *f.*
rough-shod *a.* rücksichtslos.
round *a.* rund; unverhohlen, offen; volltönend; *a* ~ *sum*, eine runde Summe *f.;* ~ *adv. & pr.* um, herum, rings; geradeheraus; ~ *s.* Runde *f.;* Salve *f.;* (Patrone) Schuß *m.;* ~ **up** *s.* Razzia *f.;* ~ *v.t.* rundmachen; umfahren; ~ *v.i.* sich runden; *to* ~ *up*, ~ *v.t.* zusammentreiben.
roundabout *a.* umgebend, Um...; ~ *adv.* rundherum; ~ *s.* Karussell *n.*
roundly *adv.* rund; geradeheraus.
roundness *s.* Rundung *f.;* Offenheit *f.*
round trip *s.* Hin- und Rückfahrt *f.*
rouse *v.t.* aufwecken; aufregen, auftreiben; ~ *v.i.* aufwachen.
rout *s.* Aufruhr *m.;* Rotte *f.;* wilde Flucht *f.;* ~ *v.t.* in die Flucht schlagen; aufreiben.
route *s.* Weg *m.;* Marschroute *f.*
routine *s.* Routine *f.;* Schlendrian *m.;* ~ *work*, laufende Arbeiten *pl.;* Routinearbeit *f.*
rove *v.i.* herumschwärmen, wandern; ~ *v.t.* durchwandern.
row *s.* Reihe *f.;* ~ *v.t. & i.* rudern; ~ *s.* Lärm *m.;* Auflauf, Streit *m.*
rowan *s.* Eberesche *f.*
row-boat *s.* Ruderboot *n.*
rowdy *s.* roher Kerl *m.;* Rowdy *m.;* ~ *a.* roh, lärmend.
rowel *s.* Spornrädchen *n.*
rowing-match *s.* Wettrudern *n.*
royal *a.*, **~ly** *adv.* königlich; prächtig.
royalist *m. s.* Royalist(in) *m.(f.)*
royalty *s.* Königtum *n.;* Krongut *n.;* Tantieme *f.*, Lizenz *f.*
r.p.m. *revolutions per minute*, Umdrehungen pro Minute, U/min.
RR *railroad*, Eisenbahn.
RSVP *répondez s'il vous plaît* (*please reply*), um Antwort wird gebeten, u.A.w.g.
rt. *right*, rechts, r.
Rt. Hon. *Right Honorable*, Hochwohlgeboren.
rub *v.t.* reiben, scheuern, abwischen; ~ *v.i.* sich durchschlagen; ~ *s.* Reibung *f.;* Hindernis *n.;* *to* ~ *one's hands together*, sich die Hände reiben.
rubber *s.* Wischtuch *n.;* Robber (im Whistspiel) *m.;* Kautschuk *m.*, Gummi *m.;* (*sl.*) Pariser *m.* (Kondom); **~s** *pl.* Gummischuhe *m.pl.;* ~ **band** *s.* Gummiband *n.;* **~-dinghy** *s.* Schlauchboot *n.;* ~ **stamp** *s.* Stempel; **~-stamp** *v.t.* abstempeln; (*fig.*) genehmigen.
rubbish *s.* Unsinn *m.;* Schutt *m.;* Kehricht *m.* & *n.*
rubbishy *a.* blödsinnig.
rubble *s.* Steinschutt *m.;* Trümmer *pl.*
rubella *s.* Röteln *pl.*
rubicund *a.* rot, rötlich.
rubric *s.* Rubrik *f.*
ruby *s.* Rubin *m.*

rudder *s.* (Steuer)Ruder *n.;* Steuer *n.*
ruddy *a.* rötlich.
rude *a.*, **~ly** *adv.* unhöflich; rüde; grob.
rudeness *s.* Grobheit *f.*, ungehöriges Benehmen *n.*
rudimentary *a.* rudimentär, Anfangs...
rudiments *s.pl.* Grundzüge *pl.;* Grundlagen *pl.*
rue *s.* Raute (Pflanze) *f.;* ~ *v.t.* bereuen; beklagen.
rueful *a.*, **~ly** *adv.* reuig, kläglich.
ruff *s.* Halskrause *f.*
ruffian *s.* roher Kerl *m.;* Raufbold *m.*
ruffianly *a.* wüst, brutal, bübisch.
ruffle *v.t.* kräuseln; zerknüllen; sträuben; durcheinanderbringen; aus der Fassung bringen; ~ *v.i.* sich kräuseln; flattern; ~ *s.* Krause, Rüsche *f.;* Gekräusel *n.;* Unruhe *f.*
rug *s.* Bettvorleger, Kaminvorleger *f.;* kleiner Teppich *m.*
rugby *s.* Rugby *n.*
rugged *a.*, **~ly** *adv.* rauh, holp[e]rig; zerklüftet.
ruin *s.* Einsturz *m.;* Ruine *f.;* Ruin *m.;* Untergang *m.;* Verderben *n.;* ~ *v.t.* zerstören; zu Grunde richten.
ruinous *a.*, **~ly** *adv.* ruinös.
rule *s.* Regel *f.;* (gerichtliche) Verfügung *f.;* Ordnung *f.;* Lineal *n.;* Maßstab *m.;* Herrschaft *f.;* ~ *of thumb,* Erfahrungsregel *f.;* ~ *of the road,* Straßenverkehrsordnung, Fahrordnung *f.;* ~ *v.t.* lin(i)ieren; regeln; verordnen; beherrschen; ~ *v.i.* herrschen; *to ~ out,* ausschließen.
ruled *a.* liniert.
ruler *s.* Herrscher(in) *m.(f.);* Lineal *n.*
ruling *s.* Gerichtsentscheidung *f.;* ~ *a.* herrschend; regierend.
rum *s.* Rum *m.*
rumble *v.i.* rumpeln, rasseln.
ruminant *s.* Wiederkäuer *m.*
ruminate *v.t. & i.* wiederkäuen; (*fig.*) grübeln.
rummage *v.t.* durchstöbern; wühlen; ~ *sale,* Ramschverkauf *m.*
rummy *s.* Rommé *n.*
rumor *s.* Gerücht *n.;* ~ *v.t.* (ein Gerücht) verbreiten, aussprengen.
rump *s.* Hinterteil *n.;* Rest *m.*
rumple *s.* Runzel *f.;* Falte *f.;* ~ *v.t.* runzeln, zerknittern.
rumpsteak *s.* Rumpsteak *n.*
rumpus *s.* (*sl.*) Krach *m.*, Trubel *m.*
run *v.i. & t.st.* laufen; eilen; verstreichen; strömen; lauten; sich erstrecken; leiten; hetzen; *to ~ down,* niederrennen; abhetzen; heruntermachen; *to ~ into,* hineinfahren in, anfahren; *to ~ into debt,* Schulden machen; *to ~ off,* davonlaufen; *to ~ on,* fortschreiten, fortsetzen; *to ~ out,* auslaufen; zu Ende gehen; sich erschöpfen; *to ~ over,* überfahren; *to ~ short,* ausgehen; *to ~ to,* sich belaufen auf; *to ~ up,* in die Höhe laufen; anwachsen lassen; hinauftreiben, steigern; errichten, aufbauen; ~ *s.* Laufen *n.;* Lauf, Gang *m.;* Andrang, Ansturm; Weidegrund *m.;* starke Nachfrage *f.;* Aufführungsperiode *(f.)* eines Stücks; Laufmasche, *f.* (*in stocking*); *the common ~,* Durchschnittstyp *m.;* ~ *on a bank,* Ansturm *(m.)* auf eine Bank; *in the long ~,* auf die Dauer.
runaway *s.* Flüchtling *m.;* Ausreißer(in) *m.(f.)*
rune *s.* Rune *f.*
rung *s.* (Leiter)Sprosse *f.*
runic *a.* runisch, Runen...
runner *s.* Läufer(in) *m. (f.);* Bote *m.;* Botin *f.;* Kufe *f.;* **~-beans** *pl.* grüne Bohnen *f.pl.;* **~-up,** Zweite *m./f.*
running *a.*, laufend; fließend; hintereinander; **~-board** *s.* (*mot.*) Trittbrett *n.;* **~ costs** *pl.* Betriebskosten *pl.;* **~ repairs** *s.* laufende Reparaturen *pl.;* **~ shoes** *pl.* Joggingschuhe *pl.;* **~ mate** *s.* Vizepräsidentschaftskandidat(in) *m.(f.);* **~ water** *s.* laufendes Wasser *n.*
runny *a.* flüssig; laufend (Nase); tränend (Auge).
runway *s.* (*avi.*) Startbahn *f.;* Landebahn *f.*
rupee *s.* Rupie *f.*
rupture *s.* Bruch *m.;* Uneinigkeit *f.;* ~ *v.i.* brechen, bersten.
rural *a.*, **~ly** *adv.* ländlich.
ruse *s.* List *f.*, Trick *m.*
rush *s.* Binse *f.;* Ansturm *m.;* Hetzerei, Hetze *f.;* Andrang *m.*, Gedränge *n.;* Sturz *m.;* **~ hour** *s.* Stoßzeit *f.;* **~ hours** *pl.* Hauptgeschäftszeiten *f.pl.;* ~ *v.i.* stürzen, schießen, rennen; rauschen; ~ *v.t.* (durch)hetzen, durchpeitschen.
rusk *s.* Zwieback *m.*
russet *a.* braunrot; ~ *s.* Rötling (Apfel) *m.*
Russia *s.* Rußland *n.*
Russian *a.* russisch, ~ *s.* Russe *m.;* Russin *f.*
rust *s.* Rost *m.;* ~ *v.i.* rosten.
rustic *a.*, **~ally** *adv.* ländlich, bäurisch; ~ *s.* Bauer *m.*
rusticity *s.* Ländlichkeit *f.*
rustle *v.i.* rauschen; säuseln; raschen.
rustler *s.* Viehdieb *m.*
rusty *a.*, **~ily** *adv.* rostig; eingerostet.
rut *s.* Spur *f.;* Geleise *n.;* Brunst *f.*, Brunft *f.;* ~ *v.t.* furchen; ~ *v.i.* brunsten.
ruthless *a.*, **~ly** *adv.* unbarmherzig.
rutted *a.* ausgefahren.
rutting-season *s.* Brunftzeit *f.*
rye *s.* Roggen *m.;* **~-grass,** Lolch *m.*

S

S, s der Buchstabe S oder s *n.*
s *second,* Sekunde, Sek.
S. *south,* Süden, S.; *Saint,* Sankt; *Society,* Verein.
S.A. *South Africa,* Südafrika.
Sabbath *s.* Sabbat *m.;* Ruhetag *m.*
sabbatical *a.* **~ term/year** Forschungssemester *n.* Forschungsjahr *n.*
saber *s.* Säbel *m.;* ~ *v.t.* niedersäbeln; **~ rattling** *s.* Säbelrasseln *n.*
sable *s.* Zobel *m.;* Zobelpelz *m.*
sabotage *s.* Sabotage *f.;* ~ *v.t.* sabotieren.
saccharin *s.* Saccharin *n.*
sacerdotal *a.* priesterlich.
sack *s.* Sack *m.;* Beutel *m.*, Tüte *f.*, (*fam.*)

Plünderung *f.;* Laufpaß *m.;* ~ *v.t.* einsacken; plündern; entlassen.
sackcloth *s.* Sackleinwand *f.*
sack race *s.* Sackhüpfen *n.*
sacrament *s.* Sakrament *n.;* heiliges Abendmahl *n.; to take the* ~, zum Abendmahl gehen.
sacred *a.*, **~ly** *adv.* heilig; ehrwürdig; ~ **cow** *s.* heilige Kuh *f.*
sacrifice *v.t. & i.* opfern; ~ *s.* Opfer *n.;* Opferung *f.;* Preisgabe *f.*
sacrificial *a.* Opfer...
sacrilege *s.* Kirchenraub, Frevel *m.*
sacrilegious *a.*, **~ly** *adv.* frevelhaft; ruchlos.
sacristan *s.* Kirchner, Küster *m.*
sacristy *s.* Sakristei *f.*
sacrosanct *a.* sakrosankt.
sad *a.*, **~ly** *adv.* traurig; trübe, ernst; dunkel; schlimm, arg.
sadden *v.t.* betrüben.
saddle *s.* Sattel *m.;* Rückenstück *n.;* ~ **horse** Reitpferd *n.;* ~ *v.t.* satteln; belasten.
saddler *s.* Sattler *m.*
sadism *s.* Sadismus *m.*
sadist *s.* Sadist(in) *m.(f.)*
sadistic *a.*, **~ally** *adv.* sadistisch.
sadness *s.* Traurigkeit, Schwermut *f.;* Ernst *m.*
safari *s.* Safari *f.*
safe *a.*, **~ly** *adv.* sicher; unversehrt; ~ *s.* Geldschrank *m.;* Safe *m.*
safe-conduct *s.* sicheres Geleit *n.;* Schutzbrief *m.*
safeguard *s.* Schutzwache *f.;* Schutz *m.;* ~ *v.t.* schützen, sichern.
safety *s.* Sicherheit *f.;* **~belt** *s.* Sicherheitsgurt *m.;* **~curtain** *s.* eiserner Vorhang *m.;* **~glass** *s.* Plexiglas *n.;* **~match** *s.* Sicherheitszündholz *n.;* **~pin** *s.* Sicherheitsnadel *f.;* **~razor** *s.* Rasierapparat *m.;* **~valve** *s.* Sicherheitsventil *n.*
saffron *s.* Safran *m.;* ~ *a.* safrangelb.
sag *v.i.* sich senken, sacken; durchhängen.
saga *s.* Heldenepos *n.;* Saga *f.*
sagacious *a.*, **~ly** *adv.* scharfsinnig.
sagacity *s.* Scharfsinn *m.*
sage *a.*, **~ly** *adv.* weise, klug; ~ *s.* Weise *m.;* (Gewürz) Salbei *f.*
sagittarius *s.* (*astr.*) Schütze *m.*
sago *s.* Sago *m.*
sail *s.* Segel *n.;* Schiff *n.;* Windmühlenflügel *m.;* ~ *v.i.* segeln; abfahren (vom Schiff); ~ *v.t.* durchsegeln; **~boat** *s.* Segelboot *n.*
sailor *s.* Matrose *m.; to be a good* ~, seefest sein.
saint *a.*, **~ly** *adv.* heilig; ~ *s.* Heilige *m./f.*
sake *s. for God's* ~, um Gotteswillen; *for the* ~ *of,* um.. .willen; *for my* ~, um meinetwillen.
salacious *a.*, **~ly** *adv.* lüstern; schlüpfrig; geil.
salad *s.* Salat *m.;* **~-dressing** Salatsoße *f.*
salamander *s.* Salamander *m.*
salami *s.* Salami(wurst) *f.*
salaried *a.* besoldet.
salary *s.* Gehalt *n.;* **~-scale** *s.* Gehaltsskala *f.*
sale *s.* Verkauf, Absatz *m.;* Ausverkauf *m.;* **~s assistant** *s.* Verkäufer(in) *m.(f.);* **~s clerk** *s.* Verkäufer(in) *m. (f.);* **~swoman** *s.* Verkäuferin *f.;* **~sman** *s.* Verkäufer *m.;* **~smanship** *s.* Verkaufstüchtigkeit, Verkaufsgewandtheit *f.; for* ~, verkäuflich.
salient *a.* springend; hervorragend.
saline *a.* salzartig; ~ *s.* Salzquelle *f.*
saliva *s.* Speichel *m.*
salivate *v.i.* speicheln.
sallow *a.* blaß; gelblich; ~ *s.* Salweide *f.*
sally *s.* Ausfall *m.;* Ausflug *m.;* witziger Einfall *m.;* ~ **forth** *v.i.* sich aufmachen; hervorbrechen.
salmon *s.* Lachs, Salm *m.*
salon *s.* Salon *m.*
saloon *s.* Saal, Salon *m.;* Kneipe *f.;* erste Klasse *f.* (Schiff); **~car** *s.* (*rail.*) Luxuswagen *m.*
salt *s.* Salz *n.;* (*fig.*) Seebär *m.;* Würze *f.;* Witz *m.;* ~ *a.*, **~y** *adv.* salzig; ~ *v.t.* (ein)salzen.
salt cellar *s.* Salzfaß *n.*
salter *s.* Salzhändler *m.*
saltpeter *s.* Salpeter *m.*
salt shaker *s.* Salzfaß *n.*
salt works *s.pl.* Saline *f.*
salty *a.* etwas salzig.
salubrious *a.* heilsam, gesund.
salubrity *s.* Heilsamkeit *f.*
salutary *a.* heilsam.
salutation *s.* Gruß *m.;* Anrede (Brief) *f.*
salute *v.t.* grüßen; ~ *s.* Gruß *m.*
salvage *s.* Bergung *f.;* Bergelohn *m.;* ~ *v.t.* bergen.
salvation *s.* Rettung, Seligkeit *f.;* **~Army,** Heilsarmee *f.*
salve *s.* Salbe *f.* ~ *v.t.* salben; lindern; bergen.
salver *s.* Präsentierteller *m.*
salvo *s.* Vorbehalt *m.;* Salve *f.*
same *pn.* derselbe, dieselbe, dasselbe; einerlei; *all the* ~, trotzdem.
sameness *s.* Gleichheit *f.*
sample *s.* Probe *f.*, Muster *n.; according to* ~, nach Muster; ~ *v.t.* eine Probe nehmen.
sampler *s.* Stick(muster)tuch *n.*
sanatorium *s.* Heilanstalt *f.*
sanctification *s.* Heiligung, Einsegnung *f.*
sanctify *v.t.* heiligen.
sanctimonious *a.*, **~ly** *adv.* scheinheilig.
sanction *s.* Bestätigung *f.*, Genehmigung *f.;* Sanktion *f.;* Zwangsmaßnahme *f.;* Gesetzeskraft *f.;* ~ *v.t.* bestätigen; genehmigen.
sanctity *s.* Heiligkeit, Reinheit *f.*
sanctuary *s.* Heiligtum *n.;* Freistätte *f.*
sand *s.* Sand *m.;* **~s** *pl.* Sandwüste; Strand *m.;* Sandbank *f.*
sandal *s.* Sandale *f.*
sandalwood *s.* Sandelholz *n.*
sandbag *s.* Sandsack *m.*
sandbox *s.* Sandkasten *m.*
sand castle *s.* Sandburg *f.*
sandpaper *s.* Sandpapier *n.*
sandstone *s.* Sandstein *m.*
sandwich *s.* belegtes Brot *n.;* Sandwich *n.;* ~ *v.t.* einklemmen; ~ **man** *s.* Plakatträger *m.*
sandy *a.* sandig; gelblichrot.
sane *a.* gesund (an Geist), vernünftig.
sangfroid *s.* Kaltblütigkeit *f.*
sanguinary *a.* blutig; blutdürstig.
sanguine *a.*, **~ly** *adv.* hoffnungsvoll.
sanitary *a.* gesundheitlich, Gesundheits...; ~ **napkin** *s.* Monatsbinde *f.*
sanitation *s.* Hygiene *f.*
sanity *s.* Gesundheit *f.;* gesunder Verstand *m.*
Santa Claus *s.* der Weihnachtsmann *m.*

sap *s.* Saft (der Bäume) *m.;* Splint *m.;* ~ *v.t. & i.* untergraben, sappen.
sapience *s.* Weisheit *f.*
sapient *a.* weise.
sapless *a.* saftlos.
sapling *s.* junger Baum, Schößling *m.*
sapper *s.* Sappeur *m.*
sapphire *s.* Saphir *m.*
sappy *a.* saftig; weich; munter.
sarcasm *s.* beißender Spott *m.;* Sarkasmus *m.*
sarcastic *a.* beißend, sarkastisch.
sarcophagus *s.* Steinsarg *m.*
sardine *s.* Sardine *f.*
sardonic *a.* sardonisch, bitter, grimmig.
sartorial *a.* Schneider...
SASE *self-addressed stamped envelope,* frankierter Rückumschlag.
sash *s.* Schärpe *f.;* Fensterrahmen *m.;* ~ **window** Schiebefenster *n.*
satanic *a.,* **~ally** *adv.* teuflisch.
satchel *s.* Schulmappe *f.;* Tasche *f.*
sate *v.t.* sättigen.
sateen *s.* Satin *m.*
satellite *s.* Satellit *m.*
satellite dish *s.* Parabolantenne *f.*
satiate *v.t.* sättigen.
satiety *s.* Sättigung *f.;* Überdruß *m.*
satin *s.* Atlas *m.;* Satin *m.*
satire *s.* Satire *f.*
satirical *a.,* **~ly** *adv.* satirisch.
satirist *s.* Satiriker(in) *m.(f.)*
satirize *v.t.* bespötteln.
satisfaction *s.* Genugtuung *f.;* Befriedigung, Freude *f.*
satisfactory *a.,* **~ily** *adv.* befriedigend.
satisfied *a.* zufrieden.
satisfy *v.t. & i.* genugtun, genügen; befriedigen; überzeugen.
satisfying *a.* befriedigend.
saturate *v.t.* (*chem.*) sättigen; durchnässen.
saturated *a.* gesättigt; durchnäßt.
Saturday *s.* Sonnabend, Samstag *m.*
Saturn *s.* Saturn *m.*
saturnine *a.* mürrisch, finster.
sauce *s.* Sauce, Soße, Tunke *f.;* Würze *f.;* **~boat** *s.* Sauciere *f.*
saucepan *s.* Kochtopf *m.,* Tiegel *m.*
saucer *s.* Untertasse *f.*
saucy *a.,* **~ily** *adv.* unverschämt; keck.
Saudi Arabia *s.* Saudi Arabien *n.*
Saudi Arabian *a.* saudiarabisch; ~ *s.* Saudi(araber) *m.,* Saudiaraberin *f.*
sauna *s.* Sauna *f.*
saunter *v.i.* schlendern; ~ *s.* Bummel *m.*
saurian *a.* Saurier...
sausage *s.* Wurst *f.*
savage *a.,* **~ly** *adv.* wild, grausam; ~ *s.* Wilde *m./f*
savagery *s.* Brutalität *f.*
savanna(h) *s.* Grasfläche *f.;* Savanne *f.*
save *v.t.* retten, bergen; schonen; sparen, ersparen; aufheben; ~ *pr.* außer, ausgenommen.
saveloy *s.* Zervelatwurst *f.*
saving *a.,* **~ly** *adv.* sparsam; ~ *s.* Rettung *f.;* Vorbehalt *m.;* Ersparnis *f.;* ~ *pr.* außer; ~ **clause,** (*jur.*) Vorbehaltsklausel *f.;* **~s bank** *s.* Sparkasse *f.;* **~s certificate** *s.* Spargutschein *m.*
Savior *s.* Erlöser, Heiland *m.;* Retter(in) *m.(f.)*
savor *s.* Geschmack *m.;* Geruch, Duft *m.;* ~ *v.i. & t.* schmecken, riechen;
savory *a.* schmackhaft; wohlriechend; scharfgewürzt; ~ *s.* Häppchen *n.*
savoy *s.* Wirsing(kohl) *m.*
savvy *a.* (*fam.*) klug; mit viel Grips.
saw *s.* Säge *f.;* Spruch *m.;* ~ *v.t.* sägen.
sawdust *s.* Sägespäne *m.pl.*
sawhorse *s.* Sägebock *m.*
sawmill *s.* Schneidemühle *f.*
Saxony *s.* Sachsen *n.*
saxophone *s.* Saxophon *n.*
saxophonist *s.* Saxophonist(in) *m.(f.)*
say *v.t. & i.st.* sagen; hersagen; erzählen.
saying *s.* Rede *f.;* Redensart *f.;* *it goes without* ~, es versteht sich von selbst.
sc., scil. *scilicet (namely),* nämlich.
scab *s.* Schorf *m.;* Krätze *f.;* Streikbrecher *m.*
scabbard *s.* Säbelscheide *f.*
scabby *a.* krätzig; schäbig.
scabies *s.* Krätze *f.*
scabrous *a.* heikel, schlüpfrig.
scaffold *s.* Gerüst, Schafott *n.;* ~ *v.t.* ein Gerüst aufschlagen; stützen.
scaffolding *s.* Gerüst *n.;* Bühne *f.*
scald *s.* Verbrühung *f.;* Brandwunde *f.;* Skalde *m.;* ~ *v.t.* brühen, verbrennen; (Milch) abkochen.
scalding hot *a.* brühheiß.
scale *s.* Waagschale *f.;* Schuppe *f.;* Kesselstein *m.;* Maßtab *m.;* Tonleiter *f.;* Stufenleiter *f.;* Gradeinteilung *f.;* *pair of* ~*s,* Waage *f.;* *on a large* ~, im Großen, auf großem Fuße; ~ *v.t.* erklettern, stürmen; abschiefern, schuppen; ~ *v.i.* abblättern.
scaled *a.* schuppig.
scaling ladder *s.* Sturmleiter *f.;* Feuerleiter *f.*
scallop *s.* Zacke *f.,* Langette *f.;* Muschel *f.;* ~ *v.t.* ausbogen.
scalp *s.* Kopfhaut *f.;* ~ *v.t.* skalpieren.
scalpel *s.* Skalpell *n.*
scaly *a.* schuppig, geschuppt.
scamp *s.* Taugenichts *m.;* Lausbub *m.;* ~ *v.t.* verpfuschen.
scamper *v.i.* rennen.
scan *v.t.* skandieren (Verse); genau ansehen, erwägen.
scandal *s.* Skandal *m.;* Schande *f.*
scandalize *v.t.* schockieren, empören.
scandalous *a.,* **~ly** *adv.* schändlich.
Scandinavia *s.* Skandinavien *n.*
Scandinavian *a.* skandinavisch; ~ *s.* Skandinavier(in) *m.(f.)*
scanner *s.* Geigerzähler *m.;* (*comp.*) Scanner *m.*
scant *a.* knapp; sparsam.
scanty *a.* sparsam, karg, knapp; gering.
scapegoat *s.* Sündenbock *m.*
scar *s.* Narbe *f.;* ~ *v.t.* eine Narbe hinterlassen; ~ *v.i.* vernarben.
scarab *s.* Käfer *m.;* Skarabäus *m.*
scarce *a.* spärlich, knapp.
scarcely *adv.* kaum.
scarcity *s.* Seltenheit, Spärlichkeit *f.;* Knappheit *f.*

scare *v.t.* scheuchen, schrecken; ~ *s.* leerer Schreck *m.*; Panik *f.*
scarecrow *s.* Vogelscheuche *f.*
scared *a.* verängstigt; Angst haben.
scaremonger *s.* Panikmacher(in) *m.(f.)*
scarf *s.* Halstuch *n.*; Kopftuch *n.*; Schultertuch *n.*
scarlet *s.* Scharlach *m.*; ~ *a.* scharlachrot; ~ **fever** *s.* Scharlachfieber *n.*
scathing *a.* beißend; scharf.
scatter *v.t.* zerstreuen, verbreiten; verstreuen; ~ *v.i.* sich zerstreuen.
scatterbrained *a.* konfus; schusselig.
scavenge *v.t.* ~ **on,** leben von; ~ **in,** herumwühlen.
scavenger *s.* Aasfresser *m.*
Sc.D. = D.Sc.
scenario *s.* Szenario *n.*
scene *s.* Bühne *f.*; Schauplatz *m.*; Szene *f.*; Begebenheit *f.*; Kulisse *f.*; Auftritt *m.*; ~ *of action,* Schauplatz *m.*
scenery *s.* Landschaft, Gegend, Szenerie *f.*; Gemälde *n.*; Bühnengerät *n.*
scenic(al) *a.* bühnenmäßig; landschaftlich, Landschafts...
scent *s.* Geruch *m.*; Witterung *f.*; Fährte *f.*; ~ *v.t.* riechen, wittern; durchduften.
scented *a.* duftend.
scepter *s.* Zepter *n.*
sceptic *a.* skeptisch; *s.* Skeptiker(in) *m. (f.)*
scepticism *s.* Skeptik *f.*; Skeptizismus *m.*
schedule *s.* Verzeichnis *n.*, Liste *f.*; Fahrplan *m.*; ~ *v.t.* aufzeichnen; *on* ~ *adv.* planmäßig, fahrplanmäßig.
scheduled *a.* planmäßig.
schematic *a.* schematisch.
scheme *s.* Plan, Entwurf *m.*; Figur *f.*, Schema *n.*; ~ *v.i.* & *t.* Pläne machen, entwerfen; Ränke schmieden.
schemer *s.* Ränkeschmied *m.*
scheming *a.* intrigant.
schism *s.* Kirchenspaltung *f.*
schismatic *a.*, **~ally** *adv.* schismatisch.
schizophrenia *s.* Schizophrenie *f.*
schizophrenic *a.* schizophren.
scholar *s.* Gelehrte *m./f.*
scholarly *a.* wissenschaftlich; gelehrt.
scholarship *s.* Gelehrsamkeit *f.*; Stipendium *n.*
scholastic *a.*, **~ally** *adv.* schulmäßig; Schul...; scholastisch; ~ **degree,** Schulabgangszeugnis *n.*
school *s.* Schule *f.*; Schulhaus *n.*; **~age,** schulpflichtiges Alter *n.*; **~attendance,** Schulbesuch *m.*; **~leaving age,** Schulentlassungsalter *n.*; ~ *v.t.* schulen, unterrichten.
school board *s.* Schulbehörde *f.*
schoolboy *s.* Schuljunge *m.*
schoolgirl *s.* Schulmädchen *n.*
schoolmaster *s.* Schullehrer *m.*
schoolmate *s.* Schulkamerad(in) *m.(f.)*
schoolmistress *s.* Lehrerin *f.*
schoolteacher *s.* Lehrer(in) *m.(f.)*
schoolyard *s.* Schulhof *m.*
school year *s.* Schuljahr *n.*
schooner *s.* Schoner (Fahrzeug) *m.*
sciatica *s.* Ischias *f.*
science *s.* Wissenschaft *f.*; Naturwissenschaft *f.*; Kenntnis *f.*
scientific *a.*, **~ally** *adv.* wissenschaftlich.
scientist *s.* (Natur) Wissenschaftler(in) *m.(f.)*
scintillate *v.i.* funkeln.
scintillating *a.* sprühend; geistsprühend.
scion *s.* Sproß *m.*, Sprößling *m.*
scissors *s.pl.* Schere *f.*
sclerosis *s.* Sklerose *f.*
scoff *v.t.* verspotten; verschlingen; ~ *s.* Hohn *m.*
scold *v.t.* & *i.* schelten, zanken.
scolding *s.* Schimpfen *n.*, Schelte *f.*
sconce *s.* kleine Laterne *f.*; Wandleuchter *m.*
scone *s.* kleiner Mürbekuchen *m.*
scoop *s.* Schaufel; Spatel *m.*; Schöpflöffel *m.*; ~ *v.t.* schaufeln, schöpfen, aushöhlen.
scoot *v.i.* (fam). rasen; die Kurve kratzen
scooter *s.* Tretroller *m.*; Motorroller *m.*
scope *s.* Spielraum *m.*, Umfang *m.*; Gesichtskreis *m.*; Zweck *m.*
scorch *v.t.* sengen, brennen; ~ *v.i.* ausdorren; *scorched earth,* (*mil.*) verbrannte Erde; ~ *s.* Brandfleck *m.*
scorching *a.* glühend heiß; sengend.
score *s.* Kerbholz *n.*, Kerbe *f.*; Zeche *f.*; Schuld *f.*; Spielstand *f.*; (*mus.*) Partitur *f.*; ~ *v.t.* einkerben; anschreiben; Punkte machen; (*mus.*) instrumentieren; gewinnen; **~board** *s.* Anzeigetafel *f.*
scorn *s.* Spott *m.*; Geringschätzung *f.*; Verachtung *f.*; ~ *v.t.* & *i.* verspotten; verachten.
scornful *a.*, **~ly** *adv.* höhnisch; verächtlich.
Scorpio *s.* (*astro.*) Skorpion *m.*
scorpion *s.* Skorpion *m.*
Scot *s.* Schotte *m.*; Schottin *f.*
Scotch *s.* Scotch Whisky. *m.*
scotch fir *s.* Föhre, Kiefer *f.*
scotch tape *s.* Klebestreifen *m.*
scot-free *a.* unversehrt, ungeschoren.
Scotland *s.* Schottland *n.*
Scots *a.* schottisch; *s.* Schottisch *n.*
Scottish *a.* schottisch.
scoundrel *s.* Schurke *m.*
scour *v.t.* & *i.* scheuern, reinigen; durchstreifen.
scourer *s.* Topfreiniger *m.*
scourge *s.* Geißel *f.*; Strafe *f.*; ~ *v.t.* geißeln, züchtigen.
scout *s.* Späher, Kundschafter *m.*; *boy* ~ *s.* Pfadfinder *m.*; *girl* ~ *s.* Pfadfinderin *f.*; ~ *v.i.* ausspähen; ~ *v.t.* zurückweisen, verspotten.
scowl *s.* finsteres Gesicht *n.*; ~ *v.i.* finster aussehen.
scraggy *a.*, **~ily** *adv.* mager; dürr.
scram *v.i.* abhauen, Leine ziehen.
scramble *v.i.* sich reißen; klettern; ~ *s.* Raffen *n.*; Gedränge *n.*; Krabbelei *f.*
scrambled eggs *s.pl.* Rühreier *n.pl.*
scrap *s.* Stückchen *n.*; Fetzen *m.*; Balgerei *f.*, Rauferei *f.*; **~s** *pl.* Überbleibsel *n.pl.*; **~iron** Schrott *m.*; ~ *v.t.* verschrotten; zum alten Eisen werfen.
scrape *v.t.* & *i.* schaben, kratzen, zusammenscharren; ~ *s.* Schürfwunde *f.*
scraper *s.* Kratzeisen, Schabeisen *n.*; Kratzbürste *f.*; Kratzer *m.*; Schaber *m.*
scrappy *a.*, **~ily** *adv.* zusammengestückelt.
scrap value *s.* Schrottwert *m.*
scratch *v.t.* kratzen; ritzen, kritzeln; ~ *s.* Riß, Ritz *m.*; Schramme *f.*

scratchy *a.* kratzend; zerkratzt.
scrawl *v.t.* kritzeln; ~ *s.* Gekritzel *n.*
scrawny *a.* mager; dürr.
scream *v.i.* kreischen, schreien; ~ *s.* Schrei *m.*
scree *s.* Schutt *m.;* Geröll *n.*
screech *v.i.* schreien, kreischen.
screen *s.* Schirm *m.;* (Kino) Leinwand *f.;* (*mil.*) Schützenschleier *m.;* Sandsieb *n.;* ~ *v.t.* schützen; sieben; (Licht) abblenden; (*fig.*) überprüfen.
screw *s.* Schraube *f.;* ~ *v.t.* schrauben; quetschen, drücken.
screwdriver *s.* Schraubenzieher *m.*
screwed up *a.* neurotisch.
screwy *a.* (*fam.*) verrückt.
scribble *v.i.* & *t.* kritzeln; ~ *s.* Gekritzel *n.*
scribbler *s.* Schmierer, Sudler *m.*
scribe *s.* Schreiber(in) *m.(f.);* Schriftgelehrte *m./f.*
scrimmage *s.* Handgemenge *n.*
scrimp *v.i.* knausern.
script *s.* (*typ.*) Schrift *f.;* Schriftart *f.;* Schreibschrift *f.;* (*Film, Radio*) Drehbuch, Manuskript *n.*
scriptural *a.* schriftmäßig, biblisch.
Scripture *s.* Heilige Schrift *f.*
script writer *s.* Drehbuchautor(in) *m.(f.)*
scrivener *s.* Schreiber *m.*
scrofula *s.* Skrofeln *f.pl.*
scrofulous *a.* skrofulös.
scroll *s.* Rolle *f.;* Schnörkel *m.*
scrounge *v.t.* stehlen, klauen, schnorren.
scrounger *s.* Schnorrer(in) *m.(f.)*
scrub *v.t.* scheuern; ~ *v.i.* sich placken; ~ *s.* Gestrüpp *n.;* Buschwerk *n.;* Gebüsch *n.*
scrubby *a.* stoppelig; stachelig.
scruffy *a.* schmuddelig.
scrumptious *a.* lecker.
scrunch *v.t.* zerknüllen; ~ *v.i.* knirschen.
scruple *s.* Bedenken *f.*, Skrupel *m.*
scrupulous *a.*, **~ly** *adv.* bedenklich, gewissenhaft, skrupulös.
scrutinize *v.t.* & *i.* forschen; prüfen.
scrutiny *s.* genaue Untersuchung *f.;* Wahlprüfung *f.*
scuba *s.* Tauchgerät *n.;* ~ **diving** *s.* (Sport) Tauchen *n.*
scud *v.i.* fortlaufen; rennen; (*nav.*) lenzen.
scuff *v.t.* verkratzen; schlurfen.
scuffle *s.* Balgerei *f.;* Handgemenge *n.;* ~ *v.i.* sich balgen.
scull *s.* Heckriemen *m.;* Skullboat *n.;* ~ *v.i.* skullen, wriggen.
scullion *s.* Küchenjunge *m.*
sculptor *s.* Bildhauer(in) *m.(f.)*
sculpture *s.* Bildhauerkunst *f.;* Skulptur *f.;* ~ *v.t.* schnitzen; formen.
scum *s.* Schaum *m.;* Abschaum, Auswurf *m.;* ~ *v.t.* abschäumen.
scurf *s.* Schuppe *f.*
scurrility *s.* grober Spaß *m.*
scurrilous *a.*, **~ly** *adv.* possenhaft; gemein, grob, zotig.
scurry *v.i.* dahineilen; ~ *s.* Hasten *n.*
scurvy *s.* Skorbut *m.*
scuttle *s.* Kohlenkasten *m.;* Luke *f.;* hastige Flucht *f.;* ~ *v.t.* (ein Schiff) durchlöchern, versenken; ~ *v.i.* flüchten.
scythe *s.* Sense *f.*
SE *southeast,* Südost, SO.
sea *s.* See *f.;* Meer *n.; at* ~, (*fig.*) ratlos.
seabed *s.* Meeresboden *m.*
seaboard *s.* Seeküste *f.*
sea chart *s.* Seekarte *f.*
seacoast *s.* Meeresküste *f.*
seafaring *a.* seefahrend.
seafood *s.* Meeresfrüchte *pl.*
sea-going *a.* seetüchtig.
sea green *s.* Meergrün *n.*
sea gull *s.* Möwe *f.*
seahorse *s.* Seepferdchen *n.*
seal *s.* Siegel, Petschaft *n.;* Bestätigung *f.;* Robbe *f.*, Seehund *m.; under my hand and* ~, unter Brief und Siegel; ~ *v.t.* & *i.* besiegeln, siegeln.
sealant *s.* Dichtungsmaterial *n.*
sea level *s.* Meeresspiegel *m.*
sealing wax *s.* Siegellack *n.*
sea lion *s.* Seelöwe *m.*
sealskin *s.* Seehundsfell *n.*
seam *s.* Saum *m.;* Nacht *f.;* Fuge *f.;* Flöz *n.*
seaman *s.* Seemann *m.*
seamanship *s.* Seemannskunst *f.*
seamless *a.* nahtlos.
seamstress *s.* Näherin *f.*
seamy *a.* gesäumt; ~ **side,** Schattenseite *f.*
sea plane *s.* Wasserflugzeug *n.*
seaport *s.* Seehafen *m.*
sear *v.t.* brennen, sengen; brandmarken; verhärten.
search *v.t.* & *i.* suchen, untersuchen, prüfen; ~ *s.* Suchen, Durchsuchen, Nachforschen *n.;* Prüfung *f.;* **~warrant** *s.* Haussuchungsbefehl *m.*
searching *a.* prüfend; forschend.
searchlight *s.* Scheinwerfer *m.*
searing *a.* brennend, stechend (Schmerz); sengend (Hitze).
sea salt *s.* Meersalz *n.*
sea shell *s.* Muschel(schale) *f.*
seasick *a.* seekrank.
seasickness *s.* Seekrankheit *f.*
seaside *s.* Strand *m.;* Küste *f.;* Seebad *n.; to the* ~, an die See.
season *s.* Jahreszeit *f.;* rechte Zeite *f.;* Saison *f.; to be in* ~, *out of* ~, saisongemäß, nichtsaisongemäß sein; ~ *v.t.* & *i.* reifen; trocknen; gewöhnen, abhärten; würzen; mildern.
seasonable *a.* zeitgemäß.
seasoned *a.* reif, abgelagert; gewürzt.
seasoning *s.* Würze *f.*
season ticket *s.* (*rail.*) Dauerkarte *f.*
seat *s.* Sitz (auch Hosensitz) *m.;* Stuhl *m.;* Lage *f.;* Schauplatz *m.;* Landsitz *m.;* Platz (Bahn, Omnibus) *m.;* ~ *v.t.* setzen; *to be* ~*ed,* sitzen; *take a* ~, nehmen Sie Platz!
seat belt *s.* Sicherheitsgurt *m.*
seated *a.* sitzend.
sea urchin *s.* Seeigel *m.*
seaward *a.* & *adv.* seewärts.
seawater *s.* Meerwasser *n.*
seaweed *s.* Tang *m.*, Alge *f.*
seaworthy *a.* seetüchtig.
Sec. *Secretary,* Sekretär(in), Sekr.; Minister, Min.
sec. *second,* Sekunde, Sek., sek.
secede *v.i.* sich trennen.
secession *s.* Spaltung *f.;* Trennung *f.*

secessionist *s.* Abtrünnige *m.;* Sonderbündler *m.*
seclude *v.t.* ausschließen, absondern.
seclusion *s.* Absonderung *f.;* Zurückgezogenheit *f.*
second *a.* der, die, das zweite; nächste; geringer; ~ **cousin,** Vetter(Base) zweiten Grades; ~ **sight,** zweites Gesicht *n.;* **on** ~ **thought,** bei nochmaliger Überlegung; ~ *s.* Sekundant *m.;* Sekunde *f.;* ~ *v.t.* beistehen, (Antrag) unterstützen.
secondary *a.*, **~ily** *adv.* nächstfolgend; untergeordnet; Neben...; ~ **circuit,** (*elek.*) Nebenstromkreis *m.;* ~ **education** *s.* höhere Bildung *f.;* ~ **school,** höhere Schule *f.*
second-best *a.* zweitbest; *come off* ~, *adv.* den kürzeren ziehen.
second-class *a.* zweitklassig, zweitrangig.
second-hand *a.* aus zweiter Hand; gebraucht; antiquarisch.
second home *s.* Zweitwohnung *f.;* Ferienhaus *n.*
secondly *adv.* zweitens.
second name *s.* Nachname *f.;* Zuname *m.*
second nature *s.* zweite Natur *f.*
second-rate *a.* zweitrangig.
second thoughts *s.pl.* *have* ~, es sich anders überlegen.
secrecy *s.* Heimlichkeit *f.;* Verschwiegenheit *f.*
secret *a.*, **~ly** *adv.* geheim, verborgen; verschwiegen; ~ **agent** *s.* Geheimagent(in) *m.(f.);* ~ **police,** Geheimpolizei *f.;* ~ **service,** Geheimdienst *m.;* ~ *s.* Geheimnis *n.;* *official* ~, Amtsgeheimnis *n.*
secretarial *a.* Sekretärs...; sekretariats...; Sekretärinnen...
secretariat *s.* Sekretariat *n.*
secretary *s.* Schriftführer(in) *m.(f.);* Sekretär *m.;* Sekretärin *f.;* ~ **of state** *s.* Außenminister(in) *m.(f.);* ~ **general** *s.* Generalsekretär(in) *m.(f.)*
secret ballot *s.* geheime Abstimmung *f.*
secrete *v.t.* absondern.
secretion *s.* Absonderung *f.*
secretive *a.* verschwiegen; geheimtuerisch.
sect *s.* Sekte *f.*
sectarian *a.* zu einer Sekte gehörig; ~ *s.* Sektierer *m.*
section *s.* Zerschneiden *n.;* Abteilung *f.;* Abschnitt *m.;* (*rail.*) Strecke *f.;* Durchschnitt *m.*
sectional *a.* Gruppen...; partikular...
sector *s.* Kreisausschnitt *m.;* (*mil.*) Geländeabschnitt *m.*
secular *a.*, **~ly** *adv.* weltlich, säkular.
secularize *v.t.* verweltlichen; säkularisieren.
secure *a.*, **~ly** *adv.* sicher; sorglos; ~ *v.t.* sichern, versichern; befestigen; sich verschaffen.
security *s.* Sicherheit, Sorglosigkeit *f.;* Schutz *m.;* Bürgschaft *f.;* **securities** *pl.* Wertpapiere *n.pl.*
sedan *s.* Sänfte *f.;* (*mot.*) Limousine *f.*
sedate *a.*, **~ly** *adv.* ruhig, gesetzt.
sedative, *a.* stillend, beruhigend; ~ *s.* Sedativum *n.;* Beruhigungsmittel *f.*
sedentary *a.* sitzend, seßhaft.
sedge *s.* Schilfgras *n.*, Binse *f.*
sediment *s.* Bodensatz *m.;* Ablagerung *f.*
sedition *s.* Aufstand *m.;* Empörung *f.*
seditious *a.*, **~ly** *adv.* aufrührerisch.
seduce *v.t.* verführen, verleiten.
seducer *s.* Verführer *m.*
seduction *s.* Verführung *f.*
seductive *s.* verführerisch.
sedulous *a.*, **~ly** *adv.* emsig, fleißig.
see *v.t.* & *i.st.* sehen; besuchen; *to* ~ *through,* durchschauen; *to* ~ *a thing through,* etwas bis ans Ende durchhalten; *to* ~ *to it,* dafür sorgen; *I'll be* ~*ing you,* auf Wiedersehen!
seed *s.* Same *m.;* Saat *f.;* ~ *v.i.* in Samen schießen, ausfallen.
seedbed *s.* (Saat)Beet *n.*
seedless *n.* kernlos.
seedling *s.* Sämling *m.*
seedy *a.* samenreich; schäbig; elend.
seek *v.t.* & *i.st.* suchen, trachten; aufsuchen.
seem *v.i.* scheinen, erscheinen.
seeming *a.*, **~ly** *adv.* scheinbar; dem Anschein nach.
seemly *a.* anständig, schicklich.
seep *v.i.* sickern.
seer *s.* Seher, Prophet *m.*
seesaw *s.* Wippe *f.*
seethe *v.t.* & *i.* sieden, kochen.
see-through *a.* durchsichtig.
segment *s.* Abschnitt *m.*
segregate *v.t.* & *i.* absondern; segregieren.
segregation *s.* Trennung *f.;* Rassentrennung *f.*
seismic *a.* seismisch.
seismometer *s.* Erdbebenmesser *m.*
seize *v.t.* ergreifen; wegnehmen; beschlagnahmen; *to be* ~*d with,* im Besitz sein von.
seizure *s.* Ergreifung *f.;* Verhaftung *f.;* Beschlagnahme *f.;* Krankheitsanfall *m.*
seldom *adv.* selten.
select *v.t.* auswählen, auslesen; ~ *a.* auserlesen.
selection *s.* Auswahl *f.;* Zuchtwahl *f.*
selective *a.* selektiv; wählerisch.
selectivity *s.* (*radio*) Trennschärfe *f.*
selenium *s.* Selen *n.*
self *n.* & *pref.* Selbst, Ich *n.;* selbst.
self-absorbed *a.* in sich selbst versunken.
self-assured *a.* selbstsicher.
self-centered *a.* ichbezogen.
self-conceit *s.* Eigendünkel *m.*
self-confidence *s.* Selbstvertrauen *n.*
self-conscious *a.*, **~ly** *adv.* befangen, gehemmt.
self-contained *a.* verschlossen; in sich vollständig.
self-control *s.* Selbstbeherrschung *f.*
self-defense *s.* selbstverteidigung; Notwehr *f.*
self-denial *s.* Selbstverleugnung *f.*
self-determination *s.* Selbstbestimmung *f.*
self-educated *a.* ~ **person** *s.* Autodidakt(in) *m.(f.)*
self-effacing *a.* zurückhaltend.
self-employed *a.* selbständig.
self-esteem *s.* Selbstachtung *f.*
self-evident *a.* offenkundig.
self-explanatory *a.* selbsterklärend; *it is* ~, es erklärt sich selbst.
self-governing *a.* autonom.
self-government *s.* Autonomie *f.;* Selbstverwaltung *f.*
self-help *s.* Selbsthilfe *f.*
self-indulgence *s.* Maßlosigkeit *f.*
self-indulgent *a.* maßlos.
self-interest *s.* Eigennutz *m.*
selfish *a.*, **~ly** *adv.* selbstsüchtig.
selfishness *s.* Selbstsucht *f.*

selfless *a.* selbstlos.
selflessness *s.* Selbstlosigkeit *f.*
self-made *a.* selbstgemacht; durch eigene Kraft emporgekommen.
self-opinionated *a.* eingebildet; rechthaberisch.
self-pity *s.* Selbstmitleid *n.*
self-portrait *s.* Selbstporträt *n.*
self-possession *s.* Selbstbeherrschung *f.*
self-preservation *s.* Selbsterhaltung *f.*
self-propelled *a.* (*mil.*) Selbstfahr...
self-raising flour *s.* Backpulvermehl *n.*
self-reliant *a.* selbstbewußt; selbstsicher.
self-respect *s.* Selebstachtung *f.*
self-respecting *a.* mit Selbstachtung.
self-restraint *s.* Selbstbeherrschung *f.*
self-righteous *a.* selbstgerecht.
self-sacrifice *s.* Selbstanfopferung *f.*
selfsame *a.* der-, die-, dasselbe.
self-service *s.* Selbstbedienung *f.*
self-styled *a.* (*ironic*) von eigenen Gnaden.
self-sufficiency *s.* Autarkie *f.*; Unabhängigkeit *f.*
self-sufficient *a.* unabhängig; autark.
self-supporting *a.* sich selbst tragend; finanziell unabhängig.
self-taught *a.* autodidaktisch; selbsterlernt.
self-will *s.* Eigenwille, Eigensinn *m.*
self-willed *a.* eigenwillig.
sell *v.t.st.* verkaufen; (*fig.*) hereinlegen; ~ *v.i.* Absatz finden, gehen; *to be sold out,* ausverkauft sein.
seller *s.* Verkäufer *m.*
selling *s.* Verkauf *m.*; Verkaufen *n.*
semantic *a.* semantisch.
semantics *s.* Semantik *f.*
semaphore *s.* optische Signale *pl.*
semblance *s.* Ähnlichkeit *f.*; Anschein *m.*
semen *s.* Samen(flüßigkeit) *m.* (*f.*); Sperma *n.*
semester *s.* Semester *n.*
semibreve *s.* ganze Note *f.*
semicircle *s.* Halbkreis *m.*
semicircular *a.* halbkreisförmig.
semicolon *s.* Strichpunkt *m.*
semiconductor *s.* Halbleiter *m.*
semi-detached *a.* halbfreistehend; ~ **house,** *s.* Doppelhaushälfte *f.*
semifinal *s.* Halbfinale *m.*
semi-finished *a.* halbfertig.
seminal *a.* grundlegend.
seminar *s.* Seminar *n.*
semiquaver *s.* Sechzehntelnote *f.*
semi-skilled *a.* angelernt.
Semite *s.* Semite *m.*, Semitin *f.*
semitone *s.* Halbton *m.*
semolina *s.* Grieß *m.*
Sen. *senior,* Senior, der Ältere, d.Ä., sen.
senate *s.* Senat, Rat *m.*
senator *s.* Senator(in) *m.*(*f.*)
senatorial *a.*, **~ly** *adv.* ratsherrlich.
send *v.t.* & *i.st.* schicken, senden; *to* ~ *for,* holen lassen.
sender *s.* Absender(in) *m.*(*f.*)
senile *a.* greisenhaft; altersschwach, senil.
senility *s.* Altersschwäche *f.*; Senilität *f.*
senior *s.* Ältere, Älteste *m.*; ~ *a.* dienstälteste, rangälteste, Ober...
senior citizen *s.* Senior(in) *m.*(*f.*)
seniority *s.* höheres Alter *n.*; Dienstalter *n.*; Altersfolge *f.*
sensation *s.* Aufsehen *n.*; Eindruck *m.*; Empfindung *f.*; Sensation *f.*
sensational *a.* Aufsehen erregend; sensationell, Sensations...
sense *s.* Sinn, Verstand *m.*; Bedeutung *f.*; Gefühl *n.*; *common* ~, gesunder Menschenverstand *m.*
senseless *a.*, **~ly** *adv.* sinnlos; unvernünftig; gefühllos, bewußtlos.
sensibility *s.* Empfindlichkeit *f.*; Empfindsamkeit *f.*
sensible *a.*, **~bly** *adv.* empfindlich, fühlbar, merkbar; reizbar; empfindsam; vernünftig, klug.
sensitive *a.*, **~ly** *adv.* empfindsam, reizbar; ~ **plant** *s.* empfindliche Pflanze *f.*
sensitivity *s.* Empfindlichkeit *f.*; Sensibilität *f.*
sensitize *v.t.* sensibilisieren.
sensory *a.* Sinnes...
sensual *a.*, **~ly** *adv.* sinnlich.
sensualist *s.* sinnlicher Mensch *m.*
sensuality *s.* Sinnlichkeit *f.*
sensuous *a.* sinnlich, die Sinne betreffend.
sentence *s.* Richterspruch, Urteil *n.*; Satz *m.*; ~ **of death,** Todesurteil *n.*; *to pass* ~, das Urteil fällen; *to serve one's* ~, seine Strafe absitzen; ~ *v.t.* verurteilen.
sententious *a.* **~ly** *adv.* moralisierend.
sentient *a.* empfindend.
sentiment *s.* Empfindung *f.*; Gefühl *n.*; Gesinnung *f.*; Meinung *f.*
sentimental *a.*, **~ly** *adv.* empfindsam, sentimental; ~ **value,** persönlicher Wert *m.*
sentimentality *s.* Rührseligheit *f.*
sentinel, sentry *s.* Schildwache *f.*; **~box,** Schilderhaus *n.*; Wachhäuschen *n.*; *line of sentries,* Postenkette *f.*
separable *a.* trennbar.
separate *v.t.* trennen; ~ *v.i.* sich trennen; ~ *a.* getrennt, einzeln; **~ly** *adv.* besonders.
separation *s.* Trennung *f.*; (*chem.*) Scheidung *f.*; Ehetrennung *f.*; ~ **allowance,** Scheidungsalimente *n.pl.*, Trennungszulage *f.*; (*mil.*) Familienunterstützung.
separatist *s.* Separatist(in) *m.*(*f.*); ~ *a.* separatistisch.
Sept. *September,* September, Sept.
September *a.* September *m.*
septennial *a.* siebenjährig; siebenjährlich.
septic *a.* septisch, Fäulnis...
septuagenarian *s.* Siebzigjährige *m.* & *f.*
sepulchral *a.* Grab..., Begräbnis...
sepulchre *s.* Grabmal *n.*; Gruft *f.*
sepulture *s.* Beerdigung *f.*; Begräbnis *n.*
sequel *s.* Folge *f.*
sequence *s.* (Reihen)folge, Ordnung *f.*
sequester, *v.t.* einziehen; absondern.
sequestration *s.* Absonderung *f.*; Beschlagnahme *f.*; Zwangsverwaltung *f.*
sequoia *s.* Mammutbaum *m.*
seraglio *s.* Serail *n.*
seraph *s.* Seraph *m.*
seraphic *a.* seraphisch.
Serb *a.* serbisch; ~ *s.* Serbe *m.*, Serbin *f.*
Serbia *s.* Serbien *n.*

serenade *s.* Ständchen *n.*
serene *a.*, **~ly** *adv.* heiter; ruhig.
serenity *s.* Heiterkeit, Gemütsruhe *f.*
serf *s.* Leibeigene *m.*
serfdom *s.* Leibeigenschaft *f.*
sergeant *s.* Sergeant *m.*; (Polizei-) Wachtmeister *m.*; **~-major** *s.* Feldwebel *m.*
serial *a.* periodisch, Lieferungs...; **~ number,** laufende Nummer *f.*; ~ *s.* Lieferungswertk *n.*, Zeitschrift *f.*
series *s.* Reihe, Folge *f.*; (*elek.*) **~ connection,** Reihenschaltung *f.*
serious *a.* ernsthaft; wichtig; **~ly** *adv.* im Ernst; *to take a thing ~ly,* etwas ernst nehmen.
seriousness *s.* Ernsthaftigkeit *f.*
sermon *s.* Predigt *f.*
serpent *s.* Schlange *f.*
serpentine *a.* schlangenförmig, geschlängelt.
serrated *a.* (*bot.*) gesägt, zackig; gezackt.
serum *s.* Blutwasser *n.*; Heilserum *n.*
servant *s.* Diener. Bediente *m.*; Magd *f.*; (Dienst) mädchen *n.*
serve *v.t.* & *i.* dienen; aufwarten, servieren; auftragen; dienlich sein; genügen; zustellen; (*tennis*) angeben, aufschlagen; *~s him right!*, geschieht ihm recht!
service *s.* Dienst *m.*; Bedienung *f.*; Dienstpflicht *f.*; Zustellung *f.*; Gefälligkeit *f.*; Nutzen *m.*; Gottesdienst *m.*; Tafelservice *n.*; (*tennis*) Aufschlag *m.*, Angabe *f.*; Verkehrsdienst *m.*; *steamship ~*, Dampferverkehr; *500 hours of ~*, 500 Stunden Arbeitsleistung (einer Maschine); *car ~*, Wagenpflege *f.*; **~ station,** Tankstelle *f.*; **~ flat,** Wohnung mit Bedienung *f.*; **~ man,** Wehrmachtsangehöriger *m.*; **~s** *pl.* öffentliche Dienste, Betriebe (auch privater Gesellschaften), öffentliche Behörden; *the (fighting) ~s, pl.* die Wehrmacht *f.*; *all ~s,* Gas, Elektrisch, etc.; ~ *v.t.* bedienen (von öffentlichen Diensten, etc.).
serviceable *a.* **~ly** *adv.* nützlich, brauchbar, verwendungsfähig.
service industry *s.* Dienstleistungsbetrieb *m.*
servile *a.*, **~ly** *adv.* unterwürfig.
servility *s.* Unterwürfigkeit *f.*
serving *s.* Portion *f.*
servitude *s.* Knechtschaft, Sklaverei *f.*
session *s.* Sitzung *f.*
set *v.t.* setzen, stellen; ordnen; (Uhr) stellen; (Edelsteine) fassen; pflanzen; *to ~ (to music),* komponieren; ~ *v.i.* untergehen (Sonne); gerinnen; *to ~ about,* an etwas gehen, anfangen; *to ~ aside,* (Urteil) aufheben; *to ~ down,* niedersetzen; aufschreiben; *to ~ forth,* dartun; ausdrücken; *to ~ in,* einsetzen; pflanzen; anfangen, eintreten; *to ~ off,* hervorheben; abreisen; *to ~ off against,* anrechnen gegen; *to ~ on,* anhetzen; angreifen; *to ~ out,* bestimmen, festsetzen; hervorheben; beginnen; aufbrechen; *to ~ the table,* den Tisch decken; *to ~ to,* anfangen, sich legen (auf); *to ~ up,* aufrichten; festetzen; sich niederlassen; *to ~ up for,* sich ausgeben für; ~ *s.* Satz *m.*; Reihe *f.*; Gespann, Paar *n.*; Spiel *n.*; Besteck *n.*; Gattung; Bande *f.*; Garnitur *f.*; Service *n.*; ~ *p.* & *a.* festgesetzt, bestimmt; geordnet; starr; versessen auf.
setback *s.* Rückschlag *m.*
settee *s.* Sofa *n.*
setting *s.* Einfassung *f.*; Ordnen *n.*; Untergang (der Sonne) *f.*; Musikbegleitung *f.*
settle *v.t.* erledigen; festsetzen; einrichten, bestimmen; regeln; schlichten; bezahlen; (eine Summe) aussetzen; *to ~ an annuity on a person,* einem eine Leibrente aussetzen; ~ *v.i.* sich setzen, sich senken; sich ansiedeln; *to ~ down,* sich niederlassen (als Arzt, etc.), sich verheiraten; ~ *s.* Bank, Truhe *f.*; *settling day,* Abrechnungstag (Börse) *m.*
settled *a.* beständig; geregelt.
settlement *s.* Entscheidung *f.*; Anordnung, Versorgung *f.*; Leibrente *f.*, Vermächtnis *n.*, Familienrente *f.*; Niederlassung, Ansiedelung *f.*; Vergleich *m.*; Rechnungsabschluß *m.*; Schlichtung *f.*; Regelung *f.*; *in ~*, als Bezahlung.
settler *s.* Ansiedler(in), Settler(in) *m.(f.)*
set-up *s.* Organisation *f.*; Aufban *m.*
seven sieben.
sevenfold *a.* & *adv.* siebenfach.
seventeen siebzehn.
seventh *a.* sieb(en)t...
seventy siebzig.
sever *v.t.* & *i.* sich trennen, abschneiden.
several *a.* verschieden; getrennt, einzeln; mehrere.
severance *s.* Abbruch *m.*; Unterbrechung *f.*; **~ pay** *s.* Abfindungsentschädigung *f.*
severe *a.*, **~ly** *adv.* streng; heftig.
severity *s.* Strenge, Härte *f.*; Ernst *m.*
sew *v.t.* & *i.* nähen, heften; **~ing kit,** Nähzeug *n.*; **~ing silk,** Nähseide *f.*
sewage *s.* Abwasser *n.*
sewer *s.* Abwasserkanal *m.*
sewerage *s.* Kanalwesen *n.*; abfließendes Wasser *n.*; Kanalbau *m.*
sewing machine *s.* Nähmaschine *f.*
sewing needle *s.* Nähnadel *f.*
sex *s.* Geschlecht *n.*
sexagenarian *s.* Sechzigjährige *m.* & *f.*
sex education *s.* Sexualerziehung *f.*
sexism *s.* Sexismus *m.*
sexist *a.* sexistisch; ~ *s.* Sexist(in) *m.(f.)*
sex life *s.* Geschlechtsleben *n.*
sex symbol *s.* Sexidol *n.*
sextant *s.* Sextant *m.*
sexton *s.* Küster *m.*; Totengräber *m.*
sexual *a.* geschlechtlich.
sexual harassment *s.* sexuelle Belästigung *f.*
sexual intercourse *s.* Geschlechtsverkehr *m.*
sexuality *s.* Sexualität *f.*
sexy *a.* (*fam.*) sexy; erotisch.
Sgt. *Sergeant,* Sergeant *m.*
shabby *a.*, **~ily** *adv.* schäbig.
shack *s.* Hütte *f.*; Baracke *f.*
shackle *v.t.* fesseln; ~ *s.* Kettenglied *n.*; **~s** *s.pl.* Fesseln *f.pl.*
shade *s.* Schatten *m.*; Schattierung *f.*; (*fig.*) Schirm *m.*; Glasglocke *f.*; Abtönung *f.*; ~ *v.t.* beschatten; schattieren; schützen.
shading *s.* Schattierung *f.*; Lichtschutz *m.*
shadow *s.* Schatten *m.*; ~ *v.t.* beschatten; schattieren; schützen; heimlich folgen.
shadowy *a.* schattig, dunkel.
shady *a.* schattig; (*fam.*) anrüchig.

shaft *s.* Schaft *m.;* Pfeil; Deichsel *f.;* Schacht *m.;* (*mech.*) Welle, Spindel *f.*
shaggy *a.* zottig; buschig.
shake *v.t.st.* (ab)schütteln, rütteln; erschüttern; *to ~ hands,* sich die Hände geben; *to ~ off,* abschütteln; ~ *v.i.* beben, wanken; (*mus.*) trillern; ~ *s.* Erschütterung *f.;* Stoß *m.;* Triller *m.;* Schütteln *n.;* (Hände) Druck *m.*
shakedown *s.* Notlager *n.*
shaky *a.* wacklig, gebrechlich.
shallop *s.* Schaluppe *f.*
shallot *s.* Schalotte *f.*
shallow *a.,* **~ly** *adv.* seicht, matt; schwach, albern; ~ *s.* Untiefe *f.*
sham *a.* unecht, nachgemacht; Schein...; ~ *s.* Täuschung *f.,* Schein *m.;* ~ *v.t. & i.* vortäuschen, betrügen.
shamble *v.i.* schlurfen.
shambles *s.pl.* Schlachthaus *n.;* Chaos *n.*
shame *s.* Scham *f.;* Schande *f.; for ~!,* pfui; ~ *v.t.* beschämen; schänden.
shamefaced *a.,* **~ly** *adv.* verschämt.
shameful *a.,* **~ly** *adv.* schändlich; beschämend.
shameless *a.,* **~ly** *adv.* unverschämt.
shampoo *v.t.* shamponieren; ~ *s.* Shampoo *n.*
shamrock *s.* weiser Klee *m.*
shandy *s.* Bier *(n.)* mit Limonade, Radler *m.*
shank *s.* Schenkel *m.;* Stengel *m.;* (*mech.*) Stiel, Schaft *m.*
shanty *s.* Hütte, Bude *f.;* **~town** *s.* Elendsviertel *n.*
shape *s.* Form, Gestalt *f.;* Modell *n.;* Wuchs *m.; in good ~,* in guter Verfassung; ~ *v.t.* bilden, gestalten; ~ *v.i.* sich gestalten.
shaped *a.* geformt.
shapeless *a.* unförmig; formlos.
shapely *a.* wohlgebildet.
share *s.* Teil, Anteil *m.;* Aktie *f.,* Anteilschein *m.; ordinary ~,* Stammaktie *f.; preferred ~,* Vorzugsaktie *f.;* Pflugschar *f.; in equal ~s,* zu gleichen Teilen; ~ *v.t.* verteilen; ~ *v.i.* teilhaben, teilnehmen.
shareholder *s.* Aktionär(in) *m.(f.)*
shark *s.* Haifisch *m.;* Gauner *m.*
sharp *a.,* **~ly** *adv.* scharf; spitzig: streng; heftig; hitzig; beißend; spitzfindig; pfiffig; genau; (*mus.*) um einen halben Ton erhöt; *to look ~,* aufpassen; *at 10 o' clock ~,* pünktlich um 10 Uhr; ~ *s.* (*mus.*) Kreuz *n.*
sharpen *v.t.* schärfen wertzen, (zu)spitzen.
sharpener *s.* Spitzer *m.;* Schleifstein *m.*
sharpness *s.* Schärfe *f.*
sharpshooter *s.* Scharfschütze *m.*
sharp-witted *a.* scharfsinnig.
shatter *v.t.* zerschmettern, zerstreuen; zerrütten; ~ *v.i.* zerfallen.
shatterproof glass *s.* Sicherheitsglas *n.*
shave *v.t.r. & st.* schaben; scheren; rasieren; placken; leicht streifen; ~ *v.i.* sich rasieren.
shaven *a.* rasiert.
shaver *s.* Rasierapparat *m.;* Rasierer *m.*
shaving *s.* Rasieren *n.;* Schnitzel *n.;* **~s** *pl.* Hobelspäne *m.pl.;* ~ **cream** *s.* Rasierkreme *f.;* ~ **soap,** ~ **stick,** Rasierseife *f.;* ~ **things** *pl.* Rasiersachen *f.pl.*
shaving-brush *s.* Rasierpinsel *m.*
shawl *s.* Umschlagetuch *n.,* Schal *m.*
she *pn.* sie; ~ *s.* Weibchen *n.*
sheaf *s.* Garbe *f.*
shear *v.t.st.* scheren; rupfen; ~ *s.* Schur *f.;* **~s** *pl.* große Schere *f.*
sheath *s.* (Schwert) Scheide *f.*
sheathe *v.t.* in die Scheide stecken; überziehen.
sheathing *s.* Umhüllung *f.;* Verkleidung *f.*
shed *s.* Schuppen *m.;* Schirmdach *n.;* ~ *v.t.* vergießen, ausschütten; abwerfen; verbreiten.
sheen *s.* Schimmer, Glanz *m.*
sheep *s.* Schaf *n.;* Dummkopf *m.*
sheepish *a.,* **~ly** *adv.* verlegen.
sheepskin *s.* Schaffell *n.*
sheer *a.* lauter, rein; senkrecht; ~ *adv.* völlig; ~ *v.i.* (*nav.*) gieren, abweichen.
sheet *s.* Bettuch *n.;* Laken *n.;* Platte *f.;* Bogen (Papier) *m.*
sheet iron *s.* Eisenblech *n.*
sheet lightning *s.* Wetterleuchten *n.*
sheet metal *s.* Blech *n.*
sheik(h) *s.* Scheich *m.*
shelf *s.* Fach *n.,* Brett *n.;* Regal *n.;* Sims *m. (& n.);* ~ **life** *s.* Haltbarkeit *f.*
shell *s.* Schale, Hülse, Muschel *f.;* Gehäse *n.;* Granate *f.;* ~ *v.t.* schälen, enthüllen, abschuppen; beschießen.
shellac *s.* Schellack *m.*
shell fish *s.* Schalentier *n.*
shell-proof *a.* bombensicher.
shelter *s.* Obdach *n.;* Schutz *m.;* Schutzraum (Luftschutz) *m.;* ~ *v.t.* decken; schützen, bergen, beherbergen; ~ *v.i.* Schutz suchen.
sheltered *a.* geschützt; bemütet.
shelve *v.t.* auf ein Regal stellen; abschieben; auf die lange Bank schieben; ~ *v.i.r.* neigen.
shelving *s.* Regale *pl.*
shepherd *s.* Schäfer, Hirt *m.*
shepherdess *s.* Schäferin, Hirtin *f.*
sherbet *s.* Sorbett *n.*
sheriff *s.* Sheriff *m.*
sherry *s.* Sherry(wein), Jerezwein *m.*
Shetland Islands *pl.* Shetlandinseln *pl.*
shield *s.* Schild *m.;* ~ *v.t.* bedecken; beschirmen.
shift *v.t.* wechseln; ausziehen; umkleiden; versetzen, wegschieben, wegschaffen; ~ *v.i.* schalten; drehen (Wind); ~ *s.* Wechsel *m.;* Ausflucht *f.;* List *f.;* Schicht *f.,* Tagewerk *m.; to make ~,* sich behelfen.
shifting *a.,* **~ly** *adv.* listig, schlau; beweglich.
shiftless *a.* hilflos, ungewandt.
shifty *a.* verschlagen.
shilling *s.* Schilling *m.*
shilly-shally *v.i.* schwanken; zaudern.
shimmer *v.i.* schimmern; *s.* Schimmer *m.*
shin *s.* Schienbein *n.*
shindy *s.* Radau, Krach *m.* Rauferei *f.*
shine *v.i.* scheinen, leuchten, funkeln; ~ *s.* Schein, Glanz *m.*
shingle *s.* Schindel *f.;* Kieselsteine *pl.* **~s** *s.pl.* Gürtelrose *f.*
shining, shiny, *a.* hell, glänzend.
ship *s.* Schiff *n.;* ~ *v.t.* schiffen; einschiffen; verschiffen; versenden.
shipboard *s.* Schiffsbord *m.*
ship-broker *s.* Schiffsmakler *m.*
ship-builder *s.* Schiffbauer *m.*

shipmate *s.* Schiffsmaat *m.*
shipment *s.* Verschiffung *f.;* Warensendung *f.;* Versand *m.*
shipowner *s.* Reeder(in) *m.(f.)*
shipper *s.* Spediteur(in) *m.(f.);* Versender, Verlader *m.*
shipping *s.* Einschiffung *f.;* Schiffsbestand *m.;* Schiffahrt *f.;* ~ **agent** *s.* Schiffsspediteur *m.;* ~-**space** *s.* Schiffsraum *m.*
shipshape *a.* in bester Ordnung.
shipwreck *s.* Schiffbruch *m.;* ~ *v.t. & i.* scheitern, stranden.
shipwright *s.* Schiffbauer *m.*
ship-yard *s.* Werft *f.*
shirk *v.t. & i.* vermeiden; sich drücken.
shirker *s.* Drückeberger *m.*
shirt *s.* Hemd *n.;* ~ **blouse** *s.* Hemdbluse *f.*
shirtsleeve *s.* Hemdsärmel *m.*
shit *s.* (*vulg.*) Scheiße *f.;* ~ *v.i.st.* scheißen; ~**ty** *a.* beschissen.
shiver *v.i.* frösteln, zittern; ~ *s.* Schauer *m.*
shivery *a.* verfroren; zitternd.
shoal *s.* Schwarm *m.;* Menge *f.;* Untiefe *f.;* ~ *a.* seicht; ~ *v.i.* wimmeln; seicht werden.
shock *s.* Stoß *m.;* Angriff *m.;* Anstoß *m.*, Ärgernis *n.;* Schock *m.*, Haarschopf *m.;* elektrischer Schlag *m.;* ~ *v.t.* anstoßen; erschüttern; Anstoß geben, verletzen, entsetzen.
shock absorber *s.* Stoßdämpfer *m.*
shocking *a.*, ~**ly** *adv.* schockierend.
shockproof *a.* stoßfest.
shock therapy *s.* Schocktherapie *f.*
shoddy *a.* schäbig; minderwertig.
shoe *s.* Schuh *m.;* Hufeisen *n.;* ~ *v.t.st.* beschuhen; beschlagen (ein Pferd).
shoe black *s.* Schuhputzer *m.*
shoe horn *s.* Schuhlöffel *m.*
shoelace *s.* Schuhlitze *f.*
shoemaker *s.* Schuhmacher *m.*
shoe polish *s.* Schuhwichse *f.*
shoeshine *s.* Schuhglanz *m.*
shoestrings *pl.* Schuhbänder *n.pl.*
shoetree *s.* Schuhleisten *m.*
shoo *v.t.* (ver)scheuchen.
shoot *v.t.st.* schießen; abfeuern; drehen (*Film*); *to ~ down,* (*avi.*) abschießen; *to ~ dead, to ~ to death,* totschießen; *to ~ a film,* einen Film aufnehmen; ~ *v.t.* hervorschießen; sprießen; daherschießen; ~ *s.* Schößling *m.;* Gleitbahn *f.*
shooting *s.* Jagd *f.;* Schuß *m.;* ~**box,** Jagdhütte *f.;* ~**gallery,** Schießstand *m.*
shooting star *s.* Sternschnuppe *f.*
shop *s.* Laden *m.;* Werkstatt *f.; to talk ~,* fachsimpeln; ~ *v.i.* einkaufen (gehen).
shop front *s.* Schaufenster *n.*
shop keeper *s.* Ladeninhaber *m.*
shoplifter *s.* Ladendieb *m.;* ~**lifting** *s.* Ladendiebstahl *m.*
shopper *s.* Käufer(in) *m.(f.)*
shopping *s.* Einkaufen *n.;* ~ **center** *s.* Einkaufszentrum *n.*
shop steward *s.* Vertrauensmann *m.;* Vertrauensfrau *f.*
shore *s.* Gestade *n.;* Strand *m.;* stützbalken *m.;* ~ *v.t.* ~ **up** abstützen.
short *a.* kurz; eng; beschränkt; *in ~,* kurzum; *to cut ~,* unterbrechen; *in ~ supply,* beschränkt verfügbar; *to be ~ of,* an etwas Mangel haben. ~**ly** *adv.* in Kürze; bald.
shortage *s.* Mangel *m.*, Knappheit *f.*
shortbread *s.* Mürbegebäck *n.*
short circuit *s.* Kurzschluß *m.*
shortcoming *s.* Mangel *m.*, Unzulänglichkeit *f.*
short cut *s.* Abkürzungsweg *m.*
shorten *v.t.* abkürzen, verkürzen; ~ *v.i.* kürzer werden.
shorthand *s.* Stenographie *f.*
short-lived *a.* kurzlebig.
shortness *s.* Kürze *f.;* Knappheit *f.*
short pastry *s.* Mürbeteig *m.*
short-sighted *a.* kurzsichtig.
short sleeved *a.* kurzärmelig.
short story *s.* Kurzgeschichte *f.*
short tempered *a.* aufbrausend.
short-term *a.* kurzfristig.
shortwave *s.* (*radio*) Kurzwelle *f.*
shot *s.* Schuß *m.;* Schußweite *f.;* Schrot *m.* or *n.;* Kugel *f.;* Aufnahme *f.* (Film; Foto).
shotgun *s.* Jagdflinte, Schrotflinte *f.*
shoulder *s.* Schulter *f.;* Seitenstreifen *m.* (Straße); *to give sb. the cold ~,* einem die kalte Schulter zeigen; ~ *v.t.* auf die Schulter nehmen, schultern; drängen, stoßen.
shoulder bag *s.* Umhängetasche *f.*
shoulder blade *s.* Schulterblatt *n.*
shoulder strap *s.* Trägerband *m.*
shout *v.i.* laut rufen; jauchzen; schreien; ~ *s.* Geschrei *n.;* Zuruf *m.*
shouting *s.* Schreien *m.;* Geschrei *n.*
shove *v.t.* schieben, stossen; ~ *s.* Schub, Stoß *m.*
shovel *s.* Schaufel *f.;* Schippe *f.;* ~ *v.t.* schaufeln.
show *v.t.* zeigen; beweisen; *to ~ round,* herumführen; ~ *v.i.* sich zeigen, erscheinen; *to ~ off,* prahlen; ~ *s.* Schau *f.;* Schauspiel *n.*, Gepränge *n.;* Anschein *m.;* Ausstellung *f.; by ~ of hands,* durch Heben der Hände (bei Wahlen) *f.; flower ~ s.* Blumenausstellung *f.;* ~**case** *s.* Schaukasten *m.;* ~**man** *s.* Schaubudenbesitzer, Aussteller *m.;* Schowman *m.;* ~**room** *s.* Ausstellungsraum *m.*
showdown *s.* endgültige Kraftprobe *f.*
shower *s.* Regenschauer *m.;* Fülle *f.;* Dusche *f.;* ~ *v.i.* schauern, regnen; ~ *v.t.* überschütten; ~ *v.i.* sich duschen.
shower-bath *s.* Brausebad *n.;* Dusche *f.*
showery *a.* regnerisch, Regen...
showground *s.* Ausstellungsgelände *n.*
showing *s.* Vorführung *f.;* Sendung *f.*
showpiece *s.* Schaustück *n.;* Paradestück *n.*
show trial *s.* Schauprozeß *m.*
showy *a.* prunkend, Aufsehen erregend.
shrapnel *s.* Schrapnell *n.*
shred *v.t.* zerfetzen; schroten; ~ *s.* Abschnitzel *n.;* Fetzen *m.*
shrew *s.* zänkisches Weib *n.;* Spitzmaus *f.*
shrewd *a.*, ~**ly** *adv.* schlau, verschlagen.
shrewdness *s.* Schlauheit *f.*
shriek *v.i.* kreischen; ~ *s.* Schrei *m.*
shrift *s. to give sb short ~,* jdn. kurz abfertigen.
shrill *a.* gellend; schrill.
shrimp *s.* Garnele *f.*, Krabbe *f.*
shrine *s.* Schrein *m.*
shrink *v.t.st.* einschrumpfen; einlaufen (Stoffe); ~ *v.t.* zusammenziehen.

shrinkage *s.* Einschrumpfen *n.*
shrive *v.t.st.* Beichte hören; ~ *v.* beichten.
shrivel *v.t.* runzeln, zusammenziehen; ~ *v.i.* einschrumpfen, sich runzeln.
shroud *s.* Hülle *f.;* Leichentuch *n.;* ~ *v.t.* einhüllen.
Shrove Tuesday *s.* Fastnachtsdienstag *m.*
shrub *s.* Staude *f.*, Strauch *m.*
shrubbery *s.* Gebüsch *n.*
shrug *v.t.* die Achseln zucken; *to* ~ *one's shoulders,* mit den Achseln zucken; ~ *s.* Achselzucken *n.*
shudder *s.* Schauder *m.;* ~ *v.i.* schaudern.
shuffle *v.t.* mischen (Karten), mengen; *to* ~ *off,* abstreifen; ~ *v.i.* schlürfend gehen, ~ *s.* Schlurfen *n.*
shun *v.t.* meiden, scheuen.
shunt *s.* Nebengleis *n.;* Nebenanschluß *f.;* ~ *v.t.* (einen Zug) auf ein Seitengeleise schieben, rangieren.
shut *v.t.* zumachen, schließen; *to* ~ *down,* (Fabrik) stillegen; *to* ~ *up,* einsperren; ~ *v.i.* sich schließen, zugehen; ~ **up,** halts Maul!
shutdown *s.* Stillegung *f.*
shutter *s.* Fensterladen *m.;* (*phot.*) Verschluß *m.*
shuttle *s.* (Weber-)schiffchen *n.;* **~-train** *s.* Pendelzug *m.;* **~-service** *s.* Pendelverkehr *m.*
shuttlecock *s.* Federball *m.*
shy *a.* **~ly** *adv.* scheu, schüchtern; ~ *v.i.* scheuen (von Pferden).
shyness *s.* Scheuheit *f.;* Schüchternheit *f.*
siamese *a.* Siamesisch.
Siberia *s.* Sibirien *n.*
sibilant *a.* zischend; ~ *s.* Zischlaut *m.*
sibling *s.* Bruder *m.;* Schwester *f.;* Geschwister *pl.*
sibyl *s.* Sibylle, Prophetin *f.*
sibylline *a.* sibyllinisch.
Sicily *s.* Sizilien *n.*
sick *a.* krank; übel; (*fig.*) ~ **of,** überdrüssig; ~ **bay,** ~ **ward** *s.* Revier *n.;* ~ **call** *s.* (*mil.*) Krankenappell *m.; to call in* ~, sich krank melden; ~ **leave** *s.* Krankenurlaub *m.*
sicken *v.t.* krank machen; ~ *v.i.* krank werden; Ekel empfinden.
sickening *a.* ekelerregend; widerlich; unerträglich.
sickle *s.* Sichel *f.*
sickly *a.* kränklich, schwächlich, siech.
sickness *a.* Krankheit, Übelkeit *f.*
sick pay *s.* Krankengeld *n.*
side *s.* Seite *f.;* Rand *m.;* Partei *f.;* (*geom.*) Schenkel (des Dreiecks); ~ *of bacon,* Speckseite *f.; to take* ~*s,* Partei nehmen; *to* ~ *with, v.i.* jemandes Partei ergreifen.
side arms *s.pl.* Seitengewehr *n.*
sideboard *s.* Anrichte *f.*
side car *s.* Beiwagen *(m.)* (des Motorrades).
side glance *s.* Seitenblick *m.*
sidelight *s.* Streiflicht *n.*
sideline *s.* Nebenverdienst *m.*, Nebenbranche *f.*
sidelong *a.* & *adv.* seitwärts.
side saddle *s.* Damensattel *m.*
sideshow *s.* Nebenattraktion *f.*
sidestep *v.i.* (*fig.*) ausweichen.
sidestroke *s.* Seitenschwimmen *n.*
side table *s.* Beistelltisch *m.*
sidetrack *v.t.* ablenken; *to* ~ *the issue,* von der wirklichen Frage ablenken.
sidewalk *s.* Bürgersteig *m.*
sideways *adv.* seitwärts.
siding *s.* Parteinahme *f.;* (*rail.*) Nebengleis *n.*
sidle *v.i.* schleichen.
siege *s.* Belagerung *f.*
sieve *s.* Sieb *n.*
sift *v.t.* sieben; sichten, prüfen.
sigh *v.i.* seufzen; ~ *v.t.* ausseufzen, beseufzen; ~ *s.* Seufzer *m.*
sight *s.* Gesicht *n.;* Sehkraft *f.;* Anblick *m.;* Sehenswürdigkeit *f.;* Visier *n.; at first* ~, auf den ersten Blick; *by* ~, vom Sehen; *in* ~, in Sicht; *to lose* ~ *of,* aus dem Gesicht verlieren; **~s** *pl.* Sehenswürdigkeiten *pl.;* ~ *v.t.* sichten, zielen.
sightseeing *s.* Besichtigung *(f.)* von Sehenswürdigkeiten.
sign *s.* Zeichen *n.;* Kennzeichen *n.;* Aushängeschild *n.;* ~ *v.t.* & *i.* unterschreiben, unterzeichnen; winken; *to* ~ *on,* sich anwerben lassen; *authorized to* ~, zeichnungsberechtigt; **~ed** 'gezeichnet' (*gez.*)
signal *s.* Zeichen *n.;* Signal *n.;* ~ **box** *s.* (*rail.*) Stellwerk *n.;* ~ **center** *s.* (*mil.*) Nachrichtenzentrale *f.;* ~ **communications** *pl.* (*mil.*) Nachrichtenwesen *n.;* **~man** *s.* (*rail.*) Signalwärter *m.;* ~ **troops** *pl.* (*mil.*) Nachrichtentruppen *pl.;* ~ *v.t.* signalisieren.
signatory *s.* Unterzeichner *m.;* ~ *a.* unterzeichnen; ~ **powers** *pl.* Signatartmächte *f.pl.*
signature *s.* Unterschrift *f.;* Zeichen, Kennzeichen *n.*
signboard *s.* Aushängeschild *n.*
signet *s.* Siegel *n.;* ~ **ring,** *s.* Siegelring *m.*
significance *s.* Bedeutung *f.;* Sinn *m.*
significant *a.,* **~ly** *adv.* bezeichnend; bedeutsam; bedeutend.
signification *s.* Bedeutung *f.*
signify *v.t.* & *i.* anzeigen; bedeuten.
sign language *s.* Zeichensprache *f.*
signpost *s.* Wegweiser *m.*
silence *s.* Ruhe *f.*, Stillschweigen *n.;* Verschwiegenheit *f.; to keep* ~, schweigen; **~!,** *i.* still!; ~ *v.t.* zum Schweigen bringen.
silencer *s.* Schalldämpfer *m.*
silent *a.,* **~ly** *adv.* schweigend; stumm; verschwiegen; *to be* ~, schweigen; ~ **movie** *s.* Stummfilm *m.;* ~ **partner** *s.* stiller Teilhaber *m.*
silent majority *s.* schweigende Mehrheit *f.*, stiller Teilhaber *m.*
Silesia *s.* Schlesien *n.*
silhouette *s.* Silhouette *f.*
silica *s.* Kieselerde *f.*
silicon *s.* Siliziun *n.*
silicone *s.* Silikon *n.*
silk *s.* Seide *f.;* Seidenzeug *n.;* **~s** *pl.* Seidenstoffe *m.pl.;* ~ *a.* seiden.
silken *a.* seiden; seidenartig, weich.
silk growing *s.* Seidenzucht *f.*
silkworm *s.* Seidenraupe *f.*
silky *a.* seiden; seidenartig.
sill *s.* Schwelle, Brüstung *f.;* Fensterbrett *n.*
silliness *s.* Dummheit *f.;* Blödheit *f.*
silly *a.,* **~ily** *adv.* einfältig, albern; ~ **season,** Sauregurkenzeit *f.*
silo *s.* Kornkeller *m.;* Kornlagerhaus *n.*, Silo *m.*

silt *v.i.* verschlammen; ~ *s.* Schlamm *m.;* Schlick *m.*

silver *s.* Silber *n.;* Silbergeld *n.;* ~ **lining,** Silberstreifen; **~-plated** *a.* versilbert; ~ *a.* silbern; ~ *v.t.* versilbern.

silversmith *s.* Silberarbeiter *m.*

silvery *a.* silbern; silberhell.

similar *a.*, **~ly** *adv.* gleichartig, ähnlich.

similarity *s.* Ähnlichkeit *f.*

simile *s.* Vergleich *m.*

similitude *s.* Ähnlichkeit *f.*

simmer *v.i.* köcheln; brodeln.

simper *v.i.* einfältig lächeln; ~ *s.* geziertes Lächeln *n.*

simple *a.*, **simply** *adv.* einfach, einzeln; einfältig.

simple-minded *a.* arglos.

simpleton *s.* Tropf *m.*, Dummkopf *m.*

simplicity *s.* Einfachheit, Einfalt *f.*

simplification *s.* Vereinfachung *f.*

simplify *v.t.* vereinfachen.

simplistic *a.* simpel.

simulate *v.t.* & *i.* nachahmen; heucheln; vorschützen.

simulated *a.* Vorgetäuscht; simuliert.

simulation *s.* Simulation *f.;* Verstellung *f.*

simultaneous *a.*, **~ly** *adv.* gleichzeitig.

simultaneous translation *s.* Simultandolmetschen *n.*

sin *s.* Sünde *f.;* ~ *v.i.* sündigen.

since *pr.* & *adv.* seit, seitdem; *long* ~, schon lange; ~ *c.* da; seit.

sincere *a.*, **~ly** *adv.* aufrichtig; *yours* ~*ly,* Ihr ergebener.

sincerity *s.* Aufrichtigkeit, Offenheit *f.*

sine *s.* (*math.*) Sinus *m.*

sinecure *s.* Sinekur *f.;* Pfründe *f.*

sinew *s.* Sehne, Flechse *f.;* Nerv *m.*

sinewy *a.* sehnig; stark.

sinful *a.*, **~ly** *adv.* sündig, sündhaft.

sing *v.t.* & *i.st.* singen, besingen.

singe *v.t.* sengen, versengen.

singer *s.* Sänger(in) *m.(f.)*

single *a.* einzeln; einfach; ledig; **~-breasted** *a.* einreihig (Anzug); ~ **combat** *s.* Zweikampf *m.;* **~-handed** *a.* ohne Hilfe; ~ **journey** *s.* Hinreise *f.;* ~ **room** *s.* einbettiges Zimmer *n.;* ~ **track** *a.* (*rail.*) eingleisig; ~ *s.* (*tennis*) Einzelspiel *n.;* ~ **out** *v.t.* absondern; aussuchen.

singleness *s.* Einzelheit *f.;* Einfachheit *f.*, Aufrichtigkeit *f.*

sing-song *s.* Singsang *m.*

singular *a.*, **~ly** *adv.* einzigartig; ungewöhnlich; ~ *s.* (*gram.*) Einzahl *f.*

singularity *s.* Einzigartigkeit *f.*, Sonderbarkeit *f.*

sinister *a.*, **~ly** *adv.* unheilvoll; schlimm, boshaft; (*her.*) link.

sink *v.t.st.* (ver)sinken; fallen; abnehmen; umkommen; ~ *v.t.* (ver)senken; unterdrücken, niederschlagen; in den Grund bohren; (Schuld) tilgen; ~ *s.* Spüle *f.;* Spülbecken *n.*

sinking *a.* sinkend; untergehend.

sinner *s.* Sünder(in) *m.(f.)*

sinuous *a.* geschlängelt, gewunden.

sinus *s.* (*anat.*) Nebenhöhle *f.;* Sinus *m.*

sinusitis *s.* Nebenhöhlenentzündung *f.*

sip *v.t.* nippen; schlürfen; ~ *s.* Schlückchen *n.*

siphon *s.* (Saug-) Heber *m.;* Siphonflasche *f.*

sir *s.* Herr (als Anrede) *m.;* Sir (Titel eines Ritters) *m.*

sire *s.* Vater *m.;* Sire *m.;* *v.t.* zeugen.

siren *s.* Sirene *f.*

sirloin *s.* Lendenbraten *m.*

sissy *s.* Weichling *m.*

sister *s.* Schwester *f.;* Nonne *f.;* Oberschwester (Krankenpflegerin) *f.;* **~-in-law** *s.* Schwägerin *f.*

sisterhood *s.* Schwesternschaft *f.*

sisterly *a.* schwesterlich.

sit *v.i.st.* sitzen; brüten; ~ *v.t.* *to ~ oneself,* sich setzen; *to ~ down,* sich setzen; *to ~ for an examination,* sich einer Prüfung unterziehen.

sitcom *s.*, **situation comedy** *s.* Situationskomödie *f.*

site *s.* Lage *f.*, Platz *m.;* Standort *m.;* ~ *v.t.* placieren, stationieren.

sitter *s.* Portraitmodell *n.*

sitting *s.* Sitzen *n.;* Sitzung *f.*

sitting room *s.* Wohnzimmer *n.*

situate *v.t.* aufstellen.

situated *a.* liegend, gelegen.

situation *s.* Lage *f.;* Zustand *m.;* Stellung, Stelle *f.;* ~ **estimate,** Lagebeurteilung *f.*, **~map,** Lagekarte *f.*, ~ **report,** Lagemeldung *f.*

six, sechs; *at ~es and sevens,* in Verwirrung.

six-footer *s.* Zwei-Meter-Mann *m.;* Zwei-Meter-Frau *f.*

sixteen, sechzehn.

sixteenth *a.* sechzehnt...

sixteenth note *s.* Sechzehntelnote *f.*

sixth *a.* sechst...

sixtieth *a.* sechzigst...

sixty, sechzig.

size *s.* Größe *f.;* Maß *n.;* Format *n.*, ~ *v.t.* nach Größenordnen; *to ~ up,* (*fam.*) einschätzen; (*paint*) grundieren.

sizeable *a.*, **~ly** *adv.* ansehnlich.

sized *a.* von gewisser Größe; geleimt.

sizzle *v.i.* zischen; brutzeln; *s.* Zischen *n.;* Brutzeln *n.*

skate *s.* Schlittschuh *m.;* Roche[n] (Fisch) *m.;* ~ *v.i.* Schlittschuh laufen.

skateboard *s.* Skateboard *n.*

skater *s.* Schlittschuhläufer(in) *m.(f.)*

skating rink *s.* Rollschuhbahn; Eisbahn *f.*

skedaddle *v.i.* davonlaufen.

skeleton *s.* Gerippe *n.;* Skelett *n.;* ~ **key,** Nachschlüssel *m.;* ~ **staff,** Minimalbesetzung *f.*

skeptic *a.* skeptisch.

sketch *s.* Entwurf *m.;* Skizze *f.;* ~ *v.t.* entwerfen, skizzieren.

sketchy *a.* flüchtig.

skew *a.* schräg; schief.

skewer *s.* (Brat)spieß *m.;* ~ *v.t.* aufspießen.

ski *s.* Ski *m.* (pl. Skier), Schi, *m.;* ~ *v.i.* skilaufen, schilaufen.

skid *s.* Hemmschuh *m.;* Kufe *f.;* ~ *v.t.* hemmen; ~ *v.i.* ausrutschen.

skier *s.* Skiläufer(in) *m.(f.)*

skiff *s.* Einer *m.* (Rudern).

skiing *s.* Skilaufen *n.;* Skisport *m.*

ski jump *s.* Sprungschanze *f.*

ski jumping *s.* Skispringen *n.*

ski lift *s.* Skilift *m.*

skill *s.* Geschicklichkeit *f.*; Fertigkeit *f.*
skilled *a.* geschickt; ausgebildet; ~ **worker,** gelernte Arbeiter(in) *m.(f.)*
skillful *a.*, ~**ly** *adv.* geschickt, erfahren.
skim *v.t.* abschäumen, (Milch) entrahmen; ~ *v.i.* flüchtig hingleiten; streifen; ~**milk** *s.* Magermilch *f.*
skimp *v.t.* knapp halten.
skimpy *a.* sparsam, karg.
skin *s.* Haut *f.*, Balg *m.*; Schale, Hülse *f.*; ~ *v.t.* häuten, abdecken; ~ *v.i.* zuheilen.
skin diving *s.* Schnorcheln *n.*
skin graft *s.* Hauttransplantation *f.*
skinny *a.* mager.
skin-tight *a.* hauteng.
skip *v.i.* springen, hüpfen; ~ *v.t.* überhüpfen; übergehen; ~ *s.* Sprung *m.*
ski pole *s.* Skistock *m.*
skipper *s.* Schiffer *m.*; Hüpfer *m.*
ski resort *s.* Skiort *m.*
skirmish *s.* Scharmützel *n.*; ~ *v.i.* plänkeln.
skirt *s.* Frauenrock, Rock *m.*; Saum *m.*; Rockschoß *m.*; Einfassung *f.*; ~ *v.t.* einfassen, besetzen; am Rande entlang gehen.
skit *s.* Stichelei, Satire, Spottschrift *f.*
skittish *a.*, ~**ly** *adv.* scheu, unstet; leichtfertig, flüchtig.
skittle *s.* Kegel *m.*; ~**alley** *s.* Kegelbahn *f.*
skulk *v.i.* lauern, herumlungern, heimlich umherschleichen.
skull *s.* Schädel *m.*; Totenkopf *m.*
skunk *s.* Stinktier *n.*; Schuft *m.*
sky *s.* (Wolken) himmel *m.*, Himmel *m.*
sky diver *s.* Fallschirmspringer(in) *m.(f.)*
skylark *s.* Feldlerche *f.*; ~ *v.i.* Possen treiben.
skylight *s.* Oberlicht *n.*; Dachfenster *n.*
skyline *s.* Kontur (einer Stadt) *f.*; Horizont *m.*
skyscraper *s.* Wolkenkratzer *m.*
slab *s.* Platte, Steinplatte *f.*; Tafel *f.*
slack *a.*, ~**ly** *adv.* schlaff, locker; nachlässig.
slacken *v.t.* schlaff werden, abspannen; nachlassen; verringern; (Kalk) löschen; ~ *v.i.* erschlaffen.
slacker *s.* Drückeberger *m.*
slacks *pl.* weite Hosen *f.pl.*
slag *s.* Schlacke *f.*
slake *v.t.* (Kalk) löschen; stillen; dämpfen.
slalom *s.* Slalom *m.*
slam *v.t.* zuschmeißen; ~ *s.* Klatsch, Schlag *m.*
slander *s.* Verleumdung *f.*; ~ *v.t.* verleumden, verunglimpfen.
slanderous *a.*, ~**ly** *adv.* verleumderisch.
slang *s.* lässige Umgangssprache *f.*; Slang *m.*
slant *a.*, ~**ly** *adv.* schief, schräg; abschüssig, ~ *v.t.* seitwärts wenden; ~ *v.i.* abfallen (von der horizontalen Linie); ~ *s.* Tendenz.
slantwise *a.* schief, schräg.
slap *v.t. & i.* schlagen, klapsen; *to ~ sb.'s face,* einem ins Gesicht schlagen; ~ *s.* Klaps *m.*
slapdash *a.* heftig; nachlässig.
slash *v.t.* hauen; (auf)schlitzen; ~ *s.* Hieb *m.*; Schlitz *m.*; Schmarre *f.*
slat *s.* Leiste *f.*; Latte *f.*; Lamelle *f.*
slate *s.* Schiefer *m.*; Schiefertafel *f.*; ~ *v.t.* mit Schiefer decken; abkanzeln; *~d for,* festgesetzt, eingesetzt für...
slattern *s.* Schlampe *f.*
slaughter *s.* Metzelei *f.*, Blutbad *n.*; ~ *v.t.* schlachten, morden.
slaughterhouse *s.* Schlachthaus *n.*
slav *s.* Slawe *m.*; Slawin *f.*
slave *s.* Sklave *m.*; Sklavin *f.*; ~ *v.i.* sich placken.
slave driver *s.* Leuteschinder *m.*; Sklaventreiber(in) *m.(f.)*
slave labor *s.* Sklavenarbeit *f.*
slaver *v.i.* geifern.
slavery *s.* Sklaverei *f.*
slavish *a.*, ~**ly** *adv.* sklavisch.
slavonic *a.* slawisch.
slay *v.t.st.* erschlagen, töten.
sled *s.*, **sledge** *s.* Schlitten *m.*; Schleife *f.*
sledgehammer *s.* Vorschlagshammer *m.*
sleek *a.*, ~**ly** *adv.* glatt; weich; ~ *v.t.* glätten.
sleep *v.t.st.* schlafen; ~ *s.* Schlaf *m.*; *to go to ~,* einschlafen; *to put to ~,* einschläfern.
sleeper *s.* Schläfer(in) *m.(f.)*; (*rail.*) Schwelle *f.*
sleeping bag *s.* Schlafsack *m.*
sleeping car *s.* (Eisenbahn) Schlafwagen *m.*
sleeping pill *s.* Schlaftablette *f.*
sleeping sickness *s.* Schlafkrankheit *f.*
sleepless *a.*, ~**ly** *adv.* schlaflos.
sleep walker *s.* Schlafwandler(in) *m.(f.)*
sleepy *a.*, ~**ily** *adv.* schläfrig, verschlafen.
sleet *s.* Schneeregen *m.*; ~ *v.i.* regnen und schneien.
sleeve *s.* Ärmel *m.*; *to laugh in one's ~,* sich ins Fäustchen lachen; *to have a plan up one's ~,* einen Plan in petto haben; *to roll up one's ~s,* die Ärmel hochkrempeln.
sleeveless *a.* ärmellos.
sleigh *s.* Schlitten *m.*
sleigh-ride *s.* Schlittenfahrt *f.*
sleight *s.* List *f.*; Kunststück *n.*; ~ **of hand,** Taschenspielerstückchen *n.*
slender *a.*, ~**ly** *adv.* schlank; dünn; spärlich, karg; schwach.
sleuth *s.* Spürhund *m.*; Detektiv *m.*
slice *s.* Schnitte, Scheibe *f.*; Slice *m.* (Tennis); ~ *v.i.* (in Scheiben) zerschneiden; schneiden (Ball).
sliced *a.* aufgeschnitten; kleingeschnitten.
slick *a.* glatt, flott.
slide *v.t.st.* gleiten, ausgleiten; schlüpfen; rutschen; ~ *v.t.* hineinschieben; ~ *s.* Gleitbahn *f.*; (*mech.*) Schlitten (Drehbank, etc.); Dia(positiv) *n.*; Rutschbahn *f.*; ~ **rule** *s.* Rechenschieber *m.*; ~ **valve** *s.* Schiebeventil *n.*
sliding door *s.* Schiebetür *f.*; ~**scale** *s.* gleitende Skala *f.*; ~ **seat,** Rollsitz *m.*
slight *a.*, ~**ly** *adv.* klein, gering; unwichtig, schwach, dünn; ~ *s.* Geringschätzung *f.*; Verachtung *f.*; ~ *v.t.* geringschätzig behandeln.; brüskieren; herabsetzen.
slim *a.* schlank, schmächtig.
slime *s.* Schleim *m.*; Schlamm *m.*
slimming *s.* Abnehmen *n.*; Kürzung *f.*
slimy *a.* schleimig; schlammig.
sling *s.* Schlag, Wurf *m.*; Schleuder *f.*; Schlinge, Binde *f.*; ~ *v.t.st.* schleudern; über die Schulter hängen.
slink *v.t.st.* schleichen.
slinky *a.* aufreizend.
slip *v.i.* gleiten, ausgleiten; (ent-) schlüpfen; ent-

fallen; ~ *v.t.* schlüpfen lassen, abreißen; loslassen; anziehen; ~ *s.* Ausgleiten *n.;* Entwischen *n.;* Versehen *n.;* Stückchen, Streifchen *n.;* Zettel *m.;* Unterrock *m.* (Kissen-)überzug *m.;* (*nav.*) Helling *f.;* ~ *of the pen,* Schreibfehler *m.;* ~ *of the tongue,* Versprecher *m.;* *to give the* ~, entwischen.
slipper *s.* Pantoffel *m.*
slippery *a.* schlüpfrig, glatt.
slipshod *a.* nachlässig; schlampig.
slipway *s.* Laufweg *m.;* Helling *f.*
slit *v.t.* aufschneiden, durchschneiden; aufschlitzen; spalten; ~ *s.* Riß *m.;* Spalte *f.*
slither *v.i.* rutschen; schlittern.
sliver *s.* Holzsplitter *m.*
slob *s.* (*sl.*) Schwein *n.*
slobber *v.i.* sabbern.
sloe *s.* Schlehe *f.*
slog *v.t.* dreschen; draufschlagen.
slogan *s.* Wahlparole *f.;* Schlagwort *n.*
sloop *s.* Schaluppe *f.*
slop *v.t.* verschütten; schwappen.
slope *s.* Abhang *m.;* Gefälle *n.;* Piste *f.;* ~ *v.i.* abfallen; ~ *v.t.* abschrägen.
sloping *a.,* **~ly** *adv.* schief, abschüssig.
sloppy *a.* schlampig; nachlässig.
slosh *v.i.* platschen; schwappen.
slot *s.* Spalte *f.,* Schlitz *m.;* ~ **machine** (Waren-, Spiel) Automat *m.*
sloth *s.* Trägheit *f.;* Faultier *n.*
slothful *a.,* **~ly** *adv.* träge, faul.
slouch *v.i.* den Kopf hängen; krumm dastehen; ~ *s.* schlaffe Haltung *f.;* latschiger Gang *m.*
slough *s.* Morast, Sumpf *m.;* Haut *f.;* Schorf *m.;* ~ *v.i.* sich häuten.
Slovak *a.* slowakisch; *s.* Slowake *m.;* Slowakin *f.*
Slovakia *s.* Slowakei *f.*
slovenly *a.* & *adv.* liederlich, schlampig.
slow *a.,* **~ly** *adv.* langsam, träge; schwerfällig, begriffsstützig; *to be* ~, (Uhr) nachgehen; **~down** *s.* Verlangsamung *f.;* **~train** *s.* Bummelzug *m.;* **~-motion picture** *s.* Zeitlupenaufnahme *f.;* ~ **down** *v.t.* verlangsamen.
slowness *s.* Langsamkeit *f.*
slow-witted *a.* schwerfällig.
slowworm *s.* Blindschleiche *f.*
sludge *s.* Matsch *m.;* Schlamm *m.*
slug *s.* Nacktschnecke *f.;* Gewehrkugel *f.;* Schlag *m.*
sluggard *s.* Faulenzer *m.;* ~ *a.* träge.
sluggish *a.,* **~ly** *adv.* langsam, träge.
sluice *s.* Schleuse *f.;* ~ *v.t.* ablassen.
slum *s.* Elendsviertel *n.*
slumber *s.* Schlummer *m.;* ~ *v.i.* schlummern.
slump *v.i.* fallen, stürzen; ~ *s.* Kurssturz *m.;* Baisse *f.*
slur *v.t.* besudeln; verleumden; (*mus.*) verschleifen; rasch darüberhingehen; ~ *s.* Beleidigung *f.;* undeutliche Aussprache *f.*
slush *s.* Schneematsch *m.;* sentimentaler Kitsch *m.*
slut *s.* Schlampe *f.*
sluttish *a.,* **~ly** *adv.* schlampig, schmutzig.
sly *a.,* **~ly** *adv.* schlau; *on the* ~, verstohlenerweise; ~ **digs** *pl.* Seitenhiebe *m.pl.*
smack *s.* Klaps *m.;* Schmatz *m.;* ~ *v.i.* schmecken; schmatzen, schnalzen; ~ *v.t.* klatschen; prügeln.
small *a.* klein, gering; dünn; ~ **hours,** frühe Morgenstunden *f.pl.;* ~ *s.* dünner Teil *m.;* ~ *of the back,* Kreuz *n.*
small arms *s.pl.* Handfeuerwaffen *f.pl.*
small change *s.* Kleingeld *n.*
smallpox *s.* Pocken *f.pl.*
small print *s.* Kleingedruckte *n.*
small-scale *a.* in kleinen Rahmen.
small screen *s.* Biedschirm (TV).
small talk *s.* Geplauder *n.*
smart *a.,* **~ly** *adv.* klug, gescheit; scharf; lebhaft; schneidig, fesch; pfiffig; elegant; *s.* Schmerz *m.;* ~ *v.i.* schmerzen; ~ **aleck** *s.* Besserwisser *m.;* ~ **ass** (*vulg.*) *s.* Klugscheißer *m.*
smarten *v.t.* herrichten; in Ordnung bringen.
smartness *s.* Schlauheit *f.;* Schick *m.*
smash *s.* Schmiß, Fall *m.;* Bankerott *m.;* ~ *v.t.* zerschmettern.
smattering *s.* oberflächliche Kenntnis *f.*
smear *v.t.* beschmieren; ~ *s.* Fleck *m.* ~ **test** *s.* Abstrich *m.*
smell *v.t.* & *i.* riechen; wittern; ~ *s.* Geruch *m.*
smelling salts *pl.* Riechsalz *n.*
smelly *a.* stinkend.
smelt *v.t.* (Erz) schmelzen.
smile *v.i.* lächeln; schmunzlen; ~ *s.* Lächeln *n.*
smirk *v.i.* grinsen; ~ *s.* Grinsen *n.*
smite *v.t.st.* schlagen, treffen; zerstören; heimsuchen.
smith *s.* Schmied *m.*
smithereens *s.pl.* Stückchen *n.pl.,* Splitter *m.*
smithy *s.* Schmiede *f.*
smitten *a.,* ~ **with,** stark verliebt, bezaubert.
smock *s.* Kittel *m.*
smog *s.* Smog *m.*
smoke *s.* Rauch *m.;* (*mil.*) Nebel; **~screen** *s.* Nebelwand *f.;* **~stack** *s.* Schornstein *m.;* ~ *v.i.* rauchen; *no smoking,* Rauchen verboten!; ~ *v.t.* rauchen; räuchern.
smoked *a.* geräuchert.
smokeless *a.* rauchlos; rauchfrei.
smoker *s.* Raucher(in) *m.(f.)*
smoking *s.* Rauchen *n.*
smoky *a.* rauchend, rauchig.
smolder *v.i.* schwelen.
smooth *a.,* **~ly** *adv.* glatt, eben; sanft, lieblich; ~ *v.t.* ebnen; polieren; mildern.
smoothness *s.* Glätte *f.;* Weichheit *f.;* Reibungslosigkeit *f.;* Geschicklichkeit *f.*
smother *v.t.* ersticken.
smudge *s.* Schmutz, Schmier *m.;* ~ *v.t.* beschmutzen, verschmieren.
smug *a.,* **~ly** *adv.* selbstgefällig.
smuggle *v.t.* & *i.* schmuggeln.
smuggler *s.* Schmuggler(in) *m.(f.)*
smuggling *s.* Schmuggelei *f.;* Schmuggel *m.*
smut *s.* Rußfleck *m.;* Schlüpfrigkeit *f.;* Getreidebrand *m.*
smutty *a.,* **~ily** *adv.* russig, schmutzig; brandig (von Gewächsen); unflätig.
snack *s.* Bissen, Imbiß *m.;* ~ **bar** *s.* Imbißraum *m.;* Schnellimbiß *m.*
snaffle *s.* Trense *f.;* **~bit,** Trensengebiß *n.*
snag *s.* Haken *m.*

snail *s.* Schnecke *f.*
snake *s.* Schlange *f.;* ~ **skin** *s.* Schlangenleder *n.*
snaky *a.* schlangenartig; gewunden.
snap *v.t.* & *i.* schnappen, abschnappen; beißen; bissig antworten; ~ **one's fingers,** mit den Fingern schnalzen; ~ *s.* Schnapp *m.;* Biß *m.;* Fang *m.;* Knall *m.;* Schnappschloß *n.;* ~ *a.* plötzlich, überraschend.
snapdragon *s.* (*bot.*) Löwenmaul *n.*
snappish *a.*, **~ly** *adv.* bissig, schnippisch.
snappy *a.*, **~ily** *adv.* schick; elegant.
snapshot *s.* Momentaufnahme *f.*, Schnappschuß *m.*
snare *s.* Schlinge *f.;* ~ *v.t.* verstricken.
snarl *v.i.* knurren; verheddern; *s.* Knurren *n.;* Knoten *m.*
snatch *v.t.* schnappen, ergreifen, an sich reißen; ~ *v.i.* haschen; ~ *s.* schneller Griff *m.;* Ruck, Hui *m.*
sneak *v.i.* kriechen; schleichen; ~ *s.* Petze *f.* Kriecher *m.*
sneaky *a.* hinterhältig.
sneer *v.i.* hohnlächeln; sticheln; grinsen; ~ *s.* Spott *m.;* Stichel *f.*
sneeze *v.i.* niesen.
snide *a.* abfällig.
sniff *v.i.* schnüffeln; schnuppern; schniefen; ~ *s.* Nasevoll *f.;* Schnuppern *n.*
snigger *v.i.* kichern.
snip *v.t.* schneiden; schnippeln; ~ *s.* Schnitt *m.;* Schnipsel *n.*
snipe *s.* Schnepfe *f.;* ~ *v.i.* aus gedeckter Stellung schießen.
sniper *s.* Heckenschütze *m.*
snippet *s.* Schnipsel *n.;* Bruchstück *n.;* Gesprächsfetzen *m.*
snitch *v.i.* ~ *on sb.*, jn. verpetzen.
snivel *v.i.* winseln; schniefen; weinerlich sein.
snob *s.* Geck *m.;* Snob *m.*
snobbery *s.* Snobismus *m.*
snobbish *a.* snobistisch.
snoop *v.i.* schnüffeln.
snooper *s.* Schnüffler(in) *m.(f.)*
snooty *a.*, **~ily** *adv.* hochnäsig.
snooze *v.i.* dösen; ~ *s.* Nickerchen *n.*
snore *v.i.* schnarchen; ~ *s.* Schnarchen *n.*
snorer *s.* Schnarcher(in) *m.(f.)*
snorkel *s.* Schnorchel *m.;* ~ *v.i.* schnorcheln.
snort *v.i.* schnaufen; schnauben.
snot *s.* (*fam.*) Rotz *m.*
snotty *a.* rotznäsig.
snout *s.* Schnauze *f.;* Rüssel *m.*
snow *s.* Schnee *m.;* ~ *v.i.* schneien; *~ed in, under,* verschneit, eingeschneit.
snowball *s.* Schneeball *m.*
snowbound *a.* eingeschneit.
snowdrift *s.* Schneewehe *f.*
snowdrop *s.* Schneeglöckchen *n.*
snowplow *s.* Schneepflug *m.*
snowshoe *s.* Schneeschuh *m.*
snow-white *a.* schneeweiß.
snowy *a.* schneeig; schneeweiß; schneereich.
snub *v.t.* zurechtweisen; brüskieren; ~ *s.* scharfe Rüge *f.;* Abfuhr *f.*
snub-nosed *a.* stupnasig.
snuff *s.* Schnupftabak *m.;* ~ *v.t.* schnupfen; (Kerze) ausdrücken.
snuff-box *s.* Schnupftabaksdose *f.*
snuffle *v.i.* schnüffeln.
snug *a.*, **~ly** *adv.* geborgen; anheimelnd, gemütlich, nett.
snuggle *v.i.* anschmiegen.
so *adv.* & *c.* so; also, folglich; daher; *~ and ~,* so und so.
soak *v.t.* einsaugen; durchnässen; einweichen; ~ *v.i.* weich werden, durchziehen; saufen.
soaking *a.* tropfnaß.
soap *s.* Seife *f.; laundry ~,* Waschseife *f.; soft ~,* Schmierseife; (*fig.*) Schmus *m.;* ~ *v.t.* einseifen.
soapbubble *s.* Seifenblase *f.*
soapflakes *pl.* Seifenflocken *f.pl.*
soap suds *s.pl.* Seifenschaum *m.*
soapy *a.* seifig; salbungsvoll.
soar *v.i.* sich aufschwingen, schweben; in die Höhe gehen.
soaring *a.* schwebend; sprunghaft ansteigend.
sob *v.i.* schluchzen; ~ *s.* Schluchzen *n.*
sober *a.*, **~ly** *adv.* nüchtern; besonnen; gesetzt; ~ *v.t.* ernüchtern; mäßigen.
sobering *a.* ernüchternd.
sobriety *s.* Nüchternheit, Mäßigkeit *f.*
soc. *society,* Gesellschaft, Verein.
so-called *a.* sogenannt.
soccer *s.* Fußball *m.*
sociable *a.*, **~bly** *adv.* gesellig.
social *a.* gesellschaftlich; gesellig; sozial; **~science,** Gesellschaftswissenschaft *f.;* **~worker,** Sozialarbeiter(in) *m.(f.)*
social class *s.* Gesellschaftsschicht *f.*
social climber *s.* Emporkömmling *m.*
Social Democrat *s.* Sozialdemokrat(in) *m.(f.)*
socialism *s.* Sozialismus *m.*
socialist *s.* Sozialist(in) *m.(f.)*
socialize *v.t.* sozialisieren, vergesellschaften.
social life *s.* gesellschaftliches Leben *n.*
society *s.* Gesellschaft *f.;* Verein *m.*
sociologist *s.* Soziologe *m.;* Soziologin *f.*
sociology *s.* Sozologie *f.*
sock *s.* Socke *f.*
socket *s.* Hülse *f.;* (Augen-, Zahn-)Höhle *f.;* (*elek.*) Steckdose *f.;* Fassung *f.*
sod *s.* Rasenstück *n.;* Sode *f.*
soda *s.* Soda *f.;* ~ **water** Sodawasser *n.*
sodden *a.* durchnäßt; aufgeweicht.
sodium *s.* (*chem.*) Natrium *n.;* ~ **chloride** *s.* Kochsalz *n.*
sodomy *s.* Sodomie *f.*
sofa *s.* Sofa *n.*
soft *a.*, **~ly** *adv.* weich, mürbe; sanft, zärtlich; leise; nachgiebig. **~!,** *i.* gemach! gelassen! sachte!; ~ **drinks** *pl.* nichtalkoholische Getränke *n.pl.;* ~ **boiled** *a.* weichgekocht
soften *v.t.* & *i.* erweichen; mildern, besänftigen; weich werden.
softener *s.* Enthärter *m.;* Weichspülmittel *n.*
soft-hearted *a.* weichherzig.
soft-spoken *a.* sanftredend.
software *s.* (*comp.*) Software *f.*
soggy *a* durchweicht, sumpfig.

soil *s.* Boden *m.;* Erdreich *n.;* Flecken *m.;* Schmutz *m.;* ~ *v.t.* besudeln, beschmutzen.
soiled *a.* schmutzig.
sojourn *s.* Aufenthalt *m.;* ~ *v.i.* sich aufhalten.
solace *s.* Trost *m.;* ~ *v.t.* erquicken, lindern, trösten.
solar *a.* Sonnen...; ~ **cell** *s.* Sonnenzelle *f.;* Solarzelle *f.;* ~ **eclipse** *s.* Sonnenfinsternis *f.;* ~ **energy** *s.* Sonnenenergie *f.*
solarium *s.* Solarium *n.*
solar plexus *s.* Solarplexus *m.*
solar system *s.* Sonnensystem *n.*
solder *v.t.* löten; ~ *s.* Lot *n.*
soldering iron *s.* Lötkolben *m.*
soldier *s.* Soldat *m.*
soldierly *a.* soldatisch.
sole *a.,* **~ly** *adv.* allein, einzig; bloß; ledig; ~ **agent** *s.* (*com.*) Alleinvertreter *m.;* ~ *s.* Sohle *f.;* Grundfläche *f.;* Seezunge *f.;* ~ *v.t.* besohlen.
solemn *a.,* **~ly** *adv.* feierlich, festlich.
solemnity *s.* Feierlichkeit *f.;* Ernst *m.*
solemnize *v.t.* feiern.
solicit *v.t.* (anhaltend) bitten; ansprechen.
solicitation *s.* Ansuchen, Anliegen *n.*
solicitor *s.* Anwalt, Notar *m.*
solicitous *a.,* **~ly** *adv.* besorgt, ängstlich; fürsorglich.
solicitude *s.* Besorgnis *f.;* Sorgfalt *f.*
solid *a.,* **~ly** *adv.* fest, gediegen; massiv, gründlich; ernst; echt; solide; ~ *s.* fester Körper *m.*
solidarity *s.* Solidarität *f.*
solidify *v.t.* verfestigen.
solidity *s.* Festigkeit, Dichtheit *f.;* Gründlichkeit, Echtheit *f.*
solid-state *s.* Festkörper *m.*
soliloquize *v.i.* ein Selbstgespräch führen.
soliloquy *s.* Selbstgespräch *n.*
solitaire *s.* Solitär(spiel) *n.;* (jewel) Solitär *m.*
solitary *a.,* **~ily** *adv.* einsam; eingezogen; **~confinement,** Einzelhaft *f.;* ~ *s.* Einsiedler(in) *m.(f.)*
solitude *s.* Einsamkeit *f.;* Einöde *f.*
solo *s.* Solo *n.*
soloist *s.* (*mus.*) Solist(in) *m.(f.)*
solstice *s.* Sonnenwende *f.*
soluble *a.* auflösbar; lösbar.
solution *s.* Auflösung *f.;* Lösung *f.*
solve *v.t.* lösen; erklären; (be)heben.
solvency *s.* Zahlungsfähigkeit *f.*
solvent *a.* zahlungsfähig; ~ *s.* Lösungsmittel *n.*
somber *a.* dunkel, düster.
some *a.* ein paar, manch; ein bißchen, einige, etliche, irgendein; etwas, ein wenig; ungefähr; ~ **body,** jemand, einer; **~how,** irgendwie; **~thing,** etwas; **~time,** einst, vormals; **~times,** zuweilen; **~what,** etwas; **~where,** irgendwo.
somersault *s.* Purzelbaum *m.;* Salto *m.*
somnambulism *s.* Schlafwandeln *n.*
somnambulist *s.* Schlafwandler(in) *m.(f.)*
somnolent *a.* schläfrig.
son *s.* Sohn *m.;* **~-in-law,** Schwiegersohn *m.*
sonata *s.* Sonate *f.*
song *s.* Gesang *m.;* Lied *n.; for a ~,* spottbillig.
sonic *a.* Schall...; **~boom** *s.* Überschallknall *m.*
sonnet *s.* Sonett *n.*
sonorous *a.,* **~ly** *adv.* resonant.
soon *adv.* bald; früh; gern; *as ~ as,* sobald (als).
sooner *adv.* eher, früher; lieber
soonest *adv.* ehestens.
soot *s.* Ruß *m.;* **~ed up,** *a.* verrußt.
soothe *v.t.* besänftigen, lindern.
soothsayer *s.* Wahrsager *m.*
sooty *a.* rußig.
sop *s.* eingetunkter Bissen *m.;* (*fig.*) Köder *m.;* ~ *v.t.* eintunken.
sophism *s.* Trugschluß *m.*
sophist *s.* Sophist *m.*
sophistical *a.,* **~ly** *adv.* sophistisch.
sophisticated *a.* kultiviert; anspruchsvoll; subtil; hochentwickelt.
sophistry *s.* Spitzfindigkeit *f.*
sophomore *s.* Student(in) im zweiten Studienjahr.
soporific *a.* einschläfernd.
soprano *s.* Sopran *m.;* Sopranistin *f.*
sorcerer *s.* Zauberer *m.;* Hexer *m.*
sorceress *s.* Hexe *f.;* Zauberin *f.*
sorcery *s.* Zauberei *f.*
sordid *a.,* **~ly** *adv.* schmutzig; gemein.
sore *a.* wund; schmerzhaft, empfindlich; ~ *s.* ~ **spot,** wunder Punkt *m.;* wunde Stelle *f.*
sorely *adv.* schmerzlich, in hohem Grade; dringend.
sorrel *a.* rötlich; ~ *s.* Rotfuchs *m.;* Sauerampfer *m.*
sorrow *s.* Kummer *m.,* Sorge *f.*
sorrowful *a.,* **~ly** *adv.* traurig.
sorry *a.,* traurig, betrübt; erbärmlich, armselig; *I am ~,* es tut mir leid.
sort *s.* Gattung, Sorte, Art *f.; out of ~s,* verstimmt; nicht in Form; ~ *v.t.* sortieren.
sort code *s.* Bankleitzahl *f.*
sortie *s.* Ausfall, Einsatz *m.*
so so *a.* (*fam.*) so la la.
sot *s.* Trunkenbold *m.*
sought-after *a.* begehrt; gesucht.
soul *s.* Seele *f.* **~destroying** *a.* nervtötend, geisttötend.
soulful *a.* gefühlvoll.
soulmate *s.* Seelenverwandte *m./f.*
soul-searching *s.* Gewissensprüfung *f.*
sound *a. & adv.,* **~ly** *adv.* gesund, fest, stark, tüchtig; ~ *s.* Schall, Laut, Klang *m.;* Sund *m.;* Sonde *f.;* Schwimmblase (eines Fisches) *f.;* **~film** *s.* Tonfilm *m.;* ~ **insulation** Schalldämpfung *f.;* ~ *v.i.* klingen, tönen, lauten; ~ *v.t.* ertönen lassen; sondieren, ausforschen; loten; *to ~ the lungs,* die Lungen abhorchen.
sound barrier *s.* Schallmauer *f.*
sounding board *s.* Resonanzboden *m.*
soundless *a.* klanglos.
soundness *s.* Gesundheit *f.;* Vernünftigkeit *f.;* Gründlichkeit *f.*
soundproof *a.* schalldicht.
soundtrack *s.* (*film*) Tonspur *f.;* Filmmusik *f.*
soundwave *s.* Schallwelle *f.*
soup *s.* Suppe, Fleischbrühe *f.*
sour *a.,* **~ly** *adv.* sauer, herb, bitter; mürrisch; ~ *v.t.* sauer machen; (*fig.*) verbittern; ~ *v.i.* sauer werden.
source *s.* Quelle *f.;* Ursprung *m.; ~ of supply,* Bezugsquelle *f.*
sourpuss *s.* Miesepeter *m.*

souse *v.t.* eintauchen.
south *s.* Süden *m.;* ~ *a. & adv.* südlich, gegen Süden.
South Africa *s.* Südafrika *n.*
South African *a.* südafrikanisch; ~ *s.* Südafrikaner(in) *m.(f.)*
South America *s.* Südamerika *n.*
South American *a.* südamerikanisch; ~ *s.* Südamerikaner(in) *m.(f.)*
southbound *a.* in Richtung Süden.
southeast *s.* südosten *m.;* ~ *a.* südöstlich.
southeastern *a.* südöstlich.
southerly *a.* südlich.
southern *a.* südlich.
southerner *s.* Bewohner(in) des Südens; Südstaatler(in) *m.(f.)*
southernmost *a.* südlichst.
South Pole *s.* Südpol *m.*
South Seas *s.* Südsee *f.*
southward *adv.* südwärts.
southwest *s.* Südwesten *m.;* ~ *a.* südwestlich.
southwester *s.* Südwestwind *m.*
souvenir *s.* Andenken *n.*
sovereign *a.* souverän; ~ *s.* Souverän *m.*, Landesherr *m.*
sovereignty *s.* Oberherrschaft *f.;* Souveränität *f.*
sow *s.* Sau *f.;* Trog *m.;* ~ *v.t. & r. st.* säen.
sowing machine *s.* Sämaschine *f.*
soybean *s.* Soyabohne *f.*
spa *s.* Bad *n.*, Badeort *m.*
space *s.* Raum *m.;* Zeitraum *m.;* Weltraum *m.;* Weilchen *n.;* Strecke, Frist *f.;* ~ *v.t.* (Druck) sperren; *single* ~*d* einzeilig (Schreibmaschine); *double-*~*d,* zweizeilig.
space: **~age** *s.* Weltraumzeitalter *n.;* **~bar** *s.* Leertaste *f.;* **~craft** *s.* Raumfahrzeug *n.;* **~flight** *s.* Raumflug *m.;* **~saving** *a.* raumsparend; **~ship** *s.* Raumschiff *n.;* **~shuttle** *s.* Raumfähre *f.;* **~station** *s.* Weltraumstation *f.;* **~suit** *s.* Weltraumanzug *m.*
spacious *a.*, **~ly** *adv.* geräumig.
spade *s.* Spaten *m.;* **~s,.** Grün, Pik (in der Karte) *n.;* **~work** *s.* Vorarbeit *f.*
Spain *s.* Spanien *n.*
span *s.* Spanne *f.;* Gespann *n.;* Spannweite *f.;* ~ *v.t.* spannen, (aus)messen.
spangle *s.* Flitter *m.*, Paillette *f.;* ~ *v.t.* übersäen.
Spaniard *s.* Spanier(in) *m.(f.)*
spaniel *s.* Wachtelhund *m.*
Spanish *a.* spanisch; *s.* Spanier(in) *m.(f.)*
spank *v.t.* durchwichsen; klapsen; ~ *v.i.* tüchtig ausschreiten.
spanking *s.* Tracht Prügel *f.*
spanner *s.* Schraubenschlüssel *m.; adjustable* ~ Engländer *m.*
spar *s.* Sparren *m.;* Scheinhieb *m.;* (*min.*) Spat *m.;* ~ *v.i.* boxen.
spare *v.t. & i.* sparen, scheuen; entbehren; (ver)schonen, Nachsicht haben; erübrigen; ~ *a.* sparsam, spärlich; mager; überzählig; ~ *s.* Ersatzteil *m.;* **~part** *s.* Ersatzteil *m.;* **~room** *s.* Fremdenzimmer *n.;* **~wheel** *s.* Ersatzrad *n.*
sparing *a.*, **~ly** *adv.* sparsam, spärlich.
spark *s.* Funke *m.;* ~ *v.i.* Funken sprühen.
sparkle *s.* Funkeln *n.;* Glitzern *n.;* ~ *v.i.* funkeln; perlen (vom Wein); sprühen; *sparkling wine,* Schaumwein *m.*
spark plug *s.* Zündkerze *f.*
sparrow *s.* Sperling *m.;* **~-hawk,** Sperber *m.*
sparse *a.*, **~ly** *adv.* spärlich; dünn.
Spartan *a.* spartanisch; ~ *s.* Spartaner(in) *m.(f.)*
spasm *s.* Krampf *m.*
spasmodic *a.* krampfartig.
spastic *s.* Spastiker(in) *m.(f.);* ~ *a.* spastisch.
spate *s.* Hochwasser *n.;* (*fig.*) Flut *f.*
spatial *a.* räumlich.
spatter *v.t.* bespritzen; besudeln.
spatula *s.* Spachtel *f.*
spavin *s.* (Pferdekrankheit) Spat *m.*
spawn *s.* Laich *m.;* Rogen *m.;* Brut *f.;* ~ *v.i.* laichen; ~ *v.t.* ausbrüten.
spay *v.t.* sterilisieren (weibliche Tiere).
speak *v.t. & i.st.* sprechen, reden.
speaker *s.* Sprecher(in), Redner(in) *m.(f.);* Präsident(in) *m.(f.)* des Unterhauses; (*elek.*) Lautsprecher *m.*
speaking *s.* sprechen *n.*
speaking tube *s.* Sprachrohr *n.*
spear *s.* Speer, Spieß *m.*, Lanze *f.*
spearhead *s.* (*mil.*) Spitze *f.*
spearmint *s.* grüne Minze *f.*
special *a.*, besonder, eigen; vorzüglich; **~correspondent,** Sonderberichterstatter *m.;* ~ **diet,** Diät *f.;* ~ **train** *s.* Extrazug, Sonderzug *m.;* **~ly** *adv.* besonders.
specialist *s.* Fachmann *m.*, Fachfrau *f.;* Spezialist(in) *m.(f.)*
specialize *v.i.* (*in*) als Spezialfach betreiben; spezialisieren.
special offer *s.* Sonderangebot *n.*
specialty *s.* Besonderheit, Eigenheit *f.;* Sonderfach *n.*
specie *s.* Metallgeld *n.*
species *s.* Art, Gattung *f.;* Gestalt *f.*
specific *a.*, **~ally** *adv.* eigen, eigenartig; bestimmt; spezifisch; ~ **gravity,** spezifisches Gewicht *n.*
specification *s.* namentliche Angabe *f.;* (Patent-) Beschreibung *f.*
specify *v.t.* einzeln angeben.
specimen *s.* Probe *f.*, Muster *n.;* Exemplar *n.;* **~copy,** Frei-, Probeexemplar *n.*
specious *a.*, **~ly** *adv.* trügerisch.
speck *s.* Fleck *m.;* Fleckchen *n.;* ~ *v.t.* flecken, sprenkeln.
speckle *s.* Fleckchen, Tüpfelchen *n.;* ~ *v.t.* flecken, sprenkeln.
spectacle *s.* Schauspiel *n.;* Anblick *m.;* **~s** *pl.* Brille *f.;* ~ **frame,** Brillengestell *n.*
spectacular *a.* spektakulär.
spectator *s.* Zuschauer(in) *m.(f.)*
specter *s.* Gespenst *n.*
spectral *a.* gespenstig; Spektral...
spectrum *s.* Spektrum *n.*
speculate *v.i.* nachsinnen, grübeln; spekulieren.
speculation *s.* Betrachtung *f.;* Nachsinnen *n.;* Vermutung *f.;* Spekulation *f.*
speculative *a.*, **~ly** *adv.* forschend; unternehmend, spekulativ.
speculator *s.* Spekulant(in) *m.(f.)*
speculum *s.* (*med.*) Spiegel *m.*
speech *s.* Rede *f.;* Sprache *f.; freedom of* ~, Redefreiheit *f.; to deliver a* ~, eine Rede halten.
speechday *s.* Schlußfeier (Schule) *f.*

speech defect *s.* Sprachfehler *m.*
speechless *a.* sprachlos.
speed *v.i.* sich beeilen, eilen; glücken; ~ *v.t.* beschleunigen, befördern; *to ~ up,* beschleunigen; ~ *s.* Eile *f.*; gute Erfolg *m.*; Geschwindigkeit *f.*; **~limit** *s.* Höchstgeschwindigkeit *f.*; **~boat** *s.* Schnellboot *n.*
speeding *s.* zu schnelles Fahren; Geschwindigkeitsüberschreitung *f.*
speedometer *s.* Geschwindigkeitsanzeiger *m.*
speed trap *s.* Geschwindigkeitskontrolle *f.*
speedy *a.*, **~ily** *adv.* eilig, schnell.
spell *v.t. & i.* buchstabieren; (richtig) schreiben; bedeuten; *to ~ out,* entziffern, enträtseln; *to ~ out a number,* eine Zahl ausschreiben; ~ *s.* Zauber *m.*; kurze Zeit *f.*; Weile *f.*
spellbound *a.* (fest)gebannt; verzaubert.
spelling *s.* Buchstabieren *n.*; Rechtschreibung *f.*; **~bee** *s.* Rechtschreibwettbewerb *m.*; **~book** Fibel *f.*; **~mistake** *s.* Rechtschreibfehler *m.*
spelt *s.* Spelz, Dinkel *m.*
spend *v.t. & i.st.* verwenden; ausgeben; verschwenden; Aufwand machen; erschöpfen; (Zeit) zubringen.
spendthrift *s.* Verschwender(in) *m.(f.)*
spent *a.* erschöpft, kraftlos.
sperm *s.* Samen *m.*
sperm whale *s.* Pottwal *m.*; Sperma *n.*
spew *v.t.* ausspeien.
sphere *s.* Kugel *f.*; Erd-, Himmelskugel *f.*; Bereich, Wirkungskreis *m.*
spherical *a.*, **~ly** *adv.* kugelförmig.
spice *s.* Gewürz *n.*; Anflug, Beigeschmack *m.*; ~ *v.t.* würzen.
spick-and-span *adv.* blitzblank; funkelnagelneu.
spicy *a.* würzig, pikant, scharf.
spider *s.* Spinne *f.*; **~web** *s.* Spinnennetz *n.*
spidery *a.* spinnenförmig.
spigot *s.* Zapfen, Hahn *m.*
spike *s.* Spitze *f.*; langer Nagel; Kornähre *f.*; ~ *v.t.* festnageln; (ein Geschütz) vernageln.
spiky *a.* spitz; stachielig.
spill *v.t.r. & st.* verschütten, vergießen.
spillage *s.* Verschütten *n.*; Verschüttetes *n.*
spin *v.t.* spinnen; wirbeln; ~ *v.i.* kreiseln, sich drehen.
spinach *s.* Spinat *m.*
spinal *a.* Rückgrat...; ~ **column** *s.* Wirbelsäule *f.* **~cord,** Rückenmark *n.*
spindle *s.* Spindel *f.*; Stengel *m.*
spindly *a.* spindeldürr.
spin drier *s.* Wäscheschleuder *f.*
spin-dry *v.t.* schleudern.
spine *s.* Rückgrat *n.*; Dorn *m.* Stachel *m.*; Buchrücken *m.*
spine-chilling *a.* gruselig.
spineless *a.* (*fig.*) rückgratlos.
spinnaker *s.* Spinnaker *m.* (Segel).
spinning: **~mill** Spinnerei *f.*; **~top** *s.* Kreisel *m.*; **~wheel** *s.* Spinnrad *n.*
spin-off *s.* Abfallprodukt *n.*; (positiver) Nebeneffekt *m.*
spinster *s.* ledige Frau, alte Jungfer *f.*
spiny *a.* stachelig; dornig.
spiral *a.*, **~ly** *adv.* spiralförmig; gewunden, schneckenförmig; ~ *s.* Schneckenlinie *f.*, Spirale *f.*; ~ **staircase** *s.* Wendeltreppe *f.*
spire *s.* (Kirch)turm *m.*, Turmspitze *f.*; Turm *m.*
spirit *s.* Geist *m.*; Seele *f.*; Gespenst *n.*; Lebhaftigkeit, Energie *f.*; Gemütsart *f.*; **~s** *pl.* Lebensgeister *m.pl.*, gute Laune *f.*; geistige Getränke *n.pl.*; *in high ~s,* munter; *in low ~s,* verstimmt; ~ *v.t. to ~ away,* hinwegzaubern.
spirited *a.*, **~ly** *adv.* geistreich; lebhaft, mutig, feurig.
spiritism *s.* Spiritismus *m.*
spiritless *a.*, **~ly** *adv.* mutlos.
spirit-level *s.* Wasserwaage *f.*
spirit of wine *s.* Weingeist *m.*
spiritual *a.*, **~ly** *adv.* geistig; geistlich.
spiritualism *s.* Spiritualismus *m.*
spit *v.t. & i.st.* spucken; fauchen; aufspießen; ~ *s.* Bratspieß *m.*; schmale Landzunge *f.*
spite *s.* Groll *m.*; Verdruß *m.*; *in ~ of,* trotz; ~ *v.t.* ärgern.
spiteful *a.*, **~ly** *adv.* boshaft, feindselig.
spitfire *s.* Brausekopf, Hitzkopf *m.*
spitting image *s. the ~,* wie aus dem Gesicht geschnitten.
spittle *s.* Speichel *m.*
spiv *s.* Schwarzhändler(in) *m.(f.)*; Schieber *m.*
splash *v.t.* bespritzen; ~ *s.* Spritzfleck *m.*; *to make a ~,* Aufsehen erregen.
splash-board *s.* Spritzbrett *n.*
splat *v.i.* klatschen.
splay *v.t.* spreizen (Finger).
spleen *s.* Milz *f.*; üble Laune *f.*
splendid *a.*, **~ly** *adv.* glänzend, prachtvoll.
splendor *s.* Glanz *m.*; Pracht *f.*
splice *v.t.* spleißen, einfügen.
splint *s.* Schiene *f.*; *v.t.* schienen.
splinter *s.* Splitter *m.*; **~-proof** *a.* splittersicher; ~ *v.t.* splittern.
split *v.t.st.* spalten; ~ *v.i.* bersten; zerspringen; ~ *s.* Spalt, Riß *m.*; ~ **second** *s.* Sekundenbruchteil *m.*
splutter *v.i.* herauspoltern; sprudeln, prusten.
spoil *v.t.* rauben, plündern; verderben, verwüsten; (Kinder) verziehen; ~ *v.i.* verderben; ~ *s.* Beute *f.*
spoilsport *s.* Spielverderber(in) *m.(f.)*
spoilt *a.* verzogen.
spoke *s.* Speiche *f.*; Sprosse *f.*
spokesman *s.* Sprecher *m.*
spokesperson *s.* Sprecher(in) *m.(f.)*
spokeswoman *s.* Sprecherin *f.*
sponge *s.* Schwamm *m.*; ~ *v.t.* wegwischen; ~ *v.i.* in sich saugen; schmarotzen; *to throw in the ~,* die Flinte ins Korn werfen
sponge cake *s.* Biskuitkuchen *m.*
sponger *s.* Schmarotzer *m.*
spongy *a.* schwammig.
sponsor *s.* Sponsor(in) *m.(f.)*; Geldgeber(in) *m.(f.)*; Bürge *m.*, Bürgin *f.*; ~ *v.t.* fördern, organisieren; *~ing member,* förderndes Mitglied *n.*
sponsored *a.* gesponsert; finanziell gefördert.
sponsorship *s.* Sponsorschaft *f.*; Unterstützung *f.*
spontaneity *s.* Freiwilligkeit *f.*
spontaneous *a.*, **~ly** *adv.* spontan
spoof *s.* Veralberung *f.*; Parodie *f.*
spook *s.* Geist *m.*; Gespenst *n.*
spooky *a.* gespenstisch.
spool *s.* Spule *f.*; ~ *v.t.* spulen.

spoon *s.* Löffel *m.;*
spoon feed *v.t.* füttern; (*fig.*) alles vorkauen.
sporadic *a.* sporadisch.
spore *s.* (*bot.*) Spore *f.*
sport *s.* Sport *m.;* Spiel *n.;* Scherz, Zeitvertreib *m.;* (*fig.*) Spielball *m.;* ~ *v.t. & i.* spielen; scherzen, belustigen; zur Schau tragen.
sporting *a.* sportlich; sport...
sportsman *s.* Sportsmann *m.*, Sportler *m.*
sportsmanship *s.* Sportlichkeit *f.*
sportswear *s.* Sportskleidung *f.*
sportswoman *s.* Sportlerin *f.*
sporty *a.* sportlich; sportbegeistert.
spot *s.* Platz *m.;* Stelle *f.;* Stück Land *n.;* Fleck *m.;* Spot *m.* (TV); ~ *v.t.* flecken, sprenkeln; genau erkennen; im voraus vestimmen.
spotless *a.* fleckenlos; unbefleckt.
spotlight *s.* Scheinwerferlicht *n.*
spotted *a.* gepunktet; getüpfelt; ~ **fever,** Fleckfieber *n.*
spotty *a.* fleckig, befleckt.
spouse *s.* Gatte *m.*, Gattin *f.*
spout *s.* Rinne *f.;* Tülle *f.;* Wasserstrahl *m.;* Wasserhose *f.;* ~ *v.t. & i.* (aus) spritzen; deklamieren.
sprain *v.t.* verstauchen; ~ *s.* Verstauchung *f.*
sprat *s.* Sprotte *f.*
sprawl *v.i.* sich spreizen, räkeln; (*bot.*) wuchern.
spray *s.* Gischt *m.;* Spray *n./m.;* Strauß *m.* (Blumen); ~ *v.t.* zerstäuben; (Metall) spritzen; sprühen.
spray gun *s.* Spritzpistole *f.*
spread *v.t. & i.* (sich) ausbreiten; (be)decken; ~ *s.* Ausdehnung *f.;* Verbreitung *f.;* ~**sheet** *s.* Arbeitsblatt *n.*
spree *s.* Jux *m.;* Zecherei *f.;* Einkaufsorgie *f.*
sprig *s.* Sproß, Sprößling *m.*
sprightly *a.* lebhaft, munter.
spring *v.t.st.* springen; entspringen, aufsprießen; entstehen; ~ *v.t.* sprengen; aufstöbern; ~ *s.* Sprung *m.;* Leck *n.;* Quelle *f.;* Springbrunnen *m.;* Frühling *m.;* Springfeder *f.*
spring board *s.* Sprungbrett *n.*
spring mattress *s.* Sprungfedermatratze *f.*
spring-tide *s.* Springflut *f.*
springy *a.* elastisch, federnd.
sprinkle *v.t. & i.* (be)sprengen; ausstreuen.
sprinkler *s.* Sprinkler *m.*
sprinkling *s.* dünne Schicht *f.*
sprint *s.* Kurzstreckenlauf, Sprint *m.;* ~ *v.i.* rennen; sprinten.
sprinter *s.* Kurzstreckenläufer(in), Sprinter(in) *m.(f.)*
sprite *s.* Schrat *m.;* Gespenst *n.*
sprout *v.i.* sproßen; ~ *s.* Sprößling *m.;* *Brussels ~s, pl.* Rosenkohl *m.*
spruce *a.*, ~**ly** *adv.* nett; geputzt; ~ *s.* Fichte *f.;* ~ *v.t.* (*v.i.* sich) herausputzen.
sprung *a.* gefedert; *well-~*, gut gefedert.
spry *a.* munter, lebhaft.
spud *s.* Kartoffel *f.*
spume *s.* Schaum *m.;* ~ *v.i.* schäumen.
spunk *s.* Mumm *m.*
spur *s.* Sporn, Stachel *m.;* Antrieb *m.;* Ausläufer einer Bergkette *m.;* ~ *v.t.* (auch *fig.*) anspornen; ~ *v.i.* eilen.
spurious *a.*, ~**ly** *adv.* unecht; unaufrichtig; zweifelhaft.
spurn *v.t.* verschmähen; ~ *v.i.* ausschlagen; verschmähen.
spurt *v.i.* spritzen; ~ *s.* plötzliche Anstrengung *f.*, Ruck *m.*
sputter *v.i.* sprudeln; ~ *v.t.* sprudelnd ausstoßen; ~ *s.* Gesprudel *n.*
spy *s.* Späher, Spion *m.;* ~ *v.i. & t.* (aus)spähen.
Sq. *Square,* Platz *m.*
sq. *square,* Quadrat...
squabble *v.i.* zanken, Hähdel suchen; ~ *s.* Streit, Wortwechsel *m.*
squad *s.* Schar *f.* Gruppe *f.;* Trupp *m.*
squadron *s.* Schwadron *f.;* (*nav.*) Geschwader *n.;* (*avi.*) Staffel *f.;* (*avi.*) ~ **leader,** *s.* Staffelkapitän *m.*
squalid *a.* schmutzig.
squall *s.* laute Schrei *m.;* Windstoß *m.;* Bö *f.;* ~ *v.i.* laut schreien.
squalor *s.* Schmutz *m.*
squander *v.t.* verschwenden; vergeuden.
square *a.* viereckig, rechtwinklig; passend; quitt; redlich; ~ **deal,** ehrliche Behandlung; ~ *s.* Viereck, Quadrat *n.;* viereckiger Platz *m.;* Feld (Schach) *n.;* Winkelmaß *n.;* *10 inches ~*, 10 Zoll im Quadrat; ~ *v.t.* viereckig machen; regeln, anpassen, ausgleichen; (*math.*) ins Quadrat erheben; ~ *v.i.* passen; übereinstimmen; ~ **measures** *pl.* Flächenmasse *n.pl.;* ~ **brackets** *pl.* eckige Klammern *pl.*
square-built *a.* vierschrötig.
squash *v.t.* zerquetschen; ~ *s.* Brei *m.*, Gedränge *n.;* Fruchtsaft *m.;* Kürb *m.*
squat *v.i.* kauern, sich ansiedeln; ~ *a.* kauernd; stämmig.
squatter *s.* Besetzer(in) *m.(f.)*
squawk *v.i.* krähen; kreischen; keifen.
squeak *v.i.* quieken, schreien; ~ *s.* Quieken *n.;* Schrei *m.*
squeal *v.i.* schreien, winseln, kreischen
squeamish *a.*, ~**ly** *adv.* wählerisch; empfindlich.
squeeze *v.t.* drücken, pressen, quetschen; ~ *v.i.* sich (durch)drängen; ~ *s.* Druck *m.;* Quetschung *f.;* Gipsabguß *m.*
squelch *v.i.* glucksen.
squib *s.* Frosch (Feuerwerk) *m.;* Spottgedicht *n.*
squid *s.* Kalmar *m.*
squint *v.i.* schielen; ~ *a.* schielend.
squint[ing] *s.* Schielen *n.*
squire *s.* (*obs.*) Schildknappe *m.;* Landedelmann *m.;* (Land)junker *m.*
squirm *v.i.* sich winden.
squirrel *s.* Eichhörnchen *n.*
squirt *v.t.* spritzen; ~ *s.* Spritzer *m.;* Wasserstrahl *m.*
Sr. *sister,* eccl. (Ordens) Schwester; *senior,* Senior, der Ältere, d.Ä., sen.
Sri Lanka *s.* Sri Lanka *n.*
Sri Lankan *a.* srilankisch; ~ *s.* Srilanker(in) *m.(f.)*
S.S. *Saints,* Heilige *pl.*
S.S. *steamship,* Dampfer *m.*
SSE *south-southeast,* Südsüdost, SSO.
SSW *south-southwest,* Südsüdwest, SSW.
St. *Saint,* Heilige *m.;* *Street,* Straße *f.*
STA *scheduled time of arrival,* planmäßige Ankunftszeit.

Sta. *Station,* Bahnhof, Bhf.
stab *s.* Stich *m.;* Stoß *m.;* Wunde *f.;* ~ *v.t. & i.* erstechen, stechen.
stabbing *s.* Messerstecherei *f.; a.* stechend.
stability *s.* Beständigkeit *f.*, Stabilität *f.*
stabilization *s.* Stabilisierung *f.;* ~ **fund,** Währungsausgleichfonds *m.*
stabilize *v.t.* stabilisieren.
stable *a.* fest, dauerhaft; beständig; stabil (Währung); ~ *s.* Stall *m.*
stack *s.* Schober, Stapel *m.;* (Gewehr-) Pyramide *f.;* ~ *v.t.* aufschichten.
stadium *s.* Stadion *n.*
staff *s.* Stab, Stock *m.;* (General)stab *m.;* Personal *n.;* die fünf Notenlinien *pl.;* **~,** *v.t.* mit Personal versehen.
stag *s.* Hirsch *m.;* (Börse) Konzertzeichner *m.*
stage *s.* Gerüst *n.;* Bühne *f.;* Schauplatz *m.;* Etappe *f.*, Stadium *n.;* Stufe *f.;* Poststation *f.; to go on the ~,* zur Bühne gehen; ~ *v.t.* inszenieren, veranstalten.
stage box *s.* Proszeniumsloge *f.*
stagecoach *s.* Postkutsche *f.*
stage direction *s.* Bühnenanweisung *f.*
stage fright *s.* Lampenfieber *n.*
stage manager *s.* Bühnenleiter *m.*
stagger *v.i.* wanken, taumeln; schwanken; ~ *v.t.* verblüffen; staffeln; **~ed holidays,** *pl.* gestaffelte Ferien *pl.;* ~ *s.* (*avi.*) Staffelung (der Flügel) *f.*
staggering *a.* erschütternd; beunruhigend.
stagnant *a.* stillstehend, stockend.
stagnate *v.i.* stillstehen, stocken.
stagnation *s.* Stillstand *m.;* Stockung *f.;* Stagnation *f.*
staid *a.* gesetzt, ernsthaft.
stain *s.* Flecken *m.;* Beize *f.;* Makel *m.;* ~ *v.t.* beflecken; färben; **~ed glass,** buntes Glas *n.*, Glasmalerei *f.*
stainless *a.* unbefleckt; rostfrei; **~steel** *s.* Edelstahl *m.*
stair *s.* Stufe *f.;* **~s** *pl.* Treppe *f.*
staircase *s.* Treppe *f.;* Treppenhaus *n.*
stairway *s.* Treppenaufgang *m.*
stake *s.* Pfahl *m.;* Einsatz (im Spiel) *m.; at ~,* auf dem Spiele; ~ *v.t.* aufs Spiel setzen.
stalactite *s.* Stalaktit *m.*
stalagmite *s.* Stalagmit *m.*
stale *a.* alt, altbacken; schal, geistlos;
stalemate *s.* Patt *n.;* Stillstand; *n.* ~ *v.t.* patt setzen; (*fig.*) lahmlegen.
stalk *s.* Stengel, Federkiel *m.;* gravitätischer Schritt *m.;* ~ *v.t. & i.* einherschreiten; stolzieren, beschleichen; verfolgen.
stall *s.* Stall *m.;* Stand *m.*, Box *f.* (im Stall); Sperrsitz *m.;* Chorstuhl *m.;* ~ *v.t.* zum Stehen bringen; ~ *v.i.* abwürgen (Motor).
stallion *s.* Hengst *m.*
stalwart *s.* stark, mutig; ~ *s.* treue Anhänger(in) *m.(f.)*
stamen *s.* Staubfäden *m.pl.*
stamina *s.* Ausdauer *f.*
stammer *v.i.* stammeln, stottern.
stammerer *s.* Stammler *m.*
stamp *v.t.* stampfen; stempeln, prägen; mit einer Marke versehen, (Brief) frankieren; *to ~ out,* austreten, unterdrücken; ~ *s.* Stampfe *f.;* Stempel *m.;* Gepräge *n.;* Abdruck *m.;* Briefmarke *f.*, Marke *f.;* ~ **collector,** Briefmarkensammler *m.;* ~ **pad,** Stempelkissen *n.*
stampede *s.* wilde Flucht *f.;* ~ *v.i.* (in wilder Flucht) davonstürmen; ~ *v.t.* in wilde Flucht jagen.
stanch *v.i.* & t. stillen, abbinden.
stand *v.i.* stehen; aufstehen, stellen;verhalten; gelten; kosten, zu stehen kommen; ~ *v.t.* stellen; aushalten, vertragen; standhalten; *to ~ by,* dabeistehen; *to ~ for,* eintreten für; *to ~ up,* aufrecht stehen; *to ~ up to,* aushalten; ~ *s.* Ständer *m.;* (*phot.*) Stativ *n.;* Stand *m.;* Gestell, Gerüst *n.;*
standard *s.* Standarte *f.;* Ständer *m.;* Pfosten *m.;* Eichmaß *n.;* Maßstab *m.*, Regel, Richtschnur *f.*, Norm *f.;* Münzfuß *m.; gold ~,* Goldstandard *m.;* ~ **of living,** Lebenshaltung *f.;* ~ **operating procedure** (SOP), (*mil.*) vorschriftsmäßiges Verfahren *n.;* ~ *a.* musterhaft, normal, klassisch.
standardize *v.t.* normieren.
standing *p. & a.* stehend, bleibend, beständig; ~ *s.* Stand, Platz *m.;* Rang *m.;* Dauer *f.;* Stellung *f.; of long (old) ~,* von lange her.
standing order *s.* Dauerauftrag *m.*
standing room *s.* Stehplatz *m.*
standpoint *s.* Standpunkt *m.*
standstill *s.* Stillstand *m.*
stand-up *a.* regelrecht (vom Faustkampf); ~ **collar,** Stehkragen *m.*
stanza *s.* Stanze *f.;* Strophe *f.*
staple *s.* Heftklammer *f.;* **~,** *v.t.* klammern, mit einer Heftklammer versehen; **~goods** *pl.*, Grundnahrungsmittel *n.*
stapler *s.* Hefter *m.*, Heftmaschine *f.*
star *s.* Stern *m.;* grosser Schauspieler, Star *m.;* ~ *v.t. & i.* besternen; eine Hauptrolle spielen; **~s and stripes,** Sternenbanner *n.*
starboard *s.* Steuerbord *n.*
starch *s.* Stärke (zur Wäsche) *f.;* ~ *v.t.* stärken.
stardom *s.* Starruhm *m.*
stare *s.* starrer Blick *m.;* Staunen *n.;* ~ *v.i.* anstarren.
starfish *s.* Seestern *m.*
staring *a.* starrend.
stark *a.*, **~ly** *adv.* kraß; öde; völlig; nackt (Wahrheit).
starlight *s.* Sternenlicht; ~ **night,** Sternennacht *f.*
starling *s.* Star (Vogel) *m.*
starlit *a.* sternklar.
starred *a.* gestirnt.
starry *a.* sternig; sternhell.
start *v.i.* (*rail.*) abgehen; (*Sport*) starten; anfangen; ~ *v.t.* aufjagen; stutzig machen; aufwerfen (Fragen); beginnen; (*mech.*) in Gang bringen, anlassen; (*Sport*) ablaufen lassen; ~ *s.* Abfahrt *f.;* Beginn *m.;* Vorsprung *m.*
starter *s.* Anreger *m.;* (*Sport*) Starter *m.;* (*mech.*) Anlasser *m.;* (Rennen) Teilnehmer(in) *m.(f.)*
startle *v.t.* erschrecken, überraschen.
startling *a.* erstaunlich; überraschend.
starvation *s.* Verhungern *n.;* ~ **wages** *pl.* Hungerlohn *m.*
starve *v.i.* Not leiden, verhungern; ~ *v.t.* verhungern lassen, aushungern.
state *s.* Zustand *m.;* Stand, Rang *m.;* Staat *m.;* Aufwand *m.;* **~-aided** *a.* staatlich unterstützt; **~-owned** *a.* im Staatsbesitz; *lying in ~,* Auf-

bahrung *f.*; ~ *v.t.* stellen, festsetzen; dartun, vortragen, erklären, sagen.

stately *a.* stattlich, prächtig; stolz.

statement *s.* Angabe, Aussage *f.*; Überschlag, Bericht *m.*, Angabe *f.*; ~ **of account** *s.* (Rechnungs) Auszug *m.*

state-of-the-art *a.* auf dem neuesten Stand der Technik stehend.

statesman *s.* Staatsmann *m.*

statesmanlike *a.* staatsmännisch.

statesmanship *s.* Regierungskunst *f.*

stateswomen *s.* Staatsfrau *f.*

static *a.* statisch, gleichbleibend; ~ *s.* atmosphärische Störung *f.*

station *s.* Stand *m.*; Stelle *f.*; Amt *n.*; Rang *m.*; Standort *m.*; Bahnhof *m.*; ~*s of the cross*, Kreuzwegstationen *pl.*; ~ *v.t.* hinstellen; (*mil.*) stationieren.

stationary *a.* feststehend

stationer *s.* Schreibwarenhändler(in) *m.(f.)*

stationery *s.* Schreibwaren *f.pl.*

stationmaster *s.* Bahnhofsvorsteher(in) *m.(f.)*

station wagon *s.* Kombiwagen *m.*

statistic(al) *a.* statistisch.

statistician *s.* Statistiker(in) *m.(f.)*

statistics *s.pl.* Statistik *f.*

statue *s.* Statue *f.*

statuette *s.* Statuette *f.*

stature *s.* Leibesgröße *f.*; Wuchs *m.*; Statur *f.*

status *s.* Lage *f.*; Status *m.*

statute *s.* Satzung *f.*; Gesetz *n.*; Parlamentsakte *f.*

statutory *a.* gesetzmäßig; ~ **corporation,** Körperschaft des öffentlichen Rechts; ~ **declaration,** eidesstattliche Erklärung *f.*

staunch *a.* zuverlässig, treu; standhaft, fest.

stave *v.t. to* ~ *in*, den Boden ausschlagen; *to* ~ *off*, abwehren.

stay *v.t.st.* stillstehen, bleiben, warten; sohnen; ~ *v.t.* aufhalten, durchhalten; ~ *s.* Aufenthalt *m.*

stay-at-home *s.* häuslicher Mensch *m.*

staying power *s.* Durchhaltevermögen *n.*

STD *Scheduled time of departure*, planmäßige Abfahrtszeit.

stead *s.* Stelle *f.*; Platz *m.*; *in his* ~, an seiner Stelle; *in* ~ *of*, statt.

steadfast *a.*, ~**ly** *adv.* fest, standhaft.

steady *a.*, ~**ily** *adv.* fest, standhaft; beständig; ~ *v.i. sich* beruhigen; ~ *v.i.* sich beruhigen; stabilisieren.

steak *s.* Steak *n.*

steal *v.t.st.* stehlen; ~ *v.i.* schleichen.

stealth *s.* Heimlichkeit *f.*; *by* ~, verstohlen.

stealthy *a.* verstohlen, heimlich.

steam *s.* Dampf *m.*; ~ *v.t.* dämpfen; ~ *v.i.* dampfen.

steamboat *s.* Dampschiff *n.*

steam engine *s.* Dampfmaschine *f.*; Dampflokomotive *f.*

steamer *s.* Dampfer *m.*; Dämpfer *m.*

steam iron *s.* Dampfbügeleisen *n.*

steam navigation *s.* Dampfschiffahrt *f.*

steam pressure gauge *s.* Dampfdruckmesser *m.*

steamroller *s.* Dampfwalze *f.*

steamship *s.* Dampfschiff *n.*

steam tug *s.* Schleppdampfer *m.*

steamy *a.* dunstig; feucht.

steel *s.* Stahl *m.*; ~ *v.t.* stählen; ~ **cabinet** *s.* Stahlschrank *m.*; ~**engraving** *s.* Stahlstich *m.*; ~ **frame** *s.* Eisenkonstruktion *f.*; ~ **helmet** *s.* Stahlhelm *m.*; ~ **wool** *s.* Stahlwolle *f.*

steely *a.* stählern; stahlhart.

steelyard *s.* Schnellwaage *f.*

steep *a.*, ~**ly** *adv.* jäh, steil; (*fam.*) übertrieben; ~ *v.t.* eintunken, einweichen; *to* ~ *sb. in*, versenken.

steepen *v.i.* steiler werden.

steeple *s.* Kirchturm *m.*

steeple-chase *s.* Hindernisrennen *n.*

steer *v.t. & i.* steuern; ~**ing column** *s.* (*mot.*) Lenksäule *f.*; ~**ing lock** *s.* Lenkradschloß *n.*; ~**ing wheel** *s.* Steuerrad *n.*

steerage *s.* Lenkung *f.*; Zwischendeck *n.*; ~-**passenger,** Zwischendeckpassagier *m.*

steersman *s.* Steuermann *m.*

stellar *a.* gestirnt, Sternen...

stem *s.* Stiel, Stengel *m.*; Stamm *m.*; ~ *v.t.* stemmen, ankämpfen; sich widersetzen.

stench *s.* Gestank *m.*

stencil *s.* Schablone *f.*, Matrize *f.*

stenographer *s.* Stenograph(in) *m.(f.)*

stenography *s.* Stenographie *f.*

stentorian *a.* überlaut.

step *v.i.* schreiten, treten; ~ **up** *v.t.* antreiben; *to* ~ *in*, sich ins Mittel legen; ~ *s.* Schritt, Tritt, Gang *m.*; Fußstapfe *f.*; Stufe *f.*; Trittbrett *n.*; ~ **by** ~, Schritt für Schritt; *to fall into* ~ *with*, in gleichen Schritt fallen mit; *to keep* ~ *with*, Schritt halten mit; *to take* ~*s*, Schritte tun, Maßnahmen ergreifen; ~ **ladder** *s.* Trittleiter *f.*; ~ *a.* Stief... (Bruder, etc.).

steppe *s.* Steppe *f.*

stepping stone *s.* Steinstufe *f.*; (*fig.*) Sprungbrett *n.*

stereo *s.* Stereoanlage *f.*; Stereo *n.*

stereophonic *a.* stereophon.

stereoscope *s.* Stereoskop *n.*

stereoscopic *a.* stereoskopisch.

stereotype *s.* Stereotyp *n.*; ~ *a.* Stereotyp... (*typ.*); (*fig.*) abgedroschen, stereotyp; ~ *v.t.* stereotypieren; unveränderlich festlegen.

sterile *a.* unfruchtbar; steril.

sterility *s.* Unfruchtbarkeit *f.*

sterilization *s.* Sterilisation *f.*; Sterilisierung *f.*

sterilize *v.t.* keimfrei machen; sterilisieren.

sterling *s.* Sterling *m.*; *a pound* ~, ein Pfund Sterling; ~ *a.* echt, zuverlässig.

stern *a.*, ~**ly** *adv.* ernst, starr; streng, grausam; ~ *s.* (*nav.*) Heck *n.*

stertorous *a.* röchelnd, schnarchend.

stethoscope *s.* Stethoskop *n.*

stew *s.* Eintopf *m.* geschmortes Fleisch *n.*; ~ *v.t.* schmoren, dämpfen; ~*ed fruit*, Kompott *n.*

steward *s.* Verwalter(in) *m.(f.)*; Steward *m.*

stewardess *s.* Stewardess *f.*

stg. *sterling*, Sterling.

stick *s.* Stock, Stecken *m.*; Stange *f.*; ~ **of wood,** Holzscheit *n.*; ~ *v.t.* stecken, ankleben; *to* ~ *together*, zusammenleimen; zusammenkleben; ~ *v.i.* stocken; sich anhängen; *to* ~ *at nothing*, vor nichts zurückscheuen; *to* ~ *to*, beharren bei.

sticker *s.* Aufkleber *m.*

stick-in-the-mud *s.* (*fam.*) Trantüte *f.*; Rückschrittler(in) *m.(f.)*

stickleback *s.* Stichling *m.*
stickler *s.* Verfechter *m.;* Eiferer *m.*
stick-up *s.* Überfall *m.*
sticky *a.* klebrig.
stiff *a.,* **~ly** *adv.* steif; staff; schwierig; hartnäckig.
stiffen *v.t.* versteifen; stärken; ~ *v.i.* steif werden, erstarren.
stiffness *s.* Steifheit *f.*
stifle *a.* ersticken.
stifling *a.* erstickend; stickig; drückend.
stigma *s.* Brandmal *n.;* Schande *f.*
stigmatize *v.t.* brandmarken.
stile *s.* Zauntritt *m.*
still *a.* still, ruhig; ~ *adv.* stets, noch, immer noch; ~ *c.* doch, indessen; ~ *v.t.* stillen, beruhigen.
stillbirth *s.* Totgeburt *f.*
stillborn *a.* totgeboren.
still life *s.* (*fig.*) Stilleben *n.*
stillness *s.* Bewegungslosigkeit *f.*
stilt *s.* Stelze *f.*
stilted *a.* hochtrabend, gespreizt.
stimulant *a.* anregend; ~ *s.* Reizmittel *n.*
stimulate *v.t.* anspornen, anreizen.
stimulation *s.* Stimulierung *f.;* Anregung *f.*
stimulative *a.* anreizend, antreibend.
stimulus *s.* Antrieb, Sporn *m.;* Reizmittel *n.*
sting *v.t.st.* stechen; schmerzen; anstacheln; (*fig.*) kränken; ~ *s.* Stachel *m.;* Stich *m.;* Biß *m.;* Spitze *f.*
stinging nettle *s.* Brennessel *f.*
stingy *a.,* **~ily** *adv.* karg, geizig.
stink *v.t.st.* stinken; ~ *s.* Gestank *m.*
stink bomb *s.* Stinkbombe *f.*
stipend *s.* Besoldung *f.;* Stipendium *n.*
stipulate *v.t.* vereinbaren, bedingen; *as ~d,* wie vereinbart.
stipulation *s.* Auflage *f.;* Übereinkunft *f.;* Bedingung *f.*
stir *v.t.* regen, bewegen; aufrühren, schüren; umrühren; ~ *v.i.* sich regen; aufstehen; ~ *s.* Regung *f.;* Lärm, Aufruhr *m.;* Getümmel *n.*
stirring *a.* aufregend, bewegt; mitreißend.
stirrup *s.* Steigbügel *m.*
stitch *v.t. & i.* stechen; heften; säumen; ~ *s.* Stich *m.;* Masche *f.*
stn *station,* Bahnhof, Bhf.
stoat *s.* Hermelin *n.*
stock *s.* Stock, Stamm, Klotz *m.;* (Gewehr-)Schaft *m.;* Grundstock *m.;* Vorrat *m.;* Lager *n.;* Aktie; Aktien pl., (Stamm-)Kapital *n.;* Herkunft *f.;* Inventar *n.; in ~,* auf Lager; ~ **taking,** Bestandsaufnahme *f.;* **~-in-trade,** *s.* Betriebsvorrat *m.* (auch *fig.*); ~ *v.t.* versehen mit; auf Lager haben.
stockade *s.* Palisade *f.*
stock breeder *s.* Viehzüchter(in) *m.(f.)*
stockbroker *s.* Börsenmakler(in) *m.(f.)*
stock exchange *s.* (Fonds-) Börse *f.*
stockholder *s.* Aktionär *m.*
stocking *s.* Strumpf *m.*
stock market *s.* Börsengeschäft *n.*
stockpile *s.* Vorrat *m.;* ~ *v.t.* einen Vorrat sammeln.
stock-still *a.* unbeweglich.
stocky *a.* stämmig.
stodgy *a.* füllend, unverdaulich.
stoic *s.* Stoiker(in) *m.(f.)*
stoical *a.,* **~ly** *adv.* stoisch, standhaft.
stoicism *s.* Gleichmut *m.*
stoke *v.t.* schüren, heizen.
stoker *s.* Heizer(in) *m.(f.)*
stole *s.* Stola *f.*
stolid *a.,* **~ly** *adv.* dumm, dickhäutig.
stomach *s.* Magen *m.;* Bauch *m.;* ~ for, Lust *(f.)* zu; ~ **ache,** Bauchweh *n.;* ~ *v.t.* sich gefallen lassen; vertragen.
stone *s.* Stein, (Obst-)Kern *m.;* Gewicht *(n.)* von 14 Pfund; ~ *a.* steinern; ~ *v.t.* steinigen; auskernen; *a ~'s throw,* eine kurze Entfernung.
Stone Age *s.* Steinzeit *f.*
stone-blind *a.* stockblind.
stone-dead *a.* mausetot.
stone-deaf *a.* stocktaub.
stone-fruit *s.* Steinobst *n.*
stonemason *s.* Steinmetz *m.*
stoneware *s.* steingut *n.*
stony *a.* steinig; steinern; steinhart.
stool *s.* Schemel *m.;* Stuhl *m.*
stoop *v.i. sich* sich bücken; ~ *s.* Bücken *n.;* Herablassung *f.*
stop *v.t.* (ver)stopfen; hemmen, hindern; versperren; (Zahn) füllen; (Zahlungen) einstellen; *to ~ payment on a check,* einen Scheck sperren; ~ *v.i.* stillstehen; anhalten; stehenbleiben; aufhören; *to ~ at a hotel,* in einem Hotel absteigen; ~ *s.* Stillstand *m.;* Klappe *f.;* Pause *f.;* Unterbrechung, Hemmung *f.;* Verbot *n.;* Eden *n.;* Haltestelle *f.;* **~!,** *i.* halt!
stopcock *s.* Absperrhahn *m.*
stopgap *s.* Notbehelf *m.*
stoplight *s.* rote Ampel *f.*
stopover *s.* Fahrtunterbrechung *f.;* Aufenthalt (im Bahnhof) *m.*
stoppage *s.* Verstopfung *f.;* Stillstand *m.;* Zahlungseinstellung *f.*
stopper *s.* Stöpsel *m.;* ~ *v.t.* zustöpseln.
stopwatch *s.* Stoppuhr *f.*
storage *s.* Lagern, *n.;* Lagerung *f.;* ~ **charge,** Lagergebühr *f.;* ~ **battery** *s.* Akkumulator *m.*
store *s.* Vorrat, Proviant *m.;* Fülle *f.;* Laden *m.;* ~ **room** *s.* Vorratskammer *f.; to put in ~,* einlagern; *~s,* Warenhaus *n.;* Vorräte *m.pl.; military ~s,* Kriegsvorräte *pl.;* Magazin *n.;* ~ *v.t.* speichern, (Möbel) einlagern; (Schiff) verproviantieren.
storehouse *s.* Lagerhaus *n.;* Schatzkammer *f.*
storekeeper *s.* Magazinaufseher *m.;* Lagerist(in) *m.(f.)*
stork *s.* Storch *m.*
storm *s.* Sturm (auch *mil.*) *m.;* Gewitter *n.;* Aufruhr *m.;* ~ *v.t. & i.* (be)stürmen; wüten.
stormy *a.* stürmisch; ungestüm.
story *s.* Geschichte *f.;* Erzählung *f.;* Lüge *f.;* Stock(werk) *n.,* Geschoß *n.,* Etage *f.;* **~teller** *s.* Erzähler *m.;* Flunkerer *m.*
stout *a.,* **~ly** *adv.* stark; standhaft, wacker, tapfer; wohlbeleibt; ~ *s.* dunkles Bier *n.*
stove *s.* Ofen *m.;* Herd *m.*
stovepipe *s.* Ofenrohr *n.*
stow *v.t.* stauen; schichten, packen.
stowage *s.* Stauen *n.;* Stauraum *m.;* Packerlohn *m.*
stowaway *s.* blinder Passagier *m.*

straddle *v.i.* mit gespreizten Beinen stehen; sich rittlings setzen.
straggle *v.i.* verstreut stehen; hinterherzockeln; wuchern (von Pflanzen).
straggler *s.* Nachzügler *m.*
straighforward *a.* freimütig.
straight *a. & adv.*, **~ly** *adv.* gerade; unmittelbar, direkt; **~ on, ~ ahead,** geradeaus; *to put ~*, in Ordnung bringen; **~ away** *adv.* sofort, gleich.
straighten *v.t.* gerade, straff machen; *to ~ out*, in Ordnung bringen; *to ~ up*, aufrichten.
straight face *s.* unbewegtes Gesicht *n.*
strain *v.t.* spannen, strecken; quetschen, durchseihen; anstrengen; verstauchen; übertreiben; ~ *v.i.* anstrengen; ~ *s.* Anstrengung *f.*; Spannung *f.*; Inanspruchnahme *f.*; Verstauchung *f.*; Neigung *f.*; Tonart *f.*, Klänge *pl.*; Stamm *m.*, Klasse, Familie *f.*; Art *f.*
strained *p. & a.* gespannt; gezwungen.
strainer *s.* Filtriertrichter *m.*; (Tee)Seiher *m.*; Sieb *n.*
strait *a.*, **~ly** *adv.* eng, knapp, genau, streng; schwierig; **~jacket** *s.* Zwangsjacke *f.*; **~laced** *a.* prüde; ~ *s.* Enge, *f.*; Meerenge *f.*; **~s** *pl.* Verlegenheit, Klemme *f.*
straiten *v.t.* verengen; in Verlegenheit setzen.
straitness *s.* Enge *f.*; Strenge *f.*; Einschränkung *f.*; Verlegenheit *f.*
strand *s.* Strand *m.*; Strähne *f.*; (*fig.*) Ader *f.*; ~ *v.i.* stranden.
strange *a.*, **~ly** *adv.* fremd; seltsam.
stranger *s.* Fremde *m./f.*; Ausländer(in) *m.(f.)*
strangle *v.t.* erdrosseln; erwürgen.
stranglehold *s.* Würgegriff *m.*
strangulate *v.t.* abschnüren.
strangulation *s.* Erdrosselung *f.*
strap *s.* Riemen, Gurt *m.*; Strippe *f.*; (*mil.*) Achselschnur *f.*; **~-hanger** *m.* (*fam.*) Stehplatzinhaber(in) *m.(f.)*; ~ *v.t.* mit Riemen fest machen.
strapping *a.* stämmig *f.*; stramm.
stratagem *s.* Kriegslist *f.*; Schachzug *m.*
strategic *a.* strategisch.
strategist *s.* Stratege *m.*; Strategin *f.*
strategy *s.* Kriegskunst *f.*; List *f.*
stratify *v.t.* schichten.
stratosphere *s.* Stratosphäre *f.*
stratum *s.* Lage, Schicht *f.*
straw *s.* Stroh *n.*; Strohhalm *m.*
strawberry *s.* Erdbeere *f.*
straw-cutter *s.* Häckselschneidemaschine *f.*
stray *v.i.* irregehen; umherstreifen; ~ *a.* verirrt, verlaufen.
streak *s.* Strich, Streifen *m.*; Strähne *f.*
streaker *s.* Blitzer(in) *m.(f.)*
streaky *a.* streifig; durchwachsen (Speck).
stream *s.* Bach *m.*; Wasserlauf *m.*; Strom *m.*; ~ *v.i.* strömen, fließen.
streamer *s.* Wimpel *f.*; (flatterndes) Band *n.*; Papierschlange *f.*
streamlined *a.* Stromlinien...
street *s.* Straße, Gasse *f.*
streetcar *s.* Straßenbahnwagen *m.*
street-lamp *s.* Straßenlaterne *f.*
street lighting *s.* Straßenbeleuchtung *f.*
street vendor *s.* Straßenverkäufer *m.*
strength *s.* Stärke, Kraft *f.*; *on the ~ of*, auf Grund von; ~ **report,** (*mil.*) Stärkenachweisung *f.*
strengthen *v.t.* (ver)stärken; befestigen; ~ *v.i.* stark werden.
strenuous *a.*, **~ly** *adv.* tapfer, wacker; tätig, eifrig;
anstrengend.
stress *s.* Nachdruck *m.*; Gewicht *n.*; Hauptton *m.*; Anspannung *f.*, Druck *m.*; ~ *v.t.* betonen.
stretch *v.t. & i.* (sich) strecken, (aus)dehnen, anstrengen; übertreiben; ~ *s.* Ausdehnung, Strecke *f.*; Überanspannung *f.*; Anstrengung *f.*; *at a ~*, in einem Zuge, ununterbrochen.
stretcher *s.* Tragbahre *f.*; Spanner *m.*; **~bearer** *s.* Krankenträger *m.*
strew *v.t.st.* streuen, bedecken.
stricken *a.* betroffen (von); heimgesucht.
strict *a.*, **~ly** *adv.* eng; straff; genau; streng; *~ly speaking*, streng genommen.
strictness *s.* Strenge *f.*
stricture *s.* Tadel *m.*; Kritik *f.*
stride *s.* (weiter) Schritt *m.*; ~ *v.i.st.* schreiten.
strident *a.* kreischend; schrill.
strife *s.* Streit *m.*; Wettstreit *m.*
strike *v.t. & i.* schlagen, stossen; treffen; rühren, bewegen; auffallen; (Flagge) streichen; (Zelt, Lager) abbrechen; (Handel) abschließen; die Arbeit einstellen, streiken; *to ~ a balance*, den Saldo ziehen; *to ~ a match*, Zündholz anzünden; *to ~ a mine*, auf eine Mine laufen; *to ~ off, out*, ausstreichen; *to ~ a person off the list*, einen von der Liste streichen; *to ~ a chord*, eine Saite anschlagen; *to ~ up*, (Lied) anstimmen; ~ *s.* Arbeitseinstellung *f.*, Streik *m.*; *on ~*, streikend; **~ballot** *s.* Urabstimmung *f.* **~breaker** *s.* Streikbrecher *m.*
striker *s.* Streikende *m./f.*
striking *a.*, **~ly** *adv.* auffallend, ergreifend; treffend; ~ **distance,** Reichweite *f.*; ~ **power,** Schlagkraft *f.*
string *s.* Bindfaden *m.*; Schnur *f.*; Sehne *f.*; Saite *f.*; Reihe *f.*; ~ *v.t.* besaiten; aufreihen.
string band *s.* Streichorchester *n.*
stringency *s.* Strenge *f.*; Knappheit *f.*
stringent *a.* streng; zusammenziehend; bindend.
stringy *a.* faserig.
strip *v.t.* abstreifen; berauben; ~ *v.i.* sich auskleiden; ~ *s.* Streifen *m.*
stripe *s.* Streifen *m.*; (*mil.*) Tresse *f.*
striped *a.* gestreift.
strip lighting *s.* Neonbeleuchtung *f.*
stripling *s.* Bürschchen *n.*
striptease *s.* Striptease *m.*
stripy *a.* gestreift.
strive *v.t.st.* streben; kämpfen um; sich bemühen.
stroke *s.* Streich, Schlag, Stoß *m.*; Schlag (der Uhr) *m.*; Schlaganfall *m.*; Strich *m.*; Zug, Federstrich *m.*; Kolbenhub *m.*; ~ *v.t.* streichen; streicheln.
stroll *v.i.* herumstreifen, herumschlendern; ~ *s.* Spaziergang *m.*
stroller *s.* Bummler(in) *m.(f.)*; Buggy *m.*
strong *a.*, **~ly** *adv.* stark, kräftig; tüchtig, streng, nachdrücklich; *40 men ~*, 40 Mann hoch; ~ **drinks,** *pl.* alkoholische Getränke *n.pl.*
strongbox *s.* Geldschrank *m.*
stronghold *s.* Feste *f.*; Bollwerk *n.*

strong language *s.* derbe Ausdrucksweise *f.*
strong-minded *a.* willensstark.
strongroom *s.* Stahlkammer *f.*
structural *a.*, **~ly** *adv.* strukturell, baulich.
structure *s.* Bau *m.;* Bauart, Einrichtung *f.*
struggle *v.i.* kämpfen, sich anstrengen; ringen; sich sträuben; ~ *s.* Sträuben *n.;* Kampf *m.;* Zuckung *f.;* ~ *for life,* Kampf *(m.)* ums Dasein.
strum *v.t.* klimpern.
strut *v.i.* stolzieren, ~ *s.* Stützbalken *m.*, Strebe *f.*
strychnine *s.* Strychnin *n.*
stub *s.* Stumpf, Klotz *m.;* Kontrollabschnitt *m.;* ~ *v.t.* (an)stoßen.
stubble *s.* Stoppel *f.*
stubborn *a.*, **~ly** *adv.* steif, unbiegsam, hart; standhaft; hartnäckig.
stubbornness *s.* Sturheit *f.;* Hartnäckigkeit *f.*
stucco *s.* Stuck *m.*
stud *s.* Knaufnagel *m.;* Knopf, Hemdenknopf *m.;* Ständer *m.;* Gestüt *n.;* Zuchthengst *m.;* ~ *v.t.* beschlagen; (*fig.*) besetzen.
studbook *s.* Zuchtbuch *n.*
student *s.* Student *m.;* Gelehrte *m.*
studied *a.*, **~ly** *adv.* gelehrt; studiert; gekünstelt.
studio *s.* Atelier *n.;* (*radio*) Senderaum *m.;* (*film*) Aufnahmeatelier *n.*
studious *a.*, **~ly** *adv.* beflissen, fleißig; bedacht; geflissentlich.
study *s.* Studium *n.;* Studierstube *f.;* Studie *f.;* ~ *v.i.* studieren; nachsinnen, sich befleißigen; ~ *v.t.* einstudieren; genau untersuchen.
stuff *s.* Stoff *m.;* Zeug *n.;* Gerät *n.;* Unsinn *m.;* Plunder *m.;* ~ *v.t.* (aus)stopfen; füllen.
stuffing *s.* Füllung *f.;* Füllsel *n.*
stuffy *a.* stickig; spießig.
stultify *v.t.* lähmen, verdummen.
stumble *v.i.* stolpern; stocken.
stumbling block *s.* Stolperstein *m.;* Hindernis *n.*
stump *s.* Stumpf *m.;* (Zigarren)stummel *m.;* ~ *v.t.* stampfen; tappen.
stumpy *a.* gedrungen.
stun *v.t.* betäuben, verdutzen.
stunning *a.* erstaunlich; (*fam.*) toll.
stunt *v.t.* am Wachstum hindern; ~ *s.* (*sl.*) Kraftanstrengung *f.;* (Zeitung) Werbetrick *m.;* Sensation *f.;* Kunststück *n.*
stupefaction *s.* Betäubung *f.*
stupefy *v.t.* betäuben, verblüffen.
stupendous *a.*, **~ly** *adv.* erstaunlich.
stupid *a.*, **~ly** *adv.* dumm, albern; langweilig.
stupidity *s.* Dummheit *f.;* Torheit *f.*
stupor *s.* Erstarrung *f.;* Staunen *n.*
sturdy *a.*, **~ily** *adv.* derb, stark; stabil; stämmig.
sturgeon *s.* Stör *m.*
stutter *v.i.* stottern; ~ *s.* Stottern *n.*
sty *s.* Schweinestall *m.*
sty(e) *s.* Gerstenkorn (am Auge) *n.*
style *s.* Stil *m.;* Schreibart *f.;* Machart, Aufmachung *f.;* Titel *m.;* ~ *v.t.* entwerfen
stylish *a.* elegant, modisch.
stylist *s.* Designer(in) *m.(f.)*
stylistic *a.* stilistisch.
styptic *a.* blutstillend.
suasion *s.* Überredung *f.;* *moral* ~, gutes Zureden *n.*
suave *a.* mild, sanft; verbindlich.
suavity *s.* Lieblichkeit, Anmut *f.*
subcommittee *s.* Unterausschuß *m.*
subconscious *a.*, **~ly** *adv.* unterbewußt.
subcontract *s.* Unterkontrakt *m.*
subcontractor *s.* Subunternehmer(in) *m.(f.)*
subculture *s.* Subkultur *f.*
subcutaneous *a.* unter der Haut.
subdivide *v.t.* unterteilen.
subdivision *s.* Unterabteilung *f.;* Unterteilung *f.*
subdue *v.t.* unterwerfen; dämpfen.
subdued *a.* gedämpft; ruhig.
subgroup *s.* Untergruppe *f.*
subheading *s.* Untertitel *m.*
subhuman *a.* unmenschlich.
subject *a.* unterworfen, ausgesetzt; zu Grunde liegend; ~ *to,* vorbehaltlich; ~ *to reservations,* unter Vorbehalt; ~ *s.* Untertan *m.;* Person *f.;* Gegenstand *m.*, Betreff *m.;* Subjekt *n.;* ~ **index** *s.* Sachregister *n.;* ~ **matter,** *s.* Gegenstand *m.*, Thema *n.;* ~ *v.t.* unterwerfen; aussetzen.
subjection *s.* Unterwerfung *f.*
subjective *a.* subjektiv.
subjoin *v.t.* beifügen.
subjugate *v.t.* unterjochen.
subjunctive *s.* (*gram.*) Konjunktiv *m.*
sublet *v.t.* unterverpachten, weitervermieten.
sublimate *s.* (*chem.*) Sublimat *n.*
sublime *a.*, **~ly** *adv.* erhaben, hehr, hoch; großartig.
subliminal *a.* unterschwellig.
sublimity *s.* Erhabenheit *f.*
submachine gun *s.* Maschinenpistole *f.*
submarine *a.* unterseeisch; ~ *s.* Unterseeboot *n.*
submerge *v.t.* & *i.* untertauchen; überschwemmen.
submersion *s.* Untertauchen *n.;* Überschwemmung *f.*
submission *s.* Unterwürfigkeit, Demut, Ergebung *f.;* Eingabe *f.*
submissive *a.*, **~ly** *adv.* unterwürfig.
submit *v.t.* unterwerfen; unterbreiten; ~ *v.i.* sich fügen; *s.* unterwerfen.
subnormal *a.* unterdurchschnittlich.
subordinate *a.*, **~ly** *adv.* untergeordnet; ~ **clause,** (*gram.*) Nebensatz *m.;* ~ *s.* Untergeordnete, Untergebene *m./f.;* ~ *v.t.* unterordnen.
suborn *v.t.* (zu falschem Zeugnis) verleiten.
subornation *s.* Anstiftung *f.*
subpoena *s.* Vorladung *f.;* ~ *v.t.* vorladen.
subscribe *v.t.* unterschreiben; zeichnen; ~ *v.i.* abonnieren; einwilligen.
subscriber *s.* Abonnent(in) *m.(f.)*
subscription *s.* Unterzeichnung *f.;* Abonnement *n.;* (Geld) Beitrag *m.;* *annual* ~, Jahresabonnement *n.;* *monthly* ~, Monatsabonnement *n.;* ~ **list,** Subskriptionsliste, Zeichnungsliste *f.;* *to cancel one's* ~, das Abonnement aufgeben.
subsection *s.* Unterabteilung *f.*
subsequent *a.*, nachfolgend, nachträglich; ~ **delivery,** Nachlieferung *f.;* ~ **payment,** Nachzahlung *f.;* **~ly** *adv.* nachher.
subservience *s.* Unterwürfigkeit *f.*
subservient *a.* dienlich; unterwürfig.
subside *v.i.* sinken, abnehmen; aufhören; zurückgehen.
subsidence *s.* Senkung *f.;* Sinken *n.*

subsidiary *a.* Hilfs..., helfend; ~ **company,** Tochtergesellschaft *f.;* ~ **subject,** Nebenfach *n.;* ~ *s.* Gehilfe *m./f.*
subsidize *v.t.* mit Geld unterstützen, subventionieren.
subsidy *s.* Subvention *f.*
subsist *v.i.* bestehen, auskommen; ~ *v.t.* erhalten, ernähren.
subsistence *s.* Dasein, Bestehen, Auskommen *n.;* Lebensunterhalt *m.;* ~ **allowance** *s.* Verpflegungsgeld *n.;* ~ **level** *s.* Existenzminimum *n.;* *minimum of* ~, Existenzminimum *n.*
subsoil *s.* Untergrund *m.*
subsonic *a.* Unterschall...
substance *s.* Wesen *n.;* Stoff *m.,* Substanz *f.;* Hauptinhalt *m.;* Vermögen *n.*
substandard *a.* unzulänglich.
substantial *a.,* **~ly** *adv.* wesentlich, wirklich, körperlich; nahrhaft; stark, zahlungsfähig, vermögend.
substantiality *s.* Wesenheit *f.*
substantiate *v.t.* dartun, nachweisen; erhärten.
substantive *s.* Hauptwort *n.*
substitute *v.t.* ersetzen; auswechseln; ~ *s.* Stellvertreter *m.;* Ersatzmittel *n.;* ~ **material,** Werkstoff *m.*
substitution *s.* Stellvertretung, Unterschiebung *f.*
substratum *s.* Unterlage, Grundlage *f.*
substructure *s.* Unterbau *m.*
subtenant *s.* Untermieter(in) *m.(f.)*
subterfuge *s.* Ausflucht *f.*
subterranean *a.* unterirdisch.
subtitle *s.* Untertitel *m.*
subtle *a.,* **~tly** *adv.* fein, schlau.
subtlety *s.* Schlauheit *f.,* Scharfsinn *m.*
subtotal *s.* Zwischensumme *f.*
subtract *v.t.* abziehen, subtrahieren.
subtraction *s.* Abzeihen *n.,* Subtraktion *f.*
subtrahend *s.* (*ar.*) Subtrahend *m.*
subtropical *a.* subtropisch.
suburb *s.* Vorstadt *f.;* Vorort *m.*
suburban *a.* vorstädtisch; ~ **traffic,** Vorortsverkehr *m.;* ~ **train,** Vorortszug *m.*
subversion *s.* Umsturz *m.*
subversive *a.* umstürzend; ~ **activities** *pl.* Wühlarbeit *f.*
subvert *v.t.* umstürzen, zerstören.
subway *s.* Unterführung *f.;* U-Bahn *f.,* Untergrundbahn *f.*
succeed *v.t. & i.* nachfolgen; *to ~ to an estate,* ein Vermögen erben; *to ~ to a person,* einen beerben; *to ~ in doing,* gelingen.
success *s.* Erfolg *m.,* Glück *n.*
successful *a.,* **~ly** *adv.* erfolgreich.
succession *s.* Reihenfolge, Folge, Nachfolge *f.;* Erbfolge *f.;* *in* ~, hintereinander, nacheinander; *right of* ~, Erbfolge *f.;* *~ to the throne,* Thronfolge *f.*
successive *a.* einander folgend; **~ly** *adv.* der Reihe nach.
successor *s.* Nachfolger(in) *m.(f.)*
succinct *a.,* **~ly** *adv.* gedrängt, bündig; prägnant.
succinctness *s.* Knappheit *f.;* Prägnanz *f.*
succulent *a.* saftig.
succumb *v.i.* unterliegen.
such *pn.* solcher, solche, solches; von der Art, so groß; ~ *a.* so ein; **~like,** dergleichen; ~ **as,** die, welche...; *no ~ thing,* nichts dergleichen.
suck *v.t. & i.* (ein)saugen; pumpen; ~ *s.* Saugen *n.*
sucker *s.* Saugkolben *m.,* Saugrohr *n.;* Wurzelsproß *m.;* (*fam.*) Gimpel *m.*
sucking pump *s.* Saugpumpe *f.*
suckle *v.t.* säugen, stillen.
suckling pig *s.* Spanferkel *n.*
suction *s.* Saugen *n.;* Saug...
Sudan *s.* Sudan *m.*
sudden *a.,* **~ly** *adv.* plötzlich; übereilt, hitzig; *all of a* ~, plötzlich.
suddenness *s.* Plötzlichkeit *f.*
suds *s.pl.* Seifenwasser *n.*
sue *v.i.* ansuchen; ~ *v.t.* bitten, verklagen; *to ~ for damages,* auf Schadenersatz klagen.
suede *s.* Wildleder *n.*
suet *s.* Talg *m.;* Hammelfett *n.*
suffer *v.t. & i.* leiden, ausstehen; Strafe, Schaden leiden; gestatten.
sufferable *a.,* **~bly** *adv.* erträglich; zulässig.
sufferance *s.* Duldung *f.*
suffering *s.* Leiden *n.*
suffice *v.i.* genügen; ~ *v.t.* Genüge leisten, befriedigen.
sufficiency *s.* Genüge *f.;* Zulänglichkeit *f.*
sufficient *a.,* **~ly** *adv.* hinlänglich.
suffix *v.t.* anhängen; ~ *s.* Anhängesilbe *f.*
suffocate *v.t.* ersticken.
suffocation *s.* Erstickung *f.*
suffrage *s.* Wahlstimme *f.;* Beifall *m.;* Stimmrecht *n.;* *universal* ~, allgemeine Wahlrecht *n.*
suffragette *s.* Suffragette *f.,* Stimmrechtlerin *f.*
suffuse *v.t.* übergießen; durchfluten.
sugar *s.* Zucker *m.;* ~ **tongs** *pl.* Zuckerzange *f.;* ~ *v.t.* zuckern.
sugar basin *s.* Zuckerschale *f.*
sugar cane *s.* Zuckerrohr *n.*
sugarloaf *s.* Zuckerhut *m.*
sugarplum *s.* Bonbon *n.*
sugary *a.* zuckerig.
suggest *v.t.* eingeben, beibringen, vorschlagen; einflössen.
suggestion *s.* Rat *m.,* Vorschlag *m.*
suggestive *a.* andeutend; anregend; vielsagend; schlüpfrig.
suicidal *a.* selbstmörderisch.
suicide *s.* Selbstmord *m.;* Selbstmörder *m.;* *to commit* ~, Selbstmord begehen.
suit *s.* Folge *f.;* Farbe (Karte) *f.;* Gesuch *n.;* Prozeß *m.;* Anzug *m.;* Bitte *f.;* ~ *v.t.* ordnen; passen; gefallen; geziemen; gut stehen; ~ *v.i.* übereinstimmen.
suitability *s.* Eignung *f.;* Angemessenheit *f.*
suitable *a.,* **~bly** *adv.* gemäß, angemessen, schicklich, passend.
suitcase *s.* Koffer *m.*
suite *s.* Gefolge *n.;* Hotelsuite *f.;* Zimmereinrichtung *f.*
suitor *s.* Bittsteller *m.;* Bewerber, Freier *m.*
sulfate *s.* Sulfat *n.*
sulfide *s.* Sulphid *n.*
sulfur *s.* Schwefel *m.*
sulfuric *a.* Schwefel...; ~ **acid** *s.* Schwefelsäure *f.*
sulfurous *a.,* **~ly** *adv.* schwef[e]lig.

sulfury *a.* schwefelgelb.
sulk *v.i.* schmollen.
sulky *a.*, **~ily** *adv.* schmollend, launisch.
sullen *a.*, **~ly** *adv.* düster, verdrießlich, mürrisch.
sully *v.t.* besudeln.
sultan *s.* Sultan *m.*
sultana *s.* (kernlose) Rosine *f.*, Sultanine *f.*
sultry *a.* schwül.
sum *s.* Summe *f.;* Rechenaufgabe *f.;* ~ **total,** Gesamtsumme *f.;* ~ *v.t.* zusammenzählen, rechnen; *to ~ up,* zusammenfassen, (*jur.*) Beweisaufnahme zusammenfassen.
summarize *v.t.* (kurz) zusammenfassen.
summary *a.*, **~ily** *adv.* summarisch, kurz; ~ *s.* Auszug, kurze Inhaltsangabe *f.;* ~ **jurisdiction,** ~ **proceedings,** (*jur.*) Schnellverfahren, beschleunigtes Verfahren *n.*
summer *s.* Sommer *m.;* Tragbalken *m.;* ~ **time,** Sommerzeit *f.*
summerhouse *s.* Gartenhaus *n.*
summer school *s.* Sommerkurs *m.*
summer term *s.* Sommerhalbjahr *n.*
summery *a.* sommerlich.
summing-up *s.* Zusammenfassung *f.*
summit *s.* Gipfel *m.*, Spitze *f.*
summon *v.t.* vorladen, aufrufen; (Kraft) zusammennehmen.
summons *s.* Vorladung *f.;* Aufforderung *f.*
sumptuous *a.*, **~ly** *adv.* prachtig; luxuriös.
sun *s.* Sonne *f.*
Sun. *Sunday,* Sonntag, So.
sunbathe *v.i.* sonnenbaden.
sunbeam *s.* Sonnenstrahl *m.*
sunburn *s.* Sonnenbrand *m.*
sunburnt *a.* gebräunt, verbrannt.
sundae *s.* Eisbecher *m.*
Sunday *s.* Sonntag *m.*
sunder *v.t.* trennen, absondern.
sundial *s.* Sonnenuhr *f.*
sundown *s.* Sonnenuntergang *m.*
sundry *a.* mehrere, verschiedene.
sunflower *s.* Sonnenblume *f.*
sunglasses, *pl.* Sonnenbrille *f.*
sunken *a.* versunken; (fig) eingefallen.
sunlamp *s.* Ultraviolettlampe *f.*
sunlight *s.* Sonnenlicht *n.*
sunlit *a.* sonnenbeschienen.
sunny *a.* sonnig.
sunray *s.* Sonnenstrahl *m.*
sunrise *s.* Sonnenaufgang *m.*
sunroof *s.* Schiebedach *n.;* Dachterrasse *f.*
sunset *s.* Sonnenuntergang *m.*
sunshade *s.* Sonnenschirm *m.*
sunshine *s.* Sonnenschein *m.*
sunspot *s.* Sonnenflecken *m.*
sunstroke *s.* Sonnenstich *m.*
suntan *s.* (Sonnen)bräune *f.;* **~lotion** *s.* Sonnenschutzmittel *n.*
sunup *s.* Sonnenaufgang *m.*
super *a.* (*fam.*) super.
superarabundant *a.*, **~ly** *adv.* überreichlich.
superb *a.*, **~ly** *adv.* prächtig, herrlich.
supercilious *a.*, **~ly** *adv.* anmassend.
superficial *a.*, **~ly** *adv.* oberflächlich; seicht.
superfluity *s.* Überfluß *m.*
superfluous *a.*, **~ly** *adv.* überflüssig.
superhuman *a.* übermenschlich.
superintend *v.t.* die Aufsicht führen; überwachen.
superintendence *s.* Aufsicht *f.*
superintendent *s.* Inspektor, Aufseher *m.*
superior *a.* höher; größer; vorzüglich; überlegen; ~ *s.* Obere, Vorgesetzte *m.;* ~ **authority,** vorgesetzte Behörde *f.*
superiority *s.* Überlegenheit *f.;* Vorrang *m.;* Vorrecht *n.*
superlative *a.*, **~ly** *adv.* unübertrefflich; im höchsten Grade; ~ *s.* Superlativ *m.*
superman *s.* Übermensch *m.*
supernatural *a.*, **~ly** *adv.* übernatürlich.
supernumerary *a.* überzählig; ~ *s.* Überzählige *m.;* Figurant *m.*
superpower *s.* Supermacht *f.*
superscribe *v.t.* überschreiben.
superscription *s.* Überschrift *f.*
supersede *v.t.* verdrängen; ablösen.
supersession *s.* Ersatz *m.*, Verdrängung *f.*
supersonic *a.* Überschall...
superstition *s.* Aberglaube *m.*
superstitious *a.*, **~ly** *adv.* abergläubisch.
superstore *s.* Großmarkt *m.*
superstructure *s.* Aufbau *m.;* Überbau *m.*
supervene *v.i.* hinzukommen.
supervention *s.* Hinzukommen.
supervise *v.t.* beaufsichtigen.
supervision *s.* Aufsicht *f.*
supervisor *s.* Aufseher *m.*
supervisory *a.* Aufsichts...
supper *s.* Abendessen *n.;* *the Last S~,* das letzte Abendmahl *n.*
suppl. *supplement,* Nachtrag.
supplant *v.t.* verdrängen, ausstechen.
supple *a.*, **~ly** *adv.* geschmeidig, biegsam; nachgiebig.
supplement *s.* Ergänzung *f.;* Zusatz, Anhang *m.;* Beilage (Zeitung) *f.;* ~ *v.t.* ergänzen.
supplemental, supplementary *a.* ergänzend; ~ **order,** Nachbestellung *f.*
suppliant *a.* demütig, flehend.
supplicate *v.t.* anflehen.
supplication *s.* demütige Bitte *f.*
supplier *s.* Versorger *m.*
supply *v.t.* ersetzen, ergänzen; liefern, versorgen; ~ *s.* Beschaffung *f.;* Zuschuß *m.;* Vorrat *m.;* (*mil.*) Nachschub *m.;* **~depot** *s.* Nachschublager *n.;* ~ **and demand,** Angebot *(n.)* und Nachfrage *(f.);* **~ies** *pl.* Bedarf *m.*, Vorrat *m.*
support *v.t.* unterstützen; erhalten, ernähren; tragen; bekräftigen; ~ *s.* Stütze *f.;* Unterstützung *f.;* Unterhalt *m.;* *in ~ of,* zum Beweis von.
supporter *s.* Unterstützer(in) *m.(f.);* Gönner(in) *m. (f.);* Anhänger(in) *m.(f.)*
supportive *a.* hilfreich.
suppose *v.t.* voraussetzen, vermuten.
supposedly *adv.* angeblich.
supposition *s.* Annahme *f.;* Vermutung *f.*
suppress *v.t.* unterdrücken; verhindern.
suppression *s.* Unterdrückung *f.;* Verheimlichung *f.;* Abschaffung *f.*
suppurate *v.i.* eitern.
supremacy *s.* Obergewalt *f.;* Übergewicht, Überlegenheit *f.*

supreme *a.*, **~ly** *adv.* höchst, oberst.
surcharge *s.* Zuschlag.
sure *a. & adv.*, **~ly** *adv.* sicher, gewiß, zuverlässig; *to be ~*, sicher wissen; *to make ~*, sich vergewissern; *for ~*, sicher.
surety *s.* Sicherheit *f.*; Bürge *m.*, Bürgschaft *f.*
surf *s.* Brandung *f.*
surface *s.* Oberfläche *f.*; Flächeninhalt *m.*; ~ **mail** *s.* gewöhnliche Post (nicht Luftpost) *f.*
surfeit *s.* Übermaß *n.*; Überangebot *n.*; ~ *v.t.* überfüllen; ~ *v.i.* sich übersättigen.
surfer *s.* Surfer(in) *m.(f.)*
surfing *s.* Surfen *n.*
Surg. *surgery*, Chirurgie *f.*; *surgeon*, Chirurg *m.*
surge *s.* Woge, Brandung *f.*; ~ *v.i.* wogen; steigen.
surgeon *s.* Chirurg(in) *m.(f.)*
surgery *s.* Chirurgie *f.*
surgical *a.* chirurgisch, wundärztlich.
surly *a.*, **~ily** *adv.* grob, mürrisch.
surmise *v.t.* mutmassen; ~ *s.* Vermutung *f.*
surmount *v.t.* überragen; überwinden.
surname *s.* Zuname *m.*; Nachname *m.*; ~ *v.t.* einen Zunamen geben.
surpass *v.t.* übertreffen.
surplice *s.* Chorhemd *n.*
surplus *s.* Überschuß *m.*; Überrest *m.*; ~ *a.* überzählig, überschüssig.
surprise *s.* Überraschung *f.*; *v.t.* überraschen; erstaunen.
surprising *a.*, **~ly** *adv.* erstaunlich.
surrender *v.t.* übergeben, überliefern; abreten; ~ *v.i.* sich ergeben; ~ *s.* Übergabe, Auslieferung *f.*
surreptitious *a.*, **~ly** *adv.* erschlichen, verstohlen; heimlich; ~ **passage,** gelfälschte Stelle *f.*
surrogate *s.* Ersatz *m.*
surrogate mother *s.* Leihmutter *f.*
surround *v.t.* umgeben, einschließen.
surroundings *s.pl.* Umgebung *f.*
surtax *s.* Steuerzuschlag *m.*
surveillance *s.* Überwachung *f.*
survey *v.t.* überblicken, besichtigen; ausmessen; ~ *s.* Überblick *m.*; Besichtigung, Vermessung *f.*; Riß, Plan *m.*
surveying *s.* Landvermessung *f.*
surveyor *s.* Inspektor(in) *m.(f.)*; Landvermessen(in) *m.(f.)*
survival *s.* Überleben *n.*
survive *v.t.* überleben; ~ *v.i.* übrig bleiben, noch leben, fortleben.
survivor *s.* Überlebende *m./f.*
susceptibility *s.* Empfänglichkeit *f.*; Anfälligkeit *f.*
susceptible *a.* empfänglich; empfindlich.
suspect *v.i.* Verdacht hegen, argwöhnen, besorgen; ~ *v.t.* in Verdacht haben; bezweifeln; ~ *s.* Verdächtige *m./f.*; *to be ~*, belastet sein.
suspected *a.* verdächtig.
suspend *v.t.* aufhängen; unterbrechen; suspendieren, zeitweise ausschließen; einstellen; aufschieben; absetzen.
suspenders *pl.* Hosenträger *pl.*
suspense *s.* Ungewißheit *f.*; Spannung *f.*
suspension *s.* Aufhängen *n.*; Aufschub *m.*; Einstellung *f.*; Stillstand *m.*; Suspension *f.*; *~ of payments*, Zahlungseinstellung *f.*
suspension-bridge *s.* Hängebrücke *f.*
suspicion *s.* Verdacht, Argwohn *m.*; *above ~*, über allen Verdacht erhaben.
suspicious *a.*, **~ly** *adv.* argwöhnisch; verdächtig.
sustain *v.t.* standhalten; widerstehen; stützen; aufrechthalten; (Verlust) erleiden; behaupten.
sustained *a.* anhaltend; ausdauernd.
sustenance *s.* Nahrung *f.*; Nährwert *m.*
suture *s.* Naht *f.*
suzerain *s.* Oberlehnsherr *m.*
svelte *a.* schlank.
SW *southwest*, Südwest, SW; *short wave*, Kurzwelle, KW.
swab *s.* (*med.*) Tupfer *m.*
Swabia *s.* Schwaben *n.*
swaddle *v.t.* windeln, wickeln.
swagger *v.i.* stolzieren; prahlen; großtun.
swallow *v.t.* (ver)schlucken; verschlingen; ~ *s.* Schwalbe *f.*
swamp *s.* Sumpf *m.*; ~ *v.t.* (in Morast) versenken; überschwemmen.
swampy *a.* sumpfig.
swan *s.* Schwan *m.*
swank *s.* (*fam.*) Großtuerei *f.*; ~ *v.i.* großtun, renommieren.
swanky *a.* protzig.
swansong *s.* Schwanengesang *m.*
swap *v.t.* tauschen; austauschen; ~ *s.* Tausch *m.*
swarm *s.* Schwarm *m.*; Gewimmel *n.*; ~ *v.i.* wimmeln.
swarthy *a.*, **~ily** *adv.* schwärzlich, dunkel.
swash *v.i.* plantschen.
swashbuckler *s.* Schwadroneur *m.*; Abenteurer *m.*
swastika *s.* Hakenkreuz *n.*
swat *v.t.* totschlagen (Fliege).
swatch *s.* Stoffmuster *n.*
swathe *v.t.* einhüllen.
sway *v.t.* schwenken; lenken, ~ *v.i.* schwanken; Einfluß haben, herrschen; ~ *s.* Schwung *m.*; Ausschlag (der Waage) *m.*
swear *v.t.st.* schwören; fluchen; ~ *v.t.* vereidigen; beschwören; *to ~ by*, schwören bei; *to ~ false*, falsch schwören; *to ~ in*, vereidigen.
swear word *s.* Fluchwort *m.*
sweat *s.* Schweiß *m.*; ~ *v.i.* schwitzen; ~ *v.t.* schwitzen; (*fig.*) ausbeuten, für Hungerlohn beschäftigen.
sweater *s.* Sweater *m.*, Pullover *m.*
sweatshop *s.* ausbeuterischer Betrieb *m.*
sweaty *a.* schweißig.
Swede *s.* Schwede *m.*; Schwedin *f.*
Sweden *s.* Schweden *n.*
Swedish *a.* schwedisch.
sweep *v.t.* fegen, kehren; ~ *s.* Zug, Schwung *m.*; Schleppe *f.*; Schornsteinfeger *m.*; flacher Landstrich *m.*
sweeper *s.* Straßenfeger *m.*
sweeping *a.* reißend; weitgreifend; umfassend.
sweepstake *s.* Lotterie.
sweet *a.*, **~ly** *adv.* süß; lieblich; freundlich; ~ **pea,** Edelwicke *f.*; ~ **william,** Bartnelke *f.*; ~ **tooth,** Leckermaul *n.*; ~ *s.* Süßigkeit, Lieblichkeit *f.*; Schätzchen *n.*; **~s** *pl.* Zuckerwerk *n.*
sweeten *v.t.* versüßen; milde stimmen.
sweetener *s.* Süßstoff *m.*
sweetheart *s.* Liebchen *n.*

sweetness *s.* Süßigkeit, Lieblichkeit *f.*
sweet potato *s.* Batate *f.*
sweetroll *s.* Schnecke (Gebäck) *f.*
sweet-tempered *a.* sanftmütig.
swell *v.t.st.* schwellen; zunehmen; sich blähen; ~ *v.t.* aufblasen; vergrössern; ~ *s.* Anschwellen *n.;* Erhebung *f.;* Dünung *f.;* ~ *a.* vorzüglich; aufgedonnert.
swelling *s.* Schwellung *f.*
swelter *v.i.* lechzen; vor Hitze vergehen.
swerve *v.i.* abweichen; abschweifen.
swift *a.* **~ly** *adv.* schnell, flüchtig; bereit; ~ *s.* Mauersegler *m.*
swiftness *s.* Schnelligkeit *f.*
swig *v.t.* schlucken; kippen.
swill *v.i.* & t. ausspülen; hinunterspülen.
swim *v.t.st.* schwimmen; schwindlig sein; verschwimmen; ~ *v.t.* durchschwimmen; schwemmen.
swimmer *s.* Schwimmer(in) *m.(f.)*
swimming pool *s.* Schwimmbad *n.*
swimsuit *s.* Badeanzug *m.*
swindle *v.t.* beschwindeln; erschwindeln; ~ *s.* Schwindel *m.*
swindler *s.* Schwindler(in) *m.(f.)*
swine *s.* Schwein *n.* (*meist fig.*)
swing *v.t.* schwingen, schaukeln; ~ *v.i.* sich schwingen; schwanken; sich umdrehen; baumeln; (*nav.*) schwaien; ~ *s.* Schwung *m.;* Schaukel *f.;* Spielraum *m.;* Gang *m.; in full* ~, in vollem Gang; **~-bridge,** *s.* Drehbrücke *f.;* **~ing chair** *s.* Schaukelstuhl *m.* **~(ing) door,** Pendeltür *f.;* **~ing lamp,** Hängelampe *f.*
swinish *a.,* **~ly** *adv.* schweinisch.
swipe *v.t.* (*fam.*) eindreschen; (auf) knallen.
swirl *v.i.* wirbeln; ~ *s.* Strudel *m.*
swish *v.t.* schlagen; sausen lassen.
Swiss *a.* Schweizerisch; *s.* Schweizer(in) *m.(f.)*
switch *s.* Gerte *f.;* (*rail.*) Weiche *f.;* (*elek.*) Schalter *m.;* (*elek.*) **~-gear** *s.* Schaltgerät *n.;* ~ *v.t.* hauen; (*elek.*) (um)schalten; *to* ~ *on, off,* andrehen, abdrehen.
switchback-railway *s.* Berg-und-Tal Bahn *f.*
switchboard *s.* Schalttafel *f.*, Schaltbrett *n.*
Switzerland *s.* Schweiz *f.*
swivel *s.* Drehzapfen *m.;* Drehgelenk *n.* **~bridge** *s.* Drehbrücke *f.;* **~chair** *s.* Drehstuhl *m.;* ~ *v.i.* & *t.* (sich) auf einem Zapfen drehen.
swollen *a.* geschwollen.
swoon *v.i.* in Ohnmacht fallen; ~ *s.* Ohnmacht *f.*
swoop *s.* Stoß *m.;* plötzliche Razzia *f.;* Sturzflug *m.* ~ *v.i. & t.* herabstoßen, herfallen über.
sword *s.* Schwert *n.;* Degen *m.*
swordfish *s.* Schwertfisch *m.*
swordsman *s.* Fechter *m.*
sworn *a.* beeidigt, vereidigt; ~ *to,* beschworen.
sybarite *s.* Genießer *m.*
sycamore *s.* Sykomore *f.*
sycophant *s.* Schmeichler *m.*, Kriecher *m.*
syllabic(al) *a.* silbig, Silben...
syllabication *s.* Silbentrennung *f.*
syllable *s.* Silbe *f.*
syllabus *s.* Lehrplan *m.;* Literaturliste *f.*
syllogism *s.* (Vernunft-) Schluß *m.*
sylph *s.* Luftgeist *m.*
symbiosis *s.* Symbiose *f.*
symbol *s.* Sinnbild, Symbol *n.;* graphische Zeichen *n.*
symbolical *a.*, **~ly** *adv.* sinnbildlich.
symbolize *v.t.* sinnbildlich darstellen, versinnbildlichen.
symmetrical *a.*, **~ly** *adv.* ebenmäßig; symmetrisch.
symmetry *s.* Ebenmaß *n.;* Symmetrie *f.*
sympathetic *a.* mitfühlend; (seelen)verwandt.
sympathize *v.i.* mitempfinden; übereinstimmen; sympathisieren.
sympathy *s.* Mitgefühl *n.;* Sympathie *f.*
symphönic *a.* sinfonisch; symphonisch.
symphony *s.* Symphonie, Sinfonie *f.;* ~ **orchestra** *s.* Sinfonieorchester *n.*
symptom *s.* Anzeichen *n.*
symptomatic *a.* bezeichnend.
synagogue *s.* Synagoge *f.*
synchronize *v.t.* gleichgehend machen; synchronisieren.
synchronous *a.* gleichzeitig.
syncopate *v.t.* (*mus.*) synkopieren.
syndicate *s.* Syndikat *n.*, Konzern *m.;* Konsortium *n.*
syndrome *s.* Syndrom *n.*
synod *s.* Kirchenversammlung *f.;* Synode *f.*
synonym *s.* sinnverwandtes Wort *n.;* Synonym *n.*
synonymous *a.*, **~ly** *adv.* sinnverwandt.
synonymy *s.* Sinnverwandtschaft *f.*
synopsis *s.* kurzer Abriß *m.*
syntactic *a.* syntaktisch.
syntax *s.* Syntax *f.*
synthesis *s.* Synthese *f.*
synthesize *v.t.* synthetisieren.
synthesizer *s.* synthesizer *m.*
synthetic *a.*, **~ally** *adv.* synthetisch, künstlich (hergestellt); ~ **material,** Werkstoff *m.;* ~ **petrol,** künstliches Benzin *n.;* ~ **rubber,** künstlicher Gummi *m.*
syphilis *s.* Syphilis *f.*
Syria *s.* Syrien *n.*
Syrian *a.* Syrisch; Syrer(in) *m.(f.)*
syringe *s.* Spritze *f.;* ~ *v.t.* spritzen.
syrup, sirup *s.* Syrup *m.*
system *s.* System, Lehrgebäude *n.*
systematic(al) *a.*, **~ally** *adv.* systematisch, planmäßig.
systematize *v.t.* systematisieren.
systemic *a.* systemisch.
systems analyst *s.* Systemanalytiker(in) *m.(f.)*

T

T, t der Buchstabe T oder t *n.*

t *ton,* Tonne, t.

tab *s.* Lasche *f.;* Aufhänger *m.;* Schildchen, Etikett *n.*

tabby *s.* Tigerkatze *f.*

tabernacle *s.* Tabernakel *m.*

table *s.* Tafel *f.;* Tisch *m.;* Tabelle *f.;* ~ **of contents,** *s.* Inhaltsverzeichnis. *f.;* ~ *v.t.* auf den Tisch legen.

tableau vivant *s.* lebendes Bild *n.*

tablecloth *s.* Tischtuch *n.*

table manners *s. pl.* Tischmanieren *pl.*

tablemat *s.* set *n.*

tablespoon *s.* Eßlöffel *m.;* **~ful,** *s.* Eßlöffelvoll *m.*

tablet *s.* Täfelchen *n.;* Tablette *f.;* Schreibtafel *f.*

table tennis *s.* Tischtennis *n.*

tableware *s.* Geschirr *n.*, Besteck *n.*

tabloid *s.* Boulevardzeitung *f.*

taboo *s.* Tabu *n.;* ~ *a.* verboten; tabuisiert.

tabular *a.* tabellarisch.

tabulate *v.t.* in Tabellen bringen; tabellarisch ordnen.

tachograph *s.* Fahrtenschreiber *m.*

tachometer *s.* (*mot.*) Umdrehungsmesser *m.*

tacit *a.*, **~ly** *adv.* stillschweigend.

taciturn *a.* schweigsam.

taciturnity *s.* Schweigsamkeit *f.*

tack *s.* Stift *m.;* Häkchen *n.;* Zwecke *f.;* (*nav.*) Kurs *m.;* ~ *v.t.* anheften, befestigen.

tackle, Takelwerk *n.;* Gerät *n.;* Flaschenzug *m.;* ~ *v.t.* takeln; in Angriff nehmen.

tacky *a.* klebrig; schäbig.

tact *s.* Feingefühl *n.;* Takt *m.*

tactful *a.*, **~ly** *adv.* taktvoll.

tactical *a.*, **~ly** *adv.* taktisch.

tactician *s.* Taktiker(in) *m.(f.)*

tactics *s.pl.* Kriegskunst, Taktik *f.*

tactless *a.*, **~ly** *adv.* taktlos.

tadpole *s.* Kaulquappe *f.*

taffeta *s.* Taft *m.*

tag *s.* Zettel *m.;* Anhängsel *n.;* Etikett *n.;* Schlaufe *f.;* Fangen *n.;* ~ *v.t.* anheften; anhängen.

tail *s.* Schwanz *m.;* Ende *n.;* Rockschoß *m.;* ~ **suit, tails,** Frack *m.*

tail-light *s.* Rücklicht *n.*

tailor *s.* Schneider *m.;* **~-made,** vom Schneider angefertigt; ~ *v.t. & i.* schneidern.

tailwind *s.* Rückenwind *m.*

taint *v.t.* beflecken; verderben; anstecken; verführen; ~ *s.* Flecken *m.;* Ansteckung *f.;* Verderbnis *f.*

take *v.t.st.* (mit-, an-, ein-, fest-, weg-) nehmen, empfangen; ergreifen; dafürhalten, meinen; bringen; sich gefallen lassen, einstecken; (Feuer) fangen; ~ *v.i.* gefallen, anschlagen, ansprechen; *it ~s (me) three hours,* ich brauche drei Stunden; *to ~ after,* einem nachgeraten; *to ~ down,* aufschreiben, zu Protokoll nehmen; *to ~ in,* betrügen; *to ~ in a paper,* eine Zeitung bestellen; *to ~ off,* ausziehen, (Hut) abnehmen; abfliegen; *to ~ to,* Gefallen finden an; *to ~ to heart,* sich zu Herzen nehmen; *to ~ for granted,* als erwiesen annehmen; *to ~ ill,* amiss, übelnehmen; *to ~ into account,* in Betracht ziehen; *to ~ part in,* teilnehmen an; *to ~ place,* stattfinden; *to ~ prisoner,* gefangennehmen; *to ~ a seat,* Platz nehmen; *to ~ one's time,* sich Zeit nehmen; *to ~ an examination, test,* eine Prüfung machen.

take off *s.* Abflug *m.*, Abheben *n.;* Start *m.*

taker *s.* Abnehmer(in) *m.(f.)*

taking *s.* Nehmen *n.;* Einnahme *f.;* ~ *a.* einnehmend, packend.

talc, talcum *s.* Talk *m.;* **talcum powder** *s.* Körperpuder *m.*

tale *s.* Erzählung *f.;* Märchen *n.*

tale bearer *s.* Zuträger *m.*

talent *s.* Talent *n.*, Begabung *f.*

talented *a.* talentvoll, begabt.

talk *v.i.* reden, sprechen; schwatzen; ~ *s.* Gespräch *n.;* Gerücht *n.*

talkative *a.*, **~ly** *adv.* gesprächig.

tall *a.* lang, groß; (*fig.*) geflunkert.

tallboy *s.* Kommode *(f.)* mit Aufsatz.

tallow *s.* Talg *m.;* ~ *v.t.* einschmieren.

tally *v.t.* einkerben; (*nav.*) anholen; ~ *v.i.* passen, entsprechen, stimmen; ~ *s.* Zählstand *m.; keep a ~ of,* Buch führen.

tallyho *i.* hallo!; ~ *s.* Weidruf *m.*

talon *s.* Kralle, Klaue *f.*

tambour *s.* Handtrommel *f.;* Stickrahmen; ~ *v.t.* sticken.

tambourine *s.* Tamburin *n.*

tame *a.*, **~ly** *adv.* zahm; folgsam; ~ *v.t.* zähmen; bändigen.

tamper (with) *v.i.* sich einmischen; an etwas herumpfuschen.

tampon *s.* Tampon *m.*

tan *s.* Lohe *f.;* Bräune *f.;* ~ *v.t.* lohen, gerben; bräunen; braun werden.

tandem *s.* Tandem *n.*

tang *s.* scharfer Geruch od. Geschmack *m.*

tangent *s.* Tangente *f.*

tangerine *s.* Mandarine *f.*

tangible *a.* greifbar, fühlbar.

tangle *v.t.* verwirren, verwickeln; ~ *s.* Knoten *m.*, Verwicklung *f.*

tangled *a.* verheddert; verworren.

tangy *a.* scharf; würzig.

tank *s.* Wasserbehälter *m.;* Tank *m.;* Panzer *m.;* ~ **car** *s.* (*rail.*) Kesselwagen, Tankwagen *m.;* ~ **driver** *s.* (*mil.*) Panzerfahrer *m.;* ~ *v.i.* tanken.

tankard *s.* Trinkgefäß *n.;* Krug *m.*

tanker *s.* Tanker *m.*

tanned *a.* braungebrannt.

tanner *s.* Lohgerber(in) *m.(f.)*

tannery *s.* Gerberei *f.*

tannin *s.* Gerbstoff *m.*

tantalize *v.t.* reizen; zappeln lassen.

tantalizing *a.* verlockend.

tantamount *a.* gleichwertig; gleichbedeutend.

tantrum *s.* Wutanfall *m.*, Trotzanfall *m.*

tap *s.* gelinder Schlag *m.;* Zapfen *m.;* Hahn *m.* (*mech.*) Gewindebohrer *m.;* ~ **wrench** *s.* Halter für Gewindebohrer; *on ~*, angezapft, erhältlich;

~ *v.t.* klopfen an, abklopfen; anzapfen; (Telegramme) abfangen, Telephon abhören.
tap dance *s.* Steptanz *m.*
tap dancer *s.* Steptänzer(in) *m.(f.)*
tape *s.* Kassette (Audio) *f.*; Video *n.*; (*Sport*) Zielband *n.*; (*tel.*) Papierstreifen *m.*
tape deck *s.* Kassettenrecorder *m.*; Tapedeck *n.*
tape-measure *s.* Bandmaß *n.*
taper *s.* Wachskerze *f.*; Wachsstock *m.*; ~ *v.t.* verjüngen, zuspitzen; ~ *off, v.i.* spitz zulaufen, sich verjüngen.
tape recorder *s.* Kassettenrecorder *m.*
tapestry *s.* gewirkte Tapete *f.*, Gobelin *m.*
tapeworm *s.* Bandwurm *m.*
tapioca *s.* Tapioka *f.*
taproom *s.* Schankstube *f.*
tap water *s.* Leitungswasser *n.*
tar *s.* Teer *m.*; (*fam.*) Matrose *m.*; ~ *v.t.* teeren.
tarantula *s.* Tarantel *f.*
tardy *a.*, **~ily** *adv.* langsam; träge; spät.
tare *s.* Wicke *f.*; (*com.*) Tara *f.*
target *s.* (Schieß-)Scheibe; (*mil., avi.*) Ziel *n.*; ~ **date,** Termin *m.*; ~ **practice,** Schießübung *f.*
tariff *s.* Zolltarif *m.*; **~-wall** *s.* Zollschranke *f.*
tarnish *v.t.* trübe machen; beschmutzen; ~ *v.i.* den Glanz verlieren.
tarnished *a.* stumpf; befleckt.
tarpaulin *s.* Plane *f.*; Persenning *f.*
tarragon *s.* Estragon *n.*
tarry *a.* teerig
tart *s.* Obsttörtchen *n.*; ~ *a.*, **~ly** *adv.* herb, sauer.
tartan *s.* Plaid *n.*
tartar *s.* Weinstein *m.*; Zahnstein *m.*; Tartar, Tatar *m.*
tartaric *a.* Weinstein...; ~ **acid** *s.* Weinsäure *f.*
tartlet *s.* Törtchen *n.*
task *s.* Aufgabe *f.*; *take to* ~, zur Rede stellen; ins Gebet nehmen.
task force *s.* Sonderkommando *n.*
tassel *s.* Troddel, Quaste *f.*
taste *v.t. & i.* kosten, schmecken; versuchen; (*fig.*) empfinden; ~ *s.* Probe *f.*; Geschmack *m.*; Neigung *f.*
tasteful *a.* schmackhaft, geschmackvoll.
tasteless *a.* geschmacklos.
tasty *a.* lecker.
tat: tit for ~, wie du mir, so ich dir.
tatter *s.* Lumpen *m.*; ~ *v.t.* zerlumpen, zerfetzen.
tattle *v.i.* schwatzen; tratschen; klatschen; ~ *s.* Geschwätz *n.*; Tratsch *m.*
tattoo *s.* Tätowierung *f.*; ~ *v.t.* tätowieren.
tatty *a.* schäbig, zerfleddert; mies.
taunt *v.t.* verspotten; verhöhnen; ~ *s.* Hohn, Spott *m.*
taunting *s.* Spott *m.*; ~ *a.* verhöhnend.
Taurus *s.* (*astro.*) Stier *m.*
taut *a.* straff, steif.
tauten *v.t. & i.* straff machen, sich straffen.
tautology *s.* Tautologie *f.*
tavern *s.* Wirtshaus *n.*; Schenke *f.*
tawdry *a.* geschmacklos, verkommen, verlottert.
tawny *a.* lohfarbig, gelbbraun.
tax *s.* Steuer, Abgabe *f.*; ~ *v.t.* besteuern; belasten; ~ **allowance** *s.* Steuerfreibetrag *m.* ~ **free,** steuerfrei; ~ **payer** *s.* Steuerzahler *m.*; ~ **collector** *s.* Steuereinnehmer *m.*; ~ **remission,** Steuererlaß *m.*
taxable *a.* steuerbar, steuerpflichtig.
taxation *s.* Abschätzung *f.*; Besteuerung *f.*; *exempt from* ~, steuerfrei.
taxi, taxicab *s.* Taxi *n.*; ~ **stand,** *s.* Taxistand *m.*; ~ *v.i.* (*avi.*) rollen.
taximeter *s.* Taxameter *m.*
tax office *s.* Finanzamt *n.*, Steueramt.
taxpayer *s.* Steuerzahler(in) *m.(f.)*
tax return *s.* Steuererklärung *f.*
TB *tuberculosis,* Tuberkulose, Tb(c).
tbsp. *tablespoon,* Eßlöffel, Eßl.
tea *s.* Tee *m.*; ~ **kettle** *s.* Teekessel *m.*; ~ **leaves** *pl.* Teeblätter *pl.* **~pot** *s.* Teekanne *f.*; ~ **set** *s.* Teeservice *n.*
teach *v.t. & i.* lehren, unterrichten.
teachable *a.*, **~bly** *adv.* gelehrig.
teacher *s.* Lehrer *m.*; Lehrerin *f.*
teak wood *s.* Teakholz *n.*
team *s.* Gespann *n.*; Mannschaft *f.*; ~ **work,** Zusammenspiel *n.*
team: ~ effort *s.* Gemeinschaftsarbeit *f.*; **~-mate** *s.* Mannschaftskamerad(in) *m.(f.)* ~ **spirit** *s.* Teamgeist *m.*
teamster *s.* Lastwagenfahrer(in) *m.(f.)*
tea-party *s.* Teegesellschaft *f.*
tear *s.* Träne *f.*; ~ *v.t.st.* reißen, zerreißen; ~ *v.i.* wüten; rasen; ~ *s.* Riß *m.*
teardrop *s.* Träne *f.*
tearful *a.* weinend; tränenreich; weinerlich.
tearing *s.* reißend; tobend; heftig.
tease *v.t.* necken, hänseln.
teasel *s.* Kardendistel *f.*; Karde *f.*
teaser *s.* (*fam.*) harte Nuß *f.*; *brain* ~, *s.* Denksportaufgabe *f.*
teasing *a.* neckend.
teat *s.* Zitze *f.*; Brustwartze *f.*
tea things *s.pl.* Teegeschirr *n.*
tea tree *s.* Teestrauch *m.*
technical *a.*, **~ly** *adv.* kunstmäßig, technisch; Fach...
technical consultant *s.* Fachberater *m.*
technicality *s.* technisches Detail *n.*
technician *s.* Techniker(in) *m.(f.)*
technique *s.* Technik *f.*
technological *a.* technologisch.
technologist *s.* Technologe *f.*; Technologin *f.*
technology *s.* Technologie *f.*
teddy-bear *s.* Teddybär *m.*
tedious *a.*, **~ly** *adv.* langweilig, lästig.
tedium *s.* Langweiligkeit *f.* Langeweile *f.*
teem *v.i.* wimmeln (von); strotzen; gießen.
teenager *s.* Teenager *m.*; Jugendliche *m./f.*
teens *s.pl.* Lebensjahre *(n.pl.)*, die auf teen endigen (von 13-19); Teenagerjahre *n.pl.*
teeter *v.i.* wanken; schaukeln.
teeth *s.pl.* Zähne *m.pl.*
teethe *v.i.* zahnen.
teetotaller *s.* Abstinenzler *m.*
tel. *telephone,* Telefon, Tel.
telecommunication *s.* Fernmeldeverkehr *m.*
telegram *s.* Telegramm *n.*
telegraph *s.* Telegraf *m.*; ~ *v.t.* telegraphieren.
telegraphic *a.* telegraphisch.
telegraphy *s.* Telegraphie *f.*

telepathy *s.* Telepathie *f.*
telephone *s.* Telefon *n.*, Fernsprecher *m.; ~ v.t. & i.* anrufen telephonieren; **~ booth** *s.* Telephonzelle *f.; ~* **exchange** *s.* Fernsprechamt *n.*
telephone operator *s.* Telefonist(in) *m.(f.)*
teleprinter *s.* Fernschreiber *m.*
telescope *s.* Fernrohr *n.; ~v.t. & i.* (sich) ineinanderschieben.
telescopic *a.* teleskopisch; ausziehbar.
teletext *s.* Bildschirmtext *m.;* Teletext *m.*
televise *v.t.* im Fernsehen übertragen.
television *s.* Fernsehen *n.;* **~ set** *s.* Fernsehapparat *m.*
telex *s.* Telex *n.*
tell *v.t. & i.* sagen; erzählen, melden, anzeigen; Wirkung tun; zählen; *to ~ off,* anschnauzen, abfahren lassen.
teller *s.* (Bank) Kassierer(in) *m.(f.)*
telling *a.* durchschlagend, wirkungsvoll.
tell-tale *s.* Klatschmaul *n.* ~ *a.* klatschaft; verräterisch.
temerity *s.* Tollkühnheit *f.*
temper *v.t.* mäßigen; mildern; (Stahl) tempern; ~ *s.* Gemütsstimmung *f.;* Mäßigung *f.;* Laune *f.;* Härte *f.; to keep one's ~,* die Ruhe behalten; *to lose one's ~,* heftig werden, die Fassung verlieren.
temperament *s.* Temperament *n.*
temperamental *a.,* **~ly** *adv.* launenhaft; reizbar; temperamentvoll.
temperance *s.* Mäßigkeit *f.;* Enthaltsamkeit *f.*
temperate *a.,* **~ly** *adv.* mäßig, gemäßigt; ruhig, gelassen.
temperature *s.* Temperatur *f.; to have a ~,* (leicht) Fieber haben; *to take the ~,* Temperatur messen *or* nehmen.
tempered *a. good~,* gutgelaunt; *bad ~,* schlechtgelaunt.
tempest *s.* Sturm *m.;* Ungewitter *n.*
tempestuous *a.,* **~ly** *adv.* stürmisch.
template *s.* Schablone *f.*
temple *s.* Tempel *m.;* Schläfe *f.*
temporal *a.,* **~ly** *adv.* zeitlich; weltlich; Schläfen...
temporary *a.,* **~ily** *adv.* vorübergehend; zeitweilig, vorläufig; **~ duty,** *(mil.)* zeitweiliger Dienst *m.*
temporize *v.i.* die passende Zeit abwarten; hinhalten; Zeit zu gewinnen suchen.
tempt *v.t.* versuchen, verleiten.
temptation *s.* Versuchung *f.*
tempter *s.* Versucher *m.*
tempting *a.* verlockend.
temptress *s.* Versucherin *f.*
ten *a.* zehn; ~ *s.* Zehn *f.*
tenable *a.* haltbar.
tenacious *a.* festhaltend, zähe.
tenacity *s.* Zähigkeit, Beharrlichkeit *f.*
tenancy *s.* Pacht-, Mietverhältnis *n.*
tenant *s.* Pächter, Mieter *m.*
Ten Commandments *s.pl.* die Zehn Gebote *pl.*
tend *v.t.* warten, pflegen; bedienen (Maschine); ~ *v.i.* abzielen, (zu-) neigen, tendieren.
tendency *s.* Richtung, Neigung *f.;* Tendenz *f.*
tendentious *a.* tendenziös.
tender *a.,* **~ly** *adv.* weich, zart; zärtlich, empfindlich; ~ *s.* Angebot *n.;* Wärter *m.; (rail.)* Tender *m.;* Zahlungsmittel *n.; ~ v.t.* anbieten; *to ~ one's resignation,* seine Entlassung beantragen.
tenderize *v.t.* *(cul.)* zart machen; weich klopfen.
tenderness *s.* Zartheit *f.;* Zärtlichkeit *f.;* Sorgfalt *f.*, Empfindlichkeit *f.*
tendon *s.* Sehne, Flechse *f.*
tendril *s.* Ranke *f.*, Trieb *m.*
tenement *s.* Mietshaus *n.*
tenet *s.* Satz, Grundsatz *m.;* Lehre *f.*
tenfold *a.* zehnfach.
tennis *s.* Tennisspiel *n.; ~ court,* Tennisplatz *m.*
tenon *s.* Zapfen *m.*
tenor *s.* Tenor *m.*
tense *s.* *(gram.)* Zeitform *f.*, Tempus *n.; ~ a.* angespannt; straff.
tensile *a.* dehnbar; **~ strength,** Zugfestigkeit *f.*
tension *s.* Spannung *f.*
tent *s.* Zelt *n.*
tentacle *s.* Fühler *m.*
tentative *a.* **~ly** *adv.* vorläufig; versuchsweise.
tenter-hook *s.* Spannhaken *m.; to be on ~s,* wie auf Kohlen sitzen, in Ängsten sein.
tenth *a.* zehnt...
tenuity *s.* Dünne *f.;* Zartheit *f.;* Armseligkeit *f.*
tenuous *a.* dünn, fein; unsicher, unbestimmt.
tenure *s.* Besitzrecht *n.;* Amtszeit *f.;* Dauerstellung *f.*
tepid *a.*, lau, lauwarm.
term *s.* Grenze *f.;* Ausdruck *m.;* Begriff *m.;* Termin *m.*, Frist *f.;* Trimester *n.;* **~s** *pl.* Preis *m.;* Bedingungen *pl.; prison ~,* Strafzeit *f.; inclusive ~s, pl.* Preis, in dem alles einbegriffen ist; *in ~s of numbers,* in Zahlen ausgedrückt; *to come to ~s with,* sich einigen über etw. mit jm.; *to be on good ~s with,* mit einem gut stehen; ~ *v.t.* nennen, benennen.
terminal *a.* letzt..., End...; ~ *s.* Endstück *n.;* *(elek.)* Pol, *m.*
terminate *v.t.* begrenzen; endigen; ~ *v.i.* enden.
termination *s.* Ende *n.;* Endung *f.*
terminology *s.* Terminologie *f.*
terminus *s.* Endstation *f.*
termite *s.* Termite *f.*
terrace *s.* Terrasse *f.*
terrain *s.* Gelände *n.*
terrestrial *a.,* **~ly** *adv.* irdisch.
terrible *a.,* **~bly** *adv.* fürchterlich.
terrier *s.* Terrier *m.*
terrific *a.* phantastisch, wahnsinnig, toll.
terrify *v.t.* erschrecken.
terrifying *a.* entsetzlich, erschreckend.
territorial *a.* Landes...; **~ waters** *pl.* Hoheitsgewässer *pl.; limit of ~ waters,* Hoheitsgrenze *f.*
territory *s.* Gebiet *n.;* Landschaft *f.*
terror *s.* Schrecken *m.; (fam.)*(Todes)Angst *f.*
terrorism *s.* Terrorismus *m.*
terrorist *s.* Terrorist(in) *m.(f.)*
terrorize *v.t.* terrorisieren; in Schrecken versetzen.
terry (cloth) *s.* Frottee *n.*
terse *a.,* **~ly** *adv.* glatt; bündig; knapp.
tertiary *a.* tertiär.
test *s.* Klassenarbeit *f.;* Test *m.;* Prüfung, Probe *f.; (fig.)* Prüfstein *m.;* **~ case,** Schulfall, Probefall *m.;* **~ flight,** Probeflug *m.;* **~ tube,** Reagenzglas *n.; to put to the ~,* auf die Probe stellen; ~ *v.t.*

prüfen; testen; (*chem.*) untersuchen; *to ~ the heart,* das Herz abklopfen; *to ~ the sight,* das Sehvermögen prüfen.
testament *s.* Testament *n.*, letzter Wille *m.*
testamentary *a.* testamentarisch.
testator *s.* Erblasser(in) *m.(f.)*
testicle *s.* Hode *f.*
testify (to) *v.i.* etwas bezeugen.
testimonial *s.* schriftliches Zeugnis *n.;* Empfehlung *f.*, Ehrbeweis *m.*
testimony *s.* Zeugnis *n.; to bear ~*, Zeugnis ablegen.
test paper *s.* Indikatorpapier *n.;* Prüfungsbogen *m.*
test tube *s.* Reagenzglas; **~ baby** *s.* Retortenbaby *n.*
testy *a.*, **~ily** *adv.* mürrisch, reizbar.
tetanus *s.* Starrkrampf *m.*
tetchy *a.* empfindlich.
tether *s.* Spannseil *n.;* (*fig.*) Fähigkeit *f.*, Kraft *f.; to be at the end of one's ~*, am Ende seiner Kraft sein; **~** *v.t.* anbinden.
Teutonic *a.* germanisch; teutonisch.
text *s.* Text *m.;* Bibelstelle *f.*
textbook *s.* Leitfaden *m.;* Lehrbuch *n.*
textile *a.* gewebt; Textil...; **~s** *pl.* Textilien *f.pl.*
textual *a.* textgemäß, wörtlich.
texture *s.* Beschaffenheit *f.;* Struktur *f.;* Konsistenz *f.*
Thai *a.* thailändisch; **~** *s.* Thai *m./f.*
Thailand *s.* Thailand *n.*
Thames *s.* Themse *f.*
than *c.* als.
thank *v.t.* danken; **~s** *pl.* Dank *m.*
thankful *a.*, **~ly** *adv.* dankbar.
thankless *a.* undankbar.
Thanksgiving *s.* Erntedankfest *n.*
thank-you *s.* Dankeschön *n.*
that *pn.* jener, jene, jenes; welcher, welche, welches; der, die, das; **~** *c.* daß, damit, weil.
thatch *s.* Dachstroh *n.;* Strohdach *n.;* **~** *v.t.* mit Stroh decken.
thaw *v.t. & i.* tauen, auftauen, **~** *s.* Tauwetter *n.*
the *art.* der, die, das; so, desto; **~ less,** umsoweniger.
theater *s.* Theater *s.;* Schauplatz *m.;* **~ of operations,** (*mil.*) Operationsgebiet; **~ of war,** Kriegsschauplatz *m.*
theatergoer *s.* Theaterbesucher(in) *m.(f.)*
theatrical *a.*, **~ly** *adv.* bühnenhaft, theatralisch.
thee *pn.* dir, dich.
theft *s.* Diebstahl *m.*
their *pn.* ihr, ihre.
theirs *pn.* ihr, ihre; der, die, das ihrige.
them *pn.pl.* sie, ihnen.
theme *s.* Gegenstand *m.;* Thema *n.*
theme music *s.* Titelmusik *f.*
themselves *pn.pl.* sie selbst, sich (selbst).
then *adv.* dann, alsdann, damals; *now and ~*, dann und wann; **~** *c.* dann, daher, folglich.
thence *adv.* von da, von dort, daher.
thenceforth *adv.* seitdem; von da ab.
theocracy *s.* Gottes-, Priesterherrschaft *f.*
theocratic *a.* theokratisch.
theologian *s.* Theologe *m.*
theological *a.*, **~ly** *adv.* theologisch.
theology *s.* Theologie *f.*
theorem *s.* Lehrsatz, Grundsatz *m.*
theoretical *a.*, **~ly** *adv.* theoretisch.
theorist *s.* Theoretiker(in) *m.(f.)*
theorize *v.i.* Theorien aufstellen.
theory *s.* Theorie *f.;* Lehre *f.*
theosophy *s.* Theosophie *f.*
therapeutics *s.pl.* Therapie, Heilkunde *f.*
therapist *s.* Therapeut(in) *m.(f.)*
therapy *s.* Heilverfahren *n.*, Therapie *f.*
there *adv.* da, dort, dahin; hin; *~ is, ~ are,* es gibt, es sind; *~ about,* daherum; *~after,* danach; *~by,* damit, dadurch; *~fore;* daher, folglich, also; *~from,* davon, daraus; *~in,* darin; *~of,* davon; *~on,* darauf, daran; *~to,* dazu; *~under,* darunter; *~upon,* darauf, hierauf; deswegen; *~with,* damit; *~you are,* da hast du es!
thermal *a.* Wärme..., Thermal...
thermodynamics *s.* Thermodynamik *f.*
thermometer *s.* Thermometer *n.* or *m.*
thermos-flask *s.* Thermosflasche *f.*
these *pn.pl.* diese.
thesis *s.* These *f.;* Dissertation *f.;* Doktorarbeit *f.*
they *pn.pl.* sie, diejenigen; man; es.
thick *a. & adv.*, **~ly** *adv.* dick, dicht; trübe, häufig; unklar; vertraut; **~** *s.* dicke Ende *n.;* Gewühl *n.*
thicken *v.t.* verdicken, verdichten; vermehren; **~** *v.i.* dick, trübe werden; sich verstärken.
thicket *s.* Dickicht *n.*
thickheaded *a.* strohdumm.
thickness *s.* Dicke, Dichtheit *f.;* Lage, Schicht *f.*
thick-set *a.* untersetzt, gedrungen.
thief *s.* Dieb *m.;* Räuber (am Licht) *m.*
thieve *v.i.* stehlen.
thievery *s.* Dieberei *f.*
thievish *a.*, **~ly** *adv.* diebisch.
thigh *s.* Schenkel *m.;* Lende *f.*
thimble *s.* Fingerhut *m.*
thin *a.*, **~ly** *adv.* dünn; mager, schwach; spärlich; **~ paper,** Dünndruckpapier *n.;* **~** *v.t.* verdünnen; lichten.
thine *pn.* dein; der, die, das deinige.
thing *s.* Ding *n.*, Sache *f.;* **~s** *pl.* Sachen *f.pl.*
think *v.t. & i.* r. denken, nachdenken; meinen, *to ~ over,* überlegen.
thinker *s.* Denker(in) *m.(f.)*
thinking *s.* Denken *n.*, Meinung *f.*
think tank *s.* (*fam.*) Denkfabrik *f.*
thinner *s.* Verdünnungsmittel *n.*
thirdly *adv.* drittens.
third party *s.* (*jur.*) dritte Person *f.;* **~ insurance** *s.* Haftpflichtversicherung *f.*
thirst *s.* Durst *m.;* Begierde *f.;* **~** *v.i.* dursten.
thirsty *a.*, **~ily** *adv.* durstig.
thirteen *a.* dreizehn.
thirteenth *s.* dreizehnt.
thirtieth *a.* dreißigst.
thirty *a.* dreißig.
this *pn.* dieser, diese, dies(es); **~ way!,** hierher!
thistle *s.* Distel *f.*
thither *adv.* dorthin, dahin.
thong *s.* Riemen *m.;* Peitschenschnur *f.*
thorax *s.* Brustkasten *m.*
thorn *s.* Dorn *m.*
thorny *a.* dornig; heikel.

thorough *a.* gänzlich; gründlich; **~ly** *adv.* durch und durch.
thoroughbred *s.* Vollblut *n.;* ~ *a.* vollblütig (Pferd).
thoroughfare *s.* Durchgang *m.;* Verkehrsstraße *f.*
thorough-going *a.* gründlich.
thoroughness *s.* Gründlichkeit *f.*
those *pn.pl.* diejenigen, jene.
thou *pn.* du.
though *c.* obgleich, obschon, obwohl, doch; wenn auch; *as* ~, als wenn.
thought *s.* Gedanke *m.;* Meinung *f.;* Idee *f.;* Denken *n.*
thoughtful *a.*, **~ly** *adv.* gedankenvoll; nachdenklich; achtsam, rücksichtsvoll.
thoughtless *a.*, **~ly** *adv.* gedankenlos; nachlässig.
thought-provoking *a.* anregend.
thousand *a.* tausend; ~ *s.* Tausend *n.*
thousandfold *a.* & *adv.* tausendfach.
thrash *v.t.* dreschen; prügeln; ~ **out,** eingehend erörtern.
thrashing *s.* (*fig.*) Prügel *m.*
thread *s.* Faden, Zwirn *m.;* Schraubengang *m.*, Gewinde *n.;* (Reifen) Profil *n.;* ~ *v.t.* einfädeln.
threadbare *a.* abgenutzt; abgedroschen; verschlissen.
threat *s.* Drohung *f.*
threaten *v.t.* drohen; *~ing letter,* Drohbrief *m.*
three *a.* drei.
three-dimensional *a.* dreidimensional.
threefold *a.* dreifach.
threescore *a.* sechzig
thresh *v.t.* dreschen.
threshold *s.* (Tür)Schwelle *f.*
thrice *adv.* dreimal.
thrift *s.* Sparsamkeit *f.*
thriftshop *s.* Secondhandladen *m.*
thrifty *a.* sparsam, wirtschaftlich.
thrill *v.t.* faszinieren; begeistern; ~ *v.i.* beben; schauern; ~ *s.* Schauer *m.;* Erregung *f.*
thriller *s.* Sensationsdrama *n.;* Schmöker *m.*
thrilling *a.* spannend; packend.
thrive *v.i.st.* wachsen; gedeihen.
thriving *a.*, **~ly** *adv.* blühend.
throat *s.* Schlund *m.;* Kehle *f.*, Hals *m.; to clear one's* ~, sich räuspern.
throaty *a.* kehlig.
throb *v.i.* pochen, klopfen; ~ *s.* Klopfen, Schlagen *n.*
throes *s.pl.* Qualen *f.pl.*
thrombosis *s.* Thrombose *f.*
throne *s.* Thron *m.*
throng *s.* Gedränge *n.*, Schar *f.;* ~ *v.i.* sich drängen.
throttle *s.* Drossel... ~ *v.t.* erdrosseln; (*mech.*) abdrosseln.
throttle valve *s.* Drosselventil *n.*
through *pr.* & *adv.* durch, mittels; ~ **carriage,** Kurswagen *m.* (*rail.*); ~ **train** *s.* durchgehender Zug *m.;* ~ **traffic** *s.* Durchgangsverkehr *m.; wet* ~, durchnaßt.
throughout *pr.* & *adv.* ganz durch; durchaus, überall.
throughway *s.* Schnellstraße *f.*
throw *v.t.* & *i.st.* (hin-, um-) werfen; *to* ~ *off,* von sich werfen, entsagen; *to* ~ *open,* weit öffnen; *to* ~ *out,* verwerfen; *to* ~ *over,* aufgeben; *to* ~ *up,* in die Höhe werfen; aufgeben; ~ *v.i.* sich übergeben, sich erbrechen; ~ *s.* Schlag *m.;* Wurf *m.*
thrush *s.* Drossel *f.*
thrust *v.t.* & *i.* stossen; schleudern; drücken, pressen; drängen; *to* ~ *upon,* aufdrängen; ~ *s.* Stoß, Stich, Angriff *m.*
thud *s.* dröhnender, dumpfer Schlag *m.*
thug *s.* Schläger *m.*
thumb *s.* Daumen *m.;* ~ *v.t.* durchblättern; per Anhalter fahren; *under a person's* ~, unter jemandes Gewalt.
thumbscrew *s.* Daumenschraube *f.*
thumbtack *s.* Reißnagel *m.*
thump *s.* Schlag, Stoß *m.;* ~ *v.t.* schlagen, stoßen, puffen.
thumping *a.* (*fam.*) sehr groß, kolossal.
thunder *s.* Donner *m.;* ~ *v.t.* & *i.* donnern.
thunderbolt *s.* Donnerkeil, Blitz *m.*
thunderclap *s.* Donnerschlag *m.*
thundercloud *s.* Gewitterwolke *f.*
thunderous *a.* donnernd.
thunderstorm *s.* Gewitter *n.*
thunder-struck *a.* wie vom Donner entsetzt.
Thur. *Thursday,* Donnerstag, Do.
Thursday *s.* Donnerstag *m.*
thus *adv.* so, also, in solcher Weise.
thwart *v.t.* durchkreuzen; vereiteln.
thy *pn.* dein, deine.
thyme *s.* Thymian *m.*
thyroid gland *s.* Schilddrüse *f.*
thyself *pn.* du selbst, selbst; dich, dir.
tiara *s.* Tiara *f.*
Tibet *s.* Tibet *n.*
Tibetan *a.* tibetisch; ~ *s.* Tibeter(in) *m.(f.)*
tibia *s.* Schienbein *n.*
tic *s.* nervöses Zucken *n.;* Tick *m.*
tick *s.* Zecke *f.;* Ticken *n.; on* ~, auf Pump; ~ *v.i.* ticken; ~ **off,** abhaken, markieren.
ticket *s.* Zettel *m.;* Billett *n.*, Fahrkarte *f.;* Los *n.;* Pfandschein *m.;* Wahlliste *f. n.; to take a* ~, ein Billett lösen; ~ *v.t.* einen Zettel anheften.
ticket-office *s.* Fahrkartenausgabe *f.*
tickle *v.t.* kitzeln.
ticklish *a.* kitzlig; heikel; verfänglich.
tidal *a.* Gezeiten..., Flut...; **~wave** *s.* Flutwelle *f.*
tidbit *s.* Leckerbissen *m.*
tide *s.* Gezeiten *f.pl.*, Ebbe und Flut *f.;* Flut (*fig.*) *f.; the* ~ *turns,* das Blatt wendet sich; *the turning of the* ~, Umschwung *m.;* ~ **over,** *v.t.* hinwegkommen über, überbrücken.
tidiness *s.* Ordentlichkeit *f.*
tidings *s.pl.* (*lit.*) Kunde.
tidy *a.*, **~ily** *adv.* ordentlich, niedlich, nett; ~ *v.t.* sauber machen, ordnen.
tie *v.t.* (an)binden, knüpfen; verpflichten; (*mus.*) (ver)binden; ~ **up,** zubinden; ~ **down** (*mil.*) (Kräfte) binden; ~ *s.* Knoten *m.;* Krawatte, Halsbinde *f.;* Schleife *f.;* (*mus.*) Bindung *f.;* (*Sport*) Gleichstand *m.*
tiepin *s.* Schlipsnadel, Krawattennadel *f.*
tier *s.* Reihe, Linie *f.;* Rang *m.*
tiff *s.* Zank *m.*
tiger *s.* Tiger *m.*
tight *a.*, **~ly** *adv.* fest, dicht; knapp, eng, straff;

genau; betrunken; ~ **corner,** Klemme *f.;* ~ **fitting,** eng anliegend; ~ **rope,** Drahtseil *n.;* ~ **ropewalker,** *s.* Seiltänzer(in) *m.(f.)*
tighten *v.t.* festziehen, schnüren; enger machen.
tights *s.pl.* Trikothose *pl.;* Trikot *n.*
tigress *s.* Tigerin *f.*
tile *s.* Ziegel *m.;* Kachel *f.;* Fliese *f.;* ~ *v.t.* mit Ziegeln decken; kacheln.
till *pr.* & *c.* bis; ~ *v.t.* pflügen, ackern; ~ *s.* Ladenkasse *f.*
tillage *s.* Ackern *n.;* Ackerbau *m.*
tiller *s.* Pinne *f.* Ruder *n.*
tilt *s.* Turnier *n.;* Neigung; ~ *v.t.* stoßen, überschlagen; überdecken; ~ *v.i.* turnieren; kippen, umschlagen, schwanken.
timber *s.* Bauholz *n.;* Holz *n.;* Balken *m.;* ~ **line** *s.* Baumgrenze *f.*
timberyard *s.* Holzlager *n.*
timbre *s.* Klangfarbe *f.;* Timbre *n.*
time *s.* Zeit *f.;* Zeitmaß *n.;* Mal, *n.;* Tempo *n.*, Takt *m.;* *at a* ~, zugleich; *at the same* ~, zugleich, gleichzeitig; *in* ~, rechtzeitig; mit der Zeit; *in no* ~, im Handumdrehen; *behind* ~, verspätet; *what is the* ~?, wieviel Uhr ist es? *to tell the* ~, sagen, wieviel Uhr es ist; *I am having a good* ~, es geht mir gut; ich amüsiere mich; *I am having a bad* ~, es geht mir schlecht; *high* ~, hohe, höchste Zeit; *to beat* ~, den Takt schlagen; *full-*~ *job,* volle Stelle *f.* *half-*~ *job,* halbe Stelle; *f.* ~ *v.t.* abmessen; Zeit festsetzen für.
time bomb *s.* Zeitbombe *f.*
time-consuming *a.* zeitraubend.
time fuse *s.* Zeitzünder *m.*
timekeeper *s.* Uhr *f.;* Kontrolleur *m.*
time limit *s.* Frist *f.*
timely *a.* & *adv.* (recht)zeitig.
time-signal *s.* Zeitzeichen *n.*
time-table *s.* Fahrplan *m.;* Stundenplan *m.*
time-worn *a.* abgenutzt.
timid *a.* schüchtern.
timidity *s.* Schüchternheit *f.*
timpani *s. pl.* Kesselpauke *f.*
tin *s.* Zinn *n.;* Weißblech *n.;* (Blech-) Büchse (zum Einmachen) *f.;* ~ *v.t.* verzinnen; in Büchsen einmachen.
tinder *s.* Zunder *m.*
tinfoil *s.* Stanniol *n.;* Alufolie *f.*
tinge *v.t.* färben; tönen; ~ *s.* Anstrich *m.;* Färbung *f.*
tingle *v.i.* kribbeln; prickeln.
tin hat *s.* (*fam.*) Stahlhelm *m.*
tinker *s.* Kesselflicker *m.;* ~ *v.t.* flicken; pfuschen.
tinkle *v.t.* klingen.
tin-opener *s.* Büchsenöffner *m.*
tinplate *s.* Weißblech *n.*
tinsel *s.* Lametta *n.*
tint *s.* Farbe *f.;* (Farb-) Ton *m.*, Tönung *f.;* ~ *v.t.* färben; abtönen.
tiny *a.* winzig.
tip *s.* Spitze *f.;* leichte Berührung *f.;* Wink *m.;* Trinkgeld *n.;* ~ *v.t.* bespitzen; antupfen; kippen; Trinkgeld geben.
tipple *s.* alkoholisches Getränk *n.;* ~ *v.i.* zechen.
tipsy *a.* berauscht, benebelt.
tiptoe *s.* Zehenspitze *f.;* ~ *v.i.* auf den Zehenspitzen gehen.
tiptop *a.* ausgezeichnet.
tirade *s.* Wortschwall *m.;* Scheltrede *f.*
tire *s.* Reifen *m.;* ~**gauge** *s.* Reifendruckprüfer *m.;* ~ **pressure** *s.* Reifendruck *m.;* ~ *v.t.* & *i.* ermüden; müde werden.
tired *a.* müde; überdrüssig.
tiredness *s.* Müdigkeit *f.*
tireless *a.* unermüdlich.
tiresome *a.*, -ly *adv.* ermüdend, langweilig.
tiring *a.* ermüdend; anstrengend.
tissue *s.* Gewebe *n.;* Papiertuch *n.;* Papiertaschentuch *n.*
tissue paper *s.* Seidenpapier *n.*
tit *s.* (*fam.*) Brust *f.;* Brustwarze *f.;* Meise *f.;* ~ **for tat,** wie du mir, so ich dir.
titanic *a.* titanisch.
tithe *s.* Zehnte *m.;* ~ *v.t.* zehnten.
title *s.* Titel *m.;* Name *m.;* Anspruch *m.*, Recht *n.;* ~ *v.t.* benennen.
titled *a.* adelig; betitelt.
title deed *s.* Eigentumsurkunde *f.*
title page *s.* Titelblatt *n.*
titmouse *s.* Meise *f.*
titter *v.i.* kichern; ~ *s.* Kichern *n.*
tittle *s.* Tüttelchen *n.*
tittle-tattle *s.* Geschwätz *n.*
titular *a.* Titular...
TM *trademark,* Warenzeichen, Wz.
to *pr.* zu, nach, an, auf, mit, gegen, für, um, in Ansehung, bis, vor; ~ *adv.* zu; ~ **and fro,** hin und her.
T.O. *Turn over,* umschlagen.
toad *s.* Kröte *f.*
toadstool *s.* Pilz *m.;* Giftpilz *m.*
toady *s.* Schmeichler(in) *m.(f.);* Kriecher(in) *m.(f.);* ~ *v.i.* (vor jm.) kriechen.
toast *v.t.* rösten; toasten; trinken auf; ~ *s.* geröstete Brotschnitte *f.*, Toast *m.;* Trinkspruch *m.*
toaster *s.* Toaster *m.*
tobacco *s.* Tabak *m.;* ~**pouch** Tabaksbeutel *m.*
tobacconist *s.* Tabakhändler *m.*
toboggan *s.* Rodelschlitten *m.*
today *adv.* heute.
toddle *v.i.* watscheln; herumschlendern.
toddler *s.* kleinkind *n.*
to-do *s.* Aufheben *n.*, Lärm *m.*
toe *s.* Zehe *f.;* Vorderhuf *m.*
together *adv.* zusammen; ~ **with,** samt.
togetherness *s.* Zusammengehörigkeit *f.*
toil *s.* schwere Arbeit, Mühseligkeit *f.;* ~ *v.i.* sich abarbeiten.
toilet *s.* Toilette *f.;* Putztisch *m.;* ~**bag** *s.* Kulturbeutel *m.* ~ **paper** *s.* Toilettenpapier *n.;* ~ **requisites** *pl.* Toilettenartikel *pl.;* ~ **set,** Toilettengarnitur *f.*
toilsome *a.* mühselig, mühsam.
token *s.* Zeichen *n.;* Gutschein *m.;* Marke *f.*
tolerable *a.*, ~**bly** *adv.* leidlich; annehmbar.
tolerance *s.* Duldung *f.;* Toleranz *f.* (*mech.*) zulässige Abweichung *f.*
tolerant *a.* duldsam; tolerant.
tolerate *v.t.* ertragen, dulden.
toleration *s.* Duldung, Nachsicht *f.*
toll *s.* Zoll *m.;* Läuten *n.;* ~ *v.t.* läuten.
toll bridge *s.* gebührenpflichtige Brücke *f.*
toll call *s.* gebührenpflichtiges Gespräch *n.*

tomato *s.* Tomate *f.*
tomb *s.* Grab, Grabmal *n.; ~* **stone** *s.* Grabstein *m.*
tomboy *s.* Wildfang (Mädchen) *m.*
tomcat *s.* Kater *m.*
tome *s.* Band *m.*, dickes Buch *n.*
tomfoolery *s.* Narretei *f.*
tommy gun *s.* Maschinenpistole *f.*
tomorrow *adv.* morgen.
tomtit *s.* Meise *f.*
ton *s.* Tonne (Gewicht: 1016 kg.; Schiffsmaß: 40 Kubikfuß) *f.*
tone *s.* Ton, Klang, Laut *m.; ~ v.t.* abtönen.
tongs *pl.* Zange *f.*
tongue *s.* Zunge *f.; ~* **in cheek,** scherzhaft, ~ **twister** *s.* Zungenbrecher *m.*
tonic *a.* tonisch; stärkend; ~ *s.* Stärkungsmittel *n.;* Tonikum *n.*
tonight *adv.* heute abend, heute nacht.
tonnage *s.* Tonnengehalt *m.*, Raumgehalt (Schiff) *m.*
tonsil *s.* Halsdrüse *f.*, Mandel *f.*
tonsillitis *s.* Mandelentzündung *f.*
tonsure *s.* Tonsur *f.*
too *adv.* zu, allzu; gleichfalls, auch.
tool *s.* Werkzeug, Gerät *n.*
toot *v.t. & i.* blasen, tuten.
tooth *s.* Zahn *m.*
toothache *s.* Zahnweh *n.*
toothbrush *s.* Zahnbürste *f.*
tooth filling *s.* Zahnfüllung *f.*
toothless *a.* zahnlos.
toothpaste *s.* Zahnpaste *f.*
toothpick *s.* Zahnstocher *m.*
top *s.* Gipfel, Wipfel *m.;* Spitze *f.;* Kreisel *m.;* Haupt *n.;* Obere *n.;* höchster Rang *m.; ~ a.* oberst, Haupt...; *from ~ to toe,* vom Scheitel bis zur Sohle; ~ **coat** *s.* (*Am.*) Überzieher *m.;* ~ **floor,** oberster Stockwerk *n.;* ~ **righthand corner,** obere rechte Ecke; ~ **secret** *a.* ganz geheim, *s.* (*mil.*) geheime Kommandosache; ~ **speed,** Höchstgeschwindigkeit *f.; ~ v.i.* sich erheben, hervorstechen; ~ *v.t.* übertreffen.
topaz *s.* Topas *m.*
topgallant *s.* Bramsegel *n.*
top-hat *s.* Zylinderhut *m.*
top-heavy *a.* oberlastig.
topic *s.* Gegenstand *m.*, Thema *n.*
topical *a.*, **~ly** *adv.* aktuell; örtlich, lokal.
topicality *s.* Aktualität *f.*
topless *a.* oben ohne, ohne Oberteil.
topmast *s.* Topmast *m.*
topmost *a.* oberst, höchst.
top-notch *a.* hervorragend; phantastisch.
topography *s.* Ortsbeschreibung *f.*
topping *s.* Glasur *f.;* Guß *m.*
topple *v.i.* vorwärts fallen, hinstürzen; ~ *v.t.* fällen, umstürzen.
topsail *s.* Marssegel *n.*
topsy-turvy *adv.* das unterste zu oberst.
torch *s.* Fackel *f.;* **~light procession,** Fackelzug *m.*
torment *v.t.* peinigen, martern; quälen; ~ *s.* Qual, Marter *f.*
tormentor *s.* Peiniger *m.*
tornado *s.* Wirbelsturm *m.*
torpedo *s.* Torpedo *m.;* ~ **boat** *s.* Torpedoboot *n.;* **~(boat) destroyer** *s.* Torpedo(boot)zerstörer *m.;* ~ **tube** *s.* Lanzierrohr *n.*
torpid *a.* starr; träge.
torpor *s.* Erstarrung *f.;* Trägheit *f.*
torrent *s.* Gießbach *m.;* (*fig.*) Strom *m.*
torrential *a.* strömend; reißend.
torrid *a.* (*also fig.*) brennend heiß, sengend.
torsion *s.* Drehung, Windung *f.*
tortoise *s.* Schildkröte *f.*
tortoise-shell *s.* Schildpatt *n.*
tortuous *a.* gewunden; verschlungen; kompliziert.
torture *s.* Folter *f.;* Marter *f.; ~ v.t.* foltern, martern.
torture chamber *s.* Folterkammer *f.*
Tory *s.* Tory, englischer Konservative *m.*
toss *v.t.* schleudern; losen; hochwerfen. ~ *s.* Wurf *m.;* Aufwerfen *n.* (einer Münze), Losen *n.*
toss-up *s.* Hochwerfen einer Münze; ungewisse Sache.
tot *s.* kleines Kind *n.;* Schlückchen, Gläschen *n.*
total *a.*, **~ly** *adv.* ganz, gänzlich; ~ *s.* Gesamtsumme *f.*, Gesamtbetrag *m.; ~ v.i.* sich belaufen auf; ~ **eclipse,** *s.* totale Finsternis *f.* ~ **loss,** Totalausfall *m.;* ~ **war,** totaler Krieg *m.*
totalitarian *a.* totalitär.
totality *s.* Ganze *n.*, Vollständigkeit *f.*
tote *v.t.* schleppen.
totem pole *s.* Totempfahl *m.*
totter *v.i.* wanken, wackeln.
touch *v.t.* (be)fühlen; betreffen; anstoßen, rühren, berühren; *to ~ up,* auffrischen, restaurieren; ~ *v.i.* sich berühren; sich beziehen auf; ~ **wood!** unberufen!; ~ *s.* Berührung *f.;* Gefühl *n.;* Anflug, Anstrich *m.;* (*mus.*) Anschlag *m.; to get in ~ with,* sich in Verbindung setzen mit.
touch-and-go, unsicher, gewagt.
touched *a.* gerührt.
touching *a.* rührend, treffend; ~ *pr.* betreffend, in betreff.
touchline *s.* Seitenlinie *f.*
touchstone *s.* Prüfstein *m.*
touch-type *v.i.* blindschreiben.
touchy *a.* empfindlich, reizbar.
tough *a.*, **~ly** *adv.* zäh; hart; fest; schwer.
toughen *v.t.* zäh machen; abhärten; ~ *v.i.* zäh werden.
toughness *s.* Festigkeit *f.;* Zähigkeit *f.*
tour *s.* (Rund-)Reise *f.;* Ausflug *m.; ~ v.t. & i.* (be)reisen.
tourism *s.* Tourismus *m.*
tourist *s.* Tourist(in) *m.(f.);* ~ **agent,** Reiseagent *m.;* ~ **traffic,** Fremdenverkehr *m.*
tournament *s.* Turnier *n.*
tour operator *s.* Reiseveranstalter(in) *m.(f.)*
tousled *a.* zerzaust.
tout *v.i.* Kunden locken; ~ *s.* Schlepper(in) *m.(f.);* Kundenwerber(in) *m.(f.)*
tow *s.* Werg *n.;* Schlepptau *n.; ~ v.t.* schleppen; ~ **away** *v.i.* abschleppen.
toward, towards *pr.* gegen, zu, bis an, entgegen; auf... zu.
towel *s.* Handtuch *n.;* ~ **horse,** Handtuchständer *m.; face ~,* Gesichtshandtuch *n.; roller ~,* Rollhandtuch *n.; to ~ oneself, v.t.* sich mit dem Handtuch abreiben.

tower *s.* Turm *m.;* Zwinger *m.;* Festung *f.;* ~ *v.i.* hoch ragen, sich erheben.
towering *s.* hoch aufragend.
towing-boat *s.* Schleppboot *n.*
town *s.* Ort *m.;* (Klein)Stadt *f.*
townhall *s.* Rathaus *n.*
town planning *s.* Städtebau *m.*
township *s.* Stadt-, Ortsgemeinde *f.*
townsman *s.* Städter, Bürger *m.*
tow path *s.* Leinpfad *m.*
towrope *s.* Abschleppseil *n.*
toxic *a.* giftig; toxisch.
toy *s.* Spielzeug *n.;* ~ *v.i.* spielen (Essen; Gedanken).
trace *s.* Spur, Fußtapfe *f.;* Strang *m.*, Zugseil *n.;* ~ *v.t.* nachspüren; zeichnen, entwerfen; abstecken; durchpausen.
traceable *a.* auffindbar.
trace element *s.* Spurenelement *n.*
tracer bullet *s.* Leuchtspurgeschoß *n.*
trachea *s.* Luftröhre *f.*
tracing *s.* Durchpausen *n.;* Pauszeichnung *n.;* Aufriß *m.;* ~ **paper** *s.* Pauspapier *n.*
track *s.* Spur *f.;* Fährte *f.;* Geleise *f.;* Pfad *f.;* (Panzer)Kette *f.;* Bahn *f.* (Rennen); **~ed vehicles,** *pl.* Raupenfahrzeuge *pl.;* *to be on the wrong* ~, auf der falschen Fährte sein; ~ *v.t.* der Spur folgen; *to* ~ *down,* aufspüren.
track events *s.pl.* Laufdisziplinen (Sport).
trackless *a.* spurlos, pfadlos.
track record *s.* Bahnrekord *m.*
track shoe *s.* Rennschuh *m.*
tract *s.* Gebiet *n.;* Trakt *m.;* Traktat *m.*, Flugschrift *f.*
traction *s.* Ziehen *n.;* Zug *m.;* ~ **engine,** Zugmaschine *f.*
tractor *s.* Traktor *m.*
trade *s.* Handel *m.;* Gewerbe, Geschäft *n.;* ~ *v.i.* Handel treiben; austauschen; *foreign* ~, Außenhandel *m.;* ~ **name,** Firmenname *m.;* ~ **price,** Engrospreis *m.;* ~ **school,** Gewerbeschule *f.*
trademark *s.* Warenzeichen *n.*
trader *s.* Händler(in) *m.(f.)*
tradesman *s.* Einzelhändler(in) *m.(f.);* **~'s entrance,** Lieferanteneingang *m.*
trade union *s.* Gewerkschaft *f.*
trade unionist *s.* Gewerkschaftler(in) *m.(f.)*
tradewind *s.* Passatwind *m.*
trading *s.* Handel *m.*
trading estate *s.* Gewerbegebiet *n.*
tradition *s.* Tradition *f.;* Überlieferung *f.;* Brauch *m.*
traditional *a.* **~ly** *adv.* traditionell; überliefert; herkömmlich.
traffic *s.* Handel *m.;* Verkehr *m.;* *goods* ~, Güterverkehr *m.;* *passenger* ~, Personenverkehr *m.;* **~circle,** Kreisverkehr *m.* ~ **code,** Verkehrsregeln *pl.;* ~ **jam,** Verkehrsstockung *f.;* ~ **light,** Verkehrsampel *f.;* ~ **regulation,** Verkehrsregelung *f.;* ~ **sign,** Verkehrszeichen *n.;* ~ *v.i.* Handel treiben.
tragedy *s.* Trauerspiel *n.*, Tragödie *f.*
tragic *a.*, **~ally** *adv.* tragisch.
tragicomedy *s.* Tragikomödie *f.*
trail *s.* Spur, Fährte *f.;* Pfad *m.;* ~ *v.t.* nachspüren; nachschleppen; ~ *v.i.* sich in die Länge ziehen.
trailer *s.* (*mot.*) Anhängewagen *m.*
train *s.* Schweif *m.;* Schleppe *f.;* Reihe *f.;* Gefolge *n.;* (*rail.*) Zug *m.;* ~ *v.t.* ziehen, schleppen; abrichten; ausbilden; trainieren; (Geschütz) richten; ~ *v.i.* sich trainieren.
train driver *s.* Lokomotivführer(in) *m.(f.)*
trained *a.* ausgebildet; geschult; trainiert.
trainee *s.* Auszubildende *m./f.;* Lehrling *m.*
trainer *s.* Trainer(in) *m.(f.);* Behandler(in) *m.(f.)*
train fare *s.* Fahrpreis *m.*
training *s.* Ausbildung *s.;* Training *n.;* *to be in* ~, trainieren; in Formsein; *to be under* ~, ausgebildet werden; **~center** *s.* Ausbildungsstelle *f.;* **~college** *s.* Lehrerseminar *n.;* **~ship** *s.* Schulschiff *n.*
train oil *s.* Fischtran *m.*
train service *s.* Zugverbindung *f.*
train station *s.* Bahnhof *m.*
trait *s.* Zug, *m.;* Eigenschaft *f.*
traitor *s.* Verräter(in) *m.(f.)*
traitorous *a.*, **~ly** *adv.* verräterisch.
trajectory *s.* Flugbahn *f.*
tram *s.* Strassenbahn *f.*
tramp *s.* Landstreicher(in) *m.(f.);* ~ *v.i. & t.* umherstreifen; trampeln.
trample *v.i. & t.* trampeln; *to* ~ *upon,* mit Füßen treten (*fig.*).
trampoline *s.* Trampolin *n.*
tramway *s.* Straßenbahn *f.*
trance *s.* Trancezustand *m.*
tranquil *a.* ruhig, gelassen.
tranquility *s.* Ruhe *f.*
tranquilize *v.t.* beruhigen; (*med.*) betäuben.
transact *v.t.* abmachen; verrichten (Geschäft).
transaction *s.* Geschäft *n.;* Verhandlung *f.*
transalpine *a.* jenseits der Alpen.
transatlantic *a.* transatlantisch.
transcend *v.t.* übersteigen; übertreffen; transzendieren.
transcendental *a.* transzendental.
transcontinental *a.* transkontinental.
transcribe *v.t.* abschreiben; übertragen.
transcript *s.* Abschrift *f.;* Umschrift *f.;* (*jur.*) Protokoll *n.*
transept *s.* (Kirche) Kreuzflügel *m.;* Querschiff *n.*
transfer *v.t.* übertragen; versetzen, verlegen; (Geld) überweisen; ~ *s.* Übertragung *f.;* Überweisung *f.;* Verlegung, Versetzung *f.;* *disciplinary* ~, Strafversetzung *f.;* **~paper** *s.* Umdruckpapier *n.*
transferable *a.* übertragbar.
transference *s.* Übertragung *f.*
transfiguration *s.* Verklärung *f.*
transfigure *v.i.* verwandeln; verklären.
transfix *v.t.* durchbohren.
transform *v.t.* umgestalten, verwandeln.
transformation *s.* Verwandlung *f.*
transformer *s.* (*elek.*) Transformator *m.;* **~station** *s.* Transformatorenhaus *n.*
transfusion *s.* Transfusion *f.;* Übertragung *f.*
transgress *v.t.* überschreiten, verletzen.
transgression *s.* Überschreitung *f.;* Vergehen *n.*
transgressor *s.* Übertreter(in) *m.(f.)*
tranship *v.t.* umladen.

transhipment *s.* Umladung *f.*, Umschlag *m.*; **~harbor,** Umschlagshafen *m.*
transient *a.*, **~ly** *adv.* vergänglich; vorübergehend.
transit *s.* Durchgang *m.*; (*mil.*) Durchmarsch *m.*; *in* ~, unterwegs, auf dem Transport; ~ **duty,** Durchgangszoll *m.*; ~ **trade,** Durchgangshandel *m.*; ~ **traffic,** Durchgangsverkehr *m.*
transition *s.* Übergang *m.*
transitional *a.* Übergangs...
transitive *a.*, **~ly** *adv.* (*gram.*) transitiv.
transitory *a.*, **~ily** *adv.* vorübergehend, vergänglich; flüchtig.
translate *v.t.* übersetzen; versetzen.
translation *s.* Übersetzung *f.*
translator *s.* Übersetzer(in) *m.(f.)*
translucent *a.* durchscheinend.
transmigration *s.* ~ **of souls,** Seelenwanderung *f.*
transmissible *a.* übertragbar; vererblich.
transmission *s.* Übertragung *f.*; Übersendung *f.*; (*phys.*) Fortpflanzung; (*mech.*) Transmission.
transmit *v.t.* übersenden, übertragen; (*phys.*) leiten; vererben.
transmitter *s.* (*tel.*, *radio*) Sender *m.*
transmutation *s.* Verwandlung *f.*, Umwandlung *f.*
transmute *v.t.* umwandeln.
transparency *s.* Durchsichtigkeit *f.*
transparent *a.*, **~ly** *adv.* durchsichtig.
transpire *v.t.* ausdünsten; ~ *v.i.* schwitzen; verlauten passieren
transplant *v.t.* verpflanzen; (*med.*) transplantieren; ~ *s.* Transplantat *n.*
transplantation *s.* Verpflanzung *f.*; (*med.*) Transplantation *f.*
transport *v.t.* befördern, transportieren; hinreißen, entzücken; ~ *s.* Versendung, Beförderung *f.*, Transportschiff *n.*; Transport *m.*; Entzückung *f.*; ~ **charges** *pl.* Speditionskosten *pl.*; ~ **plane,** Transportflugzeug *n.*; *Minister of* ~, Verkehrsminister *m.*
transportation *s.* Fortschaffung *f.*; Deportierung *f.*; Transport *m.*, Transportmittel *n.*
transpose *v.t.* umstellen.
transposition *s.* Umstellung *f.*
transubstantiation *s.* Wesensverwandlung *f.*; (*eccl.*) Transsubstantiation *f.*
transverse *a.*, **~ly** *adv.* schräg, quer.
transvestite *s.* Transvestit *m.*
trap *s.* Falle *f.*; Klappe *f.*; ~ *v.t.* ertappen; **~ped** *p.* eingeklemmt.
trap-door *s.* Falltür *f.*
trapeze *s.* Trapez *n.*; ~ **artist** *s.* Trapezkünstler(in) *m.(f.)*
trapper *s.* Fallensteller *m.*
trappings *s.pl.* Schmuck *m.*
trash *s.* Plunder, Abfall *m.*; (*fig.*) Blech *n.*, Unsinn *m.*; Schund *m.* Kitsch *m.*
trashcan *s.* Mülltonne *f.*
trashy *a.* Schund...; minderwertig.
trauma *s.* Trauma *n.*; Shock *m.*
travel *v.i.* reisen; sich bewegen; ~ *v.t.* bereisen; ~ *s.* Reise *f.*; *away on* ~, verreist; ~ **agency,** Reiseagentur *f.*; ~ **goods** *pl.* Reiseartikel *pl.*; ~ **order** (*mil.*) Fahrtbefehl *m.*, Fahrtausweis *m.*
traveler *s.* Reisende, Geschäftsreisende *m.*; **~s' check,** Reisescheck *m.*
traveling bag Reisetasche *f.*
travelog *s.* Reisebericht *m.*
travel sickness *s.* Reisekrankheit *f.*
traverse *s.* Querholz *n.*; (*mech.*) Querstück *n.*, Querträger *m.*, Traverse *f.*; (*fig.*) Querstrich *m.*; Quergang *m.*; ~ *v.t.* durchkreuzen; durchwandern; durchforschen; (durch)queren; ~ *a.* & *adv.* quer.
travesty *s.* Travestie *f.*; ~ *v.t.* travestieren.
trawl *v.t.* mit einem Schleppnetz fischen.
trawler *s.* Fischtrawler *m.*
tray *s.* Tablett *n.*; Ablagekorb *m.*; *ash*~, Aschenbecher *m.*
treacherous *a.*, **~ly** *adv.* verräterisch, heimtückisch.
treachery *s.* Heimtücke *f.*, Verrat *m.*
treacle *s.* Sirup *m.*
tread *v.t.* & i.st. (be)treten; ~ *s.* Schritt, Tritt *m.*; Lauffläche, (Reifen)Profil *n.*
treadle *s.* Trittbrett *n.*
treadmill *s.* Tretmühle *f.*
treason *s.* Verrat *m.*; *high* ~, *capital* ~, Hochverrat *m.*
treasonable *a.*, **~bly** *adv.* verräterisch.
treasure *s.* Schatz *m.*; ~ *v.t.* aufhäufen; wertschätzen.
treasurer *s.* Schatzmeister(in) *m.(f.)*; Leiter(in) der Finanzabteilung.
treasury *s.* Schatzkammer *f.*; Schatzamt *n.*; ~ **bill** *s.* Schatzwechsel *m.*; ~ **bond,** ~ **certificate,** Schatzanweisung *f.*
treat *v.t.* & *i.* handeln, behandeln; unterhandeln; freihalten; ~ *s.* Vergnügen *n.*; Leckerbissen *m.*; Schmaus *m.*; Genuss *m.*
treatise *s.* Abhandlung *f.*
treatment *s.* Behandlung *f.*
treaty *s.* Vertrag *m.*
treble *a.* dreifach; ~ *s.* Sopranstimme *f.*; Diskant *m.*; ~ *v.t.* verdreifachen; ~ **clef** *s.* Violinschlüssel *m.*
tree *s.* Baum *m.*
tree: **~-lined** *a.* von Bäumen gesäumt; **~top** *s.* Baumwipfel *m.*; **~trunk** *s.* Baumstamm *m.*
trefoil *s.* Klee *m.*
trellis *s.* Gitter *n.*; Spalier *n.*
tremble *v.i.* zittern; ~ *s.* Zittern *n.*
trembling *a.* zitternd; ~ *s.* Zittern *n.*
tremendous *a.*, **~ly** *adv.* schrecklich, furchtbar; ungeheuer groß.
tremor *s.* Zittern, Beben *n.*
tremulous *a.* zitternd; flackernd.
trench *s.* (Schützen-) Graben *m.*; ~ **coat,** Wettermantel *m.*
trenchant *a.* schneidend, scharf; deutlich.
trend *v.i.* verlaufen; sich entwickeln; ~ *s.* Richtung *f.*; Trend *m.*; Tendenz *f.*
trendy *a.* modisch.
trepidation *s.* Beklommenheit *f.*
trespass *v.i.* übertreten, sich vergehen; unbefugt betreten; ~ *s.* Übertretung *f.*; Eingriff *m.*; unbefugtes Betreten *n.*
tress *s.* Haarlocke *f.*
trestle *s.* Bockgestell *n.*
trial *s.* Prozeß *m.*, Gerichtsverhandlung *f.*; Versuch *m.*, Probe *f.*, Prüfung *f.*; ~ **by jury,** Schwurgerichtsverhandlung *f.*; ~ **in absentia,** Verhandlung in Abwesenheit des Angeklagten; *to be on* ~, *to stand* ~ *for,* unter Anklage stehen; *to*

bring to ~, vor Gericht stellen; ~ **run,** Probefahrt (Auto) *f.*
triangle *s.* Dreieck *n.;* Triangel *f.*
triangular *a.*, **~ly** *adv.* dreieckig.
tribal *a.* Stammes...
tribe *s.* Stamm *m.;* Sippe *f.*
tribesman *s.* Stammesangehörige *m.*
tribeswoman *s.* Stammesangehörige *f.*
tribulation *s.* Trübsal *f.*
tribunal *s.* Tribunal *n.*, Gerichtshof *m.*
tributary *s.* Nebenfluß *m.*
tribute *s.* Tribut *m.*
trice *s.* Augenblick *m.*, Nu *m.* or *n.*
trick *s.* Trick *m.;* Kniff *m.;* Streich, Betrug *m.;* Eigentümlichkeit *f.;* Kartenstich *m.; to play a person a* ~, einem einen Streich spielen; ~ *v.t.* betrügen, anführen.
trickery *s.* Betrügerei, List *f.*
trickle *v.i.* tröpfeln; ~ *s.* Getröpfel *n.*
trickster *s.* Betrüger(in) *m.(f.)*
tricky *a.* verzwickt; heikel.
tricolor *s.* Trikolore *f.*
tricycle *s.* Dreirad *n.*
trident *s.* Dreizack *m.*
tried *a.* erprobt.
triennial *a.*, **~ly** *adv.* dreijährlich.
trifle *s.* Kleinigkeit, Lappalie *f.;* Biskuit *(n.)* mit Kompott; ~ *v.i.* tändeln, spielen, scherzen.
trifling *a.*, **~ly** *adv.* geringfügig; unbedeutend.
trigger *s.* Drücker *m.* (am Gewehr).
trigonometry *s.* Trigonometrie *f.*
trike *s.* Dreirad *n.*
trilateral *a.* dreiseitig.
trill *s.* Triller *m.;* ~ *v.t.* trillern.
trillion *s.* (*US*) Billion *f.;* (*Brit.*) Trillion *f.*
trilogy *s.* Trilogie *f.*
trim *a.*, **~ly** *adv.* in Ordnung; geputzt; niedlich; ~ *s.* Putz, Besatz *m.;* Ausrüstung *f.;* ~ *v.t.* putzen; schneiden; stutzen; einfassen; (*nav.*) trimmen.
trimming *s.* Besatz *m.;* Verzierung *f.;* Beilagen *pl.*
Trinity *s.* Dreieinigkeit *f.*
trinket *s.* billiges Schmuckstück *n.*
trio *s.* Trio *n.;* Terzett *n.*
trip *v.i.* trippeln; stolpern; straucheln, fehlen; ~ *v.t. to* ~ *up,* ein Bein stellen, erwischen; ~ *s.* Fehltritt *m.;* Ausflug *m.;* Reise *f.*
tripartite *a.* dreiteilig, Dreimächte...; ~ **commission,** Dreierkommission *f.;* ~ **pact,** Dreierpakt *m.*
tripe *s.* Kaldaunen (Nahrung) *pl.;* Eingeweide *pl.*, Quatsch *m.*
triple *a.* dreifach; ~ *v.t.* verdreifachen.
triplet *s.* Drilling *m.*
triplicate *a.* dreifach; in dreifacher Ausführung; ~ *s.* Triplikat *n.; in* ~, in dreifacher Ausführung.
tripod *s.* Dreifuß *m.;* dreifüßiger Ständer *m.*
tripping *a.* leicht(füßig); munter; strauchelnd.
triptych *s.* Triptychon *n.*
tripwire *s.* Stolperdraht *m.*
trisyllable *s.* dreisilbiges Wort *n.*
trite *a.*, **~ly** *adv.* abgedroschen; banal.
triumph *s.* Triumph, Sieg *m.;* ~ *v.i.* triumphieren; siegen.
triumphant *a.*, **~ly** *adv.* triumphierend.
trivia *s.pl.* Bagatellen pl., Belanglosigkeiten *f.pl.*
trivial *a.*, **~ly** *adv.* alltäglich, platt; trivial.
triviality *s.* Plattheit *f.*, Trivialität *f.*
trivialize *v.t.* trivialisieren.
trolley *s.* Straßenbahn *f.;* Förderkarren *m.;* Handwagen *m.;* **~-bus,** elektrischer Omnibus *m.*
trollop *s.* Schlampe, Dirne *f.*
trombone *s.* Posaune *f.*
troop *s.* Haufen *m.*, Schar *f.;* Trupp *m.;* **~s** *pl.* Truppen *f.pl.;* ~ **carrier** *s.* Truppentransporter *m.;* ~ **ship** *s.* Truppentransportschiff *n.;* ~ **training ground,** Truppenübungsplatz *m.;* ~ *v.i.* sich scharen, in Scharen ziehen.
trope *s.* bildlicher Ausdruck, Tropus *m.*
trophy *s.* Siegeszeichen n; Trophäe *f.*
tropic *s.* Wendekreis *m.;* **~s,** Tropen *f.pl.*
tropical *a.*, **~ly** *adv.* tropisch; bildlich.
trot *v.i.* traben; ~ *s.* Trab, Trott *m.*
troth *s.* Treuegelöbnis *n.*
trotter *s.* Traber *m.;* Fuß *(m.)* eines Tieres.
trouble *v.t.* trüben, stören; beunruhigen; bemühen; quälen; ~ *v.i.* sich kümmern, sich Sorgen machen um; ~ *s.* Unruhe, Sorge *f.;* Kummer, Verdruß *m.;* Ärger *m.*
troubled *a.* besorgt; unruhig; bewegt.
trouble: **~free** *a.* problemlos; **~maker** *s.* Unruhestifter(in) *m.(f.);* **~shooter** *s.* Vermittler(in) *m.(f.)*
troublesome *a.*, **~ly** *adv.* beschwerlich.
trouble spot *s.* Unruheherd *m.;* Schwachstelle *f.*
trough *s.* Trog *m.;* Wellental *n.;* Tief *n.*
trounce *v.t.* haushoch besiegen.
troupe *s.* (Theater) Truppe *f.*
trousers *pl.* Hosen *f. pl.*
trousseau *s.* Aussteuer *f.*
trout *s.* Forelle *f.*
trowel *s.* Kelle *f.*
troy weight *s.* Gold- und Silbergewicht *n.*
truant *a.*, **~ly** *adv.* müßig, träge; ~ *s.* Schulschwänzer(in) *m.(f.);* Faulenzer(in) *m.(f.)*
truce *s.* Waffenstillstand *m.*
truck *s.* (*rail.*) Güterwagen *m.;* Lastwagen *m.*
truculent *a.* aufsässig; trotzig.
trudge *v.i.* stapfen; trotten.
true *a.* wahr; echt; treu, aufrichtig, redlich; richtig.
truffle *s.* Trüffel *f.*
truism *s.* Gemeinplatz *m.*
truly *adv.* wirklich, wahrhaftig; aufrichtig; *yours* ~, Ihr ergebener.
trump *s.* Trumpf *m.;* ~ *v.t.* trumpfen; *to* ~ *up,* erdichten.
trumpet *s.* Trompete *f.;* ~ *v.t.* ausposaunen.
trumpeter *s.* Trompeter(in) *m.(f.)*
truncate *v.t.* stutzen; kürzen.
truncheon *s.* Schlagstock *m.*
trundle *v.t. & i.* rollen, (sich) wälzen; ~ *s.* Rolle, Walze *f.*
trunk *s.* Stamm *m.;* Stumpf *m.;* Rumpf *m.;* Rüssel *m.;* Schrankkoffer *m.;* Kofferraum *m.*
truss *v.t.* fesseln; aufbinden; ~ *s.* Band, Bruchband *n.*
trust *s.* Vertrauen *n.;* Kredit *m.;* Obhut, Treuhand *f.;* anvertrautes Gut *n.;* Trust *m.; in* ~, zu treuen Händen; *on* ~, auf Treu und Glauben; *to take on* ~, auf Treu und Glauben hinnehmen; *breach of* ~, Vertrauensbruch *m.; position of* ~, Vertrauensstellung *f.;* ~ **company,** Treuhandgesellschaft *f.;* ~ *v.i. & t.* (ver)trauen, sich verlassen; anvertrauen.

trustee *s.* Treuhänder(in) *m.(f.)*; Kurator(in) *m.(f.)*
trustful *a.* vertrauensvoll.
trustworthy *a.* vertrauenswürdig.
trusty *a.* treu, zuverlässig.
truth *s.* Wahrheit *f.*; Wirklichkeit *f.*; Wahrhaftigkeit, Redlichkeit, Treue *f.*
truthful *a.* wahrhaftig.
try *v.t.* versuchen, sich bemühen; untersuchen, probieren, prüfen, verhören; (*jur.*) Prozeß verhandeln; *to ~ on,* anprobieren.
trying *a.* schwierig; mißlich.
tryout *s.* Erprobung *f.*
tsp. *teaspoon,* Teelöffel, Teel.
TU *trade union,* Gewerkschaft.
tub *s.* Faß *n.*; Zuber *m.*; Kübel *m.*; Badewanne *f.*
tuba *s.* Tuba *f.*
tubby *a.* rundlich; pummelig.
tube *s.* Rohr *n.*, Röhre *f.*; Schlauch (Fahrrad) *m.*; (*fam.*) die Röhre *f.* (TV).
tuber *s.* Knolle *f.*
tubercle *s.* Knötchen *n.*; Tuberkel *f.*
tuberculosis *s.* Tuberkulose *f.*
tubing *s.* Röhrenmaterial *n.*; Rohre *n. pl.*
tubular *a.* röhrenförmig.
tuck *s.* Falte *f.*; Biese *f.*; Umschlag (am Kleid) *m.*; ~ *v.t.* stecken einschlagen, einwickeln.
Tues. *Tuesday,* Dienstag, Di.
Tuesday *s.* Dienstag *m.*
tufa, tuff *s.* Tuffstein *m.*
tuft *s.* Büschel *m.* or *n.*; Quaste *f.*; ~ *v.t.* bequasten.
tug *v.t. & i.* ziehen, zerren; ~ *s.* Ziehen, Zerren *n.*; Schlepper *m.*; *seagoing ~,* Hochseeschlepper *m.*; ~ **of war,** Tauziehen *n.*
tuition *s.* Schulgeld *n.*; Unterricht *m.*; Erziehung *f.*
tulip *s.* Tulpe *f.*
tulle *s.* Tüll *m.*
tumble *v.i.* umfallen, stürzen; sich wälzen; ~ *v.t.* werfen, umwenden; zerknittern; ~ *s.* Fall, Sturz *m.*
tumble-down *a.* baufällig.
tumble dry *v.t.* im Automaten trocknen.
tumbler *s.* Trinkglas *n.*
tumid *a.* geschwollen.
tummy *s.* (*fam.*) Bauch *m.*; Bäuchlein *n.*
tumor *s.* Geschwulst *f.*; Tumor *m.*
tumult *s.* Getümmel *n.*; Aufruhr *m.*
tumultuous *a.*, **~ly** *adv.* lärmend, aufrührerisch.
tun *s.* Tonne *f.*; Faß *n.*
tuna *s.* Thunfisch *m.*
tune *s.* Ton *m.*; Melodie *f.*; Tonstück *n.*; Stimmung *f.*; *out of ~,* verstimmt; ~ *v.t.* stimmen; (*radio*) einstellen; *tuning dial s.* (*radio*) Einstellscheibe *f.*
tuneful *a.* wohlklingend; melodisch.
tuneless *a.* unmelodisch.
tuner *s.* (Klavier-), Stimmer(in) *m.(f.)*
tungsten *s.* Wolfram *n.*
tunic *s.* Tunika *f.*; Waffenrock *m.*
tuning fork *s.* Stimmgabel *f.*
tunnel *s.* Tunnel *m.*
turban *s.* Turban *m.*
turbid *a.*, **~ly** *adv.* trübe, dick.
turbine *s.* Kreiselrad *n.*, Turbine *f.*
turbot *s.* Steinbutt *m.*
turbulence *s.* Ungestüm *n.*; Aufruhr *m.*; Verwirrung *f.*
turbulent *a.*, **~ly** *adv.* aufrührerisch; stürmisch.
tureen *s.* Suppenschüssel *f.*; Terrine *f.*
turf *s.* Rasen *m.*; Rennbahn *f.*; Pferderennen *n.*
turgid *a.* geschwollen, gedunsen; schwülstig.
Turk *s.* Türke *m.*; Türkin *f.*
turkey *s.* Truthahn *m.*, Truthenne *f.*; Puter *m.*, Pute *f.*
Turkey *s.* Türkei *f.*
Turkish *a.* türkisch.
Turkish bath *s.* türkisches Bad, Schwitzbad *n.*
turmeric *s.* Kurkuma *f.*
turmoil *s.* Unruhe *f.*; Aufruhr *m.*
turn *v.t.* drehen, (um)wenden; drechseln; umlegen; ~ *v.i.* sich (um)drehen; sich verwandeln; werden; umschlagen, verderben; *to ~ down,* zurückweisen, ablehnen; (*Gas*) kleindrehen; *to ~ in,* abgeben; *to ~ off,* ablenken; abdrehen, ausdrehen; *to ~ on,* andrehen; *to ~ out,* ausfallen, sich erweisen; hinaustreiben; antreten; (Waren) herstellen; *to ~ over,* übertragen; (um) wenden, durchblättern; übergeben, überstellen; umsetzen (Waren); *please ~ over (PTO),* bitte wenden!; *to ~ round,* sich herumdrehen; *to ~ up,* aufschlagen; auftauchen, erscheinen; ~ *s.* Umdrehung, Schwenkung *f.*; Änderung *f.*; Wechsel *m.*; Streich *m.*; Neigung *f.*; Gestalt, Beschaffenheit *f.*; *a good ~,* eine Gefälligkeit *f.*; *it is your ~,* Sie sind an der Reihe; *by ~s,* wechselweise, abwechselnd.
turncoat *s.* Überläufer *m.*
turn-down, ~ collar *s.* (Klapp-) Umlegekragen *m.*
turner *s.* Drechsler *m.*; Eisendreher *m.*
turning *s.* Drechseln, Drehen *n.*; Wendung *f.*; Krümmung *f.*; Querstraße *f.*
turning-point *s.* Wendepunkt *m.*
turnip *s.* (Weiße) Rübe *f.*
turnout *s.* Gesamtertrag *m.*; Antreten *(n.)* zur Arbeit.
turnover *s.* Umsatz *m.*; ~ **tax,** Umsatzsteuer *f.*
turnpike *s.* gebührenpflichtige Straße *f.*
turnstile *s.* Drehkreuz *n.*
turntable *s.* (*rail.*) Drehscheibe *f.*; Plattenteller *m.*
turn-up *s.* Hosenaufschlag *m.*
turpentine *s.* Terpentin *m.*
turquoise, *s.* Türkis *m.*; ~ *a.* türkis.
turret *s.* Türmchen *n.*; Panzerturm *m.*
turtle *s.* Seeschildkröte *f.*; **~neck** *s.* Rollkragen
tusk *s.* Fangzahn *m.*
tussle *s.* Gerangel *n.*, Rauferei *f.*
tussock *s.* Grasbüschel *n.*
tutelage *s.* Vormundschaft *f.*; Unmündigkeit *f.*
tutelary *a.* vormundschaftlich.
tutor *s.* Hauslehrer *m.*; Lehrer *m.*; ~ *v.t.* unterrichten.
tutorial Lehr..., Lehrer..
tuxedo *s.* Smoking *m.*
twaddle *s.* Quatsch *m.*; Unsinn *m.*
twang *v.i.* schwirren; näseln; ~ *s.* näselnde Aussprache *f.*
tweak *v.t.* zwichen, kneifen.
tweed *s.* Tweed *m.* Halbtuch *n.*
tweezers *s.pl. pair of ~* Pinzette *f.*
Twelfth Night *s.* Dreikönigsfest *n.*
twelve *a.* zwölf.

twentieth *a.* zwanzigst...
twenty *a.* zwanzig.
twerp *s.* (*fam.*) Blödmann *m.*
twice *adv.* zweimal, doppelt.
twiddle *v.t.* herumdrehen an; (*fam.*) herumfummeln.
twig *s.* Zweig *m.;* Rute *f.*
twilight *s.* Zwielicht *n.;* Dämmerung *f.*
twin *s.* Zwilling *m.; a.* Doppel...; **~ bed** *s.* Doppelbett *n.;* **~ engine(d),** *a.* (*avi.*) zweimotorig.
twine *v.t.* drehen, zwirnen; ~ *v.i.* sich winden; ~ *s.* Bindfaden *m.;* Zwirn *m.;* Windung *f.*
twinge *s.* Stechen *n.;* stechender Schmerz *m.*
twinkle *v.i.* blinken, blinzeln; ~ *s.* Funkeln *n.;* Glitzern *n.;* Blinzeln.
twinkling *s. in the ~ of an eye,* im Handumdrehen.
twirl *v.t. & i.* quirlen; wirbeln; ~ *s.* Wirbel *m.;* Schnörkel *m.*
twist *v.t.* (*v.i. r.*) drehen, verdrehen, flechten, spinnen; verzerren; ~ *s.* Geflecht *n.;* Biegung *f.;* Windung *f.*
twisted *a.* verbogen; verdreht.
twitch *v.t.* zupfen, zwicken; zucken; ~ *s.* Zupfen, *n.;* Zucken *n.*
twitter *v.i.* zwitschern; kichern, zittern; ~ *s.* Gezwitscher *n.*
two *a.* zwei; **~-bit** *a.* klein; unbedeutend; **~-speed** (*mech.*) *a.* mit zwei Gängen; **~-piece suit,** zweiteiliger Anzug *m.; in ~,* entzwei.
twofold a zweifach.
two-handed *a.* zweihändig.
twosome *s.* Paar *n.;* Zweier *m.*
two-time *a.* zweimalig; ~ *v.t.* (*fam.*) untreu sein.
two-way *a.* zweibahnig; mit Gegenverkehr.
tympanum *s.* Trommelfell *n.;* Giebelfeld *n.*
type *s.* Typ, Typus *m.;* Schrift *f.;* Drucktype *f.;* ~ *v.t.* auf der Schreibmaschine schreiben, tippen.
typecast *v.t.* auf ein Rollenfach festlegen.
typescript *s.* Maschinenschrift *f.;* ~ *a.* maschinengeschrieben.
typesetter *s.* (Schrift-) Setzer(in) *m.(f.)*
typewrite *v.t. & i.* mit der Schreibmaschine schreiben, tippen.
typewriter *s.* Schreibmaschine *f.;* ~ **ribbon,** Schreibmaschinenfarbband *n.*
typhoid *s.* Typhus *m.*
typhoon *s.* Teifun *m.*
typhus *s.* Fleckfieber *n.*
typical *a.* **~ly** *adv.* typisch.
typify *v.t.* darstellen; typisch sein für; kennzeichnen.
typist *s.* Schreibkraft *f.*
typographic(al) *a.*, **~ly** *adv.* typographisch.
typography *s.* Typographie *f.*
tyrannical *a.*, **~ly** *adv.* tyrannisch.
tyrannize *v.t.* tyrannisieren.
tyranny *s.* Tyrannei *f.*
tyrant *s.* Tyrann *m.*
Tyrol *s.* Tirol *n.*

U

U, u der Buchstabe U oder u *n.*
ubiquitous *a.* allgegenwärtig.
ubiquity *s.* Allgegenwart *f.*
U-boat *s.* U-boot *n.*
udder *s.* Euter *n.*
UEFA *Union of European Football Associations,* UEFA.
UFO *unidentified flying object,* Ufo.
Uganda *s.* Uganda *n.*
Ugandan *a.* Ugandisch; ~ *s.* Ugander(in) *m.(f.)*
ugh *i.* bah pfui!
ugliness *s.* Häßlichkeit *f.*
ugly *a.* häßlich, ekelhaft.
UHF *ultrahigh frequency,* Ultrahochfrequenzbereich, UHF.
U.K. *United Kingdom,* Vereinigtes Königreich *n.,* Großbritannien.
Ukraine *s.* Ukraine *s.*
Ukrainian *a.* ukrainisch; ~ *s.* Ukrainer(in) *m.(f.)*
ulcer *s.* Geschwür.
ulcerate *v.i.* schwären; Geschwür hervorrufen.
ulterior *a.* hintergründig; geheim.
ultimate *a.*, **~ly** *adv.* letzt, zuletzt, endlich.
ultimatum *s.* Ultimatum *n.*
ultra *a.* ultra...; hyper...
ultra shortwave *s.* (*radio*) Ultrakurzwelle *f.*
ultrasonic *a.* Ultraschall...
ultrasound *s.* Ultraschall *m.*
ultraviolet *a.* ultraviolett.
umbel *s.* Dolde *f.*
umber *s.* Umbra (Farbe) *f.*
umbilical cord *s.* Nabelschnur *f.*
umbrage *s* Anstoß, Ärger *m.*
umbrella *s.* Regenschirm, Schirm *m.;* ~ **stand,** Regenschirmständer *m.*
umlaut *s.* Umlaut *m.*
umpire *s.* Schiedsrichter(in) *m.(f.)*
umpteen *a.* x-mal; zig.
umpteenth *a. for the ~ time,* zum x-sten Mal.
unabashed *a.* ungeniert; schamlos.
unabated *a.* unvermindert.
unable *a.* unfähig, unvermögend.
unabridged *a.* ungekürzt.
unaccented *a.* unbetont.
unacceptable *a.*, **~bly** *adv.* unannehmbar.
unaccommodating *a.* unnachgiebig.
unaccompanied *a.* unbegleitet.
unaccountable *a.*, **~bly** *adv.* unerklärlich.
unaccounted *a.* **~for** unauffindbar; vermißt.
unaccustomed *a.* ungewohnt; ungewöhnlich.
unacquainted *a.* unbekannt.
unadorned *a.* schmucklos.
unadulterated *a.* unverfälscht, echt.
unadventurous *a.* bieder; ereignislos; ohne Unternehmungsgeist.
unadvisable *a.* nicht ratsam, unklug.
unadvised *a.*, **~ly** *adv.* unberaten; unbesonnen.
unaffected *a.*, **~ly** *adv.* ungerührt; unbeeinflußt; ungekünstelt.
unafraid *a.* furchtlos.
unaided *a.* ohne Hilfe, allein, (Auge) bloß.
unalloyed *a.* unvermischt.

unalterable *a.*, **~bly** *adv.* unveränderlich.
unaltered *a.* unverändert.
unambiguous *a.*, **~ly** *adv.* unzweideutig.
un-American *a.* unamerikanisch; antiamerikanisch.
unanimity *s.* Einmütigkeit *f.*
unanimous *a.*, **~ly** *adv.* einmütig.
unanswerable *a.*, **~bly** *adv.* unwiderleglich.
unappetizing *a.* unappetitlich.
unappreciated *a.* unbeachtet.
unapproachable *a.* unerreicht; unzugänglich.
unapt *a.* **~ly** *adv.* untauglich, unpassend.
unarmed *a.* unbewaffnet, wehrlos.
unashamed *a.* schamlos, unverhohlen.
unasked *a.* ungefordert, ungebeten.
unassailable *a.* uneinnehmbar.
unassisted *a.* ohne Hilfe.
unassuming *a.* anspruchslos.
unaswered *a.* unbeantwortet.
unattached *a.* unverbunden.
unattainable *a.* unerreichbar.
unattained *a.* unerreicht.
unattempted *a.* unversucht.
unattended *a.* unbeaufsichtigt; unbegleitet.
unattractive *a.* unattraktiv; reizlos.
unauthentic *a.* unverbürgt.
unauthorized *a.* unberechtigt.
unavailable *a.* nicht erhältlich.
unavailing *a.* vergeblich, nutzlos.
unavenged *a.* ungerächt.
unavoidable *a.*, **~bly** *adv.* unvermeidlich.
unaware (of) *a.* ohne Kenntnis von, unbewußt; **~s** *adv.* unversehens.
unbalanced *a.* nicht im Gleichgewicht, unausgeglichen.
unbearable *a.* unerträglich.
unbeaten *a.* unbesiegt, unübertroffen.
unbecoming *a.*, **~ly** *adv.* nicht kleidsam; ungeziemend.
unbeknown(st) *a.* ohne Wissen, unbekannt.
unbelief *s.* Unglaube *m.*
unbelievable *a.* unglaublich, unglaubhaft.
unbeliever *s.* Ungläubiger *m./f.*
unbelieving *a.* ungläubig.
unbend *v.t.* geradebiegen, entspannen, nachlassen; ~ *v.i.* gemütlich werden.
unbending *a.* unbiegsam; starr.
unbiased *a.*, **~ly** *adv.* vorurteilsfrei.
unbid(den) *a.* ungebeten, freiwillig.
unbind *v.t.st.* losbinden.
unbleached *a.* ungebleicht.
unblemished *a.* unbefleckt, tadellos.
unblushing *a.* schamlos.
unbolt *v.t.* aufriegeln, öffnen.
unborn *a.* ungeboren.
unbosom *v.t.* (Herz) ausschütten.
unbound *a.* ungebunden.
unbounded *a.* unbegrenzt.
unbridle *v.t.* abzäumen; **~d** *a.* zügellos.
unbroken *a.* ungebrochen.
unbuckle *v.t.* aufschnallen.
unburden *v.t.* entlasten.
unbusinesslike *a.* nicht geschäftsmäßig; unpraktisch.
unbutton *v.t.* aufknöpfen.
uncalled, uncalled-for *a.* ungerufen; unnötig; unaufgefordert; nicht eingefordert.
uncanny *a.* unheimlich.
uncared-for *a.* vernachlässigt.
unceasing *a.* fortwährend, unaufhörlich.
unceremonious *a.* ungezwungen, einfach.
uncertain *a.*, **~ly** *adv.* ungewiß; unzuverlässig.
uncertainty *s.* Ungewißheit *f.*
unchain *v.t.* entfesseln.
unchallenged *a.* unbestritten.
unchanged *a.* unverändert.
unchanging *a.* unveränderlich, bleibend.
uncharitable *a.*, **~bly** *adv.* lieblos.
unchecked *a.* ungehindert; unkontrolliert.
unchristian *a.*, **~ly** *adv.* unchristlich.
uncivil *a.* unhöflich.
uncivilized *a.* ungesittet.
unclaimed *a.* unverlangt, nicht beansprucht; unbestellbar.
unclassified *a.* nicht klassifiziert; nicht geheim.
uncle *s.* Onkel *m.*
unclean *a.*, **~ly** *adv.* unrein.
unclothed *a.* unbekleidet.
unclouded *a.* unbewölkt; heiter.
uncoil *v.t.* abwickeln.
uncolored *a.* ungefärbt.
uncombed *a.* ungekämmt.
uncomfortable *a.*, **~bly** *adv.* unbehaglich.
uncommon *a.*, **~ly** *adv.* ungewöhnlich.
uncommunicative *a.* unkommunikativ; verschlossen.
uncomplaining *a.* nicht klagend.
uncompromising *a.* unnachgiebig.
unconcern *s.* Gleichgültigkeit *f.*
unconcerned a, **~ly** *adv.* gleichgültig; sorglos.
unconditional *a.* bedingungslos.
unconfined *a.*, **~ly** *adv.* unbegrenzt.
unconfirmed *a.* unbestätigt.
uncongenial *a.* unsympathisch; nicht zusagend.
unconnected *a.* unverbunden.
unconquerable *a.*, **~bly** *adv.* unüberwindlich.
unconquered *a.* unbesiegt.
unconscious *a.* unbewußt; bewußtlos.
unconsciousness *s.* Bewußtlosigkeit, Ohnmacht *f.*
unconsecrated *a.* ungeweiht.
unconstitutional *a.* verfassungswidrig.
unconstrained *a.*, **~ly** *adv.* ungezwungen.
uncontaminated *a.* unverschmutzt; nicht verseucht.
uncontested, uncontradicted *a.* unbestritten, unwidersprochen.
uncontrollable *a.*, **~bly** *adv.* unkontrollierbar.
uncontrolled *a.*, **~ly** *adv.* unkontrolliert.
uncontroversial *a.* nicht kontrovers.
unconventional *a.* unkonventionell.
unconvinced *a.* unüberzeugt.
unconvincing *a.* nicht überzeugend.
uncooked *a.* roh.
uncork *v.t.* entkorken.
uncorrected *a.* unberichtigt.
uncorrupted *a.* unverdorben.
uncourteous *a.*, **~ly** *adv.* unhöflich.
uncouth *a.*, **~ly** *adv.* ungeschlacht, grob.
uncover *v.t.* aufdecken; entblössen.
uncritical *a.* unkritisch.

uncrowned *a.* ungekrönt.
unction *s.* Salbung *f.;* Salbe *f.; extreme ~,* letzte Ölung *f.*
unctuous *a.* ölig, fettig; salbungsvoll.
uncultivated *a.* nicht kultiviert; ungebildet.
uncurbed *a.* ungezähmt, ausgelassen.
undamaged *a.* unbeschädigt.
undated *a.* nicht datiert.
undaunted *a.*, **~ly** *adv.* unerschrocken.
undeceive *v.t.* einem die Augen öffnen.
undecided *a.* unentschieden.
undecipherable *a.* nicht zu entzifferen.
undefeated *a.* unbesiegt.
undefended *a.* nicht verteidigt.
undefined *a.* unbestimmt.
undemanding *a.* anspruchslos.
undemonstrative *a.* zurückhaltend, ruhig.
undeniable *a.*, **~bly** *adv.* unleugbar.
under *pr. & adv.* unter; weniger, geringer; unten; **~age,** unmündig.
underbid *v.t.st.* unterbieten.
undercarriage *s.* (*avi.*) Fahrgestell *n.*
underclothing *s.* Unterzeug *n.*
undercover *a.* getarnt; verdeckt.
undercurrent *s.* Unterströmung *f.*
undercut *v.t.* unterbieten.
underdeveloped *a.* unterentwickelt.
underdevelopment *s.* Unterentwicklung *f.*
underdog *s.* Unterlegene *m./f.*
underdone *a.* nicht gar gekocht.
underestimate *v.t.* unterschätzen; ~ *s.* Unterschätzung *f.*
underexposure *s.* (*phot.*) Unterbelichtung *f.*
underfed *a.* unterernährt.
underfoot *adv.* unter den Füssen.
undergo *v.t.st.* sich unterziehen; ausstehen; erfahren.
undergraduate *s.* Student(in) *m.(f.)* vor dem Vordiplom (B.A.).
underground *a.* unterirdisch; (*rail.*) Untergrundbahn *f.;* ~ (*Movement*), politische Widerstandsbewegung *f.*
undergrowth *s.* Unterholz *n.*
underhand *a. & adv.* heimlich; hinterlistig; tückisch; (*Tennis*) Tief...
underlie *v.i.* liegen unter; zugrunde liegen.
underline *v.t.* unterstreichen.
underling *s.* (*pej.*) Untergebene *m./f.*
undermine *v.t.* untergraben.
undermost *a.* unterst.
underneath *adv.* unten, darunter; ~ *pr.* unter.
undernourished *a.* unterernährt.
underpaid *a.* schlecht bezahlt.
underpass *s.* Unterführung *f.*
underpin *v.t.* unterbauen; stützen.
underplay *v.t.* herunterspielen.
underprivileged *a.* unterprivilegiert.
underproduction *s.* Unterproduktion *f.*
underprop *v.t.* unterstützen.
underrate *v.t.* unterschätzen.
underscore *v.t.* unterstreichen.
undersell *v.t.ir.* unterbieten.
undershot *a.* unterschlächtig.
underside *s.* Unterseite *f.*
undersigned *a.* unterschrieben; *I, the ~,* der/die Unterzeichnete.
undersized *a.* unter normaler Größe.
understaffed *a.* unterbesetzt.
understand *v.t. & i.st.* verstehen; vernehmen, hören, erfahren.
understandable *a.* verständlich.
understanding *a.* verständnisvoll; ~ *s.* Verstand *m.*, Einsicht *f.;* Einverständnis *n.; to come to an ~ with,* sich verständigen mit; *on the ~ that,* unter der Voraussetzung, daß.
understate *v.t.* herunterspielen; zu gering angeben.
understatement *s.* Untertreibung *f.*, zu maßvolle Darstellung *f.*
understudy *s.* zweite Besetzung *f.*
undertake *v.t.st.* unternehmen, übernehmen; sich verpflichten, garantieren.
undertaker *s.* Leichenbestatter *m.*
undertaking *s.* Unternehmen *n.;* Betrieb *m.;* Übernahme *f.*
undertone *s.* halbleise Rede *f.;* Unterton *m.*
undertow *s.* Unterströmung *f.*
undervalue *v.t.* unterschätzen.
underwear *s.* Unterwäsche *f.*
underweight *a.* untergewichtig.
underwood *s.* Unterholz *n.*
underwrite *v.t.st.* (*com.*) unterzeichnen; versichern; unterstützen.
underwriter *s.* Versicherer, Assekurant *m.*
undeserved *a.*, **~ly** *adv.* unverdient.
undeserving *a.* unwürdig, unwert.
undesigned *a.*, **~ly** *adv.* unbeabsichtigt.
undesirable *a.* unerwünscht.
undetected *a.* unentdeckt.
undetermined *a.* unentschieden.
undeterred *a.* nicht entmutigt, unbeeindruckt.
undeveloped *a.* unentwickelt.
undigested *a.* unverdaut.
undignified *a.* würdelos.
undiminished *a.* unvermindert.
undiplomatic *a.* undiplomatisch.
undiscerned *a.*, **~ly** *adv.* unbemerkt, unentdeckt.
undiscernible *a.*, **~bly** *adv.* ununterscheidbar, unbemerklich.
undiscerning *a.* einsichtslos.
undisciplined *a.* ungeschult; zuchtlos.
undiscovered *a.* unentdeckt.
undiscriminating *a.* wahllos.
undisguised *a.* unverstellt, offen.
undismayed *a.* unverzagt.
undisputed *a.* unbestritten.
undistinguished *a.* mittelmäßig.
undisturbed *a.*, **~ly** *adv.* ungestört.
undivided *a.*, **~ly** *adv.* ungeteilt, ganz.
undo *v.t.st.* aufmachen; auflösen; zerstören; ungeschehen machen.
undoing *s.* Aufmachen *n.;* Verderben *n.*
undone *a.* unerledigt; (*fig.*) ruiniert, hin.
undoubted *a.*, **~ly** *adv.* unzweifelhaft.
undreamt-of *a.* ungeahnt.
undress *v.t.* (sich) auskleiden.
undressed *a.* unbekleidet; ausgezogen.
undrinkable *a.* untrinkbar.
undue *a.* ungebührlich; übermäßig.
undulate *v.t. & i.* wogen, wellen.
unduly *adv.* ungebührlich.
undutiful *a.*, **~ly** *adv.* pflichtvergessen.

undying *a.* unsterblich.
unearned *a.* unverdient.
unearth *v.t.* ausgraben; aufstöbern.
unearthly *a.* unirdisch, überirdisch.
uneasy *a.*, **~ily** *adv.* unruhig, ängstlich.
uneatable *a.* ungenießbar.
uneconomic *a.*, **~ally** *adv.* unwirtschaftlich.
unedifying *a.* unerbaulich.
uneducated *a.* unerzogen, ungebildet.
unembarrassed *a.* nicht verlegen.
unemotional *a.* temperamentlos.
unemployable *a.* verwendungsunfähig.
unemployed *a.* arbeitslos.
unemployment *s.* Arbeitslosigkeit *f.*; ~ **insurance,** Arbeitslosenversicherung *f.*
unencumbered *a.* unbelastet; ohne Hypotheken.
unending *a.* endlos.
unendurable *a.* unerträglich.
unenterprising *a.* nicht unternehmend.
unenviable *a.* nicht beneidenswert.
unequal *a.*, **~ly** *adv.* ungleich; unangemessen; nicht gewachsen.
unequalled *a.* unvergleichlich, unerreicht.
unequivocal *a.* unzweideutig.
unerring *a.*, **~ly** *adv.* untrüglich.
UNESCO *United Nations Educational, Scientific, and Cultural Organization,* (Organisation der Vereinten Nationen für Erziehung, Wissenschaft, und Kultur).
unessential *a.* unwesentlich.
unethical *a.* unmoralisch.
uneven *a.*, **~ly** *adv.* uneben, ungleich; ungerade.
uneventful *a.* ereignislos.
unexampled *a.* Beispiellos, unerhört.
unexceptional *a.*, **~ly** *adv.* alltäglich; durchschnittlich.
unexpected *a.*, **~ly** *adv.* unerwartet.
unexpired *a.* nicht abgelaufen, noch in Kraft.
unexplained *a.* unerklärt.
unexplored *a.* unerforscht.
unexpurgated *a.* nicht gereinigt, ungekürzt.
unfaded *a.* unverwelkt; unverschossen.
unfading *a.* unverwelklich; echt.
unfailing *a.* unfehlbar, gewiss; zuverlässig; unerschöpflich.
unfair *a.*, **~ly** *adv.* unfair; unsportlich; unbillig, unredlich; ~ **competition,** unlauterer Wettbewerb *m.*
unfaithful *a.*, **~ly** *adv.* untreu.
unfaltering *a.* nicht schwankend, sicher; fest.
unfamiliar *a.* ungewöhnt.
unfashionable *a.*, **~bly** *adv.* unmodern.
unfasten *v.t.* losmachen, losbinden.
unfathomable *a.*, **~bly** *adv.* unergründlich, unermeßlich.
unfavorable *a.*, **~bly** *adv.* ungünstig.
unfeeling *a.* gefühllos.
unfeigned *a.*, **~ly** *adv.* aufrichtig.
unfermented *a.* ungegoren; ungesäuert.
unfetter *v.t.* entfesseln.
unfilial *a.* lieb-, respektlos (Kind).
unfinished *a.* unvollendet.
unfit *a.*, **~ly** *adv.* ungeeignet; untauglich; ~ *v.t.* untüchtig machen.
unfix *v.t.* losmachen; lösen.
unflagging *a.* unermüdlich.
unflattering *a.* wenig schmeichelhaft.
unflinching *a.* unerschrocken.
unfold *v.t.* entfalten; darlegen.
unforeseeable unvorhersehbar.
unforeseen *a.* unvorhergesehen.
unforgettable *a.* unvergeßlich.
unforgivable *a.* unverzeihlich.
unforgiving *a.* unversöhnlich; nachtragend.
unforgotten *a.* unvergessen.
unfortified *a.* unbefestigt; schwach.
unfortunate *a.*, **~ly** unglücklich; leidig.
unfortunately *adv.* leider.
unfounded *a.* unbegründet; grundlos.
unfreeze *v.t.* auftauen.
unfrequented *a.* unbesucht.
unfriendly *a.* unfreundlich.
unfruitful *a.*, **~ly** *adv.* unfruchtbar.
unfulfilled *a.* unerfüllt.
unfurl *v.t.* aufspannen, entfalten (Segel).
unfurnished *a.* nicht ausgestattet (mit); unmöbliert; entblößt.
ungainly *a.* plump, ungeschickt.
ungentle *a.*, **~tly** *adv.* unsanft, grob.
ungentlemanly *a.* ungebildet; unfein.
unglazed *a.* unglasiert; unverglast.
ungodly *a.* gottlos.
ungovernable *a.*, **~bly** *adv.* unlenksam.
ungracious *a.*, **~ly** *adv.* ungnädig; ungünstig; mißfällig.
ungrammatical *a.* ungrammatisch.
ungrateful *a.*, **~ly** *adv.* undankbar.
ungrounded *a.* nicht stichhaltig.
ungrudging *a.*, **~ly** *adv.* gern, ohne Murren.
unguarded *a.*, **~ly** *adv.* unbewacht.
unguent *s.* Salbe *f.*
unguided *a.* ohne Führung; ungeleitet.
unhallowed *a.* verrucht; ungeweiht.
unhampered *a.* ungehindert.
unhandy *a.* unhandlich; ungeschickt.
unhappiness *s.* Unglück *n.*
unhappy *a.*, **~ily** *adv.* unglücklich.
unharmed *a.* unversehrt.
unharness *v.t.* abschirren.
unhealthiness *s.* Ungesundheit *f.*
unhealthy *a.*, **~ily** *adv.* ungesund.
unheard *a.* ungehört; ~ **of,** unerhört.
unheeded *a.* unbeachtet.
unheedful, unheeding *a.* unachtsam.
unhesitating *a.* ohne Zögern.
unhindered *a.* ungehindert.
unhinge *v.t.* aus den Angeln heben; (*fig.*) zerrütten; (*fig.*) aus dem Gleichgewicht bringen.
unhistoric *a.*, **~ally** *adv.* unhistorisch.
unholy *a.* unheilig, gottlos; verrucht.
unhook *v.t.* loshaken.
unhoped (for) *a.* unverhofft.
unhorse *v.t.* aus dem Sattel heben.
unhuman *a.*, **~ly** *adv.* nicht menschlich, überirdisch.
unhurt *a.* unverletzt.
unhygienic *a.* unhygienisch.
UNICEF *United Nations Children's Fund,* (Kinderhilfswerk der Vereinten Nationen).
unicorn *s.* Einhorn *n.*
unidentified *a.* nicht identifiziert.

unification *s.* Vereinigung *f.*, Vereinheitlichung *f.*
uniform *a.*, **~ly** *adv.* einförmig, gleichförmig; ~ *s.* Uniform *f.*
uniformity *s.* Gleichförmigkeit *f.*
unify *v.t.* vereinigen, vereinheitlichen.
unilateral *a.* einseitig.
unimaginable *a.* undenkbar.
unimaginative *a.* phantasielos, einfallslos.
unimpaired *a.* unvermindert; unverletzt.
unimpeded *a.* ungehemmt.
unimportant *a.* unwichtig.
unimpressed *a.* unbeeindruckt.
unimpressive *a.* eindruckslos.
unimproved *a.* unverbessert; unbenutzt (Land).
uninfluenced *a.* unbeeinflußt.
uninformed a ununterrichtet, uninformiert.
uninhabitable *a.* unbewohnbar.
uninhabited *a.* unbewohnt.
uninhibited *a.* ungehemmt.
uninitiated *a.* uneingeweiht.
uninjured *a.* unverletzt.
uninspired *a.* einfallslos.
uninspiring *a.* langweilig.
uninstructed *a.* ununterrichtet.
uninsured *a.* nicht versichert.
unintelligible *a.*, **~bly** *adv.* unverständlich.
unintended, unintentional *a.* unbeabsichtigt.
uninterested *a.* uninteressiert.
uninteresting *a.* uninteressant.
uninterrupted *a.*, **~ly** *adv.* ununterbrochen.
uninvited *a.* ungeladen.
uninviting a nicht anziehend; wenig einladend.
union *s.* Vereinigung *f.*, Bund *m.*; Verein *m.*; Verband *m.*; Gewerkschaft *f.*; **~Jack,** britische Nationalflagge *f.*
unique *a.* enzigartig.
unison *s.* Einklang *m.*; Einmütigkeit *f.*
unit *s.* Einheit *f.*
unite *v.t.* sich vereinigen.
united *a.* vereint.
United Kingdom *s.* Vereinigtes Königreich (Großbritannien).
United Nations *s.pl.* Vereinte Nationen *f.pl.*
United States (of America) *s, pl.* Vereinigte Staaten (von Amerika).
unity *s.* Einheit, Eintracht *f.*
universal *a.*, **~ly** *adv.* allgemein; allumfassend; Welt...; universal.
universe *s.* Weltall, Universum *n.*
university *s.* Universität *f.*
univocal *a.* eindeutig.
unjust *a.*, **~ly** *adv.* ungerecht.
unjustifiable *a.*, **~bly** *adv.* nicht zu rechtfertigen; unverantwortlich.
unjustified *a.* nicht gerechtfertigt.
unkempt *a.* ungekämmt.
unkind *a.*, **~ly** *adv.* unfreundlich, lieblos.
unkindness *s.* Unfreundlichkeit *f.*
unknowing *a.*, **~ly** *adv.* unwissend.
unknown *a.* unbekannt.
unlace *v.t.* aufschnüren.
unlamented *a.* unbeklagt.
unlatch *v.t.* aufklinken.
unlawful *a.*, **~ly** *adv.* ungesetzlich.
unleaded *a.* bleifrei.
unlearn *v.t.* verlernen.
unlearned *a.* **~ly** *adv.* ungelehrt.
unleavened *a.* ungesäuert.
unless *c.* wenn nicht, außer wenn.
unlettered *a.* ungelehrt.
unlicensed *a.* ohne Konzession.
unlike *a.*, **~ly** *adv.* ungleich, anders als.
unlikelihood *s.* Unwahrscheinlichkeit *f.*
unlikley *a.* & *adv.* unwahrscheinlich.
unlimited *a.*, **~ly** *adv.* unbegrenzt; unbestimmt.
unlined *a.* ungefüttert; ohne Linien.
unliquidated *a.* unbezahlt.
unlisted *a.* ~ **number** *s.* Geheimnummer *f.*
unlit *a.* unbeleuchtet.
unload *v.t.* abladen.
unlock *v.t.* aufschließen.
unlooked-for *a.* unerwartet, unvermutet.
unloving *a.* lieblos.
unlucky *a.* unglücklich.
unmanageable *a.* unlenksam, unbändig.
unmanly *a.* unmännlich.
unmannerly *a.* ungesittet, unartig.
unmanufactured *a.* unverarbeitet.
unmarked *a.* nicht gekennzeichnet.
unmarketable *a.* unverkäuflich.
unmarried *a.* unverheiratet, ledig.
unmask *v.t.* sich entlarven.
unmatched *a.* unvergleichlich.
unmeasured *a.* ungemessen.
unmentionable *a.* unaussprechlich.
unmentioned *a.* nicht erwähnt.
unmerciful *a.*, **~ly** *adv.* unbarmherzig.
unmerited *a.* unverdient.
unmethodical *a.* unmethodisch.
unmindful *a.* uneingedenk, unachtsam.
unmingled *a.* unvermischt.
unmistakable *a.* unverkennbar.
unmitigated *a.* ungemildert, völlig.
unmolested *a.* unbelästigt.
unmotherly *a.* unmütterlich.
unmounted *a.* (Bild) nicht aufgezogen; (Stein) nicht gefaßt.
unmoved *a.* unbewegt; unverändert.
unmusical *a.* unmusikalisch.
unnamed *a.* ungenannt, namenlos.
unnatural *a.*, **~ly** *adv.* unnatürlich.
unnecessary *a.* unnötig.
unnerve *v.t.* entnerven, entkräften.
unnerving *a.* entnervend.
unnoticed *a.* unbemerkt.
unnumbered *a.* ungezählt.
unobjectionable *a.* einwandfrei; unanfechtbar.
unobservant *a.* unachtsam.
unobserved *a.*, **~ly** *adv.* unbeobachtet.
unobstructed *a.* nicht verstopft; ungehindert.
unobtainable *a.* nicht erhältlich; unerreichbar.
unobtrusive *a.* unaufdringlich, bescheiden.
unoccupied *a.* unbesetzt; unbenutzt; unbebaut; unbeschäftigt.
unoffending *a.* unschädlich, harmlos.
unofficial *a.* nicht amtlich.
unopened *a.* ungeöffnet.
unopposed *a.* ohne Widerstand.
unorganized *a.* unorganisiert.
unorthodox *a.* unorthodox; unüblich.

unpack *v.t.* auspacken; aufmachen.
unpaid *a.* unbezahlt.
unpalatable *a.* ungenießbar.
unparalleled *a.* unvergleichlich.
unpardonable *a.*, **~bly** *adv.* unverzeihlich.
unparliamentary *a.* unparlamentarisch.
unpatriotic *a.* unpatriotisch.
unpaved *a.* ungepflastert.
unperceived *a.*, **~ly** *adv.* unbemerkt.
unperturbed *a.* nicht beunruhigt, gelassen.
unpick *v.t.* auftrennen.
unpin *v.t.* losheften, abnehmen.
unplanned *a.* ungeplant.
unpleasant *a.*, **~ly** *adv.* unangenehm.
unpleasantness *s.* Unannehmlichkeit *f.*; Unfreundlichkeit *f.*
unplowed *a.* ungepflügt.
unpoetical *a.*, **~ly** *adv.* unpoetisch.
unpolished *a.* unpoliert; (*fig.*) ungeschliffen.
unpolitical *a.* unpolitisch.
unpolluted *a.* sauber; nicht verschmutzt.
unpopular *a.* unbeliebt.
unpopularity *s.* Unbeliebtheit *f.*
unpractical *a.* unpraktisch.
unpractised *a.* ungeübt, unerfahren.
unprecedented *a.* beispiellos, unerhört.
unpredictable *a.* unberechenbar.
unprejudiced *a.* vorurteilsfrei; unvoreingenommen.
unpremeditated *a.* nicht vorsätzlich.
unprepared *a.* unvorbereitet.
unprepossessing *a.* nicht einnehmend.
unpretentious *a.* anspruchslos.
unpriced *a.* ohne Preisangabe.
unprincipled *a.* gewissenlos.
unprintable *a.* nicht druckreif.
unprinted *a.* ungedruckt.
unprivileged *a.* nicht bevorrechtigt.
unproductive *a.* unfruchtbar, unergiebig.
unprofessional *a.* unfachmännisch, stümperhaft; standeswidrig.
unprofitable *a.*, **~bly** *adv.* unrentabel, unnütz.
unpromising *a.* nicht vielversprechend.
unpronounceable *a.* unaussprechbar.
unpropitious *a.* ungünstig.
unproportioned *a.* unverhältnismäßig.
unprotected *a.* unbeschützt.
unproved *a.* ungeprüft; unbewiesen.
unprovided *a.* unversorgt; unvorhergesehen.
unprovoked *a.* unprovoziert, grundlos.
unpublished *a.* unveröffentlicht.
unpunctual *a.* unpünktlich.
unpunctuality *s.* Unpünktlichkeit *f.*
unpunished *a.* ungestraft.
unpurified *a.* ungereinigt.
unqualified *a.* nicht fähig, ungeeignet; unberechtigt; uneingeschränkt.
unquestionable *a.*, **~bly** *adv.* zweifellos.
unquestioned *a.* unbefragt; unbestritten.
unquestioning *a.* bedingungslos, blind.
unquiet *a.*, **~ly** *adv.* unruhig, ungestüm.
unravel *v.t.* ausfasern; entwirren.
unread *a.* ungelesen; unbelesen.
unreadable *a.* nicht lesenswert.
unready *a.*, **~ily** *adv.* nicht bereit.
unreal *a.* nicht wirklich.
unrealistic *a.* unrealistisch.
unrealizable *a.* nicht realisierbar, nicht verkäuflich.
unreasonable *a.*, **~bly** *adv.* unvernünftig; unbillig, ohne Grund.
unreasoning *a.* blind, vernunftlos.
unreclaimed *a.* nicht zurückgefordert; unangebaut; nicht gebessert.
unrecognizable *a.*, **~ly** *adv.* nicht wiederzuerkennen.
unreconciled *a.* unversöhnt.
unrecorded *a.* nicht aufgezeichnet.
unredeemed *a.* nicht losgekauft; unerlöst; ungemildert.
unreel *v.t.* abspulen; abwickeln.
unrefined *a.* ungeläutert.
unreflecting *a.* gedankenlos, unüberlegt.
unregarded *a.* unberücksichtigt.
unrelated *a.* unzusammenhängend; nicht verwandt.
unrelenting *a.* unbeugsam, unerbittlich.
unreliable *a.* unzuverlässig.
unrelieved *a.* ungemildert, ununterbrochen.
unremitting *a.* unablässig, unaufhörlich.
unremunerative *a.* uneinträglich.
unrepeatable *a.* einzigartig; einmalig.
unrepentant *a.* reuelos.
unrepresentative *a.* nicht repräsentativ.
unrequited *a.* unerwidert.
unreserved *a.*, **~ly** *adv.* rückhaltlos; nicht numeriert.
unresisting *a.* widerstandslos; wehrlos.
unresolved *a.* unentschlossen.
unresponsive *a.* teilnahmslos.
unrest *s.* Unruhe *f.*
unrestored *a.* nicht wiederhergestellt.
unrestrained *a.* unbeschränkt; zügellos.
unrestricted *a.*, **~ly** *adv.* uneingeschränkt, unbeschränkt.
unreturned *a.* nicht zurückgegeben; nicht gewählt.
unrevoked *a.* unwiderrufen.
unrewarded *a.* unbelohnt.
unrewarding *a.* unbefriedigend; undankbar.
unrig *v.t.* abtakeln.
unripe *a.* unreif.
unrivalled *a.* unvergleichlich; beispiellos.
unroll *v.t.* aufrollen.
unromantic *a.* unromantisch.
unruffled *a.* ruhig; glatt (vom Meer).
unruliness *s.* Ungebärdigkeit *f.*
unruly *a.* unlenksam, unbändig.
unsaddle *v.t.* absatteln.
unsafe *a.*, **~ly** *adv.* unsicher, gefährlich.
unsaid *a.* ungesagt.
unsalaried *a.* unbesoldet.
unsaleable *a.* unverkäuflich.
unsalted *a.* ungesalzen.
unsanctioned *a.* unbestätigt.
unsanitary *a.* unhygienisch.
unsatisfactory *a.*, **~ily** *adv.* unzulänglich, unbefriedigend.
unsatisfied *a.* unbefriedigt; unzufrieden.
unsatisfying *a.* unbefriedigend.

unsavory *a.*, **~ily** *adv.* (*fig.*) geschmacklos; unangenehm (Geruch...)
unscathed *a.* unversehrt.
unscented *a.* nicht parfümiert.
unscheduled *a.* außerplanmäßig.
unschooled *a.* ungeschult.
unscientific *a.* unwissenschaftlich.
unscramble *v.t.* entwirren.
unscrew *v.t.* losschrauben.
unscrupulous *a.* gewissenlos; skrupellos.
unseal *v.t.* entsiegeln
unseasonable *a.* unzeitig; unschicklich, unpassend; **~bly** *adv.* zur Unzeit.
unseasoned *a.* ungewürzt.
unseat *v.t.* abwerfen, absetzen.
unsecured *a.* (*com.*) ungedeckt, nicht sichergestellt; ungesichert; unbefestigt.
unseeded *a.* (*sp.*) ungesetzt.
unseemly *a.* unziemlich.
unseen *a.* ungesehen, unsichtbar.
unselfish *a.* selbstlos, uneigennützig.
unsettle *v.t.* durcheinanderbringen; verwirren.
unsettled *a.* ungeordnet; unbeständig, unsicher, veränderlich; unbezahlt.
unshackle *v.t.* entfesseln.
unshaken *a.* unerschüttert; fest.
unshaven *a.* nicht rasiert.
unsheltered *a.* unbedeckt; ungeschützt.
unshorn *a.* ungeschoren.
unshrinkable *a.*, **~ly** *adv.* nicht einlaufend (Stoff).
unshrinking *a.* unverzagt; nicht einlaufend.
unsightly *a.* unschön.
unsigned *a.* unsigniert, nicht unterzeichnet.
unskilful *a.*, **~ly** *adv.* ungeschickt, unkundig.
unskilled *a.* unerfahren; ungelernt; **~ worker,** ungelernter Arbeiter *m.*
unslaked *a.* ungelöscht.
unsociable *a.*, **~bly** *adv.* ungesellig.
unsocial *a.* unsozial.
unsoiled *a.* unbeschmutzt.
unsold *a.* unverkauft.
unsolicited *a.* unverlangt, ungefordert.
unsolved *a.* ungelöst.
unsophisticated *a.* unverfälscht; unverdorben, natürlich.
unsound *a.* ungesund; nicht stichhaltig; verdorben; nicht echt, nicht aufrichtig; *of ~ mind,* geisteskrank.
unsounded *a.* unergründet.
unsparing *a.* reichlich; schonungslos.
unspeakable *a.*, **~bly** *adv.* unsäglich.
unspecified *a.* nicht spezifiziert.
unspent *a.* unerschöpft, unverbraucht.
unspoiled *a.* unverdorben.
unspoken *a.* unausgesprochen.
unsportsmanlike *a.* nicht sportsmäßig.
unspotted *a.* unbefleckt.
unstable *a.* nicht fest, unbeständig.
unstained *a.* unbefleckt; ungefärbt.
unstamped *a.* ungestempelt, ohne Marke.
unsteady *a.*, **~ily** *adv.* unbeständig, veränderlich, wankelmütig.
unstinted *a.* ungeschmälert, freigebig.
unstrained *a.* ungezwungen.
unstressed *a.* unbelastet; (*ling.*) unbetont.
unstring *v.t.st.* abspannnen, lösen.
unstudied *a.* unstudiert; ungekünstelt.
unstuffed *a.* ungefüllt.
unsubstantial *a.* unkörperlich; wesenlos.
unsuccessful *a.*, **~ly** *adv.* erfolglos.
unsuitable *a.*, **~bly** *adv.* nicht passend.
unsuited *a.* nicht passend, ungeeignet.
unsung *a.* unbesungen.
unsure *a.* unsicher.
unsurpassed *a.* unübertroffen.
unsurprisingly *adv.* ohne Überraschung.
unsuspected *a.*, **~ly** *adv.* unverdächtig.
unsuspecting *a.* arglos, unbefangen.
unsuspicious *a.* nicht argwöhnisch.
unswayed *a.* unbeeinflußt.
unsymmetrical *a.* asymmetrisch.
untainted *a.*, **~ly** *adv.* unverdorben.
untamed *a.* ungezähmt.
untarnished *a.* ungetrübt.
untasted *a.* ungekostet, unversucht.
untaxed *a.* unbesteuert.
unteachable *a.* ungelehrig.
untempered *a.* ungemildert.
untenable *a.* unhaltbar.
untested *a.* ungeprüft.
unthankful *a.*, **~ly** *adv.* undankbar.
unthinkable *a.* undenkbar.
unthinking *a.* gedankenlos, sorglos.
unthought *a.* ~ of, unvermutet.
unthread *v.t.* ausfädeln.
untidy *a.* unordentlich, unreinlich.
untie *v.t.* aufbinden, lösen.
until *c.* bis; ~ *pr.* bis (an), bis zu.
untimely *a.* & *adv.* unzeitig, vorschnell.
untinged *a.* nicht gefärbt.
untiring *a.* unermüdet.
unto *pr.* zu, an, bis, bis an.
untold *a.* ungezählt; ungesagt.
untouchable *a.* unberührbar.
untouched *a.* unberührt, ungerührt.
untowards *a.*, **~ly** *adv.* widrig, ungünstig.
untraceable *a.* unaufspürbar.
untrained *a.* ungelernt; trainiert.
untranslatable *a.* unübersetzbar.
untravelled *a.* ungereist; unberiest.
untried *a.* unversucht; unverhört; unerprobt; unerfahren.
untrimmed *a.* ungeschmückt.
untroubled *a.* ungestört, ungetrübt.
untrue *a.* unwahr, falsch.
untruly *adv.* fälschlich.
untrustworthy *a.* unzuverlässig.
untruth *s.* Unwahrheit *f.*
untuned *a.* verstimmt; (*fig.*) verwirrt.
untwine *v.t.* aufwickeln, auftrennen.
untwist *v.t.* aufdrehen, aufflechten.
unused *a.* ungebraucht; ungewohnt.
unusual *a.*, **~ly** *adv.* ungewöhnlich.
unutterable *a.*, **~bly** *adv.* unausprechlich.
unvaccinated *a.* ungeimpft.
unvalued *a.* ungeschätzt.
unvaried *a.* unverändert.
unvarnished *a.* ungeschminkt.
unvarying *a.* unveränderlich.
unveil *v.t.* entschleiern.

unventilated *a.* ungelüftet; (*fig.*) ununtersucht, unerörtert.
unversed *a.* unbewandert.
unvisited *a.* unbesucht.
unvoiced *a.* unausgesprochen; stimmlos.
unwanted *a.* unerwünscht.
unwarranted *a.* ungerechtfertigt; unverbürgt.
unwary *a.* unbehutsam; unvorsichtig.
unwashed *a.* ungewaschen.
unwavering *a.* fest (Blick); unerschütterlich.
unwearied *a.* unermüdet.
unwedded *s.* unverheiratet.
unweighed *a.* ungewogen; unerworgen.
unwelcome *a.* unwillkommen.
unwell *a.* unwohl, unpäßlich.
unwholesome *a.* ungesund.
unwieldy *a.*, **~ily** *adv.* schwerfällig, unhandlich.
unwilling *a.* **~ly** *adv.* widerwillig.
unwillingness *s.* Unwille *m.*
unwind *v.t.st.* loswinden, abwickeln; entspannen.
unwise *a.*, **~ly** *adv.* töricht, unklug.
unwished *a.* **~ for,** unerwünscht.
unwitting *a.*, **~ly** *adv.* unwissentlich.
unwomanly *a.* unweiblich, unfraulich.
unwonted *a.* ungewohnt; ungewöhnlich.
unworkable *a.* unpraktisch.
unworldy *a.* weltfremd.
unworn *a.* ungetragen.
unworthy *a.*, **~ily** *adv.* unwürdig.
unwrap *v.t.* auswickeln.
unwritten *a.* ungeschrieben.
unwrought *a.* unbearbeitet; roh.
unyielding *a.* unnachgiebig, unbeugsam.
up *adv. & pr.* auf, aufwärts hinauf; empor, oben; *the second ~*, der zweite von unten; *it is ~ to him,* es ist seine Sache; *be ~ against,* (*fam.*) gegenüberstehen; **~ to date,** *a.* modern, auf der Höhe.
upbringing *s.* Erziehung *f.*
upgrade *v.t.* befördern, verbessern; aufbessern.
upheaval *s.* Erhebung *f.*, Aufruhr *m.*
upheave *v.t.st.* emporheben.
uphill *a.* bergauf führend, ansteigend; **~** *adv.* bergauf; aufwärts.
uphold *v.t.st.* aufrecht(er)halten; unterstützen.
upholsterer *s.* Tapezierer *m.*
UPI *United Press International,* (amerikanische Nachrichtenagentur).
upkeep *s.* Instandhaltung *f.*
uplift *v.t.* aufrichten; ~ *s.* Auftrieb geben.
upon *pr.* auf, an, bei, nach.
upper *a.* ober, höher; Ober...; **~ case** *s.* Großbuchstabe *m.;* **~ circle** *s.* (*theat.*) erste Rang *m.;* **~class** *s.* Oberschicht *f.* **~ leather** *s.* Oberleder *n.; down on one's ~s,* in zerlumpten Schuhen, heruntergekommen.
uppermost *a.* höchst, oberst.
uppity *a.* hochnäsig.
upright *a.*, **~ly** *adv.* aufrecht, gerade; aufrichtig; ~ *s.* Ständer *m.;* **~ size,** Hochformat *n.*
uprising *s.* Aufstand *m.*
uproar *s.* Aufruhr *m.;* heftige Getöse *n.*
uproarious *a.* aufrührerisch, lärmend.
uproot *v.t.* ausreißen, entwurzeln.
upset *v.t.* umstürzen; außer Fassung bringen; **~ stomach,** verdorbener Magen *m.*
upsetting *a.* erschütternd; ärgerlich.
upshot *s.* Ausgang *m.;* Ergebnis *n.*
upside *s.* Oberseite *f.;* **~ down,** das Oberste zu unterst, drunter und drüber.
upstage *v.t.* jm. die Schau stehlen.
upstairs *adv.* oben (im Hause), nach oben.
upstart *s.* Emporkömmling *m.*
upstate *a.* nördlicher Teil eines Staates.
upstream *a. & adv.* flußaufwärts.
upsurge *s.* Aufschwellen *n.;* Aufwallung *f.*
uptight *a.* nervös, reizbar; verklemmt.
upturn *s.* Aufschwung *m.*
upward(s) *adv.* aufwärts, oben; **~ of,** mehr als.
Urals *s.pl.* Ural *m.*
uranium *s.* Uran *n.*
urban *a.* Stadt..., städtisch.
urbane *a.* weltmännisch; gewandt.
urbanity *s.* Höflichkeit *f.*
urchin *s.* (kleiner) Schelm *m.*
urethra *s.* Harnröhre *f.*
urge *v.t.* treiben, drängen; eifrig betreiben; darauf bestehen.
urgency *s.* Dringlichkeit *f.*
urgent *a.*, **~ly** *adv.* dringend, heftig.
uric *a.* Harn...; **~ acid,** Harnsäure *f.*
urinate *v.i.* urinieren.
urine *s.* Urin, Harn *m.*
urn *s.* Urne *f.;* Teekessel *m.*
Uruguay *s.* Uruguay *n.*
Uruguayan *a.* uruguayisch; **~** *s.* Uruguayer(in) *m.(f.)*
us *pn.* uns.
U.S. *United States,* Vereinigte Staaten, *n.pl.*
U.S.A. *United States of America,* Vereinigte Staaten von Nordamerika; *United States Army,* Heer (*n.*) der Vereinigten Staaten.
usable *a.* brauchbar; gebräuchlich.
usage *s.* Gebrauch *m.;* Sitte *f.*
use *s.* Gebrauch, Brauch *m.;* Verwendung *f.; in ~*, üblich, gebräuchlich; *(of) no ~*, unnütz, zwecklos; *to make ~ of,* Gebrauch machen von; **~** *v.t.* gebrauchen, sich bedienen; anwenden; gewöhnen; behandeln; ausüben; *to ~ up,* aufbrauchen; **~** *v.i.* pflegen, gewohnt sein.
used *a.* gewöhnt; benutzt; gebraucht; *more widely ~*, gebräuchlicher; **~-up,** verbraucht.
useful *a.*, **~ly** *adv.* nützlich, dienlich.
usefulness *s.* Nützlichkeit *f.*
useless *a.*, **~ly** *adv.* unnütz, unbrauchbar.
user *s.* Benutzer(in) *m.(f.)*
usher *s.* Gerichtsdiener(in) *m.f.;* Platzanweiser(in) *m.(f.);* ~ *v.t.* **~ in,** einführen, anmelden.
usual *a.*, **~ly** *adv.* gebräuchlich, üblich.
usufruct *s.* Nutznießung *f.*
usurer *s.* Wucherer *m.*
usurious *a.* wucherisch.
usurp *v.t.* unrechtmäßig an sich reißen, usurpieren.
usurpation *s.* widerrechtliche Besitzergreifung, Aneignung *f.*
usurper *s.* unrechtmäßiger Machthaber, Inhaber *m.*
usury *s.* Wucher *m.*
USW *ultra short wave,* Ultrakurzwelle.
utensil *s.* Gerät, Guschirr *n.*
uterine *a.* Gebärmutter...

uterus *s.* Gebärmutter *f.*
utilitarian *s.* Utilitarier *m.;* ~ *a.* Nützlichkeits...; utilitaristisch.
utility *s.* Nützlichkeit *f.;* Nutzen *m.;* ~ *a.* Gebrauchs... (ohne Verschönerung, z.B. ~ **shirt,** ~ **furniture,** etc.); public utilities, gemeinnützige Anstalten *pl.*
utilization *s.* Nutzung *f.*
utilize *v.t.* nutzen.
utmost *a.* äußerst, höchst.
Utopia *s.* Utopia *n.*
Utopian *a.* utopisch, schwärmerhaft.
utter *a.* äußerst; gänzlich; ~ *v.t.* sprechen, äußern.
utterance *s.* Äußerung *f.*
utterly *adv.* äußerst, gänzlich, durchaus.
U-turn *s.* Wende (um 180°) *f.*
uvula *s.* Zäpfchen (im Halse) *n.*

V

V, v der Buchstabe V oder v *n.*
V *volt,* Volt, V.
v. *vide,* siehe; *verse,* Vers *m.; versus,* gegen.
vacancy *s.* Leere *f.;* freie Stelle *f.;* **~cies** *pl.* Zimmer frei.
vacant *a.* leer, erledigt; gedankenarm.
vacate *v.t.* räumen; (Amt) niederlegen.
vacation *s.* Räumung *f.;* Ferien *f.pl.*
vaccinate *v.t.* impfen.
vaccination *s.* Impfung *f.*
vaccine *s.* Impfstoff *m.*
vacillate *v.i.* wanken; schwanken.
vacuum *s.* luftleerer Raum *m.;* **~cleaner,** Staubsauger *s.;* ~ **bottle** *s.* Thermosflasche *f.*
vagabond *a.* umherstreifend; ~ *s.* Landstricher *m.*
vagary *s.* Grille, Laune *f.*
vagina *s.* (Mutter-) Scheide *f.,* Vagina *f.*
vagrancy *s.* Landstreicherei *f.*
vagrant *s.* Landstreicher(in) *m.(f.);* ~ *a.* wandernd, unstet.
vague *a.* unbestimmt, vage.
vain *a.,* **~ly** *adv.* leer, nichtig, eitel, vergeblich; *in* ~, vergebens.
vale *s.* Tal *n.*
valediction *s.* Abschied *m.*
valedictory *a.* Abschieds...
valentine *s.* Grußkarte *(f.)* am Valentinstage (14. Februar); (Valentins-) Schatz *m.*
valet *s.* Kammerdiener, Lakai *m.;* ~ **service** *s.* Reinigungsservice *n.*
valetudinarian *a.* kränklich, siech; ~ *s.* Kranke *m.*
valiant *a.,* **~ly** *adv.* tapfer, brav.
valid *a.,* **~ly** *adv.* rechtskräftig; gültig.
validate *v.t.* bestätigen; beweisen; für gültig erklären.
validity *s.* Gültigkeit *f.;* Wert *m.*
valley *s.* Tal *n.*
valor *s.* Tapferkeit *f.*
valorous *a.,* **~ly** *adv.* tapfer.
valuable *a.* schätzbar; kostbar; **~s** *pl.* Wertsachen *f.pl.*
valuation *s.* Schätzung *f.*
value *s.* Wert, Preis *m.;* ~ *v.t.* schätzen, Achtung erweisen; trassieren.
value added tax *s.* Mehrwertsteuer *f.*
valued *a.* geschätzt; wertroll.
value judgment *s.* Werturteil *n.*
valueless *a.* wertlos.
valuer *s.* Schätzer(in) *m.(f.)*
valve *s.* Ventil *n.;* Klappe *f.*
vamp *s.* Vamp *m.*
vampire *s.* Vampir *m.*
van *s.* Vorhut *f.;* Möbelwagen *m.;* Lieferwagen *m.*
vandalism *s.* Vandalismus *m.*
vandalize *v.t.* zerstören; beschädigen.
vane *s.* Wetterfahne *f.*
vanguard *s.* Vorhut *f.*
vanilla *s.* Vanille *f.*
vanish *v.i.* verschwinden, zergehen.
vanity *s.* Eitelkeit, Nichtigkeit *f.;* ~ **bag** *s.* Kosmetiktäschchen *n.*
vanquish *v.t.* besiegen.
vantage point *s.* Aussichtspunkt *m.; from my* ~ aus meiner Sicht.
vapid *a.* schal; geistlos.
vapor *s.* Dunst, Dampf *m.;* Schwaden *f.pl.*
vaporize *v.i.* verdampfen.
vaporous *a.* dunstig; nebelhaft, nichtig.
variable *a.* **~bly** *adv.* veränderlich.
variance *s.* Uneinigkeit, Mißhelligkeit *f.; to be at* ~, uneinig sein; nicht übereinstimmen.
variant *s.* Variante *f.;* ~ *a.* abweichend.
variation *s.* Veränderung *f.;* Verschiedenheit, Abweichung *f.*
varicose veins *pl.* Krampfadern *pl.*
varied *a.* mannigfaltig.
variegated *a.* bunt.
variety *s.* Mannigfaltigkeit, Abwechslung, Veränderung *f.;* Spielart *f.;* ~ **entertainment,** Varieteaufführung *f.*
various *a.* verschieden; mannigfach.
varnish *s.* Firnis *m.;* Anstrich *m.;* ~ *v.t.* firnissen, lackieren; (*fig.*) bemänteln.
vary *v.t.* (*v.i. sich*) verändern; verschieden sein, abweichen.
varying *a.* wechselnd; wechselhaft.
vascular *a.* (*med.*) Gefäß...
vase *s.* Vase *f.*
vasectomy *s.* Vasektomie *f.*
vaseline *s.* Vaselin *n.*
vassal *s.* Lehnsmann, Untertan *m.*
vassalage *s.* Lehnsverhältnis *f.*
vast *a.,* **~ly** *adv.* sehr groß, weit.
vastness *s.* Weite *f.;* ungeheure Größe *f.*
vat *s.* Faß *n.;* Bottich *m.*
VAT *value-added tax,* Mehrwertsteuer, Mwst.
Vatican *s.* Vatikan *m.*
vault *s.* Gewölbe *n.;* Gruft *f.;* Sprung *m.;* Tresorraum *m.;* ~ *v.i.* schwingen; ~ *v.t.* wölben; **~ing horse,** Pferd (Turnen).
vaulted *a.* gewölbt.

vaunt *v.t.* preisen, loben; ~ *v.i.* prahlen; sich rühmen.
VCR *video cassette recorder,* Videorecorder.
VD *veneral disease,* Geschlechtskrankheit.
veal *s.* Kalbfleisch *n.*
veer *v.i.* sich drehen; (*nav.*) (ab)fieren.
vegetable *s.* (*meist pl.*) Gemüse *n.;* ~ *a.* Pflanzen..., pflanzenartig; ~ **fat,** Pflanzenfett *n.;* ~ **kingdom,** Pflanzenreich *n.;* ~ **oil,** Pflanzenöl *n.; to be just a* ~, nur noch dahinvegetieren.
vegetarian *s.* Vegetarier(in) *m.(f.);* ~ *a.* vegetarisch.
vegetate *v.t.* dahinvegetieren.
vegetation *s.* Vegetation *f.*
vehemence *s.* Heftigkeit *f.;* Eifer *m.*
vehement *a.;* **~ly** *adv.* heftig, ungestüm.
vehicle *s.* Fuhrwerk *n.;* Träger *m.*
vehicular *a.* Fahr...
veil *s.* Schleier m; ~ *v.t.* verschleiern.
veiled *a.* verschleiert; (*fig.*) versteckt.
vein *s.* Blutader *f.;* Vene *f.;* Ader (im Holze, etc.) *f.;* Laune, Stimmung *f.;* Metallader *f.*
Velcro *s.* Klettverschluß *m.*
vellum *s.* Pergament *n.*
velocity *s.* Geschwindigkeit *f.;* Schnelligkeit *f.*
velvet *s.* Samt *m.;* ~ *a.* samten.
velveteen *s.* Plüsch *m.*
velvety *a.* samtig.
Ven. *Venerable,* Ehrwürden.
venal *a.* käuflich; korrupt.
venality *s.* Feilheit *f.;* Bestechlichkeit *f.*
vend *v.t.* verkaufen.
vender, vendor *s.* Verkäufer(in) *m.(f.)*
vendible *a.* verkäuflich.
vending-machine *s.* (Verkaufs-)Automat *m.*
veneer *v.t.* fournieren, auslegen; ~ *s.* Furnier *n.*
venerable *a.,* **~bly** *adv.* ehrwürdig.
venerate *v.t.* verehren.
veneration *s.* Verehrung *f.;* Ehrfurcht *f.*
venereal disease *s. (VD)* Geschlechtskrankheit *f.*
venetian blind *s.* Rolladen *m.* Jalousie *f.*
Venezuela *s.* Venezuela *n.*
Venezuelan *a.* venezolanisch; ~ *s.* Venezolaner(in) *m.(f.)*
vengeance *s.* Rache *f.*
vengeful *a.* rachsüchtig.
venial *a.* verzeihlich; lässlich (Sünde).
venison *s.* Wildbret *n.*
venom *s.* Gift *n.*
venomous *a.,* **~ly** *adv.* giftig; boshaft.
venous *a.* venös, Venen...
vent *s.;* Abzug *m.;* Öffnung *f.;* Schlitz *m.; to give* ~, Luft machen; ~ *v.t.* lüften.
ventilate *v.t.* lüften; erörtern.
ventilation *s.* Lüftung *f.;* Belüftung *f.*
ventilator *s.* Ventilator *m.*
ventricle *s.* Herzkammer *f.*
ventriloquist *s.* Bauchredner(in) *m.(f.)*
venture *s.* Wagnis *n.;* Unternehmung *f.;* Einsatz *m.; at a* ~, auf gut Glück; ~ *v.i. & t.* wagen; *joint* ~, *s.* Gemeinschaftsunternehmen *n.*
venturesome *a.,* **~ly** *adv.* verwegen.
venue *s.* Gerichtsstand, zuständiger Gerichtshof *m.;* Treffpunkt *m.*
veracious *a.* wahrhaft, aufrichtig.
veracity *s.* Wahrhaftigkeit *f.*
veranda(h) *s.* Veranda *f.*
verb *s.* Verb *n.,* Zeitwort *n.*
verbal *a.* **~ly** *adv.* sprachlich, mündlich.
verbatim *adv.* wörtlich; im Wortlaut.
verbiage *s.* Wortschwall *m.*
verbose *a.* wortreich, weitschweifig.
verdant *a.* grün, grünend.
verdict *s.* Entscheidung *f.;* Urteil *n.*
verdigris *s.* Grünspan *m.*
verge *s.* Rand m; Grenze *f.; on the* ~ *of,* am Rande, dicht vor; ~ *v.i.* sich neigen, grenzen, streifen.
verger *s.* Küster *m.*
verifiable *a.* nachprüfbar; verifizierbar.
verification *s.* Bestätigung *f.;* Nachprüfung *f.;* Beweis *m.*
verify *v.t.* überprüfen; bestätigen.
veritable *a.* wahr; echt; richtig.
vermicelli *s.pl.* Fadennudeln *f.pl.*
vermilion *s.* Zinnober *m.;* ~ *v.t.* rot färben.
vermin *s.* Ungeziefer *n.*
vermouth *s.* Wermut *m.*
vernacular *s.* Landessprache *f.;* ~ *a.* einheimisch, Landes...
versatile *a.* vielseitig; veränderlich.
versatility *s.* Vielseitigkeit *f.*
verse *s.* Vers *m.*
versed *a.* bewandert, erfahren.
versification *s.* Versbau *m.*
versify *v.t. & i.* reimen.
version *s.* Übersetzung *f.;* Lesart *f.;* Darstellung *f.*
versus *pr.* gegen.
vertebra *s.* Rückenwirbel *m.*
vertebral *a.* Wirbel...
vertebrate *s.* Wirbeltier *m.*
vertex *s.* Scheitelpunkt *m.;* Spitze *f.*
vertical *a.,* **~ly** *adv.* senkrecht, lotrecht.
vertigo *s.* Schwindel *m.;* Schwindelgefühl *n.*
verve *s.* Schwung *m.;* Energie *f.*
very *a.* wahr, wirklich, echt; völlig; gerade, gar; ~ *adv.* sehr; *the* ~ *same,* genau der, die, das selbe; *the* ~ *best,* der, die, das allerbeste.
vesicle *s.* Bläschen *n.*
vespers *s.pl.* Abendgottesdienst *m.*
vessel *s.* Gefäß *n.;* Fahrzeug *n.,* Schiff *n.*
vest *s.* Unterjacke *f.;* Weste *f.;* ~ *v.t.* bekleiden; verleihen.
vestal *s.* Vestalin *f.*
vested *p. & a.,* altbegründet, gesetzlich festgestellt, verbrieft; *to be* ~ *in,* jemandem zustehen; ~ **interests,** *pl.* Privatinteressen *pl.*
vestibule *s.* Vorhalle *f.*
vestige *s.* Spur *f.*
vestment *s.* Gewand *n.;* Ornat *n.*
vestry *s.* Sakristei; Gemeindeversammlung *f.;* **~-men** *pl.* Kirchenälteste *m.pl.*
vet *s.* (*fam.*) Tierarzt *m.,* Tierärztin *f.*
vetch *s.* Wicke *f.*
veteran *s.* alter Soldat *m.;* ~ *a.* erfahren.
veterinarian *s.* Tierarzt *m.,* Tierärztin *f.*
veterinary *a.* tierärztlich, veterinär.
veto *s.* Veto *n.;* Einspruch *m.;* ~ *v.t.* Einspruch erheben.
vex *v.t.* plagen, ärgern; ~ *v.i.* sich grämen.
vexation *s.* Plage *f.;* Verärgerung *f.*

vexatious *a.*, **~ly** *adv.* unausstehlich; ärgerlich; schikanös.
VHF *very high frequency,* Ultrakurzwelle, VHF, UKW.
via *pr.* über.
viability *s.* Lebensfähigkeit *f.*; Realisierbarkeit *f.*
viable *a.* lebensfähig, realisierbar.
viaduct *s.* Bahnbrücke *f.*
vial *s.* Phiole *f.*; Fläschchen *n.*
vibrant *a.* vibrierend; lebenssprühend.
vibrate *v.i.* zittern, beben, vibrieren.
vibration *s.* Schwingung *f.*, Vibration *f.*
vibrato *s.* Vibrato *n.*
vicar *s.* Pfarrer *m.*
vicarage *s.* Pfarrstelle *f.*; Pfarrhaus *n.*
vicarious *a.* stellvertretend.
vice *s.* Laster *n.*; Fehler, Mangel *m.*; Schraubstock *m.*; ~ *pr.* an Stelle von; ~ (in Zus.) Vize..., Unter...
vice-admiral *s.* Vizeadmiral *m.*
vice-chairman *s.* stellvertretende Vorsitzende *m.*
viceroy *s.* Vizekönig *m.*
vice-versa *adv.* umgekehrt.
vicinity *s.* Nachbarschaft, Nähe *f.*
vicious *a.*, **~ly** *adv.* lasterhaft; bösartig (Tier); ~ **circle,** Teufelskreis *m.*
vicissitude *s.* Wechsel(fall), Umschlag *m.*
victim *s.* Opfer *n.*
victimization *s.* Schikanierung *f.*
victimize *v.t.* schikanieren; (auf)opfern; betrügen.
victor *s.* Sieger(in) *m.(f.)*
Victorian *a.* viktorianisch.
victorious *a.*, **~ly** *adv.* siegreich.
victory *s.* Sieg *m.*
victuals *s.pl.* Lebensmittel *n.pl.*
vie *v.i.* wetteifern.
Vienna *s.* Wien *n.*
Viennese *a.* Wiener; ~ *s.* Wiener(in) *m.(f.)*
Vietnam *s.* Vietnam *n.*
Vietnamese *a.* vietnamesisch; ~ *s.* Vietnamese *m.*, Vietnamesin *f.*
view *s.* Aussicht *f.*; Ansicht *f.*; Anblick *m.*; *in ~ of,* in Hinblick auf; *with a ~ to,* mit der Absicht zu...; ~ *v.t.* besichtigen, betrachten; prüfen.
viewer *s.* Zuschauer(in) *m.(f.)* Betrachter(in) *m.(f.)*
viewfinder *s.* (*phot.*) Sucher *m.*
viewpoint *s.* Standpunkt *m.*; Sichtweise *f.*
vigil *s.* Nachtwache *f.*; Vorabend *(m.)* eines Festtages.
vigilance *s.* Wachsamkeit *f.*
vigilant *a.*, **~ly** *adv.* wachsam.
vigilantes *pl.* Bürgerwehr *f.*
vigor *s.* Stärke, Kraft *f.*; Energie *f.*
vigorous *a.*, **~ly** *adv.* kräftig, rüstig.
Viking *s.* Wikinger(in) *m.(f.)*
vile *a.*, gemein, abstoßend; (*fig.*) scheußlich.
vilify *v.t.* erniedrigen, beschimpfen.
villa *s.* Landhaus *n.*; Villa *f.*
village *s.* Dorf *n.*
villager *s.* Dorfbewohner *m.*
villain *s.* Schurke *m.*; Bösewicht *m.*
villainous *a.*, **~ly** *adv.* niederträchtig; abscheulich.
villainy *s.* Schändlichkeit, Niederträchtigkeit *f.*
vindicate *v.t.* verteidigen; rehabilitieren.
vindication *s.* Verteidigung *f.*; Rehabilitation *f.*
vindictive *a.* nachtragend; rachsüchtig.
vine *s.* Weinstock *m.*; Rebe, Ranke *f.*
vinegar *s.* (Wein-)Essig *m.*
vine grower *s.* Winzer(in) *m.(f.)*, Weinbauer(in) *m.(f.)*
vine growing *s.* Weinbau *m.*
vineyard *s.* Weinberg *m.*
vintage *s.* Weinlese *f.*; (Wein)Jahrgang *m.*; ~ *a.* erlesen; herrlich.
vintner *s.* Weinhändler(in) *m.(f.)*; Winzer(in) *m.(f.)*
viola *s.* Bratsche *f.*
violate *v.t.* verletzen; schänden.
violation *s.* Verletzung *f.*; Schändung *f.*
violence *s.* Heftigkeit, Gewalt.
violent *a.*, **~ly** *adv.* heftig; gewalttätig.
violet *s.* Veilchen *n.*
violin *s.* Violine, Geige *f.*; ~ **case** *s.* Geigenkasten *m.*
violinist *s.* Geiger(in) *m.(f.)*; Violinist(in) *m.(f.)*
violoncello *s.* Cello *n.*, kleine Baßgeige *f.*
VIP *very important person,* (prominente Persönlichkeit), VIP.
viper *s.* Viper, Natter *f.*
virago *s.* Xantippe *f.*
viral *a.* Virus...
virgin *s.* Jungfrau *f.*
virginal *a.* jungfräulich.
virginity *s.* Jungfräulichkeit *f.*
Virgo *s.* (*astr.*) Jungfrau *f.*
virile *a.* männlich, viril.
virility *s.* Männlichkeit *f.*
virtual *a.*, **~ly** *adv.* eigentlich, so gut wie.
virtue *s.* Tugend *f.*; *in ~ of,* zufolge; *by ~ of,* kraft.
virtuoso *s.* Virtuose *m.*; Virtuosin *f.*
virtuous *a.*, **~ly** *adv.* tugendhaft, sittsam.
virulence *s.* Bösartigkeit *f.*
virulent *a.*, **~ly** *adv.* giftig; bösartig.
virus *s.* (*med.*) Virus; (*fig.*) Gift *n.*
visa *s.* Sichtvermerk *m.*, Visum *n.*; ~ *v.t.* mit Sichtvermerk versehen.
vis-à-vis *pr.* gegenüber.
viscosity *s.* Zähflüßigkeit *f.*
viscount *s.* Vicomte *m.*
viscountess *s.* Vicomtesse *f.*
viscous *a.* zähflüßig; klebrig.
visibility *s.* Sichtbarkeit *f.*; Sichtverhältnisse *n. pl.*
visible *a.*, sichtbar.
visibly *adv.* sichtlich.
vision *s.* Sehkraft *f.*; Erscheinung *f.*; Vision *f.*
visionary *s.* Visionär(in) *m.(f.)*; ~ *a.* eingebildet; seherhaft.
visit *s.* Besuch *m.*; Besichtigung *f.*; ~ *v.t. & i.* besuchen; besichtigen; heimsuchen.
visitation *s.* Besuch *m.*; Besichtigung *f.*; Inspektion *f.*
visiting card *s.* Visitenkarte *f.*
visitor *s.* Besucher(in) *m.(f.)*; Sommergast *m.*; **~s' book,** Fremdenbuch *n.*, **~'s bureau,** Fremdenamt *n.*
visor *s.* Visier *n.*; Mützenschirm *m.*
vista *s.* Aussicht *f.*
visual *a.* Seh..., Gesichts...

visualize *v.t.* sich im Geiste vorstellen; ins Auge fassen.
vital *a.*, **~ly** *adv.* Lebens...; unentbehrlich, wesentlich; vital; **~s** *s.pl.* edle Teile *m.pl.*
vitality *s.* Lebenskraft *f.*; Vitalität *f.*
vitamin *s.* Vitamin *n.*; **~ pill** *s.* Vitamintablette *f.*
vitiate *v.t.* beeinträchtigen; hinfällig machen (Vertrag).
viticulture *s.* Weinbau *m.*
vitreous *a.* gläsern, glasartig.
vitriolic *a.* ätzend; giftig.
vituperate *v.t.* tadeln, schmähen.
vituperation *s.* Schmähung *f.*
vituperative *a.* schmähend.
vivacious *a.* munter, lebhaft.
vivacity *s.* Lebhaftigkeit *f.*
viva voce *adv.* mündlich.
vivid *a.*, **~ly** *adv.* lebhaft, strahlend; kräftig.
vividness *s.* Lebhaftigkeit *f.*
vivify *v.t.* beleben.
viviparous *a.* lebendige Junge gebärend.
vivisection *s.* Vivisektion *f.*
vixen *s.* Füchsin *f.*; zänkisches Weib *n.*
viz. *videlicet (namely)*, nämlich.; d.h.
vizier *s.* Wesir *m.*
V-neck *s.* V-Ausschnitt *m.*
vocabulary *s.* Wörterverzeichnis *n.*; Wortschatz *m.*
vocal *a.* Stimm..., stimmhaft; Vokal...; **~ chord,** Stimmband *n.*
vocalist *s.* Sänger(in) *m.(f.)*
vocation *s.* Neigung *f.*; Berufung *f.*; Begabung *f.*
vocational *a.* Berufs...; **~ guidance** *s.* Berufsberatung *f.*
vociferate *v.t. & i.* heftig schreien.
vociferous *s.* schreiend, brüllend.
vogue *s.* Mode *f.*
voice *s.* Stimme *f.*; *at the top of one's ~*, aus voller Kehle; **~** *v.t.* äußern; stimmhaft aussprechen; **~ box** *s.* Kehlkopf *m.*
voiced *a.* stimmhaft.
voiceless *a.* stimmlos.
void *a.* leer; ungültig, nichtig; öd; **~** *s.* Leere *f.* Öde *f.*; **~** *v.t.* (aus)leeren; räumen, aufheben; ungültig machen.
vol. *volume,* Band *m.*; *vols., volumes,* Bände *m.pl.*
volatile *a.* unbeständig; flüchtig.
volatilize *v.t.* verflüchtigen.
volcanic *a.* vulkanisch.
volcano *s.* Vulkan *m.*
volition *s.* Wille *m.*
volley *s.* Salve *f.*; **~ball** *s.* Volleyball *m.*
volt *s.* Volt *n.*
voltage *s.* (*elek.*) Spannung *f.*
volte-face *s.* Kehrtwendung *f.*
voltmeter *s.* (*elek.*) Voltmesser *m.*
voluble *a.*, **~bly** *adv.* redselig; gesprächig.
volume *s.* (Buch) Band *m.*, Masse *f.*; Umfang *f.*; Rauminhalt *m.*; (*Radio*) Lautstärke *f.*; **~ control,** Lautstärkeneinstellung *f.*
voluminous *a.*, **~ly** *adv.* umfangreich.
voluntary *a.* freiwillig; absichtlich.
volunteer *s.* Freiwillige *m./f.*; **~** *v.t.* freiwillig dienen; **~** *v.i.* sich freiwillig melden.
voluptuary *s.* Wollüstling *m.*
voluptuous *a.*, **~ly** *adv.* wollüstig; üppig.
volute *s.* Windung *f.*, Schnecke *f.*
vomit *v.i.* erbrechen; sich übergeben; **~** *v.t.* ausspeien, auswerfen; **~** *s.* Auswurf *m.*; Erbrochene *n.*
voracious *a.*, **~ly** *adv.* gefräßig, gierig.
voracity *s.* Gefräßigkeit, Raubsucht *f.*
vortex *s.* Wirbel *m.*; Strudel *m.*
vote *s.* Wahlstimme *f.*; Beschluß, *m.*; **~** *v.t. & i.* wählen, stimmen, abstimmen.
voter *s.* Wähler(in) *m.(f.)*
voting *s.* Abstimmung *f.*; **~ system** *s.* Wahlsystem *n.*
votive *a.* gelobt, Weih...
vouch *v.t.* bezeugen; verbürgen; **~** *v.i.* gewährleisten.
voucher *s.* Beleg, Schein, Gutschein *m.*
vow *s.* Gelübde, feierliches Versprechen *n.*; **~** *v.t. & i.* geloben.
vowel *s.* Selbstlaut, Vokal *m.*
voyage *s.* Reise *f.* Seereise *f.*; **~** *v.t. & i.* bereisen; zur See reisen; *~ out,* Ausfahrt, Hinfahrt *f.*
vs. *versus,* contra, gegen.
V-shaped *a.* V-förmig.
VSOP *very superior old pale,* (Qualitätsbezeichnung für 20-25 Jahre alten Weinbrand u.ä.).
vulcanize *v.t.* vulkanisieren.
vulgar *a.*, **~ly** *adv.* gemein; vulgär; pöbelhaft; landesüblich.
vulgarity *s.* Gemeinheit *f.*
vulgarize *v.t.* herabwürdigen.
vulnerable *a.* verwundbar.
vulpine *a.* fuchsartig.
vulture *s.* Geier *m.*
v.v. *verses,* Verse; *vice versa,* umgekehrt, v.v.

W

W, w der Buchstabe W oder w *n.*
W. *west,* Westen, W.
wad *s.* (Watte-) Bausch *m.*; Pfropfen *m.*; Knäuel *n.*; **~** *v.t.* wattieren.
wadding *s.* Wattierung *f.*; Futter *n.*; Füllmaterial *n.*
waddle *v.i.* watscheln, wackeln.
wade *v.t. & i.* (durch)waten.
wafer *s.* Oblate *f.*; Hostie *f.*; Eiswaffel *f.*; **~** *v.t.* mit Oblate siegeln.
waffle *s.* Waffel *f.*; Geschwafel *n.*; Faselei *f.*; **~** *v.i.* faseln; schwafeln.
waft *v.i.* wehen; ziehen; **~** *s.* Hauch *f.*
wag *v.t.* schütteln; wedeln; **~** *v.i.* wackeln; **~** *s.* Spaßvogel *m.*
wage *s.* Lohn *m.*; **~earner** *s.* Lohnempfänger *m.*; **~tariff** *s.* Lohntarif *m.*; **~** *v.t. to ~ war,* Krieg führen.
wager *s.* Wette *f.*; **~** *v.t. & i.* wetten.
wages *s.pl.* (Arbeits)Lohn *m.*
waggish *a.*, **~ly** *adv.* schalkhaft.

waggle *v.i.* wackeln, wanken.
wag(g)on *s.* Wagon, Güterwagen *m.*
wagtail *s.* Bachstelze *f.*
wail *v.t.* beklagen; ~ *v.i.* wehklagen; ~ *s.* Klage *f.* Geheul *n.*
wain *s.* (poet.) Wagen *m.*; *Charles's* ~, der grosse Bär.
wainscot *s.* Täfelung *f.*; Wandleiste *f.*; ~ *v.t.* täfeln.
waist *s.* Taille *f.*; schmalste Stelle *f.*; Damenbluse *f.*
waistband *s.* Gürtelbund *m.*; Hosen/Rockbund *m.*
waistcoat *s.* Weste *f.*
waist-deep *a.* bis zur Taille reichend.
waistline *s.* Taille *f.*
wait *v.i.* warten; aufwarten; *to keep a person ~ing*, einen warten lassen; *lie in* ~, lauern; ~ **on,** bedienen; ~ *s.* Lauer *f.*; Hinterhalt *m.*
waiter *s.* Aufwärter(in), Kellner(in) *m.(f.)*
waiting-woman *s.* Kammermädchen *n.*
waitress *s.* Kellnerin *f.*
waive *v.t.* aufgeben, verzichten (auf).
wake ~ up, *v.i. & t. st.* wachen; aufwachen; aufwecken; ~ *s.* Wachen *n.*; Kielwasser *n.*
wakeful *a.*, **~ly** *adv.* wachsam; schlaflos.
waken *v.t.* aufwecken; ~ *v.i.* aufwachen.
walk *v.t. & i.* (im Schritte) gehen; spazierengehen; im Schritt gehen lassen; ~ *s.* Gang, Schritt *m.*; Spaziergang *m.*
walkabout *s.* Bad in der Menge.
walker *s.* Fußgänger(in), Spaziergänger(in) *m.(f.)*; Geher(in) *m.(f.)*
walkie-talkie *s.* Walkie-Talkie *n.*
walking *s.* Spazierengehen *n.*; Wandern *n.*
walking shoe *s.* Wanderschuh *m.*
walking stick *s.* Spazierstock *m.*
walking tour *s.* Fußtour *f.*
Walkman *s.* Walkman *m.*
walk-on part *s.* Statistenrolle *f.*
walk-out *s.* Arbeitsniederlegung *f.*
walk-over *s.* leichter Sieg *m.*; Spaziergang *m.*
walkway *s.* Fußweg *m.*
wall *s.* Wand, Mauer *f.*; ~ *v.t.* ummauern; befestigen.; **~-to ~ carpeting** Teppichboden *m.*
wall bars *s. pl.* Sprossenwand *f.*
wallet *s.* Tasche *f.*; Brieftasche *f.*; Geldtasche *f.*
wallflower *s.* (*bot.*) Goldlack *m.*; (*fig.*) Mauerblümchen *n.*
wallop *v.t.* prügeln; schlagen; ~ *s.* Schlag *m.*
wallow *v.i.* sich wälzen; schlingern; schwelgen.
wallpainting *s.* Wandgemälde *n.*
wallpaper *s.* Tapete *f.*
wallsocket *s.* Wandsteckdose *f.*
wall-unit *s.* Hängeschrank *m.*
walnut *s.* Walnuß *f.*
walrus *s.* Walroß *n.*
waltz *s.* Walzer *m.*; ~ *v.i.* walzen.
wan *a.* blaß, bleich.
wand *s.* Stab *m.*; Gerte *f.*
wander *v.i.* wandern; schlendern; abschweifen, irre reden.
wane *v.i.* abnehmen, welken; ~ *s.* Abnahme *f.*, Verfall *m.*
wangle *v.t.* organisieren; ~ *s.* Kniff *m.*
want *v.t.* nötig haben, brauchen, Mangel haben (an); wollen; wünschen; ~ *v.i.* mangeln, fehlen; ~ *s.* Bedürfnis *n.*; Mangel *m.*; Not *f.*
wanting *s.* Mangel *m.*; Bedürfnis *n.*; ~ *a.* mangelnd, fehlend.
wanton *a.*, **~ly** *adv.* üppig, ausgelassen, mutwillig; zwecklos; liederlich, geil; ~ *s.* liederliche Person *f.*; ~ *v.i.* schäkern, schwärmen.
wantonness *s.* Mutwille *m.*; Geilheit *f.*; Üppigkeit *f.*; Zwecklosigkeit *f.*
war *s.* Krieg *m.*; ~ *v.i.* Krieg führen.
warble *v.t. & i.* wirbeln; trillern.
warbler *s.* Grasmücke *f.*
war correspondent *s.* Kriegsberichterstatter(in) *m.(f.)*
war crime *s.* Kriegsverbrechen *n.*
war criminal *s.* Kriegsverbrecher(in) *m.(f.)*
war cry *s.* Kriegsruf, Schlachtruf *m.*
ward *s.* Gewahrsam *m.*; Vormundschaft *f.*; Stadtbezirk *m.*; Mündel *f.*; (Hospital-)Saal *m.*; ~ *v.t.* bewachen; abwehren.
warden *s.* Aufseher(in) *m.(f.)*; Rektor(in) *m.(f.)*; Heimleiter(in) *m.(f.)*
warder *s.* Wächter, Hüter, Wärter *m.*
wardrobe *s.* Kleiderschrank *m.*; Garderobe *f.*
ware *s.* Ware *f.*, Geschirr *n.*
warehouse *s.* Warenlager, Magazin *n.*; ~ **clerk** *s.* Lagerist *m.*; ~ *v.t.* einlagern.
warfare *s.*, Krieg *m.*; Kriegsführung *f.*
war game *s.* Kriegsspiel *n.*
warhead *s.* Sprengkopf *m.*
wariness *s.* Vorsicht *f.*, Behutsamkeit *f.*
warlike *a.* kriegerisch, Kriegs...
warm *a.*, **~ly** *adv.* warm; eifrig; feurig, hitzig; ~ *v.t. & i.* (sich) erwärmen.
warm-blooded *a.* warmblütig.
war memorial *s.* Kriegsdenkmal *n.*
warm-hearted *a.* warmherzig.
warmonger *s.* Kriegshetzer(in) *m.(f.)*
warmth *s.* Wärme *f.*; Eifer *m.*
warm-up *s.* (*sp.*) Aufwärmen *n.*; (*fig.*) Vorbereitung *f.*; Warmlaufen *n.*
warn *v.t.* warnen, ermahnen; ankündigen, wissen lassen.
warning *s.* Warnung *f.*; Ankündigung *f.*; Bescheid *m.*; *at a minute's* ~, fristlos.
war office *s.* Kriegsministerium *n.*
warp *v.i.* sich verbiegen; *s.* verziehen; abweichen; ~ *v.t.* krümmen; ~ *s.* Weberkette *f.*; Krümmung *f.*
war paint *s.* Kriegsbemalung *f.*
warrant *s.* Durchsuchungsbefehl *m.*; Haftbefehl *m.*; ~ *v.t.* rechtfertigen.
warranty *s.* Garantie *f.*
warren *s.* Kaninchengehege *n.*
warring *a.* kriegführend.
warrior *s.* Krieger *m.*
war-risk *s.* Kriegsrisiko *n.*
warship *s.* Kriegsschiff *n.*
wart *s.* Warze *f.*
warthog *s.* Warzenschwein *n.*
wartime *s.* Kriegszeit *f.*
wary *a.* vorsichtig; schlau.
wash *v.t. & i.* (sich) waschen; bespülen; ~ *s.* Wäsche *f.*; Wellenschlag *m.*; Schwemmland *n.*; Anstrich *m.*; Spülwasser *n.*; **~basin** *s.* Waschbecken *n.*; **~day** *s.* Waschtag *m.*; **~tub** *s.* Wasch-

faß *n.*; **~up** *s.* Aufwaschen *n.*; **~ing powder** *s.* Waschpulver *n.*
washable *a.* waschbar.
wash bill *s.* Waschzettel *m.*
washed-out *a.* verwaschen; (*fig.*) abgehetzt.
washer *s.* Waschen *n.*; Waschmaschine *f.*; Dichtungsring *m.*
washing *s.* Waschen *n.*; Wäsche *f.*
washing-machine *s.* Waschmaschine *f.*
wash out *s.* Pleite *f.*; Reinfall *m.*
wasp *s.* Wespe *f.*
waspish *a.*, **~ly** *adv.* reizbar, zänkisch.
wastage *s.* Schwund *m.*
waste *v.t.* verwüsten, zerstören; verschwenden; ~ *v.i.* abnehmen; schwinden; ~ *a.* verwüstet, öde; unnütz; ~ *s.* Verwüstung *f.*; Abnahme *f.*; Auszehrung *f.*; Einöde *f.*; Vergeudung *f.*; Verschwendung *f.*; Abfall *m.*; ~ **of time,** Zeitvergeudung *f.*; ~ **land** *s.* Ödland *n.*; ~ **product** *s.* Abfallproduckt *n.*; ~ **(water)** *s.* Abwasser *n.*
waste disposal *s.* Abfallbeseitigung *f.*; Entsorgung *f.*
wasteful *a.*, **~ly** *adv.* verschwenderisch.
wastefulness *s.* Verschwendung *f.*
waste-paper *s.* Papierbfall *m.*; ~ **basket,** Papierkorb *m.*
waste-pipe *s.* Abflußrohr *n.*
wastrel *s.* Verschwender *m.*
watch *s.* Wache, Wachsamkeit *f.*; Posten *m.*; Armband- Taschenuhr *f.*; ~ *v.t.* bewachen; beobachten; aufpassen; ~ *v.i.* wachen.
watchband, watchbracelet *s.* Uhrenarmband *n.*
watchdog *s.* Wachhund *m.*
watchful *a.*, **~ly** *adv.* wachsam.
watchmaker *s.* Uhrmacher(in) *m.(f.)*
watchman *s.* Nachtwächter *m.*
watchstrap *s.* Uhrenarmband *n.*
watchtower *s.* Wachturm *m.*
watchword *s.* Losung *f.*
water *s.* Wasser *n.*; *to make,* ~ sein Wasser abschlagen; **~s** *pl.* (Heil) Brunnen *m.*; ~ *v.t.* wässern, begießen, tränken; verwässern; **~ing-can** *s.* Gießkanne *f.*
watercart *s.* Sprengwagen *m.*
water closet *s.* Wasserklosett *n.*; Toilette *f.*
water color *s.* Aquarell *n.*
watercolorist *s.* Aquarellist *m.*
watercourse *s.* Wasserlauf *m.*
watercress *s.* Brunnenkresse *f.*
water diviner *s.* Rutengänger(in) *m.(f.)*
waterfall *s.* Wasserfall *m.*
waterfowl *s.* Wassergeflügel *n.*
waterfront *s.* Ufer *n.*
water glass *s.* Wasserglas *n.*
water level *s.* Wasserstand *m.*
water lily *s.* Seerose *f.*
waterlogged *a.* wasserdurchtränkt.
water main *s.* Hauptwasserleitung *f.*
waterman *s.* Bootsführer *m.*
watermark *s.* Wasserzeichen *n.*
watermelon *s.* Wassermelone *f.*
watermill *s.* Wassermühle *f.*
water pipe *s.* Wasserrohr *n.*; Wasserpfeife *f.*
water power *s.* Wasserkraft *f.*
waterproof *a.* wasserdicht.
water rate *s.* Wassergeld *n.*
water-repellent *a.* wasserabstoßend.
water-resistant *a.* wasserundurchlässig.
watershed *s.* Wasserscheide *f.*
waterspout *s.* Dachtraufe *f.*
water supply *s.* Wasserversorgung *f.*
watertable *s.* Grundwasserspiegel *m.*
water tap *s.* Wasserhahn *m.*
water-tight *a.* wasserdicht.
watertower *s.* Wasserturm *m.*
waterways *pl.* Wasserstraßen *pl.*
waterworks *s.* Wasserwerk *n.*
watery *a.* wässerig, wasserreich.
watt *s.* (*elek.*) Watt *n.*
wattage *s.* elektrische Leistung *f.*
wave *s.* Welle, Woge *f.*; ~ *v.i.* wogen; winken; ~ *v.t.* schwingen.
wave band *s.* (*radio*) Wellenband *n.*
wavelength *s.* (*radio*) Wellenlänge *f.*
waver *v.i.* schwanken; wanken.
wavy *a.* wogend; wellig.
wax *s.* Wachs *n.*; Siegellack *n.*; Ohrenschmalz *n.*; Schusterpech *n.*; ~ *v.t.* wachsen; wichsen, bohnern; ~ *v.i.* wachsen, zunehmen; werden.
waxen *a.* wächsern, Wachs...
waxwork *s.* Wachsfigur *f.*
waxy *a.* wachsartig.
way *s.* Weg *m.*; Richtung *f.*; Bahn *f.*; Art und Weise *f.*; Verfahren *n.*; Mittel *n.*; **~s** *pl.* Benehmen *n.*; *the ~ out,* Ausgang *m.*, Ausweg *m.*; *right of ~,* Wegerecht *n.*; *by the ~,* beiläufig, übrigens; *by ~ of excuse,* als Entschuldigung; *this ~, so,* auf diese Weise; *this ~ or that,* so oder so; *to make ~ for,* ausweichen; *to lead the ~,* vorgehen, vorangehen; *to lose one's ~,* sich verlaufen; *to find one's ~,* sich zurechtfinden; *on his ~, under ~,* unterwegs.
waybill *s.* Beförderungsschein *m.*
wayfarer *s.* Wanderer *m.*, Wanderin *f.*, Reisende *m./f.*
waylay *v.t.* auflauern, überfallen.
wayside *s.* Wegrand *m.*; *by the ~,* am Wege.
way station *s.* Zwischenstation *f.*
wayward *a.*, **~ly** *adv.* eigensinnig.
W.C. *water closet,* Abort *m.*
we *pn.* wir.
weak *a.* schwach, schwächlich.
weak current *s.* (*elek.*) Schwachstrom *m.*
weaken *v.t.* schwächen, entkräften.
weak-kneed *a.* schwach; feige.
weakling *s.* Schwächling *m.*
weakly *a. & adv.* schwächlich.
weakness *s.* Schwäche, Schwachheit *f.*
weak-willed *a.* willensschwach.
weal *s.* Striemen *m.*
wealth *s.* Wohlstand *m.*, Reichtum *n.*
wealthy *a.*, **~ily** *adv.* wohlhabend, reich.
wean *v.t.* entwöhnen; abgewöhnen.
weapon *s.* Waffe *f.*
weaponry *s.* Waffen *pl.*
wear *v.t.st.* tragen; anhaben; ~ *v.i.st.* sich tragen; *to ~ off,* sich abnutzen, sich verlieren; *to ~ out,* abtragen, abnutzen; ~ *s.* Tragen *n.*; Abnutzung *f.*; Tracht *f.*; Anzug *m.*; *~ and tear,* Abnutzung *f.*; *hard ~,* starke Beanspruchung *f.*; *to have longer ~,* länger halten; *resistance to ~,* Strapa-

zierfähigkeit *f.;* **~ing apparel** *s.* Kleidungsstücke *pl.*

wearisome *a.*, **~ly** *adv.* ermüdend.

weary *a.*, **~ily** *adv.* müde, matt; überdrüssig; ~ *v.t.* ermüden; ~ *v.i.* müde werden.

weasel *s.* Wiesel *n.*

weather *s.* Wetter *n.;* Witterung *f.;* ~ **bureau** *s.* Wetterwarte *f.;* ~ **outlook,** Wetteraussichten *pl.;* ~ **permitting,** bei gutem Wetter; ~ *v.t.* der Luft aussetzen, lüften; verwittern; verblassen.

weather-beaten *a.* verwittert; wettergeerbt.

weather chart *s.* Wetterkarte *f.*

weather forecast *s.* Wetterbericht *m.*, Wettervorhersage *f.*

weather-map *s.* Wetterkarte *f.*

weatherproof *a.* wetterfest; ~ *v.t.* wetterfest machen.

weather satellite *s.* Wettersatellit *m.*

weather vane *s.* Wetterfahne *f.*

weave *v.t. & i.* weben, flechten, torkeln.

weaver *s.* Weber(in) *m.(f.)*

web *s.* Netz *n.;* Gewebe *n.;* Schwimmhaut *f.*

web-footed *a.* mit Schwimmfüssen.

wed *v.t. & i.* heiraten; ehelichen; trauen.

Wed. *Wednesday,* Mittwoch, Mi.

wedded *a.* eingetraut, verheiratet.

wedding *s.* Hochzeit *f.;* ~ **anniversary,** Hochzeitstag *f.;* ~ **gown,** Hochzeitskleid *n.;* **~ring,** Trauring *m.*

wedge *s.* Keil *m.;* ~ *v.t.* (ver)keilen; durchzwängen.

wedlock *s.* Ehe *f.;* Ehestand *m.*

Wednesday *s.* Mittwoch *m.*

wee *a.* winzig, klein.; ~ *v.i.* *(fam.)* Pipimachen.

weed *s.* Unkraut *n.;* **~s** *pl.* Unkraut *n.;* ~ *v.t.* jäten.

weeday *s.* Wochentag *m.*

weeding *s.* Unkrautjäten *n*

weedy *a.* voll Unkraut.

week *s.* Woche *f.; a ~ from tomorrow,* morgen über acht Tage; *a ~ ago yesterday,* gestern vor acht Tagen.

weekend *s.* Wochenende *n.*

weekly *a. & adv.* wöchentlich; ~ *s.* Wochenblatt *n.*

weeny *a.* *(fam.)* klitzeklein, winzig.

weep *v.i. & t.* weinen; beweinen.

weeping willow *s.* Trauerweide *f.*

weevil *s.* Rüsselkäfer *m.*

weigh *v.t.* wiegen, wägen, erwägen; schätzen; *to ~ out,* auswiegen; ~ *v.i.* wiegen, (nieder) drücken.

weighing machine *s.* Hebelwaage *f.*

weight *s.* Gewicht *n.;* Wucht *f.;* Schwergewicht *n.;* Nachdruck *m.;* ~ *v.t.* beschweren; *to carry ~ with,* viel gelten bei; *to gain ~,* zunehmen; *to lose ~,* abnehmen.

weight bridge *s.* Brückenwaage *f.*

weightless *a.* schwerelos.

weightlessness *s.* Schwerelosigkeit *f.*

weightlifting *s.* Gewichtheben *n.*

weighty *a.*, **~ily** *adv.* gewichtig; schwer.

weir *s.* Wehr *n.*

weird *a.* unheimlich, seltsam.

welcome *a.* willkommen; ~ *s.* Willkomm *m.; to bid ~,* willkommen heißen; ~ *v.t.* bewillkommen; *you are ~,* bitte!

welcoming *a.* einladend.

weld *v.t.* zusammen(schweißen).

welder *s.* Schweißer(in) *m.(f.)*

welfare *s.* Wohlfahrt *f.;* ~ **officer,** *s.* Fürsorgebeamter *m.;* ~ **state,** *s.* Wohlfahrtsstaat *m.* ~ **work,** *s.* Fürsorge, Sozialarbeit *f.*

well *s.* Quelle *f.;* Brunnen *m.;* **~s** *pl.* Heilquelle *f.;* ~ *v.i.* quellen; ~ *a. & adv.* wohl, gut; gesund; leicht; gern; *as ~ as,* so wohl als auch.

well-advised *a.* klug (Plan).

well-appointed *a.* gut ausgestattet.

well-authenticated *a.* wohlverbürgt.

well-balanced *a.* aus dusgeglichen, ausgewogen.

well-behaved *a.* Wohlerzogen.

well-being *s.* Wohlsein *n.*

well-bred *a.* anständig; gut erzogen.

well-chosen *a.* wohlgesetzt (Worte); gewählt.

well-deserved *a.* wohlverdient.

well-done *a.* durch (Braten).

well-groomed *a.* gepflegt, gut aussehend.

well-nigh *adv.* beinahe.

well-off, well-to-do *a.* wohlhabend.

well-read *a.* belesen.

well-wisher *s.* Gönner(in), Freund(in) *m.(f.)*

Welsh *a.* walisich; *s.* Waliser(in) *m.(f.)* **~-rabbit** *s.* Käse auf geröstetem Brot *m.;* ~ *v.i.* nicht bezahlen (Restaurant).

welter *v.i.* sich wälzen; ~ *s.* Wirrwarr *m.*

wend *v.i. & t.* gehen, sich wenden.

wer(e)wolf *s.* Werwolf *m.*

west *s.* Westen, Abend *m.;* ~ *a. & adv.* westlich; **~bound** *a.* in Richtung Westen.

westerly, western *a.* westlich.

westerner *s.* Abendländer(in) *m.(f.)*

westernize *v.t.* verwestlichen.

westernmost *a.* westlichst...

Westphalia *s.* Westfalen *n.*

westward *a.*, **~ly** *adv.* westwärts; westlich.

wet *a.* naß, feucht, regnerisch; ~ **paint!,** frisch gestrichen! ~ *s.* Nässe *f.;* ~ *v.t.* nässen, anfeuchten.

wether *s.* Hammel *m.*

wet-nurse *s.* Amme *f.*

whack *v.t.* tüchtig schlagen, prügeln; hauen.

whale *s.* Walfisch *m.*

whalebone *s.* Fischbein *n.*

whale-oil *s.* Tran *m.*

whaler *s.* Walfischfänger *m.*

wharf *s.* Kai *m.;* Landeplatz *m.*

what *pn.* was; welcher, welches; was für ein; *~... ~,* teils... teils.

what(so)ever *pn.* was auch (immer).

wheat *s.* Weizen *m.*

wheedle *v.t.* schmeicheln; beschwatzen.

wheel *s.* Rad, Spinnrad *n.;* Töpferscheibe *f.;* *(mil.)* Schwenkung *f.;* ~ *v.t. & i.* (sich) drehen, rollen; *(mil.)* schwenken, einschwenken; fahren; *right ~!,* *(mil.)* rechts schwenkt!; *left ~!,* *(mil.)* links schwenkt!

wheelbarrow *s.* Schubkarren *m.*

wheelchair *s.* Fahrstuhl, Rollstuhl *m.*

wheeze *v.i.* keuchen, schnaufen, röcheln.

wheezy *a.* keuchend; pfeifend.

whelp *s.* Junge *n.;* junger Hund *m.;* ~ *v.i.* Jungen werfen.
when *adv. & c.* wenn, wann, da, als; wo.
whence *adv.* woher, von wo.
where *adv.* wo, wohin; *adv.,* **~abouts,** wo ungefähr etwa; worüber, *s.pl.* **~abouts,** Aufenthalt *m.;* **~as,** da, doch, während; **~at,** wobei, woran, worauf; **~by,** wodurch, womit; **~fore,** weshalb, wofür; **~in,** worin; **~into,** worin; **~of,** wovon, woraus; **~on,** woran, worauf; **~so, ~soever,** wo auch immer; **~to,** wozu, worauf; **~upon,** worauf; **~with,** womit; **~withal,** womit auch.
wherever *adv.* wo immer, überall wo.
wherewithal *s.* Mittel *n.*
whet *v.t.* wetzen; schärfen.
whether *c.* ob.
whetstone *s.* Wetzstein, Schleifstein *m.*
whey *s.* Molke *f.*
which *pn.* welcher, welche, welches; wer, was; der, die, das.
whichever *pn.* welcher auch immer, was auch.
whiff *s.* Hauch, Luftzug *m.*
while *s.* Weile, Zeit, *f.;* ~ *v.t.* verbringen, **~away,** vertreiben; ~ *c.* indem, während, solange (als).
whim *s.* Grille *f.;* Einfall *m.*
whimper *v.i.* winseln; wimmern; ~ *s.* Wimmern *n.*
whimsical *a.,* **~ly** *adv.* grillenhaft, launenhaft.
whine *v.i.* weinen, wimmern; ~ *s.* Gewimmer *n.*
whip *s.* Peitsche, Geissel *f.;* (Parlament) Einpeitscher *m.;* Aufforderung *(f.)* an Parteimitglieder im Parlament; ~ *v.t.* peitschen, geißeln; übernähen; ~ *v.i.* springen, flitzen; **~ped cream,** *s.* Schlagsahne *f.,* Schlagrahm *m.*
whip hand *s.* Oberhand *f.*
whipping *s.* Prügel *f.;* **~top,** Kreisel *m.*
whirl *s.* Wirbel, Strudel *m.;* ~ *v.t.* wirbeln; ~ *v.i.* herumwirbeln.
whirlpool *s.* Strudel, Wirbel *m.*
whirlwind *s.* Wirbelwind *m.*
whirr *v.i.* surren; *s.* Surren *n.*
whisk *s.* Wedel *m.;* Schneebesen *m.;* ~ *v.t.* schlagen (Sahne); wischen; ~ *v.i.* schwirren, huschen.
whisker *s.* Backenbart *m.;* Schnurrhaar *n.;* Bartborste *f.*
whisky *s.* Whisky *m.*
whisper *v.t. & i.* wispern, flüstern; zuraunen; ~ *s.* Geflüster *n.*
whist *s.* Whist(spiel) *n.*
whist drive *s.* Whistturnier *n.*
whistle *v.i. & t.* pfeifen; ~ *s.* Pfeifen *n.;* Pfiff *m.;* Pfeife *f.*
whit *s.* Punkt *m.;* Kleinigkeit *f.; not a* ~, nicht im geringsten.
white *a.* weiß; bleich; rein; ~ **horse,** Schimmel *m.*
whitebait *s.* junger Hering *m.,* Sprotte *f.*
white-collar worker *s.* Büroangestellte *m./f.*
white heat *s.* Weißglut *f.*
white-hot *a.* weißglühend.
whiten *v.t.* weißen; weiß machen.
whiteness *s.* Blässe *f.;* Reinheit *f.*
whitewash *s.* Tünche *f.;* ~ *v.t.* weißen, tünchen; weiß waschen.
white wine *s.* Weißwein *m.*
whither *adv.* wohin; **~soever,** wohin auch.
whiting *s.* Weißling (Fisch) *m.;* Kreide *f.*
whitish *a.* weißlich, etwas blaß.
Whitsunday *s.* Pfingsten *n.*
whittle *v.t.* schneiden; schnitzeln.
whiz *v.i.* zischen, sausen, schwirren; ~ *s.* Zischen, Sausen *n.*
whiz kid *s.* Senkrechtstarter(in) *m.(f.)*
who *pn.* wer; welcher; der, die, das.
WHO *World Health Organization,* Weltgesundheitsorganisation, WGO.
whodunit *s.* *(fam.)* Krimi *m.*
whoever *pn.* wer auch (immer); jeder; der, die, das.
whole *a.* ganz; heil, gesund; ~ **number,** ganze Zahl *f.;* ~ *s.* Ganze *n.; on the* ~, im Ganzen.
wholefood *s.* Vollwertkost *f.*
wholehearted *a.,* **~ly** *adv.* mit ganzem Herzen.
whole note *s.* ganze Note *f.*
wholesale *a.* Groß..., im großen, Großhandels...; ~ *s.* Großhandel *m.;* ~ *a.* im großen.
wholesome *a.,* **~ly** *adv.* gesund, heilsam.
whole wheat *a.* Vollkorn...
wholly *adv.* gänzlich, völlig.
whom pron. wen; wem; den, die, dem.
whoop *s.* Schrei *m.;* Jauchzer *m.;* ~ *v.i.* jauchzen; schreien.
whooping cough *s.* Keuchhusten *m.*
whore *s.* Hure *f.*
whorl *s.* Quirl *m.;* Windung *f.*
whortleberry *s.* Heidelbeere *f.*
whose *pn.* dessen, deren; wessen.
whosever *pn.* wer auch (immer).
why *adv.* warum; weshalb.
wick *s.* Docht *m.*
wicked *a.,* **~ly** *adv.* böse; schlecht; niederträchtig.
wickedness *s.* Bosheit *f.,* Niedertracht *f.*
wicker *s.* Weidenzweig *m.;* ~ *a.* aus Zweigen geflochten, Korb...; Weiden... ~ **furniture,** *s.* Korbmöbel *pl.*
wickerwork *s.* Korbflechtwaren *pl.*
wicket *s.* Pförtchen *n.;* Schalter *m.;* **~s** *pl.* Tor *n.* (beim Kricket).
wide *a.,* **~ly** *adv.* weit; breit; fern; sehr; *far and* ~, weit und breit.
wide-angle lens *s.* Weitwinkelobjektiv *n.*
wide-awake *s.* ganz wach; pfiffig.
wide-eyed *a.* mit grossen Augen.
widen *v.t.* *(v.i. & r)* erweitern; verbreiten.
wide-open *a.* weit aufstehend, aufgerissen.
wide-ranging *a.* weitreichend; weitgehend.
widespread *a.* weit verbreitet.
widow *s.* Witwe *f.;* ~ *v.t.* zur Witwe machen.
widowed *a.* verwitwet.
widower *s.* Witwer *m.*
widowhood *s.* Witwenstand *m.*
width *s.* Weite, Breite *f.*
wield *v.t.* handhaben; schwingen.
wife *s.* Frau *f.;* Weib *n.;* Ehefrau *f.*
wig *s.* Perücke *f.*
wiggle *v.t.* hin- und herbewegen, wacheln.
wight *s.* Wicht, Kerl *m.*
wigwam *s.* Wigwam *m.,* Indianerzelt *n.*
wild *a.,* **~ly** *adv.* wild.
wildcat *s.* Wildkatze *f.*
wildcat strike *s.* wilder Streik *m.*
wilderness *s.* Wildnis *f.*
wildfire *s.* Lauffeuer *n.*

wildfowl *s.* Wildgeflügel *n.*
wildness *s.* Wildheit *f.*
Wild West *s.* der Wilde Westen *m.*
wile *s.* List, Tücke *f.;* Streich *m.*
wilful as., eigensinnig; vorsätzlich; willkürlich.
will *s.* Wille *m.;* Testament *n.;* ~ *v.i.* letztwillig verfügen.
willed *a.* gesonnen, geneigt.
willies *s.pl.* (*fam.*) Nervösitat *f.*, Nervenschwäche *f.*, *get the* ~, Zustände kommen.
willing *a.*, **~ly** *adv.* willig; willens; gern.
willingness *s.* Bereitwilligkeit f, Bereitschaft *f.*
will-o'-the-wisp Irrlicht *n.*
willow *s.* Weide *f.;* (*mech.*) Wolf *m.*
will power *s.* Willenskraft p.
willy-nilly *adv.* wohl oder übel.
wilt *v.i.* welken.
wily *a.* schlau, verschmitzt.
wimp *s.* (*fam. pej.*) Schlappschwanz *m.*
win *v.t.* & *i.st.* gewinnen; einnehmen; (be)siegen; erobern; *to* ~ *over,* gewinnen für.
wince *v.i.* zucken; zurückfahren.
winch *s.* Kurbel *f.;* Winde *f.*, Kran *m.*
wind *s.* Wind *m.;* Atem *m.;* ~ *v.t.st.* winden, wickeln; drehen, wenden; *to* ~ *up,* aufziehen (Uhr); liquidieren (Geschäfte).
windbag *s.* (*fig.*) Schaumschläger m; Schwätzer *m.*
windbreak *s.* Windschutz *m.*
windbreaker *s.* Windjacke *f.*
windfall *s.* Fallobst *n.;* (*fig.*) Glücksfall *m.*
winding *s.* Windung, Krümmung *f.;* (*elek.*) Wicklung *f.;* ~ *a.* gewunden; **~-stairs** *s.pl.* Wendeltreppe *f.*
wind instrument *s.* Blasinstrument *n.*
windlass *s.* Winde *f.*
windmill *s.* Windmühle *f.;* Windrädchen *n.*
window *s.* Fenster *n.;* ~ **cleaner** *s.* Fensterputzer *m.;* ~ **dresser** *s.* Schaufensterdekorateur(in) *m.(f.);* ~ **dressing,** Schaufensterdekoration *f.*, Aufmachung *f.*, **~shopping** *s.* Schaufensterbummel *m.*
windpipe *s.* Luftröhre *f.*
windshield *s.* (*mot.*) Windschutz, Windscheibe *f.;* **~-wiper** *s.* Scheibenwischer *m.*
windsurfing *s.* Windsurfen *n.*
windswept *a.* windgepeitscht.
windtunnel *s.* Windkanal *m.*
windward *a.* luvwärts; *s.* Luvseite *f.*
windy *a.* windig; nichtig.
wine *s.* Wein *m.*
wine cellar *s.* Weinkeller *m.*
wine list *s.* Weinkarte *f.*
wine press *s.* Kelter *f.*
winery *s.* Weinkellerei *f.*
wine tasting *s.* Weinprobe *f.*
wing *s.* Flügel *m.;* Schwinge *f.;* Kulisse *f.;* (*avi.*) Tragfläche *f.;* (*avi.*) Geschwader *n.;* **~commander** *s.* Geschwaderkommandeur *m.; on the* ~, im Fluge; ~ *v.t.* beflügeln; ~ *v.i.* fliegen.
winged *a.* geflügelt, schnell.
winger *s.* Außenstürmer(in) *m.(f.)*
wingspan, wingspread *s.* Flugelspannweite *f.*
wink *s.* Blinzeln *n.;* ~ *v.i.* (zu)blinzeln; (*fig.*) ~ *at sth.* ein Auge zudrücken bei etw.
winker *s.* Blinker *m.*
winner *s.* Gewinner(in) *m.(f.);* Sieger(in) *m.(f.)*
winning *p.* & *a.* gewinnend, einnehmend; siegreich; ~ *s.* Gewinn *m.*
winter *s.* Winter *m.*
winterize *v.t.* winterfest machen.
wintry *a.* winterlich.
wipe *v.t.* wischen, abwischen; abtrocknen; *to* ~ *out,* (*mil.*) vernichten; ~ *s.* Wischen *n.*
wiper *s.* Wischer *m.*
wire *s.* Draht *m.;* Drahtnachricht *f.;* ~ *v.t.* drahten; **~brush** *s.* Drahtbürste *f.;* **~netting** *s.* Drahtgeflecht *n.;* **~rope** *s.* Drahtseil *n.*
wiredraw *v.i.* Draht ziehen; (*fig.*) in die Länge ziehen.
wireless *a.* drahtlos; ~ *v.i.* funken; ~ *s.* Rundfunk *m.*, Radio *n.*, Funker *m.*
wire puller *s.* Marionettenspieler *m.;* (*fig.*) Drahtzieher *m.*
wire-pulling *s.* heimliche Umtriebe *pl.*, Intrigen *pl.*
wiring *s.* (elektrische) Leitungen *f.pl.*
wiry *a.* aus Draht; (*fig.*) zäh, sehnig.
wisdom *s.* Weisheit, Klugheit *f.;* **~tooth** *s.* Weisheitszahn *m.*
wise *a.* **~ly** *adv.* weise; verständig, erfahren.
wisecrack *v.i.* witzeln; *s.* Witzelei *f.*
wiseguy *s.* (*vulg.*) Klugscheißer(in) *m.(f.)*
wish *v.t.* & *i.* wünschen; ~ *s.* Wunsch *m.*
wishful *a.*, **~ly** *adv.* wünschend, sehnlich; ~ **thinking,** Wunschdenken *n.*
wishy-washy *a.* wässerig; (*fig.*) lasch, schlapp.
wisp *s.* Bündel *n.;* Büschel *n.*
wistful *a.*, **~ly** *adv.* sehnsüchtig; melancholisch.
wit *s.* Witz *m.;* Geist *m.;* witziger Kopf *m.;* Witzbold *m. to* ~, nämlich, das heißt; *to be at one's* ~ *'s end,* nicht mehr ein und aus wissen.
witch *s.* Hexe, Zauberin *f.*
witchcraft *s.* Hexerei *f.*
witchhunt *s.* Hexenjagd *f.*
with *pr.* mit, samt, bei, für, auf, an.
withdraw *v.t.st.* zurücknehmen, zurückziehen; abberufen; (Geld) abheben; ~ *v.i.* sich zurückziehen.
withdrawal *s.* Zurückziehung, Zurücknahme *f.;* Abhebung *f.*
withdrawn *a.* verschlossen, zurückgezogen.
wither *v.t.* & *i.* ausdörren, verwelken, vertrocknen, vergehen.
withered *a.* verwelkt.
withering *a.* vernichtend; sengend.
withhold *v.t.st.* zurückhalten; vorenthalten; verhindern.
within *pr.* in, innerhalb, binnen; ~ *adv.* drinnen, im Innern.
without *pr.* außerhalb, vor; ohne; ~ *adv.* außerhalb; draußen.
withstand *v.t.st.* widerstehen; standhalten.
witless *a.* geistlos; geistesgestört.
witness *s.* Zeugnis *n.;* Zeuge *m.;* ~ *box,* Zeugenbank *f.; to bear* ~, Zeugnis ablegen; *to take the* ~ *stand,* in den Zeugenstand treten; ~ *for the prosecution,* Belastungszeuge *m.;* ~ *for the defense,* Entlastungszeuge *m.;* ~ *summons,* Zeugenvorladung *f.;* ~ *v.t.* bezeugen; zugegen sein, erleben.
witticism *s.* Witz *m.*, Witzelei *f.*
wittingly *adv.* wissentlich, vorsätzlich.

witty *a.*, **~ily** *adv.* witzig; geistreich.
wizard *s.* Zauberer *m.*
wizened *a.* runzelig.
wk. *week*, Woche, Wo.; *work*, Arbeit.
wkly. *weekly*, wöchentlich.
wks. *weeks*, Wochen, Wo.
WNW *west-northwest*, West-Nordwest, WNW.
w/o *without*, ohne, o.
wobble *v.i.* wackeln; zittern.
woe *s.* Weh *n.*; Leid *n.*; **~!** *i.* weh!
woebegone *a.* jammervoll.
woeful *a.*, **~ly** *adv.* traurig; erbärmlich.
wolf *s.* Wolf *m.*
wolfish *a.* wölfisch, gefrässig.
wolfram *s.* Wolfram(erz) *n.*
woman *s.* Frau *f.*, Weib *n.*
womanhood *s.* Weiblichkeit *f.*, Fraulichkeit *f.*
womanish *a.*, **~ly** *adv.* weibisch.
womanizer *s.* Schürzenjäger *m.*
womankind *s.* weibliches Geschlecht *n.*
womanliness *s.* Weiblichkeit *f.*, Fraulichkeit *f.*
womanly *a.* fraulich, weiblich.
womb *s.* Gebärmutter *f.*
Women's Liberation *s.* Frauenbewegung *f.*
women's rights *s.pl.* Frauenrechte *pl.*
wonder *s.* Wunder *n.*; Verwunderung *f.*; ~ *v.i.* sich wundern; sich fragen, gern wissen mögen.
wonderful *a.*, **~ly** *adv.* wunderbar.
wondering *a.* staunend, fragend.
wonderland *s.* Paradies *n.*; Wunderland *n.*
wonderment *s.* Verwunderung *f.*
wondrous *a.*, **~ly** *adv.* wunderbar, außerordentlich.
wonted *a.* gewohnt; gewöhnlich.
woo *v.t.* & *i.* freien, werben; zustreben.
wood *s.* Wald *m.*; Holz *n.*
woodbine *s.* Geißblatt *n.*
woodcarver *s.* Holzschnitzer *m.*
woodcarving *s.* Holzschnitzerei *f.*
woodcut *s.* Holtzschnitt *m.*
wooded *a.* holzreich; waldig, bewaldet.
wooden *a.* hölzern; (*fig.*) steif.
wood engraver *s.* Holzschneider *m.*
woodland *s.* Waldung *f.*
woodlark *s.* Heiderlerche *f.*
woodlouse *s.* Assel *f.*
woodman *s.* Holzhacker *m.*; Förster *m.*
woodpecker *s.* Specht *m.*
woodpulp *s.* Holzzellstoff *m.*
woodruff *s.* Waldmeister (Pflanze) *m.*
woodshaving *s.* Holzspan *m.*
woodshed *s.* Holzschuppen *m.*
woodwind *s.* Holzblasinstrument *n.*
woodwool *s.* Holzwolle *f.*
woodwork *s.* Holzarbeit *f.*; Holzwerk *n.*; Täfelung *f.*
woodworker *s.* Holzarbeiter *m.*
woodworm *s.* Holzwurm *m.*
woody *a.* waldig, holzig.
wooer *s.* Freier, Bewerber *m.*
woofer *s.* Baßlautsprecher *m.*
wool *s.* Wolle *f.*
woollen *a.* wollen; **~s** *s.pl.* Wollwaren *f.pl.*
woolly *a.* wollig; verworren, unklar.
word *s.* Wort *n.*; Nachricht *f.*; ~ **for ~,** Wort für Wort; *in other* ~*s*, mit anderen Worten; ~ *v.t.* in Worte fassen.
wording *s.* Formulierung *f.*; Stil *m.*
word order *s.* Wortstellung *f.*
word processing *s.* Textverarbeitung *f.*
word processor *s.* Textverarbeitungssystem *n.*
wordy *a.* wortreich; weitschweifig.
work *s.* Arbeit *f.*; Werk *n.*; Getriebe *n.*; Handarbeit *f.*; *hours of* ~, Arbeitstunden *pl.*; **~basket,** Arbeitskorb *m.*, **~box,** Arbeitskästchen *n.* (Handarbeit); **~order** *s.* Werkstattauftrag *m.*; **~permit** *s.* Arbeitserlaubnis *f.*; **~s** *pl.* Fabrik *f.*, Werk *n.*; Getriebe, Werk *n.* (Uhr, Klavier); Schriften *f.pl.*; ~ *v.i.* arbeiten; wirken; gären; funktionieren; ~ *v.t.* bearbeiten; behandeln; arbeiten lassen; in Betrieb haben; bedienen (Handwerkszeug), arbeiten mit; *to* ~ *out*, berechnen; *to* ~ *out at*, kommen auf; *to* ~ *up*, aufarbeiten, verarbeiten.
workable *a.* bearbeitungsfähig; betriebsfähig.
workaday *a.* Alltags...; alltäglich.
workaholic *a.* (*fam.*) arbeitswütig; ~ *s.* arbeitswütiger Mensch *m.*; Arbeitstier.
workday *s.* Arbeitstag *m.*
worker *s.* Arbeiter(in) *m.(f.)*; *heavy* ~, Schwerarbeiter *m.*
workforce *s.* Beligschaft *f.*
working *a.* Arbeits...; ~ **capacity,** Leistungsfähigkeit *f.*; ~ **capital,** Betriebskapital *n.*; ~ **class,** Arbeiterklasse *f.*; ~ **day,** Arbeitstag *m.*, ~ **expenses** *pl.*, Betriebsunkosten *pl.*; ~ **hours** *pl.* Arbeitsstunden *pl.*; **~knowledge,** ausreichende Kenntnisse *f.pl.*; ~ **majority,** arbeitsfähige Mehrheit *f.*; ~ **partner,** aktiver Teilhaber *m.*
workload *s.* Arbeitslast *f.*
workman *s.* Arbeiter *m.*
workmanship *s.* Werk *n.*; Arbeit *f.*; Geschicklichkeit *f.*; Stil *m.*
workshop *s.* Werkstatt *f.*; Workshop *m.*
work-to-rule *s.* Dienst nach Vorschrift *f.*
world *s.* Welt *f.*; Erde *f.*
World Bank *s.* Weltbank *f.*
worldly *a.* weltlich, irdisch; Welt...
world power *s.* Weltmacht *f.*
world war *s.* Weltkrieg *m.*
world-wide *a.* weltweit.
worm *s.* Wurm *m.*; Gewinde *n.*; ~ *v.t.* & *i.* wühlen, bohren; sich einschleichen.
worm-eaten *a.* wurmstichig.
worm's-eye-view *s.* Froschperspektive *f.*
wormwood *s.* Wermut *m.*
worn-out *a.* abgenutzt; erschöpft.
worried *a.* besorgt; ängstlich.
worry *v.t.* sich Sorgen machen; ängstigen, plagen; ~ *s.* Quälerei *f.*, Sorge *f.*
worrying *a.* sorgenvoll.
worse *a.* & *adv.* schlechter, schlimmer, ärger; *the* ~, desto schlimmer.
worsen *v.i.* schlechter werden; verschlechtern; verschlimmern.
worship *s.* Verehrung *f.*; Ehrerbietung *f.*; Gottesdienst *m.*; ~ *v.t.* & *i.* verehren; anbeten.
worshipper *s.* Anbeter(in) *m.(f.)*; Andächtige *m.*
worst *a.* & *adv.* schlechtest, schlimmst; ~ *s.* Schlimmste, Ärgste *n.*; *to get the* ~ *of it*, den kürzeren ziehen; *if the* ~ *comes to the* ~, wenn alle Stricke reißen.
worsted *s.* Wollgarn, Kammgarn *n.*

wort *s.* Kraut *n.;* (Bier) Würze.
worth *s.* Wert *m.;* Würdigkeit *f.;* ~ *a.* wert; ~ **while,** der Mühe wert.
worthless *a.* unwürdig; wertlos.
worthy *a.*, **~ily** *adv.* würdig.
would-be *a.* vorgeblich, Schein...; Möchtegern...
wound *s.* Wunde *f.;* ~ *v.t.* verwunden.
WP *word processor,* Textverarbeitungssystem; *word processing,* Textverarbeitung.
w.p.m. *words per minute,* Wörter pro Minute.
wraith *s.* Gespenst *n.*
wrangle *v.i.* zanken, streiten; ~ *s.* Zank, Streit *m.*
wrap *v.t.* wickeln, einwickeln.
wrapper *s.* Umschlagetuch *n.;* Hülle *f.;* Kreuzband *n.;* Deckblatt *n.*
wrapping *s.* Verpackung *f.*
wrapping-paper *s.* Packpapier *n.*
wrath *s.* Zorn, *m.*
wrathful *a.*, **~ly** *adv.* zornig.
wreak *v.t.* rächen; (ver)üben.
wreath *s.* Gewinde *n.;* Flechte *f.;* Locke *f.;* Kranz *m.;* **~e** *v.t.* flechten, winden, bekränzen; ~ *v.i.* sich ringeln.
wreck *s.* Schiffbruch *m.;* Wrack *n.;* Verwüstung *f.;* Strandgut *n.;* ~ *v.t. & i.* zertrümmern; zum Scheitern bringen; scheitern.
wreckage *s.* Trümmer *pl.*
wren *s.* Zaunkönig *m.*
wrench *v.t.* heftig ziehen, entwinden; verrenken; ~ *s.* Ruck *m.;* Verrenkung *f.;* Schraubenschlüssel *m.*
wrest *v.t.* drehen, zerren; (ent)reißen; verdrehen.
wrestle *v.i.* ringen, kämpfen.
wrestler *s.* Ringer(in) *m.(f.)*
wrestling *s.* Ringkampf *m.*
wretch *s.* Elende *m.;* Schuft *m.*
wretched *a.*, **~ly** *adv.* unglücklich, elend.
wretchedness *s.* Elend *n.;* Erbärmlichkeit *f.*
wriggle *v.i.* biegen, sich winden.
wring *v.t.st.* wringen; auswringen; drücken; ~ *s.* Händeringen *n.*
wrinkle *s.* Runzel *f.;* Falte *f.;* Kniff *m.;* ~ *v.t.* runzeln; rümpfen; zerknittern; ~ *v.i.* runzelig werden, sich runzeln, knittern.
wrinkled *a.* runz(e)lig.
wrinkly *a.* runz(e)lig.
wrist *s.* Handgelenk *n.*
wrist-band *s.* Manschette *f.;* Armband *n.*
wristwatch *s.* Armbanduhr *f.*
writ *s.* Verfügung *f.;* Gerichtsbefehl *m.*
write *v.t. & i.st.* schreiben; *to ~ off,* abschreiben (Schuld); *to ~ out,* ausschreiben.
writer *s.* Schriftsteller(in) *m.(f.);* Verfasser(in) *m.(f.);* Schreiber(in) *m.(f.)*
writhe *v.t.* drehen, winden, verdrehen; ~ *v.i.* sich krümmen, sich winden.
writing *s.* Schreiben *n.;* Schrift, Urkunde *f.;* Aufsatz *m.;* Schriftstellerei *f.;* **~book,** Schreibheft *n.;* **~case,** Schreibmappe *f.;* **~desk,** Schreibtisch *m.;* **~pad, ~tablet,** Schreibblock *m.;* **~paper,** Schreibpapier *n.;* *in ~*, schriftlich.
written *a.* schriftlich; geschrieben.
wrong *a. & adv.*, **~ly** *adv.* unrecht; verkehrt; falsch; *to be ~*, unrecht haben; ~ *s.* Unrecht *n.;* Irrtum *m.;* *to put a person in the ~*, einen ins Unrecht setzen; ~ *v.t.* unrecht tun, Schaden zufügen; kränken.
wrongdoer *s.* Missetäter(in) *m.(f.)*
wrongdoing *s.* Missetat *f.*
wrongful *a.*, **~ly** *adv.* ungerecht.
wrong-headed *a.* starrköpfig.
wroth *a.* zornig.
wrought *p. & a.* gearbeitet; gewirkt; ~ **iron,** *s.* Schmiedeeisen *n.;* ~ *a.* schmeideeisern.
wry *a.*, **~ly** *adv.* ironisch; sarkastisch.
wryneck *s.* Wendehals *m.*
WSW *west-southwest,* West-Südwest, WSW.
wt. *weight,* Gewicht, Gew.

XYZ

X, x der Buchstabe X oder x *n.*
xerox *s.* Xerographie *f.*
XL *extra large,* extragroß.
Xmas *s.* (*fam.*) (*Christmas*) Weihnachten.
X-ray *s.* Röntgenstrahl *m.;* ~ **tube,** Röntgenröhre *f.*
XS *extra small,* extraklein.
xylophone *s.* Xylophon *n.*
Y, y der Buchstabe Y oder y *n.*
yacht *s.* Jacht *f.;* ~ *v.i.* mit einer Jacht fahren.
yachting *s.* Segeln *n.*
yachtsman *s.* Segler *m.*
yank *v.t.* reißen an; ~ **out** *v.t.* herausreißen.
Yankee *s.* Nordamerikaner *m.*
yard *s.* Hof *m.;* Yard *n.* (0,914 *m.*); Werft *f.*
yardstick *s.* Maßstab *m.*
yarn *s.* Garn *n.;* (*fig.*) Erzählung *f.*
yarrow *s.* Schafgarbe (Pflanze) *f.*
yawn *v.i.* gähnen; ~ *s.* Gähnen *n.*
yd. *yard,* Yard *n.*
ye *pr.* ihr, euch.
yea *adv.* ja, ja doch.
year *s.* Jahr *n.;* ~ **by ~,** Jahr um Jahr.
yearbook *s.* Jahrbuch *n.*
yearlong *a.* einjährig.
yearly *a. & adv.* jährlich.
yearn *v.i.* sich sehnen, verlangen.
yearning *s.* Sehnsucht *f.*
year-round *a.* ganzjährig.
yeast *s.* Hefe *f.*
yell *v.i.* gellen, schreien, kreischen; ~ *s.* Angstgeschrei, Gellen *n.*
yellow *a.* gelb; ~ **fever,** gelbes Fieber *n.;* ~ **pages** *s.pl.* Branchenverzeichnis *n.;* ~ *v.i.* vergilben.; ~ *s.* Gelb *n.*
yellowish *a.* gelblich.
yelp *v.i.* kläffen, bellen.
yeoman *s.* Freisasse, Pächter *m.*
yes *adv.* ja, jawohl.
yesterday *adv.* gestern.
yet *c.* doch, dennoch, aber; ~ *adv.* noch, sogar; schon; *as ~*, bisher, *not ~*, noch nicht.
yew tree *s.* Eibe *f.*
Yiddish *a.* jiddisch; ~ *s.* Jiddisch *n.*

yield *v.t.* hergeben; hervorbringen, gestatten; aufgeben, übergeben; abwerfen, einbringen; ~ *v.i.* sich ergeben; nachgeben; weichen; ~ *s.* Ertrag *m.*
Y.M.C.A. *Young Men's Christian Association,* Christlicher Verein Junger Männer, CVJM.
yodel *v.i.* jodeln; ~ *s.* Jodler *m.*
yoga *s.* Joga *n.*
yog(h)urt *s.* Joghurt *m.*
yoke *s.* Joch *n.;* ~ *v.t.* zusammenkoppeln.
yokel *s.* dummer Bauer *m.*
yolk *s.* Eidotter *n.;* Eigelb *n.*
yon, yonder *a.* jener, jene, jenes; ~ *adv.* an jenem Ort, da drüben.
yore *adv.; of* ~, ehedem, vormals.
you *pn.* Sie, du, dich, ihr, euch; man, einen.
young *a.* jung; ~ *s.* Junge *n.*
youngish *a.* jugendlich.
youngster *s.* Junge *m.*
your *pn.* euer, Ihr, dein.
yours *pn.* euer, eurig, eurige, Ihr, dein, etc.
yourself, yourselves *pn.* euch, euch selbst; ihr selbst, Sie (selbst) etc.
youth *s.* Jugend *f.;* Jugendlicher *m.* ~ **hostel** *s.* Jugendherberge *f.*
youthful *a.*, **~ly** *adv.* jugendlich.
yr. *year,* Jahr.
Yule *s.* Weihnachten *pl.*
yummy *a.* (*fam.*) lecker.
Y.W.C.A. *Young Women's Christian Association,* Christlicher Verein Junger Frauen, CFJF.
Z, z der Buchstabe Z oder Z *n.*
Zaire *s.* Zaire *n.*
Zambia *s.* Sambia *n.*
zany *a.* verrückt; blöd.
zeal *s.* Eifer *m.*
zealot *s.* Eiferer, Zelot *m.*
zealous *a.*, **~ly** *adv.* eifrig, warm, innig.
zebra *s.* Zebra *n.*
zenith *s.* Scheitelpunkt, Zenit *m.*
Zephir *s.* Zephyr, Westwind *m.*
zero *s.* Null *f.;* Nullpunkt *m.;* ~ **hour,** (*mil.*) Nullzeit *f.*, x Uhr.
zest *s.* erhöhter Geschmack, Genuß *m.;* Eifer *m.*
zigzag *s.* Zickzack *n.;* ~ *a.* zickzackförmig.
zilch *s.* rein gar nichts.
Zimbabwe *s.* Simbabwe *n.*
zinc *s.* Zink *n.*
Zionism *s.* Zionismus *m.*
Zionist *s.* Zionist(in) *m.(f.)*
ZIP code *s.* Postleitzahl *f.*
zipper *s.* Reißverschluß *m.*
zither *s.* Zither *f.*
zodiac *s.* Tierkreis *m.*
zonal *a.* Zonen...
zone *s.* Gürtel *m.;* Erdstrich *m.;* Gebiet *n.*, Zone *f.;* ~ *of occupation,* Besatzungszone *f.;* ~ *of operations,* Operationsgebiet *n.*
Zoo (=*Zoological Gardens*) *s.* Zoo *m.*
zookeeper *s.* Zoowärter(in) *m.(f.)*
zoological *a.* zoologisch.
zoologist *s.* Zoologe *m.;* Zoologin *f.*
zoology *s.* Zoologie *f.*, Tierkunde *f.*
zoom *v.i.* heranholen; vorbeisausen.
zoom lens *s.* Gummilinse *f.*, Zoom *n.*

Geographical Names

Abyssinia, Abessinien; **Abyssinian**, Abessinier, abessinisch.
Adriatic, das Adriatische Meer.
Aegean, the ~ Sea, das Ägäische Meer.
Africa, Afrika; **African**, Afrikaner, afrikanisch.
Aix-la-Chapelle, Aachen.
Albania, Albanien; **Albanian**, Albanese, albanisch.
Alexandria, Alexandrien.
Algiers, Algier.
Alps, die Alpen; **Alpine**, Alpen. . .
Alsace, Elsaß; **Alsatian**, Elsässer, elsässisch.
Amazon, der Amazonenstrom.
America, Amerika; **American**, Amerikaner, amerikanisch.
Andalusia, Andalusien; **Andalusian**, Andalusier, andalusisch.
Andes, die Anden.
Anglo-Saxon, Angelsachse; angelsächsisch.
Antilles, die Antillen.
Antioch, Antiochien.
Antwerp, Antwerpen.
Apennines, die Apenninen.
Arabia, Arabien; **Arab**, Araber; Arabian, arabisch.
Aragon, Aragonien; **Aragonese**, Aragonier, aragonisch.
Arctic Circle, Nördlicher Polarkreis.
Arctic Ocean, Nördliches Eismeer.
Ardennes, die Ardennen.
Argentina, Argentinien; **Argentine**, argentinisch.
Armenia, Armenien; **Armenian**, Armenier, armenisch.
Asia, Asien; **Asiatic**, Asiate, asiatisch.
Asia Minor, Kleinasien.
Asturias, Asturien; **Asturian**, Asturier, asturisch.
Athens, Athen; **Athenian**, Athener, athenisch.
Atlantic, das Atlantische Meer.
Australia, Australien; **Australian**, Australier, australisch.
Austria, Österreich; **Austrian**, Österreicher, österreichisch.
Avon, Avon.
Azores, die Azoren.

Bale, Basel.
Balearic, ~ **Islands**, die Balearen.
Baltic, baltisch.
Baltic, die Ostsee.
Barbadoes, die Barbaden Inseln.
Barbary, die Berberei.
Bavaria, Bayern; **Bavarian**, Bayer, bayrisch.
Belarus, Weißrußland.
Belgium, Belgien; **Belgian**, Belgier, belgisch.
Bengal, Bengalen; **Bengali**, Bengale, bengalisch.
Bessarabia, Bessarabien.
Biscay, Biskaya; **Biscayan**, Biskayer, biskayisch.
Black Forest, der Schwarzwald.
Black Sea, das Schwarze Meer.
Boeotia, Böotien.
Bohemia, Böhmen; **Bohemian**, Böhme, böhmisch.
Bosnia, Bosnien; **Bosnian**, Bosnier, bosnisch.
Bothnia, the Gulf of ~, der Bottnische Meerbusen.
Brazil, Brasilien; **Brazilian**, Brasili(an)er, brasili(ani)sch.
Britain, Great ~, Grossbritannien; **British**, britisch; **Briton**, Brite.
Britanny, die Bretagne; **Breton**, Bretone, bretonisch.
Bruges, Brügge.
Brunswick, Braunschweig.
Brussels, Brüssel.
Bulgaria, Bulgarien; **Bulgarian**, Bulgare, bulgarisch.
Burgundy, Burgund; **Burgundian**, Burgunder, burgundisch.
Burma, Birma; **Burmese**, Birmane, birmanisch.
Byzantium, Byzanz; **Byzantine**, Byzantiner, byzantinisch.

Cadiz, Cadix, Kadiz.
Calabria, Kalabrien; **Calabrian**, Calabrese, Kalabrier, kalabrisch.
California, Kalifornien; **Californian**, Kalifornier, kalifornisch.
Cambodia, Kambodscha.
Cameroon, Kamerun.
Canada, Kanada; **Canadian,** Kanadier, Kanadisch.

Canaries, **Canary Islands**, die Kanarischen Inseln.
Caribbee, the ~ Islands, die Karibischen Inseln.
Carinthia, Kärnten.
Carniola, Krain.
Carpathians, die Karpathen.
Cashmere, Kaschmir.
Caspian, the ~ Sea, das Kaspische Meer.
Castile, Kastilien.
Catalonia, Katalonien; **Catalonian**, Katalonier, katalonisch.
Caucasus, der Kaukasus.
Celt, Kelte.
Central America, Mittelamerika.
China, China; **Chinese**, Chinese, chinesisch.
Circassia, Zirkassien; **Circassian**, Zirkassier, zirkassisch.
Cleves, Kleve.
Cologne, Köln.
Constance, **Lake** ~, der Bodensee.
Copenhagen, Kopenhagen.
Cordileras, die Kordilleren.
Corsican, Korse, korsisch.
Courland, Kurland.
Cossack, Kosak.
Cracow, Krakau.
Crete, Kreta, Kandia; **Cretan**, Kreter, kretisch.
Crimea, die Krim.
Croatia, Kroatien; **Croatian**, Kroate, kroatisch.
Cyprus, Zypern.
Czech, Tscheche.
Czech Republic, Tschechien.
Czechoslovakia *s.* die Tschechoslovakei *f.*

Dalmatia, Dalmatien; **Dalmatian**, Dalmatiner, dalmatisch.
Dane, Däne; **Danish**, dänisch.
Danube, die Donau.
Dauphiny, die Dauphiné.
Dead Sea, das Tote Meer.
Denmark, Dänemark.
Dunkirk, Dünkirchen.
Dutch, holländisch; **the** ~, die Holländer; ~**man**, Holländer.

East Indies, Ostindien.
Egypt, Ägypten; **Egyptian**, Ägypter, ägyptisch.
England, England; **English**, englisch; **the** ~, die Engländer; **the ~ Channel**, der Ärmelkanal; **Englishman**, Engländer.
Estonia, Estland; **Estonian**, Estländer, estnisch.
Ethiopia, Äthiopien.
Europe, Europa; **European**, Europäer, europäisch.

Far East, der Ferne Osten.
Flanders, Flandern.
Fleming, Flamländer; **Flemish**, flämisch.
Florence, Florenz; **Florentine**, Florentiner, florentinisch.
France, Frankreich.
Franconia, Franken.
French, französisch; **the** ~, die Franzosen; ~**man**, Franzose.
Frisian, Friese, friesisch.

Gael, Gäle; **Gaelic**, gälisch.
Galicia, Galizien; **Galician**, Galizier, galizisch.
Galilee, Galiläa.
Gascony, die Gascogne; **Gascon**, Gascogner, gascognisch.
Gaul, Gallien; Gallier.
Geneva, Genf; **Genevan**, Genevese, Genfer, genferisch.
Genoa, Genua; **Genoese**, Genuese, genuesisch.
Germany, Deutschland; **German**, Deutsche, deutsch.
Ghent, Gent.
Greece, Griechenland; **Greek**, Grieche, griechisch.
Greenland, Grönland.

The Hague, den Haag.
Hainault, Hennegau.
Hanover, Hannover; **Hanoverian**, Hannoveraner, hannoverisch.
Hebrew, Hebräer, hebräisch.
the Hebrides, die Hebriden.
Heligoland, Helgoland.
Helvetia, Helvetien, die Schweiz.
Hesse, Hessen; **Hessian**, Hesse, hessisch.
Hindoo, Hindu.
Hungary, Ungarn; **Hungarian**, Ungar, ungarisch.

Iceland, Island; **Icelander**, Isländer; **Icelandic**, isländisch.
Illyria, Illyrien.
India, Indien; **the Indies**, Indien; **Indian**, Inder, indisch.
Ingria, Ingermanland.
Ionia, Ionien; **Ionian**, Ionier, ionisch.
Iraq, Irak.
Ireland, Irland; **Irish**, irisch; **the** ~, die Iren, Irländer; **Irishman**, Irländer.

Istria, Istrien.
Italy, Italien; **Italian**, Italiener, italienisch.

Japanese, Japaner, japanisch.
Jordan, Jordanien.
Judea, Judäa.

Lapland, Lappland; **Lapp**, **Laplander**, Lappe; **Lappisch**, lappländisch.
Latvia, Lettland.
Lebanon, Libanon.
Leeward Isles, die kleinen Antillen.
Leghorn, Livorno.
Leipsic, Leipzig.
Lett, lettisch; **the** ~, der Lette.
Levant, die Levante.
Liège, Lüttich.
Lisbon, Lissabon.
Lisle, Lille.
Lithuania, Litauen; **Lithuanien**, Litauer, litauisch.
Livonia, Livland; **Livonian**, Livländer, livländisch.
Lombardy, Lombardei; **Lombard**, Lombarde, lombardisch.
Lorraine, Lothringen.
Louvain, Löwen.
Low Countries, die Niederlande.
Lucerne, Luzern; **the Lake of** ~, der Vierwaldstädter See.
Lusatia, die Lausitz; **Lusatian**, Lausitzer, lausitzisch.
Lyons, Lyon.

Macedonia, Mazedonien; **Macedonian**, Mazedonier, mazedonisch.
Madeira, Madeira.
Malay, Malaie; malaiisch.
Maltese, Malteser, maltesisch.
Manxman, Bewohner der Insel Man.
Marches, die Marken.
Marseilles, Marseille.
Mayence, Mainz.
Mediterranean, das Mittelländische Meer.
Middle East, der Mittlere Osten.
Milan, Mailand.
Moldavia, die Moldau.
Molucas, die Molukken.
Mongolia, die Mongolei; **Mongol**, Mongole, mongolisch.
Moor, Maure, Mohr; **Moorish**, maurisch.
Moravia, Mähren; **Moravian**, Mähre, mährisch; **the Moravian Brethren**, die Herrnhuter.
Morocco, Marokko; **Moroccan**, Marokkaner, marokkanisch.
Moscovy, Moskovien.
Moscow, Moskau.
Moselle, die Mosel.
Mozambique, Mozambik.
Munich, München.

Naples, Neapel; **Neapolitan**, Neapolitaner, Neapeler, neapolitanisch.
Netherlands, die Niederlande.
Neu(f)chatel, Neuenburg.
Newfoundland, Neufundland.
Nice, Nizza.
Nile, der Nil.
Normandy, die Normandie; **Norman**, Normanne, normannisch.
North Africa, Nordafrika.
North America, Nordamerika.
Norway, Norwegen; **Norwegian**, Norweger, norwegisch.
Nova Scotia, Neuschottland.
Nubia, Nubien; **Nubian**, Nubier, nubisch.
Nuremberg, Nürnberg.

Orange, Oranien.
the Orcades *or* **Orkenys**, die Orkaden Inseln.
Ostend, Ostende.
Ottoman, **the** ~ **Empire**, das Osmanische Reich.
Oxonian, Oxforder.

Pacific, der Stille Ozean.
Palatinate, die Pfalz; **Palatine**, Pfälzer, pfälzisch.
Palestine, Palästina.
Patagonia, Patagonien; **Patagonian**, Patagonier, patagonisch.
Pennsylvania, Pennsylvanien.
Persia, Persien; **Persian**, Perser, persisch.
Peruvian, Peruaner, peruanisch.
Piedmont, Piemont; **Piedmontese**, Piemontese, piemontesisch.
Poland, Polen; **Pole**, Pole; **Polish**, polnisch.
Pomerania, Pommern; **Pomeranian**, Pommer, pommerisch.
Portuguese, Portugiese, portugiesisch.

Prague, Prag.
Prussia, Preußen; **Prussian**, Preusse, preussisch.
Pyrenees, die Pyrenäen.

Ratisbon, Regensburg.
Rhenish, rheinisch.
Rhine, der Rhein.

Rhineland, Rheinland.
Rhodes, Rhodos.
Rocky Mountains, das Felsengebirge.
Rome, Rom; **Roman**, Römer, römisch.
R(o)umania, Rumänien; **R(o)umanian**, Rumäne, rumänisch.
Russia, Rußland; **Russian**, Russe, russisch.

Saracen, Sarazene, sarazenisch.
Sardinia, Sardinien; **Sardinian**, Sardinier, sardinisch.
Savoy, Savoyen; **Savoyard**, Savoyarde.
Saxony, Sachsen; **Saxon**, Sachse, sächsisch.
Scandinavia, Skandinavien; **Scandinavian**, Skandinavier, skandinavisch.
Scania, Schonen.
Scheldt, die Schelde.
Scotland, Schottland; **Scottish**, schottisch; **the Scotch**, **Scots**, die Schotten; **Scotsman**, **Scot**, Schotte.
Serbia, Serbien; **Serbian**, Serbe, serbisch.
Siberia, Sibirien; **Siberian**, Sibirier, sibirisch.
Sicily, Sizilien; **Sicilian**, Sizili[an]er, sizili[an]isch.
Silesia, Schlesien; **Silesian**, Schlesier, schlesisch.
Slavonia, Slavonien; **Slavonian**, Slavonier, slavonisch.
Sound, der Sund.
South Africa, Südafrika.
South America, Südamerika.
Spain, Spanien; **Spaniard**, Spanier; **Spanish**, spanisch.
Spires, Speyer.
Styria, Steiermark; **Styrian**, Steiermärker, stei[e]risch.
Swabia, Schwaben; **Swabian**, Schwabe, schwäbisch.
Sweden, Schweden; **Swede**, Schwede; **Swedish**, schwedisch.
Switzerland, die Schweiz; **Swiss**, Schweizer, schweizerisch.
Syracuse, Syrakus.
Syria, Syrien; **Syrian**, **Syr[i]er**, syrisch.

Tagus, der Tajo.
Tangier, Tanger.
Tartary, die Tatarei; **Tartar**, Tatare, tatarisch.
Teuton, Germane, Teutone; **Teutonic**, germanisch.
Thames, die Themse.
Thermopylae, die Thermopylen.
Thessaly, Thessalien; **Thessalian**, Thessalier, thessalisch.
Thrace, Thrazien; **Thracian**, Thrazier, thrazisch.
Thuringia, Thüringen; **Thuringian**, Thüringer, thüringisch.
Translyvania, Siebenbürgen.
Trent, Trient.
Treves, Trier.
Troy, Troja; **Trojan**, Trojaner, trojanisch.
Turkey, die Türkei; **Turk**, Türke; **Turkish**, türkisch.
Tuscany, Toskana; **Tuscan**, Toskaner, toskanisch.
Tyre, Tyrus.
Tyrol, Tirol; **Tyrolese**, Tiroler, tirolisch.

Umbria, Umbrien.
United States, die Vereinigten Staaten.

Valais, Wallis.
Valtelline, Veltlin.
Vaud, Waadt, Waadtland.
Venice, Venedig; **Venetian**, Venediger, Venezianer, venezianisch.
Vesuvius, der Vesuv.
Vienna, Wien; **Viennese**, Wiener, wienerisch.
Vistula, die Weichsel.
Vosges, die Vogesen.

Wallachia, die Wallachei; **Wallachian**, Wallache, wallachisch.
Walloon, Wallone, wallonisch.
Warsaw, Warschau.
Welsh, walisisch; **the** ~, die Waliser.
West Indies, Westindien; **West Indian**, Westindier, westindisch.
Westphalia, Westfalen; **Westphalian**, Westfale, westfälisch.
Würtemberg, Württemberg.

Yugoslavia, Jugoslavien.

Zealand, Seeland.
Zimbabwe, Simbabwe.
Zuider Zee, die *or* der Zuidersee.

Table of English Strong and Irregular Weak Verbs

Present	Past Tense	Past Participle	Present	Past Tense	Past Participle
abide	abode*	abode*	**forsake**	forsook	forsaken
arise	arose	arisen	**forswear**	forswore	forsworn
awake	awoke*	awoken*	**freeze**	froze	frozen
be	was/were	been	**get**	got	got, gotten
bear	bore	borne, born	**gild**	gilt*	gilt*
beat	beat	beaten	**give**	gave	given
become	became	become	**go**	went	gone
befall	befell	befallen	**grind**	ground	ground
beget	begot	begotten	**grow**	grew	grown
begin	began	begun	**hang**	hung*	hung*
bend	bent	bent	**have**	had	had
bereave	bereft*	bereft*	**hear**	heard	heard
beseech	besought*	besought*	**heave**	hove*	hove*
bid	bade, bid	bidden, bid	**hew**	hewed	hewn*
bind	bound	bound	**hide**	hid	hidden, hid
bite	bit	bitten	**hit**	hit	hit
bleed	bled	bled	**hold**	held	held
blow	blew	blown	**hurt**	hurt	hurt
break	broke	broken	**keep**	kept	kept
breed	bred	bred	**kneel**	knelt*	knelt*
bring	brought	brought	**knit**	knit*	knit*
build	built	built	**know**	knew	known
burn	burnt*	burnt*	**lay**	laid	laid
burst	burst	burst	**lead**	led	led
buy	bought	bought	**lean**	leant*	leant*
can	could	—	**leap**	leapt*	leapt*
cast	cast	cast	**learn**	learnt*	learnt*
chide	chid*	chid(den)*	**leave**	left	left
choose	chose	chosen	**lend**	lent	lent
cleave	cleft, clove	cleft, cloven	**let**	let	let
cling	clung	clung	**lie** (liegen)	lay	lain
clothe	clad*	clad*	**light**	lit*	lit*
come	came	come	**lose**	lost	lost
cost	cost	cost	**make**	made	made
creep	crept	crept	**may**	(*subj.*) might	—
cut	cut	cut	**mean**	meant	meant
deal	dealt	dealt	**meet**	met	met
dig	dug	dug	**melt**	melted	molten*
do	did	done	**mow**	mowed	mown*
draw	drew	drawn	**pay**	paid	paid
dream	dreamt*	dreamt*	**pen** (einschließen)	pent*	pent*
drink	drank	drunk			
drive	drove	driven	**plead**	pled*	pled*
dwell	dwelt*	dwelt*	**prove**	proved	proven
eat	ate	eaten	**put**	put	put
fall	fell	fallen	**quit**	quit(ted)	quit(ted)
feed	fed	fed	**read**	read	read
feel	felt	felt	**rid**	rid, ridded	rid, ridded
fight	fought	fought	**ride**	rode	ridden
find	found	found	**ring**	rang	rung
flee	fled	fled	**rise**	rose	risen
fling	flung	flung	**rive**	rived	riven
fly	flew	flown	**run**	ran	run
forbear	forbore	forborne	**saw**	sawed	sawn*
forbid	forbade	forbidden	**say**	said	said
forego	forewent	foregone	**see**	saw	seen
foretell	foretold	foretold	**seek**	sought	sought
forget	forgot	forgotten	**sell**	sold	sold
forgive	forgave	forgiven	**send**	sent	sent

Verbs marked * are more commonly conjugated in the regular weak form.

Table of English Strong and Irregular Weak Verbs—continued

Present	Past Tense	Past Participle	Present	Past Tense	Past Participle
set	set	set	**stave**	stove*	stove*
sew	sewed	sewn*	**steal**	stole	stolen
shake	shook	shaken	**stick**	stuck	stuck
shall	(*subj.*) should	—	**sting**	stung	stung
shear	sheared	shorn*	**stink**	stank, stunk	stunk
shed	shed	shed	**strew**	strewed	strewn*
shine	shone	shone	**stride**	strode	stridden
shoe	shod	shod	**strike**	struck	struck (stricken)
shoot	shot	shot	**string**	strung	strung
show	showed	shown*	**strive**	strove	striven
shred	shred, shredded	shred, shredded	**strow**	strowed	strown
shrink	shrunk, shrank	shrunk	**swear**	swore	sworn
shut	shut	shut	**sweep**	swept	swept
sing	sang	sung	**swell**	swelled	swollen*
sink	sank, sunk	sunk	**swim**	swam	swum
sit	sat	sat	**swing**	swung	swung
slay	slew	slain	**take**	took	taken
sleep	slept	slept	**teach**	taught	taught
slide	slid	slid	**tear**	tore	torn
sling	slung	slung	**tell**	told	told
slink	slunk	slunk	**think**	thought	thought
slit	slit	slit	**thrive**	throve*	thriven*
smell	smelt*	smelt*	**throw**	threw	thrown
smite	smote	smitten	**thrust**	thrust	thrust
sow	sowed	sown*	**tread**	trod	trod, trodden
speak	spoke	spoken	**wake**	woke, waked	waked, woke[n]
speed	sped*	sped*	**wear**	wore	worn
spell	spelt*	spelt*	**weave**	wove	woven
spend	spent	spent	**weep**	wept	wept
spill	spilt*	spilt*	**wet**	wet, wetted	wet, wetted
spin	spun	spun	**will**	would	—
spit	spit, spat	spit, spat	**win**	won	won
split	split	split	**wind**	wound	wound
spoil	spoilt*	spoilt*	**work**	wrought*	wrought*
spread	spread	spread	**wring**	wrung	wrung
spring	sprung, sprang	sprung	**write**	wrote	written
stand	stood	stood			

Verbs marked * are more commonly conjugated in the regular weak form.

English Abbreviations

A., *answer,* Antwort, Antw.; *ampere,* Ampere, A.
A.B., *able-bodied,* dienstfähiger Matrose *m.*; *Bachelor of Arts,* Bakkalaureus der Philosophie.
abbr., *abbreviation,* Abkürzung, Abk.
AC, *alternating current,* Wechselstrom.
A.C., *ante Christum,* vor Christi Geburt.
a/c, *account,* Rechnung.
A.D., *anno Domini,* im Jahre des Herrn, nach Christus, n. Chr.
adj., *adjective,* Adjektiv, Adj.
Adm., *Admiral,* Admiral *m.*
adv., *adverb,* Adverb, Adv.
advt., *advertisement,* Inserat.
AFL-CIO, *American Federation of Labor & Congress of Industrial Organizations,* Gewerkschaftsverband.
AM, *amplitude modulation,* Kurz- Mittel- u. Langwelle.
a.m., *ante meridiem,* vormittags.
anon., *anonymous,* anonym.
a/o, *account of,* auf Rechnung von.
AP, *Associated Press,* amerikanische Nachrichten Agentur.
approx., *approximately,* ungefähr.
Apr., *April,* April, Apr.
apt., *apartment,* Wohnung, Wng.
arr., *arrival,* Ankunft, Ank.
ASCII, *American Standard Code for Information Interchange,* standardisierter Code zur Darstellung alphanumerischer Zeichen.
asst., *assistant,* Assistent(in), Asst.
attn., *attention (of),* zu Händen (von), z. Hdn.
Aug., *August,* August, Aug.
av., *average,* Durchschnitt.
Ave., *Avenue,* Allee.

b., *born,* geboren, geb.
B.A., *Bachelor of Arts,* Bakkalaureus der Philosophie.
B&B, *bed and breakfast,* Übernachtung mit Frühstück.
B.C., *before Christ,* vor Christus.
B.D., *Bachelor of Divinity,* Bakkalaureus der Theologie.
B/E, *bill of exchange,* Wechsel.
bk, *book,* Buch; *bank,* Bank.
B.L., *Bachelor of Law,* Bakkalaureus der Rechte.
B/L, *bill of lading,* Frachtbrief.
bl., *barrel,* Faß; *bale,* Ballen.
Blvd., *Boulevard,* Boulevard.
B.M., *Bachelor of Medicine,* Bakkalaureus der Medizin.
B.Mus., *Bachelor of Music,* Bakkalaureus der Musik.
BO, *branch office,* Filiale.
Bros., *brothers,* Gebrüder *pl.,* Gebr.
B.Sc., *Bachelor of Science,* Bakkalaureus der Naturwissenschaften.
B/W, *black and white,* schwarz-weiß, s/w.

C., *centigrade,* Grad Celsius.
c., *cent,* Cent; *century,* Jahrhundert, jh.
ca., *circa,* etwa.
Can., *Canada,* Kanada.
Capt., *Captain,* Kapitän; Hauptmann.
CB, *Citizens Band,* CB-Funk.
C.C., *City Council,* Stadtrat.
CD, *compact disk,* CD; *corps diplomatique,* diplomatisches Korps, CD.
C.E., *Civil Engineer,* Ingenieur.
cert., *certificate,* Bescheinigung.
CET, *Central European Time,* mitteleuropäische Zeit, MEZ.
cf., *confer,* vergleiche, vgl.
ch., *Chapter,* Kapitel, Kap.
CIA, *Central Intelligence Agency,* (US-Geheimdienst).
C in C, *Commander in Chief,* Oberbefehlshaber.
cl., *centiliter,* Zentiliter; *class,* Klasse, Kl.
cm., *centimeter,* Zentimeter.
Co., *Company,* Gesellschaft; *County,* Verwaltungsbezirk.
c/o, *care of,* bei, per Adresse, p.A.
C.O.D., *cash on delivery,* per Nachnahme.
Col., *Colonel,* Oberst.
col., *column,* Spalte, Sp.
cont(d)., *continued,* Fortsetzung, Forts.

CP, *Canadian Press,* (Nachrichtenagentur); *Communist Party,* Kommunistische Partei, KP.
cp., *compare,* vergleiche, vgl.
CPA, *certified public accountant,* amtlich zugelassener Wirtschaftsprüfer.
cu., *cubic,* Kubik.
CV, *curriculum vitae,* Lebenslauf.
C.W.O., *cash with order,* Barzahlung bei Bestellung.
cwt., *hundredweight,* Zentner *m.*

d., *died,* gestorben, gest.; *depth,* Tiefe, T.
DA, *deposit account,* Depositenkonto.
DC, *direct current,* Gleichstrom; *Distrikt of Columbia* (Distrikt der amerikanischen Haupstadt Washington).
D.C.L., *Doctor of Civil Law,* Doktor des bürgerlichen Rechts.
D.D., *Doctor of Divinity,* Doktor der Theologie.
D.D.S. *Doctor of Dental Surgery,* Doktor der Zahnmedizin, Dr. med. dent.
DDT, *dichlorodiphenyltrichloroethane,* Dichlordiphenyl-trichloräthan, DDT.
Dec., *December,* Dezember, Dez.
dec., decd., *deceased,* gestorben, gest.
deg., *degree,* Grad *m.*
dep., *departure,* Abfahrt, Abf.
dept., *department,* Abteilung *f.,* Abt.
Dip., dip., *diploma,* Diplom, dipl.
Dir., dir., *director,* Direktor, Dir.
disc., *discount,* Abzug *m.,* Rabatt *m.*
div., *divorced,* geschieden, gesch.; *division,* Abteilung, Abt.
DJ, *disk jockey,* Disk Jockey.
D.Litt., *Doctor of Literature,* Doktor der Literatur.
D.Mus., *Doctor of Music,* Doktor der Musik.
do., *ditto,* dito, desgleichen, dgl.
dol., *dollar,* Dollar.
doz., *dozen,* Dutzend *n.*
D.Phil., *Doctor of Philosophy,* Doktor der Philosophie.
Dpt., *department,* Abteilung *f.,* Abt.
Dr., *Doctor,* Doktor *m.,* Dr.; *drive,* Fahrweg.
D.Sc., *Doctor of Science,* Doktor der Naturwissenschaften, Dr. rer. nat.
D.V.M., *Doctor of Veterinary Medicine,* Doktor der Tiermedizin.

E., *east,* Osten, *m.,* O.
E. & O.E. *errors and omissions excepted,* Irrtümer und Auslassungen vorbehalten.
ECOSOC, *Economic and Social Council,* Wirtschafts- und Sozialrat der UN.
ECU, *European Currency Unit,* Europärische Währungseinheit.
Ed., ed., *edited,* herausgegeben, h(rs)g.; *edition,* Auflage, Aufl., *editor,* Herausgeber(in), H(rs)g.
EDP, *electronic data processing,* elektronische Datenverarbeitung, EDV.
E.E., e.e., *errors excepted,* Irrtümer vorbehalten.
e.g., *exempli gratia,* zum Beispiel.
enc(l)., *enclosure(s),* Anlage, Anl.
ESA, *European Space Agency,* Europäische Weltraumbehörde.
esp., *especially,* besonders, bes., bsd.
Esq., *Esquire,* Herrn.
est., *established,* gegründet, gegr.; *estimated,* geschätzt, gesch.
EDTA, *estimated time of arrival,* voraussichtliche Ankunftszeit.
etc., *et cetera,* usw.
ETD, *estimated time of departure,* voraussichtliche Abflug-oder Abfahrtszeit.
EURATOM, *European Atomic Energy Community,* Europäische Atomgemeinschaft, Euratom.
excl., *exclusive, excluding,* ausschließlich, ausschl.
ext., *extension,* Apparat (teleph.), App.; *external, exterior,* äußerlich, Außen . . .

F., *Fahrenheit,* Fahrenheit.
F.A., *Football Association,* Fußballverband.
FAO, *Food and Agriculture Organization,* Organisation für Ernährung und Landwirtschaft der UN.
FBI, *Federal Bureau of Investigation,* US-Bundeskriminalamt.
Feb., *February,* Februar, Feb.
fed., *federal,* Bundes. . .
fig., *figure,* Abbildungen, Abb.
fl., *floor,* Stock.
FM, *frequency modulation,* Ultrakurzwellen, UKW.
f.o.b., *free on board,* frei (Schiff).
fo., fol., *folio,* Folio.
foll., *following,* folgend, folg.

fr., *franc*, Franc, Franken.
FRG, *Federal Republic of Germany*, Bundesrepublik Deutschland, BRD.
Fri., *Friday*, Freitag, Fr.
ft., *foot, feet*, Fuß.
fth., **fthm.**, *fathom*, Klafter.
fur., *furlong*, Achtelmeile *f.*

g, *gram*, Gramm, g.
gal., *gallon*, Gallone (3,785 l).
GATT, *General Agreement on Tariffs and Trade*, Allgemeines Zoll- und Handelsabkommen.
G.B., *Great Britain*, Großbritannien.
GDP, *gross domestic product*, Bruttoinlandsprodukt, BIP.
Gen., *general*, General.
gen., *generally*, allgemein.
gm, *gram*, Gramm.
GMT, *Greenwich Mean Time*, Westeuropäische Zeit, WEZ.
GNP, *gross national product*, Bruttosozialprodukt, BNP.
Gov., *government*, Regierung; *governor*, Gouverneur.
G.P., *General Practitioner*, praktischer Arzt *m.*
G.P.O., *General Post Office*, Hauptpostamt *n.*
gr. wt., *gross weight*, Bruttogewicht.
gtd., *guar.*, *guaranteed*, garantiert.

h., **hr.**, *hour*, Stunde *f.*, **hrs.**, *hours*, Stunden; *height*, Höhe.
H.B.M., *His (or Her) Britannic Majesty*, Seine (Ihre) Majestät der König (die Königin) von Großbritannien.
hdbk, *handbook*, Handbuch.
HE, *high explosive*, hochexplosiv.
hf., *half*, halb.
H.M., *His/Her Majesty*, Seine/Ihre Majestät.
H.M.S., *His/Her Majesty's Ship*, Seiner/Ihrer Majestät Schiff.
HO, *head office*, Hauptgeschäftsstelle, Zentrale.
Hon., *Honorable*, Ehrenwert; *Honorary*, Ehren...
h.p., *horse-power*, Pferdestärke *f.*
HQ, *Headquarters*, Hauptquartier.
H.S., *High School*, höhere Schule.
ht., *height*, Höhe, H.

IATA, *International Air Transport Association*, Internationaler Luftverkehrsverband.
ib(id), *ibidem (in the same place)*, ebenda, ebd.
IBRD, *International Bank for Reconstruction and Development*, Internationale Bank für Wiederaufbau und Entwicklung.
IC, *integrated circuit*, integrierter Schaltkreis.
ICU, *intensive care unit*, Intensivstation.
ID, *identification*, Ausweis.
i.e., *id est*, das heißt, d.h.
ill., *illustration*, Abbildung, Abd.
in., *inches*, Zoll.
Inc., *incorporated*, eingetragen.
incl., *inclusive, including*, einschließlich, einschl.
inst., *instant, of the present month*, dieses Monats, d.M.
I.O.U., *I owe you*, ich schulde Ihnen; Schuldschein *m.*
IQ, *intelligence quotient*, Intelligenzquotient, IQ.
ISBN, *international standard book number*, ISBN-Nummer.
ital., *italics*, Kursivdruck *m.*
IUD, *intrauterine device*, Intrauterinpessar.
IYHF, *International Youth Hostel Federation*, Internationaler Jugendherbergsverband.

J, *Joule*, Joule, J.
J., *Judge*, Richter.
Jan., *January*, Januar, Jan.
JCD, *Juris Civilis Doctor (Doctor of Civil Law)*, Doktor des Zivilrechts.
J.P., *Justice of the Peace*, Friedensrichter *m.*
Jr., *Junior*, der Jüngere, jr., jun.
JUD, *Juris Utriusque Doctor (Doctor of Canon and Civil Law)*, Doktor beider Rechte.
Jul., *July*, Juli.
Jun., *June*, Juni.

K.C., *Knight Commander*, Komtur, Großmeister *m.*; King's Counsel, Justizrat *m.*
k., *kilogram*, Kilogramm, k, kg.
km., *kilometer*, Kilometer, km.
Kn, *knot*, Knoten, kn.
KO, *knockout*, Knockout, K.o.

kph, *kilometer(s) per hour,* Stundenkilometer, km/h.
kV, *kv, kilovolt,* Kilovolt, kV.
kW, *kw, Kilowatt,* Kilowatt, kW.

L, *large,* groß; *Lake,* See.
L., £, *libra, pound sterling,* Pfund (sterling) *n.*
l., *left,* links, l.; *line,* Zeile, z; *liter,* Liter, l.
LA, *Los Angeles.*
lat., *Latitude,* Breite *f.*
lb., *libra, pound,* Pfund *n.*
l.c., *loco citato,* am angeführten Orte.
L/C, *letter of credit,* Kreditbrief *m.*
LCD, *liquid crystal display,* Flüssigkristallanzeige.
Lieut., Lt., *Lieutenant,* Leutnant *m.*
lit., *literally,* wörtlich.
Litt.D., *Litterarum Doctor (Doctor of Letters),* Doktor der Literatur.
ll., *lines,* Zeilen, Z.
LL.D., *Legum Doctor,* Doktor der Rechte.
loc. cit., *loco citato (at the place already cited),* am angeführten Orte, a.a.O.
long., *longitude,* Länge *f.*
LP, *long playing,* Langspielplatte, LP.
l.p., *low pressure,* Tiefdruck.
Ltd., *limited (liability company),* (Gesellschaft) mit beschränkter Haftung, m.b.H.
LW, *long wave,* Langwelle, LW.

M, *medium,* mittelgroß.
m., *male, masculine,* männlich; *meter,* Meter *m.*; *mile,* Meile *f.*; *minute,* Minute *f.*, min.; *married,* verheiratet, verh.; *million,* Million, Mio., Mill.
M.A., *Master of Arts,* Magister der Philosophie.
Maj., *major,* Major.
Maj.-Gen., *major-general,* Generalmajor.
Mar., *March,* März.
masc., *masculine,* maskulin.
MBA, *Master of Business Administration,* Magister der Betriebswirtschaftslehre.
M.C., *master of ceremonies,* Zeremonienmeister, Conférencier.
M.D., *Medicinae Doctor,* Doktor der Medizin, Dr. med.
med., *medical,* medizinisch; *medium,* mittelgroß; *medieval,* mittelalterlich.
MEP, *Member of the European Parliament,* Mitglied des Europaparlaments.
Messrs., *Messieurs,* Herren.
mfd., *manufactured,* angefertigt.
mg, *milligram,* Milligramm, mg.
mo., *month,* Monat.
M.O., *Money Order,* Postanweisung *f.*
Mon., *Monday,* Montag.
mos., *months,* Monate.
MP, *Member of Parliament,* Parlamentsmitglied; *military police,* Militärpolizei.
mph, *miles per hour,* Stundenmeilen.
Mr., *Mister,* Herr.
Mrs., *Mistress,* Frau *f.*
Ms., Frau, Fräulein.
MS., *manuscript,* Handschrift *f.*, Ms.
M.Sc., *Master of Science,* Magister der Naturwissenschaften.
MSS., *manuscripts,* Handschriften.
Mt., *Mount,* Berg *m.*
mth, *month,* Monat.
Mus.D., *Doctor of Music,* Doktor der Musik.
MW, *medium wave,* Mittelwelle, MW.

N., *north,* Norden, N; *Nitrogen,* Stickstoff *m.*
n., *name,* Name; *noun,* Substantiv, Subst.; *neuter,* sächlich.
N.B., *nota bene (note well),* notabene, NB.
n.d., *no date,* ohne Datum.
N.E., *northeast,* Nordost, NO.
neg., *negative,* negativ, neg.
net., *netto,* netto.
NNE, *north-northeast,* Nord-Nordost.
NNW, *north-northwest,* Nord-Nordwest.
no., *numero,* Nummer *f.*
nos., *numbers,* Nummern.
Nov., *November,* November, Nov.
n.s., *not specified,* nicht angegeben.
NT, *New Testament,* Neues Testament, NT.
nt. wt., *net weight,* Nettogewicht.
NW, *northwest,* Nordwest.
N.Y., *New York.*
N.Z., *New Zealand,* Neuseeland.

O., *Oxygen,* Sauerstoff.
Ob., *obiit (=died),* gestorben, gest.

Oct., *October*, Oktober, Okt.
OECD, *Organization for Economic Cooperation and Development*, Organisation für wirtschaftliche Zusammenarbeit und Entwicklung.
O.H.M.S., *On His/Her Majesty's Service*, im Dienste Sr/Ihr. Majestät; Dienstsache.
o.n.o., *or nearest offer*, Verhandlungsbasis, VB.
OPEC, *Organization of Petroleum Exporting Countries*, Organisation der Erdöl exportierenden Länder.
O.T., *Old Testament*, Altes Testament, AT.
oz., *ounce*, Unze.

p., *page*, Seite.
p.a., *per annum* (*per year*), pro Jahr.
par., *paragraph*, Absatz, Abs., Abschnitt, Abschn.
PC, *Personal computer*, Personal-computer, PC; *police constable*, Schutzmann.
p.c., *postcard*, Postkarte *f.*; %, *per cent*, Prozent, %.
PD, *Police Department*, Polizeibehörde.
pd, *paid*, bezahlt, bez.
p.d., *per diem* (*by the day*), pro Tag.
PEN (*International Association of*) *Poets, Playwrights, Editors, Essayists, and Novelists*, PEN-Club, (internationaler Schriftstellerverband).
per pro, *per procurationem* (*by proxy*), per Prokura, pp.
Ph.D., *Philosophiae Doctor* (*Doctor of Philosophy*), Doktor der Philosophie, Dr. phil.
PIN *personal identification number*, (Nummer auf Scheckkarten).
Pk., *Park*, Park.
Pl., *Place*, Platz, Pl.
pl., *plural*, Plural, Pl., pl.
p.m., *post meridiem*, nachmittags.
P.O., *Post Office*, Postamt *n.*; *postal order*, Postanweisung.
P.O.B., *post office box*, Postfach, Pf.
P.O.D., *pay on delivery*, per Nachnahme; *Post Office Department*, Postministerium.
P.O.O., *Post Office Order*, Postanweisung *f.*
pop., *population*, Einwohner, Einw.
POW, *prisoner of war*, Kriegsgefangene.
pp., *pages*, Seiten *pl.*
PR, *public relations*, Öffentlichkeitsarbeit.
Pres., *President*, Präsident.
Prof., *Professor*, Professor.
P.S., *Postscript*, Nachschrift *f.*
pt., *pint*, Pinte *f.*; *part*, Teil, T.; *payment*, Zahlung.
PTA, *Parent-Teacher Association*, Eltern-Lehrer-Vereinigung.
P.T.O., *Please turn over*, bitte wenden.
Pvt., *private*, Gemeiner Soldat.

qr., *quarter*, Viertel.
quot., *quotation*, Kurs-Preisnotierung.
qt., *quart*, Quart.
qto., *quarto*, Quartformat *n.*

r., *right*, rechts, r.
RAM, *random access memory*, Direktzugriffsspeicher.
RC, *Roman Catholic*, römisch-katholisch, r.-k.
rcpt., *receipt*, Quittung *f.*
Rd, *Road*, Straße, Str.
recd., *received*, erhalten, erh.
ref., *reference*, (mit) Bezug (auf).
regd., *registered*, eingetragen.
Regt., *Regiment*, Regiment *n.*
res., *research*, Forschungs...; *residence*, Wohnsitz.
ret., retd., *retired*, im Ruhestand, i.R., außer Dienst, a.D.
Rev., *Reverend*, Ehrwürden, Hochwürden, Ehrw.
rm., *room*, Zimmer, Zi.
ROM, *read only memory*, Nur-Lese-Speicher.
r.p.m., *revolutions per minute*, Umdrehungen pro Minute, U/min.
RR, *railroad*, Eisenbahn.
RSVP, *répondez s'il vous plaît* (*please reply*), um Antwort wird gebeten, u.A.w.g.
rt., *right*, rechts, r.
Rt. Hon., *Right Honorable*, Hochwohlgeboren.

s, *second*, Sekunde, Sek.
S., *south*, Süden, S.; *Saint*, Sankt; *Society*, Verein.
$, *dollar*, Dollar.
S.A., *South Africa*, Südafrika.
SASE, *self-addressed stamped envelope*, frankierter Rückumschlag.
sc., scil., *scilicet* (*namely*), nämlich.

Sc.D. = **D.Sc.**
SE, *southeast,* Südost, SO.
Sec., *Secretary,* Sekretär(in), Sekr.; Minister, Min.
sec., *second,* Sekunde, Sek., sek.
Sen., *senior,* Senior, der Ältere, d.Ä., sen.
Sept., *September,* September, Sept.
Sgt., *Sergeant,* Sergeant *m.*
soc., *society,* Gesellschaft, Verein.
Sq., *Square,* Platz *m.*
sq., *square,* Quadrat. . .
Sr. *sister,* eccl. (Ordens)Schwester; *senior,* Senior, der Ältere, d.Ä., sen.
S.S., *Saints,* Heilige *pl.*
S.S., *steamship,* Dampfer *m.*
SSE, *south-southeast,* Südsüdost, SSO.
SSW, *south-southwest,* Südsüdwest, SSW.
St., *Saint,* Heilige *m.*; *Street,* Straße *f.*
STA, *scheduled time of arrival,* planmäßige Ankunftszeit.
Sta., *Station,* Bahnhof, Bhf.
STD, *Scheduled time of departure,* planmäßge Abfahrtszeit.
stg., *sterling,* Sterling.
stn, *station,* Bahnhof, Bhf.
Sun., *Sunday,* Sonntag, So.
suppl., *supplement,* Nachtrag.
Surg., *surgery,* Chirurgie *f.*; *surgeon,* Chirurg *m.*
SW, *southwest,* Südwest, SW; *short wave,* Kurzwelle, KW.

t, *ton,* Tonne, t.
TB, *tuberculosis,* Tuberkulose, Tb(c).
tbsp., *tablespoon,* Eßlöffel, Eßl.
tel., *telephone,* Telefon, Tel.
Thur., *Thursday,* Donnerstag, Do.
TM, *trademark,* Warenzeichen, Wz.
T.O., *Turn over,* umschlagen.
tsp., *teaspoon,* Teelöffel, Teel.
TU, *trade union,* Gewerkschaft.
Tues., *Tuesday,* Dienstag, Di.

UEFA, *Union of European Football Associations,* UEFA.
UFO, *unidentified flying object,* Ufo.
UHF, *ultrahigh frequency,* Ultrahochfrequenzbereich, UHF.
U.K., *United Kingdom,* Vereinigtes Königreich *n.*, Großbritannien.
UN, *United Nations,* Vereinte Nationen, UN.
UNESCO, *United Nations Educational, Scientific, and Cultural Organization,* (Organisation der Vereinten Nationen für Erziehung, Wissenschaft, und Kultur).
UNICEF, *United Nations Children's Fund,* (Kinderhilfswerk der Vereinten Nationen).
UPI, *United Press International,* (amerikanische Nachrichtenagentur).
U.S., *United States,* Vereinigte Staaten, *n.pl.*
U.S.A., *United States of America,* Vereinigte Staaten von Nordamerika; *United States Army,* Heer (*n.*) der Vereinigten Staaten.
USW, *ultra short wave,* Ultrakurzwelle.

V, *volt,* Volt, V.
VAT, *value-added tax,* Mehrwertsteuer, Mwst.
VCR, *video cassette recorder,* Videorecorder.
VD, *venereal disease,* Geschlechtskrankheit.
VHF, *very high frequency,* Ultrakurzwelle, VHF, UKW.
v., *vide,* siehe; *verse,* Vers *m*; *versus,* gegen.
Ven., *Venerable,* Ehrwürden.
VIP, *very important person,* (prominente Persönlichkeit), VIP.
viz., *videlicet* (*namely*), nämlich.
vol., *volume,* Band *m.*; **vols.,** *volumes,* Bände *m.pl.*
vs., *versus,* contra, gegen.
VSOP, *very superior old pale,* (Qualitätsbezeichnung für 20–25 Jahre alten Weinbrand u.ä.).
v.v., *verses,* Verse; *vice versa,* umgekehrt, v.v.

W., *west,* Westen, W.
W.C., *water closet,* Abort *m.*
Wed., *Wednesday,* Mittwoch, Mi.
WHO, *World Health Organization,* Weltgesundheitsorganisation, WGO.
wk., *week,* Woche, Wo.; *work,* Arbeit.
wkly., *weekly,* wöchentlich.
wks., *weeks,* Wochen, Wo.
WNW, *west-northwest,* West-Nordwest, WNW.
w/o, *without,* ohne, o.

WP, *word processor,* Textverarbeitungssystem; *word processing,* Textverarbeitung; *weather permitting,* wenn es das Wetter erlaubt.

w.p.m., *words per minute,* Wörter pro Minute.

WSW, *west-southwest,* West-Südwest, WSW.

wt., *weight,* Gewicht, Gew.

XL, *extra large,* extragroß.

Xmas, *Christmas,* Weihnachten *n.*

Xroads, *crossroads,* Straßenkreuzung.

XS, *extra small,* extraklein.

yd., *yard,* Yard *n.*

Y.M.C.A., *Young Men's Christian Association,* Christlicher Verein Junger Männer, CVJM.

yr., *year,* Jahr.

Y.W.C.A., *Young Women's Christian Association,* Christlicher Verein Junger Frauen, CFJF.

Days of the Week

Sunday	der Sonntag
Monday	der Montag
Tuesday	der Dienstag
Wednesday	der Mittwoch
Thursday	der Donnerstag
Friday	der Freitag
Saturday	der Sonnabend *or* der Samstag

Months

January	der Januar	**July**	der Juli
February	der Februar	**August**	der August
March	der März	**September**	der September
April	der April	**October**	der Oktober
May	der Mai	**November**	der November
June	der Juni	**December**	der Dezember

Signs

Vorsicht	Caution	**Raucher**	For smokers
Achtung	Watch out	**Nichtraucher**	For non-smokers
Ausgang	Exit		
Eingang	Entrance	**Rauchen verboten**	No smoking
Halt	Stop	**Kein Zutritt**	No admittance
Geschlossen	Closed	**Damen** (*or*) **Frauen**	Women
Geöffnet	Open		
Langsam	Slow	**Herren** (*or*) **Männer**	Men
Verboten	Prohibited		
Gesperrt	Road closed	**Abort**	Toilet
Einbahnstraße	One way street		

Weights and Measures

The Germans use the *Metric System* of weights and measures, which is a decimal system in which multiples are shown by the prefixes: Dezi- (one tenth); Zeni- (one hundredth); Milli- (one thousandth); Deka- (ten); Hekto- (hundred); Kilo- (thousand).

1 Zentimeter = .3937 inches
1 Meter = 39.37 inches
1 Kilometer = .621 mile
1 Zentigramm = .1543 grain
1 Gramm = 15.432 grain
1 Pfund (1/2 Kilogramm) = 1.1023 pounds
1 Kilogramm = 2.2046 pounds
1 Tonne = 2,204 pounds
1 Zentiliter = 2,204 pounds
1 Zentiliter = .338 ounces
1 Liter = 1.0567 quart (liquid); .908 quart (dry)
1 Kiloliter = 264.18 gallons

Useful Words and Phrases

Hello (*or*) How do you do?	Guten Tag. Grüß Gott.
Good morning.	Guten Morgen. Grüß Gott.
Good afternoon.	Guten Tag. Grüß Gott.
Good evening.	Guten Abend.
How are you?	Wie geht es Ihnen?
Fine, thanks, and you?	Gut, danke, und Ihnen?
I'm fine, too, thanks.	Auch gut, danke.
Please.	Bitte.
Thank you.	Danke schön.
You're welcome.	Bitte schön.
Pardon me.	Entschuldigen Sie, bitte. Verzeihung.
I am sorry, I made a mistake.	Es tut mir leid, ich habe mich geirrt.
Do you mind?	Macht es Ihnen etwas aus?
Good luck.	Alles Gute.
Good night.	Gute Nacht.
Good-bye.	Auf Wiedersehen.
Can you please help me?	Können Sie mir bitte helfen?
Do you understand me?	Verstehen Sie mich?
I don't understand you.	Ich verstehe Sie nicht.
Please speak slowly.	Sprechen Sie bitte langsam.
Please say it again.	Sagen Sie es bitte noch einmal.
I don't speak German very well.	Ich spreche nicht sehr gut Deutsch.
Do you speak English?	Sprechen Sie Englisch?
What do you call that in German?	Wie heißt das auf deutsch?
How do you say . . . in German?	Wie sagt man . . . auf deutsch?
What's your name, please?	Wie heißen Sie bitte?
My name is . . .	Ich heiße . . .
May I introduce . . .	Darf ich Ihnen . . . vorstellen?
What time is it?	Wieviel Uhr ist es?
How much does that cost?	Wie viel kostet das?
I would like . . .	Ich möchte gern . . .; Ich hätte gern . . .
May I see something better?	Könnten Sie mir etwas Besseres zeigen?
May I see something cheaper?	Könnten Sie mir etwas Billigeres zeigen?
It is not exactly what I want.	Es ist nicht ganz das, was ich suche.
I'd like to buy . . .	Ich möchte gern . . . kaufen.
I'd like to eat.	Ich möchte gern essen.
Where is there a good restaurant?	Wo ist hier ein gutes Restaurant?
I'm hungry (thirsty).	Ich habe Hunger (Durst).
Please give me . . .	Bitte geben Sie mir . . .
Please bring me . . .	Bitte bringen Sie mir . . .
May I see the menu?	Ich hätte gern die Speisekarte.
The check, please.	Bitte zahlen.
Is service included in the bill?	Ist das mit Bedienung?
Where is there a good hotel?	Wo ist hier ein gutes Hotel?
Please help me with my luggage.	Helfen Sie mir bitte mit meinem Gepäck.
Where can I get a taxi?	Wo bekomme (finde) ich eine Taxe?
What is the fare to . . . ?	Was kostet die Fahrt nach (bis) . . .?
Please take me to this address.	Bitte bringen (fahren) Sie mich zu dieser Adresse.
Please let me off at . . .	Bitte halten Sie . . .
I am lost.	Ich habe mich verlaufen (verfahren).
I have a reservation.	Ich habe . . . reserviert.
Where is the men's (ladies') room?	Wo ist die Toilette, bitte?
How do I get to the station?	Wie komme ich zum Bahnhof?
Where can I check my baggage?	Wo ist die Gepäckaufbewahrung?
Is this a non-stop flight?	Ist dies ein direkter Flug?
I'm sick.	Ich bin krank.
I need a doctor.	Ich brauche einen Arzt.
Where is the nearest drugstore?	Wo ist die nächste Drogerie?
Where is the next pharmacy?	Wo ist die nächte Apotheke?

Useful Words and Phrases

Is there any mail for me?	Ist Post für mich da?
Where can I mail this letter?	Wo kann ich diesen Brief einstecken?
I want to send a fax.	Ich möchte gern ein Fax schicken.
Where is the nearest bank?	Wo ist die nächste Bank?
Where can I change money?	Wo kann ich hier Geld wechseln?
Do you accept travelers checks?	Nehmen Sie Reiseschecks?
May I have the bill, please?	Könnte ich bitte die Rechnung haben?
Right away.	Sofort.
Help!	Hilfe!
Please call the police.	Rufen sie bitte die Polizei.
Who is it?	Wer ist dort?
Come in.	Herein.
Just a minute!	Einen Augenblick, bitte!
Hello (*on telephone*).	Hier . . . (*say your name*).
Look out!	Vorsicht! Achtung!
Hurry.	Schnell.
As soon as possible.	So bald wie möglich.
To the right.	Rechts.
To the left.	Links.
Straight ahead.	Gerade aus.

Food Terms

apple	Apfel
asparagus	Spargel
bacon	Speck
banana	Banane
beans	Bohnen
beer	Bier
bread	Brot
butter	Butter
cake	Kuchen
carrot	Mohrrübe
cauliflower	Blumenkohl
celery	Sellerie
cheese	Käse
chicken	Huhn
chocolate	Schokolade
coffee	Kaffee
cookie	Keks
cream	Sahne
cucumber	Gurke
dessert	Nachtisch
duck	Ente
egg	Ei
fish	Fisch
fowl	Geflügel
fruit	Frucht, Obst
goose	Gans
grape	Weintraube
grapefruit	Pampelmuse
ham	Schinken
ice cream	Sahneeis
juice	Saft
lamb	Lammfleisch
lemonade	Limonade
lettuce	Kopfsalat
lobster	Hummer
meat	Fleisch
milk	Milch
mushroom	Pilz
noodle	Nudel
nuts	Nüsse
orange	Apfelsine
pastry	Gebäck
peach	Pfirsich
pear	Birne
pepper	Pfeffer
pie	Obstkuchen
pineapple	Ananas
pork	Schweinefleisch
potato	Kartoffel
rice	Reis
salad	Salat
salmon	Lachs
salt	Salz
sandwich	belegtes Brot
shrimp	Garnele
soup	Suppe
spinach	Spinat
steak	Beefsteak
strawberry	Erdbeere
sugar	Zucker
tea	Tee
tomato	Tomate
trout	Forelle
turkey	Truthahn
veal	Kalbfleisch
vegetable	Gemüse
water	Wasser
wine	Wein

Decimals

Instead of a decimal point, a comma is used:
English: 3.82 "three point eight two"
German: 3,82 "drei Komma acht zwei"

Fractions

the half; half a pound	die Hälfte; ein halbes Pfund
one and a half	anderthalb, eineinhalb
the third; two-thirds	das Drittel; zweidrittel
the fourth; three-fourths	das Viertel; dreiviertel
the fifth; four-fifths	das Fünftel; vierfünftel

Numerals

Cardinal		**Ordinal**	
1	eins	**1st**	erst-
2	zwei	**2nd**	zweit-
3	drei	**3rd**	dritt-
4	vier	**4th**	viert-
5	fünf	**5th**	fünft-
6	sechs	**6th**	sechst-
7	sieben	**7th**	sieb(en)t-
8	acht	**8th**	acht-
9	neun	**9th**	neunt-
10	zehn	**10th**	zehnt-
11	elf	**11th**	elft-
12	zwölf	**12th**	zwölft-
13	drcizehn	**13th**	dreizehnt-
14	vierzehn	**14th**	vierzehnt-
15	fünfzehn	**15th**	fünfzehnt-
16	sechzehn	**16th**	sechzehnt-
17	siebzehn	**17th**	siebzehnt-
18	achtzehn	**18th**	achtzehnt-
19	neunzehn	**19th**	neunzehnt-
20	zwanzig	**20th**	zwanzigst-
21	einundzwanzig	**21st**	einundzwanzigst-
30	dreißig	**30th**	dreißigst-
32	zweiunddreißig	**32nd**	zweiunddreißigst-
40	vierzig	**40th**	vierzigst-
43	dreiundvierzig	**43rd**	dreiundvierzigst-
50	fünfzig	**50th**	fünfzigst-
54	vierundfünfzig	**54th**	vierundfünfzigst-
60	sechzig	**60th**	sechzigst-
65	fünfundsechzig	**65th**	fünfundsechzigst-
70	siebzig	**70th**	siebzigst-
76	sechsundsiebzig	**76th**	sechsundsiebzigst-
80	achtzig	**80th**	achtzigst-
87	siebenundachtzig	**87th**	siebenundachtzigst-
90	neunzig	**90th**	neunzigst-
98	achtundneunzig	**98th**	achtundneunzigst-
100	hundert	**100th**	hunderst-
101	hunderteins	**101st**	hunderterst-
202	zweihundertzwei	**202nd**	zweihundertzweit-
1,000	tausend	**1,000th**	tausendst-
1,000,000	eine Million	**1,000,000**	millionst-